ROBERT NORTH S.J.

ELENCHUS OF BIBLICA

1992

EDITRICE PONTIFICIO ISTITUTO BIBLICO
ROMA 1995

ROBERT NORTH S.J.

ELENCHUS OF BIBLICA

1992

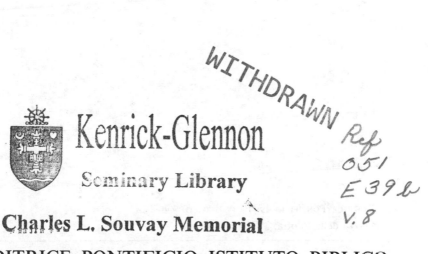

EDITRICE PONTIFICIO ISTITUTO BIBLICO
ROMA 1995

EDITRICE PONTIFICIO ISTITUTO BIBLICO
Piazza della Pilotta, 35 – 00187 Roma

Finito di stampare il 22 dicembre 1995
Tipografia Poliglotta della Pontificia Università Gregoriana
Piazza della Pilotta, 4 – 00187 Roma

This volume was published with the appreciated help of

The Catholic Biblical Association of America
defraying three percent of the annual massive production-cost

Deutsches Archäologisches Institut, Abteilung Rom

Bibliothèque de l'École Française de Rome

Milwaukee Marquette University Library and Jesuit Community

Saint Louis University Library and Jesuit Community

Gregorian University Press (Pasquale PUCA, director) and Library

---

AA	Ann Arbor	Lp	Leipzig
Amst	Amsterdam	Lv(N)	Leuven (L-Neuve)
B	Berlin	LVL	Louisville KY
Ba/BA	Basel/Buenos Aires	M/Mi	Madrid/Milano
Barc	Barcelona	Mkn/Mp	Maryknoll/Minneapolis
Bo/Bru	Bologna/Brussel	Mü	München
CasM	Casale Monferrato	N	Napoli
CinB	Cinisello Balsamo	ND	NotreDame IN
C	Cambridge, England	Neuk	Neukirchen/Verlag
CM	Cambridge, Mass.	NHv / Nv	New Haven / Nashville
Ch	Chicago	NY	New York
ColMn	Collegeville MN	Ox	Oxford
Da: Wiss	Darmstadt, WissBuchg	P/Pd	Paris/Paderborn
DG	Downers Grove IL	Ph	Philadelphia
Dü	Düsseldorf	R/Rg	Roma/Regensburg
E	Edinburgh	S/Sdr	Salamanca/Santander
ENJ	EnglewoodCliffs NJ	SF	San Francisco
F	Firenze	Shf	Sheffield
FrB/FrS	Freiburg-Br/Schw	Sto	Stockholm
Fra	Frankfurt/M	Stu	Stuttgart
Gö	Göttingen	T/TA	Torino/Tel Aviv
GR	Grand Rapids MI	Tü	Tübingen
Gü	Gütersloh	U/W	Uppsala/Wien
Ha	Hamburg	WL	Winona Lake IN
Heid	Heidelberg	Wmr	Warminster
Hmw	Harmondsworth	Wsb	Wiesbaden
J	Jerusalem	Wsh	Washington
K	København	Wsz	Warszawa
L	London	Wu/Wü	Wuppertal/Würzburg
LA	Los Angeles	Zu	Zürich

Please recall:

To separate a subtitle
from its title

we use a SEMICOLON (;)

where the original
varyingly uses
full-stop, colon, or new line

PRICE of books
is rounded off

($13 for 12.95;
less often £20 for 19.90;
DM 40 for 39,50)

to take account of
conciseness and inflation.

Note Lm 50 = Lire it. 50.000

Index systematicus – Contents

Progress toward full computerization

With this issue a further step has been taken toward more complete computerization. As an experiment, with the help and stimulus of dynamic colleague J.-N. ALETTI, the Index of numbers 2000 to 4000 was prepared on our own computer, and turned out so successfully that it could be incorporated into the present printed Index. We thereupon set about making a further experiment: a complete camera-ready copy of a portion of next year's Index (the numbers 7000 to 10,000 which had already been edited). This experiment also turned out to be fully acceptable. We are now going on to make the entire camera-ready Index for the volume 9 (1993).

Meanwhile with our collaborators we are making feverish efforts to extend the full computerization to all 17,500 numbered items per volume yet to come. But having learned from some experiences of colleagues or friendly rivals (publication-date of entire issues delayed for an extra year or more because rosy hopes turned out less rosy), we are patiently waiting to have all the complications foreseen and worked out without unduly rushing things.

A welcome new rival and resource

Special attention must be called to the revitalized *Old Testament Abstracts*. With its volume 16 for 1993, under its new editor Professor C. T. BEGG, it contains a wealth of material. Especially notable is the cross-reference under each Compilation (Festschrift, Acta of Meetings, Collected Essays) showing where each item is cited in that *OTAbs* issue.

This important resource was not available to us for this present volume 8 (problems of periodicals in bindery or otherwise elusive) but will be largely and gratefully represented in our volume 9. (We would have been even more appreciative if the date could have been given with each summarized article; and especially the original date for reprints of articles sometimes twenty years older.)

We recall to our users that our own materials, from the number 7000 ('biblical theology') and on to the end, are now [since our volume 4 (1988); see our p. 3 there] the first to be edited, so that the strictly biblical sections E-F-G can contain the more recent materials meanwhile available.

New subdivisions for Paul and John

Our Table of Contents on p. 4 does not yet indicate our experimental efforts to subdivide into more compact and cognate sections. For John's Gospel, the numbering G1.3 (introduction) and G1.4 has been left unchanged, but in these sections have been introduced some still quite tentative headings (bibliographical, narrative analysis, theological, sources). [*Apocalypse/Revelation somewhat similarly.*]

For Paul, the sections G3.1-3 remain unchanged (Life – Letters – Theology) but six new sections are added: 4. style, image; 5. Apostle of the Gentiles; 6. philosophical/moral views; 7. communities and spirituality; 8. history of research; 9. observations of detail.

Normally when a book has already been mentioned, if it is given with reviews in a later ELENCHUS, it will be in the same category and subdivision, with two important exceptions: (1) materials at first put at the front in section A in order to facilitate renvoi, will in later volumes be put into the section to which they relate; and (2) when some book-review clarifies the need, they will be moved to a more suitable section.

Acronyms: **Periodica** - Series (small).
8 fig. = ISSN; *10 fig.* = ISBN; *6/7* = DissA.

Ⓐ: *arabice,* in Arabic.
AAS: Acta Apostolicae Sedis; Vaticano. 0001-5199.
AASOR: Annual of the American Schools of Oriental Research; CM.
Abh: Abhandlungen Gö Lp Mü etc.; ➤ DOG / DPV.
AbhChrJüDial: Abhandlungen zum christlich-jüdischen Dialog; Mü, Kaiser.
AbrNahr: Abr-Nahrain; Lv, Peeters.
AcAANorv: Acta ad archaeologiam et artium historiam; R, Inst. Norv.
AcAntH: Acta Antiqua; Budapest.
AcArchH/K: Acta Archaeologica; Hungarica, Budapest. 0001-5210 / København. 0065-101X.
AcArchLov: Acta archaeologica Lovaniensia; Lv.
AcClasSAfr: Acta Classica; Pretoria. 0065-1141.
Acme; Mi, Fac. Lett. Filos. 0001-494X.
AcNum: Acta Numismatica; Barc. 0211-8386.
AcPIB: Acta Pontificii Instituti Biblici: Roma.
AcPraeh: Acta Praehistorica/Archaeol.; B.
AcSum: Acta Sumerologica; Hiroshima Univ., Linguistics. 0387-8082.
Act: Actes/Acta (Congrès, Colloque).
ActIran: Acta Iranica; Téhéran/Leiden.
ActOrH/K: Acta Orientalia: Budapest. 0044-5975 / K (Soc. Or. Danica, Norveigica). 0001-6438.
ActuBbg: Actualidad Bibliográfica; Barcelona. 0211-4143.
ADAJ: Annual of the Department of Antiquities, Jordan; 'Amman.
ADPF: Association pour la diffusion de la pensée française; Paris ➤ RCiv.
Aeg: Aegyptus; Milano. 0001-9046.
ÄgAbh: Ägyptologische Abhandlungen; Wb.
ÄgAT: Ägypten und Altes Testament; Wiesbaden. 0720-9061.
AegHelv: Aegyptiaca Helvetica: Basel Univ. Äg. Sem. (Univ. Genève).
ÄgLev: Ägypten und Levante; Wien. 1015-5014.
AEM: Archives Épistolaires de Mari.
ÄthF: Äthiopische Forschungen; Stu.
AevA: Aevum Antiquum; Mi, Univ. Cattolica/ViPe.

Aevum; Milano [anche Univ. Catt.].
AfER: African Ecclesial Review; Eldoret, Kenya.
AfJB: African Journal of Biblical Studies; Ibadan.
AfO: Archiv für Orientforschung; Graz.
AfTJ: Africa Theological Journal; Arusha, Tanzania. 0856-0048.
AGJU: Arbeiten zur Geschichte Antik. Judentums und des Urchristentums; Leiden.
AIBL: Académie des Inscriptions et Belles-Lettres; P ➤ CRAI. - **AIEMA** ➤ BMosA.
AION [-Clas]: Annali (dell')Istituto Universitario Orientale [Classico] di Napoli ➤ ArchStorAnt.
AIPHOS: Annuaire de l'Institut de Philologie et d'Histoire Orientales et Slaves; Bru.
AJA: American Journal of Archaeology; Princeton NJ. 0002-9114.
AJS: Association for Jewish Studies Review; CM 0364-0094.
Akkadica; Bruxelles/Brussel.
al.: et alii, and other(s).
Alexandria, cosmology; GR. (1,1991).
ALGHJ: Arbeiten zur Literatur und Geschichte des hellenistischen Judentums; Leiden.
Al-Kibt, The Copts, die Kopten; Ha.
Altertum (Das); Berlin. 0002-6646.
AltOrF: Altorientalische Forschungen; Berlin. 0232-8461.
AmBapQ: American Baptist Quarterly; Valley Forge PA. 0015-8992.
AmBenR: American Benedictine Review; Richardton ND. 0002-7650.
Ambrosius, bollettino liturgico; Milano. 0392-5757.
America; NY. 0002-7049.
AmHR: American Historical Rev.; NY.
AmJPg: American Journal of Philology; Baltimore. 0002-9475.
AmJTPh: American Journal of Theology and Philosophy; Lawrence.
AmMessianJ: The American Messianic Jew; Ph.
AmNumM: American Numismatic Society Museum Notes; NY.
AmPhTr: Transactions of the American Philosophical Society; Ph.
AmstCah: Amsterdamse cahiers voor exegese/bijbelse theologie; Kampen.

AmstMed ➤ Mededelingen.
AmStPapyr: American Studies in Papyrology; NHv.
AnalPapyr: Analecta Papyrologica; Messina. (1,1989).
AnáMnesis: teología, Dominicos; México. (3,1991).
AnArStorAnt: Annali di Archeologia e Storia Antica.
AnASyr: Annales Archéologiques Arabes Syriennes; Damas.
Anatolica; Istanbul. 0066-1554.
AnatSt: Anatolian Studies; London.
AnAug: Analecta Augustiniana; R.
ANaut: Archaeonautica; P. 0154-1854.
AnBib: Analecta Biblica. Investigationes scientificae in res biblicas; R. 0066-135X.
AnBoll: Analecta Bollandiana; Bruxelles. 0003-2468.
AnBritAth: Annual of the British School at Athens; London.
AnCalas: Analecta Calasanctiana; Salamanca. 0569-9789.
AnCÉtRel: Annales du Centre d'Études des Religions; Bru.
AncHB: Ancient History Bulletin; Calgary/Chicago. 0835-3638.
AnChile: Anales de la Facultad de Teología; Santiago, Univ. Católica.
AnchorB[D]: Anchor Bible [Dict]; NY. ➤ 580.
AncHRes: Ancient History Resources for Teachers; Sydney. 0310-5814.
AnCist: Analecta Cisterciensia; Roma. 0003-2476.
AnClas: Annales Universitatis, sectio classica; Budapest.
AnClémOchr: Annuaire de l'Académie de théologie 'Ochrida'; Sofya.
AnCracov: Analecta Cracoviensia (Polish Theol. Soc.); Kraków. 0209-0864.
AncSoc: Ancient Society. Katholieke Universiteit; Leuven. 0066-1619.
AncW: Ancient World; Ch. 0160-9645.
AndNR: Andover Newton Review; Newton Centre MA (3,1992).
AndrUnS: Andrews University Seminary Studies; Berrien Springs, Mich. 0003-2980.
AnÉCS: Annales Économies Sociétés Civilisations; P. 0395-2649.
AnEgBbg: Annual Egyptological Bibliography; Leiden.

AnÉPH: Annuaire ➤ ÉPHÉ.
AnÉth: Annales d'Éthiopie; Addis-Ababa.
AnFac: Let: Annali della facoltà di lettere, Univ. (Bari/Cagliari/Perugia).
— Ling/T: Annal(es) Facultat(is); linguarum, theologiae.
AnFg: Anuario de Filología; Barc.
Ang: Angelicum; Roma. 0003-3081.
AnglTR: Anglican Theological Review; Evanston IL. 0003-3286.
AnGreg: Analecta (Pont. Univ.) Gregoriana; Roma. 0066-1376.
AnHArt: Annales d'histoire de l'art et d'archéologie: Bru.
AnHConc: Annuarium Historiae Conciliorum; Paderborn.
ANilM: Archéologie du Nil Moyen; Lille. 0299-8130.
AnItNum: Annali (dell')Istituto Italiano di Numismatica; Roma.
AnJapB: Annual of the Japanese Biblical Institute; Tokyo ◑ ➤ Sei-Ron.
AnLetN: Annali della Facoltà di lettere e filosofia dell'Univ.; Napoli.
AnLovBOr: Analecta Lovaniensia Biblica et Orientalia; Lv.
AnnTh: Annales Theologici; Roma.
AnOr: Analecta Orientalia: Roma.
AnOrdBas: Analecta Ordinis S. Basilii Magni; Roma.
AnPg: L'Année Philologique; P. ➤ 7,858.
AnPisa: Annali della Scuola Normale Superiore; Pisa.
AnPraem: Analecta Praemonstratensia; Averbode.
AnRIM: Annual Review of the Royal Inscriptions of Mesopotamia Project; Toronto. 0822-2525.
AnRSocSR: Annual Review of the Social Sciences of Religion; The Hague. 0066-2062.
ANRW: Aufstieg und Niedergang der römischen Welt ➤ 581.
AnSacTar: Analecta Sacra Tarraconensia; Barcelona.
AnSemClas: Annali del Seminario di Studi del Mondo Classico; N, Univ.
AnStoEseg: Annali di Storia dell'Esegesi; Bologna. 1120-4001.
AntAb: Antike und Abendland; Berlin. 0003-5696.

AntAfr: Antiquités africaines; Paris. 0066-4871.
AnTar: Antiquité tardive (IVe-VIIe s.); Turnhout (1,1993: 2-503-50328-4).
AntClas: L'Antiquité Classique; Bru.
AntClCr: Antichità classica e cristiana; Brescia.
Anthropos; 1. Fribourg/Suisse. 0003-5572. / [2. Famiglia; Roma].
Anthropotes; Roma, Città Nuova.
AntiqJ: Antiquaries Journal; London. 0003-5815.
Antiquity; Gloucester. 0003-5982.
Ant/ka: Ⓖ Anthropologiká: Thessaloniki.
AntKu: Antike Kunst; Basel. 0003-5688.
Anton: Antonianum; Roma. 0003-6064.
AntRArch: Antiqua, Rivista d'Archeologia e d'Architettura; Roma.
AnTVal: Anales de Teología, Universidad de Valencia.
AntWelt: Antike Welt; Feldmeilen.
Anvil, Anglican Ev. theol.; Bramcote, Nottingham. 0003-6226.
AnzAltW: Anzeiger für die Altertumswissenschaft; Innsbruck. 0003-6293.
AnzW: Anzeiger der österreichischen Akademie; Wien. 0378-8652.
AOAT: Alter Orient und Altes Testament: Kevelaer/Neukirchen.
AOtt: Univ. München, Arbeiten zu Text und Sprache im AT; St. Ottilien.
Apocrypha; Turnhout (1,1990).
Apollonia: Afro-Hellenic studies; Johannesburg, Rand Afrikaans Univ.
Appoint; Montréal. (25,1992).
ArabArchEp: Arabian Archaeology and Epigraphy; K. 0905-7916.
Aram: Oxford.
Arasaradi, journal of theological reflection: Tamilnadu, Madurai (3/2, 1990).
ArBegG: Archiv für Begriffsgeschichte (Mainz, Akad.); Bonn.
ArbGTL: Arbeiten zur Geschichte und Theologie des Luthertums, NF; B.
ArbKiG: Arbeiten zur Kirchengeschichte; B.
ArbNTJud: Arbeiten zum NT und zum Judentum: Frankfurt/M. 0170-8856.
ArbNtTextf: Arbeiten zur Neutestamentlichen Textforschung; B/NY.
ArbNZ: (Texte und) Arbeiten zum NT und seine Zeitgeschichte (non = TANZ), Neuk.

ArbT: Arbeiten zur Theologie (Calwer); Stu.
ArCalc: Archeologia e calcolatori; F, Univ. Siena [1 (1990) 88-7814-072-4].
ARCE ➤ J [News] AmEg.
Archaeología; Wsz. 0066-605X.
Archaeology; Boston. 0003-8113.
Archaeometry; L. 0003-813X.
ArchAnz: Archäologischer Anzeiger; Berlin. 0003-8105.
ArchAth: Ⓖ Archaiología; Athēna.
ArchBbg: Archäologische Bibliographie zu JbDAI; Berlin.
ArchClasR: Archeologia Classica; Roma. 0391-8165.
Archeo, attualità del passato; Milano.
Archéologia; (ex-Paris) Dijon, Faton. 0570-6270 ➤ Dossiers.
Archéozoologie; Grenoble (4/2,1991).
ArchEph: Ⓖ Archaiologikē Ephēmeris; Athēnai.
ArchInf: Archäologische Informationen; Bonn.
ArchMIran: Archäologische Mitteilungen aus Iran, N.F.; Berlin.
ArchNews: Archaeological News; Tallahassee FL. 0194-3413.
ArchRep: Archaeological Reports; Wmr, British Sch. Athens. 0570-6084.
Arctos, Acta Philologica Fennica; Helsinki. 0570-734X.
ArEspArq: Archivo Español de Arqueología; Madrid. 0066-6742.
ARET/S: Archivi Reali di Ebla, Testi/Studi; Roma, Univ.
Arethusa; Buffalo NY. 0004-0975.
ArFrancHist: Archivum Franciscanum Historicum; Grottaferrata.
ArGlottIt: Archivio Glottologico Italiano; Firenze. 0004-0207.
ArHPont: Archivum Historiae Pontificiae; Roma.
ArKulturg: Archiv für Kulturgeschichte; Köln. 0003-9233.
ArLtgW: Archiv für Liturgiewissenschaft; Regensburg. 0066-6386.
ArOr: Archiv Orientální; Praha. 0044-8699.
ArPapF: Archiv für Papyrusforschung; Leipzig. 0066-6459.
ArRefG: Archiv für Reformationsgeschichte; Gütersloh.
ArSSocRel: Archives de Sciences Sociales des Religions; Paris.

ArTGran: Archivo Teológico Granadino; Granada. 0210-1629.

ArztC: Arzt und Christ; Salzburg.

ASAE: Annales du Service des Antiquités de l'Égypte; Le Caire.

AsbTJ: Asbury Theological Journal; Wilmore, KY.

AshlandTJ: ... Theological J. (Ohio).

AsiaJT: Asia Journal of Theology; Bangalore. (1,1992).

ASOR: American Schools of Oriental Research; CM (diss.: Dissertation Series).

Asprenas... Scienze Teologiche; Napoli.

At[AcBol/Tor/Tosc]: Atti [dell'Accademia... di Bologna / di Torino / Toscana].

ATANT: Abhandlungen zur Theologie des Alten & Neuen Testaments; Zürich.

ATD: Das Alte Testament Deutsch. Neues Göttinger Bibelwerk; Gö.

AteDial: Ateismo e Dialogo; Vaticano.

AtenRom: Atene e Roma; Firenze. 0004-6493.

Athenaeum: Letteratura e Storia dell'antichità; Pavia.

Atiqot; J, Dept. Ant.; from 20 (1991) Eng. + 🅑. 0066-488X.

AtKap: Ateneum Kapłańskie; Włocławek. 0208-9041.

ATLA: American Theological Library Association; Evanston, IL.

Atualização; Belo Horizonte, MG.

AuCAfr: Au cœur de l'Afrique; Burundi.

AugL: Augustinus-Lexikon ➤ 582.

AugLv: Augustiniana; Leuven.

AugM: Augustinus; Madrid.

AugR: Augustinianum; Roma.

AugSt: Augustinian Studies; Villanova PA.

AulaO: Aula Orientalis; Barc.

AusgF: Ausgrabungen und Funde; B.

AustinSB: Austin (TX) Sem. Bulletin.

AustralasCR: Australasian Catholic Record; Sydney. 0727-3215.

AustralBR: Australian Biblical Review; Melbourne.

AVA: ➤ BeitAVgA.

BA: Biblical Archaeologist; CM. 0006-0895.

Babel (translation); Budapest, Akad.

BaBernSt: Basler und Berner Studien zur hist./systematischen Theologie; Bern.

Babesch: Bulletin Antieke Beschaving; Haag. 0165-9367.

BaghMit: Baghdader Mitteilungen DAI; Berlin.

BAH: Bibliothèque Archéologique et Historique (IFA-Beyrouth).

BAnglsr: Bulletin of the Anglo-Israel Archaeological Soc.; L. 0266-2442.

BangTF: Bangalore Theological Forum.

BaptQ: Baptist [Historical Soc.] Quarterly; Oxford. 0005-576X.

BArchAlg: Bulletin d'Archéologie Algérienne; Alger.

BarIlAn: Bar-Ilan Annual; Ramat-Gan. 0067-4109.

BAR: British Archaeology Reports; Ox.

BAR-W: Biblical Archaeology Review; Washington. 0098-9444.

BArte: Bollettino d'Arte; Roma.

BAsEsp[Or/Eg]: Boletín de la Asociación Española de Orientalistas / de Egiptología (2, 1990); Madrid.

BASOR: Bulletin of the American Schools of Oriental Research; Atlanta. 0003-097X.

BASP: Bulletin, American Society of Papyrologists; NY. 0003-1186.

BAusPrax: Biblische Auslegung für die Praxis; Stuttgart.

Bazmaveb (Pazmavep; Armenian); Venezia.

BBArchäom: Berliner Beiträge zur Archäometrie; Berlin. 0344-5098.

BBB: ➤ BiBasB & BoBB.

BbbOr: Bibbia e Oriente; Bornato BS.

BBelgRom: Bulletin de l'Institut Historique Belge; R. 0073-8530.

Bbg: Bibliographia/-y.

BBRes: Bulletin for Biblical Research; Annandale NY. (1,1991).

BBudé: Bulletin de l'Association G. Budé; Paris.

BBVO: Berliner Beiträge zum Vorderen Orient: Berlin, Reimer.

BCanadB/Mesop: Bulletin Canadian Society of Biblical / Mesopotamian Studies; Ottawa / Toronto 0844-3416.

BCanMedit: Bulletin of the Canad. Mediterranean Institute.

BCentPrei: Bollettino del Centro Camuno di Studi Preistorici; Brescia. 0057-2168.

BCentProt: Bulletin du Centre Protestant d'Études; Genève.
BCH: Bulletin de Correspondance Hellénique; Paris. 0007-4217.
BCILL: Bibliothèque des Cahiers de l'Institut de Linguistique; Lv/P.
BCNH-T: Bibliothèque Copte de Nag Hammadi -Textes; Québec.
BDialRel: (Bu) Pro Dialogo; Vatican.
BEcuT: Bulletin of ecumenical theology; Enugu, Nigeria.
BeerSheva: ✪ Annual: Bible/ANE; J.
BÉF: Bibliothèque des Écoles françaises d'Athènes et de Rome; R. ➤ MÉF.
BEgS: Bulletin of the Egyptological Seminar; NY.
BeitATJ: Beiträge zur Erforschung des Alten Testaments und des Antiken Judentums; Bern. 0722-0790.
BeitAVgArch: Beiträge zur allgemeinen und vergleichenden Archäologie; München, Beck.
BeitBExT: Beiträge zur biblischen Exegese und Theologie [ipsi: BET]; Frankfurt/M.
BeitEvT: Beiträge zur evangelischen Theologie; München.
BeitGbEx: Beiträge zur Geschichte der biblischen Exegese; Tübingen.
BeitHistT: Beiträge zur Historischen Theologie; Tübingen.
BeitNam: Beiträge zur Namenforschung N. F.; Heid. 0005-8114.
BeitÖkT: Beiträge zur ökumenischen Theologie; München, Schöningh. 0067-5172.
BeitRelT: Beiträge zur Religionstheologie; Wien-Mödling.
BeitSudan: Beiträge zur Sudanforschung; Wien, Univ.
Belleten (Türk Tarih Kurumu); Ankara.
Benedictina; Roma.
Berytus (Amer. Univ. Beirut); K.
BethM: ✪ Beth Mikra; Jerusalem. 0005-979X.
BÉtOr: Bulletin d'Études Orientales; Damas, IFAO.
BFaCLyon: Bulletin des Facultés Catholiques; Lyon. 0180-5282.
Bib ➤ Biblica; Roma. 0006-0887.
BibAfr: La Bible en Afrique [francophone]; Lomé, Togo.
BiBasB: Biblische Basis Bücher; Kevelaer/ Stuttgart.

BiBeit: Biblische Beiträge, Schweizerisches Kath. Bibelwerk; Fribourg.
BibFe: Biblia y Fe; M. 0210-5209.
BibKonf: Biblische Konfrontationen; Stu.
Bible Bhashyam: Kottayam. 0970-2288.
Biblica: commentarii Pontificii Instituti Biblici; Roma. 0006-0887.
Biblos 1. Coimbra; 2. Wien.
BibNot: Biblische Notizen; Bamberg. 0178-2967.
BibOrPont: Biblica et Orientalia, Pontificio Istituto Biblico; Roma.
BibTB: Biblical Theology Bulletin; South Orange NJ, Seton Hall. 0146-1079.
BibTSt: Biblisch-Theologische Studien; Neukirchen-Vluyn. 0930-4800.
BibUnt: Biblische Untersuchungen; Regensburg.
BIFAO: Bulletin de l'Institut Français d'Archéologie Orientale; Le Caire. 0255-0962.
Bijd: Bijdragen, Filosofie en Theologie; Nijmegen. 0006-2278.
BiKi: Bibel und Kirche; Stuttgart. 0006-0623.
BInfWsz: Bulletin d'Information de l'Académie de Théologie Catholique; Warszawa. 0137-7000.
BInstArch: Bulletin of the Institute of Archaeology; London. 0076-0722.
BIP[Br]: Books in Print, U.S., annual; NY, Bowker [British, L, Whitaker]; fr./it./dt.
BiRes: Biblical Research; Chicago. 0067-6535.
Biserica ... Ortodoxă; Bucureşti.
BIstFGrec: Bollettino dell'Istituto di Filologia Greca, Univ. Padova; R.
Bits and bytes review; Whitefish MT. 0891-2955.
BJG: Bulletin of Judaeo-Greek Studies; Cambridge Univ.
BJRyL: Bulletin of the John Rylands Library; Manchester. 0301-102X.
BKAT: Biblischer Kommentar AT; Neuk.
BL: Book List, The Society for Old Testament Study. 0309-0892.
BLCéramÉg: Bulletin de liaison ... céramique égyptienne; Le Caire, IFAO. 0255-0903.
BLitEc [Chr]: Bulletin de Littérature Ecclésiastique [Chronique]. Toulouse. 0007-4322 [0495-9396].

BLtg: Bibel und Liturgie; Wien-Klosterneuburg. 0006-064X.

BMB: Bulletin du Musée de Beyrouth.

BMeijiG: Bulletin Christian Research Institute Meiji Gakuin Univ.; Tokyo.

BMosA [ipsi AIEMA]: Bulletin, étude mosaïque antique; P. 0761-8808.

BO: Bibliotheca Orientalis; Leiden. 0006-1913.

BoBB: Bonner Biblische Beiträge; Königstein.

Bobolanum, teologia; Wsz. 0867-3330.

BogSmot: Bogoslovska Smotra; Zagreb. 0352-3101.

BogVest: Bogoslovni Vestnik; Ljubljana.

BonnJb: Bonner Jahrbücher.

Boreas [1. Uppsala, series]; 2. Münster, Archäologie. 0344-810X.

BProtF: Bulletin, Histoire du Protestantisme Français; Paris.

BR: Bible Review; Wsh. 8755-6316.

BRefB: Bulletin, Reformation Biblical Studies: Fort Wayne.

BritAth: Papers of the British School in Athens; L.

BritJREd: British Journal of Religious Education; London,

BRöG: Bericht der Römisch-Germanischen Kommission DAI; Mainz. 0341-9312.

BrownJudSt/StRel: Brown Judaic Studies / Studies in Religion; Atlanta.

BS ⇢ BtS.

BSAA: Boletín, Seminario Estudios Arte y Arqueología; Valladolid.

BSAC: Bulletin de la Société d'Archéologie Copte; Le Caire.

BSeptCog: Bulletin of the International Organization for Septuagint and Cognate Studies; ND.

BSignR: Bulletin Signalétique, religions; Paris. 0180-9296.

BSLP: Bulletin de la Société de Linguistique; Paris.

BSNAm: Biblical Scholarship in North America; Atlanta, SBL.

BSNEJap ⇢ Oriento.

BSO: Bulletin of the School of Oriental and African Studies; London. 0041-977X.

BSoc[Fr]Ég: Bulletin de la Société [Française] d'Égyptologie; Genève [Paris].

BSoGgIt: Bollettino della Società Geografica Italiana; R. 0037-8755.

BSpade: Bible and Spade; Ballston NY.

BStLat: Bollettino di Studi Latini; N.

BSumAg: Bulletin on Sumerian Agriculture; Cambridge. 0267-0658.

Bt: Bibliotheca/-que.

BTAM: Bulletin de Théologie Ancienne et Médiévale; Lv. ⇢ RTAM.

BtEscB/EstB: Biblioteca Escuela Bíblica; M / de Estudios Bíblicos, Salamanca.

BtETL: Bibliotheca, ETL; Leuven.

BThemT: Bibliothek Themen der Theologie; Stuttgart.

BtHumRef: Bibliotheca Humanistica et Reformatorica; Nieuwkoop, de Graaf.

BtHumRen: Bibliothèque d'Humanisme et Renaissance; Genève/Paris.

BtMesop: Bibliotheca Mesopotamica; Malibu CA.

BToday: The Bible Today; Collegeville MN. 0006-0836.

BTrans: The Bible Translator [Technical/ Practical]; Stu. 0260-0943.

BtS: Bibliotheca Sacra; Dallas. 0006-1921.

BtScRel: Biblioteca di Scienze religiose; Roma, Salesiana.

BTSt: Biblisch-theologische Studien (ex-Biblische Studien); Neukirchen.

BtStor: Biblioteca di storia e storiografia dei tempi biblici; Brescia.

BTT: Bible de tous les temps; Paris.

BtTPaid: Biblioteca Teologica; Brescia.

BTZ: Berliner Theologische Zeitschrift; Berlin. 0724-6137.

Bu[BbgB]: Bulletin [de Bibliographie Biblique; Lausanne].

BuBRes: Bulletin for Biblical Research; Annandale NY.

BudCSt: Buddhist-Christian Studies; Honolulu, Univ. 0882-0945.

Burgense; Burgos. 0521-8195.

BurHist: Buried History; Melbourne. 0007-6260.

BVieChr: Bible et Vie Chrétienne; P.

BViewp: Biblical Viewpoint; Greenville SC, Jones Univ. 0006-0925.

BW: Beiträge zur Wissenschaft vom Alten und Neuen Testament; Stuttgart.

BySlav: Byzantinoslavica; Praha. 0007-7712.

ByZ: Byzantinische Zeitschrift; München. 0007-7704.
ⓖ Byzantina; Thessaloniki.
Byzantion; Bruxelles.
ByzFor: Byzantinische Forschungen; Amsterdam.
BZ: Biblische Zeitschrift; Paderborn. 0006-2014.
BZA[N]W: Beihefte zur ➤ ZAW [ZNW].
CAD: [Chicago] Assyrian Dictionary; Glückstadt. ➤ 7,9273.
CADIR: Centre pour l'Analyse du Discours Religieux; Lyon ➤ SémBib.
Cadmo: Lisboa, Univ. 0871-9257 (1,1991).
CAH: Cambridge Ancient History²; Cambridge Univ. ➤ 583.
CahArchéol: Cahiers Archéologiques; Paris.
CahCMéd: Cahiers de Civilisation Médiévale; Poitiers.
CahDAFI: Cahiers de la Délégation Archéologique Française en Iran; Paris. 0765-104X.
CahÉv: Cahiers Évangile; Paris. 0222-8741.
CahGlotz: Cahiers du Centre G. Glotz, revue d'histoire ancienne: P, Sorbonne (4,1993: 2-7018-0074-9).
CahHist: Cahiers d'Histoire; Lyon.
CahIntSymb: Cahiers Internationaux de Symbolique; Mons, Belgique.
CahLV: Cahiers voor Levensverdieping; Averbode.
CahPhRel: Cahiers de l'École des sciences philosophiques et religieuses; Bru, Fac. S. Louis.
CahRechScRel: Cahiers de Recherche en Sciences de la Religion; Québec.
CahSpIgn: Cahiers de spiritualité ignatienne; Québec.
CahSubaq: Cahiers d'archéologie subaquatique; Fréjus. (10,1991).
CahTrB: Cahiers de traduction biblique; Pierrefitte France. 0755-1371.
CahTun: Les Cahiers (de la Faculté des Lettres) de Tunisie; Tunis.
CalvaryB: Calvary Baptist Theological Journal; Lansdale PA. 8756-0429.
CalvinT: Calvin Theological Journal; Grand Rapids MI. 0008-1795.

CalwTMg: Calwer Theologische Monographien (A: Biblisch); Stuttgart.
CamArch: Cambridge (Eng.) Archaeological Journal. 0959-7743. (1,1991).
CamCW: Cambridge Commentary on Writings of the Jewish and Christian World.
CanadCath: Canadian Catholic Review; Saskatoon.
CANAL-infos; judaïsme-christianisme anciens: P, ÉPHÉR (9,1992).
Carmel: Tilburg.
Carmelus; Roma. 0008-6673.
Carthage Conservation Bulletin; Tunis.
Carthaginensia; Murcia, Inst. Teol. 0213-4381.
CathCris: Catholicism in crisis; ND.
CathHR: Catholic Historical Review; Wsh. 0008-8080. ➤ USCatH.
Catholica (Moehler-Institut, Paderborn); Münster.
Catholicisme: Paris ➤ 584.
Catholic Studies, Tokyo ➤ Katorikku.
CathTR: Catholic Theological Review; Clayton/Hong Kong.
CathTSocAmPr: ➤ PrCTSAm [AnCTS].
CathW: Catholic World; NY.
CathWRep: Catholic World Report; SF. 1058-8159.
CATSS: Computer assisted tools for Septuagint studies: Atlanta ➤ SBL.
CBQ: Catholic Biblical Quarterly; Washington, DC. 0008-7912.
CC: La Civiltà Cattolica; R. 0009-8167.
CCAR: (Central Conference of American Rabbis) Reform Jewish Quarterly; NY. 0149-712X [from 39 (1992) for **JRefJud**].
CCGraec/Lat/Med: Corpus Christianorum, series graeca / latina / continuatio mediaev.; Turnhout.
CdÉ: Chronique d'Égypte; Bruxelles.
CEB: Commentaire évangelique de la Bible; Vaux/Seine ➤ Édifac.
Center Journal; Notre Dame.
CERDAC: (Atti) Centro di Ricerca e Documentazione Classica; Milano.
CERDIC: Centre d'échanges et de recherches sur la diffusion et l'inculturation du christianisme.
CETÉDOC: Centre de Traitement Électronique des Documents; Lv.
CGL: Coptic Gnostic Library ➤ NHS.

CGMG: Christlicher Glaube in moderner Gesellschaft; FrB.
CGrebel: Conrad Grebel Review ... Christian inquiry; Waterloo ON (Mennonite). 0829-044X (10,1992).
ChCu: Church and Culture; Vatican.
CHermProt: Centre d'Herméneutique Protestante.
ChH: Church History; Indiatlantic FL.
CHH: Center for Hermeneutical Studies in Hellenistic & Modern Culture; Berkeley.
Chiea [ChAfC]: Nairobi, Catholic Higher Institute of Eastern Africa.
CHIran: Cambridge History of Iran.
Chiron: Geschichte, Epigraphie; München.
CHistEI: ⊕ Cathedra, History of Eretz-Israel; Jerusalem.
CHist-J: Jerusalem Cathedra.
CHJud: Cambridge History of Judaism ➤ 585.
CHLC: The Cambridge history of literary criticism; C.
Chm: Churchman 1. (Anglican); London: 0009-661X / 2. (Humanistic); St. Petersburg FL: 0009-6628.
ChrCent: Christian Century; Chicago. Christus; 1. Paris; 2. México.
ChrJRel: Christian Jewish Relations; L.
ChrLit: Christianity and Literature: Carrollton GA College. 0148-3331 (42,1992).
ChrNIsr: Christian News from Israel; Jerusalem.
ChrOost: Het Christelijk Oosten; Nijmegen.
ChrSchR: Christian Scholar's Review; Houston TX.
ChrT: Christianity Today; Carol Stream IL. 0009-5761.
ChrTW: Christ to the World [= Cristo al Mondo Eng.; papal and cognate documents] Roma ... 0011-1485 (38,1993).
ChSt: Chicago Studies; Mundelein IL.
Church: NY, Nat. Pastoral Life.
ChuT: Church & Theology; L. (6,1986).
ChWoman: The Church Woman; NY. 0009-6598.
Cienie i Światło [Ombres et Lumière (revue chrétienne des personnes non pleinement habiles: AtKap 491, 2+ 183s]; Wsz.

CistSt: Cistercian Studies; ed. Getsemani KY; pub. Chimay, Belgium.
Citeaux; Achel, Belgium. 0009-7497.
Cithara: Judaeo-Christian Tradition; St. Bonaventure (NY) Univ.
CiTom: Ciencia Tomista; S. 0210-0398.
CiuD: Ciudad de Dios; M. 0009-7756.
CivClCr: Civiltà classica e cristiana; Genova. 0392-8632.
CiVit: Città di Vita; Firenze. [0]009-7632.
Claret: Claretianum; Roma.
ClasA: [formerly California Studies in] Classical Antiquity; Berkeley.
ClasB: Classical Bulletin; Ch. 0009-8137 (EAsbury Coll., Wilmore KY).
ClasJ: Classical Journal; Greenville SC. 0009-8353.
ClasMed: Classica et Mediaevalia; København. 0106-5815.
ClasOutl: The Classical Outlook; Ch [ed. Miami Univ. OH]. 0009-8361.
ClasPg: Classical Philology; Chicago. 0009-8361.
ClasQ: Classical Quarterly NS; Oxford. 0009-8388.
ClasR: Classical Review NS; Oxford. 0009-840X.
ClasWo: Classical World; Pittsburgh. 0009-8148.
CLehre: Die Christenlehre; Berlin.
Clio, studi storici; N.
CMatArch: Contributi e materiali di archeologia orientale; Roma, Univ.
CNRS: Conseil National de Recherche Scientifique; Paris.
CogF: Cogitatio Fidei; Paris.
ColcCist: Collectanea Cisterciensia; Forges, Belgique.
ColcFranc: Collectanea Franciscana; Roma. 0010-0749.
ColcT: Collectanea Theologica; Warszawa. 0137-6985.
ColcTFu: Collectanea theol. Univ. Fujen = Shenhsileh Lunchi; Taipei.
CollatVL: Collationes, Vlaams ... Theologie en Pastoraal; Gent.
Colloquium; Auckland, Sydney.
ColStFen: Collezione di Studi Fenici; Roma, Univ.
Commentary; NY. 0010-2601.
CommBras: Communio Brasiliensis: Rio de Janeiro.

CommWsh: Communio USA; Washington. 0094-2065.

CommRevue: Communio [various languages, not related to **ComSev**]: revue catholique internationale; Paris.

CommStrum: Communio, strumento internazionale per un lavoro teologico; Milano.

Communio deutsch → **IkaZ.**

ComOT: Commentaar op het Oude Testament. Kampen.

CompHum: Computers and the Humanities; Osprey FL. 0010-4817.

CompNT: Compendium rerum Iudaicarum ad NT; Assen.

Compostellanum; Santiago de Compostela.

ComRatisbNT: Comentario de Ratisbona; Barc.

ComSev: Communio; Sevilla. 0010-3705.

ComSpirAT/NT: Commenti spirituali dell'Antico / Nuovo Testamento; Roma.

ComTeolNT: Commentario Teologico del NT; Brescia.

ComViat: Communio Viatorum; Praha. 0010-7133. Suspended 33 (1990).

ConBib: Coniectanea Biblica OT/NT; Malmö.

Conc: Concilium, variis linguis; P; M; Eng. now L/Ph 0010-5236 [deutsch → IZT].

ConcordJ: Concordia Journal; St. Louis. 0145-7233.

ConcordTQ: Concordia Theological Quarterly; Fort Wayne.

Confer (Vida Religiosa); M. (32/121-4,1993).

ConsJud: Conservative Judaism; NY. 0010-6542.

Contacts/Orthodoxe, de théologie et spiritualité; P. 0045-8325.

Continuum; NY. (1,1991).

ContrIstStorAnt: Contributi dell'Istituto di Storia Antica; Milano, Univ. Catt.

Coptologia [also for Egyptology]: Thunder Bay ONT, Lakehead Univ.

CouStR: Council for the Study of Religion Bulletin; Macon GA, Mercer Univ.

CovQ: Covenant Quarterly; Chicago.

CRAI: Comptes rendus de l'Académie des Inscriptions et Belles-Lettres; P.

CreSpir: Creation Spirituality (M. Fox); San José CA. 1053-9891 (8,1992).

Cretan Studies; Amst.

CRIPEL → **SocUÉg.**

CriswT: Criswell Theological Review; Dallas.

Criterio; Buenos Aires. 0011-1473,

CritRR: Critical Review of Books in Religion: Atlanta.

CrkvaSv: Crkva u Svijetu; Split.

CrNSt: Cristianesimo nella Storia; Bologna. 0393-3598.

CroatC: Croatica Christiana; Zagreb.

CrossC: Cross Currents; West Nyack NJ. 0011-1953.

Crux: Vancouver. 0011-2186.

CSCO: Corpus Scriptorum Christianorum Orientalium; Lv. 0070-0401.

CScrN: Corpus Sacrae Scripturae Neerlandicae Medii Aevi; Leiden.

CuadFgClás: Cuadernos de Filología Clásica; M, Univ.

CuadTeol: Cuadernos de Teología; Buenos Aires.

CuadTrad: Cuadernos de Traducción y Interpretación; Barc.

CuesT: Cuestiones Teológicas; Medellín.

CuH: Culture and History; K.

CurrAr: Current Archaeology; L (11, 1993).

CurResB: Currents in research, biblical studies; Shf. 0966-7377 (1,1993).

CurrTM[iss]: Currents in Theology and Mission; St. Louis. 0098-2113.

CyrMeth: Cyrillomethodianum; Thessaloniki.

D: director: 1. (in Indice etiam *auctor*) Dissertationis; 2. Congressus, *etc.*

DAFI: Délégation Archéologique Française en Iran (Mém); Paris.

DAI: Deutsches Archäologisches Institut; Rom (nobis utilissimum), *al.* → Mi(tt).

DanTTs: Dansk Teologisk Tidsskrift; København.

DanVMed/Skr: Dansk. Videnskabornes Selskap, Hist./Fil. Meddelelser / Skriften; K.

DBS [– SDB].

DECR: Department for External Church Relations of the Moscow Patriarchate: Moskva.

DeltChr: Deltion tes christianikēs archaiologikēs hetaireias: Athēna.

DeltVM: ⑤ Deltío vivlikôn meletôn, Bulletin Études Bibliques; Athēnai.

DHGE: Dictionnaire d'Histoire et de Géographie Ecclésiastiques; P ➤ 586.

Diakonia; 1. Mainz/Wien. 0341-9592; Stu. 2. (Eastern Christianity); Scranton (26,1993).

DialArch: Dialoghi di Archeologia; Mi.

DiálEcum: Diálogo Ecuménico; Salamanca. 0210-2870.

DialHA: Dialogues d'Histoire ancienne; Besançon. 18,1 (1992): 2-251-60475-8.

Dialog; Minneapolis. 0012-2033.

DialR: Dialog der Religionen. (1,1991).

DialTP: Diálogo teológico; El Paso TX.

DictSpir: Dictionnaire/Spiritualité; P ➤ 587.

Didascalia; Rosario ARG.

Didaskalia; Lisboa.

DielB: Dielheimer Blätter zum Alten Testament [ipsi DBAT]; Heid.

Dionysius: Halifax. 0705-1085.

Direction; Fresno CA.

DiscEg: Discussions in Egyptology; Oxford. 0268-3083.

Disciple, the (Disciples of Christ); St. Louis. 0092-8372.

DissA: Dissertation Abstracts International; AA/L. -A [= US etc.]: 0419-4209 [C = Europe. 0307-6075].

DissHRel: Dissertationes ad historiam religionum (supp. Numen); Leiden.

Divinitas, Pont. Acad. Theol. Rom. (Lateranensis); Vaticano. 0012-4222.

DivThom: Divus Thomas; Bologna. 0012-4257.

DizTF: Dizionario di Teologia Fondamentale ➤ 588.

DJD: Discoveries in the Judaean Desert; Oxford.

DLZ: Deutsche Literaturzeitung; Berlin. 0012-043X.

DMA: Dictionary of the Middle Ages; NY ➤ 7,670.

DocCath: Documentation Catholique; Paris.

DoctCom: Doctor Communis; Vaticano.

DoctLife: Doctrine and Life; Dublin.

DOG: Deutsche Orient-Gesellschaft: B.

DosB: Les dossiers de la Bible; P.

DossD: Dossiers d'archéologie; Dijon.

DowR: Downside Review; Bath. 0012-5806.

DPA: Dizionario patristico e di antichità cristiane; Casale Monferrato ➤ 590.

DrevVost: ⑨ Drevnij Vostok; Moskva.

DrewG: The Drew [Theological School] Gateway; Madison NJ.

DumbO: Dumbarton Oaks Papers; CM. 0070-7546.

DutchMgA: Dutch Monographs in Ancient History and Archaeology; Amst.

ᴱ: editor, Herausgeber, a cura di.

EAfJE: East African Journal of Evangelical Theology; Machakos, Kenya.

EAsJT: East Asia Journal of Theology [combining NE & SE AJT]; Tokyo. 0217-3859.

EAPast: East Asian Pastoral Review; Manila. 0040-0564.

ÉchMClas: Échos du Monde Classique/Classical Views; Calgary. 0012-9356.

ÉchSM: Les Échos de Saint-Maurice; Valais, Abbaye.

EcOr: Ecclesia Orans; R, Anselm.

ÉcoutBib: Écouter la Bible; Paris.

EcuR: Ecumenical Review; Geneva. 0013-0790.

EDIFAC: Éditions de la Faculté libre de Théologie Évangélique; Vaux/Seine.

Editio, internationales Jahrbuch für Editionswissenschaft; Tü (7,1993).

EfMex: Efemerides Mexicanas; Tlalpan.

Egb: Ergänzungsband.

ÉglT: Église et Théologie; Ottawa.

EgVO: Egitto e Vicino Oriente; Pisa.

ÉHRel: Études d'histoire des religions.

Eikasmós, Quaderni di Filologia Classica; Bologna, Univ.

Einz: Einzelband.

EkK [Vor]: Evangelischer-katholischer Kommentar zum NT; Z/Köln; Neukirchen-Vluyn ['Vorarbeiten'].

EkkT: ⑤ Ekklēsía kaì Theología; L. Elenchos, ... pensiero antico; Napoli.

Elliniká; ⑤ Thessaloniki.

Emerita (lingüística clásica); M.

Emmanuel: St. Meinrads IN/NY. 0013-6719.

Enc. Biblica ➤ EnṣMiqr.

EncHebr: ⑨ Encyclopaedia Hebraica; J/TA.

Enchoria, Demotistik/Koptologie; Wsb.

EncIran: Encyclopaedia Iranica; L.
EncIslam: Encyclopédie de l'Islam. Nouvelle édition [+ Eng]; Leiden/P ➤ 593.
EncKat: Encyklopedia Katolicka; Lublin.
Encounter (theol.); Indianapolis.
EncRel: (1) ᴱ*Eliade* M., NY. – 2. Fi.
EnşMiqr: ❿ *Enşiqlopediya miqrā'ît,* Encyclopaedia Biblica; Jerusalem.
Entschluss: Wien. 0017-4602.
EnzMär: Enzyklopädie des Märchens; B.
EOL: Ex Oriente Lux ➤ 1.Jb/2. Phoenix.
Eos, ... philologia; Wsz. 0012-7825.
EpAnat: Epigraphica anatolica; Bonn.
ÉPHÉ[H/R]: École Pratique des Hautes-Études, Annuaire [Hist.-Pg. / Sc. Rel.]; Paris.
EpHetVyz: ❿ Ephēmeris tēs Hetaireías Vyzantinōn Spoudōn; Athēnai.
EphLtg: Ephemerides Liturgicae; R.
EphMar: Ephemerides Mariologicae; Madrid.
ÉPR: Études préliminaires aux religions orientales dans l'Empire romain; Leiden.
Eranos[/Jb]: Acta Philologica Suecana; Uppsala / Jahrbuch; Fra.
ErbAuf: Erbe und Auftrag; Beuron.
ErfTSt/Schr: Erfurter Theologische Studien/ Schriften.
ErIsr: Eretz-Israel; J. 0071-108X.
ErtFor: Ertrag der Forschung; Darmstadt, Wissenschaftliche Buchg. 0174-0695.
Erytheia, estudios biz./neogrieg.
EscrVedat: Escritos del Vedat; Valencia. 0210-3133.
EsprVie: Esprit et Vie: 1. [< Ami du Clergé]; Langres; 2. Chambray.
EstAgust: Estudio Agustiniano; Valladolid. 0425-340X.
EstBíb: Estudios Bíblicos; Madrid. 0014-1437.
EstClas: Estudios clásicos; M. 0014-1453 (34,1992).
EstDeusto: Estudios de (Universidad) Deusto; Madrid. 0423-4847.
EstE: Estudios Eclesiásticos; Madrid. 0210-1610.
EstFranc: Estudios Franciscanos; Barcelona.
EstJos: Estudios Josefinos; Valladolid.
EstLul: Estudios Lulianos; Mallorca.
EstMar: Estudios Marianos; Madrid.
EstTrin: Estudios Trinitarios; Salamanca.

EstudosB: Estudos Bíblicos; Petrópolis.
ÉtBN: Études Bibliques, Nouvelle Série; Paris. 0760-3541.
ÉtClas: Les études classiques; Namur. 0014-200X.
ÉtFranc: Études Franciscaines; Blois.
ETL: Ephemerides Theologicae Lovanienses; Leuven. 0013-9513. ➤ Bt.
ÉtPapyr: Études [Société Égyptienne] de Papyrologie; Le Caire.
ÉtPgHist: Études de Philologie et d'Histoire; Genève, Droz.
ÉTRel: Études Théologiques et Religieuses; Montpellier. 0014-2239.
ÉtTrav: Études et Travaux; Varsovie.
Études; Paris. 0014-1941.
Euhemer (❿ hist. rel.); Wsz. 0014-2298
EuntDoc: Euntes Docete; Roma.
EurHS: Europäische Hochschulschriften / Publ. Universitaires Européennes; Fra.
EurJT: The European journal of theology: Carlisle. 0960-2720.
Evangel; Edinburgh. 0265-4547.
EvErz: Der evangelische Erzieher; Frankfurt/M. 0014-3413.
EvJ: Evangelical Journal; Myerstown.
EvKL: Evangelisches Kirchenlexikon; ➤ 595.
EvKom: Evangelische Kommentare; Stuttgart. 0300-4236.
EvQ[RT]: Evangelical Quarterly [Review of Theology]; Exeter.
EvT: Evangelische Theologie, NS; München. 0014-3502.
EWest: East and West; 1. L / 2. R.
EWSp: Encyclopedia of World Spirituality; NY/L.
ExAud: Ex auditu; Princeton. 0883-0053.
Exchange, missiological/ecumenical research; Leiden, IIMO. 0166-2740 (21, 1992).
ExcSIsr: Excavations and Surveys in Israel < Ḥadašot; J. 0334-1607.
ExGG: Exegetical guide to the Greek NT; GR.
Expedition; Ph. 0014-4738.
Explor [sic]; Evanston. 0362-0876.
ExpTim: The Expository Times; Edinburgh. 0014-5246.
F&M: Faith and mission; Wake Forest NC. (10,1992).
F&R: Faith and Reason; Front Royal VA. 0098-5449.

FascBíb: Fascículos bíblicos; Madrid.
Faventia: clásica; Barc. 0210-7570.
FemT: Feminist Theology; Shf (1, 1992).
fg./fil.: filologia/co, filosofia/co.
FgNt: Filologia neotestamentaria; Córdoba, Univ. 0214-2996.
FidH: Fides et Historia; Longview TX.
FilT: Filosofia e teologia; Napoli.
FirsT: First Things (religion/public life); Denville. 1047-5141 (28,1992).
FoiTemps: La Foi et le Temps. NS; Tournai.
FoiVie: Foi et Vie; Paris. 0015-5357.
FolArch: Folia Archaeologica; Budapest. 0133-2023.
FolOr: Folia Orientalia, Polska Akademia Nauk; Kraków. 0015-5675.
Fondamenti; Brescia, Paideia.
ForBib: Forschung zur Bibel; Wü/Stu.
ForBMusB: Forschungen und Berichte, Staatliche Museen zu Berlin.
ForFF: Forum, foundations and facets; Bonner MT. 0883-4970.
ForGLProt: Forschungen zur Geschichte und Lehre des Protestantismus; Mü.
ForJüdChrDial: Forschungen zum jüdisch-christlichen Dialog; Neuk.
ForKiDG: Forschungen zur Kirchen- und Dogmengeschichte; Gö.
Fornvännen; Lund. 0015-7813.
ForRel: Forum Religion; Stu (1,1994).
ForSystÖ: Forschungen zur Systematischen & Ökumenischen Theologie; Gö.
ForTLing: Forum Theologiae Linguisticae; Bonn.
Fortunatae; revista canaria de filología; Tenerife. (1,1991).
ForumKT: Forum Katholische Theologie; Münster. 0178-1626.
FOTLit: Forms of OT Literature; GR, Eerdmans.
FraJudBei: Frankfurter Judaistische Beiträge: Fra.
FranBog: Franciscanum, ciencias del espíritu; Bogotá. 0120-1468.
FrancSt: Franciscan Studies; St. Bonaventure, NY. 0080-5459.
FranzSt: Franziskanische Studien; Pd.
FraTSt: Frankfurter Theologische Studien; Fra, S. Georgen.
FreibRu: Freiburger Rundbrief. ... christlich-jüdische Begegnung; FrB.

FreibTSt: Freiburger Theologische Studien; Freiburg/Br.
FrKf: Freikirchenforschung; Münster (1,1992).
FRL: Forschungen zur Religion und Literatur des Alten und NTs; Gö.
FrSZ[=FreibZ]: Freiburger Zeitschrift für Philosophie und Theologie; Fribourg.
Fundamentum; Basel ev. Akad. (1993).
FutUo: Il futuro dell'uomo; Firenze, Assoc. Teilhard. 0390-217X.
Ⓖ *Graece*; title/text in Greek.
GCS: Die Griechischen Christlichen Schriftsteller der ersten Jahrhunderte; B.
GdT: Giornale di Teologia; Brescia.
GeistL: Geist und Leben; Würzburg. 0016-5921.
Genava (archéologie, hist. art); Genève. 0072-0585.
GenLing: General Linguistics; University Park PA. 0016-6553.
GeogAnt: Geographia Antiqua; Firenze. 1121-8940 (1,1992).
Georgica: Jena/Tbilissi. 0232-4490.
GerefTTs: Gereformeerd Theologisch Tijdschrift; Kampen. 0016-8610.
Gerión, revista de Historia Antigua; Madrid, Univ. 0213-0181.
GGA: Göttingische Gelehrte Anzeigen; Göttingen. 0017-1549.
GItFg: Giornale italiano di filologia; Napoli. 0017-0461.
GLÉCS: (Comptes rendus) Groupe Linguistique d'Études Chamito-Sémitiques; Paris.
GLern: Glaube und Lernen; Gö.
GLeven: Geest en leven; Eindhoven.
Glotta: griech.-lat.; Gö. 0017-1298.
Gnomon; München. 0017-1417.
GöMiszÄg: Göttinger Miszellen ... zur ägyptologischen Diskussion; Göttingen. 0344-385X.
GöOrFor: Göttinger Orientforschungen; Würzburg.
GöTArb: Göttinger Theologische Arbeiten; Göttingen.
GraceTJ: Grace Theological Journal folded 12,2 (1991) p. 161.
GraecChrPrim: Graecitas Christianorum Primaeva; Nijmegen, van den Vegt.
Grail, ecumenical quarterly; Waterloo.
GreeceR: Greece and Rome; Oxford.

Greg[LA/Inf.]: Gregorianum; R, Pontificia Universitas Gregoriana [Liber Annualis / Informationes PUG].
GrOrTR: Greek Orthodox Theological Review; Boston. 0017-3894.
GrRByz: Greek, Roman and Byzantine Studies; CM. 0017-3916.
GrSinal: Grande Sinal; Petrópolis.
Gymn: Gymnasium; Heid. 0342-5231.
Ⓗ *(Neo-)hebraice*; (modern) Hebrew.
HaBeiA: Hamburger Beiträge zur Archäologie. 0341-3152.
HABES: Heidelberger Althistorische Beiträge und Epigraphische Studien: Stu.
Ḥadašôt arkeologiyôt Ⓗ [News]; J.
HalleB: Hallesche Beiträge zur Orientwissenschaft; Halle. 0233-2205.
Hamdard Islamicus [research]; Pakistan. 0250-7196.
Handes Amsorya [armen.]; Wien.
HarvSemMon/Mus: Harvard Semitic Monographs / Museum Series; CM.
HarvStClasPg: Harvard Studies in Classical Philology; CM.
HarvTR: The Harvard Theological Review; CM. 0017-8160.
HbAltW: Handbuch der Altertumswissenschaft; München.
HbAT/NT: Handbuch zum Alten/Neuen Testament; Tübingen.
HbDG: Handbuch der Dogmengeschichte; Freiburg/B.
HbDTG: Handbuch der Dogmen- und Theologiegeschichte; Göttingen.
HbOr: Handbuch der Orientalistik; Leiden.
HbRelG: Handbuch der Religionsgeschichte; Göttingen.
HbRwG: Handbuch Religionswissenschaftlicher Grundbegriffe; Stuttgart.
HDienst: Heiliger Dienst; Salzburg. 0017-9620.
HebAnR: Hebrew Annual Review; Columbus, Ohio State Univ.
HebSt: Hebrew Studies; Madison WI. 0146-4094.
Hekima; Nairobi.
Helikon (Tradizione e Cultura Classica, Univ. Messina); Roma.
Helinium; Stockholm.
Hellenika; Bochum. 0018-0084; ⇒ *Ell.*
Helmantica; Salamanca, Univ.
Henceforth; Lenox MA.

Henoch (ebraismo): Torino (Univ.).
Hephaistos, Theorie / Praxis Arch.; Ha.
HerdKor: Herder-Korrespondenz; Freiburg/Br. 0018-0645.
HerdTKom, NT: Herders Theologischer Kommentar zum NT; FrB.
Heresis; Carcassonne. 0758-3737.
Hermathena; Dublin. 0018-0750.
Hermes; Wiesbaden. 0018-0777.
HermUnT: Hermeneutische Untersuchungen zur Theologie; Tü. 0440-7180.
HervTS: Hervormde Teologiese Studies; Pretoria.
Hesperia: 1. (American School, Athens); Princeton. 0018-098X. -2. Roma. (1,1990).
Hethitica. Travaux édités; Lv.
HeythJ: Heythrop Journal; London. 0018-1196.
HistJb: Historisches Jahrbuch; Mü.
L'Histoire; Paris (151-161, 1992).
Historia; 1. Baden-Baden: 0018-2311; 2. Santiago/Chile, Univ. Católica.
History: Oxford. 0018-2648 (78,1993).
HistRel: History of Religions; Chicago. 0018-2710.
HLand[S]: Das Heilige Land (Deutscher Verein) Köln [(Schw. Verein); Luzern].
Hokhma; Lausanne. 0379-7465.
HolyL: Holy Land: J, OFM. 0333-4851 ⇒ **TerraS.**
Homoousios; Buenos Aires.
HomP: Homiletic and Pastoral Review; New York. 0018-4268.
HomRel: Homo religiosus (histoire des religions); Louvain-la-Neuve.
HorBibT: Horizons in Biblical Theology; Pittsburgh. 0195-9085.
Horizons (College Theology Society); Villanova PA. 0360-9669.
Hsientai Hsüehyüan (= Universitas); Taipei.
HSprF: Historische Sprachforschung; Göttingen. 0935-3518.
HUC|A: Hebrew Union College [+ Jewish Institute of Religion] Annual; Cincinnati.
Humanitas; 1. Brescia; 2. Tucuman.
HumT: Humanística e Teologia; Porto.
HWomenRel: History of women religious, news and notes; St. Paul MN.
Hypom: Hypomnemata; Göttingen, VR.

HZ: Historische Zeitschrift; München. 0018-2613.
IBMiss: International Bulletin of Missionary Research; Mp.
ICC: International Critical Commentary; Edinburgh.
IClasSt: Illinois Classical Studies; Urbana. 0363-1923.
IFA[O]: Institut Français d'Archéologie (Orientale, Le Caire / Beyrouth).
IglV: Iglesia Viva; Valencia/Madrid.
IJbFs: Internationale Jahresbibliographie der Festschriften; Osnabrück ➤ 2.
IJCR: International Journal of Comparative Religion; North York ON, Univ.
IkaZ: Internationale Katholische Zeitschrift [= Communio]; Rodenkirchen. 0341-8693.
IkiZ: Internationale kirchliche Zeitschrift; Bern. 0020-9252.
Immanuel (ecumenical); J. 0302-8127.
InBeitKultW/SprW/TS: Innsbrucker Beiträge zur Kulturwissenschaft / Sprachwissenschaft / Theologische Studien.
Index Jewish Studies ➤ RAMBI.
IndIranJ: Indo-Iranian Journal; (Canberra-) Leiden. 0019-7246.
IndJT: Indian Journal of Theology; Serampore.
IndMissR: Indian Missiological Review; Shillong.
IndogF: Indogermanische Forschungen; Berlin. 0019-7262.
IndTSt: Indian Theological Studies; Bangalore, St. Peter's.
InfPUG ➤ Gregoriana; R.
Interp: Interpretation; Richmond VA. 0020-9643.
IntJNaut: International Journal of Nautical Archaeology L/NY. 0305-7445.
IntJPhR: International Journal for the Philosophy of Religion; Haag.
IntJSport: International Journal of the history of sport; London.
IntRMiss: International Review of Mission; London. 0020-8582.
Iran; London. 0578-6967.
IrAnt: Iranica Antiqua; Leiden.
Iraq; London. 0021-0889.
IrBSt: Irish Biblical Studies; Belfast. 0268-6112.

Irén: Irénikon; Chevetogne. 0021-0978.
IrTQ: Irish Theological Quarterly; Maynooth. 0021-1400.
Islam, Der: Berlin. 0021-1818.
Islamochristiana; Roma, Pontificio Istituto di Studi Arabi. 0392-7288.
IsrEJ: Israel Exploration Journal; Jerusalem. 0021-2059.
IsrJBot/Zool: Israel Journal of Botany 0021-213X / Zoology 0021-2210: J.
IsrLawR: Israel Law Review; Jerusalem. 0021-2237.
IsrMusJ: Israel Museum Journal; Jerusalem.
IsrNumJ[SocB]: Israel Numismatic Journal, J [Society Bulletin: TA].
IsrOrSt: Israel Oriental Studies; Tel Aviv.
Istina; Paris. 0021-2423.
Italoellenika, rivista di cultura greco-moderna; Napoli. (2,1989).
IVRA (Jura); Napoli.
IZBG ➤ 778: Internationale Zeitschriftenschau für Bibelwissenschaft und Grenzgebiete; Pd. 0074-9745.
IZT: Internationale Zeitschrift für Theologie [= Concilium deutsch].
JAAR: Journal, American Academy of Religion; Atlanta. 0002-7189.
JACiv: Journal of Ancient Civilizations: Chang-chun, Jilin (4, 1989).
JAfAL: Journal of Afroasiatic Languages; Leiden. 0894-9824 (3,1991).
JAMin: Journal of the American Academy of Ministry (1,1992: BtS 150, 109).
J[News]AmEg: Journal [Newsletter] of the American Research Center in Egypt [ARCE]; Winona Lake IN.
JAmScAff: ➤ PerScCF.
JANES: Journal of the Ancient Near Eastern Society; NY, Jewish Theol. Sem. 0010-2016.
JanLing[Pract]: Janua Linguarum [Series Practica]; Haag / Paris.
JAOS: Journal of the American Oriental Society; NHv. 0003-0279.
JapJRelSt: Japanese Journal of Religious Studies; Nagoya.
JapRel: Japanese Religions; Tokyo.
JArchSc: Journal of Archaeological Science; London/New York.
JAs: Journal Asiatique; P. 0021-762X.

JAsAf: Journal of Asian and African Studies; Toronto / Leiden.

JaTop: Journal of Ancient Topography; Rome.

Jb: Jahrbuch [Heid, Mainz...]; Jaarbericht.

JbAC: Jahrbuch für Antike und Christentum; Münster im Westfalen.

JbBerlMus: Jahrbücher der Berliner Museen; Berlin.

JbBTh: Jahrbuch für biblische Theologie; Neukirchen.

JbEOL: Jaarbericht van het Vooraziatisch-Egyptisch Genootschap Ex Oriente Lux; Leiden.

JBEq: Journal of Biblical Equality; Lakewood CO.

JbEvHL: Jahrbuch des Deutschen Evangelischen Instituts für Altertumswissenschaft des Heiligen Landes; Firth.

JBL: Journal of Biblical Literature; Atlanta. 0021-9231.

JBlackT: Journal of Black Theology; Atteridgeville SAf.

JbLtgH: Jahrbuch für Liturgik und Hymnologie; Kassel.

JbNumG: Jahrbuch für Numismatik und Geldgeschichte; Regensburg.

JbÖsByz: Jahrbuch der Österreichischen Byzantinistik; W. 0378-8660.

JBQ: Jewish Bible Quarterly (< Dor le-Dor); Jerusalem. 0792-3910.

JbRelW: Jahrbuch für Religionswissenschaft und Theologie der Religionen; FrB (1,1993; 3-451-23267-7; DM 48: TLZ 119,973].

JChrB: Journal of the Christian Brethren Research Fellowship; Wellington NZ.

JChrEd: Journal of Christian Education; Sydney. 0021-9657.

JCS: Journal of Cuneiform Studies; CM. 0022-0256.

JDharma: Journal of Dharma; Bangalore.

JdU: Judentum und Umwelt; Frankfurt/M.

JEA: Journal of Egyptian Archaeology; London. 0307-5133.

JEarlyC: Journal of Early Christian Studies; Baltimore. 1067-6341 (1, 1993) [< SecC].

JEcuSt: Journal of Ecumenical Studies; Ph, Temple Univ. 0022-0558.

Jeevadhara; Alleppey, Kerala.

JEH: Journal of Ecclesiastical History; Cambridge. 0022-0469.

JEmpirT: Journal of empirical theology; Kampen.

JerónMg: Institución S. Jerónimo, estudios y monografías; Valencia.

JESHO: Journal of Economic and Social History of the Orient; Leiden.

JEvTS: Journal of the Evangelical Theological Society; Lynchburg VA. 0360-8808.

JewishH: Jewish History; Leiden. 0334-701X.

JFemR: Journal of Feminist Studies in Religion; Chico CA. 8755-4178.

JField: Journal of Field Archaeology; Boston, Univ. 0093-4690.

JGlass: Journal of Glass Studies; Corning, NY. 0075-4250.

JGraceEv: Journal of the Grace Evangelical Society; Roanoke TX (4,1991).

JHispT: Journal of Hispanic/Latino theology; ColMn (1,1993).

JHistId: Journal of the History of Ideas; Ph, Temple Univ. 0022-5037.

JHMR: Judaica, Hermencutics, Mysticism, and Religion; Albany, SUNY.

JhÖsA: Jahreshefte des Österreichischen Archäologischen Institutes; Wien. 0078-3579.

JHS: Journal of Hellenic Studies; London. 0075-4269.

JIndEur: Journal of Indo-European Studies; Hatticsburg, Miss.

JIntdenom: Journal, Interdenominational Theological Center; Atlanta.

JIntdis: Journal of the Society for Interdisciplinary History; CM, MIT.

JJC: Jésus et Jésus-Christ; Paris.

JJS: Journal of Jewish Studies; Oxford. 0022-2097.

JJTht: Journal of Jewish Thought and Philosophy (1,1991).

JJurPap: Journal of Juristic Papyrology; Warszawa.

JLawA: Jewish Law Annual (Oxford).

JMeditArch: Journal of Mediterranean Archeol.; Sheffield. 0952-7648.

JMedvRenSt: Journal of Medieval & Renaissance Studies; Durham NC.

JMoscPatr: [Engl.] Journal of the Moscow Patriarchate; Moscow.

JNES: Journal of Near Eastern Studies; Chicago, Univ. 0022-2968.
JNWS: Journal of Northwest Semitic Languages; Leiden.
jNsu/jOsu: JStNT supp. 0143-5108 / JStOT supp. 0309-0787: Shf.
JOrAf: Journal of Oriental and African Studies; Athens (3,1991s).
JPentec: Journal of Pentecostal Theology; Shf (1,1992).
JPersp: Jerusalem perspective.
JPrehRel: Journal of Prehistoric Religion; Göteborg. 0283-8486.
JPseud: Journal for the Study of the Pseudepigrapha; Sheffield. 0951-8207.
JPsy&C/Jud/T: Journal of Psychology & Christianity; Farmington Hills MI. 0733-4273 / ... & Judaism; NY / ... & Theology; Rosemead CA.
JQR: Jewish Quarterly Review (Ph, Dropsie Univ.); WL. 0021-6682.
JRadRef: Journal from the Radical Reform.
JRArch: Journal of Roman Archaeology; AA.
JRAS: Journal of the Royal Asiatic Society; London.
JRefJud: Journal of Reform Judaism; NY. 0149-712X.
JRel: Journal of Religion; Chicago. 0022-4189.
JRelAf: Journal of Religion in Africa; Leiden. 0022-4200.
JRelEth: Journal of Religion and Ethics; ND (ᴱRutgers). 0384-9694.
JRelHealth: The Journal of Religion and Health; New York.
JRelHist: Journal of Religious History; Sydney, Univ. 0022-4227.
JRelPsyR: Journal of Religion and Psychical Research; Bloomfield CT.
JRelSt: Journal of Religious Studies; Cleveland.
JRelTht: Journal of Religious Thought; Washington DC.
JRelTInf: Journal of Religious and Theological Information; Binghamton NY (1,1993).
JRit: Journal of ritual studies; Pittsburgh/Waterloo ON.
JRMilit: Journal of Roman Military Equipment Studies; Newcastle. 0961-3684 (1,1990).

JRomArch: Journal of Roman Archaeology: Ann Arbor MI (4,1991).
JRPot: Journal of Roman Pottery Studies: Oxford.
JRS: Journal of Roman Studies; London. 0075-4358.
JSArm: Journal of the Society for Armenian Studies; LA.
JSav: Journal des Savants: Paris.
JScStR: Journal for the Scientific Study of Religion; NHv. 0021-8294.
JSemant: Journal of Semantics; Oxford. 0167-5133.
JSemit: Journal for Semitics/Tydskrif vir Semitistiek; Pretoria, Unisa.
JSHZ: Jüdische Schriften aus hellenistischer und römischer Zeit; Gütersloh.
JSS: Journal of Semitic Studies; Manchester. 0022-4480.
JSStEg: Journal of the Society for the Study of Egyptian Antiquities [ipsi SSEA]; Toronto. 0383-9753.
JSt[HL]JTht: Jerusalem Studies in [Hebrew literature] Jewish Thought; J.
JStJud: Journal for the Study of Judaism in the Persian, Hellenistic, & Roman Periods; Leiden. 0047-2212.
JStNT/OT: Journal for the Study of NT/OT; Sheffield, Univ. 0142-064X/0309-0892. ⇒ jN/Osu. 0143-5108/ 0309-0787.
JStRel: Journal for the study of religion [formerly Religion in Southern Africa]; Pietermaritzburg, Natal.
JTS: Journal of Theological Studies; Oxford/London. 0022-5185.
JTSAfr: Journal of Theology for Southern Africa; Rondebosch.
JTrTL: Journal of Translation and Textlinguistics; Dallas (ex-OPTAT).
Judaica: Zürich. 0022-572X.
Judaism; NY. 0022-5762.
JudTSt: Judaistische Texte und Studien; Hildesheim.
JWarb: Journal of the Warburg and Courtauld Institutes; London.
JwHist: Jewish History; Haifa.
JWomen&R: Journal of Women and Religion; Berkeley.
JyskR ⇒ RJysk.
Kadmos; Berlin. 0022-7498.
Kairos 1. (Religionswiss.); Salzburg. 0022-7757. - 2. Guatemala 1014-9341.

Karawane (Die); Ludwigsburg.

Karthago (archéologie africaine); P.

KAT: Kommentar zum AT: Gütersloh.

KatBlät: Katechetische Blätter; Mü.

KatKenk: Katorikku Kenkyu < Shingaku; Tokyo, Sophia. 0387-3005.

KBW: Katholisches Bibelwerk; Stu [bzw. Österreich, Schweiz].

KeK: Kritisch-exegetischer Kommentar über das NT; Göttingen.

KerDo: Kerygma und Dogma; Göttingen. 0023-0707.

KerkT: Kerk en Theologie; Wageningen. 0165-2346.

Kernos, religion grecque; Liège.

Kerux; Escondido CA. 0888-8513.

Kerygma (on Indian missions); Ottawa. 0023-0693.

KGaku: ❶ Kirisutokyo Gaku (Christian Studies); Tokyo, 0387-6810.

KingsTR: King's College Theological Review; London.

KirSef: ❶ Kiryat Sefer, Bibliographical Quarterly; Jerusalem, Nat.-Univ. Libr. 0023-1851. ➤ Rambi.

KIsr: Kirche und Israel, theologische Zeitschrift; Neukirchen. 0179-7239.

KkKS: Konfessionskundliche und Kontroverstheologische Studien; Paderborn.

KkMat: Konfessionskundliches Institut, Materialdienst; Bensheim.

KleinÄgTexte: Kleine ägyptische Texte; Würzburg.

Kler: ❶ Klēronomia; Thessaloniki.

Klio: Berlin. 0075-6334.

KLK: Katholisches Leben und Kirchenreform im Zeitalter der Glaubensspaltung; Münster.

KölnFG: Kölner Jahrbuch für Vor- und Frühgeschichte; B. 0075-6512.

KomBeiANT: Kommentare und Beiträge zum Alten und N.T.; Düsseldorf.

Kratylos (Sprachwissenschaft); Wsb.

KřestR [TPřil]: Křest'anská revue [Theologická Příloha]; Praha.

Kristu Jyoti; Bangalore (8,1992).

KTB/KUB: Keilschrifttexte/urkunden aus Boghazköi; B, Mann/Akademie.

Ktema; Strasbourg, CEDEX.

KuGAW: Kulturgeschichte der Antiken Welt; Mainz.

KvinnerA: Kvinner i arkeologi i Norge; Bergen, Historisk Museum.

KZg: Kirchliche Zeitgeschichte; Gö.

LA: Liber Annuus; J. 0081-8933. ➤ **SBF.**

Labeo, diritto romano; N. 0023-6462.

LAeg: Lingua aegyptia; Gö/LA.

Landas: Journal of Loyola School of Theology; Manila,

Language; Baltimore. 0097-8507.

LAPO: Littératures Anciennes du Proche-Orient; Paris, Cerf. 0459-5831.

Lateranum; R, Pont. Univ. Lateranense.

Latomus (Et. latines); Bru. 0023-8856.

Laur: Laurentianum; R. 0023-902X.

LavalTP: Laval Théologique et Philosophique; Québec.

Laverna, Wirtschafts- und Sozialgeschichte; St. Katharinen. 0938-5835.

LDiv: Lectio Divina; Paris, Cerf.

LebSeels: Lebendige Seelsorge; Wü/FrB.

LebZeug: Lebendiges Zeugnis; Paderborn. 0023-9941.

Lěšonénu (Hebrew Language); J.

Levant (archeology); London.

LexMA: Lexikon des Mittelalters; Mü/Z ➤ 596.

LexTQ: Lexington [KY] Theological Quarterly. 0024-1628.

LFrühJ: Literatur und Religion des Frühjudentums; Wü/Gü.

LGB: Lexikon des Gesamten Buchwesens²; Stu ➤ 749.

LIAO: Lettre d'Information Archéologie Orientale; Valbonne, CNRS. 0750-6279.

LIMC: Lexicon iconographicum mythologiae classicae; Z. ➤ 750.

LimnOc: Limnology & Oceanography; AA.

LinceiR/Scavi/BClas: Accademia Nazionale dei Lincei. Rendiconti / Notizie degli Scavi / Bollettino Classico. 0391-8270: Roma.

LingBib: Linguistica Biblica; Bonn. 0342-0884.

Lire la Bible; P, Cerf. 0588-2257.

Listening: Romeoville IL.

LitCu: Literary currents in biblical interpretation; Louisville.

LitLComp: Literary and Linguistic Computing; Ox. 0268-1145.

LitTOx: Literature and theology; Ox.

LivLight: The Living Light (US Cath. Conf.); Huntington. 0024-5275.

LivWord: Living Word; Alwaye, Kerala.

L^m: lire (ital.) × 1000.
LoB: Leggere oggi la Bibbia; Brescia, Queriniana.
LogosPh: Logos, philos.; Santa Clara.
Logotherapie; Bremen.
LOrA: Langues orientales anciennes; Lv. 0987-7738.
LPastB: Lettura pastorale della Bibbia: Bo.
LStClas: London studies in classical philology [8, Corolla Londiniensis 1]; Amst.
Ltg.Jb: Liturgisches Jahrbuch; Münster/Wf.
Lucentum; prehistoria, arqueología e historia antigua; Alicante, Univ.
LumenK: Lumen; København.
LumenVr: Lumen; Vitoria.
LumièreV: Lumière et Vie; Lyon. 0024-7359.
Luther [Jb]; Ha. 0340-6210. - [Gö].
LuthMon: Lutherische Monatshefte; Hamburg. 0024-7618.
LuthTJ: Lutheran Theological Journal; North Adelaide, S. Australia.
LuthTKi: Lutherische Theologie und Kirche; Oberursel. 0170-3846.
LuthQ: Lutheran Quarterly; Ridgefield NJ.
LuxB: Lux Biblica; R, Ist. B. Evangelico (1,1990).
LVitae: Lumen Vitae; Bru. 0024-7324.
LvSt: Louvain Studies.
Ⓜ magyar: *hungarice*, en hongrois.
ᴹ: *mentio, de eo*; author commented upon.
Maarav; WL. 0149-5712.
MadMitt [B/F]: DAI Madrider Mitteilungen [Beiträge/Forschungen]; Mainz.
MAGA: Mitteilungen zur Alten Geschichte und Archäologie; B.
Maia (letterature classiche); Messina. 0025-0538.
MaimS: Maimonidean Studies; NY, Yeshiva Univ./KTAV (1,1990).
Manresa (espiritualidad ignaciana); Azpeitia-Guipúzcoa.
Manuscripta; St. Louis.
Mara: tijdschrift voor feminisme en theologie.
MarbJbT: Marburger Jahrbuch Theologie: Marburg (4,1992).
MaRg: Mitteilungen für Anthropologie und Religionsgeschichte; Saarbrücken.
MARI: Mari, Annales de Recherches Interdisciplinaires; Paris.

Marianum; Roma.
MariolSt: Mariologische Studien; Essen.
MarŠipri; Boston, Baghdad ASOR.
MarSt: Marian Studies; Washington.
Masaq, al-, Arabo-Islamic Mediterranean studies; Leeds (1,1988).
Masca: Museum Applied Science Center for Archaeology Journal; Ph.
MasSt: (SBL) Masoretic Studies; Atlanta.
MastJ: Master's Seminary Journal; Sun Valley, CA (1,1990).
MatDClas: Materiali e discussioni per l'analisi dei testi classici; Pisa. 0392-6338.
MatKonfInst: Materialdienst des konfessionskundlichen Instituts; Bensheim.
MatPomWykBib: Materiały pomocznicze do wykładów z biblistyki; Lublin.
Mayéutica; Marcilla (Navarra).
MDAV: Mitteilungen des Deutschen Archäologen-Verbandes; Münster.
MDOG: Mitteilungen der Deutschen Orientgesellschaft; B. 0342-118X.
Meander; Wsz Akad. 0025-6285.
Med: Mededelingen [Amst,]; Meddelander.
MeditArch: Mediterranean Archaeology; Sydney. 1030-8482.
MeditHR: Mediterranean historical review Tel Aviv Univ.; L. 0951-8967.
MeditQ: Mediterranean Quarterly; Durham NC.
MedvHum: Mediaevalia & Humanistica (Denton, N. Texas U.); Towa.
MedvSt: Mediaeval Studies; Toronto. 0076-5872.
MÉF-A [= **MélÉcFrR**]: Mélanges de l'École Française de Rome/Athènes, Antiquité. 0223-5102.
MélSR: Mélanges de Science Religieuse; Lille.
Mém: Mémoires → AIBL ... AcSc, T...
Menora: Jahrbuch deutsch-jüdische Geschichte; Mü. (1,1990).
MenQR: Mennonite Quarterly Review; Goshen, Ind.
Mensaje; Chile.
Meroit: Meroitic Newsletter / Bulletin d'informations méroitiques: Paris, CNRS.
MESA: Middle East Studies Association (Bulletin); Tucson, Univ. AZ.
MesCiv: Mesopotamian Civilization; WL.
MesopK: Mesopotamia: København.
MesopT: Mesopotamia; T (pub. F).

Mesorot [Language-tradition resear-ches]; Jerusalem.
MESt: Middle Eastern Studies; L.
Metanoia; social and cultural issues; Praha, Broż.
MetB: Metropolitan Museum Bul-letin; New York. 0026-1521.
MethT: Method and theory in the study of religion; Toronto.
Mêtis, Anthropologie grecque; P.
Mg: Monograph (-ie, -fia); → CBQ, SBL, SNTS.
MgANE: Monographs on the Ancient Near East; 1. Leiden; 2. Malibu.
MGraz: Mitteilungen der archäologi-schen Gesellschaft; Graz.
MgStB: Monographien und Studienbü-cher; Wu/Giessen.
MHistOv: Memorias de historia antigua; Oviedo, Univ. (13s,1992s).
MHT: Materialien zu einem hethitischen Thesaurus; Heidelberg.
MiDAI-A/K/M/R: Mitteilungen des Deutschen Archäologischen Insti-tuts: Athen / Kairo / Madrid / Rom 0342-1287.
MidAmJT: Mid-America Journal of Theology: Orange City, Iowa.
Mid-Stream, Disciples of Christ; In-dianapolis. – Midstream (Jewish); NY. 0026-332X.
Mikael; Paraná, Arg. (Seminario).
MilltSt: Milltown Studies (philos-ophy, theology); Dublin. 0332-1428.
Minerva: 1. filología clásica; Vallado-lid; 2. (incorporating Archaeology Today); L (1,1990).
Minos (Filología Egea); Salamanca. 0544-3733.
MiscCom: Miscelánea Comillas, estu-dios históricos; M. 0210-9522.
MiscFranc: Miscellanea Francescana; Roma (OFM Conv.).
Mishkan, a theological forum on Jewish evangelism; Jerusalem.
MissHisp: Missionalia hispanica; Ma-drid, CSIC Inst. E. Flores.
Missiology; Scottdale PA.
Mitt: Mitteilungen [Gö Septuaginta; Berli-ner Museen ...]; → MiDAI.
Mnemosyne, Bibliotheca Classica Ba-tava [+ Supplements]; Leiden.

ModChm: Modern Churchman; Leo-minster, Herf.
ModJud: Modern Judaism; Balti-more.
ModT: Modern Theology; Oxford.
MonSt: Monastic Studies; Montreal. 0026-9190.
MondeB: Le Monde de la Bible: 1. P. 0154-9049. – 2. Genève.
Monde Copte, Le: 0399-905X.
MondoB: Il mondo della Bibbia; T-Leumann, LDC (3,11-15: 1992).
Month; London. 0027-0172.
Moralia; Madrid.
MsME: Manuscripts of the Middle East; Leiden. 0920-0401.
MSVO: Materialien zu den frühen Schrift-zeugnissen des Vorderen Orients: B.
MüÄgSt: Münchener Ägyptologische Stu-dien; München/Berlin.
MüBeit[T]PapR: Münchener Beiträge zur [Theologie] Papyruskunde und antiken Rechtsgeschichte; München.
MünstHand: Münsterische Beiträge zur Antiken Handelsgeschichte; St. Katharinen. 0722-4532.
MüStSprW: Münchener Studien zur Sprachwissenschaft; Mü. → AOtt.
MüTZ: Münchener Theologische Zeitschrift; St. Ottilien. 0580-1400.
Mus: Le Muséon; LvN. 0771-6494.
MusHelv: Museum Helveticum; Basel.
MUSJ: Mélanges de l'Université Saint-Joseph (rediviva); Beyrouth [51 (1990): 2-7214-5000-X].
MuslimW: Muslim World; Hartford.
MusTusc: Museum Tusculanum; København. 0107-8062.
MuzTA: ⊕ Muzeon Ha-Areṣ NS; TA.
NABU: Nouvelles assyriologiques brè-ves et utilitaires; 0989-5671.
NachGö: Nachrichten der Akademie der Wissenschaften; Göttingen.
NarAzAfr: ⊕ Narody: Peoples of Asia and Africa; Moskva.
NatGeog: National Geographic; Wash-ington. 0027-9358.
NatGrac: Naturaleza y Gracia; S.
NBL: Neues Bibel-Lexikon; Z → 598.
NBlackfr: New Blackfriars; London. 0028-4289.
NCent: The New Century Bible Com-mentary (reedited); Edinburgh / GR.

NChrIsr: Nouvelles Chrétiennes d'I-
sraël: Jérusalem.
NDizTB: Nuovo Dizionario Teol.B ➤ 599.
NduitsGT: Nederduits-Gereformeerde
Teologiese Tydskrif; Kaapstad. 0028-
2006.
NEA: The Near East in Antiquity [1-
3, German projects; 4, final issue];
Amman (3,1992).
NedTTs: Nederlands Theologisch Tijd-
schrift; Wageningen. 0028-212X.
Neotestamentica; Pretoria; NTWerk.
Nestor, Classical Antiquity, Indiana
Univ.; Bloomington. 0028-2812.
NesTR: Near East School of Theol-
ogy Review; Beirut.
News: Newsletter: Anat[olian Stud-
ies; NHv]; Targ[umic and Cognate
Studies; Toronto]; ASOR [Balti-
more]; Ug[aritic Studies; Calgary];
➤ JAmEg.
NewTR: New theology review: Ch.
0896-4297.
NHC: Nag Hammadi Codices, Egypt
UAR Facsimile edition; Leiden.
NHL/S: Nag Hammadi Library in English
/ Studies; Leiden.
NHLW: Neues Handbuch der Literatur-
wissenschaft: Wsb, Athenaion.
Nicolaus (teol. ecumenico-patristica);
Bari.
NICOT: New International Commentary
OT; Grand Rapids, Eerdmans.
NigJT: The Nigerian Journal of Theol-
ogy; Owerri.
NIGT: New International Greek Testa-
ment Commentary; Exeter/GR.
NJBC: New Jerome Biblical Commentary
➤ .....
NOrb: NT & Orbis Antiquus; FrS/Gö.
NorJ: Nordisk Judaistik.
NorTTs: Norsk Teologisk Tidsskrift;
Oslo. 0029-2176.
NoTr: Notes on Translation; Dallas.
NOxR: New Oxford Review; Berkeley.
NRT: Nouvelle Revue Théologique;
Tournai. 0029-4845.
NS [NF]: Nova series, nouvelle série.
NSys: Neue Zeitschrift für systemati-
sche Theologie und Religionsphi-
losophie; Berlin. 0028-3517.
NT: Novum Testamentum; Leiden.
0048-1009.

NTAbh: Neutestamentliche Abhandlungen.
[N.F.]; Münster.
NTAbs: New Testament Abstracts;
CM. 0028-6877.
NTDt: Das Neue Testament deutsch; Gö.
NTS: New Testament Studies; C.
NTTools: Leiden. 0077-8842.
NubChr: Nubia Christiana; Wsz.
Nubica; Köln (1,1990).
NumC: Numismatic Chronicle; Lon-
don. 0078-2696.
Numen (History of Religions); Leiden.
Numisma; Madrid. 0029-0015.
NumZ: Numismatische Zeitschrift;
Wien. 0250-7838.
NuovaUm: Nuova Umanità; Roma.
NVFr/Z: Nova et Vetera; 1. Fribourg,
Suisse. / 2. Zamora.
NZMissW: Neue Zeitschrift für
Missionswissenschaft; Beckenried,
Schweiz. 0028-3495. ➤ NSys.
ObnŽiv: Obnovljeni Život; Zagreb.
OBO: Orbis Biblicus et Orientalis: FrS/Gö.
OEIL: Office d'édition et d'impression du
livre; Paris.
ÖkRu: Ökumenische Rundschau;
Stuttgart. 0029-8654.
ÖkTbKom, NT: Ökumenischer Taschen-
buchkommentar; Gütersloh / Würzburg.
ÖsterrBibSt: Österreichische Biblische Stu-
dien; Klosterneuburg.
Offa, ... Frühgeschichte; Neumünster.
0078-3714.
Ohio ➤ JRelSt: Cleveland.
OIAc/P/C: Oriental Institute Acquisitions
/ Publications / Communications; Ch.
OikBud: Oikumene, historia; Budapest.
Olivo (El), diálogo jud.-cr.: Madrid.
OLZ: Orientalistische Literaturzei-
tung; Berlin. 0030-5383.
OMRO: Oudheidkundige Mededelin-
gen, Rijksmuseum Oudheden; Leiden
OmT: Omnis Terra [English; also
French, Spanish ed.]; Roma (27,1993).
OneInC: One in Christ (Catholic Ecu-
menical); Turvey, Bedfordshire.
OnsGErf: Ons Geestelijk Erf; Antwer-
pen. ➤ GLeven.
OpAth/Rom: Opuscula Atheniensia / Ro-
mana; Swedish Inst.
OPTAT ➤ JTrTL.
Opus, storia economica (Siena); R.
Or: ➤ Orientalia; Roma.

OraLab: Ora et Labora; Roriz, Portugal.

OrAnt[Coll]: Oriens Antiquus [Collectio]; Roma.

OrBibLov: Orientalia et Biblica Lovaniensia; Lv.

OrChr: Oriens Christianus; Wsb.

OrChrPer[An]: Orientalia Christiana Periodica [Analecta]; R, Pontificium Inst. Orientalium Stud. 0030-5375.

OrExp: L'Orient express, informations archéologiques. (1,1991).

OrGand: Orientalia Gandensia; Gent.

Orientalia (Ancient Near East); Rome, Pontifical Biblical Institute. 0030-5367.

Orientierung; Zürich. 0030-5502.

Orient-Japan: Orient, Near Eastern Studies Annual; Tokyo. 0743-3851; cf. ❹ Oriento. 0030-5219.

Origins; Washington Catholic Conference. 0093-609X.

OrJog: Orientasi, Annual ... Philosophy and Theology; Jogjakarta.

OrLovPer[An]: Orientalia Lovaniensia Periodica [Analecta]; Lv. 0085-4522.

OrMod: Oriente Moderno; Napoli. 0030-5472.

OrOcc: Oriente-Occidente. Buenos Aires, Univ. Salvador.

OrPast: Orientamenti Pastorali; Roma.

Orpheus: 1. Catania; 2. -Thracia; Sofya (1,1990).

OrSuec: Orientalia Suecana; Uppsala.

OrtBuc: Ortodoxia; Bucureşti.

OrthF: Orthodoxes Forum; München.

OrTrad: Oral Tradition; Columbia. MO.

OrVars: Orientalia Varsoviensia; Wsz. 0860-5785.

OstkSt: Ostkirchliche Studien; Würzburg. 0030-6487.

Ostraka, rivista di antichità; Napoli. 1122-259X (1,1992).

OTAbs: Old Testament Abstracts; Washington. 0364-8591.

OTEssays: Old Testament essays; Pretoria. 1010-9919.

OTS: Oudtestamentische Studiën; Leiden. 0169-9555.

OTWerkSuidA: Die Ou Testamentiese Werkgemeenskap Suid-Afrika; Pretoria.

OvBTh: Overtures to Biblical Theology; Philadelphia.

Overview; Ch St. Thomas More Asn.

OxJArch: Oxford Journal of Archaeology; Ox. 0262-5253.

❿: *polonice,* in Polish.

p./pa./pl.: page(s)/paperback/plate(s).

PAAR: Proceedings of the American Academy for Jewish Research; Ph.

Pacifica: Australian theological studies; Melbourne Brunswick East.

PacTR: Pacific theological review: SanAnselmo, SF Theol.Sem.

Palaeohistoria; Haarlem.

PalCl: Palestra del Clero; Rovigo.

PaléOr: Paléorient; Paris.

PalSh: ❻ Palestinski Sbornik; Leningrad.

PapBritSR: Papers of the British School at Rome; London.

PAPS: Proceedings of the American Philosophical Society; Philadelphia.

PapTAbh: Papyrologische Texte und Abhandlungen; Bonn, Habelt.

PapyrolColon: Papyrologica Coloniensia; Opladen. 0078-9410.

Parabola; New York.

Paradigms; Louisville KY.

ParOr: Parole de l'Orient; Kaslik.

ParPass: Parola del Passato; Napoli. 0031-2355.

ParSpV: Parola, Spirito e Vita; Bologna.

ParVi: Parole di Vita; T-Leumann.

PasT: Pastoraltheologie; Göttingen.

PastScP: Pastoral / Sciences pastorales; psych.sociol.théol.; Ottawa.

Patr&M: Patristica et Mediaevalia; BA.

PatrByz: Patristic and Byzantine Review; Kingston NY. 0737-738X.

PatrMedRen: Proceedings of the Patristic, Mediaeval and Renaissance Conference; Villanova PA.

PatrStudT: Patristische Studien und Texte; B. 0553-4003.

PBtScB: Petite bibliothèque des sciences bibliques; Paris, Desclée.

PenséeC: La Pensée Catholique; P.

PEQ: Palestine Exploration Quarterly; London. 0031-0328.

PerAz: Peredneaziatskij Sbornik; Moskva.

Persica: Leiden.

PerScCF: Perspectives on Science and Christian Faith (replacing

JAmScAff since 39,1987); Ipswich MA. 0892-2675.
PerspRef: Perspectives, a journal of Reformed thought (7,1992).
PerspRelSt: Perspectives in Religious Studies (Baptist); Danville VA.
PerspT: Perspectiva Teológica; Belo Horizonte.
Pg/Ph: philolog-/philosoph-.
PgOrTb: Philologia Orientalis; Tbilisi. Phase; Barcelona.
PhilipSa: Philippiniana Sacra; Manila.
Philologus; B. 0031-7985.
Phoenix; Toronto. 0031-8299.
PhoenixEOL; Leiden. 0031-8329.
Phronema: Greek Orthodox; Sydney.
Phronesis; Assen. 0031-8868.
PhTh: Philosophy and Theology; Milwaukee, Marquette Univ. [7 (1992) 0-87462-559-9].
Pneuma, Pentecostal; Pasadena.
PoeT: Poetics Today; Durham NC, Duke Univ. 0333-5372 (14,1993).
PoinT: Le Point Théologique; P.
Polin: Polish-Jewish Studies; Oxford.
PontAcc, R/Mem: Atti della Pontificia Accademia Romana di Archeologia, Rendiconti/Memorie; Vaticano.
PrPeo [< *CleR*]: Priests and People; L.
PracArch: Prace Archeologiczne; Kraków, Univ. 0083-4300.
PraehZ: Praehistorische Zeitschrift; Berlin. 0079-4848.
PrakT: Praktische theologie; Zwolle.
PraktArch: ℗ Praktika, Archeology Society Athens.
PrCambPg: Proceedings of the Cambridge Philological Soc. 0068-6735.
PrCTSAm: Proceedings Catholic Theological Society of America; Villanova.
PredikOT/NT: De Prediking van het OT / van het NT; Nijkerk.
Premislia Christiana; Przemyśl.
Presbyteri; Trento.
Presbyterion; St. Louis.
PresPast: Presenza Pastorale; Roma.
Pre/Text, rhetorical theory; Arlington TX. 0731-0714 (13,1992).
PrêtreP: Prêtre et Pasteur; Montréal. 0385-8307.
Priest (The); Washington.
PrincSemB: Princeton Seminary Bulletin; Princeton NJ.

PrIrB: Proceedings of the Irish Biblical Association; Dublin.
Prism; St. Paul MN.
ProbHistRel: Problèmes de l'Histoire des Religions; Bruxelles (1,1990).
ProcClas: Proceedings of the Classical Association; London.
ProcCom: Proclamation Commentaries; Ph.
ProcGLM: Proceedings of the Eastern Great Lakes and Midwest Bible Societies; Buffalo.
ProcIsrAc: Proceedings of the Israel Academy of Sciences & Humanities; Jerusalem.
ProEc: Pro Ecclesia; Northfield MN (2,1993).
Prooftexts; Baltimore.
PrOrChr: Proche-Orient Chrétien; Jérusalem. 0032-9622.
Prot: Protestantesimo; R. 0033-1767.
ProtokB: Protokolle zur Bibel; Klosterneuburg, ÖsKBW. (1,1992).
Proyección (mundo actual); Granada.
ProySal: Proyecto Centro Salesiano de Estudios; Buenos Aires. (4,1992).
PrPg/PrehS: Proceedings of the Philological / Prehistoric Society; Cambridge.
PrSemArab: Proceedings of the Seminar for Arabian Studies; London.
Prudentia (Hellenistic, Roman); Auckland.
PrzOr[Tom/Pow]: Przegląd Orientalistyczny, Wsz: [Tomisticzny; Wsz / Powszechny, Kraków].
PT: Philosophy/Theology: Milwaukee, Marquette Univ.
PubTNEsp: Publicaciones de la Facultad Teológica del Norte de España; Burgos.
PUF: Presses Universitaires de France; P.
Qadm: Qadmoniot ℍ Quarterly of Dept. of Antiquities; Jerusalem.
Qardom, ℍ mensuel pour la connaissance du pays; Jerusalem, Ariel.
QDisp: Quaestiones Disputatae; FrB.
Qedem: Monographs of the Institute of Archaeology: Jerusalem.
QLtg: Questions Liturgiques; Lv.
QRMin: Quarterly Review [for] Ministry; Nv. 0270-9287.
QuadCatan / Chieti: Quaderni, Catania / Chieti; Univ.
QuadSemant: Quaderni di Semantica; Bologna.

QuadSemit: Quaderni di Semitistica; Firenze.

QuadUrb: Quaderni Urbinati di Cultura Classica; Urbino. 0033-4987.

Quaerendo (Low Countries: Manuscripts and Printed Books); Amst.

QuatreF: Les quatre fleuves: Paris.

QüestVidaCr: Qüestions de Vida Cristiana; Montserrat.

QumC: Qumran Chronicle; Kraków.

Ⓡ: *russice*, in Russian.

ᴿ: *recensio*, book-review(er).

RAC: Reallexikon für Antike und Christentum; Stuttgart ⇥ 600.

Radiocarbon; NHv, Yale. 0033-8222.

RAfrT: Revue Africaine de Théologie; Kinshasa/Limete.

RAg: Revista Agustiniana; Calahorra.

RAMBI: Rešimat Ma'amarim bemadda'ê ha-Yahedût, Index of articles on Jewish Studies; J. 0073-5817.

RaMIsr: Rassegna mensile di Israel; Roma. 0033-9792.

RArchéol: Revue Archéologique; Paris. 0035-0737.

RArchéom: Revue d'Archéométrie; Rennes.

RArtLv: Revue des Archéologues et Historiens d'Art; Lv. 0080-2530.

RasArch: Rassegna di archeologia; F (9,1990).

RasEtiop: Rassegna di Studi Etiopici; R/N.

RAss: Revue d'Assyriologie et d'Archéologie Orientale; Paris.

RasT: Rassegna di Teologia; Roma [ᴱNapoli]. 0034-9644.

RazF: Razón y Fe; M. 0034-0235.

RB: Revue Biblique; J/P. 0035-0907.

RBén: Revue Bénédictine; Maredsous. 0035-0893.

RBgNum: Revue Belge de Numismatique et Sigillographie; Bruxelles.

RBgPg: Revue Belge de Philologie et d'Histoire; Bru. 0035-0818.

RBBras: Revista Bíblica Brasileira; Fortaleza.

RBíbArg: Revista Bíblica; Buenos Aires. 0034-7078.

RCatalT: Revista Catalana de Teología; Barcelona, St. Pacià.

RCiv: Éditions Recherche sur les Civilisations [Mém(oires) 0291-1655]; P ⇥ ADPF.

RClerIt: Rivista del Clero Italiano; Milano. 0042-7586.

RCuClaMed: Rivista di Cultura Classica e Medioevale; R. 0080-3251.

RÉAnc: Revue des Études Anciennes; Bordeaux. 0035-2004.

RÉArmén: Revue des Études Arméniennes. 0080-2549.

RÉAug: Revue des Études Augustiniennes; Paris. 0035-2012.

REB: 1. Revista Eclesiástica Brasileira; Petrópolis. 2. ⇥ RNEB.

RÉByz: Revue des Études Byzantines; Paris.

RECAM: Regional Epigraphic Catalogues of Asia Minor [AnSt].

RechAug: Recherches Augustiniennes; Paris. 0035-2021.

RechSR: Recherches de Science Religieuse; Paris. 0034-1258.

RecTrPO: Recueil de travaux, Proche-Orient ancien; Montréal.

RefEgy: Református Egyház; Budapest. 0324-475X.

ReferSR: Reference Services Review; Dearborn MI, Univ.

RefF: Reformiertes Forum; Zürich.

RefGStT: Reformationsgeschichtliche Studien und Texten: Münster.

RefJ: The Reformed Journal; Grand Rapids. 0486-252X.

Reformatio; Zürich. 0034-3021.

RefR: Reformed Review; New Brunswick NJ / Holland MI. 0034-3072.

RefTR: Reformed Theological Review; Hawthorn, Australia. 0034-3072.

RefW: Reformed World; Geneva. 0034-3056.

RÉG: Revue des Études Grecques; Paris. 0035-2039.

RÉgp: Revue d'Égyptologie; Paris.

RÉJ: Revue des Études Juives; Paris. 0035-2055.

RÉLat: Revue des Études Latines; P.

RelCult: Religión y Cultura; M.

RelEdn: Religious Education (biblical; Jewish-sponsored); NHv.

Religion [... and Religions]; Lancaster. 0048-721X.

RelIntL: Religion and Intellectual Life; New Rochelle. 0741-0549.

RelPBeit: Religionspädagogische Beiträge; Kaarst.

RelSoc: Religion and Society; B/Haag.
RelSt: Religious Studies; Cambridge. 0034-4125.
RelStR: Religious Studies Review; Nv, Vanderbilt. 0319-485X.
RelStT: Religious Studies and Theology; Edmonton. 0829-2922.
RelTAbs: Religious and Theological Abstracts; Myerstown, Pa.
RelTrad: Religious Traditions; Brisbane. 0156-1650.
RencAssInt: Rencontre Assyriologique Internationale, Compte-Rendu.
RencChrJ: Rencontre Chrétiens et Juifs; Paris. 0233-5579.
Renovatio: 1. Zeitschrift für das interdisziplinäre Gespräch; Köln: 2. (teologia); Genova.
RepCyp: Report of the Department of Antiquities of Cyprus; Nicosia.
RépertAA: Répertoire d'art et d'archéologie; Paris. 0080-0953.
REPPAL: Revue d'Études Phéniciennes-Puniques et des Antiquités Libyques; Tunis.
REspir: Revista de Espiritualidad; San Sebastián.
ResPLit: Res Publica Litterarum; Kansas.
RestQ: Restoration Quarterly; Abilene TX.
Résurrection, bimestriel catholique d'actualité et de formation.
RET: Revista Española de Teología; Madrid.
RÉtGC: Revue des Études Géorgiennes et Caucasiennes; Paris. 0373-1537 [< Bedi Kartlisa].
RevCuBíb: Revista de Cultura Bíblica; São Paulo.
RevSR: Revue des Sciences Religieuses; Strasbourg. 0035-2217.
RExp: Review and Expositor; Louisville. 0034-6373.
RFgIC: Rivista di Filologia e di Istruzione Classica; Torino. 0035-6220.
RgStTh: Regensburger Studien zur Theologie; Fra/Bern, Lang.
RgVV: Religionsgeschichtliche Versuche und Vorarbeiten; B/NY, de Gruyter.
RHDroit: Revue historique de Droit français et étranger; Paris.

RHE: Revue d'Histoire Ecclésiastique; Louvain. 0035-2381.
RheinMus: Rheinisches Museum für Philologie; Frankfurt. 0035-449X.
Rhetorik [Jb]; Stu / Bad Cannstatt.
RHist: Revue Historique; Paris.
RHPR: Revue d'Histoire et de Philosophie Religieuses; Strasbourg. 0035-2403.
RHR: Revue de l'Histoire des Religions; Paris. 0035-1423.
RHS ➤ RUntHö; **RU** ➤ ZPrax.
RHText: Revue d'Histoire des Textes; Paris. 0373-6075.
Ribla: Revista de interpretación bíblica latinoamericana; San José CR.
RIC: Répertoire bibliographique des institutions chrétiennes; Strasbourg ➤ 6,1063.
RICAO: Revue de l'Institut Catholique de l'Afrique de l'Ouest; Abidjan. (1,1992).
RICathP: Revue de l'Institut Catholique de Paris. 0294-4308
RicStoB: Ricerche storico bibliche; Bologna. 0394-980X.
RicStorSocRel: Ricerche di Storia Sociale e Religiosa; Roma.
RIDA: Revue Internationale des Droits de l'Antiquité; Bruxelles.
RijT: Riječki Teološki Časopis; Rijeka (Fiume), Croatia. 1330-0377.
RIMA ➤ AnRIM.
RINASA: Rivista Ist. Nazionale di Archeologia e Storia dell'Arte; Roma.
RitFg: Rivista italiana di Filologia Classica.
RItNum: Rivista Italiana di Numismatica e scienze affini; Milano.
RivArCr: Rivista di Archeologia Cristiana; Città/Vaticano. 0035-6042.
RivArV: Rivista di Archeologia, Univ. Venezia; Roma.
RivAscM: Rivista di Ascetica e Mistica; Roma.
RivB: Rivista Biblica Italiana; Bologna, Dehoniane. 0393-4853.
RivLtg: Rivista di Liturgia; T-Leumann.
RivPastLtg: Rivista di Pastorale Liturgica; Brescia. 0035-6395.
RivScR: Rivista di Scienze Religiose; Molfetta.
RivStoLR: Rivista di Storia e Letteratura Religiosa; F. 0035-6573.

RivStorA: Rivista Storica dell'Antichità; Bologna. 0300-340X.
RivVSp: Rivista di Vita Spirituale; Roma. 0035-6638.
RJysk: Religionsvidenskapeligt Tidsskrift (Jysk/Jutland); Aarhus. 0108-1993.
RLA: Reallexikon der Assyriologie & vorderasiatischen Archäologie; B ➤ 601.
RLatAmT: Revista Latinoamericana de Teología; El Salvador.
RLitND: Religion and Literature; Notre Dame, Univ. 0029-1500 (24, 1992).
RNEB: revision of New English Bible.
RNouv: La Revue Nouvelle; Bruxelles. 0035-3809.
RNum: Revue Numismatique; Paris.
RoczOr: Rocznik Orientalistyczny; Warszawa. 0080-3545.
RoczTK: Roczniki Teologiczno-Kanoniczne; Lublin. 0035-7723.
RömQ: Römische Quartalschrift für Christliche Altertumskunde...; Freiburg/Br. 0035-7812.
RomOrth: Romanian Orthodox Church News, French Version [sic]; Bucureşti.
RossArkh: Rossijskaja Arkheologija [= SovArch] after 1992/2: Moskva.
RPg: Revue de Philologie, de Littérature et d'Histoire anciennes; Paris, Klincksieck. 0035-1652.
RPontAr: (Atti) Rendiconti della Pontificia Accademia Romana di Archeologia; R.
RQum: Revue de Qumrân; P. 0035-1725.
RRéf: Revue Réformée; Saint-Germain-en-Laye.
RRel: Review for Religious; St. Louis. 0034-639X.
RRelRes: Review of Religious Research; New York. 0034-673X.
RRns: The Review of Religions; Wsh. 0743-5622.
RSO: Rivista degli Studi Orientali; Roma. 0392-4869.
RSPT: Revue des Sciences Philosophiques et Théologiques; [Le Saulchoir] Paris. 0035-2209.
RStFen: Rivista di Studi Fenici: R.
RSzem: Református Szemle; Budapest.

RTAM: Recherches de Théologie Ancienne et Médiévale; Louvain. 0034-1266. ➤ BTAM.
RTBat: Revista Teológica (Sem. Batista); Rio de Janeiro.
RThom: Revue Thomiste; Toulouse/Bru. 0035-4295.
RTLim: Revista Teológica; Lima.
RTLv: Revue théologique de Louvain. 0080-2654.
RTPhil: Revue de Théologie et de Philosophie; Épalinges. 0035-1784.
RuBi: Ruch Biblijny i Liturgiczny; Kraków. 0209-0872.
RUntHö: Religionsunterricht an höheren Schulen; Dü. (RU ➤ ZPrax).
RVidEspir: Revista de vida espiritual; Bogotá.
RZaïrTP: Revue Zaïroise de Théologie Protestante.
SAA[B]: State Archives of Assyria [Bulletin]; Helsinki.
SacEr: Sacris Erudiri; Steenbrugge. Saeculum; FrB/Mü. 0080-5319.
SAfBap: South African Baptist Journal of Theology; Cape Town. 1019-7990 (2,1992).
Sales: Salesianum; Roma. 0036-3502.
Salm: Salmanticensis; S. 0036-3537.
SalT: Sal Terrae; Sdr. 0211-4569.
Sandalion (Sassari); R, Herder.
SAOC: Studies in Ancient Oriental Civilization: Ch, Univ. 0081-7554. ➤ OI.
Sap: Sapienza; Napoli. 0036-4711.
SapCro: La Sapienza della Croce; R.
SASTUMA: Saarbrücker Studien und Materialien zur Altertumskunde; Bonn. 0942-7392 (2,1992).
sb.: subscription; price for members.
SbBrno: Sborník praci filozoficke fakulty; Brno, Univ.
SBF Anal/Pub [min]: Studii Biblici Franciscani: Analecta / Publicationes series maior 0081-8971 [minor]; Jerusalem. ➤ LA.
SBL [AramSt / Mg / Diss / GRR / MasSt / NAm / SemP / TexTr]: Society of Biblical Literature: Aramaic Studies / Monograph Series / Dissertation Series / Graeco-Roman Religion / Masoretic Studies / Biblical Scholarship in North America / Seminar Papers 0145-2711 / Texts and Translations. ➤ JBL; CATSS; CritRR.

SBS [KBW]: Stuttgarter Bibelstudien; Stuttgart, Katholisches Bibelwerk.
ScandJOT: Scandinavian Journal of the Old Testament; Aarhus.
ScAnt: Scienze dell'Antichità; storia archeologia antropologia; Roma (3s,1989s).
ScEsp: Science et Esprit; Montréal. 0316-5345.
SCHN: Studia ad Corpus Hellenisticum NT; Leiden.
Schönberger Hefte; Fra.
Scholars Choice; Richmond VA.
SChr: Sources Chrétiennes; P. 0750-1978.
SCompass: Social Compass, revue internat. sociologie de la religion: Lv.
ScotBEv: The Scottish Bulletin of Evangelical Theology; E. 0265-4539.
ScotJT: Scottish Journal of Theology; Edinburgh. 0036-9306.
ScotR: Scottish Journal of Religious Studies; Stirling. 0143-8301.
ScrCiv: Scrittura [scrivere] e Civiltà; T.
ScrClasIsr: Scripta Classica Israelica; J.
ScriptB: Scripture Bulletin; London. 0036-9780.
Scriptorium; Bruxelles. 0036-9772.
ScripTPamp: Scripta theologica; Pamplona, Univ. Navarra. 0036-9764.
Scriptura; Stellenbosch. 0254-1807.
ScriptVict: Scriptorium Victoriense; Vitoria, España.
ScuolC: La Scuola Cattolica; Venegono Inferiore, Varese. 0036-9810.
SDB [= DBS]: Supplément au Dictionnaire de la Bible; Paris ➤ 602.
SDH: Studia et documenta historiae et iuris; Roma, Pont. Univ. Lateran.
SecC: Second Century ➤ JEarlyC.
Sefarad; Madrid. 0037-0894.
SEG: Supplementum epigraphicum graecum; Withoorn.
Segmenten; Amsterdam, Vrije Univ.
SelT: Selecciones de Teología; Barc.
SémBib: Sémiotique et Bible; Lyon ➤ CADIR. 0154-6902.
Semeia (Biblical Criticism) [Supplements]; Atlanta. 0095-571X.
Seminarios; Salamanca.
Seminarium; Roma.
Seminary Review; Cincinnati.
Semiotica; Amsterdam. 0037-1998.

Semitica; Paris. 0085-6037.
Semitics; Pretoria. 0256-6044.
Sens; juifs et chrétiens; Paris.
SeptCogSt: ➤ B[ulletin].
Servitium; CasM (ᴱBergamo).
SEST: South-Eastern [Baptist] Seminary Studies; Wake Forest NC.
SetRel: Sette e religioni; Bologna (2, 1992).
Sevārtham; Ranchi.
Sève = Église aujourd'hui; P. 0223-5854.
SewaneeTR: Sewanee Theological Review (ex-St.Luke's); Sewanee TN. (17, 1992).
SFulg: Scripta Fulgentina; Murcia. (1,1991s).
SGErm: ⓡ Soobščeniya gosudarstvennovo Ermitaža, Reports of the State Hermitage Museum; Leningrad. 0432-1501.
SH: Social History; London.
ShinKen: ⓞ Shinyaku Kenkyū, Studia Textus Novi Testamenti; Osaka.
ShMišpat: Shnaton ha-Mišpaṭ ha-Ivri, Annual of Jewish Law.
ShnatM: ⓖ Shnaton la-Mikra (Annual, Biblical and ANE Studies); TA.
SicArch: Sicilia archaeologica; Trapani.
SicGym: Siculorum Gymnasium; Catania.
Sidra, a journal for the study of Rabbinic literature; Ramat-Gan.
SIMA: Studies in Mediterranean Archaeology; Göteborg.
SixtC: The Sixteenth Century Journal; St. Louis (Kirksville). 0361-0160.
SkK: Stuttgarter kleiner Kommentar.
SkrifK: Skrif en Kerk; Pretoria, Univ.
SMEA: Studi Micenei ed Egeo-Anatolici (Incunabula Graeca); Roma.
SMSR: Studi e Materiali di Storia delle religioni: Roma.
SNTS (Mg.): Studiorum Novi Testamenti Societas (Monograph Series); Cambridge.
SNTU-A/B: Studien zum NT und seiner Umwelt; Linz [Periodica / Series].
SocAnRel: Sociological analysis (sociology of religion); Chicago.
SocUÉg: Sociétés Urbaines en Égypte et au Soudan; Lille.
SocWB: The Social World of Biblical Antiquity; Sheffield.

Soundings; Nashville. 0585-5462.
SovArch: ⇢ RossArkh.
Speculum (Medieval Studies); CM. 0038-7134.
SPg: Studia Philologica. 0585-5462.
SpirC, SpirNC: La Spiritualità cristiana / non-cristiana; R ⇢ 5,907.
Spiritus; Paris. 0038-7665.
SpirLife: Spiritual Life; Washington. 0038-7630.
Sprache; Wien. 0038-8467.
SR: Studies in Religion / Sciences Religieuses; Waterloo, Ont. 0008-4298.
SSEA ⇢ JSStEg.
ST: (Vaticano) Studi e Testi.
ST: Studia Theologica; K. 0039-338X.
StAäK: Studien zur altägyptischen Kultur; Hamburg. 0340-2215.
StAChron: Studies in Ancient Chronology; London. 0952-4975.
Stadion, Geschichte des Sports; Sankt Augustin. 0178-4029.
StAns: Studia Anselmiana; Roma.
StANT: Studien zum Alten und Neuen Testament; München.
StAntCr: Studi di Antichità Cristiana; Città del Vaticano.
Star: St. Thomas Academy for Research; Bangalore.
Stauròs, Bollettino trimestrale sulla teologia della Croce: Pescara.
StBEC: Studies in the Bible and Early Christianity; Lewiston NY.
StBEx: Studies in Bible and Exegesis; Ramat-Gan.
StBib: Dehon/Paid/Leiden: Studi Biblici; Bo, Dehoniane / Brescia, Paideia / Studia Biblica; Leiden.
StBoğT: Studien zu den Boğazköy-Texten; Wiesbaden.
STBuc: Studii Teologice; Bucureşti.
StCatt: Studi cattolici; Mi. 0039-2901.
StCEth: Studies in Christian Ethics; Edinburgh. 0953-9468.
StChrAnt: Studies in Christian Antiquity; Wsh.
StChrJud: Studies in Christianity and Judaism; Waterloo ON.
StClasBuc: Studii Clasice; Bucureşti.
StClasOr: Studi Classici e Orientali; R.
StCompRel: Studies in Comparative Religion; Bedfont. 0039-3622.

StDelitzsch: Studia Delitzschiana (ᴱMünster); Stuttgart. 0585-5071.
StEbl: Studi Eblaiti; Roma, Univ.
StEC: Studies in Early Christianity; NY, Garland.
StEcum: Studi Ecumenici; Verona. 0393-3687.
StEgPun: Studi di Egittologia e di Antichità Puniche (Univ. Bo.); Pisa.
StEpL: Studi Epigrafici e Linguistici sul Vicino Oriente antico; Verona.
STEv: Studi di Teologia dell'Istituto Biblico Evangelico; Padova.
StFormSp: Studies in Formative Spirituality; Pittsburgh. 0193-2478.
StGnes: Studia Gnesnensia; Gniezno.
StHistANE: Studies in the history of the ancient Near East; Leiden. 0169-9024.
StHJewishP: Studies in the History of the Jewish People; Haifa.
StHPhRel: Studies in the History and Philosophy of Religion; CM.
StHRel [= Numen Suppl.] Studies in the History of Religions; Leiden.
StIntku: Studien zur Interkulturellen Geschichte des Christentums; Fra.
StIran: Studia Iranica; Leiden. 0772-7852.
StIsVArh: Studii şi cercetări de Istorie Veche şi arheologie; Bucureşti. 0039-4009.
StItFgC: Studi Italiani di Filologia Classica; Firenze. 0039-2987.
StiZt: Stimmen der Zeit; FrB. 0039-1492.
StJudLA: Studies in Judaism in Late Antiquity; Leiden. 0169-961X.
StLatIt: Studi Latini e Italiani: R, Univ. (5,1991).
StLeg: Studium Legionense; León.
StLtg: Studia Liturgica; Nieuwendam.
StLuke ⇢ Sewanee TR.
StMiss: Studia Missionalia, Annual; Rome, Gregorian Univ.
StMor: Studia Moralia; R, Alphonsianum. 0081-6736.
StNT: Studien zum Neuen Testament; Gütersloh; STNT ⇢ Shin-Ken.
StNW: Studies of the NT and its World; E.
StOr: Studia Orientalia; Helsinki, Societas Orientalis Fennica. 0039-3282.
StOrL: Studi Orientali e Linguistici; Bologna, Univ. Ist. Glottologia.

StOrRel: Studies in Oriental Religions; Wiesbaden.
StOvet: Studium Ovetense; Oviedo.
StPatav: Studia Patavina; Padova. 0039-3304.
StPatrist: Studia Patristica; Berlin.
StPhilonAn: Studia Philonica Annual; Atlanta.
StPostB: Studia Post-Biblica; Leiden.
StPrace: Studia i Prace = Études, Wsz.
StRefTH: Studies in Reformed Theology and History; Princeton Sem. 1667-4268. (1,1993).
Streven: 1. cultureel; Antwerpen. 0039-2324; 2. S.J., Amst.
StRicOrCr: Studi e Ricerche dell'Oriente Cristiano; Roma.
StRom: Studi Romani; Roma.
Stromata (< Ciencia y Fe); San Miguel, Argentina. 0049-2353.
StRz: Studia Religioznawcze (Filozofii i Socjologii); Wsz, Univ.
StSemLgLing: Studies in Semitic Language and Linguistics; Leiden.
StSp: Studies in Spirituality; Kampen. (2,1992).
StSp (Dehoniane) → 6,854*.
StSpG (Borla) → 6,855.
StStoR̯: Studi storici e religiosi; Capua. (1,1992).
StTNeunz: Studien zur Theologie und Geistesgeschichte des Neunzehnten Jh.; Göttingen.
StudiaBT: Studia Biblica et Theologica; Pasadena CA. 0094-2022.
Studies; Dublin. 0039-3495.
StudiesBT: Studies in Biblical Theology; L.
Studium; 1. Madrid; 2. R −0039-4130.
StVTPseud: Studia in Veteris Testamenti Pseudepigrapha; Leiden.
StWarm: Studia Warmińskie; Olstyn. 0137-6624. (22s, 1992 per 1985s).
STWsz: Studia theologica Varsaviensia; Warszawa.
SubsBPont: Subsidia Biblica; R, Pontifical Biblical Institute.
SudanTB: Sudan Texts Bulletin; Ulster, Univ. 0143-6554.
Sumer (Archaeology-History in the Arab World); Baghdad, Dir. Ant.
SUNT: Studien zur Umwelt des NTs; Gö.
SUNY: State University of New York; Albany etc.

Supp.: Supplement → NT, JStOT, SEG. Supplément, Le: autrefois 'de VSp'; P.
SvEx: Svensk Exegetisk Årsbok; U.
SVlad: St. Vladimir's Theological Quarterly; Tuckahoe NY. 0036-3227.
SvTKv: Svensk Teologisk Kvartalskrift; Lund.
SWJT: Southwestern Journal of Theology; Fort Worth. 0038-4828.
Symbolae (graec-lat.); Oslo. 0039-7679.
Symbolon: 1. Ba/Stu; 2. Köln.
Synaxe; annuale, Catania.
Syria (Art Oriental, Archéologie); Paris, IFA Beyrouth.
SyrMesSt: Syro-Mesopotamian Studies (Monograph Journals); Malibu CA.
Szb: Sitzungsberichte [Univ.], phil.-hist. Klasse (Bayr.). Mü. 0342-5991.
Szolgalat ⑩ ['Dienst']; Eisenstadt, Ös.
❶: *lingua turca,* Turkish; − ᵀtranslator.
Tablet; London. 0039-8837.
TAik: Teologinen Aikakauskirja / Teologisk Tidskrift; Helsinki.
TaiwJT: Taiwan [Presbyterian Sem.] Journal of Theology; Taipei.
TAJ: Tel Aviv [Univ.] Journal of the Institute of Archaeology. 0334-4355.
TAn: Theology Annual; Hongkong.
ṬanṭurYb: Ecumenical Institute for Theological Research Yearbook; J.
TANZ: Texte und Arbeiten zum neutestamentlichen Zeitalter; Tü. non = ArbNZ.
TArb: Theologische Arbeiten; Stu/B.
Tarbiẕ ❶ (Jewish Studies); Jerusalem, Hebr. Univ. 0334-3650.
TArg: Teología; Buenos Aires.
Target, translation studies; Amst.
TAth: ❻ Theología; Athēnai.
TAVO: Tübinger Atlas zum Vorderen Orient [Beih(efte)]: Wiesbaden.
TBeit: Theologische Beiträge; Wu.
TBer: Theologische Berichte; Z/Köln.
TBR: Theological Book Review; Guildford, Surrey. (6,1993s).
TBraga: Theologica; Braga.
TBud: Teologia; Budapest, Ac. Cath.
TBüch: Theologische Bücherei. (Neudrukke und Berichte 20. Jdt.); München.
TCN: Theological College of Northern Nigeria Bulletin; Bukuru.
TContext[o]: Theology in Context; Aachen 8,1 (1991). 0176-1439 =

Teología in Contexto 1,1 (1991). 0938-3468 = **TKontext,** Theologie im Kontext 12,1 (1991). 0724-1628.

TDeusto: Teología-Deusto; Bilbao/M.

TDienst: Theologie und Dienst; Wu.

TDig: Theology Digest; St. Louis. 0040-5728.

TDNT: Theological Dictionary of the NT [< TWNT]; Grand Rapids ➤ 5,811.

TDocStA: Testi e documenti per lo studio dell'Antichità; Milano, Cisalpino.

TDOT: Theological Dictionary of the Old Testament [< TWAT] GR.

TEdn: Theological Education; Vandalia, Ohio.

TEdr: Theological Educator; New Orleans.

TEFS: Theological Education [Materials for Africa, Asia, Caribbean] Fund, Study Guide; London.

Téléma (réflexion et créativité chrétiennes en Afrique); Kinshasa-Gombe.

Teocomunicação.

Teresianum; Roma.

TerraS / TerreS: Terra Santa: 0040-3784. / La Terre Sainte; J (Custodia OFM). ➤ **HolyL.**

TEspir: Teología Espiritual; Valencia.

TEuph: Transeuphratène [Syrie perse]; P.

TEV: Today's English Version (Good News for Modern Man); L, Collins.

TEvca: Theologia Evangelica; Pretoria, Univ. S Africa.

TExH: Theologische Existenz heute; Mü. Text; The Hague. 0165-4888.

TextEstCisn: Textos y Estudios 'Cardenal Cisneros'; Madrid, Cons.Sup.Inv.

TextPatLtg: Textus patristici et liturgici; Regensburg, Pustet.

Textus, Annual of the Hebrew Univ. Bible Project; J. 0082-3767.

TFor: Theologische Forschung; Ha.

TGegw: Theologie der Gegenwart in Auswahl; Münster, Regensberg-V.

TGL: Theologie und Glaube; Pd.

THandkNT: Theologischer Handkommentar zum NT; Berlin.

THAT: Theologisches Handwörterbuch zum AT; München. ➤ 1,908.

Themelios; London. 0307-8388.

Theokratia, Jahrbuch des Institutum Delitzschianum; Leiden/Köln.

Théologiques; Montréal (1,1993).

Theológos, Ho; Fac. Teol. Palermo.

THist: Théologie Historique; P. 0563-4253.

This World; NY.

Thomist, The; Wsh. 0040-6325.

Thought; NY, Fordham. 0040-6457.

Tikkun; Oakland CA.

TimLitS: Times Literary Supplement; L.

TItSett: Teologia; Brescia (Fac. teol. Italia settentrionale).

T-Iusi: Teología, Instituto Universitario Semin. Interdioc.; Caracas.

TJb: Theologisches Jahrbuch; Leipzig.

TKontext: Theologie im Kontext; Aachen. 0724-1682. ➤ **TContext[o].**

TLima: Theologika; Lima, Univ. Incaica.

TLond: Theology; London. 0040-571X.

TLZ: Theologische Literaturzeitung; Berlin. 0040-5671.

TolkNT: Tolkning [commentarius] av Nya Testamentet; Stockholm.

TopO: Topoi Orient-Occident; Lyon. (1, 1991).

TorJT: Toronto Journal of Theology.

TPast: Theologie en pastoraat; Zwolle.

TPhil: Theologie und Philosophie; Freiburg/Br. 0040-5655.

TPQ: Theologisch-praktische Quartalschrift; Linz, Ös. 0040-5663.

TPract: Theologia Practica; München/Hamburg. 0720-9525.

TR: Theologische Revue; Münster. 0040-568X.

TradErn: Tradition und Erneuerung (religiös-liberales Judentum); Bern.

Traditio; Bronx NY, Fordham Univ.

Tradition, orthodox Jewish; NY.

Trajecta, geschiedenis van het katholieke leven; Nijmegen. (1.1992).

Transformation ... evangelical Mission/ Ethics. (10,1993).

TRE: Theologische Realenzyklopädie; Berlin ➤ 603.

TRef: Theologia Reformata; Woerden.

TRevNE: ➤ NesTR.

TRicScR: Testi e ricerche di scienze religiose; Brescia.

TrierTZ: Trierer Theologische Zeitschrift; Trier. 0041-2945.

TrinJ: Trinity Journal; Deerfield IL. 0360-3032.

TrinSemR: Trinity Seminary Review; Columbus.

TrinT: Trinity theological journal, Singapore.
TrinUn [St/Mg] Rel: Trinity University Studies in Religion, San Antonio.
Tripod; Hong Kong.
TRu: Theologische Rundschau; Tübingen. 0040-5698.
TS: Theological Studies; Baltimore. 0040-5639.
TsGesch: Tijdschrift voor Geschiedenis; Groningen.
TsLtg: Tijdschrift voor Liturgie; Lv.
TsMeditA: Tijdschrift voor Mediterrane Archeologie; Lv. (5,1992).
TStAJud: Texte und Studien zum Antiken Judentum; Tübingen. 0721-8753.
TsTKi: Tidsskrift for Teologi og Kirke; Oslo. 0040-7194.
TsTNijm ➤ **TvT**.
TStR: Texts and Studies in Religion; Lewiston NY.
TSzem: Theologiai Szemle; Budapest. 0133-7599.
TTod: Theology Today; Princeton. 0040-5736.
TU: Texte und Untersuchungen, Geschichte der altchristlichen Literatur; Berlin.
Tü [ÄgBei] ThS: Tübinger [Ägyptologische Beiträge; Bonn, Habelt] Theologische Studien; Mainz, Grünewald.
[Tü]TQ: [Tübinger] Theologische Quartalschrift; Mü. 0342-1430.
TürkArk: Türk Arkeoloji dergisi; Ankara.
TUmAT: Texte aus der Umwelt des ATs; Gütersloh ➤ 604.
TVers: Theologische Versuche; Berlin. 0437-3014.
TViat: Theologia Viatorum; SAfr.
TVida: Teología y Vida; Santiago, Chile. 0049-3449.
TvT [= TsTNijm]: Tijdschrift voor Theologie; Nijmegen. 0168-9959.
TWAT: Theologisches Wörterbuch zum Alten Testament; Stu ➤ 605.
TWiss: Theologische Wissenschaft, Sammelwerk für Studium und Beruf; Stu.
TWNT: Theologisches Wörterbuch zum NT; Stuttgart (➤ GLNT; TDNT).
TXav: Theologica Xaveriana; Bogotá.
TxK: Texte und Kontexte (Exegese); Stuttgart.

Tyche, Beiträge zur alten Geschichte, Papyrologie und Epigraphik; Wien.
Tychique (Chemin Neuf); Lyon.
TyndB: Tyndale Bulletin; Cambridge.
TZBas: Theologische Zeitschrift; Basel. 0040-5741.
UF: Ugarit-Forschungen; Kevelaer/ Neukirchen. 0342-2356.
Universitas; 1. Stuttgart. 0041-9079; 2. Bogotá. 0041-9060.
UnivT: Universale Teologica; Brescia.
UnSa: Una Sancta: 1. Augsburg-Meitingen; 2. Brooklyn.
UnSemQ: Union Seminary Quarterly Review; New York.
UPA: University Press of America; Wsh/ Lanham MD.
Update [religious trends]; Aarhus.
URM: Ultimate Reality and Meaning; Toronto.
USCathH: U.S. Catholic Historian; Baltimore. 0735-8318. (10,1992).
VAeg: Varia Aegyptiaca; San Antonio. 0887-4026.
VBGed: Verklaring van een Bijbelgedeelte; Kampen.
VComRel: La vie des communautés religieuses; Montréal.
VDI: ❻ Vestnik Drevnej Istorii; Moskva. 0321-0391.
Veleia, (pre-) historia, filología clásicas; Vitoria-Gasteiz, Univ. P. Vasco.
Verbum; 1. SVD; R; - 2. Nancy.
Veritas; Porto Alegre, Univ. Católica.
VerkF: Verkündigung und Forschung; München. 0342-2410.
VerVid: Verdad y Vida; M. 0042-3718.
VestB: Vestigia Biblica; Hamburg.
VetChr: Vetera Christianorum; Bari.
Viator, Medieval and Renaissance studies; Berkeley. 0083-5897.
Vidyajyoti (Theology); Ranchi.
VieCons: La Vie Consacrée; P/Bru.
VigChr: Vigiliae Christianae; Leiden. 0042-6032.
ViMon: Vita Monastica; Arezzo.
ViPe: Vita e Pensiero: Mi, S. Cuore.
VisLang: Visible Language; Cleveland.
VisRel: Visible Religion, annual for iconography; Leiden. 0169-5606.
VitaCons: Vita Consacrata; Milano.
Vivarium; Catanzaro (1,1993).
VivH: Vivens Homo, scienze rel.; F.

VizVrem: ❸ Vizantijskij Vremennik;
Moskva. 0136-7358.
VO: Vicino Oriente; Roma.
Vocation; Paris.
VoicesTW: Voices from the Third
World; Colombo, Sri Lanka. (15,
1992).
VoxEvca: Vox Evangelica; London.
0263-6786.
VoxEvi: Vox Evangelii; Buenos Aires.
VoxRef: Vox Reformata; Geelong,
Australia.
VoxScr: Vox Scripturae; São Paulo.
0104-0073. (2,1992).
VoxTh: Vox Theologica; Assen.
VSp: La Vie Spirituelle; Paris. 0042-
4935; ➤ Supplément. 0083-5859.
VT: Vetus Testamentum; Leiden.
0042-4935.
WDienst: Wort und Dienst; Bielefeld.
0342-3085.
WegFor: Wege der Forschung; Da, Wiss.
WeltOr: Welt des Orients; Göttingen.
0043-2547.
WesleyTJ: Wesleyan Theological
Journal; Marion IN. 0092-4245.
WestTJ: Westminster Theological
Journal; Philadelphia. 0043-4388.
WEvent: Word + Event; Stuttgart.
WienerSt: Wiener Studien; Wien.
WisLu: Wisconsin Lutheran Quarter-
ly; Mequon. (88,1991).
Wiss: Wissenschaftliche Buchhandlung; Da.
WissPrax: Wissenschaft und Praxis in
Kirche und Gesellschaft; Göttingen.
WissWeish: Wissenschaft und Weis-
heit; Mü-Gladbach. 0043-678X.
WM: Wissenschaftliche Monographien zum
Alten/Neuen Testament; Neukirchen.
WoAnt: Wort und Antwort; Mainz.
Word and Spirit; Still River MA.
WorldArch: World Archaeology; Hen-
ley.
World Spirituality ➤ EWSp.
Worship; St. John's Abbey, College-
ville, Minn. 0043-9414.
WrocST: Wrocławskie Studia Teolo-
giczne / Colloquium Salutis; Wro-
cław. 0239-7714.
WUNT: Wissenschaftliche Untersuchun-
gen zum NT: Tübingen.
WVDOG: Wissenschaftliche Veröffentli-
chungen der Deutschen Orient-Ge-
sellschaft; Berlin.

WWorld: Word and World; St. Paul.
WZ: Wissenschaftliche Zeitschrift [...
Univ.].
WZKM: Wiener Zeitschrift für die
Kunde des Morgenlandes; Wien.
0084-0076.
Xenia [latina]; R, Bretschneider. (1,
1992).
Xilotl, revista nicaraguense de teología.
Xipe-Totek, ... filosofía, ciencias, ac-
ción social; Guadalajara, Méx (1,
1992).
YaleClas: Yale Classical Studies; NHv.
Yuval: Studies of the Jewish Music Re-
search Centre [incl. Psalms]; Jerusalem.
ZäSpr: Zeitschrift für Ägyptische
Sprache und Altertumskunde; Ber-
lin. 0044-216X.
ZAHeb: Zeitschrift für Althebraistik;
Stuttgart. 0932-4461.
ZAss: Zeitschrift für Assyriologie &
Vorderasiatische Archäologie; Ber-
lin. 0048-5299.
ZAW: Zeitschrift für die Alttesta-
mentliche Wissenschaft; Berlin.
0044-2526.
ZDialekT: Zeitschrift für dialektische
Theologie; Kampen.
ZDMG: Zeitschrift der Deutschen
Morgenländischen Gesellschaft; Wies-
baden.
ZDPV: Zeitschrift des Deutschen Pa-
lästina-Vereins; Stu. 0012-1169.
ZeichZt: Die Zeichen der Zeit, Evan-
gelische Monatschrift; Berlin.
Zeitwende (Die neue Furche); Gü.
Zephyrus; Salamanca. 0514-7336.
ZEthnol: Zeitschrift für Ethnologie;
Braunschweig. 0044-2666.
ZEvEthik: Zeitschrift für Evangelische
Ethik; Gütersloh. 0044-2674.
ZfArch: Zeitschrift für Archäologie:
Berlin. 0044-233X.
ZfG: Zeitschrift für Geschichtswissen-
schaft; Berlin. 0044-2828.
ZGPred: Zeitschrift für Gottesdienst
und Predigt; Gütersloh.
Zion: ❹; Jerusalem. 0044-4758.
ZIT: Zeitschriften Inhaltsdienst Theo-
logie; Tübingen. 0340-8361.
ZKG: Zeitschrift für Kirchengeschich-
te; Stuttgart. 0044-2985.
ZkT: Zeitschrift für katholische Theo-
logie; Innsbruck. 0044-2895.

ZMissRW: Zeitschrift für Missionswissenschaft und Religionswissenschaft; Münster. 0044-3123.
ZNW: Zeitschrift für die Neutestamentliche Wissenschaft & Kunde des Alten Christentums; B. 0044-2615.
ZPapEp: Zeitschrift für Papyrologie und Epigraphik; Bonn. 0084-5388.
ZPraxRU: Zeitschrift für die Praxis des Religionsunterrichts; Stuttgart.

ZRGg: Zeitschrift für Religions- und Geistesgeschichte; Köln. 0044-3441.
ZSavR: Zeitschrift der Savigny-Stiftung (Romanistische) Rechtsgeschichte: Weimar. 0323-4096.
ZSprW: Zeitschrift für Sprachwissenschaft; Göttingen. 0721-9067.
ZTK: Zeitschrift für Theologie und Kirche; Tübingen. 0513-9147.
Zwingliana; Zürich.
Zygon; Winter Park FL. 0591-2385.

| I. Bibliographica |

A1 *Opera collecta* .1 **Festschriften,** memorials.

1 Anthologies and Festschriften: CritRR 5 (1992) 513-533, tit. pp.; – Collected essays: CBQ 54 (1992) 188-200 . 387-399 . 597-611 . 814-831; – *Epp* Eldon J., *al.*, Collected essays: JBL 111 (1992) 163-178 . 365-9 . 737-745. – *Junghans* Helmar, *al.*, Sammelschriften: LuJb 59 (1992) p. 213-5. – *Langlamet* F. (*al*), Recueils et mélanges: RB 99 (1992) 291-9 . 445-456 . 587-591 . 756-766; – Recueils et mélanges: RHE 87 (1992) 52* . 220*s . 393*s.

2 **IJbF:** Internationale Jahresbibliographie der Festschriften, ᴱZeller Otto & Wolfram, 11 (für 1990), 704+1126+491 p.; 12 (für 1991), 706+950+470 p. Osnabrück 1991, Dietrich. [AnPg 62, p. 995].

3 ABDEL-MASSIH Ernest T. [† 1992] mem.: Studies in Near Eastern culture and history, ᴱBellamy James A.: Michigan Series on the Middle East 2. AA 1991, Univ. Michigan. x-225 p. $18 [JAOS 113,159, Jeannette *Wakin*; MuslimW 83,87, M. *Sawaje*].

4 ADAMS Charles J.; Islamic studies, ᴱHallaq Wael B., *Little* Donald P. Leiden 1991, Brill. 273 p. ƒ140 [JAOS 112,360]. – ᴿSR 21 (1992) 374 (Sheila *McDonough*).

5 R[adnoti]-ALFÖLDI Maria: Die Münze; Bild-Botschaft-Bedeutung, ᴱNoeske Hans-Christoph, *Schubert* Helmut, *al.* Fra 1991, Lang. xxxii-428 p.; 39 pl.

6 ANASTASI Rosario: Syndesmos I. Catania 1991, Univ. Ist. Biz.-Neoellen. xi-208 p. [Orpheus 13, 449, E. V. *Maltese*].

7 ANDERSON Nels: **Maclean** Derry L., Religion and society in Arab Sind (Leiden 1990, Brill. x-191 p. ƒ75), noted in JAOS 112,361 as vol. 25 of a sociology series honoring Anderson.

8 ANDERSON Ray S.: Incarnational ministry; the presence of Christ in church, society and family, ᴱKettler Christian D., *Speidell* Todd H. ... 1990, Helmers Howard. 352 p. $30; pa. $17. 0-939443-21-X; -1-X [BIP 91s,3514].

9 ANGERMANN Erich: Liberalitas, 65. Gb., ᴱFinzsch N., *Wellenreuther* H.: TransatlantHistSt 1. Stu 1992, Steiner. 545 p.; ill. DM 138 [RHE 87, 393*].

10 a) ARTUK Ibrahim: ❶ Turkish Numismatic Society 20th Anniv. Istanbul
1988. viii-278 p. – ᴿIstVArh 43 (1992) 97-99 (E. *Nicolae*).
— b) AUMANN Jordan: Compendio di Teologia Spirituale, ᴱDe Cea Emeterio.
R 1992, PUST. 347 p. [Angelicum 70, 455].
— c) AVERY Peter W.: Persian and Islamic studies, ᴱMelville Charles:
Pembroke Studies 1. C 1990, Univ. Centre of ME Studies. iii-254 p. £17.
– ᴿJRAS (1991) 406s (D. O. *Morgan*).
— d) BAARLINK H., (van en voor) Christologische Perspectieven; exegetische
en hermeneutische studies. Kampen 1992, Kok. 350 p. *f* 47.50. 90-
242-6704-8 [TvT (= TsTNijm) 33,414, H. *Berflo*: '330 p.'].
11 BACHL Gottfried: Gottesgeschichten; Beiträge zu einer systematischen
Theologie, ᴱAchleitner W., *Winkler* U. FrB 1992, Herder. 463 p. DM 68.
3-451-22456-9. – ᴿLebZeug 47 (1992) 308s (F. *Courth*); TvT 33, 304
(H. E. *Mertens*).
12 BALOG Paul, ➤ 7,14*: 15. VIII. 1990 – 6. XI. 1982 [p. 1s, D. *Barag*] mem:
IsrNumJ 10 (1988s) 142 p., 22 pl. 12 art., Arabic coins.
13 BASTIEN Pierre: Mélanges de numismatique 75ᵉ anniv., ᴱHuvelin Hélène,
al. Wetteren 1987, Numismatique romaine, xxxiv-382 p ; 29 pl. [AnPg 59,
p. 970]. – ᴿLatomus 49 (1990) 769s (H. *Zehnacker*).
13* BAUSANI Alessandro, ricordo: Yad Nāma. R 1992. [RSO 66 (1992) 197].
14 BEESTON A. F. L.: Arabicus felix, luminosus Britannicus, 80th b., ᴱJones
Alan: Ox Or. Inst. Mg. 11. Reading 1991, Ithaca. vi-239 p. [OIAc 3, 13;
excerpted].
14* BEHRENS Peter mem. † 1970: Ägypten im afro-orientalischen Kontext;
Aufsätze zur Archäologie, Geschichte und Sprache eines unbegrenzten
Raumes, ᴱMendel Daniela, *Claudi* Ulrike. Köln 1991, Univ. Inst. Afrik.
439 p. DM 158 [OLZ 88, 366, I. *Hofmann*].
BEJARANO Virgilio 1988/91 ➤ 643*.
15 BELLINCIONI SCARPAT Maria, mem.: Tradizione dell'antico nelle letterature e nelle arti d'Occidente: La civiltà delle scritture 10. R 1990,
Bulzoni. xvi-663 p.; ill. [AnPg 61, p. 728]. – ᴿRÉL 69 (1991) 329-332 (J.
Chomarat).
16 BENGTSON Hermann: Hellenistische Studien; Gedenkschrift, ᴱSeibert
Jacob: MüArbAG 5. Mü 1991, Maris. 166 p.; portr.; biobibliog. 9-16
(H. II. *Schmitt*), 159-166 (W. *Schramm*). 3-925801-10-3. 9 art.; 5 infra.
16* BERGERHOF Kurt: Mesopotamica - Ugaritica - Biblica; 70. Gb.: AOAT
232. Kevelaer/Neuk 1992, Butzon & B./Neuk. x-516 p. 3-7666-9840-0 /
3-7887-1453-0 [UF 24 (1992) 502s].
17 a) BHATTACHARYA Kalidas [1911-1984] mem., Freedom, transcendence
and identity, ᴱSengupta Pradip K. Delhi 1988, Motilal-B. viii-222 p. rs
135. - ᴿJDharma 17 (1992) 268s (J. B. *Chethimattam*).
— b) BIETENHARD Hans, 75. Gb., Judaica 47,3 (1991) 121s (-184).
— c) BILANIUK Petro B. T., in Eng.: The divine life, light, and love, ᴱPil-
linger Renate, *Renhart* Erich. Graz 1992, Schnider. 344 p. biobibliog.
13-26, *Massey* Isabel [+ 57-65] 3-900993-23-8. 21 art. [TR 89, 340, tit.
pp.]. ➤ 4666.
18 a) BIRAN Avraham: Eretz-Israel 23, ᴱStern Ephraim, *Levi* Thomas E. J
1992, Israel Exploration Soc./HUC. x-159* p. + ❹ 382; portr.; bibliog.,
XIII-s ❹. Summaries 145*-159*. $40. 965-221-017-X. 23 art. infra. [RB
100, 283 & ZAW 105,350, tit. pp.; BL 93,23, A. R. *Millard*.; BAR-W
19/1,10; BO 50,723, E. van der *Steen*; OLZ 88, 153, G. *Pfeifer*].
— b) BIRKNER Hans Joachim: SCHLEIERMACHER und die wissenschaftliche

Kultur des Christentums. B/NY 1991, de Gruyter. – ᴿFilT 6 (1992) 354-8 (P. *D'Angelo*).

— *c*) BLÁZQUEZ MARTÍNEZ J. M.: Arte, sociedad, economía y religión durante el bajo imperio y la antigüedad tardía, ᴱGonzález Blanco Antonino, *al*.: Antigüedad y cristianismo 8. Murcia 1991, Univ. 582 p., 53 p. fig.; 32 p. phot. [ClasR 43, 121, S. *Barnish*].

19 *a*) BLENKINSOPP Joseph: Priests, prophets and scribes; essays on the formation and heritage of Second Temple Judaism, ᴱUlrich Eugene, *al*.: JStOT supp. 149. Sheffield 1992, Academic. 274 p.; portr.; bibliog. 258-262. £35. 1-85075-375-X [BL 93,24, L. L. *Grabbe*; TR 89, 517 & RB 105,133, tit. pp.]. 17 art.; infra. – ᴿTBR 5,3 (1992s) 20 (J. *Day*).

— *b*) BLOTH Peter C.: 'Vor Ort'-Praktische Theologie in der Erprobung, 60. Gb., ᴱBookhagen Rainer. Nürnberg 1991, Stoja. [<LuJb 59, p. 223, ≯ m204].

— *c*) BOEMER Theo: Theologie en marginalisering, ᴱHoudijk R. Baarn 1992, Gooi & S. 203 p. *f* 32.50. 90-304-0683-6 [TvT 33,310, T. *Veerkamp*].

20 BORGER Hugo, 65. Gb.: Kölner JbVFrG 23. B 1990, Mann. 759 p.; ill. [AnPg 62, p. 996, dépouillé].

20* BOSCH VILA Jacinto: Homenaje. M 1991, Inst. Juan XXIII, cooperación con el mundo árabe. I. 653 p. II. p. 654-1208. 84-338-1439-7. [BO 49, 592].

21 BRAUN René: I: De la préhistoire à Virgile; philologie, littératures et histoires anciennes; II. Autour de TERTULLIEN: textes; ᴱGranarolo Jean (*Biraud* Michèle): Nice Fac. Lett. 56. P 1990, BLettres. 282 p.; portr. / xi-248 p. [AnPg 62, p. 996; dépouillé].

22 BRECHT Martin: LUTHERS Wirkung, ᴱHauschild Wolf-Dieter. Stu 1992, Calwer. 302 p. ill.; Bibliog. 257-283, ᴱ*Peters* C. DM 128 [TR 88,431, tit. pp.] 13 art.; 3 infra.

23 BROOKE Christopher: Church and city, 1000-1500, ᴱAbulafia David, *al*. C 1992, Univ. xxiv-354 p.; 12 fig.; 1 pl., 2 plans. £55 [RHE 87, 224*; AmHR 98,994, titles; TBR 6/1, 44, D. *Hoyle*]. 0-521-35611-3.

24 BRUCH Richard: Horizonte sittlichen Handelns, 80. Gb., ᴱKönig O., *Wolkinger* A.; GrazerTSt 14. Graz 1992, InstÖkTPatr. 462 p. DM 40. [NRT 115, 424, G. *Menin*].

24* BRÜMMER Vincent, Christian faith and philosophical theology, ᴱBrink G. van der. Kampen 1992. Kok. vii-295 p. 90-390-0004-2 [TLond 96,53, A. I. *McFadyen*]. – ᴿExpTim 104 (1992s) 60 (W. D. *Hudson*).

25 BRUNNER Emil, in der Erinnerung seiner Schüler, 100 Gb., ᴱKramer Werner, *Sonderegger* Hugo. Z 1989, Theol.-V. 231 p.; 8 pl. Fs 20. [TLZ 118, 487, N. *Müller*].

25* BRUNNER-TRAUT Emma: Gegengabe, ᴱGammer-Wallert Ingrid, *Helck* Wolfgang. Tü 1992, Attempto. 377 p. 3-89308-143-7 [OIAc 3, 15; excerpted].

26 BUTLER Joseph (bishop) tercentenary essays, ᴱCunliffe Christopher. Ox 1992, Clarendon. xiv-320 p. £37.50. 0-198-26740-1. [JEH 44, 361s, W. R. *Ward*: invigorating though continuing long-standing feuds and with 'gap-inclusive corporeality' and 'Ø-ing'].

26* CAHILL P. Joseph: RelStT 12, 2s (1992).

27 CARDONA Giorgio R., ricordo: Episteme, ᴱPoli Diego: QuadLingFg 4 (1986-9). Macerata/R 1990, Univ. / Herder. 302 p. [AnPg 62, p. 996]. – ᴿBSLP 87,2 (1992) 122-5 (Françoise *Bader*).

27* CARNEY James: Sages, saints and storytellers, Celtic studies, ᴱÓ Corráin Donnchadh, *al*.; Maynooth Mg 2. Maynooth 1989, An Sagart. xvi-

472 p. 1-870684-07-9. – ᴿBijdragen 53 (1992) 214s (M. *Schneiders*); Furrow 41 (1990) 262s (D. *Ó Laoghaire*)
28 CASSANDRO Giovanni mem.: Archivi di Stato 18. R 1991, Ministero Beni Culturali. 3 vol.; 1113 p. [RHE 88,58*]
29 CAWKWELL George: Georgica, Greek studies, ᴱFlower Michael A., *Toher* Mark: Bulletin Supp. 58. L 1991, Inst. Clas. St. x-192 p.; portr. £35 pa. – ᴿClasR 42 (1992) 416-8 (H. D. *Westlake*); RÉAnc 94 (1992) 476 (P. *Brun*).
30 *a*) CEYSSENS L., Le sort de la bulle Unigenitus 1992 [RechSR 84,479, P. *Vallin*].
— *b*) CHARNEUX P.: Hellènika symmikta; histoire, archéologie, épigraphie: ÉtArchClas 7. Nancy 1991, Univ. 170 p. 8 pl. F 180. 2-86480-550-6 [AntClas 62,428, A. *Martin*: plusieurs tit. pp.].
— *c*) CHOJNACKI Stanislaus: Orbis aethiopicus, 75. Gb., ᴱScholz Piotr O., *al.* BtNubica 3. Albstadt 1992, Schuler. I. xxxiv-264 p.; portr.; bibliog. p. xvii-xx; II. p. 267-504. 3-929513-01-3; -2-1.
31 CHRIST Karl, Alte Geschichte und Wissenschaftsgeschichte, 65. Gb. ᴱKneisel P., *Losemann* V. Da 1988, Wiss. viii-537 p.; 1 pl. → 4,d126: ᴿAnzAltW 45 (1992) 66-71 (R. *Bichler*).
32 CIVIL Miguel: Velles paraules, Ancient Near Eastern Studies, 65th b., ᴱMichalowski Piotr, *al.*: Aula Orientalis 9,1s (1991). 290 p.; phot.; bibliog. 283-290 (*Jones* Charles E.), 11-13 appreciation (*Kramer* Samuel N.).
33 CLARKE Bowman L.: Logic, God and metaphysics, ᴱHarris James F.: StPhRel 15. Boston 1992, Kluwer. ix-149 p. $77. 0-7923-1454-9. 10 art. [TDig 40,74].
33* CLEVE Fredric: Academia et ecclesia, 60. Gb., ᴱKvist Hans-Olof. Åbo 1991, Akademi. xiv-268 p.; portr. 951-9498-89-3 [TLZ 118,1015, tit. pp.]. – ᴿTsTKi 63 (1992) 236s (G. *Heiene*).
34 CODOÑER C.: Mnemosynum, ᴱRamos Guerreira Agustín: ActaSalm 247. S 1991, Univ. 342 p. [AnPg 62, p. 996, dépouillé].
34* CORISH Patrick J.: Religion, conflict and coexistence in Ireland [...since the Reformation]. Comerford/Dublin 1990, Cullen/Gill&M. 360 p.; bibliog. 13 art. – ᴿStudies 81 (1992) 119-121 (T. *Morrissey*).
35 CROUZEL Henri: Recherches et tradition, mélanges patristiques, ᴱDupleix André: THist 88. P 1992, Beauchesne. xvi-339 p.; portr.; bibliog. 315-336. F 240. 2-7010-1253-8. 21 art.; 10 infra. [TR 88,519, tit. pp.; NRT 115,748, V. *Roisel*; NTAbs 37, p. 314; VigChr 47,310, titres sans pp.; ArTGran 56,342, A. *Segovia*; TvT 33,213, A. *Davids*].
36 CULLMANN Oscar: (I) Hommage [80ᵉ anniv.], ᴱPhilonenko Marc, *Trocmé* Étienne: RHPR 72,1 (1992), 126 p.; portr. (1930); 113-8, bibliog. 1972-91 (*Arnold* M.).
37 – (II) Aphieroma sta 90 chronia: DeltioVM 21,11 (1992) 112 p.; 5-41 tributes ⊚ (S. *Agourides, al.* [ZNW 84,144, tit. pp.].
38 – (III)., Mitbegründer, 90, Gb. 'gewidmet': TZBas 48,2 (1992) 207-242.
39 DAHM Karl-Wilhelm, 60. Gb.: Ethik, Wirtschaft, Kirche; Verantwortung in der Industriegesellschaft, ᴱMarhold Wolfgang. Dü 1991, Patmos. vii-432 p. DM 47 [TR 88,532, einige tit. pp.].
40 DAVID C. Robert William: 60th b., Communication, ᴱJeyaraj Jesudason: Arasaradi Journal of Theological Reflection 5 (Madurai 1992) 209 p.; portr. bibliog. 206s (E. *Mohandoss*). 20 art.; 4 infra.
41 DAVIDSON Robert: Text as Pretext, ᴱCarroll Robert P.: jOsu [= JStOT supp.] 138. Sheffield 1992, Academic. 307 p.; portr.; bibliog. p. 291s. £40. 1-85075-295-8 [RB 100,285, tit. pp.; BL 93,9, W. J. *Houston*; TR

89,517. tit. pp.; TBR 6/3,12, Katrina *Larkin*; BZ 37,299, J. *Scharbert*; ExpTim 104,277, G. Lloyd *Jones*; Interpretation 47,426, R. N. *Boyce*; JTS 44,622, R. *Mason*; RelStR 20,48, Z. *Garber*].

42 DEIST Ferdinand E.: Old Testament science and reality; a mosaic for Deist, 50th b., ᴱWessels W., *Scheffler* E. Pretoria 1992, Verba Vitae. 357 p. 0-620-17151-0. 21 art. [BL 93,25, R. P. *Carroll*, tit. pp.].

43 DELVOYE Charles, 1917-1991: Hommage à la mémoire de ~, Byzantion 62 (1992). 432 p.; phot.; biobibliog. 5-11 (Lydie *Hadermann-Misguich* ⑥); 474-544, sa dernière Chronique archéologique.

43* DEMBOWSKI Bronisław, bp.: ⑨ *Chrześcijaństwo religią zbawienia*, Le christianisme la religion du salut I-II: AtKap 118/499 (1992) 355-458; 119/500 (1992) 1-92; 93-101, Dembowski, ⑨ Rôle de l'Église en temps de changements. – 13 art., infra.

44 DÌAZ ESTEBAN Fernando: ᴱSpottorno María V., *al.*, Sefarad 52,1 (1992) 272 p.; portr.; biobibliog. 7-14.

45 DOBLIN Helga: Abeunt studia in mores; on philosophies of education and personal learning or teaching in the humanities and moral sciences, ᴱMerrill Sarah A., NY 1990, P. Lang. xxviii-362 p. – ᴿSalesianum 54 (1992) 202s (G. *Abbà*: titles, none infra).

Dublin All Hallows college anniversary symposium 1992 ➤ 598*.

46 DUBY Georges: (I) Femmes, mariages, lignages; mélanges... BtMA 1. Bru 1992, De Boeck Univ. 470 p. 11 pl. [RHE 87,484, L. *Genicot*].

47 — (II) Histoire et sociète: I. Le couple, l'ami et le prochain; II. Le tenancier, le fidèle et le citoyen; III. Le moine, le clerc et le prince; IV. La mémoire, l'écriture et l'histoire. Aix-en-Provence 1992, Univ. 226 p.; 240 p.; 214 p.; 236 p.; 5 maps. F 620. [RHE 88,58*].

48 DUNAYEVSKY Immanuel (Munya) [1906-1968] mem.: The architecture of ancient Israel, from the prehistoric to the Persian periods, ᴱKempinski Aharon. J 1992, Israel Exploration Soc. xiv-332 p.; ill., maps. $48. 965-221-013-7. 27 art., 19 infra [BL 93,33, H. *Williamson*; OLZ 88,397, A. *Strobel*].

49 DYCK Cornelius J.: Anabaptism revisited; essays on Anabaptist/Mennonite studies, ᴱKlaassen Walter. Scottdale PA 1992, Herald. 209 p. $15. 0-8361-3577-6. 13 art. [TDig 39,349; RHE 87,432*]. – ᴿArchivScSocR 78 (1992) 236s (J. *Séguy*).

50 ENGLER Rudolf: Sprachtheorie und Theorie der Sprachwissenschaft; Geschichte und Perspektiven, 60. Gb., ᴱLiver Ricarda, *al.*: TüBeitLing 355. Tü 1990, Narr. viii-337 p. [AnPg 62, p. 997, dépouillé].

51 Erfurt Univ. 600. J., Ph/th Studium 40. J.: Denkender Glaube in Geschichte und Gegenwart, ᴱErnst Wilhelm, *Feiereis* Konrad: ErfTSt 63. Lp 1992, Benno. 460 p.; 2 fig.; 7 pl. 3-7462-1017-8; pa. -08-9 [TR 88, 425]. – ᴿTGL 82 (1992) 372s (H. E. *Drobner*).

52 ERHART Hannelore : Querdenken; Beiträge zur feministich-befreiungstheologischen Diskussion. Göttingen 1992, Pfaffenweiler. 393 p. DM 34. [TLZ 118,488, Irene *Dannemann*].

53 ERNST Wilhelm: Moraltheologie im Dienst der Kirche, 65, Gb., ᴱDemmer Klaus, *Ducke* K.-H.; ErfurtTSt 64. Lp 1992, Benno. 341 p. DM 64 [TR 88,529, tit. pp.].

54 FEILZER Heinz: Wege der Evangelisierung, 65. Gb., ᴱHeinz Andreas, *Lentzen-Deis* Wolfgang, *Schneck* Ernst. Trier 1992, Paulinus. c. 360 p. 24 art.; 5 infra.

54* FINGARETTE Herbert: Rules, rituals, and responsibilities, ᴱBockover Mary I.: Critics and their Critics 7. LaSalle IL 1991, Open Court. 228 p. [RelStR 19,142, K. *Smith*].

55 FISCHER Balthasar: Gratias agamus; Studien zum eucharistischen Hochgebet, EHinz Andreas, *Rennings* Heinrich. FrB 1992, Herder. xix-545 p. DM 78 [TR 88,535; RSPT 77,128, P.-M. *Gy*, tit. pp.; TrierTZ 102,320, N. *Fohr*; TvT 33,309, H. *Wegman*; ZkT 115,378, R. *Messner*].

55* FLASH Kurt, Historiae philosophiae Medii Aevi, Studien... EMojsisch B., *Pluta* O. Amst/Ph 1991, Grüner. xxxi-561 p.; iv+p. 562-1164. *f* 300 [RHE 88,388*].

56 FLEURY Michel: Florilegium marianum [Mari en Syrie], EDurand Jean-M.: NABU Mémoire 1. P 1992, SEPOA [Société pour l'Étude du Proche-Orient ancien]. 160 p. [RB 101,298, tit. pp.; BO 49,586; JAOS 112,725; OLZ 88,137, H. *Klengel*].

57 FLUSSER David [I. 1990 ➤ 6,54] II. Messiah and Christos; studies in the Jewish origins of Christianity, 75th b., EGruenwald Ithamar, *Shaked* Saul, *Stroumsa* Gedaliahu G.: TStAJ 32. Tü 1992, Mohr. viii-240 p.; portr. DM 216. 3-16-145996-2. 16 art.; infra. [RB 100,455, tit. pp.; BL 94,139, G. *Vermes*].

57* FONTAINE Jacques: De TERTULLIEN aux Mozarabes, 70e anniv., 1. Antiquité tardive et christianisme ancien (VIe-IXe s.), EHoltz L., *al.*: Ét-AugMA 26. P 1992, ÉtAug. 374 p.; 33 pl. [RHE 88,396*].

58 FOX John: Littera et sensus; essays on form and meaning in medieval French literature [colloquium 1988... *Muir* L., in the biblical drama], ETrotter D. A. Exeter 1989, Univ. x-132 p.; ill. £19. – RSpeculum 67 (1992) 488-490 (A. E. *Knight*).

59 FRIES Heinrich: In Verantwortung für den Glauben; Beiträge zur Fundamentaltheologie und Ökumenik, 80 ans, ENeuner P., *Wagner* H. FrB 1992, Herder. 408 p. DM 78. [NRT 115,742, L. *Renwart*; TvT 33,195, A. *Willems*]. – RZkT 114 (1992) 349 (K. H. *Neufeld*).

60 GADILLE Jacques: Histoire religieuse, histoire globale, histoire ouverte, EDurand J.-D., *Ladous* R.: BtRelSocPol. P 1992, Beauchesne. 537 p.; map. F 330 [BLitEc 94.376. J.-C. *Meyer*; Greg 75,787, F. de *Lasala*; NRT 115,617, J. *Masson*; RHE 88,358, J. *Pirotte*; RHPR 73,438, E. *Goichot*; SR 22,245, G. *Martel*; TvT 33,96, J. van *Laarhoven*].

60* GAMBASIN Angelo, mem.: EBillanovich : Fonti e studi di storia veneta 17. Vicenza 1992, Pozza. xxxi-497 p. [RHE 88,396*].

61 GARCÍA CORDERO Maximiliano, en su jubilación: Salmanticensis 39,1 (1992) 5-10; portr. (G. *Pérez*; bibliog.).

62 GASCA QUEIRAZZA Giuliano: Miscellanea di studi romanzi, 65o compleanno, ECornagliotti Anna, *al.* Alessandria 1988, Orso. xxiv-1124 p. (2 vol.) 62 art.; 2 infra. – RSalesianum 54 (1992) 411s (R. *Bracchi*: titoli senza pp.).

62* GAUSSIN Pierre-Roger: Maisons de Dieu et hommes d'Église, EDuranton H., *al.*: Centre Européen de Recherches sur les Congrégations et Ordres Religieux. St-Étienne 1992, Univ. 428 p.; 6 maps. bibliog. 13-16. F 210 [RHE 88,827, G. *Hendrix*].

63 GEFFRÉ Claude: Interpréter; mélanges, EJossua Jean-Pierre, *Séd* Nicolas-Jean. P 1992, Cerf. 328 p.; portr.; biobibliog. p. 301-319. F 180. 2-204-04468-7. 14 art.; infra. [TR 88,434, tit. pp.; FilT 7,163, M. *Pagano*; TvT 33,423, M. van *Tente*; ZkT 115,180, K. H. *Neufeld*]. – RFoiTemps 22 (1992) 563s (G. *Harpigny*); VSp 146 (1992) 400-2 (C. *Boureux*).

63* GEREMEK Bronisław: ❷ Arme und Reiche; Studien aus der Geschichte der Gesellschaft und der Kultur, 60. Gb. Wsz 1992, Państwowe. 397 p. [RHE 88,396*].

64 GEVIRYAHU Haim M. I.: memorial volume, EAdler Joshua J. J 1990, World Jewish Bible Center. xi-145 p. ❸ vii-154 [CBQ 54,832].

65 GEVIRTZ Stanley [1929-1988] mem.: Let your colleagues praise you, ᴱRatner Robert J., al. = Maarav 7s (1991s) I, 301 p.; 6 pl.; portr. ... 18 + 23 art.; infra.
66 GHUL Mahmud al-, mémorial: Inscriptions sudarabiques, ᴱBron François: L'Arabie préislamique 2. P 1992, Geuthner. 123 p. 2-7053-0625-0 [OIAc 5,16, excerpted].
66* GIBSON Margaret: Intellectual life in the Middle Ages, ᴱSmith Lesley, *Ward* Benedicta. L 1992, Hambledon. xiv-322 p.; ill. £37.50. 1-85285-069-8. [JEH 44,550, A. K. *McHardy*].
67 GRAEVE Frank De: A universal faith? Peoples, cultures, religions and the Christ, ᴱCornille Catherine, *Neckebrouck* Valeer: TheolPastMg 9. Lv 1992, Peeters. 198 p. [TContext 10/2,103, H. *Hoeben*].
68 GRAUS František: Spannungen und Widersprüche, ᴱBurghartz S., al. Sigmaringen 1992, Thorbecke. 324 p.; front.; 3 maps [RHE 88,58*].
69 GREENBERG Simon, jubilee volume: ❹ Tura, studies in Jewish thought, ᴱAyali Meir. TA 1989, Oranim Centre for Jewish Studies. 391 p. 23 art.; titles only ❹.
70 GREENLEE J. Harold: Scribes and Scripture; New Testament essays, ᴱBlack David A. WL 1992, Eisenbrauns. xv-135 p.; portr.; biobibliog. ix-xv. 0-931464-70-6. [NTAbs 37, p. 433] 9 art.; infra. – ᴿFgNt 5 (1992) 216; tit. sans pp.
71 GRIFFITHS Bede: As we are one, ᴱBruteau Beatrice. L 1991, Philosophers' Exchange. 10 art. (*Teasdale* W., *Panikkar* R....), 3 poems. – ᴿCCurr 42 (1992s) 564s (F. *Middleton*).
72 GRIFFITHS J. Gwyn: Studies in Pharaonic religion and society, ᴱLloyd Alan B.: Occas. Publ. 8. L 1992, Egypt Exploration Soc. xii-261 p.; portr.; ill.; bibliog. p. 1-13. 0-85698-120-6. 21 art.; plures infra.
73 GRMEK Mirko: Maladie et maladies – histoire et conceptualisation [Sorbonne 12. déc. 1991] ᴱGourévitch Danielle: ÉPHÉ 4/5 MédvMod 70. Genève 1992, Droz. lxxii (biobibliog.) – 473 p., portr. 31 art.; 3 infra ➔ k78. – ᴿREG 105 (1992) 593s (Véronique *Boudon*).
74 GUENTHER Heinz O.: Scriptures and cultural conversations, 65th , b., ᴱKloppenborg John S., *Vaage* Leif E.: Toronto Journal of Theology 8,1 (1992) 173 p.; 3-6, biobibliog.
   GUNNEWEG A. H. J., Sola scriptura [I 1982] II 1992 ➔ 249; [not = Sola Scriptura, ᴱSchmid H. 1990/1 ➔ 7,454c].
75 HACKETT Olwen: Town and country in Roman Tripolitania: Soc. for Libyan Studies Occas. Paper 2. BAR-Int 274; Ox 1985. xvi-311 p.; 111 fig. [AnPg 57, p. 758; 62, p. 997]. – ᴿBonnJbb 190 (1990) 713-6 (M. *Euzennat*).
75* HÄNGGI Anton [Bischof]: Miteinander; für die vielfältige Einheit der Kirche, ᴱSchifferle A. Ba 1992, Herder. 396 p. DM 68. 3-451-22608-1. [NRT 116,458, L. *Volpe*; RSPT 77,131, P.-M. *Gy*: tit. pp.; TvT 33,103, T. *Brattinga*; ZkT 115,376, H. B. *Meyer*]. – ᴿStiZt 210 (1992) 359 (W. *Seibel*).
76 HÄRING Bernhard: In Christus zum Leben befreit, ᴱRömelt Josef, *Hidber* Bruno. FrB 1992, Herder. 372 p. DM 68 [TR 88,530, some tit. pp.; NRT 115,422, L. *Volpe*; TGL 83.400 H. *Gleixner*; TvT 33,203, H. *Spee*].
77 HARRISVILLE Roy A.: All things new, 70th b., ᴱHultgren Arland J., *Juel* Donald H., *Kingsbury* Jack D.: Word &World supp. 1. St. Paul 1992, Luther NW Theological Seminary. [viii-]190 p.; phot.; biobibliog. 3-30. $15. 0-9632-3890-6. 19 art.; infra. [NTAbs 37,103].

78 HAY Denys: The impact of humanism on western Europe, ᴱGoodman
   Anthony, *McKay* Angus. L 1990, Longman. xv-292 p. 11 art. [ChH 62,
   553, D. D. *Sullivan*].
79 HEESTERMAN J. C.:   Religion, state and history in South Asia, ᴱHoek
   A. W. van den: KernInstMem 5. Leiden 1992, Brill. xi-843 p.; ill. *f* 220.
80 HENRY Carl F.:   God and culture, ᴱCarson D. A., *Woodbridge* John D. GR
   1993, Eerdmans. xii-398 p. $35. 0-8028-3709-3.
81 HIMMELMANN Nikolaus: Fs., ᴱCain Hans-Ulrich, *al.*: BonnJbb Beih 47.
   Mainz 1989, von Zabern. xi-539 p. DM 225. 3-8053-1033-1. – ᴿAntClas
   61 (1992) 683s (D. *Viviers*).
82 Hinrichs Verlag (200. Jahrestag), 'Ein Geschäft recht geistiger Natur',
   ᴱGeist Lucie. Lp 1991, Neuer Sachsenverlag.   84 p.; ill.; DM 24,80. –
   ᴿOLZ 87 (1992) 14s (W. *Rau*: Erinnerungen an ALT, EISSFELDT, *al.*).
83 HÖRNER Hedwig: Hermeneumata, 60. Gb. BtKlasAltW 2/79. Heid 1990,
   Winter.   345 p. ill.; DM 180, pa.   150. 3-533-04155-7; -4-9. [AntClas
   61,413, K. *Demoen*].   – ᴿWienerSt 105 (1992) 249 (Dorothea *Weber*).
84 HOFFMAN Michael A. [1944-1990], mem.: The followers of Horus, ᴱFried-
   man René, *Adams* Barbara: Egyptian Studies Asn. Publ. 2. Oxford 1992,
   Oxbow.   xxviii-356 p.; portr.; ill.; biobibliog. ix-xxvii. 0-946897-44-1. 40
   art.; 13 infra. [OIAc 5,24].
85 HOFFMANN Erich: Mare Balticum; Beiträge zur Geschichte des Ost-
   seeraums in Mittelalter und Neuzeit, 65. Gb., ᴱParavicini W.: Kieler Hist.
   St. 36. Sigmaringen 1992, Thorbecke. xix-503 p.; 8 fig.; 15 pl.; 5 maps.
   DM 98 [RHE 87,392*].
86 HOLLENWEGER Walter J.:   Pentecost, Mission and ecumenism; essays on
   intercultural theology, ᴱJongeneed Jan A. B., *al.* Fra 1992, Lang. 376 p.;
   biobibliog. p. (5-13) 311-357 (P. N. van der *Laan*). 3-631-44010-3. 26
   art. [TContext 10/2,102, H. *Hoeben*].
87 HORNIG Gottfried: Theologie und Aufklärung, 65. Gb., ᴱMüller Wolfgang E., *Schulz* Harmut H. R. Wü 1992, Königshausen & N.   438 p.
   DM 138 [TR 88,522]. — HORST Irvin B. (& SIMONS M.) 1992 → 565.
88 HUBBARD David A.:   Studies on Old Testament theology, ᴱHubbard
   Robert L., *al.* Dallas 1992, Word.   333 p.; tributes p. 13-28; bibliog.
   279-285. 0-8499-0865-5. 14 art.; infra [RB 101,290, tit. pp.].
89 HUBBELING Hubertus G. (1923-1986), mem.: Belief in God and intellectual honesty, ᴱVeldhuis R., *al.* Assen 1990, Van Gorcum. X-205 p.
   f 49,50. 90-232-2524-4. – ᴿKerkT 42 (1991) 262s (*Veldhuis*).
90 HUIZING P. J. M.:   Studies in canon law, ᴱProvost J. H., *Walf* K.: Annua
   Nuntia Lovaniensia 32. Lv 1991, Peeters. xxlx-234 p.; Fb 1500. 90-
   6186-439-9 [NRT 115,268, L. *Volpe*]. – ᴿTPhil 67 (1922) 314s (R. *Sebott*:
   some topics without titles); TvT [= TsTNijm] 32 (1992) 116s (M.
   Wijlens).
91 HUSSEY S. S.:   LANGLAND, the mystics and the medieval English religious
   tradition, ᴱPhillips Helen, Woodbridge 1990, Boydell & B. xii-289 p.;
   portr. $73. – ᴿSpeculum 67 (1992) 774s (tit. pp.).
92 IACOANGELI Roberto, 'Humanitas' classica et 'sapientia' christiana, ᴱFelici
   S.: BIScRel 1. R 1992, LAS. 446 p.; 1 fig.; Lit. 50.000. [NRT 115,619, S.
   Hilaire; ArTGran 56,379, A. *Segovia*].
93 İNAN Jale [Mme]: Fs/Armağanı, ᴱBaşgelen Nezih, *Luggal* Mihin. İstanbul
   1989, Arkeoloji/Sanat. I. xvi-589 p.; portr.; bibliog. xvi-xvii. II. 228 pl.
   975-7538-06-X. 69 art., 7 infra.
93* ISSAWI Charles: The economic dimensions of Middle Eastern history
   [6 of the 12 art. from 1986 conference], ᴱEsfandiari Haleh, *Udovitch*

A. I. Princeton 1990, Darwin. 368 p.; 1 portr. $25. – ᴿJRAS (1992) 262-4 (R. M. *Burrell*).

94 IVERSEN Erik: The heritage of ancient Egypt, ᴱOsing Jürgen, *Nielsen* Erland K.: Niebuhr Publ. 13. K 1992, Univ. 123 p.; portr.; bibliog. p. 121s. 87-7289-140-8. 11 art.

95 JEISMANN Karl-Ernst: Geschichte und Geschichtsbewusstsein, 65. Gb., ᴱLeidinger Paul, *Metzler* Dieter. Münster 1990, Univ. 793 p.; portr.; bibliog.778-793 (*Pramme* U.). 3-87717-939-2. 28 art.; 3 infra.

95* JOHNSTONE Thomas M. [1924-83] in memoriam: A miscellany of Middle Eastern articles, ᴱIrvine E. K., *al.* Harlow 1988, Longman. xi-249 p. £39. – ᴿBSO 55 (1991) 132-4 (C. *Holes*: mostly Arabic).

96 KÁKOSY László: The intellectual heritage of Egypt, 60th B., ᴱLuft Ulrich: StAeg 14. Budapest 1992, Innova. 631 p.; bibliog. 17-25 (*Szücs* Marianna); XLVIII pl.; 7 p. corrigenda. [OIAc 5,26, excerpted]. 963-462-5428. – 69 art.; 27 infra.

97 KANTZENBACH Friedrich W.: Das Vertrauen, das Wort findet, 60. Gb., ᴱGrauvogel Gerd W., *Heieck* Andreas. Saarbrücken-Scheidt 1992, Dadder. 260 p.; ill. DM 36 [TR 88,513].

98 KANTZER Kenneth S., Doing theology in today's world, ᴱWoodbridge John D., *McComisky* Thomas E., GR 1991, Zondervan. 511 p. $25 pa. – ᴿTrinJ 13 (1992) 110-7 (P. L. *Metzger*); TTod 49 (1992s) 579 (D. G. *Bloesch*).

99 KARAGEORGHIS Vassos: Studies in honour of ∼, ᴱIoannidis G. C.: Deltion 54s. Nicosia 1992, Soc. Cypriot. Studies. ix-374 p.; LXXXVI pl.; bibliog. 7-20 [RB 100,447, tit. pp.; RÉG 106,643, H. *Cassimatis*]; 46 art.; 5 infra.

100 KAZHDAN Alexander: Homo Byzantinus, ᴱCutler Anthony, *Franklin* Simon: DumbO 46. Wsh 1992. vii-329 p.; 23 fig.; 8 plans; bibliog. 5-26. 0-88402-198-X. 29 art.; 2 infra [RHE 88,58*].

100* KEBLE John 200th b.: The English religious tradition and the genius of Anglicanism (14 Oxford Keble college lectures]. L 1992, IKON. 256 p. £18; pa. £10. 1-871805-01-5; -2-3. – ᴿExpTim 104 (1992s) 193s (C. S. *Rodd*).

101 KELLNER Hans-Jörg: Spurensuche, 70. Gb., ᴱDannheimer Hermann (*Garbsch* Jochen): MüPrähSamml Beih 3. Kallmünz 1991, Lassleben. 202 p.; portr.; 11-30 Bibliog. (*Zahlhaas* Gisela). 3-7847-5182-2. 10 art. ➔ g526.

102 *a)* KERTELGE Karl: Monotheismus und Christologie; zur Gottesfrage im hellenistischen Judentum und im Urchristentum, ᴱKlauck Hans-J.: QDisp 138. FrB 1992, Herder. 220 p. DM 48 [TR 88,518].

— *b)* KIDSON Peter: Medieval architecture and its intellectual context, ᴱFernie E., *Crossley* P. L 1990, Hambledon. 304 p.; 67 pl. [RHE 88,297*].

— *c)* KIESOW Ernst R.: Widersprechen und Widerstehen; theologische Existenz heute, 65. Gb., ᴱBeyer F.-H., *al.* Rostock 1991, Univ. Theol. Fak. 232 p.; portr. 3-86009-080-1 [TLZ 118,288, E. *Winkler*].

103 KING Edward B.: Essays, ᴱBenson Robert G., *Naylor* Eric W. Sewanee TN 1991, Univ. of the South. vi-253 p. $25. – ᴿSpeculum 67 (1992) 1063 (tit. pp.).

103* KLAASSEN Walter: Conrad Grebel Review 9,3 (1991) p. 209-353; bio/ bibliog. 213-7 (R. *Sawatsky*) / 345-351 (D. *Smucker*); Klaassen p. 331-4 on Lk 10,25-37.

104 KOESTER Helmut: The future of early Christianity,   ᴱPearson Birger A.
Mp 1991, Fortress.   xx-509 p.; bibliog.   (*Scholer* D. M.);   epilogue by
Koester p. 467-487. $40 [CBQ 55,199, Carolyn *Osiek*].   36 art.; 29 infra.
105 KORFF Wilhelm: Markierungen der Humanität, sozialethische Herausforderungen auf dem Weg in ein neues Jahrtausend, 65. Gb.,   ᴱMertens
Gerhard, *al*.   Pd 1992, Schöningh.   408 p.; Bibliog. p. 395-405.   DM 78. 23
art. [TR 88,348, tit. pp.] ⟶ k83.
106 KOTTJE Raymund: Aus Archiven und Bibliotheken, 65. Gb.,   ᴱMordek
Hubert: Freiburger Beiträge zur MA-Geschichte 3.   Fra 1992, Lang.
xi-658 p.; ill.; Bibliog. p. 617-630.   DM 129 [TR 88,430, some tit. pp.].
107 KRAABEL A. Thomas: Diaspora Jews and Judaism, essays in honor of,
and in dialogue with, ∼, ᴱOverman J. Andrew, *MacLennan* Robert S.:
SFL StHJ 41.   Atlanta 1992, Scholars.   xiii-368 p.; bibliog.   359-362;
Kraabel afterword 347-357.   1-55540-696-3.   22 art.; infra; partly reprints
of Kraabel and others. [BL 93,142, G. *Vermes*; NTAbs 36,443; Religion
23,288, G. *Harvey*].
108 KREMER Klaus: Transzendenz; zu einem Grundwort der klassischen
Metaphysik, 65. Gb.,   ᴱHonnefelder Ludger, *Schüster* Werner.   Pd 1992,
Schöningh.   317 p.; 297-301 bibliog. DM 98 [TR 88,527, some (11) tit. pp.].
109 KRIKORIAN Mesrob K., Bischof: Chalcedon und die Folgen, 60. Gb.,
ᴱKirchschläger R., *Stirnemann* A.   Innsbruck 1992, Tyrolia.   506 p.; 16
fig. DM 89 [NRT 115,744, L.-J. *Renard*].
110 KUCAŁA Marian: Roczniki Humanistyczne 39s,6 (Językoznawstwo 1991s).
Lublin, KUL.   237 p.; phot.; bibliog. p. 7-24 (Z. *Galecki*).
111 KÜHN Ulrich, 60. Gb.:   Veritas et communicatio; ökumenische Theologie
auf der Suche nach einem verbindlichen Zeugnis,   ᴱFranke Heiko.   Gö
1991, Vandenhoeck & R.   377 p.; Bibliog. 365-375 (*Möller* M.). DM 98.
[TR 88,529, einige (14) tit. pp.]; p. 310-320, *Pannenberg* W.
112 KUNG Joan [† 1987] mem.:   Nature, knowledge and virtue,   ᴱPenner Terry,
Kraut Richard: Apeiron 22/4.   Edmonton 1989, Academic.   xii-233 p.
$45; pa. $20. – ᴿClasR 42 (1992) 84s (Pamela M. *Huby*).
112* KUSS Otto († 1991 aet. 86) mem. (no mention on cover or title-pages):
Theologie im Werden;   Studien zu den theologischer Konzeptionen im
NT,   ᴱHainz Josef (p. 11-19).   Pd 1992, Schöningh.   464 p., portr.
DM 38.   3-506-73903-4 [BZ 37,317, Hanneliese *Steichele*].   19 art.; plures
infra.
113 LABHARDT André, 80ᵉ anniv.:   MusHelv 48,4 (1991) 213-344.
114 LABOURDETTE Marie-Michel, O.P.:   Un maître en théologie: RThom 92,1
(1992).   428 p.; portr.; biog.   17-51 + bibliog. p. 388-425 (*Donneaud*
Henry) [NRT 115,452, L. *Volpe*; Divinitas 37,84-95, D. *Vibrac*]. – ᴿEspr-
Vie 102 (1992) 444-7 (P. *Jay*).
115 LAMBRECHT Jan: 'Sharper than a two-edged sword', 65th b.,   ᴱKoperski
Veronica, *Bieringer* William: Louvain Studies 17,2s (1992) 101-314; portr.;
biobibliog. 103-130.
116 ŁANOWSKI Georgio septuagenario: Eos 78 (1990). 450 p.; portr. [AnPg 62,
p. 998].
117 LARUE Rodrigue: Mélanges,   ᴱTremblay Florent: Univ. Québec Cahiers
d'Études Anciennes 25.   Trois-Rivières.   283 p.; portr. [AnPg 62, p. 998;
dépouillé].
117* LAVIN Irving, 60th b.:   IL 60, Essays,   ᴱLavin Marilyn.   NY 1990, Italica.   xviii-284 p., portr.; ill. $45.   12 art. [Speculum 68,287]; 31-44, *Spiro*
Marie, Pegasos and the seasons in a fragment from Caesarea Maritima;
1-29, *Clarke* John R., Notes ... houses of Roman Italy 100 BCE-235 CE.

118 LESLAU Wolf: Semitic studies, 85th b., ᴱKaye Alan S. [xxi-xxxv], Wsb 1991, Harrassowitz ➤ 7,93. I. lxviii-889 p.; portr.; bibliog. xxxv-lxvi (*Devens* Monica S.: 300 items + index); II. p. 891-1719; front. 3-447-03168-9. 128 art.; 84 infra [LA 43,536, M. *Pazzini* & A. *Niccacci*]. − ᴿLešonenu 57 (1992s) 175-182 (J. *Blau* ❻, omitted in English index to fasc. 2).

118* LÉVÊQUE Pierre G., Religion, ᴱMactoux Marie-M., *Geny* Évelyne: Ann. Besançon 463. P 1992, BLettres. xxx-292 p. ill. 2-251-60463-4 [Latomus 52,941, J. *Debergh*).

119 a) LEVINSON Nathan P. & Pnina N.: Aus zweier Zeugen Mund, ᴱSchoeps Julius H. Gerlingen 1992, Bleicher. 272 p. DM 48 [TR 88,529].

— b) LEVY Bernard S.: Mediaevalia 15 (SUNY 1993 for 1989) 370 p.; phot. 0361-946X. 19 art., 3 infra.

— c) LEYSER Karl: Warriors and churchmen in the high Middle Ages, ᴱReuter T. Rio Grande 1992, Hambledon. xxiii-232 p. $55 [RHE 88,399*].

— d) Liège, Univ. 175ᵉ anniv.: Serta Leodiensia secunda, Liège 1992, Univ. Département des Sciences de l'Antiquité. xviii-468 p. [Kernos 6,399].

— e) The LIGHTFOOT centenary lectures [† 1889], ᴱThompson David M. (*Hengel* M., *Barrett* C.K., *Dunn* J.D.G.) = Durham Univ. Journal special c. 1992. £5. − ᴿExpTim 104 (1992s) 128 (C.S. *Rodd*).

120 LOCHER Gottfried W.: Reformiertes Erbe, 80. Gb., ᴱOberman Heiko A., al. = Zwingliana 19,1s (1991s). Z 1992s, Theol.-V. xii-475 p., color phot.; vii-390; Bibliog. 361-376 (G.W. *Locher*ᴶ): 3-290-10903-8; -4-6. 29 + art.; infra. [BProtF 139,308; 140,317; RelStR 19,268, R. *Kolb*; RHE 88, 58*.231*; TLZ 118,1013, J. *Rogge*].

121 LOCHMAN Jan Milič: [Mt 6,9] Das universale Gebet; Studien zum Unservater, 70. Gb., ᴱSeybold Klaus: TZBas 48,1 (1992). 206 p.; 187-206, Bibliog. seit 1961 (*Becker* Stefan P.). [NTAbs 36,428]. 17 art.; 14 infra.

LOON Maurits van, Natural phenomena, colloquium 1989/92 ➤ 727*.

122 LOURDAUX Guillaume: Serta devota, 1. Devotio Windesheimensis, ᴱVerbeke W., al.: MedvLovSt 20. Lv 1992, Univ. x-452 p.; 2 fig.; 8 facsim. [RHE 87, 394*].

123 LYON Bruce: Law, custom, and social fabric in medieval Europe, ᴱBachrach Bernard S., *Nicholas* David: StMdvCu 28. Kalamazoo 1990, Univ. xxvi-304 p. − ᴿSpeculum 67 (1992) 768s (tit. pp.).

124 MARCHASSON Yves †, Histoire et culture chrétienne; hommage à mgr. ∼, ᴱLedure Y.: Cultures et Christianisme 1. P 1992, Beauchesne. xvi-268 p. [RHE 88,372; NRT 115,618, N. *Plumat*; RHPR 73,302, P. *Maraval*).

125 MARTIMORT A.: 1991, his own articles, ➤ 279 [RSPT 76,170, P.-M. *Gy*, tit. pp.; observations].

126 MARTIN Ralph P.: Worship, theology and ministry in the early Church, ᴱWilkins Michael J., *Paige* Terence: JStNT supp 87. Shf 1992, Academic. 335 p.; portr.; 21-32 vita, bibliog. (*Losie* Lynna A. + 33-36, *Allen* L.G. £45. 1-85075-417-9 [RB 105,136, tit. pp.; TR 88,519]. 17 art.; infra. − ᴿExpTim 104 (1992s) 330 (S, H. *Travis*).

127 MATCZAK Sebastian A.: The wisdom of faith, ᴱThompson Henry O. Lanham MD 1989, UPA. xxi-168 p.; portr.; bibliog. xi-xix. 0-8191-7436-X. 10 art.

†28 MEŃ Alexander [1935-1990] in mem.: Kirchen im Kontext unterschiedlicher Kulturen; auf dem Weg ins dritte Jahrtausend, ᴱFelmy Karl C. (*Heller* W. Red.). Gö 1991, Vandenhoeck & R. 1031 p., Bibliog. 35s. DM 340 [TR 88,529].

129 MESTERS Carlos: Métodos para ler a Bíblia = Estudos Bíblicos 32 (1991) 109 p.
130 MEYER Ben F.:   Self-definition and self-discovery in early Christianity, a study in changing horizons, EHawkin David J., *Robinson* Tom: StBeC 26. Lewiston NY 1990, Mellen. 261 p. $90. 10 art. [TDig 40,87].
131 MICHEL Jacques-Henri: Héritage indo-européen et survivances sélectives: Ludus magistralis 22, 65.67. Bru 1991, Centre F. Peeters. [AnPg 62, p. 998, dépouillé but no pp.].
132 MILIK Józef T.: Intertestamental essays, EKapera Zdzisław J.: Qumranica Mogilanensia 6s. Kraków 1992, Enigma. 347 p.; portr. [26 art. infra (pars I)]. 83-900504-0-4. [ZAW 105,528, tit. pp.; NTAbs 37, p. 147; JStJud 24,107, F. *García Martínez*, tit. pp. résumés; BL 94,142, T. H. *Lim*].
133 MILLS Watson E., founder: PerspRelSt 19,1 (1992), 95 p.
134 MOUTSOPOULOS Evanghelos A.: Methexis, études néo-platoniciennes. Athènes 1992, CIEPA. P. 182-192, *Places* Édouard des, DAMASCIUS et les Oracles chaldaïques [AcPIB 9,778].
135 MUÑOZ IGLESIAS Salvador: Christus natus, 75° aniversario, EFuente Adánez Alfonso de, *Muñoz León* Domingo: Estudios Bíblicos 50 (1992, 577 p.; portr.; bibliog. 565-573. 0014-1437. 30 art.; infra. [NTAbs 37, p. 426: 16 art. on infancy + 14].
136 NASTAINCZYK Wolfgang: Basiskurse im Christsein, EAngel Ferdinand, *Hemel* Ulrich.   Fra 1992, Lang.   461 p.; Bibliog. p. 446-458. DM 99 [TR 88,350, some tit. pp.] → 4937.
137 NEIRYNCK Franz: The four Gospels 1992, 65th b., ESegbroeck F. Van, *al.*: BtETL 100.   Lv 1992, Univ./Peeters. I. xvii-690 p.; II. p.-1720; III. p. 1721-2668. Fb 5000.   3-47 bibliog. (G. Van *Belle*, *al.*); 49-89 appreciations.   125 art., infra [TR 88,427 & RB 100,272, tit. pp.; ETL 68,385, C. M. *Tuckett*; ExpTim 104,248, E. *Best*; NTAbs 37, p. 273; RHPR 73,191, J.-C. *Ingelaere*; RThom 93,319s, L. *Devillers*; RTLv 24,507s, A. *Wénin*; BL 94,153, C. *Hickling*].
138 NIEDERLÄNDER Hubert: Fs 70. Gb., EJayme Erik, *al.*: Rechtsvergleichende. und Wirtschaftsrechtliche Studien 20. Hcid 1991, Winter. x- 495 p. [AnPg 62, p. 999, dépouillé]. RZSav-R 109 (1992) 725-8 (J. M. *Rainer*).
138* NOSSOL Alfons, bp.: ⊕ Veritati et caritati, w służbie teologii i pojednania (im Dienst der Theologie und der Einheit), 60. Gb., EJaskóły Piotr: Inst. Ekum. KUL 6.   Opole 1992, Św. Krzyż.   509 p. 83- 85035-40-5. 50 art. [TR 89,338, tit. (⊕ + T) pp., along with many other compilations (tit. pp.), several on the reunification of Europe].
139 NURI C. A. [− SCHNUR H. C.]: Pegasus devocatus [+ opuscula inedita], ETournoy G., *Sacré* T.: HumLov supp 7. Lv 1992, Univ. x-272 p.; portr. [RHE 87,394*].
139* NYGREN E. Herbert: The whole counsel of God, EHouse Paul R., *Heth* William A.   Upland 1991, Taylor Univ. 171 p. [JEvTS 36,543, D. *Bruce*: 7 art., 4 biblical: House on Jer. 1; Pitts R. on Pharisee origins; Heth on Paul the widower, 1 Cor 7,7; Helyer L. 'The OT and the undergraduate'].
140 ORSI Paolo, in memoria I-II = Klearchos 27s,105-112 (1985s). 154 p.; 195 p.; ill. [AnPg 62, p. 999, dépouillé].
140* OTZEN Benedikt, 60 år: Studier i Jesajabogen, ERosendal Bent: Bibel og historie 12. Århus 1989, Aarhus Univ. 127 p. Dk 148 [→ 5,148; DanTTs 52,4 (1989)]: RNorTTs 93 (1992) 58-60 (H. M. *Barstad*).
141 a) PADOUX André: Ritual and speculation in early Tantrism, EGoudrian Teun: SUNY Tantric. Albany 1992. xv-359 p. 0-7914-0898-1 [Religion 23,292s, J. *Brockington*].

— *b*) PALLOTTINO Massimo: Miscellanea etrusca e italica, 80° compleanno: ArchClas 43. R 1991, Bretschneider. L-1322 p. (2 vol.) 0391-8165 [AntClas 62,555, B. *Bouloumié*].

— *c*) PASCAL Ernest, hommage à la mémoire, ᴱ**Finette** Lucien: ÉtAnc Cah 23s. Québec 1990, Univ. Laval. 518 p. – ᴿPhoenix 46 (1992) 292-4 (M. *Lebel*).

— *d*) PÉPIN Jean: *Sophiēs maiētores*, 'chercheurs de sagesse', ᴱ**Goulet-Cazé** Marie-Odile, *Madec* G., *O'Brien* D.: Coll.ÉtAug, Ant. 131. P 1992, Inst.ÉtAug. xxiv-715 p.; portr. 2-85121-117-X [VigChr 47,311, tit. pp.].

142 PETRÁŇ Josef, 60. Gb. [čeh], ᴱ**Beneš** Z., *al.* Praha 1991, ČSAV. 583 p. [RHE 88,59*].

143 PIERCE Richard H. (dedicated to): ᴱSkarsten Roald, *al.*, Understanding and history in arts and sciences: Acta Hum. Univ. Bergen, 1. Oslo 1991, Solum. 195 p. 82-560-0762-1 [OIAc 3,38, excerpted].

144 PIÉTRI Charles, historien et chrétien; recueil des articles parus dans Les Quatre Fleuves. P 1992, Beauchesne [RHE 88,59*].

145 PILLORGET René & Suzanne: Études d'histoire européenne, ᴱ**Viguerie** Jean de: Société française d'histoire des idées et d'histoire religieuse. Angers 1990, Univ. 317 p. – ᴿRBgPg 70 (1992) 551-3 (G. *Livet*).

146 *a*) PINBORG Jan, mem.: De ortu grammaticae; studies in medieval grammar and linguistic theory, ᴱ**Bursill-Hall** G. I.: AmstHistLangSt. (47 ⊁ 6,140) 43. Amst/Ph 1990, Benjamins. x-372 p. $100 [Manuscripta 36,153, titles sans pp.; Speculum 68,1243, tit. pp.].

— *b*) PINCHAS Shlomo: Jubilee I-II: Jerusalem Studies in Jewish Thought [? 8 (1989)] 9 (1990).

— *c*) PINELL I PONS Jordi, Psallendum; miscellanea di studi, ᴱ**Scicolone** I.: StudAnselm 105. R 1992, S. Anselmo. 374 p.; portr. Lit. 75.000 [RHE 88,270*].

147 PLACES Édouard des (90th b., July 23, 1990): Platonism in late antiquity, ᴱ**Gersh** Stephen, *Kannengiesser* Charles: Christianity and Judaism in Antiquity 8. ND 1992, Univ. 258 p.; portr.; ix-xii bibliog. since ÉPR 90 (1981) xi-xix. 0-268-01513-9. 16 art.; 11 infra [NTAbs 37, p. 304].

148 *a*) PONSICH Michel: Alimenta: Gerión anejos 3. M 1991, Univ. Complutense. 383 p.; ill.; maps. [AnPg 62, p. 999, dépouillé].

— *b*) POULSSEN Niek: Stromen uit Eden; Genesis 1-11 in Bijbel, joodse exegese en moderne literatuur, ᴱ**Verdegaal** C., *Weren* W. Boxtel/Brugge 1992, KBS/Tabor. 288 p. 90-6173-488-6; -6597-455-5 [CollatVL 23,215 (N. *Bonte*); TvT 33,410, N. *Tromp*].

— *c*) POWER David N., O.M.I., A promise of presence, 60th b., ᴱ**Downey** Michael, *Fragomeni* Richard. Wsh 1992, Pastoral. ix-325 p. $25. 0-912405-92-9. 13 art. on liturgy [TDig 40,286; ÉglT 24,309, K. C. *Russell*; Horizons 21,202, Ellen M. *Leonard*; NewTR 6/4, 108, Helen *Rolfson*].

149 PREUSS Horst Dietrich: Alttestamentlicher Glaube und biblische Theologie, 65. Gb., ᴱ**Hausmann** Jutta, *Zobel* Hans-Jürgen. Stu 1992, Kohlhammer. 376 p.; portr.; Bibliog. 373-6. DM 120. 3-17-011079-9. 37 art., infra [TR 89,384, J. *Becker* & TLZ 118,205, tit. pp.; ActuBbg 30,196, J. *Boada*; TüTQ 172,243, W. *Gross*]. – ᴿExpTim 104 (1992s) 299s (R. *Coggins*, also on ᶠHERRMANN S., 1991).

149* PRINZ Friedrich, Mönchtum, Kultur und Gesellschaft; Beiträge zum Mittelalter, 60. Gb., ᴱ**Haverkamp** Alfred, *Heit* Alfred. Mü 1989, Beck. xx-323 p. DM 122 [TR 89,492, H. *Lutterbach*].

150 *a*) RADFORD C. A. Raleigh: The archaeology and history of Glastonbury Abbey, 90th b., ᴱ**Abrams** Lesley, *Carley* James P. Rochester NY

1991, Roydell. vii-351 p. [Manuscripta 36,148, titles sans pp.]: *Ridly* Felicity, Glastonbury, Joseph of Arimathea and the Grail in John HARDYNG's Chronicle.

— *b*) RADKE G.: Présence de TACITE, ᴱ**Chevallier** Raymond, *Poignault* Rémy: Caesarodunum 26 bis. Tours 1992, Piganiol. 294 p. 2-86906-049-1 [Latomus 52,932, P. *Duroisin*].

— *c*) RASKOLNIKOFF Mouza: Des Anciens et des Modernes, ᴱ**Demougin** Ségolène; pref. *Nicolet* Claude: HistAncMédv 23. P 1990, Sorbonne. viii-193 p. [RÉAnc 94,477, P. *Arnaud*].

151 RAYAN Samuel: Bread and breath, ᴱ**John** T. K.: JesuitTForum 5. Anand 1991, Gujarat-SP. xii-336 p. $12; pa. $10 [NRT 115,926, P. *Detienne*; Vidyajyoti 56,439]. – ᴿKristu Jyoti 8,2 (Bangalore 1992) 70-72 (J. *Putti*).

152 RECCHIA Vincenzo: Invigilate lucernis 11 (1989), Univ. Bari. 519 p. Lit. 50.000. 22 art. [RBgPg 71,123, J. *Schamp*: spécialiste de GRÉGOIRE le Grand].

ᶠRENDTORFF Trutz, 60. Gb. Kolloquium 1991/2 → 610 *c*.

153 RICE Eugene F.ᴶ, Renaissance society and culture, ᴱ**Monfasani** John, *Musto* Ronald G. NY 1991, Italica. xxiv-309 p. $55 [Manuscripta 36, 157, titles sans pp.]. – ᴿCathHR 78 (1992) 290s (G. A. *Brucker*).

153* RIONDATO Ezio: Ethos c cultura, ᴱ**Berti** E., *al.* Padova 1991, Antenore. xx-1279 p. Lit. 120.000 [CC 144/4, 205s, G. *Pirola*].

154 RIPOLL PERELLO E.: Homenaje: Espacio, tiempo y forma, Revista Univ. Madrid 1988. 442 p. [AnPg 61, p. 731].

155 ROMANO VENTURA David: Sefarad 52,2 (1992), 277-543; portr.; bio-bibliog. 279-289.

156 RUBIO FERNÁNDEZ Lisardo, II: Cuadernos de Filología Clásica 21. M 1988, Univ. Complutense. 380 p. [AnPg 62, p. 1000; dépouillé].

RUDHARDT Jean: Orphisme 1989/91 → 675*b*.

158 RYCKMANS Jacques, Études sud-arabes. 1991. – ᴿSyria 69 (1992) 485 (H. de *Contenson*).

159 SAIER Oskar, Erzb.: Gemeinsam Kirche sein; Theorie und Praxis der Communio, ᴱ**Biemer** Günter, *al.*: Univ. FrB. FrB 1992, Herder. 443 p. [TR 88,513; TvT 33,200, W. *Boelens*]. DM 68. 3-451-22879-3.

160 SAKELLARIOU M. B.: Poikila: Meletemata 10. Athens/P 1990, National Research / de Boccard. 106 p.; 220 fig. 960-7994-75-1. 20 art. [RB 100,449, tit. pp.].

161 SALESIANI Torino; Fac. Teol. 25° anno: Teologia e vita, studi, ᴱ**Ferasin** Egidio: BtScRel 102. R 1992, LAS. 274 p. Lit. 35.000. 88-213-0242-3. 9 art., 3 infra.

162 ŠAŠEL Jaro, memorial essays: Šašlov zbornik: Arheolški Vestnik 41 (Ljubljana 1990). 773 p.; portr.; ill., maps [AnPg 62, p. 1000, dépouillé].

163 SAUER Georg: Zur Aktualität des Alten Testaments, 65. Gb., ᴱ**Kreuzer** Siegfried, *Lüthi* Kurt. Fra 1992, Lang. 373 p.; portr.; Bibliog. p. 355-370 (Melitta *Schwinghammer*). 3-631-44045-6. 28 art.; 27 infra [ZAW 104,317, tit. pp.; TLZ 118,719, A. *Meinhold*; VT 43,573, H. G. M. *Williamson*].

164 SAXER Victor, mons.: Memoriam Sanctorum venerantes, 70° anniversario: StAntCr 48. Vaticano 1992, Pont. Ist. Arch. Cr. xliv-798 p.; bibliog. xiii-xliv (*Maestri* Gabriella). 88-85991-09-2. 53 art.; 7 infra [TR 88,519; CC 144/3, 329, A. *Ferrua*].

165 SCHASCHING Johannes: Der Mensch ist der Weg der Kirche, ᴱ**Schambeck** Herbert, *Weiler* Rudolf. B 1992, Duncker & H. xiii-456 p. DM 228 [TR 88,531, einige tit. pp. (Soziallehre)].

165* SCHLATTER Adolf 1852-1938: Paulus und das antike Judentum, ᴱHengel
M., *Heckel* U.: WUNT 58. Tü c. 1992, Mohr. xiii-475 p. DM 248. 3-
16-145795-1. – ᴿExpTim 104 (1992s) 269 (E. *Best*).
166 *a*) SCHLIEMANN Heinrich; 100. Todesjahr: Grundlagen und Ergebnisse
moderner Archäologie, ᴱHerrmann Joachim. B 1992, Akademie. 405 p.;
ill. 3-05-001853-4.
— *b*) SCHRADER Wiebke: Akropolis I-II, ᴱBerlinger Rudolf, *al.*: Perspektiven
der Philosophie 16s. Amst 1990s, Rodopi. 307 p.; 468 p. [AnPg 61,
p. 731; 62, p. 1000].
— *c*) SCHRAG Martin H.: Within the perfection of Christ; essays on peace
and the nature of the Church, ᴱBrensunger Terry, *Sider* E. Moris. Nap-
panee IN 1990, Evangel. vi-266 p.; ill. [AnPg 62, p. 1000].
— *d*) SCHRÖER Alois: Ecclesia monasteriensis; Beiträge zur Kirchengeschichte und religiösen Volkskunde Westfalens. 65. Gb., ᴱHaas Raimund:
GeschKu 7. Münster 1992, Regensberg. 435 p. DM 48 pa. [TR 89,493,
M. *Hänsel-Hohenhausen*].
167 SCHÜLE Wilhelm, 60. Gb.: ᴱ(Otto-Herman ohne Familienname, p. 3)
Vorgesch. Seminar Marburg. Internationale Archäologie 1. Buch am
Erlbach 1991, Leidorf. 355 p.; Portr.; Bibliog. 15-17. 3-924734-02-X. 29
art.; 3 infra.
168 *a*) SCHUON Frithof: Religion of the heart, ᴱNasr Seyyed H., *Stoddart*
William. Wsh 1991, Foundation for Traditional Studies.
— *b*) SCHWAIGER Georg: Papsttum und Kirchenreform, historische Beiträge,
65. Gb., ᴱWeitlauff Manfred, *Hausberger* Karl. St. Ottilien 1990, EOS.
xx-812 p. DM 98. 3-88096-481-5 [RelStR 19,270, P. *Misner*].
— *c*) SCOTT Nathan A.: Morphologies of faith, ᴱGerhart Mary, *Yu* Anthony
C. Atlanta 1992, Scholars [LitTOx 7,217, W. G. *Doty*].
169 SECKLER Max: Fides quaerens intellectum; Beiträge zur Fundamentaltheologie, 65. Gb., ᴱKessler Michael, *al.* Tü 1992, Francke. xvi-639 p.
DM 78 [TR 88,527, einige (32) tit. pp.].
170 SEIBT Ferdinand: (I) Von Aufbruch und Utopie, Perspektiven einer neuen
Gesellschaftsgeschichte des MAs; 65. Gb., ᴱLundt B., *Reimöller* H. Köln
1992, Böhlau. x-455 p. DM 98 [RHE 88,59*].
171 SEIBT Ferdinand: (II) Westmitteleuropa, Ostmitteleuropa; Vergleiche und
Beziehungen, 65. Gb., ᴱEberhard W.: Carolinum 70. Mü 1992, Oldenbourg. 403 p.; maps. DM 148 [RHE 88,231*].
171* SEILE Martin: Tragende Tradition, 65. Gb., ᴱFreund Annegret, *al.* Fra
1992, Lang. [vi-]219 p.; Portr.; Bibliog. 211-7. 3-631-44992-5. 14 art.; 4
infra.
ᶠSIEBERT Rudolf J.: Frankfurt School; Dubrovnik papers 1992 → 610*b*.
172 SIMON René: Actualiser la morale; 80ᵉ anniv., ᴱBelanger Rodrigue,
Plourde Simonne. P 1992, Cerf. 512 p.; Portr.; bibliog. (*Desrosiers* R.),
F 150 [LavalTP 49,331, C. *Boissinot*; NRT 115,424, L. *Volpe*]. – ᴿEsprVie
102 (1992) 653s (P. *Daubercies*).
SMITH Morton: Colloquium on JOSEPHUS, Pisa 1992 → *d*174 (rapporto).
173 SMITH T. C.: Perspectives on contemporary New Testament questions,
ᴱMcKnight Edgar V. [= PerspRelSt 29,4]. Lewiston NY 1992, Mellen.
100 p. (= p. 353-454), 357-367, *Ashcraft* M. on Smith (bibliog.) + 6
art., 5 infra. 0-7734-2852-6 [TBR 6/1,10, L. *Houlden*].
174 SÖLLNER Alfred: Geschichtliche Rechtswissenschaft; ars tradendo inno-
vandoque aequitatem sectandi; 60. Gb. ᴱKöhler Gerhard, *al.* Giessen
1990, Brühlscher-V. 689 p. – ᴿZSav-R 109 (1992) 728-731 (W. *Schubert*).
SPEIJER's Sanskrit syntax c. 1886 → 694*c*.

175 SPITZ Lewis W.: The harvest of humanism in central Europe, ᴱFleischer
Manfred P. St. Louis 1992, Concordia. 389 p. $20. 0-570-04560-6. 13
art. [TDig 39,364; JTS 44,414, A. McGrath; RelStR 19,360, J. L. Farthing].
176 STEINTHAL Hermann: Schola Anatolica: Uhland-Gymnasium. Tü 1989,
Osiander. 557 p. [AnPg 62, p. 100, dépouillé].
177 STICKLER Alphonsus M., card.: Studia in honorem, ᴱCastillo Lara R. I.:
StTIC 7. R 1992, LAS. xxviii-627 p.; 2 pl. Lit. 70.000 [RHE 87,221*;
NRT 115,765, L. Volpe].
177* STOTT John [I. → 7,149a; II. → 7,149b] III. The Gospel in the modern
world, ᴱEden Martyn, Wells David F. Leicester 1991, Inter-Varsity.
279 p. £15. – ᴿTBR 5,1 (1992s) 17; TLond 95 (1992) 216s (I. Smith-
Compton: evangelicals but not all in agreement).
178 STRAUSS Gerald: Germania illustrata; essays on early modern Germany,
ᴱFix Andrew C., Karant-Nunn Susan C. Kirksville MO 1992, SixtC.
xxiv-274 p. $35. 13 art. [RelStR 19,269, R. Kolb: indispensable for ec-
clesiastical concerns].
179 STROMMENGER Eva: (I) Von Uruk nach Tuttul, ᴱHrouda Barthel, al.:
MüVorderasSt 12. Mü 1992, Profil. 206 p.; 85 pl.; Bibliog. 11-12 (W.
Nagel). 3-89019-305-6 [OIAc 3,39]. 25 art.; 15 infra. – (II) 65. Gb.:
AcPraeh 24 (1992); Biobibliog. 9s, portr. (Kay Kohlmeyer); 11-15 (W.
Nagel).
179* Suisse, 700ᵉ anniv. [→ 6,327]: Peuple parmi les peuples; dossier pour
l'animation biblique, ᴱCamponovo Oddo, al. Essais bibliques 18. Genève
1990, Labor et Fides. 240 p. 2-8309-0622-5. – ᴿOTAbs 15 (1992) 93s
(D. B. Sharp: essays looking to the role of Christianity in the history of
the Swiss Confederation); RBiArg 53 (1991) 183s (R. Krüger).
180 a) SZÁDECZKY-KARDOSS Samuel, 70th b.: ActaAntArch supp. 7. Szeged
1988, Univ. 69 p.; ill. [AnPg 62, p. 1000, dépouillé].
— b) SZEMERÉNYI Oswald: Historical philology; Greek, Latin, and Romance, 75. Gb., ᴱBrogyanyi Béla, Lipp Reiner: Curr. Ling. Theory 87.
Amst 1992, Benjamins. xi-386 p. 90-272-3586-4. – 24 art., 3 infra [Ét-
Clas 61,143-6, L. Isebaert].
— c) TALMAGE Frank [25.V.1938-10.VII.1988] memorial volume, ᴱWalfish
Barry. Haifa 1992s, Univ. I. 349 p.; bibliog. 31-39 (Cohen Susan S.) + ☉
98; 965-311-014-4; II. 316 p. + ☉ 27 p. = Jewish History 6,1s; 0334-
701X. 20 + 19 art.; 19 infra (I, 283-297, Fackenheim E. on Talmud).
181 TALMON Shemaryahu: 'Shaʿarei Talmon', studies in the Bible, Qumran,
and the Ancient Near East, ᴱFishbane Michael, al. WL 1992, Eisenbrauns. xliʌ-431 p. + ☉ 165*; portr.; bibliog. xxv-xlix. 0-931464-61-7. 32
art. + 17 ☉ (summaries xv-xxiii); infra. [ZAW 104,459 & RB 99,756, tit.
pp.; BL 93,11-13, M. Knibb; ETL 68,804, J. Lust, tit. sans pp.].
181* TAYLOR John: Church and chronicle in the Middle Ages, ᴱWood I.,
Loud G. A. L 1991, Hambledon. xxvi-270 p. £36. [RHE 88,231*; JEH
44,339, Barbara Harvey].
182 THOMAS Edit B. zum Gedenken, ᴱBuschhausen Helmut, Weber Ekkehard:
Römisches Österreich 17s (1989s). Wien 1991, Österr. Ges. Archäologie.
291 p.; 31 pl. [AnPg 62, p. 1000, dépouillé].
183 TOUBER Anthonius H.: Daz ir dest werder sint, 60. Gb., ᴱQuak Arend,
Vermeyden Paula: AmstBeitÄltere Germanistik 30. Amst 1990, Rodopi.
203 p. – ᴿBeiNam 27 (1992) 422-4 (L. de Grauwe: 15 art.; NT-Joseph,
127-137, Wildenberg-de Kroon G. van den; Thomas 33-49, Kuné C.; Veronica 159-167, Zweinenber-Tönnies N.; Longinus im Passionspiel 3-13,
Dauven-von Kippenberg G.).

183* TRACY David: Radical pluralism and the truth; David Tracy and the hermeneutics of religion, 50th b., ᴱJeanrond Werner G., *Rike* Jennifer L. NY 1991, Crossroad. xxvii-296 p. $34.50 [RelStR 19,149, M. S. *Cladis*].

184 TRENTINI Johannes B.: Echo, Beiträge zur Archäologie des mediterranen [Ephesos, Hermon, Ba'al Zephon] und alpinen Raumes; 80. Gb. ᴱOtto Brinna, *Ehrl* Friedrich: InBeiKuW 27. Innsbruck 1990, Inst. Spr-W. 335 p.; portr. 3-8124-146-0. 32 art.; 10 infra.

184* TROMP Nico: Gelukkig de mens; opstellen over Psalmen, exegese en semiotiek, ᴱBeentjes P. Kampen 1991, Kok 267 p. ƒ50 pa. 90-242-3068-5. — NTAbs 37,106.

185 TURRADO TURRADO Argimiro: Augustinus minister et magister: RAg 33 (1992) 1093 p. [RHE 87,52*] = Historia Viva 4. M 1992, Augustinus. 1101 p. (2 vol.) biobibliog. 13-47 (*Lazcano* Rafael). 84-86898-11-0 [RHE 88,308, tit. pp.; Angelicum 70,463, B. *Degórski*, tit. pp.; Carthaginensia 9, 410-2 (P. *Chavero Blanco*); RCu 39,182, P. *Langa*; Salesianum 55,598]. – ᴿRET 52 (1992) 366s (M. *Gesteira*).

185* UDINA I MARTORELL Frederic [I 1987, 197 p.; II. 1988, 348 p. III 1990, 264 p.]. IV. Barc 1992, Mediaevalia. 514 p.; 3 fig.; 2 maps [RHE 88,397*].

UFFENHEIMER Benjamin, Justice and righteousness: jOsu 137, 1990/2 → 499.

186 VALLS I TABERNER Ferran: Literature, culture, and society of the Middle Ages... centenary of his birth, 9, ᴱMartínez López Miguel. Barc 1989, Univ. IV + p. 2535-2771. – ᴿSpeculum 67 (1992) 246 (tit. pp.).

187 VANDERSLEYEN Claude: Amosiadès, ᴱObsomer Claude, *Oosthoek* Ann-Laure. LvN 1992, Univ. Catholique. 373 p. 2-87209-203-X [OIAc 5,37, excerpted].

188 VIGIL PASCUAL Marcelo, La historia en el contexto de las ciencias humanas y sociales, ᴱHidalgo de la Vega María J.: EstHistorGeog 61. S 1989, Univ. 301 p.; ill. [AnPg 61, p. 732; 62, p. 1001].

189 VIGNAUX Paul [1904-1987] mém.: Lectionum varietates, ᴱJolivet J., *al.*: ÉtPhMédv 65. P 1991, Vrin. 342 p. F 375. – ᴿRechSR 80 (1992) 257-260 (F. *Ruello*).

VILAR HUESO Vicente: En torno a la Biblia; arqueología, exégesis e historia: 1992 → 325.

191 VOLP Rainer: Anstösse – Theologie im Schnittpunkt von Kunst, Kultur und Kommunikation, ᴱMöller I. Da 1991, Beispiel. 189 p.; (color.) ill. 3-923974-07-8 [TLZ 118,207, G. *Strohmaier-Wiederanders*].

192 WEBB R. K.: Religion and irreligion in Victorian society, ᴱDavis R. W., *Helmstadter* R. J. L 1992, Routledge. ix-205 p.; portr. 0-415-07625-0 [TBR 6/2,15, G. *Howes*].

193 WENDEHORST Alfred: 65. Gb., ᴱSchneider J., *Rechter* G. = JbFränkische Landesforschung 52 (Neustadt 1992) xvi-400 p.; 53 (1992) viii-452 p.; ill. [RHE 87,394*].

193* WESENER Gunter, 60 Gb.: Vestigia iuris Romani, ᴱKlingenberg G., *al.* Graz 1992, Leykam. [RHE 88,397*; ZSav-R 110,466, H. *Lange*].

194 WESTERMARK Ulla: Florilegium numismaticum, ᴱNilsson Harald: Numismatiska Meddelanden 38. Sto 1992, Svenska Numismatiska Föreningen. 382 p. – ᴿRBgNum 138 (1992) 176-180 (P. *Naster*).

195 WILL Robert: Mélanges: Cah. alsaciens d'archéologie 32. Strasbourg 1989, Soc. conserv. monum. Alsace. 363 p.; ill. [RHE 88,59*].

196 WOLF William J. mem.: No easy peace; ᴱHeyward Carter, *Phillips* Sue. Lanham MD 1992, UPA. xv-248 p. [AnglTR 75,417, Ellen K. *Wondra*].

197 WOLFF Hans-Walter: Was ist der Mensch...? Beiträge zur Anthropologie des Alten Testaments, 80. Gb., ᴱCrüsemann Frank, *al.* Mü 1992,

Kaiser. 255 p. 3-459-01933-6. 17 art., infra [TR 88,250, tit. pp.; RechSR 84,270, J. *Briend*; TLZ 118,723, E.-J. *Waschke*; TvT 33,413, M. *Vervenne*; ZkT 115,88, R. *Oberforcher*].
198 WOUDE Adam S. van der, I [II-III → 503s]: The Scriptures and the Scrolls, 65th b., ᴱ**García Martínez** F., *al.*: VT supp. 49. Leiden 1992, Brill, xiii-285 p.; portr.; 9 pl.; bibliog. p. 228-268. *f* 100 ($55). 9-0040-9746-5 [TR 88 (1992) 515, tit. pp.; BL 93,14, G. H. *Jones*]. – 19 art., infra.
199 XIBERTA Bartolomé M. [1897-1967]: In mansuetudine sapientiae (Jac 3:13), ᴱ**Valabek** Redemptus M. R 1990, ᵀInstitutum Carmelitanum. 328 p. 88-7288-013-0. – ᴿActuBbg 29 (1992) 84s (A. *Borrás*).
200 ZIADEH Farhat J.: Islamic law and jurisprudence, ᴱ**Heer** Nicholas. Seattle 1990, Univ. Washington. xvi-234 p. $30. – ᴿJAOS 112 (1992) 522s (Susan A. *Spectorsky*); JRAS (1992) 264s (I. R. *Netton*).

A1.2   Miscellanea *unius* auctoris.

201 **Abel** Karlhans,   Aus dem Geistesleben des frühen Prinzipats; Horaz-Seneca-Tacitus.   Marburg 1991, auct.   iii-184 p. [AnPg 62, p. 1001, dépouillé].
202 **Abramowski** Luise,   Formula and context; studies in early Christian thought: CS 365.   Aldershot 1992, Variorum.   x-300 p. [RHE 87,254*; NTAbs 37, p. 299; TBR 6/2,44, M. *Elliott*]. 0-86078-288-3.   18 art.; 7 < German.
203 **Accame** Silvio,   Scritti minori: SL 172-4.   R 1990, Storia e Letteratura. xvi 1542 p. (3 vol. 4 indcx; bibliog. ix-xvi). [AnPg 62, p. 1001].
204 **Adinolfi** Marco, [→ d147], Il Verbo uscito dal silenzio; temi di cristologia biblica: Collana biblica.   R 1992, Dehoniane.   190 p. Lit. 20.000.   88-396-0424-3 [RB 100,291, tit. pp.; NRT 115,621, L. *Renwart*].
205 [Rodríguez] **Adrados** Francisco,   Nuevos estudios de lingüística indoeuropea: Emerita anejos 37.   M 1988, Cons. Sup. Inv.   x-623 p. – ᴿBSLP 87,2 (1992) 132-4 (A. *Christol*, '1987'); Salesianum 54 (1992) 823s (R. *Gottlieb*).
206 *a)* **Alinei** Mario,   Dal totemismo al cristianesimo popolare; sviluppi semantici nei dialetti italiani ed europei: FgLing 4.   Alessandria 1984, Orso. x-165 p. – ᴿSalesianum 54 (1992) 616 (R. *Gottlieb*).
— *b)* **Altmann** Alexander,   The meaning of Jewish existence; theological essays, 1930-39, ᴱ*Ivry* Alfred L.   Hanover 1991, Brandeis Univ.   xlvii-169 p. $45 [JRel 73,442s, M. *Fishbane*].
— *c)* **Amaladoss** Michael,   Walking together; the practice of inter-religious dialogue [12 revised reprints]: Jesuit Theological Forum 11/7. Anand 1992, Gujarat-SP.   185 p. $8.50; pa. $6.50 [TDig 40,253; NRT 116,599, J. *Masson*].
— *d)* **Amberg** Ernst-Heinz [65. Gb.], Zur Erkenntnis der Wahrheit kommen, ᴱ*Petzoldt* M. Lp 1992, Ev-VA.   301 p. DM 78.   3-374-01403-8 [TLZ 118,1006, H. *Fischer*].
207 *a)* **Aus** R. D.,   Barabbas and Esther and other studies in the Judaic illumination of earliest Christianity: SFla SHJud 54. Atlanta 1992, Scholars. xii-205 p. $60; sb. $40. 1-55540-753-6 [BL 93,130, C. *Hickling*: 'in other studies in'; also 'Judiasm'; modus operandi reminiscent of DERRETT; Barabbas tortuously; NTAbs 37, p. 282]. 9 art.
— *b)* **Bayer** Oswald,   Autorität und Kritik; zur Hermeneutik und Wissenschaftstheorie [14 art. 1975-91 + 1]. Tü 1991, Mohr.   x-225 p. DM 59

pa. 3-16-145742-0 [ActuBbg 30,64, J. *Boada*; JRel 73,423s, J. C. *O'Flaherty*; LuthQ 7,99, K. *Huizing*].
— c) **Beardslee** W. A., Margins of belonging 1991 ➤ 7,176; 16 art. by Beardslee, ᴱ*Cunningham* [AmJTP 14,212-7, R. *Farmer*].

208 **Ben-Chorin** S., Theologia Judaica; [28 meist kurze] gesammelte Aufsätze II [I. c. 1983], ᴱ*Lenzen* H. Tü 1992, Mohr. viii-309 p. DM 128. 3-16-145801-X [BL 93,130, N. *de Lange*: one apparent ineditum on Rosenzweig as Bible translator; TLZ 118,593, S. *Schreiner*].

209 **Bernardi** Aurelio, Pietas loci; riflessioni sulla religiosità antica e altri saggi di storia romana [reprints 1946-87]. Athenaeum Bt 15. Como 1991, New Press. 218 p. [AnPg 62, p. 1002].

210 **Betz** Heinz-Dieter, Synoptische Studien; gesammelte Aufsätze 2. Tü 1992, Mohr. ix-322 p. DM 178 [TR 88,516]. 3-16-145936-9.

210* **Biffi** Inos, Figure medievali della teologia I [< TItSett]. Mi 1992, Jaca. xv-399 p. Lit. 45.000. – ᴿLetture 47 (1992) 669-671 (Paola *Müller*).

211 **Bingen** Jean, Pages d'épigraphie grecque; Attique, Égypte (1952-1982): EpigBru 1. Bru 1991, Epigraphica Bruxellensia. xx-188 p.; portr.; map; bibliog. xv-xx [AnPg 62, p. 1002].

212 **Blank** Josef [1926-89], Studien zur biblischen Theologie, ᴱ*Mahoney* Robert: SBAufs 13. Stu 1992, KBW. 282 p. DM 49. – 3-460-06151-0 [NTAbs 37, p. 292; SNTU-A 18,252, P. *Arzt*; TLZ 118,914s, E. *Schweizer*].

213 **Blau** Joshua, Studies in Middle Arabic and its Judaeo-Arabic variety. J 1988, Magnes. 482 p. – ᴿJAfAs 3 (1991s) 67-71 (B. *Hary*).

214 **Blázquez** José María, Religiones en la España antigua [reprints]: Historia ser. menor. M 1991, Cátedra. 445 p. [AnPg 62, p. 1002].

215 **Bobrinskoy** Boris, Communion du Saint-Esprit [articles depuis 1959], ᴱ*Clément* Olivier: Spiritualité orientale, 56. Bellefontaine 1992, Abbaye. 485 p. F 128. – ᴿEsprVie 102 (1992) 676 (P. *Jay*).

216 **Bonnard** André, ᴱ*Seylaz* Jean-Luc, J'ai pris l'humanisme au sérieux; de Davel à Aristophane; préf. *Chauvy* Michel. Lausanne 1991, Aire. 118 p. [AnPg 62, p. 1002].

217 a) **Bradley** Keith R., Discovering the Roman family; studies in Roman social history [5 revised + 3 new]. NY 1991, Oxford-UP. xi-216 p. 0-19-505858-5 [AntClas 62,251, Marie-T. *Raepsaet-Charlier*] ➤ k159c. – ᴿClasW 86 (1992s) 171 (R. *Rousselle*); RelStR 18 (1992) 326 (B. J. *Malina*).
— b) **Braun** René, Approches de TERTULLIEN [24 reprints, 2 inédits]. P 1992, Inst. Ét. Aug. 343 p. 2-85121-133-4 [RSPT 77,622, G. M. de *Durand*].
— c) **Brizzi** Giovanni, CARCOPINO, Cartagine e altri scritti: Pubbl. 11. Sassari 1989, Univ. 179 p. Lit. 30.000. 6 art. [Latomus 52,221, J. *Debergh*].

218 **Brock** Sebastian, Studies in Syriac Christianity; history, literature and theology: CS 357. L 1992, Variorum. X-308 p. $68. 0-86078-305-7 [NTAbs 36,441].

219 **Brown** R. Allen † 1989, Castles, conquest and charters; collected papers. Woodbridge 1989, Boydell & B. vi-387 p.; ill. $86. – ᴿSpeculum 67 (1992) 385-7 (R. V. *Turner*).

220 **Brueggemann** Walter, Old Testament theology; essays on structure, theme, and text, ᴱ*Miller* Patrick D. Mp 1992, Fortress. xviii-318 p. 0-8006-2537-4 [BL 93,160]. 1 ined. + 14; 4 infra.

220* **Brundage** James A., The Crusades; Holy War and Canon Law [19 art. 1959-86]: CS 338. Aldershot 1991, Variorum. 302 p. 0-86078-291-3 [TBR 6/2,84, Anna S. *Abulafia*].

221 **Bruun** Patrick, [for his 70th b., his 1954-88] Studies in Constantinian numismatics: Acta 12. R 1991, Inst. Finlandiae. xiii-211 p. – ᴿRivArCr 68 (1992) 367-370 (C. *Noviello*).

222 **Buck** August, Studien zu Humanismus und Renaissance [1981-90], ᴱ*Guthmüller* Bodo: Wolfenbütteler RenF 11. Wsb 1991, Harrassowitz. 538 p. [AnPg 62, p. 1003].

223 *a*) **Busi** Giulio, Il succo dei favi; studi [1984-92] sull'umanesimo ebraico: BtHebraea 1. Bo 1992, Fattodarte. 129 p.

— *b*) **Casel** Odo, 'Auf dass alle eins seien', Joh 17,21; die Mysterienlehre und der Dialog mit der Ostkirche, ausgewählte Texte, ᴱ*Krahe* M. J. Wü 1988, Echter. 135 p. – ᴿOstkSt 41 (1992) 334s (H. M. *Biedermann*).

— *c*) **Castro** Emilio, A passion for unity; [8] essays on ecumenical hope and challenges. Geneva 1992, WCC. xi-94 p. $8. 2-8254-1089-6 [TDig 40, 259: WCC secretary-general 1985-92].

224 **Chaunu** Pierre, L'apologie pour l'histoire [recensions 1985-7]. P 1988, Téqui. 618 p. – ᴿRHE 87 (1992) 873 (R. *Aubert*).

224* **Childs** Brevard S., Biblical theology of the Old and New Testaments; theological reflections on the Christian Bible. L 1992, SCM. xxii-745 p. £20. 0-334-00114-5 [TvT 33,413, L. *Grollenberg*]. ↠ 9322.

225 **Christ** Karl, Geschichte und Existenz: KLKuWBt 34. B 1991, Wagenbach. 88 p. [AnPg 62, p. 1003, dépouillé].

225* **Cobb** John B.ᴶ, Can Christ become good news again?, ᴱ*Polk* David. St. Louis 1991, Chalice. x-189 p. [JRel 73,273, J. A. *Bracken*].

226 **Cohen** Gerson D., Studies in the variety of rabbinic cultures. Ph 1991, Jewish Publ. xvii-332 p. – ᴿJJS 43 (1992) 164-6 (D. *Frank*).

226* **Collins** Adela Y., The beginning of the Gospel [reprints on Mark]. Mp 1992, Fortress. 160 p. $15 pa. [BToday 31,252].

227 **Connolly** Peter, No bland facility; selected writings on literature, religion and censorship, ᴱ*Murphy* James H. Gerrards Cross 1992, C. Smythe. 239 p. £19.60. – ᴿFurrow 42 (1991) 732-4 (A. *Martin*).

228 **Contreni** J. J., Carolingian learning, masters and manuscripts: CS 363. Aldershot 1992, Variorum. x-333 p.; 7 fig. [RIIE 87,220*].

229 **Crüsemann** Frank, Die Tora; Theologie und Sozialgeschichte des alttestamentlichen Gesetzes. Mü 1992, Kaiser. 494 p. DM 98 [TR 88,515; TvT 33,291, A. van *Wieringen*].

230 **Curran** Charles E., The living tradition of Catholic moral theology [1989-91]. ND 1992, Univ. xiii-265 p. $28. 0-268-01296-2 [TDig 40,157].

231 **Cutler** Anthony, Imagery and ideology in Byzantine art: CS 358. Aldershot 1992, Variorum. x-324 p.; portr. 0-86078-313-8. 12 art.

232 **Daube** David, Collected studies in Roman law, ᴱ*Cohen* David, *Simon* Dieter: Ius commune Sond 54. Fra 1991, Klostermann. x-722 p.; p. 724-1480 [AnPg 62, p. 1003, dépouillé].

233 **Delēbanēs** A. D. [1918-88], ⊖ The Sermon on the Mount and Lord's prayer [reflections of a physician]. Athenai 1990, Basilopoulos. 182 p.; portr. 960-7100-28-X [NTAbs 36,421].

234 **Della Corte** Francesco, Opuscula 12 (1977-89): D.AR.FI.CL.ET NS 133. Genova 1990, Univ. 306 p. [AnPg 62, p. 1003].

235 **Desroches** H., Hommes et religions; histoires mémorables [< 1972s]. P 1992, Quai Voltaire. 174 p. F 95 [NRT 115,627, A. *Harvengt*].

235* **Dillon** John, The golden chain; studies in the development of Platonism and Christianity: CS 333. Aldershot 1990, Variorum. xii-332 p. £43.50. 28 reprints [ClasR 43,93, H. J. *Blumenthal*].

236 a) **Dinkler** Erich [6.V.1909-28.V.1981; al.], Im Zeichen des Kreuzes; Aufsätze, ᴱMerk Otto, Wolter Michael: BZNW 61. B 1992, de Gruyter. x-578 p. 3-11-013017-3 [RB 100,291, tit. pp.; BZ 37,154s, R. Schnackenburg]. – ᴿGymnasium 99 (1992) 565s (R. Klein). – Plures infra.

— b) **Donfried** Karl P., The dynamic Word; NT insights for contemporary Christians 1981 ⇒ 63,185: ᴿDeltioVM 65-75 (S. Agourides, Ⓖ).

— c) **Duby** Georges, Femmes 1992 ⇒ 46.

— d) **Dulles** Avery, The craft of theology; from symbol to system [12 reorganized items]. NY/Dublin 1992, Crossroad/Gill & M. xi-228 p. £9 [America 168/2,19, B. Cooke; RelStR 19,52, J.R. Sacks]. – ᴿExpTim 104 (1992s) 220 [R. Butterworth: competent, moderate; lacking perhaps rightly a certain sense of adventure).

— e) **Dumézil** Georges, Apollon sonore, et autres essais; vingt-cinq esquisses de mythologie: BtScHumaines. P 1987 = 1982, Gallimard. 258 p. 2-07-021426-6.

237 **Dus** J., Theokratische Demokratie des alten Israel. Fra 1992, Lang. x-148 p. [OLZ 88,290, E. Osswald, dubious].

238 **Eco** Umberto, Semiótica y filosofía del lenguaje [1976-80; Einaudi 1984],ᵀ: Palabra en el Tiempo 196. Barc 1990, Lumen. 364 p. – ᴿScripTPamp 24 (1992) 1068-1073 (J.A. García Cuadrado).

239 a) **Elliott** J.K., Essays and studies in NT textual criticism: FgNt Est 3. Córdoba 1992, Almendro. 172 p. 84-86077-92-3. 12 reprints 1969-86 + p. 17-43, 'Can we recover the original text of the NT?' [RB 100, 290, tit. pp.; NRT 115,904, X. Jacques]. – ᴿActuBbg 29 (1992) 195s & FgNt 5 (1992) 209-211 (J. O'Callaghan).

— b) **Everman** Welch D., Who says this? The authority of the author, the discourse, and the reader: Crosscurrents, Modern Critique. Carbondale 1988, Southern Illinois Univ. xvii-142 p. $18. – ᴿLitTOx 5 (1991) 131-3 (Gwendolyn S. Sell).

— c) **Faivre** Alexandre. Ordonner la fraternité; pouvoir d'innover et retour à l'ordre dans l'Église ancienne. P 1992, Cerf. 560 p. F 299 [Études 378, 137, P. Vallin].

240 a) **Ferrua** Antonio, Scritti vari di epigrafia e antichità cristiane, ᴱCarletti Carlo, al.: InscrChrItaliae subs. 3. Bari 1991, Edipuglia. xiv-382 p. [AnPg 62, p. 1003]. Lit. 70.000. – ᴿCC 143 (1992,1) 295s (F.P. Rizzo).

— b) **Finance** Joseph de, En balbutiant l'indicible [2 inedita + 11]. R 1992, Pont. Univ. Gregoriana. viii-242 p. [Angelicum 70,584-7, G. Vansteenkiste].

— c) **Finley** M.I., On a perdu la guerre de Troie; propos et polémiques sur l'Antiquité [1968],ᵀ. P 1990, BLettres. 234 p. – ᴿCahHist 36 (1991) 49s (J. Rougé).

241 **Forte** Bruno, Sui sentieri dell'Uno; saggi di storia della teologia. CinB 1992, Paoline. 296 p. – ᴿAsprenas 39 (1992) 599s (O. Di Grazia).

241* **Fowler** James W., Weaving the new creation; stages of faith and the public church. SF c.1991, Harper. 204 p. $18. – ᴿChrCent 109 (1992) 102s (P.L. Blackwell: seven essays, perhaps not quite as illuminatingly interwoven as he hopes).

242 **Freydank** Helmut, Beiträge zur mittelassyrischen Chronologie und Geschichte: SchrGKAO 21. B 1991, Akademie. 228 p. DM 164. 3-05-001814-3 [BO 49,586].

242* **Fries** Heinrich, Es bleibt die Hoffnung; Kirchenerfahrungen [6 Art., teils neu]. Z 1991, Benziger. 221 p. DM 30. – ᴿStiZt 210 (1992) 285 (W. Seibel); TGL 82 (1992) 375 (K. Hollmann).

243 **Gadamer** Hans-Georg, Gesammelte Werke VII, Griechische Philosophie 3. Plato im Dialog. Tü 1991, Mohr. viii-472 p. [AnPg 62, p. 1004; 56, p. 781: V, viii-386 p.; VI, 341 p., 1985].

244 *a*) **García Martínez** Florentino, Qumran and apocalyptic; studies on the Aramaic texts from Qumran [7 art., infra < Spanish 1980-7]: Studies on the Texts of the Desert of Judah 9 [8 was 1975]. Leiden 1992, Brill. xvi-233 p. *f* 115. 90-04-09586-1 [BL 93,134, G. J. *Brooke*; RechSR 84,301, A. *Paul*]. – ᴿBAR-W 18,6 (1992) 66 (H. *Shanks*).

— *b*) **Gill** Robin, Christian ethics in secular worlds. E 1991, Clark. xvii-159 p. £10. 0-567-29198-7 [EvQ 65,287s, D. *Atkinson*].

— *c*) **Goddijn** W., Democratie en christendom; veertig jaar sociologie van kerk en godsdienst [9 art. 1954-88]. Kampen 1991, Kok Agora. 179 p. *f* 35 [TvT 33,113, J. *Sloot*].

— *d*) **Görg** Manfred, Studien zur biblisch-ägyptischen Religionsgeschichte [15 reprints]: SBAuf 14. Stu 1992, KBW. 283 p. DM 49. 3-460-06141-3 [ZAW 105,525 tit. pp.]. 15 art.

— *e*) **Görg** Manfred, Aegyptiaca – Biblica; Notizen und Beiträge zu den Beziehungen zwischen Ägypten und Israel [< BibNot]: ÄgAT 11. Wsb 1991, Harrassowitz. viii-368 p. 3-447-02670-2 [ZAW 105,141].

245 **Gold** David L., Jewish linguistic studies. Haifa 1989, Univ. 273 p. – ᴿJQR 83 (1992s) 285-9 (P. *Wexler*: verbose, digressive; idiosyncratic terminology).

246 **Gonda** Jan (1905-1991), Selected studies [I-V 1975], VI/1s: Utrecht Univ. Indology dept. Leiden 1991, Brill. xxiv-542 p.; x-581 p., Bibliog. (*Heilijgers* D.). *f* 550 [OLZ 88,72, W. B. *Bollée*].

247 *a*) **Grässer** Erich, 65. Gb., Aufbruch und Verheissung; Gesammelte Aufsätze zum Hebräerbrief, ᴱ**Evang** Martin, *Merk* Otto: BZNW 65. B 1992, de Gruyter. viii-367 p.; Bibliog. 318-336. 3-11-013669-4. – p. 1-99 < TRu 30; + 10 reprints + 1 ineditum, infra.

— *b*) **Griffith** Sidney H., Arabic Christianity in the monasteries of ninth century Palestine: CS 380. Aldershot/Brooklyn VT 1992 [OrChrPer 59, 272, V. *Poggi*].

— *c*) **Grimes** Ronald L., Ritual criticism; case studies in its practice, essays on its theory. Columbia 1990, Univ. S. Carolina. xvi-270 p. – ᴿSR 21 (1992) 98s (Ellen *Badone*).

— *d*) **Gruber** Mayer I., The motherhood of God and other studies: SFL St-Jud 57. Atlanta 1992, Scholars. xv-282 p. 1-55540-763-3. 14 art., 4 infra.

— *e*) **Gruen** Erich S., Culture and national identity in republican Rome: StClasPg 52. Ithaca NY 1992, Cornell. xiii-347 p. $37.50 [RelStR 19,352, W. J. *Tatum*].

— *f*) **Guelluy** Robert, Si tu connaissais: Spiritualité. LvN 1991, Duculot. 171 p. – ᴿETL 68 (1992) 185s (J. *Étienne*).

248 **Gummere** John F., Words & c [46 micro-essays on language]. Wauconda IL 1990, Bolchazy-Carducci. xiii-128 p. $16. 0-86516-239-5. – ᴿClasW 85 (1991s) 116 (H. V. *Bender*: erudite and entertaining).

249 **GUNNEWEG** Antonius H. J., † 17.V.1992, Sola Scriptura II. Aufsätze zu ATlichen Texten & Themen [presented without explanation or reference (exc. p. 191) as continuation of Sola Scriptura I, ᶠ1983 ➤ 64,181; but not related to the compilation Sola Scriptura, ᴱ*Schmid* H. 1990/1 ➤ 7,454c], ᴱ*Höffken* Peter. Gö 1992, Vandenhoeck & R. 202 p.; 191-3, Bibliog. seit 1987. DM 48. 3-525-58158-0. 2 inedita infra, + reprints. [BL 93,15, R. N. *Whybray*; TvT 33,291, A. *Schoors*: title not Biblische Theologie 1993 as printed (insert correction)].

250 **Harl** Marguerite, La langue de Japhet; quinze études [1960-92] sur la Septante et le grec des chrétiens. P 1992, Cerf. 290 p.; ill. F 150. 2-204-04640-2 [RB 100,288, tit. pp.; ETL 68,406, J. *Lust*].

250* **Heckel** M., Gesammelte Schriften: JusEc 38. Tü 1992, Mohr. 1265 p. (2 vol.). DM 198. – ᴿZevEth 36 (1992) 226-9 (W. *Huber*).

251 **Henry** Marie Louise, ᴱ*Janowski* Bernd, *Noort* Edward, Hüte dein Denken und Wollen; alttestamentliche Studien, mit einem Beitrag zur feministischen Theologie: BtTSt 16. Neuk 1992. 224 p. 3-7887-1379-8. – 5 art.

251* **Herman** József, Du latin aux langues romanes, ᴱ*Kiss* Sándor. Tü 1990, Niemeyer. vi-392 p.; bibliog. 378-385 [AnPg 61, p. 734].

252 *a)* **Herms** Eilert, Erfahrbare Kirche; Beiträge zur Ekklesiologie. Tü 1990, Mohr. 258 p. DM 49. – ᴿLuthMon 31 (1992) 45 (G. *Wagner*); TLZ 117 (1992) 52-54 (G. *Wenz*).

— *b)* **Hertzberg** Arthur, Jewish polemics [27 revised reprints]. NY 1992, Columbia Univ. xiv-259 p. $28. 0-231-07842-0 [TDig 40,272; FirsT 31,43, D. *Novak*).

— *c)* **Hidal** Sten, Israel och Hellas; [10 reprint] studier kring Gamla testamentet och dess verkningshistoria: Religio 27. Lund 1988, Teologiska Institutionen. 130 p. 0280-5723. – ᴿSvEx 57 (1992) 117s (P. *Stille*).

253 **Hill** William J., Search for the absent God; tradition and modernity in religious understanding [14 reprints since 1970], ᴱ*Hilkert* M. Catherine. NY 1992, Crossroad. xv-224 p. $27.50. 0-8245-1114-X [TDig 40,68; Horizons 20,359, M. *Barnes*].

254 **Hinchliff** P., God and history; aspects of British theology 1875-1914. Ox 1992, Clarendon. [ix-] 267 p. £32.50 [RHE 87,451*].

254* **Hoerber** Robert G., Studies in the New Testament. Cleveland 1991, Biblion. 114 p. – ᴿConcordJ 18 (1992) 50-58 (H. A. *Moellering*: 'fabulosa farrago', not pejoratively).

255 **Hornung** Erik, Idea into image; essays on ancient Egyptian thought, ᵀ*Bredeck* Elizabeth. NY 1992, Timken. 209 p. 0-943221-11-0 [OIAc 5,25].

255* **Houlden** J. L., Bible and belief [12 NT studies, mostly reprinted] 1991 ➤ 7,212*: ᴿChurchman 106 (1992) 278-280 (D. *Spanner*: negative view of Gospel historicity — and of God's role); TBR 5,1 (1992s) 12 (J. *Barton*); TLond 95 (1992) 207s (P. *Baelz*: intellectually radical, spiritually conservative).

256 **Hubert** Jean, Nouveau recueil d'études d'archéologie et d'histoire: Mém. École des Chartes 29. Genève 1985, Droz. ix-635 p.; ill. [AnPg 57, p. 762].

257 **Jacobsohn** Helmuth, Gesammelte Schriften, ᴱ*Jungraithmayr* Herrmann: Collectanea 43. Hildesheim 1992, Olms. xii-177 p. 3-487-09564-5 [OIAc 5,25, excerpted].

258 **Jaki** Stanley L., The only chaos and other essays. Lanham MD 1990, UPA. 278 p. $35; pa. $19.75. – ᴿHomP 92,10 (1991s) 70-73 (R. *Dennehy*, also on his 1990 Science and creation).

258* **Jonas** Hans, Dalla fede antica all'uomo tecnologico; saggi filosofici [1974], ᵀ*Bettini* G. Bo 1991, Mulino. 481 p. – ᴿEuntDoc 45 (1992) 132-4 (P. *Miccoli*).

259 **Kermode** Frank, The uses of error [a selection of his book-reviews]. CM 1991, Harvard Univ. 432 p. $25. – ᴿChrCent 108 (1991) 727s (R. *Kaftan*) [LitTOx 5 (1991) 247s (D. *McKenzie*) on his Appetite for poetry 1989 ➤ 6,256].

260 **Klauck** Hans-Josef, Gemeinde zwischen Haus und Stadt; Kirche bei Paulus. FrB 1992. 128 p. DM 24,80. – ᴿGeistL 65 (1992) 395 (P. *Imhof*).

261 **Klaus** (Swalq) Natan, ⊖ ʿ*Iyyûnîm*, Essays in biblical literature. TA 1990, Am Oved. 965-13-0710-2 [OIAc 3,26].

262 **Knaus** H., Studien zur Handschriftenkunde; ausgewählte Aufsätze, ᴱ*Achten* G. Mü 1992, Saur. 297 p.; ill. DM 148 [RHE 88,187*].

263 **Koch** A. C. F., Tussen Vlaanderen en Saksen, 1923-90, ᴱ*Kruisheer* J. G.: Middeleeuwse studies en bronnen 29. Hilversum 1992, Verloren. 320 p.; ill. [RHE 88,58*].

264 **Köves-Zulauf** Thomas, Kleine Schriften, ᴱ*Heinrichs* Achim. Heid 1988, Winter. viii-415 p.; Bibliog. 461-3 [AnPg 59, p. 977].

265 **Kopperschmidt** Josef, Rhetorica; [7] Aufsätze zur Theorie, Geschichte und Praxis der Rhetorik: PhTSt 14. Hildesheim 1985, Olms. 229 p. 3-487-07693-4.

265* **Kühn** Ulrich: Veritas et communicatio; ökumenische Theologie auf der Suche nach einem verbindlichen Zeugnis, 60 Gb. ᴱ*Franke* H., *al.* Gö 1992, Vandenhoeck & R. 377 p. DM 98. 3-525-56116-4 [NTAbs 37, p. 110].

266 **Labruna** Luigi, Adminicula² [reprints 1962-89]. N 1991, Jovene. xii-413 p. [AnPg 62, p. 1005].

267 **LaCapra** Dominick, Soundings in critical theory. Ithaca NY 1991, Cornell Univ. [xi-]213 p.

268 **Lana** Italo, Sapere, lavoro e potere in Roma antica; present. *Casavola* Franco: Opere giuridiche e storiche 3. N 1990 Jovene. xvi-539 p. [AnPg 61, p. 735].

269 **Lanata** Giuliana, Esercizi di memoria. Bari 1989, Levange. 150 p.; ill. [AnPg 62, p. 1005].

270 *a)* **La Penna** Antonio, Tersite censurato, e altri studi di letteratura fra antico e moderno. Pisa 1991, Nistri-Lischi. 469 p. [AnPg 62, p. 1005].

— *b)* LAUER Quentin: **Ibana Rainer** R. A., A Lauer reader [10 art. + bibliog.]; the Ateneo collection. Manila 1991, Atenco. 128 p. – ᴿLandas 6 (1992) 125s (F. E. *Reilly*).

— *c)* **Lévêque** P.: Mélanges 6, religion, ᴱ*Mactoux* Marie-Madeleine, *Geny* Évelyne: Univ. Besançon HistAnc 113. P 1992, BLettres. xxix-292 p.; 11 fig.; 4 maps [ClasR 43,463, Gillian *Clark*].

271 **Lindars** Barnabas, Essays on John, ᴱ*Tuckett* C. M.: SNTS Auxilia 17. Lv 1992, Univ./Peeters. xvii-233 p. Fb 1000. 90-6186-520-4 / 90-6831-444-0 [RTLv 24,508, J. *Ponthot*].

272 **Lloyd** G. E. R., Methods and problems in Greek science [15 reprints 1960-89 + 3]. C 1991, Univ. xiv-457 p. £45. 0-521-37419-7 [ClasR 43, 415, H. B. *Gottschalk*]. – ᴿAntClas 61 (1992) 506-8 (Liliane *Bodson*).

273 **Loewenstamm** Samuel E. † 1987, From Babylon to Canaan; studies in the Bible and its oriental background [sequel to 1980 collection AOAT 204], ᴱ*Avishur* Yitzhak, *Blau* Joshua: Perry Foundation. J 1992, Hebrew Univ. xvii-497 p. $37. [RB 100,451, tit. pp.; OLZ 88,514, M. *Heltzer*].

274 **Lohfink** Norbert F., The inerrancy of Scripture and other essays [= Christian meaning of OT (Milwaukee 1968, Bruce) < Siegeslied 1965], ᵀ*Wilson* R. A. Berkeley CA 1991, BIBAL. [xi-] 169 p. 0-941037-20-7 [BToday 31,382; TDig 40,369].

275 **Lowick** Nicholas, ᴱ*Cribb* Joe, *a)* Islamic coins and trade in the medieval world; – *b)* Coinage and history of the Islamic world: CS 318. 311. Aldershot 1990, Variorum. xii-300 p.; xviii-260 p. £41.50; £38. – ᴿJSS 37 (1992) 132-6 (Elizabeth *Savage*).

275* **Luttrell** Anthony, The Hospitallers of Rhodes and their Mediterranean world [19 reprints]: CS 360. Aldershot 1992, Variorum. ix-324 p. 0-86078-307-3. – ᴿTBR 5,3 (1992s) 68 (D. *Abulafia*).

276 **McBrien** Richard P., Report on the Church; Catholicism after Vatican II [syndicated newspaper articles since 1976]. SF 1992, Harper. xix-263 p. $19. 0-06-065336-1 [TDig 40,75].

276* **Maccarrone** Michele †, Romana Ecclesia cathedra Petri [20 art., ital.], ᴱ*Zerbi* Piero, *al.*: Italia sacra 47s. R 1991, Herder. lxxvi-419 p. (2 vol.). [CC 144/4, 312, M. *Fois*]. – ᴿRivStoLR 28 (1992) 591-606 (O. *Capitani*, on Daniela *Gionta* bibliography of Maccarrone).

277 **Malcovati** Enrica, Florilegio critico di filologia e storia [reprints < Athenaeum 1920-81]: Athenaeum Bt 14. Como 1990, New Press. 183 p.; 159-183 bibliog. (*Magnino* D.) [AnPg 62,p. 1006].

277* **Mansfeld** Jaap, Studies in the historiography of Greek philosophy [18 reprints 1979-1989]. Assen 1990, Van Gorcum. x-482 p. ƒ175 [ClasR 43,187; R. I. *Winton*].

278 **Marinone** Nino, Analecta graeco-latina: Univ. Torino. Bo 1990, Pàtron. xvi-470 p. [AnPg 61, p. 735].

279 **Martimort** Aimé-G., Mirabile laudis canticum; mélanges liturgiques. R 1991, Liturgiche. 388 p. Lᵐ 15. [CrNSt 13,245, Maria *Paiano*; RSPT 76,170]. – ᴿBLitEc 93 (1992) 421s (R. *Cabié*).

280 **Martini** Carlo M., Comunicare nella Chiesa e nella società; lettere, discorsi e interventi 1990. Bo 1991, Dehoniane. 667 p. Lᵐ 37. [RasT 34, 140s, G. *Mattai*] – ᴿRivB 40 (1992) 376-8 (G. *Bruni*).

281 **Masson** Olivier, Onomastica graeca selecta, ᴱ*Dobias* Catherine, *Dubois* Laurent. (Nanterre) Paris 1990, Univ.-X. xvi-348 p.; p. 351-680 [AnPg 61, p. 735]. – ᴿBeiNam 27 (1992) 416-8 (J. L. *García Ramón*).

282 **Matzel** Klaus, [27, 1962-89] Gesammelte Schriften, ᴱ*Löhr* Rosemarie, *al.* Heid 1990, Winter. xiv-786 p. DM 340 (300). – ᴿIndogF 97 (1992) 265-270 (Evelyn *Frey*).

283 **Mᴀᴢᴀʀ** Benjamin, Biblical Israel — state and people [14 art. since 1946; for 85th b., supplementing 1986 Early Biblical Period], ᴱ*Aḥituv* Shmuel. J 1992, Hebrew Univ. 175 p., ill. $25. 965-223-797-3. [BL 93,18s, J. R. *Bartlett*; OIAc 5,29]. 4 art. previously published only in Hebrew, infra.

284 **Meisner** Joachim Kard., Wider die Entsinnlichung des Glaubens; Gedanken zur Re-Evangelisierung Europas. Graz 1990, Styria. 140 p. 13 art. – ᴿScripTPamp 23 (1991) 733s (A. *Viciano*).

285 **Moberly** R. W. L., From Eden to Golgotha; essays in biblical theology: SFla HistJud 52. Atlanta 1992, Scholars. xii-157 p. $60; sb. $40. 1-55540-749-8 [BL 93,111, 'Moberley' but correctly on same page; 8 reprints 1985-92 + 1 ineditum]. 5 infra. – ᴿExpTim 104 (1992s) 375 (R. *Tomes*).

286 **Moeller** Bernd, Die Reformation und das Mittelalter; kirchenhistorische Aufsätze, ᴱ*Schilling* J. Gö 1991, Vandenhoeck & R. 366 p. DM 98. 3-525-58156-4. [RHPR 73,344, M. *Lienhard*]. 19 art. – ᴿTvT [= TsT-Nijm] 32 (1992) 199s (J. van *Laarhoven*).

287 **Moltmann** Jürgen, History and the triune God [essays since 1980], ᵀ*Bowden* John. NY 1992, Crossroad. xx-204 p. $27.50 [RelStR 19,53, Kathryn *Tanner*]. – ᴿTS 53 (1992) 765s (J. A. *Bracken*: 'God the Father' when properly understood has little or no connection with patriarch).

288 *a)* **Müller** Hans-Peter, Mensch-Umwelt-Eigenwelt; gesammelte Aufsätze zur Weisheit Israels [2 inedita + 8 reprints]. Stu 1992, Kohlhammer. 244 p. DM 128. 3-17-012200-2.

— *b*) **Muffs** Yochanan, Love and joy; law, language and religion in ancient Israel. NY 1992, Jewish Theol. Sem. [distr. CM, Harvard]. xxvii-240 p. $30. 0-674-53931-1. 8 art. [TDig 40,281].
— *c*) **Munier** Charles, Autorité episcopale et sollicitude pastorale IIe-VIe siècles [28 art. 1978-90]: CS 341. Aldershot, Hampshire 1991, Variorum. viii-305 p. [LavalTP 49,548, P.-H. *Poirier*].
— *d*) **Nelson** James B., Body theology. Louisville 1992, W-Knox. 216 p. $13 pa. [Horizons 20,361s, R. E. *Long*].
— *e*) **Neusner** Jacob, The twentieth century construction of 'Judaism'; [13] Essays on the religion of Torah in the history of religion: SFLHJud 32. Atlanta 1991, Scholars. xiii-373 p. $75. 1-55540-645-9 [NTAbs 37, p. 312].
289 *a*) **ONG** Walter [80th b.; 24 art.], Faith and contexts, I. Selected essays and studies, 1953-1991; II. Supplementary studies, 1946-1989, ^E*Farrell* Thomas J., *Soukup* Paul A.: SFla-Rochester-St. Louis Studies on Religion and the Social Order. Atlanta 1992, Scholars. lv-238 p.; 255 p. $75, sb. $50 each; both $150; sb. $90. 1-55540-766-8; -7-6 [TDig 39,378: 'wisdom literature of the highest order; his essays about faith and culture are a light to the world' (J. *Neusner*)]. – ^RCommonweal 199,20 (1992) 13-18 (D. *Toolan*: The Ong show).
— *b*) **Outler** Albert C. [1908-1989], The Wesleyan theological heritage, essays ^E*Oden* Thomas C., *Longden* Leicester R. GR 1991, Zondervan. 267 p. 0-310-75471-2. – 14 art.
— *c*) **Packer** J. I., Among God's giants [Puritans; 6 reprints + 1956-69 papers]. Eastbourne c. 1991, Kingsway. 447 p. £10. 0-86065-452-4 [EvQ 65,282-5, A. C. *Clifford*].
290 **Parry** Adam M., The language of Achilles and other papers. Ox 1989, Clarendon. xiii-334 p.; ill. [AnPg 60, p. 879].
290* **Pinckaers** Servais, La parola e la coscienza. T 1991, SEI. x-250 p. Lit. 24.000 [CC 144/1,610, F. *Cultrera*].
291 *a*) **Polotsky** H. J., Ausgewählte Briefe [to] ^E*Ullendorff* Edward (contributions from *Irvine* A. K., *Bronowski* Yoram): Äthiopische Forschungen 34. Stu 1992, Steiner. 145 p. DM 88. 3-515-06066-9 [BL 93,21, J. F. A. *Sawyer*].
— *b*) **Portillo** Alvaro del, Vocation et mission du prêtre [7 reprints, 2 interviews]. P 1991, Laurier. 144 p. [RThom 93,171, J.-M. *Fabre*: the author is successor of ESCRIVÁ as Prelate of Opus Dei, and an important collaborator of Vatican II Presbyterorum ordinis].
— *c*) **Power** David N., A promise of presence. 1992 [ÉglT 24,309, K. C. *Russell*].
— *d*) **Pricoco** Salvatore, Monaci, filosofi e santi; saggi di storia della cultura tardoantica [14 art.]: Armarium 1. Soveria Mannelli 1992, Rubbettino. 395 p. Lit. 35.000 [RHE 88,516, A. de *Vogüé*].
292 **Pulbrook** Martin, Studies in Greek and Latin authors. Maynooth 1987, Univ. 95 p. [AnPg 61, p. 716].
293 **Quacquarelli** Antonio, Le radici patristiche della teologia di Antonio ROSMINI [8 reprints]: VetChr quad 22. Bari 1991, Edipuglia. x-159 p. – ^RAngelicum 69 (1992) 273 (B. *Degórski*).
294 **Räisänen** Heikki, Jesus, Paul and Torah; collected essays [1 ineditum + 9 from The Torah and Christ 1986], ^T*Orton* D. E.: JStNT supp 43. Sheffield 1992, Academic. 286 p. 1-85075-237-0 [RB 100,457, tit. pp.].
295 **Raskolnikoff** Mouza, Des anciens et des modernes, ^E*Demougin* Ségolène, préf. *Nicolet* Claude: HistAncMédv 23. P 1990, Sorbonne-I. viii-193 p. [AnPg 62, p. 1008].

296 **Ratzinger** Joseph, Wendezeit für Europa? Diagnosen und Prognosen zur Lage von Kirche und Welt [6 grossenteils Reprints]. Einsiedeln 1991, ²1992, Johannes. 128 p. DM 24. 3-89411-302-2. – ᴿMüTZ 43 (1992) 383 (W. W. *Müller*); TGL 82 (1992) 259s (D. *Hattrupp*).

296* **Renner** Frumentius. Verkannte Kostbarkeiten des NTs; literarkritische Studien. St. Ottilien 1992, EOS. 168 p. DM 24,80. 3-88096-648-6 [TR 89,166].

297 **Ricœur** P., Dal testo all'azione; saggi di ermeneutica [1970-1985, parte in Ermeneutica 1977], ᵀ*Grampa* G. Mi 1989, Jaca. 394 p. Lit. 46.000. – ᴿAsprenas 39 (1992) 305s (P. *Cacciapuoti*).

298 **Rivarolo** José Luis, La formación lingüística de Hispanoamérica [10 art.]. Lima 1990, Univ. Católica. 254 p. – ᴿPáginas 17,1 (1992) 119s (L. *Andrade*).

299 **Romano** Domenico, LUCREZIO e il potere, ed altri saggi sulla letteratura tardorepubblicana ed augustea: Sisyphos 1. Palermo 1990, Grifo. 300 p. [AnPg 62, p. 1008]. – ᴿOrpheus 12 (1991) 601s (G. *Polara*).

300 **Rosenthal** Franz, [1. ⇥ 7,254] 2. Greek philosophy in the Arab world: CS 322. Aldershot 1990, Variorum. x-287 p. – ᴿOrChr 76 (1992) 273-5 (P. *Kunitzsch*).

301 **Rudolph** Kurt, Geschichte und Probleme der Religionswissenschaft [18 updated reprints 1965-90]: StHRel 53. Leiden 1992, Brill. 446 p. ƒ220 [TR 88,525; Numen 40, 189, J. *Waardenburg*]. 90-04-09503-9.

301* **Ruijgh** Cornelis J., Scripta minora ad linguam graecam pertinentia, ᴱ*Bremer* J. M., *al.* Amst 1991, Gieben. xxiv-871 p. ƒ250. 90-5063-065-0 [AntClas 62,369s, Y. *Duhoux*].

302 **Sacon** K. K. † 1990 aet. 59, ◉ Collected works I. Scholarly articles [12]. Tokyo 1992, Kyōbunkan. 403 p. Y 8500 [BL 93,23, D. T. *Tsumura*, titles in English; pp.].

302* **Sanders** Gabriel, Lapides memores [1968-87] païens et chrétiens face à la mort; le témoignage de l'épigraphie funéraire latine, ᴱ*Donati* Angela, *al.*: Epigrafia e antichità 11. Faenza 1991, Lega [AnPg 62, p. 1008].

303 *a)* **Santiago-Otero** Horacio, Fe y cultura en la Edad Media: MedvHum 4. M 1988, Centro de Estudios Históricos [AnPg 61,p. 237].

— *b)* **Saranyana** Josep-Ignasi, Teología profética [latino-] americana; díez estudios [1987-91] sobre la evangelización fundante. Pamplona 1991, Univ. Navarra. 271 p. [RHE 88,661, G. I. *Rodríguez*]. – ᴿBurgense 33 (1992) 313s (N. *López Martínez*).

— *c)* **Schall** James V., Religion, wealth and poverty [27 reprints]. Fraser Inst. 202 p. $15 pa. [CanadCathR 11/3,27s, A. F. *McKee*].

— *d)* **Scheffczyk** Leo, Glaube in der Bewährung, GesSchr 3. St. Ottilien 1991, EOS. 592 p. – ᴿForKT 8 (1992) 211-4 (M. *Seybold*).

— *e)* **Schlette** Heinz R., (60. Gb.) Konkrete Humanität, ᴱ*Brosseder* J., *al.* Fra 1991, Knecht. 487 p. DM 168. 3-7820-0623-3 [TLZ 118,433, G. *Hornig*; Orientierung 57, 231-5 . 249-252, K. *Wenzel*: 'Philosophieren im Modus der Melancholie'].

304 **Schmidt-Wiegand** Ruth, Stammesrecht und Volkssprache; [ihre] ausgewählte Aufsätze zu den Leges barbarorum, ᴱ*Hüpper* Dagmar, *Schott* Clausdieter, *al.* Weinheim 1991, VCH Acta Humaniora. x-546 p. – ᴿBonnJbb 192 (1992) 759-761 (K. H. *Schmidt*).

305 **Schneider** Gerhard, Jesusüberlieferung und Christologie; neutestamentliche Aufsätze 1970-1990: NT supp 67. Leiden 1992, Brill. ix-391 p. ƒ182. 90-04-09555-1 [RB 100,131, tit. pp.; TPQ 141,296, A. *Fuchs*]. 18 art.; 3 infra (1 ineditum).

306 **Schottroff** W., Das Reich Gottes und der Menschen; Studien über das Verhältnis der christlichen Theologie zum Judentum: AbhCJDialog 19. Mü 1991, Kaiser. 235 p. DM 3-459-01881-X. – ᴿTvT 32 (1992) 111 (W. *Logister*).

306* **Schreiner** Josef, Leben nach der Weisung Gottes: GesSchr II, 70.Gb., ᴱ*Zenger* E. Wü 1992, Echter. 402 p. DM 68. [BZ 37,307, J. *Scharbert*; TPQ 141,398, F. *Hubmann*].

307 **Schwartz** Daniel R., Studies in the Jewish background of Christianity [5 inedita + 10 < ❻]: WUNT 60. Tü 1992, Mohr. xii-304 p. DM 178. 3-16-145798-6 [RB 100,288, tit. pp., Christiane *Saulnier* †; BL 94,151, P. R. *Davies*; NTAbs 36,452; TLZ 118,600, K.-W. *Niebuhr*]. – ᴿArTGran 55 (1992) 341s (A. *Segovia*).

307* **Schwartz** Howard E., People of the body; Jews and Judaism from an embodied perspective. Albany 1992, SUNY. 401 p. $59.50; pa. $20 [BToday 31,246].

308 **Seeligmann** I. L., Studies in biblical literature, ᴱ*Hurvitz* A., *al.* J 1992, Magnes. 521 p. – ᴿHenoch 14 (1992) 326s (A. *Rofé*, brevissimo).

309 **Serra** Aristide, Nato da donna... (Gal 4,4); ricerche bibliche su Maria di Nazaret (1989-1992. Mi/R 1992, CENS/Marianum. 405 p. Lit. 50.000. 6 art. [2 senza indizio di anteriore stampa]. 5 infra.

310 **Smelik** K. A., Converting the past; [5; Eng.] studies in ancient Israelite and Moabite historiography: OTS 28. Leiden 1992, Brill. viii-209 p. *f*95. 90-04-09480-6 [BL 93,43, A. G. *Auld*, detailed; ZAW 105,537, M. *Köckert*: five revised articles from the Dutch].

311 **Smith** Huston, [19, 1957-89] Essays on world religions, ᴱ*Bryant* M. Darrol. NY 1992, Paragon. xxx-290 p. $23. 1-55778-447-7 [TDig 40,87; JRel 73,441, G. *D'Costa*].

311* **Solomon** Norman, Judaism and world religion [reprints + inedita]. xv-295 p. £40. 0-333-54162-6 [TBR 6/2,102s, R. *Coggins*].

312 **Sourvinou-Inwood** Christiane, 'Reading' Greek culture; texts and images, rituals and myths. Ox 1991, Clarendon. vi-315 p.; ill. [AnPg 62, p. 1009; RclStR 19,353, W. M. *Calder*ᴵᴵᴵ is not impressed].

313 **Stanton** Graham N., A Gospel for a new people; studies in Matthew. E 1992, Clark. xiv-424 p. £15 [TR 88,516]. 0-567-09535-5. [RB 100,132, tit. pp.; incl. 8 inedita].

314 **Stein** Robert H., Gospels and tradition; studies on redaction criticism of the synoptic gospels [9; 3 < diss. on Mark]. GR 1991, Baker. 204 p. $13. 0-8010-8326-5 [TDig 39,387: Transfiguration a misplaced Resurrection account].

314* **STERN** M.: Studies in Jewish history, the Second Temple period, ᴱ*Gafni* M., *al.* J 1991, Yad Ben Zvi. 670 p. $45. 965-217-094-1 [JStJud 24, 143s, M. *Mach*: all in English, two from Hebrew, none updated].

315 **Stevenson** Kenneth W., Worship, wonderful and sacred mystery [11 art.]. Wsh 1992, Pastoral. viii-219 p. $15. 0-912405-90-2 [TDig 40,188].

316 **Stroumsa** Gedaliahu G., Savoir et salut; gnoses de l'Antiquité tardive: Patrimoines. P 1992, Cerf. 404 p. F 299. 3-204-04385-0 [RB 100,134, tit. pp.; RHPR 73,308, P. *Maraval*; JTS 44,709, S. *Lieu*: publishers omitted subtitle 'Traditions juives et tentations dualistes dans le Christianisme'].

317 **Stylianopoulos** Theodore, The good news of Christ; essays on the Gospel, sacraments and Spirit. Brookline MA 1991, Holy Cross Orthodox. xii-232 p. $15 pa. [CBQ 54,617; CritRR 5,532, tit. pp.: 7 reprints + 1 ineditum].

317* **Subilia** Vittorio,   La parola che brucia; meditazioni bibliche.   T 1991, Claudiana.   176 p. L^m 17.   88-7016-151-X [FilT 7,183s, G. *Zarone*].

318 **Syme** Ronald,   Roman papers [IV, 1988 → 4,269],   ^EBirley Anthony R.; [V...] VI-VII.   Ox 1991, Clarendon.   472 p.; p. 473-710, ill.   [AnPg 62, p. 1009: vol. VII all inedita, dépouillé].

319 **Taveneaux** Renè,   Jansénisme et Réforme catholique; recueil d'articles; préf. *Bluche* François.   Nancy 1992, Univ.   xi-210 p. F 180 [RHE 88,257, B. *Neveu*].

320 **Thévenot** Xavier,   Compter sur Dieu; études de théologie morale [12 reprints 1983-91]: Recherches morales.   P 1992, Cerf.   315 p. F 145.   2-204-04497-0. – ^REsprVie 102 (1992) 650s (P. *Daubercies*: 'facies esthétique de toute éthique'); TvT 32 (1992) 433 (J. *Dijkman*).

321 **Trever-Roper** Hugh,   From Counter-Reformation to Glorious Revolution [14 reprints + 1 ineditum]. Ch 1992, Univ.   xvi-331 p. $25.   0-226-81230-8 [TDig 40,189].

322 **Vahanian** Gabriel,   L'utopie chrétienne.   P 1992, D-Brouwer.   329 p. F 128 [TLZ 118,171, F. *Lienhard*].

323 **Vernant** Jean-Pierre,   Figures, idoles, masques; conférences, essais et leçons du Collège de France.   P 1990, Julliard.   247 p. F 100 pa. – ^RClasR 42 (1992) 87s (R. *Parker*).

323* **Vidal-Naquet** Pierre,   Les Juifs, la mémoire et le présent II.   P 1991, Découverte.   322 p. – ^RArchivScSocR 78 (1992) 264 (M. *Löwy*).

324 **Vilanova** Evangelista,   La fe cristiana entre la sospecha y la inocencia [organized reprints]: Nuevos desafios.   Estella 1990, VDivino.   276 p. 84-7151-672-1. – ^RRET 52 (1992) 247s (M. *Gesteira*).

325 **Vilar Hueso** Vicente,   En torno a la Biblia, estudios, ^ECollado Bertomeu Vicente: Valentina 29.   Valencia J 1992, Fac. Teol. Ferrer/Casa de Santiago.   693 p.   84-604-4705-7.   His own chronicles of Holy Land excavation, encyclopedia-articles, etc.

326 **Vischer** Lukas,   Gottes Bund gemeinsam bezeugen; Aufsätze zu Themen der ökumenischen Bewegung.   Gö 1992, Vandenhoeck & R.   309 p. DM 48 [TR 88,435].

326* **Vögtle** A.,   Anpassung oder Widerspruch; von der apostolischen zur nachapostolischen Kirche, ^EOberlinner L.   FrB 1992, Herder.   155 p. DM 24,80 [RHE 88,231*].

327 a) **Wallace** W. A.,   GALILEO, the Jesuits and the medieval ARISTOTLE: CS 346.   Aldershot 1992, Variorum.   xiv-336 p. [RHE 87,221*].

— b) **Ward** Benedicta,   Signs and wonders; saints, miracles and prayers from the 4th century to the 14th: CS 361.   Aldershot 1992, Variorum.   xiv-300 p.   0-86078-316-2 [JTS 44,497, G. *Gould*]. – ^RTBR 5,2 (1992s) 46 (Carolyne *Larrington*).

— c) **Ward-Perkins** J. B.,   Marbles in antiquity, ^EDodge Hazel, *Ward-Perkins* Bryan: Arch. Mg. 6.   L 1992, British School at Rome.   xii-180 p.; 141 fig.; 2 pl. [RArchéol, 93,144, B. *Holtzmann*].

328 **Webster** Graham,   Archaeologist at large.   L 1991, Batsford.   iv-230; 30 fig. £25. – ^RGreeceR 39 (1992) 108 (B. A. *Sparkes*: not for the scholar).

329 a) **Weder** Hans,   Einblicke ins Evangelium; exegetische Beiträge zur neutestamentlichen Hermeneutik, GesAufs 1980-91.   Gö 1992, Vandenhoeck & R.   493 p. DM 64 [TR 88,516; NRT 115,903, X. *Jacques*; SNTU A-18, 249, M. *Hasitschka*; TvT 33,414, P. *Chatelion Counet*].

— b) **Weinberg** Joel,   The citizen-temple community [7 art. 1972-7, updated + new final chapter], ^TSmith-Christopher Daniel L.: JStOT supp.

151. Shf 1992, JStOT. 145 p. £25. 1-85075-395-X [TBR 6/1,14, M. *Boda*; BL 94,102, W. *Johnstone*].
— *c*) **Westphal** Merold, HEGEL, freedom, and modernity [13 art. 1971-89]. Albany 1992, SUNY. xvii-295 p. $19 pa. [JRel 73,416, J. *Fitzer*].
330 **Wiegmann** Hermann, *a*) Von PLATONS Kritik zur Postmoderne. Bielefeld 1989, Aletheia. 132 p. [AnPg 60, p. 881; dépouillé]. – *b*) Rhetorik und ästhetische Vernunft. Bielefeld 1990, Aisthesis. 159 p. – ᴿRhetorik 10 (1991) 183-6 (J. *Kopperschmidt*) [AnPg 62, p. 1010].
331 **Wilfred** Felix, Sunset in the east? Asian challenges and Christian involvement; Asian Theological Search 2. Madras 1991, Univ. 358 p. [TContext 10/2,92, G. *Evers*].
332 WRIGHT G. R. H., Obiter dicta. L 1992, Aquiline. vi-239 p. [OIAc 5,40, excerpted].
333 **Wright** N. T., The climax of the Covenant; Christ and the Law in Pauline theology [...some inedita]. E 1991, Clark. xiv-316 p. £20. 0-567-09594-0. – ᴿExpTim 103 (1991s) 282s (S. E. *Porter*); TLond 95 (1992) 299 (J. *Ziesler*: technical essays hopefully conjoined toward a Pauline theology).

A1.3 *Plurium compilationes* biblicae.

334 ᴱ**Abel** Olivier, **Smith** Françoise, Le livre de traverse; de l'exégèse biblique à l'anthropologie: Patrimoines. P 1992, Cerf. 291 p. F 135. 2-204-047-00-7 [RB 100,453, compilation 'mal appelée symposium'; tit. pp.].
335 ᴱ**Amos** Thomas L., *al.*, De ore Domini; preacher and word in the Middle Ages: SMC 27. Kalamazoo 1989, Univ. Medv. Inst. xiv-269 p. $33; pa. $16. – ᴿSpeculum 67 (1992) 243 (tit. pp.).
336 ᴱ**Anderson** Janice C., **Moore** Stephen D., Mark and method; new approaches in biblical studies. Mp 1992, Fortress. viii-176 p. 0-8006-2655-9. 5 art. besides Mark.
336* ᴱ**Bauckham** Richard, *al.*, Jesus 2000; die faszinierendste Gestalt der Geschichte; damals, heute, morgen. Wu 1991, Brockhaus. 239 p.; ill. 3-417-24623-7 [ActuBbg 30,197, J. *Boada*].
337 **Berger** Klaus (177-225, Visionsberichte), *al.*, Studien und Texte zur Formgeschichte: TANZ 7. Tübingen 1992, Francke. vi-233 p. DM 78 [TR 88,518, tit. pp.]. 3-7720-1886-6. 3 other art.
338 ᴱ**Bianchi** Enzo, La parola diventa preghiera: ParSpV 25 (1992) 326 p. Lit. 18.500. 17 art.; 10 infra.
339 ᴱ**Bianchi** Enzo (*Barbaglio* Giuseppe, *al.*), Le Genti nel piano di salvezza: ParSpV 26 (1992). 271 p. Lit. 18.500. 17 art.; 12 infra.
340 ᴱ**Bienkowski** Piotr, Early Edom and Moab; the beginning of the Iron Age in southern Jordan: Sheffield Archaeological Mg 7. Sheffield 1992, Collis. xiii-202 p.
341 ᴱ**Black** David A., Linguistics and New Testament interpretation; essays on discourse analysis. Nv 1992, Broadman. 319 p.
341* ᴱ**Black** David A., *Dockery* David S., New Testament criticism and interpretation 1991 → 7,292*: ᴿExpTim 103 (1991s) 310 (E. *Franklin*: not quite up to 'NT Interpretation' 1977).
342 **Blough** Neal, *al.*, Jésus-Christ aux marges de la Réforme: JJC 54. P 1992, Desclée-Bégédis. 257 p. [Irénikon 65 (1992) 297].
343 ᴱ**Bodine** Walter R. [p. 1-6; 89-105], Linguistics and biblical Hebrew. WL 1992, Eisenbrauns. x-323 p. 0-931464-55-2 [OIAc 5,15]. – 18 art., infra.

ᴱBroer Ingo, (*Taeger* Jens-W., *al.*), Jesus und das jüdische Gesetz 1992
➤ 458*d*.
345 ᴱCharlesworth James H., Jesus and the Dead Sea Scrolls: AnchorB
Reference Library. NY 1992, Doubleday. xxxvii-370 p.; ill. 0-385-
24683-6 [OIAc 5,17].
346 *a*) ᴱClifford Richard J., *Collins* John J., Creation in the biblical traditions: CBQ Mg 24. Wsh 1992, Catholic Biblical Association. vi-151 p.
0-915170-23-X. 8 art.; infra.
— *b*) ᴱCohen, Jeremy Essential Papers on Judaism and Christianity in
conflict, from late antiquity to the Reformation [➤ 7,345]. NYU/Col-
umbia Univ. 1991. xv-578 p. $60; pa. $25. – ᴿRelStR 18 (1992) 346 (R.
Stacey).
— *c*) ᴱCohn-Sherbok Dan, Torah and revelation: Problems in Contemporary Jewish Theology. Lewiston NY 1992, Mellen. viii-243 p. $70
[RelStR 19,363, M. *Verman*].
347 ᴱCoote Robert B., Elijah and Elisha in socioliterary perspective: SBL
Semeia studies. Atlanta 1992, Scholars. xiii-156 p. $45; pa. $30. 1-55540-
708-0; -9-9 [RB 100,129, tit. pp.].
348 ᴱCulpepper R. Alan, *Segovia* Fernando F., The Fourth Gospel from a
literary perspective: Semeia 53. Atlanta 1991, Scholars. v-212 p. 7 art.,
infra; responses, *Beutler* Johannes, 191-202; *Tolbert* Mary Ann, 203-212.
349 ᴱDexinger Ferdinand, *Pummer* Reinhard, Die Samaritaner: WegF 604.
Da 1992, Wiss. viii-477 p. 3-534-08557-4 [OIAc 5,19, excerpted]. 1
Dexinger ineditum + 20 reprints [A. *Crown*, M. *Delcor*, G. E. *Wright*, F.
Cross, al.].
350 ᴱDunnavant Anthony L., Poverty and ecclesiology; nineteenth-century
evangelicals in light of liberation theology. ColMn 1992, Glazier/Litur-
gical. 104 p. $8 [Encounter 54,432, D. *Bundy*].
351 *a*) ᴱEpp Eldon J., *Fee* Gordon D., Studies in the theory and method of
New Testament textual criticism: StDoc 45. GR 1992, Eerdmans. xiv-
414 p. $40.
— *b*) ᴱFabris Rinaldo, La Bibbia nell'epoca moderna e contemporanea. Bo
1992, Dehoniane. 412 p. Lit. 42.000. – ᴿLetture 47 (1992) 759s (G. R-
avasi).
— *c*) ᴱFatum I., *Nielsen* E., Fortolkning som formidling; om den bibelske
eksegeses funktion [8 Copenhagen Univ. exegetes]: Forum for bibelsk
eksegese 3. K 1992, Museum Tusculanum. 135 p. Dk 154. 87-7289-
158-0 [BL 93,80, K. *Jeppesen*].
— *d*) ᴱFewell Danna N., Reading between texts; intertextuality and the
Hebrew Bible [13 art., most from SBL 'Reading, Rhetoric' section]:
LitCurrBInt. Louisville 1992, W-Knox. 285 p.; bibliog. 257-271. 0-
664-25393-8. [BL 93,81, R.P. *Carroll*, tit. pp.; Encounter 54,430, J.L.
Berquist]. – ᴿExpTim 104 (1992s) 375s (also R.P. *Carroll*).
— *e*) Figures du NT chez les Pères: CahBPatr 3. Strasbourg 1991, Centre
d'An/Doc. Patr. 234 p. – ᴿStPatav 39 (1992) 465s (G. *Segalla*).
— *f*) Flesher P.V.M., Targum studies 1. Textual and contextual studies in
the Pentateuchal targums: SFlaHJud 55. Atlanta 1992, Scholars. ix-
155 p. $60. 1-55540-754-4 [NTAbs 37, p.304].
352 ᴱGalea Michael, *Ciarlò* John, St. Paul in Malta; a compendium of
Pauline studies [WEHNERT J. 1990 & 1991, GUILLAUMIER P. (p. 53-114),
PULLICINO J.C., SANT C. (p. 39-59): all against WARNECKE H. 1987 &
1991]. Malta 1992, Veritas. 132 p. [CC 144/3, 196s, E.G. *Farrugia*]. –
ᴿMeliT 43,1 (1992) 92-94 (J.J. *Kilgallen*: good drawn out of the pain

caused by Warnecke's honest presentation, itself only an aspect of current opposition to historicity of Acts-Malta which A. SUHL prematurely claimed will never revive).

353 ᴱ**Goldberg** Harvey E., Judaism viewed from within and from without; anthropological studies. Albany 1987, SUNY. x-352 p.; ill. 0-88706-354-3; pa. -6-X. – 9 art.

354 ᴱ**Hallamish** Moshe, *Ravitsky* Aviezer, ❿ *E. I. ba-hagut...* La Terre d'Israël dans la pensée juive médiévale. J 1991, Yad Ben Zvi. viii-356 p. 14 art. – ᴿRÉJ 151 (1992) 403s (G. *Freudenthal*).

355 ᴱ**Hamm** Berndt, *Weth* Rudolf [present.], *al.*, Volk Gottes, Gemeinde und Gesellschaft: JbBT 7. Neuk 1992, Neuk.-V. x-434 p. 3-7887-1433-6. 16 art., infra.

356 ᴱ**Hay** D. M., Both literal and allegorical; studies in PHILO of Alexandria's Questions and Answers on Genesis and Exodus: BrownJudSt 232. Atlanta 1991, Scholars. xiii-256 p. $60. 1-55540-632-7 [NTAbs 36,294].

357 ᴱ**House** Paul R., Beyond form criticism; essays in Old Testament literary criticism: Sources for Biblical and Theological Study 2. WL 1992, Eisenbruns. xvi-448 p. 0-931464-65-X [BL 93,87, J. *Barton*: excellent selection]. – ᴿExpTim 104 (1992s) 245s (C. S. *Rodd*).

357* ᴱ**Jobling** David, *Pippin* Tina, Ideological criticism of biblical texts: Semeia 59. Atlanta 1992, Scholars. vii-249 p. $20; sb. $15. 0095-571X [BL 94,90, H. S. *Pyper*].

358 *a)* ᴱ**Jost** Renate, *al.*, Auf Israel hören; Sozialgeschichtliche Bibelauslegung. Luzern 1992, Exodus. 160 p., 8 maps. DM 29,80 [TLZ 117,737].

— *b)* ᴱ**Krondorfer** Björn, Body and Bible; interpreting and experiencing biblical narratives. Ph 1992, Trinity. xi-209 p. 1-56338-048-X. – 11 art., infra.

— *c)* **Lagrée** Michel, *al.*, Figures du démoniaque hier et aujourd'hui. Bru 1992, Fac. Univ. S. Louis. F 156 [Études 379,138s, R. *Marlé*: conclusion de C. DUQUOC ne prétend pas décider l'existence de Satan ou non].

359 ᴱ**Levin** I., ❿ Studies in the works of Abraham IBN EZRA: Teʿuda 8. TA 1992, Univ. Rosenberg Jewish Studies. viii-214 p.; Eng. xvi p. [RB 100,458, tit. pp.].

359* ᴱ**Muratore** Saturnino, Israele e le genti [ristampe < RasT]. R 1991, A.V.E. 180 p. Lit. 18.000. – ᴿCC 143 (1992,3) 353 (S. M. *Katunarich*).

360 ᴱ**Neusner** Jacob, *a)* The Pharisees and other sects: Origin of Judaism 2,1s (out of 20; 24 reprints, 5 by Neusner). NY 1990, Garland. xix-517 p.; xviii-536 p. $150 both. – ᴿCritRR 5 (1992) 525-7 (tit. pp.).

— *b)* The literature of formative Judaism; the midrash-compilations (20 reprints by 14 authors); History of the Jews in the first century of the common era [34 reprints from 25 authors; vol. (17 and) 11 of 21 projected]: Origins of Judaism 11/1 (8). NY 1990, Garland. xvii-678 p. [JBL 112,365 & 749, tit. pp.].

361 **O'Donnell** Anne, Biblical interpretation in the age of Thomas MORE: Moreana 106s ('W. Tyndale' 1991). vi-202 p. – ᴿRHE 87 (1992) 914s (R. *Aubert*).

362 ᴱ**Olender** Maurice, The languages of Paradise; race, religion and philosophy in the nineteenth century [Les langues du Paradis; Aryens et Sémites, un couple providentiel 1989 → 6,9804*],ᵀ. CM 1992, Harvard Univ. xiii-193 p. 0-674-51952-6 [OIAc 3,32].

363 ᴱ**Ollenburger** Ben C., *a)* The flowering of Old Testament theology; a reader in twentieth-century OT theology, 1930-1990: Sources for Biblical and Theological Study 1. WL 1992, Eisenbrauns. xii-547 p. [CBQ 54,

616]. 0-931464-62-5. – ᴿBtS 149 (1992) 485 (E. H. *Merrill*). – *b*) So wide a sea; essays on biblical [and its relation to Mennonite] systematic theology. Elkhart IN 1991, Inst. Mennonite. 145 p. $10. 24 art. – ᴿHorBT 14 (1992) 182-4 (U. *Mauser*); TTod 50 (1992s) 500s (J. *Hanson*).

364 ᴱ**Parker** Kim I., [Destructive atheistic] Liberal democracy and the Bible. Lewiston NY 1992, Mellen. v-187 p. £30. 0-7734-9154-6 [TBR 6/1,13, N. *Adams*].

365 ᴱ**Saperstein** Marc, Essential papers on Messianic movements and personalities in Jewish history: Essential Papers on Jewish Studies. NYU 1992. xii-580 p. $60; pa. $25. 0-8147-7942-5; -3-3 [TDig 40,61]. 22 art.; 6 infra.

367 ᴱ**Shanks** *Hershel*, *a*) Christianity and rabbinic Judaism; a parallel history of their origins and early development. Wsh 1992, BAR / L 1993, SPCK. xxii-380 p. 6 pl. £15. 0-281-04625-5. – ᴿTBR 5,3 (1992) 67 (N. R. M. de *Lange*). – *b*) Understanding the Dead Sea Scrolls [22 art. < BAR-W]. NY 1922, Random. 336 p. $23. – ᴿTTod 49 (1992s) 548.550 (J. H. *Charlesworth*).

Suggs M. Jack, *al.*, The Oxford Study Bible ['features 22 indispensable articles on the biblical world'] 1992 → 1891.

368 ᴱ**Swartley** Willard M., The love of enemy and nonretaliation in the NT. Louisville 1992, W-Knox. 336 p. $30. 0-664-25354-7. – ᴿExpTim 104 (1992s) 282 (N. *Clark*: mostly not on Mt 5).

369 **Wall** Robert W., *Lemcio* Eugene E., The New Testament as canon; a reader in canonical criticism [14 of their own articles organized as chapters]: JStNT supp 76. Shf 1992, Academic. 376 p. £45; pa. £33.75. 1-85075-374-1 [RB 100,456, tit. pp.]. – ᴿExpTim 104 (1992s) 282 (W. *Moberly*: stimulating; but does not the very notion of canon include OT?).

370 ᴱ**Wimbush** Vincent L., Discursive formations, ascetic piety and the interpretation of early Christian literature I-II: Semeia 57s, Atlanta 1992, Scholars. 160 p., 156 p.

371 ᴱ**Yoder** Perry B., *Swartley* Willard M., The meaning of peace [German essays on *shālôm* and *eirēnē* mostly never published in English], ᵀ*Sawatsky* Walter: Mennonite Studies in Peace and Scripture. Louisville 1992, W-Knox. xxi-289 p. $20. 0-664-25312-1 [TDig 40,76].

A1.4   *Plurium compilationes* **theologicae.**

371* ᴱ**Abromeit** Heidrum, *Wewer* Göttrik, Die Kirchen und die Politik; Beiträge zu einem ungeklärten Verhältnis. Opladen 1989, Westdeutscher-V. vi-297 p. DM 35. 3-531-12079-4 [TLZ 118,450, W. *Huber*].

372 **Anati** E., *Boyer* R., *al.*, Le origini e il problema dell'homo religiosus. Mi 1989, Jaca. 325 p. – ᴿKatKent 31 (1992) 189-194 (R. *López Silonis* ❿).

373 ᴱ**Anderson** G. H., *al.*, Mission in the 1990s [1989s reprints]. GR 1991, Eerdmans. 80 p. – ᴿJDharma 17 (1992) 70s (P. *Areeplackal*).

374 *a*) ᴱ**Antes** P., Grosse Religionsstifter; Zarathustra, Mose [W. H. *Schmidt*], Jesus, Mani, Muḥammad, Nanak, Buddha, Lao Zi. Mü 1992, Beck. 242 p. DM 40. – ᴿZAW 104 (1990) 446s (U. *Schorn*).

— *b*) ᴱ**Arens** W., *Karp* Ivan, Creativity of power; essays on cosmology and action in African societies. Wsh 1989, Smithsonian. 315 p. 0-98774-617-5 [JRelAf 23,175, J. L. *Matory*].

— *c*) ᴱ**Austin** Gerald, Fountain of life. Dublin 1992, Columba. ix-249 p. £21.50. 0-91205-85-6. – ᴿExpTim 104 (1992s) 58 (G. S. *Wakefield*: 'a symposium' with no date or place indicated, 'by some of the world's best liturgists').

— *d*) ᴱ*Bach* Alice, Ad feminam: UnSemQ 43,1-4 (60th anniversary volume, 1989).

375 ᴱ**Badone** Ellen, Religious orthodoxy and popular faith in European society. Princeton 1990, Univ. vii-230 p. $40; pa. $13. – ᴿCritRR 5 (1992) 312-5 (L. N. *Primiano*: enlightening because by anthropologists).

375* ᴱ**Battafarano** Italo M., Begrifflichkeit und Bildlichkeit der Reformation: Forschungen zur europäischen Kultur 5. Bern 1992, Lang. 241 p. DM 54. 3-261-04528-0. 7 art. [TR 89,344].

376 ᴱ**Baum** Gregory, *Ellsberg* Robert, The logic of solidarity; commentaries on Pope JOHN PAUL's encyclical 'On social concerns' [1987]. Mkn 1989, Orbis. xv-232 p. $15. – ᴿPacifica 5 (1992) 108-111 (B. *Duncan*).

377 ᴱ**Benner** David G., Psychology and religion [52 art. < Baker Encyclopaedia of Psychology 1985). GR 1988, Baker. 343 p. $13. 0-8010-0947-2. – ᴿEvangel 9,2 (1991) 30 (S. C. *Parks*).

377* ᴱ**Berry** R. J., Real science, real faith. Eastbourne 1991, Monarch. 218 p. £9 [PerScCF 45,63s, R. H. *Bube*].

378 *a*) ᴱ**Bianchi** Euegene C., *Ruether* Rosemary R., A democratic Catholic Church [13 art.], NY 1992, Crossroad. 262 p. $24. 0-8245-1186-7 [TDig 40,158].

— *b*) ᴱ**Bianchi** L., *Randi* F., Filosofi e teologi; la ricerca e l'insegnamento nell'Università medievale. Bergamo 1989, Lubrina. 279 p. Lit. 32.000. – ᴿRasT 33 (1992) 112s (A. *Orazzo*: 'di tipo antologico').

— *c*) ᴱ**Browning** Don S., *Schüssler Fiorenza* Francis, HABERMAS, modernity, and public theology. NY 1992, Crossroad. vi-258 p. $25 [ÉglT 24, 472-4, K. R. *Melchin*].

379 **Brümmer** Vincent, Interpreting the universe as creation. Kampen 1991, Kok Pharos [NVFr 67,225].

380 *a*) ᴱ**Burrell** David, *Landau* Yehezkel, Voices from Jerusalem; Jews and Christians reflect on the Holy Land. NY 1992, Paulist. vi-176 p. 0-8091-3270-2 [TDig 39,391].

— *b*) BUTLER Joseph: moral and religious thought; tercentenary essays, ᴱ*Cunliffe* Christopher, Ox 1992, Clarendon. xiv-320 p. 0-19-826740-1 [TBR 6/2,48, S. *Plant*: an excellent collection].

— *c*) ᴱ**Card** Claudia, Feminist ethics. Lawrence 1991, Univ. Kansas. 300 p. [RelStR 19,61, P. *Lauritzen*: an excellent selection].

381 ᴱ**Cohn-Sherbok** Dan, *a*) World religions and human liberation: Faith meets faith. Mkn 1992, Orbis. $40; pa. $17. 0-88344-796-7; -5-9 [TDig 40,94; RelStR 19,58, J. B. *Cobb*].

— *b*) Using the Bible today; contemporary interpretations of Scripture: Canterbury papers 3. L 1991, Bellew. xi-203 p. £14 pa. 0-947792-95-3; pa. -4-5 [TBR 6/2,21, Jane *Charman*: 20 discussion-starting essays].

— *c*) The Salman RUSHDIE controversy in interreligious perspective. Lewiston NY 1990, Mellen. 151 p. – ᴿTLond 95 (1992) 464 (G. *D'Costa*: a very good collection).

382 ᴱ**Colpe** Carsten, *al.*, Spätantike und Christentum; Beiträge zur Religions- und Geistesgeschichte der griechisch-römischen Kultur und Zivilisation der Kaiserzeit. B 1992, Akademie. 280 p. 3-05-002004-0. 14 art.; 8 infra.

383 **Communio** Rivista Internazionale (anche Eng. franç. etc.; deutsch = IkaZ), 1992; **121**. Io sono il Signore Dio tuo. 117 p. – **122**. La pedagogia cristiana. 122 p. **123**. Le chiese orientali. 122 p. – **124**. La nuova

evangelizzazione, EGueriero E.: 112 p. – **125**, Individualismo e solidarietà, 111 p. – **126**. Henri de Lubac, 111 p. Milano, Jaca (anche P, Rio, Wsh ecc.).

384 Concilium, Internationale Zeitschrift für Theologie 28 (1992) [auch fr. Eng. usw.] **1**. EAlberigo G., Ngindu Mushete, Auf dem Weg zur Afrischen Synode; – **2**. EGreinacher N., Mette N., Das neue Europa; – **3**. EKüng H., Moltmann J., Fundamentalismus als ökumenische Herausforderung; – **4**. EDuquoc C., Floristán C., Gott, wo bist du?; – **5**. EProvost J., Walf K., Demokratisierung der Kirche, ein Tabu?; – **6**. EGeffré C., Jossua J.-P., Die Moderne auf dem Prüfstand. 537 p. [je c. DM 90]. Mainz, Grünewald [Eng. L/Ph etc.].

385 a) EDal Covolo Enrico, Triacca Achille M., La missione del Redentore; [20] studi sull'enciclica missionaria di GIOVANNI PAOLO II. T-Leumann 1992, LDC. 320 p. Lit. 26.000 [CC 144/4,521, J. Dupuis].

— b) EDayton Donald W., Johnston Robert K., The variety of American evangelicalism. GR/Knoxville 1991, Inter-Varsity/Univ. Tennessee. viii-285 p. $40; pa. $20. 0-8208-1754-9 [AndrUnS 31,64, W. Widden]. – RThemelios 18,1 (1992s) 34 (C. Blomberg).

— c) EDelumeau J., La religion de ma mère; les femmes et la transmission de la foi: Histoire. P 1992, Cerf. 387 p.; 10 fig. F 200 [RHE 87,440*].

386 EDoré J., Introduction à l'étude de la théologie³ I [➤ 7,350b]. P 1991, Desclée. 651 p.; 476 p. – 2-7189-0591-1 [NRT 115,577, R. Escol]. – vol. 3 has a subtitle, Le travail du théologien. 1992. 476 p. 2-7189-0591-3.

387 EDussel Enrique, The Church in Latin America 1492-1992. Tunbridge Wells/Mkn 1992, Burns & O/Orbis. x-501 p. $50. /0-88344-820-3 [TDig 40,156].

388 EEngemann Wilfried, Volp Rainer, Gib mir ein Zeichen; zur Bedeutung der Semiotik für theologische Praxis und Denkmodelle: Arbeiten zur praktischen Theologie 1. B/NY 1992, de Gruyter. xi-264 p. DM 148. 17 art. [TR 88,533, tit. pp.].

388* EFaivre Antoine, Needleman Jacob, Modern esoteric spirituality. NY 1992, Crossroad. 419 p. $49.50 [CCurr 43,549, Mary F. Bednarowski].

389 EFigueroa Deck Allan, Frontiers of Hispanic theology in the United States. Mkn 1992, Orbis. 174 p. [TContext 10/2,95, R. Fornet-Betancourt].

389* EFowler James W., al., Stages of faith and religious development; implications for Church, education and society. L 1992, SCM. 280 p. £17.50. 0-334-02520-6. – RExpTim 104 (1992s) 30 (E. B. Mellor: good, especially Moran G., Hull J.).

390 EFurger Franz, Wiemeyer Joachim, Christliche Sozialethik im weltweiten Horizont: Univ.InstSozW 25. Münster 1992, Aschendorff. vi-101 p. DM 28 [TR 88,532].

391 a) EGetz Lorine M., Ruy Costa O., Struggles for solidarity; liberation theologies in tension [13 art.]. Mp 1992, Fortress. 171 p. $11. 0-8006-2528-5 [TDig 39,388].

— b) EGoizueta Roberto S., We are a people! Initiatives in Hispanic American theology. Mp 1992, Fortress. xxi-164 p. [JHispT 1/1,98, Jeanette Rodríguez].

— c) EGolser K., Verantwortung für die Schöpfung in den Weltreligionen. Innsbruck 1992, Tyrolia [TLZ 118,214].

392 EGosman M., Bakker H., Heilige oorlogen; een onderzoek naar historische en hedendaagse vormen van collectief religieus gewelt. Kam-

pen/Kapellen 1991, Kok/Pelckmans. 260 p. Fb 795. 90-242-7714-0 / 90-289-1598-2. – ᴿTvT 32 (1992) 216 (A. van *Iersel*).

392* ᴱGottlieb G., *Barceló* P., Christen und Heiden in Staat und Gesellschaft des II. bis IV. Jhts.; Gedanken und Thesen zu einem schwierigen Verhältnis: Schr. Univ. Augsburg Philos. 44. Mü 1992, Vogel. [vi-]212 p.; 24 fig. [RHE 88,232*].

393 *a*) ᴱGraf Friedrich W., *Tanner* Klaus, Protestantische Identität heute. Gü 1992, Mohn. 304 p. DM 58 pa. [TR 88,529].

— *b*) ᴱGreen Ronald M., Religion and sexual health; ethical, theological, and clinical perspectives [13 art.]: Theology and Medicine 1. Boston 1992, Kluwer. xiv-232 p. $79. 0-7823-1752-1 [TDig 40,287].

— *c*) ᴱHardelin Alf, In quest of the Kingdom; ten papers on medieval monastic spirituality: BtPrac Kyrkovetenskaplige studier 48. Sto 1991, Almqvist & W. 284 p. [TR 89,116, J. *Sudbrack*: klar, nützlich].

394 *a*) ᴱHall Christine, The deacon's ministry. ... 1991, Gracewing. 206 p. £8. 8-85244-182-7. – ᴿExpTim 103 (1991s) 285 (Ruth B. *Edwards*: 8 Anglicans, 2 Roman Catholics, 1 Orthodox; some with slightly antiquarian flavour).

— *b*) ᴱHead Thomas, *Landes* Richard, [+ 11 *al*.] The peace of God; social violence and religious response in France around the year 1000. Ithaca NY 1992, Cornell Univ. 364 p.; 3 maps [RHE 88,833, P. *Riché*].

— *c*) ᴱHerzog F., *Grosscurth* R., Kirchgemeinschaft im Schmelztiegel — Anfang einer neuen Ökumene? Anfragen und Dokumente aus der United Church of Christ (USA). Neuk 1989. 176 p. DM 19,80. – ᴿOrientierung 56 (1992) 10-12 (J. *Brosseder*: eine bemerkenswerte Publikation).

395 ᴱHessel Dieter T., After nature's revolt; eco-justice and theology [10 art.]. Mp 1992, Fortress. x-218 p. $15. 0-8006-2532-3 [TDig 40,49].

396 *a*) ᴱHillenbrand Karl, Priester heute; [... DREWERMANN gegenüber] Anfragen, Aufgaben, Anregungen. Wü 1990, Echter. 256 p. DM 29. – ᴿZkT 114 (1992) 366 (J. *Thorer*).

— *b*) ᴱHinlicky Paul, Different voices, shared voices; male and female in the Trinitarian community. Delhi/NY 1992, American Lutheran Publicity Bureau. 96 p. $5. – ᴿLuthQ 7 (1993) 356-8 (J. T. *Pless*: disproves synod officials' 'there is no organized movement toward women's ordination').

— *c*) ᴱHöhn Hans-Joachim, Theologie, die an der Zeit ist; Entwicklungen — Positionen — Konsequenzen. Pd 1992, Schöningh. 233 p. DM 38 pa. 3-506-73936-0. 9 art. [TR 89,344] ➤ B33.

— *d*) ᴱHolloway Julia B., *al*., Equally in God's image; women in the Middle Ages. NY 1990, Lang. xiii-336 p.; 5 fig.; 20 pl. $55 [Speculum 68,1248, tit. pp.] 16 art.; p. 122-8, *Barr* Jane, The Vulgate Genesis and St. JEROME's attitude to women.

— *e*) ᴱJuergensmeyer Mark, Violence and the sacred in the modern world [GIRARD R.: Journal of terrorism 3/3]. L 1992, F. Cass. 155 p. £24. 0-7146-3456-5 [TBR 6/1,50, G. *Pattison*].

— *f*) ᴱKaplan Lawrence, Fundamentalism in comparative perspective. Amherst 1992, Univ. Massachusetts. viii-184 p. – ᴿRRelRes 34 (1992s) 184s (F. J. *Lechner*: J. COLEMAN treats 'Catholic integralism as a fundamentalism').

— *g*) ᴱKatz Steven T., Mysticism and language [10 original essays, including M. *Idel*, N. *Smart*, E. *Cousins*, B. *McGinn*]. NY 1992, Oxford-UP. viii-262 p. 0-19-505455-5.

397 ᴱKerber Walter, *Müller* Johannes, Soziales Denken in einer zerrissenen Welt; Anstösse der katholischen Soziallehre in Europa ['Sammelband']: QDisp 136. FrB 1991, Herder. 232 p. 3-451-02136-6. 18 art.

398 ᴱKimel Alvin F.ᴶ, Speaking [+ of: TDig 40,292] the Christian God; the Holy Trinity and the challenge of feminism. GR/Leominster 1992, Eerdmans/Gracewing. x-337 p. £13. 0-8028-0612-0 / 0-85244-213-0. – ᴿTBR 5,2 (1992s) 40 (Jane *Charman*: overall negative).

399 *a*) ᴱ*Lacey* Michael J., Religion and twentieth-century American intellectual life. C 1989, Univ./W. Wilson Center. 214 p. – ᴿRTPhil 124 (1992) 105s (K. *Blaser*).

— *b*) ᴱ*Levack* Brian P., Witchcraft, magic, and demonology [198 reprints]. NY 1992, Garland. 12 vols. $710 [RelStR 19,269, R. M. *Golden*: first-rate articles, indispensable for libraries].

— *c*) ᴱ*Linzey* Andrew, *Wexler* Peter, Fundamentalism and tolerance; an agenda for theology and society: Canterbury papers 4. L 1991, Bellew. viii-184 p. £14 pa. 0-947792-75-9; pa. -4-0 [TBR 6/2,20, G. *Howes*: not really on fundamentalism, or tolerance either].

— *d*) ᴱ*Lippy* Charles H. [cf. ➤ 4,853 ... 7,730], Twentieth century shapers of American popular religion. Westport 1989, Greenwood. xxv-494 p. $65. – ᴿJEvTS 35 (1992) 119s (J. A. *Patterson*: too Chicagoan).

400 ᴱ*Loades* Ann, *Rue* Loyal D., Contemporary classics in philosophy of religion [27 recently published]. La Salle IL 1991, Open Court. $50; pa, $20. 0-8126-9168-7; -9-5 [TDig 39,357].

401 *a*) ᴱ*Lohmann* Martin, Christliche Perspektiven; Bestandsaufnahme für eine Kirche von morgen. Pd 1990, Schöningh. 190 p. – ᴿLebZeug 46 (1991) 148s (G. *Risse*).

— *b*) ᴱ*Macciocchi* M. A., Le donne secondo WOJTYŁA, ventinove chiavi di lettura della Mulieris dignitatem; + intervista *Cossiga* F. Mi 1992, EP. 420 p. Lit. 30.000. – ᴿRasT 33 (1992) 709s (P. *Vanzan*).

— *c*) ᴱ*McGowan* A. T. B., Women elders in the Kirk? Fearn c. 1991, Christian Focus. £3.50 [EvQ 65,61, R. *Higham*: pleads chiefly for respecting the conscience of those opposed].

402 **McKim** Donald K., Major themes in the Reformed tradition [37 art., some inedita]. GR 1992, Eerdmans. 447 p. $35. 0-8028-0428-4 [TDig 39,371].

402* ᴱ**Makselon** Józef, ❷ Psychologia dla teologów. Kraków 1990, Akad. Teol. – ᴿAtKap 117 (1991) 149-151 (W. *Szewsczyk*).

403 ᴱ**Malony** H. Newton, *Southard* Samuel, Handbook of religious conversion [... in various religions; in theology, psychology, literature; only one personal case-study]. Birmingham AL 1992, Religious Education. vi-314 p. $22. 0-89135-086-1 [TDig 40,165].

404 ᴱ**Marty** Martin E., *Appleby* R. Scott, Fundamentalisms observed [vol. 1 of 5]: American Academy of Arts and Sciences Fundamentalism project, 1. Ch 1992, Univ. xvi-872 p. $40. 0-226-50877-3 [TDig 39,61]. – ᴿChrCent 109 (1992) 426-9 (R. *Wuthnow*), further p. 46-8.

405 ᴱ**Mattioli** U., Donna e cultura; studi e documenti nel III anniversario della 'Mulieris dignitatem'. Genova 1991, Marietti. xii-278 p. Lit. 35.000. – ᴿBStLat 22 (1992) 352-5 (C. *Magazzù*).

405* ᴱ**Mattioli** Umberto (p. 11-16 . 51-79 . 365-379), La donna nel pensiero cristiano antico: Saggi e Ricerche. Genova 1992, Marietti. 399 p. Lit. 45.000. 88-211-9468-X. – ᴿBStLat 22 (1992) 296-316 (C. *Magazzù*).

406 ᴱ**Mechels** Eberhard, *Weinrich* Michel, Die Kirche im Wort; Arbeitsbuch zur Ekklesiologie. Neuk 1992. 269 p. 3-7887-1426-3 [TLZ 118,957, F. *Mildenberger*].

407 ᴱ**Meyendorff** John, The primacy of Peter; essays in ecclesiology and the early Church. Crestwood NY 1992 [= 1963 + *Kesich* V.], St. Vladimir. 182 p. 0-88741-125-6.

407* ᴱMeyers Eleanor S., Envisioning the new city; a reader on urban ministry. Louisville 1992, W-Knox. 361 p. $23 [Encounter 54,218, J. *Mulholland*].

408 ᴱMieth Dietmar, Christliche Sozialethik im Anspruch der Katholischen Soziallehre; Tübinger Beiträge [aus Monographien] zur Katholischen Soziallehre: Studien zur theologischen Ethik 41. FrS/FrB 1992, Univ./ Herder. 183 p. DM 42 [TvT 33,430, T. *Veerkamp*]. 3-7278-0817-9 / 3-451-22941-2. 7 art.; 2 infra.

409 *a*) ᴱMojzes Paul, *Swidler* Leonard, Christian mission and interreligious dialogue [Cardinal Josef Tomko's reply to 10 Catholic and 7 Protestant reactions to Tomko's 1988 Rome address 'Missionary challenges to the theology of salvation']: Religions in dialogue 4. Lewiston NY 1990, Mellen. 279 p. $60. 0-88964-520-7 [TDig 39,356].

— *b*) ᴱMontefiore Hugh, The Gospel and contemporary culture. L 1992, Mowbray. 182 p. £12 pa. 0-264-67259-3. – ᴿExpTim 103 (1991s) 313 (D. B. *Forrester*: stimulating on Newbigin's debate about the Christian mission in the contemporary West); TLond 95 (1992) 393s (D. *Jasper*).

— *c*) ᴱMoser Dietz-Rüdiger, Glaube im Abseits; Beiträge zur Erforschung des Aberglaubens. Da 1992, Wiss. 496 p. DM 89. 3-534-07781-4 [ActuBbg 30, 216s, J. *Boada*].

410 ᴱMüller Hans Martin, Kulturprotestantismus; Beiträge zu einer Gestalt des modernen Christentums. Gü 1992, Mohn. 396 p. DM 128. 15 art. [TR 88,343, tit. pp.] 2 infra.

411 ᴱNeuberger Julia, *White* John A., A necessary end; attitudes to death [12 art.]. L 1991, Macmillan. 178 p. £11. 0-333-48276-X. – ᴿExpTim 103 (1991s) 348 (R. *Lunt*: absence of a sense of the soul and of divine judgment; aim to die well rather than be kept alive officiously by medics).

411* ᴱOelmüller Willi, Worüber man nicht schweigen kann; neue Diskussionen zur Theodizeefrage. Mü 1992, Fink [FilT 7,435].

412 ᴱPeden Creighton, *Axel* Larry E., God, values, and empiricism; issues in philosophical theology. Macon 1989, Mercer Univ. 252 p. $32. – ᴿInterpretation 46 (1992) 95s (J. E. *Miller*).

413 ᴱPeter-Raoul Mar, *al.*, Yearning to breathe free; liberation theologies in the U. S. Mkn 1991, Orbis. xii-242 p. $17. – ᴿCurrTMiss 19 (1992) 301s (E. *Utto-Galarneau* praises; a mixture: reports, poetry, autobiography ...).

413* ᴱPieterse Jan P. N., Christianity and hegemony; religion and politics on the frontiers of social change. NY 1992, Berg. xı-321 p. 0-85496-749-4. – ᴿTBR 5,2 (1992s) 39 (G. *Howes*: on USA hegemony and the role of Christianity in its legitimation and maintenance).

414 ᴱRaab Peter, Psychologie hilft glauben; durch seelisches Reifen zum spirituellen Erwachen; Berichte, Erfahrungen, Anregungen: Tb 1704. FrB 1990, Herder. 240 p. DM 16. – ᴿRTLv 23 (1992) 218 (P. *Weber*: de collaborateurs compétents).

414* ᴱRamey Robert H.ᴶ, *Johnson* Ben C., Living the Christian life; a guide to Reformed spirituality. Louisville 1992, W-Knox. 181 p. $13. 0-664-25286-9 [Interpretation 47,434s, Ellen L. *Babinsky*).

415 ᴱRatzinger J., *Henrici* P., Credo, ein theologisches Lesebuch [< Communio 1973-92]. Köln 1992, Communio. 398 p. DM 42 [NRT 115,620, A. *Toubeau*].

416 ᴱRawlyk George A., The Canadian Protestant experience, 1760-1990. Burlington 1990, Welch. 252 p. – ᴿTorJT 7 (1991) 297-9 (I. *Manson*).

417 a) ᴱReeves M., Prophetic Rome in the High Renaissance period (Oxford-Warburg Studies). Ox 1992, Clarendon. xiv-433 p.; 16 fig. $50 [RHE 87,258*].
— b) ᴱRodríguez Saturnino, Pasado y futuro de la Teología de la liberación; de Medellín a Santo Domingo [antología]: Horizonte. Estella 1992, VDivino. 350 p. pt. 1900. 84-7151-793-0 [ActuBbg 30,218, J. Boada].
— c) ᴱRosa Mario, Clero e società nell'Italia contemporanea. Bari 1992, Laterza. 334 p. Lit. 50.000 [CC 144/3; 318s, G. Armando].
418 ᴱSanz Valdivieso R., Biblia y cristología (1984), Unidad y diversidad (1956), Interpretación de los dogmas (1991): Publ 7. Murcia 1992, Inst. Teol. Franciscano. 275 p. 84-86042-05-2. – ᴿActuBbg 29 (1992) 200s (J. O'Callaghan).
418* ᴱScharlemann Robert P., Theology at the end of the century; a dialogue on the postmodern. Charlottesville 1990, Univ. Virginia. 160 p. [JAAR 61,154, Mary I. Bockover].
419 ᴱSchütte Heinz, Einig in der Lehre von der Rechtfertigung! mit einer Antwort an Jörg BAUR. Pd 1990, Bonifatius. 83 p. – ᴿTZBas 48 (1992) 300s (H. J. E. Beintker).
419* ᴱSchumaker John F., Religion and mental health [24 contributors]. NY 1992, Oxford-UP. viii-320 p. $45. 0-19-506985-4 [TDig 40,287].
420 ᴱShaw William, Praise disjoined; changing patterns of salvation in 17th-century English literature: Seventeenth-century texts and studies 2. NY 1991, Lang. $51. 0-8204-1460-3 [TDig 39,380]. 17 art.: SHAKESPEARE, MILTON, JOHNSON, DONNE...
421 ᴱSievernich M., al., Conquista und Evangelisation, 500 Jahre Orden in Lateinamerika. Mainz 1992, Gruenewald. 486 p.; 9 fig.; 4 maps. [RHE 88,178*].
421* ᴱSobel Zvi, Beit-Hallaḥmi Benjamin, Tradition, innovation, conflict; Jewishess and Judaism in contemporary Israel. Albany 1991, SUNY. viii-316 p. $18 pa. – ᴿJScStR 31 (1992) 223s (Mareleyn Schneider).
422 a) ᴱThomas J. Mark, Visick Vernon, [5 essays, first by N. Gottwald] God and [... Reagan-Bush] capitalism; prophetic critique of market economy. Madison WI 1991, A-R Editions. 103 p. 0-89579-251-6. – ᴿExpTim 103 (1991s) 251s (S. Booth-Clibborn: easier to grumble than to come up with a plan).
— b) ᴱTraniello F., Cultura cattolica e vita religiosa tra Ottocento e Novecento [10 reprints]: BtStoria Contemporanea. Brescia 1991, Morcelliana. 331 p. [CrNSt 14,449, R. Simonato].
— c) ᴱUlrich Hans G., Evangelische Ethik; Diskussionsbeiträge zu ihrer Grundlegung und ihren Aufgaben [15 Aufsätze seit 1945 mit Wertung]: TBü 83. Mü 1990, Kaiser. 460 p. DM 38 [TR 89,146-150, E. Arens].
423 L'uomo indoeuropeo e il sacro: Trattato di antropologia del sacro 2. Mi 1991, Jaca/Massimo. xvii-304 p. [Ries J., al.]. – ᴿSalesianum 54 (1992) 776 (R. Gottlieb).
423* ᴱVandermeer Philip R., Swierenga Robert P., Belief and behavior; essays in the new religious history. New Brunswick 1991, Rutgers Univ. xii-236 p. $38; $15 pa. [ChH 62,585, P. Williams: 'new', deflating Perry MILLER; and useful, at least as a start].
424 ᴱVecsey Christopher, Religion in native North America. Moscow ID 1990, Univ. Idaho. xxiii-201 p. $23. – ᴿCritRR 5 (1992) 400 (K. M. Morrison).
425 a) ᴱVoss-Goldstein C., Goldstein H., Schwestern über Kontinente — Aufbruch der Frauen; Theologie der Befreiung in Latein-Amerika und

feministische Theologie hierzulande. Dü 1991, Patmos. 111 p. DM 19,80. 3-491-77672-4. – ᴿTvT 32 (1992) 205 (Harriet van der *Vleuten*).
425* ᴱVroom H. M., De God van de filosofen en de God van de Bijbel; het christelijk Godsbeeld in discussie. Zoetermeer 1991, Meinema. 174 p. *f* 27.50. 90-21-13563-9. – ᴿNedTTs 46 (1992) 261s (G. van den *Brink*: a good idea to rescue PASCAL's waning influence).
426 ᴱWheeler Barbara G., *Farley* Edward, Shifting boundaries; contextual approaches to the structure of theological education. Louisville 1991, W-Knox. 328 p. $20. 0-664-25172-2. – ᴱExpTim 104 (1992s) 26 (G. *Slater*).
427 ᴱWilmer Haddon, 20/20 visions; the futures of Christianity in Britain. L 1992, SPCK. x-154 p. £10 pa. – ᴿTLond 95 (1992) 394s (H. *Montefiore*).
427* ᴱWils Jean-Pierre, *Mieth* Dietmar. Grundbegriffe der christlichen Ethik: UTb 1648. Pd 1992, Schöningh. 301 p. DM 29,80 pa. 3-506-99419-0 [TR 89,332-4, A.-P. *Rathmann*].
428 ᴱWind James P., *al.*, Clergy ethics in a changing society [14 invited essays: M. *Marty*, W. *May*, L. *Gilkey*...]: Chicago Park Ridge Center for the Study of Health, Faith, and Ethics. Louisville 1991, Westminster-Knox. $19. 0-664-25161-7 [TDig 39,356].
428* ᴱWoznicki Andrew N., The dignity of the human person; essays on the Christian humanism of John Paul II [SF Polish parish on occasion of his 1987 visit]. SF 1987, Society of Christ. xvi-174 p. [RThom 93,153, P. *Jobert*].

A1.5   *Plurium compilationes* philologicae *vel* archaeologicae.

429 *a*) ᴱAssmann Alcida, Weisheit; Archäologie der literarischen Kommunikation 3. Mü 1991, Fink. 571 p. – ᴿTGL 82 (1992) 148 (G. *Fuchs*: '1971').
— *b*) ᴱAttfield Robin, *Wilkins* Barry, International justice and the Third World; studies in the philosophy of development. L 1992, Routledge. ix-207 p. 0-415-06924-6; pa -5-4 [TBR 6/1, 57, C. *Elliott*).
— *c*) ᴱBaker F., *Thomas* J., Writing the past in the present. Lampeter 1990, St. David's college. 215 p.; 31 fig. £6.50. 0-905265-25-5. – ᴿAntiquity 66 (1992) 803-8 (C. *Gosden*, also on three cognates).
— *d*) ᴱBouchindhomme Christian, *Rochlitz* Rainer, 'Temps et récit' de Paul RICŒUR en débat: Procope. P 1990, Cerf. 216 p. 7 art. [LavalTP 49,149, J.-G. *Nadeau*].
— *e*) ᴱBrunner-Traut Emma, Die grossen Religionen des Alten Orients und der Antike. Stu 1992, Kohlhammer. 176 p. DM 25 [ZAW 105,526, tit. pp.] 3-17-011976-1.
— *f*) ᴱCalder William M.ᴵᴵᴵ, Werner JAEGER [1888-1961] reconsidered: IL-Clas supp 3. Atlanta 1992, Scholars. viii-325 p. $45 pa. [RelStR 19,351, W. E. *Bunge*: his classics pinnacle now largely ignored because he made petty compromises with shifting culture politics].
ᴱChavalas Mark W., *Hayes* John L., New horizons in the study of ancient Syria: BtMesop 25. 1992 → 705*.
430 ᴱDi Cesare Mario A., Reconsidering the Renaissance. Binghamton NY 1992, MedvRenTSt. 528 p. $40 [SixtC 24,958s, R. C. *Evans*].
430* ᴱDunn Francis M., *Cole* Thomas, Beginning in classical literature: Yale Clas 29. C 1992. Univ. 245 p. –ᴿRÉG 105 (1992) 619s (A. *Billault*).
431 ᴱEndesfelder Erika, Probleme der frühen Gesellschaftsentwicklung im Alten Ägypten. B 1991, Univ. Institut für Sudanarchäologie. 168 p. 3-86165-004-X [OIAc 3,20, excerpted].

432 ᴱFoley John M., Oral-formulaic theory; a Folklore casebook⁵ [189-225:
...and biblical studies, *Culley* Robert C.]. NY 1990, Garland. xvii-405 p.
$45. – ᴿSpeculum 67 (1992) 512 (tit. pp.).

433 *a*) ᴱGardin Jean-Claude, *Peebles* Christopher S., Representations in archaeology. Bloomington 1992, Indiana Univ. xii-395 p. 0-253-20709-6
[OIAc 3,21, excerpted].

— *b*) ᴱGoodman L. E., Neoplatonism and Jewish thought [18 art.]: Studies
in Neoplatonism 7. Albany 1992, SUNY. xiii-454 p. $57.50; pa. $19.
0-7914-1339-X [NTAbs 37,144].

— *c*) ᴱGordon Cyrus H., *Rendsburg* Gary A., Eblaitica; essays on the Ebla
archives and Eblaite language. WL 1992, Eisenbrauns. ix-158 p. 0-
911-46477-3. 6 art.; infra ➤ e735.

434 ᴱHaas Jonathan, The anthropology of war [9 art.]. C 1990, Univ. xiv-
242 p. £30. – ᴿAnthropos 87 (1990) 268-271 (A.P. *Vayda*).

435 ᴱHerzog Reinhart, *al.*, Restauration und Erneuerung; die lateinische
Literatur von 284 bis 374 n.Chr.: HbAltW 8/5. Mü 1989, Beck. xxix-
559 p. DM 238. – ᴿJbAC 34 (1991) 164s (G. J. M. *Bartelink*).

436 ᴱHoesterey Ingeborg, Zeitgeist in Babel, the postmodernist controversy.
Bloomington 1991, Indiana Univ. xv-269 p. 0-253-32835-7; pa. -20611-
1. 17 art. (on literary criticism, music etc.).

437 ᴱKnapp A. Bernard, Archaeology, Annales and Ethnohistory: New
Directions in Archaeology. C 1992, Univ. xvi-152 p. 0-521-41174-2
[OIAc 3,27].

438 ᴱLenz Ilse, *Luig* Ute, Frauenmacht ohne Herrschaft; Geschlechterver-
hältnisse in nichtpatriarchalischen Gesellschaften. B 1990, Orlanda.
350 p. DM 44. – ᴿAnthropos 87 (1992) 284-6 (E. W. *Müller*).

439 ᴱMcCarthy George E., MARX and ARISTOTLE; nineteenth-century
German social theory and classical antiquity [12 inedita]. Savage MD
1992, Rowman & L. x-379 p. $22.50 [RelStR 19,354, Antonia *Tripolitis*:
useful].

440 ᴱRidder-Symoens Hilde de, Universities in the Middle Ages: A history of
the university in Europe 1. C 1992, Univ. xviii-506 p. £60 [RHE 88,230,
J. *Paquet*].

442 ᴱSiems Andreas K., Sexualität und Erotik in der Antike [13 reprints
1907-1981; 4 updated to 1988, bibliography only to 1983]: WegFor 605.
Da 1988, Wiss. vi-456 p. – ᴿAnzAltW 45,1 (1992) 124-6 (H. *Kuch*);
Gnomon 64 (1992) 577-9 (P. *Guyot*: anregend).

443 ᴱWard William A., *Jankowsky* Martha S., The crisis years; the 12th
century B.C. from beyond the Danube to the Tigris. Dubuque 1992,
Kendall/Hunt. xiv-208 p. 0-8403-7148-9 [OIAc 3,41, excerpted].

ᴱYoung Gordon D., Mari in retrospect; fifty years of Mari and Mari
studies 1991 ➤ 739.

A2 **Acta** *congressuum* 1. **biblica** [*Notitiae,* **reports** ➤ Y7.2].

446 Attualità dell'Apocalisse: Convegni S. Spirito 8. Palermo 1992, Augustinus. 119 p. Lit. 20.000 [NRT 115,793, L. J. *Renard*].

447 Attualità della Lettera ai Romani. R 1989. [*Rossano* P., *Penna* R., ...]. –
ᴿLateranum 58 (1992) 573s (R. *Gelio*).

448 ᴱAuneau J., L'enseignement de l'Écriture Sainte / Teaching the Scriptures: Revue annuelle sur la formation des prêtres 18. P 1992, S. Sulpice.
380 p. F 100. 0337-7418. – 24 art.; 17 infra.

448* ᴱBarker William S., *Godfrey* W. Robert, Theonomy; a Reformed critique [... current applicability of OT law]. GR 1990, Zondervan. 413 p. [RefTR 51,37].

449 **Biale** David, From intercourse to discourse; control of sexuality in rabbinic literature: CHH 62. Berkeley 1992, Univ. California. [iv-] 70 p. 0-89242-063-4.

450 Bible et Informatique: Actes du colloque international [1. 1985/6 ➤ 4,389 (ᴱ*Poswick* R. F.)] – 2. Jérusalem, 9-13 juin 1988: Méthodes, outils. résultats; Travaux de Linguistique Quantitative (ᴱ*Muller* C.) 43. P/Genève 1989, Champion/Slatkine. 655 p. 2-05-101027-7. 35 art.; ...

450* Informatique 3ᵉ: ᴱSchweizer Harald, *al.*, Actes du Troisième Colloque International Bible et Informatique; interprétation, herméneutique, compétence informatique: Tübingen, 26-30 août 1991: Debora 7. P/Genève 1992, Champion-Slatkine: 661 p.; drawings. 2-05-101195-8. 34 art.; 25 infra.

451 The Bible in the new evangelization; IV plenary assembly of the World Catholic Federation for the biblical apostolate, Bogotá 27 June - 6 July 1990. Stu 1992, Catholic Biblical Federation. 256 p.

452 BIBLIA: L'umile grandezza di Mosè: Castiglione della Pescaia, 24-27 gennaio 1991. Settimello Fi 1992, Biblia. 259 p. 9 art., infra.

453 – L'Aldilà nella Bibbia; Firenze, 13-14 aprile 1991. Settimello 1992, Biblia. 248 p. 8 art.; infra.

454 [*Marenghi* Franco present.]., BIBLIA/Accademia Italiana della Cucina: Il cibo e la Bibbia: Prato 2-3 maggio 1992: Accad. Quad. 9. R 1992, Accad. It. Cucina. 127 p.; ill. 8 art.; infra.

455 – ᴱTroia Pasquale, La musica e la Bibbia, Biblia/Acc. Chigiana, Siena 24-26 agosto 1990. R 1992, Garamond. [xii-] 490 p. Lit. 70.000. 19 art., 5 infra.

456 – ᴱVerdon Timothy, L'arte e la Bibbia; immagine come esegesi biblica; Atti del Convegno internazionale di studi Venezia 14-16 ott. 1988. Settimello FI 1992, BIBLIA. 290 p. 16 art.; infra.

457 ᴱBlau Joshua, *Reif* Stefan C., Genizah research after ninety years; the case of Judaeo-Arabic [3d Congress Cambridge 13-16 July 1987]: Or. Pub. 47. C 1992, Univ. xiv-176 p. 0-521-41773-2 [OIAc 3,14]. 21 art.; 4 infra.

457* [*Bolgiani* Franco, storia del gruppo], Letture cristiane dei Libri Sapienziali; XX incontro di studiosi della antichità cristiana, 9-11 maggio 1991: St.Eph.Aug. 37. R 1992, Inst. Patristicum Augustinianum. 547 p. 34 art.; plures infra. – ᴿBStLat 22 (1992) 356-360 (T. *Piscitelli*).

458 *a*) ᴱBori Pier Cesare, Atti del IX seminario di 'Studi sulla letteratura esegetica cristiana e giudaica antica', Bologna-Idice 16-18 ottobre 1991]: AnStoEseg 9,2 (1992) 341-678.

– *b*) ᴱBoschi Bernardo G., [p. 5s; 27-40] Pentateuco come Torah; storiografia e normatività religiosa nell'Israele antico [➤ 7,1707]: Atti del VI convegno di studi veterotestamentari [Assoc. Biblica Italiana, Prato 11-13.IX.1989]: RicStoB 3,1 (1991), 114 p. 7 art.

– *c*) ᴱBrinner William M., *Rischin* Moses, Like all the nations?, The life and legacy of Judah L. MAGNES [symposium Berkeley, Oct. 12-14, 1982; 14 art.]. Albany 1987 SUNY. xvi-241 p. $39.50; pa. $13. 0-88706-507-4; -8-2. – ᴿCCAR 39,4 (1992) 72 (L. *Sussman*).

– *d*) ᴱBroer Ingo, [p. 7-12. 61-103] Jesus und das jüdische Gesetz [Fünftes theol. Symposium Siegen]. Stu 1992, Kohlhammer. 223 p. DM 50. 3-17-011835-8 [T. *Holtz*, J. *Maier*, G. *Dautzenberg*, *al.*: NTAbs 36, p. 419]. – ᴿExpTim 104 (1992s) 247s (E. *Best*).

459 ᴱBrooke George J., *Lindars* Barnabas, International Symposium on the Septuagint and its relation to the Dead Sea Scrolls and other writings (Manchester 1990): SBL SeptCog. Atlanta 1992, Scholars. viii-657 p. 17 art., infra.

460 ᴱBroshi M., al., ➋ The scrolls of the Judaean desert; forty years of research [Symposium Jerusalem June 23-24, 1987]. J 1992, Bialik Inst./ Israel Exploration Soc. xii-204 p. $22. 965-342-577-3 [JStJud 24,139, M. *Mach*].

460* — ᴱDimant Devorah, *Rappaport* Uriel, The Dead Sea Scrolls — forty years of research [Haifa-TA conference 1988]. Leiden 1992, Brill. 370 p. *f*180 [BAR-W 19/3, 72s, H. *Shanks*].

461 ᴱBusi Giulio, Viaggiatori ebrei; Berichte jüdischer Reisender vom Mittelalter bis in die Gegenwart; Atti del Congresso europeo AISG, San Miniato 4-5 nov. 1991: AISG StT 9. Bo 1992, Associazione Italiana per lo Studio del Giudaismo. 159 p.

462 *Caquot* André, présent. [*Vesco* Jean-Luc, postface 319-322], Naissance de la méthode critique; colloque du centenaire de l'École biblique et archéologique française de Jérusalem. P 1992, Cerf. 349 p. F 200. 2-204-04465-2. 31 art.; infra. [RB 100,454, tit.pp.].

463 ᴱCharlesworth James H., [p. 3-35] The Messiah; developments in earliest Judaism and Christianity: First Princeton Symposium on Judaism and Christian origins [1987]. Mp 1992, Fortress. xxix-597 p.; group photo. 0-8006-2563-3. 25 art.; infra. [PrincSemB 15,204, D. *Flusser*].

464 **Cowdell** S., al., Reading the Bible; a symposium [Univ. Queensland]: St Mark's Review 147-210 (Canberra 1991) 210 [NTAbs 36,308].

464* ᴱDas Somen, Weakness of power and power of weakness; seeking clarity, credibility and solidarity [1890 Synod of the Church of North India]. Delhi 1990, ISPCK. 82 p. rs. 15 [TBR 6/2, 64, J. *Katz*: revised Bible studies].

465 ᴱDenaux Adelbert, John and the Synoptics [39th Colloquium Biblicum Lovaniense, Aug. 7-9, 1990]: BtETL 101. Lv 1992, Univ./Peeters. xxii-696 p. 90-6186-498-4 / 90-6831-320-7. [RB 100,296, tit. pp.; SNTU A-18, 260, A. *Fuchs*]. 38 art.; infra. – ᴿExpTim 104 (1992s) 248 (E. *Best*).

466 ᴱDotan Aron, Proceedings of the Ninth Congress of the International Organization for Masoretic Studies 1989: SBL MasoreticSt. 7. Atlanta 1992, Scholars. xii-129 + 33* p. 1-55540-740-4 [OIAc 3,19; BL 94,45, J. *Barr*].

467 ᴱDunn James D. G., Jews and Christians; the parting of the ways, A.D. 70 to 135; the second Durham-Tübingen Research Symposium on earliest Christianity and Judaism (Durham, September 1989): WUNT 66. Tü 1992, Mohr. x-408 p. 3-16-145972-5. 13 art.; infra.

467* ᴱErnst Michael, Mächte des Bösen bei Johannes und Paulus: Tagung Assistenten an Biblischen Lehrstuhlen Österreich, Wien 27.-29. Sept. 1990 = Protokolle zur Bibel 1,2 (1992) 77-113.

468 ᴱEslinger Lyle, Canadian society of biblical studies, bulletin and abstracts 53 (1992s). 80 p.; p. 59-80, membership list; 47-58, members' publications; 18-28, 1992 presidential address, *Wilson* Stephen G., The salvation of the Jews in early Christian literature.

469 ᴱFrank Olof, al., Postsekulariserat interregnum? Från tro och vetande till vetenskap och mystik; antologi. Åsak 1990, Delsbo. 404 p. – ᴿSvTKv 67 (1991) 147s (B. *Hanson*).

470 **Geoltrain** Pierre, al., présent., La fable apocryphe: ÉPHÉR, Paris 1986: Apocrypha 1s (1990s). 314 p.; 299 p., XIV pl. 12 + 11 art.; infra. – ᴿSNTU A-17 (1992) 274-6 (P. *Arzt*).

471 ᴱHaas P. J., Recovering the role of women; power and authority in rabbinic Jewish society [seminar Vanderbilt 1991]: SFʟHJud 59. Atlanta 1992, Scholars. v-132 p. $50. 1-55540-765-X [NTAbs 37,p. 305].

472 ᴱHaim Abraham, Society and community; proceedings of the Second International Congress for research of the Sephardi and Oriental Jewish heritage, Jerusalem 1984. J 1991, Misgav Yerushalayim. xi-225 p. + ⊕ x-296 p. 965-296-017-9. 15 art. + ⊕ 23; none infra.

473 ᴱHainz Josef, Theologie im Werden; Studien zu den theologischen Konzeptionen im NT. Pd 1992, Schöningh. 463 p. DM 38 pa. [TR 88,516, tit. pp.].

474 ᴱHaudebert Pierre, Le Pentateuque, débats et recherches; XIVᵉ congrès de l'ACFÉB, Angers 2-6 sept. 1991: LDiv 151. P 1992, Cerf. 270 p. F 155. 3-204-04550-0 [RB 100,455, tit. pp.]. 9 art., infra.

475 a) ᴱJordan Mark D., Emery Kentᴶ, Ad litteram; authoritative texts and their medieval readers [1989 conference; glossa ordinaria + 12 al.]: ConfMedvSt 3. ND 1992, Univ. viii-380 p. $40. 0-268-00632-6 [TDig 40,253].

— b) ᴱKvist H.-O., Bibelauslegung und Gruppenidentität. Åbo 1992, Akademi [TLZ 118,298].

— c) ᴱLevine Leo I., The Galilee in late antiquity [international conference at Kibbutz Ha-Naton, Aug. 13-15, 1989; 20 art.]. NY 1992, Jewish Theol. Sem. [distr. Harvard]. xxiii-410 p. $35. 0-674-34113-9 [TDig 40,269; NTAbs 37, p. 306, topics, authors].

— d) ᴱLewis Bernard, Niewöhner Friedrich, Religionsgespräche im Mittelalter: Wolfenbütteler MASt 4. Wsh 1992, Harrassowitz. 388 p. DM 148 pa. 3-447-03349-5. 22 art. [TR 89,343 tit. pp.]. → 1424*.

476 ᴱLieu Judith, North J., Rajak Tessa, The Jews among the pagans and Christians in the Roman Empire [London Univ. Institute of Classics seminars 'to correct the distorted view of Christianity as the only truly significant event ...']. L 1992, Routledge. xxii-201 p. £30. 0-415-04972-5 [BL 93, 139, L. L. Grabbe]. – ᴿExpTim 103 (1991s) 376 (J. G. Snaith).

477 ᴱLoades Ann, McLain Michael, Hermeneutics, the Bible and literary criticism [1989 conference at a place not indicated, largely on Austin Farrer]: StLitRel. Basingstoke 1992. xi-199 p. 0-333-53959-1. 10 art.; 8 infra.

477* ᴱLohse Eduard, Verteidigung und Begründung des apostolischen Amtes (2 Kor 10-13) [Roma S. Paolo, 25.-30. Sept. 1989]: Mg Benedictina Bib/ök 11. R 1992, St. Paul vor den Mauern. 160 p. Lit. 30.000. 88-85374-01-8. – 7 art.; infra.

478 ᴱLovering Eugene H., Society of Biblical Literature [127th 1991 → 7, 446], 128th Annual Meeting Nov. 21-24, 1992, San Francisco, Seminar Papers 31. Atlanta 1992, Scholars. ix-706 p. 1-55540-769-2. 45 art.; infra.

479 ᴱLuz Ulrich, La Bible, une pomme de discorde; un livre unique — différents chemins d'approche [dialogue Fédération protestante suisse]; ᵀAnderfuhrer Jean; Essais bibliques 21. Genève 1992, Labor et Fides. 148 p. Fs 25 [NRT 115,785, A. Toubeau]. 2-8309-0675-6. – ᴿEsprVie 102 (1992) 619 (É. Cothenet: Luz avoue 'Selon la doctrine réformée, la Bible est claire, univoque et compréhensible ... mais la réalité se présente très différemment').

480 ᴱMayer Bernhard, Christen und Christliches in Qumran?: Eichstätter Studien 32. Rg 1992, Pustet. 268 p.; ill. – ᴿTR 88 (1992) 515 (tit. pp.).

481 ᴱMiegge Mario ['direttore' p. 6, present. *Pesce* Mauro; ma cf. p. 163n, *Bori* P. C.], Letture della Bibbia e pensiero filosofico e politico moderno, Atti II Convegno [Forlì 8-10.VI.1991]: AnStoEseg 9,1 (1992) 7-337.

482 ᴱMorris Paul, *Sawyer* Deborah, A walk in the garden; biblical iconography and literary images of Eden [17 (of the 21) 1987 Lancaster symposium papers, plus two others]: JStOT supp 136. Sheffield 1992, JStOT. 327 p. £40; pa. £30. 1-85075-338-5 [RB 100, 285, tit. pp.].
ᴱMuller Charles, Actes du troisième colloque international Bible et Informatique 1991 → 450*.

482* ᴱMuzzarelli M. G., *Todeschini* C., La storia degli ebrei nell'Italia medievale, tra filologia e metodologia [Univ. Bologna/Trieste ott. 1988]: Romagna Documenti 29. Bo 1990, Zanini. 128 p. – ᴿHenoch 14 (1992) 347s (M. *Perani*).

483 *a)* ᴱNeuhaus Dietrich, Teufelskinder oder Heilsbringer; die Juden im Johannes-Evangelium [Tagung]: Arnoldshainer Texte 64. Fra 1990, Haag & H. viii-182 p. 3-89228-492-X [TLZ 118,229, W. *Wiefel*].

— *b)* ᴱOduyoye Mercy A., *Kanyoro Musimbi* R. A., The will to arise; women, tradition, and the Church in Africa [Circle for Concerned African Theologians]. Mkn 1992, Orbis. 230 p. $17. 0-88344-782-7 [JRelAfr 23,359, Helen *Callaway*].

484 ᴱOllenburger Ben C., *al.*, The flowering of OT theology [...symposium]: Sources for biblical and theological study 1. WL 1992, Eisenbruns. 547 p. $29,50. – ᴿThemelios 18,3 (1992s) 23 (J. *Goldingay*).

484* ᴱOort J. van, *Wickert* U., Christliche Exegese zwischen Nicaea und Chalcedon [Tagung Berlin Jan. 1991]. Kampen 1992, Kok Pharos. 226 p. 90-242-3067-5. 9 art.; 3 infra.

485 ᴱPadovese Luigi [p. 13-17], Atti del [I. 1990/1 → 7,451] II simposio di Efeso su S. Giovanni Apostolo [13-15.V.1991]. Turchia, la Chiesa e la sua storia, 3: Cappuccini Parma. R 1992, Antonianum; Ist. Francescano di Spiritualità. 228 p. Lit. 28.000. 13 art.; 10 infra. – ᴿPrOrChr 41 (1991) 435 (P. *Ternant*, 1). → g333.

486 ᴱPannenberg W., *Schneider* T., Verbindliches Zeugnis, 1. Kanon – Schrift – Tradition [seit 1986]: Dialog der Kirchen 7/1. FrB/Gö 1992, Herder/VR. 399 p. DM 58 [NRT 115,902, X. *Jacques*].

487 *a)* ᴱParsons Mikeal C., *Tyson* Joseph B., CADBURY, KNOX, and TALBERT; American contributions to the study of Acts [1987 SBL meeting] SBL NAm. Atlanta 1992, Scholars. x-264 p. $40; pa. $25. 1-55540-653-X; -4-8 [RB 100,297, tit. pp.].

— *b)* ᴱPenna Romano, Il Giovannismo alle origini cristiane; Atti del III convegno di studi neotestamentari [Assoc. Biblica Italiana, Prato 14-16.IX.1989]: RicStoB 3,2 (1991). 175 p. 9 art.; infra.

— *c)* ᴱPerdue Leo G., *Gilpin* W. Clark, The voice from the whirlwind; interpreting the Book of Job [SBL 1989 Anaheim section]. Nv 1992, Abingdon. 264 p. $17 [p. 185-207, *Girard* R., Job as a failed scapegoat: TorJT 10,111, J. L. *McLaughlin*].

— *d)* Peregrinatio EGERIAE, Atti del Convegno Internazionale nel centenario del Codex Aretinus 405, Arezzo 23-25.X.1987. Città di Castello 1990, Tibergraph. 368 p.

488 ᴱReventlow H., *al.*, Historische Kritik und biblischer Kanon in der deutschen Aufklärung, Wolfenbüttel 10.-14. Dez. 1985: WFor 41. Wsb 1988. vii-293 p. – ᴿCrNSt 13 (1992) 457-9 (E. *Walravens*).

489 ᴱSamuelson N. M., Studies in Jewish philosophy; collected essays of the

Academy of Jewish philosophy, 1980-1985: Studies in Judaism. Lanham
MD 1987, UPA. – ᴿHenoch 14 (1992) 207s (B. *Chiesa*).

490 ᴱSanna Ignazio, La teologia per l'unità d'Europa (Riconciliare l'uomo
con se stesso, coi suoi simili, con la creazione), convegno Pont. Univ.
Lateranense: Lateranum 58,1 (1992) 1-328 (309-328, *Martini* Carlo Maria,
Cristianesimo ed Europa).

491 ᴱSchenker Adrian, Studien zu Opfer und Kult im Alten Testament, mit
einer Bibliographie (*Rosset* V.) 1969-1991 zum Opfer in der Bibel [Tagung
Fribourg/S Sept. 1990]: ForAT 3. Tü 1992, Mohr.   viii-162 p. DM 128.
3-16-145967-9 [ZAW 105,538, tit. pp.; BL 93,116, G.J. *Wenham*: tit. pp.
'alternatives to MILGROM']. 6 art., infra. – ᴿSNTU A-17 (1992) 266-8 (A.
Fuchs); SvEx 58 (1993) 179-181 (H. *Bengtsson*).

492 ᶠSCHLATTER Adolf, 1852-1938: Paulus [Missionar und Theologe] und
das antike Judentum, Symposium Tübingen 26.-29. Sept. 1988, ᴱHengel
Martin, *Heckel* Ulrich ⇒ 7,437: WUNT 58. Tü 1991, Mohr.   475 p.
DM 248.   3-16-14595-1 [RB 100,298, tit. pp.].

492* ᴱSchrijver E.G.L., The literary analysis of Hebrew texts; papers
read at a symposium held at the Juda Palache Institute, University of
Amsterdam (5 February 1990): Publ. Palache Inst. 7. Amst 1992. 121 p.
90-71396-07-X. – ᴿJStJud 23 (1992) 286-8 (J. van *Ruiten*).

493 *a*) ᴱSchunck Klaus-Dietrich, *Augustin* Mathias, Goldene Äpfel in sil-
bernen Schalen, XIII congress, International Organization for the Study
of the Old Testament [kleinere Beiträge], Leuven 1989: BeitErfAJ 20. Fra
1992, Lang.   [iv-] 179 p.   3-631-42185-0.

— *b*) ᴱSerra Aristide, *Valentini* Alberto, I Vangeli dell'infanzia I-II; XXXI
Settimana biblica nazionale Roma 10-14 sett. 1990: RicStoB 4,1s (1992)
141 p.; 168 p.   16 art.; infra.

— *c*) ᴱSmith Diana R., *Salinger* Peter S., Hebrew studies; BSO colloquium
on resources in Europe, London 11-13 Sept. 1989: BrLibr OccasP 13. L
1991, British Library.   xii-252 p.   £25.   0-7123-0220-0 [BL 94,163, J.F.
Elwolde].

— *d*) ᴱSollano Raija, Paimentolaisten Uskonnosta Kirkkolaitokseksi [⇒ 7,
456 sans ᵀ],Von Nomadenreligion zu Kircheninstitution [Vorlesungsreihe
Helsinki 1988]. Helsinki 1991, Suomen Eksegeettisen Seuran Julkaisuja 55.
vii-133 p. [TLZ 118,297, M. *Nissinen*].

494 SOTS bulletin for 1992: **67th** Winter Meeting, London 17-19 Dec. 1991:
Mayes A.D.H., presidential address, On describing the purpose of
Deuteronomy; – *Tomes* F.R., The reason for the Syro-Ephraimite war; –
Chalcraft D.J., For a sociological imagination in OT studies; *McKay*
Ms. H.A., When did the Sabbath become a day of worship?; – *Bartlett*
J.R., Edom; – *Carroll* R.P., Shadows on the text; the crowd behind
and the crowd in front of the Hebrew Bible... sociological; – *Rodd* C.S.,
OT ethics; problems and principles. – **68th** Summer Meeting, Dublin 13-16
July 1992: *Lohfink* N., The voices in Dt 2; – *McNamara* M., Irish
biblical apocrypha; – *McConville* J.G., Time, space, and 'place' in Dt; –
Cathcart K.J., Dt 13 and 28 at the Neo-Assyrian and Aramaic treaties; –
Jones G.H., From Abijam to Abijah; – *Dennis* T.J., Exodus 1:15-21, a
midwife's tale; – *Morgan* D.F., From wisdom to Torah; the pedagogy of
the Sages; – *Hengel* M., The Scriptures and their interpretation in Second
Temple Judaism; – *Kaufman* S., Dating the language of the Palestinian
Targums.

495 ᴱSternberg Thomas, Neue Formen der Schriftauslegung? [Tagung
Münster; *Dohmen* T. 13-74; *Söding* T. 75-130; *Jacob* C. 131-163]: QDisp

140. FrB 1992, Herder. 168 p. 3-451-02140-4. 3 art.; infra. [GeistL 66, 233s, J. *Sudbrack*; TGL 83, 228, J. *Ernst*; TvT 33,407, J. *Holman*].

496 Symposium between Talmud and Torah; the law of talion [Ex 21; Lev 24; Baba Kamma 83b]: S'Vara, a Journal of Philosophy and Judaism 2,1 (1991) [JStJud 23 (1992) 338s, 11 art. cited].

496* ᴱTal Abraham, *Florentin* Moshe, Société d'Études Samaritaines, First International Congress, Tel Aviv, April 11-13, 1988. TA 1991, Univ. Rosenberg School for Jewish Studies. 235 p. + ⊕ 19. 29 art.; 6 infra.

497 ᴱTamani G., Tipografi ebrei a Soncino 1483-1490; Atti del convegno 12.VI.1988 / catalogo della mostra. Soncino CR, ed. 158 p. / 95 p. – ᴿHenoch 14 (1992) 348-351 (M. *Perani*).

498 ᴱTrebolle Barrera Julio, *Vegas Montaner* Luis, The Madrid Qumran congress; proceedings of the international congress on the Dead Sea Scrolls, Madrid 18-21 March, 1991: Studies on the Texts of the Desert of Judah, 11. Leiden 1992, Brill. xxv-362 p., 8 pl.; p. 363-683, pl. 9-25. 90-04-09769-4; -70-8. – 35 art.; infra. [In OTAbs 17, p. 374-417, J. A. *Fitzmyer* gives very long and detailed analyses of all these articles].

499 ᶠUFFENHEIMER Benjamin, 70th b.: Justice and righteousness, biblical themes and their influence [TA-Bochum 2d symposium, Bochum 19-21 June 1990], ᴱReventlow Henning, *Hoffmann* Yair: JStOT supp 137. Shf 1992, JStOT. 258 p.; portr. £45; sb. £33. 1-85075-339-3 [BL 93,21, J. G. *Snaith*; JTS 44,620, H. *Mowvley*]. 15 art.; infra.

500 Valle Carlos del, present., The First International Conference on the Social Sciences and Second Testament interpretation, Valladolid 6-8 May 1991: BibTB 22,2s (1992) 51-95; ...

500* ᴱVanderKam J. C., 'No one spoke ill of her' [< 1989 SBL Pseudep. group + *al.*]. Essays on Judith: Early Judaism 22. Atlanta 1992, Scholars. vi-98 p. $25; pa. $15 [ZAW 105,533, M. *Köckert*, tit. pp.].

501 Vanni Ugo, L'esegesi tra teologia e prassi: Gregorianum 73 (Atto Accademico 1992) 593-5 [-745, 8 *al.*, infra].

501* ᴱVeijola Timo, The Law in the Bible and its environment [50th anniversary meeting]: Publ. 51. Helsinki/Gö 1990, Finnish Exegetical Society/Vandenhoeck & R. 186 p. 95-1921-706-1. – ᴿNedTTs 46 (1992) 342 (J. S. *Vos*, under NT).

502 ᴱWood Diana, Christianity and Judaism, Ecclesiastical History Society 1991-summer + 1992-winter meeting: Studies in Church History 29. Ox 1992, Blackwell. xvii-493 p.; ill. 0-931-18497-X. – 32 art.; 7 infra.

502* World Catholic Federation for the Biblical Apostolate, Fourth plenary assembly, The Bible in the new evangelization [...history and norms of the federation]. Bogotá July 1990. Stu 1992, Catholic Biblical Federation. 256 p.

503 ᶠWOUDE Adam S. van der: [I → 198] II. [Symposium Groningen, Sept. 1985] Profeten en profetische geschriften: ᴱGarcía Martínez F., *Geus* C. H. J. de, *Klijn* A. F. J. Kampen/Nijkerk 1992, Kok/Callenbach. 180 p.; portr.; biog. 9-13; bibliog. 167-173. 90-242-4036-0. 13 art.; infra.

504 — III. Sacred History and sacred texts in early Judaism; a symposium in honour of A. S. van der WOUDE [Groningen 1992], ᴱBremmer J. N., *García Martínez* F.: Contributions to Biblical Exegesis and Theology 5. Kampen 1992, Kok Pharos. 183 p. 90-390-0015-8. 5 art., infra [ZAW 105, 535, tit. pp.; BL 93,8, L. *Grabbe*; ETL 69,156, J. *Lust*; JStJud 24,83, E. *Tov*].

A2.3 **Acta congressuum theologica** [reports → Y7.4].

505 a) ᴱAlberigo Giuseppe, *Melloni* Alberto, Per la storicizzazione del Vaticano II: CrNSt 13,3 (1992) 473-641. 8 art.

— b) **Allchin** A. M., al., A fearful symmetry; the complementarity of men and women in ministry [3 years meetings]. L 1992, SPCK. vii-56 p. £4. 0-281-04651-4. – ᴿTBR 5,3 (1992s) 58s (Phoebe *Russell*).

— c) ᴱ**Allsopp** Michael E., *Burke* Ronald R., J. H. NEWMAN, theology and reform [Omaha Creighton Univ. symposium]. NY 1992, Garland. xl-261 p. $45. 0-8153-0384-X [TD 40,275; TBR 6/2,46, G. *Rowell*: worthwhile despite some undervaluing of Anglicanism].

506 Anders NYGREN som teolog och filosof: Symposiet [100. Gb., Lund 15.XI.1990]: Religio 36. Lund 1991, Teologiska Institutionen. 146 p. – ᴿSvTKv 67 (1991) 198s (B.-Å. *Månsson*).

507 a) ᴱ**Anderson** H. George, al., The one mediator, the Saints, and Mary: Lutherans and Catholics in dialogue, 8. Mp 1992, Augsburg. 392 p. $12. 0-8066-2579-1 [TDig 40,180].

— b) ᴱ**Arzt** Thomas, al., Unus mundus; Kosmos und Sympathie; Beiträge zum Gedanken der Einheit von Mensch und Kosmos. Fra 1992, P. Lang. 465 p. DM 78 pa. 3-631-44494-1 [TR 89,337, tit. pp.].

— c) ᴱ**Atcek** Naim S., *Ellis* Marc H., *Ruether* Rosemary R., Faith and the Intifada; Palestinian Christian voices: First International Symposium on Palestinian Liberation Theology, Tantur March 1990. Mkn 1991, Orbis. xv-207 p. $14. 0-88344-808-4 [OIAc 39,360; BToday 31,182].

— d) Atti del IX Congresso Tomistico internazionale, 3. Antropologia tomistica; 4. Etica, sociologia e politica; 5. Problemi teologici. Vaticano 1991, Editrice. 444 p./454 p./415 p. Lit. 50.000 ciascuno. – ᴿDocCom 45 (1992) 77-80 . 192-5 . 294-9 (D. *Vibrac*).

508 a) ᴱ**Aubert** Jean-Marie, *Couvreur* Gilles, Mission et dialogue interreligieux [cours Univ. Lyon 1989s]. Lyon 1991, Profac. 217 p. 2-85317-042-X. – ᴿÉTRel 67 (1992) 635 (J.-F. *Zorn*).

— b) **Bagrowicz** Jerzy, al., ● Congrès des théologues de l'Europe du centre et de l'est [Lublin 11-15 août]: AtKap 118,494 (1992) 1-92.

— c) ᴱ**Ball** Ian, The earth beneath; a critical guide to green theology. L 1992, SPCK. vii-216 p. £15. 0-281-04601-8. ᴿExpTim 104 (1992s) 252s (J. *Reynolds*).

509 **Barker** E., al., présent., Religion et ordre économique, Actes du 21ᵉ Conférence Internationale de Sociologie des Religions (Maynooth 1991): Social Compass 39,1 (1992) 169 p. 14 art. (rather on church finances than on improving the overall economic order).

510 ᴱ**Bauberot** Jean, Pluralisme et minorités religieuses, Colloque CNRS/ÉPHÉR [Paris 10-11 oct. 1989]: BLÉPHÉR 116. Lv 1991, Peeters. viii-159 p. 90-6831-314-2. 20 art.; 9 infra ➤ m3.5.

510* ᴱ**Beek** Heribert van, Sharing life; official report of the WCC World Consultation on Koinonia; sharing life in a world community; Escorial Oct. 1987. Genève 1989, WCC. x-149 p. Fs 16,50 [RTLv 24,100, A. de *Halleux*].

511 ᴱ**Beinert** Wolfgang, Glaube als Zustimmung; zur Interpretation kirchlicher Rezeptionsvorgänge [Tagung 1990]: QDisp 131. FrB 1991, Herder. 168 p. DM 36. – ᴿMüTZ 43 (1992) 383s (W. W. *Müller*); TPhil 67 (1992) 304s (G. *Schmidt*).

512 a) ᴱ**Beinert** Wolfgang, 'Katholischer' Fundamentalismus; häretische Gruppen in der Kirche? [Kath. Akad. Bayern]. Rg 1991, Pustet. 175 p. DM 26,80. – ᴿMüTZ 43 (1992) 137 (G. L. *Müller*).

— b) BELLARMINO e la controriforma; Atti del simposio (15-18 ott. 1986). Sora FR 1990, Centro Petrarca. xxiv-1016 p.; ill. – ᴿCC 143 (1992,2) 313s (G. *Mellinato*).

— c) Saint BERNARD de Clairvaux et la recherche de Dieu, Colloque Tou-
louse/SMDésert 25-27 janvier 1991: BLitEc 93.1 (1992) 1-196.
513 ᴱBertrand Dominique [Lobrichon Guy, présent. p. 13-31], BERNARD de
Clairvaux; histoire, mentalités, spiritualité; colloque de Lyon-Citeaux-
Dijon: SChr 380. P 1992, Cerf. 751 p.; 12 pl. 9 maps. F 292. 2-204-
04677-9. 24 art.; 4 infra [RHE 87,438*].
514 a) ᴱBiderman Shlomo, Scharfstein Ben-Ami, Interpretation in religion
[conference Tel Aviv, June 1990): Philosophy and Religion 2. Leiden
1992, Brill. xi-290 p. 90-04-09519-5. 14 art.; 7 infra [TR 88,345, tit. pp.].
— b) ᴱBödeker Hans-Erich, al., Le livre religieux et ses pratiques; études
sur l'histoire du livre religieux en Allemagne et en France à l'époque
moderne [Tagung Max-Planck Inst. 1988]: Veröff.101. Gö 1991, Vandenhoeck && R. 415 p. DM 86. 3-525-35638-2. 20 art. [TLZ 118,947,
W. Engemann].
— c) ᴱBrodeur Raymond, al., La dynamique symbolique; l'apport d'une
catéchèse pour ceux qui ne peuvent pas suivre [Colloque Québec sept.
1987]: Théologies pratiques 1. Québec 1990, Univ. Laval. x-308 p. [TR
89,408s, R. Sauer].
515 ᴱBrowning Don S., Schüssler Fiorenza Francis, HABERMAS, modernity,
and public theology [Chicago Univ. Divinity School conference 1989 + 2].
NY 1992, Crossroad. vi-258 p. $25. 0-8245-1107-7 [TDig 40,66: Haber-
mas took part (final paper ➤ 8618)].
516 ᴱBrümmer Vincent, Interpreting the universe as creation; a dialogue
of science and religion [Florida 2d consultation, Utrecht]: Studies in
Philosophical Theology 4. Kampen 1991, Kok. vii-148 p. 90-242-
3207-4. – ᴿExpTim 104 (1992s) 29s (R. Boyd); JTS 43 (1992) 824s
(D. A. Pailin); RHPR 72 (1992) 497 (G. Siegwalt).
517 BRUNNER Emil, Symposium zum 100. Gb.: Theologie und Ökonomie; zu
einem spannungsvollen Verhältnis, ᴱRuh Hans. Z 1992, Theol.-V. 224 p.
DM 32. 3-290-10873-2 [TR 88,532; TvT 33,312s, G. Manenschijn].
518 a) ᴱBühler Pierre, Karakash Clairette, Science et foi font système; une
approche herméneutique: Inst. Rech. Herm. Syst. 1988-90 / FacT 8.
Neuchâtel 1992, Univ. 215 p. 2-8309-0666-7. – 4 art.
— b) Butturini G., al., La teologia africana ed il Sinodo per l'Africa [Verona
15-19 sett. 1991]. Bo 1991, EMI, 160 p. Lit. 14.000. – ᴿRasT 33 (1992)
711-3 (Antonietta Marini Mansi).
— c) ᴱBuzzetti C., Cimosa M., I giovani e la lettura della Bibbia: BtScR 104.
R 1992 LAS. 219 p. Lit. 25.000 [NRT 115,786].
519 ᴱCalabuig Ignazio M., Atti del convegno internazionale 'Maria in San
Bernardo e nella tradizione cistercense' [Roma Fac. Marianum, 21-24 ott.
1991]: Marianum 54 (1992) 1-428; 17-38, bibliog. (Danieli Silvano M.).
520 Capital, a moral instrument? [financiers-theologians meetings, Edinburgh
Univ.]. ... 1992, St. Andrew. x-79 p. £5.50. 0-86153-149-3. – ᴿExpTim
103,9 2d-top choice (1991s) 258-260 (C. S. Rodd).
521 a) ᴱCaquot A., Canivet P., Ritualisme et vie intérieure; religion et culture; colloques 1985 et 1987 Soc. Renan: Point 52. P 1989 Beauchesne.
194 p. – ᴿLavalTP 48 (1992) 454s (L. Painchaud).
— b) ᴱCarter John R., Of human bondage and divine grace; a global testimony [Hamilton NY Colgate Univ. Jan. 1981; 12 art., varying religions'
concept of grace]. La Salle IL 1992, Open Court. xvii-330 p. $57; pa. $22.
0-8126-9170-9; -1-7 [TDig 40,283].
— c) ᴱCecolin Romano, Sacerdozio e mediazioni; dimensioni della media-
zione nell'esperienza della Chiesa: Simposio 1987 poi convegno, Ist. Li-

turgia Pastorale Padova.   Padova 1991, S. Giustina.   445 p. Lit. 40.000. –
ᴿCC 143 (1992,4) 526-8 (G. *Ferraro*).

522 CERTEAU Michel de, ou la différence chrétienne; Actes du colloque,
ᴱGeffré Claude: CogF 165.   P 1991, Cerf.   182 p.   F 115 [TR 88,434,
tit. pp.].

523 *a*) ᴱChipenda Jose B., *al.*, The Church of Africa; towards a theology of
reconstruction: All Africa Conference of Churches, Nairobi 1990: African
Challenge 2.   Nairobi 1991, AACC.   63 p. [TContext 10/2, 90, H. *Janssen*].

— *b*) Christian Hope in Europe's future; proceedings of the Catholic Theological Asn of Great Britain, Leeds 1991 = NBlackf 73.1 (1992) 80 p.

— *c*) **Chrostowski** Waldemar, present., ℗   The Church and Jews and Judaism, 3d symposium, Warszawa 11-12.IV.1991, 'Reality, symbolism, and
theology of Auschwitz': ColcT 62,2 (1992) 5-8 (-158), Eng. 159-164.

— *d*) ᴱ**Chrostowski** Waldemar, ℗ Dzieci jednego Boga [children of the one
God]; praca zbiorowa uczestników seminarium naukowego w Spertus
College of Judaica w Chicago (1989): Kościół a Żydzi i Judaizm 2.   Wsz
1991, Akademia Teologii Katolickiej.   418 p. – ᴿColcT 62,2 (1992) 179-
187 (M. *Horoszewicz*, ℗).

— *e*) ᴱ**Cole** Eve B., *Coultr ap-McQuinn* Susan,   Explorations in feminist
ethics; theory and practice [Duluth Oct. 1988].   Bloomington 1992, Indiana Univ.   £28.50; pa £12.   0-253-31384-8; -20697-9 [TBR 6/3, 8, Alison *Pryce*].

524 **Colombo** G., present., Cristianesimo e religione (gennaio 1992): Disputatio
4.   Mi 1992, Glossas.   233 p. Lit. 32.000 [NRT 115,627, L.-J. *Renard*].

525 [**Colombo** G., discours d'ouverture et de clôture p. 246-293], PAOLO IV e il
rapporto Chiesa-mondo al Concilio; Colloquio internazionale di studio,
Roma 23-24 sett. 1989; Ist. Paulo VI, 11.   Brescia 1991.   xviii-350 p. Lit.
50.000. – ᴿRTLv 23 (1992) 396s (J. *Famerée*).

526 [**Colombo** G., present.; ᴱ*Angelini* G. ↦ 7,464] *Brambilla* F. G., *al.*,   Il
prete; identità del ministero e oggettività della fede [raduno Fac. Teol.
N-Italia]: Disputatio 2.   Mi 1990, Glossas.   235 p. Lit. 30.000 [NRT 115,
293, L. *Volpe*].

528 ᴱ**Connell** George B., *Evans* C. Stephen,   Foundation of KIERKEGAARD's
vision of community; religion, ethics and politics in Kierkegaard [St. Olaf
college, Northfield MN, June 1988].   Atlantic Highlands NJ 1992, Humanities.   xxii-245 p. $45.   0-391-03724-2. 13 art. [TDig 39,262].

529 ᴱ**Coste** René, *Ribaut* Jean-Pierre,   Sauvegarde et gérance de la création
[Actes du Colloque Pax Christi sept. 1990].   P 1991, D-Brouwer.   290 p. –
ᴿEsprVie 102 (1992) 158s (F. *Mabille*).

530 ᴱ**Coyle** Kevin J., 'De moribus ... Manichaeorum' di AGOSTINO: Settimana Pavese 7.   Palermo 1991.   213 p. 7 art. – ᴿRÉLat 70 (1992) 325s (J.
Fontaine: Coyle in text, Koyle in title and index).

530* Cultura negra y teología [Rio julio 1985, 25 negros, 5 blancos]. San José
CR 1986, DEI.   178 p.   99-77904-29-4 [ActuBbg 30,64s, T. de *Balle*].

531 ᴱ**Daly** R. J.,   Origeniana quinta; papers of the Vth international Origen
congress, Boston College. 14-18 Aug. 1989: BtETL 105. Lv 1992, Univ./
Peeters.   xvii-635 p. Fb 2700 [NRT 115,781, V. *Roisel*; RSPT 77,619,
G.-M. de *Durand*].

532 ᴱ**Danies** Rupert E., The truth in tradition; a Free Church symposium.   L
1992, Epworth.   89 p. £6.50.   0-7162-0479-7. – ᴿExpTim 103 (1991s) 378
(J. L. *Houlden*: somewhat rigid but no longer sola scriptura).

532* ᴱ**Dawe** Donald G., *Fule* Aurelia,   Christians and Jews together; voices
from the conversation [Presbyterian 1987 assembly and 1989 mandate]. ...

1991, Presbyterian Theology and Worship. 171 p. $8 [Interpretation 47,210, J. H. *McKeithen*].
533 ᴱ**Dekker** G., *Gäbler* K. U., Secularisatie in theologisch perspectief [Amst VU colleges]. Kampen 1988, Kok. 173 p. ƒ32.50. 90-242-3045-4. – ᴿBijdragen 53 (1992) 219s (W. G. *Tillmans*).
533* ᴱ**Demson** David, *Webster* John, Hans Frei and the future of theology [Barth Society, Toronto June 1990]: ModT 8,2 (1992).
534 ᴱ**Despland** Michel, *Vallée* Gérard, Religion in history; the word, the idea, the reality [1989 conference on W. C. Smith; 11 art. Eng., 7 français]: ÉdSR 13. Waterloo 1992. ix-252 p. $25. 0-88920-211-7 [TDig 40,83; ÉglT 24,324, P.-A. *Turcotte*].
535 ᴱ**Deutsch** Eliot, Culture [... religion] and modernity; East-West perspectives [conference 1989]. Honolulu 1991, Univ. Hawaii. xvii-641 p. 0-8248- 1378-7 [Numen 40,195, S. *Biderman*].
536 ᴱ**Dierkens** A., Le libéralisme religieux [Bruxelles mai 1992]: ProbHistRel 3/1992. Bru 1992, Univ. 218 p. Fb 750 [NRT 115,777, P. *Évrard*].
536* ᴱ**Di Liegro** Luigi, *Pittau* Franco, Per conoscere l'Islâm; cristiani e musulmani nel mondo di oggi [Caritas diocesana di Roma, 11-15 marzo 1991]. CasM 1991, Piemme. 244 p. Lit. 28.000 [CC 144/1,413s, G. *Caprile*].
537 ᴱ**Doré** J., Les cent ans de la Faculté de Théologie; Actes du colloque déc. 1990, Centenaire Fac. T., Inst. Catholique: SciencesTR 1. P 1992, Beauchesne. 391 p. F 198 [RHE 87,281*].
538 ᴱ**Druart** Thérèse-Anne, *Rasevic* Mark, Religions and the virtue of religion: Proceedings of the American Catholic Philosophical Association 65 (1991). Wsh 1992, Catholic Univ. of America. 308 p. 0-918090-25-2.
539 ᴱ**Durand** J.-D., L'observation quantitative du fait religieux; Colloque de l'Association Française d'Histoire religieuse contemporaine, P-Sorbonne 27.IX.1990. Lille 1992, Univ. III. 129 p. F 90 [RHE 87,168*].
540 **Etchegaray** Roger card., présent., Une terre pour tous les hommes; la destination universelle des biens; Actes du colloque international organisé par le Conseil pontifical 'Justice et Paix'. P 1992, Centurion. 158 p. F 160. 2-227-31580-6 [CC 144/1,518, J. *Joblin*].
541 ᴱ**Fabella** Virginia, *Lee* Peter H. K., *Suh Kwang-Sun* David, Asian Christian spirituality; reclaiming traditions [Seoul meeting July 1989]. Mkn 1992. 159 p. $17 [TDig 39,350; RelStR 19,57, R. H. *Drummond*]. – ᴿTTod 49 (1992s) 579 (R. I. *Sano*).
542 ᴱ**Fallon** Timothy P., *Riley* Philip B., Religion in context; recent studies in Lonergan ['begun' at 1984 Santa Clara symposium; cf. Religion and culture 1987 → 3,668]: CTS Resources in Religion 4. Lanham MD 1988, UPA. xiv-201 p. $41; pa. $19.75. – ᴿCritRR 5 (1992) 499-501 (W. E. *Conn*).
543 ᴱ**Farina** M., *Mazzarello* M. L., Gesù il Signore; la specificità di Gesù in un tempo di pluralismo religioso [raduno Auxilium, Roma 29.IV-3.V. 1992]: Prisma 12. R 1992, LAS. 243 p. Lit. 25.000 [NRT 115,744, A. *Toubeau*].
544 ᴱ**Fatio** O., Les Églises face aux sciences du Moyen Âge au XXᵉ siècle: Actes du Colloque de la Commission Internationale d'Histoire ecclésiastique comparée, Genève août 1989. Genève 1991, Droz. 177 p. – ᴿRHPR 72 (1992) 497s (G. *Siegwalt*).
545 ᴱ**Felici** Sergio, La formazione al sacerdozio ministeriale nella catechesi e nella testimonianza di vita dei Padri: Convegno di studio e aggiornamento, Roma 15-17 marzo 1990: BtScR 98. R 1992, LAS(alesianum). 288 p. Lit. 35.000. 88-253-0239-3. – 14 art., 2 infra.

545* ᴱFelici Sergio, Sacerdozio battesimale e formazione teologica ... Padri [convegno R. 14-16.III.1991]: BtScRel 99. R 1992, LAS [ÉglT 24,316s; G. *Hudon*, aussi sur Ministeriale 1990/2).
546 Femmes en mission: Actes de la XIᵉ session du Crédic, St.-Flour 27-31 août 1990. Lyon 1991, Art-Histoire. 370 p. F 170. 17 femmes + 6. – ᴿEsprVie 102 (1992) 73-75 (sr. E. *Germain*).
547 ᴱFinan T., *Twomey* V., The relationship between Neoplatonism and Christianity; Proceedings of the first conference at Maynooth 1990. Blackrock 1992, Four Courts. viii-170 p. [RHE 88,121*].
547* ᴱFloyd Wayne W., *Marsh* Charles, Theology and the practice of responsibility; essays on Dietrich BONHOEFFER [Sixth annual Bonhoeffer Conference NY Union 1992]: UnSemQ 46 (1992). v-309 p. 19 art., 3 infra.
548 ᴱFolscheid Dominique, Maurice BLONDEL, une dramatique de la modernité; Actes du colloque, Sém. S. Luc, Aix-en-Provence, mars 1989. P 1990, Presses Universitaires. – ᴿRechSR 80 (1992) 436-8 (P. *Olivier*).
549 *a*) ᴱFornet-Betancourt Raúl, Theologien in der Sozial- und Kulturgeschichte Lateinamerikas [32 scholars in Bru COELI project]: Die Perspektive der Armen 1. Eichstätt 1992, Diritto. 237 p.; 353 p. (+ vol. 3) [TContext 10/2,94s, *ipse*].
— *b*) ᴱForte Bruno (p. 29-35), Teologia e storia [convegno Napoli 18.II. 1992]: BtTNapoletana. N 1992, D'Auria. 117 p. Lit. 20.000. 88-7092-051-8. – 8 art.; ↠ b870.
— *c*) Fox Matthew, *al.*, Creation spirituality and the dreamtime [1990 Melbourne Creation Spirituality workshop]. Newton NSW 1991, Millenium. 94 p. – ᴿStudies 81 (1992) 110-2 (L. *Greene*: enthusiasm).
d) ᴱFraser Colin, *Gaskell* George, The social psychological study of widespread beliefs [Colloquium Cambridge 1985]. Ox 1990, Clarendon. xvi-230 p. – ᴿArchivScSocR 80 (1992) 259-263 (J.-P. *Deconchy*).
— *e*) ᴱFurger F., *Wiemeyer* J., Christliche Sozialethik im weltweiten Horizont [Symposium Münster 1991]: InstChrSozW 25. Münster 1992, Aschendorff. vi-101 p. DM 28. 3-402-04533-8 [TvT 33,312, G. *Manenschijn*].
550 ᴱGafo Fernández Javier, Etica y ecología: Dilemas éticos de la medicina actual 5 [VII Seminario de Bioética, M]. M 1991, Univ. Comillas. 214 p. 84-87840-05-1. – ᴿActuBbg 29 (1992) 142 (V. *Trius*).
551 [ᴱGesteira Garza Manuel,] Dios y el problema del mal; Actas de la 3ᵃ Semana de Teología, Madrid, 19-21 sept. 1990: RET 51,2s (1991) 149-385. 8 art., 5 infra.
552 ᴱGifford Paul, New dimensions in African Christianity: All African Council of Churches, Mombasa 1991: African Challenges 3. Nairobi 1992, AACC. 215 p. [TContext 10/3,100, H. *Janssen*].
552* ᴱGiogia M., La teologia spirituale [seminario S. Luigi, Napoli 1-2 maggio 1990]. R 1991, A.V.E. 293 p. – ᴿRelCu 38 (1992) 486 (L. *Marín de San Martín*).
553 ᴱGira Dennis, Religions en dialogue; Institut de Science et de Théologie des Religions, 6-20 février 1990: RICathP 38 (1991) 5-82; p. 63-82, *Geffré* C., Théologie chrétienne et dialogue interreligieux.
554 *a*) ᴱGisel Pierre, *al.*, Albrecht RITSCHL, la théologie en modernité; entre religion, morale et positivité historique [colloque Lausanne]. Genève 1991, Labor et Fides. 223 p. F 129. 2-8309-0745-4. – ᴿÉTRel 67 (1992) 607 (A. *Gounelle*).
— *b*) ᴱGoizueta Roberto S., We are a people ! [1990 conference, 6 art.]; initiatives in Hispanic American theology. Mp 1992, Fortress. xxi-164 p. 0-8006-2577-3. – ᴿTBR 5,3 (1992s) 32s (J. *Lowerson*).

— c) ᴱGonzález Justo L., Out of every tribe and nation; Christian theology at the ethnic round table [Methodist 1988-90]. Nv 1992, Abingdon. 128 p. $17. 0-687-29860-1 [TBR 6/2,42, A. *Laande*].

— d) ᴱGort Jerald D., *al.*, On sharing religious experience; possibilities of interfaith mutuality [Amst Free Univ. April 1990]: Currents of Encounter 4. GR 1992, Eerdmans. xi-304 p. $28 pa. [JRel 73,302, S. M. *Heim*].

555 ᴱGregory Peter N., Sudden and the gradual — approaches to enlightenment in Chinese thought [1981 conference]. Delhi 1991, Motilal-B. 474 p. – ᴿJDharma 17 (1992) 157-9 (B. V. *Venkatakrishna*: ten excellent essays).

556 ᴱGuggisberg Hans R., *al.*, La liberté de conscience (XVIᵉ-XVIIᵉ siècles), Actes du colloque de Mulhouse et Bâle 1989: ᴱÉtPgHist 44. Genève 1991, Droz. 375 p. – ᴿRHE 87 (1992) 923s (J.-F. *Gilmont*).

557 a) ᴱHaas P. J., Recovering the role of women; power and authority in rabbinic Jewish society [1991 seminar; 4 papers on the biblical world, 2 modern]: SFLStJud 59. Atlanta 1992, Scholars. 132 p. $35. 1-55540-765-X [BL 93,136, T. *Rajak*].

— b) ᴱHamnett Ian, Religious pluralism and unbelief; studies critical and comparative [Colston meeting, Bristol 1988]. L 1990, Routledge. viii-279 p. £30. – 5 art. – ᴿArchivScSocR 78 (1992) 231 (J. *Séguy*).

— c) Harrak A., Contacts between cultures; West Asia and North Africa: 33d international congress of Asian and North African Studies, Toronto, August 15-25, 1990, 1 [2. S. Asia ᴱKoppedrayer K.; 3s. Eastern Asia, ᴱLuk Hung-Kay B.]. Lewiston NY 1992, Mellen. xiv-493 p. 0-7734-9200-3. 87 art.; 16 infra.

— d) ᴱHarskamp A. van, Verborgen God of lege Kerk? Theologen en sociologen over secularisatie [colloque Univ. Amsterdam juin 1990]. Kampen 1991, Kok. 158 p. ƒ32,30 [RTLv 24,403, P. *Weber*].

— e) Hastings Adrian [on MILINGO], *al.*, African medicine in the modern world: Seminar 27. E 1986, Univ. Centre of African Studies. 219 p. $10 [JRelAf 23,95, Toyin *Falola*: all show respect for African healers, except for children].

— f) ᴱHaug Walter, Mieth Dietmar, Religiöse Erfahrung: historische Modelle in christlicher Traditio [Symposion Reimer-Stiftung]. Mü 1992, Fink. 469 p. DM 120. 3-7705-2749-6 [TGL 83,491, G. *Fuchs*].

558 ᴱHead T., Landes R., The peace of God; social violence and religious response in France around the year 1000. Ithaca NY 1992, Cornell Univ. xv-364 p. 3 maps [RHE 88,61*].

559 ᴱHeering J. P., *al.*, De gelijkenis van de verloren Vader; Beschouwingen over Van GENNEPs boek [1989] 'De terugkeer van de verloren Vader' [Studiedag 28 mei 1990]. Nijkerk 1991, Callenbach. 174 p. ƒ32,50. 90-266-0255-3. – ᴿTvT 32 (1992) 206 (Teije *Brattinga*: death prevented van Gennep's planned participation).

560 ᴱHeron Alasdair, The forgotten Trinity [BBC Doctrine commission, 10 papers]. L 1991, BBC. 208 p. £16. 0-85169-124-2. – ᴿExpTim 103 (1991) 348 (V. *White*: dialogue, enthusiasm; Jane *Williams* transforms 'The fatherhood of God' rather than reinforcing patriarchy; but there is no sustained epistemological basis amid the ten talks).

561 ᴱHeuclin J., Mentalités religieuses et révolution française, Colloque Lille Fac. Lettres 12-13 mai 1989: MélSR 48,1s (1991). 130 p.

562 ᴱHewitt Haroldᴶ, Problems in the philosophy of religion; critical studies of the work of John HICK [conference April 1989]. L c.1991, Macmillan. xvi-246 p. – ᴿRelSt 28 (1992) 581s (M. *Wynn*).

563 ᴱHöver Gerhard, al., Die Würde des Menschen; die theologisch-anthropologischen Grundlagen der Lehre Papst Johannes Pauls II [Tagung Kath. Akad. Rottenburg-Stuttgart 1984]: Entwicklung und Frieden wiss. 41. Mainz/Mü 1986, Grünewald/Kaiser. 176 p. DM 24.50 [TR 88,416, M. *Spieker*].

564 ᴱHoltrop P. N., *Jelsma* A. J., Terwijl zij onderweg daarover spraken ... Gedachten over de opstanding [Geref. Colloquium Kampen 1990s]: Cah 73. Kampen 1991, Kok. 141 p. ƒ30. 90-242-6589-4. – ᴿTvT 32 (1992) 431 (M. Van *Tente*).

565 ꜰHORST Irvin B.: Menno SIMONS, a reappraisal [March 1990 seminar], 450th anniversary of Fundamentboek; ᴱBrunk Gerald R. Harrisburg VA 1992, Eastern Mennonite college. xvi-215 p. [Simons research survey; Horst bibliog.] $20 [TDig 39,373; ChH 62,400, J. H. *Yoder*; SixtC 24,496, E. J. *Furcha*].

566 ᴱHoutepen A., De verscheidenheid verzoend? [meeting on FRIES-RAHNER Einigung 1983]: IIMO 26. Leiden/Utrecht 1989, Interuniversitair Instituut voor Missiologie en Oecumenica. 258 p. ƒ29.50. 90-6495-204-3. – ᴿBijdragen 53 (1992) 451s (J. E. *Vercruysse*).

567 *a*) ᴱHünermann Peter, *Scannone* Juan Carlos, América Latina y la doctrina social de la Iglesia [first 2 volumes of 5 on Latin American-German dialogue program]. Buenos Aires 1992, Paulinas. 286 p.; 392 p. [TContext 10/2, 101s, R. *Fornet-Betancourt*].

— *b*) ᴱHughes Kathleen, *Francis* Mark K., Living no longer for ourselves; liturgy and justice in the nineties [Ch Cath. Theological Union dispute]. ColMn 1991, Liturgical. 208 p. $13 [TLZ 118,446, K.-H. *Bieritz*].

— *c*) ᴱHurtado Larry, Goddesses in religions and modern debate [Manitoba Univ. 1987-8]. Atlanta 1990, Scholars. 227 p. $30. 1-55540-549-5. – 7 art. [Interpretation 47,178, M. S. *Moore*]. ᴿSR 21 (1992) 124 (Pamela D. *Young*).

— *d*) ᴱIntrovigne Massimo, Spiritismo e nuove religioni: Seminario internazionale Foggia 1988. T-Leumann 1989, L.D.C. 248 p. Lit. 15.000. – ᴿDocCom 44 (1991) 200s (D. *Vibrac*).

— *e*) ᴱJames Robison B., *Dockery* David S. [dialogue 1989-91], Beyond the impasse? Scripture, interpretation, and theology in Baptist life. Nv 1992, Broadman. 319 p. $16 pa. 0-8054-6036-5 [TDig 40,256].

568 ᴱJedrej M. C., *Shaw* R., Dreaming; religion and society in Africa [Cosmology Society, Edinburgh 1986]: StRelAf 7. Leiden 1992, Brill. 194 p. ƒ95. – ᴿNRT 114 (1992) 792s (J. M.: on dreams).

569 Jelsma A., *Clemens* T., 5 al., Kerk en Verlichting, Windesheim 18.XI. 1989. Zwolle 1990, Stichting Windesheim. 127 p. ƒ18,50. 90-800537-1-6. – ᴿTvT 32 (1992) 201 (T. *Schoof*).

569* ᴱJohn Jeffrey, Living tradition [7 art., < York conference 1991]. L 1992, Darton-LT. 136 p. £6. 0-232-51981-1. – ᴿExpTim 104 (1992s) 93 (R. *Lunt*: reviving Anglo-Catholicism).

570 ᴱJuergensmeyer Mark, Violence and the sacred in the modern world [< (after) Guggenheim conference 1989] = Journal of Terrorism and Political Violence 3/3 (1990). L 1992, Cass. 155 p. $29.50 [Bulletin COV & R 5,12].

571 *a*) ᴱKaplan Lawrence, Fundamentalism in comparative perspective [1988 CCNY conference, *Marty* M., al.]. Amherst 1992, Univ. Massachusetts. viii-184 p. $25; pa. $11. 0-87023-797-7; -8-5 [TDig 39,362].

— *b*) ᴱKelsay John, *Johnson* James T., Just war and jihad; historical and theoretical perspectives on war and peace in western and Islamic traditions [< conferences]. Westport CT 1991, Greenwood. viii-254 p. $45 [JRel 73,281s, R. B. *Miller*: companion to 1990 Cross, crescent and sword].

— c) ᴱ**Kerssemakers** J. H.., Sex and religion; religious issues in sexological treatment, sexological issues in pastoral care [1991 Amsterdam world-conference]. Amst 1992, Rodopi. 128 p. 90-5183-376-8 [TvT 33,434, Anke *Hoenkamp-Bisschops*).

— d) ᴱ**Kinnamon** Michael, World council of churches; Signs of the Spirit, official report, Seventh Assembly, Canberra, Australia, 7-20 February 1991. Geneva / GR 1992, WCC / Eerdmans. xiv-396 p. $27.50 pa. [RelStR 19,336, J. T. *Ford*: canberra is an aboriginal word for 'meeting-place'].

572 ᴱ**Kippenberg** Hans G., *al.*, Concepts of person in religion and thought [Groningen Working Group]: Religion and Reason 37. B 1990, de Gruyter. x-410 p. DM 168. – ᴿJRel 72 (1992) 472s (S. *Collins*).

573 ᴱ**Klauck** Hans-Josef, Monotheismus und Christologie; zur Gottesfrage im hellenistischen Judentum und im Urchristentum [Tagung Luzern 17.-22. März 1991]: QDisp 138. FrB 1992, Herder. 230 p. 3-451-02138-2 [BtS 37,195, D. *Zeller*; TLZ 118,292, G. *Haufe*]. 7 art.; infra.

573* ᴱ**Kochanek** Herrmann, Reinkarnation oder Auferstehung; Konsequenzen für das Leben. FrB 1992, Herder. 288 p. DM 46. 3-451-22866-1 [TR 89,436].

574 ᴱ**Kosinski** Renate B., *Szell* Timea, Images of sainthood in medieval Europe [14 art., 1987 Bernard College conference]. Ithaca NY 1991, Cornell Univ. vi-315 p. $30; pa. $9. 0-8014-2507-7; -9745-0 [TDig 40,168].

575 ᴱ**Kulisz** Józef, ❷ Jesuits in central and eastern Europe past and present [symposium Warsaw 18-20 April 1991, Jesuits also from Hungary, Czechoslovakia, Romania, France]: Bobolanum 3 (1992) 7-9 . 81s ❷ + Eng.).

576 *Lagrée* Michèle, *al.*, Figures du démoniaque, hier et aujourd'hui [session février-mars 1991]: Publ. 55. Bru 1992, Fac. Univ. Saint-Louis. 155 p.; p. 31-61, *Crouzel* H., dans ORIGÈNE. 2-8028-0083-3.

576* ᴱ**Lamberigts** Matthieu, *Soetens* Claude, À la veille du Concile Vatican II; vota et réactions en Europe et dans le catholicisme oriental [colloques LvN 1989 – Houston 1991 (G. *Alberigo* project, Hist. Vat. II)]; Instrum. Theol. 9. Lv 1992, Fac. Théol. viii-277 p. 90-73683-06-8 [TvT 33,99, J. *van Laarhoven*]. – ᴿETL 68 (1992) 487s (R. *Boudens*).

577 ᴱ**Lambrecht** Jan, *Collins* Raymond F., God and human suffering [< Hoelang nog, Lv 28s.X.1987, Amersfoort 1988]: TheolPastMg 3. Lv 1989, Peeters. xi-247 p. 90-6831-210-3. 10 art.; 4 infra.

578 **Lanne** Emmanuel, Présentation du Colloque de Chevetogne 1992, Les Églises orientales catholiques et l'Œcuménisme: Irénikon 65,3 (1992) 307-324, conclusions 440-8.

578* ᴱ**La Rocca** Tommaso, Thomas MÜNTZER e la rivoluzione dell'uomo comune [colloquio Univ. Ferrara 5-6 maggio 1989]; préf. *Miegge* M. T 1990, Claudiana. 205 p. – ᴿETL 68 (1992) 172s (R. *Boudens*: rapprochement un peu artificiel avec la théologie de la libération).

579 ᴱ**Legrand** H., *al.*, a) Iglesias locales y catolicidad, Actas del Coloquio internacional de Salamanca, 2-7 abril 1991. S 1992, Univ. 782 p. – b) Colloquium, The local church and catholicity, Salamanca 2-7.IV.1991 (ᵀ). Jurist 58,1 (1992). 586 p. 31 art.; 3 infra.

580 **Leuba** Jean-Louis, Reflects de l'Épiphanie [1 art., Rome 1974 + 5 des journées d'études de l'Université S. Jean de Jérusalem fondée par Henry *Corbin*, 1976-86]: Lieux théologiques 17. Genève 1990, Labor et Fides. 128 p. F 99. 2-8309-0594-6. – ᴿÉTRel 67 (1992) 632s (L. *Gagnebin*).

580* **Levesque** Joseph présent., L'annonce de Jésus-Christ et la rencontre des religions (colloque 17-20 sept. 1991): RICathP 42 (1992) 125-176. 3 art.

581 ᴱ**Lewis** B., *Niewöhner* F., Religionsgespräche im Mittelalter, XXV. Wolfenbütteler Symposium 11.-15. Juni; W-MA Studien 4. Wsb 1992, Harrassowitz. 388 p. [RHE 88,86*].

581* ᴱ**Limouris** Gennadios, The place of the woman in the Orthodox Church and the question of the ordination of women; Interorthodox Symposium, Rhodes 30.X-2.XI.1988. Katerini 1992, Tertios. 346 p. – ᴿTAth 63 (1992) 353s (E. A. *Theodorou,* ©).

582 [ᴱ**Lobato** Abelardo], Etica e società contemporanea; III Congresso SITA [Aquinas]; R 24-28 sett. 1991. Vaticano 1992, Editrice. 372 p.; 433 p.; 398 p. – ᴿActuBbg 29 (1992) 176-183 (E. *Forment*).

583 ᴱ**Locatelli** Giancarlo, *a)* Il primato del vescovo di Roma; una problematica ecumenica, Bari 27-29 maggio 1990; – *b)* Cattolici ed ortodossi a Bari, 10 anni di dialogo, 16-17 dicembre 1991: Colloquio IX; X: Nicolaus 19 (1992) 1-169 / 171-324.

585 ᴱ**Longère** Jean, L'abbaye parisienne de Saint-Victor au moyen âge; XIII Colloque d'Humanisme médiéval de Paris (1986-8): Bibliotheca Victorina 1. Turnhout 1991, Brepols. 336 p.; 4 fig.; map. – ᴿRHE 87 (1992) 802 (A. *Haquin*).

586 [*Lustiger* card., présent.] Science et Foi, Colloque La Croix-L'Événement, 1 février 1992: Questions en débat. P 1992, Centurion. 215 p. F 99 [NRT 115,778, P. *Évrard*]. – ᴿEsprVie 102 (1992) 576s (P. *Jay*).

586* ᴱ**Lużny** Ryszard, ❷ Chrześcijański Wschód... The Christian East and Polish culture [Lublin KUL symposium 12-14 Oct. 1983]. L 1989, KUL. 398 p. – ᴿEurJT 1 (1992) 189s (G. *Bray*).

587 ᴱ**McGhee** Michael, Philosophy, religion and the spiritual life [14 papers from Liverpool 1991 conference]: Royal Institute of Philosophy supp 32. C 1992, Univ. iv-257 p. $20 pa. 0-521-42196-9 [TDig 40,284]. – ᴿExpTim 104 (1992s) 310s (P. *Byrne*).

588 ᴱ**McWilliam** Joanne, AUGUSTINE, from rhetor to theologian [Toronto Trinity college. 1600th anniversary conference]. Waterloo 1992, W. Laurier Univ. x-237 p. 0-88920-203-6. 15 art.; 5 infra [LavalTP 49,551, Anne *Pasquier*; TorJT 10,135, J. K. *Coyle*; VigChr 47,283, J. den *Boeft*].

589 ᴱ**Madden** Lawrence J., The awakening Church; 25 years of liturgical renewal [Wsh Georgetown Univ. 1988, 10 art.]. ColMn 1992, Liturgical. x-141 p. $10. 0-8146-2031-0 [TDig 40,51].

590 ᴱ**Madden** Lawrence J., The Joseph CAMPBELL phenomenon [myth-study in America; Wsh Georgetown Univ. Liturgy Center 1991; 9 art.]; implications for the contemporary Church. Wsh 1992, Pastoral. viii-153 p. $11 pa. 0-912405-89-9 [TDig 40,70].

590* Masculinidad y feminidad [en la Biblia...] en la Patrística [coloquio Inst. de Ciencias para la Familia]. Pamplona 1989, Univ. Navarra. 344 p. – ᴿRechSR 80 (1992) 293s (Y.-M. *Duval*).

591 ᴱ**Mate** Reyes, *Niewöhner* Friedrich, El precio de la 'invención' de América [III Encuentro Hispano-Alemán (Cáceres-Wolfenbüttel 1990]: Pensamiento crítico-utópico 68. Barc 1992, Anthropos. 254 p. 84-7658-349-4 [ActuBbg 30,107s, A. *Borràs*].

592 ᴱ**Mattioli** Umberto [p. 5-30], Donna e culture; studi e documenti nel III anniversario della 'Mulieris dignitatem' [Centro Ebraismo e Cristianesimo, Univ. Bologna 15 nov. 1989]. Genova 1991, Marietti. xii-278 p. Lit. 35.000. – ᴿSMSR 58 (1992) 389-393 (Concetta *Aloe Spada*).

593 ᴱMaurice M. A., *Noorda* S., De onzekere zekerheid des geloofs; beschouwingen in het spanningsveld van geloven en denken [Amsterdam VU 110 Anniv.]. Zoetermeer 1991, Meinema. 171 p. ƒ27,50. 90-211-3564-7. – ᴿTvT 32 (1992) 323s (B. *Vedder*).

593* ᴱ*Mechoulan* Henry, Puissance de la raison et rémanence de la foi au XVIIᵉ siècle [séminaire]: RSPT 76,1 (1992) 2-116.

594 *a*) ᴱMelchiorre Virgilio, Maschio-femmina; nuovi padri e nuove madri [Convegno CSIF 1991]. CinB 1992, Paoline. 224 p. Lit. 26.000 [CC 144/1, 614, E. *Flumeri*].

— *b*) MÉN Aleksandr (1935-1990) mem., Kirchen im Kontext unterschiedlicher Kulturen [Symposion Ev. Akad. Tutzing Mai 1990]. ᴱ(Red.) **Heller** W., ᴱ(Hg.) *Felmy* K. C. + 4. Gö 1991, Vandenhoeck &R. 1031 p. 3 fig.; portr. DM 340. 3-525-85936-8 [TLZ 118,815, P. *Gerlitz*].

— *c*) ᴱMeniel Patrice, Animal et pratiques religieuses; les manifestations matérielles; Actes du Colloque international de Compiègne 11-13 novembre 1988: Anthropologica sp. 3. P 1989, L'Homme et l'Animal. 198 p.; ill. 0994-7213. 22 art.; 2 infra.

— *d*) ᴱMilano Andrea, Misoginia; la donna vista e malvista nella cultura occidentale [Seminario interdisciplinare Univ. Potenza, 19 art.]. R 1992, Dehoniane. 612 p. [Teresianum 44,739, B. *Goya*].

595 ᴱMoltmann-Wendel Elisabeth, Frau und Mann; alte Rollen – Neue Werte [Studientag Kath. Akad. Freiburg]; FrAkSchr 2. Dü 1991, Patmos. 151 p. DM 22,80. 3-491-72245-4. – ᴿTvT 32 (1992) 427 (M. de *Haardt*).

596 ᴱMoreschini C., *Menestrina* G., GREGORIO Nazianzeno teologo e scrittore: Trento IstScRel 17. Bo 1992, Dehoniane. 252 p. [RHE 88,262*].

596* ᴱMorris Rosemary, Church and people in Byzantium: 20th Symposium Manchester 1986. Birmingham UK 1990, Univ. x-286 p. £14. 14 art. – ᴿRÉByz 50 (1992) 299s (A. *Failler*: tit. pp.).

597 ᴱMüller-Fahrenholz Geiko, *Pannenberg* W., *al.*, Christentum in Lateinamerika [kath. Akad. Bayern & ev. Akad. Tutzing 7.-9. Juni 1991]. Rg 1992, Pustet. 175 p. DM 34. – ᴿMüTZ 43 (1992) 370-3 (G.-L. *Müller*).

598 ᴱMuratore S., Teologia e filosofia; alla ricerca di un nuovo rapporto [Napoli 1989]. R 1990, A.V.E. – ᴿAntonianum 67 (1992) 444s (L. *Oviedo*).

598* ᴱMurphy James H., New beginnings in ministry [All Hallows College, Dublin, 150th anniv. symposium]. Dublin 1992, Columba. 188 p. 1-85607- 057-3. – ᴿExpTim 104 (1992s) 251s (A.*Lovegrove*).

599 [Nagy Stanisław, présent.] Congrès des théologiens de l'Europe du centre et de l'est, Lublin 11-15.VIII. [1991]: AtKap 118,497 (Feb. 1992) 1-93.

600 ᴱNaro Cataldo, Il discorso della Chiesa sulla società; Atti del convegno di studio, S. Cataldo (Caltanissetta) 4-6.X.1991: Studi Cammarata 2. Caltanissetta 1992, Sciascia. 350 p. Lit. 35.000. – ᴿHo Theológos 10 (1992) 115-120 (A. *Lipari*).

601 ᴱNeuhaus Richard J., Theological education and moral formation [5 of the 25 participants; 100 p. summary by P. *Stallsworth*; Rowan *Greer* on 4th cent.]: Encounter 15. GR 1992, Eerdmans. x-235 p. $19 pa. 0-8028-0215-X [TDig 39,290].

602 ᴱNiewiadomski József, *Palaver* Wolfgang, Dramatische Erlösungslehre, ein Symposion [SCHWAGER R., GIRARD R.]: InnsbTSt 38. Innsbruck 1992, Tyrolia. 386 p. 22 art., infra [TR 88,528, tit. pp.; GeistL 66,399s, M. *Herzog*].

603 ᴱObayashi Hiroshi, Death and afterlife; perspectives of world religions [Rutgers lecture series 1987s]: Contributions to the Study of Religion 33. NY 1992, Greenwood. xxii-209 p. 0-313-27906-3. 13 art.; 8 infra.

604 EOduyoye Mercy Amba, *Musimbi* R. A. Kanyoro, The will to arise; women, tradition, and the Church in Africa [First biennial institute of Catholic women, Ghana 1989; 12 art. + 1 Muslim]. Mkn 1992, Orbis. 230 p. $17. 0-88344-782-7 [TDig 40,93].

604* EOikonomidis N., ⒼByzantium in the 12th century (canon law, government and society); two Athens symposia, 20-22.X.1989 and 19-21.X.1990. Athena 1991, Society for Byzantine and Postbyzantine Studies. 620 + 13 p. – RTAth 63 (1992) 374s (P. B. *Paschos*: tit. pp.).

605 Ed'Onorio Joël-Benoît, La laïcité au défi de la modernité; Actes du Xe Colloque Nationale des Juristes Catholiques, Paris nov. 1989; préf. *Poupard* Paul. P 1990, Téqui. 247 p. F 110. – RGregorianum 73 (1992) 557s (J. *Joblin*); RevSR 66 (1992) 374s (R. *Epp*).

606 *a*) EPapandreou Damaskinos, L'icone dans la théologie de l'art 1990: RRTLv 23 (1992) 387s (A. de *Halleux*).

— *b*) EPathil Kunchena, Religious pluralism; an Indian Christian [R. Cath.] perspective [Indian Theol. Asn. 1988s, 13 art.]. Delhi 1991, ISPCK. x-349 p. rs. 75 [TBR 6/2, 97, R. S. *Sugirtharajah*].

— *c*) PAUL VI et la vie internationale; journées d'études, Aix-en-Provence, 18-19 mai 1990. Brescia/R 1992, Ist. Paolo VI/Studium. xi-225 p. Lit. 35.000 [CC 144/3, 328s, G. *Caprile*].

— *d*) Per una cultura dell'Europa unita; lo studio dei Padri della Chiesa oggi; Atti dei colloqui di Torino e Roma (30-31 ott. 1991). T 1992, SEI. vi-101 p. – RVetChr 29 (1992) 425s (A. *Isola*).

607 Peretto E., La mariologia nell'organizzazione delle discipline teologiche; collocazione e metodo; Atti dell'8° Simposio Internazionale Mariologico (Roma, 2-4 ottobre 1990). R 1992, Marianum. 527 p. Lit. 70.000 [NRT 115,582, L.-J. *Renard*].

607* EPerrone Lorenzo, Il cuore indurito del faraone; ORIGENE e il problema del libero arbitrio [incontro Univ. Pisa 1991]: Origini 3. Genova 1992, Marietti. x-152 p. Lit. 34.000. 88-211-9585-6 [RTLv 24,389, A. de *Halleux*: VigChr 47,399, P. J. van der *Eijk*].

EPetit Jean-Claude, *Breton* Jean-Claude, Jésus-Christ universel? 1989/90 ➔ b72.

608 EPitassi Maria-Cristina, [99-118 sur TURRETTINI], Apologétique 1680-1740; sauvetage ou naufrage de la théologie? [Actes Genève Inst. Hist. Réf. juin 1990]: Univ. Publ. 15. Genève 1991, Labor et Fides. 129 p. 2-8309-0644-6. – RActuBbg 29 (1992) 213s (J. *Boada*); ÉTRel 67 (1992) 288-290 (H. *Bost* appelle 'magistrale' la réponse de F. LAPLANCHE p. 119-128 'à la question posée', mais les plusieurs citations sont tout-à-fait ambivalentes); TvT 32 (1992) 317s (T. *Schoof*).

608* EPotestà Gian Luca, Il profetismo GIOACHIMITA tra Quattrocento e Cinquecento; Atti del III Congresso, S. Giovanni in Fiore, 17-21 sett. 1989: Opere/Strum 3. Genova 1991, Marietti. 520 p.; 16 pl. [RHE 88, 870, G. M. *Colombás*].

609 [non = 526]... Il prete nella Chiesa oggi [in Italia: Camaldoli-Arezzo ott. 1990]: Ricerche personali. Bo 1992, Dehoniane. 141 p. – RTeresianum 43 (1992) 515s (M. *Caprioli*).

610 *a*) ERauch Albert, *Imhof* Paul, Das Dienstamt der Einheit in der Kirche; Primat – Patriarchat – Papsttum [Symposium Regensburg Juli 1989]. St. Ottilien 1991, EOS. 505 p. DM 38. – RTR 88 (1992) 489s (W. *Ivanov*).

— *b*) EReimer A. James, The influence of the Frankfurt school [HABERMAS, ADORNO, APEL, GADAMER 1927] on contemporary theology [21 papers from 15 annual Dubrovnik seminars]: Critical Theory and the Future of

Religion. Lewiston NY 1992, Mellen. xv-342 p. £40. 0-7734-9169-4 [TBR 6/1,36, C. *Elliott*: ᶠSIEBERT R. J.]. – ᴿCGrebel 11 (1992) 299-301 (S. *Rahn*).
— *c*) ᶠRENDTORFF Trutz, 60. Gb.: Protestantische Identität heute, Kolloquium Tutzing 1991, ᴱGraf Friedrich W., *Tanner* Klaus. Gü 1992, Mohn. 304 p. DM 58. 3-579-00278-3 [TLZ 118,285, G. *Winkler*].
612 ᴱRichter K., Das Konzil war erst der Anfang; die Bedeutung des II. Vatikanums für Theologie und Kirche [13 Vorträge, Münster 1989/90]. Mainz 1991, Grünewald. 244 p. DM 34. 3-7867-1541-6. – ᴿNRT 114 (1992) 112 (A. *Toubeau*); TvT 32 (1992) 423 (P. van *Leeuwen*).
613 ᴱRies Julien, Le civiltà del Mediterraneo e il sacro, ᵀ*Telaro* Maria Giulia. Mi 1992, Jaca/Massimo, 371 p. 99-16-40298-9 / 88-7030-373-X [*Lebrun* N., *Gimbutas* M., *Bianchi* U., *Sordi* M.].
613* ᴱRittner R. (*Walter* N., *al.*), Eschatologie und jüngstes Gericht [Jahrestagung 1990 TKAB]: Fuldaer Hefte 32. Hannover 1991, Luther. 103 p. DM 19,80. 3-7859-0624-2 [TLZ 118,961, B. *Hildebrandt*].
614 ᴱRockefeller Steven C., *Elder* John C., Spirit and nature; why the environment is a religious issue; an interfaith dialogue [Symposium 1990, Vermont Middleburg College]. Boston 1992, Beacon. xii-226 p. $30; pa. $16. 0-8070-7708-9; -9-7 [TDig 40,88].
614* ᴱRossi Philip J., *Wren* Michael J., Kant's philosophy of religion reconsidered [Marquette Univ. conference, Milwaukee 1987]. Bloomington 1991, Indiana Univ. 240 p. $25 [RelStR 19,40, R. R. *Williams*].
615 ᴱRostagno S., BARTH contemporaneo (convegno 31 ott.-2 nov. 1986, Fac. Valdese, Roma): FacV 16. T 1990, Claudiana. 256 p. Lit. 35.000. – ᴿStPatav 38 (1991) 662s (E. R. *Tura*).
616 ᴱRouner Leroy S., Human rights and the world's religions [Boston Univ. 12-lecture series]. ND 1988, Univ. 220 p. $27. – ᴿJAAR 60 (1992) 177-180 (M. M. *Ellison*).
616* ᴱRublack Hans-Christoph, Die lutherische Konfessionalisierung in Deutschland; wissenschaftliches Symposion des Vereins für Reformationsgeschichte [Gö-Reinhausen 7.-10.IX.1988]: Schriften 197. Gü 1992, Mohn. 594 p. DM 98. 3-579-01665-2 [TGL 83,232, Barbara *Hallensleben*].
617 ᴱRuderman David B., Preachers of the Italian ghetto [16th-17th century; Yale 1990 faculty seminar]. Berkeley 1992, Univ. California. $32. 0-520-07735-0 [TDig 40,182].
618 ᴱRuggieri Giuseppe, La cattura della fine; variazioni dell'escatologia in regime di cristianità [seminar Bologna]: TRScRel 7. Genova 1992, Marietti. xxxi-281 p. Lit. 35.000. 88-211-6728-3 [JEH 44,548, Marjorie *Reeves*: not 'Geneva'].
619 ᴱRunyon Theodore, Theology, politics, and peace [Emory conference, Atlanta Apr. 1988: MOLTMANN, J. CARTER...]. Mkn 1989, Orbis. xxi-199 p. $17 pa. – ᴿCritRR 5 (1992) 455s (R. L. *Holmes*).
620 ᴱSalmann E., La teologia mistico-sapienziale di Anselm STOLZ [1900-1942, Symposium S. Anselmo centenario, 20-21.V.1987]; StudAnselm 100. 125 p. Lit. 25.000. 5 art. – ᴿMüTZ 43 (1992) 138-40 (M. *Schulz*).
620* ᴱSartori Luigi, *Nicoletti* Michele, Teologia politica [Trento 17-18.V. 1989]. Bo 1991, Dehoniane. – ᴿFilT 6 (1992) 371 (L. *Borelli*: A. *Rizzi* sull'Esodo).
621 *Scaer* David P., Law and Gospel in Lutheran theology [*Bloesch* Donald G., Reformed; *Estep* W. R. (Ana-)Baptist; *Clutter* Ronald T., Brethren; *Dayton* Donald W., Wesleyan]; Ev.Theol.Soc.Midwest meeting, Winona

Lake March 20-21, 1992: GraceTJ 12,2 (1991! last issue) 163-180 [181-9-215-233-243].

622 ᴱSchreiter Robert J., Faces of Jesus in Africa [2 mostly Bantu/Catholic Christology conferences]. Mkn 1991, Orbis. xiii-181 p. $17. – ᴿRelStR 18 (1992) 315 (P. C. *Hodgson*).

622* ᴱSchwöbel Christoph, *Gunton* Colin E., Persons, divine and human; King's College [weekly research seminars] essays in theological anthropology. E 1992, Clark. 165 p. £17. 0-567-09584-4. – ᴿExpTim 104 (1992s) 125 (S. *Rudman*); RefTR 51 (1992) 111 (M. *Thompson*).

623 ᴱShadid W. A. R., *Koningsveld* P. S. van, The integration of Islam and Hinduism in western Europe [conference Leiden 12-14.IX.1990]. Kampen 1991, Kok. viii-254 p. – ᴿÉglT 23 (1992) 458-461 (T. *Mooren*).

624 ᴱSnodgrass Klyne, Worship [Ch North Park Sem. Symposium Oct. 9-11, 1992]: ExAud 8 (1992) 11 art., infra.

625 ᴱStacpoole Alberio, *Pinnock* G. & J., Mary in doctrine and devotion, Ecumenical Soc. BVM, Liverpool 1989. Dublin 1990, Columba. 160 p. – ᴿMarianum 53 (1991) 298-303 (K. *Duffy*).

626 ᴱStruppe Ursula, *Weismayer* Josef, Öffnung zum Heute; die Kirche nach dem Konzil [Wiener Theologische Kurse 40-Jahr-Vortragsreihe. Innsbruck 1991, Tyrolia. 136 p. Sch 148 pa. – ᴿZkT 114 (1992) 221 (H. *Rotter*).

626* Sulle cose prime e ultime: Convegno S. Spirito 7. Palermo 1991, Augustinus. 88 p. Lit. 18.000. – ᴿETL 68 (1992) 477 (A. de *Halleux*: mince).

627 ᴱTavernier Johan De, *Vervenne* Marc, De mens; verrader of hoeder van de schepping? [Aug. 1990]: Nikè. Lv 1991, Acco. 264 p. Fb 620. – ᴿCollatVL 22 (1992) 213s (B. *Houdart*); Streven 59 (1992s) 666s (L. *Anckaert*).

628 ᴱThoaria José J., *al.*, La Iglesia en la sociedad española, del Vaticano II al año 2000 [Inst. Sup. pastoral 25 años, Madrid]. Estella 1990, VDivino. 347 p. – ᴿSalT 78 (1990) 559s (J. A. *García*).

629 ᴱThompson T. A., Mariological Society May 30-31, 1990 / May 1991 (240 p. $12): Marian Studies 41s. Dayton 1990, Univ. [NRT 115,313, L.-J. *Renard*; TLZ 118,683, H. *Beinker*].

629* Trenton Giuseppe, *al.*, 'Centesimus annus'; verso le 'cose nuove' del terzo millennio: StPatav 39/1 (simposio 1992) 3-25 [-131].

630 ᴱTriacca A. M., *Pistoia* A., La prédication liturgique et les commentaires de la liturgie; Conférences Saint-Serge 38, Paris 25-28 juin 1990: BtEphLtg subs. 65. R 1992, Ed. Liturgiche. 295 p. Lit. 50.000 [TR 88,439, tit. pp.].

630* ᴱTrotta Giuseppe, Gerusalemme [convegno ACLI 1990 + *al.*] ➤ 7, d349: ᴿProtestantesimo 47 (1992) 172 (P. *Ribet*).

631 ᴱValentini Donato, La teologia; aspetti innovatori e loro incidenza sulla ecclesiologia e sulla mariologia [convegno Salesiani 3-7 gennaio 1988]: BtScR 85. R 1989, LAS. 374 p. – ᴿMarianum 54 (1992) 475s (M. *Semeraro*).

631* ᴱVaporis Nomikos M., Hellenic/Holy Cross Conference, Christian faith facing science, education and politics: GrOrTR 37,1s (1992). ix-103 p. 10 art. 3 infra ➤ 2094.

632 a) *Vaucelles* Louis de, Quelques hypothèses sur les acquis historiques et le devenir présent de la laïcité [= Masses Ouvrières nov. 1990, 83-94]; – b) *Guasco* Maurilio, Les reclassements du catholicisme italien devant l'évolution de la société; – c) *Bauberot* Jean, L'importance de la laïcité dans les transformations internes du protestantisme français; – d) *Azria*

Régine,   Formes et effets de la sécularisation au sein du judaïsme français; – e) *Maïla* Joseph,   Pluralité des représentations et des discours au sein de l'Islam: 'Univers religieux dans une culture laïque', CNRS 11-12 mai 1990 = RICath P 41 (1992) 7-17 / 59-70 / 29-41 / 43-58 / 19-28.

633 Vie monastique et inculturation à la lumière des traditions et situations africaines; Actes du colloque international Kinshasa, 19-25 février 1989. Kinshasa 1989, Archidiocèse / Aide Inter-Monastères. 445 p. – ᴿETL 68 (1992) 183s (A. *Vanneste*).

633* [ᴱViguerie J. de] Le Jugement, le ciel et l'enfer dans l'histoire du christianisme; Actes de la douzième rencontre d'histoire religieuse, Fontevraud 14-15 oct. 1988.   Angers 1989, Univ. 224 p.; 8 fig. F 170. – ᴿRHE 87 (1992) 876 (J.-P. *Hendrickx*).

634 **Wassermann** C., *al.*,   The science and theology of information [3d European conference, Genève March 1990]: Univ. Publ. Theol. 16. Genève 1992, Labor et Fides.   337 p. F 178.   2-8309-0663-3. – ᴿÉTRel 67 (1992) 612 (A. *Gaillard*).

634* ᶠWATANABE Morimichi, Nicholas of CUSA, in search of God and Wisdom, American Cusanus Society papers 1981-8, ᴱ**Christianson** Gerald, *Izbicki* Thomas M.   Leiden 1991, Brill.   298 p. *f* 140. – ᴿSixtC 23 (1992) 845s (E. E. *Mather*).

635 ᴱ**Wiederkehr** Dietrich,   Wie geschieht Tradition? Überlieferung im Lebensprozess der Kirche [Tagung 1990]: QDisp 133.   FrB 1991, Herder. x-176 p. DM 49 pa. – ᴿTGL 82 (1992) 374s (W. *Beinert*); ZkT 114 (1992) 217s (K. H. *Neufeld*).

636 ᴱ**Wiessner** Gernot, *Klimkeit* Hans-Joachim,   Studia manichaica; 2. Internat. Kongress zum Manichäismus, 6.-10. August 1989, Bonn-St. Augustin: StOrRel 23.   Wsb 1992, Harrassowitz.   xiv-400 p. DM 90 [TR 88,526; VigChr 47,294, J. van *Oort*].

636* ᴱ**Williams** Michael A., *al.*,   Innovation in religious traditions; essays in the interpretation of religious change [Seattle Washington Univ. research seminar 1988]: Religion and Society 31.   B 1992, Mouton de Gruyter. viii-373 p.   3-11-012780-6 [TDig 40,273]. 10 art.; 3 infra.

637 Wisje końca świata w literaturze [de fine mundi in litteratura]; materiały i konferencje, Sympozjum ❷ 23-25.IV.1990.   Szczecin 1992, Univ. → 9305.

ᴱ**Wood** Diana,   Christianity and Judaism; papers read at the 1991 summer meeting and the 1992 winter meeting of the Ecclesiastical History society: Studies in Church History 29 1992 → 502.

638 ᴱ**Wood** Diana,   The Church and the arts; EcclHist Soc. 1990 & 1991: Studies in Church History 28.   Ox 1992, Blackwell. xvii-585 p.; 93 fig.; 8 (colour.) pl. £37.50.   0-631-18043-5 [JEH 44,697, P. *Binski*].

639 ᴱ**Yuhaus** Cassian,   The Catholic Church and American culture; reciprocity and change, [St. Paul Catholic college presidents 1988].   NY 1990, Paulist. – ᴿPerspRelSt 19 (1992) 246-250 (A. M. *Manis*, also on B. LEONARD's Baptist convention).

639* ᴱ**Ziegenaus** Anton,   Maria und der Heilige Geist [Tagung Augsburg 1989]: MariolSt 8.   Rg 1991, Pustet.   91 p. 3-7917-1298-5. – ᴿForKT 8 (1992) 315s (P. C. *Düren*).

A2.5   *Acta* **philologica** *et historica* [reports → Y7.6].

640 *a*) Acta symposii latini de lingua latina vinculo Europae, Paris Inst. Finn. 25-27 oct. 1991. Bru 1992, Melissa. 189 p. [ClasR 43,212, R. P. H. *Green*].

— *b*) ᶠADRIANI Achille, Giornate di studio [Roma] 26-27.XI.1989, ᴱStucchi Sandro, *Bonanno Aravantinos* Margherita: StudiMisc 28. R 1991, Bretschneider. xii-305 p. 88-7062-725-X. 15 art., 2 infra.

641 [ᴱAlbini Umberto, *Gigante* Marcello, Giornate Pisane, Atti del IX Congresso FIEC [Fédération Internationale des Associations des Études Classiques] 24-30 Ag. 1989, I-II: StItFgC 85,1s [= 3/10] (1992) XI-714 p.; p. 715-1201, 39 art. + 44 colloquia.
Antibes Rencontre 9 Tissage 1988/9 ➤ 710*d*.

642 ᴱAsztalos Monica, *al.*, Knowledge and the sciences in medieval philosophy 1987. Helsinki 1990, Finnish Soc. Missiology. I. v-284; II.; III. viii-701 p. [HeythJ 34,325s, Sabetai *Unguru*].

643* ᶠBEJARANO Virgilio, treballs en honor de ~; Actes del IXᵉ simposi de la Secció Catalana de la SEEC, St. Feliu de Guixols, 13-16 d'abril de 1988, ᴱFerreres Lambert. Barc 1991, Univ. I. 487 p.; II. p. 489-914. [AnPg 62, p. 995; dépouillé].

644 ᶠBERCHEM Denis van: Nourrir la plèbe; Actes du colloque Genève 28-29.IX.1989, ᴱGiovannini Adalberto: SchwBeitAltW 22. Ba 1991, Reinhardt. viii-200 p. 3-7245-0743-7. 8 art., 6 infra ➤ U28. – ᴿRÉLat 70 (1992) 353s (J.-C. *Richard*).

644* ᴱBiraud Michèle, Études de syntaxe du grec classique; recherches linguistiques et applications didactiques: Actes du premier Colloque international de Didactique de la Syntaxe du grec classique, 17, 18, 19 avril 1991, Univ. Nice: Publ. Fac. Lettres 7. Nice 1992. 180 p. [ClasR 43,318, S. C. *Colvin*].

645 ᴱBonnet Corinne, *Jourdain-Annequin* Colette, Héraclès; d'une rive à l'autre de la Méditerranée, bilan et perspectives; Actes de la Table Ronde de Rome, 15-16 septembre 1989: Études 28. R 1992, Institut Historique Belge. 361 p.; ill. – 90-74461-01-8.

645* ᴱBrownrigg I. L., Medieval book production; assessing the evidence; Proceeding of the Second Conference of the Seminar in the history of the book to 1500, Oxford, July 1988. Los Altos Hill CA 1990, Red Gull. xv-200 p.; 123 fig.; 33 facsim.; 5 pl. – ᴿDeutsches Archiv für Erforschung des Mittelalters 48 (1992) 732s (G. *Silagi*) [RHE 88,449*].

646 ᴱBudick Sanford, *Iser* Wolfgang, Language of the unsayable; the play of negativity in literature and literary theory [1986 Jerusalem conference, notably DERRIDA]. – ᴿLitTOx 5 (1991) 408-410 (M. *Buning*).

647 ᴱCalder William M.ᴵᴵᴵ, *Demandt* Alexander, Eduard MEYER, Leben und Leistung eines Universalhistorikers [Kolloquium Bad Homburg 1987]: Mnemosyne supp. 112. Leiden 1990, Brill. ix-537 p.; portr. 18 art. – ᴿGnomon 64 (1992) 569-572 (K. *Christ*).

647* ᴱCampanile Enrico, Rapporti linguistici e culturali tra i popoli dell'Italia antica (Pisa, 6-7 ott. 1989): Testi Linguistici 17. Pisa 1991, Giardini. 188 p.; map. – ᴿLatomus 51 (1992) 912-4 (M. *Lejeune*).

648 ᴱCavallo G., *al.*, Scritture, libri e testi, nelle aree provinciali di Bisanzio; Atti del seminario di Erice (18-25 sett. 1988): BtMedvUman Univ. Perugia 5. Spoleto 1991, Centro Medioevo. xii-416 p.; p. 417-842; 53 fig., 53 facsim, 212 pl., map. [Aevum 66,463, C. M. *Mazzucchi*; RHE 88,353*].

648* ᴱCeccanti Melania, *Castelli* Maria Cristina, Il codice miniato, rapporti tra codice, testo e figurazione [... restauro codici]: Atti del III Congresso di Storia della Miniatura, StDoc 7. F 1992, Olschki. xiv-492 p.; (color.) ill. (index p. 471-480). 88-222-4004-9.

649 Colloque de la Société des professeurs d'histoire ancienne (Nantes-Angers 24-26 mai 1991): RÉAnc 94,1s (1992). 123 p.

649* ᴱColpe Carsten, al., Spätantike und Christentum; Beiträge zur Religions- und Geistesgeschichte der griechisch-römischen Kultur und Zivilisation der Kaiserzeit [Berlin Univ. Interdisziplinäre Vorlesung; Jahr nicht erwähnt, nur 'verzögert']. B 1992, Akademie. 280 p. 3-05-002004-0. 14 art., infra.

650 La conversión de Roma; cristianismo y paganismo [ciclo 1988 Sevilla]. M 1990, Clásicas. 292 p. – ᴿMemHistAnt 11s (1990s) 351-3 (Mercedes García Martínez).

650* Cottier Georges, Starobinski Jean, présent., Les usages de la liberté: Rencontre de Genève 32, 1989. Neuchâtel 1990, La Baconnière. 324 p. Fs 45. – ᴿÉtClas 60 (1992) 161 (Nathalie Frogneux).

651 ᴱCurčić Slobodan, Mouriki Doula, The twilight of Byzantium; aspects of cultural and religious history in the Late Byzantine Empire: Colloquium Princeton 8-9 May 1989. Princeton 1991, Univ. xx-281 p.; $39 [Manuscripta 36,159, titles sans pp.].

652 ᴱDomenicy Marc, Dor Juliette, al., Phonological Reconstruction [Atti 3º Simposio, Liège 4-5 dic. 1987]: Belgian Journal of Linguistics 3. Bru 1988, Univ. 183 p. – ᴿSalesianum 54 (1992) 825s (R. Sabin: titoli senza pp.).

653 a) Dramaturgie et actualité du théâtre antique, Actes du Colloque International de Toulouse, 17-19 oct. 1991: Pallas 38 (1992). 419 p. 0031-0387. 37 art.; 2 infra.

— b) ᴱFerre Lola, al., La ciencia en la España medieval; musulmanes, judíos y cristianos, Actas VII Congreso Internacional, Granada sept. 1991. Granada 1992, Univ. 288 p. 84-86848-39-X [BL 94,137, J. F. Elwolde].

— c) ᴱGallo Italo, PLUTARCO e le scienze; Atti del IV convegno plutarcheo, Genova (Bocca di Magra) 22-25 aprile 1991: I libri di Giano. Genova 1992, Sagep. 434 p. 88-7058-452-6. 22 art.; 4 infra.

654 ᴱGazda Elaine K., (Haeki Anne E.), Roman art in the private sphere; new perspectives on the architecture and decor of the domus, villa, and insula [College Art Association meeting Boston Feb. 1987, 6 papers]. AA 1991, Univ. Michigan. 156 p. (32 of photos). $39.50. 0-472-10196-X. – ᴿClasW 86 (1992s) 148s (Paul Rehak: excellent).

654* ᴱGély Suzanne, Sens et pouvoirs de la nomination [name-giving] dans les cultures hellénique et romaine, II. Le nom et la métamorphose [18 art., dont 4 d'une table ronde 18.I.1990 sur le nom, 6 d'une autre 2.II.1989 sur l'Utopie de PLATON]: Séminaire d'études des mentalités antiques. Montpellier 1992, Univ. 325 p. – ᴿRÉAnc 94 (1992) 478s (Lucienne Deschamps).

655 Giannantoni Gabriele, present., Sesto EMPIRICO e il pensiero antico, CNR Sestri Levante 28.V-1.VI.1991: Elenchos 13 (1992). 366 p.

655* ᴱGigante Marcello, VIRGILIO e gli Augustei: congrès Castel d'Oro 17-19 nov. 1989. N 1990, Giannini. 284 p. – [AntClas 62, 318-321, P.-J. Dehon].

656 a) ᴱHägg Robin, Nordquist Güllog C., Celebrations of death and divinity in the Bronze Age Argolid: (ᶠPERSSON A.), Proceedings of the Sixth International Symposium at the Swedish Institute of Athens, 11-13 June 1988: SvInstA 40, 1990 ⇒ 7,641*: ᴿAntClas 61 (1992) 474-6 (J. Driessen).

— b) Hamesse J., présent., Rencontres de cultures dans la philosophie médiévale; traductions et traducteurs de l'antiquité tardive au XIVᵉ siècle: Lv TCongrès 11. Cassino 1990, Univ. viii-402 p.; 8 fig. Fb 1750. 18 art.

— c) ᴱIliescu M., Marxgut W., Latin vulgaire, latin tardif; Actes du IIIᵉ colloque internat. sur le latin vulgaire et tardif (Innsbruck, 2-5 sept. 1991). Tü 1992, Niemeyer. x-368 p. DM 158 [RHE 88,193*].

— d) ᴱJenkyns Richard, The legacy of Rome; a new appraisal. Ox 1992, Univ. xi-479 p.; 32 pl. £25 [ClasR 43,150, E.J. *Kenney*: successor to ᴱBAILEY C. 1923].

657 ᴱJouan F., *Motte* A., Mythe et politique, Actes du Colloque de Liège, sept. 1989: BtLett 257. P 1990, BLettres. 325 p.; 5 fig. – ᴿRÉLat 69 (1991) 336 (A. *Thill*).

658 ᴱKellens Jean, *Dor* Juliette, La reconstruction des laryngales [Liège 4-5.XII.1987]: Univ. Liège Bt ph/L 253. P 1990, BLettres. 181 p. 7 art. – ᴿAulaO 10 (1992) 156-8 (P. *Villar*).

659 ᴱKlagge James C., *Smith* Nicholas D., Methods of interpreting PLATO and his dialogues [Virginia State Univ. March 1985]: StAnc-Phil supp. Ox 1992, UP. vii-280 p. £35. 8 art. [ClasR 43, 439, G. B. *Kerferd*].

659* ᴱKonstan David, Documenting gender; women and men in non-literary classical texts [meetings Brown Univ. 28-29 Oct. 1988 'Women and ancient medicine' and AmPgAsn Baltimore Jan. 1989]: Helios 19,1s (1992) 174 p.; ill. 9 art., 2 infra.

660 ᴱKudlien Fridolf, *Durling* Richard J., GALEN's method of healing, 1982 Symposium [Kiel]: StAncMed 1. Leiden 1991, Brill. viii-205 p. ƒ110. – ᴿClasR 42 (1992) 170s (H. *King*).

661 ᴱKugel James L., Poetry and prophccy; the beginning of a literary tradition [1986 Harvard conference]. Ithaca NY 1990, Cornell Univ. xii-251 p. $35; pa. $13. 0-8014-9568-7. 10 art.; p.45-55 Kugel, David the Prophet; p.36-44 *Cooper* Alan, Imagining prophecy [OTAbs 15, p.474]. – ᴿClasR 42 (1992) 200s (K. W. *Grandsen*).

662 ᴱKugler H., (*Michael* E.), Ein Weltbild vor Columbus; die Ebstorfer Weltkarte; interdisziplinäres Colloquium 1988. Weinheim 1991, VCH. 408 p.; 145 fig.; foldout map. DM 158 [RHE 88,17*].

663 ᴱLatacz Joachim, Zweihundert Jahre HOMER-Forschung, Rückblick und Ausblick [Kolloquium Basel Aug. 1989 ... p.30ss, Homerarchäologie nach SCHLIEMANN]: Colloquia Raurica 2. Stu/Lp 1991, Teubner. xii-552 p.; 41 fig. – ᴿGnomon 64 (1992) 481-493 (T. *Krischer*). ➤ 715.

663* ᴱLétoublon Françoise, La langue et les textes en grcc ancien, Actes du Colloque Pierre Chantraine (Grenoble 5-8 sept. 1989). Amst 1992, Gieben. viii-369 p.; portr. 90-5063-066-9. 24 art.; 2 infra

664 ᴱLinders Tullia, *Alroth* Brita, Economics of cult in the ancient Greek world; Uppsala Symposium 1990: Boreas 21. U 1992, Almqvist & W. 99 p. 91-554-3031-7. – 10 art.

665 ᴱLonis Raoul [his art. p.255-270, not as Index omitting *Mossé* C. 271-7], L'Étranger dans le monde grec II, Colloque 2 sur l'Étranger, Nancy 19-21 sept. 1991. Nancy 1992, Presses Univ. 333 p. F 180. 2-86480-619-3. 14 art.; 2 infra.

666 ᴱLópez Aurora, *al.*, La mujer en el mundo mediterráneo antiguo [curso interdisciplinar abril 1989]. Granada 1990, Univ. 248 p. – ᴿHabis 22 (1991) 479-482 (Mercedes *Serrato Garrido*).

666* ᴱLópez-Ferez Juan-Antonio, GALENO; obra, pensamiento e influencia; coloquio internacional Madrid, 22-25 de marzo de 1988. M 1991, Univ. a distancia. 370 p. 84-362-2661-5 [AntClas 62,418s, Danielle *Gourévitch*].

667 ᴱMaclean Ian, *al.*, The political responsibility of intellectuals [Wien, Institut für die Wissenschaften vom Menschen]. C 1990, Univ. xviii-312 p. 0-521-39179-2; -859-2 [TBR 6/1, 56, I. *Markham*: A. *Montefiore* disagreement with P. *Winch* superb].

668 EMaddoli Gianfranco, STRABONE e l'Italia antica (Acquasparta maggio 1987). N 1988, Ed. Scientifiche. 366 p. – RLatomus 51 (1992) 253 (P. *Thollard*).

669 EMattei Jean-François, La naissance de la raison en Grèce; Actes du Congrès de Nice, mai 1987. P 1990, PUF. vii-438 p. – RRÉG 105 (1992) 594-6 (J.-F. *Balaudé*).

669* EMolho Anthony, *al.*, City-states in classical antiquity and medieval Italy; Athens and Rome, Florence and Venice: Brown Univ. colloquium 1989. Stu 1991, Steiner. 648 p.; 49 fig. DM 118 [ClasR 43,123, F. *Millar*].

670 EMoreau Alain, L'initiation; Actes du Colloque international, Montpellier 11-14 avril 1991. Montpellier 1992, Univ. Paul-Valéry. I. 323 p.; II. 318 p. 2-905397-45-4 both. 22 + 18 art.; 3 infra.

671 EMotte André, L'élément orgiastique dans la religion grecque ancienne: IIIe colloque international du CERGA [Centre d'étude de la religion grecque antique], Tripolis 17-19 mai 1991: Kernos 5 (1992) 1-220. 2-251-66257-5; pa.-X. 14 art.

671* EMudry P., *Pigeaud* J., Littérature, médecine, société; les écoles médicales à Rome [colloque Lausanne 1986]: Publ. Fac. Lettres 22. Nantes 1991, Univ. 322 p.; 200 fig. 18 art. [RBgPg 71,134, R. *Chevallier*].

672 a) EMüller Carl W., *al.*, Zum Umgang mit fremden Sprachen in der griechisch-römischen Antike; Kolloquium der Fachrichtungen Klassische Philologie der Univ. Leipzig und Saarbrücken, 21.-22.XI.1989 in Saarbrücken: Palingenesia 36. Stu 1992, Steiner. viii-252 p., p. 233-252 Bibliog. 500 items (J. *Werner, al.*), 3-515-05852-4. 15 art.; 4 infra.

— b) Naldini M., present., La letteratura patristica nei secoli IV e V riferentesi alla persona umana [in]: Atti dell'Accademia Romanistica costantiniana, VIII convegno internazionale, Napoli/Perugia 1990, Ed. Scientifiche/Univ. 768 p. Lit. 100.000. 88-7104-529-7 [Latomus 52,189s, R. *Delmaire*].

— c) EOelkers Jürgen, *Wegenast* Klaus, Das Symbol — Brücke des Verstehens [Symposium Bern Sept. 1989]. Stu 1991, Kohlhammer. 228 p. DM 50. – RTGL 82 (1992) 473 (K. *Hollmann*).

— d) EPalaima Thomas G., *al.*, Studia Mycenaea [18th Eirene Congress, Budapest Aug. 1988]: Živa Antika Mg 7. Skopje 1989. 193-vii p. $30 (Austin, Texas Univ.). – RMinos 25s (1990s) 455-9 (Ruth *Palmer*).

— e) EPani Mario, Continuità e trasformazione fra Repubblica e Principato: Bari 27-28.I. 1989: Univ. Bari Ant. 8. Bari 1991, Edipuglia. 314 p. [ClasR 43,112, Catharine *Edwards*].

— f) EPowell Anton, Roman poetry and propaganda in the age of Augustus [< London Classical Society seminar]. L 1992, Bristol Classical. ix-181 p.; 8 fig. [ClasR 43,296, R. *Nisbet*].

673 EProntera Francesco, Geografia storica della Grecia antica: IV incontro perugino di storia della storiografia, Acquasparta 29.V.-1.VI.1989. Bari 1991, Laterza. 287 p. Lit. 44.000. 88-420-3837-2. 14 art., 3 infra. – RRÉG 105 (1992) 602s (J.-N. *Corvisier*).

674 ERawson Beryl, Marriage, divorce, and children in ancient Rome [Canberra 1988]. Canberra 1992, Humanities Research Centre. xiv-252 p.; 10 fig.; 9 pl. 0-19-814918-2. 9 art.; 2 infra.

675 a) ERich John, The city in late antiquity: [Leicester-Nottingham conference-series 1986-8, 2 (1. was City & country, EWallace-Hadrill]: Studies

in ancient society 3. L 1992, Routledge. x-204 p. – 0-415-06855-X. 8 art.; 1 infra ➤ g354.

— b) ᶠRUDHARDT Jean: Orphisme et Orphée, ᴱBorgeaud Philippe: Recherches et rencontres 3. Genève 1991, Droz. 293 p. 15 art.; 2 infra [AnPg 62, p. 1000; AntClas 62,305s, Vinciane *Pirenne-Delforge*; ClasR 43,309-312, R. *Gordon*: also less approvingly on BÖHME R.].

— c) ᴱSabbah Guy, Le latin médical; la constitution d'un langage scientifique; réalités et langage de la médecine dans le monde romain; Actes du IIIᵉ colloque international 'Textes médicaux latins antiques' (Saint-Étienne 11-13 sept. 1989): Centre Palerme Mém. 10. S.-Étienne 1991, Univ. 438 p. F 200. 2-86272-016-X. – ᴿLatomus 51 (1992) 935s (L. *Rippinger*).

676 **Santori** Claudio segr., Atti del convegno internazionale sulla Peregrinatio Egeriae, nel centenario della pubblicazione del Codex Aretinus 405 (già Aretinus VI,3), Arezzo 23-25 ott. 1987. Arezzo 1990, Accademia Petrarca. 370 p. 18 art., 12 infra.

676* ᴱSchousboe Karen, *Larsen* Mogens T., Literacy and society [K Univ. Center for Research in the Humanities meeting]. K 1989, Akademisk. 87-500-2784-0. – ᴿDiscEg 20 (1991) 101-6 (M. *Megally*: shows influence of J. GOODY, E. A. HAVELOCK, W. J. ONG).

677 ᴱSlavazzi Fabrizio, al., Milano capitale, 'felix temporis reparatio', Atti Milano 8-11.III.1990/1992 ➤ 706.

677* ᴱStadter Philip A., PLUTARCH and the historical tradition [1989 Oxford International Plutarch Society conference]. L 1992, Routledge. viii-188 p.; 2 fig. £35 [ClasR 43,29, J. *Moles*].

678 ᴱSvartvik Jan, Directions in corpus linguistics ['the use of large collections of text available in machine-readable form' p. 7]; proceedings of Nobel Symposium 82, Stockholm 4-8 Aug. 1991: TrendsLingStMg 65. B 1992, Mouton de Gruyter. xii-487 p. 3-11-012826-8. 17 art.

679 a) ᶠTRENDALL A. D.: Greek colonists and native populations; symposium Canberra 1985, ᴱDescœudres J. Canberra/Ox 1990, Humanities Research Centre / Clarendon. xxxix-704 p.; 161 fig.; 54 pl. £85. ᴿClasR 42 (1992) 143-5 (Z. H. *Archibald*).

— b) ᴱVauchez André, Les textes prophétiques et la prophétie en Occident (XIIᵉ-XVIᵉ siècle); [Jean de Roquetaillade; ... Hildegarde, Jeanne d'Arc]: Actes de la Table Ronde, URA 1011 CNRS, Chantilly 30-31.V.1988. R 1990, École Française. 395 p. [RHE 88,837, D. *Verhelst*].

— c) ᴱVerdon Timothy, *Henderson* John, Christianity and the Renaissance; image and religious imagination in the quattrocento [1985 Tallahassee/ Florence symposium]. NY 1990, Syracuse Univ. xxii-611 p. $55; pa. $10. 24 art. [ChH 62,552s, Meredith J. *Gill*: high praise].

— d) ᴱVitolo G., *Mottola* F., Scrittura e produzione documentaria nel Mezzogiorno longobardo, Atti del convegno, Badia di Cava, 3-5 ott. 1990. 502 p.; 146 fig. Lit. 65.000. – ᴿStudi Storici 33 (1992) 907-917 (L. *Miglio*) [RHE 88,187*].

— e) ᴱVogt-Spira Gregor, Strukturen der Mündlichkeit der römischen Literatur [Tagung]: ScriptaOralia 19, A4. Tü 1990, Narr. 320 p. DM 84. 3-8293-4473-0 [Latomus 52, 165, J. *Dangel*].

— f) ᴱWallis Richard T., *Bergman* Jay, Neoplatonism and Gnosticism [Oklahoma Univ. 1984 conference, International Society for Neoplatonic Studies]. Albany 1992, SUNY. xi-531 p. $20 [ClasR 43,307s, H. J. *Blumenthal*].

680 ᴱWood Mark, *Queiroga* Francisco, Current research on the Romanization of the western provinces; meeting Oxford 13-14.XI.1989: BAR-S 575. Ox 1992, BAR. vi-121 p. 0-86054-728-0. 10 art.; → k277.

A2.7 *Acta* orientalistica.

681 ᴱBusi Giulio, Viaggiatori ebrei; Berichte jüdischer Reisender vom Mittelalter bis in die Gegenwart: Atti del Congresso europeo dell'Assoc. Italiana per lo Studio del Giudaismo, San Miniato 4-5 nov. 1991; StT 9. Bo 1991, Assoc. ISG. 159 p. 10 art.; 3 infra.

682 ᴱCameron Averil, *Conrad* Lawrence I., The Byzantine and Early Islamic Near East, 1. Problems in the literary source material, Workshop 1: StL-AntEIslam 1. Princeton 1992, Darwin. xiv-428 p. 0-87850-080-4 [OIAc 5,16].

682* ᴱCanivet P., *Rey-Coquais* J.-P., La Syrie de Byzance à l'Islam, viiᵉ-viiiᵉ s., Actes du colloque internat. Lyon/Paris 11-15 sept. 1990: Publ. 137. Damas 1992, Inst. Français. xx-367 p.; ill. [RHE 88,253*].

683 ᴱCharpin D., *Joannès* F., La circulation des biens, des personnes et des idées dans le Proche-Orient ancien; Actes de la 38ᵉ Rencontre Assyriologique Internationale, Paris 8-10 juillet 1991. P 1992, RCiv. 416 p. 2-86538-228-1. – 40 art.; 32 infra.

684 ᴱDemarée R. J., *Egberts* A., Village voices; proceedings of the Symposium 'Texts from Deir el-Medîna and their interpretation', Leiden May 31-June 1, 1991: Publ. 13. Leiden 1992, Centre of Non-Western Studies. vii-147 p. 90-73782-16-3. – 8 art. + bibliog.

685 ᴱDévényi Kinga, *Iványi* Tamás, Proceedings of the colloquium on Arabic grammar, Budapest 1-7 September 1991: The Arabist 33. Budapest 1991, Eötvös Univ. 375 p. $45 [JAOS 112,728].

686 *a)* ᴱEid Mushira, Perspectives on Arabic Linguistics; papers from the First / Second Symposium [Univ. Utah 1987/8]: AmstStLing 63.72. Amst/Ph 1990, Benjamins. xiii-293 p.; $97 / xiv-330 p.; $74. – ᴿJAOS 112 (1992) 143 (M. G. *Carter*).

— *b)* ᴱComrie Bernard, *Mushira* Eid, Perspectives on Arabic Linguistics III: papers from the Third Annual Symposium: AmstCurrLing 80. Amst/Ph 1991, Benjamins. xii-274 p. $40 [JAOS 112,728].

686* ᴱDomergue Claude, *al.*, Spectacula I. Gladiateurs et amphithéâtres; Actes du colloque, Lattes 26-29 mai 1987. Lattes 1990, Imago. 316 p. F 180. 2-9501-1586-8. – ᴿNikephoros 4 (1991) 288-291 (Augusta *Hönle*).

687 ᴱEllis Maria D., Nippur at the centennial: Rencontre Assyriologique Internationale 35, Philadelphia 1988: Kramer Occas. Publ. 14. Ph 1992, Univ. Museum. xix-368 p.; portr.; ill.; p. 337-365 bibliog. (*Bregstein* Linda B., *Schneider Tammi* J.). 0-884171-01-4. – 23 art.; infra.

688 ᴱFortin Michel [*Grayson* A. Kirk, present.], The origin of prophecy; seers, soothsayers, and prophets in the cradle of civilization: Symposium 21 Sept. 1991]: BCanadMesop 23 (1992) 7-44. 5 art. → 3644.

689 ᴱFrancfort H. P., Nomades et sedentaires en Asie centrale; apports de l'archéologie et d'ethnologie; Actes du colloque franco-soviétique, Alma Ata Kazakhstan, 17-26 octobre 1987. P 1990, CNRS. 240 p. 2-222-04427-8 [OIAc 3,31, excerpted].

690 ᴱGodlewski Włodzimierz, Coptic Studies; Acts of the Third International Congress, Warsaw 20-25 August 1984 → 7,617, Wsz 1990, Éd. Scientifiques. 506 p.; ill. 83-01-07663-1. 63 art.; 15 infra.

691 ᴱHaas Volkert, Aussenseiter und Randgruppen [altorientalischer Gesellschaften, 3. Konstanzer Symposion, 5.-8. Juni 1989]: Xenia 32. Konstanz 1992, Univ. 237 p. 3-87940-429-1. 10 art., infra.

692 ᴱKedar B. Z.,   The Horns of Ḥaṭṭin; Proceedings of the 2d Conference Crusades–Latin East, J/Haifa 2-6 July 1987. J/L 1992, Yad
BenZvi / Variorum. 368 p.; 91 fig.; 12 pl.; 10 maps + foldout [RHE
87,398*].

692* ᴱKhalidov A. B., Archaeographia orientalis (Proceedings of a conference
on Oriental archival documents, Leningrad 1-4 March 1988). Moskva
1990, Akademia Nauk. 204 p. – ᴿJRAS (1991) 394s (J. M. *Rogers*).

693 ᴱMawet F., *Talon* P., D'Imhotep à Copernic; astronomie et mathé-
matiques des origines orientales au Moyen Âge; Actes du colloque Université Libre de Bruxelles 3-4 novembre 1989: Lettres Orientales 2. Lv
1992, Peeters. 158 p. 90-6831-421-3. 6 art. on Babylonian astronomy
+ 2 infra ➤ g708.

694 *a*) 'Militia Christi' e crociata nei secoli XI-XIII; Atti della XI Settimana,
Mendola 28 ag.-1 sett. 1989. Mi 1992, ViPe. xii-858 p.; 2 fig. Lit.
130.000 [RHE 87,398*].
— *b*) ᴱRassart-Debergh Marguerite, *Ries* Julien, [I. ᴀᴛʏᴀ Aziss, mém.; II.
Lᴇꜰᴏʀᴛ Louis T. (1879-1959), mém.], Actes du IVᵉ Congrès Copte, Louvain-la-Neuve 5-10 septembre 1988: Publ. 40s. LvN 1992, Univ. Catholique Inst. Orientaliste. I. Art et archéologie, xviii-231 p.; II. De la linguistique au Gnosticisme, xi-503 p. 33 art.; 6 infra, 22 al. ➤ vol. 9.
— *c*) Sᴘᴇɪᴊᴇʀ's Sanskrit syntax centennial [14 art. from USA symposia 1986
and 1987], Studies in Sanskrit syntax, ᴱHock Hans H. Delhi 1991,
Motilal Banarsidass. xi-244 p.; bibliog. *Deshpande* M. M. rs. 180. – ᴿBSO
55 (1992) 141s (J. C. *Wright*).

695 ᴱTapper Richard, Islam in modern Turkey; religion, politics and literature in a secular state [London symposium 1988]. L 1991, Tauris.
v-314 p. £35. 1-85043-321-6. 11 art. [BO 50,289, J. M. *Landau*]. – ᴿRel-
StR 18 (1992) 348 (G. *Yocul*).

695* ᴱVersteegh Kees, *Carter* Michael G., Studies in the History of Arabic
Grammar II: Proceedings of the 2d symposium on the history of Arabic
grammar, Nijmegen 27 April-1 May 1987: StHistLangSc 56. Amst/Ph
1990, Benjamins. x-319 p. $66 [JAOS 112,730].

696 ᴱVogelzang Marianna E., *Vanstiphout* Herman L. J., Mesopotamian epic
literature; oral or aural [1990 Groningen workshop]. Lewiston NY 1992,
Mellen. xi-320 p. [RelStR 19,343, D. I. *Owen*: first major inroad of
Pᴇʀʀʏ-Lᴏʀᴅ Hᴏᴍᴇʀ methods].

696* ᴱWexler Albrecht, *Hammerschmidt* Ernst, Proceedings of the 32d international congress for Asian and North African Studies, Hamburg 25-
30 Aug. 1986: ZDMG Supp. 9. Stu 1992, Steiner. lxxvii-719 p.; 3-515-
04808-1. 15 sections, numerous brief summaries; 16 panels.

697 — ᴱHarrak A., [I. West Asia and North Africa] Contacts between
cultures; Selected papers from the 33d international congress of Asian and
North African Studies, Toronto Aug. 15-25, 1990. Vol. 1 [of 4] xiv-493 p.
0-7734-92003. 84 art.; 10 infra.

698 Zinguer Ilana, Miroirs de l'altérité et voyages au Proche Orient; Colloque international de l'Institut d'Histoire et de Civilisation Française
de l'Université de Haifa 1987. Genève 1991, Slatkine. 307 p. 2-05-
101155-9 [OIAc 3,42, excerpted].

A2.9   *Acta* **archaeologica** [reports ➤ T7.8].

699 AIA 1991: 93d annual meeting of the Archaeological Institute of
America, 27-30 Dec. 1991: AJA 96 (1992) 327-376: some 200 summaries
with index; a few infra.

700 *a*) ᴱ**Altan** C. T., Homo edens [colloquio Verona aprile 1987]. Mi 1989, Diapress. 350 p. – ᴿAevum 65 (1991) 189 (G. *Amiotti*).
— *b*) ᴱ**Assmann** J., Die Erfindung des inneren Menschen. Gü c. 1992, Mohn [TLZ 118,936 sans date].
— *c*) ᴱ**Barman** Lawrence M., The art of Amenhotep III; Symposium Cleveland Museum of Art 20-21 Nov. 1987. Cleveland/Bloomington 1990, with Indiana Univ. Press. xii-92 p.; 27 pl. 8 art.; 3 infra. 0-940717-01-8.

701 **Bartoloni** Gilda, *al.*, Anathema; regime delle offerte e vita dei santuari nel Mediterraneo antico, Roma, 15-18 giugno 1989 = ScAnt 3s (1989s, stampato dic. 1991). 927 p. 62 art.; 13 infra.

702 *a*) **Bienkowski** Piotr (p. 1-12.99-112), Early Edom and Moab; the beginning of the Iron Age in southern Jordan; Colloquium Liverpool, 9-12 May 1991: ShfArchMg 7. Shf 1992, Collis. xiii-202 p.; ill. 0-906090-45-8. – 16 art., infra.
— *b*) ᴱ**Bietak** Manfred, The Bronze Age in the Eastern Mediterranean; Acts of the Second International Colloquium on Absolute Chronology [High, Middle or Low 2], 12-15.VIII.1990, Haindorf, N-Austria: Ägypten und Levante 3 (1992) 159 p. 19 art.; 13 infra.
— *c*) ᴱ**Bodson** Liliane, *Libois* Roland, L'histoire des connaissances zoologiques et ses rapports avec la Zoologie, l'Archéologie, la Médecine vétérinaire, l'Ethnologie: (i) 4 mars 1989; (ii) Contributions, 17 mars 1990. Liège 1990s, Univ. iv-75 p., Fb 275; iii-123 p., Fb 450 [RBgPg 71,129, P. *Fontaine*].

703 ᴱ**Brink** Edwin C. M. van den, The Nile Delta in transition; 4th-3rd Millennium B.C., Proceedings of the seminar, Cairo 21-24 Oct. 1990, Netherlands Inst. J 1992, Israel Exploration. xix-484 p.; ill. maps. 95-221-015-3. – 40 art.; plures infra.

703* Bulletin de la Société Française d'Archéologie Classique 24 (1990s) = RArchéol (1992) 169-218.

704 Carthage et son territoire dans l'antiquité: Histoire et archéologie de l'Afrique du Nord, Cong. 113 des Soc. savantes, Strasbourg 5-9 avril 1988, I. P 1990, CTHS. 257 p.; ill. F 250. 2-7355-0201-5. – ᴿAntClas 61 (1992) 744-7 (J. *Debergh*).

705 ᴱ**Charlesworth** James H., *Weaver* Walter P., What has archaeology to do with faith?: Faith and scholarship colloquies. L/Ph 1992, SCM/Trinity. xi-116 p. $14 pa. 1-56338-038-2 [TDig 40,192; OIAc 3,16].

705* ᴱ**Chavalas** Mark W., *Hayes* John L., New horizons in the study of ancient Syria: BtMesop 25. Malibu 1992, Undena. x-232 p.; map. 0-89003-334-2; pa. -3-4. – 8 art.; infra.

706 ᴱ[Sena] **Chiesa** Semma, *Arslan* Ermanno A., [→ 677 ᴱ*Slavazzi*] Felix temporis reparatio; Atti del convegno archeologico internazionale, Milano Capitale dell'Impero Romano, 8-11 marzo 1990. Mi 1992, ET. 469 p.; ill. 31 art.; 4 infra.

707 ᴱ**Cleere** H. F., Archaeological heritage management in the modern world: One World 9. L 1989, Unwin Hyman. xxiv-318 p.; 26 fig. $60. 0-04-445028-1. – ᴿAJA 96 (1992) 166 (Brona G. *Simon*).

708 ᴱ**Courtils** Jacques, *al.*, De Anatolia antiqua I. Travaux et recherches de l'Institut Français d'Études Anatoliennes: Bt 32. P 1991, J. Maisonneuve. 344 p. [OIAc 1,14, excerpted].

709 ᴱ**Cowan** C. Wesley, *Watson* Patty Jo (*al.*), The origins of agriculture; an international perspective [Symposium Los Angeles 1985]: Smithsonian Archaeological Inquiry. Wsh 1992, Smithsonian Institution. xvi-224 p. 0-87474-990-3; pa. -1-3. 10 art.; → k18.

709* ᴱDescœudres Jean-Paul, The archaeology of the Aeolian islands; proceedings of the conferences held at the universities of Melbourne and Sydney on 28/29 May and 5 June, 1992: Mediterranean Archaeology 5s (1992s) 1-47.

710 a) ᴱElizbarashvili I. (+ 4 al.), IV. Symposium international sur l'art géorgien. Tbilisi 1983.

— b) ᴱEuzennat Maurice, L'armée romaine d'Afrique et la IIIᵉ légion Auguste: Table Ronde Lourmarin, 12-13.IX.1989: AntAfr 27 (1991) 17-19 (-149).

— c) ᴱFacchini Fiorenzo, al., La religiosità nella preistoria [< Meeting Rimini 1988]: Di fronte e attraverso 287. Mi 1991, Jaca. 112 p. [Salesianum 55,581, R. Bratky].

— d) ᴱFeugère Michel, Rolley Claude, La vaisselle tardorépublicaine en bronze; Table Ronde CNRS, Lattes 26-28 avril 1990 (UPR 290, GDR 196 Dijon). Dijon 1991, Univ. Bourgogne. viii-201 p. – ᴿRArchéol (1993) 151s (R. Adam).

— e) Fickes Jean-Luc [introd. 13-17s synthèse], Tissage, corderie, vannerie; approches archéologiques, ethnologiques, technologiques: 9ᵉ rencontres Antibes 20-22 oct. 1988, CNRS. Juan-les-Pins 1989, Musée/APDCA. 317 p. F 140. 2-904110-10-5. 27 art., 6 infra.

f) ᴱGaraffo S., La villa romana di Piazza Armerina, Univ. Catania IV Riunione Arch. Class. 23.IX-1.X.1983: Cronache d'Archéologia 23 (1984). Catania 1988, Univ. 200 p. – ᴿBMosAnt (= AIEMA) 13 (1990s) 361-373 (N. Duval, très détaillé).

711 ᴱGeertman H., Jang J.J. De, Munus non ingratum; proceedings of the int. symposium on VITRUVIUS' 'De Architectura' and the Hellenistic and Republican architecture, Leiden 20-23.I.1987: Babesch supp. 2. Leiden 1989, 239 p.; ill.

712 Ghicideanu Ion, présent., Le colloque 'Dépôts en pré- et protohistoire', 28-29.IV.1992, Bucureşti (en roumain): (Sc)IstVArh 43,4 (1992) 335-9 [-431].

713 ᴱHackens Tony, Navies and commence of the Greeks, the Carthaginians and the Etruscans in the Tyrrhenian Sea: symposium Ravello Jan. 1987: PACT 20 (1988). Strasbourg 1990, Conseil de l'Europe. 512 p.; ill. Fb 4000. 36 art., 7 infra.

713* ᴱHauck Karl, Der historische Horizont der Götterbild-Amulette aus der Übergangsepoche von der Spätantike zum Frühmittelalter: Colloquium 28.11-1.12.1988, Bad Homburg: AbhGö 200. Gö 1992, Vandenhoeck & R. 582 p. 53 pl. 3-525-82587-0. 20 art.; ➤ e127.

714 ᴱHeres Huberta, Kunze Max, Die Welt der Etrusker, internationales Kolloquium, Berlin 24.-26. Okt. 1988. B 1990, Akademie. 369 p.; 70 pl. – ᴿSalesianum 54 (1992) 364-6 (R. della Casa: in occasione di una mostra; titoli senza pp.).

715 ᴱHerrmann Joachim, Heinrich SCHLIEMANN; Grundlagen und Ergebnisse moderner Archäologie 100 Jahre nach Schliemanns Tod [Internationale Tagung Berliner Akademie. 405 p. 3-05-01853-4. 47 art.; 10 infra. ➤ 663.

716 ᴱHicks Sheila, al., Airborne particles and gases, and their impact on the cultural heritage and its environment; Ravello Dec. 12-13, 1989 and Dec. 14-16, 1990; PACT 33. Strasbourg 1991, Council of Europa. 287 p.; ill. Fb 3000. 0257-8727.

717 ᴱHoepfner Wolfram, Schwandner Ernst-Ludwig, Hermogenes und die hochhellenistische Architektur; Internationales Kolloquium in Berlin,

28.-29. Juli 1988. Mainz 1990, von Zabern. ix-127 p.; 115 fig. DM 78. –
RClasR 42 (1992) 147s (R. A. *Tomlinson*).
718 EHoffmann Adolf, *al.* (*Schwandner* E., *Hoepfner* W. ...), Bautechnik der
Antike; Internationales Kolloquium in Berlin vom 15.-17. Februar 1990,
DAI/SemKlasArch: DAI Architekturreferat Disk. 5. Mainz 1991, von
Zabern. x-265 p.; ill. 3-8053-1245-8 [OIAc 3,24, excerpted].
719 EJohnson Janet H., Life in a multi-cultural society; Egypt from Cambyses to Constantine; symposium with Fourth International Congress of
Demotists, Chicago Oriental Institute, September 4-8, 1990: SAOC 51. Ch
1992, Univ. Or. Inst. xxvii-514 p. 0-918986-84-2 [OIAc 5,26, excerpted].
720 ELaffineur Robert, *Basch* Lucien, Thalassa; l'Égée préhistorique et la
mer; Actes de la troisième Rencontre égéenne internationale de l'Univ.
de Liège, station de recherches sous-marine et océanographiques, Calvi,
Corse (23-25 avril 1990): Aegaeum 7. Liège 1991, Univ. HistArtGrèce.
322 p.; 65 p. [OIAc 5,28].
720* ELaurens Annie-France, *Pomian* K., L'anticomanie; la collection d'antiquités aux 18e et 19e siècles [Colloque Montpellier 1988]: Civilisations et
sociétés 86. P 1992, ÉPHÉ soc. 351 p.; ill. 25 art. [RStFen 21,249, E.
Acquaro].
721 ELeahy Anthony, Libya and Egypt c. 1300-750 B.C. [London Centre of
Near and Middle Eastern Studies 1990]. L 1990, School Or-Af.St. viii-
200 p.; 8 fig. 0-7286-0174-5. – RBO 49 (1992) 701-3 (J. von *Beckerath*).
722 ELe Guen-Pollet Brigitte, *Pelon* Olivier, La Cappadoce méridionale
jusqu'à la fin de l'époque romaine; état de recherches: Actes du colloque
d'Istanbul, Institut Français d'Études Anatoliennes, 13-14 avril 1987. P
1991, RCiv. 90 p.; 15 pl. 2-86538-225-7 [OIAc 3,28].
ELevine Lee I., The Galilee in Late antiquity 1989/92 ➤ 475c.
723 ELong Austin, *al.*, Proceedings of the 14th international radiocarbon
conference, Tucson May 20-24, 1991: Radiocarbon 34/3 (1992) xxiv +
p. 277-942. 88 art., 1 infra.
724 *Lordkapanidze* O. D., (p. 8-29) *al.*, Ⓖ The Black Sea Littoral in the
7th-5th centuries B.C.; literary sources and archaeology: Black Sea Littoral
Symposium 5, Vani 1987. Tbilisi 1990, Metsniereba. 479 p. 28 art. Ⓖ (or
Georgian) + 15; infra.
725 EMcGovern P. E., *Notis* M. D., Cross-craft and cross-cultural interactions in ceramic [American Ceramic Soc. 89th Annual Meeting,
Pittsburgh 27-28 April 1987]: Ceramics and Civilization 4. Westerville OH
1989, Amer. Ceramic Soc. 387 p.; 201 fig. $73. 0-916094-48-0. – RAJA
96 (1992) 168-170 (Martha S. *Joukowski*).
726 EMastino Attilio, L'Africa romana; Atti del VII / VIII / IX Convegno:
Sassari 15-17 dic. 1989 / Cagliari 14-16 dic. 1990 / Nuoro 13-15 dic. 1991.
Sassari 1990/1/2, Gallizzi, (1989/90) 1096 p. (2 vol.) Lit. 60,000 [AION 51
(1991) 97-107 (F. *Vattioni*)] – (1990/1) 637 p.; p. 639-1178 [70 art.; 4 infra]
– (1991/2) 1152 p.; 248 pl. [AtenRom 38,141, tit. pp.].
727 EMaxfield Valerie A., *Dobson* Michael J., Roman frontier studies 1989,
XVth international congress. Exeter 1991, Univ. viii-312 p.; ill. –
RBonnJbb 192 (1992) 650-3 (K. *Wachtel*).
727* EMeijer Diederik J. W., Natural phenomena; their meaning, depiction
and description in the Ancient Near East [Amst symposium July 6-8,
1989; FLoon Maurits van]: Verh. Ned. Akad. lett. 152. Amst 1992,
North-Holland. viii-306 p. 0-444-85759-1. – 12 art.; 4 infra.
728 EMellars P., *Stringer* C., The human revolution; behavioral and
biological perspectives on the emergence of modern humans [Cambridge

1987]. E 1989, Univ. 800 p. 34 art. – ᴿCamArch 1,1 (1991) 140-4 (P. *Rowley-Conwy*).

728* ᴱ**Mertens** Jozef, *Lambrechts* Roger, Comunità indigene e problemi della romanizzazione nell'Italia centro-meridionale (IV-III° sec. av. J.-C.; Colloque international, 50ᵉ anniv. Academia Belgica, 1-3 fév. 1990: ÉtPg 29. Bru/R 1991, Inst. Hist. Belg. 252 p.; 70 fig.; 1 plan. [RBgPg 71,202, R. *Chevallier*].

729 ᴱ**Mudry** Philippe, *Pigeaud* Jackie, Les écoles médicales à Rome; Actes du 2ème Colloque international sur les textes médicaux latins antiques, Lausanne, Sept. 1986: (Univ. Nantes) Univ. Lausanne, Lettres XXXIII. Genève 1991, Droz. 319 p. 18 art.; 2 infra ➤ k55. – ᴿBStLat 22 (1992) 93-99 (Paola *Migliorini*).

729* ᴱ**Pochmarski** Erwin, Akten des 1. internationalen Kolloquiums über Probleme des Provinzialrömischen Kunstschaffens, Graz 27.-30. April 1989, I: MittGraz (Arch. Ges. Steiermark) 3s (1989s). 172 p.; 57 pl. 13 art.; 2 infra.

730 *Porada* Edith, present., Chronologies in Old World Archaeology; archaeological seminar at Columbia University 1989s]: JANES 21 (1992) 117s(-172).

731 ᴱ**Quirke** Stephen, Middle Kingdom studies [colloquium 'The Residence and the regions', Cambridge Darwin College, April 1988]. New Malden, Surrey 1991, SIA. 152 p.; 5 fig.; 2 pl. £22. 1-872561-02-0 [BO 50,117, W. K. *Simpson*: important].

732 ᴱ**Randsborg** Klaus [1991 ➤ 7,d299; 1989 ➤ 6,b985], The birth of Europe; archaeology and social development in the first millenium A.D. [colloquium R 1987]: Anal. Inst. Danici 16. R 1989, Bretschneider. 192 p. – ᴿRArchéol (1992) 166-8 (O. *Buchsenschutz*).

733 **Rizakis** A. D., *Archaia*... Achaia und Elis in der Antike; Akten des 1. Internationalen Symposiums, Athen, 19.-21. Mai 1989: Meletemata 13. Athen 1990 [RB 100,449, tit. pp.].

734 ᴱ**Roberts** Charlotte A., *al.*, Burial archaeology; current research, methods and developments [Bradford Univ. conference, May 1988]: BAR-BS 211. Ox 1989. x-293 p.; 56 fig. £18. 0-86054-671-3. – ᴿAJA 96 (1992) 166s (Brenda J. *Baker*).

735 Sesto congresso internazionale di Egittologia, Torino 1-8 sett. 1991 [➤ 7,624], Atti I. [Archeologia]. T 1992. xxx-685 p.; 19 color. pl. 95 art.; 32 infra [Aegyptus 73,281-4, Patricia *Piacentini*].

736 ᴱ**Shaath** Shawqi, Studies in the History and Archaeology of Palestine (Proceedings of the First International Symposium on Palestine Antiquities) [Aleppo University 1981 (Damascus Palestine Archaeological Center = ALECSO), I...] II. Aleppo 1985, Univ. 190 p. + 191-249, pl.; Ⓐ 123 p. + 127-132. 21 art. + Ⓐ 8; infra. – III (1988) 360 p.; 83 fig.; 18 art. [➤ vol.9].

737 ᴱ**Tomasevic-Buck** Teodora, *al.*, Rei cretariae romanae fautorum acta 31s (Congressus 17 ticinensis 1990). Como 1992, New Press. 622 p. 34 art.

738 ᴱ**True** Marion, *Podany* Jerzy, Small bronze sculpture from the ancient world; Getty Museum symposium March 16-17, 1989. Malibu 1990, Getty Museum. 284 p. 0-89236-176-X [OIAc 3,40, excerpted].

738* ᴱ**Vandenabeele** Frieda, *Laffineur* Robert, Cypriote terracottas; proceedings of the First International Conference of Cypriote Studies, Bru-Liège-Amst 29.V-1.VI.1989. Publ. aussi Leventis (Nicosia) 1991. 262 p. 9963-560-12-1 [OIAc 3,40, excerpted].

739 ᴱYoung G. D., Mari in retrospect; fifty years of Mari and Mari studies.
[AOS symposium, Ch. 1983]. WL 1992, Eisenbrauns. xvi-346 p. $32.50.
0-931464-28-5. – ᴿBCanadMesop 24 (1992) 55-57 (D. Bonneterre, franç.;
Eng. en face: starts 'Under the somewhat unclear title' / 'Sous le titre, on
ne peut plus clair').
740 ᴱZaghloul Muna, al., Sites and settlement in Jordan [Fourth Conference,
Lyons Maison de l'Orient]. Amman/Lyons 1992, Dept. Antiquities/Univ.
& Maison de l'Orient Méditerranéen. 421 p. + ❹ 19 p. 60 art.; infra.
740* ᴱZeist W. van, Progress... 'Result of 20 years of International Work
Group for Palaeoethnobotany'. Rotterdam c. 1990, Balkema, ix-350 p.;
88 fig. [Syria 68 (1991) 481].

A3   Opera consultationis – Reference works   .1 plurium separately infra.

741 AnchorBD: The Anchor Bible Dictionary, ᴱFreedman David N. (Herion
Gary A., al.), '1000 contributors, 6 million words'. NY 1992, Doubleday.
I. A-C, lxxviii-1232 p.; II. D-G, xxxv-1190 p.; III. H-J, xxxii-1135 p.; IV.
K-N, xxxv-1162 p.; V. O-Sh, xxxiv-1230 p.; VI. Si-Z, xxxv-1176 p.; ill.;
endmaps. $360. 0-385-19351-3; -60-2; -61-0; -62-9; -63-7; -90-X. –
ᴿBAR-W 18,5 (1992) 10.12.14 (H. Shanks); ChrSchR 22 (1992s) 418-420
(R. W. Wall: unhesitatingly prefers to IDB); ETL 68 (1992) 428-432 (F.
Neirynck, misspelled p. 673s; Index volume awaited 1993); ExpTim 104,4
top choice (1992s) 97-100 (C. S. Rodd); TBR 5,2 (1992s) 9s (W. J.
Houston: superlative despite some slackness of editorial control); UF 24
(1992) 503-6 (O. Loretz: some twenty flaws).
742 ANRW: Aufstieg und Niedergang der Römischen Welt, II. Principat,
ᴱHaase W. [33,4s; 36,4 ➤ 7,659]: 26,1, Religion; vorkonstantinisches
Christentum; NT Sachthemen. xxv-812 p. 33,5s, Sprache und Literatur, 5
(1991) Allgemeines und 2. Jh.: TACITUS (cont.) / SUETONIUS / 6. PLU-
TARCH: p. 3263-3959 / 3963-4915. – 36,5s, Philosophia, einzelne /
Doxographica: 3248-3792 + 25* / 3793-4411. B 1992, de Gruyter.
DM 578; 470; 640; 392; 422. 3-11-010223-4; -2793-8; -3489-6; -2794-6;
3699-6. – ᴿAntClas 61 (1992) 404s (P.-J. Dehon, 333); 459-464 (O.
Ballériaux, 36/2s); 483-5 (Marie-T. Raepsaet-Charlier, 18/3s); AnzAltW 43
(1990) 35-39 & 45 (1992) 3-15 (G. Radke, 16/3; 18/2-4); Gnomon 64
(1992) 256-8 (S. Borzsák, 33/2); Gymnasium 99 (1992) 467-471 (F. Bömer,
33/3-6); RechSR 84 (1993) 481-3 (M. Fédou, 33/5; 26/1); RÉLat 69 (1991)
254-6 (H. Zehnacher, 36/3); StPatav 38 (1991) 165-170 (F. Mora, 18,2;
ZSav-R 107 (1990) 669-681 (D. Nörr: 11/1; 20/2; 25/4-6; 36/2); 108 (1991)
624-634 (D. Nörr: 10/1; 18/2; 33/1); 109 (1992) 733-740 (D. Nörr, 18/3s;
33/2; 36/3).
743 Aug-L: Augustinus-Lexikon, ᴱMeyer Cornelius (Chelius Karl H.) [I,4,
1990 ➤ 7,660]: I,5s, Bellum-Ciuitas Dei, 641-960. Basel 1992, Schwabe.
3-7965-0925-8. – ᴿAntClas 61 (1992) 431s (H. Savon); Gnomon 64 (1992)
357-9 (J. Ramminger); Gregorianum 73 (1992) 565s (F.-A. Pastor, 4);
Helmantica 43 (1992) 275-7 (J. Oroz); RÉLat 69 (1991) 265s (J.-C.
Fredouille); RTPhil 124 (1992) 98s (É. Junod).
744 CAH: Cambridge Ancient History² [7,2, ᴱWalbank F. W., al. 1989
➤ 7,662]: 3/2, The Assyrian and Babylonian Empires, and other states of
the Near East, from the eighth to the sixth centuries B.C., ᴱBoardman J.,
al. C 1991, Univ. xix-906 p.; 51 fig.; 16 maps. 0-521-22717-8. – ᴿAnt-
Clas 61 (1992) 582-4 (Marie-T. Raepsaet-Charlier, 8); Gnomon 64 (1992)
604-9 (J. Wiesehöfer, 4); HZ 253 (1991) 158-160 (C. Meier); JRAS (1991)

262s (J. *Curtis*, 4); RÉLat 69 (1991) 274-281 (J.-C. *Richard*, 7/2; 8); Phoenix 46 (1992) 190-5 (R. A. *Billows*, 7,2: not homogenized enough).
746 Catholicisme, ᴱ**Mathon** G., *al.* 13 [fasc. 59-] 1991 → 7,664: ᴿÉTRel 67 (1992) 151 (A. *Gounelle*, 58s: surtout Révélation, Royaume; discutablement ROBINSON J. A. T., Reveil; mais Revues seules catholiques); RHE 87 (1992) 241s (R. *Aubert*, 59); EsprVie 102 (1992) 700-2 (R. *Desvoyes*, 52-61); Gregorianum 73 (1992) 358s. 554 (J. *Galot*, 57s); RHPR 72 (1992) 314 (P. *Maraval*, 54-58).
746* **CHIran:** Cambridge History of Iran, ᴱ**Gershevitch** I. → 1,885... 6,834: ᴿArOr 60 (1992) 320s (M. *Shaki*, 6).
747 **CHJud:** The Cambridge History of Judaism, 2. ᴱ**Davies** W. D., *Finkelstein* L. 1989 → 5,884... 7,665: ᴿCBQ 54 (1992) 389-391 (H. W. *Basser*); JHS 112 (1992) 206s (B. *McGing*: born old); OLZ 87 (1992) 155-160 (E. *Otto*: solid); ZkT 114 (1992) 94 (R. *Oberforcher*, 2).
748 **DHGE:** Dictionnaire d'Histoire et de Géographie Ecclésiastiques; ᴱ**Aubert** R. [24,138 → 7,667]: 24, **138**, 1990. Herlet-Herzog, 1-256; – **139s**, 1991, -Hoffmann, -768s; – **141**, -Honolulu, -1024; -**142**, -Housseau, -1280. P 1992, Letouzey & A. F 66 chaque. 2-7063-0181-3, vol. 24. – ᴿAnBoll 110 (1992) 206s (J. van der *Straeten*, 132-7); EsprVie 102 (1992) 75-78 (G. de *Pasquier*, 139s).
749 **DictSpir:** Dictionnaire de Spiritualité, ᶠ**Raycz** A., *al.* [15,**99-101** → 7,668]. 16,**102s**, Ubald-Vide, 1-576. P 1992, Beauchesne. – ᴿBLitEc 93 (1992) 426 (S. *Légasse*, 102s); Gregorianum 73 (1992) 163s (M. *Ruiz Jurado*, 92-98); Irénikon 65 (1992) 796s (E. *Lanne*, 102s); Marianum 54 (1992) 489-491 (L. *Gambero*, 99-103); OrChrPer 58 (1992) 637-9 (V. *Poggi*, 102s); RET 51 (1991) 99s. 393-5 (M. *Gesteira Garza*, 115-8); RHE 87 (1992) 242. 539 (R. *Aubert*, 99-101; 112s); RHPR 72 (1992) 312s (M. *Chevallier*, 95-101); VSp 146 (1992) 239-242 (J.-H. *Nicolas*, 91-101).
750 **DizTF** [1990 → 6,837*; 7,669]: ᴱ**Latourelle** R., *Fisichella* R., Dictionnaire de Théologie Fondamentale. P/Montréal 1992, Cerf/Bellarmin. – ᴿCC 143 (1992,2) 426s (F. *Lambiasi*); Lateranum 57 (1991) 616-620 (C. *Dotolo*).
750* — ᵀᴱ**Pié i Ninot** Salvador, Diccionario de Teología Fundamental. M 1992, Paulinas. 1669 p. 84-285-1460-7. – ᴿEstE 67 (1992) 251s (J. J. *Alemany*).
751 **DMA:** Dictionary of the Middle Ages, ᴱ**Strayer** Joseph R. [12,1989; 13, index] → 7,670.
752 **DPA:** ᴱ**Di Berardino** Angelo → 7,671*a*: — Dictionnaire encyclopédique du christianisme ancien, ᵀᴱ*Vial* François, 1990 → 6,839; 7,671*b*: ᴿDLZ 113 (1992) 419s (J. *Irmscher*); RICathP 37 (1991) 187-195 (M. *Quesnel*, *al.*).
753 — Diccionario patrístico y de la antigüedad cristiana: Verdad e Imagen 97s, 1991s → 7,671*d*: ᴿAugM 37 (1992) 389-394 (J. *Oroz Reta*: indispensable); Christus 57,9s (Méx 1992) 82; Carthaginensia 8 (1992) 938-943 (F. *Martínez Fresneda*, también sobre BtPatr 13-15); RET 52 (1992) 243-5 (E. *Tourón*).
754 **DPA** [→ 4,793... 7,671]: Encyclopedia of the early Church, ᴱ**Di Berardino** A., ᵀᴱ*Walford* Adrian [NY 1991 → 7,672*c*]; also C 1992, Clarke. xxv-1130 p. (2 vol.). – ᴿChH 61 (1992) 393s (R. M. *Grant*: authoritative but interesting); RHE 87 (1992) 437 (D. *Bradley*); Tablet 246 (1992) 751 (M. *Walsh*); TLZ 117 (1992) 756s (J. *Irmscher*: post-1980 bibliography added by W. FREND); Worship 66 (1992) 563-5 (R. K. *Seasoltz*).
755 **EncIran** (not = CHIran → 746*): Encyclopedia Iranica, ᴱ**Yarshater** Ehsan [V,6 → 7,761]: V,8, Clothing – Coffee. Costa Mesa 1992, Mazda. P. 785-896 [+ frontmatter]. 0-939214-80-6 [-79-2: < OIAc 5,40].

756 **EncIslam:** Encyclopedia of Islam[2], [E]**Bosworth** C. E., *al.* [117s, 1991 → 7,672]: VII,123s, Mukawkis-Musa, p. 513-640; 125s, Musa-Mutammin, p. 641-768. Leiden 1992, Brill. 90-04-09537-3; -91-8 [OIAc 3,14].

757 **EvKL:** Evangelisches Kirchenlexikon[3], [E]**Fahlbusch** Erwin, *al.* [II, G-K 1989, xi-1534 col.; III, 1990, 1-408 → 7,676] III. L-R. Gö 1992, Vandenhoeck & R. ix-1738 col. 3-525-50132-3; -7-4. – [R]ÉglT 22 (1991) 380-2 (L. *Laberge*, 2); EvT 52 (1992) 546-9 (M. *Beintker*, 2).

758 **ExWNT:** Exegetisches Wörterbuch zum NT[2], [E]**Balz** H. [[1]1978-83 → 60,880... + bibliographic supplements]. Stu 1992, Kohlhammer. I. *Aaron-Enoch*, xxxiii-1150 col.; II. *ex-opsōnion*, viii-1380; III. *pagideúo-ōphélimos*, viii-1242 + 24* (index). DM 599, pa. 298 [NTAbs 37, p. 263s]. 3-17-011205-8; pa. -1-X. – [R]Interpretation 46 (1992) 204 (J. D. *Kingsbury*, Eng. 1 → 7,699).

759 **GLAT:** Grande lessico dell'Antico Testamento, [E][*Botterwick* G. J.] *Ringgren* H., *al.*, [TWAT → 770], [TE]*Catastini* A., *Contini* R., I, Brescia 1988, Paideia. xvi-1119 p. Lit. 195.000. 88-394-0416-3. – [R]ParVi 37 (1992) 224-6 (Ida *Zatelli*).

760 **LexÄg:** Lexikon der Ägyptologie, [E]**Helck** W., VII. Indices [Lfg. 52 → 6,848] Lfg. 55-57 (-VII,8) 545-828 (+ Eng. & French cue-words). 3-447-03216-2; -58-8; -59-6.

761 **LexMA:** Lexikon des Mittelalters, [E]**Giertz** Gernot [for V. 1991 → 7,681 gives Lfg. 3-5 and 8; not 6 or 7]. We now have found reference to 'VIII' (? for VI but omitting Leeuw-Lukas) Lfg. 1, Lukasbilder-Märchen, col. 1-224; and Lfg. 2, Marchettus-Medina, col. 225-448. Mü 1992, Artemis. 3-7608-8851-8; -2-6. – [R]ColcFran 62 (1992) 695-7 (O. *Schmucki*, 5); HZ 253 (1991) 717s (E. *Boshoff*, 4); JbÖsByz 41 (1991) 316s (W. *Hörandner*, 4).

762 **NBL:** Neues Bibel-Lexikon, [E]**Görg** M., *Lang* B., [I. 1991 → 7,682]; II. Lfg **6**, Haar-Herr, col. 1-128; 1991. – Lfg **7**, -Jesus, -322, 1992; **8**, Jesaja [col. 317-322 wiederholt]-Klage, 1992. – 3-545-23057-0; -8-9; -9-7. – [R]SNTU A-17 (1992) 244 (A. *Fuchs*, 1,1); TLZ 117 (1992) 264.734s (R. *Stahl*, 1,5; 2,6); ZAW 104 (1992) 303 (H.-C. *Schmitt*, Lfg 4-6); ZkT 114 (1992) 188s (J. M. *Oesch*, Lfg 4s).

763 **NDizTB:** Nuovo dizionario di teologia biblica, [E]**Rossano** P., *al.* 1990 → 6,852; 7,683: [R]Lateranum 58 (1992) 497-9 (S. *Lanza*).

764 **RAC:** Reallexikon für Antike und Christentum, [E]**Dassmann** Ernst [XV, 117-121, 1991 → 7,684]: **122s**, Homilie-Honorar, 161-480; – **124**, -Horoskop, -640; – **125**, -Hund, -800. Stu 1992, Hiersemann. 3-7772-9202-8; -16-8; -23-1. – [R]JTS 43 (1992) 637-647 (C. P. *Bammel*, 105-112: notes Hermeneutik, J. *Pépin*; Hesekiel, E. *Dassmann*; Hexaemeron, J. van *Winden*; also Heilig, Herr-, and much on gnosis); VigChr 46 (1992) 307-9 (J. C. M. van *Winden*, 116-120); ZKG 103 (1992) 242-258 (W. *Schneemelcher*, 99-115).

765 **RLA:** Reallexikon der Assyriologie, [E]**Edzard** Dietz O., *al.*, 7 (1990) → 6,853*; 7,685: [R]OLZ 87 (1992) 38s (H. *Klengel*, 7,5-8); TLZ 117 (1992) 420-2.737-9 (H. *Seidel*, 13s).

766 **SDB:** Supplément au Dictionnaire de la Bible, [E]**Briend** Jacques, *Cothenet* Édouard [XI, 64s 1990 → 7,686]: XII, 66, Satan (et démons) – Scribes. P 1992, Letouzey et Âne. Col. 1-256. F 300 [[R]RB 100,299s, R. J. *Tournay*, 63,64A; 101,138].

767 **TDOT:** Theological dictionary of the Old Testament [TWAT → 770], [T]*Green* D., 6, 1990 → 6,856; 7,689: [R]CBQ 54 (1992) 516 (R. E. *Murphy*, 6: largely on N. LOHFINK, *yaraš*).

768 **TRE:** Theologische Realenzyklopädie, ᴱMüller Gerhard, *al.* [21. 1991
➤ 7,690]; 22. Malaysia-Minne. B/NY 1992, de Gruyter. 796 p. DM 396.
3-11-013463-2. – ᴿBtHumRen 54 (1992) 823-8 (I. *Hazlett*, 18-20); CiuD
204 (1991) 271 (J. M. *Ozaeta*, 20) & 205 (1992) 764-6 (21); DLZ 113
(1992) 119-122 (G. *Wendelborn*, 20); JEH 42 (1991) 463s (O. *Chadwick*);
NRT 114 (1992) 455s (A. *Harvengt*, 21); Protestantesimo 47 (1992) 133
(J. A. *Soggin*, 21); RHPR 72 (1992) 311 (J. F. *Collange*, 20); TRu 57
(1992) 448-450 (E. *Grässer*, 18-21).
769 **TUmAT:** Texte aus der Umwelt des Alten Testaments [2/6, 1991; 3/1,
1990 ➤ 7,691]: 3/2, Weisheitstexte II, ᴱBurkard Günter, *al.* Gü 1991,
Mohn. p. 189-347. 3-579-00073-X. – ᴿBL (1992) 115s (W. G. *Lambert*);
VT 42 (1992) 139 (J. N. *Postgate*, 2,5).
770 **TWAT:** Theologisches Wörterbuch zum Alten Testament, ᴱFabry H.,
Ringgren H. [VII. 1-6, 1990 ➤ 6,859] 6s, *rāṣāh - šebaᶜ*. Stu 1992, Kohlhammer. Col. 641-1016. 3-17-012667-9 (vol. VII). – ᴿNRT 114 (1992)
103s (J.-L. *Ska*, 7/3-5).

A3.3   *Opera consultationis biblica non excerpta infra – not subindexed.*

771 ᴱButler Trent C., Holman Bible dictionary 1991 ➤ 7,697: ᴿBtS 149
(1992) 375s (R. D. *Ibach:* dazzling graphics).
772 ᴱCoggins R. J., Houlden J. L., A dictionary of biblical interpretation
1990 ➤ 6,865; 7,698: ᴿCBQ 54 (1992) 388s (G. S. *Sloyan:* overall fine,
some pieces excellent: though the editors must start by lamenting
'overcommitted scholars, defaulting contributors, resistance to the editors'
guidelines'); TorJT 7 (1991) 264-6 (J. S. *Kloppenborg*); TsTKi 62 (1991)
67-70 (Terje *Stordalen*).
773 **Cohn-Sherbok** Dan, The Blackwell dictionary of Judaica. Ox 1992,
Blackwell. xviii-597 p.
774 **Day** A. Colin, Roget's Thesaurus of the Bible. SF/L 1992, Harper
Collins / Marshall Pickering. [viii-]927 p. £25 [TDig 39,358: $28;
thumb-indexed $30; 0-06-061773-X; -2-1; BR 9/1,11, E. *Johnson*].
775 [**Born** A. van den...] Dictionnaire encyclopédique de la Bible, ᴱBogaert
P.-M., *al.*, Maredsous 1987 ➤ 3,888... 6,864. ᴿBijdragen 53 (1992) 425
(L. *Dequeker*).
775* Dizionario culturale della Bibbia [franç. P (1990) Nathan, senza autori],
ᵀScala M. A.; ᴱColombo D. T 1992, SEI. xvi-309 p. 88-05-05354-X
[Salesianum 55,791s, R. *Bracchi*].
776 ᴱDouglas J. D., Tanney Merrill C., The NIV compact dictionary of the
Bible [< ¹1967, ²1987]. GR 1989, Zondervan. xxix-672 p. $13 [JEvTS
37,134s, M. R. *Fairchild*].
— b) **Elwell** Walter A., Baker Encyclopedia of the Bible 1989 ➤ 5,933; 6,667a:
ᴿCalvinT 26 (1991) 434-7 (G. N. *Knoppers:* helpful despite shortcomings).
— c) Enciclopedia illustrata della Bibbia. CinB 1991, Paoline. – ᴿBbbOr 34
(1992) 58-60 (Cristina *Vertua*).
777 **ExWNT** [➤ 758] Eng.: Exegetical dictionary of the NT, ᴱBalz H.,
Schneider G., 1, ᵀHoward V. P., *Thompson* J. W. 1990 ➤ 6,868; 7,
699: ᴿCurrTMiss 19 (1992) 294s (E. *Krentz*, 1); IndTSt 28 (1991) 184-6
(L. *Legrand:* veiled western exegetical presuppositions).
778 ᴱGreen Joel B., McKnight Scot, Marshall I. Howard, Dictionary of Jesus
and the Gospels. [GR/] Leicester 1992, Inter-Varsity. xxv-934 p. £30.
0-8308-1777-8 / 0-85110-646-3 [NTAbs 36,421]. – ᴿExpTim 103,12 2d-top
choice (1991s) 353s (C. S. *Rodd*).

779 Das grosse Bibellexikon [Illustrated Bible dictionary 1962/80, ᵀᴱBurkhard
    Helmut, *al.* Wu/Giessen 1987-9, Brockhaus / Brunnen. xvi-500 p.; p. 501-
    1104; p. 1105-1750. DM 296. – ᴿZkT 114 (1992) 186-8 (R. *Oberforcher*:
    apologetisch).
780 ᴱHarrison Roland K., Encyclopedia of biblical and Christian ethics²ʳᵉᵛ
    [only 'AIDS' and 'homelessness' added to ¹1987]. Nv 1992, Nelson.
    [viii-]472 p. 0-8407-3391-7.
781 Hennig K., Jerusalemer Bibel-Lexikon [= Illustrated dictionary and
    concordance 1986],ᵀ. Stu-Neuhausen 1989, Hänssler. xv-387 p.; ill.
    DM 128. – ᴿTGgw 35 (1992) 127-133 (H. *Giesen,* auch über GÖRG,
    NEGEV).
781* ᴱKuen A., Nouveau dictionnaire biblique²ʳᵉᵛ [¹1961]. St-Légier 1992,
    Emmaüs. 1372 p.; ill.; 8 maps. Fs 120. 2-8287-0043-7 [NTAbs 37, p. 267].
782 Lurker Manfred, Dizionario delle immagini e dei simboli biblici [³1987],
    ᵀᴱRavasi Gianfranco, 1990 ➤ 7,875; Lit. 36.000. 88-215-2018-8 [NTAbs
    36,256]. – ᴿCC 143 (1992,1) 87s (G.-L. *Prato*); RClerIt 72 (1991) 395s (C.
    Ghidelli); StCattMi 36 (1992) 91s (U. *De Martino*); StPatav 38 (1991) 207s
    (G. *Segalla*); Teresianum 43 (1992) 291s (V. *Pasquetto*).
783 Monloubou Louis, Diccionario bíblico compendiado, ᵀ*Montes* Miguel
    1991 ➤ 7,704: ᴿLumenVr 41 (1992) 477s (F. *Ortiz de Urtaran*).
784 Monloubou Louis, Breve dizionario biblico [1989 ➤ 5,955], ᵀ*Masini*
    Mario: LoB 3.12. Brescia 1992, Queriniana. 282 p. Lit. 30.000. 88-
    399-1692-X.
785 Müller Paul G., Lessico della scienza biblica [1985] 1990 ➤ 6,880; 7,705:
    Lit. 30.000: ᴿCC 143 (1992,2) 621s (G. L. *Prato*).
786 ᴱNegev Avraham, ᵀᴱ*Rosenthal-Heginbottom* R., Zwickel W., Archäo-
    logisches Bibellexikon 1991 ➤ 7,706b: DM 120: ᴿBLtg 65 (1992) 124s (R.
    Wenning).
787 ᴱPanimolle Salvatore A., Dizionario di spiritualità biblico-patristica; i
    grandi temi della S. Scrittura per la 'Lectio Divina', I. R 1992, Borla. I.
    350 p. Lit. 30.000. – II. 277 p. 88-263-0912-4; -60-4 [CC 144/4, 418, E.
    Cattaneo].
788 Richards L. O., [author of all 5000 articles], The Revell Bible dictionary.
    1990 ➤ 6,882*; 1168 pages, color photos on nearly every page; 13 color
    maps. $30 [BA 55,150].
788* Riet Rob van, Prisma van de Bijbelse persoonsnamen. Utrecht 1990,
    Spectrum. 234 p. Fb 295. – ᴿStreven 58 (1990s) 659 (P. *Beentjes*).
789 ᴱSchoeps J. H., Neues Lexikon des Judentums: Gü 1992, Bertelsmann.
    495 p.; ill. DM 128 [RHE 87,424*]. – ᴿOLZ 87 (1992) 541s (L. *Wächter*:
    DM 98).

A3.5   *Opera consultationis* **theologica** *non excerpta infra.*

790 Adams Hannah, A dictionary of all religions and religious denomi-
    nations; Jewish, Heathen, Mahometan, Christian, ancient and modern
    [1817], intr. *Tweed* Thomas A.: AAR Classics in Religious Studies 8.
    Atlanta 1992, Scholars. xli-376 p.
791 ᴱAncilli Ermanno † 1988, Dizionario enciclopedico di spiritualità²ʳᵉᵛ
    [1975] 1990 ➤ 7,710: ᴿAnnTh 6 (1992) 135-151 (A. *Blanco*).
792 ᴱAndresen C., *Denzler* G., Dizionario storico del cristianesimo. CinB
    1992, Paoline. 790 p. – ᴿComSev 25 (1992) 479s (M. *Sánchez*).
793 Assfalg Julius, *al.*, Petit dictionnaire de l'Orient chrétien 1991 ➤ 7,711:
    ᴿPrOrChr 41 (1991) 437s (P. *Ternant*: adaptation).

793* ᴱAtiya Aziz S., The Coptic encyclopedia 1991 → 7,712: ᴿPrOrChr 41 (1991) 438s (M. P. *Martin*).
794 ᴱBäumer Remigius, *Scheffczyk* Leo, Marienlexikon [I-III, 1988-91 → 4,819 ... 7,713], IV. Laitha-Orange. St. Ottilien 1992, ᴇᴏs. 703 p. [RHE 88,186*].
795 ᴱBautz F. W. & Traugott, Biographisch-bibliographisches Kirchenlexikon [1s]. 3. Jedin-Kleinschmidt. Herzberg 1992, Bautz. xxxviii-1598 col. [TR 88,513].
796 Beinert W., Diccionario de teología dogmática, ᵀ*Gancho* C., 1990 → 7,714: ᴿLumenVr 40 (1991) 320s (F. *Ortiz de Urtaran*: 'Beinart'); Salmanticensis 39 (1992) 173s (A. *González Montes*); StPatav 39 (1992) 477s (C. *Corsato*).
797 Bowden John, Who's who in theology, from the first century to the present [over 900 names alphabetically]. NY 1992, Crossroad. viii-152 p. $19. 0-8245-1150-6 [TDig 39,353].
798 Bradley Martin B., *al.*, Churches and church membership in the United States 1990, an enumeration by region, state and county based on data reported for 133 church groupings. Atlanta 1992, Glenmary. xx-456 p., foldout map. $36 (extra maps $8 each). 0-914422-22-7 [TDig 40,156].
799 ᴱBurkhardt H., Swarat U., *al.*, Evangelisches Lexikon für Kirche und Gemeinde, 1. Wu 1992, Brockhaus. xii-660 p. DM 98. 3-417-24641-5 [TLZ 118,717, E. *Winkler*].
800 ᴱCancik Hubert, *al.*, Handbuch religionswissenschaftlicher Grundbegriffe 1s, 1988/90 → 5,897; 6,893; – II. Apokalyptik-Geschichte 500 p. DM 98. – ᴿActuBbg 29 (1992) 28s (J. *Boada*); StPatav 39 (1992) 203-6 (F. *Mora*); TLZ 117 (1992) 261-3 (K. W. *Tröger*).
801 Christophe P., Vocabulaire historique de culture chrétienne [2000 mots]. P 1991, Desclée. 313 p. F 125. – ᴿNRT 114 (1992) 454 (B. *Joassart*).
802 Clifton Chas S., Encyclopedia of heresies and heretics. Santa Barbara 1992, ABC-Clio. xvii-156 p.; ill. $50. 0-87436-600-3 [TDig 40,261].
802* Cohn-Sherbok Dan, A dictionary of Judaism and Christianity 1991 → 7,718*: ᴿMonth 253 (1992) 150 (Clare *Jardine*).
803 Cully Iris V. & Kendig B., Harper's encyclopedia of religious education 1990 → 6,897; 7,719: ᴿNewTR 5,1 (1992) 104s (F. S. *Tebbe*); RelStR 18 (1992) 36 (R. T. *O'Gorman*).
804 ᴱDyck Cornelius J., *Martin* Dennis D., The Mennonite encyclopedia [1-4, 1955-9, ²1969-73], 5 [updating]. Scottdale PA 1990, Herald. 961 p. $80. – ᴿSixtC 23 (1992) 355-7 (H. W. *Pipkin*).
805 Ebraismo, cristianesimo, islam; dizionario comparato delle religioni monoteistiche [= Lexikon religiöser Grundbegriffe],ᵀ. CasM 1991, Piemme. xlv-665 p. Lit. 70.000. – ᴿCC 143 (1992,4) 325s (E. *Farahian*).
806 ᴱEicher Peter, Neues Handbuch theologischer Grundbegriffe. Mü 1991, Kösel. 438 + 431 + 452 + 440 + 428 p. DM 98. 3-446-20338-4 [TvT 33,289, E. *Borgman*].
806* ᴱEicher Peter, ᵀᴿ*Francesconi* G., Enciclopedia teologica. Brescia 1991, Queriniana. 1201 p. Lit. 130.000. – ᴿAsprenas 39 (1992) 116 (P. *Pifano*).
807 ᴱElwell Walter A., The concise Evangelical dictionary of theology [1984], abridged ᴱ*Toon* Peter. GR 1991, Baker. xix-569 p. $20. 0-8010-3210-5 [TDig 39,257].
808 ᴱFerguson Everett, (*McHugh* Michael P., *al.*), The encyclopedia of early Christianity 1990 → 6,907; 7,723: ᴿBA 55 (1992) 46s (E. *Krentz*); ChH 62 (1993) 243s (H. *Chadwick*: commissioned by American societies of Church History and Patristics); HomP 91,7 (1990s) 74-76 (W. G. *Most*);

JEvTS 36 (1993) 107s (J. E. *McGoldrick*); RestQ 33 (1991) 106-8 (A. J. *Malherbe*).

809 ᴱFink Peter E., The new dictionary of sacramental worship 1990
➤ 7,724: ᴿTS 53 (1992) 372-4 (J. D. *Laurance*); ZkT 114 (1992) 369s
(H. B. *Meyer*: 160 Autoren, darunter 30 Frauen).

810 Harris Ian, *al.*, Contemporary religions; a world guide. L 1992, Longman [Detroit: Gale]. xii-511 p. $175. 0-582-08695-7 [TDig 40,157].

811 ᴱHinnells John R., Who's who of world religions. NY 1992, Simon & S.
xvi-560 p. $75. 0-13-952946-2 [TDig 39,294].

812 ᴱHunter Rodney J., *al.*, Dictionary of pastoral care and counseling. Nv
1990, Abingdon. 1346 p. £48. 0-687-10761-X. – ᴿExpTim 104 (1992s)
184s (S. *Pattison*: good).

813 ᴱKazhdan Alexander P., The Oxford dictionary of Byzantium 1991
➤ 7,727: ᴿByZ 84s (1991s) 512-4 (J. *Kader*); ChH 61 (1992) 241-3 (C. A.
Frazee); IkiZ 82 (1992) 274-6 (E. *Hammerschmidt*); JTS 43 (1992) 718s (A.
Louth); RÉByz 50 (1992) 313-5 (A. *Failler*); RelStR 18 (1992) 57 (A. T.
Kraabel) & 271-5 (J. J. *Yiannis*); Speculum 68 (1993) 1151s (J. *Rossow*);
TS 53 (1992) 749-752 (G. T. *Dennis*). ➤ 837.

814 Kelly J. F., The concise dictionary of early Christianity. ColMn 1992,
Liturgical. vii-203 p. [RHE 88,60*; NTAbs 37, p. 306].

815 ᴱLudlow Daniel H., Encyclopedia of Mormonism. NY 1992, Macmillan. 4 vol., lxxxviii-1848 p. + vol. 5 (corrected editions of The Book
of Mormon etc.) viii-485 p. $340. 0-02-904040-X [TDig 39,159]. ➤ b125;
b117.

816 McKim Donald, Encyclopedia of the Reformed faith. St. Andrew/
Louisville 1992, Univ./W-Knox. 448 p. £20. 0-7512-0660-5 / US 0-664-
21882-2 [RelStR 19,84, D. R. *Janz*; TDig 39,159]. – ᴿExpTim 104 (1992s)
92s (G. *McFarlane*).

817 Melton J. Gordon, *Köszegi* Michael A., Religious information sources; a
worldwide guide: RelInf Systems 2 / RefLibr Humanities n° 1593. NY
1992, Garland. xxiii-569 p. $75. 0-5153-0859-0 [TDig 39,373].

818 Mondin B., Dizionario enciclopedico di filosofia, teologia e morale 1989
➤ 7,735a: ᴿSacDoc 35 (1990) 98-105 (R. *Coggi*: buono).

819 ᴱMusser Donald W., *Price* Joseph L., A new handbook of Christian
theology [1958, A handbook... ᴱHalverson Marvin, *Cohen* A.; only 4 of
the authors retained, now 137 for 148 articles]. Nv 1992, Abingdon. 525 p.
$20. 0-687-27802-3 [TDig 40,78].

820 *a)* ᴱNyssen Wilhelm, *al.*, Handbuch der Ostkirchenkunde ²1989 ➤ 7,738:
ᴿTR 88 (1992) 479-482 (A. *Basdekis*, 2).

— *b)* O'Collins G., *Farrugia* E., Concise dictionary of theology 1991 ➤ 7,737:
ᴿNBlackf 73 (1992) 134-6 (R. *Ombres*); Themelios 17,3 (1991s) 31 (T.
Lane: concise, good).

— *c)* ᴱPoupard Paul, Dictionnaire des religions³ [Grande diz. 1992 ➤ 7,740].
P 1993, PUF. xvi-1098 p.; p. 1099-2218. 2-13-045967-6: -8-4 (from 1 ed.,
but date 1993).

821 Rzepkowski Horst, Lexikon der Mission; Geschichte, Theologie, Ethnologie. Graz 1992, Styria. 470 p. DM 140 [RHE 87,344*]. 3-222-12052-8.

822 Spitzing Günter, Lexikon byzantinisch-christlicher Symbole; die Bilderwelt Griechenlands und Kleinasiens 1988 ➤ 5,968: ᴿTR 88 (1992) 294s
(W. *Gessel*).

823 ᴱWilliamson William B., An encyclopedia of religions in the United
States; one hundred religious groups speak for themselves. NY 1991,
Crossroad. xii-359 p. $35. 0-8245-1094-1 [TDig 39,360].

824 **Zoffoli** Enrico, Dizionario del cristianesimo. R 1992, Synopsis. x-188 p. Lit. 60.000 [CC 144/1,205, A. *Ferrua*]. – ^RDivinitas 36 (1992) 275s (D. *Composta*).

A3.6   Opera consultationis philologica et generalia.

825 **Becker** Udo, Il Lexikon der Symbole. FrB 1992, Herder. 352 p. DM 98. 3-451-22483-6 [TGL 83,256s, W. *Beinert*].

825* **Biedermann** Hans, Dictionary of symbolism (Knaurs 1989), ^T*Hulbert* James. NY 1992, Facts on File. xi-465 p. 0-8160-2593-2.

826 **Briggs** Ward W., *Calder* William W.^{III}, Classical scholarship, a biographical encyclopedia. NY 1990, Garland. xxiv-534 p.; 48 ill. – ^RClasR 42 (1992) 174-7 (H. D. *Jocelyn*).

826* ^E**Bright** William, International encyclopedia of linguistics 1-4. Ox 1992, UP. xvi-429 p.; viii-440 p.; viii-456 p.; viii-482 p. $395 [Language 69, 138-142, R. *Hudson*].

827 ^E**Brunner** Otto, *al.*, Geschichtliche Grundbegriffe; historisches Lexikon zur politisch-sozialen Sprache in Deutschland VI. Stu 1990, Klett-Cotta. xv-954 p. – ^RTPhil 67 (1992) 283-5 (H. J. *Sieben*).

828 ^E**Buchwald** Wolfgang, *al.*, Dictionnaire des auteurs grecs et latins de l'antiquité au moyen âge [Tusculum-Lexikon], ^T*Berger* Jean Denis, *Billen* Jacques: Petits Dictionnaires Bleus. Turnhout 1991, Brepols. xxiii-898 p. 2-503-50016-1 [AntClas 62,255; BLitEc 94,351, G. *Passerat*; CC 144/4, 519, G. *Cremascoli*].

829 **Bussmann** Hadumod, Lexikon der Sprachwissenschaft² [¹1983]. Stu 1990, Kröner. 904 p. DM 42. – ^RHistSprF 104 (1991) 315s (Inge *Milfull*).

829* ^E**Chastagnol** André, *al.*, L'année épigraphique 1989. P 1992, PUF. 366 p. 2-13-044333-8 [Latomus 52,210-3, R. *Chevallier*].

830 *a)* **Chevalier** Jean, *Gheerbrant* Alain, Dizionario dei simboli; miti, sogni, costumi, gesti, forme, figure, colori, numeri: BtUniv. [1969], ^T*Sordi* Italo. Mi 1992 = 1986, Rizzoli. XXXVII-561 p.; 606 p. 88-17-14508-4; -9-2.

— *b)* ^E**Collinge** N. E., An encyclopaedia of language. L 1990, Routledge. xvii-1011 p. $80. – ^RJIndEur 20 (1992) 183-5 (E. C. *Polomé*); Language 68 (1992) 200-2 (Jane H. *Hill*).

— *c)* **Crystal** David, The Cambridge encyclopedia of language 1991 ➤ 7,747; $25 pa. (half the price of 1987 hardback). – ^RLanguage 68 (1992) 422 (P. T. *Daniels*: top value).

— *d)* ^E**Gibb** H. A. R., *Kramers* J. H., Shorter encyclopedia of Islam: Royal Netherlands Academy, 3d impression. Leiden 1991 = 1953, Brill. viii-671 p.; ill. 90-04-00681-8.

831 ^E**Goulet** Richard, Dictionnaire des philosophes antiques 1, 1989 ➤ 6,930: ^RBSO 54 (1991) 234s (C. *Burnett*: much for the orientalist); ClasR 41 (1991) 376s (M. B. *Trapp*).

832 ^E**Hausmann** Franz J., *al.*, Wörterbücher, dictionaries... ein internationales Handbuch zur Lexikographie, 5,1s. B 1989s, de Gruyter. lii-1056; 1057-2337 p. DM 740 + 880. – ^RIndogF 97 (1992) 259-265 (E. *Eggers*).

833 ^E**Jacob** André, L'univers philosophique: Encyclopédie Philosophique Universelle 1. P 1989, PUF. xxxii-1997 p. 2-13-043-038-4.

834 **LIMC:** Lexicon iconographicum mythologiae classicae, ^E**Kahil** Lilly, V, 1990 ➤ 7,750: ^RAJA 96 (1992) 384s (Brunilde S. *Ridgway*, 5); AntClas 61 (1992) 648s (C. *Delvoye*, 5); RBgPg 70 (1992) 266-8 (R. *Lambrechts*, 5).

834* — **Lochin** Catherine, Index [alphabétique par site] des mosaïques du volume IV de LIMC (Eros-Herakles): BMosAnt 13 (1990s) 464-477.

835 ᴱLipsitz Edmond Y., World Jewish directory. Downsview ON 1991, JESL educational project. I. 141 p.; II. 267 p. 0-0691-2647-6.
835* ᴱMartin René, Dictionnaire culturel de la mythologie gréco-romaine. P 1992, Nathan. 296 p.; 8 pl. 2-09-180074-0 [Latomus 52,246, J. *Marneffe*].
836 ᴱMattéi Jean-François, Les Œuvres philosophiques; dictionnaire: Encyclopédie philosophique universelle 3. P 1992, PUF. XXXII-2190; -4616 p. 2-13-044-443-5.
837 Nicol Donald M., A biographical dictionary of the Byzantine Empire. L 1991, Seaby. xxviii-156 p. – ᴿByZ 84s,1 (1991s) 137s (G. *Makris*); RÉByz 50 (1992) 313 (J.-C. *Cheynet*: utile, très clair). ➤ 813.
838 Olderr Steven, Reverse symbolism dictionary; symbols listed by subject. Jefferson NC 1992, McFarland. ix-181 p. 0-89950-561-9.
839 ᴱRobbins V. K., Ancient quotes and anecdotes 1989 ➤ 5,963; 7,752: ᴿTorJT 7 (1991) 285-7 (Mechtilde *O'Mara*).
840 Tosi Renzo, Dizionario delle sentenze latine e greche; 10.000 citazioni dall'antichità al Rinascimento nell'originale e in traduzione con commento storico letterario e filologico: BtUniv. Mi 1992, Rizzoli. xxix-891 p. 88-17-14516-9: i. modi: fama, calunnia, chiacchiere.

A3.8   *Opera consultationis* **archaeologica** *et* **geographica**.

841 Adamec Ludwig W., Historical dictionary of Afghanistan: Asian Historical Dictionaries 5. Metuchen NJ 1991, Scarecrow. xiv-376 p. 0-8108-2491-4 [OIAc 5,13].
842 Allgemeines Künstlerlexikon; die bildenden Künstler aller Zeiten und Völker 6. Avogaro-Barbieri. Mü 1992, Saur.
ᴱAmadasi Guzzo Maria Giulia, al., Dizionario della civiltà fenicia 1992 ➤ e653.
843 David Rosalie & Antony E., A biographical dictionary of ancient Egypt. L 1992, Seaby. xxvi-179 p. 1-85264-032-4 [OIAc 5,18].
844 Henze Dietmar, Encyklopädie der Entdecker und Erforscher der Erde [3/14, 1991 ➤ 7,757], 3/15, Motoro-Osborn. Graz 1992, Akad. 127 p. [DLZ 114,249, K.-R. *Biermann*].
845 ᴱ[*Wessel* Klaus], **Restle** Marcell, Reallexikon zur byzantinischen Kunst [1,1966; 2. 1971; 3. 1978] 4. Lfg. 25-32, Kathedra bis Kreta. 5, Lfg. 33s, Kreuz, -igung. [1991; 320 col.]. Stu 1990, Hiersemann. 628 p.; 329 fig. DM 490. 3-7772-8018-1; -9029-7. – ᴿJbÖsByz 42 (1992) 411s (H. *Hunger*, 4, double the interval since vols. 1-3).
846 ᴱWirth K. A., Reallexikon der deutschen Kunstgeschichte: Band 8, Lfg. 85-96, Fensterrose-Firnis. Mü 1987, Beck. 1520 col. – ᴿTLZ 117 (1992) 450-5 . 523-529 . 615-622 (Erika *Dinkler-von Schubert*) [114 (1989) 754s, Band 7].
847 ᴱYarshater Ehsan, Encyclopaedia Iranica 3s, 1989s ➤ 7,761: ᴿJRAS (1992) 83s (C. *Melville*, 3s).

A4   **Bibliographiae,** computers .1 **biblicae.**

848 *Auneau* Joseph, Bulletin biblique: MaisD 192 (1992) 139-147 [ɢɪʟʙᴇʀᴛ M., ɢʀᴇʟᴏᴛ P. ....].
849 Baeck Institute New York Catalog of the Archival Collection: Schr. L. Baeck Inst. 47. Tü 1990, Mohr. xv-412 p. – ᴿSalesianum 54 (1992) 572 (R. *Vicent*).
850 Berichte über [9] Dissertationen [im Gang]: ZAW 104 (1992) 465s.

851 **Boccaccini** Gabriele, Portraits of Middle Judaism in scholarship and arts; a multimedia catalog from Flavius JOSEPHUS to 1991: Henoch Quad. 6. T 1992, Zamorani. xxix-238 p. 88-7158-021-4.

852 *Brauer* Bernd, *al.*, Bibliographische Dokumentation; lexikalisches und grammatisches Material: ZAHeb 5 (1992) 91-112 [113s, neu entdeckte Texte, *Loersch* Sigrid; 115, Qumran, *Lichtenberger* H.].

852* **Brown** Roy, MacBible 2.0/2.4, Software for Bible study and research on the Apple Macintosh, Greek NT / NRSV with Apocrypha [and] Biblia Hebraica Stuttgardensia: GR 1990, Zondervan. $200 / $100 + 200 [Bijdragen 54,330, E. *Eynikel*, Eng.: high praise].

853 ᴱBrunelli C., *al.*, La Palestina nella produzione e stampa italiana, 1475-1900: Univ. Venezia Eurasiatica 11. F 1989, Le Monnier. 308 p. – ᴿOrChrPer 57 (1991) 463s (V. *Poggi*).

854 *Claassen* Walter T., Models of information in biblical information systems: ⮞ 450*, Informatique 3ᵉ 1991/2, 513-522.

855 *Coggins* Richard J., Recent continental OT literature [8 books, most infra]: ExpTim 103 (1991s) 295-300.308-310 (German).

856 La cultura ebraica nell'editoria italiana (1955-1990), repertorio bibliografico, ᴱ*Padellaro* Angela: Libri e Riviste d'Italia Quad. 27. R 1992, Ministero Beni Culturali. [vi-] 482 p.

856* *Evans* C.A., Jesus [− Life of Jesus research, streamlined and updated]: IBR 5. GR 1992, Baker. 152 p. $10. 0-8010-3218-0 [NTAbs 37, p.436].

857 *Fernández Tejero* Emilia, *Fernández Marcos* Natalio, *al.*, Elenco de artículos de revistas: Sefarad 51 (1991) 221-243.477-492.

858 **Fitzmyer** Joseph A., An introductory bibliography for the study of Scripture³: SubsBPont 3,1990 ⮞ 6,968; 7,773: ᴿLavalTP 48 (1992) 138 (Odette *Mainville*), TRu 57 (1992) 224 (L. *Perlitt*).

Fitzmyer J. A., *Kaufman* S. A., An Aramaic bibliography 1, 1992 ⮞ 9573.

859 *a)* ᴱ*Geoltrain* Pierre, *al.*, Bibliographie générale [des Apocryphes uniquement du NT]: Apocrypha 1 (Turnhout 1990) 13-67.

— *b)* *Giustozzi* Enzo, Biblia e informática: RBiArg 54,46 (1992) 97-116.

— *c)* *Gotenburg* Erwin, Bibelwissenschaft [Theologische Bibliographie]: TR 88 (1992) 13-16 [-88]. 161-4 [-176]. 249-252 [-264]. 337-340 [-352]. 425-8 [-440]. 513-6 [-536]. A magnificent resource!

860 **Grossfeld** Bernard, A bibliography of Targum literature 3, 1990 ⮞ 6,971: ᴿBO 49 (1992) 490s (M. J. *Mulder*).

860* *a)* *Heather* Michael A., *Rossiter* B. Nick, A generalized database management approach to textual analysis; – *b)* *Schweizer* Harald, The predication-model as a component of a semantic and pragmatic content-analysis: ⮞ 450, Informatique 2, 1988/9, 517-535 / 538-562.

861 *Heintz* Jean-Georges, Les figures de l'AT et leurs exégètes; Chronique d'AT III: RHPR 72 (1992) 473-496.

862 *Hughes* John J., Computers and the Bible: BR 7,3 (1991) 38-41.

863 **Hupper** William G., An index to English periodical literature on the Old Testament and ancient Near Eastern studies [I. 1987 ⮞ 3,966; II. 1988; III-IV. 1990] V: ATLA 21. Metuchen NJ 1992, Scarecrow. xlix-707 p. $72.50. 0-8108-[1984-8; -2126-5; -2319-5; 2393-4] -2618-6 [TDig 40,273].

864 **IZBG**: Internationale Zeitschriftenschau für Bibelwissenschaft und Grenzgebiete, ᴱ**Lang** Bernhard, *al.*, 37 (for 1990s). Düsseldorf 1992, Patmos. xiv-394 p.; 2527 items, with summary in German or (about half) English.

864* *Kaestli* J.-D., Herméneutique – Méthodes, Évangiles et Actes des Apôtres: Bulletin de Bibliographie Biblique 3 (Lausanne 1991) 1-81; 1000+ items [< NTAbs 37,14].

865 *Kealy* Seán P., Bible reading for the 1990s: Furrow 41 (1990) 639-644.
866 *McCullough* J.C., Index: Irish Biblical Studies 13 (1991) 211-228 (only authors vol. 1-6); 14 (1992) 31-49 (authors vol. 7-13; titles vol. 1-13).
867 **May** David M., Social scientific criticism of the New Testament, a bibliography: Nat. Asn. Baptist Profs. Rel. Bibliog. 4. Macon GA 1991, Mercer Univ. xv-91 p. 0-86554-392-5.
868 **Minor** Mark, Literary-critical approaches to the Bible; an annotated bibliography. West Cornwall CT 1992, Locust Hill. xxxi-520 p. $50 [BL 93,92: D. *Clines*: rich, indispensable; 2252 items with summaries].
868* Mir Biblij ❻, The world of the Bible [United Bible Societies quarterly 1/1 Moscow c. 1992] and similar recent ventures: BTrans 43 (1992) 353-5.
869 *Parunak* H. Van Dyke, Computers and biblical studies: → 741, An-chorBD 1 (1992) 1112-1124; 5 fig.
870 *Perrone* Lorenzo, *al.*, Bibliografia generale di storia dell'interpretazione biblica; esegesi, ermeneutica, usi della Bibbia 5 (1992): AnStoEseg 9 (1992) 291-318. 627-636 [611-616 utilità del lavoro).
871 *a*) *Piñero* Antonio, New Testament philology bulletin 9/10; – *b*) *Godoy* Rufino, Libros recibidos (comentados): FgNt 5 (1992) 89-117. 219-247 / 123-131. 251-6.
872 *Poswick* R. Ferdinand, Centre 'Informatique et Bible' (CIB-Maredsous); repository, archives, data base, what else?: ZAHeb 5 (1992) 87-90.
873 **Powell** Mark A., *al.*, The Bible and modern literary criticism; a critical assessment and annotated bibliography: BbgIndRelSt 21. NY 1992, Greenwood. xvii-470 p. [NTAbs 37, p. 432]. – ᴿETL 68 (1992) 432s (F. *Neirynck*, also on MINOR).
873* *Raab* Hamutal, Indexes to articles, words and subjects in Volumes 36 (1971s) – 50 (1985s): Lešonenu 54,1 (1989s) ❻ 90 p.
874 *Scholer* David M., Bibliographia gnostica supplementum XX: NT 34 (1992) 48-89.
875 *Senior* Donald [NT], *Stuhlmueller* Carroll [OT]. The Bible in review: BToday 30 (1992) 54-59. 183-9. 314-7 with a portrait newer than p. 10 / 118-125. 251-6. 309-313. 379-383.
876 *Silva* Moisés, Notes on computing; Nota bene, the research processor: WestTJ 53 (1991) 183-8.
      Specht Günther, Wissensbasierte Analyse althebräischer Morphosyntax; das Expertensystem AMOS: AOtt 35, 1990 → 9384.
876* *Taradach* Madeleine, Butlettí bibliogràfic, Judaïsme [SCHWARZFUCHS S. 1991; MECHOULAN H. 1991; VERMES P. 1992; BUBER M. 1991]: RCatalT 17 (1992) 277-288.
877 *a*) *Tov* Emanuel, Achievements and trends in computer-assisted biblical studies; – *b*) *Bühler* David A., Implementation of hypermedia in biblical studies; limits and possibilities; – *c*) *Claassen* Walter T., User needs and information systems in biblical studies → 450, Informatique 2, 1988/9, 33-60 / 167-176 / 209-221.
878 *Vattioni* Francesco, Saggio di bibliografia semitica 1990-1991: AION 52 (1992) 155-220.
879 *Vernet* André, (*Genevois* Anne-Marie), La Bible au Moyen Âge; bi-bliographie. P 1989, CNRS. 131 p. F 96. 2-222-04343-3. – ᴿÉTRel 67 (1992) 599 (H.*Bost*); Heresis 19 (1992) 91s (G. *Gonnet*); Speculum 67 (1992) 497s (Laura *Light*: excellent).
880 Verzeichnis der Beiträge 26-60 (1985-91): BibNot 63 (1992) 72-90.
881 **Zannoni** Arthur E., The Old Testament, a bibliography: OTSt 5. ColMn 1992, Liturgical. x-277 p. $18. 0-8146-5658-7.

881* Zeitschriftenüberblick: Judaica 48 (1992) 56-62.124-8.189-192.252-6.
882 ZAW 104 (1992) 112-141.263-289.428-441, Zeitschriftenschau (*Wanke* G.): 141-162.289-317.441-465, Bücherschau (*Schmitt* H.-C.). – ZNW 83 (1992) 149-151.286-289 (Zts).
883 ZIMMERLI Walther, Bibliographie 1976-89: TLZ 118 (1993) 1095-8 (J. *Motte*).

A4.2 Bibliographiae theologicae.

884 AMBERG Ernst-Heinz, 65. Gb.: TLZ 117 (1992) 554-6 (P. *Amberg*).
884* *Bach* T., *al.*, (Deutscher Verband evangelischer Büchereien), Handwörterbuch der evangelischen Büchereiarbeit². Gö 1992, Ausschuss für bibliothekarische Arbeitshilfe. Ohne Seitennummer.
885 BALTHASAR H. U. v., Bibliographie 1925-1990²ʳᵉᵛ. (**Capon** Cornelia) 1990 ➤ 7,801: ᴿMüTZ 42 (1991) 283s (M. *Tiator*).
886 *Bertuletti* Angelo, *al.*, Schede bibliografiche [Problemi metodologici]: TItSett 17 (1992) 351-441 [343-351].
887 Bibliographia œcumenica / Significant ecumenical journals: EcuR 44 (1992) 170-3.274-6.373s.529-531 / 164-9.271-3.368-372.523-8.
888 Bibliographie: Ostkirchliche Studien 41 (1992) 80-104.225-272.349-381.
888* Bibliographie 1990 und 1991 zur Geschichte der Freikirchen: FrKF 1 (1992) 23-.. [< ZIT 92,774].
890 Bibliographikon deltion (*xenoglōsson*): TAth 63 (1992) 848-865.
891 **Blasi** Anthony J., *Cuneo* Michael W., The sociology of religion; an organizational bibliography [i.e. of religious denominations]. NY 1990, Garland. xx-459 p. – ᴿSR 21 (1992) 123 (Lorne *Dawson*: companion to their Issues).
891* Bollettino bibliografico: RivLtg 79,6 (1992) 739-873, 81 scritti.
892 *Bondolfi* Alberto, (*Deckers* Daniel), Auswahlliteratur zu den Debatten um die Eroberung Amerikas: FreibZ 39 (1992) 472-500.
892* **Borgman** Erik, Promoties in de theologie: TvT 32 (1992) 85-89. 188-190.301-5.
893 *Brunet* Étienne, Le vocabulaire religieux dans trois siècles de littérature française: ➤ 450, Informatique 2, 1988/9, 147-164.
894 **Carman** John, *Juergensmeyer* Mark, A bibliographic guide to the comparative study of ethics [also India, China] 1991 ➤ 7,802: ᴿTS 53 (1992) 576-8 (J. *Kelsay*: its usefulness outweighs its unwieldiness).
895 Chronique religieuse; I. Relations entre les Communions; II. Chronique des Églises: Irénikon 65 (1992) 63-98.215-246.499-524 / 99-147. 247-288.525-583.
895* *De Klerk* Peter, Calvin bibliography 1991 / 1992: CalvinT 26 (1991) 389-411; 27 (1992) 326-352.
896 *Durand* G.-M. de, Bulletin de patrologie: RSPT 76 (1992) 117-154. 617-639: plures infra; en outre ᶠSCHNEEMELCHER 1989, 620-3; *Braun* sur TERTULLIEN 1990, 632s.
897 [*Dupuy* B.], Chronique œcuménique des périodiques: Istina 36 (1991) 115-128.211-213 (Bible), 213-224.442-445.
898 **Epp** Eldon J., Critical review of books in religion 5. Atlanta 1992, Scholars. [vi-] 553 p. 0894-8860. Books reviewed here are (a) chiefly those momentarily too numerous to review in JAAR or JBL: and (b) those of interest in more than one field [editors' note p. iii.].
899 a) *Fares* D.J., *al.*, Fichero de revistas latinoamericanas: Stromata 47 (1991) 427-476; 427-9, Indice de revistas; 442-6, S. Escritura. – b) *Fi-*

gueroa P. M., Fichero de revistas latinoamericanas: Stromata 48 (1992) 451-512; siglas 451-3; 473s, S. Escritura.

899* *Give* Bernard de, *al.*, Bulletin de spiritualité monastique: ColcCist 54 (1992) [141]-[268] (numérotation à part).

900 *Gonzalez* Javier, 25 years of Philippiniana Sacra; author/topical indexes 1966-1990: PhilipSa 26 (1991) 113-158.

900* **Gray** John, Àshe, traditional religion and healing in sub-Saharan Africa and the diaspora; a classified international bibliography [6000 items]: Bibliog. Afro-American & African 24. Westport 1989, Greenwood. 518 p. 0-313-26500-3 [JRelAfr 23,292, A. *Walls*].

901 *Gryson* Roger, Une nouvelle base de données textuelles; la 'CETEDOC library of Christian texts': RHE 87 (1992) 417-423.

902 *Gy* Pierre-Marie, Bulletin de liturgie: RSPT 76 (1992) 155-176.

903 *Häussling* Angelus A., *al.*, Der Gottesdienst der Kirche: ArLtgW 34 (1992) 208-283 (-312).

904 *Harman* Christine M., Cumulative Index volumes I-L [1942-92]: Reformed Theological Review. Doncaster, Victoria 1993. $15 (US; A$12 in Australia).

905 E*Haverals* M., Bibliographie: RHE 87 (1992) 1*-166*. 167*-347*. 349*-500*; 8243 items; + recensions 500*-538*; tables 539*-608*.

906 **Heiser** W. Charles, Theology Digest book survey: TDig 39 (1992) 45-92. 147-194. 249-295. 348-394 [very many infra; informative summaries].

907 *Henkel* W., *Metzler* J., Bibliographia missionaria 48 (1984) 375 p.; 49 (1985) 373 p.; 50 (1986) 410 p.; 51 (1987) 336 p.; 52 (1988) 408 p.; 53 (1989) 381 p.; 54 (1990) 399 p. [NRT 115,930, J. *Masson*].

907* **IATG: Schwertner** Siegfried, Internationales Abkürzungsverzeichnis für Theologie und Grenzgebiete; Zeitschriften, Series, Lexika, Quellenwerke mit bibliographischen Angaben[2rev] [[1]1974], auch in TRE. B 1992, de Gruyter. xli-488 p. DM 158 [SNTU A-18,1245].

908 Index international des dissertations doctorales en théologie et en droit canonique présentées en 1991: RTLv 23 (1992) 522-596; p. 537-541, AT; 542-8, NT; 524-533, par institutions [plusieurs diss. citées dans notre volume 7; ici vous trouverez celles de RTLv 24].

909 Indian Theological Studies 28,1 (1991) 1-114, Index I-XXVI (1962-89), with some statistical reflections p. 1s.

910 [Innsbruck] Dissertationen im Jahre 1991/2: ZkT 114 (1992) 498-504.

911 Interpretation, Index 1987-91: Richmond 1992, Interpretation. $4 [Interp 46,367 adv.].

911* JPsy&&Chr, Index 1-10 (1982-91): 11 (1992) 99-120.

912 JRit, cumulative index 1-6 (1987-92): 6,2 (1992) 161-175.

912* E*Junghans* Helmar, *al.*, Lutherbibliographie 1992: LuJb 59 (1992) 210-264; 213-5, Sammelschriften.

913 KANTZENBACH Friedrich W. [➤ 97], Schriftenverzeichnis 1982-92: ZRGg 44 (1992) 274-282.

914 **Kepple** Robert J., *Muether* John R., Reference works for theological research[3] [[1]1978; [2]1981]. Lanham MD 1992, UPA. xiv-250 p. $49.50; pa. $24.50. 0-8191-8564-7; -5-5 [TDig 39,172: 800+ titles (double 1978); mostly not duplicating Catholic *McCabe* J. 1989 ➤ 5,1061].

915 *Kraft* Robert A., Offline; computer assisted research: CouSR 21,2 (1992) 57-62.

916 LEÓN Luis de, Bibliografia: RAg 31 (1990) 3-278.

917 *Lumpe* Adolf, Bibliographie: AnHConc 22 (1990) 504s / 23 (1991) 413-5 / 24 (1992) 247-272.

918 MAU Rudolf, 65. Gb.: TLZ 117 (1992) 234-8 (H.-P. *Hasse*).
919 ᴱ*Nadolski* Bogusław, *al.*, Biuletyny: ColcT [→ 7,813s] 1992: 62/1, 99-171; 62/2, 99-174; 62/3, 91-177; 62/4, 89-145.
920 OROZCO Alonso de, Bibliografía fundamental: CiuD 204 (1991) 205-254 (R. *Lazcano*).
921 **Palmer** Bernard, Gadfly for God; a history of the [Anglican] Church Times. L 1991, Hodder & S. 354 p.; 8 pl. £18. 0-340-53818-X [TBR 6/1, 47, M. *Atkinson*].
922 Pelas revistas: REB [37 (1967) 248-252, elenco de revistas; siglas] 52 (1992) 249-256. 505-512. 781-4. 1028-33.
922* *Razzino* Giuseppe, *al.*, Dai sommari [table of contents; titles only, no summary] delle riviste: FilT 5 (1991) 552-575; 6 (1992) 505-528.
923 Recension des Revues: RSPT 76 (1992) 177-206. 337-362. 511-544. 667-688.
924 Recent dissertations in religion [completed]: RelStR 18 (1992) 170-5, infra (or chiefly in vol. 7) [in progress 153-9, not here cited].
925 Revista de Revistas: RET 51 (1991) 112-139. 408-424. 523-538 / 52 (1992) 105-115. 250-262. 371-390. 501-526.
926 *Rostagno* Sergio, Rassegna di teologia sistematica: Protestantesimo 47 (1992) 230-4. 301-312 [235-9. 313-8 pastorale, *Genre* Ermanno].
927 *Ruello* Francis, Bulletin d'histoire des idées médiévales: RechSR 80 (1992) 238-263; 22 livres.
928 *Russell* Kenneth C., *Schlitt* Dale M., Thèses de doctorat, doctoral dissertations 1932-1991 [Ottawa St. Paul Univ.]: ÉglT 23 (1992) 91-110.
930 *a*) *Sans* R., *Oliver* F., Publicaciones sobre América, sentido y orientación; – *b*) *Galindo García* A., Actualidad de la doctrina social de la Iglesia; boletín bibliográfico: Carthaginensia 8 [1992, 'América, variaciones de futuro (II)' con numeración de páginas continuada desde I = 7, 1991] 889-907 / 909-922.
931 SCHMIED Augustin, Veröffentlichungen 1962-92: TGgw 35 (1992) 307-314 (J. *Römelt*).
933 Studi ecumenici 1983-1990 (compendi di tutti gli articoli): StEcum 8 (1990) 445-574; indice d'autori 575-581.
934 Studies in Religion, Index vol. 1-20: SR 20,4 (1991) 419-558 [< ᴢɪT 92,415].
936 TContext 9 (1992) [= Theologie im Kontext 13 (1992)]; — (now also in Spanish) TContexto: Teología en Contexto, ᴱEvers Georg: 2,2 (Aachen 1992) 133-134 libros; 119-132 resúmenes; 13-118 revista de revistas; 147-161 congresos, 0724-1682.
937 Theologie 1989; Nederlandse theologische proefschriften in 1989, een totaaloversicht met samenvattingen. Gorinchem 1990, Narratio. 151 p. *f*30. 90-2563-063-7. – ᴿTvT [= TsTNijm] 32 (1992) 191 (T. *Schoof*: not exactly the information one seeks in a book, with RTLv etc. available).
938 Theologische Examensarbeiten [BR, Österreich, Schweiz]: ZMissRW 75 (1991) 71-79.
939 **Thomas** Norman E., *al.*, Selected annual bibliography: Missiology 19 (1991) 105-8 (contextualization); 245-8 (women in missions); 365-8 (third world urban); 495-8 (the Gospel and our North American culture).
939* Travaux de doctorat NS 13. LvN 1992, Univ. Catholique.
940 *Trevijano Etcheverría* Ramón, Bibliografía patrística hispano-luso-americana VII (1989-1990): Salmanticensis 39 (1992) 79-129.
940* Union dissertations and joint degree dissertations with Columbia University 1990-1992: UnSemQ 45 (1991) 252-5.

941 *a) Vidal* Marciano, *Miranda* Vicente, Panorama 1990, la moral en las
   revistas: Moralia 13 (1991) 265-296; – *b) Miranda* Vicente, 1990: 14 (1992)
   195-252.
941* Vita Consacrata, Indice delle Annate 1965-1992: 38 (1992) 879-1196.
942 *Völker* Alexander, Literaturbericht zur Liturgik: JbLtgHymn 33 (1990s)
   239-246.
943 *Wal* J. van der, Literatuur rond de herdenking van 100 jaar 'Rerum
   novarum': TvT 32 (1992) 408-411.
944 *Walls* A. F., Bibliography on mission studies: IntRMiss 80 (1991)
   133-154 . 271-295 . 449-469 / 81 (1992) 139-167 . 329-353 . 495-518 .
   623-649.
945 *Werblowsky* R. J. Z., Book survey: Numen 39 (1992) 109-147 (59
   books).
946 Who's Who in religion⁴. Wilmette IL 1992s, Marquis/Reed. xvi-480 p.
947 ᴱ*Wijnen* Leo van, *Staring* Adrianus, Bibliographia carmelitana annualis
   1989 / 1990 / 1991: Carmelus 37 (1990) 285-455 / 38 (1991) 285-477 / 39
   (1992) 249-480.
948 **ZIT**: Zeitschriften Inhaltsdienst Theologie. Tübingen 1992, Universität.
   804 p. (12 Fasz., each with its own index) + 128 p. Register (of all 12).
   Photocopied table of contents of an immense number of worldwide
   (European-language) theological periodicals.
   Žitnik Maksimilian, Sacramenta, bibliographia internationalis 1992 ➤ 7908.

A4.3   *Bibliographiae* **philologicae** *et* **generales.**

949 Althistorische Dissertationen [nur deutsche]: Chiron 22 (1992) 505-8.
950 **Berschin** Walter, Die Palatina in der Vaticana; eine deutsche Bibliothek
   in Rom. Da 1992, Wiss. 176 p.; 131 (color.) fig. 3-534-12093-0.
950* Bibliographie für Buch- und Bibliothekwesen: Biblos 40 (W 1991)
   23-31 . 86-94 . 140-8 . 210-216; – 41 (1992) 32-38 . 85-91 . 159-162 . 218-224.
951 Bibliographische Beilage: Gnomon 64 (1992) 1, Fasz. 1, *1-36*; 2, Fasz. 3,
   37-80; 3, Fasz. 5, *81-124*; 4, Fasz. 7, *125-166*. – [Fasz. 1, p. 85-91: 1992 zu
   erwartende Neuerscheinungen des deutschsprachigen Buchhandels].
952 **Ceresa** Massimo, Bibliografia dei fondi manoscritti della Biblioteca Vaticana (1981-1985): ST 342. Vaticano 1991, Biblioteca. xlv-695 p. 88-
   210-0633-6.
953 ᴱ**Chastagnol** A., *al.*, L'Année épigraphique [➤ 7,862] 1990s pour 1987s:
   ᴿRÉLat 69 (1991) 314s (P. *Grimal*).
954 *Cockshaw* Pierre, *Manning* Eugène, Bulletin codicologique: Scriptorium
   46 (Bru 1992) 1*-60* . 61*-166*. ➤ 966*b*.
955 *Courcier* Jacques, Bulletin de philosophie des sciences; l'intelligence artificielle: RSPT 76 (1992) 457-482.
956 *a) Cupaiolo* Giovanni, Notiziario bibliografico, I. autori; – *b)* Rassegna
   delle Riviste: BStLat 22 (1992) 189-232 . 457-481 / 110-188 . 364-456.
957 *Dierse* Ulrich, *Hülsewiesche* Reinhold, Bibliographie: ArBegG 35 (1992)
   292-329.
958 *Doukellis* Panagiotis, Chronique 1992 [PÉREZ J., ANNEQUIN J., esclavage; GUILLEMIN J., *al.*, cadastres; LAUBENHEIMER F., amphores]: Dial-
   HA 18,2 (1992) 261-270 [-301-325-345].
959 *Figge* Udo L., Computersemiotik: ZSemiot 13,3s ('Zeichen in der Ma-
   thematik' 1991) 321-330.
959* *Forstner* Karl, Die wissenschaftliche Bibliothek heute und morgen:
   Biblos 40 (1991) 72-76.

960 GADAMER: *Aguirre Oraa* José M.,   Bibliografía de y sobre Hans-Georg Gadamer: ScripV 39 (1992) 300-345.

961 **Garvie** A. F.,   *Hine* H. M.,   Classical Review New Series Index, vol. I-XXXVI (1950-1986). – Ox 1990, Univ.   397 p.

962 *Gauthier* P., *al.*,   Bulletin épigraphique: RÉG 105 (1992) 435-547.

963 **Gordon** W.   Terrence,   Semantics, a bibliography, 1986-1991.   Metuchen NJ 1992, Scarecrow.   ix-281 p.

964 *a) Greisch* Jean,   Bulletin de philosophie herméneutique; comprendre et interpréter; – *b) Jossua* Jean-Pierre,   Bulletin de théologie littéraire: RSPT 76 (1992) 281-310 / 311-336.

965 *a) Groves* J. Alan,   Correction of machine-readable texts by means of automatic comparison; help with method; – *b) Hardmeier* Christof, Computer concordance able to dialogue; a tool of text analysis and its influence on OT research: ➤ 450, Informatique 2, 1988/9, 271-297 / 309-317.

966 *a)* **Gullath** Brigitte,   Wie finde ich altertumswissenschaftliche Literatur? Klassische Philologie, Mittel- und Neulatein, Byzantinistik, Alte Geschichte und Klassische Archäologie: Orientierungshilfen 23.   B 1990, A. Spitz.   346 p. DM 58 [ÉtClas 61,165, P. *Pietquin*].

— *b) Hendrix* Guido, *al.*,   Bulletin codicologique: Scriptorium 45,2 (1991) 105*-196*.   ➤ 954.

— *c)* Journal des Savants, Tables 1939-1988: JSav 1990 supp.   P 1990, de Boccard.   128 p.

967 **Krause** Jens-Uwe,   Die Familie und weitere anthropologische Grundlagen: Bibliographie zur Römischen Sozialgeschichte 1 / HeidAltHBeit 11.   Stu 1992, Steiner.   xii-260 p.   DM 68.   3-515-06044-8 [AntClas 62,247].

968 **Lassère** Jean-Marie,   Tables générales de l'Année Épigraphique VIII série (1961-1980). P 1992, PUF.   652 p. F 960.   213-044186-1.

969 *Libera* Alain de,   Bulletin d'histoire de la logique médiévale: RSPT 76 (1992) 640-666.

970 ᴱ**Meyer** Horst,   Bibliographie der Buch- und Bibliothekgeschichte 6, 1986.   Bad Iburg 1988, auct.   604 p. – ᴿBtHumRen 54 (1992) 266-7 (J.-F. *Gilmont*).

971 *Peters* Martin, *al.*,   Indogermanische Chronik 34: IndogF 84,2 (1988ss) 253-1035.

971* *Piszczek* Zdzisław,   Bibliografia Polska 1987: Meander 46 (1991) 347-415.

972 *Rassegna bibliografica:*   Ivra 40 (1989) 207-422 / 41 (1990) 273-448.

973 **Roozenbeek** Herman, **SEG** (Supplementum epigraphicum graecum), consolidated index for volumes XXVI-XXXV (1976-1985).   Amst 1990, Gieben.   viii-592 p. *f* 100.   90-5063-037-5. – ᴿAntClas 61 (1992) 526 (A. *Martin*: bon); ClasR 42 (1992) 230s (P. M. *Fraser*).

974 *Schreiner* Peter, *Scholz* Cordula,   Bibliographische Notizen und Mitteilungen: ByZ 84s (1991s) 152-324 (2191 items). 551-665 (3808 items).

974* *Teyssier* mme. M.-L.,   Tables 64 (1986) à 68 (1990): RÉLat 69 (1991) 347-372.

975 *Veranstaltungen* [-Vorschau]: ZSemiot 13 (1991) 181-200 [-206]. 419-438 [-443]; 14 (1992) 149-174 [-183]. 287-309 [311-6]. 437-466 [-472].

975* **Vérilhac** Anne-Marie, *al.*,   La femme dans le monde méditerranéen [I. 1985] II, La femme grecque et romaine, bibliographie [3300 titres 1875-1986]. Lyon 1990, Maison de l'Orient.   214 p. F 125 [RBgPg 71,133, S. *Byl*].

976 *Wolff* Hartmut, *al.*,   Aus Zeitschriften und Sammelbänden: HZ 254 (1992) 230-272. 514-548. 792-829.
977 Zeitschriftenschau: Anthropos 87 (1992) 331-348. 665-667.

A4.4   *Bibliographiae* orientalisticae.

978 *Balconi* Carla, *al.*, Bibliografia metodica [+ Testi recentemente pubblicati]: Aegyptus 72 (1992) 215-287, indice 288-294 [161-198].
978* **Conti** Giovanni, *al.*,   Index of Eblaic texts (published or cited): Quad-Semit, Materiali 1. F 1992, Univ. xxii-202 p. [BL 94,23].
979 *Deller* K., *Klengel* H.,   Keilschriftbibliographie 51: Orientalia 61 (1992) 1*-119*.
   Desreumaux A.,   Repertoire... manuscrits syriaques 1991 ➤ 9599.
981 Discussions in Egyptology, Index of articles, nos. 1-21 (1985-1991) [alphabetical by author]: DiscEg 22 (1992) 97-127.
982 *Khater* A.,   Index des Tomes XXI-XXX (1971-1991): BSACopte 30 (1991) 126-142.
983 *Leemans* Wilhelmus F.,   Bibliography of books and publications on the Ancient Near East: JbEOL 32 (1991s) 5-11.
984 MOSCATI Sabatino,   Bibliografia degli scritti 1943-1991, ᴱ*Chiesa* Giovanna: Bo Mg Studi Egittologici e di Antichità Puniche: min. 3. Pisa 1992, Giardini. [viii–] 59 p. portr.
985 **OIAc:** Oriental Institute Research Archives acquisitions list, with an indexed list of essays, articles and reviews, ᴱ**Jones** Charles E., 3s (1992); 5s (1992s). Ch 1992s, Univ. Oriental Institute. 442 p. / 396 p.
986 *Plas* Dirk van der,   IEDS — ein integriertes ägyptologisches Datenbanksystem; IED — eine internationale ägyptische Datenbank: ZäSpr 119 (1992) 38-43.
987 **Roman** Stephan,   The development of Islamic library collections in Western Europe and North America: Libraries and Librarianship in the Muslim World. L 1990, Mansell. xii-259 p. £40. – ᴿJRAS (1992) 256s (B. C. *Bloomfield*).
987* *Samir Khalil* S., Bibliographie copte à l'époque médiévale (1982-1988): ➤ 694*b*, Copte IVᵉ (1988/92) 2,82-85.
988 **Seecombe** Ian J., Syria: World Bibliog. 73. Ox 1987, Clio, xxxii-341 p., map. £45. – ᴿSyrie 69 (1992) 228s (T. *Bianquis*: rien sur Ugarit).
989 **Strijp** Ruud,   Cultural anthropology of the Middle East; a bibliography: HbOrientalistik 1/10/1. Leiden 1992, Brill. I. xxvi-565 p. 90-04-09604-3.
989* *Thissen* Heinz-Josef,   Demotische Literaturübersicht XIX/XX: Enchoria 19s (1992s) 181-213.
990 **ZVOr:** Zeitschriftverzeichnis Orient. Tübingen 1991, Universitätsbibliothek. 448 p. [OIAc 3,40].

A4.5   *Bibliographiae* archaeologicae.

991 *Acquaro* G. *al.*, Bibliografia 20 (1991): RStFen 20 (1992) 203-238; indice 239-242.
992 *Blanchard-Latreyte* Christine, *Dollfus* Geneviève, Bibliographie annuelle générale: Paléorient 17,2 (1991) 181-202; 18,2 (1992) 159-180.
993 Bulletin analytique d'architecture du monde grec: RArchéol (1992) 273-365: 455 items, followed by alphabetical indication of their sites.
994 *Bush* Louise K. (bibliographer), Checklist: JGlass 34 (1992) 166-224.

995 *Calmeyer* Peter, Archäologische Bibliographie 1991: ArchMIran 25 (1992) 165-377.

996 *a) Charpin* Dominique, L'usage de l'informatique dans l'UPR 193 (CNRS) [Mari et le Proche-Orient Antique]; – *b) Schretter* Manfred, Der Einsatz von EDV für das Projekt 'Sumerisches Lexikon' am Institut für Sprachen und Kulturen des Alten Orients an der Universität Innsbruck: Akkadica 79s (1992) 31-42 / 43-49.

997 *Christophe* J., Bibliographie AIEMA 1988s: BMosAnt 13 (1990s) 2-351.

998 *Decker* Wolfgang, *Hermann* Werner, Jahresbibliographie zum Sport im Altertum 1991: Nikephoros 4 (1991) 221-246; meist gr.-röm.; Ägypten p. 224; Alter Orient 225.

998* ᴱHerrmann Werner, *Neudecker* Richard, *al.*, Archäologische Bibliographie 1991 / 1992. B 1992s, de Gruyter. lii-575 p. / xl-484 p. 0341-8308.

999 *Jursa* M., *al.*, Register Assyriologie: AfO 38s (1991s) 282-429 (430-462, Bibliographie Mesopotamien).

1000 Levant, Author index to volumes I-XXIV: 24 (1992) 228-240.

1001 *MacKa*y D. Bruce, A comprehensive index to Biblical Archaeologist volumes 36-45 (1973-1982). Atlanta c. 1990, ASOR POB 15399. $10.

1002 Numismatic Literature 125s (1991) / 127s (1992): AmNumSoc.

1003 *Parola del Passato*, Indice 1-45 (1946-90): ParPass 46,257 supp. N 1991, Macchiaroli, 128 p.

1004 **Parry** Donald W., *Ricks* Stephen D., *Welch* John W., A bibliography on temples of the ancient Near East and Mediterranean world arranged by subject and author: ANE TSt 9. Lewiston NY 1991, Mellen. xi-311 p.; 2700+ items. $70. 0-7734-9775-7 [TDig 40,61].

1005 *a) Rolfe* Elizabeth, The Mariner's Mirror, index to volumes 56-65 / 66-70 / 71-75 (*Dolley* Cecilia): – L 1981/6/90, National Maritime Museum. 96 p. £4. – *b) Law* Derek, *al.*, Bibliography for 1991; 36 unnumbered pages.

1006 *Rolley* Claude, Les bronzes grecs et romains, recherches récentes XIV. Ateliers et centres de production XV. Petites statues; XVI. Ustensiles: RArchéol (1992) 381-395; 5 fig.

1007 ᴱScandaliato Ciciani Isotta, Le edizioni del XVII secolo: BtArcheol-StoArte supp. R 1983/6, Ist. Poligrafico.

1007* ᴱ*Symonds* R. P., Roman pottery bibliography: JPot 5 (1992) 127-160.

1008 **Whitcomb** Donald S., Introduction to Islamic archaeology; a preliminary bibliography of sites and artifacts; typescript deposited for consultation. Ch 1992, Oriental Inst. 222 p. [OIAc 2,29].

1009 **Wilfong** Terry G., Women in the ancient Near East; a select bibliography of recent sources: OIAc supp 2. Ch 1992, Univ. v-42 p. [OIAc 3,42].

II. Introductio

B1 *Introductio* .1 *tota vel VT* – **Whole Bible or OT.**

1010 **Albrektson** B., *Ringgren* H., En bok om Gamla testamentet⁵ [¹1969]. Malmö 1992, Gleerup. 254 p. 91-40615-42-1 [BL 93,71].

1011 L'Antico Testamento e le culture del tempo. R 1990, Borla. 622 p. Lit. 60.000. – ᴿProtestantesimo 47 (1992) 133s (E. *Noffke*, senza menzione di qualsiasi nome).

1012 **Arenhoevel** D., Introduzione all'AT 1989 ➔ 6,1154; 7,918: ᴿParVi 35 (1990) 464 (A. *Rolla*).

1013 ᴱ**Auneau** J., Les Psaumes et les autres Écrits: PetiteBtScB AT 5. P
1990, Desclée. 476 p. – ᴿNRT 114 (1992) 101s (J.-L. *Ska*).
1013* **Barr** James, The Bible in the modern world. L/Ph 1990 = 1973,
SCM/Trinity. xiv-193 p. 0-334-00113-7. – ᴿChurchman 105 (1991) 78-80
(D. *Spanner*: the new preface is unfair to conservative evangelicals).
1014 **Barth** Christopher, God with us; a theological introduction to the Old
Testament 1991 ⮞ 7,919: ᴿBtS 149 (1992) 246s (E. H. *Merrill*); ÉTRel 67
(1992) 273s (Françoise *Smyth*); ExpTim 103 (1991s) 153 (J. *Goldingay*:
rather a very fine theological midrash on Israel's own story); Grace TJ 12
(1991) 279s (J. J. *Lawlor*); LA 41 (1991) 556s (A. *Niccacci*); Themelios 19,1
(1993s) 21 (B. *Charette*); TTod 49 (1992s) 135s (R. N. *Boyce*).
1015 *a*) **Beasley** James R., An introduction to the Bible 1991 ⮞ 7,923: TBR
5,3 (1992s) 17 (A. *Bergquist*).
— *b*) ᴱ**Beyerlin** W., Testi religiosi per lo studio dell'AT, ᵀᴱ*Jucci* E.: AT
supp 1. Brescia 1992, Paideia. 376 p. Lit. 50.000 [Asprenas 40, 115, V.
Scippa].
— *c*) **Bič** Miloš, Ze světa Starého zakona (World of the OT). Praha I. 1985,
II. 1989, Kalich. 370 p. + p. 371-799. Kčs 65 + 71. – ᴿArOr 60 (1992)
178-181 (S. *Segert*).
1016 *a*) **Bonora** Antonio, [Libri di] Introduzione generale alla Bibbia [MAN-
NUCCI V. 1981]; – *b*) **Vignolo** Roberto, Nodi di una concezione teologica
della Bibbia [Introd.]: TItSett 17 (1992) 236-247 / 248-280...
1017 **Campbell** Antony F., The study companion to OT literature; an approach to the writings of pre-exilic and exilic Israel: OTSt 2, 1989
⮞ 6,1159; 7,926: ᴿAustralBR 38 (1990) 63-69 (R. G. *Jenkins*); CBQ 54
(1992) 315s (B. C. *Ollenburger*: delightful prose; notable OT areas frankly
omitted).
1018 **Cappelletto** Gianni, In cammino con Israele; introduzione all'AT I. Padova 1991, Messaggero. 214 p. Lit. 18.000. – ᴿCC 143 (1992,3) 101s (D.
Scaiola); Lateranum 58 (1992) 491s (G. *Deiana*); ParVi 37 (1992) 223s (T.
Lorenzin).
1018* **Ceresko** Anthony R., Introduction to the Old Testament; a liberation
perspective. Mkn 1992, Orbis. 336 p. $19 pa. [ConcordJ 19,288-290,
H. D. *Hummel* sees in this book the tendencies which he likes least in
Maryknoll and divided American Catholicism].
1019 **Coggins** R. J., Introducing the OT 1990 ⮞ 6,1161; 7,928: ᴿBtS 149
(1992) 487s (R. E. *Averbeck*); Interpretation 46 (1992) 86 (E. A. *Martens*).
Coote Robert B. & Mary P., Power, politics, and the making of the Bible
1990 ⮞ k165.
1020 *a*) **Dohmen** Christoph, Führer in ein unbekanntes Land; neue Einleitung
ins AT: BiKi 47 (1992) 52-54.
— *b*) **Drane** John, Introducing the OT 1987 ⮞ 4,1065... 6,1163: ᴿConcordTQ 55 (1991) 228s (P. L. *Schrieber*, favorable).
— *c*) **Duggan** Michael, The consuming fire; a Christian introduction to
the Old Testament. SF 1991, Ignatius. xx-671 p. $30 pa. [CBQ 54,613].
– ᴿCanadCathR 10,9 (1992) 32s (Barbara E. *Organ*).
1021 *Freedman* David N., The symmetry of the Hebrew Bible [1991 Oslo
Mowinckel lecture]: ST 46 (1992) 83-108.
1022 **González Etchegaray** J., *al.*, Introducción al estudio de la Biblia, 1. La
Biblia en su entorno [ᴱ*Sánchez Caro* J. M. ⮞ 7,952] 1990 [VI. Sinop/Hc
⮞ 4522]: ᴿCompostellanum 36 (1991) 234-6 (J. *Precedo Lafuente*); RET
51 (1991) 515-8 (P. *Barrado Fernández*); TLZ 117 (1992) 491-4 [W. *Negel*:
wertlos ohne Register).

1023 *Gottlieb* Isaac B., Sof Davar, biblical endings [... to stories, units, entire books, larger cycles]: Prooftexts 11 (1992) 213-224.

1024 **Gottwald** Norman K., The Hebrew Bible, a socio-literary introduction 1985 ➤ 5,1144; 6,1167: ᴿTR 88 (1992) 456s (L. *Schwienhorst-Schönberger*).

1024* **Hauer** Christian E., *Young* William A., An introduction to the Bible; a journey into three worlds². ENJ 1990, Prentice-Hall. xxii-278 p. – ᴿRelStT 11,1 (1991) 48-50 (J. L. *Bazett-Jones*).

1025 **Hill** Andrew E., *Walton* John H., A survey of the Old Testament [evangelical college text] 1991 ➤ 7,937: ᴿAndrUnS 30 (1992) 170s (F. *Tan*); OTAbs 15 (1992) 277 (C. T. *Begg*).

1026 **Hinson** David F., The books of the Old Testament²ʳᵉᵛ [¹1974]: OT Introduction 2, TEF Study Guide 10. L 1992, SPCK. xiv-210 p.; 21 fig.; map. 0-281-04564-X (-5-8 3d world); [TBR 6/2,25, M. J. *Boda*: ideal clarity for 2d-language English-users].

1027 ᴱ**Jagersma** H., *Vervenne* M., Inleiding in het Oude Testament. Kampen 1992, Kok. 322 p. *f* 52,50. 90-242-6832-X [TvT 33,408, N. *Tromp*]. – ᴿStreven 59 (1992s) 1325s (P. *Beentjes*).

1028 **Kaiser** Otto, Grundriss der Einleitung in die kanonischen und deuterokanonischen Schriften des ATs 1. Die erzählenden Werke. Gü 1992, Mohn. 3-579-00058-6 [BL 93,89; ZAW 105,530, ersetzt nicht frühcrcs ¹1969 ⁵1985].

1028* **Laffey** Alice L., Wives, harlots, and concubines; the OT in feminist perspective 1990 ➤ 6,1173; 7,939 [= 1988 ➤ 4,1075]: ᴿModern Churchman 34,2 (1992s) 54s (Alison & Paul *Joyce*: on the whole judicious; U. S. title better).

1029 ᴱ**Lafontaine** R., *al.*, L'Écriture, âme de la théologic 1989/90 ➤ 6,541. ᴿNRT 114 (1992) 105s (D. *Luciani*).

1030 **Lambiasi** Francesco, La Bibbia, introduzione generale: Manuali di base 1, 1991 ➤ 7,940: ᴿAsprenas 39 (1992) 587 (V. *Scippa*); CC 143 (1992,4) 430s (G. *Giachi*).

1031 **Lang** Bernhard, Die Bibel, eine kritische Einführung: Uni 1954, 1990 ➤ 6,1175: ᴿBiKi 47 (1992) 177 (F. J. *Stendebach*); BLtg 64 (1991) 173s (J. M. *Oesch*); Carthaginensia 8 (1992) 924 (R. *Sanz Valdivieso*); DielB 27 (1991) 284s (B. J. *Diebner*); TLZ 117 (1992) 735s (Ingo *Baldermann*).

1032 *Lemaître* Henri, Bible et milieu cultural: RICAO 1s (1992) 69-78 [< TContext 10/1, p. 20].

1032* *a) Lemche* Niels P., Det gamle Testamente som en hellenistisk bog; – *b) Nielsen* Eduard, En hellenistisk bog?: DanTTs 55 (1992) 81-101 / 161-174 [< ᴢɪᴛ 92,680].

Loretz O., Ugarit and the Bible 1990 ➤ b441*.

1034 **Mahnke** Hermann, Die biblische Botschaft im Überblick; Altes Testament, Neues Testament: Lesen und Verstehen 1s / Biblisch-theologische Schwerpunkte 8s. Gö 1992, Vandenhoeck & R. I. AT, xv-285 p.; 18 fig.; II. NT, xvi + p. 287-559; 14 fig. 3-525-61289-3; -90-7.

1034* **Marshall** Celia B., A guide through the Old Testament. Louisville 1989, W-Knox. 158 p. $15 pa. [ConcordTQ 57,145s, A. F. *Steinmann*: good as a workbook, but approach is critical and not even updatedly so].

1035 **Matthews** Victor H., *Benjamin* Don C., OT parallels: laws and stories 1991 ➤ 7,942: ᴿBA 55 (1992) 154 (J. A. *Dearman*); CBQ 54 (1992) 754s (B. F. *Batto*); ÉglT 23 (1992) 271 (W. *Vogels*); TLZ 117 (1992) 591s (D. *Vieweger*).

1036 **Mertens** Heinrich A., Manual de la Biblia, ᵀ*Gancho* C., 1989 ➤ 6,1176; 7,943: ᴿLumenVr 40 (1991) 207s (F. *Ortiz de Urtaran*); TVida 33 (1991) 322s (E. *Pérez-Cotapos L.*).

1037 **Mickelsen** A. Berkeley & Alvera M., Understanding Scripture; how to read and study the Bible² [¹1982]. Peabody MA 1992, Hendrickson. xi-141 p. 0-943575-84-2 [NTAbs 37, p. 107].

1038 ᴱ**Mulder** M., *al.*, Mikra 1988 ➤ 4,317 ... 7,944: ᴿJJS 43 (1992) 142s (P. R. *Davies*); JPseud 7 (1990) 122-6 (Carol *Newsom*); RÉJ 151 (1992) 223s (J.-C. *Attias*); TLZ 117 (1992) 181-3 (D. A. *Koch*); TRu 57 (1992) 439-441 (L. *Perlitt*).

1038* **Ohler** Annemarie, Studying the OT 1985 ➤ 1,1198 ... 6,1178*: ᴿChurchman 106 (1992) 72 (G. *Bray*).

1039 *Petersen* David L., Hebrew Bible Form Criticism [the seven of the projected 24 FOTLit]: RelStR 18 (1992) 29-33.

1040 **Pilch** John J., Introducing the cultural context of the Old [also New] Testament: Hear the Word! 1, 1991 ➤ 7,947: ᴿBibTB 22 (1992) 180 (J. F. *Craghan*: high praise).

1041 ᴱ**Propp** W. H., *al.*, The Hebrew Bible and its interpreters 1986/90 ➤ 6,550: ᴿInterpretation 46 (1992) 307s (P. K. *Hooker*); LA 41 (1991) 551-5 (A. *Niccacci* & M. *Pazzini*).

1042 **Ravasi** Gianfranco, AT Introduzione 1991 ➤ 7,959: ᴿAsprenas 39 (1992) 108s (S. *Cipriani*); CC 143 (1992,2) 526s (G. L. *Prato*).

1043 **Rendtorff** R., Introduzione all'AT 1990 ➤ 6,1180; 7,950: ᴿLateranum 58 (1992) 494-7 (R. *Gelio*); ParVi 36 (1991) 391s (A. *Rolla*); Protestantesimo 47 (1992) 242-4 (B. *Ramírez*); RivB 40 (1992) 229-232 (L. *Monari*); STEv 4 (1992) 64-66 (V. *Bernardi*).

1044 **Rogerson** J., *Davies* P., The OT world 1989 ➤ 5,1163 ... 7,951: ᴿBO 49 (1992) 464-470 (O. *Keel*).

1045 [ᴱ*Sanchez Caro* J. M.] Introducción I., ᴱ*Artola* A., Biblia y palabra de Dios 1989 ➤ 5,1447 ... 7,952: ᴿCompostellanum 36 (1991) 236s (J. *Precedo Lafuente*); RBiArg 53 (1991) 163-7 (R. *Krüger*).

1046 **Schmidt** W., *Thiel* W., *Hanhart* R., Altes Testament [storia; archeologia ...; Eng. ➤ 7,954]: ⁴1989 ➤ 5,1116: ᴿProtestantesimo 47 (1992) 245 (J. *Hobbins*: mancanze).

1047 **Schultz** Samuel J., The Old Testament speaks⁴ 1990 ➤ 7,953: ᴿNewTR 4,4 (1991) 91s (L. R. *Hoppe*: aimed at Christians, but unhelpfully historicizing).

1048 **Sicre** José Luis, Introducción al Antiguo Testamento. Estella 1992, VDivino. 299 p.; ill., maps. 84-7151-778-7.

1049 **Soggin** J. A., Introduction to the OT³ 1989 ➤ 5,1170 ... 7,957: ᴿChrSchR 20 (1990s) 327s (D. E. *Burke*); ConcordTQ 56 (1992) 54s (C. W. *Mitchell*: admirable summary of 'scientific objectivity' but avoids and even warns against Christocentric reading); VT 42 (1992) 281 (H.G.M. *Williamson*).

1050 ᴱ**Stachowiak** L., ℗ Wstęp do Starego Testamentu [OT Introd.]. Poznań 1990, Pallottinum. 495 p. – ᴿColcT 62,4 (1992) 177s (J. *Warzecha*, ℗).

1051 ᴱ**Stone** Michael E., Rock inscriptions and graffiti project Is Inscriptions 1-3000 / -6000. SBL Resources for Biblical Study 28s. Atlanta 1992, Scholars. 282 p.; 244 p.; each $30; sb./pa. $20.

1052 **Tarazi** Paul N., The Old Testament, an introduction, I. Historical traditions. Crestwood NY 1991, St. Vladimir. xii-173 p. $10. 0-88141-105-1 [TDig 40,189].

1053 **Van Gemeren** Willem, The progress of redemption; the story of salvation from creation to the New Jerusalem. GR 1988, Zondervan. 544 p. $20. – RWestTJ 53 (1991) 147-9 (J. *Worgul*).

1054 **Walton** John H., Ancient Israelite literature in its cultural context; a survey of parallels between biblical and Ancient Near Eastern texts 1989 ➔ 6,1186; 7,938; RAndrewsUnS 30 (1992) 179-181 (P.D. *Duerksen*); CalvaryB 7,1 (1991) 66 (C. E. *McLain*); WestTJ 53 (1991) 355-7 (R. S. *Hess*).

1055 **Zenger** Erich, Das erste Testament; die jüdische Bibel und die Christen. Dü 1991, Patmos. 208 p. DM 26,80. – REvKomm 25 (1992) 491s (R. *Boschert-Kimmig*); KIsr 7 (1992) 99-101 (J. *Kirchberg*).

B1.2 'Invitations' to Bible or OT.

1056 **Andrew** M. E., Responding in community; reforming religion ... Dunedin NZ 1990, Univ. Otago. 180 p. $25. 0-9597629-1-4 [OTAbs 15,268].

1057 **Arnoldshaimer Konferenz**, Votum: Das Buch Gottes, elf Zugänge zur Bibel. Neuk 1992, Neuk.-V. 186 p.

1058 **Bagot** J.-P., *Barrios-Aucher* D., De Bijbel dichter Bij iedereen, TEEvenhuis G. Boxtel/Turnhout 1991, KBS/Brepols. 430 p. Fb. 1166. – RCollatVL 22 (1992) 109 (H. *Hoet*).

1059 **Barton** John, What is the Bible? 1991 ➔ 7,962: RTablet 246 (1992) 749s (G. *O'Collins*); TLond 95 (1992) 296s (T. *Wright*).

1060 **Beauchamp** Paul, Leggere la Sacra Scrittura oggi 1990 ➔ 6,1192; 7,963: RCC 143 (1992,1) 304s (D. *Scaiola*); ParVi 36 (1991) 399 (C. *Ghidelli*).

1061 **Beauchamp** P., Hablar de Escrituras Santas; perfil del lector actual de la Biblia [1987]T. Barc 1989, Herder. 136 p. – RCiuD 204 (1991) 268 (J. *Gutiérrez*).

1062 **Berkeley** A., *Mickelsen* Alvera M., Understanding Scripture. Peabody MA 1992, Hendrickson. 141 p. $10 [BToday 31,120].

1062* *a*) *Biser* Eugen, Die Bibel als Medium; zur medienanalytischen Schlüsselfunktion der Theologie; – *b*) *Krauss* Heinrich, Biblische Geschichten für das Fernsehen; zum Projekt einer Verfilmung des ATs: LebZeug 45 (1990) 95-106 / 129-138.

1063 *a*) **Bockmuehl** Klaus, †, Listening to the God who speaks, reflections on God's guidance from Scripture and the lives of God's people, EYanni Kathryn. ... 1990. Helmers-H. 176 p. $8. 0-939-44318-X. – RCrux 28,2 (1992) 43s (D. *Stewart*).

— *b*) **Breton** Stanislas, Libres commentaires [lieux scripturaires d'intérêt philosophique]: La nuit surveillée. P 1990, Cerf. 166 p. – [LavalTP 49, 582, J. *Paradis*].

— *c*) EBrooks R., *Collins* J. J., Hebrew Bible or OT? 1989/90 ➔ 6,579*: RLivLight 28,2 (1991s) 190s (C. *Begg*).

1064 **Brown** R. E., Responses to 101 questions on the Bible 1991 ➔ 6,1194; 7,964: RBR 7,1 (1991) 9s (H. *Shanks*: candid and unbiased); Interpretation 46 (1992) 90s (J. C. *Purdy*: good); RCatalT 17 (1992) 291s (F. *Raurell*); LivLight 28,4 (1991s) 362 (G. P. *Weber*).

1064* **Brueggemann** Walter, Interpretation and obedience; from faithful reading to faithful living: 1991 ➔ 7,186: RCurrTMiss 19 (1992) 128 (J. R. *Seraphine*: fireworks of lively interpretation).

1065 **Comte** Fernand, Les grandes figures bibliques: Les compacts. P 1992, Bordas. 256 p. [Études 378,140, P. *Gibert*, très défavorable].

1066 **Corston** John B., Journey under God; a student guide to the Old Testament. St. John's Newf. 1990, Breakwater. 162 p. $13. – ᴿCatholic World 234 (1991) 35s (L. *Boadt*, also on DRANE J.).

1067 **Cunningham** Phillip J., Exploring Scripture; how the Bible came to be. NY 1992, Paulist. xiv-216 p. $11. 0-8091-3295-8 [BL 93,78, B. P. *Robinson*: college chaplaincy talks, less out-of-date for NT than for OT; NTAbs 36,410].

1068 **Daiber** Karl-Fritz, *Lukatis* Ingrid, Bibelfrömmigkeit als Gestalt gelebter Religion: TArbB 6. Bielefeld 1991, Luther. 308 p. DM 48. – ᴿLuth-Mon 31 (1992) 331 (G. *Wegner*).

1069 **Davidson** R., A beginner's guide to the Old Testament. E 1992, St. Andrew. x-148 p. £5.50. 0-7152-0637-0 [BL 93,78, E. B. *Mellor*: delightful; partly from articles in Life and Work].

1069* **Deissler** Alfons, Con Dios paso a paso; textos clave del AT [Gehen mit Gott < Christ in der Gegenwart 1989], ᵀ*Minguez* Dionisio: Surcos. Estella 1992, VDivino. 214 p. 84-7151-788-4 [ActuBbg 30,38, I. *Riudor*].

1070 *Ehle* Paulo, A Bíblia como instrumento de transformação e poder popular: REB 52 (1992) 433-6.

1071 *Espiau de la Maëstre* A., P. CLAUDEL et la Bible; le charisme du poète et du prophète; ÉtClas 60 (1992) 313-320.

1071* ᴱ**Fabris** Rinaldo, La Bibbia nell'epoca moderna e contemporanea. Bo 1992, Dehoniane. 412 p. Lit. 42.000. – ᴿLetture 47 (1992) 759s (G. *Ravasi*: mancanze).

1072 **Fowl** Stephen E., *Jones* L. Gregory, Reading in communion; Scripture and ethics in Christian life. GR 1991, Eerdmans. 164 p. $14. – ᴿCurr-TMiss 19 (1992) 215s (R. *Hütter*).

1073 **[Lane]** Fox Robin, The unauthorized version; truth and fiction in the Bible. L 1991 → 7,970; Penguin pa. £9; 0-14-011432-7; – ᴿChurchman 106 (1992) 367-9 (D. *Spanner*); NY Times Book Review (June 7,1992) 13 (J. P. *Meier*); Tablet 246 (1992) 45 (N. *King*: a very good book; p. 70, protest by Sir David *Goodall*); TLond 95 (1992) 297s (R. P. *Carroll*: well-informed and perceptive atheist).

1074 **[Lane]** Fox R., Verità e invenzione nella Bibbia, ᴿ*Spinelli* Donatella & Piero. Mi 1992, Rizzoli. 518 p. 88-17-84221-4.

1074* **[Lane]** Fox Robin, De Bijbel, waarheid en verdichting. Amst/Antwerpen 1991, Agon/Distybo. 508 p. Fb 1190. 90-5157-104-6. – ᴿStreven 59 (1992s) 659 (P. *Beentjes*); TvT 32 (1992) 414 (L. *Grollenberg*).

1075 **Frör** Hans, Wie eine wilde Blume; biblische Liebesgeschichten: Tb 73. Mü 1990, Kaiser. 108 p. DM 16,80 pa. – ᴿTsTKi 62 (1991) 295s (Terje *Stordalen*).

1076 *a)* **Gibert** Pierre, L'Antico Testamento, guida di lettura; – *b)* **Morgen** Michèle, Il Nuovo Testamento. Brescia 1990, Queriniana. 128 p.; 109 p. Lit. 15.000 ciascuno. – ᴿCC 143 (1992,2) 218s (G. *Giachi*).

1077 **Girlanda** Antonio, Antico Testamento, iniziazione biblica. CinB 1992, Paoline. 318 p.

1078 *a)* **Goldbrunner** J., Corso biblico 1. AT; 2. NT; 3. Chiesa. Brescia 1990. Queriniana. 110 p.; 116 p.; 140 p. Lit. 15.000 ognuno. – ᴿParVi 36 (1991) 390 (C. *Ghidelli*).

— *b)* **Goldsworthy** Graeme, According to plan; the unfolding revelation of God in the Bible. Leicester 1991, Inter-Varsity. 320 p. £6. – ᴿThemelios 18,1 (1992s) 30 (G. *Grogan*).

— *c)* **Goosen** Louis, Van Abraham tot Zacharia 1990 → 6,872: ᴿStreven 58 (1990s) 950 (G. *Groot*).

1079 **Grelot** Pierre, Leggere la Bibbia [brani scelti]. CasM 1990, Piemme. 480 p. Lit. 29.500. – ᴿProtestantesimo 47 (1992) 144 (G. *Scuderi*).

1080 **Hampsch** John H., Glad you asked; Scriptural answers for our times. Huntington IN 1992, Our Sunday Visitor. 155 p. $7. 0-87973-466-3 [TDig 39,363].

1080* **Jacobs** Andrés, *a)* Fichas de formación bíblica; – *b)* Iniciación a la reflexión teológica; lectura creyente de la realidad; fichas de formación. Lima 1988/91, MIEC-JECL. / 148 p. – ᴿPáginas 17,1 (1992) 118s (Ana *Gispert-Sauch*).

1081 **Kamin** Sarah, Jews and Christians interpret the Bible. J 1991, Hebrew Univ. 68* + 99 + 8 p.

1082 **King** Thomas M., Enchantments 1989 → 6,1643*: ᴿGregorianum 73 (1992) 357s (R. *Faricy*).

1083 *Knoch* O., Die Bedeutung der Bibel für die europäische Kultur: LebZeug 47,1 (Pd 1992) 41-50 [< ZIT 92,228].

1084 **Kuhn** Johannes, Heilsame Begegnungen; Gotteserfahrungen im ANT. Stu 1991, Quell. 108 p. DM 12,80. [ErbAuf 68,249].

1085 **Levenson** Jon D., Sinai and Zion; an entry into the Jewish Bible 1985 → 1,1234 ... 3,1191: ᴿJAAR 60 (1992) 344s (D. C. *Hester*).

1085* **Lukefahr** Oscar, A Catholic guide to the Bible. 1992, Liguori. 208 p. £6 [BToday 31, 383].

ᶠ**Luz** Ulrich, La Bible, une pomme de discorde 1992 → 479.

1086 **Lys** Daniel, Treize énigmes de l'AT 1988 → 4,1125 ... 7,977: ᴿMasses Ouvrières 445 (1992) 103s (J.-M. *Carrière*).

1087 **McIlhone** J. P., The word made clear. Ch 1992, T. More. 222 p. $17 pa. 0-88347-268-6 [NTAbs 36,413].

1088 **Magonet** Jonathan, A Rabbi's Bible 1991 → 7,978: ᴿTLond 95 (1992) 46s (J.F.A. *Sawyer*: wide-ranging witty and critical comments; one essay is 'How a donkey reads the Bible').

1089 **Manigne** Jean-Pierre, Les figures du temps. P 1991, Cerf. 176 p. – ᴿBrotéria 135 (1992) 357 (F. *Pires Lopes*).

1090 [*Maraval* P. présent.] Figures de l'AT chez les Pères. P 1989, Centre Analyse de Patristique. 316 p. F 145. 2-906805-01-7. – ᴿStPatav 38 (1991) 447-9 (C. *Corsato*).

1091 *Morla* Víctor, Biblia y racionalidad: LumenVr 40 (1991) 209-233.

1092 *Pardes* I., Countertraditions in the Bible. CM 1992, Harvard Univ. 194 p. $30 [TS 53,602].

1093 *Pastore* Corrado, Leer la Biblia desde la vida: Nuevo Mundo 156s (Caracas 1992) 225-231.

1093* *Peters* F. E., Judaism, Christianity, and Islam; the classical texts and their interpretation, 1. [history] From covenant to community; 2. [revelation, Scripture]. The word and the law and the people of God; 3. [temples, theology]. The works of the Spirit 1990 → 6,1219: ᴿBSO 55 (1992) 195 (A. *Rippin*: successful companion to his 1982 Children of Abraham).

1094 Le petit guide de la Bible [4 British, 1 Canadian, 1 moralist, 1984]. Méry/P 1992, Sator/Médiaspaul. 352 p.; 150 fig.; 18 maps [NRT 115,142].

1095 **Power** John, L'Antico Testamento, storia di salvezza [Dublin 1989], ᵀ*Nardelli* Annalisa. CinB 1992, Paoline. 202 p.

1095* **Quilici** Alain, La Voix du bonheur; petit chemin pour traverser la Bible à l'intention des débutants: Lumière, Vérité. P 1992, Fayard. 234 p. [RThom 93,168, J.-G. *Ranquet*].

1096 ᴱ**Radday** Y., *Brenner* A., On humour and the comic in the Hebrew Bible 1990 → 6,367; 7,963*; ᴿHenoch 14 (1992) 327s (P. *Capelli*); JTS 43

(1992) 154 (D. F. *Murray*: just about limited to sardonic names); TLZ 117 (1992) 35-38 (W. *Herrmann*); VT 42 (1992) 133s (R. P. *Gordon*).

1097 **Raucoule** Jules C., Le Dieu de la Bible assistant des 'décideurs' [officials]: Rediviva. Nîmes 1992, Lacour. 102 p. – ᴿEsprVie 102 (1992) 308 (L. *Monloubou*: plutôt des 'décidés', ceux qui n'ont aucun droit à la décision et dont le sort est réglé par les autres).

1098 *Ravasi* Gianfranco, La bellezza nella Bibbia: RivScR 5 (1991) 17-27.

1099 *Ritt* Hubert, [*al.*], Das eine Wort und die vielen Wörter [...im Gottesdienst]: BLtg 64 (1991) 130-5 (–164].

1100 **Rohr** Richard, *Martos* Joseph, Das entfesselte Buch; die Lebenskraft des ATs, 1990 ➤ 7,984: ᴿLebZeug 45 (1990) 156 (R. *Jungnitsch*).

1100* **Schramm** Warner, present., Das Buch Gottes; elf Zugänge zur Bibel; ein Votum des Theologischen Ausschusses: Arnoldshainer Konferenz. Neuk 1992, Neuk.-V. 186 p. 3-7887-1415-8.

1101 *Schreiner* Josef, Theologie lehren und lernen in alttestamentlicher Sicht: ➤ 52, ᶠErfurt 1992, 244-259.

1102 **Sheppard** Gerald T., The future of the Bible; beyond liberalism and literalism. Toronto 1990, United Church. xii-147 p. – ᴿSR 21 (1992) 115 (D. *MacLachlan*).

1102* **Sloyan** Gerard S., So you mean to read the Bible! ColMn 1992, Liturgical. 68 p. $4 [BToday 31, 249: 'tips for absolute beginners' – 'who have tried and given up'].

1103 **Sorger** Karlheinz, *Gartmann* Michael, Was in der Bibel wichtig ist; Grundthemen des Alten und Neuen Testaments. Mü 1992, Kösel. 158 p. – ᴿMiscFranc 92 (1992) 615s (J. *Imbach*, riserve).

1104 **Steinwede** Dietrich, Kommt und schaut die Taten Gottes; die Bibel in Auswahl, nacherzählt. Gö 1992, Vandenhoeck & R. 208 p.; color. ill. (Nachweis p. 207). 3-525-61235-4.

1104* *Tabor* James D., Reflections on the Hebrew Bible [more attractive than his 'Christian traditions'] and the New Testament: JRefJud 37,3 (1990) 35-38 (39-41, response, *Signer* Michael A.).

1105 *a) Tambasco* Anthony J., Quodlibetalia biblica [prophets; God of wrath?; how Christ atones; was Jesus revolutionary?]; – *b) O'Grady* John, More about the Bible [... covenant; NT pluralism? who wrote the Gospels?]: ChSt 31 (1992) 282-9 / 316-324.

1105* **Visotzky** Burton L., *a)* Reading the Book; making the Bible a timeless text. NY 1991, Doubleday. [x–] 240 p. 0-385-41294-0. – *b)* Reading with the Rabbis; making the Bible a timeless text: ChrCent 108 (1991) 931-5.

1106 *a) Weinberg* Joel P., The perception of 'things' and their production in the OT historical writings; – *b) Weinfeld* Moshe, The phases of human life in Mesopotamian and Jewish sources: ➤ 19, ᶠBLENKINSOPP J. 1992, 174-181 / 182-9.

1107 ᴱ**Williams** Michael E., The storyteller's companion to the Bible. Nv 1992, Abingdon. I. Gen. 201 p. II. Ex-Jos, also 201 p. III. Jg-Kgs. 187 p. – 0-687-39670-0; –1-9; –2-7.

1108 *Zovkić* Mato, Sacra Scriptura in scriptis fundatricis Ordinis Carmelitarum (croatice): BogSmot 62,3s (1992) 262-294.

B1.3 *Paedagogia biblica* – **Bible-teaching techniques.**

1108* **Berg** Horst K., Ein Wort wie Feuer; Wege lebendiger Bibelauslegung 1991 ➤ 7,991: ᴿBiKi 47 (1992) 174s (R. *Baumann*); TR 88 (1992) 456-8 (D. *Dormeyer*); TsTKi 63 (1992) 221 (T. *Stordalen*).

1109 *Biesinger* Albert, Orientierungen für Glaubensdidaktik und Jugendpastoral [KULD L.; FOWLER J.; SILLER H.; BUMILLER M.]: TüTQ 172 (1992) 318-323.

1110 ᴱBissoli C., Giovani e Bibbia; per una lettura esistenziale della Bibbia nei gruppi giovanili [< Note di pastorale giovanile, Salesiani-Roma]. Torino 1991, LDC. 267 p. – ᴿRuBi 45 (1992) 47 (R. *Kempiak*).

1111 **Bobrowski** Jürgen, Bibliodramapraxis. Ha-Rissen 1991, EB. 235 p. DM 20. – ᴿEvKomm 25 (1992) 614-6 (W. *Teichert*).

1113 **Borgonovo** G., *al.*, Il testo biblico; per un approccio scolastico. T 1990, SEI. 176 p. Lit. 19.000. – ᴿViPe 74 (1991) 390s (C. *Ghidelli*, anche su 3 altri della collana).

1114 **Brereton** Virginia L., Training God's army; the American Bible school, 1880-1940; 1990 ➤ 6,1233*: ᴿChH 61 (1992) 425-7 (W. V. *Trollinger*).

1114* *Cromhout* Frans, De Bijbel met jongeren [...niemands privé-bezit]: Streven 58 (1990s) 579-586.

1115 **Dunbar** Colin A., The Bible instructor; [Adventist] manual for the training of lay Bible instructors: diss. Andrews, ᴰ*Kilcher* D. Berrien Springs MI 1992. 434 p. 92-25974. – DissA 53 (1992s) 2314-A.

1116 **Flader** Steven L., Journaling as a method of Bible study: diss. United Theol. Sem. ᴰ*Rust* Renee, 1989. 124 p. 92-21955. – DissA 53 (1992s) 1178-A.

1117 *a) Flossmann* Karel, Die Bibelbewegung in Böhmen und Mähren; – *b) Hohnjec* Nikola, ... in Kroatien; – *c) Aliulis* Vaclovas, ... in Litauen; – *d) Nagy* Josef, ... Siebenbürgen (Rumänien); – *e) Maga* Ján, *Packa* Vojtech, ... Slowakei; – *f) Rozman* Francè, ... Slowenien; – *g) Tarjáni* Béla, ... Ungarn; – *h) Kudasiewicz* Józef, *al.*, ... Polen: BLtg 65 (1992) 203s / 205-7 / 207-9 / 219-222 / 223-7 / 227s / 230-4 / 209-219.

1118 *Harris* Maria, *Moran* Gabriel, Catechetical language and religious education: TTod 49 (1992s) 21-30.

1118* *Haynes* Stephen, Relearning to read; reflections on teaching Scripture to university students: Modern Churchman 34,1 (Manchester 1992s) 34-41.

1119 *Höffken* Peter, Das Alte Testament in der Religionspädagogik der 80er Jahre: VerkF 36,1 (1991) 72-101: hundert Bücher, Register S. 107.

1120 *Holleran* J. Warren, The Bible and the ongoing education of priests: The Priest 48,5 (1992) 43-46.

1120* *Johns* J. D. & Cheryl B., Yielding to the Spirit; a Pentecostal approach to group Bible study: JPentT 1,1 (Shf 1992) 109-134 [< ZIT 92,749].

1121 ᴱKogler Franz. Tägliche Begegnung mit dem Wort Gottes; Bibelleseplan nach der katholischen Bibelleseordnung, Lesejahr II. Linz 1991, auct. 190 p. DM 9,80. – ᴿBLtg 65 (1992) 123s (B. *Kranemann*).

1122 *a) Kremer* Jacob ➤ 1170 [StiZt (1992) 75-90]. Non v'è parola di Dio senza parola d'uomo; riflessioni per l'«Anno con la Bibbia» 1992; ᵀColombi Giulio: HumBr 47 (1992) 850-873.

— *b)* ᴱKrondorfer Björn, Body and Bible; interpreting and experiencing biblical narratives [by play or biblio-drama]. Ph 1992, Trinity. 218 p. $20 [BToday 31,382].

— *c) McVann* M., The teacher and the taught; reflections after the fact: Listening 27 (Romeoville IL 1992) 195-205 [< NTAbs 37,167].

1123 **Marshall** Michael, The Gospel connection; a study in evangelism for the nineties. L 1990, Darton-LT. 290 p. £10 pa. – ᴿTLond 95 (1992) 217s (*Bernard* SFF: passionate; dubious who will connect).

1124 *Martín Barrios* J. L., *a*) La dimensión bíblica de la pastoral catequética en España desde el Concilio Vaticano II hasta nuestros días; – *b*) La Sagrada Escritura en los catecismos de la comunidad cristiana: Teología y catequesis 35s (1990) 373-388 / 399-434 [< RET 52,259].

1125 *Martini* Carlo, Teaching the Scriptures to a diocese [< Catholic Biblical Federation Bulletin 19]: PrPeo 6 (1992) 225-9.

1126 **Mesters** Carlos, 'Seht, ich mache alles neu'; Bibel und Neuevangelisierung: Tb 6. Stu 1991, KBW. 128 p. 3-460-11006-6.

1127 **Pikaza** X., *Sánchez Cruz* G., Nueva Biblia de los pobres; catequesis bíblica en imágenes. Bilbao 1991, Desclée de Brouwer 333 p. – ᴿRelCu 38 (1992) 116 (J. A. *Nistal*).

1128 **Pranjić** Marko, Biblija u katehezi. Zagreb 1992, Katehetski salezijanski centar. 139 p. – ᴿBogSmot 62 (1992) 312-4 (A. *Rebić*).

1129 **Roop** E. F., Let the rivers run; stewardship and the biblical story: Library of Christian stewardship. GR 1991, Eerdmans. xii-108 p. $10. 0-8028-0809-0 [BL 93,115, R. *Hammer*: homiletic rather than critical].

1129* **Roos** Klaus, Habt ihr keine Ohren, um zu hören? Reiz-Texte zur Bibel für Predigt und Gruppenarbeit. Mainz 1990, Grünewald. 128 p. DM 19,80. – ᴿBLtg 64 (1991) 50-52 (Susanne *Warmuth*).

1130 *Schelander* Robert, Der Streit um das Alte Testament im christlichen Religionsunterricht: ➤ 163, ᶠSAUER G., Aktualität 1992, 305-315.

1131 **Schinzer** Reinhard, Spielräume in der Bibel; Anregungen für den Umgang mit der Bibel in Gruppen 1989 ➤ 6,1243; 7,998: ᴿLuthTK 15 (1991) 185s (M. *Schätzel*); Protestantesimo 47 (1992) 342s (U. *Eckert*); TsTKi 62 (1991) 297 (T. *Grevbo*).

1132 *Schlüter* Richard, Erwachsenenkatechese heute — ein Bildungsprozess im Glauben? Zur gegenseitigen Abhängigkeit von Kirchen- und Katecheseverständnis: TGL 82 (1992) 46-72.

1133 **Scott** Marina sr., Picking the 'right' Bible study program [92 programs commended, 15 specially]. Ch c. 1992, ACTA. $15. 0-87946-063-6 [TDig 39,286]. – ᴿPrPeo 6 (1992) 486 (H. *Wansbrough*).

1134 *Stefani* Piero, Per una cultura biblica in Italia; l'associazione laica Biblia: RClerIt 73 (1992) 44-49.

1135 **Ubillus** José A., Alrededor de la Biblia; encuentros con la Palabra para las comunidades de base: Nuevos Horizontes 2. Lima 1991, Paulinas. 118 p. – ᴿRTLim 25 (1991) 310s (U. *Berges*).

1135* **Van Ness** Patricia W., Transforming Bible study with children; a guide for learning together. Nv 1991, Abingdon. 126 p. 0-687-42502-6. – ᴿTBR 5,1 (1992s) 37 (G. *Miles*).

1136 *Weinrich* Michael, [*al.*] Religionspädagogik in der Bewährung; Konsolidierungen, Innovationen und Verlegenheiten: VerkF 37,1 (1992) 17-48 [zahlreiche Publikationen, auch 3-77; Register 78].

1137 *a*) *Witherup* R. D., The role of Scripture studies in the intellectual formation of future priests; – *b*) *Lothamer* J. W., The study of the Bible in U.S. Catholic seminaries; six seminary curricula compared; – *c*) *Noye* I., L'enseignement de l'Écriture Sainte à Saint-Sulpice; – *d*) *Bouchaud* C., L'enseignement de l'Écriture Sainte dans les 'ratio' nationales; – *e*) *Auffret* P., *al.*, L'enseignement de l'Éc. S. au séminaire S. Irénée de Lyon; – *f*) *Hunter* A. Vanlier, Introducing OT studies in the seminary: ➤ 442, Ens. Écr. 1992, 240-255 / 72-90 / 28-37 / 58-71 / 92-108 / 116-125.

1138 *Ziemer* J., Die Bibel als Sprachhilfe; zum Bibelgebrauch in den Kirchen

während der 'Wende' im Herbst 1989: PastT 81 (Gö 1992) 280-291
[< ZIT 92,533].

B2.1 Hermeneutica.

1139 **Arens** Edmund, Christopraxis; Grundzüge theologischer Handlungstheorie [HABERMAS J., Kommunikatives Handeln]: QDisp 139. FrB 1992,
Herder. 174 p. 3-451-02139-0.

1140 *Balthasar* Hans Urs von, Il problema del 'senso spirituale' nella Sacra
Scrittura [1952], ᵀ*Fedeli* Carlo: ⟶ 383, Communio 126 (1992) 82-87.

1140* **Bayer** Oswald, Autorität und Kritik; zu Hermeneutik und Wissenschaftstheorie. Tü 1991, Mohr. x-225 p. DM 59 pa. – ᴿLuthMon 31 (1992) 93
(U. *Asendorf*) & 70-73, interviews; TLZ 117 (1992) 770s (C. *Gestrich*).

1141 *Beal* Timothy K., Ideology and intertextuality; surplus of meaning and
controlling the means of production: ⟶ 351*d*, Reading between texts
1992) 27-39; glossary 21-24.

1141* **Bengoa Ruiz de Azua** Javier, De HEIDEGGER a HABERMAS; hermenéutica y fundamentación última en la filosofía contemporánea: BtTFil
195. Barc 1992, Herder. 211 p. pt 1698. 84-254-1803-8 [ActuBbg 30,
114s, E. *Forment*].

1142 ᵀᴱ**Berner** Christian, F.D.E. SCHLEIERMACHER, Herméneutique 1987
[⟶ 3,1287; 6,1316: both indicating as translator *Simon* M.]: ᴿRTLv 23
(1992) 87s (E. *Brito*) [his 21 (1990) 235-7 was on ᵀ*Simon* 1987].

1142* **Betti** Emilio, Teoria generale dell'interpretazione, ᴱ*Crifò* G. Mi 1990,
Giuffrè. 1113 p. – ᴿEuntDoc 44 (1991) 326s (P. *Miccoli*).

1143 *Biffi* Inos, Esegesi scientifica ed esegesi allegorica; un divario inperti-
nente: TItSett 17 (1992) 3-15.

1144 **Bori** Pier Cesare, L'interprétation infinie; l'herméneutique chrétienne ancienne et ses transformations, ᵀ*Vial* F., 1991 ⟶ 7,1011: ᴿÉTRel 67 (1992)
120s (H. *Bost*: passionnant); RechSR 80 (1992) 140-2 (B. *Sesboüé*); RHR
209 (1992) 313s (J. *Le Brun*); RThom 92 (1992) 854s (G. *Narcisse*).

1144* **Bori** Pier Cesare, Per un consenso etico tra culture; tesi di una lettura
secolare delle scritture ebraico-cristiane. Genova 1991, Marietti ... ᴿAn-
StoEseg 9 (1992) 247-258 (M. Cristina *Laurenzi*: che significa 'esperienza'
nella fede biblica?) & 259-268 (M. *Miegge*: apologia inattuale del
sintagma ermeneutico 'storico-dialettico').

1145 **Bosetti** Elena, La tenda e il bastone; figure e simboli della pastorale
biblica: Narrare la Bibbia 1, CinB 1992, Paoline. 158 p.; 73 fig.
Lit. 22.000. 88-215-2493-0.

1145* **Bruns** G.I., Hermeneutics ancient and modern. NHv 1992, Yale
Univ. xii-318 p. $37.50. 0-300-05450-5. [NTAbs 37, p.426].

1146 ᴱ**Burrows** Mark S., *Rorem* Paul, ⟶ 7,58, ᶠFROEHLICH K., Biblical
hermeneutics in historical perspective. 1991. – ᴿRLitND 24,2 (1992) 77-81
(Mary *Gerhart*). ⟶ 1159.

1146* **Canevet** Mariette, *Adnès* Pierre, *al.*, Les sens spirituels [articles du
DictSpir.]. P ... Beauchesne. 175 p. [BLitEc 94,380s, J. *Abiven*, aussi sur
'Phénomènes extraordinaires').

1147 *Cervellin* Luigi, 'Per Scripturae secretum' (Serm. XXXIX, 34); l'interpretazione della Scrittura nei sermoni di MASSIMO di Torino: Salesianum 54 (1992) 763-772.

1148 **Chau Wai-Shing**, The letter and the spirit; a history of interpretation
from ORIGEN to LUTHER: diss. Luther NW Theol Sem.; ᴰ*Nestingen* J.
1990. 317 p. 92-24507. – DissA 53 (1992s) 1185-A.

1149 *Christoffersen* Svein A.,   Skriften, bekjennelsen og hermeneutikken [HEGSTAD H.]: NorTTs 93 (1992) 199-321.
1149* **Corrington** Robert S.,   The community of interpreters; on the hermeneutic of nature and the Bible in the American philosophical tradition: Studies in American Hermeneutics 3, 1987 ➤ 4,1185:   RChH 59 (1990) 592-4 (D. R. *Sharp*).
1150 **Cowley** R. W.,   Ethiopian biblical interpretation 1989 ➤ 4,1186 ... 7,1012, RBSO 55 (1992) 561s (S. *Uhlig*); Irénikon 65 (1992) 150 (E. *Lanne*).
1151 **Dawson** David,   Allegorical readers and cultural revision in ancient Alexandria. Berkeley 1992, Univ. California. xi-341 p. 0-520-07102-6.
1152 **Dockery** David S.,   Biblical interpretation then and now; contemporary hermeneutics in the light of the early Church. GR 1992, Baker. 247 p. $15 pa. 0-8010-3010-2 [NTAbs 37, p. 427; TDig 40,263].
1152* *a) Dohmen* Christoph,   Vom vielfachen Schriftsinn — Möglichkeiten und Grenzen neuerer Zugänge zu biblischen Texten; – *b) Jacob* Christoph, Allegorese; Rhetorik, Ästhetik, Theologie: ➤ 495, Neue Formen? 1992, 13-74 / 131-163.
1153 *a) Dupuy* Bernard, 'Au commencement était le sens'; l'herméneutique d'Edith STEIN; – *b) Greisch* Jean,   Le 'poème de l'histoire', un modèle herméneutique de l'histoire de la philosophie et de la théologie: ➤ 63, FGEFFRÉ C., Interpréter 1992, 173-189 / 141-172.
1154 *a) Ebach* Jürgen,   Vergangene Zeit und Jetztzeit; Walter BENJAMINS Reflexionen als Anfragen an die biblische Exegese und Hermeneutik; – *b) Sauter* Gerhard,   Die Kunst des Bibellesens; – *c) Räisänen* Heikki,   Die Wirkungsgeschichte der Bibel; eine Herausforderung für die exegetische Forschung; – *d) Berger* Klaus [*Weder* Hans], Meine Hermeneutik: EvT 52,4 (1992) 288-308 / 347-359 / 337-347 / 309-319 . 332-5 [319-331 . 336].
1155 **Ebeling** Gerhard,   Evangelische Evangelienauslegung; eine Untersuchung zu LUTHERS Hermeneutik³ʳᵉᵛ [¹1942 Diss; ²1962]. Tü 1991, Mohr. 560 p. DM 158. 3-16-145665-3 [TLZ 118,646, C. *Gestrich*].
1155* **Edgerton** W. Dow,   The passion of interpretation: LitCuBInt. Louisville 1992, W-Knox. 160 p. 0-664-25394-6. – RTBR 5,3 (1992s) 17 (L. *Houlden*).
1156 *a) Eslinger* Lyle,   Inner-biblical exegesis and inner-biblical allusion; the question of category [FISHBANE M. 1985]: VT 42 (1992) 47-58.
— *b) Farthing* John L.,   Ecumenical hermeneutics; Newman SMYTH [1843-1925] and the Bible: AmJTP 11 (1990) 216-232.
— *c) Fee* Gordon D.,   Issues in evangelical hermeneutics; hermeneutics and the nature of Scripture: Crux 26,2 (1990) 21-26 [26/3, 35-42, authorial intentionality; NT imperatives; 27/1, 12-20, role of tradition].
1157 *a) Ford* David,   Hans FREI and the future of theology; – *b) Hunsinger* George,   H. Frei as theologian; the quest for generous orthodoxy [*Webster* John, reply]; – *c) Lowe* Walter, H. Frei and phenomenological hermeneutics [*Demson* David, reply]; – *d) Schner* Georg, The eclipse of biblical narrative; analysis and critique [*Marshall* Bruce, reply]; – *e) Schwartzentruber* Paul, The modesty of hermeneutics; the theological reserves of H. Frei [*Placher* William, reply]: ➤ 533*, ModT 8,2 (1990/2) 203-214 / 103-128 [–132] / 133-142 [–148] / 149-172 [–179] / 181-195 [197-201].
1158 *Frei* Hans W.,   Conflicts in interpretation: TTod 49 (1992s) 344-356.
1159 FFROEHLICH K.,   Biblical hermeneutics, EBurrows M. ... 1991 ➤ 7,58 (supra ➤ 1146): RExpTim 104 (1992s) 187s (A. C. *Thiselton*: several items, especially two Froehlich reprints, suited for workshops).

1160 **Frye** Northrop, The double vision; language and meaning in religion [lectures given shortly before his death]. Toronto 1991, Univ. 88 p. $10. – RTTod 49 (1992s) 140s (W. *Wink*).

1161 *a) Geffré* Claude, De l'herméneutique des textes à l'herméneutique biblique; – *b) Beaude* Pierre-Marie, Exégèse contemporaine et sens de la Bible: ➤ 462, Naissance 1990/2, 279-283 / 245-253.

1162 **Girard** M., Les symboles dans la Bible. 1991. – RÉglT 23 (1992) 427s (W. *Vogels*).

1163 *Girardet* Giorgio, Hermeneutica biblica, rassegna: Protestantesimo 47 (1992) 96-102.

1164 *Günther* Hartmut, 'Allein die Schrift' — nötige Bemerkungen zum Verständnis der Heiligen Schrift und zum Umgang mit ihr: LuthTK 16 (1992) 58-66 [< ZIT 92,364].

1164* **Hahn** Eberhard, Schriftauslegung im Spannungsfeld von Impetus und *skándalon* [CRÜSEMANN F.]: KerDo 38 (1992) 71-79.

1165 **Halivni** David W., Peshat and derash; plain and applied meaning in rabbinic exegesis. NY 1991, Oxford-UP. vii-749 p. 0-19-506065-2. – RCritRR 5 (1992) 365-7 (G. A. *Anderson*: how texts support contrary practice); Tarbiz 61 (1991s) 583-592 (A. *Sagi*, **Ⓗ**, under surname 'Weiss').

1165* *a) Harder* Lydia, Biblical interpretation; a praxis of discipleship? [Jn 13 & 12 footwashings; feminism]; – *b) Barrett* Lois Y., *May* Melanie A., *al.*, Anabaptist women: CGrebel 10 (1992) 17-32 / 1-16.33-48 (–66); 209-226, responses.

1166 *a) Hardmeier* Christof, Computer-assisted perception of texts and its hermeneutic relevance; – *b) Berleur* Jacques, Langage naturel et intelligence artificielle; quelques réflexions épistémologiques: ➤ 450*, Informatique 3e 1991/2, 365-376 / 377-395.

1166* *Hess* Richard S., New horizons in hermeneutics; a review article (THISELTON A. 1991): Themelios 18,2 (1992s) 22-24.

1167 **Hoy** David C., Il circolo hermeneutico [1978], T. Bo 1990, Mulino. 218 p. – RLuntDoc 44 (1991) 328s (P. *Miccoli*).

1167* **Jeanrond** Werner G., *a)* Theological hermeneutics; development and significance 1991 ➤ 7,1027: RTLond 95 (1992) 380-2 (S. D. *Moore*: timely, important).
— *b)* Text and interpretation as categories of theological thinking, T *Wilson* Thomas J. 1988 ➤ 2,7910 ... 5,8814: RLitTOx 5 (1991) 239-241 (G. C. *Bruce*).

1168 **Johnson** Elliot E., Expository hermeneutics; an introduction 1990 ➤ 6,1284: RChrCent 107 (1990) 911s (I. J. *Hesselink*); TrinJ 13 (1992) 251s (D. *Huffman*).

1168* *Johnston* Paul I., REU reconsidered; the concept of Heilsgeschichte in the hermeneutic of J. M. Reu and J.C.K. von HOFMANN: ConcordJ 18 (St. Louis 1992) 339-360 [< NTAbs 37,166].

1169 *a) Kasher* Asa, Philosophical reinterpretation of Scripture; – *b) Stroumsa* Gedalyahu G., Moses' Riddles; esoteric trends in patristic hermeneutics; – *c) Werblowsky* R.J.Z., Religion as interpretation; – *d) Kiener* Ronald C., SAADIA and the Sefer Yetsirah; translation theory in classical Jewish thought: ➤ 514*a*, Interpretation 1990/2, 9-37 / 229-248 / 1-7 / 169-179.

1169* *Klemm* D. E., Subjectivity and divinity in biblical hermeneutics: LitTOx 6 (1992) 239-253 [< NTAbs 37,166].

1170 a) *Körtner* Ulrich H. J.,   Geist und Buchstabe; – b) *Nicol* Martin, '... durch einen Spiegel in einem dunklen Wort': Zeitwende 63,4 ('Die Bibel lesen, aber wie?' 1992) 193-206 / 207-220 [< ZIT 92,700].

1170* *Kremer* Joseph, Kein Wort Gottes ohne Menschenwort; Überlegungen zum 'Jahr mit der Bibel 1992': StiZt 210 (1992) 75-90. ➤ 1122.

Kugel James L., In Potiphar's house; the interpretive life of biblical texts 1990 ➤ E29.

1171 *Lanza* Sergio, L'ermeneuta della Scrittura e il catecheta della Chiesa: RivPastLtg 29,5 (1991) 25-30.

1172 **Larkin** William J.ᴶ, a) Culture and biblical hermeneutics; interpreting and applying the authoritative word in a relativistic age 1988 ➤ 4,1216; 5,1273: ᴿCalvaryB 7,1 (1991) 61s (G. H. *Lovik*).

— b) Culture, Scripture's meaning, and biblical authority; critical hermeneutics for the 90's: BuBRes 2 (WL 1992) 171-8 [< NTAbs 37,167].

1172* *Leschert* D., A change of meaning, not a change of mind; the clarification of a suspected defection in the hermeneutical theory of E. D. HIRSCHᴶ: JEvTS 35 (1992) 183-7 [< NTAbs 37,167].

1173 **Lieb** Michael, The visionary mode; biblical prophecy, hermeneutics, and cultural change. Ithaca NY 1991, Cornell Univ. xi-362 p. $36.50. – ᴿCithara 31,2 (1991s) 46s (L. E. *Frizzell*).

1173* **Mabee** Charles, Reading sacred texts through American eyes; biblical interpretation as cultural critique: Studies in American Biblical Hermeneutics 7. Macon 1991, Mercer Univ. ix-128 p. $25; pa. $17. – ᴿRel-StR 18 (1992) 353 (J. F. *Craghan*).

1174 **Macky** Peter W., The centrality of metaphors to biblical thought; a method for interpreting the Bible: StBeC 19, 1990 ➤ 6,1296: ᴿÉglT 22 (1991) 367 (W. *Vogels*); Interpretation 46 (1992) 416 (W. A. *Beardslee*); TLZ 117 (1992) 585-7 (Kirsten *Nielsen*); TvT 32 (1992) 106 (P. *Chatelion Counet*).

1175 **Maier** Gerhard, a) Biblische Hermeneutik²ʳᵉᵛ. Wu 1991, Brockhaus. 404 p. DM 50 [EurJT 2,181, K.-H. *Schlaudraff*]; – b) What is spiritual exegesis?: EvRT 16 (Exeter 1992) 143-151 [< NTAbs 36,311].

1175* *Mancini* R., Comunicazioni come ecumene; il significato antropologico e teologico dell'etica comunicativa. Brescia 1991, Queriniana. 152 p. Lit. 15.000. – ᴿRasT 33 (1992) 715s (G. *Mattai*: vedute di APEL K., HABERMAS J.).

1176 *Meagher* Patrick, Hermeneutics for today [TUCKETT C. 1987]: Vidyajyoti 56 (1992) 662-674.

1177 **Morfino** Mauro, Leggere la Bibbia con la vita; le letture esistenziali della Parola; un aspetto comune all'ermeneutica rabbinica e patristica 1990 ➤ 6,1303; Lit. 20.000: ᴿAsprenas 39 (1992) 129-131 (A. *Petti*).

1178 **Morgan** R., *Barton* J., Biblical interpretation (corrected reprint) 1989 ➤ 4,1231 ... 7,1041: ᴿHeythJ 33 (1992) 204s (D. *Way*); LvSt 17 (1992) 71s (R. F. *Collins*).

Muller Richard A., The study of theology; from biblical interpretation to contemporary formulation 1991 ➤ 7136*.

1179 *Mura* Gaspare, Ermeneutica e verità; storia e problemi della filosofia dell'interpretazione. R 1991, Città Nuova. – ᴿFilT 6 (1992) 369s (M. *Vannini*); Lateranum 58 (1992) 529-533 (P. *Coda*).

1180 **Murtonen** A., Reality and the Bible; prolegomena to a multidimensional interpretation of the Bible. Melbourne / Tallarook 1991, auct. vii-223 p. A$12. – ᴿAbrNahr 30 (1992) 176s (J.F.A. *Sawyer*: rambling memoir of a likable linguist-pastor); AustralBR 40 (1992) 69-71 (H. A. *Stamp*).

1181 **Nethöfel** Wolfgang, Theologische Hermeneutik; vom Mythos zu den Medien: BeitSysT 9. Neuk 1992. x-346 p. DM 79. 3-7887-1400-X [TLZ 118,863, G. *Isermann*].

1182 *Nickerk* B. van, *Aarde* A. G. van, Holistiese verstaan teenoor analitiese verstaan in Bybelse hermeneutiek: HervTSt 47 (1991) 1042-1057 [< NTAbs 36,312].

1183 **Noguez** Armando, Palabra de vida; liberación de la letra que mata; hermenéutica y teología bíblica desde América Latina [12 reprints] Villa Coapa Méx 1992, CAM. 231 p.

1183* *Onetto* Fernando, El problema hermenéutico: RBibArg 54 (1992) 219-230.

1184 **Osborne** Grant R., The hermeneutical spiral; a comprehensive introduction to biblical interpretation. DG 1991, InterVarsity. 488 p. $25. 0-8308-1272-5 [NTAbs 36, p. 414]. – ᴿThemelios 18,1 (1992s) 30s (C. L. *Blomberg*).

1185 ᴱ**Pacomio** L. (*La Potterie* I. de), L'esegesi cristiana oggi 1991 → 7,323. 1033*: ᴿBenedictina 39 (1992) 491-5 (M. *Serretti*).

1186 **Polka** Brayton, Truth and interpretation; an essay in thinking. NY 1990, St. Martin's. xliv-164 p. – ᴿSR 21 (1992) 469s (B. *Alton*).

1187 *a*) *Polka* Brayton, Interpretation and the Bible; the dialectic of concept and content in interpretative practice; – *b*) *Forsman* Rodger, Revelation and understanding; a defence of tradition; – *c*) *Klemm* David, The autonomous text, the hermeneutical self, and divine rhetoric: → 477, Hermeneutics 1989/92, 27-45 / 46-68 / 3-26.

1187* *a*) *Porton* Gary G., Midrasch; die Rabbinen und die hebräische Bibel, ᵀ*Noth* Isabelle; – *b*) *Stemberger* Günter, Narrative Theologie im Midrash: → 17*c*, ᶠBIETENHARD H., Judaica 47,3 (1991) 123-139 / 155-167.

1188 *Posner* Roland [*al.*], Zitat und Zitieren von Äusserungen, Ausdrücken und Kodes: ZSemiot 14,1s ('Zitat und Zitieren' 1992) 3-16 [-140, *al.*]; fasc. 3 'Zitat, Text und Intertext'.

1188* *Richard* P., Hermenéutica bíblica india; Senderos 42 (Costa Rica 1992) 51-70 [< Stromata 49,267].

1189 *Rogerson* J. W. [*Jeanrond* Werner G.] Interpretation, history of [of biblical hermeneutics]: → 741, AnchorBD 3 (1992) 424-433 [-443].

1190 *Russell* D. S., 'Countdown'; arithmetic and anagram in early biblical interpretation: ExpTim 104 (1992s) 109-113.

1191 *Seebass* Horst, Interpretation statt Hermeneutik [fast hundert Bücher; Register p. 70s]: VerkF 36,2 (NT 1991) 3-26.

1192 *a*) *Signer* Michael A., Peshat, sensus litteralis, and sequential narrative; Jewish exegesis and the school of St. Victor in the twelfth century: → 180*c*, Mem. TALMAGE F., 1 (1992s) 203-216.
— *b*) *Slate* C. Philip, The culture concept and hermeneutics: Encounter 53 (1992) 135-146.
— *c*) *Smith* F. LaGard, The cultural church; winds of change and the call for a 'New Hermeneutic'. Nv 1992, 20th Century Christian. 237 p. $10 [RestQ 35,113-6, M. S. *Moore*: principal concern in recent RestQ poll].
— *d*) *Sontag* F., The metaphysics of biblical studies: JEvTS 35 (1992) 189-192 [< NTAbs 37,170].

1193 *Theissen* Gerd, L'herméneutique biblique et la recherche de la vérité religieuse: → 518, Science et foi 1988/92, 135-154.

1194 **Thiselton** Anthony C., New horizons in hermeneutics; the theory and practice of transforming biblical reading. GR/L 1992, Eerdmans/Harper Collins. xii-703 p. $30. 0-310-51590-4 / 0-551-02448-8. – ᴿExpTim 104

(1992s) 186s (R. *Morgan*: lucid erudition, not *just* updating on the experts); TrinJ 13 (1992) 250 (D. J. *Moo*: technical).
1194* **Thomas** J. D., Harmonizing hermeneutic; applying the Bible to contemporary life. Nv 1991, Gospel advocate. x-109 p. $6 [RestQ 35,61s, R. *Dudrey*: a welcome call for peace among Restorationist interpreters].
1195 **Velde** Roger G. van de, Text and thinking; on some roles of thinking in text interpretation: Research in Text Theory 18. B 1992, de Gruyter. xv-328 p. 3-11-013250-8.
1196 *a)* **Wallace** Mark I., The second naiveté; BARTH, RICOEUR and the New Yale theology 1990 → 6,1323: ᴿJRel 72 (1992) 449-451 (D. *Pellauer*: 'second naiveté' is Ricoeur's term for 'belief that comes after criticism'); JTS 43 (1992) 772-4 (D. *Fergusson*); LuthQ 7 (1993) 347s (M. *Mattes*).
— *b)* *White* Erin, Between suspicion and hope; Paul Ricœur's vital hermeneutic: LitTOx 5 (1991) 311-321.
— *c)* **Zilles** Urbano, A significação dos símbolos cristianos. Porto Alegre 1990, EDIPUCRS. 72 p. – ᴿTeocomunicação 20,89 (1990) 295s (J. *Paviani*).
— *d)* **Zuck** Roy B., Basic Bible interpretation. Wheaton IL 1991, Victor. 324 p. $19. – ᴿBtS 149 (1992) 101s (M. L. *Bailey*).

B2.2 **Structuralismus biblicus** (generalior → J9.4).

1197 **Dosse** François, Histoire du structuralisme, 2. Le chant du cygne, 1967 à nos jours. P 1992, Cerf. 587 p. – ᴿHumTeol 13 (1992) 251s (B. *Domingues*).
1198 **Hart** Kevin, The trespass of the sign, deconstruction ... 1989 → 6,9939: ᴿPacifica 4 (1991) 105-8 (J. *Honner*).
1199 ᴱ**Jobling** David, *Moore* Stephen D., Poststructuralism as exegesis: Semeia 54. Atlanta 1992, Scholars. ix-255 p. $15. 0095-571X [BL 93,88, R. P. *Carroll*].
1200 **La Capra** Dominick, Soundings in critical theory. Ithaca NY 1991, Cornell Univ. [xi–] 213 p. 0-8014-2322-8; pa. –9573–5.
1200* *Lambert* Len M., Structuralist modelling and computer modelling of the biblical text: → 450, Informatique 2, 1988/9, 325-341.
1201 **Lescow** Theodor, Das Stufenschema; Untersuchungen zur Struktur alttestamentlicher Texte: BZAW 211. B 1992, de Gruyter. x-282 p. 3-11-103768-2.
1201* *a)* *Long* T.M.S., Deconstruction and biblical studies in South Africa; – *b)* *West* G., Interesting and interested readings; deconstruction, the Bible, and the South African context: Scriptura 42 (1992) 50-64 / 35-49 [< NTAbs 37, p. 326].
1202 *a)* *McKeever* Kerry, How to avoid speaking about God; poststructuralist philosophers and biblical hermeneutics; – *b)* *Klemm* David E., Subjectivity and divinity in biblical hermeneutics: LitTOx 6 (1992) 228-238 / 239-253 [< ZIT 92,559].
1203 **Patte** Daniel, The religious dimensions of biblical texts; GREIMAS's structural semiotics and biblical exegesis: Semeia Studies, 1990 → 7,1064: ᴿCBQ 54 (1992) 364-6 (W. A. *Vogels*: semiotic analysis and religious conclusions fine but not for the public at which he aims); JStOT 55 (1992) 126 (J. Sue *Campbell*: not for the faint-hearted); TLZ 117 (1992) 105s (R. *Stahl*).

B2.4 *Analysis* **narrationis** *biblicae* (generalior → J9.6).

1203* *Agua* Agustín del, Die 'Erzählung' des Evangeliums im Lichte der Derasch Methode: → 17b, ᶠBIETENHARD H., Judaica 47,3 (1991) 140-154.

1204 **Alter** R., L'arte della narrativa biblica [1981] [T]1990 ➤ 6,1336; 7,1067: [R]ParVi 37 (1992) 219-222 (S. *Migliasso*).

1205 **Bar-Efrat** Shimon, Narrative art in the Bible: JStOT supp 70, 1989 ➤ 5,1312 ... 7,1068: [R]BZ 36 (1992) 300s (J. *Scharbert*).

1206 **Beauchamp** Paul, Le récit, la lettre et le corps; essais bibliques[2rev] [[1]1982]: CogF 114. P 1992, Cerf. 321 p. 2-204-04662-0.

1207 **Bonsen** J., Verhalen van opstanding; praktijk en hermeneutiek [diss.] Kampen 1991, Kok. 207 p. *f*35. 90-242-6530-4. – [R]TvT [31,187] 32 (1992) 194 (P. *Chatelion Counet*: PROPP-GREIMAS and BATAILLE-ALT-HUSSER; regrettably no poststructuralism or reader-oriented exegesis).

1208 [E]**Bühler** P., *Habermacher* J.-F., La narration; quand le récit devient communication 1988 ➤ 4,a911 ... 7,1069: [R]EstE 67 (1992) 244s (M. *Benéitez*).

1209 **Crenshaw** James L., Old Testament story and faith; a literary and theological introduction. Peabody MA 1992, Hendrickson. viii-472 p. $20 [CBQ 54,613]. 0-94357-91-5. – [R]ExpTim 104 (1992s) 55 (J. G. *Snaith*: a good read; not technical, though with some footnotes); RBibArg 54 (1992) 247 (J. S. *Croatto*).

1210 **Culley** Robert C., Themes and variations; a study of action in biblical narrative: SBL Semeia. Atlanta 1992, Scholars. viii-190 p. $45; pa. $30. 1-55540-757-9; –8-7 [NTAbs 37,104; ZAW 105,520].

1211 **Dennis** Trevor, Lo and behold! the power of OT storytelling 1991 ➤ 7,1071: [R]BL (1992) 67 (R. P. *Carroll*).

1211* *Detweiler* Robert, Parerga; homely details, secret intentions, veiled threats [response to Mieke BAL's presentation of her Murder and Difference (1988) here p. 11-19]: LitTOx 5 (1991) 1-10.

1212 *Es* J.J. van, De macht van verhalen [Predikantendag Kampen, sept. 1989]: GerefTTs 91 (1991) 65-97.

1213 **Exum** J. Cheryl, Tragedy and biblical narrative; arrows of the Almighty. C 1992, Univ. xiv-206 p. 0-521-41073-8 [OIAc 5,20]. – [R]ExpTim 104 (1992s) 153s (G. G. *Nicol*).

1214 *Fowell* Danna N., *Gunn* David M., Narrative, Hebrew: ➤ 741, AnchorBD 4 (1992) 1023-7 (no Greek or other).

1215 *Frein* Brigid C., Fundamentalism and narrative approaches to the Gospels: BibTB 22 (1992) 12-18.

1215* *Goldingay* John, How far do readers make sense? Interpreting biblical narrative: Themelios 18,2 (1992s) 5-9; 9s, ample bibliography.

1216 *Greenstein* Edward L., Humor and wit, OT: ➤ 741, AnchorBD 3 (1992) 330-3; *al*. NT, Egypt, Mesopotamia.

1216* *a*) *King* Michael Λ., Flesh on dry bones; combining doctrine and story; – *b*) *Sawatsky* Rodney J., – The quest for a Mennonite hermeneutic; – *c*) *Keener* Carl S. [*Weaver* Alain E.], Some reflections on Mennonites and postmodern thought: CGrebel 11 (1993) 37-45 / 1-20 / 47-61 [63-76]; responses 171-185.

1217 **Labuschagne** C. J., Vertellen met getallen; functie en symboliek van getallen in de bijbelse oudheid. Zoetermeer 1992, Boeken-C. 135 p. *f*21.50. 90-239-0895-3. – [R]Streven 59 (1992s) 1237 (P. *Beemtjes*); TvT 32 (1992) 411 (Λ. *Schoors*).

1217* *Ledbetter* Mark, Virtuous intentions; the religious dimension of narrative 1989 ➤ 7,9756: [R]LitTOx 5 (1991) 125s (D. *Jasper*); Thought 66 (1991) 333s (J. *Kotva*).

1218 **Licht** Jacob, La narrazione nella Bibbia. [Storytelling, J 1986], [T]Dell'Aversano Carmen: StBPaid 101. Brescia 1992, Paideia. 195 p., 88-394-0482-1 [BL 94,93, M. *Richardson*: outdated].

1219 **Meier** Samuel A., Speaking of speaking; marking direct discourse in the Hebrew Bible: VTSup 46. Leiden 1992, Brill. xvi-383 p. *f* 175.

1219* *Oosthuizen* M. J., Narrative analysis in the OT — some challenges and prospects: JNWS 18 (1992) 145-161.

1220 *Pawlowski* Zdzisław, ❷ The narrative criticism [hermeneutyczna metoda opowiadania] in the contemporary exegesis: ColcT 62,1 (1992) 5-18; Eng. 18.

1220* *Polak* Frank H., Epic formulae in biblical narrative; frequency and distribution: ➤ 450, Informatique 2, 1988/9, 437-488.

1221 **Powell** Mark A., What is narrative criticism?: GuidesBSchNT, 1990 ➤ 6,1349; 7,1079: ᴿBtS 149 (1992) 112s (N. *Nelson*: best available); CritRR 5 (1992) 238-241 (E.V. *McKnight*); Interpretation 46 (1992) 328.330 (R. H. *Hiers*); TLZ 117 (1992) 587s (K.-W. *Niebuhr*).

1221* **Schleifer** Ronald, *al.*, Culture and cognition; the boundaries of literary and scientific inquiry [...narrative structures]. Ithaca 1992, Cornell Univ. xxiii-269 p. 0-8014-2632-4; pa. –1–3.

1222 ᴱ**Silberman** Lou H., Orality, aurality, and biblical narrative 1987 ➤ 3, 363: ᴿJRel 72 (1992) 425 (J. *Tabor*).

1223 **Ska** Jean-Louis, 'Our fathers have told us'; introduction to the analysis of Hebrew narratives: SubsBPont 13, 1990 ➤ 6,1352; 7,1081: ᴿCBQ 54 (1992) 768 (B. O. *Long*: more useful as a quick reference tool); ETL 68 (1992) 150s (J. *Lust*: speaks of object, structure, result, resolution; but deliberately not 'semiotics', 'structuralism', 'symbol', 'sign'); OTAbs 15 (1992) 107 (Mary K. *Deeley*); RivB 40 (1992) 91-93 (G. *Ravasi*: eccellente); RTLv 23 (1992) 378 (J.-C. *Haelewyck*: surtout histoire, temps, trame, narrateur, lecteur, personnage, point de vue); ZAW 104 (1992) 160 (H. C. *Schmitt*).

1223* **Sternberg** Meir, The poetics of biblical narrative 1985 ➤ 2,935 ... 5, 1332: ᴿThemelios 16,3 (1990s) 21s (R.W.L. *Moberly*).

1224 *Swanston* Hamish F.G., [title p. 155]: Christians telling stories [p. 145: Theology and narrative]: NBlackf 73 (1992) 155-164.

1225 **Toohey** Peter, Reading epic; an introduction to the ancient narratives. L 1992, Routledge. xiii-248 p. 0-415-04227-5; pa. –8–3.

1226 **Vanhoozer** Kevin J., Biblical narrative in the philosophy of Paul Ricœur; a study in hermeneutics and theology 1990 ➤ 6,1356; 7,1083: ᴿCritRR 5 (1992) 492-4 (L. S. *Mudge*: 'postscript to Bultmann'); JRel 72 (1992) 451 (J. Van den *Hengel*); RelSt 27 (1991) 426-8 (D. R. *McGaughey*); RelStR 18 (1992) 220 (M.J. *Wallace*); Salesianum 54 (1992) 795 (R. *Vicent*); TLond 95 (1992) 50s (F. *Watson*); TsTKi 62 (1991) 224s (T. *Stordalen*); WestTJ 54 (1992) 200-2 (R. E. *Otto*).

1227 *Vartanen* Tuija, Issues of text typology; Narrative — a 'basic' type of text?: Text 12 (1992) 293-310.

1228 **Watts** James W., Psalm and story; inset hymns in Hebrew narrative: JStOT supp 139. Shf 1992, Academic. 246 p. 1-85075-343-1. – ᴿExpTim 104 (1992s) 278 (J. *Eaton*).

B2.6   *Critica reactionis lectoris* – **Reader-response criticism.**

1228* *Frey* Jörg, Der implizite Leser und die biblischen Texte: TBeit 23 (1992) 266- ... [< ZIT 92,698].

1229 *Lategan* Bernard C., Reader response theory: ➤ 741, AnchorBD 5 (1992) 625-8 [644-647-650, Redaction criticism OT (*Barton* John) / NT (*Stein* Robert H.)].

1230 **McKnight** Edgar V., Post-modern use of the Bible; the emergence of reader-oriented criticism 1988 ➤ 5,1340 ... 7,1087: ᴿJRel 72 (1992) 102s (D. *Landry*).

B3   *Interpretatio ecclesiastica* .1 Bible and Church.

1231 *Alcedo Ternero* Antonio, El 'Nuevo catecismo de la Iglesia católica', entre la 'fidelidad al depósito' y la iniciación cristiana: ComSev 25 (1992) 359-378.

1232 **Alves** Herculano, Documentos da Igreja sobre a Bíblia. Lisboa 1991, Difusora Bíblica. 438 p. – ᴿHumTeol 13 (1992) 256s (A. *Couto*).

1232* **Ammerman** Nancy T., Bible believers; fundamentalists in the modern world 1987 ➤ 4,1289; 5,1346: ᴿRRelRes 32 (1990s) 179s (R. E. *Beckley*).

1233 *Auza* Bernardito C., Noninfallible magisterium, religious assent and theological dissent: PhilipSa 26 (1991) 339-380.

1233* **Barton** John, People of the Book? 1988 ➤ 4,1294...6,1365: ᴿChrSchR 20 (1990s) 188-190 (R. W. *Wall*).

1234 *Bavaud* Georges, Lorsque l'accès de l'Écriture était rendu difficile aux laïcs; la sévérité des prescriptions de l'Église catholique: ÉchSM 22 (1992) 39-48 [157-165].

1235 ᴱ**Beinert** Wolfgang, Glaube als Zustimmung; zur Interpretation kirchlicher Rezeptionsvorgänge [Tagung 1990]: QDisp 131, 1991 ➤ 7,467: ᴿTLZ 117 (1992) 296s (M. *Ulrich*).

1236 ᴱ**Beinert** Wolfgang, 'Katholischer' fundamentalismus; häretische Gruppen in der Kirche? Rg 1991, Pustet. 176 p. DM 26,80. 3-7917-1286-1. – ᴿActuBbg 29 (1992) 46-49 (J. *Boada*); NorTTs 93 (1992) 185 (O. *Tjørhom*).

1237 *Bendroth* Margaret L., Fundamentalism and femininity; points of encounter between religious conservatives and women, 1919-1935: ChH 61 (1992) 221-233.

1238 *Biffi* Inos, Il teologo e il magistero: StCattMi 35 (1991) 305-311.

1238* *Billé* Louis-Marie, Le Catéchisme pour adultes des évêques de France: NRT 114 (1992) 21-34.

1239 **Boone** Kathleen C., The Bible tells them so ᴰ1989 ➤ 5,1351 ... 7,1093: ᴿChrSchR 21 (1991s) 217-220 (T. M. *Dorman*); JEvTS 35 (1992) 552-4 (also T. M. *Dorman*).

1239* **Bradley** Robert J., The [Trent] Roman Catechism ᴰ1991 ➤ 7,1093: ᴿScripTPamp 24 (1992) 350s (R. *Pellitero*).

1240 *Brosseder* Johannes [*Hüffmeier* Wilhelm], Lehramt, katholisch [evangelisch]: ➤ 757, EvKL 3 (1992) 60-66 [–70].

1240* **Brueggemann** Walter, Biblical perspectives on evangelism; living in a three-storied universe. Nv 1991, Abingdon. 139 p. $13 pa. [SewaneeTR 37, 199-201, D. J. *Schlafer*].

1241 *Buckley* Francis J., Liberating the university; a commentary on Ex corde Ecclesiae: Horizons 19 (1992) 99-108.

1242 **Burke** Cormac, Autorità e libertà nella Chiesa 1989 ➤ 7,1095*b*; ᴿAngelicum 69 (1992) 585s (J. F. *Castaño*).

1243 *Burkhard* John, Sensus fidei; meaning, role and future of a teaching of Vatican II [... KASPER W. 1970, 'What is truly normative is the entire life of the whole Church']: LvSt 17 (1992) 18-34.

1243* **Cappelli** Piero, Comunicazione; crisi della Chiesa? Per un'analisi socio-religiosa dei linguaggi e della struttura della Chiesa cattolica. Genova

1992, Marietti. xx-160 p. Lit. 55.000 [CC 144/3,337s. E. *Baragli*: né gradevole né giovevole).

1244 *Cansi* Bernardo, O catecismo para a Igreja universal (pequena história de sua gènese): REB 52 (1992) 603-626.

1245 **Carroll** Robert P., Wolf in the sheepfold: the Bible as a problem for Christianity ➤ 7,966; also Ph 1991, Trinity. 168 p. $15. 1-56338-024-2. – ᴿChurchman 106 (1992) 165-8 (D. *Spanner*: 'he deconstructs himself by his extravagance'); ExpTim 103 (1991s) 99 (C. S. *Rodd*: 'My puzzlement comes in trying to decide what Carroll actually believes'); NBlackf 73 (1992) 576-8 (H.F.G. *Swanston*); Themelios 18,2 (1992s) 30s (R. S. *Hess*: the Bible has indeed been 'tamed by the middle class'); TLond 95 (1992) 47s (R. *Coggins*); TTod 49 (1992s) 124s (W. A. *Brueggemann*).

1246 Catechismo della Chiesa Cattolica. Vaticano 1992, Libreria. 788 p.

1247 *Cazelles* Henri, La Commission Biblique Pontificale et ses activités: RICathP 37 (1991) 173-7.

1248 *Chrostowski* Waldemar, ❷ L'identité et la mission des hautes écoles catholiques: PrzPow 846 (1992) 275-281.

1249 ᴱ**Cohen** Norman J., The fundamentalist phenomenon; a view from within, a response from without 1990 ➤ 6,591; 7,1098: ᴿPerspRelSt 19 (1992) 246-250 (A. M. *Manis*).

1249* *Composta* Dario, L'indice dei libri proibiti [...l'abolizione 1966; la conseguenza]: EuntDoc 45 (1992) 375-407.

1250 **Curran** Charles E., Catholic higher education, theology, and academic freedom 1990 ➤ 7,1101: ᴿCanadCathR 10,5 (1992) 27-29 (J. M. *Rist*); LivLight 28,3 (1991s) 282s (H. A. *Buetow*); NewTR 5,1 (1992) 102-4 (J. M. *Huels*).

De Bert Betty A., Ungodly women [fundamentalism antifeminist from the start] 1990 ➤ 9028.

Denzinger-Hünermann, Enchiridion symbolorum ... de rebus fidei et morum 1991 ➤ k554.

1251 *Dola* Tadeusz, ❷ Difficult questions; the Church dimension of theology [Instructio 24.V.1990]: AtKap 117 (1991) 168-180.

1252 **Dozier** Verna J., The dream of God [... demystifying the institutional Church]. Boston 1991, Cowley 160 p. $10. 1-56101-046-4. – ᴿAnglTR 74 (1992) 404s (Fredrica H. *Thompsett*).

1253 *a) Fernández Mora* H., La palabra de Dios en la Iglesia; – *b) Giraldo* N., Escritura y interpretación; – *c) Correa* G., La palabra de Dios y la historia; – *d) Ospina* R., Palabra de Dios y fe: Cuestiones Teológicas Medellín 47 (1990) 117-165 / 85-105 / 57-84 / 39-48 [< Stromata 47,442].

1254 *a) [Fernández] Ramos* Felipe, La evangelización cristiana; – *b) Ramos Guerreira* Julio A., El hombre, tema del diálogo Iglesia-Mundo: StLeg 33 (1992) 11-49 / 75-96 [219-243, en Pablo VI: *Martínez* Exiquio].

1254* *a) Flores d'Arcais* Paolo, Pacifismo [... Golfo], papismo, fondamentalismo; la santa alleanza conto la modernità: Micromega 4,2 (1991) 7-32; – *b) Rizzi* Armido, Modernità e pace; un dibattito con Micromega: RasT 33 (1992) 49-74.

1255 *Franco* Ricardo, Texto y fundamentalismo; tendencias fundamentalistas en el catolicismo: EstE 67 (1992) 51-72.

1256 *Frieling* Reinhard, Instrumentalisierte Freiheit der Theologie? Bemerkungen eines evangelischen Theologen zur römischen 'Instruktion über die kirchliche Berufung des Theologen' (Mai 1990): ZTK 88 (1991) 121-138.

1257 *a)* **Garhammer** Erich, Seminaridee und Klerusbildung bei Karl August Graf von Rᴇɪsᴀᴄʜ; eine pastoralgeschichtliche Studie zum Ultramon-

tanismus des 19. Jhts: MüKHist 5. Stu 1990, Kohlhammer. 310 p. DM 29. – ᴿStiZt 210 (1992) 62-64 (L. *Mödl*: Lehramt und Theologie — ein aktueller Konflikt).
— *b*) **Green** Michael, Evangelism through the local Church. L 1990, Hodder & S. xii-574 p. £13. – ᴿThemelios 18,2 (1992s) 32 (S. *Leeke*, a country vicar: enthusiastic).
— *c*) ᴱ**Guerrero** Fernando, El magisterio pontificio contemporáneo; colección de encíclicas y documentos desde León XIII a Juan Pablo II: I. Sagrada Escritura...; II. Evangelización...: BAC maior 38, M 1991, Católica. 1012 p.; 1038 p. [Angelicum 70,451-5, T. *Stancati*].
1258 ᴱ**Hadden** Jeffrey K., *Shupe* Anson, Secularization and fundamentalism reconsidered: Religion and the political order 3. NY 1989, Paragon. xi-320 p. $25. – ᴿJScStR 30 (1991) 126 (R. *Perrin*).
1258* *Haręzga* Stanisław, ❷ La *parrhesia* biblique et son actualité à la lumière de l'encyclique 'Redemptoris missio': AtKap 118 (1992) 293-306.
1259 *Hart* D. G., The fundamentalist origins of the American Scientific Affiliation: PerspScCF 43 (1991) 238-247 [249-258 *Haas* J. W., Early links with Moody Institute].
1259* *Healy* Gerald W., Dissent, virtue or vice? [McCORMICK R. 1989]· Landas 4 (Manila 1990) 95-109; p. 99 '90% of American moral theologians should seek employment elsewhere' (É. *Gagnon*, cardinal heading a Vatican commission).
1260 *Herlyn* Okko, Unterweisung — eine neu wahrzunehmende Dimension von Gemeindeaufbau: ZTK 88 (1991) 272-286.
1261 *a*) *Herman* Zvonimir I., Exegesis contemporanea in Ecclesia; – *b*) *Hohnjec* Nikola, S. Scriptura in ecclesiis [diversis]: BogSmot 61 (Dei Verbum 25 Anniv., 1991) 252-265 croatice; 265 riassunto ital. / 359-367 croat.; 268 Eng. summary.
1262 **Hoffmann** Paul, Das Erbe Jesu und die Macht in der [intoleranten, bürokratischen kath.] Kirche; Rückbesinnung auf das NT: ToposTb 213. Mainz 1991, Grünewald. 155 p. DM 10. 3-7867-1588-2 [TLZ 118,739, J. *Roloff*: zornig aber sachlich].
1263 *a*) *Hohnjec* Nikola, *Fućak* M. Jerko, Ecclesia coram S. Scriptura in tempore praeterito; – *b*) *Vojnović* Tadej, ... tempore hodierno: BogSmot 61 (Dei Verbum 25. Anniv. 1991) 173-185 (croat.; Eng. 185). 186-204 (croat.) / 205-213.
1264 *Horvath* Tibor [ᴱURM], Some recommendations for the new Roman Catholic universal catechism (anent America 162,189-219]: AsiaJT 5 (1991) 391-6.
1265 ᴱ**Hünermann** Peter, *Mieth* Dietmar, Streitgespräch um Theologie und Lehramt 1991 ➤ 7,359b ('über T & L'): ᴿActuBbg 29 (1992) 68s (J. *Boada*).
1266 **Illanes** José Luis, Teología y Facultades de Teología. Pamplona 1991, Univ. 413 p. – ᴿScripTPamp 24 (1992) 311-4 (C. *Izquierdo*).
1267 *Izquierdo* César, [KASPER W. CTI 1990], El dogma y su interpretación: ScripTPamp 23 (1991) 893-919.
1268 *a*) *Jensen* Peter, The teacher as theologian in theological education; – *b*) *Harman* Allan M., The place of the biblical languages in the theological curriculum: RefTR 50 (1991) 81-90 / 91-97.
1269 *a*) *Jean Paul* II, Ex corde Ecclesiae 25.IX.1990 [universités]; – *b*) son histoire, *Guiberteau* Paul; – *c*) réflexions, *Colin* Pierre: RICathP 37 (1991) 15-43 / 3-11 / 45-49.

1270 *Karrer* Leo, Prophetischer Protest; Erklärungen und Petitionen als Instrumente der Meinungsäusserung in der Kirche: Diakonia 23 (1992) 96-103.
1271 **Kaufman** Philip S., Why you can disagree ... 1989 → 5,1348; 6,1399: ᴿFurrow 42 (1991) 734-6 (P. *Connolly*); HomP 91,5 (1990s) 73-76 (V. *Foy*: a damaging attack).
1272 *Kellstedt* Lyman, *Smidt* Corwin, Measuring fundamentalism; an analysis of different operational strategies: JScStR 30 (1991) 259-278.
1273 *a) Kennedy* Leonard A., The theologians' revolt; dissent aims to create a new church; – *b) Zimmermann* Anthony, How proportionalism corrupts moral theology [*Gula* R., *Curran* C. ...]: HomP 91,2 (1990s) 54-56 / 26-32.45.
1274 ᴱ**Kienzler** Klaus, Der neue Fundamentalismus 1990 → 7,1131: ᴿActuBbg 29 (1992) 44-46 (J. *Boada*).
1275 *Kienzler* Klaus, Religiöser Fundamentalismus — Rettung oder Gefahr: LebZeug 45 (1990) 56-66.
1276 *King* Geoffrey, Responding to Christian fundamentalism: EAPast 27 (1990) 330-6.
1276* *King* N., What is a biblical truth?: Scripture in Church 23,89 (Dublin 1992) 114-8 [< NTAbs 37, p. 166].
1277 *Klein* Nikolaus, Das Engagement geht weiter [L. Boff; eine Konfliktgeschichte von 20 Jahren; Strafmassnahmen ...]: Orientierung 56 (1992) 149-151.
1277* *Kloppenburg* Bonaventura, A libertade na investigação teológica: Teocomunicação 20,88 (1990) 107-116.
1278 ᴱ**Kochanek** Hermann, Die verdrängte Freiheit; Fundamentalismus in den Kirchen. FrB 1991, Herder. 280 p. DM 39. – ᴿZkT 114 (1992) 101s (K. H. *Neufeld*).
1278* *a) Komonchak* Joseph A., The authority of the Catechism of the Catholic Church; – *b) Jensen* Joseph, Beyond the literal sense; the interpretation of Scripture in The Catechism; – *c) Clark* Douglas K., On 'Englishing' The Catechism: LivLight 29,4 (1992s) 39-49 / 50-60 / 13-28.
1279 **Küng** Hans, Liberté du chrétien, ᵀ*Évrard* Jean, *Rochais* Henri: Foi vivante 273. P 1991 = 1967, D-Brouwer/Cerf. 230 p. [RTLv 24,241, R. *Guelluy*: paisible; climat de Vatican II].
1279* *Läpple* Alfred, Der Fundamentalismus — Ursprung — Theologie — Wertung: KlerusB 72 (Mü 1992) 157-162.
1280 **Lathuilière** Pierre, Peut-on parler d'un fondamentalisme catholique? Signification ecclésiologique des mutations du conservatisme catholique en France depuis Vatican II: diss. ᴰ*Denis* H. Lyon 1992. 888 p. – BICLyon 99s (1992) 102; RTLv 24, p. 569.
1281 **Lawrence** Bruce B., Defenders of God; the fundamentalist revolt against the modern age 1989 → 6,1404: ᴿArchivScSocR 80 (1992) 313s (É. *Poulat*); ChrCent 107 (1990) 913-5 (R. V. *Pierard*); ChrSchR 21 (1991s) 201s (W. *Corduan*); JScStR 30 (1991) 216s (Nancy *Nason-Clark*); Religion 22 (1992) 279-283 (W. *Shepard*: application of 'fundamentalism' to Islam unfortunate); 284s reply; RelStR 18 (1992) 36 (L. J. *Biallas*).
1282 *Lefebvre* Marcel, Quelle est la mission du théologien?: ÉglT 22 (1991) 177-190.
1282* *Librach* Clifford E., Strange coincidence; the intersection of Reform Judaism and [fundamentalist] evangelical Christianity: JRefJud 38,1 (1991) 17-29.
1283 *Logister* Wiel, Vrijmoedigheid in geloof en theologie; reflecties bij de

vaticaanse instructie over de theologie: TvT 32 (1992) 3-30; 30, Forthrightness in faith and theology.

1284 **Longfield** Bradley J., The Presbyterian controversy; fundamentalists, modernists, and moderates 1991 ➤ 7,1138: ᴿCalvinT 26 (1991) 486-8 (J. H. *Kromminga*); JRel 72 (1992) 594s (G. T. *Miller*); TrinJ 13 (1992) 239-241 (J. *Fea*).

1285 *McBrien* Richard P., Conflict in the Church; redefining the center: America 167 (1992) 78-81.

1286 *McCormick* R. A., *McBrien* R. P., Theology as a public responsibility: America 165 (1991) 184-189 . 203-206 > Theologie in öffentlicher Verantwortung, ᵀ*Heierle* Werner: Orientierung: 56 (1992) 16-21.

1287 *a) McGovern* Thomas, Magisterium, Scripture and Catholic exegetes; – *b) Spencer* Robert B., Faith and reason in Bible reading: HomP 91 (1990s) 10,11-19 . 11s, 24-32.71 / 62-70.

1288 *McManus* William E., [retired bishop; the new Code implies] The right of Catholics to govern the Church: America 167 (1992) 374-8.

1289 *McLachlan* Douglas R., Maintaining the foundation, rebuilding the superstructure: CalvaryB 8,2 (1992) 40-57 [Kirsopp Lᴀᴋᴇ 1925 'the Bible and the *corpus theologicum* of the Church is on the Fundamentalist's side'].

1290 *Marlé* René, Un catéchisme [index p. 579 'Le catéchisme'] de l'Église catholique: Études 377 (1992) 689-695.

1291 **Marsden** George M., Understanding fundamentalism and evangelicalism 1991 ➤ 7,1142: ᴿAsbTJ 47,1 (1992) 105s (R. J. *Green*); ChH 61 (1992) 468s (Phyllis D. *Airhart*); TTod 49 (1992s) 249s (J. W. *Lewis*).

ᴱ**Marty** M., *Appleby* R., Fundamentalisms observed 1992 ➤ 404.

1292 **Marty** Martin E., *Appleby* R. Scott, The glory and the power; the fundamentalist challenge to the modern world. Boston 1992, Beacon. viii-225 p. $30; pa. $15. 0-8070-1216-5; –7–3 [TDig 40,279].

1293 **Mattai** Giuseppe, Magistero e teologia (alle radici di un dissenso) 1989 ➤ 5,1390; 6,1409: ᴿCiuD 205 (1992) 268-270 (V. *Gómez*).

1293* *Melina* Livio, Coscienza, libertà e Magistero: ScuolaC 120 (1992) 152-171.

1294 *Mertes* Klaus, Fondamentalismo e religione: CC 133 (1993,2) 116-129.

1294* *Mesters* Carlos, La Biblia en la nueva evangelización (Apoc 21,5): RBiArg 53 (1991) 1-28.

1295 *Meuleman* G.E., Theologie aan de Universiteit: GerefTTs 91 (1991) 1-27.

1295* *Mitchell* P., Recovering a biblical understanding of the Church's teaching ministry: Journal of Theology 95 (Dayton 1991) 50-60.

1296 **Naud** A., Il magistero incerto [1987 ➤ 5,1397], ᵀ*Crespi* P.: BtTContemp 62. Brescia 1990, Queriniana. 232 p. Lᵐ 25. 88-399-0362-3: ᴿStPatav 38 (1991) 410-2 (E. R. *Tura*).

1297 ᴱ**Neuhaus** R. J., Biblical interpretation in crisis; the Rᴀᴛᴢɪɴɢᴇʀ conference on Bible and Church 1989 ➤ 6,m203; 7,1150: ᴿAtKap 118,497 (1992) 153-8 (Z. *Pawlowski*, ❷).

1298 **Örsy** Ladislas, The Church, learning and teaching; magisterium, assent, dissent, academic freedom 1987 ➤ 4,1346 ... 7,1159: ᴿRTLv 23 (1992) 114s (M. *Simon*: mieux parler d'un magistère fidèle à la Révélation; 'infaillible' est négatif et sinistre).

1299 **O'Meara** Thomas F., Fundamentalism, a Catholic perspective 1990 ➤ 6,1422; 7,1160: ᴿPerspRelSt 19 (1992) 116-9 (A. *Neely*, also on Cᴀʟʜᴏᴏɴ R. M. 1988).

1300 **Osmer** Richard R., A teachable spirit; recovering the teaching office in the Church 1990 ➤ 6,1423: ᴿInterpretation 46 (1992) 71s (R. *Maas*); RelStR 18 (1992) 219 (Elizabeth F. *Caldwell*).

1301 **Pfürtner** Stephan H., Fundamentalismus; die Flucht ins Radikale: Spektrum 4031. FrB 1991, Herder. 222 p. DM 18,80 pa. – RTGL 82 (1992) 145s (W. *Beinert*).

1302 **Rawlyk** G. A., Champions of the truth; fundamentalism, modernism, and the [Canadian] maritime Baptists [Mt. Allison Univ. Bell Lectures 1987s]. Montreal 1990, McGill-Queen's Univ. xv-116 p. – RChH 61 (1992) 431s (W. M. *Patterson*); TorJT 8 (1992) 345s (M. *Parent*).

1302* *Reese* Thomas, Reactions to the Catechism for the universal Church; a bibliographical survey: LivLight 27,1 (1990s) 151-7 (130-150 *al.*).

1303 **Riesebrodt** Martin, Fundamentalismus als patriarchalische Protest-bewegung 1990 → 7,1168: RActuBbg 29 (1992) 214s (J. *Boada*); ArchivScSocR 78 (1992) 255 (J. *Séguy*: informé, brillant, suggestif).

1304 Rome's new catechism: ChrCent 109 (1992) 1126s.

1305 *Sansom* Dennis L., What is a Christian university? [FISHER B. 1989; DE JONG A. 1990; OSMER R. 1990]: → 133, FMILLS W., PerspRelSt 19 (1992) 87-95.

1306 a) *Schmid* Georg, Thesen zum evangelikalen Fundamentalismus; – b) *Stobbe* Heinz-Günther (kath.), Fundamentalismus und Kirchenzucht: UnSa 47 (1992) 38-42 / 19-28.

1307 *Schmitz* H. a) Probleme ... b) Problèmes et conflits dans l'enseignement supérieur ecclésiastique, THiebel J. L.: RDroit Canon 42,1 (1992) 1-50 / 51-97.

1308 *Schützeichel* Heribert, Der Gehorsam in der Kirche: TrierTZ 101 (1992) 190-205.

1309 a) *Segalla* Giuseppe, La lettura fondamentalista della Bibbia; – b) *Tura* Ermanno R., Tratti fondamentalisti nel tradizionalismo cattolico; – c) *Trentin* Giuseppe, Fondamentalismo e diritto alla libertà di coscienza e di religione [*al.* ebrei, Islam]: StPatav 39 (1992) (487-) 493-500 / 533-5 / 537-40 [517-531.501-515].

1310 **Segundo** Juan Luis, Qu'est-ce qu'un dogme? Liberté évangélique et vérité normative; préf. *González Faus* J. I., TGuibal F.: CogF 169. P 1992, Cerf. 534 p. F 299. – RÉtudes 377 (1992) 713s (R. *Marlé*).

1311 **Segundo** J. L., El dogma que libera 1989 → 7,1176: RSalT 78 (1990) 73-78 (A. *Torres Queiruga*).

1312 **Segundo** Juan Luis, The liberation of dogma. Mkn/L 1992, Orbis / Fowler-Wright. 307 p. £15. 0-88344-804-1. – RExpTim 104 (1992s) 250 (D. *Brown*: relentless critique of Church authority; he himself expects to be condemned; but fails to see the sociological aspect of purgatory or Marian dogmas as response to felt human need).

1313 *Sheets* John R., The vocation of the theologian in the Church: Priest 47,1 (1991) 12-16.

1314 *Sieben* Hermann J., Consensus, unanimitas und maior pars auf Konzilien, von der Alten Kirche bis zum Ersten Vatikanum: TPhil 67 (1992) 192-229.

1315 **Silva** Moisés, Has the Church misread the Bible? 1987 → 3,1365 ... 7,1177: RPerspRelSt 19 (1992) 229-232 (M. E. *Deal*, also on J. Deotis ROBERTS, *al*).

1316 **Simon** Maurice, Un catéchisme universel pour l'Église catholique, du Concile de Trente à nos jours; BtETL 103. Lv 1992, Univ./Peeters. xiv-461 p. Fb 2200. 90-6186-492-5 / P 90-6831-342-8 [NRT 115,454, A. *Toubeau*].

1317 **Slenczka** Reinhard, Kirchliche Entscheidung in theologischer Verant-wortung; Grundlagen — Kriterien — Grenzen. Gö 1991, Vandenhoeck

& R. 280 p. DM 48. – ᴿTLZ 117 (1992) 778s (H.-G. *Pöhlmann*: nicht disputativ, sondern assertorisch/ 'prophetisch').

1318 **Spong** John S., Rescuing the Bible from fundamentalism; a bishop rethinks the meaning of Scripture 1991 ➤ 7,1178: ᴿAnglTR 74 (1992) 89-95 (W. T. *Stevenson*); JRelTht 48,1 (1991) 85s (K. *Davis*); ChrCent 108 (1991) 559-561 (L. J. *Averill*).

1319 *Sweeney* Douglas A., Fundamentalism and the neo-evangelicals: Fides et historia 24 (1992) 81-96 [< ᴢɪᴛ 92,646].

1320 *a) Sweeney* James, The decade of evangelisation; has Catholicism changed? – *b) Tanner* Norman, Medieval Christendom [model won't do] and the restoration of a Christian society [not 'restorisation' as p. 457]; – *c) Turner* Geoffrey, Evangelisation and the ghost of Lᴇꜱꜱɪɴɢ; – *d) Barnes* Michael, Evangelisation and the other; response and responsibility: Month 253,12 (Catholic Theological Asn Conference 1992) 461-6 / 467-472 / 473-8 / 479-485.

1321 ᴱ**Swidler** L., *Connor* P., 'Alle Katholiken haben das Recht ...' Freiheitsrechte in der Kirche [1988 ➤ 7,1180],ᵀ. Mü 1990, Kösel. 190 p. DM 26,80. 3-466-36193-1. – ᴿTvT 32 (1992) 313 (W. *Boelens*).

1322 *a) Tábet* Miguel Angel, Verso una fondamentazione dell'esegesi cattolica; – *b) Cirillo* Antonio, La teologia e il teologo in recenti scritti III: AnnTh 6 (1992) 367-389 / 401-429.

1323 *Theobald* Michael, Schriftzitate in kirchlichen Dokumenten: TüTQ 172 (1992) 307-9.

1324 **Thils** Gustave, *Schneider* Theodor, Glaubensbekenntnis und Treueid; Klarstellungen zu den 'neuen' römischen Formeln für kirchliche Amtsträger 1990 ➤ 7,1184: ᴿMüTZ 43 (1992) 143-5 (P. *Krämer*); TLZ 117 (1992) 386s (A. *Stein*).

1325 **Thomas** Hans, 'Katholischer Fundamentalismus'; zum Mechanismus einer akademischen Debatte: ForKT 8 (1992) 261-277.

1326 *Timm* Hermann, Der Wurzelboden des Fundamentalismus: EvKomm 25 (1992) 329-332 [< ᴢɪᴛ 92,357].

1327 *Tosato* Angelo, Magistero pontificio e Sacra Scrittura: Anthropotes 8 (1992) 239-272.

1328 *Tremblay* Réal, 'Donum veritatis' [Instruction sur la vocation ecclésiale du théologien, 24.V.1990], un document qui donne à penser: NRT 114 (1992) 391-411.

1329 **Trollinger** William V.ᴶ, God's empire; William B. Rɪʟᴇʏ and midwestern fundamentalism. Madison 1990, Univ. Wisconsin. 203 p. – ᴿArchivScSocR 78 (1992) 276s (Danièle *Hervieu-Léger*).

1330 *a) Tuohey* John F., The Congregation for the Doctrine of the Faith and homosexuality ['by calling on "conscientious" persons to engage in direct discrimination, it has rewritten the rules of moral theology']; – *b) Doyle* Dennis M., Communion ecclesiology and the silencing of Bᴏꜰꜰ: America 167 (1992) 136-8 / 139-143.

1330* *Vilanova* Evangelista, Magistero 'pastorale' [differente da quello strettamente dottrinale] nel postconcilio: RCatalT 17 (1992) 105-132; Eng. 132.

1331 **Villefranche** H. de, La Bible sur le terrain; écriture-tradition-magistère: Cah.Éc.Cathédrale 4. P 1992, Mame. 88 p. [NRT 115,787].

1331* *Vitoria Cormenzana* Javier, Los conflictos en la Iglesia: SalT 80 (1992) 775-784 (–810 *al.*, sociales, familia).

1332 ᴱ**Werbick** Jürgen, *a)* Offenbarungsanspruch und fundamentalistische Versuchung 1991 ➤ 7,1194: ᴿActuBbg 29 (1992) 320s (J. *Boada*); ZkT

114 (1992) 102-4 (K. H. *Neufeld*); – *b*) Vom entscheidend und unterscheidenden Christlichen [... Umbrüche, Fundamentalismus]. Dü 1992, Patmos. 174 p. DM 28,80 [TR 89,406, K. J. *Lesch*].

1332* *White* Robert A., Twenty years of evolution in the Church's thinking about communication: Communicatio Socialis 25 (Pd 1992) 248-262 [< ZIT 92,590].

1333 *Zilles* Urbano, A constituição apostólica sobre as universidades católicas: Teocomunicação 21,93 (1991) 271-279: 'the universality of expression inevitably will give rise to varying interpretations'.

1333* **zu Eltz** Johannes, Lehrstuhlbesetzung und Beanstandung am Fachbereich katholische Theologie der Universität Mainz: Bischöflicher Stuhl 1988 ➤ 7,1196: ᴿTR 88 (1992) 228s (K. J. *Rivinius*).

B3.2 *Homiletica* – The Bible in preaching.

1334 **Achtemeier** Elizabeth R., Nature, God, and pulpit. GR 1992, Eerdmans. x-206 p. $17. 0-8028-3706-9 [TDig 40,253].

1334* **Achtemeier** Elizabeth, So you're looking for a new preacher; a guide for pulpit nominating committees. GR 1991, Eerdmans. 64 p. $6. 0-8028-0596-5 [ExpTim 104 (1992s) 190].

1335 **Achtemeier** Elizabeth, Preaching from the OT 1989 ➤ 6,1499; 7,1197: ᴿCalvinT 26 (1991) 430-3 (S. *Greidanus* recommends despite queries).

1336 *Achtemeier* Elizabeth, From exegesis to proclamation: ➤ 88, ᶠHUBBARD D., OT 1992, 47-61.

1337 **Bailey** Raymond, *a*) Jesus the preacher 1990 [➤ 6,1450; 7,1198*]; 122 p.; $8. – *b*) Paul the preacher. Nv 1991, Broadman. 126 p. $8. 0-8054-60 [07-1] 35-7. – ᴿRExp 89 (1992) 102-4 (R. *Lovett*; P. S. *Wilson*).

1338 **Bailey** Raymond + 6 others, Hermeneutics for preaching; approaches to contemporary interpretations of Scripture. Nv 1992, Broadman, 223 p. 0-8054-1016-3.

1339 *Baldovin* John F., Biblical preaching in the liturgy: StLtg 22 (1992) 100-118 [< TR 88,536].

1340 **Barth** K., Homiletics 1991 ➤ 7,1199: ᴿMid-Stream 31,1 (1992) 62-64 (D. E. *Stevenson*); RExp 89 (1992) 299 (R. *Bailey*).

1340* **Bonhoeffer** Dietrich, La parole de la prédication; cours d'homilétique à Findenwalde [Werke 4]. Genève 1992, Labor et Fides. 101 p. [LavalTP 49,157. E. *Joós*: platitudes; notes des étudiants].

1341 **Bos** R., Identificatie-mogelijkheden in preken uit het Oude Testament: geref. diss. Kampen, ᴰ*Runia* K. Kampen 1992, Kok. xiii-373 p. 90-242-6702-1. – TvT 32 (1992) 304.

1342 *Boshoff* P. E., *Aarde* A. G. van, Teorie en praktyk van die prediking in die Nuwe Testament; Walter SCHMITHALS aan die woord: HervTSt 47 (1991) 901-919 [930-949; < NTAbs 36,309].

1343 **Brueggemann** Walter, Finally comes the poet 1989 ➤ 6,1454; 7,1207: ᴿCritRR 5 (1992) 83-85 (M. *Ragness*: title from WHITMAN's 'Leaves of grass').

1344 **Bullard** Chris R., Gospel preaching as Christian hagadah; story as a preaching mode: diss. Fuller Theol. Sem., ᴰ*Anderson* R. Pasadena 1982. 155 p. 92-13597. – DissA 52 (1991s) 4359-A.

1344* **Burghardt** Walter J., Dare to be Christ; homilies for the nineties. NY c1992, Paulist. 214 p. $17.50 pa. [CanadCathR 11/5,29, A. *Cylwicki*].

1345 **Buttrick** D. G., The mystery [of the Resurrection] and the Passion; a homiletic reading of the biblical traditions. Mp 1992, Fortress. x-246 p. $15 pa. 0-8006-2550-1 [NTAbs 36,420].

1346 **Buttrick** David, Homiletic, moves and structures 1987 ➤ 3,1376 [not as] 6,1424: ᴿBijdragen 53 (1992) 335s (J. *Besemer*).

1347 **Chautard** Guy, Les petits chiens sous la table ['L'homélie plaide non-coupable' 1985, plus articles réunis sans accord de ce prêtre de Toulouse]. Laval 1991, Siloé. 117 p. F 75. – ᴿEsprVie 102 (1992) 223s (P. *Jay*: une liberté de penser malgré les impératifs des slogans).

1348 ᴱCox James W., Best sermons [2.1989 ➤ 5,1426; 3.1990 ➤ 7,1210]; 4. SF 1991, Harper. 263 p. $18. 0-06-061614-8. – ᴿRExp 89 (1992) 567 (M. *Graves*: includes G. BEASLEY-MURRAY, B. METZGER, K. STENDAHL, E. ACHTEMEIER, W. BURGHARDT ...).

1349 **Craddock** Fred B., Prêcher [Preaching 1985], ᵀ*Rebeaud* Jean-F.: Pratiques 4. Genève 1991, Labor et Fides. 229 p. – ᴿÉglT 23 (1992) 284s (M. *Lefebvre*); RTPhil 124 (1992) 167-176 (P.-A. *Betten*: rend bien la vivacité de style de l'original).

1350 **Cunningham** David S., Faithful persuasion; in aid of a rhetoric of Christian theology. ND 1992, Univ. xvii-312 p. $30. 0-268-00984-8 [TDig 40,59: not specifically preaching].

1350* **Daiber** K.-F., Predigt als religiöse Rede; homiletische Überlegungen im Anschluss an eine empirische Untersuchung: Predigen und hören 3. Mü 1991, Kaiser. 458 p. DM 98 3-459-01909-3 [TvT 33,315, R. *Cornelissen*].

1351 *Deuel* David C., *a*) An Old Testament pattern for expository preaching; – *b*) Suggestions for expositional preaching of OT narrative: Master's TheolJ 2 (Sun Valley CA 1991) 125-138 / 45-60 [< OTAbs 15,315].

1352 **Dingemans** G. D.J., Als hoorder onder de hoorders; een hermeneutische Homiletiek. c. 1991. ᴿPrakT 19 (Zwolle 1992) 276-9 (J. W. *Besemer*).

1353 *Dingemans* G.D.J., Ontwikkelingen in de homiletiek; een overzicht van recente literatuur: NedTTs 46 (1992) 124-131.

1354 **Drewermann** Eugen, Dass alle eins seien; Predigten zwischen Himmelfahrt und Dreifaltigkeitsfest. Dü 1992, Patmos. 200 p. DM 30. – ᴿTGL 82 (1992) 506 (K. *Hollmann*).

1355 **Edgerton** W. D., The passion of interpretation: Literary currents in Bible interpretation. Louisville 1992, W-Knox. 160 p. $20. 0-664-25394-6 [BL 93,79, J. *Barton*: rather homiletic reflections on 'stories' like Gen 22 & Lk 24].

1356 **Ferraro** Giuseppe, Nel nome del Padre; commento esegetico alle lettere festive; schemi di predicazione, anno A. CasM 1992, Piemme. 437 p. Lit. 45.000. – ᴿCC 143 (1992,4) 635s (M. *Simone*).

1357 **Friedenberg** Robert V., 'Hear, O Israel!'; the history of American Jewish preaching, 1654-1970. Tuscaloosa 1989, Univ. Alabama. XII-177 p. – ᴿCCAR 39,2 (1992) 76-78 (H. C. *Perelmuter*); JQR 83 (1992s) 461-3 (H. A. *Sosland*).

1358 **Greidanus** Sidney, The modern preacher and the ancient text 1988 ➤ 3,1432 ... 7,1219: ᴿEvangel 9,1 (1991) 30 (T. P. *Letis*: a bit naive and tedious; misunderstands CHILDS).

1359 *Gross* Engelbert, Kerygma; der Prediger, der Religionslehrer und der Seelsorger im Drama des Wortes: GeistL 65 (1992) 87-102.

1360 **Gross** Nancy L., A re-examination of recent homiletical theories in light of the hermeneutical theory of Paul RICŒUR: diss. Princeton Theol. Sem. ᴰ*Long* T. 1992. 232 p. 92-29018. – DissA 53 (1992s) 1545-A.

1360* **Hamilton** D. L., Homiletical handbook. Nv 1992, Broadman. 207 p. $15 pa. 0-8054-1626-9 [NTAbs 37, p. 266].

1361 **Hermelink** Jan, Die homiletische Situation [< Diss 1991 ➤ 7,1221]; Zur jüngeren Geschichte eines Predigtproblems: ArbPastT 24. Gö 1992,

Vandenhoeck & R.   311 p. DM 52.   3-525-62331-3 [TLZ 118,663-5, W. *Gräb*].

1361* *Hilkert* Mary C., Bearing wisdom; the vocation of the preacher: Sp-Tod 44,2 (final issue, 1992) 143-160.

1362 **Hirschler** Horst, Biblisch predigen 1988 ➤ 4,1379:   ᴿBijdragen 53 (1992) 227s (J. *Besemer*).

1363 *Holgate* A., Making the text our own [in preparing a sermon]: ExpTim 104 (1992s) 232-6.

1364 *Hoppe* Leslie J., Preaching from apocalyptic texts: NewTR 5,4 (1992) 61-65.

1365 *Immink* F.G., Hermeneutik en retoriek in de predikkunde — twee homiletische modellen: TRef 34,1 (1992) 29-50 [< GerefTTs 92,197].

1366 **Jabusch** Willard F., The spoken Christ; reading and preaching the transforming Word 1990 ➤ 6,1469*:   ᴿWorship 65 (1991) 474s (W. *Skudlarek*).

1367 **Jennings** Margaret, The 'ars componendi sermones' [praedicandi, concionandi] of Ranulph HIGDEN O.S.B.: DavisMelvTS 6.   Leiden 1991, Brill. lxix-82 p. ƒ80 [RHE 88,247, D. *Poirel*].

1367* *Jensen* Richard A., Reviews of current literature on preaching: Dialog 31 (1992) 196-9.

1368 ᴱ**Klein** George L., Reclaiming the prophetic mantle; preaching the Old Testament faithfully. Nv 1992, Broadman. 315 p. 0-8054-6020-9.

1368* *Laan* Jaap van der, Die Predigt als 'neues Wort'; über den Beitrag Ernst LANGERS zur Theorie und Praxis der Predigt: BTZ 9 (1992) 202-216.

1369 **McClure** John S., The four codes of preaching [... first: Scripture]; rhetorical strategies. Mp 1991, Augsburg-F. 201 p. $15. – ᴿTTod 49 (1992s) 274.276 (D. S. *Jacobsen*).

1370 **McSwain** Stephen B., Basic Bible sermons on spiritual living. Nv 1991, Broadman. 127 p. $5. 0-8054-2274-9. – ᴿRExp 89 (1992) 435 (C. *Bugg* commends this 'gifted young minister').

1370* *Marshall* I. Howard, Preaching from the New Testament: a) ScotBEv 9,2 (1991); – b) EvRT 17 (1993) 405-420.

1371 **Miller** Charles E., Ordained to preach; a theology and practice of preaching. Staten Island NY 1992, Alba. x-236 p. $13. 0-8189-0637-5 [TDig 40,176: Vincentian 35-year-long teacher of homiletics].

1372 *Mohler* R. Albertᴶ, 'Faithfully proclaim the truth' an interview with John F. MACARTHUR: Preaching 5 (Nov. 1991) 2-10 [< BtS 149 (1992) 238s (T. S. *Warren*).

1373 **Nicholls** Mike, C. H. SPURGEON; the pastor evangelist [19th cent.]. L 1992, Baptist Historical Soc. 183 p. $8. 0-903166-17-8. – ᴿExpTim 104 (1992s) 64 (C. S. *Rodd*, noting on p. 63 also published sermons by EVANS S.; HOULDEN L.; KEE A.).

1374 *Niebergall* Alfred, Histoire de la prédication [< RGG³ 1961, 516-530], ᵀ*Carrel-Conod* Sylvie & Serge: Hokhma 48 ('Prêchez!' 1991) 43-64.

1375 **Norén** Carol M., The woman in the pulpit. Nv 1991, Abingdon. 176 p. $13. 0-687-45893-5. – ᴿRExp 89 (1992) 583s (Amy L. *Mears*).

1376 **Olivar** Alexandre, La predicación cristiana antigua: BtHerderTf 189, 1991 ➤ 7,1227:   ᴿAnVal 17 (1991) 184s (F. T.); LumenVr 40 (1991) 535s (F. *Ortiz de Urtaran*); RelCu 37 (1991) 740s (P. *Langa*); Teresianum 43 (1992) 525s (M. *Diego Sánchez*).

1377 *Otto* Gert, Predigt (-lehre): ➤ 757, EvKL 3 (1992) 1305-17.

1377* *Prakash* Surya [➤ 7,1232 *Surya* P.], Sermon preparation; biblical preaching, methodological issues and perspectives: BangaloreTF 23 (1991) 25-37 [< TContext 10/1, p. 29].

1378 *Reingrabner* Gustav, Zur Predigt alttestamentlicher Texte im evangelischen Gottesdienst: ➤ 163, FSAUER G., Aktualität 1992, 291-303.

1378* **Rice** Charles L., The embodied word; preaching as art and liturgy. Ph 1991, Fortress. 144 p. [LuthQ 7,109, D. D. *Shellaway*].

1379 **Saperstein** Marc, Jewish preaching 1200-1800: 1989 ➤ 6,1489; 7,1230: RJAAR 60 (1992) 180-2 (N. A. *Stillman*).

1380 **Schlafer** David J., Surviving the sermon; a guide to preaching for those who have to listen, Boston 1992, Cowley. 132 p. $11. 1-56101-064-2 [TDig 40,186].

1381 **Shearlock** David J., The practice of preaching. 1990, Churchman. 128 p. £5.50. – RExpTim 104 (1992s) 156s (C. S. *Rodd*: splendid).

1382 *Stiefel* Robert E., Preaching to all the people; the use of Jungian typology and the Myers-Briggs type indicator in the teaching of preaching and in the preparation of sermons: AnglTR 74 (1992) 175-202.

1382* *Stookey* Laurence H., MARCION, typology, and lectionary preaching: Worship 66 (1992) 251-262.

1383 **Theissen** Gerd, *a*) Die offene Tür 1990 ➤ 6,1495: RRTPhil 124 (1992) 201s (Muriel *Schmid*).; *b*) The open door [25 biblical sermons]. L 1991, SCM. xii-191 p. £10 pa. – RTLond 95 (1992) 301 (Frances M. *Young*).

1384 **Troeger** Thomas H., The parable of ten preachers. Nv 1992, Abingdon. 128 p. $10. – RSewaneeTR 36 (1992s) 443s (D. *Schlafer*).

1384* *Van Horn* Roger E., Pew rights; for people who listen to sermons. GR 1992, Eerdmans. xiv-162 p. $15 [PrincSemB 14,219, L. W. *Farris*].

1385 *Waznak* Robert P., The homily fulfilled in our hearing: Worship 65 (1991) 27-37.

1386 *Willhite* Keith, Audience relevance in expository preaching: BtS 149 (1992) 355-369.

1387 **Willimon** William H., Last laugh. Nv 1991, Abingdon. 160 p. $15. 0-687-45598-7. – RRExp 89 (1992) 299s (B. J. *Leonard*: for preaching).

B3.3 **Inerrantia, inspiratio** [Revelatio ➤ H1.7].

1389 **Abba** R., The nature and authority of the Bible²*rev* [¹1958]. C 1992, Clarke. vi-383 p. £13. 0-227-67912-1 [BL 93,100, R. *Davidson*].

1390 *Adam* Albrecht, Ein Schriftsteller als Träger göttlicher Botschaft? Vom Anspruch und Selbstverständnis biblischer und ausserbiblischer Literatur: LuthTK 15 (1991) 90-105.

1390* *Aldwinckle* R., The authority of Scripture in recent Yale theology: McMasterJT 3,1 (Hamilton 1992) 47-74 [< NTAbs 37,2].

1391 **Alonso Schökel** Luis, A Palavra inspirada, a Bíblia à luz da ciência da linguagem [La palabra inspirada ³1986]. TStela Conçalves Maria: Biblica Loyola Subsidios 9. São Paulo 1992, Loyola. 271 p. 85-15-00492-5.

1391* *Amit* Yairah, 'The Glory of Israel does not deceive or change his mind'; on the reliability of narrator and speakers in biblical narrative: Prooftexts 12 (1992) 201-212.

1392 *Begbie* Jeremy, Who is this God? — Biblical inspiration revisited: TyndB 43 (1992) 259-283.

1393 EBlaisdell Charles R., Conservative, moderate, liberal; the biblical authority debate 1989/90 ➤ 6,514*; 0-8272-0455-8: RInterpretation 46 (1992) 306 (D. K. *McKim*).

1393* *Borg* Marcus J.,   Different ways of looking at the Bible; 'God's story' or a 'human composition'? ... BR 8,4 (1992) 7.13.
1394 **Bourgeois** H., *al.*, La cause des Écritures; l'autorité des écritures en christianisme. Lyon 1989, Profac. 127 p. 2-85317-038-1 [ActuBbg 30, 57s, X. *Alegre*].
1394* *Brown* Raymond E.,   Communicating the divine and human in Scripture: Origins 22,1 (Wsh 1992s) 1.3-9.
1395 **Chauvet** P.,   Parole de Dieu; Écriture, tradition, magistère: Cah.Éc. Cathedrale 1. P 1992, Mame. 80 p. F 45. – ᴿNRT 114 (1992) 632 (L.-J. *Renard*).
1395* ᴱ**Conn** Harvie M.,   Inerrancy and hermeneutics; a tradition, challenge and debate [3d symposium at Ph Westminster Seminary since its secession from Princeton Seminary 1940] 1989 ➤ 5,388; 7,1238: ᴿConcordTQ 56 (1992) 312s (R. F. *Surburg*: not the hermeneutics of the Westminster Confession or the Westminster Seminary founders); JEvTS 35 (1992) 241-4 (R. J. *Erickson*).
1396 *Culbertson* Philip,   Known, knower, and knowing; the authority of Scripture in the Episcopal Church: AnglTR 74 (1992) 144-174.
1397 *Delivuk* John A.,   Inerrancy, infallibility, and Scripture in [J. Rᴏɢᴇʀs, 1967] The Westminster confession of faith: WestTJ 54 (1992) 349-355.
1398 *Dixon* Richard D., *al.*,   Biblical authority questions; two choices in identifying conservative Christian subcultures: Sociological Analysis ... Religion 53,1 (Wsh 1992) 63-72 [< zɪᴛ 92,349].
1399 *a) Felder* Cain H.,   Afrocentrism and biblical authority; – *b) Ringe* Sharon H.,   The word of God may be hazardous to your health; – *c) Beker* J. Christiaan,   The authority of Scripture; normative or incidental: TTod 49 (1992s) 357-366 / 367-375 / 376-382.
1400 *a) Fogarty* Gerald,   Scriptural authority (Roman Catholicism) [*al.* Judaism, Eastern Orthodoxy, Early Medieval Church, Reformation]; – *b) Reventlow* H. Enlightenment; – *c) Brueggemann* W., Post-critical: ➤ 741, AnchorBD 5 (1992) 1023-6 [1017-23.1026-35] / 1035-49 / 1049-56.
1401 *a)* **Gabel** Helmut,   Inspirationsverständnis im Wandel; theologische Neuorientierung im Umfeld des Zweiten Vatikanischen Konzils. Mainz 1991, Grünewald. 251 p. DM 48. – ᴿBLtg 65 (1992) 67s (B. J. *Hilberath*); TGL 82 (1992) 380s (W. *Beinert*); TvT 32 (1992) 327 (W. *Logister*).
— *b)* **Goodrick** Edward W.,   Is my Bible the inspired Word of God? 1988 ➤ 5,1455: ᴿJEvTS 35 (1992) 240s (T. F. *Bulick*).
— *c) Hanson* P. D.,   Biblical authority today: Dialog 31 (St. Paul 1992) 176-180 [< NTAbs 37,4].
— *d) Hart* D. G.,   A reconsideration of biblical inerrancy and the Princeton Theology's alliance with fundamentalism: ChrSchR 20 (1990s) 362-376.
1401* *a) Höhn* Hans-J.,   Distanz und Dissens; Theologie zwischen Moderne und Postmoderne; – *b) Scobel* Gert. Postmoderne für Theologen? Hermeneutik des Widerstreits und Bildende Theologie: ➤ 396c, Theologie, die an der Zeit ist 1992, 11-15 / 175-229; – *c) Johnston* Paul I.,   Johann Michael Rᴇᴜ [c. 1930] and inerrancy: ConcordTQ 56 (1992) 145-185 (p. 169 'maddening consistency of his inconsistency').
1402 *a) Loughlin* Gerard,   Making it plain; Austin Fᴀʀʀᴇʀ and the inspiration of Scripture; – *b) Delferth* Ingolf,   The stuff of revelation; Austin Farrer's doctrine of inspired images; – *c) Hauge* Hans,   The sin of reading; Austin Farrer, Helen Gᴀʀᴅɴᴇʀ and Frank Kᴇʀᴍᴏᴅᴇ on the poetry of St. Mark: ➤ 477, Hermeneutics 1989/92, 96-112 / 71-95 / 113-128.

1403 **Maranesi** Pietro, Il concetto di 'Verbum inspiratum' in S. BONA-VENTURA: diss. Pont. Univ. Gregoriana, D*Adnès* P. Roma 1992, 473 p. – RTLv 24, p. 554.

1403* *Oberkampf de Dabrun* Serge, Sola Scriptura et l'unité de l'Église [... LECERF Auguste 1872-1943]: Hokhma 49 (1992) 23-27.

1404 *Petzoldt* Martin, Schriftprinzip und Bekenntnishermeneutik; Überlegungen zur Confessio Augustana [... OBST M. 1989]: TLZ 117 (1992) 161-8.

1405 *Sánchez Mielgo* Gerardo, Inspiración e interpretación de la Escritura en la luz de la 'Dei Verbum' del Concilio Vaticano II: EscrVedat 21 (1991) 7-49.

Schniedewind Wm. M., Prophecy ... inspiration in Chronicles D1992 → 3021.

1406 *Schümmer* Léopold, Quelques remarques sur l'autorité de l'Écriture dans l'Église des années 1990: RRéf 43,2 (1992) 5-10 [< ZIT 92,298].

1407 *Stöhr* Martin, The authority of the Word of God: RefW 42,1 (Geneva 1992) 4-10 [< ZIT 92,274]; 11-16, *Smyth-Florentin* Françoise, fundamentalism.

1407* **Woods** Lauric, The Bible; God's word. ColMn 1993, Liturgical. 92 p. $10 [BToday 31,385].

1408 *Wright* J. Robert, The official position of the Episcopal Church on the authority of Scripture: AnglTR 74 (1992) 348-361.478-489.

B3.4 **Traditio.**

1409 *Apecechea Perurena* Juan, La tradición, principio de progreso en la Iglesia: LumenVr 40 (1991) 1-44.

1410 *Bruckberger* R.-L., La tradition catholique à l'intérieur du monde moderne: PeCa 259 (1962) 27-35.

1411 **Bunnenberg** Johannes, Lebendige Treue zum Ursprung; das Traditionsverständnis Yves CONGARS 1989 → 5,1474 ... 7,1257: RRThom 92 (1992) 549-552 (F. *Gaboriau*).

1412 *Chmiel* Jerzy, P Paradosis; interpretacja tradycji i hermeneutyka biblijna: RuBi 45 (1992) 1-5.

1412* *Farrugia* Mario, Cercando una tradizione viva; la riscoperta della Parathēkē: RasT 33 (1992) 404-426.

1413 *a) Fine* Lawrence, The unwritten Torah, Judaism's oral teachings; – *b) Jordan-Smith* Paul, And the Word was made flesh; origins of the Christian Mass: Parabola 17,3 ('Oral Tradition' 1992) 65-70 / 85-90 [plus 14 other short items].

1414 *Gardeil* Pierre, Écriture, tradition, Corps livré: NRT 114 (1992) 251-260.

1415 *Grelot* Pierre, La tradition apostolique: RB 99 (1992) 163-204; Eng. 163s.

1415* *Haarbeck* Ako, Glaubwürdiges Zeugnis der Gemeinde: TBeit 23 (1992) 241-8 [< ZIT 92,697].

1416 **Hanegraaff** J., Rondom de mondelinge traditie: Met de Torah is het begonnen 1990 → 7,1260: RKerkT 42 (1991) 264 (P. A. *Elderenbosch*).

1416* *Harakas* Stanley S., 'Tradition' in Eastern Orthodox thought: Chr-SchR 22 (GR 1992) 144-165 [< ZIT 93,133].

1417 *Hoover* Arlie J., Christ and Columbus on tradition: RestQ 34,1 (Abilene 1992) 51–... [< ZIT 92,296].

1418 **Kelber** W. H., Tradition orale et Écriture 1991 → 7,1263: RCarthaginensia 8 (1992) 932s (R. *Sanz Valdivieso*).

1419 *Lilie* Frank, HEIDEGGERS Forderung nach einer Destruktion der Tradition: NSys 34 (1992) 315-325; Eng. 325.
1420 **Lods** Marc, 80. Gb., Protestantisme et tradition de l'Église, 30 ans réimprimés ᴱ*Pérés* J.-N., *Dubois* J.-D.: Patrimoines Christianisme 1988 ➤ 5,299: ᴿZKG 103 (1992) 370-3 (W. *Erdt*).
1421* *a) McWilliam* Joanne, Tradition before the future; – *b) Samuelson* Norbert M., Tradition from a Jewish perspective: TorJT 9 (1992) 51-66 / 27-50.
1421 **Schori** Kurt, Das Problem der Tradition; eine fundamentaltheologische Untersuchung. Stu 1992, Kohlhammer. 370 p. DM 74. 3-17-011542-1. – ᴿTGL 82 (1992) 373s (W. *Beinert*); TvT 32 (1992) 429s (W. *Logister*).
1422 ᴱ**Wiederkehr** Dietrich, Wie geschieht Tradition? [Tagung Vierzehnheiligen (Franken) 24.-28. Sept. 1990]: QDisp 133. FrB 1991, Herder. x-176 p. 3-451-02133-1; p. 45-68 *Hünermann* Peter; 89-110 *Pottmeyer* Hermann J., + 3 *al.* – ᴿTvT 32 (1992) 430s (W. *Logister*).

B3.5 Canon.

1422* *Balch* David L., The canon; adaptable and stable, oral and written; critical questions for KELBER and RIESNER: ForumFF 7 (1991) 183-205.
1423 **Balge** R. D., The Bible through the ages, 1. The canon of Scripture: WisLu 88 (Mequon 1991) 280-293 [< NTAbs 36,307].
1424 **Beckwith** R., OT canon of NT Church 1985 ➤ 1,1472 ... 6,1547: ᴿJPseud 5 (1989) 111-3 (J. C. *VanderKam*).
1424* *Ben-Shammai* Haggai. The Karaite controversy; Scripture and tradition in early Karaism: ➤ 475*d*, Religionsgespräche 1992, 11-26.
1425 *Brooks* James A., CLEMENT of Alexandria as a witness to the development of the New Testament canon: SecC 9 (1992) 41-55.
1426 *Claramont Llácer* F., La relación entre la Sagrada Escritura y la Iglesia en la relección 'De sacro canone et de ejus sensibus' de Domingo de SOTO, con el texto inédito de la misma: AnVal 16,31 (1990) 63-106 [< RET 51,408].
1427 **Dohmen** Christoph, *Oeming* Manfred, Biblischer Kanon, warum und wozu? Eine Kanontheologie: QDisp 136. FrB 1992, Herder. 132 p. DM 36. [TR 88,425] 3-451-02137-4.
1428 **Hahnemann** Geoffrey M., The Muratorian Fragment and the development of the canon [dated 375]; – *a)* diss. Oxford 1987. 369 p. BRD-96174. – DissA 53 (1992s) 842-A; – *b)* OxTheolMg. Ox 1992, Clarendon. xi-237 p. $50. 0-19-826341-4 [TDig 40,271].
1428* *a) Hallo* William W., The concept of canonicity in cuneiform and biblical literature; a comparative appraisal; – *b) Hoskisson* Paul Y., Emar as an empirical model of the transmission of canon: ➤ 7,334*, Canon 1990/1, 1-19 / 21-32.
1429 *Jörns* K.-P., Liturgy, cradle of Scripture: StLtg 22,1 (Rotterdam 1992) 17-34 [< NTAbs 37,1].
1429* *Kevers* Paul, De canon van de heilige Schrift; absolute norm of inspirerende richtlijn? Tijdschrift voor geestelijk leven 47 (1991) 210-....
1430 *a) Lang* B. *al.*, Kanon: ➤ 762, NBL II, 8 (1992) 440-450.
— *b) Linebarger* John M., History meets theology; three recent books about the canon [BRUCE F.; METZGER B.; MCDONALD L.]: Crux 27,3 (1991) 34-37.
— *c)* **McDonald** Lee M., The formation of the biblical canon 1988 ➤ 4,1446 ... 7,1275: ᴿCrux 26,4 (1990) 42s (D. *Stewart*).

1431 **Meade** David G., Pseudonymity and canon 1986 ➤ 2,1040 ... 7,1276: RNedTTs 46 (1992) 161s (J. *Smit Sibinga*); ScripTPamp 23 (1991) 1073s (J. M. *Casciaro*).
1432 **Metzger** Bruce, Canon of the NT 1987 ➤ 3,1456 ... 7,1277: RCurr-TMiss 19 (1992) 59s (E. *Krentz*); JAAR 60 (1992) 350-5 (A. C. *Sundberg*); ZkT 114 (1992) 208s (R. *Oberforcher*).
1433 **Morgan** Donn F., Between text and community; the 'Writings' in canonical perspective 1990 ➤ 6,1564*; 7,1278: RAnglTR 74 (1992) 96-8 (M. H. *Floyd*); CBQ 54 (1992) 119 (J. J. *Collins*); JAAR 60 (1992) 562-7 (L. H. *Feldmann* warmly admires his sensitive approach to Jewish-Christian dialogue).
1434 *Ohlig* Karl-Heinz, Canon scripturarum [deutsch]; ➤ 743, AugL 1,5s (1992) 713-724.
1435 EPannenberg Wolfhart, *Schneider* Theodor, Verbindliches Zeugnis, I. Kanon, Schrift, Tradition: Dialog der Kirchen 7. Gö 1992, Vandenhoeck & R. 399 p. DM 50. 10 art. [TR 88,529 tit. pp.; *Steck* O., *Frank* K. S., *Lohse* B., *Fries* H., *Kasper* W.; ➤ 1807, Hengel M.].
1436 EReventlow H., *al.*, Historische Kritik und biblischer Kanon in der deutschen Aufklärung 1988 ➤ 5,602; 6,1567: RJEH 43 (1992) 155 (W. R. *Ward*).
1437 *Skeat* T. C., IRENAEUS and the four-gospel canon: NT 34 (1992) 194-9.
1437* *Topping* Richard R., The canon and the truth; Brevard CHILDS and James BARR on the Canon and the historical-critical method: TorJT 8 (1992) 239-260.
Wall R., *Lemcio* E., The NT as canon 1992 ➤ 369.
1438 **Ziegenaus** A., Kanon 1990 ➤ 6,1575; 7,1290: RScripTPamp 23 (1991) 706 (A. *Viciano*); TPQ 140 (1992) 191 (A. *Fuchs*).

B4 *Interpretatio humanistica* – .1 **The Bible and man: health, toil, age.**

1438* *Abu Byung Mu*, A biblical view of the refugee problem: RefW 41 (1990s) 214-224.
1439 **Betz** Georg, Wenn der Menschlichkeit die Luft ausgeht; eine biblische Therapie gegen den Notstand in Krankenhaus und Altenpflege. FrB 1990, Herder. 176 p. DM 22. – RBiKi 47 (1992) 122 (Kalle *Schmitz*).
1439* **Armerding** Hudson T., The heart of godly leadership. Wheaton IL 1992, Crossway. 220 p. $15. 0-89107-675-1 [TDig 40,150].
1440 **Castro** S., La bellezza en la Biblia: RevEspir 204 (1992) 253-270 [< NTAbs 37, p. 233].
1440* **Corneau** Guy, Absent fathers, lost sons; the search for masculine identity. Boston 1991, Shambhala. [CGrebel 11,294s, B. *Balmer*].
1441 **Cotterell** Peter, Mission and meaninglessness; the Good News in a world of suffering and disorder. L 1990, SPCK. xii-332 p. £13 pa. – RTLond 95 (1992) 469s (H. *Willmer*).
1441* **Culbertson** Philip, New Adam; the future of male spirituality. Mp 1992, Fortress. 183 p. $11 [BToday 31,54].
1442 *Dupré* Louis, On being a Christian teacher of humanities: ChrCent 109 (1992) 452-5.
1443 *Gaiser* Frederick J., The emergence of the self in the Old Testament; a study in biblical wellness: HorBT 14 (1992) 1-29 ['used by permission'].
1444 **Grenholm** Carl-Henric, Arbetets mening; en analys av sex teorier om arbetets syfte och värde: AcUniv Social Ethics 11. U 1988, Univ. 531 p. – RSvTKv 67 (1991) 99-101 (G. *Collste*).

1444* **Hauerwas** Stanley, Naming the silences; God. medicine and the problem of suffering. GR 1991, Eerdmans. 154 p. [RestQ 35,48-51, D. *Brown*].

1445 **Hurding** Roger, The Bible and counselling. L 1992, Hodder & S. xii-228 p. £10. 0-340-51742-5. – ᴿTBR 5,2 (1992s) 35s (A. *Browne*).

1445* *Ibaronia* Francisco, Teología del dolor en la Biblia: REspir 49 (1990) 197-228.

1446 *a) Janzen* Waldemar, The theology of work from an OT perspective; – *b) Shillington* V. George, A NT perspective on work: Conrad Grebel Review 10,2 (1992) 121-138 / 139-155 [329-340, responses].

1447 *Kaiser* Otto, 'Und dies sind die Geschlechter ...' Alt und Jung im Alten Testament: ➤ 163, ᶠSAUER G., Aktualität 1992, 29-45.

1448 **Kysar** Robert, Called to care; biblical images for social ministry 1991 ➤ 7,1300: ᴿChrCent 108 (1991) 824; CritRR 5 (1992) 451-3 (J. R. *Levison*); CurrTMiss 19 (1992) 296s (E. *Utto-Galarneau*).

1449 **Larchet** Jean-Claude, Théologie de la maladie: Théologies. P 1991, Cerf. 148 p. – ᴿBLitEc 93 (1992) 349s (J.-J. *Fauconnet*: 'réactions de l'homme moderne' plutôt que théologie).

1449* **Levoratti** A. J., Grandeza y miseria del trabajo humano: Nuevo Mundo 39 (Buenos Aires 1990) 3-40 [< Stromata 48,474].

1450 *Lohfink* Norbert, Die Bibel und die Armen — drei Lesehilfen für Ordensleute: Ordens-Korrespondenz (1992,4) 385-392.

1451 *Luyten* Jos, Perspectives on human suffering in the Old Testament: ➤ 577, Suffering 1987/9, 1-30.

1452 **McDermott** John M., La sofferenza umana nella Bibbia [The Bible on human suffering], ᵀ*Martorana* H.: PiccBtT 9, 1990 ➤ 7,1302: ᴿAngelicum 69 (1992) 123s (S. *Jurić*, ma non 'The Bible of human suffering').

1453 **Matto** Michele S., The twelve steps in the Bible; paths to wholeness for adult children. NY 1991, Paulist. v-172 p. $8 [CBQ 54,615].

1453* *Moftah* Ramses, Lebenszeit in alttestamentlichen Zahlwortspielen [Ps 89,10; Gn 50,3.26; Ex 2,22]: BSACopte 30 (1991) 121-6.

1454 **Moore** Robert, *Gillette* Douglas, *a)* The king within; accessing the king in the male psyche. NY 1992, Avon. 336 p. ill. 0-380-72068-7; – *b)* King, Warrior, Magician, Lover; rediscovering the archetypes of the mature masculine. SF 1990 (pa. 1981), Harper. 192 p. $17; pa. $10. 0-06-250597-1; -606-4; – *c)* ᵀ*Poppe* Thomas, König, Krieger, Magier, Liebhaber; die Stärken des Mannes: Männer in Bewegung. Mü 1992, Kösel. 207 p. 3-466-34285-6 [ActuBbg 30,141, J. *Boada*].

1456 **Mulders** P. J., Arbeid om te leven en arbeidsleven; een theologisch-ethische verkenning van het fenomeen 'arbeid' in het bijzonder bij C. J. DIPPEL, A. T. van LEEUWEN, Hanna ARENDT en E. F. SCHUMACHER. Haag 1991, Boeken-C. 411 p. *f* 59. 90-239-1044-3. ᴿTvT [31,318 diss.] 32 (1992) 114 (G. *Manenschijn*).

1456* **Payne** Franklin E.ᴶ (M. D.), Making medical decisions. Escondido 1989, Hosanna. 178 p. – ᴿJEvTS 35 (1992) 560 (S. *Vantassel*).

1457 **Richard** L., What are they saying about the theology of suffering? [... BRUEGGEMANN W., Bible]. NY 1992, Paulist. 163 p. $8. 0-8091-3347-4 [NRT 115,467; NTAbs 37, p. 247].

1458 **Romaniuk** Kazimierz, ℗ Biblijna teologia odpoczynku [of leisure]. Wsz 1992, Loretanek. 102 p.

1458* *Schottroff* Willy, Alter als sociales Problem in der hebräischen Bibel: ➤ 197, ᶠWOLFF H. W., Wer 1992, 61-77.

1459 *Schröer* Henning, Biblischer Blick auf die Medien: EvKomm 25 (1992) 721-4 [< ZIT 92,746].

1460 *Schwab* Claude, A pleine vie; jalons bibliques pour naître, vivre et mourir. Aubonne 1989, Moulin. 100 p. – ᴿProtestantesimo 47 (1992) 144s (B. *Costabel*).

1460* *Thompson* W. G., Men [males] and the Gospels: CathW 235,3 (1992) 104-111 [< NTAbs 37,16].

1461 *Thorbjørnsen* Svein-Olaf, Nyere boker om arbeid [ᴱFAHLBUSCH W., *al.*, Werk ist nicht alles; Versuche zu einer Ethik der Zukunft 1987; BRAKELMANN G., Zur Arbeit geboren? 1988; NEFF W. S., Work and human behaviour³ 1985]: TsTKi 63 (1992) 227-230.

1462 **Volf** Miroslav, Work in the Spirit; a pneumatological understanding of work [U. S. subtitle 'toward a theology of work']. Ox c. 1992, U.P. 252 p. $32.50. [TDig 39,192]. – ᴿChrCent 109 (1992) 307s (J. *Banks*); TLond 95 (1992) 226s (R. *Preston*); TTod 49 (1992s) 270.2.4 (Amy P. *Pauw*).

1463 *Winkler* Klaus, Lachen und Weinen: → 757, EvKL 3 (1992) 1-3.

B4.2 *Femina, familia*; **Woman in the Bible** [→ H8.8s].

1464 **Angelini** Giuseppe, Il figlio; una benedizione, un compito: Sestante 1. Mi 1991, ViPe. 207 p. Lit. 22.000. 88-343-3871-5. – ᴿActuBbg 29 (1992) 60s (M. *Cuyás*; ¿qué es hijo, madre, engendrar?); CC 143 (1992,3) 218 (también M. *Cuyás*).

1465 **Archer** Léonie J., Her price is beyond rubies: JStOT supp 60, 1990 → 6,1590; 7, 1310: ᴿCritRR 5 (1992) 352-4 (Kathleen E. *Corley*: inadequate use of sources research); JAOS 112 (1992) 162s (D. J. *Gilner*); JRS 82 (1992) 282 (Catharine *Edwards*).

1465* **Asciutto** Liborio, Eva e le sue sorelle; la Bibbia al femminile. Bo 1992, Dehoniane. 256 p. Lit. 22.000 [CC 144/3, 442s, A. *Ferrua*].

1466 **Aynard** Laure, La Bible au féminin: LDiv 138, 1990 → 7,1311: ᴿÉglT 23 (1992) 129-131 (Barbara A. *Bozak*)

1467 **Bach** Alice, The pleasure of her text 1990 → 6,1592: ᴿInterpretation 46 (1992) 317.320 (L. *Rowlett*).

1468 ᴱ**Bal** Mieke, Anti-Covenant 1989 → 5,625 ... 7,1313: ᴿPacifica 5 (1992) 223-6 (Anne E. *Gardner*).

1469 **Beyerle** Stefan, Feministische Theologie und alttestamentliche Exegese; Versuch einer Bestandsaufnahme zur Methodik: BibNot 59 (1991) 7-11.

1470 *a) Bird* Phyllis A., Israelite religion and the faith of Israel's daughters; reflections on gender and religious definition; – *b) Day* Peggy L., Why is Anat a warrior and hunter?; – *c) Jobling* David, Feminism and 'mode of production' in ancient Israel; search for a method: → 7,67*, ᶠGOTTWALD N., 1991, 97-108 / 141-6 / 239-251 [< OTAbs 15, p. 140.142,145].

1471 **Brown** Cheryl A., No longer be silent; Jewish portraits of biblical women; studies in Pseudo-PHILO's Biblical Antiquities and JOSEPHUS's Jewish Antiquities: [diss. Graduate Theological Union, ᴰEndres J. G., Berkeley 1989]: Gender and the biblical tradition. Louisville 1992, W-Knox. 240 p. $18 pa. 0-664-25294-X [NTAbs 36, p. 441: Philo fairer]. – ᴿExpTim 104 (1992) 94s (C. S. *Rodd*; good); JStJud 23 (1992) 249s (P. W. van der *Horst*).

1471* *Bycel* Lee T., 'To reclaim our voice'; an analysis of representative contemporary feminist Passover haggadot: CCAR 40, 160 (1993) 55-71.

1472 **Chalier** Catherine, As matriarcas (Sara, Rebeca, Raquel & Lia). Petrópolis 1992, Vozes. 224 p. – ᴿREB 52 (1992) 762s (V. da *Silva*).

1473 **Ciccarelli** Bruno, Le donne della Bibbia [some 100 very short items]. Catania 1992, Marino. 246 p.

1474 **Darr** Katheryn P., Far more precious than jewels; perspectives on biblical women 1991 ➤ 7,1315: ᴿCritRR 5 (1992) 507-9 (Sharon P. *Jeansonne*).

1475 ᴱ**Day** Peggy L., Gender and difference 1989 ➤ 5,391 ... 7,1316: ᴿRExp 89 (1992) 106s (Pamela J. *Scalise*).

1476 **Dijk-Hemmes** F. van, Sporen van [Traces de] vrouwenteksten in de Hebreeuwse Bijbel: diss. ᴰ*Bal* M. Amsterdam 1992. 383 p. – TvT 33,82; RTLv 24, p. 543.

1477 **Eisenstein** Zillah R., The female body and the law. Berkeley 1989, Univ. California. 235 p. $10. – ᴿChrCris 51 (1991s) 69s (Mary C. *Segers*).

1478 **Engelken** K., Frauen ᴰ1990 ➤ 6,1606; 7,1317: ᴿBijdragen 53 (1992) 201s (P. C. *Beentjes*); TR 88 (1992) 286-8 (E. *Otto*).

1479 *Eskenazi* Tamara C., Out from the shadows; biblical women in the postexilic era: JStOT 54 (1992) 25-43.

1479* *a*) *Exum* J. Cheryl, Murder they wrote; ideology and the manipulation of female presence in biblical narrative; – *b*) *Tolbert* Mary Ann, Protestant feminists and the Bible; on the horns of a dilemma: UnSemQ 43 (1989) 19-39 / 1-17.

1480 *a*) *Foulkes* Pamela A., Images of family life in the Scriptures; – *b*) *Scarfe* Mary E., Myths and models of the family; – *c*) *Digby-Baker* Janet, The family and abuse; a personal view; – *d*) *Whitehead* James D. & Evelyn E., Re-imagining the masculine: Way 32 (1992) 83-92 / 93-103 / 123-133 / 113-122.

1481 **Frymer-Kensky** Tikva, In the wake of the goddesses; women, culture, and the biblical transformation of pagan myth. NY 1992, Free Press. xi-292 p. $25. 0-02-910800-4 [OIAc 2,19]. – ᴿBR 8,3 (1992) 11s (R. S. *Hendel*); FirsT 27 (1992) 50-52 (J. D. *Levenson*).

1482 **Gill** Deborah Menken, The female prophets; gender and leadership in the biblical tradition: diss. Fuller Theol. Sem., ᴰ*Martin* R. Pasadena 1991. xxiii-292 p. 91-35883. – OIAc 5,22.

1483 *Gimbutas* Marija, The language of the goddess [... matriarchal societies] 1989 ➤ 6,d599: ᴿAJA 96 (1992) 170s (W. *Barnett*).

1484 *Gluzman* Michael, The exclusion of women from Hebrew literary history: Prooftexts 11 (1991) 259-278.

1485 **Grassi** Joseph, Children's liberation; a biblical perspective 1991 ➤ 7, 1310: ᴿCritRR 5 (1992) 89-91 (Elizabeth S. *Malbon*: good idea, strained realization).

1486 **Green** Elizabeth [pastora; non traduzione], Dal silenzio alla parola; storie di donne nella Bibbia: PiccBtT 26. T 1992, Claudiana. 80 p. Lit. 13.000. 88-7016-158-7 – ᴿBbbOr 34 (1992) 123-5 (Cristina *Vertua*).

1486* *Hollis* Karyn, Literacy theory, teaching composition, and feminist response: Pre/Text 13,1s ('Marxism and rhetoric' 1992) 103-115.

1487 *Horst* P. van der, Notities bij het thema: vrouwen in het vroege Jodendom: KerkT 43 (1992) 113-129 [< ZAW 104,435].

1488 *Jeansonne* Sharon P., The women of Genesis 1990 ➤ 6,1612; 7,1322: ᴿBA 55 (1992) 159s (Patricia C. *Wood*); BtS 149 (1992) 376s (R. B. *Chisholm*: careful, sensitive); IndTSt 28 (1991) 332-4 (M. D. *Ambrose*); IrBSt 14 (1992) 199s (Clare *Amos*: flat, monochrome; no Eve); JRel 72 (1992) 423s (Kathleen *Waller*).

1489 **Karssen** Gien, Frau, Mensch und Mutter in der Bibel (1 Mose 2,23): Telos 318. Stu 1988, Hänssler. 206 p. 3-7751-0582-4.

1490 **Kramer** Ross S., Her share of the blessings; women's religions among pagans, Jews, and Christians in the Greco-Roman World. Ox 1992, UP. ix-275 p.; 1 fig. £22.50 [ClasR 43, 314-6, R. *Hawley*]. 0-19-406686-3.

1491 **Kuzmack** Linda G., Woman's cause; the Jewish woman's movement in England and the United States, 1881-1933. Columbus 1990, Ohio State Univ. xiv-280 p. – ᴿJQR 83 (1992s) 403s (Dianne *Ashton*).

1492 **Lacocque** André, The feminine unconventional: OvBT 1990 ➤ 6,1614; 7,1323: ᴿCBQ 54 (1992) 531s (Sharon P. *Jeansonne*); CritRR 5 (1992) 146s (Katharine D. *Sakenfeld*); Horizons 19 (1992) 310 (D. *Bergant*); Interpretation 46 (1992) 316s (Phyllis *Trible*: the masculine conventional); IrBSt 13 (1991) 229s (Katherine P. *Meyer*); SpTod 43 (1991) 384s (Pheme *Perkins*); TTod 49 (1992s) 254.256 (Carolyn J. *Pressler*); VT 43 (1993) 574s (Katharine J. *Dell*: 'La Coque').

1493 **Lacocque** André, Subversives ou Un pentateuque de femmes: LDiv 148. P 1992, Cerf. 191 p.

1493* *Larson* Lyle E., Defining the family in a biblical perspective; Crux 28,4 (1992) 39-44 [< NTAbs 37, p. 235].

1494 ᴱ**Levine** Amy-Jill, 'Women like this'; new perspectives on Jewish women in the Greco-Roman world 1991 ➤ 7,317: ᴿCBQ 54 (1992) 827s (R. *Doran*, tit.pp.; tension between the last two methodological essays and the rest of the book).

1495 **Ljung** Inger, Silence or suppression 1989 ➤ 7,1325: ᴿCBQ 54 (1992) 751s (Alice L. *Laffey*); CritRR 5 (1992) 511-3 (Naomi *Steinberg*); ÉTRel 67 (1992) 98s (Françoise *Smyth*); Interpretation 46 (1992) 213s (C. M. *Carmichael*); NedTTs 46 (1992) 156s (P. B. *Dirksen*); RevSR 66 (1992) 355s (B. *Renaud*); SvTKv 67 (1991) 40s (S. *Norin*); TLZ 117 (1992) 110s (G. *Begrich*); TR 88 (1992) 288-290 (Irmtraud *Fischer*).

1496 *Mahlke* Hans-Peter, Die Frau in der Öffentlichkeit — ein Beitrag zur hermeneutischen Frage in der Geschichte selbständiger evang.-luth. Kirchen in Deutschland: LuthTK 16 (1992) 1-28.

1496* **Mollenkott** Virginia R., Women, men and the Bible² 1988 ➤ 5,1540: ᴿJEvTS 35 (1992) 238s (Madelyn M. *Johnson*).

1497 **Mulack** Christa, Natürlich weiblich; die Heimatlosigheit der Frau im Patriarchat. Stu 1990, Kreuz. 272 p. DM 29,80. – ᴿLuthMon 30 (1991) 328 (Ulrike *Schelander*).

1498 **Ohler** Annemarie, Mutterschaft in der Bibel. Wü 1992, Echter. 272 p. DM 29,80 [TLZ 117, 737].

ᴿ**Pantel-Schmitt** [also as Schmitt-Pantel] Pauline, Histoire des femmes 1. L'antiquité ➤ d123.

1498* **Pfäfflin** E., Frau und Mann; ein symbolkritischer Vergleich anthropologischer Konzepte in Seelsorge und Beratung. Gü 1992, Mohn. 184 p. DM 58. 3-579-00251-1 [TvT 33,101s, H. de *Groot-Kopetzky*].

1499 **Phipps** William E., Assertive biblical women: Contributions in Women's Studies 128. Westport CT 1992, Greenwood. xii-171 p. 0-313-28498-9.

1500 **Pikaza** X., La mujer en las grandes religiones. Bilbao 1991, D-Brouwer. 187 p. – ᴿBibFe 18 (1992) 140s (A. *Salas*).

1501 **Pissarek** Anna H., **Ferchl** Annamaria, Die Rekonstruktion von Frauengeschichte in der hebräischen Bibel; Bericht von einem Versuch, den Ansatz E. Schüssler Fiorenzas in diesem Bereich anzuwenden: ProtokB 1,1 (1992) 68-73.

1502 **Plaskow** Judith, Standing again at Sinai 1990 ➤ 6,1625; 7,1336: ᴿJEvTS 35 (1992) 422s (D. J. *Evearitt*); Midstream 38,2 (1992) 42-44 (A. J. *Yuter*).

1502* **Plaskow** Judith, Und wieder stehen wir am Sinai; eine jüdisch-fe-
ministische Theologie [1990 ➤ 6,1625], ᵀ*Merz* V. Luzern 1992, Exodus.
318 p. DM 46. 3-905575-67-1 [TLZ 118, 829, Helga *Weippert*].

1503 **Ravel** Edeet, The application of biblical laws to women by rabbis of
the Tannaitic period: diss. McGill, ᴰ*Levy* B. Montréal 1992. – SR 21
(1993) 496.

1504 ᴱ**Schmidt** Eva Renate, *al.*, Feministisch gelesen; 32 ausgewählte Bi-
beltexte für Gruppen, Gemeinden und Gottesdienste I-II. Stu 1988s. je
296 p. – ᴿDielB 27 (1991) 299s (B. J. *Diebner*).

1504* **Sered** Susan S., Women as ritual experts; the religious lives of elderly
Jewish women in Israel: Amer. Folklore Soc. NY 1992, Oxford-UP.
xi-174 p. $30. [RelStR 19, 367s, Rachel *Simon*].

1505 **Toorn** K. van der, Van haar wieg [ᵀ1994 JStOT], 1987 ➤ 3,1518; 5,1545:
ᴿVT 42 (1992) 421s (J. A. *Emerton*).

1506 ᴱ**Uglione** Renato, La donna nel mondo antico 1988/9 ➤ 4,699 ... 7,609:
ᴿRÉG 105 (1992) 596-8 (H. *Cassimatis*).

1507 ᴱ**Umansky** Ellen M., *Ashton* Dianne, Four centuries of Jewish women's
spirituality; a sourcebook. Boston 1992, Beacon. [RelStR 19, 84, Vanessa
L. *Ochs*].

1508 **Wegner** Judith R., Chattel or person? The status of women in the
Mishnah 1988 ➤ 4,b177 ... 7,1339: ᴿRelStR 28 (1992) 13-14 (Judith
Hauptmann) & 14-18 (Karen L. *King*).

1509 **Wehr** Demaris S., JUNG and feminism; liberating archetypes 1987 ➤ 5,
8962: ᴿJAAR 60 (1992) 572-4 (Elizabeth *Willems*).

1510 **Weiler** G., Das Matriarchat im alten Israel 1989 ➤ 6,1633; 7,1340: ᴿBO
49 (1992) 826-8 (Jopie *Siebert-Hommes*).

1511 **Winter** Mariam T., Women of the Hebrew Scriptures [I. ➤ 9194], II.
Woman witness; a feminist lectionary and Psalter. NY 1992, Crossroad.
xii-372 p.; ill. (Craighead M.). $17. 0-8245-1141-7. [CBQ 54,838].

B4.4 *Exegesis litteraria* – **The Bible itself as literature.**

1512 **Alter** Robert, The world of biblical literature. NY 1991, Basic. 225 p.
$23. 0-465-09255-1 [TDig 40, 149]. – ᴿBR 8,3 (1992) 11 (M. *Fishbane*);
ChrCent 109 (1992) 812-5 (E. F. *Campbell*).

1513 ᴱ**Alter** R., *Kermode* F., The literary guide to the Bible 1987 ➤ 3,324 ...
7,1342 (1990 pa.) ᴿInterpretation 46 (1992) 181s (D. *Jobling*: damning intentions fortunately not adhered to); MilltSt 29 (1992) 158-164 (P. *Rogers*).

1514 **Carbonetto** Arturo, Poesia epica della Bibbia. R 1990, Vivere In. 322 p.
Lit. 40.000. – ᴿStCattMi 36 (1992) 863 (G. A. *Brunelli*).

1515 *Daecke* Sigurd M., Die enteignete Bibel; die Heilige Schrift als Gegenstand weltlicher Kultur und Kritik: EvKomm 25 (1992) 575-8.

1516 **Frye** Northrop, Words with power 1991 ➤ 7,1342*: ᴿJRel 72 (1992)
478s (E. J. *Ziolkowski*); Parabola 16,1 (1991) 135-8 (P. *Jordan-Smith*);
RLitND 24,2 (1992) 83-90 (J. C. *Meagher*).

1517 *Hamlin* Cyrus, The Bible and literature / the Bible as literature; biblical
hermeneutics and the rise of literary criticism in American culture [...
FRYE N. vs. BLOOM H.]: ➤ 481, AnStoEseg 9 (1992) 163-190.

1518 **Jasper** David, The study of literature and religion 1989 ➤ 7,1343:
ᴿCritRR 5 (1992) 74-76 (L. D. *Bouchard*); RelStT 11,2 (1991) 79-81
(D. W. *Atkinson*).

Jemielity Thomas, Satire and the Hebrew Prophets: LitCurrBInt. 1992
➤ 3614.

1520 **Jens** Walter, *Küng* Hans, Literature and religion; PASCAL, GRYPHIUS, LESSING, HÖLDERLIN, NOVALIS, KIERKEGAARD, DOSTOYEVSKY, KAFKA [Dichtung und Religion 1985 ➤ 3,1550; ital. 1989 ➤ 5,a652]; ᵀ*Heinegg* Peter. NY 1991, Paragon. x-308 p. $23. – ᴿChrCent 108 (1991) 945s (J. *Sykes*); CritRR 5 (1992) 76-79 (E. J. *Ziolkowski*).

1521 *Josipovici* Gabriel, The Book of God; a response to the Bible 1988 ➤ 4,1073 ... 7,1344: ᴿEvQ 64 (1992) 180-3 (A. G. *Newell*).

1522 *Kuschel* Karl-Josef, Theologen und ihre Dichter; Analysen zur Funktion der Literatur bei Rudolf BULTMANN und Hans Urs von BALTHASAR: TüTQ 172 (1992) 98-116.

1523 **Longman** T., Literary approaches to Biblical interpretation 1987 ➤ 4,1529; 7,1345: ᴿ*Furrow* 41 (1990) 64s (S. P. *Kealy*, also on POYTHRESS V.); JEvTS 35 (1992) 244 (D. L. *Turner*).

1524 *Mędala* Stanisław, ℗ Sacra Scriptura in cultura mundi hodierni [FRYE N.; STOTT-COOTE ...]: RuBi 44,4 (1991) 90-99.

   Minor Mark [**Powell** Mark], Bibliographies; literary-critical approach to the Bible 1992 ➤ 868.

1525 **Prickett** Stephen, *Barnes* Robert, The Bible: Landmarks of world literature, 1991 ➤ 7,1347: ᴿBR 8,6 (1992) 15 (J. *VanderKam*).

1526 *Schmitt* Hans-C. [*Paulsen* Henning], Literaturgeschichte AT [NT]: ➤ 757, EvKL 3 (1992) 128-133 [–138] (–149 + 117-128, *al.*).

1527 ᴱ**Schwartz** Regina, The book and the text; the Bible and literary theory 1990 ➤ 6,371: ᴿChrCent 108 (1991) 439s (M. G. *Williams*); JRel 72 (1992) 103s (B. *Britt*: valuable); LitTOx 6 (1992) 90-92 (Lynn *Poland*: alternative to ALTER-KERMODE proscriptions).

1528 *Stordalen* Terje, 'Bible and [= as] literature' in recent OT research: TsTKi 63 (1992) 113-128.

1529 **Wilder** Amos N., The Bible and the literary critic. Mp 1992, Fortress. $13. 0-8006-2436-X. – ᴿAnglTR 74 (1992) 106s (A. R. *Marmorstein*); Month 253 (1992) 203-5 (Mary E. *Mills* applies to GIBLIN *al.*).

B4.5 Influxus biblicus in litteraturam profanam, *generalia*.

1530 ᴱ**Cohen** David, *Heller* Deborah, Jewish presence in English literature. ⸗Montreal 1990, McGill-Queen's Univ. viii-134 p.

1531 **Cousins** Anthony D., The Catholic religious poets from SOUTHWELL to CRASHAW; a critical history. Westminster MD 1992, Christian Classics. xiii-204 p. $25 pa. 0-7220-1570-4 [TDig 40,262].

1532 **Detweiler** Robert, Religious readings of contemporary fiction; breaking the fall. SF 1989 ➤ 5,1560*; $25. 0-06-061891-4. – ᴿRExp 89 (1992) 133 (W. L. *Hendricks* praises in a single long boomingly emphasized sentence).

1533 **Fiddes** Paul S., Freedom and limit; a dialogue between literature and Christian doctrine. NY 1991, St Martins ➤ 7,1359; also L 1992, Macmillan. £40. 0-333-49142-4. – ᴿExpTim 103,11 2d-top choice (1991s) 323s (C. S. *Rodd*); TLond 95 (1992) 463 (D. *Mackenzie*); TTod 49 (1992s) 412 (Cleo M. *Kearns*).

1534 **Finkelman** Louis, The romantic vindication of Cain; a study of sympathetic presentations of Cain by seven major Romantic poets in England [... BLAKE, BYRON, COLERIDGE ...] and France: diss. City Univ., ᴰ*Feder* Lillian. NY 1992. 593 p. 92-24810. – DissA 53 (1992s) 1151-A.

1535 **Finkelstein** Bluma, L'écrivain juif et les Évangiles 1991 ➤ 5,1360: ᴿNRT 114 (1992) 131s (D. *Luciani*); ZkT 114 (1992) 96s (R. *Oberforcher*).

1536 *Fischler* Brakha, ❻ [The historical dictionary project] The use of a biblical literary quotation in some early Modern Hebrew sources: Lešonenu 56 (1991s) 153-161; Eng., III.

1537 **Forshey** Gerald E., American religious and biblical [cinema] spectaculars: Media and Society. Westport CT 1992, Praeger. xii-202 p. $45. 0-275-93197-8 [TDig 40,162].

1538 ᴱ**Frontain** Raymond J., *Wojcik* Jan, Old Testament women in western literature. Conway 1991, Univ. Central Arkansas. xi-301 p. $29. 0-944436-12-9 [TDig 39,377].

1539 **Giles** Paul, American Catholic arts and fiction; culture, ideology, aesthetics: Cambridge Studies in American Literature and Culture. C 1992, Univ. ix-547 p. $65. 0-521-41777-5 [TDig 40,164: 'fictions'].

1540 *Gorak* Jan, The making of the modern canon [not biblical but (English) literature]; genesis and crisis of a literary idea [E. SAID open-inclusive, against E. GOMBRICH (& T. S. ELIOT); Northrop FRYE and biblical KERMODE midway]. L 1991, Athlone. 309 p. £35. – ᴿTLond 95 (1992) 135s (M. *Brett*).

1541 ᴱ**Jeffrey** David L., *a)* A dictionary of biblical tradition in English literature. GR 1992, Eerdmans. xxxii-960 p. $80. 0-8028-3634-8 [TDig 40,158; NTAbs 37, p. 266]. – *b)* Mistakenly 'logocentric'; centering poetic language in a Scriptural tradition: RLitND 22, 2s ('Religious thought and contemporary critical theory' 1990) 33-46.

1541* **Jossua** Jean-Pierre, Pour une histoire religieuse de l'expérience littéraire: Religions 16. P 1985/90. Beauchesne. 300 p., 284 p. [RTPhil 125,307s, S. *Molla*].

1542 *a)* *Lermen* Birgit, Biblische Texte in der deutschen Gegenwartsliteratur; – *b)* *Langenhorst* Georg, Die literarische Wiederentdeckung Jesu in Romanen der achtziger Jahre; Jesus im modernen Roman: StiZt 210 (1992) 529-543 / 751-761 . 819-830.

1543 ᴱ**Link** Franz, Paradeigmata [-dig- → 6,355*] literarischer Typologie des ATs, I. von den Anfängen bis zum 19. Jahrhundert; 2. 20. Jh.: Schr-LitWiss 5/1s. B 1989, Duncker & H. 510 p.; p. 511-953. DM 198 + 160. – ᴿTLZ 117 (1992) 176-9 (E.-J. *Waschke*).

1544 **Manlove** Colin N., Christian fantasy, from 1200 to the present [... DANTE, MILTON] ND 1992, Univ. x-356 p. $33. 0-268-00790-X [TDig 40,173].

1544* *Ostriker* Alicia, A Word made flesh; the Bible and revisionist women's poetry: RLitND 23,3 ('Reconstructing the Word; spirituality in women's writing' 1991) 9-26.

1545 *a)* [*Parkinson*] **Zamora** Lois, Writing the Apocalypse; historical vision in contemporary U. S. and Latin American fiction. C 1989, Univ. x-233 p. £25. – ᴿLitTOx 5 (1991) 129s (C. *Lock*).

— *b)* **Pifano** Paolo, Tra teologia e letteratura; inquietudine e ricerca del sacro negli scrittori contemporanei. CinB 1990, Paoline. [CC 144/3, 250-3, F. *Castelli*].

— *c)* **Pozzoli** Luigi, Vincerà la parola; tra scrittori e profeti. Bo 1990, EDB [CC 144/3, 247-250 F. *Castelli*: 'La letteratura interpella la teologia'].

— *d)* *Reist* John S.ᴶ, An aesthetics of openness; Christianity and literature: → 133, ᶠMILLS W., PerspRelSt 19 (1992) 73-85.

1546 **Simon** Ulrich, Pity and terror; Christianity and tragedy. NY 1989, St. Martin. 128 p. $35. 0-312-03237-4. – ᴿScotJT 45 (1992) 255-7 (G. S. *Wakefield*).

1546* **Sommavilla** Guido, Uomo, diavolo e Dio nella letteratura contemporanea. CinB 1991, Paoline. [CC 144/3, 252-5, F. *Castelli*: redattore delle riviste Letture e Communio].

1547 *Whittaker* John R., French romantic poets' rediscovery of the Bible: ScripB 22,1 (1992) 2-8.

1547* **Wood** Ralph C., The comedy of redemption; Christian faith and comic vision in four American novelists 1988 ↠ 4,1547; 5,1570: ᴿLitTOx 5 (1991) 126-8 (S. R. *Haynes*).

B4.6 *Singuli auctores* – **Bible-influence on individual authors.**

1548 *a*) ALEICHEM: *Nave* Yudith, Y. D. BERKOWITZ's rendition of Sholem Aleichem's 'Song of Songs' (1911); a study of its structure and Hebrew translation: HebAnR 11 (1987) 319-329.

— *b*) BACHMANN: **Habbel** Marie-Luise, 'Diese Wüste hat sich einer vorbehalten'; biblisch-christliche Motive, Figuren und Sprachstrukturen im literarischen Werk Ingeborg Bachmanns: Münsteraner TAbh. Altenberge 1992, Oros. 236 p. DM 35 [TR 89, 428, G. *Langenhorst*].

— *c*) **Barnes** Julian, A history of the world in 10 1/2 chapters [...Noah; a pilgrimage to Ararat; Jonah; 1520 French excommunication of a group of insects; self-styled apocalypse survivor...]. NY/L 1989, Knopf/Cape. – ᴿLitTOx 5 (1991) 220-233 (G. *Salyer*).

1549 BLAKE: **Chauvin** Danièle, L'œuvre de William Blake; apocalypse et transfiguration. Grenoble 1992, Ellug. 286 p. F 175 [RSPT 77,290, J.-P. *Jossua*].

1549* *Sturrock* June, Blake and the women of the Bible: LitTOx 6 (1992) 23-32.

1550 **Yoder** Richard P., Significant events; language and narrative in Blake's 'Jerusalem': diss. Duke, ᴰ*Glockner* R. Durham NC 1992. 261 p. 92-27061. – DissA 53 (1992s) 1531-A.

1551 BORON: **Hand** Sophie, Fusing the Biblical and the Arthurian; a study of Robert de Boron's poetic craft in the 'Joseph d'Arimathie' and the 'Merlin': diss. Wisconsin, ᴰ*Kelly* D. Madison 1992. 268 p. 92-11616. – DissA 53 (1992) 804-A.

1552 BUNYAN: **Stachniewski** John, [Bunyan...]. The persecutory imagination; English Puritanism and the literature of religious despair. Ox 1991, Clarendon. xii-400 p. £45. 0-19-811781-7. – ᴿJTS 43 (1992) 749-753 (G. S. *Wakefield*).

1552* **Batson** Beatrice, John Bunyan's Grace Abounding and The Pilgrim's Progress; an overview of literary studies, 1960-1987: NY 1988 ↠ 5,1578: ᴿRLitND 23,1 (1991) 81-86 (Nancy *Arneson*, also on B. *Collmer*'s and N. *Keeble*'s Bunyan).

1553 **Wakefield** Gordon, Bunyan the Christian. L 1992, Collins Fount. x-143 p. £18. 0-00-215995-3. – ᴿExpTim 103 (1991s) 352 [C. S. *Rodd*]; TLond 95 (1992) 386s (J. M. *Gordon*).

1554 CERVANTES: *Jones* Troy M., ERASMIAN biblicism in Don Quixote: RestQ 34 (1992) 31-50 [< ZIT 92, 296].

1554* CHAUCER: *Cigman* Gloria, Chaucer and the goats of creation: LitTOx 5 (1991) 162-180.

1555 DONNE: **McNeese** Eleanor J., Eucharistic poetry; the search for presence in the writings of John Donne, Gerard M. HOPKINS, Dylan THOMAS and Geoffrey HILL. Cranbury 1992, Bucknell Univ. 241 p. $38.50. 0-8387-5205-5 [TDig 39,371].

1555* *Holmes* M. Morgan, Out of Egypt; John Donne and the quest for apocalyptic re-creation: ChrLit 42,1 (1992) 25-40.

1556 a) DOSTOJEVSKY: *Hegedüs* Lorant, Jesus and Dostoevsky: EurJT 1,1 (Devon 1992) 49-62 [< ZIT 92,487].
— b) ELIOT G.: *Bonaparte* Felicia, Carrying the Word of the Lord to the Gentiles; Silas Marner and the translation of Scripture into a secular text: RLitND 23,2 (1991) 39-60.
— c) EMERSON: **Hodder** Alan D., Emerson's rhetoric of revelation; 'Nature', the reader, and the apocalypse within. 1989, Penn State Univ. xiv-170 p. $23.50. – ᴿRLitND 23 (1991) 105-113 (J. *Loving*, also on four other Emerson studies).

1557 FIELDING: *Wiles* John K., Storytellers and their vocation; [H. Fielding's] Tom Jones and the inspiration and authority of Scripture: Persp-RelSt 19 (1992) 291-309.

1558 GREENE: **Bjerg** Svend, Litteratur og teologi; transfigurationer — omkring Graham Greene. Århus 1989, Anis. 174 p. – ᴿSvTKv 67 (1991) 52s (Helen *Anderson*).

1559 HAWTHORNE: **McCarthy** Judith A., Hawthorne [Scarlet Letter], Puritanism, and the Bible; T. S. ELIOT [Knowledge; Cocktail Party]: diss. Rutgers, ᴰ*Gibson* D. New Brunswick NJ 1992. 114 p. 92-19950. – DissA 53 (1992s) 496-A.

1559 HELIAND: **Murphy** G. Ronald, The Saxon Savior; the Germanic transformation of the Gospel in the ninth-century Heliand 1989 ➤ 6, 1985: ᴿSpeculum 67 (1992) 457-9 (D. N. *Yeandle*).

1561 HERBERT: **Bingham** Mark E., The Bible in [George] Herbert's 'Church': diss. N. Carolina, ᴰ*McQueen* W. Chapel Hill 1992. 463 p. 93-02501. – DissA 53 (1992s) 3219-A.

1561* **Sherwood** Terry G., [Hymnist George] Herbert's prayerful art. Toronto 1989, Univ. 190 p. $45 [JEvTS 36, 534, D. T. *Williams*].

1562 *Wakefield* Gordon S., God and some English poets, 1. George Herbert; 2. Robert BROWNING; 3. Gerard M. HOPKINS: ExpTim 104 (1992s) 201-5 / 263-7 / 328-332.

1562* HOPKINS: *Lichtmann* Maria R., The incarnational aesthetic of Gerard Manley Hopkins: RLitND 23,1 (1991) 37-50.

1563 KAFKA: *Wasserman* Martin, Kafka's 'The new attorney'; a therapeutic poem offering a Jewish way to face death: Cithara 31,1 (1991s) 3-15.

1564 LANGLAND: a) **Harwood** Britton J., Piers Plowman and the problem of belief. Toronto 1992, Univ. xii-237 p. $60. 0-8020-5799-3 [TDig 40,67: he wrote not to teach but to find faith].
— b) *Cox* Catherine S., Langland's Christian Narcissus; self-reflexive 'Mesure' in Piers Plowman B: ChrLit 42,1 (1992) 5-23.
— c) **Godden** Malcolm, The making of Piers Plowman. L 1990, Longman. xii-215 p. £22; pa. £14. – ᴿLitTOx 5 (1991) 332-7 (S. *Hussey*, also on 4 cognates).
— d) **Raabe** Pamela, Imitating God; the allegory of faith in 'Piers Plowman'. Athens 1990, Univ. Georgia. 196 p. $30 [RelStR 19, 152, Barbara *Newman*]. – ᴿRLitND 23,1 (1991) 99s (Patti *Quattrin*).
— e) *Ryan* Thomas A., [PiersP] Scripture and the prudent ymaginatif: Viator 23 (1992) 215-230.

1565 LE GUIN: *Donaldson* Mara A., Prophetic and apocalyptic eschatology in Ursula Le Guin's The farthest shore and Tehanu: Semeia 60 (1992) 111-122.

1566 LOCKE: **Foster** David J., John Locke's critique of the Bible in the 'First treatise of government': diss. Toronto 1991. 386 p. DANN-69298. – DissA 53 (1992s) 2963-A.

1567 MELVILLE: *Taylor* Mark L., Ishmael's (m)other; gender, Jesus, and God in Melville's Moby Dick: JRel 72 (1992) 325-350.

1568 MILTON: *a*) **Leonard** John, Naming in Paradise; Milton and the language of Adam and Eve. Ox 1990, Clarendon. x-304 p. £30. – ᴿLitTOx 5 (1991) 234-9 (W. *Myers*, also on C. GROSE 1988; Regina SCHWARTZ 1989).

— *b*) *Lieb* Michael, The book of M., [echo of BLOOM H., Book of J], Paradise Lost as revisionary text: Cithara 31,1 (1991), 28-35.

— *c*) ᴱ**Loewenstein** David, *Turner* James G., Politics, poetics and hermeneutics in Milton's prose. C 1990, Univ. xiv-282 p. £30 [HeythJ 34, 116s, D. *Haskin*].

— *d*) *Luckett* Richard, Milton, John (1608-1674), ᵀ*Schwöbel* Christoph: ➤ 768, TRE 22 (1992) 753-759.

— *e*) **Parisi** Hope A., Abiding in the native element; John Milton and feminist theology: diss. City Univ., ᴰ*Wittreich* J. NY 1992. 254 p. 92-24846. – DissA 53 (1992s) 1166s-A.

— *f*) **Radzinowicz** Mary Ann, Milton's epics and the Book of Psalms. Princeton 1989, Univ. xvii-227 p. $32.50. – ᴿRLitND 23,1 (1991) 85-91 (S. M. *Fallon*: 'deeply satisfying'; also on three cognates).

1569 PEARL: *Clopper* Lawrence M., Pearl and the consolation of Scripture: Viator 23 (1992) 231-245.

1570 SHAKESPEARE, **Carlson** Donald T., [1 Cor 13; Lk 8,22-11,4] 'Charity never falleth away'; 'The Tempest' and Shakespeare's poetic of biblical allusion: diss. Dallas 1991. 284 p. 92-16269. — DissA 53 (1992s) 156-A.

1571 **Marshall** Cynthia, Last things and last plays; Shakespearean eschatology. Carbondale 1991, Southern Illinois Univ. xvi-143 p. $24.50 [RelStR 19, 152, D. *Stump*].

SHAKESPEARE, MILTON, JOHNSON, DONNE: ➤ 420.

1572 WANG MENG: *Gálik* Marián, Wang Meng's mythopoetic vision of Golgotha and Apocalypse: AION 52 (1992) 61-82.

1572* YEATS: *Swain* Stella, The problem of belief in Yeats' A Vision; text and context: LitTOx 5 (1991) 198-219.

B4.7 *Interpretatio athea, materialistica, psychiatrica.*

1573 *Belzen* J. A. van, 'De eeuw der psychologie' — ook in de theologie?: NedTTs 46 (1992) 320-333.

1574 **Arraj** James, Jungian and Catholic? The promises and problems of the Jungian-Christian dialogue. Chiloquin OR 1991, Inner Growth. 122 p. $10. 0-914073-06-0 [TDig 39,251].

1575 — **Bonnette** Lucie, Le fondement religieux de la pensée de Jung. Montréal 1986, Fides. 111 p. – ᴿLavalTP 48 (1992) 134-6 (R. *Richard*).

1576 — **Kaempf** Bernard, Réconciliation; psychologie et religion selon Carl Gustav Jung. P 1991, Cariscript. 320 p. – ᴿRevSR 66 (1992) 345s (R. *Mengus*).

[Amado] **Lévy-Valensi** Éliane A., Job; réponse à Jung 1991 ➤ 3336.

1578 **Braekers** M., Begrijpt U wat U leest? De veelzinnigheid van bijbel-
verhalen. Averbode/Kampen 1991, Altiora/Kok. 196 p. Fb 545. 90-
317-0871-2 / 90-242-6141-4. – ᴿTvT 32 (1992) 191 (J. *Bonsen*: a psy-
chotherapist on 'conversation' between reader and text).

1579 **Bucher** Anton A., Bibel-Psychologie; psychologische Zugänge zu biblischen Texten. Stu 1992, Kohlhammer. 200 p. DM 34. 3-17-012007-7
[TLZ 118,491, W. *Rebell*; TR 89,156, J. *Goldbrunner*].

1580 **Christian** Carol, In the spirit of truth; a reader in the work of [recently
popular founder of Clinical Theology Association] Frank LAKE. L 1991,
Darton-LT. xv-176 p. £13. 0-232-51931-5. – ᴿExpTim 103 (1991s) 92s
(D. G. *Deeks*: 'reads like a coherent book'; audacious and compelling
ideas about Cross and Spirit for mental health).

1581 **Crummett** Alan W., Biblical self-esteem and psychopathology; a
psychological/theological integration: diss. Western Michigan, ᴰ*Geisler* J.,
1991. 179 p. 92-16460. – DissA 53 (1992s) 532-A.

1582 DREWERMANN: *Bagrowicz* Jerzy, *Oko* Dariusz, ❷ Autour de l'affaire de
Drewermann: AtKap 119 (1992) 102-114.

1583 *Barrett* Richard J., The bishop as ordinary teacher of the faith; notes
on the Drewermann affair: Monitor Ecclesiasticus 117 (R 1992) 231-...
[< ZIT 92,601].

1584 ᴱ**Benedikt** Bernadette, *Sobel* Alfred, Der Streit um Drewermann; was
Theolog[inn]en und Psycholog[inn]en kritisieren: Theologische Anfragen.
Wsb 1992, Sobel. 172 p. DM 34. 3-9802928-2-7 [TLZ 118,615, W. *Rebell*,
auch über Sobels 1992 Bibliog.].

1585 *Biser* Eugen, Der Indikator; Gründe und Folgen des Falles Drewermanns: StiZt 210 (1992) 291-6.

1586 *Boventer* Hermann, Der Fall Drewermann als Lehrstück: Renovatio 48
(Köln 1992) 154-161 [< ZIT 92,567].

1587 *Brosseder* Johannes, Worüber gestritten werden sollte [Drewermann]:
Orientierung 56 (1992) 61-65.

1588 **Drewermann** Eugen, La Parole qui guérit [Wort des Heils, interviews
1989], ᵀ*Bagot* Jean-Pierre, 1991 ➤ 7,1398: ᴿBLitEc 93 (1992) 348s (L.
Monloubou: les uns acceptent, les autres moins); ÉTRel 67 (1992) 137s (J.
Ansaldi: 'Drewermann; narcissisme contre exégèse'); RTLv 23 (1992) 216-8
(P. *Weber*: salutaire malgré une agressivité étonnante).

1589 — *Karakash* Clairette, La psychanalyse au secours de la Bible: RTPhil
124 (1992) 177-188.

1590 **Drewermann** Eugen, La peur et la faute; psychanalyse et morale I. P
1992, Cerf. 148 p. F 95. 2-204-04517-9. – ᴿÉTRel 67 (1992) 614 (J.
Ansaldi: incontestablement meilleur que La parole qui guérit).

1591 ᴱ**Eicher** P., Der Klerikerstreit 1990 ➤ 7,1402: ᴿGeistL 64 (1991) 79s (J.
Sudbrack: ein ärgerliches Buch; D.s Freunde schaden ihm mehr als seine
Gegner).

1592 — ᴱ**Eicher** P., La controversia sui chierici, la sfida di E. Drewermann:
GdT 203. Brescia 1991, Queriniana. 260 p. Lit. 28.000. – ᴿStPatav 38
(1991) 150-3 (E. R. *Tura*).

1593 **Fehrenbacher** Gregor, Drewermann verstehen — eine kritische Hinführung 1991 ➤ 7,1403: ᴿTPhil 67 (1992) 612-5 (P. *Knauer*).

1594 **Gestrich** Reinhold, Eugen Drewermann — Glauben aus Leidenschaft;
eine Einführung in seine Theologie. Stu 1992, Quell. 141 p.; 7 fig. DM
16,80. 3-7918-1917-8 [NTAbs 37, p. 265].

1595 *Giustiniani* Pasquale, Eugen Drewermann; una lettura in prospettiva filosofica: Sapienza 45 (1992) 205-9.

1596 *Hünermann* Peter, Bishops and theologians [... a poll shows more Germans supporting Drewermann than his bishop]: Tablet 246 (1992) 1450 [< TüTQ 172].

1597 **Jeziorowski** Jürgen, Eugen Drewermann — der Streit um den Glauben geht weiter: Tb 1301. Gü 1992, Mohn. 126 p. 3-579-01301-7.

1598 *Julien* Philippe, Drewermann devant l'angoisse de l'homme: Études 376 (1992) 539-547.

1599 *Knoch* Otto, Die Botschaft der Bibel — und die Aufgabe der Kirche — in der Deutung von E. Drewermann: Klerusblatt 72 (Mü 1992) 91-... [< ZIT 92,265].

1599* **Kreiner** Armin, Ende der Wahrheit? Zum Wahrheitsverständnis in Philosophie und Theologie. FrB 1992, Herder. viii-608 p. DM 78 pa. [TR 89,122, P. *Schmidt-Leukel*: über POPPER, HABERMAS ...; aber auch 'der Streit um Drewermann ist ein Streit um den Wahrheitsanspruch von Glaubenssätzen und theologischen Aussagen').

1600 *Labooy* G.H., Van R. BULTMANN naar L. GOPPELT; een kritische bespreking van de hermeneutik van E. Drewermann: KerkT 42 (1991) 126-144.

1601 **Marcheselli-Casale** Cesare, Il caso Drewermann; psicologia del profondo, un nuovo metodo per leggere la Bibbia? 1991 → 7,1405: ᴿAsprenas 39 (1992) 241-255 (P. *Giustiniani, al.*, con replica), Letture 47 (1992) 86s (G. *Sommavilla*).

1602 *a) Müller* Gerhard L., Neue Ansätze zum Verständnis der Erlösung; Anfragen an E. Drewermann; – b) Werbick Jürgen, Gottesoffenbarung in der 'Sprache der Seele'; Eugen Drewermanns Herausforderung der herkömmlichen Fundamentaltheologie: MüTZ 43 (1992) 51-73 / 17-38 [75-105 Dokumente, Erzb. J. *Degenhardt, al.*; cf. *Rick* H. → 1603*].

1603 **Reinders** Angela M.T., Entmythologisierung — Der Mythos als Schlüssel; christliche Verkündigung in zwei konträren Programmen; BULTMANN und Drewermann: KerDo 38 (1992) 138-147; Eng. 148.

1603* ᴱ**Rick** H.J., für das erzbischöfliche Generalvikariat Paderborn, Dokumentation zur jüngsten Entwicklung um Dr. Eugen Drewermann. Pd 1991, Bonifatius. 367 p. DM 29,80 [MüTZ 43,105].

1604 *Rossi* Giacomo, Il male, l'angoscia e la colpa; risposte della morale e risposte della fede; riflessioni in margine al caso Drewermann: CC 144 (1993,4) 27-42.

1604* *Schellong* Dieter, Drewermann und die Folgen: Junge Kirche 53 (1992) 503s.

1605 *Schrodt* Christoph, 'Eugen Drewermann, ein neuer Prophet?' [nur teils]: Fundamentum (1993,3) 67-80.

1605* *a) Splett* Jörg, Eugen Drewermann — worum es wirklich geht; – b) *Seeliger* Hans R., Historische Kritik oder psychologisches Verstehen? Zu einer falschen Alternative im Denken E. Drewermanns: TPhil 67 (1992) 381-404 / 405-412.

1606 *Sudbrack* Josef, Ein Brückenschlag zum Anliegen Drewermanns [Lehrbefugnis vom kath. Erzbischof Paderborns entzogen]: GeistL 65 (1992) 46-66; p. 51, 'Dokumentation' enttäuschend.

1607 FREUD: **Hessing** Jakob, Der Fluch des Propheten; drei Abhandlungen zu Sigmund Freud. Dü 1989, Rheda-Wiedenbrück. 349 p. – ᴿTRu 57 (1992) 431-8 (N. *Slenczka*).

1608 **Rice** Emanuel, Freud and Moses 1990 ➤ 7,1414: RJRel 72 (1992) 481s (M. *Gresser*).

1609 **Sprengnether** Madelon, The spectral mother; Freud, feminism, and psychoanalysis: Ithaca NY 1990, Cornell Univ. xiii-264 p. $12 [RelStR 19,110].

1610 **Yerushalmi** Yosef H., Freud's Moses; Judaism terminable and interminable 1991 ➤ 7,1415: RAmHR 97 (1992) 1178s (S. L. *Gilman*); ChrCent 109 (1992) 495.7 (R. *Beum*); CritRR 5 (1992) 395-7 (Lucy *Bregman*).

1611 **Früchtel** Ursula, Mit der Bibel Symbole entdecken 1991 ➤ 7,1018: RTGL 82 (1992) 159s (K. *Hollmann*).

1612 **Gassmann** Lothar, Das anthroposophische Bibelverständnis [R. STEINER, *al.*]: ev. Diss. DBeyerhaus P. Tübingen 1992. 361 p. – RTLv 24, p. 571.

1612* *a) Gennrich* Alfred, Religionspsychologische Lernprozesse in der Bibel und im heutigen Unterricht; – *b) Gascard* Johannes R., Zur Auflösung von Psychotherapie in Religion; – *c) Stein* Herbert, Die Psychologie des vorchristlichen Kreuzes und die christliche Kreuzestheologie: Archiv für Religionspsychologie 20 (Gö 1992) 124-133 / 100-113 / 150-169.

1613 **Gibert** P., Le récit biblique de rêve; essai de confrontation analytique: Profac bibl. 3, 1990 ➤ 6,1708: RNRT 114 (1992) 943 (Y. *Simoens*: dernier chapitre Mt 1, 20-25, fonction du rêve pour dire la conception virginale).

1613* *Gladson* Jerry, *Plott* Charles, Unholy wedlock? The peril and promise of applying psychology to the Bible: JPsy&Char 10 (1991) 54-64.

1614 *Hill* Peter C., The interface between psychology and Christianity; assessing the role of the specialty journal: JPsy & Chr 10 (1991) 5-11.21-23 [12-20 *al.*, responses].

1615 **Jaschke** Helmut, 'Aus der Tiefe rufe ich, Herr, zu Dir!'; Psychotherapie aus den Psalmen: Tb 1603. FrB 1990, Herder. 127 p. DM 10. – RBiKi 47 (1992) 236s (S. *Cibulka*).

1616 *Körtner* Ulrich, Zurück zum vierfachen Schriftsinn? Tiefenpsychologie und geistliche Exegese: TBeit 23 (1992) 249-265 [< ZIT 92,698].

1617 **McGrath** Joanna [clinical psychologist] & Alister E., The dilemma of self-esteem; the Cross and Christian confidence. Wheaton IL 1992, Crossway. 156 p. $9. 0-89107-676-X [TDig 40,172; EvJ 11,91, W. S. *Sailer*].

1618 **Oates** Wayne E., Temptation; a biblical and psychological approach 1991 ➤ 7,1419*: RCurrTMiss 19 (1992) 217s (J. R. *Seraphine*).

1619 *Rossi* Giacomo, Letture psicanalitiche della Bibbia [BALMARY M. 1991]: CC 143 (1992,4) 476-487.

1620 *Trendelkamp* Maria, 'Krank sein' und 'Heil werden' in biblischen Geschichten; Impulse aus der tiefenpsychologischen Bibelauslegung für die Religionspädagogik; ein Werkstattbericht: ZPraxRU 22 (1992) 13-16 [< ZIT 92,128].

1621 *a) Vitz* Paul C., Narratives and counseling; – *b) Anderson* Ray S., Response to Vitz; perspectives from biblical anthropology; – *c) Reck* James R., *Banks* James W., Christian anti-psychology; hints of an historical analogue: JPsy&T 20,1 (1992) 11-27 / 28-33 / 3-10 [< ZIT 92,401].

B5 **Methodus exegetica.**

1622 *a) Adam* A.K.M., The future of our allusions [exegetes' orientation is unduly historical, not literary]; – *b) Powell* Mark A., What is 'literary' about literary aspects?; – c) *Parsons* Mikeal C., ... of Gospels and Acts: ➤ 478, SBL Sem 31 (1992) 5-13 / 41-50 / 15-40.

1623 a) *Aletti* Jean-Noël, Exégèse biblique et sémiotique; quels enjeux? – b) *Ska* Jean-Louis, La 'nouvelle critique' et l'exégèse anglo-saxonne; – c) *Gibert* Pierre, Vers une intelligence nouvelle du Pentateuque?: RechSR 80,1 (Courants et problèmes d'exégèse 1992) 9-28 / 39-53 / 55-80; Eng. 6-8.

1624 a) *Aletti* Jean-Noël, Problèmes de composition et de structure dans la Bible; positions et propositions; – b) *Gibert* Pierre, Nouveau regard sur les formes littéraires; le 'principe d'icônie' [... n'importe quel écrit reflète l'image de son milieu]; – c) *Gisel* Pierre, De quelques déplacements dans le champ exégétique; regards d'un théologien: ➤ 462, Naissance 1990/2, 213-230 / 205-211 / 255-263.

1625 ᴱ**Backus** Irena, *Higman* Francis, Théorie et pratique de l'exégèse; Actes du troisième colloque international sur l'histoire de l'exégèse biblique au XVIᵉ siècle (Genève, 21 août – 2 septembre 1988): ÉtPgH 43, 1990 ➤ 6,511: ᴿBtHumRen 54 (1992) 827s (I. *Hazlett*); TLZ 117 (1992) 263s (R. *Kieffer*).

1626 **Blake** Norman F., An introduction to the language of literature. L 1990, Macmillan. vi-152 p. 0-333-45410-3; pa. –1-1.

1626* *Bothma* Theo J.D., Hypermedia [p. 329; 'hypertext' p. 660] as information model in studying biblical languages and cultures: ➤ 450*, Informatique 3, 1991/2, 329-350.

1627 *Boyer* Mark G., (author of the monthly 'Homily Backgrounds'), How important is the context of Scripture? an exercise in literary criticism: The Priest 47,10 (1991) 17-22.

1628 **Brett** Mark G., Biblical criticism in crisis? The impact of the [CHILDS] canonical approach on OT studies 1991 ➤ 7,1425f: ᴿBL (1992) 101s (J. *Barr*: charitable; maybe unacceptable); CritRR 5 (1992) 116-9 (D. *Patrick*); JTS 43 (1992) 135-141 (also J. *Barr*: valuable and powerful though sometimes misreading Childs and overlooking BARTH; but his proposal of a GADAMER approach might produce more division than the union he seeks); ModT 8 (1992) 403s (Ben C. *Ollenburger*); RCatalT 17 (1992) 290s (F. *Raurell*); TLund 95 (1992) 135 (R. E. *Clements*); TS 53 (1992) 339s (J. J. *Collins*); TvT 32 (1992) 411 (J. *Holman*).

1629 **Brichto** Herbert C., Toward a grammar of Hebrew poetics; tales of the prophets. Ox 1992, UP. xv-298 p. £27.50. 0-19-506911-0 [BInterp 1, 373, P. *Joyce*].

1630 *Briggs* Sheila, The deceit of the sublime; an investigation into the origins of ideological criticism of the Bible in early nineteenth-century German biblical studies [de WETTE, BAUR...]: Semeia 59 ['Ideological criticism of biblical texts' 1992] 1-23.

1631 ᴱ**Brooks** R., *Collins* J., Hebrew Bible or OT? 1989/90 ➤ 6,519*: ᴿJRel 72 (1992) 100s (G. A. *Anderson*: 'responses' not indicated as such).

1632 *Bruce* Gregory C., ['The school of thought known variously and problematically as postmodernism'] Cracks in the walls of the postmodern monastery; bibliographic leak or ruin?: CritRR 5 (1992) 1-32; bibliog. 32-38.

1633 *Brueggemann* Dale A., Brevard CHILDS' canon criticism; an example of post-critical naiveté: JEvTS 32 (1989) 311-326 [< OTAbs 15,141].

1634 *Bryan* Christopher, The preachers and the critics; thoughts on historical criticism: AnglTR 74 (1992) 37-53.

1635 **Cave** Terence, Recognitions; a study in poetics. Ox 1990, Clarendon. xiii-530 p. 0-19-815849-1; pa. –163–2.

1636 *a) Conroy* Charles, Reflections on the present state of Old Testament studies; – *b) Prato* Gian Luigi, Antico Testamento e culture coeve; dal rifiuto illusorio all'assimilazione vitale: → 501, Gregorianum 73 (1992) 597-609 / 697-717.

1637 *Damon* Cynthia, Aesthetic response and technical analysis in the rhetorical writings of DIONYSIUS of Halicarnassus: MusHelv 48 (1991) 33-58.

1638 *Deck* Scholastika, Wortstatistik — ein immer beliebter werdendes exegetisches Handwerkzeug auf dem (mathematischen) Prüfstand [Exkurs von Diss. 1991, ForBi 67]: BibNot 60 (1991) 7-12.

1639 *Delorme* Jean, Analyse sémiotique du discours et étude de la Bible (1990): SémBib 66 (1992) 37-44.

1640 *Dohmen* Christoph, Es geht ums Ganze; aktuelle Tendenzen in der alttestamentlichen Wissenschaft: HerdKor 46 (1992) 81-87.

1641 **Eagleton** Terry, The ideology of the aesthetic. Ox 1990, Blackwell. [vi–] 426 p. 0-631-16301-8; pa. –2–6.

1642 *a) Ernst* Josef, Bibelexegese im Umbruch [(Bethel–) Paderborn 1.VII. 1992], katholische Thesen [... DREWERMANN E.]; – *b) Lindemann* Andreas, Evangelische Reaktionen: TGl 82 (1992) 457-463.469 / 464-8.

1643 *Freedman* David N., The symmetry of the Hebrew Bible ST 46 (1992) 83-108 [computerized word-count and letters per word].

1644 **Gassmann** Lothar, Das anthroposophische Bibelverständnis; eine kritische Untersuchung unter besonderer Berücksichtigung der exegetischen Veröffentlichungen von Rudolf STEINER, Friedrich RITTELMEYER, Emil BOCK und Rudolf FRIELING: Diss. Tübingen 1991. 361 p. – TLZ 117,879.

1645 **Glatt** David A., A chronological displacement in biblical and related literatures: diss. Pennsylvania, ᴰTigay J. Ph 1991. xiv-340 p. 92-11936. – OIAc 5,22.

1646 *a) Guillet* Jacques, Le sens de l'écriture; exégètes d'autrefois, recherches d'aujourd'hui [de LUBAC]; – *b) Sesboüé* Bernard, Le surnaturel chez Henri de Lubac; un conflit autour d'une théologie: RechSR 80 (1992) 358-372 / 373-408; Eng. 325s [327-344.345-358, *Sommet* J.; *Valadier* P.: de Lubac 1896-4.IX. 1991].

1647 *Hahn* Eberhard, Schriftauslegung im Spannungsfeld von Impetus und *skándalon*: KerDo 38 (1992) 71-79.

1648 *Hegstad* Harald [in Norwegian], The Word of God as an exegetical object: TsTKi 62 (1991) 261-274; Eng. 274.

1648* **Hens-Piazza** Gina, Socio-rhetorical exegesis of selected biblical texts; a study in method: diss. Union. NY 1992. — UnSemQ 45 (1991) 254.

1649 *Jensen* Jørgen S., Retorisk kritik: DanTTs 55 (1992) 262-279 [< ZIT 92,745].

1650 *Knight* Douglas A., Tradition history: → 741, AnchorBD 6 (1992) 633-8.

1651 *a) Lentzen-Deis* Fritzleo, Metodi dell'esegesi tra mito, storicità e comunicazione; prospettive 'pragma-linguistiche' e conseguenze per la teologia e la pastorale; – *b) Costacurta* Bruna, Esegesi e lettura credente della Scrittura; – *c) Marchesi* Giovanni, L'esegesi e l'evangelizzazione della nuova Europa: → 501, Gregorianum 73 (1992) 731-7 / 739-745 / 719-730.

1651* *Letis* Theodore, Brevard CHILDS and the Protestant dogmaticians; a window to a new paradigm of biblical interpretation: Churchman 105 (1991) 261-277.

1652 ᴱLevering Mariam, Rethinking Scripture; essays from a comparative perspective 1989 → 5,695: ᴿHistRel 32 (1992) 199-201 (R. *Campany*); RelStT 11,1 (1991) 50s (K. *Hamilton*).

1653 **Linnemann** Eta,   Historical criticism of the Bible; methodology or
ideology?, ᵀ*Yarbrough* Robert W. 1990 ➤ 5,1730; 7,1436: ᴿAndrUnS 30
(1992) 171-4 (R. M. *Johnston*); CalvaryB 7,1 (1991) 62s (G. H. *Lovik*
recommends); ChrSchR 22 (1992s) 106-9 (G. A. *Boyd*); JEvTS 35 (1992)
101s (D. B. *Clendenin*); RelStR 18 (1992) 140: C. *Bernas*, sympathy but
no); TrinJ 13 (1992) 95-98 (A. J. *Köstenberger*).

1654 **Luck** Georg, Humor: ➤ 764, RAC, 16,125 (1992) 753-773.

1655 *McDonald* Peter J., Discourse analysis and biblical interpretation:
➤ 343, Linguistics/BH 1992, 153-175.

1656 *McEvenue* Sean, Mandala [diagrama budista para la meditación] para
un comentario bíblico: RBibArg 54,47 (1992) 155-162.

1657 *Martini* Carlo M., La práctica de la lectio divina en la pastoral bíblica
[Roma, Gregoriana 13.XIII.1990; 25° año Dei Verbum]: RBiArg 54,46
(1992) 85-96.

1658 *a) Mealand* Donald L.,   On finding fresh evidence on old texts;
reflections on results in computer-assisted biblical research; – *b) Conner*
Patrick W., Hypertext in the last days of the book; – *c) Renear* Allen,
Representing text on the computer; lessons for and from philosophy:
BJRyL 74,3 ('Computers and the Humanities' 1992) 67-88 [53-66 *alískõ*
➤ 9888] / 7-24 / 221-248.

1659 **Meynet** Roland, L'analyse rhétorique; une nouvelle méthode pour
comprendre la Bible 1989 ➤ 5,1642 ... 7,1440: ᴿÉTRel 67 (1992) 117s
(Danielle *Ellul*); Foi Temps 22 (1992) 282s (A. *Wénin*); ScEspr 44 (1992)
97s (P. *Letourneau*).

1660 **Meynet** Roland, L'analisi retorica, ᵀ*Sembrano* Lucio: BtBiblica 8. Brescia 1992, Queriniana. 295 p. Lit. 35.000. 88-399-2008-0.

1661 *a) Müller* Hans-Peter, Bedarf die alttestamentliche Theologie einer philosophischen Grundlegung? – *b) Waschke* Ernst-Joachim, Die Einheit der
Theologie heute als Anfrage an das AT — ein Plädoyer für die Vielfalt:
➤ 149, ꟳPREUSS H. 1992, 342-351 / 331-341.

1662 *Neugebauer* Johannes, 'Extreme Exegese' — am Text vorbei? Anregungen zu einer thematisch orientierten Auslegung: BibNot [53 (1990) 68-99,
Williams B.] 57 (1991) 26 29.

1664 **Patrick** Dale, *Scult* Allen, Rhetoric and biblical interpretation: JStOT
supp 82, 1990 ➤ 6,1736; 7,1441: ᴿCBQ 54 (1992) 332s (B. *De Pinto*);
Interpretation 46 (1992) 102 (D. *Jobling*, reserves); CritRR 5 (1992) 155-7
(D. *Bland*); JQR 83 (1992s) 193 (Adele *Berlin*).

1665 *Pollard* J. Paul, Recent trends in biblical interpretation: RestQ 34 (1992)
65-81 [< NTAbs 37, p. 7].

1666 **Powell** Mark A., *al.*, The Bible and modern literary criticism; a critical
assessment and annotated bibliography: BibliogIndRelSt 22. NY 1992,
Greenwood. xv-469 p. $65. 0-313-27546-7 [TDig 39,380].

1667 *Preuss* Horst D., Paradigmenwechsel? [Oᴛᴛo E. in OrBibChr 1991]:
BibNot 60 (1991) 33-39.

1668 **Raffelt** Albert, Proseminar Theologie; Einführung in die wissenschaftliche Arbeiten und die theologische Bücherkünde⁵ʳᵉᵛ (wiederum). FrB
1992, Herder. 255 p. DM 30 [TLZ 118,208; ⁴ᴿ111,654; ¹ᴿ102,21].

1669 *Ravasi* Gianfranco, Bibbia e semiotica: RClerIt 73 (1992) 181-191.

1670 **Reboul** Olivier,   Introduction à la rhétorique; théorie et pratique: Premier Cycle 1. P 1991, PUF. 238 p. F 79. 2-13-043917-9. – ᴿÉTRel 67
(1992) 598s (E. *Cuvillier*: plaisir de découvrir des figures comme anta-
naclase, apodioxie, aposiopèse, chleuasme, corax, épanalepse...).

1670* **Refoulé** F., *Dreyfus* F., Quale esegesi oggi nella Chiesa? [< Le Supplément 1974; RB 1975-6-8...] ᵀᴱ*De Benedittis* Giorgio. préf. *Vanhoye* A.: Sussidi Biblici 38-41. Reggio Emilia 1992s, San Lorenzo. I, 133 p.; II. p. ii + 135-305. Lit. 22.500 ciasc.

1671 *a*) *Rüger* Hans-Peter, Oral tradition in the Old Testament; – *b*) *Talmon* Shemaryahu, Oral tradition and written transmission, or the heard and the seen word in Judaism of the Second Temple period; – *c*) *Alexander* Philip S., Orality in Pharisaic-rabbinic Judaism at the turn of the eras; – *d*) *Andersen* Ørvind, Oral tradition: ➤ 7,460*b*, ᴱ*Wansbrough* H., Jesus and the oral Gospel tradition 1989/91, 107-120 / 121-158 / 159-184 / 17-58.

1672 *Schobinger* Jean-Pierre, Operationale Aufmerksamkeit in der textimmanenten Auslegung: FreibZ 39 (1992) 5-28.

1673 *a*) *Seidel* Bodo, Über die notwendige Ergänzung der historisch-kritischen Arbeit durch die forschungsgeschichtliche Überprüfung exegetischer Theoriebildung; – *b*) *Beyse* Karl-Martin, Hebräisch-Unterricht und biblische Realienkunde: ➤ 7,164*a*, ᶠWALLIS Gerhard, Überlieferung und Geschichte (Halle 1990) 52-71 / 105-9.

1674 *Seitz* Christopher R., The changing face of Old Testament studies: ChrCent 109 (1992) 932-5.

1675 *Söding* Thomas, Historische Kritik und theologische Interpretation; Erwägungen zur Aufgabe und zur theologischen Kompetenz historisch-kritischer Exegese: TGL 82 (1992) 199-231.

1676 *a*) *Söding* Thomas, Geschichtlicher Text und Heilige Schrift – Fragen zur theologischen Legitimität historisch-kritischer Exegese; – *b*) *Jacob* Christoph, Allegorese, Rhetorik, Ästhetik, Theologie; – *c*) *Dohmen* Christoph, Vom vielfachen Schriftsinn; Möglichkeit und Grenzen neuerer Zugänge zu biblischen Texten: ➤ 495, Neue Formen? 1992, 75-130 / 131-163 / 13-74.

1676* *Staudinger* H., Die geistesgeschichtliche und wissenschaftstheoretische Basis und Problematik der sogenannten historisch-kritischen Methode; ein Beitrag zur angemessenen Interpretation biblischer Texte: Renovatio 48 (1992) 189-203 [< NTAbs 37, p. 328].

1677 **Stenger** W., Biblische Methodenlehre 1987 ➤ 3,1617: ᴿSNTU A-17 (1992) 246-8 (A. *Fuchs*).

1678 **Stenger** Werner, Metodologia biblica [Biblische Methodenlehre 1987], ᵀ*Gatti* Enzo: GdT 205. Brescia 1991, Queriniana. 350 p. Lit. 32.000. – ᴿGregorianum 73 (1992) 544s (G. *Marconi*).

1679 **Stenger** W., Los métodos de la exégesis bíblica: BtTeol 14, 1990 ➤ 7,1448: ᴿActuBbg 29 (1992) 201s (X. *Alegre*), ComSev 25 (1992) 121 (M. de *Burgos*); RTLim 25 (1991) 491s (U. *Berges*).

1680 *Stordalen* Terje, Eksegese og systematikk; til spørsmålet om teologiens enhet: TsTKi 62 (1991) 113-129; Eng. 129.

1681 *a*) *Thayer* D.D., The state of Scriptural studies; a philosopher's puzzlement; – *b*) *Barré* M.L., The contribution of Sulpicians in America to the advancement of biblical scholarship; – *c*) *Vidal* M., Qu'est devenu l'argument d'Écriture?; – *d*) *Holleran* J.W., The Bible and the ongoing education of priests: ➤ 448, Ens.Écr. 1992, 223-239 / 38-47 / 193-204 / 263-272 [48-57, *Cazelles* M., interview].

1681* **Thomas** Rosalind, Literacy and orality in ancient Greece [... and Roman world]: Key themes in ancient history. C 1992, Univ. xii-201 p. £32.50; pa. £11. 0-521-37346-8; –742–0 [BL 94,129, M. *Goodman*: wideranging].

1682 **Vickers** Brian, In defense of rhetoric. NY 1989 = 1988, Oxford-UP. 528 p. $29 pa. 0-19-811791-4. – ᴿMnemosyne 45 (1992) 537-544 (J. *Wisse*).

1683 ᴱWarner Martin, The Bible as rhetoric; studies in biblical persuasion and credibility. 1990 ➤ 6,561; 7,333c: ᴿChrCent 108 (1991) 240s.243 (J.H. *Burtness*: 9 British + 2); RelStR 18 (1992) 225 (C. *Bernas*); TorJT 7 (1991) 269-271 (I. *Friesen*).
1683* *Watson* Duane F., Rhetorik, ᵀ*Starke* E.; ➤ 757, EvKL 3 (1992) 1650-4.
1684 **Weber** H.R., Esperimenti di studio biblico; nuovi metodi e tecniche: PiccolaBtT 20. T 1989, Claudiana. 240 p. Lit. 24.000. – ᴿParVi 36 (1991) 316s (C. *Ghidelli*).

III. Critica Textus, Versiones

D1 **Textual Criticism.**

1685 [Ant–] **Adourukis** Y.B., ⊕ *Epigraphikē* ... Greek-Christian epigraphy². Athena 1988. 200 p. – ᴿTAth 63 (1992) 879-883 (C. *Charalabakis*, ⊕).
1686 *Balge* R.D., The Bible through the ages; II. The text of Scripture: Wisconsin LuthQ 89,1 (Mequon 1992) 47-58 [< NTAbs 36, p. 312].
1687 **Banks** Doris H., Medieval manuscript bookmaking; a bibliographic guide. Metuchen NY 1989, Scarecrow. xvii-282 p.; 2 maps. $29.50. – ᴿSpeculum 67 (1992) 371s (Laura *Light*: unreliable; use BOYLE L. 1984, which is not in her bibliography).
1688 *Bar-Ilan* M., ⊕ The transition from scroll to codex and its mark upon the reading of the Torah: Sinai 107 (1990s) 242-254 [< JStJud 24,172].
1689 **Barthélemy** Dominique, Critique textuelle de l'Ancien Testament [I-II, 1982-6, ➤ 63,1720 ... 6,1749]. III. Ézéchiel, Daniel et les 12 Prophètes: OBO 50/3. FrS/Gö 1992, Univ./VR. ccxliii-1150 p. Fs 350. 2-8271-0574-8. – ᴿExpTim 104 (1992s) 300 (R.J. *Coggins*); RivB 40 (1992) 334-8 (B. *Ognibeni*).
1690 [ᴱ**Beit-Arié** Malachi] Users' guide, microfilmed manuscripts catalog. J 1989, Nat./Univ. Library. 41 p.; ⊕ 1-23,42-48. – ᴿHenoch 14 (1992) 364-6 (M. *Perani*).
1691 ᴱ**Blanchard** A., Les débuts du codex 1985/9 ➤ 5,778; 6,1757: ᴿArPapF 38 (1992) 67s (G. *Poethke*); JEA 78 (1992) 349s (J.D. *Thomas*).
1692 **Blanck** Horst, Das Buch in der Antike: ArchäolBt. Mü 1992, Beck. 246 p.; 121 fig. 3-406-36686-4 [OIAc 5,15].
1693 ᴱ**Cambiano** Giuseppe, *al.*, Lo spazio letterario della Grecia antica; I. La produzione e la circolazione del testo, 1. La polis. R 1992, Salerno. 621 p.; 44 fig. 88-8402-002-1. 20 art. sulla letteratura classica.
1694 **Canart** Paul, Paleografia e codicologia greca, una rassegna bibliografica: Littera antiqua 7. Vaticano 1991, Scuola di Paleografia. 131 p. – ᴿRÉByz 50 (1992) 299 (P. *Géhin*).
1695 *Canart* Paul, *al.*, Remarques préliminaires sur les matériaux utilisés pour la règlure en couleur dans les manuscrits grecs et latins: Scriptorium 45 (Bru 1991) 205-225.
1696 ᴱ**Deroche** François, Les manuscrits du Moyen-Orient; essais de codicologie et de paléographie (Actes du Colloque d'Istanbul, 26-29 mai, 1986). P 1989. 143 p.; 31 pl. – ᴿJRAS (1991) 393s (J.M. *Rogers*).
1697 *Dorandi* Tiziano, Fünf buchtechnische Miszellen [citations from PLATO, CATULLUS, CICERO and PLINY about book-production]: ArPapF 38 (1992) 39-45.

1698 *Dupuy* Bernard, Pourquoi les chrétiens ont-ils préféré le codex au rouleau pour la copie de leurs Écritures? : Istina 37 (1992) 67-73.

1699 *Edwards* A.S.G., From manuscript to print [BANKS D., *al.*]: MedvHum 19 (1992) 183-8.

1700 **Eleuteri** Pacio, *Canart* Paul, Scrittura greca nell'umanesimo italiano: Documenti sulle arti del libro 16. Mi 1991, Polifilo. 204 p.; 4 fig.; 82 pl. Lit. 260.000 [ClasR 43,147, N. G. *Wilson*].

1700* *Epp* Eldon J., New Testament papyrus manuscripts and letter carrying in Greco-Roman times: ➤ 104, ᶠKOESTER H. 1991, 35-36.

1701 *Esch* Arnold, Fehlleistungen in mittelalterlichen Texten: Deutsches Archiv für Erforschung des Mittelalters 48,1 (Köln 1992) 175-8 [< ZIT 93,31].

1702 Fälschungen im Mittelalter 1986/8 ➤ 4,1662* ... 7,1464: ᴿHZ 253 (1991) 432-8 (H. *Müller*).

1703 ᴱ**Gamillscheg** E., *al.*, Repertorium der griechischen Kopisten 2, 1989 ➤ 6,1779; 7,1466: ᴿJbÖsByz 42 (1992) 403-5 (F. *Winkelmann*).

1704 **Garel** Michel, D'une main forte; [148] manuscrits hébreux des collections françaises: exposition 1991s. P 1991, Bibliothèque Nationale. 207 p. – ᴿRÉJ 151 (1992) 386-392 (Marie-Thérèse *Gousset*).

1705 ᴱ**Garzya** Antonio, Metodologie della ricerca sulla tarda antichità: Atti del Convegno (Napoli, 16-18 ott. 1987) 1989 ➤ 6,735: ᴿCC 143 (1992,1) 408s (G. *Cremascoli*).

1706 *Geyer* Angelika, Die Genese narrativer Buchillustration; der Miniaturenzyklus zur Aeneis im Vergilius Vaticanus: FraWissBeit KuW 17. Fra 1989, Lang. 255 p. – ᴿGGA 244 (1992) 187-206 (R. *Warland*); Gnomon 64 (1992) 507-510 (F. *Rickert*).

1707 ᴱ**Grant** John N., Editing Greek and Latin texts 1987/9 ➤ 6,738; 7,1467: ᴿAnz AltW 45 (1992) 54-56 (R. *Kassel*).

1708 **Greetham** D.C., Textual scholarship; an introduction: RefLib Humanities 1417. NY 1992, Garland. xx-539 p.; 150 fig. $36 [RelStR 19,250, (L. J. *Greenspahn*: all you didn't even know you wanted to know; with clarity, grace, and evenhandedness).

1709 ᴱ**Hamesse** Jacqueline, Les problèmes posés par l'édition critique des textes anciens et médiévaux [18 auteurs]: Textes, Études, Congrès 13. LvN 1992, Univ.Inst.Mdv. xiii-522, 25 pl.

1710 ᴱ**Heide** A. van der, *Voolen* E. van, The Amsterdam Mahzor 1989 ➤ 5,1672: ᴿSpeculum 67 (1992) 227s (N. *Roth*).

1711 **Hindman** Sandra, Printing the written word; the social history of books, circa 1450-1520 [Northwestern Univ. conference, Evanston April 1987]. Ithaca 1991, Cornell Univ. xii-331 p. [SixtC 24,706s, R. W. *Clement*].

1712 **Horst** Koert van der, Illuminated ... mss Utrecht. 1989. ᴿCiuD 205 (1992) 794-6 (M. *González Velasco*).

1713 **Hunger** Herbert, Schreiben und lesen in Byzanz 1989 ➤ 5,1673 ... 7,1473: ᴱEmerita 60 (1992) 351-4 (Inmaculada *Pérez Martín*).

1714 **Lemaire** Jacques, Introduction à la codicologie 1989 ➤ 5,1675 ... 7,1475: ᴿBtHumRen 52 (1990) 696s (E. *Poulle*); Speculum 67 (1992) 182-4 (R. G. *Dennis*).

1715 *Lewis* Naphtali, Papyrus in classical antiquity, an update: CdÉ 67 (1992) 308-318.

1716 **Lowden** John, The Octateuchs; a study in Byzantine manuscript illustration. University Park 1992, Penn State Univ. xxi-140 p.; 179 fig. $49.50. – ᴿRelStR 18 (1992) 320 (J. *Guttmann*).

1717 **McCormick** Michael, Five hundred unknown glosses from the Palatine Virgil (Ms. Pal.Lat. 1631): ST 343. Vaticano 1992, Bt. [ix–] 118 p.; 16 pl. 88-210-0635-2.

1718 *Margain* Jean, Aspects de la critique [textuelle] biblique ancienne: ÉTRel 67 (1992) 83-86.

1719 **Mayr-Harting** Henry, Ottonian book illumination; an historical study, I. Themes. L/NY 1991, H. Miller / Oxford-UP. 271 p.; ill $85. – ᴿManuscripta 35 (1991) 231s (M. B. *McNamee*).

1720 *a) Ott* Wilhelm, Transcription errors, variant readings, scholarly emendations; software tools to master them; – *b) Weitzman* Michael P., The analysis of manuscript traditions; Isaiah (Peshitta version) and Matthew: ➤ 450, Informatique 2, 1988/9, 419-434 / 641-652.

1721 **Perani** Mauro, Frammenti di manoscritti e libri ebraici a Nonantola: Archiv.Sto. 1. Nonantola 1992, Comune / A. Ausilio. 217 p.; 67 pl.

1722 **Pestman** P. W., The new papyrological primer 1990 ➤ 7,1485: ᴿEnchoria 19s (1992s) 235s (W. M. *Brashear*); JAOS 112 (1992) 542s (J. J. *Farber*); JStJud 23 (1992) 128s (A. *Hilhorst*).

1723 *a) Pontani* Anna, Le maiuscole greche antiquarie di Giano Lascaris; per la storia dell'alfabeto greco in Italia nel [millc] '400; – *b) Tedeschi* Carlo, L'unciale usuale a Roma e nell'arca romana in alcune iscrizioni graffite: ScrCiv 16 (1992) 77-227 / 313-330.

1724 **Randall** Lilian M. C., *al.*, Medieval and Renaissance manuscripts in the Walters Art Gallery, I. France 875-1420. Baltimore 1989, Johns Hopkins Univ. 432 p. $85. 0-8018-2869-4. – ᴿScriptorium 45 (Bru 1991) 306s (M. *Huglo*).

1725 *Resnick* Irven M., The codex in early Jewish and Christian communities: JRelHist 17,1 (Sydney 1992) 1-17 [< ᴢɪᴛ 92,712].

1726 **Richler** B., Hebrew manuscripts, a treasured legacy; *Brody* R. on Cairo Genizah. Cleveland/J 1990, Ofeq Inst. 165 p.; ill. (16 color); – ᴿHenoch 14 (1992) 366-8 (M. *Perani*).

1727 ᴱ**Rück** Peter, Pergament; Geschichte, Struktur, Restaurierung, Herstellung: Historische Hilfswissenschaften 2. Sigmaringen 1991, Thorbecke. 430 p.; 251 fig. DM 240. [ErbAuf 68,256].

1727* *Scanlin* Harold P., The presuppositions of HOTTP [text project ➤ BARTHÉLEMY 1-3] and the translator: BTrans 43 (1992) 101-116 [missing last ten bibliography items supplied p. 355].

1728 **Schott** Siegfried, (1897-1971), ᴱ(wife) Erika, Bücher und Bibliotheken im alten Ägypten; Verzeichnis der Buch- und Spruchtitel und der Termini technici; Wortindex *Grimm* A.: MainzAkad. Wsb 1990, Harrassowitz. 553 p. ➤ 6,e591: ᴿHenoch 14 (1992) 325s (M. *Zonta*).

Seider Richard, Paläographie der griechischen Papyri 3/1/1, 1990 ➤ a10.

1730 *Vendrell Peñaranda* M., Estudio de los códices de la Biblioteca Nacional de Paris, ms 8093, y de la Biblioteca Universitaria de Leiden, ms. Voss F 111: Helmantica 43 (1992) 147-201 [RHE 87,176*].

1731 ᴱ**Weiser** R., ⊕ Books from Sefarad. J 1992, Nat./Univ. Library. 157 p. (Eng. vii-xi). – ᴿHenoch 14 (1992) 352s (M. *Perani*).

1732 **Wisselink** W. E., Assimilation as a criterion for the establishment of the text ... Mt Mk Lk ᴰ1989 ➤ 5,1750: ᴿEvQ 64 (1992) 268-271 (J. N. *Birdsall*: disappointing).

1733 **Wright** David H., Codicological notes on the Vergilius Romanus (Vat.lat. 1867): ST 345. Vaticano 1992, Biblioteca. 138 p.; 41 fig. 88-210-0641-7.

1734 *Würthwein* E., AT; *Aland* K., NT: Handschriften der Bibel: ➤ 762, NBL II, 6 (1991) 31-35-41.

1735 *Zaluska* Yolanta, L'enluminure cistercienne au XIIᵉ siècle: ↠ 512c, BERNARD 1992, 271-285.

1735* ᴱZatelli Ida, La Bibbia a stampa da Gutenberg a Bodoni [↠ 7,1588; ma include anche stampa ebraica e greca; e il numero di pagine è 222, non 22]: Biblioteca Medicea Laurenziana & Nazionale, ott.-nov. 1991; iconologia *Mino* Gabriele. F 1991. 222 p.; ill. 88-7038-214-1.

D2.1 *Biblia hebraica,* Hebrew text.

1736 ᴱAdler Israel, [microfilm] ⊕ *Qaṭalog*... Catalogue of the Jack MOSSERT collection [5600 fragments of the Cairo Jewish community, unused since his death in 1934]. J 1990, National and University Library. 16 + 407 + 30 p. [Relatively few biblical, checked by I. YEIVIN]. – ᴿJQR 83 (1992s) 197s (R. *Brody*).

1737 *Allan* Nigel, A typographical odyssey; the 1505 Constantinople Pentateuch [2d earliest Nahmias and Turkey printed work, including Onqelos, Rashi, Kimḥi, the 5 scrolls]: JRAS (1991) 343-351 + 3 fig.

1738 *a) Bajard* Jean, *Juste* Yolanda, Massora electronica; approche quantitative de la Bible hébraïque; – *b) Cassuto* Philippe, Isomorphie consonantique et hétéromorphie vocalique: ↠ 450, Informatique 2, 1988/9, 99-133; Eng. 107-9 / 177-208.

1739 *Barthélemy* Dominique, Les ruines de la tradition des Soferim dans le manuscrit d'Alep; la gageure de Shelomoh BEN BUYA'A: RB 99 (1992) 7-39; Eng. 7s.

1740 ᴱBreuer Mordechai, ⊕ The Masorah Magna to the Pentateuch by Shemuel BEN YA'AQOV (MS Lᴹ). NY 1992, Lehmann Found. 821 p.; Eng. lvi p. – ᴿLešonenu 56 (1991s) 269-283; Eng. VII (Y. *Ofer*).

1741 **Cassuto** P., Qeré-Ketib et listes massorétiques dans le manuscrit B 19, 1989 ↠ 6,1830: ᴿBO 49 (1992) 470s (D. *Barthélemy*); ÉglT 23 (1992) 132s (L. *Laberge*).

1742 *Chiesa* Bruno, Textual history and textual criticism of the Hebrew Old Testament: ↠ 498, MQumran 1 (1991/2) 257-272.

1743 *Crown* Alan D., The Abisha scroll 3000 years old?: BR 7,5 (1991) 12-21 [BtS 149 (1992) 240-2 (R. A. *Taylor*)].

1744 *Deist* Ferdinand E., 'Canonical criticism', Reformed theology and developments in the textual criticism of the First Testament: JNWS 18 (1992) 37-47.

1745 *Foley* C. M., The formation of the Jewish Scriptures; 1. The Hebrew text; 2. (*Magennis Feidlimidh* T.) The Greek text: CanadCathR 10,8s (1992) 7-15 / 10/9, 5-9.

1746 *Geoffroy* Bérénice, Manuscrits hébreux à la Bibliothèque Nationale: Archéologia 274 (1991) 28-33; ill.

1747 *Goshen-Gottstein* M. H. †, The development of the Hebrew text of the Bible; theories and practice of textual criticism: VT 42 (1992) 204-213.

1748 *a) Goshen-Gottstein* Moshe, Editions of the Hebrew Bible — past and future; – *b) Kamin* Sarah, The theological significance of the *Hebraica veritas* in JEROME's thought; – *c) Tov* Emanuel, Interchanges of consonants between the Masoretic text and the Vorlage of the Septuagint; – *d) Ulrich* Eugene, The canonical process, textual criticism, and later stages in the composition of the Bible: ↠ 181, Sha'arei TALMON 1992, 221-242 / 243-253 / 255-266 / 267-291.

1749 **Khan** Geoffrey, Karaite Bible manuscripts 1990 ↠ 6,1834: ᴿJQR 83 (1992s) 244-6 (L. *Nemoy*).

1750 **Miletto** G., L'Antico Testamento ebraico nella tradizione babilonese; i frammenti della Genizah: Henoch Quad. 3. T 1992, Zamorani. xi-308 p. Lit. 50.000. 88-7158-013-3 [BL 93,155, J. *Barr*: well done, important; proves older roots of scribal variants].

1751 *Millard* Alan, Were words separated in ancient Hebrew writing? [yes, sometimes by dot as in Siloam inscription; by space in square script after the exile]: BR 8,3 (1992) 45-47.

1752 *Minkoff* Harvey, The Aleppo codex; ancient Bible from the ashes [amid 40 Torah scrolls drenched in kerosene and set afire in 1947; but three-fourths of it (588 pages) were saved, and after ten years smuggled into Turkey and then Israel by Mordecai Fahham; the lost portions include Gn 1,1 to Dt 28,17; Qoh Est Lam Dan Ez-Neh]: BR 7,4 (1991) 22-27 . 38-40.

1753 **Mynatt** Daniel S., The 'sub loco' notes in the Torah [Leningrad Masorah Parva] of the Biblia Hebraica Stuttgartensia: diss. Southern Baptist Theol. Sem. 1992, D*Kelley* P. 410 p. 93-03766. — DissA 53 (1992s) 3565s-A.

1754 **Penkower** Jordan S., New evidence for the Pentateuch text in the Aleppo Codex: Sources & Studies 6. Ramat Gan 1992, Bar-Ilan Univ. 144 p.

1755 E**Pérez Castro** Federico, *al.*, El Códice de Profetas de El Cairo Tomo VIII, índice alfabético de sus Masoras: TEstCisn 51. M 1992, Cons. Sup. Inv., Inst.Fg. 317 p. 84-00-07256-1 [BL 93,51, P. *Wernberg-Møller*].

1756 *Rabe* Norbert, On the scope of Old Testament textual criticism: → 450*, Informatique 3e 1991/2, 283-306 (-314, comments).

1757 **Richter** Wolfgang, Biblia hebraica transcripta [for computer] 1-3, Gen-Dt: AOtt 33,1-3, 1991 → 7,1505: R BL (1992) 56 (C. S. *Rodd*: bewildered, but time will tell); OLZ 87 (1992) 51s (R. *Stahl*).

1758 D**Richter** Wolfgang, Biblia hebraica[1] transkribiert [für Computer 1-4, 1991 → 1757]; 5. 1-2 Sam, 585 p. DM 63; − 6. 1-2 Kön, 569 p. DM 63; − 7. Jes. 433 p. DM 48; − 8. Jer, 497 p. DM 58; − 9. Ezech, 433 p. DM 48; − 10. Kleine Proph. 357 p. DM 43; − 11. Pss, 589 p. DM 78; − 12. Ijob + Sprüche, 389 p. DM 48; − 13. Megillot, 253 p. DM 34; − 14. Dan Esra Neh, 341 p. DM 42; − 15. 1-2 Chr, 491 p. DM 68; (Egb) 16. Sirach, 140 p. DM 24,80. 3-88096-585-4; -86-2; -87-0; -88-9; -89-7; -90-0; -91-9; -92-7; -93-5; -97-8; -95-1; -96-X [TR 89,185]. − R TLZ 117 (1992) 903 (W. *Herrmann*).

1759 E**Sed-Rajna** Gabrielle, Lisbon Bible 1482 (British Library Or. 2626). TA 1988, Nahar Miskal. 408 p. $100. − R BR 7,1 (1991) 9 (J. *Gutmann*).

1760 *Sirat* Colette, Par l'oreille et par l'œil; la Bible hébraïque et les livres qui la portent: → 180c, Mem. TALMAGE F. 1 (1992s) 233-249; 5 fig.

1761 **Tov** Emanuel, Textual criticism of the Hebrew Bible [1989],T. Mp/ Assen 1992, Fortress/VanGorcum. xl-456 p.; 30 pl. 0-8006-2687-7 / 90-232-2712-3 [BL 93,53, L. L. *Grabbe*, not his 1981 Septuagint handbook but an expansion of his 1989 Hebrew Bible textual criticism → 7,1508]. − R VT 42 (1992) 566-8 (Meira *Pollack*, on ❻).

1761* *Tov* E., A new understanding of the Samaritan Pentateuch in the wake of the discovery of the Qumran scrolls: → 496*, Congress 1988/91, 293-303.

1762 **Wonneberger** R. ❶ Leitfaden zur Biblia Hebraica Stuttgartensia [1984], T*Matsuda* Isaku. Tokyo 1992, Seishochūkai Kankōkai. 220 p. Y 4000 [BL 93,55, D. T. *Tsumura*].

1763 *Woude* A. S. van der, Pluriformity and uniformity; reflections on the transmission of the text of the OT: ➤ 504, ᶠWOUDE Symposium 1992, 151-169.

D2.2 Targum.

1764 *Alexander* Philip S., Targum, Targumim: ➤ 741, AnchorBD 6 (1992) 320-331.
Cathcart K., *Gordon* R., Targum of the minor prophets 1989 ➤ 3953.
1765 ᴱ**Flesher** Paul V. M., Targum studies, 1. Textual and contextual studies in the Pentateuch Targums: SFL StJud 55. Atlanta 1992, Scholars. ix-154 p. 1-55540-754-4.
1766 **Grelot** Pierre, What are the Targums? Selected texts, ᵀ*Attanasio* S. ColMn 1992, Liturgical/Glazier. 144 p. $12 pa. 0-8146-5644-7 [NTAbs 37,145; BL 93,161].
1767 **Grossfeld** Bernard, A bibliography of targum literature 3. NY 1990, Sepher-Hermon. xx-91 p. $39.50. – ᴿCBQ 54 (1992) 529 (D. M. *Colomb*).
1768 *Hayward* C. T. R., Inconsistencies and contradictions in Targum Pseudo-Jonathan; the case of Eliezer and Nimrod: JSS 37 (1992) 31-55.
1769 **Klein** Michael L., [1600] Targumic manuscripts in the Cairo Genizah collections. C 1992 Univ. xvi-138 p.; 24 fig. 0-521-42076-8 [BL 93,50, K. J. *Cathcart*; OLZ 88,160, G. *Stemberger*].
1770 **Levine** Etan, The Aramaic version of the Bible; contents and context: BZAW 174, 1988 ➤ 4,1706 ... 7,1523: ᴿJAOS 112 (1992) 324s (M. J. *Bernstein*); NedTTs 46 (1992) 71s (P. W. van der *Horst*).
1771 ᴱ**McNamara** Martin, The Aramaic Bible; 1A, Neofiti I Gn; 1B, ᴱ*Maher* Michael, Ps-Jon Gn: ColMn 1992, Glazier/Liturgical [= E, Clark edition ➤ 2008*]. xiv-271 p.; xiv-208 p. $65 each. 0-8146-5476-2; -92-4 [TDig 39,250, noting also in the series: 10. *Harrington-Saldarini*, Former Prophets 1987; 11. *Chilton* B., Isa 1987; 15. *Mangan* C., Job, *al*., 1991; 18. *Grossfeld* B., Esther 1991].
1772 **Samely** Alexander, *a*) The interpretation of speech in the Pentateuch targums; a study of method and presentation in targumic exegesis, with special regard to Pseudo-Jonathan: diss. Oxford 1989. 229 p. BRD-97306. — DissA 53 (1992s) 2415-A.
— *b*) The interpretation of speech in the Pentateuch Targum; a study of method and presentation in Targumic exegesis: TStAJ 27. Tü 1992, Mohr. xi-203 p. DM 128. 3-16-145643-2. – ᴿTBR 5,2 (1992s) 12 (R. *Coggins*).
1773 **Shinan** Avigdor, The embroidered Targum; the Aggadah in Targum Pseudo–Jonathan of the Pentateuch: Perry Foundation. J 1992, Hebrew Univ. 237 p. $17. 965-223-811-2.
1774 **Sperber** Alexander [new pref. *Gordon* R. P.], The Bible in Aramaic I-IVab. Leiden, Brill reprint of 1957-73 (compiled 1920-50). xxii-357 p.; x-331 p.; xi-505 p.; viii-205 p.; xv-417 p. 90-04-09575-6; -76-4; -77-2; 78-0; 79-9; (ALL)-80-2 [NTAbs 36, p.483; BL 93,52, C. *Hayward*]. – ᴿJStJud 23 (1992) 290 (F. *Garcia Martinez*).

D3.1 *Textus graecus* – Greek NT.

1775 **Aland** K. & B., Il testo del NT [1982]: CommStoEseg NT, Strum 2. Genova 1987, Marictti. xii-372 p. Lit. 55.000 ➤ 4,1712: ParVi 36 (1991) 314-6 (G. M. *Vigna*).

1776 **Aland** B., H. Kunst Stiftung, Bericht 1988-91. Mü 1992. 122 p. [NTAbs 36, p. 409].
Aland K., Text und Textwert 1-4, 1991 ➤ 6049 [7,5158].
1778 *Amphoux* Christian-B., [➤ 1798] Les manuscrits du Nouveau Testament; du livre à la parole: ÉTRel 67 (1992) 345-357.
1779 *Birdsall* J. Neville, The recent history of NT textual criticism (from WESTCOTT and HORT, 1881, to the present): ➤ 742, ANRW 2,26,1 (1992) 99-197.
1780 *Botha* P. J. J., Die teks van die Nuwe Testament [PETZER J. H. 1990]; steeds 'n vraagstuk in die Nuwe-Testamentiese wetenskap: Theologia Evangelica 25,2 (Pretoria 1992) 2-18 [< NTAbs 37,173].
1781 **Comfort** P. W., The quest for the original text of the NT. GR 1992, Baker. 200 p.; 11 pl., map. $12 pa. 0-8010-2566-4 [NTAbs 37, p. 264].
1782 **Comfort** Philip W., Early manuscripts and modern translations of the New Testament 1990 ➤ 6,1852; 7,1528: ᴿBR 8,4 (1992) 16 (B. M. *Metzger*); ÉTRel 67 (1992) 283 (C. B. *Amphoux*); Themelios 17,3 (1991s) 29 (P. M. *Head*).
1783 **Donalies** E., Die Augsburger Bibelhandschrift und ihre Überlieferung; Untersuchung und Text der vier Evangelien. Münster/NY 1992, Waxman. xvi-276 p. [RHE 88,28*].
1784 **Elliott** J. K., A bibliography of Greek NT manuscripts 1989 ➤ 5,1738 ... 7,1529: ᴿETL 68 (1992) 161s (F. *Neirynck* supplies the 'unfortunately' missing concordance to Van HAELST).
Elliott J. K., Essays and studies in NT textual criticism 1992 ➤ 239.
1785 *Foti* Maria Bianca, Il vangelo miniato di Parma e la biblioteca del monastero *in lingua Phari*: Koinonia 16,1 (1992) 75-84 + 6 pl. (testo greco).
1786 *Karavidopoulos* John, The origin and history of the terms 'Evangelistarion' and 'Evangeliarion': OrthF 7 (1993) 177-183.
1787 **Kilpatrick** G. D. †, ᴱ*Elliott* J. K., Essays and studies in NT textual criticism (69 art.): BtETL 96, 1990 ➤ 6,257. ᴿExpTim 104 (1992s) 220 (J. N. *Birdsall* welcomes this hearing for views differing from his own; but protests Elliott's overstating of his own Luke-editorship); FgNt 5 (1992) 81-83 (J. *Heimerdinger*); JTS 43 (1992) 210-4 (D. C. *Parker*: his method has sometimes been regarded as aberrant); NT 34 (1992) 201-7 (I. A. *Moir*).
1788 — *Rodgers* Peter R., The new eclecticism ... in appreciation of G. D. KILPATRICK: NT 34 (1992) 388-397.
1789 **Merk** Augustinus, ¹¹*O'Callaghan* J., Novum Testamentum graece et latine: Scripta PIB 65. R 1992, Pontificio Istituto Biblico. 47*-877 p.; maps. 88-7653-597-7.
1790 **Merk** A., *Barbaglio* G., Nuovo Testamento greco e italiano 1990 ➤ 6,1870; Lit. 50.000: ᴿCC 143 (1992,1) 305 (G. *Giachi*).
1791 **Metzger** Bruce M., The text of the NT; its transmission, corruption, and restoration³ [= ²1968 + 36 p. update]. NY 1992, Oxford-UP. ix-310 p. $17. 0-19-507297-9. [RelStR 19,163, B. D. *Ehrman*: tops].
1792 **Parker** David C., Codex Bezae, an early Christian manuscript and its text [Gospels-Acts, bilingual]. C 1992, Univ. xxiii-349 p.; 25 pl. £50 [RHE 87,175*]. 0-521-40037-6. – ᴿExpTim 104 (1992s) 57 (J. N. *Birdsall*); RivB 40 (1992) 493-5 (G. *Ravasi*: d'importanza soprattutto per gli Atti).
1793 ᴱ**Petersen** William L., Gospel traditions in the second century: 1988/9 ➤ 6,549: ᴿCBQ 54 (1992) 396s (H. C. *Kee*).

1794 **Petzer** Kobus [J. H.], Die teks van die Nuwe Testament: 'n inleiding in die basiese aspekte van die teorie en praktyk van die tekskritiek van die NT: HervTSt supp. 2, 1990 → 6,1873: ᴿNedTTs 46 (1992) 164s (A. F. J. *Klijn*: uitstekend).

1795 *Ralston* T., The majority text and Byzantine origins: NTS 38 (1992) 122-137 [his name is Timothy J., not R as in NTS (letter of 4.III.1992)].

1796 **Robinson** A. M., *Pierpont* W. G., The New Testament in the original Greek according to the Byzantine/Majority textform. Atlanta 1991, Original Word. – ᴿFgNt 5 (1992) 79-81 (J. *Wenham*).

1797 *Ross* J. M., Floating words; their significance for textual criticism [single words or short phrases in differing location likelier to be interpolated than whole sentences]: NTS 38 (1992) 153-6.

1798 [*Vaganay* Léon] **Amphoux** Christian-B., An introduction to NT textual criticism 1991 → 7,1536: ᴿTBR 5,1 (1992s) 12 (J. *Houlden*).

D3.2 *Versiones graecae* — **VT, Septuaginta etc.**

1799 *Amir* Y., ⓓ The two faces of the miracle story concerning the translation of the Septuagint [contradictory use of the same details in PHILO, Ps-JUSTIN and bMeg 9a as in Ps-ARISTEAS]: BethM 38,133 (1992s) 183-6 [< JStJud 24,342].

1800 *a)* **Brock** Sebastian P., To revise or not to revise; attitudes to Jewish biblical translation; – *b)* **Hanhart** Robert, The translation of the Septuagint in light of earlier traditions and subsequent influences; – *c)* *Aejmelaeus* Anneli, Septuagintal translation techniques, a solution to the problem of the tabernacle account: → 459, Septuagint 1990/2, 301-338 / 339-379 / 381-402.

1801 **Carbone** Sandro P., *Rizzi* Giovanni, Le Scritture ai tempi di Gesù; introduzione alla LXX e alle antiche versioni aramaiche; pref. *Le Déaut* Roger: Testi e Commenti 1. Bo 1992, Dehoniane. 154 p. Lit. 18.000. 88-10-20554-5.

1802 *a)* *Collins* Nina L., 281 BCE, the year of the translation of the Pentateuch into Greek under Ptolemy II; – *b)* *Grabbe* Lester L. The translation technique of the Greek minor versions; translations or revisions?: – *c)* *Hanson* A. T., The treatment in the LXX of the theme of seeing God: → 459, Septuagint 1990/2, 403-503 / 505-556 / 557/568.

1803 **Cousin** Hugues, La Biblia griega, los Setenta: Documentos en torno a la Biblia 21. Estella 1992, VDivino. 115 p. 84-7151-722-8. – ᴿRET 52 (1992) 492s (P. *Barrado Fernández*).

1803* ᶠHANHART R., Studien zur Septuaginta, ᴱ**Fraenkel** D. 1990 → 6,70: ᴿÉglT 23 (1992) 425s (L. *Laberge*).

1804 **Harl** Marguerite, *al.*, La Bible grecque des Septante 1988 → 4,1732 ... 6,1883: ᴿRÉAug 38 (1992) 180s (É. *Cothenet*).

1805 *Harl* Marguerite, La Septante et la pluralité textuelle des Écritures; le témoignage des Pères grecs: → 402, Naissance 1990/2, 231-243.

1806 **Haverling** Gerd, Studies on SYMMACHUS 1988 → 7,1545: ᴿIndogF 97 (1992) 283-5 (Otta *Wenskus*: erster Eindruck 'Meisterwerk').

1807 *Hengel* Martin, *a)* Die Septuaginta als 'christliche Schriftensammlung' und das Problem ihres Kanons: → 1435 supra, Kanon 1992, 34-127; – *b)* Die Septuaginta als von den Christen beanspruchte Schriftensammlung bei Justin und den Vätern vor Origenes: → 467, Parting 1989/92, 39-84.

1808 **Olofsson** Staffan, The LXX version: ConBib AT 30, 1990 → 6,1887; 7,1548: ᴿBiblica 73 (1992) 582-5 (Marguerite *Harl*, aussi sur son God is my rock ➤ 9482); ETL 68 (1992) 149s (J. *Lust*); JTS 43 (1992) 158s (H. F. D. *Sparks*, also on his simultaneous God is my rock); Salesianum 54 (1992) 584s (M. *Cimosa*); SvEx 57 (1992) 119-121 (Anneli *Aejmelaeus*, auch und besonders über God is my rock); ZAW 104 (1992) 304 (H. C. *Schmitt*).

1809 *Peters* Melvin K. H., Septuagint: ➤ 741, AnchorBD 5 (1992) 1093-1104.
1810 *Rex* Richard, St. John FISHER's treatise on the authority of the Septuagint: JTS 43 (1992) 55-72; Latin text 73-116.
1811 **Salvesen** Alison, SYMMACHUS in the Pentateuch 1991 ➤ 7,1551: ᴿJJS 43 (1992) 145-7 (P. S. *Alexander*); JSS 37 (1992) 113-6 (C. T. R. *Hayward*); JTS 43 (1992) 562s (H. F. D. *Sparks*).
1812 *Scher* Timothy P. The perfect indicative in Septuagint Genesis: BSept-Cog 24,1 (1991) 14-24 [➤ ZIT 92,511].
1813 **Schmidt** W., Untersuchungen zur Fälschung historischer Dokumente bei Ps-ARISTAIOS... 1986 ➤ 4,3098: ᴿVT (1992) 275s (W. *Horbury*).
1814 *Simotas* Panagiotis, ☉ Untranslated Hebrew words of the OT in the ancient translations of AKYLA, THEODOTION and SYMMACHUS: TAth 63 (1992) 37-65 . 226-254.
1815 *a*) *Tov* Emanuel, The contribution of the Qumran scrolls to the understanding of the LXX; – *b*) *Ulrich* Eugene C., The Septuagint manuscripts from Qumran; a reappraisal of their value: ➤ 459, Septuagint 1990/2, 11-47 / 49-80.
1816 *Veltri* Giuseppe, Der Fasttag in Erinnerung an die Entstehung der Septuaginta und die Megillat Taanit Batra: FraJudBei 19 (1991s) 63-72 [-94; < ZAW 105,286].
1817 *Wevers* John W., The earliest witness to Jewish exegesis: ➤ 180*, Mem. TALMAGE F., 1 (1992s) 115-127.

D4 Versiones orientales.

1818 *Birdsall* J. Neville, *al.*, Versions; ancient: ➤ 740, AnchorBD 6 (1992) 788-813 (813-6 Catholic, *Collins* R. F.; 816-829 English, *Lewis* Jack P., including Catholic col. 825 and 828, but Wyclif and Authorized/King James, also by Lewis, separately p. 830-4 (Modern Era 842-851, *Grether* Herbert G.).
1819 **Boismard** M.-É., (*Lamouille* A.) Le diatessaron; de TATIEN à JUSTIN: ÉtBN 15. P 1992, Gabalda. 171 p. – ᴿRÉG 105 (1992) 636 (A. *Wartelle*).
1820 *Dirksen* P. B., The Peshitta and textual criticism of the OT: VT 42 (1992) 376-390.
1821 **Falla** Terry C., A key to the Peshitta gospels I, 1991 ➤ 7,1556: ᴿÉT-Rel 67 (1992) 113s (A.-G. *Martin*); JSS 37 (1992) 105s (A. *Salvesen*); NT 34 (1992) 308s (D. J. *Lane*); OrChr 76 (1992) 252s (H. *Kaufhold*).
1822 **Lane** D. J., *al.*, Lev (Nm Dt Jos): The OT in Syriac according to the Peshitta 2, 1991 ➤ 7,1561: ᴿBL (1992) 46 (S. P. *Brock*).
1823 *Luke* K., Targumisms in the Peshitta version of the Pentateuch: Bible Bhashyam 16 (1990) 52-64.
1824 **Sörries** Reiner, Die syrische Bibel von Paris BN syr 341; eine früh-christliche Bilderhandschrift aus dem 4. Jht. Wsb 1991, Reichert. 104 p.; ill.

1825 *Aranda Pérez* Gonzalo, Autour de la version sahidique du Nouveau Testament; s'agit-il d'une tradition textuelle unique? Étude des manuscrits M 569 et Bodmer XIX: ➤ 690, 3d Coptic, 1984/90, 21-26.

1826 *Bethge* Hans-Gebhard,   Fragmente eines sahidischen Manuskriptes des
  Matthäus- und Johannes-Evangeliums in der British Library (Ms. Or.
  14149 [13-27]); ein Zwischenbericht: ➤ 694*b*, IVe Copte 1988/92, 2,
  245-253.
  Diebner B. J., *Kasser* R., Ha Papyrus Bil. 1, [CtLamEces] 1989 ➤ 3406.
1828 *Luke* Kuriakose,   The Coptic versions of the Bible: Living Word 98
  (Kerala 1992) 251-269 [TContext 10/2,33].
1829 *a) Nagel* Peter,   The present state of work in the edition of the Sahidic
  version of the Old Testament; – *b) Kasser* Rodolphe,   À propos des
  caractéristiques lexicales des dialectes coptes dans divers textes bibliques:
  ➤ 690, 3d Coptic 1984/90, 281s / 187-194.
1830 *Nagel* Peter,   Coptology and biblical text research (1980-1988): ➤ 694*b*,
  Copte IVe (1988/92) 2,237-244.
1831 **Schmitz** Franz-Jürgen, *Mink* G.,   Liste der koptischen Hss 1/2/2, 1991
  ➤ 7,1566;   DM 158   [I. 499 p.;   II. xii + p. 451-1279;   3-11-012255-3;
  -3015-7]:   RCC 143 (1992,3) 102s (M. *Erbetta*); Enchoria 19s (1992s)
  237-241 (K. *Schüssler*); NRT 114 (1992) 742 (X. *Jacques*); NT 34 (1992)
  400-2 (J. K. *Elliott*).

1832 **Mathews** Thomas F., *Sanjian* Avedis K.,   Armenian Gospel iconography; the tradition of the Glajor Gospel: DumbOStud. 29. Wsh 1991.
  xxii-246 p.; 16 color pl. 0-88402-183-1 [JbÖsByz 43,483, H. *Buschhausen*].
1833 **Renoux** Charles,   Le lectionnaire arménien de Jérusalem en Arménie I,
  1989 ➤ 6,1909:   RMuséon 105 (1992) 203-6 (B. *Coulie*).

1834 *Matschavariani* Elene,   Die Rolle des Schreibers in den illuminierten
  georgischen Handschriften des Mittelalters: JbÖsByz 42 (1992) 229-232;
  4 pl.

1835 **Shehadeh** Haseeb,   The Arabic translation of the Samaritan Pentateuch
  1, 1989 ➤ 5, 1771:   RSefarad 51 (1991) 471-3 (L. F. *Girón*); VT 42 (1992)
  277s (W. *Johnstone*).

1836 **Griepentrog** Wolfgang,   Synopse der gotischen Evangelientexte: MüSt-
  SprW Beih 14, 1988 ➤ 4,1764; 7,1570:   RBSLP 86,2 (1991) 175s (C. de
  Lamberterie).

D5   **Versiones latinae.**

1837 **Almar** Knud P.,   Inscriptiones latinae; eine illustrierte Einführung in die
  lateinische Epigraphik: ClasSt 14.   Odense 1990, Univ. 569 p. 87-
  7492-701-9.
1838 **Bischoff** Bernhard,   Latin palaeography, antiquity and the Middle Ages,
  TÓ Cróinin Dáibhí, *Ganz* David; 1990 ➤ 6,1915; 7,1572:   RPhoenix 46
  (1992) 297s (D. *Brearley*: noting printing-flaws which have been meanwhile corrected in a reissue).
1839 *Bogaert* P.-M., *Gryson* R.,   Centre de recherches sur la Bible latine
  [Louvain]; rapport d'activités 1991: RTLv 23 (1992) 283-8.

1840 Bulletin de la Bible latine 6/12: RBén 102 (1992) [309-340].
1841 **Cavallo** Guglielmo, Codex purpureus rossanensis: Guide illustrate 1. R 1992, Salerno ed. 91 p.; 16 color. pl. 88-8402-097-2.
1842 *Elliott* J. K., The translations of the New Testament into Latin; the Old Latin and the Vulgate: → 742, ANRW 2,26,1 (1992) 198-245.
1843 **Hälvä-Nyberg** Ulla, Die Kontraktionen auf den lateinischen Inschriften Roms und Afrikas: AnnAcFenn 49, 1988 → 4,a722.g839: ᴿWienerSt 105 (1992) 254-8 (Michaela *Zelzer*).
1844 ᴱ**Kötzsche** Dietrich, Das Evangeliar Heinrichs 1989 → 6,1929: ᴿHZ 253 (1991) 735-7 (J. *Fried*).
1845 ᴱ**Labriola** A., *Smeltz* J., Biblia pauperum 1990 → 6,1930; 7,1581: ᴿRExp 89 (1992) 117 (W. L. *Hendricks*: 1470 'comic book' of 120 panels, suited for today's biblical illiteracy).
1846 **McNamara** Martin, Studies on the text of early Irish Latin Gospels: InstrPatr 20,1990 → 6,1932: ᴿRHE 87 (1992) 260s (P.-M. *Bogaert*).
1847 **McNamara** M., The Echternach and MacDurnan gospels; some common readings and their significance: Peritia 6s (Galway 1987s) 217-222 [< RHE 88,372*].
1848 *McNamara* Martin, Non-Vulgate readings of Codex AMB I.61 sup.; 1. The Gospel of Matthew: SacrEr 33 (1992s) 183-257.
1849 *Popović* Vladislav, Du nouveau sur les Évangiles de Split: BrSocAntFr (1990) 275-293; 19 fig.
1850 *Rittmueller* Jean, Ms. Vat. Reg. Lat. 49 reviewed; a new description and a table of textual parallels with the Liber quaestionum in euangeliis: SacrEr 33 (1992s) 259-305.
1851 **Sevrugian** Petra, Der Rossano-Codex und die Sinope-Fragmente; Miniaturen und Theologie; Diss. Heidelberg, ᴰ*Brenk* B.: McKunstW 35. Worms 1990, Werner. 198 p.; 24 pl. – ᴿDielB 27 (1991) 300s (B. J. *Diebner*).

D5.5 *Citationes apud Patres* — **the Patristic Bible.**

1852 Biblia Patristica, index des citations et allusions bibliques dans la littérature patristique. 5. BASILE de Césarée, GRÉGOIRE de Nazianze, GRÉGOIRE de Nysse, AMPHILOQUE d'Iconium, 1991 → 7,1589; 3-222-04591-6 [Bijdragen 54,436s, M. *Parmentier*, Eng.: also on SIEBEN, Homilien 1991].
1853 *Fee* Gordon D., The use of Greek patristic citations in NT textual criticism; the state of the question: → 742, ANRW 2,26,1 (1992) 246-265.
1854 **Jarrett** Paul D., EUSEBIUS of Caesarea and the text of the Gospels: diss. SW Baptist Theol. Sem. 1992, ᴰ*Cranford* L. 266 p. 92-31661. — DissA 53 (1992s) 1960-A.
1855 **McLean** Bradley H., Citations and allusions to Jewish Scripture in early Christian and Jewish writings through 180 C.E. Lewiston NY 1992, Mellen. [vi-] 138 p. 0-7734-9430-8. [NTAbs 36, p. 414].
1856 **Sieben** H. J., Kirchenvaterhomilien Repertorium 1991 → 7,1598: ᴿOrChrPer 58 (1992) 627s (V. *Ruggieri*); ZkT 114 (1992) 223 (S. C. *Kessler*).

D6 **Versiones modernae** .1 *romanicae*, **romance.**

1857 ᴱ**Blum-Cuny** Pascale, Blaise de VIGENÈRE, Le Psautier de David torné en prose mesurée ou vers livres (1588), I. P 1991, Le Miroir Volant. 594 p. F 285. – ᴿEsprVie 102 (1992) 210 (L. *Monloubou* y trouve une

certaine herméneutique, mais n'indique pas quels psaumes sont compris dans ce 'vol. I').
1858 **Bogaert** P.-M., Les Bibles en français 1991 ➤ 7,1600: ᴿEsprVie 102 (1992) 12-14 (É. *Cothenet*); Foi Temps 22 (1992) 378-380 (C. *Focant*); RTLv 23 (1992) 489-492 (J. *Ponthot*).
1859 *Camus* Jean, La traduction de la Bible en français fundamental: RICAO 1s (1992) 79-81 [< TContext 10/1, p. 20].
1860 *a) Chédozeau* Bernard, Problèmes idéologiques de la traduction des textes sacrés en France aux XVIIᵉ et XVIIIᵉ siècles; – *b) Philonenko* Marc, La traduction des écrits intertestamentaires aujourd'hui: ➤ 462, Naissance 1990/2, 125-130 / 147-154.
1861 **Delforge** Frédéric, La Bible en France et dans la francophonie; histoire, traduction, diffusion 1991 ➤ 7,1602: ᴿÉTRel 67 (1992) 475 (H. *Bost*).
1862 **Jean-Nesmy** Claude, *Solms* Élisabeth de, Bible chrétienne; les quatre évangiles. P c.1980, Sigier/Desclée. – ᴿPeCa 244 (1990) 80-83 (Y. *Daoudal*).
1863 *Raurell* Frederic, La veritas hebraica del traductor André CHOURAQUI: EstFranc 93 (1992) 107-129.

1864 ᴱ**Guijarro** Santiago, La Biblia: La Casa de la Biblia. M 1992, Sígueme/PPC/VDivino/Atenas. 1934 p. pt. 2400. – ᴿHelmantica 43 (1992) 448-450 (S. *García-Jalón*).
1865 ᴱ**Guijano** Santiago, *Salvador* Miguel, La Biblia; traducción totalmente revisada con amplias notas e introducciones; aprobada por la Conferencia Episcopal Española. S 1992, Sígueme. xiii-1934 p.; maps. 84-7151-776-0. – ᴿActuBbg 29 (1992) 26s (J. *O'Callaghan*).
1866 ᴱ**Fernández Lago** J, *Torres Queiruga* A., A Biblia [en gallego]. Vigo 1989, SEPI. – ᴿCompostellanum 36 (1991) 233s (J. *Precedo Lafuente*).
1867 *Carrasquero Martínez* Otto, Las versiones castellanas de la Biblia: RBiArg 53 (1991) 35-95 (-118, otras lenguas romances).

1868 **Barbieri** Edoardo, Le Bibbie italiane del Quattrocento e del Cinquecento; storia e bibliografia ragionata delle edizioni in lingua italiana dal 1471 al 1600: Grandi Opere 4. Mi 1992, Bibliografica. 498 p.; vol. of pl. 885 fig. Lit. 400.000. 88-7075-257-7. – ᴿRHE 87 (1992) 816-821 (J.-F. *Gilmont*).
1869 Bibbia TOB [Traduction Œcuménique 1975, ²ʳᵉᵛ1987] edizione integrale [mantenendo la forma italiana approvata dalla Conferenza dei vescovi, ma notando ovunque diverge dalla TOB; l'ordine dei libri è quello della TOB]. T-Leumann 1992, LDC. 2491 p.; 16 maps [CC 144,195s, D. *Scaiola*].
1870 ᴱ**Ghirlanda** A., La Bibbia, nuovissima versione dai testi originali (4 vol.); Vangelo e Atti degli Apostoli. CinB 1992, Paoline. 605 p., maps.
1871 Parola del Signore; la Bibbia, traduzione interconfessionale in lingua corrente. T-Leumann / R 1986, L.D.C. / Alleanza bibl. univ. AT 1323 p.; NT 482 p. 15 maps. 88-01-14828-2.

D6.2   *Versiones anglicae* — **English Bible translations.**

1872 **Cassirer** Heinz W. († 1979), ᴱ*Weitzman* Ronald, God's new covenant, a NT translation 1989 ➤ 6,1811; 7,1609: ᴿHeythJ 33 (1992) 207s (L. *Swain*); RestQ 33 (1991) 53-55 (J. P. *Lewis*).

1873 *Collins* Michael F.,   Ronald KNOX — a forgotten legend: The Priest 48,6s (1992) 39-42 . (,7) 29-33.
1874 ᴱ**Daniell** David, [William] TYNDALE's Old Testament, being the Pentateuch of 1530, Joshua to 2 Chronicles of 1537, and Jonah; in modern spelling. L 1992, Yale Univ. xxxviii-643 p.; 2 pl. £25. – ᴿExpTim 104 (1992s) 308s (C. S. *Rodd*); RHE 87 (1992) 915s (D. *Bradley*).
1875 **Doane** A. N.,   The Saxon Genesis; an edition of the West Saxon Genesis B and the Old Saxon Vatican Genesis. Madison 1991, Univ. Wisconsin. 416 p. $45. 0-299-12800-8. – ᴿTBR 5,2 (1992s) 53 (Carolyne *Larrington*).
1876 *Dowd* Sharyn,   Helen B. MONTGOMERY's Centenary Translation of the NT (1924); characteristics and influences: PerspRelSt 19 (1992) 133-150.
1877 **Hargreaves** Cecil,   A translator's freedom; modern English Bibles and their language: BiblicalSem 22. Shf 1993, JStOT. 206 p. £12.50. 1-85075-400-4 [TBR 6/3, 17, H. *Finlay*].
1878 *Jacobs* E. C.,   King James's translators; the Bishops' Bible New Testament revised: The Library 6/14 (1992) 100-126: 8 facsim. [< RHE 87,191*].
1879 **Lawton** David,   Faith, text and history; the Bible in English [summarized]. Hemel Hempstead / Charlottesville 1990, Harvester / Univ. Virginia. x-203 p. £35. [LitTOx 7,307, J. *Barton*, compares with similar/better PRICKETT-BARNES]. – ᴿRelStR 18 (1992) 323 (L. J. *Greenspoon*).
1880 **Lewis** Jack P.,   The English Bible from KJV to NIV; a history and evaluation² [= ¹1981 + RNEB, NRSV] 1991 ⮞ 7,1618: ᴿBR 8,5 (1992) 15 (B. D. *Ehrman*).
1881 ᴱ**Lindberg** Conrad,   The Middle English Bible; 1. Prefatory epistles of St. Jerome; 2. The Book of Baruch; 3. The Book of Judges. Oslo 1978/85/89, Univ. 172 p.; 174 p.; 505 p. ⮞ 5,1814: ᴿSpeculum 67 (1992) 713-6 (Mona L. *Logarbo*).
1882 *Minkoff* Harvey,   *a*) How Bible translations differ: BAR-W 18,2 (1992) 66-68; 70s, table of study Bibles; – *b*) How to buy a Bible: BR 8,2 (1992) 40s; 42s. tabular chart of 26 Study Bibles in English.
1883 ᵀᴱ**Murphy** G. Ronald,   The Heliand, the Saxon Gospel. NY 1992, Oxford-UP. xviii-238 p, $38, pa. $15. 0-19-507375-4; -6-2 [TDig 40,272].
1884 **NIV:** *Martin* Robert P.,   Accuracy of translation and the NIV; the primary criterion in evaluating Bible versions. Carlisle 1989. Banner of Truth. vi-89 p. $7 pa. – ᴿConcordTJ 56 (1992) 316s (T. O. *Letis*: much-needed sensible evaluation, but weak in Appendix C); JEvTS 35 (1992) 231-5 (M. W. *Holmes*; best-selling Bible; also on RADMACHER-HODGES critique).
1885 **NRSV:** 1990 ⮞ 7,1622: ᴿBibTB 22 (1992) 34-37 (P. J. *Griffin*, J. T. *Walsh*).
1886 *Carson* D. A.,   A review of the New Revised Standard Version: RefTR 50 (1991) 1-11; many detail queries.
1887 *Metzger* Bruce M.,   The New Revised Standard Version: ⮞ 70, ᶠGREENLEE J., Scribes 1992, 111 [20 English words not previously used; 12 samples of unsexed language, none touching the Deity].
1888 *Stek* John H.,   The New Revised Standard Version; a preliminary assessment: CalvinT 26 (1991) 80-99.
1889 **Metzger** B. M., *Murphy* R. E.,   The new Oxford annotated Bible NRSV, with the Apocrypha 1991 ⮞ 7,1627: ᴿCBQ 54 (1992) 568s (Alice L. *Laffey* recommends, though cost is double Nelson's); Churchman 105 (1991) 360s (D. *Allister*: beautifully produced; 'it is just a pity about the contents').

1890 **RNEB:** Revised [New] English Bible, ᴱMcHardy W. D., 1989 ➤ 5,1820
...7,1630:   ᴿJNWS 18 (1992) 209-218 (W. *McKane*); JTS 43 (1992)
545-550 (J. *Barton* compares with NRSV: 'both are translations of a Bible
that does not actually exist'); LitTOx 5 (1991) 322-7 (S. *Prickett*: also on
Daniell's Tyndale and NJB 1985).
1891 — ᴱSuggs M. Jack, *al.*, The Oxford Study Bible; Revised English
Bible with the Apocrypha. NY 1992, Oxford-UP. xxviii-192* [19
general articles] – 1597 p.; 14 maps. $38.   0-19-529001-1 [TDig 39,150].
1891* — *Bratcher* Robert G., The Revised English Bible [...considerably
more conservative than idiosyncratic NEB]: BTrans 43 (1992) 342-8.
1892 **Rashkow** Ilona N., Upon the dark places; anti-Semitism and sexism in
English renaissance Bible translation. Shf 1991, Almond. 180 p. $50. –
ᴿBR 8 (1992) 13.50 (Jane *Schaberg*).
1893 **Robertson** Edwin, Makers of the English Bible. C 1990, Lutterworth.
322 p. – ᴿEvQ 64 (1992) 189s (P. *Ellingworth*).
1894 **Throckmorton** Burton H.ᴶ, The Gospels and the letters of Paul; an
inclusive-language edition. Cleveland 1992, Pilgrim. $16. [HorBT 15,98s,
J. A. *Walther*: unfavoring].
1895 **Wauck** M. A., The Alba House Gospels; so you may believe. NY 1992,
Alba. xvii-282 p. $13 pa. 0-8189-0625-1 [NTAbs 37,123].

D6.3   *Versiones germanicae* – **Deutsche Bibelübersetzungen.**

1896 ᵀᴱ*Bonola* Gianfranco, Quale lingua per la Parola? S. Kʀᴀᴄᴀᴜᴇʀ,
[critica di] M. Bᴜʙᴇʀ e F. Rᴏꜱᴇɴᴢᴡᴇɪɢ [Die Schrift, das Buch im
Anfang 1925] sulla Bibbia in tedesco: ➤ 481, AnStoEseg 9 (1992)
203-236; Eng. 5.
1897 **Deissler** Alfons, *al.* [ᵀChütz Ulrich), Neue Jerusalemer Bibel; Ein-
heitsübersetzung mit dem Kommentar der Jerusalemer Bibel. FrB 1985,
Herder. xviii-1878 p. – ᴿTAth 63 (1992) 183-5 (P. *Simotas*, Ⓖ).
1898 *a*) Ebbinghaus Ernst A., Ulfila(s) [no] or Wulfila? – *b*) *Schlerath*
Bernfield, Lateinisch *latro* und *fur* in den germanischen Bibelübersetzungen: HistSprF 104 (1991) 236-8 / 224-235.
1899 **Himmighofer** Traudel, Die Zürcher Bibel bis zum Tode Zᴡɪɴɢʟɪꜱ
(1551); ev. Diss. ᴰ*Benrath* G. Mainz 1992. – RTLv 24, p. 555.
1900 *Hövelmann* Hartmut, Lᴜᴛʜᴇʀꜱ Bibelkonzept und unsere Lutherbibel:
LuthTK 15 (1991) 138-155.
1901 *Riedlinger* Rudolf, Welchen Grundtext übersetzte Martin Luther für
seine Deutsche Bibel? [kaum griechisch, noch weniger hebräisch): Jb-
ÖsByz 42 (1992) 325-330.
1902 ᵀ**Stier** F., Das NT, ᴱ*Reeb* E., *al.*, 1989 ➤ 6,1988; 7,1642:   ᴿGeistL 64
(1991) 396s (F. J. *Steinmetz*).
1903 *Stutz* E., Die noch ungelösten Rätsel des Speyerer Wulfila-Fragments:
Bibliothek und Wissenschaft 25 (Wsb 1991) 1-14 [< RHE 87,357*].
1905 *Zink* Jörg, Die Bibel-Übersetzungen von Walter Jᴇɴꜱ [Mt 1972, Mk
1990, Lk 1991, Jn 1988 Stu, Radius]: EvKomm 25 (1992) 295-7.

D6.4   **Versiones nordicae** *et variae.*

1905* ᴱ**Jaakke** A. W. G., *Tuinstra* E. W., Om een verstaanbare bijbel; Nederlandse bijbelvertalingen na de Statenbijbel. Haarlem/Bru 1990, Bijbelgenootschap. 403 p. *f* 59,50. 90-6126-914-8. – ᴿNcdTTs 46 (1992) 228
(A. van der *Kooij*).

1906 [**Weren** W. J. C. coordinator] Het Nieuwe Testament; Willibrordvertaling, Herziene uitgave. Den Bosch/Lv 1992, KBStichting/VlaamseBS. xiv-428 p. ƒ42,50. – ᴿBijdragen 54 (1993) 407-428; Eng. 429 (J. *Lambrecht*; title 'Willibrord Herzien' = 'revised'; in text sometimes 'de herziene Willibrord', i.e. Ep-Rev from 1975 Willibrord; but Gospels-Acts is revision of a new 1987 translation).

1907 *Goulder* Michael, Translation and exegesis; some reflections on the Swedish NT translations of 1917 and 1981: SvEx 57 (1992) 102-114.

1908 ᴱ**Hansson** Gunnar, Bible reading in Sweden; studies related to the translation of the New Testament 1981: AcU PsSocRel 2. U 1990, Almqvist & W. 171 p. – ᴿSalesianum 54 (1992) 539-543 (C. *Buzzetti*: 'l'uso effettivo della Bibbia; un esempio di indagini e riflessioni').

1909 Nowy Testament; nowy przekład na współczesny język polski. Wsz 1991, Brytyjskie i Zagraniczne Towarzystwo Biblijne. – ᴿRuBi 45 (1992) 45s (J. *Chmiel*: ekwiwalencja dynamiczna; no names mentioned).

1910 **Matual** D., Toʟsᴛoʏ's [union and] translation of the Gospels; a critical study. Lewiston NY 1992, Mellen. x-202 p. $70. 0-7734-9502-9 [NTAbs 37,118].

1911 *Wächter* Otto, Das Miroslav Evangeliar, oder die beste aller Restaurierungsmöglichkeiten: Biblos 40 (1991) 201-4; 1 fig.

1912 **Sant** Carmel, Bible translation and language; essays into the history of Bible translation in Maltese: MelT supp 2. Zabbar, Malta 1992, Veritas. xii-343 p.

D7   *Problemata vertentis* – **Bible translation techniques.**

1913 ᴱ**Beer** Jeannette, Medieval translators and their craft 1989 ➤ 7,1651*: ᴿSpeculum 67 (1992) 106-8 (P. *Cherchi*).

1914 ᴱ**Contamine** Geneviève, Traduction et traducteurs au Moyen Âge 1986/9 ➤ 6,727*a; 7,1656: ᴿBtHumRen 54 (1992) 578-580 (S. *Bamforth*); RÉJ 151 (1992) 401s (E. *Nicolas*); Speculum 67 (1992) 1062 (tit. pp.).

1915 **Copeland** Rita, Rhetoric, hermeneutics and translation in the Middle Ages; academic traditions and vernacular texts: StMedvLit 2. C 1991, Univ. xiv-295 p. £35. – ᴿLitTOx 6 (1992) 293s (G. R. *Evans*); Manuscripta 36 (1992) 56s (J. J. *Murphy*).

1916 ᴱ**Gibaud** H., Problèmes / traduction 1986/8 ➤ 4,486: ᴿÉglT 23 (1992) 273s (L. *Laberge*).

1917 **Greenstein** E. L., Essays on biblical method and translation 1989 ➤ 5,269 ... 7,1658: ᴿJQR 83 (1991) 264-7 (H. P. *Scanlin*).

1918 *Lejogne* Jean-Claude, To what extent can a version of the Bible be ideologically marked? (on the basis of a comparison of 4 versions in 3 languages): ➤ 450, Informatique 2, 1988/9, 343-373.

1919 **Leupin** Alexandre, Barbarolexis; medieval writing and sexuality, ᵀ*Cooper* Kate M. CM 1989, Harvard Univ. 261 p. £28. – ᴿHeythJ 33 (1992) 117s (G. R. *Dunstan*: a translation which does not implement the claim that translation is a correctional operation).

1920 ᴱ**Louw** Johannes P., Meaningful translation; its implications for the reader. NY 1991, United Bible Societies. 111 p. – ᴿRBiArg 54,45 (1992) 54-56 (A. J. *Levoratti*).

1921 **Niranjana** Tejaswini, Siting translation; history, post-structuralism, and the colonial context. Berkeley 1992, Univ. California. xi-203 p. $35; pa. $13 [RelStR 19,328, J. E. *Cort*].

1922 **Olofsson** Staffan, Guds ord och människors språk; en bok om bibelöversättning. Uppsala 1986, EFS. 199 p. 91-7080-721-3. – ᴿSvEx 57 (1992) 141-3 (Kerstin *Bergman*).

1923 *Olofsson* Staffan, Consistency as a translation technique: ScandJOT 6,2 (1992) 14-30.

1924 ᴱ**Pieterman** K. G., Elementen van bijbelvertalen [seminar]. Haarlem 1992, Ned. Bijbelgenootschap. 142 p. 90-6126-724-2 [TvT 33,289, W. *Weren*].

1925 *Rosenhouse* Judith, *Cohen* Ariel M., The passive in Arabic, Hebrew and English and machine translation: LitLComp 5,1 (1990) 9-18.

1925* *a*) *Salevsky* Heidemarie, Theory of Bible translation and general theory of translation; – *b*) *Corro* Anicia del, The use of figurative language: BTrans 42 (1991 in ➤ 7,1666 as a special issue 2A) 101-114 / 114-127.

1926 *Schneider* B., ❶ The order and number of books of the Bible especially in modern printed editions: *Seisho Honyaku Kenkyū* (The study of Bible translating) 25 (1991) 27-59 [< OTAbs 15,16].

1927 *Shiffman* Yair, ❸ Shem Tov FALAQUERA's method of translation: Lešonenu 56 (1991s) 223-240; Eng. III.

1928 **Steiner** George, After Babel; aspects of language and translation[2] [¹1975]. Ox 1992, UP. xxii-538 p. 0-19-212300-9; pa. -82874-6.

1929 **Stine** Philip C., Bible translation and the spread of the Church, the last 200 years: Studies in Christian Mission 2, 1990 ➤ 6,556; *f* 75: ᴿInterpretation 46 (1992) 434s (H. M. *Goodpasture*); IntRMiss 81 (1992) 131s (D. *O'Connor*); NRT 114 (1992) 589s (J. *Masson*); Salesianum 54 (1992) 374s (C. *Buzzetti*).

Stine P. C., *Wendland* E. R., Bridging the gap; African traditional religion and Bible translation 1990 ➤ 8900.

1929* Student exam boners: BTrans 43 (1922) 247 [... Jesus rowed into Jerusalem on a donkey; the tenth leopard when he saw he had lost his spots went back to say thank you ...].

1930 *Thomas* R. L., Dynamic equivalence; a method of translation or a system of hermeneutics?: Master'sSemJ 1 (1990) 149-175 [< NTAbs 38, p. 12].

1930* *Verhoeven* Cornelis, De onmogelijkheid van het vertalen: Streven 59 (1992s) 701-710.

1931 *Willi-Plein* Ina, Heilige Schrift oder Heilige Übersetzung — zur theologischen Relevanz hebraistischer Forschung und Lehre: BibNot 60 (1991) 48-58.

Young Frances, The art of performance; towards a [pre-translation] theology of Holy Scripture 1990 ➤ 7105*.

D8 *Concordantiae, lexica specialia* – **Specialized dictionaries, synopses.**

1933 *Bajard* Jean, *Poswick* R.-Ferdinand, Une concordance analytique de la Traduction Oecuménique de la Bible française (T.O.B.); réflexions méthodologiques: ➤ 450*, Informatique 3ᵉ 1991/2, 263-282.

1934 *a*) **Goodrick** E. W., *Kohlenberger* J. R., The NIV exhaustive concordance. GR 1990, Zondervan. xxii-1853 p., $50. 0-310-43690-7. – *b*) **Kohlenberger** J. R., The NRSV concordance unabridged 1991 ➤ 7,1578: ᴿBL (1992) 14s (A. G. *Auld*).

1935 **Rinaldi** Giancarlo, Biblia Gentium 1989 ➤ 5,1872... 7,1680: ᴿJEH 43 (1992) 333 (W. H. C. *Frend*: documents also in English, but English scholarship not adequately represented); RHPR 72 (1992) 326s (D. A. *Bertrand*); VetChr 29 (1992) 215-220 (S. *Leanza*).

1936 Nelson's Concordance of Bible phrases [= ²Phrase Concordance of the Bible 1986]. Nv 1992, Nelson. vii-741. $20. 0-8407-4262-2 [NTAbs 37, p. 269: 48 items 'word of God' spares seeking 900 'word' + 4500 'God'].

1937 Quick Verse Bible concordance [IBM-based computer program]. Hiawatha ɪᴀ 1990, Parsons. $35. – ᴿCurrTMiss 19 (1992) 55 (R. W. *Klein* praises and explains its merits).

1938 *Talstra* Epp, The production of a syntactically orientated concordance of biblical Hebrew texts: ➤ 450, Informatique 2, 1988/9, 563-580.

| IV. ➤ K1 | V. Exegesis generalis VT vel cum NT |

D9 **Commentaries on the whole Bible or OT.**

1939 ᴱ**Bergant** Dianne (OT), *Karris* Robert J. (NT), The Collegeville Bible Commentary based on the NAB ➤ 5,1876 ... 7,1881a; now in 2 vol. ColMn 1992, Liturgical. OT xvi-858 p.; $20. 0-8146-2210-0; -1-0. – ᴿChrCent 107 (1990) 158.160 (Allene S. *Phy-Olsen*).

1940 ᴱ**Carpenter** Eugene E., [NT ᴱ*McCown* Wayne], Asbury Bible Commentary. GR 1992, Zondervan. 1246 p. $38. 0-310-39460-9 [BL 93,56, J. *Goldingay*].

1940* ᴱ**Elwell** Walter A., Evangelical commentary of the Bible 1989 ➤ 6, 2032: ᴿSTEv 4 (1992) 64 (G. *Emetti*).

1941 **Federici** T., Per conoscere lui 1989 ➤ 3,216 ... 7,1682: ᴿRivPastLtg 28,3 (1990) 82-84 (E. *Lodi*).

1942 ᴱ**Gaebelein** F. E., Expositor's Bible Commentary, NIV [5, 1991 ➤ 7, 1683] 3. Deuteronomy–2 Samuel. GR 1992, Zondervan. xvi-1104 p. $38, 0-310-36450-7. ➤ Dt, *Kalland* E. S.; Jos, *Madvig* D. H.; Jg, *Wolf* H.; Ruth, *Huey* F. B.; 1-2 Samuel, *Youngblood* R. F. – ᴷBtS 149 (1992) 115s (T. C. *Constable*, 2).

1943 ᴱ**Guthrie** Donald, *Motyer* J. Alec, Kommentar zur Bibel; AT und NT in einem Band [1970], ᵀ*Baldero* G. Wu 1992, Brockhaus. xvi-996 + 630 p.; 4 maps. 3-417-24615-6.

1944 ᴱ**Mays** John L., Harper's Bible commentary 1988 ➤ 4,1895 ... 7,1685: ᴿConcordTQ 56 (1992) 315s (C. A. *Gieschen*: valuable chiefly in showing how texts are currently being interpreted — fortunately mostly in the 'final form').

1945 ᴱ**Newsom** Carol A., *Ringe* Sharon H., The women's Bible commentary. L/Louisville 1992, SPCK/W-Knox. xix-396 p. $20. 0-281-04581-X / 0-664-21922-5. – ᴿExpTim 104 (1992s) 216s (C. S. *Rodd*: not a section-by-section 'commentary'; important); FirsT 28 (1992) 56-59 (Charlotte *Allen*).

1946 **NJBC**: New Jerome Biblical Commentary, ᴱ**Brown** R. E., *al.*, 1989 ➤ 5,384 ... 7,1686: ᴿETL 68 (1990) 426-8 (F. *Neirynck*, apparently the only non-Anglophone contributor).

1947 — The New Jerome Bible handbook [outlines and abridgments of introductory materials from NJBC]. L 1992, Chapman. vii-456 p.; ill.; maps. 0-225-66642-1.

1948 **Owens** John J., Analytical key to the OT [1. Gen-Jos 1990 ➤ 6,2038; 3. Ezra – Song of Solomon 1991 ➤ 7,1688] 2. – ᴱRExp 89 (1992) 101s (A. J. *Glaze*, 1) & 411s (R. L. *Cate*, 3).
1949 ᴱ**Senior** Donald, The Catholic Study Bible-NAB ➤ 6,2039; 7,1620: NY 1990, Oxford-UP. xiii-577-1174-477 p. £18. – ᴿCanadCathR 10,7 (1992) 28s (J. S. *Kloppenborg*); ETL 68 (1990) 426s (F. *Neirynck*: tit. pp. of a dozen special articles; Senior and co-editor Gᴇᴛᴛʏ are Louvain-trained); HeythJ 33 (1992) 441s (L. *Swain*); HomP 91,9 (1990s) 77s (W. G. *Most*).
1950 Stuttgarter Erklärungsbibel; die Heilige Schrift nach der Übersetzung M. Lᴜᴛʜᴇʀs mit Einführungen und Erklärungen. Stu 1992, Deutsche Bib. Ges. 1626 + 118 p. DM 110; pa. 78. 3-438-01111-5. – ᴿEvKomm 25 (1992) 530-3 (H. *Wilckens*); LuthTK 16 (1992) 148 (S. *Förster*).

VI. Libri historici VT

E1   **Pentateuchus, Torah** . *Textus, commentarii.*

1951 **Astås** R., An Old Norse biblical compilation; studies in Stjörn [= Gen 1 - Ex 18, under Dominican influence; with a prologue and three pious insertions]: AmerUnivSt 7/109. Fra 1991, Lang. x-251 p. £22. 0-9204-1585-4 [BL 93,47, G. W. *Anderson*: from the author's larger work in Norwegian].
1952 **Blenkinsopp** Joseph, The Pentateuch; an introduction to the first five books of the Bible: AnchorBRef. L/NY 1992, SCM/Doubleday. 273 p. £17.50. 0-334-02253-3. – ᴿExpTim 104 (1992s) 277 (R. N. *Whybray*: not theological, perhaps unduly); TBR 5,3 (1992s) 20 (Katrina *Larkin*).
1952* *Chiesa* Bruno, *Lockwood* Wilfrid, Al-Qɪʀǫɪsᴀ̄ɴɪ's newly-found commentary on the Pentateuch; the [Fɪʀᴋᴏᴠɪč] commentary on Gen 12: Henoch 14 (1992) 153-177; facsim. 178s; ital. 180.
1953 *Friedman* Richard E., Torah (Pentateuch): ➤ 741, AnchorBD 6 (1992) 604-622.
1954 **Hanegraaff** J., Met de Torah is het begonnen, III. Rondom de mondelinge traditie. Nijkerk 1990, Callenbach. 370 p. *f* 54.50. 0-266-0219-7 [sic in]: ᴿBijdragen 53 (1992) 426 (E. *Eynikel*).
1955 *a*) *Briend* Jacques, Lecture du Pentateuque et hypothèse documentaire; – *b*) *Margain* Jean, Le Pentateuque samaritain; – *c*) *Beauchamp* Paul, Le Pentateuque et la lecture typologique: ➤ 474, ACFÉB 14, 1991/2, 9-32 / 231-240 / 241-259.
1956 **Goulet** Richard, La philosophie de Moïse 1987 ➤ 3,1849 ... 6,2044: ᴿIstina 37 (1992) 323s (B. *Dupuy*); RHPR 72 (1992) 213s (D. A. *Bertrand*).
1957 **Kraus Reggiani** C., *al.*, Filone, La filosofia mosaica 1987 ➤ 5,1893 ... 7,1693: ᴿRÉJ 150 (1991) 186 (Mireille *Hadas-Lebel*); RevSR 66 (1992) 365s (M. *Canevet*); VT 42 (1992) 135s (W. *Horbury*).
1958 **McEvenue** Sean, Interpreting the Pentateuch 1990 ➤ 6,2067: ᴿBL (1992) 78 (J. W. *Rogerson*: tries to show how the authors challenged their world).
1959 Nᴀʜᴍᴀɴɪᴅᴇs, Commentary on the Pentateuch, with vocalization. J 1992, A. Blum. I. Gn. 222 p. II. Ex. 202 p. III. Lev 143 p.; Num to p. 209; Dt. to p. 251.

1960 *Römer* Thomas,   L'école de Heidelberg a 15 ans; à propos de deux ouvrages sur une nouvelle approche de la formation du Pentateuque [RENDTORFF R., 1990 'expose de manière impitoyable et avec beaucoup d'ironie les incohérences et faiblesses' de JEPD; BLUM E. 1990, son élève]: ÉTRel 67 (1992) 77-81.
1961 *Sailhamer* John H. [→ 1996],   The Mosaic law and the theology of the Pentateuch: WestTJ 53 (1991) 241-261.
1962 *Seebass* Horst,   Vor einer neuen Pentateuchkritik? [ᴱPury A. de 1989, *al.*]. TR 88 (1992) 177-186.
1963 ᵀᴱ**Vredenburg** J.,   De Thora. Amst 1991, Nederlands-Israëlitisch Kerkgenotschap. ƒ145. 90-71727-17-3 [Bijdragen 54,202s, J. van *Ruiten*].

A1   *Pentateuchus*   .2   **Introductio; Fontes JEDP.**

1964 *Abela* Anthony,   Umberto CASSUTO's The documentary hypothesis; thirty years later: MeliT 43,1 (1992) 61-68.
1964* a) *Beauchamp* Paul,   La lecture typologique et le Pentateuque; – b) *Chauvet* Louise-Marie, La singularité du rapport chrétien à la Bible: MaisD 190 (1992) 51-73 / 142-154.
1965 **Berge** Kåre,   Die Zeit des Jahwisten... Vätertexte: BZAW 186, ᴰ1990 → 6,2048; 7,1697: ᴿBZ 36 (1992) 316s (P. *Mommer*); CBQ 54 (1992) 102s (R. B. *Coote*: 950 B.C., somewhat overrelying on 'Israel's nomadic past'), ÉTRel 67 (1992) 589s (T. *Römer*); NedTTs 46 (1992) 157s (B. *Becking*); Syria 69 (1992) 479s (A. *Caquot*); TR 88 (1992) 21-23 (C. *Dohmen*).
1966 (ᵀ*Rosenberg* David),   The book of J interpreted by **Bloom** Harold 1990 → 6,2055; 7,1698: ᴿBR 7,1 (1991) 8s (D. *Halpern*); JSS 37 (1992) 308s (L. I. *Yudkin*); LitTOx 6 (1992) 86-89 (W. L. *Reed*); Parabola 16,1 (NY 1991) 114, 116-8 (Judith *Hauptman*); UnSemQ 45 (1991) 138-142 (E. M. *Good*: on 'Bloom's book': praise for his readiness to be disastrously wrong).
1967 (ᵀ*Rosenberg* David),   **Bloom** Harold,   Het boek van J.   Amst 1992, Waterland. 327 p. ƒ44,50. – ᴿStreven 59 (1992s) 1140s (P. *Beentjes*: 'de Bijbel geschreven door een vrouw?').
Blum Erhard, Studien zur Komposition des Pentateuch: BZAW 168, 1990: in accord with its title, this work has been widely acclaimed as a new global theory of Pentateuch authorship; but we continue to class it with the passages which it claims to focus, Ex 1-14 → 2487.
1967* *Briend* Jacques,   La composition du Pentateuque entre hier et aujourd'hui: → 462, Naissance 1990/2, 197-204.
1968 **Campbell** Antony F., *O'Brien* Mark A., Sources of the Pentateuch; texts, introductions, annotations. Mp 1992, Fortress. xix-266 p.
1968* a) *Clines* David J. A.,   Images of Yahweh; God in the Pentateuch; – b) *Bush* Frederic W.,   Images of Israel; the people of God in the Torah; – c) *Kaiser* Walter C.,   Images for today; the Torah speaks today: → 88, ᶠHUBBARD D., OT 1992, 79-98 / 99-115 / 117-132.
1969 **Coote** Robert B., *Ord* David R., The Bible's first history [J, under David] 1989 → 7,1700: ᴿCBQ 54 (1992) 108-110 (W. L. *Humphreys*: somewhat Marxist along with other recently-queried assumptions); JAOS 112 (1992) 316-9 (J. *Van Seters*: written for believers, not for scholarly dialogue).
1969* *Friedman* Richard E.,   Is everybody a Bible expert? Not [BLOOM H., ROSENBERG D.] the authors of The book of J ['the text that they are calling J is not J, and the words of that text are not the words of the Bible']: BR 7,2 (1991) 16-18.50s.

1970 *Geller* Stephen A., Blood cult; toward a literary theology of the priestly work of the Pentateuch: Prooftexts 12 (1992) 97-124.

1971 **Krapf** Thomas M., Die Priesterschrift und die vorexilische Zeit [KAUF-MANN Y.: P vor D und von J & E unabhängig; diss. Berlin, ᴰ*Welten* P.]: OBO 119. FrS/Gö 1992, Univ./VR. xx-364 p. Fs 96. 3-7278-0815-2 / VR 3-525-53753-0 [BL 94,109, J. W. *Rogerson*]. – ᴿTüTQ 172 (1992) 327s (W. *Gross*).

1972 *a)* *Milgrom* Jacob, Priestly ('P') source: ➤ 741, AnchorBD 5 (1992) 454-461 (-486, Primeval History, *Kikawada* Isaac M.).

— *b)* *Nicholson* E. W., Pentateuch (-forschung), ᵀ*Voorgang* D.: ➤ 757, EvKL 3 (1992) 1115-20.

— *c)* **Pola** Thomas, Der Umfang der ursprünglichen Priesterschrift; Beobachtungen zur Literarkritik und Traditionsgeschichte von Pg: ev. Inaug. – Diss. Tübingen 1992. 428 p. – RTLv 24, p. 543; TLZ 118,560s.

1973 ᴱ**Pury** Albert de, Le Pentateuque en question 1986/9 ➤ 5,601 ... 7,1703: ᴿAugM 37 (1992) 198s (P. *Orosio*); BZ 36 (1992) 129-131 (H. *Engel*); ÉglT 22 (1991) 209-211 (L. *Laberge*); Protestantesimo 47 (1992) 146-8 (J. *Hobbins*); ScripB 22,1 (1992) 18s (L. *Swain*); VSp 146 (1992) 242-4 (J. *Asurmendi*); VT 42 (1992) 131s (H. G. M. *Williamson*).

1974 *Pury* Albert de, Yahwist ('J') source: ➤ 741, AnchorBD 6 (1992) 1012-1020.

1975 **Rendtorff** Rolf, The problem of the process of transmission: jOsu 89, 1990 ➤ 6,2070: ᴿInterpretation 46 (1992) 308.310 (G. A. *King*); JTS 43 (1992) 142-5 (R. J. *Coggins* begins with a rundown on Rendtorff's 1977 preliminary, from which his view that Pentateuch exegesis can only begin from the final form of the text is a significant advance; SCULLION's translation slightly less 'golden' than his WESTERMANN Gn); VT 42 (1992) 137 (J. A. *Emerton*).

1976 *Seitz* Christopher R., WELLHAUSEN goes to Yale [cover: Looking for the Jahwist, Harold BLOOM's 'book of J']: ChrCent 108 (1991) 111-4: 'drained of any religious sentiment'.

1976* **Silva** Jorge Luis da, The implications of the Arad Temple for the question of dating P: MA diss. Andrews, ᴰ*Storffell* J. Berrien Springs MI 1992. vi-156 p. AA 13-48183. – OIAc 5,18.

1977 **Van Seters** John, Prologue to history; the Yahwist as historian in Genesis, Z/Louisville 1992, Theol.-V./W-Knox. xviii-354 p. DM 75 pa. [TR 88,514]. 0-664-21967-5. – ᴿExpTim 104 (1992s) 277s (R. *Coggins*: post-Deuteronomistic).

E1.3   *Pentateuchus,* themata.

1978 *Ben Zvi* Ehud, The closing words of the Pentateuchal books; a clue for the historical status of the book of Genesis within the Pentateuch: Bib-Not 62 (1992) 7-10.

1978* **Biondi** Albano, L'esegesi biblica di frate Marin MERSENNE [Quaestiones celeberrimae in Genesim 1623]: ➤ 481, AnStoEseg 9 (1992) 35-52; Eng. 3.

1979 ᴱ**Brekelmans** C., *Lust* J., Pentateuchal and Deuteronomistic studies, IOSOT XIII Leuven 1989/90 ➤ 6,518: ᴿJSS 37 (1992) 95s (T. *Collins*: only 15 of the 52 short papers of the first two days, and 7 of the 38 on the 3d; the 23 major papers are to appear in the normal VTS); RivB 40 (1992) 112-4 (A. *Bonora*); RB 99 (1992) 448 (tit. pp.); RTLv 23 (1992) 379s (P.-M. *Bogaert*); ZAW 104 (1992) 305 (tit. pp.).

1980 *Croatto* J. Severino, ¿Como releer la Biblia desde su contexto socio-político? Ejercicio sobre algunos temas del Pentateuco: RBiArg 53 (1991) 193-212.
Crüsemann Frank,   Tora 1992 ➤ 229.
1981 *Fanuli* Antonio, A guerra do Pentateuco [WHYBRAY R. N. 1987 < RivB 37 (1989) 469-485],[T]: RBBras 8 (1991) 21-46 [104-160.195-240; -289-308, outras recensões, todas de C. *Minette de Tillesse*].
1981* **Feldstern** Bruce A., ⊕ Shet Harofel BEN YEFET's 'Hemat hahemda' to Genesis; critical edition with commentary and introduction: diss. Jewish Theol. Sem., [D]*Dimitrovsky* H., 1992. 407 p. 92-34483. – DissA 53 (1992s) 2855s-A.
1982 *a*) *García López* Félix,   Dalla Torah al Pentateuco; – *b*) *Cardellini* Innocenzo,   Dalla Legge alla Torah; – *c*) *Garbini* Giovanni,   Torah e Mosè; – *d*) *Prato* Gian Luigi,   L'esclusivismo jahwista alle origini storico-religiose della Torah; – *e*) *Vivian* Angelo,   Il concetto di Legge nel 'Rotolo del Tempio': ➤ 458*b*, Pentateuco 1989/91, RicStoB 3 (1991) 11-26 / 57-81 / 83-96 / 41-55 / 97-114.
1983 **Gorman** Frank H.[J],   The ideology of ritual... P [D]1990 ➤ 6,2059; 7,1709: [R]CBQ 54 (1992) 526s (B. E. *Shafer*: most welcome, despite bad editing); CritRR 5 (1992) 137s (G. A. *Anderson*: refreshing, not always critical).
1984 **Grünwaldt** Klaus,   Exil und Identität; Beschneidung, Passa und Sabbat in der Priesterschrift [ev. Diss. Bonn, [D]*Seebass* H.]: BoBB 85. Fra 1992, Hain. x-254 p. DM 88.   3-445-09148-X [ZAW 105,527, M. *Köckert*].
1985 **Halpern** Baruch, The first historians; the Hebrew Bible and theology 1988 ➤ 4,d139... 7,1711: [R]BR 7,6 (1991) 8s (M. D. *Coogan*); RelStT 11,1 (1991) 58s (H. W. *Basser*).
1986 [E]**Havazzelet** M.,   Zechariah BEN SOLOMON-RAFE,   Midrash ha-Ḥefeẓ, On the Pentateuch I. J 1990, Kook. 403 p.
1987 **Ide** A. F.,   Moses, making of myth and law; the influence of Egyptian sex, religion and law on the writing of the Torah. Las Colinas TX 1992, Monument. vi-393 p. $25 pa.   0-930383-273 [NTAbs 37, p. 305].
1988 **Jenson** Philip P.,   Graded holiness; a key to the Priestly conception of the world: jOsu 106. Shf 1992, Academic. 281 p. £35; pa. £26.25.   1-85075-360-1 [TR 89,99-101, H. *Reventlow*].
1989 **Lacocque** André,   Subversives, ou Un Pentateuque de femmes [The feminine unconventional 1990 ➤ 1493], [T]*Veugelen* Claude: LDiv 148.   P 1992, Cerf. 191 p. F 135 [CBQ 55,210]. 2-204-04481-4.
1990 **Mann** Thomas W.,   The book of the Torah; the narrative integrity of the Pentateuch 1988 ➤ 4,1928... 7,1714: [R]ConcordTQ 56 (1992) 45-47 (D. O. *Wenthe*: readable, rich).
1992 *Minette de Tillesse* Caetano, *a*) Teología da Biblia; o que será?: RBBras 8 (1991) 81-95; *b*) O colofão do Javista? 95-104; – *c*) Tradição de Cadés, 179-190; – *d*) ... do Sinai, 190-3 [-4 Qadesh?]; *e*) Matrimonio e Aliança, 255-264; – *f*) O sexo na Biblia, 264-8; – *g*) O nascimento de 'Escritura', 268-273.
Moberly Walter (R. W. L.),   The OT of the OT; patriarchal narratives and Mosaic Yahwism: OvBT 26, 1992 ➤ 7017.
1993 *Müller* Augustin R.,   Ein Missbrauch des Wortes Transkription: BibNot 63 (1992) 42s [STEURER R. 1989 ➤ 7,1641].
1995 *Rodd* C. S.,   [Torah] Your teacher: ExpTim 104 (1992s) 114-6.
1996 **Sailhamer** John H. [➤ 1961],   The Pentateuch as narrative; a biblical-theological commentary: Library of Biblical Interpretation.   GR

1992, Zondervan. xxii-522 p. $40 [BL 93,68, R. P. *Gordon*: Moses wrote all; the 613 Maimonidean prescriptions are given in appendix].
1998 **Schmidt** Ludwig,   Väterverheissungen und Pentateuchfrage [BLUM E. 1984; KÖCKERT M. 1988]: ZAW 104 (1992) 1-27.
1999 **Visotzky** Burton L., [➤ 7,9974*] Reading the book; making the Bible a timeless text. NY 1991, Doubleday. 240 p. $12. – ᴿTS 53 (1992) 586 (A. J. *Saldarini*: racy midrashic approach to some pentateuchal narratives).

E1.4   **Genesis; textus, commentarii.**

2000 **Belkin** Samuel *zal.*, ᴱ*Hurvitz* Elazar, ❺ The Midrash of Philo — the oldest recorded midrash, written in Alexandria by PHILO (c. 20 B.C.E.-45 C.E.) before the formulation of Tannaitic literature, I. Genesis II-XVII [Questions and Answers etc. from Armenian and Greek] 1989 ➤ 6,2075: ᴿJStJud 23 (1992) 100-5 (Naomi G. *Cohen*).
2001 *Ben-David* Israel, ❺ [anon. Gn 1 - Ex 29,43] A Karaite scholar's inquiries on biblical grammar and accentuation: Lešonenu 56 (1991s) 119-136; Eng. ii.
2002 ᵀᴱ**Davis** Avrohom,   Genesis, linear, with RASHI commentary ᵀ*Kleinkaufman* Avrohom.   Hoboken 1991, KTAV.   ix-575 p. $25.50.   0-88125-389-8 [JStOT 59,128, J. F. *Elwolde*: attractive and usable, but with defectively-proofread pointing].
2003 **Delius** Hans-Ulrich,   Die Quellen von M. LUTHERs Genesisvorlesung: BeitEvT 111.   Mü 1992, Kaiser.   96 p. DM 70 [TR 88,431].
2004 **Hamilton** Victor,   Gn 1-17, NICOT 1990 ➤ 6,2082; 7,1725:   ᴿAndrUnS 30 (1992) 86-88 (D. *Merling*); BL (1992) 52 (J. C. L. *Gibson*); CalvaryB 7,1 (1991) 61 (C. E. *McLain*: some unusual views); GraceTJ 12 (1991) 286-8 (D. G. *Barker*).
2005 *a) Hendel* Ronald S., Genesis, book of; – *b) Scullion* John J., narrative of: ➤ 741, AnchorBD 2 (1992) 923-41-63.
2006 **Hill** Robert C.,   St. John CHRYSOSTOM, Homilies on Genesis 46-67: Fathers 87. Wsh 1992, Catholic Univ. v-288 p. [RHE 88,30*]. 0-8132-0074-1.
2007 ᴱ**Katzenellenbogen** M. L.,   Torat Ḥayyim [Miqra'ot gedolot, Bible rabbinique]: J, Moçad Kook.   Genèse 1986, 6+25+358, 6+312 p.; - Exode 1987, 7+314, 6+444 p.; - Lév. 1987, 6+456 p. – ᴿRHR 209 (1992) 73 (S. *Schwarzfuchs*).
2008 ᵀ**Korsak** Mary P.,   At the start – Genesis made new: EurS LvCah 124. Lv 1992, European Association for the Promotion of Poetry.   xiii-201. Fb 695 [RTLv 24,386s, J. *Vermeylen*, lyric praise].
2008* ᵀᴱ**McNamara** Martin,   Targum Neofiti 1, Genesis: Aramaic Bible 1A. E 1992, Clark.   xiv-271 p. 0-567-09458-8. ➤ 1771.
2009 ᵀᴱ**Maher** M.,   Targum Pseudo-Jonathan, Genesis: Aramaic Bible 1B. ColMn/E 1992, Liturgical/Clark.   xiv-208 p. $65. 0-8146-5492-4 [NTAbs 37,149]. E 0-567-09608-4.
2010 **Neusner** Jacob,   Confronting creation; how Judaism reads Genesis; an anthology of Genesis Rabbah 1991 ➤ 7,1727:   ᴿJStJud 23 (1992) 125-8 (G. *Stemberger*).
2011 ᴱ**Petit** Françoise,   La chaîne sur la Genèse I (1-3): Traditio exegetica graeca 1, 1991 ➤ 7,1728:   ᴿETL 68 (1992) 448s (A. de *Halleux*); RHE 87 (1992) 784-6 (Nicole *Zeegers*).

2013 **Ravasi** Gianfranco, Il libro della Genesi: Guide spirituali all'Antico Testamento. R 1991, Città Nuova. cap. I. 1-11, 175 p. Lit. 15.000. 88-311-3731-X.

2014 **Ravasi** Gianfranco, El libro del Génesis (1-11), I. [T]*Villanueva* Marciano. Barc/M 1992, Herder/Ciudad Nueva. 216 p. [Stromata 49,224]. 84-254-1812-7.

2015 **Ruppert** Lothar, Genesis, ein kritischer und theologischer Kommentar I (1-11,26): ForBi 70. Wü 1992, Echter. x-536 p. DM 64. 3-429-01451-4 [TLZ 118,1029, H. *Seebass*].

2015* **Sacks** Robert D., A commentary on the book of Genesis: ANE TSt 6, 1990 ➤ 6,2087; $80. – [R]CalvaryB 7,1 (1991) 64s (C. E. *McLain*: influenced by MAIMONIDES via Leo STRAUSS; useless for lack of documentation).

2016 **Sarna** Nahum M., Genesis: JPS Torah comm. 1989 ➤ 5,1932; 6,2088: [R]JRefJud 38,2 (1991) 81-83 (L. J. *Greenspoon*, also on MILGROM's Lev.).

2017 **Scullion** John J., Genesis; a commentary for students, teachers, and preachers: OT Studies 6. ColMn 1992, Glazier. 384 p. $20 [BToday 31, 249]. 0-8146-5659-5.

2018 **Soggin** J Alberto, Genesi 1-11: CommStoEseg 1/1, 1991 ➤ 7,1729: [R]RBibArg 54,47 (1992) 171-3 (J. S. *Croatto*).

2019 [E]**Sylwan** A., Petrus CANTOR, Glossae super Genesim, Prologus et Capitula 1-3: GrLatGoth 55. Göteborg 1992, Univ. lxxxviii-104 p.; 3 pl. 91-7346-246-2. – [R]NRT 114 (1992) 785 (A. *Harvengt*).

2020 **Westermann** C., Genesi (breve) 1989 ➤ 7,1734: [R]RivB 40 (1992) 100-3 (A. *Ranon*).

2020* **Youngblood** Ronald F., The book of Genesis, an introductory commentary[2] [[1]1976-80]. GR 1991, Baker. 311 p. [RelStR 19,66, H.T.C. *Sun*].

E1.5 *Genesis, themata.*

2021 **Breukelman** F. H., Bijbelse Theologie 1/2, de theologie van het boek Genesis; het eerstelingschap van Israël temidden van de volkeren op de aarde als thema van 'het boek van de verwekkingen van Adam, de mens'. Kampen 1992, Kok. 226 p. ƒ42.50. 90-242-6181-3 [TvT 33,291s, A. *Schoors*].

2022 **Brisman** Leslie, The voice of Jacob; on the composition of Genesis 1990 ➤ 6,2098; 7,1736: [R]CritRR 5 (1992) 119-121 (R. E. *Friedman*: a hypothesis which the laudable efforts of this English professor to acquire the needed biblical skills do not suffice to defend); JQR 83 (1992s) 417s (R. S. *Hendel*: semi-BLOOMIAN); LitTOx 6 (1992) 86-89 (W. L. *Reed*); RelStR 18 (1992) 50 (W. L. *Humphreys*: playful, incomplete).

2023 [T]**Cox** Everett, In the beginning / Now these are the names (➤ 2,1729; 5,2352). NY 1983/6, Schocken. xxxvii-211 p. / 230 p. – [R]JRefJud 37,1 (1990) 95-98 (M. A. *Sweeney*).

2024 **Erffa** Hans M. von, Ikonologie der Genesis: Die christlichen Bildthemen aus dem AT und ihre Quellen 1, 1989 ➤ 6,2099; 7,1736: [R]TZBas 48 (1992) 295s (C. *Dohmen*).

2025 **Garrett** Duane A., Rethinking Genesis; the sources and authorship of the first book of the Pentateuch. GR 1991, Baker. 273 p. $14 pa. 0-8010-3837-5. – [R]CalvaryB 8,1 (1992) 69-71 (C. E. *McLain*); Crux 28,2 (1992) 41s (T. *Williams*); GraceTJ 12 (1991) 284-6 (J. J. *Lawlor*); RExp 89 (1992) 571s (J. D. W. *Watts*).

2026 *Hyman* Ronald T., Fielding [*i.e.*, dealing with (the 21)] 'why' questions in Genesis: HebAnR 11 (1987) 173-183.

2027 *Kraft* Robert, *al.*, Computer assisted identification and reconstruction of fragmentary manuscripts (papyri, leather, paper): Chester Beatty Greek papyrus 5 (Genesis) = Rahlfs 962: ➤ 450, Informatique 2, 1988/9, 319-321 (-324).

2028 *a) Nicol* George G., Story-patterning in Genesis; – *b) Evans* Christopher F., Criticism and tradition; – *c) Carroll* Robert P., The discombobulations of time and the diversities of text; notes on the Rezeptionsgeschichte of the Bible: ➤ 41, [F]DAVIDSON R., Text as pretext 1992, 215-233 / 106-128 / 61-85.

2029 **Prewitt** Terry J., The elusive covenant; a structural-semiotic reading of Genesis 1990 ➤ 6,2104: [R]BL (1992) 85 (R. P. *Carroll*: high praise); CritRR 5 (1992) 162-4 (D. *Jobling*); JRel 72 (1992) 276s (F. E. *Greenspahn*: better than many in its genre).

2030 **Radday** Y. T., **Shore** H., Genesis; an authorship-study in computer-assisted statistical linguistics: AnBib 103, 1985 ➤ 1,1982... 4,1970: [R]VT 42 (1992) 134s (G. I. *Davies*).

2031 **Ralph** Margaret N., Discovering OT origins; the books of Genesis, Exodus and Samuel [answers to U. S. high-school questions]: Discovering the Living Word. NY 1992, Paulist. vi-319 p. $13. 0-8091-3322-9 [BL 93,93, E. B. *Mellor*: UK concerns rather different].

2032 **Rogerson** J. W., Genesis 1-11: OTGuides 1991 ➤ 7,1744: [R]Interpretation 46 (1992) 192s (E. *Achtemeier*); VT 42 (1992) 140 (J. A. *Emerton*: somewhat neglects GUNKEL, SKINNER, S. DRIVER).

2033 **Steinmetz** Devorah, From father to son... Gn 1991 ➤ 7,1746: [R]Encounter 53 (1992) 97s (L. K. *Handy*).

2034 **Thompson** T. L., The origin tradition of ancient Israel I GnEx 1987 ➤ 3,1917... 7,1748: [R]VT 42 (1992) 286-8 (J. A. *Emerton*: must be taken seriously, though open to some same criticisms he directs at others).

2035 **Turner** Laurence A., Announcements of plot in Genesis: JStOT supp 96, 1990 ➤ 6,2109: [R]BZ 36 (1992) 311s (H. *Seebass*); CritRR 5 (1992) 169-171 (R. S. *Hendel*: some odd conclusions); VT 42 (1992) 423s (R. P. *Gordon*).

2036 **White** Hugh C., Narration and discourse in the book of Genesis 1991 ➤ 7,1752; £35: [R]BR (1992) 95s (R. P. *Carroll*: beautiful); ÉTRel 67 (1992) 448 (T. *Römer*); TLond 95 (1992) 51s (T. *Dennis*: a very fine book despite almost impenetrable style).

E1.6   **Creatio,** *Genesis 1s.*

2036* **Aaron** David H., Polemics and mythology; a commentary on chapters 1 and 8 of Bereshit Rabbah: diss. Brandeis, [D]*Fox* M. Boston 1992. 479 p. 92-17471. – DissA 53 (1992s) 187-A.

2037 *a) Batto* Bernard F., Creation theology in Genesis; – *b) Di Vito* Robert A., The demarcation of divine and human realms in Genesis 2-11; – *c) Clifford* Richard J., Creation in the Psalms; – *d) Tobin* Thomas J., Interpretations of the creation of the world in PHILO; – *e) Cook* Joan E., Creation in 4 Ezra; the biblical theme in support of theodicy: ➤ 346, Creation 1992, 16-38 / 39-56 / 57-69 / 108-128 / 129-139.

2037* *Bonora* Antonio, Creazione e libertà umana in Genesi 1-11: Ambrosius 67 (1991) 441-454.

2038 *a) Boschi* Bernardo G., Creazione nella Bibbia; terminologia – contenuti – modi espressivi; – *b) Strumia* Alberto, Il problema della creazione e le cosmologie scientifiche; – *c) Coggi* Roberto, Considerazioni teologiche sulla storia del cosmo e dell'uomo; – *d*) *Lorenzini* Mirella, La creazione secondo i Testimoni di Geova: DivThom 95,3 (1992) 9-30 / 82-94 / 116-138 / 139-142.

2038* **Brito** Emilio, La création selon SCHELLING; Universum: BtETL 80, 1987 ➤ 4,1980: ᴿETL 68 (1992) 175s (M. *Vetö*).

2039 ᴱ**Burrell** D., *McGinn* B., God and creation 1990 ➤ 6,584*: ᴿJRel 72 (1992) 444-6 (D. F. *Duclow*).

2040 *Clouser* Roy A., Genesis on the origins of the human race: PerspScCF 43 (1991) 2-13.

2041 *a*) *David* Robert, Prolégomènes à l'étude écologique des récits de Gn 1-11; – *b*) *Thériault* Jean-Yves, La portée écologique de la notion paulinienne de la création; – *c*) *Vogels* Walter, The God who creates is the God who saves; the Book of Wisdom's reversal of the biblical pattern: ÉglT 22 (1991) 275-291 / 293-313 / 315-335.

2042 **Eberlein** Karl, Gott der Schöpfer – Israels Gott²ʳᵉᵛ [¹1986 < Diss. Erlangen 1984]: BeitErfAJ 5, 1989 ➤ 2,1423... 7,1759: ᴿTLZ 117 (1992) 175s (S. *Wagner*).

2043 **Ferrucci** Franco, La création, autobiographie de Dieu [1988 ➤ 6,2119], ᵀ*Sarrabayrouse* Alain. P 1990, Payot. 354 p. – ᴿFoiTemps 21 (1991) 278-287 (J.-F. *Grégoire*).

2044 *Fretheim* Terence E., Creator, creature, and co-creation in Genesis 1-2: ➤ 77, ꟳHARRISVILLE R., All things new 1992, 11-20.

2045 *[Gertz* M. C.] **Ebbesen** Sten, *Mortensen* L. B., Andreae Sunonis filii [SUNESEN] Hexaemeron 1983-8 ➤ 5,1959; 6,2116: ᴿRHE 87 (1992) 465s (R. *Hissette*); SvTKv 66 (1992) 86-88 (A. *Piltz*).

2045* *a*) *Gibert* Pierre, La pluralité des concepts de création [Gn 1/2s]; – *b*) *Martelet* Gustave, Ce que créer veut dire: Études 376 (1992) 811-8 / 819-829.

2046 *Hendel* Ronald S., Worldmaking in ancient Israel [as seen by Canaan villagers, not escaped from Egypt, p. 9]: JStOT 56 (1992) 3-18.

2047 *Herrmann* Wolfram, Jahwe und sein Kampf gegen das Meer [... früh als Schöpfer anerkannt]: ➤ 192, ꟳWALLIS G., Überlieferung 1990 (➤ 7,164*a*).

2048 *Hudson* W. D., God revealed in creation [... central to PANNENBERG W., Syst I, 1992]: ExpTim 104 (1992s) 46-48.

2048* *Ibal* Bernard, Création, séparation et amour [... BEAUCHAMP P. 1969]: RevSR 66 (1992) 333-343.

2049 **Jaki** Stanley L., Genesis 1 through the ages. Ch 1992, T. More. xiii-319 p. $17; pa. $10. 1-897713-00-2 [CanadCathR 11/11, 22s, M. *Doughty*].

2049* **Jewett** Paul K., God, creation, and revelation. GR 1991, Eerdmans. xix-535 p. $30. – ᴿTrinJ 13 (1992) 225-9 (M. A. *Cook*).

2050 **Kochanek** Piotr, La fisiologia dell'‹Esamerone› di San BASILIO: diss. Pont. Univ. Gregoriana 3848, ᴰ*Sprokel* N. Roma 1992. 316 p. – RTLv 24, p. 551.

2050* **Leeuw** M. van der, Het scheppingsverhaal herschapen; een kritische analyse. Delft 1990, Eburon. 162 p. 90-5166-154-1. – ᴿNedTTs 46 (1992) 229 (P. B. *Dirksen*: not critical but speculative).

2051 *a*) *Nicolas* Jean-Hervé, Être créé: RThom 92 (1992) 609-641.

— *b*) **Nothomb** Paul, Les récits bibliques de la création: Vers la Seconde Alliance. P 1991, Différence. 220 p. F 120. – ᴿÉtudes 376 (1992) 281s (P. *Gibert*).

— *c*) ᵀᴱ**Ozilou** M., S. BONAVENTURE, Les six jours de la création. P 1991, Desclée/Cerf. 556 p. F 240. – ᴿÉtudes 376 (1992) 137 (R. *Marlé*).

2052 **Ross** Allen P., Creation and blessing 1988 → 4,1952*; 5,1931: ᴿVT 42 (1992) 142 (J. A. *Emerton*: good).
2053 **Samuelson** Norbert M., The first seven days; a philosophical commentary on the creation of Genesis: SFL StJudaism 61. Atlanta 1992, Scholars. [viii-] 186 p. 1-55540-768-4.
2054 **Vannier** Marie-Anne, Creatio / AUGUSTIN ᴰ1991 → 7,1780: ᴿArT-Gran 55 (1992) 358s (A. *Segovia*); AugM 37 (1992) 397-9 (J. *Ortali*); RSPT 76 (1992) 633-7 (G. M. de *Durand*); TS 53 (1992) 748s (R. J. *Teske*); WienerSt 105 (1992) 275-8 (Hildegund *Miller*).
2055 **Vogels** Walter, [Gen 1-11] Nos origines: L'horizon du croyant. Ottawa 1992, Novalis. 196 p. [BLitEc 94,344-6, L. *Monloubou*].
2056 ᵀ*Wolters* Al, [1932 G. C.] AALDERS on Genesis 1 and 2: CalvinT 26 (1991) 155-164.

2056* **Brown** William P., Structure, role and ideology in the Hebrew and Greek texts of Genesis 1:1-2:3; diss. Emory, ᴰ*Hayes* J. Atlanta 1992. 479 p. 92-04807. – OIAc 3,15.
2057 *Waltke* Bruce K., The literary genre of Genesis, chapter one: Crux 27,4 (1991) 2-10.
2057* **Young** Edward J., Studies in Genesis I (1964), ᴱ*Kik* J. M.: Int. Libr. Bibl. Stud. GR c.1991, Baker. 105 p. $1.50.
2058 *Rooker* Mark F., Genesis 1/1-3; creation or re-creation? [WALTKE B. 1974]: BtS 149 (1992) 316-323 . 411-427.
2058* *Görg* Manfred, Zur Struktur von Gen 1,2: BibNot 62 (1992) 11-15.
2059 *Fischer* Dick, The days of creation; hours or eons? PerspScCF 42 (1990) 15-22 [180s, *Siemens* David F., comment; 182-4, reply].
2060 **Tsumura** David T., The earth and the waters in Genesis 1 and 2: JStOT supp 83, 1989 → 5,1978... 7,1793: ᴿBZ 36 (1992) 119s (D. *Mathias*); CurrTMiss 19 (1992) 303 (H. M. *Niemann*); VT 42 (1992) 422s (H. G. M. *Williamson*).
2061 a) **Schüngel-Straumann** Helen, Ruaḥ bewegt die Welt, Gottes schöpferische Lebenskraft in der Krisenzeit des Exils: SBS 151. 111 p. DM 35. 3-460-04511-6 [TR 89,166].
— b) *Görg* M., *raqîaᶜ* 'Himmelsgewölbe' [Gen 1,6]: → 770, TWAT 7,6s (1992) 688-675.
— c) *Seely* Paul H., The firmament and the water above; I. the meaning of *raqiaᶜ* in Gen 1:6-8; II. the water above: WestTJ 53 (1991) 227-240; 54 (1992) 31-46.
— d) *O'Loughlin* Thomas, Aquae super caelos (Gen 1:6-7); the first faith-science debate [BASIL, AMBROSE...]?: MillSt 29 (1992) 92-114.
2062 a) *Sasson* Jack M., Time... to begin [world's history begins with the fourth day]; – b) *Gordon* Cyrus H., 'This time' (Genesis 2:23): → 181, Shaᶜarei TALMON 1992, 183-194 / 47-51.

Gen 1,26: imago Dei:

2063 a) *Andersen* Kirsten M., 'Imago Dei' and desire in Genesis 1-3: to eat or not to eat, or rather to eat or what to eat; – b) *Edgar* Andrew, KANT's two interpretations of Genesis: LitTOx 6 (1992) 254-267 / 280... [< ZIT 92,560].
2064 *Amjad-Ali* Christine, [Gen 1,26] Power and the image of God: Al-Mushir 34 (1992) 45-50 [< TContext 10/1, 50].

2064* *Beek* A. van de,   De mens het beeld van God — of omgekeerd: KerkT 43 (1992) 310-321.
2065 **Børresen** Kari E.,   Image of God and gender models 1991 ➤ 7,472: ᴿRHE 87 (1992) 788-792 (Alice *Dermience*).
2066 **Boer** Harry R.,   An ember still glowing; humankind as the image of God 1990 ➤ 6,2147:   ᴿThemelios 18,1 (1992s) 31 (B. W. *Wilson*).
2067 *Dahar* Gilbert,   L'exégèse de Genèse 1,26 dans les commentaires du XIIᵉ siècle: RÉAug 38 (1992) 124-153.
2068 *Emmett* Peter A.,   The image of God and the ending of life: AsbTJ 47,1 (1992) 53-62.
2069 *Golub* Ivan,   *Čovjek*... Homo imago Dei – amicus Dei: BogSmot 60 (1990) 106-111 (+ 121-3).
2070 *a*) *Greenhalgh* Stephen,   Creative partnership in Genesis [WESTERMANN C. 1,26 'plural of deliberation' unduly closes off debate]: ScripB 22,1 (1992) 9-14.
— *b*) ᵀᴱ**Hamman** Adalbert G.,   L'uomo immagine somigliante di Dio [56 brani da AT-NT-Padri]. Letture Cristiane del primo millennio. Mi 1991, Paoline. 310 p. Lit. 30.000. – ᴿCC 143 (1992,4) 323s (M. *Farrugia*).
— *c*) *Hess* Richard S. [Fakhariyah 1979] Eden, a well-watered place; [&] are the image of God and the likeness of God different concepts?: BR 7,6 (1991) 28-33; ill.
— *d*) *Hughes* Philip E.,   The true image... in Christ 1989 ➤ 6,7174 [not 1174!]; 7,1809:   ᴿJDharma 16 (1991) 306s (sr. *Thaijasa*); RefTR 49 (1990) 34s (R. C. *Doyle*).
2071 *Hunter* David G.,   The paradise of patriarchy; AMBROSIASTER on woman as (not) God's image: JTS 43 (1992) 447-469.
2072 **Jónsson** Gunnlaugur A.,   The image of God; ConBib OT 26, 1988 ➤ 4,2017... 6,2115:   ᴿBZ 36 (1992) 292s (G. *Dautzenberg*).
2072* *Lamau* Marie-Louise,   L'homme à l'image de Dieu chez les théologiens et spirituels du XIIᵉᵐᵉ siècle: MélSR 48 (1991) 203-214; Eng. 214.
2073 *Parodi* Massimo,   'Imago ad similitudinem'; i termini di immagine e somiglianza nel Monologion di ANSELMO [anche di Dio, ma non menzionando Adam]: RÉtAug 38 (1992) 337-354.
2073* *Tångberg* Arvid,   Selvbilde og Guds bilde: TsTKi 63 (1992) 181-192 [in Norwegian; Eng. 192: Gen 1,26-28 against Egypt-Mesopotamia background confirms the modern self-concept as independence].
2074 *Wilson* R. Ward, *Blomberg* Craig L.,   The image of God in humanity; a biblical-psychological perspective: Themelios 18,3 (1992s) 8-15.

2075 **Cohen** Jeremy, [Gen 1,28] 'Be fertile...' 1989 ➤ 5,1992; 7,1815:   ᴿCBQ 54 (1992) 517s (E. J. *Fisher*: the 'fall' not so different in Jewish and Christian interpretation); CCAR 39,1 (1992) 67-69 (J. *Klein*); CritRR 5 (1992) 124-6 (Judith R. *Baskin*); Speculum 67 (1992) 398-400 (J. A. *Brundage*).
2075* *Anderson* Bernhard W., [Gen 1,28; Dt 30,19], 'Subdue the earth'; what does it mean?: BR 8,5 (1992) 4.10.
2076 *a*) *Uehlinger* Christoph,   Vom dominium terrae zu einem Ethos der Selbstbeschränkung; – *b*) *Zenger* Erich, 'Du kannst das Angesicht der Erde erneuern' (Ps 104,30); – *c*) *Baumann* Barbara,   Schöpfungsglaube und Umweltzerstörung; – *d*) *Langer* Gerhard,   Pflanzen, Schützen und Bewahren; eine ökologische Ethik der Rabbinen: BLtg 64 (1991) 59-74 / 75-86 / 92-100 / 86-92.
2077 *a*) *Bonora* Antonio,   L'uomo coltivatore e custode del suo mondo in Gn

1-11; – *b*) *Colzani* Gianni, Teologia ed ecologia; dalla sfida all'incontro: Credere Oggi 12/70 (1992) 18-29 / 42-53.

2078 *a*) *Rendtorff* Rolf, Some reflections on creation as a topic of OT theology; – *b*) *Weinfeld* Moshe, The phases of human life in Mesopotamian and Jewish sources; – *c*) *Weinberg* Joel P., The perception of 'things' and their production in the OT historical writings: ➤ 19*a*, ᶠBLENKINSOPP J., Priests 1992, 204-212 / 182-9 / 174-181.

2079 *Rodinò* Netina, La decima parola della Creazione (Gen. 1,29), un messaggio di non-violenza: RasT 33 (1992) 243-260.

E1.7   *Genesis 1s:*   **Bible and myth** [➤ M3.8].

2080 **Batto** Bernard F., Slaying the dragon; mythmaking in the biblical tradition. Louisville 1992, W-Knox. viii-248 p. 0-664-25353-9 [TBR 6/2,26, Jill *Harries*].

2080* *Bilolo* M., Concepts et expressions égyptiens relatifs à la création; importance et actualité en égard à l'héritage gréco-biblique: GöMiszÄg 131 (1992) 13-19.

2081 **Bottéro** J., *Kramer* S. N., Lorsque les dieux faisaient l'homme; mythologie mésopotamienne. P 1989 ➤ 5,1996; 6,2171: ᴿBCanadMesop 22 (1991) 53s (D. *Bonneterre*, ᵀ*Wilding* Linda).

2081* *Bottéro* Jean, L'anthropogonie mésopotamienne et l'élément divin en l'homme: ➤ 157, ᶠRUDHART J., Orphisme 1991, 211-225.

2082 *a*) **Ceccherelli** Ignazio M., Fermati, o sole! [sfondo cosmico di Gn Es...]. Bornato BS 1992, Sardini [BbbOr 34,113].

— *b*) **Dalley** Stephanie, Myths from Mesopotamia; creation, the flood, Gilgamesh and others: World's Classics, 1989 ➤ 5,1997... 7,1821: ᴿBR 8,2 (1992) 12s (R. S. *Hendel*); ÉtClas 60 (1992) 75 (Corinne *Bonnet*).

— *c*) **Fischbach** S. M., Totenerweckungen – zur Geschichte einer Gattung: ForBi 69: Wü 1992, Echter. 345 p. – ᴿArTGran 55 (1992) 529 (A. S. *Muñoz*).

Frymer-Kensky Tikva, In the wake of the goddesses; women, culture, and the biblical transformation of pagan myth 1991 ➤ 9114.

— *d*) **Furley** David, Cosmic problems; [2 inedita + 16] essays on Greek and Roman philosophy of nature 1989 ➤ 6,233: ᴿRÉLat 70 (1992) 302-4 (C. *Lévy*).

2083 **Görg** Manfred, Mythos, Glaube und Geschichte; die Bilder des christlichen Credo und ihre Wurzeln im Alten Ägypten. Dü 1992, Patmos. 189 p. – ᴿMiscFranc 92 (1992) 616s (J. *Imbach*: 'Görig').

2083* *Gombrich* Richard, The Buddha's book of Genesis? [DAVIDS T. 1921]: IndIranJ 35 (1992) 159-178.

2084 **Hughes** Jeremy, Secrets of the times; myth and history in biblical chronology [D & P; myth meaning 'schematic'; Oxford diss.]: jOsu 66. Shf 1990, Academic. xii-315 p. 1-85075-178-1. – ᴿHeythJ 33 (1992) 129s (B. P. *Robinson*).

2085 **Kramer** Samuel N., *Maier* John, Myths of Enki, the crafty god 1989 ➤ 5,2007; 7,1826: ᴿBO 49 (1992) 773-7 (Hannes D. *Galter*); CBQ 54 (1992) 114s (W. J. *Moran*: mildly queries Maier's 'fugitive god' and 'saturnine way').

2085* *Lambert* W. G., The relationship of Sumerian and Babylonian myth as seen in accounts of creation: ➤ 683, Circulation 1991/2, 129-135.

2086 **Leeming** D. A., The world of myth; an anthology. Ox 1990, UP. xvi-362 p. £12 pa. 0-19-507475-0 [BL 93,17, L. L. *Grabbe*].

2086* **Leick** G., A dictionary of Ancient Near Eastern mythology [Mesopotamia, Syria, Anatolia, without Egypt. NY 1991, Routledge. xiv-199 p.; 44 fig. $50. 0-415-00762-3 [BL 93,123].

2087 ᴱ**Mensen** Bernhard, Die Schöpfung in den Religionen 1990 → 7,538: ᴿZkT 114 (1992) 107 (K. H. *Neufeld*: auch über Ökologie und Technologie).

2088 **Pettazzoni** Raffaele † 1959, Miti e leggende, ᴱ*Filoramo* G. T 1990, UTET. xxvi-158 p.; xxii-176 p. – ᴿRivStoLR 28 (1992) 693 (C. *Gianotto*).

2088* *Rosner* Victor (1911-1985), Myths from Chota Nagpur retold, ᴱ*Clarysse* L.: Sevartham 17 (1992), 129 p.

2089 *Russell* D. S., Interpreting Scripture; myth and remythologizing: ExpTim 104 (1992s) 356-9.

2090 **Stannard** Brendan, The cosmic conquest; a systems study in Indo-European myth, cult and cosmogony. Southport UK 1992, CARIB. 304 p. 0-9508-9471-0 [OIAc 3,39].

2091 *Wettengel* Wolfgang, Bilder der Schöpfung [aus dem Urgewässer, in Ägypten]: AntWelt 23 (1992) 281-6; 9 fig.

2092 *Weisberg* David B., Loyalty and death; some Ancient Near Eastern metaphors [... Enuma Eliš]: → 65, Mem. GEVIRTZ S., Maarav 7 (1991) 253-267.

2093 *Zandee* J. †, The birth-giving creator-god in ancient Egypt: → 72, ᶠGRIFFITHS J. G. 1992, 169-185.

E1.8   *Gen 1s, Jos 10,13 ...* :   **The Bible, the Church, and Science.**

2094 *a) Adamantides* Achilles G., Science and faith; – *b) Harakas* Stanley S., Orthodox Christianity facing science; – *c) Papagiannis* Michael D., Can science search for God?: → 631*, Holy Cross, GrOrTR 37 (1992) 1-6 / 7-15 / 17-33.

2094* *Albright* John R., God and the pattern of nature; a physicist considers cosmology: ChrCent 109 (1992) 711-4.

2095 **Amrhein** Eva-Maria, **Brungs** Robert, The vineyard; scientists in the Church. St. Louis 1992, TEST Faith/Science Press. vii-146 p. $10 pa. 0-9625-4315-2 [TDig 39,249].

2096 *Banet* Robert A., The fall of the house of DARWIN: HomP 93,1 (1992s) 70-... [< ZIT 93,110].

2097 **Banner** Michael, The justification of science and the rationality of religious belief 1990 ➤ 6,2194; 7,1836: ᴿHeythJ 33 (1992) 95s (P. *Avis*); JRel 72 (1992) 288s (W. J. *Wainwright*); RelSt 27 (1991) 421s (E. J. *Love*); TPhil 67 (1992) 133s (F. *Rickens*).

2098 **Barbour** I. G., Religion in an age of science 1990 → 6,2195: ᴿChrCent 109 (1992) 459s (S. M. *Heim*); Evangel 10,1 (1992) 29s (J. C. *Sharp*: good but not much TORRANCE; and be wary of the theological perspective); Horizons 19 (1992) 179s (T. B. *Ommen*); TvT 32 (1992) 108s (R. *Munnik*).

2099 **Barbour** Ian G., Ethics in the age of technology [Gifford Lectures 2d set, continuing Religion in an age of science]. L 1992, SCM. 312 p. £17.50. 0-334-00408-X. – ᴿExpTim 104,10 top choice (1992s) 257s (C. S. *Rodd*).

2100 **Beale** Graham, Evolution and a creator? 1991 → 7,1839: ᴿChrSchR 22 (1992s) 319-322 (S. *Rice*: severe).

2100* **Bergold** Ralph, Der Glaube vor dem Anspruch der Wissenschaften; der Dialog zwischen Naturwissenschaft und Theologie am Beispiel von Schöpfungsglauben und Evolutionstheorie [Diss. Münster 1988]: EurHS 23/437. Fra 1991, Lang. 140 p. DM 95. – ᴿTGL 82 (1992) 270s (D. *Hattrup*).

2101 **Berra** Tim M., Evolution and the myth of creationism; a basic guide to the facts in the evolution debate 1990 ➤ 7,1840: ᴿPerspScCF 44 (1992) 203s (S. *Rice*).

2102 ᴱ**Berry** R. J., Real science, real faith [16 scientists]. Eastbourne 1991, Monarch. 224 p. £9 pa. 1-85424-125-7. – ᴿTBR 5,1 (1992s) 9 (I. *Bird*).

2103 **Beukel** A. van den, More things in heaven and earth; God and the scientists. L 1991, SCM. 166 p. £8.50. 0-334-02504-4. – ᴿExpTim 104 (1992s) 127 (C. S. *Rodd* ambiguously: 'what it feels like to be a Christian scientist').

2104 **Bird** W. R., The origin of species revisited I, 1989 ➤ 6,2201; 7,1841: ᴿPerspScCF 44 (1992) 61s (L. D. *Thurman*).

2105 **Blackwell** Richard J., GALILEO, BELLARMINE and the Bible 1991 ➤ 7,1843: ᴿCanadCathR 10,2 (1992) 26s (W. R. *Carroll*, also on RE-DONDI P.); CathHR 78 (1992) 120-2 (W. A. *Wallace*); Manuscripta 35 (1991) 247s (F. D. *Grande*); NBlackf 73 (1992) 524 (A. *McGrath*); NRT 114 (1992) 618 (P. *Evrard*); TS 53 (1992) 150s (M. F. *McCarthy*).

2106 *Boné* Édouard, Hominisatie en humanisatie; zin en toekomst van de menselijke evolutie?: Streven 58 (1990s) 800-815.

2107 **Bowden** M., Science vs. evolution. Kent 1991, Sovereign. xiv-238 p. £8. – ᴿThemelios 18,3 (1992s) 32s (J. *Drane*).

2108 **Bowler** Peter J., The non-Darwinian revolution; reinterpreting a historical myth. Baltimore 1988, pa. 1992, Johns Hopkins Univ. 238 p. $13 pa. [PerScCF 45,198, J. D. *Thurman*].

2109 **Brandmüller** Walter, Galileo e la Chiesa; ossia il diritto ad errare. Vaticano 1992, Libreria. 226 p. Lit. 35.000 [CC 144/3, 310s, J. *Casanovas*].

2110 ᴱ**Bresch** Carsten, *al.*, Kann man Gott aus der Natur erkennen? Evolution als Offenbarung: QDisp 125, 1990 ➤ 6,394*: ᴿLebZeug 46 (1991) 311s (H. *Lenz*); TPhil 67 (1992) 468-470 (R. *Koltermann*).

2111 **Brooke** John H., Science and religion; some historical perspectives: History of Science series. C 1991, Univ. x-422 p.; 40 fig. £27.50; pa. £11. 0-5212-3961-3; -8374-4. – ᴿJTS 43 (1992) 797-800 (D. A. *Pailin*: pleasingly readable though with American spelling like 'center'); NedTTs 46 (1992) 263 (W. B. *Drees*); Protestantesimo 47 (1992) 347s (P. *Comba*); TLond 95 (1992) 230 (P. *Byrne*).

ᴱ**Brümmer** Vincent, Interpreting the universe as creation 1991 ➤ 516.

2112 *Brungs* Robert A., Science – democracy – Christianity: Thought 64 (1989) 377-398.

2113 ᴱ**Bühler** Pierre, *Karakash* Clairette, Science et foi font système; une approche herméneutique: Lieux théologiques 21. Genève 1992, Labor et fides. 215 p. 2-8309-0666-7 [RHPR 73,456s, G. *Siegwalt*].

2114 *a*) *Buijs* Joseph A., Religion, science, and philosophy; how are they compatible?: RelStT 11,1 (1991) 27-38.

— *b*) **Capra** Fritjof, *Steindl-Rast* David, Wendezeit im Christentum; Perspektiven für eine aufgeklärte Theologie. Bern 1991, Scherz. 286 p. DM 38. – ᴿTGL 82 (1992) 159 (K. *Hollmann*).

— *c*) **Caron** Anthime, La science change-t-elle la foi?: PremièreBtCRel. P 1991, Mame. 64 p. – ᴿRICathP 41 (1992) 190-2 (J. *Doré*).

2115 **Casti** John L., Paradigms lost; images of man in the mirror of science. NY 1989, Morrow. 450 p. $23. – ᴿPerspScCF 44 (1992) 64s (J. W. *Burgeson*).

2115* *Castillo* Norberto, Unique obsessions; behind scientific discoveries: PhilipSa 26 (1991) 51-65.

2116 *Chavée* Daniel, La création, lieu de rencontre entre science et théologie: FoiTemps 21 (1991) 5-21.
2117 **Clayton** Philip, *a)* Explanation from physics to theology 1989 ➤ 5,2034: ... 7,1850: ᴿZygon 27 (1992) 225-231 (J. W. *Robbins*).
—*b)* Rationalität und Religion; Erklärung in Naturwissenschaft und Theologie, ᵀ*Laube* M., Vorw. *Pannenberg* W. Pd 1992, Schöningh. xv-256 p. DM 68. 3-506-71881-9 [TLZ 118,761-3, C. *Pentz*].
2118 **Clements** Tod S., Science vs. religion. Buffalo 1990, Prometheus. 264 p. £17. 0-87975-593-8. – ᴿTBR 5,1 (1992s) 9 (W. F. *Clocksin*).
2119 **Close** Frank, Das Ende; Vom Schicksal des Weltalls [Catastrophe and the fate of the universe 1988],ᵀ. Fra 1989, Umschau. 260 p. – ᴿTPhil 87 (1992) 145s (R. *Koltermann*).
2119* **Coyne** George V., Implicazioni filosofiche e teologiche delle nuove cosmologie: CC 143 (1992,4) 343-352.
2120 **Davies** Paul, The mind of God [final word of HAWKING's Brief history of time]; the scientific basis for a rational world. NY 1992, Simon & S. 254 p. $22. – ᴿTablet 246 (1992) 440 (J. *Cornwell*); TLond 95 (1992) 396 (J. *Polkinghorne*: a significant phenomenon); TS 53 (1992) 770-2 (J. F. *Haught*: important despite Platonic notion of existence).
2120* **Deane-Drummond** Celia, God and Gaia [LOVELOCK J. 1988]; myth or reality: TLond 95 (1992) 277-285.377s, protest of H. *Montefiore*.
2121 **Degler** Carl N., The search for human nature; the decline and revival of Darwinism in American social thought. NY 1991, Oxford-UP. 432 p. $25. – ᴿCithara 31,2 (1991s) 49s (S. *O'Mara*).
2122* **Desmond** Adrian, *Moore* James, DARWIN 1991 ➤ 7,1855; 0-7181-3430-3: ᴿMonth 253 (1992) 152 (K. *O'Callaghan*).
2123 **Desmond** Adrian, The politics of evolution; morphology, medicine, and reform in radical London. Ch 1989, Univ. x-503 p. $35. – ᴿChH 61 (1992) 258s (J. D. *Root*).
2123* *di Rovasenda* Enrico, San TOMMASO e la scienza fisica: SacDoc 36 (1991) 688-697.
2124 **Drees** Willem B., Beyond the big bang 1990 ➤ 5,2039 ... 7,1856: ᴿJRel 72 (1992) 603s (J. R. *Albright*); PerspScCF 44 (1992) 144 (M. *Kuehn*); TTod 49 (1992s) 439s (R. J. *Russell*).
2125 ᴱ**Drees** W. B., Theologie en natuurwetenschap; op zoek naar een snark [Lewis CARROLL figment]: StLevensbeschouwing. Kampen 1992, Kok. 88 p. 90-242-6864-8 [TvT 33,311, T. *Brattinga*].
2125* *Drees* Willem B., Potential tensions between cosmology and theology; ➤ 516, Interpreting 1991, 65-89 [ᴿNVFr 67 (1992) 225-234 (J.-M. *Portas*)].
2126 **Ellul** Jacques, The technological bluff, ᵀ*Bromiley* G. W., 1990 ➤ 7, 1857*: ᴿCGrebel 9 (1991) 89-91 (D. *Huron*); CritRR 5 (1992) 434-7 (R. R. *Reno*: mad misanthrope or seer?).
2127 **Eve** Raymond A., *Harrold* Francis B., The creationist movement in modern America. Boston 1991, Twayne. xii-294 p. $36; pa $12. – ᴿJSc-StR 31 (1992) 238s (A. *Shupe*).
2128 **Finocchiaro** Maurice A., The GALILEO affair 1989 ➤ 5,2041 ... 7,1858: ᴿChH 60 (1991) 393s (C. B. *Kaiser*).
2129 **Galleni** Lodovico, Scienza e teologia; proposte per una sintesi feconda: GdT 209. Brescia 1992, Queriniana. 196 p. Lit. 18.000. – ᴿAsprenas 39 (1992) 601s (P. *Cacciapuoti*).
2130 **Gilkey** Langdon, Religion and the scientific future; reflections on myth, science, and theology: ROSE [Reprints of scholarly excellence] 2. Macon 1982, Mercer Univ. = Harper 1970. xii-193 p. 0-86554-030-6.

2131 **Guitton** Jean (con *Bogdanov* Grichka e Igor), Dio e la scienza [1991
➤ 7,1864], ᵀ*Spranzi* M., *Giorello* G. Mi 1992, Bompiani. 137 p. Lit.
29.000. – ᴿLetture 47 (1992) 667s (C. *Maroni*); LVitae 47 (1992) 229-237
(J. *Courcier*: 'le succès d'un mauvais livre').

2132 **Haffner** P., Creation and scientific creativity; a study in the thought of
S. L. JAKI. Front Royal VA 1991, Christendom. 205 p. – ᴿAnnTh 6
(1992) 485-7 (T. *Kennedy*).

2132* *Haikola* Lars, Skapelse och försyn (WILES M.) i ljuset av modern vetenskap: SvTKv 67 (1991) (113-) 122-9.

2133 ᴱ**Hammacher** Klaus, *al.*, Transzendentalphilosophie und Evolutionstheorie: Fichtestudien 4. Amst 1992, Rodopi. 270 p. *f* 80 [TGL 83,397-
9, B. *Dieckmann*].

2134 **Harris** Errol E., Cosmos and Theos; ethical and theological implications
of the anthropic cosmological principle. Atlantic Highlands NJ 1992,
Humanities. xviii-221 p. $35. 0-391-03744-7 [TDig 40,66; RelStR 19,51s,
P. *Hodgson*]. – ᴿÉglT 23 (1992) 291s (J. R. *Pambrun*).

2135 **Harris** Marvin, Antropologia culturale [Eng.²], ᵀ. Bo 1990, Zanichelli.
xvi-454 p. – ᴿSalesianum 54 (1992) 152s (R. *Sabin*: 'Lo spazio pre-
ponderante concesso ... all'evoluzionismo delle forme ha in parte svuotato
di senso le reali divergenze').

2136 *Hasker* William, Evolution and Alvin PLANTINGA: PerspScCF 44
(1992) 150-162; 258-263, Plantinga reply, On rejecting the theory of
common ancestry.

2137 **Hawking** S. W., A brief history of time. NY 1988, Bantam. 198 p. $19
➤ 6,2222; 7,1865: ᴿPerspScCF 42 (1990) 47-52 (P. *Hammond*).

2137* **Hawking** Stephen W., Anfang oder Ende? [Is the end in sight for
theoretical physics? 1980]. Pd 1991. 48 p. DM 9,80. – ᴿTGL 82 (1992)
489s (D. *Hattrup*).

2138 *a) Hefner* Philip, Can a theology of nature be coherent with scientific
cosmology? – *b) Norris* Russell B.ᴶ, Metaphor, myth, and cosmology; –
c) Albright John R., The end of the world; a scientific view of Christian
eschatology: Dialog 30 (St. Paul 1991) 267-272 / 273-8 / 279-283.

2138* ᴱ**Heller** Michał, *Zyciński* Józef, Dylematy ewolucji. Kraków 1990,
Pol. Tow. Teol. 188 p. – ᴿAntonianum 67 (1992) 451-3 (R. M. *Olejnik*).

2139 ᴱ**Herrmann** Joachim, *Ullrich* Herbert, Menschwerdung; Millionen Jahre
Menschheitsentwicklung — natur- und geisteswissenschaftliche Ergebnisse. B 1991, Akademie. 778 p.; 207 fig.; 80 pl. – ᴿTPhil 67 (1992) 470-
2 (C. *Kummer*).

2140 **Hitchcock** John, The web of the universe; JUNG, the 'new physics' and
human spirituality. NY 1991, Paulist. ix-243 p. $15. 0-8091-3267-2. –
ᴿTBR 5,1 (1992s) 29 (C. *Elliott* does not think it as successful as W.
WINK declares).

2141 *Hübner* Jürgen, Naturwissenschaft und Theologie: ➤ 757, EvKL 3
(1992) 648-656.

2141* **Jaki** Stanley L., The purpose of it all ➤ 7,1868: E 1990, Scottish
Academic. xi-294 p. 0-7073-0631-0. – ᴿGregorianum 73 (1992) 772s
(J. M. *McDermott*).

2142 **Jaki** S. L., Scientist and Catholic, P. DUHEM. Front Royal VA 1991,
Christendom. – ᴿHomP 92,11s (1991s) 86s (J. S. *Robertson*); JEH 43
(1992) 498s (P. *McPartlan*).

2143 **Jaki** Stanley L., Pierre DUHEM homme de science et de foi: Scientifiques et croyants 4, 1990 ➤ 7,1869: ᴿArchivScSocR 80 (1992) 309s (É.
Poulat).

2144 *Jaki* Stanley L.,   Christ and science: *a*) DowR 110 (1992) 110-130; – *b*) EuntDoc 45 (1922) 93-114.

2145 *John Paul II* [Oct. 31, 1992 to Pontifical Academy of Sciences],   Lessons of the GALILEO case: Origins 22 (1992s) 369.371-4 (-5, *Poupard* P.).

2146 **Johnson** Phillip E.,   DARWIN on trial [in recent U.S. courts]. Wsh/DG 1991, Regnery/InterVarsity. 195 p. $20. – ᴿBtS 149 (1992) 245s (R.A. *Pyne*: his (lawyer's) lack of scientific training helps him to a firm judgment on evolution's weaknesses); HomP 92,10 (1991s) 76s (Edith *Myers*); PerspScCF 44 (1992) 140-2 (L.D. *Thurman* & O. *Gingerich*); 249-252, comment of J.L. *Wiester*; 283s, Gingerich reply; SciAm 267,1 (1992) 118-121 (S. *Gould*: severe).

2146* *Kaelin* E.-Jean,   La dérive gnostique de Jean GUITTON [Dieu et la science; P 1991, Grasset]: NVFr 67 (1992) 64-69.

2147 **Kaiser** Christopher B.,   Creation and the history of science [→ 7,1871*]: GR/E 1991, Eerdmans/Marshall Pickering. 316 p. 0-8028-0197-8 / 0-551-02008-3. – ᴿExpTim 103 (1991s) 317 (J.H. *Brooke*); PerspScCF 44 (1992) 178-185 (H.J. *Van Till*); TrinJ 13 (1992) 104s (L. Russ *Bush*); TTod 49 (1992s) 98s (W. van *Huyssteen*).

2148 *Kellner* Hans., *al.*, 'Wenn ich sehe die Himmel, diener Finger Werk...'; Informationen, Bilder und Materialien zur neuen kosmologischen Frage: Forum Religion 2 (Stu 1992) 2-14 [< ᴢɪᴛ 92,333].

2149 *Knobelsdorf* Christian von,   Wissenschaft, Wirklichkeit und Religion; Thesen: Deutsches Pfarrerblatt 92 (Essen 1992) 231-4 [< ᴢɪᴛ 92,397].

2150 **Koch** T.,   Das göttliche Gesetz der Natur; zur Geschichte des neuzeitlichen Naturverständnisses und zu einer gegenwärtigen theologischen Lehre von der Schöpfung: TSt 136. Z 1991, Theol.-V. 101 p. Fs 15. 3-290-10133-9. – ᴿTvT 32 (1992) 207 (W.B. *Drees*).

2150* *a*) *Kozhamathadam* Job,   Cosmology without God? [HAWKING S.W.]; – *b*) *Ambrose* M. Devadass,   Cosmic experience of God according to Genesis II: IndTSt 28 (1991) 119-131 / 155-165.

2151 **Lamoureux** Denis,   Between The Origin of Species and The Fundamentals; toward a historiographical model of reaction to Darwinism over the first fifty years: diss. St. Michael's, ᴰ*Wiebe* D. Toronto 1991. – SR 21 (1992) 495.

2152 **Landa** Judah,   Torah and science. Hoboken 1991, KTAV. 361 p. $39.50. 0-88125-320-0 [RelStR 19,85, D.H. *Gordis*]. – ᴿExpTim 104 (1992s) 63 (C.S. *Rodd*).

2152* **Lazorthes** G.,   Croyance et raison; de la recherche scientifique à l'interrogation spirituelle. P 1991, Centurion. 219 p. – ᴿScEsp 44 (1992) 383s (M. *Maesschalck*).

2153 **Lecourt** Dominique,   L'Amérique entre la Bible et DARWIN. P 1992, PUF. 230 p. F 148 [Études 378,134, P. *Valadier*].

2154 *Le Poidevin* Robert,   Creation in a closed universe, or, Have physicists disproved the existence of God?: RelSt 27 (1991) 39-48.

2155 **Lindberg** David C.,   The beginning of western science; the European scientific tradition in philosophical, religious, and institutional context, 600 B.C. to A.D. 1450. Ch 1992, Univ. 474 p. 116 fig. $57; pa. $20 [PerScCF 45,196s, P.K. *Wason*].

2156 **Livingstone** David N.,   The preadamite theory and the marriage of science and religion: AmPhTr 82/3. Ph 1992, American Philosophical Soc. x-81 p.; 8 fig. 0065-9746.

2157 **Loder** James E., *Neidhardt* W. Jim, The Knight's move; the relational logic of the Spirit in theology and science. Colorado Springs 1992, Helmers & H. 350 p. $25 [RefR 47,64, H. *Buis*].
2158 **Lonchamp** J.-P., La création du monde. P 1990, D-Brouwer. 142 p. [RThom 93,451, J.-M. *Maldamé*].
2158* **Lüke** Ulrich, Evolutionäre Erkenntnislehre und Theologie: Universitas. Stu 1990, Wiss.V. 223 p. – ᴿLebZeug 46 (1991) 312s (H. *Lenz*).
2159 **McCrady** Edward, Seen and unseen; a biologist views the universe. Sewanee 1990. Univ. of the South. 351 p. [JEvTS 36,412, D. *Englin*].
2160 **MacKay** Donald M. † 1987, Behind the eye [brain-microscope; < 1986 Gifford Lectures], ᴱ*MacKay* Valerie. Ox/CM 1991, Blackwell. 288 p. $25. – ᴿPerspScCF 44 (1992) 49-54 (W. R. *Thorson*: 'An I behind the eye') & 55-60 (J. W. *Haas*).
2161 **Malherbe** Jean-François, Le langage théologique à l'âge de la science 1985 → 1,9595... 4,a843: ᴿTR 88 (1992) 217s (K. J. *Tossou*).
2162 **Marcozzi** Vittorio, Alla ricerca dei nostri predecessori; compendio di paleoantropologia. CinB 1992, Paoline. 144 p. Lit. 18.000. – ᴿBbbOr 34 (1992) 118s (D. *Sardini*); CC 143 (1992,4) 525s (M. *Alessandri*).
2163 ᴱ**Margenau** Henry, *Varghese* Roy A., Cosmos, bios, theos; [60 invited] scientists reflect on science, God and the origins of the universe, life, and homo sapiens. La Salle ɪʟ 1992, Open Court. xiv-285 p. $39; pa. $18. 0-8126-9185-7; -6-5 [TDig 40,157].
2164 **Martin** Russell N. D., Pierre DUHEM; philosophy in the work of a believing physicist. LaSalle ɪʟ 1991, Open Court. xii-274 p. – ᴿArchiv-ScSocR 80 (1992) 317s (É. *Poulat*).
2165 *Mayaud* Pierre-Noël, Une 'nouvelle' affaire GALILÉE: RHistSciences 45,2s (P 1992) 162-230 [< RSPT 77,590].
2166 *Miccoli* Paolo, Teologia e science umane: EuntDoc 44 (1991) 381-417.
2167 *a)* ᴱ**Miller** James B., *McCall* Kenneth E., The Church and contemporary cosmology. Pittsburgh 1990, Carnegie Mellon Univ. 400 p. $14 pa. 0-88-748-1019. – ᴿInterpretation 46 (1992) 428-430 (D. W. *Hall*); PerspScCF 44 (1992) 145s (R. H. *Bube*).
— *b)* **Minois** Georges, L'Église et la science; histoire d'un malentendu, I. De saint AUGUSTIN à Galilée → 6,2241; II. De GALILÉE à JEAN-PAUL II. P 1990s, Fayard. 484 p.; 526 p. F 150 + 160. – ᴿEsprVie 102 (1992) 39-43 (G. *Viard*).
— *c)* **Miranda** J.P., Apelo a la razón; teoría de la ciencia y crítica del positivismo. S 1988, Sígueme. 508 p. – ᴿREspir 49 (1990) 159 (E. *García*).
— *d)* **Miranda** J.P., La revolución de la razón; el mito de la ciencia empírica. S 1991, Sígueme. 382 p. – ᴿREspir 51 (1992) 208s (T. *Polo*).
2168 **Moreland** J.P., Christianity and the nature of science 1988 → 5,2077*; 6,2243: ᴿGraceTJ 12 (1991) 309-311 (J. *Morrison*); Themelios 17,1 (1991s) 32s (Pattie *Pun*).
2169 **Mortensen** Viggo, *a)* Teologi og naturvidenskab; hinsides restriktion og ekspansion. 1989.
— *b)* ᴱGud og naturen; kan der etableras en dialog mellem teologi og naturvidenskap? K 1990, Munksgaard. 135 p. – ᴿSvTKv 66 (1990) 49-59 & 187s (H. *Görman*).
— *c)* *Moss* Christopher, A glimpse of creation: Tablet 246 (1992) 539s.
— *d)* *Muratore* Saturnino, Il principio antropico [BARROW J. 1986, *al.*] tra scienza e metafisica: RasT 33 (1992) 21-48 . 154-197 . 261-300.
2170 **Murphy** Nancey, Theology in the age of scientific reasoning. Ithaca ɴʏ 1990, Cornell Univ. xi-215 p. $28. – ᴿChrSchR 22 (1992s) 94-96 (S. M.

Heim); JAAR 60 (1992) 173s (J. W. *Jones*); JRel 72 (1992) 601s (E. A. *Yonan* starts and ends 'impressive'); TPhil 67 (1992) 299s (F. *Ricken*).

2171 *Mutschler* Hans-Dieter, Mythos 'Selbstorganisation': TPhil 67 (1992) 86-108.

2172 **Nebelsick** Harold P. † 1989, The Renaissance, the Reformation and the rise of science. E 1992, Clark. xxi-237 p. $30 [PrincSemB 14,305, W. B. *Drees*]. – ᴿExpTim 104 (1992s) 310 (C. A. *Russell*: edited by his daughter and son-in-law).

2173 *Neidhardt* W. Jim, Theology and science at the frontiers [ᴱTorrance T., 12 vols. 1985-1990]: TTod 50 (1993s) 449-455.

2174 **Oakes** Edward T., Final causality; a response: TS [52 (1991) 289-329, *Mooney* C., Theology and science] 53 (1992) 534-544.

2175 **Olding** Alan, Modern biology and natural theology. L c. 1991, Routledge. xxii-181 p. £30. – ᴿRelSt 28 (1992) 425s (D. A. *Pailin*).

2176 **Onimus** Jean, TEILHARD de Chardin et le mystère de la Terre: Espaces Libres 21. P 1991, A. Michel. 224 p. F 45. – ᴿBrotéria 135 (1992) 350s (F. *Pires Lopes*); Christus 39 (P 1992) 94 (G. *Lepoutre*).

2177 **Paul** Erich R., Science, religion, and Mormon cosmology. Urbana 1992, Univ. Illinois. xi-272 p. $30. 0-252-01895-8 [TDig 40,181].

2178 **Peacock** Roy E., A brief history of eternity 1990 → 7,1890: ᴿPerspScCF 44 (1992) 187s (F. P. *Lollar*) &188 (D. *Ratcliff*).

2179 **Peacocke** Arthur, Theology for a scientific age 1990 → 7,1892: ᴿTS 53 (1992) 790s (J. F. *Salmon*: good).

2180 *a)* **Pedersen** Olaf, The book of nature [1990s Kraków lectures]. Vatican 1992, Observatory. $10 [ND]. 0-268-00690-3 [TDig 40,284]. – ᴿTablet 246 (1992) 780 (P. *Hodgson*).

— *b)* *Pérez de Laborda* Alfonso, Big bang y dogma cristiano de la creación: Salmanticensis 39 (1992) 379-386.

— *c)* ᴱ**Peters** Ted, Cosmos as creation; theology and science in consonance [9 Protestants] 1989 ► 6,443: ᴿRelStR 18 (1992) 317 (W. *Falla*).

2181 *a)* *Plantinga* Alvin, When faith and reason clash; evolution and the Bible; – *b)* *Van Till* Howard A. (*al.*), Responses: ChrSchR 20,1 ('symposium' 1991s) 8-32 . 80-109 / 33-45 (-79).

2182 *a)* **Polkinghorne** John, Reason and reality — the relationship between science and theology 1991 ► 7,1897: ᴿChurchman 106 (1992) 181-3 (D. *Spanner*: a fine book; some reserves); Tablet 246 (1992) 1229s (P. *Hodgson*); Themelios 18,3 (1992s) 31s (*Kai Man Kwan*); TLond 95 (1992) 231s (I. H. *Jórysz*: apologetic rather than rigorous on the relation).

— *b)* **Polkinghorne** John, Science and creation; the search for understanding 1988 ► 5,2085 ... 7,1888: ᴿEvangel 9,2 (1991) 31 (S. *Williams*: some lacks).

— *c)* **Polkinghorne** John, The way the world is; the Christian perspective of a scientist. L 1992 = 1983, SPCK/Triangle. 130 p. £5. – ᴿStreven 59 (1992) 1237s (J. *Haers*).

— *d)* *Polkinghorne* John, Reckonings in science and religion: AnglTR 74 (1992) 376-380.

2183 *a)* *Polkinghorne* John, Spiritual growth and the scientific quest; – *b)* *Thompson* Ross, Scientific and religious understanding; – *c)* *Russell* Robert J., Finite creation without a beginning: Way 32 (1992) 252-7 / 258-267 / 268-280.

2184 *Poupard* Paul, L'affaire Galilée; les conclusions d'une enquête [pontificale]: EsprVic 102 (1992) 683-5.

2184* **Prigogine** Ilia, *Stengers* Isabelle, La nouvelle alliance. P 1979, Gallimard. – ᴿBCentProt 44,2 (1992) 3-30 (G.P. *Widmer*) & 11-24 (C. *Wassermann*, 'La temporalisation de l'espace').

2185 **Redondi** Pietro, GALILEO heretic 1987 ➤ 5,2091; 6,2255: ᴿCanadCathR 10,2 (1992) 27s (W.E. *Carroll*).

2186 **Ruether** Rosemary R., Patriarchy and creation; feminist critique of religious and scientific cosmologies: Feminist Theology (Shf 1992s, 2) 57-69 (-112, earth-healing) [< ZIT 93,203].

2186* *Ruiz de la Peña* Juan Luis, Dios y el cientifismo resistente [... DAWKINS R., HAWKING S.]: Salmanticensis 39 (1992) 217-243; Eng. 243.

2187 ᴱ**Russell** Robert J., *al.*, Physics, philosophy and theology; a common quest for understanding [Vatican Observatory conference] 1988 ➤ 5,2095; 6,682: ᴿCritRR 5 (1992) 437-9 (J.F. *Ollom*: as good an account of the issues as seems possible today); ÉglT 22 (1991) 263s (J.R. *Pambrun*).

2188 *Sappington* A.A., New scientific concepts and Christian beliefs: JPsy& Chr 10 (1991) 40-47.

2190 a) *Schmitz-Moormann* Karl, Theology in an evolutionary mode; – b) *Galleni* Lodovico, Relationships between scientific analysis and the world view of P. TEILHARD de Chardin; – c) *Carloye* Jack C., The existence of God and the creation of the universe: Zygon 27 (1992) 133-152 / 153-166 / 167-185.

2191 a) **Schroeder** Gerald L., Genesis and the Big Bang; the discovery of harmony between modern science and the Bible. NY 1992, Bantam. xi-212 p. $10 pa. [PerScCF 45,66s, D.F. *Siemens*].
— b) **Seely** Paul H., Inerrant wisdom; science and inerrancy in biblical perspective 1988 ➤ 6,2263: ᴿAustralBR 38 (1990) 91s (P. *Rule*: defends 'sapiential' but not 'factual' inerrancy).
— c) *Serrão* Daniel, As grandes questões antropológicas provocadas pelo desenvolvimento científico e tecnológico: HumTeol 13 (1992) 163-176.

2192 **Shea** William, La révolution galiléenne [1977], ᵀ*Gandt* François de. P 1992, Seuil. 456 p. F 320 [Études 378,117-9, F. *Russo*, aussi sur 3 semblables].

2193 *Shults* F. LeRon, A theology of chaos; an experiment in postmodern theological science: ScotJT 45 (1992) 223-235.

2194 **Shumaker** Wayne, Natural magic and modern science; four treatises, 1590-1657: MedvRTSt 63. Binghamton 1989, SUNY. 233 p. $18. – ᴿJRel 72 (1992) 305s (I. P. *Culianu*).

2195 **Sitchin** Zecharia, Genesis revisited; is modern science catching up with ancient knowledge? Santa Fe, 1991, Bear. 343 p. $22 [PerScCF 45,65s, E.O. *Bowser*].

2195* *Snoke* David W., Toward a unified view of science and theology: JAmScAff 43 (1991) 166-173.

2196 *Soontiëns* Frans, Evolution, teleology and theology: Bijdragen 53 (1992) 394-406; Eng. 406.

2197 a) *Spradley* Joseph L., Changing views of science and the Scripture; Bernard RAMM and the American Scientific Affiliation: PerspScCF 44 (1992) 2-8.
— b) *Sterling* Gregory E., Creatio temporalis, aeterna, vel continua? [... HAWKING S.]; an analysis of the thought of PHILO of Alexandria: StPhilonAn 4 (1992) 15-41.
— c) *Stoeger* William R., Theology and the contemporary challenge of the natural sciences: ProcCathTSAm 46 (1991) 21-43 (-48 response, *Johnson* Elizabeth A.).

— d) *Taylor* Howard,   Watchmakers are not blind [DAWKINS Richard, The blind watchmaker (Penguin 1988) title from W. *Paley*: explains complexity of nature from mindless natural selection]: Evangel 10,1 (1992) 26-29.

2198 *Testa Bappenheim* Italo,   Creazionismo ed evoluzionismo, oggi: BbbOr 34 (1992) 1-12.

2198* **Thomas** Nicholas,   Out of time; history and evolution in anthropological discourse: Studies in Social Anthropology. C 1989, Univ.   149 p. – RTsTKi 62 (1991) 73 (Terje *Stordalen*).

2199 **Tilby** Angela,   Science and the soul – new cosmology, the self and God [< her television series]. L 1992, SPCK.   275 p.   £13.   0-281-04579-8. – RExpTim 104 (1992s) 156 (J. *Polkinghorne*: good despite title); Tablet 246 (1992) 1130 (C. *Moss*).

2200 **Torrance** Thomas F.,   Senso del divino e scienza moderna, TDel Re Giuseppe.   Vaticano 1992, Editrice.   395 p. – RScripTPamp 24 (1992) 1065-8 (M. *Artigas*).

2201 *Torresani* Alberto,   Caso GALILEO, ultimo atto: StCattMi 36 (1992) 809-812.

2202 TEVan Helder Albert,   Galileo GALILEI, Sidereus nuncius or The sidereal messanger [1610].   Ch 1989, Univ.   xii-127 p. – RTPhil 67 (1992) 431-3 (A. *Radl*).

2203 **Van Till** Howard J., *al.*,   Portraits of creation 1990 ➤ 7,1918:   RCalvinT 26 (1991) 271-3 (C. B. *Kaiser*); JDharma 17 (1992) 58 (J. *Chiramattel*).

2204 *Van Till* Howard J., *Johnson* Phillip E.,   God and evolution; an exchange: FirsT 34 (1993) 32-38-41.

2205 **Vloet** Johan Van der,   Schaduw van God; christelijk scheppingsgeloof en nieuwste wetenschap. Antwerpen 1992, Hadewijch.   Fb498. – RStreven 59 (1992s) 1234 (J. *Haers*).

2206 *Wassermann* Christoph,   La théologie de l'expiation dans un monde relativiste; quelques aspects de la recherche interdisciplinaire entre physique et théologie après EINSTEIN: RTPhil 124 (1992) 41-60.

2207 **Wenner** V.,   Die Bibel zwischen Wissenschaft und Theologie; welche Glaubens- und Erkenntnislehre heute?   FrS 1989, Paulus.   249 p. – RBZ 36 (1992) 114 (J. *Becker*).

2208 **Wright** Richard T.,   Biology through the eyes of faith; Christian College coalition.   SF 1989 ➤ 6,2275; 0-06-069695-8:   RThemelios 18,2 (1992s) 33 (B. E. *Collis*).

2208* **Yanase** Michael,   Meeting God through science, TJohnston William.   Tokyo 1991, Sophia Univ.   114 p. – RPhilipSa 26 (1991) 506-8 (N. *Castillo*).

2209 *Yob* Iris M.,   Religious metaphor and scientific model; grounds for comparison: RelSt 28 (1992) 475-485.

2210 **Zabilka** Ivan L.,   Scientific malpractice; the creation/evolution debate.   Lexington 1992, Bristol.   160 p. $9 pa. [BToday 31,251].

2211 *Zoffoli* Enrico, *a*) Il tomismo di GALILEO: SacDoc 37 (1992) 196-220; – *b*) Galileo; fede nella ragione, ragioni della fede: SacDoc 35,3s intero (1990) 255-433; – *c*) Il fondamentale tomismo di Galileo: DocCom 44 (1991) 130-147.

E1.9   *Peccatum originale,*   **The Sin of Eden,** *Genesis 2-3.*

2212 *Andersen* Kristen M., 'Imago Dei' and desire in Genesis 1-3; to eat or not to eat, or rather to 'eat or what to eat: LitTOx 6 (1992) 254-267.

2213 *Anderson* Gary A.,   The penitence narrative in the [recently published Armenian and Georgian] Life of Adam and Eve: HUCA 63 (1992) 1-38.

2214 *Aranda Pérez* Gonzalo, Gen 1-3 en las homilías del Beato Josemaría ESCRIVÁ DE BALAGUER: ScripTPamp 24 (1992) 895-919
2215 *Barker* Kenneth S., The devil made me do it [as T-shirt slogan]: ExpTim 104 (1992s) 118-120.
2216 **Barr** James, Garden of Eden [Bristol Read-Tuckwell lectures, really on immortality and resurrection; Gn 2s does not teach a Fall]. L 1992, SCM. xiii-146 p. £10. 0-334-00531-0 [EurJT 2,179, G. *McConville*].
2217 *Barzel* Alexander, Concrete relationship in history; an interpretation of the origin and status of evil of Eden story: URM 14 (1991) 210-229.
2217* *Batto* Bernard F., Paradise reexamined: ➤ 7,334*, Canon 1990/1, 33-66.
2218 *Baudry* Gérard-Henry, Le Péché originel dans les pseudépigraphes de l'AT: MélSR 49 (1992) 163-192; Eng. 192.
2218* *Bourguet* Daniel, L'homme ou bien Adam?: ÉTRel 67 (1992) 323-7.
2219 *a*) *Cañellas* Gabriel, La sexualidad; visión de las religiones antiguas; – *b*) *Gallego* Epifanio, ... aporte de los relatos de la creación; – *c*) *Valle* José Luis del, ... simbología matrimonial en los escritos proféticos; – *d*) *Martín Juárez* Miguel A., ... aporte de los escritos sapienciales; – *e*) *Salas* Antonio, ... aporte del 'corpus' paulino; – *f*) *Quelle Parra* Constantino, ... de la tradición sinóptica; – *g*) *Sáenz de Santa María* Miguel, ... del cuarto evangelio: BibFe 18,52 (1992) 5-20 / 21-36 / 37-50 / 51-66 / 67-91 / 92-113 / 114-135.
2220 *Castilla y Cortázar* Blanca, ¿Fue creado el varón antes que la mujer? Reflexiones en torno a la antropología de la creación: AnnTh 6 (1992) 319-366.
2221 **Chiesa** B., Creazione e caduta 1989 ➤ 5,2131; 7,1926: ᴿRTPhil 124 (1992) 197 (A. *Moda*).
2222 *a*) **Clines** David J. A., What does Eve do to help? 1990 ➤ 6,213; 7,1927: ᴿCritRR 5 (1992) 121-4 Peggy L. *Day*); Themelios 17,3 (1991s) 24 (W. *Moberly*).
— *b*) **Colemonts-Vroninks** Elsy, De l''hominisation' à l''humanisation'; lecture des encycliques sociales à la lumière du paradoxe sotériologique révélé en Gn 1-2: Mémoire ᴰ*Schooyans*. LvN 1991s. – Mémoires de licence LvN 1991s: RTLv 24,142.
— *c*) *Conrad* Richard, Making sense of original sin: PrPeo 6 (1992) 109-113.
— *d*) *Cutsinger* James S., A knowledge that wounds our nature: JAAR (1992) 465-491.
2223 **Day** P. L., An adversary in heaven, *śāṭān* 1988 ➤ 4,2167 ... 7,1929: ᴿBZ 36 (1992) 295 (H. *Niehr*).
2223* *Delumeau* Jean, *a*) La nouvelle érudition (XVIᵉ-XVIIᵉ siècles) et le paradis terrestre: JSav (1991) 289-306; – *b*) Le paradis terrestre [subsistant encore sur notre terre d'après S. Thomas d'AQUIN] se trouvait-il à l'Équateur?: CRAI (1991) 135-144.
2224 **Díaz** Carlos, En el jardín de Edén. S 1991, ed. S. Sebastián. 155 p. – ᴿSalmanticensis 39 (1992) 163s (J. L. *Ruiz de la Peña*).
2224* *Dohmen* C., Ebenbild Gottes oder Hilfe des Mannes? Die Frau im Kontext anthropologischer Aussagen von Gen 1-3: Jb für christliche Sozialwissenschaften 34 (1991) 152-164 [< ZAW 105,509].
2225 Engel und Dämonen, eine Handreichung für die Verkündigung, Österreichische Theologische Kommission: Christlich pädagogische Blätter 105, 3 (Mai 1992) 106ss.
2226 **Fohr** S. D., Adam and Eve; the spiritual symbolism of Genesis and Exodus 1986 ➤ 3,2094; 0-8191-5268-4: ᴿJStOT 55 (1992) 119s (Athalya *Brenner*: value, despite some trends).

2227 *García Andrade* Carlos, El pecado original como respuesta cristiana al origen del mal moral: ➤ 551, RET 51 (1991) 215-236.
2228 **Garrett** Susan B., The demise of the devil... in Luke's writings 1989 ➤ 5,5036 ... 7,1938*: HeythJ 33 (1992) 86 (Mary E. *Mills*); TorJT 7 (1991) 273-5 (J. V. *Kozar*).
2228* **González Núñez** A., Adán y Eva; el hombre y su porvenir 1990 ➤ 6, 2305: ᴿRelCu 37 (1991) 127 (M. A. *Martín Juárez*).
2229 *Gottschalk* Alfred, The image of man in Genesis and the Ancient Near East: ➤ 65, Mem. GEVIRTZ S., Maarav 7 (1991) 131-140.
2230 *a) Grey* M., Moet Eva nog altijd schuldig blijven? Het Genesisverhaal herlezen; – *b) Geel* J., *Klijn* T., De stad van vrouwen; een gesprek over feministische theologie: Mara 4,3 (1991) 37-45/4-16 [< GerefTTs 91,188].
2231 **Grübel** I., Die Hierarchie der Teufel; Studien zum christlichen Teufelsbild und zur Allegorisierung des Bösen in Theologie, Literatur und Kunst zwischen Frühmittelalter und Gegenreformation [Diss.]: KuGF 13. Mü 1991, Tuduv. 325 + 46 p.; ill. DM 60 [RHE 87,428*].
2232 **Hauke** Manfred, Heilsverlust in Adam; Stationen griechischer Erbsündenlehre; IRENÄUS – ORIGENES – Kappadozier [Diss. Augsburg 1991 ➤ 7,1942]: KkTSt 58. Pd 1992, Bonifatius. 850 p. DM 128. 3-87088-718-4 [TGL 83,509s, D. *Hattrup*].
2233 *Hayward* C. T. R., The figure of Adam in Pseudo-PHILO's Biblical Antiquities: JStJud 23 (1992) 1-20.
2234 *a) Humbrecht* Thierry-Dominique, Le péché originel selon le Père Labourdette; – *b) Nicolas* Jean-Hervé, La volonté salvifique de Dieu contrariée par le péché; – *c) Bonino* Serge-Thomas, Le thomisme du Père Labourdette: ➤ 114, ꜰLABOURDETTE M., RThom 92,1 (1992) 153-176 / 177-196 / 88-122.
2234* **Kelly** Henry A., The devil at baptism 1985 ➤ 1,7208 ... 4,8716: ᴿRevSR 66 (1992) 360s (M. *Metzger*).
2235 **Koch** Robert, Die Sünde im Alten Testament. Fra 1992, Lang. 171 p. 3-631-44657-8.
2236 *Kowalski* A., Perfezione e giustizia di Adamo...: OrChrAnal 232, 1989 ➤ 5,2148 ... 7,1947: ᴿCrNSt 13 (1992) 207-9 (M. *Aveta*).
2237 *Kübel* Paul, Zur Entstehung der Paradieserzählung: BibNot 65 (1992) 74-85.
2238 **Levison** John R., Portraits of Adam in early Judaism: JPseud supp 1, 1988 ➤ 4,2192 ... 7,1940: ᴿJSS 37 (1992) 106-9 (G. J. *Brooke*); RB 99 (1992) 300s (J. *Murphy-O'Connor*).
2239 *Levison* John R., Early Judaism looks at Adam: BToday 30 (1992) 372-7.
2240 **Lipscomb** W. Lowndes, The Armenian apocryphal Adam literature [diss. 1983]: Univ. Pennsylvania Armenian 8. Atlanta 1990, Scholars. vi-288 p. $30. – ᴿJAOS 112 (1992) 501s (S. P. *Cowe*).
2240* **Louth** Andrew, The wilderness of God [Bible ch. 2, between Eden and New Jerusalem; the rest on FOUCAULD, JULIAN, SURIN, T. S. ELIOT]. L 1991, Darton-LT. x-166 p. £9 pa. – ᴿTLond 95 (1992) 303 (C. *Stewart*).
2241 *Louys* Daniel, Le jardin d'Éden; mythe fondateur de l'Occident: Lire la Bible 95. P 1992, Cerf. 225 p. F 100 [ÉglT 24,135s, W. *Vogels*]. 2-204-04539-X. – ᴱEsprVie 102 (1992) 204 (L. *Monloubou*).
2242 *Mannucci* Valerio, [Gen 1-3; Job, Qoh...] Il problema del male; 'modelli' di soluzione nell'Antico Testamento: VivH 3 (1992) 195-223; Eng. 223.
2243 ᴱ**Marchioni** Cristina, GIORDANO DA PISA [OP 1260-1310] Sul terzo capitolo del Genesi: RivStoLR BtTDoc 13. F 1992, Olschki. xxi-312 p. 88-222-3915-6.

2244 *Mense* Josef,   Gen 1-2 als politische Ballade; historisch-kritische Methode im Unterricht: KatBlät 117 (1992) 51-59 [< ZIT 92,124].
2245 **Michell** John,   The dimensions of paradise; the proportions and symbolic numbers in ancient cosmology.   SF 1988, Harper & R.   216 p. $20. – ᴿChH 60 (1991) 86s (I. P. *Culianu*).
2246 *a) Miscall* Peter D.,   Jacques DERRIDA in the Garden of Eden; – *b) Amit* Yairah,   Biblical utopianism; a mapmaker's guide to Eden; – *c) Brown* Schuyler,   Sin and atonement; biblical imagery and the experience of evil: UnSemQ 44,1s ('After the garden' 1990s) 1-9 / 11-17 / 151-6.
2248 *Moberly* R. W. L.,   *a)* Did the serpent get it right [< JTS 39 (1988) 1-27]; – *b)* Abraham's righteousness [< VTS 42 (1990) 103-130]: – *c)* [Gen 22] The earliest commentary on the Akedah [< VT 38 (1988) 302-323]; – *d)* Story in the OT [< Themelios 11 (1986) 77-82]; – *e)* 'Old Testament'; the propriety of the term for Christian theology [< TLond 95 (1992) 26-32] (+ 3 others; all 'slightly modified'):   ➤ 285, From Eden to Golgotha: SFLStJud 52 (Atlanta 1992, Scholars) 1-27 / 29-53 / 55-73 / 105-118 / 135-140 [-157].
2249 *a) Moltmann* Jürgen,   Zwölf Bemerkungen zur Symbolik des Bösen; – *b) Schmidt* Werner H.,   Gott und Böses; Hinweise auf das AT; – *c) Baumbach* Günther,   Die Funktion des Bösen in neutestamentlichen Schriften; – *d) Bjerg* Svend,   Judas als Stellvertreter des Satans; – *e) Schloz-Dürr* Adelbert,   Der traditionelle kirchliche Exorzismus im Rituale Romanum — biblisch-systematisch betrachtet; – *f) Rehberger* Claudia,   Die Verteufelung der Frau als Hexe in den Hexenverfolgungen des späten Mittelalters und der frühen Neuzeit; – *g) Krieg* Carmen,   Die Wiederkehr des Teufels? Satanismus heute: EvT 52,1 ('Wohin mit dem Teufel?' 1992) 2-6 / 7-22 / 23-42 / 42-55 / 56-65 / 65-75 / 76-86.
2249* *Moltmann* Jürgen,   Twelve comments on the symbolism of evil [i. The 'devil' is a mythic figure which serves to fixate diffuse anxieties in the face of monstrous atrocities (and) can achieve exploratory and exorcistic significance, < EvT 52 (1992) 2-6 > ᵀᴱ*Asen* B. A.: TDig 40,235-8].
ᴱ**Morris** Paul, *Sawyer* Deborah,   A walk in the garden; biblical, iconographical and literary images of Eden 1992 ➤ 482.
2250 *Neufeld* Ernest,   On the trail of original sin: Midstream 38,4 (1992) 29-31.
2250* **Nielsen** Kirsten,   *a)* Satan — den fortabte søn? Fredriksberg 1992, Religionspaedagogisk.   163 p.   Dk 168 pa. – ᴿTsTKi 63 (1992) 221-3 (T. *Stordalen*: spennend). – *b) šāṭān* 'Satan, Widersacher':   ➤ 770, TWAT 7,6s (1992) 745-751.
2251 *Norris* Richard A.,   The little engine that could; a musing on two recent studies of early Christianity [PAGELS E., Adam, Eve and the serpent; BROWN P., The body and society]:   UnSemQ 44,1s ('After the garden' 1990s) 19-30.
2252 *O'Loughlin* Thomas,   Adam's burial at Hebron; some aspects of its significance in the Latin traditions: PrIrB 15 (1992) 66-88.
2253 **Ormerod** Neil,   Grace and disgrace; a theology of self-esteem, society and history.   Newtown NSW 1992, Dwyer.   x-212 p. £7 pa. 0-85574-428-6 [TDig 39,378]. – ᴿTBR 5,2 (1992s) 27 (M. *Northcott*: on original sin).
2254 **Pagels** Elaine,   Adam, Eve, and the serpent 1988 ➤ 4,2203 ... 7,1959: ᴿPerspScCF 44 (1992) 208 (J. B. *Armstrong*).
2254* **Pagels** Elaine,   Adam, Eva und die Schlange; die Theologie der Sünde. Reinbek 1991, Rowohlt.   352 p. DM 44. – ᴿLuthMon 31 (1992) 282s (W. *Metz*).

2255 *Peters* Ted, *a*) Satan's friends [... Satanism] and enemies: Dialog 30 (St. Paul 1991) 303-313; – *b*) The selling of Satan in popular literature: ChrCent 108 (1991) 458-462.

2256 *Peursen* C. A. van, Onomatopeeën en de taal van Adam; de rol van LEIBNIZ' 'lingua adamica': Tijdschrift voor Filosofie 54 (1992) 241-254 [< RSPT 77,162].

2257 **Phipps** William E., Genesis and gender; biblical myths of sexuality and their cultural impact 1989 ➤ 6,2334: ᴿCCAR [new name of JRefJud] 39,1 (1992) 79s (Beth D. *Davidson*: Christian, feminist, convincing); JEvTS 35 (1992) 268s (R. *Lambert*).

2258 *Ravasi* Gianfranco, Hermeneutical comments on Gn 2-3 [< IkaZ 20 (1991) 294-304], ᵀᴱ*Asen* B. A.: TDig 39 (1992) 241-7.

2259 ᴱ**Robbins** G. A., Gn 1-3...: StWomenR 27 (1988): ᴿVT 42 (1992) 138 (J. A. *Emerton*).

2260 *Ruiz de la Peña* Juan L., Pecado original; la década de los ochenta: StOvet 17 (1989) 6-23.

2261 **Russell** J. B., Il diavolo nel mondo antico [1977 ➤ 65,1911], ᵀ*Cezzi* F., 1989 ➤ 6,2341 (Lit. 32.000): ᴿBbbOr 34 (1992) 189s (E. *Jucci*).

2262 **Salas** Antonio, Los orígenes; del Edén a Babel, M 1992, Paulinas. 150 p. [Iter 4/2, 153s, J.-P. *Wyssenbach*).

2262* *Sanni* Amidu, The original sin in Arabic poetics [Adam on Cain]: BSO 55 (1992) 9-15.

2263 **Sayés** José Antonio, Antropología del hombre caído 1991 ➤ 7,7155*: ᴿAugM 37 (1992) 415s (J. A. *Galindo*), Burgense 33 (1992) 571s (P. *Cervera*); CiuD 205 (1992) 763s (J. M. *Ozaeta*); EsprVie 102 (1992) 300 (J. *Galot*); Salmanticensis 39 (1992) 164-6 (J. L. *Ruiz de la Peña*); ScripTPamp 24 (1992) 297-304 (L. F. *Mateo-Seco*); Teresianum 43 (1992) 548 (F. *Javier Sancho*).

2263* *Sayés* José A., El pecado original en Santo TOMÁS: Burgense 32 (1991) 325-341.

2264 *Scheffczyk* Leo, Zur christozentrischen (christokephalen) Interpretation der Erbsünde: ➤ 51, ᶠErfurt 1992, 343-356.

2264* **Schönborn** Christoph, *al.*, Zur kirchlichen Erbsündenlehre; Stellungnahmen [GÖRRES Albert, SPAEMANN R.] zu einer brennenden Frage: Kriterien 87, 1991 ➤ 7,1970: ᴿErbAuf 68 (1992) 75s (U. J. *Plaga*: warum ist der Mensch böse? die Evolution zwingt ihn hierzu nicht, p. 14); TGL 82 (1992) 480s (D. *Hattrup* disapproves the new Denzinger 'Ursünde' for 'Erbsünde').

2265 *Schwager* Raymund, Der vom Himmel gefallene Satan; wer oder was ist der Teufel?: TGgw 35 (1992) 255-264.

2265* *Sfameni Gasparro* Giulia, La donna nell'esegesi patristica di Gen 1-3: ➤ 405, *Mattioli* U., Donna 1992, 17-50.

2266 *Spaemann* Heinrich, Erbsünde in biblischer Sicht: GeistL 65 (1992) 212-220.

2267 **Stewart** Charles, Demons and the devil; moral imagination in modern Greek culture 1991 ➤ 7,1973: ᴿAnthropos 87 (1992) 629s (Ulrike *Krasberg*); TS 53 (1992) 792 (Irena *Makarushka*: *exotika* in their relation to Orthodox Christianity).

Stone Michael E., A history of the literature of Adam and Eve: SBL EarlyJud 3, 1992 ➤ a258.

2269 *a*) *Stone* Michael E., New discoveries relating to the Armenian Adam books; – *b*) *Robinson* Stephen E., The Testament of Adam, an updated Arbeitsbericht: JPseud 5 (1989) 101-9 / 95-100.

2270 *a)* *Stordalen* Terje, Man, soil, garden; basic plot in Genesis 2-3 reconsidered; – *b)* *Dragga* Sam, Genesis 2-3, a story of liberation: JStOT 53 (1992) 3-26 / 55 (1992) 3-13.

2271 *Suchocki* Marjorie H., Original sin revisited: Process Studies 20 (1991) 233-... [< ZIT 92,720].

2273 *a)* *Tate* Marvin E., [Job 1s; Nm 22; Zech 3,1-7; 1 Chr 21; briefly Gn 1-3 ...]: – *b)* *Hinson* E. Glenn, Historical and theological perspectives on Satan; – *c)* *Hendricks* William L., Giving the devil his due; a visual approach; – *d)* *Wink* Walter, Demons and DMins; the Church's response to the demonic; – *e)* *Thornton* Edward E., Fragmentation anxiety and the balm of Gilead; a pastoral care perspective on Satanism; – *f)* *Allen* W. L., Matthew 4:1-11, the devil at the crossroads: RExp 89 (1992) 461-474 / 475-487 / 488-501; 2 fig. / 503-513 / 515-526 / 529-533.

2274 *Temiño Saiz* Angel, Nuestra solidaridad con Cristo y con Adán; el pecado original y los dogmas marianos: Burgense 32 (1991) 9-40.

2275 *Thériault* Jean Yves, Le parcours de l'Adam dans le jardin: SémBib 67 (1992) 13-36; 68 (1992) 15-34.

2276 ᴱVerdegaal C., *Weren* W., Stromen uit Eden; Genesis 1-11 en bijbel, joodse exegese en moderne literatuur. Brugge/Boxtel 1992, Tabor/KBS. 298 p. – ᴿStreven 59 (1992s) 1141 (P. *Beentjes*).

2276* *a)* *Vermes* Geza, Genesis 1-3 in post-biblical Hebrew and Aramaic literature before the Mishnah; – *b)* *Alexander* Philip S., Pre-emptive exegesis; Genesis Rabbah's reading of the story of creation: JJS 43 (1992) 221-229 / 230-245.

2277 *a)* *Winling* Raymond, Péché originel et rédemption dans l'œuvre de N. S. BERGIER; contribution à l'histoire des idées au XVIIIᵉ siècle: RevSR 66 (1992) 297-317.

— *b)* **Wolde** Ellen J. van, A semiotic analysis of Gn 2-3, 1989 → 6,2357; 7,1987: ᴿVT 42 (1992) 573s (J. A. *Emerton*).

— *c)* **Zimmermann** Anthony F., Original sin; where doctrine meets science. –

— *d)* The religion of Adam and Eve. NY 1990s, Vantage. xviii-264 p. $17 / xv-159 p., $15. 0-533-08740-4; -869-0. – ᴿVidyajyoti 56 (1992) 632-4 (G. V. *Lobo*).

2278 *Hoevels* Fritz Erik, [Gen 2,4-3,24] Das Tabu der Nacktheit: System ubw, Zeitschrift für klassische Psychoanalyse 2 (1984) 86-114 (3-922774-91-1) = The hidden psychology of nudity, in his Collected Papers (New Delhi 1993).

2279 **Marlière** Frédéric, 'Et ils virent qu'ils étaient nus' 1989 → 6,2325; 7,1955: ᴿPeCa 251 (1991) 70-73 (J. *Bacon*).

2280 *Tamez* E., De macht van naaktheid: Mara 3,3 (1990) 5-12 [< GerefTTs 9,163].

2280* *Zimmermann* Anthony, Naked but not ashamed: The Priest 48,9 (1992) 47-54: IRENAEUS more congenial than AUGUSTINE.

2281 *Stordalen* Terje, Genesis 2,4; restudying a *locus classicus*: ZAW 104 (1992) 163-177: a unit; what follows is not a creation-story but what happened some time *after* creation.

2281* *Azzali Bernardelli* Giovanna, La componente dotta nell'esegesi tertullianea di Gen 2,7: → 458, AnStoEseg 9,2 (1992) 387-396; Eng. 342.

2282 *Boulnois* Marie-Odile, Le souffle et l'Esprit; exégèses patristiques de l'insufflation originale de Gn 2,7 en lien avec celle de Jn 20,22: RechAug 24 (1989) 3-37.

2282* *Fernández Ardanaz* Santiago: A la búsqueda del paradigma original del hombre; Gen. 1,27 y 2,7 en los pensadores cristianos del s. II: ScripV 38 (1991) 80-113.

2283 *Adamo* David T.,   Ancient Africa and Genesis 2:10-14:   JRelTht 49,1 (1992) 33-43 [< ZIT 92,685].

2284 *Güttgemanns* Erhardt, [Gn 2,18-25]: Die Sprache Adams und Evas: LingB 67 (1992) 83-114; Eng. 114.

2284* *Barton* Peter F.,   Das Alte Testament und die Kirchengeschichte [i. Welche Sprache sprachen Adam und Eva; ii. Clan (Lamech)...]: ➤ 163, FSAUER G., Aktualität 1992, 145-154.

2285 *Hess* Richard S.,   The roles of the woman and the man in Genesis 3: Themelios 18,3 (1992s) 15-19.

2285* *Albertz* Rainer,   'Ihr werdet sein wie Gott' (Gen 3,5): ➤ 197, FWOLFF H. W., 'Was ist der Mensch...?' 1992, 11-27.

2286 a) *Shore* Eliezer,   The tree at the heart of the garden: Parabola 14,3 (1989) 38-43.

— b) *Wosk* Yosef J.,   Two trees planted in the midst of an enigmatic garden; a four-dimensional study of Genesis 2:8-9: diss. Boston Univ. 1992, ᴰ*Mason* H. 318 p. 92-21850. – DissA 53 (1992s) 846-A.

2286* *Müller* H.-P.,   Weisheitliche Deutungen der Sterblichkeit; Gen 3,19 und Pred 3,21; 12,7 im Licht antiker Parallelen ➤ 288a, Mensch-Umwelt 1992, 220-233.

2287 **Anderson** Jeffrey S.,   The nature and function of curses in the narrative literature of the Hebrew Bible: diss. Vanderbilt, ᴰ*Knight* D. Nv 1992. 288 p. 93-00043. – DissA 53 (1992s) 2854s-A.

2287* *Laeuchli* Samuel,   The expulsion from the garden and the hermeneutics of play [< Religious Traditions 14 (1991) 1-57]: ➤ 358b, Body and Bible 1992, 27-56.

E2.1   **Cain ut Abel**; *gigantes, longaevi; Genesis 4s.*

2288 *Albans* Keith R., [Gn 4,1-16] As in Cain: ExpTim 104 (1992s) 371s.

2289 *Ceccherelli* Ignazio M., [Gen 4,1-16] Caino, storia di una vita che abbraccia millenni: BbbOr 34 (1992) 93-112.

2290 *Fournet* Jean-Luc,   Une éthopée [exercice de rhétorique] de Caïn dans le Codex des Visions de la Fondation Bothmer: ZPapEp 92 (1992) 253-266.

2291 a) *Komenda* Bettina, al., [Gn 4,1-16] Wie schuldig ist Kain? Zur Wirkungsgeschichte der biblischen Erzählung; – b) *Dieckmann* Bernhard, Schuld abladen; der Sündenbock und die anderen: KatBlätt 117 (1992) (523-) 532-7 / 456-464 [< ZIT 92,530].

2292 a) *Pirani* Alix,   Cain and Abel; a case for family therapy? [< European Judaism]; – b) *Wink* Walter,   Bible study and movement for human transformation: ➤ 358b, Body and Bible 1992, 145-158 / 120-132.

2293 **Quinones** Ricardo J.,   The changes of Cain; violence and the lost brother in Cain and Abel literature.   Princeton 1991, Univ. viii-284 p. 0-691-06883-6; pa. -1502-3.

2294 *Ratner* Robert J.,   Cain and Abel, and the problem of paradox: JRefJud 37,4 (1990) 9-20.

2295 *Spina* Frank A.,   The 'ground' for Cain's rejection (Gen 4); ʾ*dāmāh* in the context of Gen 1-11: ZAW 104 (1992) 319-332.

2296 *Vogels* Walter,   Caïn; l'être humain qui devient une non-personne (Gn 4,1-16): NRT 114 (1992) 321-340.

2297 *Hocherman* Yaakov, ❺ Notes to [Gen 4,1; 6,3; 22,6; 27,40]: BethM 36 (1990s) 20-28 (119-123) [< OTAbs 15,35, transcription 'Hocherman', not Hookerman ➤ 6,2374; and fuller details].

2298 **Peters** U., [Gn 4,22] Wie der biblische Prophet Henoch zum Buddha wurde [Diss. 1983 ᴰ*Klimkeit* H.]. Sinzig 1989, St Meinrad. ix-219 p., 14 pl. 3-927593-07-9 [NTAbs 36,451].

2298* *Hess* Richard S., Lamech in the genealogies of Genesis: BuBRes 1 (1991) 21-27.

2299 *Kugel* James, [Gn 4,23; 5,28] Why was Lamech blind?: HebAnR 12 (1990) 91-103.

2300 *Seidel* Hans, Genesis 4,19-21 und der Ursprung der Kultur: ➤ 7,164*a*, ꟳWALLIS G., Überlieferung und Geschichte (Halle 1990) 23-34.

2301 **Ward** Peter D., [Gn 5,21] On Methuselah's trail; living fossils and the great extinctions. 1992, Freeman. 212 p. – ᴿPerspScCF 44 (1992) 271s (*G. C. Mills*).

2301* *Dexinger* Ferdinand, Jüdisch-christliche Nachgeschichte von Gen 6,1-4: ➤ 163, ꟳSAUER G., Aktualität 1992, 155-175.

2302 *Savasta* Carmelo, Genesi [6,] 3a-c e Genesi 6,3d*-e; proposta di una nuova collocazione: BbbOr 34 (1992) 171-8.

E2.2 *Diluvium*, **The Flood**; Gilgameš (Atraḫasis); **Genesis 6 ...**

2302* *Alster* Bendt, Court ceremonial and marriage in the Sumerian epic 'Gilgamesh and Huwawa': BSO 55 (1992) 1-8.

2303 ᵀᴱ**Bottéro** Jean, L'épopée de Gilgameš, le grand homme qui ne voulait pas mourir: L'aube des peuples. P 1992, Gallimard. 299 p.; ill.; maps. F 160. 2-07-072583-9.

2304 **Couliano** I. P., Out of this world; otherworldly journeys from Gilgamesh to Albert Einstein. Boston 1991, Shambhala. xvi-287 p. $15 pa. – ᴿParabola 16,4 (1991) 94 . 98 . 101 (Carol *Zaleski*).

2305 **Dux** Günter, Liebe und Tod im Gilgamesch-Epos; Geschichte als Weg zum Selbstbewusstsein des Menschen. W 1992, Passagen. 98 p. 3-85165-003-4 [OIAc 5,19].

2306 *Edzard* Dietz O., Gilgameš XI 65-69: ➤ 118, ꟳLESLAU W., Semitic 1991, 392-6; Teil II, ZAss 81 (1992) 156-233; 'Teil III folgt'.

2307 **Ferry** David, Gilgamesh; a new rendering in English verse; pref. *Moran* William L. NY 1992, Farrar-SG. xi-99 p. 0-374-16227-1 [OIAc 3,20].

2308 *Hallo* William W., Information from before the flood; antediluvian notes from Babylonia and Israel: ➤ 65, Mem. GEVIRTZ S., Maarav 7 (1991) 173-181.

2309 **Jackson** Danny P., The epic of Gilgamesh; pref. *Biggs* Robert D. Wauconda ɪʟ 1992, Bolchazi-Carducci. xxvi-96 p.; ill. (*Kapheim* Thom), 0-86516-252-2 [OIAc 5,25].

2310 **Kluger** Rivkah S., The archetypal significance of Gilgamesh, ᴱ*Kluger* H. Yehezkel. Einsiedeln 1991, Daimon. 238 p. [JAOS 112,726].

2310* *Lim* Timothy H., The chronology of the Flood story in a Qumran text (4Q252): JJS 43 (1992) 288-298.

2311 **McCall** Henrietta, Mesopotamian myths [... Gilgamesh]: The Legendary Past, L 1990 ➤ 6,b90; also Austin 1990, Univ. Texas. 80 p.; 34 fig.; map. $8 pa. 0-292-75130-3. – ᴿClasW 85 (1991) 734s (Shelly P. *Haley*).

2312 ᵀᴱ**Malbran-Labat** Florence, Gilgamesh: Documents autour de la Bible (0993-510X). P 1992 = 1982, Cerf. 78 p. 2-204-04526-8 [OIAc 5,28].

2312* a) *Moran* William L., The epic of Gilgamesh; a document of ancient humanism; – b) *Silva* Aldina da, La symbolique des rêves et des vêtements dans les mythes sur Dumuzi: BCanadMesop 22 (1991) 15-22 / 31-35.

2313 *Moreno* G. Jaime, La literatura mesopotámica antigua [... Gilgameš]: TVida 33 (1992) 237-254.

2313* **Pettinato** Giovanni, *al.*, La saga di Gilgamesh. Mi 1992, Rusconi. 430 p. Lit. 32.000 [Letture 48,177s, G. *Ravasi*].

2314 **Van Nortwick** Thomas, Somewhere I have never travelled; the second self and the hero's journey in ancient epic. NY 1992, Oxford-UP. xv-204 p. 0-19-507149-2.

2315 *Vanstiphout* H. L. J., [Gilgameš] The craftsmanship of *Sīn-leqi-unninnī*: OrLovPer 21 (1990) 45-79.

2315* *Vulpe* Nicola, Gilgamesh and the specific nature of poetry: → 557*, Contacts 1990/2, 153-9.

2316 *Geller* Stephen A., Some sound and word plays in the first tablet of the Old Babylonian Atramhasis epic: → 180c, Mem. TALMAGE F., 1 (1992s) 63-70.

2317 *Westhuizen* J. P. van der, Some further possible restorations to Atra-ḫasīs: Akkadica 78 (1992) 18-25.

2317* **Bailey** Lloyd R., Noah 1989 → 5,2216... 7,2002: ᴿBR 7,2 (1991) 13 (M. *Brettler*).

2318 **Cazeaux** Jacques, La trame et la chaîne; II. Le cycle de Noé dans PHI-LON: ArbLHJ 20, 1989 → 5,2217; 7,2004: ᴿStPhilonAn 4 (1992) 153-6 (M. *Alexandre*); VigChr 46 (1992) 83-87 (J. *Dillon*).

2318* **Deurloo** K., *Zuurmond* R., De dagen van Noach; de verhalen rond de vloed in Schrift en oudste traditie (bijdrage, *Apeldoorn* Margreet van). ƒ34.50. 90-259-4444-2. – ᴿDielB 27 (1991) 276s (B. J. *Diebner*); TvT 32 (1992) 412 (J. *Holman*).

2319 ᴱ**Dundes** Alan, The flood myth 1988 → 4,224b... 7,2005: ᴿJAOS 112 (1992) 164s (L. R. *Bailey*).

2321 *Kikawada* Isaac M., Noah and the Ark: → 741, AnchorDB 4 (1992) 1123-31 (-32, *Bailey* Lloyd R., the Ark... survival).

2322 *Jacobson* Howard, 4Q252; addenda: JJS [43 (1992) 288, T. *Lim* on Flood] 44, 118-120 (-121-6, 1 fig., Lim).

2323 *Siemens* David F., [More] problems with Flood geology: PerspScCF 44 (1992) 169-174. 228-235.

2324 *Tomasino* Anthony J., History repeats itself; the 'fall' and Noah's drunkenness: VT 42 (1992) 128-130.

2325 **Millard** M., [Gn 9] Die Noachidischen Gebote; zur Endgestalt der Bibel, ihrer inner- und nachbiblischer Auslegung: Diss. Mag. Heid 1989. 110 p. – ᴿDielB 27 (1991) 233s (B. J. *Diebner*).

2326 *Mello* Alberto, La diaspora necessaria, Gen 10-11: → 339, ParSpV 26 (1992) 9-23.

2327 *Christensen* Duane L., Nations [not on Gn 10; largely on NT *goyim*]: → 741, AnchorBD 4 (1992) 1037-1049 [1031-37, Nationality and political identity, *Liverani* Mario].

2328 a) *Mazzinghi* Luca, Unità e diversità della famiglia nella 'tavola dei popoli' (Gen 10); – b) *Rizzi* Armido, 'L'unità del genere umano'; alla ricerca di un concetto; – c) *Rocchetta* Carlo, Introduzione... Nota

bibliografica: VivH 3,1 (1992) 27-43; Eng. 43 / 9-26; Eng. 26 / 5-9.
63-82.

2328* *Heller* B., [Gn 10,9] Namrud: ➤ 756, EncIslam² 7 (1992) 953s.

2329 *a*) **Klengel-Brandt** Evelyn, Der Turm von Babylon² [¹1982]; Legende und Geschichte eines Bauwerkes. Lp 1992, Koehler & A. 191 p.; 10 color. pl. [OIAc 5,27].

— *b*) *Launay* Marc B. de, Babel [... et la traduction; verset par verset]: ➤ 462, Naissance 1990/2, 267-278.

— *c*) *Noël* Damien, [*al.*], [Gn 10] La tour de Babel, un texte énigmatique: MondeB 71 ('Babylone' 1991) [2-]30s.

2330 **Uehlinger** Christoph, Weltreich und 'eine Rede'... Gn 11,1-9: OBO 101, 1990 ➤ 5,2238 ... 7,2036: ᴿBL (1992) 93s (J. A. *Emerton*); ÉTRel 67 (1992) 267s (Françoise *Smyth*); ExpTim 103 (1991s) 297s (R. J. *Coggins*); JBL 111 (1992) 321-3 (M. H. *Floyd*); TLZ 117 (1992) 169-272 (E.-J. *Waschke*); TR 88 (1992) 365-7 (H. *Seebass*).

2330* *Dokurno* Wacław, ❷ The universality of the Noahic covenant: ColcT 62,4 (1992) 5-24; Eng. 24.

2331 *Emerton* J. A., The source analysis of Genesis XI 27-32: VT 42 (1992) 37-46: still 28-30 J, 27 . 31-32 P.

E2.3   Patriarchae, Abraham; *Genesis 12s.*

2332 *Ceccherelli* Ignazio M., Abramo, padre di una moltitudine di genti: BbbOr 34 (1992) 159-169.

2333 *Collin* Matthieu, Une tradition ancienne dans le cycle d'Abraham?: ➤ 474, ACFÉB 1991/2, 209-228.

2334 **Deurloo** K., De vader van het landvolk; exegetische vertelsels over Abraham. Baarn 1992, Ten Have. 137 p. Fb 498. – ᴿCollatVL 22 (1992) 440 (H. *Hoet*).

2335 **Hansen** G. Walter, Abraham in Galatians: JStNT supp 20, ᴰ1989 ➤ 7,2040: ᴿJTS 43 (1992) 614s (G. N. *Stanton*: claimed kin to the 12 out of 43 *thaumázō* papyri in which the rebuke is followed by a request).

2336 **Harrisville** Roy A., The figure of Abraham in the Epistles of St. Paul; in the footsteps of Abraham [< diss. Union, Richmond 1990]. SF 1992, Mellen Univ. xiv-314 p. £40. 0-7734-9841-9. – ᴿTBR 5,3 (1992s) 28 (R. *Morgan*).

2336* *Hinkelammert* F. J., La fe de Abraham y el Edipo occidental: Ribla 3 (1989) 59-105 [< Stromata 47,444].

2337 **Köckert** Matthias, Vätergott und Väterverheissungen ... ALT: FRL 142, 1988 ➤ 4,8023: ᴿTsTKi 63 (1992) 219s (M. *Sæbø*); VerkF 36,21 (1991) 101-3 (H. *Seebass*).

2338 **Maatti** Émile, *Rocalve* Pierre, *Hamidullah* Mohammed, Abraham: La chêne de Mambré, trois voix monothéistes [ᴱ*Laudenbach* Annie]. P 1992, Centurion. 168 p. F 100. – ᴿÉtudes 378 (1993) 426 (J. *Thomas*: aussi sur 'Le pardon' et 'Prier' dans la même nouvelle série).

2339 *Millard* A. R., Abraham: ➤ 741, AnchorBD 1 (1992) 35-41.

2340 **Moberly** R. W. L., [➤ 7017] Genesis 12-50: OTGuides. Sheffield 1992, JStOT. 112 p. £6. 1-85075-371-7.

2341 **Nielsen** E., Abrahams historie; en historisk-kritisk kommentar til Genesis 11,26-25,11. K 1992, MusTusc. 152 p. Dk 140. 87-7289-201-3 [BL 93,42, K. *Jeppesen*: shows concern for new trends].

2341* *O'Brien* Mark A., [Gen 12,...] The story of Abraham and the debate over the source hypothesis [BLUM E. 1984]: AustralBR 38 (1990) 1-17, presidential address Melbourne 1989.

2342 *Schreiner* Josef, Zur Theologie der Patriarchenerzählungen in Gen 12-36: ➤ 149, ᶠPREUSS H., At. Glaube 1992, 20-34.

2343 **Siker** Jeffrey S., Disinheriting the Jews; Abraham 1991 ➤ 7,2048: ᴿEncounter 53 (1992) 291s (R. J. *Allen*); Mid-Stream 31,2 (1992) 163s (F. A. *MacDonald*); TS 53 (1992) 382 (L. E. *Frizzell*).

2344 *Thompson* John L., The immoralities of the patriarchs in the history of exegesis; a reappraisal of CALVIN's position: CalvinT 26 (1991) 9-46.

2345 ᴱ**Dierkens** Alain, Apparitions et miracles [Colloque 1991]: ProbHistRel 2. Bru 1991, Univ. 190 p. – ᴿRHPR 72 (1992) 315s (P. *Maraval*).

2346 *Kottackal* Joseph, The call of Abraham and faith-formation in the Book of Genesis: Bible Bhashyam 16 (1990) 69-78.

2347 *Zwickel* Wolfgang, *a*) [Gn 12; 26; 35] Die Altarbaunotizen im Alten Testament: Biblica 73 (1992) 533-546; – *b*) Der Altarbau Abrahams zwischen Bethel und Ai (Gen 12f), ein Beitrag zur Datierung des Jahwisten: BZ 36 (1992) 207-219.

2348 *Talstra* Epp, [Gn 12...] Text, grammar and computer; the balance of interpretation and calculation: ➤ 450*, Informatique 3ᵉ 1991/2, 135-149.

2349 *Vlachos* L. S., [Gen 12...] Ⓖ The phrase 'Do not think greatly' [... CHRYSOSTOM]: TAth 63 (1992) 255-285 . 451-500.

2350 *Launderville* Dale, Divine encounter and obedient response: BToday 30 (1992) 73-79.

2351 *Espinel* José Luis, [Gn 12,3] Israel y la bendición de Abrahán para todas las gentes: ➤ 135, ᶠMUÑOZ IGLESIAS S., EstBib 50 (1992) 411-422.

2352 *Alexander* T. D., [Gn 12,10...] Are the wife/sister incidents of Genesis literary compositional variants? [VAN SETERS J., WESTERMANN C. inconclusive]: VT 42 (1992) 145-153. ➤ 2375*.

2353 **Brock** Sebastian P., *Hopkins* Simon, [Gn 12,10-20 + Gn 20], A verse homily on Abraham and Sarah in Egypt; Syriac original with early Arabic translation: Muséon 105 (1992) 87-146.

2354 *Hoffmeier* James K., The wives' tale of Genesis 12 [&] 20 & 26 and the covenants at Beer-Sheba: TyndB 43,1 (1992) 81-99.

2355 *Firestone* Reuven, Prophethood, marriageable consanguinity, and text; the problem of Abraham and Sarah's kinship relationship and the response of Jewish and Islamic exegesis: JQR 83 (1992s) 331-347.

2355* *McKinlay* Judith E., [Gn 12/20] Dead spots or living texts? A matter of biblical reading: Pacifica 5 (1992) 1-16.

2356 *a*) *Rashkow* Ilona N., Intertextuality, transference, and the reader in/of Genesis 12 and 20; – *b*) *Penchansky* David, Staying the night; intertextuality in Genesis and Judges; – *c*) *Hawk* L. Daniel, Strange houseguests; Rahab, Lot, and the dynamics of deliverance; – *d*) *Davis* Ellen F., Job and Jacob; the integrity of faith: ➤ 351d, Reading 1992, 57-73 / 77-88 / 89-97 / 203-224.

E2.4 **Melchisedech, Sodoma;** *Genesis 14.*

2357 *Bernhardt* Karl-Heinz, *al.*, Melchisedek: ➤ 768, TRE 22 (1992) 414-7 [-420, *Willi* Thomas, Judentum; -421, *Balz, Horst*, NT].

2357* *Cohen* Chaim H., Genesis 14:1-11 – an early Israelite chronographic source: ➤ 7,334*, ᴱ**Younger** K., Canon 1990/1, 67-107.

2358 **Loader** J.A., A tale of two cities, Sodom and Gomorrah in the OT, early Jewish and early Christian traditions 1990 ➤ 6,2419: ᴿCBQ 54 (1992) 752s (D. *Bundy*); ÉglT 23 (1992) 261s (W. *Vogels*); ExpTim 103 (1991s) 142 (C.S. *Rodd*: impressive research); JStJud 23 (1992) 118-122 (J. van *Ruiten*); LvSt 17 (1992) 408s (Lieve *Teugels*); TvT 32 (1992) 311 (A. *Schoors*); ZAW 104 (1992) 300 (H.C. *Schmitt*).

2359 a) *Moorsel* Paul van, Treasures from Baramous with some remarks on a Melchizedek scene; – b) *Helderman* Jan, Melchisedek, Melchisedekianer und die koptische Frömmigkeit: ➤ 694b, Copte IVᵉ (1988/92) 1,171-7; 8 fig. / 2,402-415.

2360 *Kruse* Heinz, ❷ Who is Melchizedek? KatKenk 31 (1992) 1-21; Eng. i-iv.

2360* *Grelot* Pierre, De l'Apocryphe de la Genèse aux Targoums; sur Genèse 14,18-29: ➤ 132, ᶠMɪʟɪᴋ J. 1992, 77-90.

2361 *Gianotto* Claudio, 'Melkisedeq benedisse Abram' (Gen 14,18-20): ➤ 339, ParSpV 26 (1992) 25-45.

2362 *Sedgwick* Colin J., [Heb 7,11-28] Melchizedek the mystery man: ExpTim 104 (1992s) 213s.

2362* *Vivian* Angelo †, ᴱ*Sacchi* Paolo [< AISG 1990], I movimenti che si oppongono al Tempio; il problema del sacerdozio di Melchisedeq: Henoch 14 (1992) 97-111; Eng. 111s.

E2.5 **The Covenant** (alliance, Bund); *Foedus, Genesis 15...*

2363 *Firestone* Reuven, Abraham; the first Jew or the first Muslim? Text, tradition, and 'truth' in interreligious dialogue: ᴄᴄᴀʀ 39,1 (1992) 17-28.

2363* **Hays** John D., An exegetical and theological study of the Abrahamic covenant in a canonical context: diss. SW Baptist Theol. Sem. 1992. 285 p. 92-23536. – DissA 53 (1992s) 842s-A.

2364 **Ha** John, Genesis 15: BZAW 181, ᴰ1989 ➤ 5,2272... 7,2058: ᴿNed-TTs 46 (1992) 58s (B. *Becking*); TR 88 (1992) 185s (K. *Grünwaldt*: Fragezeichen).

2364* **Kreuzer** Siegfried, Die Frühgeschichte Israels... [Gn 15; Dt 26,5-9; Jos 24,2-13; ev. Hab.-D 1987 Wien] 1989 ➤ 5,2274... 7,2060: ᴿJAOS 112 (1992) 704s (R.S. *Hendel*).

2365 **Mölle** Herbert, Genesis 15...: ForBi 62, 1988 ➤ 4,2309... 7,2061: ᴿBiblica 73 (1992) 568-575 (M. *Köckert*); CBQ 54 (1992) 535-7 (R. *Gnuse*).

2366 **Nordheim** Eckhard von, Die Selbstbehauptung Israels in der Welt des Alten Orients; religionsgeschichtlicher Vergleich anhand von Gen 15/22/28, dem Aufenthalt Israels in Ägypten, 2 Sam 7, 1 Kön 19 und Psalm 104: OBO 115. FrS/Gö 1992, Univ./VR. 220 p. Fs 59. 3-7278-0792-X / 3-525-53749-2 [BL 93,112, J.R. *Porter*: Fra Hab-Schrift; 4 of the 5 chapters already published].

2367 a) *Wächter* Ludwig, Erwägungen zur Redaktionsgeschichte; Theologie und Text von Genesis 15; – b) *Zobel* Hans-Jürgen, Geschichte und Überlieferung; die Theologie Israels und Judas; – c) *Soggin* J. Alberto, Gedanken zur Vor- und Frühgeschichte Israels und Judas: ➤ 7,164a, ᶠWᴀʟʟɪs G., Überlieferung und Geschichte, ᴱ*Obst* H. (Halle 1990) 121-132 / 7-22 / 83-92.

2367* **Karavites** Peter (Panayiotis), (*Wren* Thomas), Promise-giving and treaty-making; HOMER and the Near East: Mnemosyne supp. 119, Leiden 1992, Brill. x-324 p. 90-04-09567-5.

2368 *Rendsburg* Gary A., Notes on Genesis XV [,1 Janus parallelism; ,20 Amorites]: VT 42 (1992) 266-272.

2368* *Vania Proverbio* Delio, Gen. XV,19-21 = Jub. XIV,18; note miscellanee: Henoch 14 (1992) 261-271; Eng. 272.

2369 **Firestone** Reuven, Journeys in holy lands; the evolution of the Abraham-Ishmael legends in Islamic exegesis 1990 ➤ 6,2433; 7,2066: ᴿBSO 55 (1992) 122-4 (A. *Rippin*: complaints); JQR 83 (1992s) 290-2 (Aviva *Schussman*); RHR 209 (1992) 77s (G. *Monnot*).

2370 **Knauf** Ernst A., [Gn 16s] Ismael²ʳᵉᵛ [¹1985 diss.] 1989 ➤ 4,d97 ... 7,b14: ᴿCBQ 54 (1992) 327s (V. H. *Matthews*: new material isolated).

2371 **Wormhoudt** Arthur A. [translator of 33 items from Arabic in BIP], Blessing of Ishmael and Esau. Auct. – ᴿTBR 5,3 (1992s) 82 (C. *Holes*).

2372 *Hoppe* Klaus D., Psychoanalytische Bibelauslegung; das Beispiel der Hagar-Ismael Überlieferung: WegMensch 43 (1991) 323-334.

2373 *Mothes* Pierre, Le fils de la migrante; note exégétique sur Genèse 16[,12]: ÉTRel 67 (1992) 67-70.

2373* **Teubal** Savina J., Hagar the Egyptian; the lost tradition of the matriarchs 1990 ➤ 6,2434: ᴿBR 8,6 (1992) 13s (Ilona N. *Rashkow*); Interpretation 46 (1992) 310 . 312 (Susan *Ackerman*).

2374 *Niehoff* M., [Gn 17s ... 37,29s] Do biblical characters talk to themselves? Narrative modes of representing inner speech in early biblical fiction. JBL 111 (1992) 575-595.

2375 *Propp* William H., [Gen 17:10-14] The origins of infant circumcision in Israel: HebAnR 11 (1987) 355-370.

2375* *Ronning* John, [Gen 17,17] The naming of Isaac; the role of the wife/sister episodes in the redaction of Genesis: WestTJ 53 (1991) 1-27.

2376 *Regt* L. J. de, [Gn 18,1-15 ...] Participant reference in some biblical Hebrew texts: JbEOL 32 (1991s) 150-172.

2377 *Welten* Peter, [Gn 18,1] Mamre: ➤ 768, TRE 22 (1992) 11-13.

2378 *Beuken* W. A. M., Gen 18:21; an overview of the problems of interpretation and an attempt at translation: JbEOL 32 (1991s) 141-9.

2379 *Ben Zvi* Ehud, The dialogue between Abraham and ʏʜᴡʜ in Gen. 18. 23-32; a historical-critical analysis: JStOT 53 (1992) 27-46.

2380 *Matthews* Victor H., Hospitality and hostility in Genesis 19 and Judges 19: BibTB 22 (1992) 3-11.

2381 *Rothchild-Laeuchli* Evelyn, [Gen 19,26; Lk 17,32] Lot's wife looks back; biblical stories as therapy and play. ➤ 358b, Body and Bible 1992, 191-201.

2382 *Gargano* Innocenzo, (Gen 19,30ss) 'Lot si rifugiò nella grotta con le sue due figlie', Oʀɪɢᴇɴᴇ: ➤ 339, ParSpV 26 (1992) 215-231.

2383 **Bouwman** Gijs, [Gen 18] De Zonde van Sodom; ontstaan en verstaan van een bijbelverhaal. Hilversum 1990, Gooi en S. 141 p. ƒ24. – ᴿStreven 58 (1990s) 659 (P. *Beentjes*).

Loader J. A. [Gen 18,16 - 19,20] A tale of two cities, Sodom and Gomorrah in the OT ... 1990 ➤ 2358.

2383* *Smith* Carol, [Gen 19,30s; 2 Sam 13] Stories of incest in the Hebrew Bible; scholars challenging text or text challenging scholars?: Henoch 14 (1992) 227-242; ital. 242.

2384 *Weisman* Zeev, ❿ Ethnology, etiology, genealogy, and historiography in the tale of Lot and his daughters (Genesis 19:31-38): ➤ 181, Shaʿarei Tᴀʟᴍᴏɴ 1992, 43*-62*; Eng. xvii.

2385 *Tarlow* Peter E., *Want* E. Cleve, Bad guys, textual errors, and wordplays in Genesis 21;9-10: JRefJud 37,4 (1990) 21-29.

E2.6 **The ʿAqedâ;** *Isaac, Genesis 22 ...*

2386 **Agus** Aharon (Ronald), The binding of Isaac and Messiah; law, martyrdom and deliverance in early rabbinic religiosity. Albany 1988,

SUNY. xi-327 p. 0-88706-735-2, pa. -6-0. – ᴿCCAR 38,3 (henceforth for JRefJud 1991) 73-75 (L. M. *Barth*).

2387 *Bakker* W. F., Ⓢ *Thysia tou Avraam, ameses skēnikes hodēgies*: Cretan Studies 3 (1992) 1-19.

2388 *Stroumsa* Gedaliahu G., Herméneutique biblique et identité; l'exemple d'Isaac [... Agéda]: RB 99 (1992) 529-543; Eng. 529, patristic perceptions of identity as figura/exemplum.

2389 **Edgerton** W. D., [Gn 22; Lk 34,13-35] The passion of interpretation: LitCurBInt. Louisville 1992, W-Knox. 160 p. $20. 0-664-25394-6 [NTAbs 37, p. 265].

2390 *Martin-Achard* Robert, Isaac, ᵀ*Prendergast* Terrence; ⇥ 741, AnchorBD 3 (1992) 462-470.

2390* *Bandstra* Barry L., Word order and emphasis in biblical Hebrew narrative; syntactic observations on Genesis 22 from a discourse perspective: ⇥ 343, Linguistics/BH 1992, 109-124.

2391 *Pleins* J. David, [Gn 22; 1 Sam 17] Son-slayers and their sons: CBQ 54 (1992) 29-38.

2393 *Faucher* Alain, Quand Dieu apprend sa leçon; Gn 22,1-19: Appoint 25 (Montréal 1992) 1-19.

2394 **Hinkelammert** Franz J., Der Glaube Abrahams und der Ödipus des Westens; Opfermythen im christlichen Abendland, ᵀᴱ*Arntz* Norbert. Münster 1989, Liberación. 224 p. DM 27,80. – ᴿBLtg 64 (1991) 121-3 (M. *Bongardt*).

2395 *Milman* Yoseph, The sacrifice of Isaac and its subversive variations in contemporary Hebrew protest poetry: RLitND 23,2 (1991) 61-83.

2396 *Bader* Winfried, *a)* The agents in Gen 22: 1-14; – *b)* Data base functions in TUSTEP [Gen 22]: ⇥ 450*, Informatique 3ᵉ 1991/2, 49-76 / 449-470.

2397 **Tschuggnall** Peter, Das Abraham-Opfer als Glaubensparadox; bibeltheologischer Befund — literarische Rezeption — KIERKEGAARDs Deutung [Diss. Innsbruck 1989]: EurHS 23/399, 1990 ⇥ 7,2081: ᴿBL (1992) 113 (P. R. *Davies*); TLZ 117 (1992) 31s (W. v. *Kloeden*).

2398 *Tschuggnall* Peter, Der gebundene Isaak; 'Isaaks Opferung' in der modernen jüdischen Literatur: ZkT 114 (1992) 304-316.

2399 *Azwalus* Y., Ⓢ Gen 22,6 *ma'akelet*: BethM 37,130 (1991s) 199-201.

2400 *Schwantes* M., *a)* [Gen 22,12] No extiendas tu mano contra el niño (observaciones sobre Génesis 21 y 22); – *b)* 'Era un niño': RIBLA 10 (1991) 27-45 / 14 (1993) 41-52 [< Stromata 49,290].

2401 **Schmid** H., Die Gestalt des Isaak; ihr Verhältnis zur Abraham- und Jakobtradition: ErtFor 274, 1991 ⇥ 7,2086*: ᴿBL (1992) 89 (R. J. *Coggins*); ZAW 104 (1991) 308 (H.-C. *Schmitt*).

2402 *a)* *Fields* Weston W., [Gen 19; Jos 2; Jg 19s] The motif 'night as danger' associated with three biblical destruction narratives; – *b)* *Fishbane* Michael, [Gen 26,16; Cant 4,15] The well of living water; a biblical motif and its ancient transformations; – *c)* *Soggin* J. Alberto, [Gen 36,1-7] Jacob in Shechem and in Bethel: ⇥ 181, Shaʿarei TALMON 1992, 17-32 / 3-16 / 195-8.

E2.7   **Jacob** and Esau; ladder-dream; *Jacob, somnium, Genesis 25 ...*

2403 **Dicou** B., [Gn 25-36] Jakob en Esau, Israël en Edom; Israël tegenover de volken in de verhalen over Jakob en Esau in Genesis en in de grote profetieën over Edom [diss. Amst 1990]. Voorburg 1990 ⇥ 7,2096; ƒ 39,50:

ᴿBijdragen 53 (1992) 426s (E. *Eynikel*); DielB 27 (1991) 278s (B. J. *Diebner*); NedTTs 46 (1992) 338s (A. van der *Kooij*).

2403* *Clerc* Danielle, *al.*, Jacob, les aléas d'une bénédiction; Gn 25-35, dossiers pour l'animation biblique: Essais Bibliques 20. 179 p.; map. 2-8309-0671-3.

2404 *Krondorfer* Björn, *a*) Jacob, Esau and the crisis of male identity; investigations into the seriousness of play; – *b*) The whole gamut of experience; historical and theoretical reflections on play: ➤ 358*b*, Body and Bible 1992, 175-190 / 5-26.

2405 *Schwartz* Susan, Brothers of choice, chosen brothers; Rama/Bharata, Jacob/Esau: LitTOx 6,1s (1992) 11-22 [< ᴢɪᴛ 92,362].

2406 *Weisman* Zeev, [Gen 25-36], The interrelationship between J and E in Jacob's narrative; theological criteria: ZAW 104 (1992) 177-197.

2407 *Görg* Manfred, [Gen 25,15] Zur Heimat der Ituräer: BibNot 64 (1992) 7-9.

2408 **Hendel** Ronald S., The epic of the patriarchs ... Jacob ᴰ1987 ➤ 5,2308 ... 7,2092: ᴿJNES 51 (1992) 226s (D. *Pardee*).

2409 **Boecker** Hans Jochen, 1. Mose 25,12 - 37,1; Isaak und Jakob: Z BK AT 1/3. Z 1992, Theol.-V. 152 p. 3-290-10862-7 [ZAW 105,519, M. *Köckert*].

2410 *Freund* Joseph, ❻ Gen 25,22: BethM 37,130 (1991s) 267-274.

2411 *Ska* Jean-Louis, Sommaires proleptiques en Gn 27 et dans l'histoire de Joseph: Biblica 73 (1992) 518-527.

2412 **Martini** Carlo M., [Gn 28,12] Jacob's dream; setting out on a spiritual journey, ᵀ*Lane* R. ColMn 1992, Liturgical. 79 p. $5. 0-8146-2000-0 [NTAbs 37, p. 456].

2413 **Neeb** John, Gen 28,12; the function of a biblical text in early Jewish and Christian communities: diss. St. Michael's, ᴰ*Walters* S. Toronto 1991. 320 p. DANN-68808. ➤ 7,2117: SR 21 (1992) 495; DissA 53 (1992s) 2856-A.

2414 **Sherwood** Stephen K., 'Had God not been on my side' ... Gn 29,1-32,2, ᴰ1990 ➤ 6,2475: ᴿBiblica 73 (1992) 108-112 (B. *Dicou*); BL (1992) 1991 (D. J. A. *Clines*); CBQ 54 (1992) 767 (J. T. *Walsh*: 'unrevised' not seen as a disadvantage).

2415 *Walters* Stanley D., Jacob narrative: ➤ 741, AnchorBD 3 (1992) 598-608.

2416 *Beyerle* Stefan, [Gn 30,18 ...] Der Name Issachar: BibNot 62 (1992) 51-60.

E2.8   Jacob's wrestling; the Angels; *lucta, Angelus/malʾak Gn 31* ...

2417 *Beck* Heinrich, Triadische Engel-Ordnungen; frühchristlicher und mittelalterlicher Ansatz; i. Das Glaubensmysterium des drei-einen Gottes als archetypisches Ordnungsprinzip und die Angemessenheit seiner Vermittlung durch Engel; ii. Dɪᴏɴʏsɪᴜs; iii. Bᴏɴᴀᴠᴇɴᴛᴜʀᴀ: TPhil 67 (1992) 321-355.

2418 *Clark* Stephen R. L., Where have all the angels gone?: RelSt 28 (1992) 221-234.

2419 **Daniélou** Jean, Les anges et leur mission: Essais. P 1990 [imprimatur 1951], Desclée. 173 p. 2-7189-0471-2. – ᴿÉTRel 67 (1992) 606s (O. *Abel*).

2420 *Fleury* Philippe, L'ange comme figure messianique dans la philosophie de l'histoire de Walter Bᴇɴᴊᴀᴍɪɴ: ArchivScSocR 78 (1992) 169-177; Eng. 169.

2420* **Godwin** M., Ángeles, una specie en peligro de extinción. Barc 1991, Robin. 235 p. – ᴿRelCu 38 (1992) 337 (M. *Arranz Rodrigo*: 'angel' would ultimately mean 'recognizing the angelic aspect in ourselves and others').

2421 **Hierzenberger** Gottfried, Die Boten Gottes — Helfer der Menschheit, biblisch gesehen. Innsbruck 1990, Tyrolia. 256 p. DM 29 [ErbAuf 68 (1992) 425].

2422 *Hofius* Otfried, Gemeinschaft mit den Engeln im Gottesdienst der Kirche; eine traditionsgeschichtliche Skizze: ZTK 89 (1992) 172-196.

2423 **Lavatori** Renzo, Gli angeli, storia e pensiero: Dabar 41. Genova 1991, Marietti. 294 p. – [R]RivStoLR 28 (1992) 645s (M. *Pesce*).

2424 **Mach** Michael, Entwicklungsstadier des jüdischen Engelglaubens in vorrabinischer Zeit [Diss. TA 1987, [D]*Gruenwald* I.]: TStAJud 34. Tü 1992, Mohr. xvii-457 p. [TR 88,516; NTAbs 37, p. 307]. DM 168. 3-16-145937-7.

2424* **Marconcini** B., *al.*, Angeli e demoni: CTSys. 11. Bo 1991, Dehoniane. 429 p. Lit. 40.000 [NRT 115,621, L. *Renwart*: relecture dans un esprit de critique constructive].

2425 *Merling Alomía* B., Los ángeles en el contexto extrabíblico veterotestamentario; un estudio exegético y comparativo: TLima 3 (1988) 166-183; 4 (1989) 44-99. 118-205 [< OTAbs 15,1].

2426 *Micaelli* Claudio, L'angelologia di GREGORIO Magno tra Oriente e Occidente [finora cauto; 'angelo nella S. Scr. una funzione, non una natura', Tert. carm. 14,3]: Koinonia 16,1 (1992) 35-51.

2426* **Rofé** Alexander, Israelite belief in angels in the pre-exilic period as evidenced by biblical traditions: diss. Hebrew Univ., [D]*Seeligmann* I. L. J 1969. English summary, xxiii p. [OIAc 3,36].

2427 *Schwank* Benedikt, Vergessene Engel?: ErbAuf 68 (1992) 67-71.

2428 *Stone* Michael E., Some Armenian angelological and uranographical texts: Muséon 105 (1992) 147-157.

2428* **Ströter-Bender** Jutta, Engel; ihre Stimme, ihr Duft, ihr Gewand und ihr Tanz: Symbole 1988 ➤ 6,2489; DM 29,80: [R]LuthMon 29 (1990) 234 (Roswitha *Flitner*).

2429 *Spanier* Ktziah, [Gn 31,19] Rachel's theft of the Teraphim; her struggle for family primacy: VT 42 (1992) 404-412.

2429* **Lockwood** Peter F., Gulls and grace; the significance of Genesis 32-34 for the literary and theological coherence of the Jacob cycle: diss. Luther NW Theol. Sem. 1991, [D]*Throntveit* M. 254 p. 92-24506. – DissA 53 (1992s) 1184-A.

2430 **Massenet** Michel, [Gen 32] Jacob ou la fraude 1991 ➤ 7,2112: [R]EsprVie 102 (1992) 92 (L. *Monloubou*: une méthode différente de lire la Bible); LA 41 (1991) 565-7 (A. *Mello*); LavalTP 48 (1992) 307 (Aldina *da Silva*: beau).

2430* *Marcel T. Bona,* Jacob at Jabbok (Gen 32: 23-33): IndTSt 29 (1992) 206-222.

2431 *Weber* Beat, 'Nomen est omen'; einige Erwägungen zu Gen 32,23-33 und seinem Kontext: BibNot 61 (1992) 76-83.

2432 **Rogerson** John, [Gen 32,22-32] Wrestling with the angel; a study in historical and literary interpretation: ➤ 477, Hermeneutics 1989/92, 131-144.

2432* *Bailey* Clinton, [Gen 34] How desert culture helps us understand the Bible; bedouin law explains reaction to rape of Dinah: BR 7,4 (1991) 14-21 . 38.

2433 *Kugel* James, [Gn 34] The story of Dinah in the Testament of Levi; HarvTR 85 (1992) 1-34.

2434 **Sheres** Ita, Dinah's rebellion; a biblical parable for our time 1990 ↠ 6,2491; 7,2113; $18: ᴿRelStR 18 (1992) 50 (W. L. *Humphreys*).

2434* *Baarda* Tjitze, The Shechem episode in the Testament of Levi; a comparison with other traditions: ↠ 504, ᶠWOUDE A. van der, Symposium 1992, 11-73.

2435 *Waskow* Arthur, [Gen 34 ...] God's body, the midrashic process, and the embodiment of Torah: ↠ 358*b*, Body and Bible 1992, 133-144.

2436 *Knopf* Tilmann, [Gen 35,16-20; 1 Sam 10,2] Rahels Grab, eine Tradition zu dem TNK: DielB 27 (1991) 73-137; 7 fig. [115 Mutter Rahel – Mutter Maria; 129, Mutter des Hirten-Messias ...].

E2.9   **Joseph**; Jacob's blessings; *Genesis 37; 39-50.*

2437 *Boecker* Hans Jochen, Überlegungen zur Josephsgeschichte: ↠ 149, ᶠPREUSS H. 1992, 35-45.

2437* *Davila* James R., New Qumran readings for the Joseph story (Genesis 37-50): ↠ 498, MQumran 1 (1991/2) 167-175; pl. 1.

2438 *Feldman* Louis H., JOSEPHUS' portrait of Joseph: RB 99 (1992) 379-417. 504-528; franç. 379. 504.

2439 *Gauthier-Walter* M. D., Sources iconographiques du cycle de Joseph à la cathédrale de Poitiers: Cah. Civ. Médv. 34,1 (1991) 141-158 [< RSPT 76,180].

2440 **Grimm** Alfred, Joseph und Echnaton, Thomas MANN und Ägypten. Mainz 1992, von Zabern. 468 p.; 277 fig. 3-8053-1418-3 [OIAc 5,23].

2440* *Hassán* Iacob M., Versión manuscrita de la copia sefardí La castidad de José: ↠ 44, ᶠDÍAZ ESTEBAN F., Sefarad 52 (1992) 123-130.

2441 **Humphreys** W. Lee, Joseph and his family 1988 ↠ 4,2375 ... 6,2301: ᴿBR 7,2 (1991) 13s (M. *Brettler*).

2441* *Ibañez Arana* Andrés, Sobre la datación de la historia de José (Gn 37-50): ScripV 38 (1991) 338-386.

2442 ᵀᴱ*Isaac* E., The Ethiopic History of Joseph: JPseud 6 (1990) entire, 1-125.

2442* **Kebekus** Norbert, Die Joseferzählung ᴰ1990 ↠ 6,2502: ᴿZAW 104 (1992) 152 (H. C. *Schmitt*).

2443 *Knibb* Michael A., A note on 4Q372 [about Joseph though not named] and 4Q390: ↠ 198, ᶠWOUDE A. van der, VTSupp 49 (1992) 164-177.

2443* **Longacre** Robert E., Joseph 1989 ↠ 5,2334; 6,2505: ᴿBL (1992) 77s (R. J. *Coggins*).

2444 **Niehoff** Maren, The figure of Joseph in post-biblical Jewish literature. ArbGAntJ 16. Leiden 1992, Brill. 178 p. ƒ90. 90-04-09556-X [JStJud 24,123 7, L. H. *Feldman*].

2445 **Redford** Donald B.., Hyksos [*Weinstein* J., archaeology]: ↠ 741, AnchorBD 3 (1992) 341-4 [-8].

2446 **Schweizer** Harald, Die Josefsgeschichte; Konstituierung des Textes 1991 ↠ 7,2122: *Knipping* Burkhard R., Textwahrnehmung 'häppchenweise'; Bemerkungen zu H. Schweizers 'Die Josefsgeschichte' und zu seiner Literarkritik [TüTQ 168 (1988) 23-43]: BibNot 62 (1992) 61-95; Replik 63 (1992) 52-57.

2447 **Wills** Lawrence M., [Joseph, but more on Daniel, Esther] The Jew in the court of the foreign king; ancient Jewish court legends [diss. Harvard, ᴰ*Strugnell* J.]: HarvDissR 26, 1990 ↠ 6,2518: ᴿCBQ 54 (1992)

137s (P. D. *Miscall*]; CritRR 5 (1992) 177-9 (J.J. *Collins*: refreshing, elegantly written); OTAbs 15 (1992) 109 (R. A. *Taylor*),

2448 *Maloney* Elliott C., [Gen 37,1-36; 1 Sam 16] Teenagers in the Bible: BToday 30 (1992) 202-7.

2449 *Becking* Bob, 'They hated him even more'; literary technique in Genesis 37,1-11: BibNot 60 (1991) 40-47; 1 fig.

2450 *a) Bos* Johanna W. H., An eyeopener at the gate; George COATES and Genesis 38; – *b) Kinnamon* Michael, The teaching ministry of George Coates; – *c) Dietlein* Damian, The scholarship...; – *d*) Coates bibliography: LexTQ 27 (1992) 119-123 / 97-99 / 100-104 / 132-5.

2450* **Bach** Alice H., 'I shall stir up thy mistress against thee!' Getting at the woman's story in Genesis 39: diss. Union. NY 1992. – UnSemQ 45 (1991) 254.

2451 **Kugel** James L., [Gen 39,1] In Potiphar's house; the interpretive life of biblical texts [also Gen 4,29; Ps 137...] 1990 → 6,2504; 7,2126: RChrCent 108 (1991) 600s (M. A. *Sweeney*); NewTR 4,4 (1991) 97s (J. T. *Townsend*: rabbinic exegesis).

2451* *Gnuse* Robert, [Gn 40s] The Jewish dream interpreter in a foreign court... JPseud 7 (1990) 29-53 [→ 7,2129 '29-35'].

2452 *Oswald* Wolfgang, [Gen 40] Research in text grammar and database system JOSEF: → 450*: Informatique 3e 1991/2, 575.

2452* **Tábet Balady** Miguel Angel, Los comentarios de A. IBN EZRA, M. BEN NAHMAN y Y. ABRABANEL a las bendiciones de Jacob (Gn 49,1-28) [diss. Salamanca]. S 1991, Univ. Pontificia. 232 p. – RAntonianum 67 (1992) 437s (M. *Nobile*).

E3.1 **Exodus event and theme;** *textus, commentarii.*

2453 *Amjad Ali* Christine, The faith of Exodus: al-Mushir 54 (1992) 12-17.

2454 *Bokser* B. M., Messianism, the Exodus pattern, and early rabbinic Judaism: → 463, Messiah 1987/92, 239-260.

2455 TCastaño Félix Ángel, ORÍGENES, Homilías sobre el Éxodo, intr. *Danieli* M. Ignazia: BtPatr 17. – M 1992, Ciudad Nueva. 228 p. pt. 1900. 84-86987-39-3. – RComSev 25 (1992) 457s (M. *Sánchez*).

2555* *Daoust* J. [< *Manns* Frédéric, TerreS janv. 1992]. Lire la Bible en Église; l'Éxode: EsprVie 102 (1992) 439-441 & 518-521.

2456 TEDrazin Israel, Targum Onkelos to Exodus 1990 → 7,2135: RBL (1992) 46 (R. P. *Gordon*); Salesianum 54 (1992) 793s (R. *Vicent*).

2456* *Feinman* Peter, Drama of the Exodus: BR 7,1 (1991) 26-35; ill.

2457 **Fretheim** Terence E., Exodus: Interpretation comm. 1991 → 7,2137: RBL (1992) 50 (W. *Johnstone*: continuance of creation, not intervention; green tinge); CritRR 5 (1992) 131-3 (T. S. *Dozeman*: good, 'but one suspects that other less creation-oriented and more liberationist readings are also present'); Interpretation 46 (1992) 410s (B. S. *Childs*); TS 53 (1992) 338s (J. P. M. *Walsh*).

2458 **Goldberg** Michael, Jews and Christians; getting our stories straight; the Exodus and the Passion-Resurrection 1985 → 1,2381; 2,1730: RJRefJud 37,4 (1990) 74-77 (M. A. *Signer*).

2459 **Guillén Torralba** Juan, Éxodo: MensajeAT 2. Estella 1992, VDivino. 208 p.

2460 *Hoffman* Yair, O Éxodo em Oseias e Amós [< VT 39 (1989) 169-182],T: RBBras 8 (1991) 241-255.

2461 **Holladay** Carl R.,   Fragments ... 2 ... Ezekiel the tragedian: SBL Pseud 12, 1989 ➤ 5,b678 ... 7,2140:   ᴿCritRR 5 (1992) 367-9 (B. Z. *Wacholder*); StPhilonAn 4 (1992) 128-133 (N. *Walter*).

2462 **Houtman** C.,   Exodus I-II 1986/9 ➤ 5,2356 ... 7,2142:   ᴿBZ 36 (1992) 114s (J. *Becker*); ETL 68 (1992) 407-9 (M. *Vervenne*, Eng.).

2463 **Isabelle de la Source** sr.,   ➤ 6,2539*; 7,2143: Le cycle de Moïse (Ex Lév Nm Dt): Lire la Bible avec les Pères 2. P/Montréal 1990, Médiaspaul/Paulines. 253 p. F 85. 2-7122-0372-0 / 2-89039-423-9. – ᴿRB 99 (1992) 621 (J. *Taylor*).

2464 **Jacob** Benno (1869-1945),   The second book of the Bible; Exodus, ᵀᴱ*Jakob* Walter (*Elman* Yaakov).   Hoboken 1992, ᴋᴛᴀᴠ.   xxxv-1099 p. $69.50.   0-88125-028-7 [BR 9/2, 12-14, W. *Propp*].

2466 *Kathanar* Vazhuthanapally O.,   Exodus and faith formation: Bible Bhashyam 16 (1990) 141-155.

2467 **Kelm** George L.,   Escape to conflict; a biblical and archaeological approach to the Hebrew exodus and settlement in Canaan.   Fort Worth 1991, 'IAR'.   280 p. $17.   – ᴿBAR-W 18,6 (1992) 8.10 (M. D. *Coogan*: uncritically conservative).

2468 ᵀᴱ**Le Boulluec** Alain, *Sandevoir* Philippe,   L'Exode: Bible d'Alexandrie 2, 1989 ➤ 6,2541; 7,2146:   ᴿCBQ 54 (1992) 116s (J. W. *Olley*: 'Le Boullec', also p. 209); LavalTP 48 (1992) 447s (Anne *Pasquier*); RÉAug 38 (1992) 181s (E. *Cothenet*).

2469 **Leder** Arie,   The structure of the Book of Exodus and its relationship to Genesis: diss. Knox College, ᴰ*Walters* S. Toronto 1992. – SR 21 (1992) 494.

2469* **Loewenstamm** S. E.,   The evolution of the Exodus tradition [◉ 1987 < diss. 1968], ᵀ*Schwartz* Baruch J.   J 1992, Magnes. 310 p. $27.   965-223-784-1 [ZAW 105,532, M. *Köckert*].

2470 *Loretz* Oswald,   Exodus, Dekalog und Ausschliesslichkeit Jahwes im Amos- und Hosea-Buch in der Perspektive ugaritischer Poesie: UF 24 (1992) 217-248.

2471 *Lott* Anastasia sr.   Exodus as a soteriological paradigm; journey – struggle – hope – covenant fulfilment: AfER 32 (1990) 29-41.

2472 **Magnante** A.,   La teologia dell'Esodo nei Salmi ᴰ1991 ➤ 7,2147*: ᴿEuntDoc 45 (1992) 116-8 (G. *Ettorri*).

2472* *a*) *Marti* Kurt,   Bundesgenosse Gott; Versuche zu 2. Mose 1-14²ʳᵉᵛ. Z 1992, Jordan.   96 p. Fs 19,80. – ᴿOrientierung 56 (1992) 253 (N. *Klein*).
— *b*) Oʀɪɢᴇɴᴇs, Homilías sobre el Éxodo. M 1992, Ciudad Nueva. 228 p. – ᴿAugM 37 (1992) 414s (E. *Ayape*).

2473 **Rao** O. M.,   Let my people go [four studies for NE India Baptist council]. Delhi 1991, ISPCK.   73 p. rs. 15.   81-7214-002-9. – ᴿTBR 5,1 (1992s) 10 (R. *Hooker*).

2474 *Rendsburg* Gary A.,   The date of the Exodus and the conquest/resettlement; the case for the 1100s: VT 42 (1992) 510-527 [> BtS 150,359s, E. H. *Merrill*].

2074* *Rizzi* Armido,   Esodo; un paradigma teologico-politico. Fiesole 1990, Cultura della Pace.   159 p. Lit. 18.000. – ᴿCC 143 (1992,1) 304 (G. L. *Prato*); StPatav 39 (1992) 259 (G. *Trentin*).

2475 **Sarna** Nahum M.,   Exodus, JPS comm. 1991 ➤ 7,2150:   ᴿVT 42 (1992) 142 (J. A. *Emerton*); ZAW 104 (1992) 457 (H. C. *Schmitt*).

2476 *Sarna* Nahum M.,   Exodus, book of: ➤ 741, AnchorBD 2 (1992) 689-701 (-8, event, *Kitchen* K. A.).

2477 *Sperber* Daniel,   ◉ [29] Greek words in *Sefer Rushaina* to Exodus: Lešonenu 56 (1991s) 143-6; Eng. III.

2478 **Spreafico** Ambrogio, Il libro dell'Esodo: Guide spirituali all'AT. R 1992, Città Nuova. 182 p. Lit. 17.000. 88-311-3734-4 [CC 144/4, 620s, D. *Scaiola*].

2479 ᴱ**Terian** Abraham, PHILON d'Alexandrie, Quaestiones et solutiones in Exodum I et II e versione armeniaca et fragmenta graeca: Œuvres 34c. P 1992, Cerf. 297 p. F 269. 2-204-04312-5 [BL 94,155, N. de *Lange*].

2479* ᴱ**Vervenne** M., Exodus, verhaal en leidmotief: [? T(ijdschrift voor) G(e-schiedenis)] 114s. Lv 1989, Acco. 175 p. ƒ25,75. 90-33421-80-1. – ᴿNed-TTs 46 (1992) 55s (B. *Becking*: JAGERSMA, LUST).

2480 **Wevers** John W.: Text history of the Greek Exodus: Mitteilungen des Septuaginta-Unternehmens 21. Gö 1992, Vandenhoeck & R. 280 p. DM 254, sb. 215. 3-525-82479-3 [BL 93,54, W. *Johnstone*].

2481 **Wevers** J. W., Notes on the Greek text of Exodus: SeptCog 30, 1990 ➤ 6,2555; 7,2154: ᴿCBQ 54 (1992) 339-341 (B. G. *Wright*).

ᴱ3.2 **Moyses** – Pharaoh, Goshen – *Exodus 1...*

2481* *Abu Assāf* ᶜ*Ali* A., ❹ The prayer of Moses among Midianites and Israelites: ➤ 736, ᴱ*Shaath* S., Palestine 1981/5, 61-66.

2482 **Alonso Schökel** Luis, *Gutiérrez* Guillermo, La mission de Moïse; méditations bibliques [1989 ➤ 5,2372], ᵀ*Macina* Menahem. Tournai 1992, Desclée. 152 p. 2-71890-594-8.

2483 **Alonso Schökel** Luis, Moses, biblische Betrachtungen [La misión de Moisés 1989 ➤ 5,2372], ᵀ*Beyrink* Hans. Mü 1992, Neue Stadt. 182 p. 3-87996-285-5.

2484 *Alves dos Santos* Fabio, De Moisés ao evento Jesus: Teocomunicação 20,88 (1990) 117-124.

2485 [*Basch*] *Moreen* Vera, Moses, God's shepherd; an episode from a Judeo-Persian epic: Prooftexts 11 (1991) 107-130.

2486 *Beegle* Dewey M., Moses OT: ➤ 741, AnchorBD 4 (1992) 905-918 [-920 NT; *Gillman* Florence M.; 905-8, Mosaic covenant, *Guinan* Michael D.; 920-2, Testament of Moses, *Priest* John E.].

2486* *a*) *Bianchi* Enzo, Mosè nella tradizione cristiana; – *b*) *Verdon* Timothy, Mosè, Cristo e il potere divino: ➤ 452, Mosè 1991/2, 63-86 / 183-214.

2487 **Blum** Erhard, [Ex 1-14...] Studien zur Komposition des Pentateuch: BZAW 189, 1990 ➤ 6,2527; 7,2135: ᴿBLitEc 93 (1992) 332-5 (J.-M. *Husser*, aussi sur deux autres); Carthaginensia 8 (1992) 925s (R. *Sanz Valdivieso*); CBQ 54 (1992) 312s (J. *Blenkinsopp*); ExpTim 103 (1991s) 295s (R. J. *Coggins*); JBL 111 (1992) 122-4 (J. *Van Seters*: significant); NedTTs 46 (1992) 158s (C. *Houtman*); RivB 40 (1992) 493-9 (I. *Cardellini*); TR 88 (1992) 17-21 (H. *Seebass*).

2487* **Boer** P. A. H. de, Egypt in the Old Testament; some aspects of an ambivalent assessment [diss. Oxford 1975, Univ. Roma 1981; ineditum], Selected Studies ᴱ*Duin* C. van: OTS 27, 1991 (➤ 7,180) 152-167 [< Henoch 14 (1992) 325, J. A. *Soggin*].

2488 *a*) *Cimmino* Franco, La politica di Ramesse II a potenziamento del Delta; – *b*) *Alfi* Mostafa El-, Une triade de Ramsès II (Statue Caire JE 45975): ➤ 735, Sesto Eg. 1991/2, 107-112 / 167-170 + phot.

2488* *Crocker* P. T., *a*) Pharaoh Merenptaḥ's Israelite campaign; new evidence [YURCO F.]; – *b*) Biblical individuals on seal impressions [1 Chr 6,13; Jer 36,9]: BurHist 27 (1991) 14-19 / 19s (< OTAbs 15,163].

2489 **Davies** Gordon F., Israel in Egypt; reading Exodus 1-2: JStOT supp 135. Shf 1992, JStOT. 204 p. £30; sb. £22.50. 1-85075-337-7. – ᴿExp-Tim 104 (1992s) 217 (G. G. *Nicol*).

Dörrfuss Ernst M.,   Mose in den Chr., Garant theokratischer Zukunftserwartung, ᴰ1992 → 3011.

2490 *Feldman* Louis, JOSEPHUS' portrait of Moses: JQR 82 (1991s) 285-328; 83 (1992s) 7-50. 301-330.

2490* *Hardmeier* Christof,   Die Erinnerung an die Knechtschaft in Ägypten; sozialanthropologische Aspekte des Erinnerns in der hebräischen Bibel: → 197, ᶠWOLFF H. W., Wer ist? 1992, 133-152.

2491 *Heller* B., Musa: → 756, EncIslam² 7 (1992) 638s.

2491* **Jaeger** David K., [Ex 2-14; Jg 6-8; 13-15; 1 Sam 9-11; 13s; 16s] The initiatory trial theme of the hero in Hebrew Bible narrative: diss. Iliff, ᴰ*Peterson* D. Denver 1992. 225 p. 92-20097. – DissA 53 (1992s) 843-A.

2492 *Jensen* Robin M., Moses imagery in Jewish and Christian art; problems of continuity and particularity: → 478, SBL Sem. 31 (1992) 389-418.

2493 **Martini** Carlo M.,   Through Moses to Jesus 1988 → 4,2460: ᴿLandas 3 (Manila 1989) 132-4 (T. H. *Green*).

2493* **Mélèze-Modrzejewski** J.,   Les Juifs d'Égypte, de Ramsès II à Hadrien 1991 → 7,2165: ᴿAegyptus 72 (1992) 206-211 (Anna *Passoni dell'Acqua*); CdÉ 67 (1992) 379-383 (Thérèse *Liebman-Frankfurt*); RÉJ 151 (1992) 207-9 (Mireille *Hadas-Lebel*).

2494 ᴱ*Musurillo* Hubert, GREGORII Nysseni De vita Moysis: Opera 7/1. Leiden 1991 = 1964, Brill. 145 p. ƒ120.   ᴿMüTZ 43 (1992) 465s (T. *Böhm*).

2494* a) *Renaud* Bernard, Moïse et le monothéisme; – b) *Palayret* Nadine, Akhénaton, l'edorateur du disque solaire; l'art amarnien [*Kanawaty* Monique, les lettres]; – c) *Barbotin* Christophe, Les Ramessides [*Brihaye* Pierrick, Thoutmosis III]; – d) *Lemaire* André, Les Hébreux en Égypte: MondeB 78 ('L'Égypte et la Bible au Louvre' 1992) 14s / 6-11 [12s] / 16-21 [3-5] / 22-25.

2495 *Siebert-Hommes* Jopie, Die Geburtsgeschichte des Mose innerhalb des Erzählungszusammenhangs von Exodus I und II: VT 42 (1992) 398-404.

2496 *Slenczka* Notger,   Moses und Ödipus [HESSING J., Freud 1989]: TRu 57 (1992) 431-8.

2496* a) *Soggin* J. Alberto,   Alla ricerca di Mosè; – b) *Natoli* Salvatore, Esodo e rivoluzione; – c) *Flores d'Arcais* Francesco,   Vita e vicende del liberatore; – d) *Luzzatto* Amos,   Mosè dal Midrash a Buber: → 452, Mosè 1991/2, 89-98 / 149-179 / 9-59 / 239-259.

2497 *Tapia* Elizabeth S., [Ex 1,8-22] The story of the Shiphrah and Puah; disobedient or subservient women?: CTC Bulletin 10,2s (Hong Kong 1991) 44s [< TContext 10/1, p. 27].

2498 *Weems* Renita J.,   The Hebrew women are not like the Egyptian women; the ideology of race, gender and sexual reproduction in Exodus 1: Semeia 59 (1992) 25-34.

2498* *Zobel* Hans-Jürgen, [Ex 'Hebräer'] 'Israel' in Ägypten: → 163, ᶠSAUER G., Aktualität 1992, 109-117.

2499 *Naor* Menahem, ⊙ Ex 2,1: BethM 37,130 (1991s) 260-3.

2500 a) *Barclay* John M.G.,   Manipulating Moses; Exodus 2:10-15 in Egyptian Judaism and the New Testament; – b) *Johnstone* William, The two theological versions of the Passover pericope in Exodus; – c) *McKay* Heather A., From evidence to edifice; four fallacies about the Sabbath: → 41, ᶠDAVIDSON R., Text as pretext 1992, 28-46 / 160-178 / 179-199.

2500* *Carniti* Cecilia, *wajjēdaᶜ ʾĕlōhîm* (Es 2,25): 'e Dio li riconobbe'?: Gregorianum 73 (1992) 337s.

2501 *a) Fanuli* Antonio, 'Ora va, io ti mando' (Es 3,10); – *b) Cortese* Enzo, La missione nell'AT: ParVi 35,1 (Missione/Preludi 1990) 15-23 / 7-14 (24-44, *al.*).
2502 *Gewalt* Dietfried, [Ex 4,10; 6,12.30] Die 'Sprachfehler' des Mose: DielB 27 (1991) 8-16.
2503 *Görg* Manfred, [Mutter Moses Ex 6,20; Nm 26,59] Jochebed und Isis: BibNot 61 (1992) 10-14.
2504 *Stroumsa* Gedaliahu G., Moses' riddles; esoteric trends in patristic hermeneutics: ➤ 514, Interpretation 1992, 229-248.
2505 *Tottoli* Roberto, Il bastone di Mosè mutato in serpente nell'esegesi e nelle tradizioni islamiche: AION 51 (1991) 225-243 ...

E3.3   **Nomen divinum, Tetragrammaton;**   *Exodus 3,14* ... **Plagues.**

2505* *Baumgarten* Joseph M., A new Qumran substitute for the divine name [*ʿôn* (? power) *hû*] and Mishnah Sukkah 4,!; JQR 83 (1992s) 1-5.
2506 *a) de Blois* Kees [authorship acknowledged p. 402], How to translate the Name; – *b) Osborn* Noel D., The Name; when does it make a difference? : – *c) Slager* Donald J., The use of divine names in Genesis; – *d) Wendland* Ernst B., Yahweh – the case for [(Chi-)Chewa] *chauta*, 'Great-[God]-of-the-Bow'; – *e) Achumi* Nitoy, Translation of 'God' and 'Lord' in some [NE-India] Naga Bibles; – *f) Rai* Benjamin, What is his name? translation of divine names in some major North Indian languages; – *g) Hatton* H., Thailand: BTrans 43,4 (1992) 403-414 / 415-422 / 423-9 / 430-8 / 438-443 / 443-6 / 446-8.
2506* *Boespflug* François, Uno spettacolo straordinario; la teofania del 'roveto ardente' nell'arte occidentale (XII-XVI secolo): ➤ 677c, Arte 1988/ 92, 133-150.
2507 **Cramer-Naumann** Samuel, Gott als geschehende Geschichte; die elohistische Interpretation JHWHs als des Kommenden im *'hyh 'šr 'hyh* von Ex 3,14: Diss. ᴰ*Herrmann* S. Bochum 1992. 492 p. – RTLv 24, p. 540; TR 89,77.
2507* *Croatto* J.S., La relectura del nombre de Yahwe (reflexiones herme-néuticas sobre Ex 3,1-15 y 6,2-13): Ribla 4 (1989) 7-17 [< Stromata 47,443].
2508 **Fischer** Georg, Jahwe unser Gott... Ex 3-4: OBO 91, 1989 ➤ 5,2390 ... 7,2170: ᴿBZ 36 (1992) 128s (H. D. *Preuss*); Gregorianum 73 (1992) 340-2 (G. L. *Prato*); ZkT 114 (1992) 79-91 (A. *Stiglmair*).
2508* **Harrison** Simon J., Stealing people's names; history and politics in a [Melanesian] Sepik River cosmology: StSCAnthrop 71. C 1990, Univ. xv-217 p. £27.50. – ᴿAnthropos 87 (1992) 274-6 (P. *Roscoe*).
2509 *Knobloch* Johann, Die Ehrfurcht vor dem Namen Gottes: BeiNam 27 (1992) 1s.
2510 **Kohata** Fujiko, J & P in Ex 3-14: BZAW 166, 1986 ➤ 2,1776 ... 5,2391: ᴿOLZ 87 (1992) 546s (G. *Wallis*); VerkF 36,1 (1991) 103-6 (K. *Grünwaldt*; Anfragen, die 'den Wert des Buches wenig trüben').
2510* *Lombardini* Pietro, Il Dio di Mosè: ➤ 452, Mosè 1991/2, 101-123.
2511 **Luzi** Pietro, La passione del nome di Dio nella storia della salvezza. T 1991, LDC. 296 p. Lit. 22.000. – ᴿParVi 37 (1992) 52-54 (M. *Galizzi*).
2512 *Malachi* Zvi, ❻ [*qamūṣ* 'ineffable' as liturgical-hymn name for God]: Lešonenu 56 (1991s) 137-141; Eng. ii-iii.
2513 **Peursen** C. van, De Naam die geschiedenis maakt; het geheim van de bijbelse Godsnamen: Interacties. Kampen 1991, Kok. 160 p. ƒ32,50. 90-242-3477-8 [TvT 93,99, M. Van *Tente*].

2514 *Rohrbacher-Sticker* Claudia, Die Namen Gottes und die Namen Metatrons; zwei Geniza-Fragmente zur Hekhalot-Literatur: FraJüdBeit 19
(1991s) 95-168 [< JStJud 24,96].
2515 *Rose* Martin, Names of God in the OT: ➤ 741, AnchorBD 4 (1992)
1001-1011.
2515* **Gimaret** D., Les noms divins en Islam 1988 ➤ 4,b997: ᴿHenoch 14
(1992) 203-5 (B. *Chiesa*).
2516 **Scholem** Gershom, Il nome di Dio e la teoria del linguaggio della
Kabbala [1972], ᵀ*Antinolfi* Gabriella.
2516* *Seow Choon-Leong,* The ineffable name of Israel's God: BR 7,6
(1991) 49s.

2517 *Stern* Philip D., [Ex 3,8,17] The origin and significance of 'the land flow-
ing with milk and honey' [Ugarit KTU 1,6,III,14]: VT 42 (1992) 554-7.
2518 *Schmitt* Hans-Christoph, Das sogenannte vorprophetische Berufungs-
schema; zur 'geistigen Heimat' des Berufungsformulars von Ex 3,9-12; Jdc
6,11-24 und 1 Sam 9,1-10,16: ZAW 104 (1992) 202-216.
2519 *Ogden* G.S., [Ex 3,14 + 13t] Idem per idem; its use and meaning:
JStOT 53 (1992) 107-120.
2520 a) *Wal* A.J.O. van der, 'Hij is het, die ons Zijne vriendschap biedt', Ex
3:14 nogmaals gelezen; – b) *Beentjes* P.C., De vertaling van drie cruciale
woorden in Exodus 3,14: Ter Herkenning 19,2 (1991) 109-114 / 115-8
[< GerefTTs 91,188].
2521 *Ska* Jean-Louis, Récit et récit métadiégétique en Ex 1-15; remarques
critiques et essai d'interprétation de Ex 3,16-22: ➤ 474, ACFÉB 14,
1991/2, 135-171.
2522 *Garr* W. Randall, The grammar and interpretation of Exodus 6:3: JBL
111 (1992) 385-408.
2523 *Brottier* Laurence, L'épisode des fléaux d'Égypte (Ex 7-11), lu par PHI-
LON d'Alexandrie et les Pères Grecs: RechAug 24 (1989) 39-64.
2524 ᴱ**Hunger** Herbert, Prochoros KYDONOS' Übersetzungen ... Ps.-AUGU-
STINUS, De decem plagis Aegyptiorum: Wiener St. 14. W 1990, Österr.
Akad. 96 p. Sch. 210 [Speculum 68,805s, F. *Kianka*].
2525 a) *Miscall* Peter D., [Ex 1-15] Biblical narrative and categories of the fantastic; – b) *Manlove* Colin, The Bible in fantasy; – c) *Zipes* Jack, The messianic power of fantasy in the Bible: Semeia 60 (1992) 39-51 / 91-110 / 7-21.
2526 ᴱ**Perrone** Lorenzo, [Ex 7,3] Il cuore indurito del faraone; ORIGENE e il
problema del libero arbitrio: Origini 3. Genova 1992, Marietti. 152 p.
[Teresianum 44,723, M. *Diego Sánchez*].
2527 *Cartun* Ari M., 'Who knows ten?' The structural and symbolic use
of numbers in the ten plagues; Exodus 7:14-13:16: UnSemQ 46,1 (1991)
65-112.

E3.4 *Pascha, sanguis, sacrificium:* **Passover, blood, sacrifice,** *Ex 11* ...

2528 *Martola* N., Om studiet av påskhaggadan [since 1845]: Nordisk
Judaistik 11,1s (Åbo 1990) 85-90) [Judaica 47,179; his Commentary on the
Passover Haggadah (svensk 1987) is awaited].
Boyarin Daniel, [Ex 13-18] Intertextuality 1990 ➤ a506.
2529 *Shea* William H., La ruta del Éxodo, desde Rameses hasta Sinai: TLima
6 (1991) 272-313 [< OTAbs 15, p. 357].
2530 **Bauer** U.F.W., *Kol ha-debarim ha-elleh,* All diese Worte; Impulse zur
Schriftauslegung aus Amsterdam, expliziert an der Schilfmeererzählung in

Exodus 13,17-14,31: EurHS 21/442, 1991 ➤ 7,2190: ᴿDielB 27 (1991) 272-5 (B. J. *Diebner*).

2530* *Brooks* Simcha, [Ex 13,21] The Medinet Habu inscription and the Red Sea narrative: BInstArch 28 (1991) 151s.

2531 **Brenner** Martin L., The song of the sea, Ex 15:1-21: BZAW 195, 1991 ➤ 7,2193: ᴿArTGran 55 (1992) 322-6 (A. *Torres*); ÉTRel 67 (1992) 268s (T. *Römer*: bon, mais ne mentionne pas SKA J.-L. 1986; et parle de J/E/P comme si rien ne s'était passé); ZkT 114 (1992) 91s (G. *Fischer*: klar, nicht immer überzeugend).

2532 **Goverts** K. D., Het lied van de Doortocht; een bijbels-theologische en liturgische studie n.a.v. Exodus 15,1-18 [... oorlogen van JHWH; is de hebreeuwse bijbel en oorlogsboek?]: diss. Amsterdam, ᴰ*Deurloo* K. A., 1992. 566 p. – TvT 32 (1992) 301; RTLv 24, p. 541.

2533 *Janzen* J. Gerald, [Ex 15,1.21] Song of Moses, song of Miriam; who is seconding whom?: CBQ 54 (1992) 211-220.

2534 *Mello* A., Cantico del Mare; dall'evento alla sua celebrazione: dal testo alla sua interpretazione: ➤ 338, ParSpV 25 (1992) 7-26.

2535 *Meynet* Roland, Le cantique de Moïse et le cantique de l'Agneau (Ap 15 et Ex 15): Gregorianum 73 (1992) 19-46; Eng. 47; 8 planches (texte disposé par phrases).

2536 *Barré* Michael L., 'My strength and my song' in Exodus 15:2: CBQ 54 (1992) 623-637.

2537 *Bietak* Manfred, Der Ursprung des Baʿal Zephon Kultes in Ägypten: ➤ 184, ᶠTRENTINI J. B., Echo 1990, 37-44; 2 fig.

2537* **Burden** Terry L., The wilderness traditions in the Hebrew Bible; kerygma and community of faith: diss. Southern Baptist Theol. Sem. 1992, ᴰ*Watts* J. 332 p. 92-23283. – DissA 53 (1992s) 841s-A.

2538 **Propp** W. H., Water ᴰ1987 ➤ 5,2417; 6,2648: ᴿVT 42 (1992) 131 (J. A. *Emerton*).

2538* *De Benedetti* Paolo, Il capitolo delle mormorazioni; dai cocomeri d'Egitto al vitello d'oro: ➤ 452, Mosè 1991/2, 127-145.

2539 **Schart** Aaron, Mose und Israel im Konflikt... OBO 98, 1990 ➤ 6,2647; 7,2196: ᴿBiblica 73 (1992) 412-6 (Fujiko *Kohata*); CBQ 54 (1992) 542-4 (J. G. *Williams*: differentiation so fine suggests mythical origin).

2540 *Herrmann* Wolfram, Ex 17,7 und die Frage nach der Gegenwart JHWHs in Israel: ➤ 149, ᶠPREUSS H. 1992, 46-55.

2540* **Couto** António J. da Rocha, *a*) A aliança do Sinai como núcleo lógico-teológico central do Antigo Testamento [diss. R, Urbaniana]. Valadares 1990, Missões. 307 p. – ᴿHumTeol 13 (1992) 253-5 (J. *Carreira das Neves*). – *b*) A significativa ausência do Sinai nos sumários históricos de Israel: HumTeol 12 (1991) 315-323.

2541 **Tronina** Antoni, ❷ Bóg przybywa z Synaju. Lublin 1989, KUL. 180 p. – ᴿFolOr 27 (1990) 271s (E. *Lipiński*: excellent).

2541* **Renaud** Bernard, La théophanie du Sinaï, Ex 19-24: CahRB 30, 1991 ➤ 7,2208: ᴿEsprVie 102 (1992) 158s (L. *Monloubou*: semble un dinosaure parmi les exégètes modernes, mais son anachronisme n'est qu'apparent).

2542 *Zyl* Danie C. van, Exodus 19:3-6 and [= as] the kerygmatic perspective of the Pentateuch: OTEssays 5 (1992) 264-271.

E3.5   **Decalogus, Ex 20 = Dt 5; Ex 21ss; Ancient Near East Law.**

2543 **Brooks** Roger, The spirit of the ten commandments 1990 ➤ 6,2654: ᴿAndrUnS 30 (1992) 80s (A. J. *Greig*); CritRR 5 (1992) 359-361 (T. *Kleven*: clear); JRel 72 (1992) 424 (Y. *Elman*).

2543* **Carmichael** Calum M., The origins of biblical law [...Dt 1985
➤ 1,2482]; the Decalogues and the Book of the Covenant. Ithaca NY
1992, Cornell Univ. xvi-253 p. $31.35. 0-8014-2712-6 [BL 93,104, A.
Phillips].

2544 **Chill** Abraham, The mitzvot; the commandments and their rationale. J
1990, Keter. xxxiv-508 p., all Eng. 0-7065-1463-7.

2544* **Crüsemann** Frank, Die Tora; Theologie und Sozialgeschichte des
alttestamentlichen Gesetzes. Mü 1992, Kaiser. ix-496 p. DM 79. 3-459-
01953-0 [TLZ 118,903, E. *Otto*].

2545 **Gatti** Guido, Una legge che libera; il decalogo nella catechesi: StR-
Catechetica 15. T-Leumann 1991, LDC. 176 p. – ᴿSalesianum 54 (1992)
821s (P. *Carlotti*).

2546 **Giovanni Paolo II**, I dieci comandamenti [quarta visita in Polonia], ᴱ*Del
Rio* Domenico. CinB 1992, Paoline. 125 p. Lit. 12.000. – ᴿBbbOr 34
(1992) 122s (Cristina *Vertua*).

2547 *Kaiser* Otto, The law as center of the Hebrew Bible: ➤ 181, Shaᶜarei
TALMON 1992, 93-103.

2547* **Kealy** Sean P., The vision of the Ten Commandments, charter of
freedom: The Living Flame 33. Dublin 1989, Avila Centre. 112 p.
0-86088-45-1. – ᴿCarmelus 38 (1991) 253 (L. P. *Rogge*).

2548 **Loza** José, Las palabras de Yavé, estudio del decálogo 1989 ➤ 5,2434;
7,2204: ᴿRBibArg 54 (1992) 249s (J. S. *Croatto*).

2548* *Mannucci* Valerio, Le dieci parole: ➤ 452, Mosè 1991/2, 217-236.

2549 **Mesters** Carlos, Befreit – gebunden; die 10 Gebote; das Bundesbuch
1989 ➤ 6,2658*: ᴿZMissRW 75 (1991) 242-5 (L. *Schwienhorst-Schönberger*).

2549* *a*) *Muszyński* Henryk bp., ℗ 'Dix paroles simples de Dieu' appelées
'Dix commandements'; – *b*) *Bajda* Jerzy, ℗ Tu ne tueras pas: AtKap 117
(1991) 221-233 / 251-260.

2550 **Niehr** Herbert, Rechtsprechung in Israel; Untersuchungen zur Geschichte der Gerichtsorganisation im AT...: SBS 130, 1987 ➤ 3,2430;
5,2473: ᴿTLZ 117 (1992) 24s (M. *Köckert*).

2551 *a*) *Otto* Eckart, Der Dekalog als Brennspiegel israelitischer Rechtsge-
schichte; – *b*) *Crüsemann* Frank, Das Gerecht im Tor — eine staatliche
Rechtsinstanz; – *c*) *Herrmann* Siegfried, Weisheit im Bundesbuch; eine
Miszelle zu Ex 23,1-9: ➤ 149, ᶠPREUSS H. 1992, 59-68 / 69-79 / 56-58.

2551* *a*) ᴱ**Ozilou** M., S. BONAVENTURE, Les dix commandements: Œuvre de
S. B. P 1992, Desclée/Cerf. 205 p. F 110 [NRT 115,469, L. V.].

— *b*) **Peters** Albrecht, ᴱ*Seebass* Gottfried, Kommentar zu LUTHERs Ka-
techismen, 1. Die Zehn Gebote; Luthers Vorreden, 1990 ➤ 7,2307; 3-
525-56180-6: ᴿLuthTK 15 (1991) 86s (H. P. *Mahlke*) [16 (1992) 50, H.
Günther über 2. Der Glaube 1991].

2552 **Renaud** Bernard, La théophanie du Sinaï Ex 19-24...: CahRB 30, 1991
➤ 7,2208, F 348: ᴿBL (1992) 86 (W. *Johnstone*); JTS 43 (1992) 550-5
(also W. *Johnstone*); RHPR 72 (1992) 192s (P. de *Robert*); ZAW 104 (1992)
305s (H.-C. *Schmitt*).

2554 **Schmitt** Werner H., (*Delkurt* Holger, *Graupner* Axel), Die zehn Gebote im Rahmen alttestamentlicher Ethik: ErtFor 281. Da c. 1992, Wiss.
3-534-10007-7 [TR 89,166].

2556 **Schreiner** Josef, I dieci comandamenti nella vita del popolo di Dio.
Brescia 1991, Queriniana. 123 p. Lit. 16.000. – ᴿBbbOr 34 (1992) 117s
(G. *De Virgilio*); RClerIt 72 (1991) 703s (C. *Ghidelli*).

2557 *Smith* Louis, Original sin as 'envy'; the structure of the biblical deca-
logue: Dialog 30 (St. Paul 1991) 227-230.

2557* *Weinfeld* Moshe, What makes the Ten Commandments different?:
BR 7,2 (1991) 34-41.

2558 *Diebner* Bernd J., Anmerkungen zum sogenannten 'Bilderverbot' in
der Torah: DielB 27 (1991) 48-57 (253-270 Biblia Hebraica Anmerkungen).

2558* **Keel** Othmar, Das Recht der Bilder gesehen zu werden; drei Fallstudien zur Methode der Interpretation altorientalischer Bilder: OBO 122.
FrS/Gö 1992, Univ./VR. xiv-307 p.

2559 *a) Luzzatto* Amos, L'aniconismo ebraico tra immagine e simbolo; – *b)*
Nolli Gianfranco, Il silenzio iconografico nell'AT e la parola come so-
stituto; – *c) Verdon* Timothy, Arte, natura, Bibbia; estetica e etica nella
cultura giudeo-cristiana; – *d) Ravasi* Gianfranco, '...*Kī tŏb*'; Dio vide
che era bello; – *e) Givone* Sergio, Apocalipsis [= rivelazione; non libro
NT] cum figuris: ➤ 456, Arte 1988/92, 87-101 / 79-85 / 31-42 / 43-78 /
25-30.

2559* *Maser* Peter, 'Du sollst dir kein Bildnis machen!' Judentum, Christentum und Islam in der Auseinandersetzung um die Bilder: Beit.
Würtemb. KG 90 (1990) 31-37 [< TLZ 118,148].

2560 **Patrich** J., The formation of Nabatean art; prohibition of a graven image
1990 ➤ 6,2666: ᴿBL (1992) 119 (J. F. *Healey*); JRS 82 (1992) 279 (Judith
McKenzie).

2561 **Prigent** Pierre, Le Judaïsme et l'image: TStAntJ 24, 1990 ➤ 6,2665;
7,2211: ᴿAntonianum 67 (1992) 536-8 (M. *Nobile*); BLitEc 93 (1992)
330s (M. *Delcor*); Gregorianum 73 (1992) 747-750 (G. L. *Prato*); JBL 111
(1992) 712-4 (P. C. *Finney*); Salesianum 54 (1992) 374 (R. *Vicent*); TLZ
117 (1992) 272 (S. *Vollenweider*).

2461* **Rordorf** Bernard, Tu ne feras pas d'image [... asservissement au visible
p. 424]; prolégomènes à une théologie de l'amour de Dieu: CogF 167. P
1992, Cerf. 197 p. F 130. – ᴿEsprVie 102 (1992) 568 (P. *Jay*).

2562 **Schroer** Silvia, In Israel gab es Bilder: OBO 74, 1987 ➤ 3,2404...
5,2448: ᴿBASOR 285 (1992) 85s (Ziony *Zevit*).

2563 *Gruber* Mayer I., *a)* The source of the biblical sabbath; – *b)* Women in
the cult according to the Priestly Code [1983]: ➤ 247*d*, Motherhood of
God 1992, 111-9 / 49-68.

2564 *Hasel* Gerhard F., Sabbath: ➤ 741, AnchorBD 5 (1992) 849-856 [857-
861, sabbatical year, *Wright* Christopher J. H.].

2564* *a) Klinghardt* Matthias, '...auf dass du den Feiertag heiligest'; Sabbat
und Sonntag im antiken Judentum und frühen Christentum; – *b) Rend-*
torff Rolf, Die Entwicklung des altisraelitischen Festkalenders: ➤ 7,465*,
Fest 1988/91, 206-233 / 185-205.

2565 *Laberge* Léo, Sabbat, étymologie et origines; étude bibliographique: Sc-
Espr 44 (1992) 185-204.

2565* **Spier** Erich, Der Sabbat 1989 ➤ 5,2449...7,2215: ᴿLuthMon 30 (1991)
41 (A. *Silbermann*).

2566 ᴱ**Trotta** Giuseppe, Il sabato nella tradizione ebraica: Attendendo l'aurora. Brescia 1991, Morcelliana. 180 p. Lit. 20.000. – ᴿAsprenas 39
(1992) 588s (O. *Di Grazia*).

2567 *Waschke* Ernst-Joachim, Das Sabbatgebot und die Frage nach der
zeitlichen Ansetzung des Dekalogs: ➤ 7,174*a*, ᶠWALLIS G., Überlieferung
1990, 73-81.

2568 *Sandt* H. van de, [Ex 20,13-17 = Dt 5,17-21] Didache 3.1-6; a transformation of an existing Jewish hortatory pattern: JStJud 23 (1992) 21-41.

2569 **Dorff** Elliott, The covenant; the transcendent thrust in Jewish law: JLawA 7 (1988) 68-96 [< OTAbs 15,3].

2569* **Marshall** Jay W., Israel and the Book of the Covenant; an anthropological approach to biblical law: diss. Duke, ᴰ*Bailey* L. Durham NC 1992. 336 p. 92-37877. – DissA 53 (1992s) 2413-A.

2570 **Osumi** Yuichi, Die Kompositionsgeschichte des Bundesbuches Exodus 20,22b - 23,33 [Diss. Bethel 1989 ᴰ*Crüsemann* F.]: OBO 105, 1991 ➤ 7,2218: ᴿBL (1992) 82 (W. *Johnstone*); TüTQ 172 (1992) 145s (W. *Gross*); ZAW 104 (1992) 304s (H.-C. *Schmitt*).

2570* **Schenker** Adrian, Verbannung und Widerstand; bibeltheologische Untersuchung zum Strafen Gottes und der Menschen, besonders im Lichte von Ex 21s; SBS 139. Stu 1990, KBW. 110 p. 3-460-04591-1. – ᴿIndTSt 29 (1992) 370-3 (A. R. *Ceresko*).

2571 **Schwienhorst-Schönberger** Ludger. Das Bundesbuch: BZAW 188, 1990 ➤ 6,2675; 7,2220: ᴿBL (1992) 89s (W. *Johnstone*); BLtg 65 (1992) 244s (C. *Dohmen*); BO 49 (1992) 478-480 (W. *Johnstone*); CBQ 54 (1992) 765s (T. B. *Dozeman*); JBL 111 (1992) 126-8 (W. *Brueggemann*).

2572 *Avraham* Nahum, ◍ *Emet* in the Book of the Covenant, Ex 21, 7-11: BethM 37,131 (1991s) 289-301.

2573 **Houtman** C., Het altaar als asielplaats ... Ex 21:12-14, 1990 ➤ 6,2683: ᴿBL (1992) 106 (G. I. *Davies*).

2574 *Brueggemann* Walter, *a*) [Ex 22,21-27 ...] Bodied faith and the body politic [ineditum]; – *b*) The rhetoric of hurt and hope; ethics odd and crucial [< Annual of the Society of Christian Ethics (1989) 73-92]: ➤ 220, OTTheology 1992, 67-94 / 45-66.

2575 *Kleer* Martin, *Kröger* Maria, [Ex 22,25; Dt 24,10] Das gepfändete Gewand; Untersuchungen zum sozialen und rechtlichen Kontext des im Ostrakon von Mesad Heschavjahu dargestellten Konfliktfalles: BibNot 61 (1992) 38-50.

2575* *Horst* Pieter W. van der, 'Gij zult van goden geen kwaad spreken'; de Septuaginta-vertaling van Exodus 22:27(28), haar achtergrond en invloed: NedTTs 46 (1992) 192-8; Eng. 226.

2576 **Barbiero** Gianni, [Es 23,4 ...] L'asino del nemico: AnBib 128, ᴰ1991 ➤ 7,2224: ᴿBiblica 73 (1992) 263-5 (A. *Schenker*); BL (1992) 99s (W. G. E. *Watson*: forces reevaluation of OT ethics); NRT 114 (1992) 99s (J.-L. *Ska*); ParVi 37 (1992) 146-8 (A. *Rolla*); RivB 40 (1992) 338-344 (I. *Cardellini*: meritevole; un po' pesante a causa delle digressioni); VetChr 29 (1992) 227-9 (A.-S. *di Marco*).

2577 **Hoevels** Fritz Erik, [Ex 23,19 ...] Ein jüdisches Speisetabu und sein Geheimnis: System ubw, Zeitschrift für klassische Psychoanalyse 11,1 (1993) 63-85 [3-98484-700-X] = A Jewish food taboo and its secret, in **Hoevels**, Collected Papers on Psychoanalysis of Religion (New Delhi 1993, Indian Atheist publishers; 175 p.; 81-7374-001-1).

2578 *Labuschagne* C. J., [Ex 23,19 ...] 'You shall not boil a kid in its mother's milk'; a new proposal for the origin of the prohibition: ➤ 198, ᶠWOUDE A. van der, VTSupp 49 (1992) 6-17.

2579 **Draï** Raphaël, Le mythe de la loi du talion; une introduction au droit hébraïque. Aix-en-Provence 1991, Alinéa. 270 p. – ᴿArchivScSocR 80 (1992) 256s (Doris *Bensimon*).

2580 *Osumi* Yuichi, Brandmal für Brandmal; eine Erwägung zum Talionsgesetz im Rahmen der Sklavenschutzbestimmungen [< (unveröffentlichter) ᶠCRÜSEMANN F. 1988, 73-92]: AnJapB 18 (1992) 3-30.

2581 **Bultmann** Christoph, Der Fremde im antiken Juda; eine Untersuchung zum sozialen Typenbegriff *gēr* und seine Bedeutungswandel in der alttestamentlichen Gesetzgebung [Diss. Göttingen 1990, ᴰ*Smend* R.]: FRL 153. Gö 1992. 235 p. 3-525-53834-0.

2582 *Cardellini* Innocenzo, Stranieri ed 'emigrati-residenti' in una sintesi di teologia storico-biblica: RivB 40 (1992) 129-181; Eng. 181.

2583 *a)* **Brin** Gershon, The development of some laws in the Book of the Covenant; – *b)* **Falk** Zeev W., Law and ethics in the Hebrew Bible; – *c)* *Frey* Christofer, The impact of the biblical idea of justice on present discussions of social justice; – *d)* *Raiser* Konrad, Reflections about social justice within the ecumenical movement; – *e)* *Reventlow* Henning. Righteousness as order of the world; some remarks towards a programme; – *f)* *Hoffman* Yair, The creativity of theodicy [*Schatz-Uffenheimer* R. on M. LUZZATTO]: ➤ 499, Justice 1990/2, 60-70 / 82-90 / 91-104 / 154-162 / 163-172 / 117-130 [173-190].

2583* *a)* *Greenberg* Moshe, Biblical law; establishing a moral order [< ᴱ*Firmage* E., *al.*, Religion and law 1990 ➤ 6,526, with reaction of *Welch* J. there]: BR 7,3 (1991) 42-45.

— *b)* *Greengus* Samuel, Law: ➤ 741, AnchorBD 4 (1992) 242-252 (-4, forms, *Sonsino* R.; 254-265, NT-period Judaism, *Sanders* E. P.).

2584 *Houten* Christiana Van, The alien in Israelite law: JStOT supp 107, 1991 ➤ 7,2231: ᴿÉTRel 67 (1992) 452s (D. *Lys*: seul *gêr*, seul Pent.); ExpTim 103 (1991s) 308 (C. S. *Rodd*: attractively written and most valuable).

2585 **Klinck** Dennis R., The word of the Law. Ottawa 1992, Carleton Univ. xiii-458 p.

2586 *Koluthara* Varghese, The Old Testament concept / Gospel understanding of law: Living Word 98 (1992) 42-58. 83-93 (207-222).

2587 *a)* *Levinson* Bernard M., The human voice in divine revelation; the problem of authority in biblical law; – *b)* *Jaffee* Martin S., Halakhah in early rabbinic Judaism; innovation beyond exegesis, tradition before Oral Torah; – *c)* *Waldman* Marilyn R., *Baum* Robert M., Innovation as renovation; the 'prophet' as an agent of change: ➤ 636*, Innovation 1988/92, 35-71 / 109-142 / 241-284.

2588 **Muffs** Yochanan, Love and joy; law, language and religion in ancient Israel. NY 1992, Jewish Theol. Sem. xxvii-240 p. 0-674-53931-1 [OIAc 5,30; excerpted].

2588* **Rakover** Nahum, ⊕ A bibliography of Jewish law; modern books, monographs and articles in Hebrew, II. J 1990, Library of Jewish Law. 586 p.

2589 **Veijola** Timo, The Law in the Bible and in its environment: Publ. Finnish Exeg. Soc. 51, 1990 ➤ 6,560: ᴿTsTKi 62 (1991) 228s (T. *Stordalen*).

2590 **Viberg** Åke, Symbols of law; a contextual analysis of legal symbolic acts in the Old Testament [diss. Lund, ᴰ*Mettinger* T.]: ConBib OT 34. Sto

1992, Almqvist & W. x-206p. Sk 172. 91-22-01477-2 [JStOT 60,124, P. R. *Davies*: useful]. – ᴿVT 42 (1992) 568 (J. A. *Soggin*).

2591 *Welten* Peter, Asyl im Widerstreit; zur Geschichte von Vorstellung und Praxis [... Babylon; Israel]: BTZ 9 (1992) 217-230.

2592 **Westbrook** Raymond, Property and the family in biblical law: JStOT supp 113. 177 p. £22.50. 1-85075-271-0 [5 reprints + 142-164, The Dowry; 118-141, Undivided inheritance; < OTAbs 15, p.477.322s; BL 93,117, A. *Phillips*] – ᴿÉTRel 67 (1992) 453s (D. *Lys*: livre d'un juriste, se lie comme un roman); Themelios 18,2 (1992s) 25 (R. S. *Hess*).

2593 **Westbrook** Raymond, Studies in biblical and cuneiform law 1988 ⇒ 4, 2568 ... 6,2699: ᴿVT 42 (1992) 431s (J. N. *Postgate*); ZSav-R 107 (1990) 417-433 (R. *Yaron*).

2594 *Aartun* Kjell, Ein Zeugnis ugaritischer Rechtsprechung (702 [KTU 3.9]: 1-21): StEpL 7 (1990) 59-73.

2595 *Donbaz* V., *Sauren* H., NI 2553+2565, a missing link of the Hammurabi law-code: OrLovPer 22 (1991) 5-26 + 2 pl.; 1 facsimile.

2595* *Fontanille* Isabelle, Les lois hittites, traduction, commentaire: Ktema 12 (1987) 209-255.

2596 *Greengus* Samuel, Filling gaps; laws found in Babylonia and in the Mishna but absent in the Hebrew Bible: ⇒ 65, Mem. GEVIRTZ S., Maarav 7 (1991) 149-171.

2597 *Hengstl* J., 'Soll und Haben' in einer altassyrischen familienrechtlichen Urkunde: ZAss 82 (1992) 212-220.

2597* a) *Hengstl* Joachim, Die neusumerische Eintrittsehe; – b) *Yaron* Reuven, Zu babylonischen Eherechten: ZSav-R 109 (1992) 31-50 / 51-99.

2598 *Otto* Eckart, a) Die Bedeutung des altorientalischen Rechtsgeschichte für das Verständnis des Alten Testaments: ZTK 88 (1991) 139-168; – b) Der reduzierte Brautpreis; Ehe- und Zinsrecht in den Paragraphen 18 und 18a des Kodex Ešnunna: ZSav-R 109 (1992) 475-481.

2599 *Owen* D. I., *Westbrook* R., Tie her up and throw her into the river; an Old Babylonian inchoate marriage on the rocks [legal practice]: ZAss 82 (1992) 202-7; 2 facsimiles with photo.

2600 *Röllig* W., Hammurapi: ⇒ 762, NBL II,6 (1991) 22-24.

2600* *Saporetti* Claudio, Le più antiche leggi: Mesopotamia, Egitto, Ittiti, Bibbia... Archeo 7,84 (1992) 69-109.

2601 *Sjöberg* Åke W, Was there a Sumerian version of the laws of Hammurabi?: ⇒ 32, CIVIL M., AulaO 9,1 (1991) 219-223 + 2 pl.

2602 *Shupak* Nili, A new source for the study of the judiciary and law of ancient Egypt, 'The tale of the eloquent peasant': JNES 51 (1992) 1-18.

2603 **Stone** Elizabeth C., *Owen* David I., Adoption in Old Babylonian Nippur and the archive of Mannum-mešu-liṣṣur: Mesopotamian Civilizations 3; 1991 ⇒ 7,2249: ᴿJCS 43s (1991-3) 124-130 (M. van de *Mieroop*).

E3.6 Cultus, Exodus 24-40.

2604 **Brinkman** Johan M., The perception of space in the Old Testament; an exploration of the methodological problems of its investigation, exemplified by a study of Exodus 25 to 31 [geref. Diss. Kampen 1992, ᴰ*Moor* J. C. de]. Kampen 1992, Kok Pharos. 271 p. 90-390-0003-4. – TvT 32.303; RTLv 24, p. 540.

2604* *Vanhoye* Albert, [Es 24,8; Mt 14,24] Il sangue dell'alleanza nel NT: CC 143 (1992,1) 118-132.

2605 a) *De Benedetti* Paolo, [Es 24,12] Videro Dio e mangiarono e bevvero; – b) [*Natale*] *Terrin* Aldo, Il pasto sacro e il pasto sacrificale nella storia comparata delle religioni; – c) *Goria* Giovanni, Il linguaggio dei cibi; – d) *Sierra* Sergio, La cucina della Bibbia; le regole alimentari ebraiche, la Kasherut: → 454, Cibo 1992, 9-21 / 22-37 / 38-51 / 105-115.

2605* *Hendrix* Ralph E., The use of *miškān* and *ōhel môʿēd* in Exodus 25-40: AndrUnS 30 (1992) 3-13 [123-138, A literary structural overview].

2606 *Friedman* Richard E., Tabernacle: → 741: AnchorBD 6 (1992) 292-300.

2606* *Horowitz* Wayne, Hurowitz Victor (Avigdor), [Ex 28,30 + 6 times] Urim and Thummim in light of a psephomancy ritual fom Assur (LKA 137): JANES 21 (1992) 95-115.

2607 **Koester** Craig R., The dwelling of God; the Tabernacle in the OT/ Int/NT: CBQ Mg 22, ᴰ1989 → 5,2500 ... 7,2256: ᴿCBQ 54 (1992) 356s (R. J. *Daly*: claim that the tabernacle was more favorably viewed than the Temple is sometimes a bit forced); TLZ 117 (1992) 495 (E. *Bammel* wants more on 'feast of tabernacles' and Rechabites).

2607* *Milgrom* Jacob, Seeing the ethical within the ritual: BR 8,4 (1992) 6 . 13.

2608 *Renaud* Bernard, La formation de Ex 19-40; quelques points de repère: → 474, ACFÉB 14, 1991/2, 101-133.

2609 **Utzschneider** Helmut, Das Heiligtum und das Gesetz...: OBO 77, 1988 → 4,2604 ... 7,2257: ᴿJBL 111 (1992) 515-7 (D. G. *Schley*).

2610 **Vicent Saera** Rafael, Interpretaciones de la fiesta de Sukkot en el judaismo antiguo, desde el texto bíblico al targum y midrás: diss. PIB 1992, ᴰ*Le Déaut*. – Biblica 73 (1992) 432.

2611 *Gane* Roy, [Ex 25,30; Nm 4,7] 'Bread of the presence' and 'Creator in residence': VT 42 (1992) 179-203.

2612 *Nowack* Horst, Untersuchungen über die materialtechnischen Aspekte des Altars Ex 27: BibNot 63 (1992) 62-71.

2613 ᴱ**Anderson** G. A., *Olyan* S. M., Priesthood and cult in ancient Israel: JStOT supp 125, 1991 → 7,288: ᴿThemelios 18,3 (1992s) 24s (P. *Jenson*).

2614 *Spencer* John R., Aaron, Aaronites: → 741, AnchorBD 1 (1992) 1-6.

2615 *Gosse* Bernard, L'expiation-rançon d'Ex 30,11-16: BibNot 63 (1992) 26-29.

2616 *Houtman* C., On the function of the holy incense (Exodus XXX 34-8) and the sacred anointing oil (Exodus XXX 22-33): VT 42 (1992) 458-465.

2617 **Zwickel** Wolfgang, Räucherkult...: OBO 97, ᴰ1990 → 6,2721; 7,2358: ᴿCBQ 54 (1992) 550s (G. A. *Anderson*); JBL 111 (1992) 138s (D. P. *Wright*).

2618 *Ahuvia* Avraham, ❺ Ex 32,22: BethM 37,131 (1991s) 302-4.

2619 *Hakohen* David, ❺ Ex 32,22: BethM 37,129 (1991s) 131-6.

2620 a) *Brooke* George J., The Temple Scroll and LXX Exodus 35-40; – b) *Schiffman* L. H., The Septuagint and the Temple Scroll; shared 'Halakhic' variants: → 459, Septuagint 1990/2, 81-106 / 277-297.

ᴱ**Schenker** Adrian, Studien zu Opfer und Kult im AT 1992 → 491.

E3.7 Leviticus.

2621 *Harlé* P., *Pralon* D., Le Lévitique: Bible d'Alexandrie 3, 1988 → 4,2613 ... 6,2739: ᴿRÉAug 38 (1992) 182 (E. *Cothenet*).

2622 **Hartley** John E., Leviticus: Word comm. 4. Dallas 1992, Word. lxxiii-496 p. $25. 0-8499-0203-7 [TDig 39,295].

2623 *a) Levine* Baruch A., Leviticus; – *b) Rehm* Merlin D., Levites and priests: ➤ 741, AnchorDB 4 (1992) 297-310-321.

2623* **Milgrom** Jacob, Leviticus 1-16: AnchorB 3, 1991 ➤ 7,2270: ᴿBR 8,4 (1992) 17 (J. *Vander Kam*); Claretianum 32 (1992) 506s (J. *Sánchez Bosch*); ETL 68 (1992) 409s (J. *Lust:* mainly redaction-criticism).

2624 *Neusner* J., *Chilton* B. D., Uncleanness; a moral or an ontological category in the early centuries A.D.?: BuBRes 1 (WL 1991) 63-88 [< NTAbs 37,93].

2624* **Noth** Martin, Levitico [1962], ᵀ1989 ➤ 6,2740; Lit. 30.000: ᴿProtestantesimo 47 (1992) 136 (J. *Hobbins*).

2625 **Peter-Contesse** René, *Ellington* John, A translator's handbook on Leviticus 1990 ➤ 6,2741: ᴿSalesianum 54 (1992) 160s (C. *Buzzetti*).

2626 *Razzano* Micaël, La notion biblique de sainteté; étude du Lévitique: RRéf 42,1 (1992) 23-30 [< ZIT 92,299]; p. 29 'Pierre' BEAUCHAMP.

2627 **Sabar** Yona, *Sefer Vajjikra...* Lv in Jewish-Aramaic ... of Zakho. J 1990, Magnes. xv-149 + 8 p. ⦿ 37. [ZAW 106,169, S. *Segert*]. – ᴿJSS 37 (1992) 330s (S. E. *Fox*).

2627* **Scherman** Nosson, *Goldwurm* Hersh, Vayikra, Leviticus; a new translation with a commentary anthologized from Talmudic, Midrashic and Rabbinic sources: ArtScroll Tanach. Brooklyn 1989s, Mesorah. I. xiii-338 p.; II. xlix-to p. 570. 0-89906-370-5; –2-1; pa. –1-3; –3-5.

2628 *Soggin* J. A. Leviticus / Numeri: ➤ 757, EvKL 3 (1992) 82 / 800-2.

2629 *Visotzky* B. L., Anti-Christian polemics in Leviticus Rabba: PAAR 66 (1990) 29-49 [< JStJud 24,365].

2630 **Knierim** Rolf P., Text and concept in Leviticus 1:1-9; a case in exegetical method: ForAT 2. Tü 1992, Mohr. vii-125 p. 3-15-145859-1.

2630* *Lipiński* Edward, *maqlūta'*, [holocauste, akkad.], *qinīta* [bête à sacrifier], *plug qduš* [viande pour les sacrifiants] à Palmyre: ➤ 132, ᶠMILIK J. 1992, 305-311.

2631 *Katchen* Aaron L., [Lv 2,13] The covenantal salt of friendship: ➤ 180c, Mem. TALMAGE F. 1 (1992s) 167-180.

2632 *Schenker* Adrian, [Lv 5ss; 17s] Die Anlässe zum Schuldopfer Ascham: ➤ 491, Opfer 1992, 45-66.

2632* *Porta* Pietro C., L''Omelia sul Levitico 5,1'; ORIGENE e RUFINO a confronto: Orpheus 13,1 (1992) 52-76.

2633 *a)* **Harrington** Hannah K. [Lev 11, Ex 12], The biblical foundations of the impurity systems of the Qumran sectarics and the Rabbis: diss. California. Berkeley 1992, 331 p. 93-04933. – DissA 53 (1992s) 3564s-A.

— *b) Milgrom* Jacob, [Lev 11,3; Dt 14,6...] Food and faith; the ethical foundations of the biblical diet laws: BR 8,6 (1992) 5.10.

— *c) Tamulénas* John, Översättningen av fågellistorna i Lev 11:13-19 och Deut 14:11-18: SvEx 57 (1992) 28-59.

2634 *a) Tov* Emanuel, [Lev 14-17] 4QLevᵈ (4Q26); – *b) Neusner* Jacob, How the Bavli shaped rabbinic discourse; the case of Sifra: ➤ 198, ᶠWOUDE A. van der, VTSupp 49, 1992, 1-5; pl. 1-2 / 204-216.

2634* *Massonnet* Jean, [Lev 16] Kippour, jour de pardon dans le judaïsme ancien [*Kessler* Colette, Rosh Hashanah]: MondeB 79 (1992) 41-47 [–51].

2635 **Kufulu Mandunu** Joseph, [Lev 16] Das 'kindoki' im Licht der Sündenbocktheologie; Versuch einer christlichen Bewältigung des Hexenglaubens in Schwarz-Afrika: Diss. ᴰ*Schwager* R. Innsbruck 1992. 334 p. – RTLv 23,564.

2635* *Nash* Stanley, [Lev 16] Two poles of the Yom Kippur experience in AGNON: Prooftexts 11 (1991) 297-302.

2636 *Chiu* Andrew, [Lev 17-26] Aspects related to the 'Holiness School' and 'Priestly Torah' [*Knohl* I.]: AsiaJT 5 (1991) 55-57.

2636* *Luciani* Didier, 'Soyez saints, car je suis saint'; un commentaire de Lévitique 19: NRT 114 (1992) 212-236.

2637 *Crüsemann* F., Heiligkeitsgesetz: ➤ 762, NBL II, 6 (1991) 93-96.

2638 *a) Sun* Henry T. C. [Lv 17-26] Holiness Code; – *b) Wright* David P. OT [*Hodgson* Robert NT]; Holiness; ➤ 741, AnchorBD 2 (1992) 254-7 / 237-240 [–254].

2639 *Neudecker* Reinhard, *a)* 'And you shall love your neighbor as yourself — I am the Lord' (Lev 19,18) in Jewish interpretation: Biblica 73 (1992) 496-517; franç. 517; – *b)* Nächster ➤ 768, TRE.

2640 *Groot van Houten* Christiana de, Remember that you were aliens; a traditio-historical study: ➤ 19*a*, ꜰBLENKINSOPP J., Priests 1992, 224-240.

2641 *Gerstenberger* Erhard S., 'Er soll dir heilig sein'; Priester und Gemeinde nach Lev 21,1-22,9: ➤ 197, ꜰWOLFF H. W., Wer ist? 1992, 194-210.

2642 *a) Amit* Yairah [Lev 25], The Jubilee law; an attempt at instituting social justice; – *b) Aḥituv* Samuel, [Nm 26...] Land and justice: ➤ 499, Justice 1990/2, 47-59 / 11-28.

2643 *Chaney* Marvin L., [Lev 25...] Debt easement in Israelite history and tradition: ➤ 7,67*, ꜰGOTTWALD N., 1991, 127-139.

2644 *Fager* Jeffrey A., Land tenure in the biblical jubilee; a moral world view: HebAnR 11 (1987) 59-68.

2645 **Wright** Christopher J. H., God's people in God's land ᴰ1990 ➤ 6,2762; 7,2292: ᴿCalvaryB 7,1 (1991) 67 (C. E. *McLain*); RestQ 34 (1992) 116s (T. *Willis*).

2645* *Wright* Christopher J. H., Jubilee, year of: ➤ 741, AnchorBD 3 (1992) 1025-30.

2646 *Zohar* Zvi, The consumption of sabbatical year produce in biblical and rabbinic literature: ➤ 353, Judaism 1987, 75-107.

2646* *Hubbard* Robert L.ᴶ, [Lv 25,33] The Go'el in ancient Israel; theological reflections on an Israelite institution: BuBRes 1 (Annandale NY 1991) 3-19.

2647 *Sperber* D., [Lev 26,3-46] ❺ A note on the Palestinian division of the reading of the Levitical cases: Sidra 8 (1990) 119s [< JStJud 23,335].

2647* *Fleishman* Joseph, [Lev 27,1-8 ...] The age of legal maturity in biblical law: JANES 21 (1992) 35-48.

E3.8 *Numeri;* **Numbers, Balaam.**

2648 **Jagersma** H., Numeri, deel 3: PredikOT 1990 ➤ 7,2299: ᴿCBQ 54 (1992) 529s (C. T. *Begg*).

2648* *Jastram* Nathan, The text of 4QNumᵇ: ➤ 498, MQumran 1 (1991/2) 177-198.

2649 **Maier** Gerhard, Das vierte Buch Mose: Wu Studienbibel 1986 ➤ 5, 2536: ᴿDielB 27 (1991) 390s (B. J. *Diebner*).

2650 **Milgrom** Jacob, Numbers JPS 1990 ➤ 6,2768: ᴿCritRR 5 (1992) 148-150 (D. T. *Olson*: splendid, despite 'peculiar view of redaction criticism'); TLZ 117 (1992) 115-8 (S. *Schreiner*).

2651 *Milgrom* Jacob, Numbers, book of: ➤ 741, AnchorBD 4 (1991) 1146-55 [1139-96, *Friberg* Jöran, Numbers and counting].

2652 **Scharbert** Josef, Numeri: NEchter 27. Wü 1992, Echter. 144 p. DM 24. 3-429-01429-8 [ActuBbg 30,203, J. *Boada*].

2653 *Hill* David F., [Nm 1; 26] The half-tribe of Manasseh: ExpTim 104 (1992s) 140s.

2654 *Adutwum* Ofosu, [Nm 5,11] The suspected adultress; ancient Israelite and traditional Akan treatment: ExpTim 104 (1992s) 38-42.

2655 **Cartledge** T. W., [Nm 6; 15; 30...] Vows in the Hebrew Bible and the Ancient Near East [diss. Duke 1989]: jOsu 147. Shf 1992, JStOT. 221 p. £30. 1-85075-359-8 [BL 93,104, R. E. *Clements*: good].

2656 *Mulzer* Martin, Die griechische Variante zu Num 6,27 in der Synagogeninschrift von Thessalonike: BibNot 62 (1992) 38-40.

2657 *Crocker* P. T., [Nm 13...] Spies and spying in biblical times: BurHist 27 (1991) 76-82 [< OTAbs 15, p. 142].

2658 *Noort* E., De naamsverandering in Num. 13:16 als facet van het Jozuabeeld: ➤ 503, Symposium A. van der WOUDE 1985/92, 55-70.

2659 *Beltrán Torreira* F.-M., [Nm 16,24] Notas en torno a una sanción religiosa de época visigoda (la maldición de Core, Datan y Abirón): Heresis 16 (1991) 21-35 [< RHE 88,93*].

2660 *Milgrom* Jacob, [Num 19] The priestly laws of sancta contamination: ➤ 181, Shaᶜarei TALMON 1992, 137-146.

2661 *Neusner* Jacob, [Nm 19,10] Mr. MACCOBY's red cow, Mr. SANDERS's Pharisees – and mine: JStJud [21 (1990) 60ss] 23 (1992) 81-98.

2662 *McCane* Byron R., [Num 19:11-22; Mt 23,27s] Is a corpse contagious? Early Jewish and Christian attitudes toward the dead: ➤ 478, SBL Sem 31 (1992) 378-388.

2663 *Knauf* Ernst A., [Num 20s; 33] Mount Hor and Kadesh Barnea: BibNot 61 (1992) 22-26.

2663* **Fearer** Timothy L., [Num 21; 32-35; Ex 17] Wars in the wilderness; textual cohesion and conceptual coherence in Pentateuchal battle traditions: diss. Claremont, ᴰ*Knierim* R. 1992. 609 p. 92-38845. – DissA 53 (1992s) 3945-A.

2664 *McNamara* Martin, Early exegesis in the Palestinian Targum (Neofiti), Numbers chapter 21: SNTU A-16 (1991) 127-149.

2665 **Greene** John T., [Num 22-24] Balaam and his interpreters; a hermeneutical history of the Balaam traditions: BrownJudSt 244. Atlanta 1992, Scholars. xii-229 p. $60; sb. $40. 1-55540-690-4 [TDig 40,65: down through modern writers].

2665* *Dion* Paul E., Balaam l'Araméen d'après de nouveaux documents akkadiens du VIIIᵉ siècle: ÉglT 22 (1991) 85-87.

2666 ᴱ**Hoftijzer** J., *Kooij* G. van der, The Balaam text 1989/91 ➤ 7,440: ᴿBASOR 288 (1992) 92s (W. J. *Fulco*); BO 49 (1992) 824 (E. *Lipiński*); JJS 37 (1992) 305-8 (A. R. *Millard*).

2666* *Jobsen* A., Bileam, profeet tussen Israël en de volken: VBGed. Kampen 1991, Kok. 108 p. *f* 18,50. – ᴿNedTTs 46 (1992) 341 (P. B. *Dirksen*).

2667 **Moore** Michael S., The Balaam traditions SBL diss 113, 1990 ➤ 6,2790: 7,2315: ᴿCBQ 54 (1992) 330s (M. A. *Throntveit*).

2668 *Layton* Scott C., Whence comes Balaam? Num 22,5 revisited: Biblica 73 (1992) 32-61; franç. 61: Aramean deported by Neo-Assyrians to an East-Jordan Ammonite river.

2669 **Boudreau** George R., [Num 25,2] A study of the traditio-historical development of the Baal of Peor tradition: diss. Emory, ᴰ*Miller* J. M. Atlanta 1992. vii-372 p. 91-27591. – OIAc 3,14.

2670 *Toker* Naftali, [Num 27,17...] ➊ Shepherds' guilt as a type in the shepherds' parables: BethM 36 (1990s) 29-41 [< OTAbs 15,17].

2670* *Ellington* John, The troublesome parentheses in Numbers 32.38: BTrans 43 (1992) 241-4.

E3.9 Liber Deuteronomii.

2671 **Braulik** Georg, Deuteronomium [I (1-16,17) 1986 ➤ 2,1922] II. 16,18-34,12: NEchter 28. Wü 1992, Echter. 136 p. DM 28.   3-429-01442-5 [BL 93,55, J. W. *Rogerson*].

2672 **Christensen** Duane L., Deuteronomy 1-11: Word comm. 6A. Dallas 1991, Word. lxii-223 p. $25.   0-8499-0294-3 [TDig 39,295].

2673 **Dogniez** Cécile, *Harl* Marguerite, Le Deutéronome; traduction du texte grec de la Septante, introduction et notes: Bible d'Alexandrie 5. P 1992, Cerf. 364 p. F 185. – ᴿETL 68 (1992) 411-3 (J. *Lust*); VSp 146 (1992) 723 (J. *Asurmendi*).

2673* *a) Duncan* Julie A., Considerations of 4QDtʲ in light of the 'All Souls Deuteronomy' and Cave 4 Phylactery texts; – *b) White* Sidnie A., 4Q364 & 365 [some Gn 2 through Dt 19], a preliminary report: ➤ 498, MQumran 1 (1991/2) 199-215 / 217-228.

2674 **Fraade** Stephen D., From tradition to commentary; Torah and its interpretation in the Midrash Sifré to Deuteronomy 1991 ➤ 7,2326*: ᴿCritRR 5 (1992) 363-5 (B. E. *Nielsen*); JStJud 23 (1992) 108-111 (E. *Cortes*); Prooftexts 12 (1992) 188-192 (E. *Segal*).

2675 ᴱ**Hendrickx** H., Gedenk uw bevrijding; de profetische bibelboeken van Deuteronomium tot Koningen, een werkboek: Bijbelkollektief van Kristenen voor het Socialisme. Lv 1989, KvS. 199 p. Fb 400. 90-800162-2-5. – ᴿTvT 32 (1992) 306s (M. *Vervenne*).

2675* *Kalland* Earl S., Deuteronomy: ➤ 1942, Expositor's Bible Comm. 3 (1992) 1-235.

2676 **Labuschagne** C. J., Deuteronomium deel 2: PredikOT, 1990 ➤ 7, 2328: ᴿCBQ 54 (1992) 530s (C. T. *Begg*); KerkT 43 (1992) 75 (B. *Becking*).

2677 **Miller** Patrick D.ᴶ, Deuteronomy: Interpretation Comm. 1990 ➤ 6, 2810; 7,2330: ᴿCBQ 54 (1992) 757s (H. T. C. *Sun*: stimulating and consistently successful).

2678 **Weinfeld** Moshe, Deuteronomy 1-11: AnchorB 5, 1991 ➤ 7,2337: ᴿBR 8,4 (1992) 17.58s (J. *VanderKam*); ETL 68 (1992) 410s (J. *Lust*); ÉTRel 67 (1992) 448s (J. *Rennes*: p.236 véritable monographie sur le Décalogue; abondante bibliographie, 58 titres de lui-même); TS 53 (1991) 545-7 (S. *McEvenue*).

2679 **Weitenberg** J. J. S., *Leeuw van Weenen* A. de, Lemmatized index of the Armenian version of Deuteronomy: SeptCog 32. Atlanta 1990, Scholars. xii-96 p. $20; pa. $15. – ᴿCBQ 54 (1992) 547s (E. G. *Mathews*, also on Stone 4Ezra).

2680 *Braulik* Georg, Haben in Israël auch Frauen geopfert? Beobachtungen am Deuteronomium [(nur) nicht ausgeschlossen]: ➤ 163, ᶠSauer G., Aktualität 1992, 19-28.

2680* **Johnson** David D., Deuteronomy as the constitution of Israel's emergent society: diss. Dallas Theol. Sem., 1992, ᴰ*Merrill* E. 93-03918. – DissA 53 (1992s) 3251-A.

2681 **Lohfink** Norbert, Studien zum Dt: SBAuf 8,1990 ↠ 6,265: ᴿBijdragen 53 (1992) 323 (P. C. *Beentjes*); RelStR 18 (1992) 325 (C. T. *Begg*).

2681* *a) Lohfink* Norbert, Deutéronome et Pentateuque; état de la recherche, ᵀ*Kuntzmann* Raymond; – *b) Römer* Thomas, Le Deutéronome à la quête des origines: ↠ 474, ACFÉB 14, 1991/2, 35-64 / 65-98.

2682 *Lohfink* Norbert, Opfer und Säkularisierung im Deuteronomium: ↠ 491, Opfer 1990/2, 15-43, gegen *Weinfeld* M.

2683 *Nicholson* Ernest, Deuteronomy's view of Israel: ↠ 7,141, ᶠSoGGIN J. A., 1991, 191-203.

2684 *Nielsen* E., Lov og rett [Gesetz und Recht]: DanTTs 55 (1992) 1-14 [< ZAW 104,431].

2685 **Regt** L. J. de, A parametric model for syntactic studies ... Dt 1-30, ᴰ1988 ↠ 4,2696 ... 7,2333: ᴿBL (1992) 86 (J. C. L. *Gibson*); JNES 51 (1992) 160 (E. *Cruz-Uribe*).

2686 **Römer** Thomas, Israels Väter: OBO 99, 1990 ↠ 6,2817; 7,2335: ᴿBiblica 73 (1992) 112-6 (C. T. *Begg*: impressive, but somewhat too much and too little); DielB 27 (1991) 295-7 (B. J. *Diebner*); WeltOr 23 (1992) 180-3 (E. *Blum*).

2686* — **Lohfink** N. [*Römer* T.], Die Väter Israels: OBO 111, 1991 ↠ 7,2336: ᴿExpTim 103 (1991s) 374 (R. *Coggins*: a draw); TüTQ 172 (1992) 145 (W. *Gross*).

2687 **Weinfeld** Moshe, Deuteronomy and the Deuteronomistic school [reprint of Oxford 1972]. WL 1992, Eisenbrauns. xviii-467 p. 0-931464-40-4 [OIAc 3,41].

2688 *Weinfeld* Moshe, Deuteronomy, book of: ↠ 741, AnchorDB 2 (1992) 168-183.

2688* **Wilson** Ian, Divine presence in Deuteronomy [< diss. Cambridge 1992]: TyndB 43 (1992) 403-6.

2689 **Zobel** Constantin, Prophetie und Deuteronomium; die Rezeption prophetischer Theologie durch das Dt [Diss. Halle 1990, ᴰ*Wallis* G.]: BZAW 199. B/NY 1992, de Gruyter. ix-267 p. DM 108. 3-11-012838-1. – ᴿÉT-Rel 67 (1992) 590s (T. *Römer*); ZAW 104 (1992) 465 (H.-C. *Schmitt*).

2690 **Slater** Susan, 'I have set the land before you'; a study of the rhetoric of Deuteronomy 1-3: diss. McGill, ᴰ*Culley* R. Montreal 1991. 279 p. DANN-73313. – DissA 53 (1992s) 4360-A; SR 21,494.

2691 *Christensen* Duane L., [Dt 1,1-6] New evidence for the Priestly redaction of Deuteronomy: ZAW 104 (1992) 197-201.

2691* **Johnston** Edgar O., Syntax and emphasis in Deuteronomy 4-11: diss. Annenberg. Ph 1991. 268 p. 92-30468. – DissA 53 (1992s) 2348-A.

2692 **Achenbach** Reinhard, [Dt 5-11] Israel zwischen Verheissung und Gebot [Diss. Göttingen 1989, ᴰ*Perlitt* L. ↠ 5,2587, wrongly 'Aschenbach']: EurHS 23/422, 1991 ↠ 7,2342; 3-631-43847-8: ᴿBL (1992) 97s (G. H. *Jones*).

2693 *Amit* Yairah, [Dt 5...] ⊕ 'We are here, all alive': BethM 37,131 (1991s) 313-9.

2693* **Ibáñez Arana** Andrés, Deuteronomio 5 y la redacción del Deuteronomio: ScripV 38 (1991) 114-188 . 225-248.

2694 *Olson* Dennis T., Temptations and trials in Deuteronomy 6-11, Luke 4, and Luke 22-24; the significance of a recurring three-fold pattern: ➤ 77, FHARRISVILLE R., All things new 1992, 21-28.

2695 *Veijola* Timo, a) Das Bekenntnis Israels; Beobachtungen zur Geschichte und Theologie von Dtn 6,4-9: TZBas 48 (1992) 369-381; – b) Höre Israel; der Sinn und Hintergrund von Deuteronomium VI 4-9: VT 42 (1992) 528-541.

2696 *Lohfink* Norbert, Deuteronomy 6:24 *lᵉḥayyotenû* 'to maintain us': ➤ 181, Shaʿarei TALMON 1992, 111-9.

2697 *O'Connell* Robert H., Deuteronomy VII 1-26; asymmetrical concentricity and the rhetoric of conquest: VT 42 (1992) 248-265.

2698 *Giles* Terry, Knowledge as a boundary in the organization of experience, Deut 8:3,16: IrBSt 13 (1991) 155-169.

2699 *O'Connell* Robert H., Deuteronomy IX 7 - X 7,10-11; panelled structure, double rehearsal and the rhetoric of covenant rebuke: VT 42 (1992) 492-509.

2699* *Jones* Ray C.ᴶ, Deuteronomy 10:12-22, expository: Interpretation 46 (1992) 281-5.

2700 **Langer** G., Von Gott erwählt Dt 12, ᴰ1989 ➤ 5,2590; 6,2832: ᴿAtKap 116 (1991) 185s (Z. *Kowalska*).

2701 **Reuter** Eleonore, Kultzentralisation; zur Entstehung und Theologie von Dtn 12: kath. Diss. ᴰ*Hossfeld*: Bonn 1992. – TR 89,78.

2702 *Seebass* Horst, [Dt 12...] Vorschlag zur Vereinfachung literarischer Analysen im dtn Gesetz: BibNot 58 (1991) 83-98.

2703 *Niehaus* Jeffrey, [Dt 12,5] The central sanctuary; where and when? [1991 Tyndale OT Lecture]: TyndB 43,1 (1992) 3-30.

2704 **Herman** M., [Dt 14; Lev 27,30] Tithe as gift; the institution in the Pentateuch and in the light of Mauss's prestation theory: Distinguished Diss. SF 1991, Mellen. xviii-188 p. $70. 0-7734-9959-8 [BL 93,107, A. D. H. *Mayes*].

2705 *Brodie* Thomas, Fish, temple tithe, and remission; the God-based generosity of Deuteronomy 14-15 as one component of Matt 17:22 - 18:35: RB 99 (1992) 697-718; franç. 697.

2706 **Hamilton** Jeffries M., Social justice and Deuteronomy; the case of Deuteronomy 15: SBL diss. 136 (Princeton 1990, ᴰ*Miller* P.). Atlanta 1992, Scholars. xiii-168 p. $32; sb./pa. $21. 1-55540-747-1; pa. -8-X. – ᴿExpTim 104 (1992s) 346 (C. S. *Rodd*).

2707 *Hamilton* Jeffries M., [Dt 15,1-11] Ha-areṣ in the shemitta law: VT 42 (1992) 214-222.

2708 *Morrow* William, The composition of Deut 15:1-3: HebAnR 12 (1990) 115-131.

2709 a) *Kessler* Rainer, Die Rolle des Armen für Gerechtigkeit und Sünde des Reichen; Hintergrund und Bedeutung von Dtn 15,9; 24,13.15; – b) *Strauss* Hans, 'Armut' und 'Reichtum' im Horizont biblischer, vor allem alttestamentlicher Aussagen: ➤ 197, FWOLFF H. W., Wer ist? 1992, 153-163 / 179-193.

2710 *Rodd* C.S., [Dt 18,15-22; Acts 3,11-26] 'Forth-tellers' or [still rather] 'fore-tellers': ExpTim 104 (1992s) 16-18.

2711 *Carrière* J.-M., L'organisation des lois en Dt 19-26; les lois sur le mariage: NRT 114 (1992) 519-532.

2712 *Stulman* Louis, [Dt 19-22] Sex and familial crimes in the D-code; a witness to mores in transition: JStOT 53 (1992) 47-63.

2713 *Otto* Eckart,   Das Verbot der Wiederherstellung einer geschiedenen Ehe; Deuteronomium 24,1-4 im Kontext des israelitischen und jüdischen Eherechts: UF 24 (1992) 301-312.

2713* *Laney* J. Carl,   Deuteronomy 24:1-4 and the issue of divorce: BtS 149 (1992) 3-15.

2714 *Nicol* George G.,   [Dt 26,1-11; Mt 5,17-26] The offering of life: ExpTim 103 (1991s) 369s.

2715 *Bonora* Antonio,   Dalla storia e dalla natura alla professione di fede e alla celebrazione (Dt 26,1-15): ➤ 338, ParSpV 25 (1992) 27-39.

2716 *Lohfink* Norbert,   Dtn 28,69 – Überschrift oder Kolophon?: BibNot 64 (1992) 40-51 [*Rooy* H. van, 1988].

2716* **Lenchak** Timothy A.,   A rhetorical-critical and theological study of Dt 29,30: diss. Pont. Univ. Gregoriana, ᴰ*Conroy* C.   R 1992. Extr. 3806: 131 p. – RTLv 24, p. 542.

2717 *Bonora* Antonio,   Israele popolo eletto e disperso tra le genti (Dt 30,1ss): ➤ 339, ParSpV 26 (1992) 47-56.

2717* **Britt** Brian M.,   The Hebrew Bible as sacred text in Deut. 31-34 and the philosophy of Walter BENJAMIN: diss. ᴰ*Fishbane* M.   Ch 1992. – RTLv 24, p. 540.

2718 *Cooper* Alan,   [Dt 32] An extraordinary sixteenth-century biblical commentary, Eliezer Ashkenazi on the Song of Moses: ➤ 180c, Mem. TALMAGE F., 1 (1992s) 129-150.

2719 *Loewenstamm* S. E., a) The death of Moses (1976); – b) The Testament of Abraham and the texts concerning Moses' death (1976); – c) The story of Moses' birth (1980): ➤ 273, From Babylon 1992, 136-166 / 167-173 / 201-221.

E4.1   *Origo Israelis in Canaan; Deuteronomista;*   **Liber Josue.**

2720 **Alt** Albrecht,   Essays on Old Testament history and religion, ᵀ*Wilson* R. A. (1966). Sheffield 1989, JStOT. x-274 p. £11. – ᴿCBQ 54 (1992) 101s (M. S. *Moore*: approach now part of the standard histories; reprint fully justified).

2721 **Boschi** Bernardo G.,   Le origini di Israele nella Bibbia tra storia e teologia; la questione del metodo e la sfida storiografica: RivB supp 20, 1989 ➤ 6,b351:   ᴿParVi 36 (1991) 69-71 (P. *Borbone*).

2722 *Coggins* R. J.,   The origins of Israel [survey]: TBR 5,2 (1992s) 4s.

2723 **Coote** Robert B.,   Early Israel, a new horizon 1990 ➤ 6,2852; 7,2362: ᴿBL (1992) 42 (A. D. H. *Mayes*); BtS 149 (1992) 114s (E. H. *Merrill*); HeythJ 33 (1992) 442s (J. *Mulrooney*); Horizons 19 (1992) 126-8 (R. *Gnuse*, also on his Power, politics); JBL 111 (1992) 319-321 (D. C. *Hopkins*); OTEssays 5 (1992) 394-6 (N. van der *Westhuizen*); RB 99 (1992) 769s (J. M. de *Tarragon*); TorJT 7 (1991) 266-8 (B. *Halpern*); WestTJ 54 (1992) 175-8 (R. S. *Hess*).

2724 **Davies** Philip R.,   In search of 'Ancient Israel' ['The emergence of Israel', as THOMPSON T., but also where and how was the biblical literature written]: jOsu 148. Shf 1992, Academic. 172 p.; £22.50; sb. £18.75. 1-85075-380-6 [BL 93,39, K. W. *Whitelam*: provocative, on the confusions which theology has generated].

2725 *Dever* William G.,   Unresolved issues in the early history of Israel; toward a synthesis of archaeological and textual reconstructions: ➤ 7,67*, ᶠGOTTWALD 1991, 195-208.

2726 **Dus** Jan, Israelitische Vorfahren ... ALT: EurHS 23/404, 1991 ➤ 7,2365: ᴿBL (1992) 43 (I. W. *Provan*); ÉglT 23 (1992) 262-4 (L. *Laberge*).
2727 ᴱ**Freedman** D. N., *Graf* D. F., Palestine in transition; the emergence of ancient Israel 1983 ➤ 64,262 ... 3,f738: ᴿHenoch 14 (1992) 193s (Piera *Arata Mantovani*).
2728 *Frendo* Anthony J., Five recent books on the emergence of ancient Israel [AHLSTRÖM G. 1986; COOTE-WHITELAM 1987; FINKELSTEIN I. 1988; KASWALDER P. 1990; STIEBING W. 1991]: PEQ 124 (1992) 144-151.
2728* *Gottwald* Norman, Surgimiento del pueblo de Israel [conferencia Univ. Javeriana, Bogotá 15.III.1989]: TXav 41 (1991) 185-197.
2729 *Halpern* Baruch, Sociological comparativism and the theological imagination; the case of the Conquest: ➤ 181, Shaʿarei TALMON 1992, 53-67.
2730 *Halpern* Baruch, Settlement of Canaan: ➤ 741. AnchorBD 5 (1992) 1120-43.
2731 *Herrmann* Siegfried, Observations on some recent hypotheses pertaining to early Israelite history [LEMCHE N. 1988], ᵀ*Cryer* F. H.: ➤ 499, Justice 1990/2, 105-116.
2731* **Hostetter** Edwin C., Nations mightier and more numerous; the biblical view of the peoples that the ancient Israelites encountered in acquiring the Promised Land: diss. Johns Hopkins, ᴰ*McCarter* P. K. Baltimore 1992. 263 p. 92-16575. – DissA 53 (1992s) 194-A.
2732 *Kempinski* Aharon, How profoundly Canaanized were the early Israelites?: ZDPV 108 (1992) 1-7.
Kreuzer Siegfried, Die Frühgeschichte Israels 1989 ➤ 2364*.
2733 ᴱ**Laperrousaz** E.-M., La protohistoire d'Israël 1990 ➤ 7,2371: ᴿÉTRel 67 (1992) 276 (T. *Römer*: désarroi de l'historien face à cette période 'fondatrice'); RTLv 23 (1992) 76-81 (J.-C. *Haelewyck*); Salesianum 54 (1992) 157s (R. *Vicent*).
2734 **Lemche** Niels P., The Canaanites and their land; the tradition of the Canaanites: JStOT supp 110, 1991 ➤ 7,b17: ᴿETL 68 (1992) 151s (J. *Lust*); ÉTRel 67 (1992) 100s (D. *Lys*: an imposing work, though perhaps not without some vicious circles); JBL 111 (1992) 695-7 (Diana *Edelman*).
2735 **Lemche** N. P., Ancient Israel, a new history of Israelite society 1988 ➤ 4,d98 ... 7,b329: ᴿJNES 51 (1992) 312-4 (Diana *Edelman*).
2736 **Lemche** N. P., Early Israel: VTSup 37, 1985 ➤ 2,1955 ... 7,237.
McNutt Paula M., The forging of Israel ᴰ1990 ➤ d620.
2737 **Nordheim** E. von, Die Selbstbehauptung Israels in der Welt des Alten Orients: OBO 115. FrS/Gö 1992, Univ./VR. 214 p. – ᴿJNWS 18 (1992) 226-8 (F. *Deist*: on Israelite religion).
2738 **Rösel** Hartmut N., Israel in Kanaan; zum Problem der Entstehung Israels: BeitErfAJ 11. Fra 1992, Lang. 150 p. $36.80. 3-631-43456-1 [OIAc 2,26].
2739 *Rösel* Hartmut N., Die Entstehung Israels; Evolution oder Revolution? [SBL Wien 1990]: BibNot 59 (1991) 28-32.
2740 *Seebass* Horst, Dialog über Israels Anfänge; zum Evolutionsmodell von N. P. LEMCHE 1985: ➤ 149, ᶠPREUSS H., At Glaube 1992, 11-19.
2741 *Silberman* Neil A., Who were the Israelites? Archaeology 45,2 (1992) 22-30.

2742 **Arx** U. von, Amphiktyonie (Zwölfer 1) 1990 ➤ 7,2359: ᴿBL (1992) 41 (A. G. *Auld*: does not recognize that words for tribe oftener mean objects and date near 4th cent.).

2743 *Herrmann* Siegfried, Was bleibt von der Jahwe-Amphiktyonie?: TZ-Bas 48 (1992) 304-314.
2744 *McKenzie* Steven L., Deuteronomistic history: ➤ 741, AnchorDB 2 (1992) 160-8.
2745 *Moenikes* Ansgar, Zur Redaktionsgeschichte des sogenannten Deuteronomistischen Geschichtswerks: ZAW 104 (1992) 333-348.
2746 **Noth** Martin, The Deuteronomistic history[2] [= [1], but with translation more homogenized with The Chronicler's History (also Sheffield); and the whole text has been reset with the notes at the foot of each page]. Sheffield 1991, Academic. 156 p. [ETL 68,149, J. *Lust*].
2747 **O'Brien** Mark, The Deuteronomistic history hypothesis...: OBO 92, 1989 ➤ 5,2602... 7,2386 (-istic!): [R]Pacifica 5 (1992) 219-221 (N. *Habel*).

2748 *Boling* Robert G., Joshua / Judges, book of: ➤ 741, AnchorBD 3 (1992) 1002-1014 / 1107-1117.
2749 **Görg** Manfred, Josua: NEchter 26, 1991 ➤ 7,2377: [R]BL (1992) 51s (A. *Curtis*).
2750 *Greenspoon* Leonard, The Qumran fragments of Joshua; which puzzle are they part of and where do they fit?: ➤ 459, Septuagint 1990/2, 159-194.
2751 Joshua ❹ Annotated critical translation from the original languages by the Studium Biblicum Franciscanum. Tokyo 1991, Chuo Shuppansha. vi-180 p.
2752 **Koorevaar** H.J., De opbouw van het boek Jozua 1990 ➤ 6,2868: [R]CritRR 5 (1992) 143s (M. *Kessler*); NRT 114 (1992) 100s (J.-L. *Ska*).
2752* *Madvig* Donald H., Joshua: ➤ 1942 supra, Expositor's Bible Comm. 3 (1992) 237-371.
2753 *Murrs* Rick R., Joshua, a model for Church leaders: BToday 30 (1992) 267-270.
2753* **Merchant** Moelwyn, Jesha. Swansea 1987, C. Davies. 426 p. £11. 0-7154-0684-1. – [R]Churchman 106 (1992) 360-2 (O. *Thomas* recommends).
2754 **Ottosson** Magnus, Josuaboken, en programskrift for davidisk restauration 1991 ➤ 7,2387 (not 'für'): [R]BL (1992) 83s (J.R. *Porter*); Divinitas 36 (1992) 193 (T. *Stramare*).
2755 **Schäfer-Lichtenberger** Christina, Josua und Salomo; eine Studie zu Autorität und Legitimität des Nachfolgers im Alten Testament: Hab.-Diss. [D]*Rendtorff* R. Heidelberg 1992. – RTLv 24, p. 543.
2756 *Tov* Emmanuel, 4Q Josh[h] ➤ 132, [F]MILIK J. 1992, 205-212; pl. 1.

2757 *a*) *Sacchi* Paolo, Giosuè 1,1-9; dalla critica storica a quella letteraria; – *b*) *Rofé* Alexander, Ephraimite versus Deuteronomistic history; – *c*) *Ringgren* Helmer, Early Israel; – *d*) *Wallis* Gerhard, Israel: Namen, Land und Volk: ➤ 7,141, [F]SOGGIN J.A., Storia 1991, 237-253 / 221-235 / 217-220 / 281-292.
2758 **Felber** Anneliese, Ecclesia ex gentibus congregata; die Deutung der Rahabepisode (Jos 2) in der Patristik: Diss. Graz 85. Graz 1992, Univ. 10*-197 p. DM 25. 3-7041-9045-4. – [R]ErbAuf 68 (1992) 425 (B. *Schwank*); TPhil 67 (1992) 591s (H.J. *Sieben*).
2759 *Hertog* Cornelis G. den, Ein Wortspiel in der Jericho–Erzählung (Jos. 6)?: ZAW 104 (1992) 99s.

2760 *Luria* Ben-Zion, ❹ *Oṣar beth H´* Jos 6,22:   BethM 37,130 (1991s) 238-240.
2761 **Younger** K. Lawson^J, [Jos 9-12] Ancient conquest accounts: JStOT supp 98, 1990 ➤ 6,b404; 7,2596:   ᴿBiblica 73 (1992) 116-9 (H. *Engel*); BO 49 (1992) 480s (J. A. *Soggin*: wichtig; offene Fragen); CBQ 54 (1992) 342s (J. S. *Rogers*: 'most poorly proofread work I have read'); JBL 111 (1992) 115-7 (A. J. *Hauser*); RB 99 (1992) 299s (J.-M. de *Tarragon*).
2762 *Sutherland* Ray K., Israelite political theories in Joshua 9:   JStOT 53 (1992) 65-74.
2763 *Rowlett* Lori, [Josh 10...] Inclusion, exclusion and marginality in the book of Joshua: JStOT 55 (1992) 15-23.
2764 *Margalit* Baruch, The day the sun did not stand still; a new look at Joshua 8-15:   VT 42 (1992) 466-491.
2765 **Cortese** Enzo, Josua 13-21, ein priesterschriftlicher Abschnitt im deuteronomistischen Geschichtswerk [kath. Hab.-D. Wien]: OBO 94, 1990 ➤ 7,2398:   ᴿBO 49 (1992) 481 (J. A. *Soggin*: wichtig); RivB 40 (1992) 500-4 (P. *Tagliacarne*).
2766 *Vargon* Shmuel, [Jos 15...] Gedud, a place name in the Shephelah of Judah: VT 42 (1992) 557-564.
2767 *Görg* Manfred, [Jos 19,5] Zur Diskussion um die Lage von Scharuhen: BibNot 58 (1991) 17-19.
2768 *Ben Zvi* Ehud, [Josh 21] The list of the Levitical cities: JStOT 54 (1992) 77-106.
2769 **Anbar** Moshé, Josué et l'Alliance de Sichem (Josué 24:1-28): BeitBExT 25. Fra 1992, Lang. 163 p. 3-631-45018-4.
2770 **Koopmans** William T., Joshua 24 as poetic narrative: JStOT supp 93, 1990 ➤ 6,2880; 7,2404:   ᴿCBQ 54 (1992) 328s (K. L. *Younger*); JTS 43 (1992) 555-7 (J. A. *Soggin*).

E4.2   *Liber Judicum:*   Richter, Judges.

2771 ᵀᴱ**Danieli** Maria Ignazia, ORIGENE, Omelie sui Giudici: Collana TestP 101. R 1992, Città Nuova. 172 p. 88-311-3101-X.
2772 **Dirksen** P. B., Richteren: Tekst en Toelichting. Kampen 1990, Kok. 120 p. *f* 19,75. 90-242-5323-3. – ᴿTvT 32 (1992) 307 (M. *Vervenne*).
     Dus Jan, Theokratische Demokratie des alten Israel; fünf Studien zur Geschichte Israels 1992 ➤ 237.
2773 **Hamlin** E. J., Judges; at risk... 1990 ➤ 6,2887; 7,2408:   ᴿHorBT 14 (1992) 75s (R. G. *Bowman*); RefTR 50 (1991) 69s (B. *Webb*).
2774 **Webb** B., Book of Judges 1987 ➤ 3,2638... 7,2411: ᴿVT 42 (1992) 429s (R. P. *Gordon*).
2775 **Wilcock** Michael, The message of Judges; grace abounding: The Bible Speaks Today. Leicester 1992, Inter-Varsity. 175 p. 0-85510-972-1.
2775* *Wolf* Herbert, Judges: ➤ 1942 supra, Expositor's Bible Comm. 3 (1992) 373-506.

2776 **Amit** Yaira, ❹ The book of Judges; the art of editing;   EnṣMiqrait Library 6. J 1992, Bialik. xii-396 p. 965-342-592-7.
2777 **Becker** Uwe, Richterzeit und Königtum: BZAW 192, ᴰ1990 ➤ 6,2883: ᴿBL (1992) 62 (A. G. *Auld*); BO 49 (1992) 828-831 (P. B. *Dirksen*); ExpTim 103 (1991s) 296s (R. J. *Coggins*); JBL 111 (1992) 517-9 (M. *Brettler*); TLZ 117 (1992) 825s (K. *Zobel*).
2778 *Beem* Beverly G., The minor judges; a literary reading of some very short stories: ➤ 7,334*, Canon 1990/1, 147-172 [109-146, *Younger* on Jg. 4s].

2779 *Fensham* Frank C., Literary observations on historical narratives in sections of Judges: ➤ 7,141, FSOGGIN J. A., Storia 1991, 77-87.
2780 **Klein** Lilian R., Triumph of irony... Jg 1988 ➤ 4,2763 ... 6,2888: RScripB 22,1 (1992) 24 (R. *Duckworth*).

2781 *Penchansky* David, [Jg 2,10-23] Up for grabs; a tentative proposal for doing ideological criticism: Semeia 59 (1992) 35-41.
2782 *Hon* Saul, ⊕ Jg 3,26: BethM 37,130 (1991s) 235-7.
2783 *Horst* P. W. van der, [Jg 4s] Deborah and Seila in Ps.-PHILO's Liber antiquitatum biblicarum: ➤ 57, FFLUSSER D., Messiah 1992, 111-7 [Deborah 2575 words; Jg 4s 786, reduced to 497 by misogynist Josephus (FELDMAN); Seila is the name given to Jephtha's daughter Jg 11,27s].
2784 *Matthews* V., *Benjamin* D., [Jg 4,17-22] Jael: host or judge?: BToday 30 (1992) 291-6.
2785 *Urbrock* William G., a) [Jg 5] ⊕ Sisera's people in the song of Deborah: BethM 37,131 (1991s) 305-312; – b) Sisera's mother in Judges 5 and Haim GOURI's 'Immo': HebAnR 11 (1987) 423-434.
2786 **Gibert** Pierre [Jg 6-8] Vérité historique... Gédéon 1990 ➤ 6,2901; 7,2425: RCBQ 54 (1992) 523s (B. *MacDonald*); FoiTemps 22 (1992) 281s (A. *Wénin*).
2786* *Tanner* J. Paul, [Jg 6-8] The Gideon narrative as the focal point of Judges: BtS 149 (1992) 146-161.
2787 *Fokkelman* Jan P., Structural remarks on Judges 9 and 19: ➤ 181, Sha'arei TALMON 1992, 33-45.
2788 *Marcus* David, [Jg 11,7] The legal dispute between Jephthah and the Elders: HebAnR 12 (1990) 105-114.
2789 **Kaswalder** Pietro A., La disputa diplomatica di Iefte (Gdc 11,12-28); la ricerca archeologica in Giordania e il problema della conquista: SBF Anal 29, 1990 ➤ 6,2908; 7,2433: RCBQ 54 (1992) 325s (R. *North*); RivB 40 (1992) 103-5 (F. *Dalla Vecchia*).
2790 *Landers* Solomon, [Jg 11,39] Did Jephthah kill his daughter?: BR 7,4 (1991) 28-31. 42 [no; he consigned her to an isolated life as virgin].
2791 *Loon* Gertrud J. M. van, The iconography of Jephthah; a wallpainting in the sanctuary of the old church of St. Anthony's monastery near the Red Sea: ➤ 694b, Copte IVe (1988/92) 1,115-122 + 1 fig.
2791* *Ellington* John, More on shibboleth (Judges 12,6) [adding LXX Stachys]: BTrans 43 (1992) 244s.
2792 *Faber* Alice, [Jg 12,6] Second harvest; *šibbolet* revisited (yet again): JSS 37 (1992) 1-10.
2793 *Mazar* A., *Kelm* G. L., Au pays de Samson, la Timna biblique: MondeB 68 (1991) 42-46.
2794 *Jonker* Louis C., Samson in double vision; Judges 13-16 from historical-critical and narrative perspectives: JNWS 18 (1992) 49-66; 2 fig.
2795 *Reinhartz* Adele, [Jg 13] Samson's mother; an unnamed protagonist: JStOT 55 (1992) 25-37.
2796 *Römheld* K. F. D., Von den Quellen der Kraft (Jdc 13): ZAW 104 (1992) 28-52; Eng. 52.
2797 **Bader** Winfried, [Jg 14,11-19] Textual analysis with the help of TUSTEP [Tü Univ. System of Text Processing Programs]: ➤ 450, Informatique 2, 1988/9, 75-86.
2798 **Bal** Mieke, Death and dissymmetry [Jg 16,4; 12,34] 1988 ➤ 5,2682; 6,2912: RLitTOx 5 (1991) 327s (D. *Jasper*).

2799 *Wilcock* Michael, a) All the right procedures; Judges 17:1-18:31; – b) All the wrong attitudes; Judges 19:1-20:48:   Evangel 10,2 (1992) 3-5; 10/3,66-68.

2800 *Malamat* Avraham, ❸ '... After the manner of the Sidonians... and how [at Dan] they were far from the Sidonians...' (Judges 18:7): ➤ 18, ᶠBɪʀᴀɴ A., ErIsr 23 (1992) 194s; Eng. 153*.

2801 *Amit* Yaira, [Jg 19-21] ❸ The Gibeah concubine passage as *polemos simui* [blind, veiled] against Saul's kingship: BethM 37,129 (1991s) 109-118 ➤ 7,2436.

2802 *Satterthwaite* P. E., a) Some Septuagintal pluses in Judges 20 and 21: BSeptCog 24,1 (1991) 25-35 [< ᴢɪᴛ 92,511]; – b) Narrative artistry in the composition of Judges XX 29ff: VT 42 (1992) 80-89.

E4.3   **Liber Ruth**, *'V Rotuli'*, the Five Scrolls.

2803 *Bohlen* Reinhold, a) Feministische Exegesen der Rutrolle; Versuch eines kritischen Dialogs mit ihren Autorinnen: ➤ 54, ᶠFᴇɪʟᴢᴇʀ H., 1992, 13-30; – b) Die Rutrolle; ein aktuelles Beispiel narrativer Ethik des Alten Testaments: TrierTZ 101 (1992) 1-19.

2804 ᴱ**Cabezudo Melero** Enrique,   Historia episódica; Rut, Tobías, Judit y Ester; texto (La Casa de la Biblia) y comentario.   Estella 1992, VDivino. 207 p.

2805 **Fewell** Danna N., **Gunn** David M.,   Compromising redemption... Ruth 1990 ➤ 6,2920; 7,2442: ᴿAnglTR 74 (1992) 98s (P. H. *Reardon*); CBQ 54 (1992) 522s (Barbara *Green*); CritRR 5 (1992) 130s (Katharine D. *Sakenfeld*: high standard radical reinterpretation); JQR 83 (1992s) 191s (A. *Berlin*: a modern midrash); TTod 49 (1992s) 135s (Johanna W. H. *Bos*).

2806 **Frevel** Christian,   Das Buch Rut: NStu AT 6.   Stu 1992, KBW.   176 p. 3-460-07061-7.

2807 **Gow** Murray D.,   The book of Ruth; its structure, theme and purpose. Leicester 1992, Apollos.   240 p. £19.   0-85111-765-1 [TBR 6/2,29, R. *Mason*]; WestTJ 53 (1991) 149-151 (R. *Whitekettle*).

2808 **Hubbard** R.,   The Book of Ruth: NICOT 1989 ➤ 4,2793* ... 7,2445: ᴿThemelios 17,1 (1991s) 21s (F. W. *Bush*).

2808* *Huey* F. B.ᴶ,   Ruth: ➤ 1942 supra, Expositor's Bible Comm. 3 (1992) 509-549.

2809 ᴱ**Martel** Gérard de,   Commentaria in Ruth e codicibus Genoufensi 45 et Clagenfurtensi 13: CCMed 81.   Turnhout 1990, Brepols. 460 p. Fb 5500. 2-503-03811-5 (-2-3 pa.). – ᴿCBQ 54 (1992) 520 (J. R. *Davila*); JEH 43 (1992) 146s (M. *Gibson*); Speculum 67 (1992) 404s (G. R. *Evans*), & 656 (D. *Ganz*, Répertoires).

2810 **Martel** Gérard de,   Répertoire des textes latins relatifs au livre de Ruth (VIIᵉ-XVᵉ s.): InstrPatr 18.   Steenbrugge/Dordrecht 1990, S. Pieter/Academic.   273 p. – ᴿRÉAug 38 (1992) 212s (G. *Dahan*).

2810* *Rebera* Basil A.,   Translating a text to be spoken and heard; a study of Ruth 1 [two-thirds of the book is dialogue]:   BTrans 43 (1992) 230-8.

2811 **Waard** J. De, **Nida** E. A.,   Manuel du traducteur pour le livre de Ruth, ᵀᴱ*Peter-Contesse* R. Stu 1990, Alliance Biblique Universelle. 155 p. – ᴿSalesianum 54 (1992) 369s (C. *Buzzetti*, anche su Psalms).

2812 *Walfish* Barry,   An annotated bibliography of medieval Jewish com-

mentaries on the Book of Ruth in print and in manuscript: → 180c, Mem.
TALMAGE F. 1 (1992s) 251-271.

2813 *Miller-McLemore* Bonnie J., [Ruth 1,14]   Returning to the 'Mother's
house'; a feminist look at Orpah: ChrCent 108 (1991) 428-430.
2814 *Loader* J.A.,   Ruth 2-7 — an old crux: JTydSem 4 (1992) 151-9 [ends
'this is her residence, her home in a sense'].

E4.4 **1-2 Samuel.**

2815 **Anderson** Arnold A.,   2 Samuel: Word Comm. 11, 1989 → 5,2704...
7,2455: ᴿRefTR 49 (1990) 106s (J. *Woodhouse*); Themelios 18,1 (1992s)
25 (J.R. *Vannoy*); WestTJ 54 (1992) 370-2 (B.L. *Johnson*).
2816 **Brueggemann** Walter,   1-2 Samuel: InterpC, 1990 → 6,2941; 7,2457:
ᴿCBQ 54 (1992) 106s (R. *Gnuse*: 'not a scholarly work', though valuable
and familiar with scholarship); Interpretation 46 (1992) 296-8 (L. *Williamson*: 'the commentator as artist').
2817 **Dinesen** P.,   Samuelsbøgerne og Kongebøgerne fortolket, K 1992, Det
Danske Bibelselskab. 151 p. Dk 140. 87-7523-303-7 [BL 93,58, K. *Jeppesen*: 'inspired by modern exegesis, looks upon the totality of the four
books as one book'].
2818 *Endres* John C., [Proposal for] A new parallels version of Samuel, Kings,
Chronicles: ForumFF 8 (1992) 31-43.
2819 *Fernández* **Marcos** Natalio, *Busto Saiz* Ramón, El texto antioqueno de
la Biblia griega I, 1-2 Samuel 1989 → 5,2711... 7,2461: ᴿCBQ 54 (1992)
110s (L.J. *Greenspoon*: outstanding experts); ComSev 24 (1991) 103s (M.
de *Burgos*).
2820 *Flanagan* James W., Samuel, book of 1-2 [*Brueggemann* Walter, Narrative and theology]: → 741, AnchorBD 5 (1992) 957-965[-973].
2821 **Gressmann** Hugo, *al.*, Narrative and novella in Samuel [1906-1923],
ᴱ*Gunn* D.: jOsu 116, 1991 → 7,2462: ᴿBL (1992) 72 (I.W. *Provan*); CBQ
54 (1992) 746s (W. *Lee Humphreys*).
2822 **Polzin** Robert, Samuel and the Deuteronomist, II. I Samuel 1990 → 5,
2719 ... 7,2467: ᴿCalvinT 26 (1991) 257-261 (G.N. *Knoppers*); ConcordTQ 56 (1992) 210-2 (H.D. *Hummel*); WestTJ 54 (1992) 368-370
(B.L. *Johnson*).
2823 **Richter** Wolfgang, 1 und 2 Samuel, BHᵗ 5: MüUniv ArbO. St. Ottilien
1991, EOS. 585 p. DM 63.
2824 **Schroer** Silvia, Die Samuelbücher: NStu AT 7. Stu 1992, KBW.
224 p.; 33 fig.; 10 maps. DM 38. 3-460-07071-4 [ZAW 105,536, M.
Köckert].
2825 **Spek** Wouter van der, *a*) De messias in de Hebreeuwse Bijbel; over het
eerste Samuëlboek: Diss. Amsterdam 1992, ᴰ*Deurloo* K. 168 p. – TvT 32
(1992) 301; RTLv 24, p. 543; – *b*) De messias in de Hebreeuwse Bijbel;
over het eerste Samuelboek. Gorinchem 1992, Narratio. 168 p. ƒ 39,50. –
ᴿStreven 59 (1992s) 1326 (P. *Beentjes*).
2826 **Taylor** Bernard A., The Lucianic manuscripts of 1 Reigns, I. Majority text [diss. ᴰ*Tsevat* M., HUC 1989]: HarvScmMg 50. Atlanta
1992, Scholars. xxiii-110 p. $27; sb. $18. 1-55540-785-4 [NTAbs 37,
p. 317].
2827 **Trebolle Barrera** Julio, Centena Sm-Rg 1989 → 5,2723; 6,2953: ᴿCBQ
54 (1992) 335s (R.H. *McGrath*).

2828 *Verheij* A. J. C., [Sam-Kgs/Chr (4 synopses already published)] Criteria for parallels; a grass roots synoptic problem: ⇒ 450, Informatique 2, 1988/9, 591-603.

2829 ᵀᴱVogüé Adalbert de, GRÉGOIRE le Grand, Commentaire sur le premier livre des Rois [1 Sam]: SChr 351, 1989 ⇒ 6,2954; 7,2468: ᴿEsprVie 102 (1992) 615 (Y.-M. *Duval*); RÉAug 37 (1991) 179-181 (M. *Doucet*); RechSR 80 (1992) 304s (aussi Y.-M. *Duval*).

2830 **Wonneberger** Reinhard, Redaktion: Studien zur Textfortschreibung im AT, entwickelt am Beispiel der Samuel-Überlieferung: FRL 156. Gö 1992, Vandenhoeck & R. xviii-377 p. DM 128. 3-525-53837-5 [BL 93,99, H. G. M. *Williamson*: stimulating radical conclusions; assumes confidence in our ability to identify authorial intention].

2830* *Youngblood* Ronald F., 1, 2 Samuel: ⇒ 1942 supra, Expositor's Bible Comm. 3 (1992) 551-1104.

2831 **Zijl** A. H. van, I Sam II: PredikOT 1989 ⇒ 5,2725; 7,2470: ᴿBijdragen 53 (1992) 203s (Tamis *Wever*); KerkT 42 (1991) 263s (B. *Becking*); NedTTs 46 (1992) 59s (P. B. *Dirksen*).

2832 *Ackerman* James S., Who can stand before YHWH, this holy God? A reading of 1 Samuel 1-15: Prooftexts 11 (1991) 1-24.

2833 *Feldman* Louis H., Josephus' portrait of Samuel: AbrNahr 30 (1992) 103-141.

2834 **Martini** Carlo M., Samuel profeta religioso y civil: Servidores y Testigos 51, 1991 ⇒ 7,2464: ᴿComSev 25 (1992) 121s (F. *Sánchez*).

2835 *Wénin* André, Le personnage biblique de Samuel (1 Samuel 1-12): CahPhRel 7 (1990) 147-154.

2836 *Rendtorff* Rolf, [1 Sam 1] Die Geburt des Retters: ⇒ 7,141, ᶠSOGGIN J. A., Storia 1991, 205-216.

2837 *Tsevat* Matitiahu, [1 Sam 1,11] Was Samuel a Nazirite?: ⇒ 181, Shaᶜarei TALMON 1992, 199-204.

2838 *Catastini* Alessandro, Ancora sul nazireato di Samuele: 4Q Samᵃ: EgVO 14s (1991s) 155-8.

2839 **Eichenberg** Tobias, Gotteserfahrung und Gotteslob; ein Beitrag zur persönlichen Frömmigkeit im AT anhand der Gebete Hannas, Hiskias und Daniels: diss. Naumburg, ᴰMeinhold A. 1992. – RTLv 24, p. 541.

2840 **Becker-Spörl** Silvia, 'Und Hanna betete, und sie sprach...'; literarische Untersuchungen zu 1 Sam 2,1-10: Textw/Informatik 2. Tü 1992, Francke. x-163 p. DM 68. 3-7720-1951-X [OIAc 3,13].

2841 *Gosse* Bernard, L'interprétation des livres de Samuel à partir des psaumes en 1 Sam. II 1-10: BbbOr 34 (1992) 145-153.

2842 **Adair** James R.ᴶ, A methodology for determining the textual variants which are relevant for reconstructing the original text of the OT: a case study of 1 Samuel 3: diss. SW Baptist Theol. Sem. 1992, 354 p. 92-23534. DissA 53 (1992s) 841-A.

2843 *Gitay* Yehoshua, [1 Sam 4-6] Reflections on the poetics of the Samuel narrative; the question of the Ark narrative: CBQ 54 (1992) 221-230.

2844 *Deist* Ferdinand E., [1 Sam 4,4] 'By the way, Hophni and Phinehas were there'; an investigation into the literary and theological functions of Hophni, Phinehas and Shiloh in 1 Samuel 1-4: JNWS 18 (1992) 25-35.

2845 *Gordon* R. P., The meaning of the verb šwy [rapid/hostile motion] in the Targum to 1 Samuel 5-6: VT 42 (1992) 395-7

2846 a) *Lust* Johan, [1 Sam 5,6 ...] *Edra* and the Philistine plague; – b) *Gordon* Robert P., The problem of haplography in 1 and 2 Samuel; – c) *Polak* Frank H., Statistics and textual filiation; the case of 4QSamᵃ/LXX (with a note on the text of the Pentateuch): ➤ 459, Septuagint 1990/2, 569-597 / 131-158 / 215-276.

2847 *Wallace* R.S., The Ark comes home; an exposition of 1 Samuel 6:1-7:1; – Evangelism, an exposition of 1 Samuel 7:2-4; – National leadership, 1 Samuel 7:4-11; – ... – The days of Samuel, 1 Samuel 7:12-17: Evangel 1991s, 9/1, 2-4 / 9/2, 2-6 / 9/3, 2-4 [9/4 ...] / 10/1, 2-6.

2848 *Fouts* David M., Added support for reading '70 men' [without asyndetic 50,000] in 1 Samuel VI 19: VT 42 (1992) 394.

E4.5   *1 Sam 7 ... Initia potestatis regiae,*   **Origins of kingship.**

2849 **Brettler** Marc Z., God is king [diss. 1986 ᴰ*Sarna* N.] 1989 ➤ 5,2733 ... 7,2472: ᴿBA 55 (1992) 158 (R.D. *Miller*: ambitious and successful); BZ 36 (1992) 135-7 (H. *Irsigler*); JBL 111 (1992) 120-2 (P.D. *Miller*).

2850 *Cazelles* Henri, Sacral kingship: ➤ 741, AnchorBD 5 (1992) 863-6.

2851 *Halperin* Bilha, ❾ From the kingship of God to a king of flesh and blood: BethM 37,130 (1991s) 219-234.

2852 ᴱ**Halpern** Baruch, *Hobson* Deborah W., Law and ideology in monarchic Israel: JStOT supp 124, 1991 ➤ 7,436: ᴿTLZ 117 (1992) 827-830 (E. *Otto*).

Kessler Rainer, Staat und Gesellschaft im vorexilischen Juda 1992 ➤ k207.

2853 **Long** V. Philips, The reign and rejection of King Saul; a case for literary and theological coherence: SBL diss. 118 (Cambridge 1987) 1989 ➤ 5,2738; 7,2484: ᴿCBQ 54 (1992) 117s (R.C. *Culley*: scenes; is there a deeper structure?); JQR 83 (1992s) 411s M. *Brettler*: related to R. MOBERLY 1983 and to conservative Tyndale House).

2854 *Mazar* Benjamin, Kingship in ancient Israel [< *Ben-Gurion* D., Types of leadership 1973, 27-35], ᵀ: ➤ 283, Biblical Israel 1992, 55-66; p. 63 n. 17 read 'McCarthy'.

2855 *Nürnberger* Klaus, The royal-imperial paradigm in the Bible and the modern demand for democracy; an exercise in soteriological hermeneutics: JTSAfr 81 (1992) 16-34.

2856 **Polish** David, Give us a king; legal-religious sources of Jewish sovereignty 1989 ➤ 7,045*ᵢ ᴿ𝄴ᴀᴿ [I RefJud from] 38,3 (1991) 80-82 (D. *Ellenson*); RelStR 18 (1992) 71 (Jody E. *Myers*: largely on medieval preference for God alone as king).

2857 *Whitelam* Keith W., King and kingship: ➤ 741, AnchorBD 4 (1992) 40-48 [69-83, Book of Kings, *Holloway* Steven W.].

2858 **Edelman** Diana V., King Saul in the historiography of Judah: JStOT supp 121, 1991 ➤ 7,2482: ᴿÉTRel 67 (1992) 592-4 (D. *Lys*).

2859 *Edelman* Diana V., Saul: ➤ 741, AnchorBD 5 (1992) 989-999.

2860 **Berges** Ulrich, Die Verwerfung Sauls: ForBi 61, 1989 ➤ 6,2985; 7,2483: ᴿÉTRel 67 (1992) 95s (T. *Römer*); RB 99 (1992) 596s (F. *Langlamet*).

2861 *Naʾaman* Nadav, The pre-Deuteronomistic story of King Saul and its historical significance: CBQ 54 (1992) 638-658.

2862 *Schunck* Klaus-Dietrich, König Saul — Etappen seines Weges zum Aufbau eines israelitischen Staates: BZ 36 (1992) 195-206.

2863 **Popović** Anto,   The election-rejection of Saul (1 Sam 9,1-11,15; 13,7b-15a: diss. Pont. Ist. Biblico, ^D*Pisano* S. R 1992. – AcPIB 9,807.861s; RTLv 24, p. 543.
2864 *Jacobsen* Howard, The judge Bedan (1 Samuel XII 11): VT 42 (1992) 123s.
2865 *Ram* Hayyim, ✪ 1 Sam 14,47 (*mg'*): BethM 37,130 (1991s) 275-281, map.

E4.6   *1 Sam 16 ... 2 Sam: Accessio Davidis.* David's Rise.

2866 *Auld* A. Graeme, *Ho* Craig Y.S., The making of David and Goliath: JStOT 56 (1992) 19-39.
2866* **Bosetti** E., La tenda e il bastone; figure e simboli della pastorale biblica. Mi 1992, Paoline. 159 p. L^m 22. 88-215-2493-9. – ^RBL 93,27, R. P. R. *Murray*: Jacob-Moses-David in a rather reciprocal pastoralism with women; relevance to kingship noted tardily).
2867 **Brueggemann** Walter, [David's rise] Power, providence, and personality; biblical insights into life and ministry 1990 ⇒ 6,2941*: ^RCBQ 54 (1992) 741s (K. M. *Craig*); Interpretation 46 (1992) 208 (M. *Newman*).
2868 **Flanagan** James W., David's social drama, a hologram ... 1988 ⇒ 4,2855 ... 7,2488: ^RBR 7,3 (1991) 14 (N. K. *Gottwald*).
2869 *Haglund* Erik, Kung David och exodus: SvEx 57 (1992) 60-85.
2870 *Howard* David M.^J, David: ⇒ 741, AnchorBD 2 (1992) 40-49 (52-67, city of, *Tarler* David, *Cahill* Jane M.).
2871 **Veijola** Timo, David, Ges. St. 1990 ⇒ 6,315; 7,2494: ^RBZ 36 (1992) 313-6 (P. *Mommer*); RB 99 (1992) 448s (tit. pp.).
2872 **Tang** M.J., David, koning van Israël; een biografie. 's-Gravenhage 1990. 95 p. ƒ19,50. 90-2391-474-0. – ^RNedTTs 46 (1992) 230 (P.B. *Dirksen*: leesbar).

2873 **Bierling** V., Giving Goliath his due; new archaeological light on the Philistines [fairer to the non-Israelites]; pref. *Maier* P.L. GR 1992, Baker. 281 p. $15. 0-8010-1018-7 [BL 93,25, J.R. *Bartlett*].
2874 *Kooij* Arie van der, The story of David and Goliath; the early history of the text [BARTHÉLEMY D., *al.*, 1986]: ETL 68 (1992) 118-131.
2874* *Schuller* Eileen, A preliminary study of 4Q373 and some related (?) fragments [still likelier a David (-Goliath, as BAILLET) than a Moses-Og battle (as TALMON) apocryphon]: ⇒ 498, MQumran 2 (1991/2) 515-530.
2875 *Nelson* William B.^J, 1 Samuel 16-18 and 19:8-10, a traditio-historical study: diss. – HarvTR 85 (1992) 499s.
2876 *Magonet* Jonathan, [1 Sam 16 David, *al.*] The biblical roots of Jewish identity; exploring the relativity of exegesis [... 'Hebrews, Jews, or just plain human beings']: JStOT 54 (1992) 3-24.
2877 *Tsumura* David T., *Ḥᵃmor leḥem* (1 Samuel XVI 20): VT 42 (1992) 412-4: a donkey-load of bread.
2878 *Marinberg* Evyatar, ✪ The war of David and Goliath (1 Sam 17): BethM 37,130 (1991s) 245-259.
2879 *Fernández* Víctor M., Benjamin, querido de Yavé (Dt 33,12) y la alianza con David (1 Sam 18,3); una explicación sobre la preeminencia de Judá: RBiArg 53 (1991) 213-6.
2880 **Riepl** Christian, Sind David und Saul berechenbar? Von der sprachlichen Analyse zur literarischen Struktur von 1 Sam 21 und 22: kath. Diss. ^D*Seidl* T. München 1992. 400 p. – RTLv 24, p. 543.

2881 *Langlamet* François, 1 Samuel 13 – 2 Samuel 1?: FOKKELMAN et le prêtre de Nob (1 Sam 21,2-7): RB 99 (1992) 631-675; Eng. 631.

2881* *Zwickel* W., [1 Sam 21,2...] Nahurim und Nob: BibNot 61 (1992) 84-93.

2882 *Bloch-Smith* Elizabeth M., [1 Sam 28; Isa 8,19...] The cult of the dead in Judah; interpreting the material remains: JBL 111 (1992) 213-224.

2883 **Zangara** Vincenza, [1 Sam 28; Mt 17,3 → 7,4229; ... EVODIO] Exeuntes de corpore; discussioni sulle apparizioni dei morti in epoca agostiniana: Bt RivStoLR 1. Firenze 1990, Olschki. xviii-225 p. Lᵐ 45. – ᴿOrpheus 13,1 (1992) 165-8 (Beatrice *Marotta Mannino*).

2884 *Görg* Manfred, [1 Sam 30,30 ʿatak] Der biblische Name des Kupferminengebiets von Timna: BibNot 65 (1992) 5-8.

2885 **Fokkelman** J. P., Narrative art III. Throne and city (ii Sam 2-8 & 21-24) 1990 → 6,3008; 7,2511: ᴿBijdragen 53 (1992) 429s (P. C. *Beentjes*); TLZ 117 (1992) 345-8 (H. J. *Stoebe*).

2886 *Malul* M., David's curse of Joab (2 Sam 3:29) and the social significance of *mḥzyq bplk* ['effeminate']: AulaO 10 (1992) 49-67.

2887 *Martini* Carlo M., [2 Sam 5,1...] L'esperienza dell'alleanza: Ambrosius 67 (1991) 313-323.

2888 **Floss** J., David und Jerusalem... 2 S 5,6-9: 1987 → 3,2738; 6,3010: ᴿTR 88 (1992) 190 (G. *Hentschel*).

2888* *Kleven* T., Hebrew style in 2 Samuel 6: JEvTS 35 (1992) 294-314 [< ZAW 105,511].

2889 **Seow** C. L., [2 Sam 6,14] Myth... David's dance 1989 → 5,2777: ᴿSyria 69 (1992) 231s (A. *Caquot*).

2890 **Jones** Gwilym H., [2 Sam 7; 12] The Nathan narratives: JStOT supp 80, 1990 → 7,2517: ᴿCritRR 5 (1992) 110-3 (R. G. *Bowman*).

2891 **Hentschel** Georg, Gott, König und Tempel; Beobachtungen zu 2 Sam 7,1-17: ErfTSch 22. Lp 1992, Benno. xii-99 p. DM 32 [TR 88, 514]. 3-7462-1001-1.

2892 *Cayuot* André, Un point difficile du discours de la Téqoïte (ii Samuel 14,13-15): → 7,141, ᶠSOGGIN J. A., Storia 1991, 15-30.

2892* a) *Linafelt* Tod, [1 Sam 25] Taking women in Samuel; readers/responses/responsibility; – b) *Willey* Patricia K., [2 Sam 11-14] The importunate woman of Tekoa and how she got her way; – c) *Lasine* Stuart, Reading Jeroboam's intentions; intertextuality, rhetoric, and history in 1 Kings 12; – d) *Garcia-Trefo* Francisco O., The fall of the house; a carnivalesque reading of 2 Kings 9 and 10 [< JStOT 46 (1990) 47-65]; – e) *Granowski* Jan J., Jehoiachin at the king's table; a reading of the ending of the second book of Kings: → 351d, Reading 1992, 99-113 / 115-131 / 133-152 / 153-171 / 173-188.

2893 *Althann* Robert, Uriah: → 741, AnchorBD 6 (1992) 767-9.

2894 *Stansell* Gary, Honor and shame in the David narratives: → 197, ᶠWOLFF H. W., Wer ist? 1992, 94-114.

2895 **Bailey** Randall C., David in love and war, 2 Sam 10-12: JStOT supp 75, 1990 → 6,3019: 7,2510: ᴿCritRR 5 (1992) 110-2 (R. G. *Bowman*); RB 99 (1992) 729-750 (F. *Langlamet*).

2895* *Hentschel* Georg, Die Kriege des friedfertigen Königs David (2 Sam 10,1-11; 12,28-31): → 7,164a, **Wallis** G., Überlieferung 1990, 49-58.

2896 **Jensen** Hans J. L., [2 Sam 11...; R. GIRARD's] Desire, rivalry and collective violence in the 'Succession Narrative': JStOT 55 (1992) 39-59.

2897 *Sailhamer* J. H., 2 Samuel 11:1-4 and a data base approach to the analysis of Hebrew narrative; → 450*, Informatique 3, 1991/2, 99-124.

2898 *Hentschel* Georg, Davids ungewöhnliches Verhalten (2 Sam 12,15b-25): ➤ 51, ᶠErfurt 1992, 203-215.

2899 *Hansen* Tracy, [2 Sam 13,1] My name is Tamar [< PrPeo Sept. 1990]: TLond 95 (1992) 370-6.

2900 *Althann* Robert, The meaning of *arbaʿim šanâh* in 2 Sam 15,7: Biblica 73 (1992) 248-252.

2901 *Görg* Manfred, [2 Sam 15,19] Ittai aus Gat: BibNot 60 (1991) 20-23.

2902 *Cartun* Ari M., [2 Sam 17,24] Topography as a template for David's fortunes during his flight before Avshalom: JRefJud 38,2 (1991) 17-34.

2903 *Smith* John H., Thomas WATSON, Absalom...: Renaissance Latin Drama in England 2/5. Hildesheim 1988, Olms. iv-38 p. – ᴿLatomus 51 (1992) 457s (Perrine *Galand-Hallyn*: also on 6; 7 Iephte; 8-10).

2905 *Margalith* Othniel, A note on *Šālîšîm* [2 Sam 23... Ug. ṭlt 'metal' in sense of 'armoured']: VT 42 (1992) 266.

2906 *Weinfeld* Moshe, [2 Sam 21,6] The census in Mari, in ancient Israel and in ancient Rome: ➤ 7,141, ᶠSOGGIN J. A., Storia 1991, 293-8.

E4.7 *Libri Regum;* **Solomon, Temple: 1 Kings...**

2907 **Cogan** M., *Tadmor* H., II Kings: AnchorB 11, 1988 ➤ 4,2952; 5,2842: ᴿRB 99 (1992) 770-2 (F. J. *Gonçalves*).

2908 ᴱ**Fernández Marcos** Natalio, *al.*, El texto antioqueno de la Biblia griega, II. 1-2 Reyes: TEstCisn 53. M 1992, Cons. Nac. Inv. Inst. Fg. lxxi-161 p. 84-00-07235-3 [BL 93,49, A. G. *Salvesen*].

2909 **McKenzie** Steven L., The trouble with Kings: VTS 42, 1991 ➤ 7,2534: ᴿBL (1992) 78s (I. W. *Provan*: unduly detailed); CurrTMiss 19 (1992) 132.4 (R. W. *Klein*); JNWS 18 (1992) 229s (F. E. *Deist*); Themelios 18,3 (1992s) 23s (R. S. *Hess*).

2910 **Miller** Clyde M., 1-2 Kings: Living-Word comm. 7. Abilene 1992, ACU. xii-484 p. $28 [RestQ 35,121s, M. P. *Graham*, unenthusiastic].

2911 **Moreno Hernández** Antonio, Las glosas de Vetus Latina en las Biblias Vulgatas Españolas 1-2 Reyes: TEstCisn 49. M 1992, ConsNac InstFg. 462 p. 84-00-07261-8.

2912 **Rice** Gene, 1 Kings; Nations under God 1990 ➤ 6,3053; 7,2535*: ᴿHorBT 14 (1992) 90s (J. T. *Willis*); OTEssays 5 (1992) 298-300 (W. *Vosloo*).

2913 **Richter** Wolfgang, 1 und 2 Könige: Biblia Hebraica transcripta 6 / Univ. Mü AOtt 33. St. Ottilien 1991, EOS. 569 p. DM 63.

2914 **Rogers** Jeffrey Scott, Synchronism and structure in 1-2 Kings and Mesopotamian chronographic literature: diss. Princeton Theol. Sem. 1992, ᴰRoberts J. 345 p. 93-00243. – DissA 53 (1992s) 3252-A.

2915 **Taylor** Bernard A., The Lucianic manuscripts of 1 Reigns, 1. Majority text [diss. HUC, ᴰTsevat M.]: HarvSemMg 50. Atlanta 1992, Scholars. I. xxiii-110 p. 1-55540-785-4.

2915* *Trebolle Barrera* Julio, A preliminary edition of 4QKings (4Q54): ➤ 498, MQumran 1 (1991/2) 229-246; pl. 8.

2916 **Weinberg** Joel, The citizen-temple community [7 reprints], ᵀSmith-Christopher David L.: jOsu 151. Shf 1992, Academic. 145 p. 1-85075-395-X.

2917 *Körner* Regina, Märchenmotive bei König Salomo (1 Kön 1-11): BibNot 62 (1992) 25-31.

2918 **Parker** Kim Ian, Wisdom and law in the reign of Solomon. Lewiston NY 1992, Mellen. 127 p. 0-7734-2356-7.

2919 *Parker* Kim I., Solomon as philosopher king? The nexus of law and wisdom in 1 Kings 1-11: JStOT 53 (1992) 75-91.

2920 *Duval* Danièle, Salomon sage ou habile? dans le texte massorétique et dans la Septante (1 R 2,12-11,43 et 3 R 2,12-11,43): RevSR 66 (1992) 213-232.

2921 **Carr** David M. [1 Kgs 3,2-15] From D to Q; a study of early Jewish interpretations of Solomon's dream at Gibeon [< diss. Claremont]: SBL mg 44. Atlanta 1991, Scholars. xii-257 p. $30 pa. 1-55540-528-2; -9-0. – RBL (1992) 65 (A. G. *Auld*); ETL 68 (1992) 413s (J. *Lust*: misleadingly uses D for 'deuteronomistic history' and Q for the/a Quelle of the *New Testament*; belabors what he calls 'sunegesis'); JBL 111 (1992) 704s (S. L. *McKenzie*).

2922 *Lasine* Stuart, [1 Kgs 3:16-27; Dan 13] Solomon, Daniel, and the detective story; the social functions of a literary genre: HebAnR 11 (1987) 247-266.

2923 *Burns* John B., [1 Kgs 4,26] Solomon's Egyptian horses and exotic wives: ForumFF 7,1s (1991) 29-44.

2924 *Gosse* Bernard, La sagesse et l'intelligence de Salomon en 1 Rois 5,9: BibNot 65 (1992) 12-14 (15-18 en 1 Rois 5,21).

2925 *Dreher* C.A., [1 R 5,13] Salomón y los trabajadores: Ribla 5s (1990) 15-25 [< *Stromata* 47,444].

2925* *Görg* Manfred, Noch einmal zu śdrt in 1 Kön 6,9: BibNot 57 (1991) 14-16; 60 (1991) 24-26, eine Revision. *sdbt* statt *sdrt*.

Templum, 1 Reg 6s:

2926 **Bissoli** Giovanni, La corrispondenza fra tempio celeste e terrestre nella letteratura giudaica antica e neotestamentaria: diss. Pont. Ist. Biblico 1993, DLe Déaut R. – AcPIB 9,9 (1992s) 808; sunto 855s.

2927 *Ritmeyer* Leen, Locating the original Temple mount: BAR-W 18,2 (1992) 24-45.64s; ill. [18,4 (1992) 17 corrects the claim that the original Temple Mount was 145 acres, the size of 24 football fields; it is now 35 acres, 5120 × 5150 ft., double the original 500-cubit-square Temple Mount].

2928 *Weippert* Helga, [1 Kön 7,27-39] Die Kesselwagen Salomos: ZDPV 108 (1992) 8-41; 18 fig.

2929 **Hurowitz** Victor (Avigdor), I have built you an exalted house; Temple building in the Bible in the light of Mesopotamian and Northwest Semitic writings [< diss.]: JStOT supp 115. Sheffield 1992, JStOT. 398 p. £35; sb. £26.25. 1-85075-282-6. – EExpTim 104 (1992s) 185s (J. F. *Healey*).

2930 *Peter* C.B., The temple of Jerusalem in historico-theological perspective: DeltioVM 21,11 (1992) 86-100.

2931 *Fritz* Volkmar, Die Kapitelle der Säulen des salomonischen Tempels: → 18, FBIRAN A., ErIsr 23 (1992) 36*-42*; 3 fig.

2932 *Zevit* Ziony, [1 Kgs 5,6-9] Timber for the Tabernacle; text, tradition and realia: → 18, FBIRAN A., ErIsr 23 (1992) 136*-143*.

2933 **Kaufman** Asher S., ⊕ The Temple of Jerusalem, I. Tractate Middot. J 1991; Har Ye'ra'eh. viii-102 p. 965-379-0013. – RJStJud 23 (1992) 117s (D. *Sperber*).

2934 *Meyers* Carol, Temple; Jerusalem: → 741, AnchorBD 6 (1992) 350-368 (369-372 Egypt, *Ward* W.; 372-8, Mesopotamia, *Robertson* J.F.; 376-380 Syro-Palestine, *Dever* W.; 380-2, Greco-Roman, *Cole* Susan G.).

2935 **Parry** Donald W., The significance of graded Temple space; the Temple of Herod model: diss. Utah 1992. 388 p. 92-28119. – DissA 53 (1992s) 1961-A.

2936 *Heutger* N., Der biblische Granatapfel [aus Elfenbein, der bisher 'einzige Überrest des salomonischen Tempels']: JbEvHL 3 (1991) 87-90 [< ZAW 105,507].

2937 *Sheppard* Gerald T., The relation of Solomon's wisdom to biblical prayer: ➤ 74, ᶠGUENTHER H., TorJT 8 (1992) 7-27.

2938 *Virgulin* Stefano, La preghiera di Salomone per la consacrazione del Tempio (1 Re 8): ➤ 339, ParSpV 25 (1992) 41-51.

2939 *McConville* J. G., 1 Kings VIII 46-53 and the Deuteronomic hope: VT 42 (1992) 67-79.

2940 *Görg* Manfred, [1 Kön 9,15 gegen 2 Sam 5,9?] Die Darstellung königlicher Baumassnahmen in Israel und Assur: BibNot 59 (1991) 12-16; 1 pl.

2941 *Ben Zvi* Ehud, Once the lamp has been kindled ... A reconsideration of the meaning of the MT *nîr* in 1 Kgs 11:36; 15:4; 2 Kgs 8:19 and 2 Chr 21:7: AustralBR 39 (1991) 19-30.

2942 *Luciani* Ferdinando, Il significato e la funzione sintattica di *lāleket* in 1 Re 12,24b: RivB 40 (1992) 257-297.

2943 *McFall* Leslie, Has the chronology of the Hebrew Kings finally been settled?: Themelios 17,1 (1991s) 6-11: yes, THIELE revised.

2944 **Barnes** W. H., Studies in the chronology of the Divided Monarchy 1991 ➤ 7,2557: ᴿBtS 149 (1992) 488s (E. H. *Merrill*).

2945 *Talshir* Zipora, Is the alternate tradition of the division of the kingdom (3 Kgdms 12:24a-z) non-deuteronomistic?: ➤ 459, Septuagint 1990/2, 599-621.

2946 *Hocherman* Yaakov, [1 Kgs 15,18... *šōḥad*] ➊ Does the concept of bribery have a positive side?: BethM 36 (1990s) 220-2 [< OTAbs 15, p. 145].

2947 *Galpaz* Pnina, The reign of Jeroboam and the extent of Egyptian influence: BibNot 60 (1991) 13-19.

2948 *Mullen* E. Theodoreᴶ, [1 Kgs 14s; 2 Kgs 12-24] Crime and punishment; the sins of the king and the despoliation of the treasuries: CBQ 54 (1992) 231-248.

2248* *Feldman* Louis H., [1 Kgs 6,29-22,40, ➊ 140 lines, ➋ 527 lines, Ant 8,316-420, 672 lines] JOSEPHUS' portrait of Ahab: ETL 68 (1992) 368-384.

2949 a) *Trebolle Barrera* Julio, Crítica textual de 1 Re 22,35; aportación de una nueva lectura de la Vetus Latina; – b) *Busto Saiz* José Ramón, El testimonio textual de la Políglota Complutense para la edición del texto luciánico en 3 y 4 Reyes; – c) *Spottorno* Maria Victoria, Flavio JOSEFO, técnicas de adaptación del texto bíblico (1 Re 3,16-28): ➤ 44, ᶠDÍAZ ESTEBAN F., Sefarad 52 (1992) 235-243 / 49-58 / 227-234.

2950 *Reviv* Hanoch, ➊ Military elite and politics; dismal episodes in the history of the Northern Kingdom: ➤ 181, Shaʿarei TALMON 1992, 93*-97*; Eng. xx.

E4.8   *1 Regum 17-22: Elias,* **Elijah.**

2951 a) *Todd* Judith A., The pre-deuteronomistic Elijah cycle; – b) *Hill* Scott D., The local hero in Palestine in comparative perspective: ➤ 347, Elijah 1992, 1-35 / 37-73.

2952 *Poirot* E., La fête du saint prophète Élie dans la liturgie byzantine: Ec-Orans 9 (1992) 173-199.

2953 **Jobsen** A., [1 K 16-2 K 10] Izebel en Achab: VBGed. Kampen 1990, Kok. 148 p. ƒ19,50. 90-2424-972-4. – ᴿNedTTs 46 (1992) 231 (C. van *Leeuwen*); Streven 58 (1990s) 752 (P. *Beentjes*).

2954 **Hauser** Alan J., *Gregory* Russell, [1 Kgs 17-19] From Carmel to Horeb; Elijah in crisis: JStOT supp 85, 1990 ➤ 6,3068; 7,2562*: ᴿCBQ 54 (1992) 747s (E. T. *Mullen*: new interpretive possibilities); ETL 68 (1992) 152s (J. *Lust*).

2955 Un Groupe, Le passage du témoin; étude du cycle d'Élie (1 R. 17-19,21 et 2 R. 1-2): SémBib 65 (1992) 19-41.

2956 **Woods** Fred E., [1 Kgs 17s] Water and storm; polemics against Baalism in the deuteronomistic history: diss. Utah, ᴰ*Lenowitz* H. Salt Lake City 1991. vii-193 p. 92-11543. – OIAc 5,40.

2957 *Seger* Joe D., [1 Kgs 18:21] Limping about the altar: ➤ 18, ᶠBᴵʀᴀɴ A., ErIsr 23 (1992) 120*-127*; 3 fig.

2958 *Throntveit* Mark A., 'Show 'em who's boss!' A sermon on 1 Kings 18:30-40 and 1 Corinthians 1:18-25: ➤ 77, ᶠHᴀʀʀᴵꜱᴠᴵʟʟᴇ R., All things new 1992, 29-32.

2959 *Alonso Díaz* José, [1 R 19] El derrumbamiento espiritual de Elías y su oración en Horeb: StOvet 20 (1992) 139-158.

2960 *Willmes* Bernd, Eine folgenreiche Begegnung (1 Reg 19,19-21): BibNot 60 (1991) 59-93.

2961 **Briend** Jacques, [Moïse, Samuel; 1 R 19,1-18 Élie] Dieu dans l'Écriture: LDiv 150. P 1992, Cerf. 136 p. 2-204-04570-5. ➤ 7002.

2962 **Masson** Michel, [1 Rois 19,12] Élie ou l'appel du silence: Parole présente. P 1992, Cerf. 238 p. F 120. 2-204-04379-6. – ᴿEsprVie 102 (1992) 413-5 (L. *Monloubou*, aussi sur deux de Bᴇʟʟᴇꜰᴏɴᴛᴀᴵɴᴇ sur Élie); LA 41 (1991!) 567s (A. *Mello*).

2963 *Van Winkle* D. W., 1 Kings 20-22 and true and false prophecy: ➤ 9493, IOSOT-B 1989/92, 9-23.

2964 *Revell* E. J., Language and interpretation in 1 Kings 20: ➤ 180c, Mem. Tᴀʟᴍᴀɢᴇ F., 1 (1992s) 105-113.

2965 **Cloete** Jan P., Teksbetekenis [textual meaning] en kanoniese betekenis; 'n empiriese studie aan de hand van 1 Konings 21: diss. ᴰ*Deist* F. Pretoria 1992. 307 p. – RTLv 24, p. 571.

2966 *Turiot* Cécile, [1 Rois 21], Nécessaire retour vers les figures: SémBib 66 (1992) 3-14.

2967 **Walsh** Jerome T., Methods and meanings; multiple studies of 1 Kings 21: JBL 111 (1992) 193-211.

2968 *Lifschitz* Nili, *Biger* Gideon, [1 Kgs 21,1] ⓪ Naboth's 'vineyard' — grapes or olives?: BethM 37,129 (1991s) 119-121.

E4.9   **2 Reg 1... *Elisaeus .. Ezechias, Josias.***

2969 *a*) *Rentería* Tamis H., The Elijah-Elisha stories; a socio-cultural analysis of prophets and people in 9th c. B.C.E. Israel; – *b*) *Bergen* Wesley J., The prophetic alternative — Elisha and the Israelite monarchy: ➤ 347, ᴱ*Coote* R., Elijah/Elisha 1992, 127-137 / 75-126.

2969* *Wendland* Ernst R., Elijah and Elisha; sorcerers or witch doctors?: BTrans 43 (1992) 213-223.

2970 **Moore** Rick D., God saves; lessons from the Elisha stories: JStOT supp 95, 1990 ➤ 6,3081; 7,2576: ᴿETL 68 (1992) 153 (J. *Lust*); JTS 43 (1992) 150s (H. *Mowvley*); ZAW 104 (1992) 155 (H. C. *Schmitt*).

2971 **Reinhold** Gotthard G. G., Die Beziehungen Altisraels zu den aramäischen Staaten 1989 → 7,2577: ᴿBZ 36 (1992) 305-8 (W. *Thiel*); NorTTs 93 (1992) 57 (H. B. *Barstad*); VT 42 (1992) 136 (J. A. *Emerton*: richly documented).

2972 *Rösel* Hartmut N., 2 Kön 2,1-18 als Elija- oder Elischa-Geschichte?: BibNot 59 (1991) 33-36.

2973 *Long* Burke O., [2 Kgs 4:8-37] The Shunammite woman; in the shadow of the prophet? BR 7,1 (1991) 12-19. 42.

2974 *Görg* Manfred, [4 Kön 4,12 Giezi] Gehasi, 'Gazellenhirsch': BibNot 56 (1991) 15s.

2975 **Ziolkowski** Jan M., Jezebel, Norman Latin 1989 → 7,2573*: ᴿGnomon 64 (1992) 680-3 (T. A.-P. *Klein*); Speculum 67 (1992) 508-510 (M. *Herren*).

2976 *a) Greenfield* Jonas C., Doves' dung and the price of food; the topoi of II Kings 6:24 - 7:2; – *b) Liverani* Mario, Kilamuwa 7-8 e II Re 7; – *c) Lemaire* André, La stèle de Mécha et l'histoire de l'ancien Israël; – *d) Lipiński* Edward, Jéroboam II et la Syrie: → 7,141, ᶠSOGGIN J. A., Storia 1991, 121-6 / 177-183 / 143-169 / 171-6.

2977 *Tropper* M., [2 Kgs 7,13] ⊕ Reaction to the article 'between Judah and Israel': BethM [1988] 37,129 (1991s) 137-144; 145, answer, *Luria* B.

2978 **Mulzer** Martin, Jehu schlägt Joram; Text- literatur- und strukturkritische Untersuchung zu 2 Kön 8,25-10,36 [Diss. Bamberg ᴰ*Irsigler* H.: Mü ArbO 37. St. Ottilien 1992, EOS. xi-414 p. DM 48 [TR 88,514]. 3-88096-537-4.

2979 **Breytenbach** Johan H., The kingship of Jehu; an investigation into the possibility of a justifiable reconstruction of its history [in Afrikaans]: diss. ᴰ*Oberholzer* J. Pretoria 1992. – DissA 53 (1992s) 1545-A.

2980 **Schearing** Linda Sue, [2 Kgs 11s] Models, monarchs and misconceptions; Athaliah and Joash of Judah: diss. Emory, ᴰ*Hayes* J. Atlanta 1992, 280 p. 92-31503. – DissA 53 (1992s) 1962-A; RTLv 24, p. 543.

2981 *Zakovitch* Yair, ⊕ 'Elisha died ... He came to life and stood up' (2 Kings 13: 20-21); a short 'short story' in exegetical circles: → 181, Shaʿarei TALMON 1992, 53*-62*; Eng. xvii.

2982 *Day* John, The problem of 'So, king of Egypt' in 2 Kings XVII 4: VT 42 (1992) 289-301.

2983 **Lowery** Richard H., The reforming kings; cults and society in First Temple Judah: JStOT supp 120, 1991 → 7,2583 [not 'cult']: ᶠÉTRel 67 (1992) 591s (D. *Lys*); JBL 111 (1992) 697-9 (R. D. *Nelson*); Themelios 18,3 (1992s) 24 (R. S. *Hess*).

2984 *Bordreuil* Pierre, *Israel* Felice, [2 Rois 17,17; 19,2] A propos de la carrière d'Elyaqim; du page au majordome (?): Semitica 41s (1991s) 81-87; 2 fig.

2984* *Delcor* Mathias, La divinité Ashima de Samarie en 2 R 17,30 et ses survivances: → 496*, Congress 1988/91, 33-48.

2985 **Camp** Ludger, Hiskija... 2 Kön 18-20, ᴰ1990 → 5,2866 ... 7,2587: ᴿZkT 114 (1992) 189-191 (J. M. *Oesch*).

2986 *Catastini* A., Isaia ed Ezechia. 2 Re 18-20, 1989 → 5,2860: ᴿHenoch 14 (1992) 328-331 (N. *Fernández Marcos*, español).

  Hardmeier C., Prophetie im Streit, 2 Reg 18-20: BZAW 187, ᴰ1990 → 3820.

2987 **Jong** S. de, Het verhaal van Hizkia en Sanherib; een synchronische en diachronische analyse van II Kon. 18,13 - 19,37 (par. Jer 36-37): diss. Amst VU 1992, ᴰ*Leene* H. x-280 p. – TvT 32 (1992) 302; RTLv 24, p. 541.

2988 *Feldman* Louis H., Josephus' portrait of Hezekiah: JBL 111 (1992) 597-610.

2989 **Provan** Iain W., Hezekiah... BZAW 172, 1988 ► 4,2979 ... 7,2590:   ᴿRB
99 (1992) 574-581 (F. J. *Gonçalves*).
2990 *Rendsburg* Gary A., Baasha of Ammon [at Qarqar, Shalmaneser III
monolith 2,95: rather than Amana as FOHRER E. RLA 1,328]: JANES 20
(1991) 57-61.
2991 **Becking** Bob, The fall of Samaria; an historical and archaeological
study: StHistANE 2. Leiden 1992, Brill. xvi-153 p. $48.75.   90-04-
09633-7 [RelStR 19,158, C. T. *Begg*].
2992 *Spieckermann* Hermann, [2 K 21] Manasse: ► 768, TRE 22 (1992)
36-39.
2993 **Dorp** Jacob van, Josia; de voorstelling van zijn koningschap in II Koningen 22-23: diss. ᴰ*Leeuwen* C. van. Utrecht 1991. x-252 p. – TvT 32
(1992) 305. – ᴿETL 68 (1992) 414s (W. A. M. *Beuken*).
2994 **Laato** Antti, Josiah and David redivivus; the historical Josiah and
the messianic expectations of exilic and postexilic times: ConBib OT 33.
Sto 1992, Almqvist & W. x-416 p. 91-22-01475-0 [TLZ 118,390-3, J. A.
Soggin].
2995 *a*) *Koch* Klaus, [2 Kön 22s] Gefüge und Herkunft des Bericht über die
Kultreformen des Königs Josias; – *b*) *Thiel* Winfried, Jahwe und Prophet
in der Elisa-Tradition: ► 149, ᶠPREUSS H., 1992, 80-92 / 93-103.
2996 *Suzuki* Yoshihide, A new aspect on occupation policy by King Josiah;
assimilation and codification in view of Yahwism: AnJapB 18 (1992)
31-61.
2997 *Conrad* Edgar W., [2 Kgs 22s] Heard but not seen; the representation of
'books' in the OT: JStOT 54 (1992) 45-59.
2998 *Elayi* J., New light on the identification of the seal of priest Ḥanan, son
of Ḥilqiyahu (2 Kings 22): BO 49 (1992) 680-5.
2999 *Knoppers* Gary N., [2 Kgs 23,25] 'There was none like him'; incom-
parability in the books of Kings: CBQ 54 (1992) 411-431.
3000 **Tagliacarne** Pierfelice, 'Keiner...' 2 Kön 22s, ᴰ1989 ► 5,2870; 7,2599:
ᴿBZ 36 (1992) 121s (W. *Thiel*); OLZ 87 (1992) 543-6 (R. *Stahl*); TLZ
117 (1992) 28-31 (E.-J. *Waschke*); ZkT 114 (1992) 83s (J. *Oesch*).
3001 *Naʾaman* Nadiv, Nebuchadrezzar's campaign in year 603 BCE: BibNot
62 (1992) 41-44.
3002 **Wiseman** D. J., Nebuchadrezzar and Babylon [1983 Schweich Lectures,
1985 ► 1,2908] paperback, Ox 1991, UP. 142 p.; viii pl. £10. 0-19-
726100-0 [BL 93,46].
3003 **Sack** R. H., Images of Nebuchadnezzar; the emergence of a legend.
Selinsgrove / Toronto 1991, Susquehanna Univ. / Assoc.Univ.Pr. 143 p.
$27.50. 0-945636-35-0 [BL 93,127, L. L. *Grabbe*: intended as a companion
to WISEMAN for later periods].

E5.2   *Chronicorum libri* – **The books of Chronicles.**

3004 **Cavedo** R., 1-2 Cronache Esdra e Neemia: LoB 1.9s, 1991 ► 7,2605:
ᴿAsprenas 39 (1992) 109s (A. *Rolla*); RivB 40 (1992) 353-5 (A. *Minissale*).
3005 **De Vries** Simon J., 1-2 Chr: FOTLit 11, 1989 ► 5,2880 ... 7,2606: ᴿBijdragen 53 (1992) 203 (P. C. *Beentjes*, also on HALS R., Ezek); BO 49
(1992) 484-6 (P. B. *Dirksen*); WestTJ 53 (1991) 357-9 (A. H. *Konkel*).
3006 **Then** Reinhold, [Chr-Aussicht] 'Gibt es denn keinen mehr unter den
Propheten?': BeitErfAJ 22, ᴰ1990 ► 6,3127: ᴿRelStR 18 (1992) 51
(M. A. *Sweeney*).

3007 *Verheij* Arian, Die hebräischen Synopsen [Chr-Kön] als Hilfsmittel beim sprachlichen Vergleich paralleler Texte: VT 42 (1992) 90-102 [VANNU-TELLI still as good as any].

3008 **Abadie** Philippe, La figure de David dans les livres des Chroniques; de la figure historique à la figure symbolique: diss. Inst.Cath. & Sorbonne, ᴰ*Meslin* M. P 1990 [➤ 6,3137, 'Aradie' (faux, aussi Index); RTLv juste]. – RICathP 37 (1991) 231-3 (J. *Briend*).

3009 **Ackroyd** Peter R., The Chronicler in his age [1967-88, 3 inedita + reprints]: JStOT supp. 101, 1991 ➤ 7,2604: ᴿJTS 43 (1992) 147 (R. *Mason*); TLZ 117 (1992) 424-6 (R. *Stahl*).

3010 **Dörrfuss** Ernst M., Mose in den Chronikbüchern — Garant theokratischer Zukunftserwartung: Diss. ᴰ*Welten* P. B 1992. 347 p. – RTLv 24, p. 541.

3011 **Duke** Rodney K., The persuasive appeal of the Chronicler: JStOT supp 88, 1990 ➤ 6,3119; 7,2607: ᴿÉTRel 67 (1992) 96s (J.-P. *Sternberger*); Interpretation 46 (1992) 312.314 (M. A. *Throntveit*); Themelios 18,2 (1992s) 26 (M. J. *Selman*); TLZ 117 (1992) 109s (J. *Weinberg*).

3012 **Graham** Matt P., The utilization of 1-2 Chr in the reconstruction of history, 19th cent.: SBL diss 116, 1990 ➤ 6,3120; 7,2610: ᴿCBQ 54 (1992) 321s (G. N. *Knoppers*: valuable despite bypassed questions).

3013 **Japhet** S., Ideology of Chr ᴰ1989 ➤ 5,2884 ... 7,2631: ᴿNedTTs 46 (1992) 62s (P. B. *Dirksen*).

3014 **Kalimi** Isaac, The books of Chronicles, a classified bibliography 1990 ➤ 6,3124: ᴿBO 49 (1992) 482-4 (P. B. *Dirksen*).

3015 **McEntire** Mark H., The function of sacrifice in Chronicles, Ezra, and Nehemiah: diss. Southern Baptist Theol. Sem. 1992, ᴰ*Keown* G. 179 p. 93-02765. — DissA 53 (1992s) 3565-A.

3016 **Mason** Rex, Preaching the tradition 1990 ➤ 6,3125; 7,2613: ᴿAndr-UnS 30 (1992) 91-93 (J. M. *Wright*); JRel 72 (1992) 93-95 (S. *Weitzman*); Salesianum 54 (1992) 789s (R. *Vicent*); ScotJT 45 (1992) 420s (R. W. *Moberly*).

3017 *Nel* H. W., Die Kronis se perspektief van God in 1 en 2 Kronieke: JTydSem 4 (1992) 98-113; Eng. 98.

3018 **Pomykala** Kenneth E., [Chr Zech ...] The Davidic dynasty tradition in early Judaism; its background, context, and function: diss. Claremont, ᴰ*Sanders* J. 1992. 405 p. 92-38869. — DissA 53 (1992s) 2853s-A.

3019 **Raison** Stephen J., From theocracy to kingdom; royalist hope in Chronicles: diss. Westminster Theol. Sem., ᴰ*Dillard* R. 1992. 352 p. 92-31646. — DissA 53 (1992s) 2414-A.

3020 **Ruffing** Andreas, Jahwekrieg als Weltmetapher; Studien zu Jahwekriegstexten des chronistischen Sondergutes [< kath. Diss. Bochum 1991, ᴰ*Berg* ➤ 7,2614]: SBB 24. Stu 1992, KBW. 402 p. DM 49. 3-460-00241-7.

3021 **Schniedewind** William M., Prophets, prophecy, and inspiration; a study of prophecy in the Book of Chronicles: diss. Brandeis, ᴰ*Brettler* M. Boston 1992. 313 p. 92-29483. — DissA 53 (1992s) 1962-A.

3022 **Throntveit** M. A., When kings speak ... Chr 1987 ➤ 3,2849 ... 5,2892: ᴿVT 42 (1992) 288 (R. P. *Gordon*).

———————

3023 **Kartveit** M., Motive und Schichten der Landestheologie in 1. Chronik 1-9: ConBib OT 28, ᴰ1989 ➤ 5,2895 ... 7,2617: ᴿBZ 36 (1992) 116 (J. *Becker*).

3024 *Galil* Gershon, [1 Chron 7,20-27] The Chronicler's genealogies of Ephraim: BibNot 56 (1991) 11-14.

3025 **Oeming** Manfred, Das wahre Israel ... 1 Chr 1-9: BW 128, ᴰ1990 ➤ 6,3131; 7,2618: ᴿBijdragen 53 (1992) 323s (P.C. *Beentjes*); CBQ 54 (1992) 123s (M.P. *Graham*: amplest to date, though not using W. Osborne's 1979 Dropsie diss.; denies that Ezra-N is by a different author, or that 1-9 is a later addition); JBL 111 (1992) 701s (S. *De Vries*); TPQ 140 (1992) 185s (Borghild *Baldauf*).

3026 *Lorenzin* Tiziano, L'uso di un procedimento esegetico analogo all'*al tiqré* in 1 e 2 Cronache [primo esempio: 1 Cr 2,17 cita 2 Sam 17,25 'israelita' come 'ismaelita'; 28 altri]: RivB 40 (1992) 67s.

3027 **Gabriel** Ingeborg, Friede über Israel ... 1 Chr 10 - 2 Chr 36 [diss. Wien 1988, ᴰ*Braulik* G.]: ÖsBS 10, 1990 ➤ 5,2898; 6,3135: ᴿCritRR 5 (1992) 133-5 (M.P. *Graham*: 'Iranian model for David's relationship with his warriors').

3028 *Pisano* Stephen, Mibhar son of Hagri [1 Chr 11,38 reading preferable to 2 Sam 23,36]: ➤ 741, AnchorBD 4 (1992) 805.

3029 a) *Hanson* Paul D., 1 Chronicles 15-16 and the Chronicler's views on the Levites; – b) *Japhet* Sara, The Israelite legal and social reality as reflected in Chronicles; a case study: ➤ 181, Sha'arei Talmon 1992, 69-77 / 79-91.

3030 *Wright* John W., From center to periphery; 1 Chronicles 23-27 and the interpretation of Chronicles in the nineteenth century: ➤ 19a, ꜰBlenkinsopp J., Priests 1992, 20-42.

3031 *Perez* Maaravi, ⑩ The commentary of R. Jehuda Ibn Bal'am to 2 Chronicles 8:16-34:6: HUCA 63 (1992) ⑩ 1-17; Eng. 1.

3032 **Steiner** Vernon J., [2 Chr 16] The Asa narrative and the Chronicler's exegetical method; intertextuality and the question of relevance in the proclamation of OT narrative texts: diss. Trinity Ev. Divinity School 1992. 351 p. 92-33314. — DissA 53 (1992s) 2415-A.

3033 *Davies* Philip R., Defending the boundaries of Israel in the Second Temple period; 2 Chronicles 20 and the 'Salvation Army': ➤ 19a, ꜰBlenkinsopp J. 1992, 43-54.

3034 **Strübind** Kim, Tradition als Interpretation in der Chronik; König Josaphat als Paradigma chronistischer Hermeneutik und Theologie: BZAW 201, 1991 ➤ 6,3144; 7,2628: ᴿETL 68 (1992) 415s (J. *Lust*); ExpTim 103 (1991s) 309s (R. *Coggins*); ZAW 104 (1992) 463 (H.-C. *Schmitt*).

3035 a) *Sugimoto* Tomotoshi, Chronicles as independent literature; – b) *Kleinig* J.W., The divine institution of the Lord's song in Chronicles [II. 29,25...]. JStOT 55 (1992) 61-74 / 75-83.

3036 *Delcor* Mathias, Le récit de la célébration de la Pâque au temps d'Ézéchias d'après 2 Chr 30 et ses problèmes [midrash basée sur 2 Chr 35]: ➤ 491, Opfer 1990/2, 93-105; deutsch 106.

3036* *Nobile* Marco, La Pasqua del re Ezechia (2 Cr 30): Antonianum 67 (1992) 177-197; Eng. 177.

3037 **Eves** Terry L., The role of Passover in the Book of Chronicles; a study of 2 Chronicles 30 and 35; diss. Annenberg, ᴰ*Geller* S. Ph 1992. 349 p. 93-07389. — DissA 53 (1992s) 4358s-A.

3038 *Anbar* Moshe, [2 Chr 33,18] 'Mot en vedette' (Stichwort) en vue d'une correction: BibNot [48 (1989) 7] 63 (1992) 7-11.

3039 *Carroll* Robert P., [2 Chr 36,17-21] The myth of the empty land: Semeia 59 (1992) 79-93.

E5.4   *Esdrae libri (etiam 3-5)* – **Ezra, Nehemiah.**

3040 **Becker** J., Esra/Nehemia: NEchter 25, 1990 ➤ 6,3147; 7,2631: ᴿBLtg 65 (1992) 189s (M. *Oeming*); CBQ 54 (1992) 512s (J. W. *Wright*: not only holds Chr authorship but doubts prior Ez-N sources).

3041 **Bedford** Peter R., Temple and community in early Achaemenid Judea: diss. ᴰ*Ahlström* G. Ch 1992. vii-298 p. — OIAc 3,13.

3042 **Blenkinsopp** Joseph, Ezra-Nehemiah 1988 ➤ 4,3032 ... 7,2632: ᴿBijdragen 53 (1992) 324 (P. C. *Beentjes*); ConcordTQ 55 (1991) 221s (C. *Mitchell*).

3043 **Carter** Charles E., A social and demographic study of post-exilic Judah: diss. Duke, ᴰ*Meyers* E. Durham NC 1992. xvi-409 p. 92-27042. — OIAc 5,16.

3044 **Hoglund** Kenneth G., Achaemenid imperial administration in Syria-Palestine and the missions of Ezra and Nehemiah [diss. Duke]: SBL diss 125. Atlanta 1992, Scholars. xii-275 p. $45; sb./pa. $30. 1-55540-456-1; -7-X [TDig 40,167].

3045 *a) Lee* Peter, A land no longer desolate? The return from Babylon as paradigm of our changing situation; – *b) Wittenberg* Gunther H., Processes of change in the life of Israel; an OT perspective: Missionalia 20 (Pretoria 1992) 88-98 / 75-87.

3046 *North* Robert, Ezra/Nehemiah: ➤ 741, AnchorBD 2 (1992) 726-8 / 4, 1068-71 (2, 731-742, Ezra-Nehemiah books, *Klein* Ralph W.).

3047 **Smith** Daniel L., The religion of the landless 1989 ➤ 5,2923; 7,2640: ᴿBR 7,1 (1991) 37s (H. G. M. *Williamson*); VT 42 (1992) 280 (also *Williamson*).

3048 *Williamson* H. G. M. Palestine, administration of (Persian): ➤ 741, AnchorBD 5 (1992) 81-86 [68-81 Assyro-Babylonian, *Machinist* Peter; 86-90, Postexilic Judean officials, *North* Robert; 91-99, *al.* Ptolemaic/ Seleucid/ Roman].

_____

Bigvai Ezra 2,14 ... cf. Bagoas, *Barag* D. 1992 ➤ 3081.

3049 *Luria* Ben-Zion, ❶ Ezra 4,23: BethM 37,129 (1991s) 99-101.

3050 *Koch* Klaus, [Ezra 8,32-34] Ezra and Meremoth; remarks on the history of the High Priesthood: ➤ 181, Shaʿarei TALMON 1992, 105-110.

_____

3050* *Baltzer* Klaus, Moses servant of God and the servants; text and tradition in the prayer of Nehemiah (Neh 1,5-11): ➤ 104, ᶠKOESTER H. 1991, 121-130.

3051 *Feldman* Louis H., JOSEPHUS' portrait of Nehemiah: JJS 43 (1992) 187-202.

3052 *Tollefson* Kenneth D., *Williamson* H. G. M., Nehemiah as cultural revitalization; an anthropological perspective: JStOT 56 (1992) 41-68.

3052* *Croatto* J. S., La deuda en la reforma social de Nehemías; un estudio de Nehemías 5:1-19: Ribla 55 (1990) 27-37 [< Stromata 47,443].

3053 *Heltzer* Michael, [Neh 5,15] Again on some problems of the Achaemenid taxation in the province of Judah: ArchMIran 25 (1992) 169-171.

3054 *McKenzie* Kathryn, [Neh 6,14] Noadiah, the woman prophet: CTC Bulletin 10,3 (Hong-Kong 1991) 37-40 [< TContext 10/1, p. 27].

3055 *McFall* Leslie, [Neh 8,9] Was Nehemiah contemporary with Ezra in 458 B.C.?: WestTJ 53 (1991) 263-293.

3056 *Segert* Stanislav, History and poetry; poetic patterns in Nehemiah 9:5-37: → 7,141, ^FSOGGIN J. A., Storia 1991, 255-265.
3057 *Holmgren* Frederick C., Faithful Abraham and the ^c*ᵃmānâ* covenant, Nehemiah 9,6 - 10,1: ZAW 104 (1992) 249-254.

3058 **Berger** Klaus, *al.*, Synopse des Vierten Buches Esra und der syrischen Baruch-Apokalypse: TANZ 8. Tü 1992, Francke. [viii-] 287 p. DM 68. [TR 88,515]. 3-7720-1861-0; pa. -87-4.
3059 *Hilhorst* A., [LXX Esdras *a*] The speech on truth in 1 Esdras 4,34-41: → 198, ^FWOUDE A. van der, VTSupp 49 (1992) 135-153.
3060 ^{TE}**Klijn** A. Frederik J., Die Esra-Apokalypse (IV. Esra) nach dem lateinischen Text unter Benutzung der anderen Versionen: GCS. B 1992, Akademie. xxxv-129 p. [NTAbs 37, p. 306]. 3-05-000565-3.
3061 *Mędala* Stanisław, The original language of 4 Esdras: → 132, ^FMILIK J. 1991, 313-326.
3062 *Talshir* Zipora & David, ⊕ The original language of the story of the three youths (1 Esdras 3-4) [Aramaic or at least Semitic]: → 181, Sha‘arei TALMON 1992, 63*-75*; Eng. xviii.
3063 *Drint* Adriana, The Mount Sinai Arabic version of IV Ezra: OrChrPer 58 (1992) 401-422.
Longenecker B. W., Eschatology... 4 Ezra, Rom 1,11: jNsu 57, 1991 → 6254.
3064 **Stone** Michael E., Fourth Ezra, a commentary: Hermeneia 1990: → 6, 3168; 7,2662: ^RAndrUnS 30 (1992) 93-95 (A. *Thompson*); BL (1992) 57s (M. A. *Knibb*); CritRR 5 (1992) 92s (R. W. *Thomson*); Interpretation 46 (1992) 322.324 (J. C. *VanderKam*); JBL 111 (1992) 333-5 (A. *Thompson*: in preparation since 1965; best since B. VIOLET 1910 & 1924); RB 99 (1992s) 302s (J. *Murphy-O'Connor*); SecC 9 (1992) 121-4 (F. J. *Murphy*: a delight).
3065 **Bergren** Theodore A., Fifth Ezra [= 2 Esdras 1s+4 Ezra+6 Ezra < diss. Ph ^D*Kraft* R.] 1990 → 6,3167; 7,2659: ^RCBQ 54 (1992) 143s (R *Doran*); JBL 111 (1992) 336-8 (B. *Wright*).
3066 *Geoltrain* Pierre, Remarques sur la diversité des pratiques discursives apocryphes; l'exemple de 5 Esdras: → 470, Apocrypha 2 (1991) 17-30.

E5.5   **Libri Tobiae, Judith, Esther.**

^E**Cabezudo Melero** Enrique, Tobias Judit Ester 1992 → 2804.
3067 **Deselaers** Paul, Das Buch Tobit; Geistliche Schriftlesung AT 11. Dü 1990, Patmos. 248 p. DM 47; sb. 40. – ^RBLtg 64 (1991) 118s (G. *Fuchs*); GeistL 66 (1993) 232s (M. *Schneider*); TR 88 (1992) 190s (C. *Dohmen*).
3068 **Gross** Heinrich, Tobit, Judit: NEchter 19, 1987 → 3,2900 ... 6,3172: ^RBijdragen 53 (1992) 205s (Tamis *Wever*).
3069 *Levine* Amy-Jill, *a*) Diaspora as metaphor; bodies and boundaries in the book of Tobit: → 107, ^FKRAABEL A. T. 1992, 105-117; – *b*) Tobit; teaching Jews how to live in the Diaspora: BR 8,4 (1992) 42-51.64; ill.
3070 *Marangon* Antonio, Il libro di Tobia: RClerIt 73 (1992) 448-456.
3071 *Moore* Carey A., Scholarly issues in the Book of Tobit before Qumran and after; an assessment: JPseud 5 (1989) 65-81.
3072 **Rabenau** Merten, Studien zum Buch Tobit: Diss. ^D*Kaiser* O. Marburg 1992s. — RTLv 24, p. 543.

3073 *Engel* Helmut, 'Der HERR ist ein Gott, der Kriege zerschlägt'; zur Frage

der griechischen Originalsprache und der Struktur des Buches Judit:
➤ 493*a*, IOSOT-B 1989/92, 155-168.

3074 **Hellmann** Monika, Judit — eine Frau im Spannungsfeld von Autonomie und göttlicher Führung [< Diss. Bochum ᴰ*Berg* W.]: EurHS 23/ 444. 249 p.; 26 fig. $45.80. 3-631-44145-2 [NTAbs 37, p. 305].

3075 *Moore* Carey A., Judith, book of: ➤ 741, AnchorBD 3 (1992) 1117-1125.

3076 **Ploeg** J. P. M. van der, The book of Judith (daughter of Merari), Syriac text with translation and footnotes: Mōrān ʿEthʿō 3, 1991 ➤ 7,2669: ᴿOrChr 76 (1992) 253 (H. *Kaufhold*).

3077 *Ploeg* J. P. M. van der, Some remarks on a newly found Syriac text of the book of Judith: ➤ 198, ᶠWOUDE A. van der, VTSupp 49 (1992) 125-134.

3078 **Labouérie** G., Judith... contre le totalitarisme 1991 ➤ 7,2668: ᴿEspr-Vie 102 (1992) 211s (L. *Walter*: 7,26 'le peuple succombe à la tentation du pacifisme': prises de position qui font réfléchir).

ᴱ**VanderKam** James C., 'No one spoke ill of her'; essays on Judith 1992 ➤ 500*.

3079 **Priotto** Michelangelo, Il discorso di Achior, Gdt 5,5-21: ➤ 339, ParSpV 26 (1992) 87-98.

3080 *a*) **Roitman** A. D., Achior in the book of Judith; his role and significance; – *b*) *Caponigro* M. S., Judith; holding the tale of HERODOTUS; – *c*) *Moore* Carey A., Why wasn't the book of Judith included in the Hebrew Bible? – *d*) *Stone* N., Judith and Holofernes; – *e*) *Levine* A. J., Sacrifice and salvation; otherness and domestication; – *f*) *White* S. A., In the steps of Jael and Deborah: ➤ 500*, Judith 1989/92, 31-46 / 47-60 / 61-72 / 73-94 / 17-30 / 5-16.

3081 *Barag* D., ❺ [Jdt 12,11] A coin of Bagoas with a representation of God on a winged wheel: Qadmoniot 25 (1992) 97-99; 4 × 2 fig.

3082 *Börner-Klein* Dagmar, Der Ester-Midrasch in Meg 10B-17A, ein typischer Diaspora-Midrasch?: Henoch 14 (1992) 273-280; Eng. 281.

3083 ᴱ**Busi** G., La istoria di Purim io ve racconto. Rimini 1987, Luisé. 107 p.; 2 fig. – ᴿHenoch 14 (1992) 353s (A. *Vivian*).

3084 *Cavedo* Romeo, Il libro di Ester: RClerIt 73 (1992) 360-8.

3085 **Fox** Michael V., Character and ideology in the book of Esther: St-PersOT 1991 ➤ 7,2672: ᴿExpTim 103 (1991s) 374s (P. R. *Davies*: a full-scale commentary in disguise).

3086 **Fox** M., The redaction of Esther 1991 ➤ 7,2673: ᴿBL (1992) 70s (D. J. A. *Clines*); ETL 68 (1992) 416s (J. *Lust*); WestTJ 54 (1992) 372-4 (Karen H. *Jobes*).

3087 *Fox* Michael V., The redaction of the Greek alpha-text of Esther: ➤ 181, Shaʿarei TALMON 1992, 207-230.

3088 **Hary** Benjamin H., Multiglossia in Judeo-Arabic, with an edition, translation, and grammatical study of the Cairene Purim Scroll: ÉtJudMédv 14. Leiden 1992, Brill. xvii-359 p. 90-04-09694-9.

3089 *Lacocque* André, Haman in the book of Esther: HebAnR 11 (1987) 207-222.

3090 *Mosala Itumeleng* J., The implications of the text of Esther for African women's struggle for liberation in South Africa: Semeia 59 (1992) 129-137.

3091 *Nolan* Myles, Esther in the New Testament [5:3 = Mk 6:22s]: PrIrB 15 (1992) 60-65.
3092 *Rosenheim* Judith, Fate and freedom in the scroll of Esther: Prooftexts 12 (1992) 125-149.
3093 **Wynn** Kerry H., The sociohistorical contexts of the recensions of Esther: diss. Southern Baptist Theol. Sem., [D]*Smothers* T. Louisville 1991. ix-326 p. 91-12511. — OIAc 3,42.
3094 *Yamauchi* Edwin M., Mordecai, the Persepolis tablets, and the Susa excavations: VT [41 (1991) 129-136, CLINES D.] 42 (1992) 272-5.

3095 *Galarneau* Charlene A. + 7 *al.*, [Esther 4,16] 'If *I* perish, *we* perish'; a collective [and feminist] interpretation of competition: UnSemQ 45 (1991) 1-15 [17-49, *Dimen* Muriel].

E5.8 *Machabaeorum libri,* **1-2 [-4] Maccabees.**

3096 **Bar-Kochva** Bezalel, Judas Maccabaeus 1989 ➤ 5,2960...7,2682: [R]Crit-RR 5 (1992) 94-97 (G. E. *Sterling*); JHS 112 (1992) 208s (R. *Taylor*).
3097 **Bickerman** Elias J., Gli Ebrei in età greca 1991 ➤ 7,2683: [R]Protestantesimo 47 (1992) 323s (E. *Noffke*).
3098 **Derfler** Steven L., The Hasmonean revolt; rebellion or revolution: AneTSt 5, 1989 ➤ 5,2962; 6,3198: [R]BL (1992) 42 (L. L. *Grabbe*: simplistic, ignores BRINGMANN); JQR 83 (1992s) 419-421 (A. *Kasher*).
Droge Arthur J., *Tabor* James D., A noble death; suicide and martyrdom among Jews and Christians in antiquity 1992 ➤ 7423.
3099 **Harrington** Daniel J., The Maccabean revolt 1988 ➤ 4,3092...7,2688: [R]ConcordTQ 56 (1992) 216s (J. A. *Kellerman*: good apart from several errors in his late dating of Daniel).
3099* *Hodgson* Robert[J], Translating 1 Maccabees for children: BTrans 43 (1992) 117-124.
3100 **Kampen** John, Hasideans... 1-2 Mcb [D]1989 ➤ 4,3093...6,3206: [R]Austral-BR 40 (1992) 73s (Anne E. *Gardner*).
3101 **Latchmann** Georges, Une étude de l'acculturation des Juifs en Judée de 175 av. J.-C. à 70 ap. J.-C. en relation à l'observance des lois de pureté comme variable: diss. Laval 1991. 364 p. DANN 71601. — DissA 53 (1992s) 4434-A.
3102 **Martín Nieto** Evaristo, Los libros de los Macabeos, comentario [texto: Casa de la Biblia]: MensajeAT 11. S 1992, Sígueme. 215 p. 84-301-1186-7 más 3 ed.
3102* **Momigliano** Arnaldo, Alien wisdom; the limits of Hellenization. C 1990 pa. = [1]1978, Univ. vii-176 p. [R]ÉtClas 60 (1992) 175 (C. *Bonnet*).

3103 *Sisti* A., [I Mcb 1,15.48.60s] Il valore della circoncisione al tempo dei Maccabei: LA 42 (1992) 33-48.
3103* *Hall* Robert G., [I Mcb 1,15] Epispasm, circumcision in reverse; for nearly 600 years, some Jews tried to remove the mark of the covenant: BR 8,4 (1992) 53-57; ill.
3104 *Philonenko* Marc, 'Jusqu'à ce que se lève un prophète digne de confiance' (1 Maccabées 14,41): ➤ 57, [F]FLUSSER D., Messiah 1992, 95-98.
3105 [E]**Henten** J. W. van, [2/4 Mcb] Die Entstehung der jüdischen Martyrologie 1989 ➤ 5,a99; 6,533; 7,2705: [R]JJS 43 (1992) 312-5 (C. R. A. Murray-Jones).

3106 *Stern* Menahem, *zal.* ☉ 'Antioch[ians 2 Mcb 4,9] in Jerusalem'; the polis and the rise of Menelaus: Zion 57 (1992) 233-246; Eng. XIX.

3107 *Curty* Olivier, À propos de la parenté entre Juifs et Spartiates: Historia 41 (1992) 246-8.

3108 **Klauck** H. J., 4. Makkabäerbuch JSHZ 3/6, 1989 ↠ 5,2979; 7,2708: ᴿFranzSt 72 (1990) 371 (Helga *Rusche*).

3109 **Kraus Reggiani** Clara, 4 Maccabei: CommStoEseg supp 1. Genova 1992, Marietti. 166 p. 88-211-8040-9.

| **VII. Libri didactici VT** |

E6.1   *Poesis*   *.1 metrica,*   **Biblical versification.**

3110 **Alonso Schökel** Luis, Manuale di poetica ebraica 1989 ↠ 5,2982 ... 7, 2711: ᴿParVi 35 (1990) 390s (C. *Carniti*).

3111 **Alonso Schökel** Luis, Antología de poesía bíblica hebrea bilingüe. Zaragoza 1992, Delegación diocesana de catequesis. 657 p.; (color.) ill. 84-604-4421-X. pt. 5000.

3112 **Alter** Robert, The art of biblical poetry, 1985 (Clark 1990) ↠ 1,2978 ... 7,2712: ᴿAustralBR 39 (1991) 54-56 (B. *Rutherford*); HeythJ 33 (1992) 85s (R. *Althann*); ScotJT 45 (1992) 407s (Francesca *Murphy*).

3113 *Berlin* Adele, Azariah DE' ROSSI on biblical poetry: Prooftexts 12 (1992) 175-183.

3114 *Berlin* Adele, Parallelism: ↠ 741, AnchorBD 5 (1992) 155-162.

3115 **Brichto** Herbert C., Toward a grammar of biblical poetics; tales of the prophets. NY 1992. xv-298 p, [JAOS 112,725]. 0-19-506911-0.

3116 **Culbertson** Diana, The poetics of revelation. Macon 1989, Mercer Univ. xii-189 p. $17. – ᴿPerspRelSt 19 (1992) 328-333 (J. D. *Sykes*, also on BOOTH W. 1988 & BRYANT D. 1989).

3117 *Del Valle* Carlos, Cuestiones de métrica cuantitativa hebrea: RÉJ 151 (1992) 141-7.

3118 **Dickens** Owen P., A study of rhetorical devices in Ugaritic verse: diss. Brandeis. Boston 1992. 455 p. 92-29461. — DissA 53 (1992s) 1499-A; OIAc 5,19.

3119 [Scott] *Meisami* Julie, Arabic poetics revisited [*Kanazi* G. 1989; content rather than versification]: JAOS 112 (1992) 254-68.

3120 a) *Paul* Shalom M., Polysensuous polyvalency in poetic parallelism; – b) *Polak* Frank H., ☉ *Wayyištaḥᵃwû*, group formulas in biblical prose and poetry: ↠ 181, Shaʿarei TALMON 1992, 147-163 / 81*-91*; Eng. xix.

3121 **Petersen** David L., *Richards* Kent H., Interpreting Hebrew Poetry: GuidesBSch. Mp 1992, Fortress. x-117 p. $7. 0-8006-2625-7 [BL 93, 157, W. G. E. *Watson*].

3122 **Rousseau** Françoise, [↠ 7,2719] La poétique fondamentale du texte biblique; le fait littéraire d'un parallélisme élargi et omniprésent: Recherches NS 20. Montréal/P 1989, Bellarmin/Cerf. 280 p. 2-89007-672-5 / P 2-204-00562-3. – ᴿÉglT 22 (1991) 220-2 (W. *Vogels*); SR 21 (1992) 222s (P. *Letourneau*).

3123 *Sternberg* Meir, Biblical poetics and sexual politics; from reading to counterreading [defense of his Poetics of Biblical Narrative against FEWELL and GUNN]: JBL [110 (1991) 193-212] 111 (1992) 463-488.

3124 *Watson* Wilfred G. E., Number parallelism in Mesopotamian texts: ➤ 65, Mem. GEVIRTZ S., Maarav 7 (1991) 241-252.

E6.2 **Psalmi, textus.**

3125 *Blum-Cuny* Pascale, Traduire le sacré; le Psautier de Blaise de VIGE-NÈRE: BtHumRen 54 (1992) 441-9.
3126 *Corrigan* K., Visual polemics in the IXth-cent. Byzantine psalters. C 1992, Univ. 324 p.; 113 fig. £50 [RHE 88,140*].
3127 *Cook* Johann, On the relationship between 11QPs[a] and the Septuagint on the basis of the computerized data base (CAQP): ➤ 459, Septuagint 1990/2, 107-130.
3128 *Hannay* Margaret P., 'Wisdome the Wordes'; [*Lok* A., *Sidney* (Herbert) M.] Psalm translation and Elizabethan women's spirituality: RLitND 23,3 (1991) 65-82.
3129 *Jensen* Joseph, Report on NAB Psalter revision: CBQ 54 (1992) 724-6.
3130 **Koster** Albert. Vieringen, een woord-voor-woord vertaling uit het Hebreeuws van het boek der psalmen. Eindhoven 1991, auct. 153 p. *f*24.50 [Bijdragen 54,431, A. van *Wieringen*].
3131 Der Landgrafenpsalter Stu LandesBt HB II 24, Faksimile. Graz/Bielefeld 1992, Akad.-VA/Regional-G. 384 p. DM 5560 [ErbAuf 68,424].
3132 *a)* **Santucci** Luigi, La poesia nella Bibbia; – *b)* *Paredi* Angelo, Nota storica sui Salteri milanesi del IX secolo: Miniature altomedievali lombarde 1s / Fontes ambrosiani 59. Mi 1978, Banco Ambrosiano. 179 p.; 54 (color.) pl.
3133 [E]**Schmeisser** Martin, Das Buch der Psalmen; ein Eschbacher Bilderpsalter in acht Bänden [je ca. 20 Psalmen]. Z/Lp 1990, Theol.-V. / Thomas. [ca. DM 32 sb.] I (1-21) 52 p.; II (22-41) p. 53-100; III. (42-59) -148; IV (60-72) -189; V (73-89) -244; VI (90-106) -296; VII (107-119) -344; VIII (120-150) -392. 3-88671-091-2; -2-0; -3-9; -4-7; -5-5; -6-3; -7-1; -8-X. – [R]BiKi 47 (1992) 233 (R. *Russ*).
3134 **Stork** Dieter, Die Psalmen — neu gelesen; I (1-75), Zukunft, die heute beginnt; II (76-150), Mein Lachen in der Angst: STb 12.14. Stu 1992, KBW. je 158 p. DM 16,80. – [R]BiKi 47 (1992) 237 (S. *Cibulka*).
3135 **Wagenaar** C., Het boek der psalmen naar de Septuagint 1988 ➤ 7,2733: [R]CollatVL 22 (1992) 97 (F. *Lefevre*).
3136 **Zuber** Beat, Die Psalmen; eine Studienübersetzung unter besonderer Berücksichtigung des hebräischen Tempus: DielBl Beih 7. Heid 1986. 216 p. DM 12,50. – [R]BiKi 47 (1992) 235 (Verena *Lenzen*).

E6.3 **Psalmi, introductio.**

3136* *Brière* J., Une expérience d'initiation aux Psaumes: ➤ 448, Ens.Écr. 1992, 126-133.
3137 **Day** John, Psalms: SOTS (Guide). Sheffield 1990, JStOT (Ithaca NY, Cornell). 159 p. $10 pa. 1-85075-703-8 [TDig 38,354]. – [R]ETL 68 (1992) 422s (A. *Schoors*); SvTKv 67 (1991) 135s (F. *Lindström*).
3138 *Limburg* James, Psalms, book of: ➤ 741, AnchorBD 5 (1992) 522-536.
3139 *a)* *McCann* J. Clinton[J], The Psalms as instruction; – *b)* *Wilson* Gerald H., The shape of the Book of Psalms; – *c)* *Sheppard* Gerald T., Theology and the Book of Psalms; – *d)* *Smith* Mark S., The Psalms as a book for pilgrims: Interpretation 46 (1992) 117-128 / 129-142 / 143-155 / 156-166.

3140 *Milhau* Marc, Différentes versions de titres ou de versets de psaumes rapportées par HILAIRE de Poitiers, Tractatus super Psalmos: RBen 102 (1992) 24-43.
3141 **Millard** Matthias, Die Komposition des Psalters, ein formgeschichtlicher Ansatz: Diss. ᴰ*Rendtorff* R. Heidelberg 1992. – RTLv 24, p. 542.
3142 **Neveu** Louis, Au pas des psaumes 3, 1991 ➔ 7,2742: ᴿEsprVie 102 (1992) 210 (L. *Monloubou* s'avoue myope).
3143 **Raabe** Paul R., Psalm structures; a study of psalms with refrains [diss. ᴰ*Freedman* D.]: jOsu 104, 1990 ➔ 7,2743: ᴿThemelios 18,2 (1992s) 26 (B. *Weber*, hesitant); TLZ 117 (1992) 179-181 (H. *Reventlow*).
3144 **Seybold** Klaus, Introducing the Psalms, ᵀ*Dunphy* R. Graeme 1989 ➔ 7, 2746: ᴿCBQ 54 (1992) 518s (W. A. *Young*: verbose, obtuse; but upper level); IndTSt 29 (1992) 373-5 (A. R. *Ceresko*); Interpretation 46 (1992) 190.192 (J. C. *McCann*); ScotJT 45 (1992) 113s (S. E. *Gillingham*); ScripB 22/1 (1992) 22 (W. G. E. *Watson*).
3145 *Seybold* Klaus, Psalmen: ➔ 757, EvKL 3 (1992) 1366-73.
3146 **Simon** Uriel, Four approaches to the Book of Psalms; from Saadiah Gaon to Abraham Ibn Ezra [Ⓗ 1982]ᵀ 1991 ➔ 7,2747: ᴿJudaica 48 (1992) 53s (S. *Schreiner*: gelungen); Prooftexts 11 (1991) 303-7 (Adele *Berlin*); RB 99 (1992) 597s (R. J. *Tournay*).
3147 *Vesco* Jean-Luc, L'approche canonique du Psautier: RThom 92 (1992) 482-502.

E6.4   **Psalmi, commentarii.**

3147* **Alonso Schökel** Luis, *Carniti* Cecilia, *a*) Salmos I (1-72), traducción, introducciones y comentario: Nueva Biblia Española. Estella 1992, VDivino. 942 p. 84-7151-667-5. – *b*) I salmi I, ᵀᴱ*Nepi* Antonio: Commenti Biblici. R 1992, Borla. 1068 p. 88-263-0904-3. – ᴿRBibArg 54,47 (1992) 173-6 (A. *Ricciardi*).
3148 **Beaucamp** Évode, Dai Salmi al 'Pater'; commento teologico-spirituale al Salterio. CinB 1991, Paoline. 1150 p. Lit. 48.000. – ᴿRivScR 6 (1992) 211-4 (P. *Fragnelli*).
3149 ᴱ**Boese** Helmut, Anonymi [7. Jh.] Glosa Psalmorum ex traditione seniorum, I. Praefatio und Psalmen 1-100: VLatGesch 22. FrB 1992, Herder. 32*-471 p. 3-451-22682-0 [BL 93,47, S. P. *Brock*].
3149* **Bouma** H., In de schaduw van de psalmen [elke psalm origineel herschreven]. Kampen 1990, Kok. 175 p. Fb 590. – ᴿCollatVL 22 (1992) 99 (J. de *Kesel*).
3150 **Bratcher** Robert G., *Reyburn* William D., A translator's handbook on the Book of Psalms 1991 ➔ 7,2753: ᴿBL (1992) 49 (G. W. *Anderson*); CBQ 54 (1992) 733-740 (A. R. *Ceresko*: 10 years in the making);
3151 ᵀᴱ**Cattani** Luigi, KIMḤI David, Commento ai Salmi: Tradizione d'Israele 6. R 1991, Città nuova. I. (1-50) 417 p. Lᵐ 48. 88-311-4913-X. – ᴿCC 143 (1992,4) 525s (G. L. *Prato*).
3152 **Craven** Toni, The book of Psalms: Message of Biblical Spirituality 6. ColMn 1992, Liturgical. 172 p. £8 [BL 93,160] . 0-8146-5564-4; pa. -72-6.
3153 **Curti** Carmelo, EUSEBIANA I, In Pss 1987 ➔ 5,249...7,2755: ᴿMélSR 48 (1991) 187s (M. *Spanneut*).
3154 **Daur** Klaus-D., ARNOBII in Pss: CCLat 25, 1990 ➔ 6,3266; 7,2756: ᴿJTS 43 (1992) 693-701 (W. *Kinzig* enumerates many errors or lacks in the apparatus); VigChr 46 (1992) 438-440 (J. den *Boeft*).

3155 *Folliet* Georges, L'itinéraire heureux d'un manuscrit des Énarrationes in Psalmos (Évreux B. M. 131): RÉAug 37 (1991) 321-333.

3156 **Gerstenberger** E., Psalms I, 1988 ➤ 4,3117... 6,3258: ᴿScripB 22,1 (1992) 22s (B. *Croft*); Themelios 17,1 (1991s) 22s (T. *Longman*).

3156* **Gross-Díaz** Theresa J., The Psalms commentary of GILBERT of Poitiers [sic]; from lectio divina to the lecture room: diss. Northwestern, ᴰ*Lerner* R. Evanston 1992. 279 p. 93-09367. – DissA 53 (1992s) 4043-A.

3157 **Hossfeld** Frank-Lothar, *Zenger* Erich: Psalmen I (1-50): NEchter. Wü c. 1992, Echter. 318 p. 3-429-01503-0. – ᴿBiKi 47 (1992) 230s (J. *Schreiner*).

3157* **Katsumura** Hiroya, ❹ Shihen chūkai... Leaf Commentary, [34] Psalms. Tokyo 1992, Nihon Kirisutokyōdan Shuppankyoku. 354 p. Y 2000 [BL 93,63, D. T. *Tsumura*].

3158 **Kinzig** Wolfram, In search of ASTERIUS / Psalms ᴰ1990 ➤ 6,3269; 7,2760*: ᴿJTS 43 (1992) 249-252 (S. G. *Hall*: a masterpiece of orderly presentation); MüTZ 43 (1992) 376-8 (T. *Böhm*).

3159 **Kraus** H. J., Ps 60-150. ᵀ*Oswald* 1989 ➤ 5,3026... 7,2761: ᴿScotJT 45 (1992) 404s (Susan *Gillingham*).

3160 **Marti** Kurt, Die Psalmen Davids; Annäherungen. Stu 1991, Radius. I. 1-41, 192 p.; II. 42-72, 160 p.; III. 73-106, 192 p. je DM 26. – ᴿBiKi 47 (1992) 234s (T. *Steiger*: kritisch, eigenartig; TGL 82 (1992) (K. *Holl-mann*).

3160* **Nielsen** Eduard, 31 udvalgte salmer. Frederiksberg 1990, Anis. 144 p. – ᴿSvTKv 67 (1991) 135 (F. *Lindström*).

3161 **Pollack** Aharon, ❺ *Al Hasetumot Bamizmor*, Commentary on the Psalms. J 1991, Nezer. xx-556 p. 965-222-230-5.

3162 ᵀᴱPrinzivalli Emanuela, ORIGENE, Omelie sui Salmi 36-38: BtPatr 18. F 1991, Nardini. 510 p. Lit. 48.000. 88-404-2020-7. – ᴿAsprenas 39 (1992) 275s (L. *Fatica*). BLitEc 93 (1992) 225-7 (H. *Crouzel*).

3163 **Quesson** Noël, The spirit of the Psalms 1990 ➤ 7,2806: ᴿCBQ 54 (1992) 519s (W. A. *Young*: omission of Ps 23 & 139 in a collection of 'best-known' psalms is rather startling).

3164 **Spurgeon** Charles H. (1834-1892), The treasury of David; containing an original exposition of the book of Psalms, a collection of illustrative extracts from the whole range of literature. [Toronto 1892, Funk & W.]. Peabody MA, Hendrickson. $60. 7 vol. in 3: I (Ps 1-57) iv-458 p.; II (58-110) iv-484 p.; III, v-475 p. 0-917006-25-9 (all).

3165 **Tate** Marvin E., Psalms 51-100: WordComm 20, 1990 ➤ 6,3264*b*; 7, 2762*: ᴿEvJ 10 (1992) 40-42 (D. A. *Dorsey*, delighted); TLZ 117 (1992) 498-500 (H. *Seidel*); VT 42 (1992) 420s (J. D. *Ray*).

3166 **Waaijman** Kees, *Aarnink* Letizia, Psalmenschrift [10 vol.]: Psalm [1-11, 1988 ➤ 5,3036] 12-16 / 17-29. Kampen 1989, Kok. viii-80 p. / viii-96 p. *f* 24,50 each. – ᴿStreven 58 (1990s) 471 (P. *Beentjes*).

3166* **Waaijman** Kees, Psalmen om het uitroepen van de Naam: VBGed. Kampen 1991, Kok. 192 p. – ᴿCollationesVL 22 (1992) 216s (E. *Eynikel*; his tenth and last); Streven 58 (1990s) 175 (P. *Beentjes*).

3167 ᵀᴱWalsh P. G., CASSIODORUS, Explanations of the Psalms [1, 1990 ➤ 7, 2764] 2-3: Ancient Christian Writers [51] 52; 53. NY 1991s, Paulist/ Gracewing. [vi-618 p.] 528 p.; vi-543 p. [$37] $35 each. 0-8091-0441-5; -4-X; -5-8. – ᴿBL (1992) 49s (R. P. R. *Murray*).

3168 **Williams** Donald M., Psalms 73-150: Communicator's comm. 14, 1989 ➤ 6,3280*: ᴿCBQ 54 (1992) 341s (M. D. *Futato*: useful little homilies and personal experiences).

3169 **Zenger** Erich,   Ich will die Morgenröte wecken 1991 ↠ 7,2767:   RBiKi 47 (1992) 232 (S. *Gerstenberger*); TLZ 117 (1992) 599s (H. *Seidl*); TüTQ 172 (1992) 241s (W. *Gross*).

E6.5   **Psalmi, themata.**

3169* a) *Althann* Robert,   The Psalms of vengeance against their Ancient Near Eastern background; – b) *Nel* P. J.,   Parallelism and recurrence in Biblical Hebrew poetry; a theoretical proposal: JNWS 18 (1992) 1-11 / 135-143.

3170 **Baldermann** Ingo,   Wer hört mein Weinen? Kinder entdecken sich selbst in den Psalmen³ [¹1986]: Wege des Lernens 4.   Neuk 1992.   132 p.; 4 color. pl.   3-7887-1253-8 [TLZ 118,260, R. *Degen*].

3171 *Bozak* Barbara A.,   Suffering and the psalms of lament: ÉglT 23 (1992) 325-338.

3172 **Brueggemann** Walter,   Abiding astonishment; Psalms, modernity, and the making of history: LitCuB 1991 ↠ 7,2771:   RCBQ 54 (1992) 740s (M. S. *Moore*: few historians will find it convincing, despite its theological acumen).

3173 a) *Coetzee* J. H.,   A survey of research on the psalms of lamentations; – b) *Hunter* J.,   How can we lament when we are glad? A comment on genre in poetic texts: OTEssays 5 (1992) 151-174 / 175-183.

3174 *Cook* Stephen L.,   Apocalypticism and the Psalter: ZAW 104 (1992) 82-99.

3175 **Davidson** Robert,   Wisdom and worship [Ps. 32; 34; 49; 73... 1989 E. Cadbury lectures].   L/Ph 1990, SCM/Trinity.   148 p. $13 pa. – RInterpretation 46 (1992) 193s (J. L. *Crenshaw*).

3176 *Davis* Eli,   The Psalms in Hebrew medical amulets: VT 42 (1992) 173-8.

3177 **Dhanaraj** Dharmakkan,   Theological significance of the motif of enemies in selected psalms of individual lament [13; 3; 54; 5; 56; 59; 140; 143; 71; in excursus 64]: OrBibChr 4.   Glückstadt 1992, Augustin.   xii-311 p. DM 94.   3-87030-153-8 [BL 94,106, A. H. W. *Curtis*].

3179 **Ferris** Paul W.,   The genre of communal lament in the Bible and the Ancient Near East [< diss. Dropsie]: SBL diss. 127.   Atlanta 1992, Scholars.   xvii-190 p.   1-55540-542-8 [OIAc 5,21].

3180 *Gelander* Shamai,   Convention and originality; identification of the situation in the Psalms: VT 42 (1992) 302-316.

3181 a) *Gerstenberger* Erhard S.,   Der Schrei der Psalmisten, 'Wo ist Gott?'; – b) *Cattin* Yves,   Die Metapher Gott, THimmelsbach A.: (↠ 384) IZT (Concilium) 28 (1992) 288-295 / 319-329.

3182 *Hawkins* Roderick A.,   The imprecatory psalms: CalvaryB 8,1 (1992) 39-56.

3183 EHeider Anne H.,   LE JEUNE Claude [1530-1600], Dodecacorde, comprising twelve psalms of David set to music according to the twelve modes: RecResMusRen 74-76.   Madison WI 1989, A-R.   xxx-92 p.; xi + p. 93-191; xii + p. 192-310. – RSixtC 23 (1992) 368s (D. C. *Nichols*).

3184 **Jauss** Hannelore,   Tor der Hoffnung D1991 ↠ 7,2778:   RÉglT 23 (1992) 268s (W. *Vogels*).

3185 **Jauss** Hannelore, al.,   Die Melodie des Glaubens; Psalmen: Bibelauslegung für die Praxis 9.   Stu 1991, KBW.   160 p.   3-460-25091-7.

3186 *Ladaria* Luis F.,   Adán y Cristo en los Tractatus super Psalmos de San HILARIO de Poitíers: Gregorianum 73 (1992) 97-122; Eng. 122.

3187 *Levine* Herbert,   The dialogic discourse of Psalms: ↠ 400, Hermeneutics 1989/92, 145-161.

3188 *Pezhumkattil* Abraham, Israel's faith reflected in the Psalms: Bible Bhashyam 16 (1990) 156-172.
3189 **Rasmussen** Tarald, Inimici Ecclesiae... in LUTHERS Dictata 1989 → 7, 2785: ᴿBijdragen 53 (1992) 329s (T. *Bell*).
3190 **Rendsburg** Gary A., Linguistic evidence for the northern origin of selected psalms [9s and 33 others] 1990 → 6,3306; 7,2786: ᴿBL (1992) 138 (L. L. *Grabbe* welcomes but queries the methodology; BSO 55 (1992) 543s (J. C. L. *Gibson*); CBQ 54 (1992) 126-9 (Z. *Zevit* queries 9 assumptions); ÉglT 23 (1992) 267s (L. *Laberge*); ETL 68 (1992) 423s (A. *Schoors*: Phoenician scribes wrote the Temple-building account? p. 29); JAOS 112 (1992) 702-4 (D. *Pardee*: data inadequate); RB 99 (1992) 458s (R. J. *Tournay*).
3191 **Ridderbos** N. H., † 1981, Psalmenstudie; Prof. Dr. Nic. H. Ridderbos en het boek der Psalmen [12 art. 1950-75]. Kampen 1991, Kok. 208 p. ƒ34,50. 90-2424-966-X. – ᴿNedTTs 46 (1992) 340s (P. B. *Dirksen*).
3192 *Smith* Mark E., The theology of the redaction of the Psalter; some observations: ZAW 104 (1992) 408-412.
3193 *Totev* T., Un psaume de la Bible dans une inscription de Preslav en langue grecque: ÉBalk 28,2 (1992) 83-86; 2 fig. [RHE 88,19*].
3194 *Urbina* P. A., Los Salmos de David en la 'Subida del Monte Carmelo' [JUAN C.]: ScripTPamp 22 (1991) 939-959.
Waaijman Kees, Psalmen om het uitroepen van de naam 1991 → 3166*.
3196 *Walton* J. H., Psalms; a cantata about the Davidic covenant: JEvTS 34 (1991) 21-31 [< ZAW 104,270].
Watts James W., Psalm and story; inset hymns in Hebrew narrative ᴰ1992 → 1228.

E6.6 *Psalmi: oratio, liturgia* – Psalms as prayer.

3197 **Arminjon** Blaise, Sur la lyre à dix cordes 1990 → 6,3215; 7,2796: ᴿRev-SR 66 (1992) 353s (B. *Renaud*: commentaire spirituel).
3198 **Asensio** Félix, La oración en los Salmos; la antítesis 'justo-impio': Fac-TNE 56, 1991 → 7,2797: ᴿSalmanticensis 39 (1992) 298 (M. *García Cordero*); ScripTPamp 24 (1992) 332s (A. *García-Moreno*).
3199 *Beeck* Franz J. van, Israel's God, the Psalms, and the city of Jerusalem; life experience and the sacrifice of praise and prayer: Horizons 19 (1992) 219-239.
3200 **Brueggemann** Walter, Israel's praise 1988 → 4,3205... 7,2799: ᴿAndr-UnS 30 (1992) 81-83 (C. R. *Holmes*); RestQ 33 (1991) 50s (J. T. *Willis*); Worship 66 (1992) 463-5 (J. *Jensen*).
3201 ᴱ**Bruijn** J. de, *Heijting* W., Psalmzingen in de Nederlanden van de zestiende eeuw tot heden. Kampen 1991, Kok. 326 p.; ill. – ᴿArchivSc-SocR 78 (1992) 223s (W. *Frijhoff*).
Craven Toni, The book of Psalms: Message of Biblical Spirituality 6, 1992 → 3152.
3203 *Fischer* Balthasar, Zur relecture chrétienne des Psalters im patristischen Zeitalter; ein Bericht [RONDEAU M. 1982/5; TRUBLET J. 1986²]: JbAC 34 (1991) 159-163.
3204 *Gerstenberger* Erhard S., Lieder von Freiheit und Leben; die Psalmen in den Basisgemeinden Lateinamerikas: BiKi 47 (1992) 214-9.
3205 **Gilbert** Maurice, Les louanges du Seigneur 1991 → 7,2802: ᴿÉglT 23 (1992) 270 (W. *Vogels*); EsprVie 102 (1992) 209s (L. *Monloubou*: excellent, mais donne l'impression de commenter des mots ou formules plutôt que le

poème lui-même, et n'indique pas deux rapports importants avec la liturgie); LVitae 47 (1992) 236 (L. *Partos*); RTLv 23 (1992) 83 (P.-M. *Bogaert*: 'il réussit le prodige de nous donner en toute clarté un commentaire simple' des 90 psaumes).

3206 **Gilbert** Maurice,   Ogni vivente dia lode al Signore; commento dei Salmi delle domeniche e delle feste [I. 1991 ➤ 7,2802*b*] 2-3. R 1992, Apostolato della Preghiera. 298 p.; 296 p.; 415 p. Lit. 24.000 ciascuno. – ᴿCC 143 (1992,4) 641s (D. *Scaiola*).

3207 **Goulder** Michael,   The prayers of David (Ps 51-72): JStOT supp 102, 1990 ➤ 6,3332:   ᴿCBQ 54 (1992) 527s (J. C. *McCann*: collections and order of psalms in them the key of interpretation); Interpretation 46 (1992) 190 (J. L. *Mays*); JBL 111 (1992) 527s (M. L. *Barré*); JTS 43 (1992) 805 (E. W. *Nicholson*: not dull; startling, perhaps scandalous); TLZ 117 (1992) 348-350 (H. *Seidel*).

3208 *Hinz* Günther, *Völker* Alexander,   Vom Singen der Psalmen; ein Werkstattbericht: JbLtgHymn 33 (1990s) 1-94; Eng. 94.

3209 **Huonder** Vitus,   Die Psalmen in der Liturgia horarum [Hab.-Diss.]: StFrib NF 74.   FrS 1991, Univ.   307 p. [RSPT 77,127, P.-M. *Gy*].

3210 **Lewis** C. S.,   Das Gespräch mit Gott; Gedanken zu den Psalmen² [¹1959], Vorw. *Zenger* E.   Z 1992, Benziger.   204 p. DM 19,80. – ᴿBiKi 47 (1992) 232s (Maria *Russ*).

3211 *Lohfink* Norbert, Psalmengebet und Psalterredaktion [Gastvorlesung Mainz 17.I.1991]: ArLtgW 34 (1992) 1-22.

3212 *a) Lohfink* Norbert,   Der Psalter und die christliche Meditation; die Bedeutung der Endredaktion für das Verständnis des Psalters; – *b) Russ* Maria,   Psalmen beten in Gemeinschaft; – *c) Füglister* Notker,   Die Verwendung des Psalters zur Zeit Jesu; der Psalter als Lehr- und Lebensbuch: BiKi 47 (1992) 195-200 / 188-194 / 201-8.

3213 *Lohfink* Norbert,   The Psalter and Christian meditation [... Bedeutung der Endredaktion < ArLtgW 34 (1992) 1-22; BiKi 47 (1992) 195-200], ᵀᴱ*Asen* B. A.: TDig 40, 133-9.

3214 *Molina* Mario A.,   La salmodía del día de Pascua, salmodía del domingo: Phase 31 (1991) 125-147.

3215 **Mowinckel** Sigmund,   The Psalms in Israel's worship, ᵀ*Ap-Thomas* D. R. [Blackwell 1962]: Biblical Seminar 14.   Shf 1992, Academic.   xxxi-246 + [viii-] 243 p.   0226-4984 [OIAc 3,31].

3216 *a) Murphy* Roland,   The Psalms and worship; – *b) Hardy* Daniel W., Worship as the orientation of life to God; – *c) Hustad* Donald P., Doxology, a biblical triad [response, *Best* Harold M.]: ➤ 624, Worship, ExAud 8 (1992) 23-31 / 55-71 / 1-16 [17-21].

3217 *Oakes* Edward T.,   The Psalms as Christian prayer: America 166 (1992) 208s.

3218 **Peterson** Eugene H.,   Answering God; the Psalms as tools for prayer. SF 1989, Harper.   151 p. $14. – ᴿCrux 26,4 (1990) 42s (D. *Stewart*).

3219 **Premk** Francka,   Kocenine slovenskik Psalmov [ᵀTRUBAN P. 1566; DALMATIN J. 1594; Ps 119 + 30 autres]. Ljubljana 1992, Trubarjevo.   752 p. $49 [RB 100,608, R. J. *Tournay*].

3220 [Vroon] **Rienstra** Marchiene,   Swallow's nest; a feminine reading of the Psalms.   L/GR 1992, Gracewing/Eerdmans/Friendship.   xx-257 p. £13. 0-85241-214-8 / 0-8028-0624-4 / 0-377-00248-8. – ᴿExpTim 104 (1992s) 246 (J. *Eaton*: beautifully produced; for prayer).

3220* *Schmidt-Lauber* Hans-Christoph,   Verchristlichung der Psalmen durch das Gloria Patri?:   ➤ 163, ᶠSAUER G., Aktualität 1992, 317-329.

3221 *Sedgwick* Colin J., Preaching from the Psalms [... prayers]: ExpTim 103 (1991s) 361-4.
3222 **Tournay** R.J., Seeing and hearing God with the Psalms 1991 → 7,2812: ᴿJTS 43 (1992) 808 (D. R. *Jones*: densely learned summation of 50 years' study); TLZ 117 (1992) 904-6 (M. *Sæbø*).
3223 **Trigo** Pedro, Salmos [modernos] de vida y fidelidad; oraciones desde el compromiso por la liberación: Betania 50, 1989 → 6,3343: ᴿHumTeol 12 (1991) 419s (F. *Rosas Magalhães*).
3224 **Valles** Carlos G., Praying together; psalms for contemplation. Anand 1989, GJPrakash. 344 p. – ᴿBibleBhashyam 16 (1990) 133s (C. *Velamparampil*).
3225 **Vincent** Monique, S. AUGUSTIN maître de prière... EnPs 1990 → 6, 3338; 7,2814: ᴿEsprVie 102 (1992) 681s (Y.-M, *Duval*); Gregorianum 73 (1992) 366s (M. *Ruiz Jurado*); RelCu 37 (1991) 735 (P. *Langa*); RHR 209 (1992) 308s (J. *Doignon*); RSPT 76 (1992) 148-151 (G.-M. de *Durand*); Teresianum 43 (1992) 293s (M. *Diego Sánchez*).
3226 **Wahl** Otto, Lieder der Befreiten; [10] Psalmen beten heute. Mü 1989, Don Bosco. 142 p. DM 19.80. ᴿBiKi 47 (1992) 238 (Jutta *Drewnick*); TPQ 140 (1992) 195s (Borghild *Baldauf*).

E6.7 *Psalmi: versiculi* – Psalms by number and verse.

3227 *Buber* Martin, Die Wege; Psalm I in Text und Deutung [< ?]: BiKi 47 (1992) 181-3.
3228 **Mattioli** Anselmo, Beatitudini [45 AT in dieci gruppi] e felicità nella Bibbia d'Israele. F-Prato 1992, Città Nuova. 361 p. Lᵐ 70 [Antonianum 68,564s, M. *Nobile*].
3229 *Gosse* Bernard, Le Psaume 2 et l'usage rédactionnel des oracles contre les nations à l'époque post-exilique: BibNot 62 (1992) 18-24.
3230 *Norton* Gerard J., Psalm 2:11-12 and modern textual criticism: PrIrB 15 (1992) 89-111.
3231 *Sarna* Nahum M., Legal terminology in Psalm 3:8: → 181, Sha'arei TALMON 1992, 175-181.
3232 **Kinzig** Wolfram, Erbin Kirche,... Ps 5,1 ASTERIUS 1990 → 6,3350: ᴿBL (1992) 75 (R.P.R. *Murray*); CritRR 5 (1992) 335-7 (M. *Slusser*: excellent, both sober and adventurous); TLZ 117 (1992) 609s (H.G. *Thümmel*).
3233 *da Silva* A.A., 'n Poëtiese analise van Psalm 6: OTEssays 5 (1992) 206-224.
3234 **Duin** C. van, [Ps 6;88] 'Zal het stof u loven?' Weerlegging van de individualistische uitleg van woorden voor dood en onderwereld in de psalmen 1989 → 5,3099: ᴿDielB 27 (1991) 280 (B.J. *Diebner*); TvT 32 (1992) 91s (P. *Kevers*).
3235 **Auffret** Pierre, Quatre Psaumes et un cinquième; étude structurelle des Psaumes 7-10 et 35. P 1992, Letouzey & Â. 273 p. F 340. 2-7063-0187-2.
3236 *Limburg* James, Who cares for the earth? Psalm Eight and the environment: → 77, ᶠHARRISVILLE R., All things new 1992, 43-52.
3237 *Crüsemann* Frank, Die Macht der kleinen Kinder; ein Versuch, Psalm 8,2b.3 zu verstehen: → 197, ᶠWOLFF H. W., Wer ist der Mensch 1992, 61-78.
3238 *Stroumsa* Sarah, 'What is man?'; Psalm 8:4-5 in Jewish, Christian and Muslim exegesis [reflects attitude to Christology; 1984 > ᶠ*Braude* W.]: Henoch 14 (1992) 283-290; ital. 291.

3239 ᴱLifschitz Daniel, Perché, Signore, te ne stai lontano? Salmi 9 e 10: La tradizione ebraica e cristiana commenta i Salmi 4. T-Leumann 1992, Elle Di Ci. 255 p. 88-01-14895-X.

3240 *Auffret* Pierre, 'Maintenant je me lève'; étude structurelle du psaume 12: ÉglT 23 (1992) 159-176.

3241 *Dellazari* Romano, Salmo 15: Teocomunicação 22,97 (Porto Alegre 1992) 385-396 [< TContext 10/2, 61].

3242 *Hodge* Carleton T., [Ps 16; 56-60] Mikram: → 118, ᶠLESLAU W., Semitic 1991, 634-644.

3243 *Chaillot* G., Le psaume 19 lu par Jean-Jacques OLIER: → 448, Ens.Écr. 1992, 18-27.

3244 *Deurloo* K. A., Psalm 19; riddle and parable: → 493*a*, IOSOT-B 1989/92, 93-100.

3245 *Egan* Miguel, El Salmo 19 [Vlg, segundo Cristobal COLÓN] y el descubrimiento de América: RBibArg 54 (1992) 231-6.

3246 *Davis* Ellen F., Exploding the limits; form and function in Psalm 22: JStOT 53 (1992) 93-105.

3247 *Tostengard* Sheldon, Psalm 22: Interpretation 46 (1992) 167-170.

3248 *Gordon* Edwin, [Ps 23] The Good Shepherd, the ideal for the priest: HomP 92,3 (1991s) 23-30 [< ZIT 92,54].

3249 *Weiss* Meir, ❸ Psalm 23; the Psalmist on God's care: → 181, Shaʿarei TALMON 1992, 31*-41*; Eng. xvi.

3250 *Herr* Larry G., An off-duty archaeologist looks at Psalm 23: BR 8,2 (1992) 44-51; 8/4, 10s letters of Elizabeth *Miel*, G. W. *Buchanan*.

3251 *Jacobson* Diana L., A literary and theological exploration of appeals to the Creator in Psalms 24, 33, and 74: diss. Union. NY 1990. — UnSemQ 45 (1991) 252.

3252 *Auffret* Pierre, 'En raison de ton Nom, ʏʜᴡʜ, tu pardonneras ma faute'; étude structurelle du psaume 25: ÉglT 22 (1991) 5-31.

3253 *Lohfink* Norbert, [Ps 25...] Der neue Bund und die Völker: KIsr 6 (1991) 115-133.

3254 *Freedman* David N., Patterns in Psalms 25 and 34: → 19*a*, ᶠBLENKINSOPP J., Priests 1992, 125-138.

3255 **Eriksson** Lars Olov, 'Come...' Ps 34: 1991 → 7,2834: ᴿThemelios 18,3 (1992s) 25 (B. *Weber*).

3256 *Hurvitz* Avi, ṣaddīq = 'wise' in biblical Hebrew and the wisdom connections of Ps 37: *a*) → 493*a*, IOSOT-B 1989/92, 109-112; – *b*) (fuller) ❸ → 181, Shaʿarei TALMON 1992, 131*-135*; Eng, xxii.

3257 *Hossfeld* Frank-Lothar, *Zenger* Erich, 'Selig, wer auf die Armen achtet' (Ps 41,2); Beobachtungen zur Gottesvolk-Theologie des ersten Davidpsalters: → 355, JbBT 7 (1992) 21-50.

3258 **Raabe** P. R., [Ps 42s; 46; 49; 56s; 59] Psalm structures: jOsu 104. Shf 1990, Academic. 240 p. £30; sb. £22.50. 1-85075-262-1. – ᴿBL (1992) 86 (R. J. *Coggins*: dubious).

3259 *Auffret* Pierre, 'Pourquoi dors-tu, Seigneur?' Étude structurelle du Psaume 44: JANES 21 (1992) 13-33.

3260 *Crow* Loren D., The rhetoric of Psalm 44: ZAW 104 (1992) 394-401.

3261 **Paulus** Beda, Paschasius RADBERTUS, Expositio in Ps XLIV: CCMed 94, 1991 → 7,2838: ᴿRBén 102 (1992) 378s (L. *Wankenne*).

3261* *Doignon* Jean, L'Incarnation; la vraie visée du Ps 44,8 sur l'onction du Christ chez HILAIRE de Poitiers: RTLv 23 (1992) 172-7; Eng. 295.

3262 *Hacker* Joseph R., ❸ 'If we have forgotten the name of our God' (Psalm 44:21); interpretation in the light of the realities in medieval Spain: Zion 57 (1992) 247-274; Eng. XIX-XX.

3263 *Wallis* Gerhard, A note on Ps 45,7a: ➤ 198, ᶠWOUDE A. van der, VTSupp 49 (1992) 100-3.

3264 *Monloubou* Louis, Les Psaumes poèmes de croyants; Ps 48: EsprVie 102 (1992) 319s.

3264* *Suda* Max Josef, [Ps 50,7G 33-mal zitiert] Psalm 51.7 als Belegstelle für AUGUSTINS Erbsündenlehre: ➤ 163, ᶠSAUER G., Aktualität 1992, 187-198.

3265 *Mosis* Rudolf, Die Mauern Jerusalems; Beobachtungen zu Ps 51,20f: ➤ 149, ᶠPREUSS H. 1992, 201-215.

3266 *Vermeylen* Jacques, Une prière pour le renouveau de Jérusalem; le psaume 51: ETL 68 (1992) 257-283.

3267 *Opitz* Peter, 'Asperges me Domine hyssopo, et mundabor'; Beobachtungen zu [J.] SADOLETS und CALVINS Exegese von Psalm 51 als Frage nach dem 'proprium' reformierter Schriftauslegung: ➤ 120, ᶠLOCKER G., Zwingliana 19,2 (1992) 297-313.

3268 ᴱ**Deun** Peter Van, MAXIMI Confessoris opuscula exegetica duo [... Ps 59] 1991 ➤ 7,2848*: ᴿJbÖsByz 42 (1992) 365-7 (H. *Hunger*); JTS 43 (1992) 269s (L. R. *Wickham*); TLZ 117 (1992) 198 (G. *Haendler*).

3269 *Weber* Beat, Ps 62,12-13; Kolometrie, Zahlenspruch und Gotteswort: BibNot 65 (1992) 44-46.

3270 *Bazaq* Yaaqov, ❺ Ps 67, *ereṣ nātenāh yᵉbūlāh*: BethM 37,131 (1991s) 326-338.

3271 **Beyerlin** Walter, Im Licht der Traditionen; Psalm lxvii und cxv, ein Entwicklungszusammenhang: VT supp 45. Leiden 1992, Brill. 152 p. ƒ100 [TR 88,338],

3272 *Wahl* Harald-Martin, Psalm 67; Erwägungen zu Aufbau, Gattung und Datierung: Biblica 73 (1992) 240-7.

3272* **Tillmann** Norbert, 'Das Wasser bis zum Hals!' Gestalt, Geschichte und Theologie des 69. Psalms: Münsteraner TAbh 20. Altenberge 1992, Oros. 345 p. DM 55 pa. 3-89375-066-5 [TLZ 118,737].

3273 *Jobling* David (guest editor), Deconstruction and the political analysis of biblical texts; a Jamesonian reading of Psalm 72 [JAMESON Fredric, The political unconscious; narrative as a socially symbolic act; Ithaca NY 1981, Cornell Univ.]: Semeia 59 (Ideological criticism of biblical texts 1992) 95-127; p. 227-237, recorded 1990 conversation with Jameson; p. 239-249, bibliog.

3274 *Nielsen* E., Ps 73 [in Danish exegesis 1900-1984]: ➤ 351c, ᴱ*Fatum* I. 1992.

3275 *Zenger* Erich, Psalm 73 als christlich-jüdisches Gebet: BiKi 47 (1992) 184-7.

3276 *Monloubou* Louis, Les Psaumes poèmes de croyants; Psaume 73/74: EsprVie 102 (1992) 104s, 620s.

3277 *Auffret* Pierre, La droite du Très-Haut; étude structurelle du Psaume 77: ScandJOT 6,1 (1992) 92-122.

3278 *Carroll* Robert P., Salmo 78 (77); vestigios de uma polémica tribal [< VT 21 (1971) 133-150],ᵀ: RBBras 8 (1991) 161-179.

3279 **Hiebert** Paula S., Psalm 78; its place in Israelite literature and history: diss. Harvard, ᴰ*Cross* F. CM 1992, 279 p. 92-25790. — DissA 53 (1992s) 1547-A; HarvTR 85 (1992) 497.

3280 *Lohfink* Norbert, Noch einmal *ḥōq ûmišpāṭ* (zu Ps 81,5f): Biblica 73 (1992) 253s.

3281 *Auffret* Pierre, Dieu juge; étude structurelle du Psaume 82: BibNot 58 (1991) 7-12.

3282 *Scholem* [Šalom] Avraham, Ps 86,2 ❺: BethM 37,129 (1991s) 181.

3283 *Caquot* André, Observations sur le Psaume 89: Semitica 41s (1991s) 133-158.

3284 *Glessmer* Uwe, Das Textwachstum von Ps 89 und ein Qumranfragment: BiNot 65 (1992) 55-73.

3285 *Floyd* Michael H., Psalm LXXXIX, a prophetic complaint about the fulfillment of an oracle: VT 42 (1992) 442-457.

3287 *Schmidt* Werner H., 'Der Du die Menschen lässest sterben'; exegetische Anmerkungen zu Ps 90: ➤ 197, ᶠWOLFF H. W., Wer ist? 1992, 115-130.

3288 *Davis* Ellen F., Psalm 98; rejoicing in judgment: Interpretation 46 (1992) 171-175.

3289 **Scoralick** Ruth, Trishagion... Ps 99: SBS 138, 1989 ➤ 5,3144...7,2861: ᴿBiblica 73 (1992) 577s (Bruna *Costacurta*); IndTSt 29 (1992) 376s (A. R. *Ceresko*); VT 42 (1992) 276 (H. G. M. *Williamson*).

3290 **Brüning** Christian, Mitten im Leben vom Tod umfangen; Ps 102 als Vergänglichkeitsklage und Vertrauenslied [Diss. Salzburg, ᴰ*Füglister* N. 1990 ➤ 6,3400]: BoBB 84. Fra 1992, Hain. iii-434 p. DM 98. 3-445-09147-1.

3291 *Chien* Philip, ☉ Psalm 104 and its contemporary meaning: ColcFuJen 93 (1992) 311-319.

3292 *Hoffman* Yair, ☉ Psalm 104; a literary examination: ➤ 181, Shaᶜarei TALMON 1992, 13*-24*; Eng. xv.

3293 *Howard* Virgil, Psalm 104: Interpretation 46 (1992) 176-180.

3294 *a) Johnson* Elliott E., Hermeneutical principles and the interpretation of Psalm 110; – *b) Bateman* Herbert W.ᴵⱽ, Psalm 110:1 and the New Testament: BtS 149 (1992) 428-437 / 438-453.

3295 *Burba* Klaus, Psalm 114; wir singen ihn täglich; ein Beitrag zu LUTHERS Gesangbuch: Luther 62 (1991) 12-20.

3296 *Prinsloo* W. S., Psalm 114; it is Yahweh who transforms the rock into a fountain: JNWS 18 (1992) 163-176.

3297 *Lifschitz* Barkiyyahu, ☉ Ps *qṭ'z* (116,14) *nōder*: BethM 37,129 (1991s) 146-9.

3297* *Elanskaya* A. I., A Fayumic text of Psalm 118, 50-52.62-67.74-77 (the Ms.I.1.b. 637 of the Pushkin Museum of Fine Arts): BSACopte 30 (1991) 25-28.

3298 **Milhau** Marc, HILAIRE Ps 118 II: SChr 347, 1988 ➤ 4,3309...7,2869: ᴿLatomus 51 (1992) 683s (J. *Oroz*).

3299 *Botha* P. J., The function of the polarity between the pious and the enemies in Psalm 119: OTEssays 5 (1992) 253-263.

3300 **Soll** Will, Psalm 119; matrix, form, and setting: CBQ Mg 23, 1991 ➤ 7,2870: ᴿBL (1992) 92 (J. H. *Eaton*: more admiring than DUHM); JStOT 55 (1992) 121 (P. R. *Davies*: calling Jehoiachin author is irrelevant); RB 99 (1992) 598 (R. J. *Tournay*); TLZ 117 (1992) 743-5 (P. D. *Miller*).

3301 ᴱ**Deurloo** K. A., *al.*, Voor de kinderen van Korach; dramatiek en liturgische gestalte van de Psalmen, 2. De liederen van opgang, de psalmen 120-134 / 3. De koning komt, de psalmen 90-100. Amst 1989/91, 129-xxxii p. / 124-xxxvi p. – ᴿDielB 27 (1991) 277s (B. J. *Diebner*).

3302 **Willis** John T., Psalm 121 as a wisdom poem: HebAnR 11 (1987) 435-451.

3303 *Prinsloo* G. T. M., Analysing Old Testament poetry; an experiment in methodology with reference to Psalm 126: OTEssays 5 (1992) 225-251,

3304 *Dobberahn* Friedrich E., [Ps 126,5] 'Los que siembran entre lágrimas cosecharán entre canciones'; al rescate de la memoria ambiental popular de la Mesopotamia antigua: RBiArg 54,45 (1992) 1-14.

3305 *Auffret* Pierre, YHWH est juste; étude structurelle du Ps 129: StEpL 7 (1990) 87-96.

3306 *Sedlmeier* Franz, 'Bei dir, da ist die Vergebung, damit du gefürchtet werdest'; Überlegungen zu Psalm 130:   Biblica 73 (1992) 473-495; franç. 495.

3307 *Laato* Antti, Psalm 132 and the development of the Jerusalemite/Israelite royal ideology: CBQ 54 (1992) 49-66.

3308 *Amir* Yehoyada, ❻ KROCHMAL and Psalm 137:   Tarbiz 61 (1991s) 527-544; Eng. VI.

3309 *Rendsburg* Gary A. & Susan L., Physiological and philological notes to Psalm 137: JQR 83 (1992s) 385-399.

3310 *Linafelt* Tod, Psalm 138; thanksgiving and the relentless imagination of Israel: Paradigms 8,1s (1992s) 1-9.

3311 *Holman* Jan, Psalm 139 (TM) and Psalm 138 (LXX), a semiotic comparison: ⮞ 493*a*, IOSOT-B 1989/92, 113-121.

3312 *Karasszon* Dezsö, Bemerkungen zu Psalm 146: ⮞ 493*a*, IOSOT-B 1989/92, 123-7.

3313 *Sedgwick* Colin J., The message of the Psalmists, 12. Praise the Lord! Pss 148-150: ExpTim 103 (1991s) 209s.

3314 *Mancini* Renata, Note sul Salmo 151 [G Lat Syr Qumran]: RSO 65 (1991) 125-9.

3315 *Eshel* E. al., Qumran Ps 154...: IsrEJ 42 (1992) 199-229.

E7.1 **Job, *Textus, commentarii.***

3316 ᴱ**Ahrend** Moshe M., Joseph KARA, Commentary on Job, based on manuscripts and first printings. J 1988, Mosad Kook. 193 p. ❻.

3317 **Bonora** Antonio, Giobbe, il tormento di credere; il problema e lo scandalo del dolore. Padova 1990, Gregoriana. 156 p. Lᵐ 16. – ᴿAsprenas 39 (1992) 437s (V. *Scippa*); HumBr 47 (1992) 758-760 (R. *Celada Ballanti*).

3318 **Bräumer** Hansjörg, Das Buch Hiob, erklärt: Studienbibel AT. Wu 1992, Brockhaus. I. (Kap. 1-19) 320 p. 3-417-25221-0.

3319 **Clines** David J.A., Job 1-20: Word comm. 17, 1989 ⮞ 5,3173 ... 7,2877: ᴿCBQ 54 (1992) 316-8 (D. *Penchansky:* encyclopedic, but untenably defends artistic unity of the whole); ChrSchR 22 (1992s) 334s (E.R. *Smick*); ConcordJ 18 (1992) 219s (C.W. *Mitchel:* little for the Christian; HABEL somewhat better); EvQ 64 (1992) 253-5 (D. *Schibler:* without peer); RefTR 49 (1990) 112s (W.J. *Dumbrell:* excellent; will challenge intrenched views); RestQ 34 (1992) 178s (R.R. *Marrs*); ScotJT 45 (1992) 419s (P. *Joyce*); Themelios 18,1 (1992s) 25s (E.B. *Smick;* valuable, but a commentary is not a group-discussion manual).

3320 *García* Crisógono, Fray Luis de LEÓN, obras (I-III] IV. El libro de Job: RelCu 37 (1991) [9-48.171-250.367-444] 603-626.

3321 **Good** Edwin M., In turns of tempest 1990 ⮞ 6,3432: ᴿBtS 149 (1992) 117s (R.B. *Zuck:* good except refers to 'the god'); CBQ 54 (1992) 524-6 (G. *Vall:* p.viii, 'I no longer answer when someone addresses me as a theologian'); CritRR 5 (1992) 135-7 (D. *Penchansky*); JTS 43 (1992) 151-3 (J.B. *Job:* several bees in his bonnet: *elohim* always 'god' with small g no more Jewish than Christian; G.M. HOPKINS is a hero of his; all in all bizarre in comparison with judicious CLINES); UnSemQ 45 (1991) 133-8 (Claudia V. *Camp*); ZAW 104 (1992) 149s (H.M. *Wahl*).

3322 ᵀᴱ**Goodman** L.E. SAADIA comm. Job. Theodicy 1988 ⮞ 5,3178 ... 7, 2879: ᴿSpeculum 67 (1992) 217-9 (M.A. *Signer*).

3323 **Gutiérrez** G., On Job 1987 ⮞ 3,3165 ... 6,3453: ᴿIndTSt 29 (1992) 223-233 (A.R. *Ceresko*).

3324 ᴱHagedorn U. & D., J. CHRYSOSTOMOS/Hiob 1990 ⇒ 6,3435a; 7,2881: ᴿAntonianum 67 (1992) 538s (M. *Nobile*); ClasR 42 (1992) 187s (W.H. C. *Frend*); JTS 43 (1992) 254s (L. R. *Wickham*).

3324* **Lobato Fernández** Juan Bautista, El libro de Job, comentario: MensajeAT 18. S 1992; Sígueme. 148 p. 84-301-1187-5.

3325 *Pace* Umberto, I LXX di Giobbe; metodologia della versione greca e possibilità di datazione attraverso l'analisi delle tecniche di traduzione: Acme 45 (1992) 5-24.

3326 *Richler* Benjamin, Ranneinu TAM's 'lost' commentary on Job: ⇒ 180c, Mem. TALMAGE F. 1 (1992s) 191-202.

3327 **Rodd** C.S., The book of Job: Epworth (Narrative) comm. 1990 ⇒ 6, 3438: ᴿCBQ 54 (1992) 540 (A.A. *Di Lella*: popularization at its best); CritRR 5 (1992) 164s (Jane A. *Morse:* many gems, but seems to be fighting its own conclusion); Interpretation 46 (1992) 410s (C. R. *Seitz*).

3328 *Schlafer* David J., The book of Job and the Tao Te Ching as antidotes to 'preachy' preaching: AnglTR 74 (1992) 370-5.

3329 ᴱSiniscalco Paolo, GREGORIO Magno Opere 1/1, Commento morale a Giobbe, ᵀ*Gandolfo* Emilio. R 1992, Città Nuova. 716 p. [Teresianum 44, 283, M. *Diego Sánchez*].

3330 *Ṣmuda* Joseph, ❿ 'Small *iyyub*' in the light of big 'Job': BethM 37,129 (1991s) 157-169.

3331 ᵀᴱSorlin H., Jean CHRYSOSTOME, commentaire sur Job: SChr 346.348, 1988 ⇒ 4,3337 ... 7,2885: ᴿJbÖsByz 42 (1992) 355-7 (W. *Lackner*); RechSR 80 (1992) 129s (B. *Sesboüé*, aussi sur HAGEDORN U. & D.).

3332 **Szpek** Heidi M., Translation technique in the Peshitta to Job; a model for evaluating a text with documentation from the Peshitta to Job [diss. Wisconsin, ᴰ*Fox* M. Madison 1991. 309 p. 92-09336. – DissA 53 (1992s) 845s-A]: SBL diss. 137. Atlanta 1992, Scholars. xv-329 p. $30; sb./pa. $20. 1-55540-761-7; –2-5.

3333 **Vogels** Walter, Job: Belichting 1989 ⇒ 6,3442: ᴿBijdragen 53 (1992) 205 (W.A.M. *Beuken*).

3334 **Wiersbe** Warren W., *a*) Be patient [Job]; – *b*) Be satisfied [Eces]. Wheaton IL 1991/0, Victor. 155 p., $8 / 136 p., $7. – ᴿBtS 149 (1992) 249 (R. B. *Zuck*).

E7.2 *Job: themata*, **Topics** ... *Versiculi*, **Verse-numbers.**

3335 *Alexander* Jon, Job considered as a conversion account: SpTod 42 (1990) 126-140.

3336 **[Amado] Lévy-Valensi** Éliane, Job; réponse à Jung: Parole présente. P 1991, Cerf. 347 p. F 175. 3-204-04345-1. – ᴿEsprVie 102 (1992) 93s (L. *Monloubou*); ÉTRel 67 (1992) 624 (F. *Guillaume*); LavalTP 48 (1992) 291-5 (R. *Valois*); PrOrChr 41 (1991) 182s (P. *Ternant*).

3337 *Barge* Laura, Job's Travail of creation in HOPKINS' poetry: Cithara 31, 1 (1991s) 36-45.

3337* *a*) *Ciccarese* Maria Pia, Una esegesi 'double face'; introduzione alla Expositio in Iob del presbitero Filippo [ms. sec. 16; < Origene]; – *b*) *Perani* Mauro, *Somekh* Albert, Frammenti ebraici di un commento medievale sconosciuto a Proverbi e Giobbe; – *c*) *Savigni* Raffaele, L'interpretazione dei libri sapienziali di RABANO Mauro; tradizione patristica e 'moderna tempora': ⇒ 458a, AnStoEseg 9,2 (1992) 483-492 / 589-608; Heb. 609s / 557-587; Eng. 343s.

3338 **Calati** Benedetto, *al.*,   Le provocazioni di Giobbe; una figura biblica nell'orizzonte letterario: Punti critici 1. Genova 1992, Marietti. 120 p. 88-211-9830-6. 8 altri art. (*Ravasi* G., *Quinzio* S. ...) present. *Salvarani* Brunetto.

3339 *Coggi* Roberto,   La prova morale dell'immortalità dell'anima nel commento di S. Tommaso al libro di Giobbe [= 7,2888*]: DivThom 95,1 (1992) 157-163.

3340 *Crenshaw* James L., Job, book of: ⇒ 741, AnchorBD 3 (1992) 858-868 (-9 targums, *Zuckerman* B.; –111 Testament of, *Spittler* Russell F.).

3341 **Dell** Katharine J.,   The book of Job as sceptical literature: BZAW 197, D1991 ⇒ 5,3190 ... 7,2893: RBL (1992) 86 (J. H. *Eaton*); ExpTim 103 (1991s) 215 (C. S. *Rodd*); JTS 43 (1992) 557-9 (J.C.L. *Gibson*); TLZ 117 (1992) 266s (W. *Herrmann*); VT 42 (1992) 415-420 (T.N.D. *Mettinger*); ZkT 114 (1992) 84s (J. M. *Oesch*).

3342 **Fuchs** Gisela,   Der Mythos vom Chaoskampf in der Hiobdichtung; Rezeption und Umdeutung einer altorientalischen Tradition: Diss. D*Schmidt* W. H. Bonn 1992. 320 p. – RTLv 24, p. 541.

3343 **Jong** A.T.M. de,   Weerklank van Job; over geloofstaal in bijbellessen [... met behulp van J. R. *Searle*]: kath. diss. Nijmegen, D*Ven* J. A. van der. Kampen 1990, Kok. 352 p. 90-242-6504-5. – TvT 31 (1991) 91.

3344 *Fuente* Alfonso de la, Job y el Siervo de Yahvé; dos interpretaciones del sufrimiento: ⇒ 551, RET 51 (1991) 237-251.

3345 **García-Moreno** Antonio, Sentido del dolor en Job 1990 ⇒ 7,2894: RETL 68 (1992) 424 (A. *Schoors*: not on Job but on Juan de Pineda); Salmanticensis 38 (1991) 370s (G. *Pérez*).

3346 *a) Gavaler* Campion P., The transformation of Job; – *b) Janecko* Benedict, The wisdom tradition and mid-life: BToday 30 (1992) 208-212 / 213-7.

3347 **Girard** René,   Job, idol en syndebok. Fredriksberg 1990, Anis. 184 p. Dk 188. – RNorTTs 92 (1991) 14 (A. *Kapelrud*).

3348 — *Hoerschelman* Paul-Gerhard, Das Ende der Gewalt; René GIRARDS Hiob [⇒ 7,2895]: LuthMon 31 (1992) 23-26 [< ZIT 92,15].

3349 **Gosling** Frank, The syntax of Hebrew poetry; an examination of the use of tenses in poetry, with reference to Job 3/1 - 42/6: diss. St. Andrews 1992. 536 p. – RTLv 24, p. 541: 'D*Coxow* P. N.'.

3350 *Gowan* Donald E., Reading Job as a 'wisdom script': JStOT 55 (1992) 85-96.

3351 *Greenberg* Moshe, ❾ Did Job really exist? An issue of medieval exegesis: ⇒ 181, Shaʿarei TALMON 1992, 3*-11*; Eng. xv.

3352 *Kutsch* Ernst, Hiob und seine Freunde; zu Problemen der Rahmenerzählung des Hiobbuches: ⇒ 163, FSAUER G., Aktualität 1992, 73-83.

3353 **Loades** A. L.,   Kant and Job's comforters 1985 ⇒ 4,k228*; 7,2901: RJAAR 60 (1992) 558-560 (R. *Meerbote*).

3354 **Martini** Carlo M., Avete perseverato con me nelle prove; riflessioni su Giobbe 1990 ⇒ 6,3458: RRivScR 5 (1991) 509s (S. *Ramirez*: anche su Martini, Davide).

3355 **Martini** Carlo M.,   Wer in der Prüfung bei mir bleibt; von Ijob zu Jesus 1991 ⇒ 7,2908: RTPhil 67 (1992) 317s (M. *Grenzer*); TPQ 140 (1992) 194s (J. *Hörmandinger*).

3356 **Moretto** G.,   Giustificazione e interrogazione; Giobbe nella filosofia: Filosofia e sapere storico. N 1991, Guida [FilT 7,391].

3357 *Müller* Hans-Peter, Theodizee? Anschlusserörterungen zum Buch Hiob: ZTK 89 (1992) 249-279.

3358 **Nash** Richard T., Job's misconception; a critical analysis of the problem of evil in the philosophical theology of Charles HARTSHORNE: diss. ᴰWillaert B. Leuven 1991. iv-211 p. – LvSt 17 (1992) 392s.

3359 **Penchansky** David, The betrayal of God; ideological conflict in Job: LitCu 1990 ➤ 6,3463; 7,2904: ᴿCBQ 54 (1992) 537s (A. A. Di Lella); CritRR 5 (1992) 157-160 (Jane A. Morse: this dissonantal reading might be beneficial).

3360 **Perdue** Leo G., Wisdom in revolt; metaphorical theology in the book of Job: JStOT supp 112, 1991 ➤ 7,2905: ᴿBL (1992) 109 (J. H. Heaton: gives 'book of Jacob' in title); CritRR 5 (1992) 160-2 (J. B. Burns: basis Job 3, 'destabilization of metaphor'); JTS 43 (1992) 807s (K. Aitken: closely argued but fresh and readable).

3361 Potter Harry, Rebel against the light; Job or God: ExpTim 103 (1991s) 198-201.

3362 **Reyburn** William D., A handbook on the book of Job: Helps for Translators. NY 1992, United Bible Societies. ix-806 p. $13. 0-8267-0117-5.

3363 **Safire** William, The first dissident; the Book of Job in today's politics. NY 1992, Random. xxix-304 p.; 16 pl. [Blake W.] . 0-679-41755-9.

3364 Sánchez B. Galo, Job o el sufrimiento abierto al misterio: TXav 41 (1991) 173-183.

3365 Schlobin Roger, Prototype horror; the genre of the book of Job: Semeia 60 (1992) 23-38.

3366 **Schultz** Karl A., Where is God when you need him? Sharing stories of suffering with Job and Jesus; from easy answers to hard questions. NY 1992, Alba. xix-184 p. $10 pa. 0-8189-0023-5 [TDig 39,383].

3367 Simundson Daniel J., Job and his ministers: ➤ 77, ᶠHARRISVILLE R. 1992, 33-41.

3368 Smith Gary V., Is there a place for Job's wisdom in OT theology? TrinJ 13 (1992) 3-20.

3369 **Turoldo** David M., ᴱLevi Abramo, La parabola di Giobbe: Quaderni di Ricerca. Mi 1992, CENS (Cooperativa Editrice Nuova Stampa). 347 p.

3370 **Wolde** E. van, Meneer en mevrouw Job; Job in gesprek met zijn vrouw, zijn vrienden en God. Baarn 1991, Ten Have. 166 p. ƒ27,50. 90-259-4486-X. – ᴿTvT 32 (1992) 413 (N. Tromp).

3371 ᴱ**Zuck** Roy B., Sitting with Job; selected studies on the book of Job [34-art. anthology]. GR 1992, Baker. 488 p. $23. 0-8010-9936-6 [TDig 39,385].

3372 **Zuckerman** Bruce, Job the silent 1991 ➤ 7,2917: ᴿBL (1992) 92 (D.J.A. Clines: 'counterpoint' to Y. PERETS' Yiddish Bontsye, stupid rather than pious); TS 53 (1992) 138s (F. L. Moriarty).

3373 Nielsen Kirsten, [Job 1s] Whatever became of you, Satan? or, A literary-critical analysis of the role of Satan in the book of Job: ➤ 493a, IOSOT-B 1989/92, 129-134.

3374 Chiolerio Marco, Giobbe invoca la morte; paura o desiderio? (Giobbe 3,3-26): Teresianum 43 (1992) 27-52.

3375 **Course** John E., Speech and response; a rhetorical analysis of the introductions to the speeches of the book of Job (chs. 4-24): diss. St. Michael's, ᴰSheppard G. Toronto 1990. iv-273 p. 0-315-60419-0. – OIAc 5,18.

3376 **Cotter** David W., A study of Job 4-5 in the light of contemporary literary theory [diss. R., Gregoriana 1989, ᴰCox D. SBL diss 124. Atlanta 1992, Scholars. xi-259 p. 1-55540-464-2; pa –5-0.

3377 *Brin* Gershon,   Job V 3 — textual test case; the translator's limits of consideration: VT 42 (1992) 391-3.

3378 **Funke-Reuter** Andreas,   Septuaginta-exegetische Studien am Beispiel von Hiob 9 und 10: Diss. Leipzig. 1992. vii-171 p. – TLZ 118,458.

3379 *Puhvel* Jaan, [Job 9,9; 36,18; Am 5,8] Names and numbers of the Pleiad; ➤ 118, ᶠLᴇsʟᴀᴜ W., Semitic 1991, 1243-7.

3380 *Sokolow* Moshe,   Taʿufâ ... The vicissitudes of Rᴀsʜɪ's commentary to Job 11:17:   JANES 18 (1986) 87-89.

3381 *Jacobs* Irving, [Job 13,15] The historical and ideological implications of Mishnah Sotah 5:5: JStJud 23 (1992) 227-243.

3381* **Gross** Carl,   Notes on the meaning of Job 16,20:   BTrans 43 (1992) 236-241.

3382 **Christo** Gordon E.,   The eschatological judgment in Job 19: 21-29; an exegetical study: diss. Andrews, ᴰ*Doukhan* J.   Berrien Springs 1992. 274 p. – AndrUnS 30 (1992) 157; DissA 53 (1992s) 1183-A.

3383 *Gasperini* Lidio, [Job 19,25s] Su un epitafio catinense con ripresa scritturistica: CivClasCr 13,1 (1992) 63-69; facsim.

3384 *Geyer* J. B.,   Mythological sequence in Job XXIV 19-20:   VT [39 (1989) 480-4, J. B. *Burns*] 42 (1992) 118-120.

3385 *Küchler* Max,   Gott und seine Weisheit in der Septuaginta (Ijob 28; Spr 8): ➤ 573, QDisp 138, 1991/2, 118-143.218-224.

3386 **Smith** William C.,   The function of chapters 29-31 in the Book of Job: diss. Southern Baptist Theol. Sem. 1992, ᴰ*Tate* M. 372 p. 92-23288. – DissA 53 (1992s) 845-A.

3387 *Dailey* Thomas F.,   'Wondrously far from me'; the wisdom of Job 32, 2-3:   BZ 36 (1992) 261-4.

3388 **Diewert** David A., [Job 32-37] The composition of the Elihu speeches; a poetic and structural analysis: diss. Toronto 1991. 639 p. DANN-66090. – DissA 53 (1992s) 528-A (no summary).

3389 **Mende** Theresia,   Durch Leiden zur Vollendung; die Elihureden im Buch Ijob (32-37) ᴰ1990 ➤ 7,2926:   ᴿCBQ 54 (1992) 755s (R. E. *Murphy:* leaves some questions); ZAW 104 (1992) 302 (M. *Witte*).

3390 *Wahl* Harald-Martin,   a) Seit wann gelten die Elihureden (Hi 32-37) als Einschub? Eine Bemerkung zur Forschungsgeschichte: BibNot 63 (1992) 58-61 [Eɪᴄʜʜᴏʀɴ, in seiner Einleitung erst ³1803, aber schon 1787 in Rezension von Mɪᴄʜᴀᴇʟɪs]. – b) Ein Beitrag zum alttestamentlichen Vergeltungsglauben am Beispiel von Hiob 32-37:   BZ 36 (1992) 250-5.

3391 *Crenshaw* James L.,   When form and content clash; the theology of Job 38:1-40:5 ➤ 346, Creation 1992, 70-84.

3392 *Cowe* S. Peter, [Job 37s] An Armenian Job fragment from Sinai and its implications: OrChr 76 (1992) 123-157.

3393 *Caquot* A.,   Le Léviathan de Job 40,25-41,26: RB 99 (1992) 40-69; Eng. 40.

3394 **Whitney** Kenneth W.ᴶ [➤ 9461],   Two strange beasts; a study of traditions concerning Leviathan and Behemoth in Second Temple and early rabbinic Judaism [4 Esra 6,47-52; 2 Apc. Baruch 29,4; 1 Enoch 60,7-9.24]: diss. Harvard. CM 1992. 293 p. 92-25791. – DissA 53 (1992s) 1550-A.

3395 *a)* *Gibson* J.C.L.,   A new look at Job 41,1-4 (English 41,9-12); – *b)* *Hunter* Alastair G.,   Could not the universe have come into existence 200 yards to the left? A thematic study of Job; – *c)* *Pyper* Hugh,   The reader in pain; Job as text and pretext: ➤ 41, ᶠDᴀᴠɪᴅsᴏɴ R., Text as pretext 1992, 129-139 / 140-159 / 234-255.

3396 *Shelley* John C.ᴶ.,   Job 42:1-6; God's bet and Job's repentance: RExp 89 (1992) 541-6 [461-475, *Tate* M., Job 1-2 ➤ 2273a].

3397 *a) Wagner* Siegfried, Theologischer Versuch über Ijob 42,7-9(10a); – *b) Seidel* Hans, Ijob, der Patron der Musiker: ⇥ 149, ᶠPREUSS H. 1992, 216-224 / 225-232.

E7.3 *Canticum Canticorum,* Song of Songs, Das Hohelied, *Textus, comm.*

3398 **Alonso Schökel** Luis, El cantar² 1990 ⇥ 6,3492:   ᴿActuBbg 29 (1992) 194 (J. *O'Callaghan).*
3399 *Andiñach* Pablo R., Midras Cantar de los Cantares Rabba [ᴱ*Girón Blanc* 1991]: RBibArg 54,47 (1992) 163-9.
3400 *Artola* Antonio M., El desposorio espiritual del alma consagrada con Cristo; lectura del Cantar de los Cantares desde las vivencias del alma consagrada. Deusto-Bilbao 1992, Pasionistas. 168 p. – ᴿTeresianum 43 (1992) 545 (B. *Goya).*
3401 ᵀᴱ**Bouchet** C., *Devailly* M., GRÉGOIRE de Nysse, Le Cantique des Cantiques: Les Pères dans la foi. P 1992. Migne. 332 p. F 150 [Études 378, 138, M. *Fédou].*
3402 ᴱ**Brésard** Luc, *Crouzel* Henri (*Borret* Marcel), ORIGÈNE, Commentaire sur le Cantique des Cantiques Is: SChr 375s. P 1991, Cerf. I. 471 p.; II. p. 487-820. F 256. 2-204-04397-4; –513-6. – ᴿEsprVie 102 (1992) 603 (Y.-M. *Duval);* EstE 67 (1992) 246 (C. *Granado);* ETL 68 (1992) 451s (A. de *Halleux);* JTS 43 (1992) 673-5 (R. E. *Heine,* 1); VigChr 46 (1992) 412-7 (J.C.M. van *Winden).*
3403 **Deckers-Dijs** Mimi, Hooglied: Belichting 1989 ⇥ 7,2938*a:* ᴿBijdragen 53 (1992) 427a (A. *Schoors,* also on NEGENMAN J., Prediker 1988).
3404 — *Bekkenkamp* J., Het Beste over het Hooglied? Mimi Deckers-Dijs' commentar onder de loep: Mara 3,4 (1990) 31-38; rejoinder 4,2 (1991) 45-47 [< GerefTTs 91,63.115].
3405 **Deckers-Dijs** M., [⇥ 7,2938*b]* Begeerte in Bijbelse liefdespoëzie, een semiotische analyse van het Hooglied [diss.]. Kampen 1991, Kok. 315 p. 90-242-3160-4. – TvT 32 (1992) 191s (E. van *Wolde).*
3406 ᴱ**Diebner** B. J., *Kasser* R., Hamburger Papyrus bil. 1 [Ct Lam Eces] 1989 ⇥ 5,1765; 7,1565:   ᴿLavalTP 48 (1992) 450-2 (P.-H. *Poirier).*
3407 ᵀᴱ**Falchini** Cecilia, GUGLIELMO di Saint-Thierry, Commento al Cantico dei Cantici 1991 ⇥ 7,2940:   ᴿAsprenas 39 (1992) 444s (L. *Fatica);* CC 143 (1992,4) 425s (A. *Orazzo).*
3408 **Falk** Marcia, Song of Songs 1990 ⇥ 6,3498*;* 7,2941:   ᴿNewTR 5,4 (1992) 79s (Dianne *Bergant).*
3409 ᴱ**Garbini** Giovanni, Cantico dei Cantici: BiblicaTS 2. Brescia 1992, Paideia. 358 p. 88-394-0480-5. – ᴿAntonianum 67 (1992) 534-6 (M. *Nobile:* non solo filológico; una visione del tutto).
3410 **Hamburger** Jeffrey F., The Rothschild Canticles; art and mysticism in Flanders and the Rhineland circa 1300: 1990 ⇥ 7,2944: ᴿJRel 72 (1992) 429-431 (M. *Camille);* Manuscripta 35 (1991) 233s (M. B. *McNamee).*
3411 ᴱ**Kamin** Sarah, *Saltman* Avrom, Secundum Salomonem, 13th c. commentary 1989 ⇥ 5,3243 ... 7,2946:   ᴿJEH 43 (1992) 471s (A. A. *Macintosh).*
3412 **König** Hildegard, APPONIUS, Die Auslegung zum Lied der Lieder; die einführenden Bücher 1-3 und das christologisch bedeutsame Buch 9: VLatGesch 21. FrB 1992, Herder. 112*-302 p. [RHE 87,199*] 3-451-21935-2.
3413 **Mulder** M. J., Hooglied, een praktische Bijbelverklaring. Kampen 1991, Kok. 77 p. ƒ18,50. – ᴿStreven 59 (1992) 1046 (P. *Beentjes).*

3414 **Murphy** Roland E.,   The Song of Songs ... Hermeneia comm. 1990
→ 7,2951:   ᴿCarmelus 39 (1992) 197s (K. *Waaijman*); CBQ 54 (1992)
758-761 (M. H. *Pope:* role of Murphy has been seminal in its history of
interpretation); Interpretation 46 (1992) 298-302 (also M. H. *Pope*); TS 53
(1992) 547s (W. J. *Fulco*).

3415 **Neri** U.,   El Cantar de los Cantares 1.   Bilbao 1988, D-Brouwer. –
ᴿCompostellanum 36 (1991) 237s (J. *Precedo Lafuente*).

3416 **Neusner** J.,   Song of Songs Rabbah 1-2, 1989 → 7,2952:   ᴿAbrNahr 30
(1992) 177-9 (L. F. *Girón-Blanc*).

3417 **Ravasi** Gianfranco,   Il Cantico dei Cantici; commento e attualizzazione:
Testi e Commenti 4.   Bo 1992, Dehoniane.   895 p. Lit. 80.000; pa. 60.000.
88-10-20552-9.

3418 ᴱ**Schulz-Flügel** Eva,   Canticum canticorum, 1. Einleitung: VLat 10/3,
Lfg. 1.   FrB 1992, Herder.   80 p.   3-451-00101-2 [BL 93,54, J. *Barr*].

3419 **Stadelmann** Luis,   Love and politics; a new commentary on the Song
of Songs.   NY 1992, Paulist.   x-243 p. $10.   0-8091-3290-7. – ᴿTBR 5,3
(1992s) 22 (R. *Coggins* is not convinced).

3421 ᵀᴱ**Vrégille** B. de, *Neyrand* L.,   APPONIUS, In Canticum Canticorum ex-
positio: CCL 19, 1988 → 2,2445 ... 6,3494*b*:   ᴿRechSR 80 (1992) 276-8
(Y.-M. *Duval:* très belle édition); RivStoLR 28 (1992) 168s (Maria Pia
Ciccarese).

3422 **Zakovitch** Yair, ⓗ *Shir ha-Shirim* ... The Song of Songs, introduction
and commentary: Mikra le-Yisrael. TA 1992, Am Oved. x-148 p. [OIAc
5,40].

E7.4   **Canticum**, *themata, versiculi.*

3423 *Andiñach* Paulo R.,   Crítica de Salomón en el Cantar de los Cantares:
RBiArg 53 (1991) 129-156.

3424 *Astell* Ann W.,   The Song of Songs in the Middle Ages 1990 → 6,3513:
ᴿSpeculum 67 (1992) 367-371 (L. *Besserman*, also on E. Ann MATTER),

3425 *Brenner* Athalya,   A note on Bat-Rabbîm (Song of Songs VII 5): VT 42
(1992) 113-5.

3426 *Calloud* Jean,   Esquisse; propositions pour une interprétation raisonnée
du Cantique des Cantiques: SémBib 65 (1992) 43-60.

3427 ᴱ**Ceresa-Gastaldo** A.,   Realtà e allegoria nell'interpretazione del Cantico:
D.AR.FI.CL.ET 12 [1988; Genova 1989 → 6,3522]: ᴿÉtClas 60 (1992) 75s (X.
Jacques).

3428 **Contreras Molina** F.,   Revelación de amor; a zaga del Cantar de los
Cantaresᵀ.   M 1991, PPC.   100 p. – ᴿRelCu 38 (1992) 126.

3429 *Elliott* M. Timothea sr.,   The literary unity of the Canticle ᴰ1989
→ 5,3259 ... 7,2959: ᴿÉglT 22 (1991) 211-3 (L. *Laberge*); Helmantica 42
sup (1991) 393s (S. *García-Jalón*).

3430 *Engammare* Max,   'Qu'il me baise des baisers de sa bouche'; interprétation et usage du Cantique des cantiques dans la première moitié du
XVIᵉ siècle: diss. Genève 1992. 750 p. – RTLv 24, p. 541.

3431 *Engammare* Max,   Der *sensus litteralis* des Hohen Liedes im Refor-
mationszeitalter; interessante Indizien am Rande der Exegese: ArRefG 83
(1992) 5-29; Eng. 30.

3432 *García* Crisógono,   Fray Luis de LEÓN, las Odas y el Cantar de los
Cantares: RelCu 38 (1992) 3-23.

3433 *Girón Blanc* L. F.,   *a)* Aproximación a la lengua de Šir ha-Širim Rabbâ y
modelo de edición; – *b)* Exégesis y homilética en Cantar de los Cantares

Rabba: Miscelánea de Estudios Árabes y Hebraicos 37s (1988s) 249-272
/ 40 (1991) 33-54 [< JStJud 24,362].
3434 *Hunt* Patrick N., Subtle paronomasia in the Canticum Canticorum;
hidden treasures of the superlative poet: ➤ 493*a*, IOSOT-B 1989/92,
147-154.
3435 *Keel* O., Hoheslied: ➤ 762, NBL II, 7 (1992) 183-192.
3436 *McGinn* Bernard, With 'the kisses of the mouth'; recent works on the
Song of Songs [MURPHY R., MATTER E., ASTELL A. ...]: JRel 72 (1992)
269-275.
3437 *Marcus* Ivan G., The Song of Songs in German Ḥasidism and the
school of RASHI; a preliminary comparison: ➤ 180*c*, Mem. TALMAGE F. 1
(1992s) 181-9.
3438 **Matter** E. Ann, The voice of my beloved 1990 ➤ 6,3528; 7,2963: ᴿJEH
43 (1992) 337s (P. *Cramer:* 'too little about BERNARD, and if we are to
have BAKHTINE, too little about Bakhtine'); RBén 102 (1992) 243s (L.
Wankenne).
3439 **Pelletier** A.-M., Lectures du Cantique: AnBib 121, 1989 ➤ 5,3264 ...
7,2964: ᴿTeresianum 43 (1992) 525s (M. *Diego Sánchez*); VigChr 46
(1992) 422-7 (A. *Bastiaensen*).
Stubenrauch Bertram, Der heilige Geist bei APPONIUS; zum theologischen
Gehalt einer spätantiken Hoheliedauslegung 1991 ➤ 7610.
3440 ᴱ**Verduin** M., UDEMANS Godefridus Cornelisz c. 1581-1649, Canticum
Canticorum, Het Lied der Liederen; een onderzoek naar de betekenis, de
functie en de invloed van de bronnen van de Kanttekeningen bij het
Hooglied in de Statenbijbel van 1637 [diss. ᴰ*Graafland* C.], Utrecht 1992,
De Banier. 841 p.; portr. – TvT 33,85; RTLv 24, p. 559. 90-336-0313-6.
3441 **Wade** Theodore E.ᴶ, The Song of Songs; tracing the story of the Church.
Auburn CA 1992, Gazelle. 64 p. $6. 0-930192-27-3. – ᴿTBR 5,3 (1992s)
22 (M. *Boda*).
3442 *Webb* Barry, The Song of Songs; a love poem and as Holy Scritpture:
RefTR 49 (1990) 91-99.
3443 **Yannaras** Christos, Variazioni sul Cantico dei Cantici: Quaderni di Ricerca. Mi 1992, CE Nuova Stampa. 131 p.

––––––––––

3444 *Maier* Johann, Io sono nera e/ma graziosa; Ct 1,5-6 nella antica tradizione giudaica, ᵀ*Gentile* Carlo: ➤ 457*, Letture Sap 1991/2, 305-348.
3445 *Lombard* Denis, Le Cantique des Cantiques (3,6-5,1): SémBib 66 (1992)
45-52.
3446 *Garbini* Giovanni. Turris Davidica (Cantico 4,4) [originally a reference
to the Pharos of Alexandria, changed 100 A.D. to make the poem acceptable for the canon]: ParPass 45 (1990) 188-191 [< JStJud 23,329].
3447 *Girón* Luis F., Cantar de los Cantares Rabbá 4,7-8; edición crítica:
➤ 44, ᴱDÍAZ ESTEBAN F., Sefarad 52 (1992) 103-112.
3448 *Landy* Francis, [Ct 4,8] In defense of JAKOBSON: JBL [109 (1990) 385-
401, *Zevit* Z.] 111 (1992) 105-113.
3449 *Mulder* Martin J., Does Canticles 6,12 make sense?: ➤ 198, ᶠWOUDE
A. van der, VTS 49 (1992) 104-113.

E7.5 *Libri sapientiales* – **Wisdom literature.**

3450 *Alster* Bendt, Early Dynastic proverbs and other contribution to the
study of literary texts from Abū Ṣalābīkh: AfO 38s (1991s) 1-51; 8 fig.

3451 **Berger** Klaus,   Die Weisheitsschrift aus der Kairoer Geniza 1989
→ 6,3546a; 7,2973:   ᴿBijdragen 53 (1992) 430 (P. C. *Beentjes*); StPhilonAn
4 (1992) 141-4 (M. *Küchler* compares RÜGER).

3452 **Berndt** Rainer, ANDREAE de Sancto Victore,   Expositiones historicae in
libros Salomonis: Opera 3, CCMed 53B, 1991 → 7,2976; auch Hab.-Diss.
St. Georgen, ᴰ*Lohr* (TR 89,75): ᴿRHE 87 (1992) 463-5 (D. *Poirel*).

3453 a) *Bjornard* Reidar B., Aging according to the wisdom literature; – b)
Perelmuter Hayim G., The strength of the elders: BToday 30 (1992)
330-4 / 347-352.

3454 *Blumenthal* Elke,   Zur Wiederherstellung zweier ägyptischer Weisheitslehren [HELCK W. 1984]: OLZ 87 (1992) 229-238.

3455 **Brunner** Hellmut,   Die Weisheitsbücher der Ägypter; Lehren für das
Leben [= ²Altäg. Weisheit 1988]. Z 1991, Artemis.   528 p.   3-7608-
1062-4. – ᴿDiscEg 19 (1991) 99-102 (R. B. *Parkinson*).

3456 **Cimosa** Mario, Temi di Sapienza biblica: Piccola BtT 8,   1989 → 6,3277;
7,2979: – ᴿParVi 37 (1992) 149-151 (G. *Boggio:* una Introduzione, anche
ai Salmi).

3457 *Cimosa* Mario, L'umanesimo dell'amore nei Sapienziali: ParVi 37 (1992)
86-93.

3458 **Clements** R F.,   Wisdom for a changing world; wisdom in OT theology
(Bailey Lectures 2). 1990 → 6,3548; 7,2980: ᴿCBQ 54 (1992) 319s (Camilla
Burns); Interpretation 46 (1992) 88.90 (Mary C., *Berglund*).

3459 **Clements** Ronald E.,   Wisdom in theology [1989 Didsbury lectures + 2
art.]. Carlisle UK / GR 1992, Paternoster / Eerdmans. 188 p. $17. 0-8028-
0576-0 [TDig 40,353].

3460 **Davidson** Robert,   Wisdom and worship   1990 → 6,3550; 7,2981: ᴿCBQ
54 (1992) 742s (R. J. *Clifford:* judicious); CritRR 5 (1992) 126s (R. C. *Van
Leeuwen*).

3461 *Delkurt* Holger, Grundprobleme alttestamentlicher Weisheit: VerkF 36,
1 (1991) 38-71: 50 Bücher; Register S. 107.

3462 **Denning-Bolle** Sara,   Wisdom in Akkadian literature; expression, instruction, dialogue: MedEOL 28. Leiden 1992, Ex Oriente Lux. xiii-199 p.
*f*45.   90-72690-04-4 [OIAc 5,18].

3463 *Dietrich* Manfried, 'Ein Leben ohne Freude...'; Studie über eine Weis-
heitskomposition aus den Gelehrtenbibliotheken von Emar und Ugarit:
UF 24 (1992) 9-29.

3464 *Dietrich* M., *Loretz* O., Die Weisheit des ugaritischen Gottes El im
Kontext der altorientalischen Weisheit: UF 24 (1992) 31-38.

3465 **Eaton** John,   The contemplative face of OT wisdom in the context of
world religions 1989 → 6,3350*; 7,2984:   ᴿCBQ 54 (1992) 319s (Camilla
Burns).

3466 ᴱ**Eynikel** E.,   Wie wijsheid zoekt, vindt het leven; de Wijsheidsliteratuur
van het OT [colleges UTP Heerlen]. Lv/Boxtel 1991, Acco/KBS.   165 p.
*f*28,75.   90-334-2603-X. – ᴿTvT 32 (1992) 309 (N. *Tromp*).

3467 ᴱ**Gammie** J. G., *Perdue* L. G., The sage 1990 → 6,336: ᴿBtS 149 (1992)
120 (R. B. *Zuck*).

3468 **Goedicke** Hans,   Wisdom of Any VII, 12-27: RÉgp 43 (1992) 75-85:
Maxims 26 & 27 make one unit on theological ideals.

3469 *Irmscher* Johannes,   La fortuna dei libri sapienziali dell'AT a Bisanzio:
→ 457*, Letture Sap 1991/2, 55-63 [–85, al., monachesimo].

3470 **Jasnow** Richard,   A late period hieratic wisdom text (P. Brooklyn 47.
218.135 [< diss. Chicago 1988]: SAOC 52. Ch 1992, Univ. Or.Inst.
xviii-219 p.; 20 fig. 0-918986-85-0 [OIAc 3,25].

3471 a) *Kieweler* Hans V.,   Prophetie und Weisheit; – b) *Micskey* [p. 241 &
   372; Misckey p. 15] Koloman, Hoffnung und Weisheit: ➤ 163, ᶠSAUER
   G., Aktualität 1992, 47-55 / 241-8.

3472 **Kottsieper** Ingo,   Die Sprache der Aḥiqarsprüche: BZAW 194, ᴰ1990
   ➤ 6,3563; 7,2991:   ᴿBL (1992) 136 (R. P. *Gordon*).
   Lips Hermann von,   Weisheitliche Traditionen im NT 1990 ➤ 4152.

3473 **Lux** Rüdiger,   Die Weisen Israels; Meister der Sprache, Lehrer des
   Volkes, Quelle des Lebens. Lp 1992, Ev.-VA. 179 p.; ill. DM 22,80.
   3-374-01407-0 [TLZ 118,824, H.-D. *Preuss*].

3474 *Mack* Burton L.,   The Christ and Jewish wisdom: ➤ 463, Messiah
   1987/92, 192-221.

3475 **Maire** Thierry,   Ainsi parle la sagesse; microstructure et macrostructure
   des enseignements dans le Proche-Orient ancien. Chevroux 1992, auct.
   317 p., spiral-bound.

3476 **Matthews** Caitlin,   Sophia, goddess of wisdom; the divine feminine from
   black goddess to world soul. L 1991, Mandala. viii-387 p. £8. 0-04-
   440590-1 [TBR 6/3,85, Una *Kroll*].
   Momigliano Arnaldo,   Alien wisdom; the limits of Hellenization 1990
   ➤ 3102*.

3477 **Murphy** R. E.   The tree of life 1990 ➤ 6,3567; 7,2997: ᴿBtS 149 (1992)
   118s (R. B. *Zuck*); CritRR 5 (1992) 150-3 (L. G. *Perdue:* more judicious
   than recent approaches); Interpretation 46 (1992) 183s (D. *Bland*); TS 53
   (1992) 382 (F. L. *Moriarty*).

3478 *Murphy* Roland E.,   Wisdom in the OT: ➤ 741, AnchorBD 6 (1992)
   920-931 (–45, of Ben Sira, *Di Lella* A.).

3479 a) *Murphy* Roland E.,   Images of Yahweh; God in the Writings; – b)
   Goldingay John,   Images of Israel; the People of God in the Writings; – c)
   Johnston Robert K.,   Images for today; learning from OT wisdom: ➤ 88,
   ᶠHUBBARD D., OT 1992, 189-204 / 205-221 / 223-239.

3480 **Rüger** Hans P.,   Die Weisheitsschrift der Kairoer Geniza ...: WUNT 53,
   1991 ➤ 7,3002:   ᴿJBL 111 (1992) 705-7 (J. J. *Collins*); Judaica 48 (1992)
   51s (S. *Schreiner*).

3481 **Sandelin** K.-G.,   Wisdom as nourisher 1986 ➤ 2,2488* ... 6,3570: ᴿRÉJ
   151 (1992) 399-401 (A. *Sérandoun*).

3482 **Synowiec** Juliusz S., ℗ Mędrcy Izraela [Les sages d'Israël], ich pisma i
   nauka. Kraków 1990, Franciszkanów. 286 p. – ᴿColcT 62,4 (1992)
   178-180 (J. *Warzecha* ℗).

3483 a) *Thompson* Henry O.,   Biblical wisdom [title differently p. iii]; – b)
   James Theodore,   Wisdom, faith and reason; – c) *Öztürk* Yasar N.,   The
   wisdom of Islam in Sufism: ➤ 127, ᶠMATCZAK S.,   Wisdom of faith 1989,
   101-127 / 63-79 / 79-90.

3484 a) *Tuilier* André,   Les livres sapientiaux et le canon de l'AT dans l'Église
   ancienne; – b) *García Bazán* Francisco,   El uso de los libros sapienciales
   en el Códice de Jung (CNH 1); – c) *Malachi* Zvi,   The influence of
   biblical wisdom literature on the writings of Nag Ḥammadi's Gnostics:
   ➤ 457*, Letture Sap. 1991/2, 19-34 / 35-48 / 49-54.

3485 *Vanstiphout* H.L.J.,   The Mesopotamian debate poems 2: AcSum 14
   (1992) 339-367.

3486 *Veltri* Giuseppe,   Mittelalterliche Nachahmung weisheitlicher Texte; Da-
   ticrung und Herkunft der sog. 'Weisheitsschrift aus der Kairoer Geniza':
   TRu 57 (1992) 405-430.

3487 **Weeks** S.D.E., The nature and influence of early Israelite wisdom: diss. Oxford 1991. – RTLv 24, p. 543.

E7.6   **Proverbiorum liber,** *themata, versiculi.*

3488 **Alonso Schökel** Luis, *Vilchez Lindez* José, I proverbi 1988 → 4,3475: ᴿParVi 35 (1990) 222s (M. *Cimosa*).

3489 **Bonora** Antonio, Proverbi Sapienza: LoB 1.14, 1990 → 7,3007: ᴿCC 143 (1992,1) 309 (G.L. *Prato*); ParVi 36 (1991) 230s (G. *Torta*); Riv-PastLtg 29,2 (1991) 83s (L. *Della Torre*).

3490 **Farmer** Kathleen H., Who knows what is good? Pv Eces 1991 → 7,3009: ᴿBibTB 22 (1992) 180s (Betty Jane *Lillie*); BL (1992) 70 (R.B. *Salters*); BtS 149 (1992) 119s (R.B. *Zuck*); CBQ 54 (1992) 745s (L.F. *Asma*); HorBT 14 (1992) 85s (Kathleen M. *O'Connor*); RB 99 (1992) 599 (R.J. *Tournay*); Vidyajyoti 56 (1992) 375-7 (R.H. *Lesser*).

3491 ᵀᴱ**Géhin** Paul, ÉVAGRE, Scholies aux Proverbes: SChr 340, 1987 → 3,3254 ... 7,3010: ᴿJbAC 34 (1991) 176s (W.A. *Bienert*).

3492 **Goldberg** Louis, Savoring the wisdom of Proverbs. Ch 1990, Moody. 218 p. $9 pa. – ᴿBtS 149 (1992) 377s (R.B. *Zuck*).

3493 **Hubbard** David A., Proverbs: Communicator's comm. 154, 1989 → 5, 3312; 7,3012: ᴿBtS 149 (1992) 248s (R.B. *Zuck*); CBQ 54 (1992) 112s (L. *Boadt*: full information).

3494 ᴱ**Isoz** C. Claire, Sanson de Nanteuil, Les proverbes de Salemon 1-2: Anglo-N 44s. L 1988, Anglo-Norman Text Soc. vii-183 p., front.; 175 p.: ᴿSpeculum 67 (1992) 1039s (Mary B. *Speer*: 3d volume eagerly awaited).

3495 **Meinhold** Arndt, Die Sprüche 1991 → 7,3014: ᴿBL (1992) 53 (W. *McKane*).

3496 **Michaud** Robert, Proverbi e Giobbe, storia e teologia: Parole di vita 1990 → 7,3015: ᴿRivScR 5 (1991) 495s (P. *Fragnelli*).

3497 **Morla Asensio** Víctor. Proverbios: El Mensaje del AT 19. Estella 1992, VDivino. 209 p.

3498 **Plöger** O., Sprüche 1984 → 1,3344; 2,2505. ᴿTsTKi 62 (1991) 67 (M. *Sæbø*).

3499 **Schneider** Théo R., The sharpening of wisdom; OT Proverbs in translation: OTEssays supp. 1. Pretoria 1992, OTSSA (OT Soc. SAfr.) xvii-260 p. 0-86981-784-1.

3500 **Boström** Lennart, The God of the Sages ... Prov: ConBib OT 29, 1990 → 6,3578; 7,3017: ᴿCBQ 54 (1992) 313s (J.A *Gladson*); CritRR 5 (1992) 115s (D.C. *Snell*); Interpretation 46 (1992) 194 (D.F. *Morgan*); JRel 72 (1992) 580s (W.L. *Humphreys*); NedTTs 46 (1992) 159s (L.A. *Snijders*); SvEx 57 (1992) 115-7 (J. *Bergman*); TsTKi 62 (1991) 159s (Terje *Stordalen*).

3501 **Delkurt** Holger, Ethische Einsichten in der alttestamentlichen Spruchweisheit: Diss. ᴰ*Schmidt* W. Bonn 1992. 176 p. – RTLv 24, p. 541; TR 89,78.

3502 *a)* **Frickel** Josef, Zu HIPPOLYTS Kommentar zu den Proverbia; – *b)* **Hamblenne** Pierre, Sapientia salomonienne et virtus romaine; convergences et écarts entre les Prouerbes (X-XXIX) et les Sententiae di PUBLILIUS Syrus; – *c)* **Prinzivalli** Emanuela, L'uso dei Proverbi nella cultura

asiatica da Giustino a Metodio di Olimpo: ➤ 457*, Letture Sap 1991/2, 179-185 / 145-164 / 165-177.
3503 *Giese* Ronald L.ᴶ, Qualifying wealth in the Septuagint of Proverbs: JBL 111 (1992) 409-425.
3504 *Grieshammer* Reinhardt, Zum Gebrauch griechischer Wörter in koptischen Übersetzungen der Proverbia Salomonis: DielB 27 (1991) 58-72.
3505 *Heintz* Jean-Georges, La Sagesse égyptienne d'Aménemopé et le livre biblique des Proverbes, vus par l'égyptologue Eugène DRIOTON: Ktema 14 (1989) 19-29.
3506 **Sailler** Ronald M., *Wyrtzen* David, The practice of wisdom; a topical guide to Proverbs. Ch 1992, Moody. 171 p. $16 [BtS 150, 372, R.B. *Zuck*: relevance for today]. 0-8024-6896-9.
3507 **Steiert** Franz-Josef, Die Weisheit Israels — ein Fremdkörper im AT? Eine Untersuchung zum Buch der Sprüche auf dem Hintergrund der ägyptischen Weisheitslehren [Diss. Fr 1988]: FreibTSt 143, 1990 ➤ 6,3573; 7,3019: ᴿBZ 36 (1992) 318s (Jutta *Hausmann*); JBL 111 (1992) 134-7 (M. V. *Fox*); TvT 32 (1992) 91 (N. *Tromp*: Spr 10-29).
3508 ᵀᴱVisotzky Burton L., The midrash on Proverbs: Yale Judaica 27. NHv 1992, Yale Univ. 169 p. $28.50. 0-300-05107-7 [TDig 39,373]. – ᴿRelStR 18 (1992) 344 (J. T. *Townsend*).
3509 **Washington** Harold C., Wealth and poverty in the 'Instruction of Amenemope' and the Hebrew Proverbs; a comparative study in the social location and function of Ancient Near Eastern wisdom literature: diss. Princeton Theol. Sem., ᴰ*Seow* C. 1992. viii-344 p. 92-29028. – OIAc 5,39; DissA 53 (1992s) 1549-A.
3510 **Wehrle** Josef, Sprichwort und Weisheit; Studien zur Syntax und Semantik der *tob* ... *min-* Sprüche im Buch der Spruchwörter: kath. Hab.-Diss. München, ᴰ*Görg* M. 1992. - TR 89,76.
3511 **Whybray** R. N., Wealth and poverty in Prov 1990 ➤ 6,3591; 7,3021: ᴿCritRR 5 (1992) 126-8 (R. C. *Van Leeuwen*: valuable, but with unresolved criteria); ETL 68 (1992) 424s (W. A. M. *Beuken*); ÉTRel 67 (1992) 97s (D. *Lys*); RestQ 34 (1992) 245s (1992) 245s (M. S. *Moore*); VT 42 (1992) 571s (Katharine J. *Dell*).

3512 *Gilbert* Maurice, Le discours menaçant de Sagesse en Proverbes 1,20-33: ➤ 7,141, ᶠSOGGIN J. A., Storia 1991, 99-119.
3513 *a*) *Michel* Diethelm, Proverbia 2 — ein Dokument der Geschichte der Weisheit; – *b*) *Meinhold* Arndt, Der Umgang mit dem Feind nach Spr 25,21f; – *c*) *Gunneweg* Antonius H. J. †, Weisheit, Prophetie und Kanonsformel; Erwägungen zu Proverbia 30,1-9; – *d*) *Hausmann* Jutta, Beobachtungen zu Spr 31,10-31: ➤ 149, ᶠPREUSS H. 1992, 233-243 / 244-252 / 253-260 / 261-6.
3514 *McLain* Charles E., [Prov 2,16-19...] The sage and the seductress, I. A background study; II. an exegetical study: CalvaryB 8,1 (1992) 1-23; 8/2,1-39.
3515 *Giese* Ronald L.ᴶ, Strength through wisdom and the bee in LXX-Prov 6,8ᵃ⁻ᶜ: Biblica 73 (1992) 404-411.
3516 *Yee* Gale A., The theology of creation in Proverbs 8:22-31: ➤ 346, Creation 1992, 85-96.
3517 *Doignon* Jean, HILAIRE de Poitiers commentateur de Proverbes 8,26-30: ➤ 457*, Letture Sap. 1991/2, 201-7.

3518 **Panikkar** Raimon, [Prov 9,9] A dwelling-place for wisdom, ᵀ*Kidder* Annemarie S. Louisville c. 1992, W-Knox. vi-179 p. $13. 0-664-25362-4 [TBR 6/3,85, J. *Katz*].

3519 **Westermann** Claus, [Prov 10-20; 25-29] *a*) Forschungsgeschichte 1991 ➤ 7,3028: ᴿZAW 104 (1992) 315 (O. *Kaiser*). – *b*) Wurzeln der Weisheit 1990 ➤ 6,3597; 7,3029: ᴿÉglT 23 (1992) 127s (W. *Vogels*); JBL 111 (1992) 529-531 (M. V. *Fox:* a strong book with some weak theses).

3520 *a*) *Whybray* R. N., Thoughts on the composition of Proverbs 10-29; – *b*) *Crenshaw* James L., Prohibitions in Proverbs and Qoheleth: ➤ 19a; ᶠBLENKINSOPP J., Priests 1992, 102-114 / 115-124.

3521 **Parker** Don, Syntactic and poetic structures in Proverbs 10:1-23:16: diss. UCLA, ᴰ*Segert* S. 1992. 464 p. 93-10883. – DissA 53 (1992s) 4360-A.

3522 *Hildebrandt* Ted, Motivation and antithetic parallelism in Proverbs 10-15: JEvTS 35 (1992) 433-444.

3523 **Hausmann** Jutta, Studien zum Menschenbild der älteren Weisheit (Spr 10ff): ev. Hab.-Diss. ᴰ*Preuss*. Neuendettelsau 1992. – TR 89,76.

3524 *Ninow* Friedbert, Von gestohlenem Brot und Kieselsteinen; einige Über-legungen zu Spr 20,17: BibNot 63 (1992) 44-46.

3525 **Römheld** Diethard, Wege ... Pv 22-24: BZAW 184, ᴰ1989 ➤ 6,3600*; 7,3034: ᴿBZ 36 (1992) (J. *Scharbert*); NedTTs 46 (1992) 54s (L. A. *Snijders*); ZkT 114 (1992) 89s (J. M. *Oesch*).

3526 *a*) *Sitompul* Adelbert A., Urbilder von Glück und Segen (Spr 22,4); Versuch einer ethnologischen Annäherung; – *b*) *Westermann* Claus, Das gute Wort in den Sprüchen; ein Beitrag zum Menschenverständnis der Spruchweisheit: ➤ 197, ᶠWOLFF H. W., Wer? 1992, 78-93 / 243-255.

3527 **Nzambi** Philippe Dinzolele, Proverbes bibliques et proverbes kongo; étude comparative de Proverbia 25-29 et de quelques proverbes kongo: Religionswissenschaft 5. Fra 1992, Lang. 767 p. 3-631-44827-9.

3528 **Van Leeuwen** R. C., Context and meaning ... Prov 25-27, ᴰ1988 ➤ 4, 3905 ... 6,3602: ᴿJSS 37 (1992) 316-9 (W. *McKane*).

3529 *Gottlieb* Claire, The words of the exceedingly wise; Proverbs 30-31: ➤ 7,334*, Canon 1990/1, 277-298.

3530 *Cavalcanti* Elena, L'aquila, il serpente, la nave, il giovane; l'interpre-tazione tipologica di Prov 30:18-20: 457*, Letture Sap. 1991/2, 187-200.

3531 **(Levine) Katz** Yael, *Midreshei Eshet Ḥayil*; a study of the smaller Midrashim on 'A woman of valor' (Proverbs 31:10-31): diss. Bar-Ilan, ᴰ*Tabori* J. Ramat-Gan 1992. 433 p. – RTLv 24, p. 544.

3532 *Magazzù* Cesare, L'elogio della 'donna forte' (Prov. 31,10-31) nell'in-terpretazione patristica: ➤ 457*, Letture Sap 1991/2, 213-224.

3533 *Waegeman* Maryse, The perfect wife of Proverbia 31,10-31: ➤ 493*a*, IOSOT-B 1989/92, 101-7.

E7.7 *Ecclesiastes* – **Qohelet,** *themata, versiculi.*

3534 **Bonora** A., Qohelet, la gioia e la fatica di vivere: LoB 1.15, 1987 ➤ 3,3281; 6,3605: ᴿParVi 35 (1990) 391-3 (M. *Milani*).

3535 **Bonora** Antonio, Il libro di Qoèlet: Guide Spirituali all'Antico Testa-mento. R 1992, Città Nuova. 175 p. 88-311-3733-6.

3537 **Hubbard** D. A., Ecclesiastes, Song of Songs: Communicator's Comm. Dallas 1991, Word. 351 p. $20. – ᴿBtS 149 (1992) 378 (T. L. *Constable*).

3538 **Jarick** John, GREGORY Thaumaturgos' paraphrase of Ecclesiastes ᴰ1990 ➤ 6,3624; 7,3048: ᴿJTS 43 (1992) 241-3 (K. W. *Noakes*); TLZ 117 (1992) 193s (H. G. *Thümmel*).

3539 ᴱLabate A., Catena Hauniensis [... DIONYSII Alexandrini] in Ecclesiasten: CCG 24. Turnhout 1992, Brepols. xl-302 p. Fb 5300. – ᴿNRT 114 (1992) 763s (A. *Harvengt*).

3540 — *Labate* Antonio, Il recupero del 'Commentario all'Ecclesiaste' di DIONIGI Alessandrino attraverso le catene bizantine: Koinonia 16,1 (1992) 53-74.

3541 *Manns* Frédéric, Le Targum de Qohelet – Manuscrit Urbinati I, traduction et commentaire: LA 42 (1992) 145-198.

3542 **Murphy** Roland E., Ecclesiastes: Word comm. 23A. Dallas 1992, Word. lxxxiv-170 p. $25. 0-8499-0222-3 [TDig 40,281].

3543 **Ravasi** G., Qohelet 1988 ➤ 4,3531 ... 6,3638: ᴿParVi 36 (1991) 231s (M. *Cimosa*).

3544 **Sánchez** (Manuel) Diego, El comentario al Eclesiastés de DÍDIMO Alejandrino; exégesis y espiritualidad [diss. 1989 R, Inst. Patr. Aug.] R 1991, Teresianum. 308 p. – ᴿRelCu 37 (1991) 741s (P. *Langa*).

3545 **Tidball** Derek, That's life! Realism and hope for today from Ecclesiastes. Leicester 1989, Inter-Varsity. 191 p. £4 pa. 0-85110-778-8. – ᴿEvangel 10,2 (1992) 29s (C. M. *Cameron*, disappointed); – ScripTPamp 24 (1992) 1091s (A. *Viciano*).

3546 **Whybray** R. N., Ecclesiastes 1989 ➤ 6,3645: ᴿRefTR 49 (1990) 107s (W. J. *Dumbrell*).

3547 *a*) *Carny* Pin'has, Theodicy in the Book of Qohelet; – *b*) *Amir* Yehoshua, Measure for measure in talmudic literature – and in the Wisdom of Solomon: ➤ 499, Justice 1990/2, 71-81 / 29-46.

3548 **Ellul** J., Reason for being; a meditation on Ecclesiastes [La raison d'être],ᵀ. GR 1990, Eerdmans. 306 p. $19. – ᴿOTEssays 5 (1992) 301-4 (J. A. *Loader*, Afrikaans).

3549 *Gianto* Agustinus, The theme of enjoyment in Qohelet [< IOSOT 1992]: Biblica 73 (1992) 328-332.

3550 *Jong* Stephan de, A book on labour; the structuring principles and the main theme of the Book of Qohelet: JStOT 54 (1992) 107-116.

3551 *Klopfenstein* Martin A., Kohelet und die Freude an Dasein: ➤ 7,174*a*, ꟳWALLIS G., Überlieferung 1990, 93-103.

3552 **Lange** Armin, Weisheit und Torheit bei Kohelet und in seiner Umwelt [Diss. Münster + Stellungnahme zu D. *Michel* 1989]: EurHS 23/433. Fra 1991, Lang. xii-196 p. DM 63 pa. 3-631-43889-3 [TLZ 118,22, T. *Krüger*).

3553 **Lavoie** Jean-Jacques, La pensée de Qohélet; étude exégétique et intertextuelle: Héritage et projet 49. Québec 1992, Fides. 300 p. 2-7621-1623-6.

3554 *Lavoie* Jean-Jacques, À quoi sert-il de perdre sa vie à la gagner? Le repos dans le Qohelet: ScEsp 44 (1992) 331-347.

3555 *a*) *Leanza* Sandro, L'esegesi patristica di Qohelet; da MELITONE di Sardi alle compilazioni catenarie; – *b*) *Sicari* Alberto, La dottrina della 'doppia creazione' nelle Omelie sull'Ecclesiaste di GREGORIO di Nissa; – *c*) *Savigni* Raffaele, Il commentario di ALCUINO al libro dell'Ecclesiaste e il suo significato nella cultura carolingia: ➤ 457*, Letture Sap 1991/2, 237-250 / 251-264 / 275-303.

3556 *a*) *Lux* Rüdiger, Der 'Lebenskompromiss' — ein Wesenszug im Denken Kohelets; – *b*) *Schmidt* Werner H., 'Wie kann der Mensch seinen Weg verstehen?' Weisheitliche Lebenserfahrung — ein Gespräch mit H. D. Preuss; – *c*) *Fabry* Hans-Josef, Der Makarismus — mehr als eine

weisheitliche Lehrform; Gedanken zu dem neu-edierten Text 4 Q 525:
➤ 149, FPREUSS H. 1992, 267-278 / 287-297 / 362-371.
3558 **Michel** Diethelm,   Untersuchungen zur Eigenart des Buches Qohelet:
BZAW 183, 1989 ➤ 5,3350 ... 7,3062:   RBZ 36 (1992) 301s (J. *Scharbert*).
3559 *Quacquarelli* Antonio,   La lettura patristica di Qoêlet: VetChr 29 (1992)
5-17.
3559* *Raurell* Frederic,   Dimensione etico-pedagogica della provocazione nel
'Qohelet':   Laurentianum 33 (1982) 375-402.
3560 **Schoors** Antoon,   The Preacher sought to find pleasing words; a study of
the language of Qoheleth: OrLovAnal 11. Lv 1992, Univ./Peeters.   xiv-
258 p. Fb 1750.   90-6831-376-2 [RB 100,609, R. J. *Tournay*].
3561 *Sekine* Seizo,   Qohelet als Nihilist: AnJapB 17 (1991) 3-54.
3562 **Streza** Sergio,   Storia dell'esegesi del libro dell'Ecclesiaste nei Padri (fino
a Origene): diss. Pont. Univ. Gregoriana,   DCrouzel H.   Roma 1992.
439 p. Extr. 3872: 153 p. – RTLv 24, p. 552.
3563 *Templeton* Douglas A.,   A 'farced epistol' as a sinking sun of David;
Ecclesiastes and Finnegan's Wake; the sinoptic view: ➤ 41, FDAVIDSON
R., Text as pretext 1992, 282-290.
3564 *Vílchez* José,   Lengua original de Qohélet: ➤ 135, FMUÑOZ IGLESIAS S.,
EstBib 50 (1992) 553-564.

3565 *McKenna* John E., [Qoh 1,2] The concept of *hebel* in the book of Ecclesiastes: ScotJT 45 (1992) 19-28.
3566 **Schwienhorst-Schönberger** Ludger,   Nicht im Menschen selbst gründet
das Glück (Koh 2,24); Kohelet im Spannungsfeld jüdischer Weisheit und
hellenistischer Philosophie: kath. Hab.-Diss. DZenger.   Münster 1992.
TR 89,76.
3567 *Mateo Seco* Lucas F.,   [Ecl 3,2] *Ho eúkairos thánatos*; consideraciones en
torno a la muerte en las homilias al Eclesiastés de GREGORIO de Nisa:
ScripTPamp 22 (1991) 921-937.
3567* *Müller* Hans-Peter,   Mensch — Umwelt — Eigenwelt; Weisheitliche
Wirklichkeitswahrnahme und Anthropologie [inceditum mit 8 Reprints]:
➤ 288a, Mensch-Umwelt 1992, 69-99 [220-233. Qoh 3,21; 12,7 ➤ 2886*].
3568 *Bianchi* Francesco,   'Essi non hanno chi li consoli' (Qo 4,1):   RivB 40
(1992) 299-307.
3569 *Qimron* Elisha, Ⓗ *še-taqqīp* (Qoh 6:10) — an unnoticed Aramaism:
Lešonenu 56 (1991s) 117; Eng. 1.
3570 *Krüger* Thomas,   'Frau Weisheit' in Koh 7,26?:   Biblica 73 (1992)
394-403.
3571 *Gómez Aranda* Mariano,   Ecl[es] 12,1-7 interpretado por Abraham IBN
'EZRA: ➤ 44, FDÍAZ ESTEBAN F., Sefarad 52 (1992) 113-121.
3571* *Dohmen* Christoph,   Der Weisheit letzter Schluss? Anmerkungen zur
Übersetzung und Bedeuting von Koh 12,9-14: BibNot 63 (1992) 12-18.

E7.8   *Liber Sapientiae* – **Wisdom of Solomon.**

3572 **Busto Saiz** José R.,   La justicia es inmortal; una lectura del Libro de la
Sabiduría de Salomón: PresTeol 69. Sdr 1992, Sal Terrae.   166 p.   84-
293-1069-X [ActuBbg 30,193, J. *Vives*]: – RSalT 80 (1992) 835s (P. *Luis
Ruiz*).
3573 **Pock** Johann I.,   Sapientia Salomonis; HIERONYMUS' Exegese des
Weisheitsbuches im Lichte der Tradition [Diss. 89, DMarböck J.   Graz

1992. 378 p. – RTLv 24, p. 542]. Graz 1992, Technische Univ.-V. viii-442 p. DM 32. 3-7041-9049-7.

3574 **Scarpat** Giuseppe, Libro della Sapienza 1, 1989 ➤ 5,3377; 7,3077: ᴿBiblica 73 (1992) 270-2 (E. *della Corte*); CBQ 54 (1992) 764s (D. *Winston*); EstE 67 (1992) 116 (J. *Vílchez*); Irénikon 65 (1992) 148 (E. *Lanne*); ParVi 37 (1992) 391-3 (A. *Ranon*); RBgPg 70 (1992) 205s (É. des *Places*); RFgIC 120 (1992) 94-97 (A. *Colonna*); VT 42 (1992) 143 (N.R.M. de *Lange*).

3574* — *Passoni Dell'Acqua* Anna, Alcune osservazioni sugli *hápax legómena* del Libro della Sapienza [... SCARPAT G., 1989]: RivB 40 (1992) 459-465.

3575 **Sisti** Adalberto, Il libro della Sapienza; introduzione, versione. Assisi 1992, Porziuncola. 423 p.

3576 **Vilchez Lindez** José, Sabiduría 1990 ➤ 6,3661: ᴿAngelicum 69 (1992) 557-9 (J. *Garcia Trapiello*); Biblica 73 (1992) 421-4 (G. *Scarpat*); CritRR 5 (1992) 171s (C. T. *Begg*); EstE 67 (1992) 101s (J. R. *Busto Saiz*); JTS 43 (1992) 809 (R. *Hayward*: excels in summarizing neatly the views of other scholars); NRT 114 (1992) 102s (J.-L. *Ska*); RBiArg 53 (1991) 174s (P. *Andiñach*); RelCu 37 (1991) 736 (M. A. *Martín Juárez*); RET 51 (1991) 513-5 (P. *Barrado Fernández*); Salmanticensis 38 (1991) 371-3 (G. *Pérez*); ScripTPamp 24 (1992) 678s (G. *Aranda*).

3577 **Vílchez Líndez** J., Sapienza 1990 ➤ 6,3661b [non = Sabiduría BAC 293, 1969 ampliato]: ᴿParVi 36 (1991) 393s (G. *Torta*); RivB 40 (1992) 105-7 (M. *Priotto*).

3578 ᴱ**Hentschel** Georg, *Zenger* Erich, Lehrerin der Gerechtigkeit 1988/91 ➤ 7,3075: ᴿAntonianum 67 (1992) 431s (M. *Nobile*).

3579 *Kolarcik* Michael, Creation and salvation in the Book of Wisdom: ➤ 346, Creation 1992, 97-107.

3580 *a) Lilla* Salvatore, La Sapienza di Salomone tra Stoicismo e Neoplatonismo; – *b) Mazzanti* Angela M., La Sapienza e FILONE d'Alessandria; questioni antropologiche: ➤ 457*, Letture Sap. 1991/2, 505-522 / 523-531.

3581 *Poniży* Bogdan, High-priestly ministration of Aaron according to the Book of Wisdom: ➤ 493a, IOSOT-B 1979/92, 135-145.

3582 *Seeley* David, Narrative, the righteous man and the philosopher; an analysis of the story of the *díkaios* in Wisdom 1-5: JPseud 7 (1990) 55-78.

3583 *a) Foubert* Jean, Ad gloriam corporis; au delà de Sagesse 9,15, 'corpus quod corrumpitur adgravat animam' [AUGUSTIN] (Confessions VII 17,23); – *b) Madec* Goulven, Augustin et PORPHYRE; ébauche d'un bilan des recherches et des conjectures: ➤ 141d, ᶠPÉPIN J., Sophiēs maiētores 1992, 383-402 / 367-382 [les 40 autres art. sont surtout sur PLOTIN].

3584 *Beentjes* Pancratius C., 'You have given a road in the sea'; what is Wisdom 14,3 talking about?; ETL 68 (1992) 137-141.

3585 *Chrostowski* Waldemar, ⊘ Wisdom 14,7-12 as the conclusion of the condemnation of idol worship and the false divinization of human works: ColcT 62,1 (1992) 19-29; Eng. 30.

E7.9 *Ecclesiasticus, Siracides;* **Wisdom of Jesus Sirach.**

3586 *Beentjes* P. C., The book of Ben Sira in Hebrew; preliminary remarks towards a new text edition and synopsis: ➤ 450*, Informatique 3ᵉ 1991/2, 471-485.

3586* **Hahn** Ferdinand, Einige notwendige Bemerkungen zu zwei Texteditionen [1. Sirach: SAUER G., JSHZ 3/5 folgt dem Hebräischen von VATTIONI F., wo wenigstens zwei Traditionen vermischt sind; – 2. Didache]: VerkF 36,2 (NT 1991) 64-69.

3587 **Minissale** Antonio, Il Siracide; confronto tra testo ebraico e versione greca alla luce del metodo midrascico targumico: diss. Pont. Ist. Biblico, ᴰ*Le Déaut* R. R 1992. 406 p. – AcPIB 9/8, 685 & 731; Biblica 73,432; RTLv 24, p. 542.

3588 **Samaan** Kamil W., Sept traductions arabes de Ben Sira [diss. 1990, ᴰ*Gilbert* M.]: AcPIB 9,9 (1992s) 854s (summarium].

3589 **Skehan** P. W., *Di Lella* A. A., Wisdom of Ben Sira: AnchorB 39, 1987 ➤ 3,3329 ... 6,3674: VT 42 (1992) 278s (J. A. *Emerton*).

3590 **Thiele** Walter, Sirach (Ecclesiasticus) [Lfg 1s, 1989 ➤ 7,3095] Lfg 4, Sir 3,31-7,30: VLatBeuron 11/2. FrB 1992, Herder. p. 241-320. 3-451-00427-5.

3591 **Wright** B. G., No small difference 1989 ➤ 5,3395 ... 7,3097: ᴿAustralBR 38 (1990) 72s (Pamela A. *Foulkes*); JQR 83 (1992s) 279 (J. A. *Soggin*); JSS 37 (1992) 99s (A. *Salvesen*); RivB 40 (1992) 232-5 (A. *Minissale*); Salesianum 54 (1992) 796s (M. *Cimosa*).

3592 **Bohlen** Reinhold, Die Ehrung der Eltern bei Ben Sira; Studien zur Motivation eines familienethischen Grundwertes in frühhellenistischer Zeit: TrierTSt 51. Trier 1991, Paulinus. 434 p. DM 98. – ᴿTrierTZ 101 (1992) 80 (R. *Mosis*).

3593 **Burton** Keith W., Sirach and the Judaic doctrine of creation: diss. Glasgow 1987. 271 p. BRDX-97157. – DissA 53 (1992s) 2412-A.

3594 *Hayward* Robert, The New Jerusalem in the wisdom of Jesus Ben Sira: ScandJOT 6,1 (1992) 123-138.

3595 **Kieweler** Hans Volker, Ben Sira zwischen Judentum und Hellenismus; eine Auseinandersetzung mit Th. MIDDENDORP [Stellung 1973]: BeitErfAJ 30. Fra 1992, Lang. 296 p. Fs 34. 3-631-45019-2 [OIAc 5,27].

3596 **Michaud** Robert, Ben Sira et le judaïsme 1988 ➤ 4,3562; 5,3389: ᴿRiv-ScR 5 (1991) 267 (P. *Fragnelli*).

3597 *Petraglio* Renzo, Figli e padri; lettori, copisti e traduttori cristiani di Ben Sirac: ➤ 457*, Letture Sap 1991/2, 489-504.

3598 **Wischmeyer** Oda. Die Kultur des Buches Jesus Sirach: Hab.-Diss. ᴰ*Theissen* G. Heidelberg 1992s. – RTLv 24, p. 543.

3599 *Beentjes* Pancratius C., 'How can a jug be friends with a kettle?' [Sir 13,2c RNEB]; a note on the structure of Ben Sira chapter 13: BZ 36 (1992) 87-93.

3600 *Prockter* L. J., 'His yesterday and yours today' (Sir 38:22); reflections on Ben Sira's view of death: Journal of Semitics 1 (1989) 193-203 [< JStJud 23,160].

3601 *Raurell* Frederic, Ecli 45,1-5; la 'doxa de Moisès': RCatalT 17 (1992) 1-42; Eng. 42.

VIII. Libri prophetici VT

E8.1 **Prophetismus.**

3602 **Alonso Schökel** Luis, *Gutiérrez* G., Mensajes de profetas 1991 ➤ 7,3102: ᴿBibFe 18 (1992) 136s (A. *Salas*).

3603 *Álvarez Valdés* Ariel, El enfrentamiento entre profetas y falsos profetas: RBiArg 53 (1991) 217-229.

3604 *Barton* John, [*Böcher* Otto] Propheten, Prophetie, AT [NT]: ⇥ 757, EvKL 3 (1992) (1335–) 1339-45 [–49].

3605 a) *Boogaart* Thomas A., The world of the prophets revisited; – b) *Paarlberg* John, Contemporary prophetic voices; the cries of the poor and the groans of creation: RefR 46 (1992s) 5-21 / 35-51.

3606 **Boyer** Paul S., When time shall be no more; prophecy belief in modern American culture [really 'apocalyptic belief', 'sequence of events that herald the end of the world']: Studies in cultural history. CM 1992, Harvard Univ. xiv-568 p. $30. 0-674-05128-X [TDig 40,153].
   Brichto Herbert C., ... tales of the prophets 1992 ⇥ 3115.

3607 **Davson** J., Critical and conservative treatments of prophecy in nineteenth-century Britain: diss. Oxford 1991. – RTLv 24, p. 557.

3608 **Evitt** Regula M., Anti-Judaism and the medieval Prophet Plays; exegetical contexts for the 'Ordines Prophetarum': diss. Virginia 1992. 324 p. 92-37469. – DissA 53 (1992s) 2807s-A.

3609 a) *Geus* C.H.J. de, Wie waren de profeten?; – b) *Ploeg* J.P.M. van der, Het zelfbewustzijn der profeten; – c) *Hilhorst* A., De benaming grote en kleine profeten; – d) *Hospers* J.H., Het woord *nabi* in de ostraka van Lakis: ⇥ 503, Symposium A. van der WOUDE 1985/92, 20-27 / 28-42 / 43-54 / 9-13.

3610 *Günther* Hartmut, 'Die Propheten mit Ernst und Nutz lesen und gebrauchen'; Beobachtungen zu LUTHERS Verständnis der Propheten: Luth-TK 15 (1991) 50-67.

3611 **Heschel** A.J. ❶ The prophets 1962, ᵀ*Moriizumi* Koji. Tokyo 1992, Kyōbunkan. 451 + 22 p. Y 5000 [BL 93,87].

3612 *Holt* Else K., Paradigmer [KUHN Y.] og profeter: DanTTs 55 (1992) 15-27 [< ZAW 104,431].

3613 *Jaramillo Rivas* Pedro, La injusticia y la opresión en el lenguaje figurado de los profetas [dis. Gregoriana, R 1986, ᴰ*Conroy* C.]: JerónMg 26. Estella 1992, VDivino. xvii-128 p. 84-7151-857-0.

3614 **Jemielity** Thomas, Satire and the Hebrew prophets: LitCurrBInt. Louisville 1992, W-Knox. 255 p. $18. 0-664-25229-X. – ᴿExpTim 104 (1992s) 217; BL (1993) 88 (R.P. *Carroll*).

3615 *Jemielity* Thomas, The prophetic character; good, heroic and naive: Lit-TOx 5 (1991) 37-48.

3616 **Kozioł** Stanisław, ❷ Symbolika małzenska ... La symbolique matrimoniale et familiale dans les oracles prophétiques: diss. ᴰ*Homerski* J. Lublin 1992. 151 p. – RTLv 24, p. 542.

3617 *Kurichianil* John, Prophets were men of faith: Bible Bhashyam 16 (1990) 79-94.

3618 **Lieb** Michael, The visionary mode; biblical prophecy, hermeneutics and cultural change. Ithaca NY 1991, Cornell Univ. 362 p. $32.50. 0-8014-2273-6 [Interpretation 47, 198s, P.L. *Tite*].

3619 *Malamat* Abraham, New light from Mari (ARM xxvi) on biblical prophecy (III-IV) ⇥ 7,141, ᶠSOGGIN J.A., 1991, 185-190.

3620 [*Martins*] *Terra* João E., A profecia no Antigo Testamento: RCuBíb 14,55s (1990) 120-141.

3621 *Miller* Patrick D., Toward a theology of leadership; some clues from the Prophets: AsbTJ 47,1 (1992) 43-50.

3622 **Nugent** Brigid P., JEROME'S Prologues to his Commentaries on the Prophets: diss. Texas, ᴰ*Parker* D. Austin 1992. 470 p. 92-25689. – DissA 53 (1992s) 1148s-A.

3623 **Overholt** Thomas W., Channels of prophecy; the social dynamics of prophetic activity 1989 ➤ 5,3438 ... 7,3116: ᴿHeythJ 33 (1992) 443s (W. D. *Lindsey*); Interpretation 46 (1992) 196 (G. *Gerbrandt*); JRel 72 (1992) 92s (Susan *Ackerman*, also on J. BARTON 1988).

3624 **Pongutá** Silvestre, Por medio de los Profetas; una presentación: Cuad-Bib 1. Caracas 1990, Asoc. Bib. Salesiana. 156 p. 980-6035-32-1 [Actu-Bbg 30,199, X. *Alegre* S.].

3625 **Rofé** Alexander, Storie di profeti; la narrativa sui profeti nella Bibbia ebraica; generi letterari e storia: BtStorB 8, 1991 ➤ 7,3120: ᴿBL (1992) 87 (J. R. *Porter*); ÉTRel 67 (1992) 269 (Jeanne M. *Léonard*: érudit et vivant); RivB 40 (1992) 479-492 (P. *Rota Scalabrini*).

3626 *Satran* David, Biblical prophets and Christian legend; the lives of the prophets reconsidered: ➤ 57, ᶠFLUSSER D., Messiah 1992, 143-9.

3627 *Schmitt* John J., Prophecy, preexilic Hebrew: ➤ 741, AnchorBD 5 (1992) 482-9 [-495 postexilic, *Barton* J.; 477-482, ANE, *Huffmon* Herbert B.; 495-501, early Christian, *Boring* M. Eugene].

3628 *Sevrugian Petra*, Prophetendarstellungen in der frühchristlichen Kunst: FrühMaS 26 (1992) 65-81.

3629 **Sicré** José L., I profeti d'Israele e il loro messaggio [antologia] 1989 ➤ 5,3446; Lit. 20.000: ᴿCC 143 (1992,1) 307 (D. *Scaiola*); ParVi 36 (1991) 71-73 (A. *Rolla*).

3630 **Sicre Díaz** José Luis, Profetismo en Israel; el profeta, los profetas, el mensaje: Teología 572. Estella 1992, VDivino. 572 p. 84-7151-7809. – ᴿRET 52 (1992) 93-95 (P. *Barrado Fernández*).

3631 **Sicre** José L., **Castillo** José M., **Estrada** Juan A., La Iglesia y los profetas 1989 ➤ 5,3447 ... 7,3123: RBiArg 53 (1991) 121-3 (R. *Krüger*).

3632 *Sivatte* Rafael de, Crítica profética a los imperialismos y a la religión nacionalista de Israel: Christus 56,4s (Méx 1990) 83-91.

3633 **Sklba** Richard J., Pre-exilic prophecy; words of warning, dreams of hope: MessageBSpir 3, 1990 ➤ 6,3732: ᴿBL (1992) 91s (J. H. *Eaton*).

3634 **Stacey** W. O., Prophetic drama in the OT 1990 ➤ 7,3126: ᴿVT 42 (1992) 283 (R. P. *Gordon*).

3635 *Stuhlmueller* Carroll, The prophet-mystic and justice and peace: Philip-Sa 26 (1991) 381-400.

3636 **Tan** Paul L., A pictorial guide to biblical prophecy. Garland TX 1991, Bible Communications. 413 p. $30. – ᴿBtS 149 (1992) 344 (J. F. *Walvoord*: a book without precedent).

3637 **Vogels** Walter, Les prophètes: L'Horizon du Croyant 1990 ➤ 7,3129: ᴿTorJT 7 (1991) 268s (P. E. *Dion*).

3638 **Walvoord** John F., Major biblical prophecies; 37 crucial prophecies that affect you today. GR 1991, Zondervan. 450 p. $20. – ᴿBtS 149 (1992) 374s (J. A. *Witmer*).

3639 **Ward** James M., Thus says the Lord; the message of the prophets. Nv 1991, Abingdon. 282 p. $18 pa. 0-687-41902-6 [TDig 39,392].

3640 *a) Watts* John D. W. Images of Yahweh; God in the Prophets; – *b) Allen* Leslie C., Images of Israel; the People of God in the prophets; – *c) Armerding* Carl C., Images for today; word from the Prophets: ➤ 88, ᶠHUBBARD D., OT 1992, 135-147 / 149-168 / 169-186.

3641 *Weis* R. D., Oracle: ➤ 741, AnchorBD 5,28: RSV 'and most' only for *maśśa'* [*nᵉ'ûm* not mentioned].

3642 **Westermann** Claus, Basic forms of prophetic speech 1991 = c. 1966 ➤ 7,3132: ᴿExpTim 103 (1991s) 343 (H. *Mowvley*: the unqualified references to 'covenant', 'amphyctiony' [sic] and 'corporate personality' betray its age).

3643 **Westermann** C.,   Prophetic oracles of salvation 1991 ➤ 7,3131:   ᴿGrace-
TJ 12 (1991) 292-4 (M. A. *Grisanti*).
3644 *a) Wevers* John W.,   Ecstatic vs. literary prophets in ancient Israel; – *b)*
Williams Ronald J.,   Soothsayers and oracles in ancient Egypt; – *c) Biggs*
Robert D.,   The Babylonian prophecies; – *d) Charpin* Dominique,   Le
contexte historique et géographique dans les textes retrouvés à Mari; – *e)*
Peters Celeste A.,   The Mesopotamian astrologers' universe; celestial and
terrestrial: ➤ 688, BCanadMesop 23 (1991/2) 9-13 / 15s / 17-20 / 21-31 /
33-44; 7 fig.; franç. 33.
3645 *a) Zobel* Hans-Jürgen,   Das Schöpfungshandeln Jahwes im Zeugnis der
Propheten; – *b) Jeremias* Jörg,   Umkehrung von Heiltraditionen im AT:
➤ 149, ᶠPREUSS H. 1992, 191-200 / 309-320.

E8.2   Proto-Isaias, *textus, commentarii.*

3646 **Chilton** B. D.,   The Isaiah targum 1987 ➤ 3,3400 ... 6,3745:   ᴿSNTU
A-17 (1992) 273s (A. *Fuchs*).
3647 *Gordon* Robert P.,   'Isaiah's wild measure', R. M. McCHEYNE [hymn of
1834, an early recognition following LOWTH that the prophets are mainly
poetry]: ExpTim 103 (1991s) 235-7.
3648 ᵀᴱ**Goshen-Gottstein** Moshe,   ❺ Judah ben Samuel IBN BALʿAM,
Commentary on Isaiah; the Arabic original according to MS Firkowitch
(Hebr-Arab I 1377) with a Hebrew translation, notes and introduction.
Ramat Gan 1992, Bar-Ilan Univ. 267 p.; Eng. v-vii. 965-226-125-4.
3649 **Gryson** Roger,   Esaias [fasc. 4-7: ➤ 7,3133] 8s: VLat 12, 19 [89-91]: JTS
43 (1992) 631s (J. K. *Elliott*: strenuous work; some fascinating nuggets
and purple patches).
3649* **Jacob** Edmond, Ésaïe 1-12, 1987 ➤ 3,3403 ... 7,3135. – ᴿRBiArg 53
(1991) 172-4 (A. *Ricciardi*).
3650 *Kooij* Arie van der,   The Old Greek text of Isaiah in relation to the
Qumran texts of Isaiah; some general comments: ➤ 459, Septuagint
1990/2, 195-213.
3651 **Montagnini** F.,   Isaia 1-39: LoB 1.18, 1990 ➤ 7,3138:   ᴿRivPastLtg 28,4
(1990) 72s (L. *Della Torre*).
3652 **Stachowiak** Lech,   ❺ Das Buch Jesaja. Übersetzung, Einleitung und
Kommentar: PismoŚ SNT. Lublin 1991, KUL. 293 p. [TR 89,518].
3653 **Watts** John D. W.,   Isaiah 1-33: Word **Comm** 24, 1985 ➤ 2,2632; 6,3772
[themes 1989 ➤ 5,3481]: ᴿCritRR 5 (1992) 175-7 (J. J. *Schmitt*: a striking
tour de force); RTLv 23 (1992) 83-85 (J. *Vermeylen*).
3654 **Widyapranawa** S. H.,   The Lord is savior; faith in national crisis ... Isa
1-39: 1990 ➤ 6,3762; 7,3141:   ᴿCBQ 54 (1992) 136s (J. A. *Dearman*);
HeythJ 33 (1992) 330 (R. E. *Clements*).
3655 *Zijl* J. B. van,   The British Library ms Or. 2211 of SAADIA Gaon's
Arabic translation of Isaiah: JSS 37 (1992) 57-63.

E8.3   [Proto-] Isaias 1-39, *themata, versiculi.*

3656 **Cassel** J. David,   CYRIL of Alexandria and the science of the grammarians; a study in the setting, purpose, and emphasis of Cyril's 'Commentary on Isaiah': diss. Virginia 1992, ᴰ*Wilken* R. 251 p. 92-37576. –
DissA 53 (1992s) 2852-A.
3657 **Conrad** Edgar W.,   Reading Isaiah: OvBT 1991 ➤ 7,3143:   ᴿBtS 149
(1992) 249s (E. H. *Merrill*); JBL 111 (1992) 699-701 (R. J. *Clifford*); TS 53

(1992) 587 (D. B. *Sharp*: 'first synthetic presentation we have of the Book of Isaiah' but not clear to whom his 'community' refers).

3658 *Cook* Johann, The dichotomy of IQIsa: ➤ 132, FMILIK J. 1992, 7-24.

3659 **Deck** Ulrike [Scholastika], Die Gerichtsbotschaft Jesajas; Charakter und Begründung: ForBi 67, 1991 ➤ 7,3144: RArTGran 55 (1992) 327s (A. *Segovia*).

3660 **Doorly** William J., Isaiah of Jerusalem, an introduction. NY 1992, Paulist. 187 p. $10 pa. [BToday 31,185; TDig 40,61]. 0-8091-3337-7.

3661 *a) Forbes* A. Dean, A critique of statistical approaches to the Isaiah authorship problem; – *b) Wieringen* Archibald van, Analogies between the Second and Third Isaiah; a computer assisted analysis: ➤ 450*, Informatique 3ᵉ 1991/2, 531-545 / 629-641.

3662 **Günzler** Helmut, *a)* Der Versuch einer Synthese von historisch-kritischer und biblizistisch-pneumatischer Auslegung in August H. Franckes Jesajavorlesung (1709-1721). Magdeburg 1979. – *b)* FRANCKE, Introductio specialis in Jesaiam: dazu *Peschke* Erhard, Zur Jesajavorlesung Franckes; TLZ 117 (1992) 321-334.

3663 *a) Haag* Ernst, Die Frohbotschaft von der Heilsoffenbarung Gottes nach dem Buch Jesaja; zur Vorgeschichte des Begriffes 'Evangelium' im Neuen Testament; – *b) Günther-Schüttler* Heinz, Rückgabe der Aufgabe? Bilder vom Volk Gottes im Dienst evangelisierender Verkündigung: ➤ 54, FFEILZER H., Wege der Evangelisierung 1992, 31-48 / 49-62.

3664 **Høgenhaven** Jesper, Gott und Volk bei Jesaja 1988 ➤ 4,3673 ... 6,3765: RRTLv 23 (1992) 497 (J. *Vermeylen*); TLZ 117 (1992) 666s (S. *Wagner*).

3665 *Lee Ki-Rak*, Structure and themes of the Book of Isaiah: Catholic Theology and Thought 8 (Seoul Catholic University 1992) 179-202 [< TContext 10/2, 47].

3666 **Mosley** Harold R., The concept of faith in Isaiah 1-39: diss. Baptist Theol. Sem., DBailey D. W. New Orleans 1992. 175 p. 93-11818. – DissA 53 (1992) 4360-A.

3667 **Nielsen** Kirsten, There is hope for a tree; the tree as metaphor in Isaiah, TCrowley C. & F.: JStOT supp 65, 1989 ➤ 5,3491 ... 7,3147: RBZ 36 (1992) 109-112 (Helga *Weippert*).

3668 *Seitz* Christopher R., Isaiah, book of: ➤ 741, AnchorBD 3 (1992) 472-488 (-490 ch. 24-27, little apocalypse, *Millar* Wm. R.; 490-501, 2d Isaiah, *Clifford* Richard J.; 501-7, 3d, Seitz).

3669 *a) Sheppard* Gerald T., The book of Isaiah; competing structures according to a late modern description of its shape and scope [SEITZ C., *al.*]; – *b) Carr* David M., What can we say about the tradition history of Isaiah? A response to Christopher Seitz's Zion's final destiny: ➤ 478, SBL Sem 31 (1992) 549-582 / 583-597.

3670 ETalstra Epp, *Wieringen* A. van, A prophet on the screen; computerized description and literary interpretation of Isaianic text: Applicatio 9. Amst 1992, VU. [vi–] 148 p. 90-5383-120-7.

3671 **Wegner** Paul D., An examination of kingship and messianic expectation in Isaiah 1-35 [< diss. London]. Lewiston NY 1992, Mellen. xiii-397 p. 0-7734-2354-0 [TRB 6/1,16, R. *Coggins*].

3672 *Gosse* Bernard, Isaïe 1 dans la rédaction du livre d'Isaïe: ZAW 104 (1992) 52-66.

3673 **Holmyard** Harold R[III], Mosaic eschatology in Isaiah, especially chapters 1 [and] 28-33: diss. Dallas Theol. Sem. 1992, [D]*Chisholm* R. 303 p. 93-03916. – DissA 53 (1992s) 3250s-A.

3674 *Sweeney* Marvin A., Structure and redaction in Isaiah 2-4: HebAnR 11 (1987) 407-422.

3675 *Magonet* Jonathan, [Is 2,2 rivers flow upstream] Isaiah's mountain, or the shape of things to come: Prooftexts 11 (1991) 175-181.

3676 *Alonso Fontela* Carlos, Una breve nota marginal de Alfonso de ZAMORA sobre *laḥpor perôt* (Is 2,20): ⇒ 44, [F]DÍAZ ESTEBAN F., Sefarad 52 (1992) 29-32.

3677 *Greger* Barbara, *Pethîgîl* in Jes 3,24: BibNot 61 (1992) 15s.

3677* a) *Miscall* Peter D., Isaiah [4...]; new heavens, new earth, new book; – b) *Gunn* David M., Samson of sorrows; an Isaianic [42ss] gloss on Judges 13-16]: ⇒ 351*d*, Reading 1992, 41-56 / 225-253.

3678 a) *Emerton* J.A., The translation of Isaiah 5,1; – b) *Ruiten* J. van, The intertextual relationship between Isa 11,6-9 and Isa 65,25; – c) *Beuken* W.A.M., Isa 29,15-24, perversion reverted, [T]*Doyle* B. ⇒ 198, [F]WOUDE A. van der, VTSupp 49 (1992) 18-30 / 31-74 / 43-64.

3679 *Roberts* J.J.M., [Is 5,11; 27s...] Double entendre in First Isaiah: CBQ 54 (1992) 39-48.

3680 *Auret* Adrian, [Is 6,1-9,6]. The theological intent of the use of the names of God in the eighth-century Memoir of Isaiah: OTEssays 5 (1992) 272-291.

3681 *Irvine* Stuart A., [Isa 6,1 – 9,6; BUDDE K.], The Isaianic Denkschrift; reconsidering an old hypothesis: ZAW 104 (1992) 216-230.

3682 **Irvine** Stuart A., Isaiah, Ahaz and the Syro-Ephraimite crisis: SBL diss 123, 1990 ⇒ 6,3783; [R]CBQ 54 (1992) 748s (J.A. *Dearman*: fresh, valuable); ETL 68 (1992) 154s (J. *Lust*); JBL 111 (1992) 519-521 (M.A. *Sweeney*).

3683 **Conrad** Edgar W., [Is 6 vision 'a book within a book']. Mp 1991, Fortress. 185 p. $13. 0-8006-1560-3. – [R]ExpTim 103 (1991s) 244s (D. *Stacey*: literary approach good except for sniping at historico-critical, which 'has alienated itself from western culture in general' p. 26, absurd).

3684 *Müller* H.P., Sprachliche und religionsgeschichtliche Beobachtungen zu Jesaia 6: ZAHeb 5 (1992) 163-185.

3685 *Gosse* Bernard, Isaïe VI et la tradition isaïenne: VT 42 (1992) 340-9.

3686 **Wagner** Renate, Textexegese als Strukturanalyse ... Jes 6,1-11: AOtt 32, 1989 ⇒ 5,3510; 6,3163: [R]CBQ 54 (1992) 135s (L. *Laberge*: p. 185-210 for exegetes); WeltOr 23 (1992) 183-6 (H. *Schweizer*); ZkT 114 (1992) 84 (J.M. *Oesch*).

3687 **Evans** C., To see ... Is 6,9s [D]1989 ⇒ 5,3512; 7,3167: [R]RExp 89 (1992) 413s (D.E. *Gerland*).

3688 *Kellenberger* Edgar, Heil und Verstockung; zu Jes 6,9f bei Jesaja und im Neuen Testament: TZBas 48 (1992) 268-275.

3689 *Sonnet* Jean-Pierre, Le motif de l'endurcissement (Is 6,9-10) et la lecture d' 'Isaïe': Biblica 73 (1992) 208-239; Eng. 239.

3690 *Cazelles* Henri, [Is 7], La guerre syro-éphraïmite dans le contexte de la politique internationale: ⇒ 7,141, [F]SOGGIN J.A., Storia 1991, 31-48.

3691 **Werlitz** J., Geschichte und Heil in Isa 7,1-17; 29,1-8 Studien zur literarkritischen Methode [diss. Ausgburg, [D]*Kilian*]: BZAW 204. B 1992, de Gruyter. x-351 p. DM 138. 3-11-013488-8. – [R]ExpTim 104 (1992s) 218 (R. *Coggins*: after half on W. RICHTER theory, treats with excursus 28 basic controversies on Immanuel).

3692 *Lemche* N.P., Isa 7,14 [and a comparison between efficacy of exegesis teaching in the 1960s & 1990s]: → 351*c*, ᴱ*Fatum* J., 1992.

3693 *Most* William G., The problem of Isaiah 7:14: Faith & Reason 18,2 (1992) 181-199.

3694 *Jensen* Joseph, Immanuel: → 741, AnchorDB 3 (1992) 392-5.

3695 *Vieweger* Dieter, 'Das Volk, das durch das Dunkel zieht ...' Neue Überlegungen zu Jes (8,23*abb*) 9,1-6: BZ 36 (1992) 77-86.

3696 *Wegner* Paul D., A re-examination of Isaiah IX 1-6: VT 42 (1992) 103-112.

3697 *Reeth* J.M.F. Van, [Isa 11,1]. Le prophète musulman en tant que *nāṣir* Allâh et ses antécédents; le 'nazōraios' évangélique et le Livre des Jubilés: OrLovPer 23 (1992) 251-274: p. 257-265, Jesus as Nazaréen, related to Isa 11,1; relation to Abraham and Teraḥ discussed not only in Jubilees but also in the Apocalypse of Abraham and in some Syriac writers.

3698 *Steck* Odil H., '... ein kleiner Knabe kann sie leiten'; Beobachtungen zum Tierfrieden in Jesaja 11,6-8 und 65,25: → 149, ᶠPREUSS H. 1992, 104-113.

3699 **Fabiny** Tibor, The lion and the lamb; figurism and fulfilment in the Bible, art and literature. Basingstoke 1992, Macmillan. xlv-164 p.; 4 pl. 0-333-53952-4. – ᴿTBR 5,2 (1992s) 38 (G. *Pattison*: applies N. FRYE).

3700 *a) Prinsloo* Willem S., Isaiah 12; one, two, or three songs?: *b) Wodecki* Bernard, The religious universalism of the pericope Isa 25:6-9: → 493*a*, IOSOT-B 1989/92, 25-33 / 35-47.

3701 **Boshoff** François J., A survey into the theological function of the oracles against the nations in the Old Testament with special reference to Isaiah 13-23: diss. [in Afrikaans], ᴰ*Oberholzer* J. Pretoria 1992. – DissA 53 (1992s) 1555s-A.

3702 **Gosse** Bernard, Isaïe 13,1-14,23 ... et oracles contre les nations: OBO 78, 1988 → 4,3691 ... 7,3176: ᴿÉTRel 67 (1992) 270 (D. *Bourget*).

3703 *Görg* Manfred, 'Dämonen' statt 'Eulen' in Jes 13,21: BibNot 62 (1992) 16s.

3704 *Gosse* Bernard, *a)* Isaïe 14,24-27 et les oracles contre les nations du livre d'Isaïe; – *b)* L'emploi de *ṣ'ṣ'ym* dans le livre d'Isaïe: BibNot 56 (1991) 17-21 / 22-24.

3705 *Gosse* Bernard, Isaïe 17,12-14 dans la rédaction du livre d'Isaïe: BibNot 58 (1991) 20-23.

3706 *Virgulin* Stefano, 'Benedetto l'Egitto, mio popolo' (Is 19,16-25): → 339, ParSpV 26 (1992) 57-66.

3707 *Geyer* John B., The night of Dumah (Isaiah XXI 11-12): VT 92 (1992) 317-339.

3708 **Greggs** Gilbert A., [Is 24-27] Priest, prophet, and apocalyptic; the authoring of identity in the period of the Restoration: diss Yale, ᴰ*Wilson* R. NHv 1991. 428 p. 92-18785. – DissA 53 (1992s) 535-A: RTLv 24, p. 541: 'priesthood, prophecy ...'.

3709 **Johnson** Dan G., From chaos to restoration ... Isa 24-27: JStOT supp 61, 1988 → 4,3696 ... 6,3797: ᴿBZ 36 (1992) 294 (G. *Dautzenberg*).

3709* *Pagán* Samuel, Apocalyptic poetry; Isaiah 24-27: BTrans 43 (1992) 314-325.

3710 **Nakamura** Catherine L., Monarch, mountain, and meal; the eschatological banquet of Isaiah 24:21-23; 25:6-10*a*: diss. Princeton Theol. Sem. 1992, ᴰ*Roberts* J. 307 p. 92-29022. – DissA 53 (1992s) 1547-A.

3711 *Routledge* Robin L. The siege and deliverance of the city of David in Isaiah 29:1-8: TyndB 43,1 (1992) 181-190.

3712 *Dicou* Bert, Literary function and literary history of Isaiah 34: BibNot 58 (1991) 30-45.
3713 **Poythress** Diane M., Johannes OECOLAMPADIUS' exposition of Isaiah chapters 36-37: diss. Westminster Theol. Sem. 1992, ᴰ*Davis* D. 816 p. 92-24636. – DissA 53 (1992) 1187-A.
3714 *Ognibeni* Bruno, Achaz o no Achaz; a proposito del testo di Is 38,8 [CATASTINI A. 1983; TREBOLLE J. 1986...]: RivB 40 (1992) 77-86.
3715 *Hoffer* Vicki, An exegesis of Isaiah 38.21: JStOT 56 (1992) 69-84.

E8.4 **Deutero-Isaias 40-52**: *Commentarii, themata, versiculi.*

3716 **Barstad** H. M., A way ... 2-Ex in 2-1sa 1989 ➤ 6,3804; 7,3190: ᴿZAW 104 (1992) 292 (Ulrike *Schorn*).
3717 **Beaucamp** Évode, Le livre de la consolation d'Israël; Isaïe 40-55: Lire la Bible 93, 1991 ➤ 7,3191: ᴿBL (1992) 48 (A. *Gelston*); Gregorianum 73 (1992) 752s (J. *Galot*); ÉTRel 67 (1992) 450s (D. *Lys*: regrette 'Yahvé' et 'Isaïe' pour Ésaïe selon l'accord œcuménique TOB); VSp 146 (1992) 244s (J. *Asurmendi*).
3718 **Birch** Bruce C., Singing the Lord's song ... Isa 40-55, 1990 ➤ 6,3806: ᴿCBQ 54 (1992) 104 (R. J. *Clifford*: 1981 spiritual growth study for Methodist women; successful).
3719 *Gelston* A., Universalism in Second Isaiah [SOTS presidential address 2.I.1991]: JTS 43 (1992) 377-398.
3720 *Gottwald* Norman K., Social class and ideology in Isaiah 40-55; an Eagletonian rendering [EAGLETON Terry, Criticism and ideology; L 1976, New Left]: Semeia 59 (1992) 43-57 (responses 59-71, *Milbank* J.; 73-78, *Newsom* Carol).
3721 *Gruber* Mayer I., *a*) The motherhood of God in Second Isaiah [1981]; – *b*) The Hebrew *qᶜdēšāh* and her Canaanite and Akkadian cognates [1978]: ➤ 247*e*, Motherhood of God 1992, 3-15 / 17-47.
3722 **Hermisson** Hans-Jürgen, Deuterojesaja: BK AT 11 [Lfg. 7, 1987 ➤ 6, 3810] Lfg 8, Jes 45,18-47,15; Lfg. 9, Jes 47,2-48,11: Neuk 1991s. P. 81-160 / 161-240. 3-7887-1258-9 beide.
3723 **Koole** J. L., Jesaja II² (49-55). Kampen 1990, Kok. 359 p. *f*85. – ᴿKerkT 42 (1991) 353s (C. van *Leeuwen*).
3724 **Kratz** Reinhard, Kyros im Dt-Jes-B 1991 ➤ 7,3199: ᴿBL (1992) 75 (A. *Gelston*); TLZ 117 (1992) 745-7 (T. *Krüger*); TvT 32 (1992) 412 (A. *Schoors*); ZAW 104 (1992) 448s (H.-C. *Schmitt*).
3725 **Laato** Antti, The servant of YHWH and Cyrus; a reinterpretation of the exilic messianic programme in Isaiah 40-55: ConBib OT 35. Sto 1992, Almqvist & W. x-307 p. 91-22-01529-9.
3726 *Marconcini* Benito, La salvezza contemplata nel Secondo Isaia: ➤ 338, ParSpV 25 (1992) 53-66.
3727 *Ranon* Angelo, L'universalismo della salvezza nel Secondo Isaia: ParVi 35 (1990) 94-103.
3728 **Matheus** Frank, Singt dem Herrn ein neues Lied; die Hymnen Deuterojesajas [< Form und Funktion, Diss. Heidelberg 1987, ᴰ*Rendtorff* R.]: SBS 141. Stu 1990, KBW. 192 p. – ᴿIndTSt 29 (1992) 368s (A.R. *Ceresko*).
3729 *Stone* Bebb W., Second Isaiah; prophet to patriarchy: JStOT 56 (1992) 85-99.

3730 *Seidl* Theodor, Offene Stellen in Jesaja 40,1-8; ein methodenkritischer Vergleich: ➤ 493*a*, IOSOT-B 1989/92, 49-56.

3731 **Farfan Navarro** Enrique,   El desierto transformado; una imagen deu-
teroisaiana de regeneración [dis. Isa 41,17-20 ... 1991 ➤ 7,3192]: AnBib
130. R 1992, Pontificio Istituto Biblico. 304 p. Lit. 35.000. 88-7653-
130-0.

3732 *Sorg* Theo,   Vom Dienst der Knechte Gottes (Jes. 42,1-4): TBeit 22 (Wu
1991) 169-173 [< ZIT 91,585].

3733 *a*) *Schmitt* Hans-Christoph,   Erlösung und Gericht; Jes 43,1-7 und sein
literarischer und theologischer Kontext; – *b*) *Baltzer* Klaus,   Stadt-Tyche
oder Zion-Jerusalem; die Auseinandersetzung mit den Göttern der Zeit bei
Deuterojesaja: ➤ 149, ᶠPREUSS H. 1992, 120-131 / 114-9.

3734 *Stassen* S. L.,   Die rol van Egypte, Kus en Seba in Jesaja 43:3 en 45:14:
JTydSem 4 (1992) 160-180; Eng. 160.

3735 *Hutter* Manfred,   'Asche' und 'Trug'; eine antizoroastrische Polemik in
Jes 44,20:   BibNot 64 (1992) 10-13.

3736 **Gross** Walter, *Kuschel* Karl-Josef,   'Ich schaffe Finsternis und Übel!' Ist
Gott verantwortlich für das Übel?   Mainz 1992, Grünewald.   234 p. DM
38. [TGL 83,484-6, N. *Fischer*].

3737 *Deroche* Michael,   Isaiah XLV 7 and the creation of chaos?:   VT 42
(1992) 11-21.

3738 *Gaiser* Frederick J.,   'Remember the former things of old'; a new look at
Isaiah 46:3-13: ➤ 77, ᶠHARRISVILLE R., All things new 1992, 53-63.

3739 *Deléani* Simone,   Un emprunt d'AUGUSTIN à l'Écriture: 'Redite prac-
varicatores ad cor' (Isaïe 46,8*b*): RÉAug 38 (1992) 39-49.

3740 *Holter* Knut,   *a*) Die Parallelismen in Jes 50,1ab*a* — im hebräischen und
syrischen Text: BibNot 63 (1992) 35s; – *b*) A note on *šᵉbi / šᵉbît* in
Isa. 52,2: ZAW 104 (1992) 106s.

3741 *Hofius* Otfried,   Zur Septuaginta-Übersetzung von Jes 52,13b: ZAW 104
(1992) 107-110.

E8.5   *Isaiae 53ss, Carmina Servi* YHWH: **Servant-Songs.**

3742 *Brown* John Pairman,   Prometheus, the Servant of Yahweh, Jesus; legitimation and repression in the heritage of Persian imperialism: ➤ 7,67*,
ᶠGOTTWALD N. 1991, 109-125.

3743 **Jonge** Marinus de,   Jesus, the Servant-Messiah.   NHv 1991, Yale Univ.
viii-115 p. $18.50.   0-300-04849-1. – ᴿJTS 43 (1992) 159s (A. E. *Harvey*:
limited to a narrow selection of Jewish and Christian writings).

3744 *Steck* Odil H.,   Gottesvolk und Gottesknecht in Jes 40-66: ➤ 355, JbBT 7
(1992) 51-75.

3745 *Eynikel* Erik,   Die Liederen van de lijdende Dienaar van Jahwe (Jes
42,1-4; 49,1-6; 50,4-9; 52,13-53,12): CollatVL 22 (1992) 115-127.

3746 *Jostein* Ådna,   The Lord's Servant in Is. 53 described as the triumphant
Messiah: TsTKi 63 (1992) 81-94 [in Norwegian: Eng. 94].

3747 **Glassner** Gottfried,   Vision eines auf Verheissung gegründeten Jerusalem; textanalytische Studien zu Jesaja 54 [Diss. 1990, ᴰ*Füglister* N., durch
Egger W. Gal.-Seminar reorientiert]: ÖsBSt 11.   Klosterneuburg 1991,
ÖsKBW.   277 p. DM 39. – ᴿErbAuf 68 (1992) 248 (B. *Schwank*); TLZ
117 (1992) 900-2 (R. *Stahl*, vergleicht mit R. KRATZ).

E8.6   [Trito–]   **Isaias 56-66.**

3748 **Beuken** W.A.M.,   Jesaja III A-B: PredikOT 1989 ➤ 6,3843; 7,3221:
ᴿBZ 36 (1992) 116-8 (J. *Becker*); CBQ 54 (1992) 514s (C. T. *Begg*: 'sum-
mations' odd).

3749 *Beuken* W.A.M., Trito-Jesaja; profetie en schriftgeleerdheid: ➤ 503, Symposium A. van der WOUDE 1985/92, 71-85.
3750 **Emmerson** Grace I., Isaiah 56-66: OT Guides. Shf 1992, Academic. 117 p. £6. 1-85075-382-2.
3751 **Steck** Odil H., Der Abschluss der Prophetie im AT; ein Versuch zur Frage der Vorgeschichte des Kanons: BTSt 17. Neuk 1991. 198 p. – ᴿTüTQ 172 (1992) 147s (W. *Gross*, auch über sein 3-Jes).
3752 **Steck** O. H., Studien Tritojesaja; BZAW 203, 1991 ➤ 7,3225: ᴿExpTim 104 (1992s) 298 (R. J. *Coggins*).

3753 *Lewis* Theodore J., Death cult imagery in Isaiah 57: HebAnR 11 (1987) 267-284.
3754 *Du Preez* Ron, Linguistic links between verses 12 and 13 of Isaiah 58: AndrUnS 30 (1992) 115-121.
3755 *Kellermann* Ulrich, Tritojesaja und das Geheimnis des Gottesknechts; Erwägungen zu Jes 59,21; 61,1-3; 66,18-24: BibNot 58 (1991) 46-82.
3756 **Langer** Birgit, Gott als 'Licht' in Israel und Mesopotamien ... Jes 60,1-3.19f, 1989 ➤ 5,3580 ... 7,3227: ᴿBA 36 (1992) 112s (H. D. *Preuss*); TPhil 67 (1992) 268 (H. *Engel*).
3757 **Ruiten** Jacobus van, Een begin sonder einde; de doorwerking van Jesaja 65:17 in de intertestamentaire literatuur en het NT [diss. Amst Cath. Theol. Univ. 1990 ➤ 6,3858]. Sliedrecht 1990, Merweboek. vii-247 p. ƒ35. – ᴿCBQ 54 (1992) 549s (M. E. *Biddle*: cumbersome).

E8.7 **Jeremias.**

3758 **Bonora** Antonio, Geremia uomo dei dolori: Fratelli nostri. Padova 1992, Gregoriana. 144 p. Lit. 19.000. [BbbOr 34,126]. 88-7706-108-1.
3759 **Brueggemann** Walter, To pluck up ... Jer 1-25, 1988 ➤ 4,3746 ... 7,3232: ᴿRefTR 49 (1991) 37s (M. D. *Raiter*).
3760 **Brueggemann** W., To build ... Jer 26-52, 1991 ➤ 7,3233: ᴿBtS 149 (1992) 378 (E. H. *Merrill*: 'sub-evangelical points of view here and there', notably Jer 31,31-34); GraceTJ 12 (1991) 281-4 (R. D. *Patterson*: good, except in part for evangelicals); Mid-Stream 31,4 (1992) 378-380 (R. D. *Miller*).
3761 **Clements** R. E., Jeremiah: Interpretation Comm. 1988 ➤ 4,3749 ... 7,3234: ᴿAnglTR 74 (1992) 381-3 (D. F. *Morgan*, also on HOLLADAY II); JEvTS 35 (1992) 250s (R. D. *Spender*).
3762 **Craigie** Peter C. † [1-8,3], *Kelley* P. H., *Drinkard* J. F.ᴶ, Jeremiah 1-25: Word Comm. 26. Dallas 1991, Word. xlvii-389 p. $25. 0-8499-0225-8 [BL 93,57, W. *McKane*].
3763 **Holladay** William J., Jeremiah 2 (26-52). Hermeneia 1989 ➤ 5,3591 ... [6,3867; not 'Jeremias'] 7,3235: ᴿBiblica 73 (1992) 575-7 (P. *Bovati*); JEvTS 35 (1992) 407-410 (D. A. *Dorsey*); RB 99 (1992) 772-6 (F. J. *Gonçalves*, 1s).
3764 **Jones** Douglas R., Jeremiah (RSV): NCent. GR 1992, Eerdmans. 557 p. 0-551-02048-2.
3765 **McKane** W., ICC Jeremiah 1-25, 1986 ➤ 3,2728 ... 6,3869: ᴿRB 99 (1992) 776-781 (F. J. *Gonçalves*, à *suivre*).
3766 **Oosterhoff** B. J., Jeremia, vertaald en verklaard I (1-10): CommOT. Kampen 1990, Kok. 335 p. ƒ79,50. 90-2420-837-8. – ᴿGerefTTs 92 (1992) 47-51 (A.J.O. van der *Wal*); NedTTs 46 (1992) 232 (B. *Becking*).
3767 **Pain** Alan, I am Jeremiah, Eastbourne 1990, Kingsway. 155 p. £3. 0-86065-722-1. – ᴿChurchman 105 (1991) 179s (A. *Maughan*).

3768 *Piovanelli* Pierluigi, Le texte de Jérémie utilisé par Flavius JOSÈPHE
Ant.X: Henoch 14 (1992) 11-35; Eng. 35s.
3769 **Reynolds** Blair, Jean CALVIN, Sermons on Jeremiah: TStRel 46, 1990
➤ 6,3872: ᴿRelStR 18 (1992) (D. K. *McKim*); RHE 87 (1992) 290 (J.-F.
Gilmont: notably shorter than on Micah); SixtC 23 (1992) 182-4 (B.
Armstrong, also on Micah).
3770 *Ribera* Joseph, La puntuación babilónica del Targum de Jeremías en
relación con la del texto hebreo: ➤ 44, ꟾDÍAZ ESTEBAN F., Sefarad 52
(1992) 201-8.
3771 **Schneider** D., Der Prophet Jeremias⁴ʳᵉᵛ. Wu 1991, Brockhaus. 367 p. –
ᴿZAW 104 (1992) 309 (G. *Wanke*).

3772 *Althann* Robert, Jeremiah (person) / Josiah / Jehoahaz / Shallum /
Shemaiah / Zedekiah: ➤ 741, AnchorBD 3 (1992) 684 / 1015-8 / 660 /
5,1154 / 1199-1201 / 1068-1071 [AcPIB 9,775].
3773 **Bak Dong Hyun**, Klagender Gott ... Jer: BZAW 193, 1990 ➤ 6,3876;
7,3244: ᴿBL (1992) 61 (R. P. *Carroll*); BO 49 (1992) 832s (R. *Oosterhoff*);
JBL 111 (1992) 324-6 (A.R.P. *Diamond*: insufficiently imaginative); RivB
40 (1992) 111s (A. *Bonora*).
3774 *Balbinot* Marcos A., Para reconhecer [p. 397; p. 297 para conhecermos]
Jeremias como profeta: Teocomunicação 22,97 (1992) 397-409.
3775 *Becking* Bob, Jeremia's beeld van God en zijn strijd tegen de goden-
beelden: KerkT 43 (1992) 280-290.
3776 **Dobraczyński** Jan, Los elegidos de las estrellas; la misión profética de
Jeremías. M 1991, Arcaduz. 387 p. – ᴿBurgense 33 (1992) 570 (P. *Are-
nillas*: novelista); RelCu 38 (1992) 339.
3777 *Fernández-Martos* José Mª., Jeremías 'casi' aprendió a orar en el dolor:
SalT 80 (1992) 115-133.
3778 **Ferry** Joëlle, Illusions et salut dans la prédication prophétique de Jérémie: diss. ᴰ*Briend* J., Inst. Cath. Paris 1992. – RTLv 24, p. 541.
3779 **Herrmann** Siegfried, Jeremia, der Prophet und das Buch: ErtFor 271,
1990 ➤ 6,3880 [not 'Jeremias']; DM 45: ᴿBL (1992) 73s (R. P. *Carroll*);
ZAW 104 (1992) 296 (G. *Wanke*).
3780 *King* Philip J., Archaeology and the book of Jeremiah: ➤ 18, ꟾBIRAN
A., ErIsr 23 (1992) 95*-99*.
3781 *Lundbom* Jack R., Jeremiah / book of: ➤ 741, AnchorBD 3 (1992)
684-698 / 707-721 (additions to, 698-706, *Moore* Carey A.).
3782 *Lurz* F., Jeremia in der Liturgie der Alten Kirche: EcOrans 9 (1992)
141-171.
3783 *McConville* J. Gordon, Jeremiah, prophet and book: Themelios 17,1
(1991s) 12-16.
3784 **Mazurel** Johannes W., De vraag naar de verloren broeder; terugkeer en
herstel in de boeken Jeremia en Ezechiël: diss. Amsterdam 1992, ᴰ*Deurloo*
K. xxiii-243 p. – TvT 32 (1992) 301; RTLv 24, p. 542.
3785 *Moore* Michael S., Jeremiah's identity crisis: RestQ 34 (1992) 135-150
[< ZIT 92, 568].
3786 **Seitz** C.R., Theology in conflict... Jeremiah ᴰ1989 ➤ 5,1622...7,3253: ᴿAr-
TGran 55 (1992) 343s (J.L. *Sicre*); Bijdragen 53 (1992) 87 (P.C. *Beentjes*).
3787 *Trapp* Thomas, Jeremiah; the other side of the story: ➤ 197, ꟾWOLFF
H. W., Wer ist? 1992, 229-242.
3788 **Unterman** J., From repentance to redemption: jOsu 54, 1987 ➤ 3,3543
... 6,3888: ᴿVT 42 (1992) 424 (R. P. *Gordon*).

3789 **Watts** James W., Text and redaction in Jeremiah's oracles against the nations: CBQ 54 (1992) 432-447.
3790 **White** Reginald E. O., The indomitable prophet; a bibliographical commentary on Jeremiah; the man, the time, the book, the tasks. GR 1992, Eerdmans. x-194 p.; map. 0-8028-0529-9.

3791 **Young** Theron R., The syntactic construction of poetic units in Jeremiah 1-10: diss. Wisconsin, ᴰ*Schoville* K. Madison 1991. 575 p. 92-05574. – DissA 53 (1992s) 479-A.
3792 *Wanke* Gunther, Jeremias Berufung (Jer 1,4-10); exegetisch-theologische Überlegungen zum Verhältnis von individueller Äusserung und geprägtem Gut anhand eines Einzeltextes: → 149, ᶠPREUSS H., 1992, 132-144.
3793 *McHatten* Mary Timothy, Turn from your wickedness [Jer 1,6 'The call came to an unsuspecting boy']: BToday 30 (1992) 80-83.
3794 **Borges de Sousa** Agabo, Studien zum Menschenverständnis in Jer 2-6 aus einer lateinamerikanischen Perspektive; ein Beitrag zur Anthropologie des Jeremiabuches: Diss. Bethel, ᴰ*Crüsemann* F. Bielefeld 1992. – RTLv 24, p. 572; TLZ 118,691; TR 89,97.
3795 **Biddle** Mark E., A redaction history of Jeremiah 2,1-4,2, ᴰ1990 → 6, 3890; 7,3261: ᴿTZBas 48 (1992) 292s (B. *Huwyler*).
3796 *Barbiero* Gianni, kî ʿal kol ʾēlleh (Ger 2,34*bb*); una lettura contestuale: RivB 40 (1992) 183-191.
3797 *Steiner* Richard C., A colloquialism in Jer. 5:13 from the ancestor of Mishnaic Hebrew: JSS 37 (1992) 11-26.
3798 *Miller* Dana R., Found, a folio of the lost full commentary of John CHRYSOSTOM on Jeremiah [6,2-4]: HarvClasPg 94 (1992) 379-385.
[Jer 7; 44] **Ackerman** Susan, Under every green tree 1992 → b411.
3799 **Mottu** Henry, Geremia [11 ... (1985)] 1990 → 6,3900; 7,3266: ᴿParVi 37 (1992) 228s (G. *Castello*).
3800 **Smith** Mark S., The laments of Jeremiah and their contexts; a literary and redactional study of Jeremiah 11-20: SBL Mg 42, 1980 → 6,3903; ᴿBL (1992) 92 (R. P. *Carroll*: high praise); CBQ 54 (1992) 768-780 (W. L. *Holladay*: engaging but too technical for the beginner and too brief for the scholar); ÉglT 23 (1992) 264s (L. *Laberge*); ETL 68 (1992) 155s (J. *Lust*: suggestive rather than solid); JBL 111 (1992) 323s (A.R.P. *Diamond*); JSS 37 (1992) 314s (A.H.W. *Curtis*).
3801 **Pohlmann** K.-F., Die Ferne Gottes ... Jer 11...: BZAW 179, 1989 → 5, 3647 ... 7,3265: ᴿBLitEc 93 (1992) 336-8 (M. *Delcor*, aussi sur son Ézéch); Protestantesimo 47 (1992) 136s (D. *Garrone*).
3802 *Römer* Thomas, Les 'anciens' pères (Jér 11,10) et la 'nouvelle' alliance (Jér 31,31): BibNot 59 (1991) 23-27.
3803 *Malamat* Abraham, ❸ 'If you race with foot-runners and they exhaust you' (Jeremiah 12:5): → 181, Shaʿarei TALMON 1992, 77*-79*; Eng. xviii.
3804 *a*) *Fretheim* Terence E., The repentance of God; a study of Jeremiah 18: 7-10; – *b*) *Davies* Philip R., Potter, prophet and people; Jeremiah 18 as parable: HebAnR 11 (1987) 81-92 / 23-33.
3805 *Magonet* Jonathan, [Jer 20,7-18] Jeremiah's last confession; structure, image and ambiguity: HebAnR 11 (1987) 303-317.
3806 *Sedgwick* Colin J., [Jer 20, 7-13]. The loneliness of the long-serving prophet: ExpTim 104 (1992s) 304s.

3807 **Smelik** K.A.D., Het gezicht van de twee vijgenkorven; de plaats van hoofdstuk 24 binnen het boek Jeremia [Inaug. prot. fac. Brussel]. Kampen 1991, Kok. 48 p. ƒ10. 90-242-6103-1. – ᴿDielB 27 (1991) 301 (B.J. *Diebner*); TvT 32 (1992) 90 (A. *Schoors*: een model).

3808 **Goldman** Yohanan, [Jér 25-33] Prophétie et royauté au retour de l'exil; les origines littéraires de la forme massorétique du livre de Jérémie [diss. Fribourg 1989]: OBO 118. FrS/Gö 1992, Univ./VR.   xiii-259 p.   3-7278-0814-4 / 3-525-53752-2 [OIAc 3,22].

3809 **Stipp** Hermann-Josef, Jeremia im Parteienstreit [< 'J. und die judäische Nobilität', Diss. ᴰ*Gross*, Tübingen 1991 ↠ 7,3274]; Studien zur Textentwicklung von Jer 26,36-43 und 45 als Beitrag zur Geschichte Jeremias, seines Buches und judäischer Parteien im 6. Jahrhundert: BoBB 82. Fra 1992, Hain.   ix-390 p.   3-445-09145-5.

3810 *Büsing* Gerhard, Ein alternativer Ausgangspunkt zur Interpretation von Jer 29: ZAW 104 (1992) 402-8.

3811 **Bozak** Barbara A., Life 'anew' ... Jer 30-31: AnBib 122, ᴰ1991 ↠ 7,3276: ᴿJTS 43 (1992) 559-562 (R.P. *Carroll*: 'both excellent *and* thought-provoking'); ZkT 114 (1992) 90s (G. *Fischer*).

3812 *McKane* William, Jeremiah 30,1-3, especially 'Israel': ↠ 198, ꟻWOUDE A. van der, VTSupp 49 (1992) 65-73.

3813 *Brown-Gutoff* Susan E., The voice of Rachel in Jeremiah 31; a calling to 'something new': UnSemQ 45 (1991) 177-190 [< ZIT 93,219].

3814 *Mendecki* Norbert, Stammt Jer 31,10-14 aus der Schule Deuterojesajas?: ↠ 493a, IOSOT-B 1989/92, 57-67.

3815 *Leene* Hendrik, Jeremiah 31,23-26 and the redaction of the Book of Comfort: ZAW 104 (1992) 349-364.

3816 *Graafland* Cornelis, Alter und neuer Bund; CALVINS Auslegung von Jeremia 31,31-34 und Hebräer 8,8-13: ↠ 120, ꟻLOCHER 1s, Zwingliana 19,2 (1992) 127-145.

3816* *Lohfink* Norbert, [Jer 31,31] Der neue Bund und die Völker: KIsr 6 (1991) 115-133.

3817 *Browning* Daniel C., [Jer 32,6-15] Contracts, deeds, and their containers: BIL 16,3 (1990) 62-66 [< OTAbs 15,3].

3818 **Fortuna** Mariola, ⊕ The Rechabite ideal of nomadic life Jer 35,1-10: StBib 6. Wsz 1991, Akademia. [TLZ 118, 495s, J. *Rohde*, auch über WOJCIECHOWSKI M. im selben Band].

3819 **Mulder** M.J., De Rekabieten in Jeremia 35; fictie, secte of stroming?: Cah 68. Kampen 1990, Kok. 37 p. ƒ12.50. 90-2424-874-4. – ᴿNedTTs 46 (1992) 229 (B.J. *Oosterhoff*).

3820 **Hardmeier** Christof, Prophetie im Streit ... 2 Reg 18-20; Jer 37-40: BZAW 187, ᴰ1990 ↠ 7,3916: ᴿGerefTTs 91 (1991) 57-59 (J. *Renkema*); RivB 40 (1992) 345-9 (S.P. *Carbone*); TR 88 (1992) 367-372 (L. *Camp*); ZkT 114 (1992) 189-194 (J.M. *Oesch*).

3821 *Knauf* Ernst A., Jeremia XLIX 1-5; ein zweites Moab-Orakel im Jeremia-Buch: VT 42 (1992) 124-8.

3822 **Reimer** David J., 'A horror among the nations'; the oracles against Babylon in Jeremiah 50-51: diss. Oxford. 1989. 334 p. BRD-96864. – DissA 53 (1982s) 1548-A.

3823 *Luke* K., [Jer 51,27] Ararat, Minni and Ashkenaz: IndTSt 29 (1992) 185-205.

3824 *Edwards* Ormond, The year of Jerusalem's destruction; 2 Addaru 597 B.C. reinterpreted [H. CAZELLES 1983 found 15 experts favoring Jer 52,29 586 B.C., 16 favoring Jer 52,12 587 B.C.; – solution: Nebukadnezzar around this time *changed* Babylonian practice]: ZAW 104 (1992) 101-6.

E8.8 **Lamentationes,** *Threni;* **Baruch.**

3825 **Abrego de Lacy** José María, *al.,* Lamentaciones, Cantar de los Cantares, Eclesiastés, Sabiduria: El Mensaje del AT 21. Estella 1992, VDivino. 234 p.

3826 *Alarcón Sainz* Juan José, Vocablos griegos y latinos en el Targum de Lamentaciones: ➤ 44, FDíAZ ESTEBAN F., Sefarad 52 (1992) 15-19; Eng. 19.

3827 **Bartoli** M., La caduta di Gerusalemme; il Commento al Libro delle Lamentazioni di Pietro di Giovanni OLIVI: NStStor 12. R 1991, Ist. Medio Evo. lxxii-99 p. – ᴿColcFr 62 (1992) 733s (P. *Accrocca*) [RHE 88,45*].

3828 *Bosman* Hendrik J., Two proposals for a structural analysis of Lamentations 3 and 5: ➤ 450*, Informatique 3ᵉ 1991/2, 77-98.

3829 **Dobbs-Allsopp** Frederick W., Weep, O daughter of Zion; a study of the city-lament genre in the Hebrew Bible [Mesopotamian parallels not only to Lam]: diss. Johns Hopkins, ᴰ*Hillers* D. Baltimore 1992, 296 p. 92-29315. – DissA 53 (1992s) 1546-A.

3830 *Gous* I.G.P., A survey of research on the book of Lamentations: OTEssays 5 (1992) 184-205.

3831 *Heater* Homerᴶ, Structure and meaning in Lamentations: BtS 149 (1992) 304-315.

3832 *Ḥemiel* H., ❹ Lam *pešaṭ* and *deraš:* BethM 37,131 (1991s) 360-375.

3833 **Hillers** Delbert E., Lamentations²ʳᵉᵛ [¹1972]: AnchorB 7A. NY 1992, Doubleday. xiv-175 p. 0-385-26407-0.

3834 *Krašovec* Jože, The source of hope in the book of Lamentations, ᵀ*Ceh* Anne: VT 42 (1992) 223-233.

3835 **Neusner** J., Lam Rabbah: BrownJudSt 192, 1989 ➤ 6,3922: ᴿAbr-Nahr 30 (1992) 179-190 (H.-E. *Steller*, preparing a new edition).

3836 **Provan** Iain, Lamentations: NCent 1991 ➤ 7,3250: ᴿBL (1992) 55 (R. B. *Salters*); BTrans 43 (1992) 349s (G. S. *Ogden*); BtS 149 (1992) 489-491 (H. *Heater*: some perhaps dissents).

3837 **Reyburn** William D., A handbook on Lamentations: Helps for Translators. NY 1992, United Bible Societies. ix-166 p. $9. 0-8267-0124-8.

3838 *Turner* Mary D., Daughter of Zion; lament and restoration: diss. Emory ᴰ*Newsom* C. Atlanta 1992. – RTLv 24, p. 543.

3839 **Westermann** C., Die Klagelieder 1990 ➤ 6,3924; 7,3292: ᴿVT 42 (1992) 570 (H.G.M. *Williamson*).

3840 *Monloubou* Louis, Un poème de croyant; la Lamentation 3: EsprVie 102 (1992) 304s.

3841 *Harrelson* Walter, Wisdom hidden and revealed according to Baruch: ➤ 19*a*, FBLENKINSOPP J., Priests 1992, 158-171.

3842 *Wes* Marinus A., Mourning becomes Jerusalem; Josephus, Jesus the son of Ananiás, and the Book of Baruch (1 Baruch): ➤ 524, FWOUDE A. van der, Symposium 1992, 119-150.

3843 **Wright** J. Edward, The cosmography of the Greek Apocalypse of Baruch and its affinities: diss. Brandeis, ᴰ*Fishbane* M. Boston 1992. 433 p. 92-29491. – DissA 53 (1992s) 1545-A.

3844 **[Kabasele] Mukenge** André,   La supplique collective de Ba(ruch) 1,15-3,8; traditions et réécriture: diss. LvN 1992, ᴰ*Bogaert* P.   381 p. – RTLv 24,141.542.

3845 **Murphy** F.J.,   The structure and meaning of Second Baruch 1985 ➤ 1,3629 ... 5,3674:   ᴿJQR 83 (1992s) 252s (L.J. *Prockter*).

3846 **Willett** Tom W.,   Eschatology in the theodicíes of 2 Baruch and 4 Ezra: JPseud supp 4, 1989 ➤ 5,3677 ... 7,3296:   ᴿJQR 83 (1992s) 268s (L.H. *Schiffman*); RB 99 (1992) 301s (J. *Murphy-O'Connor*).

3847 *Frasson* Martina,   La struttura dei cieli in 3 Baruc [apc. greca]; uno studio filologico: Henoch 14 (1992) 137-144; Eng. 144.

3848 *Picard* Jean-Claude,   'Je montrerai d'autres mystères, plus grands que ceux-ci ...'; notes sur 3 Baruch et quelques écrits apparentés: Canal-infos [Centre d'analyse pour l'histoire du Judaïsme hellénistique et des origines chrétiennes] 8 (1991) 17-40 [< JStJud 23,314].

E8.9   **Ezechiel:** *Textus, commentarii; themata, versiculi.*

3849 **Allen** Leslie C.,   Ezek 20-48: Word Comm 29, 1990 ➤ 6,3932:   ᴿBiblica 73 (1992) 579-581 (T. *Krüger*); BtS 149 (1992) 120s (H. *Heater:* forceful, but unsatisfactory on the dead bones ch. 37); CBQ 54 (1992) 736s (H. *Gossai*); RCatalT 17 (1992) 289s (F. *Raurell*); WestTJ 53 (1991) 360s (I. *Duguid*).

3850 **Blenkinsopp** Joseph,   Ezekiel: InterpComm 1990 ➤ 6,3934; 7,3299:   ᴿCalvinT 26 (1991) 238-241 (W.T. *Koopmans*); CritRR 5 (1992) 113-5 (Carol A. *Newsom:* a model); Interpretation 46 (1992) 69s (R.L. *Braun*).

3851 ᵀᴱ**Borret** Maurice,   ORIGÈNE, Homélies sur Ézéchiel: SChr 352, 1989 ➤ 5,3680 ... 7,3300:   ᴿLavalTP 48 (1992) 471s (Anne *Pasquier*); RBgPg 70 (1992) 212-4 (J. *Schamp*); RHPR 72 (1992) 331 (D.A. *Bertrand*).

Lieb Michael,   The visionary mode [Ezechiel chariot-vision of God] 1991 ➤ 3618.

3852 **Maarsing** B.,   Ezechiël II: PredikOT 1988 ➤ 4,3832 ... 7,3301:   ᴿKerkT 42 (1991) 170 (B. *Becking*).

3853 **McGregor** Leslie J.,   The Greek text of Ezekiel; an examination of its homogeneity: SBL SeptCog 18, ᴰ1985 ➤ 1,3647 ... 5,3685:   ᴿJQR 83 (1992s) 440-4 (G. *Marquis*; reserves).

3854 *Recchia* Vincenzo,   I moduli espressivi dell'esperienza contemplativa nelle Omelie su Ezechiele di GREGORIO Magno; schemi tropi e ritmi: VetChr 29 (1992) 75-112.

3855 **Savoca** Gaetano,   Il libro di Ezekiele: Guide spirituali AT.   R 1991, Città Nuova. 142 p. Lit. 12.000.   88-311-3732-8. – ᴿCC 143 (1992,3) 103s (D. *Scaiola*).

3856 ᴱ**Signer** Michael A.,   ANDREAS de S. Victore, Expositio in Ezechielem: Opera 6 / CCMed 53E.   Turnhout 1991, Brepols.   lxxxiv-203 p. – ᴿJTS 43 (1992) 739s (G.R. *Evans*); RBén 102 (1992) 380 (L. *Wankenne*).

3857 **Vawter** B.,   *Hoppe* L.,   Ezekiel, a new heart 1991 ➤ 7,3303:   ᴿAntonianum 67 (1992) 432-4 (M. *Nobile*); BL (1992) 94s (P.M. *Joyce*); CBQ 54 (1992) 770 (I.M. *Duguid*); NewTR 5,4 (1992) 78s (L. *Boadt*).

──────

3858 *Boadt* Lawrence, Ezekiel, book of: ➤ 741, AnchorBD 2 (1992) 711-722.

3859 **Bodi** Daniel,   The book of Ezekiel and the poem of Erra [diss. NY Union 1987]: OBO 104, 1991 ➤ 7,3305; 3-7278-0731-8/VR 3-525-53736-0:   ᴿAfO 38s (1991s) 242-253 (W. von *Soden:* good); BL (1992) 63 (P.M. *Joyce*); ÉTRel 67 (1992) 451s (J.-P. *Sternberger:* important); RÉJ 151 (1992) 181s

(J. *Margain*); RHR 209 (1992) 301 (A. *Caquot*); TLZ 117 (1992) 496-8
(H. *Reventlow*); TüTQ 172 (1992) 146s (W. *Gross*); TvT 32 (1992) 90s (A.
Schoors: kritische zin, teveel fouten).

3860 *Brooke* Georg J.,   Ezekiel in some Qumran and New Testament texts:
➤ 498, MQumran 1 (1991) 317-337.

3861 **Brueggemann** Walter, Hopeful imagination; prophetic voices in exile [Ezek
36,22-32; Jer 30,12-17; Isa 54,1-17]. L 1992, SCM. x-147 p. 0-334-02528-1.

3862 **Burke** Dennis L.,   Style and rhetoric in Ezekiel; a syntactical approach:
diss. Annenberg. Ph 1992. 173 p. 93-07368. – DissA 53 (1992s) 4358-A.

3863 *Cutler* Anthony,   Pas oîkos *Israēl*; Ezekiel and the politics of resurrection in tenth-century Byzantium: ➤ 100, [F]KAZHDAN A., DumbO 46
(1992) 47-58; 8 fig.

3864 *Dimant* Devorah,   a) The apocalyptic interpretation of Ezekiel at Qumran: ➤ 57, [F]FLUSSER, Messiah 1992, 31-51; – b) New light from Qumran
on the Jewish pseudepigrapha – 4Q390 [4Q385-391 were originally considered by her, following Strugnell, as a single Ezekiel-apocryphon]:
➤ 498, MQumran 2 (1991/2) 405-448; pl. 24-25.

3865 **Hals** Ronald M.,   Ezekiel: FOTLit 19, 1989 ➤ 5,3693 ... 7,3308:   [R]JEv-
TS 35 (1992) 410s (A. *Luc*); Themelios 17,1 (1991s) 23s (L. C. *Allen*).

3866 **Joyce** Paul,   Divine initiative and human response in Ezekiel 51: jOsu
51, [D]1989 ➤ 5,3694 ... 7,3323:   [R]CBQ 54 (1992) 113s (W. E. *Lemke*).

3867 **Krüger** T.,   Geschichtskonzepte im Ezechielbuch: BZAW 180, [D]1989
➤ 5,3696 ... 7,3310:   [R]Antonianum 67 (1992) 142-4 (M. *Nobile*); RivB 40
(1992) 349-353 (L. *Monari*).

3868 **Pohlmann** Karl-Friedrich.   Ezechielstudien; zur Redaktion des Buches
und zur Frage nach den ältesten Texten: BZAW 202. B 1992, de Gruyter.
ix-274 p. 3-11-012976-0. – [R]ETL 68 (1992) 418s (J. *Lust*); ZAW 104
(1992) 454s (H.-C. *Schmitt*).

3869 **Rooker** Mark F.,   Biblical Hebrew in transition ... Ezek: JStOT supp 90,
[D]1990 ➤ 6,3950; 7,3313:   [R]CBQ 54 (1992) 540-2 (E. *Ben Zvi*: dubious; a
similar situation exists in other books); JBL 111 (1992) 521-3 (D. I.
Block); JSS 37 (1992) 87s (D. *Pardee*: good); VT 42 (1992) 140s (R. P.
Gordon: on the whole convincing).

3870 *Miller* James E.,   The thirtieth year of Ezekiel 1:1: RB 99 (1992)
488-503; franç. 488.

3871 *Lieb* Michael,   Ezekiel's inaugural vision as Jungian archetype:
Thought 64 (1989) 116-129.

3872 *Kingsley* Peter, [Ezek 1,26s] Ezekiel by the Grand Canal; between Jewish
and Babylonian tradition: JRAS (1992) 339-346.

3873 *Thomasson* Jacques de,   Acte-signes ou actes magiques? — Ez 2-5 et
šurpu: BibNot 64 (1992) 18-25.

3874 **Ohnesorge** Stefan,   Jahwe gestaltet sein Volk neu; zur Sicht der Zukunft
Israels nach Ez 11,14-21; 20,1-44; 36,16-38; 37,1-14.15-28 [kath. Diss.
München 1990, [D]*Schreiner* J.]: ForBi 64,   1991 ➤ 7,3318:   [R]TLZ 117
(1992) 596-8 (E. *Osswald*); TüTQ 172 (1992) 60s (W. *Gross*); ZAW 104
(1992) 304s (F. *Fechter*).

3875 *Wahl* Harald-Martin,   Noah, Daniel und Hiob in Ezechiel XIV 12-20
(21-3); Anmerkungen zum traditionsgeschichtlichen Hintergrund: VT 42
(1992) 542-553.

3876 **Galambush** Julia,   [Ezek 16; 23] Jerusalem in the book of Ezekiel; the
city as Yahweh's wife [diss. Emory 1991, [D]*Hayes* J.]: SBL diss. 130.
Atlanta 1992, Scholars. xiii-181 p. $60; pa. $20. 1-55540-755-2; –6–0
[BL 93,60, P. M. *Joyce*).

3877 *Görg* Manfred, Ein verkanntes Wort für die 'Hebamme' in Ez 16,4 [*mš'y*]: BibNot 58 (1991) 13-16.

3878 **Chrostowski** Waldemar, ❷ A prophet confronting history, Ezechiel 16,20.23 + Septuagint [< diss. Wsz 1986]. Wsz 1991, Akad. Teol. Kat. 268 p. – ᴿRuBi 44 (1991) 157 (J. *Chmiel*).

3879 *Odell* Margaret S., The inversion of shame and forgiveness in Ezekiel 16.59-63: JStOT 56 (1992) 101-112.

3880 **Matties** Gordon H., Ezekiel 18, ᴰ1990 ➤ 6,3965: ᴿBL (1992) 80 (P.M. *Joyce*, detailed); ÉglT 23 (1992) 125s (W. *Vogels*); ETL 68 (1992) 419s (J. *Lust*); JBL 111 (1992) 523-5 (L.C. *Allen*); RelStR 18 (1992) 138 (M.A. *Sweeney*).

3881 *Darr* Kathryn P., [Ezek 20,1-44; 16,1-63; 23,1-49] Ezekiel's justifications of God; teaching troubling texts: JStOT 55 (1992) 97-117.

3882 *Allen* Leslie C., The structuring of Ezekiel's revisionist history lesson (Ezekiel 20:3-31): CBQ 54 (1992) 448-462.

3883 *Horst* P.W. van der, 'Laws that were not good'; Ezekiel 20:25 in ancient Judaism and early Christianity: ➤ 504, ᶠWOUDE A. van der, Symposium 1992, 94-118.

3884 **Sedlmeier** Franz, Studien zu Komposition und Theologie von Ezechiel 20 [Diss. Eichstätt, ᴰ*Mosis* R.]: SBB 21, 1990 ➤ 6,3966; 7,3324: ᴿJBL 111 (1992) 525-7 (G. *Matties:* 'a commentary on a massive scale'); ZAW 104 (1992) 458 (H.-C. *Schmitt*).

3885 **Fechter** Friedrich, Bewältigung der Katastrophe [Ez 25-29]: BZAW 208, Diss. 1991 ➤ 7,3307]: B 1992, de Gruyter. x-350 p. – ᴿExpTim 104 (1992s) 343 (R. *Coggins*).

3886 *Barr* James, 'Thou art the Cherub'; Ezekiel 28,14 and the post-Ezekiel understanding of Genesis 2-3: ➤ 19*a*, ᶠBLENKINSOPP J., Priests 1992, 213-223.

3887 *a) Boadt* Lawrence. The function of the salvation oracles in Ezekiel 33 to 37; – *b) Rooker* Mark F., Ezekiel and the typology of biblical Hebrew: HebAnR 12 (Columbus 1990) 1-21 / 133-155.

3888 *Sloan* Ian B., [Ezek 34,25; 37,36] Ezekiel and the covenant of friendship: BibTB 22 (1992) 149-154.

3889 *Seitz* Christopher R., Ezekiel 37: 1-4 [... valley of bones]: Interpretation 46 (1992) 53-56.

3890 *Block* Daniel I., Gog in prophetic tradition; a new look at Ezekiel XXXVIII 17: VT 42 (1992) 154-172.

3891 **Patton** Corinne L., Ezekiel's blueprint for the Temple of Jerusalem: diss. Yale, ᴰ*Wilson* R. NHv 1991. 200 p. 92-21348. – DissA 53 (1992s) 845-A.

3892 **Stevenson** Donna I., The vision of transformation; the territorial rhetoric of Ezekiel 40-48: diss. Graduate Theological Union, ᴰ*Chaney* M. Berkeley 1992. 201 p. 93-05975. – DissA 53 (1992s) 3566-A:

3893 *Tuell* Steven S., The law of the Temple in Ezekiel 40-48 [diss. Richmond Union, ᴰ*McBride* D.]: HarvSemMg 49. Atlanta 1992, Scholars. x-194 p. $30; pa. $20. 1-55540-717-X [OIAc 3,40].

3894 *Dijkstra* Meindert [Ezek 43,13-17] The altar of Ezekiel; fact or fiction?: VT 42 (1992) 22-36; 2 fig.

E9.1 Apocalyptica VT.

3895 **Aalen** Sverre, † 1980, ᴱ*Rengstorf* K. Heilsverlangen ... apokalypt. [De-litzsch-Vorlesungen 1974]; Vorw. *Baasland* F. [Aalen-Biog.] 1990 ➤ 6, 3970: ᴿTLZ 117 (1992) 114 (S. *Schreiner*).

3896 **Addison** Erin H., When history fails; apocalypticism in the ancient Mediterranean world diss. California, ᴰ*Pearson* B. Santa Barbara 1992. 373 p. 92-37785. – DissA 53 (1992s) 3568-A.

3897 *a*) *Alexander* Philip S., Late Hebrew apocalyptic; a preliminary survey; – *b*) *Herr* Moshe D., Les raisons de la conservation des restes de la littérature juive de l'époque du Second Temple: → 470, Apocrypha 1 (1990) 197-217 / 219-230.

3898 ᴱ**Althaus** Heinz, Apocalittica ed escatologia; senso e fine della storia [1985/7 4 art. deutsch → 3,579] ᵀ*Colombo* G., ᴱ*Canobbio* Giacomo. Brescia 1992, Morcelliana. 176 p. Lit. 20.000. 88-372-1453-7. – ᴿStPatav 39 (1992) 657s (G. *Segalla*).

3898* L'apocalyptique, Sèvres 17-28 sept. 1990: 1991 → 7,413: ᴿLVitae 47 (1992) 237 (L. *Partos*).

3899 **Cerutti** Maria Vittoria. Antropologia [nel senso generale filosofico/teologico] e apocalittica: Storia delle Religioni 7, 1990 → 7,3331: ᴿJStJud 23 (1992) 105-8 (P. *Sacchi*: intelligent, profond, stimulant — mais pas la méthode de Sacchi).

3900 ᴱ**Collins** J., *Charlesworth* J., Mysteries ... Apocalyptic since 1979: 1989/91 → 7,425: ᴿETL 68 (1992) 425s (J. *Lust*).

3901 **Cook** Stephen L., Apocalypticism and prophecy in post-exilic Israel; the sociological settings of the apocalyptic sections of Ezekiel, Joel and 1-Zechariah: diss. Yale, ᴰ*Wilson* R. – RTLv 24, p. 540 sans date.

3902 *Croatto* J.S., Apocalíptica y esperanza de los oprimidos (contexto socio-político y cultural del género apocalíptico): Ribla 7 (1990) 9-24 [8 (1991) 39-53; < Stromata 47,443].

3903 **Delcor** M., Studi sull'apocalittica: StBPaid 77, 1987 → 3,212 ... 5,3720: ᴿParVi 36 (1991) 67s (S. *Rolla*).

3904 *Frerichs* Wendell W., What is new in Old Testament apocalyptic?: → 77, ᶠHARRISVILLE R., All things new 1992, 75-86.

3905 ᴱ**Kappler** C., Apocalypses 1987 → 3,3625 ... 7,3334: ᴿJJS 43 (1992) 316-8 (C.R.A. *Murray-Jones:* critical).

3906 **Körtner** Ulrich H.J., Weltangst und Weltende; eine theologische Interpretation der Apokalyptik [Hab.-Diss. Bethel 1987]. Gö 1988 → 4,3867 ... 6, 3978: ᴿZkT 114 (1992) 199-202 (R. *Oberforcher*, mit Genuss und Freude).

3907 *Lüthi* Kurt, Apokalyptik als heutiges Lebensgefühl: → 163, ᶠSAUER G., Aktualität 1992, 201-217.

3908 *Paul* André, De l'Apocalyptique à la théologie: RechSR 80 (1992) 165-186; Eng. 161s.

3909 **Placanica** A., Segni dei tempi; il modello apocalittico nella tradizione occidentale. Venezia 1990, Marsilio. 343 p. – ᴿEuntDoc 45 (1992) 126s (P. *Miccoli*).

3910 *Ronchi de Michelis* Laura, Apocalittica, profetismo e idea della storia; LUTERO e MÜNTZER: → 481, AnStoEseg 9 (1992) 19-34; Eng. 3.

3911 **Russell** D.S., Divine disclosure; an introduction to Jewish Apocalyptic. L 1992, SCM. 164 p. £10. 0-334-01977-X [TDig 40,288]. – ᴿExpTim 104 (1992s) 55s (C.S. *Rodd:* reliable).

3912 *Russell* D.S., L'apocalittica giudaica [1964 ³1980], ᵀᴱ*Borbone* P.G.: BtT 23, 1991 → 7,3338: ᴿStPatav 39 (1992) 656s (G. *Segalla*).

3913 **Sacchi** Paolo, L'apocalittica giudaica e la sua storia: BtCuRel 55, 1990 → 6,3984; 7,3339: ᴿBL (1992) 88 (P.R. *Davies*); ExpTim 103 (1991s) 298s (R.J. *Coggins*); Henoch 14 (1992) 196-201 (B. *Marconcini*); ParVi 36 (1991) 65-67 (A. *Rolla*); RHPR 72 (1992) 211 (P. *Prigent*); RivB 40 (1992) 107-9 (G. *Castello*); VivH 3 (1992) 410-2 (B. *Marconcini*).

3914 *Villanueva* Carol, Características de la literatura apocalíptica: RBibArg 54 (1992) 193-217.

E9.2 **Daniel:** *Textus, commentarii; themata, versiculi.*

3915 *Cathcart* Kevin J., Daniel, especially the additions, and Chester Beatty-Cologne papyrus 967: PrIrB 15 (1992) 37-41.
3916 **Cowe** S. Peter, The Armenian version of Daniel: ArmenTSt 9. Atlanta 1992, Scholars. xviii-490 p. $65. 1-55540-687-4 [AndrUnS 31, 242s, J. E. *Miller*].
3917 *García Martínez* Florentino, *a)* 4QPseudo Daniel Aramaic and the Pseudo-Danielic literature [< AulaO 2 (1983) 193-208], T; – *b)* The prayer of Nabonidus; a new synthesis [< Sefarad 40 (1980) 5-25]: ➤ 244*a*, Qumran/Aramaic 1992, 137-161 / 116-136.
3918 **Goldingay** J. E., Daniel: WordComm 30, 1989 ➤ 4,3880 ... 7,3342: RThemelios 17,2 (1991s) 18s (R. A. *Taylor*).
3919 **Grelot** P., Le livre de Daniel [... lecture chrétienne]: CahÉv 79. P 1992, Cerf. 68 p. F 30. 0222-9714. [NTAbs 36, p. 446].
3920 **MacRae** Allan A., The prophecies of Daniel. Singapore 1991, Christian Life. 275 p. $10 [BtS 150, 374, J. A. *Witmer*].
3921 **Phillips** John, *Vines* Jerry, Exploring the book of Daniel 1990 ➤ 7,3342*: RBtS 149 (1992) 121s (J. F. *Walvoord*).
3922 **Russell** D. S., Daniel, an active volcano 1989 ➤ 5,3741; 7,3343: RCBQ 54 (1992) 130 (P. J. *Griffin:* merits consideration though closer to Christian spiritual reading than to commentary).
3923 *Schmitt* Armin, Die griechischen Danieltexte ('Th'' und O') und das Theodotionproblem: BZ 36 (1992) 1-29.
3924 *Slutzberg* E., ⊕ The nature and exegetical purpose of the commentary of R. SAADIA Gaon on the Book of Daniel: PAAR 66 (1990) 5-15⊕ [< JStJud 24,365].

3925 **Bennett** Boyce M., [Dan Rev...] An anatomy of revelation; prophetic visions in the light of scientific research. Harrisburg PA 1990, Morehouse. xiv-118 p. – RCBQ 54 (1992) 513s (X. J. *Harris:* admits parapsychology sheds only a dim light on the biblical texts).
3926 *Colless* Brian E., Cyrus the Persian as Darius the Mede in the book of Daniel: JStOT 56 (1992) 113-126.
3927 **David** Pablo S., The composition and structure of the Book of Daniel; a synchronic and diachronic reading: diss. DLuyten J. Lv 1991. liii-397 p. – TvT 32,189; LvSt 17,391; RTLv 24, p. 540.
3928 **Davies** P. R., Daniel: OTGuide, 1985 ➤ 1,3692 ... 5,3746: RTLZ 117 (1992) 108s (K. *Koch*).
3929 *Feldman* Louis H., Josephus' portrait of Daniel: Henoch 14 (1992) 37-94; ital. 95s.
3930 **Ferch** Arthur J., The Son of Man in Daniel 7, D1983 ➤ 64,3683 ... 1,3718: RBijdragen 54 (1992) 89 (J. van *Ruiten*).
3931 *a)* *Gese* Hartmut, Das medische Reich im Geschichtsbild des Danielbuches — eine hermeneutische Frage; – *b)* *Sæbø* Magne, Eschaton und Eschatologie im AT — in traditionsgeschichtlicher Sicht: ➤ 149, FPREUSS H. 1992, 289-308 / 321-330.
3932 **Kratz** Reinhard G., Translatio imperii ... Dan: WM 63, D1991 ➤ 7,3352: RJBL 111 (1992) 702-4 (J. J. *Collins*).

3933 *Raurell* Frederic, The book of Daniel in light of recent findings (XL Colloquium Biblicum Lovaniense 1991) [en castellano]: EstFranc 93 (1992) 157-160.

3934 **Stefanovic** Zdravko, Correlations between Old Aramaic inscriptions and the Aramaic section of Daniel [diss. Andrews 1987; 315 p.]: jOsu 129. Shf 1992, JStOT. 128 p. £27.50; sb. £20. 1-85075-351-2 [BL 93, 158, A. P. *Hayman*].

3935 *Stefanovic* Zdravko, Daniel, a book of significant reversals: AndrUnS 30 (1992) 139-150.

[Dan 1-9 ...] **Wills** Lawrence M., The Jew in the court of the foreign king 1990 ➤ 2447.

3936 *Rappaport* U., Apocalyptic vision and preservation of historical memory [... Dan 2]: JStJud 23 (1992) 217-226.

3937 *Koch* Klaus, Der 'Märtyrertod' als Sühne in der aramäischen Fassung des Asarja-Gebetes Dan 3,38-40: ➤ 602, Erlösungslehre 1991/2, 119-134.

3938 *Mastin* B. A., The meaning of $h^a l\bar{a}$' at Daniel IV 27: VT 42 (1992) 234-247.

3939 *Otzen* Benedikt, [Dan 7s] Michael and Gabriel; angelological problems in the book of Daniel: ➤ 198, ᶠWOUDE A. van der, VTS 49 (1992) 114-124.

3940 **Bryan** David J., Cosmos, chaos and the Kosher mentality; the roots and rationale of zoomorphic imagery in the animal apocalypse [1 Enoch 85-90], the Testament of Naphtali and Daniel 7: diss. Oxford 1989. 369 p. BRD-96857. – DissA 53 (1992s) 1553-A.

3941 *Patterson* Richard D., The key role of Daniel 7: GraceTJ 12 (1991) 245-261.

3942 *Haag* Ernst, Zeit und Zeiten und ein Teil einer Zeit (Dan 7,25); eine eschatologische Zeitangabe in apokalyptischer Gestalt: TrierTZ 101 (1992) 65-68.

3943 *Roscupp* J. E., Prayer relating to prophecy in Daniel 9,4-19: Master's-SemJ 3 (1992) 47-72 [< JStJud 24,361].

3944 **Kalafian** Michael, [Dan 9,24-27] The prophecy of the seventy weeks of Daniel [comparative data on pre/amillennialism without indicating a preference]. Lanham MD ᴰ1991, UPA. 259 p. $20 [BtS 150,243, J. D. *Pentecost*; NTAbs 37, p. 135].

3945 **Matheny** J. & Marjorie, The 70 weeks of Dan 9,24-27. Brevard NC 1990, Jay. 133 p. $7 pa. – ᴿBtS 149 (1992) 491 (J. A. *Witmer*).

3946 *Brückner* Annemarie, [Dan 10,13] Michaelsverehrung: ➤ 768, TRE 22 (1992) 717-724.

3947 *Gardner* Anne E., The way to eternal life in Dan 12:1e-2, or how to reverse the death curse of Genesis 3 [presidential address, Melbourne 1991): AustralBR 40 (1992) 1-19.

3948 *Carlini* Antonio, *Bandini* Michele, P. Bodmer XLVII; un acrostico alfabetico tra Susanna-Daniele e TUCIDIDE: MusHelv 48 (1991) 158-168; 2 pl.

3949 *Moore* Carey A., [Dan 13] Susanna, a case of sexual harassment in ancient Babylon: BR 8,3 (1992) 20-29. 52; ill.

3950 **Steussy** Martha Jane M., 'Gardens in Babylon'; narrative and faith in the Greek legends of Daniel: diss. Vanderbilt, ᴰCrenshaw J. Nv 1992. 280 p. 92-31009. – DissA 53 (1992s) 1962-A.

3951 *Collins* John J., [Dan 14 Vulg.; 13 G] 'The king has become a Jew'; the perspective on the Gentile world in Bel and the snake: ➤ 107, F KRAABEL A. T. 1992, 335-345.
3952 *Perraymond* Myla, Abacuc e il cibo soterico; iconografia e simbolismo (Dan 14,33-39): SMSR 58 (1992) 249-274.

E9.3   *Prophetae minores,* Dōdekaprophētōn ... Hosea, Joel.

3953 **Cathcart** Kevin J., *Gordon* Robert P., The targum of the minor prophets: [E*McNamara* M.] Aramaic Bible 14, 1989 ➤ 5,3780: R CBQ 54 (1992) 108 (S. A. *Kaufman*: by far the best translation in the series, though introduction is inadequate).
3954 **House** Paul R., The unity of the Twelve 1990 ➤ 6,4030; 7,3377: R CBQ 54 (1992) 323s (Julia M. *O'Brien*): CritRR 5 (1992) 142s (K. M. *Craig:* impact); ScripB 22,1 (1992) 23s (T. *Collins*); TLZ 117 (1992) 426s (K. *Koch*).
3956 *Kasser* Rodolphe, Le pap. Vat. Copto 9, codex des Petits Prophètes (note préliminaire sur la variété subdialectale *B74* de ce témoin 'bohaïrique ancien', IVe s.): ➤ 694*b*, IVe Copte 1988/92, 2, 64-73.
3957 **Simon** Uriel, A. IBN EZRA'S ... Hosea Joel Amos 1989 ➤ 6,4046: R BZ 36 (1992) 124s (J. *Maier*); CBQ 54 (1992) 131 (Z. *Garber*: splendid, though indexes put off to vol. 3).
3958 **Simon** Uriel, *al.,* ⊕ Deux commentaires de R. Abraham IBN EZRA sur les Douze. Ramat Gan 1989, Bar-Ilan Univ. – R Teùda 8 (1992) 207-214 (Yosefa *Rachman*).
3959 **Tov** E., (*Kraft* R. A., *Parsons* P. J.), The Greek minor prophets scroll from Nahal Haver (BHev XIIgr), the Seiyâl collection I [including the fragments from N. Hever belonging to the document published by D. BARTHÉLEMY Devanciers 1963 from find site vaguely designated as wadi Seiyal): DJD 8, 1990 ➤ 6,4033; 7,3380: R CBQ 54 (1992) 334s (H. *Gossai*); JAOS 112 (1992) 541 (B. *Taylor*); JBL 111 (1992) 532-5 (L. H. *Schiffman*); JStJud 23 (1992) 140-2 (A. *Hilhorst*); TLZ 117 (1992) 588-591 (O. *Munnich*: contains the fragments published by LIFSHITZ G. and chiefly BARTHÉLEMY B. 1963; Tov announces another work on the relation of this 'Recension-R' to TM and other LXX texts).

3959* **Beeby** H. D., Grace abounding: Hosea 1989 ➤ 5,3786 ... 7,3382: R DTrans 43 (1992) 350s (N. D. *Osborn*).
3960 **Borbone** Pier Giorgio, Il libro del profeta Osea [< diss. Torino] 1990 ➤ 6,4036; 7,3383: R CBQ 54 (1992) 737s (J. F. *Craghan*: demonstrates need of a new critical edition of the entire Bible); JSS 37 (1992) 93-95 (A. *Gelston* notes the English of the introduction by Luisa *Paglieri* p. 39-64).
3961 **Boshoff** W. S., Yahweh as God of nature; elements of the concepts of God in the book of Hosea: JNWS 18 (1992) 13-24.
3962 **Carbone** Sandro P., *Rizzi* Giovanni, Il libro di Osea, secondo il testo ebraico masoretico, secondo la tradizione greca detta dei Settanta, secondo la parafrasi aramaica del Targum: Testi e Commenti 1. Bo 1992, Dehoniane. 295 p. 88-10-20555-3.
3963 **Daniels** Dwight R., Hosea and salvation history: BZAW 191, D 1990 ➤ 7,3384: R Biblica 73 (1992) 265-270 (H.-D. *Neef*); BL (1992) 66 (G. I. *Emmerson*); BO 49 (1992) 833-5 (H. *Haag*); JBL 111 (1992) 326s (W. E. *March*); NedTTs 46 (1992) 338 (C. *van Leeuwen*).

3964 **Davies** G. I., Hosea (RSV): NCent. L/GR 1992, Marshall Pickering / Eerdmans. 315 p. $20. 0-8028-0656-2 [TDig 40,158].
3965 **Doorly** W. J., Prophet of love ... Hosea 1991 ➤ 7,3385: ᴿÉglT 23 (1992) 266s (W. *Vogels*).
3966 *Fuller* Russell, Textual traditions in the Book of Hosea and the Minor Prophets: ➤ 498, MQumran 1 (1991/2) 247-256.
3967 **Holt** Else K., Hosea og historien. Traditionerne om Israels fortid og deres teologiske betydning i Hoseabogen: diss. Aarhus 1990. 163 p. – ST 46 (1992) 69.
3968 **Jung** Johannes, Die Beziehungen zwischen den Prophetenbüchern Hosea und Jeremia: ev. Diss. ᴰ*Hermisson* H.-J. Tübingen 1992. 265 p. – RTLv 24, p. 541; TLZ 118,367.
3969 *Kruger* P. A., Yahweh and the gods in Hosea: JTydSem 4 (1992) 81-97.
3970 *Lemche* Niels P., The God of Hosea: ➤ 19a, ᶠBLENKINSOPP J., Priests 1992, 241-257.
3971 ᵀᴱ**Lipshitz** Abe, The commentary of Rabbi Abraham IBN EZRA on Hosea 1988 ➤ 4,3923; 6,4042: ᴿJQR 83 (1992s) 280-2 (M. *Sokolow*, also on SIMON/IBN Ezra 1989).
3972 **McComiskey** Thomas E., The Minor Prophets; an exegetical and expository commentary. GR 1992s, Baker, I. Hosea, Joel, and Amos; x-509 p. $30. 0-8010-6285-3 [TDig 40,76].
3973 **Naumann** T., Hoseas Erben: BW 131, 1991 ➤ 7,3388: ᴿBL (1992) 81 (G. I. *Davies*); TvT 32 (1992) 308 (A. van *Wieringen*); ZAW 104 (1992) 452 (W. *Werner*).
3974 *Nobile* Marco, Il valore strutturante e teologico di 'šwb' e 'yšb' nel libro di Osea; un tentativo di esegesi linguistico-strutturale: Antonianum 67 (1992) 472-491; Eng. 472.
3975 **Simian-Yofre** Horacio, El desierto de los dioses; teología e historia en el libro de Oseas. Córdoba 1992, Almendro. 286 p. 84-8005-007-1.

3976 a) *Schmidt* Ludwig, Bemerkungen zu Hosea 1,2-9 und 3,1-5; – b) *Stahl* Rainer, 'Deshalb trocknet die Erde aus und verschmachten alle, die auf ihr wohnen ...' Der Versuch einer theologiegeschichtlichen Einordnung von Hos 4,3: ➤ 149, ᶠPREUSS H. 1992, 155-165 / 166-173.
3977 *Mulzer* Martin, Zur Funktion der *gml*-Aussage in Hosea 1,8a: BibNot 65 (1992) 35-39.
3978 *Dyrness* William A., Environmental ethics and the covenant of Hosea 2: ➤ 88, ᶠHUBBARD D., OT 1992, 263-278.
3979 *Whitt* William D., The divorce of Yahweh and Asherah in Hos 2,4-7.12ff: ScandJOT 6,1 (1992) 31-67.
3980 *Olyan* Saul M., 'In the sight of her lovers'; on the interpretation of *nablût* in Hos 2,12 [either 'misconduct' or 'degeneration']: BZ 36 (1992) 255-261.
3981 **Nissinen** Martti, Prophetie, Redaktion und Fortschreibung im Hoseabuch; Studien zum Werdegang eines Prophetenbuches im Lichte von Hos 4 und 11: Diss. ᴰ*Veijola* T. Helsinki 1991. 406 p. – RTLv 24, p. 542: > AOAT 231.
3982 *Woude* Adam S. van der, Bemerkungen zum historischen Hintergrund von Hosea 5:8 – 6:6: ➤ 7,141, ᶠSOGGIN J. A., Storia 1991, 299-308.
3983 *Kruger* Paul A., The divine net in Hosea 5,12: ETL 68 (1992) 132-6.
3983* *Krause* Deborah, A blessing cursed; the prophet's prayer for barren womb and dry breasts in Hosea 9: ➤ 351d, Reading between texts 1992, 191-202.

3984 *Pury* Albert de, Osée 12 et ses implications pour le débat actuel sur le Pentateuque: ➤ 474, ACFÉB 1991/2, 175-207.
3985 *a) Franklyn* Paul N., Oracular cursing in Hosea 13; – *b) Peckham* Brian, The composition of Hosea: HebAnR 11 (1987) 69-80 / 331-353.

3986 *Dreher* C. A., *a)* La economía en el libro de Joel; – *b)* Las uvas del vecino: – *c)* Josué ¿modelo de conquistador? RIBLA 10 (1991) 71-82 / 14 (1993) 23-39 / 12 (1992) 49-67 [< Stromata 49,290].
3987 **Findley** Thomas J., Joel, Amos, Obadiah: Wycliffe Exegetical Comm. 1990 ➤ 7,3407: ᴿJEvTS 36 (1992) 405-7 (G. V. *Smith*).
3988 *Hiebert* Theodore, Joel, book of: ➤ 741, AnchorBD 3 (1992) 873-880.
3989 **Lloyd** Richard R.ᴵᴵᴵ, Preaching and the literary genre of prophetic drama in the Book of Joel: diss. Southern Baptist Theol. Sem., ᴰ*Cox* J. 1992. 299 p. 92-23286. – DissA 53 (1992s) 844-A.
3990 **Meer** W. van der, Oude woorden ... Joël 1989 ➤ 5,3821 ... 7,3410: ᴿBZ 36 (1992) 117s (J. *Becker*); CritRR 5 (1992) 143-6 (M. *Kessler*).
3991 **Pettus** David D., A canonical-critical study of selected traditions in the Book of Joel: diss Baylor 1992. 255 p. 93-07206. – DissA 53 (1992s) 3946-A.
3992 *Prinsloo* Willem S., The unity of the Book of Joel: ZAW 104 (1992) 66-81.
3993 **Wheeler** Raymond D., The development of repentance in Joel; a reader-response approach: diss. Southern Baptist Theol. Sem. 1992, ᴰ*Smothers* T. 228 p. 92-28428. – DissA 53 (1992s) 1549s-A.
3994 *Andiñach* Pablo R., The locusts in the message of Joel: VT 42 (1992) 433-441.
3995 *Leeuwen* C. van, *a)* The 'northern one' in the composition of Joel 2, 19-27: ➤ 198, ᶠWOUDE A. van der, VTS 49 (1992) 85-99. – *b)* De *mōrè liṣdāqā* in Joël 2:23: ➤ 503, Symposium van der Woude 1985/92, 86-99.
3996 *Stahl* R. [Joel 4,10] Abrüstung; Gedanken eines Alttestamentlers zu einer Überlebensfrage: Kirchliche Hochschule Lp Judentum 5 (1992) 3-17 [< ZAW 105,511].

E9.4 **Amos.**

3997 **Andersen** F., *Freedman* D., Amos: AnchorB 24A, 1989 ➤ 5,3827 ... 7,3412: ᴿBijdragen 54 (1993) 89s (J. van *Ruiten*); ETL 68 (1992) 156s (J. *Lust*); Gregorianum 73 (1992) 140-4 (C. *Conroy*).
3998 **Fleischer** Gunther, Von Menschenverkäufern ... Amos: BoBB 74, 1989 ➤ 5,3834; 7,3434: ᴿBZ (1992) 131-5 (W. *Thiel*: anregend, unentbehrlich).
3999 **Hasel** Gerhard F., Understanding the book of Amos: Basic Issues in Current Interpretation 1991 ➤ 7,3418: ᴿConcordJ 18 (1992) 408-410 (H. D. *Hummel*: Hasel may be like ROWLEY the major bibliographer of his era); GraceTJ 12 (1991) 289s (R. B. *Chisholm*).
4000 *Mowvley* Harry, Which is the best commentary? XVI. Amos and Hosea: ExpTim 103 (1991s) 364-8: 'best of breed' easier to judge than 'best of show'; mid-range SOGGIN; small Epworth (author not named); big 'Anchor Bible worst in terms of user-friendliness'.
4001 **Paul** Shalom M., Amos: Hermeneia comm. 1991 ➤ 7,3425: ᴿBL (1992) 84 (A. G. *Auld*); BtS 149 (1992) 492s (R. S. *Chisholm*); Henoch 14 (1992) 331s (J. A. *Soggin*); TS 53 (1992) 737-9 (R. J. *Clifford*; good sense and literary sensitivity; unmatched for lexical analysis).

4002 **Rösel** Hartmut N., ❸ The book of Amos, ➤ 7,3428: Haifa Univ. Naharija 1990, Aḥ. 316 p. 965-267-038-3: ᴿCBQ 54 (1992) 762s (M. A. *Sweeney*: 'makes a major contribution by placing the composition of the book prior to the exile'); VT 42 (1992) 139s (R. P. *Gordon*).

4003 *Aerathedathu* Thomas, The challenge of the Indian situation and the relevance of Amos' teaching for India: Indian Journal of Spirituality 4 (1991) 279-298.

4004 *Auneau* Joseph, De la justice d'Amos à la justice de Paul: VSp 146 (1992) 307-322.

4005 *Burger* J. A., Amos, a historical-geographical view: JTydSem 4 (1992) 130-150.

4006 **Carroll** R. Mark D., Contexts for Amos; prophetic poetics in Latin American perspective: [diss. ᴰ*Rogerson* J.]: JStOT supp 132. Shf 1992, Academic. 362 p. £40 / £30. 1-85075-297-4 [TDig 40,155].

4007 *Dietrich* Walter, ᴊʜᴡʜ, Israel und die Völker beim Propheten Amos: TZBas 48 (1992) 315-328.

4008 *Dorsey* David A., Literary architecture and aural structuring techniques in Amos: Biblica 73 (1992) 305-330; franç. 330.

4009 a) *Eslinger* Lyle, The education of Amos; – b) *Landy* Francis, Vision and poetic speech in Amos: HebAnR 11 (1987) 59-68.

4010 *Gillingham* Susan, 'Who makes the morning darkness?'; God and creation in the Book of Amos: ScotJT 45 (1992) 165-184.

4011 *Loretz* Oswald, Die Entstehung des Amos-Buches im Licht der Prophetien aus Mari, Assur, Ishchali und der Ugarit-Texte; Paradigmenwechsel in der Prophetenbuchforschung: UF 24 (1992) 179-215.

4012 *Maggioni* Bruno, Il profeta Amos; RClerIt 73 (1992) 590-9.

4013 **Polley** Max E., Amos and the Davidic empire 1989 ➤ 5,3841 ... 7,3437: ᴿJNES 51 (1992) 314s (Diana *Edelman*); RelStR 18 (1992) 51s (M. A. *Sweeney*).

4014 **Pungumbu** Lody, L'intervention sociale d'Amos — une contribution à l'étude de la mission prophétique en Afrique aujourd'hui: diss. Bru 1992. – RTLv 24, p. 543.

4015 **Reimer** Haroldo, Richtet auf das Recht! Studien zur Botschaft des Amos: SBS 149. [TR 88,426]. Stu 1992, KBW. 256 p. DM 50. 3-460-04491-8.

4016 a) *Reimer* H., Agentes y mecanismos de opresión y explotación en Amós; – b) *Gallazzi* S., Mis hijos y yo caminaremos en la Alianza de nuestros padres; – c) *Winters* A., La sangre derramada por Manasés: ʀɪʙʟA 12 (1992) 69-81 / 11 (1992) 87-104 / 65-74 [< Stromata 49,291].

4017 **Rosenbaum** Stanley N., Amos of Israel, a new interpretation ➤ 7,3429: Macon/Lv 1990, Mercer Univ. / Peeters. xii-129 p. $25. – ᴿCBQ 54 (1992) 129s (D. *Carr*); Interpretation 46 (1992) 86s (M. E. *Polley*: original insights); JRel 72 (1992) 277s (J. S. *Kaminsky*); TorJT 8 (1992) 188s (B. P. *Irwin*); RelStR 18 (1992) 137 (Z. *Garber*, not so clear as to who holds what on 'northern origin'); VT 42 (1992) 141s (R. P. *Gordon*).

4018 **Shelly** Patricia J., Amos and irony; the use of irony in Amos' prophetic discourse: diss. Iliff. Denver 1992. 184 p. 92-26113. – DissA 53 (1992s) 1548s-A.

4019 *Thompson* Michael E. W., Amos — a prophet of hope?: ExpTim 104 (1992s) 71-76.

4020 *Willoughby* Bruce E., Amos: ➤ 741, AnchorBD 1 (1992) 203-212.

4021 **Witaszek** Gabriel, ❷ *Prorocy Amos i Micheasz* ... in face of social injustice. Tuchów 1992, Redemptorystów. 222 p.

4022 *Köckert* Matthias, Das Gesetz und die Propheten in Amos 1-2: ➤ 149, FPREUSS H. 1992, 145-154.

4023 *Ogden* Kelly, [Am 1,1s]. The earthquake motif in the Book of Amos: ➤ 493*a*, IOSOT-B 1989/92, 69-80.

4024 *a*) *Garbini* Giovanni, La 'deportazione di Salomone' (Amos 1,6-11); – *b*) *Auld A.* Graeme, Amos and apocalyptic; vision, prophecy, revelation; – *c*) *Clements* Ronald E., Amos and the politics of Israel: ➤ 7,141, FSOGGIN J. A., Storia 1991, 89-98 / 1-13 / 49-64.

4025 *a*) *Steinmann* Andrew E., The order of Amos's oracles against the nations 1:3-2:16; – *b*) *Giles* Terry, A note on the vocation of Amos in 7:14: JBL 111 (1992) 683-9 / 690-2.

4026 *Dangl* Oskar, [Am 3,9-15]. Comparison of different OT-methodologies: ➤ 450*, Informatique 3e, 1991/2, 151-180.

4027 *Daniel* Jerry L., At ease in a place of action; Amos 6:1-7: RestQ 34 (Abilene 1992) 170-2 [< ZIT 92,568].

4028 **Manakatt** Mathew, A judgement narrative and two pairs of visions (Amos 7,1 - 8,3): diss. Pont. Univ. Gregoriana, DConroy C. R 1992. Extr. 3882: 112 p. – InfPUG 25/124,27; RTLv 24, p. 542.

E9.5 **Jonas.**

4029 **Chieregatti** Arrigo, Giona, lettura spirituale: Conversazioni Bibliche. Bo 1992, Dehoniane. 71 p. 88-10-70927-6.

4030 *Feldman* L. H., Josephus' interpretation of Jonah: AJS 17,1 (CM 1992) 1-29 [< NTAbs 37,90].

4031 **Golka** F. W., Jona: Calwer BK 1991 ➤ 7,3442: RBLtg 65 (1992) 243s (L. *Schwienhorst-Schönberger*).

4031* **Lacocque** A. & P., Jonah 1990 ➤ 6,4096: RCBQ 54 (1992) 532-4 (J. *Limburg*).

4032 TEPavia Nicoletta, GIROLAMO, Commento al libro di Giona: TPatr 96. R 1992, Città Nuova. 113 p.

4033 **Sasson** Jack M., Jonah ...: AnchorB 24B, 1990 ➤ 6,4102; 7,3449: RInterpretation 46 (1992) 314.316 (R. *Gnuse*); JBL 111 (1992) 130-4 (G. M. *Landes* compares with LACOCQUE).

4034 **Folker** Siegert, PS.-PHILON, Über Jona (Fragment) und Über Simson: Drei (aber ohne De Deo) hellenistisch-jüdische Predigten 2: WUNT 61. Tü 1992, Mohr. ix-416 p. 3-16-145758-7. – RAntonianum 68 (1993) 399-401 (M. *Nobile*: non continuazione del vol. i, 1980, bensí commentario sulle altre due prediche).

4035 **Simon** Uriel, ❻ Jonah, introd. comm.: Mikra le-Yiśra'el. TA 1992, 'Am 'Oved. xii-96 p. [OIAc 5,35].

4036 *Adamo* David T., Universalism in the book of Jonah: DeltioVM 21,12 (1992) 41-50; ❻ 50-51.

4037 *Brzegowy* Tadeusz, ❷ *a*) Dieu veut sauver tous les hommes: message religieux du livre de Jonas: AtKap 119 (1992) 203-213; – *b*) La dimension prophétique du livre de Jonas: ColcT 62,3 (1992) 5-20; franç. 20.

4038 *a*) *Cottini* Valentino, Giona, una vicenda emblematica; – *b*) *Boggio* Giovanni, I profeti, ambasciatori di Dio: ParVi 35 (1990) 104-110 / 86-93.

4039 *Davis* Adam B., What the poet of [Middle English] 'Patience' really did to the Book of Jonah: Viator 22 (1991) 267-278.

4040 *Krüger* Thomas, Literarisches Wachstum und theolǫgische Diskussion im Jona-Buch: BibNot 59 (1991) 57-88.

4041 *Lescow* Theodor, Die Komposition des Buches Jona: BibNot 65 (1992) 29-34.

4042 **Muthengi** Julius K., Missiological implications of the Book of Jonah; an African perspective: diss. Trinity Ev. Divinity School 1992. 276 p. 92-33319. – DissA 53 (1992s) 2424-A.

4043 *Rutschowscaya* Marie-Hélène, La tapisserie au Jonas du Musée du Louvre: DielB 27 (1991) 179-193 + 8 fig.

4044 *Davis* Edward B., A whale of a tale; fundamentalist fish stories [BARTLEY swallowed by a whale and came out alive: Moody Bible Institute Monthly, Sept. 1930]: PerspScCF 43 (1991) 224-237.

4045 *Lemanski* Jay, Jonah's Nineveh: ConcordJ 18 (1992) 40-49.

4046 *Scalabrini* Patrizio R., *Facchinetti* Giacomo. Ninive, la grande città; Giona: ➤ 339, ParSpV 26 (1992) 67-85.

4047 *Hamblenne* P., Relectures de philologue sur le 'scandale' du lierre/ricin (Hier. In Jon. 4,6): Euphrosyne NS 16 (1988) 183-223 [< JStJud 24,352].

E9.6 *Michaeas,* **Micah.**

4048 **Alfaro** Juan I., Justice and loyalty ... Micah 1989 ➤ 5,3980 ... 7,3454: RJEvTS 35 (1992) 252s (M. A. *Grisanti*).

4049 **Renaud** Bernard, Michée-Sophonie-Nahum 1987 ➤ 3,3740 ... 7,3461: RVT 42 (1992) 136s (J. A. *Emerton*).

4050 **Reynolds** Blair, Jean CALVIN, Sermons on Micah: TStRel 47, 1990 ➤ 6,4114: RRHE 87 (1991) 290 (J.F. *Gilmont*: no notes or index).

4051 **Schibler** Daniel, Le livre de Michée: ComEv 11, 1989 ➤ 5,3885 ... 7,3463: RCBQ 54 (1992) 333s (S. B. *Reid*: succinct, cautious); ETL 68 (1992) 159 (J. *Lust*: authenticity of Mi 2,12s is *extra chorum* defended, from 2 Chr 30,16, despite its absence in Kings); EvQ 64 (1992) 77 (Joyce *Baldwin*).

4052 **Schuman** N. A., Micha: VBGed, 1989 ➤ 5,3886; 7,3463: RGerefTTs 91 (1991) 180-2 (A.J.O. van der *Wal*).

4053 **Timm** S., Micah zwischen den Mächten; Studien zu historischen Denkmälern und Texten: ÄgAT 17. Wsb 1989, Harrassowitz, viii-516 p.: DM 128. – RVT 42 (1992) 288 (J. A. *Soggin*: highly original and well informed).

4054 **Wolff** H. W., Micah [BK] TStandel G.: Augsburg Continental Comm. 1990 ➤ 6,4123: RVT 42 (1992) 574s (J. A. *Emerton*).

4055 *Carroll* R. P., Night without vision; Micah and the prophets: ➤ 198, FWOUDE A. van der, VTS 49 (1992) 74-84.

4056 **Hagstrom** D. G., Coherence of Micah D1988 ➤ 4,4002 ... 7,3455: RAustralBR 38 (1990) 69s (M. A. *O'Brien*); ETL 68 (1992) 159s (J. *Lust*).

4057 *Labuschagne* C. J., Opmerkelijke compositietechnieken in het boek Micha: ➤ 503, Symposium van der WOUDE 1985/92, 100-116.

4058 *Otto* Eckart, Micha/–buch: ➤ 768, TRE 22 (1992) 695-704 [704-7 Micha ben Jimla, *Beyerle* Stefan, *Grünwaldt* Klaus].

4059 *Pennybacker* Albert M.J, The two Micahs; reflections on integrity in ministry: LexTQ 27 (1992) 33-42.

4060 **Stansell** Gary, Micah and Isaiah, ᴰ1988 ➤ 4,4010 ... 7,3464: ᴿAustralBR 38 (1990) 70-72 (M. A. *O'Brien*); VT 92 (1992) 283s (H.G.M. *Willamson*).

4061 *Luker* Lamontte M., Beyond form criticism; the relation of doom and hope oracles in Micah 2-6: HebAnR 11 (1987) 285-301.

4062 **Niccacci** Alviero, Un profeta tra oppressori e oppressi ... Mi 2: SBF Anal 27, 1989 ➤ 5,2889; 7,3467: ᴿCBQ 54 (1992) 331s (J. L. *Sullivan*); ETL 68 (1992) 420s (A. *Schoors*).

4063 *Anderson* Bernhard W., [Mi 4,1-5 = Is 2,2-5]. A worldwide pilgrimage to Jerusalem: BR 8,3 (1992) 14.16.

4064 *Jeremias* Jörg, Tau und Löwe (Mi 5,6f): ➤ 197, ᶠWOLFF H. W., Wer ist? 1992, 221-7.

E9.7 *Abdias, Sophonias* ... Obadiah, Zephaniah, Nahum.

4065 **Baker** D. *al.*, Obadiah, *al.*, 1988 ➤ 6,4127: ᴿBTrans 42 (1991) 149s (D. J. *Clark*); JEvTS 35 (1992) 251s (R. D. *Spender*).

4066 **Cogan** Mordechai, ❹ Obadiah, introd. comm.: Mikra 1ᵉ-Yiśra'el [bound with *Simon* U., ❹ Jonah ➤ 4035]. xii-96 p. [OIAc 5,17].

4067 *Snyman* S. D., *Yom* (ʏʜᴡʜ) in the Book of Obadiah: ➤ 493*a*, IOSOT-B 1989/92, 81-91.

4068 **Wehrle** Josef, Prophetie und Textanalyse ... Ob 1-21: AOtt 28, 1987 ➤ 3,3750 ... 5,3899: ᴿVT 42 (1992) 568s (J. A. *Emerton*).

4069 **Ben Zvi** Ehud, Historical-critical study of Zephaniah [< diss. Emory, ᴰ*Tucker* G.]. B 1992, de Gruyter. xi-390 p. 311-002837-3. ➤ 7,3469]. – ᴿBL (1992) 62s (A. *Gelston*: caution); ETL 68 (1992) 421s (J. *Lust*); ExpTim 103 (1991s) 216 (R. *Mason*).

4070 **Robertson** O. Palmer, The books of Nahum, Habakkuk and Zephaniah: NIntComm 1990 ➤ 6,4138: ᴿCritRR 5 (1992) 166-9 (J. D. *Nogalski* compares with SEYBOLD, noting also CLARK-HATTON); Interpretation 46 (1992) 87s (J. C. *McCann*); RestQ 34 (1992) 61s (J. P. *Lewis*); Themelios 18,2 (1992s) 26s (D. W. *Baker*); VT 42 (1992) 138s (J. A. *Emerton*); WestTJ 54 (1992) 178s (J. *Worgul*).

4071 **Seybold** Klaus, Nahum Habakuk Zephanja: Z BK. Z 1991, Theol.-V. 134 p. DM 28,80. 3-280-10134-7. – ᴿBL (1992) 90 (R. A. *Mason*); VT 42 (1992) 277 (J. A. *Emerton*); ZAW 104 (1992) 309 (H.-C. *Schmitt*).

4072 **Seybold** Klaus, Profane Profetie; Studien zum Buch Nahum 1989 ➤ 5,3914: ᴿIndTSt 29 (1992) 156-162 (A. R. *Ceresko*, detailed).

4073 *Sweeney* Marvin A., Concerning the structure and generic character of the Book of Nahum: ZAW 104 (1992) 364-377.

E9.8 *Habacuc, Habakkuk.*

4074 *Carrez* Maurice, Ambakoum Septante [en français]: RHPR 72 (1992) 129-141; Eng. presentation 229.

4075 **Hahlen** Mark A., The literary design of Habakkuk: diss. Southern Baptist Theol. Sem. 1992, ᴰ*Watts* J. 216 p. 93-03763. – DissA 53 (1992s) 3564-A.

4076 **Leigh** Ben Y., A rhetorical and structural study of the Book of Habakkuk: diss. Golden Gate Baptist Theol. Sem., ᴰ*Tang* S. 1992. 237 p. 92-24780. – DissA 53 (1992s) 1184-A.

4077 *Seybold* Klaus, Habakuk 2,4 und sein Kontext: ➤ 163, ᶠSᴀᴜᴇʀ G., Aktualität 1992, 99-107.

4078 *Passoni Dell'Acqua* Anna, Lo scarabeo in Ab 2,11: RivB 40 (1992) 3-66; Eng. 66: ➊ hapax *kāpîs* 'girder' > LXX *kántharos* 'wood-worm', but early taken as an image of resurrection as in Egypt.

4079 *Copeland* Paul E. [Hab 3,2 RSV]. The midst of the years: ➤ 41, ᶠDᴀᴠɪᴅsᴏɴ R., Text as pretext 1992, 91-105.

E9.9 *Aggaeus*, **Haggai** – *Zacharias*, **Zechariah** – *Malachias*, **Malachi.**

4080 **Bauer** Lutz, Das Haggai-Sacharja-Maleachi-Korpus und Aspekte seiner ökonomischen Theorie: Diss. Bethel. ᴰ*Crüsemann* F. Bielefeld 1992. – TR 89,77.

4081 *Christensen* D. L., Impulse and design in the book of Haggai: JEvTS 35 (1992) 445-456 [< ZAW 105,511].

4082 **Craig** Thomas D., [HagZecMal, Isa 66]. The return of ʏʜᴡʜ and Yahwists; metaphor and social drama in Second Temple prophetic texts: diss. Vanderbilt, ᴰ*Barr* J. Nv 1991. 170 p. 92-30907. – DissA 53 (1992s) 1958s-A.

4083 **Feltes** Heinz, Traditionsgeschichtliche Ansätze zum 'Messianismus' bei Haggai und Sacharja; ein Beitrag zur alttestamentlichen Literatur- und Religionsgeschichte wie zur messianischen Theologie nebst einem sozialgeschichtlichen Kapitel: Hab.-Diss. ᴰ*Ruppert.* Freiburg/Br 1992. – TR 89.75.

4084 *Kasser* Rodolphe, *Quecke* Hans, *Bosson* Nathalie, Le second chapître d'Aggée en bohaïrique B 74: Orientalia 61 (1992) 169-204.

4085 **Meyers** C. & E., Haggai, Zechariah 1-8: AnchorB 25-B, 1987 ➤ 3,3781 ... 7,3489: ᴿBijdragen 53 (1992) 205 (Tamis *Wever*).

4086 **Tollington** J. E., Continuity and divergence; a study of Haggai and Zechariah 1-8 in relation to earlier OT prophetic literature: diss. Oxford 1991. – RTLv 24, p. 543.

4087 **Butterworth** Mike, Structure and the book of Zechariah [diss.]. Sheffield 1992, JStOT. 325 p. £45; sb. £33.75. 1-85075-293-1. – ᴿExpTim 104 (1992s) 246s (R. *Mason* finds this more acceptable than most structural-chiastic efforts).

4088 *a) Duarte* Raúl, La escatologia (Segundo Isaias, Zacarias y Ageo); el futuro como medio de discernir y de actuar; – *b) López Rivera* Francisco, Proyecto de Dios y discernimiento; la prospectiva profética; – *c) Díaz Valencia* Héctor, Proyecto de Dios y discernimiento en el Apocalipsis: Christus 56,4s (Méx 1990) 63-65 / 53-62 / 66-70.

4089 *Hartle* J. A., The literary unity of Zechariah: JEvTS 35 (1992) 145-157 [< ZAW 105,511].

4090 *Meyers* Carol & Eric [1-8]. *Petersen* David [9-16], Zechariah, book of: ➤ 741, AnchorBD 6 (1992) 1061-5-7.

4091 *Kline* Meredith G., [Zech 1,18-21] Messianic avenger: Kerux 7,1 (1992) 20-36.

4092 **Wong Chan-Kok,** The interpretation of Zechariah 3,4 and 6 in the NT and early Christianity: diss. Westminster 1992, ᴰ*Poythress* V. 240 p. 92-24642. – DissA 53 (1992s) 1184-A.

4093 **Redditt** Paul L., [Zc 4,6-10; 6,9-15; 3,1-10: the only passages mentioning Zerubbabel or Joshua]: Zerubbabel, Joshua, and the night visions of Zechariah: CBQ 54 (1992) 249-259.

4094 *Reventlow* Henning Graf, Tradition und Aktualisierung in Sacharjas siebentem Nachtgesicht Sach 6,1-8: → 149, ᶠPREUSS H. 1992, 180-190.

4095 *Schwarz* Günther, 'Keinen Lohn für das Vieh'? (Sacharja 8,10c): Bib-Not 65 (1992) 42s.

4096 **Larkin** Katrina J. A., The eschatology of Second Zechariah: diss. ᴰ*Knibb* M. London 1992. – RTLv 24, p. 542.

4097 **Person** Raymond F., Deuteronomic redaction in the postexilic period; a study of Second Zechariah: diss. Duke, ᴰ*Meyers* E. Durham NC 1991. 340 p. 92-20310. – DissA 53 (1992s) 528-A.

4098 *Laubscher* Frans D., The king's humbleness in Zechariah 9:9; a paradox?: JNWS 18 (1992) 125-134.

4099 *Gordon* R. P., Inscribed pots and Zechariah XIV 20-1: VT 42 (1992) 120-3.

4100 *Brzegowy* T., ❾ The triple ideal of the prophet Malachi: Homo Dei (1991,4) 15-26 [< RuBi 45,50].

4101 *Hastoupis* Athanasios P., ❻ The book of Malachi: TAth 63 (1992) 18-27.

4102 *Hill* Andrew E., Malachi, book of: ➤ 741, AnchorBD 4 (1992) 478-483.

4103 *Meinhold* Arndt, Maleachi/-buch: ➤ 768, TRE 22 (1992) 6-11.

4104 **O'Brien** Julia, Priest and Levite in Malachi: SBL diss 121 (Duke, ᴰ*Meyers* E.) 1990 ➤ 7,3499: ᴿBL (1992) 82 (R. A. *Mason*); CBQ 54 (1992) 761s (P. L. *Redditt*: Malachi a *rîb* dated 605-500); JBL 111 (1992) 327-9 (Beth *Glazier-McDonald*: valuable though the real subject is effect of acceptance of JEPD on our reading of Malachi); JSS 37 (1992) 315s (R. *Mason*: care with flair); TLZ 117 (1992) 267-9 (A. *Meinhold*).

4105 *Glazier-McDonald* Beth, *Mal'ak habberît*; the messenger of the covenant in Mal 1,1: HebAnR 11 (1987) 93-104.

4105* *Keller* C.-A. [Mal 1,6-14], Religionswissenschaftliche Betrachtungen zu Maleachis Kritik an der Opferpraxis seiner Zeit: ➤ 491, Opfer 1990/2, 79-91.

4106 **Utzschneider** Helmut, Die Schriftprophetie und die Frage nach dem Ende der Prophetie; Überlegungen anhand von Mal 1,6-2,16: ZAW 104 (1992) 377-394.

> ## IX. NT Exegesis generalis

ꜰ1.1 **New Testament Introduction.**

4107 **Aguirre Monasterio** Rafael, *Rodríguez Carmona* Antonio, Evangelios sinópticos y Hechos de los Apóstoles: (Inst. S. Jerónimo) Introducción al estudio de la Biblia 6. Estella 1992, VDivino. 404 p. 84-7151-730-2. – ᴿRET 52 (1992) 493-7 (P. *Barrado Fernández*).

4108 a) *Alexandre* Manuel[J], The Chreia in Greco-Roman education; – b) *Dangel* Jacqueline, Les discours chez TACITE; rhétorique et imitation créatrice: Ktema 14 (1989) 159-168 / 291-300.

4109 **Aune** David E., The NT in its literary environment 1987 = C 1988, J. Clarke ⇒ 3,3801 ... 6,4164: [R]ColcT 62,1 (1992) 177-180 (M. *Wojcie-chowski*, ❷).

4110 **Baird** William, History of New Testament research I. From Deism to Tübingen. Mp 1992, Fortress. xxii-450 p. $42. 0-8006-2626-5. – [R]ExpTim 104 (1992s) 309 (D. *Hill*).

4111 **Baldermann** Ingo, Der Himmel ist offen; Jesus aus Nazareth, eine Hoffnung für heute 1991 ⇒ 7,3504: [R]BiKi 47 (1992) 176s (M. *Helsper*: gelungener narrativer Versuch wie THEISSENS und SCHWAGERS).

4112 [E]**Barrett** C. K., [TE]*Thornton* Claus-J., Texte zur Umwelt des Neuen Testaments[2rev]: Uni-Tb 1591. Tü 1991, Mohr. xxxiv-413 p. 3-16-145619-X. [Salesianum 55,597, R. *Vicent*).

4113 **Beilner** Wolfgang, Sehnsucht nach dem Evangelium [= Massstab Evangelium 1987]: 3-222-11735-7.

4114 *Beker* J. C., Integration and integrity in NT studies; ChrCent 109 (1992) 515-7.

4115 *Berger* Klaus, Neutestamentliche Texte im Lichte der Weisheitsschrift aus der Geniza von Alt-Kairo: ⇒ 742, ANRW 2,26,1 (1992) 412-428.

4116 a) *Berger* Klaus, Die Bedeutung von Elementen des antiken Herrscherkultes für Liturgie und Eschatologie des Christentums im 1. Jahrhundert; – b) *Petersmann* Hubert, Springende und tanzende Götter beim antiken Fest: – c) *Chaniotis* Angelos, Gedenktage der Griechen; ihre Bedeutung für das Geschichtsbewusstsein griechischer Poleis: ⇒ 429a, Fest 1988/91, 146-154 / 123-145.

4117 [F]BOERS Hendrikus W., Text and Logos; the humanistic interpretation of the NT, [E]**Jennings** T., 1990 ⇒ 6,26: [R]Neotestamentica 26 (1992) 250-2 (P.J.J. *Botha*).

4118 a) *Botha* P.J.J., Greco-Roman literacy as setting for New Testament writings; – b) *Botha* J., The ethics of NT interpretation: Neotestamentica 26 (1992) 195-215 / 169-194.

4119 **Carson** D. A., *Moo* D. J., *Morris* L., An introduction to the NT. GR 1982, Zondervan. 537 p. $25. 0-310-51940-3 [NTAbs 36, p.410]. – [R]ChrCent 109 (1992) 497s (D. A. *de Silva*); Themelios 18,3 (1992s) 25s (C. L. *Blomberg*).

4120 *Chiarazzo* Rosario, Introduzione al NT 1991 ⇒ 7,3510: [R]Asprenas 39 (1992) 438s (A. *Rolla*).

4121 *Chrostowski* Waldemar, ❷ Compendia rerum iudaicarum ad Novum Testamentum [[E]*Safrai* S., al., I/1a, I/1b; II/1 (*Mulder*, Mikra); II/2 (*Stone*); II/3a; III/2 (*Tomson*)]: ColcT 62,4 (1992) 147-176.

4123 **Collins** Raymond F., Introduction to the New Testament[2] [[1]1983]. L 1992, SCM. xxix-449 p. 0-334-02105-7.

4124 **Conzelmann** Hans † 1989, Gentiles, Jews, Christians; polemics and apologetics in the Greco-Roman world [Heiden 1981]. [T]*Boring* M. Eugene. Mp 1992, Fortress. xxxvii-390 p. $38 [CBQ 55,802, J. S. *Siker*].

4125 **Davids** Peter H., [72] more hard sayings of the NT. DG 1991, InterVarsity ⇒ 7,3514; = L 1992, Hodder & S. 311 p. £8. – 0-340-56895-X. – [R]TBR 5,2 (1992s) 16 (L. *Houlden*).

4126 **Davies** Stephen L., The New Testament, a contemporary introduction 1988 ⇒ 4,4081 ... 6,4176: [R]RExp 89 (1992) 115s (D. S. *Dockery* does not recommend).

4127 **Delorme** Jean,   Au risque de la parole; lire les Évangiles: 1991 ➤ 7,195: ᴿRBiArg 54,45 (1992) 51-53 (A. J. *Levoratti*).

4128 **Dicharry** Warren,   Human authors of the NT I 1990 ➤ 6,4177:   ᴿFurrow 43 (1992) 253-5 (F. *Magennis*).

4129 **Di Giacomo** James J., *Walsh* John J.,   Christian discovery; the road to justice [i. nature of religious experience; ii. story of Jesus; iii. meaning of membership in his body the Church]. Mkn 1992, Orbis.   ix-225 p. $11. 0-88344-807-6 [TDig 40,159].

4130 *Dormeyer* D.,   Metaphor, history and reality in the NT: Scriptura 40 (Stellenbosch 1992) 18-29 [< NTAbs 37, p. 164].

4131 **Downing** F. Gerald,   Cynics and Christian origins.   E 1992, Clark.   xi-377 p.   0-567-09613-0.

4132 *Dunn* J.D.G.,   The question of anti-Semitism in the New Testament writings of the period: ➤ 467, Jews and Christians 1989/92.

4133 **Epp** E., *MacRae* G.,   The NT and its modern interpreters 1989 ➤ 5,394 ... 7,3518:   ᴿNT 34 (1992) 293s (J. K. *Elliott*).

4134 **Evans** Craig A.,   Noncanonical writings and New Testament interpretation.   Peabody MA 1992, Hendrickson.   xv-281 p.   0-943575-95-8.

4135 **Fahner** C.,   De grondtext van het Nieuwe Testament, gedecodeerd, geanalyseerd en van Nederlandse equivalenten voorzien, 1. De vier evangeliën; 2. Handelingen, de brieven en Openbaring; tekstverwerking *Gent* A. van. Utrecht 1992, De Banier. I. 933 p. II. 1012 p. 90-336-0330-6 both.

4135* **Fee** Gordon D.,   Gospel and Spirit in NT hermeneutics.   Peabody MA 1991, Hendrickson.   157 p. $10. – ᴿSWJT 35,2 (1992s) 44 (T. D. *Lea*).

4136 **[Fernández] Ramos** Felipe,   El Nuevo Testamento 1988s ➤ 6,4182; 7,3521:   ᴿIter 4,2 (1992) 151s (J.-P. *Wyssenbach*).

4137 *a*) *Gempf* Conrad,   Pseudonymity and the New Testament; – *b*) *Parsons* Mikeal C.,   Appendices in the NT: Themelios 17,2 (1991s) 8-10 / 11-13.

4138 **Grelot** P., (*Dumais* M.),   Homélies sur l'Écriture à l'époque apostolique [relecture AT dans NT]: IntrodNT 8, 1989 ➤ 5,g657 ... 7,3526:   ᴿGregorianum 73 (1992) 342-5 (E. *Farahian*): RICathP 37 (1991) 207-210 (J.-F. *Desclaux*); RThom 91 (1991) 308-310 (L. *Devillers*).

4139 **Grelot** Pierre,   Homilías sobre la Escritura en la época apostólica, ᵀ*Arias* Isidro: BtSEscr 193.   Barc 1991, Herder.   300 p. pt. 3000; pa. 2500   84-254-1751-1; -0-3. – ᴿActuBbg 29 (1992) 55s (J. *O'Callaghan*); LumenVr 41 (1992) 480s (U. *Gil Ortega*); Phase 32 (1992) 356s (J. *Latorre*); SFulg 1 (1991s) 163-6 (J. M. *García*).

4140 **Grelot** P.,   Omelie sulla Scrittura nell'età apostolica [Introduction critique 7, 1989]ᵀ, R 1990, Borla.   300 p. – ᴿParV 37 (1992) 153s (C. *Doglio*); RivB 40 (1992) 239 (G. *De Virgilio*: la priorità della predicazione come condizione della formazione della Scrittura).

4141 **Grelot** Pierre, *al.*,   La liturgie dans le Nouveau Testament ➤ 7,8207: IntrNT 9.   P 1991, Desclée.   363 p. F 185.   2-7189-0540-9. – ᴿÉTRel 67 (1992) 598 (B. *Coyault*: beaucoup sur Jn 1,1-18; peu sur Paul).

4142 **Hall** David R.,   The seven pillories of wisdom 1990 [➤ 7,3556 but really on NT criticism]: ᴿCBQ 54 (1992) 566s (C. *Mercer*: a useful warning overstated); Churchman 106 (1992) 371s (D. *Watson*: CHESTERTON's mantle; 'the *whole* structure of form-criticism is built on sand').

4143 *a*) *Harrington* Daniel J.,   New Testament study and ministry of the Word; – *b*) *Cahill* Michael,   Coping with hypotheses; a strategy in regard to the historical Jesus: ChSt 31 (1992) 117-129 / 130-141.

4145 *Horst* Pieter W. van der,   Das Neue Testament und die jüdischen Grabinschriften aus hellenistisch-römischer Zeit: BZ 36 (1992) 161-173.

4146 **Huppenbauer** Markus, Mythos und Subjektivität; Aspekte neutesta-
mentlicher Entmythologisierung im Anschluss an Rudolf BULTMANN und
Georg PICHT [Diss. Zürich 1991, ᴰ*Weder* H.].: HermUnT 31. Tü 1992,
Mohr. xii-226 p. 3-16-146015-4. – ᴿArchScSocRel 84 (1992) 281 (W.
Frijhoff).

4147 **Jonge** H.-J. de, Visionaire ervaring en de historische oorsprong van het
christendom [Inaugural Leiden 17.II.1992]. Leiden 1992, Rijks Universiteit. 31 p. [Origin of Christianity is to be sought not in the Resurrection but in the belief before his death that God's Reign had come in
Jesus].

4148 *a*) *Kelber* Werner H., Die Anfangsprozesse der Verschriftlichung im
Frühchristentum; – *b*) *Klijn* A.F.J., Die Entstehungsgeschichte des Neuen
Testaments: ➤ 742, ANRW 2,26,1 (1992) 3-62 / 64-97.

4149* ᴱ**Kertelge** K., Metaphorik und Mythos im NT: QDisp 126, 1990
➤ 7,4049: ᴿFreibZ 39 (1992) 209-211 (D. *Kosch*); TPQ 140 (1992) 190
(K. M. *Woschitz*).

4150 **Knoch** O., Das NT in seinen grossen Gestalten; 41 Glaubens- und Lebensgeschichten, mit einer Erklärung wichtiger neutestamentlicher Begriffe. Mainz 1992, Grünewald. 136 p. DM 26,80. 3-7867-1638-2 [NTAbs
37, p. 266].

4151 **Lagrange** Marie-Joseph, The Gospel of Jesus Christ [1928], ᵀ*Ginns*
Reginald 1938, reprint. Bangalore 1992, Theological. xxv-350 p.

4152 **Lips** Hermann von, Weisheitliche Traditionen im NT: WM 64, ᴰ1990
➤ 6,3564; 7,2992: ᴿBZ 36 (1992) 155-7 (H.-J. *Klauck*); CBQ 54 (1992)
180s (L. W. *Hurtado*); TPQ 140 (1992) 188 (O. B. *Knoch*); TvT 32 (1992)
416 (W. *Weren*).

4153 **Lund** N. W. †, Chiasmus in the NT [1942] ᴱ*Scholer* D. M., *Snodgrass*
K. R. Peabody MA 1992, Hendrickson. XXX-428 p. $15 pa. 0-943575-
92-3 [NTAbs 36, p. 413].

4154 ᴱ**McKnight** Scot, Introducing NT interpretation 1989 ➤ 7,357: ᴿAsb-
TJ 47,1 (1992) 97s (M. R. *Mulholland*).

4155 **Maier** Paul L., In the fulness of time; a historian looks at Christmas,
Easter, and the early Church. SF 1991, Harper. [BR 8/3,13].

4156 *a*) *Malherbe* Abraham J., Hellenistic moralists and the NT; – *b*) *Colish*
Marcia L., Stoicism and the NT; an essay in historiography; – *c*) *Balch*
David L., Neopythagorean moralists and the NT household codes:
➤ 742, ANRW 2,26,1 (1992) 267-333 / 334-379 / 380-411.

4157 *a*) *Marshall* I. Howard, The parousia in the New Testament — and
today; – *b*) *Ellis* E. Earle, Pseudonymity and canonicity of NT documents; – *c*) *Hawthorne* Gerald F., Faith, the essential ingredient of effective Christian ministry: ➤ 126, ᶠMARTIN R., 1992, 194-211 / 212-224
/ 249-259.

4158 *Marucci* Corrado, Die Haltung der neutestamentlichen Schriftsteller gegenüber dem römischen Reich: ZkT 114 (1992) 317-326.

4159 **Marxsen** Willi, Jesus and the Church; the beginnings of Christianity,
ᵀ*Devenish* P. E. Ph 1992, Trinity. xxxv-179 p. $17 pa. 1-56338-053-6
[NTAbs 37, p. 456].

4160 **Meyer** Ben F., Christus faber; the master builder and the house of God:
Princeton TheolMg 29. Allison Park PA 1992, Pickwick. x-300 p. $27.50
pa. 1-55635-014-7 [NTAbs 37, p. 119].

4161 **Migliore** Franzo, Introduzione al NT: Armarium 3. Soveria M., Catanzaro 1992, Rubbettino. 309 p.; 3 maps. Lᵐ 30. 88-7284-077-5 [NTAbs
37, p. 268].

4163 **Müller** Peter, In der Mitte der Gemeinde, Kinder im NT [1992 HabD Mü]. Neuk 1992. 447 p. 3-7887-1423-9 [TLZ 118,93; 838s, W. *Vogler*).

4165 *a*) *Murawski* Roman, ℗ Le caractère évangélique de la catéchèse; – *b*) *Haręzga* Stanisław, ℗ La *parresia* biblique et son actualité à la lumière de l'encyclique 'Redemptoris missio': AtKap 118,498 (1992) 181-193 / 293-305.

4168 **Murphy** Frederick J., The religious world of Jesus. Nv c. 1991, Abingdon. 406 p. $25 pa. – ᴿAmerica 166 (1992) 220 (D. J. *Harrington*, amid 27 'Books on the Bible').

4171 **Newbigin** Lesslie, Truth to tell; the Gospel as public truth. L 1991, SPCK. 90 p. £6. – ᴿThemelios 18,1 (1992s) 32 (S. *Williams*: justly hard on DESCARTES) & 18,2 (1992s) 20s (J. *Corrie*, conference report).

4172 **Newsome** J. D., Greeks, Romans, Jews; currents of culture and belief in the NT world. Ph 1992, Trinity. xiv-475 p.; 4 maps. $30. 1-56338-037-4 [NTAbs 37, p. 313].

4173 **Patten** P. & R., The world of the early Church, a companion to the NT. Lewiston NY 1991, Mellen. ix-263 p. $70. 0-88946-598-3 [NTAbs 36, p. 451].

4174 ᴱ**Pedersen** Sigfred, Skriftsyn og metode; om den nytestamentlige hermeneutik: DansKommNT 1. Aarhus 1989, Univ. 386 p. – ᴿSvTKv 67 (1991) 87s (II. *Ulfgard*).

4174* *a*) *Perkins* Pheme, New Testament Christologies in Gnostic transformation; – *b*) *Pearson* Birger A., Pre-Valentinian Gnosticism in Alexandria; – *c*) *Pagels* Elaine H., The 'mystery of marriage' in the Gospel of Philip revisited: → 104, ᶠKOESTER H. 1991, 433-441 / 455-466 / 442-454.

4175 **Piettre** Monique, Le [33] parole 'dure' del Vangelo. Brescia 1991, Queriniana. 131 p. Lit. 15.000. – ᴿParVi 36 (1991) 369s (L. *Cilia*).

4176 ᴱ**Piñero** Antonio, Orígenes del cristianismo; antecedentes y primeros pasos 1989/91 → 7,453: ᴿÉTRel 67 (1992) 471 (E. *Cuvillier*: 'travail impressionnant ... qui manifeste la vitalité de la recherche biblique de haut niveau de l'autre côté des Pyrénées'); Gerión 10 (1992) 334s (S. *Montero*); JStJud 23 (1992) 285s (F. *García Martínez*).

4177 **Puskas** Charles B., An Introduction to the New Testament. Peabody MA 1989, Hendrickson. 297 p. 0-913573-45-0. – ᴿExpTim 103 (1991s) 310 (E. *Franklin*: clear, partial); Neotestamentica 26 (1992) 542s (J. C. de *Smidt*); RBibArg 54,47 (1992) 182s (R. *Krüger*).

4178 **Reese** James M., The student's guide to the Gospels: Good News Studies 24. ColMn 1992, Liturgical. 150 p. 0-8146-5689-7 [NTAbs 36, p. 426].

4178* *a*) *Rudolph* Kurt, Early Christianity as a religious-historical phenomenon; – *b*) *Georgi* Dieter, Reflections of a NT scholar on PLUTARCH's tractates De Alexandri magni fortuna aut virtute; – *c*) *Smith* Dennis E., The Messianic banquet reconsidered; – *d*) *Cameron* Ron, The Gospel of Thomas and Christian origins; – *e*) *Malherbe* Abraham J., 'SENECA' on Paul as letter writer: → 104, ᶠKOESTER H., The Future of Early Christianity 1992, 9-19 / 20-34 / 64-73 / 381-392 / 414-421.

4179 **Russell** D. S., Poles apart; the Gospel in creative tension. Louisville 1991, W-Knox. $11. 0-7152-0646-X. – ᴿRExp 89 (1992) 109 (A. A. *Trites*).

4180 *Sand* A., 'Abba-Vater' — Gotteserfahrung und Gottesglaube Jesu: Renovatio 48 (1992) 204-218 [< NTAbs 37, p. 341].

4181 **Sawicki** Marianne, The Gospel in history ... Christian education 1988 → 4,h691; 5,g649: ᴿIrTQ 56 (1991) 327s (J. *McDonagh*).

4182 **Schmidt** Peter, Woord van God — Boek van Mensen; inleiding tot de
Evangeliën en Handelingen. Averbode/Boxtel 1991, Altiora/KBS. 216 p.
90-317-0847-X / 90-6173-499-1. – RBijdragen 53 (1992) 432s (W. G.
Tillmans, f 43,30); Streven 58 (1990s) 657 (P. *Beentjes*); TvT 32 (1992) 311
(F. van *Helmond, f* 29,70).

4183 *Schmidt* Thomas E., The penetration of barriers and the revelation of
Christ in the Gospels: NT 34 (1992) 229-246.

4184 **Schneemelcher** W., Il cristianesimo delle origini [1981] 1987 ➤ 6,k14:
RScripTPamp 23 (1991) 1068s (G. *Aranda*).

4185 **Schneiders** Sandra M., The revelatory text, NT 1991 ➤ 7,3555: RAngl-
TR 74 (1992) 503s (Phyllis *Zagano*); ChrCent 109 (1992) 848s (L. S.
Mudge); Church 8,3 (1992) 54s (P. *Dinter*); Horizons 19 (1992) 288-294
(W. M. *Thompson*) & 294-7 (Susan A. *Ross*) & 297-300 (J. *Koenig*) &
300-2 (Mary *Gerhart*); 303-9, Schneiders' response; RRel 51 (1992) 934s
(Susan *Wood*); TTod 49 (1992s) 414-6 (M. *Cahill*: exceptionally clear).

4186 TESchröder Heinrich O., P. Aelius ARISTIDES, Heilige Berichte 1986
➤ 7,3555*; RAnzAltW 43 (1990) 165-7 (H. *Niedermayr*).

4187 **Schweizer** Eduard, Theologische Einleitung in das NT 1988 ➤ 5,3997 ...
7,3556: RDeltioVM 21,12 (1992) 63-68 (S. *Nauakos* Ⓖ); NedTTs 46
(1992) 63s (M. de *Jonge*).

4188 **Schweizer** Eduard, A theological introduction to the New Testament
[1988 ➤ 5,3997]. TDean O.C. Nv 1991, Abingdon. 191 p. $19. 0-687-
41469-5 [TDig 40,186].

4189 **Schweizer** Eduard, Introduzione teologica al Nuovo Testamento, T(*Sacchi*) Balestrieri Anna: NT supp 2. Brescia 1992, Paideia. 203 p. 88-394-
0479-1.

4189* **Segalla** Giuseppe, Panoramas del Nuevo Testamento [1989 ➤ 5,3999;
6,4226],T: Estudios Bíblicos. Estella 1989, VDivino. 487 p. 84-7151-597-0.

4190 ESevrin J. M., The NT in early Christianity 1986/9 ➤ 5,606 ... 7,3557:
RIstina 37 (1992) 322s (B. *Dupuy*).

4191 **Stein** Robert H., Difficult passages in the NT 1990 ➤ 7,3559: RJPsy &
Chr 11 (1992) 207 (J. A. *Gladson*).

4192 **Strecker** Georg, Literaturgeschichte des Neuen Testament: Uni-Tb 1682.
Gö 1992, Vandenhoeck & R. 300 p. DM 35. 3-8252-1682-9 [TvT 33,292,
J. *Negenman*].

4193 *Strecker* Georg, Das Göttinger Projekt 'Neuer Wettstein' [NT back-
ground-materials]: ZNW 83 (1992) 245-252.

4194 ESwartley Willard M., The love of enemy and nonretaliation in the NT:
Studies in peace and Scripture. Louisville 1992, W-Knox. x-136 p. 0-664-
25354-7.

4195 **Talbert** Charles H., Learning through suffering; the educational value
of suffering in the NT and its milieu. ColMn 1991, Glazier/Liturgical.
92 p. $7. – RBR 8,6 (1992) 14 (Elizabeth *Johnson*); CBQ 54 (1992) 804s
(D. *Mosser*); CritRR 5 (1992) 244-7 (R. P. *Meye*).

4196 **Tanner** Robert C., *al.*, Toward understanding the NT2rev [11932]. Salt
Lake City 1990, Signature. xii-462 p. $20. – RCritRR 5 (1992) 247s (D. L.
Barr: Jesus 'probably' was sent to school at age six, p. 14, 'and we are
treated to a little summary of what school-life was like').

4197 **Teeple** Howard M., How did Christianity really begin? A his-
torical-archeological approach. Evanston IL 1992, Religion and Ethics
Institute. xx-601 p. $30. 0-914384-04-X [TDig 39,389].

4198 **Thomas** Johannes, Der jüdische PHOKYLIDES; formgeschichtliche Zugänge zu Pseudo-Phokylides und Vergleich mit der neutestamentlichen

Paränese: NOrb 23. FrS/Gö 1992, Univ./VR. xvii-534 p. 3-7278-0834-9 / VR 3-525-53925-8.
4199 ᴱToit A. B. du, Handleiding by die Nuwe Testament, 6. Die Johannesevangelie; Hebreeërs tot Openbaring; inleiding en teologie. Pretoria 1988, Kerk-B. xiii-314 p. 0-7987-0563-9. – ᴿNedTTs 46 (1992) 164s (A.F.J. *Klijn*).
4200 **Unger** Merrill F. † 1980, *White* William, Nelson's expository dictionary of the NT + **Vine** W. E, † 1949, An expository dictionary of NT words with their precise meaning for English readers. Nv 1992, Nelson. xviii-755 p. $20. 0-8407-7559-8 [TDig 40,295].
4201 *Veldsman* D. P., Remembering as socio-historic dynamic of religious experience [... BULTMANN]: Scriptura 42 (1992) 1-16 [< NTAbs 37, p. 329].
4202 ᶠVERMES G., Essays on Jewish and Christian literature and history, ᴱ**Davies** P. 1990 → 6,183: ᴿJSS 43 (1992) 136-140 (E. P. *Sanders*: T. RAJAK stars on Hellenism; J. BARR scintillating on the inevitability of hypocrisy in any serious religion).
4203 **Vielhauer** Philip, Historia de la literatura cristiana primitiva; introducción al NT, los Apócrifos y los Padres Apostólicos [¹1975 ⁵1989], ᵀ*Olasagasti* M., al.: BtEstB 72. S 1991, Sígueme. 865 p. – ᴿActuBbg 29 (1992) 60s (J. *Boada*): CiuD 205 (1992) 240-2 (J. *Gutiérrez*); ComSev 24 (1991) 273s (M. de *Burgos*); LumenVr 41 (1992) 478s (U. *Gil Ortega*); RET 52 (1992) 234-7 (E. *Tourón*); TVida 33 (1991) 322s (E. *Pérez-Cotapos L.*).
4204 **Vögtle** Anton, *Oberlinner* Lorenz, Anpassung oder Widerspruch? Von der apostolischen zur nachapostolischen Kirche. FrB 1992, Herder. 160 p. DM 24,80. [TGL 83,100s, J. *Ernst*].
Wall Robert W., *Lemcio* Eugene E., The New Testament as canon 1992 → 369.
4205 **Weeks** Norman, The test of love; a revaluation of the NT. Buffalo 1992, Prometheus. 322 p. $26. 0-87975-741-8 [NTAbs 37, p. 298; TBR 6/2, 31, G. *Howes*: no future for Christianity; exasperating].
4206 **Wehrli** Eugene S., Gifted by their Spirit; leadership roles in the NT. Cleveland 1992, Pilgrim. vi-124 p. 0-8298-0920-1.
4207 **Welburn** Andrew, The beginnings of Christianity; Essene mystery, Gnostic revelation and the Christian vision. E 1991, Floris. viii-351 p.; 11 fig. £20. 0-86315-122-1 [NTAbs 37,158].
4208 [*Williams* James G., 'Neither here nor there' ... wisdom/apocalyptic: ForumFF 5 (1989) 7-30]; 7 (1991) 243-260, *Seeley* David response, Here and there.
4209 **Wright** N. T., The New Testament and the People of God: Christian origins and the question of God, 1. Mp/L 1992, Fortress/SPCK. xix-535 p. $17. 0-8006-2681-8 / UK 0-281-04593-3 [NTAbs 37, p. 273].
4210 **Zilles** Urbano, Profetas, apóstolos e evangelistas. Porto Alegre 1992, EDIPUCRS. 96 p. – ᴿTeocomunicação 22 (1992) 601s (R. A. *Ullmann*).

F1.2   *Origo Evangeliorum*, the origin of the Gospels.

4211 *a) Berger* Klaus, Zur Diskussion um die Gattung Evangelium; formgeschichtliche Beiträge aus Beobachtungen an PLUTARCHS 'Leben der zehn Redner'; – *b) Schmithals* Walter, Die Bedeutung der Evangelien in der Theologiegeschichte bis zur Kanonbildung; – *c) Strecker* Georg, Schriftlichkeit oder Mündlichkeit der synoptischen Tradition? Anmerkungen zur formgeschichtlichen Problematik¡: → 137, ᶠNEIRYNCK F., Four Gospels 1992, 121-7 / 129-157 / 159-172.

4212 **Burridge** R.A., What are the Gospels? A comparison with Graeco-Roman biography [< diss. 1989, Nottingham ᴰ*Casey* M.]: SNTS mg 70. C 1992, Univ. xiii-292 p. £35. 0-521-41229-3. – ᴿPloutarchos, Journal of the international Plutarch society 9 (1992) 7 (F. *Brenk*); SewaneeTR 36 (1992s) 173s (C. *Bryan*); TS 53 (1992) 780s (B. *Fiore*).

4213 **Deardorff** J.W., The problems of NT Gospel origins; a Glasnost approach. SF 1992, Mellen Univ. ix-228 p. $70. 0-7734-9807-8 [NTAbs 37, p. 275].

4214 *a) Ellis* E. Earle, The making of narratives in the Synoptic Gospels; – *b) Dunn* James D.G., John and the oral gospel tradition; – *c) Holtz* Traugott, Paul and the oral gospel tradition; – *d) Meyer* Ben F., Some consequences of Birger GERHARDSSON's account of the origins of the Gospel tradition: → 7,460*b*, ᴱ*Wansborough* H., Jesus and the oral Gospel tradition 1989/91, 310-333 / 351-379 / 280-393 / 424-440.

4215 *Farkasfalvy* Denis, The presbyters' witness on the order of the Gospels as reported by CLEMENT of Alexandria: CBQ 54 (1992) 260-270.

4216 *Feuillet* André, La date de composition et les caractéristiques de chacun des quatre Évangiles: Divinitas 36 (1992) 3-18.

4217 **Gerhardsson** Birger, Evangeliernas förhistoria². Lund 1988 [= 1977 + tillägg], Novapress. 88 p. – ᴿSvTKv 67 (1991) 194 (S.Y. *Rudberg*).

4218 **Jeanne d'Arc,** Les Évangiles, les quatre. P 1992, Desclée-B. 623 p. F 32. – ᴿLVitae 47 (1992) 239 (P. *Mourlon Beernaert*).

4219 ᴱ**Hahn** F., Zur Formgeschichte des Evangeliums. Da 1985, Wiss. xi-484 p. DM 69,40. – ᴿSNTU A-17 (1992) 257-261 (O. *Schwankl*).

4220 ᵀᴱ**Kiernikowski** Zbigniew. Komentarze i marginalia Biblii Jerozolimskiej do Ewangelii. Gniezno 1992, Gaudentium. 387 p. 83-85654-06-2.

4221 **Klijn** A.F.J., Jewish-Christian gospel tradition [+ 56 texts]: VigChr supp 17. Leiden 1992, Brill. vii-156 p. *f* 80. 90-04-09453-9 [NTAbs 36, p. 448]. – ᴿRÉJ 151 (1992) 190-3 (S. *Mimouni*); Salmanticensis 39 (1992) 404-7 (R. *Trevijano*); VigChr 46 (1992) 435-7 (P.W. van der *Horst*).

4222 **Koester** Helmut, Ancient Christian gospels; their history and development 1990 → 6,4246; 7,3570: ᴿCBQ 54 (1992) 159-161 (E.V. *Gallagher*: good observations lacking synthesis); ChrCent 108 (1991) 784s (W.R. *Schoedel*); CurrTMiss 19 (1992) 291s (E. *Krentz*: useful but leaves some questions unanswered); ÉTRel 67 (1992) 278-280 (C.-B. *Amphoux*: cours magistral pour le doctorat honoris causa à Genève 1990); JTS 43 (1992) 220-5 (R.M. *Wilson*: magisterial); NT 34 (1992) 207s (J.K. *Elliott*); RelStR 18 (1992) 290-5 (R.A. *Horsley*); Themelios 18,2 (1992s) 29s (P. *Head*).

4223 **Koester** H., Bovon F., Genèse de l'Écriture chrétienne 1991 → 7,3536: ᴿSalmanticensis 39 (1992) 289-302 (R. *Trevijano*).

4224 **Moloney** F.J., The living voice of the Gospel: The Gospel Today 1986 → 3,3839 ... 6,3986: ᴿRivB 40 (1992) 248s (G. *Zevini*).

4225 **Moloney** Francis J., Quattro vangeli, una parola, ᵀ*Fissore* Stefano: Religione. T 1992, SEI. 198 p. Lit. 25.000. 88-05-05182-9. – ᴿParVi 37 (1992) 471 (M. *Làconi*).

4226 **Moore** Robert G., The Gospel and narrative performance; the critical assessment of meaning-as-correspondence in D.F. STRAUSS and R. BULTMANN: diss. Rice, ᴰ*Kelber* Werner H. 1992. 199 p. 92-34440. – DissA 53 (1992s) 2413-A.

4227 **O'Grady** J.F., The four gospels and the Jesus tradition 1989 → 5,4015 ... 7,3572: ᴿScripB 22,1 (1992) 26s (K. *Grayston*).

4228 *Pérez Herrero* F., Origen y formación de los Evangelios; tres postulados de la historia de las formas actualmente en entredicho: Burgense 33 (1992) 9-47.

4229 ᴱ**Petersen** W. L., Gospel traditions 1989 ➤ 6,549: ᴿSalmanticensis 39 (1992) 306-8 (R. *Trevijano*).

4230 **Ranon** Angelo, Da Gesù ai Vangeli: IntrodNT 1. Padova 1990, Messaggero. 251 p. Lit. 18.000. 89-250-0012-X [NTAbs 37, p. 120]. – ᴿCC 143 (1992,3) 99s (D. *Scaiola*); RivScR 5 (1991) 505 (A. *Resta*).

4231 *Roth* Wolfgang, *a*) The evangelists' narrative strategies; – *b*) The six vessels of John; – *c*) Elisha's mantle and the Gospel of Mark; – *d*) Moses and Matthew: BToday 30 (1992) 175-180 / 241-5 / 297-301 / 362-6.

4232 **Stanton** Graham N., The Gospels and Jesus: Oxford Bible Series [10 volumes planned] 1989 ➤ 5,4016 ... 7,3575: ᴿAustralBR 38 (1990) 74-77 (J. *Painter*); TLZ 117 (1992) 193 (C. *Burchard*).

4233 **Stoldt** Hans-Herbert, Aenigma fundamentale evangeliorum: EurHS 23/ 416. 297 p. DM 89 [TR 88,518].

4234 **Vasiliadis** Petros V. ⓖ *Hermeneia* ... Interpretation of the Gospels. Thessaloniki 1990, Pournaras. 302 p. – ᴿTAth 63 (1992) 867-9 (E. D. *Theodorou*, ⓖ).

4235 ᴱ**Wansbrough** H., Jesus and the oral Gospel tradition: JStNT supp 64, 1991 ➤ 7,460*b*; £40; sb. £30. 1-85075-329-6. – (plures art. infra): ᴿExpTim 103 (1991s) 311 (M. *Casey*).

F1.3   **Historicitas,** *chronologia* **Evangeliorum.**

4236 **Doig** K. F., New Testament chronology. SF 1991, EMText. xxiv-401 p.; 31 charts. 0-7734-9920-2 [NTAbs 36, p. 411].

4237 *Dulles* Avery, Historians and the reality of Christ [... MEIER J.]: First Things 38 (NY 1992) 20-25 [< NTAbs 37,184].

4238 *Glasswell* M. E., The Gospels as history: Metanoia 3 (Praha 1993) 104-112; franç. 112. (235-244 as proclamation).

4239 **Grelot** P., Los Evangelios y la historia: BtSEscr 179, 1987 ➤ 4,4147 ... 6,4259 (not '1979'): ᴿCiuD 204 (1991) 259s (J. *Gutiérrez*).

4240 **Grelot** P., Le parole di Gesù Cristo: IntrNT 7, 1988 ➤ 5,4027; 6,4261: ᴿStPatav 38 (1991) 195-9 (G. *Leonardi*).

4241 **Kee** Howard C., What can we know about Jesus? 1990 ➤ 6,4262*; 7,3579: ᴿHorizons 19 (1992) 129s (J. *Carmody*: dispensed from theology; though editor of a series taking too little notice of theological claims).

4242 **Kee** Howard C., ¿Qué podemos saber sobre Jesús? ᵀ*Godoy* Rufino: Entorno al Nuevo Testamento 16. Córdoba 1992, Almendro. 158 p. 84-8005-001-2.

4243 *Krieger* Klaus-Stefan, Die Problematik chronologischer Rekonstruktionen zur Amtszeit des Pilatus: BibNot 61 (1992) 27-32.

4244 **Kulisz** Józef, ⓞ Jezus w świetle historii. Wsz 1989, Akad.Teol. 68 p. – ᴿColcT 62,3 (1992) 188s (J. *Królikowski*, ⓞ).

Mitchell Stephen, The Gospel according to Jesus; a new translation and guide to his essential teaching for believers and unbelievers 1991 ➤ 4322.

4246 **Thiede** C., *a*) Jesus, life or legend? 1990. – *b*) Gesù, storia o leggenda? Grandi religioni 6. Bo 1992, Dehoniane. 180 p. Lit. 18.000. 88-10-60406-8 [NTAbs 37, p. 122].

4247 *Ulrichsen* J. H., Har evangeliernas Jesus levt? Några tankar kring en artikel av A. ELLEGÅRD [Lychnos 1990: Jesus never existed] och dess bakgrund hos A. DREWS och G. A. WELLS: Religion och Bibel 51 (Lund 1992) 51-61 [< NTAbs 37,166].

F1.4 *Jesus historicus* — **The human Jesus.**

4248 **Asz** Szalom, Mąz z Nazaretu, [T]*Friedman* Michael: Bt Pisarzy Żydowskich. Wrocław 1990, Dolnośląsk. 800 p. – [R]PrzPow 847 (1992) 481-4 (W. *Chrostowski*, ❷).

4249 **Beilner** Wolfgang, Die Jesus-Tradition der synoptischen Evangelien: Vermittlung 27. Salzburg 1992. 138 p. [Für Studenten, nicht im Handel].

4250 **Bellet** Maurice, Christ: JJC 42. P 1990, Desclée. 316 p. – [R]FoiTemps 21 (1991) 84s (B. *Lobet*).

4251 **Betz** O., Was wissen wir von Jesus?[2rev] [[1]c. 1965]: TVG. Wu 1991, Brockhaus. 144 p. DM 29,80. 3-417-29535-1 [NTAbs 37, p. 273].

4252 **Blanchard** John, Will the real Jesus stand up? Darlington 1989, Evangelical. 192 p. £3 pa. 0-85234-258-6. – [R]Churchman 105 (1991) 81s (R. *Cook*).

4253 **Blough** Neal, al., J. C. aux marges de la Réforme: JJC 54. P 1992, Desclée. 237 p. – [R]EsprVie 102 (1992) 462-4 & 622s (P. *Jay*).

4254 **Boers** Hendrikus, Who was Jesus? The historical Jesus and the synoptic gospels 1989 ⤐ 5,4037 ... 7,3589: [R]CritRR 5 (1992) 179-181 (M. J. *Borg*: a few sensational claims; much of the Jesus tradition is simply not treated); Interpretation 46 (1992) 198.200 (E. *Krentz*).

4255 *a) Borg* Marcus J., New understandings of Jesus and motives for contemporary evangelism; – *b) Harvey* A. E., Is NT study still interesting?: Sewanee TR 36 (1992s) 136-151 / 11-16.

4256 **Bowden** John, Jesus, the unanswered questions 1989 ⤐ 4,4157 ... 6,4272: [R]Commonweal 119,2 (1992) 28-30 (L. T. *Johnson*, also on MEAGHER, Truing).

4257 *a) Broer* Ingo, Jesus und das Gesetz; Anmerkungen zur Geschichte des Problems und zur Frage der Sündenvergebung durch den historischen Jesus; – *b) Taeger* Jens-W., Der grundsätzliche oder ungrundsätzliche Unterschied: ⤐ 344, Jesus & Gesetz 1992, 61-104 / 13-35.

4258 *a) Bühler* Pierre, Vraiment homme? Une question séculaire; – *b) Perrot* Charles, L'énigme néotestamentaire; des figures de Jésus à sa particularité historique; – *c) Sublon* Rolland, Jésus, le sexe, le rire et le travail; – *d) Duquoc* Christian, Révélation de Dieu et effacement de l'humanité de Jésus: LumièreV 41,210 ('Jésus; l'énigme de son humanité' 1992) 5-15 / 17-26 / 43-51 / 81-89.

4259 *Cascioli* Lino, Il figlio dell'uomo. R 1991, Il Parnasso. 216 p.; ill. Lit. 150.000. – [R]CC 143 (1992,4) 642 (G. *Caprile*: '150.000').

4260 *Charlesworth* J. H., Jesus research; a paradigm shift for New Testament scholars: AustralBR 38 (1990) 18-32 + 18ab, page of significant corrigenda included.

4261 **Chevalley** Bernard, La pédagogie de Jésus. P 1992, Desclée. 152 p. 2-7189-0566-2 [Masses Ouvrières 449,114, X. *Durand*].

4262 **Cooke** Bernard J., God's beloved; Jesus' experience of the transcendent. Ph 1992, Trinity. viii-131 p. $14. 1-56338-020-X [NTAbs 36, p. 420].

4263 **Crossan** John D., The historical Jesus; the life of a Mediterranean Jewish peasant 1991 ⤐ 7,3596: [R]America 166 (1992) 198s (J. P. *Meier*); CCurr 42 (1992s) 246-250 (Mary C *Boys*, also on MEIER and SCHNEIDERS); Commonweal 119,8 (1992) 25s (L. T. *Johnson*); FgNt 5 (1992) 85s (J. *Mateos*); TBR 5,3 (1992s) 36 (Morna D. *Hooker*: like SCHWEITZER, grandly demonstrates the impossibility of ever discovering the historical Jesus); TLond 95 (1992) 452s (G. *Stanton*: relies too heavily on the parables); TrinJ 13 (1992) 230-9 (C. A. *Evans*: stimulating); TTod 49 (1992) 398-407 (K. *Nickle*, also on MEIER J.).

4264 *Crossan* John D., The life of a Mediterranean Jewish peasant: ChrCent 108 (1991) 1194-1200 (–1204 interview; Crossan ends: Jesus thanks him for not falsifying his message, but says that is not enough).

4265 **Cunningham** Philip A., Jesus and the evangelists 1988 ➤ 4,4166 ... 7, 3597: ᴿScripTPamp 23 (1991) 710s (J. M. *Casciaro*).

4266 *Cunningham* Lawrence S., Who is Jesus and what does he want? [MEIER J., SLOYAN G. and 4 others]: Commonweal 119,2 (1992) 41-44.

4267 **Daniel-Rops**, Jesús en su tiempo. M 1990, Palabra. 631 p. – ᴿRelCu 37 (1991) 128 (M. A. *Martín Juárez*: clásico, pero los años pasan).

4269 **Dimont** Max J., Appointment in Jerusalem; a search for the historical Jesus 1991 ➤ 7,3598: ᴿAmerica 166 (1992) 41s (Pheme *Perkins*: ill-founded theories).

4270 **Dunn** James, Jesus' call to discipleship: Understanding Jesus today. C 1992, Univ. ix-141 p. $23; $8. 0-521-41434-2; –2481-X [TDig 40,160].

4271 **Eckardt** A. Roy, Reclaiming the Jesus of history; Christology today. Mp 1992, Fortress. xii-297 p. $30. 0-8006-2513-7 [NTAbs 36, p. 436]. – ᴿEncounter 53 (1992) 414-6 (P. M. *Van Buren*).

4272 **Edwards** David L., The real Jesus; how much can we believe? L 1992, Harper Collins. 276 p. $7 pa. 0-00-627637-7 [NTAbs 37, p. 276]. – ᴿTablet 246 (1992) 1575 (J. *Galvin*).

4273 **Ellul** Jacques, Si tu es le Fils de Dieu; souffrances et tentations de Jésus. Z/P 1991, Brockhaus / Centurion. 110 p. F78 pa. 3-417-26659-9 / 2-227-31575-X [NTAbs 37, p. 276].

4274 **Evans** Craig A., Life of Jesus research; an annotated bibliography 1989 ➤ 7,772: ᴿCBQ 54 (1992) 347s (M. E. *Boring*: choices somewhat subjective, accuracy good but not absolute).

4275 **Feneberg** Wolfgang, Jesus — der nahe Unbekannte 1990 ➤ 6,4283: ᴿGeistL 64 (1991) 397s (J. *Steiner*: faszinierend).

4276 *Feuillet* André, La connaissance de Jésus d'après la double tradition synoptique et johannique: Divinitas 36 (1992) 103-118.

4277 *Fitzmyer al.*, BAR-W 18,5 (1992) 19/2, 13 letter of A. *Wallenstein* against Hellenization in four articles.

4278 **Fredriksen** Paula, From Jesus to Christ 1988 ➤ 6,4242: ᴿCBQ 53 (1991) 321s (Karen A. *Barta*: very literate, a master teacher); JRel 71 (1991) 258s (J. D. *Tabor*); RelStT 10,2 (1990) 86s (S. G. *Wilson*).

4279 *Fredriksen* Paula, De Jésus aux Christs; les origines des représentations de Jésus dans le Nouveau Testament, ᵀ*Fortier-Masek* Marie-Odile: Jésus depuis Jésus. P 1992, Cerf. 345 p. F 165. 2-204-04480-6.

4280 *Fredriksen* Paula, Who do you say I am?: Books and Religion 19,1 (NY 1992) 17s. 27s. [MEIER J., untrue to his sources; CROSSAN J., a cheerful romp; CASEY M. clearer and more honest: < NTAbs 37, p. 17].

4281 *[Funk* Robert W.]. The Jesus Seminar, voting records, – *a*) sorted by Gospels, by weighted average; – *b*) sorted by grouped parallels, by weighted average; – *c*) sorted by clusters, by weighted average; – *d*) sorted alphabetically by title: ForumFF 6,3s (1990) 245-298 / 299-352 / 7,1 (1991) 51-104 / 105-158: four of the six tables [1-2 published in 6,1s].

4282 *Georgi* Dieter, The interest in Life of Jesus theology as a paradigm for the social history of biblical criticism: HarvTR 85 (1992) 51-83.

4283 **Gill** A., Life on the road; the Gospel basis for a messianic lifestyle. Scottdale PA 1992 = 1989, Herald. 334 p. $12. 0-8361-3588-1 [NTAbs 37, p. 378].

4284 **Giorgianni** Gianni, Gesù a rischio; un confronto con la radicalità del Vangelo. CinB 1991, Paoline. 138 p. Lit. 10.000 [CC 144/1,408s, G. *Giachi*: dir. 'Orizzonti cristiani' della Radio Vaticana].

4285 **Gnilka** Joachim, Jesus von Nazaret ➤ 6,4289; 7,3600: ᴿActuBbg 29 (1992) 197 (X. *Alegre*). BLtg 65 (1992) 119-121 (T. *Söding*); BZ 36 (1992) 138-140 (J. *Schlosser*); KerkT 42 (1991) 354s (G. de *Ru*); MüTZ 42 (1990s) 395-401 (R. *Schnackenburg*); SNTU A-16 (1991) 293 (A. *Fuchs*); StPatav 38 (1991) 614-6 (G. *Segalla*); TGegw 35 (1992) 68s (H. *Giesen*); TPQ 140 (1992) 78s (C. *Niemand*); ZkT 114 (1992) 209s (M. *Hasitschka*); ZMiss-RW 75 (1991) 237s (J. *Kuhl*).

4286 *Gnilka* J., Jesus Christus: ➤ 762, NBL II, 8 (1992) 320-338.

4287 *González Faus* José I., La autoridad en Jesús: SalT 78 (1990) 247-268.

4288 **Grant** M., Jesus; an historian's review of the Gospels. NY 1992, Collier. 272 p. $12 [BR 9/3,55, E. *Johnson*].

4289 *a) Guerra* Santiago, Jesús, hombre libre; – *b) Pikaza* Xabier, Cautividades de ayer y esclavitudes de hoy; caminos de liberación: REspir 51 (1992) 419-447 / 473-502.

4290 **Guthrie** Michael D., Discovering the life of Christ; a [12-week] biographical study approach to the life of Jesus Christ utilizing the four Gospels: diss. United Theol. Sem. 1992, ᴰ*Snyder* H. 305 p. 92-33343. – DissA 53 (1992s) 2412-A.

4291 **Harrington** Wilfrid J., The Jesus story 1991 ➤ 7,3603: ᴿAustralasCR 69 (1992) 512s (B. *Byrne*: a 'deadening' approach that proves only how superior the Gospel narrative style is).

4292 **Harvey** N. P., The morals of Jesus [hardly of interest to him]. L 1991, Darton-LT. 112 p. £7. 0-232-51926-9 [NTAbs 36, p. 422].

4293 **Herr** W. A., In search of Christian wisdom; rediscovering how Jesus taught. Ch 1991, T. More. 106 p. $12. 0-88347-221-X [NTAbs 36, p. 422].

4294 *Holland* Scott, The problems and prospects of a 'sectarian ethic'; a critique of the HAUERWAS reading of the Jesus story: CGrebel 10 (1992) 157-168.

4295 *a) Homerski* J., ⓟ Misja Jezusa w planie zbawienia [salvation]; – *b) Kudaszewicz* J., ⓟ J.-C. pośrednikiem Objawienia [medium of revelation]; – *c) Langkammer* H. ⓟ Consciousness of his divine mission; – *d) Teklak* Z., ⓟ Who is Jesus Christ: AtKap 118, 499 (1992) 417-431 / 432-447 / 406-416 / 364-384 (–405).

4296 **Houlden** J. L., [L King's College Lectures] Jesus, a question of identity. L 1992, SPCK. 136 p. £6 pa. 0-281-04573-9 [NTAbs 36, p. 422]. – ᴿExpTim 103,10 2d-top choice (1991s) 290s (C. S. *Rodd*: is every image of Jesus a self-image, like the distasteful Dürer cover?); TBR 5,1 (1992s) 21s (C. C. *Rowland*); TLond 95 (1992) 382s (J. *Drury*: not-easy stocktaking of the resources of Christology).

4297 *Houlden* J. L., Jesus before faith; portrait of a peasant Jewish Cynic? [MEIER J.; CROSSAN J.: WILSON A.]: TimesLitSupp [25 Sept 1992] 27 [< NTAbs 37, p. 185].

4298 **Imbach** Josef, ¿De quién es Jesús? Su significación para judíos, cristianos y musulmanes [Wem gehört J.?]. ᵀ*Villanueva* Marciano. Barc 1991, Herder. 270 p. 84-254-1748-1. – ᴿActuBbg 29 (1992) 70 (J. *Boada*); AugM 37 (1992) 200 (J. *Anoz*); Burgense 33 (1992) 569s (G. *del Pozo Abejón*).

4299 **Jonge** Marinus de, Jezus als Messias; hoe hij zijn zending zag. Boxtel/ Brugge 1990, KBS/Tabor. 128 p. ƒ 33. 90-61734-60-6 / 90-6597-404-0. – ᴿNedTTs 46 (1992) 70s (A.F.J. *Klijn*).

4300 **Joubert** S., Van werklikheid tot werklikheid; die interpretasie en interkulturele kommunikasie van Nuwe-Testamentiese waarden: Scriptura 41 (Stellenbosch 1992) 55-65 [< NTAbs 37, p. 166].

4301 **Kähler** Martin, Il cosiddetto Gesù storico e l'autentico Cristo biblico [1892, con altro saggio 1896]. N 1992, D'Auria. 154 p. [CC 144/4, 617s, V. *Fusco*, anche su OMODEO A.², *al*.].

4302 *Karrer* Martin, Der lehrende Jesus; neutestamentliche Erwägungen: ZNW 83 (1992) 1-20.

4303 *Kee* Howard C., [➤ 4241] Changing modes of leadership in the NT period: [➤ a21] Social Compass 39 (1992) 241-254; franç 251.

4304 **Kesich** V., The Gospel image of Christ²ʳᵉᵛ [¹c. 1978]. Crestwood NY 1992, St. Vladimir. 214 p. $10 pa. 0-88141-102-7 [NTAbs 37, p. 279].

4305 ᴱ**Klappert** B. *al*., Jesusbekenntnis und Christusnachfolge: Tb 115. Mü 1992, Kaiser. 93 p. DM 12,80. 3-459-01925-5 [NTAbs 37, p. 136].

4306 **Knoch** Otto, Das NT [*Maiberger* P. 1990, AT] in seinen grossen Gestalten; 41 Glaubens- und Lebensgeschichten; mit einer Erklärung wichtiger neutestamentlicher Begriffe. Mainz 1992. Grünewald. 196 p. DM 26,80 pa. [TR 89,106, K. *Scholtissek*].

4307 **Kroll** G., Auf den Spüren Jesu¹⁰ 1988 ➤ 4,4179 ...: ᴿScripTPamp 23 (1991) 708 (K. *Limburg*).

4308 *a*) *Lascaris* André, Die Einmaligkeit Jesu, ᵀ*Brinkmann* M.; – *b*) *Knauer* Peter, Rivalität und Nächstenliebe: ➤ 602, Dramatische Erlösungslehre 1991/2, 213-226 / 201-212.

4309 **Lemcio** Eugene S., The past of Jesus in the Gospels: SNTS Mg 60. C 1991, Univ. xiv-189 p. £25. – ᴿTR 87 (1991) 445-7 [H. *Giesen*: zweifältige Zeitrechnung; anregend (oder) provozierend].

4310 *Lenoci* Michele, Gesù profeta e maestro: ParVi 36 (1991) 326-335 [-369, *al*., Messia, Servo, sacerdote].

4310* **Lentzen-Deis** Fritzleo, *al*., Images of Jesus; contributions to biblical method, ᵀᴱ*Pascual* Henry. Bombay 1988, St. Paul. 102 p. ɪs. 35. – ᴿBible Bhashyam 16 (1990) 131-3 (C. *Velamparampil*).

4311 **Macquarrie** John, Jesus Christ in modern thought 1990 ➤ 7,7479: ᴿHorizons 19 (1992) 139-141 (W. P. *Loewe*).

4312 *Madec* Goulven, Christus: ➤ 743, AugL 1,5s (1992) 645-908.

4313 **Maqsood** R. W. [= *Kendrick* Rosalyn], The separated ones; Jesus, the Pharisees and Islam. L 1991, SCM. xiii-194 p. £10. 0-334-02498-6 [NTAbs 36, p. 449].

4314 *Marchesi* Giovanni. Il discepolato di Gesù; vocazione, sequela e missione: CC 143 (1992,3) 131-144.

4315 **Marguerat** Daniel, L'homme qui venait de Nazareth; ce qu'on peut aujord'hui savoir de Jésus. Aubonne 1990. Poulin. 212 p. [RTPhil 125, 105s, F. *Amsler*]. – ᴿRHPR 72 (1992) 200s (C. *Grappe*: vif; moins bien sur la Passion).

4316 **Marsh** Clive, Albrecht RITSCHL and the problem of the historical Jesus. Lewiston NY 1992, Mellen. xxiv-236 p. $70 [TR 88,343].

4317 **Mateos** Juan, L'utopia di Gesù. Assisi 1991, Cittadella. 210 p. – ᴿTeresianum 43 (1992) 291 (V. *Pasquetto*).

4318 **Mateos** Juan, *Camacho* Fernando, Jesus e a sociedade de seu tempo. São Paulo 1992, Paulinas. 171 p. [Teocomunicação 23, 443s].

4319 *Mesters* Carlos,   La práctica evangelizadora de Jesús: Christus 57,4 (Méx 1992) 36-42.
4320 *Meyer* Ben F.,   (→ 4160) 'Phases' in Jesus' mission: Gregorianum 73 (1992) 5-17; franç. 17.
4321 *a) Meyer* Ben F.,   Jesus Christ; – *b) Wright* N.T.,   Quest for the historical Jesus; – *c) Riches* John,   Actual words of Jesus; – *d) Borg* Marcus J.,   Teaching of Jesus; – *e) Bauckham* Richard,   Worship of Jesus; – *f) Brashler* James A.,   Brothers and sisters of Jesus: → 741. AnchorBD 3 (1992) 773-796-802-804-812-819-820.
4322 **Mitchell** Stephen,   The Gospel according to Jesus; a new translation and guide to his essential teachings for believers and unbelievers. L c. 1991, Harper-Collins. $23. – [R]BR 8,5 (1992) 13-15 (Elizabeth *Johnson*); ChrCent 109 (1992) 307 (R. *Large*); Tablet 246 (1992) 584 (G. *O'Collins*, also on CROSSAN and HOULDEN).
4323 *O'Collins* Gerald, *Kendall* Daniel,   The faith of Jesus: TS 53 (1992) 403-423.
4324 **Omodeo** Adolfo [1889-1848],   Gesù il Nazoreo [1927],   [E]*Sciuto* F.E.: Armarium 2. Soveria Mannelli 1992, Rubbettino.   188 p.; 5 pl. Lit. 20.000.   88-7384-075-9 [NTAbs 37, p. 282].
4325 *Orsatti* Mauro,   La coscienza che Gesù aveva di se stesso: ParVi 36 (1991) 246-257.
4326 **Painter** John,   Theology as hermeneutics; Rudolf BULTMANN's interpretation of the history of Jesus.   Sheffield 1987, Almond.   xiv-265 p. $15. – [R]CurrTMiss 19 (1992) 54 (W.C. *Linss*).
4327 **Pelikan** J.,   Jésus au fil de l'histoire; sa place dans l'histoire de la culture, [T]*Malamoud* Catherine. P 1989, Hachette.   302 p. F 168. – [R]RHR 209 (1992) 212-4 (F. *Blanchetière*).
4328 **Pelikan** Jaroslav,   Jesús a través de los siglos; su lugar en la historia de la cultura[T].   Barc 1989, Herder. 303 p. – [R]CiuD 204 (1991) 265s (J. *Gutiérrez*).
4329 **Perkins** Pheme,   Jesus as teacher: Understanding Jesus Today 1990 → 6,4315:   [R]CBQ 54 (1992) 788s (J. *Winkler*, also on the other three volumes); ScotJT 45 (1992) 118s (D.C. *Parker*, also on KEE and TIEDE).
4330 **Pikaza** Xabier,   La figura de Jesús; profeta, taumaturgo, rabino, Mesías: El mundo de la Biblia.   Estella 1992, VDivino. 249 p. pt. 1200 [NRT 115,103, L. *Renwart*].   84-7151-812-0.
4331 **Renan** Ernst,   Vie de Jésus (1867 sans commentaire). P 1992. – [R]Études 377 (1992) 268s (J. *Guillet* 'travail consciencieux et prolongé'). Abréa en titre (diffusion Seuil)/Arléa en texte, sans pp. ou prix.
4332 — *Barret* Philippe,   Ernest RENAN; tout est possible, même Dieu. P 1992, Bourin. 186 p. F 110. – [R]Études 377 (1992) 572 (R. *Marlé*).
4333 *Rodríguez Roca* José A.,   La experiencia creyente de Jesús: RET 52 (1992) 349-356.
4334 **Ross** C. Randolph,   Common sense Christianity 1989 → 5,4082:   [R]JEvTS 35 (1992) 127-9 (B. *Demarest*: aims to show that much of Christian belief is just plain wrong).
4335 *Sand* Alexander,   'Abba-Vater'; Gotteserfahrung und Gottesglaube Jesu: Renovatio 48 (Köln 1992) 204-218 [< ZIT 92,755].
4335* *Sanders* E.P.,   Jesus in historical context: TTod 50 (1993s) 429-448.
4336 *Schmid* Peter F.,   'Ecce homo! Seht, was für ein Mensch!' Anthropologische Voraussetzungen für die Begegnung mit Jesus: Diakonia 23,1 (1992) 5-12 [-60, verschiedenartige Jesusbilder].
4337 **Schwager** Raymund,   Dem Netz des Jägers entronnen; das Jesusdrama nacherzählt 1991 → 7,3628:   [R]ActuBbg 29 (1992) 58s (J. *Boada*).

4338 **Schweitzer** Albert, Investigación sobre la vida de Jesús [1906], ᵀ*Rodelas* Juan Miguel: Clásicos de la ciencia biblica 4/1. Valencia 1990, Inst. S. Jerónimo. 379 p. – ᴿActuBbg 29 (1992) 75s (J. *Boada*); LumenVr 41 (1992) 56s (F. *Ortiz de Urtaran*).

4339 **Schweizer** Eduard, Gesù Cristo; l'uomo di Nazareth e il Signore glorificato, ᵀ*Tomasetto* Domenico, ᴱ*Gloer* Hulitt: PiccCollMod 69. T 1992, Claudiana. 164 p. Lit. 18.000. 88-7016-162-5.

4340 **Segundo** Juan Luis, An evolutionary approach to Jesus 1988 ➤ 5,7441; 7,3629: ᴿLexTQ 27 (1992) 92s (W. R. *Barr*); WestTJ 53 (1991) 159-161 (R. *Letham*).

4341 **Senior** Donald, Jesus, a Gospel portrait²ʳᵉᵛ. NY 1992, Paulist. iii-161 p. 0-8091-3338-5.

4342 *Senior* Donald, Understanding Jesus; a man of his time: Church 9,4 (1993) 5-11.

4344 **Theissen** Gerd, L'ombre du Galiléen 1988 ➤ 5,4092 ... 7,3633: ᴿIstina 37 (1992) 324-6 (B. *Dupuy*, aussi sur Lokalkolorit).

4345 **Theissen** Gerd, La sombra del Galileo 1988 ➤ 4,4217 ... 7,3635: ᴿRET 52 (1992) 98 (M. *Gesteira*).

4346 **Wilson** A. N., Jesus. L/NY 1992, Sinclair-Stevenson / Norton. xviii 269. £15. 0-393-03087-3. – ᴿFurrow 44 (1993) 455s (A. *Doyle*: not new but clearly put); Tablet 246 (1992) 1198s (H. *Chadwick*: 'Jesus did not know himself to be the second Person of the Trinity' is a proposition which in those terms is tolerable to an instructed Catholic).

4347 **Wright** Chris, What's so unique about Jesus? Eastbourne c. 1990, Marc. 125 p. £2.50. 1-85424-114-1. – ᴿChurchman 105 (1991) 182 (J. *Bournon*).

4348 **Zahrnt** Heinz, Jesus de Nazaré. Petrópolis 1992, Vozes. 252 p. [REB 52,100s].

4349 **Zahrnt** Heinz, Gesù, una vita, Mi 1990, Rizzoli. ᵀ*Fiorillo* M. 269 p. Lit. 28.000. – ᴿRivScR 5 (1991) 502-4 (A. *Resta*); StPatav 38 (1991) 205-7 (G. *Segalla*).

F1.5 *Jesus et Israel* – **Jesus the Jew.**

4350 *Anderlini* Gianpaolo, Chi è questo Gesù di Nazareth? ['ebreo e per sempre', Nostra Aetate 1985]: BbbOr 34 (1992) 129-144.

4351 **Aron** Robert, Así rezaba Jesús de niño. Bilbao 1988, D-Brouwer. – ᴿCompostellanum 36 (1991) 238s (J. *Precedo Lafuente*).

4352 *Baarda* T., al., Jodendom en vroeg christendom; continuiteit en discontinuiteit 1991 ➤ 7,415a: ᴿCollationes VL 22 (1992) 108s (J. de *Kesel*).

Bartolini Elena, al., Gesù ebreo per sempre 1991 ➤ a707.

4353 **Berlin** George L., Defending the faith; nineteenth-century American Jewish ... 1989 ➤ 5,4104; 6,4335: ᴿJAAR 60 (1992) 543-5 (R. G. *Goldy*).

4354 **Brewer** D. Instone, Techniques and assumptions in Jewish exegesis before 70 CE [diss. Cambridge]: TStAJ 30. Tü 1992, Mohr. xiii-299 p. DM 198. – ᴿSNTU A-17 (1992) 272s (A. *Fuchs*).

4355 *Buth* R., Language use in the first century; spoken Hebrew in a trilingual society: JTransTLing 5 (Dallas 1992) 298-312 [< NTAbs 37,174].

4356 **Calimani** Riccardo, Gesù ebreo 1990 ➤ 7,3644: ᴿAsprenas 39 (1992) 271s (G. *Jossa*); StPatav 38 (1991) 151-164 (G. *Leonardi*: 'Gesù solo un pio ebreo?').

4357 **Casey** P. M., From Jewish prophet to Gentile God 1991 ⇒ 7,3645: ^RIr-
BSt 14 (1992) 192-8 (J. C. *O'Neill*).
4358 ^E**Charlesworth** James H., Jesus' Jewishness 1991 ⇒ 7,294: ^RWorship 66
(1992) 367-9 (M. S. *Kogan*).
4359 **Charlesworth** James H., Jesus within Judaism 1988 ⇒ 4,4225 ... 7,3646:
^RColcT 62,1 (1992) 175-7 (W. *Chrostowski* ❾); JQR 83 (1992s) 194-6
(A. J. *Blasi*); JTS 43 (1992) 576-8 (D. *Cohn-Sherbok*: fivefold agenda).
4360 **Chilton** Bruce, Profiles of a rabbi ... Jesus: Brown JudSt 177, 1989
⇒ 5,4410; 7,3847: ^RJQR 83 (1992s) 401s (W. *Adler*).
4361 **Chilton** Bruce, The temple of Jesus; his sacrificial program within a
cultural history of sacrifice [Ezek; Jos.F. ... GIRARD]. Univ.Park 1992,
Penn. State Univ. xli-209 p. $34.50. 0-271-00824-5 [TDig 40,156].
4362 *Defelix* Chantal, Jésus face aux enjeux d'Israël; le messianisme et la loi:
LumièreV 41 (1992) 27-42.
4363 *de Lacey* D. R., In search of a Pharisee [prefers modified NEUSNER
model to E. P. SANDERS]: TyndB 43 (1992) 353-372.
4364 **Dunn** James D. G., The partings of the ways 1991 ⇒ 7,3650: ^RChrCent
109 (1992) 657s (J. T. *Pawlikowski*); ExpTim 103,8 top choice (1991s)
225-7 (C. S. *Rodd*); NBlackf 73 (1992) 461s (T. J. *Gorringe*); Themelios
18,3 (1992s) 28s (I. H. *Marshall*); TvT 32 (1992) 417 (J. *Negenman*).
4365 **Edwards** David D., Jesus and the Temple; a historico-theological study
of Temple motifs in the ministry of Jesus: diss. SW Baptist Theol. Sem.
1992. 287 p. 92-31658. – DissA 53 (1992s) 1959-A.
4366 **Flusser** David, Das Christentum, eine jüdische Religion 1990 ⇒ 6,
4345: ^RActuBbg 29 (1992) 65s (J. *Boada*); CritRR 5 (1992) 195-8 (J. H.
Charlesworth).
4367 **Flusser** David, Il cristianesimo, una religione ebraica [1990],^T. CinB
1992, Paoline. 164 p. Lit. 14.000. [VivH 4, 195, L. *Mazzinghi*].
4368 **Flusser** David, Het Christendom, een joodse religie, 1991 ⇒ 7,3682:
^RStreven 59 (1991s) 468s (P. *Beentjes*).
4369 *a) Frankemölle* Hubert, Die Entstehung des Christentums aus dem Judentum; – *b) Zenger* Erich, Wie soll die Kirche die jüdische Bibel lesen?;
– *c) Vorgrimler* Herbert, Israel und Kirche vor dem gemeinsamen Bun-
desgott: RUHöh 35 (Dü 1992) 25-35 / 1-24 / 36-47 [< ZIT 92,271].
4370 **Freyne** Sean, Galilee, Jesus and the Gospels; literary approaches and
historical investigations 1988 ⇒ 4,4238 ... 7,3655: ^RScotJT 45 (1992) 117s
(D. C. *Parker*); ZkT 114 (1992) 205 (R. *Oberforcher*: nothing like it in
German, even BÖSEN W. 1985).
4371 **Harrison** John P., Did Jesus teach obedience to the Law?: diss. Edinburgh 1992. 320 p. – RTLv 24, p. 547.
4372 **Hengel** Martin, The 'Hellenization' of Judaea 1989 ⇒ 6,4351; 7,3657:
^RColcT 62,1 (1992) 181s (M. *Wojciechowski*, ❾).
4373 *a) Holtz* Traugott, 'Ich aber sage euch'; Bemerkungen zum Verhältnis
Jesu zur Tora; – *b) Müller* Karlheinz, Beobachtungen zum Verhältnis
von Tora und Halacha in frühjüdischen Quellen; – *c) Maier* Johann,
Beobachtungen zum Konfliktpotential in neutestamentlichen Aussagen
über den Tempel: ⇒ 344, Jesus & Gesetz 1992, 135-145 / 105-134 /
173-213.
4374 *Jenkins,* The Pharisees: Scripture in Church 23 (Dublin 1989) 106-9
[< NTAbs 37, p. 251].
4375 **Jonge** Marinus de, Jesus, the Servant-Messiah [Yale Shaffer lectures
1989 echoing title of T. MANSON's 1939, Cambridge Univ. 1953]. NHv
1991, Yale Univ. viii-115 p. $16. – ^RCBQ 54 (1992) 775s (C. A. *Evans*).

4376 **Karrer** Martin, Der Gesalbte; die Grundlagen des Christustitels: FRL 151, ᴰ1991 ➤ 7,3662; ᴿBL (1992) 75 (J. R. *Porter*); BZ 36 (1992) 146-8 (J. *Schnackenburg*); ÉTRel 67 (1992) 470 (J. *Cousin*); ExpTim 103 (1991s) 274s (E. *Best*); SNTU A-16 (1991) 194 (H. *Giesen*).

4377 *Keith* Kevin, The background of the NT; diversity in first-century Judaism and its contemporary implications: ➤ 115, ᶠLAMBRECHT J., LvSt 17 (1992) 131-151.

4378 *a) Kosch* Daniel, Jesus der Jude — zehn Thesen; – *b) Rendtorff* Rolf, Identifikation mit Israel?; – *c) Ehmann* Johannes, Solidarität mit dem Staat Israel?: KIsr 7 (1992) 74-82 / 136-144 / 149-180.

4379 [*Lang* B.] *Kampling* R., Judentum im NT: ➤ 762, NBL II, 8 (1992) [404–] 408-412.

4380 **Lapide** Pinchas, Jesus — ein gekreuzigter Pharisäer?: Tb 1427. Gü 1990, Mohn. 121 p. DM 16,80. – ᴿLuthMon 29 (1990) 473s (S. von *Kortzfleisch*).

4381 **Lee** Bernard J., The Galilean Jewishness of Jesus 1988 ➤ 4,4250 ... 7,3664: ᴿCalvinT 26 (1991) 429s (T. R. *Wolthuis*); Gregorianum 73 (1992) 757s (J. *Dupuis*).

4382 **Lenhardt** P., *Collin* M., La Torah orale des pharisiens; textes de la tradition d'Israël: CahÉv supp. ➤ 6,4362: P 1990, Cerf. 115 p. F 45. 0222-9706 [NTAbs 35,266].

4383 **Lenhardt** Pierre, *Collin* Matthieu, La Tora oral de los fariseos; textos de la tradición de Israel: Documentos en torno a la Biblia. Estella 1991, VDivino. 114 p. 84-7151-734-5 [NTAbs 35, p. 266]. – ᴿRET 52 (1992) 237-241 (E. *Tourón*).

4383* *McGarry* M., The meaning of the Messiah: Thought 67 (1992) 385-398 [< NTAbs 38, p. 71: the challenge is to seek a meaning for the Christian Messiah who is at the same time the Jew Jesus].

4384 *McNamara* Martin, The language situation in first century Palestine; Aramaic and Greek: PrIrB 15 (1992) 7-36.

4385 **Manns** Frédéric, Le Judaïsme; milieu et mémoire du Nouveau Testament: SBF 36. J 1992, Franciscan. 263 p.; bibliog. p. 237-242.

4386 *Manns* F., Israël et l'Église; un problème d'héritage: Didaskalia 21 (1991) 3-16 [< NTAbs 37, p. 235].

Marquardt Friedrich W., Das christliche Bekenntnis zu Jesus, dem Juden, eine Christologie 1-2, 1990s ➤ 7540.

4388 **Meier** John P., A marginal Jew; rethinking the historical Jesus I, 1991 ➤ 7,3667: ᴿAmerica 166 (1992) 42s (Pheme *Perkins*); BR 5,3 (1992) 10s (M. *Borg*); cf. 5/4, 17 (E. *Johnson*: 'Meier has been challenged for over a decade on his ... view that Matthew's Jesus abrogates the OT Law'); ChrCent 109 (1992) 489-493 (D. L. *Bartlett*, also on CROSSAN, Peasant); Claretianum 32 (1992) 504s (J. *Sánchez Bosch*); Commentary 93,4 (1992) 54.56.58 (H. *Maccoby*); Commonweal 119,8 (1992) 24s (L. T. *Johnson*); ÉTRel 67 (1992) 463s (E. *Cuvillier*); ExpTim 103 (1991s) 282 (D. *Catchpole*: a breath of fresh air); HomP 92,7 (1991s) 70s (J. R. *Sheets* despite reserves, awaits hopefully the second volume); Mid-Stream 32, 1 (1993) 103-6 (M. E. *Boring*); NRT 115 (1993) 101s (L. *Renwart*); SewaneeTR 36 (1992s) 171-3 (R. H. *Fuller*, also on CROSSAN); TLond 95 (1992) 384s (B. *Capper*); TS 53 (1992) 739-742 (D. *Senior*: classic method; the Christ of faith is distinct not only from the 'historical' Jesus, the limited and fragmentary portrayal reconstructible from the evidence; but also from the 'real' Jesus); TTod 49 (1992s) 398-407 (K. F. *Nickle*, also on CROSSAN 1991); TvT 32 (1992) 416s (L. *Grollenberg*).

4389 *Mimouni* Simon C., Le judéo-christianisme ancien dans l'historiographie du XIXeme et XXeme siècle: RÉJ 151 (1997) 419-428.

4390 **Neusner** Jacob, Jews and Christians; the myth of a common tradition 1991 ➤ 7,3673: ^RInterpretation 46 (1992) 416.8 (C. M. *Williamson*); TLond 95 (1992) 140s (C.J.A. *Hickling*: perhaps best understood as autobiography); TS 53 (1992) 384 (A. J. *Saldarini*).

4391 **Pelletier** Marcel, Les Pharisiens, histoire d'un parti méconnu: Lire la Bible 86, 1990 ➤ 6,4377; 7,3679: ^RMélSR 48 (1991) 248s (G.-H. *Baudry*); NRT 114 (1992) 128s (N. *Plumat*).

4392 **Perelmuter** Hayim G., Siblings; rabbinic Judaism and early Christianity at their beginnings 1989 ➤ 5,4146 ... 7,3680: ^RCalvinT 26 (1991) 224-7 (J.A.D. *Weima*); ChH 60 (1991) 527 (A. J. *Springer*).

4393 *Perrot* Charles, Les milieux juifs du Nouveau Testament: ➤ 462, Naissance 1990/2, 157-160.

4394 **Petuchowski** Jakob J., The Torah, the Rabbis, and the early Church: AnglTR 74 (1992) 216-224.

4395 **Pixner** Bargil, With Jesus through Galilee according to the Fifth Gospel [i.e. soil of the Holy Land], ^T*Botha* Christa, *Foster* David. Rosh Pina 1992, Corazin. 136 p. 965-434-001-1.

4396 **Poorthuis** M., De joodse groeperingen ten tijde van Jezus; oorsprong, inhoud, en relatie tot Jezus 1989 ➤ 7,3681: ^RNedTTs 46 (1992) 163s (P. W. van der *Horst*).

4397 *Pritz* Ray, Nazarene Jewish Christianity [diss. Hebrew Univ.]. J c. 1990, Magnes. – Jerusalem Perspective 3,5 (1990) 3.

4398 *Riggans* W., The Jewish reclamation of Jesus and its implications for Jewish-Christian relations: Themelios 18,1 (1992s) 9-16.

4399 *Rottenberg* Isaac C., A re-judaized Jesus?: Perspectives, a journal of Reformed thought 7/10 (1992) 18–...

4400 *Sacchi* Paolo, Riflessioni sul problema della formazione culturale di Gesù: Henoch 14 (1992) 243-258; Eng. 259s.

4401 *Saldarini* Anthony J., Pharisees/Scribes ➤ 741, AnchorBD 5 (1992) 289-303 / 1012-6.

4402 **Sanders** E.P., Jesus and Judaism 1985 ➤ 1,4028 ... 6,4382: ^RColcT 62,4 (1992) 183-6 (M. *Wojciechowski*, **ⓟ**).

4403 **Sanders** E. P., Judaism, practice and belief 63 BCE – 66 CE. L/Ph 1992, SCM/Trinity. xix-580 p. £40; pa. £20. 0-334-02469-2, –70-6 / 1-56338-016-1, -5-3. – ^RBR 8,6 (1992) 12s (Shaye J. D. *Cohen*); ExpTim 1st choice 103,10 (1991s) 289s (C. S. *Rodd*: Sanhedrin a mirage; Pharisees not so influential); PrPeo 6 (1992) 256 (H. *Wansbrough*).

4404 **Schelkle** K. H., Israele nel NT 1991 ➤ 7,3690: ^RLateranum 58 (1992) 499s (R. *Penna*).

4405 **Schwartz** Daniel R., Studies in the Jewish background of Christianity: WUNT 60. Tü 1992, Mohr. xii-304 p. DM 178 [TR 88,281]. 3-16-145798-6.

4406 *Scott* J. J., The Jewish backgrounds of the NT; Second Commonwealth Judaism in recent study: ArchBW 1,2 (1991) 40s. 43-49 [< NTAbs 37, p. 417].

4407 **Simon** Marcel, *Benoît* André, Le judaïsme et le christianisme antique d'Antiochus Épiphane à Constantin² [= ¹1968 + bibliog.]: NClio. P 1991, PUF. 360 p. F 148. 2-13-043881-4. – ^RÉTRel 67 (1992) 473 (E. *Cuvillier*).

4408 *Soden* Hans von, Jesus der Galiläer und das Judentum: Deutsches Pfarrerblatt 92 (1992) 427-9 [from 1942, with 9 others from every 10 years since its founding].

4409 **Stegner** William R., Narrative theology in early Jewish Christianity [GERHARDSSON-style form criticism, not 'narrative criticism' as currently understood] 1989 ➤ 6,9882; 7,3694: ᴿAsbury TJ 46,1 (1991) 125-7 (M.A. *Powell*).

4410 **Swidler** Leonard, Der umstrittene Jesus [Yeshua, a model for moderns 1988 ➤ 4,4273], (gekürzt). Stu 1991, Quelle. 143 p. DM 24,80. 3-7918-1418-4. – ᴿEvKomm 25 (1992) 309s (A. *Malessa*: 'historisiert'); KIsr 7 (1992) 101s (J. *Kirchberg*); TGL 82 (1992) 141s (J. *Ernst*).

4411 **Testa** Emanuele, The faith of the Mother Church; an essay on the theology of the Judeo-Christiansᵀ; SBF min 32. J 1992, Franciscan. xvii-236 + 41 p.; 52 fig. [RHE 87,395*].

4412 **Wilson** Marvin R., Our father Abraham 1989 ➤ 5,4160 ... 7,3698: ᴿPacifica 5 (1992) 228s (E.J. *Fisher*).

4413 **Zeitlin** Irving M., Jesus and the Judaism of his time 1988 ➤ 4,4278 ... 7,3699: ᴿInterpretation 46 (1992) 84.86 (A.J. *Saldarini*).

F1.6   *Jesus in Ecclesia* – **The Church Jesus.**

4414 *Bühlmann* Walbert, Jesus von Nazaret und die Praxis der Kirche: Diakonia 23 (1992) 46-50; ≽ Jesus of Nazareth and church praxis, TDig 39 (1992) 127-130 (B.A. *Asen*).

4416 **Dotolo** Carmelo, Gesù di Nazaret; il problema storico e la fede cristiana. Bo 1990, Dehoniane. 136 p. Lit. 11.000. – ᴿRivScR 5 (1991) 504 (A. *Resta*).

Goergen Donald J., The Jesus of Christian history: Theology of Jesus 3, 1992 ➤ 7522.

4418 **Gudorf** Christine E., Victimization; examining Christian complicity. Ph 1992, Trinity. 124 p. $14. 1-56338-044-7 [TDig 40,65 ... misuse of authoritative revelation; romanticizing of victims and 'option for the poor' ...].

4419 *a*) *Hanc* Wojczech, ❷ Jésus vivant dans l'Église; – *b*) *Balter* Lucjan, ❷ Jésus le bâtisseur de l'Église; – *c*) *Góralczyk* Paweł, ❷ Les valeurs humaines apportées par Jésus: ➤ 43*, ᶠDEMBOWSKI B., AtKap 119 (1992) 55-68 / 42-54 / 69-79.

4420 **Hatch** S.A., Jesus of Nazareth, Messiah and Son of God: Journal from the Radical Reformation 1,3 (Marrow GA 1992) 4-13 [< NTAbs 37,18].

4420* **O'Carroll** Michael, Verbum caro; an encyclopedia on Jesus, the Christ. ColMn 1992, Liturgical/Glazier. x-201 p. $35. 0-8146-5017-1 [TDig 39,377].

4421 **Reymond** Robert L., Jesus: divine Messiah. Phillipsburg NJ 1990, Presbyterian & R. ix-347 p. $18. – ᴿThemelios 18,1 (1992s) 33 (C. *Blomberg*).

4422 *a*) *Teklak* Czesław, ❷ Qui est Jésus-Christ? [... au marxisme]; – *b*) *Langkammer* Hugolin, ❷ La conscience de la mission divine de Jésus; – *c*) *Homerski* Jósef, ❷ La mission de Jésus dans le plan du salut: ➤ 43*, ᶠDEMBOWSKI B., AtKap 118 (1992) 364-384 [385-405] / 406-416 / 417-431.

4423 **Weber** E.-H., Le Christ selon T. d'AQUIN: JJC 35, 1988 ➤ 6,7485; 7,3711: ᴿAngelicum 69 (1992) 130s (G.M. *Salvati*).

F1.7   *Jesus 'anormalis'*: **to atheists, psychoanalysts, romance...**

4424 *Arnaldez* Roger, Gesù nel pensiero musulmano [1988 ➤ 4,4298],ᵀ: Problemi e dibattiti 16. CinB 1990, Paoline. 207 p. Lit. 16.000. – ᴿAsprenas 39 (1992) 149-151 (G. *Ragozzino*); Lateranum 57 (1991) 623-5 (G. *Ancona*); StPatav 39 (1992) 253s (C. *Saccone*).

4426 **Böll** Heinrich, Ansichten eines Clowns 33. Mü 1981; Opiniones de un payaso[12], [T]Casas Lucas, *Barral* Seix. Barc 1986. – [R]Lumen Vr 41 (1992) 68-92 (G. *del Pozo*: 'El Evangelio frente a la Ley').

4427 **Bowman** Frank P., Il Cristo delle barricate, 1789-1848 [1967 ➤ 3,4045], [T]*Reali* S.: Gesù dopo Gesù. Brescia 1991, Morcelliana. 414 p. – [R]Salesianum 54 (1992) 569 (C. *Semeraro*).

4428 **Boyer** R., Il Cristo dei barbari; il mondo nordico (IX-XIII secolo) [1987],[T] *Reali* S.: Gesù dopo Gesù 2. Brescia 1992, Morcelliana. 162 p. – [R]ArTGran 55 (1992) 396s (A. *Segovia*).

4429 **Breech** James, Jesus and postmodernism 1989 ➤ 5,4175; 7,3712: [R]HeythJ 33 (1992) 88 (J. P. *Galvin*).

4430 **Bruce** F. F., Ausserbiblische Zeugnisse über Jesus (1974), [T]1991 ➤ 7, 3713: [R]SNTU A-16 (1991) 252 (A. *Fuchs*). TLZ 117 (1992) 121s (G. *Haufe*).

4430* *Bruce* F. F., Gesù visto dai contemporanei; le testimonianze non bibliche 1989 ➤ 6,4402*; 7,3714: [R]RivStoLR 28 (1992) 430s (Giuliana *Iacopino*).

4431 **Brunner** Constantin, Our Christ; the revolt of the mystical genius [Unser Christus oder Das Wesen des Genius 1921]. Assen 1990, Van Gorcum. xii-492 p. *f*87,50 [NRT 115,102, L. *Renwart*].

4432 [E]**Cameron** R., The apocryphal Jesus and Christian origins: Semeia 40. Atlanta 1990, Scholars. iv-176 p. – [R]Salmanticensis 39 (1992) 302-6 (R. *Trevijano*).

4433 **[Castra] De Knibbs** Dina, Models of the cosmic Christ; a critical analysis and perspective: diss. Calvin Sem., [D]*Bolt* J. GR 1991. vi-206 p. – CalvinT 26 (1991) 508s.

4434 *Charbonneau-Lassay* Louis, Christ the hunter and the hunted [< Bestiary 1991], [T]*Dooling* D.: Parabola, the magazine of myth and tradition 16,2 (NY 1991) 23-25.

4435 *Eckert* Jost, Der Christ der Zukunft — ein Mystiker? Neutestamentliche Orientierungspunkte: ➤ 54, [F]FEILZER H., 1992, 63-78.

4436 *Elizalde* Ignazio, La alegoría, Jesucristo capitán, antes de San Ignacio: Manresa 63 (1991) 239-246.

4437 *Guillaume* Baudouin, 'La dernière tentation du Christ' [film] ou le blasphème intégral: PeCa 249 (1990) 44-65.

4438 *Hoepner* Barbara, Jesus in der Gestalt einer Frau?: Junge Kirche 53 (1992) 542s.

4439 **Lee** David N., Speculative Christ and cosmic Christ; comparison and analysis of the Christologies of G.W.F. HEGEL and Pierre TEILHARD de Chardin: diss. SW Baptist Theol. Sem. 1992, [D]*Kirkpatrick* D. 285 p. 92-31663. – DissA 53 (1992s) 1968-A.

4440 **Malaparte** C. [1898-1957]. Il Cristo proibito, [E]*Martellini* L., Napoli 1992, ESI. [CC 144/9, 220-232, F. *Castelli*].

4441 **Mauch** U., Der listige ['tricky'] Jesus. Z 1992, Theol.-V. 103 p. Fs 18. 3-290-10861-9 [NTAbs 37, p. 281].

4442 **Messadié** Gerald, Ein Mensch namens Jesus. Mü 1989, Droemer. 751 p. DM 44. – [R]BiKi 47 (1992) 62s (K. *Schmitz*).

4443 *Messiha* Hishmat, Jesus Christ in Coptic antiquities; his life and symbols: ➤ 694*b*, Copte IVe (1988/92) 127-134; 6 fig.

4444 *Milet* Jean, Les philosophes face au Christ; à propos du Colloque de la Faculté de Philosophie de l'Université catholique de Lyon (1990): EsprVie 102 (1992) 385-399.

4445 *Niel* Jean-Baptiste, Ceci est mon sang. P 1992, Julliard. 258 p. F 100. – [R]RSPT 77 (1993) 310s (J.-P. *Jossua*: rencontre d'un jeune homme avec douze autres, homosexuelle mais peut-être comme figure de l'attirance personnelle, enfin un ultime repas à perpétuer toujours).

4446 **Notovitch** Nicolas, La vie inconnue de Jésus-Christ [... Kashmir]: Toulouse 1991 = ⁵1894, Basileus. – ᴿEsprVie 102 (1992) 86-89 (M. *Delahoutre*).

4447 ᴱ**Patterson** David, The Gospel according to TOLSTOY. Tuscaloosa 1992, Univ. Alabama. xi-155 p. 0-8173-0590-4.

4448 **Pope-Levison** Priscilla A., *Levison* John R., Jesus in global contexts. Louisville 1992, W-Knox. 232 p. $18 [RelStR 19,335, D. W. *Musser*]. – ᴿEncounter 54 (1993) 449s (I. *McCrae*).

4449 **Rhodes** Ron, The counterfeit Christ of the New Age movement [< diss. Dallas 1986]. GR 1990, Baker. 255 p. $12 pa. – ᴿBtS 149 (1992) 104 (J. R. *Brady*: may force solidifying Christology as Gnosticism did, p. 24).

4450 **Risse** Günther, 'Gott ist Christus, der Sohn der Maria'; eine Studie zum Christusbild im Koran: Begegnung 2, 1989 ➤ 5,4204; 7,3735: ᴿOrChrPer 58 (1992) 605s (E. G. *Farrugia*); OstkSt 41 (1992) 77s (Eva M. *Synek*).

4451 **Robinson** Neal, Christ in Islam and Christianity; the representation of Jesus in the Qur'ān and the classical Muslin commentaries 1991 ➤ 7,3736: ᴿBSO 55 (1992) 321-3 (A. *Rippin*, also on *McAuliffe* J. 1991).

4452 **Salibi** K., Who was Jesus? pa. [= 1988 A conspiracy in Jerusalem]. L 1992, Tauris. viii-200 p.; 4 fig. £10. 1-85043-562-6 [NTAbs 37, 284].

4453 **Saramago** José, O Evangelho segundo Jesus Cristo, romance; 1991, ➤ 7,3739; 972-201-052-8: ᴿActaBbg 29 (1992) 29 (1992) 186-8 (M. *Longa Pérez*); HumTeol 13 (1992) 73-81 (C. do C. *Silva*: O evangelho segundo Jesus Cristo ou o Kakangélion); Orientierung 56 (1992) 189-192 (A. *von Brunn*).

4454 **Stroker** William D., Extracanonical sayings of Jesus [266 plus parallels]: SBL Resources 18, 1989 ➤ 5,4210: ᴿCBQ 54 (1992) 174s (M. E. *Boring*); Salmanticensis 38 (1991) 237s (R. *Trevijano*).

4455 *Thiede* Werner, Der kosmische Christus und sein Jesus; ein christologischer Paradigmenwechsel?: DtPfarrB 92 (Essen 1992) 191-4 [< ZIT 92,329].

4456 **Tilliette** X., Le Christ de la philosophie 1991 ➤ 7,3744: ᴿScEspr 44 (1992) 247-251 (M. *Maesschalck*); ScripTPamp 24 (1992) 1084s (L. F. *Mateo-Seco*).

4457 *Tilliette* Xavier, Il Cristo dei non-credenti: RasT 33 (1992) 123-136.

4458 *Trocmé* Étienne, Un christianisme sans Jésus-Christ? [SNTS presidential address 1991]: NTS 38 (1992) 321-336.

4459 *Villanueva* Carlos, El mensaje de Jesús y la literatura apocalíptica: RBiArg 54,45 (1992) 15-25.

4460 **Weiland** P. J., Ein Messias aus Galiläa; was Christen nicht wissen — aber sollten — mit 1300 Bezugshinweisen im 'ABC der Gedankeninhalte'. Thalwil 1989, ³1991. 544 p. – ᴿDielB 27 (1991) 303 (B. J. *Diebner*).

4461 **Wessels** J., Images of Jesus / non-European 1990 ➤ 7,3748: ᴿJDharma 17 (1992) 56s (S. *Athappily*).

4462 **Wessels** A., Immagini di Gesù nelle culture non europee [1986: Eng. 1990 7,3748]ᵀ: GdT 211. Brescia 1992, Queriniana. 195 p. Lit. 20.000 [NRT 115,581, L.-J. *Renard*]. – ᴿHumTeol 13 (1992) 414s (B. *Domingues*).

4463 *Wills* Elizabeth, Christ as eternal companion; a study in the Christology of Shusaku ENDO: ScotJT 45 (1992) 85-100.

4464 **Wolff** Hanna, Gesù psicoterapeuta: Nuovi saggi 45. Brescia 1990, Queriniana. 192 p. Lit. 16.000. – RParVi 36 (1991) 317s (C. *Ghidelli*).

F2.1 *Exegesis creativa* – **innovative methods.**

4465 **Bailey** James L., *Vander Broek* Lyle D., [Thirty] Literary forms in the New Testament; a handbook. Louisville 1992, W-Knox. 219 p. $15 pa. 0-664-25154-4 [BL 93,71, D. *Clines*; TDig 39,252]. – RExpTim 103 (1991s) 375 (N. *Clark*: good); RefR 46 (1992s) 178s (S. *Van Dop*).

4466 *Bartnicki* Roman, ℗ Strukturalizm i semiotyka w badaniach nad Ewangeliami: RuBi 45 (1992) 6-20.

4467 **Berger** K., Formgeschichte des NTs 1984 ➤ 65,3705; 1,4115: RCarthaginensia 8 (1992) 926-9 (R. *Sanz Valdivieso*, también sobre su Einführung 1987 & p. 930s, Hermeneutik 1988).

4468 **Blount** Brian K., Beyond the boundaries; cultural perspective and the interpretation of the NT: diss. Emory, DBoers H. Atlanta 1992. 511 p. 92-24390. – DissA 53 (1992s) 1182-A; RTLv 24, p. 545.

4469 *Caba* José, Métodos exegéticos no estudo actual do Novo Testamento: Brotéria 135 (1992) 295-302.

4470 *a) Caba* José, Métodos exegéticos en el estudio actual del Nuevo Testamento; – *b) Becker* Karl J., Der Gebrauch der Heiligen Schrift in der dogmatischen Theologie; – *c) Rasco* Emilio, La 'Parola vivente' (Eb 4,12); dallo studio alla vita: ➤ 501, Gregorianum 73 (1992) 611-669 / 671-687 / 689-695.

4471 **Byrskog** S., Nya testamentet och forskningen; några aktuella tendenser inom den nytestamentliga exegetiken: Religio 39. Lund 1992, Teologiska Inst. 62 p. 0280-5723.

4472 **Conzelmann** H., *Lindemann* A., Interpreting the NT [⁸1985], TSchatzmann S. S. Peabody MA 1988, Hendrickson. 389 p. – EExpTim 103 (1991s) 310 (E. *Franklin*); Neotestamentica 26 (1992) 532s (H. S. *Theron*); RBibArg 54,47 (1992) 180-2 (R. *Krüger*).

4473 **Egger** Wilhelm, Lecturas del Nuevo Testamento; metodología lingüística histórico-crítica [1987 ➤ 3,4096], TERuiz Garrido Constantino. Estella 1990, VDivino. 283 p. pt. 2100. 84-7151-685-3. – RActuBbg 29 (1992) 195 (X. *Alegre*); ComSev 25 (1992) 121 (M. de *Burgos*); RBibArg 54,47 (1992) 177-180 (R. *Krüger*); ScripTPamp 24 (1992) 1089s (V. *Balaguer*).

4474 *a) Götke* E. Tøjner, Eksegese og forkyndelse; J. D. CROSSANS lignelseteori og dens teologiske implikationen; – *b) Tronier* H., Spørgsmålet om hermeneutisk kongruens i Pauluseksegesen; – *c) Engberg-Pedersen* T., Om en adækvat Pauluseksegese; – *d) Davidsen* O., Den strukturelle Adam/Kristustypologi; om Romerbrevets grundfortælling; – *e) Jensen* J. S., Om en ny vej i evangelienforskning: DanTTs 55 (1992) 175-190 / 191-208 / 209-216 / 241-261 / 262-279 [ZNW 84,145].

4475 **Grant** Patrick, Reading the Gospel 1989 ➤ 5,3966; 6,4185: RLitTOx 5 (1991) 330s (P. S. *Fiddes*; postmoderns stress openness of meaning in texts; Grant tries to reconcile that with a certain 'closure' in them coming from claims of historical truth).

4476 EHartin P. J., *Petzer* J. H., Text and interpretation; new approaches in the criticism of the NT 1991 ➤ 7,307: RNeotestamentica 26 (1992) (J. H. *Hunter*).

4477 *a) Lemcio* E. E. The Gospels and canonical criticism [< BibTB 11 (1981) 114-122]; – *b) Wall* R. W., The Acts of the Apostles in canonical

context [< BibTB 18 (1988) 16-24]; – c) *Wall*, The problem of the multiple letter canon in the NT [< HorBT 8 (1988) 1-31]; – d) *Wall*, The
Apocalypse of the NT in canonical context [ineditum]: ➤ 369, NT Canon
1992, 28-47 / 110-128 / 161-183 / 274-298 [+ 10 other reprints of the two
authors organized as chapters].

4478 *Lentzen-Deis* Fritzleo, Evangelientext als Handlungsmodell; pragmalingui-
stische Methoden in der Exegese: Missio 7 (1992) 8-16 [< AcPIB 9/8, 656].

4479 *Lüdemann* Gerd, Die Religionsgeschichtliche Schule und ihre Konsequenzen für die neutestamentliche Wissenschaft: ➤ m719, ᴱMüller H.,
Kulturprotestantismus 1992, 311-338.

4480 **Mack** Burton L., Rhetoric and the NT 1990 ➤ 6,4446; 7,3759: ᴿAngl-
TR 74 (1992) 383-7 (F. W. *Hughes*, also on his Patterns of persuasion
1989 ➤ 4859 infra); ConcordJ 18 (1992) 93-5 (J. W. *Voelz*: good); Interpretation 46 (1992) 202.204 (also J. W. *Voelz*); Neotestamentica 26
(1992) 546s (J. N. *Vorster*).

4481 ᴱ**McKnight** Edgar V., Reader perspectives on the NT: Semeia 48, 1989
➤ 5,1341: ᴿCurrTMiss 19 (1992) 58 (D. *Rhoads*).

4482 **Mateos** J., Método de análisis semántico aplicado al griego del NT 1989
➤ 5,9575: ᴿComScv 24 (1991) 106s (M. *de Burgos*); StPatav 38 (1991)
195 (G. *Segalla*).

4483 *Meier* John P., The testimonium; evidence for Jesus outside the Bible:
BR 7,3 (1991) 20-25.45.

4484 *Mercer* C., Modern interpretation of the NT: retrospect and prospect:
Faith & Mission 10,1. Wake Forest NC 1992) 34-44 [< NTAbs 38, p. 6].

4485 *Mouson* Jean †, Initiation à la lecture critique des Évangiles: Faculté
Ouverte Religion et Laïcité Cah. 4, 1990 ➤ 7,3762: ᴿTvT 32 (1992) 92
(H. *Welzen*).

4486 *Price* Robert M., Is there a place for historical criticism?: RelSt 27
(1991) 371-388.

4487 ᴱ**Raffelt** A., Begegnung mit Jesus? Was die historisch-kritische Methode leistet: FreibAkad 1, 1991 ➤ 7,325b; 3-491-77370-9: ᴿTvT 32
(1992) 193 (H. *Welzen*).

4488 **Renner** Frumentius, Verkannte Kostbarkeiten des Neuen Testamentes;
literarkritische Studien. St.Ottilien 1992, EOS. 158 p. 3-88096-648-6.

4489 *Rossman* Parker, *Kirby* Richard, Christians and the world of computers;
professional and social excellence in the computer world. L/Ph 1990,
SCM/Trinity. 173 p. $13 pa. 0-334-023468-4. – ᴿInterpretation 46 (1992)
220 (N. B. *Houk*, editor of ChurchBytes, the Church computing magazine,
Durham NC).

4490 *Stamps* D. L., Rhetorical criticism and the rhetoric of New Testament
criticism: LitTOx 6 (1992) 268-279 [< NTAbs 37, p. 170].

4491 *Stanton* Graham N., a) Redaction criticism; the end of an era? [ine-
ditum]; – b) Literary criticism, ancient and modern [ineditum]: ➤ 313,
Studies in Mt 1992, 23-53 / 54-84.

F2.2   *Unitas VT-NT:* **The Unity of the Two Testaments.**

4492 **Beauchamp** Paul, L'un et l'autre Testament, 2. Accomplir les Écritures
1990 ➤ 6,4555; 7,3770: ᴿCBQ 54 (1992) 310s (M. *Kolarcik*); CritRR 5
(1992) 81-83 (W. A. *Vogels*); TPhil 67 (1992) 269 (J. *Beutler*).

4493 a) *Beauchamp* Paul, Présentation d'un schéma de cours; la notion d'"accomplissement'; – b) *Pelletier* A. M., Accès nouveaux à une lecture ecclésiale des Écritures: ➤ 448, Ens.Écr. 1992, 180-192 / 160-179.

4494 *Bock* D., El uso del Antiguo Testamento en el Nuevo: Kairós 10 (Guatemala 1992) 49-70 [< NTAbs 37, p. 69].

4495 ᴱ**Bratcher** Robert G., Old Testament quotations in the New Testament³ʳᵉᵛ [¹1961]: Helps for Translators. L 1987, United Bible Societies. xi-88 p. 0-8267-0031-4.

4595* *Clowney* E. P., The unfolding mystery; discovering Christ in the OT 1990 ➤ 7,3733: ᴿSTEv 4 (1992) 67s (M. *Clemente*).

4496 *a*) *Corsani* Bruno, Le citazioni dai cosiddetti 'libri storici' negli scritti del Nuovo Testamento; – *b*) *Gunneweg* Antonius H. J., Das alte und das neue Israel; zur Frage nach der historischen Kontinuität: ➤ 7,141, ꟻSOGGIN J. A., Storia 1991, 65-76 / 127-142.

4497 *a*) *Dantine* Johannes, Das Verhältnis der beiden Testamente in der neueren Dogmatik; – *b*) *Schmalstieg* Olaf, Das andere Sehen; systematisches Interesse an hebräischer Tradition: ➤ 163, ꟻSAUER G., Aktualität 1992, 229-239 / 259-267.

4498 *De Martino* Umberto, 'Logos endiathetos'; prospettiva verso l'Incarnazione: StCattMi 36 (1992) 492-4.

4499 **Ellis** E., The OT in early Christianity 1991 ➤ 7,198: ᴿSvEx 57 (1992) 134-6 (T. *Fornberg*).

4500 **Eppler** Wilhelm, Die Sicht des Alten Testaments in den neueren protestantischen Theologien des Neuen Testaments: ev. Diss. ᴰ*Stuhlmacher* P. Tübingen 1991. 393 p. — RTLv 24, p. 546.

4501 **Feuillet** André, Accomplissement des prophéties 1991 ➤ 7,3775: ᴿNV-Fr 67 (1992) 75-77 (M.-T. *Huguet*).

4502 **Fuller** D. P., The unity of the Bible; unfolding God's plan for humanity. GR 1992, Zondervan. 508 p. $20. 0-310-53300-7 [NTAbs 37, p. 134].

4503 *Fuller* Daniel P., The importance of a unity of the Bible: ➤ 88, ꟻHUBBARD D., OT 1992, 63-75.

4504 *Guinot* J. N. [méthodologie/typologie des Pères], *al.*, Figures de l'AT chez les Pères 1989 ➤ 7,3781: ᴿLavalTP 48 (1992) 448s (S. *Painchaud*); RÉAug 37 (1991) 162s (J. *Doignon*); RechSR 80 (1992) 135s (B. *Sesboüé* sur Guinot).

4505 *a*) *Hengel* Martin, Jesus, der Messias Israels; zum Streit über das 'messianische Sendungsbewusstsein' Jesu; – *b*) *Mach* Michael, Christus mutans; zur Bedeutung der Verklärung Jesu im Wechsel von jüdischer Messianität zur neutestamentlichen Christologie; – *c*) *Stroumsa* Gedaliahu G., The early Christian fish symbol reconsidered [*Nun*, surname of Joshua = Jesus]: ➤ 57, ꟻFLUSSER D., Messiah 1992, 155-176 / 177-198 / 199-205.

4506 **Heyer** C. J. den, Een Bijbel — twee testamenten; de plaats van Israël in een Bijbelse Theologie: Verkenning en Bezinning 1, 1990 ➤ 7,3782: 90-242-2276-1: ᴿStreven 58 (1990s) 660 (P. *Beentjes*); TvT 33 (1993) 90 (K. *Waaijman*).

4507 *a*) *Hidal* Sten, Från messianiskt skriftbevis till ny perikopserie; Strövtåg i kyrkans användning av Gamla testamentet; – *b*) *Andersson* Torsten, De gammaltestamentliga texterna i Den svenska evangelieboken — några notiser; – *c*) *Cöster* Henry, Det icke-kristna folkets historia som kyrkans kanon; om Gamla testamentet i den systematiska teologin; – *d*) *Grenholm* Cristina, Gamla testamentet i kristen predikan; – *e*) *Sæbø* Magne, De vises Gud [BOSTRÖM L. 1990]: SvTKv 67 (1991) 2-6 / 7-16 / 17-22 / 23-30 / 31-39.

4508 *Hübner* Hans, NT (OT quotations in the), ᵀ*Schatzmann* S.: ➤ 741, AnchorBD 4 (1992) 1096.

4509 **Jonge** Marinus de,   Jesus, the Servant-Messiah 1991 ➤ 7,3786:   ᴿChr-
Cent 108 (1991) 889s (J.D. *Kingsbury*); JBL 111 (1992) 718s (M.J.
Borg).
4510 *a*) *Jonge* M. de,   Jezus als profetische zoon van David; – *b*) *Kippenberg*
H.G.,   Het charisma van het Davididengeslacht in de Joodse, vroeg-chri-
stelijke en gnostische godsdienstgeschiedenis van Palestina: ➤ 503, Symposium van der WOUDE 1985/92, 157-166 / 133-156.
4511 *Juel* D.H.,   NT reading of the Old; norm or nuisance?   Dialog 31
(1992) 181-9 [< NTAbs 37, p.73].
4512 *Katz* Paul,   Bedeutung und Vermittlung von Hebräischkenntnissen zum
Verständnis des NTs: ZAW 104 (1992) 412-427.
4513 **McLean** Bradley H.,   Citations and allusions to Jewish Scripture in early
Christian and Jewish writings through 180 C.E.   Lewiston NY 1992,
Mellen.   138 p. $49 [TorJT 9,266, M.P. *Knowles*].
4514 **Martin** Francis,   Narrative [OT] parallels to the NT 1988 ➤ 4,4379:
ᴿAustralBR 38 (1990) 73s (B.R. *Doyle*).
4515 **Neusner** Jacob,   Christian faith and the Bible of Judaism; the Judaic
encounter with Scripture 1987 ➤ 4,4255 ... 7,3791:   ᴿTLZ 117 (1992)
908 (P. von der *Osten-Sacken*: Rabbinismus auch für Christen richtungs-
weisend).
4516 **Poythress** Vern,   The shadow of Christ in the law of Moses.   Brentwood
TN 1991, Wohlgemuth & Hyatt.   422 p. $12 [JPsy&Chr 12,3785, B.B.
Hayton].
4517 **Rebell** Walter,   Erfüllung und Erwartung; Erfahrungen mit dem Geist
des Urchristentums.   Mü 1991, Kaiser.   196 p. – ᴿTvT 63 (1992) 223-5
(M. *Synnes*).
4518 *Riggans* Walter,   Jesus and the Scriptures [Mk 2,1-12 / Dt 18; — Mt 28,
11 / Dt 15,11]: Themelios 16,2 (1990s) 15s.
4519 **Zenger** Erich,   Das Erste Testament; die jüdische Bibel und die
Christen. Dü 1991, Patmos.   208 p. DM 26,80 pa. – ᴿBLtg 65 (1992)
187-9 (C. *Dohmen*); TüTQ 172 (1992) 57-59 (W. *Gross*, mit Lob auch
für N. *Lohfink*).

F2.3   *Unitas interna* – **NT** – **Internal unity.**

4520 **Reumann** John,   Variety and unity in NT thought 1991 ➤ 7,3797:
CurrTMiss 19 (1992) 377 (E. *Krentz*); LuthMon 31 (1992) 426 (E. *Lohse*:
gelehrt und doch verständlich); Salesianum 54 (1992) 792s (J.J. *Bartolomé*); TLond 95 (1992) 137 (J.L. *Houlden*); TR 88 (1992) 460s (O.B.
Knoch); TvT 32 (1992) 193 (L. *Grollenberg*).
4521 **Russell** D.S.,   Poles apart; the Gospel in creative tension 1990 ➤ 6,4221;
7,3552:   ᴿInterpretation 46 (1992) 414.416 (P.E. *Thompson*).

F2.5   *Commentarii* – **Commentaries on the whole NT.**

4522 **Aguirre Monasterio** R., *Rodríguez Carmona* A.,   Evangelios sinópticos
y Hechos: Introd. 6.   Estella 1992, VDivino.   404 p. – ᴿRBibArg 54,47
(1992) 183-7 (R. *Krüger*); Teresianum 43 (1992) 540 (V. *Pasquetto*).
4523 ᴱ**Karris** Robert J.,   The Collegeville Bible Commentary [➤ 1939 supra],
New Testament.   ColMn 1992, Liturgical..
4524 ᵀᴱ**Martin** Lawrence T., *Hurst* David,   BEDE the Venerable, Homilies
on the Gospels: Cistercian Studies 110s.   Kalamazoo 1991, Cistercian.
xxx-252 p.; vi-290 p. $60 each; pa. $25 [Manuscripta 36,149].

4524* ᴱReeve Anne, *Screech* M. A., Erasmus' annotations to the NT: AcRomCor 1990 ➤ 6,4578*b*; 7,3801: ᴿSixtC 22 (1991) 596 (M. H. *Hoffmann*).
4525 **Servotte** H., Wegen naar het Woord; interpretaties van evangelieteksten. Averbode 1991, Altiora. 184 p. Fb. 545. – ᴿCollatVL 22 (1992) 208 (J. De *Kesel*).
4526 ᵀᴱ**Simonetti Abbolito** Giuseppina, BEDA, Omelie sui Vangeli. R 1990, Città Nuova. 141 p. Lit. 45.000. – ᴿCC 143 (1992,2) 315 (E. *Cattaneo*).

X. Evangelia

F2.6   **Evangelia Synoptica;** *textus, synopses, commentarii.*

4527 *a)* **Elliott** J. K., Printed editions of Greek Synopses and their influence on the Synoptic Problem; – *b)* **Aland** Barbara, Das Zeugnis der frühen Papyri für den Text der Evangelien: ➤ 137, ᶠNEIRYNCK F., Four Gospels 1992, 337-357 / 325-335.
4528 **Funk** Robert W., New Gospel parallels 1s, 1990 ➤ 6,4243: ᴿBibTB 22 (1992) 40 (B. B. *Scott*); CBQ 54 (1992) 561s (Patricia M. *McDonald*: fine new layout; RSV replaced by Scholars Version, 'more accessible to most students', including Mk 1,41 'Okay — you're clean' and 'Son of Adam').
4529 **Gądecki** Stanisław, Wstęp (introductio) do Ewangelii Synoptycznych. Gniezno 1992, Gaudentinum. 378 p.
4530 **Neirynck** F., Minor agreements 1991 ➤ 7,3806: ᴿNT 34 (1992) 412s (J. K. *Elliott*).
4531 **Poppi** Angelico, Sinossi dei quattro Vangeli I²-II 1990/88 ➤ 7,3806: ᴿRBBras 9 (1992) 259s (C. *Minette de Tillesse*); ETL 68 (1992) 437-9 (F. *Neirynck*).
4532 **Sanders** E. P., & (his wife) *Davies* Margaret, Studying the Synoptic Gospels 1989 ➤ 5,4289; 6,4591: ᴿCBQ 54 (1992) 374s (R. L. *Mowery*: S. was 'teaching' at Oxford and D. 'lecturing' at Bristol; targeted audience fluctuates); CurrTMiss 19 (1992) 64 (E. *Krentz*); RelStT 11,1 (1991) 46-48 (M. *Desjardins*); Themelios 17,1 (1991s) 26s (I. H. *Marshall*).

F2.7   *Problema synopticum:* **The Synoptic Problem.**

4534 *Asgeirsson* John M., *Robinson* James M., The international Q project work sessions 12-14 July, 22 November 1991 [texts here in Greek and English]: JBL 111 (1992) 500-8.
4535 **Carruth** Shawn, Persuasion in Q; a rhetorical critical study of only Q [Lk] 6:20-49: diss. Claremont 1992, ᴰ*Robinson* J. M. 341 p. 92-23319. — DissA 53 (1992s) 1182s-A.
4536 *Catchpole* David R., The beginning of Q; a proposal [whether Jesus' baptism or John's appearance in KLOPPENBORG]: NTS 38 (1992) 205-221.
4537 *a) Catchpole* David R., The question of Q; – *b) Rhys* Howard, Examples of redaction by the Evangelists: SewaneeTR 36 (1992s) 33-44 / 103-122.
4538 *Downing* F. Gerald, A paradigm perplex; Luke, Matthew and Mark [both SANDERS-DAVIES and GOULDER solutions have a major defect]: NTS 38 (1992) 15-36.

4539 *a*) **Dungan** David L., Two-Gospel hypothesis; – *b*) *Boismard* M.-E., Two-Source hypothesis, ᵀ*Prendergast* T., ➤ 741, AnchorBD 6 (1992) 671-9-682.

4540 *Huggins* Ronald V., Matthean posteriority; a preliminary proposal: NT 34 (1992) 1-22.

4541 **Johnson** Sherman E., The GRIESBACH hypothesis and redaction criticism: SBL mg 41. Atlanta 1991, Scholars. vii-1072 p. – ᴿAustralBR 40 (1992) 82-84 (D. C. *Sim*); ETL 68 (1992) 436s (F. *Neirynck*: 'a very readable book, with a sound conclusion', preferring Two-Source).

4542 **Kloppenborg** J. S., The formation of Q 1987 ➤ 3,4184 ... 5,4297: ᴿRelCu 38 (1992) 615s (A. *Moral*).

4543 **Kloppenborg** J., *al.*, Q Thomas reader 1990 ➤ 6,4599: ᴿBR 7,1 (1991) 10s (J. A. *Fitzmyer*); TorJT 8 (1992) 336-9 (H. *Guenther*).

4544 *Kosch* Daniel, Q und Jesus: BZ 36 (1992) 30-58.

4545 **Linnemann** Eta, Is there a synoptic problem? Rethinking the literary dependence of the three Gospels, ᵀ*Yarbrough* Robert W. GR 1992, Baker. 219 p. $11 [ConcordJ 19,280s, E. H. *Kiehl*; TDig 40,172].

4546 *Moreland* Milton C., *Robinson* James M., The international Q project work sessions 31 July-2 August, 20 November 1992: JBL 112 (1993) 500-6.

4547 *Robinson* James M., A critical text of the Sayings Gospel Q: ➤ 36, ᶠCULLMANN O., RHPR 72 (1992) 15-21; 21s, sample, the Lord's Prayer Lk 11,2-4.

4547* *a*) *Robinson* James M., The Q trajectory; between John and Matthew via Jesus; – *b*) *Horsley* Richard, *Logoi prophētōn*? reflections on the genre of Q; – *c*) *Doran* Robert, The divinization of disorder; the trajectory of Matt 8:20 / Luke 9:58 / Gos. Thom, 86: ➤ 104, ᶠKOESTER H. 1991, 173-194 / 195-209 / 210-219.

4548 *a*) *Robinson* James M., The Sayings Gospel Q; – *b*) *Zeller* Dieter, Eine weisheitliche Grundschrift in der Logienquelle? – *c*) *Jacobson* Arland D., Apocalyptic and the Synoptic Sayings Source Q: ➤ 137, ᶠNEIRYNCK F., Four Gospels 1992, 361-388 / 389-401 / 403-419.

4549 *Scholer* David M., Q bibliography supplement III, 1992: ➤ 478, SBL Sem. 31 (1992) 1-4.

4550 **Schüling** Joachim, Studien zum Verhältnis von Logienquelle und Markusev.: ForBi 65. Wü 1991, Echter. 252 p. DM 39. – ᴿBiblica 73 (1992) 276-9 (F. G. *Downing*); TR 88 (1992) 376s (T. *Söding*).

4551 **Stein** Robert H., *a*) The Synoptic Problem; an introduction 1987 ➤ 3,4189 ... 6,4613; – *b*) Gospels and tradition; studies on redaction criticism of the Synoptic Gospels. GR 1991, Baker. 204 p. – ᴿETL 68 (1992) 434-6 (F. *Neirynck*).

4552 **Throckmorton** Burton H.ᴶ, Gospel parallels; a comparison of the Synoptic Gospels with alternative readings from the manuscripts and noncanonical parallels²ʳᵉᵛ (NRSV) [¹1949]. Nv 1992, Nelson. xl-212 p. $16. 0-8407-7484-2 [TDig 40,152].

4553 **Wenham** John, Redating Mt Mk Lk; a fresh assault on the Synoptic Problem 1991 ➤ 7,3585: ᴿEurJT 1 (1992) 185s (I. H. *Marshall*); NT 34 (1992) 200s (J. K. *Elliott*); Tablet 246 (1992) 750 (P. *Fitzgerald-Lombard*); TLond 95 (1992) 53s (M. *Goulder*).

F2.8 *Synoptica: themata.*

4554 *Bailey* Kenneth E., Informal controlled oral tradition and the synoptic gospels: AsiaJT 5 (1991) 34-54.

4555 *Bartnicki* Roman, ❷ The origin of the Synoptic Gospels in the light of the statements of the Church's Fathers [w świetle tradycji starożytnego Kościoła]: ColcT 62,4 (1992) 25-42; Eng. 42s.

4556 *Casciaro* José María, Contribución al estudio de los discursos de Jesús en los sinópticos: ➤ 135, ᶠMUÑOZ IGLESIAS S., EstBib 50 (1992) 395-409.

4557 ᴱ**Dungan** David L., The interrelations of the Gospels 1984/90 ➤ 6,524: ᴿChurchman 105 (1991) 362s (J. *Wenham*: no solution); JTS 51 (1992) 180-2 (D. *Wenham*: the galaxy could agree on only 4 points out of 19); TvT 32 (1992) 92s (W. *Weren*).

4558 **Ebersohn** Michael, Das Nächstenliebegebot in der synoptischen Tradition: Diss. ᴰ*Lührmann* D. Marburg 1992. — RTLv 24, p. 546.

4559 *a) Kloppenborg* John S., The theological stakes in the Synoptic Problem; – *b) Hooker* Morna D., The Son of Man and the synoptic problem; – *c) Chilton* Bruce D., The Son of Man, human and heavenly; – *d) Hoffmann* Paul, QR und der Menschensohn; eine vorläufige Skizze: ➤ 137, ᶠNEIRYNCK F., Four Gospels 1992, 93-120 / 189-201 / 203-218 / 421-456.

4560 *a) Lampe* Stephen J., Authority and power in the Synoptics; – *b) Bergant* Dianne, Power; a blessing or a curse?: BToday 30 (1992) 271-6 / 260-6.

Malina Bruce, *Rohrbaugh* R.L., Social science commentary on the Synoptic Gospels 1992 ➤ k220.

4561 **Marx** W.G., Proof positive; a fresh look at Synoptic origins. Lima OH 1992, Fairway. 117 p. $14.50 pa. 1-55673-462-X [NTAbs 37, p. 117].

4562 *Meadors* Edward P., The orthodoxy of the 'Q' sayings of Jesus: TyndB 43 (1992) 233-257.

4563 **Piper** R.A., Wisdom in the Q-tradition 1989 ➤ 5,4518; 7,3828: ᴿCrNSt 13 (1992) 421-7 (P. *Hoffmann*).

4564 *Ronning-Ronen* Halvor, Word statistics and the minor agreements of the synoptic gospels: ➤ 450, Informatique 2, 1988/9, 501-516.

4565 *Stein* Robert H., The Matthew-Luke agreements against Mark; insights from John: CBQ 54 (1992) 482-502.

4566 **Theissen** Gerd, The Gospels in context; social and political history in the Synoptic tradition 1991 ➤ 7,3831; 0-567-09602-5; pa. -29602-1: ᴿTS 53 (1992) 548-550 (F.J. *Matera*).

4567 **Theissen** G., Lokalkolorit ... synopt: NOrb 8, 1989 ➤ 5,4317 ... 7,3831: ᴿNedTTs 46 (1992) 68s (P.W. van der *Horst*); RHPR 72 (1992) 198-200 (C. *Grappe*: fort agréable); RivB 40 (1992) 358-360 (V. *Fusco*: 'il lettore rimane stupito dalla quantità di dati ricavabili dalle fonti coeve'); TorJT 9 (1993) 139s (S. *Carruth*); TR 88 (1992) 108-110 (K. *Scholtissek*).

F3.1   **Matthaei evangelium:** *textus, commentarii.*

4568 **Beare** F.W. [† 1986], Il vangelo secondo Matteo; commento [1981],ᵀ. R 1990, Dehoniane. 643 p. – ᴿRivB 40 (1992) 242-5 (M. *Làconi*: fra le affermazioni strane 'la teologia crucis manca').

4569 **Blomberg** Craig L., Matthew: New American Commentary 22. Nv 1992, Broadman. 464 p. 0-8054-0122-9 [NTAbs 37, p. 273].

4570 **Bruggen** Jacob van, Matteüs; het evangelie voor Israël: CommNT 3. Kampen 1990. Kok. 510 p ƒ72. 90-24208-15-7. – ᴿKerkT 42 (1991) 257s (G. de *Ru*); NedTTs 46 (1992) 236s (H. *Welzen*); Streven 59 (1991s) 175s (P. *Beentjes*).

4571 **Bruner** Frederick D., The Christbook [Mt 1-12]; The Churchbook [Mt 13-28]: Mt comm (but not Word Comm.). Waco 1987/90, Word.

xxx-475 p.; xx-p. 477-1127. – ᴿCurrTMiss 19 (1992) 299s (E. *Krentz*);
RefTR 51 (1992) (D. *Peterson*, 2).
4572 **Davies** W. D., *Allison* Dale C., ICC Mt 1988 ➤ 4,4439 ... 7,3833: ᴿCalvinT 26 (1991) 424s (T. R. *Wolthuis*); ÉTRel 67 (1992) 455-7 (E. *Cuvillier*:
excellent, petites réserves); JTS 43 (1992) 162-6 (I. H. *Jones*); RExp 89
(1992) 113s (D. S. *Dockery*); ScotJT 45 (1992) 408s (C. *Tuckett*).
4573 **Drewermann** Eugen, Das Matthäusevangelium, Bilder der Erfüllung
I (1-7). Olten 1992, Walter. 848 p. 3-530-16891-21. – ᴿHerdKor 46
(1992) 194 (U. *Ruh*) [272-8 K. *Nientiedt*, 'Fall D.']; MüTZ 43 (1992)
239-250 (G. L. *Müller*: just taped Sunday sermons, but evoking quite
dense comment).
4574 — *Ernst* Josef, Anmerkungen zum 'Matthäus-Roman' von Eugen
DREWERMANN: TGL 82 (1992) 352-8.
4575 **Fischer** B., Varianten zu Matthäus 1988 / Markus 1989 / Lukas 1990
➤ 4,4460 ... : ᴿRET 51 (1991) 111 (M. *Gesteira*).
4576 **Gardner** Richard B., Matthew: Believers Church Bible comm. 1991 ➤ 7,
3836: ᴿCritRR 5 (1992) 200-2 (F. W. *Burnett*: excellent, user-friendly);
GraceTJ 12 (1991) 298s (D. L. *Turner*); TLZ 117 (1992) 749 (Ingo *Broer*).
4577 **Gnilka** Joachim, MtEv II (14-28) 1988 ➤ 4,4440 ... 7.3837: ᴿMüTZ 43
(1992) 113s (T. *Böhm*).
4578 **Green** M., Matthew for today 1989 ➤ 6,4646*: ᴿWestTJ 54 (1992)
183-5 (N. E, B. *Hofstetter*).
4579 **Harrington** Daniel J., The Gospel of Matthew; Sacra Pagina 1, 1991
➤ 7,3838: ᴿETL 68 (1992) 439-441 (F. *Neirynck*, ample description
without evaluation).
4580 **Howard** George, The Gospel of Matthew ... Hebrew [IBN SHAPRUT
c. 1400) 1987 ➤ 3,4215 ... 5,4328; 0-86554-250-3: ᴿJTS 43 (1992) 166-69
(W. *Horbury*: often confused with the renditions of S. MÜNSTER 1537 or
J. du TILLET 1555).
4581 **Kilgallen** John J., A brief commentary on the Gospel of Matthew.
Lewiston NY 1992, Mellen. ix-231 p. $70. 0-7734-2350-8 [NTAbs 37,
p. 280].
4582 ᴱ**Löfstedt** B., SEDULIUS Scottus, Kommentar zum Evangelium nach
Matthäus [i-x, 1989 ➤ 6,4648]: xi,2 bis Schluss: VLatG (14) 19, 1991
➤ 7,3839: ᴿLatomus 51 (1992) 658s (J. *Meyers*, 1); RHE 87 (1992) 794s
(R. *Étaix*, 2).
4583 **Luz** Ulrich, Matthew 1-7; a commentary 1989 ➤ 5,4333 ... 7,3841:
ᴿAustralBR 40 (1992) 88s (J. *Painter*); JBL 111 (1992) 539-542 (D. A.
Hagner); ScotJT 45 (1992) 114-6 (C. M. *Tuckett*).
4584 **Madigan** Kevin J., Peter OLIVI's 'Lectura supra Matthaeum' in medieval exegetical context: diss. ᴰMcGinn B. Chicago 1992. RTLv 24,
p. 553.
4585 **Mali** Franz, Das 'Opus imperfectum in Mt' und sein Verhältnis zu den
Mt-Kommentaren von ORIGENES und HIERONYMUS [Diss.]: InnTSt 34.
Innsbruck 1991, Tyrolia. 397 p. Sch 410. – ᴿTPhil 67 (1992) 590s (H. J.
Sieben).
4586 **Meier** J. P., Matthew, Gospel of: ➤ 741, AnchorBD 4 (1992) 622-641
[618-622, *Duling* D., Matthew].
4587 **Montague** George T., Companion God, a cross-cultural commentary on
Mt 1989 ➤ 5,4334* ... 7,3845: ᴿCBQ 54 (1992) 361-3 (Barbara E. *Bowe*:
not as cross-culturally satisfying as OVERMAN).
4588 **Morris** Leon, The Gospel according to Matthew: Pillar NT comm.
GR/Leicester 1992, Eerdmans/Inter-Varsity. xviii-781 p. $40. 0-8028-

3696-8 / 0-85111-338-9 [CBQ 55, 814-6, J. D. *Kingsbury*: deep faith, out-dated historicizing].

4589 **Ravasi** Gianfranco, Das Evangelium nach Matthäus; Einführung und Erklärungen. Mü 1992, Neue Stadt. 152 p. DM 24,80. 3-87996-280-4. – ᴿTGL 83 (1993) 498 (J. *Ernst*).

4590 **Schuman** N. A., Al deze woorden; over het evangelie van Mattheüs. Haag 1991, Meinema. 200 p. ƒ26,90. – ᴿStreven 59 (1991s) 175s (P. *Beentjes*).

4591 **Smith** R. H., Matthew: Augsburg 1989 ➤ 5,4338...7,3847: ᴿSvTKv 67 (1991) 53s (S. *Byrskog*).

4592 **Stoll** B., Drei karolingische Matthäus-Kommentare (*Claudius* von Turin, *Hrabanus* Maurus, Ps.-*Beda*) und ihre Quellen zur Bergpredigt: MittellateinJ 26 (1991) 36-55 [< RHE 88,43*].

4593 **Tassin** Claude, L'évangile de Matthieu, commentaire pastoral 1991 ➤ 7,3848: ᴿRICathP 41 (1992) 202-4 (M. *Quesnel*).

4594 ᵀᴱ**Vogt** Hermann-J., ORIGENES, Der Kommentar zum Evangelium nach Matthäus: BiblGrLit [18.] 30. Stu [I. 1983 ➤ 64,4205]; II. 1990 ➤ 6,4658; DM 270 (beide): ᴿBijdragen 53 (1992) 438 (M. *Parmentier*, Eng.); TR 88 (1992) 94s (L. *Lies*).

4595 **Wiles** James W., A reconstruction and evaluation of the Matthean text of John CHRYSOSTOM: diss. SW Baptist Theol. Sem., ᴰ*Roark* M. 1992. 93-11171. — DissA 53 (1992s) 4361-A.

F3.2 **Themata** *de Matthaeo*.

4597 **Bauer** David R., Structure of Mt: jNsu 31, ᴰ1988 ➤ 4,4456 ... 6,4661: ᴿCurrTMiss 19 (1992) 56s (E. *Krentz*).

4598 **Beilner** Wolfgang, Exegetisches Material zum Matthäusevangelium: Vermittlung 15. Salzburg 1992, nicht im Handel. 384 p.

4599 *Bellinzoni* Arthur J., The Gospel of Matthew in the second century [... supports against his teacher KOESTER the revised MASSAUX which he is editing in English]: SecC 9 (1992) 197-258 [*Farmer* W., 193-6]; responses by *Everding* H. E., 259-263; *Nardoni* Enrique, 265-270; *Farkasfalvy* D., 271-5.

4600 **Bottini** Claudio, *Adinolfi* Marco, ᴱ*Corona* Raimondo, Il vangelo secondo Matteo, lettura esegetico-esistenziale: IV Settimana Biblica Abruzzese, 3-8.VII.1989. L'Aquila 1990, Curia O.F.M. 183 p.

4601 *a) Broer* Ingo, Versuch zur Christologie des ersten Evangeliums; – *b) Dormeyer* Detlev, Mt 1,1 als Überschrift zur Gattung und Christologie des Matthäus-Evangeliums; – *c) Carlston* Charles E., Christology and Church in Matthew; – *d) Edwards* Richard A., Characterization of the disciples as a feature of Matthew's narrative; – *e) Collins* Raymond F., Matthew's *entolai*; towards an understanding of the commandments in the First Gospel: ➤ 137, ᶠNEIRYNCK F., Four Gospels 1992 (2) 1251-82 / 1361-83 / 1283-1304 / 1305-23 / 1325-48.

4602 *Burnett* Fred W., Exposing the anti-Jewish ideology of Matthew's implied author; the characterization of God as father: Semeia 59 (1992) 155-191.

4603 *Carter* Warren, Kernels and narrative blocks; the structure of Matthew's Gospel: CBQ 54 (1992) 463-481.

4604 **Charette** Blaine, The theme of recompense in Matthew's Gospel [diss. Shf, ᴰ*Lincoln* A.]: jNsu 78. Shf 1992, Academic. 184 p. 1-85075-385-7.

4605 *Combrink* H.J.B., Reference and rhetoric in the Gospel of Matthew: Scriptura 40 (Stellenbosch 1992) 1-17 [< NTAbs 37, p. 189].

4606 **Deladrière** Valentin, Admirons le message en Matthieu en harmonies septénaires: Libre Parole 28, 9ss. Bru 1992, auct. 95 p.

4607 *Duling* Dennis C., Matthew's plurisignificant 'Son of David' in social science prospective; kinship, kingship, magic, and miracle: BibTB 22 (1992) 99-116.

4608 **Ernst** Josef, Matteo, un ritratto teologico [Patmos 1989 → 5,4355], ᵀ*Proch* Umberto. Brescia 1992, Morcelliana. 190 p. Lit. 20.000. 88-372-1460-X. – ᴿSalesianum 55 (1992) 792s (J. J. *Bartolomé*).

4609 **France** R. T., Matthew evangelist and teacher 1989 → 5,4159: ᴿJEvTS 35 (1992) 424-6 (S. *McKnight*).

4609* **Gargano** I., Iniziazione alla 'Lectio divina'; indicazioni metodologiche con l'esemplificazione di alcuni brani presi dal Vangelo secondo Matteo: Conversazioni bibliche. Bo 1992, Dehoniane. 144 p. Lᵐ 20. 88-10-70932-2 [NTAbs 38, p. 119].

4610 **Gradara** R., Matteo, il Vangelo della comunità. Bo 1992, Dehoniane. 92 p. Lit. 7.000. 88-10-70585-8 [NTAbs 37, p. 378].

4611 *Hagner* Donald A., Righteousness in Matthew's theology: → 126, ᶠMARTIN R., Worship 1992, 101-120.

4612 *Howard* George, A note on Codex Sinaiticus and SHEM-TOB's Hebrew Matthew: NT 34 (1992) 46s.

4613 **Howell** David B., Matthew's inclusive story ...: jNsu 42, ᴰ1990 → 6, 4674; 7,3857: ᴿCBQ 54 (1990) 570s (R. A. *Edwards*); CritRR 5 (1992) 218-220 (R. M. *Fowler*); TLZ 117 (1992) 189-191 (U. *Luz*).

4614 *Kingsbury* Jack D., Matthäusevangelium, ᵀ*Voorgang* D.: → 757, EvKL 3 (1992) 341-3.

4615 **Kupp** David D., Matthew's Emmanuel Messiah; a paradigm of presence for God's people: diss. ᴰ*Stanton* G. Durham UK 1992. 309 p. – RTLv 24, p. 547.

4616 **Kynes** William L., A Christology of solidarity; Jesus as the representative of his people in Matthew [→ 7,3861, diss. Cambridge 1986, ᴰ*Hooker* Morna]. Lanham MD 1991, UPA. xiii-247 p. $42.50; pa. $27. 0-8191-8097-1; –8-6 [NTAbs 36, p. 422].

4617 **Massaux** Édouard, Influence of Mt I, [ᴰ1950], ᵀ*Belvalle* N., *Hecht* Suzanne 1990 → 7,3866: ᴿRExp 89 (1992) 428s (A. A. *Trites*).

4618 **Menninger** Richard E., The relationship between Israel and the Church in the Gospel of Matthew: diss. Fuller Theol. Sem. Pasadena 1991. 329 p. 92-12726. – DissA 53 (1992s) 534-A.

4619 *Mora* Vincent, La symbolique de la création dans l'Évangile de Matthieu [sept montagnes, Mt 4,1-11; 5,1-12; 15,29-39; 17,1-9; 21,1-17; 27,32-44; 28,16-20; ensuite la mer, le bestiaire, les signes cosmiques]: LDiv 144, 1991 → 7,3868: ᴿEsprVie 102 (1992) 213-5 (L. *Walter:* clair même pour les débutants, mais profond pour le spécialiste); PrOrChr 41 (1991) 177s (P. *Ternant*); ScEspr 44 (1992) 231s (M. *Girard*); TvT 32 (1992) 312 (L. *Grollenberg*).

4620 *Müller* Mogens, The Gospel of St. Matthew and the Mosaic Law — a chapter of a biblical theology: ST 46 (1992) 109-120.

4621 *Orton* W., The understanding scribe 1989 → 5,4374 ... 7,3871: ᴿJQR 83 (1992s) 184-6 (W. *Adler*); ScripB 22,1 (1992) 25s (H. *Wansbrough*).

4622 **Overman** J. Andrew, Matthew's Gospel and formative Judaism ᴰ1990 → 6,4687; 7,3872: ᴿBibTB 22 (1992) 42s (S. *Joubert*); Interpretation 46 (1992) 200s (M. I. *Wegener*); NewTR 5,3 (1992) 107s (D. J. *Harrington*); NT 34 (1992) 294-7 (R.A.J. *Gagnon*); RB 99 (1992) 607-9 (B. T. *Viviano*); TorJT 8 (1992) 191s (M. P. *Knowles*).

4623 **Page** Homer A., An investigation of the concept of reward in the Gospel of Matthew: diss. Baptist Theol. Sem., ᴰ*Simmons* B. New Orleans 1991. 206 p. 92-16457. – DissA 53 (1992s) 185-A.

4624 **Paglia** Vincenzo, Il volto di Dio; riflessioni sul Vangelo di Matteo: BtUniv 57. Mi 1991, Rizzoli. 299 p. Lᴹ 12. 88-17-11557-6.

4625 **Pennington** M. Basil, [30 Mt meditations] Call to the center 1990 ➤ 6,8232: ᴿCurrTMiss 19 (1992) 52 (T. *Hubert*).

4626 *Powell* Mark A., The plot and subplots of Matthew's Gospel: NTS 38 (1992) 187-204.

4627 *a) Powell* Mark A., Toward a narrative-critical understanding of Matthew; – *b) Kingsbury* Jack D., The plot of Matthew's story; – *c) Baker* David R., The major characters of Matthew's story; their function and significance; – *d) Snodgrass* Klyne R., Matthew's understanding of the Law; – *e) Stanton* Graham N., The communities of Matthew: Interpretation 46 (1992) 341-6 / 347-356 / 357-367 / 368-378 / 379-392.

4628 **Quesnel** Michel, Jésus-Christ selon saint Matthieu; synthèse théologique: JJC 47, 1991 ➤ 7,3837: ᴿCBQ 54 (1992) 584s (R. *Doran:* first-world Christian; does not explain why he holds Mt 5,18-20 to mean that only the ethical precepts remain valid); RICathP 40 (1991) 298s (C. *Perrot*); VSp 146 (1992) 396 (H. *Cousin*).

4629 *Riley* H., The first gospel [proto-Mt]. Macon 1992, Mercer Univ. vi-130 p. $25. 0-86554-409-3 [NTAbs 37, p. 284]. – ᴿSWJT 35,3 (1992s) 45 (H. A. *Brehm*, unconvinced).

4630 *Sand* Alexander, *a)* 'Schule des Lebens'; zur Theologie des Matthäusevangeliums – *b)* Die Logia Jesu, die vier Evangelien und der Kanon der ntl Schriften: ➤ 112*, Mem. Kuss O. 1992, 57-82 / 125-141.

4631 **Shr Yichou,** Three dimensions of community in the Gospel of Matthew: righteousness, compassion, and worship: diss. Southern Baptist Theol. Sem. 1992, ᴰ*Ward* W. 240 p. 92-28427. – DissA 53 (1992s) 1549-A.

4632 *Sloyan* Gerard, Preaching Matthew; book roundup: Church 8,4 (1992) 51s.

4633 *Smith* Robert H., Matthew's message for insiders; charisma and commandment in a first-century community: Interpretation 46 (1992) 229-240.

4634 *a) Smith* Robert., Interpreting Matthew today; – *b) Danker* Frederick W., God with us; Hellenistic Christological perspectives in Matthew; – *c) Rhoads* David, The Gospel of Matthew; the two ways, hypocrisy and righteousness; – *d) Luz* Ulrich, Matthew's anti-Judaism; its origin and contemporary significance; – *e) Krentz* Edgar, More than many lessons; on preaching Matthew: CurrTMiss 19 (1992) 424-432 / 433-9 / 453-461 / 405-415 / 440-452.

4635 *a) Standaert* Benoît, L'évangile selon Matthieu; composition et genre littéraire; – *b) Allison* Dale C., Matthew; structure, biographical impulse, and the Imitatio Christi; – *c) Stanton* Graham N., Matthew; *bíblos, euangélion,* or *bíos? – d) Dunn* James D.G., Matthew's awareness of Markan redaction: ➤ 137, ᶠNEIRYNCK F., Four Gospels 1992, (2) 1223-50 / 1203-21 / 1187-1201 / 1349-59.

4636 *Stanton* G.N., Matthew's Christology and the parting of the ways: ➤ 467, Jews & C., 1989/92, 99-116.

4637 *Stanton* Graham N., *a)* Matthew's Gospel and the Damascus Document in sociological perspective [ineditum]; – *b)* Synagogue and church [ineditum]: ➤ 313, Studies in Mt 1992, 85-107 / 113-145.

4638 **Stock** Klemens, Gesù annuncia la beatitudine ... Mt 1989 ➤ 5,4387: ᴿCC 143 (1992,1) 306 (D. *Scaiola*).

4639 **Tisera** Guido, Univeralism according to the Gospel of Matthew: diss.
Pont. Univ. Gregoriana, ᴰ*Stock* K. Roma 1992. 525 p.; Extr. 3900,
105 p. – RTLv 24, p. 550.

4640 **Trilling** W., Il vero Israele; studi sulla teologia di Matteo. CasM 1992,
Piemme. 219 p. [VivH 4,191, S. *Dianich*].

4641 *Weber* Beat, Schulden erstatten – Schulden erlassen; zum matthäischen
Gebrauch einiger juristicher und monetärer Begriffe: ZNW 83 (1992)
253-6.

4642 **Williams** Allen, The relation of narrative time to the plot of Matthew's
Gospel: diss. Baptist Theol. Sem., ᴰ*Stevens* G. New Orleans 1992. 195 p.
92-33502. – DissA 53 (1992s) 2415-A.

4643 **Wong Kun-Chun,** Interkulturelle Theologie und multikulturelle Gemeinde im Matthäusevangelium; zum Verhältnis von Juden- und Hei-
denchristen im ersten Evangelium [Diss. Heidelberg 1991 ➤ 7,3881; Titel
leicht verändert]: NOrb 22. FrS/Gö 1992, Univ./VR. [viii–] 223 p. 3-
7278-0821-7 / VR 3-525-55923-1.

4644 **Wouters** Armin, '... wer den Willen meines Vaters tut'; eine Untersuchung zum Verständnis vom Handeln im Mt.-ev. [kath. Diss. Mü 1990,
ᴰ*Laub* F.]: BUnt 23. Rg 1992, Pustet. 458 p. [TR 88,517] 3-7917-1307-8.
– ᴿBLitEc 93 (1992) 403s (S. *Légasse*).

4645 **Wrege** Hans T., Das Sondergut des Mt-Ev: Z Werkkomm. Z 1991,
TVZ. 143 p. Fs 36. 3-290-10136-3. – ᴿTvT 32 (1992) 311s (W. *Berflo*).

F3.3   *Mt 1s* (*Lc 1s* ➤ F7.5) *Infantia Jesu* – **Infancy Gospels.**

4646 **Aus** R. D., Weihnachtsgeschichte usw. 1988 ➤ 4,4220; 6, 4708: ᴿSNTU
A-16 (1991) 223 (A. *Fuchs*).

4647 *Borg* Marcus J., The first Christmas; I am a Christian who does not
believe in the virgin birth, nor in the star of Bethlehem, nor in the journey
of the wisemen: BR 8,6 (1992) 4.10.

4648 *Brown* Raymond E., Infancy narratives in the NT Gospels: ➤ 741,
AnchorBD 3 (1992) 410-415.

4649 **Casalini** Nello, Libro dell'origine di Gesù Cristo ... Matt 1-2: SBF
Anal 28, 1990 ➤ 6,4706; 7,3886: ᴿCBQ 54 (1992) 114s (S. B. *Marrow*;
significantly concludes with a list of 'revealed facts' distinguished from
'historical facts' by the earliest Church).

4650 *Crouch* James E., How early Christians viewed the birth of Jesus: BR
7,5 (1991) 34-38; 8/1,6, answer to J. *Bragança*, 'How did the Virgin Birth
get so popular?'.

4651 *Cruz Hernández* Miguel, ➤ 1991 [o] 1993, ¿Dos mil años del nacimiento
de Jesús de Nazaret?: RelCu 38 (1992) 61-70.

4652 **Drewermann** Eugen, De la naissance des dieux à la naissance du Christ;
une interprétation des récits de la nativité de Jésus d'après la psychologie
des profondeurs [1986], ᵀ*Feisthauer* Joseph. P 1992, Seuil. 306 p. 2-02-
014399-2.

4653 **Ferreira Martins** José Miguel, A família de Jesus segondo os evangelhos
da infancia: diss. Pamplona 1992. 340 p. – RTLv 24, p. 546.

4654 **Fuller** R., He that cometh 1990 ➤ 6,4710; ᴿAnglTR 74 (1992) 101-4
(R. E. *Kahl:* companion and corrective to R. E. *Brown*).

4655 *Masini* Mario, I Vangeli dell'infanzia di Gesù; traguardi e prospettive:
Marianum 54 (1992) 451-460.

4656 **Muñoz Iglesias** Salvador, Nacimiento e infancia de Jesús en san Mateo:
Evangelios de la Infancia 4 / BAC 509. M 1990, Católica. xvi-443 p. –

ᴿCBQ 54 (1992) 794s (F. *Martin*, also on 1 ➤ 7,4498*); ComSev 24 (1991) 104s (M. de *Burgos*, I y 4); Gregorianum 73 (1992) 146-8 (G. *Marconi*, anche su I); RBiArg 54 (1992) 117-120 (R. *Krüger*); ScripTPamp 24 (1992) 335s (J. M. *Casciaro*).

4657 **Pérez Rodríguez** Gabriel, La infancia de Jesús 1990 ➤ 7,3893: ᴿScrip-TPamp 24 (1992) 679s (J. M. *Ferreira-Martins*).

4658 **Schnackenburg** R., ¿Dios ha enviado a su Hijo? El misterio de Navidad. Barc 1992, Herder. 93 p. – ᴿPhase 32 (1992) 535 (J. *Aldazábal*).

4659 **Schönborn** Christoph, Noël, quand le mythe devient réalité. P 1991, Desclée. 80 p. F 65. – ᴿEsprVie 102 (1992) 346 (P. *Rouillard:* commence avec une méditation contre The myth of God incarnate 1977, qui aujourd'hui semble viser plutôt DREWERMANN).

4660 **Spong** John S., Born of a woman; a bishop rethinks the birth of Jesus. SF 1992, Harper. – ᴿBR 8,6 (1992) 15 (Elizabeth *Johnson*); Tablet 246 (1992) 1598-1602 (B. *Daley*).

Urbaniak-Walczak Katarzyna, Die 'conceptio per aurem' ... Marienbild in Ägypten 1992 ➤ e40.

4660* **Wolfe** R., Light on Jesus' birth and boyhood [like Nicholas of Myra = 'Santa Claus', the unconcern of the Synoptics for the real facts has been covered over by successive layers of falsity]. Lewiston NY 1990, Mellen. vii-160 p. $50. 0-88946-739-0 [NTAbs 38, p. 126: he wrote in 1990 'Studies in the Life of Jesus; a liberal approach'].

4661 *Moloney* Francis J., Beginning the Gospel of Matthew; reading Matthew 1:1 – 2:23: Salesianum 54 (1992) 341-359.

4662 *a) Aarde* Andries G. Van, The Evangelium Infantium [Mk 10,13-16], the abandonment of children, and the infancy narrative in Matthew 1 and 2 from a social-scientific perspective; – *b) Weaver* Dorothy J., Power and powerlessness; Matthew's use of irony in the portrayal of political leaders: ➤ 478, SBL Sem. 31 (1992) 435-453 / 454-466.

4663 *a) Nolan* Brian M., Rooting the Davidic Son of God of Matthew 1-2 in the experience of the Evangelist's audience; – *b) Vilar Hueso* Vicente, Notas marginales de san Juan de Ribera a Mt 1-2; – *c) Pérez Rodríguez* Gabriel, Dimensión existencial de Mt 1-2; Lc 1-2: ➤ 135, ꟳMUÑOZ IGLESIAS S., EstBib 50 (1992) 149-156 / 305-316 / 161-175.

4664 *Pesch* Rudolf, 'Er wird Nazoräer heissen'; messianische Exegese in Mat 1-2: ➤ 137, ꟳNEIRYNCK F., Four Gospels 1992, 1385-1401.

4665 *Barbaglio* Giuseppe, Le genti nella genealogia di Mt 1,1-17: ➤ 339, ParSpV 26 (1992) 101-110.

4666 *Bruns* J. Edgar, The priestly lineage of Mary and Jesus reconsidered: ➤ 17c, ꟳBILANIUK P., The divine life 1992, 57-65.

4667 *a) Klassen-Wiebe* Sheila, Matthew 1:18-25; – *b) Senior* Donald, Matthew 2:1-12; expository: Interpretation 46 (1992) 392-395-398.

4668 *Bauer* Johannes B., 'Josef gedachte Maria heimlich zu verlassen' (Mt 1,19; AscIs 11,3): ➤ 38, ꟳCULLMANN O., TZBas 48 (1992) 218-220.

4669 *Parrinder* Geoffrey, Son of Joseph; the parentage of Jesus. E 1992, Clark. £9. 0-567-29213-4. – ᴿTablet 246 (1992) 1598-1602 (B. *Daley*).

4670 *Chorpenning* Joseph F., St. Joseph's pilgrimage of faith; John Paul II's apostolic exhortation Guardian of the Redeemer: CommWsh 20 (1993) 188-194.

4671 **Schaberg** Jane,   The illegitimacy of Jesus 1987 ⇒ 3,4273 ... 6,4731:
   ᴿJAAR 60 (1992) 358-361 (Mary H. *Schertz*); RExp 89 (1992) 107s
   (Molly T. *Marshall:* illuminating despite provocative title).
4672 *Daley* Brian,   Born of a virgin [...*pace* PARRINDER G., SPONG J. S.]:
   Tablet 246 (1992) 1598-1602.
4673 *Hattrup* Dieter, Neues von der Jungfrauengeburt: TGL 82 (1992) 249-255.
4674 *a) Lumbala* François K.,   La conception virginale de Jésus; une lecture
   africaine; – *b) Granger* Émile,   Est né de la Vierge Marie: LumièreV 41
   (1992) 53-59 / 61-70.
4675 **Müller** Gerhard L.,   Was heisst, Geboren von der Jungfrau Maria?:
   QDisp 119, 1989 ⇒ 5,4413; 6,4727: ᴿMarianum 54 (1992) 467-9 (H.
   Moll).
4676 *Pixner* Bargil,   Maria im Hause Davids; Tempelrolle und Jungfrauengeburt: GeistL 64 (1991) 41-51.
4677 **Montefiore** Hugh,   The womb and the tomb. L 1992, Collins.   189 p.
   £6. – ᴿExpTim 103 (1991s) 313 (T.J. *Gorringe:* somewhat unsatisfying
   further reflections on the House of Bishops document on Virgin Birth and
   Resurrection which he signed in 1986).
4678 **Fournée** J.,   Histoire de l'Angelus; le message de l'Ange a Marie.   P
   1991, Téqui.   55 p. – ᴿArTGran 55 (1992) 329s (A. *Segovia*).
4679 *Zeller* Dieter, Geburtsankündigung und Geburtsverkündigung [≅ ANRW
   2,26 (1987)]: TANZ 7 (1992) 59-134.
4680 *Lawrence* John,   Publius Sulpicius Quirinius and the Syrian census:
   RestQ 34 (1992) 193-205.
4681 *Humphreys* Colin J.,   The star of Bethlehem, a comet in 5 BC and the
   date of Christ's birth [< JRoyalAstronS 32 (1991) 389-407]: TyndB 43,1
   (1992) 31-56.
4682 *Mauny* Michel de,   Les sages-femmes de la Sainte-Vierge ['ventrières'
   dans certaines scènes de la Nativité]: PeCa 255 (1991) 29-33.
4683 *Agourides* Suvas,   The birth of Jesus and the Herodian dynasty; an
   understanding of Matthew, chapter 2: GrOrTR 37 (1992) 135-146.
4684 *Legrand* L.,   Angels' songs or Rachel's dirge; a Christmas meditation.
   IndTSt 29 (1992) 281-290.
4685 *a) Soares-Prabhu* George M.,   Jesus in Egypt; a reflection on Mt
   2:13-15.19-21 in the light of the Old Testament; – *b) Trebolle Barrera*
   Julio,   El relato de la huida y regreso de Egipto (Mt 2,13-15a.19-21);
   estructura y composición literaria; – *c) Alonso Schökel* Luis, Notas de
   Antiguo Testamento a los Evangelios de la Infancia: ⇒ 135, ꟳMUÑOZ
   IGLESIAS S., EstBib 50 (1992) 225-249 / 251-260 / 13-18.
4686 **Quéré** France,   Jésus enfant: JJC 35. P 1992, Desclée.   253 p. [NRT
   115,889, L. *Renwart*].
4687 **Gutiérrez** José Ignacio,   La Santa Pareja de Nazaret, una hipótesis de
   investigación.   Barquisimeto 1992, Mencey. 391 p. [EstJos 47,119, J. A.
   Carrasco].
4688 **Molinari** F., *Hennessy* A.,   The vocation and mission of Joseph and
   Mary.   Dublin 1992, Veritas.   59 p. £3. 1-85390-149-0 [NTAbs 37,118].

F3.4 *Mt 3 ... Baptismus Jesu,* **Beginning of the Public Life.**

4689 *Ahirika* Edwin A.,   The theology of the Matthean baptism narrative:
   Bible Bhashyam 18 (1992) 131-9.
4690 *Allison* Dale C.,ᴶ,   The baptism of Jesus and a new Dead Sea Scroll:
   BAR-W [17,6 (1991) 65] 18,2 (1992) 58-60; ill.

4691 **Backhaus** Knut, Die 'Jüngerkreise' des Täufers Johannes; eine Studie zu den religionsgeschichtlichen Ursprüngen des Christentums [Diss. Paderborn 1989, ᴰ*Ernst* J.]: PdTSt 19, 1991 ➤ 7,3913; ᴿBZ 36 (1992) 267s (D. *Kosch*); JTS 43 (1992) 583s (E. *Bammel*); TGL 82 (1992) 138-140 (J. *Hainz*); TLZ 117 (1992) 909-911 (J. *Becker*); TvT 32 (1992) 197s (P.J. *Farla*).

4692 **Castellano** Antonio, L'esegesi di ORIGENE e di ERACLEONE alle testimonianze del Battista: diss. Salesianum, ᴰ*Bergamelli* F. Roma 1991. Extr. 284: 62 p. – RTLv 24, p. 551.

4693 **Ernst** Josef, Johannes der Täufer: BZNW 53, 1989 ➤ 5,4433 ... 7,3915: ᴿBijdragen 53 (1992) 209s (J. *Lambrecht*); JBL 111 (1992) 144-6 (W. *Wink:* sober and informative); RB 99 (1992) 459s (J. *Murphy-O'Connor*); TR 88 (1992) 110-3 (F.W. *Horn*).

4693* *Hollenbach* Paul W., John the Baptist: ➤ 741, AnchorBD 3 (1992) 887-899.

4694 **Lupieri** E., Giovanni Battista fra storia e leggenda 1988 ➤ 4,4537 ... 7,3918: ᴿGregorianum 73 (1992) 152s (R. *Fisichella*).

4695 **Lupieri** Edmondo, Giovanni e Gesù; storia di un antagonismo: Uomini e religioni, Oscar 60. R 1991, Mondadori. 254 p. Lᵐ 12. 88-04-34762-7. – ᴿHenoch 12 (1992) 201-3 (P. *Sacchi*).

4696 *Lupieri* Edmondo F., John the Baptist in New Testament traditions and history: ➤ 742, ANRW 2,26,1 (1992) 430-461.

Meier John P., John the Baptist [Lk 3,10-14 ...] in Josephus 1992 ➤ d187.

4697 **Metzsch** Friedrich A. von, Johannes der Täufer; seine Geschichte und seine Darstellung in der Kunst ➤ 6,4138: Mü 1989, Callwey. 224 p.; 197 phot. + 23 color. DM 49,80: ᴿLuthMon 30 (1991) 235 (Roswitha *Flitner*); TrierTZ 101 (1992) 160 (E. *Sauser*).

4698 **Ottillinger** A., Vorläufer, Vorbild oder Zeuge? Zum Wandel des Täuferbildes im Johannesevangelium [kath. Diss. München 1991, ᴰ*Laub* F.]: TheolR 45. St.Ottilien 1991, EOS. vi-315 p. DM 33. 3-88096-845-4 [NTAbs 37,282].

4699 *Vigne* Daniel, Christ au Jourdain; le baptême de Jésus dans la tradition judéo-chrétienne: ÉtBN 16. P 1992, Gabalda. 362 p. F 430. 2-85021-055-2 [TR 89,167; BLitEc 94,349-351, R. *Cabié*].

4700 a) *Walter* Nikolaus, [Mt 3] Mk 1,1-8 und die 'agreements' von Mt 3 und Lk 3; Stand die Predigt Johannes des Täufers in Q?; – b) *Légasse* Simon, L'autre 'baptême' (Mc 1,8; Mt 3,11; Lc 3,16; Jn 1,26.31-33); – c) *Tuckett* Christopher M., The temptation narrative in Q: ➤ 137, ꟳNEIRYNCK F., Four Gospels 1992, 457-478 / 257-273 / 479-507.

4701 **Webb** Robert L., John the Baptizer and prophet: jNsu 62, 1991 ➤ 7,3919: ᴿCBQ 54 (1992) 807s (D.J. *Harrington:* solid); ÉTRel 67 (1992) 464 (E. *Cuvillier:* solide); JTS 43 (1992) 582s (W. *Wink:* superb).

4702 *Zilles* Urbano, Quem foi João Batista? Teocomunicação 22,96 (1992) 279-283.

4703 *Baarda* T., 'He holds the fan in his hand ...' (Mt 3:12, Lk 3:17) and Philoxenus: Muséon 105 (1992) 63-86.

4704 **Ellul** Jacques, Si tu es le Fils de Dieu; souffrances et tentations de Jésus. P 1991, Centurion. 110 p. – ᴿEsprVie 102 (1992) 79s (P. *Jay*).

4705 **Laeuchli** Samuel, Jesus und der Teufel; Begegnung in der Wüste; Imagination, Spiel und Therapie in der Versuchungsgeschichte; *Rothchild-*

Laeuchli Evelyn, klinische Beiträge.   Neuk 1992, Neuk.-V.   vi-161 p.
DM 38 [EvKomm 25,615]. 3-7887-1393-3.

4706 **Storniolo** Ivo,   Las tentaciones de Jesús.   Buenos Aires 1990, Paulinas.
64 p. – ᴿRBiArg 53 (1991) 124-6 (M. *Egan*).

4707 **Yan [Yang] Seung Ai,**   The original intention of the longer version of the
temptation story of Jesus as a Jewish story of God's testing of the
righteous man Jesus: diss. ᴰ*Betz* H. Chicago 1992. – RTLv 24, p. 550.

4708 **McMurry** Berta W.,   Testing in the wilderness; a comparative study of
Matt. 4:1-11 in the light of Deut 6-8 and midrashic interpretations: diss.
SW Baptist Theol. Sem. ᴰ*Urrey* T. 1992. 280 p. 93-11169. – DissA 53
(1992s) 4369-A.

4709 *Schwarz* Günther,   *Tò pterýgion toû hieroû* (Mt 4,5 / Lk 4,9): BibNot 61
(1992) 33-35 (Temple-atrium roof).

F3.5   Mt 5 ... Sermon on the Mount [... plain, Lk 6,17].

4710 **Bauman** Clarence,   The Sermon on the Mount; the modern quest for its
meaning 1985 ⇒ 1,4321: ᴿRelStR 18 (1992) 141 (C. *Mercer*).

4711 **Beilner** Wolfgang,   Die Fleischtöpfe Israels [= Der Christ in Staat und
Gesellschaft, oder die FI 1982 (Bergpredigt, Ökumene ...)]: Vermittlung 5.
Salzburg 1992. 210 p. 3-222-11392-0.

4712 *Betz* Hans Dieter,   Sermon on the mount (plain): ⇒ 741, AnchorBD 5
(1992) 1106-12.

4713 *Brooks* J.A., (*al.*), Sermon on the Mount: CriswellTJ 6,1 (1992) 15-28
(3-14 / 25-42 / 43-56 / 57-72 / 73-89) [< NTAbs 37, p. 348ss].

4714 **Derrett** J.D.M.,   The ascetic discourse; an explanation of the Sermon on
the Mount 1989 ⇒ 5,4451; 6,4762: ᴿGrazBeit 18 (1992) 300 (K. *Niederwimmer:* unkonventionell, anregend).

4715 **Drewermann** E.,   De Bergrede; beelden van vervulling; toelichting op
Mattheüs 5, 6 en 7.   Zoetermeer 1992, Meinema. 296 p. ƒ42,50. 90-
211-3582-5 [TvT 33,415, H. *Berflo*].

4716 **Entrich** Manfred,   Die Bergpredigt als Ausbildungsordnung; der katechetische Entwurf einer 'ratio formationis' bei ALBERT dem Grossen:
StSeelsorge 10. Wü 1992, Echter. xxiv-347 p. DM 48 [TR 88,522].

4717 **Fernández Lago** José,   *a)* El monte en las homilías de ORÍGENES: diss.
Pont. Univ. Gregoriana, ᴰ*Orbe* A.   Roma 1992. 377 p.; Extr 3901: 80 p. –
RTLv 24, p. 551; – *b)* La montaña, en las Homilías de ORÍGENES: Coll-
ScCompostellana 7.   Compostela 1993, Inst.Teol. 248 p. 84-7009-377-0.

4718 *Flusser* David,   'Den Alten ist gesagt'; zur Interpretation der sog. An-
tithesen der Bergpredigt: Judaica 48 (1992) 35-39.

4719 **Guelich** Robert,   The Sermon on the Mount; a foundation for understanding. Dallas 1992, Word. 451 p. 0-8499-0110-3; pa. -3310-2.

4720 *a) Holtz* Traugott,   'Ich aber sage euch'; Bemerkungen zum Verhältnis
Jesu zur Tora; – *b) Müller* Karlheinz,   Beobachtungen zum Verhältnis
von Tora und Halacha in frühjüdischen Quellen: ⇒ 344, Gesetz 1992,
135-145 / 105-134.

4721 **Krämer** Michael,   Die Überlieferungsgeschichte der Bergpredigt; eine
synoptische Studie zu Mt 4,23-7,29 und Lk 6,17-49: Deutsche Hochschulschriften 433. Egelsbach 1992, Hänsel-Hohenhausen. xxiv-246 p.
[TR 88,516]. 3-89349-433-2.

4722 **Kühlwein** K.,   Familienbeziehung und Bergpredigt-Weisungen [Diss.
Fra St.-Georgen, ᴰ*Lay* R. 1991]: EurHS 23/435. Fra 1992, Lang. 347 p.
$61.80. 3-631-44199-1 [NTAbs 37, p. 280].

4723 **Lohfink** G., Per chi vale ...? 1990 ➤ 7,3935. – ᴿParVi 36 (1991) 335s (C. *Ghidelli*, anche su VENETZ H.); Teresianum 43 (1992) 288s (V. *Pasquetto*).

4724 *a) McEleney* Neil, The sermon on the mount, then and now; – *b) Day* Martin, The ten commandments in their contexts: LivLight 27,1 (1990s) 30-35 / 17-29.

4725 **Massey** Isabel Ann, Interpreting the Sermon on the Mount in the light of Jewish traditions as evidenced in the Palestinian targums of the Pentateuch; selected themes. Lewiston NY 1991, Mellen. xx-309 p. $60. 0-88946-784-6. [TDig 40,174].

4726 **Mateos** J., El sermón del monte / Comentario al Ev. de Marcos: Biblia y pueblo 4s. México c.1991, Centro de Reflexión Teológica [Christus 57/5,91, con 8 títulos más].

4726* *Müller* Mogens, The Gospel of St. Matthew and the Mosaic Law — a chapter of a biblical theology: ST 46 (1992) 109-120.

4727 ᴱ**Nash** S., The Sermon on the Mount [north/south, white/black, male/ female Baptist] studies and sermons: Kerygma and Church. Greenville SC 1992, Smith & H. x-182 p. $11. 1-88-0837-06-4 [NTAbs 37, p. 440].

4728 *Raiter* Michael, Doers of the greater righteousness; the righteousness of the Sermon on the Mount: RefTR 49 (1990) 1-10.

4729 *Römelt* Josef, Normativität, ethische Radikalität und christlicher Glaube; zur theologisch-ethischen Hermeneutik der Bergpredigt: ZkT 114 (1992) 293-303.

4730 **Schweizer** Eduard, Il discorso della montagna (Matteo, cap. 5-7), ᵀ*Fiorillo* Michele 1991 ➤ 7,3941: ᴿAngelicum 69 (1992) 270s (S. *Jurič*); BbbOr 34 (1992) 57s (G. *De Virgilio*); CC 143 (1992,3) 453s (D. *Scaiola*).

4731 *a) Songer* Harold S., The Sermon on the Mount and its Jewish foreground; – *b) Trites* Allison A., (Mt 5:3-12; 7:13-27) The blessings and warnings of the Kingdom; – *c) Stassen* Glen H., Grace and deliverance in the Sermon on the Mount; – *d) Allen* Loyd, The Sermon on the Mount in the history of the Church; – *e) Borchert* Gerald L., Matthew 5:48; perfection and the sermon; – *f) Tilley* W. Clyde, Matthew 7:13-27: RExp 89 (1992) 165-177 / 179-196 / 229-244 / 245-262 / 265-9 / 271-8.

4732 *Stanton* G., Interpreting the Sermon on the Mount [ineditum] ➤ 313, Studies in Mt. 1992, 285-306, [also 307-325 (1987)].

4733 *Stefanovic* Zdravko, 'One greater than the Temple'; the Sermon on the Mount in the early Palestinian liturgical setting: AsiaJT 6,1 (1992) 108-116 [< TContext 16/1, p. 29].

4734 *a) Stevens* G. L., Understanding the Sermon on the Mount; its rabbinic and NT context; – *b) Ray* C. A., The beatitudes; challenging worldviews: TEdr 46 (1992) 83-95 [125-132 *Simmons* B. E.] / 97-104 [105-123 *al.*]; < NTAbs 37, p. 192s].

4735 **Stott** John R. W., The message of the Sermon on the Mount; Christian counter-culture: The Bible Speaks Today. Leicester 1992, Inter-Varsity. 238 p. 0-85110-970-5.

4736 **Tilley** W. C., The surpassing righteousness; evangelism and ethics in the Sermon on the Mount. Greenville SC 1992, Smith & H. x-170 p. $11. 1-880837-03-X [NTAbs 37, p. 443].

4737 *a) Tolar* William B., The Sermon on the Mount from an exegetical perspective; – *b) Greenfield* Guy, The ethics of the Sermon on the Mount; – *c) Lea* Thomas D., Understanding the hard sayings of Jesus;

– *d) Nelson* Jimmie L., Preaching values in the Sermon on the Mount; – *e)* bibliography: SWJT 35,1 (1992s) 4-12 / 13-19 / 20-27 / 28-33 / 34-38.

F3.6 Mt 5,3-11 (Lc 6,20-22) Beatitudines.

4738 ᵀᴱ**(Penati) Bernardini** Anna, GREGORIO di Nissa, Commento al NT; le Beatitudini ed altri scritti: Cultura e culture. R 1992, Coletti. 181 p. 88-7626-808-9.

4739 *a) Fitzmyer* Joseph A., A Palestinian collection of beatitudes; – *b) Gerhardsson* Birger, The Shemaᶜ in early Christianity: → 137, ᶠNEI-RYNCK F., Four Gospels 1992, 509-515 / 275-293.

4740 **Hamm** M. Dennis, The beatitudes in context; what Luke and Matthew meant: Glazier-Zc. ColMn 1990, Liturgical. 120-xvii p. $7. – ᴿPersp-RelSt 29 (1992) 340s (F. S. *Spencer*, also on TALBERT C. 1991).

4741 *a) Molari* Carlo, L'intreccio ideale delle Beatitudini; – *b) Rossi de Gasperis* Francesco, Le beatitudini del Vangelo secondo Matteo; – *c) D'Agostino* Francesco, La povertà scandalo e beatitudine; – *d) Galot* Jean, Sofferenza e beatitudine; – *e) Balducci* Ernesto, Beati i miti perché erediteranno la terra; → 7,416, ᴱ**Ballis** G., Il mondo dell'uomo nascosto; le Beatitudini 1990/1, 5-20 / 21-38 / 39-47 / 49-61 / 63-90. – ᴿCC 143 (1992,3) 543 (G. *Giachi*).

4742 *Pierrard* Pierre, Les Béatitudes, une école de lâcheté?: VSp 146 (1992) 343-352.

4743 *Viviano* Benedict T., *a)* Beatitudes found among Dead Sea Scrolls [4Q535, *Puech* E., RB 138 (1991) 80-86: like and unlike Mt/Lk]: BAR-W 18,6 (1992) 53-55.66; – *b)* Eight beatitudes from Qumran [*Puech* E., RB 1991]: BToday 31 (1993) 219-224.

4744 *Nin* Manuel, Il commento di Giovanni il Solitario a Mt. 5:3: The Harp 5 (Kerala 1992) 29-37 [TContext 10/2,28].

4745 *Nordstokke* Kjell, [Mt 5,4] 'Salige er de fattige i ånden ...': NorTTs 92 (1991) 157-169: 'poor' in liberation-theology perspective.

4745* *Turocchi* Stefano, 'Beati i miti ...'? (Mt 5,5); appunti in margine alla versione in lingua corrente della beatitudine della mitezza: VivH 3,1 (1992) 83-98; Eng. 99.

4746 *Beutler* Johannes, [Mt 5,9 ...] Peacemaking, peacemakers: → 741, AnchorBD 5 (1992) 212s.

4747 *Chilton* Bruce, [Mt 5,23; 23,15-24: Temple still standing] Forgiving at and swearing by the Temple: ForumFF 7,1s (1991) 45-50.

4748 *Sélis* Claude, [Mt 5,31; 19,1-12; Mc 10,1-12; 1 Cor 7,8-16]. La répudiation dans le Nouveau Testament: LumièreV 41,206 ('Fidélité et divorce' 1992) 39-49.

4749 *Force* Paul, Encore les incises de Matthieu! [5,32; 19,9 sur le divorce]: BLitEc 94 (1993) 315-327; Eng. 327 (a scribal blunder).

4750 **Keener** Craig, [Mt 5,32] 'And marries another'. Peabody MA 1991, Hendrickson. – ᴿAndrUnS 31 (1993) 72-74 (A. *Valenzuela*); Themelios 18,3 (1992s) 31 (P. M. *Head*).

4751 **Collins** Raymond F., Divorce in the New Testament: Good News Studies 38. ColMn 1992, Liturgical. xv-389 p. $20. 0-8146-5691-9.

4752 *Wink* Walter, Neither passivity nor violence; Jesus' third way (Matt 5:38-42 ‖ Luke 6:29-30): ForumFF 7,1s (1991) 5-28.

4753 *Steinhauser* Michael G., The violence of [military] occupation; Matthew 5:40-41 and Q [cynic rather than Jewish milieu]: → 74, [F]GUENTHER H., TorJT 8 (1992) 18-37.

4754 *Williams* Samuel F.[J], Matthew 5:43-48 (expository): RExp 89 (1992) 389-395.

4755 *Cooper* Burton, [Mt 5,48 'perfect']. The disabled God: TTod 49 (1992s) 173-182.

F3.7 *Mt6,9-13 (Lc11,2-4)* **Oratio Jesu,** Pater Noster, **Lord's Prayer** [→ H1.4].

4756 [TE]**Aalders** G.J.D., ORIGENES, Het gebed [het Onze Vader]: Kerkvaderteksten met commentaar 8. Bonheiden 1991, Abdij Bethlehem. 137 p. 90-71837-35-1. – [R]TvT 32 (1992) 198 (F. van de *Paverd:* feilen; 'popularisieren door vertalen' een illusie).

4757 *Apecechea Perurena* Juan, Comentario del Padre Nuestro de Joaquín LIZARRAGA: VI (La tercera petición): ScripV 38 (1991) 387-411.

4758 **Ayo** Nicholas, The Lord's Prayer; a survey theological and literary. ND 1992, Univ. xiv-258 p. $30. 0-268-01291-1 [TDig 40,51; BToday 31,58].

4759 *Bivin* D. [Mt 6,9-13...]. Prayers for emergencies: JPersp 5,2 (1992) 16s.

4760 **Boers** Arthur P., Lord, teach us to pray; a new look at the Lord's Prayer. Scottdale PA 1992, Herald. $10. 0-8361-3583-0 [TDig 40,152].

4761 [E]**Callahan** Johannes, GREGORII Nysseni, De oratione dominica, de beatitudinibus: Opera 7/2, Leiden 1992, Brill. lii-180 p. 90-04-09598-5 [VigChr 47,93, J.C.M. Van *Winden*].

4762 **Chevalier** Max-Alain †, [E]*Chevalier* Marjolaine, *Viallaneix* Paul: Relire le Notre-Père. P c.1992, Réforme. 50 p. F 20. – [R]EsprVie 102 (1992) 410 (É. *Cothenet* recommande vivement).

4763 *Garland* David E., The Lord's Prayer in the Gospel of Matthew: RExp 89 (1992) 215-228.

4764 **Jeong Woo Kim,** The function and meaning of the Lord's Prayer in the Sermon on the Mount: diss. Calvin Sem., [D]*Holwerda* D. c. 1991 – CalvinT 26 (1991) 509s.

4765 **John** of Taizé, Praying the Our Father today. Wsh 1992, Pastoral. 64 p. $7. 0-912405-91-0 [TDig 40,70].

4766 *Juel* D., [Mt 6,9s] The Lord's prayer in the gospels of Matthew and Luke: PrincSemB supp 2 (1992) 56-70 [< NTAbs 37,25].

4767 **Kretz** Louis, 'Vater unser'; das Christentum im Widerspruch zu Jesus. Olten 1992, Walter. 195 p. DM 27,50. 3-530-49002-4. – [R]ActuBbg 29 (1992) 211 (J. *Boada*).

4768 *a) Lienhard* Marc, LUTHER et CALVIN commentateurs du Notre Père; – *b) Philomenko* Marc, La troisième demande du 'Notre-Père' et l'hymne de Nabuchodonosor: → 36, [F]CULLMANN O., RHPR 72 (1992) 73-88 / 23-31; Eng. 125s.

4769 **Lochman** Jan M., The Lord's prayer [1988], [T]1990 → 6,4819: [R]Interpretation 46 (1992) 206 (A. C. *Winn*).

4770 **Lorenz** Erika, Das Vaterunser der TERESA von Avila, Anleitung zur Kontemplation. FrB 1987, Herder. 94 p. DM 12,80. 3-451-20971-3. – [R]FranzSt 72 (1990) 93s (L. *Lehmann*).

4771 *a) Ott* Heinrich, Das universale Gebet; – *b) Buri* Fritz, Gebot und Gebet; – *c) Gerber* Uwe, Beten als Vatererfahrung; – *d) Schmidt* Martin A., Thomas von AQUINO zu Matthäus 6,9/10; – *e) Hammer* Karl, Predigt über die erste Bitte des Unservaters; – *f) Gäbler* Ulrich, Das Vaterunser in der Basler Reformation; – *g) Müller* Christoph, Unservater-Paraphrasesn; ein Beitrag zur (praktisch-) theologischen Hermeneutik: ➤ 121, FLOCHMAN J., TZBas 48 (1992) 7-14 / 15-21 / 33-45 / 46-55 / 56-61 / 118-126 / 163-186.

4772 *Perotti* Pier Angelo, Commento al 'Pater noster' (Mt 6,9-13; Lc 11,2-4): Maia 44 (1992) 91-96.

4773 **Ronchi** Ermes, Il cantico del cuore. Bornato BS c. 1991, Sardini. Lit. 20.000 [BbbOr 34,52, adv.].

4774 **Sabugal** Santos, Il Padrenuestro [1981, con numerose aggiunte], TNicolosi M. 1988 ➤ 4,4610 ... 7,3971: RSalesianum 54 (1992) 198 (W. *Turek*).

4775 **Stritzky** Maria-Barbara von, Studien ... des Vaterunsers 1989 ➤ 5,4503; 7,3973: RRechSR 80 (1992) 154s (B. *Sesboüé*).

4776 *Urbanek* Ferdinand, 'Vater im Himmel'; das alte Vaterunser in sprachlicher Neuauflage: LingBib 66 (1992) 39-54.

4777 *a) Cullmann* Oscar, Beten und Sorgen; zur vierten Bitte des Vaterunsers; – *b) Blaser* Klauspeter, Prédication sur Matthieu 6,11, 'Donne-nous aujourd'hui notre pain de jour!'; – *c) Brändle* Rudolf, Die fünfte Bitte in der Auslegung GREGORS von Nyssa; – *d) Jenni* Ernst, Kausativ und Funktionsverbgefüge; sprachliche Bemerkungen zur Bitte, 'Führe uns nicht in Versuchung'; – *e) Stoebe* Hans-Joachim, Überlegungen zur sechsten Bitte; – *f) Willi Plein* Ina, Die Versuchung steht am Schluss; Inhalt und Ziel der Versuchung Abrahams Gen 22; – *g) Seybold* Klaus, Zur Vorgeschichte der liturgischen Formel 'Amen': ➤ 121 FLOCHMAN J., TZBas 48 (1992) 62-64 / 65-69 / 70-76 / 89-99 / 100-108 / 109-117.

4778 *a) Portinari* Folco, Dacci oggi il nostro pane; – *b) Garrone* Daniele, Il vino nella Bibbia; – *c) Bonora* Antonio, La simbologia biblica del mangiare e del bere; gioia e sapienza: ➤ 454, BIBLIA 1992, 52-64 / 65-75 / 76-87.

4779 *Bartolomé* Juan J., O Dios o mammona (Mt 6,24; Lc 16,13); para un discernimiento evangélico sobre la primacia social del capital: ProyCSE 4,13 (1992) 333-345 [< Stromata 49,492].

4780 **Bursey** Ernest J., [Mt 7,15-33 ...]. Exorcism in Matthew: diss. Yale, DMalherbe A. NHv 1992. 242 p. 93-06936. – DissA 53 (1992s) 3564-A; RTLv 24, p. 546.

4781 *a) Fleddermann* Harry T., The demands of discipleship; Matt 8,19-22 par. Luke 9,57-62; – *b) Schlosser* Jacques, Le logion de Mt 10,28 par. Luc 12,4-5; – *c) Boring* M. Eugene, [Mt 12 ...] The Synoptic Problem; 'minor' agreements and the Beelzebul pericope; – *d) Friedrichsen* Timothy A., [Mt 13 ...] 'Minor' and 'major' Matthew-Luke agreements against Mk 4,30-32; ➤ 137, FNEIRYNCK F., Four Gospels 1992, 541-561 / 621-631 / 587-619 / 649-676.

4782 **Hengel** Martin, [Mt 8,21s] Sequela c carisma ... Mt 8,21s, 1990 ➤ 6,4833; 7,3985: RRivStoLR 28 (1992) 694s (Gabriella *Dogliani Saladini*), Salesianum 54 (1992) 371s (J. J. *Bartolomé*).

4783 **Kingsbury** Jack D., The stilling of the storm (Matthew 8:23-27): ➤ 77, FHARRISVILLE R. 1992, 101-8.

4784 *Bauerschmidt* Frederick C., [Mt 8,23s ||, 'a misreading']. The wounds of Christ: LitTOx 5 (1991) 83-100.

F4.1 *Mt 9-12; Miracula Jesu* – **The Gospel miracles**

4785 *Adinolfi* M., L'esorcismo di Gesù in Mc 1,21-28 e i quattro esorcismi di APOLLONIO riferiti da FILOSTRATO: LA 42 (1992) 49-65.

4786 *Billault* Alain, Un sage en politique; APOLLONIOS de Tyane et les empereurs romains: ➤ 657, Mythe et politique 1989/90, 23-32.

4787 **Cornwell** John, Powers of darkness — powers of light [alleged miracles and apparitions]. L 1991, Viking. 395 p. A$45. – ᴿAustralasCR 69 (1992) 47-51 (B. *Lucas*).

4788 *Davies* Brian, Miracles [... proving a religion true?]: New Blackf 73 (1992) 102-120.

4789 ᴱ**Dierkens** Alain, Apparitions et miracles [Colloque international Bru mai 1991]: ProbHistRel 1991/2, 1991 ➤ 7,488: ᴿRTLv 23 (1992) 407s (R. *Guelluy:* haute qualité scientifique et objectivité).

4790 *a) Dunn* James D. G., La possession démoniaque et l'exorcisme dans le NT [< Churchman 94,210-225], ᵀ*Rochat* D., *Sordet* J.; – *b) Ansaldi* Jean, Diableries et naissance d'un sujet devant Dieu [répliques *Koschafjee* Shafique, *Desplanque* Christophe, *Rochat* D. & N.; *Sordet* Jean-Michel]: Hokhma 51 (1992) 34-52 / 53-59 [–65-68-71-75].

4791 **Fischbach** Stephanie M., Totenerweckungen; zur Geschichte einer Gattung [kath. Diss. Würzburg 1991 ➤ 7,3991]: ForBi 69. Wü 1992, Echter. xiv-345 p. DM 48. 3-429-01427-1.

4792 **Geisler** Norman L., Miracles and the modern mind; a defense of biblical miracles. GR 1992, Baker. 163 p. $11. 0-8010-3847-3 [NTAbs 37, p. 135].

4793 **Gerhardsson** Birger, Jesu maktgärningar i Matteusevangeliet. Lund 1991, Novapress. 135 p. – ᴿSvTKv 67 (1991) 136-8 (Helge K. *Nielsen*).

4794 **Greer** Rowan S., Fear of freedom ... miracles 1989 ➤ 5,4546 ... 7,3994: ᴿChH 60 (1991) 92-94 (E. *Ferguson*).

4795 **Jividen** Jiminy, Miracles: from God or man? Abilene TX 1987, Christian Univ. 163 p. – ᴿPerspScCF 43 (1991) 54 (R. *Ruble:* NT from God; currently from frauds).

4796 **Kahl** Werner, Synoptic miracle narratives in their religious-historical setting; a religionsgeschichte comparison from a structural perspective: diss. Emory, ᴰ*Boers* H. Atlanta 1992. – RTLv 24, p. 547.

4797 *Kassel* Maria, Wunder geschehen in uns — oder gar nicht; zur tiefenpsychologischen Exegese von biblischen Wundergeschichten: CLehre 45 (1992) 135-9 [< ZIT 92,260].

4798 *Kee* Howard C., Medicina, milagro y magía en tiempos del Nuevo Testamento [1986 ➤ 2,3468], ᵀ*Valiente Mallá* J.: Grandes Temas del Nuevo Testamento 2. Córdoba 1992, Almendro. 228 p. 84-8005-005-5.

4799 **Koskenniemi** Erkki, Der philostrateische APOLLONIOS 1991 ➤ 7,3997: ᴿCritRR 5 (1992) 298-300 (L. H. *Martin:* against misconstruing the Vita Apollonii as a challenge to Christianity).

4800 *Lang* Marijke H. de, John TOLAND en Hermann S. REIMARUS over de wonderen in het Oude Testament: NedTTs 46 (1992) 1-9.

4801 **Langer** Heidemarie, Vielleicht sogar Wunder; Heilungsgeschichten im Bibliodrama. Z 1991, Kreuz. 183 p. DM 24,80 [EvKomm 25,615].

4802 *Latourelle* René, The miracles of Jesus 1988 ➤ 4,4652 ... 7,3998: ᴿPerspScCF 42 (1990) 187 (D. K. *Pace:* felt like an outsider amid Catholic jargon).

4803 **Latourelle** R., Milagros 1990 ➤ 6,4855*b*; 7,4000: ᴿLumenVr 40 (1991) 106 (F. *Ortiz de Urtaran*).

4804 **McCready** William, Signs of sanctity; miracles / GREGORY 1989 ➤ 5, 4558 ... 7,4002: ᴿTR 88 (1992) 38-40 (H. *Lutterbach*); ZkT 114 (1992) 231s (K. H. *Neufeld:* 'man sollte sich vom Titel nicht verleiten lassen, hier einen Beitrag zur fundamentaltheologischen Diskussion um Taten, Zeichen und Wunder zu suchen').

4805 **Maillot** Alphonse, I miracoli di Gesù, ᵀ*Bert Revel* Delia; Parola per l'uomo d'oggi: T 1990, Claudiana. 176 p. Lit. 19.000. – ᴿAsprenas 39 (1992) 272-4 (V. *Scippa:* pastore Riformato ex-scienziato; scorrevole).

4806 **Mills** Mary E., Human agents of cosmic power: jNsu 41, 1990 ➤ 6,4680*; 7,4003: ᴿCBQ 54 (1992) 167s (R. D. *Chesnutt*); ScripB 22,1 (1992) 28s (K. *Grayston*).

4807 **Neyton** André, Le merveilleux religieux dans l'Antiquité; aspects choisis. P 1991, Letouzey & A. 128 p. F 95. – ᴿEsprVie 102 (1992) 668 (M. *Delahoutre:* 'Quel beau sujet d'étude!' – gâché par un esprit rationaliste).

4808 *Obeng* E. A., The significance of the miracles of resuscitation and its implication for the Church in Africa: Bible Bhashyam 18 (1992) 83-95.

4809 **Padilla** Carmen, Los milagros de la 'Vida de APOLONIO de Tiana'; morfología del relato y géneros afines 1991 ➤ 7,4005: ᴿBLitEc 93 (1992) 355s (S. *Légasse*); FgNt 5 (1992) 87 (J. *Peláez*); RBibArg 54 (1992) 191s (J. P. *Martín*).

4810 *Remus* Harold E., Miracle NT [*Zakovitch* Yair, OT]: ➤ 741, AnchorDB 4 (1992) 856-869 [845-856].

4811 *Scarre* G., TILLOTSON and HUME on miracles: DowR 110 (1992) 45-65.

4812 ᵀᴱ**Torrell** Jean-Pierre, *Bouthillier* Denise, PIERRE le Vénérable, Livre des merveilles de Dieu (De miraculis): Vestigia 9. FrS/P 1992, Univ./Cerf. 302 p. [RTLv 24,225-7, A. de *Halleux*].

4813 **Williams** T. C., The idea of the miraculous; the challenge to science and religion 1990 ➤ 6,4870: ᴿRelSt 27 (1991) 562s (E. L. *Schoen*).

4814 *Wolter* Michael, Inschriftliche Heilungsberichte und neutestamentliche Wundererzählungen: ➤ 337, ᴱ*Berger* K., TANZ 7 (1992) 135-175.

4815 **Herrenbrück** Fritz, [Mt 9,10...] Jesus und die Zöllner: WUNT 2/41, 1990 ➤ 6,4873; 7,4014: ᴿJBL 111 (1992) 338-340 (B. *Chilton:* a fine work blemished by a tendency toward historicism); RB 99 (1992) 463s (J. *Murphy-O'Connor:* good but fails to use Ephesus 'fishermen's *teloneion*' or to contrast the differing tax-situations of Judea and Galilee); TLZ 117 (1992) 430-2 (W. *Vogler*).

4816 *Fuchs* Albert, [Mt 9,18-26] Schrittweises Wachstum; zur Entwicklung der Perikope Mk 5,21-43 par Mt 9,18-26 par Lk 8,40-56: SNTU A-17 (1992) 5-53.

4817 **Trummer** Peter, [Mk 5,25-34] Die blutende Frau; Wunderheilung im NT 1991 ➤ 7,4015: ᴿSvEx 57 (1992) 127-9 (S. *Byrskog*); TPQ 140 (1992) 190s (O. B. *Knoch*); TvT 32 (1992) 198 (A. van *Schaik*); ZkT 114 (1992) 212s (M. *Häsitschka*).

4818 **Grilli** Massimo, Comunità e missione; le direttive di Matteo; indagine esegetica su Mt 9,35 – 11,1 [diss. PIB 1991 ᶠ*Lentzen-Deis* F. ➤ Biblica 73,452]: EurHS 23,458. Fra 1992, Lang. 361 p. 3-631-44587-3.

4819 **Weaver** Dorothy J., [Mt 9,35-11,1] Matthew's missionary discourse ᴰ1990 ➤ 6,4876; 7,4017: ᴿCBQ 54 (1992) 184-6 (G. A. *Phillips*); CurrTMiss 19 (1992) 61s (E. *Krentz*); JBL 111 (1992) 146-8 (Janice C. *Anderson:* useful companion to K. BARTA's Mt 10,34, ᴰMarquette 1979).

4820 *Fuchs* Albert, [Mt 10,1-14] Die synoptische Aussendungsrede in quellenkritischer und traditionsgeschichtlicher Sicht: SNTU A-17 (1992) 77-168.

4821 *Schwarz* Günther, [Mt 10,2] *Philippon kaì Bartholomaîon?*: BibNot 56 (1991) 26-30.

4822 *Schwarz* Günther, *a)* [Mt 10,10] *Tês trophês autoû* oder *tês misthoû autoû?* [*tês* mit *misthôu* (sic) im Titel, auch im Text von Lk 10,7]: BibNot 56 (1991) 25; – *b)* 'Seiner Nahrung' oder 'seines Lohnes'? (Mt 10,10e / Lk 10,7c): BibNot 65 (1992) 40s [wieder *tês misthôu*: Lk 10,7].

4823 *Häfner* Gerd, Gewalt gegen die Basileia? Zum Problem der Auslegung des 'Stürmerspruches' Mt 11,12: ZNW 83 (1992) 21-51.

4824 *Franzmann* Majella, [Mt 11,18s] Of food, bodies, and the boundless reign of God in the Synoptic Gospels: Pacifica 5 (1992) 17-31.

4825 **Cho Tae Yeon**, The Son of Man came eating and drinking (Matt 11:19); a study of the table fellowship in Qumran and Q: diss. Drew, ᴰ*Dey Lala* K. K. Madison NJ 1992. 257 p. 92-33180. – DissA 53 (1992s) 1958-A.

4826 *Denaux* Adelbert, The Q-Logion Mt 11,27 / Lk 10,22 and the Gospel of John: ➤ 465, CLv 39, 1990/2, 163-199.

4827 *Charette* B., 'To proclaim liberty to the captives'; Matthew 11.28-30 in the light of OT prophetic expectation: NTS 38 (1992) 290-7.

4828 *Luke* K., The Syriac text of Matthew 11:29b and John 1:32-33: Bible Bhashyam 16 (1990) 250-267.

4829 *Volf* Miroslav, [Mt 12,43] When the unclean spirit leaves: EurJT 1,1 (Devon 1992) 13-24. [< ᴢɪᴛ 92,487].

4830 *Meier* John P., [Mt 12,46 ...] The brothers and sisters of Jesus in ecumenical perspective [CBA presidential address, Los Angeles Aug. 10, 1991]: CBQ 54 (1992) 1-28 [obscure in the 'hierarchy of truths'; relation to the foundation of Christian faith remote].

F4.3   **Mt 13 ...** *Parabolae Jesu* — **the Parables.**

4831 **Blomberg** Craig L., Interpreting the parables 1990 ➤ 6,4894; 7,4032 ('Bomberg'): ᴿAndrUnS 30 (1992) 78-80 (S. *Kubo*); BZ 36 (1992) 141s (B. *Heininger*); JEvTS 35 (1992) 254-6 (D. B. *Clendenin,* also on WENHAM D. 1989).

4832 **Bucher** Anton A., Gleichnisse verstehen lernen; strukturgenetische Untersuchungen zur Rezeption synoptischer Parabeln: Praktische Theologie im Dialog 1990 ➤ 6,4898; 7,4035: ᴿSNTU A-16 (1991) 247 (*Huemer*); TLZ 117 (1992) 831-4 (W. *Engemann,* C. *Kähler,* severe).

4833 **Capon** Robert F., The parables of judgment [of the Kingdom 1885 ➤ 7,4037; of grace 1988]. GR 1989, Eerdmans. vi-181. $16. – ᴿBibTB 22 (1992) 37s (W. R. *Herzog,* also on 3 cognate works).

4834 *Castro* J. M., *Waardenburg* F., Orar desde las parábolas; apuntes para un diálogo entre agnósticos, creyentes y posmodernos: Almogaren 4 (1989) 127-140 [< RET 51,112].

4835 *Cook* Michael L., Jesus' parables and the faith that does justice: Studies in the Spirituality of Jesuits 24/5. St. Louis 1992, [Univ.] Seminar on Jesuit Spirituality. 35 p. [< NTAbs 37, p. 187].

4836 *Crossan* J. Dominic, Parable: ➤ 741, AnchorBD 5 (1992) 146-152.

4837 *a)* *D'Angelo* T. P., The rabbinic background of the parables of Jesus; – *b)* *Pascuzzi* M., Rediscovering the cultural heritage of Jesus: Catholic World 235 (1992) 63-67 / 78-83 [< NTAbs 36,325.328].

4838 **Donahue** John R., The Gospel in parable 1988 ➤ 4,4700 ... 7,4041: ᴿRelStT 11,1 (1991) 51-53 (P. J. *Cahill*); RestQ 33 (1991) 243-5 (A. *Black,* also on BLOMBERG C.).

4839 *Dschulnigg* Peter, Rabbinische Gleichnisse und Gleichnisse Jesu; ein Vergleich aufgrund der Gleichnisse aus Pcsiqta de Rab KAHANA: Judaica 47 (1991) 185-197.

4840 *Estrada* Bernardo, A century of interpreting parables; the legacy of Adolf JÜLICHER [SBL Rome meeting 1991]: AnnTh 6 (1992) 93-111.

4841 **Fisher** Neal F., The parables of Jesus^{2rev} [glimpses of the New Age ^{1}1986], glimpses of God's reign 1990 ➤ 6,4906; 7,4044: ^{R}AnnTh 6 (1992) 153-5 (B. *Estrada*).

4842 ^{TE}**Friedlander** Colette, Galand de REIGNY [12^e s.], Parabolaire: SChr 378. P 1992, Cerf. 471 p. 2-204-04602-7.

4843 **García-Lomas** Santiago, Jesús les contó esta parábola; parábolas para trabajar en grupo. M 1992, Paulinas. 130 p. 84-285-1455-0. – ^{R}ActuBbg 29 (1992) 349s (F. de P. *Solá*); EstE 67 (1992) 110s (G. *Higuerra*).

4844 *a) Gerhardsson* Birger, Illuminating the Kingdom; narrative meshalim in the Synoptic Gospels; – *b) Aune* David E., Oral tradition and the aphorisms of Jesus; – *c) Reisner* Rainer, Jesus as preacher and teacher: ➤ 7,460*b*, ^{E}**Wansbrough** H., Jesus and the oral Gospel tradition 1989/91, 266-309 / 211-265 (+ 59-106) / 185-210.

4845 *a) Gesteira Garza* Manuel, 'Christus medicus'; Jesús ante el problema del mal; – *b) Romero Pose* Eugenio, El problema del mal en la primera teología cristiana: ➤ 551, RET 51 (1991) 253-300 / 301-329.

4846 **Hall** Douglas J., Steward, a biblical symbol come of age^{2rev} [^{1}1982]. GR 1990, Eerdmans. $15 pa. 0-8028-0472-1. – ^{R}CGrebel 10 (1992) 109-111 (A. *Kreider*).

4847 *Harnisch* Wolfgang, Language of the possible; the parables of Jesus in the conflict between rhetoric and poetry [Atlanta lecture 1991, ^{T}*Kahl* W., *al.*]: ST 46 (1992) 41-54.

4848 **Harnisch** Wolfgang, Las parábolas 1989 ^{T}1989 ➤ 5,4621 ... 7,4046: ^{R}RBiArg 53 (1991) 119-121 (U. *Schoenborn*); RET 52 (1992) 95s (E. *Tourón*); TVida 33 (1992) 323s (E. *Pérez-Cotapos L.*).

4849 **Hermans** C., Wie werdet Ihr die Gleichnisse verstehen? Empirisch-theologische Forschung zur Gleichnisdidaktik: ThEmpirie 12. Kampen/ Wenheim 1990, Kok/DeutschStV. 236 p. 90-242-3110-8 / 3-89271-277-8. – ^{R}CollatVL 22 (1992) 441 (B. *Roebben*); KerkT 43 (1992) 257s (A. K. *Ploeger*); TvT 32 (1992) 336 (J. *Bulckens*).

4850 **Kähler** Christoph, Gleichnisse Jesu als Poesie und Therapie; Versuch eines integrativen Zugangs zum Kommunikativen Aspekt der Gleichnisse Jesu: Hab.-Diss. ^{D}*Walter*. Jena 1992. – TR 89,75.

4851 **Kalas** J. Ellsworth, Parables from the back side; stories with a twist [... perspective on a minor or overlooked character in the story]. Nv 1992, Abingdon. 111 p. $9.25. 0-687-30062-2. – ^{R}RExp 89 (1992) 582 (C. *Bugg* regrets only that some anonymous characters are given nicknames).

4852 **Kemmer** Alfons, Le parabole di Gesù; come leggerle, come comprenderle [1981], ^{TE}*Montagnini* Felice: StBPaid 93. Brescia 1990, Paideia. 158 p. 88-394-0451-1 [Salesianum, 55,594, C. *Bissoli*].

4853 ^{E}**Kertelge** Karl, Metaphorik und Mythos im NT: QDisp 126, 1990 ➤ 6,350: ^{R}TGL 82 (1992) 140s (J. *Ernst*).

4854 **Kim Duk Ki**, A postmodern ethical-political interpretation of Jesus' sayings and parables in light of DERRIDA, FOUCAULT, and RICŒUR: diss. Drew, ^{D}*Doughty* D. Madison NJ 1992. 348 p. 92-33185. – DissA 53 (1992s) 1960-A.

4855 **Krech** V., Vom Verkündigen und Verstehen der verborgenen Dinge; Konturen einer Hermeneutik biblischer Rede im Spannungsfeld von Text und Rezeption am Beispiel neutestamentlicher Parabeln: Diss.mag. Heid 1991, ^{D}*Berger* K. 144 p. – DielB 27 (1991) 282s (B. J. *Diebner*: 'Magister auf RICŒURS Spuren').

4856 **Lambrecht** Jan, Nieuw en oud uit de schat; parabels in het Matteüs-
evangelie. Lv/Boxtel 1991, Acco/KBS. 294 p. ƒ47,50; Fb 795. 90-334-
2432-0 / -6173-500-9. – ᴿCollatVL 22 (1992) 323s (M. *Steen*); Streven 59
(1992s) 659 (P. *Beentjes*).
4857 **Lambrecht** Jan, Out of the treasure; the parables in the Gospel of
Matthew: TheolPastMg 10. Lv/GR 1992, Peeters/Eerdmans. 272 p.
Fb 695 [TvT 33,185, S. *Noorda*]. 90-6831-161-1. – ᴿLvSt 17 (1992)
409-411 (D. J. *Harrington*).
4858 **McArthur** Harvey K., *Johnston* Robert M., They also taught in parables
1990 ➤ 6,4910; 7,4052: ᴿCritRR 5 (1992) 378-380 (B. B. *Scott:* rabbis'
parables held to reinforce conventional values, while those of Jesus were
'subversive').
4859 **Mack** Burton L., *Robbins* Vernon K., Patterns of persuasion in the
Gospels 1989 ➤ 5,4628: ᴿCBQ 54 (1992) 162s (M. A. *Powell*); JRel 72
(1992) 97s (S. *Cory:* sees plenty of subtlety); LexTQ 26 (1991) 30-32
(Sharyn E. *Dowd*); TorJT 7 (1991) 280-2 (W. *Braun*).
4861 **Pérez-Cotapos Larraín** Eduardo, Parábolas; diálogo y experiencia; el
método parabólico de Jesús según Dom Jacques DUPONT: diss. Roma, Pont. Univ. Gregoriana, ᴰ*Rasco* E. Santiago/Chile 1991, Alfabeta.
272 p.
4862 *Pérez-Cotapos L.* Eduardo, Las parábolas de Jesús; su sentido y ade-
cuada interpretación: TVida 33 (1992) 165-178.
4863 **Perkin** J.R.C., Introduction to the parables and preaching: Mc-
MasterJT 3,1 (Hamilton 1992) 5-16 [< NTAbs 37,22].
4864 **Rau** Eckhard, Reden in Vollmacht: FRL 149, ᴰ1990 ➤ 6,4919: ᴿCBQ
54 (1992) 586s (J. *Plevnik*); NedTTs 46 (1992) 235s (J. *Smit Sibinga*).
4865 *Roloff* Jürgen, Das Kirchenverständnis des Matthäus im Spiegel seiner
Gleichnisse: NTS 38 (1992) 337-359.
4866 *Schneller* Thomas, Gottesreich und Menschenwerk; ein Blick in Gleichnisse Jesu: WissWeis 54 (1991) 81-95.
4867 **Scott** Bernard B., Hear then the parable 1989 ➤ 5,4632 ... 7,4061:
ᴿCBQ 54 (1992) 377s (J. D. *Crossan*); Themelios 17,1 (1991s) 25s (C. L.
Blomberg: good except for five presuppositions).
4868 *Sevrin* Jean-Marc, La rédaction des paraboles dans l'Évangile de
Thomas: ➤ 694*b*, 4ᵉ Copte (1988/92) 2,343-354.
4869 *Stern* R.C., Preaching the parables of Jesus: Church 8,4 (NY 1992)
19-24 [< NTAbs 37,188].
4870 **Thoma** C., *Lauer* S., Die Gleichnisse der Rabbinen [I. ...] II. Von der
Erschaffung der Welt bis zum Tod Abrahams, Bereschit Rabba 1-63:
JudChr 13. Fra 1991, Lang. 426 p. £39. 3-261-04396-2 [BL 93,151, R.
Loewe].
4871 ᴱ**Thoma** C., *Wyschograd* M., Parable and story 1987/9 ➤ 5,610; 6,5002;
7,a12: ᴿScripB 22,1 (1992) 19s (R. C. *Fuller*).
4872 **Ulonska** Herbert, Der geschenkte Augenblick; ein Gleichnisbuch 1991
➤ 7,4065: ᴿTLZ 117 (1992) 433s (G. *Sellin*).
4873 **Venetz** H.-J., Von Klugen und Dummen; Waghalsigen [bold] und
Feigen und von einem beispielhaften Gauner [rogue]; [12] Gleichnisse Jesu
für heute. Dü 1991, Patmos. 168 p. DM 24,80. 3-491-72248-9.
4874 **Vonck** Pol, Understanding 42 Gospel parables² [¹1981]: Spearhead
110s. Eldoret 1990, Gaba. xii-128 p. $5. – ᴿAfER 32 (1990) 119s (B. K.
Zabajungu).
4875 **Vouga** François, Formgeschichtliche Überlegungen zu den Gleichnissen
und zu den Fabeln der Jesus-Tradition auf dem Hintergrund der hel-

lenistischen Literaturgeschichte: → 137, FNEIRYNCK F., Four Gospels 1992, 173-187.
4876 **Weder** Hans, Metafore del Regno; le parabole di Gesù; ricostruzione e interpretazione, TGarra G., EFusco Vittorio. Brescia 1991, Paideia. 389 p. Lit. 50.000. [CC 144/3,87-89, D. Scaiola]; – RRClerIt 73 (1992) 467-470 (F. Riva).
4877 **Westermann** Claus, The parables 1990 → 6,4922; 7,4068: RAndrUnS 30 (1992) 181s (S. Kubo); AnnTh 6 (1992) 155-7 (B. Estrada); AustralBR 40 (1992) 80-82 (Rikki Watts); IndTSt 28 (1991) 187s (L. Legrand); Interpretation 46 (1992) 324 (R. A. Harrisville); NewTR 5,1 (1992) 94-96 (Celia Deutsch).
4878 **Winton** Alan F., The Proverbs of Jesus; issues of history and rhetoric: jNsu 35, 1990 → 6,4923; 7,4069: RBZ 36 (1992) 269s (M. Ebner); CBQ 54 (1992) 186s (C. E. Carlston: four varying kinds of wisdom); JTS 43 (1992) 160-2 (R. A. Piper).

4879 Baarda Tjitze, PHILOXENUS and the parable of the fisherman; concerning the diatessaron text of Mt 13,47-50: → 137, FNEIRYNCK F., Four Gospels 1992, 1403-23.
4880 Hultgren Arland J., Things new and old at Matthew 13:52: → 77, FHARRISVILLE R., All things new 1992, 109-117.
4881 Cotter Wendy J., [Mt 13,31s] The parables of the mustard seed and the leaven; their function in the earliest stratum of Q: → 74, FGUENTHER H., TorJT 8 (1992) 38-51.
4882 **Totten** Michael R., [Mt 14,13-21 ...] The center of Jesus' ministry; the miraculous feeding as Christological instruction: diss. Golden Gate Baptist Theol. Sem. DBrooks O. – 1992. 223 p. 93-07336. – DissA 53 (1992s) 4361-A.
4882* Magne Jean, Les récits de la multiplication des pains [... P. Rolland]: EphLtg 106 (1992) 477-525.

F4.5   Mt 16 ... Primatus promissus – The promise to Peter.

4883 Agua Augustín del, Derás narrativo del sobrenombre de 'Pedro' en el conjunto de Mt 16,17-19; un caso particular de la escuela exegética de Mateo: Salmanticensis 39 (1992) 11-33; Eng. 33.
4884 **Allison** Dale C., Peter and Cephas; one and the same: JBL [109 (1990) 463-474, Ehrman B.] 111 (1992) 489-495.
4885 **Brändle** Rudolf, Petrus und Paulus als nova sidera [Cullmann O. 1952, ²1985]: → 38, FCULLMANN, TZBas 48 (1992) 207-217.
4886 **Caragounis** Chrys C., Peter and the Rock: BZNW 58, 1990 → 5,4654 .. 7,4082: RBijdragen 53 (1992) 88s (H. Hoet: arguments fort valables); NedTTs 46 (1992) 63 (J. N. Sevenster); RHPR 72 (1992) 201s (C. Grappe); TR 88 (1992) 29s (A. Sand).
4886* **Carrasco Rouco** Alfonso, Le primat de l'évêque de Rome; étude sur la cohérence ecclésiologique et canonique du primat de juridiction. Fribourg 1990. – RCrNSt 13,1 (1992) 191-200 (J.M.R. Tillard).
4887 **Claudel** Gérard, La confession de Pierre, trajectoire d'une péricope évangélique: EtBN 10, D1988 → 4,4741 ... 7,4083: RRB 99 (1992) 261-287 (F. Refoulé).
4888 **Deproost** Paul-Augustin, L'apôtre Pierre dans une épopée du Ve siécle; l'Historia apostolica d'ARATOR 1990 → 7,4084: RAugM 37 (1992) 421 (J. Mazas).

4889 *Donfried* Karl P., Peter: ➤ 741, AnchorDB 5 (1992) 251-263.
4890 **Feuillet** André, La primauté de Pierre: Essai. P 1992, Desclée. 103 p. F 68. – ᴿEsprVie 102 (1992) 575 (P. *Jay*).
4891 *a) Ghiberti* Giuseppe, L'Apostolo Pietro nel Nuovo Testamento; la discussione e i testi; – *b) Bauckham* Richard J., The martydom of Peter in early Christian literature: ➤ 742, ANRW 2,26,1 (1992) 462-538 / 539-595.
4892 **Jeffers** James S., Conflict at Rome [on 1 Clement and claims of primacy, not Romans or Mt 16,18] 1991 ➤ 7,4087: ᴿAnglTR 74 (1992) 387s (R. M. *Grant*); CathHR 78 (1992) 267s (T. M. *Finn*); JBL 111 (1992) 731s (Carolyn *Osiek*); TS 53 (1992) 181 (Patricia M. *McDonald*); TTod 49 (1992s) 283 (C. S. *Wansink*).
4893 *a) Karavidopoulos* Jean, Le rôle de Pierre et son importance dans l'Église du NT; problématique exégétique contemporaine; – *b) Tillard* Jean-Marie. La présence de Pierre dans le ministère de l'évêque de Rome: ➤ 583, Nicolaus 19 (1992) 13-29 / 55-76.
4894 **Nau** Arlo J., Peter in Matthew; discipleship, diplomacy, and dispraise ... with an assessment of power and privilege in the Petrine office; pref. *Marty* M. Good News St 36. ColMn 1992, Liturgical/Glazier. xvi-184 p.; 2 fig.; map. $13 pa. – 0-8146-5700-1 [CBQ 55,816s, D. J. *Harrington*].
4895 *a) Ratzinger* Joseph, Il primato di Pietro e l'unità della Chiesa; – *b) Minnerath* Roland, Il primato del vescovo di Roma nel primo millennio; rassegna bibliografica; – *c) Vian* Paolo, La chiesa romana e la cattedra di Pietro (M. *Maccarrone*): Divinitas 36 (1992) 207-221 / 259-262 / 263-270.
4896 *Ratzinger* Joseph, Il primato di Pietro e l'unità della Chiesa: EuntDoc 44 (1991) 157-176.
4897 *Santos* Manoel A., Possibilidades e límites do primado pontificio: Teocomunicação 22,95 (1992) 57-91.
4898 **Schatz** Klaus, Der päpstliche Primat 1990 ➤ 6,4947; 7,4093: ᴿBurgense 32 (1991) 579s (E. *Bueno*).
4899 **Schatz** Klaus, La primauté du pape; son histoire des origines à nos jours [1990], ᵀ*Hoffmann* Joseph. P 1992, Cerf. 288 p. F 140 [RHE 88, 205, B. *Neveu*] 2-204-04461-X. – ᴿÉtudes 377 (1992) 137s (R. *Marlé*).
4900 *Sharkey* Sarah Ann, [... Lk 22,32] Peter's call to conversion: BToday 30 (1992) 84-89.

4901 *Refoulé* François, Le parallèle Matthieu 16/16-17 — Galates 1/15-16 réexaminé: ÉTRel 67 (1992) 161-175.
4902 *a) Grappe* Christian, Mt 16,17-19 et le récit de la Passion; – *b) Minnerath* Roland, L'exégèse de Mt 16,18-19 chez TERTULLIEN: ➤ 36, ᶠCULLMANN O., RHPR 72 (1992) 33-40 / 61-72; Eng. 125.
   Sebastiani Lilia, Tra/Sfigurazione 1992, tratta Maria di Magdala, non Mt 17 ➤ 9076.
4903 **Veniamin** C., The Transfiguration of Christ in Greek patristic literature, from IRENAEUS of Lyons to Gregory PALAMAS: diss. Oxford 1992. – RTLv 24, p. 578.
4904 *Schwarz* G., *Anoíxas tò stóma autoû?* (Matthäus 17.27): NTS 38 (1992) 138-141.
4905 *Quine* Jay A., [Mt 18,15-20; 1 Cor 5,1-15; allaying fears of] Court involvement in Church discipline: BtS 149 (1992) 60-73.223-238 [bottom line: every case studied that was allowed to go to the jury was decided against the disciplining church].

4906 *Cacitti* Remo, [Mt 18,16-30 ‖] 'Ad caelestes thesauros'; l'esegesi della pericope del 'giovane ricco' nella parenesi di CIPRIANO di Cartagine: Aevum 65 (1991) 151-169 ...

4907 *O'Callaghan* José, Dos minucias textuales en Mt (18,19.35): Emerita 60 (1992) 111-4.

4908 **Buckley** Thomas W., [Mt 18,22] Seventy times seven; judgment and forgiveness in Matthew: GlazierZc 1991 → 7,4108: RCritRR 5 (1992) 184-6 (Amy-Jill *Levine:* articulate, even elegant; but snippet-like disrupted argument).

4909 *Cranfield* C.E.B., [Mt 18,23-35] The parable of the unmerciful servant: ExpTim 104 (1992s) 339-341.

4910 *Branden* A. Van den, Mt. 19,1-12 dans une perspective historique: BbbOr 34 (1992) 65-82.

4911 *Dewey* Arthur J., The unkindest cut of all? Matt 19:11-12: ForumFF 8 (1992) 113-122.

4912 *Kertsch* M., L'esegesi di Mt 19,11-12 in GREGORIO Nazianzeno e Giovanni CRISOSTOMO: → k801, Gregorio Naz. 1992,103-114.

4913 *Beck* Edmund †, [Mt 19,16-22] Der syrische Diatessaronkommentar zur Perikope vom reichen Jüngling: OrChr 76 (1992) 1-45.

4914 *Harrington* Daniel J., The rich young man in Mt 19,16-22; another way to God for Jews?: → 137, FNEIRYNCK F., Four Gospels 1992, 1425-33.

F4.8   **Mt 20** ... *Regnum eschatologicum* — **Kingdom eschatology.**

4915 **Hezser** Catherine, Lohnmetaphorik ... Mt 20,1-16 [< Diss. Heidelberg 1955, DTheissen G.] → 6,4969: RJBL 111 (1992) 340s (R. H. *Gundry*); SNTU A-16 (1991) 213 (A. *Fuchs*); TLZ 117 (1992) 911-4 (C. *Kähler*).

4916 *Lambrecht* Jan, ⊖ The workers in the vineyard (Mt. 20,1-16): ColcFuJen 92 (1992) 159-177 [< TContext 10/1, p. 26].

4917 *Theobald* Michael, Die Arbeiter im Weinberg (Mt 20,1-16); Wahrnehmung sozialer Wirklichkeit und Rede von Gott: → 408, Sozialethik 1992, 107-128.

4918 *Zwick* Reinhold, Die Gleichniserzählung als Szenario, dargestellt am Beispiel der 'Arbeiter im Weinberg' (Mt 20,1-15): BibNot 62 (1992) 53-89 + 3 fig.

4919 *Elliott* John H., Matthew 20:1-15; a parable of invidious comparison and evil eye accusation: → 500, BibTR 22 (1992) 52-65.

4920 *Tevel* J. M., The labourers in the vineyard; the exegesis of Matthew 20,1-7 in the early Churh: VigChr 46 (1992) 356-380.

4921 *Brock* S.P., A [Syriac] palimpsest folio of Matt 20:23-31 (Peshitta) in Sinai Ar. 514 ('Codex arabicus'): Orientalia 61 (1992) 102-105; 1 facsim.

4922 **Nieviarts** Jacques, L'entréc de Jésus à Jérusalem; lecture de Mt XXI, 1-17; approche narrative et théologique de la christologie de Matthieu: diss. Toulouse 1992. – RTLv 24, p. 548.

4923 *Krüger* René, Humilde, montado en un burrito; Mateo 21,1-11 y el recurso escriturístico: RBiArg 54,46 (1992) 65-83.

4924 **Bratcher** R.G., That troublesome *kaí* in Matthew 21:5: NotTr 6,2 (1992) 14s [< NTAbs 37, p. 351].

4925 a) *Kallemeyn* Harold, Un Jésus intolérant; méditation sur Mt 21:12-17; – b) *Wells* Paul, Quand faut-il cesser d'être tolérant?; – c) *Bergèse* Daniel, Convictions chrétiennes et tolérance; – d) *Willaime* Jean-Paul, Quelques réflexions sociologiques sur protestantisme et tolérance: RRéf 43,3 (1992) 85ss / 7-14 / 15-22 / 23ss [< ZIT 92,498].

4926 *Söding* Thomas, [Mt 21,12-17 ||] Die Tempelaktion Jesu: TrierTZ 101 (1992) 36-64.

4927 *Simonetti* Manlio, [Mt 21,12s; Gv 2,14s] ORIGENE e i mercanti nel Tempio; – *b) Pelland* Gilles, À propos d'une page d'Origène, In Jn 2,16-18: ➤ 35, FCROUZEL H., Recherches 1992, 271-284 / 189-198.

4928 *Tilly* Michael, [Mt 21,12; Zech 14,21] Kanaanäer, Händler und der Tempel in Jerusalem: BibNot 57 (1991) 30-36.

4929 *Hart* Henry S. [Mt 21,16...] Hosanna in the highest: ScotJT 45 (1992) 283-301.

4930 *Schwarz* Günther, Jesus und der Feigenbaum am Wege (Mk 11,12-14.20-25 / Mt 21,18-22): BibNot 61 (1992) 36s.

4931 *Buzzetti* Carlo, [Mt 22] Per l'attualizzazione di una parabola; la guida di due applicazioni precedenti, un criterio e un esempio: RivB 40 (1992) 193-212.

4932 *Wrembek* Christoph, Das Gleichnis vom königlichen Hochzeitsmahl und vom Mann ohne hochzeitliches Gewand; eine geistlich-theologische Erwägung zu Mt 22,1-14: GeistL 64 (1991) 17-40.

4933 *Cuvillier* Elian, [Mt 22,22] Marc, JUSTIN, [Év.] Thomas et les autres; variations autour de la péricope du denier à César: ÉTRel 67 (1992) 329-344.

4934 *Saldarini* Anthony J., Delegitimation of leaders in Matthew 23: CBQ 54 (1992) 659-680.

4935 **Becker** Hans-J., Auf der Kathedra des Mose; rabbinisches-theologisches Denken ... Mt 23,1-12, 1990 ➤ 7,4123: ᴿCBQ 54 (1992) 141-3 (B. T. *Viviano:* workmanlike dissertation, but not serene in tone); TLZ 117 (1992) 428-432 (Ingo Broer).

4937 *a) Jaschke* Helmut, Einer ist euer Lehrer (Mt 23,8.10); die 'Didaktik Jesu' als Anfrage an die Religionspädagogik; – *b) Zwergel* Herbert, 'Erinnern' und 'Gehen in Spuren' — vom Wiedergewinnen der hermeneutischen Kraft biblischer und geschichtlicher Fragen in religiösen Bildungsprozessen; – *c) Ott* Rudi, Biblisches Erzählen; eine unverzichtbare Form religiöser Bildung: ➤ 136, FNastainczyk W., Basiskurse 1992, 311-9 / 300-310 / 333-350.

4938 **Will** Édouard, Orrieux Claude, [Mt 23,15] 'Prosélytisme juif'? Histoire d'une erreur. P 1992, BLettres, 398 p. – ᴿRHPR 72 (1992) 318s (A. *Benoît*).

4939 **Del Verme** Marcello, [Mt 23,23 ...] Giudaismo e NT, il caso delle decime 1989 ➤ 5,4687* ... 7,4127: ᴿGregorianum 73 (1992) 751s (G. *Marconi*); JJS 43 (1992) 322s (M. *Goodman*); Koinonia 15 (1991) 75s (R. *Maisano*); Orpheus 13 (1992) 483-5 (Maria Laura *Astarita*); RivStoLR 27 (1991) 333s (V. *Fusco*); StPatav 39 (1992) 461s (G. *Segalla*).

4940 **Gray** James R., [Mt 24s] Prophecy on the Mount [of Olives]. Chandler AZ 1991, Berean. 141 p. – ᴿBtS 149 (1992) 250s (J. F. *Walvoord*).

4941 **Reiser** Marius, [Mt 24s] Die Gerichtspredigt Jesu [kath. Hab-D Tü 1989] 1990 ➤ 6,4988; 7,4128*: ᴿCBQ 54 (1992) 371s (D. J. *Harrington* mentions many texts; Mt 22-25 barely); JBL 111 (1992) 143s (B. *Chilton:* an important task, but with pre-BACHER rabbinica, and FLUSSER ignored); KIsr 7 (1992) 102s (J. *Kirchberg*); SNTU A-17 (1992) 261s (A. *Fuchs*); TR 88 (1992) 382-4 (L. *Oberlinner*).

4942 **Riniker** Christian, Die Gerichtsverkündigung Jesu: Diss. ᴰ*Luz* U. Bern 1992. 567 p. – RTLv 24, p. 549.

4943 **Majernik** Jan, The parable of the servant left in charge in Mt 24, 45-51: diss. Antonianum. Roma 1992. – RTLv 24, p. 548.

4944 *Engemann* Josef, [Mt 25,31-46] Zur Schönheit des Teufels im raven-natischen Weltgerichtsbild: ➤ 164, [F]SAXER V., Memoriam 1992, 335-351; 5 fig.

4945 **Frahier** Louis-Jean, a) Le jugement du Fils de l'homme; implications éthiques du récit eschatologique en Mt 25,31-46; diss. InstCath, [E]*Doré* J.; RICathP 39 (1991) 203; – b) Le jugement dernier; implications éthiques pour le bonheur de l'homme (Mt 25,31-46): RechMorSynthèses. P 1992, Cerf. 430 p. F 150. 2-204-04498-0 [RTLv 24,491-8, H. *Wattiaux:* 'la théologie morale entre l'Écriture et la raison'].

4946 **Gray** Sherman W., The least of my brothers, Mt 25,31-46: [D]1989 ➤ 7,4138: [R]AustralBR 40 (1992) 84-87 (D. C. *Sim*); CurrTMiss 19 (1992) 295s (W. C. *Linss*); JRel 72 (1992) 96s (G. *Robbins*).

4947 *Herrmann* Volker, Anmerkungen zum Verständnis einiger Paralleltexte zu Mt 25,31ff aus der altägyptischen Religion: BibNot 59 (1991) 17-22.

F5.1   *Redemptio,* Mt 26, *Ultima coena;* **The Eucharist** [➤ H7.4].

4948 **Barth** M., Riscopriamo la Cena del Signore 1990 ➤ 6,4998b; 7,4145b: [R]StPatav 38 (1991) 412-415 (E. R. *Tura*).

4948* a) *Baumann* Urs, 'Gedenken' und 'Erinnern'; Nachdenken über die Zukunft des ökumenischen Abendmahlgesprächs; – b) *Kirchschläger* Walter, Eucharistie als gefeierte Gemeinschaft; – c) *Friemel* Franz G., Recht auf Eucharistie; – d) *Ahlers* Reinhild, Eucharistie und Kirche: TPQ 140 (1992) 3-19 / 20-26 / 27-34 / 35-40.

4949 **Bernier** P., Eucharist; meal or sacrifice?: Emmanuel 98 (1992) 64-69. 76. 136-141. 164 [< NTAbs 36, p. 381].

4950 **Berquist** Jon L., Ancient wine, new wineskins; the Lord's Supper in Old Testament perspective. St. Louis 1991, Chalice. vii-180 p. $14 pa. [CBQ 54,612].

4950* **Bishop** J., Some bodies; the Eucharist and its implications. Macon 1992, Mercer Univ. xvi-244 p. $35. 0-86554-401-9 [NTAbs 38, p. 135: the Eucharist is a parable by which six forms of bodiliness can be recognized [but] Jesus' purpose was to transmit his entire identity.

4951 **Brooks** Peter N., [2]*Collinson* Patrick, Thomas CRANMER's doctrine of the Eucharist. L 1992, Macmillan. xxvii-195 p. £29.50. 0-333-54541-9. – [R]ExpTim 103 (1991s) 312 (J. *Frederick*).

4952 **Byron** B. F., Sacrifice and symbol; a new theology of the Eucharist for Catholic and ecumenical consideration: Faith and Culture 19. Sydney 1991, Manly Catholic Inst. xvi-160 p. A$18. – [R]Gregorianum 73 (1992) 354s (R. *Faricy*).

4953 *Chazelle* Celia, Figure, character, and the glorified body in the Carolingian Eucharistic controversy: Traditio 47 (1992) 1-36.

4954 **Collins** Mary, Eucharist and Christology revisited; the Body of Christ [12th Aquinas Institute Lecture, St. Louis University, Jan. 28,1993 (sic) unabridged]: TDig 39 (1992) 321-332.

4955 **David** Thomas J., The clearest promises of God; the development of CALVIN's eucharistic theology: diss. [D]*Schreiner* S. Chicago 1992. – RTLv 24, p. 562.

4956 *Davies* Glenn N., The Lord's Supper for the Lord's children: RefTR 50 (1991) 12-20.

4957 **DeConcini** Barbara, Narrative remembering [... Eucharist]. NY 1990, UPA. xv-292. $36.50. – [R]CritRR 5 (1992) 69-71 (R. C. *Wood*: philosophically analytic with some oddnesses).

4958 *Derrett* J.D.M., Unappreciated legal aspects of the Eucharist [... covenant means contract]: DowR 110 (1992) 161-176.
4959 **Di Sante** Carmine. Pane e perdono; l'Eucaristia, celebrazione della solidarietà. T 1992, LDC. 168 p., Lit. 11.000 [CC 144/4,416, G. *Giachi*].
4960 **Di Sante** Pasquale, Cena pasquale ebraica ed eucaristia cristiana: ➤ 380*b*, Cibo 1992, 89-104.
4961 *Dunn* J.D.G., Whatever happened to the Lord's Supper? EpworthR 19,1 (1992) 35-48 [< NTAbs 37, p. 72].
4962 **Galot** Jean, L'Eucharistie, repas de foi et d'amour. Lv 1991, Sursum. 146 p. Fb 505. – ᴿLVitae 47 (1992) 115 (L. *Partos*).
4963 *Galot* Jean, Les paroles eucharistiques de Jésus: EsprVie 102 (1992) 161-7.
4964 **Gesteira Garza** Manuel, La Eucaristía, misterio de comunion²ʳᵉᵛ: Verdad e Imagen 123. S 1992, Sígueme. 717 p. 84-301-1164-6. – ᴿREspir 51 (1992) 359s (S. *Fernández*); RET 52 (1992) 362s (A. de la *Fuente Adanez*).
4965 **Giraudo** Cesare, Eucaristia per la Chiesa 1989 ➤ 5,4714 ... 7,4158: ᴿCrNSt 13 (1992) 428-432 (E. *Mazza*); Lateranum 57 (1991) 257-9 (M. *Semeraro*); Salmanticenses 38 (1991) 107-9 (J. *López Martín*, también sobre BÉKÉS, SAYÉS).
4966 *Grasso* Giacomo, Validità, oggi [*Biffi* I.], del trattato sull'Eucaristia di san Tommaso d'AQUINO: Angelicum 69 (1992) 55-68.
4967 **Hellwig** Monika K., The Eucharist and the hunger of the world²ʳᵉᵛ [¹1976; here added 'Hunger for freedom and dignity' and 'The Eucharist and world peace']. KC 1992, Sheed & W. x-85 p. $9. 1-55612-561-5 [TDig 40,166].
4968 **Hönig** Elisabeth, Die Eucharistie als Opfer ...: KeKSt 54, 1989 ➤ 5, 4721; 6,7777: ᴿColcT 62,1 (1992) 183-5 (S. *Napiórkowski*, 𝍐); TR 88 (1992) 139s (auch S. C. *Napiórkowski*).
4969 **Holeton** David R., La communion des tout-petits enfants; étude du mouvement eucharistique en Bohème vers la fin du Moyen Age: B.E.L. Subsidia 50. R 1989, Liturgiche. 324 p. Lit. 50.000. – ᴿEsprVie 102 (1992) 350s (P. *Rouillard*: auteur anglican canadien important).
4970 *Kandler* Karl-Hermann, LUTHER und die Frage nach dem Hausabendmahl: Luther 62 (1991) 21-27.
4971 **Kaufmann** Thomas, Die Abendmahlstheologie der Strassburger Reformatoren bis 1528 [Diss. Gö 1991 ➤ 7,4162]: BeitHistT 81. Tü 1992, Mohr. viii-497 p. DM 218 [TR 88,343].
4972 *Kelleher* Margaret Mary, The communion rite; a study of Roman Catholic liturgical performance [à la V. TURNER]: JRit 5,2 (1991) 99-122.
4973 **Killinger** Keith A., Hoc facite; the role of the words of institution in the Lutheran understanding and celebration of the Lord's Supper in the sixteenth century: diss. 1992, Lutheran School of Theology, ᴰ*Hendel* K. 348 p. 92-30461. – DissA 53 (1992s) 1972-A.
4974 *a) Kobayashi* Nobuo, The meaning of Jesus' death in the 'Last Supper' traditions; – *b) Kloppenborg* John S., Exitus clari viri, the death of Jesus in Luke: ➤ 74, ᶠGUENTHER H., TorJT 8 (1992) 95-105 / 106-120.
4975 **Kollmann** Bernd, Ursprung und Gestalten der frühchristlichen Mahlfeier [Diss. Gö]: GöTArb 43. Gö 1990, Vandenhoeck & R. 296 p. DM 62. – ᴿJBL 111 (1992) 733-5 (H. *Taussig*); ZkT 114 (1992) 367s (H. B. *Meyer*).
4976 *Kuttianimattathi* Jose, Transubstantiation as a new creation: Kristu Jyoti 8,1 (1992) 67-75 (+ 8/3,1-17).

4977 a) Lang Bernhard, The roots of the Eucharist in Jesus' praxis; – b) Chilton Bruce, The purity of the Kingdom as conveyed in Jesus' meals: → 478, SBL Sem. 31 (1992) 467-472 / 473-488.

4978 Leithart Peter J., What's wrong with transubstantiation? An evaluation of theological models: WestTJ 53 (1991) 295-324.

4979 Léon-Dufour Xavier, Sharing the eucharistic bread 1986 → 3,4620 ... 7,4165 [ConcordTQ 56,39-41, A. Just].

4980 Löhe Wilhelm, Abendmahlspredigten (1866), EWittenberg Martin: Ges-WEgb 1. Neuendettelsau 1991, Freimund. 183 p. 3-7726-0157-X. – RLuth-TK 16 (1992) 90-92 (R. Eles).

4981 Macy Gary, The banquet's wisdom; a short history of the theologies of the Lord's Supper. NY 1992, Paulist. iv-218 p. $13. 0-8091-3309-1 [TDig 40,279; RelStR 19,169, D. R. Janz]. – RTBR 5,2 (1992s) 28 (Jill Pinnock).

4982 Magne Jean, Les récits de la Cène et la date de la Passion: EphLtg 105 (1991) 185-236; lat. 185 [non 145-236 comme → 7,4167].

4983 Margerie B. de, Vous ferez ceci 1989 → 5,4730 ... 7,4168: RMélSR 48 (1991) 251-3 (B. Rey).

4984 Marini A., La celebrazione eucaristica presieduta da Sant'AGOSTINO 1989 → 5,g845; 7,4169: REcOrans 7 (1990) 102-4 (B. Studer).

4985 Martín Ramos Nicasio, La presencia eucarística según Edward SCHIL-LEBEECKX: CommSev 24 (1991) 19-56 [→ 7,4169*] & 167-196. 355-386.

4986 Medina Carpintero Benito, Eucaristía y comunión en la eclesiología de Henri de LUBAC: ComSev 25 (1992) 167-212.

4987 Meyer Hans B., Eucharistie; Geschichte, Theologie, Pastoral: HbLtgW 4, 1989 → 6,5025; 7,4170: REcOrans 7 (1990) 236-242 (B. Neunheuser); TR 88 (1992) 62-64 (A. Gerhards); ZkT 114 (1992) 71-75 (R. Kaczynski).

4988 Moloney F. J., A body broken for a broken people 1990 → 7,4171: RCBQ 54 (1992) 793 (P. Zilonka).

4989 Moloney Francis, La Eucaristía como presencia de Jesús para los rotos [< Pacifica 2 (1989) 151-174],T: Phase 31 (1991) 183-202.

4990 Nichols Aidan, The Holy Eucharist; from the NT to Pope John Paul II: Oscott 6. Dublin / SF 1991, Veritas / Ignatius. 153 p. $17 pa. 0-85390-182-2 [TDig 39,376]. RStudies 81 (1992) 237-9 (R. Moloney).

4991 Nubiola Ramon, Union with God through the Eucharist. Anand 1987, Gujarat-SP. x-120 p. rs 13. – RBible Bhashyam 16 (1990) 193s (J. Poovanikunnel).

4992 O'Toole Robert F., Last Supper: → 741, AnchorBD 4 (1992) 234-241 [p. 362-372, Klauck D., Lord's Supper, the ritual meal of the early Churches].

4993 Paprocki Henryk, Le mystère de l'eucharistie; genèse et interprétation de la liturgie eucharistique byzantine. TLhoesi F. P 1992, Cerf. 556 p. F 290 [Études 378,423s, R. Marlé].

4994 Porro C., L'Eucaristia; tra teologia e storia [→ 7,5031 'tra storia e teologia']. CasM 1989, Piemme. 232 p. – RLateranum 57 (1992) 268s (F. Marinelli).

4995 Power David N., The sacrifice we offer 1987 → 3,4625 ... 7,4177: RAnHConc 24 (1992) 234-8 (K. Ganzer).

4996 Power David N., The eucharistic mystery; revitalizing the tradition. NY/Dublin 1992, Crossroad/Gill & M. xiii-370 p. $30. 0-8245-1220-0 [TDig 40,285].

4997 Rehm Johannes, Das Abendmahlsgespräch; römisch-katholische und evangelisch-lutherische Kirche im Dialog: Diss. DMoltmann J. Tübingen 1992. 323 p. – RTLv 24, p. 588; TLZ 118,562s.

4998 **Rempel** John D., The Lord's Supper in Anabaptism; a study in the Christology of HUBMAIER, Pilgram MARPECK and Dirk PHILIPS. Scottdale c. 1992, Herald. [CGrebel 12,103, S. *Holland*].

4999 *Ruano de la Haza* Pedro-Alejandro, El sacramento de la Eucaristía en san AGUSTÍN: AugM 37 (1992) 145-168.

5000 **Rubin** Miri, Corpus Christi; the Eucharist in late medieval culture. C 1991, Univ. xv-432 p. – ᴿTS 53 (1992) 566-8 (J. F. *Baldovin:* a book that has long needed to be written).

5001 *Smith* Barry D., *a*) The chronology of the Last Supper: WestTJ 53 (1991) 29-45; – *b*) The more original form of the words of institution: ZNW 83 (1992) 166-186.

5002 *Szablewski* Marian, Public character of the Eucharist in the early Church: AustralasCR 69 (1992) 395-401.

5003 **Tilliette** Xavier, La Semaine Sainte des philosophes: JJC 53. P 1992, Desclée. 156 p. F 125 [NRT 115, 96, L. *Renwart*]; – ᴿEsprVie 23 (1992) 568s (P. *Jay*); RTLv 23 (1992) 493s (É. *Gaziaux:* notablement HEGEL).

5004 *Vanhoye* Albert ❷ [Mt 26,28], Il sangue dell'alleanza nel NT [CC 143 (1992/1) 118-132], ᵀ*Schmidt* Grzegorz: PrzPow 848 (1992) 11-27.

5005 **Walker** Michael †, Baptist at the table [diss.]. L 1992, Baptist Historical Society. 212 p. £6. 0-903166-16-X. – ᴿExpTim 104 (1992s) 188s (M. D. *Atkins*; stands on its own merits, not just as piety for untimely demise).

5006 *Zimmer* Christoph, Sakrament und Simulation; zur Semiotik der eucharistischen 'Realpräsenz': LingBib 67 (1992) 5-28; Eng. 28.

F5.3 **Mt 26,30 ... ‖** *Passio Christi*; **Passion-narrative.**

5007 **Balthasar** H.U.v., Theologie der drei Tage. Einsiedeln 1990, Johannes. 272 p. DM 42. 3-89411-031-7. – ᴿGregorianum 73 (1992) 756 (R. *Fisichella*).

5008 — **Seward** J., The mysteries of March. L 1991, Collins. xxi-186 p. [Furrow 42/91,597].

5009 **Brown** R. E., La passione nei Vangeli: Meditazioni 72, Brescia 1988, Queriniana. 120 p. Lit. 9.000. – ᴿParVi 35 (1990) 75s (C. *Ghidelli*).

5010 **Garland** David E., One hundred years of study on the Passion Narratives: NAmBap Bibliog 3, 1989 ⇒ 6,5051; 7,4190 [RTLv 24,214, J. *Ponthot*].

5011 *Gnilka* Christian, Der neue Sinn der Worte; zur frühchristlichen Passionsliteratur: FrühMaS 26 (1992) 32-54.

5012 *Grayston* K., Dying we live 1991 ⇒ 6,5053; 7,4192: ᴿBR 8,4 (1992) 14s (Elizabeth *Johnson*); CBQ 54 (1992) 350s (J. P. *Heil:* informative; some flaws); Interpretation 46 (1992) 66s (R. P. *Martin*); JEcu St 29 (1992) 117 (G. S. *Sloyan*); TLond 95 (1992) 210-2 (J. C. *O'Neill:* he holds the death of Christ is not an act of atonement and is not concerned with forgiveness of sin).

5012* **Heil** John P., The death and resurrection of Jesus; a narrative-critical reading of Matthew 26-28. Mp 1991, Fortress. xi-126 p. $10 pa. 0-8006-2514-5 [NTAbs 36,422]. – ᴿJStNT 47 (1992) 127 (C. M. *Tuckett:* parallels are admitted only with other parts of Mt).

5013 **Kiehl** Erich H., The passion of our Lord. GR 1990, Baker. 224 p. – ᴿCalvinT 26 (1991) 247-250 (R. A. *Argall:* severe).

5014 **Messori** V., Patì sotto Ponzio Pilato? Un'indagine sulla Passione e morte di Gesù. T 1992, SEI [Salesianum 55,725-738, A. *Strus*).

5015 **Myllykoski** Matti, Die letzten Tage Jesu Mk-Jn 1991 → 7,4197: ᴿBZ 36 (1992) 271s (R. *Schnackenburg*); TLZ 117 (1992) 432s (W. *Vogler*).
5015* **Padovano** Anthony T., Scripture in the streets; reflections on Holy Week; contemporary spirituality. NY 1992, Paulist. 76 p. $6 [PerspRelSt 20,204 (W. *McWilliams*).
5016 *Senior* Donald, The death of Jesus and the birth of a new world; Matthew's theology of history in the Passion narrative: CurrTMiss 19 (1992) 416-423.
5017 *Soards* Marion J., Oral tradition before, in, and outside the canonical Passion narratives: → 7,460b, ᴱ**Wansbrough** H., Jesus and the oral Gospel tradition 1989/91, 334-350.
5018 *Spiazzi* Raimondo, Le passioni e la passione di Cristo in San Tommaso d'Aquino: SacDoct 37 (1992) 5-34.
5019 *Willert* N., [Mt 26-28] Kristologien; Mattæus' passionsfortælling; litterære og sociologiske aspekter: DanTTs 54 (1991) 241-260 [< NTAbs 37, p. 352].

5020 *Hamilton* John, The chronology of the Crucifixion and Passover: Churchman 106 (1992) 323-338 [< ᴢɪᴛ 93,5; NTAbs 37, p. 342].
5021 *Hinz* Walther, Jesu Sterbedatum: ZDMG 142 (1992) 53-56 [139 (1989) 302-9, April 30, ᴀ ᴅ 28: month and year correct, but it must have been a Friday, therefore April 27].
5022 *Humphreys* Colin J., *Waddington* W.G., The Jewish calendar, a lunar eclipse and the date of Christ's crucifixion: TyndB 43 (1992) 331-351: Friday April 3, A.D. 33 [born c. April 20, 5 B.C.].
5023 **Reinbold** Wolfgang, Der älteste Bericht über den Tod Jesu; literarische Analyse und historische Kritik der Passionsdarstellungen der Evangelien: Diss. ᴰ*Lüdemann* G. Göttingen 1992s. – RTLv 24, p. 549.
5024 *Stanton* Graham N., Once more, Mt 25,31-46 [ineditum]: → 313, Studies in Mt 1992, 207-231.
5025 *Alonso* José, El misterio de Getsémani en el plan de los Ejercicios de S. Iɢɴᴀᴄɪᴏ: Manresa 64 (1992) 43-63.
5026 *Eibach* Ulrich, Die Versuchung, das Böse durch Macht zu besiegen (Mt. 26,36-46): TBeit 23 (1992) 57-61 [< ᴢɪᴛ 92,301].

5027 **Anderson** Ray S., The Gospel according to Judas. Colorado Springs c. 1992, Helmers & Howard. $16 [Interp 46,85 adv.].
5028 **Dieckmann** Bernhard, Judas als Sündenbock; eine verhängnisvolle Geschichte von Angst und Vergeltung 1991 → 7,4207*; ᴅᴍ 38: ᴿTGL 82 (1992) 158s (K. *Hollmann*); TR 88 (1992) 198s (H.-J. *Klauck*).
5029 *a) Dieckmann* Bernhard, Judas als Doppelgänger Jesu? Elemente und Probleme der Judastradition; – *b) Oberlinner* Lorenz, 'Wer kann sich in Wahrheit auf Gott berufen?' Ein Plädoyer für die Gegner Jesu: → 602, Dramatische Erlösungslehre 1991/2, 227-242 / 37-48.
5030 *a) Klauck* Hans-Josef, Judas der 'Verräter'? Eine exegetische und wirkungsgeschichtliche Studie; – *b) Lémonon* Jean-Pierre, Ponce Pilate; documents profanes, Nouveau Testament et traditions ecclésiales: → 742, ANRW 2,26,1 (1992) 717-740 / 741-778.
5031 **Maccoby** Hyam, Judas Iscariot and the myth of Jewish evil. NY/L 1992, Macmillan / Free Press Halban. $23. 0-02-919555-1 [NTAbs 36, p. 423]; – ᴿCommentary 94,4 (1992) 56.58s (J. D. *Levenson*).
5032 *Niemand* Christoph, Zur Funktion der Judasgestalt in den Evangelien: → 467*, ProtokB 1 (1992) 85-99.

5033 **Teichert** Wolfgang, Jeder ist Judas; der unvermeidliche Verrat. Stu 1990, Kreuz. 142 p. – ᴿLebZeug 47 (1992) 230-234 (Verena *Lenzen*, auch über JENS W. 1975 ⁵1990; KLAUCK H. 1987; DIECKMANN B. 1991).

5034 *a) Dautzenberg* Gerhard, Über die Eigenart des Konfliktes, der von jüdischer Seite im Prozess Jesu ausgetragen wurde; – *b) Maier* Johann, Beobachtungen zum Konfliktpotential in neutestamentlichen Aussagen über den Tempel: ⇥ 344, Gesetz 1992, 147-172 / 173-213.

5035 ᴱ**Kertelge** K., Der Prozess gegen Jesus ...: QDisp 112, 1987/8 ⇥ 4,491* ... 7,4215: ᴿSalesianum 54 (1992) 159 (C. *Bissoli*).

5036 **Medema** H. P., Het proces tegen Jezus. Vaassen 1990, auct. 168 p. ƒ27,50. – ᴿNedTTs 46 (1992) 239 (J. *Smit Sibinga*).

5037 *Prendergast* Terrence, Trials of Jesus: ⇥ 741, AnchorBD 6 (1992) 659-663.

5038 **Romano** Davide, Il processo di Gesù; appunti per la collocazione storico-giuridica degli avvenimenti relativi al processo ed alla condanna di Gesù di Nazareth: Ricerche 1. Bari 1992, Palomar. 325 p.

5039 *Gillman* Florence M., The wife of Pilate (Matthew 27:19): ⇥ 115, ᶠLAMBRECHT J., LvSt 17 (1992) 152-165.

5040 *Sullivan* Desmond, New insights into Matthew 27:24-25 [blood-guilt]: NBlackf 73 (1992) 453-7 (not anti-Semitic).

5041 **Shantz** Susan D., The stations of the Cross; a calculated trap. London 1991, Univ. W. Ontario. 183 p. – ᴿRRelRes 34 (1992s) 382s (M. *Komechak*); [SR 22,141, Maureen *Korp:* how four Ontario artists represent the tradition; inadequately worked out].

5042 *Sticca* Sandro, The Via Crucis; its historical, spiritual and devotional context: ⇥ 119*b*, ᶠLEVY B., Mediaevalia 15 (1989) 93-126.

5043 **Blumenstein** John M., An exegetical study of Matthew 27:38-54 [events while Jesus was on the Cross]: diss. Union Theol. Sem. Richmond 1991. 178 p. 92-26628. – DissA 53 (1992s) 1545-A.

5044 *Schwarz* Günther, *Kathelein* oder *sōsōn* (Mk 15,36 / Mt 27,49) [Syr. -mḥ- in beiden: Mt *mḥ*ᵓ Aph. Part. ῾am Leben erhaltend᾽ besser als Mk *mḥt*, Abs.Inf. < *nḥt* ῾herabzuholen᾽]: BibNot 64 (1992) 17.

5045 *Aichele* G., Two fantasies on the death of Jesus [Mk & Gospel of Peter]: Neotestamentica 26 (1992) 485-498; 499-503, *Smit* J. A. comment; 503-5 reply.

5046 **Barth** Gerhard, Der Tod Jesu Christi im Verständnis des Neuen Testaments. Neuk 1992. viii-176 p. DM 38 [TR 88,518]. 3-7887-1410-7.

5047 **Gourgues** Michel, Le crucifié: JJC 38, 1989 ⇥ 5,4789; 6,4191: ᴿÉglT 22 (1991) 222s (N. *Bonneau*).

5048 *Hübner* Hans, Kreuz und Auferstehung im NT, 2. Zur Kreuzesthematik: TRu 57 (1992) 58-82.

5049 *Seeley* D., Jesus' death in Q: NTS 38 (1992) 223-234.

5050 *Wells* Paul, Entre ciel et terre; les dernières paroles de Jésus [sur la croix]: RRéf 41, 166 entier (1990) 179 p.

5051 **Wright** Tom, The crown and the fire; meditations on the Cross and the life of the Spirit. L 1992, SPCK. 106 p. £5 pa. – ᴿTLond 95 (1992) 131s (Ruth *Etchells*).

5052 **Ledrus** Michel [21.XII.1899-20.VIII.1983], Alla scuola del 'ladrone' penitente, present. *Federici* G.-C., *Rendina* S. R 1992, Apost. Preghiera. 159 p. Lit. 13.000. 88-7357-115-8.

5053 *García García* Luis, [Jn 19,40; Lc 24,127] 'Lienzos' no 'vendas' en la sepultura de Jesús: Burgense 32 (1991) 557-567.

5054 *Senior* Donald, Matthew's account of the burial of Jesus (Mt 27,57-61): ➤ 137, ᶠNEIRYNCK F., Four Gospels 1992, 1433-48.

Zangara V., Exeuntes de corpore ... apparizioni [su 1 Sm 28; Mt 17,3 *al.*, anziché Mt 27,53] 1990 ➤ 2883.

5055 **Kee** Alistair, From bad faith to good news; [Edinburgh 1990] reflections on Good Friday and Easter. L/Ph 1991, SCM/Trinity. xii-147 p. $16. – ᴿCurrTMiss 19 (1992) 129 (Lynna A. *Kauppi*); TLond 95 (1992) 130s (P. *Bates*).

F5.6   **Mt 28 ‖ :   Resurrectio.**

5056 *Ayán Calvo* Juan José, El tratado de san JUSTINO sobre la Resurrección: RÁg 31 (1990) 591-614.

5057 **Barlone** Sandro, Le apparizioni del Risorto agli Undici, natura e funzione secondo tre recenti disegni cristologici: diss. Pont. Univ. Gregoriana 1991, No. 6914, ᴰ*O'Collins* G. – InfPUG 119/23,14. Excerptum 96 p.

5058 **Bartolomé** Juan José, La resurrección de Jesús; experiencia y testimonios neotestamentarios: Folletos Biblicos 3. Caracas 1992, AsnBíblica Salesiana. 48 p. 980-6035-64-X.

5059 *Berkhof* A. W., Geding over de Opstanding: KerkT 42 (1991) 279-283 [-339, *al.*].

5060 **Bonsen** Jan, Verhalen van opstanding [resurrection-accounts]; praktijk en hermeneutik: diss. Bruxelles 1991, [ᴰ*Roon* R. van. – RTLv 24, p. 545]. Kampen 1991, Kok. 207 p. Fb 700. – ᴿCollatVL 22 (1992) 212s (V. *Draulans*).

5061 **Carson** Mary C., And they said nothing to anyone; a redaction-critical study of the role and status of women in the crucifixion, burial and resurrection stories of the canonical and apocryphal Gospels: diss. Newcastle 1990. BRDX-96298. – DissA 53 (1992s) 842-A.

5062 **Caba** José, Cristo, mia speranza, è risorto 1988 ➤ 4,4906; 6,5102*b*: ᴿRivLtg 79 (1992) 117s (G. *Crocetti*).

5063 **Chupungco** Anscar J., Shaping the Easter feast. Wsh 1992, Pastoral. vii-186 p. [Landas 7,239-241, J. T. *Meehan*].

5064 **Craig** William I., Knowing the truth about the Resurrection. AA 1988, Servant. 153 p. $8 pa. – ᴿHomP 91,6 (1990s) 74-76 (Sean *Donnelly*).

5066 *Geense* Adriaan, La résurrection; révélation de la dimension transcendante de l'humain: LumièreV 41 (1992) 71-80.

5067 *Kendall* Daniel, *O'Collins* Gerald, The uniqueness of the Easter appearances: CBQ 54 (1992) 287-307.

5068 *Klumbies* Paul-Gerhard, 'Ostern' als Gottesbekenntnis und der Wandel zur Christusverkündigung: ZNW 83 (1992) 157-165.

5069 *Kremer* Jacob, War das Grab Jesu leer? Die Evangelien vom leeren Grab und das christliche Leben: BiKi 47 (1992) 163 nur.

5070 **Lash** N., Easter in ordinary 1990 (not specifically on Easter) ➤ 5,7019 ... 7,7126: ᴿLivLight 28,1 (1991s) 90 (W. *Au*).

5071 **Marxsen** Willi, Jesus and Easter 1990 ➤ 6,5118; 7,4247: ᴿRelStT 11,1 (1991) 43s (C.H.H. *Scobie*).

5072 **Nicolas** Marie-Joseph, Teologia della Risurezione [1982],ᵀ, TeolFilos. Vaticano 1989, Editrice. Lit. 52.000. – ᴿDocCom 44 (1991) 90-92 (D. *Vibrac*).

5073 **O'Collins** Gerald, Jesus risen; an historical, fundamental, and systematic examination of Christ's Resurrection 1987 → 3,4718 ... 6,5124*a*: ᴿCalvinT 26 (1991) 168s (R. J. *Feenstra*).

5074 **Scholla** Robert W., Recent Anglican contributions on the resurrection of Jesus (1945-1987): diss. Pont. Univ. Gregoriana, N. 3895, ᴰ*O'Collins* G. Roma 1992. 304 p. – RTLv 24, p. 577.

5075 *Soosten* Joachim von, Unde suspirat cor; Überlegungen zur Auferweckung Jesu Christi als Versprechen: EvT 52 (1992) 478-497.

5076 **Vos** Jac, zn Anthonie, Het is de Heer! De opstanding voorstellbaar. Kampen 1990. 90-242-2294-X. – ᴿKerkT 42 (1991) 355s (J. *Verheul*).

5077 *Wakefield* G. S., [Mt 28,1-10] Easter with St. Matthew [adds 'novelistic' features to Mk, and other problems; no one knows what really happened, but we need not be disturbed]: ExpTim 104 (1992s) 179s.

5078 *a*) *Weaver* Dorothy Jean, Matthew 28:1-10; expository: – *b*) *Campbell* Cynthia M., Matthew 28:16-20: Interpretation 46 (1992) 398-402-405.

5079 *Abraham-Williams* Gethin, [on Mt 28,11-15] Easter correspondence [a refreshingly candid skeptical letter from believers to Jesus about the Resurrection, and his admittedly less effective reply]: ExpTim 104 (1992s) 181s.

5080 **Arias** Mortimer, *Johnson* Alan, [Mt 28,16-20] The great commission; biblical models for evangelism. Nv 1992, Abingdon. 142 p. $13. [PrincSemB 15,75, R. S. *Armstrong*].

5080* *Davies* William D., *Allison* D. C., Matt. 28:16-20; texts behind the text: → 36, ꟳCULLMANN O., RHPR 72 (1992) 89-98.

5081 *Hiebert* D. Edmond, An expository study of Matthew 28:16-20: BtS 149 (1992) 338-354.

5082 *Scaer* David P., The relation of Matthew 28:16-20 to the rest of the Gospel: ConcordiaTQ 56 (Fort Wayne 1992) 245-266 [< ᴢɪᴛ 92,552].

5083 *Finkbeiner* Douglas, An examination of 'Make disciples of all nations' in Matthew 28:18-20: CalvaryB 7/1 (1991) 12-42; 7/2, 1-10.

5084 *Coleman* R. S., [Mt 28,19s] The promise of the Spirit for the great commission: EvRT 16 (1992) 271-283 [< NTAbs 37, p. 71].

5085 *Chmiel* Jerzy, ❷ Mt 28,19; model strukturalny (aktancjalny), semantyczny, teologiczny, liturgiczny: RuBi 44 (1991) 127-89.

5086 *Ferrua* P. Valerio, [Mt 28,19] Dal battesimo cristologico a quello trinitario; una conferma nella Didache?: – *a*) Salesianum 54 (1992) 223-230; – *b*) → 161, Salesiani 1992, 153-160.

5087 **Duck** Ruth C., Gender and the name of God; the trinitarian baptismal formula 1991 → 7,4256: ᴿTTod 49 (1992s) 524-533 (J. F. *Kay*).

5087* **Hartman** L., 'Auf den Namen des Herrn Jesus'; die Taufe in den neutestamentlichen Schriften: SBS 148. Stu 1992, KBW. 164 p. ᴅᴍ 40. 3-460-04481-0 [NTAbs 38, p. 137].

5088 *Kay* James F., [Mt 28,19] In whose name? Feminism and the trinitarian baptismal formula [*Duck* R. 1991 → 7060 'invites Christians to abandon the one thing we share']: TTod 49 (1992s) 524-533.

5089 *a*) *Kruse* H., ❶ [Mt 28,20 vs. 15,24] Jesus and the mission; –) *Akano* Yoshiyuki, ❶ The ethical teaching of Mt 25,31-46: Kat Kenk 31 (1992) 197-209; Eng. i-iii / 337-361; Eng. xi-xiv.

F6.1 **Evangelium Marci** – *Textus, commentarii.*

5090 **Chouraqui** André, La Bible traduite et commentée: Marcos (L'évangile selon Marc). ... 1992, Lattès. 280 p. F 135. [Études 378,425, G. *Duchêne*].

5091 **Cole** R. Alan, Mark 1989 ➤ 5,4856; 7,4260: ᴿRefTR 50 (1991) 72s (A. E. *Bird*).

5092 **Drewermann** Eugen, Das Markusevangelium 1987s ➤ 4,4956 ... 7,4261: ᴿZkT 114 (1992) 207s (R. *Oberforcher:* presented as commentary, but rather homily-snatches, as jacket-subtitle 'Bilder von Erlösung': fascinating and not to be overlooked).

5093 **English** Donald, The message of Mark; the mystery of faith: The Bible Speaks Today. Leicester/DG 1992, Inter-Varsity. 254 p. $13. 0-85110-968-3 / US 0-8308-1231-8 [NTAbs 37, p. 277].

5094 **Fausti** Silvano, Ricordi o racconti di Vangelo; la catechesi narrativa di Marco. Mi 1990, Ancora. 557 p. Lᵐ 45. – ᴿCC 143 (1992,1) 308s (D. *Scaiola*).

5095 **Festugière** A. J., [† 1982] La bonne nouvelle de Jésus selon Marc, ᴱ*Saffrey* H.-D. P 1992, Cerf. 87 p.; portr. F 48. 2-204-04598-5 [NTAbs 37, p. 437].

5096 **Georgeot** J.-M., Évangile selon saint Marc 1-3, 1988s ➤ 5,4859 ... 7,4265: ᴿÉglT 22 (1991) 94-96 (W. *Vogels*).

5097 **Guelich** Robert A. [† 1991], Mark 1 – 8:26: Word Comm. 34a, 1989 ➤ 5,4863 ... 7,4266: ᴿCritRR 5 (1992) 212-4 (Adela Y. *Collins:* successfully 'mediates the best of current international thinking on Mark to present-day readers'); EvQ 64 (1992) 171-4 (K. E. *Brower*); Themelios 17,1 (1991s) 24s (L. W. *Hurtado*).

5098 **Heil** John P., The Gospel of Mark as a model for action; a reader-response commentary. NY 1992, Paulist. x-396 p. $20 [BToday 31,252]. 0-8091-3148-X.

5099 **Hooker** Morna, The Gospel according to St. Mark 1991 ➤ 7,4268; £16: ᴿCrux 28,3 (1992) 47s (R. *Beaton*); ExpTim 104 (1992s) 151s (C. S. *Rodd*); RefTR 51 (1992) 112 (P. *Bolt*).

5100 **Humphrey** Hugh M., 'He is risen!' A new reading of Mark's Gospel. NY 1992, Paulist. vi 184 p.; map. $12 pa. 0-8091-3302-4 [TDig 40,69]. – ᴿExpTim 104 (1992) 344s (Meg *Davies:* unimpressed).

5101 **Hurtado** L., Mark 1983/9 ➤ 6,5154; 7,4268*: ᴿRelStT 11,1 (1991) 53s (Margaret Anne *Moore*).

5102 **Iersel** Bas van, Reading Mark, 1989 ➤ 5,4865; 7,4269: ᴿAustralBR 38 (1990) 78 (B. R. *Doyle:* valuable though badly proofread).

5102* **Maggioni** Bruno, Il racconto di Marco⁷: Bibbia per tutti. Assisi 1991, Cittadella. 219 p. Lᵐ 15. 88-308-0312-X.

5103 **Mann** C. S., Mark: AnchorB 22, 1986 ➤ 2,3736 ... 7,4272: ᴿRelStT 11,1 (1991) 40s (A. E. *Milton*).

5104 *Minette de Tillesse* Caetano, Evangelho segundo Marcos, nova tradução estruturada; análise estrutural e teológica: RBBras 9,1s (Fortaleza 1992) 1-240 [3s, p. 247-549, recensões: NTAbs 37, p. 281].

5105 **Peatman** William, The beginning of the Gospel [Mk]. ColMn 1992, Liturgical. 61 p. $5 [BToday 31,255].

5106 **Senft** Christophe, L'Évangile selon Marc 1991 ➤ 7,4274: ᴿÉTRel 67 (1992) 278 (Isabelle *Parlier*).

5107 **Taylor** D. B., Mark's Gospel as literature and history. L 1992, SCM. xii-388 p. £13. 0-334-00974-X [TvT 33,294, B. van *Iersel*].

5108 **Valette** Jean, L'Évangile de Marc; parole de puissance, message de vie; commentaires. P 1986, Les Bergers et les Mages. I. xi-319 p.; II. 309 p. 2-85304-068-2; –9-0.

5109 **Zuurmond** Rochus, NT aethiopice 1/2, Gospel of Mark in Geez: Aeth-

For 27, 1989 ➤ 6,1906; 7,4277: ᴿBSO 55 (1992) 124-6 (M. A. *Knibb*); EvQ 64 (1992) 170s (J. N. *Birdsall*).

F6.2 *Evangelium Marci,* **Themata.**

5110 *Achtemeier* Paul J., Mark, Gospel of: ➤ 741, AnchorBD 4 (1992) 541-557.

5111 **Adinolfi** Marco, *Bottini* Claudio, *al.,* ᴱ*Corona* Raimondo, Il Vangelo secondo Marco, lettura esegetico-esistenziale: II Settimana Biblica Abruzzese, luglio 1987. L'Aquila 1987, Curia O.F.M. 206 p.; ill.

ᴱ**Anderson** Janice C., *Moore* Stephen D., Mark and method; new approaches in biblical studies 1992 ➤ 336.

5112 *a) Anderson* Janice C., *Moore* Stephen D., The lives of Mark; – *b) Fowler* Robert M., Reader-response criticism; figuring Mark's reader; [+ 4 *al.*]: ➤ 336, Mark & Method 1992, 1-22 / 50-83 [–161].

5113 **Attinger** Daniel [di Bose], Evangelo secondo san Marco; il paradosso della debolezza di Dio. R 1991, Nuove Frontiere. 176 p. [CC 144/1, 197s, D. *Scaiola*].

5114 *Baarda* T., The etymology of the name of the evangelist Mark in the 'Legenda Aurea' of Jacobus a VORAGINE: Nederlands Archief voor Kerkgeschiedenis 72 (1992) 1-12 [< ZIT 92,217].

5115 **Baarlink** H., Bist du der Christus, der Sohn des Hochgelobten? Implizite und explizite Christologie im Markusevangelium: KamperCah 74. Kampen 1992, Kok. 92 p. *f* 26. 90-242-6668-8 [NTAbs 37, p. 433].

5116 **Balaguer** Beltrán V. El yo-testigo en el evangelio de San Marcos (perspectiva estructural): dis. Pamplona 1991. 250 p. – ᴿRCatalT 16 (1991) 423-5 (E. *Cortès*).

5117 *Balaguer* V., Testimonio y tradición en san Marcos 1990 ➤ 7,4279 (no 1900): ᴿBurgense 33 (1992) 301s (F. *Pérez Herrero*); RivB 40 (1992) 361s (V. *Fusco:* validità malgrado mancanze); ScripTPamp 23 (1991) 695-702 (J. M. *Casciaro*).

5118 *Bartolomé* Juan J., El evangelio de Marcos; un manual de formación para seguidores de Jesús: Phase 30 (1990) 397-411.

5119 **Barton** Stephen, Discipleship and family ties according to Mark and Matthew: diss. ᴰ*Stanton* G. London 1992. 243 p. – RTLv 24, p. 545.

5120 **Biguzzi** Giancarlo, 'Yo destruiré este templo'; el templo y el judaismo en el Evangelio de Marcos: Grandes Temas de NT 1. Córdoba 1992, Almendro. 200 p. 84-86077-94-X. – ᴿActuBbg 29 (1992) 192s (J. *O'Callaghan*); RBibArg 54 (1992) 241-4 (A. J. *Levoratti*).

5121 **Blackburn** Barry, Theios anēr and the Markan miracle traditions: WUNT 2/40, 1991 ➤ 7,4284: ᴿCBQ 54 (1992) 774s (H. C. *Kee*); ComSev 24 (1991) 423s (M. de *Burgos*); ÉTRel 67 (1992) 105s (Isabelle *Parlier*); JBL 111 (1992) 720-2 (G. E. *Sterling*); SNTU A-16 (1991) 216 (A. *Fuchs*); TLZ 117 (1992) 351-3 (B. *Kollmann*); TR 88 (1992) 377-9 (D. *Zeller*).

5122 **Bravo Gallardo** Carlos, Galilea año 30; para leer el evangelio de Marcos. Córdoba 1991, Almendro. 178 p. – ᴿPhase 32 (1992) 168s (J. *Latorre*); RBiArg 54 (1992) 60-62 (A. J. *Levoratti*).

5123 *Breytenbach* Cilliers, Gesamtdarstellungen zum Markusevangelium: VerkF 36,2 (1991) 50-55; 55-64 *Hahn* Ferdinand, Streit um [O. HOFIUS' Rezension von Breytenbachs] 'Versöhnung'.

5124 *Breytenbach* Cilliers, Markusevangelium: ➤ 757, EvKL 3 (1992) 294-6.

5125 **Broadhead** Edwin K., Teaching with authority; miracles and Christology in the Gospel of Mark: jNsu 74. Shf 1992, Academic. 235 p.

£32.50; sb. £23.50.   1-85075-366-0. – ᴿ κpTim 104 (1992s) 218s (Meg *Davies*).
5126 *Broadhead* Edwin K., Christology as polemic and apologetic; the priestly postrait of Jesus in the Gospel of Mark: JStNT 47 (1992) 21-34.
5127 **Burdon** Christopher, Stumbling on God; faith and vision in Mark's Gospel. GR 1990, Eerdmans. xii-110 p. $9; also L 1989, SPCK; £6, ➤ 6,5176:   ᴿCritRR 5 (1992) 181s (C. C. *Black:* salutary; 'both the academy and the church have tried to tame Mark's subversive little book').
5128 *Cadwallader* Alan H., The hermeneutics of purity in Mark's Gospel; considerations for the AIDS debate: Pacifica 5 (1992) 145-169.
5129 **Camery-Hoggatt** Jerry, Irony in Mark's Gospel; text and subtext: SNTS mg 72. C 1992, Univ. xiii-219 p. £30. 0-521-41490-3 [TDig 40, 55]. – ᴿExpTim 104 (1992s) 342 (B. G. *Powley*).
5131 **Collins** A. Yarbro, The beginnings of the Gospel; probings of Mark in context. Mp 1992, Fortress. xii-171 p. $11 pa. 0-8006-2622-2 [NTAbs 37, p. 445].
5132 **Cotter** Wendy J., The Markan sea miracles; their history, formation, and function in the literary context of Greco-Roman antiquity: diss. St. Michael's ᴰ*Guenther* H. Toronto 1991. 528 p. 0-315-68807-6 (DANN-68807). – DissA 53 (1992s) 2855-A; SR 21 (1992) 494.
5133 *Diebner* Bernd J., Wie kam der hl. Markus Evangelista nach Ägypten, und warum kam er nach Venedig?: DielB 27 (1991) 203-224.
5134 **Dillmann** Rainer, Christlich handeln in der Nachfolge Jesu ... Mk 1989 ➤ 6,5181; 7,4292:   ᴿTPQ 140 (1991) 192s (S. *Stahr*).
5135 *Dormeyer* Detlev, O evangelho de Marcos; uma biografia querigmática e historiográfica: RBBras 7 (1990) 98-125; Zusammenfassung 97.
5136 *Dowd* Sharyn E., The Gospel of Mark as ancient novel [TOLBERT M. 1989]: LexTQ 26 (1991) 53-59.
5137 *Ernst* Josef, Das sogenannte Messiasgeheimnis — kein 'Hauptschlüssel' zum Markusevangelium: ➤ 112*, Mem. KUSS O. 1992, 21-56.
5138 **Fander** Monika, Die Stellung der Frau in Mk ᴰ1989 ➤ 5,4896; 7,4297: ᴿCBQ 54 (1992) 149-151 (J. *Topel*); CritRR 5 (1992) 194s (Joanna *Dewey*).
5139 **Fowler** R., Let the reader understand 1991 ➤ 7,4300:   ᴿTS 53 (1992) 742-4 (J. R. *Donahue*).
5140 *Fowler* Robert M., Reader-response criticism; figuring Mark's reader: ➤ 336, Mark & method 1992, 50-83 [*al.*].
5141 **France** R. T., Divine government; God's kingship in the Gospel of Mark 1990 ➤ 6,5187; 7,4301:   ᴿEvQ 64 (1992) 72s (I. H. *Marshall*).
5142 **Friedrichsen** Timothy, The Matthew-Luke agreements against Mark, 1974-1991: diss. ᴰ*Neirynck* F. Leuven 1992. vii-316 p. + cumulative list, vi + 312 p. – LvSt 17 (1992) 405-7.
5143 *Fuchs* Albert, Aufwind für Deuteromarkus [LUZ U. 1990]: SNTU A-17 (1992) 55-76.
5144 **Gundry** Robert H., Mark, a commentary on his apology for the Cross. GR 1992, Eerdmans. iv-106 p. $60.
5145 a) *Hamerton-Kelly* Ray, Die 'Menschenmenge' und die Poetik des Sündenbocks im Markusevangelium, ᵀ*Jenewein* B.: – b) *Baudler* Georg, Christliche Gotteserfahrung und das Sakrale; der Aufweis positiver Gotteserfahrung in der Religions- und Menschheitsgeschichte als (religionspädagogisch und pastoral) notwendige Ergänzung zu einer Neuinterpretation christlichen Glaubens im Licht der Theorie GIRARDS: ➤ 602, Dramatische Erlösungslehre 1991/2, 49-67 / 275-281.

5146 *Iersel* Bas van, De thuishaven van Marcus: TvT 32 (1992) 125-142; Eng. 142.
5147 **Kalajainen** Larry R., Speaking plainly, seeing clearly ...: ᴰ1991 ↠ 7,4304 [not 'seeking clearly' as RTLv 24, p. 547: 'ᴰ*Dey*' as RelStR].
5148 **Kampling** Rainer, Israel unter dem Anspruch des Messias; Studien zur Israelthematik im Markusevangelium [Hab.-Diss. Münster 1991]: SBB 25. Stu 1992, KBW. X-259 p. DM 49. 3-460-00251-4 [TLZ 118,925s, D. *Lührmann*].
5149 **Kingsbury** J. D., Conflict in Mark 1989 ↠ 5,4908 ... 7,4306: ᴿNeotestamentica 26 (1992) 533s (E. van *Eck*); RestQ 34 (1992) 179s (A. J. *McNicol*).
5150 **Kingsbury** J. D., Conflicto en Marcos; Jesús, autoridades, discípulos 1991 ↠ 7,4307: ᴿBurgense 33 (1992) 303s (F. *Pérez Herrero*).
5151 *Krieger* Klaus-Stefan, Die Herodianer im Markusevangelium — ein neuer Versuch ihrer Identifizierung [Anhänger des Antipas für den politischen status quo]: BibNot 59 (1991) 49-56.
5152 *Legrand* L., The Good Shepherd in the Gospel of Mark: IndTSt 29 (1992) 234-255.
5153 **Lüdemann** Gerd, Texte und Träume, ein Gang durch das Markusevangelium in Auseinandersetzung mit E. Drewermann: Bensheimer Hefte 71. Gö 1992, Vandenhoeck & R. 280 p. DM 29,80. 3-525-87159-7 [TLZ 118,313, G. *Theissen*].
5154 **Malbon** Elizabeth S., Narrative space and mythic meaning in Mark [Harper 1986 ↠ 2,3769] = Biblical Sem. 13. Shf 1991, JStOT. xvii-212 p.; 17 fig. £15. 1-85075-711-9. – ᴿExpTim 103 (1991s) 375s (J. M. *Court:* carries forward R. Lightfoot 1938).
5155 *Manns* Frédéric, Le thème de la maison dans l'évangile de Marc: RevSR 68 (1992) 1-17.
5156 **Marcus** Joel, The way of the Lord; Christological exegesis of the Old Testament in the Gospel of Mark. Louisville 1992, W-Knox. xv-240 p. [NTAbs 37, p. 280]. 0-664-21949-7.
5157 *Marcus* Joel, The Jewish War and the Sitz im Leben of Mark: JBL 111 (1992) 441-462.
5158 **Marshall** Christopher D., Faith as a theme in Mark's narrative [diss. London 1985]: SNTS Mg 64, 1989 ↠ 5,4920 .. 7,4314: ᴿCBQ 54 (1992) 164s (N. *Elliott*).
5159 **Miller** Dale & Patricia, The Gospel of Mark as midrash: SBeC 21, 1990 ↠ 6,5205; 7,4319: ᴿÉglT 22 (1991) 213s (N. *Bonneau*); ÉTRel 67 (1992) 457s (P. *Myers:* bon, mais pas des plus sérieux).
5160 *a)* **Milne** Douglas J. W., Mark, the Gospel of servant discipleship; – *b)* *France* R. T., The beginning of Mark: RefTR 49 (1990) 20-29 / 11-19.
5161 *Minette de Tillesse* Caetano, *a)* O segredo messiánico em Mc; – *b)* A fonte de Lógia; – *c)* Uma tradicião batista?; – *d)* Recensões: RBBras 7 (1990) 6-40 / 157-206 / 213-248 / 61-96.133-156.195-212.275-297.
5162 *Minor* Mitzi, The women of the Gospel of Mark and contemporary women's spirituality: SpTod 43 (1991) 134-141.
5163 **Monshouwer** D., *a)* Markus en de Torah; een onderzoek naar de relatie tussen het evangelie en de synagogale lezingen in de eerste eeuw: diss. Kampen 1987 ↠ 3,4797; – *b)* Markus en drie jaar Torah; het evangelie gelezen als de jaargangen schrifuitleg 1989 ↠ 6,5159*: ᴿDielB 27 (1991) 291s (B. J. *Diebner*).
5164 **Moore** Stephen D., Mark and Luke in poststructuralist perspectives [Derrida, Lacan, Foucault]; Jesus begins to write. NHv 1992, Yale Univ. xix-192 p. $25. 0-300-05197-2 [TDig 40,77].

5165 *Moore* Stephen D., [Mk] Illuminating the Gospels without the benefit of color; a plea for concrete criticism: JAAR 60 (1992) 257-279.

5166 **Mutombo-Mukendi,** L'apport théologique du Fils de l'Homme dans le deuxième Évangile: diss. Bruxelles 1992. – RTLv 24, p. 548.

5167 **Myers** Ched, Binding the strong man ... Mk 1988 ➤ 4,4994 ... 7,4322: ᴿCalvinT 26 (1991) 182-6 (D. *Deppe*).

5168 **Neiynck** F., *al.*, The gospel of Mark, a cumulative bibliography 1950-1990: BtETL 102. Lv 1992, Univ./Peeters. xii-717 p. Fb 2700 [NT 35, 299-301, J. K. *Elliott*: in 40 years, 10,000 titles by 3000 authors, including 80 by Neirynck plus reviews].

5168* *Neirynck* Frans, The Gospel of Mark 1950-1990 [BtETL 102 (1992)], supplement [items from (general biblical literary criticism) bibliographies of M. POWELL and M. MINOR, both 1992: alphabetical list of authors with reference only to M or P number]: ETL 68 (1992) 397-9.

5169 *a*) *Orchard* Bernard, Mark and the fusion of traditions; – *b*) *Ellis* E. Earle, The date and provenance of Mark's Gospel; – *c*) *Donahue* John R., The quest for the community of Mark's Gospel; – *d*) *Best* Ernest, Mark's readers; a profile; – *e*) *Goulder* Michael D., A Pauline in a Jacobite church: ➤ 137, ᶠNEIRYNCK F., Four Gospels 1992 (2) 779-800 / 601-815 / 817-838 / 839-858 / 859-875.

5170 **Peatman** W., The beginning of the Gospel; Mark's story of Jesus. Col Mn 1992, Liturgical. 61 p. $5. 0-8146-2068-X [NTAbs 37, p. 283].

5171 *Perón* Juan Pablo, El lenguaje de Jesús en el Evangelio de Marcos: Iter 3,1 (Caracas 1992) 23-38.

5172 **Plöbst** Markus J., Der Anbruch des Reiches Gottes in den Dämonen-austreibungen des Markusevangeliums; eine historisch-kritische Unter-suchung der Perikopen Mk 1,21-28; 5,1-20; 7,24-30; 9,14-29 und ihre theologische Aussage: Diss. ᴰZeilinger F. Graz 1992. 452 p. – RTLv 24, p. 549.

5173 **Puente Ojea** Gonzalo, El Evangelio de Marcos; del Cristo de la fe al Jesús de la historia. M 1992, Siglo Veintiuno. xiii-129 p. 84-323-0743-2.

5174 **Räisänen** Heikki, The 'Messianic secret' [1976 updated and incor-porating his 1973 Parabeltheorie], ᵀ*Tuckett* Christopher: StNW 1990 ➤ 6,5210; 7,4326: ᴿCBQ 54 (1992) 798s (Q. *Quesnell*: updating with some 70 recent works successful); JBL 111 (1992) 341-3 (Adela Y. *Collins*).

5175 **Reichert** Jean-Claude, Réalité mystérique et fonction initiatique dans l'Évangile de Marc; une initiation chrétienne par le mystère de la foi: diss. cath. ᴰ*Winling* R. Strasbourg 1992. 326 + 104 p. – RTLv 24, p. 576.

5176 **Robbins** Vernon K., Jesus the teacher; a socio-rhetorical interpretation of Mark² [= ¹1984 + introduction]. Mp 1992, Fortress. xliv-249 p. 0-8006-2595-1.

5177 **Roth** W., Hebrew Gospel; cracking the code of Mark 1989 ➤ 4,5007 ... 6,5214: ᴿNeotestamentica 26 (1992) 242s (W. S. *Vorster*).

5178 *a*) *Schenk* Wolfgang, Sekundäre Jesuanisierungen von primären Pau-lus-Aussagen bei Markus; – *b*) *Minette de Tillesse* Caetano, Structure théologique de Marc; – *c*) *Petersen* Norman R., 'Literarkritik', the new literary criticism and the Gospel according to Mark; – *d*) *Oyen* Geert Van, Intercalation and irony in the Gospel of Mark: ➤ 137, ᶠNEIRYNCK F., Four Gospels 1992 (2) 877-904 / 905-933 / 935-948 / 949-974.

5179 **Scholtissek** Klaus, Die Vollmacht Jesu; traditions- und redaktionsge-schichtliche Analysen zu einem Leitmotiv markinischer Christologie: NT-

Abh NF 25. Münster 1992, Aschendorff. xii-340 p. DM 98. 3-402-04773-X.
5180 *Sellew* Philip., Aphorisms of Jesus in Mark; a stratigraphic analysis: ForumFF 8 (1992) 141-160.
5181 **Shiner** Whitney T., 'Follow me!' Narrative and rhetorical functions of the disciples in the Gospel of Mark, Greek philosophical biographies, and the 'Wisdom of Ben Sira': diss. Yale, ᴰ*Meeks* W. NHv 1992. 438 p. 93-09004. – DissA 53 (1992s) 3946s-A.; [RTLv 24, p. 550 gives title: Sages and followers; a study of the literary role of disciples in the gospel of Mark and the literature of the time].
5182 **Stock** Klemens, On the way with Jesus; Spiritual Exercises according to the Gospel of Mark [< Emmaus in Manresa, the Bible and the Exercises ➤ 7433*b* (Anand 1992) GujaratSP] 25-72 [AcPIB 9,781].
5183 **Stock** Klemens, Gesù, la buona notizia; il messaggio di Marco 1990 ➤ 6,5219: ᴿCC 143 (1992,3) 98s (D. *Scaiola*).
5184 **Tafi** Angelo, *Zanella* Danilo, Evangelizzatori con Marco evangelista: In ascolto. T-Leumann 1990, Elle DiCi. 128 p. – ᴿRivLtg 79 (1992) 121s (G. *Crocetti*).
5185 **Taylor** David B., Mark's Gospel as literature and history. L 1992, SCM. xii-388. £13. 0-334-00974-X. – ᴿTBR 5,3 (1992s) 25 (J. L. *Houlden:* a trained amateur, thus more accessible for some).
5186 *a*) *Telford* William R., The pre-Markan tradition in recent research (1980-1990); – *b*) *Breytenbach* Cilliers, Vormarkinische Logientradition; Parallelen in der urchristlichen Briefliteratur; – *c*) *Schweizer* Eduard, Markus, Begleiter des Petrus?; – *d*) *Rolland* Philippe, Marc, lecteur de Pierre et de Paul: ➤ 137, ᶠNEIRYNCK F., Four Gospels 1992, (2) 693-723 / 725-749 / 751-773 / 775-8.
5187 **Theissen** Gerd, Texte und Träume [DREWERMANN E., Mk]. Gö 1992, VR. 277 p. DM 30. 3-525-87159-7. ᴿExpTim 104 (1992s) 248 (E. *Best*).
5188 **Thompson** Mary R., The role of disbelief in Mark 1989 ➤ 5,4942; 7,4338: ᴿPerspRelSt 19 (1992) 119s (D. O. *Via*, also on BECK B. Lk 1989).
5189 **Tolbert** Mary Ann, Sowing the Gospel ... Mk 1989 ➤ 5,4943; 7,4339: ᴿCBQ 54 (1992) 382-4 (C. C. *Black*; judicious, eloquent, unlike her view of Mark as 'fairly crude'); CurrTMiss 19 (1992) 303s (D. *Rhoads*); HeythJ 33 (1992) 331s (Marion *Smith*); JRel 72 (1992) 95s (Elizabeth S. *Malbon*); LitTOx 5 (1989) 328-330 (D. B. *Gowler*).
5190 **Vogt** Theo, Angstbefähigung und Identitätsbildung im Markusevangelium: Diss. ᴰ*Theissen* G. Heidelberg 1992s. – RTLv 24, p. 550.
5191 **Wegener** Mark I., Antidote to failure; the readers' response to Mark's story of Jesus and his disciples; a literary critical study of Mark's Gospel: diss. Lutheran School of Theology 1992, ᴰ*Krentz* E. 476 p. 92-30467. – DissA 53 (1992s) 1962-A.
5192 **Williams** Joel F., Other followers of Jesus; the characterization of the individuals from the crowd in Mark's Gospel: diss. Marquette, ᴰ*Edwards* R. Milwaukee 1992. 331 p. 93-06007. – DissA 53 (1992s) 3947-A.

F6.3 **Evangelii Marci versiculi 1,1 ...**

5193 *Lambrecht* Jan, John the Baptist and Jesus in Mark 1.1-15; Markan redaction of Q?: NTS 38 (1992) 357-384.
5194 **Kuthirakkattel** Scaria, The beginning of ... Mk: AnBib 123, ᴰ1990 ➤ 6,5231; 7,4348: ᴿBiblica 73 (1992) 279s (V. *Fusco*); JBL 111 (1992) 722-4 (W. M. *Swartley:* high praise).

5194* *Coote* Robert B., Mark 1.1, *archē* 'scriptural lemma': ⇥ 41, ᶠDA-
VIDSON R., Text as pretext 1992, 86-90.
5195 *De Santis* Luca, Mc 1, 1, studio di traduzione: Angelicum 69 (1992)
175-192.
5196 *a*) *Giblin* Charles H., The beginning of the ongoing Gospel (Mk
1,2-16,8); – *b*) *Boismard* M.-Émile, Étude sur Mc 1,32-34; – *c*) *Hanhart*
Karel, Son, your sins are forgiven, Mk 2,5; – *d*) *Merklein* Helmut, Die
Heilung des Besessenen von Gerasa (Mk 5,1-20), ein Fallbeispiel für die
tiefenpsychologische Deutung E. DREWERMANNS und die historisch-kritische Exegese; ⇥ 127, ᶠNEIRYNCK F., Four Gospels 1992 (2) 975-985 /
987-995 / 997-1016 / 1017-37.
5197 *Juel* Donald H., The baptism of Jesus (Mark 1:9-11): ⇥ 77, ᶠHAR-
RISVILLE R. 1992, 119-126.
5198 *Dörrfuss* Ernst M., 'Wie eine Taube'; Überlegungen zum Verständnis
von Mk 1,10 [< ᶠ*Dietzfelbinger* 1989, 35-42]: BibNot 57 (1991) 7-13.
5199 *Ulansey* David, [Mk 1,10] Heavens torn open; Mark's powerful metaphor explained [< JBL 1991]: BR 7,4 (1991) 32-37.
5200 *Puthussery* Paul S., 'Repent and believe the Gospel' (Mk 1,15): Bible
Bhashyam 16 (1990) 95-113.
5201 *Lee Yeong-Heon*, ❽ Exegetical study on Mk 1:21-28; Sinhak Jonmang 98
(Kwangju 1992) 2-24 [< TContext 10/2,51].
5202 *Mateos* Juan, Algunas notas sobre el evangelio de Marcos (IV) [1,24;
2,6; 3,20]: FgNt 5 (1992) 61-68.
5203 *Kazmierski* Carl R., Evangelist and leper; a socio-cultural study of
Mark 1.40-45: NTS 38 (1992) 37-50.
5204 *Broadhead* Edwin K., Mk 1,44; the witness of the leper: ZNW 83
(1992) 257-265.
5205 *Parlier* Isabelle, L'autorité qui révèle la foi et l'incrédulité; Marc 2/1-
12: ÉTRel 67 (1992) 243-7.
5206 *Maartens* Pieter J., [Mk 2,18-22] Interpretation and meaning in a conflict
parable: LingB 67 (1992) 61-82; Eng. 82.
5207 *Halsema* J. H. van, Aren plukken op de sabbat (Mc. 2:23-28): KerkT 42
(1991) 210-7.
5208 **Roure** Damià, Jesús y la figura de David en Mc 2,23-26: AnBib 124,
ᴰ1990 ⇥ 6,5238; 7,4351: ᴿActuBbg 29 (1992) 199s (X. *Alegre*); AulaO
10 (1992) 166s (L. *Diez Merino*); CBQ 54 (1992) 169-171 (V. P. *Branick*:
not so clear that David as prophet had any special authority over the
law); EstE 67 (1992) 102s (J. *O'Callaghan*) & 220-3 (E. *Cortés*);
ScripTPamp 24 (1992) 333s (A. *García-Moreno*).
5209 *Syx* Raoul, Jesus and the unclean spirit; the literary relation between
Mark and Q in the Beelzebul controversy (Mark 3:20-30 par): ⇥ 115,
ᶠLAMBRECHT J., LvSt 17 (1992) 166-180.
5210 *Wayne* James C., Mark 3:20-30; mission and counter-mission or
'learning to live outside!': RExp 89 (1992) 535-9.
5211 *Sabin* Marie, Reading Mark 4 as midrash: JStNT 45 (1992) 3-26.
5212 *Heil* John P., Reader-response and the narrative context of the parables
about growing seed in Mark 4:1-34: CBQ 54 (1992) 271-286.
5213 **Henaut** Barry W., Oral tradition behind the written Gospel text? Mark
4:1-34 and the problem of textuality: diss. ᴰ*Guenther* H. Toronto 1992.
432 p. DANN-73732. – DissA 53 (1992s) 4359-A; SR 21 (1992) 494.
5214 **Beavis** Mary Ann, Mark's audience ... 4,11s, ᴰ1989 ⇥ 5,4975; 7,4354:
ᴿTorJT 9,121s (W. *Braun*).

5215 *a) Steinhauser* Michael G.,   The sayings of Jesus in Mark 4:21-22.24b-25;
– *b) Hedrick* Charles W.,   On missing mountains; Mark 11:22b-23 / Matt
21:21 and parallels; – *c) Kea* Perry V.,   Salting the salt, Q [Lk] 14:34-35
and Mark 9:49-50:   ForumFF 6,3s (1993 for 1990) 197-217 / 219-237 /
239-244.

5216 *Aichele* George, [Mk 4,26-29; 6,17-20] Two theories of translation with
examples from the Gospel of Mark: JStNT 47 (1992) 95-116.

5217 *Frick* Eckhard,   Der Besessene von Gerasa; ein Bibliodrama zu Mk
5,1-20:   GeistL 64 (1991) 385-393.

5218 *[Skard] Dokka* Trond,   En fortolkning av Mk 5,21-43 med synoptisk
sammenlikning: NorTTs 93 (1992) 149-162.

5219 *Vattioni* Francesco,   Varia semitica, v. [Giairo Mc 5,22; ... nome Pe-
ph(r)asménos]: AION 52 (1992) 451-4.

5220 **Selvidge** Marla J.,   Woman, cult and miracle recital ... Mk 5:24-34: 1990
➤ 6,5254; 7,4256:   ᴿHeythJ 33 (1992) 446s (Marion *Smith*); JTS 43 (1992)
169-171 (R. E. *Watts:* constantly overstated).

5221 **Reiser** Marius,   Die blutflüssige Frau; Weisen der Vergegenwärtigung
biblischer Texte am Beispiel von Mk 5,25-34:   ErbAuf 68 (1992) 48-56.
➤ 4817.

5222 *Ilan* Tal, [Mc 6,3] 'Man born of woman ...' (Job 14:1); the phenomenon
of men bearing metronyms at the time of Jesus: NT 34 (1992) 23-45.

5223 *a) Focant* Camille,   La fonction narrative des doublets dans la section
des pains (Mc 6,6b – 8,26); – *b) Iersel* Bas M. F. van,   Kaì ēthelen pa-
relthe̅in autoús — another look at Mk 6,48d; – *c) Dautzenberg* Gerhard,
Elija im Markusevangelium; – *d) Delorme* Jean,   Dualité, dissection critique et signification, Mc 9,14-29; – *e) Kirchschläger* Walter,   Bartimäus
— Paradigma einer Wundererzählung (Mk 10,46-52 par.); – *f) Collins*
Adela Y.,   The eschatological discourse of Mark 13; – *g) Verheyden* Josef,
Persecution and eschatology, Mk 13,9-13: ➤ ꟳNEIRYNCK F.,   Four Gospels (2) 1039-63 / 1065-76 / 1077-94 / 1095-1104 / 1105-23 / 1125-40 /
1141-59.

5224 *Hofrichter* Peter, [Mk 6,30-44 (8,1-10); Lk 9,12-17] Von der zweifachen
Speisung des Markus zur zweifachen Aussendung des Lukas; die Aus-
einandersetzung um die Heidenmission in der Redaktionsgeschichte der
Evangelien: ➤ 112* Mem. KUSS O.,   Theologie im Werden 1992, 143-155.

5225 *Cuvillier* Elian,   Tradition et rédaction en Marc 7:1-23:   NT 34 (1992)
169-192.

5226 *Räisänen* Heikki,   Jesus and the food laws; reflections on Mark 7.15
[< JStNT 16 (1982) 79-100]: ➤ 294, Jesus, Paul and Torah 1992, 127-148.

5227 *Aichele* George, [Mk 7,18-23; 3,22-27 ...] The fantastic in the discourse of
Jesus: Semeia 60 ('Fantasy and the Bible' 1992) 53-66 (1-6, editors' introduction, with Tina *Pippin*); 123-8 bibliog.

5228 *a) Schramm* Tim F., [Mk 7,24-30] Bibliodrama in action; reenacting a
New Testament healing story, ᵀ*Elston* Gerhard; – *b) Martin* Gerhard M.,
The origins of bibliodrama and its specific interest in the text [1985
+ 1989], ᵀ*Krondorfer* B.; – *c) Rhoads* David,   Performing the Gospel of
Mark; – *d) Driver* Tom F.;   Performance and biblical reading; its power
and hazard: ➤ 358*b*, Body and Bible 1992, 57-84 / 85-101 / 102-119 /
159-174.

5229 *Smith* Mahlon H., [Mk 8-10] To judge the Son of Man; the Synoptic
sayings: ForumFF 7 (1991) 207-242 (an actual phrase 'to judge the Son of
Man' seems nowhere cited]).

5230 *Hulmes* Edward, [Mk 8,27] 'The people of the Book' and the question of
Jesus: TLond 95 (1992) 334-343.

5231 *Waldenfels* Hans, [Mk 8,27] 'Fur wen halten mich die Menschen?' Gedenken an Jesus Christus: GeistL 64 (1991) 365-381.

5232 *Aichele* George[J], [Mk 8,31] Jesus' frankness: ➤ 478, SBL Sem. 31 (1992) 695-706.

5233 **Runacher** Caroline, La guérison de l'épileptique, Marc 9,14-29: kath. diss. [D]*Schlosser* J. Strasbourg 1992. 565 p. – RTLv 24, p. 549; RevSR 67/2,107.

5234 *Link* C., Exegetical study of Mark 9:49: NotTr 6,4 (1992) 21-35 [< NTAbs 37, p. 256].

5235 *La Verdiere* E., [Mk 10,13-20] Children / wealth and the Kingdom of God: Emmanuel 98 (1992) 78-84.130-5.164 / 220-227.

5236 **Fusco** Vittorio, [Mc 10,17-31] Povertà e sequela: StBPaid 94, 1991 ➤ 7,4370: [R]Biblica 73 (1992) 425s (S. *Légasse*); CBQ 54 (1992) 563s (P. *Rogers*); CC 143 (1992,3) 499-503 (C. *Marucci*); Lateranum 58 (1992) 492s (R. *Penna*); ParVi 37 (1992) 152s (B. *Moriconi*); Salesianum 54 (1992) 158 (J. J. *Bartolomé*); StPatav 38 (1991) 656 (G. *Segalla*); Teresianum 43 (1992) 311s (B. *Moriconi*).

5237 *Sänger* Dieter, Recht und Gerechtigkeit in der Verkündigung Jesu; Erwägungen zu Mk 10,17-22 und 12,38-34: BZ 36 (1992) 179-194.

5238 *Sayer* Josef, 'Eher geht ein Kamel durch ein Nadelohr, als dass ein Reicher in das Reich Gottes gelangt' (Mk 10,25); Situationsanalyse ... in einem Elendsviertel Limas: MüTZ 43 (1992) 327-345.

5239 *Schmidt* Thomas E., Mark 10.29-30; Matthew 19.29, 'Leave houses ... and region'?: NTS 38 (1992) 617-620.

5240 *Reardon* Patrick H., The Cross, sacraments and martyrdom; an investigation of Mark 10:35-45: StVlad 36 (1992) 103-115.

5242 *Duff* Paul B., [Mk 11] The march of the divine warrior [Zech 14; Ex 15, Jg 5 ...] and the advent of the Greco-Roman king; Mark's account of Jesus' entry into Jerusalem: JBL 111 (1992) 55-71.

5243 *Clark* A., [Mk 11,12-25] The interpretation of the cursing of the fig-tree pericope in Mark's gospel: CGST Journal 12 (Hong Kong 1992) 96-114 [< NTAbs 37,32].

5244 *Kienle* Bettina von, Mk 11,12-14.20-25, der verdorrte Feigenbaum: BibNot 57 (1991) 17-25.

5245 *Miller* Robert J., [Mk 11,15-17] Historical method and the deeds of Jesus; the test case of the Temple demonstration: ForumFF 8 (1992) 5-30.

5246 *Smith* Barry D., Objections to the authenticity of Mark 11:17 reconsidered: WestTJ 54 (1992) 255-271.

5247 **Dowd** Sharyn E., Prayer, power ... Mk 11,22, [D]1988 ➤ 4,5059 ... 7,4378: [R]AustralBR 38 (1990) 79 (M. *FitzPatrick*).

5248 *Risch* Andreas, [Mk 12,28] Die Frage nach dem wichtigsten Gebot: Klerusblatt 72 (Mü 1992) 83s [< ZIT 92.265].

5249 *Buzzard* A., [Mk 13] The Markan apocalypse; the core of the Christian message in the light of its background in Daniel: JRadRef 1,3 (Morrow GA 1992) 23-37 [< NTAbs 37, p. 33].

5250 **Geddert** Timothy J., Watchwords Mk 13, [D]1989 ➤ 5,5003; 7,4385: [R]Interpretation 46 (1992) 76-78 (R. D. *Witherup*); Themelios 17,2 (1991s) 20s (D. *Wenham*); TR 88 (1992) 462s (R. *Pesch*).

5251 *Myers* Paul, Marc 13; une lecture synchronique: ÉTRel 67 (1992) 481-492.

F6.8 Passio secundum Marcum, 14,1 ... [➤ F5.3].

5252 *a) Delorme* Jean, Sémiotique et lecture des évangiles – à propos de Mc 14,1-11; – *b) Standaert* Benoît, Lecture rhétorique d'un écrit biblique [Mc ...]: ➤ 462, Naissance 1990/2, 161-174 / 187-194.

5253 **Johnson** Steven R., [Mk 14,51s] The identity and significance of the *neaniskos* in Mark: ForumFF 8 (1992) 123-139.
5254 *Ruprecht* L. A., Mark's tragic vision; Gethsemane: Religion & Literature 24,3 (ND 1992) 1-25 [< NTAbs 37, p. 357].
5255 *Heil* John P., The progressive narrative pattern of Mark 14,53 – 16,8: Biblica 73 (1992) 321-358; franç. 358.
5256 *Munro* W., Women disciples; light from Secret Mark: JFemStRel 8,1 (1992) 47-64 [< NTAbs 37, p. 29].
5257 *Borse* Udo, Der Mehrheitstext Mk 15,27f.32c; die Kreuzigung Jesu zwischen zwei Räubern als Schrifterfüllung: SNTU A-17 (1992) 169-194.
5258 **Caza** Lorraine, [Mc 15,34] 'Mon Dieu, mon Dieu, pourquoi m'as-tu abandonné?' comme Bonne Nouvelle de Jésus-Christ, Fils de Dieu, comme Bonne Nouvelle pour la multitude: Recherches NS 24. Montréal/P 1989, Bellarmin-Cerf. 546 p. $35. – ᴿÉglT 22 (1991) 92s (L. *Laberge*).
5259 **Escaffre** Bernadette, Traditions concernant Élie et le rôle de prophète dans le récit de la crucifixion de Marc: diss. Pont. Ist. Biblico, ᴰ*Swetnam* J. R 1992. – AcPIB 9,808.857s.; RTLv 24, p. 546.
5259* *a) Mirecki* Paul A., The antithetic saying in Mark 16:16; formula and redactional features; – *b) Sellew* Philip, *Secret Mark* and the history of canonical Mark; – *c) Collins* Adela Y., The apocalyptic Son of Man sayings: ➤ 104, ꜰKOESTER H. 1991, 229-241 / 242-257 / 220-8.

XII. Opus Lucanum

F7.1 *Opus Lucanum* – **Luke-Acts.**

5260 *a) Barrett* C. K., The Third Gospel as a preface to Acts? Some reflections; – *b) Gundry* Robert H., Matthean foreign bodies in agreements of Luke with Matthew against Mark; evidence that Luke used Matthew; – *c) Kingsbury* Jack D., The Pharisees in Luke-Acts; – *d) Moessner* David P., The meaning of *kathexēs* in the Lukan prologue as a key to the distinctive contribution of Luke's narrative among the 'many': ➤ 137, ꜰNEIRYNCK F., Four Gospels 1992, 1451-66 / 1467-95 / 1497-1512 / 1513-28.
5261 *Bovan* François, Studies in Luke-Acts; retrospect and prospect: HarvTR 85 (1992) 175-196.
5262 **Brawley** Robert L., Centering on God; method and message in Luke-Acts: LitCu 1990 ➤ 6,5304; 7,4400: ᴿCBQ 54 (1992) 553s (Marie-Eloise *Rosenblatt*); CritRR 5 (1992) 182-4 (Beverly R. *Gaventa:* from BARTHES); RB 99 (1992) 610 (J. *Taylor*).
5263 **Crowe** Jerome, Wealth and poverty in Luke's writings: AustralasCR 69 (1992) 343-355.
5264 **Crump** D. M., Jesus the intercessor; prayer and Christology in Luke-Acts [diss. Aberdeen, ᴰ*Marshall* I. H.]: WUNT 2/49. Tü 1992, Mohr. xiv-295 p. DM 124 [NTAbs 37, p. 274]. 3-16-145821-4.
5265 **Darr** John, On character building; the reader and the rhetoric of characterization in Luke-Acts. Louisville 1992, W-Knox. 208 p. $16. 0-664-25117-X. – ᴿExpTim 104 (1992s) 219 (Judith *Lieu*).
5266 *a) Darr* John A., Discerning the Lukan voice; the narrator as character in Luke-Acts; – *b) Fitzmyer* Joseph A., The use of the Old Testament in Luke-Acts; – *c) Tyson* Joseph B., Torah and Prophets in Luke-Acts; temporary or permanent: ➤ 478, SBL Sem. 31 (1992) 255-265 / 524-538 / 539-548.

5267 **Dauer** Anton, Beobachtungen zur literarischen Arbeitstechnik des Lukas [Lk 24,12.24 ... ob in Reden neue Elemente auftauchen, p. 11]: BoBB 79. Fra 1990, Hain. 171 p. DM 54 pa. 3-445-09135-8. – ᴿRHPR 72 (1992) 202s (C. *Grappe*); SNTU A-16 (1991) 226 (F. *Kogler*); TLZ 117 (1992) 186s (M. *Rese*).

5268 **Esler** Philip, Community and gospel in Luke-Acts; the social and political motivations of Lucan theology 1987 ➤ 3,4908 ... 6,5311: ᴿPersp-RelSt 19 (1992) 342s (D. M. *Blair*, also on Bʀᴀᴡʟᴇʏ R. 1990).

5269 **Gillman** John, Possessions ... Lk-Acts 1991 ➤ 7,4409: ᴿCritRR 5 (1992) 204s (J. B. *Chance:* clear, insightful).

5270 **Gowler** David B., Host ... Pharisees in Luke/Acts [diss. Southern Baptist, ᴰ*Culpepper*] 1991 ➤ 7,4410 (not 'Gower'): ᴿRExp 89 (1992) 110 (S. *Sheeley*).

5271 *a) Jegen* Carol F., Lucan reflections on aging; – *b) Stockhausen* Carol K., Paul's theology of aging: BToday 30 (1992) 335-340 / 341-6.

5272 *Johnson* Luke T., Luke-Acts, book of: ➤ 741, AnchorBD 4 (1952) 403-420 (397-402, *Plümacher* Eckhard, Luke; 402s, as theologian, *Marshall* I. Howard).

5273 **Kim Hees-Song,** Die Geisttaufe des Messias; eine kompositionsgeschichtliche Untersuchung zu einem Leitmotiv des lukanischen Doppelwerks; ein Beitrag zur Theologie und Intention des Lukas: Diss. ᴰ*Burchard*. Heidelberg 1992. – RTLv 24, p. 547.

5274 **Koet** Bart, Five studies on interpretation of Scripture in Luke-Acts ᴰ1989 ➤ 5,5043 ... 7,4413: ᴿBijdragen 53 (1992) 89s (J. van der *Meij*: three republished from here; important); TR 88 (1992) 291s (W. *Radl*).

5275 *Liu* P., ☺ The reliability, distinctives and objectives of the Lucan writings: CGST (Hong Kong) 12 (1992) 48-81 [< NTAbs 37, p. 34].

5276 ᴱ**Luomanen** Petri, Luke-Acts 1991 ➤ 7,318: ᴿTLZ 117 (1992) 755s (J. *Roloff*).

5277 *Méhat* André, [Lc 19,40-44; 21,20-24 se refèrent aux événements de –586, non + 70]: Les écrits de Luc et les événements de 70, problèmes de datation: RHR 209 (1992) 149-180; Eng. 149: Lc daté 60, Actes 64.

5278 **Neipp** Bernadette, Rembrandt et la narration lucanienne ou l'exégèse d'un peintre; au-delà de la parole... le geste ... [sic]: diss. Lausanne 1992, [iv–] 163 p.; photocopy ill.

5279 ᴱ**Neyrey** Jerome H., The social world of Luke-Acts; models of interpretation 1991 ➤ 7,450: ᴿExpTim 103 (1991s) 344s (S. C. *Barton:* stress on models a challenge); NorTTs 93 (1992) 167-174 (Inger M. *Lindboe:* interessante modeller — metodiske svakheter); TLond 95 (1992) 208s (L. *Houlden:* a very worthwhile protest against anachronism and ethnocentricity).

5280 **Park Sung Kun,** The influence of 2 and 4 Maccabees for the concept of piety in Luke-Acts: diss. SWBaptist Theol. Sem. 1992. 278 p. 92-23543. – DissA 53 (1992s) 855-A:

5281 **Pilgrim** Walter E., The death of Christ in Lukan soteriology: diss. Princeton Theol.Sem. 1971, ᴰ*Beker* J. xi-413 p.

5282 *a) Pilgrim* W. E., Luke-Acts and a theology of creation; – *b) Powell* M. A., Salvation in Luke-Acts; – *c) Saldarini* A. J., ... Luke-Acts for Jewish-Christian dialogue; – *d) Tannehill* R. C., What kind of king?...: WWorld 12,1 (1992) 51-58 / 5-10 / 37-42 / 17-22 [< NTAbs 36, p. 344s].

5283 **Punayar** Sebastian, Luke's Christological use of the Old Testament; a study on the special Lucan quotations: diss. Pont. Univ. Gregoriana, ᴰ*Rasco* E. R 1992s. xvii-145 p. extract.

5284 ᶠRASCO Emilio, Luca-Atti, ᴱMarconi G., *O'Collins* G. 1991 → 7,124:
ᴿRasT 33 (1992) 232s (G. *Ferraro*).

5285 **Reinhardt** Wolfgang, Das Wachstum des Gottesvolkes; sprachliche,
theologische und historische Untersuchungen zum 'Wachsen der Kirche'
im lukanischen Doppelwerk auf dem Hintergrund des Alten Testaments
und mit einem Ausblick in die frühpatristische Literatur: Diss. ᴰ*Haacker*
K. Wuppertal 1992s. – RTLv 24, p. 549.

5287 **Salo** K., Luke's treatment of the Law, a redaction-critical investigation:
Annales 57. Helsinki 1991, Acad. Scientiarum Fennica. 337 p. 951-41-
0634-2 [NTAbs 37, p. 441].

5288 *Schneider* Gerhard, Literatur zum lukanischen Doppelwerk; Neuerscheinungen 1990/91: TR 88 (1992) 1-18.

5289 *Selvidge* Marla J., Alternate lifestyles and distinctive careers; Luke's
portrait of people in transition: SewaneeTR 36 (1992s) 91-103.

5290 **Sheeley** Steven M., Narrative asides in Luke-Acts: jNsu 72. Shf 1992,
JStOT. 204 p. £27.50; sb. £20. 1-85075-352-0 [TDig 40,187]. – ᴿSWJT
35,3 (1992s) 45 (H. A. *Brehm:* outstanding logic, lucid writing).

5290* **Shelton** James B., Mighty in word and deed; the role of the Holy Spirit
in Luke-Acts ᴰ1991 → 7,4426; ᴿExpTim 104 (1992s) 88 (N. *Clark*).

5291 **Stegemann** Wolfgang, Zwischen Synagoge und Obrigkeit; zur historischen Situation der lukanischen Christen: FRL 152, 1991 → 7,4427:
ᴿCBQ 54 (1992) 803s (R. L. *Mowery*); ExpTim 103 (1991s) 271s (E.
Best); TvT 32 (1992) 314s (L. *Grollenberg*).

5292 **Sterling** Gregory E., Historiography and self-definition; Josephos, Luke-
Acts and apologetic historiography [diss. Graduate Theological Union,
ᴰ*Donahue* J. R., Berkeley 1989]: NT supp 64. Leiden 1992, Brill. xv-
500 p. [TR 88,517]. 90-04-09501-2.

5293 **Sweetland** Dennis M., On journey with Jesus; discipleship according to
Luke-Acts: Glazier Good News 25. ColMn 1990, Liturgical. 261 p. $15.
– ᴿCBQ 54 (1992) 590s (M. *Cahill*); CritRR 5 (1992) 243s (S. M. *Sheeley*).

5294 **Tannehill** Robert C., The narrative unity of Luke-Acts; 1. Luke 1986 →
2,3901; 2. Acts 1990 → 6,5499; 7,4641: ᴿBibTB 22 (1992) 43s (R. L. *Mowery*, 2); BtS 149 (1992) 251s (D. E. *Malick*, 2: significant though weak on
historicity); CBQ 54 (1992) 380-2 (W. S. *Kurz*, 2: his good common-sense
may not please radical deconstructionists); RB 99 (1992) 609s (J. *Taylor*).

5295 *Turner* Max, The spirit of prophecy and the power of authoritative
preaching in Luke-Acts; a question of origins: NTS 38 (1992) 66-88.

5296 **Tyson** J. B., Images of Judaism in Luke-Acts. Columbia 1992, Univ. S.
Carolina. xiv-218 p. $30. 0-87249-794-1 [TDig 39,391]. – ᴿExpTim 104
(1992s) 89s (C. K. *Barrett*).

5297 *Wallis* E. E., The first and second epistles of Luke to Theophilus:
Journal of Translation and Textlinguistics 5 (Dallas 1992) 225-251
[< NTAbs 37, p. 34].

5298 **Weatherly** Jon A., Jewish responsibility for the Cross in Luke-Acts:
diss. Aberdeen 1991. 498 p. BRDX-98281. – DissA 53 (1992s) 846-A.

5299 **Włodarczyk** S., ❷ Realizacja zbawienia 'dziś' w Chrystusie; *sēmeron* w
soteriologii Łukasza [Hab.-Diss.]. Lublin 1989, KUL. 160 p. – ᴿRuBi 45
(1992) 46 (J. *Chmiel,* ❷).

F7.3 **Evangelium Lucae** – *Textus, commentarii.*

5300 *Amphoux* Christian-B., Les premières éditions de Luc, II. L'histoire du
texte au IIᵉ siècle: ETL [67 (1991) 312-327] 68 (1992) 38-48.

5301 ᵀAugrain Charles, L'Évangile sans frontières; l'Évangile de Luc. P 1992, Médiaspaul. xi-115 p.; xiii-115 p.; xi-115 p.; x-117 p.; ix-117 p.

5302 **Bovon** François, Das Evangelium nach Lukas I (1-9): EkK 3/1, 1989 ➤ 5,5057; 6,5340: ᴿJTS 43 (1992) 172-4 (I. H. *Marshall*: bulkier than FITZMYER, less repetitive than NOLLAND); ZkT 114 (1992) 206s (R. *Oberforcher*).

5303 **Bovon** François, L'Évangile selon saint Luc 1-9: CommNT 3a, 1991 ➤ 5,5057...7,4438: ᴿÉTRel 67 (1992) 458s (E. *Cuvillier*); VSp 146 (1992) 397s (H. *Cousin*).

5304 ᴱCorona Raimondo, Il Vangelo secondo Luca, lettura esegetico-esistenziale (*Adinolfi* M., *Bottini* C., *al.*), I Settimana Biblica Abruzzese, 24-29.VI.1985. L'Aquila 1988, Curia O.F.M. 263 p.; 50 fig.

5305 **Craddock** Fred B., Luke: Interpretation Comm 1990 ➤ 6,5341; 7,4441: ᴿCritRR 5 (1992) 190-2 (J. B. *Green*: plays on the assumption that a pastor starts to prepare his next Sunday sermon by heavy reading on Monday and Tuesday; this volume is suited — but will perhaps then not be needed — for Wednesday); HorBT 14 (1992) 187s (D. *Senior*); Interpretation 46 (1992) 91 (D. L. *Matson*); PerspRelSt 19 (1992) 243-6 (D. M. *Blair*).

5306 **Delebecque** E., L'évangile de Luc²ʳᵉᵛ. P 1992, Klincksieck. – ᴿEsprVie 102 (1992) 617s (É. *Cothenet*).

5307 **Evans** C. E., Saint Luke: TPI comm. 1990 ➤ 6,5344; 7,4443: ᴿCBQ 54 (1992) 559s (R. F. *O'Toole*: enjoyable and informative, but limited; and claims LkAc for non-Christians, datable only between 75 and 130); ScotJT 45 (1992) 116s (M. *Goulder*).

5308 **Fischer** Bonifatius, Varianten zu Lukas: VLatGesch 17, 1990 ➤ 6,5362; 7,4444: ᴿZKG 103 (1992) 121s (R. *Haacke*).

5309 **Goulder** Michael D., Luke, a new paradigm: jNsu 20, 1989 ➤ 5,5066... 7,4445: ᴿJTS 43 (1992) 176-180 (J. *Muddiman*: 'new' means Mt created Q himself); WestTJ 53 (1991) 363-5 (F. S. *Spencer*).

5310 **Graumann** Thomas, Christus interpres; die Einheit von Auslegung und Verkündigung in der Lukaserklärung des AMBROSIUS von Mailand: Diss. ᴰ*Aland* B. Münster. 354 p. – RTLv 24, p. 551 sans date.

5311 **Johns** Eric, *Major* David, Witness in a Gentile world; a study of Luke's Gospel. 1991, Lutterworth. 168 p. £9. 0-7188-2802-X. – ᴿExpTim 104 (1992s) 152 (C. S. *Rodd*: slight).

5312 **Johnson** Luke T., The Gospel of Luke: Sacra Pagina 1991 ➤ 7,4446; $30: ᴿETL 68 (1992) 441s (F. *Neirynck*); TR 88 (1992) 1s (G. *Schneider*).

5313 **Nolland** John, Luke 1-9,20: Word Comm 35A, 1989 ➤ 5,5071... 7,4451: ᴿCBQ 54 (1992) 363s (F. W. *Danker* objects to 'pagan' but uses 'verbiage' unflatteringly); PerspRelSt 19 (1992) 121-3 (D. O. *Via*); RefTR 50 (1991) 38s (D. *Peterson*); Themelios 17,2 (1991s) 19s (M. *Nola*); WestTJ 53 (1991) 361-3 (C. L. *Blomberg*).

5314 **Rossé** Gérard, Il Vangelo di Luca, commento esegetico e teologico: Collana Scr. R 1992, Città Nuova. 1060 p. 88-311-3615-1.

5315 **Sabourin** Léopold, L'évangile de Luc 1985 ➤ 1,4946...5,5073 [= R 1992, Pont. Univ. Gregoriana]: ᴿTLZ 117 (1992) 41 (F. *Bovon*, non Boron: intelligent et pratique).

5316 **Sáez** C., Una edición comentada del Evangelio de San Lucas de principios del siglo IX: Anuario de Estudios Medievales 21 (Barc 1991) 537-547; 13 fig. [RHE 87,176*].

5317 ᵀᴱSieben Hermann-Josef, ORIGENES, In Lucam homiliae [I, 1-25, 1991 ➤ 7,4452] II. 26-39 & 91 griech, Fragmente: Fontes Christiani 4. FrB

1992, Herder. viii p. 276-536. – ᴿTR 88 (1992) 93 (L. *Lies*); TüTQ 172 (1992) 314s (H. J. *Vogt*).

5317* **Smith** L., *Raeper* W., Luca, un vangelo per oggi [1989], ᵀ*Gatti* E.: Capire la Bibbia. Bo 1991, Dehoniane. 345 p. Lᵐ 30 pa. 88-10-80689-1 [NTAbs 38, p. 124].

5318 **Stein** R. H., Luke; New American Comm. 24. Nv 1992, Broadman. 642 p. $25. 0-8054-0124-5 [NTAbs 37, p. 442].

5319 **Stock** Klemens, *a*) Gesù la bontà di Dio; il messaggio di Luca: Bibbia e preghiera 10. R 1991, Apostolato della Preghiera. 184 p. – ᴿCC 143 (1992,3) 457 (D. *Scaiola*). – *b*) Jésus, la bonté de Dieu; le message de Luc [1984], ᵀ*Vassière* M. Tournai 1992, Desclée. 136 p. 2-7189-0591-3. [AcPIB 98 (1991s) 660]. – ᴿVSp 146 (1992) 728s (H. *Cousin*: passages de Luc propres ou du cycle liturgique).

5320 **Talbert** C., Reading Luke 1982 ➤ 64,4881, now 1990 ➤ 7,4453; 0-281-04494-5: ᴿExpTim 104 (1992s) 152 (C. S. *Rodd*).

5322 **Walter** Jens, Und ein Gebot ging aus; das Lukas-Evangelium. Stu 1991, Radius. 160 p. 3-87173-826-3. – ᴿActuBbg 29 (1992) 56 (J. *Boada*).

F7.4   *Lucae themata*   – **Luke's Gospel, topics.**

5323 **Aletti** Jean-Noël, L'arte di raccontare Gesù Cristo; la scrittura narrativa del vangelo di Luca, ᵀ*Sembrano* L.: BtB 7, 1991 ➤ 7,4458; Lᵐ 30; 88-399-2007-2: ᴿHumBr 47 (1992) 761s (A. *Bodrato*); ParVi 37 (1992) 383-6 (S. *Migliasso*); RClerIt 73 (1992) 387-390 (F. *Riva*, anche su *Alter* R.); RivB 40 (1992) 217-228 (R. *Vignolo*: 'Arte di raccontare — gioia di leggere').

5324 **Aletti** Jean-Noël, El arte de contar a Jesucristo; lectura narrativa del evangelio de Lucas, ᵀ*Ortiz García* Alfonso: BtEstB 77. S 1992, Sígueme. 230 p. 84-301-1191-3.

5325 *Bartolomé* Juan J., Lucas, la salvación como historia: Phase 31 (1991) 415-430.

5326 **Beilner** Wolfgang, Exegetisches Material zum Lukasevangelium: Vermittlung 17. Salzburg 1992, nicht im Handel. 366 p.

5327 **Beydon** France, En danger de richesse; le chrétien et les biens de ce monde selon Luc 1989 ➤ 5,5083: ᴿProtestantesimo 47 (1989) 328 (D. *Mazzarella*: pasteur Réformé à Chartres).

5328 *Bovon* François, Lukasevangelium: ➤ 757, EvKL 3 (1992) 188-191. *Demel* Sabine, Jesu Umgang mit Frauen nach Lk 1991 ➤ 9029.

5329 *Dermience* Alice, L'évangile de Luc; bonne nouvelle pour les pauvres: FoiTemps 22 (1992) 57-72.

5330 **Diefenbach** Manfred, Die Komposition des 'Lukasevangeliums' unter Berücksichtigung antiker Rhetorikelemente: Diss. ᴰ*Mödl* L. Bern 1992. 341 p. – RTLv 24, p. 546: > FraTSt 43.

5331 **Donders** Sjef, Bijbels bezien, Lucas; meditaties... Brugge 1991, Tabor. 158 p. Fb 590. – ᴿCollatVL 22 (1992) 328 (N. *Vangansbeke*).

5332 **Dongell** Joseph R., The structure of Luke's Gospel: diss. Union Theol. Sem. Richmond 1991. 371 p. 92-36275. — DissÅ 53 (1992s) 2855-A.

5333 *Ernst* Josef, *a*) Das evangelisch Katholische und das katholisch Evangelische im Lukasevangelium; ein ökumenisches Modell? – *b*) Lukas und das kirchliche Glaubensbekenntnis: ➤ 112*, Mem. Kᴜss O. 1992, 83-103 / 105-124.

5334 **Estrada** Sergio A., A critique of liberationist exegesis of the Gospel of Luke as reflected in the writings of José MIGUEZ BONINO, Leonardo BOFF, and Gustavo GUTIÉRREZ: diss. SW Baptist Theol. Sem. 1992, ^D*Lea* T. 304 p. 92-31659. — DissA 53 (1992s) 1959-A.

5335 **Fitzmyer** J. A., Luke the theologian 1989 ➤ 5,5034 ... 7,4406:   ^RBR 7,1 (1991) 11.36 (J. T. *Sanders*); Furrow 41 (1990) 194s (J. *McEvoy*); HeythJ 33 (1992) 208s (J. J. *Kilgallen*).

5336 **Fitzmyer** J. A., Luca teologo; aspetti del suo insegnamento.   Brescia 1991, Queriniana.   192 p. – ^RAnnTh 6 (1992) 462-5 (B. *Estrada*); RClerIt 73 (1992) 62s (C. *Ghidelli*).

5337 **Heininger** Bernhard,   Metaphorik, Erzählstruktur und szenisch-dramatische Gestaltung in den Sondergutgleichnissen bei Lukas [Diss. ^D*Klauck* H., Würzburg 1989]: NTAbh 34, 1991 ➤ 7,4483:   ^RCBQ 54 (1992) 784-6 (R. *Norton*); JTS 43 (1992) 584-8 (J. L. *Nolland*: thoroughly worthwhile); NRT 114 (1992) 744s (X. *Jacques*); RBibArg 54 (1992) 187-9 (R. *Krüger*).

5338 **Hogan** Frances,   Words of life from Luke.   L 1991, Collins.   320 p. £3.50. – ^RFurrow 43 (1992) 59s (J. *Byrne*).

5339 *Johnson* Luke T.,   How St. Luke affirms/challenges the world: PrPeo 6 (1992) 202-6 / 280-4.

5340 **Kingsbury** Jack D.,   Conflict in Luke 1991 ➤ 7,4467:   ^RCBQ 54 (1992) 790s (F. *Danker*); NewTR 5,4 (1992) 81 (D. *Senior*: sequel to Mk 1989); WestTJ 54 (1992) 374-6 (S. E. *Porter*).

5341 **Kingsbury** Jack D.,   Conflicto en Lucas; Jesús, autoridades, discípulos [1991 ➤ 7,4467], ^T*Godoy* Rufino: En torno al Nuevo Testamento 15. Córdoba 1992, Almendro.   236 p.   84-8005-002-0.

5342 *Koester* Helmut,   Luke's Holy Land and Jesus' company: Only in Luke do we find a group of women among Jesus' followers who parallel the 12 male disciples; if Luke reflects any prejudice, it is against people who are wealthy and comfortable: BR 8,3 (1992) 15.52.

5343 *Liu* Peter,   Did the Lucan Jesus desire voluntary poverty of his followers?:   EvQ 64 (1992) 291-317.

5344 *Mosetto* Francesco,   Cristo ieri e oggi nelle Homiliae in Lucam di ORIGENE: *a*) Salesianum 54 (1992) 283-307; – *b*) ➤ 161, Salesiani 1992, 213-237.

5345 **Mueller** John L.,   The Lucan prayer of forgiveness and selected pastoral theologies of forgiveness; a critical dialogue: diss. Duquesne. Pittsburgh 1992.   246 p.   92-22346. — DissA 53 (1992s) 844-A.

5346 **Neale** David A.,   None but the sinners; religious categories in the Gospel of Luke [diss. Sheffield]: jNsu 58, 1991 ➤ 7,4473:   ^RAustralBR 40 (1992) 78s (R. *Boid*); JTS 43 (1992) 589-594 (B. *Capper*: holds with M. SMITH and NEUSNER that the Pharisees were not the dominant religious authority, but a fringe numbering 1% of the population); Themelios 18,2 (1992s) 28s (J. B. *Green*).

5347 **Nebe** G.,   Prophetische Züge ... Lukas: BW 127, ^D1989 ➤ 5,5098 ... 7,4474:   ^RBijdragen 53 (1992) 208s (B. J. *Koet*); Protestantesimo 47 (1992) 148s (E. *Ferrario*).

5348 ^E**Neirynck** F.,   L'évangile de Luc² 1989 ➤ 5,5099 ... 7,4475:   ^RJTS 43 (1992) 171s (J. *Nolland*: the ¹1973 essays were all in French, the seven added ones are all in English); TR 88 (1992) 290s (W. *Radl*).

5349 **Petzke** Gerd,   Sondergut Lk 1990 ➤ 6,5373; 7,4476:   ^RJBL 111 (1992) 724-6 (R. L. *Brawley*).

5350 *Philipose* John,   *Kurios* in Luke; a diagnosis: BTrans 43 (1992) 325-333.

5351 **Schnackenburg** Rudolf, [Lc ...] El camino de Jesús.   Estella 1991, VDivino.   123 p. – ^REstE 67 (1992) 113-5 (J. L. *Larrabe*).

5352 *Sellew* Philip, Interior monologue as a narrative device in the parables of Luke: JBL 111 (1992) 239-253.

5353 *Shoemaker* Mel, Good news to the poor in Luke's Gospel: WeslTJ 27,1s (1992) 181-205.

5354 *Spencer* A. B., 'Fear' as a witness to Jesus in Luke's Gospel: BuBRes 2 (WL 1992) 59-73 [< NTAbs 37, p. 200].

5355 [Richter] **Reimer** J., Frauen in der Apostelgeschichte des Lukas; eine feministisch-theologische Exegese [Diss. Kassel 1990, ᴰ*Schottroff* L.]. Gü 1992, Mohn. 284 p. DM 98. 3-579-00092-6 [NTAbs 37, p. 283].

5356 **Rius-Camps** Josep, El éxodo del hombre libre; catequesis sobre el Evangelio de Lucas. Córdoba 1991, Almendro. 364 p. – ᴿRBiArg 54,45 (1992) 43s (R. *Krüger*: 'Ruis-Camps').

5357 **Rius i Camps** J., L'Exode de l'home lliure... Lluc. Barc 1989, Claret. 198 p. – ᴿPhase 30 (1990) 171s (J. *Latorre*).

5358 **Rius-Camps** Josep, L'esodo dell'uomo libero; catechesi sul Vangelo di Luca, ᵀ*Pistocchi* Bruno. R 1992, Borla. 301 p. 88-263-0930-2.

5359 *a) Trudinger* P., The historical Jesus; two recent issues for consideration; – *b) Blackburn* J. R., Prophecies fulfilled in the Gospels: Faith and freedom 45,1s (Ox 1992) 26-32 / 43-48 [< NTAbs 37, 181.188].

5360 *Tsutsui* Kenji, Das [Lk-]Evangelium MARCIONS; ein neuer Versuch der Textrekonstruktion: AnJap 18 (1992) 67-132.

5361 **Zedda** Silverio, Teologia della salvezza nel Vangelo di Luca: StBDeh 18, 1990 ⇒ 7,4485: ᴿRivB 40 (1992) 245s (R. *Mela*).

F7.5 *Infantia, cantica* – **Magnificat, Benedictus: Luc. 1-3.**

5362 **Coleridge** Mark, The birth of the Lukan narrative; narrative as Christology in Luke 1-2: diss. Pont. Ist. Biblico, ᴰ*Aletti* J. Rome 1992. 472 p. – AcPIB 9/8, 685 & 729; Biblica 73 (1992) 432; RTLv 24, p. 546.

5363 *Coleridge* Mark, [Lk 1s] In defence of the other; deconstruction and the Bible: Pacifica 5 (1992) 123-144.

5364 Ó **Fearghail** F., The introduction to Luke-Acts: AnBib 126, ᴰ1991 ⇒ 7,4486: ᴿRivB 40 (1992) 364-7 (A. *Rolla*); StPatav 39 (1992) 240s (G. *Segalla*).

5365 **Drewermann** Eugen, De la naissance des dieux à la naissance du Christ. P 1992, Seuil. 306 p. F 140. – ᴿÉtudes 376 (1992) 696s (J. *Thomas*: théologiens et exégètes disqualifiés).

5366 *Kelly* Joseph F., BEDE's exegesis of Luke's infancy narrative: ⇒ 119*b*, ᶠ*Levy* B., Mediaevalia 15 (1989) 59-70.

5367 **Landry** David T., 'Promises, promises': the literary function of the birth stories in Luke-Acts: diss. Vanderbilt, ᴰ*Tolbert* Mary Ann. Nv 1992. 478 p. 93-00059. — DissA 53 (1992s) 2856-A.

5368 *a) Manicardi* Ermenegildo, Redazione e tradizione in Lc 1-2; – *b) Cavalletti* Sofia, Il metodo derashico nei racconti lucani dell'infanzia; – *c) Valentini* Alberto, I cantici in Lc 1-2; – *d) Peretti* Elio, Letture apocrife dell'annuncio lucano a Maria; – *e) Prete* Benedetto, Il genere letterario di Lc 1,26-38; – *f) Serra* Aristide, I pastori al presepio; riflessioni su Lc 2,8-20 alla luce dell'antica tradizione giudaico-cristiana; – *g) Zedda* Silverio, La gioia in Lc 1-2 [e resto del Vangelo], 3-24 e nel libro degli Atti; Termini e contesto antico-testamentario: ⇒ 492*b*, RicStoB 4,2 (1990/2) 13-53 / 5-12 / 81-108 / 133-151 / 109-151 / 153-168.

5369 *Shuler* Philip L., *a*) Luke 1-2; – *b*) (with others) Narrative outline of the composition of Luke according to the Two Gospel hypothesis: ➤ 478, SBL Sem. 31 (1992) 82-97 / 98-120.
Muñoz Iglesias Salvador, Evangelio de la Infancia 1-4 ➤ 4656.
5370 **Panier** L., La naissance... Lc 1-2, 1991 ➤ 7,4489: ᴿArTGran 55 (1992) 339s (A. *Segovia*); RBiArg 54,45 (1992) 49 (A. J. *Levoratti*); ScEsp 44 (1992) 362-6 (J.-Y. *Thériault*); VSp 146 (1992) 727s (A. *Gueuret*).
5371 **Berlingieri** G., Il lieto annuncio... del Precursore Lc 1,5-25, 1991 ➤ 7,4490: ᴿArTGran 55 (1992) 332 (A. *Segovia*).
5372 *Green* Joel B., The social status of Mary in Luke 1,5-2,52; a plea for methodological integration [Malina B., Neyrey J.]: Biblica 73 (1992) 457-471; franç. 472.
5373 *Orbán* A. P., Die Versifikation von Lk 1,5-80 in den Evangeliorum libri quattuor des Juvencus; eine Analyse von Juvenc. 1,1-132: ZNW 83 (1992) 224-244.
5374 *Croatto* J. Severino, La anunciación a la luz de la teología de la alianza; María como antitipo di David: RBibArg 54,47 (1992) 129-139.
5375 *Mussner* Franz, Das 'Semantische Universum' der Verkündigungsperikope (Lk 1,26-38): Catholica 46 (1992) 228-239.
5376 **Chappuis-Juillard** Isabelle, Le temps des rencontres, quand Marie visite Élisabeth (Luc 1). Aubonne 1991, Moulin. 83 p. [CBQ 54,613].
5377 *a*) *Fuente Alfonso* Isabel de la, 'Llena de Espíritu Santo'; Lc 1,41 a la luz de la tradición rabínica; – *b*) *Díez Merino* Luis, Trasfondo semítico de Lucas 1-2; – *c*) *Aranda Pérez* Gonzalo, Los relatos evangélicos de la concepción y nacimiento de Jesús en los escritos de Nag Hammadi; – *d*) *Muñoz León* Domingo, Derás y historia; la distinción entre acontecimiento-base y artificio literario en los relatos derásicos [Muñoz Iglesias, Evangelios de la Infancia I-IV]; – *e*) *Agua* Agustín del, El mundo del midrás/derás; investigaciones recientes: ➤ 135, ᶠMuñoz Iglesias S., EstBib 50 (1992) 73-92 / 35-72 / 19-34 / 123-148 / 319-334.
5378 *Stock* Klemens, *a*) Von Gott berufen und von den Menschen seliggepriesen; die Gestalt Marias in Lukas 1,26-56: GeistL 64 (1991) 52-63. – *b*) ⊗ The vocation of Mary (Lk 1,26-38): Sinhak Jonmang 96 (Kwang-Ju 1992) 2-26 [< TContext 10/1, p. 49].
5379 *Kaut* Thomas, Befreier... Magnifikat, Benediktus: BoBB 77, ᴰ1990 ➤ 6,5392: ᴿCBQ 54 (1992) 574s (C. H. *Talbert*).
5380 *Laurentin* René, Magnificat, action de grâces de Marie. P 1991, Desclée-B. 210 p. F 89. – ᴿVSp 146 (1992) 136 (Janine *Feller*).
5381 **Lohfink** N., Lobgesänge der Armen; Studien zum Magnifikat: SBS 143, 1990 ➤ 6,3301: ᴿIndTSt 28 (1991) 335-7 (L. *Legrand*); JBL 111 (1992) 710-2 (Eileen *Schuller*: Hodayot section dominates); ZAW 104 (1992) 300s (H. C. *Schmitt*).
5382 *a*) *Luzárraga* Jesús, [Lc 1,58...] Las versiones siríacas del Magnificat; – *b*) *O'Callaghan* José, Detalle crítico en Lc 2,11; – *c*) *Simón Muñoz* Alfonso, La 'permanencia' de Israel; una nueva lectura de Lc 2,34a; – *d*) *Martínez Fernández* Francisco Javier, Un canto arameo a la encarnación del Hijo de Dios; San Efrén el Sirio, himno De Nativitate III: ➤ 135, ᶠMuñoz Iglesias S., EstBib 50 (1992) 103-122 / 157-160 / 191-223 / 475-491.
5383 **Valentini** A., Il Magnificat [diss. PIB 1983] 1987 ➤ 3,4993... 5,5121: ᴿCiuD 204 (1991) 260s (J. *Gutiérrez*).
5384 **Maestri** William F., Mary, model of justice; reflections on the Magnificat. NY 1987, Alba. viii-89 p. $5. 0-8189-0511-5. – ᴿCarmelus 37 (1990) 234s (L. P. *Rogge*).

5385 *Rickers* Folkert, 'Die Niedrigen aber hebt er empor und richtet sie auf'; unterschiedliche Bibelauslegungen und didaktische Überlegungen zum Magnifikat (Lk 1,46-55): JbRPäd 8 (Neuk 1992) 155-178 [233-254 (255...) Religionspädagogik, Literaturbericht 1990 (1991, *Heimbrock* H.); < ZIT 93,112].

5386 **Manns** Frédéric, Une prière juive reprise en Luc 1,68-69: EphLtg 106 (1992) 162-6 [< RHE 87, 192*].

5387 *a) Vanhoye* Albert, L'intérêt de Luc pour la prophétie en Lc 1,76; 4,16-30 et 22,60-65; – *b) Koet* Bart J., Simeons Worte (Lk 2,29-32. 34*c*-35) und Israels Geschick; – *c) Wilcox* Max, Luke 2,26-38 'Anna bat Phanuel, of the tribe of Asher, a prophetess'; a study of midrash in material special to Luke: → 137, ᶠNEIRYNCK F., Four Gospels 1992, 1529-48 / 1549-69 / 1571-9.

5388 *Morris* Royce L.B., Why *Augoustos*? A note to Luke 2.1: NTS 38 (1992) 142-4.

5389 *Serra* Aristide, Pastori al presepio; riflessioni su Lc 2,8-20 alla luce dell'antica tradizione giudaico-cristiana: → 309, Nato da donna 1992, 7-95.

5390 *a) Kellermann* Ulrich, Jesus — das Licht der Völker; Lk 2,25-33 und die Christologie im Gespräch mit Israel; – *b) Stegemann* Ekkehard, Welchen Sinn hat es, von Jesus als Messias zu reden?: KIsr 7 (1992) 10-27 / 28-44.

5391 *Panimolle* Salvatore A., Gesù salvezza e luce; la preghiera di fronte al compimento (Lc 2,29-32): → 338, ParSpV 25 (1992) 85-100.

5392 *a) Valentino* Alberto, [Lc 2,41-52], La rivelazione di Gesù dodicenne al Tempio; – *b) Rodríguez Carmona* Antonio, Jesús comienza su vida de adulto (Lc 2,41-52); – *c) González Echegaray* Joaquín, Las tres ciudades de los Evangelios de la Infancia de Jesús; Nazaret, Belén y Jerusalén: → 135, ᶠMUÑOZ IGLESIAS S., EstBib 50 (1992) 261-304 / 177-189 / 83-102.

5394 *Prete* B., Il battesimo di Gesù secondo il racconto di Lc 3,21-22: LA 42 (1992) 67-84.

F7.6 Evangelium Lucae 4,1...

5395 *a) Brawley* Robert J., Canon and community; intertextuality, canon, interpretation, Christology, theology, and persuasive rhetoric in Luke 4,1-13; – *b) Robbins* Vernon K., [Luke 7,36-50...] Using a socio-rhetorical poetics to develop a unified method; the woman who anointed Jesus as a test case: → 478, SBL Sem. 31 (1992) 419-434 / 302-319.

5396 **Morris** Joseph A., Irony and ethics in the Lukan narrative world; a narrative rhetorical reading of Luke 4:14-30: diss. Graduate Theological Union, ᴰ*Boyle* J. Berkeley 1992. 307 p. 93-05969. — DissA 53 (1992s) 3565-A.

5397 *Pergnier* Maurice, (*Levin* Saul), An accidental displacement of text in Chapter 4 of Luke [verse 31-44 for 14 (or 16)-30]: → 119*b*, ᶠLEVY B., Mediaevalia 15 (1993 for 1989) 1-5.

5398 **Noorda** S., Historia vitae magistra: een beoordeling... Lc 4,16-30: 1989 → 7,4512: ᴿKerkT 42 (1991) 78s (G. de *Ru*).

5399 **Shin Kyo-Seon** Gabriel, Die Ausrufung des endgültigen Jubeljahres durch Jesus in Nazaret... Lk 4,16-30: EurHS 23/378, ᴰ1989 → 6,5410*a*: ᴿTR 88 (1992) 291-3 (W. *Radl*: kaum mehr als der Stand der Forschung); SNTU 17-A (1992) 264-6 (M. *Hasitschka*).

5400 *Siker* Jeffrey S., 'First to the Gentiles'; a literary analysis of Luke 4:16-30: JBL 111 (1992) 73-90.

5401 *Bergant* Dianne, [Lk 4,21] 'Fulfilled in your hearing' [... reinterpretation within Scripture]: NewTR 5,3 (1992) 78-85.

5402 *Morgen* Michèle, Jésus descendit à Capharnaüm; il étonne par la puissance de sa parole (Lc 4, 31-32 et ses sources): RevSR 66 (1992) 233-248.

5402* *Bock* Darrell L., The Son of Man in Luke 5:24: BuBRes 1 (1991) 109-121.

5403 *Biser* Eugen, [Lk 5,37] Wohin mit dem neuen Wein? Zur Frage der Aktualisierung der christlichen Botschaft: MüTZ 43 (1992) 161-172.

5404 *Immerwahr* Henry R., [Lk 5,37] New wine in ancient wineskins; the evidence from Attic vases: Hesperia 61 (1992) 121-132; pl. 29-32.

5405 *Rodd* C. S., There you've lost me [taking Lk 6,27s literally means catastrophe as in the film 'Heaven's Above']: ExpTim 103 (1991s) 302s.

5406 *Vattioni* Francesco, Varia semitica IV [Lc 7,5 Nabatei; *šnh*; *aklas, ʾchthō-rodlapsou*]: AION 52 (1992) 299-308.

5407 *Imbach* Josef, [Lk 7,36-50] Die Türe nicht zuschlagen; eine Jesusbegegnung als Lehrstück für zwischenmenschliche Beziehungen: GeistL 64 (1991) 7-16.

5408 *Lafon* Guy, [Lc 7,36-50] Le repas chez Simon: Études 377 (1992) 651-660.

5409 *Resseguie* James L., [➤ 7.4523], Luke 7:36-50; making the familiar seem strange: Interpretation 46 (1992) 285-290.

5410 *Saxer* Victor, [Lc 7,36-50 ...] Marie-Madeleine dans les évangiles; 'la femme coupée en morceaux': RThom 92 (1992) 674-701. 818-833 [... d'autres femmes, historiquement distinctes d'elle, mais littérairement confondues].

5411 *Sanders* James A,. [Lk 7,40-42 *charizomai* for Dt/Lv *aphiēmi*] Sins, debts and jubilee release: ➤ 41, FDAVIDSON R., Text as pretext 1992, 273-281.

5412 *a) Delobel* Joël, Lk 7,47 in its context; an old crux revisited; – *b) Gourgues* Michel, Regroupement littéraire et équilibrage théologique; le cas de Lc 13,1-9; – *c) Tannehill* Robert C., The Lukan discourse on invitations (Luke 14,7-24); – *d) Räisänen* Heikki, The prodigal son and his Jewish Christian brother (Lk 15,11-32); ➤ 137, FNEIRYNCK F., Four Gospels 1992, 1581-90 / 1591-1602 / 1603-16 / 1617-36.

5413 *Centelles* Jorge, [Lc 9,28-36] La Transfiguración en San Lucas y 'la elección ignaciana': Manresa 64 (1992) 65-70.

5414 **McClane** Curtis D., Moving toward involvement; Jesus' ministry pronouncement at Nazareth as a paradigm for community outreach: diss. Drew, DGross C. Madison NJ 1992. 434 p. 92-29515. – DissA 53 (1992s) 3561s-A.

F7.7   *Iter hierosolymitanum – Lc 9,51 ...* – **Jerusalem journey.**

5415 **Moessner** David P., Lord of the banquet ... travel narrative, Lk 9,51s, D1989 ➤ 5,5153 ... 7,4529: RBibTB 22 (1992) 41s (J. *Topel*); NT 34 (1992) 101s (L.T. *Johnson*); TorJT 8 (1992) 174-8 (J. *Plevnik*).

5416 **Thekemury** Pius, Discipleship and attitudes to possessions according to the Lukan travel narrative: diss. Innsbruck, DHasitschka M. 1991s. – ZkT 114 (1992) 503s.

5417 *Baarlink* Heinrich, Die zyklische Struktur von Lukas 9.43b-19.28: NTS 38 (1992) 481-506.

5418 *Braun* Willi, The historical Jesus and the mission speech in Q [= Lk] 10:2-12: Forum FF 7 (1991) 279-319.

5419 *Røsæg* Nils A., A new exegesis of the 'mission speech' (Lk 10,2-12 ‖; 9,1-6 ‖): TsTKi 63 (1992) 161-179 [in Norwegian; Eng. 179].

5420 *Hills* Julian V., Luke 10.18 — who saw Satan fall? JStNT 46 (1992) 25-40 [the demons, not Jesus].

5421 **Phillips** Gary A., 'What is written? How are you reading?' Gospel intertextuality and doing Lukewise; a writerly reading of Lk 10:25-37 (and 38-42): ➤ 478, SBL Sem. 31 (1992) 266-301.

5422 **Légasse** S., [Lc 10,25] Et qui? *agape* 1989 ➤ 5,5160 ... 7,4536: ᴿLaval-TP 48 (1992) 139s (Odette *Mainville*); RB 99 (1992) 606s (B. T. *Viviano*: 'almost perfect theological poise').

5423 *Díaz Marcos* Cipriano, [Lk 10,30-35] El buen samaritano, ese insensato: SalT 78 (1990) 385-394.

5424 *Lona* Horacio, La historia del Buen Samaritano; observaciones sobre la ética de Jesús: ProyCSE 4,13 (Buenos Aires 1992) 307-332.

5425 *Oakman* Douglas, Was Jesus a peasant? Implications for reading the Samaritan story (Luke 10:30-35): BibTB 22 (1992) 117-125 [< NTAbs 37, p. 203].

5426 *Kilgallen* John J., A suggestion regarding *gar* in Luke 10,42: Biblica 73 (1992) 255-8.

5427 *Anderson* David, [Lk 11,5-8] Appraisal and interpretation of the Friend at midnight: CalvaryB 8,1 (1992) 24-38.

5428 a) *Schürmann* Heinz, QLk 11,14-36 kompositionsgeschichtlich befragt; – b) *März* Claus-Peter, Das Gleichnis vom Dieb; Überlegungen zur Verbindung von Lk 12,39 par Mt 24,43 und 1 Thess 5,2.4; – c) *Catchpole* David R., [Lk 7] The centurion's faith and its function in Q; – d) *Suhl* Alfred. [... Lk 22] Die Funktion des Schwertstreichs bei der Gefangennahme Jesu: ➤ 137, ᶠNEIRYNCK F., Four Gospels 1992, 563-586 / 635-648 / 517-540 / 295-323.

5429 *Nebe* Gottfried, Das *éstai* in Lk 11,36 — ein neuer Deutungsversuch: ZNW 83 (1992) 108-114.

5430 *Hultgren* Arland J., Jesus and gnosis; the saying on hindering others in Luke 11:52 and its parallels: ForumFF 7 (1991) 165-182.

5431 **Visonà** G., Citazioni patristiche ... Lc 12,49: AnBib 125, 1990 ➤ 7,4548: ᴿArTGran 55 (1992) 559s (A. *Segovia*); CC 143 (1992,1) 305s (A. *Ferrua*).

5432 *Franco-Martínez* César-Augusto, Lc 12,50; ¿Angustia de Jesús ante su muerte?: ➤ 135, ᶠMUÑOZ IGLESIAS S., EstBib 50 (1992) 423-441.

5433 *O'Toole* Robert F., Some exegetical reflections on Luke 13,10-17 [... SCHÜSSLER FIORENZA E.]: Biblica 73 (1992) 84-107; franç. 107.

5434 **York** John O., [Lk 13,30] The last shall be first; the rhetoric of reversal in Luke: jNsu 46, ᴰ1991 ➤ 7,4550: ᴿCBQ 54 (1992) 812s (M. *Olsthoorn*); CritRR 5 (1992) 261-3 (D. L. *Tiede*); EvQ 64 (1992) 277-9 (R. *Shirock*); JTS 43 (1992) 174-6 (E. *Franklin*); TLZ 117 (1992) 126s (M. *Rese*).

5435 a) *Braun* Willi, Symposium or anti-symposium? Reflections on Luke 14:1-24; – b) *Kozar* Joseph V., Absent joy; an investigation of the narrative pattern of repetition and variation in the parables of Luke 15; ➤ 74, ᶠGUENTHER H., TorJT 8 (1992) 70-84 / 85-94.

5436 **Ostaszewski** Andrzej, L'immagine di Dio presentata nelle tre parabole del vangelo di Luca: diss. Pont. Univ. Gregoriana, ᴰ*Lentzen-Deis* F., Roma 1992. 376 p.; Extr, 3833: 75 p. – RTLv 24, p. 548.

5437 **Bailey** Kenneth E., Finding the lost; cultural keys to Luke 15: Scholarship Today. St. Louis 1992, Concordia. 232 p. $16 pa. [NTAbs 36, p. 418]. – ᴿConcordJ 18 (1992) 420 (E. H. *Kiehl*).

5438 *Kiehl* Erich H., 'The Lost' parables in Luke's Gospel account: ConcordJ 18 (1992) 244-258.

5439 *Durber* Susan, [Lk 15] The female readers of the parables of the lost: JStNT 45 (1992) 59-78.

5439* *Mangatt* George, [Lk 15,2] Jesus' option for sinners: Bible Bhashyam 18 (1992) 208-220.

5440 *Gourgues* Michel, Le père prodigue (Lc 15,11-32); de l'exégèse à l'actualisation: NRT 114 (1992) 3-20.

5440* *Peretti* Antonio, La parabola del figliol prodigo ovvero l'amore oltre la giustizia: Studium 88 (R 1992) 555-563.

5441 *Poffet* Jean-Michel, [Lc 15...] La patience de Dieu; essai sur la miséricorde: Essai. Tournai/P 1992, Desclée/Bégédis. 190 p. F 75. – ᴿVSp 146 (1992) 726s (H. *Cousin*).

5442 *Depnerin* Wilfried, Transaktionsanalyse als Interpretationshilfe für biblische Texte; das Gleichnis vom Verlorenen Sohn transaktionsanalytisch betrachtet: WegMensch 43 (1991) 335-346.

5443 *Frot* Yves, [Lc 15,11-32] Nota sur l'utilisation de la parabole de l'Enfant Prodigue dans l'œuvre de Saint AUGUSTIN: → 164, ᶠSAXER V. 1992, 443-8.

5444 **Nouwen** Henri J. M., The return of the Prodigal Son; a meditation on fathers, brothers, and sons. L/NY 1992, Darton-LT/Doubleday. [xvi-] 142 p. $25. / 0-385-41867-1 [TDig 40,79].

5445 *Brown* Colin, [Lk 16,1-13] The unjust steward; a new twist?: → 126, ᶠMARTIN R., Worship 1992, 121-145.

5446 **Ireland** D. J., Stewardship and the Kingdom of God; an historical, exegetical and contextual study of the unjust steward in Luke 16:1-13 [diss. Westminster, ᴰSilva M. 1989]: NT supp 70. Leiden 1992, Brill. xi-233 p. *f* 150. 90-04-09600-0 [NTAbs 37, p. 279: TvT 33,415, S. *Noorda*].

5447 *Koester* Helmut, [Lk 16,1-13...] Finding morality in Luke's disturbing parables: BR 8,5 (1992) 10.

5448 *Beavis* Mary Ann, Ancient slavery as an interpretative context for the New Testament servant parables with special reference to the Unjust Steward (Luke 16:1-8): JBL 111 (1992) 37-54.

5449 *Monat* Pierre, [Lc 16,8] L'exégèse de la parabole de 'L'intendant infidèle' du IIe au XIIe siècle: RÉAug 38 (1992) 89-123.

5450 **Hintzen** Johannes, Verkündigung und Wahrnehmung; über das Verhältnis von Evangelium und Leser am Beispiel Lk 16,19-31 im Rahmen des lukanischen Doppelwerkes [Diss. → 7,4566]: BoBB 81. Fra 1991, Hain. [xii-] 404 p. 3-445-09144-7.

5451 *a) Piper* Ronald A., Social background and thematic structure in Luke 16; – *b) Hartman* Lars, Reading Luke 17,20-37; – *c) Fusco* Vittorio, 'Point of view' and 'implicit reader' in two eschatological texts (Lk 19,11-28; Acts 1,6-8); – *d) Dauer* Anton, Lk 24,12 — ein Produkt lukanischer Redaktion?: → 137, ᶠNEIRYNCK F., Four Gospels 1992, 1637-654 / 1663-75 / 1677-96 / 1697-1716.

5452 *Houzet* Pierre, Les serviteurs de l'Évangile (Luc 17,5-10) sont-ils inutiles? ou un contresens traditionnel: RB 99 (1992) 335-372; Eng. 335.

5453 **Dagron** Alain, Aux jours du Fils de l'Homme; essai sur le service de la parole, Luc XVII 1 à XVIII 8, lecture sémiotique et propositions théologiques 1990 → 7,4569; 2-905601-01-9: ᴿRHPR 72 (1992) 203 (C. *Grappe*).

5454 *Schwarz* Günther, [Lk 17,20] *Ouk... metà paratērēseōs?*: BibNot 59 (1991) 45-48.

5455 *Lebourlier* Jean, [Lc 17,21] *Entòs hymōn*; le sens 'au milieu de vous' est-il possible?: Biblica 73 (1992) 259-262.

5456 *Downing* F. Gerald, The ambiguity of 'the Pharisee and the toll-collector' (Luke 18:9-14) in the Greco-Roman world of late antiquity: CBQ 54 (1992) 80-99.

5456* *Porter* Stanley E., 'In the vicinity of Jericho'; Luke 18:35 in the light of its Synoptic parallels: BuBRes 2 (1992) 91-104.

5457 *O'Toole* Robert F., [Lk 19,...] Zacchaeus / Cleopas / Theophilus: ➤ 741, AnchorBD (1992) 6,1032s / 6,1063s / 6,511s.

5458 *Vos* Geerhardus, [Lk 19,10] Seeking and saving the lost: Kerux 7 (1992) 1-19.

5459 *Borg* Marcus J., Luke 19:42-44 and Jesus as Prophet?: ForumFF 8 (1992) 99-112.

F7.8 **Passio** – *Lc 22...*

5460 **Kraus** Jonathan D. B., Symposium scenes in Luke's Gospel with special attention to the Last Supper: diss. Vanderbilt, [D]*Patte* D. Nv 1991. 271 p. 92-30921. — DissA 53 (1992s) 1960-A.

5461 *Nash* Robert N.[J.] Luke 22:14-34 (expository): RExp 89 (1992) 397-401.

5462 **Nelson** Peter K., Leadership and discipleship; a study of Luke 22:24-30: diss. British Academic Awards 1991. 330 p. BRDX-96113. – DissA 53 (1992s) 844-A.

5463 *Brown* Raymond E., The Lucan authorship of Luke 22: ➤ 478, SBL Sem. 31 (1992) 154-164,

5464 *Crump* David, [Lk 22,31s echoing 10,18] Jesus, the victorious scribal-intercessor in Luke's gospel: NTS 38 (1992) 51-65.

5465 *Dupont* Jacques, [Lc 23] Gesù salvatore: ParVi 36 (1992) 270-277.

5466 a) *Garrett* S. R., The meaning of Jesus' death in Luke; – b) *Jervell* J., God's faithfulness... Lk-Acts: WWorld 12,1 (1992) 11-16 / 29-36 [< NTAbs 36,343].

5466* *Tiede* David L., Contending with God; the death of Jesus and the trial of Israel in Luke-Acts: ➤ 104, [F]KOESTER H., 1991, 301-8.

5467 *Petzer* Jacobus H.. Anti-Judaism and the textual problem of Luke 23:24: FgNt 5 (1992) 199-203.

5468 *Untergassmair* Franz G., Der Spruch vom 'grünen und dürren Holz' (Lk 23,31): SNTU A-16 (1991) 55-87.

5469 a) *Talbert* Charles H., The place of the Resurrection in the theology of Luke; – b) *Johnson* Luke T., Luke 24:1-11 the not-so-empty tomb: Interpretation 46 (1992) 19-30 / 57-61.

5470 *Riedel* Ingrid, Die Emmaus-Geschichte als Trauer-Weg; Erschliessung eines Textes mit bibliodramatischen Elementen: JbRPäd 8 (Neuk 1992) 89-100 [< ZIT 93,111].

5471 *Gilbert* Maurice, A six-day retreat with the disciples of Emmaus, Luke 24,13-35: Emmaus in Manresa; the Bible and the Exercises [Gujarat-SP 1992) 10-24 [AcPIB 9,776].

5472 *Rosica* T. M., In search of Jesus; the Emmaus lesson: Church 8,1 (NY 1992) 21-25 [< NTAbs 36,350].

5473 *Greinacher* Norbert, [Lk 24,23 ...] Bekehrung durch Eroberung; kritische Reflexion auf die Kolonisations- und Missionsgeschichte in Lateiname-

rika: Diakonia 23 (1992) 109-113; > Eng. Conversion through conquest:
TDig 39 (1992) 121-5 [B. A. *Asen*].
5474 *Flusser* David, Wie in den Psalmen über mich geschrieben steht (Lk
24,44): Judaica 48 (1992) 40-42.

XII. Actus Apostolorum

F8.1 **Acts** – *Text, commentary, topics.*

5475 **Adinolfi** Marco, *Bottini* Claudio, ᴱ*Corona* Raimondo, Gli Atti degli
Apostoli; lettura esegetico-esistenziale: III Settimana Biblica Abruzzese,
4-9.VIII. 1988. L'Aquila 1990, Curia O.F.M. 286 p.
5476 **Boismard** M., *Lamouille* A., Les Actes des deux apôtres 1990 → 6,5466;
7,4598: ᴿRTLv 23 (1992) 218-220 (C. *Focant*); TR 88 (1992) 26-28 (G. D.
Kilpatrick, ᵀ*Woestmann* Annegret).
5477 *Co* Maria Anicia, The major summaries in Acts; Acts 2,42-47; 4,33-35;
5,12-16; linguistic and literary relationship: ETL 68 (1992) 49-85.
5478 **Dumais** Marcel, Communauté et mission; une lecture des Actes des
Apôtres pour aujourd'hui. Relais Études 10. P 1992, Desclée. 210 p.
2-7189-0587-5. – ᴿEsprVie 102 (1992) 618s (É. *Cothenet:* en note regrette le caractère déductif du document sur l'Église comme communion
→ 8138).
5479 **FLANDERS** Henry J.: With steadfast purpose; essays on Acts in honor of
→ 6,47*, ᴱ**Keathley** Naymond H. Waco 1990, Baylor. xi-345 p. (biog.
Pitts W. L.). $20. – ᴿRelStR 18 (1992) 141 (C. *Bernas*). 15 art.
5480 **Hackett** H. B., Commentary on Acts. GR 1992 = 1982, Kregel.
341 p.; map. $22. 0-8254-2749-5; pa. -8-7 [NTAbs 37, p. 278].
5481 *Heimerdinger* Jenny, *Levinsohn* Stephen, The use of the definite article
before names of people in the Greek text of Acts with particular reference
to Codex Bezae: FgNt 5 (1992) 15-44; español 44.
5482 **Hemer** Colin J. † 1987; ᴱ*Gempf* Conrad, The Book of Acts in the setting of Hellenistic history: WUNT 49, 1989 → 5,5231 ... 7,4615: ᴿCBQ
54 (1992) 156-8 (A. T. *Kraabel:* valuable despite important problems not
treated); CrNSt 13 (1992) 202-4 (R. *Fabris*); JStNT 46 (1992) 119 (Loveday *Alexander*); NedTTs 46 (1992) 234s (P. W. van der *Horst*).
5483 **Johnson** Luke T., The Acts of the Apostles: Sacra Pagina comm. 5.
ColMn 1992, Liturgical/Glazier. xiv-568 p. $30. 0-8146-5807-5 [TDig
40,185].
5484 **Kampen** L. van, Apostelverhalen; doel en compositie: diss. Utrecht.
1990, Sliedracht. 338 p. ƒ45. – ᴿKerkT 43 (1992) 256s (J. *Helderman*).
5485 **Kee** H. C., Good news ... Theology of Acts 1990 → 6,5480; 7,4616:
ᴿCritRR 5 (1992) 229-231 (C. R. *Matthews*); CurrTMiss 19 (1992) 300s
(Lynn A. *Kauppi*); Encounter 53 (1992) 94s (Beverly R. *Gaventa*); Furrow
42 (1991) 393 (S. *Quinlan:* lucid); Interpretation 46 (1992) 326.328 (P. W.
Walaskay); RelStT 11,2 (1991) 100s (B. W. *Henaut*).
5486 *Kee* Howard C., The Jews in Acts: → 107, ᶠKRAABEL A. T. 1992,
183-195.
5487 **Kilgallen** John, A brief commentary on the Acts of the Apostles 1988
→ 4,5238: ᴿLivLight 27,2 (1990s) 180s (J. *Winkler,* also on his Luke
1988).
5488 **Kistemaker** Simon J., Exposition of the Acts 1990 → 7,4617: ᴿTR 88
(1992) 6 (G. *Schneider*).

5489 a) **Loning** Karl, Das Gottesbild der Apostelgeschichte im Spannungsfeld von Frühjudentum und Fremdreligionen; – b) *Gnilka* Joachim, Zum Gottesgedanken in der Jesusüberlieferung: ➤ 573, Monotheismus 1991/2 88-117 / 144-162.

5490 **Lüdemann** G., Early Christianity ... Acts, commentary 1989 ➤ 5,5327 ... 7,4623: ᴿCrNSt 13 (1992) 201s (R. *Fabris*).

5491 **Marchesi** Giovanni, Il Vangelo da Gerusalemme a Roma; l'origine del cristianesimo negli Atti degli Apostoli: Supersaggi 1991 ➤ 7,4625: ᴿNRT 114 (1992) 746 (X. *Jacques*).

5492 **Marshall** I. Howard, The Acts of the Apostles: NT Guides. Sheffield 1992, JStOT. 112 p. £6. 1-85075-372-5 [Themelios 19/2,30, B.J. *Dodd:* priorities other than sociological].

5493 ᵀᴱ**Martin** Lawrence T., Venerable BEDE, Commentary on the Acts of the Apostles: Cistercian Studies 117. Kalamazoo 1989, Cistercian. xxxv-214 p. $30; pa. $15. 0-87907-617-8. – ᴿCanadCathR 10,1 (1992) 26 (M. G. *Steinhauser*).

5494 **Moria** Thaddeus A., The community of goods in Acts, a Lukan model of Christian charity [diss. Rome, Urbanianum, ᴰ*Sisti* A.]. Secunderabad c. 1991, Amruthavani. 178 p. – ᴿIndTSt 29 (1992) 162-4 (P. A. *Sampathkumar*).

5495 *Palmer* Darryl W., Acts and the historical monograph: TyndB 43 (1992) 373-388.

ᴱ**Parsons** Mikael C., *Tyson* Joseph B., CADBURY-KNOX-TALBERT on Acts 1992 ➤ m654.

5496 **Pesch** Rudolf, Atti degli Apostoli [1986 ➤ 2,4037], ᵀ*Filippi* Emilio, al.; ᴱ*De Lorenzi* Lorenzo: Commenti e studi biblici. Assisi 1992, Cittadella. 1087 p. 88-308-0508-4.

5497 **Polhill** J. B., Acts: NewAmC 26. Nv 1992, Broadman. 574 p.; 4 maps. $25. 0-8054-0126-1 [NTAbs 37, p. 283].

Richter-Reimer Ivoni, Frauen in der Apg 1992 ➤ 9072.

5498 **Rius-Camps** Josep, Commentari als Fets dels Apòstols, I. 'Jerusalem'; configuració de l'esglesia judeocreient (Ac 1,1 – 5,42): Col·lectània Sant Pacià 43. Barc 1991, Fac.Teol. Catalunya/Herder. 312 p. – ᴿRCatalT 17 (1992) 292-4 (J. *Montserrat i Torrents*).

5499 *Ross* J. M., The spelling of Jerusalem in Acts: NTS 38 (1992) 474-6.

5500 ᵀᴱ**Schrader** Richard J., al., ARATOR's On the Acts of the Apostles. Atlanta 1987, Scholars. 104 p. – ᴿResPublica Litterarum 13 (Kansas U. 1990) 295-7 (R. *Cecire*).

5501 **Segalla** G., Carisma e istituzione ... Atti 1991 ➤ 7,4640: ᴿCC 143 (1992,3) 456s (D. *Scaiola*); RivPastLtg 30,5 (1992) 74s (P. *Rota Scalabrini*).

5502 **Stott** John R. W., The Spirit, the Church, and the world; the message of Acts 1990 [➤ 6,5498, different (? title)]: ᴿCalvinT 26 (1991) 265-8 (J. *Westerhof*).

5503 **Strange** W. A., The problem of the text of Acts: SNTS Mg 71. C 1992, Univ. 258 p. £30. 0-521-41384-2. – ᴿExpTim 104 (1992s) 23 (C. K. *Barrett:* an excellent first book).

Tannehill Robert C., The narrative unity of ... Acts 1990 ➤ 5294.

5504 *Tyson* Joseph B., Authority in Acts: BToday 30 (1992) 279-283.

5505 **Verheij** W. A., De geest wijst wegen in de tijd; Lucas' theologie des woords in het Evangelie (een ecclesiologische Christologie) en Handelingen (een christologische ecclesiologie). Kampen 1991, Kok. 611 p. f45. 90-24282-70-5. – ᴿNedTTs 46 (1992) 166s (J. *Smit Sibinga:* far-fetched).

5506 **Wylie** Amanda Lee B., John CHRYSOSTOM and his [55] homilies on the Acts of the Apostles; reclaiming ancestral models for the Christian people: diss. Princeton Theol. Sem. 1992, ᴰ*McVey* Kathleen E. 287 p. 92-29030. – DissA 53 (1992s) 1553-A.

5507 **Yrigoyen** Charles, Acts for our time: Lay Bible Studies. Nv 1992, Abingdon. [vi-] 104 p. 0-687-00771-2.

5508 **Zettner** Christoph, Amt, Gemeinde und kirchliche Einheit in der Apostelgeschichte des Lukas [kath. Diss. Bochum]: EurHS 23/423. Fra 1991, Lang. lviii-434 p. DM 99. 3-631-43818-4. [TLZ 118,619, *J. Roloff*].

F8.3 *Ecclesia primaeva Actuum:* **Die Urgemeinde.**

5509 **Brown** R. E., Le chiese degli apostoli; indagine esegetica sulle origini dell'ecclesiologia, ᵀ*Bell* Graham, *Caffaro* Enzo. CasM 1992, Piemme. 189 p. Lᵐ 30. [VivH 4,189, S. *Dianich*].

5510 **Cwiekowski** F. J., The beginnings of the Church 1988 ➤ 4,5279 ... 7,4648: ᴿScripTPamp 23 (1991) 1070s (G. *Aranda*).

5511 **Feldtkeller** Andreas, Das entstehende Heidenchristentum im religiösen Umfeld Syriens zur Prinzipatszeit; ein Beitrag zum Verhältnis von Urchristentum und Religionsgeschichte: Diss. ᴰ*Theissen* G. Heidelberg 1992. – RTLv 24, p. 346.

5512 **Grappe** Christian, D'un Temple à l'autre; Pierre et l'Église primitive de Jérusalem: Ét(R)HPR. P 1992, PUF. 371 p. F 380. 2-13-043628-5. – ᴿBLitEc 93 (1992) 405s (S. *Légasse:* en partant de Max WEBER).

5513 **Guillet** Jacques, Las primeras palabras de la fe; de Jesús a la iglesia: Buena Noticia 11. Estella 1982, VDivino. 173 p. 84-7151-329-3.

5514 **Hall** Stuart G., Doctrine and practice in the early Church. L 1991, SPCK / GR 1992, Eerdmans. x-262 p. /0-8028-0629-5.

5515 **Hoffmann** Paul, Das Erbe und die Macht der [... paulinischen, charismatischen] Kirche; Rückbesinnung auf das NT: ToposTB 213. Mainz 1991, Grünewald. 152 p. DM 9,80. – ᴿErbAuf 68 (1992) 74 (va).

5516 *Jauregui* José A., Concepto de evangelización y su práctica en las primeras comunidades cristianas: LumenVr 41 (1992) 409-418.

5517 **Kirchschläger** Walter, Die Anfänge der Kirche; eine biblische Rückbesinnung 1990 ➤ 6,5221; 7,4653: ᴿAtKap 117 (1991) 148s (M. *Marczewski*); BLtg 65 (1992) 90s (T. *Söding*); LebZeug 46 (1991) 149 (A. *Weiser*); RB 99 (1992) 614 (J. *Taylor:* whole NT, not just Acts); TPQ 140 (1992) 190 (K. M. *Woschitz*).

5518 **Klauck** Hans-Josef, Gemeinde zwischen Haus und Stadt; Kirche bei Paulus. FrB 1992, Herder. 128 p. DM 22,80. 3-451-22620-0. [TLZ 118, 401, E. *Schweizer*].

5519 *Klauck* H.-J., 'Urbane Frömmigkeit?' in den paulinischen Gemeinden: Lebendige Seelsorge 43,1 [Wü 1992] 20-26 [< NTAbs 36, p. 362].

5520 **Lüdemann** G., Early Christianity ... Acts 1989 ➤ 3,5103 ... 6,5483*b*: ᴿRelStT 11,2 (1991) 85s (D. *Fraikin*).

5521 **MacDonald** Margaret Y., The Pauline churches ᴰ1988 ➤ 4,5296 ... 7,4654: ᴿBibTB 22 (1992) 143 (N. *Elliott*).

5522 *Mangatt* George, Believing community according to the Acts of the Apostles: Bible Bhashyam 16 (1990) 173-181.

5523 **Marchesi** Giovanni, Il Vangelo da Gerusalemme a Roma; l'origine del cristianesimo negli Atti: BtUniv 43, 1991 ➤ 7,4625: ᴿRB 99 (1992) 614 (J. *Taylor*).

5524 a) *Marconcini* Benito, La comunità testimone (Ap); – b) *Bosetti* Elena, Esortazione ai presbiteri; – c) *Valentini* Alberto, La formazione dell'uomo in Cristo; – d) *Dal Covolo* Enrico, Sacerdozio ministeriale e sacerdozio comune nei primi tre secoli: ParVi 36,3 ('Una comunità ministeriale' 1991) 166-174 / 175-184 / 185-194 / 195-207.

5525 *Mimouni* Simon C., Pour une définition nouvelle du Judéo-Christianisme ancien ['juifs qui ont reconnu la messianité de Jésus, qui ont reconnu ou qui n'ont pas reconnu la divinité du Christ', p. 184]: NTS 38 (1992) 161-186.

5526 a) *Morris* Leon, The Saints and the Synagogue; – b) *Stanton* Graham, Aspects of early Christian and Jewish worship; PLINY and the Kerygma Petrou: ➤ 126, FMARTIN R., Worship 1992, 39-52 / 84-98.

5527 *Munier* Charles, Le témoignage du Livre des Actes sur l'initiation chrétienne: ➤ 164, FSAXER V., Memorian 1992, 587-597.

5528 **Pagé** Jean-Guy, L'Église à son printemps: Brèches théologiques 9. Montréal/P 1990, Paulines / Médiaspaul. 425 p. $24. – REglT 22 (1991) 382s (A. *Peelman*).

5529 **Rius-Camps** Josep, De Jerusalén a Antioquía; génesis de la Iglesia cristiana ... Hch 1-12, 1989 ➤ 5,5246; 6,5497: RRBiArg 53 (1991) 177-180 (R. *Krüger*).

5530 **Sabourin** Léopold, Protocatholicisme et ministères; commentaire bibliographique. Montréal 1989, Bellarmin. 521 p. – RSR 21 (1992) 114 (L. *Painchaud*).

5531 **Schenke** Ludger, Die Urgemeinde 1990 ➤ 6,5527; 7,4660: RÉTRel 67 (1992) 111s (G. *Wagner*); LebZeug 46 (1991) 149-151 (A. *Weiser*); ZKG 103 (1992) 110s (W. *Schmithals*):

5532 *Scobie* Charles H. H., Israel and the nations [... in the NT]; an essay in biblical theology: TyndB 43 (1992) 283-305.

5533 *Suhl* Alfred, Der Beginn der selbständigen Mission des Paulus; ein Beitrag zur Geschichte des Urchristentums: NTS 38 (1992) 430-447.

5534 **Taylor** Nicholas, Paul, Antioch and Jerusalem; a study in relationships and authority in earliest Christianity [diss. Durham 1990, DDunn J.]: jNsu 66. Sheffield 1992, JstOT. 271 p. £32.50; sb. £24.50. 1-85075-331-8 [TLZ 118,233, J. *Becker*]. – RExpTim 104 (1992s) 23 (J. *Proctor*).

5535 a) *Vargas-Machuca* Antonio, Jesús, ¿fundador del cristianismo?; – b) *Salas* Antonio, Génesis de la experiencia cristiana; – c) *Rius-Camps* Josep, Orígenes del cristianismo; perspectiva de Lucas (Hch I-XII); – d) *Piñero* Antonio, Cristianismo y gnosticismo; fijando fronteras; – e) *Sánchez Díaz* Carlos J., La religión cristiana; decantando doctrinas: BibFe 18,54 (1992) 301-312 / 313-360 / 361-406 / 407-428 / 429-457.

5536 *Volz* Carl A., Pastoral life and practice in the early Church 1990 ➤ 6,5531: RRelStT 11,2 (1991) 103-5 (H. O. *Maier*).

5537 **Wander** Bern, Trennungsprozesse zwischen 'frühem Christentum' und Judentum im 1. Jahrhundert n. Ch.: Diss. DBerger K. Heidelberg 1992. – RTLv 24, p. 550.

F8.5 **Ascensio, Pentecostes; ministerium Petri** – *Act 1 ...*

5538 *Walsh* Brian J., *Keesmaat* Sylvia C., Reflections on the Ascension: TLond 95 (1992) 193-200.

5539 *Weissenbuehler* Wayne, Acts 1:1-11 [Ascension]: Interpretation 46 (1992) 61-65.

5540 **Wilcke** Karin, Christi Himmelfahrt; ihre Darstellung in der europäischen Literatur von der Spätantike bis zum ausgehenden Mittelalter: BeitÄltLitG, 1991 ➤ 7,4673*: ᴿStiZt 210 (1992) 861s (W. *Loggen*).

5541 *Ellis* E. E., 'The end of the earth' (Acts 1:8): BuBRes 1 (WL 1991) 123-132 [Spain not Rome; < NTAbs 37, p. 47].

5542 **Co** M. Aricia, The composite summaries in Acts 2-5; a study of Luke's use of summary as a narrative technique: diss. Lv 1990, ᴰ*Delobel* J. liv-420 p. – TvT [= TsTNijm] 32,88.

5543 *Constant* P., Forme textuelle et justesse doctrinale de l'AT dans le Nouveau; la citation du Psaume 16 dans le discours d'Actes 2: Baptist Review of Theology 2,1 (Gormley ON 1992) 4-15 [< NTAbs 37, p. 47].

5544 *a)* *Fabris* Rinaldo, La Pentecoste e le genti; At 2,1-47; – *b)* *De Lorenzi* Lorenzo, 'Iddio non è parziale' At 10,34c: ➤ 339, ParSpV 26 (1992) 127-140 / 141-174.

5545 *Jarvis* Peter G., [Acts 2,1-13] What was Luke getting at? [not a realist account of the past, but a vision of a future when people from every nation will hear and understand God's word]: ExpTim 103 (1992s) 240s.

5546 *Dominy* Bert B., Spirit, Church, and mission; theological implication of Pentecost: SWJT 35,2 (1992s) 34-39.

5547 *Mitchell* Alan C., The social function of friendship in Acts 2:44-47 and 4:32-37: JBL 111 (1992) 255-272.

5548 *Webber* Randall C., 'Why were the heathen so arrogant?' The socio-rhetorical strategy of Acts 3-4: BibTB 22 (1992) 19-25.

5549 *Juel* D., Hearing Peter's speech in Acts 3; meaning and truth in interpretation: WWorld 12,1 (1992) 43-50.

5549* **Carrón Pérez** J., El Mesías escondido y su manifestación; tradición literaria y trasfondo judio de Hch 3,19-26 [dis. Burgos 1985]: Fac. Burgos. M 1991. 165 p. – Carthaginensia 9, 477 (R. *Sanz Valdivieso*).

5550 *Carrón Pérez* Julián, El significado de *apokatástasis* en Hch 3,21: ➤ 135, ᶠMuñoz Iglesias S., EstBib 50 (1992) 375-394.

5551 *Pietras* Henryk, ℗ [Act 3,21] L'*apokatástasis* secondo i Padri della Chiesa; la speranza della salvezza o l'amnestia universale: ColcT 62,3 (1992) 21-41; ital. 41.

5552 **Schubert** Judith M., The image of Jesus as the Prophet like Moses in Luke-Acts as advanced by Luke's reinterpretation of Dt 18:15,18 in Acts 3:22 and 7:37; diss. Fordham, ᴰ*Giblin* C. H. NY 1992. 307 p. 92-23825.

5553 *Culpepper* Hugo, Acts 4,12 (expository): RExp 89 (1992) 85-87.

5554 *Barbi* Augusto, La preghiera della comunità perseguitata (At 4,23-31): ➤ 338, ParSpV 25 (1992) 101-115.

5555 *Olsen* Glenn W., One heart and one soul (Acts 4.32 and 34) in Dʜuoᴅᴀ's 'Manual': ChH 61 (1992) 23-33.

5555* *a)* *Bartchy* S. Scott, Community of goods in Acts; idealization or social reality; – *b)* *Betz* Hans D., The Sermon on the Mount in Matthew's interpretation: ➤ 104, ᶠKoester H. 1991, 309-318 / 258-275.

5556 *Barton* Stephen C., The comunal dimension of earliest Christianity; a critical survey of the field: JTS 43 (1992) 399-427.

5557 *O'Toole* Robert F., *a)* Ananias [Acts 5,1; + 9,10; 23,1; Tob 5,13; Judith 8,1]; – *b)* Sapphira: ➤ 741, AnchorBD 1 (1992) 224s / 5,980s.

5558 **Brehm** Harold A., [Acts 6s] The role of the 'Hellenists' in Christian origins; a critique of representative models in light of an exegetical study of Acts 6-8: diss. SW Baptist Theol. Sem. 1992. 295 p. 92-31652. – DissA 53 (1992s) 1957s-A.

5559 **Hill** Craig C., [Acts 6,1-8,4] Hellenists and Hebrews; reappraising division within the earliest church [diss. Oxford, ᴰ*Sanders* E.]. Mp 1992, Fortress. x-237 p. $25. 0-8006-2506-6 [NTAbs 36, p. 264]. – ᴿComSev 25 (1992) 271s (M. de *Burgos*); JStNT 48 (1992) 127 (C. M. *Tuckett*).

5560 *Dombrowski* Bruno W. W., Synagōgē in Acts 6:2: ➤ 132, ᶠMɪʟɪᴋ J. 1992, 53-65.

5561 *Tsitsigos* Spyros K., Ⓖ What was the task of the seven deacons?: DeltioVM 21,12 (1992) 52-58.

5562 **Légasse** Simon, Stephanos; histoire et discours d'Étienne dans les Actes des Apôtres: LDiv 147. P 1992, Cerf. 262 p. F 130. 2-204-04383-4. [NTAbs 36, p. 403]. – ᴿEsprVie 102 (1992) 409s (E. *Cothenet*); ScEspr 44 (1992) 230s (P.-É. *Langevin*); TvT 32 (1992) 415 (W. H. *Berflo*).

5563 **White** John P., Lucan composition of Acts 7:2-53 in the light of the author's use of OT texts: diss. SW Baptist Theol. Sem. 1992, ᴰ*Cranford* L. – DissA 53 (1992s) 1978-A.

5564 *Boespflug* François, 'Voici que je contemple les cieux ouverts ...' (Ac 7,55s); sur la lapidation d'Étienne et sa vision dans l'art médiéval (IXᵉ-XVIᵉ siècles): RevSR 66 (1992) 263-295; 12 fig.

5565 *Gow* Murray D., [Act 8,4s; 5,1s] Simony — an evangelical virtue [... 'Spirit's presence in the life of the church in the way people are liberated from their attachment to material possessions']: Evangel 9,2 (1991) 26-29.

5566 *Papp* Benjamin, [Acts 8:26-40] The Finance Minister's journey: ExpTim 103 (1991s) 276s.

5567 **Spencer** F. Scott, [Acts 8,(4-) 26-40] The portrait of Philip in Acts; a study of roles and relations [diss. Durham, ᴰ*Dunn* J.]: jNsu 67. Sheffield 1992, Academic. 320 p. £30; sb. £22.50. 1-85075-340-7. – ᴿExpTim 104 (1992s) 219s (I. H. *Marshall*).

5568 *Spencer* F. Scott, [Acts 8,26-40] The Ethiopian eunuch and his Bible; a social-science analysis: BibTB 22 (1992) 155-165.

5569 *Das* A. Andrew, Acts 8[,39] Water, baptism, and the Spirit: ConcordJ 19 (1993) 108-135.

5570 **Sabugal** S., La conversione di S. Paolo [Análisis exegético sobre...]. R 1992, Dehoniane. 351 p. Lᵐ 35. ᴿAsprenas 39 (1992) 591s (G. *Di Palma*).

5570* **Carpinelli** Francis, A source- and redaction-critical analysis of the three accounts of Paul's Damascus experience, Acts 9:1-19; 22,3-16; 26,9-18: diss. Regis College, ᴰ*Plevnik* J. Toronto 1992. – SR 22,537.

5571 *Witherup* Ronald D. [Acts 9,22.26] Functional redundancy in the Acts of the Apostles; a case study: JStNT 48 (1992) 67-86.

5572 (Congo Jorge) **Casimiro,** Etapas do nascimento duma igreja segundo o episódio de Cornélio (Act. 10,1-11,18); dinámica do encontro em Cristo: diss. Urbaniana, ᴰ*Virgulin* S. R 1992. xiv-308 p.

5573 **Łukasz** Czesław, Evangelizzazione e conflitto; indagine sulla coerenza letteraria e tematica della pericope di Cornelio (At 10,1-11,18); diss. Pont. Ist. Biblico, ᴰ*Kilgallen* J. R 1992. – AcPIB 9,808.858s; RTLv 24, p. 548.

5574 *Esler* Philip F., [Acts 10:44-48] Glossolalia and the admission of Gentiles into the early Christian community: BibTB 22 (1992) 136-142.

5575 *Sanders* Jack T., [Acts 11,19-26] Jewish Christianity in Antioch before the time of Hadrian; where does the identity lie?: ➤ 478, SBL Sem. 31 (1992) 346-361.

5576 *Greet* Kenneth G., [Acts 12] Meanwhile [... some hedging on the angel-miracles]: ExpTim 104 (1992s) 117s.

F8.7   Act 13 ... *Itinera Pauli,* Paul's Journeys.

5577 *Tremolada* Pierantonio, Paolo fondatore e pastore (Atti): ParVi 36,1 ('Figure ministeriali nel NT' 1991) 35-44 (6-34.86-132, *al.*).

5578 **Eck** J. van, Paulus en de koningen; politieke aspecten van het boek Handelingen. Franeker 1989, van Wijnen. 143 p. *f*22.50. 90-5194-014-9. – ᴿNedTTs 46 (1992) 162 (J. *Smit Sibinga*).

5579 *Ellul* Danielle, Antioche de Pisidie; une prédication ... trois credos? (Actes 13,13-43): FgNt 5 (1992) 3-14; Eng. 14.

Taylor Nicholas, Paul, Antioch and Jerusalem 1992 ➤ 5534.

5581 **Won** Rodney M., Paul's contextual approach for evangelizing the Jews and the Gentiles against the background of Acts 13:16-41 and Acts 17:22-31: diss. SWBaptist Theol. Sem. 1992. 272 p. 92-23546. – DissA 53 (1992s) 557-A.

5582 **Meierding** Paul, [Ac 14,1s] Jews and Gentiles; a narrative and rhetorical analysis of the implied audience in Acts: diss. Luther NW Theol. Sem. 1992. 358 p. 93-11101. – DissA 53 (1992s) 4359s-A.

5583 *Slater* Thomas B., The possible influence of LXX Exodus 20:11 on Acts 14:15: AndrUnS 30 (1992) 151s.

5584 *Suggit* John N., 'The Holy Spirit and we resolved ...' (Acts 15-28): JTSAf 79 (1992) 38-48 [< TContext 10, p. 18].

5585 *Nolland* John, Acts 15; discerning the will of God in changing circumstances: Crux 27,1 (1991) 30-34.

5586 *Jefford* Clayton N., Tradition and witness in Antioch; Acts 15 and Didache 6: ➤ 173, ᶠSMITH T., PerspRelSt 29,4 (1992) 409-419.

5587 *Garcia-Viana* Caro L.F., El concilio de Jerusalén como experiencia sinodal de la Iglesia primitiva: Almogaren 3,5 (1990) 63-78 [< RET 51,408].

5588 *Sanders* Jack T., [Acts 15 ...] Circumcision of Gentile converts, the root of hostility: BR 7,1 (1991) 20-25.44.

5589 *Taylor* Justin, Ancient texts and modern critics; [Didascalia Apostolorum shows awareness of three problems in] Acts 15,1-34: RB 99 (1992) 373-8; franç. 373.

5590 *Sandt* Huub van de, An explanation of Acts 15.6-21 in the light of Deuteronomy 4.29-35 (LXX): JStNT 46 (1992) 73-97.

5591 *Gillman* John, Hospitality in Acts 16: ➤ 115, ᶠLAMBRECHT J., LvSt 17 (1992) 181-196.

5592 **Adinolfi** Marco, ➤ d147, [Atti 16,8 ...] Ellenismo e Bibbia 1991 ➤ 7,171: ᴿAsprenas 39 (1992) 590s (A. *Rolla*, sull'unico inedito, 'Sogni di S. Paolo negli Atti; confronto con ERODOTO').

5594 *Pellicia* Flora, Pablo y Lucas, ayer, hoy y mañana: RBiArg 54,45 (1992) 27-41.

5595 **Wehnert** Jürgen, [Apg 16,10 ...] Die Wir-Passagen 1989 ➤ 5,5333 ... 7,4710: ᴿTLZ 117 (1992) 363-5 (C. *Burchard*).

5596 **Thornton** Claus-Jürgen, Der Zeuge des Zeugen [Diss. Tü 1989 ᴰ*Hengel* M.]: WUNT 56, 1991 ➤ 7,4711: ᴿBZ 36 (1992) 274-6 (R. *Schnackenburg*); ExpTim 103 (1991s) 272 (E. *Best*); TR 88 (1992) 9s (G. *Schneider*).

5596* *Proctor* John, [Acts 17:22-34] The Gospel from Athens; Paul's speech before the Areopagus and the Evangel for today: Evangel 10,3 (1992) 69-72.

5597 *Sciberras* Paul, [Acts 17,22-31] The figure of Paul in the Acts of the Apostles; the Areopagus speech: MeliT 43,1 (1992) 1-15.

5598 *Sabugal* Santos, El kerigma de Pablo en el Areópago ateniense (Act 17,22-31); análisi histórico-tradicional: RAg 31 (1990) 505-534.

5599 **Tapweti-Taduggoronno** Irmiyah N.A., Paul in Athens, the Athenian agora: diss. Harvard, ᴰ*Koester* H. CM 1992. 92-38307. – HarvTR 85 (1992) 503; DissA 53 (1992s) 3947-A.

5600 *Edwards* M.J., Quoting ARATUS; Acts 17,28: ZNW 83 (1992) 266-9.

5601 *Cox* William C., [Act 18,18-23] When Paul got a haircut: ExpTim 103 (1991s) 337-9.

5602 *Murphy-O'Connor* Jerome, [Acts 18,18...] Prisca and Aquila, traveling tentmakers and church builders: BR 8,6 (1992) 40-51.62; ill.

5603 *Slingerland* Dixon, SUETONIUS Claudius 25.4, Acts 18, and Paulus OROSIUS' Historiarum adversus paganos libri VII; dating the Claudian expulsion(s) of Roman Jews: JQR 83 (1992s) 127-144.

5604 *Ross* J.M., The extra words in Acts 18:21: NT 34 (1992) 247-249.

5605 *Lampe* Peter, Acta 19 im Spiegel der ephesischen Inschriften: BZ 36 (1992) 59-76.

5606 *Cunningham* Richard, [Acts 19; 1 Cor 16,9] Wide open doors and many adversaries: RExp 89 (1992) 89-98.

5607 *Strange* W.A., The text of Acts 19.1: NTS 38 (1992) 145-8.

5608 **Martini** Carlo, [Acts 20,18-38] After some years; reflections on the ministry of the priest. Dublin/SF 1991, Veritas/Ignatius. 125 p. $10. 1-85390-038-9 [TDig 39,372].

5609 *Plümacher* Eckhard, Eine THUKYDIDESreminiszenz in der Apostelgeschichte (Act 20,33-35 – Thuk. II 97,3f.): ZNW 83 (1992) 270-275.

5610 *Viviano* Benedict T., *Taylor* Justin, Sadducees, angels, and resurrection (Acts 23:8-9): JBL [109 (1990) 493-7, DAUBE D.] 111 (1992) 498-8: nowhere else is it attested that the Sadducees deny angels; and here also they deny only human survival after death either as *angelos* or as *pneuma*.

ᴱGalea Michael, *al.*, St. Paul in Malta; a compendium of Pauline studies [against WARNECKE]. 1992 → 352.

5611 **Warnecke** Heinz [Die tatsächliche Romfahrt, ᴰ1987 → 3,5226 ... 6,5611], + *Schirrmacher* Thomas, [p.181-255, Plädoyer für die historische Geschichtlichkeit der Apg und der Pastoralbriefe] War Paulus wirklich auf Malta? Theologie für die Gemeinde. Stu 1992, Hänssler. 255 p. 3-7751-1617-6.

5612 *Metallinos* Georgios A., ⊝ Paul and Cephallonia [WARNECKE H.): Kleronomia 21 (1989) 207-215.

5613 *Suhl* Alfred, Zum Titel *prôtos tês nēsou* (Erster der Insel) Apg 28,7: BZ 36 (1992) 220-6.

5614 **Johnson** Rockford A., [Ac 28,26] The narrative function of the quotation of Isaiah 6,9-10 and the concomitant hear-see motif in the Book of Acts: diss. SW Baptist theol. sem. 1992. 282 p. 92-23537. – DissA 53 (1992s) 843-A.

XIV. Johannes

Gl *Corpus Johanneum* .1 **John and his community.**

5615 **Bull** Klaus-Michel, Gemeinde zwischen Integration und Abgrenzung; ein Beitrag zur Frage nach dem Ort der johanneischen Gemeinde(n) in der

Geschichte des Urchristentums [Diss. Rostock 1990s ➤ 7,4723]: BeitBExT 24. Fra 1992, Lang. XV-257 p. DM 77 pa. 3-631-44135-5 [NTAbs 37, p. 274].

5616 **Eckle** W., Den der Herr liebhatte — Rätsel um den Evangelisten Johannes; zum historischen Verständnis seiner autobiographischen Andeutungen [Diss.Tü 1991, ᴰ*Hommel* H.]. Ha 1991, Kovać. x-258 p. DM 49,50. 3-925630-72-4 [NTAbs 37, p. 276].

5617 **Ernst** J., Johannes, ein theologisches Portrait. Dü 1991, Patmos. 137 p. DM 19,80. 3-491-77709-7 [NTAbs 37, p. 436].

5618 **Ernst** Josef, Juan, retrato teológico ᵀ*Ruiz-Garrido* Constantino. Barc 1992, Herder. 190 p. pt. 1553. 84-254-1810-3. – ᴿActuBbg 30 (1992) 194 (J. *O'Callaghan*).

5619 **Grassi** Joseph A., The secret identity of the beloved disciple [... adopted son of Jesus]. NY 1992, Paulist. 135 p. $8. 0-8091-3121-8. – ᴿBR 8,5 (1992) 49 (Elizabeth *Johnson*).

5620 ᴱ**Kaestli** J.-D., *al.*, La communauté johannique 1990 ➤ 6,538*; 7,4727: ᴿCBQ 54 (1992) 193s (C. R. *Koester:* tit.pp.; comments); ChH 60 (1991) 525s (A. J. *Springer*); NedTTs 46 (1992) 69s (M.J.J. *Menken*); RivStoLR 27 (1991) 334-340 (Giuliana *Iacopino*).

5621 *Koester* Helmut, The story of the Johannine tradition: Sewanee TR 36 (1992s) 17-32.

5621* *a) Kraabel* A. Thomas, The God-fearers meet the beloved disciple; – *b) Tanzer* Sarah J., Salvation is *for* the Jews; secret Christian Jews in the Gospel of John; – *c) Lohse* Eduard, The Revelation of John and Pauline theology; – *d) Hills* Julian V., A genre for 1 John: ➤ 104, ᶠKOESTER H. 1991, 276-284 / 285-300 / 358-366 / 367-377.

5622 *a) La Potterie* Ignace de, Anticristi e Anticristo; la scissione nella comunità giovannea e il suo senso cristologico; – *b) Studer* Basil, Spiritualità giovannea in AGOSTINO: ➤ 485, Efeso II 1991/2, 131-151 / 73-86.

5623 *a) La Potterie* Ignace de, Il discepolo che Gesù amava; – *b) Philippe* Marie-Dominique, Jean le Théologien — l'Évangile des rencontres personnelles; – *c) Mara* Maria Grazia, Presenza della tradizione giovannea nelle prime comunità cristiane: ➤ 7,451, Efeso I, 1990/91, 33-55 / 57-74 / 111-127.

5624 *a) McHugh* John, 'In him was life' — John's Gospel and the parting of the ways; – *b) Rowland* Christopher, The parting of the ways; the evidence of Jewish and Christian apocalyptic and mystical material; – *c) Chester* Andrew, The parting of the ways; eschatology and Messianic hope: ➤ 467, Parting 1989/92, 123-158 / 213-237 / 239-313.

5625 **Painter** John, The quest for the Messiah; the history, literature and theology of the Johannine community 1991 ➤ 7,245: ᴿExpTim 103 (1991s) 345 (J. M. *Lieu*).

5626 **Pryor** John W., John, evangelist of the covenant people; the narrative and themes of the Fourth Gospel. L/DG 1992, Darton-LT/InterVarsity. ix-234 p. $20 pa. 0-232-51938-2 / 0-8308-1762-X [TDig 40,182]. – ᴿExpTim 104 (1992s) 154 (S. S. *Smalley*).

5627 **Puthenkandathil** Eldho, 'Philos' a designation for the Jesus-disciple relationship; an exegetico-theological investigation of the term in the Fourth Gospel: Diss. Pont. Univ. Gregoriana, ᴰ*Caba* J. Roma 1992. 388 p.; extr. 3942. – InfPUG 25/124,27; RTLv 24, p. 549.

5628 **Quast** Kevin, Peter and the Beloved Disciple ... community in crisis 1989 ➤ 5,5354 ... 7,4730: ᴿThemelios 17,2 (1991s) 21s (D. A. *Carson* is not convinced).

5629 **Rensberger** David, Overcoming the world; politics and community in the Gospel of John 1989 ➤ 7,4731: ᴿScotJT 45 (1992) 410s (C. *Warner*); Themelios 17,1 (1991s) 27s (D. A. *Carson:* U.S. title Johannine faith and liberating community).

5630 *Schenke* Ludger, Das johanneische Schisma [1 Jn 2,18s; 4,1s] und die 'Zwölf' (Johannes 6.60-71): NTS 38 (1992) 105-121.

5631 **Schnelle** Udo, *a*) Antidoketische Christologie im JEv; FRL 144, 1987 ➤ 3,5237 ... 6,5628: ᴿTsTKi 62 (1991) 293s (H. *Kvalbein*). – *b*) Antidocetic Christology in the Gospel of John; an investigation of the place of the Fourth Gospel in the Johannine School [1987], ᵀ*Maloney* Linda M. Mp 1992, Fortress. xi-275 p. $33. 0-8006-2592-7 [NTAbs 37, p.284]; – ᴿExpTim 104 (1992) 344 (D. *Wenham*); TBR 5,3 (1992) 25 (T. *Williams*).

5632 *a*) *Segalla* Giuseppe, 'Il discepolo che Gesù amava' e la tradizione giovannea; – *b*) *Panimolle* Salvatore, Identità e storia della comunità giovannea; 'status quaestionis'; – *c*) *Grech* Prospero, La comunità giovannea nei cc. 7 e 8 del Vangelo di Giovanni; – *d*) *Fabris* Rinaldo, Tensioni e divisioni nella comunità giovannea; Vangelo e Lettere: ➤ 481, Giovannismo 1989 = RicStoB 3,2 (1991) 11-35 / 37-57 / 59-68 / 69-80.

5633 **Stowasser** Martin, Johannes der Täufer im Vierten Evangelium; eine Untersuchung zu seiner Bedeutung für die johanneische Gemeinde [Diss. Wien 1991 ➤ 7,4735]: ÖsBSt 12. Klosterneuburg 1992, ÖsKBW. [viii-] 271 p. ᴅᴍ 37. 3-85396-084-7. – ➤ 4691.

5634 **Wahlde** Urban C. von, The Johannine commandments ... 1 Jn/Tradition 1990 ➤ 6,5633; 7,4237: ᴿBiblica 73 (1992) 130-5 (G. *Segalla*); CBQ 54 (1992) 182s (J. E. *Bruns*); RTLv 23 (1992) 380-2 (J.-P. *Kaefer:* outil indispensable d'une recherche passionnante).

G1.2 **Evangelium Johannis:** *textus, commentarii.*

5635 **Barrett** C. K., Das Evangelium nach Johannes [1955, ²1978], ᵀ1990 ➤ 6,5637; 7,4739: ᴿLuthMon 30 (1991) 94 (E. *Lohse*); TLZ 117 (1992) 120s (P. *Pokorný*).

5636 **Beasley-Murray** George E., John: WordC 36, 1987 ➤ 3,5243 ... 6,5362: ᴿBtS 149 (1992) 122s (W. H. *Harris*); ÉglT 22 (1991) 96-98 (M. *Gourgues*).

5637 ᵀᴱ**Berrouard** M.-F., S. AUGUSTIN, Homélies sur l'évangile de Saint Jean 34-43 / 44-54: Œuvres 73ab. P 1988s, Brepols. 539 p.; 555 p. je Fb 1900 ➤ 4,5411* ... 7,4740: ᴿEsprVie 102 (1992) 681 (Y.-M. *Duval*); RHE 87 (1992) 154-6 (M. *Testard*); TR 88 (1992) 389s (C. *Mayer*).

5638 ᵀᴱ**Blanc** Cécile, ORIGÈNE, Commentaire sur Saint Jean V (28, Jn 11, 39-57; 32, Jn 13,2-33): SChr 385. P 1992, Cerf. 392 p. F 324. 2-204-04678-7 [NRT 115,431, V. *Roisel*].

5639 ᵀᴱ**Bougerol** Jacques Guy, San BONAVENTURA, Commento al Vangelo di Giovanni: 7 vol. in 2. R 1990s, Città Nuova. 406 p.; 472 p.; ill. Lit. 70.000 ognuno. [CC 144/3,314s; A. *Orazzo*; p.316 sui Sermoni domenicali].

5640 **Carson** D. A., The Gospel according to John: Pillar comm. 1991 ➤ 7, 4743; $30: ᴿBtS 149 (1992) 122 (W. H. *Harris*); CBQ 54 (1992) 555s (J. E. *Bruns*); CritRR 5 (1992) 186-9 (F. F. *Segovia:* spirited and learned defense of traditional sound interpretation); GraceTJ 12 (1991) 296-8 (J. D. *Colwell*); RefTR 51 (1992) 69s (D. *Peterson*); TvT [= TsTNijm] 32 (1992) 194s (S. van *Tilborg:* een heel eigen positie); WestTJ 54 (1992) 376s (M. *Silva*).

5641 **Clancy** F.G.J., St. AUGUSTINE of Hippo on Christ, his Church, and the Holy Spirit; a study of the 'De Baptismo' and the 'Tractatus in Iohannis Evangelium': Diss. Oxford 1992. – RTLv 24, p. 551.

5642 ^E**Corona** Raimondo, Il Vangelo secondo Giovanni; lettura esegetico-esistenziale (*Bottini* C.; *Adinolfi* M., *al.*): Settimana Biblica Abruzzese, 3-7.VII.1990. L'Aquila 1991, Curia O.F.M. 318 p.

5643 **Delebecque** É., Év/Epp de Jean: CahRB 23.25 ➤ 3,5250 ... 7,4745: ^RPeCa 244 (1990) 84s (Y. *Daoudal*).

5644 **Ehrman** Bart D., *Fee* Gordon D., *Holmes* Michael W., The text of the Fourth Gospel in the writings of ORIGEN, 1 (of 2): SBL NT GkF 3. Atlanta 1992, Scholars. x-499 p. $45; sb./pa. $30. 1-55540-788-9; –9–7 [NTAbs 37, p. 276].

5645 **Fabris** Rinaldo, Giovanni; Commenti Biblici. R 1992, Borla. 1150 p. 88-263-0870-5. – ^RLetture 47 (1992) 865s (G. *Ravasi*); StPatav 39 (1992) 653s (G. *Segalla*).

5646 **Fatica** Luigi, I commentari a Giovanni di TEODORO M. e di CIRILLO A. 1988 ➤ 4,5418 ... 7,4746 (4746*): ^RRÉAug 37 (1991) 174-7 (J. N. *Guinot*).

5647 **Fischer** Bonifatius: Varianten zu Johannes: VLatGesch 18, 1991 ➤ 7, 4747: ^RJTS 43 (1992) 633-5 (J. K. *Elliott:* further shows that the Neo-Vulgata often has shaky Latin-text support in its desire to provide a Latin counterpart to NESTLE-ALAND²⁶).

5648 **Gargano** L., 'Lectio divina' su [Mt 1989; Mc Lc 1991] il Vangelo di Giovanni I: Conversazioni bibliche. Bo 1992, Dehoniane. 168 p. Lit. 20.000. 88-10-78930-6 [NTAbs 37, p. 277].

5649 ^{TE}**Garzón Bosque** Isabel, *Garcia-Jalón* Santiago, Juan CRISÓSTOMO, Homilías sobre el Evangelio de San Juan; introd. *Viciano* Alberto; notas *Zanna* Alfredo del: BtPatr 15. M 1991, Ciudad Nueva. 354 p. 84-86987-33-4. – ^RScripTPamp 24 (1992) 684s (M. *Merino*).

5650 **Grayston** Kenneth, The Gospel of John: Narrative [= Epworth] Comm 1990 ➤ 6,5645: ^RCritRR 5 (1992) 205-7 (G. M. *Burge:* continues trustworthy Epworth Preacher's comm. tradition); JTS 43 (1992) 813s (J. C. *Fenton:* extraordinarily lively and creative).

5651 **Hunt** Desmond, [Jn 1-9] More than we can ask or imagine. Toronto 1992, Anglican. 96 p. $10. 0-924846-43-6. – ^RExpTim 104 (1992s) 22 (F. *Franklin:* reflections, sometimes refreshing).

5652 ^{TE}**Jeanne d'Arc** sr., Év. selon Jean 1990 ➤ 6,5647: ^RRÉG 105 (1992) 634 (A. *Wartelle*).

5653 **Kilgallen** John J., A brief commentary on the Gospel of John. Lewiston NY 1992, Mellen. xxii-253 p. 0-7734-2346-X.

5654 **Koen** Lars, The saving Passion ... CYRIL A., John 1991 ➤ 7,4955: ^RExpTim 103 (1991s) 377 (Frances M. *Young*); RSPT 76 (1992) 628-632 (G.-M. de *Durand*).

5655 **Kreitzer** Larry, The Gospel according to John: Oxford Regents Park College study guides (first to appear) 1990. 123 p. £5. 0-951-81040-5. – ^RExpTim 104 (1992s) 22 (F. *Franklin*).

5656 **Léon-Dufour** X., Lecture II (5-12) 1990 ➤ 3,5359 ... 5,4749: ^RBiblica 73 (1992) 427-9 (J. *Beutler:* the up-to-date outlooks are chiefly in the various 'concluding reflections'); VSp 146 (1992) 247 (H. *Cousin*).

5657 **Léon-Dufour** Xavier, Lettura dell'Evangelo secondo Giovanni I (1-4) 1990 ➤ 6,5650c: ^RLaurentianum 33 (1992) 229-231 (L. *Martignani*); Lateranum 57 (1991) 595s (R. *Penna*); RivB 40 (1992) 249-252 (L. *Cilia*).

5658 **León-Dufour** X., Lectura del Ev. de Jn 5-12. S 1992 ➤ 6,5650b; 7,4750: Sígueme. 402 p. – ^RREspir 51 (1992) 536s (S. *Castro*).

5660 **Marchadour** Alain, L'Évangile de Jean, commentaire pastoral. P 1992, Centurion-Novalis. 264 p. F 135. – ^RBLitEc 93 (1992) 404 (S. *Légasse*); EsprVie 102 (1992) 244 (É. *Cothenet*); Études 376 (1992) 712s (P. *Gibert*).

5661 **Pasquetto** Virgilio, Abbiamo visto la sua gloria; lettura e messaggio del Vangelo di Giovanni. R 1992, Dehoniane. 278 p. [Teresianum 44,741s, B. *Moriconi*].
5662 **Reynier** C., L'évangile selon saint Jean. P 1991, Médiasèvres. 43 p. [NRT 115, 198, Y. *Simoens*].
5663 **Schenke** L., Das Johannesevangelium; Einführung — Text — dramatische Gestalt: Urban-TB 446. Stu 1992, Kohlhammer. 230 p. DM 28. 3-17-011925-5 [NTAbs 37, p. 284].
5664 **Servotte** Herman, Johannes litterair; de geest van de letter in het vierde evangelie. Averbode / Boxtel 1992, Altiora / KBStichting. 119 p. Fb 390. – ᴿStreven 59 (1992s) 1046s (P. *Beentjes*).
5665 *Spada* C. A., Aspetti della polemica antimarcionita nel Commento al Vangelo di Giovanni: ➤ 531, Origeniana V, 1989/92, 85-91.
5666 *a) Studer* Basil, I 'tractatus in Ioannem' di Sant'AGOSTINO; – *b) Speigl* Jakob, Il Vangelo di Giovanni, la 'primizia' dei commenti neotestamentari d'ORIGENE; – *c) Rossano* Piero, Ipotesi di un 'corpus ephesinum Novi Testamenti': ➤ 7,451, Efeso I, 1990/91, 135-146 / 129-134 / 17-31.
5667 **Talbert** Charles H., Reading John; a literary and theological commentary on the Fourth Gospel and the Johannine Epistles: Reading the NT. NY 1992, Crossroad. xv-284 p. $24. 0-8245-1179-4 [TDig 40,89].
5668 **Tasker** R.V.G., The Gospel according to St. John; an introduction and commentary. Tyndale NT. Leicester/GR 1992 = 1960, Inter-Varsity/Eerdmans. 237 p. 0-85111-853-4 / GR 0-8028-1403-4.
5669 **Voigt** Gottfried, Licht — Liebe — Leben; das Evangelium nach Johannes: BibT Schwerpunkte 6. Gö 1991, Vandenhoeck & R. 296 p. DM 38. – ᴿTvT 32 (1992) 313 (A. van *Diemen:* verstaanbar, sympatiek).
5670 **Wallace** R. S., The Gospel of John, chapters 1-11; pastoral and theological studies. E 1991, Scottish Academic. 216 p. £7.50. 0-7073-0700-7. – ᴿExpTim 104 (1992s) 22 (E. *Franklin*).
5671 *Wengert* Timothy J., Caspar CRUCIGER Sr.'s 1546 'Enarratio' on John's Gospel; an experiment in ecclesiological exegesis: ChH 61 (1992) 60-73.
5672 *Wyrwa* Dietmar, AUGUSTINS geistliche Auslegung des Johannesevangeliums: ➤ 483*, ᴱ*Oort* J. van, 1991/2, 185-216.

G1.3 **Introductio** in *Evangelium Johannis.*

5673 **Ashton** John, Understanding the Fourth Gospel 1991 ➤ 7,4769: ᴿAngl-TR 74 (1992) 504-6 (S. B. *Marrow*); DeltioVM 21,11 (1992) 113-122 (S. *Agourides*, ☺); HeythJ 33 (1992) 332-4 (W. A. *Meeks:* a deeply learned and cultured writer); JTS 43 (1992) 594-600 (D. M. *Smith:* successfully most ambitious work since DODD; most important figure of the interval was BULTMANN, from whom HOSKYNS was not so very far off — nor Ashton from Hoskyns); RelStR 18 (1992) 328s (also D. M. *Smith*); ScotJT 45 (1992) 245-251 (B. *Lindars* †); SWJT 35,2 (1992s) 45 (G. L. *Munn* praises, while continuing to hold firmly that the gospel was written by the Apostle John for the purpose expressed in 20,31); TLond 95 (1992) 385s (J.D.G. *Dunn:* erudite and elegant); TS 53 (1992) 744-6 (R. E. *Brown:* 'gives primacy to the understanding of John through the optic of his stages of development'); TvT [= TsTNijm] 32 (1992) 195 (P. *Chatelion Counet:* inspirerend en geïnspireerd).
5674 **Bauer** Bruno, Kritik der evangelischen Geschichte des Johannes. NY 1990, Olms. xiv-440. DM 108. – ᴿSWJT 35,1 (1992s) 55 (E. E. *Ellis:* akin to SIMONIS W. 1990).

5675 **Beasley-Murray** George R., John: Word **Themes** 1989 ➤ 5,5388:   RJEv-
TS 35 (1992) 534s (W. H. *Vermillion*).
5676 **Burge** Gary M., Interpreting the Fourth Gospel. GR 1992, Baker.
185 p. [NTAbs 37, p. 274].
5677 *Hofrichter* B., Johannesevangelium: ➤ 762, NBL II, 8 (1992) 359-369.
5678 *Kieffer* René, Det gåtfulla Johannesevangeliet: SvTKv 67 (1991) 109-112.
5679 *Kysar* Robert, John, epistles of / gospel of: ➤ 741, AnchorBD 3 (1992)
900-912-931.
5680 **Lindars** Barnabas [➤ 271], John: NTGuides 1990 ➤ 6,5676; 7,4782:
RChurchman 106 (1992) 72-74 (D. *Spanner*); Interpretation 46 (1992)
78.80 (M. *Rissi*); ScripB 22/1 (1992) 25 (K. *Grayston*).
5681 *Osiek* Carolyn, With John for the long haul [different from Synoptics
and less concrete; excluded from lectionary cycle]: NewTR 5,1 (1992)
76-80.
5682 **Schenke** Ludger, *al.*, Das Johannesevangelium; Einführung — Text —
dramatische Gestalt, Übersetzung: UrbanTb 446. Stu 1992, Kohlhammer. 230 p.

Bibliographica – **Johannine research.**
5683 *Boer* M. C. de, Narrative criticism, historical criticism, and the Gospel
of John: JStNT 47 (1992) 35-48.
5684 *Edwards* Ruth B., John and the Johannines [BROWN R. E., BARRETT
C. K. ...]: BTrans 43 (1992) 140-151.
5685 *a) Grossi* Vittorino, Nota d'insieme sulla presenza della letteratura
giovannea nella Chiesa di Roma dei primi secoli; – *b) Siniscalco* Paolo,
Giovanni nella catechesi della Chiesa antica: ➤ 485, Efeso II, 1991/2,
87-112 / 173-186.
5686 **Hengel** Martin, The Johannine question 1989 ➤ 5,5397* ... 7,4777:
RAustralBR 38 (1990) 80-83 (J. *Painter*); CBQ 54 (1992) 351-3 (F. E.
Segovia: professedly on authorship of Jn & 1-3 Jn, but ultimately including Apc); ScotJT 45 (1992) 411-3 (S. S. *Smalley*).
5687 *Jackson* Rogers W., The future of the Fourth Gospel: CurrTMiss 19
(1992) 277-280.
5688 *a) Merkel* Helmut, Frühchristliche Autoren über Johannes und die
Synoptiker; – *b) Jonge* Henk J. de, The loss of faith in the historicity of
the Gospels; H. S. REIMARUS (ca. 1750) on John and the Synoptics; – *c)
Verheyden* J., P. Gardner SMITH and 'the turn of the tide'; – *d) Dowell*
Thomas M., Why John rewrote the Synoptics; – *e) Roth* Wolfgang,
Mark, John, and their Old Testament codes: ➤ 465, CIv 39, 1990/2,
403-8 / 409-421 / 423-452 / 453-7 / 458-465.
5689 *a) Neirynck* F., John and the Synoptics 1975-1990; – *b) Barrett* C. K.,
The place of John and the Synoptics within the early history of Christian
thought; – *c) Thyen* Hartwig, Johannes und die Synoptiker; auf der
Suche nach einem neuen Paradigma zur Beschreibung ihrer Beziehungen
anhand von Beobachtungen an Passions- und Ostererzählungen: ➤ 465,
CLv 39, 1990/2, 3-26 / 63-79 / 81-107.
5690 *a) Pacomio* Luciano, Per un contributo alla teologia della storia; appunti; – *b) Siniscalco* Paolo, Giovanni nella catechesi della Chiesa antica;
– *c) Grossi* Vittorino, Nota d'insieme sulla presenza della letteratura
giovannea nella Chiesa di Roma dei primi secoli; – *d) Nobile* Marco,
Alcune note al riguardo del problema storico-religioso del Vangelo di S.
Giovanni: ➤ 485, Efeso 2, 1991/2, 153 [poi 152 di fronte, poi]– 154-172 /
173-186 / 87-112 / 19-28.

5691 **Panimolle** Salvatore A., Gesù di Nazaret nell'ultimo evangelo e nei primi scritti dei Padri: StudiRicB, 1990 ➤ 6,5739: ᴿCritRR 5 (1992) 236-8 (M. *Lattke:* carefully produced); Lateranum 58 (1992) 536s (G. *Ancona*); ParVi 37 (1992) 72s (C. *Burini*); ScripTPamp 24 (1992) 1089 (A. *García-Moreno*).

5692 *Pryor* John W., JUSTIN Martyr and the Fourth Gospel: SecC 9 (1992) 153-169.

5693 **Rábanos Espinosa** R., *Muñoz León* D., Bibliografía joánica 1990 ➤ 6, 5684: ᴿCBQ 54 (1992) 368s (S. B. *Marrow:* 'The question is not whether the advent of the computer doomed bibliographies to extinction, but simply how long it will take'; this kind will be first to fall, with its all-alphabetical classifying); CiuD 204 (1991) 261s (J. *Gutiérrez*); RBiArg 54,45 (1992) 44-46 (A. J. *Levoratti*).

5694 **Schmithals** Walter, Johannesevangelium und Johannesbriefe; Forschungsgeschichte und Analyse: BZNW 64. B 1992, de Gruyter. x-473 p. DM 168. 3-11-013560-4. – ᴿETL 68 (1992) 166-8 (F. *Neirynck*).

5695 **Sloyan** Gerald S., What are they saying about John? 1991 ➤ 7,4792: ᴿCBQ 54 (1992) 801s (R. D. *Witherup*, also on SENIOR D. and KAUFMAN P., all fine); CritRR 5 (1992) 241s (Marianne *Meye Thompson*).

5696 **Smith** D. Moody, John among the Gospels; the relationship in twentieth-century research. Mp 1992, Augsburg-Fortress. xiii-210 p. $13. 0-8006-2530-7. – ᴿETL 68 (1992) 442-4 (F. *Neirynck*); ExpTim 104 (1992s) 153s (S. S. *Smalley*).

5697 *a*) *Smith* D. Moody, The problem of John and the Synoptics in light of the relation between apocryphal and canonical gospels; – *b*) *Weder* Hans, Von der Wende der Welt zum Semeion des Sohnes; – *c*) *Kieffer* René, Jean et Marc; convergences dans la structure et dans les détails: ➤ 465, CLv 39, 1990/2, 147-162 / 127-145 / 109-125.

5698 *Walter* Louis, Regards sur la recherche johannique [KAESTLI J. al., 1987-90; ᴱMARCHADOUR A., ACFÉB 1989/90]: EsprVie 102 (1992) 215-220.

G1.4 *Themata de evangelio Johannis* – **John's Gospel, topics.**

5700 **Brodie** Thomas L., The quest for the origin of John's Gospel; a source-oriented approach. NY 1993, Oxford-UP. x-194 p.

5701 *Dennison* James T.ᴶ, The structure of John's Gospel — the present state of the question: Kerux 7,1 (1992) 37-42.

5702 *Farmer* Craig S., The Johannine signs in the exegesis of Wolfgang MUSCULUS [1497-1563]: diss. Duke, ᴰ*Steinmetz* D. Durham NC 1992. 363 p. 92-37858. – DissA 53 (1992s) 3421-A.

5703 *Fortna* Robert T., The fourth gospel and its predecessor 1988 ➤ 4,5454 ... 7,4772: ᴿAustralBR 38 (1990) 84s (M. *FitzPatrick:* no real answer to criticisms of his 1970 Gospel of Signs); IndTSt 28 (1991) 337-9 (L. *Legrand*); Themelios 17,1 (1991s) 27 (G. M. *Burge*); TLZ 117 (1992) 34-39 (H. *Thyen*).

5704 *a*) *Hainz* Josef, Neuere Auffassungen zur Redaktionsgeschichte des Johannesevangeliums; – *b*) *Hofrichter* Peter, Das Joh.-ev. in der religionsgeschichtlichen Forschung und die Literarkritik des Prologs; – *c*) *Lütgehetmann* Walter, Die Hochzeit von Kana — der Anfang der Zeichen Jesu: ➤ 112*, Mem. KUSS O., Theologie im Werden 1992, 157-176 / 219-246 / 177-197.

5705 **Mlakuzhyil** G., The Christocentric literary structure of the Fourth Gospel: AnBib 117, ᴰ1987 ➤ 3,5286 ... 7,4785: ᴿRivB 40 (1992) 346-8 (G. *Zevini*).

5706 *a*) *Pasquetto* Virgilio, Prospettive redazionali del quarto Vangelo; – *b*) *Filoramo* Giuseppe, Il Vangelo di Giovanni fra gnosi e gnosticismo; – *c*) *Gianotto* Claudio, Il commento di ERACLEONE al Vangelo di Giovanni; – *d*) *Iacopino* Giuliana, Temi giovannei in un testo gnostico, il Secondo discorso del grande Seth (NH VII, 2): ➤ 487*b*, Giovannismo 1989: RicStoB 3,2 (1991) 81-105 / 123-160 / 107-122 / 161-175.

5707 **Ruckstuhl** E., *Dschulnigg* P., Stilkritik und Verfasserfrage im Joh,-Ev.; die johanneische Sprachmerkmale auf dem Hintergrund des NTs und des zeitgenössischen hellenistischen Schrifttums: NOrb 17, 1991 ➤ 7,4790: ᴿETRel 67 (1992) 459s (P. *Kneubühler*).

5708 **Schuchard** Bruce G., Scripture within Scripture; the interrelationship of form and function in the explicit Old Testament citations in the Gospel of John: SBL diss. 133 [Richmond Union 1991, ᴰ*Rissi* M.]. Atlanta 1992, Scholars. xvii-174 p. $40; sb./pa. $25. [NTAbs 37, p. 285].

5709 *a*) *Vanni* Ugo, Il 'segno' in Giovanni; – *b*) *Valgiglio* Ernesto, Aspetti stilistici del quarto Vangelo: ➤ 7,423, Giovanni 1989/91, 39-58 / 59-119.

5710 **Wahlde** Urban C. von, The earliest version of John's Gospel 1989 ➤ 5,5410 ... 7,4799: ᴿJBL 111 (1992) 148-150 (R. T. *Fortna*).

Intuitiones de scopo auctoris – **Narrative Analysis.**

5711 *a*) *Ferrando* Miguel A , Filosofía y evangelio de Juan; – *b*) *Villegas* M. Beltrán, Filosofía y teología en la Biblia; – *c*) *Vergara* O. Roberto, Filosofía y teología: TVida 33 (Santiago de Chile 1992) 27-34 / 13-25 / 5-11.

5712 *a*) *Gorgulho* Maria Laura, Lendo a Bíblia na dinâmica de João, 'O amor de Deus pelos homens'; – *b*) *Ternay* Henri de, *al.*, Uma leitura global da Bíblia na dinâmica da Aliança: EstudosB 33 (1992) 9-30 / 31-40.

5713 **Grenier** Brian, St. John's gospel; a self-directed retreat. Homebush NSW c. 1991, St. Paul. 251 p. A$17. 0-949080-46-2 [AustralasCR 69,135 adv].

5714 **Hanson** Anthony T., † 1991, The prophetic Gospel; a study of John and the OT 1991 ➤ 7,4725: ᴿBZ 36 (1992) 272-4 (R. *Schnackenburg*); CBQ 54 (1992) 780s (J. P. *Heil*); ExpTim 103 (1991s) 216s (Judith *Lieu*); JTS 43 (1992) 185-7 (J. *Ashton:* learned, stimulating, often exasperating); NBlackf 73 (1992) 291-4 (Meg *Davies*); NT 34 (1992) 403-6 (M.J.J. *Menken*); TLond 95 (1992) 300 (K. *Grayston:* where did John get his extra material and his own Christology?).

5715 **Hasitschka** Martin, Sozialgeschichtliche Anmerkungen zum Johannesevangelium: ProtokB 1,1 (1992) 59-67.

5716 **Hopkins** Anthony D., A narratological approach to the development of faith in the Gospel of John: diss. Southern Baptist Theol. Sem. ᴰ*Culpepper* R. 1992. 290 p. 93-02764. – DissA 53 (1992s) 3565-A.

5717 **Kieffer** René, Le monde symbolique de saint Jean: LDiv 137, 1989 ➤ 5,5440 (non 5540 comme 7,4822): ᴿActuBbg 29 (1992) 57 (X. *Alegre*); Carmelus 38 (1991) 212-5 (J. *Velasco Arenas*); TLZ 117 (1992) 279s (H. *Weder*).

5718 *a*) *Marty* François, L'signe, épreuve du croire; le livre qui fait foi; – *b*) *Genuyt* François, L'économie des signes; – *c*) *Lemonon* Jean-Pierre, Chronique johannique (1981-1992): LumièreV 41,209 ('Les signes et la Croix chez saint Jean' 1992) 5-18 / 19-35 / 95-104.

5719 *Moloney* Francis J., Who is 'the reader' in/of the Fourth Gospel?: AustralBR 40 (1992) 20-33.

5720 *Rand* J.A. du, Johannine perspectives; Introduction to the Johannine writings, I. Pretoria 1991, Orion. xii-409 p. 0-7987-0601-3 [NTAbs 37, p. 113].

5721 **Ravasi** G. F., Il Vangelo di Giovanni [10 conferenze S. Fedele]. Bo 1989, Dehoniane. 118 p.; 121 p. Lit. 10.000 ognuno. – ᴿProtestantesimo 47 (1992) 324s (R. *Marchetti*).

5722 **Ravindra** Ravi, The Yoga of the Christ in the Gospel according to St. John. Shaftesbury, Dorset 1990, Element. 234 p. $16 pa. – ᴿParabola 16,1 (1991) 132-5 (J. *George*).

5723 *Reim* Günter, Nordreich — Südreich; der vierte Evangelist als Vertreter christlicher Nordreichstheologie: BZ 36 (1992) 235-240.

5724 **Stibbe** Mark W.G., John as storyteller; narrative criticism and the Fourth Gospel [diss. Nottingham]: SNTS mg 73. C 1992, Univ. xiii-214 p. £30 0-521-41524-1. – ᴿExpTim 104 (1992s) 22 (S. E. *Porter:* the right questions).

5725 **Waldstein** Michael M., The mission of Jesus in John; probes into the 'Apocryphon of John' and the Gospel of John: diss. Harvard, ᴰ*Koester* H. CM 1992. [xiv–] 306 p.

5726 **Wilton** Murray R., Witness as a theme in the Fourth Gospel: diss. Baptist Theol. Sem., ᴰ*Stevens* G. New Orleans 1992. 205 p. 93-11809. – DissA 53 (1992s) 4361-A.

Theologica.

5727 **Beasley-Murray** George R., Gospel of life; theology in the Fourth Gospel (1990 Pasadena-Fuller Payton lectures) 1991 ⇒ 7,4803: ᴿExpTim 104 (1992s) 90 (L. *Kreitzer*); JStNT 48 (1992) 123 (E. S. *Christianson*).

5728 **Beilner** Wolfgang, Johanneische Theologie: Vermittlung 28. Salzburg 1992, nicht im Handel. 148 p.

5729 **Boismard** M.-E., Moïse ou Jésus... Christologie 1988 ⇒ 5,5416... 7,4804 ᴿJTS 43 (1992) 184 (J. *Ashton:* useful approach to his theories, but with much 'crazy logic' and hardly anything new).

5730 *a) Caragounis* Chrys C., The Kingdom of God in John and the Synoptics; realized or potential eschatology; – *b) Jonge* Marinus de, The radical eschatology of the Fourth Gospel and the eschatology of the Synoptics; some suggestions; – *c) Geiger* Georg, Die *egō eimi*-Worte bei Johannes und den Synoptikern; eine Rückfrage nach dem historischen Jesus: ⇒ 465, CLv 39, 1990/2, 473-480 / 481-7 / 466-472.

5731 **Cassidy** Richard J., John's Gospel in new perspective; Christology and the realities of Roman power. Mkn 1992, Orbis. xi-132 p.; 2 maps. $40; pa. $19. 0-88344-841-6; –18-1 [NTAbs 37, p. 274].

5732 **Dorado** Guillermo, Moral y existencia cristiana en el IV Evangelio y en las Cartas de Juan 1989 ⇒ 5,5434; 6,5707: ᴿEstE 67 (1992) 230s (J. *Iturriaga:* gran erudición y valor pedagógico).

5733 **Harrington** Daniel J., John's thought and theology; an introduction: Glazier Good News Studies 33. Collegeville MN 1990, Liturgical. 120 p. $9. 0-89453-796-2 [TDig 38,360]. – ᴿCritRR 5 (1992) 215-7 (Sandra M. *Schneiders:* fine, but reticent about the symbolic).

5734 *Heever* A.A. van den, Theological metaphorics and the metaphors of John's Gospel: Neotestamentica 26 (1992) 89-100.

5735 *Loader* William, The Christology of the Fourth Gospel 1989 ⇒ 5,5446 ... 7,4834: ᴿCiuD 205 (1992) 756s (J. *Gutiérrez*); RefTR 49 (1990) 102s (P. T. *O'Brien*).

5736 *Luzarraga* Jesús, Eternal life in the Johannine writings, ᵀ*Anadon* Silvia: ComND 18 (1991) 24-34.

5737 *Meye Thompson* Marianne, Signs and faith in the Fourth Gospel: Bulletin for Biblical Research 1 (WL 1991) 89-108 [< NTAbs 37, p.41].

5738 **Morris** Leon, Jesus is the Christ; studies in the theology of John 1989 ➤ 5,5450 ... 7,4831: ᴿJEvTS 35 (1992) 535s (D.C. *Stoutenburg*); RExp 89 (1992) 111 (D.S. *Dockery:* for conservatives).

5739 [Santos] *Silva* B. A escatologia do ... / O simbolismo no Evangelho de João: Atualizaçao 20 (1991) 99-118 / 22,107-131.

5740 **Stimpfle** Alois, Blinde sehen; die Eschatologie im ... Joh-Ev: BZNW 57, 1990 ➤ 6,5753; 7,4844: ᴿCBQ 54 (1992) 378-380 (B.D. *Ehrman*); JBL 111 (1992) 150-2 (C.R. *Koester*).

5740* ᴱ**Toit** A.B. du, Handleiding by die Nuwe Testament, 6. Die Johannesevangelie, Hebreërs on Openbaring, inleiding en teologie [= Guide to the NT] 1990, N.G. Kerk-B. 314 p. – ᴿNeotestamentica 26 (1992) 241s (E.A.C. *Pretorius*).

5741 **Trumbower** Jeffrey A., Born from above; the anthropology of the Gospel of John [< diss. Chicago 1989]: HermUntT 29. Tü 1992, Mohr. 176 p. DM 138. 3-16-145806-0. – ᴿExpTim 104 (1992s) 90 (L. *Kreitzer*, largely soteriology, diminishing human responsibility); JStNT 48 (1992) 124 (M. *Stibbe:* through Gnostic spectacles).

5741* *a)* **Vellanickal** Matthew, Christ, Spirit and the Church in the ...; – *b)* *Gabriel* A., Faith and rebirth in the Fourth Gospel: Bible Bhashyam 16 (1990) 234-249 / 205-215.

5742 **Willett** M.E., Wisdom Christology in the Fourth Gospel [< diss. Southern Baptist 1985, ᴰ*Polhill* J.] SF 1992, Mellen Research Univ. x-194 p. $70. 0-7734-9947-4 [NTAbs 37, p.444].

Particularia — **Observations of detail.**

5743 **Augenstein** Jörg, Das Liebesgebot im Corpus Johanneum: Diss. ᴰ*Thyen* H. Heidelberg 1992. 215 p. – RTLv 24, p.545.

5744 *Bertschausen* R.B., [Jesus' riddles in John] Turning the world upside down: Unitarian Universalist 46,3s (Boston 1991) 49-59 [< NTAbs 37,40].

5745 *Booth* S.C., Marking of peak in the Gospel of John: NotTr 6,3 (1992) 18-26 [< NTAbs 37, p.361].

5746 **Burkett** Delbert, The Son of Man in the Gospel of John: jNsu 56, 1991 ➤ 7,4806: ᴿÉTRel 67 (1992) 597 (P. *Kneubühler*, 'pas convaincu du bien-fondé de la méthode'); HorBT 14 (1992) 178s (D.R.A. *Hare*).

5747 **Collins** R.F., These things ... 4th Gospel (12 reprints 1976-89): 1990 ➤ 7,193: ᴿInterpretation 46 (1992) 411 (M. *Rissi*).

5748 **Davies** Margaret, Rhetoric and reference in the Fourth Gospel: jNsu 69. Shf 1992, Academic. 412 p. £45. 1-85075-345-8. – ᴿExpTim (1992s) 309 (S.S. *Smalley:* 'off-putting title').

5749 **Ferraro** Giuseppe, La gioia di Cristo nel quarto vangelo 1988 ➤ 4,5488 ... 6,5710: ᴿEstE 67 (1992) 242s (M. *Benéitez*); Salesianum 54 (1992) 785 (D. *Marzotto*).

5750 *Harder* Raymond G., The rendering of Greek participles in the Peshitta Gospel of John: ➤ 450, Informatique 2, 1988/9, 299-307.

5751 *Hasitschka* Martin, Dämonen und Teufel bei Johannes: ProtokB 1 (1992) 79-84.

5752 **Heiligenthal** Roman, Ist der Antijudaismus konstruktiv für das Christentum? Zum sog. Antijudaismus im Johannesevangelium: DtPfarrB 92 (Essen 1992) 187-190 [< zɪᴛ 92,329].

5753 *Howard* George, A note on Sʜᴇᴍ-Toʙ's Hebrew Matthew and the Gospel of John: JStNT 47 (1992) 117-126.

5754 **Karris** Robert J., Jesus and the marginalized in John's Gospel: GlazierZc 1990 → 6,5719: ᴿCBQ 54 (1992) 786s (Mary C. *Boys:* unlike KEALY, fulfills the mandate of the series); StPatav 39 (1992) 654s (G. *Segalla*).

5755 **Kaufman** Philip S., The beloved disciple; witness against anti-Semitism 1991 → 7,4820: ᴿCritRR 5 (1992) 227s (G. M. *Burge:* now 82, became Catholic and Benedictine 50 years ago).

5756 *Kysar* R., The Gospel of John and [i.e. not is but nurtures] anti-Jewish polemic: Explorations 6,2 (Ph 1992) 3s [< NTAbs 37, p. 41].

5757 *McHugh* John, 'In him was life'; John's Gospel and the parting of the ways: → 467, Jews & Christians 1989/92, 123-158.

5758 **Manns** Frédéric, L'Évangile de Jean et le Judaïsme: SBFAnal 33. J 1991, Franciscan. $45 [TR 88,251].

5758* *Marzotto* Damiano, L'unità della famiglia umana nel vangelo di Giovanni: VivH 3 (1992) 45-61 [63-82, bibliog. *Rocchetta* Carlo].

5759 **[Meye] Thompson** M., The humanity of Jesus in the Fourth Gospel 1988 → 4,5523 ... 7,4846: ᴿVidyajyoti 56 (1992) 53s (P. *Meagher*).

5760 *a) Painter* John, Quest stories in John and the Synoptics; – *b) Bammel* Ernst, Die Tempelreinigung bei den Synoptikern und im Johannesevangelium: → 465, CLv 39, 1990/2, 498-506 / 507-513.

5761 *[Silva] Santos* Bento, O amor no quarto evangelho: RBBras 7 (1990) 41-60.

5762 **Scott** Martin, Sophia and the Johannine Jesus: jNsu 71. Shf 1992, Academic. 276 p. £35; sb. £26. 1-85075-356-3. – ᴿExpTim 104 (1992s) 280 (Ruth B. *Edwards:* arose out of R. E. *Brown's* view of women's role in the Johannine church; perhaps overstated).

5763 *Sieg* Franciszek, Eigentliche Präpositionen als gebundene Morpheme der Substantive im Evangelium nach Johannes und in der Offenbarung des Johannes: FgNt 5 (1992) 135-166; español 165s; Eng. 166.

5764 **Stevens** John L., Conflict in the Fourth Gospel; its relation to an understanding of Messiah: diss. Baptist Theol. Sem., ᴰ*Simmons* B. New Orleans 1991. 185 p. 92-16458. – DissA 53 (1992s) 185-A.

G1.5 **Johannis Prologus 1,1 ...**

5765 *Abramowski* Luise, Der Logos in der altchristlichen Theologie: → 382, *Colpe,* Spätantike 1992, 189-201.

5766 **Harris** Elizabeth, Prologue and Gospel; a study in the theology of the Fourth Gospel: diss. ᴰ*Stanton* G. London 1992. 305 p. – RTLv 24, p. 547: > SNTS mg.

5767 **Mensch** J. R., The beginning of the Gospel according to St. John; philosophical reflections: AmerUnivSt 5/121. NY 1992, Lang. xi-219 p. $41. 0-8204-1583-9 [NTAbs 37, p. 281].

5768 **Pronzato** Alessandro, Un Vangelo per cercare, Giovanni [cap. 1 solo] 1986 → 2,4155: ᴿTeresianum 43 (1992) 285 (V. *Pasquetto*).

5769 **Reinhartz** Adele, The Word in the world; the cosmological tale in the Fourth Gospel: SBL mg 45. Atlanta 1992, Scholars. x-155 p. $40; sb./ pa. $26. 1-55540-798-6; -9-4 [NTAbs 37, p. 283].

5770 *Saxby* Harold, The time-scheme in the Gospel of John [ch. 1]: ExpTim 104 (1992s) 9-13.

5771 *Scarpat* Giuseppe, Prologo di Giovanni e Sapienza di Salomone: → 7, 423, Giovanni 1989/91, 7-37.

5772 *Schoneveld* Jacobus,   Die Thora in Person; eine Lektüre des Prologs des Johannesevangeliums als Beitrag zu einer Christologie ohne Antisemitismus: Klsr 6 (1991) 40-52.

5773 *a) Theobald* Michael,   Gott, Logos und Pneuma; 'trinitarische' Rede von Gott im Johannesevangelium; – *b) Hofrichter* Peter,   Logoslehre und Gottesbild bei Apologeten, Modalisten und Gnostikern; johanneische Christologie im Lichte ihrer frühesten Rezeption: → 573, QDisp 138, 1991/2, 41-87 / 187-217.

5774 *a) Goulder* Michael D.,   John 1,1-2,12 and the Synoptics; appendix Jn 2,13-4,54; – *b) Hofrichter* Peter,   Johannesprolog und lukanische Vorgeschichte: → 465, CLv 39, 1990/2, 201-237 / 488-497.
5775 **Miller** Ed. L.,   Salvation-history in ... Jn 1:3/4, 1989 → 5,5490 ... 7,4866: ᴿJBL 111 (1992) 542-4 (D. M. *Smith*).
5775* *a) Clemente* Matteo,   La vera luce che illumina ogni uomo (Gv 1.9); – *b) Bolognesi* Pietro,   Unicità e pluralismo; – *c) Ramirez* Antonino,   Prospettive unitarie dell'evangelismo radicale italiano; – *d) Jones* Hywel R., La sfida ecumenica, ᵀ*Walker* D.:   – *e) Castellina* Paolo, New Age e coscienza moderna: STEv 4 (1992) 99-114 / 115-126 / 127-134 / 140-151 / 152-177.
5776 *a) Lockmann* Paulo,   João Batista, a testemunha (Jo 1,19-34); – *b) Garmus* Ludovico,   Para que todos tenham vida em abundância (Jo 10,1-18); – *c) Konings* Johan,   Literatura sobre o Evangelho de João em edição brasileira: EstudosB 33 (1992) 41-48 / 49-60 / 61-80.
5777 **Gunawan** Henricus P.,   Jesus the new Elijah according to the Fourth Gospel; a logical consequence of John 1:21 [diss. Angelicum]. Malang, Indonesia 1990, B. Karmel.   vii-182 p. – ᴿCarmelus 39 (1992) 199-202 (H. *Welzen*).
5778 *Sandy* D. Brent,   [Jn 1,29] John the Baptist's 'Lamb of God' affirmation in its canonical and apocalyptic milieu: JEvTS 34 (1991) 447-460 [< BtS 149 (1992) 460s (H. *Heater*)].
5779 *Panier* Louis,   Cana et le Temple; la pratique et la théorie; une lecture sémiotique de Jean 2:   LumièreV 41 (1992) 37-54.
5780 **Lütgehetmann** Walter,   Die Hochzeit Joh 2, ᴰ1990 → 6,5796; 7,4875: ᴿCBQ 54 (1992) 577-9 (G. W. *Buchanan:* 402 p. on 11 verses); Marianum 54 (1992) 463-5 (O. da *Spinetoli*); TGgw 35 (1982) 70s (H. *Giesen*).
5781 **Serra** Aristide, E c'era 1989 → 6,301: ᴿBible Bhashyam 18 (1992) 126 (J. *Kottackal*); Lateranum 57 (1991) 229-231 (M. *Semeraro*).
5782 *Serra* Aristide,   *a)* 'Vi erano là sei giare ...' Gv 2,6 alla luce di antiche tradizioni giudaico-cristiane relative ai 'sei giorni' della creazione [< Marianum 53 (1981) 433-508]; – *b)* 'Ma lo sapevano i servi che avevano attinto l'acqua' Gv 2,9c e le tradizioni biblico-giudaiche sul pozzo di Beer (Num 21,16-30) [< ᶠ*Koehler* H., 1991, 157-196]; – *c)* 'Quanto il Signore ha detto, noi lo faremo'; nuove ricerche sugli echi di Es 19,8 e 24,3.7 come formula di alleanza [< ᶠ*Besutti* G. 1991, 51-89]: → 309, Nato di donna 1992, 141-188 / 189-265 / 97-140.
5783 *Trudinger* P.,   [Jn 2,1-11; 4,1-42] Of women, weddings, wells, waterpots and wine! Reflections on Johannine themes: St. Mark's Review 151 (1992) 10-16 [< NTAbs 37, p. 363].
5784 *Schwarz* Günther,   *Anà metrētas dúo ē treis*? (Joh 2,6):   BibNot 62 (1992) 45.
5785 *a) Matson* Mark A.,   [Jn 2,14-17] The contribution to the Temple Cleansing in the Fourth Gospel; – *b) Richardson* Peter,   Why turn the

tables? Jesus' protest in the Temple precincts: ➤ 478, SBL Sem. 31 (1992) 489-506 / 507-523.

G1.6   Jn 3ss ... Nicodemus, Samaritana.

5786 **Létourneau** Pierre, Jésus, Fils de l'Homme et Fils de Dieu; Jean 2,23-3,36 et la double christologie johannique [diss. 1990 ➤ 7,4884]: Recherches NS 27. P/Montréal 1992, Cerf/Bellarmin. 274 p. 2-89007-022-0.

5787 **Kiessel** Marie-Élisabeth, Le sens baptismal de la formule 'naître d'eau et d'Esprit' (Jn 3,5): Mémoire ᴰ*Sevrin* J.-M. LvN 1991s – Mémoires de licence LvN 1991s: RTLv 24,142.

5788 *Schwarz* Günther, [Joh 3,8] 'Der Wind weht, wo er will'? [vielmehr 'Der Geist inspiriert...']: BibNot 63 (1992) 47s.

5789 *a) Morgen* Michèle, Jean 3 et les évangiles synoptiques; – *b) Boismard* M.-É., Jean 4,46-54 et les parallèles synoptiques: ➤ 465, CLv 39, 1990/2, 514-522 / 239-259.

5790 *García-Moreno* Arturo, [Jn 4] Adorar al Padre en espíritu y verdad: ScripTPamp 23 (1991) 785-835.

5791 **Boers** Hendrikus, Neither on this mountain ... Jn 4, 1988 ➤ 4,5560 ... 7,4890: ᴿAustralBR 38 (1990) 83s (M. *FitzPatrick*).

5792 **Botha** G. Eugene, Jesus and the Samaritan woman; a speech act reading of Joh 4,1-42, ᴰ1991 ➤ 7,4891: ᴿExpTim 103 (1991s) 376 (R. *Morgan:* careful and sensible application of new linguistic theory); Neotestamentica 26 (1992) 545s (J. P. *Louw*); Themelios 18,3 (1992s) 26 (L. J. *Kreitzer*).

5793 **Johnson** David H., Our father Jacob; the role of the Jacob narrative in the Fourth Gospel compared to its role in the Jewish Bible and in the writings of early Judaism: diss. Trinity Ev. Divinity School 1992. 291 p. 92-33310. – DissA 53 (1992s) 2413-A.

5794 **Link** Andrea Hildegard, 'Was redest du mit ihr?' Eine Studie zur Exegese-, Redaktions- und Theologiegeschichte von Joh 4,1-42 [kath. Diss. Fra 1992, ᴰ*Hainz* J. 437 p. – RTLv 24, p. 548]: BibUnt 24. Rg 1992, Pustet. x-437 p. 3-7917-1353-1.

5795 **Schwab** C., Une femme en Samarie; le récit d'une rencontre bouleversante 1990 ➤ 6,5819: ᴿProtestantesimo 47 (1992) 150 (Berta *Subilia*).

5796 *a) Rennert* Jürgen, Joh 4,5-30, Versuch einer Bibelarbeit; – *b) Bindemann* Walther, Im Dickicht von Feindbildern und Vorurteilen: ZeichZt 45 (1991) 96-98 / 91-95 [< ᴢɪᴛ 92,636].

5797 *Prest* Loring A., [Jn 4,18] The Samaritan woman: BToday 30 (1992) 367-371.

5798 *Serra* Aristide, 'E rimase lì ... nel luogo dove si trovava due giorni'; l'emerologia di Gv 4,40.43 e 11,6 nei Padri e negli autori moderni: ➤ 135, ᶠMᴜÑᴏᴢ Iɢʟᴇꜱɪᴀꜱ S., EstBib 50 (1992) 493-520.

5799 *Stimpfle* Alois, Das 'sinnlose *gár*' in Joh 4,44; Beobachtungen zur Doppeldeutigkeit im Johannesevangelium: BibNot 65 (1992) 86-96.

5800 *Staley* Jeffrey L., Stumbling in the dark, reaching for the light; reading character in John 5 and 9: ➤ Semeia 53 (1991) 55-80.

5801 *Gaeta* Giancarlo, [Jn 5,17; 8,37-42] Il Figlio immagine della volontà del Padre; l'interpretazione Oʀɪɢᴇɴɪᴀɴᴀ della cristologia giovannea: ➤ 458, AnStoEseg 9,2 (1992) 349-363; Eng. 341.

G1.7   **Panis Vitae** – *Jn 6* ...

5802 *Beauchamp* Paul, [Jn 6] Le signe des pains: LumièreV 41 (1992) 55-67.

5803 *Beutler* Johannes, Zur Struktur von Johannes 6: SNTU A-16 (1991) 89-104 [< TR 88,251].

5804 *Green* Lowell C., Philosophical presuppositions in the Lutheran-Reformed debate on John 6: ConcordTJ 56 (1992) 17-37 [< ZIT 92,355].

5805 *a*) *Konings* Johan, The dialogue of Jesus, Philip and Andrew in John 6,5-9; – *b*) *Vouga* François, Le quatrième évangile comme interprète de la tradition synoptique; Jean 6: ➤ 465, CLv 39, 1990/2, 523-534 / 261-279.

5806 *Manus* U.C., Jn 6:1-15 and its Synoptic parallels; an African approach toward the solution of a Johannine critical problem: JIntdenom 19,1 (1991s) 47-71 [< NTAbs 38, p. 42].

5807 *Packer* J.I., [Jn 6,44] 'Nul ne peut venir à moi si le Pére qui m'a envoyé ne l'attire'; le salut biblique et l'annonce de l'Évangile [préface d'une édition de John OWEN, reprise 1991], ᵀ*Coste* André: RRéf 43,5 (1992) 1-20.

5808 *Farrell* Shannon-Elizabeth, *a*) Seeing the Father (Jn 6,46; 14,9): ScEspr 44 (1992) 1-23.159-182; franç. 24.183; – *b*) Seeing the Father (Jn 6:46; 14:9), III. Eschatological seeing and memorial seeing: ScEspr 44 (1992) 307-329; franç. 329.

5809 *Wessel* Friedhelm, 'Der Mensch' in der Verteidigungsrede des Nikodemus Joh 7,51 und das 'Ecce Homo': SNTU A-17 (1992) 195-214.

5810 *O'Day* Gail R., John 7:53-8.11; a study in misreading: JBL 111 (1992) 631-640.

5811 *Simonetti* Manlio (Jn 8,20) ORIGENE e la povera vedova; commento a Giovanni XIX, 7-10 (40-58): RivStoLR 27 (1991) 475-481.

5812 ᴱ**Beutler** J., *Fortna* R., The shepherd discourse of John 10, 1985/91 ➤ 7,417: ᴿÉTRel 67 (1992) 280s (E. *Cuvillier*, aussi sur COLLINS, These things, JTS 43 (1992) 182-4 (D.M. *Smith*); Neotestamentica 26 (1992) 248s (H.A. *Lombard*); StPatav 39 (1992) 627-9 (G. *Segalla*).

5813 *Ghidelli* Carlo, [Gv 10] Gesù pastore: ParVi 36 (1991) 278-284.

5814 *a*) *Kysar* Robert, Johannine metaphor — meaning and function; a literary case study of John 10:1-18; – *b*) *Wuellner* Wilhelm, Putting life back into the Lazarus story and its reading; the narrative rhetoric of John 11 as the narration of faith: ➤ 348, Semeia 53 (1991) 81-111 / 113-152.

5815 *Bretherton* Donald J., Lazarus of Bethany; resurrection or resuscitation?: ExpTim 104 (1992s) 169-173.

5816 **Byrne** Brendan, Lazarus: GlazierZc 1991 ➤ 7,4926: ᴿCritRR 5 (1992) 224-7 (R.A. *Culpepper*, also on KARRIS & COLLINS Zc, all admirable); Pacifica 5 (1992) 324s (F.J. *Moloney*).

5817 *Lindars* Barnabas † 21 X 1991, Rebuking the spirit; a new analysis of the Lazarus story of John 11: NTS 38 (1992) 89-104.

5818 *a*) *Lindars* Barnabas, Rebuking the Spirit; a new analysis of the Lazarus story of John 11; – *b*) *Busse* Ulrich, Johannes und Lukas; die Lazarusperikope Frucht eines Kommunikationsprozesses; – *c*) *Dauer* Anton, Spuren der (synoptischen) Synedriumsverhandlung im 4. Evangelium [Joh 10; 18...]; – *d*) *Dunderberg* Ismo, Zur Literarkritik von Joh 12,1-11: ➤ 465, CLv 39, 1990/2, 542-7 / 281-306 / 307-339 / 558-570.

5819 **McVoy** Heather Jo, Those whom Jesus loved; the development of the paradigmatic story of Lazarus, Mary, and Martha through the medieval period: diss. Florida State, ᴰ*Moore* W. 1992. 260 p. 92-33294. – DissA 53 (1992s) 2424-A.

5820 *Thyen* Hartwig, Vom Tod zum Leben; Intertextualität in der Erzählung von der Auferweckung des Lazarus (Johannes 11,1 - 12,19): DielB 27 (1991) 138-158.

5821 *Minear* Paul S., [Jn 11,25s] The promise of life in the Gospel of John: TTod 49 (1992s) 485-499.

5822 **Cilia** Lucia,   La morte di Gesù e l'unità degli uomini (Gv 11,47-53; 12,32); contributo allo studio della soteriologia giovannea [diss. ᴰ*De Santis* L., Angelicum 1990]: RivB supp. 24. Bo 1992, Dehoniane. 167 p. Lit. 26.000. 88-10-30212-5 [NTAbs 37, p. 113].

5823 *a) Wagner* Josef,   Die Erweckung des Lazarus — ein Paradigma johanneischer Theologiegeschichte; – *a) Link* Andrea,   Botschafterinnen des Messias; die Frauen des vierten Evangeliums im Spiegel johanneischer Redaktionsgeschichte: ➤ 112*, Mem. Kuss O., Theologie im Werden 1992, 199-217 / 247-278.

5824 *a) Breytenbach* Cilliers, *Mnemoneuein;* das 'Sich-Erinnern' in der urchristlichen Überlieferung; die Bethania-Episode (Mk 14,3-9 / Jn 12,1-8) als Beispiel; – *b) Menken* Maarten J. J.,   The quotations from Zech 9,9 in Mt 21,5 and in Jn 12,15; – *c) Segovia* Fernando F., [... Jn 12,12-19] The journey(s) of Jesus to Jerusalem; plotting and Gospel intertextuality: ➤ 465, CLv 39, 1990/2, 548-557 / 571-8 / 535-541.

5825 *Zevini* Giorgio,   'Vogliamo vedere Gesù' (Gv 12,20-36); l'universalità salvifica di Gesù Cristo secondo Giovanni: ➤ 339, ParSpV 26 (1992) 111-126.

5826 *Rodriguez* Pedro,   Omnia traham ad meipsum; il significato di Giovanni 12,32, nell'esperienza di mons. Escrivá de Balaguer: AnnTh 6 (1992) 5-34.

5827 *Giblin* Charles H.,   Mary's anointing for Jesus' burial-resurrection (John 12,1-8): Biblica 73 (1992) 560-4 [> BtS 150, 494s, W. H. *Harris*].

5828 *Martín Nieto* Evaristo, [Jn 12,28] La glorificación del Nombre de Dios en el IV evangelio: StLeg 32 (1991) 65-99.

5829 **Kühschelm** Roman,   Verstockung ... Joh 12,35-50 [kath. Hab-Diss. Wien]: BoBB 76, 1990 ➤ 6,5856; 7,4940: ᴿZkT 114 (1992) 211s (M. *Hasitschka*).

G1.8   Jn 13 ... Sermo sacerdotalis et Passio.

5830 **Thomas** John C.,   Footwashing in Jn 13: JStNT supp 61, 1991, ➤ 7, 4943: ᴿÉTRel 67 (1992) 460 (P. *Kneubühler* accepte comme rite, même si non comme purification des péchés postbaptismaux); RelStR 18 (1992) 330 (D. M. *Smith*).

5831 *Tripp* David,   Meanings of the foot-washing; John 13 and Oxyrhynchus Papyrus 840 [a Pharisee accuses the disciples of not washing ('feet' supplied)]: ExpTim 103 (1991s) 237-9.

5832 *a) Culpepper* R. Alan,   The Johannine hypodeigma; a reading of John 13: 1-38; – *b) O'Day* Gail R., 'I have overcome the world' (John 16:33); narrative time in John 13-17: ➤ 348, Semeia 53 (1991) 133-152 / 153-166.

5833 *a) Bammel* Ernst,   Die Abschiedsrede des Johannesevangeliums und ihr jüdischer Hintergrund; – *b) Draper* J. A.,   The sociological function of the Spirit/Paraclete in the farewell discourses in the Fourth Gospel; – *c) Durand* J. A.,   A story and a community; reading the first farewell discourse (John 13,31-14,31) from narratological and sociological perspectives; – *d) Suggit* J. N., John 13-17 viewed through liturgical spectacles; – *e) Wendland* E. R.,   Rhetoric of the Word, an interactional discourse analysis of the Lord's prayer of Jn 17 and its communicative implications: Neotestamentica 26 (1992) 1-12 / 13-29 / 31-45 / 47-58 / 59-88.

5834 **Kurz** William S.,   Farewell addresses in the NT 1990 ➤ 7,4094: ᴿNewTR 5,1 (1992) 96s (C. *Osiek:* a neglected topic); PerspRelSt 29 (1992) 342s

(F. S. *Spencer:* too hastily skips between what is being said 'to them' and 'to us').

5835 **Segovia** Fernando F., [Jn 13,31 - 16,33] The farewell of the Word; the Johannine call to abide. Mp 1991, Fortress. xvi-341 p. $28 [TR 88,517; TDig 39,286]. 0-8006-2486-6.

5836 **Winter** Martin, Das Vermächtnis Jesu und die Abschiedsworte der Väter; gattungsgeschichtliche Untersuchung der Vermächtnisrede im Blick auf Joh 13-17: ev. Hab.-Diss. *DStegemann.* Neuendettelsau 1992. – TR 89,76.

5837 *Derrett* J.D.M., Impurity and idolatry; John 13,11; Ezekiel 36,25: BbbOr 34 (1992) 87-92.

5838 *Beutler* Johannes, [Jn 14,27] Peace not of this world? [wrong: < GeistL 63 (1990) 165-175], TEAsen B. A.: TDig 39 (1992) 131-5.

5839 **Breck** John, Spirit of truth; the Holy Spirit in Johannine tradition, 1. The origins of Johannine pneumatology 1991 → 7,4949: ROrChrPer 59 (1992) 596s (V. *Ruggieri*); PatrPyzR 11 (1992) 95-97 (H. O. *Thompson*).

5841 *Mara* Maria Grazia, Il giovanneo Paraclito, Spirito di verità, in alcune interpretazioni del cristianesimo antico: → 485, Efeso II, 1991/2 123-9 [19-27 *Nobile* M., 153-172 *Pacomio* L.: appunti sulla storia].

5842 *Bolt* Peter, What fruit does the vine bear? Some pastoral implications of John 15:1-8: RefTR 51 (1992) 11-19.

5843 *Schwarz* Günther, 'In der Welt habt ihr Angst'? [richtiger mit Syr 'werdet ihr durch Menschen Bedrängnis haben']: BibNot 63 (1992) 49-51.

5844 *Arnold* Matthieu, 'Prenez courage, j'ai vaincu le monde'; l'emploi de Jn 16,33 dans les lettres de LUTHER: PosLuth 40 (1992) 121-147 [< ZIT 92,366].

5845 *a) Schenk* Wolfgang, Die Um-Codierungen der matthäischen Unser-Vater-Redaktion in Joh 17; – *b) Létourneau* Pierre, Le quatrième évangile et les prédictions de la Passion dans les Évangiles synoptiques: → 465, CLv 39, 1990/2, 587-607 / 579-586.

5846 *Ricca* Paolo, Giovanni 17,21: StEcum 9 (1991) 49-54.

5847 *Zevini* Giorgio, La preghiera del Figlio al Padre (Gv 17): → 338, ParSpV 25 (1992) 117-137.

5848 **Leone** Cosimo, La morte di Gesù e il dono dello Spirito (Gv 19,28-37): diss. Pont. Univ. Gregoriana, DRasco E. – Roma 1992. 706 p. – RTLv 24, p. 548.

5849 **Derrett** J.D.M., The victim; the Johannine passion narrative re-examined. Shipston 1992, Drinkwater [BbbOr 34,87].

5850 **La Potterie** Ignace de, The hour of Jesus; the Passion and Resurrection of Jesus according to John; TMurray Gregory. NY c.1991, Alba. 190 p. $13 pa. – RCanadCathR 10,1 (1992) 25 (S. F. *Miletic*); HomP 91,6 (1990s) 76s (J. R. *Sheets* praises).

5851 *a) Brownson* James V., Neutralizing the intimate enemy; the portrayal of Judas in the Fourth Gospel; – *b) Staley* Jeffrey L., Reading with a passion; John 18:1-19:42 and the erosion of the reader [... autobiographical]: → 478, SBL Sem 31 (1992) 51-60 / 61-81.

5852 TELivrea Enrico, NONNO/Giovanni Canto XVIII, 1989 → 6,5651; 7, 4751: RJbÖsByz 41 (1991) 320-3 (H. *Hunger*); Koinonia 16,1 (1992) 87-93 (F. *Vian*).

5853 *Vicent Cernuda* Antonio, [Jn 18,37] Nacimiento y verdad de Jesús ante Pilato: → 135, FMUÑOZ IGLESIAS S., EstBib 50 (1992) 537-551.

5854 **Urbán** Ángel, El origen divino del poder ... Jn 19,11a: FgNt Est 2, D1989 → 5,5602 ... 7,4962: RCBQ 54 (1992) 384s (J. C. *Turro*); ComSev

24 (1991) 105s (M. de *Burgos*); ÉTRel 67 (1992) 461 (E. *Cuvillier*); Salesianum 54 (1992) 377s (R. *Farina*).

5855 *a*) **Sabbe** Maurits, The trial of Jesus before Pilate in John and its relation to the Synoptic Gospels; – *b*) *Karavidopoulos* Jean, L'heure de la crucifixion de Jésus selon Jean et les Synoptiques; Mc 15,25 par rapport à Jn 19,14-16: ➤ 465, CLv 39, 1990/2, 341-385 / 608-613.

5856 **Blanquart** Fabien, Le premier jour; étude sur Jean 20: LDiv 148, 1991 ➤ 7,4972: RespirVie 102 (1992) 411s (É. *Cothenet:* clair mais un peu trainant); ÉTRel 67 (1992) 596s (P. *Kneubühler*); RBiArg 54,45 (1992) 50s (A. J. *Levoratti* enuncia claramente los nueve problemas); TvT 32 (1992) 415 (A. van *Diemen*).

5857 *Segovia* Ferdinand F., *a*) The final farewell of Jesus; a reading of John 20:30 - 21.25; – *b*) The journey(s) of the word of God; a reading of the plot of the Fourth Gospel: ➤ 348, Semeia 53 (1991) 167-190 / (1-) 23-54.

5858 **Dietzfelbinger** C., Johanneischer Osterglaube: ThSt 138. Z 1992, Theol.-V. 79 p. Fs 15. 3-290-10868-6 [NTAbs 37, p. 113].

5859 *García García* Luis, [Jn 20,5] 'Lienzos', no 'vendas', en la sepultura de Jesús: Burgense 32 (1991) 557-567.

5860 **Gangemi** Attilio, I racconti post-pasquali nel Vangelo di San Giovanni, I. Gesù si manifesta a Maria Maddalena (Gv 20,1-18); II. Gesù appare ai discepoli (Gv 20,19-31): Documenti e Studi di Synaxis 2.4. Acireale 1989s, Galatea. 287 p.; 294 p. – RRivB 40 (1992) 252s (L. *Cilia*); RivStoLR 28 (1992) 431s (Giuliana *Iacopino*).

5861 *a*) *Craig* William L., The disciples' inspection of the empty tomb (Lk 24,12.24; Jn 20,2-10); – *b*) *Standaert* Benoît, Jean 21 et les Synoptiques; l'enjeu interecclésial de la dernière rédaction de l'évangile; – *c*) *Bammel* Caroline P., The first Resurrection appearance to Peter; John 21 and the Synoptics; – *d*) *Fortna* Robert T., Diachronic/synchronic; reading John 21 and Luke 5: ➤ 465, CLv 39, 1990/2, 614-9 / 632-643 / 620-631 / 387-399.

5862 *Okure* Teresa, [Jn 20,11-18] The significance today of Jesus' commission to Mary Magdalene: IntRMiss 81 ('Women in Mission' 1992) 177-188.

5863 *Perrone* Antonio, *De Palma* Elisabetta, [Gv 20,11-19] Maria di Magdala al sepolcro nel quarto vangelo: RivScR 5 (1991) 381-400.

5864 *Simenel* Philippe, Les deux anges de Jean 20/11-12: ÉTRel 67 (1992) 71-76.

5865 *Perkins* Pheme, 'I have seen the Lord' (John 20:18); women witnesses to the Resurrection: Interpretation 46 (1992) 31-41.

5866 *a*) *Duplantier* Jean-Pierre, Le pasteur et l'écrivain; lecture de Jean 21; – *b*) *Zumstein* Jean, Le signe de la croix [... 'un fait surprenant: la croix et la résurrection ne sont jamais considérées comme des signes dans Jn']: LumièreV 41 (1992) 83-94 / 68-82.

5867 *a*) *Ellis* Peter F., The authenticity of John 21; – *b*) *Breck* John, John 21; appendix, epilogue or conclusion?; – *c*) *Franzmann* M., *Klinger* M., The call stories of John 1 and John 21: StVlad 36 (1992) 17-25 / 27-49 / 7-15.

5868 **Welck** Christian, Erzählte 'Zeichen'; die johanneischen Wundergeschichten literarisch untersucht, mit einem Ausblick auf Joh. 21: Diss. Bethel, DLindemann A. Bielefeld 1992. – RTLv 24, p. 550; TLZ 118,691.

5869 *Wiarda* Timothy, John 21.1-23; narrative unity and its implications: JStNT 46 (1992) 53-71.

5870 *Schenk* W., Interne Structurierungen im Schluss-Segment Johannes 21: *syngraphē* + *satyrikon / epilogos*: NTS 38 (1992) 507-530.

G2.1   Epistolae Johannis.

5871 **Anderson** J. L., An exegetical summary of 1, 2, and 3 John [for translators]. Dallas 1992, Summer Inst. Linguistics. 272 p. $6.25 pa. 0-88312-827-6 [NTAbs 37, p. 445].

5872 **Dalbesio** Anselmo, Quello che abbiamo udito e veduto ... 1 Gv: RivB supp 22, 1990: ↠ 6,5912; 7,4980: ᴿEstFranc 93 (1992) 177-9 (F. *Raurell*); Gregorianum 73 (1992) 345s (G. *Ferraro*); Laurentianum 33 (1992) 227-9 (L. *Martignani*); RivLtg 79 (1992) 119-121 (G. *Crocetti*); Teresianum 43 (1992) 287 (V. *Pasquetto*).

5873 *Dalbesio* Anselmo, L'esperienza ecclesiale nella 1 Gv alla luce del suo contesto storico: ↠ 485, Efeso II 1991/2, 55-71.

5874 *Ghiberti* Giuseppe, Genesi e ambiente vitale delle lettere giovannee: ↠ 487*b*, Giovannismo 1989 – RicStoR 3,2 (1991) 107-122.

5875 *Hansford* K. I., The underlying poetic structure of 1 John: JTrans-TLing 5,2 (Dallas 1992) 126-174 [< NTAbs 37, p. 63].

5876 **Lieu** Judith M., The theology of the Johannine epistles: NTTheol, 1991 ↠ 7,4984: ᴿNedTTs 46 (1992) 346 (M. de *Jonge*); TLZ 117 (1992) 837 840 (G. *Strecker:* series initiated by J.D.G. DUNN); TvT 32 (1992) 197 (S. van *Tilborg*); ZkT 114 (1992) 213s (M. *Hasitschka*).

5877 **Loader** William, The Johannine epistles: Epworth comm. L 1992, Epworth. xxxiii-108 p. [NTAbs 37, p. 449]. 0-7162-0480-4.

5878 *Mannucci* Valerio, La 'trilogia' teo-logica di Giovanni ['Dio è Spirito / luce / amore']: RClerIt 72 (1991) 180-9.

5879 [Meye] **Thompson** Marianne, 1-3 John: IVP comm. DG/Leicester 1992, Inter-Varsity. 168 p. $15. 0-8308-1819-7 / UK 0-85111-671-X [NTAbs 37,132].

5880 **Schnackenburg** Rudolf, The Johannine epistles; introduction and commentary [1951, ⁷1984], ᵀ*Fuller* Reginald & Ilse. Tunbridge Wells 1992, Burns & O. xv-320 p. £35. 0-86012-206-9 [NTAbs 37, p. 131]. – ᴿTBR 5,3 (1992s) 30 (M. *Bockmuehl*).

5881 **Smith** D. Moody, 1-3 John: Interpretation comm. 1991 ↠ 7,4988: ᴿHorBT 14 (1992) 180s (R. *Kysar*).

5882 **Strecker** G., Die Joh-briefe 1989 ↠ 5,5623 ... 7,4990: ᴿActuBbg 29 (1992) 202s (X. *Alegre*).

5883 *a*) **Studer** Basil, Spiritualità giovannea in AGOSTINO (osservazioni sul commento agostiniano sulla Prima Ioannis); – *b*) *Dalbesio* Anselmo, L'esperienza ecclesiale nella 1 Gv alla luce del suo contesto storico; *c*) *La Potterie* Ignace de, Anticristi e Anticristo; la scissione nella comunità giovannea e il suo senso cristologico: ↠ 485, Efeso 2, 1991/2, 55-71 / 131-151.

5884 **Vogler** Werner, Die Briefe des Johannes: Hab.-Diss. ᴰ*Weiss*. Greifswald 1992. – TR 89,75.

5885 **Vouga** François, Die Johannesbriefe 1990 ↠ 5,5623 ... 7,4990: ᴿBiblica 73 (1992) 280-6 (G. *Strecker*); JBL 111 (1992) 356s (D. *Rensberger*); TLZ 117 (1992) 195 (U. *Schnelle*).

5886 **Jenks** Gregory C., The origins and early development of the Antichrist myth: BZNW 59, 1991 ↠ 7,4995: ᴿCBQ 54 (1992) 572-4 (W. *Adler*); CritRR 5 (1992) 222s (B. *McGinn:* good against BOUSSET, but puts origins too late); JTS 43 (1992) 652-7 (C. E. *Hill*); SecC 9 (1992) 124-6 (D. *Frankfurter*).

5887 **Sbaffoni** Fausto, Testi sull'Anticristo, secoli I-II/III: BtPatr 21 F 1992, Nardini. 230 p. / 227 p. – ᴿMiscFranc 92 (1992) 611-3 (M. *Baldini*); Sapienza 45 (1992) 342-4 (anche M. *Baldini*).

5888 *Sproston* Wendy E., [1 Jn 1,1 + 6t] Witnesses to what was *ap' archês*; 1 John's contribution to our knowledge of tradition in the Fourth Gospel: JStNT 48 (1992) 43-65.

5889 *Luke* G., [Koran 24,35, (not) 1 Jn 1,5] God is light: IndTSt 28 (1991) 166-183.

5890 *Baylis* Charles P., The meaning of walking 'in the darkness' (1 John 1:6): BtS 149 (1992) 214-222.

5891 *Curtis* E. M., The first person plural in 1 John 2:18-27: EvJ 10,1 (Myerstown PA 1992) 27-36 [< NTAbs 36, p. 375].

5892 *Black* David A., An overlooked stylistic argument in favor of *pánta* in 1 John 2:20: FgNt 5 (1992) 205-8.

5893 *Morland* Kjell A., [1 Joh 4,1-6] To reveal and reject false teachers: TsTKi 63 (1992) 95-112 [in Norwegian; Eng. 112].

5894 [*Meye*] *Thompson* Marianne, Intercession in the Johannine community; 1 John 5,16 in the context of the Gospel and Epistles of John: ➤ 126, ᶠMᴀʀᴛɪɴ R. 1992, 225-245.

G2.3 *Apocalypsis Johannis* – **Revelation: text, introduction.**

5895 ᴱ**Argyriou** Astérios, ⑥ Zacharie Gᴇʀɢᴀɴᴏs, Exégèse de l'Apocalypse de Jean le Théologien (1622). Athena 1991, Artos Zōēs. 302 p. [RHPR 73,201, P. *Prigent*].

5896 **Campo Hernández** Alberto del, Comentario al Apocalipsis de Aᴘʀɪɴɢɪᴏ de Beja 1991 ➤ 7,5003: ᴿRBiArg 54 (1992) 121s (J. P. *Martín*); Salmanticensis 39 (1992) 438s (R. *Trevijano*).

5897 **Charlier** Jean-Pierre, Comprendre l'Apocalypse: Lire la Bible 89s ➤ 7, 5005: ᴿPrOrChr 41 (1991) 181s (P. *Ternant:* écarte un peu vite 'l'archéologie du texte').

5898 ᵀᴱ**Courreau** D., *Bouquet* S., L'Apocalypse expliquée par Cᴇ́sᴀɪʀᴇ d'Arles [et] Scolies attribuées à Oʀɪɢᴇ̀ɴᴇ; intr. *La Potterie* I. de, *Hamman* A. G.: Les pères dans la foi, 1989 ➤ 5,5646 ... 7,5006: ᴿRechSR 80 (1992) 303s (Y.-M. *Duval*).

5899 ᵀᴿ**Delebecque** Édouard † 26.I.1990, L'Apocalypse de Jean. P 1992, Mame. 268 p. [NTAbs 37, p. 287]. 3-7289-0463-4. – ᴿEsprVie 102 (1992) 408s (É. *Cothenet*); RÉG 105 (1992) 635s (A. *Wartelle*).

5900 *Dulaey* Martine, Jᴇ́ʀᴏ̂ᴍᴇ 'éditeur' du Commentaire sur l'Apocalypse de Vɪᴄᴛᴏʀɪɴ de Poetovio [Pannonia]: RÉAug 37 (1991) 199-236.

5901 **Efird** James M., Revelation for today; an apocalyptic approach. Nv 1989, Abingdon. 139 p. $10 pa. – ᴿAndrUnS 30 (1992) 84s (K. A. *Strand*); LexTQ 27 (1992) 91s (S. *Thaler*).

5902 **Fallon** Michael, The Apocalypse; a revelation that history is graced; a commentary. Eastwood NSW, Australia 1992, Parish Ministry. 183 p.; map. 1-875463-00-3.

5903 **Fauvarque** B., Les Apocalypses de la bibliothèque de Cambrai. Cambrai 1991, Soc. d'émulation. ci-65 p.; ill. [RHE 88,140*].

5905 **Giblin** Charles H., The book of Revelation; the open book of prophecy: Glazier Good News 34, 1991 ➤ 7,5008: ᴿCritRR 5 (1992) 202s (W. *Wink:* Holy War notion; brings us to the edge of promise, but others will have to take us across); ExpTim 104 (1992s) 238 (C. S. *Rodd:* sensitive, helpful); NBlackf 73 (1992) 521s (A.R.C. *Leaney*); TLZ 117 (1992) 834s (J.-W. *Taeger* regrets that he did not aim at a 'large-scale' commentary); TPhil 67 (1992) 585s (J. M. *McDermott*, Eng.).

5906 **Giesen** Heinz, *al.*, Ermutigung zum Christsein; Offenbarung [9 indicated authors]: BAusPrax 27. Stu 1992, KBW. 143 p. 3-460-25271-5.

5907 **Gonzalez** Catherine & Justo, Vision at Patmos; a study in the Book of Revelation: Lay Bible. Nv 1979 = 1977, Abingdon. 121 p. 0-687-43774-1. ᴿTBR 5,1 (1992s) 15.

5908 **Hughes** Philip E. † 1990, Book of Revelation 1990 ⇢ 7,5011: ᴿCalvinT 26 (1991) 290s (A. J. *Bandstra*); CritRR 5 (1992) 220-2 (M. R. *Mulholland:* Amillennial, inadequately sociological); EvQ 64 (1992) 279-282 (R. *Shirock*); ExpTim 104 (1992s) 237s (C. S. *Rodd*); TrinJ 13 (1992) 106-8 (D. A. *de Silva*); WestTJ 54 (1992) 379s (R. *Letham*).

5909 **Jeremiah** David, *Carlson* C.C., Escape the coming night [Rev. comm.]. Dallas 1990, Word. 240 p. $9. – ᴿBtS 149 (1992) 124 (J. F. *Walvoord:* thrilling).

5910 *Marion* Denis, Apocalypse ou révélation de Jésus-Christ XII: EsprVie 102 (1992) couv.-227s ('suite de la p. 256, 2ᵉ partie', non vérifiable).

5911 *Mazzaferri* Fred, Commentaries on Revelation; a translator's guide: BTrans 42 (1991) 133-9.

5912 **Mounce** Robert H., What are we waiting for? Commentary on Revelation. GR 1992, Eerdmans. x-141 p. $11. 0-8028-0613-9 [NTAbs 36, p. 434].

5913 **Schüssler Fiorenza** Elisabeth, Revelation; vision of a just world: Proclamation Comm. Mp 1991, Fortress. 150 p. $10. 0-8006-2510-2. – ᴿExpTim 104 (1992s) 238 (C. S. *Rodd:* clearly far removed from the older style of commentary).

5914 **Sinclair** Scott G., Revelation — a book for the rest of us. SF 1992, BIBAL. 156 p. £13. 0-941037-19-3 [TDig 40,187]. – ᴿExpTim 104 (1992s) 281 (J. M. *Court:* for those interested neither in academic facts nor in speculations about when the world will end); SewaneeTR 36 (1992s) 174s (D. R. *Ruppe*).

5915 *Stanley* John E., Some words on the Bible's last word; an assessment of four recent commentaries on Revelation [BORING M.; MULHOLLAND M., SCHÜSSLER FIORENZA E., WALL R.]: ChrSchR 22 (1992) 291-6.

5916 **Thomas** R. L., Revelation 1-7. Exegetical Comm. Ch 1992, Moody. xxvii-524 p. 0-8024-9265-7.

5917 **Thompson** Leonard L., The book of Revelation; apocalypse and empire [against GAGER and SCHÜSSLER-FIORENZA] 1990 ⇢ 6,5935; 7,5019: ᴿAnglTR 74 (1992) 231-3 (R. A. *Whitacre*, also on HUGHES P.); JRel 72 (1990) 98s (Adela Y. *Collins:* a genuine contribution); TLZ 117 (1992) 512-4 (J. *Zengenberg:* unconvincing).

5918 **Vögtle** Anton, Il libro dei sette sigilli; commento all'Apocalisse di Giovanni, ᵀ: In ascolto. T-Leumann 1990, ElleDiCi. 189 p. – ᴿRivLtg 79 (1992) 122s (G. *Crocetti*).

5919 **Wall** Robert W., Revelation: NIntB 1991 ⇢ 7,5022: ᴿExpTim 104 (1992s) 238 (C. S. *Rodd*).

5920 **Wilcock** Michael, The message of Revelation; I saw Heaven opened: The Bible Speaks Today. Leicester 1992, Inter-Varsity. 240 p. 0-85110-964-0.

G2.4 *Apocalypsis, Revelation, topics.*

5921 *Agourides* Savas, The apocalypse of St. John (a text of mellontological or mainly paraenetical character?): DeltioVM 21,11 (1992) 70-85.

5922 **Altenbaumer** James E.,   The salvation myth in the hymns in Revelation: diss. Emory, ᴰ*Robbins* V. Atlanta 1992. 343 p. 92-24382. – DissA 53 (1992s) 1182-A: RTLv 24, p. 545.

5923 **Altizer** T.J.J.,   Genesis and apocalypse; a theological voyage toward authentic Christianity. Louisville 1991, W-Knox. 192 p. 0-664-21932-2. – ᴿJRel 72 (1992) 605s (Lissa *McCullough:* authentic Christianity is apocalyptic Christianity).

5924 **Beagley** Alan J.,   The 'Sitz im Leben' of the Apocalypse with particular reference to the role of the Church's enemies [Diss. Fuller 1983]: BZNW 50, 1987 ➤ 3,5494 ... 5,5659: ᴿTR 88 (1992) 117s (O. *Böcher*).

5925 **[Turley von] Burkalow** James, † 1959, A study of St. John's Revelation, ᴱ*Burkalow* Anastasia von (his daughter; first of several manuscripts she is preparing). Pittsburgh 1990, Dorrance. v-270 p. $13. – ᴿCritRR 5 (1992) 248-250 (R. *Farmer:* good on structure, otherwise outdated and allegorizing).

5926 *Collins* Adela Y.,   Revelation, book of: ➤ 741, AnchorBD 5 (1992) 694-708.

5927 **Contreras Molina** Francisco, El Señor de la vida; lectura cristológica del Apocalipsis: BtEstB 76. S 1991, Sígueme. 383 p. – ᴿBibFe 18 (1992) 147s (A. *Salas*); LumenVr 41 (1992) 385 (F. *Ortiz de Urtaran*).

5928 **de Silva** David A.,   The social setting of the Revelation to John; conflicts within, fears without: WestTJ 54 (1992) 273-302.

5928* *a)* de Silva David A.,   The Revelation to John; a case study in apocalyptic propaganda and the maintenance of sectarian identity; – *b)* *Sanders* Jack T.,   Christians and Jews in the Roman Empire; a conversation with Rodney STARK: SocAnalysis 53 (Wsh 1992) 375-396 / 431-446 [447s, rejoinder].

5929 **Gentry** Kenneth L.,   Before Jerusalem fell; dating the book of Revelation. Tyler 1989, Institute for Christian Economics. xv-489 p. – ᴿJEvTS 35 (1992) 545s (R. *Ludwigson*); JTS 43 (1992) 816 (J.P.M. *Sweet*).

5930 **Guimond** John,   The silencing of Babylon; a spiritual commentary on the Revelation of John 1991 ➤ 7,5009: ᴿCritRR 5 (1992) 214s (J. C. *Wilson:* rather 'Silencing of Revelation'; unmitigated eisegesis); ExpTim 104 (1992s) 238 (C. S. *Rodd:* not intended as exegesis).

5931 **MacKenzie** Robert K.,   The ethnic background of John the Seer; an examination of the language, scriptural allusions, and distinctive motifs of the Apocalypse: diss. McGill, ᴰ*Wisse* F. Montreal 1992. – SR 21 (1992) 494.

5932 **Michaels** J. Ramsey,   Interpreting the Book of Revelation: Guides to NT Exegesis 7. GR 1992, Baker. 150 p. $10. 0-8010-6293-4 [NTAbs 37, p. 289].

5933 *Moberly* Robert B.,   When was Revelation conceived? [69 A.D. at Patmos]: Biblica 73 (1992) 376-393; franç. 393.

5934 **Mendel** A. P. (1927-88), Vision and violence. AA 1992, Univ. Michigan. v-322 p. $30. 0-472-10275-3 [NTAbs 37, p. 150: 'universal devastation' varyingly foreseen in western culture is less central to the Bible than a humane 'repair of nature'].

5935 **Montague** G. T.,   The Apocalypse; understanding the book of Revelation and the end of the world. AA 92, Servant. 246 p. ill., map. [NTAbs 34, p. 128] 0-89283-746-2.

5936 *Pikaza* Xabier,   Apocalipsis de Juan; origen y fin de la violencia: Carthaginensia 8 (1992) 609-639.

5938 **Prévost** Jean-Pierre, Pour lire l'Apocalypse. P/Outremont QU 1991, Cerf/ Novalis. 160 p. F 100. 2-204-04395-8. – ᴿAugM 37 (1992) 411s (J.

Anoz); EsprVie 102 (1992) 212s (L. *Walter*); ÉTRel 67 (1992) 470s (E. *Cuvillier*).

5939 *Ravasi* Gianfranco, L'Apocalisse secondo i Testimoni di Geova: RCler-It 72 (1991) 30-40.

5940 *Sand* Alexander, Mahnung, Trost und Verheissung; die Prophetenrede der Joh-Apokalypse: ➤ 112*, Mem. Kuss O., 1992, 433-448.

5941 **Spivey** Steven W., The implications of the Book of Revelation for Karl BARTH's doctrine of election as presented in the 'Church Dogmatics': diss. Baylor 1991. 271 p. 93-09329. – DissA 53 (1992s) 4370-A.

5942 *Stevens* R. Paul, Poems for people in distress; the Apocalypse of John and the contemplative life: Themelios 18,2 (1992s) 11-14.

5943 **Stock** Klemens, Das letzte Wort hat Gott; Apokalypse als Frohbot-schaft[2]. Innsbruck 1992, Tyrolia. 158 p. [AcPIB 9/8,660].

5944 *a*) *Thompson* Leonard L., Mooring the Revelation in the Mediterra-nean; – *b*) *Ruiz* Jean-Pierre, Betwixt and between on the Lord's Day; liturgy and the Apocalypse: ➤ 478, SBL Sem. 31 (1992) 635-653 / 654-672.

5945 *Vanni* Ugo, L'Apocalisse; ermeneutica, esegesi, teologia 1988 ➤ 4,5676 ... 7,5936: R Angelicum 69 (1992) 425-7 (G. *Marcato*); Salesianum 54 (1992) 161 (R. *Sabin*).

5946 **Weber** Hans-Ruedi, The way of the lamb; Christ in the Apocalypse; Lenten meditations: Risk Book. Genève 1988, WCC. 58 p. Fs 8. [RTLv 24,88, J. *Ponthot*].

Structura; **genre, research history.**

5947 *Adinolfi* Marco, Le similitudini dell'Apocalisse e l'interpretazione di VITTORINO di Petovio: ➤ 485, Efeso II, 1991/2, 41-53.

5948 *Bøe* Sverre, The use of the Old Testament in Revelation [in Norwegian with a survey of recent treatments]: TsTKi 63 (1992) 253-268; Eng. 269.

5949 E **Emmerson** Richard K., *McGinn* Bernard, The Apocalypse in the Middle Ages. Ithaca NY 1992, Cornell Univ xiii-428 p.

5950 *Mathewson* Dave, Revelation in recent genre criticism; some impli-cations for interpretation: TrinJ 13 (1992) 193-213.

5951 **Mazzaferri** Frederick D., The genre of the Book of Revelations from a source-critical perspective [diss. Aberdeen 1986]: BZNW 54, 1989 ➤ 5, 5683; 6,5959: R Bijdragen 53 (1992) 325s (J. *Lambrecht:* Australian; the high quality we would expect); CBQ 53 (1991) 143s (R. *Morton*).

5952 **Rakoto** Modeste E., Unity of the letters and vision in the Revelation of John: diss. Lutheran School of Theology 1991, D*Linss* W. 258 p. 92-30464. – DissA 53 (1992s) 1961s-A.

5953 *Thomas* R.L., Literary genre and hermeneutics of the Apocalypse: Master's SemJ 2,1 (1991) 79-97 [< NTAbs 38, p. 67].

5954 **Zager** Werner, Begriff und Wertung der Apokalyptik in der neutesta-mentlicher Forschung 1989 ➤ 6,3987: [ev. Diss. Mainz 1988, D*Bran-denburger* E.].

Theologica.

5955 *Boring* M. Eugene, Narrative Christology in the Apocalypse: CBQ 54 (1992) 702-723.

5956 *Corsini* Eugenio, Appunti per una lettura teologica dell'Apocalisse: ➤ 485, Efeso 2, 1991/2, 187-205.

5957 *Harrington* Wilfrid, Positive eschaton only; *Revelation* and universal salvation: PrIrB 15 (1992) 42-59.

5958 *Hohnjec* Nikola,   Die Christologie in der Offenbarung des Johannes: BogSmot 62,3s (1992) 239; 216-238 hrvatsk.

5959 **Raguse** Hartmut,   Psychoanalytische und theologische Auseinandersetzung mit E. DREWERMANNS Auslegung der Apokalypse des Johannes: Diss. ᴰ*Stegemann*. Basel 1992. – TR 89,77; RTLv 24, p. 600.

5960 ᴱ**Rogers** C. R., *Jeter* J. R.,   Preaching through the Apocalypse; sermons from Revelation. St. Louis 1992, Chalice. ix-165 p. $16 pa.   0-8272-2944-5 [NTAbs 37, p. 450].

5961 *Shin Kyo-Seon,* Exegetical study on Revelation [... Christology]: Sinhak Jonmang 99 (Kwangju 1992) 2-54 [< TContext 10/2,51].

5962 **Thomas** R. L.,   The Kingdom of Christ in the Apocalypse: Master's SemJ 3 (1992) 117-140 [< NTAbs 37, p. 385].

5963 **Toribio** Fernando,   El 'venir' de Dios en el Apocalipsis; uso exegético-teológico del verbo 'erchesthai' en la literatura joánica: diss. Pont. Univ. Gregoriana, 3927, ᴰ*Vanni* U. Roma 1992. 572 p. – RTLv 24, p. 550.

Particularia – **Observations.**

5964 *a) Burtness* J. H., 'The Lamb who was slain has begun his reign, Amen'; texts from the Revelation to John for the Sundays of Easter: WWorld 12,2 (1992) 182-7; – *b) Pagán* S.,   El Apocalipsis de Juan y la Iglesia hispana: Apuntes 12,1 (Dallas 1992) 3-12 [both < NTAbs 36,376].

5965 *Byrd* James P.ᴶ,   The slave spiritual as apocalyptic discourse: PerspRelSt 19 (1992) 199-201.204-216.

5966 *Cook* Cornelia,   The language of likeness in the Apocalypse: NBlackf 73 (1992) 472-486.

5967 *a) Guthrie* Donald,   Aspects of worship in the Book of Revelation; – *b) Stanton* Graham,   Aspects of early Christian and Jewish worship; PLINY and the Kerygma Petrou: ⇒ 126, ᶠMARTIN R., Worship 1992, 70-83 / 84-98.

5968 **Harȩzga** Stanisław, ⦿ Błogosławieństwa [beatitudines] Apokalipsy: Attende lectioni 17. Katowice 1992, Św. Jacka. 151 p. 83-7030-046-4.

5969 **Huelskoetter** John M.,   The social function of the Book of Revelation: diss. Baptist Theol. Sem., ᴰ*Simmons* B. New Orleans 1992. 192 p. 92-33846. – DissA 53 (1992s) 2412s-A.

5970 *Kealy* Séan P.,   At a loss when facing the Book of Revelation [rather a critique of then-current apocalyptic than a justification for J. F. WALVOORD's million-copy Armageddon, oil, and the Middle East crisis; or Pat ROBERTSON's quarter-million The new millennium): BToday 30 (1992) 29-32.

5971 *Le Grys* Alan,   Conflict and vengeance in the Book of Revelation: ExpTim 104 (1992s) 76-80.

5972 *Martens* M.,   Key terms in the Book of Revelation: NotTr 6,1 (1992) 23-43 [< NTAbs 37, p. 385].

5973 *a) Meye Thompson* Marianne,   Worship in the Book of Revelation; – *b) Gowan* Donald E.,   Worship as divine-human encounter; in Scripture and in contemporary experience; – *c) Hadidian* Dikran Y.,   Anthropocentric to theocentric; worship in American churches in the 20th century; – *d) Murphy* Larry G.,   African American worship and the interpretation of Scripture: ⇒ 624, Ex Aud 8 (1992) 45-54 / 73-84 / 107-112 / 95-105.

5974 **Pippin** Tina,   Death and desire; the rhetoric of gender in the Apocalypse. Louisville 1992, W-Knox. 144 p. $19.   0-664-25157-9 [NTAbs 37, p. 290]. – ᴿExpTim 104 (1992s) 281s (D. S. *Russell:* useful if or because admittedly biased; 'victimage', 'scapegoating' bewilder).

5975 *Pippin* Tina,   Eros and the end; reading for gender in the Apocalypse of John: Semeia 59 (1992) 193-210 (responses 211-7, *Robbins* V.; 219-225, *Schaberg* Jane).
5976 *Selvidge* Maria J.,   Powerful and powerless women in the Apocalypse: Neotestamentica 26 (1992) 157-167.

G2.5   *Apocalypsis,* Revelation 1,1 ...

5977 **Woschitz** Karl M.,   Erneuerung aus dem Ewigen; Denkweisen — Glaubensweisen in Antike und Christentum nach Offb. 1-3, 1987 ➤ 3,5588 ... 6,5975: ᴿTR 88 (1992) 118s (O. *Böcher*).
5978 a) *Adinolfi* Marco,   I cristiani 'sacerdoti' secondo Apc. 1,6; 5,10 e 20,6 nella interpretazione di TERTULLIANO; – b) *Corsini* Eugenio,   Per una nuova lettura dell'Apocalisse: ➤ 7,451, Efeso I, 1990/91, 99-109 / 75-97.
5979 *Toribio* J. F.,   La recepción de Dn 7,13 en Ap 1,7:   Mayéutica 18,45 (Marcilla 1992) 9-56 [< NTAbs 37, p. 227].
5980 **Hagedorn** D.,   P. IFAO II 31 [ᴱ*Wagner* G.,   Papyrus grecs de l'IFAO II, 1971, 47s]: Johannesapokalypse 1,13-20: ZPapEp 92 (1992) 243-7.
5981 a) *Boring* M. Eugene,   The voice of Jesus in the Apocalypse of John; b) *Beale* G. K,   The interpretative problem of Rev. 1:19:   NT 34 (1992) 334-359 / 360-387.
5982 *Pilch* John J.,   Lying and deceit in the letters to the seven churches; perspectives from cultural anthropology: BibTB 22 (1992) 126-135.
5983 *Klauck* H.-J.,   [Apk 2,12] Das Sendschreiben nach Pergamon und der Kaiserkult in der Johannesoffenbarung: Biblica 73 (1992) 153-182; franç. 182.
5984 *Prigent* Pierre,   Lettre à l'Église de Pergame: MondeB 77 (1992) [< EsprVie 102 (1992) 647-9 (J. *Daoust*)].
5985 *Grayston* K.,   [Rev 4-6] Heaven and hell: a door opened in Heaven: EpworthR 19 (1992) 19-26 [< NTAbs 37,64].
5986 **Davis** R. D,,   The heavenly court judgment of Revelation 4-5.   Lanham MD 1992, UPA.   vii-296 p. $42.50.   0 8191 8613-9 [NTAbs 37, p. 125]. – ᴿExpTim 104 (1992s) 155s (D. S. *Russell:* 'a telescope' compared to MEALY's 'microscope').
5987 *Rochat* Didier,   [Apc 4s] La vision du trône; une clé pour pénétrer l'Apocalypse: Hokhma 49 (1992) 1-21.
5988 a) *Míguez* N. O.,   Las víctimas en el Apocalipsis; estudio de Apc 5 tras 500 años de incorporación de América al dominio occidental; – b) *Nogueira* P. A. de Souza,   La realización de la justicia de Dios en la historia: RIBLA 12 (1992) 167-185 / 11 (1992) 112-121 [< Stromata 49,292].
5989 a) *Sorger* Karlheinz,   [Apk 5,1] 'Das Buch mit den sieben Siegeln'; Einführung / Bilderwelt der Apokalypse; – b) *Chmielus* Augustinus,   Zwei Bilder zur Apokalypse; – c) *Richter* Irmhild,   Das Zelt Gottes unter den Menschen und die neue Stadt ... Apk 21: ZPraxRU 22 (1992) 82-89 / 100-2 / 92-95 [< ZIT 92,534s].
5990 **Vögtle** Anton,   Il libro dei sette sigilli: In Ascolto 49.   T-Leumann 1990, LDC.   192 p.   Lᵐ 12.   88-01-13593-9. – ᴿParVi 37 (1992) 155s (C. *Doglio*).
5991 *Steinmann* Andrew E.,   The tripartite structure of the sixth seal, the sixth trumpet, and the sixth bowl of John's Apocalypse (Rev 6:12-7:17; 9:13-11:14; 16:12-16): JEvTS 35 (1992) 69-79.
5992 **Ulfgard** Håkan,   Feast and future; Rev 7:9-17 and the Feast of Tabernacles 1989 ➤ 5,5713 ... 7,5074:   ᴿJTS 43 (1992) 623s (J.P.M. *Sweet*; modest, well-informed, surely correct); WestTJ 53 (1991) 156-9 (Karen H. *Jobes*).

5993 *Nielsen* Kirsten, [Rev 7,14-17] Shepherd, lamb, and blood; imagery in the OT, use and reuse: ST 46 (1992) 121-132.

5994 **Paulien** Jon, Decoding ... Rev 8:7-12, 1988 ➤ 7,5076: ᴿJBL 111 (1992) 358-361 (G. K. *Beale:* interesting but limited).

5995 *a) Horn* Friedrich W., Die sieben Donner; Erwägungen zu Offb 10; – *b) Schille* Gottfried, Der Apokalyptiker Johannes und die Edelsteine (Apk 21): SNTU A-17 (1992) 215-229 / 231-244.

5996 *Pippin* Tina, [Apc 12 ...] The heroine and the whore; fantasy and the female in the Apocalypse of John: Semeia 60 (1992) 67-82 (83-89, response, *Dewey* Joanna).

5997 *Robinson* Andrew, [Rev 13] Identifying the beast; Samuel HORSLEY and the problem of papal [or? Napoleonic] AntiChrist: JEH 43 (1992) 592-607.

5998 *Bohak* Gideon, [Rev 13,18] Greek-Hebrew gematrias in 3 Baruch and in Revelation: JPseud 7 (1990) 119-121.

5999 **Ruiz** Jean-Pierre, Ezekiel in... Apc 16,17-19,10: EurHS 23/376, 1989 ➤ 5, 5718 ... 7,5084: ᴿCBQ 54 (1992) 171s (R. *Morton:* valuable, readable).

6000 **Reichelt** Hansgünter, [Apc 17.7 ...] Angelus interpres; Texte in der Johannes-Apokalypse: Diss. ᴰ*Vogler* W. Leipzig 1992. – RTLv 24, p. 549.

6001 *Lupieri* Edmondo, [Rev 17,9-11] The seventh night; visions of history in the Revelation of John and the contemporary apocalyptic: Henoch 14 (1992) 113-132; ital. 132.

6002 *Kraybill* J. Nelson, Cult and commerce in Revelation 18: diss. Union Theol. Sem. Richmond 1992. 244 p. 92-25335. – DissA 53 (1992s) 1183s-A.

G2.7 **Millenniarismus,** *Apc 20 ...*

6003 ᴱ**Blaising** Craig A., **Bock** Darrell L., Dispensationalism, Israel, and the Church. GR 1992, Zondervan. 402 p. $20 pa. 0-310-34611-8 [TDig 40,263].

6004 **Boyer** Paul, When time shall be no more; prophecy belief in modern American culture. CM 1992, Harvard Belknap press. xiv-468 p. $30. [ChH 62,452-4, J. A. *Carpenter:* how premillennial beliefs have shaped public attitudes].

6005 ᴱ**Campbell** Donald K., *Townsend* Jeffery L., A case for premillennialism; a new consensus. Ch 1992, Moody. 290 p. $22. – ᴿCalvaryB 8,2 (1992) 68s (C. E. *McLain*).

6006 **Crutchfield** Larry, The origins of dispensationalism [< diss. Drew]. Lanham ᴍᴅ 1992, UPA. 236 p. $22.50. – ᴿBtS 149 (1992) 497s (R. P. *Lightner*).

6007 **Gerstner** John, Wrongly dividing the word of truth: a critique of dispensationalism. Brentwood ᴛɴ 1991, Wolgemuth & H. – ᴿBtS 149 (1992) 121-145.259-278 (J. A. *Witmer:* bitter abusive diatribe).

6008 — *Turner* David L., 'Dubious evangelicalism?' A response to John GERSTNER's critique of dispensationalism [1991]: GraceTJ 12 (1991 top of page '1992') 263-277.

6009 **Hill** Charles, Regnum caelorum [... millenarianism in the early Church]. Ox 1992, Clarendon. 236 p. £27.50. 0-19-826738-X. – ᴿExpTim 104 (1992s) 285 (G. *Bostock*).

6010 *Matheson* Iain G., The end of time; a biblical theme in [Roman Catholic Olivier] MESSIAEN's Quartet: ➤ 41, ᶠDAVIDSON R., Text as pretext 1992, 200-214.

6011 *Mattison* M. J., A revised hermeneutic of premillennialism: Journal from the Radical Reformation 1,2 (Morrow GA 1992) 24-29 [< NTAbs 36, p. 380].

6012 **Rosenthal** Marvin J., [Rev 20,11-15...] The pre-wrath rapture of the Church. Nv 1990, Nelson. – ᴿBtS 148 (1991) 90-111 (G. B. *Stanton*); CalvaryB 7,2 (1991) 38-55 (R. *Piserchia*: 'for 30 years a confirmed pretribulationist, he now believes that the Church will have to endure the persecution of the Antichrist') & 56-65 (P. *Piccolo*, on use of Joel 2,31; Mal 4,5).

6013 — **Karleen** Paul S., The pre-wrath rapture of the Church; is it biblical? Langhorne PA 1991, BF.

6014 **St. Clair** Michael J., Millenarian movements in historical context. NY 1992, Garland. 373 p. – ᴿRRelRes 34 (1992s) 379s (J. *Kaplan*).

6015 **Showers** Ronald E., There really is a difference! A comparison of covenant and dispensational theology. Bellmawr NJ 1990, Friends of Israel. 225 p. $6 pa. – ᴿBtS 149 (1992) 498s (R. B. *Zuck*).

6016 *Snyder* Barbara W., How millennial is the millennium? A study in the backround of the 1000 years in Revelation 20: EvJ 9,2 (1991) 51-...

6067 **Stanton** Gerald B., Kept from the hour²ʳᵉᵛ [¹1956 diss.]. Miami Springs FL 1991, Schoettle. 423 p. $9 pa. – ᴿBtS 149 (1992) 244 (J. F. *Walvoord:* clear faith in a pretribulational Rapture).

6018 *Strecker* Georg, *a*) Chiliasmus und Doketismus in der Johanneischen Schule: KerDo 38 (1992) 30-45; Eng. 45s. – *b*) Chiliasm and docetism in the Johannine school: AustralBR 38 (1990) 45-61.

6019 **Grenz** Stanley J., [Apc 20] The millennial maze; sorting out evangelical options. DG 1992, InterVarsity. 284 p. $12. 0-8308-1757-3. – ᴿCrux 28,3 (1992) 46s (T. *Williams*).

6020 **Mealy** J. Webb, After the thousand years; resurrection and judgment in Revelation 20. Sheffield 1992, Academic. vii-296 p. £35; sb. £26.25. 1-85075-363-6 [TDig 40,174]. ᴿExpTim 104 (1992s) 156 (D. S. *Russell*).

6021 *Nardi* C., GREGORIO Magno interprete di Apocalisse XX: ➤ 7,501*, Gregorio 1990/1, 267-283.

6022 *Poythress* Vern S., Genre and hermeneutics in Rev 20:1-6: JEvTS 36 (1993) 41-54.

6023 *Doglio* Claudio, Compimento della storia e liturgia in Ap 21: ➤ 336, ParSpV 25 (1992) 139-154.

6024 *Álvarez Valdés* Ariel, [Apc 21,1-4] La nueva Jerusalén del Apocalipsis; sus raices en el AT; el período de la 'Jesusalén reconstruida': RBibArg 54,47 (1992) 141-153.

6025 *Nereparampil* Lucius, [Rev 21,22] New worship and new Temple: Bible Bhashyam 16 (1990) 216-233.

| XIII. Paulus |

G3.1 Pauli biographia.

6026 **Bartaglio** Giuseppe, Pablo de Tarso y los orígenes cristianos ᵀ*Ortiz García* A: BEB 65, 1989 ➤ 6,6005*b*; 7,5099: ᴿLumenVr 40 (1991) 527s (J. M. *Arróniz*).

6027 **Baslez** Marie-Françoise, Saint Paul 1991 ➤ 7,5100: ᴿDialHA 18,1 (1992) 302-5 (P. *Lévêque*); RB 99 (1992) 440 (J. *Murphy-O'Connor*); RÉLat 70 (1992) 381s (Y. *Le Bohec*); RHPR 72 (1992) 203s (E. *Trocmé*).

6028 *Betz* Hans D., Paul: → 741, AnchorDB 5 (1992) 186-201 [–202, Paul's nephew, Acts 22,16, *O'Toole* Robert].

6029 **Breton** Stanislas, S. Paolo, un ritratto filosofico [1988], ᵀ1990 → 6,6012: ᴿParVi 37 (1992) 309s (E. *Franco*, anche su KERTELGE K., SCHELKLE K.).

6030 **Dicharry** Warren, Human authors of the NT, 2. Paul and John. ColMn 1992, Liturgical. 253 p.; 7 maps. $13 pa. 0-8146-2099-X [NTAbs 37, p. 104].

6031 **Dreyfus** Paul, Saint Paul. 1990. – ᴿRB 99 (1992) 613s (J. *Taylor*).

6032 *Durand* Xavier, Vies de Saint Paul [DREYFUS P. 1990; BASLEZ M., LÉGASSE S., SAFFREY H. 1991]: Masses Ouvrières 445 (1992) 107-111.

6033 **Feneberg** Wolfgang, Paulus der Weltbürger; eine Biographie. Mü 1992, Kösel. 312 p. DM 40. 3-466-20357-0 [NTAbs 36, p. 431]. – ᴿGeistL 65 (1992) 395-7 (J. *Steiner*).

6034 **Hengel** Martin, The pre-Christian Paul 1991 → 7,5119: ᴿNBlackf 73 (1992) 458s (Morna *Hooker*); TLond 95 (1992) 138s (J. *Barclay* contrasts with 'slapdash' MACCOBY 1991); UnSemQ 45 (1991) 142-8 (A. F. *Segal*, also on MACCOBY); Vidyajyoti 56 (1992) 560s (P. *Meagher*).

6035 **Hengel** Martin, Il Paolo precristiano, ᵀ*Pontaglio* Giovanni: StBPaid 100. Brescia 1992, Paideia. 204 p. 88-394-0478-3.

6036 *Hengel* M. (*Deines* M.). Der vorchristliche Paulus: → 492, SCHLATTER-Symposium 1988/91, 177-291 (–293 Diskussion).

6037 **Hildebrandt** Dieter, Saulus / Paulus, ein Doppelleben 1989 → 6,6028: ᴿLuthMon 29 (1990) 572 (D. *Aschenbrenner*).

6038 **Hildebrandt** Dieter, Saulo-Pablo, una doble vida 1991 → 7,5120; ᵀ*Gancho* Claudio: ᴿLumenVr 41 (1992) 400s (U. *Gil Ortega*).

6039 **Hubaut** Michel A., Paul de Tarse: BtHistChr 18, 1989 → 5,5757 ... 7,5123: ᴿÉglT 22 (1991) 217s (N. *Bonneau*); MélSR 48 (1991) 190-2 (L. *Derousseaux*).

6040 *Langenhorst* Georg, Neues und Altes vom 'selbsternannten Apostel' [MESSADIÉ G., *al.*]: Orientierung 56 (1992) 247-250.

6041 **Légasse** Simon, Paul apôtre; essai de biographie critique 1991 → 7, 5129: ᴿBiblica 73 (1992) 586-9 (S. B. *Marrow*); ÉTRel 67 (1992) 469 (G. *Wagner:* standard); Foi Temps 22 (1992) 376s (C. *Focant*); RB 99 (1992) 440-4 (J. *Murphy-O'Connor*, also on BASLEZ); RBiArg 53 (1991) 175-7 (A. J. *Levoratti*); RHPR 72 (1992) 204 (E. *Trocmé*, aussi sur SANDERS); Salesianum 54 (1992) 583s (J. J. *Bartolomé*).

6042 **Messadié** Gérald, Ein Mann namens Saulus, Roman [1991 → 7,5136]. ᵀ*Choma* A., *Kienast* W. Mü 1992, Droemer Knaur. 640 p. DM 44.

6043 **Mesters** Carlos, Una entrevista con el Apóstol Pablo. Bogotá 1991, Paulinas. 64 p. – ᴿIter 3,1 (1992) 134s (J. P. *Perón*).

6044 *Moda* Aldo, Paolo prigioniero e martire [< conferenze ÉPHÉ 1971s, poi ᴰ1981]: BbbOr 34 (1992) 179-183.193-252 ...

6045 *Rolland* Philippe, Discussions sur la chronologie paulinienne [DREYFUS P. 1990; LÉGASSE S., BASLEZ M. 1991 ...]: NRT 114 (1992) 870-889.

6046 *Roloff* Jürgen, Paulus: → 757, EvKL 3 (1992) 1088-97.

6047 **Sánchez Bosch** Jordi, Nascut a temps; una vida de Paul, l'Apòstol: Eines 10. Barc 1992, Claret. 263 p. 84-7263-760-3.

6048 **Sanders** E. P. Paul 1991 → 7,5148: ᴿJTS 43 (1992) 600-5 (N. T. *Wright:* clearest available); Salesianum 54 (1992) 585s (J. J. *Bartolomé*).

G3.2 **Corpus paulinum;** *generalia, technica epistularis.*

6049 **Aland** K. *al.*, Text und Textwert 2/1, Die paulinischen Briefe 1991 → 7,5158: ᴿEnchoria 19s (1992s) 231s (H. J. *Klauck*); RÉG 105 (1992) 286 (J. *Irigoin*, 1-3).

6050 *Aletti* Jean-Noël, La *dispositio* rhétorique dans les épîtres pauliniennes; propositions de méthode: NTS 38 (1992) 385-401.

6051 **Carena** Carlo, S. Paolo, Le lettere 1990 ➤ 6,6058; 7,5163: ᴿRivStoLR 27 (1991) 519-523 (F. *Bolgiani*); StPatav 38 (1991) 202s (G. *Segalla*).

6052 ᴱ**Cugusi** Paolo, Corpus epistularum latinarum papyris tabulis ostracis servatarum (CEL): PapyrFlor 23. F 1992, Gonnelli. I. Textus p. 261; XXII pl.; II. commentarius 406 p.

6053 *Greenwood* H. H., St. Paul revisited; a computational result; LitLComp 7 (1992) 43-47; 5 fig. (clusters).

6054 **Neumann** Kenneth J., The authenticity of the Pauline Epistles in the light of stylistic analysis: SBL diss 120 (Toronto, ᴰ*Hurd* J.) 1990 ➤ 6, 6065: ᴿCBQ 54 (1992) 795s (T. A. *Bergren*); JBL 111 (1992) 550-3 (E. *Krentz*).

6055 *Pardee* Dennis, *Dion* Paul E., *Stowers* Stanley K., Letters: Hebrew / Aramaic / Greek-Latin: ➤ 741, AnchorBD 4 (1992) 282-85-90-93.

6056 **Ranon** Angelo, S. Paolo: Vita e lettere. NT II. Padova 1991, Messaggero. 250 p. Lit. 18.000. 88-250-0076-6. – ᴿCC 143 (1992,3) 452s (D. *Scaiola*); Gregorianum 73 (1992) 346s (G. *Marconi*).

6057 **Richards** E. Randolph, [Rom 16:22] The secretary in the letters of Paul [diss, SW Baptist (Fort Worth, *pace* p. 605), ᴰ*Ellis* E.]: WUNT 2/42, 1991, ➤ 7,5156: ᴿBiblica 73 (1992) 286-8 (R. *Penna*); ÉTRel 67 (1992) 109s (É. *Cuvillier*); JTS 43 (1992) 618-620 (H. D. *Betz*, severe: full of errors and guesswork; it is he who needed a secretary); NT 34 (1992) 300-2 (J.A.D. *Weima*); RHPR 72 (1992) 206s (C. *Grappe*); TLZ 117 (1992) 915-7 (A. *Lindemann*).

6058 **Schmidt** Peter, In vrijheid, trouw en hoop; inleiding tot Paulus, de Katholieke Brieven en de Apocalyps. Averbode / Boxtel 1992, Altiora / KBStichting. 270 p. Fb 795. – ᴿStreven 59 (1992s) 1046 (P. *Beentjes*: Ghent sem. prof.).

6059 **Schreiner** Thomas R., Interpreting the Pauline epistles: Guides to NT Exegesis 5, 1990 ➤ 6,6075 ... 7,5180: ᴿAsbTJ 47,1 (1992) 98-101 (M. R. *Mulholland*); EvQ 64 (1992) 175-8 (R. *Shirock*).

6060 *Söding* Thomas, Zur Chronologie der paulinischen Briefe; ein Diskussionsvorschlag: BibNot 56 (1991) 31-59.

6061 **Taatz** Irene, Frühjüdische Briefe; die paulinischen Briefe im Rahmen der offiziellen religiösen Briefe des Frühjudentums: NOrb 16, 1992 ➤ 7, 5182: ᴿRelStR 18 (1992) 330 (A. J. *Malherbe*); RHPR 72 (1992) 205s (C. *Grappe*); TLZ 117 (1992) 193s (M. *Karrer*).

6062 **Thekkekara** Mathew, The face of early Christianity; a study of the Pauline letters 1988 ➤ 6,6080: ᴿBible Bhashyam 16 (1990) 199s (M. *Kizhakeerunjanil*); IndTSt 28 (1991) 339s (L. *Legrand*).

6063 **Trobisch** David, Die Entstehung der Paulusbriefsammlung ...: NOrb 10, 1989 ➤ 5,5810 ... 7,5183: ᴿBO 49 (1992) 580-2 (P. J. *Tomson*); MüTZ 43 (1992) 254s (J. *Gnilka*: originell, hypothesenfreundlich, lesbar).

6064 *Vouga* François, Der Brief als Form der apostolischen Autorität: ➤ 337, TANZ 7 (1992) 7-58.

6065 **Wente** Edward F., Letters from ancient Egypt 1990 ➤ 6,6085: ᴿAustralBR 40 (1992) 65s (H. A. *Stamp*).

G3.3 Pauli theologia.

6066 *Barrett* C. K., Paulus als Missionar und Theologe: ➤ 492, SCHLATTER-Symposium 1988/91, 1-15.

6067 ᴱBassler Jouette M., Pauline theology 1, 1991 ➤ 7,290: 0-8006-2488-2.
267-289 bibliographies; 16 art.; infra (1992) [JBL 112,557, tit. pp.]. –
ᴿExpTim 103 (1991s) 346 (J.M.G. *Barclay*).

6068 **Beilner** Wolfgang, Die Theologie des Paulus: Vermittlung 26. Salzburg
1992, nicht im Handel. 152 p.

6069 *a*) *Beker* J. Christiaan, Recasting Pauline theology; the coherence-con-
tingency scheme as interpretative model; – *b*) (response) *Achtemeier* Paul
J., Finding the way to Paul's theology: ➤ 6067, Pauline Theology 1
(1991) 15-24 / 25-36.

6070 **Capes** D. B., OT Yahweh texts in Paul's Christology [diss. SW Baptist
Sem, Fort Worth 1990, ᴰ*Ellis* E.]: WUNT 2/47. Tü 1992, Mohr. –
vii-220 p. 3-16-145819-2. – ᴿArTGran 55 (1992) 326s (A. *Segovia*);
SNTU A-17 (1992) 268s (A. *Fuchs*).

6071 **Cousar** Charles B., A theology of the Cross; the death of Jesus in the
Pauline letters [selected passages from the seven chief epistles]: OvBT 1990
➤ 6,6094; 7,5188: ᴿCBQ 54 (1992) 147s (J. P. *Heil*); CritRR 5 (1992)
188-190 (C. J. *Roetzel:* considerable strengths); Horizons 19 (1992) 132s
(D. *Burton-Christie*); Interpretation 46 (1992) 73 (R. C. *Tannehill*).

6072 **Davis** Christopher A., 'The truth which is the Gospel'; the coherent
center of Paul's theology: diss. Union Theol. Sem. ᴰ*Achtemeier* P. Richmond 1992. 697 p. 92-22443. – DissA 53 (1992s) 1183-A.

6073 *Dumbrell* William, Justification in Paul, a covenantal perspective: Ref-
TR 51 (1992) 91-101.

6074 **Ellis** E. Earle, Pauline theology; ministry and society 1989 ➤ 5,5819 ...
7,5191: ᴿJEvTS 35 (1992) 541-3 (D. B. *Capes*); RefTR 50 (1991) 37s (D.
Peterson); StPatav 38 (1991) 203 (G. *Segalla*); WestTJ 53 (1991) 367-370
(J.A.D. *Weima*).

6075 **Fitzmyer** Joseph A., Paul and his theology 1988 ➤ 4,5820 ... 7,5193:
ᴿÉglT 22 (1991) 215-7 (N. *Bonneau*); JEvTS 35 (1992) 261s (D. C.
Stoutenburg: thoroughly modern).

6076 **Fitzmyer** Joseph A., According to Paul; studies in the theology of the
Apostle. NY 1992, Paulist. xi-177 p. $13.

6077 *Hainz* Josef, Gemeinde des Gekreuzigten; Skizze zur paulinischen Ekklesiologie: ➤ 112*, Mem. Kᴜss O. 1992, 329-349.

Hamerton-Kelly R. G., Sacred violence; Paul's hermeneutic of the Cross
1992 ➤ 7824.

6078 **Horn** F. W., Das Angeld des Geistes; Studien zur paulinischen Pneumatologie [Hab.-Diss. Gö 1986]: FRL 154. Gö 1992, Vandenhoeck & R.
478 p. DM 148. 3-525-53835-9. – ᴿExpTim 104 (1992s) 269 (E. *Best*).

6079 *Horn* Friedrich W., Wandel im Geist; zur pneumatologischen Begründung der Ethik bei Paulus: KerDo 38 (1992) 149-170; Eng. 170.

6080 **Howell** Don N.ᴶ, The theocentric character of Pauline theology: diss.
Dallas Theol. Sem. 1992, 331 p. 93-03917. – DissA 53 (1992s) 3251-A.

6081 *a*) *Hübner* Hans, Zur gegenwärtigen Diskussion um die Theologie des
Paulus [MERKLEIN H.; SANDERS E. P.; BEKERS J., BECKER J.]; – *b*) *Hainz*
Josef, Vom 'Volk Gottes' zum 'Leib Christi'; biblisch-theologische Per-
spektiven paulinischer Theologie: ➤ 355, JbBT 7 (1992) 399-413 / 145-164.

6082 **Kertelge** Karl, 'Giustificazione' in Paolo 1991 ➤ 7,5198: ᴿCC 143
(1992,2) 311-3 (D. *Scaiola*); MüTZ 43 (1992) 135 (G. L. *Müller*); RivB 40
(1992) 116 (A. *Bonora:* appendice dei molti titoli frattanto pubblicati);
Salesianum 54 (1992) 583 (J. J. *Bartolomé*).

6083 *Kottackal* Joseph, Life in the Spirit according to Paul: Bible Bhashyam
18 (1992) 18-33.

6084 **Kreitzer** L. Joseph, Jesus and God in Paul's eschatology 1987 ➤ 3,5648 ... 7,5199: ᴿJJS 43 (1992) 320-2 (C.R.A. *Murray-Jones*).

6085 **Langkammer** Hugolin, ❷ Teologia św. Pawła: TeolNT 2. Lublin 1992. KUL. 106 p. 83-228-0291-9 [TR 89,519].

6086 **Limbeck** Meinrad, Mit Paulus Christ sein; Sachbuch zur Person und Theologie des Apostels Paulus 1989 ➤ 6,6033: ᴿBiKi 47 (1992) 175 (Kelle *Schmitz*).

6087 **Martin** R.P., Reconciliation, a study in Paul's theology 1989 = 1981 + appendix. – ᴿNeotestamentica 26 (1992) 538s (F.S. *Malan*).

6088 *Nebe* Gottfried, Righteousness in Paul, ᵀ*Cathey* Paul: ➤ 499, Justice 1990/2, 131-153.

6089 **Newman** Carey C., [1 Cor 9,1 ... Ezek 1] Paul's glory-Christology, tradition and rhetoric: NT supp 69. Leiden 1992, Brill. xviii-305 p. *f* 160. 90-04-09463-6. – ᴿJStJud 23 (1992) 257-260 (P.W. van der *Horst*, also on GARLINGTON D. 1991; WILSON W. 1991).

6090 **Nichols** David R., The strength of weakness, the wisdom of foolishness; a theological study of Paul's theologia crucis: diss. Marquette, ᴰ*Kurz* W. Milwaukee 1992. 224 p. 92-27132. – DissA 53 (1992s) 1195-A.

6091 *O'Grady* John F., Paul and justification: ChSt 31 (1992) 66-80.

6092 **Scott** James M., Adoption as sons of God; an exegetical investigation into the background of *huiothesia* in the Pauline corpus [< ev. diss. Tübingen 1989, ᴰ*Stuhlmacher* P. ➤ 7,5240]: WUNT 2/48. Tü 1992, Mohr. xv-353 p. DM 79. 3-16-145895-8 [TDig 40,290].

6093 **Seeley** David, The noble death; Graeco-Roman martyrology and Paul's concept of salvation: JStNT supp 28, ᴰ1990 ➤ 6,6116 ... 7,5208: ᴿCBQ 54 (1992) 172-4 (J. *Gillman*); Interpretation 46 (1992) 74.76 (M.L. *Soards*); JBL 111 (1992) 544-6 (J.D. *Tabor*).

6094 **Seifrid** Mark A., Justification by faith; the origin and development of a central Pauline theme: NT supp 68. Leiden 1992, Brill. xiv-310 p. *f* 170. 90-04-09521-7 [NTAbs 37, p. 291].

6095 **Sinclair** Scott G., Jesus Christ according to Paul; the Christologies of Paul's undisputed epistles and the Christology of Paul ➤ 5,5834 [diss. 1986, Graduate Theological Union]: BIBAL mg 1. Berkeley 1988. vi-150 p. $13 pa. 0-941037-08-8.

6096 **Yorke** Gosnell, The Church as the Body of Christ in the Pauline corpus 1991 ➤ 7,5213: ᴿEvQ 64 (1992) 286s (A. *Perriman*).

6097 **Zdziarstek** Roman S., ❷ Chrystianologia [the Christianology] świętego Pawła, I. Aspekt ontyczny. Kraków 1989, Polskie Towarzystwo Teologiczne. 276 p. – ᴿColcT 62,3 (1992) 189-192 (J. *Królikowski*, ❷).

G3.4 *Pauli stylus et modus operandi* – Paul's image.

6098 *Alves* Herculano, Cristocentrismo em S. Paulo: HumTeol 13 (1992) 277-315.

6099 **Arzt** Peter, Bedrohtes Christsein; zu Eigenart und Funktion eschatologisch bedrohlicher Propositionen in den echten Paulusbriefen [kath. Diss. Salzburg 1991, ᴰ*Beilner* W.]: BeitBExT 26. Fra 1992, Lang. 294 p. 3-631-45097-4.

6100 *Asensio* Félix, Los colaboradores de Pablo: Burgense 33 (1992) 329-380.

6101 **Beker** J. Christian, The triumph of God; the essence of Paul's thought 1990 ➤ 6,6009; 7,5104: ᴿCurrTMiss 19 (1992) 139 (Lynn A. *Kauppi*: translation of Der Sieg Gottes, which in turn was abridgedᵀ of Paul the

Apostle 1980); HorBT 14 (1992) 77s (D.M. *Hay*); HumTeol 12 (1991) 143s (A. *Couto*); Interpretation 46 (1992) 201s (E. *Best:* the English adds to the 1988 German a 1989 Interpretation article); ScotJT 45 (1992) 121s (Frances M. *Young*, also on ZIESLER); TorJT 8 (1992) 190 (L. Ann *Jervis*); TrinJ 13 (1992) 215s (M.A. *Seifrid*); Vidyajyoti 56 (1992) 119s (P. *Meagher*).

6102 **Blasi** A., Making charisma ... Paul 1991 ➤ 7,5106: ᴿRRelRes 33 (1990s) 377s (C.D. *Bradfield*).

6103 *Bony* P., L'enseignement de saint Paul dans un séminaire; articulation avec d'autres aspects de la formation: ➤ 448, ᴱ*Auneau*, Ens.Écr. 1992, 134-145.

6104 *a) Buzzetti* Carlo, La coscienza missionaria di Paolo; – *b) Valentini* Alberto, L'annuncio anima della missione; – *c) Barbaglio* Giuseppe, Le lettere di Paolo, strumento della missione; – *d) Heriban* Jozef, La catena dei missionari: ParVi 35,5 (S. Paolo e la missione 1990) 326-334 / 335-341 / 342-350 / 351-361.

6105 **Carson** D.A., A call to spiritual reformation; priorities from Paul and his prayers. GR 1992, Baker. 230 p. 0-8010-2569-9. [NTAbs 37,125].

6106 **Castelli** Elizabeth A., Imitating Paul; a discourse of power < diss. Claremont: LitCuB 1991: ➤ 7,5112: ᴿAnglTR 74 (1992) 520-2 (P.T. *Coke*); BZ 36 (1992) 279-281 (C. *Heil*); CCurr 43 (1993s) 130-3 (G. *Aichele*, also on FOWLER R. 1991); Encounter 53 (1992) 292-4 (R.J. *Allen*); ExpTim 104 (1992s) 281 (J.M. *Court*); JRel 72 (1992) 581s (Margaret M. *Mitchell*); Mid-Stream 31,3 (1992) 272-4 (W.R. *Baird*); SWJT 35,1 (1992s) 61 (B.K. *Putt:* multiple readings).

6107 **Goodwin** Mark J., Conversion to the living God in diaspora Judaism and Paul's letters: diss. Yale, ᴰ*Malherbe* A. New Haven. – RTLv 24, p. 547 sans date.

6108 **Klumbies** P.-G., Die Rede von Gott bei Paulus in ihrem zeitgeschicht-lichen Kontext [< diss. Bethel. 1988, ᴰ*Lindemann* A.]: FRL 155. Gö 1992, Vandenhoeck & R. 289 p. DM 98. 3-525-53836-7 [NTAbs 37, p. 448].

6109 *a) Lambrecht* Jan, Paul and suffering; – *b) Michiels* Robrecht, Jesus and suffering — the suffering of Jesus: ➤ 577, Suffering 1987/9, 47-67 / 31-45.

6110 *Lips* Hermann von, Paulus und die Tradition; Zitierung von Schrift-worten, Herrenworten und urchristlichen Traditionen [150 Publikationen; Register S. 70]: VerkF 36,2 (1991) 27-49.

6111 **Mödritzer** Helmut, Selbststigmatisierung im Neuen Testament und seiner Umwelt: Diss. ᴰ*Theissen* G. Heidelberg 1992s. – RTLv 24, p. 548.

6112 **Neyrey** Jerome H., Paul, in other words 1990 ➤ 6,6066; 7,5175: ᴿAngl-TR 74 (1992) 100s (D.J. *Horton*); BA 55 (1992) 159 (S.M. *Sheeley:* exciting, challenging, sociological / anthropological model; CBQ 54 (1992) 583s (N. *Elliott:* important counterbalance to traditional theology, despite Christian ethnocentrism of some of the 'maps'); ChrCent 108 (1991) 891 (W.R. *Stegner:* illuminating despite some overstating); JBL 111 (1992) 726-8 (J.L. *Jaquette:* criticisms not meant to detract); LivLight 28,1 (1991s) 91s (F. *Gillman*).

6113 **Oechslen** B., Kronzeuge Paulus 1990 ➤ 6,6109; 7,5203: ᴿTvT 32 (1992) 94 (H. van de *Sandt*).

6114 *Omanson* Roger L., Acknowledging Paul's quotations: BTrans 43 (1992) 201-213.

6115 **Pagels** Elaine H., The Gnostic Paul; gnostic exegesis of the Pauline letters. Ph 1992 (pa. = 1975), Trinity. xii-180 p. $15. 1-56338-039-0 [NTAbs 36, p. 434].

6116 **Pak Yeong-Sik** James, Paul as a missionary ... contemporary Jewish texts ᴰ1991 ⇥ 7,5140: ᴿLuthTK 15 (1991) 180 (V. *Stolle*).

6117 **Pastor Ramos** Federico, Pablo, un seducido por Cristo 1991 ⇥ 7,5141: ᴿRBibArg 54 (1992) 244-6 (N. O. *Miguez*).

6118 **Peace** Richard V., The conversion of the Twelve in the light of St. Paul's conversion; toward a biblical definition of conversion: diss. Natal S. Africa 1990. – DissA 53 (1992s) 3562-A.

6119 *Pelicia* Flora, San Pablo evangelizador y el poder interior: RBiArg 53 (1991) 157-162.

6120 **Penna** Romano, Paolo di Tarso; un cristianesimo possibile: Univ Teologia 7. CinB 1992, Paoline. 190 p. Lᵐ 15. 88-215-2360-9. – ᴿLateranum 58 (1992) 610 (*ipse*); RivScR 6 (1992) 457 (G. *Ricchiuti*).

6121 **Pereira** Francis, Gripped by God in Christ; the mind and heart of St. Paul. Bombay 1990, St. Paul. 160 p. rs 35. – ᴿJDharma 17 (1992) 61.

6122 **Pillette** Bard M., Paul and his fellow workers; a study in the use of authority: diss. Dallas Theol. Sem. 1992, ᴰHeater H. 412 p. 93-03920. – DissA 53 (1992s) 3251s-A.

6123 *Sampley* J. Paul. From text to thought world; the route to Paul's ways: ⇥ 6067, Pauline Theology 1 (1991) 3-14.

6124 **Sandnes** Karl O., [Gal 1,15s...] Paul — one of the prophets?: WUNT 2/43, 1991 ⇥ 7,5149: ᴿBiblica 73 (1992) 120-2 (R. *Penna*); RB 100 (1993) 310 (J. *Murphy-O'Connor*); TvT 32 (1992) 195s (H. van de *Sandt*).

6125 **Segal** Alan F., Paul the convert 1990 ⇥ 6,6049; 7,5150: ᴿCBQ 54 (1992) 588-590 (A. J. *Saldarini:* very fine despite several reserves); ChrCent 107 (1990) 1000s (J. C. *Wilson*); DanTTs 55 (1992) 28-35 (T. *Engberg-Pedersen*) [< NTAbs 37, p. 370]; EvQ 64 (1992) 61-74 (C. C. *Newman:* transforming images of Paul); Interpretation 46 (1992) 184-7 (R. B. *Hays:* 'not the Paul I know'); JRel 72 (1992) 484 (A. J. *Droge*); JTS 43 (1992) 191-6 (M. *Bockmuehl*); TLond 95 (1992) 209s (G. *Stanton:* one of the finest).

6126 *Smit* Joop, Het andere gezicht van Paulus: Streven 59 (1992s) 771-8.

6127 **Stanley** Christopher D., Paul and the language of Scripture; citation technique in the Pauline epistles and contemporary literature [diss. Duke 1990, ᴰSmith D. M. ⇥ 6,6078a]: SNTS mg 74. C 1992, Univ. xii-396 p. £40. 0-521-41925-5. – ᴿExpTim 104 (1992s) 379 (G. J. *Brooke*).

6128 *Stuhlmacher* P., Das Christusbild der Paulus-Schule; eine Skizze: ⇥ 467, Jews & C 1989/92, 159-175.

6129 **Tambasco** A., In the days of Paul 1991 ⇥ 7,5152: ᴿLvSt 17 (1992) 76s (R. F. *Collins*, also on his Atonement).

6130 *a) Tronier* Henrik, Spørgsmålet om hermeneutisk kongruens i Paulus-eksegesen; – *b) Engberg-Pedersen* Troels, Om en adækvat Pauluseksegese: DanTTs 55 (1992) 102-122.121-208 / 209-216 [< zɪᴛ 92,680].

6131 **Via** Dan O.ᴶ, Self-deception and wholeness in Paul and Matthew 1990 ⇥ 6,6169; ᴿCBQ 54 (1992) 806s (Mary Ann *Getty*); CritRR 5 (1992) 250-3 (L. *Steffen:* some issues); TLZ 117 (1992) 435-7 (G. *Sellin*); TorJT 7 (1991) 287s (S. *Brown*).

6132 **Ziesler** John, Pauline Christianity 1991 ⇥ 7,5248: ᴿSalesianum 54 (1992) 587s (J. J. *Bartolomé*).

G3.5 Apostolus Gentium [⇥ G4.6, Israel et Lex / Jews & Law].

6133 *Barclay* J.M.G., The Jewish missionary to the Gentiles [WRIGHT N. 1992; HENGEL M., MACCOBY H. 1991]: L Times Literary Supp. (May 8 1992) 2612 [< NTAbs 37, p. 49].

6134 **Becker** Jürgen, Paulus, Apostel der Völker 1989 → 6,5739; 7,5101:
ᴿBLtg 65 (1992) 121-3 (T. *Söding*); ÉTRel 67 (1992) 468s (G. *Wagner*).

6135 *Engberg-Pedersen* Troels, Den jødiske Paulus — og den græske: Dan-
TTs 55 (1992) 28-35 [< ᴢɪᴛ 92,285].

6136 **Gerleman** Gillis, Der Heidenapostel; ketzerische Erwägungen 1989 → 5,
5751; 7,5114: ᴿJTS 43 (1992) 606s (N. T. *Wright:* holds Paul's 'solid
food' is a defense of pagan myths as a subversion of Christian teachings).

6137 **Hays** Richard B., Echoes of Scripture in the letters of Paul 1989
→ 5,5795 ... 7,5170: ᴿJBL 111 (1992) 155-7 (Carol L. *Stockhausen:* seven
quite utilizable criteria); HeythJ 33 (1992) 87 († F. F. *Bruce*); TorJT 8
(1992) 332s (Patricia M. *Stortz*).

ᴱHengel M., Heckel U., Paulus und das antike Judentum 1988/91 → 492
(7,437).

6139 *Hooker* M. D., Paul — apostle to the Gentiles: EpworthR 18,2 (1991)
79-89 [< NTAbs 37, p. 50].

6140 *Kruse* Colin G., The price paid for a ministry among Gentiles; Paul's
persecution at the hands of the Jews: → 126, ᶠMARTIN R., 1992, 360-372.

6141 **Laato** Timo, Paulus und das Judentum; anthropologische Erwägungen
1991 → 7,5127: ᴿJStNT 47 (1992) 128 (C. M. *Tuckett:* normative SAN-
DERS 1977 does not take into account that Paul's view of human nature's
capabilities is radically pessimistic, Judaism's optimistic); KIsr 7 (1992)
103s (J. *Kirchberg*).

6142 **Niebuhr** Karl-Wilhelm, Heidenapostel aus Israel; die jüdische Identität
des Paulus nach ihrer Darstellung in seinen Briefen: WUNT 62. Tü 1992,
Mohr. xi-234 p. DM 188. 3-16-145892-3. – ᴿExpTim 104 (1992s) 268s
(E. *Best:* Gal 1,13s; Phlp 3,5s; 2 Kor 11, 22s; Röm 11,1).

6143 ᴱ**Perelmuter** Hayim, Wuellner Wilhelm, Paul the Jew; Jewish/Christian
dialogue [GTU student papers plus useful data]: HermSt 60. Berkeley
1990, Center Herm.St. vi-89 p. – ᴿCBQ 54 (1992) 168s (Florence M.
Gillman: very badly edited).

6144 *Räisänen* Heikki, Paul's call experience and his later view of the Law
[p. 7: intended to fill a gap in Paul and the Law 1983 ²1987, and to reply
to S. KIM and G. KLEIN]: → 294, Jesus, Paul and Torah 1992, 15-47 [with
7 reprints already in The Torah and Christ 1986, partly from German].

6145 *Stegner* William R., A Jewish Paul [NEYREY J.]: AsbTJ 47,1 (1992) 89-95.

6147 [→ 6330] *Tomson* Peter J., Halachische brieven uit de oudheid; Qumran
[MMT], Paulus en de Talmoed: NedTTs 46 (1992) 284-301.

G3.6 *Pauli fundamentum* **philosophicum** *et* **morale.**

6148 *Basevi* Claudio, San Paolo misogino?: StCattMi 35 (1991) 402-411.

6149 **Baumert** Norbert, [→ 9021] Frau und Mann bei Paulus; Überwindung
eines Missverständnisses. Wü 1992, Echter. 448 p. DM 39 [NTAbs 38,
p. 127]. 3-429-01407-7. – ᴿGeistL 65 (1992) 394s (P. *Imhof*); TGL 82
(1992) 365s (W. *Beinert*); TPhil 67 (1992) 581s (H. *Giesen*).

6150 **Fredrickson** D., Free speech in Pauline political theology: WWorld 12
(1992) 345-351 [< NTAbs 37, p. 220].

6151 **Holloway** J. O., *peripateō* as a thematic marker for Pauline ethics [diss.
SWBaptist, Fort Worth, ᴰ*Greenfield* G.]. SF 1992, Mellen Univ. viii-
264 p. 0-7734-9943-1 [NTAbs 37, p. 288].

Keener Craig S., Paul, women and wives 1992 → 9053.

6152 **Maccoby** Hyam, Paul and Hellenism 1991 → 7,5132: ᴿJJS 43 (1992)
153-6 (C. R. A. *Murray-Jones*); NT 34 (1992) 297-9 (Nina L. *Collins*).

6153 *Merritt* H.W., Paul and the individual; a study in Pauline anthropology: JIntdenom 18 (Atlanta 1990s) 31-60 [< NTAbs 37, p. 370].

6154 **Muller** E.C., Trinity and marriage in Paul 1990 ⇒ 6,6108; 7,5202: ᴿTvT 32 (1992) 95 (L. *Visschers*).

6155 *Nikopoulos* B.E., The legal sense of *arrhabōn* in the letters of Paul: DeltioVM 21,12 (1992) 28-40.

6156 **Pitassi** M.C., Le philosophe et l'Écriture, LOCKE / Paul 1990 ⇒ 6,6069: ᴿCrNSt 13 (1992) 235-8 (M. *Micheletti*).

6157 *Roth* Catharine P., Platonic and Pauline elements in the ascent of the soul in GREGORY of Nyssa's dialogue on the soul and resurrection: VigChr 46 (1992) 20-30.

6158 **Sampley** J. Paul, Walking between the times; Paul's moral reasoning 1991 ⇒ 7,5239: ᴿExpTim 103 (1991s) 376s (M. B. *Thompson*); RelStR 18 (1992) 317 (R. C. *Sparks*).

6159 *Schnabel* E.J., Wie hat Paulus seine Ethik entwickelt? Motivationen, Normen und Kriterien paulinischer Ethik: EurJT 1 (1992) 63 ... [< ZIT 92,488].

6160 **Strong** Leslie T.ᴵᴵᴵ, The significance of the 'knowledge of God' in the epistles of Paul: diss. Baptist Theol. Sem., ᴰ*Stevens* G. New Orleans 1992. 155 p. 92-27158. – DissA 53 (1992s) 1549-A.

6161 *Vassiliadis* Petros, Equality and justice in classical antiquity and in Paul; the social implications of the Pauline collection: StVlad 36 (1992) 51-59.

G3.7 *Pauli* communitates *et* spiritualitas.

6162 **Branick** Vincent P., The house church in the writings of Paul 1989 ⇒ 5,5843: ᴿPerspRelSt 29 (1992) 341s (F. S. *Spencer*).

6163 **Cruz** Hieronymus, Christological motives 1990 ⇒ 6,6126 [3-631-42857-X]; 7,5222: ᴿIndTSt 28 (1991) 340-3 (L. *Legrand*).

6164 **Ebner** M., Leidenslisten 1991 ⇒ 7,5223: ᴿStreven 59 (1992s) 753s (P. *Beentjes*, ook over SCHRAGE W. 1 Kor); TPhil 67 (1992) 580s (N. *Baumert*).

6164* [Schiefer] **Ferrari** Markus, [1 Cor 4] Die Sprache des Leids in den paulinischen Peristasenkatalogen [Diss. Marburg, ᴰ*Gnilka* J. ⇒ 6,6164] Stu: BB 23, 1991, KBW. xi-510 p. DM 49. 3-460-00231-X. – ᴿLuthTK 16 (1992) 145s (H. *Brandt*).

6165 **Gebauer** Roland, Das Gebet bei Paulus; forschungsgeschichtliche und exegetische Studien [Diss. Erlangen ᴰ*Merk* O.] 1989 ⇒ 6,6129: ᴿTLZ 117 (1992) 356 (K. *Haacker*).

6166 **Georgi** Dieter, Theocracy in Paul's praxis and theology [< 1987 conference]; ᵀ*Green* D. 1991 ⇒ 7,5194: ᴿCBQ 54 (1992) 777s (P. *Rogers*); ExpTim 103 (1991s) 311 (J. *Proctor:* good, but would Paul agree 'his crime was an active one, an act of political aggression' p. 104?).

6167 *Harris* B.F., St. Paul and the public reputation of the churches: RefTR 50 (1991) 50-58.

6168 *Meagher* P., Paul and mission: Vidyajyoti 56 (1992) 250-9.

6169 **Monloubou** Louis, Oración y evangelización; San Pablo y la oración [S. Paul et la prière, LDiv 110, 1982 ⇒ 63,5731; 2-204-01786-8, Cerf]: Buena Noticia 14. Estella 1983, VDivino. 160 p. 84-7151-365-X.

6170 *Moore* W. Ernest, 'Outside' and 'Inside'; Paul and Mark [SCHILLEBEECKX: Pharisees, Essenes, and all groupings within Judaism tended to divide or exclude; Jesus was always pro, never anti]: ExpTim 103 (1991s) 331-6.

6171 **Perkins** William J.[J], A sociological exegesis of Pauline paraeneses pertaining to the formation of the community of believers in Rom, 1-2 Cor, Gal, 1-2 Thess: diss. Baylor 1992, 196 p. 93-07295. – DissA 53 (1992s) 3946-A.

6172 **Reck** Reinhold, Kommunikation und Gemeindeaufbau; eine Studie [Lektüre der Paulusbriefe...] zu Entstehung, Leben und Wachstum Paulinischer Gemeinden in den Kommunikationsstrukturen der Antike [kath. Diss. [D]*Klauck* H., Würzburg 1990]: SBB 22. Stu 1991, KBW. 354 p. DM 39. – [R]BZ 36 (1992) 149-152 (A. *Weiser*).

6173 *Roetzel* Calvin J., Oikumene and the limits of pluralism in Alexandrian Judaism and Paul: ➤ 107, [F]KRAABEL A. T., 1992, 163-182.

6175 *Stuhlmacher* Peter, Das Christusbild der Paulus-Schule — eine Skizze: ➤ 467, Parting 1989/92, 159-175.

Taylor Nicholas, Paul, Antioch and Jerusalem; a study in relationships and authority in earliest Christianity, [D]1922 ➤ 5534.

6176 *Teliercio* Giuseppe, Nuove creature in Cristo; con Paolo alla scuola del Maestro: Meditazioni per la vita 8. CinB 1990, Paoline. 186 p. L[m] 10. – [R]Protestantesimo 47 (1992) 142s (L. *De Lorenzi*).

6177 *Thuruthumaly* Joseph, *a*) Renewal of life in St. Paul: Bible Bhashyam 16 (1990) 114-128. – *b*) Mysticism in Pauline writings: Bible Bhashyam 18 (1992) 140-152.

6178 **Tobin** Thomas H., The spirituality of Paul 1987 ➤ 3,5713; 4,5898: [R]LexTQ 25 (1990) 59s (Sharyn E. *Dowd*).

6179 *Vellanickal* Matthew, Faith experience and ecclesial life according to St. Paul: Bible Bhashyam 16 (1990) 182-192.

G3.8 *Pauli receptio,* **history of research.**

6180 [E]**Babcock** William S., Paul and the legacies of Paul [1987 meeting] 1990 ➤ 6,510: [R]AndrUnS 30 (1992) 77s (H. *Weiss*); Interpretation 46 (1992) 412 (Rebecca H. *Weaver*); TLZ 117 (1992) 274-7 (W. *Klaiber*, tit.pp. comment).

6181 *Balás* David L., The use and interpretation of Paul in IRENAEUS's five books Adversus haereses: SecC 9 (1992) 27-39.

6182 **Beker** J. Christiaan, Heirs of Paul; Paul's legacy in the NT and in the Church today. Mp 1991, Augsburg Fortress [➤ 7,5102]; also E 1992, Clark. 146 p. £10. 0-567-29214-2. – [R]ExpTim 103 (1991s) 311s (D. *Hill*: clear and persuasive); TBR 5,3 (1992s) 27s (D. *Horrell*).

6183 *Braet* H., La réception médiévale de l'Apocalypse paulinienne; une réécriture de l'au-delà: ➤ 62, [F]GASCA QUIERAZZA G. 1988...

6184 **Caleo** M., L'Apostolo e il filosofo, San Paolo 'letto' da Karl BARTH [Röm 1932, ital. 1974]. N 1989, LER. 309 p. Lit. 25.000. – [R]Asprenas 39 (1992) 289s (P. *Giustiniani*).

6185 **Cecchini** Francesca, Il Paolo di ORIGENE; contributo alla storia della recezione delle epistole paoline nel III secolo: Verba Seniorum NS 11. R 1992, Studium. 225 p. 88-382-3646-1 [BLitEc 94,134 H. *Crouzel*].

6186 *De Bruyn* Theodore S., CONSTANTIUS the tractator, author of an anonymous commentary on the Pauline epistles? [FREDE H. 1973, mostly from Budapest]: JTS 43 (1992) 38-54.

6187 [E]**Feld** Helmut, Johannes CALVIN, Commentarii in Pauli Epistolas: Opera 2/16. Genève 1992, Droz. lviii-487 p. [ActuBbg 30,223, A. *Borràs*].

6188 **Heither** Theresia, Translatio religionis; die Paulusdeutung des ORIGENES: BoBKG 16, 1990 ➤ 6,6206: [R]ETL 68 (1992) 170s (D. *Bundy*).

6189 **Luedemann** Gerd, Opposition to Paul 1989 ➤ 5,5765 ... 7,5130: ᴿAngl-
TR 74 (1992) 104-6 (R. I. *Pervo*); JPsy&Chr 10 (1991) 89-92 (J. H. *Ellens*).
6190 **Noormann** Rolf, Paulus in frühchristlicher Zeit; Studien zu Rezeption,
Verständnis und Wirkung paulinischer Theologie im Werk des IRAENÄUS
von Lyon: Diss. ᴰ*Wickert* U. Berlin 1992, 679 p. – RTLv 24, p. 552.
6191 *Pollastri* Alessandra, Osservazioni sulla presenza del corpus paolino nelle Quaestiones di AGOSTINO su Deuteronomio, Giosuè e Giudici: ➤ 458,
AnStoEseg 9,2 (1992) 425-466; Eng. 342.
6192 *Rodd* C. S., Recent commentaries C. The Pauline epistles: ExpTim 104
(1992s) 173-8: 15, several infra; p. 177 expresses dismay at the emergence
of several new commentary-series, and suspicion that the 'commentary' itself is an outdated genre.
6193 *a) Tronier* H., Spørgsmålet om hermeneutisk kongruenz i Pauluseksegesen 2. Allegorisk og typologisk hermeneutik; – *b) Engberg-Pedersen* T.,
Om en adaeqvat Pauluseksegese [contra Tronier]: DanskTTs 55 (1992)
191-208 / 209-216 [< NTAbs 37, p. 213].
Viciano A., Cristo ... salvación ... TEODORETO / paulinas 1990 ➤ k838.
6195 *Viciano* Alberto, Das Bild des Apostels Paulus im Kommentar zu den
paulinischen Briefen des THEODORET von Kyros: ZNW 83 (1992) 138-148.
6196 **Way** David V., The lordship of Christ; Ernst KÄSEMANN's interpretation of Paul's theology [< diss. Oxford, ᴰ*Ashton* J.]: TMg, 1991
➤ 7,5211: ᴿCritRR 5 (1992) 253s (R. *Scroggs:* clear 'long-needed guide
to this craggy giant', though ultimately favoring E. P. SANDERS); JTS 43
(1992) 319 (J. *Riches:* his influence waned since his 1973 Romans and
un-theology of E. P. SANDERS and THEISSEN; but he is also too open for
conservative defenses against them).

G3.9 *Themata particularia de Paulo,* **details.**

6197 *Godin* André, Une libido, au sens élargi de l'apôtre Paul: VSp 146 (1992)
483-494.
6198 **[Gundry] Volf** Judith M., Paul and perseverance; staying in and falling
away ᴰ1990 ➤ 6,6131; 7,5225: ᴿCalvinT 26 (1991) 273-7 (A. J. *Bandstra*);
CBQ 54 (1992) 178-180 (W. *Willis*), RefTR 50 (1991) 70s (P. *O'Brien*).
6199 **Hofius** Otfried, Paulusstudien: WUNT 51, 1989 ➤ 5,280 ... 7,5229:
ᴿTLZ 117 (1992) 600s (H. *Hübner*).
6200 **Hooker** Morna D., From Adam to Christ; essays on Paul 1990 ➤ 6,249:
ᴿJTS 43 (1992) 196-8 (V. P. *Furnish:* some queries).
6201 **Leonarda** S., Gioia / Paolo 1988 ➤ 4,6241 ... 7,5232: ᴿCiuD 204 (1991)
263s (J. *Gutiérrez*); RTPhil 124 (1992) 360s (R. *Petraglio*).
6202 **Merklein** Helmut, Studien zu Jesus und Paulus 1987 ➤ 3,257: ᴿTLZ
117 (1992) 125s (C. *Burchard*, 'durch meine Schuld zu spät').
6202* *Oss* Douglas A., A note on Paul's use of Isaiah: BuBRes 2 (1992)
105-112.
6203 **Zeller** Dieter, *Charis* bei Philon und Paulus: SBS 142, 1990 ➤ 6,6174:
ᴿJBL 111 (1992) 548-550 (D. *Winston*).

G4 **Ad Romanos** .1 *Textus, commentarii.*

6204 **Aland** Barbara, *Juckel* Andreas, Die paulinischen Briefe, 1. Römer und
1 Kor: NT syr 2 / ArbNtTextf 14, 1991: ➤ 7,5249: ᴿJBL 111 (1992)
555-8 (W. L. *Peterson*); NT 34 (1992) 398-400 (J. K. *Elliott*).
6205 **Bindemann** Walther, Theologie im Dialog; ein traditionsgeschichtlicher

Kommentar zu Römer 1-11 [Hab.-D. Rostock]. Lp 1992, Ev.-V. 300 p.; ill. DM 120 [TR 88,517; NTAbs 37, p. 445]. 3-374-01390-2.

6206 **Boice** James M.,   Romans.   GR 1991s, Baker.   I. 500 p. [501-512 index]; II. p. x + 503-1021. 0-8010-1002-0; -3-9.

6207 ᵀᴱ**Buzzi** Franco,   M. LUTERO, La lettera ai Romani 1991 ➤ 7,5250: ᴿDivinitas 36 (1992) 91s (B. *Gherardini*); ETL 68 (1992) 461s (J. E. *Vercruysse*, Eng.); FilT 6 (1992) 479s (S. *Sorrentino*); Lateranum 58 (1992) 523-6 (I. *Sanna*).

6208 — **Brambilla** Franco G.,   La prima versione integrale delle Lezioni sulla Lettera ai Romani (1515-6) di LUTERO [ᵀᴱ*Buzzi* F. 1991]: ScuolC 120 (1992) 536-548.

6209 *Deidun* Tom,   James DUNN and John ZIESLER on Romans in new perspective: HeythJ 33 (1992) 79-84.

6210 **Díaz Sánchez-Cid** J. R., Justicia ... ORÍGENES Rom. ᴰ1991 ➤ 7,5252: ᴿSalmanticensis 39 (1992) 415-8 (R. *Trevijano*); ScripTPamp 24 (1992) 621-6 (A. *Viciano*).

6211 **Dunn** James D. G.,   Romans 1-8/9-16: Word Comm. 38AB, 1988/91 ➤ 4,5904 ... 7,5253: ᴿConcordTQ 56 (1992) 44s (P. E. *Detering*: helpful here and there, but with objectionable Christology); CurrTMiss 19 (1992) 299 (E. *Krentz*); ExpTim 104 (1992s) 174 (C. S. *Rodd*, also on EDWARDS J., BLACK M., MOULE H.); RelStR 20 (1990s) 309-311 (K. *Snodgrass*); ScripB 22,1 (1922) 27s (H. *Wansbrough*).

6212 **Edwards** James R.,   Romans: NIntBC 6, 1992 ➤ 7,5254: ᴿJStNT 47 (1992) 127s (P. H. *Kern:* conservative, lucid, readable; but citation of a few Greek words in transliteration will annoy).

6213 ᵀᴱ**Gavigan** J., *al.*, The Navarre Bible; Romans and Galatians. Dublin/ New Rochelle 1991, Four Courts / Scepter. 212 p. $20; pa. $13. – ᴿHomP 92,4 (1991s) 71-73 (W. G. *Most:* series policy on the Gospels less successful here).

6214 **Gregory** Charles D.,   THEODORE of Mopsuestia's commentary on Romans; an annotated translation: diss. Southern Baptist Theol. Sem., 1992, ᴰ*Polhill* J. 157 p. 93-10418. – DissA 53 (1992s) 3945s-A.

6215 **Grenholm** Christina,   Romans interpreted ... BARTH *al.* ᴰ1990 ➤ 6,6181; 7,5256:   ᴿCritRR 5 (1992) 207-210 (D. A. *Carson:* not much hermeneutical sophistication; E. P. SANDERS only briefly noticed); NedTTs 46 (1992) 165s (R. *Roukema*); SvEx 57 (1992) 138-141 (E. *Larsson*).

6216 **Hammond Bammel** Caroline P., Röm/ORIGENES 1990 ➤ 7,5257:   ᴿCBQ 54 (1992) 552s (W. R. *Schoedel*); RET 51 (1991) 405s (M. *Gesteira*).

6216* **Haulotte** Edgar, [notes d'auditeur cours 1979] Lettre aux Romains. P 1991, Médiasèvres. 126 p.; bibliog. de Haulotte. F 85. – ᴿVSp 146 (1992) 248s (H. *Cousin*).

6217 ᵀᴱ**Heither** Theresia, ORIGENES, Commentarii in Epistulam ad Romanos [I. 1990] II. (3.-4. Buch): Fontes Christiani 2. FrB 1992, Herder. 320 p. DM 50; pa. 38. – ᴿBijdragen 53 (1992) 438s (M. *Parmentier*) Eng.: unfortunate that 'he' was unwilling to wait for Mrs. Hammond Bammel's critical edition 1990); TR 88 (1992) 91s (L. *Lies*); TS 53 (1992) 141-3 (B. E. *Daley*); TüTQ 172 (1992) 312s (H. J. *Vogt*).

6218 **Heither** Theresia, 'Translatio religionis'; die Paulusdeutung des ORIGENES in seinem Kommentar zum Römerb. 1990 ➤ 6,6206; 7,5276: ᴿZKG 103 (1992) 116-8 (A. *Lindemann*).

6219 *Hüber* Hans, Römerbrief: ➤ 757, EvKL 3 (1992) 1676-80.

6220 **Hughes** R. Kent, Romans; righteousness from heaven. Westchester IL 1991, Crossway. 339 p. $13. – ᴿBtS 149 (1992) 123 (J. W. *Reed:* brief data also on his Mk Eph Col, to help preaching).

6221 ᴱJunack K., al., Rom 1-2 Kor auf Papyrus: ArbNTTextF 12, 1989 ➤ 7,5259: ᴿRelStR 18 (1992) 330 (B. D. *Ehrman*).

6222 **Kruijf** T. de, Paulus, Rom 1990 ➤ 7,5260: ᴿTvT 32 (1992) 94s (L. *Visschers*).

6223 **Moo** Douglas, Romans 1-8, 1991 ➤ 7,5262*: ᴿJStNT 45 (1992) 123 (S. E. *Porter:* gives conservatives, but also others, a fair view of alternative positions); Themelios 18,1 (1992s) 29 (K. *Snodgrass*).

6224 **Morris** Leon, The epistle to the Romans 1988 ➤ 4,5911; 6,6188: ᴿJEvTS 35 (1992) 539s (S. E. *Porter:* all that evangelicals would expect); RefTR 51 (1992) 31s (D.J.W. *Milne*).

6225 ᵀᴱ**Pani** Giancarlo, Martin Lᴜᴛᴇʀᴏ, Lezioni sulla lettera ai Romani 1991 ➤ 7,5263: ᴿCC 143 (1992,2) 627s (J. E. *Vercruysse*); STEv 4 (1992) 198s (P. *Bolognesi:* ed. Bᴜᴢᴢɪ simultanea).

6226 **Penna** Romano, Una fede per vivere; seguendo il filo della Lettera ai Romani: Frammenti di saggezza biblica 9. CinB 1992, Paoline. 204 p. – ᴿLateranum 58 (1992) 610 (ipse).

6227 **Pongutá** H. Silvestre, El Evangelio de Dios; una lectura de Romanos 1-5 en el V centenario de la primera evangelización: CuadB 4. Caracas 1992, Asn Bíblica Salesiana. [xii–] 265 p. 980-6035-86-0.

6228 **Reller** Jobst, Mose Bᴀʀ Kᴇᴘʜᴀ und seine Paulinenauslegung nebst Edition und Übersetzung des Kommentars zum Römerbrief: Diss. ᴰ*Murtikainen* J. Göttingen 1992s. – RTLv 24, p. 544.

6229 **Rolland** Philippe, À l'écoute de Rom 1991 ➤ 7,5265: ᴿÉTRel 67 (1992) 465 (Danielle *Ellul:* projet fort intéressant; vocabulaire à expliciter ou abandonner; 18 lignes sur le judaïsme inadmissibles); LavalTP 48 (1992) 138s (Odette *Mainville*); PrOrChr 41 (1991) 178s (P. *Ternant*).

6230 **Rossi** Margherita M., Teoría e metodo esegetici in S. Tommaso d'AQᴜɪɴᴏ; analisi del 'Super epistolas Sancti Pauli lectura ad Romanos' c. I, 1,6: diss. Pont. Univ. Angelicum, ᴰ*De Santis* I. Roma 1991. 312 p.

6231 **Roukema** Riemer, The diversity of laws in Oʀɪɢᴇɴ's commentary on Romans 1988 ➤ 5,5915; 6,6215: ᴿRechSR 80 (1992) 113 (B. *Sesboüé*; p. 108 & index 'Roumeka').

6232 **Schmidt-Lauber** Gabriele, Lᴜᴛʜᴇʀs Vorlesung über den Römerbrief 1515/16; ein Vergleich zwischen Luthers Manuskript und den studentischen Nachschriften: Diss. ᴰ*Lohse* B. Hamburg 1992s. – RTLv 24, p. 556.

6233 **Stancari** Pino, Commento alla Lettera ai Romani [lezioni 1989s]: Alle Querce di Mamre. Mi 1992, ᴄᴇɴs, [Coop. Ed. Nuova Stampa]. 208 p.

6234 **Stuhlmacher** P., Der Brief an die Römer 1989 ➤ 5,5901; 7,5266: ᴿTsTKi 62 (1991) 323s (R. *Hvalvik*).

6235 **Theobald** Michael, Römerbrief: Stuttgarter Kleiner Kommentar NT 6. Stu 1992, KBW. I. 320 p. 3-460-15361-X.

6236 **Wilckens** Ulrich, La carta a los Romanos I. ᵀ*Martínez de Lapera* Víctor A.: BtEB 61, 1989 ➤ 6,6195; 7,5269: ᴿLumenVr 40 (1991) 529s (J. M. *Arróniz*); TVida 33 (1992) 321s (M. A. *Ferrando*).

6237 **Ziesler** John, Paul's letter to the Romans: TPI comm 1989 ➤ 5,5903 ... 7,5270: ᴿCBQ 54 (1992) 385s (M. *Cahill*); Furrow 41 (1990) 195s (J. *McEvoy*); Themelios 17,2 (1991s) 22 (M. B. *Thompson*).

G4.2 *Ad Romanos: themata,* **topics.**

6238 **Aletti** J.-N., Comment Dieu est-il juste? 1991 ➤ 7,5271: ᴿBLitEc 93 (1992) 252s (S. *Légasse*); JTS 43 (1992) 360 (J. A. *Ziesler:* has he proved too much? does anyone construct a work as intricately as this? nevertheless important); MondeB 75 (1992) 64 (C. *Perrot*); RivB 40 (1992) 367-9 (R. *Penna:* eccellente); RTPhil 124 (1992) 361 (Muriel *Schmid*).

6239 *Aletti* Jean Noël [Rom 1,16s] Comment Paul voit la justice de Dieu en Rm., enjeux d'une absence de définition: Biblica 73 (1992) 359-375; Eng. 375.

6240 *Barnett* Paul, bp., Revelation in its Roman setting: RefTR 50 (1991) 59-64 + 1 plan; 3 maps.

6241 *a) Crutchley* David, The purpose of Romans; a relief offering and relief letter; – *b) André* Ellis, Preaching on Romans: SAfBap 2 (1992) 1-22 / 92-102.

6242 ᴱ**Donfried** K. P., The Romans debate²ʳᵉᵛ 1991 ➤ 7,298 [JBL 112,745, tit.pp.]: ᴿExpTim 103 (1991s) 246 (D. *Hill:* 13 new essays and all skilfully chosen and presented); IndTSt 29 (1992) 164-6 (L. *Legrand*); Neotestamentica 26 (1992) 245s (M. A. *Kruger*); NRT 114 (1992) 748s (X. *Jacques*); Themelios 18,3 (1992s) 26s (E. *Adams*); TLZ 117 (1992) 754s (P. *Pokorný*); WissWeis 54 (1991) 223s (H.-J. *Klauck*).

6243 *Eckert* Jost, *a)* Zur Erstverkündigung des Paulus; – *b)* Das paulinische Evangelium im Widerstreit: ➤ 112*, Mem. Kᴜss O., Theologie im Werden 1992, 279-299 / 301-328.

6244 **Elliott** Neil, The rhetoric of Romans: jNsu 45, 1990 ➤ 5,5908 ... 7,5274: ᴿInterpretation 46 (1992) 412 (A. C. *Wire*); JTS 43 (1992) 607-9 (W. *Dabourne*).

6245 *Gestrich* Christoph, Der Römerbrief des Paulus und wir heute: ZeichZt 45,3 ('Akzent Mitbürger anderen Glaubens' 1991) 86-90 [< ZIT 92,636].

6246 **Jervis** L. Ann, The purpose of Romans; a comparative letter structure investigation: jNsu 55, 1991: ➤ 7,5277: ᴿÉTRel 67 (1992) 281 (E. *Cuvillier*); JBL 111 (1992) 729s (A. G. *Patzia*); TLZ 117 (1992) 835-7 (K. *Haacker:* student of R. *Longenecker*); TorJT 8 (1992) 305-8 (K. *Quast*, also on W. Hᴀɴsᴇɴ's Galatians).

6247 *Myers* Charles D.ᴶ, Romans, epistle to the: ➤741, AnchorBD 5 (1992) 816-830 [also *al.* Rome; Roman Empire; Rome, Christian monuments / attitudes to].

6248 **Nsengiyumva** François-Vincent, L'Épître aux Romains comme éclairage sur les relations entre l'Occident et le Tiers-Monde: diss. ᴰ*Gourgues* M. Ottawa 1992. 462 p. – RTLv 24, p. 548.

6249 *Oroz Reta* J., Tres lecturas y una conversión ... Rom: AugM 37 (1992) 245-272 [273-302, *Basevi* C., Rom 8].

6250 **Simonis** Walter, Der gefangene Paulus 1990 ➤ 6,6216; 7,5288: ᴿJEvTS 35 (1992) 104s (M. *Silva:* will confirm the view of some that academics can prove anything); TPhil 67 (1992) 269-271 (N. *Baumert*).

6251 *Sontag* Frederick, Bᴀʀᴛʜ, Romans and feminist theology; the problem of God's freedom [a/b ➤ 7,5289]; – *c)* AsiaJT 6,1 (1992) 117-129.

6252 **Vouga** F., Ce Dieu qui m'a trouvé ... Rom 1990 ➤ 7,5291: ᴿProtestantesimo 47 (1992) 325s (Berta *Subilia*).

6253 **Wedderburn** A.J.M., The reasons for Romans 1988 ➤ 4,5926 ... 7,5293: ᴿAustralBR 38 (1990) 85-90 (N. M. *Watson*); RefTR 49 (1990) 33s (D.J.W. *Milne*); Salesianum 54 (1992) 162s (J. J. *Bartolomé*); Vidyajyoti 56 (1992) 561-3 (P. *Meagher*).

G4.3 *Naturalis cognitio Dei* ... **Rom 1-4.**

6254 **Longenecker** Bruce W., Eschatology and the covenant, 4 Ezra/Rom 1-11: jNsu 57, 1991 ➤ 7,5296: ᴿBL (1992) 124 (C.J.A. *Hickling*); ÉTRel

67 (1992) 281s (E. *Cuvillier*); JSS 37 (1992) 101s (B. *Lindars*); JTS 43 (1992) 187-190 (H. *Räisänen:* perceptive).
6256 *Greene* John T., Christ in Paul's thought; Romans 1-8: JRelTht 49,1 (1992) 44-58.
6257 **Moores** John, Enthymematic argument in Romans 1-8, viewed against the background of semiology: diss. London. 231 p. – RTLv 24, p. 548, sans date.
  Pongutá H. Silvestre, El Evangelio de Dios; una lectura de Romanos 1-5 en el V centenario de la primera Evangelización: 1992 ➤ 6227.
6258 *Reid* Marty L., A rhetorical analysis of Romans 1:1-5:21 with attention to the rhetorical function of 5:1-21: PerspRelSt 19 (1992) 255-272.
6259 **Davies** Glenn N., Faith and obedience in Romans ... 1-4: jNsu 39, ᴰ1990 ➤ 6,6219; 7,5297: ᴿCBQ 54 (1992) 345s (B. *Fiore*); TLZ 117 (1992) 670-2 (H. *Hübner*); Themelios 17,3 (1991s) 26s (P. M. *Head*).
6260 **Rogers** Eugene F., A theological procedure in the 'Summa Theologiae'; 'sacra doctrina est scientia' 9.1 and ch. 1 of the 'In Romanos' with a comparison to Karl BARTH: diss. Yale, ᴰ*Lindbeck* G. NHv 1992. 387 p. 93-06967. – DissA 53 (1992s) 4270-A.
6261 *a) Jewett* Robert, Ecumenical theology for the sake of mission; Romans 1:1-17 + 15:14 - 16:24; – *b) Cosgrove* Charles H., The justification of the other; an interpretation of Rom 1:18-4:25; – *c) Wright* N.T., Romans and the theology of Paul: ➤ 478, SBL Sem. 31 (1992) 589-612 / 613-634 / 184-213.
6262 *Bray* Gerald, The Gospel (Romans 1:1-17); – Man's guilt (Romans 1:18-32); – God's Judgement (Romans 2:1-16); – The Jews and the Law (Romans 2:17-3:8); Man's righteousness and God's salvation (Romans 3:9-13); Evangel 1991s: 9/1, 5-8 / 9/2, 7-9 / 9/3, 5-8 / 10-1, 6-10 / 10-2, 5-9.
6263 **Eskola** Timo, *Messias ja Jumalan poika* ... Messiah and Son of God; a tradition-critical study of the Christological clauses in Romans 1:3,4 [diss. ᴰ*Aejmelaeus* L.] Helsinki 1992. 226 p.; Eng. p. iii. RTLv 24, p. 546. 951-9217-11-8.
6264 *a) Toit* Andries B. du, Romans 1,3-4 and the Gospel tradition; a re-assessment of the phrase *katà pneúma hagiosúnēs*; – *b) Bieringer* Reimund, Traditionsgeschichtlicher Ursprung und theologische Bedeutung der *hypèr*-Aussagen im Neuen Testament: ➤ 137, ꟳNEIRYNCK F., Four Gospels 1992, 249-256 / 219-248.
6265 *Álvarez Verdes* Lorenzo, Nacido de la estirpe de David según la carne; contenido semántico del sintagma *katà sôma* en Rom 1,13: ➤ 135, ꟳMUÑOZ IGLESIAS S., EstBib 50 (1992) 335-358.
6266 *Bonneau* Normand, Stages of salvation history in Romans 1:16-3:26: ÉglT 23 (1992) 177-194.
6267 **Kyomya** Michael A. S., The use of Habakkuk 2:4 in Romans 1:17: Diss. Dallas Theol.Sem. 1991, ᴰ*Lowery* D. 210 p. 92-14486. – DissΛ 53 (1992s) 528-A.
6268 *Turner* John M., [Rom 1,17] Mature living: ExpTim 104 (1992s) 84-86.
6269 *Pitta* Antonio, Solo i pagani oggetto dell'ira di Dio? (Rm 1,18-32): ➤ 339, ParSpV 26 (1992) 175-189.
6270 *Mussner* Franz, *Nooumena*; Bemerkungen zum 'Offenbarungsbegriff' in Röm 1,20: ➤ 169, ꟳSECKLER M., Fides 1992, 137-146.
6271 **Henriksen** Jan-Olav, Nature as norm; the concept of nature discussed with reference to Romans 1,24-27 [in Norwegian]: TsTKi 62 (1991) 95-111; Eng. 112.

ᴱ**Bresch** Carsten, *al.*, Kann man Gott aus der Natur erkennen? QDisp 125, 1990 ➤ 2110.

6273 *Holness* Peter, [Rom 1,26s; 1 Cor 6,9; 1 Tim 1,10] Homosexuality; a thorny issue re-examined: SAfBap 2 (1992) 23-35 [no, but with compassion].

6274 *Carras* George P. Romans 2,1-29; a dialogue on Jewish ideals: Biblica 73 (1992) 183-207; franç. 207.

6275 **Garlington** D. B., [Rom 2,13] 'The obedience of faith' ... WUNT 2/38, 1991 ➤ 7,5304: ᴿTvT 32 (1992) 415s (L. *Visschers*).

6276 *Garlington* D. B., [Rom 2,13] The obedience of faith in the letter to the Romans, II. The obedience of faith and judgment by works: WestTJ 53 (1991) 47-72.

6277 *Slater* Graham, [Rom 3] How God puts us right with him: ExpTim 104 (1992s) 14s.

6278 *Feneberg* Wolfgang, [Röm 3,3.31] 'Vernichten' oder 'entmachten'? Bemerkungen zu dem paulinischen Vorzugswort *katargeîn:* KIsr 6 (1991) 53-60.

6279 *Dunn* James D. G., [Gal 2,16; Rom 3,20]: Yet once more – 'the works of the Law'; a response: JStNT [43 (1991) 89-101, CRANFIELD C.] 46 (1992) 99-117.

6280 **Campbell** Douglas A., The rhetoric of righteousness in Romans 3.21-26: jNsu 65. Sheffield 1992, JStOT. 272 p. £35; sb. £26.25. 1-85075-294-X. – ᴿExpTim 103 (1991s) 346s (C.E.B. *Cranfield:* neatly structured, perhaps overstated).

6281 **Kraus** Wolfgang, Der Tod Jesu als Heiligtumsweihe ... Röm 3,25: WM 66, 1991 ➤ 7,5306: ᴿLuthTK 16 (1992) 89s (V. *Stolle*).

6282 *Lincoln* Andrew T., Abraham goes to Rome; Paul's treatment of Abraham in Romans 4: ➤ 126, ᶠMARTIN R., 1992, 163-179.

G4.4 *Peccatum originale; redemptio cosmica:* **Rom 5-8.**

6283 *Pulcini* Theodore, In right relationship with God; present experience and future fulfillment, an exegesis of Romans 5:1-11: StVlad 36 (1992) 61-85.

6284 *Davidsen* O., [Rom 5,12-21] Den strukturelle Adam/Kristus-typologi; om Romerbrevets grundfortælling: DanTTs 55 (1992) 241-261 [< NTAbs 37, p. 216].

6285 *a) Kertelge* Karl, The sin of Adam in the light of Christ's redemptive act according to Romans 5:12-21; – *b) Wiedenhofer* Siegfried, The main forms of contemporary theology of original sin; both ᵀ*Waldstein* Michael; – *c) Henrici* Peter, The philosophers and original sin, ᵀ*Verhalen* Peter: ComND 18 (1991) 502-513 / 514-529 / 489-501.

6286 **Malelel** Augustin B., Die Heilsverfahrung bei den Basaa in Südkamerun im Lichte des Römerbriefes 5,12-21: Diss. ᴰ*Oberlinner* L. Freiburg/Br 1992. 317 p. – RTLv 24, p. 597.

6287 **Mascellani** Elisa, Prudens dispensator verbi; Romani 5,12-21 nell'esegesi di CLEMENTE Alessandrino e ORIGENE: Univ Milano, FacLettF 10, 1990 ➤ 7,5314: ᴿETL 68 (1992) 171s (D. *Bundy*).

6288 *Pratscher* Wilhelm, Die ekklesiologische Dimension der Adam-Christus-Typologie (Röm 5,12-21): ➤ 163, ᶠSAUER G., Aktualität 1992, 133-142.

6289 *Vives* Josep, [Rom 6,1s ...] Bautizados en la muerte y resurrección de Jesucristo: SalT 78 (1990) 121-130.

6290 **Gillman** F. M., A study of Rom 6,5a, United to a death like Christ's [Diss. DLambrecht J., Lv 1982]. SF 1992, Mellen. xix-404 p. $90. 0-7734-9946-6 [NTAbs 37, p. 447].

6291 **Lambrecht** J., Het verscheurde 'ik' en zijn bevrijding; Paulus in Romeinen 7 en 8. 's-Hertogenbosch 1992, KBS. 144 p. 90-334-2696-X. [TvT 33,416, P. J. Farla].

6292 **Lambrecht** Jan, The wretched 'I' and its liberation; Paul in Romans 7 and 8: LvTPastMg 14. LvN 1992, Peeters. 165 p. Fb 695. 90-6831-436-X [TR 89,518].

6293 **Baaij** Peter, Paulus over Paulus; exegetische studie over Rom 7: diss. Bruxelles 1992. – RTLv 24, p. 545.

6294 **Gladden** Philip K., Romans 7 in the context of the sources of Pauline theology: diss. Union Theol. Sem. DAchtemeier P. Richmond 1992. 359 p. 92-22444. – DissA 53 (1992s) 1183-A.

6295 *Schwartz* Robert C., Not complaining about obscurity; Romans 7 and the identity of 'I': SewaneeTR 36 (1992s) 123-135.

6296 *Seifrid* Mark A., The subject of Rom 7:14-25: NT 34 (1992) 313-333.

6297 *Kreitzer* Larry, R. L. STEVENSON's Strange case of Dr. Jekyll and Mr. Hyde and Romans 7:14-23; images of the moral duality of human nature: LitTOx 6,2 (1992) 125-145 [< ZIT 92,363].

6298 *a) Huggins* Ronald V., Alleged classical parallels to Paul's 'What I want to do I do not do, but what I hate, that I do' (Rom 7:15); – *b) Gordon* T. David, Why Israel did not obtain Torah-righteousness; a translation note on Rom 9:32: WestTJ 54 (1992) 153-161 [ZNW 83 (1992) 389 'parables'] / 163-6.

6299 *Basevi* Claudio, Las citas de la Escritura, como recurso de estilo; estudio en los Sermones de san AGUSTÍN sobre Rom 8: AugM 37 (1992) 273-301.

6300 *Rodd* Cyril S., [Rom 8,1-11] Flesh and spirit [King Alfred said translation can be 'word for word' and 'meaning for meaning'; both are useful]: ExpTim 104 (1992s) 146s.

6301 *Burtness* James H., Law and life; a new invitation to an old problem [Rom 8,1 4; BONHOEFFER]: → 77, FHARRISVILLE R. 1992, 155-164.

6302 *a) Wiid* Jack, The 'adopting spirit' in Romans 8:15; – *b) Mathie* Rex, Providence and Romans 8:28; a preacher's personal theodicy: SAfBap 2 (1992) 44-49.50-65.

6303 **Christoffersson** Olle, The earnest expectation of the creature; the flood-tradition as matrix of Rom 8:18-27: ConBib NT 23, 1990 → 6,6347; 7,5323: RCBQ 54 (1992) 145s (Beverly R. Gaventa); SvEx 57 (1992) 129-134 (C. Cavallin).

6304 *a) Lederer* Josef, Geisterfahrung des Priesters; zu Röm 8,19-27; – *b) Braun* Karl, Zur Spiritualität des Diözesanpriesters: KlerusB 72 (Mü 1992) 135s / 131ss.

G4.6 *Israel et Lex;* **The Law and the Jews,** *Rom 9-11.*

6305 **Berger** Klaus, Gottes einziger Ölbaum; Betrachtungen zum Römerbrief. Stu 1990, Quell. 279 p. DM 32. – RLuthMon 30 (1991) 377 (E. Lohse).

6306 **Campbell** W. S., Paul's Gospel in an intercultural context; Jew and Gentile in the Letter to the Romans: StIntK 69, 1991 → 7,5329: ScotJT 45 (1992) 415s (I. H. Marshall; his own collected essays here reviewed by R. T. France); TvT 32 (1992) 196 (H. van de Sandt).

6307 *Campbell* D. A., The meaning of *pístis* and *nómos* in Paul; a linguistic and structural perspective: JBL 111 (1992) 91-103.

6308 **Cassirer** Heinz W., Grace and law; St. Paul, KANT, and the Hebrew prophets 1988 ⇥ 4,5959 ... 7,5330: ᴿÉTRel 67 (1992) 619s (D. *Müller*).

6309 *Dorsey* David A., The Law of Moses and the Christian; a compromise: JEvTS 34 (1991) 321-334 [< BtS 149 (1992) 370s (R. A. *Pyne:* tacitly, rightly, supports dispensationalists)].

6310 **Dunn** J., Jesus, Paul and the Law ... Mk/Gal 1990 ⇥ 6,226; 7,5334: ᴿAndrUnS 30 (1992) 166s (S. *Kubo*); CBQ 54 (1992) 391s (Mary Ann *Getty-Sullivan*); JJS 43 (1992) 147-150 (C.R.A. *Murray-Jones*); ScotJT 45 (1992) 119-121 (H. *Räisänen*).

6311 — *Silva* Moisés, The law and Christianity; DUNN's new synthesis [1990]: WestTJ 53 (1991) 339-353.

6312 **Elliott** Neil, The rhetoric of Romans; argumentative constraint and strategy in Paul's dialogue with Judaism: jNsu 45, 1990 ⇥ 6,6202: ᴿTLZ 117 (1992) 673-5 (K.-W. *Niebuhr*).

6312* *a*) *Faessler* Marc, La racine et la greffe; – *b*) *Bovon* François, Paul aux côtés d'Israël et des Nations; – *c*) *Banon* David, L'Alliance irrevocable; – *d*) *Chalier* Catherine, Le Royaume chez F. ROSENZWEIG; – *e*) *Gross* Benjamin, Israël, une mutation d'identité?; – *f*) *Ucko* Hans, Le dialogue judéo-chrétien; diagnostic et pronostic: BCentProt 44,7s (1992) 22-26 / 6-16 / 17-21 / 27-33 / 34-41 / 42-51.

6313 **Gaston** Lloyd, Paul and the Torah 1987 ⇥ 4,196 ... 7,5336: ᴿConcordTQ 55 (1991) 218-221 (H. A. *Moellering*); TorJT 7 (1991) 275-7 (P. *Richardson*).

6314 *Goedt* Michel De, [Rom 9-11] La véritable 'question juive' pour les chrétiens; une critique de la théologie de la substitution [des chrétiens au peuple juif]: NRT 114 (1992) 237-250.

6315 **Harrington** D. J., Paul on the mystery of Israel: Zch. ColMn 1992, Liturgical. 103 p. $8. 0-8146-5035-X [NTAbs 37, p. 288].

6316 **Johnson** E. Elizabeth, The function of wisdom and apocalyptic traditions in Romans 9-11 [diss. Princeton, ᴰBeker J.C.] 1989 ⇥ 5,5965 ... 7,5337: ᴿAustralBR 40 (1992) 89-91 (D. C. *Sim*); Carthaginensia 8 (1992) 936 (R. *Sanz Valdivieso*).

6317 *a*) *Manicardi* Ermenegildo, Legge, coscienza e grazia nell'insegnamento paolino; – *b*) *Boschi* Bernardo G., Coscienza e Sacra Scrittura: DivThom 95,2 ['La coscienza morale e l'evangelizzazione oggi', Convegno Bologna 6-7.V: 1992) 12-52 / 172-6.

6317* *Martens* Elmer A., Embracing the law; a biblical theological perspective [... Rom 9-11]: BuBRes 2 (1992) 1-28.

6318 **Martens** John, The superfluity of the law in PHILO and Paul; a study in the history of religions: diss McMaster, ᴰWesterholm S., 1991. – SR 21 (1992) 494.

6319 **Martin** Bruce L., Christ and the Law in Paul: NT supp 62, ᴰ1989 ⇥ 6,6276; 7,5344: ᴿStPatav 39 (1992) 462s (G. *Segalla*).

6320 ᴱMuratore Saturnino, Israele e le genti. R 1991, A.V.E. 180 p. Lᵐ 18. ᴿAsprenas 39 (1992) 589s (S. *Cipriani*).

6321 **Oss** Douglas A., Paul's use of Isaiah and its place in his theology with special reference to Romans 9-11: diss. Westminster Theol.Sem. ᴰSilva M. 1992. 230 p. 92-31645. – DissA 53 (1992s) 2413s-A.

6322 **Osten-Sacken** Peter von der, Die Heiligkeit der Tora ... bei Paulus 1989 ⇥ 5,5973: ᴿFranzSt 72 (1990) 373-5 (P. *Kampling*).

6323 **Panimolle** S. A., La libertà ... dalla legge ... 1988 → 6,6280; 7,5346*: ᴿSalesianum 54 (1992) 791s (P. *Merlo*).

6324 *Pinto* C. O., As citações de Isaías em Romanos 9-11; um teste para as técnicas hermenêuticas paulinas: VoxScr 1,1 (1991) 19-32 [< NTAbs 37, p. 217].

6325 *Pitchers* Alrah, Paul's understanding of the place of the Law: SAfBap 2 (1992) 36-43.

6326 *Räisänen* Heikki, a) Freiheit vom Gesetz im Urchristentum: ST 46 (1992) 55-67; – b) Freedom from the law in early Christianity, ᵀᴱ*Asen* B. A.: TDig 40 (1992) 43-48.

6326* ᴱ**Richardson** P., *Westerholm* S., Law ... Torah/Nomos in post-biblical Judaism and early Christianity 1991 → 7,5351: ᴿTorJT 7 (1991) 282-5 (S. *Mason*).

6327 **Sanders** E. P., Paolo, la legge e il popolo giudaico 1989 → 6,6285; 7,5352: ᴿParVi 36 (1991) 468-470 (E. *Franco*).

6328 *Tamez* E., La elección como garantía de la inclusión (Romanos 9-11): RIBLA 12 (1992) 153-166 [< Stromata 49,293].

6329 **Thielman** Frank, From plight to solution ...: NT supp 61, 1989 ▸ 5, 5979; 7,5356: ᴿCBQ 54 (1992) 165-7 (E. *Hensell*, also on MARTIN B. L.); Interpretation 46 (1992) 80.82 (K. *Snodrass*); Themelios 17,1 (1991s) 30 (D. A. *Carson*).

6330 **Tomson** Peter J., Paul and the Jewish law; halakha in the letters of the apostle to the Gentiles: CompRJ 3/2, 1990 ▸ 7,5357: ᴿAndrUnS 30 (1992) 177-9 (H. *Weiss*); CBQ 54 (1992) 805s (J. C. *Turro*: scholarly, daring); CiuD 205 (1992) 757s (J. *Gutiérrez*); GerefTTs 91 (1991) 185s (J. S. *Vos*); JJS 43 (1992) 157-160 (T. H. *Lim*).

6331 *a) Trummer* Peter, Zwischen Gesetz und Freiheit; Anmerkungen zu einer Antinomie bei Jesus und Paulus; – b) *Taeger* Jens-W., Der grund-sätzliche oder ungrundsätzliche Unterschied; Anmerkungen zur gegen-wärtigen Debatte um das Gesetzverständnis Jesu: ▸ 458d, Gesetz 1992, 37-60 / 13-35.

6332 *Versteeg* J. P., Kerk en Israël volgens Romeinen 9-11: TRef 34,2 (1991) 151-169 [< GerefTTs 91,189].

6333 *Villapadierna* Carlos de, Obras de la ley y ley de Cristo según San Pablo: StLeg 32 (1991) 13-41.

6334 *a) Weder* Hans, Rechtfertigung aus Glauben; eine Überlegung zum springenden Punkt der paulinischen Theologie; – b) *Seebass* Horst, Recht und Gesetz im AT; : c) *Lindemann* Andreas, Gerechtigkeit Gottes bei Paulus; zu drei neuen Paulusbüchern: Glaube und Lernen 7,1 (Gö 1992) 28-36 / 17-27 / 82– ... [< ZIT 92,261].

6335 **Wright** N. T., Climax of the covenant; Christ and the Law in Pauline theology 1991 ▸ 7,5364: ᴿChurchman 106 (1992) 74s (G. *Bray*).

6336 *Buzzard* A., Paul's apocalyptic Gospel as a challenge to contemporary Christianity; a commentary on Romans 10:6-17 [< JRadRef 2/2, 27-40; NTAbs 37, p. 373].

6337 *Glancy* Jennifer, Israel vs. Israel in Romans 11:25-32: UnionSemQ 45,3s (1991) 191-203 [< NTAbs 37, p. 373].

6338 **Carbone** Sandro P., La misericordia universale di Dio in Rom 11,30-32 [diss J/R ᴰ*Buscemi* A. ▸ 6,6299]: RivB supp. 23. Bo 1991, Dehoniane. 301 p. 88-10-30211-7.

6339 a) *Carbone* Sandro P., La misericordia universale di Dio in Rm 11,30-32; – b) *Orsatti* Mauro, Le opere della misericordia: ParVi 37 (1992) 166-176 / 94-102.

G4.8 **Rom 12 ...**

6340 **Thompson** Michael B., Clothed with Christ ... Rom 12-15; jNsu 59, ᴰ1991 ➤ 7,5372: ᴿChurchman 106 (1992) 359s (R. T. *France:* a rare dissertation; common sense and accuracy); Themelios 18,3 (1992s) 27 (G. N. *Davies*).

6341 *Dawn* Marva J., The hilarity of community; Romans 12 and how to be the Church. GR 1992, Eerdmans. xvi-303 p. $17 pa. 0-8028-0657-0.

6342 *Ridgway* John K., 'By the mercies of God' — mercy and peace in Romans 12: IrBSt 14 (1992) 170-191.

6343 *Sandnes* Karl-Olav, [in Norwegian]; Rom 12; 1 Cor 12] 'Body and members' in St. Paul and ancient texts [PLUTARCH, Hierocles] on *philadelphia:* TsTKi 62 (1991) 17-26; Eng. 26.

6344 *Probst* Alain, 'Soyez transformés par le renouvellement de l'intelligence' (Romains 12:2): RRéf 42 (1991) 43-48 [page-headings 'Calvinisme et philosophie'].

6345 **Wilson** Walter T., Love without pretense; Romans 12,9-21 and Hellenistic-Jewish wisdom literature: WUNT 2/46. Tü 1991, Mohr. ix-262 p. DM 74. 3-16-145756-0. – ᴿArTGran 55 (1992) 345 (A. *Segovia*).

6346 *Łach* Jan, ❸ 'Rejoicing in hope' (Rom 12,12): RuBi 45 (1992) 21-24.

6347 [*Yoder*] *Neufeld* T. R., Romans 13 in our day: ➤ 103*, ᶠKLAASSEN W., CGrebel 9 (1991) 315-320.

6348 *Cuvillier* Élian, Soumission aux autorités et liberté chrétienne; exégèse de Romains 13,1-7: Hokhma 50 (1992) 29-48.

6349 *Denova* Rebecca I., Paul's letter to the Romans, 13,1-7; the Gentile-Christian response to civil authority: Encounter 53 (Indianapolis 1992) 201-229 [< NTAbs 37, p. 55].

6350 *Hale* Frederick, Romans 13:1-7 in South African Baptist social ethics: SAfBap 2 (1992) 66-83.

6351 **Oosterhuis** T. J., The 'weak' and the 'strong' in Paul's epistle to the Romans; an exegetical study of Romans 14,1 - 15,13: diss. ᴰ*Van Elderen* B. Amsterdam 1992 [RTLv 24, p. 548]. 295 p. – TvT 33,179.

6352 **Ettorri** Giuseppe, Paolo liturgo del Cristo Gesù per l' 'obbedienza delle nazioni'; teologia di Romani 15,16: diss. Pont. Univ. Urbaniana, ᴰ*Federici* T. R 1992. xxxix-63 p. estratto.

6353 **Giorgi** Dieter, [Rom 15,25-31...] Remembering the poor; the history of Paul's collection for Jerusalem [diss. 1965], ᵀ*Racz* Ingrid. Nv 1992, Abingdon. 232 p. $18 pa. 0-687-36117-6 [TDig 40,63].

6354 a) *Gnako* Celestin, Romains 15, 18-21; – b) *Nare* Laurent, Témoignage et kérygme dans les Actes des Apôtres: Ricao 1s (Revue de l'Inst. Cath. de l'Afrique de l'Ouest, 1992) 35-53 / 5-33 [< TContext 10, p. 19].

6355 **Vose** Noel, Women in ministry with special reference to Romans 16: SAfBap 2 (1992) 84-91.

6356 *Ernst* Michael, Die Funktionen der Phöbe (Röm 16,1f) in der Gemeinde von Kenchreai: ProtokB 1 (1992) 135-147.

6356* a) *Petersen* Norman R., On the ending(s) to Paul's letter to Rome; – b) *Nickelsburg* G. W. E., The incarnation Paul's solution to the universal human predicament; – c) *Schenke* Hans-M., Four problems in the life of Paul reconsidered; – d) *Meeks* Wayne A., The Man from Heaven in

Paul's letter to the Philippians: ➤ 104, ᶠKOESTER H. 1991, 337-347 / 348-357 / 319-328 / 329-336.

G5.1 Epistulae ad Corinthios (I vel I-II) – Textus, commentarii.

6357 **Merklein** Helmut, Der erste Brief an die Korinther: ÖkTbNT 7/1. Gü/Wü 1992, Mohn/Echter. 335 p. DM 44. 3-579-00511-1 [TLZ 118, 119, C. *Wolff*].

6358 **Schenk** Wolfgang, *al.*, Gemeinde im Lernprozess; die Korintherbriefe: Bibelauslegung für die Praxis 22. Stu 1979, ²1980, KBW. 160 p. DM 22,80. 3-460-25221-9. – ᴿLingBib 66 (1992) 123-6 (J. *Winkel;* 126n ᴱwhy now).

6359 **Schrage** Wolfgang, 1Kor 1-6, EkK 7, 1991 ➤ 7,5386: ᴿBZ 36 (1992) 277-9 (J. *Hainz*).

6360 **Snyder** G. F., First Corinthians: A Faith Community Commentary. Macon 1992, Mercer Univ. ix-267 p. 0-86554-393-3 [NTAbs 37, p. 451].

6361 **Talbert** Charles H., Reading Corinthians 1987 ➤ 3,5851 ... 7,5388; SPCK 1990; 0-281-04493-7: ᴿExpTim 104 (1992s) 175 (C. S. *Rodd*).

6362 **Watson** Nigel, The first epistle to the Corinthians. L 1992, Epworth. 189 p. £8. 0-7162-0481-9 [NTAbs 37, p. 451]. – ᴿExpTim 104 (1992s) 21 (N. *Clark:* a miracle of compression, like W. LOADER's 1-3 Jn in the same New Epworth Preacher's comm.).

G5.2 1 & 1-2 ad Corinthios – Themata, topics.

6363 **Balthasar** Hans Urs von, Paul struggles with his congregation; the pastoral message of the letters to the Corinthians [Paulus ringt 1988] ᵀ*Bojarska* Brigine L. SF 1992, Ignatius. 90 p. $7. 0-89870-386-7.

6364 **Chow Kin-Man** John, Patronage and power; studies on social networks in Corinth: *a)* diss. Durham, UK 1991. 289 p. BRD-98088. – DissA 53 (1992s) 3637-A; – *b)* jNsu 75. Shf 1992, J8tOT. 230 p. £32.50; sb. £24.50. 1-85075-370-9.

6365 *Hillmer* M. R., Knowledge, New Age, Gnosticism and First Corinthians: McMasterTJ 3,1 (Hamilton 1992) 18-38 [< NTAbs 37, p. 55].

6366 **Mitchell** Margaret, Paul and the rhetoric of reconciliation, 1 Cor: HermUnT 28, 1991 ➤ 7,5399: ᴿTvT 32 (1992) 313s (P. J. *Farla*).

6367 *Oster* Richard E.ᴶ, Use, misuse and neglect of archaeological evidence in some modern works on 1 Corinthians (1 Cor 7,1-5; 8,10; 11,12-16; 12,14-26): ZNW 83 (1992) 52-73.

6368 *Paige* Terence, Stoicism, *eleuthería* and community at Corinth: ➤ 126, ᶠMARTIN R. 1992, 180-193.

6369 **Probst** Hermann, Paulus und der Brief; die Rhetorik des antiken Briefes als Form der paulinischen Korintherkorrespondenz (1 Kor 8-10): WUNT 2/45. Tü 1991, Mohr. xii-407 p. DM 99. 3-16-145678-5. ᴿExpTim 104 (1992s) 268 (E. *Best*).

6370 *Rubio Miralles* F., Los signos de la predicación en 1 Corintios según san Juan CRISÓSTOMO: Scripta fulgentina 1,2 (1991) 95-126 [< RET 52,516].

6371 *Söding* Thomas, Kreuzestheologie und Rechtfertigungslehre; zur Verbindung von Christologie und Soteriologie im Ersten Korintherbrief und im Galaterbrief: Catholica 46 (1992) 31-61.

6372 *Swartz* S. M., Praising or prophesying; what were the Corinthians doing?: NotTr 6,2 (1992) 25-36 [< NTAbs 37, p. 374].

6373 *Thielman* Frank, The coherence of Paul's view of the Law; the evidence of First Corinthians: NTS 38 (1992) 235-253.
6374 **Wire** Antoinette C., The Corinthian women prophets 1990 ➤ 6,6329; 7,5406: ᴿAnglTR 74 (1992) 233-6 (N. *Elliott*); AustralBR 40 (1992) 58-63 (N. M. *Watson:* 'reconstructing the other half of the telephone conversation'); BibTB 22 (1992) 44 (Carolyn *Osiek:* creative reconstruction, needed since the written record of the ancient world is men's story); CBQ 54 (1992) 594-6 (Barbara E. *Reid*); Horizons 19 (1992) 311 (J. *Neyrey:* a hot book); Interpretation 46 (1992) 412s (Beverly R. *Gaventa*); JBL 111 (1992) 546-8 (R. *Scroggs*); NewTR 5,1 (1992) 97-99 (Marie-Eloise *Rosenblatt*); RExp 89 (1992) 284s (A. A. *Trites*); TS 53 (1992) 139-141 (A. J. *Tambasco*).

G5.3   **1 Cor 1-7:** *sapientia crucis ... abusus matrimonii.*

6376 *Clarke* Andrew D., Secular and Christian leadership in Corinth [< ...; a socio-historical and exegetical study of 1 Corinthians 1-6; diss. Cambridge 1991]: TyndB 43 (1992) 395-401.
6377 *Borghi* Ernesto, Il tema *sophia* in 1 Cor 1-4: RivB 40 (1992) 421-458.
6378 **Pogoloff** Stephen M., Logos and sophia; the rhetorical situation of 1 Corinthians 1-4 in the light of Greco-Roman rhetoric [diss. Duke, ᴰ*Smith* D. M. 1990 ➤ 7,5407]: SBL diss 134. Atlanta 1992, Scholars. xi-313 p. $30; pa. $20. 1-55540-784-6; -3-8 [TDig 40,283; CBQ 55,819s, Margaret M. *Mitchell:* rather serpentine].
6379 **Theis** Joachim, Paulus als Weisheitslehrer ... 1 Kor 1-4, ᴰ1991 ➤ 7, 5408: ᴿCarthaginensia 8 (1992) 934s (F. *Marín Heredia*); LebZeug 47 (1992) 236s (C. *Schmitt*); TPhil 67 (1992) 578s (N. *Baumert:* wertvoll; Auseinandersetzungen); TvT 32 (1992) 94s (L. *Visschers*).
6380 **Brown** Alexandra R., Transforming perception and the Word of the Cross in 1 Cor 1-2: diss. Union-Columbia. NY 1991. – UnSemQ 45,253.
6381 *Fee* Gordon D., Textual-exegetical observations on 1 Corinthians 1:2; 2:1; and 2:10: ➤ 70, ᶠGREENLEE J., Scribes 1992, 1-15.
6382 *Watson* Francis, Christ, community, and the critique of ideology; a theological reading of 1 Corinthians 1,18-31: NedTTs 46 (1992) 132-149.
6383 *Lautenschlager* Markus, Abschied vom Disputierer; zur Bedeutung von *syzētētēs* in 1 Kor 1,20: ZNW 83 (1992) 276-285.
6384 *Walker* William O.ᴶ, 1 Corinthians 2.6-16: a non-Pauline interpolation?: JStNT 47 (1992) 75-94.
6385 *Kuck* David, Paul and pastoral ambition; a reflection on 1 Corinthians 3-4: CurrTMiss 19 (1992) 174-184.
6386 **Kuck** David W., Judgement and community conflict; Paul's use of apocalyptic judgement language in 1 Corinthians 3:5 - 4:5 [diss. Yale, ᴰ*Meeks* W.]: NT supp. 66. Leiden 1992, Brill. xiii-318 p. [TR 88,75. 163]. 90-04-09510-1.
6387 *Trevijano Etcheverria* Ramón, A propósito del incestuoso (1 Cor 5-6): Salmanticensis 38 (1991) 129-153; Eng. 153.
6388 *Rosner* Brian S., Corporate responsibility in 1 Corinthians 5: NTS 38 (1992) 470-3.
6389 *Edwards* M. J., [1 Cor 5,1], Some early Christian immoralities ['Oedipean' unfounded]: AncSoc 23 (1992) 71-82.
6390 *Kistemaker* S., 'Deliver this man to Satan' (1 Cor 5,5); a case study in Church discipline: Master's SemJ 3,1 (1992) 33-46 [< NTAbs 38, p. 56].

6391 *Rosner* Brian S., A possible quotation of Test.Reuben 5:5 in 1 Corinthians 6:18A: JTS 43 (1992) 123-7.

6392 *Fauconnet* Jean-Jacques, La morale sexuelle chez saint Paul; analyse et commentaire de 1 Cor 6,12 à 7,40: BLitEc 93 (1992) 359-378.

6393 **Kirchhoff** Renate, Die Sünde gegen den eigenen Leib; Studien zu *porne* und *porneia* in 1 Kor 6,12-20 und dem soziokulturellen Kontext der paulinischen Adressaten: Diss. ᴰ*Burchard.* Heidelberg 1992s. – RTLv 24, p. 547.

6394 *Rouiller* Grégoire, Consultation conjugale; quand Paul répond aux couples (1 Corinthiens 7,1-7): ÉchSM 22 (1992) 105-120.

6395 *Lindemann* Andreas, [1 Cor 7,10 ...] Die Funktion der Herrenworte in der ethischen Argumentation des Paulus im ersten Korintherbrief: ➤ 137, ᶠNᴇɪʀʏɴᴄᴋ F., Four Gospels 1992, 677-688.

6396 *Boston* Linda, A woman's reflection on 1 Cor. 7:21-24 and 1 Cor. 14:33-35: JWomenR 9s ('Intersection of racism and sexism, Afro-American women' 1990s) 81-88.

6397 *Genton* Philippe, 1 Corinthiens 7/25-40, notes exégétiques: ÉTRel 67 (1992) 249-253.

6398 *Dolfe* K.G.E., 1 Cor 7,25 reconsidered; Paul a supposed adviser: ZNW 83 (1992) 115-8.

G5.4 *Idolothyta ... Eucharistia:* 1 Cor 8-11.

6399 *Starck* Christian, [1 Cor 6-11] Recht, Gerichte und der Geist der Liebe: EvKomm 24 (1991) 30-32.

6400 **Gordon** Jean D., A sociological exegesis of 1 Corinthians 7: diss. Knox College, ᴰ*Humphries* R. Toronto 1991. – SR 21 (1992) 494.

6401 **Probst** Hermann, Paulus und der Brief; die Rhetorik des antiken Briefes als Form der paulinischen Korintherkorrespondenz [Diss. Erlangen 1985 '1 Kor 8-10']: WUNT 2/45. Tü 1991, Mohr. xii-427 p. DM 99. 3-16-145678-5. – ᴿNRT 114 (1992) 750s (X. *Jacques*); TvT 32 (1992) 314 (J. *Smit*).

6402 *Brand* Richard, [1 Cor 8,1-13] Eating to another's taste: ExpTim 103 (1991s) 341s.

6403 **Yeo Khiok-Khng,** Rhetorical interaction in 1 Cor 8 & 10; potential implications for a Chinese cross-cultural hermeneutic: diss. Northwestern. Evanston 1992. 462 p. 93-09491. – DissA 53 (1992s) 3947-A.

6404 *De Young* J.B., [1 Cor 8,9] The source and NT meaning of *arsenokoîtai*,with implications for Christian ethics and ministry: Master's SemJ 3 (1992) 191-215 [< NTAbs 37, p. 374].

6405 *Adkin* Neil, [1 Cor 9,5] The date of St. John Cʜʀʏsᴏsᴛᴏᴍ's treatises on 'subintroductae': RBén 102 (1992) 255-266.

6406 *Brewer* D. Instone, 1 Corinthians 9.9-11; a literal interpretation of 'Do not muzzle the ox': NTS 38 (1992) 554-565.

6407 **Martin** Dale B., [1 Cor 9,19-23] Slavery as salvation 1990 ➤ 7,5647: ᴿCBQ 54 (1992) 580-2 (R. A. *Wild;* very persuasive); ChrCent 108 (1991) 379s (R. H. *Bryant*); JRel 72 (1992) 426s (J. A. *Harrill*); JSS 37 (1992) 325s (J.D.G. *Dunn*); JTS 43 (1992) 200-2 (Isobel *Combes*); Thought 66 (1991) 413 (Carolyn *Osiek*); TLond 95 (1992) 454s (S. C. *Barton*).

6408 *a) Vignolo* Roberto, Tutto a tutti (1 Cor 9,22); – *b) Ghidelli* Carlo, Sapienza cristiana e sapienza greca: ParVi 37 (1992) 341-353 / 333-340.

6409 *a) Dunn* James D. G., [1 Cor 10,16 ...] 'The body of Christ' in Paul; – *b) Paige* Terence, Stoicism, *eleutheria* and community at Corinth: ➤ 126, ᶠMᴀʀᴛɪɴ R., Worship 1992, 146-162 / 180-193.

6410 *Boyarin* Daniel, 'This we know to be the carnal Israel' [AUGUSTINE on 1 Cor 10,18 in Adv.Jud]; circumcision and the erotic life of God and Israel [< his Carnal Israel]: Critical Inquiry 18 (Ch 1992) 474-505.

6411 *Rosner* Brian S., 'Stronger than he?' The strength of 1 Corinthians 10:22b: TyndB 43,1 (1992) 171-9.

6412 *Gill* David W.J., The meat-market at Corinth (1 Corinthians 10:25): TyndB 43 (1992) 389-393.

6413 *Watson* Francis, [1 Cor 11s] Strategies of recovery and resistance; hermeneutical reflections on Genesis 1-3 and its Pauline reception: JStNT 45 (1992) 79-103.

6414 **Stichele** Caroline Vander, Authenticiteit en integriteit van 1 Kor 11,2-16; een bijdrage tot de discussie omtrent Paulus' visie op de vrouw: diss. ᴰ*Delobel* J. Leuven 1992. liii-597 p. – LvSt 17 (1992) 397s: RTLv 24, p. 550.

6415 *Basevi* Claudio, [1 Cor 11,9s] Il carisma profetico delle donne nella prima lettera ai Corinti: AnnTh 6 (1992) 35-53.

6416 *Winandy* J., Un curieux casus pendens; 1 Corinthiens 11.10 et son interprétation: NTS 38 (1992) 621-9.

G5.5 1 Cor 12s... Glossolalia, charismata.

6417 **Angel** Gervais, Delusion or dynamite? Reflections on a quarter-century of charismatic renewal. Eastbourne 1990, Marc. 191 p. £6. 1-85424-076-5. – ᴿChurchman 106 (1992) 64s (D. *Spanner*).

6418 **Bentivegna** Giuseppe, Effusione dello Spirito Santo e doni carismatici; la testimonianza di sant'AGOSTINO 1990 ➤ 6,6366; 7,5443: Lᴹ 15: ᴿAugM 37 (1992) 396s (P. *Orosio*).

6419 *Bini* Enrico, La profezia nella Chiesa secondo S. Tommaso d'AQUINO: Divinitas 36 (1992) 38-51.

6420 **Boring** M. Eugene, The continuing voice of Jesus; Christian prophecy and the Gospel tradition [revision of his 1982 Sayings of the Risen Jesus]. Louisville 1991, W-Knox. 304 p. $19. 0-664-25184-6. – ᴿChrCent 109 (1992) 248 (S.L. *Cox*); Encounter 53 (1992) 100s (R. *Pregeant*); RExp 89 (1992) 416s (A.A. *Trites*).

6421 *Cameron* Nigel M., Healing miracles and the role of the pastor [...he bears a heavy responsibility for the expectations which he raises]: Evangel 9,1 (1991) 17-19.

6422 *a) Cartledge* Mark J., Charismatic prophecy and New Testament prophecy [PACKER J.; HILL D.; GRUDEM W.; TURNER M., CARSON D.]; – *b) Wright* Nigel G., The Kansas City prophets, an assessment: Themelios 17,1 (1991s) 17-19 / 20s.

6423 *Codina* Victor, Experiencia profética ayer y hoy: Confer 31,119 ('Actualidad de la vida religiosa en Iberoamérica' 1992) 533-9.

6424 **Espinel** José Luis, Profetismo cristiano: Glosas 13. S 1990, S. Esteban. 200 p. – ᴿLumenVr 40 (1991) 202 (U. *Gil Ortega*); RTPhil 124 (1992) 202 (Carmen *Burkhalter*).

6425 *Farnell* F. David, Is the gift of prophecy for today? 1) The current debate about NT prophecy; – 2) The gift of prophecy in the Old and New Testaments; – [3.4]: BtS 149 (1992) 279-303 . 387-410 ...

6426 **Gerosa** Libero, Charisma und Recht; kirchenrechtliche Überlegungen zum 'Urcharisma' der neuen Vereinigungsformen in der Kirche [Hab.-D. Eichstätt] 1989 ➤ 7,5449; DM 42: ᴿMüTZ 43 (1992) 145-8 (W. *Aymans*: sehr zu begrüssen).

6427 **Grudem** Wayne A., The gift of prophecy in the New Testament and today [< Cambridge Univ. diss. 1978]. Westchester IL 1988, Crossway. – ᴿBtS 149 (1992) 43 (R. L. *Thomas*: prophecy rediscovered? he stretches the NT evidence in order to reconcile today's factions); CalvinT 26 (1991) 173-8 (W. P. *De Boer*); RefTR 49 (1990) 30s (G. N. *Davies*); WestTJ 54 (1992) 321-330 (D. B. *McWilliams*: 'something new under the sun?').

6428 **Hollenweger** Walter J., L'expérience de l'Esprit; jalons pour une théologie interculturelle, ᵀ*Mazellier* C., *Toscer* S.: Pratiques 5. Genève 1991, Labor et Fides. 230 p. 2-8309-0652-7 [TLZ 118,642, K. *Blaser*: 'zweifelsohne einer der originellsten Theologen der Gegenwart'].

6429 **Jefferies** Esmond, The power and the glory. L 1991, A. James. 188 p. £8. 0-85305-303-0. – ᴿChurchman 106 (1992) 285-7 (P. *May*: psychosomatic healings, not as in the Gospels).

6430 ᴱ**Lapointe** Guy, Crise de prophétisme, hier et aujourd'hui... Jacques GRAND'MAISON; Montréal 5-7 oct 1989: Héritage et projet 43, 1990 → 6,640: ᴿÉglT 22 (1991) 400s (J.-M. *Larouche*).

Miller Timothy, When prophets die; the postcharismatic fate of new religious movements 1991 → b126.

6431 **Miskotte** H. H., Pastor en profeet; over de andere kant van pastoraat. Baarn 1992, Ten Have. 213 p. ƒ35. 90-259-4475-2 [TvT 33,433, G. *Heitink*].

6432 **Neitz** Mary Jo, Charisma and community; a study of religious commitment within the charismatic renewal → 7,5461 (also) New Brunswick 1987, Rutgers Univ. xxi-294 p. 0-88738-130-8,

6433 **Rey** Bernard, *al.*, Jésus vivant au cœur du Renouveau charismatique: JJC 43, 1990 → 6,6393; F 135: ᴿÉglT 28 (1992) 141 (L. *Laberge*).

6434 **Schatzmann** S., A Pauline theology of charismata [ᴰSW Baptist 1981]. Peabody MA 1987, Hendrickson. x-117 p. $8 pa. – ᴿWestTJ 53 (1991) 365-7 (W. W. *Klein*).

6435 **Snyder** Howard A., Signs of the Spirit; how God reshapes the Church. GR 1989, Zondervan. 336 p. $15. 0-310-51541-6. – ᴿJEvTS 35 (1992) 235s (R. J. *Gore*).

6436 *a)* **Veenhof** Jan, The significance of the charismatic renewal for theology and Church; – *b)* *Hocken* Peter, Charismatic renewal in the Roman Catholic Church; reception and challenge: → 86, ᶠHOLLENWEGER W., Pentecost 1992, 289-300 / 301-9.

6437 *Wehrli* E. S., Gifted by their Spirit; leadership roles in the NT. Cleveland 1992, Pilgrim. v-124 p. $11 pa. 0-8298-0920-1 [NTAbs 37, p. 299].

6438 **White** John, When the Spirit comes to power [John WIMBER, 'Signs and wonders' movement]. L 1989, Hodder & S. 261 p. £5. – ᴿChurchman 106 (1992) 173-5 (M. *Tinker*).

6439 **Wünsche** Matthias, Der Ausgang der urchristlichen Prophetie in der frühkatholischen Kirche: Diss. ᴰ*Staats* R. Kiel 1992. — RTLv 24, p. 552.

6440 *Garcia Teijeiro* Manuel, Langage orgiastique et glossolalie: → 671, L'élément orgiastique 1991, Kernos 5 (1992) 59-69.

6440* **Carson** D. A., Showing the spirit... 1 Cor 12-14, 1987 → 3,5921... 6, 6369: also Sydney 1988, Lance: ᴿRefTR 49 (1990) 35-37 (B. *Harris*).

6441 **Lopez** Michael D., The concept of love in I Corinthians 13; an analysis of its origin, development, and other Pauline usage: diss. Fuller Theol. Sem., ᴰ*Martin* R. Pasadena 1992. 247 p. 92-17749. — DissA 53 (1992s) 533-A.

6441* *Wong* Emily, I Corinthians 13:7 and Christian hope: → 115, ᶠLAMBRECHT J., LvSt 17 (1992) 232-242.

6442 **Söding** Thomas, Die Trias Glaube, Hoffnung, Liebe bei Paulus; eine exegetische Studie [< Hab.-D.]: SBS 150. Stu 1992, KBW. 232 p. 3-460-04501-9.

6442* *Dowling* Robin, 1 Corinthians 14:1-25; mind and spirit: Evangel 9,3 (1991) 9-16 [... harm has resulted from thinking the Spirit's witness a kind of inward voice].
6443 *Maier* Walter A., An exegetical study of 1 Corinthians 14:33b-38: ConcordTQ 55 (1991) 81-104.
6443* *Reid* Barbara E., [1 Cor 14,33s; 11,2s] Problematic Paul on women: NewTR 5,1 (1992) 40-51.
6444 *Baar* M. de, [1 Cor 14,34] 'Let your women keep silence in the churches'; how women in the Dutch Reformed Church evaded Paul's admonition, 1650-1700: ➤ 6,692*, Women in the Church 1989/90, 389-401; 1 fig.

G5.6   **Resurrectio;** *1 Cor 15 ...* [➤ F5.6].

6445 *Barth* Gerhard, Zur Frage nach der in 1 Korinther 15 bekämpften Auferstehungsleugnung: ZNW 83 (1992) 187-201.
6445* **Boer** Martinus G. de, The defeat of death ... 1 Cor 15, Rom 5: jNsu 22, 1988 ➤ 4,6115 ... 6,6409: RJBL 111 (1992) 152-5 (M. A. *Plunkett*).
6446 *Bachmann* Michael, Zum 'argumentum resurrectionis' 1 Kor 15,12ff nach Christoph ZIMMER, AUGUSTIN und Paulus: LingB [65 (1991) 25-36] 67 (1992) 29-39; Antwort 40-44; Eng. 39.44.
6446* *Talbott* Thomas, [1 Cor 15,22 ...] The New Testament and universal reconciliation: ChrSchR 21 (1992) 376-394 [< BtS 149 (1992) 482 (S. R. *Spencer*: as if 'triumph' implied reconciliation)].
6447 **Olson** Mark J., IRENAEUS, the Valentinian Gnostics, and the Kingdom of God (A. H. Book V); the debate about 1 Corinthians 15:50. Lewiston NY 1992, Mellen. viii-153 p. 0-7734-2352-4 [TBR 6/1, 44, M. *Bockmuehl*].
6447* *Mertens* Herman-Emiel, [1 Kor 15,54s] Lachen op Pasen: CollatVL 22 (1992) 5-16.
6448 *Söding* Thomas, 'Die Kraft der Sünde ist das Gesetz' (1 Kor 15,56); Anmerkungen zum Hintergrund und zur Pointe einer gesetzkritischen Sentenz des Apostels Paulus: ZNW 83 (1992) 74-84.
6448* **Verbrugge** V. D., [1 Cor 16,1-2] Paul's style: diss. 1992 DCollins A. Y. ND [NTAbs 37, p. 132].

G5.9   **Secunda epistula ad Corinthios.**

6449 **Danker** F. W., II Cor 1989 ➤ 5,6131 ... 7,5488: RCurrTMiss 19 (1992) 131s (E. *Krentz*).
6450 **Jones** P., La deuxième épître de Paul aux Corinthiens: Comm. Év. 14. Vaux-sur-Seine 1992, ÉDIFAC. 191 p. F 110. 2-904407-13-6 [NTAbs 37, p. 448].
6451 **Kremer** J., 2. Kor. 1990 ➤ 6,6433: RGeistL 65 (1992) 157 (F.-J. *Steinmetz*).
6452 **Wolff** Christian, 2 Kor: ThHK 8, 1989 ➤ 6,6439; 7,5493: RBZ 36 (1992) 152-5 (G. *Dautzenberg*).
6453 **Young** Frances, *Ford* David F., Meaning and truth in 2 Corinthians 1987 ➤ 3,5999 ... 7,5494: RConcordTQ 56 (1992) 309s (C. A. *Gieschen*: qualified endorsement).

6454 **Zeilinger** Franz, Krieg und Friede in Korinth; Kommentar zum 2. Korintherbrief des Apostels Paulus; I. Der Kampfbrief, der Versöhnungsbrief, der Bettelbrief. Köln 1992, Böhlau. 339 p. DM 98 [TR 88,517; NTAbs 37, p. 291]. 3-205-05535-7.

6455 **Bosenius** Bärbel, Die 'apusia' des Apostels als theologisches Programm; der zweite Korintherbrief als Beispiel für die Brieflichkeit der paulinischen Theologie: Diss. Bethel, ᴰVouga F. Bielefeld 1992s. – RTLv 24, p. 545.

6456 **Crafton** Jeffrey A., The agency of the Apostle... 2 Cor: JStNT supp 51, ᴰ1991 ► 7,5487: ᴿCBQ 54 (1992) 586s (J. P. Heil); EvQ 64 (1992) 282s (R. P. Martin); TLZ 117 (1992) 748 (G. Schille).

6457 **Murphy-O'Connor** Jerome, Theology of 2 Cor 1991 ► 7,5490: ᴿTLond 95 (1992) 54-56 (Ruth B. Edwards: a sure guide; also on LIEU J. 1-3 Jn and LINDARS B. Heb); TZBas 48 (1992) 294s (S. H. Vollenweider); TLZ 117 (1992) 914s (C. Wolff).

6458 **Pfitzner** V. C., Strength in weakness, 2 Cor: ChiRho comm. Adelaide 1992, Lutheran. 206 p. 0-85910-623-3 [NTAbs 37, p. 129].

6459 **Sumney** Jerry L., Identifying Paul's opponents... 2 Cor: jNsu 40, 1990 ► 6,6469; 7,5514: ᴿCBQ 54 (1992) 175-7 (R. L. Tyler); JBL 111 (1992) 347-350 (S. I. Hafemann: somewhat provisional); Salesianum 54 (1992) 375s (J. J. Bartolomé); TLZ 117 (1992) 42s (C. Wolff).

6460 **Schröter** Jens, Der versöhnte Versöhner; Paulus als unentbehrlicher Mittler im Heilsvorgang zwischen Gott und Gemeinde nach 2 Kor 2,14 -7,4: Diss. ᴰBerger. Heidelberg 1992. – RTLv 24, p. 549.

6461 **Oliveira** Anacleto de, Die Diakonie der Gerechtigkeit und der Versöhnung in der Apologie des 2. Korintherbriefes; Analyse und Auslegung von 2. Kor 2,14-4,6; 5,11-6,10: NTAbh 21, ᴰ1990 ► 6,6443; 7,5501: ᴿCBQ 54 (1992) 148s (L. T. Johnson: his vigorous arguments for the GEORGI position show it ever more untenable).

6462 **Hafemann** Scott J., Suffering... 2 Cor 2:14-3:3: 1990 ► 7,6447: ᴿThemelios 17,3 (1991s) Linda L. Belleville); WestTJ 54 (1992) 185s (W. W. Klein).

6463 *Schmitt* Christoph, Das Verhältnis des Apostels Paulus zum 'Wort Gottes; '...wie aus Gott, angesichts Gottes, reden wir' (2 Kor 2,17c): LebZeug 47 (1992) 286-296.

6464 *Collins* John N., The mediatorial aspect of Paul's role as diakonos [2 Cor 3-6 8t; 10-13 3t]: AustralBR 40 (1992) 34-44.

6465 *Bochet* Isabelle, 'La lettre tue; l'Esprit vivifie', l'exégèse AUGUSTINIENNE de 2 Co 3,6: NRT 114 (1992) 341-370.

6466 **Belleville** Linda L., Reflections of glory... Moses-Doxa 2 Cor 3,12-18: JStNT supp 52, 1991 ► 7,5503: ᴿÉTRel 67 (1992) 467 (M. Carrez); ExpTim 103 (1991s) 217 (I. Torrance): JTS 43 (1992) 190s (Margaret E. Thrall).

6467 *Hafemann* Scott J., The glory and veil of Moses in 2 Cor 3:7-14; an example of Paul's contextual exegesis of the OT; a proposal: HorBT 14 (1992) 31-49.

6468 *Jongeneel* Jan A. B., [2 Kor 4,4; Kol 1,15] Christus Jezus, icoon van de onzichtbare God: KerkT 43 (1992) 270-2 [273-9, Kuiper P. C., Afscheid van de godsbeelden].

6469 *Erlemann* Kurt, Der Geist als arrabōn (2 Kor 5,5) im Kontext der paulinischen Eschatologie: ZNW 83 (1992) 202-223.

6470 **Rebell** W., Christologie und Existenz bei Paulus; eine Auslegung von
2. Kor 5,14-21: ArbT 73. Stu 1992, Calwer. 107 p. DM 34. 3-7668-
3162-3 [NTAbs 37, p. 450].

6471 **Magg** G. [1904-1986], Christus — ansonsten nichts? Neuübersetzung
des dunklen Pauluswortes 2 Kor 5,16 [< Diss. Fribourg 1939, ᴰ*Braun*
T.], ᴱ*Renner* F. St. Ottilien 1991, EOS. 86 p. DM 9,80. 3-88096-663-X
[NTAbs 37, p. 289].

6472 *Ebeling* Gerhard, [2 Kor 5,21; LUTHER 1521] 'Christus... factus est
peccatum metaphorice': ➤ 171*, ꟻSEILS M., Tragende Tradition 1992,
49-73.

6473 *Roetzel* Calvin J., [2 Cor 6,10] 'As dying, and behold we live'; death and
resurrection in Paul's theology: Interpretation 46 (1992) 5-18.

6474 *Webb* William J., [2 Cor 6,14] Unequally yoked together with unbelievers;
– *a*) Who are the unbelievers (*ápistoi*)? – *b*) What is the unequal yoke
(*heterozygoûntes*)?: BtS 149 (1992) 27-44 / 162-179.

6475 *Joubert* S., Behind the mask of rhetoric; 2 Corinthians 8 and the
intra-textual relation between Paul and the Corinthians: Neotestamentica
26 (1992) 101-112.

6476 **Betz** Hans D., 2 Korinther 8 und 9; ein Kommentar zu zwei Ver-
waltungsbriefen des Apostels Paulus [Hermeneia], ᵀ*Sibylle* Ann. Mü 1992,
Kaiser, 280 p. DM 98 [TR 88,517].

6477 *Vassiliades* Petros, [2 Cor 8] The collection revisited: DeltioVM 21,11
(1992) 43-48.

6478 *Wong* Kasper, 'Lord' in 2 Corinthians 10:17: ➤ 115, ꟻLAMBRECHT J.,
LvSt 17 (1992) 243-253.

6479 *a*) *Lohse* Eduard, Das kirchliche Amt des Apostels und das apostolische
Amt der Kirche — ökumenische Erwägungen zu 2 Kor 10-13: – *b*)
Strecker Georg, Die Legitimität des paulinischen Apostolates nach 2 Kor
10-13: ➤ 584, Verteidigung 1989/92, 129-146 / 107-128.

6480 *Loubser* J. A., A new look at paradox and irony in 2 Corinthians 10-13:
Neotestamentica 26 (1992) 507-521.

6481 *a*) *Penna* Romano, La présence des adversaires de Paul en 2 Cor 10-13;
approche littéraire; – *b*) *Sánchez Bosch* Jorge, L'apologie apostolique —
2 Cor 10-11 comme réponse de Paul à ses adversaires; – *c*) *Court* John M.,
The controversy with the adversaries of Paul's apostolate in the context of
his relations to the Corinthian congregation: ➤ 584, Verteidigung 1989/92,
6-41 / 43-63 / 87-105.

6482 *Strecker* Georg, Die Legitimität des paulinischen Apostolates nach 2
Korinther 10-13: NTS 38 (1992) 566-586.

6483 **Arzt** Peter, Gegner des Paulus als böse Mächte; Überlegungen zur
Funktionalität von 2 Kor 11,15 und Phil 3,18f: ➤ 490, Mächte, ProtokB 1
(1990/2) 101-113.

6484 *Ellingworth* Paul, Grammar, meaning, and verse divisions in 2 Cor 11,
16-29: BTrans 43 (1992) 245s.

6485 *Taylor* Justin, The ethnarch of King Aretas at Damascus; a note on
2 Cor 11,32-33: RB 99 (1992) 719-728.

6486 *a*) *Trakatellis* Demetrios. Power in weakness; exegesis of 2 Cor 12,1-13;
– *b*) *Corsani* Bruno, Forza e debolezza nella vita e nel pensiero di Paolo:
➤ 584, Verteidigung 1989/92, 87-105 / 147-159.

6487 *Leary* T. J., 'A thorn in the flesh' — 2 Corinthians 12:7: JTS 43 (1992)
530-2 [poor eyesight? MARTIAL relates to 'mcmbranes' (as 2 Tim 4,13)
more legible than cheaper wax tablets].

6488 *Ruiz* Guillermo, 'Ma puissance se déploie dans la faiblesse' (II Cor 12,9); une interprétation d'IRÉNÉE de Lyon: → 35. FCROUZEL H., Recherches 1992, 259-269.

6489 *Reiser* Marius, [2 Kor 13,5; Oxy 654; EvThom 3] Erkenne dich selbst! Selbsterkenntnis in Antike und Christentum: TrierTZ 101 (1992) 81-100; 2 fig. [*Non adhibentur* 6490-7].

G6.1   Ad Galatas.

6498 **Barclay** John, Obeying the truth... Gal: D1988 → 4,6165... 7,5523: RAustralBR 38 (1990) 90s (W. J. *Dalton*); HorBT 14 (1992) 79-84 (A. L. *Nations*); JEvTS 35 (1992) 105s (W. W. *Wessel*).

6499 **Betz** H. D., Der Galaterbrief 1988 → 4,6166; 6,6477: RFranzSt 72 (1990) 300s (R. *Kampling*).

6500 **Dalton** William J., Galatians without tears: Biblical Studies 2. Homebush NSW 1992, St. Paul. 75 p. 0-949080-79-9.

6501 *Dolbeau* François, Sermons inédits de S. AUGUSTIN prêchés en 397, 2/c, Sermo super verbis Apostoli ad Galatas: RBén 102 (1992) 44-63 [-74, de dilectione; 267-297 ...].

6502 *Hagen* Kenneth, LUTHER's approach to Scripture as seen in his 'Commentaries' on Galatians 1519-1538. Tü 1992, Mohr. xiii-210 p. DM 148 [TR 88,523].

6503 **Herman** Zvonimir I., Liberi in Cristo... Gal 1986 → 2,4803 ... 5,6172: RLateranum 57 (1991) 225s (R. *Penna*).

6504 **Longenecker** Richard N., Galatians: Word Comm 41, 1990 → 6,6492: RAsbTJ 47,1 (1992) 101s (R. D. *Rightmire*); CBQ 54 (1992) 791s (R. L. *Tyler*); JTS 43 (1992) 609-614 (T. J. *Deidun*: least plausible on the two points he puts forward as distinctive: stress on Hellenistic epistolary conventions, and eclectic treatment of Graeco-Roman rhetorical features; but very well-crafted and usable); SR 21 (1992) 103s (Margaret Y. *MacDonald*); Themelios 17,3 (1991s) 28s (T. D. *Gordon*).

6505 **Lührmann** D., Galatians [²1988], TDean O. C.; Continental Comm. Mp 1992, Fortress. x-161 p. $25. 0-8006-9618-3 [NTAbs 37, p. 449].

6506 **Marin Heredia** F., Evangelio de la gracia; carta de San Pablo a los Gálatas. Murcia 1990, Espiga. 182 p. – RStPatav 39 (1992) 241s (G. *Segalla*).

6507 **Matera** Frank J., Galatians: Sacra Pagina 9. ColMn 1992, Liturgical. xiii-252 p. $25. 0-8146-5811-3 [NTAbs 37, p. 289]. – RExpTim 104 (1992s) 175s (C. S. *Rodd*, also on LONGENECKER Word).

6508 **Sheppard** Gerald T., A commentary on Galatians by William PERKINS [1617] 1989 → 5,6181: RCalvinT 26 (1991) 231-4 (D. W. *Hall*); SixtC 22 (1991) 780-2 (C. J. *Rasmussen*).

6509 *Rizzerio* Laura, Robert GROSSETESTE, Jean CHRYSOSTOME et l'*expositor graecus* (= THÉOPHYLACTE) dans le commentaire Super epistolam ad Galatas: RTAM 59 (1992) 166-209.

6510 **Ziesler** John, Epistle to the Galatians: Epworth Conn. 122 p. £7. 0-7162-0486-X [NTS 38, p. 124]: RExpTim 104 (1992s) 280 (E. *Franklin*).

6511 *Botha* P. J. J., Letter writing and oral communication in antiquity; suggested implications for the interpretation of Paul's letter to the Galatians: Scriptura 42 (1992) 17-34 [< NTAbs 37, p. 376].

6512 **Buckel** John, Free to love; Paul's defense of Christian liberty in Galatians: LvTPmg 15. Lv 1992, Peeters. xiv-240 p. 90-6831-490-4.

6513 *Buckel* John, Paul's defense of Christian liberty in Galatians: ➤ 115, FLAMBRECHT J., LvSt 17 (1992) 254-268.
6514 *Cook* David, The prescript as programme in *Galatians*: JTS 43 (1992) 511-9.
6515 *a) Dunn* James D. G., The theology of Galatians; the issue of covenantal nomism; – *b) Gaventa* Beverly R., The singularity of the Gospel; a reading of Galatians; – *c)* (response) *Martyn* J. Louis, Events in Galatia; Modified covenantal nomism versus God's invasion of the cosmos in the singular Gospel: ➤ 6067, Pauline Theology 1 (1991) 125-146 / 147-159 / 160-179.
6516 **Ebeling** G., La verità dell'Evangelo... Gal 1989 ➤ 7,5528: RCC 143 (1992,1) 296s (D. *Scaiola*).
6517 **Howard** George, Paul, crisis in Galatia; a study in early Christian theology² [= ¹1979 + 21 p. introd.]: SNTS mg 35, 1990 ➤ 6,6487; 7,5533: RÉTRel 67 (1992) 109 (É. *Cuvillier*); JTS 43 (1992) 814s (J. P. M. *Sweet* gives the four points of his added 20 pages).
6518 **Jegher-Bucher** V., Der Galaterbrief auf dem Hintergrund antiker Epistolografie und Rhetorik; ein anderes Paulusbild: ATANT 78, 1991 ➤ 7, 5534; Fs 42: RTvT 32 (1992) 314 (J. *Smit*).
6519 *a) Lategan* B. C., The argumentative situation of Galatians; – *b) Toit* A. B. du, Alienation and re-identification as pragmatic strategies in Galatians; – *c) Vorster* J. N., Dissociation in the letter to the Galatians: Neotestamentica 26 (1992) 257-277 / 279-295 / 297-310 / 311-327 [appendix p. 1-41, *Pelser* G. M. M. *al.*, Discourse analysis of Galatians].
6520 **O'Grady** John F., Pillars of Paul's Gospel, Gal Rom. NY 1992, Paulist. v-177 p.; 4 maps, $10 pa. 0-8091-3327-X [NTAbs 37, p. 129].
6521 **Pitta** Antonio, Disposizione e messaggio della Lettera ai Galati; analisi retorico-letteraria [diss. Pont. Ist. Biblico, DAletti J. ➤ 7,5537]: AnBib 131. R 1992, PIB. 270 p. Lit. 30.000. 88-7653-131-9 [NTAbs 37, p. 290].
6522 *Söding* Thomas, Die Gegner des Apostels Paulus in Galatien; Beobachtungen zu ihrer Evangeliumverkündigung und ihrem Konflikt mit Paulus: MüTZ 42 (1991) 305-321.
6523 *Strobel* Karl, Die Galater im hellenistischen Kleinasien; historische Aspekte einer hellenistischen Staatenbildung: ➤ 16, FBENGTSON H., 1991, 101-134.
6524 **Zuurmond** Rochus, God noch gebod, bijbels-theologische notities over de brief van Paulus aan de Galaten, 1990 ➤ 7,5541; *f* 29,50. 90-25944-39-6: RNedTTs 46 (1992) 237s (J. *Smit Sibinga*: ook over *Smit* I. 1989; van *Heyer* C. 1987).

6525 *Schwarz* Günther, Zum Wechsel von 'Kephas' zu 'Petros' in Gal 1 und 2: BibNot 62 (1992) 46-50.
6526 *a) Roberts* J. H., Paul's expression of perplexity in Galatians 1:6; the force of emotive argumentation; – *b) Kertelge* K., The assertion of revealed truth as compelling argument in Gal 1:10-2:21; – *c) Gräbe* P. J., Paul's assertion of obedience as a function of persuasion: Neotestamentica 26 (1992) 329-338 / 339-350 / 351-8.
6527 *Artola* Antonio María, 'Revelar en mi a su Hijo para que le anunciara' (Gál 1,16); la dimensión inspiracional de la visión de Damasco: ➤ 135, FMUÑOZ IGLESIAS S., EstBib 50 (1992) 359-373.

6528 *a) Talbott* Thomas, [Gal 1,20] The New Testament and universal reconciliation; – *b) Lacy* Larry, Talbott on Paul as a universalist: ChrSchR
21 (1992) 362-376 / 376-395 [< ZIT 92,353].

6529 **Bartolomé** J.J., [Gal 2] El evangelio y su verdad ^D1988 ➤ 4,6188 ...
7,5545: ^RCiuD 204 (1991) 264s (J. *Gutiérrez*); ScripTPamp 23 (1991)
1034-7 (C. *Basevi*).

6530 *Walker* William O.^J, Why Paul went to Jerusalem; the interpretation of
Galatians 2:1-5: CBQ 54 (1992) 503-510.

6531 *Berge* Paul S., Peter and Cephas and Paul; God's apostolate and mission in Galatians 2:7-9: ➤ 77, ^FHARRISVILLE R. 1992, 127-137.

6532 *Schmidt* A., Das Missionsdekret in Galater 2.7-8 als Vereinbarung vom
ersten Besuch Pauli in Jerusalem: NTS 38 (1992) 149-152.

6533 *Agouridis* S., ☉ [Gal 2,11-21] The incident between Peter and Paul in
Antioch: DeltioVM [year 21, though 22 on cover, and editor's name is
sometimes latinized Agourides] 12 NS (1992) 5-27.

6534 **Knudtson** Paul R., [Gal 2,11-14] The Antioch incident; an investigation
into the hospitable character of Paul's Gospel: diss. Luther NW Theol.
Sem., ^D*Juel* D. 1992. 220 p. 93-11100. – DissA 53 (1992s) 4359-A.

6535 **Wechsler** A., Geschichtsbild und Apostelstreit ... Gal 2,11-14 ^D1991
➤ 7,5549: ^RSNTU A-17 (1992) 269-271 (A. *Fuchs*).

6536 *Hagen* Kenneth, Did Peter err? The text is the best judge; LUTHER on
Gal. 2:11: ➤ 6,133*, ^FOBERMAN H., Augustine 1990, 110-125; Zusammenfassung 125s.

6537 *Ponthot* Joseph, La 'Vérité de l'Évangile' selon l'Épître aux Galates
[2,14 ...]: FoiTemps 22 (1992) 197-212.

6538 **Bachmann** Michael, Sünder oder Übertreter; Studien zur Argumentation in Gal 2,15ff [Hab.-D. Basel]: WUNT 59. Tü 1992, Mohr. xi-
200 p. DM 148. 3-16-145706-X. – ^RArTGran 55 (1992) 320s (A. *Segovia*).

6539 *Boers* Hendrikus, [Gal 2,15] 'We who are by inheritance Jews, not from
the Gentiles, sinners': JBL 111 (1992) 273-281, towards reconciling Rom
2,13 with 3,20.

6540 *Gibson* G.S., [Gal 3,1-14] Freedom to be: ExpTim 104 (1992s) 15s.

6541 *Caneday* Ardel B., The curse of the law and the cross; works of the law
and faith in Galatians 3:1-14: diss. Trinity Ev. Divinity School 1992.
386 p. 92-33316. – DissA 53 (1992s) 2412-A.

6542 *a) Lemmer* H.R., Mnemonic reference to the Spirit as a persuasive tool
(Gal 3:1-6 within the argument, 3:1-4;11); – *b) Pelser* G.M.M., The
opposition faith and works as persuasive device in Galatians (3:6-14); – *c)
Tolmie* D.F., *hò nómos paidagōgós* ... The persuasive force of a Pauline
metaphor (Gal 3:23-26): Neotestamentica 26 (1992) 359-388 / 389-405 /
407-416.

6543 *Braswell* Joseph P., 'The blessing of Abraham' versus 'the curse of the
Law'; another look at Gal 3:10-13: WestTJ 53 (1991) 73-91.

6544 *a) Silva* Moisés, The text of Galatians; evidence from the earliest Greek
manuscripts; – *b) Dockery* David S., [Gal 3,24; 5,13-16; 2 Cor 3,7; 2,12 ...]
Life in the Spirit in Pauline thought: ➤ 70, ^FGREENLEE J., Scribes 1992,
17-25 / 49-76.

6545 *Vos* J.S., Die hermeneutische Antinomie bei Paulus (Galater 3.11-12;
Römer 10.5-10): NTS 38 (1992) 254-270.

6546 **Setiawan** Kornelius A., An exegetical study of Galatians 3:23-29 with
special reference to 3:28: diss. ^D*Bandstra* A. GR c. 1991. – CalvinT 26
(1991) 512.

6547 *Grant* Robert M., [Gal 3,28] Neither male nor female: BiRes 37 (1992) 5-14.
6548 *Rusam* Dietrich,   Neue Belege zu den *stoicheîa toû kósmou* (Gal 4,3.9; Kol 2,8.20): ZNW 83 (1992) 119-125.
6549 *a) Cronjé* J.,   The stratagem of the rhetorical question in Galatians 4:9-10 as a means towards persuasion; – *b) Malan* F. S.,   The strategy of two opposing covenants, Gal 4:21-5:1:   Neotestamentica 26 (1992) 417-424 / 425-440.
6550 *a) Hong In-Gyu*,   The Law and Christian ethics in Galatians 5-6; – *b) Pretorius* E. A. C.,   The opposition *pneûma* and *sárx* as persuasive summons (Galatians 5:13-6:10); – *c) Wessels* G. F.,   The call to responsible freedom in Paul's persuasive strategy, Galatians 5:13-6:10; – *d) Snyman* A. H.,   Modes of persuasion in Galatians 6:7-10:   Neotestamentica 26 (1992) 113-130 / 441-460 / 461-474 / 475-484.
6551 *Gench* Frances T.,   Galatians 5:1, 13-25; expository: Interpretation 46 (1992) 290-5.
6552 *Baarda* T.,   Tí éti diōkomai in Gal. 5:11; apodosis [no] or parenthesis? [yes]:   NT 34 (1992) 250-6.
6553 *North* J. L.,   Sowing and reaping (Galatians 6:7b); more examples of a classical maxim: JTS 43 (1992) 523-7.

G6.2   Ad Ephesios.

6554 **Bouttier** Michel,   L'épître de s. Paul aux Éphésiens: CommNT 9b, 1991 ► 7,5576:   ᴿActuBbg 29 (1992) 193s (X. *Alegre*); ExpTim 103 (1991s) 272s (E. *Best*: replacing MASSON); FreibZ 39 (1992) 206-8 (H.-J. *Venetz*); Gregorianum 73 (1992) 753s (J. *Galot*); RHPR 72 (1992) 207s (C. *Grappe*, aussi sur SCHNACKENBURG anglais); Salesianum 54 (1992) 581s (J. J. *Bartolomé*).
6555 **Cooper** Stephen A.,   Metaphysics and morals in Marius VICTORINUS' commentary on the Letter to the Ephesians: diss. Columbia, ᴰ*Norris* R. NY 1992.   341 p.   92-31988. – DissA 53 (1992s) 1964-A.
6556 **Foulkes** Francis,   The letter of Paul to the Ephesians² [¹1963] 1989 ► 5,6216:   ᴿJEvTS 35 (1989) 257s (J. D. *Harvey*).
6557 **Lincoln** Andrew W.,   Ephesians: Word Comm. 42, 1990 ► 6,6530:   ᴿBiblica 73 (1992) 590-4 (A. *Lindemann*); Protestantesimo 47 (1992) 326 (U. *Eckert*); Themelios 17,2 (1991s) 22s (C. E. *Arnold*); WestTJ 54 (1992) 376-8 (M. *Silva*: his rejection of Pauline authenticity disappointing).
6558 **Pokorný** Petr,   Der Brief des Paulus an die Epheser: THk NT 10s.   Lp 1992, Ev.-VA.   xxiv-265 p.   DM 45.   3-374-01389-0 [TLZ 118,611, A. *Lindemann*].
6559 Navarre Bible,   Captivity/Thess-Pastoral [1986/9].   Dublin 1992, Four Courts.   205 p., 181 p. $20 each.   1-85182-080-9; -78-7; pa. -79-5; -77-9 [NTAbs 37, p. 291].
6560 **O'Brien** Peter T.,   The epistle to the Philippians: NIGNT.   GR 1991, Eerdmans.   xi-560 p. $40.   0-8028-2392-0. – ᴿWestTJ 54 (1992) 378s (C. D. *Balzer*).
6561 *Pauselli* Maria Cristina,   Nota sugli Scholia di Gasparo CONTARINI ad Efesini e Galati: ArRefG 83 (1992) 130-153; Eng. 153.
6562 **Schlier** H.,   Carta a los Efesios 1991 ► 7,5585:   ᴿActuBbg 29 (1992) 201 (X. *Alegre*).
6563 **Schnackenburg** Rudolf,   The Epistle to the Ephesians: EkK 1991 ► 7, 5586:   ᴿExpTim 104 (1992s) 176 (C. S. *Rodd*, also on LINCOLN A.,

MARTIN R.); JStNT 45 (1992) 124s (J. *Knight*: good, but comparison with Lincoln's excellent 1991 raises questions about translating key books without updating); NRT 114 (1992s) 748s (X. *Jacques*).

6564 **Stockhausen** Carol L., Letters in the Pauline tradition; Eph...: Message of Biblical Spirituality 13, 1989 → 5,6228; 7,5888: ᴿCurrTMiss 19 (1992) 138 (Lynn A. *Kauppi*).

6565 **Arnold** Clinton E., Ephesians — power and magic: SNTS mg 63, ᴰ1989 → 5,6213 ... 7,5575: ᴿJEvTS 35 (1992) 258s (W. S. *Henderson*).

6566 *Best* Ernest, The use of credal and liturgical material in Ephesians: → 126, ᶠMARTIN R. 1992, 53-69.

6567 *Breeze* M., Hortatory discourse in Ephesians: JTransTLing 5 (Dallas 1992) 313-347 [< NTAbs 37, p. 220].

6568 *Cocchini* Francesca, La comunità di Efeso, comunità di spirituali nel commentario di Origene alla lettera agli Efesini: → 485, Efeso II, 1991/2, 113-122.

6569 *Dunn* James D. G., 'The body of Christ' in Paul [Eph... 1 Cor; Col]: → 126, ᶠMARTIN R., 1992, 146-162.

6570 *Field* Barbara, The discourses behind the metaphor 'The Church is the body of Christ' as used by St. Paul and the 'post-Paulines': AsiaJT 6,1 (1992) 88-107 [< TContext 10/1, p. 28].

6571 *Penna* Romano, Lo scopo della Lettera agli Efesini nella sua situazione storico-ecclesiale: → 485, Efeso 2, 1991/2, 29-39.

6572 **Preti** Benedetto, L'ecclesiologia della Lettera agli Efesini: SacDoc 37 (1992) 133-195.

6573 **Reynier** Chantal, Évangile et mystère; les enjeux théologiques de la lettre aux Éphésiens [< Diss Paris-Sèvres 1990, ᴰAletti J.-N.]: LDiv 149. P 1992, Cerf. 321 p. F 165. 2-204-04484-9 [NTAbs 37, p. 130].

6574 *Sellin* Gerhard, Über einige ungewöhnliche Genitive im Epheserbrief: ZNW 83 (1992) 85-107.

6575 **Eaton** Michael A., [Eph 1,13...] Baptism with the Spirit... M. LLOYD-JONES 1989 → 6,6539: ᴿEvangel 9,1 (1991) 28 (R. *Kearsley*).

6576 *Steinmetz* Franz-J., Wie weit ist es bis Ephesus? [GesAufs]; title, also of p. 24-31, ecumenical vision of the Church in Eph (2,11-15)] 1989 → 6, 6542: ᴿTPhil 67 (1992) 621s (R. *Sebott*).

6577 *Best* Ernest, Ephesians 2.11-22; a Christian view of Judaism: → 41, ᶠDAVIDSON R., Text as pretext 1992, 47-60.

6578 *Villegas* M. Beltrán, Redacción y tradición en Ef 2,11-12: TVida 33 (1992) 179-184.

6579 *White* R. Fowler, [Richard] GAFFIN and [Wayne] GRUDEM on Eph 2:20; in defense of Gaffin's cessationist exegesis: WestTJ 54 (1992) 303-320.

6580 *Hyde* James A., Ephesians 4:17-24 (expository): RExp 89 (1992) 403-7.

6581 *Giannarelli* Elena, L'esegesi patristica ad Efesini 5,20-33: → 405, Donna e cultura 1989/91, 31-58.

6582 *Morgen* M., Le sacrement du mariage dans la littérature paulinienne; Eph 5,21-33 un midrash chrétien?: Revue de Droit Canonique 42,2 (Colloque, 2 partie, 1992) 21-33 [< RSPT 77,337].

6583 **Bristow** John T., [Eph 5,22...] What Paul really said about women 1988 → 4,9889; 6,8836: ᴿJEvTS 35 (1992) 260s (E. M. *Curtis*: not much on Gal 3).

6584 ᵀᴱSfameni Gasparro G., *al.*, La coppia nei Padri [e CRISOSTOMO su Ef 5,22s ...]: Letture cristiane del primo millennio 9. Mi 1991, Paoline. 474 p. – ᴿVigChr 46 (1992) 199s (J. den *Boeft*).

6585 *Schützeichel* Heribert, Das Geheimnis des Evangeliums (Eph 6,19): ➤ 54, ᶠFEILZER H., Wege 1992, 79-89.

G6.3 Ad Philippenses.

6586 *Löser* Werner, Paulus als Apostel und Zeuge Christi; zu Erik PETER-SONS Auslegung des Philipperbriefes: Catholica 46 (1992) 240-252.

6587 **McQuay** E. P., [Phlp] Learning to study the Bible. Nv 1992, Broadman. 109 p. $10. 0-8054-8159-1 [NTAbs 37, p. 267].

6588 **Marshall** I. Howard, Epistle to the Philippians: Epworth comm. 126 p. £8. 0-7162-0485-1 [NTAbs 38, p. 131]. – ᴿExpTim 104 (1992s) 280 (E. *Franklin*).

6589 **O'Brien** Peter T., The epistle to the Philippians; a commentary on the Greek text: NIGT, 1991 ➤ 7,5607: ᴿBTrans 43 (1992) 351-3 (*I-Jin Loh*); ÉTRel 67 (1992) 466 (E. *Cuvillier*: dense, précis, informé); ExpTim 104 (1992s) 176s (C. S. *Rodd*: major); STEv 4 (1992) 199-201 (E. *Beriti*, anche su SILVA M. 1988).

6590 **Silva** Moisès, Philippians: Wycliffe Exeg. Comm. 1988 ➤ 7,5609: ᴿChr-SchR 21 (1991s) 328-330 (Scott *Hafemann*); ConcordJ 19 (1993) 415s (E. H. *Kiehl*).

6591 *Fitzgerald* John T., Philippians: ➤ 741, AnchorBD 5 (1992) 318-326 [Philippi 313-7, *Hendrix* Holland L., Philippian jailor Acts 16,23, *O'Toole* R. J. (but his Philippian slave girl is referred to slave)].

6592 **Geoffrion** Timothy C., An investigation of the purpose and the political and military character of Philippians; Paul's letter of exhortation calling citizens of Heaven to remain steadfast: diss. Lutheran School of Theology 1992, ᴰ*Krentz* Edgar. 268 p. 92-30460. – DissA 53 (1992s) 1959-A.

6593 **Greenlee** J. H., An exegetical summary of Philippians. Dallas 1992, Summer Inst. Linguistics. 288 p. $6.25. 0-88312-824-8 [NTAbs 37, p. 447].

6594 *Noordegraaf* A., Familia Dei; de functie en de betekenis van de huisgemeente in het Nieuwe Testament: TRef 35 (Woerden 1992) 183-204 [< ZIT 92,571].

6595 *O'Brien* Peter T., The Gospel and godly models in Philippians: ➤ 126, ᶠMARTIN R., 1992, 273-284.

6596 **Palmer** Earl F., Integrity in a world of pretense; insights from the book of Philippians. DG 1992, InterVarsity. 187 p. 0-8308-1736-0.

6597 *a) Perkins* Pheme, Theology for the heavenly politeuma; – *b) Stowers* Stanley K., Friends and enemies in the politics of Heaven; reading theology in Philippians: ➤ 6067, Pauline Theology 1 (1991) 89-104 / 105-121.

──────────

6598 *Reeves* Rodney R., To be or not to be? That is not the question [contents p. 253 omits 'not']; Paul's choice in Philippians 1:22: PerspRelSt 19 (1992) 273-289.

6599 *Fee* Gordon D., Philippians 2:5-11; hymn or exalted Pauline prose?: BuBRes 2 (1992) 29-46 [< NTAbs 37, p. 223].

6600 **Fowl** Stephen E., [Phlp 2,6-11 ...] The story of Christ in the ethics of Paul... hymnic material: JStNT supp 36, ᴰ1990 ➤ 6,6554; 7,5611: ᴿCBQ 54 (1992) 151-3 (M. *Kiley*: good); EvQ 64 (1992) 284s (J. *Barclay*); JTS 43 (1992) 205s (C. J. A. *Hickling*).

6601 **Hofius** O., Der Christushymnus Phlp 2,6-11: WUNT 17, 1991 = 1975 ➤ 7,5612: ᴿSNTU A-17 (1992) 271s (M. *Hasitschka*).

6602 *a*) *Martin* Ralph P. [Phil 2,6-11] Hymns in the NT; an evolving pattern of worship responses; – *b*) *Dulles* Avery, Theology and worship; the reciprocity of prayer and belief; – *c*) *Webber* Robert, The future direction of Christian worship [response, *Johnson* Todd E.]: ➤ 624, ExAud 8 (1992) 33-44 / 85-94 / 113-128 [129-133].

6603 *Söding* Thomas, Erniedrigung und Erhöhung; Erwägungen zum Verhältnis von Christologie und Mythos am Beispiel des Philipperhymnus (Phil 2,6-11): TPhil 67 (1992) 1-28.

6604 *a*) *Thekkekara* Mathew, A neglected idiom in an overstudied passage (Phil 2:6-8); – *b*) *Bieringer* Reimund, Paul's divine jealousy; the Apostle and his communities in relationship; – *c*) *Koperski* Veronica, Feminist concerns and the authorial readers in Philippians; – *d*) *Wong* Teresa, [Phil 2,5-11] Christ's mind, Paul's mind: ➤ 115, ᶠLAMBRECHT J., LvSt 17 (1992) 306-314 / 197-231 / 269-292 / 293-305.

6605 *Gibbs* Norman B. & Lee W , 'In our nature'; the kenotic Christology of Charles CHAUNCY: HarvTR 85 (1992) 217-233.

6606 *Ogliari* Donato, The kenosis theme and monastic theology: AmBenR 41 (1990) 209-221.

6607 *Harrington* D. J., [Plp 3,5] Paul the Jew: Catholic World 235 (1992) 68-73 [< NTAbs 36, p. 361].

6608 **Koperski** Veronica, The knowledge of Christ Jesus my Lord; a study of Philippians 3:8-11: diss. ᴰ*Lambrecht* J. Leuven 1991. lxviii-551 p. – TvT 32 (1992) 189; RTLv 24, p. 547; LvSt 17 (1992) 388s & extract 269-292.

6609 *Koperski* Veronica, Textlinguistics and the integrity of Philippians; a critique of Wolfgang SCHENK's arguments for a compilation hypothesis [< diss. Leuven 1991, The knowledge of Christ, Phlp 3,9-11]: ETL 68 (1992) 331-367.

6610 *Bergant* Dianne, [Phil 3,10] Spirituality of the Apostle: Emmanuel 98 (1992) 86-89 [< NTAbs 36,360].

6611 *O'Brien* Peter T., Divine provision for our needs; assurances from Philippians 4: RefTR 50 (1991) 21-29.

G6.4 Ad Colossenses.

6612 **Cothenet** Édouard, Les épîtres aux Colossiens et aux Éphésiens: CahEv 82. P 1992, Cerf. 68 p. F 30. 0222-9714 [NTAbs 37, p. 446].

6613 **Ghini** Emanuela, sr., Lettera ai Colossesi, commento pastorale 1990 ➤ 6,6578; 7,5621: ᴿAustralBR 40 (1992) 91s (A. *Jones*); Gregorianum 73 (1992) 754s (E. *Farahian*).

6614 **Harris** Murray J., Colossians and Philemon: ExGG (first of 20 projected) 1991 ➤ 7,5622: ᴿAndrUnS 30 (1992) 88s (Nancy J. *Vyhmeister*); CBQ 54 (1992) 783s (E. M. *Hensell*: good; not a commentary, though including exegetical notes on each passage, with homiletical suggestion); ExpTim 104 (1992s) 177 (C. S. *Rodd*: 'the patter of EGGNT', for pattern?).

6615 **MacArthur** John, New Testament Commentary, Colossians and Philemon. Ch 1992, Moody. vi-249 p. 0-8024-0761-7.

6616 **Pokorný** Petr, Colossians, a commentary [ThK 1987] ᵀ*Schatzmann* Siegfried S., 1991 ➤ 7,5624: ᴿCBQ 54 (1992) 796s (G. T. *Montague*: one of the finest); ExpTim 104 (1992s) 177 (C. S. *Rodd*: not easy; introduction arrangement odd; translation awkward); JTS 43 (1992) 616-8 (C. F. D. *Moule*: arduous but does not miss much); Neotestamentica 26 (1992) 536-8 (J. G. van der *Watt*); Themelios 18,3 (1992s) 27s (S. E. *Porter*).

6617 *a*) *Genest* Olivette, L'actorialisation de Jésus dans l'Épître aux Colossiens; – *b*) *Daviau* Pierrette T., Une lecture des figures de l'acteur Dieu; – *c*) *Légaré* Clément, Figure et figuratif; – *d*) *Michaud* Jean-Paul, L'ombre des Autorités et des Pouvoirs; la dimension polémique; – *e*) *Pierre* Jacques, Totalité et plénitude; une stratégie de saturation de l'espace et du temps; – *f*) *Milot* Louise, *al.*, Défi à la lecture; souffrances et soumissions: LavalTP 48,1 ('Lectures sémiotiques Col.' 1992) (3-5) 19-30 / 7-18 / 31-42 / 43-52 / 53-63 / 65-79.

6618 *Harrington* Daniel J., Christians and Jews in Colossians: ➤ 107, ᶠKRAABEL A. T., 1992, 153-161.

6619 **Hoppe** Rudolf, Der Kreuz als Triumph; Studien zur Rezeption der paulinischen Kreuzestheologie im Kolosserbrief: kath. Hab.-Diss. ᴰ*Hoffmann*. Bamberg 1992. – TR 89,75.

6620 *Hoppe* Rudolf, Theo-logie in den Deuteropaulinen (Kolosser- und Epheserbrief): ➤ 573, QDisp 138, 1991/2, 163-186.

6621 *House* H. Wayne, *a*) Heresies in the Colossian church; – *b*) The doctrine of Christ in Colossians: – *c*) *d*) awaited: BtS 149 (1992) 45-59 . 181-192 ...

6622 *Ryen* Jan Olav, [in Norwegian] Who authored Colossians? TsTKi 62 (1991) 175-185; Eng. 186.

6623 **Sappington** Thomas J., Revelation and redemption at Colossae: jNsu 53, 1991 ➤ 7,5627: ᴿÉTRel 67 (1992) 282 (E. *Cuvillier*); JTS 43 (1992) 206s (J. M. *Court*).

6624 **Wink** Walter, Engaging the powers; discernment and resistance in a world of domination. Mp 1992, Fortress. xvi-424 p. [CoV&R 6,10, J. G. *Williams*].

6625 **Pongutá** H. Silvestre, Él es imagen de Dios invisible; una lectura de Col 1: CuadBíb 3. Caracas 1992, Asn Bíblica Salesiana. 128 p. 980-6035-61-5 [NTAbs 37, p. 129].

6626 **Arnold** Clinton E., [Col 1,13; Eph 6,12] Powers of darkness; principalities and powers in Paul's letters. DG 1992, InterVarsity. 244 p. 0-8308-1336-5 [NTAbs 36, p. 430].

6627 **Dawn** Marva J. S., The concept of 'the principalities and powers' in the works of Jacques ELLUL: diss. ᴰ*Yoder* J. Notre Dame 1992. 399 p. – DissA 53 (1992s) 533-A.

6628 *O'Brien* P. T., Principalities and powers; opponents of the Church: EvRT 16 (1992) 353-384.

6629 **Hwang Chu-Loon** Andrew, Colossians 1:15-20 and Philippians 2:6-11; the semantic aspect of the nature of parallelism from the perspective of semantic Scripture analysis: diss. Westminster Theol. Sem., ᴰ*Poythress* V. 1992, 207 p. 92-24639. — DissA 53 (1992s) 1183-A.

6630 **Yorke** Gosnell L. O. R., [Col 1,18; mostly Cor Rom] The Church as the body of Christ in the Pauline corpus; a re-examination [diss. McGill 1987, ᴰ*Wright* T.]. Lanham MD 1991, UPA. xx-156 p. 0-8191-8215-X; pa. -6-8. – ᴿJTS 43 (1992) 202-5 (C. F. D. *Moule*, chiefly on 1 Cor 12).

6631 *Cahill* Michael, The neglected parallelisms in Colossians 1,24-25: ETL 68 (1992) 142-7.

6632 **Gielen** Marlis [Col 3s, Eph 5s, 1 Pt 2s] Tradition und Theologie neutestamentlicher Haustafelethik; ein Beitrag zur Frage einer christlichen Auseinandersetzung mit gesellschaftlichen Normen [Diss. Bonn 1988, D*Merklein* H.]: BoBB 75, 1990 ➤ 6,6592; 7,5639: RCBQ 54 (1992) 779s (J. H. *Elliott*: pivots on an interpretation of the 1Pt passage at variance with the argument of the letter as a whole); TLZ 117 (1992) 505-8 (C.-P. *März*); TR 88 (1992) 192-4 (E. *Lohse*).

6633 *Cranfield* C. E. B., [Col 3,1-15] Dying with Christ and being raised with Christ: Metanoia 2 (1992) 99-102; franç. 103.

6634 *Porter* Stanley E., P.Oxy. 744.4 and Colossians 3,9: Biblica 73 (1992) 565-7.

6635 *Cranfield* C. E. B. [Col 3,18-4,1] Some human relationships: ExpTim 104 (1992s) 305-7.

G6.5 *Ad Philemonem* – Slavery in NT Background.

6636 *Arzt* Peter, Brauchbare Sklaven; ausgewählte Papyrustexte zum Philemonbrief [mit griechischem Text]: ProtokB 1,1 (1992) 44-58.

6637 **Binder** Hermann, (*Rohde* Joachim), Der Brief des Paulus an Philemon: THk NT 8/2, 1990 ➤ 6,6593: RTLZ 117 (1992) 185s (W. *Vogler*).

6638 *Karrer* Martin, Philemon/Philipper: ➤ 757, EvKL 3 (1992) 1180-2.

6639 *Martens* John W., IGNATIUS [Eph 2,1] and Onesimus [Plm 13 = early bishop]; John KNOX [Philemon 1935, ²1959] reconsidered: SecC 9 (1992) 73-86: no.

6640 *Wilson* Andrew, The pragmatics of politeness and Pauline epistolography; a case study of the letter to Philemon: JStNT 48 (1992) 107-119.

6641 **Abramenko** A., Zum Fehlen von Cognomina in der Nomenklatur von Freigelassenen; der Befund der Augustalität [< Diss. Mainz 1991]: ZPapEp 93 (1992) 91-95.

6642 *Annequin* Jacques, L'esclavage et la crise des institutions à Rome; la Conjuration de Catilina de [1844, P.] MÉRIMÉE: DialHA 18,1 (1992) 37-57; Eng. 58.

6643 **Bradley** K., Slavery & rebellion 1989 ➤ 5,6293 ... 7,5641: RAmJPg 113 (1992) 119-122 (N. *Rosenstein*); Gerión 9 (1991) 322-4 (P. *López Barja de Quiroga*); Gnomon 64 (1992) 174-6 (Liselot *Huchthausen*); Phoenix 46 (Toronto 1992) 198s (J. *Vander Leest*).

6644 **Dumont** J., Servus 1987 ➤ 5,6296 ... 7,5643: RGerión 9 (1991) 329-333 (D. *Plácido*).

6645 **Klein** Richard, Die Sklaverei in der Sicht der Bischöfe AMBROSIUS und AUGUSTINUS 1988 ➤ 4,6269 ... 7,5644: RAugM 37 (1992) 186s (J. *Oroz*); JTS 43 (1992) 255-8 (A. *Lenox-Conyngham*).

6646 **Kudlien** Fridolf, Sklaven-Mentalität im Spiegel antiker Wahrsagerei: ForAntSklav 23. Stu 1991, Steiner. 189 p. – RRÉAnc 94 (1992) 508-510 (J. *Annequin*).

6647 **Marinovič** L. P., *al.*, Die Sklaverei in den östlichen Provinzen des Römischen Reiches, T*Kriz* Jaroslav, *al.*: Übersetzungen / ant. Sklaverei 5. Stu 1992, Steiner. 283 p. DM 78 [DLZ 114,299, R. *Günther*].

Martin Dale S., Slavery as salvation 1990 ➤ 6407.

6648 *Memmer* Michael, Der 'schöne Kauf' des 'guten Sklaven'; zum Sachmängelrecht im syrisch-römischen Rechtsbuch: ZSav-R 107 (1990) 1-45.

6649 *Osiek* Carolyn, Slavery in the Second Testament world: BibTB 22 (1992) 174-9.
6649* *O'Toole* Robert E., [Acts 16,16-19] Slave girl at Philippi: AnchorDB 6 (1992) 57s [58-65, slavery ANE-OT, *Dandamayev* M. A.; 65-73 NT (but page-headings 'Greco-Roman'), *Bartchy* S. S.].
6650 **Patterson** Orlando, Freedom: 1. in the making of Western culture [obverse of the history of slavery] c. 1991, Basic. 487 p. $30. – ᴿChrCent 109 (1992) 19 (T. *Volker*).
6651 **Scholl** Reinhold, Corpus der ptolemäischen Sklaventexte: ForAntSklav Beih. I. Stu 1990, Steiner. x-514 p.; p. 515-1024; p. 1025-1127. DM 198. 3-515-05711-0. – ᴿAegyptus 72 (1992) 201s (S. *Daris*); AntClas 61 (1992) 543-6 (J. A. *Straus*); ClasR 42 (1992) 164-6 (Dorothy J. *Thompson*).
6652 **Volkmann** Hans, Die Massenversklavungen der Einwohner eroberter Städte in der hellenistisch-römischen Zeit [1961], ²ʳᵉᵛ*Horsmann* Gerhard: ForschAntSkl 22. Stu 1990, Steiner. 202 p. DM 49. 3-5150-5770-6 [Latomus 52,440 J.-C. *Dumont*].
6653 ᴱ**Yuge** Tõru, *Annequin* Jacques, *Lévêque* Pierre, Le monde méditer-ranéen et l'esclavage; recherches japonaises: Ann. Univ. Besançon 426. P 1991, BLettres. 169 p.; 2 maps. – ᴿRÉAnc 94 (1992) 507s (Marie-Madeleine *Mactoux*).

G6.6 **Ad Thessalonicenses.**

6654 **Balthasar** H. U. v., Thess.- und Pastoralbriefe des hl. Paulus. FrB 1992, Johannes. 236 p. DM 28.
    ᴱ**Frede** H. J., Thess-Heb ➤ 6725s.
6655 **Hiebert** D. Edmond, 1 & 2 Thessalonians²ʳᵉᵛ [¹1982]. Ch 1992, Moody. 415 p. 0-8024-8696-7.
6656 **Iovino** P., La prima lettera ai Tessalonicesi, comm.: Scritti delle origini cristiane 13. Bo 1992, Dehoniane. 307 p. Lit. 38.000. 88-10-20613-4 [NTAbs 37,127].
6657 **Jewett** Robert, The Thessalonian correspondence; Pauline rhetoric and millenarian piety: 1986 ➤ 2,4895 ... 5,6317: ᴿCurrTMiss 19 (1992) 135s (W. C. *Linss*).
6658 **Marxsen** Willi, La prima lettera ai Tessalonicesi 1988 ➤ 4,6293 ... 7, 5659: ᴿFilT 5 (1991) 543-6 (G. *Capone*: 'Walter Marxsen').
6659 **Stott** John R. W., The message of Thessalonians 1991 ➤ 7,5667: ᴿTBR 5,2 (1992s) 22 (R. *Morgan*).
6660 **Wanamaker** Charles A., The epistles to the Thessalonians: NIGNT 1990 ➤ 6,6621; 7,5668: ᴿBiblica 73 (1992) 429s (J. *Plevnik*); CBQ 54 (1992) 183s (D. *Seeley*: useful, cogent); ComSev 24 (1991) 276 (M. de *Burgos*); Crux 28,1 (1992) 46s (M. *Bockmuehl*, also on DAVIDS 1 Pt); Interpretation 46 (1992) 413s (D. M. *Blair*); JBL 111 (1992) 350-2 (E. *Richard*); RefTR 51 (1992) 68s (G. N. *Davies*).
6661 **Williams** D. J., 1 & 2 Thessalonians: NIntBCom 12. Peabody MA 1992, Hendrickson. xii-168 p. $10 pa. 0-943575-86-9 [NTAbs 37, p. 133].

6662 **Adinolfi** Marco, 1 Thes nel mondo greco-romano: BtAntonian. 31, 1990 ➤ 6,6606; 7,5654: ᴿRB 99 (1992) 613s (J. *Taylor*).
6663 *Barclay* John M. G., Thessalonica and Corinth; social contrasts in Pauline Christianity: JStNT 47 (1992) 49-74.
6664 ᴱ**Collins** R. F., The Thessalonian correspondence 1988/90 ➤ 6,521; 7,5655: ᴿCBQ 54 (1992) 189-191 (D. R. *Bauer*: tit. pp.); JBL 111

(1992) 177s (D. M. *Scholer*); Protestantesimo 47 (1992) 141s (L. *De Lorenzi*).

6664* *Hendrix* Holland L., Archaeology and eschatology at Thessalonica: ➤ 104, ᶠKOESTER H. 1991, 107-118.

6665 *Kuhn* Heinz-W., Die Bedeutung der Qumrantexte für das Verständnis des ersten Thessalonicherbriefes; Vorstellung des Münchener Projekts Qumran & NT: ➤ 498, MQumran 1 (1991/2) 339-353.

6666 a) *Richard* Earl, Early Pauline thought; an analysis of 1 Thessalonians; – b) (response) *Bassler* Jouette M., Peace in all ways; theology in the Thessalonian letters: ➤ 6067, Pauline theology 1991, 39-51 / 71-85.

6667 **Schoon-Janssen** Johannes, Umstrittene 'Apologien'... 1 Thes Gal Phlp 1991 ➤ 7,5665: ᴿNRT 114 (1992) 751s (X. *Jacques*); StPatav 39 (1992) 211-3 (G. *Segalla*); TLZ 117 (1992) 606s (G. *Haufe*).

6668 a) *Wright* N. T., Putting Paul together again; toward a synthesis of Pauline theology [1-2 Thess. Phlp Phlm]; – b) *Scroggs* Robin. Salvation history, the theological structure of Paul's thought [1 Thess, Phlp, Gal]; – c) *Hays* Richard B., Crucified with Christ; a synthesis of the theology of 1-2 Thess, Phlm, Phlp, and Gal; d) *Lull* David J., (response) Salvation history, theology in 1 Thess, Phlm, Phlp, Gal: ➤ 6067, Pauline Theology 1 (1991) 183-211 / 212-226 / 227-246 / 247-265.

6669 **Roberts** Mark D., [1 Thes 1-3; Acts 17] Images of Paul and the Thessalonians: diss. Harvard, ᴰ*Koester* H. CM 1992. 243 p. 92-28350. – HarvTR 85 (1992) 501s; DissA 53 (1992s) 1548-A.

6670 *Goulder* Michael D., Silas in Thessalonica [1 Thes 1,1; 2 Thes 1,1: the source of the trouble there, hinted in Acts 15,30s; 17,14s]: JStNT 48 (1992) 87-106.

6671 *Ware* James, The Thessalonians as a missionary congregation; 1 Thessalonians 1,5-8: ZNW 83 (1992) 126-131.

6672 *Boyce* James L., Graceful imitation; 'imitators of us and the Lord' (1 Thessalonians 1:6): ➤ 77, ᶠHARRISVILLE R. 1992, 139-146.

6673 *Kampling* Rainer, [1 Thess 1,6; 2,19...] Freude bei Paulus: TrierTZ 101 (1992) 69-79.

6674 a) *Elias* Jacob W., 'Jesus who delivers us from the wrath to come' (1 Thess 1:10); apocalyptic and peace in the Thessalonian correspondence; – b) *Fee* Gordon D., On text and commentary in 1 and 2 Thessalonians: ➤ 478, SBL Sem. 31 (1992) 121-132 / 165-183.

6675 **Schlueter** Carol, 1 Thessalonians 2:14-16 and polemical hyperbole in Paul: diss. McMaster, 1992. ᴰ*Sanders* E. – SR 21 (1992) 495.

6676 *Baumert* Norbert, 'Wir lassen uns nicht beirren'; semantische Fragen in 1 Thess 3,2f: FgNt 5 (1992) 45-59; Eng. 59s.

6677 **Jurgensen** Hubert, Saint Paul et la Parole; 1 Thessaloniciens 4,12-5,11 dans l'exégèse moderne et contemporaine: diss. ᴰ*Trocmé* E. Strasbourg 1992. – RTLv 24, p. 547.

6678 *Collins* R., [1 Thes 4,14-18] From Good Friday to Easter; a call for metanoia: Emmanuel 98 (1992) 125-9, 147 [< NTAbs 36,361].

6679 *Jezierska* Józefa Ewa, ❷ [1 Tes 4,14-17...] L'espérance chrétienne dans la théologie de saint Paul: ColcT 62,1 (1992) 31-41; franç. 41.

6680 *Merklein* Helmut, [1 Thess 5,20] Der Theologe als Prophet; zur Funktion prophetischen Redens im theologischen Diskurs des Paulus: NTS 38 (1992) 402-429.

6681 *Pitassi* Maria Cristina, 'Anima naturaliter mortalis?' L'interpretazione lockiana di 1 Tessalonicesi 5,23: ➤ 481, Pensiero 1991/2, 87-99; Eng. 4.

6682 *Menken* M. J. J., Paradise regained or still lost? Eschatology and disorderly behaviour in 2 Thessalonians: NTS 38 (1992) 271-289.

6683 *Schmidt* Andreas, Erwägungen zur Eschatologie des 2 Thessalonicher und des 3 Johannes: NTS 38 (1992) 477-480.

6684 **Hughes** Frank W., Early Christian rhetoric and 2 Thes 1989 ➤ 5,6331 ... 7,5673: ᴿSvTKv 67 (1991) 41-43 (A. *Eriksson*, also on HOLLAND G.).

6685 *a*) *Krentz* Edgar, Through a lens: theology and fidelity in 2 Thessalonians; – *b*) *Jewett* Robert. A matrix of grace; the theology of 2 Thessalonians: ➤ 6067, Pauline Theology 1 (1991) 53-62 / 63-70.

G7 **Epistulae pastorales.**

6686 *Ellis* E. E., Die Pastoralbriefe und Paulus; Beobachtungen zu J. RO-LOFFS Kommentar über 1. Tim: TBeit 22 (1991) 208-... [< ZIT 91,585].

6687 **Guthrie** Donald, The pastoral epistles²*ʳᵉᵛ* 1990 ➤ 6,6655: ᴿBTrans 43 (1992) 154s (R. G. *Bratcher*: not much help for translators).

6688 **Knight** George W., The pastoral epistles: NIGT. GR 1992, Eerdmans. xxxiv-514 p. $40. 0-8028-2395-5 [NTAbs 37, p. 127].

6689 **Lea** T. D., *Griffin* H. P., 1-2 Timothy, Titus: NAmComm 34. Nv 1992, Broadman. 352 p. $20. 0-8054-0134-2 [NTAbs 37, p. 127].

6690 **Oden** Thomas C., 1-2 Timothy and Titus 1989 ➤ 7,5680: ᴿJEvTS 35 (1992) 259 (J. *Miller*: 'exposition, not exegesis' nor 'direct exposure to the text').

6691 **Ramos Marcos** A., 1 Timoteo, II Timoteo y Tito: Comentario biblico hispanoamericano. Miami 1992, Caribe. 415 p. [JHispT 2/1, 80, J.-P. *Ruiz*].

6692 **Schuetze** Armin W., 1-2 Tim Titus: The People's Bible. Milwaukee 1991, Northwestern. 220 p. $8 pa. – ᴿConcordJ 18 (1992) 411 (E. H. *Kiehl*: for the laity).

6693 **Towner** Philip H., The goal of our instruction 1989 ➤ 5,6346 ...7,5681: ᴿCBQ 54 (1992) 177s (R. B. *Hays*: effectively challenges post-DIBELIUS consensus that Pastorals advocate a bourgeois Christianity without eschatology); EvQ 64 (1992) 358s (M. B. *Thompson*); HeythJ 33 (1992) 334s (M. *Prior*).

6694 *Brown* Lucinda A., Asceticism and ideology; the language of power in the Pastoral Epistles: ➤ 370, Semeia 57 (1992) 77-94.

6695 *Ellis* E. Earle, The pastorals and Paul: ExpTim 104 (1992s) 45-47.

6696 **Kidd** Reggie M., Wealth and beneficence in the Pastoral Epistles: SBL diss 122, 1990 ➤ 6,6656: ᴿCBQ 54 (1992) 789s (R. J. *Karris*); JBL 111 (1992) 352-4 (G. D. *Fee*); RelStR 18 (1992) 142 (C. *Bernas*: good).

6697 *Mitchell* Margaret M., New Testament envoys in the context of Greco-Roman diplomatic and epistolary conventions; the example of Timothy and Titus: JBL 111 (1992) 641-662.

6698 *Redalié* Yann, Dieu dans l'exhortation; le salut, le temps et la morale selon les épîtres à Timothée et à Tite: diss. Genève 1992. — RTLv 24, p. 549.

6699 *Sand* Alexander, 'Am Bewährten festhalten'; zur Theologie der Pastoralbriefe: ➤ 112, Mem. KUSS O., 1992, 351-376.

6700 *Soards* Marion L.,   Reframing and reevaluating the argument of the Pastoral Epistles toward a contemporary NT theology: ➤ 173, ᶠSMITH T., PerspRelSt 29,4 (1992) 389-398.

6701 **Wolfe** Benjamin P.,   The place and use of Scripture in the Pastoral Epistles: diss. Aberdeen 1990.   366 p.   BRDX-96270. – DissA 53 (1992s) 846-A.

6702 *Wolter* Michael,   Pastoralbriefe: ➤ 757, EvKL 3 (1992) 1067-1070.

6703 *Young* Frances,   The pastoral epistles and the ethics of reading ['Is there anything *in* what we say?' STEINER G., Real presences 1989]: JStNT 45 (1992) 105-120.

G7.2   1-2 ad Timotheum.

6704 *Marshall* I. Howard,   The Christian life in 1 Timothy: RefTR 49 (1990) 81-90.

6705 *Reed* J. T.,   Cohesive ties in 1 Timothy; in defense of the epistle's unity: Neotestamentica 26 (1992) 131-147.

6706 *Hiebert* D. Edmond,   [1 Tim 2,1-4] The significance of Christian intercession: BtS 149 (1992) 16-26.

6707 *Abesamis* Carlos H.,   [1 Tim 2,4] The contextual and universal dimension of Christian theology; a NT perspective: BangaloreTF 24,3 (1992) 16-23.

6708 *Fee* Gordon D.,   The great watershed — intentionality and particularity / eternity;   1 Timothy 2:8-15 as a test case: Crux 26,4 (1990) 31-37.

6709 *Hugenberger* G. P.,   Women in church office; hermeneutics or exegesis? A survey of 1 Tim 2:8-15:   JEvTS 35 (1992) 341-360 [< NTAbs 37, p. 224].

6710 *Waltke* Bruce K.,   1 Timothy 2:8-15: unique [no; not all women silenced only to cope with local misleaders, as G. FEE] or normative [yes]? :   Crux 28,1 (Vancouver 1992) 23-27 [< NTAbs 36, p. 373].

6711 *Ferguson* Everett.   *Tópos* in 1 Timothy 2:8:   RestQ 33 (1991) 65-73.

6712 **Gritz** Sharon H.,   Paul, women teachers, and the mother goddess at Ephesus; a study of 1 Timothy 2:9-15 in light of the religious and cultural milieu of the first century [diss. SW Baptist, ᴰGideon V.]. Lanham MD 1991, UPA.   186 p. $37.50; pa. $18.75. – ᴿCritRR 5 (1992) 210s (Kathleen E. *Corley*: Pauline authorship; no prohibition of women teachers); SWJT 35,1 (1992s) 49s (J. P. *Newport*).

6713 *Bowman* Ann L.,   Women in ministry; an exegetical study of 1 Timothy 2:11-15: BtS 149 (1992) 193-213.

6714 **Kroeger** R. C. & C. C.,   I suffer not a woman; rethinking 1 Tim 2:11-15 in light of ancient evidence.   GR 1992, Baker.   253 p., 2 fig.; 2 maps. $13.   0-8010-5250-5 [NTAbs 35, p. 27]. – ᴿPresbyterion 18,1 (St. Louis 1992) 25-31; SWJT 35,2 (1992s) 51 (Ebbie C. *Smith*: valid, illuminating).

6715 *Mathews* A. [1 Tim 2,12; 1 Cor 14,34s] How many anomalies does it take to destroy a paradigm? :   Journal of Biblical Equality 4 (Lakewood CO 1992) 41-49 [< NTAbs 37, p. 67].

6716 *Lassman* Ernei,   1 Timothy 3:1-7 and Titus 1:5-9 and the ordination of women: ConcordTQ 56 (1992) 291-5.

6717 *Baugh* Steven M.,   'Savior of all people'; 1 Tim 4:10 in context: WestTJ 54 (1992) 331-340.

6718 *Lülsdorff* Raimund,   [1 Tim 5,21; 3,16] *Eklektoi ángeloi*; Anmerkungen zu einem untergegangenen Amtsbezeichnung: BZ 36 (1992) 104-8.

6719 *Campbell* Alastair, [2 Tim 4,5] 'Do the work of an evangelist': EvQ 64 (1992) 117-129.

6720 **Fick** Wendy, Les Homélies de Jean CHRYSOSTOME sur les Épîtres à Tite et Philémon: prot. diss. ^D*Maraval* P. Strasbourg 1992. 407 p. – RTLv 24, p. 563.

G8 Epistula ad Hebraeos.

6721 **Attridge** Harold W., The Epistle to the Hebrews. Hermeneia Comm. 1989 → 5,6362 ... 7,5696: ^RInterpretation 46 (1992) 67-69 (D. E. *Aune*); SvTKv 67 (1991) 44-46 (W. *Übelacker*).

6722 **Brown** Raymond [not the NJBC editor], The message of Hebrews; Christ above all: The Bible Speaks Today. Leicester/DG 1992, Inter-Varsity. 272 p. 0-85110-738-9 / US 0-87784-289-2.

6723 *Cadwallader* Alan H., The correction of the text of Hebrews towards the LXX: NT 34 (1992) 257-292.

6724 **Delitzsch** Franz, Der Hebräerbrief ¹1857, Vorwort *Michel* Otto. Giessen 1989, Brunnen. xliv-770 p. 3-7655-9225-0.

6725 **Frede** H. J., Hbr 10,28-11,37 / 11,37-13,10 / 13,10-25; Index: VetLat 25/ 2/9s. FrB 1991, Herder. p. 1477-1556. 1557-1636. – ^RJTS 43 (1992) 635-7 (J. K. *Elliott*); NRT 114 (1992) 738 (X. *Jacques*); RÉLat 70 (1992) 284s (J. *Fontaine*).

6727 **Grässer** Erich, An die Hebräer... 1-6, EkK NT 17/1, 1990 → 6,6694; 7,5702: ^RTLZ 117 (1992) 749-754 (C.-P. *März*).

6728 *Horak* Tomasz, **Θ** O nowy przekład listu do Hebrajczyków [some translation-proposals]: RuBi 45 (1992) 83-86.

6729 **Lane** William L. Hebrews: Word Comm 47AB, 1991 → 7,5708. – ^RExpTim 108 (1992s) 236 (C. S. *Rodd*: Recent Commentaries D. Heb-Rev); Themelios 18,2 (1992s) 30 (J. *Lewis*).

6730 **Navarre Bible**, Epistle to the Hebrews [RSV & Neo-Vulgate]. Dublin 1991, Four Courts. 198 p. 1-85182-070-1; pa. -69-8.

6731 **Schlossnikel** R. F., Der Brief an die Hebräer und das Corpus Paulinum... Claromontanus 1991 → 7,5717: ^RBLitEc 93 (1992) 339 (S. *Légasse*).

6732 **Stedman** R. C., Hebrews; IVP Comm. DG/Leicester 1992, Inter-Varsity. 108 p. $15. 0-8308-1815-4 / UK 0-85111-672-8 [NTAbs 37, p. 132].

6733 **Weiss** Hans-F., Der Brief an die Hebräer: KeK 1991 → 7,5725: ^RExpTim 103 (1991s) (E. *Best*: double the length of O. MICHEL 1936 which it replaces); WissWeis 54 (1991) 233-5 (H.-J. *Klauck*).

6734 *Buzzard* A., Hebrews and eschatology; the challenge of a realistic future: JRadRef 1,2 (Morrow GA 1992) 14-23 [< NTAbs 36, p. 373].

6735 **Casalini** N., Agli Ebrei; discorso di esortazione: SBF 34. J 1992, Franciscan. 459 p. $35 [NTAbs 37, p. 287].

6736 **Collins** Raymond F., Letters that Paul did not write: Glazier Good News Studies 28, 1988 → 4,6331 ... 6,6691: ^RCurrTMiss 19 (1992) 62 (E. *Krentz*).

6737 **Dunnill** John, Covenant and sacrifice in the letter to the Hebrews [diss. Birmingham 1988, ^D*Ford* D.]: SNTS mg 75. C 1992. Univ. xii-297 p. £35 [NTAbs 38, p. 129]. 0-521-43158-1.

6738 *Gratseas* George, The epistle of the Hebrews and the apostolic readings in the liturgical life of Orthodoxy: DeltioVM 21,11 (1992) 49-60.

6739 ᴱHolbrook Frank R., Issues in the book of Hebrews 1989 → 6,6698: ᴿAndrUnS 30 (1992) 90s (E. E. *Reynolds*).
6740 *Horak* Tomasz, ℗ Chrystologia listu do Hebrajczyków: ColcT 62,4 (1992) 45-57; 57, Die Christologie des Hebräerbriefes.
6741 **Hurst** Lincoln D., The Epistle to the Hebrews; its background of thought [< diss. Oxford 1982, ᴰ*Caird* G.]: SNTS Mg 65. C 1991, Univ. xiv-209 p. $39.50. 0-521-37097 [TDig 38,271]. – ᴿCBQ 54 (1992) 591s (C. R. *Koester*: no nearer to a solution of the problems): JBL 111 (1992) 160-2 (D. A. *Hagner*); RelStR 18 (1992) 142 (C. *Bernas*: bibliography stops 1982 but gnat-straining continues); TR 88 (1992) 116s (C.-P. *März*).
6742 **Isaacs** Marie E., Sacred space; an approach to the theology of the Epistle to the Hebrews; jNsu 73. Shf 1992, Academic. 253 p. 1-85075-356-3. – ᴿExpTim 104 (1992s) 155 (R. *Williamson*).
6743 **Josuttis** Manfred, Über alle Engel; politische Predigten zum Hebräerbrief. Mü 1990, Kaiser. 218 p. DM 34. – ᴿTPQ 140 (1992) 203 (J. *Hörmandinger*).
6744 *Knoch* Otto, Hält der Verfasser des Hebräerbriefs die Feier eucharistischer Gottesdienste für theologisch unangemessen?: LtgJb 42 (1992) 166-187.
6745 *Laub* Franz, Glaubenskrise und neu auszulegendes Bekenntnis; zur Intention der Hohenpriesterchristologie des Hebräerbriefs: → 112*, Mem. KUSS O., Theologie im Werden 1992, 377-396.
6746 **Lehne** Susanne, The new covenant in Hebrews: jNsu 44, 1990: ᴿCBQ 54 (1992) 360s (J. *Swetnam*: she rightly shows that what the New Covenant meant to Jeremiah is not automatically what it meant to later users of the term); RHPR 72 (1992) 209s (C. *Grappe*); SvTKv 67 (1991) 46s (W. *Übelacker*); TTod 49 (1992s) 138s (Lala K. *Dey*).
6747 **Lindars** Barnabas, The theology of the Letter to the Hebrews: NT-Theology. C 1991, Univ. xiv-155 p. £8. – ᴿTLZ 117 (1992) 840s (C.-P. *März*); TvT 32 (1992) 196s (H. *Welzen*).
6748 *McKnight* Scot, The warning passages of Hebrews; a formal analysis and theological conclusions: TrinJ 13 (1992) 21-59.
6749 *März* Claus-Peter, a) Zur Aktualität des Hebräerbriefes: TPQ 140 (1992) 160-8; – b) Vom Trost der Theologie; zur Pragmatik der christologisch-soteriologischen Reflexion im Hebräerbrief: → 51, ꟳErfurt 1992, 260-276.
6750 *Martínez de Pisón* Ramón, Acción salvífica de Jesucristo y lenguaje sacrificial-sacerdotal; ¿continuidad o ruptura en la Epístola a los Hebreos?: ComSev 25 (1992) 333-358.
6751 **Pursiful** Darrell J., The cultic motif in the spirituality of Hebrews: diss. Southern Baptist Theol. Sem. 1992, ᴰ*Polhill* J. 301 p. 93-10433. — DissA 53 (1992s) 3946-A.
6752 *Scholer* John M., Proleptic priests... Heb: jNsu 49, 1991 → 7,5718: ᴿCBQ 54 (1992) 799s (J. *Swetnam*, misquoted); EvQ 64 (1992) 359s (P. *Ellingworth*); JTS 43 (1992) 620-2 (A. S. *Browne*: good question; answer not sufficiently sensitive to metaphor); NT 34 (1992) 411 (R. *Williamson*).
6753 *Schmidt* Thomas E., Moral lethargy and the Epistle to the Hebrews: WestTJ 54 (1992) 167-173.
6754 *Stringhini* P. L., La cuestión del sacrificio en la Epístola a los Hebreos: RIBLA 10 (1991) 91-98 [< Stromata 49,293].
6755 *Trummer* P., Hebräerbrief: → 762, NBL II,6 (1991) 66-69.

6756 a) *Ebert* Daniel J.ᴵⱽ, The chiastic structure of the Prologue to Hebrews;

– *b) Jobes* Karen H., The function of paronomasia in Hebrews 10:5-7: TrinJ 13 (1992) 163-179 / 181-191.

6757 **Übelacker** Walter G., Der Hebräerbrief als Appell, I. Untersuchungen zu exordium, narratio und postscriptum (Hebr. 1-2 und 13,22-25) 1989 ➤ 5,6397 ... 7,5727: ᴿRHPR 72 (1992) 210 (C. *Grappe*); TR 88 (1992) 113-6 (F. *Laub*).

6758 **Marcenaro** Ignacio, La obediencia de Jesús; estudio sobre la plenitud humana de Cristo y el significado dogmático de su obediencia: diss. Angelicum, ᴰ*Gunten* F. von. Roma 1991. Extr. 96 p. – RTLv 24, p. 575.

6759 **Franco Martínez** César A., Jesucristo, su persona y su obra, en la carta a los Hebreos; lengua y cristología en Heb 2,9-10; 5,1-10; 4,14 y 9,27-28 [dis. Comillas]: StSem NT 1. M 1992, Ciudad Nueva / Fund. S. Justino. 421 p. 84-86987-31-8 / [NTAbs 37, p. 126]. – ᴿJStNT 48 (1992) 126 (P. *Coutsoumpos*).

6760 *a) Bruce* F. F. †, [Heb 2.9 + 11 others] Textual problems in the Epistle to the Hebrews; – *b) Kubo* Sakae, Hebrews 9:11-12; Christ's body, heavenly region, or ... ?; – *c) Black* David A., Translating New Testament poetry [Heb 1,1-4 ...]: ➤ 70, ꟳGREENLEE J., Scribes 1992, 27-39 / 97-109 / 117-127.

6761 *Mitchell* Alan C., The use of *prépein* and rhetorical propriety in Hebrews 2:10: CBQ 54 (1992) 681-701.

6762 *Yeo Khiok-Khng*, The meaning and usage of the theology of 'rest' (*katápausis* and *sabbatismós*) in Hebrews 3:7-4:13: AsiaJT 5 (1991) 2-33.

6763 **Zesati Estrada** Carlos, Hebreos 5,7-8: AnBib 113, 1990 ➤ 6,6715; 7,5731: ᴿJBL 111 (1992) 157-160 (P. *Zilonka*); RThom 92 (1992) 595 (H. *Ponsot*: information parfaitement maîtrisée); TPQ 140 (1992) 187 (C.-P. *März*).

6764 *Battaglia* Vincenzo, [Eb 5,7 ...] L'autoumiliazione e l'obbedienza del Figlio di Dio incarnato; saggio interpretativo in prospettiva soteriologica: Antonianum 67 (1992) 198-239; Eng. 198.

6765 *Wiid* J. S., The testamental significance of *diathēkē* in Hebrews 9,15-22: Neotestamentica 26 (1992) 149-156.

6766 **Cosby** Michael R., The rhetorical composition and function of Hebrews 11 in light of example lists in antiquity 1988 ➤ 4,6362 ... 7,5736: ᴿWestTJ 53 (1991) 153-5 (Karen H. *Jobes*).

6767 *Niederwimmer* Kurt, Vom Glauben der Pilger; Erwägungen zu Hebr 11,9-10 und 13-16: ➤ 163, ꟳSAUER G., Aktualität 1992, 121-131.

6768 *Díaz Mateos* Manuel, [Heb 13,8, lema escogido para la reunión en Santo Domingo] Jesucristo ayer, hoy y siempre: Páginas 17,117 (1992) 58-71.

6769 *Ortiz V.* Pedro, 'Jesucristo es el mismo ayer y hoy, y lo será por siempre' (Hb 13,8); estudio exegético: TXav 42 (1992) 441-453.

6770 *Vanhoye* Albert, 'Jesucristo ayer, hoy y siempre' según la Carta a los Ebreos: Medellín 18 (1992) 161-170 [AcPIB 9, 782].

6771 *Grässer* Erich, 'Wir haben hier keine bleibende Stadt' (Hebr 13,14); Erwägungen zur christlichen Existenz zwischen den Zeiten [unveröffentlicht], ➤ 247a, Ges. Aufs. zum Hebräerbrief 1992, 251-264.

G9.1   1-2 Petri.

6772 **Davids** Peter H., The first epistle of Peter: NICNT 1990 ➤ 6,6729; 7,5746: ᴿCBQ 54 (1992) 557-9 (H. *Fleddermann*); CritRR 5 (1992) 192s (J. R. *Michaels*: does not claim to be definitive); ConcordTQ 57 (1993) 310s (P. E. *Deterding*); Evangel 10,2 (1992) 31 (H. C. *Bigg*); ExpTim 108

(1992s) 237 (C. S. *Rodd*, praising also I. H. MARSHALL); NT 35 (1993) 305s (R. *Bauckham*); STEv 4 (1992) 73s (G. *Rizza*, S. *Traina*).

6773 **Frankemölle** H., 1-2 Pt Jud 1987 ➤ 3,6269...7,5749: ᴿSNTU A-16 (1991) 244 (A. *Fuchs*),

6774 **Hiebert** D. Edmond, 1 Peter. Ch 1992 = 1984, Moody. 369 p. 0-8024-8697-5.

6775 **Hillyer** Norman, 1-2 Peter, Jude: NIntBComm 16. Peabody MA 1992, Hendrickson. xv-297 p. $10 pa. 0-943575-87-7 [NTAbs 37, p. 288].

6776 **Houwelingen** P. H. R. van, 1 Petrus, rondzendbrief uit Babylon: Comm-NT³. Kampen 1991, Kok. 205 p. ƒ37,50. – ᴿStreven 59 (1991s) 273s (P. *Beentjes*).

6777 **Knoch** Otto, Der erste und zweite Petrusbrief; der Judasbrief: RgNT 1990 ➤ 6,6736; 7,5753: ᴿActuBbg 29 (1992) 198s (X. *Alegre*); BLitEc 93 (1992) 253s (S. *Légasse*); Carthaginensia 8 (1992) 936-8 (F. *Marín Heredia*); ExpTim 103 (1991s) 374 (E. *Best*); TLZ 117 (1992) 675-7 (C. *Wolff*); TPhil 67 (1992) 583-5 (H. *Engel*).

6778 **Marshall** I. Howard, 1 Peter: IVP comm. Leicester 1991, Inter-Varsity. – ᴿCritRR 5 (1992) 233-5 (J. R. *Michaels*: laudable flagship for a new series).

6779 **Naastepad** T. J. M., De twee Petrusbrieven: VBGed. Kampen 1991, Kok. 148 p ƒ22,90. – ᴿStreven 59 (1991s) 273s (P. *Beentjes*).

6780 Navarre Bible Catholic Epistles [1988]ᵀ. Dublin 1992, Four Courts. 240 p. $20. 1-85182-088-4; pa. 9-2 [NTAbs 37,287].

6781 **Schüssler** Karlheinz, Die katholischen Briefe in der koptischen (sahidischen) Version: CSCOr 528s. Lv 1991, Peeters. I. Text cxi-103 p., 4 pl. II. xxv-87 p. Komm. 0070-0428.

6782 **Bosetti** Elena, Il Pastore... 1 Pt 1990 ➤ 6,6727; 7,5743: ᴿBiblica 73 (1992) 126s (W. J. *Dalton*); CBQ 54 (1992) 344s (S. P. *Kealy*).

6783 **Cervantes Gabarrón** José, La Pasión de Jesucristo en la Primera Carta de Pedro; centro literario y teológico de la Carta. Estella 1991, VDivino. 434 p. – ᴿRBibArg 54 (1992) 189-191 (R. *Krüger*).

6784 **Clowney** Edmund, The message of 1 Peter; the way of the Cross. DG 1988, Inter-Varsity. 234 p. – ᴿJEvTS 35 (1992) 543s (L. *Perkins*).

6785 *Elliott* John H., Peter, first/second epistle of: ➤ 741, AnchorBD 5 (1992) 269-278 / 282-7.

6786 *Karrer* Martin, Petrus(-briefe): ➤ 757, EvKL 3 (1992) 1142-7.

6787 *Knoch* Otto B., Gab es eine Petrusschule in Rom?: SNTU A-16 (1991) 105-126.

6788 **Martin** Troy W., Metaphor and composition in 1 Peter (diss. Ch. 1990 ᴰ*Betz* H.]. Atlanta 1992, Scholars. xi-383 p. $33; pa $22. 1-55540-664-5; -5-3 [PrincSemB 14,81, S. R. *Bechtler*].

6789 **Prostmeier** Ferdinand-R., Handlungsmodelle im ersten Petrusbrief [Diss. Regensburg, ᴰ*Brox* N.] 1990 ➤ 6,6743; 7,5756: ᴿJBL 111 (1992) 553-5 (J. H. *Elliott*); TR 88 (1992) 104-8 (H. *Frankemölle*).

6790 **Reichert** Angelika, Eine urchristliche praeparatio ad martyrium... 1 Pt: BeitBExT 22, ᴰ1989 ➤ 5,6426; 7,5757: ᴿCBQ 54 (1992) 369-371 (J. H. *Elliott*: speculative).

6791 *Sang* David Ito, The New Age and an interpretation of First Peter: diss. Oxford 1988. 389 p. BRD-96180. – DissA 53 (1992s) 845-A.

6792 *Schröger* Friedrich, Wegweisung für Christen in Leiden, Diskriminierung und Verfolgung nach dem 1. Petrusbrief: ➤ 112*, Mem. KUSS O., Theologie im Werden 1992, 417-431.

6793 **Schutter** William L., Hermeneutic and composition in 1 Peter: WUNT
2/30, ᴰ1989 ➤ 5,6428; 7,5759: ᴿNedTTs 46 (1992) 64s (R. A. *Bitter*).
6794 *Shimada* Kazuhito, Is 1 Peter dependent on Ephesians? A critique of
C. L. Milton: AnJapB 17 (1991) 77-106.
6795 **Thurén** L., The rhetorical strategy of 1 Peter ᴰ1990 ➤ 6.6746; 7,5762:
ᴿBiblica 73 (1992) 122-6 (A. *Pitta*); CBQ 54 (1992) 593s (C. C. *Black*).

6796 *Martin* Troy, The present indicative in the eschatological statements of
1 Peter 1:6,8: JBL 111 (1992) 307-312.
6797 *a) Schweizer* Eduard, The priesthood of all believers; 1 Peter 2.1-10; – *b)*
Ellis E. Earle, Pseudonymity and canonicity of New Testament documents; – *c) Wilkins* Michael J., The interplay of ministry, martyrdom,
and discipleship in Ignatius of Antioch: ➤ 126, ᶠMartin R., Worship
1992, 285-293 / 212-224 / 294-315.
6798 *Prigent* Pierre, I Pierre 2,4-10: ➤ 36, ᶠCullmann O., RHPR 72 (1992)
53-60; Eng. 126.
6799 *a) Busto* José Ramón, [I Pe 2,5; Apc] Un reino de sacerdotes 'llamados a
reproducir la imagen del Hijo'; – *b) Lago* Francisco, Partícipes del oficio
real de Cristo: SalT 78 (1990) 83-92 / 107-118.
6800 *Busto* José R., [1 Pt 2,5; Rev. 1,6...] A kingdom of priests [< SalT 78
(1990) 83-92], ᵀ*Bonness* Mary Kay: TDig 39 (1992) 215-9.
6801 **Feldmeier** Reinhard, [1 Pt 2,11] *a)* Fremde in einer entfremdeten Welt;
die Erschliessung christlichen Selbstverständnisses durch die Kategorie der
Fremde im 1. Petrusbrief: ev. Hab.-Diss. ᴰ*Hengel* M. Tü 1992 [TR
89,76]. – *b)* Die Christen als Fremde; die Metapher der Fremde in der
antiken Welt, im Urchristentum und im 1. Petrusbrief: WUNT 64. Tü
1992, Mohr. xiii-264 p. 3-16-145982-2. – ᴿExpTim 104 (1992s) 269s (E.
Best: '1982').
6802 *Heiene* Gunnar, En analyse av 1 Pt 2,13-17 met henblikk på tekstens
aktualitet for politisk etikk: TsTKi 63 (1992) 17-31; Eng. 31.
6803 **Slaughter** James R., The dynamics of marriage in 1 Peter 3:1-7: diss.
Dallas Theol. Sem. 1992, ᴰ*Toussaint* S. 291 p. 93-03921. – DissA 53
(1992s) 3252-A.
6804 **Dalton** William J., Christ's proclamation to the spirits² [¹1965] 1989
➤ 5,6436: 7,5767: ᴿEvQ 64 (1992) 283s (R. P. *Martin*).
6805 *Applegate* Judith K., The co-elect woman of 1 Peter [5,13]: NTS 38
(1992) 587-604.

6806 **Bouchat** Robert A., Dating the Second Epistle of Peter [no proof prior
to 100]: diss. Baylor 1992. 281 p. 93-07284. – DissA 53 (1992s) 3945-A.
6807 **Hiebert** D. Edmond, Second Peter and Jude, an expositional commentary. Greenville 1989, Unusual. 324 p. – ᴿJEvTS 35 (1992) 544s
(L. *Perkins*).
6808 **Paulsen** Henning, Der zweite Petrusbrief und der Judasbrief: KeK NT
12/2. Gö 1992, Vandenhoeck & R. [NTAbs 37, p. 290]. 3-525-51626-6. –
ᴿExpTim 104 (1992s) 270 [E. *Best*: now agreed that 2 Pt used Jude].

G9.4   **Epistula Jacobi ...** data on both apostles James.

6810 *Edwards* Ruth B., Which is the best commentary? XV. The epistle of
James: ExpTim 103 (1991s) 262-8 can only reduce the field to 9.

6811 **Hiebert** D. Edmond, James. Ch 1992=1979, Moody. 348 p. 0-8024-8698-3.

6812 **Hitzé** P. P. A., Die brief van Jakobus: Kommentaar op die Nuwe Testament; struktuur — uitleg — boodskap. Cape Town 1990, Lux Verbi. 238 p. – [R]Neotestamentica 26 (1992) 543-5 (J. van der *Westhuizen*: first volume of the new series).

6813 **Keddie** Gordon J., The practical Christian; James simply explained. Darlington 1989, Evangelical. 239 p. £7, pa. 0-85234-261-6. – [R]Evangel 9,1 (1991) 31 (C. M. *Cameron*).

6814 **Maggioni** Bruno, La lettera di Giacomo; un itinerario di maturità cristiana: Bibbia per tutti, 1989 ➤ 5,6451: [R]RivLtg 79 (1992) 118s (G. *Crocetti*).

6815 **Marconi** G., La lettera di Giacomo 1990 ➤ 7,5784: [R]RivB 40 (1992) 371 (G. *De Virgilio*: solido ma non di uso facile; manca sostrato teologico-riflessivo).

6816 **Martin** Ralph P., James: WordC 48, 1988 ➤ 4,4604... 7,5785: [R]Churchman 105 (1991) 181s (S. *Motyer*); EvQ 64 (1992) 364s (Ruth B. *Edwards*); RefTR 49 (1990) 104s (A. *Lane*); WestTJ 54 (1992) 186-8 (D. G. *McCartney*).

6817 **Schnider** Franz, La lettera di Giacomo [1987 ➤ 3,6309], [T]Proch Umberto. Brescia 1992, Morcelliana. 248 p. Lit 30.000. – [R]StCattMi 36 (1992) 695 (U. *De Martino*: veleno razionalistico).

6818 **Adamson** James B., James, the man and his message 1989 ➤ 5,6442... 7,5772: [R]Evangel 10,2 (1992) 30s (H. *Biss*); JEvTS 35 (1992) 262-4 (J. L. *Easterwood*); RestQ 34 (1992) 124s (D. *Warden*); WestTJ 53 (1991) 151-3 (S. E. *Porter*).

6819 **Arthurs** Jeffrey D., [James:] Biblical interpretation through rhetorical criticism; augmenting the grammatical/historical approach: diss. Purdue 1992, [D]Burke D. 229 p. 93-01255. — DissA 53 (1992s) 3259-A.

6820 **Cargal** Timothy B., Restoring the diaspora; discursive structure and purpose in the Epistle of James: diss. Vanderbilt, [D]Patte D. Nv 1992. 385 p. 92-30954. — DissA 53 (1992s) 1958-A.

6821 *Crotty* Robert B., The literary structure of the letter of James: AustralBR 40 (1992) 45-57.

6822 *Fay* Siegfried C. A., Weisheit — Glaube — Praxis; zur Diskussion um den Jakobusbrief: ➤ 112*, Mem. KUSS O., Theologie im Werden 1992, 397-415.

6823 *Fernández* Víctor M., Santiago, la plenificación cristiana de la espiritualidad postexílica: RBiArg 53 (1991) 29-33.

6824 **Hartin** Patrick J., James and the Q sayings of Jesus [Pretoria diss.]: jNsu 47, 1991 ➤ 7,5782: [R]CBQ 54 (1992) 567s (J. S. *Kloppenborg*), Salmanticensis 39 (1992) 308-310 (R. *Trevijano*); Themelios 18,1 (1992s) 29s (P. M. *Head*).

6825 a) *Iovino* Paolo, La lettera di Giacomo; struttura letterario-tematica; – b) *Manfredi* Silvana, ... Ispirazione veterotestamentaria: Ho Theológos 10 (1992) 7-36 / 37-62.

6826 a) *Laws* Sophie, James, epistle of; – b) *Hagner* Donald A., James (person): ➤ 741, AnchorDB 3 (1992) 621-8 / 616-8.

6827 **Pratscher** W., Der Herrenbruder Jakobus [D]1987 ➤ 3,6305...7,5788: [R]ScotJT 45 (1992) 122s (C. K. *Barrett*); StPatav 39 (1992) 629-631 (G. *Segalla*).

6828 **Tamez** Elsa, The scandalous message of James 1990 ➤ 7,5793: ᴿChr-Cris 51 (1991s) 260s (W. *Urffer*).
6829 **Vries** Egbert de, De Brief van Jakobus; dispositie en theologie ᴰ1991 ➤ 7,5795: ᴿKerkT 43 (1992) 167 (T. *Baarda*).
6830 *Ward* R. B., James of Jerusalem in the first two centuries: ➤ 742, ANRW 2,26,1 (1992) 779-812.

6831 *Greer* A. D. C., (James 1:16-27) The mirror; the glance or the studious gaze?: ExpTim 103 (1991s) 339s.
6832 *Wolmarans* J. L. P., The tongue guiding the body; the anthropological presuppositions of James 3:1-12: Neotestamentica 26 (1992) 523-530.
6833 *Mayordomo-Morin* Moisés, Jak 5,2,3a, zukünftiges Gericht oder gegenwärtiger Zustand: ZNW 83 (1992) 132-7.

G9.6 Epistula Judae.

6834 **Bauckham** Richard, Jude and the relatives of Jesus 1990 ➤ 6.6788; 7,5800; ᴿBiblica 73 (1992) 128-130 (S. *Légasse*); BTAM 15,3 (1992) 141s (E. *Manning*); JBL 111 (1992) 354-6 (P. H. *Davids*: supplements his 1983 Word Comm.); JEH 43 (1992) 634s (S. G. *Hall*); JTS 43 (1992) 208-210 (Judith *Lieu*: careful and creative); NedTTs 46 (1992) 343s (T. van *Lopik*); Neotestamentica 26 (1992) 243-5 (S. *Joubert*); Pacifica 5 (1992) 221-3 (A. *O'Hagan*); RB 99 (1992) 460s (J. *Murphy O'Connor*: 'The four brothers — James, Joses, Jude, Simon — and two sisters — Mary, Salome — of Jesus continue to fascinate both believers and scholars'; not concerned with dogmatic debates, but notes his belief that they were children of Joseph by a prior marriage); RelStR 18 (1992) 142 (C. *Bernas*: magisterial, magnificent); TorJT 7 (1991) 271-3 (J. S. *Kloppenborg*); TvT 32 (1992) 92 (P. J. *Farla*).
6835 **Heiligenthal** Roman, Zwischen Henoch und Paulus; Studien zum theologiegeschichtlichen Ort des Judasbriefes [Hab.-Schr. Tübingen]: TANZ 6. Tü 1992, Francke. 196 p. DM 68 [TR 88,518; NTAbs 37, p. 447].
6836 *Heiligenthal* Roman, Die Weisheitsschrift aus der Kairoer Geniza und der Judasbrief: ZRGg 44 (1992) 356-361.
6837 *Philonenko* Marc, [Jude 9] Melkireša' et Melkira'; note sur les 'Visions d'Amram' [*Milik* J. 1972]: Semitica 41s (1991s) 159-162.
6838 *Renoux* Charles, [Jude 9] L'Assomption de Moïse; d'ORIGÈNE à la chaîne arménienne sur les Épîtres Catholiques: ➤ 35, ᶠCROUZEL H., Recherches 1992, 239-249.

Hoc anno non adhibentur — Nᵒ 6839-6999 — **not used this year.**

| XV. Theologia Biblica |

H1 **Biblical Theology** .1 [OT] **God.**

7000 **Birnbaum** David, God and evil 1989 ➤ 5,7001 ... 7,7001: ᴿGregorianum 73 (1992) 773s (F.-A. *Pastor*); MilltSt 29 (1992) 155-8 (T. *O'Loughlin*); TsTKi 62 (1991) 222 (J.-O. *Henriksen*).
7001 *Bloch* Ariel A., Questioning God's omnipotence in the Bible; a linguistic case-study: ➤ 118, ᶠLESLAU W., Semitic 1991, 174-188.

7002 **Briend** Jacques, Dieu dans l'Écriture: LDiv 150. P 1992, Cerf. 136 p.
7002* **Buckley** Michael J., At the origins of modern atheism 1987 ➤ 4,8010
...7,7003*: ᴿModT 8 (1992) 89-92 (J. *Milbank*: a splendid, bold endeavour).
7003 *Cameron* Charles A., A biblical approach to theodicy: Evangel 10,2 (1992) 25-29.
7004 *Cavedo* Romeo, Gli scandali dell'AT [ira di Dio]: ParVi 37 (1992) 26-35.
7005 **Cazelles** Henri, a) La Bible et son Dieu: JJC 40, 1989 ➤ 5,7010 ...
7,7005: ᴿColcT 62,3 (1992) 179-183 (J. *Warzecha* ❷); RCatalT 16 (1991) 397-403 (A. *Cruells*); RTLv 23 (1992) 82 (J.-C. *Haelewyck*).
— b) La Bibbia e il suo Dio. R 1991, Borla. 205 p. Lit. 25.000. – ᴿCC 143 (1992,3) 455s (D. *Scaiola*).
7006 **Friedlingsdorf** Karl, a) Dämonische Gottesbilder, ihre Entstehung, Entlarvung und Überwinden. Mainz 1992, Grünewald. 176 p.; 6 color. fig. DM 29,80. 3-7867-1640-4. – b) [ein Kapitel:] zu ihrer Genese und Symptomatik: GeistL 65 (1992) 187-199.
7007 *Fujita* Neil S., Biblical monolatry: BToday 30 (1992) 246-250.
7007* **García-Murga** J.R., El Dios del amor y de la paz 1991 ➤ 7,7006*: ᴿCiuD 205 (1992) 249s (J.M. *Ozaeta*).
7008 *Görg* M., Jahwe: ➤ 762, NBL II,7 (1992) 260-6.
Goldman Ari L., The search for God at Harvard 1991 ➤ a919.
7010 **Halbertal** Moshe, *Margalit* Avishai, Idolatry [versus Israel's God], ᵀ*Goldblum* Naomi. CM 1992, Harvard Univ. 299 p. $40. 0-674-44312-8 [TDig 40,165].
7011 *Hendel* Ronald S., When God acts immorally; is the Bible a Good Book?: BR 7,3 (1991) 34-37. 46. 48. 50.
7012 **Levenson** Jon D., Creation and the persistence of evil 1988 ➤ 4,8026 ...
6,7014: ᴿJNES 50 (1991) 143s (W. *Brueggemann*: important on the interface between history of Israelite religion and biblical theology).
7013 **Lodahl** Michael E., Shekhinah/Spirit; divine presence in Jewish and Christian religion: StJudChr. NY 1992, Paulist. vi-234 p. 0-8091-3311-3.
– ᴿTsTKi 62 (1991) 229s (A. *Sæbø*, deutsch).
7014 **Lohfink** N., al., Dio l'Unico: QDisp 24,1991 ➤ 7,7013: ᴿAsprenas 39 (1992) 436s (O. *Di Grazia*); RivB 40 (1992) 355-7 (A. *Rolla*).
7014* a) **McLelland** Joseph C., Prometheus rebound; the irony of atheism 1988 ➤ 7,7014*: ᴿModT 8 (1992) 92-95 (C. *Crowder*).
— b) **Marion** Jean-Luc, God without being, ᵀ*Carlson* Thomas A. Ch 1991, Univ. xxv-258 p. $32. – ᴿAnglTR 74 (1992) 400-2 (A.A. *Vogel*).
7015 *Mauser* Ulrich, One God alone; a pillar of biblical theology: PrincSemB 12 (1991) 225-265 [< ᴢɪᴛ 91,783].
7016 *Metz* Johann B., Suffering from God; theology as theodicy: Pacifica 5 (1992) 274-287.
7017 **Moberly** R.W.L., The Old Testament of the Old Testament; patriarchal narratives and Mosaic Yahwism: OvBT. Mp 1992, Fortress. xvi-234 p. $14. 0-8006-1561-X [BL 93,111, W.J. *Houston*: enviably lucid and persuasive]. – ᴿThemelios 18,2 (1992s) 3s (C. *Wright*, editorial: P for Pentateuch, patriarchs and pagans).
7018 **Moor** J.D. de, The rise of Yahwism: BtETL 91, 1990 ➤ 6,7022; 7,7016: ᴿBijdragen 53 (1992) 438s (P.C. *Beentjes*); BZ 36 (1992) 308s (H. *Niehr*); ETL 68 (1992) 400-2 (A. *Schoors*).
7019 **Mooren** Thomas, Macht und Einsamkeit Gottes; Dialog mit dem islamischen Radikal-Monotheismus: WüFMRelW 2/17. Wü/Altenberge 1991, Echter/Oros. 408 p. DM 60. – ᴿZkT 114 (1992) 350s (G. *Risse*).

Neudecker Reinhard, Die vielen Gesichter des einen Gottes 1989 / I vari volti 1990 → a769.

7020 *Scullion* John J., God (OT): → 741, AnchorBD 2 (1992) 1041-8 (NT 1048-55, *Bassler* Jouette M.).

7021 **Seebass** Horst, Il Dio di tutta la Bibbia [1982]: StBPaid 72, 1985 → 2,5056 ... 5,7030: ᴿAsprenas 39 (1992) 553-562 (V. *Scippa*).

7022 **Tilley** Terrence W., The evils of theodicy 1991 → 7,7023: ᴿJAAR 60 (1992) 570-2 (W. *McWilliams*: insightful); TS 53 (1992) 363-5 (S. *Duffy*).

7023 **Trau** Jane Mary, The co-existence of God and evil: AmerUnivSt 5/101. NY 1991, Lang. 109 p. $28. 0-8204-1380-1 [TDig 39,190].

7024 **Whitney** Barry L., What are they saying about God and evil? 1989 → 5,7036 [not Whitner]: ᴿHorizons 19 (1992) 322s (T. W. *Tilley*).

7025 **Williams** Daniel D. †1973, The demonic and the divine [< his Armstrong Lectures], ᴱ*Evans* Stacy A., 1990 → 7,7024*: ᴿExpTim 103 (1991s) 85 (D. A. *Pailin*).

Zimmer C., 'Deus' 1991 → a205

H1.3 *Immutabilitas* – **God's suffering; process theology.**

7026 *Antinucci* Lucia, Il mistero dell'eterna agonia di Dio; la proposta cristologica di François VARILLON [L'humilité de Dieu 1974; La souffrance de Dieu 1975]: Asprenas 39 (1992) 519-528.

7027 *Beardslee* William A., Process thought on the borders between hermeneutics and theology: Process Studies 19 (1990) 230-4 [< NTAbs 36,149].

7028 **Beek** A. Van de, Why? On suffering, guilt, and God, ᵀ*Vriend* John, 1990 → 7,7025: ᴿInterpretation 46 (1992) 208s (D. J. *Simundson*); RefTR 50 (1991) 112s (M. *Hill*); WestTJ 54 (1992) 188-191 (R. W. *Vunderink*).

7029 *Bouton-Parmentier* Suzanne, Comment concilier l'amour de Dieu, la souffrance et le mal? Apports de la 'process philosophy' et de la 'process theology': RevSR 66 (1992) 181-204.

7030 **Boyd** Gregory A., Trinity and process; a critical evaluation and reconstruction of HARTSHORNE's di-polar theism towards a Trinitarian metaphysics: AmerUnivSt 7/119. NY 1992, P. Lang. 424 p. $61. 0-8204-1660-6 [TDig 40,153].

7031 **Bracken** Joseph A., Society and Spirit; a trinitarian cosmology; pref. *Cobb* J. Selinsgrove / L 1991, Susquehanna Univ. / Assoc. Univ. 194 p. [TR 88,171]. $29.50. – ᴿHorizons 19 (1992) 320s (B. L. *Whitney*); Pacifica 5 (1992) 345s (J. *Honner*: scholarly but modest proposals).

7031* ᴱ**Cameron** N., The power and weakness of God; impassibility and orthodoxy 1990 → 6,586: ᴿRefTR 50 (1991) 73s (P. *Jensen*).

7032 **Case-Winters** Anna, God's power; traditional understandings and contemporary challenges [diss.] 1990 → 7,7027: ᴿTS 53 (1992) 561s (Susan A. *Ross*: process-feminist alternative to all-powerful God irreconcilable with evil and with human freedom).

7032* **Faber** Roland, Der Selbsteinsatz Gottes; zur theo-logischen Grundlegung der Rede vom 'Leiden' Gottes im Hinblick auf eine 'künftige' trinitätstheologisch letzt-fundierte Gotteslehre; kath. Diss. ᴰ*Schulte* R. Wien 1992. – RTLv 24, p. 573.

7033 **Ferguson** Sinclair B., Children of the living God. E 1989, Banner of Truth. 127 p. £2.50 pa. 0-85151-526-3. – ᴿEvangel 10,2 (1992) 31 (C. M. *Cameron*: more useful than ponderous Puritan reprints).

7034 *a) Fetz Reto* Luzius, In critique of WHITEHEAD, [T]*Felt* James W.; – *b)* *Mesle* C. Robert, Sharing a vague vision; WIEMAN's early / later critique of Whitehead: ProcSt 20 (1991) 1-9 / 23-36 . 37-53 [< ZIT 92,48].

7035 *Forte* Bruno, Le 'imperfezioni' di Dio; l''evangelium crucis' e il sacro come rovescio di Dio: Asprenas 39 (1992) 323-340.

7036 **Geffré** Claude, Passion de l'homme, passion de Dieu. P 1991, Cerf. iv-253 p. F 100 [TR 88,83].

7037 **Gonnet** Dominique, Dieu aussi connaît la souffrance 1990 ➤ 6,7039: [R]Études 374 (1991) 140 (J. *Thomas*).

7038 **Hallman** Joseph M., The descent of God; divine suffering in history and theology 1991 ➤ 7,7033*: [R]TS 53 (1992) 182s (M. R. *Tripole*: recovers many unnoticed elements of tradition).

7038* **Han In Chul,** Christianity in the making; a critical study of John B. COBB Jr's process-relational vision of Christianity: diss. Drew, [D]*Keller* Catherine. Madison NJ, 1992. 291 p. 92-33182. – DissA 53 (1992s) 1971-A.

7039 **Harrington** W. J., The tears of God; our benevolent creator and human suffering. ColMn 1992, Liturgical, 70 p. $5. 0-8146-5006-6 [NTAbs 36,437].

7039* *Kobusch* Theo, Kann Gott leiden? Zu den philosophischen Grundlagen der Lehre van der Passibilität Gottes bei ORIGENES: VigChr 46 (1992) 328-333.

7040 **Leftow** Brian, Time and eternity: StPhRel. Ithaca NY 1991, Cornell Univ. xiv-378 p. $43. – [R]TS 53 (1992) 556-8 (J. H. *Wright*).

7041 **Mesle** C. Robert, John HICK's theodicy [extract and reply]; a process humanist critique. L 1991, Macmillan. xxxiii-141 p. £35 [RelSt 28,284].

7042 **Meessen** Frank, Unveränderlichkeit und Menschwerdung Gottes [D]1989 ➤ 7,7038: [R]TLZ 117 (1992) 211-3 (Ingolf U. *Dalferth*); TvT (= TsT-Nijm) 32 (1992) 109 (H. *Häring*).

7043 *Moltmann* J., La Pasión de Cristo y el dolor de Dios [his book El Dios crucificado was in the hands of Juan Ramón MORENO when he was assassinated in El Salvador]: Carthaginensia 8 (1992) 641-655 (-659).

7044 **O'Hanlon** Gerard F., The immutability of God in the theology of H. U. von BALTHASAR 1990 ➤ 6,7048; 7,7040: [R]CritRR 5 (1992) 480-2 (P. C. *Phan*); ETL 68 (1992) 470s (E. *Brito*); ExpTim 103 (1991s) 29 (R. *Butterworth*); IrBSt 13 (1991) 233-5 (J. *Thompson*, excellent).

7045 *Pendergast* R. J., A process Christology: ScEspr 44 (1992) 45-66.

7046 *Reid* Duncan, Without parts or passions? The suffering God in Anglican thought: Pacifica 4 (1991) 257-272.

7047 *Santiago del Cura* Elena, El 'sufrimiento' de Dios en el trasfondo de la pregunta por el mal; planteamientos teológicos actuales: ➤ 551, RET 51 (1991) 331-373.

7047* *Sarot* Marcel, Suffering of Christ, suffering of God?: TLond 95 (1992) 113-9.

7048 *Schlosser* Marianne, Über das Mitleid Gottes [... BONAVENTURA]: FranzSt 72 (1990) 305-319.

7049 **Snider** Theodore M., The divine activity; an approach to 'incarnational' theology: AmerUnivSt 7/63. NY 1990, P. Lang. 416 p. – [R]Interpretation 46 (1992) 104 (R. *Crawford*: 'international').

7050 **Steen** M., Het actuele thema van de lijdende God; vooronderstellingen, illustratie en evaluatie van recent theopaschitisme: diss. Lv 1990, [D]*Willaert* B. – TvT 32,87.

7051 *a) Steen* Marc, The theme of the 'suffering' God; an exploration; – *b)* *Depoortere* Kristiaan, 'You have striven with God' (Gen. 32:28); a

pastoral-theological reflection on the image of God and suffering: ➤ 577,
Suffering 1987/9, 69-93 / 211-234.
7052 **Sweeney** Leo, Divine infinity in Greek and medieval thought; pref.
O'Brien Denis. NY 1992, Lang. xx-576 p. $53. 0-8204-1178-7 [TDig
40, 189; TR 88,526].
7052* **Ward** Keith, Divine action 1991 ➤ 7,7045*: ᴿAnglTR 74 (1992) 398-
400 (D. L. *Berry*).
7053 **Warner** Pauline, For your maker is your husband; a study of the Christian understanding of self-hood. ... 1991, Epworth. 151 p. $7. – ᴿExpTim
103 (1991s) 59 (D. *Peel*: actually an unfair polemic against process theology, which she had at first favored).
7054 *Welker* Michael, Prozesstheologie: ➤ 757, EvKL 3 (1992) 1363-6
[1360-3, -philosophie, H. *Husslik*].
7055 **Yates** John C., The timelessness of God 1990 ➤ 7,7047: ᴿTS 53 (1992)
361-3 (M. *Stebbins*: brimming with insight).
7056 **Young** Henry J., Hope in process; a theology of social pluralism. Mp
1990, Fortress. 137 p. $12 pa. 0-8006-2497-5.
7057 **Zoffoli** Enrico, Mistero della sofferenza di Dio, il pensiero di san Tom-
MASO 1988 ➤ 6,7060; 7,7048: ᴿAnnTh 6 (1992) 157-190 (Catalina *Ber-
múdez*).

H1.4 *Femininum in Deo* – **God as father and as mother** [➤ F3.7; H8.8s].

7057* **Clanton** Jann A., In whose image? God and gender. NY 1990, Crossroad. viii-135 p. $10 pa. – ᴿWestTJ 54 (1992) 202-4 (R. E. *Otto*, also on
HEINE S.).
7058 **Daly** Mary, Al di là di Dio Padre; verso una filosofia della liberazione delle donne. R 1990, Riuniti. 272 p. Lit. 40.000. – ᴿStPatav 38
(1991) 223 (G. *Segalla*: linguaggio 'trasgressivo', giudizi radicali non in-
fondati).
7059 *D'Angelo* Mary Rose, *a) Abba* and 'Father'; imperial theology and the
Jesus traditions: JBL 111 (1992) 611-630; – *b)* Theology in Mark and Q;
Abba and 'father' in context: HarvTR 85 (1992) 149-174.
  Duck Ruth C., Gender and the name of God; the trinitarian baptismal
formula 1991 ➤ 5087.
7061 *Dunkel* G. E., Vater Himmels Gattin: Sprache 34 (1990) 1-26.
7062 **Durrwell** F. X., Nuestro Padre; Dios en su misterio 1990 ➤ 6,7064;
7,7053: ᴿRET 52 (1992) 99s (E. *Tourón*).
7063 *Galot* Jean, Abba, Father, we long to see your face; theological insights
into the first person of the Trinity, ᵀ*Bouchard* Angeline. NY 1992, Alba.
xiv-233 p. $13. 0-8189-0645-6 [TDig 40,163].
7064 *Galot* Jean, Culto del Padre e festa del Padre: Vita Consacrata 28
(1992) 99-109.
7065 **Johnson** Elizabeth A., She who is; the mystery of God in feminist theological discourse. NY 1992, Crossroad. xii-316 p. $25. 0-8245-1162-X
[TDig 40,168].
7066 *Kaczor* Chris, Inclusive language and revealed truth: HomP 92,7 (1991s)
16-20: Scripture never says God is a mother.
7067 **Kulandaisamy** Julian A., God is more loving than a mother. Madras
1991, Christian Literature. xxi-101 p.
7068 **Miller** John W., Biblical faith and fathering 1989 ➤ 5,7087 ... 7,7058:
ᴿCarmelus 39 (1992) 193-6 (A. *Vella*); HomP 91,6 (1990s) 78s (R.
Gilsdorf, under the rubric 'Life with father').

7069 **Moltmann-Wendel** Elisabeth & *Moltmann* Jürgen, Als Frau und Mann von Gott reden: Tb 99. Mü 1991, Kaiser. 117 p. DM 12,80. 3-459-01894-1 [TvT 32,427, C. *Halkes*].
7070 **Moltmann** Elisabeth & Jürgen, God — his and hers. L 1991, SCM. xiii-94 p. £7. 0-334-02017-4. – ᴿExpTim 103 (1991s) 220 (Ruth B. *Edwards*); TTod 49 (1992s) 444 (P. J. *Willson*).
7070* **Montague** George T., Our Father, our Mother; Mary and the faces of God; biblical and pastoral reflections. Steubenville 1990, Franciscan Univ. 174 p. 0-940535-28-9. – ᴿCarmelus 39 (1992) 196s (L. P. *Rogge*).
7071 **Mulack** Christa, Im Anfang war die Weisheit; feministische Kritik des männlichen Gottesbildes 1988 ➤ 5,326*: ᴿLuthMon 29 (1990) 426 (J. *Jeziorowski*).
7071* **Oddie** William, What will happen to God? 1984 ➤ 65,7541 ... 5,7091: ᴿCarmelus 37 (1990) 223s (L. P. *Rogge*).
7072 **Raurell** Frederic, Der Mythos vom männlichen Gott 1989 ➤ 5,7092; 6, 7079: ᴿBZ 36 (1992) 113 (H.D. *Preuss*); LebZeug 45 (1990) 232s (F. *Courth*).
7073 *Rizzi* Armido / *Milano* Andrea, Padre: FilT 5 (1991) 435-444 / 445-462.
7074 *Samsa* Cal, Is God having an identity crisis? The Priest 48,12 (1992) 9.
7075 **Schmidhäuser** Ulrich, Soll 'Gott' nicht mehr 'Herr' genannt werden? Zum gegenwärtigen Feminismus in Gesellschaft und Kirche. Stu 1991, Radius. 147 p. DM 22. – ᴿEvKomm 25 (1992) 114s (Elisabeth *Raiser*: Vorurteil).
7076 *Soden* Wolfram von, Der Genuswechsel bei *rūᵃḥ* und das grammatische Geschlecht in den semitischen Sprachen [SCHÜNGEL-STRAUMANN H. in ᴱ*Kassel* M., Feministische Theologie 1988, 59-73, citing no grammar-work; 'die bisherige Forschung zum Genusproblem wird ignoriert']: ZAHeb 5 (1992) 57-63.
7077 **Strotmann** Angelika, 'Mein Vater bist du' (Sir 51,10); zur Bedeutung der Vaterschaft Gottes in kanonischen und nichtkanonischen frühjüdischen Schriften: FraTSt 39, 1991 ➤ 7,7044: ᴿBZ 36 (1992) 265-7 (Maria *Trautmann*: unverzichtbar); TüTQ 172 (1992) 59s (W. *Gross*); TvT 32 (1992) 309s (P. van der *Horst*); ZkT 114 (1992) 85 (J. M. *Oesch*).
7078 *Talbert* Charles H., The Church and inclusive language for God?: ➤ 175, ᶠSMITH T., PerspRelSt 29,4 (1992) 421-439.
7079 ᴱ**Wacker** M.-T., *Zenger* F., Der eine Gott und die Göttin: QDisp 135, 1991 ➤ 7,7065: ᴿExpTim 103 (1991s) 344 (R. *Coggins*).
7080 *Wenig* Margaret Moers, Gott ist eine Frau — und sie wird älter [< ᴱ*Cox* J., Best Sermons 5 (SF 1992); Yom Kippur sermon in NY Beth Am 1990], ᵀ*Krobath* Evi: EvT 52 (1992) 382-8.

H1.7   Revelatio.

7081 **Akeroyd** Richard H., Reason and revelation, from Paul to Pascal. Macon GA 1991, Mercer Univ. ix-130 p. 0-86554-386-0; pa. -405-0.
7081* ᴱ**Alonso Schökel** L., *Artola* A. M., La palabra de Dios ... Dei Verbum² 1991 ➤ 7,286: ᴿBurgense 33 (1992) 304s (F. *Pérez Herrero*); TVida 32 (1991) 326s (M. A. *Ferrando*).
7082 **Bockmuehl** Markus N. A., Revelation and mystery in ancient Judaism and Pauline Christianity [diss. Cambridge 1987]: WUNT 2/36, 1990 ➤ 6,7089; 7,7071: ᴿJBL 111 (1992) 730s (A. F. *Segal*); JJS 43 (1992) 150-3 (C. R. A. *Murray-Jones*); TLZ 117 (1992) 114s (D. *Lührmann*).
7083 **Carda Pitarch** J. M., La revelación de Dios; una realidad misteriosa que da sentido a la vida humana; Síntesis 2/3. M 1991, Atenas. 307 p. –

ᴿSalmanticensis 39 (1992) 161s (A. *González Montes*); ScripTPamp 24 (1992) 705s (Maria D. *Odero*).

7083* *Coda* Piero,   La filosofia della rivelazione di HEGEL e il postulato BARTHIANO dell'esser-Dio di Dio: Lateranum 57 (1991) 441-452.

7084 ᴱ**Elders** Léon,   La doctrine de la révélation divine de S.T. d'AQUIN, symposium Rolduc 4-5.XI.1989:   StTomistici 37, 1990 ➤ 6,607:   ᴿETL 68 (1992) 200-6 (R. *Wielockx*); ForumKT 7 (1991) 227-9 (R. *Niedermeier*).

7085 **Gioberti** V.,   Filosofia della Rivelazione,   ᴱ*Bonafede* Giulio: Opere 36. Padova 1989, Cedam.   370 p. Lit. 35.000. – ᴿAsprenas 39 (1992) 145s (A. *Ascione*).

7086 **Gorringe** T.J.,   Discerning the Spirit; a theology of revelation 1990 ➤ 7,7079:   ᴿInterpretation 46 (1992) 332 (D.C. *Murchison*).

7087 **Jewett** Paul K.,   God, creation, and revelation; a neo-evangelical theology.   GR 1991, Eerdmans.   viii-544 p. $30.   0-8028-0460-8. – ᴿPersp-RelT 19 (1992) 217-225 (F. *Humphreys*).

7087* **Kautz** John B.,   Analysis and assessment of the concept of revelation in Karl RAHNER's theology; its application and relationship to African traditional religions: diss. Fordham, ᴰ*Heaney* J.   NY 1992, 480 p.   93-00240. – DissA 53 (1992s) 3261-A.

7088 *a) Kudasiewicz* Józef, ➒ Jésus intermédiaire de la révélation; – *b) Rusecki* Marian, ➒ Dieu se révélant dans les œuvres: ➤ 43*, ꟻDEMBOWSKI B., AtKap 118 (1992) 432-447 / 448-459.

7088* *a)* **Lambiasi** Francesco,   Teologia fondamentale; la rivelazione: Alpha-omega. CasM 1991, Piemme.   142 p. Lit. 11.000. – ᴿCC 143 (1992,4) 430s (G. *Giachi*).

— *b)* **Lee Jae-Suk,**   Rivelazione; concetto fondamentale per una teologia delle religioni; confronto tra 'Uditori della Parola' di K. RAHNER e Hwa-Yom Sutra (Gandavyuna) del Buddhismo Mahayana: diss. Pont. Univ. Gregoriana, ᴰ*Fuss* Michael.   R 1992. – InfPUG 24,123 (1992) 10.

7089 *Lohfink* Norbert,   Der weisse Fleck in Dei Verbum, Artikel 12 [... relation between 'what the human author intended and expressed' and 'what God wished to communicate' ... taking into account what is nowadays called Paradigmenwechsel, Diachronie/Synchronie]: TrierTZ 101 (1992) 20-35.

7090 *Martín Velasco* Juan,   Revelación y tradición; aproximación fenomenológica desde la historia de las religiones: RET 52 (1992) 315-347.

7091 **Murad** Afonso T.,   Revelação e história; um estudo sobre o pensamento teológico de J.L. SEGUNDO: diss. Pont. Univ. Gregoriana, ᴰ*Pastor* F. Roma 1992.   336 p.; Extr. 3792, 98 p. – InfPUG 24/122,28; RTLv 24, p. 571.

7092 **Niemann** F.-J.,   Jesus der Offenbarer I-II, 1990 ➤ 7,7093:   ᴿActuBbg 29 (1992) 72s (J. *Boada*); Gregorianum 73 (1992) 349s (R. *Fisichella*).

7093 *Onaiyekan* John,   The constitution Dei Verbum after 25 years: EAPast 27 (1990) 305-329.

7094 *Patterson* Sue,   Gratuitous truth; metaphor and revelation: Colloquium 24,1 (1992) 29-43 [< zɪт 92,284].

7095 *Payne* Steven L.,   The relationship between public revelation and private revelations in the theology of Saint JOHN of the Cross: Teresianum 43 (1992) 175-215.

7095* *Porter* Jacquelyn,   The word on the cross; the function of 'theologia crucis' in Stanislas BRETON's understanding of revelation as writing: diss. ᴰ*Power* D.   Washington D.C. 1992. – RTLv 24, p. 576.

7096 **Reist** Benjamin A., Processive revelation [... the essence of Christianity differs for each epoch]. Louisville 1992, W-Knox. 205 p. $25. 0-664-21955-1 [TDig 40,183].

7097 *Resweber* Jean-Paul, Vérité révélée et liberté humaine: RevSR 66 (1992) 163-179.

7098 *Russo* Adolfo, Rivelazione e rivelazioni nel contesto delle religioni mondiali: Asprenas 39 (1992) 5-34.

7099 **Schelling** F. W. J., Philosophie de la Révélation: Épiméthée. P 1991, PUF. 400 p. F 225. 2-13-043510-6. – RÉTRel 67 (1992) 299 (J.-P. *Gabus*: 'Épithémée'; Tnon nommé].

7100 **Schmitz** Josef, La rivelazione: GdT 206, 1991 ➤ 7,7097*: RAsprenas 39 (1992) 446s (A. *Russo*).

7101 **Schmitz** Josef, La revelación 1990 ➤ 7,7097: RLumenVr 40 (1991) 321s (U. *Gil Ortega*); ScripTPamp 24 (1992) 304-8 (C. *Izquierdo*).

7101* **Steinheim** Solomon L., The revelation according to the doctrine of Judaism; a criterion [Die Offenbarung nach dem Lehrbegriffe der Synagoge 1865 EKatz Steven, 4 Bände 1980]. – REurJT 1 (1992) 163-172 (C. H. *Henry*).

7102 FSUDBRACK Josef; Gottes Nähe; religiöse Erfahrung in Mystik und Offenbarung, 65, Gb. 1990 ➤ 6,174: RTR 88 (1992) 333-6 (Marianne *Heimbach-Steins*, detailliert).

7103 **Swinburne** Richard, Revelation; from metaphor to analogy. Ox 1992, Clarendon. vii-236 p. £13. 0-19-823968-8. – RJTS 43 (1992) 777-80 (M. *Wiles*: p. 189, the happy one of Ps 137 'dashes little ones against the Rock' by destroying their evil inclinations).

7104 *Sykes* Stephen W., Offenbarung(sreligion), TSchnitker T. A.: ➤ 757, EvKL 3 (1992) 810-8.

7104* *Wanke* Joachim, Wort Gottes an Menschen unserer Zeit; 25 Jahre Offenbarungskonstitution 'Dei Verbum': ➤ 58, EErfurt 1992, 195-202.

7105 *Wilson* Jonathan R., The Gospel as revelation in Julian N. HARTT: JRel 72 (1992) 549-559.

7105* **Young** Frances, The art of performance; towards a theology of Holy Scripture 1990 ➤ 7,7103: RJTS 42 (1991) 426-8 (J. L. *Houlden*); TLond 95 (1992) 48-50 (J. *Barton*: lively though conservative).

H1.8 **Theologia fundamentalis.**

7106 **Anglin** W. S., Free will and the Christian faith. Ox 1991, Clarendon. ix-218 p. £25. 0-19-823936-X. – RJTS 43 (1992) 338-341 (P. *Helm*).

7107 **Ansaldi** Jean, L'articulation de la foi, de la théologie et des écritures: CogF 163, 1991 ➤ 7,7104; 2-204-04237-4: RTvT 32 (1992) 326 (F. *Maas*).

7108 *Brito* Emilio, La 'théologie philosophique' de SCHLEIERMACHER et la théologie fondamentale: MélSR 49 (1992) 33-42 .91-103; Eng. 103.

7109 *Camroux* Martin, The case for liberal theology: ExpTim 103 (1991s) 168-172.

7110 **Casale** U., L'avventura della fede; saggio di teologia fondamentale 1988 ➤ 5,7131: RAntonianum 67 (1992) 449 (T. *Larrañaga*); EstE 67 (1992) 470 (J. J. *Alemany*).

7111 *Chapman* Mark D., Apologetics and the religious a priori; the use and abuse of KANT in German theology 1900-20: JTS 43 (1992) 470-510.

7112 EColombo G., (*Bertuletti* A., *al.*) L'evidenza e la fede. Mi 1988, 'Glossa. – RSapienza 43 (1990) 181-196 (S. *Sorrentino*), risposta in TItSett 17 (1992) 17-31 (A. *Bertuletti*).

7113 **Davis** Caroline F., The evidential force of religious experience 1989
➤ 6,7115*: ᴿJRel 72 (1992) 129s (Pamela S. *Anderson*).

7113* *D'Costa* Gavin, The end of systematic theology: TLond 95 (1992)
324-334.

7114 ᴱ**Doré** J., Introduction à l'étude de la théologie, 1. Le Christianisme et la
foi chrétienne 1991 ➤ 7,350*b*: ᴿScEsp 44 (1992) 367-372 (R. *Latourelle*).

7114* *a) Evans* James H.ᴶ, The graduate education of future theological
faculties; – *b) McBrien* Richard P., ..., a Catholic perspective: TEdn 28,1
(1991) 85-89 / 90-94.

7115 *Fäh* Hans L., J.D. Scotus, Gegenstand und Wissenschaftscharakter
der Theologie [Ordinatio prol. 3s] lat./deutsch mit Erklärungen: FranzSt
72 (1990) 113-236.

7116 **Farrelly** M. John, Belief in God in our time; foundational theology:
Glazier Theology & Life 35. ColMn 1992, Liturgical. 381 p. $20. 0-
8146-5706-0 [TDig 39,361].

7117 **Fisichella** Rino, Introduzione alla teologia fondamentale: IntDiscT 4.
CasM 1992, Piemme. 158 p. Lit. 25.000. 88-384-1780-6 [NRT 115,519,
L. *Renwart*]. – ᴿCC 143 (1992,3) 109 (G. *O'Collins*): Gregorianum 73
(1992) 581 (*ipse*).

7118 *a) Fisichella* R., Metodo in teologia fondamentale; – *b) Rocchetta* C., Il
'novum' in teologia; spunti per un dibattito; – *c) Milano* A., 'Analogia
Christi'; sul parlare intorno a Dio in una teologia cristiana: Ricerche
Teologiche 1 (1990) 75-90 / 5-27 / 29-73 [< FilT 5,569].

7119 *Forte* Bruno, La teología como compañía, memoria y profecía; introducción al sentido y al método de la teología como historia: Verdad e
Imagen 118, 1990 ➤ 7,7117: ᴿActuBbg 29 (1992) 66s (J. *Boada*); Burgense 32 (1991) 587s (R. *Berzosa Martínez*); ComSev 24 (1991) 278s (M.
Sánchez); LumenVr 40 (1991) 526 (F. *Ortiz de Urtaran*); RET 51 (1991)
402s (E. *Tourón*); Salmanticensis 38 (1991) 97s (J.L. *Ruiz de la Peña*).

7120 *Frostin* Per, Systematic theology in a pluralistic society, ᵀ*Meakin* Christopher: ST 46 (1992) 15-27.

7121 **Gelabert** Martín, Valoración cristiana de la experiencia: Nueva Alianza
115. S 1990, Sígueme. 174 p. 84-301-1106-9. – ᴿActuBbg 29 (1992) 67s
(J. *Boada*).

7122 **Haight** Roger, Dynamics of theology 1990 ➤ 7,7120: ᴿGregorianum
73 (1992) 359s (J. *Galot*: relativise trop); JRel 72 (1992) 604s (Catherine
M. *LaCugna*); RelStR 18 (1992) 39 (J.R. *Sachs*: splendid).

7123 **Hübner** Hans, Metaphysikkritik — gemeinsames Anliegen von Philosophie und Theologie? [Topitsch Ernst, Heil und Zeit; Tü 1990, Mohr;
129 p. DM 78; pa. 48]: TLZ 117 (1992) 481-492.

7124 **Imbach** J., Breve teología fundamental, ᵀ*Villanueva* Marciano. Barc
1992, Herder. 220 p. – ᴿArTGran 55 (1992) 365 (A. *Jiménez Ortiz*);
CiuD 205 (1992) 766s (J.M. *Ozaeta*).

7125 **Knauer** Peter, Der Glaube kommt vom Hören; ökumenische Funda-
mentaltheologie⁶ʳᵉᵛ [¹1978]. FrB 1991, Herder. 448 p. DM 36 pa. – ᴿMü-
TZ 43 (1992) 258s (W.W. *Müller*); StiZt 210 (1992) 278-284 (H. *Döring*);
NRT 114 (1992) 124 (L. *Renwart*); ZkT 114 (1992) 100 (K.H. *Neufeld*).

7126 **Korsmeyer** Jerry D., A neo-classical framework for Catholic fundamental theology: diss. Duquesne, ᴰ*Thompson* W. Pittsburgh 1992. 290 p.
93-09319. – DissA 53 (1992s) 3954-A.

7126* **Kreiner** Armin, Ende der Wahrheit? Zum Wahrheitsverständnis in
Philosophie und Theologie. FrB 1992, Herder. viii-608 p. DM 78 [TR
88,434].

7127 **Kurtén** Tage, Grunder för kontextuell teologi; ett wittgensteinskt sätt att närma sig teologin i diskussion med Anders JEFFNER. Åbo 1987, Akademis. 234 p. – ᴿTsTKi 62 (1991) 222-4 (Terje *Wigen*).

7127* *Latourelle* René, Spécificité de la théologie fondamentale: ⇉ 63, ᶠGEF-FRÉ C., Interpréter 1992, 103-122.

7128 **McGrath** Alister E., The genesis of doctrine 1990 ⇉ 7,7128: ᴿChr-Cent 108 (1991) 23s (T. *Peters*); HeythJ 33 (1992) 89s (J. E. *Thiel*: applauds and modifies LINDBECK); JTS 43 (1992) 334-6 (D. *Nineham*: illuminating, badly edited); ScotJT 45 (1992) 401-3 (S. *Williams*); TS 53 (1992) 155s (Nancy C. **Ring**: simple restatement of doctrinal statements is no advance over simple restatement of Scripture); TZBas 48 (1992) 297-9 (W. *Kern*).

7129 *Maddox* Randy L., Opinion, religion and 'Catholic spirit'; John WESLEY on theological integrity: AsbTJ 47,1 (1992) 63-87.

7130 **Marquardt** F.-W., Von Elend und Heimsuchung der Theologie 1988 ⇉ 5,7148; 6,7137: ᴿProtestantesimo 47 (1992) 335-7 (B. *Rostagno*); TsTKi 63 (1992) 315s (H. *Hegstad*); ZevEth 36 (1992) 309-311 (F. *Wagner*).

7131 **Masetti** N., Orientamenti di teologia fondamentale, ad uso di studenti laici, catechisti e operatori pastorali: Testi di teologia per tutti. T-Leumann 1991, Elle Di Ci. 325 p. Lit. 18.000. – ᴿAsprenas 39 (1992) 117 (G. *Tubiello*).

7132 *Miccoli* Paolo, Teologia e scienze umane: RivScR 5 (1991) 303-334.

7133 **Michelin** Étienne, Supernaturalis; enquête sur l'emploi du mot 'surnaturel' durant des périodes antépréparatoires du second concile Vatican 1959-1962: diss. Fribourg 1992, ᴰ*Torrell* J. P. – RTLv 24, p. 558.

7134 **Migliore** Daniel L., Faith seeking understanding; an introduction to Christian theology 1991 ⇉ 7,7130: ᴿCurrTMiss 19 (1992) 219.222 (J. K. *Robbins*); ExpTim 103 (1991s) 283 (D. *Cornick*: Reformed pastor of Italian immigrants); RefTR 51 (1992) 65s (P. *Jensen*); TTod 49 (1992s) 85s (Ellen T. *Charry*); WestTJ 54 (1992) 380-2 (R. E. *Otto*).

7134* **Mikolajczyk-Thyrion** Francine, La dissertation aujourd'hui; du lieu commun au texte de réflexion personnelle: L'esprit des mots. P 1990, Duculot. 120 p. – ᴿAtKap 117 (1991) 145-7 (A. *Nowicki*).

7135 **Moltmann** Jürgen, Che cos'è oggi la teologia? [1988 ⇉ 4,8161],ᵀ: GdT 200. Brescia 1991, Queriniana. 126 p. Lit. 13.000. – ᴿEstE 67 (1992) 235-7 (María A. *Navarro Girón*); REB 52 (1992) 230-2 (C. M. *Boff*); StPatav 38 (1991) 661s (E. R. *Tura*).

7136 **Moltmann** J., ¿Qué es teología hoy? ᵀ*Olivera* Adolfo: Pedal 219. S 1992, Sígueme. 139 p. – ᴿLumenVr 41 (1992) 386 (F. *Ortiz de Urtaran*).

7136* **Muller** Richard A., The study of theology; from biblical interpretation to contemporary formulation: Foundations of Contemporary Interpretation 7, 1991 ⇉ 7,7131*: ᴿWestTJ 54 (1992) 383s (D. P. *Fuller*).

7137 **Muratore** Saturnino, Teologia e filosofia, alla ricerca di un nuovo rapporto, in dialogo con Giovanni FERRETTI: Saggi 28. R 1990, A.V.E. 318 p. Lit. 38.000. – ᴿZkT 114 (1992) 100s (K. H. *Neufeld*).

7138 **Neufeld** K. H., Fundamentaltheologie 1. Jesus — Grund christlichen Glaubens: StBuT 171. Stu 1992, Kohlhammer. 220 p. DM 28. 3-17-011123-X. – ᴿTvT [= TsTNijm] 32 (1992) 322s (W. *Logister*).

7139 **Nichols** A., The shape of Catholic theology; an introduction to its sources, principles, and history. E 1991, Clark. 374 p. £12.50 [TR 88,76]. ᴿModT 8 (1992) 98-100 (J. J. *Buckley*); PrPeo 6 (1992) 85s (N. P. *Harvey*): TvT 32 (1992) 423s (N. *Schreurs*).

7140 *Pérez de Laborda* Alfonso, La théologie comme science; théologie de la raison pure et philosophie de la raison pratique, ^T*Follon-Gambra Gutiérrez* Irène: RTLv 23 (1992) 297-320; Eng. 424.

7141 **Pié i Ninot** Salvador, Tratado de Teología Fundamental: Agape 7, 1989 ➤ 5,7162 ... 7,7137: ᴿRET 51 (1991) 507-510 (M. *Gesteira*); ScripTPamp 23 (1991) 737s (C. *Izquierdo*); TR 88 (1992) 132-4 (H. *Verweyen*).

7142 **Poppi** Antonino, Il dibattito sull'esclusione della teologia dal ruolo universitario nello Studio di Padova (1363-1806); un aggiornamento: Atti e Memorie 103,3 (1990s). Padova 1992, Coop. Tipografica. p. 41-56.

7143 **Roberts** James Deotis, A philosophical introduction to theology 1991 ➤ 7,7138: ᴿChrCent 108 (1991s) 976s (J. K. *Robbins*); ExpTim 103 (1991s) 85 (R. *Butterworth* notes 'the later Platonisms, Justine...').

7144 *Russell* John M., Apologetics the casual way; RAHNER's indirect method: *a*) JRelSt 17 (1991) 108-155; – *b*) AsiaJT 6,1 (1992) 154-168.

7145 *Schner* George P., The appeal to experience [in theology; often vaguely equivalent to '(in my) opinion']: TS 53 (1992) 40-59.

7146 **[Schüssler] Fiorenza** Francis, Fundamentale Theologie; zur Kritik theologischer Begründungsverfahren [1984 ➤ 65,5815], ^T*Hartwich* R., gekürzt: Welt der Theologie. Mainz 1992, Grünewald. 316 p. DM 48 [NRT 115, 742, L. *Renwart* hésite].

7147 **Sölle** Dorothee, Thinking about God; an introduction to theology 1991 ➤ 7,7141*; 0-334-02476-5: ᴿExpTim 103 (1991s) 94 (K. W. *Clements* admires); TGL 82 (1992) 475s (W. *Beinert* mistakes the author for his famous feminist wife).

7147* *Szymik* Jerzy, ☉ Littérature et méthodologie dans la théologie: AtKap 119 (1992) 243-251.

7148 **Thiel** John E., Imagination and authority; theological authorship in the modern tradition. Mp 1991, Fortress. xii-228 p. $25. – ᴿTS 53 (1992) 768-770 (C. M. *Wood*).

7149 **Torrance** Thomas F., Science théologique, ^T*Lacoste* J.-Y.: Théologiques 1990 ➤ 7,7143: ᴿRThom 92 (1992) 860-4 (G. *Narcisse*).

7149* **Tresmontant** Claude, I primi elementi della teologia, ^{TE}Maurizio Lucillo. Brescia 1990, Queriniana. 288 p. Lit. 25.000. – ᴿCC 143 (1992,1) 204 (G. *Ferraro*).

7150 **Verweyen** Hansjürgen, Gottes letztes Wort; Grundriss der Fundamentaltheologie 1991 ➤ 7,7145; DM 55. 3-491-71037-5: ᴿTGL 473-5 (W. *Sosna*); TLZ 117 (1992) 693-7 (Annette *Weidhas*); TvT [= TsTNijm] 32 (1992) 105 (J. *Brok*).

7151 **Vilanova** Evangelista, Para comprender la teología. Estella 1992, VDivino. 116 p.

7152 *Vroom* Hendrik M., Does theology presuppose faith?: ScotJT 45 (1992) 145-163.

7153 **Wagner** Falk, Was ist Theologie? Studien zu ihrem Begriff und Thema in der Neuzeit. Gü 1989, Mohn. 504 p. DM 148. 3-579-00180-9. – ᴿActuBbg 29 (1992) 219s (J. *Boada*). – *b*) Philosophie und Theologie: ➤ 757, EvKL 3 (1992) 1205-11.

7154 **Waldenfels** Hans, Manuel de théologie fondamentale, ^T*Depré* Olivier, ^E*Geffré* Claude: CogF 159, 1990 ➤ 7,7147: ᴿÉTRel 67 (1992) 128s (J.-D. *Kraege*); RThom 92 (1992) 864-9 (G. *Narcisse*).

7155 **Wiebe** Donald, The irony of theology and the nature of religious thought: McGill-Queen's Studies in the History of Ideas. Montreal 1991, McGill-Queen's Univ. xiv-261 p. C$ 40. – ᴿJRel 72 (1992) 455s (T. W. *Tilley*); RelSt 28 (1992) 120 (B.R. *Clack*); TS 53 (1992) 157s (M.D. *Hart*).

7156 ᴱWohlmuth Josef, Katholische Theologie heute; eine Einführung in das Studium 1990 ➤ 7,387: ᴿTvT 32 (1992) 306 (A. *Brants*).

H2.1 Anthropologia theologica – VT & NT.

7157 *Albertz* Rainer [AT], *Neudecker* Reinhard [Judentum], *Hegermann* Harald [NT], Mensch ➤ 768, TRE 22 (1992) 464-474-481-493 (-577, *al.*).

7157* *Alvarez-Suárez* Aniano, Releyendo la 'Gaudium et spes'; de la teología a la antropología: Burgense 33 (1992) 381-420.

7158 *Beauchamp* Paul, Accomplir les Écritures; un chemin de théologie biblique: RB 99 (1992) 132-162; Eng. 132 (adding anthropology to his 1977-1990 books).

7159 ᴱBernard C. A., L'antropologia dei maestri spirituali [Simposio Gregoriana, Roma 28.IV-1.V. 1989]; Spiritualità 8, 1991 ➤ 7,469: ᴿComSev 24 (1991) 451 (M. *Sánchez*).

7160 Bokwa Ignacy, Christologie als Anfang und Ende der Anthropologie; über das gegenseitige Verhältnis zwischen Christologie und Anthropologie bei Karl RAHNER; EurHS 23/381, ᴰ1990 ➤ 7,7154: ᴿActuBbg 29 (1992) 78s (J. *Boada*); TR 88 (1992) 474-6 (E. C. *Farrugia*: kritisch, positiv).

7161 Bravo Lazcano Carlos, El marco antropológico de la Fe. Bogotá 1991, Univ. Javeriana. 211 p. – ᴿTXav 41 (1991) 99-104 (G. *Neira F.*).

7162 *a) Brenk* Frederick E., Darkly beyond the glass; Middle Platonism and the vision of the soul; – *b) Blumenthal* H. J., Soul vehicles in SIMPLICIUS; – *c) Andia* Ysabel de, 'pathōn tà theîa' [Noms divins 648 B]: ➤ 147, ᶠPLACES É. des, Platonism 1992, 39-60 / 173-188 / 239-258.

7163 *Cahill* Lisa S., Can we get real about sex?: Commonweal 117 (1990) 497-9.502s.

7164 Cavarnos Constantine, Modern Greek philosophers on the human soul²ʳᵉᵛ. Belmont MA 1987, Institute for Byz. 140 p. – ᴿJAAR 59 (1991) 595-7 (G. C. *Papademetriou*).

7165 Colzani G., Antropologia cristiana; il dono e la responsabilità: Manuali di base 23. CasM 1991, Piemme. 158 p. Lit. 15.000. 88-384-1723-7. – ᴿHoTheológos 10 (1992) 107s (A. *Raspanti*).

7166 *Colzani* Gianni, Recenti manuali di antropologia teologica di lingua italiana e tedesca: VivH 3 (1992) 391-405.

7167 *Comblin* Joseph, Anthropologie chrétienne [1985 ➤ 2,5239; Eng. 1990 ➤ 7,7157], ᵀ*Puratte* Raymond; préf. *Simon* René. 265 p. F 155. 2-204-04206-4. – ᴿÉTRel 67 (1992) 613 (M. *Müller*).

7168 Ebeling Gerhard, LUTHERstudien 2/3: Die theologische Definition des Menschen; Kommentar zu Thesc 20-40, 1989 ➤ 7,7159: ᴿAntonianum 67 (1992) 151-4 (H.-M. *Stamm*); ArRefG 82 (1991) 315-9 (K.-H. *zur Mühlen*, 1-3); SvTKv 67 (1991) 91-93 (B. *Hägglund*).

7169 — *Fischer* Hermann, Luthers Sicht des Menschen im Spannungsfeld von philosophischer und theologischer Definition [*Ebeling* G., Luther De homine 1977-89]: TRu 57 (1992) 305-317.

7170 *Frankemölle* H., Menschlichkeit; Impulse aus den Evangelien zu einem Grundwert des Lebens: TJb (Lp 1990) 141-8 [< ZIT 91,654].

7171 *Frigato* Sabino, Antropologia cristologica e verità morale: Salesianum 54 (1992) 99-121.

7171* *a) Ganoczy* A., Neue Aufgaben der christlichen Anthropologie; – *b) Pannenberg* W., Anthropologie in theologischer Perspektive; philosophisch-theologische Grundlagen: TJb (1991, aus den 15 1973-1988 unter kommunistischer Zensur nicht publizierbaren) 120-131 / 209-219.

7172 *Giannoni* Paolo,   La definizione del Concilio di Vienne sull'anima: VivH 3,1 (1992) 101-118; Eng. 118.

7173 *Gire* Pierre, De l'intelligence: EsprVie 102 (1992) 489-495.

7174 **Gozzelino** Giorgio,   Il mistero dell'uomo in Cristo; saggio di proto-logia²ʳᵉᵛ [¹1985]: CorsStT. T-Leumann 1992, L.D.C.   456 p. Lit. 35.000. – ᴿAsprenas 39 (1992) 285s (P. *Pifano*); Divinitas 36 (1992) 200 [D. *Vibrac*].

7175 **Guardini** Romano,   Welt und Person; Versuche zu einer christlichen Lehre vom Menschen (1939), ᴱ*Henrich* F.   Mainz/Pd 1988, Grüne-wald/Schöningh. 196 p. DM 29,80. – ᴿTR 88 (1992) 68s (W. *Schmidt*).

7175* *Henriksen* Jan-Olav,   [in Norwegian] Whole and real human being; understanding of humanity in the anthropology of E. JÜNGEL: TsTKi 62 (1991) 27-43; Eng. 43.

7176 *Izquierdo Labeaga* José A.,   El hombre entre dos hermenéuticas [COMTE-KANT y (?) AQUINAS]:   Gregorianum 73 (1992) 523-539; Eng. 539.

7177 **Joha** Ždenko,   Christologie und Anthropologie; eine Verhältnisbe-stimmung unter besonderer Berücksichtigung des theologischen Denkens Walter KASPERS [Diss. Rom 1987]: FrTSt 148. FrB 1992, Herder. xvi-399 p. DM 88 [TR 88,524]. – ᴿTGL 82 (1992) 481 (D. *Hattrup*).

7178 *a) Kegler* Jürgen,   Beobachtungen zur Körpererfahrung in der hebräi-schen Bibel; – *b) Ogushi* Motosuke,   Ist nur das Herz die Mitte des Menschen?; – *c) Rendtorff* Rolf,   Die sündige *næfæš*: → 197, ᶠWOLFF H., ... Anthropologie 1992, 28-41 / 42-47 / 211-220.

7179 **Ladaria** Luis F.,   Introduzione alla antropologia teologica. CasM 1992, Piemme. 168 p. Lit. 25.000. 88-384-1781-4. – ᴿGregorianum 73 (1992) 583s (*ipse*).

7180 *Lategan* Bernard, [*Kruger* M. A. response], New Testament anthro-pological perspectives in a time of reconstruction: JTSAf 76 (1991) 86-94 [-96; < ZIT 91,709].

7180* **Le Breton** David,   Anthropologie du corps et modernité: Sociologie d'au-jourd'hui. P 1990, PUF. 263 p. – ᴿHumTeol 12 (1991) 413-5 (J. *Cunha*).

7181 *Lienhard* Marc,   LUTHER et sa conception de l'homme; regards sur le Commentaire de la Genèse (1536-1545): PosLuth 40 (1992) 105-120 [< ZIT 92,366].

7182 **McDermott** John M.,   The Bible on human suffering 1990 → 7,7170: ᴿPrPeo 5 (1991) 162 (B. *Robinson*).

7183 **McFadyen** Alistair I.,   The call to personhood; a Christian theory of the individual in social relationships. C 1990, Univ. xii-327 p. £35; pa. £13. 0-521-38471-0; -40929-2. – ᴿJTS 43 (1992) 332-4 (N. *Lash*: a surprising monologue from an admirer of dialogue).

7184 **Malnati** Ettore,   L'uomo pensato dalla teologia; sviluppo dell'antro-pologia teologica: (Studium Fidei) Prospettive teologiche.   Trieste 1989, LINT. 282 p. – ᴿVivH 3 (1992) 429s (M. *Meini*).

7184* *Matabosch* Antoni,   'Manuals' d'antropologia teològica en la dècada dels '80 (II) [10-22: NEUSCH M. 1985; GOZZELINO G. 1985; COMBLIN J. 1985; GONZÁLEZ FAUS J. 1987; PANNENBERG W. 1983; TRIGO P. 1988; SAHAGÚN LUCAS J. de, 1988; COLZANI G. 1988; RUIZ DE LA PEÑA J. 1983/88/91]: RCatalT 16 (1991) 405-419.

7185 *Mattei* Paul,   L'anthropologie de NOVATIEN; affinités, perspectives et limites: RÉAug 38 (1992) 235-259.

7186 *Mayer* Cornelius,   Caro – spiritus [deutsch]: → 743, AugL 1,5s (1992) 743-759.

7187 *Mondin* Battista,   L'antropologia teologica; definizione, obiettivi, punto di partenza, metodo, divisione: Sapienza 45 (1992) 113-135.

7188 **Nascentes Dos Santos** Tarsício, Introdução ao discurso antropológico de João Paulo II, Gaudium et Spes 22 e 24 no programa do atual Pontífice: diss. S. Croce. R 1992. 376 p. – ᴿScripTPamp 24 (1992) 1115s (A. *Aranda*).

7189 *Orbe* Antonio, Gloria Dei vivens homo (análisis de IRENEO, adv. haer. IV, 20, 1-7): Gregorianum 73 (1992) 205-267; franç. 268.

7190 [Hunt] **Overzee** Anne, The body divine; the symbol of the body in the works of TEILHARD de Chardin and RĀMĀNUJA: StRelTrad 2. C 1992, Univ. xv-218 p. £ 30. – ᴿJDharma 17 (1992) 160-162 (V. V. *Vineeth*: masterly).

7190* **Panteghini** Giacomo, L'uomo alla luce di Cristo; lineamenti di antropologia teologica 1990 ➤ 7,7180: ᴿCC 143 (1992,2) 629s (F. *Lambiasi*).

7191 **Pattaro** Germano [➤ 7,7181], † 1986, ᴱ*Cavedo* Romeo, La svolta antropologica. Bo 1991, Dehoniane. 677 p. – ᴿTeresianum 43 (1992) 536s (E. *Laudazi*: per specialisti).

7192 **Pesch** Otto H., Liberi per grazia; antropologia teologica: [Frei sein 1983 ➤ 65,5909]: BtTContemporanea 54. Brescia 1988, Queriniana. 609 p. Lit. 55.000. – ᴿAsprenas 39 (1992) 118s (P. *Cacciapuoti*).

7193 **Rocchetta** Carlo, Per una teologia della corporeità. T 1990, Camilliane. 289 p. – ᴿAtKap 118 (1992) 334-7 (J. *Królikowski*, ❷).

7194 **Ruiz de la Peña** Juan L., El don de Dios; antropología teológica especial: Presencia Teológica 63. M 1991, Sal Terrae 412 p. 84-293-0911. – ᴿBurgense 33 (1992) 307-310 (J. S. *Lucas*) & 572-5 (J. A. *Sayés*, la parte sobre pecado original); Carthaginensia 8 (1992) 950s (J. M. *Roncero Moreno*); Gregorianum 73 (1992) 352s (L. F. *Ladaria*); LumenVr 41 (1992) 100s (F. *Ortiz de Urtaran*); RET 52 (1992) 481-492 (A. *Revilla Cuñado*).

7195 **Ruiz de la Peña** J. L., Imagen de Dios; antropología 1988 ➤ 4,4243 ... 7,7184a: ᴿRTLv 23 (1992) 90s (E. *Brito*).

7196 *a) Sanna* Ignazio, La categoria persona e le antropologie contemporanee; – *b) Grossi* Vittorino, La categoria teologica di persona nei primi secoli del cristianesimo; l'ambito latino; – *c) Bordoni* Marcello, Il contributo della categoria teologica di persona: ➤ 490, Lateranum 58 (1992) 75-142 / 11-45 / 47-62.

7197 **Sattler** Gary R., Nobler than the angels, lower than a worm; the pietist view of the individual in the writings of Heinrich MÜLLER and August H. FRANCKE [diss. Marburg]. Lanham MD 1989, UPA. xvii-187 p. $29.75. – ᴿChH 60 (1991) 554s (E. *Lund*).

Sayés J. A., Antropología del hombre caido; el pecado original 1991 ➤ e1.9.

7198 **Schillebeeckx** E., Menschen, die Geschichte von Gott 1990 ➤ 7,7188: ᴿGeistL 65 (1992) 78 (J. *Sudbrack*); KerkT 43 (1992) 343-5 (A. *Noordegraaf*); LuthMon 31 (1992) 429 (J. *Jeziorowski*).

7199 **Schillebeeckx** Edward, L'histoire des hommes, récit de Dieu [Mensen 1989 ➤ 6,7190; Eng. ➤ 7929], ᵀ*Cornelis-Gevaert* H.: CogF. P 1992, Cerf. 382 p. F 195. – ᴿÉtudes 376 (1992) 857 (R. *Marlé*); FoiTemps 22 (1992) 564-6 (G. *Harpigny*).

7200 ᴱ**Schneider** Theodor, Mann und Frau 1989 ➤ 5,513; 7,7189: ᴿTLZ 117 (1992) 147-9 (C. *Frey*).

7201 **Schulze** Markus, Leibhaft und unsterblich; zur Schau der Seele in der Anthropologie und Theologie des hl. Thomas von AQUIN: StFrib 76. FrS 1992, Univ. 186 p. Fs 34 [TR 88,522].

7202 *a) Schwager* Raymund, Hörer des Wortes; eine empirische Anthropologie für die Theologie? (Karl RAHNER — Alfred TOMATIS — René

GIRARD); – b) Fassbender Pantaleon, Theologische Anthropologie, 'Leib-Seele-Problem' und biomedizinische Wissenschaften: ZkT 114 (1992) 1-23 / 24-42.

7203 Seifert Josef, Das Leib-Seele-Problem und die gegenwärtige philosophische Diskussion; eine systematisch-kritische Analyse. Da 1989, Wiss. xiii-327 p. – ᴿTPhil 67 (1992) 472s (R. Koltermann).

7203* Sepe Crescenzio, Persona e storia; per una teologia della persona. CinB 1990, Paoline. 218 p. Lit. 20.000. – ᴿCC 143 (1992,1) 516s (L. Pezzullo).

7204 Starke Ekkehard, Leben, biblisch-theologisch: ➤ 757, EvKL 3 (1992) 44-47 (-51 al.).

7205 Stotz Gabriele, Person und Gehirn; historische und neurophysiologische Aspekte zur Theorie des Ich bei POPPER/ECCLES. Hildesheim 1988, Olms. xiv-344 p. – ᴿTPhil 67 (1992) 144s (H. Goller: Autorin).

7205* Theron D.S., The excluded soul [principle not only of mind but of life ...]: NSys 34 (1992) 1-26; deutsch 26.

7206 Thürig Markus, Dankbarkeit, Grundform menschlicher Existenz; ein psychologischer Beitrag zur christlichen Anthropologie: Diss. Pont. Univ. Gregoriana, ᴰKiely B. Roma 1992. 452 p.; Extr. 3894, 90 p. – RTLv 24, p. 577.

7207 Vernooy D., Het lichaam is de mens als een tweede natuur; lichamelijkheid, spiritualiteit en de theologie von Thomas van AQUINO: Mara 4,2 (1991) 48-56.

Vivens Homo, (Annali, Firenze, Istituto Superiore di Scienze Religiose Galantini) 1 (1990); 2 (1991) ➤ 7184.

7208 Volf Miroslav, Work in the Spirit; toward a theology of work. NY 1991, Oxford-UP. xviii-252 p. $32.50. 0-19-506808-4 [TDig 39,192].

7209 Waschke Ernst-Joachim, 'Was ist der Mensch, dass du seiner gedenkst?' (Ps 8,5); theologische und anthropologische Koordinaten für die Frage nach dem Menschen im Kontext alttestamentlicher Aussagen: TLZ 116 (1991) 801-812.

7210 Wéber E.-A., La personne humaine au XIIIᵉ siècle; l'avènement chez les maîtres parisiens de l'acception moderne de l'homme: BtThomiste 46. P 1991, Vrin. 546 p. F 240. – ᴿNRT 114 (1992) 134s (H. Jacobs).

7211 Wehrle J., Herz, AT ➤ 762, NBL II,7 (Z 1992) 137-9 (139-141 Kampling R., NT).

7212 Zincone Sergio, Studi sulla visione dell'uomo in ambito antiocheno 1988 ➤ 5,7207; 7,7199: ᴿRÉAug 37 (1991) 173s (A. Le Boulluec); RivScR 5 (1991) 168-270 (R. Scognamiglio).

H2.8 Oecologia VT & NT – saecularitas.

7213 Allen C. Leonard, The cruciform church; becoming a cross-shaped people in a secular world. Abilene 1990, Christian Univ. $18; pa. $12. – ᴿMid-Stream 30 (1991) 402s (R. E. Osborn).

7214 Anheim Fritz E., Neuansatz in der Ökumenischen Ethik; zur Soziologie der 'konziliaren' Bewegung: EvKomm 24 (1991) 12-15.

7215 a) Arapura John G., Ahimsa in basic Hindu Scriptures, with reference to cosmo-ethics; – b) Jaini Padmanabh S., Animals as agents in Ahimsa action and spiritual life: JDharma 16,3 ('Ahimsa and Ecology' 1991) 197-210 / 269-281.

7215* Armendariz Luis M., El hombre, imagen de Dios, en el contexto de la crisis ecológica: EstE 67 (1992) 289-308.

7216 **Badke** William B., Project earth; preserving the world God created. Portland OR 1991, Multnomah. 166 p. – RGraceTJ 12 (1991) 321s (R. A. *Young*).

7217 **Baratay** Eric, L'Église et l'animal, du XVIIᵉ siècle à nos jours, en France: diss. Lyon III 1991, DLadous R. – ERHE 87 (1992) 616s (Elisabeth *Hardouin-Fugier*).

7218 a) *Becker* William H., Ecological sin; – b) *Hauerwas* Stanley, *Berkman* John, The chief end of all flesh: TTod 49 (1992s) 152-164 / 196-208.

7218* **Berry** Thomas, O sonho da terra, TAlves Ephraím F. Petrópolis 1991, Vozes. 246 p. – RREB 52 (1992) 490-2 (B. *Leers*).

7219 EBirch Charles, Liberating life; contemporary approaches to ecological theology 1988/90 ➤ 6,302 ('American' approaches; but really) WCC consultation, Annecy 10-15.IX.1988, Mkn 1990; $17; 0-88344-689-8: REcuR 41 (1992) 267s (Margrethe *Brown*); Gregorianum 72 (1991) 782s (J. T. *Bretzke*); RExp 89 (1992) 120 (W. *Hendricks*).

7220 *Birmelé* André, Ökologie: ➤ 757, EvKL 3 (1992) 820-6.

7221 **Bouma-Prediger** Steven C., Toward a new Christian theology of nature; a critical comparison of Rosemary R. RUETHER, Joseph SITTLER, and Jürgen MOLTMANN: diss. DTracy D. Chicago 1992. RTLv 24, p. 556.

7222 **Bradley** Ian, God is green 1990 ➤ 6,7205: RPacifica 112s (1991) 112s (T. *Kelly*: but GILSON not female).

7223 *Brearley* Margaret, Matthew FOX and the Cosmic Christ; Anvil 9,1 (Bristol 1992) 39-54 [< ZIT 92,217].

7224 *Bresch* Carsten, al., Kann man Gott aus der Natur erkennen? Evolution 1989/90 ➤ 7,476a: REvKomm 24 (1991) 173s (H. G. *Pöhlmann*).

7224* a) EBreuilly Elizabeth, *Palmer* Martin, Christianity and ecology; – b) ERose Aubrey, Judaism and ecology; – c) EKhalid Fazlun, O'Brien Joanne, Islam... L 1992, Cassell. £6 each (also Hinduism, Buddhism). – RTablet 246 (1992) 1403s (S. *McDonagh*).

7225 *Brinkman* Martien E., Die Herausforderung einer ökumenischen Schöpfungstheologie: UnSa 47 (1992) 218-227.

7226 **Campolo** Anthony, How to rescue the earth without worshiping nature. Nv 1992, Nelson. x-213 p. $17. 0-8407-7772-8 [TDig 40,154].

7227 ECaprioli A., *Vaccaro* L., Questione ecologica e coscienza cristiana: Gazzada quad. 9. Brescia 1988, Morcelliana. 218 p. – RSalmanticensis 39 (1992) 182-4 (J.-R. *Flecha*).

7228 **Cárcel Ortí** Vicente, ¿España neopagana? Análisis de la situación y discursos del Papa en las visitas 'ad limina' [1976-91]. Valencia 1991, Edicep. 302 p. 84-7050-281-9. REstE 67 (1992) 105-7 (M. *Revuelta*).

7229 a) *Castro* Emilio, JPIC — a conciliar process; – b) *Newbigin* Lesslie, Whose justice?: EcuR 44,3 (1992) 291-303 / 308-311.

7230 **Champouthier** Georges, Au bon vouloir de l'homme, l'animal: Médiations. P 1990, Denoël. 263 p. – RLavalTP 48 (1992) 289-291 (J.-Y. *Goffi*).

7230* *Colette* Jacques, L'expérience religieuse du monde: ➤ 63, FGEFFRÉ C., Interpréter 1992, 123-140.

7231 **Cooper** Tim, Green Christianity. L c.1991, Hodder & S. £6. – RTablet 145 (1991) 407s (S. *McDonagh*, also on BRADLEY I., FOX M.).

7232 *Coste* René, La dynamique oecuménique 'Justice, paix, sauvegarde de la création'; évaluation et prospective: EsprVie 102 (1992) 378-382.

7233 **Cummings** Charles, Eco-spirituality; toward a reverent life. NY 1991, Paulist. $10. 0-8091-3251-6 [TDig 39,257: Utah Trappist].

7233* *Daoust* J., Le dernier ami de l'homme [giant expense of maintaining pets, < *Dubranu* Didie, Science et Vie 898 (1992)]: EsprVie 102 (1992) 646s.

7234 *Davies* John A., Toward a biblical theology of the environment: Ref-TR 51 (1992) 42-49.

7235 *Delteil* Gérard, La catéchèse au défi de la sécularisation: ÉTRel 67 (1992) 417-431.

7236 ᴱ**DeWitt** Calvin B., The environment and the Christian; what can we learn from the New Testament 1991 → 7,7211* (subtitle different): ᴿRExp 89 (1992) 415 (P. D. *Simmons*: a worthy endeavor; not deep).

7239 **Drewermann** Eugen, De l'immortalité des animaux. P 1992, Cerf. 84 p. F 60. – ᴿVSp 146 (1992) 729s (J. P. *Jossua*).

7239* Ecología y creación; fe cristiana y defensa del planeta : BtSalm 139. S 1991, Univ. 339 p. – ᴿHumTeol 13 (1992) 413s (B. *Domingues*).

7240 **Edwards** Denis, Jesus and the cosmos [... RAHNER, TEILHARD]. NY 1991, Paulist. v-116 p. $7 pa. 0-8091-3221-4 [TDig 39,360]. – ᴿPacifica 5 (1992) 335-7 (R. *Anderson*).

7241 *Edwards* Denis, The integrity of creation; Catholic social teaching for an ecological age: Pacifica 5 (1992) 182-203.

7242 *a*) *Ernst* Josef, Das Heil der Schöpfung; – *b*) *Nagel* Ernst J., Schöpfungslehre im ökumenischen Gespräch: Catholica 46 (1992) 189-206 / 207-227.

7242* *a*) *Faricy* Robert, The Christian and creation; the approach of TEIL-HARD de Chardin; – *b*) *Michel* Thomas, The teaching of the Qur'an about nature: BDialRel 27 (1992) 47-57 / 90-96.

7243 **Fox** Matthew, Creation spirituality; liberating gifts for peoples of the earth. SF 1991, Harper. 155 p. $19. – ᴿAmerica 165 (1991) 97s (P. B. *Riley*); Horizons 19 (1992) 333-5 (M. *Downey*).

7244 **Gabus** Jean-Paul, L'amour fou de Dieu pour sa création. P 1991, Bergers et Mages. 150 p. F 105. 2-85304-090-9. – ᴿÉTRel 67 (1992) 295 (A. *Gounelle*: suivent trois du même genre).

7245 *Garmus* Ludovico, Bíblia e ecologia; aspectos fundamentais (Gn 1-11): Grande Sinal 46 (1992) 275-290.

7246 *George* William P., Regarding future neighbours; Thomas AQUINAS and concern for posterity: HeythJ 33 (1992) 283-306.

7247 *Gómez Hinojosa* José F., ¿Está viva la naturaleza? Apuntes para una ecología liberadora II: EfMex 9 (1991) 71-96.

7248 **Halkes** Catharina J. M., ... en alles zal worden herschapen; gedachten over de heelwording van de schepping in het spanningsveld tussen natuur en cultuur. 1989 → 6,7223; 90-259-4393-4: ᴿBijdragen 53 (1992) 331 (Freda *Dröes*).

7249 **Hall** Douglas J., The steward, a biblical symbol come of age²ʳᵉᵛ [¹1982]. GR/NY 1990, Eerdmans/Friendship. xiii-258 p. $15. – ᴿJDharma 16 (1991) 166 [P. *Kalluveettil*].

7250 **Hansson** Mats G., Human dignity and animal well-being: Uppsala Studies in Social Ethics 12. U 1991, Almqvist & W. 210 p. Sk 150. 91-554-2681-6. – ᴿExpTim 103 (1991s) 125s (R. *Rodd*: logical).

7251 ᴱ**Harskamp** A. van, Verborgen God of lege kerk; theologen en sociologen over secularisatie [Raad van Kerken Amst VU symposium 1.VI. 1990]: Studies over Levensbeschouwing. Kampen 1991, Kok. 156 p. ƒ 32.50. 90-242-3358-5. – ᴿTvT 32 (1992) 426 (P. A. van *Gennip*).

7251* *Hattrup* Dieter, Die evangelischen Räte in Ekklesiologie und Ökologie: TGL 82 (1992) 179-198.

7252 *a*) *Kehm* George H., Priest of creation; – *b*) *Rolston* Holmes ᴵᴵᴵ, Does nature need to be redeemed?: *c*) *Hudsell* Heidi, Creation theology and the doing of ethics; – *d*) *Kaiser* Christopher B., Humanity as the exegete of creation, with reference to the work of natural scientists; HorBT 14,2 (1992) 129-142 / 143-172 / 93-111 / 112-128.

7253 *a)* *Korff* Wilhelm, Wirtschaft vor der Herausforderung der Umweltkrise; – *b)* *Binswanger* Hans C., Weltwirtschaft und Ökologie: ZevEth 36 (1992) 161-174 / 192s.

7254 *Kuenning* Paul P., The case for a worldly Christianity: CurrTM 19 (1992) 42-48.

7255 **Leahy** Michael P. T., Against liberation; putting animals in perspective. NY 1991, Routledge. 273 p. $60. – ᴿRelStR 18 (1992) 319 (S. G. *Post*: against over-anthropomorphism).

7256 **Le Roux** Charl J. P., Eco-theo-logy; in search of an eco-theo-logy for the modern technical man: [Afrikaans] diss., ᴰ*Heyns* J. Pretoria 1992. DissA 53 (1992s) 1558-A.

7256* ᴱ**Lindberg** David C., *Numbers* Ronald L., God and nature; historical essays on the encounter between Christianity and science [Univ. Wisconsin conference 1981]. 1986 ➤ 2,461; 4,8275: ᴿChrSchR 21 (1991s) 198s (K. W. *Hermann*).

7257 *Linzey* Andrew, The theological basis of animal rights: ChrCent 108 (1991) 906-9.

7257* **Lüpke** Johannes, Anvertraute Schöpfung; biblisch-theologische Gedanken zum Thema 'Bewahrung der Schöpfung': Vorlagen 16. Hannover 1992, Luther. 120 p. DM 12,80. [TLZ 118,298].

7258 **McDonagh** Sean, To care for the earth; a call to a new theology 1987 ➤ 3,6696; also L 1986, Chapman. 214 p. £8. – ᴿModT 7 (1990s) 494-7 (D. *Toole*).

7259 *McPherson* James, Ecumenical discussion of the environment 1966-1987: ModT 7 (1990s) 363-371.

7260 *Maldamé* Jean-Michel, Place de l'homme dans la nature [DELÉAGE P. 1991; RUELLE D. 1991; GODDARD J. 1990, *al.*]: RThom 92 (1992) 871-891.

7261 *Migliore* Daniel L., The ecological crisis and the doctrine of creation: PrincSemB 12 (1991) 266-282 [< zɪᴛ 91,783].

7262 **Moltmann** Jürgen, Dieu dans la création; traité écologique de la création: CogF 146, 1988 ➤ 4,8282 ... 7,7245: ᴿEsprVie 102 (1992) 677s (P. *Jay*: '1985')

7263 **Moltmann** Jürgen, Reconciliation with nature: Pacifica 5 (1992) 301-311.

7264 **Montefiore** Hugh bp., Reclaiming the high ground, a Christian response to secularism 1990 ➤ 7,7240*: ᴿExpTim 103 (1991s) 125 (D. *Cornick*: lively).

7264* *a)* *Moser* António, Ecologia — perspectiva ética; – *b)* *Gudynas* Eduardo, O movimento ambientalista latino-americano; múltiplas sementes de mudança (Ética, ambiente e ecologia, uma crise entrelaçada); – *c)* *Ramos Regidor* José, Ressarcir os povos e a natureza — em busca de uma reconversão sócio-ecológica da sociedade: REB 52 (1992) 5-22 / 45-63 (64-74) / 23-44.

7365 *Muratore* Saturnino, Antropocentrismo cosmologico e antropocentrismo teologico [testatine 'Principio antropico']: CC 143 (1992,3) 236-247.

7365* **Murphy** Charles M., At home on earth; foundations for a Catholic ethic of the environment 1989 ➤ 6,7251; 7,7242: ᴿJRel 72 (1992) 293s (W. *French*).

7266 **Murray** Robert, The cosmic covenant; biblical themes of justice, peace and the integrity of creation: Heythrop Mg 7. L 1992, Sheed & W. xxv-233 p. £16. 0-7220-2750-8. – ᴿArTGran 55 (1992) 334s (A. *Segovia*);

ExpTim 103,11 top choice (1991s) 321-3 (C. S. *Rodd*: vibrant and accessible, a bit idealistic).

7267 *Nardi* Carlo, Cristianesimo primitivo e realtà terrene; note per una teologia della laicità: VivH 2 (1991) 221-241.

7268 **Nash** James A., Loving nature; ecological integrity and Christian responsibility: Churches' Center for Public Policy. Nv 1991, Abingdon. 265 p. $17. 0-687-22824-7 [TDig 39,277: 'econological'].

7269 *Nothelle-Wildfeuer* Ursula, Kirche im Kontrast oder Kirche in der Welt? Zur Grundlegung und Eigenart christlicher Weltverantwortung: MüTZ 43 (1992) 347-366.

7270 *Ormerod* Neil, Renewing the earth — renewing theology: Pacifica 4 (1991) 295-306.

7271 **Oviedo Torro** Lluis, La secularización como problema [...WEBER M.] → 7,7244; Valencia 1990, FacTFerrer. 316 p. – ᴿScripTPamp 24 (1992) 1106-9 (J. L. *Illanes*).

7271* *Padberg* Lutz E. van, Säkularisierung — das Paradigma der Neuzeit?: TBeit 22 (1991) 230-248 [< ZIT 91,653].

7272 **Parham** Robert, Living neighbors across time; a Christian guide to protecting the earth. Birmingham AL 1992, New Hope. 129 p. $7. 1-56309-042-2. – ᴿRExp 89 (1992) 420s (G. *Stassen*).

7273 *Perkins* Pheme, World, on the origin of: → 741, AnchorBD 6 (1992) 972s; there is no other article or renvoi on 'world' (secularity, secularization), nor on 'ecology', 'nature', 'dominion', 'conciliar process' nor 'creation' (only 'creatures, see zoology').

7274 **Petty** Michael W., A faith that loves the earth; the ecological theology of Karl RAHNER: diss. Vanderbilt, ᴰ*Te Selle* E. Nv 1992. 352 p. 92-30996. – DissA 53 (1992s) 1977-A.

7275 **Primavesi** Anne, From apocalypse to genesis; ecology, feminism and Christianity 1991 → 7,7246*: ᴿChrCent 109 (1992) 403-5 (H. P. *Santmire*); JTS 43 (1992) 794-7 (Clare *Palmer*); ScotJT 45 (1992) 265-8 (A. *Linzey*); Tablet 246 (1992) 748 (Ursula *King*); TLond 95 (1992) 294 (Isabel *Wollaston*).

7276 **Regenstein** Lewis G., Replenish the earth; a history of organized religion's treatment of animals and nature — including the Bible's message of conservation and kindness to animals [NY 1991 → 7,7248; also] L 1991, SCM. 304 p. £10. 0-334-01395-X. – ᴿExpTim 103 (1991s) 63 [C. S. *Rodd*: 'selective quotation, misunderstanding, sheer inaccuracy' on the Bible].

7277 *Reymond* Bernard, L'affirmation de Dieu entre sécularisation et religion: PosLuth 39 (1991) 231-246 [< ZIT 92,17].

7278 *Rhoads* David, The role of the Church in the care of the earth: CurrTMiss 18 (1991) 406-414.

7279 **Rodd** Rosemary, Biology, ethics and animals. Ox 1990, Clarendon. 272 p. £27.50. 0-19-824223-9. – ᴿExpTim 102 (1990s) 351 (G. J. *Warnock*: 'animals have interests', especially in not being killed, however humanely or for nutriment; but experimenting on whole animals is not condemned, animal food is tolerable where no other is available, or even perhaps where others did the killing).

7280 *Ross-Bryant* Lynn, Of nature and texts; nature and religion in American ecological literature: AnglTR 73 (1991) 38-50.

7281 *Rostagno* Sergio, Uomo e natura; nuovi modelli teologici; D. SÖLLE: StEcum 8 (1990) 371-5; Eng. 376.

7282 **Rowthorn** Anne,   Caring for creation; toward an ethic of responsibility. Wilton CT 1989, Morehouse.   xii-163 p. $12 pa. – RAnglTR 74 (1992) 120-2 (N. *Faramelli*).

7283 *Rubio Ferreres* José M., Símbolo religioso, razón utópica y secularización en el pensamiento filosófico de Ernst BLOCH: ComSev 24 (1991) 241-9. 387-416.

7284 ERudolph Kurt, *Rinscheide* Gisbert,   Beiträge zur Religion/Umwelt-Forschung, Eichstätt 5.-8. Mai 1988: Geographia Religionum 6s, 1989 → 6,680:   RZMissRW 75 (1991) 159s (O. *Bischofberger*).

7285 *Ruether* Rosemary R., Frauen, Männer und Tiere: EvKomm 24 (1991) 474-7 [< ZIT 91,563].

7285* *Sáez Cruz* Jesús,   Mundanidad y transcendencia de Dios en Xavier ZUBIRI: Burgense 33 (1992) 467-525.

7286 *Schäfer* Gerhard,   Vom Wort zur Antwort; Dialog zwischen Kirche und Welt in 5 Jahrhunderten; Vorw.Sorg.T.   Stu 1991, Theiss.   205 p.; ill. DM 69 [TR 88,78].

7287 **Schiwy** Günther,   Der kosmische Christus; Spuren Gottes ins Neue Zeitalter 1990 → 7,3741:   RTLZ 116 (1991) 143s (U. *Gerber*: 'kosmoästhetische Kultur', wie TIMM H.).

7287* **Schupp** Franz,   Schöpfung und Sünde 1990 → 7,7257:   RLebZeug 45 (1990) 306s (S. *Ernst*).

7288 *Seweryniak* Henryk, ❷ Les faces multiples de la sécularisation: PrzPow 856 (1992) 362-373.

7289 **Sherman** Robert J.,   The shift to modernity; Christ in the doctrine of creation in the theologies of SCHLEIERMACHER and BARTH: diss. DGerrish B. Univ. Chicago 1992. – RTLv 24, p. 577.

7290 **Sherrard** Philip,   The sacred in life and art [... a desacralized world]. Ipswich 1990, Golgonooza.   162 p. £22.50; pa. £9. – RHeythJ 33 (1992) 93s (H. *Meynell*: amid valuable insights, science and technology are unmitigated disaster).

7290* **Sobosan** Jeffrey G.,   Bless the beasts; a spirituality of animal care. NY 1991, Crossroad.   144 p. $11. – RRRel 51 (1992) 938-940 (Theresa Mancuso).

7291 **Soelle** D.,   Per lavorare e amare, una teologia della creazione [lezioni NY 1983, ECloyes S.A.],T: Nostro Tempo 49.   T 1990, Claudiana. 178 p. Lit. 22.000. – RParVi 36 (1991) 75 (C. *Ghidelli*); StPatav 39 (1992) 675-8 (G. *Dianin*).

7291* *Straarup* Jørgen,   Sekulariseringen ifrågasatt; amerikanska sociologer om religionen i USA: SvTKv 67 (1991) 182-191.

7292 *Tabournel* Jean-Simon,   Économie, écologie, éthique chrétienne [< BIC-Lyon 95 (1991) 61-74]: EsprVie 102 (1992) 33-39.

7293 **Tester** Keith,   Animals and society; the humanity of animal rights. NY 1991, Routledge.   vi-218 p. $60; pa. $16. – RAmHR 97 (1992) 1180s (H. *Ritvo*).

7294 *Trilling* W.,   Schöpfung, Gerechtigkeit und Frieden; eine biblisch-theologische Besinnung: TJb (Lp 1990) 165-177 (-339 *al.*) [< ZIT 91,654].

7295 *Tschannen* Olivier,   a) La genèse de l'approche moderne de la sécularisation; une analyse en histoire de la sociologie: Social Compass 39,2 (Lv 1992) 291-308 [< ZIT 92,395]; – b) The secularization paradigm; a systematization: JScStR 30 (1991) 395-415 [< ZIT 92,137].

7296 *Valkenberg* Pim,   'Dauwt, hemelen, gerechtigheid'; de heelheid van de schepping als werk van de Geest: TvT 32 (1992) 165-184; Eng. 184.

7297 *Van Dyke* Fred G., Ecology and the Christian mind; Christians and the environment in a new decade: JAmScAff 43 (1991) 174-184.

7298 *Vanhoye* Albert, Destination universelle des biens de la terre selon la Bible: → 540, Une terre pour tous les hommes (1992) 9-15.

7299 **Verbeek** Bernhard, Die Anthropologie der Umweltzerstörung; die Evolution und die Schatten der Zukunft. Da 1990, Wiss. viii-279 p. – ᴿTPhil 67 (1992) 146s (R. *Koltermann*).

7300 *Vernette* Jean, En France, après la sécularisation, un 'retour du religieux'? [... un vigoureux reveil des paganismes sous des formes subtiles]: EsprVie 102 (1992) 253-6.

7301 *Voss* Gerhard (kath.), Kampf und Kontemplation; gemeinsame Spiritualität im säkularisierten Kontext: UnSa 47 (1992) 188-210.

7302 *Wennberg* Robert, Animal suffering and the problem of evil: ChrSchR 21 (1991) 120-140 [< ZIT 92,70].

7303 *Wink* Walter, Ecobible; the Bible and ecojustice: TTod 49 (1992s) 465-478.

7304 *Zauner* Wilhelm, Die Verantwortung des Menschen für seine Umwelt: TPQ 140 (1992) 153-9.

7305 *Zinger* Don H., Lutheran reflections on nature; prolegomena to a theology of the environment: CurrTMiss 19 (1992) 281-7.

H3.1 *Foedus* – **the Covenant**; the Chosen People; Providence.

Biersack M., BELLARMIN, Prädestinationslehre ᴰ1989 → m301.

7306 *a) Bolognesi* Pietro, La via della salvezza nell'AT; tra dispensazionalismo e teologia dell'alleanza; – *b) Bauckham* Richard, Uno sguardo storico sull'universalismo, ᵀ*Bernardi* V.: STEv 3 (1991) 144-161 / 207-223 (-248, *Packer* J. L.).

7307 *Branon* Dave, Waking up from the American dream; Moody Monthly (Sept, 1991) 28-30: three cases in which the struggling jobless were 'supernaturally supplied' by God with job or physical needs [< BS 148 (1992) 87s (A. M. *Malphurs*)].

7307* **Brom** Luco J. van den, Gottes Welthandeln und die Schachmetapher: Glaube und Denken, JbHeimGes 3 (1990) 125-151 [< NSys 34 (1992) 220].

7308 **Bühlmann** Walbert, Les peuples élus; pour une nouvelle approche de l'élection 1986 → 2,5350; 5,7264: ᴿLVitae 46 (1991) 236s (L. *Partos*).

7308* *Couto* António, J. de R., Teologia da aliança como teologia do Antigo Testamento: HumTeol 13 (1992) 5-21.

7309 **Craig** William L., Divine foreknowledge and human freedom. Leiden 1991, Brill. xiii-360 p. f160. [not 1987 → 3,6389]: ᴿRelSt 28 (1992) 269-274 (J. M. *Fischer*); TvT [= TsTNijm] 32 (1992) 307 (H. *Rikhof*).

7310 **Dickson** Kwesi, Uncompleted mission; Christianity and exclusivism. Mkn 1991, Orbis. x-177 p. $19. 0-88344-751-7 [TDig 39,258].

7311 **Dybdahl** J., OT grace. Boise 1990, Pacific. 152 p. $17. – ᴿAndrUnS 30 (1992) 83s (J. *Doukhan*).

7312 **Ebert** Howard J., Prolegomenon to a doctrine of providence; a critical [GILKEY L., TAYLOR M., METZ J.] assessment of Karl RAHNER's contribution: diss. Marquette, ᴰ*Masson* R. Milwaukee 1992. 331 p. 93-05996. – DissA 53 (1992s) 3570-A.

7313 Évêques de France, Catéchisme pour adultes; l'alliance de Dieu avec les hommes 1991 → 7,7273: ᴿAnnTh 6 (1992) 203-9 (A. *Fernández Marzalo*).

7314 **Gerstner** John H., Wrongly dividing the word of truth; a critique of dispensationalism. Brentwood TN 1991, Wolgemuth & H. $16. – RCalvaryB 8,1 (1992) 71-73 (K. R. *Pulliam*).

7315 **Gorringe** Timothy J., God's theatre; a theology of Providence. L 1991, SCM. xi-114 p. £9. 0-334-02493-5. – RExpTim 103,1 1st choice (1991s) 1s (C. S. *Rodd*); ScripTPamp 24 (1992) 1104 (J. M. *Odero*).

7316 *a) Hanson* Paul D., War das Alte Israel einmalig? T*Fischer* Maria; – *b) Sacchi* Paolo, Das Problem des 'wahren Israel' im Lichte der universalistischen Auffassungen des Alten Orients, T*Stemberger* Günter: ⇒ 355, JbBT 7 (1992) 3-20 / 77-100.

7317 *Hasker* William, Providence and evil; three theories: RelSt 28 (1992) 91-105.

7318 **Høgenhaven** Jesper, Den gamle pagt; en introduktion til den nyere debat om pagtem i det Gamle Testamente: Tekst og Tolkning 8, 1989 ⇒ 6,7283: RSvEx 56 (1991) 123-6 (E. *Nielsen*); TsTKi 62 (1991) 70s (Terje *Stordalen*).

7319 *Hunt* David P., Middle knowledge [MOLINA] and the soteriological problem of evil: RelSt 27 (1991) 3-26.

7320 **Lohfink** Norbert, Der niemals gekündigte Bund 1989 ⇒ 5,7274; 6,7287: RBiKi 45 (1990) 60s (M. *Helsper*); BogSmot 60 (1990) 133-5 (M. *Zovkić*).

7321 **Lohfink** Norbert, The covenant never revoked 1991 ⇒ 7,7279: RCBQ 54 (1992) 753 (D. J. *Harrington*: his claim that there were not two covenants but only one is weak only on Jer 31,31: Paul did not have access to a Jer scroll, p. 36 & 64); ETL 68 (1992) 444s (A. de *Halleux*); Gregorianum 73 (1992) 750 (J. *Dupuis*); NewTR 4,4 (1991) 104-6 (E. J. *Fisher*); RefTR 51 (1992) 78 (A. M. *Harman*: MOTYER better on place of Jews in God's purposes).

7322 **Lohfink** N., La Alianza nunca derogada; reflexiones exegéticas para al diálogo entre judíos y cristianos [1989 ⇒ 5,7274], T*Arias* Isidro. Barc 1992, Herder. 136 p. pt. 896. 84-254-1775-9. – RActuBbg 29 (1992) 199 (J. *Boada*); Carthaginensia 8 (1992) 974 (R. *Sanz Valdivieso*).

7322* *a) McWilliams* David B., The covenant theology of The Westminster Confession of Faith and recent criticism; – *b) Karlberg* Mark W., Covenant theology and the Westminster tradition [WEIR D. 1990]: WestTJ 53 (1991) 109-124 / 54 (1992) 135-152.

7323 *Nehorai* Michael Z., ⊕ 'Righteous Gentiles have a share in the world to come': Tarbiz 61 (1991s) 465-487; Eng. V.

7324 *Nielsen* Eduard, 'Lov og ret' i det Gamle Testamente: DanTTs 55 (1992) 1-14 [< ZIT 92,285].

7324* *a) Patrick* Dale OT [*Shogren* Gary S. NT] Election; – *b) Dillon* John M., Providence: ⇒ 741, AnchorBD 2 (1992) 434-441[-444] / 5,520s [no article or renvoi on 'Predestination'].

7325 *Rohls* Jan, Prädestination: ⇒ 757, EvKL 3 (1992) 1282-8.

7326 **Rössler** Andreas, Steht Gotes Himmel allen offen?... der kosmische Christus 1990 ⇒ 7,7286: RActuBbg 29 (1992) 38-41 (J. *Boada*).

7326* *Sarot* Marcel, Gods volmaakte kennis: NedTTs 46 (1992) 23-33; Eng. 52.

7327 **Sohn Seock-Tae**, The divine election of Israel [< diss. 1986, NYU]. GR 1991, Eerdmans. xvi-296 p. $20. 0-8028-0545-0 [OIAc 2,27].

7328 *Wood* Charles M., The doctrine of Providence: TTod 49 (1992s) 209-224.

H3.5 *Liturgia, spiritualitas VT* – **OT prayer.**

7329 *Bollag* Michel, Die Torah hat siebzig Gesichter; ein jüdischer Beitrag zur zeitgenössischen Spiritualität: IkiZ 82 (1992) 38-49.

7330 ᴱBradshaw P., *Hoffman* L., The making of Jewish and Christian worship 1991 ⇥ 6,474:   ᴿJTS 43 (1992) 227s (K. *Stevenson*: a landmark, though Bradshaw seems to hold that the opposite of what the Fathers claimed was really happening).

7331 **Carucci Viterbi** Benedetto,   Il Qaddish: Le voci della preghiera 3. Genova 1991, Marietti. 81 p.   88-211-6939-1.

7332 **Chaze** Micheline,   L'Imitatio Dei dans le Targum et la Aggada [diss. 1977, ᴰ*Touati* C.]: Bt ÉPHÉR 97. Lv 1990, Peeters. 202 p.   90-6831- 295-2.

7333 ᵀᴱCova Gian Domenico,   Yehuda Hᴀʟᴇᴡʏ,   Non nella forza ma nello Spirito; 95 inni e poesie scelte da Franz Rᴏꜱᴇɴᴢᴡᴇɪɢ.   Genova 1992, Marietti. xxviii-214 p.   88-211-8996-1.

7334 **Di Sante** Carmine,   Jewish prayer; the origins of the Christian liturgy [1985 ⇥ 2,5358],   ᵀ*O'Connell* Matthew J.   NY 1991, Paulist.   259 p. $15. 0-8091-3207-9 [NTAbs 36,444; français 31,384]:   ᴿPrPeo 6 (1992) 358s (S. *Gross*); TS 53 (1992) 587s (L. A. *Hoffman*: not 'origins of Christian liturgy' yet 'hoping to counter Cᴀꜱᴇʟ... Christian origins in non-Jewish antecedents').

7335 **Di Sante** C. Het gebed van Israel 1989 ⇥ 7,7297:   ᴿCollatVL 22 (1992) 97s (F. *Lefevre*).

7336 ᴱFisher Eugene J.,   The Jewish roots of Christian liturgy 1990 ⇥ 6,7303; 7,7298:   ᴿMid-Stream 30 (1991) 177-9 (G. M. *Williamson*: wonderfully helpful).

Flender Reinhard,   Der biblische Sprachgesang... in Synagoge 1988 ⇥ d837.

7337 **Gammie** John G.,   Holiness in Israel 1989 ⇥ 5,7297...7,7299:   ᴿGregorianum 73 (1992) 144-6 (G. L. *Prato*).

7338 *Hammer* Reuven,   What did they bless? A study of Mishnah Tamid 5.1 [oldest surviving outline of a service]: JQR 81 (1990s) 305-324.

7339 *Kleinig* John W.,   The attentive heart / the indwelling Word; meditation in the OT: RefTR 51 (1992) 50-63 / 81-90.

7340 ᴱLevin Israel, *Sáenz-Badillos* Ángel,   Si me olvido de ti, Jerusalén...; cantos de las sinagogas de al-Andalus: Autores hebreos de al-Andalus 2. Córdoba 1992, El Almendro. 40 + 160 + 160* + 27 p.

7341 **Loopik** M. van,   Het messiaanse perspectief van de synagogale liturgische cyclus: diss. Amst VU 1992, ᴰ*Heide* A. van der.   477 p. – TvT 32 (1992) 302; RTLv 24, p. 545.

7342 **Ozorowski** Mieczysław,   Eucharistie-Beraḫa; la théologie des nouvelles prières eucharistiques à la lumière de l'euchologie juive: diss. ᴰ*Walsch* L. G. Fribourg... 1992. – RTLv 24, p. 588.

7343 *Rochettes* Jacqueline des,   Simḥat Torah! La Torah festeggiata, studiata, pregata: ⇥ 338, ParSpV 25 (1992) 67-81.

7344 *Sellès* Jean-Marie,   Écriture et parole dans le judaïsme: MaisD 190 (1992) 114-120.

7345 **Standaert** Benoît,   Les trois colonnes du monde [Torah, prière, miséricorde]; ressemblances dans l'Islam et le bouddhisme.   P 1991, Desclée. 190 p. F 125. – ᴿEsprVie 102 (1992) 160 (L. *Barney*).

7345* **Trepp** Leo,   Der jüdische Gottesdienst; Gestalt und Entwicklung.   Stu 1992, Kohlhammer. 326 p.; 1 fig.   DM 59 pa.   3-17-011077-2 [NTAbs 37, p. 157; TLZ 118, 224, K.-W. *Niebuhr*].

7346 **Vicent Saera** Rafael,   Interpretaciones de la fiesta de Sukkot en el judaismo antiguo, desde el texto bíblico al targum y midrás: diss. Pont. Ist. Biblico, ᴰ*Le Déaut* R.   Roma 1992. 226 + 185 p. – AcPIB 9/8, 685 & 733; RTLv 24, p. 545.

7347 **Zahavy** Tzvee, Studies in Jewish prayer 1990 → 7,7324: ᴿAnglTR 73 (1991) 489-491 (J. T. *Townsend*).

H3.7 *Theologia moralis VT* – OT moral theology.

7348 **Berkowitz** Adena K., The conflict between mother and child; rabbinic and legal views on the status of the fetus: diss. Jewish Theol. Sem. 1991. 159 p. 92-21889. – DissA 53 (1992s) 1968-A.

7349 **Birch** Bruce C., Let justice roll down; the Old Testament, ethics and Christian life 1991 → 7,7308: ᴿGraceTJ 12 (1991) 280s (J. J. *Lawlor*); TS 53 (1992) 736s (M. D. *Guinan*).

7350 *Cañellas* Gabriel, La preocupación social en el Antiguo Testamento: VerVid 48 (1990) 137-163.

7351 **Clemons** James T., What does the Bible say about suicide? 1990 → 6, 8314; 7,6320: – ᴿAnglTR 74 (1992) 257s (R. M. *Kawano*); ChrCris 51 (1991s) 292-4 (Sally B. *Geis*, also on Cobb J. 1991); Interpretation 46 (1992) 209s (K. *Crim*).

7352 *Davis* Dena S., Abortion in Jewish thought; a study in casuistry: JAAR 60 (1992) 313-324.

7353 *Freund* Richard A., Lying and deception in the biblical and post-biblical Judaic tradition: ScandJOT 5,1 (1991) 45-61.

7354 *Goodfriend* Elaine A., Adultery: → 741, AnchorBD 1 (1992) 81-86 [5,1144-6, Sex, *Frumer-Kensky* T: neither has a NT section (ETL 68, 429, F. *Neirynck*)].

7355 *Kuntzmann* R., Le mariage et le sacre dans l'AT: Revue de Droit Canonique 41,3 (Colloque 1991, Le mariage sacrement) 59-69.

7355* *Lesch* Walter, Ethische Argumentation im jüdischen Kontext; zum Verständnis von Ethik bei Emmanuel Levinas und Hans Jonas: FreibZ 38 (1991) 443-469.

7356 *Nysse* Richard, Moral discourse on economic justice; considerations from the Old Testament: Word + World 12 (1992) 337- ...

7357 *Parker* Simon B., The Hebrew Bible and homosexuality: QRMin 11,3 (1991) 4-19 [4,18-32 NT, *Smith* Abraham).

7358 **Prouser** Ora H., The phenomenology of the lie in biblical narrative: diss. Jewish Theol. Sem. 1991, ᴰ*Greenstein* E. 230 p. 92-17738. – DissA 53 (1992s) 592s-A.

7359 *Ravasi* Gianfranco, 'Tra di voi non vi sia nessun bisogno!'; solidarietà nel popolo di Dio dell'AT: → 383, Communio 125 (1992) 8-16.

7360 *Reinhartz* Adele, Philo on infanticide: StPhilonAn 4 (1992) 42-58.

7361 *Rosman* Murray J., ❻ Culture in the book [*Elbaum* J., Openness and insularity, in ❻ *Gies* Zev, Literature of conduct, *Hunhagût*, J 1990]: Zion 56 (1991) 321-344.

7362 **Roth** Joel, The halakhic process 1986 → 2,8252; 3,a448: ᴿRHR 209 (1992) 302s (S. *Schwarzfuchs*).

7363 *Wenham* G. J., The OT attitude to homosexuality [undeniably contrary, but why? in retention of neighboring Near East usage? rather a corollary of the description of creation]: ExpTim 102 (1990s) 359-363.

7364 **Wright** Christopher J. H., The ethical authority of the OT, a survey of approaches I-II: TyndB 43 (1992) 101-120. 203-231.

7364* a) *Wright* Chris, Ethical decisions in the Old Testament; – b) *Douma* Jochem, The use of Scripture in ethics: European Journal of Theology 1,2 (Devon 1992) 123-140 / 105-122.

7365 *a) Wright* Christopher, Le decisioni etiche dell'AT, ᵀ*Borelli* C.; – *b)*
Douma Jochem, L'uso della Scrittura nell'etica, ᵀ*Terino* J.; – *c) Murray*
John, L'etica biblica, questioni introduttive, ᵀ*Tuccillo* G.: STEv 3 (1991)
48-78 / 22-47 / 3-21.

H3.8   *Bellum et pax VT-NT* – **War and peace in the whole Bible.**

Barbaglio G., Dio violento? 1991 → 7805.
Baudler Georg, God and violence 1992 → b142*.
7366 **Beauchamp** P., *Vasse* D., La violence dans la Bible: CahÉv 76. P
1991, Cerf. 68 p. F 25. 0222-9714 [NTAbs 36,127].
7367 **Beestermöller** Gerhard, T.v. Aquin und der gerechte Krieg 1990
→ 7,7325: ᴿActuBbg 29 (1992) 236 (J. *Boada*); MüTZ 43 (1992) 124s (J.
Splett); StiZt 210 (1992) 67 (K. *Mertes*).
7368 *Berrouard* Marie-François, Bellum: → 743, AugL 1,4s (1991s) 641-645.
7369 **Crépon** Pierre, Les religions et la guerre² [¹1982]: Espaces libres 16. P
1991, Albin-Michel. 258 p. 3-226-05276-3. – ᴿÉTRel 67 (1992) 92 (J.
Argaud).
7370 *a) Curran* Charles E., The new world order and military force; – *b) Stern*
Jean M., Security and world order: NewTR 5,1 (1992) 5-18 / 19-28.
7371 **Drewermann** Eugen, Die Spirale der Angst; der Krieg und das Christentum... gegen den Krieg am Golf: Spektrum. FrB 1991, Herder.
448 p. DM 19,80 [EvKomm 24,303].
7372 **Espinel Marcos** José Luis, El pacifismo del Nuevo Testamento: Paradosis 8. S 1992, Fac. Teol. San Esteban. 239 p. 84-87557-44-9.
7373 ᴱ**Gosman** M., *al.,* Heilige oorlogen; een onderzoek naar historische und
hedendaagse vormen van kollektief religieus geweld. Kampen/Kapellen
1991, Kok/Pelckmans. 200 p. Fb 295 [TR 88,76].
7374 **Goss-Mayr** Jean & Hildegarde, La non-violenza evangelica. Molfetta
1991, Meridiana. 128 p. Lit. 15.000. – ᴿStCattMi 36 (1992) 280s (A. *Ca-
vallina*).
7375 *Gravel* Pierre, *al.,* L'origine de la violence [Oedipe, Agamemnon ...] LavalTP 48,2 (1992) 151-7 [-278, 8 art. sur 'violence': 'de pensée', de bioéthique, Royce/Jung sur la guerre; nulle part mention de R. Girard].
7376 **Heim** François, La théologie de la victoire de Constantin à Théodose:
THist 89. P 1992, Beauchesne. xv-347 p. 2-7010-1254-6.
7377 *Heimann-Koenen* Marie-Luise, War (peace) related norms and values:
ZEthnol 115 (1990) 63-66.
7378 **Hellwig** Monika K., A case for peace in reason and faith. ColMn
1992, Liturgical/Glazier. 110 p. $7. 0-8146-5834-2 [TDig 40,166].
7378* **Herr** Édouard, Sauver la paix; qu'en dit l'Église?: Chrétiens d'aujourd'hui NS 5. Namur 1991, Culture et vérité. 146 p. [RTLv 24, 383, J.
Étienne].
7379 **Hobbs** T. R., A time for war... OT, 1989 → 6,7352; 7,7334: ᴿCritRR 5
(1992) 139s (H. G. *Washington*: useful, though not new nor always critical); RB 99 (1992) 769 (J.-M. de *Tarragon*).
7380 *Humeński* Julian, ☻ A Jesuit strategist from the 17th century [Wojciech
Tylkowski 1626-95; author of 80 books on ethics; his De bono tam in
pace quam in bello is a real military textbook... duties and virtues of
officers and soldiers: a mirror of universal European practice]: Bobolanum
3 (1992) 112-141; Eng. 141.
7381 *Hunter* David G., A decade of research on early Christians and military
service: RelStR 18 (1992) 87-94.

7382 **Joblin** Joseph, La Iglesia y la guerra 1990 ➤ 7,7335: ᴿLumenVr 40 (1991) 422s (U. *Gil Ortega*); Salmanticensis 39 (1992) 186-8 (A. *Galindo García*).

7383 **Joest** Wilfried, Der Friede Gottes und der Friede auf Erden 1990 ➤ 7,7336: ᴿTRu 57 (1992) 335s (M. *Honecker*).

7384 ᴱ**Johnson** James T., *Kelsay* John, Cross, crescent and sword; the justification and limitation of war in western and Islamic tradition: CSReligion 27. Westport CT 1991, Greenwood. xviii-236 p. $43 [JAOS 112, 361]. – ᴿRRelRes 33 (1990s) 94s (Arfa *Aflatooni*).

7385 **Justenhoven** Heinz-Gerhard, Francisco de VITORIA zu Krieg und Frieden: Theologie und Frieden 5. Köln 1991, Bachem. 213 p. – ᴿActuBbg 29 (1992) 239s (J. *Boada*); MüTZ 43 (1992) 125s (J. *Splett*); StiZt 210 (1992) 67s (K. *Mertes*); TS 53 (1992) 786s (D. M. *Traboulay*).

7386 **Kang Sa-Moon,** Divine war... OT, diss. HebUniv, ᴰ*Haran* M.: BZAW 177, 473 ➤ 5,7339*... 7,7337: ᴿBO 49 (1992) 473-6 (P. D. *Miller*).

7387 *Klassen* William, Peace, NT [*Healey* Joseph P., OT]: ➤ 741, AnchorBD 5 (1992) 207-212 [206s].

7388 *Klassen* William, War: ➤ 741, AnchorBD 6 (1992) 867-75 (-76, *Davies* P. on Qumran War-scroll).

7389 **Küng** Hans, Global responsibility; in search of a new world ethic. L 1991, SCM. £13 [Tablet 145,251 adv.]

7390 *Langan* John, The just-war theory after the Gulf war: TS 53 (1992) 95-112.

7391 **Lingen** Anton van der, Les guerres de Yahvé 1990 ➤ 6,7359; 7,7339: ᴿCBQ 54 (1992) 133-5 (J. T. *Walsh*); CritRR 5 (1992) 140-2 (H. C. *Washington*: redaction criticism refined perhaps unduly); RTPhil 124 (1992) 357s (M. *Rose*); TvT 32 (1992) 308 (M. *Vervenne*).

7392 *Lohfink* N., *al.,* Violencia y pacifismo en el Antiguo Testamento [Brixen Aug. 1981] ᵀ*Albizu* José Luis, 1990 ➤ 7,7340: ᴿREspir 51 (1992) 537 (S. *Fernández*).

7393 **McNeal** Patricia F., Harder than war; Catholic peacemaking in twentieth century America. New Brunswick NJ 1992, Rutgers Univ. xiv-316 p. $40 [TDig 39,371, does not clarify whether she means harder than 'declaring' war, or harder than having one's limbs shot off..]

7394 **Mantovani** Mauro, Bellum iustum; die Idee des gerechten Krieges in der römischen Kaiserzeit [Diss. Zürich 1989]: Geist und Werk der Zeiten 7. Bern 1990, Lang. xii-149 p. – ᴿGnomon 64 (1992) 455s (Maxime *Lemosse*, franç.).

7395 **Mauser** Ulrich, The Gospel of peace; a scriptural message for today's world. Studies in Peace and Scripture. Louisville 1992, W-Knox. xii-196 p. $17 pa. 0-664-25349-0 [NTAbs 36,438]. – ᴿTTod 49 (1992s) 435s (Sue Anne S. *Morrow*).

7396 **Miller** Richard B., Interpretations of conflict; ethics, pacifism, and the just-war traditiion. Ch 1991, Univ. x-294 p. $48; pa. $18 [TR 88,172]. – ᴿChrCent 109 (1992) 311s (D. J. *Snider*).

7397 *Molnar* Thomas, La guerre juste: PeCa 258 (1992) [< EsprVie 102 (1992) 642s (J. *Daoust*)].

7398 **Oded** Bustenay, War, peace and empire; justifications for war in Assyrian royal inscriptions. Wsb 1992, Reichert. xxiv-199 p. 3-88226-217-6.

7399 *Palmer-Fernández* Gabriel, Waging modern war; an analysis of the moral literature on the nuclear arms debate; diss.: HarvTR 85 (1992) 500s.

7400 *Pawlas* Andreas, Militärseelsorge — instrumentalisierte Religion oder unabhängige Kirche unter Soldaten?: KerDo 38 (1992) 230-256; Eng. 257.

7401 **Perine** Marcelo, Philosophie et violence; sens et intention de la philosophie d'Éric WEIL [bras.], ᵀ*Buée* Jean-Michel: BtArchivesPh 52. P 1991, Beauchesne. 323 p. F 328. – ᴿEsprVie 102 (1992) 400 (P. *Gire*).

7402 **Pucciarelli** Enrico, I Cristiani e il servizio militare; testimonianze dei primi tre secoli [< diss.]: BtPatristica 9, 1987 ➤ 3,6854... 5,7348: ᴿRivStorLR 27 (1991) 189-192 (R. *Valabrega*).

7403 **Rad** Gerhard von, Holy War in ancient Israel, ᵀ*Dawn* Marva J.; bibliog. *Sanderson* Judith E., 1991 ➤ 7,7346: ᴿBL (1992) 43 (G. H. *Jones*); ExpTim 103 (1991s) 22 (C. S. *Rodd*); TTod 49 (1992) 447 (J. S. *Ackerman*); VT 42 (1992) 133 (J. A. *Emerton*: bibliography 'representative' rather of U.S. seminary interests than of war).

7403* **Ramsey** Paul, Speak up for just war or pacifism 1988 ➤ 5,7349; 6, 7369: ᴿModT 8 (1992) 95-98 (C. *Pinches*).

Rüpke Georg, Domi militiae; die religiöse Konstruktion des Krieges in Rom, ᴰ1990 ➤ b205.

7404 **Sider** Ronald J., Cristo y la violencia, ᵀ*Mejía* Martha de. Guatemala 1991, Semillas. 130 p. [Kairós/Guatemala 12,88].

7405 **Sölle** Dorothee, The window of vulnerability; a political spirituality [... militarization leads inexorably away from peace]. Mp 1990, Fortress. 156 p. $9. 0-8006-2432-7. – ᴿExpTim 103 (1991s) 29s (K. G. *Greet*).

7406 **Spiegel** Egon, Gewaltverzicht, Grundlagen einer biblischen Friedenstheologie 1987 ➤ 3,6859 ... 6,7374*; Eng. 242-6: ᴿBijdragen 53 (1992) 87s (J. *Lambrecht*).

7407 ᴱ**Tambasco** A. J., Blessed are the peacemakers 1989 ➤ 5,609 ... 7,7350: ᴿRelStR 16 (1990) 335 (T. A. *Nairn*).

7408 *Theissen* Gerd, Pax romana et pax Christi; le christianisme primitif et l'idée de paix [pour son doctorat h.c. Neuchâtel]: RTPhil 124 (1992) 61-84.

7409 *Tillich* Paul, Theology of peace [articles 1937-65], ᴱ*Stone* Ronald E. Louisville 1990, W-Knox. 190 p. $11 pa. – ᴿAnglTR 74 (1992) 245s (S. M. *Smith*).

7410 *Tulloch* John & Marian, Discourses about violence; critical theory and the 'TV violence' debate: Text 12 (1992) 183-231.

7411 **Vaillant** F., La non-violence 1991 ➤ 7,7351: ᴿNRT 114 (1992) 377 (L. *Volpe*).

7412 ᴱ**Viaud** Pierre, Les religions et la guerre [➤ 7,7353]; Judaïsme, Christianisme, Islam: Positions. P 1991, Cerf. 583 p. F 145. 2-204-04288-9. – ᴿÉTRel 67 (1992) 265s (L. *Gambarotto*); TvT 32 (1992) 216s (A. van *Iersel*).

7413 **Way** Thomas von der, Göttergericht und 'Heiliger' Krieg im Alten Ägypten; die Inschriften des Merenptah zum Libyerkrieg des Jahres 5: StArchGAltÄg 4. Heid 1992, Orient. xi-99 p.; ill.

7414 *Wénin* André, Une culture de la vie et de la paix; projet du Dieu de la Bible? FoiTemps 22 (1992) 73-84.

7415 *Wink* Walter, Beyond just war and pacifism; Jesus' nonviolent way: RExp 89 (1992) 197-214.

7416 **Wright** Cyril, *Augarde* Tony, Peace be the way; a guide to pacifist views and actions. ... 1990, Lutterworth. 178 p. £7. 0-7188-2821-6. – ᴿExpTim 103 (1991s) 55s (K. C. *Greet*).

ᴱYoder Perry B., *Swartley* Willard M., The meaning of peace; biblical studies 1992 ➤ 371.

H4.1 – Messianismus.

7416* *a)* *Alonso Díaz* José, La esperanza mesiánica; visión del Antiguo Testamento; – *b)* *Muñoz León* Domingo,... visión del Targum; – *c)* *Pikaza* Xabier,... visión del NT; – *d*)... *Folgado Flórez* Segundo,... milenarista; – *e)* *Gracio das Neves* Rui Manuel,... hoy, reto para una Iglesia profética: BibFe 18,53 (1992) 149-173 / 174-196 / 197-238 / 239-263 / 264-290.

7417 **Bauckham** Richard, MOLTMANN; messianic theology in the making 1987 ➤ 6,7382: ᴿScotJT 44 (1991) 267-9 (D. *McLoughlin*: Moltmann can really listen).

7418 *Jonge* Marinus de, Messiah: ➤ 741, AnchorBD 4 (1992) 777-788 [791-7 movements, *Horsley* Richard A].

Karrer Martin, Der Gesalbte; die Grundlagen des Christustitels: FRL 151, ᴰ1991 ➤ f15.

7419 **Poorthuis** Marcel, Het gelaat... The face of the Messiah; Emmanuel LEVINAS' Messianic Talmud lectures; translation, commentary, background: kath. diss. Utrecht, ᴰ*Peperzak* A., 1992. 299 p. – TvT 33,84; RTLv 24, p. 544.

7420 *Strauss* Hans [AT], *Stemberger* Günter [Judentum], *Burridge* Kenelm [NT, ᵀ*Schwöbel* C.], Messias, Messianische Bewegungen: ➤ 768, TRE 22 (1992) 617-622-630-638.

7421 **Van Groningen** Gerard, Messianic revelation in the Old Testament 1990 ➤ 6,7388: ᴿKerux 7/1 (1992) 43-55 (R. S. *Clark*: subjective); VT 42 (1992) 425s (R. P. *Gordon*).

7422 *a)* *Werblowsky* R. J. Zwi, Jewish messianism in comparative perspective; – *b)* *Thoma* Clemens, Entwürfe für messianische Gestalten in frühjüdischer Zeit; – *c)* *Gruenwald* Ithamar, From priesthood to messianism; the anti-priestly polemic and the messianic factor; – *d)* *Nodet* Étienne, Miettes messianiques [... haggada de Pâques; ambiguité du grec]: ➤ 57, ᶠFLUSSER D., Messiah 1992, 1-13 / 15-29 / 75-93 / 119-141.

7422* *a)* *Werblowsky* R. J. Zwi, Messianism in Jewish history [< Journal of World History 11 (1968)]; – *b)* *Schweid* Eliezer, Jewish Messianism; metamorphoses of an idea [< JQuarterly 16 (1985)]; – *c)* *Horsley* Richard A., Popular messianic movements around the time of Jesus [< CBQ 46 (1984)]; – *d)* *Smith* Morton, Messiahs; robbers, jurists, prophets, and magicians [< PAAR 44 (1977)]: ➤ 365, Essential Messianic 1992, 35 52 / 53-70 / 83-110 / 73-82.

H4.3 *Eschatologia VT* – OT hope of future life.

7423 **Droge** Arthur J., *Tabor* James D., A noble death; suicide and martyrdom among Christians and Jews in antiquity. NY 1992, Harper-Collins. xii-203 p. 0-06-062905-1.

7424 *a)* *Garrone* Daniele, Dallo Sheol alla Gerusalemme celeste; morte e vita eterna secondo la Bibbia ebraica; – *b)* *Laras* Giuseppe, Immortalità, risurrezione ed era messianica nell'ebraismo; – *c*) *Caro* Luciano, I temi dell'aldilà nella liturgia ebraica; – *d)* *Xella* Paolo, Gli abitanti dell'aldilà nel Vicino Oriente e nell'Antico Testamento: ➤ 453, Aldilà 1991/2, 9-61 / 195-210 / 241-8 / 65-104.

7425 *Gibson* George S., There must be more [what NT adds to Sheol wraiths gloating over King of Babylon 'you have become as weak as we are', Isa 14,10]: ExpTim 103 (1991s) 112-4.

7425* **Krieg** Matthias, Todesbilder im AT: ATANT 73, 1988 ➤ 4,8411; 5,7373: ᴿTsTKi 63 (1992) 306s (M. *Sæbø*).

7426 *a) Martin-Achard* Robert, Le statut des morts en Israël [Shéol; pessimiste jusqu'à 200 av. J.-C.]; – *b) Ziegler* Christiane, Les peintures des tombes [en Égypte; vie des vivants; *Bridonneau* Catherine, coutumes funéraires]: MondeB 78 (1992) 34s / 36-43 [29-33].

7426* *a) Mendenhall* George E., From witchcraft to justice; death and afterlife in the Old Testament; – *b) Goldenberg* Robert, Bound up in the bond of life; death and afterlife in the Jewish tradition: ➤ 603, Death 1988/92, 67-81 / 97-108 [125-192 *al.*, Muslim, Buddhist ...].

7427 *a) Moraldi* Luigi, L'aldilà dell'uomo nella civiltà babilonica, egizia, greca, latina, ebraica, cristiana e musulmana. Mi 1991, Mondadori. 265 p. – ᴿStPatav 39 (1992) 252s (C. *Saccone*).

– *b) Moraldi* Luigi, Nach dem Tode; Jenseitsvorstellungen von den Babyloniern bis zum Christentum, ᵀ*Hoag* Martin, 1987 ➤ 4,a118: ᴿFranzSt 72 (1990) 301 (P. H. *Daly*, Eng.).

– *c) Puech* Émile, La croyance des Esséniens en la vie future; immortalité, résurrection, vie éternelle? Histoire d'une croyance dans le judaïsme ancien: diss. Inst. Cath. ᴰ*Grelot* P. Paris 1992. 584 p. – RTLv 24, p. 544.

7427* *Steudel* Annette, 4QMidrEschat, 'a midrash on eschatology' (4Q174 + 4Q177) [both published by J. *Allegro* in 1968]: ➤ 498, MQumran 2 (1991/2) 531-541.

7428 *Veld* H van 't, [Isa 26,19; Dan 12,2] De opstanding in het Oude Testament: KerkT 42 (1991) 18-27.

7428* *Wächter* L., *šeˀôl* 'Unterwelt': ➤ 770, TWAT 7,8 (1992) 901-910.

H4.5　*Theologia totius VT* – **General Old Testament theology.**

7429 *a) Brueggemann* Walter, *a*) A convergence in recent Old Testament theologies [< JStOT 18 (1980) 2-18]; – *b*) Futures in OT theology [< HorBT 6 (1984) 1-11]: ➤ 220, OT Theology 1992, 95-110 / 111-7.

7430 *a) Childs* Brevard S., Die Bedeutung der hebräischen Bibel für die biblische Theologie, ᵀ*Dietrich* W.: TZBas 48 (1992) 382-390.

– *b) Ellul* Jacques, Ce Dieu injuste ...? Théologie chrétienne pour le peuple d'Israël. P 1991, Arléa. 203 p. F 100. – ᴿÉtClas 60 (1992) 162 (Françoise *Mies*).

– *c) Hasel* Gerhard [➤ 7437 infra], OT Theology; basic issues in the current debate ⁴ʳᵉᵛ [¹1972, ³ʳᵉᵛ1982] 1991 ➤ 7,7380: ᴿBL (1992) 105 (R. E. *Clements*); ExpTim 103 (1991s) 152s (M. G. *Brett*); LA 41 (1991) 561-3 (A. *Niccacci*); OTAbs 14 (1991) 362s (R. E. *Murphy*).

7430* *Hubbard* Robert L., Doing Old Testament theology today: ➤ 88, ᶠHUBBARD David A., Studies in OT Theology 1992, 31-46.

7431 *Lemke* Werner F./ *Morgan* Robert, Theology OT/NT: ➤ 741, Anchor-BD 6 (1992) 448-473-483 [-505, its history, *Reventlow* H.].

7432 *Lohfink* Norbert, Ein Wolkenspalt; neue Veröffentlichungen zur Religionsgeschichte Israels ['Biblische Theologie ist keine (doch braucht die) Religionsgeschichte Israels': NIEHR H., MOOR J. de, SMITH M., METTINGER T.]: ➤ 355, JbBT 7 (1992) 387-398.

7433 *Lux* Rüdiger, Die Theologie des Alten Testaments zwischen israelitischer Religionsgeschichte und Israel-Theologie; eine hermeneutische Skizze: ↠ 7,174a, FWALLIS G., Überlieferung 1990, 35-47.

7434 **Mildenberger** Friedrich, Eine Biblische Theologie in dogmatischer Perspektive 1991 ↠ 7,7385: RExpTim 103 (1991s) 309 (R. *Coggins*).

Moberly R. W. L., The Old Testament of the Old Testament; patriarchal narratives... 1992 ↠ 7017.

7435 *Müller* Hans-Peter, Bedarf die alttestamentliche Theologie einer philosophischen Grundlegung?: ↠ 149, FPREUSS H., Atl.Glaube 1992, 342-351.

7436 **Oeming** Manfred, Gesamtbiblische Theologien... seit von RAD D1985 ↠ 1,6777... 7,7387: RCBQ 54 (1992) 121s (G. F. *Hasel*).

7437 *Ollenburger* Ben C., From timeless ideas to the essence of religion; method in OT theology before 1930 [+ passages from EISSFELDT O., EICHRODT W.]: ↠ 363, Flowering 1992, 3-19 [-39]; *Martens* E. 43-57; *Hasel* G., 373-383.

7438 **Preuss** H. D., JHWHS... Handeln: Theologie des ATs I, 1991 ↠ 7,7388: RBL (1992) 109s (R. E. *Clements*: very important); ExpTim 103 (1991s) 286 (R. J. *Coggins*); TüTQ 172 (1992) 242s (W. *Gross*); TvT 32 (1992) 309 (J. *Holman*); ZAW 104 (1992) 455 (H.-C. *Schmitt*).

7439 **Preuss** H. D., Israels Weg mit JHWH: Theologie des Alten Testaments 2. Stu 1992, Kohlhammer. viii-361 p. 3 17 011075 6 [BL 93,114, R. E. *Clements*].

7440 *Ravasi* Gianfranco, La teologia biblica dell'AT: Ambrosius 67 (1991) 426-440.

7440* *Rendtorff* Rolf, Old Testament theology, Tanakh theology, or biblical theology? Reflections in an ecumenical context [Pont. Biblical Inst. McCarthy Lecture 1992]: Biblica 73 (1992) 451.

7441 *Scobie* Charles H. H., La théologie biblique; un défi [< TyndB 42 (1991)], TCarrel Sylvie & Serge: Hokhma 51 (1992) 1-32.

7441* **Sherwin** Byron L., Toward a Jewish theology; methods, problems and possibilities. Lewiston NY 1991, Mellen. 194 p. – RColcT 62,4 (1992) 180-3 (W. *Chrostowski*, ❷).

7442 *a) Veijola* Timo, Offenbarung als Begegnung; von der Möglichkeit einer Theologie des Alten Testament; – *b) Fischer* Johannes, Wie wird Geschichte als Handeln Gottes offenbar? Zur Bedeutung der Anwesenheit Gottes im Offenbarungsgeschehen: ZTK 88 (1991) 427-450 / 211-231.

7442* *Westermann* Claus, Théologie de l'AT 1985 ↠ 2,5489: RMasses Ouvrières 445 (1992) 104s (J.-M. *Carrière*).

7443 **Zuck** Roy B., A biblical theology of the Old Testament. Ch 1991, Moody. 446 p. $28. – RBtS 149 (1992) 486s (F. R. *Howe*); GraceTJ 12 (1991) 294-6 (M. A. *Grisanto*).

H5.1 Deus – NT – God [as Father ↠ H 1.4].

7444 **Arias Reyero** Maximino, El Dios de nuestra fe; Dios uno y trino: Col. Sem.LAm 5. Bogotá 1991, Consejo Episcopal. 478 p. 958-625-197-7. – RGregorianum 73 (1992) 153s (C. I. *González*).

Baudler Georg, God and violence [Erlösung vom Stiergott]; the Christian experience of God in dialogue with myths 1992 ↠ b142*.

7445 *Cacciapuoti* Pierluigi, L'identità di Dio nell'età postmoderna; metafisica e teologia tra SCIACCA [1972/90] e PANNENBERG: Asprenas 39 (1992) 563-574.

7446 **García-Murga** J. R.,   El Dios del amor y de la paz.   M 1991, Univ. Comillas.   440 p. – RCarthaginensia 8 (1992) 945s (J. M. *Roncero Moreno*: = De Deo uno et trino).

7447 **Kasper** Walter,   The God of Jesus Christ [1982 ➤ 64,6534],T.   L 1992 [= Eng. 1984 ➤ 65,6176], SCM.   x-404 p.   0-334-02029-8.

7448 **Maass** Fritz,   Vom neuen Bekenntnis zu Gott.   FrB-Denzlingen 1989, auct. (Berlinerstr. 32).   90 p. – RDielB 27 (1991) 286s (B. J. *Diebner*).

7449 **Marguerat** Daniel,   Le Dieu des premiers chrétiens: Essais Bibliques 16, 1990 ➤ 6,7426; 7,7400; 2-8309-0607-1:   RBijdragen 53 (1992) 434s (H. *Hoet*).

7450 **Martini** Carlo Maria,   Cattedra dei non credenti [... domande anche dei credenti].   Mi 1992, Rusconi.   188 p.   88-18-0109-56.

7451 **Muñoz** Ronaldo,   The God of Christians 1990 ➤ 7,7401:   RTS 53 (1992) 155 (A. J. *Tambasco*).

7452 *Schneider* Gerhard,   *a*) Gott, der Vater Jesu Christi, in der Verkündigung Jesu und im urchristlichen Bekenntnis [ineditum]; – *b*) Das Gebet des Herrn, ein 'jüdisches' Gebet [< ähnlich FRatzinger J.,   1 (1987) 405-417]; – *c*) In der Nachfolge Christi [Neufassung < ESchneider G., Anfragen 1971, 132-146]: ➤ 305, Jesusüberlieferung 1992, 3-38 / 39-51(-85) / 143-154.

7453 *Schwager* Raymund,   Dunkles im Gott Jesu Christi? oder, Der liebende Vater und der schreckerregende Richter: BiKi 46 (1991) 164-171.

7454 ESiertsema B.,   Zeg mij hoe Uw God is; Godsbeelden en mensbeelden [Amst VU 20 okt. 1990].   Kampen 1990, Kok.   168 p. *f*29,50.   90-242-7724-8. – RTvT 32 (1992) 425 (P. A. van *Gennip*).

7455 *Staehlin* Wilhelm,   Le mystère de Dieu [1970], T: Théologies, 1990 ➤ 7, 7405:   REsprVie 102 (1992) 79 (P. *Jay*).

7456 **Ven** J. A. van der,   God in Nijmegen; een theologisch perspectief [... sensus fidelium]: TvT 32 (1992) 225-248; Eng. 248s.

7457 **Vorgrimler** Herbert,   Theologische Gotteslehre: Leitfaden Theologie 3, 1985 (español 1987) ➤ 3,6954 [= ? Gotteslehre: Textus, Dogm. 2, 1989]: RActuBbg 29 (1992) 85 (J. *Boada*).

H5.2   Christologia ipsius NT.

7458 **Capes** D. B.,   Old Testament Yahweh texts in Paul's Christology [diss. SW Baptist sem. DEllis E., Fort Worth]: WUNT 2/47.   Tü 1992, Mohr. vii-220 p.   DM 69.   3-16-145819-2 [NTAbs 36,431]. – RJTS 43 (1992) 605s (L. *Kreitzer*).

7459 **Casey** P. M.,   From Jewish prophet to Gentile God; the origins and development of NT Christology [Cadbury lectures] 1991 ➤ 7,7410:   RBiblica 73 (1992) 430-4 (Pheme *Perkins*: with inadequate arguments challenges the comfortable sense that a Christology 'from below' can ground the belief of the Church); ExpTim 103, 2d top choice (1991s) 33s (C. S. *Rodd*: fierce attack on Chalcedonian theology, hard to refute); TLZ 117 (1992) 353-5 (E. *Schweizer*).

7460 **Doré** J.,   Le NT dans l'enseignement de la Dogmatique; l'exemple de la Christologie: ➤ 448, Ens.Écr. 1982, 205-222.

7461 EDupont Jacques,   Jésus aux origines de la Christologie[2], BtETL 40, 1989 ➤ 5,7423 ... 7,7411:   RRThom 92 (1992) 547-9 (M.-V. *Leroy*).

7462 **Fitzmyer** Joseph A.,   A Christological catechism; NT answers[2rev] 1991 ➤ 7,7412:   RCBQ 54 (1992) 776s (M. *Cahill*; five new questions; still the most accessible source of the 1964 Vatican Instructio); RefTR 51 (1992)

117 (-: useful Catholic summary; aggravating critical skepticism); ZkT 114 (1992) 218s (K. H. *Neufeld*: nachdrücklich empfohlen).

7463 **Fredriksen** Paula,   De Jésus aux Christs; les origines des représentations de Jésus dans le NT, [T]*Fortier-Masek* M.-O.: Jésus depuis Jésus. P 1992, Cerf. 346 p. F 165. – [R]EsprVie 102 (1992) 616s (É. *Cothenet*: p. 196 Pilate 'précurseur' et des objections plus sérieuses); Études 376 (1992) 856s (R. *Marlé*).

7464 **Habermann** Jürgen,   Präexistenzaussagen im NT [D]1990 ⟶ 6,7434; 7, 7415: [R]CBQ 54 (1992) 564-6 (R. *Scroggs*); JBL 111 (1992) 537-9 (L. W. *Hurtado*); JTS 43 (1992) 633-6 (J. D. G. *Dunn*: only one helpful point).

7465 **Heyer** C. J. den,   De Messiaanse weg, III. De Christologie van het Nieuwe Testament. Kampen 1991, Kok. 314 p. f 49,50.   90-242-2304-0. – [R]KerkT 43 (1992) 76-78 (G. de *Ru*); TvT 32 (1992) 313 (L. *Grollenberg*).

Jonge Marinus de,   Jesus, the Servant-Messiah 1991 ⟶ 4509.

7466 **Jossa** Giorgio,   Dal Messia al Cristo; le origini della cristologia 1989 ⟶ 5,7429; 7,7416*: [R]CBQ 54 (1992) 158s (V. P. *Branick*: a first-class work of scholarship); RivB 40 (1992) 239-241 (G. *De Virgilio*); RivStoLR 28 (1992) 693s (Gabriella *Dogliani Saladini*); RTPhil 124 (1992) 359s (A. *Moda*).

7467 **Lemcio** Eugene,   The past of Jesus in the Gospels: SNTS mg 68, 1991 ⟶ 7,7417: [R]ExpTim 103 (1991s) 245s (M. B. *Thompson*: how much the christological material in the gospel accounts differs from the emphases of early Christian preaching); JTS 43 (1992) 578-580 (K. *Grayston*); TvT[= TsTNijm] 32 (1992) 193 (P. J. *Farla*).

7468 *Michiels* Robrecht,   Jezus en de andere godsdiensten; twee nieuwe Christologische modellen [SCHOONENBERG P. 1991; SCHILLEBEECKX E. 1989]: CollatVL 22 (1992) 381-396.

7469 **Müller** Ulrich B.,   Menschwerdung... Doketismus: SBS 140, 1990 ⟶ 6, 7440: [R]JBL 111 (1992) 343-5 (M. *Lattke*).

7469* *Stanton* Graham N.,   Christology and the parting of the ways [ineditum]: ⟶ 313, Studies in Mt. 1992, 169-191.

7470 **Witherington** Ben [III],   The Christology of Jesus 1990 ⟶ 6,7448; 7,7420*: [R]BibTB 22 (1992) 44s (E. L. *Bode*); CBQ 54 (1992) 810s (R. J. *Miller*); ChrCent 108 (1991) 821 (R. L. *Omanson*); ExpTim 102 (1990s) 378 (L. *Houlden*: lively but old-fashioned); Horizons 19 (1992) 312s (G. S. *Sloyan*); Interpretation 46 (1992) 324. 326 (C. B. *Cousar*); JBL 111 (1992) 143 (J. R. *Michaels*); Pacifica 5 (1992) 229-232 (F. J. *Moloney*: 'middle of the road' with elegance and insight); StPatav 39 (1992) 631-4 (G. *Segalla*); TLZ 117 (1992) 277s (P. *Pokorný*); TTod 49 (1992s) 110s (M. I. *Soards*).

H5.3   *Christologia praemoderna* – **patristic through Reformation.**

7471 *Abramowski* Luise,   Was hat das Nicaeno-Constantinopolitanum (C) mit dem Konzil von Konstantinopel 381 zu tun?: TPhil 67 (1992) 481-513.

7472 *Aubineau* Michel,   Citations de l'homélie de PROCLUS, In nativitatem Salvatoris (CPG 5068), dans un florilège christologique des IVe et Ve siècles: VigChr 45 (1991) 209-222.

7472* **Bartos** Jan F.,   Gesù Cristo rivelazione di Dio nel pensiero di S. BO-NAVENTURA: Diss. Seraphicum 76, 1990 ⟶ 6,7450: [R]ColcFran 61 (1991) 378-80 (P. *Maranesi*).

7473 **Bausenhart** Guido,   *a*) In allem uns gleich ausser der Sünde; Studien zum Beitrag MAXIMOS' des Bekenners zur altkirchlichen Christologie: kath. Diss. [D]*Hünermann* P. Tübingen 1990. 364 p. – RTLv 24, p. 572. – *b*) In allem uns gleich ausser der Sünde; Studien zum Beitrag Maximos' des Bekenners zur altkirchlichen Christologie; mit einer kommentierten Übersetzung der 'Disputatio cum Pyrrho': TüStTPh 5. Mainz 1992, Grünewald. 364 p. DM 56 [TR 88,520].

7473* *Bavaud* Georges, Une controverse entre Bossuet et Jurieu sur le mystère de la génération du Verbe expliquée par les Péres de l'Église: NVFr 67 (1992) 120-132.

7474 **Blough** Neal, *al.,* Jésus-Christ [... christologies] aux marges de la Réforme: JJC 54. P 1992, Desclée. 257 p. [NRT 115, 95, L. *Renwart*].

7475 **Böhm** Thomas, Die Christologie des Arius; dogmengeschichtliche Überlegungen unter besonderer Berücksichtigung der Hellenisierungsfrage D1991 → 7,7421*: RScripTPamp 24 (1992) 1094-6 (L. F. *Mateo-Seco*); VigChr 46 (1992) 300s (E. P. *Meijering*).

7475* *Böhm* Thomas, Die Thalia des Arius; ein Beitrag zur frühchristlichen Hymnologie: VigChr 46 (1992) 334-355.

7476 **Brennecke** Hans C., Studien zur Geschichte der Homöer D1988 → 5, 7449; 6,7452: RAugR 30 (1990) 493-8 (M. *Simonetti*).

7477 *Brennecke* H. C., Homéens: → 748, DHGE XXIV, 141 (1992) 932-960.

7478 **Bruns** Peter, Das Christusbild des Aphrahats D1990 → 7,7422: RBijdragen 53 (1992) 441-3 (M. *Parmentier,* Eng., also on Grillmeier 2/2.4); RÉAug 38 (1992) 193-5 (M.-J. *Pierre*); RTLv 23 (1992) 385s (A. de *Halleux*).

7479 *Brox* Norbert, ¿Quién es Jesús? La respuesta de los primeros concilios [< Orientierung 54 (1990) 52-56], TEAlemany Rosario: SelT 30 (1991) 281-6.

7480 **Dahl** Nils A., Jesus the Christ; the historical origins of Christological doctrine, EJuel Donald H., 1991 → 6,194: RHorBT 14 (1992) 185s (P. *Pokorný*); Interpretation 46 (1992) 302-4 (W. A. *Meeks*); TR 88 (1992) 379-382 (H. *Giesen*).

7480* TEDattrino Lorenzo, Giovanni Cassiano, L'incarnazione del Signore, 1991 → 7,7427: RCC 143 (1992,2) 315s (A. *Ferrua*).

7481 **Doherty** James J., Scripture and soteriology in the Christological system of St. Cyril of Alexandria: diss. Fordham, DMeyendorff J. NY 1992. 215 p. 92-23812. – DissA 53 (1992s) 1191-A.

7482 *Farkasfalvy* Denis [Cistercian abbot], The Christological content and its biblical basis in the letter of the martyrs of Gaul: SecC 9 (1992) 5-25.

7483 **González** Carlos Ignacio, El desarrollo dogmático de los concilios cristológicos 1-2: Autores 3. Bogotá 1991, Consejo Episcopal. 693 p. 958-625-221-3. – RGregorianum 73 (1992) 582s (*ipse*).

7484 **Grillmeier** Alois, (*Hainthaler* Theresia), Jesus der Christus im Glauben der Kirche 2/2, 1989 → 5,7459 ... 7,7434: 2/4, 1990 → 6,7463*: RKatKenk 31 (1992) 182-9 (S. *Takayanagi,* 2/2 ❶); LebZeug 45 (1990) 67s & 46 (1991) 151s (F. *Courth* 2/2.4); RTLv 23 (1992) 71-74 (A. de *Halleux,* 2/4); TvT [= TsTNijm] 32 (1992) 97s (A. *Davids,* 2/2.4).

7485 **Grillmeier** Alois, Le Christ dans la tradition chrétienne [2/1, 1990 → 6, 7465; 7,7435], 3. Chalcédoine: CogF 154. P 1990, Cerf. – RAngelicum 69 (1992) 127s (A. *Wilder*); FoiTemps 21 (1991) 73-75 (G. *Harpigny*); RÉAug 38 (1992) 204s (J. *Doignon,* 2/1).

7486 **Gronchi** Maurizio, La cristologia di S. Bernardino da Siena; l'''Imago Christi' nella predicazione in volgare [diss. Pont. Univ. Gregoriana, DDupuis J. Roma 1992. 245 p.; publ. 3898, 228 p. – RTLv 24, p. 574]: TeologiaSR. Genova 1992, Marietti. 228 p. Lit. 35.000 [NRT 115,88, L. *Renwart*].

7487 **Hanson** R. P. C.,   The search for the Christian doctrine of God; the Arian controversy 1988 ➤ 4,8475 ... 7,7436:   ᴿJRel 72 (1992) 104s (D. E. *Groh*).

7487* **Haystrup** Helge,   Kristusbekendelsen i oldkirken² [¹1979]. K 1982, Reitzel. 212 p. – ᴿTsTKi 63 (1992) 68s (O. *Skarsaune*).

7488 *Head* Peter M.,   *a*) TATIAN's Christology and its influence on the composition of the Diatessaron: TyndB 43,1 (1992) 121-137; – *b*) On the Christology of the Gospel of Peter: VigChr 46 (1992) 209-224.

7489 **Henne** Philippe,   La christologie chez CLÉMENT de Rome et dans le Pasteur d'HERMAS [diss. LvN 1988, ᴰ*Halleux* A. de]: Paradosis 33.   FrS 1992, Univ.   371 p. 2-8271-0555-1.

7490 *Iammarrone* Giovanni,   Wert und Grenzen der Christologie des Johannes Duns SCOTUS in heutiger Zeit: WissWeis 52 (1989) 1-20.

7491 *Kang Phee Seng,*   The epistemological significance of *homooúsion* in the theology of Thomas F. TORRANCE: ScotJT 45 (1992) 341-366.

7492 **Kannengiesser** Charles,   Le Verbe de Dieu selon ATHANASE 1990 ➤ 7, 7438:   ᴿRSPT 76 (1992) 136-8 (G.-M. de *Durand*).

7493 *Kearsley* Roy,   The impact of Greek concepts of God on the Christology of CYRIL of Alexandria: TyndB 43 (1992) 307-329.

7494 **Ladaria** Luis F.,   La cristologia de HILARIO ...:   AnGreg 255, 1989 ➤ 5,7466 ... 7,7439:   ᴿEstE 67 (1992) 104s (G. *Higuera*); RET 52 (1992) 87-90 (M. *Gesteira*).

7495 **Lage** Dictmar,   M. LUTHER's Christology and ethics: TextStRel 45. Lewiston NY 1990, Mellen.   viii-175 p. $50.   0-88946-834-6. – ᴿJRel 72 (1992) 433s (S. H. *Hendrix*); TvT [= TsTNijm] 32 (1992) 101 (T. H. M. *Akerboom*).

7495* **Legarth** Peter V.,   Guds Tempel; tempelsymbolisme og kristologi hos IGNATIUS af Antiokia: diss. Lund 1992. 404 p. – RTLv 24, p. 547.

7496 ᵀᴱ**Lo Castro** Giovanni,   TEODOTO di Ancira,   Omelie cristologiche e mariane: TPatr 97.   R 1992, Città Nuova. 167 p. Lit. 16.000.   88-311-3097-8.

7497 **Lord** Raymond W.,   Teaching adults the meaning of 'Jesus Christ' based upon issues contained in the Chalcedonian debates. diss. Lancaster Theol. Sem. 1992, ᴰ*Freeman* D.   300 p. 92-25340. – DissA 53 (1992s) 2853-A.

7498 *McWilliam* Joanne,   The study of AUGUSTINE's Christology in the twentieth century: ➤ 588, Rhetor 1992, 183-205.

7499 *Madec* Goulven,   Christus [franç.]: ➤ 743, AugL 1,5s (1992) 846-908.

7500 *a*) *Mazas* J.,   La materia incandescente; una imagen cristológica en San CIRILO de Alejandría; – *b*) *Catelli* Giovanni,   Cristo nei Padri Apostolici: Helmantica 43 (1992) 315-328 / 297-314.

7501 ᴱ**Mazzanti** G.,   BASILIO di Cesarea, Testi cristologici.   R 1991, Borla. 202 p. – ᴿVivH 3 (1992) 439 (*ipse*).

7502 *Mazzanti* Giorgio,   Il fondamento biblico della cristologia di s. BASILIO Magno: VivH 3 (1992) 225-240; Eng. 241.

7503 ᵀᴱ**Meijering** E. P. (*Winden* J. C. M. van) ATHANASIUS, De Incarnatione Verbi 1989 ➤ 6,7475:   ᴿClasR 41 (1991) 227 (J. N. *Birdsall*).

7504 **Müller** Ulrich B.,   Die Menschwerdung des Gottessohnes; frühchristliche Inkarnationsvorstellungen und die Anfänge des Doketismus: SBS 140. Stu 1990, KBW.   136 p. 3-460-04401-2.

7404* *Petersen* William L.,   The Christology of APHRAHAT, the Persian sage; an excursus on the 17th Demonstration: VigChr 46 (1992) 241-256.

7505 **Pifarré** C.,   ARNOBIO el Joven y la Cristología del 'Conflicto' 1988 ➤ 35,7473; 6,7479:   ᴿCiuD 205 (1992) 264 (S. *Folgado Flórez*).

7505* **Sarrasin** Claude, Plein de grâce et de vérité; théologie de l'âme du Christ selon s. Thomas d'AQUIN: Théologie 4. Venasque 1992, Carmel. 352 p. F 170 [NRT 115, 887, L. *Renwart*].

7506 **Sim Jong-Hyeok** Luke, Christological vision of the Spiritual Exercises of St. IGNATIUS of Loyola and the hermeneutical principles: diss. Pont. Univ. Gregoriana, 6945, ᴰ*Dupuis* J. Roma 1992. – InfPUG 121,19.

7507 *Stead* G. Christopher, Homoousios, ᵀ*Hoheisel* Karl: ➤ 764, RAC 16, 123s (1992) 365-433.

7507* *Suttner* Ernst C., Der christologische Konsens mit den Nicht-Chalkedonensern: OstkSt 41 (1992) 3-21.

7508 **Welch** Lawrence J., Christology and the Eucharist in the thought of CYRIL of Alexandria; a reconsideration: diss. Marquette, ᴰ*Keefe* D. Milwaukee 1992. 284 p. 93-06006. – DissA 53 (1992s) 3944-A.

7509 ᵀᴱ**Wesche** Kenneth P., On the person of Christ; the Christology of Emperor JUSTINIAN. Crestwood NY 1991, St. Vladimir. 203 p. 0-88141-089-6.

H5.4 (*Commentationes de*) *Christologia* **moderna.**

Adinolfi Marco, Il Verbo uscito dal silenzio; temi di cristologia bíblica 1992 ➤ 204.

7510 **Amato** Angelo, Gesù il Signore, saggio di Cristologia: Sist 4, 1988 ➤ 5, 7481; 6,7487: ᴿTPhil 67 (1992) 619s (W. *Löser*).

7511 **Barth** Ulbrich, Die Christologie Emanuel HIRSCHS; eine systematische und problemgeschichtliche Darstellung ihrer geschichtstheologischen und subjektivitätstheoretischen Grundlagen [Hab.-Diss. Göttingen]. B 1992, de Gruyter. xvi-669 p. DM 212 [TR 88,256].

7512 **Bordoni** M., *a*) Gesù di Názaret; presenza, memoria, attesa 1988 ➤ 5, 7484: ᴿParVi 36 (1991) 73s (C. *Ghidelli*); – *b*) Gesù... cristologia sistematica 1-3, 1982-6: DivThom [(1989,3s) 317-389; (1991,4) 96-148] 95,3 (1992) 161-197 (L. *Iammarrone*).

7513 **Brambilla** F. G., La cristologia di SCHILLEBEECKX 1989 ➤ 5,7487; 7, 7453: ᴿAsprenas 39 (1991) 284s (P. *Pifano*).

7514 *Bravo* L. Carlos, ¿Que significa el título 'Hijo de Dios' (Dios), aplicado a Jesús?: TXav 41 ('Cristología y evangelización' 1991) 7-42

7514* *a*) *Buckley* James J., Adjudicating conflicting Christologies; – *b*) *Krieg* Robert, On the value of diverse Christologies. Philosophy & Theology 6 (Milwaukee 1991) 117-135 / 137-143 [145-8, *Marshall* Bruce D.].

7515 **Cantalamessa** Raniero, *a*) Gesù Cristo, il Santo di Dio, 1991. – *b*) Jesus Christ, the holy one of God, ᵀ*Neame* Alan. ColMn 1991, Liturgical. vi-166 p. $7. 0-8146-2073-6 [TDig 39,256].

7516 **Cathey** David V., David TRACY's aesthetic-phenomenological hermeneutic; implications for revisionist Christology: diss. SW Baptist Theol. Sem. 1992, ᴰ*Woodfin* Y. 274 p. 92-31654. – DissA 53 (1992s) 1941-A.

7517 **De Marchi** Sergio, La cristologia italiana da [1931 a 1979]: diss., Pont. Univ. Gregoriana, ᴰ*Fisichella* R. Roma 1992. – RTLv 24, p. 573.

7518 *Dunn* James D. G., *a*) Christology (NT); – *b*) Incarnation: ➤ 741, AnchorBD 1992, 1, 979-991 / 3, 397-404.

7519 **Duquoc** Christian, Messianisme de Jésus et discrétion de Dieu 1984 ➤ 65,6194... 3,6958: ᴿNZMissW 47 (1991) 157 (A. *Peter*).

7520 **Eckardt** A. Roy, Reclaiming the Jesus of history; Christology today. Mp 1992, Augsburg. 297 p. $30 [TR 88,347].

7521 **Erickson** Millard J.,   The Word becomes flesh; a contemporary incarnational Christology.   GR 1991, Baker.   663 p. $30.   0-8010-3208-3 [TDig 39,160]. – RCritRR 5 (1992) 470s (W. *McWilliams*).

7521* *Galot* Jean,   L'identità personale di Cristo; Verbo e Figlio: CC 143 (1992,1) 543-556.

7522 **Goergen** D. J.,   The Jesus of Christian history: A theology of Jesus 3. ColMn 1992, Liturgical.   287 p. $15 pa.   0-8146-5605-6 [NTAbs 36,437].

7523 **González** Carlos Ignacio,   Jesucristo ayer, hoy y siempre; una proposición cristológica... Bogotá 1992, Consejo Episcopal.   238 p.   958-625-233-X. – RGregorianum 73 (1992) 581s (*ipse*).

7523* *González de Cardedal* Olegario,   Boletín de Cristologia (2): Salmanticensis 38 (1991) 345-367 (BALTHASAR, TILLIETTE + 3).

7524 **Guggenberger** Engelbert, K. RAHNERS Christologie und heutige Fundamentalmoral 1990 ➤ 7,7460:   RSalesianum 54 (1992) 803s (G. *Abbà*); TPhil 67 (1992) 625s (R. *Sebott*); ZkT 114 (1992) 302-4 (A. *Batlogg*).

7525 **Habra** Georges,   La foi en Dieu incarné, I. Justification rationnelle 1989 ➤ 5,7498*:   RAustralBR 40 (1992) 68s (Rory *Boid*: polemic).

7526 **Hebblethwaite** Brian,   The Incarnation; collected essays in Christology 1987 ➤ 3,235... 7,7461:   RCritRR 5 (1992) 475s (W. J. *Abraham*).

7527 *Hinson* E. Glenn,   Historical perspectives on Christology: RExp 88 (1991) 331-342 (-397, *al.*, African / Yellow / Evangelical).

7528 **Joha** Zdenko,   Christologie und Anthropologie, eine Verhältnisbestimmung unter besonderer Berücksichtigung des theologischen Denkens W. KASPERS [... RAHNER, BALTHASAR, ALFARO, LATOURELLE]: FreibTSt 148. FrB 1992, Herder.   399 p.   DM 68 [NRT 115,99, L. *Renwart*].

7529 **Johnson** Elizabeth A.,   Consider Jesus 1990 ➤ 6,7516; 7,7467:   RJRel 72 (1992) 608-610 (T. J. *Martin*); Worship 65 (1991) 279-281 (C. *O'Regan*).

7530 **Kaiser** Alfred,   Möglichkeit und Grenzen einer Christologie 'von unten': CusanusG 11. Münster 1992, Aschendorff.   xvi-334 p.   DM 58 [TR 88,528].

7531 **Kuschel** K.-J.,   Geboren vor aller Zeit? Der Streit um Christi Ursprung D1990; 3-492-03374-1:   RTvT [= TsTNijm] 32 (1992) 208s (N. *Schreurs*).

7532 **Kuschel** Karl-Josef,   Born before all time? The dispute over Christ's origin; TBowden J. L/NY 1992, SCM/Crossroad.   xix-20+664 p. $50. 0-334-00111-0 / 0-8245-1207-3 [TDig 40,171].

7533 **Lane** Dermot A.,   Christ at the centre; selected issues in Christology 1990 ➤ 6,261; 7,7475:   RGregorianum 73 (1992) 758 (J. *Dupuis*); PerspRelSt 19 (1992) 104-6 (W. *McWilliams*); TS 53 (1992) 183 (G. M. *Fagin*).

7534 **La Tribouille** Armelle de,   La foi en Jésus-Christ: CahÉcCathédraleP 2. P 1991, Mame.   114 p. – REsprVie 102 (1992) 569 (P. *Jay*).

7535 *Leclercq* Jean,   La Christologie clunisienne au siècle de S. HUGUES: StMon 31 (1989) 267-278 [< BTAM 15,3 (1992) 179s (P. H. *Daly*)].

7536 **López Amat** Alfredo,   Jesús el ungido; Cristología: Síntesis 2/4. M 1991, Atenas.   274 p.   84-7020-298-7. – RActuBbg 29 (1992) 229 (F. de P. *Solá*).

7536* *Lorizio* Giuseppe,   Cristologia e filosofia; la lezione di Xavier TILLIETTE: Lateranum 57 (1991) 199-209.

7537 **Macquarrie** John,   Jesus Christ in modern thought 1990 ➤ 6,7473; 7,7479:   RChrCent 108 (1991) 437-9 (M. S. *Burrows*); Interpretation 46 (1992) 73s (J. C. *Livingston*); Pacifica 5 (1992) 102-4 (A. *Dutney*); TS 53 (1992) 160s (R. A. *Krieg*).

7538 **Madonia** Nicolò,   Ermeneutica e cristologia in W. KASPER: Theologia 2, 1990 ➤ 7,7480; Lit. 50.000:   RAntonianum 67 (1992) 439s (V. *Battaglia*); ETL 68 (1992) 473s (E. *Brito*); LumenVr 41 (1992) 490s (U. *Gil Ortega*).

7539 **Maldamé** Jean-Michel,   Le Christ et le Cosmos; incidences de la cosmologie moderne sur la christologie: diss. Toulouse 1991. – RTLv 24, p. 575.

7540 **Marquardt** F. M.,   Das christliche Bekenntnis zu Jesus, dem Juden, eine Christologie 2, [1. 1990 ➤ 7,7481]; 2. Mü 1991, Kaiser. ➤ 7,366:   RÉTRel 67 (1992) 608s (J.-L. *Klein*); EvKomm 24 (1991) 237-9 (P. *Pokorný,* 1); TsTKi 63 (1992) 315s (H. *Hegstad*); TvT [= TsTNijm] 32 (1992) 209 (W. *Logister,* also on PANNENBERG).

7541 **Marrone** Fortunato,   Cristo il figlio di Dio fatto uomo; l'incarnazione del Verbo nel pensiero cristologico di J. H. NEWMAN [diss. Pont. Univ. Gregoriana]: Già e non ancora 195.   Mi 1990, Jaca.   271 p. [TR 88,79].

7541* **Marshall** I. Howard,   The origins of NT Christology [2rev]. Leicester 1990, Inter-Varsity.   142 p. £8.50. – RStPatav 39 (1992) 655 (G. *Segalla*).

7542 *Mbogu* Nicholas I.,   Christology in contemporary Africa; a prolegomenon for a theology of development: AfER 33 (1991) 214-230.

7543 **Mikhael** Romanos,   Jésus comme prophète dans la christologie contemporaine de langue française: diss. Pont. Univ. Gregoriana, DGalot J. Roma 1992. 490 p.; Extr. 3838, 101 p. – InfPUG May 1992, 10; RTLv 24, p. 575.

7543* **Moioli** Giovanni † 1984, EBrambilla Franco G.,   Cristologia; proposta sistematica 1989 ➤ 7,7484; Lit. 45.000:   RCC 143 (1992,2) 101-3 (F. *Lambiasi*); Lateranum 57 (1991) 615s (G. *Ancona*).

7544 **Moltmann** J.,   Der Weg von J. C., Christologie in messianischen Dimensionen 1989 ➤ 5,7515 … 7,7486:   RFranzSt 73 (1991) 89s (F.-J. *Bäumer*).

7545 **Moltmann** Jürgen,   The way of Jesus Christ; Christology in messianic dimensions 1991 ➤ 7,7487:   RChrCent 108 (1991) 658s (D. W. *Musser*); Horizons 19 (1992) 141s (M. L. *Cook*); HomP 92,4 (1991s) 75 (J. R. *Sheets:* a lack of cohesiveness); Interpretation 46 (1992) 407-9 (J. D. *Godsey*); IntRMiss 81 (1992) 324-6 (R. S. *Sugirtharaja[h]*); JRel 72 (1992) 607s (J. A. *Colombo*); Pacifica 5 (1992) 238-240 (C. *Mostert*); TS 53 (1992) 161-3 (J. P. *Galvin*).

7545* **Moltmann** Jürgen,   Le vie di Cristo; Cristologia in dimensioni messianiche: BtTContemp 68.   Brescia 1991, Queriniana. 408 p. Lit. 45.000. – RStPatav 39 (1992) 441-4 (E. R. *Tura*).

7546 **Mueller** J. J.,   Practical discipleship; a United States Christology.   ColMn 1992, Liturgical.   175 p. $15 pa.   0-8146-5012-0 [NTAbs 36, p. 438].

7547 **N'Zilamba** Malonga V.,   Divinité et résurrection de Jésus; essai sur la christologie de Jean GUITTON: diss. Pont. Univ. Gregoriana, DGalot J. Roma 1992. 409 p.; Extr. 3829, 83 p. – InfPUG May 1992, 10; RTLv 24, p. 575.

7548 **Ocáriz-L. F.,** *Mateo-Seco* J., *Riestra* A.,   El misterio de Jesuscristo. Pamplona 1991, Univ.   452 p. – RBurgense 33 (1992) 567-9 (J. A. *Sayés*); ScripTPamp 24 (1992) 295-7 (J. *Morales*).

7549 **O'Carroll** Michael,   Verbum caro; an encyclopedia on Jesus, the Christ: Glazier.   ColMn 1992, Liturgical.   x-203 p. $35 [CBQ 55,211].

7550 **Ols** Daniel,   Le Cristologie contemporanee [SCHILLEBEECKX, RAHNER …] e le loro posizioni fondamentali al vaglio della dottrina di San TOMMASO [diss. 1990 ➤ 6,7534*]: Pont. Accad. S. Tommaso.   Vaticano 1991, Editrice.   213 p. [TR 88,78]. – RAsprenas 39 (1991) 283s (A. *Langella*): Benedictina 39 (1992) 495-7 (M. *Serretti*); ETL 68 (1992) 475-7 (A. de *Halleux:* injuste mise en question de l'orthodoxie de Rahner et Schillebeeckx); MiscFranc 92 (1992) 613-5 (L. M. *Lorusso*).

7551 *Ols* Daniel, Plénitude de grâce et vision béatifique; une voie peu fréquentée pour établir la vision béatifique du Christ durant sa vie terrestre: DocCom 44 (1991) 14-28.

7552 **Ottati** Douglas F., Jesus Christ and Christian vision 1989 → 6,7536; 7,7490: ᴿCritRR 5 (1992) 482-4 (W. P. *Loewe*).

7553 **Page** Ruth, The incarnation of freedom and love. L 1991, SCM. ix-214 p. £15. 0-334-02490-0. – ᴿExpTim 103 (1991s) 93 (T. J. *Gorringe*: 'imaginative Christology'; attractive drama-model, emphasizing relationship with creation rather than pre-existing Logos); JTS 43 (1992) 345-8 (J. L. *Houlden*: 'theologians have every right to accuse biblical scholars of lending little help; they are simply uninterested... in the theologians' enterprise'); TLond 95 (1992) 212s (Paul *Avis* wonders what post-Christian feminists will make of it); TvT 32 (1992) 328 (M. Van *Tente*: Scots feminist perspective).

7554 *Panikkar* Raimon, A Christophany for our times [... Christology not divorced from cosmology; what 'heaven' means...; Bellarmine Lecture, St. Louis University Oct. 9, 1991, unabridged]: TDig 39 (1992) 3-21.

7555 **Pavlou** Telesphora, La cristologia di Trembelas PANAGHIOTIS, un teologo greco ortodosso del nostro secolo: diss. Pont. Univ. Gregoriana, ᴰGalot J. Roma 1992. 621 p.; Extr. 3847, 179 p. – RTLv 24, p. 576.

7556 **Porro** Carlo, Gesù il Salvatore: TViva 7. Bo 1992, Dehoniane. 287 p. Lit. 30.000 [NRT 115, 896, L. *Renwart*].

7557 **Reno** R. R., Christology in political and liberation theology: Thomist 56 (1992) 291-322.

7558 **Rössler** Andreas, Steht Gottes Himmel allen offen? Zum Symbol des kosmischen Christus 1989 → 7,7286: ᴿMüTZ 42 (1991) 93-95 (P. *Schmidt-Leukel*: christologische Fragen); NZMissW 47 (1991) 319s (F. *Kollbrunner*); RHPR 72 (1992) 500s (G. *Siegwalt*).

7559 **Samartha** S., One Christ, many religions; toward a revised Christology. Faith Meets Faith. Mkn 1991, Orbis. 190 p. [TContext 10/1,97, G. *Evers*].

7560 **Scharlemann** Robert P., The reason of following; Christology and the ecstatic, I. Ch 1991, Univ. xi-214 p. $32.50. – ᴿChrCent 109 (1992) 1145s (D. *Pellauer*: biblical basis remote); TS 53 (1992) 767s (J. J. *Mueller*: good, though admittedly idiosyncratic).

7561 **Schoon** Simon, De weg van Jezus, een christologische heroriëntatie vanuit de joods-christelijke ontmoeting. Kampen 1991, Kok. 283 p. ƒ39,50. 90-242-6533-9. – ᴿKerkT 42 (1991) 357s (A. A. *Spijkerboer*).

7562 **Serenthà** Mario, Gesù Cristo ieri, oggi e sempre; saggio di cristologia 1991 → 4,8545; 7,7499: ᴿAntonianum 67 (1992) 440-3 (V. *Battaglia*).

7562* **Sesboüé** B., Gesù Cristo nella tradizione della Chiesa; per una attualizzazione del Concilio di Calcedonia 1987 → [64,6654] 5,7477: ᴿLateranum 57 (1991) 272-4 (M. *Semeraro*).

7563 *Simon* Benoît-Marie, Cristo aveva la visione beatifica?: SacDoc 35 (1990) 555-573.

7564 **Sobrino** Jon, Jesucristo liberador; lectura histórico-teológica de Jesus de Nazaret: Estructuras y procesos, rel. M 1991, Trotta. 359 p. 84-87699-20-0. – ᴿActuBbg 29 (1992) 188-191 (R. *Schwager*: muestra influjo de R. GIRARD).

7565 **Song** C. E., Jesus; the crucified people [Christology from Asian perspective, part 1 of 3] 1990 → 7,7775: ᴿCritRR 5 (1992) 490-2 (Elizabeth A. *Johnson*).

7566 **Sosna** Werner, Die Selbstmitteilung Gottes in Jesus Christus; Grundlagen und dogmatische Explikation der Christologie Herman SCHELLS

[Diss.]: PdTSt 20. Pd 1991, Schöningh. vii-319 p. DM 48. – ᴿMüTZ 43 (1992) 379s (H. *Filser*); TLZ 117 (1992) 915-7 (G. *Pfleiderer*).

7567 **Sturch** Richard, The Word and the Christ; an essay in analytic Christology 1991 ➤ 7,7507: ᴿExpTim 103 (1991s) 156 (V. *White*: closely argued, ultimately orthodox; homely analogies sometimes inept); JTS 43 (1992) 343-5 (A. *Thatcher*: fine insights 'from the middle', but few revisionists will be persuaded); RelSt 28 (1992) 123-5 (T. W. *Bartel*); TLond 95 (1992) 132s (A. *Logan*: able but not perfect defence of tradition); TvT 32 (1992) 210 (H.-E. *Mertens*).

7568 *Sugirtharajah* R. S., What do men say remains of me? Current Jesus research and Third World Christologies: AsiaJT 5 (1991) 331-7 [< ZIT 5,558]; TvT 32 (1992) 436s (F. *Peerlinck*: interdisciplinair).

7569 **Thompson** William M., Christology and spirituality 1991 ➤ 7,7510: ᴿTS 53 (1992) 776-8 (R. P. *Imbelli*: fine; a bit repetitive).

Tilliette Xavier, Le Christ de la philosophie; prolégomènes à une christologie philosophique 1990 ➤ 4456 (5003).

7570 *Willi* Hans-Peter, Theologie der Menschwerdung [PANNENBERG W., Syst. II]: TBeit 22 (1991) 332-... [< ZIT 91,789].

7571 **Wohlmuth** Josef, Jesu Weg — unser Weg; kleine mystagogische Christologie. Wü 1992, Echter. 240 p. DM 34. 3-429-01433-6. – ᴿHerdKor 46 (1992) 438s (A. S.).

7572 *Wostyn* Lode L., Doing Christology after Vatican II: EAPast 28 (1991) 253-269.

H5.5   *Spiritus Sanctus; pneumatologia*   –   The Holy Spirit.

7573 **Alanda** Antonio, Estudios de pneumatología 1985 ➤ 2,5678 ... 7,7518: ᴿRThom 92 (1992) 781 (S.-T. *Bonino*: de valeur).

7574 *Boogaert* Thomas A., Israel's experience of the Spirit: RefR 45,1 (1991) 5-21 [< ZIT 92,18].

7575 **Brooks** Gregory K., The role of the Holy Spirit in moral discernment with attention to the thought of José COMBLIN: diss. Southern Baptist Theol. Sem. 1992, ᴰSimmons P. 215 p. 92-28429. – DissA 53 (1992s) 1553-A.

7576 **Chevallier** Max-Alain, Souffle de Dieu III, 1991 ➤ 7,7523: ᴿÉTRel 67 (1992) 114s (É. *Cuvillier*); RThom 92 (1992) 759-761 (S.-T. *Bonino*); RTLv 23 (1992) 321 (A. de *Halleux*, 2); ScEspr 44 (1992) 98-100 (L. *Sabourin*).

7577 **Comblin** José, The Holy Spirit and liberation [1987], ᵀBurns Paul: Liberation & Theology 4, 1989 ➤ 5,7547 ... 7,7524: ᴿBijdragen 53 (1992) 450 (J.-J. *Suurmond*: full of wisdom, except 'Flora' for 'Fiora').

7578 **Comblin** J., Spirito Santo e liberazione [1987], ᵀᴱPompei G.: TLib 2/4. Assisi 1989, Cittadella. 243 p. Lit. 20.000. – ᴿAsprenas 39 (1992) 117s (G. *Tubiello*).

7579 *Coste* René, Théologie de l'Esprit Saint et notre responsabilité chrétienne aujourd'hui; brèves réflexions à propos de la Septième Assemblée du Conseil Œcuménique des Églises: EsprVie 102 (1992) 145-152.

7580 **Doutreleau** L., DIDYME l'Aveugle, Traité du S. Esprit: SChr 386. P 1992, Cerf. 449 p. F 166. 2-204-4601-6. [NRT 115, 432, V. *Roisel*].

7580* **Ferlay** Philippe, Dieu le Saint-Esprit 1990 ➤ 7,7527: ᴿAtKap 117 (1991) 154-7 (A. *Nowicki*).

7581 *Forte* Bruno, a) La Trinità e la 'pericoresi'; lo Spirito Santo come vita e come forza: StEcum 9 (1991) 245-267; Eng. 267; – b) Trinität und 'perichorese'; der Geist als Leben und Kraft: UnSa 46 (1991) 9-21.

7581* *Gaffin* Richard J, The gifts of the Holy Spirit: RefTR 51 (1992) 1-10.

7582 *Gisel* Pierre, Promesses et risques d'une théologie du Saint-Esprit: LavalTP 48 (1992) 351-366.

7583 *Gräbe* P. J., *Dýnamis* (in the sense of power) as a pneumatological concept in the main Pauline letters: BZ 36 (1992) 226-235.

7584 ᵀᴱ**Granado** Carmelo, CIRILO de Jerusalén, El Espíritu Santo. M 1990, Ciudad Nuova. 101 p. – ᴿCiuD 205 (1992) 256s (J. M. *Ozaeta*).

7585 *a) Hauke* Manfred, La discusión sobre el simbolismo femenino de la imagen de Dios en la pneumatología; – *b) Margerie* Bertrand de, Sobre el Espíritu Santo y la vida cristiana: ScripTPamp 24 (1992) 1005-1027 / 993-1004.

7586 **Hawthorne** Gerald F., The power and the presence; the significance of the Holy Spirit in the life and ministry of Jesus [< 1954 master's thesis]. Dallas 1991, Word. xii-264 p. $15 pa. – ᴿCritRR 5 (1992) 217s (C. A. *Evans*: mature and thoughtful, though not critical).

7587 *Horn* F. W., Holy Spirit: ➤ 741, AnchorBD 3 (1992) 260-278 (ᵀ*Elliott* D.); 278-280 bibliog.

7588 *Jackson* Pamela, CYRIL of Jerusalem's treatment of scriptural texts concerning the Holy Spirit: Traditio 46 (1991) 1-31.

7589 **Koch** Robert, Der Geist Gottes im Alten Testament. Fra 1991, Lang. 147 p. 3-631-43885-0.

7590 **Kooi** Akke Van der, Het heilige en de Heilige Geest bij NOORDMANS: diss. ᴰ*Neven* G. Kampen 1992. 342 p. – RTLv 24, p. 577.

7591 *Langella* Alfonso, Mariologia e pneumatologia; il magistero di PAOLO VI e di GIOVANNI PAOLO II: Asprenas 39 (1992) 500-518.

7592 *La Potterie* Ignace de [6 art.], *Lyonnet* Stanislas [†4 art.], La vita secondo lo Spirito condizione del cristiano: Teologia oggi 1. R 1992, A.V.E. 359 p. Lit. 32000.

7593 **McDonnell** Kilian, **Montague** George, Christian initiation and baptism in the Holy Spirit 1991 ➤ 7,7536: ᴿEsprVie 102 (1992) 349 (P. *Rouillard*); ExpTim 103 (1991s) 57 (G. *Bostock*); RHE 87 (1992) 551 (P. H. *Daly*); RThom 92 (1992) 595s (H. *Ponsot*); TS 53 (1992) 344s (R. P. *Imbelli*).

7594 *Min* Anselm K., Renewing the doctrine of the Spirit; a prolegomenon [Euro-American Seminar AAR, Kansas City Nov. 1991]: PerspRelSt 19 (1992) 183-198.

7595 **Moltmann** Jürgen, Der Geist des Lebens; eine ganzheitliche Pneumatologie. Mü 1991, Kaiser. 335 p. DM 48 [TR 88,82]. – ᴿTGL 82 (1992) 268-270 (G. *Fuchs*); TsTKi 63 (1992) 72s (J.-O. *Henriksen*).

7596 ᵀᴱ**Noce** Celestino, DIDIMO il Cieco, Lo Spirito Santo: TPatr 89, 1990 ➤ 6,7569: ᴿAsprenas 39 (1992) 595s (D. *Pennino*); Salesianum 54 (1992) 383 (S. *Felici*: pervenuto nel latino di GIROLAMO; prima versione italiana).

7597 **O'Carroll** Michael, Veni Creator Spiritus; a theological encyclopedia of the Holy Spirit. ColMn 1990, Liturgical. 235 p. $30. 0-8146 5785-0. – ᴿTS 55 (1992) 164s (J. F. *Russell*: roams idiosyncratically).

7598 **Paprocki** Henryk, La promesse du Père; l'expérience du Saint-Esprit dans l'Église orthodoxe, ᵀ*Lhoest* Françoise: Théologies, 1990 ➤ 7,7538*: ᴿRThom 92 (1992) 763 (S.-T. *Bonino*); RTLv 23 (1992) 237s (A. de *Halleux*).

7599 *Parthenios* patr. Aless., Lo Spirito Santo [Canberra 1991]: StEcum 9 (1991) 111-124.

7600 *Pedrini* Arnaldo, Simbologie e denominazioni dello Spirito Santo nella dottrina di S. Francesco di SALES, ricerca biblico-teologica: Teresianum 43 (1992) 389-416.

7601 a) *Potter* Philip, Bijbelstudies over de Heilige Geest; – b) *Brinkman* Martien, 'Kom Heilige Geest, vernieuw de hele schepping': Wereld en Zending 20,3 (Amst 1991) 7-13 / 23-31 [< ZIT 91,692].

7602 *Pratscher* Wilhelm, Pneumatologie, biblisch: → 757, EvKL 3 (1992) 1242-7 (-52, *al.*).

7603 **Rea** John, The Holy Spirit in the Bible. Altamonte FL 1989, Strang. 394 p. $20. 0-88419-261-X. – ᴿBtS 149 (1992) 109 (R. P. *Lightner*).

7604 **Rebell** W., Erfüllung und Erwartung; Erfahrungen mit dem Geist im Urchristentum. Mü 1991, Kaiser. 196 p. DM 54. 3-459-01882-8. – ᴿTvT 32 (1992) 315 (A. van *Schaik*).

7605 *Reymond* Bernard, Entre effusions, épiclèses et codes culturels; le Saint-Esprit dans le culte: RTPhil 124 (1992) 139-156.

7606 **Romerowski** Sylvain, L'œuvre du Saint Esprit ancienne et nouvelle [< diss. Westminster]. Mulhouse 1989, Centre de Culture Chrétienne. 131 p. – ᴿSTEv 3 (1991) 268s (P. *Bolognesi*).

7607 **Royo Marín** Antonio, The great unknown; the Holy Spirit and his gifts [1975], ᵀ. Sunbury PA 1991, Western Hemisphere. xvii-179 p. $13.50 pa. [TDig 40,184].

7608 *Schenk* Wolfgang, 'Heiliger Geist' — eine Simulationskategorie?: LingBib 66 (1992) 5-38; Eng. 38: the expression 'Holy Spirit' is used largely as a category of 'simulation', which makes Christianity degnerate to a 'Platonism for common people'; impression of a far-reaching forgery coinage.

7609 **Strong** Barry R., The economy of the Spirit in ecumenical perspective [diss]. R 1991, Pont. Univ. Gregoriana. xvi-536 p. – TR 88, 171.

7610 **Stubenrauch** Bertram, Der Heilige Geist bei APPONIUS; zum theologischen Gehalt einer spätantiken Hoheliedauslegung [Diss. Lateranum 1991, ᴰ*Studer* B.]: RömQ Supp 46. R 1991, Herder. xiii-256 p. 3-451-22473-9. – ᴿTGL 82 (1992) 370-2 (H. R. *Drobner*).

7611 **Thompson** John, The Holy Spirit in the theology of Karl BARTH. PrincetonTMg. Alison Park PA 1991, Pickwick. vii-211 p. $24. 0-915138-94-8. – ᴿExpTim 103 (1991s) 221 (C. *Gunton*: rightly questions ROSATO's thesis that Barth is primarily a theologian of the Spirit; anyway he is essentially Augustinian); JTS 43 (1992) 316 (T. *Gorringe*: thorough, but with less fresh air than in Rosato).

7612 **Welker** Michael, Gottes Geist; Theologie des Heiligen Geistes. Neuk 1992. 333 p. DM 31. [TR 88,347].

7613 *Wells* Harold, Holy Spirit and theology of the Cross; significance for dialogue: TS 53 (1992) 476-492.

7614 **Ziebritzki** Henning, Heiliger Geist und Weltenseele; das Problem der dritten Hypostase bei ORIGENES, PLOTIN und ihren Vorläufern: ev. Diss. ᴰ*May* G. Mainz 1992. – RTLv 24, p. 552.

H5.6 *Spiritus et Filius*; **'Spirit-Christology'**, Filioque.

7615 *Bauerschmidt* John C., 'Filioque' and the Episcopal Church: AnglTR 73 (1991) 7-25.

7616 *Callahan* Daniel F., The problem of the 'Filioque' and the letter from the pilgrim monks of the Mount of Olives; is the letter another forgery by ADÉMAR of Chabannes?: RBén 102 (1992) 75-134.

7617 **Durrwell** François-X., L'Esprit du Père et du Fils 1989 → 5,7575: ᴿAtKap 116 (1991) 542-4 (A. *Nowicki*, ●); RThom 92 (1992) 762s (S.-T. *Bonino*: répudie 'une théologie plus rationnelle que biblique').

7618 *Durrwell* F.X., Pour une christologie selon l'Esprit Saint: NRT 114 (1992) 653-677.

Eaton Michael A., Baptism with the Spirit ... Eph 1,13, 1989 ➤ 6575.

7618* *Haight* Roger, The case for Spirit Christology: TS 53 (1992) 257-287.

7619 **Hawthorne** Gerald F., The presence and the power [... of the Holy Spirit in Jesus]. Dallas 1991, Word. 264 p. 0-8499-3220-3. – ᴿBtS 149 (1992) 108s (R.P. *Lightner*: 'a definitive study of the relationship of the Holy Spirit to Jesus'); RExp 89 (1992) 106 (J. Estill *Jones*).

7620 *Huculak* Benedykt, Indole della teologia trinitaria greca [... Filioque at Florence 1431-7]: Antonianum 67 (1992) 123-141; Eng. 123.

7621 *Letourneau* Pierre, Le double don de l'Esprit et la Christologie du quatrième Évangile: ScEsp 44 (1992) 281-306.

7622 **Riaud** Alexis, *a*) L'Esprit du Père et du Fils; une étude nouvelle de l'Esprit-Saint et de la vie trinitaire. P 1984, Nouvelles éd. latines. 148 p. – *b*) Le 'Filioque'; origine et rôle de la troisième Personne de la Trinité 1989 ➤ 6,7578*: ᴿRThom 92 (1992) 761s (S.-T. *Bonino*).

7623 **Schoonenberg** Piet, De Geest, het Woord en de Zoon; theologische overdenkingen over Geest-Christologie, Logos-Christologie en drieëenheidsleer. Averbode/Kampen 1991, Altiora/Kok. 258 p. Fb 1095. – ᴿCollatVL 22 (1992) 91-95 (R. *Michiels*).

7624 **Schoonenberg** P., Der Geist, das Wort und der Sohn, eine Geist-Christologie [De Geest 1991]ᵀ. Rg 1992, Pustet. 221 p. DM 48 [NRT 115, 891, L. *Renwart*].

7625 *Wong* Joseph H.P., The Holy Spirit in the life of Jesus and of the Christian: Gregorianum 73 (1992) 57-95; franç. 95.

H5.7 *Ssma Trinitas* – **The Holy Trinity.**

7626 *Barrigar* Christian J., Protecting God; the lexical formation of Trinitarian language: ModT 7 (1990s) 299-310 [< zɪᴛ 91,604].

7627 *Beck* Heinrich, Triadische Götter-Ordnungen; klassisch-antiker und neuplatonischer Ansatz: TPhil 67 (1992) 230-245.

7627* **Boff** Leonardo, Trinità, la migliore comunità 1990 ➤ 7,7556*a*; Lit. 15.000: ᴿCC 143 (1992,1) 88s (P. *Vanzan*).

Boyd Gregory A., Trinity and process 1992 ➤ 7030.

Bracken Joseph A., Society and Spirit; a trinitarian cosmology 1991 ➤ 7031.

7628 *Brändle* Werner, Immanente Trinität — ein 'Denkmal der Kirchengeschichte'? [... ᴿᴀʜɴᴇʀ K.]: KerDo 38 (1992) 185-198; Eng. 198.

7629 *Brito* Emilio, ꜱᴄʜʟᴇɪᴇʀᴍᴀᴄʜᴇʀ et la doctrine de la Trinité; réflexions critiques: RTLv 23 (1992) 145-171 . 321-342; Eng. 295.

7630 *Buth* Randall B., Trinitarian conflict; a re-assessment of trinitarian analogies in the light of modern psychological and sociological conflict theories: ➤ 133, ꜰᴍɪʟʟs W., PerspRelSt 19 (1992) 9-37.

7631 ᵀᴱ**Cataldo** Antonio, ᴄɪʀɪʟʟᴏ di Alessandria, Dialoghi sulla Trinità: TPatr 98. R 1992, Città Nuova. 407 p. Lit. 38.000. 88-311-3098-6.

7631* **Faber** Roland, Freiheit, Theologie und Lehramt; trinitätstheologische Grundlegung und wissenschaftstheoretischer Ausblick. Innsbruck 1992, Tyrolia. 126 p. DM 22. – ᴿTGL 82 (1992) 482 (W. *Beinert*: komplizierte Diktion).

7632 **Forte** Bruno, The Trinity as history; saga of the Christian God [1985 ➤ 1,7061] 1990 ➤ 5,7591: ᴿHomP 91,7 (1990s) 71s (J.R. *Sheets*: important).

7633 **Forte** Bruno, La Trinité comme histoire 1989 ➤ 5,7590; 6,7588: ᴿRThom 92 (1992) 756-9 (S.-T. *Bonino*).

7634 **Forte** Bruno, Trinität als Geschichte; der lebendige Gott — Gott der Lebenden: G-Reihe 15. Mainz 1989, Grünewald. 224 p. DM 36. 3-7867-1404-5. ➤ 6,7589; ᵀ*Richter* Jorinde: ᴿLebZeug 45 (1990) 311-3 (H. *Lenz*, auch über SPLETT H.); RTLv 23 (1992) 370s (A. de *Halleux*).

7635 **Gironés** Gonzalo, La divina arqueología [... *archē*]... Trinidad 1991 ➤ 7,7563: ᴿCiuD 205 (1992) 248s (J. M. *Ozaeta*) & 262s (S. *Folgado Flórez*), Gregorianum 73 (1992) 549s (J. *Galot*); ScripTPamp 23 (1991) 1058s (A. *Aranda*).

7636 **Grözinger** Albrecht, Erzählen und Handeln; Studien zu einer trinitarischen Grundlegung der Praktischen Theologie: Tb 70, 1989 ➤ 6,7593; 3-459-01832-1: ᴿBijdragen 53 (1992) 336s (J. *Besemer*).

7637 **Gunton** Colin, The promise of Trinitarian theology. E 1991, Clark. x-198 p. £15 [TR 88,82]. – ᴿAnglTR 74 (1992) 396-8 (D. A. *Scott*); ExpTim 103 (1991s) 156s (R. *Butterworth*); JTS 43 (1992) 780-2 (L. *Ayres*); RefTR 51 (1992) 112s (R. C. *Doyle*); TLond 95 (1992) 133s (D. *Brown*); TS 53 (1992) 560s (P. D. *Molnar*); TTod 49 (1992s) 409s (M. L. *Raposa*).

7638 *Hammerstaedt* Jürgen, Der trinitarische Gebrauch des Hypostasisbegriffs bei ORIGENES: JbAC 34 (1991) 12-20.

7638* ᴱ**Heron** Alasdair I. C., The forgotten Trinity, 3. A selection of papers presented to the BCC study commission. L 1991, BCC. xii-196 p. £16 pa. – ᴿTLond 95 (1992) 450-2 (G. *Rowell*).

7639 **Hilberath** Bernd J., Der dreieinige Gott und die Gemeinschaft der Menschen; Orientierung zur christlichen Rede von Gott. Mainz 1990, Grünewald. 120 p. DM 20. 3-7867-1476-2. – ᴿÉTRel 67 (1992) 131 (J.-L. *Klein*).

7640 *Iammarrone* Luigi, *Polionato* Livio, Trinità come amore; la dottrina trinitaria di RICCARDO di S. Vittore: MiscFranc 92 (1992) 33-83.

7641 **Jones** L. Gregory, Transformed judgement; towards a trinitarian account of the moral life. ND 1990, Univ. xi-189 p. $23 [TD 88,172].

7641* **Kaliba** Clemens, Die Welt als Gleichnis des dreieinigen Gottes; Entwurf zu einer trinitarischen Ontologie [1952 mit Vorwort, *Beck* Heinrich]: Schriften zur Triadik und Ontodynamik 4. Fra 1991, Lang. – ᴿFreibZ 38 (1991) 495s (A. J. *Bucher*).

7642 **Kelly** Anthony, The Trinity of love 1989 ➤ 6,7595; 7,7568: ᴿPacifica 4 (1991) 229-232 (D. *Coffey*).

7643 **LaCugna** Catherine M., God for us; the Trinity and Christian life. SF 1992, Harper. xiv-434 p. $25. – ᴿTS 53 (1992) 558-560 (J. A. *Bracken*).

7644 *Lison* Jacques, L'énergie des trois hypostases divines selon Grégoire PALAMAS [d'Athos; évêque de Thessalonique † 1359: hésychasme; déification]: ScEspr 44 (1992) 67-77.

7644* *McFadyen* Alistair, The Trinity and human individuality; the conditions for relevance: TLond 95 (1992) 10-18.

7645 **Melotti** Luigi, Un solo Padre, un solo Signore, un solo Spirito; saggio di teologia trinitaria: Saggi Teol. T-Leumann 1991, Elle Di Ci. 307 p. Lit. 23.000 [TR 88,82]. – ᴿCC 143 (1992,1) 206s (G. *Ferraro*); Divinitas 36 (1992) 276s (D. *Vibrac*).

7646 **Merriel** D. Juvenal, To the image of the Trinity; a study of the development of AQUINAS' teaching. Toronto 1990, Pontifical Institute of Medieval Studies. x-266 p. – ᴿAngelicum 69 (1992) 143s (A. *Wilder*).

7647 **Moltmann** Jürgen, In der Geschichte des dreieinigen Gottes; Beiträge zur trinitarischen Theologie 1991 ➤ 7,7572: ᴿEvKomm 24 (1991) 557s (W. *Rebell*); TGL 82 (1992) 149-151 (G. *Fuchs*).

7648 **Moltmann** Jürgen, History and the triune God — contributions to trinitarian theology [In der Geschichte 1991 ➤ 7,7572], ᵀ*Bowden* John. L 1991, SPCK. 204 p. £13. 0-334-02513-3. – ᴿExpTim 103 (1991s) 249 (J. *Macquarrie*: part 2 'conversations' with AQUINAS, FIORE, BARTH ...; interesting 20-page autobiography appended).

7648* **Moltmann** Jürgen, Treenigheten och Guds rike [1980 ➤ 63,7453], ᵀ*Hemrin* Sven. Sto 1991, Verbum. 276 p. – ᴿTsTKi 63 (1992) 73s (J.-O. *Henriksen*).

7649 **Navone** John, Self-giving and sharing; the trinity of human fulfilment. ColMn c. 1992, Liturgical. 161 p. – ᴿFurrow 42 (1991) 394-6 (G. *O'Hanlon*: a collection of meditations).

7650 **O'Donnell** John J., The mystery of the triune God 1989 ➤ 4,8626 ... 7,7573: ᴿPerspRelSt 19 (1992) 100-4 (C. *Marsh*, also on 1990 PLAN-TINGA-FEENSTRA compilation).

7651 **Pikaza** Xabier, Trinidad y comunidad cristiana; el principio social del cristianismo: Koinonia 30, 1990 ➤ 7,7578: ᴿLumenVr 40 (1991) 197s (F. *Ortiz de Urtaran*); SalT 78 (1990) 885s (E. T.).

7652 **Radlbeck** Regina, Personbegriff 1989 ➤ 6,7607; 7,7579: ᴿBijdragen 53 (1992) 220 (W. G. *Tillmans*); RThom 92 (1992) 555-7 (G. *Emery*).

7653 *Ripa di Meana* Paolo, All'ascolto di un 'pensiero forte'; la dottrina tomista della Trinità: Salesianum 54 (1992) 9-39.

7654 **Rovira Belloso** Josep M., Vivir en comunión; comunión trinitaria, comunión eucarística y comunión fraterna. S 1991, Secretariado Trinitario. 187 p. – ᴿSalT 80 (1992) 875-7 (N. *Silanes*).

7655 ᴱ**Schadel** E., *al.* Bibliotheca Trinitariorum I-II, 1984-8 ➤ 65,929 ... 7, 7582: ᴿBijdragen 53 (1992) 318s (K. *Hedwig*).

7656 **Smart** Ninian, *Konstantine* Steven, Christian systematic theology in a world context. L/Mp 1991, Marshall Pickering / Fortress. 466 p. £15. 0-551-02055-5 / 0-8006-2515-3. – ᴿExpTim 103 (1991s) 157 (W. D. *Hudson*: a 'social' doctrine of the Trinity: N's erudition, K's ingenuity: 'we find it easy to talk with the Trinity for we know that she suffered alongside of us').

7657 **Tavard** Georges, La Trinité: Bref. P 1991, Cerf/Fides. 128 p. - ᴿRThom 92 (1992) 759 (S.-T. *Bonino*).

7658 **Torrance** T. F., The Trinitarian faith 1988 ➤ 4,8640 ... 7,7592: ᴿAngl-TR 73 (1991) 214-6 (D. A. *Scott*).

7659 **Twombly** Charles C., *Perichoresis* and personhood in the thought of John of DAMASCUS: diss. Emory, ᴰ*Bondi* Roberta C. Atlanta 1992. 216 p. 92-24956. – DissA 53 (1992s) 1560-A.

H5.8 *Regnum messianicum, Filius hominis* – **Messianic kingdom, Son of Man.**

7660 *Batstone* David B., Jesus, apocalyptic and world transformation: TTod 49 (1992s) 383-397.

7660* **Beyerhaus** Peter P. J., God's kingdom and the utopian error; discerning the biblical Kingdom of God from its political counterfeits. Wheaton IL 1992, Crossway. 221 p. $13. 0-89107-651-4 [TDig 40,52: essays criticizing the ecumenical movement for its development of a new type of missionary vision].

7661 **Campolo** Tony, The Kingdom of God is a party. Dallas 1990, Word. 150 p. 0-8499-0767-5. – ᴿRExp 89 (1992) 301s (D. F. *D'Amico*: well written).

7662 *Cho Kyu-Man*, The Kingdom of God in the Old Testament and in the writings of later Judaism: Catholic Theology and Thought 8 (Seoul 1992) 147-178 [< TContext 10/2, 47].

7663 *Collins* John J., The Son of Man in first-century Judaism: NTS 38 (1992) 448-466.

7664 *Duling* Dennis C., Kingdom of God [also OT]: ➤ 741, AnchorBD 4 (1992) 49-69.

7665 *Erickson* Millard J., Lordship theology; the current controversy: SWJT 13 (1991) 5-15 [< BtS 148 (1991) 360s (D. L. *Bock*)].

7666 **Habichler** A., Reich Gottes als Thema des Denkens bei KANT; Entwicklungsgeschichtliche und systematische Studie zur Kantischen Reich-Gottes-Idee [Diss. Tü ᴰ*Seckler* M.]: TüStTP 2. Mainz 1991, Grünewald. 301 p. DM 48. 3-7867-1540-8 – ᴿMüTZ 43 (1992) 259s (W. W. *Müller*); TvT 32 (1992) 201s (H. M. *Kuitert*: a must; add YOVEL Y., Kant and the philosophy of history 1980).

7667 **Hampel** Volker, Menschensohn und historischer Jesus ᴰ1990 ➤ 6,7624; 7,7601: ᴿCBQ 54 (1992) 154s (B. F. *Meyer*: abundant survey of options for theses not quite nailed down); JBL 111 (1992) 139-141 (R. H. *Fuller*); TLZ 117 (1992) 39-41 (G. *Haufe*).

7668 **Hare** Douglas R. A., The Son of Man tradition 1990 ➤ 6,7625; 7,7602: ᴿBZ 36 (1992) 143-6 (W. *Radl*); CBQ 54 (1992) 782s (A. K. M. *Adam*); ExpTim 103 (1991s) 25s (J. M. *Court*: excellent); FgNt 5 (1992) 312s (S. E. *Porter*); HeythJ 33 (1992) 447s (D. *Burkett*); Interpretation 46 (1992) 406s (P. M. *Casey*); JAAR 60 (1992) 550-3 (W. O. *Walker*); JBL 111 (1992) 535-7 (T. P. *Haverly*); JTS 43 (1992) 580-2 (Morna D. *Hooker*); TLZ 117 (1992) 357-9 (H. *Bietenhard*).

7669 ᴱ**Hengel** M., *Schwemer* A. M., Königsherrschaft Gottes 1984/91 ➤ 7, 438: ᴿArTGran 55 (1992) 333s (A. *Segovia*); TGgw 35 (1992) 71-73 (H. *Giesen*); StPhilonAn 4 (1992) 145s (D. *Zeller*); TvT 32 (1992) 194 (H. *Welzen*).

7670 **Kosch** Daniel, Die eschatologische Tora des Menschensohnes ... in Q: NOrb 12, 1989 ➤ 5,7626; 7,7609: ᴿCBQ 54 (1992) 357s (R. D. *Witherup*: skilful reconstruction, overconfident conclusions); ÉTRel 67 (1992) 107s (P. *Magne de la Croix*); TLZ 117 (1992) 191s (D. *Lührmann*); TR 88 (1992) 28s (D. *Zeller*).

7671 — *Dautzenberg* Gerhard, Tora des Menschensohnes? Kritische Überlegungen zu Daniel KOSCH: BZ 36 (1992) 93-103.

7671* *Kreuzer* Siegfried, Gottesherrschaft als Grundthema alttestamentlicher Theologie: ➤ 163, ᶠSAUER G., Aktualität 1992, 57-72.

7672 *a*) *Larsson* Edvin, [in Norwegian] Gospel with no claim? Kingdom of God and demands of God in the preaching of Jesus: TsTKi 62 (1991) 81-94.

— *b*) *Levy* B. Barry, Why Bar-nash does not mean 'I': ➤ 180*c*, Mem. TALMAGE F. 1 (1992s) 85-101.

— *c*) *Lubsczyk* Johannes, Gott offenbart das Geheimnis seines Reiches im Kommen des Menschensohnes: ➤ 32, ᶠErfurt 1992, 216-243.

7672* **Margerie** Bertrand de, Liberté religieuse et règne du Christ 1988 ➤ 4, 8662 ... 6,7630: ᴿRThom 92 (1992) 564-7 (D.-M. de *Saint-Laumer*: des réflexions intéressantes et urgentes, malgré un côté un peu superficiel et concordiste).

7673 *Moltmann* J., Primero el reino de Dios [< Herrschaft im Himmel oder auf Erden? EvKomm 22/8 (1989) 10-15], ᵀᴱ *Escrivá* M.-Dolores: SelT 30 (1991) 3-12.

7674 **Premawardhana** Shanta D. E.,   Purusa and the Son of Man; a comparative study of mythology: diss. Northwestern, ᴰ*Perry* E.   Evanston 1992. 208 p. 92-29981. – DissA 53 (1992s) 1956-A.

7675 *Richard* Jean (docteur honoris causa de Montpellier),   Royaume de Dieu et justification par grâce: ÉTRel 67 (1992) 493-) 495-524.

7676 *Ross* J. M., The Son of Man: IrBSt 13 (1991) 186-198 [< ᴢɪᴛ 91,726].

7677 **Snyder** Howard A.,   Models of the Kingdom.   Nv 1991, Abingdon. 176 p. $11.   0-687-27104-5 [TDig 39,288; RelStR 19,63, B. *Stiltner*].

7678 *Spieckermann* Hermann, [*Pratscher* Wilhelm], Reich Gottes AT [NT]: ➔ 757, EvKL 3 (1992) 1526s [1527-31].

7679 *a) Spijker* W. van 't,   Het Koninkrijk van Christus bij Bucer en bij Calvin; – *b) Koyeer* R. W. de, 'Pneumatologia': TRef 34 (Woerden 1991) 202-225 / 226-... [< ᴢɪᴛ 91,652].

7680 *a) Vaage* Leif E.,   Monarchy, community, anarchy; the Kingdom of God in Paul and Q; – *b) Barreto César* Ely E.,   The historical radicality of the Reign of God; a paradigm for our missionary efforts: ➔ 74, ꜰGuenther H., TorJT 8 (1992) 52-69 / 148-160.

7681 **Viviano** Benedict T.,   Le Royaume de Dieu dans l'histoire [1988 ➔ 4, 8671], ᵀ*Prignaud* Jean: Lire la Bible 96. P 1992, Cerf. 258 p. 2-204-04544-6.

7682 **Way** David,   The Lordship of Christ... Käsemann's/Paul (diss. Ox 1987, ᴰ*Morgan* R.) 1991 ➔ 7,7616: ᴿTS 53 (1992) 340-2 (D. J. *Harrington*).

7683 *Welker* Michael,   *a)* Das Reich Gottes: EvT 52 (1992) 497-512; – *b)* The reign of God: TTod 49 (1992s) 500-515.

7684 **Wiebe** Ben,   Messianic ethics; Jesus' proclamation of the Kingdom of God and the Church in response.   Scottdale PA 1992, Herald.   224 p. $16. 0-8361-3585-7 [TDig 40,193].

H6.1   *Creatio, sabbatum NT* [➔ E3.5]; **The Creation** [➔ E1.6; H2.8].

7685 *Bacq* Philippe,   Sabbat juif, dimanche chrétien: LVitae 47 (1992) 127-138 [-229, *al.*].

7686 **Bayer** Oswald,   Schöpfung als Anrede 1986 ➔ 2,5816... 4,8674: ᴿZev-Eth 36 (1992) 74s (H.-G. *Pöhlmann*).

7687 **Bieler** Martin,   Freiheit als Gabe; ein schöpfungstheologischer Entwurf [ev. Diss. Bern summa cum laude]: FreibTSt 145. FrB 1991, Herder. 528 p. DM 58.   3-451-22294-0. – ᴿNRT 114 (1992) 122s (L. *Renwart*); TLZ 117 (1992) 297s (R. *Becker*); TvT 32 (1992) 327 (H. M. *Kuitert*).

 Brito E.,   La création selon Schelling 1987 ➔ 2038.

7688 ᴱ**Burrell** David B., *McGinn* Bernard,   God and creation, an ecumenical symposium.. ND/Ch, Apr. 26-28, 1987:   1989 ➔ 6,584*: ᴿSpeculum 67 (1992) 770 (tit. pp.).

7688* **Chantry** Walter,   Call the Sabbath a delight. Carlisle PA 1991, Banner of Truth.   112 p. $6. – ᴿWestTJ 54 (1992) 191-3 (D. *Strickland*: detriments outweigh advantages).

 ᴱ**Clifford** Richard J., *Collins* John J.,   Creation in the biblical tradition: CBQ mg 24, 1992 ➔ 346.

7689 **Dawn** Marva J.,   Keeping the Sabbath wholly 1989 ➔ 6,7645: ᴿWestTJ 53 (1991) 168-171 (L. C. *Sibley*: good but eclectic).

7689* *Fantino* Jacques,   La création ex nihilo chez saint Irénée; étude historique et théologique: RSPT 76 (1992) 421-442; Eng. 442.

7690 *Gelabert Ballester* Martin,   La creación a la luz del misterio trinitario: EscVedat 22 (1992) 7-45.

7691 ᴱGesché A., *al.*, Création et salut: Fac.S.Louis Publ 47, 1989 ⇒ 6,411*b*; 2-8028-0068-X: ᴿFoiTemps 21 (1991) 71-73 (G. *Harpigny*): TvT [= Ts-TNijm] 32 (1992) 108 (R. *Munnik*).

7692 *Gross* Walter, Sabbat am Sonntag? Der Streit um die Sonntagsarbeit aus bibeltheologischer Sicht: ⇒ 340, Sozialethik 1992, 91-106.

7692* *Günther* Hartmut, Herrentag und Arbeitsruhe; biblisch-theologische Überlegungen zu Feier des Sonntags: LuthTKi 16 (1992) 128-138.

7693 **Gunton** Colin E., Christ and creation (Didsbury Lectures). Carlisle/GR 1992, Paternoster/Eerdmans. 127 p.

7694 *Hamm* Dennis, Reinventing the sabbath: RRel 51 (1992) 721-732.

7694* *Hawthorne* Gerald F., Faith, the essential ingredient of effective Christian ministry: ⇒ 126, ᶠMARTIN R., Worship 1992, 163-179 / 260-272 / 249-259.

7695 *Hoeps* Reinhard, Theophanie und Schöpfungsgrund; der Beitrag des Johannes Scotus ERIUGENA zum Verständnis der *creatio ex nihilo*: TPhil 67 (1992) 161-191.

7696 *Hütter* Reinhard, 'Creatio ex nihilo'; promise of the gift: CurrTMiss 19 (1992) 89-97.

7697 *a) Latorre* Jordi, Del sábado al domingo en la Escritura; – *b) Castellano Cervera* Jesús, Una espiritualidad del domingo; teología, mistagogía, compromiso: Phase 32 (1992) 453-474 / 475-490.

7698 *Leftow* Brian, Why didn't God create the world sooner?: RelSt 27 (1991) 157-172.

7699 **Link** Christian, Schöpfungstheologie, 1. in reformatorischer Tradition; 2. angesichts der Herausforderungen des 20. Jahrhunderts: HbSysT 7. Gü 1991, Mohn. xix-329 p.; xiv-267 p. DM 78 + 48. 3-579-04921-6; -2-4. – ᴿEvT 52 (1992) 86-92 (J. *Moltmann*: 'Schöpfung im Horizont der Zeit'); TvT 32 (1992) 428s (P. *Valkenberg*).

7700 *López Martín* Julián, El orígen del domingo, estado actual de la cuestión: Salmanticensis 38 (1991) 269-297; Eng. 297.

7700* **McClymond** Michael J., Creation in Jonathan EDWARDS: diss. ᴰGilpin W. Chicago 1992, – RTLv 24, p. 555.

7701 ᴱMensen Bernhard, Die Schöpfung in den Religionen 1989/90 ⇒ 7, 530: ᴿTGL 82 (1992) 359s (K. J. *Tossou*).

7702 **Oliva** Blanchette, The perfection of the universe according to AQUINAS; a teleological cosmology. Univ. Park 1992, Penn State Univ. xvii- 334 p. – ᴿAngelicum 69 (1992) 565-9 (C. *Vansteenkiste,* Eng.; '1922').

7703 *a) Piattelli* Abramo A., La teologia della creazione e il sabato; – *b) Angelini* Giuseppe, Ecologia e vangelo della creazione: ⇒ 490, Lateranum 1992, 263-9 / 271-288.

7704 *Rendtorff* Rolf, Some reflections on creation as a topic of OT theology: ⇒ 19, BLENKINSOPP J. 1992, 204-212.

7705 *Rikhof* Herwi, Reden van bestaan; over de plaats en functie van de scheppingstheologie: TvT 32 (1992) 250-271; Eng. 271.

7706 *Wohlmuth* Josef, Schöpfung bei Emmanuel LÉVINAS: ZkT 114 (1992) 408-424.

ʜ6.3 *Fides, veritas in NT* – **Faith and truth.**

7707 **Ansaldi** Jean, L'articulation de la foi, de la théologie et des Écritures: CogF 163, 1991 ⇒ 7,7642: ᴿLavalTP 48 (1992) 133s (R.-M. *Roberge*); NRT 114 (1992) 106s (G. *Navez*).

7708 **Ardusso** F., Imparare a credere; le ragioni della fede cristiana: Universa Teol 8. CinB 1992, Paoline. 212 p. Lit. 15.000 [NRT 115, 578].

7708* *Backes* Jakob, Die Glaubensanalyse ALBERTS des Grossen: FranzSt 72 (1990) 272-288.

7709 E**Beinert** W., Glaube als Zustimmung [Berlin 1990]: QDisp 131, 1991 ➤ 7,467: ᴿNRT 114 (1992) 107 (A. *Toubeau*: 'problème de la réception des décisions de l'autorité ecclésiale').

7710 **Berger** Peter, A far glory; the quest for faith in an age of credulity. NY c. 1991, Free Press. 218 p. $23. – ᴿChrCent 109 (1992) 1061-3 (W. C. *Placher*).

7711 **Birmelé** André, *Lienhard* Marc, La foi des églises luthériennes; confessions et catéchismes, ᵀ*Jundt* A. & P. 1991 ➤ 7,7646: ᴿTLZ 117 (1992) 204s (G. *Siegwalt*).

7713 **Cupitt** Don, The sea of faith 1988 ➤ 6,m124*: ᴿAnglTR 74 (1992) 225-230 (D. F. *Winslow*: deft, creative, also in the 6-program TV form).

7714 *Dagens* Claude, Foi et liberté en Europe occidentale: EsprVie 102 (1992) 503-9.

7714* **Fowler** James W., Stufen des Glaubens; die Psychologie der menschlichen Entwicklung und die Suche nach Sinn [1981]. Gü 1991, Mohn. 352 p. DM 78. – ᴿTGL 82 (1992) 385s (K. *Hollmann*).

7715 **Gisel** Pierre, L'excès du croire; expérience du monde et accès à soi. P 1990, D-Brouwer. 193 p. – ᴿLavalTP 48 (1992) 302s (M. *Viau*).

7716 **Görg** Manfred, Mythos, Glaube und Geschichte; die Bilder des Christlichen Credo und ihre Würzeln im alten Ägypten. Dü 1992, Patmos. 188 p. 3-491-77044-0. – ᴿActuBbg 29 (1992) 365 (J. *Boada*).

7717 *Guerrero* Luis, Fe luterana y fe católica en el pensamiento de KIERKEGAARD: ScripTPamp 23 (1991) 983-992.

7718 *Harle* Winfried, Der Glaube als Gottes- und/oder Menschenwerk in der Theologie M. LUTHERS: Marburger Jahrbuch, Theologie & Glaube (1992) 37-77 [< TR 88,434].

7719 E**Heim** Mark, Faith to creed; ecumenical perspectives on the affirmation of the apostolic faith in the fourth century [WCC inquiry]. GR 1991, Eerdmans. xxiii-206 p. [RelStR 18, 219, P. C. *Phan*].

7719* **Henry** Carl F. H., Toward a recovery of Christian belief 1990 ➤ 6, m141*: ᴿBtS 149 (1992) 103s (J. R. *Brady*).

7720 **Imbach** J., Kleiner Grundkurs des Glaubens. Dü 1990, Patmos. 200 p. DM 29,80. 3-491-77798-4. – ᴿWissWeis 54 (1991) 220s (W. *Dettloff*).

7721 **Jossua** Jean-Pierre, Cuestión de fe [La foi en question 1989 ➤ 6,7676], ᵀ*Diorki* S. A.: PresTeol 59. Sdr 1990, SalTerrae. 125 p. 84-293-0883-0. – ᴿActuBbg 29 (1992) 209s (J. *Boada*).

7722 **Kasper** Walter, Transcending all understanding; the meaning of Christian faith today. Harrison NY 1989, Ignatius. 124 p. $8 pa. – ᴿHomP 91,9 (1990s) 78s (J. R. *Sheets*: deep but like floating on rays of light).

7723 **Kasper** Walter, La foi au défi 1989 ➤ 6,7677: ᴿLavalTP 48 (1992) 141 (R. *Sauvageau*).

7724 **Kerr** Hugh T., The simple Gospel; reflections on Christian faith 1991 ➤ 7,7653; 0-664-25171-4: ᴿCurrTMiss 19 (1992) 219 (C. L. *Nessan*); RExp 89 (1992) 119s (Molly T. *Marshall*).

7725 **Klauck** Hans-Josef, Im Kraftfeld der Liebe; biblische Glaubensimpulse. Wü 1992, Echter. 192 p. DM 24,80.

7726 **Korsch** Dietrich, Glaubensgewissheit und Selbstbewusstsein; vier systematische Variationen über Gesetz und Evangelium [Hab.-Diss. Göttingen]: BeitHistT 76, 1989 ➤ 7,7655: ᴿTLZ 117 (1992) 56-58 (F. *Jacob*).

7726* **Kropf** R. W., Faith, security and risk. NY 1990, Paulist. 186 p. $11. –
ᴿRefTR 50 (1991) 77 (M. *Hill*).
7727 **Kuitert** H. M., Het algemeen betwijfeld christelijk geloof; een herziening.
Baarn 1992, Ten Have 300 p. *f*40. 90-259-4481-7. – ᴿTvT 32 (1992) 323
(N. *Schreurs*).
7728 — *a*) *Graafland* C., Kuiterts 'Het algemeen betwijfeld christelijk geloof'
[Baarn 1992] beoordeeld in het licht van de Gereformeerde traditie; – *b*)
Kuitert H. M., Wil de ware God opstaan; – *c*) *Logister* Wiel, Der Christologie van Kuitert nader bekeken; – *d*) *Bakker* J. T., Wat zeggen wij als
we 'scheping' zeggen; – *e*) *Häring* Hermann, De laatste zekerheid van een
verlichte theologie: GerefTTs 92,2 (Studiedag 'THUK' 19 mei rond Kuiterts boek, 1992) 76-92 / 66-75 / 107-112 / 113-120 / 93-106.
7729 **Kutschera** F. von, Vernunft und Glaube. B 1990. – ᴿTPhil 67 (1992)
263-7 (O. *Mück, zu* GÖDELS Gottesbeweis; auch p. 60-85).
7730 **Lachmann** Rainer, Grundsymbole christlichen Glaubens; eine Annäherung: BibThSchwerpunkte 7. Gö 1992, Vandenhoeck & R. 117 p. 3-
525-61288-5.
7731 *La Potterie* Ignace de, Vérité I. Écriture sainte: → 749, DictSpir 16,
102s (1992) 413-427 [-453, *al*].
7731* ᴱ**Lee** J. M., Handbook of faith. Birmingham 1990, Religious Education.
328 p. $20. – ᴿRefTR 50 (1991) 110 (M. *Thompson*: on the nature of faith).
7732 **McKinnon** Alastair, KIERKEGAARD's accounts of faith; their relative
centrality: ST 46 (1992) 147-159.
7733 **Nadeau** Marie-Thérèse, Foi de l'Église; évolution d'une formule: THist
78, 1988 → 6,7684: ᴿLavalTP 48 (1992) 464 (Anne *Pasquier*).
7734 **O'Collins** Gerald, *Venturini* Mrs. Mary, Believing. NY 1992, Paulist.
178 p. $9 pa. – ᴿThe Priest 48,5 (1992) 56 (C. *Dollen*).
7735 **Patey** Edward, Faith in a risk [–] taking God. L 1991, Darton-LT.
174 p. £9. 0-232-51936-6. – ᴿExpTim 103 (1991s) 349 (W. D. *Horton*:
acknowledging RAHNER; faith is not safety and security).
7736 **Piersiak** J. W., A study of John H. NEWMAN's idea of religious faith
[... truth, certainty]: diss. Oxford 1989. 299 p. BRD-97799. – DissA 53
(1992s) 3258-A.
7737 **Sabugal** S., Io credo 1990 → 7,7671: ᴿRivScR 5 (1991) 498-500 (R.
Scognamiglio).
7738 **Schreer** Werner, Der Begriff des Glaubens; das Verständnis des Glau-
bensaktes in den Dokumenten des Vatikanum II und in den theologischen Entwürfen K. RAHNERS und H. U. v. BALTHASARS [Diss. Tü-
bingen]: EurHS 23/448. Fra 1992, Lang. xvi-712 p. DM 119 [TR 88,432].
7739 *Splett* Jörg, Gewusst, wem wir glauben ... (Oder: Wie scharf dürfen
Atheisten denken?) [... 2. Gerechtfertigt Menschsein (Humanität ohne
Bibel?)]: MüTZ 43 (1992) 449-460 [451-5].
7740 **Thielicke** Helmut, Modern faith and thought, ᵀ*Bromiley* Geoffrey W.
GR 1990, Eerdmans. 582 p. $35. 0-8028-3685-2. – ᴿInterpretation 46
(1992) 304-6 (C. B. *Kline*: 'faith lives in ever new contexts').
7741 *Thompson* Michael E. F., The pastor's patch 4. The country town,
England [Faith in the countryside 1990]: ExpTim 103 (1991s) 4-8.
7742 ᴱ**Zerfass** Rolf, Erzählter Glaube — erzählende Kirche [Arbeitsge-
meinschaft für Homiletik 1986]: QDisp 116, 1988 → 6,710; 3-451-02116-1:
ᴿBijdragen 53 (1992) 338s (J. *Besemer*).

H6.6   *Peccatum NT* – Sin, Evil [→ E1.9].

7743 **Farley** Edward, Good and evil; interpreting a human condition 1990
→ 7,7680: ᴿAnglTR 74 (1992) 391-3 (J. A. *Carpenter*).

7743* **Fuček** Ivan, Il peccato oggi; riflessione teologico-morale. R 1991, Pont. Univ. Gregoriana. 290 p. Lit. 25.000. – RAtKap 118 (1992) 530s (J. *Królikowski*, ❷); CC 143 (1992,3) 442s (P. *Cultrera*).

7744 *Galot* Jean, La complexité du problème de la lutte entre le bien et le mal: EsprVie 102 (1992) 481-8.

7745 *Geyer* C. F., Das Böse in der Perspektive von Christentum und Neo-platonismus: PhJb 98 (1991) 233-250 [< RSPT 76,193].

7746 **Griffin** David R., Evil revisited; responses and reconsiderations. Albany 1991, SUNY. xiv-277 p. $20 [TR 88,83; RelStR 19,56, N. *Gier*].

7747 **Highfield** Ron, BARTH and RAHNER... sin and evil 1989 ➤ 6,7699; 7,7684: RETL 68 (1992) 471s (E. *Brito*).

7747* *Ligas* Giovanni, Peccato 'ferita della Chiesa'; la dimensione antiec-clesiale del peccato secondo la 'Lumen gentium': Lateranum 57 (1991) 71-107.

7748 **Millás** M. J., Pecado/BULTMANN 1989 ➤ 6,7703: RBurgense 32 (1991) 295s (G. P. *Abejón*); Phase 30 (1990) 169 (J. *Guiteras*); Salesianum 54 (1992) 598 (C. *Bissoli*).

7749 *Neven* G. W., Over de betekenis van het woord zonde voor het verstaan van het christelijk geloof [GESTRICH C., Wiederkehr des Glanzes 1990]: GerefTTs 91 (1991) 44-56.

7750 *O'Connell* Robert J., 'Involuntary sin' in the De libero arbitrio: REAug 37 (1991) 23-36.

7751 **Ohly** Friedrich, The damned and the elect; guilt in western culture [1976], TArchibald Linda. C 1992, Univ. xiv-211 p.; 12 fig. £30 [NRT 115, 419, P. *Evrard*]. 0-521-38205-3.

7752 EPeterson Michael L., The problem of evil; selected readings: Library of religious philosophy 8. ND 1992, Univ. ix-391 p. $45; pa. $20. 0-268-01514-7; -5-5 [TDig 40,82].

7752* *Sutherland* D. Dixon, A theological anthropology of evil; a com-parison in the thought of Paul RICŒUR and TEILHARD de Chardin: NSys 34 (1992) 85-100; deutsch 100.

H7 Soteriologia NT.

7753 **Barclift** Philip L., Pope LEO's soteriology; sacramental recapitulation; diss. Marquette, DCizewski Wanda. Milwaukee 1992. 269 p. 92-27115. – DissA 53 (1992s) 2420s-A, not indicating whether Leo I [yes] or XIII or?

7754 **Bayer** Oswald, Aus Glauben leben; über Rechtfertigung und Heili-gung² [= ¹1984 + 40 Anmerkungen]. Stu 1990, Calwer. 100 p. DM 14,80. – RLuthMon 31 (1992) 94 (W. *Härle*).

7755 *a*) *Beintker* Michael, Die Bedeutung der Rechtfertigungsbotschaft für das Verständnis von Freiheit heute; – *b*) *Baur* Jörg, Zur Vermittelbarkeit der reformatorischen Rechtfertigungslehre; noch einmal, Helsinki 1963 und die Folgen: ➤ 173, FSEILS M., Tragende Tradition 1992, 35-48 / 9-24.

7755* *Boersma* Hans, The Chalcedonian definition; its soteriological im-plications: WestTJ 54 (1992) 47-63.

7756 *Bremmer* J. N., The Atonement in the interaction of Jews, Greeks and Christians: ➤ 504, FWOUDE Symposium 1992, 75-93.

7757 **Cessario** Romanus, The godly image.. salvation in... AQUINAS 1990 ➤ 7,7695: RNRT 114 (1992) 766s (R. *Escol*); TS 53 (1992) 145s (R. *McInerny*).

7758 *Corsani* Bruno, La dottrina della salvezza nel Nuovo Testamento: STEv 3 (1991) 162-173.

7759 ᴱ**Crockett** William V., *Sigountos* James G., Through no fault of their own; the fate of those who have never heard. GR 1991, Baker. 278 p. $16. – ᴿBtS 149 (1992) 500s (R. P. *Richard*).

7759* *Deuser* Hermann, Rechtfertigung(-slehre): ➤ 757, EvKL 3 (1992) 1455-66.

7760 *Dunn* James D. G., The justice of God; a renewed perspective on justification by faith (Oxford Regents Park Henton Davies lecture, Jan. 1991): JTS 43 (1992) 1-22.

7761 **Dunn** John L., Jesus Christ as universal savior in the theology of Edward Sᴄʜɪʟʟᴇʙᴇᴇᴄᴋx: diss. Catholic Univ., ᴰ*Galvin* J. Washington D. C. 505 p. 92-26133. – DissA 53 (1992s) 3569-A; RTLv 24, p. 573.

7761* **Eckardt** Burnell F., Aɴsᴇʟᴍ and Lᴜᴛʜᴇʀ on the atonement: was it 'necessary'?: diss. Marquette, ᴰ*Hagen* K. Milwaukee 1991. 286 p. 92-26216. – DissA 53 (1992s) 1186-A..

7762 ᶠEɴɢᴇʟʜᴀʀᴅᴛ Paulus O.P.: Versöhnung; Versuche zu ihrer Geschichte und Zukunft, ᴱ**Eggensperger** T., *Engel* U., *Pesch* O. H: WalberbergerSt ph. 8., 1991 ➤ 7,47: ᴿActuBbg 29 (1992) 80 (J. *Boada*); MüTZ 43 (1992) 119s (W. W. *Müller*); NRT 114 (1992) 424 (A. *Toubeau*).

7763 *Ernst* Stephan, [*al.*], Neues Leben durch Jesus Christus; Skizze der christlichen Erlösungslehre: LebZeug 45 (1990) 257-271 [241-256. 272-283].

7764 *Gestrich* Christof, Unterscheidung zwischen göttlicher und menschlicher Stellvertretung; zur Präzisierung des Verständnisses des 'wunderbaren Tausches' und der 'Sündenvergebung': UnSa 46 (1991) 229-244. 272.

7765 **Giacometti** Luigi, 'È disceso agli inferi'; saggio tematico sulla soteriologia Bᴏɴᴀᴠᴇɴᴛᴜʀɪᴀɴᴀ: Coll. Assisiensis 19. Assisi 1990, Porziuncola. xx-314 p. Lit. 35.000. – ᴿColcFran 61 (1991) 380-3 (P. *Maranesi*).

7766 *Goodloe* James C.ᴵⱽ, John McLeod Cᴀᴍᴘʙᴇʟʟ [unfrocked 1831; Nature of the Atonement 1856]; redeeming the past by reproducing the atonement: ScotJT 45 (1992) 185-208.

7767 *Gunneweg* Antonius H. J., Leistung und Rechtfertigung [1984, unveröffentlicht]: ➤ 249, Sola Scriptura II (1992) 82-92.

7767* *Haag* Herbert, Die Rede vom Heil; Überlegungen eines Alttestamentlers: TüTQ 172 (1992) 81-97.

7768 **Jankiewicz** Romuald, ℗ The problem of the salvation of unbelievers according to Karl Rᴀʜɴᴇʀ: diss. ᴰ*Bartnik* C. Lublin 1992. 413 p. – RTLv 24, p. 574.

7769 **Joubert** J., Le corps sauvé: CogF 161, 1991 ➤ 7,7713: ᴿNRT 114 (1992) 109s (C. *Verdonck*).

7770 *Jüngel* Eberhard, Die Bedeutung der Rechtfertigungslehre für das Verständnis des Menschen: Luther 62 (1991) 110-126.

7771 **Kettler** Christian D., The vicarious humanity of Christ and the reality of salvation [in Küɴɢ etc.]. Lanham MD 1991, UPA. 337 p. $48.50; pa. $24.50. 0-8191-8272-9; -3-7. – ᴿExpTim 103 (1991s) 283s (D. R. *Peel*).

7772 **Kötter** Ralf, Johannes Bᴜɢᴇɴʜᴀɢᴇɴs Rechtfertigungslehre und der römische Katholizismus; Studien zum Sendbriefe an die Hamburger (1525): Diss. ᴰ*Hauschild* W. Münster ... 398 p. – RTLv 24, p. 570 sans date.

7773 **McMullen** Michael, The wisdom of God in the work of redemption; soteriological aspects of the theology of Jonathan Eᴅᴡᴀʀᴅs: diss. ᴰ*Sefton* H. Aberdeen 1992. 461 p. – RTLv 24, p. 555.

7774 *a*) *McNaughton* David, Reparation and atonement; *b*) *Brümmer* Vincent, Atonement and reconciliation; – *c*) *Gunton* Colin, Universal and particular in atonement theology: RelSt 28 (1992) 129-144 / 435-452 / 455-466.

7775 **Magill-Cobbler** Thelma I., Women and the Cross; atonement in Rosemary R. RUETHER and Dorothy SOELLE: diss. Princeton Theol. Sem. 1992. 473 p. 92-29020. – DissA 53 (1992s) 1559-A.

7776 **Martens** Gottfried, Die Rechtfertigung des Sünders – Rechtshandeln Gottes oder historisches Interpretament? Grundentscheidungen lutherischer Theologie und Kirche bei der Behandlung des Themas 'R.' im ökumenischen Kontext [< Diss. Erlangen-N.]: ForSysÖk 64. Gö 1992, VR. 426 p. DM 88 [TR 88,171].

7777 **Menke** Karl-Heinz, Stellvertretung; Schlüsselbegriff christlichen Lebens und theologische Grundkategorie [< Hab.-D. FrB]: Horizonte 29. Einsiedeln 1991, Johannes. 526 p. DM 58 [TR 88,83]. – RHerdKor 46 (1992) 99 (U. *Ruh*); TGL 82 (1992) 484-7 (G. *Fuchs*).

7778 *Milbank* John, The name of Jesus; incarnation, atonement, ecclesiology: ModT 7 (1990s) 311-334 [< ZIT 91,604].

7779 *Morales* José, La justificación en el pensamiento de J.H. NEWMAN: RAg 31 (1990) 867-888.

7780 *Newman* Paul W., Identifying with Jesus; atonement as royal metaphor: ChrCent 108 (1991) 115-7.

7781 *Nuth* Joan M., Two medieval soteriologies; ANSELM of Canterbury and JULIAN of Norwich: TS 53 (1992) 611-645.

7782 *O'Collins* Gerald G., Salvation: → 741, AnchorBD 5 (1992) 907-914.

7783 *a) Peter* C.J., Rechtfertigung durch Glauben und die Notwendigkeit eines weiteren kritischen Prinzips; – *b) Meyer* H., Rechtfertigung im ökumenischen Dialog; eine Einführung; TJb (Lp 1990) 427-438 / 373-426 [< ZIT 91,655].

7784 *a) Peters* Tiemo R., Universales Heil und particuläre Hoffnungen; die Neue Evangelisierung vor der alten Herausforderung; – *b) Lorenz* Hildegard, Die Neue Evangelisierung aus der Sicht der Bibel: Ordensnachrichten 30,5 (1991) 5-26 / 27-35.

7785 **Pröpper** Thomas, Redenzione e storia della libertà; abbozzo di soteriologia [1985 → 3,7384],T: GdT 198. Brescia 1990, Queriniana. 216 p. 88-399-0698-3. – RAsprenas 39 (1992) 285 (P. *Pifano*); EstE 67 (1992) 125s (J. *Alonso Díaz*).

7786 **Reed** Esther D., Salvation in a social context; the impact of HEGELIAN social theory on contemporary understanding of soteriology: diss. DHardy D. Durham UK 1992. 249 p. – RTLv 24, p. 580.

7787 **Röhser** Günter, Neues Testament, Prädestination und Verstockung; Untersuchungen zu ihrer Struktur in der biblisch-jüdischen, paulinischen und johanneischen Theologie: Hab.-Diss. DBerger Heidelberg 1992s. – RTLv 24, p. 549.

7788 **Salom Climent** Fernando, Una lectura teológica del Concilio Vaticano II en la frontera del Protestantismo y mundo de hoy; catolicidad y justificación. Valencia 1992, Fac. Ferrer. 195 p. [TR 88,432].

7789 **Sanders** John, No other name; an investigation into the destiny of the unevangelized 1991 → 7,7286: RRelStR 18 (1992) 315 (J.R. *Sachs*).

7790 **Sattler** Dorothea, Gelebte Busse; das menschliche Busswerk (satisfactio) im ökumenischen Gespräch [< kath. Diss. Mainz 1992, DSchneider T.]: RTLv 24, p. 576]. Mainz c. 1992, Grünewald.

7791 **Schnackenburg** Rudolf, Jesus der Erlöser; neutestamentliche Leitlinien und Perspektiven: MüTZ 43 (1992) 39-50.

7792 **Schwager** Raymund, Jesus im Heilsdrama, Entwurf einer biblischen Erlösungslehre: InnsbruckTSt 29, 1990 → 6,7742; 7,7724: RActuBbg 29 (1992) 82s (J. *Boada*); BLtg 64 (1991) 115-7 (J. *Werbick*); TLZ 117 (1992)

215 (H. *Timm*: weniger 'Entwurf' als durchgearbeitete Ausführung); TPhil 67 (1992) 300-2 (P. *Knauer*: viele sympathische Seiten); ZkT 114 (1992) 75-79 (J. *Niewiadomski*).

7793 **Schwager** Raymund, Dem Netz des Jagers entronnen; das Jesusdrama nacherzählt, Mü 1991, Kösel. 204 p. – ᴿLebZeug 46 (1991) 308 (R. *Jungnitsch*).

7793* *Seckler* Max, Theosoterik — eine Option und ihre Dimensionen; fundamentaltheologische Anfragen und Anstösse zur Soteriologie: TüTQ 172 (1992) 257-284.

7794 **Sesboüé** Bernard, Les récits du salut; JJC 51. P 1991, Desclée. 472 p. F 189. – ᴿDivinitas 36 (1992) 36 (1992) 286 (D. *Vibrac*: néglige la 'satisfaction'; présente l'Écriture 'dans un ordre surprenant et criticable').

7795 **Sesboüé** Bernard, Jésus-Christ, l'unique Médiateur, I: JCC 33, 1988 ➤ 4, 8765... 7,7725: ᴿEsprVie 102 (1992) 442-4 (P. *Jay*); Études 376 (1992) 282s (J. *Thomas*).

7796 **Sesboüé** Bernard, Jesucristo, el único mediador I. 1990 ➤ 7,7726: ᴿRET 51 (1991) 518s (M. *Gesteira*); ScripTPamp 23 (1991) 1015-8 (L. F. *Mateo-Seco*).

7697 **Sesboüé** Bernard, Gesù Cristo, l'unico Mediatore; saggio sulla redenzione e la salvezza, ᵀ*d'Anna* C.: Prospettive Teologiche 11, CinB 1990, Paoline. 456 p. Lit. 26.000. 88-215-2070-6. – ᴿCC 143 (1992,2) 97-99 (F. *Lambiasi*); Lateranum 58 (1992) 542-4 (I. *Sanna*).

7798 **Sesboüé** B., Jésus-Christ, l'unique médiateur, [I. 1988 ➤ 4,8765]; 2. Les récits du salut; proposition de théologie narrative: JJC 51. P 1991, Desclée. 472 p. F 189 [NRT 115.85]. – ᴿCC 143 (1992,2) 99s (F. *Lambiasi*); RSPT 76 (1992) 363-6 (B. *Rey*).

7799 *Splett* Jörg, Erlösung wovon? aus der Sicht philosophischer Anthropologie: MüTZ 43 (1992) 3-16.

7800 **Steindl** Helmut, Genugtuung; biblisches Versöhnungsdenken — eine Quelle für Aɴsᴇʟᴍs Satisfaktionstheorie?: StFrib 71, 1989 ➤ 5,7729... 7,7727: ᴿJTS 43 (1992) 283-6 (C. *Gunton*).

7801 *Viaux* Dominique, L'économie du salut dans les textes des fondations de messes aux XVᵉ et XVIᵉ siècles; essai théologíque: RHPR 72 (1992) 151-163; Eng. 228.

Viciano Alberto, Cristo el autor de nuestra salvación.. Tᴇᴏᴅᴏʀᴇᴛᴏ/paulina 1990 ➤ k836.

7802 **White** Vernon, Atonement and incarnation; an essay in universalism and particularity. C 1991, Univ. ix-134 p. ➤ 7,7738; £22.50; pa. £8. 0-521-40031-7; -732-X. – ᴿAnglTR 74 (1992) 246-8 (C. C. *Hefling*); ExpTim 102,12 1st choice (1990s) 353s (C. S. *Rodd*); JTS 43 (1992) 336-8 (T. *Williams*: on Christ's universality); TLond 95 (1992) 44 (D. *Brown*); TvT 32 (1992) 327s (M. Van *Tente*).

7803 *Zahrnt* Heinz, Gottes Heil oder Gottes Rache? [Sᴄʜɪʟʟᴇʙᴇᴇᴄᴋx, Menschen; Kᴇᴘᴇʟ G., Rache]: TLZ 117 (1992) 403-8.

H7.2   *Crux, sacrificium*; **The Cross; the nature of sacrifice.**

7804 *Anderson* Gary A., Sacrifice OT [*Klauck* Hans-J., NT, ᵀ*Fuller* R. H.]: ➤ 741, AnchorBD 5 (1992) 870-886 (-891).

7805 **Barbaglio** Giuseppe, Dio violento? 1991 ➤ 7,7744a: ᴿTeresianum 43 (1992) 289s (V. *Pasquetto*); ScEspr 44 (1992) 359-362 (Marc *Girard*).

7806 **Barbaglio** Giuseppe, ¿Dios violento? Lectura de las Escrituras hebreas y cristianas: EstB. Estella 1992, VDivino. 280 p. 84-7151-783-3.

7807 **Battaglia** Vincenzo, Gesù crocifisso, figlio di Dio 1991 ⇢ 7,7745: ᴿAsprenas 39 (1992) 283 (A. *Langella*: teologia della croce).

7808 *Bauckham* Richard, In defence of the crucified God [... MOLTMANN; < ᴱ*Cameron* N., Power and weakness of God]: Evangel 9,1 (1991) 13-16.

7808* **Baudler** Georg, Gott und Frau; die Geschichte von Gewalt, Sexualität und Religion. Mü 1991, Kösel. 432 p. – ᴿTGL 82 (1992) 362s (W. *Beinert*).

7809 **Bergmann** Martin S., In the shadow of Moloch; the sacrifice of children and its impact on western religions. NY 1992, Columbia. xi-347 p. $40. 0-231-07248-1. – ᴿTDig 39 (1992) 352 (W. C. *Heiser*: Jews and Christians never tolerated it, but had to continue fighting against it; and in making the sacrifice of the son Isaac/Jesus into the central religious event, built a permanent shrine to the trauma).

7810 *Blank* J., Weisst du, was Versöhnung heisst? Der Kreuzestod Jesu als Sühne und Versöhnung: TJb (Lp 1990) 13-63 [< ZIT 91,654].

Chilton Bruce, The Temple of Jesus; his sacrificial program within a cultural history of sacrifice 1992 ⇢ 4361.

7812 *Colpe* C., *al.*, Opfer: ⇢ 757, EvKL 3 (1992) 877-881 (-887).

7813 *Dangl* Oskar, Gewalt und Gewaltlosigkeit im AT [... im Lichte R. GIRARDS]: BiKi 45 (1990) 100-106.

7814 *Dinkler-von Schubert* Erika, Kreuz, I. vorikonoklastisch: Reallexikon der Byzantinischen Kunst (Stu 1991) 5,1-219. – ᴿDiclB 27 (1991) 279 (B. J. *Diebner*).

7815 **Dupuy** J. P., Le sacrifice et l'envie; le libéralisme aux prises avec la justice sociale. P 1992 [ActuBbg 29,190].

7816 **Durand** Jean-Louis, Sacrifice et labour en Grèce ancienne; essai d'anthropologie religieuse 1986 ⇢ 3,b118; 5,a838: ᴿClasPg 86 (1991) 149-151 (Anne *Burnett*).

7817 *Egmond* A. van, Het einde van de religie; René GIRARD vergeleken met Dietrich BONHOEFFER en Karl BARTH: GerefTTs 91 (1991) 232-245.

7818 *a) Fiedler* Peter, Jesus, kein Sündenbock; – *b) Williams* James G., Die Wahrheit des Opfers, ᵀ*Jeneweit* D.; *c) Pesch* Otto Hermann, Erlösung durch stellvertretende Sühne — oder Erlösung durch das Wort? Thesen und einige Kurzkommentare; – *d) Seshoüé* Bernard, Erzählung von der Erlösung; Vorschläge einer narrativen Soteriologie, ᵀ*Scherl* M.:⇢ 602, Dramatische Erlösungslehre 1991/2, 19-36 / 69-81 / 147-156 / 243-251.

7818* *a) Finet* André, Sacrifices d'alliance dans le Proche-Orient ancien; – *b) Limet* Henri, La mort du mouton de sacrifice: ⇢ 594c, Animal 1988/9, 53-58 / 59-68.

7819 *García Quintela* M. V., El sacrificio lusitano; estudio comparativo: Latomus 51 (1992) 337-354.

7820 **Girard** René, Das Heilige und die Gewalt. Z 1987, Benziger. 484 p. – ᴿTPhil 67 (1992) 474s (P. *Knauer*).

7821 **Girard** René, Der Sündenbock. Z 1988, Benziger. 305 p. – ᴿTPhil 67 (1992) 611s (P. *Knauer*).

7822 *Gittins* Anthony J., Sacrifice, violence, and the Eucharist: Worship 65 (1991) 420-435 [GIRARD invoked near the end].

7823 **Grayston** Kenneth, Dying we live; a new enquiry into the death of Christ in the NT. NY 1990, Oxford UP. x-496 p. $40. – ᴿBR 8,4 (1992) 14s (Elizabeth *Johnson*); CBQ 54 (1992) 350s (J.P. *Heil*: informative, some flaws).

7824 **Hamerton-Kelly** Robert G., Sacred violence; Paul's hermeneutic of the Cross [...GIRARD R.]. Mp 1992, Fortress. $25. 0-8006-2529-3 [TDig 39,363].

7825 **Haulotte** Edgar †, Le concept de croix: JJC 49. P 1991, Desclée. 371 p. F 169. 2-7189-0496-8. – ᴿÉTRel 67 (1992) 595s (M. *Bouttier*: exégète 'visité d'une passion lyrique'; mal rédigé mais stimulant); VSp 146 (1992) 125 (H. *Cousin*).

7826 **Hengel** Martin, Crocifissione ed espiazione BtCuRel 52, 1988 ➤ 7,7757: ᴿRivStoLR 27 (1991) 375s (Gabriella *Dogliani Saladini*).

7827 *Herzog* Markwart, a) Hingerichtete Verbrecher als Gegenstand der Heiligenverehrung; zum Kontext von René GIRARD: GeistL 65 (1992) 367-386; – b) Religionstheorie und Theologie René GIRARDS: KerDo 38 (1992) 105-136; Eng. 136s 'fruitful – untenable'.

7828 *Hoffmann* Norbert, Christus der Gekreuzigte und das Übel in der Welt; sühnetheolgische Erwägungen zum Theodizeeproblem: TGegw 34 (1991) 37-51.

7829 **Hughes** Dennis D., Human sacrifice in ancient Greece 1991 ➤ 7,7759: ᴿAJA 96 (1992) 768 (Carla M. *Antonaccio*); ClasW 86 (1992s) 169s (A. *Brumfield*).

7830 *Jouanna* Jacques, Libation et sacrifices dans la tragédie grecque: RÉG 105 (1992) 406-434.

7831 *a*) *Jouanna* Jacques, Rite et spectacle dans la tragédie grecque; re- marques sur l'utilisation dramaturgique des libations et des sacrifices; – *b*) *Moretti* Jean-Claude, Les entrées en scène dans le théâtre grec; le point de vue de l'archéologue: ➤ 653*a*, Théâtre/Pallas 38 (1991/2) 47-56; Eng. 56 / 79-106; Eng. 107.

Krenski Thomas R., Passio caritatis; trinitarische Passiologie... BALTHA- SARS ᴰ1990 ➤ m744.

7832 **McKenna** Andrew J., Violence and difference; GIRARD, DERRIDA, and deconstruction. Urbana 1992, Univ. Illinois. c. 233 p. – ᴿBulletin CoV&R 2 (1992) 10 (J. G. *Williams*).

7833 *McLean* Bradley H., The absence of an atoning sacrifice in Paul's soteriology: NTS 38 (1992) 531-553.

7834 *Marx* Alfred, Familiarité et transcendance [rejects GIRARD; sacrifice is not ritual murder but a meal expressing god's nearness and otherness]: ➤ 491, Opfer 1990/2, 1-12; deutsch 13.

7834* *Mourão* José A., A hipótesis mimética e a paixão segundo René GIRARD: HumTeol 13 (1992) 21-30.

7835 ᴱ**Oelmüller** Willi, Worüber man nicht schweigen kann; neue Diskussio- nen zur Theodizee-Frage. Mü 1992, Fink. 320 p. DM 78. 10 art. [TR 88, 526, tit. pp.]: p. 15-54, *Marquard* Odo, Exkulpationsarrangements; Be- merkungen im Anschluss an René GIRARDS soziologische Theologie des Sündenbocks; p. [?1-]14, *Spaemann* Robert, Transformationen des Sünden- fallmythos.

7836 **Palaver** Wolfgang, Politik und Religion bei Thomas HOBBES; eine Kri- tik aus der Sicht der Theorie René GIRARDS 1991 ➤ 7,7765: ᴿTR 88 (1992) 467-9 (H. *Reventlow*: Nachweise über biblische Aussagen werden oft aus allgemein-zusammenfassenden Darstellungen oder als 'mythologi- scher Mischtext' bezeichnet; wegen Girard, erhebliche Fragen); TvT [= TsTNijm] 32 (1992) 201 (A. *Lascaris*).

7837 *Palaver* Wolfgang, Thomas HOBBES' Umgang mit der Bibel; eine Inter- pretation aus der Sicht der Theorie von René GIRARD: ZkT 114 (1992) 257-273.

7838 *Peters* Ted, Atonement and the final scapegoat [GIRARD R.]: PerspRel- St 19 (1992) 151-181.

7839 *a) Reuter* Hans-Richard, Stellvertretung; Erwägungen zu einer dogmatischen Kategorie im Gespräch mit R. GIRARD und R. SCHWAGER; – *b) Arens* Edmund, Dramatische Erlösungslehre aus der Perspektive einer theologischen Handlungstheorie: ➤ 602, Symposion 1991/2, 179-199 / 165-177.

7840 **Rey** Bernard, Nous prêchons un Messie crucifié 1989 ➤ 5,7769... 7, 7766: ᴿMélSR 48 (1991) 189s (L. *Derousseaux*).

7841 *a) Schwager* Raymund, Thesen zur Erlösungslehre / Rückblick auf das Symposion; – *b) Otto* Eckart, Gewaltvermeidung und -überwindung in Recht und Religion Israels; rechtshistorische und theologische Anmerkungen eines Alttestamentlers zu R. Schwagers Entwurf einer biblischen Ersöhnungslehre; – *c) Verweyen* Hansjürgen, Offene Fragen im Sühnebegriff auf dem Hintergrund der Auseinandersetzung R. Schwagers mit Hans Urs von BALTHASAR; – *d) Galvin* John P., Zur dramatischen Erlösungslehre R. Schwagers; Fragen aus der Sicht Karl RAHNERS: ➤ 602, Dramatische Erlösungslehre 1991/2, 13-15 / 339-384 / 97-117 / 137-146 / 157-164.

7842 *Scordato* Cosimo, Edipo Re nella prospettiva di una estetica teologica: Ho Theológos 10 (1992) 63-106.

7843 *Siegwalt* Gérard, Pourquoi fallait-il qu'il meure? sur le sens de la mort du Christ: PosLuth 39 (1991) 193-210 [< ZIT 92,17].

7844 *a) Spiegel* Egon, Gründungsmord oder Wiederherstellungsmord? Sozio-theologische Anmerkungen zum Stellenwert des Opfers bei René GIRARD: – *b) Waldschütz* Erwin, Kritische Überlegungen zum Verständnis der Mimesis; – *c) North* Robert, LOHFINKS Empfehlung für Girard, ᵀmit *Plötz* K.: ➤ 602, Dramatische Erlösungslehre 1991/2, 283-306 / 307-316 / 85-95.

7845 ᴱ**Sykes** S. W., Sacrifice and redemption 1991 ➤ 7,384: ᴿExpTim 103 (1991s) 221 (B. L. *Horne*); JTS 43 (1992) 325-9 (Carolyn *Kuykendall*).

7846 **Varone** F., El Dios 'sadico', ᵀ*Garcia Abril* J., 1988 ➤ 5,7776: ᴿSalmanticensis 38 (1991) 90-94 (A. *González Montes*).

7847 **Williams** James G., The Bible, violence, and the sacred. SF 1992, Harper. 288 p. $27 [TDig 39,394]. – ᴿTTod 49 (1992s) 566, 568s (J. L. *Crenshaw*: conflict from mimetic rivalry in the whole Bible; many insights, not fully conclusive).

H7.4 **Sacramenta**, *Gratia*.

7848 **Amundsen** Arne B., Folkelig og kirkelig tradisjon; dåpsforståelser [views on baptism] i Norge særlig på 1800-tallet. Oslo 1989, Solum. 604 p. – ᴿSvTKv 67 (1991) 95-97 (K. *Genrup*).

7849 *Anderson* Herbert, *Foley* Edward, The birth of a story; infant baptism in a pastoral perspective: NewTR 4,4 (1991) 46-62.

7850 **Bausch** W., A new look at the sacraments.² Mystic CT 1983, Twenty-Third. – ᴿAustralasCR 69 (1992) 416-423 (B. *Gleeson* defends his ch. 17 on Holy Orders against charge of 'dangerous' by ten Sydney priests).

7851 *Bavaud* Georges, La destinée des enfants morts sans baptême [... espèce de martyre]: ➤ 7,85*b*, ᶠJOURNET C., NVFr 66,4 (1991) 120-133.

7852 **Béguerie** Philippe, *Duchesneau* Claude, How to understand the sacraments. L 1991, SCM. 160 p. £8.50. 0-334-02453-6 [TDig 39,150]. – ᴿExpTim 103 (1991s) 188 (K. *Stevenson*: anthropology and P. RICŒUR on symbols help).

7852* **Blanchette** Claude, Pénitence et Eucharistie 1989 → 5,7783 ... 7,7781*: ᴿColcT 62,1 (1992) 185s (S. *Sosnowski*, ❷).

7853 *Boughton* Lynne C., Sacramental theology and ritual studies; the influence and inadequacies of structuralist and mythographic approaches: Divinitas 36 (1992) 52-76.

Bourgeois Daniel, L'un et l'autre sacerdoce; essai sur les structures sacramentelles de l'Église 1991 → 8189.

7855 *Brattston* David, The forgiveness of post-baptismal sin in ancient Christianity: Churchman 105 (1991) 332-349 [< ᴢɪᴛ 92,71].

7856 **Brinkman** Martien E., Schepping en sacrament; een oecumenische studie naar de reikwijdte van het sacrament als heilzaam symbool in een weerbarstige werkelijkheid. Zoetermeer 1991, Meinema. 321 p. [TR 88,435]. ƒ 37,50. 90-211-3566-3. – ᴿTvT 32 (1992) 429 (H. E. *Mertens*).

7857 *Burns* J. Patout, Christ and the Holy Spirit in AUGUSTINE's theology of Baptism: → 588, Rhetor 1992, 161-171.

7858 **Chauvet** L. M., Símbolo y sacramento; dimensión constitutiva de la existencia cristiana [1987 → 4,8813; ital. 7,7786]. Barc 1991, Herder. 563 p. – ᴿCiuD 205 (1992) 252s (J. M. *Ozaeta*); Stromata 47 (1991) 419.

7859 *Christian* Robert, Midway between baptism and holy orders; Saint THOMAS' contribution to a contemporary understanding of confirmation: Angelicum 69 (1992) 157-173.

7860 *Colpe* Carsten, Mysterienkult und Liturgie; zum Vergleich heidnischer Rituale und christlicher Sakramente: → 649*, Spätantike 1992, 203-228.

7861 **Croce** V., Cristo nel tempo della Chiesa; teologia dell'azione liturgica, dei sacramenti e dei sacramentali. T 1992, LDC. 552 p. – ᴿAntonianum 67 (1992) 239-241 (V. *Calabrese*).

7862 **Cuschieri** Andrew J., The sacrament of reconciliation; a theological and canonical treatise. Lanham ᴍᴅ 1991, UPA. 353 p. [TDig 40,59; TR 88,435].

7863 *de Mesa* José M., Marriage is discipleship: EAPast 28 (1991) 313-396; 29 (1992).

7864 *Dinkler* Erich, *a)* Die Taufaufsagen des NTs, neu untersucht im Hinblick auf Karl BARTHS Tauflehre [< ᴱ*Viering, KB*'s Lehre 1971, 60-153]; *b)* Römer 6,1-14 und das Verhältnis von Taufe und Rechtfertigung bei Paulus [< ᴱ*De Lorenzi* L., Battesimo 1974, 83-103]: → 236, Im Zeichen des Kreuzes 1992, 39-132 / 133-153.

7865 **Duffy** Stephen J., The graced horizon; nature and grace in modern Catholic thought: Glazier Theology & Life 37. ColMn 1992, Liturgical. 247 p. $17 pa. 0-8146-5705-2 [TDig 40,159].

7866 **Emeis** Dieter, Grundkurs Sakramentenkatechese. FrB 1991, Herder. 287 p. DM 38. 3-451-22476-3. – ᴿAtKap 119 (1992) 184-6 (J. *Stefański*, ❷); LtgJb 42 (1992) 260 (A. *Schilson*); StiZt 210 (1992) 141 (R. *Bleistein*); TvT 32 (1992) 335s (J. *Bulckens*).

7867 **Espeja** Jesús, Sacramentos y seguimiento de Jesús 1989 → 5,7796; 6, 7810: ᴿAngelicum 69 (1992) 438-440 (A. *González Fuente*); LumenVr 40 (1991) 536s (U. *Gil Ortega*).

7868 **Fernández** Domiciano, The Father's forgiveness; a new look at the sacrament of reconciliation [cf. 1989 → 6,7812], ᵀ*Olmedo* Pablo, Quezon City 1991, Claretian. xiii-87 p. – ᴿEAPast 28 (1991) 189-191 (G. *King*: Trent-style confession unknown in the Church for a thousand years).

7869 **Finn** Thomas M., Early Christian baptism and the catechumenate; *a)* West and East Syria; – *b)* Italy, North Africa, and Egypt: Message of the Fathers 5s. ColMn 1992, Liturgical. xiv-218 p.; xiv-249 p. 0-8146-5345-6; -6-4; pa. -17-0; -18-9.

7870 *Gäde* Gerhard, 'Nondum considerasti, quanti ponderis sit peccatum'; ANSELMIanische Überlegungen zur gegenwärtigen Gnadenlehre: Wiss-Weis 54 (1991) 3-26.

7871 **Galindo Rodrigo** José A., Compendio de la gracia. Valencia 1991, Edicep. 414 p. – ᴿEscVedat 22 (1992) 447s (M. *Gelabert*).

7872 **Ganoczy** Alexandre, De su plenitud todos hemos recibido; doctrina de la gracia, ᵀ*Gancho* Claudio: BtTF 192, 1991 → 7,7796: ᴿCiuD 205 (1992) 250s (J. M. *Ozaeta*); LumenVr 40 (1991) 421 (F. *Ortiz de Urtaran*); StPatav 39 (1992) 444-8 (E. R. *Tura*).

7872* *a*) **García Paredes** J. C. R., Teología fundamental de los sacramentos. M 1991, Paulinas. 213 p. – ᴿBurgense 33 (1992) 310s (N. *López Martínez*).

— *b*) **Greshake** Gisbert, Geschenkte Freiheit; Einführung in die Gnadenlehre¹ʳᵉᵛ. [¹1977]. FrB 1992, Herder. – ᴿTGL 82 (1992) 378-380 (D. *Hattrup*).

7873 **Groen** Basilius J., Ter genezing van ziel en lichaam; de viering van het oliesel [*euchélaion*] in de Grieks-Orthodoxe Kerk [→ 7,7797] een wetenschappelijke proeve op het gebied van de godgeleerdheid [diss. Nijmegen]: Theologie en empirie 11. Kampen/Weinheim 1991, Kok Pharos / Dt. Studien. xvi-281 p. – ᴿETL 68 (1992) 481s (A. de *Halleux*).

7874 *Güttgemanns* Erhardt, Die Differenz zwischen Sakramenten und 'Zeichen-Körpern' bei Thomas AQUINAS (Summa theologica III quaestio 60): LingBib 65 (1991) 58-115; Eng. 116.

7875 **Hamilton** David S. M., Through the waters; baptism and the Christian life. E 1990, Clark. 136 p. £10. 0-567-29178-2. – ᴿExpTim 102 (1990s) 381 (G. T. *Eddy*).

7876 *Hartman* Lars, 'Auf den Namen des Herrn Jesus'; die Taufe in den neutestamentlichen Schriften [< ANRW 26]: SBS 148. Stu 1992, KBW. 164 p. [TLZ 118,144]. 3-460-04481-0.

7876* ᴱ**Heinz** Hanspeter, *al.*, Versöhnung in der jüdischen und christlichen Liturgie [Symposion Augsburg 2.-5. Juli 1989]: QDisp 124, 1990 → 6.625; 7,7709: ᴿLtgJb 41 (1991) 133s (M. *Kunzler*).

7877 **Hempelmann** Reinhard, Sakrament als Ort der Vermittlung des Heils: Sakramententheologie im evang.-katholischen Dialog [Diss. Heidelberg]: Kirche und Konfession 32. Gö 1992, Vandenhoeck & R. 246 p. DM 74 [TR 88,529].

7877* **Hoekema** Anthony A., Saved by grace 1989 → 6,7723; 7,7711: ᴿRefTR 50 (1991) 39s (J. P. *Wilson*).

7878 **Klär** Karl-Josef, Das kirchliche Bussinstitut von den Anfängen bus zum Konzil von Trient [Diss. Saarbrücken, ᴰ*Ohlig* K.]: EurHS 23/413. Fra 1991, Lang. 254 p. DM 77 [TR 88,340]. – ᴿZkT 114 (1992) 327-336 (R. *Messner*: nichts weniger als eine neue Methode, HARNACK/VORGRIMLER gegenüber).

7879 *Krakowiak* Czesław, ⊕ From the theology of Christian initiation (wtajemniczenia): RuBi 45 (1992) 65-74.

7880 **Kranemann** Benedikt, Die Krankensalbung in der Zeit der Aufklärung 1990 → 6,7831; 7,7803: ᴿZkT 114 (1992) 377 (H. B. *Meyer*).

7881 **Larrabe** José Luis, Bautismo y confirmación, sacramentos de iniciación cristiana 1989 → 7,7807: ᴿEstE 67 (1992) 229s (P. J. *Álvarez*).

7882 *Larrabe* José Luis, Liturgia y sacramentos en esta época postconciliar: EstE 67 (1992) 429-448.

7883 **Lerle** Johannes, Haben die Apostel Säuglinge getauft? Gross Oesingen 1990, Harms. 88 p. [TLZ 116,193].

7884 **Lies** Lothar, Sakramententheologie 1990 ➤ 6,7833; 7,7810: ᴿLtgJb 41 (1991) 63s (A. *Schilson*); MüTZ 42 (1991) 284s (T. *Böhm*). WissWeish 54 (1991) 216-8 (A. *Gerken*).

7885 **López-González** Pedro, Penitencia y reconciliación 1989 ᴰPamplona ➤ 6, 7836; 7,7811: ᴿTR 88 (1992) 202s (H. *Vorgrimler*: Arzt des Opus Dei).

7886 **McDonnell** K., *Montague* G.T., Christian initiation and baptism in the Holy Spirit 1990 ➤ 7,7536: ᴿNRT 114 (1992) 110s (A. *Toubeau*); TvT [= TsTNijm] 32 (1992) 95s (H. *Wegman*: 18% of all Catholics and 22% of all Protestants belong to the charismatic movement).

7886* **Magne** Jean, Logique des sacrements / des dogmes 1989 ➤ 5,7814; 6, 7837: ᴿLavalTP 48 (1992) 455-7 (L. *Painchaud*).

7887 *Maldonado Arenas* Luis, Los movimientos de la sacramentología: RET 51 (1991) 43-55; Eng. 43.

7888 **Margerie** Bertrand de, Du confessional en littérature [... LAMARTINE, CLAUDEL] P c. 1990, St. Paul. – ᴿPeCa 246 (1990) 90-92 (F. *Chassagne*).

7889 *Mitchell* Leonel L., The reconciliation of penitents: AnglTR 74 (1992) 25-36.

7890 **Moos** Alois, Das Verhältnis von Wort und Sakrament in der deutschsprachigen katholischen Theologie des 20. Jahrhunderts [Diss. Mainz]: KkKSt 59. Pd 1992, Bonifatius. 416 p. DM 78 [TR 88,529].

7891 **Old** Hughes O., The shaping of the Reformed baptismal rite in the sixteenth century. GR 1992, Eerdmans. xii-324 p. $45. 0-8028-3699-2 [TDig 40,79].

7892 **Osborne** Kenan B., Reconciliation and justification; the sacrament and its theology 1990 ➤ 6,7843; 7,7824: ᴿHomP 91,10 (1990s) 69-71 (J.R. *Sheets*: very debatable; hidden agenda); Worship 65 (1991) 287s (J. *Dallen*).

7893 **Philips** G., L'union personnelle avec le Dieu vivant; essai sur l'origine et le sens de la grâce créée² [¹1974]: BtETL 36, 1989 ➤ 5,7821; 6,7845: ᴿRET 51 (1991) 101-3 (M. *Gesteira*: trasfondo la 'muerte de dios' de los años 60).

7894 **Piolanti** A., I sacramenti² 1990 ➤ 6,7846; 7,7825: ᴿStPatav 39 (1992) 258s (E.R. *Tura*).

7894* *Rumianek* Ryszard, ⊘ *Bierzmowanie*... Confermazione nel concetto biblico: ColcT 62,4 (1992) 59-67; ital. 67.

7895 **Scalco** Eugenio, 'Sacramentum' et 'sacramenti res' nell'istituzione nuziale; loro impiego e significato negli scritti di AGOSTINO di Ippona: diss. Lv 1992, ᴰHaquin A. – RTLv 23 (1992) 293s.

7896 **Schenk** Wolfgang, Lima-Ökumene... gegen Taufe/Herrenmal unter einem Amtsbegriff. 1990. – ᴿTLZ 117 (1992) 546s (R. *Slenczka*).

7897 *Schlögl* Herbert, Erneuerung des Busssakramentes — auch ein Thema der Moraltheologie?: TGgw 35 (1992) 163-172.

7898 *Stefano* Frances, The evolutionary categories of Juan Luis SEGUNDO's Theology of Grace: Horizons 19 (1982) 7-30.

7899 **Swindoll** Charles R., The grace awakening. Dallas 1990, Word. xvi-311 p. $16. – ᴿBtS 148 (1991) 121s (R.A. *Pyne*).

7900 *Theissen* Gerd, Sakrament und Entscheidung; Überlegungen zu Taufe und Abendmahl im frühen Christentum: CLehre 44 (1991) 340-7 [< ZIT 91,747].

7901 [ᴱ**Thurian** M.] Baptism, Eucharist and Ministry 1982-1990 [➤ 7,7781]; report on the process and responses [synthesis of the six volumes]: Faith and Order 149. Geneva 1990, WCC. viii-160 p. Fs 15. – ᴿNRT 114 (1992) 135s (Λ. *Harvengt*).

7902 *Tranvik* Mark D., A water gracious, heavenly and divine; baptism in the Lutheran Reformation: CurrTMiss 19 (1992) 250-8.

7903 **Trigg** Jonathan D., Baptism in the theology of Martin LUTHER: diss. Durham UK 1992. – ᴿTLv 24 p. 563.

7904 *Turner* Paul, The origins of confirmation [*Kavanagh* A. ➤ 4,8825...7, 7800]: Worship 65 (1991) 320-336; response 337s.

7905 **Van Roo** William A., The Christian sacrament [baptism]: AnGreg 262. viii-196 p. Lit 25.000 [TR 88,528]. 88-7652-652-8.

7906 **Varghese** Baby, Les onctions baptismales dans la tradition syrienne: CSCOr 512/82. Lv 1989, Peeters. xxxiii-348 p. Fb 4580. – ᴿJTS 43 (1992) 712-6 (B. D. *Spinks*).

7907 **Vorgrimler** Herbert, Sacramental theology [1987 ²1990 ➤ 3,7509], ᵀ*Maloney* Linda M. ColMn 1992, Liturgical. xii-329 p. $25. 0-8146-1994-0 [TDig 40,191].

7907* **Zimmer** Siegfried, Das Problem der Kindertaufe in der Theologie M. LUTHERS; Luthers reformatorische Grundkenntnisse als Massstab für die Frage nach der Kindertaufe: Diss. Tübingen 1992. – TLZ 118, 460.

7908 **Žitnik** Maksimilijan, Sacramenta; bibliographia internationalis. R 1992, Pont. Univ. Gregoriana. 4 vol.: xxxii-1172 p.; iv-1048 p.; iv-1040 p.; 452 p. [TR 88,528]. I. A-G (17,583 items) Lit. 120.000. – ᴿCC 143 (1992,4) 432 (G. *Ferraro*).

H7.6   *Ecclesiologia, theologia missionis, laici* - **The Church.**

7908* **Aagaard** Anna Marie, Identifikation of kirken. Fredriksberg 1991, ANIS. – ᴿTsTKi 63 (1992) 74s (Ola *Tjørhom*).

7909 *Balz* Heinrich, Mission (-stheologie): ➤ 757, EvKL 3 (1992) 425-444 (-472 *al.*, Geschichte usw.).

7910 [Gomes] **Barbosa** Manuel J., A Igreja como comunhão, à luz das noções de 'mistério/sacramento' e de 'povo de Deus' no Concilio Vaticano II e no sínodo extraordinário dos bispos de 1985 [diss. Lisboa 1990]: BtHumTeol 2. Porto 1990, Univ. 173 p. – ᴿAntonianum 67 (1992) 442 (I. *Lamelas*).

7911 **Baril** Gilberte sr., Feminine face of the people of God. Slough 1992, St. Paul. 239 p. £11. – ᴿFurrow 42 (1991) 669s (Eleanor *Cunney*: on the Church's use of feminine images to describe itself).

7911* *Berentsen* Jan-Martin, [Norsk misjon] Jubileer og prinsipper... prinsipperklæringer om misjon: TsTKi 63 (1992) 129-140.

7912 *Bischofberger* Otto, Bekehrung; zum Verständnis und zur Definition aus religionswissenschaftlicher Sicht: NZMissW 46 (1990) 162-175.

7912* **Blasetti** Lorenzo, La Chiesa immagine dell'uomo, 1989 ➤ 7,7846*; Lit. 16.000: ᴿProtestantesimo 47 (1992) 165s (G. *Anziani*).

7913 **Bosch** David J. † 1992, Transforming mission; paradigm shifts in theology of mission 1991 ➤ 7,7851: ᴿGregorianum 73 (1992) 375s (J. *López-Gay*); HomP 92,4 (1991s) 70s (J. R. *Sheets*: it concludes there is no certitude on the meaning of mission); IntRMiss 81 (1992) 319-324 (*Hwa Yung*); JDharma 17 (1992) 270s (S. *Athappilly*); Vidyajyoti 56 (1992) 623-5 (G. *Gispert-Sauch*).

7913* ᴱ**Bost** Hubert, Genèse et enjeux de la laïcité 1990/0 ➤ 7,7853: ᴿProtestantesimo 47 (1992) 164s (C. *Tron*).

Bourgeois Daniel, L'un et l'autre sacerdoce 1991 ➤ 8189.

7914 **Bouyer** Louis, Parole, Église et sacrements dans le Protestantisme et le Catholicisme: Essai. P 1991, Desclée. 101 p. – ᴿAtKap 118 (1992) 519-521 (A. *Nowicki*, ⊕).

7914* **Brachlow** Stephen, The communion of Saints; radical Puritanism and separatist ecclesiology. Ox 1988, UP. viii-293 p. – ᴿScotJT 45 (1992) 421-3 (G. S. *Wakefield*).

7915 **Brashford** Robert, Mission and evangelism in recent thinking, 1974-1986 [Oxford 1989 M. Phil. thesis]: Latimer Studies 35s. Ox 1990, Latimer. 93 p. £3.50 [RefTR 51,117].

7915* **Brennan** John P., Christian mission in a pluralistic world. Middlegreen, Slough 1990, St. Paul. x-134 p. £6.50. 0-85439-326-9. – ᴿExpTim 103 (1991s) 94 (G. T. *Eddy*).

7916 *Bueno* Eloy, ¿Redescubrimiento de los laicos o de la Iglesia?: RET 51 (1991) 475-500.

7917 **Burridge** Kenelm, In the way; a study of Christian missionary endeavours. Vancouver BC 1991, UBC. xvi-307 p. $40. 0-7748-0376-2. ᴿTDig 39 (1992) 152 (W. C. *Heiser*: an anthropologist; to moderate the common view that missionaries are now passé).

7918 **Burton** Lary M., Johannine and Pauline ecclesiological metaphors; a comparative study: diss. Baptist Theol. Sem., ᴰ*Dukes* J. New Orleans 1992. 177 p. 92-27153. – DissA 53 (1992s) 1546-A.

7919 **Canobbio** G., Laici o cristiani? Elementi storico-sistematici per una descrizione del cristiano laico. Brescia 1992, Morcelliana. 322 p. Lit. 30.000. [NRT 115, 624].

7920 **Caputa** Giovanni, Il sacerdozio comune dei fedeli nelle opere teologiche di S. BEDA il Venerabile (672-735); contributo a una teologia liturgico-spirituale: Diss. Salesiana, ᴰ*Triacca* A. Roma 1991. Extr. 281, 106 p. – RTLv 24, p. 553.

7921 *Cartwright* Michael C., The pathos and promise of American Methodist ecclesiology: AsbTJ 47,1 (1992) 5-25.

7922 ᴱ**Cazelles** Henri (Commission biblique), Unité et diversité dans l'Église 1988/9 ➤ 6,520; 7,7857: ᴿEsprVie 101 (1991) 385-396 (texte) & 102 (1992) 172-5 (É. *Cothenet*: analyses détaillées); ScEsp 44 (1992) 372s (A. *Faucher*); StPatav 39 (1992) 191-201 (G. *Leonardi*: dettagliato, anche sui singoli articoli).

ᴱ**Chauvet** Patrick, 'Sacerdoce des baptisés', textes 1991 ➤ 8197.

7924 **Cheesman** Graham, Mission today. Belfast 1989, Qua Ibae Fellowship. 167 p. 0-9507657-59. – ᴿEvangel 9,1 (1991) 30 (P. *Cook*).

7925 Chiesa e missione: StUrbaniana 37, 1990 ➤ 6,588; 7,7859: ᴿAngelicum 68 (1991) 553-6 (G. *Phan Tan Thanh*).

7925* *Coda* Piero, I movimenti ecclesiali; una lettura ecclesiologica: Lateranum 57 (1991) 109-144.

7926 *Collet* Giancarlo, 'Zu neuen Ufern aufbrechen'? 'Redemptoris Missio' aus missionstheologischer Perpektive: ZMissRW 75 (1991) 161-171 (172-190, Ekklesiologie, *Waldenfels* H.; 191-209, Dialog, *Evers* G.).

7926* a) *Colombo* Domenico, Fondamenti teologici e identità della *missio ad gentes* nella Redemptoris missio; – b) *Henkel* W., I destinatari della *missio ad gentes* (cap. IV); – c) *Nunnenmacher* Eugen, 'Le missioni' — un concetto vacillante reabilitato?... dimensione geografica; – d) *Giglioni* P., ... vocabolario: EuntDoc 44 (1991) 203-223 / 225-239 / 241-264 / 265-285.

7927 **Conigliaro** Francesco, Un gioco senza / regole; chiesa-éschaton, potere-persona [... La chiesa fa le sue vittime, p. 13]: Cristianismo 11. Palermo 1992, Augustinus. 237 p. 88-246-0512-5.

7928 *Dassmann* Ernst, Kirche, geistliches Amt und Gemeindeverständnis zwischen antikem Erbe und christlichen Impulsen: ➤ 648*, Spätantike 1992, 249-269.

7929 *Davis* John R., How Church structures [... pastor as 'head'] can effectively help or hinder Church growth: Evangel 10,3 (1992) 73-83.

7929* **Dentin** Pierre, Peuple de prêtres. P 1992, Cerf. 325 p. – ᴿBLitEc 93 (1992) 424s (J. *Rigal*: vues intéressantes sans justification approfondie).

7930 **Descamps** A. †, Jésus et l'Église [17 art.] ᴱ*Houssiau* A.: BtETL 77, 1987 → 3,213; 5,7856: ᴿRThom 92 (1992) 545-7 (M.-V. *Leroy*).

7931 **Dianich** Severino, Iglesia extrovertida; investigación sobre el cambio de la eclesiología contemporánea: Verdad e imagen 114. S 1991, Sígueme. 126 p. 84-301-1142-5. – ᴿRET 52 (1992) 242 (M. *Gesteira*).

7931* **Di Luca** G., Il laico cristiano; per una definizione teologica; verso una nuova maturità, R 1989, Dehoniane. 176 p. – ᴿLateranum 57 (1991) 657s (M. *Semeraro*).

7932 **Donovan** Vincent J., The Church in the midst of creation 1989 → 7,786; also L 1991, SCM. 168 p. £8. 0-334-00165-X. – ᴿExpTim 102,10 1st choice (1990s) 289 (C. S. *Rodd*: a Catholic's arresting culture-shock at returning from the mission field to the church in America).

7933 **Dujarier** M., L'Église-fraternité, I. Les origines de l'expression 'adelphotes-fraternitas' aux trois premiers siècles du christianisme; Théologies. P 1991, Cerf. 107 p. – ᴿEsprVie 102 (1991) 600 (Y.-M. *Duval*); ETL 68 (1992) 447s (A. de *Halleux*); RHPR 72 (1992) 327 (D. A. *Bertrand*).

7934 **Estrada** Juan A., La identidad de los laicos; ensayo de eclesiologia; BtTeol 2, 1990 → 6,7686*; 7,7870: ᴿComSev 24 (1991) 109 (M. *Sánchez*); SalT 78 (1990) 803s (J. J. *Rodríguez Ponce*).

7935 *Faber* Eva-Maria, Kirche zwischen Identität und Differenz; die ekklesiologischen Ansätze von Romano GUARDINI und Erich PRZYWARA: Diss. ᴰ*Greshake* G. Freiburg/Br 1992. – RTLv 24, p. 569.

7936 *Fahey* Michael A., AUGUSTINE's ecclesiology revisited: → 588, Rhetor 1992, 173-181.

7936* *a) Fahey* Michael A., The catholicity of the Church in the NT and in the early patristic period [*Trevijano* Ramón, response]; – *b) Peri* Vittorio, Local churches and catholicity in the first millennium of the Roman tradition; – *c) Halleux* André de, The catholicity of the local church in the patriarchate of Antioch after Chalcedon: → , Jurist 52 (1992) 44-70 [-78] / 79-108 / 109-129 [-137].

7937 *Famerée* J., L'ecclésiologie d'Yves CONGAR avant Vatican II: BtETL 107. Lv 1992, Univ./Peeters. 497 p. Fb 2600 [NRT 115, 746, A. *Toubeau*].

7938 *Famerée* Joseph, L'ecclésiologie du Père Yves CONGAR; essai de synthèse critique: RSPT 76 (1992) 377-418; Eng. 419.

7939 **Favale** Agostino, *al.*, Movimenti ecclesiali contemporanei; dimensioni storiche, teologiche-spirituali ed apostoliche⁴ [¹1980]: BtScRel 92. R 1991, LAS. 601 p. Lit. 50.000. – ᴿActuBbg 29 (1992) 222 (J. *Boada*); NRT 114 (1992) 624 (A. *Toubeau*); TPQ 140 (1992) 182-4 (J. *Singer*).

7939* *Federici* Tommaso, La Chiesa in missione e il dialogo con le religioni; le difficili ottiche moderne: EuntDoc 44 (1991) 177-202.

7940 *a) Fernández-Martos* José M., Preocuparse por la Iglesia ¿Qué tipo de preocupación? – *b) Aguirre* Rafael, Iglesia-mundo, ¿marcha atrás?; – *c) Estrada* Juan A., El retorno de las 'certezas' en la Iglesia; del diálogo a la confrontación; – *d) Lucchetti Bingemer* María C., El laico y la mujer en la Iglesia; dar entrada a la 'diferencia' y a la santidad; – *e) Unciti* Manuel de, Pluralismo, libertad, corresponsabiliad; tres signaturas pendientes en el interior de la Iglesia: SalT 80 (1992) 427-435 / 437-445 / 447-455 / 457-464 / 465-478.

7941 **Flegg** Columba G., '.Gathered under Apostles'; a study of the Catholic Apostolic Church [a passé British sect]. Ox 1992, Clarendon. xvi-524 p. £50 [TR 88,529].

7942 **Forte** Bruno, The Church, icon of the Trinity; a brief study [< Bossey seminar 1983], TPaolucci Robert. Boston 1991, St. Paul. 107 p. $7. 0-8198-1482-2 [TDig 39,262].

7942* **Fuchs** E., *Grappe* C., Le droit de résister; le protestantisme face au pouvoir. Genève 1990, Labor et fides. 96 p. Fs 13. – RProtestantesimo 47 (1992) 169 (E. *Genre*).

7943 *Galot* Jean, La missione messa in questione: Vita Consacrata 28 (1992) 328-339.

7944 a) *García* José A., La Iglesia, buena noticia sobre Dios; – b) *Sobrino* Jon, La Iglesia samaritana y el Principio-Misericordia; – c) *Alemany* Jesús M., La Iglesia, casa de la libertad; – d) *Martin Velasco* Juan, Una Iglesia intelectualmente habitable: SalT 78,10 (Las 'otras notas' de la Iglesia, 1990) 651-663 / 665-678 / 679-692 / 693-706.

7945 **Garijo-Guembe** Miguel M., Gemeinschaft der Heiligen; Grund, Wesen und Struktur der Kirche 1988 ➤ 5,7871; 7,7876: RTRu 57 (1992) 188-221 (E. *Herms*: 'aus der Sicht eines katholischen Theologen').

7946 **Garijo-Guembe** Miguel M., La comunión de los santos; fundamento, esencia y estructura de la Iglesia [1988 ➤ 5,7871], TGancho Claudio: BtTF 190. 1991. – RCiuD 205 (1992) 246 (J.M. *Ozaeta*); LumenVr 41 (1992) 297s (U. *Gil Ortega*).

7947 *Garijo-Guembe* Miguel M., Communio-Ekklesiologie: UnSa 47 (1992) 323-9. 352.

7948 a) **González de Cardedal** O., Génesis de una teología de la iglesia local desde el Concilio Vaticano I al Concilio Vaticano II; – b) *Komonchak* J. A., La iglesia local y la Iglesia católica; la problématica teológica contemporánea: ➤ 579, Iglesias 1991/2, 33-78 / 559-591.

7949 **González Faus** José I., Elogio del MELOCOTÓN de Secano: La Iglesia que queremos 4. Córdoba 1992, Almendro. 202 p.

7950 **Greive** Wolfgang, Die Kirche als Ort der Wahrheit; dar Verständnis der Kirche in der Theologie K. BARTHS: ForSysÖkT 61. Gö 1991, Vandenhoeck & R. 406 p. DM 118. 3-525-56268-3. – RTR 88 (1992) 333-6 (G. *Pfleiderer*).

7951 **Hagstrom** Aurelie, The concepts of the vocation and the mission of the laity (Lumen Gentium etc.]: diss. Angelicum, DFox J. Roma 1991. Extr. 91 p. – RTLv 24, p. 569.

7952 **Hamner** J. E., The sanctifying community; the doctrine of the Church in the thought of L. S. THORNTON and E. L. MASCALL: Diss. Oxford 1991. – RTLv 24, p. 569.

7952* **Hanson** Anthony T. & Richard P. C., The identity of the Church; a guide to recognizing the contemporary Church 1987 ➤ 6,7897: RTsTKi 62 (1991) 59s (O. *Tjørhom*).

Herms Eilert, Erfahrbare Kirche; Beiträge zur Ekklesiologie 1990 ➤ 252.

7953 *Herms* Eilert, Erfahrbare Kirche [Aufsätze 1990] als soziales System; Antwort auf Rückfragen: EvT [51 (1991) 296-304, *Brandt* Sigrid] 52 (1992) 454-467 (-470, Brandt).

7954 **Hill** Charles, Mystery of life, a theology of Church. Melbourne 1990, Collins Dove. 102 p. $A 15. – RPacifica 4 (1991) 232s (J. *Wilcken*).

7955 **Hobbs** Herschel H., You are chosen; the priesthood of all believers. SF 1990, Harper & R. 123 p. $16. 0-06-252004-0. – RParadigms 8,1 (1992s) 40s (Christine *Mader*); RExp 88,2 (1991) 231 (C.B. *Bugg*: by a venerated leader).

7956 *Hollenweger* Walter J., The discipline of thought and action in mission: IntRMiss 80 ('Spirit[uality] and mission' 1991) 91-104.

7957 ᴱJenkinson William, *O'Sullivan* Helene, Trends in mission; toward the third millenium. Mkn 1991, Orbis. 419 p. $27 [JAAR 59,888]. 0-88344-766-5. – ᴿMonth 253 (1992) 107s (A. *Egan*).

7958 **Jongeneel** J.A.R., Missiologie II. missionaire theologie. Haag 1991, Boeken-C. 401 p. *f* 55. 90-239-0638-1. – ᴿIntRMiss 81 (1992) 620s (J. van *Butselaar*); TvT [27 (1987) 217] 32 (1992) 331 (A. *Camps*).

7959 **Kasper** Walter, Theology and church 1989 → 6,255a; 7,7890: ᴿAmerica 146 (1991) 66 (M. *Pacwa*).

7960 **Kasper** Walter, La théologie et l'Église: CogF 158, 1990 → 6,255b: ᴿRTLv 23 (1992) 371-4 (G. *Thils*).

7961 **Kehl** Medard, Die Kirche; eine katholische Ekklesiologie. Wü 1992, Echter. 472 p. DM 48 [TR 88,434]. – ᴿHerdKor 46 (1992) 581s (K. *Nientiedt*); StiZt 210 (1992) 645s (K. *Mertes*).

7962 *Khodr* Georges *(al.)*, Holiness as the focal point of witness: IntRMiss 80 (1991) 7-16 (-88).

7963 *a) Kim Yong-Bock*, Mission and Christ's solidarity with the people; – *b) Green* Robin, God is doing a new thing; a theological reflection on the practice of partnership: IntRMiss 80 (1991) 163-179 / 219-229.

7964 **Knoch** Wendelin, Die Frühscholastik und ihre Ekklesiologie; eine Einführung. Pd 1992, Bonifatius. 142 p. DM 16,80 pa 3-87088-702-8 [TLZ 118,150s, K.-H. *Kandler*].

7965 **Kohler** Marc-Édouard, Kirche als Diakonie — ein Kompendium. Z 1991, Theol.-V. 304 p. Fs 28. 3-290-10154-1. – ᴿÉTRel 67 (1992) 633s (B. *Reymond*).

7966 **Koschorke** Klaus, Spuren... Kirche/BASILIUS 1991 → 7,7894*: ᴿArT-Gran 55 (1992) 353s (A. *Segovia*).

7966* *a) Kühn* Ulrich, Alttestamentliches Volk Gottes und christliche Gemeinde; zu einer These R. BULTMANNS; – *b) Link* Christoph, Die Gemeinde und ihre Vertretung: → 63, ᶠSAUER G., Aktualität 1992, 271-280 / 281-290.

7967 **Lakeland** Paul, Theology and critical theory; the discourse of the Church 1990 → 6,7913: ᴿCritRR 5 (1992) 476-8 (R. R. *Burke*: need for Rome to be self-critical à la HABERMAS).

7968 *a) Lanne* Emmanuel, Aspects ecclésiologiques du dialogue théologique... catholique-orthodoxe; – *b) Galitis* Georgios, Gli aspetti ecclesiologici... cattolico-ort.: → 583, Nicolaus 19 (1992) 179-189 / 191-199.

7969 *Larrabe* José Luis, Hacia una Iglesia misionera según la 'Redemptoris missio'; un comentario teológico y catequético: EstE 67 (1992) 73-90.

7970 **Ledegang** F., Mysterium ecclesiae; Beelden voor de Kerk en haar leven bij ORIGENES: diss. ᴰ*Davids* A. Nijmegen 1992, auct. xxxiii-976 p. 90-9005-258-5. – TvT 33,83; RTLv 24, p. 569.

7971 **Legrand** Lucien, Unity and plurality; mission in the Bible 1990 → 7, 7898; also Gracewing: ᴿExpTim 103 (1991s) 94 (G. T. *Eddy*: the 'plurality' is not pluralism of religions, but inner-Bible models); Horizons 19 (1992) 133s (J. A. *Grassi*).

7971* **Legrand** Lucien, Il Dio che viene; la missione nella Bibbia [1988 → 4,8427], ᵀ*Valentino* C. R 1989, Borla. 232 p. Lit. 20.000. 88-263-0716-4. – ᴿLateranum 57 (1991) 226-8 (R. *Penna*).

7972 **Leith** John H., From generation to generation; the renewal of the Church according to its own theology and practice. Louisville 1990, W-Knox. 223 p. $15 pa. – ᴿInterpretation 46 (1992) 210, 212 (Nancy J. *Duff*: on Prebyterian decline).

7973 **Leuninger** Ernst, Wir sind das Volk Gottes! Demokratisierung der Kirche. Fra 1992, Knecht. 167 p. 3-7820-0641-0. – ᴿActuBbg 29 (1992) 273 (J. *Boada*).

7974 **Liberti** V., I laici 1988/90 ⇒ 6,542*: ᴿBurgense 32 (1991) 292 (E. *Bueno*).

7975 **Lingenfelter** Sherwood G., Transforming culture; a challenge for Christian mission: GR 1992, Baker. 218 p. $15. 0-8010-5674-8 [TDig 40,74].

7976 *Lohfink* Gerhard, Jesus und die Kirche: TJb (Lp 1990) 64-106 [< ZIT 91,654].

7977 *a)* *Losada* J., La actual eclesiología latinoamericana; – *b)* *Bougerol* J. G., Reflexiones sobre la Iglesia: Carthaginensia 8 (1982) 711-743 / 745-756.

7978 **Lutz** Jürgen, Unio und Communio... LUTHER 1990 ⇒ 6,7918: ᴿTLZ 117 (1992) 206-9 (T. *Kaufmann*); TvT [= TsTNijm] 32 (1992) 101 (T. H. M. *Akerboom*).

7978* **McMann** Duncan, Mission in unity; the Bible and missionary structures: Latimer Studies 33. L 1989, Latimer House. 20 p. £1.75. – ᴿRefTR 50 (1991) 72s (Narelle *Jarrett*: '20 p.').

7979 *a)* *Maggioni* Bruno, Missione e vangelo / e culture; – *b)* *Penna* Romano, ...e spirito; – *c)* *Ravasi* Gianfranco. ...e Chiesa; – *d)* *Marconcini* Benito, ...e mondo: ParVi 35,6 (1990) 406-412.435-441 / 413-420 / 421-7 / 428-434.

7979* *Maliekal* Francis F., 'Viis sibi notis'; an analysis of 'Ad Gentes' [1976] 7a: Salesianum 54 (1992) 705-741.

7980 **Manaranche** A., J'aime mon Église: Lumière Vérité. P 1991, Sarment/Fayard. 351 p. F 65. [NRT 115, 583, B. *Clarot*].

7980* *Marto* António, A Igreja, mistério de comunhão: HumTeol 13 (1992) 317-333.

7981 **Meier** Bertram, Die Kirche der wahren Christen; J. M. SAILER ...: MüThSt 4, ᴰ1990 ⇒ 7,7909*: ᴿTR 88 (1992) 213-6 (M. *Probst*); TvT [= TsTNijm] 32 (1992) 103 (T. *Schoof*).

7982 **Meyer zu Schlochtern** Josef, Sakrament Kirche; Wirken Gottes im Handeln der Menschen [Hab.-Diss. Bochum]. FrB 1992, Herder. 416 p. DM 58 [TR 88,434].

7983 *Mobbs* Frank, L'unique véritable église selon Vatican II [... et DULLES, TILLARD, MCBRIEN]: PeCa 250 (1991) 53-65.

7984 **Monchanin** Jules, Théologie et spiritualité missionnaires; préf. *Duperray* É. (*Gadille* J.). P 1985, Beauchesne. 214 p. F 120. – ᴿTR 88 (1992) 244 (K. J. *Tossou*).

7985 *Mondal* Asish K., The place of conversion in Christian mission: Indian Missiological Review 13,3 (1991) 17-23 [TContext 10/1, 91, G. *Evers*].

7986 **Mondin** Giovanni B., La Chiesa primizia del regno; trattato di Ecclesiologia²: CorsTSist 7. Bo 1989, Dehoniane. 511 p. 88-10-50307-4. – ᴿEstE 67 (1992) 473s (J. J. *Alemany*).

7987 *a)* *Morerod* Charles, Le Saint-Esprit dans l'ecclésiologie de C. JOURNET; – *b)* *Emonet* Pierre-Marie, L'Église, l'univers de la Rédemption; – *c)* *Cagin* Michel, Le mystère de l'Église: ⇒ 785*b*, ᶠJOURNET C., NVFr 66,4 (1991) 53-65 / 49-52 / 28-48.

7987* *Mouw* Richard J., Israel and the Church in the world: ⇒ 88, ᶠHUBBARD D., OT 1992, 243-261.

7988 **Müller** Karl, Teologia della missione; una introduzione. Bo 1991, Missionaria. 283 p. – ᴿVivH 3 (1992) 409s (S. *Dianich*).

7989 *a)* *Nardi* Carlo, 'L'uomo via della chiesa' nella Redemptor hominis e nella Centesimus annus; note storico-teologiche; – *b)* *Cioli* Gianni, Conversione, vita morale e missione della Chiesa; riflessioni teologiche sull'etica alla luce dell'ecclesiologia del Vaticano II: VivH 3,1 (1992) 153-170; Eng. 171 / 173-186; Eng. 186.

7990 **Nascimento Filho** Antonio J. de, The role of the Laity in the Roman Catholic Church analyzed from a Reformed perspective: diss. Reformed Theol. Sem. 1992, ᴰ*Long* P. 266 p. 93-00040. – DissA 53 (1992s) 3251-A.

7991 **Neckebrouck** Valeer, De stomme duivelen; het anti-missionair syndroom in de westerse Kerk 1990 ➤ 7,7916: ᴿETL 68 (1992) 184s (R. *Boudens*: 'issues in development' replaces 'missiology' in the theology curriculum).

7992 **Neuner** Peter, Der Laie and das Gottesvolk 1989 ➤ 7,7917: ᴿRelStR 18 (1992) 219 (P. C. *Phan*).

7992* *Neuner* J., Mission in Ad gentes and in Redemptoris missio: Vidyajyoti 56 (1992) 228-241.

7993 **Nichols** Aidan, Theology in the Russian diaspora; Church, Fathers, Eucharist in Nikolai AFANAS'EV (1893-1966). C 1989, Univ. xv-295 p. DM 32,50. – ᴿScotJT 45 (1992) 272s (H. M. *Boosalis*); TR 88 (1992) 487s (T. *Bremer*).

7994 *Nichols* Aidan, The appeal to the Fathers in the ecclesiology of Nicolai AFANAS'EV, I. from the Didache to Origen; II. from Cyprian to Denys; III. Byzantine canonical tradition: HeythJ 33 (1992) 125-145 . 247-266 . 415-425.

7995 *Nichtweiss* Barbara, Kirche und Reich Gottes; PETERSONS Traktat 'Die Kirche'; Catholica 46 (1992) 281-306.

7996 *Nicolas* Xavier, Une nouvelle donne [néologisme de J. GADILLE, LumièreV 205 pour une avancée dans trois directions]: Christus 39 (P 1992) 448-456.

7996* **Nkulu Kabamba** Olivier, Visions théologiques africaines de l'Église; essai d'une théologie contextuelle et critique: diss. ᴰ*Neckebrouck* V. Leuven 1992. xlii-218 p. – LvSt 17 (1992) 403s [RTLv 24, p. 569].

7997 **Nordstokke** Kjell, Ekklesiogenese; konsil og kontekstet i Leonardo BOFFS ekklesiologi [diss. Oslo 1991]. Oslo 1990, Diakonhjemmet. 307 p. – ST 46 (1992) 71.

7998 **Nwabuike** Okesie David, Sentido y alcance de los términos 'laicus' y 'saecularis' y sus afines en los escritos de S. Tomás de AQUINO: dis. ᴰ*Illanes* J. L. Pamplona 1992. 441 p. – RTLv 24, p. 554.

7998* **Parent** Rémi, A Church of the baptized; overcoming the tensions between the clergy and the laity [1987 ➤ 3,7667]; ᵀ*Arndt* Stephen W. NY 1989, Paulist. 213 p. $13. – ᴿThought 66 (1991) 95-97 (T. P. *Rausch*).

7999 *Park Jae Soon,* Jesus' table community movement and the Church: CTC Bulletin 11,1 (1992) 32-50 [summary in TContext 10/2, 78].

8000 **Pellitero Iglesias** Ramiro, La teología del laicado según Yves CONGAR: diss. ᴰ*Rodríguez* P. Pamplona 1992. 1182 p. – RTLv 24, p. 569.

8001 *Potter* Philip, (*al.*), Mission as reconciliation in the power of the Spirit; impulses from Canberra [WCC, Feb. 1991]: IntRMiss 80 (1991) 305-314 (-403).

8001* ᴱ**Pottmeyer** Hermann J., Kirche im Kontext der modernen Gesellschaft; zur Strukturfrage der römisch-katholischen Kirche [FrB Nov. 1988] 1989 ➤ 6,670* *a*: ᴿRTLv 23 (1992) 253s (P. *Weber*).

8002 *Poupard* Paul, *a*) Église et cultures; l'Évangile au coeur de l'homme et de l'humanité; – *b*) L'Église face au défis de l'an 2000: HumTeol 13 (1992) 121-140 / 141-151.

8002* *Ramos Guerreiro* Julio, El intento de fundamentación cristológica de la eclesiología en el Vaticano I: Salmanticensis 39 (1992) 325-347; Eng. 348.

8003 **Ratzinger** Joseph Kard., *a)* Zur Gemeinschaft gerufen; Kirche heute verstehen 1991 ➤ 7,7923*: ᴿAtKap 119 (1992) 357-360 (R. *Karwacki*, ❷); – *b)* La Chiesa. CinB 1991, Paoline. 144 p. – ᴿAnnTh 6 (1992) 161s (R. P. *Bucciarelli*).

8003* **Ratzinger** J., Église et théologie. P 1992, Mame. 226 p. – ᴿÉtudes 377 (1992) 282 (J. *Thomas*).

8004 **Rebeiro** Manuel, The Church as the community of the believers; Hans KÜNG'S concept of the Church as a proposal for an ecumenical theology: diss. ᴰ*Michiels* R. Leuven 1992. cxcvii-441 p. – LvSt 17 (1992) 401.

8005 *a) Recker* Robert D., Le basi bibliche della missione cristiana, ᵀ*Borelli* C.; – *b) Herm* Daniel, La dimensione comunitaria del servizio missionario, ᵀ*Secondi* B.; – *c) Finch* Paul, La relazone tra Chiesa e missione; contorni del problema: STEv 2 (1990) 7-27 / 39-46 / 47-54 (112-6, rassegna).

8006 **Rigal** Jean, Le mystère de l'Église; fondements théologiques et perspectives pastorales. P 1992, Cerf. 275 p. F 140 [TR 88,528]. – ᴿBLitEc 93 (1992) 344-6 (F. *Rausières*).

8007 *a) Rüegger* Heinz, Christus als Gemeinde existierend; Grundzüge der Sozialgestalt des christlichen Glaubens; – *b) Nayak* Anand, Die Herausforderung des christlichen Glaubens durch östliche Religionen und New Age: IkiZ 82 (1992) 50-76 / 10-24.

8008 **Sanks** T. Howland, Salt, leaven, and light; the community called Church. NY 1992, Crossroad. xi-251 p. $22. 0-8245-1175-1 [TDig 40,185].

8009 *Santiago Madrigal* J., El primer 'tractatus de Ecclesia' [Juan STOJKOVIC c, 1440, según TORQUEMADA 1450]; relectura de la doctrina de las 'Notae Ecclesiae': EstE 67 (1992) 19-50.

8010 **Schillebeeckx** E., Church, the human story of God 1990 ➤ 7,7929: ᴿJTS 43 (1992) 329-332 (A. E. *Harvey*: why he called it Church); NBlackf 73 (1992) 571-3 (F. *Kerr*); PrPeo 5 (1991) 81s (J. *Tolhurst*); LvSt 17 (1992) 65-68 (R. *Michiels*).

8011 **Schmitz** Rudolf M., Aufbruch zum Geheimnis der Kirche J. C.; Aspekte der katholischen Ekklesologie des deutschen Sprachraums von 1918 bis 1943 [Diss. Gregoriana]: MüTSt 45. St. Ottilien 1991, EOS. xi-338 p. DM 76 [TR 88,347]. – ᴿDivinitas 36 (1992) 92-94 (B. *Gherardini*).

8011* **Schreiter** Robert J., Reconciliation; mission and ministry in a changing social order [Boston Costas consultation on mission]: Boston Theol. Inst. 3. Mkn 1992, Orbis. ix-84 p. $11 pa. 0-88344-809-2 [TDig 40, 186].

8012 **Secondin** Bruno, I nuovi protagonisti; movimenti, associazioni, gruppi nella Chiesa 1991 ➤ 7,7981: ᴿAtKap 118 (1992) 344-6 (M. *Chmielewski*, ❷).

8012* **Semeraro** Marcello, *a)* Con la Chiesa nel mondo; il laico nella storia nella teologia nel magistero: Vivere In. R 1991. 221 p. Lit. 18.000. – ᴿRivScR 5 (1991) 500s (G. *Ancona*); – *b)* La Chiesa, sacramento di Cristo e dello Spirito: Lateranum 57 (1991) 55-70.

8013 **Senn** Felix, Orthopraktische Ekklesiologie? Karl RAHNERS Offenbarungsverständnis und seine ekklesiologischen Konsequenzen im Kontext der neueren katholischen Theologiegeschichte [Diss. FrS 1988]: FreibZ ÖkBeih 19, 1989 ➤ 6,7946; 7,7933: 3-7278-0651-6. – ᴿBijdragen 53 (1992) 448s (W. G. *Tillmans*).

8014 ᴱ**Seybold** Michael, Fragen in der Kirche und an die Kirche: Extemporalia 6, 1987/8 ➤ 5,517, 6,7946* : ᴿMüTZ 43 (1992) 133-5 (T. *Böhm*).

8015 *Simon* Bruno-Marie, Il mistero della Chiesa: SacDoc 35 (1990) 492-532.

8016 **Sinclair** Maurice, Ripening harvest, gathering storm [... mission on six continents]. L 1988. 252 p. £ 4. pa. 0-86065-648-9. – ᴿEvangel 9,1 (1991)

29s (G. *Palmer* gives the publisher of this 'wide-ranging and passionate book' as 'MARC/STL/CMS/EMA').

8017 *Sonnberger* Klus, *Ven* Johannes van der, Ekklesiologische Hypothesen zur kirchlichen Autorität: Bijdragen 53 (1992) 234-262; Eng. 263.

8017* *Stidsen* Catherine B., *a*) The reconception of Christianity according to William E. HOCKING; – *b*) A new kind of Christian mission: Vidyajyoti 56 (1992) 215-223 / 247-255.

8018 **Sullivan** Francis A., The Church we believe in; one, holy, catholic and apostolic 1988 ➤ 5,7920 ... 7,7937: ᴿRTLv 23 (1992) 501 (M. *Simon*: solide et d'une très grande clarté); Thought 65 (1990) 207s (S. *Babos*).

8019 **Sullivan** Francis A., Salvation outside the Church? Tracing the history of the Catholic response. L c. 1992, G. Chapman. £13. – ᴿTablet 246 (1992) 1303 (M. *Barnes*).

8020 **Tavard** George H., The Church, community of salvation: NTheolSt 1. ColMn 1992, Liturgical. 264 p. $19. 0-8146-5789-3 [NRT 115, 622, A. *Toubeau*].

8021 *a*) *Theissen* Gerd, Gruppenmessianismus; Überlegungen zum Ursprung der Kirche im Jüngerkreis Jesu; – *b*) *Klaiber* Walter, Proexistenz und Kontrastverhalten; Beobachtungen zu einer Grundstruktur neutestamentlicher Ekklesiologie: ➤ 355, JbBT 7 (1992) 101-123 / 125-144.

8021* **Thils** Gustave, Primauté et infaillibilité du Pontife romain à Vatican I... ecclésiologie: RtETL 89, 1989 ➤ 6,309; 7,7939: ᴿAngelicum 69 (1992) 128s (A. *Wilder*: not much new or original); ETL 68 (1992) 176s (M. *Simon*); RET 52 (1992) 91-93 (M. *Gesteira*).

8022 **Thornhill** John, Sign and promise; a theology of the Church for a changing world 1988 ➤ 5,7925: ᴿPacifica 4 (1991) 93-96 (M. *Putney*: a Catholic ARCIC ecclesiology).

8023 *Tihon* Paul, Retour aux missions? Une lecture de l'Encyclique 'Redemptoris missio': NRT 114 (1992) 69-86.

8024 **Uka** E. M., Missionaries go home? A sociological interpretation of an African response to Christian missions. Fra 1989, Lang. 313 p. Fs 25. – ᴿHeythJ 33 (1992) 106s (M. F. C. *Bourdillon*: Truth amid utopian elements).

8025 **Valadier** Paul, La Iglesia en proceso; catolicismo y sociedad moderna 1990 ➤ 6,7953: ᴿChristus 57,1 (Méx 1992) 57 (C. *Bravo G.*).

8026 ᴱ**Valentini** Donato, La teologia; aspetti innovatori... ecclesiologia, mariologia 1988/9 ➤ 6,703: ᴿAngelicum 69 (1992) 278-281 (T. *Stancati*); Gregorianum 73 (1992) 350-2 (R. *Fisichella*).

8026* **Van Engen** Charles, God's missionary people. GR 1991, Baker. 223 p. [RefTR 51,75].

8027 *Vanhoye* Albert, Le origini della missione apostolica nel NT: Vita consacrata 28 (1992) 694-707.

8028 *a*) *Velema* W. H., KUYPERS conceptie van de kerk als organisme kritisch bekeken; – *b*) *Loonstra* B., Het Verbond der verlossing en onze heilszekerheid: TRef 34 (Woerden 1991) 295-309 / 310-... [< ZIT 92,27].

8028* **Villar** José R., Teología de la Iglesia particular 1989 ➤ 6,7958; 7,7948: ᴿETL 68 (1992) 488-490 (J.-P. *Schouppe*). Lateranum 57 (1991) 630-2 (M. *Semeraro*).

8029 **Voss** K. P., Der Gedanke des allgemeinen Priester- und Prophetentums... Reformationszeit 1990 [Diss. Göttingen] ➤ 7,7950; DM 35; 3-417-29363-4: ᴿTvT [= TsTNijm] 32 (1992) 200s (W. *Boelens*).

8030 *Wainwright* Geoffrey, The end of all ecclesiastical order [CALVIN J.]: OneInC 27 (1991) 34-48.

8031 *Webster* John, Locality and catholicity; reflections on theology and the Church: ScotJT 45 (1992) 1-17.

8032 **Weinrich** Adele, Die Kirche in der Glaubenslehre Friedrich SCHLEIER-MACHERS. ᴰ1990 → 7,7951: ᴿRTLv 23 (1992) 88-90 (E. *Brito*).

8033 **Weiss** Paul, Gemeindekirche — Ort des Glaubens; die Praxis als Fundament und als Konsequenz der Theologie 1989 → 7,7952: ᴿTLZ 117 (1992) 542-5 (E. *Hübner*).

8034 **Wiedenhofer** Siegfried, Das katholische Kirchenverständnis; ein Lehrbuch der Ekklesiologie. Graz 1992, Styria. 381 p. DM 54. [TR 88,171]. – ᴿHerdKor 46 (1992) 390 (U. *Ruh*); TGʟ 88 (1992) 482-4 (W. *Beinert*).

8035 *Wilckens* Ulrich [ev.-Luth.], Die Stellung der Kirche im Heilsgeschehen — nach biblischer Sicht: UnSa 46 (1991) 44-64.

8036 **Wirsching** Johannes, Kirche und Pseudokirche; Konturen der Häresie 1990 → 7,7954: ᴿExpTim 102 (1990s) 333s (G. *Wainwright*).

8038 *Yarnold* Edward, The Church as communion [... RATZINGER; TILLARD (Church of Churches badly translated)]: Tablet 246 (1992) 1564s.

8039 *Zago* Marcello, La missione 'ad gentes' nella missione integrale della Chiesa: Studium 87 (R 1991) 229-236.

8040 *Zorn* Jean-François, Internationalisme missionnaire et nationalisme colonial; les enjeux d'une action apostolique qui dépasse les frontières: ÉTRel 67 (1992) 177-192.

H7.7 *Œcumenismus* – The ecumenical movement.

8041 ᴱ**Alberigo** Giuseppe, Christian unity; the council of Ferrara-Florence 1438/9-1989 [Florence 23-29 Sept. 1989] 1991 → 7,462a; Fb 3000. 90-6186-437-2 / 90-6831-318-5: ᴿCollatVʟ 22 (1992) 324s (J. *Bonny*); ETL 68 (1992) 458-460 (A. de *Halleux*); ExpTim 103 (1991s) 314s (J. A. *Newton*); Gregorianum 73 (1992) 768-770 (J. E. *Vercruysse*).

8042 **Amaladoss** Michael, Making all things new; dialogue, pluralism and evangelization in Asia. Mkn 1990, Orbis. 203 p. – ᴿTContexto 2,1 (1992) 128 (G. *Evers*).

8043 *Amaladoss* Michael, Liberation; an inter-religious project: EAPast 28 (1991) 4-33.

8044 AMALORPAVADAS D. S., mem.: Third world theologies in dialogue, 1991 → 7,5: ᴿEcuR 44 (1992) 517-520 (F. J. *Balasundaram*: 16 art., detailed).

8044* *Arinze* Francis, Dialogue and proclamation: BDialRel 26 (1991) 201-3.

8045 **Avis** Paul, Anglicanism and the Christian Church 1989 → 6,7967; 7,7963: ᴿChH 60 (1991) 582s (W. L. *Sachs*: effort to face questioning of the 'integrity of Anglicanism' by its bishop S. SYKES).

8046 **Avis** Paul, Christians in communion 1990 → 7,7964: ᴿExpTim 103 (1991s) 123 (R. *Lunt*: flamboyance of a cavalry-charge).

8047 **Baillargeon** Gaëtan, Perspectives orthodoxes sur l'Église-Communion: l'œuvre de Jean ZIZIOULAS; préf. *Tillard* J.: Brèches théologiques 6. Montréal/P 1989, Paulines/Médiaspaul. 414 p. 2-89093-458-1 [RTLv 24,78, A. de *Halleux*].

8048 **Barth** H.-M., Einander Priester sein; allgemeines Priestertum in ökumenischer Perspektive 1990 → 6,6979; 8,7968: ᴿTvT [= TsTNijm] 32 (1992) 109s (H. *Witte*).

8048* **Baur** Jörg, Einig in Sachen Rechtfertigung 1989 → 6,7970; 7,7969: — **Kühn** U., **Pesch** O. H., Rechtfertigung im Disput; eine freundliche Antwort an Baur. Tü 1991. – ᴿTGʟ 82 (1992) 498s (B. *Neumann*).

8049 **Beaupère** René, L'œcuménisme: Parcours. P 1991, Centurion/Croix. 126 p. F 62. – ᴿChristus 39 (1992) 94s (J.-B. *Baudin*).

8050 a) **Bertsch** Ludwig, Universale Kirche als Communio ecclesiarum; – b) *Suttner* Ernst C., Einheit der Ortskirchen ohne Uniatismus: TPQ 140 (1992) 109-115 / 116-122.

8051 ᴱ**Best** Thomas F., Living today towards visible unity; fifth international consultation of united and uniting churches: Faith and Order Papers 143. Geneva 1988, WCC. xii-136 p. Fs 15. – ᴿRTLv 23 (1992) 113s (A. de *Halleux*).

Beyerhaus Peter P. J., God's kingdom [against ecumenical movement transformation of missionary vision] 1992 ➤ 7660*.

8052 **Bilheimer** Robert S., Breakthrough; the emergence of the ecumenical tradition 1990 ➤ 6,6972; 7,7967: ᴿMid-Stream 30 (1991) 409s (P. C. *Rodger*).

8053 **Bizeul** Yves, L'identité protestante; étude de la minorité protestante de France: Réponses sociologiques. P 1991, Méridiens Klincksieck. 278 p. 2-86563-284-9. – ᴿÉTRel 67 (1992) 139-141 (J.-M. *Prieur*).

8054 a) *Blancy* Alain, Can the Churches convert? Should the Churches convert? – b) *Motte* Mary, Conversion; a missiological perspective: EcuR 44,4 (1992) 419-428 / 453-7.

8055 **Braybrooke** Marcus, Pilgrimage of hope; one hundred years of interfaith dialogue. L 1992, SCM. xvi-368 p. £30 [TR 88,171; TDig 39,353].

8055* *Braybrooke* Marcus, The interfaith movement; the present reality: Vidyajyoti 56 (1992) 181-193.

8056 **Brent** Allen, Cultural episcopacy and ecumenism; representative ministry in church history from the age of IGNATIUS of Antioch to the Reformation with special reference to contemporary ecumenism: Studies in Christian Mission 6. Leiden 1992, Brill. xiv-250 p. 90-04-09432-6.

8056* **Bria** Ion, The sense of ecumenical tradition; the ecumenical witness and vision of the Orthodox. Geneva 1991, WCC. viii-120 p. – ᴿOstkSt 41 (1992) 338s (B. *Plank*).

8057 *Brock* Peter, The 'no-future' generation: EcuR 44,2 ('Youth in the ecumenical movement' 1992) 179-196: p. 181 'Young people today ride a tiger. Rapidation is reality'; p. 187 cites 'within two years, 70% of [Christian teens] have left the church, never to return'.

8058 **Bruce** Steve, A house divided; Protestantism, schism, and secularization. L 1990, Routledge. vi-257 p. $40. – ᴿRRelRes 33 (1990s) 91s (D. R. *Hoge*).

8059 **Brunner** Gottlieb, Grundwerte als Fundament der pluralistischen Gesellschaft; eine Untersuchung der Positionen von Kirchen, Parteien und Gewerkschaften in der Bundesrepublik Deutschland: FreibTSt 142. FrB 1989, Herder. xi-219 p. DM 38. – ᴿTLZ 116 (1991) 217-9 (H. *Kress*).

8060 ᴱ**Burgess** Joseph A., In search of Christian unity 1991 ➤ 7,477*: ᴿTsTKi 63 (1992) 230s (O. *Tjørhom*).

8060* *Burgess* Joseph A., Ökumenische Bewegung, ᵀ*Mühlenberg* M.: ➤ 757, EvKL 3 (1992) 826-839 (-862 *al.*, Dialog usw.; 863-873, *Fahlbusch* E., Ökumenismus).

8061 **Burrows** Mark S., An 'aesthetic' of ecumenism for the divided churches: NewTR 5,1 (1992) 88-93.

8062 *Butselaar* Jan van (*al.*), Thinking locally, acting globally; the ecumenical movement in the new era: IntRMiss 81 (1992) 363-373 (-463).

8063 **Calian** Carnegie S., Theology without boundaries; encounters of Eastern Orthodoxy and western tradition. Louisville 1992, W-Knox. 130 p. $15. 0-664-25156-0 [TDig 39,355].

8064 *Cassidy* Edward J., *a*) Lutheran-Roman Catholic relations: Mid-Stream 30 (1991) 299-315; – *b*) Der Päpstliche Rat zur Förderung der Einheit der Christen im Jahre 1991: Catholica 46 (1992) 169-188.

8065 *Cazelles* Henri [➤ 7922], Unité et diversité dans l'Église en dialogue: RechSR 80 (1992) 81-84.

8066 *Ciobotea* Daniel, L'Église orthodoxe en Roumanie; son rôle passé, présent et futur: IkiZ 81 (1991) 123-132.

8067 **Coakley** J. F., The Church of the East and the Church of England; a history of the Archbishop of Canterbury's Assyrian mission. Ox 1992, Clarendon. x-422 p.; ill. £45 [TR 88,529].

8068 Comité mixte catholique-orthodoxe en France [aucun responsable nommé]. La primauté romaine dans la communion des Églises: Documents des Églises. P 1991, Cerf. 125 p. F 69. 2-204-04384-2. – ᴿÉTRel 67 (1992) 305s (J.-M. *Prieur*).

8068* Confessing the one faith...: Faith & Order 153. Geneva 1991, WCC. viii-139 p. [RelStR 19,58, J. T. *Ford*].

8069 **Cracknell** Kenneth, Mission und Dialog; für eine neue Beziehung zu Menschen anderer Glaubens [1986], ᵀ*Berger* Ulrike. Fra 1990, Lembeck. 160 p. – ᴿNZMissW 47 (1991) 321s (D. *Krieger*).

8070 **Cullmann** Oscar, Einheit durch Vielfalt ²ʳᵉᵛ 1990 ➤ 7,7995: ᴿTZBas 48 (1992) 394s (D. *Braun*).

8071 **Cullmann** Oscar, Les voies de l'unité chrétienne: Théologie. P 1992, Cerf. 100 p. F 99. 2-204-04389-3. – ᴿEsprVie 102 (1992) 220-2 (P. *Jay*: clarifications sans dépassements: 'Un texte livré au public échappe toujours plus ou moins à son auteur'); ETRel 67 (1992) 630s (J.-M. *Prieur*).

8072 *a*) *Cwiekowski* F. J., Early churches in the early Church; – *b*) *Guarino* J., The role of women...: Catholic World 235, 1406 (1992) 58-62 / 74-77 [< NTAbs 36,379s].

8073 *David* Bernard, Le mouvement œcuménique chez les catholiques [Code de Droit canonique, c. 755 'renversant la perspective de 1917']: EsprVie 102 (1992) 1-13.

8074 **De Gruchy** John W., Liberating Reformed theology; a South African contribution to an ecumenical debate. GR/Cape Town 1991. Eerdmans/ Philip. xviii-291 p. $19 [TR 88,171].

8075 **Dionne** J. Robert, The papacy and the Church; a study of praxis and reception in ecumenical perspective ᴰ1987 ➤ 3,7776... 7,8003: ᴿBenedictina 39 (1992) 267-9 (A. B. *Calkins*).

8076 **Döpmann** Hans-Dieter, Die orthodoxen Kirchen. B 1991, Union. 384 p. (32 p. photos). DM 48. 3-372-00200-8. – ᴿOstkSt 41 (1992) 216-8 (H. *Rohling*); TR 88 (1992) 482-4 (T. *Bremer*).

8076* *Döpmann* Hans-Dieter, Meinungen über den Platz der russischen Kirche in der zeitgenössischen Welt in den Vorbereitungen auf ein russisches Landeskonzil (seit 1905) und bei den kirchlichen Erneuerern nach der Revolution: OstkSt 41 (1992) 107-125.

8077 *Döring* Heinrich, Zur mangelnden Effizienz ökumenischer Theologie; soziologische Faktoren im ökumenischen Gesamtprozess: UnSa 46 (1991) 279-291. 304.

8078 *Dombes*, groupe, Pour la conversion des Églises; identité et changement dans la dynamique de la communion 1991 ➤ 7,8005: ᴿTPhil 67 (1992) 305s (P. *Knauer*).

8079 *Dupuis* Jacques, Dialogo e annuncio in due recenti documenti [Redemptoris missio 1990; Dialogo e annuncio 1991]: CC 143 (1992,2) 221-236.

8080 **Dupuy** B. [2 art.+5 *al.*; fruit de 5 ans de rencontres], La primauté romaine dans la Communion des Églises; comité mixte catholique-orthodoxe en France. P 1992, Cerf. 125 p. F 69. – ᴿEsprVie 102 (1992) 571s (P. *Jay*).

8081 *Eber* Jochen, The vision of the Pope [Erzählung, 1975], a novel by 'KNECHT Sebastian', really an ecumenical effort of Edmund SCHLINK (1903-1984): ScotJT 45 (1992) 237-243 [< ᶠ*Mildenberger* F., Zeit (1989) 7-12].

8081* *Erickson* John, *Borelli* John, Nouvelle crise au sein du dialogue orthodoxe-catholique: Œcuménisme 27,107 (1992) 22-24.34 / 25-29.

8082 *Fahlbusch* Erwin, Römisch-katholische Kirche: ➤ 757, EvKL 3 (1992) 1680-98 ➤ 8060.

8083 **Felmy** Karl C., Orthodoxe Theologie der Gegenwart; eine Einführung, 1990 ➤ 7,8011; DM 59: ᴿEvKomm 24 (1991) 431s (Friederike *Stockmann-Köckert*); TR 88 (1992) 484-7 (S. *Harkianakis*).

8084 **Frame** John M., Evangelical reunion; denominations and the Body of Christ. GR 1991, Baker. 185 p. [RefTR 51,36]. $11 pa. – ᴿBtS 149 (1992) 253s (R. A. *Pyne*).

8085 **Frieling** Reinhard, Der Weg des ökumenischen Denkens; eine Ökumeniekunde: Zugänge zur Kirchengeschichte 10 / Kleine Reihe 1564. Gö 1992, Vandenhoeck & R. 376 p. DM 25,80 [TR 88,529].

8086 *Frieling* Reinhard, Wider die ökumenische Gleichgültigkeit: UnSa 47 (1992) 289-297.

8087 **Fuchs** O., Zwischen Wahrhaftigkeit und Macht; Pluralismus in der Kirche? Fra 1990, Knecht. 217 p. DM 29,80. 3-7820-0614-3. – ᴿTvT 32 (1992) 436 (F. *Haarsma*).

8087* ᶠGASSMANN Günther, ᴱ**Meyer** Harding. Gemeinsamer Glaube und Strukturen der Gemeinschaft 1991 ➤ 7,63*: ᴿTsTKi 63 (1992) 231-3 (O. *Tjørhom*).

8088 *Geldbach* Erich, On the road to unity?: Pacifica 5 (1992) 204-218.

8089 **Girault** René, Construire l'Église une; nouveaux chemins œcuméniques 1990 ➤ 7,8019: ᴿAtKap 119 (1992) 353-5 (A. *Nowicki*, ❷).

8089* *Girault* René, Le Conseil œcuménique des Églises [WCC] à un tournant: Études 376 (1992) 831-842.

8090 ᴱ**Gort** Jerald D., On sharing religious experience; possibilities of interfaith mutuality: Currents of Encounter 5. Amst 1992, Rodopi. xi-304 p. ƒ 56 [TR 88,529].

8091 *Green* Robin, God is doing a new thing; a theological reflection on the practice of partnership: IntRMiss 80 (1991) 219-229.

8092 **Grès-Gayer** Jacques, Paris-Cantorbéry 1717-1720, le dossier d'un premier œcuménisme ... 1989 ➤ 6,8010: ᴿChII 60 (1991) 553s (T. A. *Campbell*).

8093 **Griffiths** Paul J., An apology for [interreligious] apologetics 1991 ➤ 7,8020*: ᴿCritRR 5 (1992) 274s (S. M. *Heim*); ModT 8 (1992) 404-6 (F. X. *Clooney*).

8094 *Hage* Wolfgang, Geschichte und Gegenwart der orientalischen Kirchen: TRu 57 (1992) 254-276.

8094* *Halleux* André de, La Nativité et l'Épiphanie dans le dialogue unioniste du VIIᵉ au XIVᵉ siècle: ETL 68 (1992) 5-37.

8095 *Hammerschmidt* Ernst, Die orthodoxen Kirchen Nᵒ 102-105; IkiZ 81 (1991) 77-122.201-252; 82 (1992) 77-127.233-268.

8096 **Hardjowasito** Kadarmanto, The significance of David TRACY's and George LINDBECK's theological methods for a religious education that takes dialogue among religious groups seriously: diss. 1991, Presbyterian School of Religious Education. 234 p. 92-25334. – DissA 53 (1992s) 1466-A.

8097 **Hastings** Adrian,   The theology of a Protestant Catholic 1990 ➤ 6,244: ᴿEcuR 44 (1992) 156s (G. *Kelly*).

8098 *a) Himes* Michael J.,   The ecclesiological significance of the reception of doctrine; – *b) Crowley* Paul G.,   Catholicity, inculturation and NEWMAN's sensus fidelium: HeythJ 33 (1992) 146-160 / 161-174.

8099 *Holtrop* P. N.,   Analyses van de stagnatie in de oecumene [RAISER K. 1989]:   GerefTTs 92 (1992) 121-130.

8100 *Houdart* Bernadette,   Tolerantie, zingeving en christelijke levensbeschouwing: CollatVL 22 (1992) 397-416.

8101 *Hulshof* Jan,   Christenen en de vrijheid van anderen; menschenrechten als hermeneutisch probleem in de katholieke traditie: TvT 32 (1992) 31-56; Eng. 56.

8102 *a) Jacobs* J. Y. H. A.,   Een beweging in verandering; de inzet van Belgische und Nederlandse katholieken voor de eenheid der kerken 1921-1964; – *b) Gevers* Lieve,   Vaticanum II en de lage landen; bronnen en historiografie: Trajecta 1 (1922) 67-91 / 187-205 [< TR 88,432].

8103 **Jones** Hywel R.,   Gospel and Church; an evangelical evaluation of ecumenical documents on Church unity.   Bryntirion 1990, Ev. Press of Wales.   171 p. – ᴿSTEv 3 (1991) 138 (T. *Racca*).

8104 *a) Jongeneel* Jan A. B.,   Ecumenical, evangelical and Pentecostal/charismatic views on mission as a movement of the Holy Spirit; – *b) Staples* Peter,   Ecumenical theology and Pentecostalism: ➤ 86, ᶠHOLLENWEGER W., Pentecost 1992, 231-246 / 261-271.

8105 *Jongeneel* Jan A. B.,   Oecumenische, evangelikale en pentecostale/charismatische visies op zending als beweging van de Heilige Geest: KerkT 43 (1992) 15-31.

8105* **Jünemann** Elisabeth,   Gemeinde und Weltverantwortung; eine historisch-systematische Studie zur Wahrnehmung sozialer Verantwortung durch die christliche Gemeinde [kath. Diss. Bonn 1991]: StudSeelsorge 7. – Wü 1992, Echter.   375 p. DM 48.   3-429-01430-1 [TLZ 118,456, W. *Huber*].

8106 *Kallis* Anastasios,   Orthodoxe katholische Kirchen: ➤ 757, EvKL 3 (1992) 939-951; (953-) 966-976, Orthodoxie, *Meyendorff* J., ᵀ*Hoffmann* H.

8107 **Keshishian** Aram,   Conciliar fellowship, a common goal.   Geneva 1992, WCC.   Fs 16,50. – ᴿNRT 114 (1992) 773 (A. *Harvengt*).

8107* *Knight* James,   Mission and dialogue in Asia; can we plumb the depths?   Vidyajyoti 56 (1992) 125-134.

8108 **Koch** K.,   Gelähmte Ökumene; was jetzt noch zu tun ist.   FrB 1991, Herder.   237 p. – ᴿNRT 114 (1992) 120 (A. *Harvengt*); TZBas 48 (1992) 392-4 (K. *Blaser*).

8109 *Körner* Bernhard,   Extra ecclesiam nulla salus; Sinn und Problematik dieses Satzes in einer sich wandelnden fundamentaltheologischen Ekklesiologie: ZkT 114 (1992) 274-292.

8109* **Koza** Stanisław J., ❷ Ewangelijna katolickość; zarys porównawszej [sketch of comparative] eklezjologii Friedricha HEILERA. Lublin 1987, KUL.   399 p. – ᴿAtKap 119 (1992) 176-8 (W. *Hanc*, ❷).

8110 *Kreiner* Armin,   *a*) 'Hierarchia veritatum'; Deutungsmöglichkeiten und ökumenische Relevanz; – *b*) Versöhnung ohne Kapitulation; Überlegungen zu George A. LINDBECKs 'The nature of doctrine';   Catholica 46 (1992) 1-30 / 307-321.

8111 *Krieger* David J., Bekehrung und Dialog; zur Sprechpragmatik interreligiösen Begegnungen: NZMissW 46 (1990) 267-285.

8112 **Kröger** Wolfgang, Die Befreiung des Minjung; das Profil einer protestantischen Befreiungstheologie für Asien in ökumenischer Perspektive: ÖkExH 10. Mü 1992, Kaiser. 193 p. DM 32 [TR 88,529].

8113 **Küng** Hans, Projekt d'éthique planétaire; la paix mondiale par la paix entre les religions, ᵀ*Feisthauer* J. P 1991, Seuil. F 120. – ᴿÉtudes 376 (1992) 138 (R. *Marlé*).

8114 **Kurečić** Zvonimir, 'Communio ecclesiastica'; fondamento della 'communicatio in sacris' tra cattolici e gli orientali non cattolici: diss. Pont. Univ. Gregoriana, ᴰ*Navarrete* U. Roma 1992, 398 p. – RTLv 24, p. 570.

8115 **La Hera** Eduardo de, La unidad de la Iglesia en PABLO VI (1961-1978); fundamentos teológicos y quehacer pastoral del camino de la unidad en el Papa Montini: diss. Pont. Univ. Gregoriana, ᴰ*Antón* Á. Roma 1992. 574 p.; Extr. 3916 (Palencia), 128 p. – RTLv 24, p. 569.

8116 ᴱ**Lange** Dietz, Überholte Verurteilungen? Die Gegensätze in der Lehre von Rechtfertigung, Abendmahl und Amt zwischen dem Konzil von Trient und der Reformation damals und heute. Gö 1991, Vandenhoeck & R. 136 p. DM 19,80. 3-525-56830-4. – ᴿTvT 32 (1992) 213s (G. P. *Hartvelt*); ZkT 114 (1992) 219-221 (Silvia *Hell*).

8117 *a) Larentzakis* Gregorius, Ferrara-Florenz im Urteil der heutigen Orthodoxie; – *b) Neuthen* Erich, EUGEN IV., Ferrara-Florenz und der lateinische Westen: AnHistConc 22 (1990) 199-218 / 219-234 [< 92,312].

8118 ᴱ**Lehmann** Karl, *Pannenberg* Wolfhart, Lehrverurteilungen — kirchentrennend? [I. 1986 ⇒ 3,661] II. 1989 ⇒ 6,8026: ᴿMüTZ 42 (1991) 89s (G. *Schütz*).

8119 ᴱ**Lehmann** Karl, *Pannenberg* Wolfhart, The condemnations of the Reformation era; do they still divide? ᵀ*Kohl* Margaret, 1990 ⇒ 7,8064: ᴿCritRR 5 (1992) 337s (J. T. *Ford*).

8120 ᴱ**Link** Hans-Georg, One God, one Lord, one Spirit; on the explication of the apostolic faith today [Kottayam 1984, Kinshasa, Chantilly 1985]: Faith & Order 139, 1988 ⇒ 4,382. ᴵᴵRTLv 23 (1992) 368s (A. de *Halleux*).

8121 *Löser* Werner, Papst und Konzil im Anglikanisch/Römisch-Katholischen Dialog; Erörterungen zu der katholischen Antwort auf [ARCIC I] den Schlussbericht von 1981: TPhil 67 (1992) 413-423.

8121* ᴱ**Lossky** Nicholas, al., Dictionary of the ecumenical movement. Geneve/ GR 1991 ⇒ 7,8048: ᴿCC 143 (1992,1) 571-4 (N. *Venturini*); ETRel 67 (1992) 479 (L. *Gambarotto*); ExpTim 103,8 2d-top choice (1991s) (C. S. *Rodd*); NRT 114 (1992) 117s (A. *Harvengt*); OstkSt 41 (1992) 208s (H. M. *Biedermann*).

8122 *McDonald* Kevin, Ecumenism in the Catholic Church; the present position twenty-five years after the decree: PrPeo 5 (1991) 6-14.

8123 **Maffeis** Angelo, Il ministero nella Chiesa; uno studio sul dialogo cattolico luterano (1967-1984): Rendiconti Lombardo diss. 2. Mi 1991, Glossa. 361 p. [TR 88,347].

8124 **MARON** Gottfried, Zum Gespräch mit Rom; [60. Gb., seine] Beiträge aus evangelischer Sicht. Bensheimer Hefte 69, 1998 ⇒ 5,312; 6,8032. ᴿGregorianum 73 (1992) 158 (J. E. *Vercruysse*).

8125 *Martikainen* Jouko, Wittenberg-Moskau-Rom; Johann P. KOHLs These von der ökumenischen Nähe der Orthodoxen Kirche zum Luthertum: JbNiedersächsKG 89 (1991) 229-236 [< ZIT 92,103].

8126 **Martling** Carl H., Gud i Orienten [eastern churches]. Sto 1990, Verbum. 240 p. – ᴿSvTKv 67 (1991) 140-3 (S. *Rubenson*).

8127 *Masson* Joseph, Le dialogue entre les religions; deux documents récents [Dialogue et annonce, 19.V.1991; Redemptoris missio 17.XII.1990]: NRT 14 (1992) 726-737 [... Que signifie pour l'Église le mot 'religion'? que pense l'Église de sa mission? qu'entend-elle par l'annonce? par 'dialogue'? le rapport de l'annonce et du dialogue ...].

8128 *a*) *Meyer* Harding, Pourquoi dans le document luthérien 'Face à l'unité?' (1984) a-t-on envisagé l'union de Florence comme 'exemple' d'unité?; – *b*) *Bobrinskoy* Boris, L'Uniatisme à la lumière des ecclésiologies qui s'affrontent [... *Varnalidis* S.]: ➤ 578, Chevetogne 1992, 325-338, Eng. 338 / 423-438; Eng. 439s [401-422].

8129 **Netland** Harold A., Dissonant voices; religious pluralism and the question of truth. GR/Leicester 1991, Eerdmans/Apollos. 323 p. £15. 0-8028-0602-3 / 0-85111-426-1. – ᴿExpTim 103 (1991s) 350 (K. *Cracknell*: missionary in Japan, acute but not facing the real issues).

8130 *a*) *Neusner* Jacob, Can people who believe in different religions talk together?; – *b*) *Hartin* Patrick J., Sensus fidelium; a Roman Catholic reflection on its significance for ecumenical thought: JEcuSt 28,1 (1991) 88-100 (-114, 3 responses) / 74-87.

8131 **Nichols** Aidan, Rome and the Eastern churches. E 1992, Clark. 240 p. £12.50. 0-567-29206-1. – ᴿDowR 110 (1992) 156-8 (D. *Edwards*); ExpTim 103 (1991s) 378 (H. *Chadwick*: a model of conciliation).

8131* *Nossol* Alfons, ℗ Theologische Hindernisse am Weg zur Einheit heute: ColcT 62,4 (1992) 69-77; deutsch 77s.

8132 *a*) *Nossol* Alfons, Ökumene in Bedrängnis? Theologische Hindernisse auf dem Weg der Einheit heute; – *b*) *Beinert* Wolfgang, Die katholische Kirche und der Dialog mit den Religionen [für Bischof] Nossols 60. Gb.: Catholica 46 (1992) 61-69 / 140-166.

8132* *Örsy* Ladislas, The conversion of the churches, condition of unity; a Roman Catholic perspective: America 166 (1992) 479-487.

8133 *a*) **Østnor** Lars [➤ 6,8039], Kirkens enhet; et bidrag til forståelse av norske teologers oppfatning av det økumeniske problem i mellomkrigstiden, ᴰ1990: ᴿNorTTs 92 (1991) 56-58 (N. E. *Bloch-Hoell*).
— *b*) ᴱ**Orth** G., Dem bewohnten Erdkreis Schalom; Beiträge zu einer Zwischenbilanz ökumenischen Lernens. Münster 1991, Comenius-Inst. 332 p. DM 15. – ᴿTGL 82 (1992) 500s (R. *Schlüter*).

8133* *Pannenberg* Wolfhart, Müssen sich die Kirchen immer noch gegenseitig verurteilen?; KerDo 38 (1992) 311-330; Eng. 330.

8134 *Peri* Vittorio, Le vocabulaire des relations entre les Églises d'Occident et d'Orient jusqu'au XVIᵉ siècle: Irénikon 65 (1992) 194-9; Eng. 199 ('catholic' 'orthodox' used equally for both until then).

8135 *Pickering* W. S. F., Anglo-Catholicism 1989 ➤ 6,8043; 7,8066: ᴿChH 60 (1991) 145s (R. *Kollar*); JRel 72 (1992) 116s (Ellen K. *Wondra*).

8135* *Puthiadam* Ignatius, Dialogue and proclamation; problem? challenge? grace-filled dialectic?: Vidyajyoti 56 (1992) 289-308.

8136 **Raiser** Konrad, Ökumene im Übergang? Paradigmenwechsel in der ökumenischen Bewegung? 1989 ➤ 6,8047: ᴿExpTim 102 (1990s) 332s (G. *Wainwright*).

8137 **Raiser** Konrad, Ecumenism in transition 1991 ➤ 7,8066*: ᴿExpTim 103 (1991s) 187 (J. *Kent*: a sad book; Vatican II created a conflict situation, WCC slowly marginalized by Roman Catholic and Orthodox).

8138 *Ratzinger* Joseph, Lettre aux évêques de l'Église catholique sur certains aspects de l'Église comprise comme communion (28.V.1992): EsprVie 102 (1992) 401-7.

8138* **Reardon** Martin, We believe in one holy Catholic and apostolic Church: OneInC 27 (1991) 308-319.

8139 **Rebeiro** Manuel, The Church as the community of the believers; Hans KÜNG's concept of the Church as a proposal for an ecumenical ecclesiology: diss. ᴰ*Michiels* R. Leuven 1992. cxcvii-441 p. – RTLv 24, p. 569.

8139* **Reid** Duncan, Die Lehre von den ungeschaffenen Energien; ihre Bedeutung für die ökumenische Theologie: Diss. Tübingen 1992. 241 p. – TLZ 117 (1992) 954s.

8140 *Ricca* Paolo, Taccuino ecumenico; Roma, Istanbul, Budapest e l'Europa: Protestantesimo 47 (1992) 126-132.

8140* **Rohr** Richard, Warum katholisch?ᵀ. FrB 1991, Herder. 214 p. – ᴿAtKap 118 (1992) 521-3 (L. *Górka* ❷).

8141 **Rupp** George, Commitment and community [in a pluralist world]. Mp 1989, Fortress. 117 p. – ᴿJRel 72 (1992) 283 (D. F. *Ottati*).

8142 **Ryan** Robin, The quest for the unity of the Christian Churches; a study of Karl RAHNER's writings on Christian ecumenism: diss. Catholic Univ., ᴰ*Galvin* J. Washington D.C. 1992. – RTLv 24, p. 570.

8143 *Saarinen* Risto, Ökumenische Theologie; Handbücher und Lexika: TRu 57 (1992) 392-404.

8144 **Sartori** L., L'unità dei cristiani; commento al decreto conciliare aul l'ecumenismo: La tunica inconsutile 1. Padova 1992, Messaggero. 140 p. Lit. 12.000. – ᴿStPatav 39 (1992) 634-6 (E. R. *Tura*).

8145 *Scheffczyk* Leo, Die Ehelehre Karl BARTHs unter ökumenischem Aspekt: ↠ 6,97*, ꟳMAY G., Fides et ius 1991, 389-406.

8146 **Schillebeeckx** Edward, Plaidoyer... ministères dans l'Église 1987 ↠ 3, 8008... 5,8114*: ᴿRTLv 23 (1992) 252s (M. *Simon*, avec un mot sur la critique de GRELOT).

8147 *Schilling* Johannes, *al.*, Papst(-tum): ↠ 757, EvKL 3 (1992) 1016-27 (-35).

8148 ᴱ**Schlemmer** Karl, Gottesdienst — Weg zur Einheit...: QDisp 122, 1988/9 ↠ 6,687. ᴿTLZ 117 (1992) 152-4 (K.-H. *Bieritz*).

8149 **Schlüter** Richard, Ökumenisches Lernen in der Kirchen — Schritte in die gemeinsame Zukunft; eine praktisch-theologische Grundlegung: RPPerspektiven 15. Essen 1992, Blaue Eule. 143 p. DM 32. – ᴿTR 88 (1992) 490s (K. J. *Lesch*).

8150 *Schreiner* Stefan, ❷ Vérité et tolérance dans le dialogue entre religions, ᵀ*Kleszcz* Anna, Żak Adam: PrzPow 847 (1992) 357-369.

8151 **Schütte** Heinz, Kirche im ökumenischen Verständnis; Kirche des dreieinigen Gottes 1991 ↠ 7,8078: ᴿTLZ 117 (1992) 547-9 (K. *Schwarzwäller*).

8152 **Sell** Alan P. F., A Reformed, evangelical, catholic theology; the contribution of the World Alliance of Reformed Churches, 1875-1982. GR 1991, Eerdmans. xi-304 p. $19. 0-8028-0483-7 [TDig 39,286].

8153 *Sesboüé* Bernard, Pour une théologie œcuménique: CogF 160, 1990 ↠ 7,263: ᴿArTGran 55 (1992) 377 (A. *Segovia*); BLitEc 93 (1992) 347s (A. *Dupleix*); ExpTim 102 (1990s) 333 (G. *Wainright*); Spiritus 32 (1991) 221 (M. *Oger*).

8154 *Skowronek* Alfons, ❷ Le siège de Pierre, problème œcuménique numéro 1?: PrzPow 845 (1992) 22-33; franç. 33.

8155 **Smart** Ninian, *Konstantine* Steven, Christian systematic theology in a world context. Mp/L 1991, Fortress/Marshall Pickering. 466 p. $18; £15 pa. – ᴿChrCent 109 (1992) 252s (L. J. *Hesselink*: eclectic not Christian, phenomenology not theology); TS 53 (1992) 775s (R. *Schreiter*); TLond 95 (1992) 40s (A. *Race*).

8156 *a*) *Staples* Peter, Ecumenical theology and Pentecostalism; – *b*) *MacRobert* Iain, The black roots of Pentecostalism; – *c*) *Hocken* Peter, Charismatic renewal in the Roman Catholic Church; reception and challenge: ➤ 86, ᶠHOLLENWEGER W., Pentecost 1992, 261-271 / 73-84 / 301-9.

8157 **Sullivan** Francis A., Salvation outside the Church; tracing the history of the Catholic response. NY 1992, Paulist. v-224 p. $13 [NRT 115,584, R. *Escol*].

8158 *Sullivan* Francis A., The Vatican response [AAS 74 (1982) 1063-74; Origins 21/28 (Dec. 19, 1991) 441-7] to ARCIC I [1981]: Gregorianum 73 (1992) 489-498; ital. 498.

8159 **Suttner** Ernst C., Die eine Taufe zur Vergebung der Sünde; zur Anerkennung der Taufe westlicher Christen durch die Orthodoxe Kirche im Laufe der Geschichte: Öst. Akad. ph/h Anzeiger 127. W 1991, Österr. Akad. 46 p. – ᴿOstkSt 41 (1992) 209s (H. M. *Biedermann*).

8159* *Suttner* Ernst C., Der offizielle theologische Dialog zwischen der katholischen und der orthodoxen Kirche: TPQ 139 (1991) 156-167.

8160 *Tavard* George H., A review of Anglican orders 1990 ➤ 6,8066: ᴿWorship 65 (1991) 276s (J. J. *Hughes*).

8160* *Testa* E., L'unità della Chiesa nel pluralismo; saggio di teologia biblica: LA 42 (1992) 109-144; Eng. 334.

8161 *a*) *Thangaraj* M. Thomas, Historical consciousness and inter-religious communication; – *b*) *Edappilly* John, Communication explosion and theological exploration: ➤ 40, ᶠDAVID C., Arasaradi 5 (1992) 42-50 / 1-22.

8162 **Thurian** Max, Una sola fede; in cammino verso l'unità. CasM 1992, Piemme. 190 p. – ᴿAsprenas 39 (1992) 278-280 (B. *Forte*).

8163 **Tillard** Jean-Marie Roger, Church of churches; the ecclesiology of communion [1987 ➤ 3,7911], ᵀ*De Peaux* R. C. ColMn 1992, Liturgical/ Glazier. xiii-330 p. $20 pa. 0-8146-5708-7 [TDig 39,390].

8164 **Tillard** J.-M. R., Iglesia de Iglesias, eclesiología de comunión [1987 ➤ 3,7911], ᵀ*Ortiz García* Alfonso: Verdad e imagen 113. S 1991, Sígueme. 356 p. – ᴿLumenVr 41 (1992) 383s (J. M. *Ochoa*); REspir 51 (1992) 214s (G. *Turiño*).

8164* **Tillard** J., Chiesa di chiese 1989 ➤ 5,8037... 7,8087: ᴿProtestantesimo 47 (1992) 248-250 (F. *Ferrario*).

8165 **Tillard** J.-M. R., Chair de l'Église, chair du Christ; aux sources de l'ecclésiologie de communion: CogF 168. P 1992, Cerf. 168 p. F 100. – ᴿEsprVie 102 (1992) 363-6 (P. *Jay*: 'défense et illustration de l'ecclésiologie de communion'); NRT 114 (1992) 901s (A. *Toubeau*); VSp 146 (1992) 736s (J. *Hoffmann*).

8165* *Tjørhom* Ola, [in Norwegian] Ecclesiastical offices in ecumenical light: TsTKi 62 (1991) 187-198.

8166 **Trapnell** Judson B., Bede GRIFFITHS' theory of religious symbol and practice of dialogue towards interreligious understanding: diss. ᴰ*Urubshurow* V. Washington D.C. 1992. – RTLv 24, p. 568; DissA 54, '1993'.

8167 **Trocholepczy** Bernd, Rechtfertigung und Seinsfrage; Anknüpfung und Widerspruch in der HEIDEGGER-Rezeption BULTMANNs: FreibTSt 146. FrB 1991, Herder. 170 p. – ᴿTPhil 67 (1992) 293s (R. *Sebott*).

8168 [**Ugenti** Antonio, intervista con] THURIAN Max. Una vita per l'unità 1991 ➤ 7,8085: ᴿNRT 114 (1992) 937 (B. *Clarot*).

8169 ᴱ**Urban** Hans J., *Wagner* Harald, Handbuch der Ökumenik II, 1986; III,1s 1987 ➤ 3,7918... 6,8072: ᴿBijdragen 53 (1992) 221s (A. H. C. van

Eijk); TR 88 (1992) 476-9 (R.W. *Jenson*: for a Lutheran, very 'inner-Catholic').

8170 *a*) *Varnalidis* Sotirios, Come e perché l'uniatismo può bloccare il proseguimento del dialogo cattolico-ortodosso; – *b*) *Cioffari* Gerardo, L'uniatismo; una sfida per la storiografia e l'ecumenismo; – *c*) *Tillard* Jean-Marie, La tension entre primauté du Siège romain et conciliarité; – *d*) *Papadopoulos* Antonios, L'istituzione conciliare; il suo carattere carismatico e unificatore: ➤ 583, Nicolaus 19 (1992) 201-216 / 217-258 / 275-283 / 285-296.

8171 *Wainwright* Geoffrey, Apostolic tradition as a theme in ecumenical dialogue: ➤ 173, ᶠSᴇɪʟs M., Tragende Tradition 1992, 157-171.

8172 *a*) *Wainwright* Geoffrey, Towards Eucharistic fellowship; – *b*) *Pobee* John S., Bread and wine; see of St. Aᴜɢᴜsᴛɪɴᴇ and see of St. Pᴇᴛᴇʀ; – *c*) *Thorogood* Bernard, Coming to the Lord's table; a Reformed viewpoint; – *d*) *Stephanopoulos* Robert G., Implications for the Ecumenical Movement: EcuR 44 (1992) 6-9 / 29-39 / 10-17 / 18-28.

8173 ᴱWaldenfels Hans, Begegnung der Religionen; Theologische Versuche 1 [essays 1970-80s) 1990 ➤ 7,275: ᴿTS 53 (1992) 176s (R. *Kress* considers it 'fun' to read the passages from the earlier Rᴀᴛᴢɪɴɢᴇʀ); WissWeis 54 (1991) 73s (J. *Lang*).

8174 *Wanke* J., Ökumene im Gebet — nur eine Verlegenheit? Überlegungen zum theologischen und pastoralen Stellenwert ökumenischer Gebetsinitiativen: TJb (Lp 1990) 439-... [< zɪᴛ 91,655].

8174* *Weakland* Rembert G., Crisis in Orthodox-Catholic relations; challenges and hopes: America 166 (1992) 30-35.

8175 *Willebrands* Johannes, *a*) The place of theology in the ecumenical movement; its contribution and its limits: Mid-Stream 30 (1991) 101-110; – *b*) La vocazione all'unità: Salesianum 54 (1992) 429-452.

8176 **Wind** A., Zending en oecumene in het twintigste eeuw, 2a. Van Ghana 1957/58 tot en met Uppsala 1968. Kampen 1991, Kok. 536 p. – ᴿCollatVʟ 22 (1992) 438s (J. *Bonny*).

8177 **Wolff** M.M., Gott und Mensch; ein Beitrag Yves Cᴏɴɢᴀʀs zum ökumenischen Dialog [Diss. Gregoriana]: FraTSt 38. Fra 1990, Knecht. 342 p. DM 58. 3-7820-0615-1. – ᴿTvT [= TsTNijm] 32 (1992) 105 (P. van *Leeuwen*).

8178 **Yannaras** Christos, Elements of faith; an introduction to Orthodox theology, ᵀ*Schram* Keith. E 1991, Clark. 167 p. £12.50. 0-567-29190-1. ᴿExpTim 103 (1991s) 187s (Ann *Shukman*: lively, against rationalism and Aᴜɢᴜsᴛɪɴᴇ).

8178* **Zehner** Joachim, Der notwendige Dialog; die Weltreligionen in katholischer und evangelischer Sicht: Studien zum Verstehen fremder Religionen 3. Gü 1992, Mohn. 323 p. – ᴿTGʟ 82 (1992) 476s (W. *Beinert*).

8179 *Ziegler* Joseph G., Interkommunion? Eine Orientierung: TrierTZ 101 (1992) 206-223.

8180 *Zielinsky* Vladimir, 'Afin que le monde croie...' ... un orthodoxe/ Rᴀᴛᴢɪɴɢᴇʀ 1989 ➤ 7,8101*: ᴿRTLv 23 (1992) 110-2 (A. de *Halleux*).

8181 *Zielinski* Vladimir, 'Afin que le monde croie'; réflexions sur l'œcuménisme: NRT 114 (1992) 161-185.

H7.8 **Amt** – *Ministerium ecclesiasticum.*

8182 **Areeplackal** J., Spirit and ministries; perspectives of East [Zɪᴢɪᴏᴜʟᴀs J.] and West [Cᴏɴɢᴀʀ Y.], diss. Pont. Univ. Gregoriana, Bangalore 1990 ➤ 7,8104: ᴿNRT 114 (1992) 126s (A. *Harvengt*).

8182* **Barbaini** P., Il prete e la Chiesa. T 1990, Tempi di fraternità. – ᴿProtestantesimo 47 (1992) 253s (C. *Tron*: lasciò il sacerdozio cattolico dopo
20 anni).

8183 *Baruffa* Antonio, Diventare preti, oggi; aspetti teologici e spirituali: Riv-
ScR 5 (1991) 197-215 [239-264, *Zuppa* Pio, formazione; orientamenti bi-
bliografici].

8184 *Bavaud* Georges, Comment justifier le ministère réformé; une question
importante pour les protestants français du XVIIᵉ siècle: NVFr 66 (1991)
100-112.

8185 *Beek* A. van de, Amtstheologie en salarisstructuur van de predikant:
GerefTTs 91 (1991) 195-205.

8186 **Bernier** Paul, Ministry in the Church; a historical and pastoral approach. Mystic CT 1992, Twenty-Third. ix-319 p. $17. 0-89622-536-4
[TDig 40,151].

8187 *Bloth* Peter C., Zur theologischen Diakonie-Forschung: TRu 57 (1992)
83-95.

8188 *Bouchaud* Constant, À propos de l'exhortation apostolique 'Pastores
dabo vobis' [25.III.1992]; sur la formation des prêtres dans les circon-
stances actuelles: EsprVie 102 (1992) 321-336.

8189 *Bourgeois* Daniel, L'un et l'autre sacerdoce; essai sur les structures
sacramentelles de l'Église 1991 → 7,8108: ᴿNVFr 67 (1992) 145-9 (B.-D.
de la *Soujeole*); Thomist 56 (1992) 162s (R. *Cessario*).

8190 **Bradshaw** Paul, Ordination rites in the ancient churches, east and west
1990 → 6,8088; 7,8109: ᴿHeythJ 33 (1992) 90s (K. *Stevenson*).

8191 **Brent** Allen, Cultural episcopacy and ecumenism; representative ministry in church history from the age of IGNATIUS of Antioch to the
Reformation, with special reference to contemporary ecumenism: Studies
in Christian Mission 6. Leiden 1992, Brill. 250 p. *f*110 [TR 88,519].

8192 **Burtchaell** James T., From Synagogue to Church; public services and
offices in the earliest Christian communities. C 1992, Univ. xviii-375 p.
0-521-41892-5.

8193 *Caprioli* Mario, Esortazione apostolica postsinodale 'Pastores dabo
vobis' di GIOVANNI PAOLO II [25.III.1992]; presentazione e valutazione:
Teresianum 43 (1992) 323-357.

8194 **Carrasco Rouco** Alfonso, Le primat de l'évêque de Rome 1990 → 7,
8112: ᴿGregorianum 73 (1992) 759-761 (W. *Henn*); JTS 43 (1992) 782-4
(E. J. *Yarnold*: original, important).

8195 **Casey** Michael, What are we at? Ministry and priesthood for the third
millenium: The practice of priesthood. Dublin 1992, Columba. 278 p.
[TR 88,450].

8196 *Castellucci* Erio, L'istituzione del presbiterato: SacDoc 35 (1990) 71-
97.156-194.

8197 ᴱ**Chauvet** Patrick, *al.*, Sacerdoce des baptisés, sacerdoce des prêtres;
textes 1991 → 7,7858*: ᴿBLitEc 93 (1992) 273s (J. *Rigal*); EsprVie 102
(1992) 602s (Y.-M. *Duval*); RHPR 72 (1992) 329 (W. *Fick*); RÉAug 38
(1992) 195-7 (I. *Rigolot*).

8198 **Cochini** Christian, The apostolic origins of priestly celibacy 1990
→ 7,8114*: ᴿAmerica 167 (1992) 17-19 (P. E. *Fink*: post-Constantine, not
rooted in Scripture; some uncertain grounds); EurJT 1 (1992) 173s (A. J.
Köstenberger); HomP 92,1 (1991s) 75s (J. R. *Sheets*: 'priestly celibacy has
a certain inevitability about it').

Collins John N., Diakonia 1990 → 9902.

8198* ᴱCooke Bernard, The Papacy and the Church in the United States [conference Worcester] 1989 ➤ 7,486: ᴿThought 66 (1991) 417-9 (T. P. *Rausch* 'Cook' throughout: informative but not on the title).

8199 *a*) *Dacquino* Pietro, La spiritualità biblica del presbitero; – *b*) *Sodi* Manlio, Temi biblici dei riti di ordinazione; – *c*) *Ardusso* Franco, Per una teologia del diaconato: ParVi 36 (1991) 419-431 / 438-450 / 432-7.

8200 *Dassmann* Ernst, Klerikermangel in der frühen Kirche? [eindeutig Nein]: ➤ 164, ᴱSAXER V., 1992, 183-197.

8200* *De Melo* Carlos M., Priestly celibacy and formation to celibate life I-II: Vidyajyoti 56 (1992) 23-33; III. p. 89-98.

8201 *Denaux* Adelbert, Le Synode des évêques sur la formation des prêtres (oct. 1990): FoiTemps 21 (1991) 419-439.

8202 ᴱDenzler Georg, Lebensberichte verheirateter Priester; Autobiographische Zeugnisse zum Konflikt zwischen Ehe und Zölibat: Piper 964. Mü 1989. – ᴿIkiZ 81 (1991) 133-140 (H. U. *Wili*).

8203 *Donfried* Karl Paul, Ministry; rethinking the term *diakonía*: ConcordTJ 56,1 (1992) 1-15 [< ᴢIT 92,355].

8204 **Donovan** Daniel, What are they saying about the ministerial priesthood? NY 1992, Paulist. iii-149 p. $8. 0-8091-3318-0 [TDig 40,159].

8205 **Drewermann** Eugen, Kleriker 1989 ➤ 6,8101; 7,8118: ᴿActuBbg 29 (1992) 11-24 (J. *Boada*: 'un oscuro psicograma del estado clerical').

8206 **Drilling** Peter, Trinity and [mostly] ministry. Mp 1991, Fortress. $17. 0-8006-2490-4 [TDig 40,61].

8207 **Dunn** Patrick J., Priesthood; a re-examination of the Roman Catholic theology of the presbyterate 1990 ➤ 6,8103; 7,8122: ᴿAmerica 167 (1992) 17 (P. E. *Fink*); HomP 91,5 (1990s) 71s (K. *Baker*); Worship 65 (1991) 285-7 (H. P. *Bleichner*: good; not against celibacy or for women's ordination, but dialogues too much with SCHILLEBEECKX).

8208 *Eck* E. van, 'n Sosiaal-wetenskaplike ondersoek na die 'amp' van die ouderling in die Nuwe Testament: HervTSt 47 (1991) 656-684 [< NTAbs 36,381].

8208* *Esquerda Bifet* J., Spiritualità e missione dei presbiteri segni del Buon Pastore. CasM 1990, Piemme. 188 p. – ᴿLateranum 57 (1991) 635-7 (F. *Marinelli*).

8209 *Famerée* Joseph, Au fondement des conférences épiscopales; la 'communio Ecclesiarum': RTLv 23 (1992) 343-354; Eng. 424.

8210 **Fastenrath** Elmar, Papsttum und Unfehlbarkeit; Fuldaer HSS 13. Fra 1991, Knecht. 64 p. DM 10 [TR 88,171].

8211 **Favale** A., Il ministero presbiterale 1989 ➤ 5,8064*... 7,8127: ᴿSalmanticensis 38 (1991) 110 (J. *López Martín*, también sobre A. ELBERTI).

8212 **Fengler** Jörg, Helfen macht müde; zur Analyse und Bewältigung von Burnout und beruflicher Deformation: Leben lernen 77. Mü 1991, Pfeiffer. 255 p. DM 28 pa. – ᴿTR 88 (1992) 240s (K. *Thomas* †: Psychologie-professor).

8212* *Ferraro* Giuseppe, Lettorato e accolitato, punto di arrivo e di partenza: CC 143 (1992,3) 392-402.

8213 **Fichter** Joseph H., Wives of Catholic clergy. KC c. 1992, Sheed & W. 191 p. $13 pa. – ᴿChrCent 109 (1992) 947.

8214 **Forestell** J. Terence, As ministers of Christ; the Christological dimension of ministry in the New Testament, an exegetical and theological study 1991 ➤ 7,8128: ᴿCritRR 5 (1992) 198-200 (Marie-Eloise *Rosenblatt*); LvSt 17 (1992) 78s (R. F. *Collins*).

8215 **Freitag** Josef, Sacramentum Ordinis auf dem Konzil von Trient; aus-geblendeter Dissens und erreichter Konsens [Diss. FrB]: InTSt 32. Innsbruck 1991, Tyrolia. 401 p. DM 88 [TR 88,79]. – ᴿTGL 82 (1992) 477-480 (D. *Hattrup*); ZkT 114 (1992) 440-4 (G. *Greshake*: K. Rahner-Preis, B. Welte-Preis; gibt auch über die Stellung des Papstamtes nachzudenken).

8216 **Garuti** Adriano, *a*) Il papa patriarca d'Occidente? 1990 → 6,234; 7,8130: ᴿLateranum 57 (1991) 239-241 (D. *Valentini*); RTLv 23 (1992) 208-211 (A. de *Halleux* s'oppose); – *b*) Le Pape, patriarche d'Occident? 1990 [ᵀ?]: ᴿNVFr 66 (1991) 236-240 (D. *Ols*).

8217 *Gaventa* Beverly R. and four others, The culture of seminaries: ChrCent 109 (1992) 129-155 (amid ads).

8218 *a*) *Gerlitz* Peter, *al.*, Priester(-amt/-tum); – *b*) *Dahm* Karl-Wilhelm, Pfarrer, Pfarramt: → 757, EvKL 3 (1992) 1319-21(-28) / 1147-59.

8219 *Gesché* Adolphe, Ministère et mémorial de la vérité: RTLv 23 (1992) 3-22; Eng. 144.

8220 *Gherardini* Brunero, Il card. Pietro PARENTI e la collegialità dei vescovi: Divinitas 36 (1992) 19-28.

8221 **Glaubitz** Elfriede, Der christliche Laie vom Konzil zur Bischofssynode 1987; Vergleich und Entwicklung: Diss. Pont. Univ. Gregoriana, ᴰ*Beyer* J. Roma 1992. 416 p.; Extr. 3862, 136 p. – RTLv 24, p. 569.

8222 **Greshake** Gisbert, Priester sein⁵ʳᵉᵛ. FrB 1991, Herder. 254 p. DM 38. 3-451-22432-1. – ᴿMüTZ 43 (1992) 136s (G. L. *Müller*).

8223 **Greshake** Gisbert, The meaning of Christian priesthood [Westminster MD 1989 → 6,8118]; also Blackrock 1988, Four Courts. 173 p. £6. 1-85128-002-1. – ᴿCarmelus 38 (1991) 218s (L. P. *Rogge*).

8224 **Harpigny** Guy, 'Que Dieu achève en vous ce qu'il a commencé'; l'exercice du ministère presbytéral, une réponse spécifique à l'appel à la sainteté: FoiTemps 21 (1991) 485-506 [< ᴢɪᴛ 92,48].

8225 *Heim* Manfred, Der Archidiakonat in der Geschichte: MüTZ 43 (1992) 107-111.

8226 ᴱ**Hillenbrand** Karl, Priester heute; Anfragen-Ausgaben-Anregungen 1990 ²1991 → 7,388*d*: ᴿWissWeis 54 (1991) 209s (J. *Gerwing*).

8227 **Hoenkamp-Bisschops** A., Celibaat; varianten van beleving; een verkennend onderzoek rond ambtscelibaat en geestelijke gezondheid [< 24 interviews]. Baarn 1991, Ambo. 128 p. Fb. 450. – ᴿCollatVL 22 (1992) 204s (L. *Vinken*).

8228 **Hornsby-Smith** Michael P., The changing parish; a study of parishes, priests and parishioners after Vatican II. L 1989, Routledge. 241 p. £30. – ᴿFurrow 41 (1990) 65s (J. *Weafer*: good, though omitting Ireland).

8229 **Houssiau** Albert, *Mondet* Jean-Pierre, Le sacerdoce du Christ et de ses serviteurs selon les Pères de l'Église: Cerfaux-Lefort 8, LvN 1990 → 6,8125; 7,8139: ᴿFoiTemps 21 (1991) 381s (G. *Harpigny*); Gregorianum 73 (1992) 367s (J. *Galot*); LavalTP 48 (1992) 467s (L. *Painchaud*); MaisD 192 (1992) 155-8 (J. *Puglisi*); RHPR 72 (1992) 333s (W. *Fick*); RThom 92 (1992) 941-3 (M.-V. *Leroy*).

8230 *Imhof* Paul, Aspekte des neutestamentlichen Priestertums: GeistL 64 (1991) 1-6.

8231 **Jacobs** Michael, Holding in trust; the appraisal of ministry 1989 → 7, 8141: ᴿPrPeo 4 (1990) 75s (B. *Kilroy*).

8231* *Kavunkal* Jacob, Ministry and mission; Christological considerations: Vidyajyoti 56 (1992) 641-652.

8232 *King* Geoffrey, Priests for the 21st century [East Asia symposium, 24 priests, 14-26 May 1990]: EAPast 27 (1990) 86-101.

8233 **Klauck** H.-J., Gemeinde – Amt – Sakrament 1989 ➤ 5,292: ᴿMüTZ 42 (1991) 412-5 (G. L. *Müller*).

8234 *Koffeman* Leo, Het bijzondere van het kerkelijk ambt: GerefTTs 91 (1991) 28-43.

8235 **Kolata** Dagmar, Priests — telling it like it is. Dublin c. 1992. Veritas. 216 p. £10. – ᴿFurrow 43 (1992) 180-2 (Catherine *KilBride*).

8236 *Kuhn* Hans, Spätberufung; Beobachtungen und Anmerkungen zu einem Begriff: TrierTZ 101 (1992) 224-238.

8237 ᴱ**Legrand** Hervé, Les conférences épiscopales; théologie, statut canonique, avenir 1988 ➤ 5,691 [español Naturaleza y futuro 1988 ➤ 5,690]: ᴿAntonianum 67 (1992) 156-8 (D.-M. A. *Jaeger*).

8238 ᴱ**Legrand** Hervé, *al.*, The nature and future of episcopal conferences 1988/9 ➤ 5,692: ᴿPhilipSa 26 (1991) 501s (J. *Gonzalez*).

8239 *López Martin* Julián, Ordenación para el ministerio; notas bibliográficas sobre la historia y la teología litúrgica del sacramento del Orden: Salmanticensis 39 (1992) 131-160.

8240 **Maciel** Marcial, La formación integral del sacerdote 1990 ➤ 7,8147: ᴿAngelicum 69 (1992) 133s (A. *Huerga*).

8241 **Mahoney** Donna T., Touching the face of God [should celibacy be voluntary?] .., Mercier. £10: ᴿTablet 246 (1992) 1130s (L. *Marteau*).

Maier Harry O., The social setting of the ministry... HERMAS ᴰ1991 ➤ k644.

8242 **Marinelli** F., Sacramento e ministero. CasM 1990, Piemme. 190 p – ᴿAnnTh 5 (1991) 427-9 (E. *Borda*).

8243 **Martelet** G., Théologie du sacerdoce; deux mille ans 3, 1990 ➤ 6,8141; 7,1990: ᴿCC 143 (1992,3) 548s (F. A. *Pastor*); EstE 27 (1992) 237s (María A. *Navarro Girón*); Lateranum 57 (1991) 264s (R. *Gerardi*).

8244 *Martin Nieto* E., El ministerio presbiteral en el Nuevo Testamento: Lumieira 5,14 (1990) 11-33 [< RET 51,422].

8245 *Massey* Denise McLain, [*al.*] Confronting alienation and abandonment; principles for ministry: RExp 89 (1992) 359-372 [321-358 . 373-386].

8246 *a) Mieth* Dietmar, Ehe und Priestertum; über ihre konstruktive Beziehung; - *b) Puza* Richard, Viri uxorati — viri probati; kanonistisch-historische Überlegungen; - *c) Greinacher* Norbert, Das Heil der Menschen — oberstes Gesetz in der Kirche; - *d) Hünermann* Peter, Zeit zum Handeln... Röm 14,19: TüTQ 172 (1992) 23-35 / 16-23 / 2-15 / 36-49.

8246* *Murphy-O'Connor* Jerome, Christ and ministry [Melbourne 1990 Knox Lecture]: Pacifica 4 (1991) 121-136.

8247 ᴱ**Nichol** Todd, *Kolden* Marc, Called and ordained; Lutheran perspectives on the office of the ministry. Mp 1990, Fortress. 240 p. $15. – ᴿMid-Stream 30 (1991) 294s (J. *Gros*).

8248 **Nichols** Aidan, Holy Orders; the apostolic ministry from the NT to the Second Vatican Council: Oscott 5. Dublin 1990, Veritas. 187 p. – ᴿStudies 80 (1991) 103-5 (R. *Maloney*).

8249 **Nouwen** Henri J. M., In the name of Jesus; reflections on Christian leadership [... ministry to the handicapped]. NY 1990, Crossroad. 81 p. $11. 0-8245-0915-3. – ᴿRExp 89 (1992) 303-5 (C. J. *Scalise*).

8250 **d'Onorio** Joël-Benoît, Le Pape et le gouvernement de l'Église. P 1992, Fleurus-Tarday. 616 p. – ᴿEsprVie 102 (1992) 590-2 (R. *Coste*: important).

8251 *O'Toole* Robert F., Hands, laying on of, NT: ➤ 741, AnchorBD 3 (1992) 48s (OT 47s, *Wright* D. P.).

8252 **Padovese** Luigi, I sacerdoti dei primi secoli; testimonianze dei Padri sui ministeri ordinati. CasM 1992, Piemme. 397 p. – ᴿTeresianum 43 (1992) 513 (M. *Caprioli*).

8253 **Parent** Rémi,   Prêtres et évêques; le service de la présidence ecclésiale: Théologies. P/Montréal 1992, Cerf/Paulines. 283 p. F 138. 2-204-04381-8 / 2-89039-525-1.
8254 **Peel** Donald, The ministry of the laity. Toronto 1991, Anglican Book Centre. 158 p. 0-921846-06-1. – ᴿExpTim 103 (1991s) 159 (G.W.S. *Knowles*).
8255 *Pfammatter* Josef, Neutestamentliche Perspektiven für die Dienste in der Kirche; 19 Thesen zum Dienst des Gemeindeleiters: Diakonia 23 (Mainz 1992) 162-9 [< ᴢɪᴛ 92,330].
8256 *a) Phidas* Vlassos, La notion de primauté papale dans la tradition canonique orthodoxe; – *b) Sullivan* Francis A., Per un rinnovamento del ministero del Vescovo di Roma; principio di legittima diversità, collegialità, sussidiareità; – *c) Joos* André, Les incertitudes des infaillibilités; ➤ 583, Nicolaus 19 (1992) 31-41 / 42-53 / 109-161.
8257 **Powers** William F., Free priests; movement for ministerial reform in the American Catholic Church. Ch 1992, Loyola. xviii-346 p. $17. 0-8294-0729-4 [TDig 40,182].
8257* Il prete 1990 ➤ 7,548: ᴿLateranum 57 (1991) 632s (F. *Marinelli*).
8258 **Ranke-Heinemann** Uta, Des eunuques pour le Royaume des Cieux; l'Église catholique et la sexualité, ᵀ*Thiollet* Monique: Essais. P 1990, Laffont. – ᴿFoiTemps 21 (1991) 376-380 (Alice *Dermience*).
8259 **Rausch** Thomas P., Priesthood today; an appraisal. NY 1992, Paulist. viii-139 p. $9. 0-8091-3326-1 [TDig 40,183].
8260 ᴱ**Reese** Thomas J., Episcopal conferences 1989 ➤ 6,445: ᴿLvSt 17 (1992) 82s (R. F. *Collins*).
8261 **Rice** David, Kirche ohne Priester; der Exodus der Geistlichen aus der katholischen Kirche [Shattered vows; priests who leave: 1990, Morrow; $19; 0-688-07805-2], ᵀ*Maas* Hans-Joachim. Mü 1991, Bertelsmann. 349 p. 3-570-04720-2. – ᴿActuBbg 29 (1992) 224s (J. *Boada*).
8262 *a) Rondet* Michel, Célibataires, pour qui?; – *b) Laplace* Jean, La virginité selon les premiers Pères; – *c) Guillet* Jacques, La chasteté de Jésus-Christ: Christus 39 (P 1992) 143-152 / 174-184 / 193-203.
8263 ᴱ**Ratzinger** J., *al.*, Mission et formation du prêtre 1990 ➤ 6,672b: ᴿScEsp 44 (1992) 379s (J.-G. *Pagé*).
8264 *Salvatierra* Ángel, Los nuevos ministerios: LumenVr 40 (1991) 45-75.
8265 **Saraiva Martins** J., Il sacerdozio ministeriale: StUrban 48. R 1991, Pont. Univ. Urbaniana. – ᴿTeresianum 43 (1992) 309s (M. *Caprioli*).
8266 **Schwartz** Robert M., Servant leaders of the people of God; an ecclesial spirituality for American priests 1989 ➤ 6,8160: ᴿHomP 91,5 (1990s) 76s (J. R. *Sheets*: lacks a clear theology of the priesthood).
8267 *Schweizer* R. Eduard, Ministry in the Early Church: ➤ 741, AnchorBD 4 (1992) 835-842; no article or renvoi on 'priesthood' or 'deacon/diaconate'; only to 'Levites and priests'.
8268 **Schwillus** Harald, Kleriker im Hexenprozess; Geistliche als Opfer der Hexenprozesse des 16. und 17. Jhts in Deutschland: ForFränkKTG 16. Wü 1992, Echter. 540 p. DM 64 [TR 88,255].
8269 **Seagraves** Richard, Pascentes cum disciplina; a lexical study of the clergy in the Cʏᴘʀɪᴀɴɪᴄ correspondence: Diss. *Damme* D. Van. Fr 1992. – RTLv 24, p. 552, only 'Fribourg'.
8270 *Semeraro* Marcello, Unum presbyterium cum suo Episcopo constituunt: RivScR 5 (1991) 29-67. ˙
8271 **Sieben** H.-J., Die Partikularsynode; Studien zur Geschichte der Konzilsidee: FraTSt 37. Fra 1990, Knecht. 303 p. DM 58. 3-7820-0610-0. – ᴿTvT [= TsTNijm] 32 (1992) 98 (J. van *Laarhoven*).

8272 **Sipe** A. W. Richard, A secret world; sexuality and the search for celibacy 1990 ➤ 7,8164: ᴿAmerica 164 (1991) 89s (W. W. *Meissner*, also on RICE D.).

8273 *Sipe* Richard, Double-talk on celibacy: Tablet 246 (1992) 576s. 605s.

8273* *Soares-Prabhu* George M., Christian priesthood in India today; a biblical reflection: Vidyajyoti 56 (1992) 61-88 [356-363, on Pastores dabo vobis].

8274 **Spiazzi** Raimundo, Il Papa nella Chiesa: Euntes 2. R 1991, Vivere In. 193 p. Lit. 17.500. – ᴿDivinitas 36 (1992) 280-2 (D. *Vibrac*).

8275 *Spital* Hermann J., [Bischof; Gespräch] 'Das fundamentale Problem ist nicht der Priestermangel'; zu den Veränderungen in den Seelsorgestrukturen: HerdKor 46 (1992) 70-75.

8276 *Strand* Kenneth A., Governance in the first-century Christian church in Rome; was it collegial?: AndrUnS 30 (1992) 59-75.

8277 *Thompson* William M., A theological reflection on priesthood today: The Priest 48,10 (1992) 46-53.

8278 *Thuruthumaly* Joseph, Ecclesiastical authority according to the NT: Living Word 98,1 (Alwaye 1992) 25-41.

8279 *Tinoko* Jose M., The ministry of the laity [p. 435; ministries p. 338]: PhilipSa 26 (1991) 435-450.

8280 **Turre** Reinhard, Diakonik; Grundlegung und Gestaltung in der Diakonie. Neuk 1991. 318 p. DM 48. – ᴿLuthMon 31 (1992) 136 (K. F. *Daiber*).

8281 **Unsworth** Tim, The last priests in America; conversations with remarkable men. NY 1991, Crossroad. 228 p. $20. 0-8245-1129-5. – ᴿChrCent 109 (1992) 409-411 (J. H. *Mahan*).

8282 **Vanhoye** Albert, Il sacerdozio della nuova alleanza: meditazioni. Bo 1992, Dehoniane. 78 p. 88-10-80695-6.

8282* *Weakland* Rembert desabafa 'O Papa não nos ouve' [entrevista Corriere della Sera < ADISTA 5166 (R 1992) 11s]: REB 52 (1992) 465s.

8283 **Whitehead** James D. & Evelyn E., The promise of partnership; leadership and ministry in an adult church 1991 ➤ 7,8174; 0-06-069362-2: ᴿRExp 89 (1992) 148 (E. *White*).

H8.0 *Liturgia; oratio, vita spiritualis* – NT – **Prayer.**

8284 **Abbott** Maureen, *Doyle* Joseph M., With love beyond all telling; a biblical approach to adult spiritual formation. NY 1991, Paulist. v-253 p. $15 pa. [CBQ 54,612].

8285 ᴱ**Adams** Doug, *Apostolos-Cappadona* Diane, Dance as religious studies. NY 1990, Crossroad. 256 p. $17.05. ᴿWorship 65 (1991) 468-472 (R. *Fabian*).

8286 ᴱ*Alexander* Donald L., Christian spirituality; five views of sanctification. DG 1988, InterVarsity. 203 p. $10. – ᴿBtS 148 (1991) 238s (R. P. *Richard*).

8287 **Alonso Schökel** Luis, *Gutiérrez* Guillermo Mensajes de profetas; meditaciones bíblicas. Sdr 1991, SalT. / Io pongo le mie parole sulla tua bocca; meditazioni bibliche: Bibbia e preghiera 12. R 1992, Ap. Preghiera 183 p. / 193 p. [AcPIB 9/8, 653].

8288 ᴱ**Alonso Schökel** Luis, Emaús en Manresa; Biblia y Ejercicios. 1991. – ᴿManresa 64 (1992) 204s (J. L. *Sicre*).

8289 **Alonso Schökel** L., Emmaus in Manresa: also Anand 1992, Gujarat-SP. vii-160 p.

8290 ᴱAncilli Ermanno, La preghiera; Bibbia, teologia, esperienze storiche 1900 ➤ 4,9214; Lit. 100.000; ᴿCC 143 (1992,2) 100s (G. *Mucci*).

8291 **Antoli** Miguel, La religiosidad de los cristianos; hacia un cambio deseable. Valencia 1992, Fac. Teol. Ferrer. 276 p. 84-86067-55-3. – ᴿEstE 67 (1992) 108s (G. *Higuera*).

8292 **Arnold** Fritz, Befreiungstherapie Mystik; Gotteserfahrung in einer Welt der 'Gottesfinsternis'. Rg 1991, Pustet. 211 p. 3-7917-1288-8. – ᴿActu-Bbg 29 (1992) 205s (J. *Boada*).

8293 **Arnold** Patrick M., Wildmen, warriors, and kings; masculine spirituality and the Bible. NY 1991, Crossroad. xii-240 p. $20. – ᴿAmerica 166 (1992) 414s (D. *Toolan*); RRel 51 (1992) 789s (J. A. *Tetlow*); TS 53 (1992) 599s (C. C. *Bryant*).

8293* **Baldovin** John F., The urban character of Christian worship ... stational liturgy: OrChrAnal 228, 1987 ➤ 3,8037 ... 7,8178: ᴿRechSR 80 (1992) 152s (B. *Sesboüé*).

8294 **Barton** Stephen C., The spirituality of the Gospels. L 1992, SPCK. x-161 p. 0-281-04613-1.

8295 **Beauchamp** Paul. All'inizio, Dio parla; itinerari biblici: Bibbia e Preghiera 14. R 1992, Ap. Preghiera. 260 p. Lit. 20.000. 88-7357-114-X.

8296 **Bell** Catherine, Ritual theory, ritual practice. NY 1992, Oxford-UP. xii-278 p. 0-19-506923-4; pa. -7613-3.

8296* **Bernard** Charles-A., Teologia spiritualeᴶ³ʳᵉᵛ. Mi 1988, Paoline. 582 p. – ᴿAtKap 116 (1991) 351-3 (M. *Chmielewski*); Lateranum 57 (1991) 278s (Eva C. *Rava*).

8297 *a*) **Bernard** Charles-André, *al.*, ᴱGioia Mario, Teologia spirituale, temi e problemi (29 saggi) 1990/1 ➤ 7,497. 8182: ᴿDivinitas 36 (1992) 201s (D. *Vibrac*); TItSett 17 (1992) 281-302 (Annamaria *Valli*).

8298 **Bexell** Oloph, Liturgins teologi hos Uddo L. ULLMAN [diss.]: BtTPrac 42. Sto 1987, Almqvist & W. 356 p. + deutsch 88 p. – ᴿSvTKv 67 (1991) 92-94 (L. *Eckerdal*).

8299 *Boguniowski* Józef W., ❷ Mensa Domini et Ecclesiae; refleksje teologiczne nad terminologią ołtarza katolickiego: RuBi 45 (1992) 86-90.

8300 *a*) *Bouwen* Frans, L'histoire spirituelle de l'Orient chrétien; – *b*) Špidlík Tomas, La vie spirituelle selon les anciens Pères; – *c*) *Meyendorff* Jean, Une théologie mystique: Christus 39 (P 1992) 264-274 / 275-285 / 286-293.

8301 **Bouyer** Louis, Architecture et liturgie [1967], ᵀLecourt G.: Foi vivante 276. P 1991, Cerf. 108 p. – ᴿBLitEc 93 (1992) 243-8 (J. *Rocacher*: traduction mal conseillée).

8302 *Bouyer* Louis [➤ 9927], Parole, Église et sacrements dans le protestantisme et le catholicisme [1971]. P 1991, Desclée. 102 p. F 65. – ᴿEsprVie 102 (1992) 349 (P. *Rouillard*: agressif contre les prétendues perversions post-conciliaires).

8303 **Bradshaw** P. F., The search for the origins of Christian worship. L 1992, SPCK. xii-217 p. [RHE 88,99*].

8304 **Brändle** Francisco, La oración en S. Mateo [Lucas, *Llamas* R.; Juan, *Castro* S.; Pablo, *Ródenas* Á.: REspir 49 (1990) 9-25 [27-61 / 63-94 / 95-119].

8305 **Brune** François, Pour que l'homme devienne Dieu: Horizons Spirituels. S.-Jean-de-Braye 1992, Dangles. 605 p. – ᴿRHPR 72 (1992) 498-500 (J.-C. *Larchet*: remarquable par sa richesse et sa profondeur).

8306 *a*) **Burtchaell** J. R., From synagogue to church; public services and offices in the earliest Christian communities. C 1992, Univ. xviii-375 p. £40 [RHE 87,395*].

— b) Aune D. E., Worship, early Christian: ⇥ 741, AnchorBD 6 (1992) 973-989.

8307 **Bux** Nicola, Codici liturgici latini di Terra Santa: SBF Museum 8. Fasano 1990, Schena. 145 p.; 90 ill. [TR 88,263].

8308 **Byrne** Lavinia, Traditions of spiritual guidance. L 1990, Chapman. 213 p. £9. 0-225-66616-2. – ᴿExpTim 103 (1991s) 158s (G. S. *Wakefield*: a series from 'that excellent Jesuit periodical, The Way').

8309 **Cabaniss** Allen, Pattern in early Christian worship. Macon 1991, Mercer Univ. x-112 p. $17.50. – ᴿChH 60 (1991) 524s (C. A. *Volz*); CritRR 5 (1992) 319 (C. *Kannengiesser*); RelStR 18 (1992) 313 (T. M. *Finn*).

8310 **Cantalamessa** Raniero, Jesucristo, el santo de Dios [1990 ⇥ 7,8186],ᵀ. M 1991, Paulinas. 184 p. 84-285-1412-7. – ᴿEstE 67 (1992) 103s (J. *O'Callaghan*).

8311 **Cantalamessa** Raniero, I misteri di Cristo nella vita della Chiesa. Mi 1991, Àncora. 532 p. Lit. 49.000. – ᴿCC 143 (1992,2) 425 (G. *Mucci*).

8311* **Carmody** Denise L. & John T., Prayer in World Religions ⇥ 6,a660: ᴿTsTKi 62 (1991) 312s (T. *Austad*).

8312 ᴱ**Carson** D. A., Teach us to pray; prayer in the Bible and the world. Exeter/GB 1990, Paternoster/Baker. 362 p. 0-85364-495-0 / 0-8010-2537-0. – ᴿBtS 148 (1991) 250s (T. L. *Constable*: anthology); ExpTim 102 (1990s) 383 (Dorothy *Bell*: rather heavy).

8313 **Clément** Olivier, L'hésychasme; petite introduction à l'étude: ColcCist 53 (1991) 3-19 [30-48, *d'Andia* Y., chez Isaac Syr.].

8314 **Corbon** Jean, The wellspring of worship 1988 ⇥ 5,8142: ᴿRivLtg 78 (1991) 653-5 (V. *Raffa*).

8315 ᴱ**Corsato** C., *al.*, Oranti e preghiere, dalla Bibbia e dal mondo 1991 ⇥ 7,8190: ᴿDivinitas 36 (1992) 193s (L. G—).

8316 ᴱ**Dahme** Klaus, Die evangelische Perla; das geistliche Begleitbuch einer flämischen Mystikerin des 16. Jh, ᵀ*Silesius* Angelus. Salzburg 1990, O. Müller. 220 p. DM 35. – ᴿTR 88 (1992) 36s (Louise *Gnädinger*).

8317 *Damián Gaitán* José, Jesús y la oración del cristiano: REspir 191 ('La Trinidad en nuestra oración' 1989) 221-242.

8318 **Darricau** Raymond, *Peyrous* Bernard, Histoire de la Spiritualité: Que sais-je? P 1991, PUF. 128 p. – ᴿEsprVie 102 (1992) 170s (G.-M. *Oury* conclut 'depuis 1970 dizaines de communautés nouvelles ont vu le jour', mais n'indique pas que le livre est sur l'histoire de la vie religieuse communautaire).

8319 *Debarge* Louis, De la danse sacrée à la liturgie dansante [index et tête de pages: aux liturgies dansantes]: MélSR 49 (1992) 143-159; Eng. 161.

8320 *Delahoutre* Michel, Les institutions religieuses européennes sont-elles menacées par les spiritualités orientales? : EsprVie 102 (1992) 81-85.

8321 **De Zan** Renato, *a*) S. Anafora e Todah [Giraudo C. 1981] / e Berakah [Audet J. 1966]: ParVi 36 (1991) 51-54. 140-143 [35 (1990) 198-203. 298-302. 371-5. 449-453]. – *b*) Le processioni; modelli biblici — Le deambulazioni sacre nella Bibbia: RivLtg 79 (1992) 478-495 [496-504, nel cristianesimo antico, *Beatrice* P. F.].

8322 **Dober** Hans Martin, Erfahrbare Kirche; dimensionierte Zeit und symbolische Ordnung im Kirchenjahr: ZTK 89 (1992) 222-248.

8323 **Donders** Joseph G., Scripture reflections, day by day. Mystic CT 1992, Twenty-Third. ix-374 p. $10 [CBQ 54,402].

8324 **Dürig** Walter, Das stellvertretende Gebet das Priesters; Gedanken zum Stundengebet ohne Gemeinde. St. Ottilien 1986, EOS. 58 p. DM 4,80. – ᴿTR 88 (1992) 60.62 (S. *Rau*).

8325 *Duggan* Robert D. [*al.*], Sunday Eucharist; theological reflections: ChSt 29 (1990) 209-223 [-306].

8326 **Dupré** Louis, *Saliers* Don E., Christian spirituality; post-reformation and modern: EWSp 18, 1989 ➤ 5,8151 ... 7,8194: ᴿHomP 91,6 (1990s) 72s (J. R. *Sheets*: for libraries); RExp 88 (1991) 118 (E. G. *Hinson*).

8327 **Empereur** J. L., *Kiesling* C. J., The liturgy that does justice 1990 ➤ 7, 8196: ᴿNewTR 5,1 (1992) 110-2 (J. T. *Pawlikowski*).

8328 **Flanagan** Kieran, Sociology and liturgy, re-presentations of the Holy. L 1991, Macmillan. 411 p. £50. 0-333-55079-X. – ᴿExpTim 103 (1991s) 252 (B. D. *Spinks*: a Roman Catholic who likes the sound of his own rhetoric, and does not recognize that his own church is in worse decline than the Anglican); TLond 95 (1992) 304-6 (K. *Stevenson*: severe on his smug ultra-Catholic asides; but much is perceptive and entertaining).

8329 **Fleischmann-Bisten** Walter, Evangelische Frömmigkeit: Im Lichte der Reformation 34. Gö 1991 Vandenhoeck &R. 152 p. – ᴿTLZ 117 (1992) 256s (G. *Haendler*).

8330 *Frattallone* Raimondo, Celebrare la 'metanoia' all'interno dell'esperienza cristiana: RivLtg 78 (1991) 555-581.

8331 **Galot** Jean, Il cuore di Cristo: Paralleli. Mi 1992, ADP (Ap. Preghiera) ViPe. 271 p. Lit. 25.000. 88-7357-108-5 / 88-343-3971-1.

8332 **Galot** Jean, The Eucharistic Heart 1990 ➤ 6,8198: ᴿPrPeo 4 (1990) 298s (sr. M. Cecily *Boulding*).

8333 ᵀᴱ**Ganss** George E., *al.*, Ignatius of LOYOLA, Spiritual Exercises and selected works: Classics of Western spirituality. NY 1991, Paulist. 503 p. $20 pa. 0-8091-3216-8. – ᴿRExp 89 (1992) 135 (E. G. *Hinson*: one of the most influential writings of all times).

8334 **Gelven** Michael, Spirit and existence; a philosophic inquiry into the meaning of spiritual existence. L 1990, Collins. 264 p. £15. 0-00-599201-X. – ᴿExpTim 102 (1990s) 382s (P. *Vardy*: leaves God's place and love itself ambiguous, amid good nuggets); Studies 80 (1991) 203-5 (D. *O'Grady*).

8335 *George* Raymond, present., A four-year lectionary, Joint Liturgical Group 2 [JLG-1 c. 1978 was two-year]. ... 1990, Canterbury. 30? p. £1.50. 1-85311-021-3. – ᴿExpTim 103 (1991s) 3s (C. S. *Rodd*: statistics of the revision; '30 p.').

8336 *Gesteira Garza* Miguel, Cristo, ¿'principio y fundamento' de los Ejercicios Espirituales?: MiscCom 49 (1991) 327-367.

8337 **Gilchrist** Steven C., The *orans* posture in early Christianity; a study of the body in worship: diss. Emory, ᴰ*Saliers* D. Atlanta 1992. 233 p. 92-24398. – DissA 53 (1992s) 1556s-A; RTLv 24, p. 551.

8339 *Gordon* James M., Evangelical spirituality, from the WESLEYS to John STOTT. L 1991, SPCK. 340 p. £13. 0-281-94542-9. – ᴿExpTim 103 (1991s) 253 (M. *Hennell*: very valuable and readable, but regrettably without Catholic comparisons).

8340 *Grego* Igino, L'Amen nella liturgia e nei Padri: Asprenas 39 (1992) 529-538.

8341 **Greiner** Sebastian, Gewissheit der Gebetserhörung; eine theologische Deutung. Köln 1990, Communio. 292 p. DM 44. – ᴿMüTZ 42 (1992) 419-421 (M. *Tiator*); TPhil 67 (1992) 303s (G. *Switek*).

8342 **Gy** Pierre-Marie, La liturgie dans l'histoire. P 1990, Cerf. 329 p. F 149 ➤ 6,242 (not F 349): ᴿWorship 65 (1991) 558-560 (R. A. *Duffy*).

8343 *a*) *Gy* Pierre-Marie, Bible et liturgie en dynamique œcuménique; – *b*) *Jörns* Klaus-Peter, Liturgie, berceau de l'Écriture?; – *c*) *Wainwright* Geoffrey,

'Bible et liturgie' quarante ans après DANIÉLOU; – *d*) *Bradshaw* Paul, Perspectives historiques sur l'utilisation de la Bible en liturgie; – *e*) *Clerck* Paul de, 'Au commencement était le Verbe': MaisD 189 ('Bible et Liturgie' 1992) 7-18 / 55-78 / 41-53 / 79-104 / 19-40.

8344 **Heck** Erich, Segen des dreieinigen Gottes; Heilige Schrift – Liturgie – Frömmigkeitsgeschichte: Grundgebete der Christen. Stu 1990, KBW. 160 p.; 8 fig. – ᴿTR 88 (1992) 492s (B. *Kranemann*: eine Fülle von exegetischen Informationen).

8345 *Izquierdo* A., La oración en la Biblia: Ecclesia 5 (Méx 1991) 39-56 [< Stromata 47,443].

8346 *a*) *Jörns* Klaus P., Liturgy, cradle of Scripture?; – *b*) *Bradshaw* Paul F., The use of the Bible in liturgy; some historical perspectives; – *c*) *Josuttis* Manfred, The authority of the word in the liturgy; the legacy of the Reformation: StLtg 22 (1992) 17-34 / 35-52 / 53-67 [< TR 88,536].

8347 **Jones** W. Paul, Trumpet at full moon; an introduction to Christian spirituality as diverse practice. Louisville 1992, W-Knox. [viii-] 190 p. $13. [CBQ 54,834].

8348 **Kavanaugh** John F., Following Christ in a consumer society²ʳᵉᵛ [¹1981] 1991 → 7,8214*: 0-88344-777-0: ᴿGregorianum 73 (1992) 763s (J. T. *Bretzke*).

8349 **Kavanaugh** John F., Cristiani in una società consumistica; la spiritualità della resistenza culturale. Assisi 1990, Cittadella. 256 p. Lit. 20.000. – ᴿCC 143 (1992,2) 420s (P. *Vanzan*).

8350 **Kellermann** Bill W., Seasons of faith and conscience [... discipleship for the liturgical year]. Mkn 1991, Orbis. 228 p. – ᴿBibTB 22 (1992) 40s (R. L. *Cassidy*).

8350* *Koch* Kurt, Gottesdienst und Tanz: LtgJb 42 (1992) 63-69.

8351 **Koenig** John, Rediscovering New Testament prayer: boldness and blessing in the name of Jesus. SF 1992, Harper. xi-203 p. $15. 0-06-064755-8 [TDig 40,71: NY General Theol. Sem. prof.].

8352 *Labbé* Yves, Revenir, sortir, demeurer; trois figures de l'apophatisme mystique: RThom 92 (1992) 642-673.

8353 **Lagarde** Claude & Jacqueline, Comprendre la Messe avec la Bible. P 1991, Mame. 143 p. F 135. – ᴿLVitae 47 (1992) 115s (L. *Partos*).

8354 *Lamberts* Jozef, Die spiritualiteit van de voorganger: CollatVL 22 (1992) 41-66.

8355 ᴱ**Lanza** Sergio (La Bibbia nella prassi ecclesiale), *al.*, La Bibbia nella liturgia; Atti della XV settimana di studio As. Prof. Liturgia, Sassone Frattocchie (Roma) 18-22 agosto 1986: StLtg 15. Genova 1987, Marietti. 141 p. – ᴿRivLtg 79 (1992) 113s (Antonella *Meneghetti*).

8356 **Laplace** Jean, Prayer according to the Scriptures, ᵀ*Powell* Mary Louise. Dublin/SF 1991, Veritas/Ignatius. 85 p. $8 pa. 1-85390-167-9 [TDig 39,272].

8357 **La Potterie** I. de, La preghiera di Gesù; il Messia, il Servo di Dio, il Figlio del Padre [< conferenze Boneiden, 1989], ᵀ*Berényi* Gabriella: Bibbia e Preghiera 2. R 1992, Ap. Preghiera. 165 p. 88-7357-039-9. – ᴿRivB 40 (1992) 242 (G. *Zevini*: prezioso, valido).

8358 **Lattke** Michael, Hymnus: NOrb 19, 1991 → 7,8219: ᴿJTS 43 (1992) 818 (H. *Chadwick*: the vast material he gathered for his RAC article); TLZ 117 (1992) 823-5 (G. *Schille*).

8359 **Leech** Kenneth, The eye of the storm; living spirituality in the real world. SF 1992, Harper. viii-280 p. $19. 0-06-065208-X [TDig 40,73].

8359* **Le Gall** Robert, La liturgie de l'Église; mystères, signes et figures 1990
→ 7,8220: ᴿAtKap 119 (1992) 356s (B. *Nadolski,* ❷).

8360 ᴱ**Maas** Robin, *O'Donnell* Gabriel, Spiritual traditions for the contemporary Church. Nv 1990, Abingdon. 464 p. $30. – ᴿCurrTMiss 19
(1992) 291 (T. D. *Hubert*).

8361 **Maass** Fritz, Bekenntnis zu Jesus. FrB-Denzlingen 1989. 156 p. –
ᴿDielB 27 (1991) 287s (B. J. *Diebner*: 'leben im Geiste Jesu').

8362 **MacArthur** John ᴶ, Our sufficiency in Christ. Dallas 1991, Word. 282 p.
$16. – ᴿBtS 149 (1992) 102s (R. A. *Pyne*: he is sometimes harsh and
should apply to himself 1 Cor 9,22).

8363 **McFadyen** Alistair I., The call to personhood [... transformation in
Christ]; a Christian theory of the individual in social relationships. C
1990, Univ. xii-327 p. $49.50; pa. $15. – ᴿTS 53 (1992) 365s (Jean *Porter*:
no self-love?).

8364 **McGinn** Bernard, The presence of God; a history of western Christian
mysticism, 1. The foundations of mysticism. L 1991, SCM. xxii-494 p.
[TR 88,348]. – ᴿAmHR 97 (1992) 1497s (K. F. *Morrison*); AnglTR 74
(1992) 393-6 (A. *Jones*).

8365 **Maloney** George A., Mysticism and the New Age; Christic consciousness in the new creation. NY 1991, Alba. xv-193 p. $10. – ᴿNew-
TR 5,1 (1992) 100-2 (E. *Dreyer*: staccato).

8366 **Martin** James A., Beauty and holiness; the dialogue between aesthetics
and religion. Princeton c. 1990, Univ. 222 p. $27.50. 0-691-07357-0. –
ᴿRExp 88,2 (1991) 231s (W. L. *Hendricks*: 'as abstract ideas'; but the
beauty seems to be in objects, and the holiness only or also in persons).

8367 **Martini** Carlo Maria, a) All'alba ti cerco. CasM 1990, Piemme. – b) Je
te cherche dès l'aube; une école de prière, ᵀ*Rouers* Simone. P 1992,
Centurion. 100 p. F 78. – ᴿEsprVie 102 (1992) 698 (G.-M. *Oury*, aussi
sur son Prêtres quelques années après).

8368 *Maschke* Timothy, Prayer in the Apostolic Fathers: SecC 9 (1992)
103-118.

8368* **Matanić** Atanasio G., La spiritualità come scienza; introduzione
metodologica allo studio della vita spirituale cristiana. CinB 1990,
Paoline. 194 p. – ᴿAtKap 118 (1992) 163-5 (M. *Chmielewski,* ❷).

8369 **Matta** el-Maskine [Réformateur du monachisme copte c. 1950], Prière,
Esprit-Saint et Unité chrétienne: Spiritualité orientale 48. Bégrolles-en-
Mauges 1990. 212 p. – ᴿScEsp 44 (1992) 376s (J. *Lison*: mérite).

8369* **Mazza** Enrico, Anafora eucaristica, studi sulle origini. BtEphLtg,
Subs. 62. R 1992, Liturgiche. 398 p. Lit. 50.000. 88-85918-65-4. – ᴿIrénikon 65 (1992) 586s (E. *Lanne*).

8370 **Miles** Margaret R., Practicing Christianity; critical perspectives for an
embodied spirituality 1988 → 6,8225*b*: ᴿAnglTR 73 (1991) 99-102
(Louise *Conant*).

8371 **Miquel** Pierre, Le vocabulaire de l'expérience spirituelle dans la tradi-
tion patristique grecque du ivᵉ au xivᵉ siècle: THist 86. P 1991 [= 1989],
Beauchesne. 208 p. F 195. – ᴿEsprVie 102 (1992) 566s (Y.-M. *Duval*);
RSPT 76 (1992) 623-5 (G.-M. de *Durand*); TPhil 67 (1992) 283 (H. J.
Sieben).

8372 **Mistrorigo** Antonio, Voi assetati, venite all'acqua, I. Bibbia e liturgia
nella vita dei credenti; II. Temi biblici-liturgici per un cammino di fede;
dalle origini alla monarchia in Israele; III. ... attesa e venuta del Messia.
Mi 1991, Paoline. 198 p.; 252 p.; 250 p. Lit. 15.000 + 14.000 + 14.000. –
ᴿCC 143 (1992,1) 414 s (G. *Ferraro*).

8373 **Nardone** Richard M., The story of the Christian year. NY 1991, Paulist. v-192 p. $10 pa. 0-8091-3277-X [TDig 39,375].

8374 **Navone** John, Teología del fallimento² 1988 → 4,9272; 6,1586*: RREspir 49 (1990) 160 (J. *García Rojo*).

8375 **Norman** Andrew, Silence in God. L 1990, SPCK. 142 p. £7. 0-281-04477-5. – RExpTim 102 (1990s) 383 (Dorothy *Bell*: an insight).

8376 *Pablo Maroto* Daniel de, Un proyecto de espiritualidad mundial [EWSp 13; 15; 16; 19]: REspir 48 (1989) 137-145.

8377 *Pistoia* Alessandro, Dal movimento liturgico alla riforma conciliare; un cammino da rileggere: EphLtg 106 (1992) 319-380.

8378 **Poloma** Margaret, *Gallup* George ᴶ, Varieties of prayer; a survey report. Ph c. 1991, Trinity. 142 p. $25; pa. $15. – RChrCent 109 (1992) 20s (R. *Holloway*).

8379 *Prigent* Pierre, Les orants dans l'art funéraire ancien: RHPR 72 (1992) 143-150. 259-287; Eng. 228. 379.

8380 *Principe* Walter, Pluralism in Christian spirituality: Way 32 (1992) 54-61.

8381 **Ramey** Robert H.ᴶ, *Johnson* Ben C., Living the Christian life; a guide to Reformed spirituality, Louisville 1992, W-Knox. 181 p. $13. – RTTod 49 (1992s) 432. 434s (D. L. *Guder*, also on RICE H. L. 1991).

8382 **Rice** Howard L., Reformed spirituality; an introduction for believers. Louisville 1991, W-Knox. 224 p. $15 pa. 0-664-25230-3 [TDig 39,283].

8383 *Rigo* Antonio, La preghiera di Gesù: → 338, ParSpV 25 (1992) 245-291.

8384 **Rizzi** Armido, Dio in cerca dell'uomo; rifare la spiritualità 1987 → 3,1987 (fr. 1989 → 6,8235): RFilT 5 (1991) 172-4 (A. *Canali*).

8385 **Roccasalvo** Joan L., The Eastern Catholic Churches; an introduction to their worship and spirituality: American Essays in Liturgy. ColMn 1992, Liturgical. 70 p. $5. 0-8146-2047-7 [TDig 39,382].

8385* ᴱ**Romero** C. Gilbert, Hispanic devotional piety; tracing the biblical roots: Faith & Culture. Mkn 1991, Orbis. ix-140 p. $17 pa. [RelStR 19,57, J. T. *Ford*].

8386 **Ruh** Kurt, Geschichte der abendländischen Mystik I. Mü 1990, Beck. 414 p. DM 78. – RTR 88 (1992) 200-2 (J. *Sudbrack*).

8387 **Sagne** Jean-Claude, Traité de théologie spirituelle; le secret du cœur. P 1992, Chalet/Mame. 188 p. – REsprVie 102 (1992) 353s (G.-M. *Oury*: approche différente et moins didactique que l'homonyme de C. BERNARD, 1986 → 8296* supra).

8388 **Sheldrake** Philip, Spirituality and history; questions of interpretation and method [... most of it came from now outdated male monastic origins]. L 1991, SPCK. 238 p. £15. 0-281-04511-9. – RExpTim 103 (1991s) 220s (R. *Howe*); Month 253 (1992) 30s (P. *Edwards*); TLond 95 (1992) 213s (G. *Mursell*); TS 53 (1992) 778-780 (M. *Downey*).

8389 **Skelley** Michael, The liturgy of the world; Karl RAHNER's theology of worship [... what it means to be Christians in the modern world]: Pueblo. ColMn 1991, Liturgical. 176 p. $12. 0-8146-6009-6 [TDig 40,87].

8390 *Soares-Prabhu* George M., The Jesus of faith; a Christological contribution to an ecumenical Third World spirituality: Voices from the Third World 15,1 (Colombo 1992) 46-89.

8391 **Spencer** W. & A., The prayer life of Jesus. Lanham MD 1991, UPA. xii-296 p. $30. 0-8191-7779-2. – RExpTim 102 (1990s) 377s I. H. *Marshall*: fruit of their involvement in urban and prison ministries).

8391* ᴱStevenson Kenneth, Spinks Bryan, The identity of Anglican worship. L 1991, Mowbray. x-196 p. £13 pa. – ᴿTLond 95 (1992) 306s
(Tom Baker is left thinking with RUNCIE that the 'identity' of the future
lies in capacity to handle diversity).

8392 Stock Klemens. La fede in Gesù Cristo via alla pienezza della vita,
ᵀᴱGenero Bartolomeo: RasT 33 (1992) 603-616.

8392* Taft Robert, La liturgie des Heures en Orient et en Occident; origine et
sens de l'office divin [1986 → 2,6444], ᵀPasselecq Georges: Mysteria 2. P
1991, Brepols. 390 p. – ᴿEsprVie 102 (1992) 345s (P. Rouillard); RThom
92 (1992) 944-6 (J.-M. Boudaroua); VSp 146 (1992) 559s (sr. M. Pascale).

8393 Teresa Mutter, Beschaulich inmitten der Welt; geistliche Weisungen,
ᴱDevanandi Scolozzi P.A.: Der neue Weg 10. Einsiedeln 1990, Johannes.
163 p. – ᴿZMissRW 75 (1991) 245-9 (Marianne Heinbach-Steins).

Thompson William M., Christology and spirituality 1991 → 7569.

8394 Toon Peter, Spiritual companions; introduction to the Christian classics
[100, in alphabetical order]. GR 1992, Baker. 210 p. $10. 0-8010-8904-2
[TDig 40,90].

8395 ᴱTroxell Kay, Resources in sacred dance. Petersborough NH 1991,
Sacred Dance Guild. 56 p. $12.50. – ᴿCurrTMiss 19 (1992) 129 (Deena
S. Borchers).

8396 Tyrrell Bernard J., Christointegration; the transforming love of Jesus
Christ. NY c.1990, Paulist. 146 p. $10 pa. – ᴿHomP 91,2 (1990s) 72s
(J. R. Sheets).

8397 Vallavanthara Antony, The liturgical year of the St. Thomas Christians;
attempts at restoration; a historical investigation: diss. LvN 1990. – RTLv
24, p. 92.

8399 Vanhoye Albert, Per progredire nell'amore: Bibbia e Preghiera 1. R
1988, Ap. Preghiera. 214 p. Lᵐ 12.

8400 Vanhoye Albert, Il sangue dell'alleanza; corsi di Esercizi Spirituali biblici: Sangue e Vita 10. R 1992, Unione Prez. Sangue. 128 p. [AcPIB
9/8,662]. Lᵐ 10.

8401 Vanhoye Albert, Opere di Gesù dono del Padre, meditazione biblica:
Bollettini mensili dell'Apostolato della Preghiera (1992) 5s.37s.69s. 101s.
133s.; 'Eucarestia e prossimità', supp. giugno 1991, 42-5 [AcPIB 9/8,661].

8401* Van Olst E. H., The Bible and liturgy. GR/ 1991, Eerdmans/ Gracewing. 159 p. £9. 0-8028-0306-7. – ᴿExpTim 103 (1991s) 381 (R. Howe:
'the Bible itself determines a structure of celebration').

8402 Varillon François, Vivre le christianisme; la dernière retraite du P. ~.
P 1992, Centurion. 308 p. F 120. – ᴿEsprVie 102 (1992) 678 (P. Jay,
préoccupé par la tendance à publier des bandes enrégistrées, parfois sans
autorisation de l'auteur).

8403 a) Vedant Swami Satya, Contemplative dimension of Osho [RAJANEESH]'s
vision and his work; – b) Pathrapankal Joseph, Jesus of Nazareth, paradigm par excellence; – c) MacNutt Francis S., Charismatic renewal as a
help to contemplation; JDharma 17 (1992) 5-12 / 13-24 / 38-41.

8404 Wegman Herman, Omnes circumadstantes... people in the liturgy 1900
→ 6,187 ['circumstantes']: ᴿTvT [= TsTNijm] 32 (1992) 211s (P. D'Haese).

8405 Wegman H. A. J., Riten en mythen; liturgie in de geschiedenis van het
christendom. Kampen 1991, Kok. 408 p. ƒ65. 90-242-6509-6. – ᴿTvT
32 (1992) 432s (R. Rutherford).

8406 Weiss Joseph, Jesuits and the liturgy of the hours; the tradition, its
roots, classical exponents and criticism in the perspective of today: diss.
ᴰTaft R. Notre Dame 1992. – RTLv 24, p. 563.

8406* **White** James F., Protestant worship; traditions in transition 1990 ➤ 7,8259: ᴿWestTJ 54 (1992) 193-5 (J. H. *Ball*).

8407 **Whitehead** Evelyn E. & James D., Les étapes de la vie adulte; évolution psychologique et religieuse [Christian life patterns 1979],ᵀ: Chemins spirituels. P 1990, Centurion. 268 p. – ᴿLavalTP 48 (1992) 136s (R. *Richard*); ScEspr 44 (1992) 114.

8408 *Wolz-Gottwald* Eckard, Theologie und spirituelle Erfahrung; zur Entwickung spiritueller Theologie der Gegenwart: TGgw 35 (1992) 280-293.

8409 *Wolterstorff* Nicholas, [responses, *Olson* D., *Cunningham* L., *Fishburn* J.] Justice as a condition of authentic liturgy: TTod 48 (1991s) 6-21 (-32).

8410 **Wynn** Samuel, A biblical, western European and Native American understanding of spirituality: diss. Drew, ᴰ*Gustafson* R. Madison NJ 1991. 247 p. 92-13405. – DissA 53 (1992s) 184-A.

H8.1 **Vocatio**, *vita religiosa communitatis* – *Sancti;* the Saints.

8411 *Akermann* Philippe, Histoire des monastères coptes: Christus 39 (P 1992) 376-382.

8412 *Ansaldi* Jean, 'Célibat pour Christ' et sexualité [hommage 150ᵉ anniv. Diaconesses de Reuilly]: ETRel 67 (1992) 403-415.

8413 **Barth** Hans-M., Sehnsucht nach den Heiligen? Verborgene Quellen ökumenischer Spiritualität. Stu 1992, Quell. 168 p. DM 19,80. – ᴿEv-Komm 25 (1992) 755s (K.-F. *Ruf*).

8414 **Billy** Dennis, Towards a theological spirituality of the religious life: diss. Angelicum, ᴰ*Williams* B. Roma 1992. 287 p. – RTLv 24, p. 588.

8415 **Brown** P., The body and society 1988 ➤ 4,9307... 7,8267: ᴿRSPT 76 (1992) 122-7 (G.-M. de *Durand*).

8416 **Brown** P., Il corpo e la società; uomini, donne e astinenza sessuale nei primi secoli cristiani, ᵀ. T 1992, Einaudi. 466 p. [RHE 87,396*].

8417 — *Lizzi* Rita, Sessualità castità *aoovsi* nella società tardoantica [P. *Brown* 1988]: RivStoLR 28 (1992) 105-125.

8418 **Brown** Peter, Die Keuschheit der Engel; sexuelle Entsagung, Askese und Körperlichkeit am Anfang des Christentums [The Body and Society 1986]. Mü 1991, Hanser. 605 p. DM 78. – ᴿHerdKor 64 (1992) 145 (K. *Nientiedt*).

8419 **Brown** Peter, Die Heiligenverehrung, ihre Entstehung und Funktion in der lateinischen Christenheit [1981], ᵀ*Bernard* J. 1991 ➤ 7,8267*: ᴿZkT 114 (1992) 227s (H. B. *Meyer*).

8420 **Cecconi** Dino, Fenomenologia della vocazione sacerdotale: diss. Angelicum, ᴰ*Pascucci* A. Roma 1988; estr. 1991, 250 p. – RTLv 24, p. 589.

8421 **Codina** V., Zevallos N., Vita religiosa; storia e teologia, ᵀᴱ*Pompei* G.: TeLib 4/9. Assisi 1990, Cittadella. 214 p. Lit. 22.000. – ᴿAsprenas 39 (1992) 286s (B. *Senofonte*).

8422 *Cunningham* Lawrence S., A decade of research on the saints, 1980-1990 [ᴱWILSON S., Saints and their cults 1983... declining role of thaumaturgy... feminists]: TS 53 (1992) 517-533.

8423 *Daoust* J. [< *Caffet* Silouane], Aux sources du monachisme chrétien: EsprVie 102 (1992) 180-2.

8424 ᵀᴱ**Dattrino** Lorenzo, EVAGRIO Pontico, Trattato pratico sulla vita monastica: TPatr 100. R 1992, Città Nuova. 126 p. 88-311-3100-1.

Bunge Gabriel, Akedia, la doctrine spirituelle d'ÉVAGRE le Pontique sur l'acédie 1991 ➤ 9878.

8424* **Dewar** Francis, Called or collared? An alternative approach to vocation. L 1991, SPCK. xi-124 p. £10 pa. – ᴿTLond 95 (1992) 228 (W. M. *Jacob*).

8425 **Driot** Marcel, Les Pères du désert; vie et spiritualité. P/Montréal 1991, Paulines/Médiaspaul. 160 p. F 75. – ᴿEsprVie 102 (1992) 562 (Y.-M. *Duval*).

8425* **Fros** Henryk, ❿ Saints nowadays. Kraków 1991, Ap. Modlitwy [prayer]. 240 p. – ᴿAtKap 119 (1992) 186s (I. *Werbiński*, ❿).

8426 **Garrigues** Jean-Miguel, *Legrez* Jean, Moines dans l'assemblée des fidèles à l'époque des Pères (iveͤ-viiieͤ siècle): THist 87. P 1992, Beauchesne. 230 p. F 120. – ᴿEsprVie 102 (1992) 563s (Y.-M. *Duval*).

8426* **Herzig** Annaliese, 'Ordens-Christen'; Theologie des Ordenslebens in der Zeit nach dem Zweiten Vatikanischen Konzil [Diss. Freiburg 1990, ᴰ*Greshake* G.]: StSysSpT 3. Wü 1991, Echter. 463 p. DM 68. – ᴿTGL 82 (1992) 266-8 (Barbara *Hallensleben*).

8427 **Holze** H., Erfahrung und Theologie im frühen Mönchtum; Untersuchungen zu einer Theologie des monastischen Lebens bei den ägyptischen Mönchsvätern, Johannes CASSIAN und BENEDIKT von Nursia [Diss.]: ForKDG 48. Gö 1991, Vandenhoeck & R. 311 p. DM 92 [RHE 87,440*].

8428 *a) Hunter* David G., The language of desire; CLEMENT of Alexandria's transformation of ascetic discourse; – *b) Harrison* Verna E. F., Allegory and asceticism in GREGORY of Nyssa; – *c) Torjesen* Karen Jo, In praise of noble women; asceticism, patronage and honor; – *d) Corrington* Gail P., The defense of the body and the discourse of appetite; continence and control in the Greco-Roman world: → 370, Semeia 57 (1992) 95-111 / 113-130 / 41-64 / 65-74 [131-151, *Kelsey* N., Anthony; 25-39, *Vaage* L., Cynics].

8429 *Kam* John, A cursory review of the biblical basis for monastic life: AsiaJT 6,1 (Bangalore 1992) 183-6.

8429* *Kanior* Marian, ❿ Vie monastique au Mont Athos: AtKap 119 (1992) 252-267.

8430 **Kasper** Clemens M., Theologie und Askese; die Spiritualität des Inselmönchtums von Lerins im 5. Jahrhundert: BeitGeschMönchtums 40. Münster 1991, Aschendorff. xxxii-425 p. DM 98. – ᴿMüTZ 43 (1993) 120s (W. W. *Müller*); TPhil 67 (1992) 588-590 (H. J. *Sieben*); TR 88 (1992) 206-8 (H. *Lutterbach*).

8431 *Koonammakkal* Thoma K., Early Christian monastic origins; a general introduction in the context of Syriac Orient: Christian Orient 13,3 (Kerala 1992) 139-163 [TContext 10/2,27].

8432 *Leroy* Marie-Vincent, Théologie de la vie religieuse: → 114, ᶠLABOURDETTE M., RThom 92,1 (1992) 324-343 (-372, inédits de Labourdette).

8433 **London** Mary, Unveiled; [10 persevering] nuns talking. L c.1992, Chatto & W. £10. – ᴿTablet 246 (1992) 1047 (Dorothy *Bell*).

8434 **López Amat** Alfredo, La vita consacrata; le varie forme dalle origini ad oggi. R 1991, Città Nuova. 759 p. Lit. 75.000. – ᴿBenedictina 39 (1992) 279-282 (Annamaria *Valli*).

8435 **Martínez Peque** Moisés, *a)* El Espíritu Santo y el matrimonio a partir del Vaticano II. R 1991, Antonianum. – *b)* Matrimonio y virginidad; desarrollo histórico-teológico; aportación pneumatológica a la reflexión actual sobre los estados cristianos de vida: RET 51 (1991) 57-98; Eng. 57.

8435* **Metz** J.-B., *Peters* T. R., Gottespassion; zur Ordensexistenz heute. FrB 1991, Herder. 103 p. DM 17,80. – ᴿTGL 82 (1992) 157s (M. *Skeb*).

8436 a) Monachesimo cristiano e non cristiano: Quad. de Saux 7. Mi 1990. – ᴿProtestantesimo 47 (1992) 250 (E. *Noffke*). – b) *Montan* Agostino, La vita consacrata nel mistero della Chiesa fra tradizione e rinnovamento; dal Concilio Vaticano II al Codice di diritto canonico (1983): Lateranum 57 (1991) 515-576.

8436* **Müller** Gerhard L., Gemeinschaft und Verehrung der Heiligen; geschichtliche Grundlegung der Hagiologie ᴰ1986 ➤ 3,8147: ᴿTRu 57 (1992) 103-8 (Dorothea *Wendebourg*).

8437 **Munier** Charles, Matrimonio e verginità nella Chiesa antica: Traditio Christiana 4, 1990 ➤ 6,8283: ᴿRivStoLR 27 (1991) 530-2 (R. *Lizzi*).

8438 *Pardilla* Ángel, Orizzonte biblico dell'Istruzione 'Potissimum Institutioni' [AAS 82 (1990) 470-532]: Vita Consacrata 28 (1992) 757-768.

8439 *Piacentini* Ernesto, L'infallibilità papale nella canonizzazione dei santi: Monitor Ecclesiasticus 117 (1992) 91-132.

8440 *Pieris* Aloysius, The three ingredients of authentic humanism [... his experience of the vows]: a) Month 253 (1992) 73-78.114-121; – b) Vidyajyoti 56 (1992) 1-22; – c) EAPast 28 (1991) 224-252.

8441 **Piolanti** A., La comunione dei santi e la vita eterna²: Pont. Accad. Teol. Romana. Vaticano 1992, Editrice. 693 p. Lit. 50.000. – ᴿNRT 114 (1992) 962s (L. *Renwart*).

8442 *Rabe* Susan A., Veneration of the saints in western Christianity; an ecumenical issue in historical perspective: JEcuSt 28,1 (1991) 39-62 [< ZIT 92,407].

8443 **Sánchez de Murillo** José, Sobre la excelencia humana y social de la vida religiosa. Sevilla 1991, Miriam. 128 p. – ᴿTeresianum 43 (1992) 282-4 (C. *Pérez Milla*).

8443* *Theisen* Jerome [abbot primate], The Church and the cenobium: DowR 110 (1992) 259-283.

8444 *Vanhoye* Albert, Adulti nella fede, adulti nella Chiesa: Vocazioni 8 (1991) 10-14 [AcPIB 9/8,662].

8445 **Veraja** Fabijan (mgr., sous-secrétaire), Le cause di canonizzazione dei santi. Vaticano 1992, Editrice. 192 p. Lit. 20.000. – ᴿEsprVie 102 (1992) couv. 335 (M. N.).

8446 **Vogüé** Adalbert de, Histoire du mouvement monastique dans l'Antiquité, I. Le monachisme latin, de la mort d'Antoine à la fin du séjour de Jérôme à Rome (356-385): Patrimoines Christianisme 1991 ➤ 7,8223; 2-204-04214-5: ᴿGregorianum 73 (1992) 564s (G. *Pelland*); NRT 114 (1992) 605s (L.-J. *Renard*); RHPR 72 (1992) 329 (W. *Fick*); RSPT 76 (1992) 131-4 (G.-M. de *Durand*); Teresianum 43 (1992) 301 (M. *Diego Sánchez*).

8447 **Wagenaar** C., Om met Christus te zijn; het christelijk oosters monachisme: Monastieke Cahiers 39. Bonheiden/Brugge 1990, Betlehem/Tabor. 985 p. Fb. 1995. – ᴿCollatVL 22 (1992) 103s (J. *Bonny*).

8448 *Wendebourg* Dorothea, Mönchtum: ➤ 757, EvKL 3 (1992) 516-528.

8449 ᴱ**Wimbush** Vincent L., Aascetic behavior in Greco-Roman antiquity — a sourcebook: Studies in Antiquity and Christianity 1990 ➤ 7,8297; ᴿCBQ 54 (1992) 808-810 (T. M. *Finn*); ExpTim 103 (1991s) 56s (S. *Lieu*: bold new arrangement); RExp 89 (1992) 139 (E. G. *Hinson*); StPhilonAn 4 (1992) 133-6 (D. T. *Runia*).

8450 a) *Wimbush* Vincent L., Ascetic behavior and color-ful language; stories about Ethiopian Moses; – b) *BeDuhn* Jason D., Regimen for salvation; medical models in Manichaean asceticism; – c) *Harpham* Geoffrey G., Old water in new bottles; the contemporary prospects for the study of asceticism: ➤ 370, Semeia 58 (1992) 81-92 / 109-134 / 135-148.

8451 **Woodward** Kenneth L.,   La fabbrica dei santi.   Mi 1991, Rizzoli.   491 p.
Lit. 36.000. – ᴿCC 143 (1992,3) 97s (F. *Castelli*).

8452 **Woodward** Kenneth L.,   Die Helfer Gottes; wie die katholische Kirche
ihre Heiligen macht [Making saints], ᵀ*Conrad* Gabriele, *Lohmeyer* Till R.,
Rost Christl. Mü 1991, Bertelsmann. 558 p.   3-570-06270-8. – ᴿActuBbg
29 (1992) 225s (J. *Boada*).

H8.2   Theologia moralis NT.

8453 *Arens* Edmund,   Kommunikative Ethik und Theologie [APEL K.-O.:
HABERMAS J.]: TR 88 (1992) 441-454.

8454 **Arnold** Markus,   Kontext und Moral; zur Korrelation von Weltethik
und Heilsethos [Diss.]: EurHS 23/354.   Fra 1988, Lang.   vii-309 p. – ᴿSalesianum 54 (1992) 163-5 (G. *Abbà*).

8455 *Audisio* Gabriel [*al.*],   Famille, religion, sexualité; perspectives d'hier ou
d'avenir: RHR 209,4 (1992) 339-347 [-457].

8456 *Bach* Ulrich,   Die Gemeinde Jesu Christi – Gemeinschaft von Behinder-
ten und Nichtbehinderten: Diakonie (Stu 1992,3) 133-7 [< ᴢɪᴛ 92,398].

8457 *Barilier* Roger,   Le divorce; étude biblique et pastorale: RRéf 42,5
(1991) 1-46 [< ᴢɪᴛ 92,21].

8457* **Barral-Baron** A.,   La morale: Tout simplement.   P 1992, Ouvrières.
208 p. F 85. – ᴿEsprVie 102 (1992) 315s (P. *Daubercies*: dans une société
pluraliste, il faut offrir un message plus chrétien et traditionnel).

8458 *Beckwith* Francis J.,   A critical appraisal of theological arguments for
abortion rights [i.e. the author refutes claims that the Bible actually
approves abortion or at least (MOLLENKOTT V.) does not forbid it]: BtS
148 (1991) 337-355.

8459 **Bexell** Göran,   Etiken, Bibeln och samlevenden; utformningen av en
nutidiga kristen etik, tillämpad på samlevnadsetiske frågor.   Sto 1986,
Verbum.   285 p. – ᴿSvTKv 67 (1991) 48s (H. *Fagerberg*).

8460 *Bindemann* Walther,   Gottes Recht und Menschenrechte; biblisches Ge-
rechtigkeitsethos und sozio-politische Herausforderungen der Gegenwart:
TLZ 117 (1992) 561-576.

8462 *Brox* Norbert,   Von der apokalyptischen Naherwartung zur christlichen
Tugendlehre: → 648*, Spätantike 1922, 229-248.

8463 *Canévet* Mariette,   L'humanité de l'embryon selon GRÉGOIRE de Nysse:
NRT 114 (1992) 678-695.

8464 *Castaño* José F.,   Studio esegetico-dottrinale sulle tre figure del can.
1095 ['nascita'... del vincolo matrimoniale]: Angelicum 69 (1992) 193-255
[493-517, can. 1095, reflexiones, *Burke* Cormac].

8465 *a) Chethimattam* J.B.,   Towards a world morality; – *b) Henry* Sarojini,
Social ethic of Mahatma GANDHI and Martin BUBER; – *c) Michel* Thomas,
Islamic ethical vision; – *d) Kochumuttom* Thomas,   Ethics-based society of
Buddhism: JDharma 16 ('Comparative Ethics' 1991) 317-336 / 375-386 /
398-409 / 410-420.

8466 *Cioli* Gianni,   Il cammino della teologia morale preconciliare alla luce
del rinnovamento ecclesiologico; appunti per un'indagine storica: VivH 1
(1990) 101-119.

8467 *Composta* Dario,   La schiavitù e il magistero pontificio nei secoli XV-
XVII: DocCom 45 (1992) 225-243.

8468 **D'Aquino** P.,   Storia del matrimonio cristiano alla luce della Bibbia 2.
Inseparabilità e monogamia 1988 → 5,8270; 6,8322:   ᴿAntonianum 67
(1992) 447-9 (T. *Larrañaga*).

8469 **Dannemeyer** William, Shadows in the land; homosexuality in America [... biblical data also]. SF 1989, Ignatius. 243 p. $10 pa. – RHomP 91,3 (1990s) 73s (J. M. *Grondelski*).

8470 *Davison* Beverly C., Hospitality; welcoming the stranger: AmBapQ 11 (1992) 6-21 [< ZIT 92,351].

8471 **Desclos** Jean, Libérer la morale; christocentrisme et dynamique filiale de la morale chrétienne à l'époque de Vatican II. Montréal/P 1991, Paulines/Médiaspaul. 251 p. – RScEspr 44 (1992) 233s (J.-M. *Dufort*).

8472 *Dichgans* Johannes, Der Arzt und die Wahrheit am Krankenbett; zwischen Forderung und Überforderung: ArztC 38 (1992) 13-..

8472* *Dillmann* Rainer, Aufbruch zu einer neuen Sittlichkeit; biblisch-narrative Begründung ethischen Handelns [... Mk 7,31-35; Lk 13,10-17]: TGL 82 (1992) 34-45.

8473 *Di Virgilio* Giuseppe, Rassegna, l'etica del NT: ParVi 37 (1992) 55-65.

8474 **Dowell** Susan, They two shall be one; monogamy in history and religion. L 1990, Collins Flame. 221 p. £8 pa. – RScotJT 45 (1992) 277s (Helen *Oppenheimer*); TLond 95 (1992) 67s (Anne *Borrowdale*: feminists have tended to regard marriage as a form of oppression).

8475 **Drewermann** Eugen, La peur et la faute; psychanalyse et théologie morale 1. P 1992, Cerf. 151 p. – RArTGran 55 (1992) 423-5 (C. *Dominguez Morano*).

8476 **Drewermann** Eugen, Psychanalyse et morale 2. L'amour et la réconciliation, TBagot Jean-Pierre. P 1992, Cerf. viii-186 p. F 99. 2-204- 04568-3 [RTLv 24,513, P. *Weber*: bâti sur l'estimation pessimiste p. 62 'proportion de gens nevrosés 70%'].

8477 **Drewermann** Eugen, Psychanalyse et morale, 3. Le mensonge et le suicide, TBagot Jean-Pierre. P 1990, Cerf. vi-136 p. F 90. 2-204-04569-1 [RTLv 24,514, P. *Weber*].

8478 **Duff** Nancy J., Humanization and the politics of God; the *koinonia* ethics of Paul LEHMANN. GR 1992, Eerdmans. 188 p. $22. – RTTod 49 (1992s) 544.546 (E. M. *Huenemann*).

8479 **Dussel** Enrique, Éthique communautaire: Libération. P 1991, Cerf. 256 p. F 155. 2-204-04208-0. – REsprVie 102 (1992) 94-96 (P. *Daubercies*); ÉTRel 67 (1992) 132 (M. *Muller*).

8480 *Eugene* Toinette M., African American family life; an agenda for ministry within the Catholic Church: NewTR 5,2 (1992) 33-47 (al. 6-32 on family).

8481 *Evans* Craig A., Jesus' ethic of humility [... underplayed in SCHNACKENBURG R. 1986]: TrinJ 13 (1992) 127-138.

8482 *Ewald* George R., Jesus and divorce; a biblical guide for ministry to divorced persons. Scottdale PA c. 1991, Herald. $10 [Interp 46,89 adv.].

8483 *Falgueras* Ignacio, Los grados de la sexualidad: Burgense 33 (1992) 115-141.

8484 *Feehan* Thomas, The morality of lying in St. AUGUSTINE: AugSt 21 (1990) 67-81.

8485 *Ferasin* Egidio, 'Dottrina costante' della Chiesa sulla sessualità?: Salesianum 54 (1992) 123-150 [anche in ➔ 161].

8486 **Fischer** James A., Looking for moral guidance; dilemma and the Bible. NY 1992, Paulist. iii-152 p. $10. 0-8091-3170-6.

8487 *a) Fischer* Johannes, Christliche Ethik als Verantwortungsethik?; – *b) Ringeling* Hermann, Konturen einer 'postmodernen' Moral: EvT 52,2 (1992) 114-128 / 103-114.

8488 **Ford** Norman, When did I begin? [fourteen days after conception]. Cambridge 1992, Univ. xix-217 p. 0-521-42428-3. – RExpTim 103 (1991s)

382s (J. *Wilkinson*: important, essential; by a Salesian priest concerned that only since 1974 has the Roman Catholic church committed itself to 'human person since conception').

8489 **Fowl** Stephen E., *Jones* L. Gregory, Reading in communion; Scripture and ethics in Christian life 1991 ➤ 7,8331; also L 1991, SPCK. 166 p. £13 pa. 0-281-04526-7. – ᴿExpTim 103 (1991s) 349s (R. *Preston*: lively, unconvincing; 'influence of recent tendencies... are evident'); TLond 95 (1992) 309s (J. J. N. *McDonald*).

8490 ᴱ**Freyne** Séan, Ethics and the Christian [Dublin lectures; his key essay is on the ethics of Jesus]. Dublin 1991, Columba. 156 p. £9. 1-85607-019-0. – ᴿExpTim 103 (1991s) 85s (R. G. *Jones*: fresh, 'this new magic of ethics').

8491 **Fuchs** Éric, L'éthique protestante; histoire et enjeux: Le champ éthique 19, 1990 ➤ 7,8333: ᴿSalesianum 54 (1992) 173-5 (G. *Abbà*).

8492 *Fuchs* Josef, *a)* Sittliche Selbststeuerung: StiZt 117 (1992) 553-9 > Eng. Ethical self-direction, TDig 39 (1992) 343-7 [ᵀᴱ*Asen* B. A.]; – *b)* Law and grace [< StiZt 116 (1991) 317-322], ᵀᴱ*Asen* B. A.: TDig 39 (1992) 229-233.

8493 *Fürger* Franz, Gerechtigkeit in der römisch-katholischen Soziallehre: TGgw 35 (1992) 173-9.

8494 **Gamwell** Franklin I., The divine good; modern moral theory and the necessity of God; pref. *Tracy* David. NY 1990, HarperCollins. xiv-218 p. $30. – ᴿPerspRelSt 19 (1992) 239-242 (J. C. *Shelley*: rightly extolled by RICŒUR, OGDEN, COBB).

8495 *Gatti* Guido, A proposito di opzione fondamentale ['teorema' secondo K. DEMMER, NDizTMor 1990]: Salesianum 54 (1992) 635-703.

8496 *Ghesquièreds* Louis-Étienne, Nullités et annulations de mariage; l'Église change-t-elle sa loi?: EsprVie 102 (1992) 545-552.

8496* **Gill** Robin, Christian ethics in secular worlds. E 1991, Clark. xvii-158 p. £10 pa. – ᴿTLond 95 (1992) 311 (D. *Martin*: essays).

8497 **Gillen** Erny, Wie Christen ethisch handeln und denken; die Debatte um die Autonomie der Sittlichkeit im Kontext katholischer Theologie [Diss. LvN 1987]. Wü 1989, Echter. 215 p. – ᴿSalesianum 54 (1992) 384s (G. *Abbà*).

8498 *a) González Faus* José I., Jesús y la mentira; – *b) Vives* Josep, Verdad y mentira en la Iglesia: SalT 80 (1992) 347-369 / 389-398.

8499 **Graham** Gordon, The idea of Christian charity; a critique of some contemporary conceptions. L 1990, Collins. xiv-190 p. £15. 0-00-599199-4. – ᴿExpTim 102 (1990s) 347 (R. G. *Jones*: attacks both non-directive therapy and social-religious politics, shrewdly, but giving no hearing to their practicioners); TLond 95 (1992) 69s (J. *Fuller*: limitingly philosophical).

8500 **Grecco** [TR 88,172] Richard, A theology of compromise; a study of method in the ethics of Charles E. CURRAN: AmerUnivSt 7/104. NY 1991, Lang. xi-273 p. DM 78.

8501 **Grisez** Germain, *Shaw* Russell, Fulfillment in Christ; a summary of Christian moral principles. ND 1991, Univ. xviii-456 p. – ᴿSalesianum 54 (1992) 593-5 (G. *Abbà*).

8502 **Gula** Richard M., Reason informed by faith; foundations of Catholic morality. NY 1989, Paulist. – ᴿHomP 92,5 (1991s) 74s (J. M. *Grondelski*: fundamentally flawed; follows the wrong authors).

8503 **Häring** Bernhard, Frei in Christus I-III Sonderausgabe. FrB 1989, Herder. 484 p., 561 p., 489 p. – ᴿCiuD 205 (1992) 195-204 (V. *Gómez Mier*).

8504 **Häring** B., Uitzichtloos? Pastoral bij scheiding en hertrouw; een pleidooi [1989 ⇒ 6,8337]. Averbode 1991, Altiora. 92 p. Fb 395. – ᴿCollatVL 22 (1992) 217s (J. *Jackers*).

8505 **Häring** Bernhard, La théologie morale, idées maîtresses: Recherches morales, synthèses. P 1992, Cerf. 184 p. F 120. – ᴿEsprVie 102 (1992) 317s (P. *Daubercies*).

8506 *Hamilton* Victor P., [*Collins* Raymond F.; NT]: Marriage: ⇒ 741, AnchorBD, 4 (1992) 559-569 [-572].

8507 **Hanigan** James P., Homosexuality 1988 ⇒ 4,9383... 6,8340: ᴿTLZ 116 (1991) 219s (H. *Schulz* †).

8508 **Harrison** Brian W., *a)* Religious liberty and contraception; did Vatican II open the way for a new sexual ethic? [diss. Angelicum, Rome 1987]. Melbourne 1988, John XXIII Fellowship. – *b)* Le développement de la doctrine catholique sur la liberté religieuse; un précédent pour un changement vis-à-vis de la contraception? Bouère 1988, Morin. 208 p. – ᴿRThom 92 (1992) 567-9 (D.-M. de *Saint-Laumer*: mérite du fond).

8509 **Hartfeld** H., Homosexualität im Kontext von Bibel, Theologie und Seelsorge. Wu 1991, Brockhaus. 318 p. 3-417-29368-5. – ᴿTvT 32 (1992) 438 (F.-F. *Hirs*).

8510 **Harvey** Anthony E., Strenuous commands 1990 ⇒ 7,8347: ᴿAndrUnS 30 (1992) 169s (H. *Weiss*); Interpretation 26 (1990) 432-4 (J. F. *Piper*).

8511 **Hauerwas** Stanley M., Christian existence today 1988 ⇒ 5,277; 7,8349: ᴿCritRR 5 (1992) 284-6 (T. *Reynolds*: answers GUSTAFSON).

8512 **Hilpert** Konrad, Die Menschenrechte; Geschichte, Theologie, Aktualität. Dü 1991, Patmos. 312 p. DM 50 [TR 88,172].

8513 *Hoheisel* Karl, Homosexualität: ⇒ 764, RAC XVI,123 (1992) 289-364.

8514 *Honecker* Martin, Einführung in die theologische Ethik. B 1990, de Gruyter. xxii-423 p. DM 58. 3-11-008146-6. – ᴿSvTKv 67 (1991) 145-7 (G. *Bexell*).

8515 **Houlden** J.L., Ethics and the New Testament. E 1992, Clark. x-134 p. £9.

8516 **House** Bernard, Proportionalism; the American debate and its European roots. Wsh 1987, Georgetown Univ. xii-159 p.

8517 ᵀᴱ**Hunter** David G., Marriage in the Early Church [texts]: Sources of Early Christian Thought. Mp 1992, Fortress. viii-157 p. 0-8006-2652-4.

8518 **Jacobelli** Maria Caterina, Ostergelächter; Sexualität und Lust im Raum des Heiligen [Il risus paschalis, 1990 Queriniana] ᵀ*Sommerfeld* Fortunat. Rg 1992, Pustet. 144 p. 3-7917-13175. – ᴿTGL 82 (1992) 506s (W. *Beinert* links with F. A. STROHL's 1698 ecclesiastically approved sermons Ovum paschale novum).

8519 **Jones** L. Gregory, Transformed judgment; toward a trinitarian account of the moral life. ND 1990, Univ. 208 p. $23. – ᴿJRel 72 (1992) 614 (Lois *Malcolm*).

8520 **Jonsen** Albert R., *Toulmin* Stephen, The abuse of casuistry; a history of moral reasoning 1988 = 1991 ⇒ 7,8352: ᴿAmerica 165 (1991) 492 (J. F. *Brown*).

8521 *Kaiser* W. C., New approaches to biblical ethics ['on the brink of total collapse' faced with modernity]: JEvTS 35 (1992) 289-297 [< ZAW 105,511].

8522 **Keeling** Michael, The foundations of Christian ethics. E 1990, Clark. 269 p. £10. 0-567-29180-4. – ᴿExpTim 102,9 2d-top choice (1990s) 258s (C. S. *Rodd*).

8523 **Keener** Craig S., And marries another; divorce and remarriage in the teaching of the NT 1991 ⇒ 7,8354: ᴿCritRR 5 (1992) 231-3 (C. L. *Blomberg*: first-rate scholarship).

8524 *a) Kitchens* Ted G., Perimeters of corrective Church discipline [1 Cor 5,9-13; Rom 16,17...]; – *b) Moreland* J. P., The morality of suicide; issues and options: BtS 148 (1991) 201-213 / 214-230.

8525 **Küng** Hans, Projekt Weltethos. Mü 1990, Piper. 192 p. DM 19,80. – ᴿDLZ 113 (1992) 404-8 (H. *Mohr*); LuthMon 31 (1992) 329s (R. *Ficker*); ZkT 114 (1992) 355s (H. *Rotter*).

8526 **Küng** Hans, Proyecto de una ética mundial, ᵀ*Canal Marcos* Gilberto. M 1991, Trotta. 174 p. 84-87699-12-X. – ᴿActuBbg 29 (1992) 72 (J. *Boada*); SalT 80 (1992) 79s (L. *González-Carvajal*).

8527 **Küng** Hans, Etikk for verdens fremtid. Oslo 1991, Gyldendal. 208 p. – ᴿSvTKv 67 (1991) 148s (E. *Westerberg*).

8527* **Lachner** Gabriele, Die Kirchen und die Wiederheirat Geschiedener [Diss. 1989 ➤ 6,8349*]: BeitÖkT 21. Pd 1991, Schöningh. 288 p. – ᴿOstkSt 41 (1992) 342s (E. C. *Suttner*).

8528 **Legrain** Michel, Divorciados y vueltos a casar; reflexión bíblica, teológica y pastoral. Sdr 1990, Sal Terrae. 172 p. – ᴿChristus 57,1 (Méx 1992) 57 (C. *Bravo G.*).

8529 **LeMasters** Philip, Discipleship for all believers; Christian ethics and the Kingdom of God. Scottdale PA 1992, Herald. 176 p. $13. 0-8361-3579-2 [NTAbs 36,438]. – ᴿRExp 89 (1992) 426-8 (G. *Stassen*).

8530 **Locht** P. de, Morale sexuelle et Magistère. P 1992, Cerf. 250 p. F 120. – ᴿNRT 114 (1992) 412-8 (A. *Chapelle*: 'la tradition morale catholique y est mise en question, y compris en ses fondements... compétence magistérielle...').

8531 **Lohse** (bp.) Eduard, Theological ethics of the NT, ᵀ*Boring* M. E. 1991 ➤ 4,9394... 7,8360: ᴿRExp 89 (1992) 419s (H. *Barnette*); TS 53 (1992) 550-2 (J. *Topel*).

8532 **Lohse** Eduard, Etica teologica del NT, ᵀᴱ*Soffritti* Giorgio. Brescia 1991, Paideia. 231 p. Lit. 32.000. – ᴿCC 143 (1992,4) 631-3 (P. *Cultrera*).

8533 *López Azpitarte* Eduardo, Fundamentación de la ética cristiana: BtTeol 8. M 1991, Paulinas. 460 p. pt. 2100 [TR 88,84].

8534 *McCormick* Richard A., *a)* Physician-assisted suicide; flight from compassion: ChrCent 108 (1991) 1132-4; – *b)* Moral theology in the year 2000; tradition in transition: America 166 (1992) 312-8.

8535 *McGrath* Alister E., Doctrine and ethics: JEvTS 34 (1991) 145-156 [< ᴢɪᴛ 91,562].

8536 *a) McGrath* Alister E., In what way can Jesus be a moral example for Christians?; – *b) Dorsey* David A., The law of Moses and the Christian; a compromise: JEvTS 34 (1991) 289-298 / 321-334 [< ᴢɪᴛ 91,771s].

8537 **MacIntyre** Alasdair, Three rival versions of moral inquiry 1990 ➤ 6, 8354; 7,8363: ᴿChrCent 108 (1991) 53s (T. *Volker*).

8538 **McQuilkin** Robertson, [An introduction to] Biblical ethics 1989 ➤ 7, 8366: ᴿBtS 48 (1991) 240 (R. P. *Lightner*: a gold mine).

8539 **Mahoney** John, The making of moral theology 1987 ➤ 3,8247... 6,8357: ᴿHomP 91,3 (1990s) 74-76 (T. C. *Donlan*).

8539* **Mancini** Roberto, Comunicazione come ecumene; il significato antropologico e teologico dell'etica comunicativa [ʜᴀʙᴇʀᴍᴀs]: GdT 202. Brescia 1991, Queriniana. 152 p. – ᴿHumTeol 13 (1992) 264-6 (J. T. da *Cunha*).

8540 **Marxsen** Willi, 'Christliche'... Ethik 1989 ➤ 5,8334... 7,8371: ᴿJRel 72 (1992) 582 (P. E. *Devenish*).

8541 **May** William E., *a)* Moral absolutes 1989 ➤ 5,8337: ᴿThought 66 (1991) 117s (T. R. *Kopfensteiner*); – *b)* Principios de vida moral ➤ 7,8372:

T*Sarmiento* Augusto: Ética y Sociedad. Barc 1990, EIUNSA. 270 p. – RSalesianum 54 (1992) 387-9 (G. *Abbà*).

8542 *May* William E., La retorica di HÄRING sui divorziati risposati: St-CattMi 36 (1992) 34-36.

8543 **Moore** Gareth, The body in context; sex and Catholicism. L c. 1992, SCM. £17.50. – RTablet 246 (1992) 1439s (B. *Hoose*).

8544 **Moser** Antonio, *Leers* Bernardino; Moral theology; dead ends and alternatives 1990 ➤ 7,8373*b*; $30; pa. $17. 0-88344-680-4; -65-0. – RExpTim 102 (1990s) 380s (R. G. *Jones*: unsubstantiated, incoherent, ignores Protestants).

8544* *Moxnes* Halvor, Eskatologisk eksistens; nytestamentlige bidrag til etikken: NorTTs 92 (1991) 1-13.

8545 *Müller* Gerhard L., Unauflöslichkeit der Ehe – Scheidung – Wiederheirat: MüTZ 42 (1991) 45-68.

8546 *Noonan* John T.J, Retrospective [... DEMPSEY B. versus LECKY W. got him interested in Catholic authority-claims; he now has 'little support for those theorists — mostly Marxists when I began, now mostly feminists — who see in moral doctrine and law a hidden agenda of oppression']; RelStR 18 (1992) 111s [113-117-120, comments of *Kaveny* M. Cathleen; *Buckley* William J.].

8547 **Pailin** David A., A gentle touch; from a theology of handicap to a theology of human being. L 1992, SPCK. 196 p. £12.50. 0-281-04575-5. – RExpTim 103,12 top choice (1991s) 353s (C. S. *Rodd*).

8547* *Petrà* Basilio, Tra cielo e terra; introduzione alla teologia morale ortodossa contemporanea. Bo 1992, Dehoniane. 284 p. – ROstkSt 41 (1992) 335-7 (H. M. *Biedermann*).

8548 *a*) *Pinto de Oliveira* C. J., La finalité dans la morale thomiste ... du bonheur évangélique; – *b*) *Mongillo* Dalmazio, La verità rende liberi; – *c*) *Kaczyński* Edward, La formazione morale cristiana; – *d*) *Rizzello* Raffaele, La legge morale per il bene della persona e per l'amicizia tra le persone: Angelicum 69,3 (Simposio Roma 1 apr. 1992, 'Morale fondamentale' 1992) 301-326 / 327-350 / 351-368 / 369-388.

8549 *Piva* Pompeo, Riflessioni per un'ermeneutica ecumenica dell'evento etico: StEcum 9 (1991) 9-20; Eng. 20 [8 (1990) 379-388].

8550 *Pizzorni* Reginaldo, Giustizia e 'carità' nel pensiero greco-romano, I: Sapienza 45 (1992) 233-278.

8551 **Poling** James N., The [sexual] abuse of power, a theological problem. Nv 1991, Abingdon. 224 p. $16. – RTTod 49 (1992) 572-4 (Abigail R. *Evans*: sample too limited).

8552 **Porter** Jean, The recovery of virtue; the relevance of AQUINAS for Christian ethics 1990 ➤ 7,8385; 0-664-21924-1: RExpTim 102 (1990s) 350s (G. J. *Warnock*: boldly assumes Aquinas is always right, even in his 'weird, archaic' ignoring of ARISTOTLE on some basics — but *not* on 'mental inferiority of women' p. 140).

8553 **Pozo Abejón** Gerardo del, Lex evangelica; estudio histórico-sistemático del paso de la concepción tomística e [sic en título; 'a' en R] la suareciana: BtTGran 23, 1988 ➤ 5,8352: RAngelicum 69 (1992) 283s (E. *Kaczyński*).

8554 **Prader** Joseph, Il matrimonio in Oriente e Occidente: Kanonika I. R 1992, Pont. Inst. Stud. Orientalium. X-260 p. – ROrChrPer 58 (1992) 563-9 (Urbano *Navarrete*).

8555 **Putz** Gertraud, Christentum und Menschenrechte: Salzburg Int. ForZ 40. Innsbruck 1991, Tyrolia. 449 p. [TR 88,172].

8556 **Ranke-Heinemann** Uta,   Eunuchs 1986 ➤ 5,8353; 7,8388:   ᴿAmerica 164 (1991) 350 (Jean *Porter*).

8557 **Ranke-Heinemann** Uta, Eunuchi per il regno dei cieli; la chiesa cattolica e la sessualità. Mi 1990, Rizzoli. 361 p. Lit. 35.000. – ᴿAsprenas 39 (1992) 125s (L. *Medusa*).

8558 **Riddle** John M.,   Conception and abortion from the ancient world to the Renaissance. CM 1992, Harvard Univ. x-245 p.   0-674-16875-5 [OIAc 3,36].

8559 **Riordon** Michael,   The first stone; homosexuality and the United Church.   Toronto 1990, McClelland & S.   301 p. $37. – ᴿAnglTR 74 (1992) 518-520 (R. M. *Kawano*).

8560 **Rosenberg** Roy A., *al.*,   Happily intermarried; authoritative advice for a joyous Jewish-Christian marriage.   NY 1989, Collier-Macmillan. $8. 0-02-036420-X. – ᴿRExp 88,2 (1991) 242s (Diana S. *Richmond Garland*).

8561 **Salaün** R.,   Separés, divorcés, une possible espérance.   P 1990, Nouvelle Clio.   272 p. F 98 [NRT 115,117, L. *Volpe*].

8562 **Sánchez** Urbano,   Moral conflictiva; entre la creatividad, el riesgo y la comunión: Lux Mundi 67.   S 1991, Sígueme.   396 p. [TR 88,172].

8563 **Schnackenburg** Rudolf,   El mensaje moral del NT, II. Los primeros predicadores cristianos [1988], ᵀ*Villanueva* Marciano 1991 ➤ 7,8395:   ᴿLateranum 58 (1992) 500s (R. *Penna*); LumenVr 40 (1991) 531s (J. *Querejazu*); ScripTPamp 23 (1991) 1026-9 (A. *García-Moreno*, 1s).

8564 **Schnackenburg** Rudolf,   Il messaggio morale del NT, II. I primi predicatori cristiani²ʳᵉᵛ [1988], ᵀ*Tomasoni* Francesco: CommTeolNT supp. 2. Brescia 1990, Paideia.   370 p.   88-394-0449-X. – ᴿAsprenas 39 (1992) 290s (S. *García-Jalón*, 1).

8565 *Schwab* Claude,   De la Bible à la bioéthique: ÉTRel 67 (1992) 193-204.

8566 **Segalla** Giuseppe,   Introduzione all'etica biblica del NT 1989 ➤ 6,300; 7,8398:   ᴿAustralBR 40 (1992) 79s (E. *Osborn*); ScripTPamp 23 (1991) 1065s (C. *Basevi*).

8567 ᴱ**Silva** Alvaro de, [passages from] CHESTERTON G. K.,   Brave new family.   SF c. 1990, Ignatius.   279 p. $20; pa. $12. – ᴿHomP 91,11s (1990s) 88 (J. R. *Sheets*).

8568 **Sleeper** C. Freeman,   The Bible and the moral life.   Louisville 1992, W-Knox.   181 p. $15.

8569 **Smith** J. E.,   Humanae vitae, a generation later.   Wsh 1991, Catholic Univ.   xii-426 p. – ᴿTGgw 35 (1992) 315-9 (B. *Häring*).

8570 *Starowieyski* Marek, ❷ L'avortement dans l'opinion des premiers temps du christianisme: PrzPow 855 (1992) 292-307.

8571 **Tafferner** Andrea,   Gottes- und Nächstenliebe in der deutschsprachigen Theologie des 20. Jahrhunderts [Diss. Münster]: InTSt 37.   Innsbruck 1992, Tyrolia.   336 p. DM 48 [TR 88,530].

8572 **Thévenot** Xavier [➤ 320],   La bioetica; quando la vita comincia e finisce, ᵀᴱ*Laurita* Roberto.   Brescia 1990, Queriniana.   134 p. Lit. 15.000. – ᴿCC 143 (1992,1) 625s (F. *Cultrera*).

8573 **Thévenot** X.,   Omosessualità m. 1991 ➤ 7,8404:   ᴿCC 143 (1992,3) 319-321 (F. *Cultrera*).

8574 *Thraede* Klaus,   Homonoia (Eintracht): ➤ 764, RAC XVI, 123s (1992) 176-289.

8575 *Trigg* Joseph W.,   What do the Church Fathers have to tell us about sex? [... their concerns and presuppositions about personhood were different]: AnglTR 74 (1992) 18-24.

8575* *Valadier* Paul, Une morale sans exceptions?: Études 377 (1992) 67-76.

8576 *Viscuso* Patrick, The theology of marriage in the Rudder [Pedalion 1800] of NIKODEMOS the Hagiorite: OstkSt 41 (1992) 187-207.
8576* **Walker** Nigel, Why punish? Ox 1991, UP. xiv-168 p. £8 pa. – RMonth 253 (1992) 31 (J. *Mullens*); TLond 95 (1992) 128-130 (L. *Scarman*: high praise).
8577 *Wattiaux* Henri, La famille a-t-il un avenir?: EsprVie 102 (1992) 529-544 + couv. 266-9.
8578 **Wiebe** Ben, Messianic ethics; Jesus' proclamation of the Kingdom of God and the Church in response. Waterloo ONT 1992, Herald. 224 p. 0-8361-3585-7.
8579 *Wiebering* Joachim, Evangelische Ethik zwischen Tradition und Spontaneität [FREY C., *al.*]: TLZ 116 (1991) 161-172.
8580 **Wiemeyer-Faulde** Cornelia, Ethik und christlicher Glaube; Beiträge zur Diskussion um das Proprium einer christlichen Ethik von Basil MITCHELL, Keith WARD und John MACQUARRIE [Diss. Münster]: MünsteranerTA 11. Altenberge 1990, Telos. 194 p. DM 27,80 [TR 88,84].
8581 **You** Alain, La loi de gradualité; une nouveauté en morale?: Sycomore. P 1991, Lethielleux. 198 p. F 89. – REsprVie 102 (1992) 651s (P. *Daubercies*); NRT 114 (1992) 264s (A. *Mattheuws*).
8582 **Zion** William B., Eros and transformation, sexuality and marriage; an Eastern Orthodox perspective. Lanham MD 1992, UPA. xvi-376 p. 0-8191- 8647-3; pa. -8-1.

H8.4 *NT ipsum de reformatione sociali* – **Political action in Scripture.**

8583 *Alana* Olu E., Reconsidering the poor by Gospel norms: AfER 32 (1990) 193-200.
8584 *Amberg* Ernst-Heinz, Enzyklika und Denkschrift; neue Beiträge zur christlichen Sozialethik: TLZ 117 (1992) 241-252.
8585 [Carneiro de] **Andrade** Paulo F., Fe e política; o uso da sociologia na teologia da libertação. São Paulo 1991, Loyola. 311 p. – RREB 52 (1992) 487s (C. M. *Boff*).
8586 **Arens** Edmund, *al.*, Erinnerung, Befreiung, Solidarität; BENJAMIN, MARCUSE, HABERMAS und die politische Theologie 1991 ➤ 7,8413*: RTPhil 67 (1992) 616-8 (M. *Möhring-Hesse*: theories from outside theology are often ground into hamburger and served up with a theological sauce in the dry bread of a theological treatise).
8587 **Assmann** Hugo, *Hinkelammert* Franz J., A idolatria do mercado; ensaio sobre economia e teologia; Teologia e libertação 5/5. São Paulo 1989, Vozes. 456 p. – RActuBbg 29 (1992) 165-9 (J. I. *González Faus*).
8588 *a)* *Bartolomé* Juan J., Jesús ante el dinero; 'nadie puede servir a dos señores'; – *b)* *Rojo* Eduardo, Mitos y verdades de las sociedades desarrolladas; los riesgos de olvidar los 'demonios' del capitalismo: SalT 78 (1990) 449-459 / 408-424.
8589 **Bassler** Jouette M., God and mammon; asking for money in the New Testament. Nv 1991, Abingdon. 144 p. $10 pa. 0-687-14962-2. – RRExp 89 (1992) 286-8 (P. D. *Duerksen*).
8590 **Bauckham** Richard, The Bible in politics 1989 ➤ 6,8415; 7,8414: RCBQ 54 (1992) 139-141 (R. J. *Miller*: creative insights; some evasions).
8591 *Baum* Gregory, *Vaillancourt* Jean-Guy, Église catholique et modernisation politique: LavalTP 48 (1992) 433-446.
8591* **Billingsley** K. L., From mainline to sideline; the social witness of the National Council of Churches. Lanham MD 1990, Ethics and Pub-

lic Policy Center. ix-220 p. $16.50 pa. – ᴿWestTJ 53 (1991) 382s (R. E. Otto).

8592 *Braidfoot* L., Church, state and salt; a biblical reflection: TEdr 45 (NO 1992) 107-116 [< NTAbs 36,382].

8593 **Bruce** Steve, The rise and fall of the New Christian Right; conservative Protestant politics in America 1978-1988. Ox 1990, Clarendon. 210 p. $34.50. 0-19-827861-6. – ᴿRExp 89 (1992) 118s (B. J. *Leonard*).

8593* *a*) *Burrell* David B., An introduction to [MILBANK J.], Theology and social theory; – *b*) *Coles* Roman, Storied others and the possibilities of caritas; Milbank and neo-Nietzschean ethics; – *c*) *Lash* Nicholas, Not exactly politics or power? – *d*) *Louglin* Gerard, Christianity at the end of the story or the return of the master-narrative; – *e*) *Kerr* Fergus, Rescuing Girard's argument?: ModT 8,4 ('Special focus on Milbank' 1992) 319-329 / 331-351 / 353-364 / 365-384 / 385-399.

8594 ᴱ**Cerillo** Augustus ᴶ, *Dempster* Murray W., Salt and light; evangelical political thought in modern America. GR 1989, Baker. 175 p. $12. 0-8010-2536-2. – ᴿRExp 89 (1992) 131 (D. S. *Dockery*: includes C. HENRY and J. FALWELL, but also all other positions fairly).

8595 **Chewning** Richard C., *al.*, Business through the eyes of faith 1990 ➤ 7,8417: ᴿNewTR 4,4 (1991) 109s (S. *Priest*).

8596 **Collier** Jane, The culture of economism; an exploration of barriers to faith-as-praxis [diss. Birmingham]. Fra 1990, Lang. xii-407 p. Fs 90. – ᴿMilltSt 29 (1992) 150-4 (P. *Riordan*).

8597 *Dahm* Karl-Wilhelm, Wenn der Markt zum 'Sündenbock' wird; kritische Rückfragen an die theologischen Kritiker der Marktwirtschaft: ZEvEth 36 (1992) 276-290.

8598 *a*) *Díaz Marcos* Cipriano, Del utilitarismo mercantilista a la gratuidad evangélica; – *b*) *Alfaro* María Elena, 'El pozo y los camellos'; como pasar del individualismo a la experiencia de una fraternidad solidaria: SalT 80 (1992) 587-604 / 645-657.

8599 *Dieterich* Veit-Jakobus, 'Alle sollen essen, trinken, sich kleiden und Gott preisen ...' Zur Frage der sozialen Gerechtigkeit bei Johann Amos COMENIUS (1592-1670): EvT 52 (1992) 512-526.

8600 *Doré* Joseph, Dans un monde en progrès, la croissance des pauvretés: EsprVie 102 (1992) 497-509.

8601 **Dorrien** Gary J., Reconstructing the common good; theology and the social order 1990 ➤ 6,8426: ᴿJRel 72 (1992) 459s (P. N. *Williams*).

8601* **Drinan** Robert F., The fractured dream; America's divisive moral choices. NY 1991, Crossroad. x-217 p. $20 [RelStR 19,62, T. H. *Donlin-Smith*].

8602 *Dulles* Avery, Religion and the transformation of politics [... 'when the bishops intervene in controversial questions of a secular character they stir up opposition to themselves from within the Church and undermine their own authority to teach and govern']: America 167 (1992) 296-301.

8602* **Durand** A., La cause des pauvres; société, éthique et foi: Théologies. P 1991, Cerf. 179 p. F 110. 2-204-04390-7. – ᴿTvT 32 (1992) 433s (J. *Jans*: voor, niet over, de armen).

8603 **Elliott** Michael C., Freedom, justice, and Christian counter-culture 1990 ➤ 7,8427: ᴿInterpretation 46 (1992) 212s (S. H. *Moore*: for activists).

8604 **Erlander** Lillemore, Faith in the world of work [< diss.]. U 1991, Almqvist & W. 190 p. 91-554-2714-6. – ᴿExpTim 103 (1991s) 158 (A. *Hurst*: almost exciting drama; conflicting visions of the role of the Church, Canterbury as well as Rome).

8605 *Everett* William J., Biblical bases for modern politics: Bangalore Theol. Forum 23 (1991) 3-24 [< TLZ 118,456].

8606 **Fabris** Rinaldo, La scelta dei poveri nella Bibbia 1989 ➤ 6,8429: ᴿTeresianum 43 (1992) 287 (V. *Pasquetto*: risposta non 100% soddisfacente).

8607 **Fabris** Rinaldo, La opción por los pobres en la Biblia [1989], ᵀ*Ortiz García* Alfonso: Horizonte. Estella 1992, VDivino. 229 p. 84-7151-792-2.

8608 ᴱ**Fornet-Betancourt** R., Verändert der Glaube die Wirtschaft? Theologie und Ökonomie in Lateinamerika: ThDritW 16. FrB 1991 Herder. 189 p. DM 32. 3-451-22413-5. – ᴿHerdKor 64 (1992) 145s (A. *Foitzik*); TvT 32 (1992) 432s (J. *Van Nieuwenhove*).

8609 **Frosini** G., Impegno cristiano; per una teologia della politica: Universa-Teol 4. CinB 1992, Paoline. 293 p. Lit. 15.000 [NRT 115,578].

8609* *a) Furger* Franz, Christliche Werte und Normen in der Politik; – *b) Kaufmann* F.-X., Wie weit reichen die christlichen Wurzeln des Rechts- und Sozialstaats? Ein Beitrag zum Verstehen der Moderne; – *c) Kerber* Walter, Katholische Soziallehre und Wirtschaftswissenschaft [*Senft* J., Zwei Enzykliken]: TJb (1991) 392-409 / 381-391 / 423-431 [-441].

8610 **Gay** Craig M., With liberty and justice for whom? The recent evangelical debate over capitalism. GR 1992, Eerdmans. 276 p. $20. – ᴿTTod 49 (1992s) 569s.572 (C. R. *Strain*).

8611 **Gauly** Thomas M., Katholiken; Machtanspruch und Machtverlust 1991 ➤ 6,m66*b; 7,g889: ᴿTGL 82 (1992) 153 (W. *Beinert*).

8612 *Giers* Joachim, *a)* Neue Strukturen der 'sozialen Gerechtigkeit': Salesianum 54 (1992) 743-762: ≅ *b)* 'Partizipation' und 'Solidarität' als Strukturen der Sozialen Gerechtigkeit: ➤ 105, ᶠKᴏʀꜰꜰ W., 1992...

8613 **Gillman** J., Possessions and the life of faith: Zch. ColMn 1991, Liturgical. 120 p. $7. 0-8146-5675-7 [NTAbs 36,263].

8613* *Gire* Pierre, Le christianisme est-il une idéologie? ou les dangers qui guettent le christianisme: EsprVie 102 (1992) 299-303 [après 289-298, *Evenou* Jean, Liturgie et unité culturelle de l'Europe].

8614 *Gismondi* Gualberto, Contestualizzazione, liberazione e nuova evangelizzazione nel contesto asiatico (riflessioni sul dibattito filippino 1965-1980): Antonianum 67 (1992) 360-413; Eng. 360.

8615 **González** Justo L., Faith and wealth; a history of early Christian ideas on the origin, significance, and use of money 1990 ➤ 6,8436; 7,8433: ᴿCathHR 78 (1992) 97s (B. *Ramsey*); JRel 72 (1992) 278s (L. W. *Countryman*); RelStR 18 (1992) 333 (E. V. *Gallagher*: clear).

8616 *González-Carvajal Santabarbara* Luis, Los dineros de la Iglesia ante el Evangelio: SalT 80 (1992) 179-187.

8616* *González-Montes* Adolfo, A teologia política contemporânea perante a doutrina social da Igreja: HumTeol 13 (1992) 21-42.

8617 **Gordon** Barry, The economic problem in biblical and patristic thought: VigChr supp 6, 1989 ➤ 7,8434: ᴿCBQ 54 (1992) 349s (T. M. *Finn*: also on J. Gᴏɴᴢᴀʟᴇᴢ, less reliable); RSPT 76 (1992) 120-2 (G.-M. de *Durand*).

8617* **Grosfeld** Jan, ❷ Religia i ekonomia. Wsz 1989, Pax. 244 p. – ᴿAtKap 117 (1991) 140-2 (K. *Grabski*, ❷).

8618 *a) Grosser* Alfred, Ethik und Politik in und für Europa heute; – *b) Kaufmann* Franz-X., Gesellschaftliche Entwicklungen in Europa als Herausforderung an die katholische Universitäts-Theologie; – *c) Lehmann* Karl, Zur Aufgabe der Theologie in der gegenwärtigen Kirche; Anmerkungen zur Situation der Theologie nach der Europa-Sondersynode: TGL 82,3 (Tagung Pd 26.-28.I, 1992) 302-312 / 313-328 / 287-301.

8618* *Habermas* Jürgen, Transcendence from within, transcendence in this world: ➤ 515, Public theology 1988/92, 226-250.
8619 **Hancock** Ralph C., CALVIN and the foundations of modern politics. Ithaca NY 1989, Cornell Univ. xvii-221 p. $26.50. – RWestTJ 54 (1992) 195s (R. *Letham*).
8619* **Harries** Richard (bp. Oxford), Is there a Gospel for the rich? The Christian in a capitalist world. L 1992, Mowbray. ix-182 p. £13. 0-264-67276-3. – RTablet 246 (1992) 778 (C. *Moss*).
8620 *a*) **Hay** Donald A., Economics today; a Christian critique 1989 ➤ 6,8442; 7,8437: RRefTR 48 (1990) 108s (Kim *Hawtrey*).
— *b*) *Heiene* Gunnar, [➤ g91] Den menneskelige stat; The human state; Eivind BERGGRAV's political anthropology and ethics [dissertation Oslo 1991]; summary and criticisms of *Schjørring* Jens H., *Montgomery* Ingun: TsTKi 63 (1992) 33-45 / 47-57; Heiene's Replikk 61-64 (3-16, A new world ethic or particular moral traditions?, in Norwegian, on KÜNG H., MACINTYRE A.).
— *c*) **Hilton** Boyd, The age of atonement; the influence of evangelicalism on social and economic thought, 1795-1865: 1988 ➤ 5,k303; 7,8438: RRefTR 49 (1990) 105s (M. *Hill*).
— *d*) *Hogan* Trevor, The social imagination of radical Christianity [DOR-RIEN G. 1989; ROWLAND C. 1988]: Pacifica 5 (1989) 67-83.
8621 **Iosso** Christian T., A Church for the lean years; towards an economic ethic for the future life and witness of mainline Protestantism: diss. Union Theol. Sem., DRasmussen L. New York 1990. – RTLv 24, p. 598.
8622 **Jensen** Gordon A., The significance of LUTHER's Theology of the Cross for contemporary political and contextual theologies: diss. St. Michael, DMcSorley H. Toronto 1992. 360 p. – RTLv 24, p. 557.
8623 **Jones** Arthur, Capitalism and Christians; tough Gospel challenges in a troubled world economy. NY 1992, Paulist. R 25 [SAfBap 3,113, F. *Hale*].
8623* **Jüchen** Aurel von, Wie politisch war Jesus Christus?: Anstösse zur Friedensarbeit, 1. Hildesheim 1990, Olms. 132 p. DM 17,80. 3-487-09371-5 [NTAbs 36,117].
8624 **Kässmann** M., Die eucharistische Vision; Armut und Reichtum als Anfrage an die Einheit der Kirche in der Diskussion des Ökumenischen Rates [< ev. Diss. Bochum]. Mü/Mainz 1992, Kaiser/Grünewald. 392 p. DM 78. 3-459-01936-0 / 3-7867-1608-0. – RTvT 32 (1992) 431s (Teije *Brattinga*).
8625 *Kaufman* Peter I., Redeeming politics: Studies in Church and State 3, 1990 ➤ 7,8444: RJRel 72 (1992) 432s (G. W. *Olsen*).
8626 *Kavanaugh* John F., *a*) Christ's Kingdom and cultural resistance; riches and poverty in contemporary life; – *b*) Media and moral discernment; consumer ideology: MilltSt 30 (1992) 27-37 / 38-42.
8627 **Kealy** Seán, Jesus and politics: GlazierZc 1990 ➤ 6,8446: RCritRR 5 (1992) 228s (W. *Wink*: silent on Ireland, but ultimately hints a Catholic 'just war' position).
8627* *King* Ursula, The spiritual, personal and political religion in global perspective: Vidyajyoti 56 (1992) 151-169.
8628 **Klinger** Elmar, Armut, eine Herausforderung Gottes; der Glaube des Konzils und die Befreiung des Menschen 1990 ➤ 7,8446: RTR 88 (1992) 312s (H. *Fries*).
8629 *Kreck* Walter, 'Gemeinwohl und Eigennutz'; kritische Anmerkungen zur Wirtschaftsdenkschrift der E(v.) K(irche) D(eutschlands) [Gü c. 1992, Mohn]: EvT 52 (1992) 92-99.

8629* **Kysar** Robert, Called to care. Mp 1991, Fortress. ix-165 p. $12. 0-8006-2470-X. – ᴿExpTim 103 (1991s) 190 (A. *Le Grys*: over-optimistic use of Scripture to replace charity with justice).

8630 **Laot** L., Catholicisme, politique, laïcité 1990 → 7,8450: ᴿArTGran 55 (1992) 366s (J. *Camacho*).

8631 **Lapide** Pinchas, Jesus, das Geld und der Weltfrieden. Gü 1991, Mohn. 155 p. DM 26,80. – ᴿLuthMon 31 (1992) 474 (W. D. *Mauritz*: incorrigible world-improver).

8632 **Lehmann** Paul, Christologie und Politik; eine theologische Hermeneutik des Politischen, 1987 → 3,8343; 4,9478: ᴿEvKomm 24 (1991) 175s (F. *Herzog*).

8634 *López Rivera* Francisco [AT], *Balderas* Gonzalo [NT], La Biblia y el tratado de libre comercio: Christus 57,2 (Méx 1992) 7s . 9-12.

8635 *Lutzenberger* José A., O modelo liberal-consumista perante o desafio ecológico: REB 52 (1992) 128-136.

8636 **McCarthy** George E., *Rhodes* Royal W., Eclipse of justice; ethics, economics, and the lost traditions of American Catholicism [critique of U.S. Catholic bishops 1986]. Mkn 1992, Orbis. vi-298 p. $25. 0-88344-806-8 [TDig 39,370].

8636* *a) Majka* József, ❷ L'Église devant le capitalisme et le communisme; – *b) Sieg* József, ❶ La pastorale polonaise devant d'actuels besoins de la rééducation nationale: AtKap 116 (1991) 231-246 / 247-258.

8637 **Mardonés** José M., Capitalismo y religión; la religión política neoconservadora. Sdr 1991, Sal Terrae. 295 p. – ᴿChristus 57,8 (Méx 1991) 59s (C. *Bravo G.*); Iter 3,1 (1992) 127-130 (F. *Moracho*).

8638 **Meeks** M. D., God the economist 1989 → 5,8429 ... 7,8457: ᴿHorizons 19 (1992) 142s (P. L. *Quinn*).

8639 *a) Melé* Domènec, Empresa y economía del mercado a la luz de la 'Centesimus Annus'; – *b) Cattaneo* Arturo, La valorización del capitalismo en la CA: ScripTPamp 24 (1992) 221-239 / 259-271.

8640 *Metz* J. B., *Kroh* W., Politische Theologie: → 757, EvKL 3 (1992) 1261-6.

8641 **Milbank** John, Theology and social theory; beyond secular reason. Ox 1990, Blackwell. vii-443 p. $65. – ᴿAnglTR 74 (1992) 512-4 (A. K. M. *Adam*: erudite, vigorous); ScotJT 45 (1992) 125s (L. *Ayres*: an important book with a grand scope); → 8593*; m850*.

8642 *Mitchell* Joshua, The equality of all under the One in Luther and Rousseau; thoughts on Christianity and political theory: JRel 72 (1992) 351-365.

8643 **Molnar** Thomas, Twin powers; politics and the sacred 1988 → 5,8431: ᴿJRel 72 (1992) 135s (Christine F. *Hinze*).

8643* *Moreira* J.M.L., Igualitarismo económico e relativismo moral, na óptica de Hayek [A. F., The fatal conceit, Ch 1989]: HumTeol 13 (1992) 341-354.

ᴱ**Müller** J., *Kerber* W., Soziales Denken in einer zerrissenen Welt: QDisp 136, 1991 → 408*.

8644 **Mützenberg** G., L'éthique sociale dans l'histoire du Mouvement œcuménique: Histoire et société 23. Genève 1992, Labor et Fides. 137 p. – ᴿNRT 114 (1992) 773s (L.-J. *Renard*).

8645 **Nebechukwu** Augustine U., The prophetic mission of the Church in the context of social and political oppression in Africa: AfER 33 (1991) 264-280.

8645* *Østnor* Lars, Poverty and wealth as subject in theological ethics [Hallesby O. 1928; Smith Axel 1984; all in Norwegian]: TsTKi 63 (1992) 207-218.

8646 ᴱd'Onorio Joël-Benoît, JEAN-PAUL II et l'éthique politique: Ét. Inst. Église-État. P 1992, Éd. Univ. 212 p. – ᴿEsprVie 102 (1992) 605s (R. *Coste*).

8647 *a*) *Osiek* Carolyn, Jesus and money, or — did Jesus live in a capitalist society? — *b*) *Rosenblatt* Marie-Eloise, Mission and money in the NT: ChSt 30 (1991) 17-28 / 77-98.

8648 **Pelletier** Denis, Aux origines du tiers-mondisme catholique; de l'utopie communautaire au développement harmonisé; économie et humanisme du Père LEBRET: diss. Lyon II, 1992, ᴰ*Fouilloux* É. – RHE 87 (1992) 617-620 (H. *Puel*).

8649 *Pikaza* Xabier, El hombre bíblico y la ruptura de fronteras: SalT 78 (1990) 815-832.

8649* *Pinho Ferreira* Manuel de, A Igreja e a comunidade política na obra de D. António FERREIRA GOMES: HumTeol 12 (1991) 263-281.

8650 ᴱ**Pirotte** Jean, *Derroitte* Henri, Églises et santé dans le Tiers Monde [LvN 1989 Lebbe colloquium]. 1991 ➤ 7,543*b*; *f*95. 90-04-09470-9: ᴿExpTim 103 (1991s) 379 (A. *Shorter*: 'the healing power of God is not ultimately at the disposal of the churches', C. GRUNDMANN); Gregorianum 73 (1992) 771s (J. *Joblin*).

8651 **Pospischil** Hans T., Der solidarische Umgang mit Eigentum und Einkommen in christlichen Gemeinschaften und Gruppen: FreibTSt 124. FrB 1990, Herder. xiii-416 p. DM 48. – ᴿTLZ 117 (1992) 228-230 (J. *Langer*).

8652 **Preston** Ronald H., Religion and the ambiguities of capitalism. L 1991, SCM. 182 p. £12.50 pa. 0-334-02305-X. – ᴿAnglTR 74 (1992) 402-4 (J. S. *Moore*); ExpTim 103,9 top choice (1991s) 257s (C. S. *Rodd*); TLond 95 (1992) 312 (J. *Gladwin*).

8653 **Regnier** Jérôme, Chrétiens dans la cité [... la politique]: L'Horizon du Croyant 11, 1990 ➤ 7,8468: ᴿMélSR 48 (1991) 192s (L. *Debarge*).

8654 **Reich** Robert B., The work of nations; preparing ourselves for 21st century capitalism. NY 1991, Knopf. 320 p. $24. – ᴿChrCent 108 (1991) 1003-8.

8655 **Reumann** John, Stewardship and the economy of God: Library of Christian Stewardship. GR/Indianapolis 1992, Eerdmans/Ecumenical Center CS. xiv-157 p. $13 pa. [CBQ 55,211].

8656 **Rostig** Dittmar, Bergpredigt und Politik; zur Struktur und Funktion des Reiches Gottes bei Leonhard RAGAZ [Diss. Lp]: EurHS 23/419. Fra 1991, Long. 276 p. DM 69. 3-631-43577-0. – ᴿActuBbg 29 (1992) 215s (J. *Boada*).

8657 **Salemink** T., Katholieke Kritiek op het Kapitalisme 1891-1991. Amersfort 1991, Acco. 279 p. – ᴿCollatVL 22 (1992) 333s (F. *Pottie*).

8658 **Santa Ana** Julio de, La práctica económica como religión; crítica teológica a la economía política. SanJosé CR 1991, DEI. 138 p. [TContext 10/1,104, R. *Fornet-Betancourt*].

8659 **Schall** James V., Religion, wealth, and poverty 1990 ➤ 7,8473: ᴿHomP 92,4 (1991s) 75-77 (J. M. *Grondelski*).

8659* **Sawyer** Frank, The poor are many; political ethics in the social encyclicals, Christian democracy, and Liberation Theology in Latin America: diss. ᴰ*Manenschijn* G. Kampen 1992. 199 p. – TvT 32,303; RTLv 24, p. 585.

8660 **Schooyans** Michel, La dérive totalitaire du libéralisme. P 1991, Éd. Univ. 358 p. F 150. – ᴿEsprVie 102 (1992) 425-8 (H. *Wattiaux*: 'Économie, démographie et développement').

8661 **Schuck** Michael J., That they be one; the social teaching of the papal encyclicals 1740-1989. Wsh 1991, Georgetown Univ. xii-224 p. 0-87840-489-9. – ᴿGregorianum 73 (1992) 576s (S. *Bernal R.*).

8661* **Seidler** Victor J., The moral limits of modernity; love, inequality and oppression. Basingstoke 1991, Macmillan. xiv-250 p. £40. – ᴿTLond 95 (1992) 218s (G. *Howes*: KIERKEGAARD's 'equality' prescinds from the everyday conditions of power and subordination).

8662 *Sitter-Liver* Beat, Neuvermessung des Rechts- und Staatsdiskurses; zu Otfried HOFFES Theorie der politischen Gerechtigkeit [Fra 1987]: FreibZ 38 (1991) 83-109.

8662* **Spicciani** Amleto, Capitale e interesse tra mercatura e povertà dai secoli XIII-XV. R 1990, Jouvence. 262 p. – ᴿJRel 72 (1992) 584s (J. *Kirshner*).

8663 **Spiegel** Y., Wirtschaftsethik und Wirtschaftspraxis — ein wachsender Widerspruch? Stu 1992, Kohlhammer. 238 p. DM 35. 3-17-011732-7. – ᴿTvT 32 (1992) 433 (G. *Manenschijn*).

8664 **Stevenson** W. Taylor, Soul and money; a theology of wealth. NY 1991, Episcopal Center. 162 p. $10. – ᴿAnglTR 73 (1991) 485-7 (D. M. *Barney*).

8665 **Sutherland** John R., Going broke; bankruptcy, business ethics, and the Bible. Scottdale PA c.1991, Herald. $10 [Interp 46,89 adv.].

8666 **Sutor** Bernhard, Politische Ethik; Gesamtdarstellung auf der Basis der christlichen Gesellschaftslehre. Pd 1991, Schöningh. 338 p. DM 38. – ᴿHerdKor 46 (1992) 194 (D. *Seeber*).

8667 *Thomas* Owen C., Public theology and counter-public spheres [TRACY D.]: HarvTR 85 (1992) 453-466.

8668 **Tinder** Glenn, The political meaning of Christianity; the prophetic stance 1989 ➤ 6,8484; 7,8483: ᴿCurrTMiss 19 (1992) 293s (R. *Hütter*); GraceTJ 12 (1991) 312; RRel 51 (1992) 636s (L. *Cervantes* agrees with NYTimes praise).

8668* *a) Tudela* Juan A., Destino universal de los bienes; propiedad y trabajo; – *b) Sanchis* Antonio, La pobreza y el derecho a los bienes de la tierra: EscrVedat 21 (1991) 255-286 / 287-302.

8669 **Valarché** Jean-Marie, Nos Papes ont-ils une doctrine économique? FrS 1991, Univ. – ᴿNVFr 67 (1992) 152-4 (E. *Rossi di Montelera*).

8669* *a) Vanhoye* Albert, Destination universelle des biens de la terre selon la Bible; – *b) González* Carlos I., Aspects patristiques: ➤ 540, Une terre 1991/2, 9-15 / 16-31.

8670 *Verstraeten* Johan, Business-Ethick, een christelijk-ethisch perspectief: CollatVL 22 (1992) 67-89.

8671 *Vives* Josep, M. NOVAK [El espíritu del capitalismo democrático BA 1983 = Eng. 1982], ¿Una ideología del capitalismo?: ActuBbg 29 (1992) 5-11.

8671* **Waterman** A. M. C., Revolution, economics and religion; Christian political economy, 1798-1833. C 1991, Univ. 309 p. £35. – ᴿTLond 95 (1992) 220s (E. *Norman*: 'a polemical book about polemical books').

8672 **Weigel** George, Freedom and its discontents; Catholicism confronts modernity [... capitalist ethic]. Wsh 1991, Ethics and Public Policy Center. xii-179 p. $20. 0-89633-158-X [TDig 40,92].

8673 **Wheeler** Sondra E., The New Testament on possessions; a test of ethical method: diss. Yale, ᴰ*Hays* E. New Haven ... – RTLv 24, p. 550 sans date.

8674 *Williams* D. T., Poverty; an integrated Christian approach: JTSAf 77 (1991) 47-57 [< ZIT 92,79].

H8.5 **Theologia liberationis latino-americana.**

8674* **Altmann** Walter, LUTHER and liberation; a Latin American perspective, ᵀ*Solberg* Mary. Mp 1991, Fortress. xi-146 p. [RelStR 19,58, D. R. *Janz*].

8675 *Álvarez Gandara* Miguel, Doloroso avance de la Iglesia de América Latina: Christus 57,660s (Méx 1992) 50-55 [résumé TContext 10/2,79].

8676 *Bagnati* Claudio, L'evangelizzazione del Nuovo Mondo; due studi su Pedro de CÓRDOBA [MEDINA M. 1987] e Bartolomé de LAS CASAS [PÉREZ FERNÁNDEZ I. 1989]: Asprenas 39 (1992) 101-106.

8677 **Baker** Christopher J. [Scripture-teacher turned Lima missionary] Covenant and liberation; giving new heart to God's endangered family: EurUnivSt 23/411. NY 1991, Lang. xvii-357 p. $62 pa. 3-631-43479-0 [TDig 39,149].

8678 *Bastian* Jean-Pierre, *al.*, *a*) How Protestantism has developed in Latin America; – *b*) 500 years of Christianity in Latin America: Social Compass 39 (1992) 323-354 (-463; bibliog. 465-496 / 543-551 (499-583).

8679 **Batstone** David B., From conquest to struggle; Jesus of Nazareth in Latin America 1991 ➤ 7,8494: ᴿAnglTR 74 (1992) 250-3 (J. L. *Kater*); IntRMiss 80 (1991) 444-7 (S. G. *Mackie*).

8680 **Belli** Humberto, *Nash* Ronald H., Beyond liberation theology. GR 1992, Baker. 206 p. $13. 0-8010-1022-5 [TDig 40,51].

8681 *a*) *Beozzo* José Oscar, 500 anos de evangelização da América Latina; – *b*) *Boff* Leonardo, O conflito dos modelos de evangelização para a América Latina: REB 52 (1992) 282-316 / 344-364.

8682 *Boero* Mario, Teología de la liberación y teología progresista; encuentros, diferencias y tareas en continentes distintos: EstFranc 93 (1992) 253-279.

8683 **Boff** Clodovis, Théorie et pratique; la méthode des théologies de la libération ➤ 7,8500* [< diss. c. 1975], ᵀʳᵉᵛ*Rath* N. M.: CogF 157. P 1990, Cerf. 404 p. F 239. 2-204-04093-2. – ᴿÉTRel 67 (1992) 616s (C. *Izard*).

8684 **Boff** Leonardo, Faith on the edge; religion and marginalized existence. SF 1989, Harper. 212 p. $20. – ᴿHomP 91,4 (J. V. *Schall*: 'socialism or how to make the poor poorer'); Vidyajyoti 56 (1992) 328s (G. V. *Lobo*).

8685 **Boff** Leonardo, New evangelization; good news to the poor, ᵀ*Barr* Robert R. Mkn 1992, Orbis. vi-128 p. $14. 0-88344-778-9 [TDig 39,353].

8686 *Boff* Leonardo, La nueva evangelización; perspectiva de los oprimidos. Sdr 1991, Sal Terrae. 162 p. – ᴿChristus 57,1 (Méx 1992) 57 (C. *Bravo G.*).

8687 **Boff** Leonardo, Nuova evangelizzazione; prospettiva degli oppressi. Assisi 1991, Cittadella. 160 p. Lit. 15.000. – ᴿCC 143 (1992,1) 199-201 (P. *Vanzan*).

8688 **Boff** Leonardo, Gott kommt früher als der Missionar; Neuevangelisierung für eine Kultur des Lebens und der Freiheit. Dü 1991, Patmos. 148 p. DM 29,80. 3-491-77040-8. – ᴿTvT 32 (1992) 331s (R. G. van *Rossum*).

8689 ᴱ**Boff** Leonardo, *Elizondo* Virgil, The voice of the victims [< Concilium Special]. L 1991, SCM. 151 p. £9. 0-334-02412-9. – ᴿExpTim 103 (1991s) 351 [C. S. *Rodd*: 'cruelty of the conquerors led to the death of 90 percent of the population... still lives on in Latin America'].

8690 [Boff] **Pixley** J., *Boff* C., Les pauvres; choix prioritaire 1990 → 6,8500; 7,8498: ᴿNRT 114 (1992) 115 (L. *Volpe*).

8690* *Borobio* D., Principales agentes en la evangelización de América durante il siglo XVI según Jerónimo de MENDIETA: Carthaginensia 8 (1992) 661-689.

8691 **Brown** Robert M., G. GUTIÉRREZ; an introduction to liberation theology [as a stage play]. Mkn 1990, Orbis. 224 p. $10 pa. – ᴿMissiology 19 (1991) 235s (J. R. *Blue*).

8692 *Burns* Peter, The problem of [left-wing non-Marxist] socialism in liberation theology: TS 53 (1992) 493-516.

8693 **Candelaria** Michael S., Popular religion and liberation; the dilemma of liberation theology. Albany c. 1991, SUNY. 189 p. $39.50; pa. $13. – ᴿChrCent 108 (1991) 378s (P. *Berryman*: contrasts SCANNONE and SOBRINO).

8694 ᴱ**Castillo** Fernando, Die Kirche der Armen in Lateinamerika; eine theologische Hinführung 1987 → 6,8512: ᴿNZMissW 46 (1990) 75s (S. *Herbst*).

8694* **Cipolini** Pedro C., Sacramento de salvação integral; a teologia da Igreja dos Pobres na América Latina 1980-1990: diss. Pont. Univ. Gregoriana, ᴰ*Pastor* F. A. Roma 1992. 459 p.; Extr. 3826, 129 p. – RTLv 24, p. 568.

8695 ᴱ**Collet** Giancarlo, Der Christus der Armen; das Christuszeugnis der [12; 1975-84] lateinamerikanischen Befreiungstheologen, ᵀ*Berz* A., *al.*, 1988 → 5,452: ᴿTLZ 116 (1991) 303s (R. *Frieling*).

8696 **Comblin** José, Retrieving the human: Theology and Liberation. Mkn 1990, Orbis. 295 p. $15. 0-88344-657-X. – ᴿExpTim 102 (1990s) 381 (R. J. *Elford* cites, 'It is extremely difficult to allow the poor to exercise their own discernment. A long clerical tradition in the Roman Catholic Church finds priests the most qualified to exercise discernment in the name of the poor').

8697 *Connors* Michael, The experience of God in history; a personal journey into liberation spirituality: Grail 7,4 (1991) 48-..

8698 **Costas** Orlando E. †, [→ 5,863; ind.!] Liberating news; a theology of contextual evangelization. GR 1989, Eerdmans. 182 p. $13. 0-8028-0364-4. – ᴿRExp 88 (1991) 112s (D. F. *D'Amico*).

8699 **Dagmans** Ferdinand, Liberation and ethics; an inquiry into the foundation of a Christian ethics of liberation: diss. ᴰ*Burggraeve* R. Lv 1991. lii-373 p. – RTLv 24, p. 539.

8700 *Delgado* Mariano, LAS CASAS und seine Gegner; ein Blick in die 'politischen Theologien' des 16. Jahrhunderts: StiZt 210 (1992) 841-854.

8701 *Duquoc* Christian, *al.*, L'invention des Amériques et la missiologie: RechSR 80,4 (Évangile et terres nouvelles 1992) (491-) 611-624; Eng. 485-490 ('the discovery of...').

8702 *a) Durán* Juan G., La primitiva evangelización mexicana; métodos e instrumentos pastorales; – *b) García* Ruben D., La 'primera evangelización' y sus lecturas; desafíos a la 'nueva evangelización': TArg 27 (1990) 33-72 / 111-152.

8703 **Dussel** Enrique, Prophetie und Kritik; Entwurf einer Geschichte der Theologie in Lateinamerika → 7,8511 [< Hipótesis, Bogotá 1986, erweitert], ᵀ*Hermans* K. FrS 1989, Exodus. 157 p. DM 26,80. – ᴿNZMissW 46 (1990) 230s (J. *Baumgartner*); TLZ 116 (1991) 209s (H.-J. *Prien*: 'ein anregender Beitrag aus katholischer Sicht ... Untertitel freilich kaum gerecht').

8704 a) *Eggensperger* Thomas, *Engel* Ulrich, Bartolomé de LAS CASAS, Blick in Geschichte und Gegenwart; – b) *Goldstein* Horst, Die andauernde Conquista; lateinamerikanische Perspektiven: RUHöh 34,6 ('Las Casas und die Conquista' 1991) 352-361 / 362-373 (-388, *al.*).

8705 **Eggensperger** T., *Engel* U., Bartolomé de LAS CASAS: a) Dominikaner – Bischof – Verteidiger der Indios: Topos Tb 207. Mainz 1991, Grünewald, 154 p. DM 12,80. 3-7867-1547-5; – b) Bisschop – politicus – Dominicaan, ᵀ*Spoor* C. Kampen/Averbode 1992, Kok/Altiora. 126 p. ƒ22,50. 3-0342-6645-9 / 90-317-0964-6. – ᴿTvT 32 (1992) 419s (R. G. van *Rossum*).

8706 **Ellacuría** I., *Sobrino* J., Mysterium liberationis 1990 ➤ 7,8513: ᴿComSev 24 (1991) 276-8 (M. *Sánchez*); SalT 78 (1990) 883s (J. A. *García*); ScripTPamp 24 (1992) 317-323 (L. F. *Mateo-Seco*)

8706* **Ellul** Jacques, ᵀ*Hanks* Joyce M., Jesus and MARX; from Gospel to ideology 1988 ➤ 4,4307: ᴿThought 64 (1989) 412s (G. *Baum*).

8707 a) *Estrada* Juan A., Interpelaciones éticas y sociopolíticas de la teología de la liberación; – b) *González Dorado* Antonio, La nueva evangelización en América Latina: EstE 67 (1992) 361-396 / 397-427.

8708 a) *Fernandez* Eleazar S., Hermeneutics and the Bible in liberation theology; a critique from other companions in the struggle; – b) *Therukattil* George, The resurrection of Jesus and human liberation: Vidyajyoti 56 (1992) 385-402 / 403-412.

8708* **Fornet-Betancourt** Raúl, Philosophie und Theologie der Befreiung 1988 ➤ 5,8505*; 7,8517: ᴿTR 88 (1992) 158-160 (A. *Lienkamp*).

8709 **Forrester** Kevin L., An analysis and critique of the relationship between faith and ideologies in the work of Juan Luis SEGUNDO: diss. Catholic Univ. ᴰ*Power* D. Wsh 1992. 412 p. 92-17081. – DissA 53 (1992s) 189s.

8709* *Frades Gaspar* Eduardo, El uso de la Biblia en Fray Bartolomé de LAS CASAS: Iter 3,2 (Caracas 1992) 95-135.

8710 **Friedemann** Cristián J., Religiosidad popular entre Medellín y Puebla; antecedentes y desarrollo. Santiago, Chile 1990, Univ. Anales 41. 306 p. [TLZ 118,77, H.-J. *Prien*].

8711 **Galdino Feller** Vitor, O Deus da revelação; a dialética entre revelação e libertação ... [diss.]: Fe e realidade 24. São Paulo 1988, Loyola. 321 p. ᴿEstE 67 (1992) 234s (María Ángeles *Navarro Girón*).

8712 **Galindo** Florencio, El protestantesimo fundamentalista; una experiencia ambígua para América Latina [diss. Fra St-Georgen]: Estella 1992, VDivino. 419 p. [TContext 10/1,103, R. *Fornet-Betancourt*].

8713 a) *Galli* Carlos M., Evangelización, cultura y teología; el aporte de J. C. SCANNONE a una teología inculturada; – b) *Seibold* Jorge R., Nuevo punto de partida en la filosofia latinoamericana; las grandes etapas de la filosofia inculturada de J. C. Scannone: Stromata 47 (1991) 205-216 / 193-204.

8714 *García* Rubén D., El choque de dos 'grandes'; el franciscano Fray Toribio MOTOLINÍA († 1569) contra el dominico Fray Bartolomé de LAS CASAS († 1566); un símbolo de la dialéctica Conquista/Evangelización en el siglo XVI: ProyectoCSE 4 (1992) ... 135-227. 357-392.

8715 *Gesché* Adolphe, La théologie de la libération du mal: LVitae 47 (1992) 281-299. 451-464.

8716 ᴱ**Getz** I. M., *Costa* R. O., Struggles for solidarity; liberation theologies in tension. Mp 1992, Fortress. 171 p. [NRT 115,626, J. M.].

8717 **Girardi** Giulio, La túnica rasgada; la identidad cristiana, hoy, entre liberación y restauración, ᵀ*Velasco* Rufino: PresTeol 62. Sdr 1991, Sal

Terrae. 485 p. 84-293-09010-1. – ᴿActuBbg 29 (1992) 208s (J. *Boada*: polémico).

8718 ᴱ**Goodpasture** H. M., Cross and sword ... in Latin America 1989 ➤ 6,8535; 7,8521: ᴿJRel 72 (1992) 119s (Susan E. *Ramirez*); Missiology 19 (1991) 353s (P. E. *Pierson*).

8718* **Gutiérrez Cuervo** Rafael, Cristo hombre perfecto; el seguimiento de Cristo como compromiso con la justicia et las obras de José GONZÁLEZ FAUS S.J.: diss. Pont. Univ. Gregoriana, ᴰ*Demmer* K. Roma 1992. 364 p.; Extr. 3814, 108 p. – RTLv 24, p. 574.

8719 ᶠGUTIÉRREZ G., The future of liberation theology, ᴱ**Ellis** M., *al.*, 1988/9 ➤ 5,671: ᴿBijdragen 53 (1992) 98s (A. van der *Helm*); ScotJT 44 (1991) 417s (J. *Draper*: important).

8720 **Gutiérrez** G., Gott oder das Gold ... LAS CASAS [1989 ➤ 5,8515], ᵀ1990 ➤ 6,8538; 7,8524: ᴿLuthMon 31 (1992) 189 (J. *Jeziorowski*).

8721 **Gutiérrez** Gustavo, Dieu ou l'or des Indes occidentales; Las Casas ou la conscience chrétienne (1492-1992). P 1992, Cerf. 164 p. F 118. – ᴿEsprVie 102 (1992) 187-191 (R. *Costa*: indignation parfois injuste; 'réponse' de JEAN-PAUL II).

8722 **Gutiérrez** G., The God of life [1982 ²1989 ➤ 7,8528], ᵀ*O'Connell* Matthew J. Mkn 1991, Orbis. xviii-214 p. $14 pa. 0-88344-760-6 [TDig 39,265]. – ᴿChrCent 109 (1992) 161 (J. F. *Stanley*).

8723 **Gutiérrez** Gustavo, Theologie der Befreiung, ᵀ*Goldstein* Horst, 1992 [¹⁰ʳᵉᵛAuflage]. – ᴿMüTZ 43 (1992) 368-370 (G. L. *Müller*).

8724 *Gutiérrez* Gustavo, Bartolomé de LAS CASAS, defender of the Indians: Pacifica 5 (1992) 263-273.

8725 **Hennelly** Alfred T., Liberation theology, a documentary history 1989 ➤ 6,8544; 7,8528: ᴿETL 68 (1992) 81s (V. *Neckebrouck*); HeythJ 33 (1992) 92 (M. J. *Walsh*: many mentions of DUSSEL, none of COMBLIN, to whom Dussel attributed the origin of the movement); Pacifica 4 (1991) 113s (A. *Hamilton*: splendid, indispensable); ScripTPamp 23 (1991) 740s (L. F. *Mateo-Seco*).

8726 **Höfte** Bernard, Bekering en bevrijding; de betekenis van de Latijns-amerikaanse theologie van de bevrijding voor een theologische basistheorie 1990 ➤ 6,8548: Studien over kerkopbouwkunde 2; ƒ39,50: ᴿBijdragen 53 (1992) 98 (T. C. de *Kruijf*).

8726* *Horoszewicz* Michał, ❷ Rok 1492 i jego zamorskie dziedzictwo [overseas inheritance] w teologii 'Concilium': ColcT 62,3 (1992) 147-177.

8727 **Kee** Alistair, MARX and the failure of liberation theology 1990 ➤ 6,8552; 7,8537: ᴿIntRMiss 80 (1991) 438-442 (Marcella *Althaus-Reid*).

8728 **Kern** Bruno, Fundamental-Theologie im Horizont des Marxismus; zur Geschichte der Marxismusrezeption in der lateinamerikanischen Theologie der Befreiung [Diss. Fribourg/S (Laval, Titel kaum anders ➤ 7,8538)]. Mainz 1992, Grünewald. 396 p. [TContext 10/1,99, R. *Fornet-Betancourt*].

8729 *Lemasters* Philip, 'Theology from the underside of history' [GUTIÉRREZ G.] as a critical theory of theology: ➤ 133, ᶠMILLS W., PerspRelSt 19 (1992) 39-52.

8730 Let my people live; faith and struggle in Central America: Calvin Center. GR 1988, Eerdmans. 271 p. $10. – ᴿRExp 88 (1991) 282s (B. J. *Leonard*).

8731 **Levine** Daniel H., Popular voices in Latin American Catholicism: Studies in Church and State, Princeton 1992, Univ. xxii-403 p. $49.50; pa. $19. 0-691-08754-7; -2459-6 [TDig 40,74].

8732 *Libánio* João B., *a*) Panorama da teologia da América Latina nas últimos 20 años: PerspTeol 24 (1992) 147-192; – *b*) La Iglesia latinoamericana a las puertas de Santo Domingo: Christus 57,655s (Méx 1992) 43-47 [TContext 10/1,87, R. *Fornet-Betancourt*, both].

8733 *López Hernández* Eleazar, Aportes de los indígenas al CELAM IV: Diakonia 16,61 (1992) 115-121 [TContext 10/1,87, R. *Fornet-Betancourt*].

8734 *Lowe Ching* Theresa, Latin American theological method and its relevance to Caribbean theology: Caribbean Journal of Religious Studies 12,1 (Kingston 1991) 4-28 [résumé TContext 10/2,86].

8735 **Lynch** Edward A., Religion and politics in Latin America; liberation theology and Christian democracy 1991 → 7,8547: R AnglTR 74 (1992) 253-5 (Phyllis *Zagano*); HomP 92,3 (1991s) 76.78 (J. V. *Schall*); RRelRes 33 (1990) 285 (P. E. *Lampe*).

8736 **MacCormack** Sabine, Religion in the Andes; vision and imagination in early colonial Peru, 1 [of 2]. Princeton 1991, Univ. xv-488 p. $39.50. 0-691-09468-3 [TDig 39,370].

8737 **McGovern** Arthur F., Liberation theology and its critics 1989 → 6,8560; 7,8549: R Interpretation 46 (1992) 94s (D. *Diekema*); LvSt 17 (1992) 87s (Lieven *Boeve*).

8738 **McKelway** Alexander J., The freedom of God and human liberation [1987 Princeton lectures] 1990 → 7,8550; $9: R ExpTim 103 (1991s) 154 (J. *Milbank*: for those who have 'acquired a taste for the gossipy idiom of the worst of American academic production, which consists mainly of pasting together utterly unremarkable quotations').

8739 *Mahecha* Guidoberto, On some recent publications on Latin American Protestantism [MARTIN D. 1990; STOLL D. 1990]: IntRMiss 81 (1992) 605-612.

8740 **Marlé** René, Introduzione alla teologia della liberazione [1988 → 4, 9603], TECanobbio Giacomo. Brescia 1991, Morcelliana. 154 p. Lit. 20.000. – R CC 143 (1992,1) 197s (C. I. *González*).

8741 *Mateo-Seco* Lucas F., Teología de la liberación y doctrina social de la Iglesia: ScripTPamp 23 (1991) 505-513 [435-530 *al.*, Centenario de la Rerum Novarum].

8742 *a*) *Merino* J. A., Antropología franciscana y liberación; – *b*) *Tapia* B., Identidad del franciscanismo en la América Latina del futuro; – *c*) *Boff* L., Nueva evangelización; el Evangelio sin poder; la Utopía franciscana en América Latina como impulso para una nueva evangelización: Carthaginensia 8 (1992) 757-772 / 773-837 / 857-888.

8743 *a*) *Metz* J.-B., Teología e Iglesia en Latinoamérica; elementos proféticos en el cristianismo actual; – *b*) *Tamayo Acosta* J. J., Presente y futuro de la teología de la liberación [< ital. Adista 25]; – *c*) *Tornos* A., ¿Hacia el descubrimiento y valorización positiva de lo característico de Latinoamérica?: Carthaginensia 8 (1992) 481-501 / 503-592 / 593-608 [Page-numbering of this volume 8 begins with 481, presumably because it is called 'América, variaciones de futuro (II)'].

8744 **Metz** Johann B., *Bahr* Hans-Eckhard, Augen für die anderen; Lateinamerika — eine theologische Erfahrung. Mü 1991, Kindler. 160 p. DM 19.80. – R MüTZ 42 (1992) 418s (G. L. *Müller*).

8745 *a*) *Moll* Peter G., Liberating liberation theology; towards independence from dependency theory; – *b*) *Villa-Vicencio* Charles, Liberating Christology for liberation; – *c*) *de Gruchy* John W., Liberating Reformed theology: JTSAf 78 (1992) 25-40 / 15-24 / 84-.. [< ZIT 92,290].

8746 *a*) *Müller* Karl, The part is not the whole; 500 years of evangelization [must take into account efforts of church and state to rectify the injustices: < Ordenskorrespondenz 33,1 (1992) 23-30]; – *b*) *Peter* Anton, LAS CASAS and liberation theology [< NZMissW 48,1 (1992) 1-14]; – *c*) *Fornet-Betancourt* Raul, The future of Latin American Catholicism [< StiZt 116 (1991) 254-260]: TDig 39 (1992) 103-6 / 107-116 / 117-120 [ᵀᴱ*Asen* B. A.].

8747 **Musto** Ronald G., Liberation theologies; a research guide: LibrSocSc 507. NY 1991, Garland. xlvii-581 p. $70 [TR 88,82; TDig 40,78].

8748 **Nealen** Mary Kaye, The poor in the ecclesiology of Juan Luis SE-GUNDO: AmerUnivSt 7/113. NY 1991, Lang. 190 p. [TR 88,432].

8749 **Nessan** Craig L., Orthopraxis or heresy 1989 ➤ 6,8574; 7,8562: ᴿHorizons 19 (1992) 150-3 (R. S. *Goizueta*, also on 'superb' McGOVERN).

8750 *a*) *Neuner* Peter, Theologie der Befreiung — was ist das? – *b*) *Codina* Victor, Theologie und Glaube in Lateinamerika, ᵀ*Eder* Hans; – *c*) *Gutiérrez* Gustavo, Die Kirche der Armen [< Eng. ᵀ*Böhm* Thomas]: MüTZ 42 (1991) 110-120; 1 color. fig. / 121-140 / 141-150.

8751 *Nickoloff* James B., Liberation theology and the Church [GUTIÉRREZ G. 1990 & ᶠ1989; McGOVERN A., SIGMUND P., DUQUOC C.]: RelStR 18 (1992) 8-12.

8751* **O'Brien** John, Theology and the option for the poor. ColMn 1992, Liturgical. 167 p. $13 [RelStR 19,58, J. R. *Suchs*].

8752 *Ogle* Catherine, Bible and liberation; friend or foe; some issues in feminist and liberation theologies: Way 31 (1991) 236-247.

8753 ᴱ**Parish** Helen R., ᵀ*Sullivan* Francis J., LAS CASAS Bartolomé de, The only way: Sources of American spirituality. NY 1992, Paulist. vi-281 p. $23. 0-8091-0367-2. – ᴿGregorianum 73 (1992) 770s (J. *Wicks*); TS 53 (1992) 786 (T. H. *Sanks*).

8754 ᴱ**Pérez Fernández** Isacio, Bartolomé de LAS CASAS, Brevísima relación de la destrucción de África, preludio de la destrucción de las Indias: Los Dominicos y América 3. S 1989, S. Esteban. 218 p. – ᴿTArg 27 (1990) 235-7 (M. A. *Poli*).

8755 *Pérez Fernández* Isacio, La última generación española de denigradores del Padre LAS CASAS [BORGES P.: PEREÑA L.; LA CIERVA R. de, todos 1990]: (inutilidad de su actitud reaccionaria): Studium 31 (M 1991) 27-61.

8756 **Peter** Anton, Befreiungstheologie und Transzendentaltheologie; Enrique DUSSEL und Karl RAHNER im Vergleich 1988 ➤ 6,8581; ᴿTLZ 116 (1991) 547s (J. *Althausen*).

8757 *Pettegrew* Larry D., Liberation theology and hermeneutical preunderstandings: BtS 148 (1991) 274-287.

8758 *Piepke* J. G., Befreiungstheologie nach 'Centesimus annus': TGegw 35 (1992) 3-19.

8759 **Pope-Levison** Priscilla, Evangelization from a liberation perspective: AmerUnivSt 7/79. NY 1991, P. Lang. xii-201 p. $36. 0-8204-1169-8 [TDig 39,281].

8759* **Prien** Hans-Jürgen, Evangelische Kirchenwerdung in Brasilien: Luth. Kirche Gesch. 10. Gü 1989, Mohn. 640 p. – ᴿREB 52 (1992) 227-9 (M. N. *Dreher*).

8760 *Prien* Hans-J. [*Collet* Giancarlo], Lateinamerika [Theologie]: ➤ 757, EvKL 3 (1992) 16-26 (-31 Konzile, *al*.) [33-38].

8761 *Rodriguez Maradiaga* Oscar, 'Die wahre Entdeckung Amerikas steht noch in den Anfängen': HerdKor 46 (1992) 27-32.

8761* *Roux López* Rodolfo R. de, Le rêve messianique de la première évangélisation, ᵀ*Malley* François: LumièreV 41,208 ('1492; l'invention des Amériques' 1992) 29-37.

8762 **Rowland** Christopher, *Corner* Mark, Liberating exegesis 1990 → 7,8573: ᴿCBQ 54 (1992) 373s (Barbara E. *Reid*); EstudosB 33 (1992) 81-86 (H. de *Ternay*); HorBT 13 (1991) 79-82 (L. W. *Countryman*); ScotJT 45 (1992) 423-5 (J. I. H. *McDonald*).

8762* a) *Rowland* Christopher, How the poor can liberate the Bible; – b) *Brading* David, B. LAS CASAS, prophet of justice: PrPeo 6 (1992) 367-371 / 386-9.

8763 *Salvatierra* Ángel, Teología de la liberación; contenido y aportes: LumenVr 40 (1991) 135-181.

8764 **Scannone** Juan Carlos, Evangelización, cultura y teología. Buenos Aires 1990, Guadalupe. 286 p. – ᴿTXav 41 (1991) 211s (Ana Isabel *González B.*).

8765 **Scannone** Juan Carlos, Nuevo punto de partida de la filosofía latinoamericana. Buenos Aires 1990, Guadalupe. 256 p. – ᴿRTLv 23 (1992) 212-4 (E. *Brito*).

8766 a) *Scannone* Juan Carlos, Der nichtverstandene Andere; zum Gedächtnis der 500 Jahre Evangelisierung Lateinamerikas; – b) *Boff* Leonardo, Herausforderung nach 500 Jahren Evangelisierung; eine lateinamerikanische Perspektive; – c) *Suess* Paulo, Zur Geschichte und Ideologie von Sklaverei und Sklavenbefreiung in Brasilien: MüTZ 43 (1992) 265-277 / 279-291 / 293-313.

8767 *Scannone* J. C., a) Les défis actuels de l'évangélisation en Amérique Latine: NRT 114 (1992) 641-652; – b) Nueva modernidad adveniente y cultura emergente en América Latina; reflexiones filosóficas y teológico-pastorales: Stromata 47 (1991) 145-192.

8768 *Shaull* Richard, Latin America; three responses to a new historical situation: Interpretation 46 (1992) 261-270.

8768* **Sherman** Amy L., Preferential option; a Christian and neoliberal strategy for Latin America's poor. GR 1992, Eerdmans. x-230 p. $18 pa. 0-8028-0642-2 [TDig 40,187].

8769 a) *Sievernich* Michael, 'Geschichtserinnerung' in der Theologie der Befreiung; – b) *Bernecker* Walther L., Von der Reconquista zur Conquista; Spanien im ausgehenden 15. Jht; – c) *Eggensperger* Thomas, Kampf um Gerechtigkeit in Spanien; die andere Seite des LAS CASAS: Wort und Antwort 32 (Mainz 1991) 159-165 / 148-153 / 172-7 [< ZIT 91,722].

8770 **Sigmund** Paul E., Liberation theology at the crossroads; democracy or revolution? 1990 → 6,8597; 7,8581: ᴿCritRR 5 (1992) 488-490 (A. K. *Min*).

8771 **Smith** Christian, The emergence of liberation theology; radical religion and social movement theory. Ch 1991, Univ. xiv-300 p. $15. – ᴿTS 53 (1992) 589s (T. L. *Schubeck*: a sociologist's view).

8772 **Sobrino** Jon, Jesucristo liberador; lectura histórico-teológica de Jesús de Nazaret. M 1991, Trotta. 350 p. 84-87699-21-9. – ᴿSalT 80 (1992) 259-261 (R. de *Sivatte*); EstE 67 (1992) 232-4 (Maria Ángeles *Navarro Girón*); TR 88 (1992) 405-8 (R. *Schwager*: shows also that it is better for Latin-American and European theology to cooperate).

8773 **Sobrino** Jon, El principio misericordia; Bajar de la cruz a los pueblos crucificados: PresTeol 67. Sdr 1992, Sal Terrae. 267 p. 84-293-1063-0. – ᴿActuBbg 29 (1992) 316s (J. *Vives*).

8774 *Sobrino* Jon, a) Awakening from the sleep of inhumanity, ᵀ*Planas*

Dimas; ChrCent 108 (1991) 364-370; – b) First world, third world; sin and grace [< Salford Cathedral Paul VI memorial lecture]: Tablet 246 (1992) 419-421.

8775 **Sölle** Dorothee, Gott im Müll; eine andere Entdeckung Lateinamerikas. Mü 1992, Deutsch-Tb-V. 176 p. DM 9,80. – RLuthMon 31 (1992) 279 (U. *Tietze*).

8775* **Spykman** Gordon, *al.*, Let my people live; faith and struggle in central America. GR 1988, Eerdmans. $13 pa. 0-8028-0373-3. – RJDharma 17 (1992) 63-65 (M. C. *Teekoy*).

8776 **Stefano** Frances, The absolute value of human action in the theology of Juan Luis SEGUNDO. Lanham MD 1992, UPA. xxxi-298 p. $42.50. 0-8191-8511-6 [TDig 39,387].

8777 **Stoll** David, Is Latin America turning Protestant? The politics of evangelism 1990 → 6,8602 ['of evangelical growth']: RTS 53 (1992) 172-4 (J. P. *Fitzpatrick*: warns sects of 'the clear and present danger of being manipulated by the U.S. government' but warns Catholics that the spiritual appeal of fundamentalism is more powerful).

8779 ESunderlin George, Bartolomé de LAS CASAS, a selection of his writings. Mkn 1992, Orbis. $13 pa. 0-88344-790-8.

8780 **Tamayo-Acosta** J. A., Para comprender la teología de la liberación 1989 → 5,8569; 6,8603: RComScv 24 (1991) 109s (M. *Sánchez*).

8781 **Taylor** Mark K., Remembering Esperanza; a cultural-political theology for North American praxis. Mkn 1992, Orbis. $30. 0-88344-642-1. – RJRel 72 (1992) 610s (Anne *Carr*).

8781* **Vattathara** Mathachan, The methodology of Latin American liberation theology; towards an understanding and a critical evaluation of its relation to Marxism: diss. DSchrijver G. De. Leuven 1992. xxxiv-300 p. – LvSt 17 (1992) 400s; RTLv 24, p. 540.

8782 **Wimberly** John W., Grace and the human condition in the theology of Juan Luis SEGUNDO: diss. Catholic Univ., DFord J. Wsh 1992. 321 p. 92-17095. – DissA 53 (1992s) 191s-A.

8783 **Wit** J. H. de, Leerlingen van de armen; een onderzoek naar de betekenis van de Latijnsamerikaanse volke lezing van de Bijbel in de hermeneutische ontwerpen en de exegetische praktijk van C. MESTERS, J. S. CROATTO en M. SCHWANTES: diss. Amst VU, DLeene H. xvi-383 p. 90-5383-027-8. – TvT 32,85.

H8.6 *Theologiae emergentes* – 'Theologies of' emergent groups.

8784 EAbraham K. C., Third world theologies, commonalities and divergences 1986/90 → 6,565; 7,8591: RBDialRel 26 (1991) 130-6 (T. *Michel*, also on the 11 other volumes of Maryknoll 'Faith meets faith' series); ExpTim 103 (1991s) 54 (G. *D'Costa*).

8785 **Agbeti** J. K., West African Church history II. Christian missions and theological training 1842-1970. [< diss. 1969]. Leiden 1991, Brill. xv-261 p. ƒ85. 90-04-09100-9. – RTvT [= TsTNijm] 32 (1992) 202 (J. *Heijke*).

8786 EAlberts Louw, Chikane Frank, The road to Rustenberg [Transvaal Nov. 1990]; the Church looking forward to a new South Africa. Cape Town 1991, Struik. 286 p. [TContext 10/2, 101, H. *Janssen*].

8787 **Amafili** Emenike Leo, The celebration of the Eucharist with an African face; from adaptation rooted in the western world to inculturation into the African/Igbo sacrificial setting: diss. DSchrijver G. de. Leuven 1992. xxxix-376 p. – TvT 32 (1992) 189: RTLv 24, p. 572.

8788 **Amaladoss** Michael, Making all things new; dialogue, pluralism and evangelization in Asia. Mkn 1990, Orbis. x-203 p. $19. – ᴿMissiology 19 (1991) 485s (J. H. *Kroeger*).

8789 **Barboza** Francis P., Christianity in Indian dance forms: Sri GaribDass 114. Delhi 1990, Sri Satguru. xiii-240 p. rs. 300. – ᴿAnthropos 87 (1992) 563s (Judy *Van Zile*).

8790 **Bertsch** Ludwig, Laien als Gemeindeleiter: ein afrikanisches Modell 1990: → 7,8599: ᴿTLZ 117 (1992) 633-5 (J. *Althausen*); TvT 32 (1992) 110 (J. *Heijke*).

8790* **Batumalai** S., An introduction to Asian theology. Delhi 1991, ISPCK. xii-457 p. rs 45. 81-7214-015-0. – ᴿVidyajyoti 56 (1992) 380s (A. *Kullu*).

8791 **Biernatzki** William E., Roots of acceptance; the intercultural communication of religious meanings: Inculturation 13. R 1991, Pont. Univ. Gregoriana. 186 p. 88-7652-640-4. – ᴿGregorianum 73 (1992) 167-9 (J. T. *Bretzke*).

8792 *Blaser* Klauspeter, Martin Luther KING, précurseur de la théologie noire [*Molla* S.]: RTPhil 124 (1992) 427-434.

8793 **Bloom** Harold, The American religion; the emergence of a post-Christian nation. NY c. 1992, Simon & S. 288 p. $22. – ᴿChrCent 109 (1992) 545-8 (M. E. *Marty*); Commonweal 119/10 (1992) 26-28 (E. T. *Oakes*).

8794 **Bujo** Bénézet, African theology in its social context [deutsch], ᵀO'Donohue John: Faith & Cultures. Mkn 1992, Orbis. 143 p. $17. 0-88344-805-X [TDig 40,54; TContext 10/2,90, H. *Janssen*].

8795 *Bujo* Bénézet, 'Des prêtres noirs s'interrogent'; une théologie issue de la négritude: NZMissW 46 (1990) 286-297.

8796 *a) Camps* Arnulf, Das dritte Auge; von einer Theologie in Asien zu einer asiatischen Theologie; – *b) Pulsfort* Ernst, Die liturgische Inkulturation des Christentums in Indien seit dem Zweiten Vatikanum; – *c) Daneel* Martinus I., Towards a sacramental theology of the environment in African independent churches: ZMissRW 75 (1991) 1-21 / 22-36 / 37-65.

8797 *a) Carmo Cheuiche* Antônio do, Evangelización e inculturación; – *b) Kloppenburg* Bonaventura, El sincretismo afro-brasileño como desafío a la evangelización: ScriptTPamp 24 (1992) 57-72 / 101-112.

8798 **Carmody** Brendan P., Conversion and Jesuit schooling in Zambia. Leiden 1992, Brill. xxix-179 p. *f* 80. 90-04-09428-8. – ᴿExpTim 103 (1991s) 379 (A. *Shorter*: valuable).

8799 **Carrier** Hervé, Évangélisation et développement des cultures: Studia Socialia NS 4. R 1990, Gregoriana. 380 p. Lit. 32.000. – ᴿNRT 114 (1992) 588 (G. *Navez*).

8800 **Carrier** Hervé, Lexique de la culture, pour l'analyse culturelle et l'inculturation. Tournai 1992, Desclée. 441 p. Fb 1199. 2-7189-0593-X. – ᴿGregorianum 73 (1992) 776 (*ipse*).

8801 **Carrier** Hervé, Vangelo e cultura da Leone XIII a Giovanni Paolo II [Évangile et cultures]: ᵀMarchesi A.: Vangelo e culture. R 1990, Città Nuova. 224 p. – ᴿSalesianum 54 (1992) 193s (C. *Semeraro*).

8802 *Chandrahanthan* A.J.V., Evangelization in the multi-cultural and pluri-religious context of Sri Lanka: ZMissRW 75 (1991) 133-146.

8803 **Chidester** David, Religions of South Africa [post-missionary; indigenous only briefly]: Library of religious beliefs and practices. NY 1992, Routledge. xvi-286 p. $24.50. 0-415-04780-3 [TDig 39,356].

8804 *Chupungco* Anscar J., Inculturation and the organic progression of the liturgy: EcOrans 7 (1990) 7-21.

8805 **Cipollini** Antonietta, Per una teologia africana autenticamente cristiana; rapporto fede-cultura nella teologia africana; il caso di Camerun: diss. Pont. Univ. Gregoriana, R 1992, ᴰ*Wolanin* A. – RTLv 24, p. 565.

8806 *Comerford* Patrick, Zephania KAMEETA; Namibia's black [Lutheran] liberation theologian: DocLife 41 (1991) 133-141.

8807 **Cone** James H., The spirituals and the blues [African-American religion]. Mkn 1991 = 1972, Orbis. ix-141 p. $14. – ᴿChrCent 109 (1992) 199.201 (T. G. *Poole*: reissue well-advised); CritRR 5 (1992) 61s (J. M. *Spencer*).

8808 **Cone** James H., La noirceur de Dieu [God of the oppressed 1975], ᵀ*Jean* M., *Philibert* J. 1989 → 6,6830: ᴿRTPhil 124 (1992) 104s (K. *Blaser*).

8809 **Costas** Orlando E., Liberating news; a theology of contextual evangelization 1989 → 7,8610: ᴿEvangel 10,1 (1992) 31s (P. *Neilson*).

8810 **Cox** James L., The impact of Christian missions on indigenous cultures; the 'real people' and the unreal Gospel: Studies in the History of Missions 4. Lewiston NY 1991, Mellen. viii-261 p. $60. 0-88946-072-8 [TDig 40,59].

8811 *Dagens* Claude, Le christianisme dans l'histoire; le temps des origines et notre temps [... l'inculturation de la foi]: NRT 114 (1992) 801-815.

8812 *Daneel* M. L., African Christian theology and the challenge of earthkeeping: NZMissW 47 (1991) 129-141. 225-246.

8813 *Daughtry* Herbert, The beloved community; a historical overview of the black church's participation in the struggle of African people for freedom: Drew Gateway 61,1 (1991) 29-...

8814 **Davis** Cyprian, The history of black Catholics in the US 1990 → 6,8634; 7,8611: ᴿAmerica 164 (1991) 422-4 (Stephen *Ochs*); p. 395-420, interviews with 5 of the 13 U.S. black bishops); AndrUnS 30 (1992) 164s (R. *Dederen*); HomP 92,7 (1991s) 76s (J. R. *Sheets*: discrimination diminished under pressure from Rome).

8815 **Deck** Allan F., The second wave; [U.S.] Hispanic ministry and the evangelization of cultures. NY 1989, Paulist. 191 p. $10. 0-0891-3042-4. – ᴿRExp 88 (1991) 116s (D. F. *D'Amico*).

8816 **Derroitte** Henri, Le Christianisme en Afrique entre revendication et contestation; analyse de 25 revues de théologie et de pastorale en Afrique francophone subsaharienne (1969-1988): diss. ᴰ*Simon* M. LvN 1992. xvi-830 p., 513 p. – RTLv 23,422s; 24, p. 557 et extr. p. 38-59.

8817 *Derroitte* Henri, Expériences missionnaires belges au Zaïre: RTLv 23 (1992) 41-70; Eng. 144.

8818 **Dohi** Akio, *al.,* Japan: Theologiegeschichte der Dritten Welt, Tb 107. Mü 1991, Kaiser. 215 p. [TContext 10/2,94; G. *Evers*].

8819 *a) Dupuy* Bernard, Aux origines de l'Église syrienne-orthodoxe de l'Inde; – *b) Dvornik* François, mgr., Églises nationales et Église universelle [< Eastern Churches Quarterly 5 (1943) 172-219], ᵀ*Delmotte* Marguerite: Istina 36 (1991) 53-61 / 9-52.

8820 ᴱ**Ellsberg** Robert, GANDHI on Christianity. Mkn 1991, Orbis. xxiii-117 p. $11 pa. – ᴿAnglTR 74 (1992) 524-6 (B. *Smith*).

8821 **Elolia** Samuel Kiptalai, Christianity and culture in Kenya; an encounter between the Africa Inland Mission and the Marakwet belief systems and culture: diss. ᴰ*Klein* M., St. Michael. Toronto 1992. 285 p. – RTLv 24, p. 560.

8822 *England* John C., The earliest Christian communities in Southeast and Northeast Asia; an outline of the evidence available in seven countries before A.D. 1500: Missiology 19 (1991) 203-215.

8823 **Etukuri** M., Towards an Indian Christology of liberation; a critical analysis of the Christology of Jan SOBRINO in a GANDHIAN perspective: diss. Leuven 1991, ᴰ*Schrijver* G. De. xliv-434 p. – TvT 32 (1992) 188.
ᴱ**Felder** Cain H., Stony the road 1991 ➤ m632.

8825 **Fujita** Neil S., Japan's encounter with Christianity; the Catholic mission in pre-modern Japan. NY 1991, Paulist. viii-294 p. $14. – ᴿTS 53 (1992) 389s (B. L. *Wren*).

8826 **George** Francis E., Inculturation and ecclesial communion, culture and Church in the teaching of Pope John Paul II, ᴰ1990 ➤ 7,8623; 88-401-8051-6: ᴿGregorianum 73 (1992) 762s (A. *Wolanin*).

8827 **Gerwin van Leeuwen** J.A.G., Fully Indian — authentically Christian: Nijmegen Univ. Kerk en Theologie in Context. Kampen 1990, Kok. xv-357 p. – ᴿJDharma 16 (1991) 168 [P. *Kalluveettil*: a history of D. S. AMALORPAVADASS' Bangalore foundation NBCLC 1967-1982].

8828 **Gichure** Peter I., Contextual theology; a contribution to theological method: diss. ᴰ*Willaert* B. Leuven 1992. xliii-365 p. – LvSt 17 (1992) 398s; RTLv 24, p. 595.

8828* ᴱ**Gilliland** Dean S., The Word among us; contextualizing theology for mission today 1989 ➤ 6,8650: ᴿRefTR 50 (1991) 111s (N. *Foster*).

8829 *Goldman* Gerard, Preface to a local theology; the Murinbata case [Port Keats, N. Australia aborigines]: Nelen Yubu 50 (1992) 30-43 [TContext 10/1, 85, H. *Janssen*].

8830 **Gray** Richard, Black Christians and white missionaries 1990 ➤ 7,8626: ᴿColcFran 61 (1991) 434 (B. *Vadakkekara*); HeythJ 33 (1992) 461s (A. *Shorter*); IntRMiss 81 (1992) 618-620 (P. *Jenkins*); Tablet 246 (1992) 515s (A. *Hastings*).

8831 **Greeley** A. M., The Catholic myth; the behavior and beliefs of American Catholics. NY 1991, Scribners. 322 p. $22. – ᴿAmerica 164 (1991) 604-6 (V. R. *Yanitelli*).

8832 *Griffin* P., Schooled and unschooled biblical exegetes in the African American religious experience, 1865-1900: Journal of the Interdenominational Theological Center 17,1s (Atlanta 1989s) 31-53 [< NTAbs 36,319].

8833 *Gubuan* Woodrow, The basic Christian communities in the Church in the Philippines: diss. Pont. Univ. Angelicum, ᴰ*Christian* R. – Roma 1989. 229 p. – RTLv 24, p. 560.

8834 **Hall** Douglas J., Thinking the faith; Christian theology in a North American context 1989 ➤ 5,8611 ... 7,8627: ᴿCritRR 5 (1992) 473-5 (Anna *Case-Winters*); CurrTMiss 19 (1992) 305s (C. L. *Nessan*).

8835 **Harding** Vincent, Hope and history; why we must share the story of the movement. Mkn 1990, Orbis. xii-249 p. $11 pa. – ᴿCritRR 5 (1992) 63s (D. *De Leon*: rambling 'responsibilities of the black scholar to the community').

8836 *Harrisville* Roy A., Reading the Bible in the American context: WWorld 12,2 (1992) 165-172 [< NTAbs 36,309].

8837 **Hastings** A., African Catholicism ²1989 ➤ 5,276 ... 7,8628: ᴿNewTR 5,1 (1992) 107s (A. J. *Gittins*).

8838 **Hesselgrave** David J., Communicating Christ cross-culturally; an introduction to missionary communication² [¹1978, 15 printings]. GR 1991, Zondervan. 672 p. $22. 0-310-36811-1 [TDig 39,266].

8839 *Hiebert* Paul G., Beyond anti-colonialism to globalism: Missiology 19 (1991) 263-281.

8840 *Hillman* Eugene, Maasai religion and inculturation: LvSt 17 (1992) 351-376 > TDig 39 (1992) 335-341 [*Asen* B. A.].

8841 **Hodgson** Janet, *Kothare* Jay, Vision quest; native spirituality and the Church in Canada. Toronto 1990, Anglican. 213 p. $19. – ᴿTorJT 7 (1991) 303s (M. *Stogre*).

8842 *Holifield* E. Brooks, Nordamerikanische Theologie, ᵀ*Ruprecht* A.: ➤ 757, EvKL 3 (1992) 775-783.

8843 **Hood** Robert E., Must God remain Greek? Afro cultures and God-talk 1990 ➤ 7,8631*; $15; 0-8006-2449-1: – ᴿExpTim 103 (1991s) 93s (A. C. *Ross*: 'To free Christ from Europe', including North America, intellectual strait-jacket).

8843* *Hovland* Thor H., Fundamental problems in African theology, particularly concerning Christology: TsTKi 63 (1992) 193-205 [in Norwegian; Eng. 205].

8844 *a)* *Hunsberger* George R., The NEWBIGIN gauntlet; developing a domestic missiology for North America; – *b)* *West* Charles C., Gospel for American culture; variations on a theme by Newbigin; – *c)* *Watson* David L., Christ all in all; the recovery of the Gospel for North American evangelism: Missiology 19 (1991) 391-408 / 431-442 / 443-460 [< ᴢɪᴛ 92,64].

8845 **Jackson** Alvin A., An exegetical and homiletical study of Blacks in the Bible: diss. Eastern Baptist Theol. Sem. 1992. 173 p. 92-27182. – DissA 53 (1992s) 1960-A.

8846 *a)* *Ishida* Yoshiro, The role of liberal theology in Japan at the turn of this century [c. 1901]; – *b)* *Sherer* James A., [not a relative], A pioneer Lutheran missionary in Japan; James A. B. SCHERER [1870-1944]: Curr-TMiss 19 (1992) 357-363 / 326-338 [322-373 *al.*, on American Lutheran mission to Japan 1892-1992].

8847 **Jesudasan** Ignatius, GANDHIAN theology of liberation 1987 ➤ 65,7339 ... 7,8632*: ᴿBible Bhashyam 16 (1990) 195s (G. *Mangalapilly*: splendid; translated into several languages).

8848 **Kabongo-Mbaya,** L'Église du Christ au Zaïre; formation et adaptation du protestantisme en situation de dictature: Hommes et Sociétés. P 1992, Karthala. 467 p.; 12 pl.; 4 maps. F 170. – ᴿRHE 87 (1992) 856-8 (M. *Spindler*).

8849 **Kidangean** Xavier, Family and priesthood in the Syro-Malabar church: diss. Pont. Univ. Angelicum, ᴰ*Thottakara* A. Rome 1992. 91 p. – RTLv 24, p. 560.

8850 **Kochuparampil** X., Evangelization in India; a theological analysis of the missionary role of the Syro-Malabar church in the light of Vatican II and post-conciliar documents: diss. ᴰ*Leijssen* L., Leuven 1991. lix-426 p. – TvT 32 (1992) 188s.

8851 *Kwon Jin-Kwan,* Minjung theology and its future task for people's movement; a theological reflection on the theme of religion, power and politics in the Korean context: CTC-Bulletin 10,2 (1991) 16-22 [TContext 10/1,86, G. *Evers*].

8852 **Lambert** Tony, The resurrection of the Chinese church. L 1991, Hodder & S. 328 p. £8. 0-340-54997-1. – ᴿExpTim 103 (1991s) 379 (H. D. *Beeby*: one Chinese reaction: 'Did it ever die?').

8852* *a)* *Lambino* Antonio B., Dialogue, discernment, deeds; an approach to Asian challenges today; – *b)* *Kroeger* James H., Apostolic spirituality; aware we are sent: Landas 4 (1990) 147-160 / 161-181.

8853 *La Torre* Jesús de, La comunidad eclesial con rostro amerindígena: Iter 3,1 (Caracas 1992) 39-60.

8854 *Loader* Bill, Biblical perspectives on issues of multiculturalism and inculturation: Colloquium 24,1 (Sydney 1992) 3-13 [< ᴢɪᴛ 92,284].

8855 a) *Lobinger* Fritz, Afrikaner suchen sich in der Bibel; – b) *Janssen* Hermann, Zwischen Mythos und Bibel: KatBlätt 117 (Mü 1992) 380-3 / 392-7 [< ZIT 92,402].

8856 **Luker** Ralph E., The social gospel in black and white; American racial reform 1885-1912: Studies in Religion. Chapel Hill 1991, Univ. N. Carolina. 410 p. $40. 0-8078-1978-6. – ᴿCathHR 78 (1992) 476s (D. M. *Reimers*).

8857 *Lumembu* Leonard K., Inculturation in action; African rites and liturgies: SEDOS 23,5 (1991) 133-8 [< TContexto 2/1,110].

8858 **Luzbetak** Louis J., Chiesa e culture; nuove prospettive di antropologia della missione [1963 ²1989 ➤ 5,8627 ... 7,8644], ᵀ. Bo 1991, Missionaria. 524 p. Lit. 57.000. – ᴿBenedictina 39 (1992) 497-502 (G. *Anelli*).

8859 **Mabee** C., Reading sacred texts through American eyes; biblical interpretation as cultural critique: Studies in American Biblical Hermeneutics 7. Macon 1991, Mercer Univ. ix-128 p. $25; pa. $17. 0-86554-385-2; -403-4 [NTAbs 36, 256].

8860 *Madey* Johannes, La Chrétienté de Saint-Thomas en Inde; Églises catholiques et orthodoxes: Irénikon 65 (1982) 24-41; Eng. 41 [451-461, *Wybrew* Hugh].

8860* a) *Madtha* William, Dalit theology, voice of the oppressed; – b) *Massey* James, Christian Dalits, a historical perspective; – c) *Vadakumchery* J., The original inhabitants of India, victims of written traditions ['tribals' the major portion of the 'dalits', 'the bottom of Indian society']: JDharma 16 (1991) 74-92 / 44-60 / 33-43.

8861 *Masiá* Juan, Nueva evangelización o nueva inculturación: MiscCom 49 (1991) 505-519.

8862 *Meliá* Bartolomeu, Indigenous cultures and evangelization; challenges for a liberating mission: IntRMiss 81 (1992) 557-568 (al. 525-601).

8863 *Mercado* Leonardo N., The Filipino face of Christ: PhilipSac 27,79 (1992) 91-103 [TContext 10/1, 90, G. *Evers*].

8864 a) *Mercado* Leonardo N., Inculturation and the biblical apostolate; – b) *Mercado* Edwin E., Emerging images of the Asian Church: PhilipSa 26 (1991) 37-49 / 77-94.

8864* *Milligan* Mary, The Bible as formative in a basic Christian community of Brazil: Studies in Formative Spirituality 13 (1992) 145-....

8865 **Moffett** Samuel H., A history of Christianity in Asia, 1. Beginnings to 1500. SF 1992, Harper. xxvi-560 p.; maps. $45. 0-06-065779-0 [TDig 40,77].

8866 **Mosala** Itumeleng J., Biblical hermeneutics and Black theology in South Africa 1989 ➤ 7,8689: ᴿCBQ 54 (1992) 582s (A. *Moyo*); Missiology 19 (1991) 236 (P. L. *Capp*).

Mueller John J., Practical discipleship; a United States Christology 1992 ➤ 7546.

8867 *Mulder* Niels, Localization and Philippine Catholicism: Philippine Studies 40,2 (1992) 240-254 [TContext 10/1, 90, G. *Evers*].

8868 **Musopole** Augustine Chingwala, On being-human in Africa; a critical evaluation of an African view of humanity in writings of John Mʙɪᴛɪ: diss. Union Theol. Sem., ᴰCone J. New York 1991. – RTLv 24, p. 507.

8868* **Neckebrouck** V., La terza chiesa e il problema della cultura. CinB 1990, Paoline. 130 p. – ᴿLateranum 57 (1991) 266-8 (M. *Semeraro*).

8869 **Nijno** Joseph K., al., Communicating the Gospel message in Africa today: Spearhead 120. Eldoret 1992, Gaba. 69 p. [TContext 10/2, 100, H. *Janssen*].

8870 *Nkwoka* A.O., Jesus as eldest brother (Okpara); an Igbo paradigm for Christology in the African context: Evangel 10,3 (1992) 84-92.

8871 **Nolan** Albert, Dieu en Afrique du Sud [1988 ➤ 6,8700]: Théologies. P 1991, Cerf. 293 p. F 160. 2-204-04318-4. – ᴿEsprVie 102 (1992) 110-2 (P. *Jay* admire la condamnation de W. WINK, La troisième voie de Jésus); ÉTRel 67 (1992) 145-7 (Anne-Marie *Goguel*).

8872 *Nyamiti* Charles, *a*) The Incarnation viewed from the African understanding of person III: Chiea 7 (Nairobi 1991) 29-52 [< TContexto 2/2, 20]; – *b*) My approach to African theology: Chiea 7,4 (1991) 35-53 [TContext 10/1,85, H. *Janssen*].

8873 **Okolo** Chukwudum B., The liberating role of the Church in Africa today: Spearhead 119. Eldoret 1991, Gaba. 83 p. [TContext 10/2, H. *Hoeben*].

8874 *Osei-Bonsu* Joseph, Biblically/theologically based inculturation: AfER 32 (1990) 346-359.

8875 **Parappally** Jacob, Emerging Christology in the Indian context; a critical study of the development, context, and contemporary attempts of R. PANIKKAR and S. KAPPEN to articulate a relevant Christology in the Indian context: diss. ᴰ*Greshake* G. Freiburg/Br 1992. 375 p. – RTLv 24, p. 576.

8876 **Persaud** Winston D., The theology of the Cross and MARX's anthropology; a view from the Caribbean. NY 1991, P. Lang. 295 p. 0-8204-1409-3. – ᴿExpTim 103 (1991s) 188 (A. *Kee*: black theology owes much to earlier Caribbean activists).

8877 **Pieris** Aloysius, El rostro asiático de Cristo; notas para una teología asiática, ᵀᴱ*Sánchez-Rivera* Juan M.: Verdad e Imagen 119, 1991 ➤ 7, 8678: ᴿLumenVr 40 (1991) 412s (U. *Gil Ortega*).

8878 **Pieris** Aloysius, Une théologie asiatique de la libération [1988 ➤ 5, 8655],ᵀ. P 1990, Centurion. 232 p. F 140. – ᴿLVitae 46 (1991) 116 (P. *Tihon*, répétée 234).

8879 **Porter** Muriel, Land of the Spirit? [Terra Australis S. Spiritus] the Australian religious experience. Geneva/Melbourne 1990, WCC/Joint Board of Christian Education. xi-102 p. A$11. – ᴿPacifica 4 (1991) 327-335 (Veronica *Brady*).

8880 **Poupard** Paul, L'Église au défi des cultures [15 art. depuis 1979] 1989 ➤ 6,8709: ᴿScEsp 43 (1991) 117 (G. *Langevin*).

8881 *Poupard* Paul card., La nouvelle évangélisation; l'inculturation au cœur de la mission [Colloque œcuménique, Berne 20 mars 1992): EsprVie 102 (1992) 225-233 [234-9, *Foley* John P., extraits d'Aetatis novae sur les communications sociales].

8882 **Pulsfort** Ernst, Christliche Ashrams in Indien 1989 ➤ 6,8712: ᴿNZMiss-W 47 (1991) 171s (F. *Frei*).

8883 **Rader** Dick A., Christian ethics in an African context; a focus on urban Zambia: Amer Univ St 7/128. NY 1991, Lang. xii-201 p. DM 69 [TR 88,84].

8884 **Raison-Jourde** Françoise, Bible et pouvoir à Madagascar au XIXᵉ siécle; invention d'une identité chrétienne et construction de l'État. P 1991, Karthala. 844 p. – ᴿÉtudes 377 (1992) 715s (F. *Noiret*).

8885 **Reid** David, New wine; the cultural shaping of Japanese Christianity: Nanzan Studies 2. Berkeley 1991, Asian Humanities. 199 p. [TContext 10/2, 93, G. *Evers*].

8886 **Rogers** Delores J., The American empirical movement in theology [Mordecai KAPLAN, B. MELAND]: EurUnivSt 7/70. NY 1990, Lang. viii-246 p. $47.50: ᴿCritRR 5 (1992) 484-6 (Emanuel S. *Goldsmith*).

8887 ᴱRuggieri G., Église et histoire de l'Église en Afrique; Actes du Colloque de Bologne, 1988 ➤ 6,681; 7,8687: ᴿNRT 114 (1992) 591 (J. *Masson*); ZMissRW 75 (1991) 88-90 (K. J. *Tossou*).

8888 **Schineller** Peter, A handbook on inculturation 1990 ➤ 6,8723: ᴿHomP 92,3 (1991s) 72s (Faith A. *Strop*); Mid-Stream 30 (1991) 94s (J. *Gros*, also on GITTINS A.).

8889 **Schlegelberger** Bruno, Unsere Erde lebt; zum Verhältnis von altandiner Religion und Christentum in den Hochanden Perus: NZMissW Supp 41. Immensee 1992. 350 p. [TR 88,525].

8889* ᴱSchneider Franz, Inkulturation — nur für die dritte Welt? Tagung, 1990. Erfurt 22.-27. Juli: LtgJb 41 (1991) 1-5 [-52, *al.*]; p. 73-87, *Schaeffler* Richard, Kultur und Kult.

8890 *Schotte* John P. [secr. for Synod of Bishops], The Church in Africa and her evangelizing mission toward the year 2000: AfER 33,1s (1991) 1-100.

8891 ᴱSchreiter Robert J., Faces of Jesus in Africa: Faith & Cultures. Mkn 1991, Orbis. xiii-181 p. $17 pa. 0-88344-768-1 [TDig 39,261]. – ᴿNewTR 5,4 (1992) 85s (J. G. *Donders*); RExp 89 (1992) 578s (H. J. *Mugabe*); Tablet 246 (1992) 1106s (A. *Shorter*).

8891* *Simpson* Theo, Theology in context: TLond 95 (1992) 343-353.

8892 *Skhakhane* Jerome, African spirituality: Grace and Truth 10,3s (Hilton SAf 1991) 148-155 [< TContexto 2,1 (1992) 119].

8893 *Smit* D. J., The Bible and ethos [... more socially influential than ethics] in a new South Africa. Scriptura 37 (1991) 51-67 [< NTAbs 36,9].

8894 *Smith* Jane I., Globalization in theological education. QRMin 11,2 (1991) 61-75 [3, 41-57, *Deschner* John; 4, 63-80, *Meeks* W. Douglas].

8895 *a)* *Smolicz* J. J., The essential tension between modernity and tradition; Asian cultural heritage and scientific development; – *b)* *Mercado* Leonardo N., The Filipino image of God: PhilipSa 26 (1991) 179-192 / 401-415.

8896 **Spijker** G. van 't, Les usages funéraires et la mission de l'Église; une étude anthropologique et théologique des rites funéraires au Rwanda [diss. VU]. Kampen 1990, Kok. [TContext 10/2,96, H. *Hoeben*: Presbyterian]: ᴿNedTTs 46 (1992) 171s (G. J. van *Butselaar*).

8897 *Spindler* M., L'usage de la Bible dans le discours politique malgache depuis l'indépendance (1960-1990): ➤ 60, ᶠGADILLE J., Histoire religieuse 1992, 199-220.

8898 **Stanley** Brian, The Bible and the flag; Protestant missions and British imperialism in the nineteenth and twentieth centuries. Leicester 1990, Inter-Varsity. 212 p. £11. – ᴿMissiology 19 (1991) 478s (A. C. *Smith*).

8899 *Starkloff* Carl F., Aboriginal cultures and the Christ: TS 53 (1992) 288-312.

8900 ᴱStine P. C., *Wendland* E. R., Bridging the gap; African traditional religion and Bible translation: UBS Mg 4. NY 1990, United Bible Societies. 224 p. – ᴿSalesianum 54 (1992) 586s (C. *Buzzetti*: anche tit.pp.).

8901 **Stockton** Eugene D., Landmarks; a spiritual search in a southern land. Eastwood NSW, Parish Ministry. 127 p. A$10,50 pa. – ᴿPacifica 4 (1991) 111s (D. *Edwards*: towards a distinctively Australian spirituality).

8902 ᴱSugirtharajah Rasiah S., Voices from the margin; interpreting the Bible in the Third World, 1991 ➤ 7,330: ᴿModT 8 (1992) 315-7 (G. *West*); Studies 81 (1992) 112s (Gesa *Thiessen*); TLond 95 (1992) 45s (C. *Rowland*).

8903 *a)* *Sundermeier* Theo, Inkulturation und Synkretismus; Probleme einer Verhältnisbestimmung; – *b)* *Koschorke* Klaus, Kontextualität und Uni-

versalität als Problemstellungen der Kirchengeschichte; – *c*) *Feldtkeller*
Andreas, Der Synkretismus-Begriff im Rahmen einer Theorie von Ver-
hältnisbestimmungen zwischen Religionen; – *d*) *Brück* Michael von, Religionswissenschaft und interkulturelle Theologie; – *e*) *Rzepkowski* Horst,
'Religionen, Religiosität und christlicher Glaube' [Arnoldsheimer Konferenz, Gü 1991] und 'Redemptoris missio'; ein Vergleich: EvT 52,3 ('Synkretismus und Inkulturation', 1992) 192-209 / 209-224 / 224-245 / 245-261
/ 262-276.

8904 *a*) *Sundermeier* Theo, Inkulturation als Entäusserung; – *b*) *MacRobert*
Iain, The black roots of Pentecostalism: → 86, FHOLLENWEGER W., Pentecost 1992, 209-214 / 73-84.

8904* ETaylor William D., Internationalising missionary training; a global
perspective. Exeter/GR 1991, Paternoster/Baker. 286 p. [RefTR 51,118].

8905 **Tehindrazanarivelo** Emmanuel D., Vers une christologie contemporaine;
une perspective ancestrale: diss. St. Michael, DLaporte J.-M. Toronto
1992. 423 p. – RTLv 24, p. 577.

8906 **ter Haar** Gerrie, Spirit of Africa... abp. MILINGO. – c. 1992. RMonth
253 (1992) 194-8 (Mona *Macmillan*); Tablet 246 (1992) 740s (P. *Ka-
lilombe*).

8907 *Tinker* George E. [an Osage], Spirituality, native American priesthood,
sovereignty and solidarity: Voices from the Third World 15,1 (1992) 22-45
[résumé TContext 10/2,80].

8908 **Trompf** Garry W., Melanesian religion. C 1991, Univ. xi-283 p. $54.50.
0-521-38306-4 [TDig 39,191].

8909 *Tuwere* Sevati, Emerging themes for a Pacific [... Fiji] theology: Pa-
cificJT 2,7 (1992) 49-55 [TContext 10/1, 89, H. *Janssen*].

8910 EUka E. M., Readings in African traditional religion; structure, meaning, relevance, future. Bern 1991, Lang. 391 p. Fs 80 [TR 88,526].

8911 *a*) *Uzukwu* F. E., African symbols and Christian liturgical celebration; –
b) *Healey* Joseph G., Inculturating the Holy Week liturgy in East Africa:
Worship 65 (1991) 98-112 / 112-125.

8912 **Van Rheenen** Gailyn, Communicating Christ in animistic contexts
[Kenya 1973-6]. GR 1991, Baker. 342 p. $15. 0-8010-9312-0 [TDig
39,292].

8913 *Wachege* N., African inculturation, liberation theology: Chiea 8,1 (1992)
43-56 [TContext 10/1, 84, H. *Janssen*].

8914 **Walker** TheodoreJ, Empower the people; social ethics for the African-
American Church: Turner Studies in Black Religion 5. Mkn 1991,
Orbis. x-132 p. $16 pa. 0-88344-777-1. – RGregorianum 73 (1992) 555-
7 (J. T. *Bretzke*).

8915 *Wang* Weifan, The pattern and pilgrimage of Chinese theology: Chinese Theological Review (Holland MI 1990) 30-54 [< TContexto 2/2,120].

8916 *Wendland* Ernst, 'Who do people say I am?' Contextualizing Christology in Africa: AfJevT 10,2 (1991) 13-32 [TContext 10/1,84, H.
Janssen].

8917 *Wernhart* Karl R., Altes Testament und Schwarzafrika: → 163, FSAUER
G., Aktualität 1992, 219-226.

8918 **West** Gerald O. Biblical hermeneutics of liberation; modes of reading
the Bible in the South African context 1991 → 7,8713: RSAfBap 2 (1992)
103s (D. *Walker*); TContexto 21 (1992) 127 (H. *Janssen*).

8919 **Wilfred** Felix [kath], *Thomas* M. M. [prot.], Indien: Theologiegeschichte
der Dritten Welt 3, Tb-108. München 1992, Kaiser. 353 p. [TContext
10/2, 93, G. *Evers*].

8920 *Wilfred* Felix, Die Option für die Armen und die Option der Armen; Überlegungen aus einer asiatischen Perspektive: ZMissRW 75 (1991) 257-273.
8921 **Williams** C. Peter, The ideal of the self-governing church; a study in Victorian missionary strategy. Leiden 1990, Brill. 293 p. *f* 148. 90-04-09188-2. – ᴿExpTim 103 (1991s) 184 (P. *Cotterell*: important; on H. VENN and E. STOCK, ignoring R. ALLEN and J. NEVIUS; favors euthanasia of mission and segregation of expatriate from native Christians).
8922 *Wilson* David D., The minister [and his wife, in Panama] working overseas: ExpTim 103 (1991s) 99-104.
8923 **Young** Henry J., Hope in process; a theology of social pluralism. Mp 1990, Fortress. 157 p. $12. 0-8006-2397-5. – ᴿExpTim 103 (1991s) 54 (G. *D'Costa*).
8924 **Zemale** Terese J., Christian witness through small communities [Nairobi ...]: Spearhead 121. Eldoret 1992, Gaba. [TContext 10/2, 96, H. *Janssen*].
8925 *Zi Zhu*, The transformation of a Chinese theologian; T. C. CHAO's journey from humanism to theocentrism, ᵀ*Wickeri* Janice: ChineseTR (1991) 77-102 [TContext 10/1, 86, G. *Evers*].

H8.7 *Mariologia* — The mother of Jesus in the NT

8926 ᴱ**Anderson** H. George, The one mediator, the saints, and Mary: Lutherans and Catholics Dialogue 8. Mp 1992, Augsburg Fortress. 397 p. $12 [TR 88,529].
8927 ᴱ**Bäumer** R., *Scheffczyk* L., Marienlexikon I-II 1988s ➤ 794 [5,917*; 7, 8723]: ᴿEstFran 62 (1992) 366-9 (O. *Schmucki*).
8927* **Basetti-Sani** G. Maria e Gesù ... nel Corano 1989 ➤ 7,8724: ᴿStPatav 39 (1992) 439-441 (C. *Saccone*).
8928 *Bellagamba* Tony, Mary and mission today: African Christian Studies 5 (1989) 19-45; > ᵀᴱ*Pascual* Eduard: SelT 30 (1991) 333-348.
8929 **Biegger** Katharina, 'De invocatione BMV', PARACELSUS und die Marienverehrung: Kosmosophie 6, 1990 ➤ 7,8728; 308 p.; 8 pl. DM 78: ᴿTLZ 117 (1992) 71-3 (M. *Beumers*).
8930 **Bruckberger** R.-L., Marie Mère de Jésus-Christ. P 1991, Fayard. – ᴿPeCa 254 (1991) 88-91 (Y. *Daoudal*).
8931 *Buckley* Gerald A., Mary, the alternative to feminism: HomP 91,8 (1990s) 11-16.
8932 **Bur** Jacques, Pour comprendre la Vierge Marie dans le mystère du Christ et de l'Église. P 1992, Cerf. 185 p.; ill. – ᴿMarianum 54 (1992) 469s (J. *Stern*).
8933 **Calero** Antonio M., María en el misterio de Cristo y de la Iglesia: EstTeol 1. M 1990, CCS. 433 p. – ᴿMarianum 53 (1991) 275-7 (D. *Fernández*).
8934 **Cantalamessa** Raniero, Maria uno specchio per la Chiesa² 1990 ➤ 6, 8754; 7,8731: ᴿAtKap 118 (1992) 333s (J. *Królikowski* ❷); Lateranum 57 (1991) 620s (G. *Ancona*); Salesianum 54 (1992) 380-2 (S. *Palumbieri*).
8935 **Cantalamessa** Raniero, María espeja de la Iglesia: Lo eterno y el tiempo 6. Valencia 1991, Edipec. 283 p. – ᴿScripTPamp 24 (1992) 1111s (J. L. *Bastero*).
8936 **Carroll** Michael P., Madonnas that maim; popular Catholicism in Italy since the fifteenth century. Baltimore 1992, Johns Hopkins Univ. xii-202 p. $35. 0-8018-4299-9 [TDig 40,56: a sociologist's statistics].
8937 **Clayton** Mary, The cult of the Virgin Mary in Anglo-Saxon England: Studies ASE 2, 1990 ➤ 7,8736: ᴿJAAR 60 (1992) 337s (Lynda L. *Coon*).

8938 **Courth** Franz, Maria, die Mutter des Herrn; Leitfaden für Hörer der Mariologievorlesung. Vallendar 1991, Theol. Hochschule der Pallottiner. iv-131 p. 3-222-11994-5. – [R]Marianum 53 (1991) 667s (L. *Gambero*); TvT 32 (1992) 214 (M. Van *Tente*).

8939 [E]**Courth** Franz, Mariologie: Texte zur Dogmatik 6. Graz 1991, Styria. 272 p. – [R]Marianum 53 (1991) 287-290 (L. *Gambero*); TLZ 117 (1992) 872s (H. *Kirchner*).

8940 **De Fiores** Stefano, María en la teología contemporánea, [T]*Ortiz García* Alfonso, 1991 → 7,8738: [R]ActuBbg 29 (1992) 79 (F. de P. *Solá*): LumenVr 40 (1991s) 410s (F. *Ortiz de Urtaran*); REspir 51 (1992) 186s (G. *Turiño*).

8941 **De Fiores** Stefano, Maria madre di Gesù; sintesi storico salvifica: CTeolSist 6. Bo 1992, Dehoniane. 399 p.; ill. – [R]Marianum 54 (1992) 465-7 (B. *Forte*).

8942 **Donadeo** Maria, Inno acatisto in onore della Madre di Dio: Le voci della preghiera 2. Genova 1991, Marietti. 104 p.; 1 fig. 88-211-6937-5.

8943 [E]**Donnelly** Doris, Mary, woman of Nazareth [ND June 1988; 8 art.] 1989 → 6,523; 7,8739: [R]Marianum 53 (1991) 675-9 (K. *Duffy*).

8944 **Durrwell** François-Xavier, Marie; méditation devant l'Icône. P/Montréal 1990, Médiaspaul/Paulines. 123 p. F 57. – [R]Marianum 53 (1991) 313-5 (G. *Gharib*).

8945 *D'Urso* Giacinto, Gesù e Maria in cielo; occhi negli occhi: SacDoc 35 (1990) 5-39.

8946 *Fahlbusch* E., *Napiórkowski* Stanisław, Mariologie → 757, EvKL 3 (1992) 283-8-294 (274-283, Marienverehrung, *al.*).

8947 [E]**Felici** Sergio, La Mariologia nella catechesi dei Padri 1989 → 5,8711 ... 7,8743: [R]Angelicum 69 (1992) 125s (Nella *Filippi*); Asprenas 39 (1992) 594s (L. *Fatica*); RivStoLR 27 (1991) 376s (F. *Trisoglio*); Salmanticensis 38 (1991) 101s (E. *Llamas*).

8948 **Forderer** Manfred, Königin ohne Tod in den Himmel aufgenommen; das Siegel der göttlichen Offenbarung; Vorw. Bischof Rudolf *Graber*. Stein/Rhein 1988, Christiana. 325 p. DM 18 pa. – [R]TR 88 (1992) 316s (S. C. *Napiórkowski*: Mariologie des Herzens).

8949 **Forte** Bruno, Maria, Mutter und Schwester des Glaubens, [T]*Huber* Mara. Z 1990, Benziger. 291 p. – [R]LebZeug 45 (1990) 233s (F. *Courth*).

8950 **Forte** B., Maria, la donna icona[2] 1989 → 5,8712 ... 7,8743: [R]Carmelus 38 (1992) 213-5 (E. R. *Carroll*); RivPastLtg 28,3 (1990) 81s (E. *Lodi*).

8951 **Galot** Jean, Maria, la donna nell'opera della salvezza. R 1991, Pont. Univ Gregoriana. xvi-440 p. Lit. 39.000 [TR 88,171].

8952 **Galot** J., Vivere con María nella vita consacrata[2] [< VConsacr 1980-6] 1987 → 4,195: [R]Claretianum 31 (1991) 370s (J. *Rovira*).

8953 **Gambero** Luigi, Maria nel pensiero dei Padri della Chiesa: Alma Mater 5, 1991 → 7,8744: [R]ArTGran 55 (1992) 350s (A. *Segovia*); Asprenas 39 (1992) 286 (P. *Pifano*); Marianum 53 (1991) 267s (B. *Amata*).

8953* *Gessel* W. M., Die Jerusalemer Marientradition, archäologisch und literarisch betrachtet: JbEvHL 3 (1991) 51-55.

8954 [E]**Gharib** G. *al.*, Testi mariani del primo millennio, 3. [E]*Gambero* L., Padri ed altri autori latini. 1990 → 7,8748: [R]Asprenas 39 (1992) 592-4 (L. *Fatica*) Marianum 53 (1991) 265s (P. *Langa*); NRT 114 (1992) 430s (V. *Roisel*, 2s).

8955 [E]**Gharib** G., *al.*, Testi mariani IV. Orientali. R 1991, Città Nuova. – [R]StPatav 38 (1991) 414-6 (C. *Corsato*).

8956 **Gössmann** E.v., *Bauer* D. R., Maria — für alle Frauen oder über alle Frauen? 1887/9 ➤ 5,669 ... 7,8752: ᴿLebZeug 45 (1990) 154 (F. *Courth*).

8957 **González** Carlos I., Maria, evangelizada y evangelizadora; Mariología II. TSem 4/2. Bogotá 1988, CELAM. 489 p. – ᴿCarmelus 38 (1991) 227s (E. R. *Carroll*).

8958 *González* Carlos I., Mariologia I. 1988 ➤ 4,9809; 5,8725: ᴿParVi 36 (1991) 75 (Maria *Ko*).

8959 **Gorski** Horst, Die Niedrigkeit seiner Magd; Darstellung und theologische Analyse der Mariologie M. LUTHERS als Beitrag zum gegenwärtigen lutherisch/römisch-katholischen Gespräch [Diss. Hamburg, ᴰ*Pesch* O.]: EurHS 23/... Fra 1987, Lang. 297 p. – ᴿMarianum 54 (1992) 492s (F. *Courth*).

8960 **Grass** Hans [ev.], Traktat über Mariologie: MarbTSt 30. Marburg 1991, Elwert. vii-116 p. DM 28 [TLZ 118, 178, F. *Jacob*).

8961 **Grassi** C., Giuliano GUIZZELMI [1446-1518], Historia della cintola della Vergine Maria. Prato 1990, Soc. Storia Patria. 184 p. [GitFg 45/1, 151, D. *Simoncini*].

8962 **Haile** Getatchew, The Mariology of Emperor ZÄR'A Yá'aqov of Ethiopia; texts and translations: OrChrAnal 242. R 1992, Pont. Inst. Studiorum Orientalium. xii-210 p. 88-7210-292-8.

8963 *Herzig* Anneliese, Maria — hoffnungslos entferntes Ideal oder Schwester im Glauben?: Ordenskorrespondenz 33 (1992) 65-76; > Mary — hopeless ideal or sister in faith?, ᵀᴱ*Asen* B. A.: TDig 39 (1992) 209-213.

8964 *Himes* Mary, What ever happened to Mary? [... disappeared from view since challenged in Vatican II]: NewTR 5,4 (1992) 70-75.

8965 *Hurty* Kathleen S., Mary, LUTHER, and the quest for ecumenical images: Mid-Stream 30 (1991) 60-74.

8966 ᴱ**Hyland** John, Mary in the Church [Athlone July 1984, centenary of Marist Brothers in Ireland] 1989 ➤ 6,629*; ᴿMarianum 54 (1992) 476-8 (W. T. *Brennan*).

8967 **Kniazeff** Alexis, La Mère de Dieu dans l'Église orthodoxe: Théologies 1990 ➤ 6,8781; 7,8761: ᴿEsprVie 102 (1992) 470-2 (B. *Billet*); TR 88 (1992) 50s (W. *Beinert*).

8967* **Kudasiewicz** Józef, ❷ Matka Odkupiciela [of the Redeemer]. Kielce 1991, Jedność. 298 p. – ᴿAtKap 119 (1992) 173-6 (T. *Lewandowski* ❷).

8968 *Langkammer* Hugolin, ❷ Maryja w Nowym Testamencie. Gorzów 1991, Diecez. 204 p. – ᴿRuBi 45 (1992) 47 (J. *Chmiel* ❷).

8969 **La Potterie** I. de, Maria nel mistero dell'alleanza: Dabar 6, 1988 ➤ 4, 9834 ... 6,8784: ᴿParVi 35 (1990) 156s (M. Cecilia *Visentin*); RivLtg 79 (1992) 114-7 (G. *Crocetti*: di grande valore); Vidyajyoti 56 (1992) 679s (J. *Neuner*).

8970 **La Potterie** Ignace de, Mary in the mystery of the Covenant [¹1985 ➤ 6,8782], ᵀ*Buby* Bertrand. NY 1992, Alba. 266 p. [AcPIB 9,779].

8971 **Larrañaga** I., The silence of Mary [1979], ᵀ*Gaudet* V. Boston 1991, St. Paul. 230 p. $13. 0-8198-6911-2 [NTAbs 36, 423].

8972 **Laurentin** René, A short treatise on the Virgin Mary, [ital. 1987 ➤ 5, 8741*a*], ᵀ*Neumann* C. Washington NJ 1991, AMI. xx-391 p. $15. – ᴿHomP 92,6 (1991s) 72s (D. Q. *Liptak*: a masterpiece).

8973 **Laurentin** René, Je vous salue Marie. P 1989, D-Brouwer. 128 p. F 52. – ᴿEsprVie 102 (1992) 465 (B. *Billet*).

8974 *Limouris* Gennadios, La Theotókos ... nella tradizione e fede della Chiesa Ortodossa: StEcum 9 (1991) 277-284; Eng. 284 (341-351, inni).

8975 **López Melús** Francisco M., Coloquios con María. Onda 1992, Amacar. 214 p. ᴿREspir 51 (1992) 365 (F. *Antolín*).

8976 **López Melús** Francisco M., María de Nazareth, la verdadera discípula 1991 ► 7,8766: ᴿActuBbg 29 (1992) 97s (F. *de P. Solá*: reune la erudición con la devoción); Angelicum 69 (1992) 561-3 (J. *Salguero*: hermoso); LumenVr 41 (1992) 407 (F. *Ortiz de Urtaran*); Religión y Cultura 38 (1992) 342 (J. *Teixidor*); REspir 51 (1992) 203s (G. *Turiño*).

8977 *Maccagnan* Valerio, La vocación del cristiano y la vocación de María: ► EfMex 9,2 (1991) 355-369.

8978 **Macquarrie** John, Mary for all Christians 1991 ► 7,8767: ᴿPrPeo 5 (1991) 347 (sr. M. Cecily *Boulding*: of more value than much from Catholic sources); RRel 51 (1992) 469s (B. A. *Buby*); Vidyajyoti 56 (1992) 680s (J. *Neuner*).

8979 *Madigan* Shawn, Do Marian festivals image 'that which the Church hopes to be'?: Worship 65 (1991) 194-207.

8980 **Maeckelberghe** Els, Desperately seeking Mary 1991 ► 7,8768: ᴿLvSt 17 (1992) 414s (Susan K. *Roll*).

8981 *Maeckelberghe* E., Eva en Maria; psychoanalyse en de tweedeling in goed en kwaad: Mara 5,1 (1991) 15-23 [< GerefTTs 91,188].

8982 **Maggi** Alberto M., Nostra Signora degli eretici 1988 ► 5,8746; 6,8791: ᴿMarianum 52 (1990) 408-410 (G. *Barbaglio*).

8983 **Maggi** A., Notre Dame des hérétiques 1990 ► 7,8792: ᴿEsprVie 102 (1992) 467s (B. *Billet*).

8984 **Maillot** Alphonse, Marie ma soeur; la femme dans le NT (et au début du christianisme) 1990 ► 6,8866: ᴿEsprVie 102 (1992) 466s (B. *Billet*: remarques fort judicieuses, mais dans une perspective strictement biblique, rien sur Assomption, Conception, Corédemption); RB 99 (1992) 612s (J. *Taylor*: on women's ministries).

8985 **Manns** Frédéric, Le récit de la Dormition de Marie (Vatican grec 1982), contribution à l'étude des origines de l'exégèse chrétienne: SBF pubbl. 33. J 1989, Franciscan. 255 p.; 15 foldouts, 19 facsimiles. – ᴿJbÖsByz 42 (1992) 423 (G. *Tsigaras*).

8986 *Mauny* Michel de, Essai d'iconologie mariale: PeCa 259 (1992) 42-55.

8987 **Meehan** Bridget M., Exploring the feminine face of Mary; a prayerful journey. KC 1992, Sheed & W. xii-102 p. $9. – ᴿFurrow 43 (1992) 643-5 (S. *O'Riordan*).

8988 *Melvin* Edward J., The [Marian] miraculous medal and Sacred Scripture [1977]: The Priest 47,12 (1991) 44-49.

8989 **Michaud** J.-P., Marie des Évangiles: CahÉv 77. P 1991, Cerf. 66 p. F 25. 0222-9714 [NTAbs 36,266].

8990 **Michaud** Jean-Paul, María de los evangelios: CuadB 77. Estella 1992, VDivino. 74 p.

8991 **Minelli** Stefano M., Mariologia biblica I, 1989 ► 7,8771: ᴿMarianum 53 (1991) 263-5 (M. *Làconi*: riserve; non che cosa intendevano comunicare gli scrittori sacri, ma le maturazioni successive della Chiesa).

8992 **Moioli** Giovanni, † X.1984, Il mistero di Maria, ᴱ*Castenetto* Dora: Contemplatio 2. Mi 1989, Glossa. 143 p. – ᴿMarianum 52 (1990) 448-451 (P. *Sartor*).

8993 **Pazdan** Mary M., Mary, mother of Jesus: ► 741, AnchorBD 4 (1992) 584-6.

8993* *Pek* Kazimierz, ❷ Mariologia jako problem ekumeniczny [sympozjum Lublin 21-23.X]: AtKap 116 (1991) 330-4.

8994 **Pelikan** Jaroslav,   Eternal feminines; three theological allegories in DANTE's Paradiso [Mary, Wisdom, Beatrice]. New Brunswick 1990, Rutgers Univ. 144 p. $14. 0-8135-1602-1; pa. -03-X. – ᴿRExp 89 (1992) 429 (W. L. *Hendricks*).

8995 ᴱ**Peretto** Elio,   Aspetti della presenza di Maria, 7° simp. internaz. R 21-23.VI.1988, R/Bo 1989 ► 5,721:   ᴿCarmelus 38 (1991) 223-5 (F. *Candelori*); Marianum 53 (1991) 303-8 (P. *Sartor*).

8996 **Perry** N., *Echeverría* L.,   Under the heel of Mary 1988 ► 5,8760 ...7,8776:   ᴿChH 60 (1991) 571s (D. G. *Schultenover*; a sneering but useful book).

8997 ᴱ**Petri** H.,   Divergenzen in der Mariologie 1989 ► 5,723; 7,8777:   ᴿCarmelus 38 (1991) 225-7 (E. R. *Carroll*).

8998 **Pinckaers** Servais,   La grâce de Marie; commentaire de l'Ave Maria. P 1990, Médiaspaul. 112 p. F 57. – ᴿEsprVie 102 (1992) 466s (B. *Billet*).

8999 *Quéré* France,   Marie et la femme dans le NT: Foi Temps 22 (1992) 330-341.

9000 *Räisänen* Heikki, [*al.*] Maria/Marienfrömmigkeit NT: ► 768, TRE 22 (1992) 115-9 [–161; 137-143 ev., *Frieling* R.: 143-8 kath., *Courth* F.].

9001 [**Rostagno** S., *al.*] Maria nostra sorella 1988 ► 7,8781:   ᴿMarianum 54 (1992) 493-7 (G. M. *Bruni*).

9002 *Rostagno* Sergio, Marie, modèle du rapport de l'être humain avec Dieu [discours pour son doctorat honoris causa, Montpellier]: ÉTRel 67 (1992) 227-242.

9003 **Salgado** J.-M.,   La maternité spirituelle de la Très Sainte Vierge: St-Tomist 36, 1990 ► 7,8782:   ᴿSalmanticensis 38 (1991) 103-5 (E. *Llamas* también sobre PERETTO y BIFET).

Schleifer Aliah,   Maryam in Islam ᴰ1991 ► b612.

9004 *Singleton* John,   The Virgin Mary and religious conflict in Victorian Britain [B. D. diss. Edinburgh 1989]: JEH 43 (1992) 16-34.

9005 **Stancati** T.,   La situazione della Mariologia in Italia; il I convegno dell'Associazione Mariologica Interdisciplinare [Poggio di Roio AQ, 9-12 ott. 1991]: Angelicum 69 (1992) 257-265.

9006 **Stirnemann** H.,   Marjam 1989 ► 6,8821; 7,8787: ᴿLebZeug 45 (1990) 153s (F. *Courth*).

9006* **Suenens** Léon-Joseph, ❷ Kim ona jest? Synteza mariologii: BtMaryjna 5. Wsz 1988, Marianów. 141 p. – ᴿAtKap 116 (1991) 192-4 (J. *Królikowski* ❷).

9007 **Tavard** George H.,   The forthbringer of God; St. BONAVENTURE on the Virgin Mary. Ch 1989, Franciscan Herald. viii-187 p. $10. – ᴿColcFran 61 (1991) 383s (J. L. *Haas*).

9008 **Trettel** G.,   La Vergine Maria in S. CROMAZIO: Centro StR 21, 1991 ► 7,8788:   ᴿSalesianum 54 (1992) 809s (E. dal *Covolo*).

9009 **Turoldo** David M., *Fabretti* Nazareno, La Bibbia di Maria; miniature del XV-XVI secolo [Modena BT. Estense]. CinB 1991, Paoline]. 310 p. Lit. 48.000. – ᴿBbbOr 34 (1992) 125 (Cristina *Vertua*).

9010 *Wagner* Marion, Maria — Mutter und Mittlerin; die Marienenzyklika Papst JOHANNES PAULS II. und der ökumenische Dialog über Maria: TrierTZ 101 (1992) 172-189.

9011 *Witaszek* G., ❷ Maryja — mesjańska Gebirah: Homo Dei (1991,4) 35-42 [< RuBi 45,50].

9012 ᴱ**Ziegenaus** Anton,   Maria und der Heilige Geist; Beiträge zur pneumatologischen Prägung der Mariologie; 1988: Mariolog. St. 8. Rg 1981, Pustet. 91 p. DM 28 pa. 3-7917-1298-5. – ᴿMarianum 54 (1992) 471-3 (H. *Moll*).

9013 **Zimdars-Swartz** Sandra L., Encountering Mary; from La Salette to Medjugorje 1991 ➤ 7,8795: ᴿRHE 87 (1992) 847s (A. *Vergote*: fort bien informé).

9014 **Zmijewski** Josef, Die Mutter des Messias; Maria in der Christusverkündigung des NTs, eine exegetische Studie. Kevelaer 1989, Butzon & B. 186 p. – ᴿMarianum 53 (1991) 660-2 (O. *da Spinetoli*).

9015 *Zmijewski* Josef, Maria im Neuen Testament: ➤ 742, ANRW 2,26,1 (1992) 596-716.

9016 **Zoccali** V., Maria di Nazaret, la vergine madre: Ist.Sup.Sc.Rel. Reggio Calabria 1990, Jason. 320 p. – ᴱDocCom 44 (1991) 199s (M. *Pangallo*).

H8.8 *Feminae NT* – Women in the NT and later Church.

9017 **Aspegren** Kerstin, The male woman 1990 ➤ 6,8827; 7,8796: ᴿCritRR 5 (1992) 309-311 (Virginia *Burrus*: incomplete); JEH 43 (1992) 335s (Judith *Lieu*); JTS 43 (1992) 231-4 (Verna E. F. *Harrison*); RechSR 80 (1992) 271s (Y.-M. *Duval*: difficile de juger ce livre posthume inachevé).

9018 *Atkinson* Colin & Jo B., Subordinating women; Thomas BENTLEY's use of biblical women in 'The monument of matrones' (1582): ChH 60 (1991) 289-300.

9019 **Atwood** Richard, Mary Magdalene in the NT gospels and early tradition. EurHS 23/457. Fra 1992, Lang. 246 p. DM 56 [TR 88,518].

9020 **Aynard** Laure, La Bible au féminin...: LDiv 138, 1990 ➤ 6,8829; 7,8798: ᴿGregorianum 73 (1992) 155s (J. *Galot*).

Baril Gilberte, The feminine face of the people of God; biblical symbols of the Church as bride and mother 1992 ➤ 7911.

9021 **Baumert** Norbert, *a)* Antifeminismus bei Paulus? Einzelstudien: ForBi 68. Wü 1992, Echter. 484 p. DM 56. 3-429-01450-6. – ᴿArTGran 55 (1992) 321s (A. S. *Muñoz*); – *b)* Frau und Mann bei Paulus 1992 ➤ g36.

9022 *Blasberg Kuhnke* M., Jesus — wie Frauen ihn sehen; Jesusbilder und christologische Aspekte feministischer Theologie: Diakonia 23,1 (1992) 24-32 [< NTAbs 36,370].

9022* *a)* *Brunsch* Wolfgang, Zum Verständnis der Frau in den koptischen Apophthegmata Patrum; – *b)* W*essetzky* Vilnos, Remarks on the character of the Coptic view of history; – *c)* *Naguib* Saphinaz-Amal, 'Fille du Dieu', 'épouse du Dieu'. 'mère du Dieu' ou la métaphore féminine: ➤ 96, ᶠKÁKOSY L. 1992, 85-93 / 615-7 / 437-447.

9023 **Clark** Elizabeth A., Ascetic piety and women's faith; essays in late ancient Christianity [2 inedita + 11]: Studies in Women and Religion 20, 1987 ➤ 3,204 ... 7,8806: ᴿCritRR 5 (1992) 506s (Mary Ann *Donovan*).

9024 *Coakley* John, Gender and the authority of friars; the significance of holy women for thirteenth-century Franciscans and Dominicans: ChH 60 (1991) 445-460.

9025 **Condren** Mary, The serpent and the goddess; women, religion and power in Celtic Ireland 1990 ➤ 7,8807: ᴿStudies 79 (1990) 432-5 (D. *Flanagan*).

9026 *Corley* Kathleen E., A place at the table; Jesus, women and meals in the Synoptic Gospels [only promiscuous and slaves in Greco-Roman background]: diss. Claremont, ᴰMack B., 1992. 251 p. 92-20595. – DissA 53 (1992s) 842-A.

9027 *D'Angelo* Mary Rose, Re-membering Jesus; women, prophecy, and resistance in the memory of the early churches: Horizons 19 (1992) 199-218.

9028 **De Berg** Betty A., Ungodly women; gender and the first wave of American fundamentalism 1990 ➤ 7,8808: ᴿChH 61 (1992) 467s (Nancy A. *Hardesty*); SWJT 34,2 (1991s) 62s (G. *Greenfield*: a warning for our Baptist crisis).

9029 *Demel* Sabine, Jesu Umgang mit Frauen nach dem Lukasevangelium [kath. Diplomarbeit Eichstätt ᴰ*Mayer* B.]: BibNot 57 (1991) 41-95.

9030 **Demers** Patricia, Women as interpreters of the Bible. NY 1992, Paulist. vi-181 p. $13. 0-8091-3291-5 [TDig 39,358; NTAbs 36,411].

9030* **Disselkamp** Gabriele, Christiani senatus lumina; die Religionszugehörigkeit römischer Frauen der Oberschicht im Rom des 4. und 5. Jahrhunderts und ihr Anteil an der Christianisierung der stadtrömischen Senatsaristokratie: kath. Diss. Bochum 1992, ᴰ*Geerlings* W. 414 p. – RTLv 24, p. 551.

9031 *Dunde* Siegfried R., Mann [... kann nicht getrennt von der Frauenfrage diskutiert werden]: ➤ 768, TRE 22 (1992) 51-56.

9032 **Elkins** Sharon K., Holy women of twelfth-century England. Chapel Hill 1988, Univ. NC. xx-244 p. £21.25. – ᴿEngHR 107 (1992) 171 (Henrietta *Leyser*).

9033 *Elliger* Katharina, Sexualität — ihre biblische Begründung, die kirchliche Tradition und Norm und die gelebte Wirklichkeit: RUntHöh 34 (1991) 234-243 [< ᴢɪᴛ 91,684].

9034 *Ettlinger* Gerard H., Church fathers and desert mothers; male and female in the early Church: America 164 (1991) 558-565.

9035 *Fander* Monika, Frauen im Urchristentum am Beispiel Palästinas: ➤ 355, JbBT 7 (1992) 165-185.

9036 *a) Fander* Monika, Frauen in der Nachfolge Jesu; die Rolle der Frau im Markusevangelium; – *b) Moltmann-Wendel* Elisabeth, Wie leibhaft ist das Christentum? Wie leibhaft können wir sein?; – *c) Martin* Gerhard M., Körperbild und Leib Christi: EvT 52,5 (1992) 413-432 / 388-401 / 402-413.

9037 *Field-Bibb* Jacqueline, From deaconess to bishop; the vicissitudes of women's ministry in the Protestant Episcopal Church in the USA: HeythJ 33 (1992) 61-78.

9038 **Furlong** Monica, A dangerous delight — women and power in the Church. L 1991, SPCK. 162 p. £8. 0-281-04551-8. – ᴿExpTim 103 (1991s) 351 (Deborah F. *Sawyer* does not hint what the 'delight' is; the book centres on the ordination of women); Tablet 246 (1992) 74 (P. *Sheldrake*); TLond 95 (1992) 229 (E. *James* also approves ordaining women, but as an issue more complex than she sees).

9039 — *Kirk* Geoffrey [Anglican priest], A furlong too for: Tablet 246 (1992) 36-39 [66s, *Barnes* Donald, rejoinder (favoring women's ministry).

9040 **Garzonio** Marco, Gesù e le donne 1990 ➤ 7,8811; 191 p.; Lit. 29.000: ᴿStCattMi 35 (1991) 278 (P. *Di Sacco*),

9041 **Gentili** Antonio, Si vous ne devenez comme des femmes; symboles religieux du feminin [ital (³1991) ➤ 4,9974]ᵀ, 1991 ➤ 7,8811: ᴿCC 143 (1992,4) 528s (P. *Vanzan*).

9042 *Gerl* Hanna-Barbara, Neues zum Thema 'Frau und Kirche': TGgw 35 (1992) 82-90.

9043 **Gillman** Florence M., Women who knew Paul: Glazier-Zc. ColMn 1992, Liturgical. 95 p. $7. 0-8146-5674-9 [TDig 39,264].

9044 *a) Goldenberg* Naomi (interview), Gender equality and religion; – *b) Thuravackal* Jose, The male-female symbolism in religious literature; – *c) Dupuy* Elaine. The women's movement; a two-hundred year synopsis: JDharma 16 (1991) 156-183 / 115-124 / 125-142.

9045 **Grey** Mary, Feminism, redemption and the Christian tradition [< diss. Louvain] 1990 ➤ 6,8851; 7,8812: ᴿHorizons 19 (1992) 156s (Mary A. *O'Neill*).

9046 **Hoffman** Daniel L., The status of women and Gnosticism in IRENAEUS and TERTULLIAN: diss. Miami Univ. 1992, ᴰ*Yamauchi* E. 325 p. 93-09091. – DissA 53 (1992s) 4042-A. ➤ a807.

9047 **Hourcade** Janine, L'église est-elle misogyne? Une vocation féminine, antique et nouvelle 1990 ➤ 7,8815: – ᴿRTLv 23 (1992) 262s (P. *Weber*).

9048 **Ibarra Benlloch** Martín, Mulier fortis; la mujer en las fuentes cristianas (280-313) [diss. Zaragoza]: MgHistAnt 6 1990 ➤ 7,8816: ᴿOrpheus 13,1 (1992) 193s (Vincenza *Milazzo*); RivStoLR 28 (1992) 695-7 (F. *Trisoglio*).

9049 **Jaubert** Annie, Les femmes dans l'Écriture: Foi Vivante. P 1992, Cerf. 138 p. – ᴿEsprVie 102 (1992) 686-8 (E. *Germain*).

9050 **Kazhdan** A. P., *Talbot* A. M., Women and Iconoclasm: ByZ 84s (1991s) 391-508.

9052 *Kee* Howard C., The changing role of women in the early Christian world: TTod 49 (1992s) 225-238 (239-242, *Burrus* Virginia, response, Blurring the boundaries).

9054 **Keener** Craig S., Paul, women and wives; marriage and women's ministry in the letters of Paul. Peabody MA 1992, Hendrickson. xviii-350 p. 0-943575-96-6.

9056 **Kenneally** James K., The history of American Catholic women. NY 1991, Crossroad. 286 p. $25. – ᴿAmerica 164 (1991) 384s (Alice L. *Laffey*); ChrCent 108 (1991) 568.

9057 **Kvam** Kristen E., LUTHER, Eve, and theological anthropology; reassessing the reformer's response to the Frauenfrage: diss. Emory, ᴰ*Lowe* W. Atlanta 1992. 303 p. 92-24407. – DissA 53 (1992) 1193-A; RTLv 24, p. 574.

9058 **Kwok Pui-Lan**, Chinese women and Christianity 1860-1927 [diss.]. Atlanta 1992, Scholars. 225 p. [TContext 10/1, 101, G. *Evers*].

9059 *Lu Delfa* Rosario, La donna nella Chiesa; la situazione di ieri e la 'questione' di oggi [< S. Cataldo 6-7 XII 1992; Acta atteso]: Ho Theológos 10 (1992) 151-175.

9059* *Leonardi* G., Apostoli al femminile 1991 ➤ 7,8820*: ᴿStPatav 39 (1992) 656 (G. *Segalla*).

9060 **Lindboe** Inger Marie, Women in the NT, a select bibliography 1990 ➤ 6,8864; 7,8821: ᴿCBQ 54 (1992) 577 (Carolyn *Osiek*: 717 entries plus indices).

9061 **MacHaffie** Barbara J., Readings in her story; women in Christian tradition. Mp 1992, Fortress. xvi-238 p. $13 pa. 0-8006-2575-7 [TDig 40,75].

9062 *MacKinnon* Donald M., The *icon Christi* [... as bar to women's ordination] and Eucharistic theology: TLond 95 (1992) 109-113.

9063 ᴱ**Marshall** Sherrin, Women in Reformation and Counter-Reformation Europe; private and public worlds. Bloomington 1989, Indiana Univ. 215 p. $35; pa. 11. – ᴿChH 60 (1991) 548s (Charmasie J. *Blaisdell*: a rich variety of original essays).

9064 **Martimort** Aimé G., Deaconesses; an historical study [1982 ➤ 63,7571], ᵀ*Whitehead* Kenneth D. 1987 ➤ 3,8879; 0-89870-114-7: ᴿHomP 91,2 (1990s) 74-76 (R. M. *Nardone*).

9065 *Mattioli* Umberto, Donne del Vangelo; linee di esegesi: ➤ 405, La donna nel pensiero cristiano antico 1992, 51-78 (365-379).

9066 *a*) *Milne* Pamela J., Feminist interpretations of the Bible, then [Sarah & Angelina GRIMKE; Elizabeth C. STANTON ...] and now; the Bible has frequently been used as a weapon to oppress women; – b) *Trible* Phyllis, If the Bible's so patriarchal, how come I love it?: BR 8,5 (1992) 38-43.52 / 44-47.55; ill.

9067 **Moloney** F., La donna prima tra i credenti 1989 → 7,8829*: ᴿParVi 37 (1992) 159s (I. *Zedde*).

9068 **Mourlon Beernaert** Pierre, Marthe, Marie et les autres; les visages féminins de l'Évangile: Écritures 5. Bru 1992, LVitae. 256 p. Fb 520. – ᴿLVitae 47 (1992) 458s (L. *Partos*).

9068* **Neipp** Bernadette, Marie Madeleine... malentendu 1991 → 7,8831: ᴿProtestantesimo 47 (1992) 140s (B. *Subilia*).

9069 **Pikaza Ibarrondo** Xabier, La mujer en las grandes religiones [< Dignidad de la mujer y fe cristiana, Jornadas de teología, S 1991, Univ.]: Cristianismo y Sociedad. Bilbao 1991, D-Brouwer. 197 p. – ᴿRET 51 (1991) 398-401 (Felisa *Elizondo Aragón*).

9070 *Rapisarda* Grazia, Ancora sull'esegesi biblica di CROMAZIO di Aquileia; le figure femminili: → 458, AnStoEseg 9,2 (1992) 519-535.

9071 *Recio Veganzones* A., Maria Magdalena, protagonista de la escena 'Mulieres ad sepulcrum Domini' en la iconografia sepulcral de Occidente (siglos IV-V): → 164, ᶠSAXER V., Memoriam 1992, 667-688; 19 fig.

9072 **Richter-Reimer** Ivoni, Frauen in der Apostelgeschichte des Lukas; eine feministisch-theologische Exegese [Diss. Kassel]. Gü 1992, Mohn. 272 p. DM 98 [TR 88,517].

9073 **Salisbury** Joyce E., Church Fathers, independent virgins 1991 → 7,8839: ᴿAmHR 97 (1992) 1498s (J. H. *Lynch*); CathHR 78 (1992) 434s (G. H. *Ettlinger*); ClasW 86 (1992s) (Mary Ann *Rossi*).

9074 *Schaberg* Jane, How Mary Magdalene became a whore: BR 8,5 (1992) 30-37.51s; ill.

9075 **Schüssler Fiorenza** Elisabeth, In memoria di Lei 1990 → 6,8888; 7,8840: ᴿRivB 40 (1992) 319-326 (Cettina *Militello*).

9076 **Sebastiani** Lilia, Tra/Sfigurazione; il personaggio evangelico di Maria di Magdala e il mito della peccatrice redenta nella tradizione occidentale: Nuovi Saggi 58. Brescia 1992, Queriniana. 301 p. Lᵐ 28. 88-399-0958-3.

9077 *Serra* Aristide, La 'Mulieris dignitatem', consensi e dissensi [< Marianum 53 (1991) 144-182]: → 309, Nato da donna 1992, 267-308.

9078 **Shephard** Amanda, Gender and authority in sixteenth-century England; the debate about John KNOX's 'First blast of the trumpet against the monstrous regiment of women': diss. Lancaster UK. 1990. 450 p. BRDX-98243. – DissA 53 (1992s) 4108-A.

9079 *Sturrock* June, BLAKE and the women of the Bible: LitTOx 6,1 (1992) 23-32 [< ZIT 92,363].

9080 *Tanasar* Constance J., Women in the mission of the Church — theological and historical perspectives: IntRMiss 81 ('Women in Mission' 1992) 189-200 (–318, *al.*).

9081 **Thompson** John L., John CALVIN and the daughters of Sarah; women in regular and exceptional roles in the exegesis of Calvin, his predecessors, and his contemporaries [diss. Durham]: TravHumRen 259. Geneva 1992, Droz. xiii-308 p. Fs 65 [TR 88,431].

9081* **Thurston** Bonnie B., The widows 1989 → 6,8894; 7,8845: ᴿCurrTMiss 19 (1992) 56 (A. *Weisner*).

9082 **Tucker** Ruth A., Guardians of the great commission; the story of women in modern missions. GR 1988, Zondervan. 278 p. $15 pa. – ᴿWestTJ 53 (1991) 176s (M. *Ortiz*).

9082* **Valerio** Adriana, Cristianesimo al femminile 1990 ➤ 7,8847: ᴿProtestantesimo 47 (1992) 169s (Letizia *Tomassone*); RasT 33 (1992) 223-230 (Cloe *Taddei Ferretti*); RivStoLR 28 (1992) 429s (R. *Lizzi*).

9083 *Willen* Diane, Godly women in early modern England; Puritanism and gender: JEH 43 (1992) 561-580.

9084 **Witherington** Benᴵᴵᴵ, Women and the genesis of Christianity 1990 ➤ 6,8897; 7,8851: ᴿChrCent 108 (1991) 339s (Patricia *Wilson-Kastner*; CritRR 5 (1992) 259-261 (Deirdre *Good*: closes discussions which he should open).

9085 **Witherington** Benᴵᴵᴵ, Women in the earliest churches: SNTS Mg 59, 1988 ➤ 6,8898; 7,8852: ᴿMnemosyne 45 (1992) 279-281 (L. de *Blois* & E. A. *Hemelrijk*).

H8.9 *Theologia feminae* – **Feminist theology.**

9086 *Alexandre* Dolores, Mujeres en la hora undécima: Fe y Sec 10, 1990 ➤ 7,8854: ᴿMiscCom 49 (1991) 306 (ipsa).

9087 ᴱ**Bekkenkamp** J., *al.*, Proeven van [Nederland] vrouwenstudies theologie: IIMO 32. Leiden 1991, IIMO. 309 p. ƒ39,50. 90-6495-245-0. – ᴿTvT 32 (1992) 424 (Hedwig *Meyer-Wilmes*).

9088 **Bennett** Anne M. [1903-86], From woman-pain to woman-vision, ᴱ*Hunt* Mary E. 1989 ➤ 6,8905; 7,8858: ᴿCritRR 5 (1992) 504-6 (June *O'Connor*).

9089 ᴱ**Berger** Teresa, *Gerhards* Albert, Liturgie und Frauenfrage; ein Beitrag zur Frauenforschung aus liturgiewissenschaftlicher Sicht: Pietas liturgica 7, 1990 ➤ 7,340a: – ᴿRSPT 76 (1992) 167-170 (P.-M. *Gy*, tit.pp.; comments); TLZ 117 (1992) 150-2 (C. *Grethlein*).

9089* **Bingemer** Maria Clara L., O segredo feminino do mistério (ensaios de teologia na ótica da mulher). Petrópolis 1991, Vozes. 180 p. – ᴿREB 52 (1992) 1002s (Tereza *Cavalcanti*).

9090 *Blasberg-Kuhnke* Martina, Jesus — wie Frauen ihn sehen; Jesusbilder und christologische Aspekte feministischer Theologie: Diakonia 23,1 (W/ Mainz 1992) 24-32; > Jesus as women see him, ᵀᴱ*Asen* B. A.: TDig 39 (1992) 205-8.

9091 *Børresen* Kari E., The ordination of women; to nurture tradition by continuing inculturation: ST 46 (1992) 3-13.

9092 *Brauner* Gerburg / *Eisenbeiser-Engelbrecht* Iris, Zulassung der Frau zum Priesteramt — warum nicht?: RUntHöh 244-253 [< ᴢɪᴛ 91,684].

9093 **Brock** Rita N., Journeys by heart 1988 ➤ 5,8860: ᴿJAAR 60 (1992) 328-331 (Mary Z. *Strange*).

9094 ᴱ**Brotherton** Anne, The voice of the turtledove; new Catholic women in Europe. NY 1992, Paulist. x-217 p. $13 pa. 0-8091-3307-5 [TDig 40,191].

9095 **Buitink-Heijblom** M. A., Feminisme, een bijbels-kritische benadering. Kampen 1992, Kok. 136 p. Fb 530. – ᴿCollatVᴸ 22 (1992) 439 (Veerle *D-raulans*).

9096 *a) Cady* Linell E., Theories of religion in feminist theologies; – *b) Lindsey* William D., The social gospel and feminism: American Journal of Theology and Philosophy 13,3 (Sept. 1992) 183-193 / 195-210.

9097 **Cameron** Deborah, Feminism and linguistic theory² [¹1985]. L 1992, Macmillan. x-247 p. 0-333-55888-X; pa. -9-8.

9098 **Carson** Anne, Goddesses and wise women; the literature of feminist spirituality, 1980-1992; an annotated bibliography. Freedom ᴄᴀ 1992,

Crossing. 247 p. $40. 0-89594-536-3 [TDig 40,56: continuation of her 1986 bibliography 1833-1985].

9099 **Chinnici** R., Can women re-image the Church? NY 1992, Paulist. 110 p. $7 [TS 53,602].

9100 **Chopp** Rebecca, The power to speak; feminism, language, God 1989 ➤ 5,8866 ... 7,8863: ᴿHorizons 19 (1992) 153s (Morny *Joy*); JAAR 60 (1992) 150-3 (Martha J. *Reineke*).

9101 **Chung Hyun Kyung**, Struggle to be the sun again; introducing Asian women's theology [ᴰ1989 ➤ 5,8867 (Chung Kyun)]. Mkn 1990, Orbis. xiii-146 p. $15. – ᴿGregorianum 73 (1992) 356s (J. T. *Bretzke*; provocative, like her prayer at Canberra 1991); LvSt 17 (1992) 415s (A. *Daniel*).

9102 **Clanton** J. A., In whose image? God and gender. L 1991, SCM. vii-135 p. £7. 0-334-02080-8. – ᴿTvT 32 (1992) 325s (M. de *Haardt*).

9103 **Crysdale** Cynthia S. W., LONERGAN and feminism: TS 53 (1992) 234-256.

9104 **Cunneen** Sally, Mother Church; what the experience of women is teaching her. NY 1991, Paulist. iii-222 p. $12 pa. – ᴿHorizons 19 (1992) 329s (Mary H. *Snyder*).

9104* *Delmas* Clement, Il y a cent ans ... L'éveil du féminisme, une interpellation à l'Église: BLitEc 93 (1992) 307-328.

9105 *Dewey* Joanna, Feminist readings, Gospel narrative and critical theory: BibTB [18 (1988) 130-6, missing in W. KELBER's 'Five Ways'] 22 (1992) 167-173.

9106 ᴱ**Dornbusch** Sanford M., *Strober* Myra H., Feminism, children, and the new families. NY 1988, Guilford. 366 p. $19. 0-89862-514-9. – ᴿRExp 89 (1992) 433 (Diana S. R. *Garland*).

9107 **Dumas** Monique, Les droits des femmes. Montréal/P 1992, Paulinas/Médiaspaul. 132 p. – ᴿEsprVie 102 (1992) 510s (E. *Germain*).

9108 **Edwards** Ruth B., The case for women's ministry 1989 ➤ 6,8943; 7,8871: ᴿScotJT 45 (1992) 270-2 (Denise *Newton*).

9109 **Fabella** V., *Park Sun Ai* Lee, We dare to dream 1990 ➤ 6,406: ᴿHorizons 18 (1991) 338s (Letty M. *Russell*); Pacifica 4 (1991) 100-2 (Maryanne *Confoy*).

9110 **Field-Bibb** Jacqueline, Women towards priesthood; ministerial politics and feminist praxis 1991 ➤ 7,8874: ᴿAmerica 167 (1992) 19 (Nancy C. *Ring*); ExpTim 102,11 2d-top choice (1990s) 322s (C. S. *Rodd*); LvSt 17 (1992) 68s (R. F. *Collins*); TvT 32 (1992) 330 (C. *Halkes*).

9111 **Finson** Shelley D., Women and religion; a bibliographic guide to Christian feminist liberation theology. Toronto 1991, Univ. xix-207 p. $70. 0-8020-5881-7 [TDig 39,162].

9112 **Fortune-Wood** Janet, The relationship between Christology and the position of women in the Church of England from a feminist theological perspective: diss. Exeter 1991. 467 p. BRDX-95845. — DissA 53 (1992s) 533-A.

9113 **Frantz** Nadine P., Theological hermeneutics; Christian feminist biblical interpretation and the Believers' Church tradition: diss. Chicago 1992. – RTLv 24, p. 557.

9114 **Frymer-Kensky** Tikva, In the wake of the goddesses; women, culture, and the biblical transformation of pagan myth. NY 1991, Free Press. 250 p. $25. 0-02-910800-4. – ᴿChrCent 109 (1992) 556s (J. *Pulling*).

9115 ᴱ**Fuchs** Gotthard, Männer; auf der Suche nach einer neuen Identität. Dü 1988, Patmos. 164 p. – ᴿZkT 114 (1992) 336-340 (Herlinde *Pissarek-Hudelist*).

9116 *Fulkerson* M. M., Contesting feminist canons; discourse and the problem of sexist texts: JFemStR 7,2 (Atlanta 1991) 53-73 [< NTAbs 36,151].

9117 *a) Geense-van Ravenstein* A., Zoals God nieuw maakt; een gesprek met Mercy ODUYOYE; – *b) Wilde* J. de, Zoeken naar nieuwe vormen; Doreen HAZEL over zwarte feministische theologie in Nederland; – *c) Horst* P. W. van der, Sara's zaad: Mara 3,3 (1990) 33-39 / 25-32 / 44-52 [< GerefTTs 91,63].

9117* *a) Genest* Olivette, Le NT répond-il à la question du ministère des femmes?; – *b) McPherson* Janet, Une décennie œcumenique; les Églises solidaires des femmes, ᵀ*Bonnette* Élise: Œcuménisme 26,103 (Montréal 1991) 26-29 / 30s.

9118 **Globig** Christine, Frauenordination im Kontext lutherischer Ekklesiologie: Diss. ᴰ*Woelfel* E. Kiel 1992. 215 p. – RTLv 24, p. 569.

9119 ᴱ**Gössmann** E., *al.*, Wörterbuch der feministischen Theologie 1991 ➤ 7,8882: ᴿEvKomm 25 (1992) 367 (Irma *Driesen*); HerdKor 46 (1992) 534 (K. *Nientiedt*); TGL 82 (1992) 375-7 (G. *Fuchs*): TvT 32 (1992) 324 (C. *Halkes*).

9120 **Goldenberg** Naomi R., Returning words to flesh; feminism, psychoanalysis, and the resurrection of the body 1990 ➤ 6,8955: ᴿCritRR 5 (1992) 429-431 (Diane *Jonte-Pace*).

9121 **Grabowski** John S., Theological anthropology and gender since Vatican II; a critical appraisal of recent trends in Catholic theology: diss. Marquette, ᴰ*Keefe* D. Milwaukee 1991. 413 p. 92-26318. – DissA 53 (1992s) 1191s-A.

9122 *Grant* Jacqueline, White women's Christ and black women's Jesus 1989 ➤ 7,3722: ᴿJRel 72 (1992) 284s (Toinette *Eugene*).

9122* — *Green* Elizabeth E., Liberazione, ermeneutica, storia; un'introduzione alla teologia femminista di Elisabeth SCHÜSSLER FIORENZA: Protestantesimo 47 (1992) 289-300.

9123 *Grey* Mary, Feministische Theologie als uitdaging voor de europese cultuur on de christelijke traditie, ᵀ*Schepers* Lieve: CollatVl 22 (1992) 279-293 [227-278, *Ungerer* Werner, al., Europese identiteit].

9124 **Halkes** Catharina, New creation; Christian feminism and the renewal of the earth, ᵀ*Romaniuk* Catherine. L 1991, SPCK. 177 p. £11. 0-281-04539-9. – ᴿExpTim 103 (1991s) 286 (Daphne *Hampson* didn't know what to make of it; it falls apart into too many topics).

9125 **Hampson** Daphne, Theology and feminism 1990 ➤ 6,8960; 7,8884: ᴿAnglTR 74 (1992) 118-120 (Patricia *Wilson-Kastner*); EcuR 44 (1992) 157s (Janet *Crawford*).

9126 *Hartnagel* Timothy F., Feminism and religious behavior; GREELEY [A. & DURKIN M.] revisited in Western Canada: RRelRes 33 (1991) 153-168 [< ZIT 92,20].

9127 *Herzog* Kristin, Die Frauenbewegung in Peru und die Theologie der 'Ersten Welt': EvT 52 (1992) 433-451.

9127* *Hill* Christopher, The ordination of women in the context of Anglican/Roman Catholic dialogue: Month 253 (1992) 6-11.

9128 *a) Hill* Christopher, ℗ L'ordination des femmes à la lumière du dialogue anglicano-catholique, ᵀ*Okuljar* Ewa; – *b) Humeński* Julian, ℗ La place de la femme dans l'Eglise orthodoxe: PrzPow 855 (1992) 267-284 / 285-291.

9128* ᴱ**Holloway** Richard, Who needs feminism? Men respond to sexism in the Church 1991 ➤ 7,359a: ᴿTLond 95 (1992) 152s (Jane *Williams*: it seems to answer 'men do'; but women do more).

9129 *Hunga* T. M., Women liberation in and through the Bible; the debate and the quest for a new feminist hermeneutics: African Christian Studies 6,4 (Nairobi 1990) 33-49 (< NTAbs 36,152].

9130 **Hunt** Mary E., Fierce tenderness; a feminist theology of friendship. NY 1991, Crossroad. xii-204 p. $23; pa. $12. - ᴿChrCent 108 (1991) 659s (B. A. *De Berg*); ChrCris 51 (1991s) 202-4 (Kathleen *Sanda*); CritRR 5 (1992) 509-511 (Sharon H. *Ringe*: begins 'Everyone has friends, but by reading contemporary theology one would never know it').

9131 *Jong* Saskia de, De bijbel; nummer één of gepasseerd station? Bijdrage van de exegese in feministisch perspektief: PrakT 19,2 (Zwolle 1992) 185-192 [< ZIT 92,404].

9132 **Joseph** Alison, Through the devil's gateway; women, religion and taboo 1990 ➤ 7,8896: ᴿScotJT 45 (1992) 274s (Susan F. *Parsons*).

9132* ᴱ**Jost** R., *Kubera* U., Befreiung hat viele Farben [➤ 7,359*]: feministische Theologie als kontextuelle Befreiungstheologie: Tb 534. Gü 1991, Mohn. 175 p. DM 24,80. 3-579-00534-X. - ᴿTvT 32 (1992) 329 (Els *Maeckelberghe*).

9133 *Kaminski* Phyllis H., 'Reproducing the world'; Mary O'BRIEN's theory of reproductive consciousness and repercussions for feminist incarnational theology: Horizons 19 (1992) 240-262.

9134 **Kassian** M., The feminist Gospel. Wheaton IL 1992, Crossway. 287 p. $12 [TS 53,602; TDig 39,367].

9135 *Kaye* E., A turning-point in the ministry of women; the ordination of the first woman to the Christian ministry in England in September 1917: ➤ Women in the Church 1989/90, 505-512.

9136 **Keller** Catherine, Der Ich-Wahn; Abkehr von einem lebensfeindlichen Ideal, ᵀ*Wisselinck* Erika. Stu 1989 [= Gü 1993, Mohn, unter dem Titel 'Penelope verlässt Odysseus; auf dem Weg zu neuen Selbsterfahrungen']. - ᴿEvT 52 (1992) 451-4 (Hildegund *Keul*: 'ein Buch über Sexismus, Separatismus und das neue Selbst der Frauen').

9137 **Klotz** V., 'Mit dir, statt gegen dich'; ein feministisch-theologischer Beitrag zur relationalen Selbstvergewisserung der Frauen in einer androcentrischen Kultur: EurHS 23/392. Fra 1990, Lang. 513 p. Fs 103. 3-631-42850-2. - ᴿTvT 32 (1992) 324s (Hedwig *Meyer-Wilmes*).

9138 **Korte** A., Een passie voor transcendentie; feminisme, theologie en moderniteit in het denken van Mary DALY: diss. ᴰ*Houtepen* A. Nijmegen 1992. xviii-424 p. - TvT 32 (1992) 304; RTLv 24, p. 540.

Lacocque André, Subversives, ou Un Pentateuque de femmes, ᵀ*Veugelen* Claude: LDiv 148, 1992 ➤ 1989.

9138* *La Cugna* Catherine M., Catholic women as ministers and theologians: America 167 (1992) 238-248.

9139 **Lee-Linke Sung Hee**, Frauen gegen Konfuzius; Perspektiven einer asiatisch-feministichen Theologie: Siebenstern 530. Gü 1991. 224 p. [TContext 10/2,99, G. *Evers*].

9140 *Lee-Pollard* Dorothy A., Feminism and spirituality; the role of the Bible in women's spirituality: Way 32 (1992) 23-32.

9141 **Loades** Ann, Feminist theology, a reader 1990 ➤ 7,8898: ᴿHorizons 19 (1992) 153s (Mary Anne *Mayeski*); Interpretation 46 (1992) 214.216 (Lisa S. *Cahill*).

9142 *McFague* Sallie, An earthly theological agenda [HMC]: ChrCent 108 (1991) 12-15.

9143 ᴱ**McInerny** Ralph, The Catholic woman [8 lectures by women]. Harrison NY 1991, Ignatius. 131 p. $12. - ᴿHomP 92,9 (1991s) 77s (L. *Kennedy*).

9144 *Maillard* Christine, Le divin et la féminité; à propos de la sophiologie de Carl G. JUNG: RHPR 72 (1992) 427-437 (–444, annexe, L'exclusion des femmes de l'ordination; un point de vue psychologique); Eng. 521.

9145 *Mankowski* Paul, Womanhood; its champions, its enemies: HomP 92,2 (1991s) 12-21.

9146 *Martin* Francis, Feminist hermeneutics; an overview: ComND 18 (1991) 144-163.398-424.

9147 *Martineau* Suzanne, Ministères féminins dans la communion anglicane: EsprVie 102 (1992) couv. 331-3.

9148 **Mayeski** Marie Anne, Women, models of liberation. L 1991, Collins. 234 p. £6 pa. – R Furrow 43 (1992) 116-9 (Mary *Condren*).

9149 **Meyer-Wilmes** Hedwig, Rebellion auf der Grenze; Ortsbestimmung feministischer Theologie 1989 ➤ 6,8987; 7,8902: R TR 88 (1992) 310-2 (Eva *Schmetterer*, Ursula *Waldingsbrett*).

9150 **Miles** Margaret M., Carnal knowing 1989 ➤ 7,8989: R AnglTR 73 (1991) 345-7 (Flora A. *Keshgegian*); JAAR 60 (1992) 171-3 (Diane *Apostolos-Cappadona*).

9151 **Militello** Cettina, Donna in questione; un itinerario ecclesiale di ricerca: TSaggi. Assisi 1992, Cittadella. 303 p. Lit. 25.000 [NRT 115, 584, L. *Volpe*].

9152 *Milligan* Mary, The Bible as formative in a basic Christian community of Brazil: Studies in Formative Spirituality 13 (1992) 145-000.

9153 E Moll Helmut, The Church and women 1988 ➤ 5,492; 7,368.8991: R HomP 92,1 (1991s) 73s (J. R. *Sheets*: the discussion has reached a standstill).

9154 E **Moltmann-Wendel** Elisabeth, *Kegel* Günter, Feministische Theologie im Kreuzfeuer; der Streit um das 'Tübingen Gutachten'; Dokumente-Analysen-Kritiken: Siebenstern 536. Gü 1992, Mohn. 208 p. DM 24,80. 3-579-00536-7 [TLZ 118, 161, U. *Gerber*].

9155 *Moltmann-Wendel* Elisabeth, [Women's] Self-love and self-acceptance: Pacifica 5 (1992) 288-300.

9156 *a) Nanchen* Gabrielle, Genre, feminin; espèce, humaine; – *b) Louis* Éric, Différences, indentités, destins; regards d'hommes; – *c) Graessle* Isabelle, Homme et femme il les créa: BCentProt 43,5s (1991) 3-8 / 9-24 / 25-44.

9157 **Neuberger** Julia, Whatever's happening to women? promises, practices and pay-offs. L c.1991, Kyle Cathie. £10. – R Tablet 246 (1992) 203 (Rachel *Billington*: sense of woman as wife and mother).

9158 **Neuer** Werner, Man and woman in Christian perspective, T *Wenham* Gordon J. Wheaton IL 1991, Crossway. 199 p. $10 pa. 0-89107-606-9. – R RExp 89 (1992) 579s (Molly T. *Marshall*, also on PIPER/GRUDEM: emphasis on what is 'natural' without attention to the new voices).

E **Newsom** Carol A., *Ringe* Sharon H. The women's Bible commentary 1992 ➤ 1945 supra.

9160 *O'Neill* Maura, Women speaking, women listening; women in interreligious dialogue 1990 ➤ 6,8997; 7,8905; $15. 0-88344-697-9. – R ExpTim 103 (1991s) 61s (G. *D'Costa*, also on SWIDLER L. 1990); Horizons 19 (1992) 174s (Jane *Stier*); RExp 89 (1992) 121s (Molly T. *Marshall*).

9161 *a) Persons* Susan, Feminist reflections on embodiment and sexuality; – *b) Cotter* Jim, Same-sex relationships [response *Atkinson* David]: Studies in Christian Ethics 4,2 (E 1991) 16-28 / 29-37 [–41; < ZIT 91,674].

9162 E **Piper** J., *Grudem* W., Recovering biblical manhood and womanhood 1991 ➤ 7,375: R BibTB 22 (1992) 143s (T. R. *Hobbs*: erudite but with some weaknesses, and 19 of the 22 authors are male).

9163 ᴱPomeroy Sarah B., Women's history and ancient history [12 art.] 1991
→ 7,405; $40: pa. $14; 0-8078-1949-2; –4310-5. – ᴿClasW 85 (1991s) 726s
(Kathryn *Gutzwiller*); GreeceR 39 (1992) 247 (P. *Walcot*: women deserve
better).

9163* *Redmond* Walter, Eine Logik der religiösen Hoffnung: TGʟ 82 (1992)
414-438.

9164 **Redmont** Jane, Generous lives; American Catholic women today. NY
1992, Marrow. 381 p. $23. 0-688-06707-7 [TDig 40,183].

9165 ᴱRosenblatt Marie-Eloise, Where can we find her? Searching for
women's identity in the new Church [conversations about weaknesses in
bishops' first draft] 1991 → 7,377c: ᴿNewTR 5,1 (1992) 109s (Mary E.
Hines).

9165* *a*) *Rosenblatt* Eloise-Marie, A new look at Scripture through women's
eyes; – *b*) *Hilliard* Maureen, Following the path to feminist spirituality; –
c) *Chinnici* Rosemary, Angry, yet faithful; how women cope with their
non-responsive church: CathW 234 (1991) 248-253 / 270-274 / 244-7.

9166 **Scanzoni** Letha D., *Hardesty* Nancy A., All we're meant to be; biblical
feminism for today³ʳᵉᵛ [¹1974 'A biblical approach to women's liberation']. GR 1992, Eerdmans. xiv-426 p. 0-8028-0654-6.

9167 ᴰScherzberg Lucia, Sünde und Gnade in der feministischen Theologie
ᴰ1991 → 7,8992: ᴿETRel 67 (1992) 610s (Arina van de *Kerk*); TvT 32
(1992) 428 (Els *Maeckelberghe*).

9168 *Scherzberg* Lucia, 'Schuld' und 'Sünde' in der feministischen Theologie: UnSa 46 (1991) 208-213; Eng. 'Guilt' and 'sin' in feminist theology,
ᵀᴱ*Asen* B. A.: TDig 39 (1992) 201-4.

9169 ᴱSchmitt-Pantel Pauline, A history of women from ancient goddesses
to Christian saints. CM c. 1992, Harvard. 572 p. $30. – ᴿChrCent 109
(1992) 752 (Edna H. *Hong*).

9170 **Schneider-Böcklen** Elisabeth, *Vorländer* Dorothea, Feminismus und
Glaube. Mainz/Stu 1991, Grünewald/Quell. 148 p. 3-7867-1579-3 [TLZ
118, 161, Gerlinde *Strohmaier-Wiederanders*].

9171 **Schneiders** Sandra, Beyond patching 1991 → 7,8923: ᴿPacifica 5 (1992)
539-541 (Christine B. *Burke*).

9172 **Schüssler Fiorenza** Elisabeth, Bread not stone 1984 → 1,8622; now E
1990, Clark → 7,8925. – ᴿBL (1992) 111 (G. I. *Emmerson*); Furrow 42
(1991) 602 (Linda *Hogan*: since 1984 it has reigned supreme); HeythJ 33
(1992) 205s (Mary *Grey*: British edition of 1984 'classic': the past reality
discloses itself only from the committed questions we put to it).

9173 **Schüssler Fiorenza** Elisabeth, But she said; feminist practices of biblical
interpretation. Boston 1992, Beacon. x-262 p. $24. 0-8070-1214-9 [TDig
40,86].

9174 *Schussler-Fiorenza* Elisabeth, Feminist hermeneutics: → 741, AnchorBD
2 (1992) 783-791.

9176 ᴱSilva Sergio (SELADOC), La mujer. S 1990, Sígueme. 362 p, 84-301-
1119-0. – ᴿGregorianum 73 (1992) 355s (J. *Villegas*).

9176* *a*) *Smith* Karen E., The role of women in Baptist missions; – *b*) *Watts*
John D. W., Baptists and the transformation of culture; – *c*) *Lorensen*
Thorwald, Baptists and the challenge of religious pluralism; – *d*) *Lotz*
Denton, Baptists facing the third millennium: RExp 89 (1992) 35-48 /
11-21 / 49-69 / 71-82.

9177 *a*) *Soskice* Janet M., Women's problems; – *b*) *Murphy-O'Connor* Jerome,
St. Paul promoter of the ministry of women: PrPeo 6 (1992) 301-6 /
307-311 [–340, *al.*].

9177* **Soskice** Janet M., After Eve; women, theology, and the Christian tradition. L 1990, Marshall Pickering. 178 p. £6. 0-551-02039-3. 10 art. – ᴿExpTim 103 (1991s) 63 [C. S. *Rodd*].

9178 **Steinem** Gloria, Revolution from within, a book of self-esteem. ... c. 1991, Blooomsbury. £18. – ᴿTablet 246 (1992) 203 (Rachel *Billington*: women are tired of fighting for so little gain).

9178* ᴱ**Strahm** Doris, *Strobel* Regula, Vom Verlangen nach Heilwerden; Christologie in feministisch-theologischer Sicht. Fr 1991, Exodus. 240 p. Fs 30. – ᴿOrientierung 56 (1992) 130-3 (D. *Sölle*); TGL 82 (1992) 377s (W. *Beinert*).

9179 **Tamez** Elsa interviews 15 male Liberation Theologians, Against machismo, ᴱ*Eagleson* John. Oak Park ɪʟ 1987, Meyer Stone. 148 p. – ᴿIntRMiss 81 (1992) 497-482 (Priscilla *Pope-Levison*: less relevant than FABELLA).

9180 *Taves* Ann, Women and gender in American religion(s) [TUCKER C. 1990; BRAUDE A. 1989, *al.*]: RelStR 18 (1992) 263-270.

9181 **Thistlethwaite** Susan B., Sex, race, and God 1990 → 6,9020; 7,8931: also L, Chapman; 0-225-66612-X: ᴿExpTim 102 (1990s) 379 (Ann *Loades*); RExp 89 (1992) 117s (Molly T. *Marshall*); ScotJT 45 (1992) 273s (Susan F. *Parsons*).

9182 **Toon** Peter, Let women be women [... and not priests]. ... 1990, Gracewing. 121 p. £4. 0-85244-191-6. – ᴿExpTim 103 (1991s) 26 (Ruth B. *Edwards*: sincere but unfair; cites by name supporters but not opponents).

9183 **Tucker** E. A., Women in the maze; [30] questions and answers on biblical equality. DG 1992, InterVarsity. 276 p. $10 pa. 0-8308-1307-1 [NTAbs 36,439].

9184 *Untener* Kenneth, Forum, the ordination of women; can the horizons widen? Worship 65 (1991) 50-59 (451-461, *Sheets* J. R.); Responses, 256-262, 263-8, *Meyer* Charles R., *Butler* Sarai [482-508, *Legrand* H., < ᶠ*Gy*].

9186 **Van Wijk-Bos** Johanna W. H., Reformed and feminist; a challenge to the Church. Louisville 1990, W-Knox. 132 p. $11 pa. 0-664-25194-3. – ᴿTTod 49 (1992s) 142s (D. L. *Migliore*).

9187 *Viladesau* R., Could Jesus have ordained women? Reflections on Mulieris dignitatem: Thought 67,264 (1992) 5-20 [< NTAbs 36,381].

9188 **Wagner-Rau** Ulrike, Zwischen Vaterwelt und Feminismus; eine Studie zur pastoralen Identität von Frauen [Diss. Kiel]. Gü 1992, Mohn. 222 p. DM 68 [TR 88,534].

9189 *Walker* David, Are opponents of women priests sexists?: Churchman 105 (1991) 326-331 [< ᴢɪᴛ 92,71].

9190 **Wallace** Ruth A., They call her pastor; a new role for Catholic women: Religion, culture, and society. Albany 1992, SUNY. x-204 p. $49.50; pa. $17. 0-7914-0926-0 [TDig 40,192: 20 U.S. Catholic parishes administered by women (of whom 11 are nuns)].

9191 *Watson-Franke* Maria-Barbara, Masculinity and the 'Matrilineal Puzzle': Anthropos 87 (1992) 475-488.

9192 **Welch** Sharon D., A feminist ethic of risk 1989 → 6,9028: ᴿJAAR 60 (1992) 821-5 (Christine F. *Hinze*).

9193 **White** Erin, *Tulip* Marie, Knowing otherwise; feminism, women, and religion. Melbourne 1991, Lovell. xvii-179 p. – ᴿPacifica 5 (1992) 120s (Margaret *Heagney*).

9194 **Winter** Miriam T., *a*) WomanWord; a feminist lectionary and psalter; – *b*) Women of the NT. NY 1990, Crossroad. $17; 0-8245-1054-2; – *c*) WomanWisdom, a feminist lectionary and psalter; Women of the Hebrew Scriptures. NY 1991s, Crossroad. xv-367 p.; xii-372 p. $17 each, pa. 0-8245-1100-X; –41-7 [TDig 39,193].

9194* *a*) *Wootton* Janet, The priesthood of all believers — is this what you want?; – *b*) *Fageol* Suzanne, Women in the Church; claiming our authority; – *c*) *Thomas* Ronwyn G., Authority in the Church; fraudulent fabrication, larceny from the laity; – *d*) *Pinsent* Pat, Christian feminism in the seventeenth century; – *e*) *Davies* David P., Women priests — the theological imperative: Feminist Theology 1,1 (Sheffield 1992) 74-79 / 10-26 / 27-57 / 58-73 / 89-93 [< ZIT 93,136].

9195 **Young** Pamela D., Feminist theology / Christian theology; in search of method. Mp 1990, Fortress. 132 p. 0-8006-2402-5. – ᴿExpTim 103 (1991s) 287 [C. S. *Rodd*].

9196 **Zappone** Katherine, The hope for wholeness — a spirituality for feminists. Mystic CT 1991, Twenty-Third. 195 p. £10. 0-89622-495-3. – ᴿExpTim 103 (1991s) 351 (Deborah F. *Sawyer*: owes much to Christianity, goes far beyond it).

H9 **Eschatologia NT,** *spes, hope.*

9196* *Agourides* Savas, The middle state of the souls in the orthodox oriental eschatology: DeltioVM 21,11 (1992) 61-69.

9197 [Sardos] *Albertini* Lino, L'Au-delà existe; un témoignage exceptionnel rigoureusement documenté [best-seller italien]; recours d'un avocat à un médium pour localiser le corps de son fils disparu. P 1991, Filipacchi. 252 p. F 119. – ᴿEsprVie 102 (1992) 222s (P. *Jay*: 'curé de Trieste' et 'anonyme du Vatican' cités suggèrent que l'Église approuve).

9198 *Ambaum* Jan, An empty hell? The restoration of all things? BALTHASAR's concept of hope for salvation, ᵀ*Dodds* Michael J.: ComND 18 (1991) 35-52.

9199 **Ancona** Giovanni, Il significato escatologico cristiano della morte 1990 ➤ 6,9032; 7,8937: ᴿDivinitas 36 (1992) 285 (D. *Vibrac*); Letture 46 (1991) 476s (A. *Carrara*).

9200 *Ancona* Giovanni, Sull'escatologia cristiana; rassegna bibliografica: RivScR 5 (1991) 477-491.

9201 **Arregui** Jorge Vicente, El horror de morir; el valor de la muerte en la vida humana. Barc 1992, Tibidabo. 405 p. – ᴿScriptTPamp 24 (1992) 1074-7 (L. F. *Mateo-Seco*).

9202 **Aubert** Jean-Marie, Et après... Vie ou néant? essai sur l'au-delà 1991 ➤ 7,8939: ᴿChristus 39 (P 1992) 94 (Hélène *Polissard*); EsprVie 102 (1992) 587s (P. *Jay*).

9203 **Baarlink** Heinrich, Die Eschatologie der synoptischen Evangelien: BW 120, 1986 ➤ 2,7141 ... 4,a53: ᴿProtestantesimo 47 (1992) 149s (G. *Conte*).

9203* *Baarlink* H., Eschatologie en hermeneutik: TRef 35,1 (Woerden 1992) 29-... [< ZIT 92,235].

9204 *Bachl* Gottfried, Der Tod, die Bilder und die Hoffnung: GeistL 65 (1992) 134-141.

9205 *Baudler* Georg, Jesus und die Hölle; zum religionspädagogischen und pastoralen Umgang mit den Bildern der Gehenna: TGegw 34 (1991) 163-174.

9206 **Becker** Jürgen, La resurrezione dei morti nel cristianesimo primitivo [1976], ^T*Casciari* Antonio: StBPaid 97. Brescia 1991, Paideia. 208 p. 88-394-0469-4.

9207 *Bokwa* Ignacy, ⊕ Die universale Heilshoffnung bei Hans Urs von BALTHASAR: ColcT 62,4 (1992) 79-88; deutsch 88.

9208 **Bowker** John, The meanings of death 1991 → 7,8943: ^RExpTim 103 (1991s) 189s (M. *Forward*: bypasses Islam); RelStR 18 (1992) 311 (D. W. *Musser*); TvT 32 (1992) 214s (M. van *Knippenberg*).

9209 *Brandenburger* Egon, Gerichtskonzeptionen im Urchristentum und ihre Voraussetzungen: SNTU A-16 (1991) 5-54.

9210 **Bregman** Lucy, Death in the midst of life; perspectives on death from Christianity and depth psychology: Christian Explorations in Psychology. GR 1992, Baker. 248 p. $13. 0-8010-1017-9 [TDig 39,354].

9211 *Brown* Montague, AQUINAS on the resurrection of the body: Thomist 56 (1992) 165-199.

9212 **Camporesi** Piero, The fear of hell; images of damnation and salvation in early modern Europe. Univ. Park PA 1991, Penn. State Univ. ix-221 p. [TR 88,78].

9213 *Caspar* Philippe, Éléments pour une eschatologie du zygote: RThom 92 (1992) 460-481.

9214 *Cockburn* David, The evidence for reincarnation: RelSt 27 (1991) 199-207.

9215 **Coggan** Donald, God of hope. L 1991, Collins. 159 p. £5. 0-00-627587-7. – ^RExpTim 103 (1991s) 313 (R. *Lunt*: a Bible study with an eye impressively on the modern world).

9216 **Condrau** Gion, Der Mensch und sein Tod; certa moriendi condicio. Z 1991, Kreuz. 480 p.; ill. 3-368-00109-2. – ^RActuBbg 29 (1992) 169-176 (J. *Boada*).

9217 **Cooper** John W., Body, soul, and life everlasting; biblical anthropology and the monism-dualism debate 1989 → 5,8984...7,8948: ^RRefTR 49 (1990) 110s (M. *Hill*); STEv 3 (1991) 133-5 (P. *Finch*); WestTJ 53 (1991) 161-3 (R. A. *Clouser*).

9218 **Couture** Agnès, La réincarnation; théorie, science ou croyance? Montréal/Paris 1992, Paulines/Médiaspaul. 357 p. – ^REsprVie 102 (1992) 623 (J. *Vernette*).

9219 **Couture** André, La réincarnation: L'Horizon du Croyant. Ottawa 1992, Novalis. 181 p. 2-89088-578-X [RTLv 24,519, J. *Scheuer*, aussi sur son étude bibliographique avec M. *Saindon*].

9220 **Criswell** W. A., Eschatology: Great Doctrines of the Bible. GR 1982, Zondervan. 153 p. $13. – ^RCalvaryB 7,2 (1991) 67 (J. M. *Garber*, mentioning eight other titles in his series).

9221 **Cupitt** Don, The time being. L c.1992, SCM. £10. – ^RTablet 246 (1992) 746 (G. *Daly*).

9222 **Daley** Brian, The hope of the early Church; a handbook of patristic eschatology, 1991 → 7,8950: ^RExpTim 103 (1991s) 89s (H. *Chadwick*: excellent); Irénikon 65 (1992) 152s (E. *Lanne*); JEH 43 (1992) 141 (G. *Gould*); RHPR 72 (1992) 328s (W. *Fick*); RThom 92 (1992) 943s (D. *Cerbelaud*); TPhil 67 (1992) 279s (H. J. *Sieben*); TLond 95 (1992) 142s (R. *Bauckham*); TS 53 (1992) 746-8 (Joanne *McWilliam*); TvT 32 (1992) 199 (A. *Lascaris*).

9223 **Davis** Stephen T., Death and afterlife. NY 1989, St. Martin's. – ^RPerspRelSt 19 (1992) 236-9 (N. *Chaney*, also on COOPER J. 1989).

9224 **Deissler** Alfons,   Was wird am Ende der Tage geschehen? biblische
Visionen der Zukunft 1991 ➤ 7,8951:   ᴿExpTim 103 (1991s) 152 (R.
Coggins); MüTZ 42 (1991) 190-2 (G. L. *Müller*).

9225 *Disse* Jörge,   La temporalité dans l'eschatologie de Jésus selon la
'Dramatique divine' de H. U. v. BALTHASAR: RTLv 23 (1992) 439-471;
Eng. 607.

9226 **Durrwell** François-X.,   Le Christ l'homme et la mort: Maranatha 26.
Montréal/P 1991, Paulines/Médiaspaul.   109 p.   F 69. – ᴿEsprVie 102
(1992) 585-7 (P. *Jay*).

Duval Yvette,   Auprès des saints corps et âme; l'inhumation 'ad sanctos'
1988 ➤ g639.

9227 *Fackre* Gabriel,   I believe in the resurrection of the body: Interpretation
46 (1992) 42-52.

9228 **Feder** Angela,   Reinkarnationshypothese in der New-Age-Bewegung
1991 ➤ 7,8957:   ᴿZkT 114 (1992) 107s (K. H. *Neufeld*).

9229 *Fernández Ardanaz* Santiago,   'Thánatos' en CLEMENTE de Alejandría:
ScripV 38 (1991) 249-301.

9229* **Finger** Thomas N.,   Christian theology, an eschatological approach
1989 ➤ 2,7164; 6,9058:   ᴿRefTR 50 (1991) 108s (R. C. *Hill* does not want
to damn with faint praise).

9230 **Frahier** Louis-Jean,   Le jugement dernier; implications éthiques pour le
bonheur de l'homme; préf. (archévêque de Bordeaux) *Eyt* [Diss. P Inst.
Cath.].   P 1992, Cerf.   428 p.   F 150. – ᴿEsprVie 102 (1992) 654s (P. *Daubercies*).

9231 *Friedli* Richard,   La réincarnation; une approche en anthropologie culturelle comparée: ZMissRW 75 (1991) 97-116.

9232 *Frosini* Giordano,   Dove va oggi l'escatologia?: VivH 2 (1991) 197-219.

9232* **Geisler** Norman L.,   In defense of the resurrection.   Lynchburg 1991,
Quest.   131 p. $10 [RefTR 51,115] ➤ 7,4239.

9233 ᴱ**Gerhards** Albert,   Die grössere Hoffnung der Christen...:   QDisp 127,
1990 ➤ 6,411a; 7,8963:   ᴿLebZeug 46 (1991) 309s (S. *Ernst*); TLZ 117
(1992) 145-7 (F. *Beisser*); WissWeish 54 (1991) 78-80 (V. *Clemens*).

9234 **Gilmore** John,   Probing heaven; key questions on the hereafter.   GR
1989, Baker.   466 p. $15.   0-8010-3833-2. – ᴿRExp 89 (1992) 112s (D. S.
Dockery).

9235 **Girard** Jean-Michel,   La mort chez Saint AUGUSTIN; grandes lignes de
l'évolution de sa pensée, telle qu'elle apparaît dans ses traités [diss.
ᴰ*Wermelinger* O.]: Paradosis 34.   FrS 1992, Univ.   251 p.   2-8271-0594-2.

9236 **Gounelle** André, *Vouga* François,   Après la mort qu'y a-t-il?   Les
discours chrétiens sur l'au-delà: Théologies, 1990 ➤ 7,8964:   ᴿEsprVie
102 (1992) 588s (P. *Jay*); RTLv 23 (1992) 250s (R. *Guelluy*).

9237 **Gozzelino** Giorgio,   Lineamenti di escatologia.   T-Leumann 1992, Elle
Di Ci.   143 p.   Lit. 11.000 [TR 88,171].

9238 *Gozzelino* Giorgio,   Problemi e compiti dell'escatologia contemporanea;
come parlare dell'escatologia oggi: *a*) Salesianum 54 (1992) 79-98; – *b*)
➤ 161, Salesiani 1992, 81-100.

9239 **Guillen Preckler** Fernando,   Ven, Señor Jesús; hacia lo definitivo; meditaciones sobre el sentido escatológico de los grandes valores humanos:
Mundo y Dios 29.   S 1990, Secr. Trinitario.   130 p. – ᴿTeresianum 43
(1992) 533s (F. *Javier Sancho*).

9240 **Gulkin** David P.,   An investigation of dispensational premillennialism;
an analysis and evaluation of the eschatology of John F. WALVOORD:

diss. Andrews, ^D*La Rondelle* H.   Berrien Springs MI 1992.   471 p.   92-25977. – DissA 53 (1992s) 1186-A.

9241 **Haas** Alois M., Todesbilder in Mittelalter; Fakten und Hinweise in der deutschen Literatur. Da 1989, Wiss.   vii-299 p.   DM 59.   3-534-06719-3. – ^RWissWeis 54 (1991) 76s (C. *Auffarth*).

9242 **Harris** Murray J., From grave to glory; resurrection in the New Testament; including a response to Norman L. GEISLER [p. 337-458]. GR 1990, Zondervan.   xxviii-29 + 493 p.   0-310-51991-8. – ^RRefTR 51 (1992) 115s (I. *Smith*).

9243 **Hattrup** Dieter, Eschatologie. Pd 1992, Bonifatius.   352 p.   DM 32 [TR 88,347]. – ^RTR 88 (1992) 408-412 (H. *Vorgrimler*: banal adversary-portrayal and other deficiencies).

9244 **Hildebrand** Dietrich von, † 1977, Jaws of death, gate of heaven [Über den Tod],^T.   Manchester NH 1991, Sophia.   xiv-148 p. $15.   0-918477-10-7 [TDig 39,192].

9245 **Hill** Charles E., Regnum caelorum; patterns of future hope in early Christianity. Ox 1992, Clarendon.   xvii-236 p. [TR 88,519].

9246 **Hoekema** Anthony A., The Bible and the future. GR 1991, Eerdmans. xi-343 p.   0-8028-3516-3.

9247 *House* H. Wayne, Resurrection, reincarnation, and humanness: BtS 148 (1991) 131-150.

9248 a) *Hughes* Philip E., Conditional immortality [< his True Image p. 402-7]; – b) *Packer* James I., The problem of eternal punishment; – c) *Bray* Gerald, Hell; eternal punishment or total annihilation?: Evangel 10,2 (1992) 10-12 / 13-19 / 19-24.

9249 *Imbach* Joseph, La dottrina sui 'novissimi'; messaggio di minaccia o lieta novella?: Studium 87 (R 1991) 15-35.

9250 *Karrer* Martin, Parousie: → 757, EvKL 3 (1992) 1059-61.

9251 *Kearney* [as corrected p. 449] John, Saint THOMAS on death, resurrection, and personal identity: Angelicum 69 (1992) 3-22.

9252 a) *Keck* Leander E., Death and afterlife in the New Testament; – b) *Obayashi* Hiroshi, Death and eternal life in Christianity: → 603, Death 1988/92, 83-96 / 109-123.

9253 **Kehl** Medard, Escatología [1988 → 2,7179],^T: Lux Mundi 70. S 1992, Sígueme.   386 p.   84-301-1169-7. – ^RRET 52 (1992) 497-9 (E. *Tourón*).

9254 **König** Adrio, The eclipse of Christ in eschatology 1989 → 5,9008 ... 7,8978: ^RRExp 89 (1992) 111s (D. S. *Dockery*: intriguing).

9255 ^E**Lambrecht** J., *Kenis* L., Leven over de dood heen; verslagboek van een interdisciplinair Leuvens colloquium [III. 1990] 1990 → 6,638*; 7,8979: ^RRTLv 23 (1992) 251 (P. *Weber*).

9256 **Lang** B., *McDannell* C. [= 9262, reversed!] Der Himmel; eine Kulturgeschichte des ewigen Lebens [1988 → 4,a106].^T: Suhrkamp 1586. Fra 1990.   578 p. – ^RDielB 27 (1991) 283s (B. J. *Diebner*: 'a history not of heaven but of the images used to describe it' p. 9).

9257 **Lannert** Berthold, Die Wiederentdeckung der nt. Eschatologie durch J. WEISS: TANZ 2, 1989 → 7,8981: ^RTLZ 116 (1991) 188-190 (W. *Wiefel*); TR 88 (1992) 127-131 (G. *Wenz*).

9258 a) *Léon-Dufour* Xavier, Oltre la morte; – b) *Ricca* Paolo, Il giudizio universale e la risurrezione dei morti; – c) *Poletto* Giannina, La fine del mondo nelle ipotesi della scienza; – d) *Frugoni* Chiara, La scoperta del macabro nel medioevo: → 453, Aldilà 1991/2, 213-238 / 143-184 / 107-139 / 187-192.

9259 **Lincoln** Andrew T., Paradise now and not yet, C ᴰ1981 ➤ 62,8377; = GR 1991 pa, Baker. xi-277 p. $15. 0-8016-5672-1 [NTAbs 36,276].

9260 **Logister** W., Reincarnatie; de vele kanten van een oud en nieuw geloof 1900 ➤ 6,9078; 90-209-1865-X: ᴿTvT 32 (1992) 214 (M. Van *Tente*).

9261 **Lohmann** Hans, Drohung und Verheissung; exegetische Untersuchungen zur Eschatologie bei den Apostolischen Vätern: BZNW 55, 1989 ➤ 5,9016 ... 7,8983: ᴿCBQ 54 (1992) 161s (J. S. *Sikes*: significant).

9262 **McDannell** Colleen, *Lang* Bernhard [➤ 9256], Heaven, a history 1988 ➤ 4,a106 ... 7,8985: ᴿParabola 14,3 (1989) 108.110 (Peggy R. *Ellsberg*).

9263 **MacGregor** Geddes, Images of afterlife; beliefs from antiquity to modern times. NY 1992, Paragon. xi-231 p. $22. 1-55778-396-9 [TDig 40,173].

9264 *Macintosh* J. J., Reincarnation ...: RelSt [25 (1989) 153-165; 26 (1990) 483-491 . 501-4 (*Noonan* H.; *Daniels* C.)] 28 (1992) 235-251.

9265 **McKeating** Colm, Eschatology in the Anglican sermons of John H. NEWMAN: diss. Pont. Univ. Gregoriana, ᴰ*Sharkey* M. Roma 1992. 413 p.; Extr. 3817, 362 p. – RTLv 24, p. 558.

9266 **Marguerat** Daniel, Vivre avec la mort; le défi du Nouveau Testament² [¹1987]. Aubonne 1991, Moulin. 83 p.

9267 *Maritano* Mario, GIUSTINO Martire di fronte al problema della metempsicosi (Dial. 4,4-7 e 5,5): Salesianum 54 (1992) 231-281.

9268 *Martin* Raymond, Survival of bodily death; a question of values: RelSt 28 (1992) 165-184.

9269 *Matar* Nabil I., The Anglican eschatology of Thomas TRAHERNE: AnglTR 74 (1992) 289-303.

9270 *Mauny* Michel de, L'enfer et les enfers: PeCa 256 (1992) [< EsprVie 102 (1992) 376-8, J. *Daoust*].

9271 **Milazzo** G. Tom, The protest and the silence; suffering, death, and biblical theology. Mp 1992, Fortress. xiii-182 p. 0-8006-2526-9.

9272 **Mondin** Battista, Preesistenza sopravvivenza reincarnazione 1989 ➤ 6, 9088: ᴿSalesianum 54 (1992) 169s (S. *Palumbieri*).

Moraldi Luigi, Nach dem Tode 1987 ➤ 7427a.

9274 **Murphy** Marie, New images of the last things; Karl RAHNER on death and life after death 1988 ➤ 5,9028; 6,9089: ᴿPerspRelSt 19 (1992) 328 (Molly T. *Marshall*: unfavoring, compared to GRENZ's PANNENBERG ➤ 9341 infra).

9275 *Neusner* Jacob, How is 'eternity' to be understood in the theology of Judaism?: ScotJT 45 (1992) 29-43.

9276 *Niewiadomski* Józef, Hoffnung im Gericht; soteriologische Impulse für eine dogmatische Eschatologie: ZkT 114 (1992) 113-126.

9277 *Noemi* C. Juan, Interrogantes sobre 'Algunas cuestiones actuales de escatología': TVida 33 (1992) [193-] 225-235.

9278 *O'Donnell* John, God's justice and mercy; what can we hope for? [Melbourne Knox lecture 1991]: Pacifica 5 (1992) 84-96.

9279 *a) Osiek* Carolyn, Fullness of life [p. 135, 'there is no clear evidence that the ancient Israelites believed in any kind of real survival after death']; – *b) Rogers* Patrick, The death of Jesus; – *c) Moeser* Annelies G., The death of Judas [< diss.]: BToday 30 (1992) 133-7 / 138-144 / 145-152.

9280 **Ott** Ludwig †, ᴱ*Naab* E., Eschatologie in der Scholastik: HbDg 4/7b, 1990 ➤ 6,9096; 7,8993*: ᴿColcFranc 61 (1991) 364s (B. de *Armellada*); TLZ 116 (1991) 211s (K.-H. *Kandler*).

9280* *Otto* Randall E., The eschatological nature of MOLTMANN's theology: WestTJ 54 (1992) 115-133.

9281 **Pago** Annegret, 'Behold he comes with clouds'; Untersuchungen zur eschatologischen Dichtung in der englischen Literaturgeschichte des 17. und 18. Jahrhunderts: Münsteraner MgEngLit 9. Fra 1992, Lang. 355 p. 3-631-45023-0.

9282 **Panteghini** Giacomo, L'orizzonte speranza; lineamenti di escatologia cristiana: Strumenti ScRel. Padova 1991, Messaggero. 251 p. [TR 88,347].

9283 **Paxton** F. S., Christianizing death 1990 → 7,8994: ᴿJRel 72 (1992) 583s (Celia M *Chazelle*: careful).

9284 *Pérez Tapias*, Más allá del optimismo y del pesimismo; la 'esperanza paradójica' de Erich FROMM: EstE 67 (1992) 309-329.

9285 ᴱ**Pfammatter** J., *Christen* E., Hoffnung über den Tod hinaus: TBer 19, 1990 → 7,8995: ᴿSalmanticensis 39 (1992) 169s (J. L. *Ruiz de la Peña*).

9286 **Piolanti** Antonio, La comunione dei santi e la vita eterna². Vaticano 1992, Pontificia Accademia Teologica Romana. 693 p. Lit. 50.000. – ᴿAngelicum 69 (1992) 563-5 (A. *Huerga*); CiuD 205 (1992) 761s (J. M. *Ozaeta*); Divinitas 36 (1992) 271-4 (R. M. *Schmitz*).

9287 **Pokorný** Petr, Die Zukunft des Glaubens; sechs Kapitel über Eschatologie: ArbT 72. Stu 1992, Calwer. 105 p. DM 34 [TR 88,528].

9288 *Poupin* Roland, La réincarnation, l'antiquité et la Bible: RRéf 43,2 (1992) 45- ... [< ZIT 92,299].

9289 **Pozo** Cándido, Teología del más allá³ [¹1970, ²1980]: BAC 282. M 1992, Católica. xxxi-597 p. 84-7914-051-8.

9290 ᴱ*Pozo* C., Alcune questioni attuali riguardanti l'escatologia [Comm. Teol.]: CC 143 (1992,1) 458-494.

9291 ᴱ*Pozo* Candido *al.*, Commissio theologica internationalis 1990, De quibusdam quaestionibus actualibus circa eschatologiam: Gregorianum 73 (1992) 395-435.

9292 **Ratzinger** J., Eschatologie⁶ 1990 → 7,8997: ᴿMüTZ 42 (1991) 415s (G. L. *Müller*).

9293 **Rhymer** Joseph, The end of time; eschatology of the New Testament. Middlegreen, Slough 1992, St. Paul. 157 p. 0-85439-404-2.

9294 **Richards** Jeffrey J., The promise of dawn; the eschatology of Lewis Sperry CHAFER [diss. Drew]. Lanham MD 1991, UPA. viii-259 p. $27.50 pa. – ᴿBtS 149 (1992) 243s (J. A. *Witmer*: good).

9295 **Robillard** Edmond, Reincarnation, illusion or reality? ᵀ*Whitehead* K. D. NY 1991, Alba. xi-182 p.; 6 pl. $10. 0-8189-0432-1 [TDig 39,284].

9296 *Rosenthal* Marvin J., Imminence; does the Bible teach an any-moment rapture?: Zion's Fire (Aug. 1990) 3-9 [< BtS 148 (1991) 358s (J. A. *Witmer*); further 90-110 (G. B. *Stanton*), 387-398 (J. A. *McLean*)].

9297 *Roukema* R., Reïncarnatie in de Oude Kerk (I): GerefTTs 92 (1992) 199-218.

9298 *Sattler* Dorothea, Erlösen durch Strafen? Zur Verwendung des Strafbegriffs im Kontext der christlichen Lehre von Heil und Erlösung: Catholica 46 (1992) 89-113.

9299 *a)* *Saward* John, The flesh flowers again; St. BONAVENTURE and the aesthetics of the Resurrection; – *b)* *Buchanan* George W., [B. F.] MEYERS's support for WEISS's eschatology: DowR 110 (1992) 1-29 / 83-96.

9300 *Schall* James V., Life everlasting: HomP 92,9 (1991s) 15-22.

9301 *Scharen* Hans, Gehenna in the Synoptics: BtS 149 (1992) 324-337. 454-470.

9302 **Schoenborn** Christoph, La vie éternelle. P 1992, Mame. 192 p. – ᴿEsprVie 102 (1992) 572-4 (P. *Jay*: mérites; coquilles).

9303 *Sciattella* Marco, Il sabato eterno come immagine escatologica in alcuni Padri e scrittori cristiani d'Occidente: Divinitas 36 (1992) 230-258.

9304 *a) Senior* Donald, The end of the world; – *b) Boadt* Lawrence, OT images of the end; – *c) Bowe* Barbara E., Like a thief in the night; – *d) Carroll* John T., The end in the Synoptics: BToday 30 (1992) 4-10 / 11-16 / 17-23 / 24-28.

9305 *Sieg* Franciszek, ℗ Cechy... Traits of the apocalyptic writings of the NT period and the question of their origin in varying evaluation: → 637, Wizje 1990/2, 1-17 (offprint).

9306 *Solignac* Aimé, Caelum [franç.]: → 743, AugL 1,5s (1992) 698-702.

9307 **Steiger** Johann A., Bibel-Sprache; Welt und Jüngster Tag bei Johann Peter HEBEL; Erziehung zum Glauben zwischen Überlieferung und Aufklärung: Diss. ᴰ*Eisinger* W. Heidelberg 1992. 320 p. – RTLv 24, p. 558.

9308 *Tabarroni* A., Visio beatifica e Regnum Christi nell'escatologia di Giovanni XXII: → 618, La cattura della fine 1992, 123-149.

9309 **Thiede** Werner, Auferstehung der Toten — Hoffnung ohne Attraktivität? Grundstrukturen christlicher Heilserwartung und ihre verkannte religionspädagogische Relevanz: ForSysÖk 65. Gö 1991, Vandenhoeck & R. xii-437 p. – ᴿTR 88 (1992) 317s (G. *Wenz*).

9309* *a) Threinen* Norman J., Friedrich BRUNN, Erweckung ['Revival'] und konfessionelles Luthertum; – *d) Rothfuchs* Wilhelm, Umkehr und Erweckung im Neuen Testament: LuthTKi 16 (1992) 29-47 / 103-137.

9310 **Tornos** Andrés, Escatología [I. 1989 → 5,9057], II: Textos 11. M 1991, Univ. Comillas. 263 p. – ᴿCiuD 205 (1992) 247 (J. M. *Ozaeta*); RET [49,323] 51 (1991) 387-393 [E. *Tourón del Pié*]; Salmanticensis 39 (1992) 166-9 (J. L. *Ruiz de la Peña*).

9311 **Tourón del Pié** Eliseo, Escatología cristiana; aproximación catequética: Textos de Teología 11. M 1990, Inst. Sup. Catequética San Pío X. 208 p. 84-7221-272-6. – ᴿRET 52 (1992) 243s (M. *Gesteira*).

9311* *Uytfanghe* Marc Van, Les Visiones du très haut Moyen Âge et les récentes 'expériences de mort temporaire'; sens ou non-sens d'une comparaison [I. ᶠSANDERS G. 1991, 447-481] 2. SacrEr 33 (1992s) 135-182.

9312 ᴱ**Wagner** Harald, (*Kruse* Torsten), Ars moriendi; Erwägungen zur Kunst des Sterbens: QDisp 118, 1989 → 5,763; DM 38: ᴿZkT 114 (1992) 365s (W. *Guggenberger*).

9313 **Walls** Jerry L., Hell; the logic of damnation: Library of religious philosophy 9. ND 1992, Univ. 182 p. $27. 0-268-01095-1 [TDig 40,192].

9314 *Walter* Nikolaus, [*al.*], Die Botschaft vom jüngsten Gericht im Neuen Testament: in, Eschatologie und jüngstes Gericht: Bekenntnis 32 [Hannover 1991, Luther; 103 p.] 10-48 [TR 88,435].

9315 **Walther** Christian, Eschatologie als Theorie der Freiheit; Einführung in neuzeitliche Gestalten eschatologischen Denkens: TBtTöpelmann 48, 1991 → 7,9018: ᴿTLZ 117 (1992) 691-3 (G. *Wenz*).

9315* **Wheeler** Michael, Death and the future life in Victorian literature and theology → 7,9021: ᴿCommonweal 119,1 (1992) 20-22 (Elizabeth *Beverly*).

9316 **Witherington** Ben, Jesus, Paul, and the end of the world; a comparative study in NT eschatology. DG 1992, InterVarsity. 306 p. $20 pa. – 0-8308-1759-X [NTAbs 36,429].

9317 *Woschitz* K.M.,   Ersehntes und erschlossenes Leben; Skizzen zum biblischen Thema 'ewiges Leben':   TJb (Lp 1990) 149-163 [< ZIT 91,654].

H9.5   *Theologia totius* [V-] *NT*   –   **General [O-] NT theology.**

9318 *a) Auld* A. Graeme,   Can a biblical theology also be academic or ecumenical? – *b) Riches* John K.,   Towards a biblical theology; von Balthasar's The glory of the Lord: → 41, FDAVIDSON R. 1992, 13-27 / 256-272.

9319 **Beeck** F.J. van,   God encountered I, 1989 → 5,9067...7,9025:   RCatholic World 234 (1991) 178s (J.T. *Ford*); HomP 91,1 (1990s) 77-79 (J.R. *Sheets*: good, but); ProcCathTheolAm 46 (1991) 141s (R.P. *Imbelli*); Thomist 56 (1992) 141-5 (G. *Rocca*).

9320 **Beilner** Wolfgang,   Grundlegung einer neutestamentlichen Theologie: Vermittlung 25.   Salzburg 1992; nicht im Buchhandel.   186 p.

9321 **Casalini** Nello,   I misteri della fede; teologia del NT: SBF Anal. 32, 1991 → 7,9027:   RLetture 46 (1991) 851s (G. *Ravasi*).

9322 **Childs** Brevard S.,   [→ 224*] Biblical theology of the Old and New Testaments; theological reflection on the Christian Bible.   L 1992, SCM. xxii-745 p. £20.   0-334-00114-5 [BL 93,104, J.W. *Rogerson*: important fundamental issues].

9323 **Coleridge** Mark,   Biblical theology and beyond: AustralasCR 69 (1992) 437-445.

9324 **Dunn** James D.G., *Mackey* James P.,   New Testament theology in dialogue, Christology and ministry 1988 → 3,9161...6,9134:   RRExp 89 (1992) 423 (Molly T. *Marshall*).

9325 EEicher P.,   Neue Summe Theologie 1-3, 1988s → 5,458*...7,9031: RStPatav 39 (1992) 213-7 (L. *Sartori*).

9326 EElwell W.A.,   Topical analysis of the Bible, NIV.   GR 1991, Baker. xiii-893 p. $40.   0-8010-3205-9 [NTAbs 36,253].

9326* **Eppler** Wilhelm,   Die Sicht des Alten Testaments in den neueren protestantischen Theologien des Neuen Testaments.   Diss. Tübingen 1989. 393 p. – TLZ 118,457.

9327 [**Schüssler**] **Fiorenza** F., *Galvin* J.,   Systematic theology 1991 → 7,379: RCommonweal 119,3 (1992) 30s (L.S. *Cunningham*); Horizons 19 (1992) 109-112 (B. *Cooke*) & 112-4 (Mary Ann *Hinsdale*) & 116-9 (P.C. *Hodgson*); 120-1-5 (Galvin/Fiorenza responses); PrPeo 6 (1992) 360 (J. *Tolhurst*).

9328 **Garrett** James L.J,   Systematic theology; biblical, historical and evangelical 1990 → 7,9032:   RChrCent 108 (1991) 597.599 (S. *Grenz*); GraceTJ 12 (1991) 308s (R.T. *Clutter*); Interpretation 46 (1992) 96.98 (G. *Fackre*).

9329 **Gnilka** Joachim,   Teologia del Nuovo Testamento [1989 → 5,9073], TGatti Enzo: BtBib 9.   Brescia 1992, Queriniana. 180 p. Lit. 25.000. 88-399-2009-9.

9330 **Güttgemanns** Erhardt,   Gegenstand, Methode und Inhalt einer Theologie des Neuen Testaments: LingBib 66 (1992) 55-112; Eng. 112s.

9331 **Hedlund** Roger E.,   The mission of the Church to the world; a biblical theology.   GR 1991, Baker.   300 p. – RGraceTJ 12 (1991) 316s (P.A. *Beals*).

9332 **Hübner** Hans,   Biblische Theologie des NTs 1. Prolegomena 1990 → 6, 9138; 7,9034:   RBZ 36 (1992) 281-3 (J. *Gnilka*); ComSev 24 (1991) 424s

(M. *de Burgos*); ExpTim 102 (1990s) 269s (E. *Best*: enticing); Gregorianum 73 (1992) 149 (G. *O'Collins*); SNTU A-16 (1991) 189 (*Niemand*); StPatav 38 (1991) 652-4 (G. *Segalla*).

9333 **Kittel** Gisela, Der Name über alle Namen; biblische Theologie, 1. AT 1989 ➤ 6,9140; 2. NT 1989s ➤ 7,9035: ᴿCBQ 54 (1992) 326s (M. C. *Lind*, 1); TLZ 117 (1992) 111s (S. *Wagner*) & 124s (T. *Holtz*).

9334 **Kreck** Walter, Dommatica evangelica; le questioni fondamentali: NStT-SolaScr 11, 1986 ➤ 4,a157; 88-7016-049-1: ᴿAntonianum 67 (1992) 542s (R. *Giraldo*).

9335 *Lang* Friedrich, Gesetz und Gerechtigkeit Gottes in biblisch-theologischer Sicht: TBeit 22 (Wu 1991) 195-207 [< ᴢɪᴛ 91,585].

9336 **Mildenberger** Friedrich, Biblische Dogmatik; eine Biblische Theologie in dogmatischer Perspektive [1. 1991 ➤ 7,9042]; 2. Ökonomie als Theologie. Stu 1992, Kohlhammer. 433 p. 3-17-011082-9. – ᴿTGL 82 (1992) 381s (W. *Beinert*, 1).

9337 **Motte** Jochen, Gesamtbiblische Theologie nach Walther ZIMMERLI; Darstellung und Würdigung der alttestamentlichen Theologie W.Z.s und der sich aus ihr ergebenden Perspektive zum Neuen Testament in systematisch-theologischer Sicht: Diss. ᴰ*Klappert* B. Wuppertal 1992. 351 p. – RTLv 24, p. 542.

9338 **Pannenberg** Wolfhart, Systematische Theologie [1. 1988 ➤ 5,9087]; 2. Gö 1991, Vandenhoeck & R. 564 p. DM 98. – ᴿActuBbg 29 (1992) 231s (J. *Boada*); Gregorianum 73 (1992) 552-4 (J. *O'Donnell*); LuthMon 30 (1991) 563 (W. *Sparn*); TGL 82 (1992) 151s (W. *Beinert*); TR 88 (1992) 353-360 (G. L. *Müller*); TsTKi 62 (1991) 309-311 (J.-O. *Henriksen*).

9339 **Pannenberg** Wolfhart, Teologia sistematica I [1988 ➤ 5,9087], ᵀ*Pezzetta* Dino: BtTeolContemp 67. Brescia 1990, Queriniana. 535 p. Lit. 55.000. – ᴿETL 68 (1992) 462s (E. *Brito*); FilT 6 (1992) 455-466 (F. *Costa*); REB 52 (1992) 229s (C. *Boff*).

9340 **Pannenberg** W. An introduction to systematic theology 1991 ➤ 7,9045: ᴿPacifica 5 (1992) 329-331 (C. *Mostert*); TTod 49 (1992s) 557s.560 (J. E. *Loder*).

9341 — **Grenz** Stanley J., Reason for hope; the Systematic Theology of W. PANNENBERG. NY c. 1990, Ox-UP. 279 p. $34.50. – ᴿChrCent 108 (1991) 338s (D. S. *Cunningham*).

9342 **Räisänen** Heikki, Beyond NT theology, a story and a programme [J. GABLER, D. F. STRAUSS, W. WREDE saw the need] 1990 ➤ 6,9149; 7, 9046: ᴿInterpretation 46 (1992) 83s (J. D. *Kingsbury*); JTS 43 (1992) 626-630 (N. T. *Wright*); StPatav 38 (1991) 170-4 (G. *Segalla*).

9343 ᴱ**Reumann** John, The promise and practice of biblical theology 1991 ➤ 7,326: ᴿExpTim 103 (1991s) 346 (J. *Goldingay*: rather in the sense of 'theological interpretation of scripture in general' and distinct also from the 'postwar biblical theology movement' now much proclaimed dead).

9344 *Scobie* Charles H. H., Three twentieth century biblical theologies [BURROWS M. 1946; TERRIEN S. 1978; SEEBASS H. 1982]: HorBT 14 (1992) 51-69.

9345 **Siegwalt** Gérard, Dogmatique pour la catholicité évangélique [1, 1986 ➤ 3,6581; 2/1, 1991 ➤ 7,9048] 4. P c. 1993, Cerf: ᴿIrénikon 65 (1992) 207-214 (J. P. *Gaber*).

9346 **Stuhlmacher** Peter, Biblische Theologie des Neuen Testaments, I. Grundlegung; von Jesus zu Paulus. Gö 1992, Vandenhoeck & R. xi-419 p. 3-525-53595-3.

9347 *Via* Dan O., New Testament theology; historical event, literary text, and the locus of revelation: ➤ 175, ᶠSMITH T., PerspRelSt 29,4 (1992) 369-388.

XVI. Philologia biblica

J1 **Hebraica** .1 *grammatica*

9347* *a*) *Andersen* Francis I., *Forbes* A. Dean, Methods and tools for the study of OT syntax; – *b*) *Dyk* J. W., Variation in the functioning of the Hebrew participle; a computer-assisted study of syntactical shift; – *c*) *Vervenne* Marc, Hebrew verb form and function; a syntactic case study with reference to a linguistic data base: ➤ 450, Informatique 2, 1988/9, 61-72 / 255-263 / 605-640.

9348 **Beall** Todd S., *Banks* William A., *al.*, OT parsing guide [Gen-Esther 1986] Job-Malachi. Ch 1990, Moody. xii-299 p. $30. 0-8034-631[5-0]; -6-9. – ᴿTrinJ 13 (1992) 217-221 (R. *Giesse*, also on OWENS).

9348* *Blau* Joshua, ⊕ An excellent adaptation of a well-known Hebrew grammar [JOÜON-MURAOKA]: Lešonenu 56 (1991s) 163-174; Eng. iv-v.

9349 *a*) *Blau* Joshua, ⊕ On the multilayered structure of Biblical Hebrew in the light of Modern Hebrew; – *b*) *Ben-David* Israel, ⊕ The capacity of grammatical patterns to generate contextual and pausal forms in biblical Hebrew; – *c*) *Ornan* Uzzi, ⊕ The basic factors of a Hebrew word; – *d*) *Dotan* Aron, ⊕ From Masora to grammar, the beginnings of grammatical thought in Hebrew; – *e*) *Eldar* Ilan, ⊕ HAYYŪJ's grammatical analysis; – *f*) *Goldenberg* Esther, ⊕ Medieval linguistics and good Hebrew; – *g*) *Merkin* Reuven, ⊕ Ben-Yehuda's dictionary: Lešonenu 54,2-4 (The Hebrew Language Year, 1990) 103-114 / 279-288 / 247-268 / 155-168 / 169-181 / 183-216 / 311-323 .

9349* *Bodine* Walter R., *a*) The study of linguistics and biblical Hebrew; – *b*) How linguists study syntax [1987]: ➤ 343, Linguistics/BH 1992, 1-5 / 89-107.

9350 **Cohen** David, L'aspect verbal. P 1989, PUF. 272 p. F 180. – ᴿBSLP 86,2 (1991) 93-96 (S. *Patri*).

9351 **Deiana** Giovanni, *Spreafico* Ambrogio, Guida allo studio dell'Ebraico biblico 1990 ➤ 6,9156; 7,9054: ᴿCBQ 54 (1992) 743s (R. *Althann*); ParVi 37 (1992) 318 (A. *Rolla*); StCattMi 35 (1991) 473 (U. *De Martino*).

9352 **Eskhult** Mats, Studies in verbal aspect and narrative technique in biblical Hebrew prose 1990 ➤ 6,9158; 7,9056: ᴿBSLP 86,2 (1991) 247s (J. *Margain*); CBQ 54 (1992) 520-2 (R.J. *Owens*); JAOS 112 (1992) 487s (M. *O'Connor*); OLZ 87 (1992) 543s (G. *Begrich*); SvEx 56 (1991) 120s (B. *Johnson*); ZDMG 142 (1992) 163s (D. *Blohm*).

9353 *a*) *Florentin* Moshe, ⊕ The disappearance of the internal passive and the status of *Nipᶜal* and *Nitpaᶜel* in the Samaritan tradition and Mishnaic Hebrew; – *b*) *Becker* Dan, ⊕ 'The *Paᶜūl*, the *Pōᶜel* of which has not been specified' according to R. Yonah BEN JĀNĀḤ; – *c*) *Kuzar* Ron, ⊕ The nominal impersonal; a part of speech or a syntactic construction?: Lešonenu 56 (1991s) 201-211 / 213-221 / 241-8; Eng. I-IV.

9354 **Freedman** David N., *al.*, Studies in Hebrew and Aramaic orthography [follow-up to 1986 San Diego meeting]: BJudSDiego 2. WL 1992, Eisenbruns. xii-329 p. 0-931464-63-3.

9355 *Geller* Stephen A., Cleft sentences with pleonastic pronoun; a syntactic construction of biblical Hebrew and some of its literary uses: JANES 20 (1991) 15-33.

9355* *Gevirtz* Stanley, Of syntax and style in the 'Late Biblical Hebrew' — 'Old Canaanite' connection [features hitherto considered late are increasingly being identified in early Phoenician, Ugaritic, Amarna Akkadian, and Israelian Hebrew]: JANES 18 (1986) 25-29.

9356 **Glinert** Lewis. The joys of Hebrew [pathetic or humorous phrases of modern Hebrew]. NY 1992, Oxford. xii-292 p. 0-19-507424-6.

9357 *Goerwitz* Richard L., The accentuation of the Hebrew jussive and preterite: JAOS 112 (1992) 198-203.

9358 *a) Hoftijzer* J., A preliminary remark on the study of the verbal system in classical Hebrew; – *b) Greenberg* Joseph H., The Semitic 'intensive' as verbal plurality; a study of grammaticalization; – *c) Corrá* Alan D., Hebrew – some modest proposals; – *d) Revell* E. J., Conditional sentences in biblical Hebrew prose; – *e) Tsujita* Kyoji, The retrospective pronoun as direct object in relative sentences in biblical Hebrew: → 118, ᶠLESLAU W., Semitic 1991, 645-651 / 576-587 / 245-251 / 1278-90 / 1577-82.

9359 *Irsigler* H., Hebräisch: → 762, NBL II,6 (1991) 69-81.

9360 **Jamieson-Drake** D. W., Scribes and schools [ᴰ1988 → 6,9163]: JStOT supp 109. Sheffield 1991, Almond. 240 p. £30. 1-85075-275-3. – ᴿBL (1992) 34s (A. R. *Millard*, severe: many omissions, especially Arad); JSS 37 (1992) 319-321 (R. *Tomes*).

9361 *Joosten* Jan, Biblical Hebrew wᵉqāṭal and Syriac hwā qāṭel expressing repetition in the past: ZAHeb 5 (1992) 1-14.

9362 *a) Kedar* Benjamin, ❸ The interpretation of rhetorical questions in the Bible; – *b) Kogut* Simcha, ❸ The authority of Masoretic accents in traditional biblical exegesis; – *c) Morag* Shelomo, ❸ The structure of semantic and associative fields in biblical Hebrew and classical Arabic: → 181, Shaʿarei TALMON 1992, 145*-152* / 153*-165* / 137*-143*; Eng. xxiii.

9363 **Kelley** Page H., Biblical Hebrew, an introductory grammar. GR/ Leominster 1992, Eerdmans / Fowler Wright. xiv-453 p. £20. 0-8028-0598-1 [BL 93,154, J. F. *Healey*: deserves to be tried in class]. – N.B. OIAc 5,26 lists as 'Kenney'.

9364 **Klein** George L., The meaning of the Niphal in biblical Hebrew: diss. Annenberg. Ph 1992. 356 p. 93-07370. – DissA 53 (1992s) 4298-A.

9364* **Köhn** Rosemarie, Hebraisk grammatikk⁴. Oslo 1990, Univ. 198 p. Nk 190. – ᴿNorTTs 93 (1992) 244-7 (Ebbe *Knudsen*).

9365 *Krüger* Thomas, Belegt das Ostrakon KAI 200 einen narrativen Gebrauch der Verbform wᵉqatal im Althebräischen?: BibNot 62 (1992) 32-37.

9366 **Lambdin** Thomas O., Lehrbuch Bibel-Hebräisch, ᵀᴱSiebenthal H. von, 1990 → 6,9167; 7,9067: ᴿTZBas 48 (1992) 290s (I. *Willi-Plein*).

9367 — **Williamson** H., Annotated key to LAMBDIN's Introd. BH 1987 → 3,9231: ᴿVT 42 (1992) 432 (Judith M. *Hadley*).

9368 **Lettinga** J. P., Grammatik des biblischen Hebräisch; Hilfsbuch; Lesestücke; Vokabular, Verbalparadigmen [c. 1977]ᵀ. Basel 1992, Immanuel. xii-211 p.; viii-84+23 p. Fs 54,80. 3-95201-386-2 [BL 93,154, L. L. *Grabbe* (Dutch 1978, 140; French 1981, 133)].

9369 *Levi* Jaakov, Die Inkongruenz 1987 → 3,9209 ... 7,9068: ᴿJQR 81 (1990s) 501-3 (P. B. *Zuber*).

9370 **McFall** Leslie, The enigma of the Hebrew verbal system [diss. Cambridge]. Sheffield 1982, Almond. xiv-259 p. – ᴿJAOS 112 (1992) 693-6 [P. T. *Daniels* (nothing on why now): merits a more careful reedition].

9371 **Mendes** Paulo, Noções de Hebraico Bíblico: São Paulo 1983, Vida Nova. – ᴿRCuBíb 14,55s (1990) 168s (J. M. *Terra*).

9372 **Meyer** Rudolf, Hebräische Grammatik; bibliog. Nachwort, *Rüterswörden* Udo. B 1992, de Gruyter. 533 p. 3-11-013694-5 [OIAc 5,28].

9373 *Muraoka* Takamitsu, Much ado about nothing? A sore point or two of Hebrew grammarians [... shewa was basically absence of vowel]: JbEOL 32 (1991s) 131-140.

9374 **Nash** Peter T., The Hebrew *Qal* active participle; a non-aspectual narrative backgrounding element: diss. ᴰ*Pardee* D. Chicago 1992. viii-173 p. – OIAc 3,31.

9375 **Niccacci** Alviero, Syntax of the verb 1990 → 6,9173; 7,9072: ᴿCritRR 5 (1992) 153s (S. A. *Meier*: translation also a revision; as in ESKHULT, 'there are as many printing errors as there are pages'); ÉTRel 67 (1992) 103s (Jeanne-M. *Léonard*: lutte contre la cacophonie actuelle des traductions); ExpTim 102 (1990s) 313 (J. C. L. *Gibson* compares to ROOKER M., ESKHULT M.).

9376 **Niccacci** Alviero, Lettura sintattica della prosa ebraico-biblica [applicazione di WEINRICH H. 1978; SCHNEIDER W. ⁵1982]: SBF Anal 31, 1991 → 7,9071: ᴿAbrNahr 30 (1992) 190-2 (T. *Muraoka*); CiuD 204 (1991) 255s (J. *Gutiérrez*); RivB 40 (1992) 235s (G. *Ravasi*).

Owens John J., Analytical key to the OT I-IV, 1989-92 → 1948.

9377 *Payne* Geoffrey, Functional sentence perspective; theme in biblical Hebrew: ScandJOT 5,1 (1991) 62-82.

9378 *Pinto León* Adolfo, Aprendendo a repetir hebreo: EfMex 9,3 (1991) 345-354.

9378* *Qimron* Elisha, ⊕ Interchangeability of ṣere and pataḥ in Biblical Hebrew and 'Philippi's Law': Lešonenu 56 (1991s) 111-5; Eng. i.

9379 **Rattray** Susan, The tense-mood-aspect system of biblical Hebrew, with special emphasis on 1 and 2 Samuel: diss. California. Berkeley 1992. 169 p. 93-05048. – DissA 53 (1992) 3508-A.

9380 a) *Rendsburg* Gary A., Morphological evidence for regional dialects in ancient Hebrew [1988]; – b) *Garr* W. Randall, The linguistic study of morphology: → 343, Linguistics/BH 1992, 65-88 / 49-64.

Rooker Mark F., Biblical Hebrew in transition... Ezek ᴰ1990 → 3869.

9381 a) *Sarfatti* Gad B., ⊕ Reflexive pronouns and pronouns of identity in Hebrew; – b) *Betser* Zvi, ⊕ The extended use of Hufʿal in responsa Hebrew: Lešonenu 56 (1991s) 341-351 / 319-339; Eng. III/II.

9381 *Schramm* Gene, al., Hebrew: → 741, AnchorBD 4 (1992) 203-214.

9382 **Siebesma** P. A., The function of the niphal: StSemNeer 28, 1991 → 7,9079: ᴿJTS 43 (1992) 563s (W. *Watson*).

9383 *Sinclair* Cameron, The valence of the Hebrew verb: JANES 20 (1991) 63-81.

9384 **Specht** Günther, Wissensbasierte Analyse althebräischer Morphosyntax; das Expertensystem AMOS: AOtt 35, 1990 → 6,9075: ᴿCBQ 54 (1992) 771s (J. A. *Groves*, also on VERHEIJ I.); ZkT 114 (1992) 81s (J. M. *Oesch*, auch über ECKARDT W. 1987).

9385 *Talshir* David, ⊕ Prosthetic aleph: Lešonenu 56 (1991s) 285s.

9386 **Verheij** A. J. C., Verbs and numbers; a study of the frequencies of the Hebrew verbal tense forms in the books of Samuel, Kings, and

Chronicles: StSemNeerl 28, 1990 ➤ 6,9176: ᴿBL (1992) 141 (J. *Barr*: he shows that Sam/Kgs differ from each other as well as from Chron); TüTQ 172 (1992) 245s (W. *Gross*); ZAW 104 (1992) 313s (H. W. *Hoffmann*).

9387 *Verheij* Arian, Stems and roots; some statistics concerning the verbal stems in the Hebrew Bible [... JENNI-WESTERMANN THAT 2,542]: ZAHeb 5 (1992) 64-71: p. 68 'The number for verbal forms of any particular stem in a specific text is statistically correlated with the squared number of verbal roots used in that stem in that text'.

9388 **Volgger** David. Notizen zur Phonologie des Bibelhebräischen [Diplomarbeit Salzburg]: Mü Univ. AOtt 36. St. Ottilien 1992, EOS. xii-132 p. DM 24,80. 3-88096-536-6 [OIAc 5,38].

9389 **Waldman** Nahum M., The recent study of Hebrew 1989 ➤ 5,9117... 7,9085: ᴿJAOS 112 (1992) 318-320 (G. A. *Rendsburg*: several proposals).

9390 **Waltke** B. K., *O'Connor* M., An introduction to biblical Hebrew syntax 1990 ➤ 6,9178; 7,9086: ᴿCBQ 54 (1992) 338s (E. M. *Cook*: grammatical functions, not constructions); CritRR 5 (1992) 172-4 (Z. *Garber*: too much for a year, but an indispensable research tool); JTS 43 (1992) 357s (Judith M. *Hadley*: stresses usableness over completeness); SvEx 56 (1991) 118s (Gunnel *André*); VT 42 (1992) 428s (J. A. *Emerton*).

9390* **Williams** Ronald J., Hebrew syntax, an outline². Toronto 1988, Univ. x-122 p.

9391 **Yardeni** Ada, ❶ The book of Hebrew script. J 1991, Carta. 291 p.; 235 fig. – ᴿRÉJ 151 (1992) 213s (Colette *Sirat*).

9392 *Young* Ian, The style of the Gezer Calendar and some 'archaic biblical Hebrew' passages: VT 42 (1992) 362-375.

9393 *Zohori* Menahem, *a*) The absolute infinitive and its uses in the Hebrew language; – *b*) The metathesis and dual forms in the Hebrew language; – *c*) The passive forms, their uses and frequency in biblical Hebrew. Israel 1990, 183 p.; 1991, 70 p.; 1992, 158 p.

9394 *Zuber* Beat, Das 'Nun paragogicum' [HOFTIJZER J. 1985]: DielB 27 (1991) 17-45.

J1.2 Lexica et inscriptiones hebraicae; later Hebrew.

9395 **Albeck** Orly, ❶ Formal analysis by syntactic and syntacto-semantic tools of standard Hebrew written in Israel: diss. Bar-Ilan, ᴰ*Kaddari* M. Ramat-Gan. 307 p. – RTLv 24, p. 544 sans date.

9396 **Alonso Schökel** Luis, Diccionario bíblico 1, 1990 ➤ 7,9089: ᴿCarthaginensia 8 (1992) 923 (R. *Sanz Valdivieso*); RelCu 37 (1991) 554 (M. A. *Martín Juárez*, 1); RivB 40 (1992) 331-3 (A. *Spreafico*, 1-7: i nomi propri saranno messi alla fine).

9397 **Andersen** F. I., *Forbes* A. D., The vocabulary of the OT 1989 ➤ 5,9120 ... 7,9093: ᴿRivB 40 (1992) 329s (G. *Odasso*: per una conoscenza morfolessica propria di ogni libro).

9398 *Azcárraga* María J. de, La masora y el intercambio de laríngeas: ➤ 44, ᶠDÍAZ ESTEBAN F., Sefarad 52 (1992) 33-38.

9399 ᴿBaltsan Hayim, Webster's New World Hebrew dictionary; Hebrew-English, English-Hebrew [entirely in the order of the Latin alphabet]. NY 1992, Prentice Hall. xxx-829 p. 0-13-944547-1.

9399* *Barr* James, Hebrew lexicography; informal thoughts: ➤ 343, Linguistics/BH 1992, 137-151.

9400 *Breuer* Yoḥanan, ❸ *Paṭṭᵉruha — piṭruha*; Babylonian Hebrew and its influence on the interpretation of the Mishnah during the Tannaitic period: Lešonenu 56 (1991s) 11-21; Eng. i.

9400* *Clines* David J. A., The new dictionary of classical Hebrew: ➤ 493a, IOSOT-B 1989/92, 169-175; 176-9 sample pages.

9401 **Davies** G. I., *al.*, Ancient Hebrew inscriptions; corpus and concordance 1991 ➤ 7,9097: ᴿExpTim 103 (1991s) 340s (J. C. L. *Gibson*: there is no epigraphy without tears).

9401* *a) Dijkstra* M., Schrijvers en scholing in Oud-Israël; – *b) Janssen* J. J., Schooljongens in het oude Egypte; – *c) Krispijn* T. J. H., Naar school in het oude Mesopotamië; – d) *Hout* T. van den, Een augur voor 25 sikkels; iets over opleiding bij de Hettieten: Phoenix EOL 38,3 (1992) 34-50; 2 fig. + 1 color. / 13-20; 3 fig. / 21-33; 2 fig. / 6-12.

Horbury W., *Noy* D., Jewish inscriptions of Graeco-Roman Egypt 1992 ➤ 9982.

9402 **Horst** P. W. van der, Ancient Jewish epitaphs; an introductory survey of a millennium of Jewish funerary epigraphy (300 BCE-700 CE): ContrBExT 2. Kampen 1991, Kok. 179 p. 90-242-3307-0 [NTAbs 36,305]. – ᴿBA 56 (1993) 163 (B. R. *McCane*); Biblica 73 (1992) 437s (D. J. *Harrington*); ETL 68 (1992) 403s (A. *Schoors*); RÉJ 151 (1992) 377-9 (G. *Nahon*).

9403 *Jacobson* Howard, Nonnulla onomastica [improving WUTZ F., TU 41, 1914]: JTS 43 (1992) 117 only.

9404 *Jeyaraj* Jesudason B., Naming and renaming as communication in ancient Israel: ➤ 40, ᶠDAVID C., Arasaradi 5 (1992) 158-169.

9405 *Kedar-Kopfstein* Benjamin, Leicht verzerrt; Bibelhebräisch im Spiegel des Neuhebräischen: ZAHeb 5 (1992) 72-86.

9406 **Klein** Ernest, A comprehensive etymological dictionary of the Hebrew language for readers of English 1987 ➤ 5,9141; 6,9199: ᴿRExp 89 (1992) 105s (T. G. *Smothers*).

9407 **Layton** Scott C., Archaic features of Canaanite personal names in the Hebrew Bible; HarvSemMg 47, ᴰ1990 ➤ 6,9202; 7,9107: ᴿBiblica 73 (1992) 273-6 (S. *Morin*: wichtig; CBQ 54 (1992) 749-751 (W. J. *Fulco*); JBL 111 (1992) 315-7 (Frank L. *Benz*); Syria 69 (1992) 480s (A. *Caquot*); TLZ 117 (1992) 350s (M. S. *Smith*, Eng.).

9408 *Marlowe* W. Creighton, A summary evaluation of Old Testament Hebrew lexica, translations, and philology in light of key developments in Hebrew lexicographic and Semitic linguistic history: GraceTJ 12,1 (1991) 3-20.

9409 **Meier** Samuel A., Speaking of speaking; marking direct discourse in the Hebrew Bible: VTS 46. Leiden 1992, Brill. xvi-383 p. 90-04-09602-7.

9410 **Miller** Cynthia L., Reported speech in biblical and epigraphic Hebrew; a linguistic analysis: diss. ᴰ*Dahlstrom* Amy. Chicago 1992. ix-376 p. – OIAc 3,31.

9411 **Murtonen** A., Hebrew in its West-Semitic setting; a comprehensive survey of non-Masoretic dialects and traditions, I-A 1986 ➤ 2,7306; 7,9114; I-B 1988s ➤ 6,9208s; II. 1990 ➤ 6,9210: ᴿBL (1982) 137 (J. C. L. *Gibson* foreseen content reduced; still a massive and useful work); JSS 37 (1992) 310-2 (P. *Wernberg-Møller*); OLZ 87 (1992) 410s (W. *Herrmann*).

9412 *Ólafsson* Sverrir, Late biblical Hebrew; fact or fiction? [POLZIN R. 1976; term first used by KUTSCHER Y. 1974]: ➤ 132, MILIK J. 1992, 135-146 ['fiction; but we can change that to fact if we want to'].

9413 *Pazzini* M., Grammatiche e dizionari di ebraico-aramaico in italiano; catalogo ragionato: LA 42 (1992) 9-32; Eng. 333.

9414 **Pérez Fernández** Miguel, La lengua de los sabios, I. Morfosintaxis: Jeron BtMidrásica 13. Estella 1992, VDivino. 421 p. 84-7151-841-4 [BL 93,157, J. F. *Elwolde*: Tannaitic Hebrew grammar for classroom].

9415 **Renz** Johannes, Die althebräischen Inschriften: Text, Kommentar und zusammenfassende Erörterungen: Diss. ᴰ*Sonner* H. Kiel 1992s. – RTLv 24, p. 544.

9416 **Reymond** Philippe, Dictionnaire d'Hébreu et d'Araméen bibliques 1991 ⇥ 7,9120: ᴿRÉJ 151 (1992) 216 (Madeleine *Petit*); Syria 69 (1992) 481s (J. *Margain*).

9417 **Ridzewski** Beate, [Vorislamisch-] Neuhebräische Grammatik auf Grund der ältesten Handschriften und Inschriften [grossenteils Qumran; Diss. Heidelberg 1990, ᴰ*Schall* A.]: HeidOrSt 21. Fra 1992, Lang. xviii-201 p. DM 67. 3-631-43695-5 [BL 93,157, J. A. *Emerton*].

9418 *Smelik* K. A. D., The literary structure of the Yavneh-Yam ostracon: IsrEJ 42 (1992) 55-62.

9419 [**Koehler**] **Stamm** J., *al.*, Hebräisches und Aramäisches Lexikon³ Lfg. 4, 1990 ⇥ 7,9095: ᴿJSS 37 (1992) 88-93 (W. von *Soden*: eine gewaltige Arbeit); TLZ 117 (1992) 830s (G. *Pfeifer*, Lfg. 4).

9420 ᴱ**Stone** Michael E., Rock inscriptions and graffiti project; catalogue of inscriptions; Inscriptions 1-6000: SBL Resources 28s. Atlanta 1992, Scholars. I. 1-3000; 282 p. II. 244 p. 1-5540-790-0; -3-5 [ZAW 105,535, M. *Köckert*].

9421 *Swiggers* P., The Bet-Shemesh 'Abecedary': ⇥ 118, LESLAU W., Semitic 1991, 1520-7.

9422 *Tilley* Maureen A., Typological numbers [7; 12; 40]; taking a count of the Bible: BR 8,3 (1992) 48s.

9423 **Tur-Sinai** Naphtali H. ✪ Lachish Ostraca, ²*Ahituv* Shmuel [¹1940]. J 1987, Bialik / Isr. Expl. Soc. xi-274 p. $20. – ᴿBASOR 285 (1992) 83-85 (B. *Halpern*).

9424 **Wexler** Paul, *a)* The schizoid nature of modern Hebrew; a Slavic language in search of a Semitic past. Wsb 1990, Harrassowitz. 140 p. – ᴿZDMG 142 (1992) 164s (D. *Blohm*). – *b)* Explorations in Judeo-Slavic linguistics. Leiden 1987, Brill. xix-286 p. *f* 160. – ᴿBSO 54 (1991) 150s (L. *Glinert*).

J1.3 **Voces** ordine alphabetico *consonantium* **hebraicarum.**

9425 *ebyon:* Pleins J. David, Poor, poverty OT: ⇥ 741, AnchorBD 5 (1992) 402-414: distinguishes *ebyon* 'the beggarly poor'; *dal* 'the poor peasant farmer'; *mahsôr* 'the lazy poor'; *raš* 'political and economic inferiority'; *'ani* 'the injustice of oppression'; 414-424, NT, *Hanks* Thomas D.

9426 *'bl: Clines* David J. A., Was there an *'bl* II 'be dry' in classical Hebrew?: VT 42 (1992) 1-10 [not really; variant of 'mourn'].

9427 **'ôb:* [Job 32,19] *Rubiato* M. J., *al.*, Recipientes bíblicos III: Sefarad 51 (1991) 145-161; Eng. 162.

9428 *ah: Görg* Manfred, *'h*, 'Seele' im biblischen und nichtbiblischen Hebräisch: BibNot 63 (1992) 19-25.

9429 *'ah*, *'asūk: Rubiato* M., *al.*, Recipientes bíblicos 4: Sefarad 51 (1991) 369-387; 2 fig.; Eng. 387: both hapax, Jer 36,22s brazier; 2 Kgs 4,2 body-oil measure.

9430 *Barkay* Gabriel, The world's oldest poorbox [bowl with paleohebraic inscription *'hk* on inside ⇥ 7,9134]: BAR-W 18,6 (1992) 48-50; ill.

9431 *ʾel:* **Brin** Gershon, The [elohim] superlative in the Hebrew Bible, additional cases: VT 42 (1992) 115-8.

9432 *elep:* **Fouts** David M., The use of large numbers in the Old Testament, with particular emphasis in the use of *ʾelep*: diss. Dallas Theol. Sem. 1992. 233 p. 93-03913. – DissA 53 (1992s) 3250-A.

9433 *im:* **Creason** M., The syntax of *îm* and the structure of the Marseilles Tanff: RStFen 20 (1992) 143-159.

9434 *ʾašer:* **Wyk** W.C. Vanᴶ, The syntax of *ʾašer* in Hebrew investigated anew: JTydSem 4 (1992) 200-9.

9435 *bᵉ:* **Jenni** Ernst, Die hebräischen Präpositionen, Band I. Die Präposition Beth. Stu 1992, Kohlhammer. 398 p. DM 149. 3-17-01177-1 [BL 93,153, J.C.L. *Gibson*]. – ᴿTüTQ 172 (1992) 328s (W. *Gross*).

9436 *bᵉhēmôt* [➔ 9461], **Hermann** Wolfram, [Hi 40,15] Eine notwendige Erinnerung: ZAW 104 (1992) 262-4.

9438 *bôʾ:* **Gelio** Roberto, Le anomalie sintattiche di certe forme verbali derivate dalla radice *bwʾ* e le opportunità di una differente lettura: Lateranum 58 (1992) 331-355.

9439 **Lingen** Anton van der, *bwʾ yṣʾ* ('to go out and to come in') as a military term [= 'go to war' as commander]: VT 42 (1992) 59-66.

9440 *bārāʾ:* **Finley** Thomas J., Dimensions of the Hebrew word for 'create' (*bārāʾ*): BtS 148 (1991) 409-423.

9441 *bārak:* **Taylor** John B., The theology of blessing in the Hebrew Scriptures: diss. UK Open University 1992. 361 p. BRDX-97604. – DissA 53 (1992s) 3253-A.

9442 *gam:* **Merwe** C.H.J. Van der, Pragmatics and the translation value of *gam*: JTydSem 4 (1992) 181-199.

9443 **Merwe** C. van der, The Old Hebrew particle gam ... Gn-2Kg: AOtt 34, 1990 ➔ 6,9242; 7,9146: ᴿCBQ 54 (1992) 336s (G. *Vall*).

9444 *yôn:* **Touitou** Elazar, ❸ *kᵉgônēnû* = *kᵉmônû*, a neologism created by RASHI: Lešonenu 56 (1991s) 317s; Eng. II.

9445 *gēr:* **Greger** Barbara, Beobachtungen zum Begriff *gēr*: BibNot 63 (1992) 30-34.

9446 *dābār:* **Schneider** Wolfgang, *Dabar* bedeutet 'S[ache]' [Jer 35,17]: BibNot 58 (1991) 24-28.

9447 *dam:* **Prassel** Richard C.ᴶ, An examination of the biblical metaphor of 'blood' in light of some contemporary studies on violence [it means both life and death, and serves to express human violence toward the divine]: diss. Southern Baptist Theol. Sem., 1992, ᴰ*Ward* W., 290 p. 93-10431. – DissA 53 (1992s) 3956-A.

9448 *zônâh:* **Schulte** Hannelis, Beobachtungen zum Begriff der Zônä im AT: ZAW 104 (1992) 255-262.

9449 *ḥgb:* **Olmo Lete** G. del, Ug. *ḥgb* und *slḥ* como material sacrificial: AulaO 10 (1992) 151-4.

9450 *ḥaṭṭā:* **Hutter** Manfred, Die Verwendung von hethitisch *waštul* in historischen Texten im Vergleich mit akkadisch *ḥīṭu* [Sünde]: ➔ 683, Circulation 1991/2, 221-6.

9450* *ḥamtu, maru:* **Lambert** W.G., The reference of ∼ in lexical lists: ZAss 81 (1991) 7-9.

9451 *ḥesed:* **Clark** Gordon R., *ḥesed* — a study of a lexical field: AbrNahr 30 (1992) 34-54.

9452 *Dase* Heike, Der *ḥesed* der Mesopotamischen Frauen und seine Bedeutung für die Heilsgeschichte Israels: DielB 26 (1989s) 162-172.

9453 *ṭôb:* González Lamadrid Antonio, Apuntes sobre *ṭôb/yāṭab* y su traducción en las Biblias modernas: → 135, ᶠMuÑoz Iglesias S., EstBib 50 (1992) 443-456.

9453* *yad:* Ackroyd P., Hand: → 762, NBL II, 6 (1991) 25-27.

9454 *yārāʾ:* Merwe C.H.J. Van der, Is there any difference between *yārāʾ mi-penê, yārāʾ min,* and *yārā et?*: JNWS 18 (1992) 177-193: *et* no threat; *mippᵉnē* immediate threat.

9455 *yēš:* Putnam Frederic C., Representation of the Hebrew predicators of existence in the Septuagint: diss. Annenberg. Ph 1991. 478 p. 92-30470. – DissA 53 (1992s) 2414-A.

9456 *kabbîr:* Rendsburg Gary A., Kabbîr in biblical Hebrew; evidence for style-switching and addressee-switching in the Hebrew Bible: JAOS 112 (1992) 649-651.

9457 *kalāʾum, narum:* Rawi Farouk N.H. al-, Two Old Akkadian [Sulayma; Diyāla] letters concerning the offices of ~ : ZAss 82 (1992) 180-184+2 facsim.; 2 pl.

9458 *kippēr:* Laato Antti, The eschatological act of *kippēr* in the Damascus Document: → 132, ᶠMilik J. 1992, 91-107.

9459 *ktym:* Dion P.-E., Les KTYM de Tel Arad; Grecs ou Phéniciens?: RB 99 (1992) 70-97; Eng. 70 [could have been Greeks].

9460 *lôʾ/lô:* Ognibeni Bruno, Tradizioni orali di lettura e testo ebraico della Bibbia... 17 ketiv *lôʾ* / qere *lô,* 1989 → 4,2547... 7,9162: ᴿBZ 36 (1992) 125-7 (J. *Maier*); RivStoLR 27 (1991) 374 (G. *Miletto*); Sefarad 51 (1991) 468-470 (M.J. de *Azcárraga*).

9461 *Leviathan:* Whitney K., Two strange beasts; a study of traditions concerning Leviathan and Behemoth in Second Temple and Early Rabbinic Judaism: diss. – HarvTR 85 (1992) 503s.

9462 *MṬL* (Gn 27,28.39 *m-* could be preformative rather than preposition): Lešonenu 56 (1991s) 298s (I. *Ben-David,* ❸); Eng. I.

9463 *moṭâh:* Zwickel Wolfgang, *moṭah* = 'Jochhaken' [Lv 26,13; Jer 27,8]: BibNot 57 (1991) 37-40; 2 fig.

9464 *mrlh:* Vattioni Francesco, A proposito di mrlh [*mare+elahê* su altare a quattro corni]: EpAnat 18 (1991) 96.

9465 *māṣāʾ:* Tzadka Yitzhak, ❸ *'Maṣaʾ iššâ maṣa ṭob';* a semantic-syntactic analysis of *maṣaʾ:* Lešonenu 56 (1991s) 353-360. Eng. V.

9466 *met:* Durand Jean-Marie, L'emploi des toponymes dans l'onomastique d'époque amorrite; (1) les noms en *mut* ['worker, warrior, male']: StEpL 8 (1991) 81-97.

9467 *mt:* Tropper Josef, Samʾalisch *mt* 'wahrlich' und das Phänomen der Aphärese im Semitischen: Orientalia 61 (1992) 448-453.

9468 *-na:* Kaufman Stephen A., An emphatic plea for [*-na* meaning] please: → 65, Mem. Gevirtz S., Maarav 7 (1991) 195-8.

9469 *NGR:* 9 biblical occurrences could be rather *grr* conjugated as Aramaic: Lešonenu 56 (1991s) 293 (I. *Ben-David,* ❸); Eng. I.

9470 *NDW* (*ndr*), *bll* (*bhl, byl,* ʾ*bl*)...: Masson Michel, Quelques parallélismes sémantiques en relation avec la notion de 'couler': → 118, ᶠLeslau W., Semitic 1991, 1024-41.

9471 *nādar:* Cartledge Tony W., Vows in the Hebrew Bible and the Ancient Near East [diss. Duke, ᴰ*Meyers* E.]: JStOT supp 147. Sheffield 1992, Academic. 221 p. 1-85075-359-8.

9472 *NZH:* Sperling David, Aramaic *nzh* and Akkadian *nesû* ['depart']: → 65, Mem. Gevirtz S., Maarav 7 (1991) 229-239.

9473 *nzl:* Watson Wilfred G. E., An enigmatic expression in Ugaritic: Abr-Nahr 30 (1992) 172-5.

9474 *nîr:* Ben Zvi Ehud, Once the lamp has been kindled; a reconsideration of the meaning of the MT *nîr:* AustralBR 39 (1991) 19-30 [< ZIT 92,238].

9475 *seren:* Garbini Giovanni, On the origin of the Hebrew-Philistine word *séren:* ⇥ 118, FLESLAU W., Semitic 1991, 516-520.

9476 *'anaw:* Dawes Stephen B., Humility; whence this strange notion? [WENGST K. Eng. 1988]: ExpTim 103 (1991s) 72-75.

9477 *pānîm:* Knight Teman W.[III], The presence of God in the OT: diss. Baptist Theol. Sem., DBailey D. New Orleans 1992. 212 p. 92-27155. – DissA 53 (1992s) 1547-A.

9478 *Soden* W. von, Zur Herkunft von hebr. *p^enîmāh* 'hinein, (dr)innen' und *p^enîmî* 'innerer': UF 24 (1992) 311s.

9479 *ṣedeq* [⇥ 499], Scullion J. J., Righteousness OT: ⇥ 741, AnchorBD 5 (1992) 724-736 [-742-773, Reumann J. NT etc.].

9480 *Lenzen* Verena, 'Gerechtigkeit' — in der hebräischen Sprachtradition: LebZeug 46 (1991) 49-55.

9482 *ṣur:* Olofsson Staffan, God is my rock 1990 ⇥ 6,9279: RBZ 36 (1992) 309-311 (W. Schenk); TLZ 117 (1992) 508-510 (A. Aejmelaeus).

9483 *ṣāpôn:* a) O'Connor M., Cardinal-direction terms in biblical Hebrew; – b) Rosén Ḥaiim B., Some thoughts on the system of designation of the cardinal points in ancient Semitic languages: ⇥ 118, FLESLAU W., Semitic 1991, 1140-57 / 1337-44.

9484 *qēn:* Barr James, Is Hebrew *qēn* 'nest' a metaphor? [Gen 6,14 ark-rooms]: ⇥ 118, FLESLAU W., Semitic 1991, 150-161.

9485 *qrb:* Schweizer Harald, Sprachkritik als Ideologiekritik... qrb 1991 ⇥ 7,9188: RTLZ 117 (1992) 344s (W. Engemann).

9486 *rûaḥ:* a) Sekki Arthur E., The meaning of ruaḥ at Qumran: SBL diss 110, 1989 ⇥ 5,9239; 7,9192: RCBQ 54 (1992) 544-6 (Maurya P. Horgan: flawed and outdated). – b) Dreytza M., Der theologische Gebrauch von Ruaḥ 1990 ⇥ 7,9190: RNedTTs 46 (1992) 230s (P. B. Dirksen).

9486* *rāḥôq:* Gelio Roberto, Rilievi sul tema biblico-orientale della lontananza e relative implicazioni teologiche: Lateranum 57 (1991) 3-26.

9487 *rîb:* Bovati Pietro, Ristabilire la giustizia: AnBib 110, D1986 ⇥ 2,7458... 7,9194: RRB 99 (1992) 597 (F. Langlamet, aussi sur BOECKER H.); ZSav-R 107 (1990) 683s (S. H. Siedl: 'selten habe ich ein Buch mit so grosser Freude gelesen wie dieses').

9488 *r^epā'îm:* Pitard Wayne T., A new edition of the 'Rāpi'ūma' texts: KTU 1.20-22: BASOR 285 (1992) 33-77; 22 fig.

9489 RQM: Vattioni Francesco, A proposito della radice *rqm* [ital. ricamo]: StEpL 7 (1990) 129-131.

9490 *rāṣāh,* 'Gefallen [joy] (haben)': ⇥ 770, TWAT 7,6s (1992) 641-652 (H. M. Barstad).

9491 *rāṣaḥ* 'töten': ⇥ 770, TWAT 7,6s (1992) 652-663 (F.-L. Hossfeld).

9492 *rṣp ṣprm:* RStFen 20 (1992) 93s (G. Garbini).

9493 *rāṣaṣ* 'zerschmettern': ⇥ 770, TWAT, 7,6s (1992) 663-5 (H. Ringgren).

9494 *rāqad* 'tanzen': ⇥ 770, TWAT 7,6s (1992) 665-9 (M. J. Mulder).

9495 *rāśā',* 'Frevler': ⇥ 770, TWAT 7,6s (1992) 675-683 (H. Ringgren).

9495* *ræšæp* 'Feuer': ⇥ 770, TWAT 7,6s (1992) 684-690 (M. Mulder).

9496 *ræšæt,* 'Netz': ⇥ 770, TWAT 7,6s (1992) 690-2 (P. Mommer).

9497 *śāba'* 'satt werden': ⇥ 770, TWAT 7,6s (1992) 693-704 (G. Warmuth).

9498 *śābar* 'hoffen': ⇥ 770, TWAT 7,6s (1992) 704-6 (K.-M. Beyse).

9499 *śāgab* 'Zuflucht': ⇥ 770, TWAT 7,6s (1992) 706-9 (H. Ringgren).

9500 *śādæh* 'Feld': → 770, TWAT 7,6s (1992) 709-718 (G. *Wallis*).
9501 *śôś* / *śyś* 'Freude': → 770, TWAT 7,6s (1992) 721-9 (H.-J. *Fabry*).
9502 *śāḥaq* 'lachen': → 770, TWAT 7,6s (1992) 730-745 (R. *Bartelmus*).
9502* Klaus Nathan, ❿ *miśḥaqē lāśōn* in the Bible: BethM 37,129 (1991s)
    170-181.
9503 *śê[j]bah,* '(hohes) Alter': → 770, TWAT 7,6s (1992) 751-7 (H. J. *Fabry*).
9504 *śîḥah* 'Nachdenken': → 770, TWAT 7,6s (1992) 757-761 (J. *Hausmann*).
9505 *śîm* 'setzen': → 770, TWAT 7,6s (1992) 761-781 (G. *Vanoni*).
9506 *śākal, maśkîl* 'Einsicht': → 770, TWAT 7,6s (1992) 781-795 (K. *Koenen*).
9507 *śākār* 'Lohn(arbeiter)': → 770, TWAT 7,6s (1992) 795-801 (É. *Lipiński*).
9508 *śᵉmô'l* 'links': → 770, TWAT 7,6s (1992) 804-8 (D. *Kellermann*).
9509 *śāmaḥ, śimḥāh* 'Freude': → 770, TWAT 7,6s (1992) 808-822 (G. *Vanoni*).
9510 *śānēʾ, śinʾâh* 'Hass': → 770, TWAT 7,6s (1992) 828-839 (É. *Lipiński*).
9511 *śāpâh* 'Lippe': → 770, TWAT 7,6s (1992) 840-9 (B. *Kedar-Kopfstein*).
9512 *śaq* 'Sack, Trauerkleidung': → 770, TWAT 7,6s (1992) 849-855 (W.
    Thiel).
9513 *śar* 'Beamter': → 770, TWAT 7,6s (1992) 855-879 (H. *Niehr*).
9514 *śārîd* 'Rest, remnant': → 770, TWAT 7,6s (1992) 879-882 (B. *Kedar-Kopfstein*).
9515 *śārap* 'Verbrennen': → 770, TWAT 7,6s (1992) 882-891 (U. *Rüterswörden*).
9516 *šāʾab* 'schöpfen': → 770, TWAT 7,6s (1992) 891-4 (H. *Schmoldt*).
9517 *šāʾag* 'brüllen': → 770, TWAT 7,7s (1992) 895-8 (A. *Graupner*).
9518 *šāʾāh* 'Getöse': → 770, TWAT 7,8 (1992) 898-901 (K.-M. *Beyse*).
9519 *šāʾāl* 'fragen': → 770, TWAT 7,8 (1992) 910-926 (N. F. *Fuchs*); *šᵉʾôl*
    → 7428*.
9520 *šaʾᵃnān* 'ruhig': → 770, TWAT 7,8 (1992) 827-9 (W. *Thiel*).
9521 *šāʾap* 'schnappen': → 770, TWAT 7,8 (1992) 929-931 (P. *Maiberger* †).
9522 *šāʾar* ['Fleisch'] 'Rest, übrig bleiben': → 770, TWAT 7,8 (1992) [931-3, H.
    Ringgren] 933-950 (R. E. *Clements*).
9523 *šᵉbî* 'Kriegsgefangenschaft': → 770, TWAT 7,8 (1992) 950-8 (B. *Otzen*).
9524 *šᵉbût* 'Wiederherstellung': → 770, TWAT 7,8 (1992) 958-965 (M. *Ben-Yashar*, M. *Zipor*).
9525 *šæbæṭ* 'Stab, Stamm': → 770, TWAT 7,8 (1992) 966-974 (H.-J. *Zobel*).
9526 *šābaᶜ* 'Eid': → 770, TWAT 7,8 (1992) 974-1000 (L. *Kottsieper*).
9527 *šebaᶜ* 'sieben': → 770, TWAT 7,8 (1992) 1000-1027 (E. *Otto*).
9528 *šdmt*: *Wyatt* N., A new look at Ugaritic *šdmt* [*Sarment*, juice-producing
    shoot of the vine; rather than 'terrace': also in Dt 32,32; Isa 16,8 ...]: JSS
    37 (1992) 149-153.
9529 *škm*: *Janowski* Bernd, Rettungsgewissheit... am Morgen ᴰ1989 → 5,
    9245 ... 7,9200: ᴿTRu 57 (1992) 180-7 (L. *Perlitt*, al.).
9530 *škn*: *Buccellati* Giorgio, A note on the *muškēnum* as a 'homesteader':
    → 65, Mem. GEVIRTZ S., Maarav 7 (1991) 91-100. – *šᵉkînâ* → 7013.
9530* *šāpān*: *Görg* Manfred, Von der 'Bergmaus' zum 'Klippdachs' [*Diebner*
    B.]: BibNot 65 (1992) 9-11.

J1.5   *Phoenicia, ugaritica* – **North-West Semitic** [→ T5.4].

9531 a) *Ahlström* Gösta W. †, The Nora inscription and Tarshish; – b)
    Zuckerman Bruce, The Nora puzzle: → 65, GEVIRTZ S. mem., Maarav 7
    (1991) 41-49 / 296-301; 5 fig.; 2 pl.
9532 *Arnaud* Daniel, Contribution de l'onomastique du Moyen-Euphrate à la
    connaissance de l'Émariote: StEpL 8 (1991) 23-46.

9533 **Aufrecht** Walter E., A corpus of Ammonite inscriptions 1989 ➤ 6,9367; 7,9204: ᴿBL (1992) 25s (J. C. L. *Gibson*); JAOS 112 (1992) 489s (S. *Segert*).

9534 *Bonnet* Corinne, La terminologie phénico-punique relative au métier de lapicide et à la gravure des textes: StEpL 7 (1990) 111-127.

Bordreuil P., *al.*, Bibliothèque RS, textes 1991 ➤ e708.

9535 **Bordreuil** P., *Pardee* D., *al.*, La trouvaille épigraphique de l'Ougarit, I. Concordance: RasShamra 5, 1989 ➤ 6,9368; 7,9205: ᴿOLZ 87 (1992) 256-8 (W. *Herrmann*); RStFen 20 (1992) 194s (P. *Xella*).

9536 *Bordreuil* Pierre, Flèches phéniciennes inscrites: RB 99 (1992) 205-213; Eng. 205; 2 fig.; pl. II-III.

9536* *a*) *Bordreuil* Pierre, Vingt ans d'épigraphie transjordanienne; – *b*) *Macdonald* Michael, The distribution of Safaitic inscriptions in northern Jordan: ➤ 740, Jordan 4 (1992) 185-9 / 303-7 [❹ 5-14, *Khraysheh* Fawwaz Al-].

9537 *Brooks* Simcha, Pregnant women (*rḥmt*) in the Moabite inscription: BInstArch 14,28 (1991) 149s.

9538 **Caquot** A., Textes ougaritiques [I. 1976] II. avec *Tarragon* Jean-Michel de, *Cunchillos* Jesús-Luis, Textes rituels, correspondence: LAPO 14, 1989 ➤ 5,9253; 7,9209: ᴿÉTRel 67 (1992) 454s (D. *Lys*); JAOS 112 (1992) 125-7 (B. A. *Levine*).

9539 *a*) *Colonna* Giovanna, 'Tempio' e 'santuario' nel lessico delle lamine di Pyrgi; – *b*) *Amadasi Guzzo* Maria Giulia, Per una classificazione delle iscrizioni fenicie di dono: ➤ 701, ScAnt 3s (1989s) 197-216; 9 fig. / 831-843.

Creason S., The syntax of *'im* and the structure of the Marseille tariff 1992 ➤ 9433: RStFen 20 (1992) 143-159.

9541 *Cross* Frank M., An inscribed arrowhead of the eleventh century BCE in the Bible Lands Museum in Jerusalem ['the corpus ... 11th cent. Old Canaanite and Linear Phoenician scripts continues to grow']: ➤ 18, ᶠBIRAN A., ErIsɪ 23 (1992) 21*-26*; 1 fig.; table of signs.

9542 **Cunchillos** Jesús-Luis [➤ e711s] (*Vita* Juan-Pablo): Banco de datos filológicos semíticos noroccidentales, I/1, Textos ugaríticos. M 1992, Inst Fg. (B-OrAnt). xxi-906 p. 84-00-04790-7.

9542* *Edzard* Dietz H., Arbiter, ein punisches Lehnwort?: ZSav-R 108 (1991) 286 nur.

9543 *a*) *Hens-Piazza* Gina, Repetition and rhetoric in Canaanite epic; a close reading of KTU 1.14 III 20-49; – *b*) *Márquez-Rowe* J., Summaries of Ugaritic texts and some new reading suggestions: UF 24 (1992) 103-112 / 259-262.

9544 **Huehnergard** J., *a*) Ugaritic vocabulary in Semitic transcription: HarvSemSt 1987 ➤ 3,9468 ... 7,9214: ᴿLešonenu 56 (1991s) 185-194 (D. *Sivan*, ❸); Eng. vi. – *b*) The development of the third person suffixes in Phoenician: ➤ 65, Mem. GEVIRTZ S., Maarav 7 (1991) 183-194.

9545 **Izre'el** Shlomo, *Singer* Itamar, The general's letter ... RS 20-33: 1990 ➤ 6,e308: ᴿBLitEc 93 (1992) 250s (M. *Delcor*); BO 49 (1992) 406-8 (R. R. *Stieglitz*); RSO 66 (1992) 221s (M. *Liverani*).

9546 **Knoppers** Gary N., 'The god in his temple'; the Phoenician text from Pyrgi as a funerary inscription: JNES 51 (1992) 105-120; facsim.

9547 *a*) *Knudesen* Ebbe E., Amorite grammar; a comparative statement; – *b*) *Israel* Felice, Some conservative features of Phoenician in the light of geographical linguistics: – *c*) *Zevit* Ziony, How do you say 'noble' in

Phoenician, biblical Hebrew, and in Ugaritic?: ➤ 118, ᶠLESLAU W., Semitic 1991, 866-885 / 729-745 / 1704-15.
9547* *Krahmalkov* C. R., Phoenician 'yt and 't: RSO 66 (1992) 227-231.
9548 *Lemaire* André, Notes d'épigraphie nord-ouest sémitique: Semitica 40 (1991) 39-54; 29 fig.
9548* **Levi della Vida** G., *Amadasi Guzzo* Maria Giulia, Iscrizioni puniche della Tripolitania (1927-1967) 1987 ➤ 3,e371; 7,8217: ᴿRSO 65 (1991) 341-3 (R. *Contini*).
9549 **Margalit** Baruch, The Ugaritic poem of AQHT: BZAW 182, 1989 ➤ 5,9267*... 7,9219: ᴿBLitEc 93 (1992) 249s (M. *Delcor*); TR 88 (1992) 363s (O. *Loretz*: hidden biblical premises).
9550 **Mohamed** Amgud M., ⊕ A handbook of Phoenician [survey in Hebrew; 25 texts with translation] in the Arabic language: diss. ᴰ*Levine* B. NYU 1992. 244 p. 92-22903. – DissA 53 (1992s) 788-A.
9551 **Negev** Avraham, Personal names in the Nabatean realm: Qedem 32. J 1991, Hebrew Univ. xii-228 p. 0333-5844.
9552 *O'Connor* M., Diction and the ancient Northwest Semitic inscriptions: ➤ 557*, Contacts 1990/2, 108-114.
9553 *Olmo Lete* Gregorio de, Receta mágica para un enfante enfermo (KTU 1,124): ➤ 44, ᶠDÍAZ ESTEBAN F., Sefarad 52 (1992) 187-192.
9554 **Pardee** Dennis, Les textes para-mythologiques 1988 ➤ 4,a349... 7,9224: ᴿArOr 60 (1992) 86s (J. *Pečirková*); OLZ 86 (1991) 283-5 (W. *Herrmann*).
9555 *Pardee* Dennis, RS 24.643; texte et structure: Syria 69 (1992) 153-170.
9556 *a*) *Pardee* Dennis, The structure of RS 1.002; – *b*) *Voigt* Rainer, On voicing and devoicing in Ugaritic; – *c*) *Arbeitman* Yoël L., Ugaritic pronominals in the light of morphophonemic economy; – *d*) *Dietrich* M., *Loretz* O., Ugaritisch ʿašr, āširūma und äthiopisch ʿaššara: ➤ 118, ᶠLESLAU W., Semitic 1991, 1181-96 / 1619-1631 / 82-106 / 309-327.
9557 *Pitard* Wayne T., The shape of the ʿayin in the Ugaritic script: JNES 51 (1992) 261-8 + 6 (double) fig.
9558 *Pope* Marvin H., A resurvey of some Ugaritic-Hebrew connections: ➤ 65, Mem. GEVIRTZ S., Maarav 7 (1991) 199-206.
9558* **Renfroe** Fred, Arabic-Ugaritic lexical studies: AbhLitAltSyrPal 5. Münster 1992, Ugarit-Verlag. xii-198 p. 3-927120-09-X [OIAc 3,36).
9559 **Rin** Svi & Shifra, ⊕ The third column of Acts of the Gods; a revised paraphrase of the Ugaritic poetry with Tiberian vocalization. Ph 1992, INBAL.
9559* *a*) *Röllig* Wolfgang, Die phönizische Sprache; Bemerkungen zum gegenwärtigen Forschungsstand [< Atti del I Congresso Fen/Pun (Roma 1983) 375-385 Eng.]; – *b*) *Sznycer* Maurice, Die punische Literatur [< ArchViva 1/2 (1968s) 141-8]: ➤ e696, Karthago 1992, 76-94 / 321-340.
9560 *a*) *Sader* Hélène, Nouvelle inscription punique découverte au Liban [*Maʿmura* S Tyr]; – *b*) *Salem* Ali, Un abécédaire punique trouvé à Carthage; – *c*) *Sznycer* Maurice, Brèves remarques sur les anthroponymes libyques dans les inscriptions néopuniques de Mididi (Tunisie); – *d*) *Masson* Olivier, Encore l'urne phénicienne A. P. Cesnola de *Kition*: Semitica 41s (1991s) 107-116; 3 fig. / 117-121; 3 fig. / 123-131 / 101-5; 2 fig.
9560* **Segert** Stanislav, A basic grammar of the Ugaritic language 1984 ➤ 65,7912... 5,9272: ᴿAfO 38s (1991s) 196-8 (H. *Hirsch*).
9561 **Sivan** Daniel, *Cochavi-Rainey* Zipora, West-Semitic vocabulary in Egyptian script of the 14th to the 10th centuries BCE [in English]: Beer-Sheva 6. Beersheba 1992, Ben-Gurion Univ., Negev. xii-93 p. [OIAc 5,35]. 0334-2255.

9562 *Tropper* Josef, Das ugaritische Verbalsystem; Bestandsaufnahme der Formen und statistische Auswertung: UF 24 (1992) 313-337.
9563 *Vattioni* Francesco, Numido-punica; *a*) divagazioni sul nome di Giugurta; – *b*) punico o libico?: AION 51 (1991) 61-64. 319-331.
9564 *Watson* Wilfred G. E., *a*) Imagery in a Ugaritic incantation; – *b*) More on preludes to speech in Ugarit: UF 24 (1992) 367s / 361-6.
9565 *Watson* Wilfred G. E., The particle *p* in Ugaritic: StEpL 7 (1990) 75-86.
9565* *Yon* Marguerite, *Sznycer* Maurice, A Phoenician victory trophy at Kition: RepCyp (1992) 157-165; 3 fig.; pl. 51.
9566 *Young* Ian, [Isa 15s; 21,11s] The diphthong **ay* in Edomite [*layl* > *lēl* as *qaws* > *qôs*]: JSS 37 (1992) 27-30.
9567 *Zadok* Ran, Notes on the West Semitic material from Emar: AION 51 (1991) 113-137.

J1.6 Aramaica.

9568 *a*) *Aggoula* Basile, Studia aramaica III; – *b*) *Cussini* Eleonora, Two Palmyrene Aramaic inscriptions in American collections: Syria 69 (1992) 391-472 / 423-429.
9569 *Arata Mantovani* Piera, I papiri di Samaria (1 SP) [12 items from her Iscrizioni aramaiche in preparation]. RivB 40 (1992) 87-89.
9569* *Ben-David* Israel, ❹ The Aramaic noun pattern *ᵃpʿulāʾ* with ayin ayin roots — *apaʿāʾ*: Lešonenu 56 (1991s) 23-25; Eng. II.
9570 *a*) *Brock* Sebastian P., Some notes on dating formulae in Middle Aramaic inscriptions and in early Syriac manuscripts; – *b*) *Davis* Michael P., *Stuckenbruck* Loren T., Notes on translation phenomena in the Palmyrene bilinguals; – *c*) *Lemaire* André, La stèle araméenne d'Assouan (RES 439,1806), nouvel examen: ➤ 132, ᶠMILIK J. 1992, 263-264 / 265-283 / 289-303.
9570* *a*) *Cook* E. M., Qumran Aramaic and Aramaic dialectology; – *b*) *Díez Merino* L., The adverb in Qumran Aramaic; – *c*) *Fassberg* S. E., Hebraisms in the Aramaic documents from Qumran; – *d*) *Muraoka* T., The verbal rection in Qumran Aramaic; – *e*) *Qimron* E., Pronominal suffix *-kāh* in Qumran Aramaic; – *f*) *Wise* M. O., Accident and accidence; a scribal view of linguistic dating of the Aramaic scrolls from Qumran; – *g*) *Greenfield* Jonas C., with Qimron, The Genesis Apocryphon col. XII; – *h*) with *Sokoloff* M., The contribution of Qumran Aramaic to the Aramaic vocabulary ➤ 9586: ᴱ*Muraoka* T., Studies in Qumran Aramaic, Abr-Nahrain supp 3 (Lv 1992, Peeters; vii-167 p.; 90-6831-419X) 1-21 / 22-47 / 48-69 / 99-118 / 119-123 / 124-167 / 70-77 / 70-98.
9571 *Cook* Edward M., An Aramaic incantation bowl from Khafaje: BASOR 285 (1992) 79-81; 1 fig.
9571* **De Caen** Vincent J. J., A revised bibliography of the Samalian dialect of Old Aramaic: TargCogNews supp. 6. Toronto 1991, Univ. 18 p. [OIAc 2,17].
9572 **Fassberg** Stephen A., A grammar of the Palestinian Targum fragments from the Cairo Genizah [diss. 1983]: HarvSemSt 38, 1990 ➤ 6, 9397: ᴿJBL 111 (1992) 707s (B *Grossfeld*); LA 41 (1991) 571s (M. *Pazzini*).
9573 **Fitzmyer** Joseph A., *Kaufman* Stephen A., (*al.*) An Aramaic bibliography 1. Old, official, and biblical Aramaic: Lexicon Project. Baltimore 1992, Johns Hopkins Univ. XVI-349 p. $56. 0-8018-4318-X [TDig

39,262]. – ᴿOLZ 87 (1992) 547-552 (J. *Oelsner*; initial good impression marred by misprints).
9574 *Greenfield* Jonas C., *a*) The Aramaic legal texts of the Achaemenian period: ➤ Syrie perse 1989, TEuph 3 (1990) 85-92; – *b*) Some glosses on the Sfire inscriptions: ➤ 65, Mem. GEVIRTZ S., Maarav 7 (1991) 141-7.
9575 *a*) *Greenfield* Jonas C., The verb for washing in Aramaic; – *b*) *Tsereteli* K. G., About the states of nouns in Aramaic; – *c*) *Sabar* Yona, The Hebrew Bible vocabulary as reflected through traditional oral Neo-Aramaic translations; – *d*) *Pennacchietti* Fabrizio A., Gli allomorfi della flessione preteritale del dialetto neoaramaico orientale di Hertevin (Turchia) in prospettiva storica; – *e*) *Morag* S., Graded isoglosses in East-Aramaic: ➤ 118, ᶠLESLAU W., Semitic 1991, 588-594 / 1571-6 / 1385-1401 / 1197-1202 / 1085-99.
9576 *Harrak* Amri, Des noms d'année en araméen?: WeltOr 23 (1992) 68-74.
9577 ᴱHeinrichs Wolfhart, Studies in Neoaramaic: HarvSemSt 36, 1990 ➤ 6,9401; 7,9240: ᴿBO 49 (1992) 835-8 (H. L. *Murre-Van den Berg*); ZDMG 141 (1991) 431s (C. *Correll*).
9578 *Hillers* Delbert R., *Cussini* Eleonora, Two readings in the [Palmyrene Aramaic and Greek] caravan inscription Dunant, Baalshamin, No. 45: BASOR 286 (1992) 35-37; 1 facsimile.
9579 ᵀᴱJones G. Lloyd, Robert WAKEFIELD, On the three languages [1524] 1989 ➤ 7,9244: ᴿGnomon 64 (1992) 554-7 (J. *Ijsewijn*).
9579* **Kara** Yechiel, Babylonian Aramaic in the Yemenite manuscripts of the Talmud; orthography, phonology and morphology of the verb: Language Traditions Project 10. J 1983, Hebrew Univ. IV-396+43p. 0333-5143.
9580 *Kaufman* Stephen A., Aramaic: ➤ 741, AnchorDB 4 (1992) 173-8.
9580* *Klingbeil* G. A., The onomasticon of the Aramaic inscriptions of Syria-Palestine during the Persian period: JNWS 18 (1992) 67-86; bibliog. 87-94.
9581 *Kotansky* Roy, *Naveh* J., *Shaked* S., A Greek-Aramaic silver amulet from Egypt in the Ashmolean museum: Muséon 105 (1992) 5-23; photo.
9582 *Macuch* Rudolf, Some lexicographical problems of Jewish Palestinian Aramaic [SOKOLOFF M. dictionary 1990]: BSO 55 (1992) 205-230.
9583 *Martínez Borobio* Emiliano, 'Erigir una estatua' en las antiguas dedicaciones arameas: ➤ 44, ᶠDÍAZ ESTEBAN F., Sefarad 52 (1992) 173-9; Eng. 180.
9584 **Morag** Shelomo, ❸ *Aramit* ... Babylonian Aramaic; the Yemenite tradition; historical aspects and transmission; phonology; the verbal system. J 1988, Ben-Zvi. x-389p. 965-235-023-0: ᴿJQR 83 (1992s) 223-5 (Y. *Kara*); JSS 37 (1992) 328s (G. *Khan*).
9585 *Müller-Kessler* Christa, Christian-Palestinian Aramaic fragments in the Bodleian library: JSS 37 (1992) 207-221.
9586 ᴱMuraoka T., Studies in Qumran Aramaic: AbrNahr supp. 3. Lv 1992, Peeters. viii-167p. Fb 1800. 90-6831-419-X [BL 93,156, L. L. *Grabbe* describes the valuable contents ➤ 9570*].
9587 *Naveh* Joseph, *a*) ❸ Hebrew versus Aramaic in the epigraphic finds of the Second Temple – Bar Kokhba period: Lešonenu 56 (1991s) 301-316; Eng. II; – *b*) Aramaic ostraca and jar inscriptions from Tell Jemmeh: ʿAtiqot 21 (1992) 49-53; 1 fig.
9588 **Odiahu** Daniel I., The Aramaic inscriptions of Hatra: diss. Wales 1990. 590p. BRDX-95925. – DissA 53 (1992s) 514-A.
9589 *Pennacchietti* Fabrizio A., Le due iscrizioni aramaiche inedite dell'edificio A di Hatra: Mesop-T 27 (1992) 199-205; 2 fig. + fot. 15s.

9590 ᵀᴱ**Porten** Bezalel, *Yardeni* Ada, Textbook of Aramaic documents from ancient Egypt, 2. Contracts 1989 ➤ 5,9307 ... 7,9248: ᴿCBQ 54 (1992) 124-6 (J. A. *Fitzmyer*: valuable despite some dissatisfactions; 3. Literary-historical, and 4. Ostraca awaited; 1. Letters was 1986 ➤ 2,7529): JEA 78 (1992) 344 (J. B. *Segal* accepts some of the corrections of his 1983 edition).

9591 *Porten* Bezalel, *Yardeni* Ada, Three unpublished Aramaic ostraca: ➤ 65, Mem. GEVIRTZ S., Maarav 7 (1991) 207-227; 4 pl.

9592 *Puech* Émile, La stèle de Bar-Hadad à Melqart et les rois d'Arpad: RB 99 (1992) 311-334; 2 fig.; pl. XV-XVI: Eng. p. 311.

9593 **Rosenthal** F., Grammaire de l'araméen biblique [⁸1988] ᵀ*Hébert* P. P 1988, Beauchesne. 134+96 p. – ᴿHelmantica 43 (1992) 469s (S. *García-Jalón*).

9594 **Sokoloff** M., A dictionary of Jewish Palestinian Aramaic of the Byzantine period 1990 ➤ 6,9414; 7,9250: ᴿAbrNahr 30 (1992) 191-201 (K. *Beyer*); AulaO 10 (1992) 167-170 (L. *Díez Merino*); Biblica 73 (1992) 434-7 (J. A. *Fitzmyer*); BL (1992) 140s (R. P. *Gordon*); CritRR 5 (1992) 386s (M. J. *Bernstein*: a superior tool; he is now widening the horizon); JRAS (1992) 255s (E. *Ullendorff*: queries 'trivia'); Muséon 105 (1992) 387s (J.-C. *Haelewyck*); Orientalia 61 (1992) 11s (Deirdre *Dempsey*); VT 42 (1992) 281s (H. G. M. *Williamson*).

9595 **Steyl** C., 'n Beknopte Grammatika van Bybelse Aramees: Reeks C5. Bloemfontein 1982, Oranje-Univ. iii-93 p. 0-86886-143 [only].

9595* *Tal* A., The lexicon of Samaritan Aramaic and its problems: ➤ 496*, Congress 1988/91, 347-355 (*Florentin* M., *Talshir* D. ❹ 7-17 / 1-6.

9596 *Ustinova* Yulia, *Naveh* Joseph, A Greek-Palmyrene Aramaic dedicatory inscription from the Negev: ʿAtiqot 22 (c. 1992) 91-96; 1 fig.

9597 **Yadin** Y., *al*, Aramaic and Hebrew ostraca: Masada I, 1989 ➤ 7,9252: ᴿOLZ 87 (1992) 153-5 (P. G. *Pfeifer*, also on II. COTTON H.); PEQ 125 (1993) 84 (J. F. *Healey*).

9597* *Borbone* Pier Giorgio, *Mandracci Francesco*, Another way to analyze Syriac texts; a simple powerful tool to draw up Syriac computer aided concordances: ➤ 450, Informatique 2, 1988/9, 135-145.

J1.7 Syriaca.

9598 *Botha* P. J., The rhetoric function of polarity in one of EPHREM the Syrian's hymns on the Church: JSemit 3 (1991) 188-201.

9599 **Desreumeaux** A., Répertoire des bibliothèques et des catalogues de manuscrits syriaques 1991 ➤ 7,890: ᴿMuséon 105 (1992) 283-302 (C. *Detienne*: nombreuses additions); OrChr 76 (1992) 244-252 (H. *Kaufhold*: zahlreiche Beobachtungen); REByz 50 (1992) 301s (P. *Géhin*).

9600 **Gignoux** Philippe, Incantations magiques syriaques 1987 ➤ 3,9543 ... 7,9257: ᴿLA 41 (1991) 599s (M. *Pazzini*).

9601 *Harrak* Amir, Pagan traces in Syriac Christian onomastica: ➤ 557*, Contacts 1990/2, 318-323.

9602 *Joosten* Jan, *a*) Two West Aramaic elements in the Old Syriac and Peshitta Gospels [*slb* 'cross, crucify'; *Etnasra* 'the Twelve']: BibNot 61 (1992) 17-21; – *b*) The negation of the non-verbal clause in early Syriac: JAOS 112 (1992) 584-8.

9603 **Levi della Vida** Giorgio, PITAGORA, BARDESANE e altri studi siriaci, ᴱ*Contini* Riccardo. Univ. Roma, St. Or. 8. R 1989, Bardi. xxi-194 p. – ᴿZDMG 142 (1992) 380 (H. *Daiber*).

9604 **Selb** Walter, Sententiae syriacae, Glossar 1990 ➤ 7,9265: ᴿAbrNahr 30 (1992) 192-5 (L. *Van Rompay*); ZSav-R 109 (1992) 602-615 (R. *Yaron*).

9605 *a*) *Spitaler* Anton, Das Femininum des Zahlwortes für 'zwei' im Hebräischen und für 'sechs' im Syrischen; – *b*) *Troupeau* Gérard, Réflexions sur l'origine syriaque de l'écriture arabe: ➤ 118, ᶠLESLAU W., Semitic 1991, 1493-8 / 1562-70.

9606 **Teixidor** J., BARDESANE d'Édesse; la première philosophie syriaque. P 1992, Cerf. – ᴿRÉJ 151 (1992) 371-4 (S. C. *Mimouni*).

9607 *Vattioni* Francesco, Una nuova [1979] iscrizione siriaca a Edessa (Urfa) [mosaico di Brsmy', casa per i figli e il fratello]: Henoch 14 (1992) 133-6.

J2.1 **Akkadica** (sumerica).

9608 *Alster* Bendt, Two Sumerian short tales reconsidered: ZAss 82 (1992) 186-201.

9609 *Arnold* Bill T., An early neo-Babylonian formula from Uruk [such as can serve in default of author or date]: JAOS 112 (1992) 383-7.

9609* *Caplice* Richard J., Akkadian: ➤ 741, AnchorDB 4 (1992) 170-3 ➤ a60.

9610 *a*) *Charpin* Dominique, Les malheurs d'un scribe ou l'inutilité du Sumérien loin de Nippur; – *b*) *Artzi* Pinhas, Nippur elementary schoolbooks in the 'West'; – *c*) *Joannès* Francis, Les archives de Ninurta-Aḫḫê-Bullit: ➤ 687, Nippur 1988/92, 7-27; 3 fig. / 1-5 / 87-100.

9610* *a*) *Deventer* H. J. M. Van, *Huÿssteen* P. J. J. Van, The orthography and phonology of the Akkadian texts from Ḫatti found at Ugarit; – *b*) *Prinsloo* G. T. M., Poetic conventions in an Old-Babylonian hymn to Ištar: JTydSem 4 (1992) 35-50 / 1-21.

9611 **Englund** B. K., *Grégoire* J.-P., (*Matthews* R. J.), The proto-cuneiform texts from Jemdet Nasr, I. Copies, transliterations and glossary: Materialien zu den frühen Schriftzeugnissen des Vorderen Orients 1. B 1991, Mann. 220 p.; 91 pl. DM 148. 3-7861-1646-6 [BL 93,30].

9612 *Foster* Benjamin R., On authorship in Akkadian literature: AION 51 (1991) 17-32.

9613 **Gianto** Agustinus, Word order variation in the Akkadian of Byblos ᴰ1989; StPohl 15, 1990 ➤ 6,9448; 7,9277: ᴿBO 49 (1992) 329-357 (A. F. *Rainey* (praise, also for 'superb' computer-presentation; several proposals); Orientalia 61 (1992) 148-151 (S. *Izre'el*).

9614 **Gelb** Ignace J., *Steinkeller* Piotr, *Whiting* Robert M.ᴶ, Earliest land tenure systems in the Near East; ancient kudurrus: OIP 24. Ch 1991, Univ. Or. Inst. x-166 p. (2 vol.).

9615 **Hayes** John L., A manual of Sumerian grammar and texts: ARTANES 5. Malibu 1990, Undena. viii-311 p.; ill. $34.50. – ᴿMesop-T 27 (1992) 297-300 (K. *Volk*); OLZ 87 (1992) 136-148 (G. J. *Selz*: both less and more than the title promises).

9615* **Hecker** K., Rückläufiges Wörterbuch des Akkadischen 1990 ➤ 7,9278: ᴿArOr 60 (1992) 302s (B. *Hruška*).

9616 **Huÿssteen** P. J. J. van, Western peripheral Akkadian features and Assyrianisms in the Emar letters: JNSW 18 (1992) 185-207.

9616* *Izre'el* Shlomo, On the person-prefixes of the Akkadian verb: JANES 20 (1991) 35-56.

9617 *a*) *Jacobsen* Thorkild, The term ensi; – *b*) *Finkel* Irving L., Muššu'u, Qutāru, and the scribe Tanittu-Bēl; – *c*) *Farber* Gertrud, Konkret, kollektiv, abstrakt?; – *d*) *Michalowski* Piotr, Negation as description;

the metaphor of everyday life in early Mesopotamian literature: ➤ 32, ᶠCIVIL M., AulaO 9,1 (1991) 113-121; 8 fig. / 91-104 / 81-90 / 131-6.
9618 *Kilmer* Anne D., Sumerian and Akkadian names for designs and geometric shapes: ➤ 641, Artistic 1988/90, 83-91; 12 fig.
9619 **Kraus** R. F., Sonderformen akkadischer Parataxe 1987 ➤ 3,9583; 6, 9459: ᴿZAss 81 (1991) 150s (W. *Sommerfeld*).
9620 *Krispijn* T. J. H., The early Mesopotamian lexical lists and the dawn of linguistics: JbEOL 32 (1991s) 12-22.
9621 *Langenmayr* Arnold, Sprachpsychologische Untersuchung zur sumerischen 'Frauensprache' (eme-sal): ZAss 82 (1992) 208-211.
9621* **Longman** Tremper ᴵᴵᴵ, Fictional Akkadian autobiography; a generic and comparative study 1991 ➤ 7,9284: ᴿJRAS (1992) 429-431 (Stephanie *Dalley*: dangers lie in wait for immature Assyriologists)
9622 a) *Malbran-Labat* F., Le 'passif' en akkadien; - b) *Diakonoff* I. M., On plene-spelling in Akkadian; - c) *Huehnergard* John, Further South Semitic cognates to the Akkadian lexicon; - d) *Meltzer* Tova, The deictic nature of *alāku* in Akkadian; - e) *Soden* Wolfram von, Deminutiva [sic] nach der Form *qutail* > *qutīl* und vergleichbar vierkonsonantige Bildungen im Akkadischen; - f) *Izre'el* Shlomo, Reflections on the Amarna recension of Adapa: ➤ 118, ᶠLESLAU W., Semitic 1991, 977-990 / 295s / 690-713 / 1042-5 / 1488-92 / 746-772.
9624 *Malul* Meir, Şillam paţārum, 'to unfasten the pin'; copula carnalis and the formation of marriage in ancient Mesopotamia: JbEOL 32 (1991s) 66-86.
9625 *Maul* Stefan M., Neues zu den 'Graeco-babyloniaca': ZAss 81 (1991) 87-107.
9626 *Mayer* Werner R., Das 'gnomische Preteritum' im literarischen Akkadisch: Orientalia 61 (1992) 373-399.
9627 **Moran** William L., The Amarna letters, edited and translated [= franç. 1987 ➤ 3,e766]. Baltimore 1992, Johns Hopkins Univ. xlvii-393 p.; map. 0-8018-4251-4. ➤ g122
9628 a) *Muntingh* L. M., The role of the scribe [*mar bīt tuppim*] according to the Mari texts; a study of terminology; - b) *Westhuizen* J. P. Van der, Morphology and morphosyntax of the verb in the Amqi Amarna letters / Verbless sentences in the Amqi Amarna letters: JTydSem 3 (1991) 21-53 / 54-84 & 4 (1992) 117-129.
9629 *Neumann* Hans, Ein Brief an König Šulgi in einer späten Abschrift: AltOrF 19 (1992) 29-39; 1 pl.
9630 **Oberhuber** Karl, Sumerisches Lexikon zu G. REISNER, Hymnen (1896) 1990 ➤ 6,9462; 7,9285: 3-85124-144-4; Sch 1600. - ᴿBO 49 (1992) 764-772 (K. *Volk*).
9631 a) *Pomponio* Francesco, Le sventure di Amar-Suena; - b) *Talon* Philippe, Le mythe d'Adapa: StEpL 7 (1990) 3-14 / 43-57.
9632 ᶠREINER Erica, Language ... ᴱ**Rochberg-Halton** F., al., 1987 ➤ 3,136: ᴿAfO 38s (1991s) 187-193 (H. *Hirsch*); JAOS 112 (1992) 122-5 (Brigitte *Groneberg*, meist zu LAMBERT).
9633 *Römer* W. H. P., Beiträge zum Lexikon des Sumerischen: BO 49 (1992) 317-329.
9634 a) *Saporetti* Claudio, *Ghiroldi* Angelo, Per una rielaborazione dell'onomastico medio-assira; - b) *Stol* Marten, Old Babylonian personal names: StEpL 8 (1991) 181-190 / 191-212.
9635 *Schmitt* Rüdiger, Assyria grammata und ähnliche; was wussten die Griechen von Keilschrift und Keilinschriften?: ➤ 672, Fremdspr. 1989/ 92, 21-35.

9636 **Schretter** Manfred K., Emesal-Studien; Sprach- und literargeschichtliche Untersuchungen zur sogenannten Frauensprache des Sumerischen: Ges. Geist. W. 69. Innsbruck 1990, Univ. Inst. Spr. W. 297 p. Sch 640. – ᴿOLZ 87 (1992) 382-5 (J. A. *Black*).

9637 **Soden** Wolfram von, Introduzione all'orientalistica antica [1985 ⇥ 1, 9116], ᵀᴱ*Mora* Clelia: StVOA 1, Lit. 35.000. 1989 ⇥ 5,357 ... 7,9290: ᴿAntonianum 67 (1992) 147s (M. *Nobile*).

9638 **Steible** H., Die neusumerischen Bau- und Weihinschriften: Freib-AltorSt 9. Stu 1991, Steiner. xv-430 p.; vii-359 p. + XXIV pl., DM 146. 3-515-04250-4. – ᴿBL (1992) 121 (W. G. *Lambert*).

9639 *Testen* David, A trace of [1894 J.] ʙᴀʀᴛʜ's preradical *i in Akkadian: JNES 51 (1992) 131-3.

9640 **Ungnad** Arthur, ⁵ʳᵉᵛ*Matouš* Lubor, Akkadian grammar (1965, ⁵1969): SBL Resources 30. Atlanta 1992, Scholars. xix-185 p. $40; sb./pa. $25. 1-55540-800-1; pa. 1-X.

9641 ᴱ**Vogelzang** Marianna E., *Vanstiphout* Herman L. J., Mesopotamian epic literature; oral or aural? Lewiston ɴʏ 1992, Mellen. xi-320 p. 0-7734-9538-X.

9641* *Westenholz* Aage, The phoneme /o/ in Akkadian: ZAss 81 (1991) 10-19.

9642 *a) Yoshikawa* Mamoru, Sumerian genitival construction / Valency-change system / Verbs of agentive-oriented infixation; – *b) Watanabe* Kazuko, Segenswünsche für den assyrischen König in der 2. Person (2): AcSum 14 (1992) 403-6 . 395-402 . 379-394 / 369-373 + 4 fig.

J2.7 Arabica.

9642* *a) Abdel Haleem* M. A. S., Grammatical shift for rhetorical purposes; *iltifāt* and related features in the Qur'ān; – *b) Henkin* Roni, The three faces of the Arabic participle in Negev Bedouin dialects; continuous, resultative, and evidential: BSO 55 (1992) 407-432 / 433-444.

9643 **Abed Shukri** B., Aristotelian logic and the Arabic language in ᴀʟ-ꜰᴀ̄ʀᴀ̄ʙꞮ̄. Albany 1991, ꜱᴜɴʏ. xvi-201 p. – ᴿZDMG 142 (1992) 382-4 (H. *Daiber*).

9643* **Agius** Dionysius, The study of Arabic in Malta 1632 to 1915 [1980], ᵀ*Borg* Vinċenz P., ᴱ*Geraci* Francine. Lv 1990, Peeters. xii-52 p. – ᴿJRAS (1992) 259s (Farida *Abu-Haidar*).

9644 **Åkesson** Joyce, Aḥmad ʙ. ʿAʟꞮ̄ ʙ. Mᴀꜱʿᴜᴅ on Arabic morphology, *marāḥ al-Arwāḥ*, I. The strong verb, *as-saḥīḥ*: StOrLund 4. Leiden 1990, Brill. xxx-100 p. + ❹ 25. ƒ75. – ᴿJAOS 112 (1992) 711s (W. *Smyth*: mystical enthusiasm for the reasons behind language).

9645 **Bar-Asher** Moshé, La composante hébraïque du judéo-arabe algérien (communautés de Tlémcen et Aïn-Témouchent). J 1992, Magnes. 184 p. – ᴿLešonenu 56 (1991s) 269-283; Eng. VI-VII (A. *Maman*).

9646 *Behnstedt* Peter, Noch einmal zum Problem der Personalpronomina *-henne* (3 Pl.), *-kon* (2 Pl.) und *-hon* (3 Pl.) in den syrisch-libanesischen Dialekten: ZDMG 141 (1991) 235-252.

9647 *a) Blau* Joshua, On some misspelt, misunderstood and wrongly transmitted vocables in medieval Judeo-Arabic; – *b) Bar-Asher* Moshe, Hebrew elements in North-African Judeo-Arabic; alternations in meaning and form; – *c) Rendsburg* Gary A., Parallel developments in mishnaic Hebrew, colloquial Arabic, and other varieties of spoken Semitic; – *d) Hary* Benjamin, On the use of *'ilā* and *li* in Judeo-Arabic texts; – *e) Pia-*

menta Moshe, Hypothetical sentences in Jerusalem Arabic; – *f*) *Rosenhouse* Judith, Two unstable phonemes in Israeli Hebrew and colloquial Arabic, ʿAleph and ʿAyin: ➤ 118, ᶠLᴇsʟᴀᴜ W., Semitic 1991, 162-173 / 128-149 / 1265-77 / 595-608 / 1203-19 / 1345-63.

9648 **Cadora** Frederic J., Bedouin, village and urban Arabic; an ecolinguistic study: StSemLLing 18. Leiden 1992, Brill. xiv-168 p. 90-04-09627-2.

9649 **Chahristan** Kamil, Aspects of phrases and clauses in Syrian [Arabic, as p. 3510-A] within the framework of head-driven phrase structure grammar: diss. N. Wales. Bangor 1991. 309 p. BRDX-98164. – DissA 53 (1992s) 3509-A.

9649* **Coussonnet** Patrice, Pensée mythique, idéologie et aspirations sociales dans un conte [ʿAli du Caire] des Mille et une nuits. Le Caire 1989, IFAO. viii-68 p.; 6 pl. – ᴿJRAS (1991) 282-4 (R. *Irwin*).

ᴱ**Dévényi** K. 1991 ➤ 685; ᴱ**Eid** M. 1987/90 ➤ 686, Arabic linguistics.

9650 *Ditters* Everhard, A modern standard Arabic sentence grammar [Netherlands project]: BÉtOr 43 (1991) 197-222; franç. 223.

9651 **Endress** Gerhard, *Gutas* Dimitri, A Greek and Arabic lexicon; materials for a dictionary of the medieval translations from Greek into Arabic: HbOr 1/11. Leiden 1992, Brill. I. 30* + 96 [+ 20] p. 90-04-09494-6 [OIAc 3,20].

9652 *Ernst* Carl W., The spirit of Islamic calligraphy [Bābā Shāh Iꜱꜰᴀʜᴀɴɪ, *Ādāb al-mašq* c. 1580, ᴱ*Šufi*ʾ M. 1967 = 1950]: JAOS 112 (1992) 279-286.

9653 **Feghali** Habaka J., (*Kaye* Alan S.) Moroccan Arabic reader. ... 1989, Dunwoody. xiv-143 p. – ᴿBSO 54 (1991) 370 (C. *Holes*: for rather advanced learners).

9654 ᴱ**Fischer** Wolfdietrich, Grundriss der arabischen Philologie, 3.-Supp. Wsb 1992, Reichert. xii-299 p. 3-88226-214-1.

9655 Gʜᴜʟ Mahmoud † 1983, Arabian Studies, Symposium at Yarmouk Univ. Dec. 8-11, 1984, ᴱ**Ibrahim** Moawiyah M.: Univ. Publ. Archaeol. 2, 1989 ➤ 6,801: ᴿJAOS 112 (1992) 139-141 (J. A. *Bellamy*).

9656 **Günther** Sebastian, Quellenuntersuchungen zu den 'Maqātil aṭ-Ṭālibiyyīn' des Abū 'l-Faraǧ al-Iꜱꜰᴀʜᴀɴɪ (gest. 356/967); ein Beitrag zur Problematik der mündlichen und schriftlichen Überlieferung in der mittelalterlichen arabischen Literatur: ArabTSt 4. Hildesheim 1991, Olms. 249 p. DM 45. – ᴿJAOS 112 (1992) 710s (S. *Leder*: limits).

9656* ᵀ**Haddawy** Husain, The Arabian Nights, based on the text edited by Mahsin Mᴀʜᴅɪ. NY 1990, Norton. xxvi-428 p. $17. – ᴿBSO 55 (1992) 330s (H. T. *Norris*).

9657 **Holes** Clive, Gulf Arabic: Croom Holm descriptive grammars. L 1990, Routledge. xvi-302 p. £45. – ᴿBSO 54 (1991) 369s (B. *Ingham*).

9658 *Ingham* B., Subordinate clauses of time and condition in [Sinai, Jordan] bedouin dialects: BSO 54 (1991) 42-62.

9659 **Jarrar** Maher, Die Prophetenbiographie im islamischen Spanien; ein Beitrag zur Überlieferungs- und Redaktionsgeschichte [12 'prophets' from the east]: Diss. Tü, EurHS 3/404. Fra 1989, Lang. ix-363 p. DM 74. 3-631-42087-0. – ᴿZDMG 141 (1991) 435 (E. *Wagner*).

9659* **Johnstone** Barbara, Repetition in Arabic discourse; paradigms, syntagms, and the ecology of language: Pragmatics and beyond NS 18. Amst/Ph 1991, Benjamins. xii-130 p. ⌡65. – ᴿBSO 55 (1992) 556s (C. *Holes*).

9660 **Khan** Geoffrey, Arabic papyri; selected materials from the Khalili collection: StKhalili 1. L 1992, Oxford-UP. 254 p. 0-19-727500-1.

9661 **Kunitzsch** Paul,   Die Plejaden in den Vergleichen der arabischen Dichtung: Szb 1992/4. Mü 1992, Bayerische Akad. 185 p.; ill. 3-7696-1566-2.

9662 *a) Larcher* Pierre,   D'une grammaire l'autre; catégorie d'adverbe et catégorie de *maf ūl muṭlaq*; – *b) Gonegai* Abdelkader,   La syntaxe des constructions relatives restrictives en arabe : BÉtOr 43 (1991) 139-159 / 161-195.

9663 *a) Lentin* Jérôme,   À propos de la valeur 'intensive' de la IIème forme verbale en arabe syrien; modalité et expressivité; vers un renouvellement du système verbale; – *b) Caubet* Dominique,   The active participle as a means to renew the aspectual system; a comparative study in several dialects of Arabic; – *c) Diem* Werner,   Vom Altarabischen zum Neuarabischen; ein neuer Ansatz; – *d) Fischer* Wolfdietrich,   What is Middle Arabic? [largely Jewish and Christian users]: ➤ 118, ᶠLESLAU W., Semitic 1991, 891-916 / 209-224 / 297-308 / 430-6.

9664 ᴱ**Mahdi** Muhsin,   The thousand and one nights (Alf Layla wa-Layla), from the earliest known sources, Arabic text edited with introduction and notes. Leiden 1984, Brill. I. text, xii + 708 p.; II. viii + 111 p. + ❹ 308 p. 90-04-07429-5: -30-9.

9665 **Malina** Renate,   Zum schriftlichen Gebrauch des Kairinischen Dialekts anhand ausgewählter Texte von Saʿdaddīn WAHBA: IslamkUnt 111.   B 1987, Schwarz. 218 p. 3-922968-59-7. – ᴿBO 49 (1992) 526-8 (C. H. M. *Versteegh*).

9666 **Mitchell** T. F.,   Pronouncing Arabic, I. Ox 1990, Clarendon. xii-167 p. $50. 0-19-815151-9. – ᴿBO 49 (1992) 523-6 (K. *Versteegh*: useful, though closer to Koran-recitation than to the obvious norm of TV-news); JAOS 112 (1992) 137s (A. S. *Kaye*).

9667 **Nishio** Tetsuo,   A basic vocabulary of the Bedouin Arabic dialect of the Jbāli tribe (Southern Sinai): Studia Sinaitica 1 / Studia Culturae Islamicae 43.   Tokyo 1992, Institute for the Study of Languages and Cultures of Asia and Africa. xviii-238 p.

9667* **Owens** Jonathan,   Early Arabic grammatical theory; heterogeneity and standardization: StHistLangSc 53/9.   Amst/Ph 1990, Benjamins. xvi-294 p. *f* 110. – ᴿBSO 55 (1992) 546s (G. *Khan*).

9668 **Palva** Heikki,   Artistic colloquial Arabic; traditional narratives and poems from al-Balqā' (Jordan); transcription, translation, linguistic and metrical analysis: Studia Orientalia 69.   Helsinki 1992, Finnish Oriental Society. 191 p. 951-9380-18-3.

9669 *Peled* Yishai,   ʿamal and *ibtidāʾ* in medieval Arabic grammatical tradition: AbrNahr 30 (1992) 146-171.

9670 **Piamenta** Moshe,   Dictionary of post-classical Yemeni Arabic. Leiden 1991, Brill. I. '-š, xxiv-274p.; II. s-y, p. 275-541. *f* 165. – ᴿJAOS 112 (1992) 537s (A. S. *Kaye*); JRAS (1992) 257s (R. B. *Serjeant*); ZDMG 142 (1992) 378s (W. *Diem*).

9671 **Ricks** Stephen D.,   Lexicon of inscriptional Qatabanian: StPohl 14, 1989 ➤ 5,9385 ... 7,9318: ᴿZDMG 141 (1991) 176s (W. W. *Müller*).

9672 **Robin** Christian,   Inabba', Haram, Al-Kāfir, Kamma et Al-Ḥarashif; fascicule A, les documents; fascicule B, les planches: Inventaire des inscriptions sudarabiques 1.   P 1992, de Boccard. 221 p.; vol. of 60 pl.

9673 *Rosenhouse* Judith,   The occurrence of the passive in some [Galilee, Sinai] bedouin dialects: JAfAs 3 (1991s) 9-21.

9674 **Sabuni** A.,   Wörterbuch (arab.); die 2000 häufigsten Wörter. Hamburg 1988, Buske.

9675 **Said** Edward W., Orientalisme. T 1991, Bollati-B. 198 p. Lit. 60.000. – RStPatav 39 (1992) 254-6 (C. *Saccone*).

9676 **Schall** Anton, Elementa arabica [deutsch] 1988 → 4,a443 ... 7,9319: RJSS 37 (1992) 348s (C. *Holes*).

9677 **Tairan** Salem A., Die Personennamen in den altsabäischen Inschriften; ein Beitrag zur altsüdarabischen Namengebung: Texte und Studien zur Orientalistik 8. Hildesheim 1992, Olms. [viii-]265 p. 3-487-09665-X.

9678 *Tarrier* Jean-Michel, À propos de sociolinguistique de l'arabe; présentation de quelques difficultés: BÉtOr 43 (1991) 1-15.

9679 **Tillisi** Kalifa M., Dizionario italiano-arabo (una edizione studentesca). Beirut 1986, Librairie du Liban. 400 p.

9680 EUllmann Manfred, Wörterbuch der klassischen arabischen Sprache: DMG mit Akademien Gö Heid Mü Mainz, Band 2., Lfg. 20. Wsb 1991, Harrassowitz. xvii + p. 1187-1267. [OIAc 3,40].

EVersteegh Kees, *Carter* Michael G., Studies in the history of Arabic grammar II, 1987/90 → 695*.

9681 **Voigt** Rainer M., Die infirmen Verbaltypen des Arabischen und das Biradikalismus-Problem: AkMainz 39, 1988 → 4,a488 ... 7,9325: RWeltOr 23 (1992) 187-193 (E. A. *Knauf*).

9681* **Walther** Wiebke, Tausendundeine Nacht: Einführungen 31. Mü 1987, Artemis. 174 p. DM 19,80. – RJRAS (1991) 280-2 (R. *Irwin*).

9682 *Wittig* Sabine, Zur semantischen und syntaktischen Struktur ornativer und kombinativer Beförderungsverben im modernen Arabischen: ArOr 60 (1992) 1-15; Eng. 14s.

J3 Aegyptia.

9682* *a*) *Andrews* Carol A. R., Unpublished demotic texts in the British Museum; – *b*) *Aguizy* Ola el-. About the origins of early demotic in lower Egypt; – *c*) *Martin* Cary J., Demotic contracts as evidence in a court case?; – *d*) *Porten* Bezalel, Aramaic-demotic equivalents; who is the borrower and who the lender?; – *e*) *Roccati* Alexander, Writing Egyptian; scripts and speeches at the end of Pharaonic civilization: → 719, Life 1990/2, 9-14 / 91-94; 8 pl. / 217-220 / 259-264 / 291-4.

9683 FASSFALG Julius: Lingua restituta orientalis, ESchulz R., ...: ÄgAT 20, 1990 → 6,8*; ROrChr 76 (1992) 275-279 (H. *Kaufhold* adds an index to the cited mss.).

9684 *Baskakov* Alexej, Zur Geschichte der Erforschung des ägyptischen Vokalismus in der UdSSR : WeltOr 23 (1992) 5-14.

9685 **Bierbrier** M. L., The British Museum hieroglyphic texts 11, 1987 → 6, 9505: RCdÉ 67 (1992) 293-5 (E. *Graefe*).

9686 **Bradshaw** Joseph, The imperishable stars of the northern sky in the Pyramid Texts. L 1990, auct. 38 p. [OIAc 3,15].

9687 **Bresciani** Edda, Il mito dell'occhio del sole; i dialoghi filosofici tra la Gatta Etiopica e il Piccolo Cinocefalo: Testi VOA 1, eg. 3. Brescia 1992, Paideia. 77 p. 88-394-0471-6.

9688 *Brier* Bob, Napoleon's missing oracle papyrus [H. KIRCHENHOFFER hoax]: NewsAmEg 155 (1991) 5-9.

9689 *Caminos* Ricardo A., On ancient Egyptian mummy-bandages: Orientalia 61 (1992) 337-353; pl. XLI-XLV.

9690 *Cannuyer* Christian, Encore le naufrage du Naufragé: BSÉg 14 (Genève 1990) 15-21.

9691 *Chappaz* Jean-Luc, Répertoire annuel [de 400 mots égyptiens sur] des figurines funéraires 4: BSocÉg 15 (Genève 1991) 115-127.

9692 *Daoust* J., CHAMPOLLION, l'homme qui fit parler les Pharaons [< *Lebeau* R., Notre histoire 86, 1992; polémique contre T. *Young*]: EsprVie 102 (1992) 375s.

9693 **Davies** W. V., Egyptian Hieroglyphs 1987 → 3,9672 ... 6,9517: ᴿCdÉ 66 (1991) 156s (B. van de *Walle* †).

9693* *Davoli* Paola, Geroglifici al computer; HyperScribe: StEgPun 9 (1991) 51-58; 5 fig.

9694 *Dochniak* Craig C., The Horus Falcon's wings on the seated statue of Khafre as a zoomorphic substitute for the Ka hieroglyph: VarAeg 8 (1992) 69-73; 4 fig.

9695 **Fischer-Elfert** Hans-W., Literarische Ostraka der Ramessidenzeit in Übersetzung 1986 → 3,9674 ... 7,9343: ᴿCdÉ 67 (1992) 271s (J. *López*).

9696 **Fischer-Elfert** Hans-W., Die satirische Streitschrift des Papyrus Anastasi I, 1986 → 6,9523; 7,9344: ᴿCdÉ 67 (1992) 267-270 (M. *Green*).

9697 *Fischer-Elfert* Hans W., Synchrone und diachrone Interferenzen in literarischen Werken des Mittleren und Neuen Reiches: Orientalia 61 (1992) 354-370.

9698 ᵀᴱ**Foster** John L., Echoes of Egyptian voices; an anthology of ancient Egyptian poetry: Classical Culture 12. Norman 1992, Univ. Oklahoma. xxiii-134 p.; 1 pl. 0-8061-2411-3.

9698* *a*) *Gasse* Annie, Les ostraca hiératiques littéraires de Deir el-Medīna; nouvelles orientations de la publication; – *b*) *Janssen* J. J., Literacy and letters at DM; – *c*) *Demarée* R. J., 'Royal riddles'; – *d*) *Heel* Koen D. van, Use and meaning of the Egyptian term *w3ḥ mw* [pouring water]: → 684, Village voices 1991/2, 51-70; 18 fig. / 81-94 / 9-18; 2 fig. / 19-30.

9699 **Goedicke** Hans, Old hieratic paleography 1988 → 6,9526; $84. 0-9613805-4-3: ᴿBO 49 (1992) 367-374 (Paule *Posener-Kriéger*, de nombreuses corrections).

9700 **Goedicke** Hans, Studies in 'The instructions of King Amenemhet I for his son': VarAeg supp. 2. San Antonio 1988, Van Siclen. 78 p. (text); vol. of 51 pl. 0-933175-15-9.

9701 *Goedicke* Hans, Readings VIII. The right to sustenance; / IX. Thutmosis's IV's request for divine guidance: VarAeg 8 (1992) 75-84 / 85-92.

9702 **Hoch** James E., Semitic words in Egyptian texts of the New Kingdom and Third Intermediate Period: diss. Toronto. 1991. 689 p. DANN-73780. – DissA 63 (1992s) 4297-A.

9703 *a*) *Hodge* Carleton T., Consonant Ablaut in Egyptian; – *b*) *Good* William, On the reading of *Nfr.nfrw. Ỉtn Nfrt.i.ti*; – *c*) *Nibbi* Alessandra, A note on *t3 šm'w* [answering her 'totally negative critic' K. KITCHEN]: DiscEg 23 (1992) 15-22 / 13s / 39-44.

9704 ᵀᴱ**Hornung** Erik, Gesänge vom Nil. Z 1990, Artemis. 204 p. 3-7608-1040-3 [OIAc 2,21].

9705 *Jansen-Winkeln* Karl, Zur Schreibung des Pseudopartizips in den Pyramidentexten: BSocÉg 15 (Genève 1991) 43-56.

9706 **Johnson** Janet H., Thus wrote 'Onchsheshonqy 1986 → 2,7615 ... 7,9348*: ᴿCdÉ 67 (1992) 70-72 (M. *Chauveau*).

9707 *Junge* Friedrich, 'Emphasis' ... 1989 → 5,9433: ᴿAfO 38s (1991s) 244s (W. *Brunsch*); JAOS 112 (1992) 330-2 (L. *Depuydt*: high quality, some queries).

9708 **Kaplony-Heckel** Ursula, Ägyptische Handschriften 3, 1986 → 2,7617*; 7,9352: ᴿCdÉ 67 (1992) 68-70 (H. De *Meulenaere*).

9709 ᴱKlengel H., *Sündermann* W., Ägypten ... Probleme der Edition 1987/91 ⟶ 7,619: ᴿOLZ 87 (1992) 15s (H.-O. *Feistel*).

9710 **Koch** Roland, Die Erzählung des Sinuhe 1990 ⟶ 6,9534: ᴿBO 49 (1992) 698s (C. *Cannuyer*).

9711 **Lichtheim** Miriam, Maat in Egyptian autobiographies and related studies: OBO 120. FrS/Gö 1992, Univ./VR. 211 p. 3-7278-0846-2 / VR 3-525-53754-9.

9712 **Loprieno** Antonio, Topos und mimesis; zum Ausländer in der ägyptischen Literatur 1988 ⟶ 4,a484; 5,9440: ᴿJAOS 112 (1992) 134s (D. B. *Redford*); OLZ 87 (1992) 19-23 (U. *Luft*).

9713 **Lüddeckens** Erich, *al.*, Demotisches Namenbuch I. Lfg, 11, h3-nfr-htp-b3st.t: MainzAkad. Wsb 1992, Reichert. p. 769-848. 3-88226-559-0 [OIAc 5,28].

9714 **Lüscher** Barbara, Totenbuch Spruch 1. nach Quellen des Neuen Reiches 1986 ⟶ 4,a487: ᴿCdÉ 66 (1991) 165s (A. De *Caluwe*).

9715 **Magee** D. N. E., *Malek* J., A checklist of transcribed hieratic documents in the archives of the Griffith Institute [adds to the already-published ČERNÝ papers (p. 1-40) also those of GARDINER, GUNN, PEET, GRIFFITH (41-58)]. Ox 1991, Ashmolean. 64 p. – ᴿDiscEg 24 (1992) 51-57 (J. J. *Janssen* adds missing data on already-published Černý ostraca).

9716 **Menu** Bernadette, Petit lexique de l'égyptien hiéroglyphique à l'usage des débutants. P 1991, Geuthner. 311 p. F 175. 2-7053-0638-2. ᴿDiscEg 24 (1992) 67s (Barbara *Watterson*: less complete than FAULKNER but handier to use).

9717 **Munro** Irmtraut, Untersuchungen zu den Totenbuch-Papyri 1988 ⟶ 6, 9538; 7,9353: ᴿJNES 51 (1992) 151s (H. *Goedicke*).

9718 *Nibbi* Alessandra, Some questions for M. YOYOTTE: DiscEg [1 (1985) 17-26, her proposal that *Djahy* means Delta and *t3 mhw* only a part of it] 24 (1992) 29-42; map: his ÉPHÉR Annuaire 28 (1989s) 181-3 'finds no positive point whatsoever' in her 'dogmatique nubienne / fantasmagoriques incidences'.

9719 **Parkinson** R. B., *a*) The tale of the eloquent peasant. Ox 1991, Ashmolean Griffith Inst. xliii-97 p. 0-90041-660-2; – *b*) Literary form and the Tale of the eloquent peasant: JEA 78 (1992) 163-178.

9719* **Parkinson** R. B., Voices from Ancient Egypt; an anthology of Middle Kingdom writings. L 1991, British Museum. 160 p., ill. 0-7141-0961-4 [OIAc 3,33].

9720 *Parkinson* Richard, *Quirke* Stephen, The coffin of Prince Herunefer and the early history of the Book of the Dead: ⟶ 72, ᶠGRIFFITHS J. G. 1992, 37-51; 1 fig.; pl. II-IV.

9721 **Patanè** Massimo, Les variantes des Textes des Pyramides à la basse époque. Genève 1992, auct. v-58 p. [OIAc 3,33].

9722 ᶠPOLOTSKY H., Essays on Egyptian grammar (symposium 1985) Yale EgSt 1, 1986 ⟶ 4,711 ... 7,9357: ᴿCdÉ 67 (1992) 66-68 (M. *Malaise*).

9723 **Posener** Georges, Le papyrus Vandier [a Neo-Egyptian story, reconstituted with the help of a Book of the Dead text on the back]: BtGén 7, 1985 ⟶ 1,9216; 5,9444; F 168: ᴿCdÉ 66 (1991) 159-162 (Fayza *Haikal*).

9724 **Quack** Joachim F., Studien zur Lehre für Merikare: GöOrF 4/23. Wsb 1992, Harrassowitz. 200 p. 3-447-03226-X [OIAc 3,34].

9725 *Quack* Joachim F., Ein demotischer Ausdruck in aramäischer Transkription: WeltOr 23 (1992) 15-20.

9725* *Ray* J.D., Are Egyptian and Hittite related?: → 72, ᶠGRIFFITHS J.G. 1992, 124-136.
9726 *Reineke* Walter F., Zur Entstehung der ägyptischen Bruchrechnung: AltOrF 19 (1992) 201-211.
9727 **Renaud** Odette, Dialogue du désespéré 1991 → 7,9360: ᴿOLZ 87 (1992) 520-2 (H. *Goedicke*).
9728 *Roccati* Alessandro, *a*) La polionomia nella civiltà egizia: StEpL 8 (1991) 171-4; – *b*) I vocaboli allogeni nella lingua egizia: StEgPun 9 (1991) 13-18.
9729 ᴱ**Rosati** G., Libro dei morti; i papiri torinesi di Tachered e Isiemachbit: TestiVOA 1991 → 7,9361: ᴿParVi 37 (1992) 226-8 (A. *Rolla*).
9730 **Schade-Busch** Mechthilde, Zur Königsideologie Amenophis' III.; Analyse der Phraseologie historischer Texte der Voramarnazeit [Diss. Mainz 1988, ᴰ*Gundlach* R.]. HildÄgBeit 35. Hildesheim 1992, Gerstenberg. xix-391 p. 3-8067-8128-1.
9731 **Schenkel** Wolfgang [→ 7,9365], Tübinger Einführung in die klassisch-ägyptische Sprache und Schrift. Tü 1991, auct. 303 p. [OIAc 3,37].
9732 **Schlott** Adelheid, Schrift und Schreiben im Alten Ägypten 1989 → 5, 9446; 7,9366: ᴿVT 42 (1992) 144 (J.D. *Ray*).
9733 *Schmitz* Johanna, Impressionen der Wirklichkeit (Petosiris, Inschrift Nr. 61,31-41): CdÉ 67 (1992) 41-55.
9734 **Schneider** Thomas, Asiatische Personennamen in ägyptischen Quellen des Neuen Reiches: OBO 114. FrS/Gö 1992, Univ./Vandenhoeck & R. [xiv-] 482 p. Fs 125. 3-7278-0806-3 / 3-525-53748-4 [BL 93,127, K.A. *Kitchen*].
9735 **Simpson** William K., Personnel accounts of the Early Twelfth Dynasty Papyrus Reisner IV, transcription and commentary; indices I-IV; palaeography IV/F,G (*Der Manuelian* Peter). Boston 1986, Museum of Fine Arts. 47 p.; 33 pl. + Reisner portr. 0-87846-261-9.
9736 **Sturtewagen** Christian, The funerary papyrus Palau Rib. Nr. Inv. 250, 1991 → 7,9371: ᴿDiscEg 21 (1991) 73-75 (Carol A.R. *Andrews* hopes that this will be an opening to Spanish collections).
9737 *a*) *Vercoutter* Jean, Le déchiffrement des hiéroglyphes égyptiens 1680-1840; – *b*) *Goelet* Ogdenᴶ, W3d-wr and lexicographical method; – *c*) *Goedicke* Hans, *Imn nb nswt t3wy*, Amon lord ...; – *d*) *Israelit-Groll* Sarah, The *di.s tm.s stp* formations in poetic late Egyptian; – *e*) *Vandersleyen* Claude, *Inepou*; un terme désignant le roi avant qu'il ne soit roi: → 96, ᶠKÁKOSY L., Intellectual heritage of Egypt 1992, 579-586 / 205-214 / 197-203 / 563-6
9738 **Vernus** Pascal, Future at issue; tense, mood and aspect in Middle Egyptian; studies in syntax and semantics: Yale EgSt 4, 1990 → 7,9375: ᴿOLZ 87 (1992) 377-380 (W. *Schenkel*).
9738* **Vernus** Pascal, Le surnom au Moyen Empire...: StPohl 13, 1986 → 2,7632 ... 5,9454: ᴿOLZ 87 (1992) 125-7 (U. *Luft*).
9739 ᴱ**Vleeming** S.P., Aspects of demotic lexicography 1984/7 → 4,715 ... 7,9376: ᴿCdÉ 66 (1991) 157-9 (D. *Devauchelle*).
9739* *Vycichl* Werner, L'Égyptien et les langues négro-africaines: RSO 66 (1992) 193-6.
9740 **Ward** William A., Essays on feminine titles ... 1986 → 2,7633 ... 6,9558: ᴿCdÉ 67 (1992) 265-7 (H. De *Meulenaere*).
9741 **Winand** Jean, Études de néo-égyptien, 1. La morphologie verbale: Aegyptiaca Leodiensia 2. Liège 1992, Centre Informatique Ph/Lett. x-591 p.

9742 **Zaghloul** El-Hussein O. M., Frühdemotische Urkunden aus Hermupolis: Bulletin 2. Cairo 1985, Ain Shems Univ. Center of Papyrological Studies. v-120 p., ❹ 5 p.; 19 pl. [OIAc 2,30].

9743 **Zauzich** Karl-Theodor, Hieroglyphs without mystery; an introduction to ancient Egyptian writing, ᵀᴱRoth Ann M. Austin 1992, Univ. Texas. xii-121 p. 0-292-79804-0 [OIAc 5,40].

9744 **Browne** G. M., Old Nubian texts from Qasr Ibrim II, 1989 ➤ 5,9463; 7,9379: ᴿJSStEg 19 (1989) 112 (P. L. *Shinnie*).

9745 *Browne* Gerald M., GRIFFITH's Old Nubian sale: Orientalia 61 (1992) 454-8.

9746 *Werner* Roland, Der Stand der Erforschung der nubischen Sprachen [BROWNE G. 1989]: OLZ 87 (1992) 507-515.

J3.4 Coptica.

9747 **Blanchard** Monica J., Henri HYVERNAT (1958-1941), Coptic scholar; library exhibit. Wsh 1992, Catholic University of America. 31 p. [OIAc 5,15].

9748 *Brunsch* Wolfgang, Verzeichnis der [142 photographisch] aufgenommenen koptischen und griechischen Inschriften aus dem Koptischen Museum [Magazinräumen; Stelen] in Alt-Kairo: ArPapF 38 (1992) 47-60.

9749 **DuQuesne** Terence, A Coptic initiatory invocation (PGM IV 1-25) [another ➤ m65]; an essay in interpretation with critical text, translation and commentary: OxCommEg 2. Thame/Oxon 1991, Darengo. 107 p. £30. 1-871266-11-4 [Supplement in DiscEg 20 (1991) 5-18]. – ᴿDiscEg 24 (1992) 65s (A. *Roccati*, ital.).

9750 *Gregorius* Anba, Greek loan words in Coptic: BSACopte 30 (1991) 77-92 (§ 150-178, conjunctions).

9751 **Hasitzka** Monika R. M., Corpus Pap. Raineri 12, Koptische Texte 1987 ➤ 3,9714... 7,9389: ᴿCdÉ 67 (1992) 389s (L. *Depuydt*); ZSav-R 108 (1991) 636-9 (J. *Hengstl*, auch über HARRAUER H. 13/9; FANTONI G. 14/10).

9752 **Hasitzka** Monika R. M., Neue Texte zum Koptisch-Unterricht: Nat.-B. Papyrussammlung Mitt. 18. W 1990, Hollinek. 343 p. iv-143 pl. – ᴿOrientalia 61 (1992) 479-481 (W. *Brunsch*).

9753 *a) Kasser* Rodolphe, Prééminence de l'alphabet grec dans les divers alphabets coptes; première partie, propos liminaires; – *b*) *Vycichl* Werner, CHAMPOLLION et la langue copte: BSocEg 15 (Genève 1991) 57-68 / 101-6.

9754 *McBride* Daniel R., The development of Coptic; late-pagan language of synthesis in Egypt: JSStEg 19 (1989) 89-111.

9755 *Proverbio Delio* Vania, Le recensioni copte del miracolo di Doroteo e Teopista; testimonia Vaticani: Orientalia 61 (1992) 78-91.

9756 *Quecke* Hans, Eine koptische alphabetische Akrostichis: Orientalia 61 (1992) 1-9.

9757 *Vis* Henri De, Homélies coptes de la Vaticane I-II [= 1922-9 + préf. *Rosentiehl* Jean-Marc]: CahBtCopte 5s. Lv 1990, Peeters. 220 p.; 315 p. 90-6831-213-8; –4-6 [OIAc 2,17].

9758 *Vogüé* Adalbert de, Le texte copte du chapitre XVIII de l'Histoire Lausiaque, l'édition d'AMÉLINEAU et le manuscrit: Orientalia 61 (1992) 459-462.

9759 *Warga* Richard G., A Coptic stela from Oxford Ms: CdÉ 67 (1992) 189-191; photos.

J3.8 Æthiopica.

9760 a) *Ambros* Arne A., A computer-assisted survey of Ethiopic verb-patterns based on W. LESLAU's Concise dictionary of Geʿez; – b) *Correll* Christoph, Gedanken zur nichtpossessiven Determination mit Hilfe von Possessivsuffixen im Altäthiopischen und Amharischen; – c) *Daniels* Peter T., Ha, La, Ḥa or Hôi, Lawe, Ḥaut? The Ethiopian letter-names; – d) *Devens* Monica S., On the laryngeal rules in Geʾez: ➤ 118, ᶠLESLAU W., Semitic 1991, 56-71 / 252-267 / 275-288 / 289-294.

9761 **Böhm** Gerhard, Die Sprache der Aethiopen im Lande Kusch: Veröff. 47. W 1988, Univ. Inst. Afr. 206 p. [OIAc 3,14].

9762 *Goldenberg* Gideon, Comparative dictionary of the Ethiopic language [LESLAU W. 1987]: JAOS 112 (1992) 78-87.

9763 a) *Goldenberg* Gideon, 'Oneself', 'one's own', and 'one another' in Amharic; – b) *Gragg* Gene, 'Also in Cushitic'; how to account for the complexity of Geʿez-Cushitic lexical interactions?; – c) *Hudson* Grover A., A and B-type verbs in Ethiopian and Proto-Semitic; – d) *Kapeliuk* Olga, Definiteness and indefiniteness in Amharic: ➤ 118, ᶠLESLAU W., Semitic 1991, 531-549 / 570-5 / 679-689 / 809-820.

9763* **Haile** Getatchew, Catalogue of Ethiopian manuscripts microfilmed 9, 3301-4000: ➤ 7,9401*: ᴿJRAS (1992) 252s (R. *Pankhurst*: called EMMI by the experts).

9764 **Haile** G., *Amare* M., Beauty of the creation 1991 ➤ 7,9401: ᴿJRAS (1992) 253-5 (R. *Pankhurst*).

9764* **Kane** Thomas L., Amharic English dictionary. Wsb 1990, Harrassowitz. I. xxvi-1088 p.; II. p. 1089-2351. DM 298. 3-447-02871-8 [OLZ 88, 203, S *Uhlig*, also on POLÁČEK Z.]. – ᴿZDMG 142 (1992) 378 (E. *Wagner*).

9765 **Leslau** W., Concise dictionary of Geʿez 1989 ➤ 6,9584: ᴿOLZ 87 (1992) 405s (S. *Uhlig*).

9766 a) *Loewenstamm* Jean, Vocalic length and centralization in two branches of Semitic (Ethiopic and Arabic); – b) *Drewes* J.A., Some features of epigraphical Ethiopic; – c) *Avanzini* Alessandra, Linguistic data and historical reconstruction: between Semitic and Epigraphic South Arabian; – d) *Amsalu Akilu*, The influence of Arabic on Wollo Amharic; – e) *Ricci* Lanfranco, Iscrizioni paleoetiopiche; – f) *Richter* Renate, Functional verbs and functional verb constructions in Amharic; – g) *Rundgren* Frithiof, On the form of the texteme in Tigriña: ➤ 118, ᶠLESLAU W., Semitic 1991, 949-965 / 382-391 / 107-118 / 72-81 / 1291-1311 / 1312-22 / 1363-9.

9767 **Neugebauer** Otto, Chronography in Ethiopic sources 1989 ➤ 5,9486; 7,9403*: ᴿOLZ 87 (1992) 406-8 (S. *Uhlig*).

9767* **Pankhurst** Richard, A social history of Ethiopia; the northern and central highlands from early medieval times to the rise of Emperor Téwodros II. Addis Ababa / Kings Ripton 1990, Univ./ELM. xii-171 p.; ill. £15. – ᴿJRAS (1992) 61-63 (C.F. *Beckingham*).

9768 a) *Raz* Shlomo, Semitic South Ethiopic; the definite future revisited; – b) *Podolsky* Baruch, The Schewa vowel in Amharic; – c) *Poláček* Zdeněk, Several notes on text connectors in Amharic; – d) *Kane* Thomas L., Some observations on Amharic idioms; – e) *Kaye* Alan S., Etymology, etymological method, phonological evolution, and comparative Semitics; Geʿez (classical Ethiopic)? egr and colloquial Syro-Palestinian Arabic *?ᵉžr* 'foot' one last time: ➤ 118, ᶠLESLAU W., Semitic 1991, 1248-64 / 1220-5 / 1226-32 / 794-808 / 826-849.

9769 *Ricci* Lorenzo, Wolf LESLAU e la lessicografia etiopica: RasEtiop 34 (1990) 169-206.

9769* **Six** Veronica, ᴱ*Hammerschmidt* Ernst, Äthiopische Handschriften 2, Bayer. Staatsbt, 1989 ➤ 6,9586: ᴿJRAS (1991) 264s (M. A. *Knibb*).

9770 **Uhlig** Siegbert, Äthiopische Paläographie: ÄthFor 22, 1988 ➤ 4,a550 ... 7,9408: ᴿOrChr 76 (1992) 260-6 (M. *Kropp*).

9771 **Ullendorff** E., From the Bible to Cerulli 1990 ➤ 6,313: ᴿOLZ 87 (1992) 269s (J. *Oelsner*).

J4 Anatolica.

9772 *a*) *Archi* Alfonso, Un sigillo con iscrizione in geroglifico ittita; – *b*) *Salvini* Mirjo, Collezioni di sigilli reali ittiti; – *c*) *Haas* Volkert, Hethitologische Miszellen; – *d*) *Carruba* Onofrio, Die Endungen auf –*ti* des hethitischen Mediums: SMEA 29 (1992, next after 24/1984: p. 5) 13s; 2 fig. / 149-158; 2 fig.; 1 pl. + 1 color. / 99-109 / 15-31.

9773 **De Martino** Stefano, Die mantischen Texte: SMEA CIIurrit 1/7. R 1992, Bonsignori. xv-159 p. – ᴿMesop-T 27 (1992) 306s (A. M. *Jasink*).

9774 *De Martino* Stefano, Il ductus come strumento di datazione nella filologia ittita: ParPass 47,244 (1992) 81-98.

9775 **Friedrich** Johannes, *Kammenhuber* Anneliese, Hethitisches Wörterbuch I (Lfg. 1-8) 1975-84; II, Lfg. 9s, 1988 ➤ 6,9595*; 7,9415: ᴿSalesianum 54 (1992) 826s (R. *Sabin*).

9776 **Girbal** Christian, Beiträge zur Grammatik des Hattischen: EurHS 21/50, 1986 ➤ 5,9493: ᴿZAss 81 (1991) 160-4 (E. *Neu*).

9777 *Girbal* Christian, *a*) Zum hurritischen Vokabular; – *b*) Das hurritische Antipassiv· SMEA 29 (1992) 159-169 / 171-182.

9778 **Güterbock** H.G., *Hoffner* H., Hittite dictionary [➤ 6,9599], L.-N. Ch 1989, Univ. Or. Inst. xxx-477 p. – ᴿZAss 81 (1991) 108-119 (D. O. *Edzard*).

9779 **Hagenbuchner** Albertine, Die Korrespondenz der Hethiter 1-2: Texte der Hethiter. 15s. 1989 ➤ 5,9498 ... 7,9417*: ᴿBO 49 (1992) 804-815 (F. *Starke*: unzufrieden).

9780 ᴱ*Imparati* Fiorella, Quattro studi ittiti: Eothen 4. F 1991, ELITE. 187 p. [OIAc 5,25].

9781 **Kronasser** Heinz, Etymologie der hethitischen Sprache 2, 1987 ➤ 3, 9775 ... 7,9421: ᴿOLZ 87 (1992) 531s (J. *Gebhardt*).

9782 **Luraghi** Silvia, Old Hittite sentence structure ᴰ1990 ➤ 6,9604: ᴿBSLP 87,2 (1992) 179-182 (Françoise *Bader*).

9783 **Marazzi** Massimiliano, Il cosiddetto geroglifico anatolico; spunti e riflessioni per una definizione [< ScrCiv 15 (1991) 31-77].

9784 **Mayrhofer** M., Etymologisches Wörterbuch 1,9 p. 637-716. Heid 1991, Winter: ᴿBSLP 87,2 (1992) 170-5 (Françoise *Bader*).

9785 **Neumann** Günter, System und Ausbau der hethitischen Hieroglyphenschrift: NachGö p/h 1992/3. Gö 1992, Vandenhoeck & R. 26 p.

9786 **Nyland** Ann, Penna and Parh in the Hittite horse training texts: JNES 51 (1992) 293-6.

9787 **Otten** H., *Rüster* C., Die hurritisch-hethitische Bilingue 1990 ➤ 6,9610: ᴿOrientalia 61 (1992) 122-141 (G. *Wilhelm*: mit Wörtern, Grammemen, Indices).

9788 **Puhvel** Jaan, Hittite etymological dictionary 1s, 1984 ➤ 65,8133...3, 9759: ᴿZAss 82 (1992) 149s (E. *Neu*).
9789 **Rüster** Christel, *Neu* Erich, Hethitisches Zeichenlexikon... Boğazköy 1989 ➤ 5,9510...7,9425: ᴿBO 49 (1992) 450-3 (H. *Freydank*); JAOS 112 (1992) 127-9 (R. H. *Beal*); OLZ 87 (1992) 255 (L. *Jakob-Rost*); ZDMG 142 (1992) 159s (G. *Wilhelm*).
9790 *Salvini* Mirjo, *a)* Betrachtungen zum hurritisch-urartäischen Verbum: ZAss 81 (1991) 120-132; – *b)* Note su alcuni nomi di persona hurriti: StEpL 8 (1991) 175-180.
9791 **Starke** Frank, Untersuchungen zur Stammbildung des keilschrift-luwischen Nomens 1990 ➤ 6,9613; DM 268: ᴿOLZ 87 (1992) 532-5 (J. *Tischler*).
9792 **Tischler** Johann, Hethitisches etymologisches Glossar [Lfg 4, 1983 ➤ 2, 7673] II, Lfg. 7, 'N' InBeitSprW 20. Innsbruck 1991, Univ. Inst. SprW. p. 245-355. 3-85124-631-4 [OIAc 3,40]. – III, Lfg. 8, 'T, D/1', 1991, 170 p. [OIAc 2,28: –20-2].
9793 *a) Wegner* Ilse [➤ b410], Die selbständigen Personalpronomina des Hurritischen; – *b) Wilhelm* Gernot, Hurritische Berufsbezeichnungen auf –*li*: SMEA 29 (1992) 227-237 / 239-244 (–253).
9794 **Weitenberg** Joseph J. S., Die hethitischen u-Stämme 1984 ➤ 65,8138... 2,7675: ᴿZAss 81 (1991) 155-7 (H. *Eichner*).
9795 **Yoshida** Daisuke, Die Syntax des althethitischen substantivischen Genitivs: Texte der Hethiter 13, 1987 ➤ 3,9764...7,9429: ᴿOLZ 87 (1992) 48s (J. *Gebhardt*).
9796 **Yoshida** Kazuhiko, The Hittite mediopassive endings in-ri: Unt-Indog-SK 5, 1990 ➤ 6,9618: ᴿBSLP 86,2 (1991) 134-141 (G.-J. *Pinault*); BSO 55 (1992) 138s (Gillian R. *Hart*); OLZ 87 (1992) 392-6 (J. *Tischler*).

9797 ᴱ**Hazai** György, Handbuch der türkischen Sprachwissenschaft I: BtOr-Hung 31, 1990 ➤ 7,9430; ᴿFolOr 27 (1990) 237-254 (M. *Stachowski*).
9797* **Sinor** Denis, Essays in comparative Altaic linguistics: Uraic-Altaic Studies 143. Bloomington IN 1990, Research Institute for Inner Asian Studies. x-454. – ᴿJRAS (1991) 445-7 (C. *Heywood*).
9798 **Zieme** Peter, Die Stabreimtexte der Uiguren von Turfan und Dunhuang; Studien zur alttürkischen Dichtung: BtOrHung 33. Budapest 1991, Akad. 450 p. DM 68. – ᴿOLZ 87 (1992) 1-13 (J. P. *Laut*: 'ein Handbuch der alttürkischen Dichtung').

J4.4 Phrygia, Lydia, Lycia.

9799 *Blümel* Wolfgang, Einheimische Personennamen in griechischen Inschriften aus Carien: EpAnat 20 (1992) 7-33; Özet 34.
9800 *Brixhe* Claude, Étymologie populaire et onomastique en pays bilingue [...Cilicie]: RPg 65 (1991) 67-81.
9801 **Bryce** Trevor R., The Lycians in literary and epigraphic sources 1986 ➤ 2,b843...5,g243: ᴿAnzAltW 43 (1990) 184-6 (Edith *Specht*).
9802 *Bryce* Trevor R., Dynastic rule in ancient Lycia [epigraphic and numismatic data on HERODOTUS 1,176]: ➤ 557*, Contacts 1990/2, 7-13.
9803 **Gusmani** Roberto, Lydisches Wörterbuch Lfg 1-3, 1980-6 ➤ 2,7679 ...7,9438: ᴿSalesianum 54 (1992) 618s (R. *Gottlieb*).
9804 **Hodot** René, Le dialecte éolien d'Asie; la langue des inscriptions, VIᵉ s.a.C.-IVᵉ s.p.C.: RCiv Mém 88, 1990 ➤ 7,9439; F 248: ᴿBSLP 87,2

(1992) 184-6 (Catherine *Dobias-Lalou*); Kratylos 37 (1992) 187s (M. *Meier-Brügger*).
9805 *Neu* Erich,   Etruskisch — eine indogermanische Sprache Altanatoliens?: HistSprF 104 (1991) 9-28.
9806 *Melchert* H. Craig,   The third person present in Lydian: IndogF 97 (1992) 31-54.

J4.8   Armena, georgica.

9807 **Coulie** Bernard,   Répertoire des bibliothèques et des catalogues de manuscrits arméniens: CCOr. Turnhout 1992, Brepols.   xiii-266 p.
9808 *Gragg* Gene,   Subject, object, and verb in Urartian; prologue to typology: ➤ 32, ^FCIVIL M., AulaO 9,1 (1991) 105-112.
9809 **Minassian** Martiros [➤ 7,1568] Études arménologiques.   Genève 1992, Fond. Ghoukassiantz.   1052 p.
9810 *Morani* Moreno,   Pour une histoire du génitif arménien: Muséon 105 (1992) 303-319.
9811 *Pisowicz* Andrzej,   Les traits distinctifs des consonnes occlusives et affriquées dans l'arménien classique: FolOr 27 (1990) 189-198 [185-8, J. *Greppin* on Zuřna].
9812 *Salvini* Mirjo,   *a*) Nuovi confronti fra hurrico e urarteo: SMEA 29 (1992) 217-225; – *b*) Il segno LIŠ nel cuneiforme urarteo: Orientalia 61 (1992) 160s; pl. VI.

9813 *Tsereteli* Konstantin,   Relazioni linguistiche semitico-georgiane: Rend. Lombardo 125,1 (1991) 61-72.

J5   **Graeca**   .1 *grammatica, onomastica* [Inscriptiones ➤ J5.4].

9814 **Adrados** F., *al.*,   Diccionario griego-español Is 1980/6   ➤ 2,7689 ... 4,a579*: ^RJbÖsByz 42 (1992) 336-340 (E. *Trapp*).
9815 **Avotins** Ivars,   On the Greek of the novels of JUSTINIAN; a supplement to LIDDELL-SCOTT-JONES together with observations on the influence of Latin on legal Greek: AltWTSt 21.   Hildesheim 1992, Olms-Weidmann.   xiii-246 p.   3-487-09543-2.
9816 *Bauer*-**Aland**, Wörterbuch 1988 ➤ 4,a579 ... 7,9447:   ^RBSLP 86,2 (1991) 155-7 (M. *Janse*); NedTTs 46 (1992) 104-8 (A. *Hilhorst*); ZkT 114 (1992) 214s (R. *Messner*).
9816* **Bechtel** Friedrich [➤ 65,160*], † 1924, Die historischen Personennamen des Griechischen bis zur Kaiserzeit.   Hildesheim 1982 = 1917, Olms.   xvi-637 p.   3-487-00497-6.
9817 **Beetham** Frank,   An introduction to NT Greek; a quick course in the reading of koiné Greek. L 1992, Bristol Classical.   xv-374 p.   1-85399-338-7.
9818 **Biville** Frédérique,   Les emprunts du latin au grec, approche phonétique I, 1990 [^DSorbonne 1983] ➤ 7,9452:   ^RBSLP 87,2 (1992) 229-232 (O. *Masson*); ÉtClas 60 (1992) 92s (H. *Leclercq*); IndogF 97 (1992) 278-281 (Otta *Wenskus*).
9819 **Black** David A.,   Learn how to read New Testament Greek.   Nv 1992, Broadman.   xii-211 p.
9820 **Bubeník** Vít,   Hellenistic and Roman Greece as a sociolinguistic area 1989   ➤ 7,9454*:   ^REmerita 60 (1992) 338s (A. *Striano Corrochano*); Kratylos 37 (1992) 79-85 (R. *Coleman*).
9821 *Calcante* Cesare M.,   Due modelli di descrizione dell'ordine delle parole; DIONIGI d'Alicarnasso e il *Perì hýpsous*:   StClasOr 41 (1991) 299-309.

9822 *Christol* Alain, Dérivation synchronique, dérivation diachronique dans le verbe grec: RPg 65 (1991) 89-98.

9823 *Cignelli* Lino, *Bottini* G. Claudio, L'articolo nel greco biblico: LA 41 (1991) 159-199; Eng. 491.

9824 **Cole** T., The origins of rhetoric in ancient Greece: AncSocHist. Baltimore 1991, Johns Hopkins Univ. xiv-192 p. $30. – ᴿMnemosyne 45 (1992) 387-392 (D. M. *Schenkeveld*).

9825 **Conde Moreno** María Isabel, Tema de frase bimembre in griego antiguo y sus implicaciones para las nociones de 'sujeto' y 'casos' [diss. ᴰ*García Calvo* A.]. M 1988, Univ. Complutense. 435 p. – ᴿSalesianum 54 (1992) 824s (R. *Gottlieb*).

9825* *de Lacey* D. R., Word order and emphasis; a study in *koinē* Greek: ➤ 450, Informatique 2, 1988/9, 223-242.

9826 *Drexhage* Hans-Joachim, Feminine Berufsbezeichnungen im hellenistischen Ägypten: MünstHand 11,1 (1992) 70-79; franç. Eng. 79.

9827 **Duhoux** Yves, Le verbe grec ancien; éléments de morphologie et de syntaxe historiques: ʙᴄɪʟʟ 61. LvN 1992, Peeters. 549 p. 90-6831-387-8.

9828 **Fanning** Buist M., Verbal aspect in NT Greek 1990 ➤ 6,9659; 7,9460: ᴿExpTim 103 (1991s) 54 (H. *Guite*: must there not be a commonsense limit to the number of levels?); JBL 111 (1992) 714-8 (D. H. *Schmidt* compares ᴘᴏʀᴛᴇʀ S. 1989); JSS 37 (1992) 102-5 (D. *Bain*); NT 34 (1992) 102-4 (J. K. *Elliott*); TLZ 117 (1992) 187-9 (K.-W. *Niebuhr*); WestTJ 54 (1992) 179-183 (M. *Siva*, also on ᴘᴏʀᴛᴇʀ S.).

9829 **Friberg** Barbara & Timothy, O Novo Testamento, grego-analítico [1981]. São Paulo 1987, Vida Nova. – ᴿRCuBíb 14,55s (1990) 159-161 (J. M. *Terra*).

9830 **Guillemette** Pierre, The Greek New Testament analyzed 1986 ➤ 5, 9564; fr. ➤ 6,9666; deutsch 1988 ➤ 6,9667: ᴿSTEv 3 (1991) 131 (P. *Bolognesi*).

Harl Marguerite, La langue de Japhet... grec des chrétiens 1992 ➤ 250.

9831 **Hoerber** R. G., Studies in NT 1991 ➤ 7,210d: — *Moellering* H. A., Fabulosa farrago: ConcordJ 18,1 (1992) 50-58: Hoerber holds Greek basically identical from Homer through *koiné*.

9832 **Jacquinod** Bernard, Le double accusatif en grec, d'Homère à la fin du Vᵉ siècle avant J.-C.: BtCILL 50, 1990 ➤ 7,9464; Fb 900. 90-6831-194-8: ᴿAntClas 61 (1992) 444-6 (D. *Donnet*); BSLP 87,2 (1992) 182-4 (G. *Lazard*); ClasR 42 (1992) 96s (Gillian R. *Hart*).

9833 *a*) *Kimball* Sara E., The origin of the Greek *k*-perfect; – *b*) *Sicking* G.M.J., The distribution of aorist and present tense stem forms in Greek, especially in the imperative: Glotta 69 (1991) 141-153 / 14-43. 154-170.

9834 **Lamberterie** C. de, Les adjectifs grecs en -*ys*, sémantique et comparaison: BCILL 54s. LvN 1990, Peeters. – ᴿBSLP 86,2 (1991) 145-9 (L. *Dubois*; Françoise *Bader*).

9835 *Larsen* I., *a*) Notes on the function of *gár, oûn, mén, dé, kaí,* and *té* in the Greek NT; – *b*) Quotations and speech introducers in narrative texts; – *c*) Word order and relative prominence in NT Greek: NotTr 5,1 (1991) 35-47 (1-28 *Titrud* J. on *kai*) / 55-60 / 29-34 [< NTAbs 36,313ss].

9836 *Ledgerwood* L. W.ᴵᴵᴵ, [ɢʀɪᴄᴇ H. P. 1975, 1978]. What does the Greek first class conditional imply? Gricean methodology and the testimony of the ancient Greek grammarians: GraceTJ 12,1 (1991) 99-118.

9837 **Lillo** Antonio, The ancient Greek numeral system; a study of some problematic forms 1990 ➤ 7,9468: ᴿBSLP 86,2 (1991) 150s (Françoise *Bader*).

9838 **Louw** Johannes P., *Nida* Eugene A., Greek-English...NT semantic domains 1988 ➤ 4,2617...7,9470: ᴿFgNt 5 (1992) 167-188 (J.A.L. *Lee*, Eng., 188s español).

9839 ᴱ**Lust** J., *Eynikel* E., *Hauspie* K., A Greek-English lexicon of the Septuagint, I. A-I. Stu 1992, Deutsche Bibelgesellschaft. liii-217 p. DM 38. 3-438-05125-7 [BL 93,155, L.L. *Grabbe*: based on RAHLFS; Cambridge and Göttingen apparatus not systematically recorded].

9840 *Lust* J., A concise dictionary of the Septuagint [project]: ETL 68 (1992) 188-194.

9841 *McKay* K.L., Time and aspect in NT Greek: NT 34 (1992) 209-228.

9842 **Martin** R.A., Syntax criticism 1987/9 ➤ 6,9687: ᴿRHR 209 (1992) 304-8 (A. *Méhat*).

9843 **Mateos** J., Método de análisis semántico... NT 1989 ➤ 5,9575: ᴿHelmantica 43 (1992) 261s (S. *García-Jalón*); StPatav 38 (1991) 195 (G. *Segalla*).

9844 **Metzger** Bruce, Lexical aids for students of New Testament Greek³ 1989 ➤ 6,9780, now also E 1990, Clark. 100 p. £5. 0-567-29182-0 [Exp-Tim 103,95].

9845 **Molendijk** Arie, Le passé simple et l'imparfait; une approche REI-CHENBACHIENNE. Amst 1990, Rodopi. 279 p. – ᴿBSLP 87,2 (1992) 263-7 (Zlatka *Guentchéva*).

9846 **Mugler** Alfred, Tempus und Aspekt als Zeitbeziehungen [< Diss. Mü 1986]: Studien zur theoretischen Linguistik 9. Mü 1988, Fink. 297 p. DM 78. – ᴿKratylos 37 (1992) 31-45 (Ana *Agud*).

9846* *Mussies* Gerard, Greek: ➤ 741, AnchorBD 4 (1992) 195-203.

9847 *Niccacci* Alviero, Dall'aoristo all'imperfetto, o dal primo piano allo sfondo; un paragone tra sintassi greca e sintassi ebraica: LA 42 (1992) 85-108; Eng. 334.

Nida E., *Louw* J., Lexical semantics NT 1992 ➤ a129.

9849 *Passoni Dell'Acqua* Anna, I prestiti latini nella *koinē* greca d'Egitto e di Palestina; osservazioni su Il lessico latino nel greco d'Egitto di S. DARIS [Aegyptus 40 (1960) 177-314 e PapyrCastroct 3, 1971]: RivB 40 (1992) 309-317.

9850 *Penna* Romano, Lessicografia neotestamentaria: Lateranum 57 (1991) 577-581.

9851 **Porter** Stanley E., Idioms of the Greek New Testament: Biblical Languages, Greek 2. Sheffield 1992, JStOT. 339 p. $46.75; pa. $19.50. 1-85075-357-1; -79-2 [TDig 40,181].

9852 ᴿ**Porter** S.E., The language of the NT, classic essays 1991 ➤ 7,324; ᴿNT 34 (1992) 311s (J.K. *Elliott*).

9853 **Porter** Stanley E., Verbal aspect in the Greek of the NT 1989 ➤ 5, 9581...7,9481: ᴿCBQ 54 (1992) 366s (F.T. *Gignac*: enlightening); CiuD 205 (1992) 754s (J. *Gutiérrez*).

9854 *Porter* Stanley E., Keeping up with recent studies, IV. Greek language and linguistics: ExpTim 103 (1991s) 202-8.

9855 **Rehkopf** Friedrich, Griechisch-deutsches Wörterbuch zum Neuen Testament. Gö 1992, Vandenhoeck & R. xi-140 p. 3-525-50118-8.

9856 **Rienecker** Fritz, *Rogers* Cleon, Chave lingüística do N.T., ᵀ*Chown* Gordon, *Zabatiero* Júlio. São Paulo 1985, Vida Nova. – ᴿRCuBíb 14,55s (1990) 161s (J.M. *Terra* compares to ZERWICK).

9857 **Rijksbaron** A., *al.*, In the footsteps of Raphael KÜHNER [gr. Syntaxe Amst, 150. Anniv.] Colloquium 1986/8 ➤ 6,765: ᴿAnzAltW 45 (1992) 61-66 (M. *Kienpointner*].

9858 **Robinson** Thomas A., Mastering Greek vocabulary 1990 ➤ 6,9696: ᴿRThom 92 (1992) 593s (L. *Devillers*: severe; mixes roots).

9859 **Romaniuk** Kazimierz, ❷ *Mały słownik ...* Small metaphorical-exegetical dictionary of the NT. Wsz 1992, Archidiecezji. 123 p. 83-85706-01-1. **Sieg** F., Präpositionen als Morpheme 1992 ➤ 5763.

9860 **Spicq** C., Lexique théologique du NT [1 vol.; 350 art.]. FrS/P 1991, Univ. / Cerf. 1668 p. ➤ 7,9488; Fs 86. 2-8271-0564-0 / 2-204-04494-6 [NTAbs 36,258]. – ᴿEsprVie 102 (1992) 3-couv. (E. *Vauthier*).

9861 **Swetnam** James, An introduction to the study of New Testament Greek: SubsBPont 16. R 1992, Pontificio Istituto Biblico. I. Lessons, 488 p. II. Key, lists, 328 p. Lit. 52.500. 88-7653-600-0.

9862 ᶠTAILLARDAT Jean, Hediston logodeipnon 1988 ➤ 5,190: ᴿRÉLat 70 (1992) 420-2 (Frédérique *Biville*).

9863 **Trapp** E., *al.*, Studien zur byzantinischen Lexikographie: ByzVindob. 18. W 1988. 222 p. – ᴿByzantina 16 (1991) 433-8 (Nike *Papatriadaphyllou-Theodoridi*).

9864 **Tucker** Elizabeth F., The creation of morphological regularity; early Greek verbs in -éō ...: HSprF ErgH 35, 1990 ➤ 7,9706: ᴿSalesianum 54 (1992) 617s (R. *Gottlieb*).

9865 **Van Voorst** Robert E., Building your NT Greek vocabulary 1990 ➤ 6,9707; 7,9491: ᴿSalesianum 54 (1992) 161s (R. *Sabin*: si basa sulle più aggiornate pubblicazioni scientifiche).

9866 **Verboomen** Alain, L'imparfait périphrastique dans l'Évangile de Luc et dans la Septante; contribution à l'étude du système verbal du grec néotestamentaire: Acad. Belgique, Fonds Draguet 10. Lv 1992, Peeters. xiv-92 p. Fb 800.

9867 *Weissengruber* Franz, Zum Verbalaspekt im Griechischen des Neuen Testament: SNTU A-16 (1991) 169-177 [< ZIT 92,309] (*Fuchs* A p. 151-168).

9868 *a) Werner* Jürgen, Zur Fremdsprachenproblematik in der griechisch-römischen Antike; – *b) Franke* Peter R., Dolmetschen in hellenistischer Zeit; – *c) Schöpsdau* Klaus, Vergleiche zwischen Latenisch und Griechisch in der antiken Sprachwissenschafl; – *d) Weis* Rudolf, Zur Kenntnis des Griechischen im Rom der republikanischen Zeit: ➤ 672, Fremdsprachen 1989/92 1-20 / 85-96 / 115-136 / 137-142.

9869 **Windekens** A. J. van, Dictionnaire étymologique complémentaire de la langue grecque 1986 ➤ 7,9494: ᴿArGlotIt 76 (1991) 210-2 (C. A. *Mastrelli*).

9870 **Windham** Neal, NT Greek for preachers and teachers; five areas of application 1991 ➤ 7,9495; 0-8191-8325-3: ᴿCritRR 5 (1992) 257s (D. D. *Schmidt*: useful features and aim, but misuses semantic domains); ExpTim 103 (1991s) 310s (H. *Guite*: not a manual for beginners; good on how an apparatus criticus is made).

9871 **Woodard** Roger D., On interpreting morphological change; the Greek reflexive pronoun 1990 ➤ 6,9712: ᴿClasR 42 (1992) 213s (A. C. *Moorhouse*); Kratylos 37 (1992) 73-76 (C. *Brixhe*).

J5.2 **Voces graecae** (*ordine alphabetico* **graeco**).

9872 *aga-* 'great(ly)': RPg 65 (1991) 195-218 (G.-J. *Pinault*).

9873 *agápē*: *Söding* Thomas, Das Wortfeld der Liebe im paganen und biblischen Griechisch; philologische Beobachtungen an der Wurzel *agap-*: ETL 68 (1992) 284-330.

9874 *agroikía:* *Traina* G., Sul termine *agroikía* nelle iscrizioni di Asia Minore: AnPisa 20 (1990) 791-6.

9875 *adelphótēs:* **Dujarier** Michel, L'Église-fraternité; I. Les origines de l'expression 'adelphótēs-fraternitas' aux trois premiers siècles du christianisme: Théologies. P 1991, Cerf. 111 p. F 85. – ᴿRTLv 23 (1992) 384s (Marie-André *Houdart*).

9876 *aítion:* **Valverde Sánchez** Mariano, El aítion en las Argonáuticas de APOLONIO de Rodas, estudio literario [dis. 1986, ᴰ*García López* J.]: Col. Mayor 17. Murcia 1989, Univ. 346 p. – ᴿHabis 22 (1991) 469s (A. *Villarrubia*).

9877 *aiōn:* **Zuntz** Günther [➤ d374], Aiōn im Römerreich 1991/3 ➤ 7,9499; 3-533-04387-8: ᴿRÉLat 70 (1992) 392s (R. *Chevallier* 'Zunth' aussi index).

9878 *akēdía:* **Bunge** Gabriel, Akédia; la doctrine spirituelle d'ÉVAGRE le Pontique sur l'acédie: Spiritualité orientale 52. Bellefontaine 1991, Abbaye. 138 p. – ᴿEsprVie 102 (1992) 138s (P. *Jay*); RHPR 72 (1992) 336s (J. C. *Larchet*).

9888 *halískō:* **Bergren** Theodore A., **Kraft** Robert A., *Halískō* (*haliskomai*) in Greek Jewish Scriptures; profile of a difficult Greek verb: BJRyL 74,3 (1992) 53-66.

9889 *Amazōn:* RPg 65 (1991) 229-241 (M. *Tichit*).

9890 *anaginōskō:* **Slusser** Michael, Reading silently in antiquity: JBL [109 (1990) 16s] 111 (1992) 499 only.

9891 *anámnēsis:* **Ginn** Richard J., The present and the past; a study of anamnesis [... OT; NT]: Princeton Theol Mg 20. Allison Park PA 1989, Pickwick. 92 p. – ᴿTorJT 7 (1991) 307-9 (P. *Wagner*).

9892 *ánemos* / anima [IE *ani– piuttosto 'vuoto, inanis']: BbbOr 34 (1992) 17s; *Ceccherelli* Ignazio M., Nomi [non propri; 26 sostantivi], origini e significati, p. 13-51.

9893 *apeithéō:* **Thibaut** André, L'infidélité du peuple élu; apeithō entre la Bible hébraïque et la Bible latine 1988 ➤ 4,a657; 7,9502*: ᴿRÉAug 37 (1991) 159s (G. *Dorival*); RHE 87 (1992) 252 (P.-M. *Bogaert*).

9894 *arketós:* **Schwarz** Günther, Arketón [... Mt 10,25: 'möglich', nicht 'es genüge']: BibNot 58 (1991) 29.

9895 *Assyría:* **Frye** Richard N., Assyria and Syria, synonyms: JNES 51 (1992) 281-5.

9896 *-assō,* verb-ending: RPg 65 (1991) 219-227 (Françoise *Skoda*).

9897 *auktoritas:* **Freyburger-Galland** Marie-Laure, DION Cassius et l'etymologie; *auctoritas* et *augustus:* RÉG 105 (1992) 237-246.

9898 *geláō:* **Arnould** Dominique, Le rire et les larmes dans la littérature grecque d'Homère à Platon (ᴰ1987) 1990 ➤ 7,9506: ᴿAmJPg 113 (1992) 448-452 (D. *Lateiner:* title correctly here, but 'Le rire et les armes' in Contents before p. 1 and p. 319); RBgPg 70 (1992) 194s (L. *Jerphagnon*).

9899 *dé:* **Buth** R., 'And' or 'but' – so what? JPersp 4,2 (1991) 13-15 [< NTAbs 36, 11: *dé* means 'but' rather than 'and', but is less used in NT than in secular Greek].

9900 *déxios:* **Liou-Gille** Bernadette, 'Dexter' et 'sinister' et leurs équivalents [ambiguity not due to Greek influence, or Babylonian or Egyptian either]: Glotta 69 (1991) 194-201.

9901 *deutereúō:* **Blomqvist** Jerker, **Olsson** Britt, Bedeutung und Konstruktion von deutereúō: Eranos 90 (1992) 11-21.

9902 *diakonía:* **Collins** John N., Diakonía; re-interpreting the ancient sources 1990 ➤ 6,9729; 7,8115. 9508; $45: ᴿAnglTR 74 (1992) 108-110

(J. R. *Wright*); ClasW 85 (1991s) 146s (D. J. *Constantelos*); JTS 53 (1992) 198-200 (K. *Grayston*: enjoyably discursive); Tablet 246 (1992) 865s (T. *Radcliffe*); TTod 49 (1992s) 440. 442 (P. G. *Craighill*).

9903 **díkē:** *Coulet* Corinne, Réflexions sur la famille de *díkē* dans l'Enquête d'HÉRODOTE: RÉG 105 (1992) 371-384.

9904 **dýnamis: Barnes** Michael R., The power of God; the significance of 'dynamis' in the development of GREGORY of Nyssa's polemic against EUNOMIUS of Cyzicus: diss. St. Michael, ᴰRist J. Toronto 1992, 549 p. – RTLv 24, p. 550.

9905 **ekeînos,** *autós: Elliott* J. K., New Testament linguistic usage: ➤ 70, ᶠGREENLEE J., Scribes 1992, 41-48.

9906 **eumarēs:** *Blanc* Alain, La distribution des biens et des maux; *eumarēs* et la racine **smer* –; RÉG 105 (1992) 548-556.

9907 **ēthos: Wisse** Jakob, Ethos and pathos from Aristotle to Cicero. Amst 1989, Hakkert. xv-170 p. – ᴿGnomon 64 (1992) 579-583 (E. *Schütrumpf*).

9908 **ētoi:** *Sijpesteijn* P. J., The meanings of *ētoi* in the papyri: ZPapEp 90 (1992) 241-250 [... 'and especially'].

9909 **theosebēs:** *Murphy-O'Connor* Jerome, Lots of God-fearers? *theosebeîs* in the Aphrodisias inscription: RB 99 (1992) 418-424; franç. 418.

9910 **thlîpsis:** RPg 65 (1991) 169-178 (F. *Mawet*).

9911 *Mawet* Francine, Du grec thlîpsis à l'arménien nelut'iwn: CdÉ 66 (1991) 245-9.

9912 **thymós: Caswell** Caroline P., A study of thumos in early Greek epic: Mnemosyne supp. 114, 1990 ➤ 7,9514: ᴿJHS 112 (1992) 177 (M. M. *Willcock*: deplorable proofreading).

9913 **Ioudaios:** *Pritz* Ray, Who is a Jew in the Gospels?: Jerusalem Perspective 3,5 (1990) 5s.

9914 **Italía: Gély** Suzanne, Le nom d'Italie, mythe et histoire, d'Hellanicos à Virgile [... terre des veaux]. Genève 1991, Slatkine. 532 p. – ᴿRÉAnc 94 (1992) 489 (Lucienne *Deschamps*); RÉLat 70 (1992) 335 (Dominique *Briquel*).

9915 *Molinos Tejada* Maria Teresa, La particule modale *ka* dans la littérature dorienne: RÉG 105 (1992) 328-348.

9916 **kairós: Bielecki** Stanisław, ❷ Nowotestamentalne ujęcie terminu Kairos: RuBi 45 (1992) 57-65.

9917 **kálamos: Krengel** Elke, **Speck** Paul, *Kalamon syntomia;* zu griechischen Bezeichnungen für *tesserae:* RheinMus 134 (1991) 196-202; 5 fig.

9918 **káranos** = *kýrios:* Glotta 69 (1991) 173s (D. *Testen*).

9919 **koimáomai: Jackson** Paul N., The concept of eschatological sleep; an investigation of *koimaomai* in the NT: diss. SW Baptist Theol. Sem. ᴰCorley B. 1992. 307 p. 93-11165. – DissA 53 (1992s) 4359-A.

9920 **koinós,** koinóō: FgNt 5 (1992) 69-78 (J.D.M. *Derrett*).

9920* **ktistēs:** *a) Follet* Simone, Hadsien ktistès kaì oikistès; lexicographie et realia; – *b) Chadwick* John, Semantic history and Greek lexicographie: ➤ 663*, Langue 1989/92, 241-254 / 281-8.

9921 **kōs:** *Lillo* Antonio, Ionic kōs, hókōs, hópōs, Thessalian kis; a phonetic problem of analyzable compounds: Glotta 69 (1991) 1-13.

9922 **lásanon:** *Papadopoulos* John K., *Lásana*, tuyères, and kiln firing supports: Hesperia 61 (1992) 203-221; 8 fig.; pl. 47-51.

9923 **mathētēs:** *Richards* Lawrence O., The disappearing disciple; why is the use of 'disciple' limited to the Gospels and Acts?: EvJ 10, 1 (1992) 3– ...

9924 **mantis:** *Casevitz* Michel, Mantis, le vrai sens: RÉG 105 (1992) 1-18.

9925 **mártyr:** *Ranft* Patricia, The concept of witness in the Christian tradition from its origin to its institutionalization: RBén 102 (1992) 9-23. **memnōn** ➤ 9947.

9926 **mouliōn:** *Tanrıver* Cumhur, Some new texts regarding occupations [*mouliōn* muleteer; *naúarchos, gymnasíarchos, philósophos* ...]: EpAnat 18 (1991) 79-82; Özet 82.

9927 **mystērion:** **Bouyer** Louis, The Christian mystery; from pagan myth to Christian mysticism 1990 ➤ 6,9750; 7,8184.9525: ᴿCathHR 78 (1992) 94s (J. A. *Wiseman*). Interpretation 46 (1992) 216 (Rebecca H. *Weaver*: mysticism not to be relegated).

9928 **nekrothaptēs,** vespa/vespillo: RheinMus 134 (1991) 403s (J. *Knobloch*).

9929 **némō:** *Jordan* Borimir, The *naukraroi* of Athens and the meaning of *némō*: AntClas 61 (1992) 60-79.

9930 **nêtta:** *Rix* Helmut, Nochmals griech. *nêtta* / *nêssa* / *nâssa*: HistSprF 104 (1991) 186-198.

9931 **nin:** *Lillo* Antonio, Thessalian *mademina*, Aeolic *îa*, Homeric *min*, Doric *nin*: IndogF 97 (1992) 55-64.

9932 **opēdós:** *Meier-Brügger* Michael, a) Zu griechisch *opēdós* ['Begleiter']; – b) Verbaute lokale Genetive im Griechischen; *éraze, thýraze, chamāze; Erébeusphi; phóōsde*: Glotta 69 (1991) 171s. / 44-47.

9933 **orgē:** *Crockett* W. V., Wrath that endures forever: JEvTS 34 (1991) 195-202 [< NTAbs 36,47].

9934 *Motte* André, *Pirenne-Delforge* Vinciane, Le mot et les rites; aperçu des significations de *órgia* et de quelques dérivés: ➤ 671, Kernos 5 (1991/2) 119-140.

9935 **hósios:** *Rici* Marijana, Hosios kai dikaios; nouveaux monuments: EpAnat [18 (1991) 1-20; 19 (1992) 71-102] 20 (1992) 95-100; pl. 9-10; p. 100 Özet [p. 143-7 ein frühes Zeugnis, *Petzl* G.].

9936 **parástasis** [late meaning 'arrival' = *parousía*]: CdÉ 66 (1991) 303-7 (B. *Boyaval*).

9937 **páredros:** *Ciraolo* Leda J., The warmth and breath of life; animating physical object *páredroi* in the Greek Magical Papyri: ➤ 478, SBL Sem. 31 (1992) 240-254.

9938 **pémpō:** *Di Marco,* Angelico Salvatore, Pémpō; per una ricerca del 'campo semantico' nel NT: RivB 40 (1992) 385-419; Eng. 419: use with 'go' does not prevail over 'see, know, speak'.

9939 **plêthos:** **Olsen** Birgit A., The proto-Indo-European instrument noun suffix *-tlom* and its variants. K 1988, Munksgaard. – ᴿLatomus 51 (1992) 659 (Francine *Mawet*).

9940 **pneûma:** *Brottier* Laurence, Sur quelques définitions de *pneumatikós* chez Jean CHRYSOSTOME: RÉAug 38 (1992) 19-28.

9941 **potamós,** étymologies antiques: RPg 65 (1991) 185-193 (J.-L. *Perpillou*).

9942 **prín:** *Wilson* John R., Negative *prín* clauses and the rhetoric of Achilles: Glotta 69 (1991) 175-183.

9943 **pŷr:** **Kienle** Bettina von, *Pyr*; die sprachliche Entfaltung einer Wortfelddimension in den Synoptikern, im Liber antiquitatum biblicarum und im 4. Esra: Diss. ᴰ*Burchard*. Heidelberg 1992. – RTLv 24, p. 547.

9944 **sébō:** dans PLATON II: RBgPg 70 (1992) 35-52 (A. *Cheyns*).

9945 **spéos:** RPg 65 (1991) 179-184 (M. *Meier-Brügger*).

9946 **syngnōmē:** **Metzler** Karin, Der griechische Begriff des Verzeihens: WUNT 2/44, 1991 ➤ 7,9539: ᴿClasR 42 (1992) 460s (H. *Yunis*).

9947 **téktōn:** *Kastner* Wolfgang, Téktōn-mémnōn; zu den Wurzeln *tek-* und *men-* im Griechischen: MusHelv 48 (1991) 65-85.

9948 *hypó:* **Villey** L., Soumission; thème et variations aux temps aposto-liques; la fonction d'une préposition *hypò:* THist 91. P 1992, Beauchesne. 530 p. F 198 [NRT 115, 749, V. *Roisel*].

9949 *hypomonē,* patient persistence: **Pisarek** Stanisław, Cierpliwa wytrwa-lość, *hypomonê/eîn* w NT. Katowice 1992, Św. Jacka. 360 p. [RB 100,631].

9950 *phantasía:* **Watson** Gerard, Phantasia in classical thought. Galway 1988, Univ. xiii-176 p. – ᴿGnomon 64 (1992) 348-350 (Deborah K. W. *Modrak*).

9951 *phóbos* – *éleos* (ARISTOTELES, Poetica): **Kerkhecker** Arnd, Furcht und Mitleid: RheinMus 134 (1991) 288-310.

9952 *phrēn:* **Mastrelli** Carlo A., Per l'etimologia di gr. *phrēn* e *osphraínomai:* ArGlotIt 76 (1991) 153-8.

9953 **Chaldaîos:** *Wong Chan-Kok,* PHILO's use of Chaldaioi [1. astrol-ogists; 2. Mesopotamians; 3. Hebrew(s)]: StPhilonAn 4 (1992) 1-14.

9954 *cháris:* **Zeller** Dieter, Charis bei PHILON und Paulus 1990 ➤ 6,6174: ᴿStPhilonAn 4 (1992) 174s (D. M. *Hay*).

9955 *psychē, noós:* **Jahn** Thomas, Zum Wortfeld 'Seele-Geist' im der Sprache Homers: Zetemata 83, 1987 ➤ 5,9644: ᴿClasR 42 (1992) 3-5 (A. A. *Long:* his most important findings concern *thymós, phrēn, kēr/kradiē* ...); Phoenix 45 (1991) 66-68 (Shirley D. *Sullivan*).

J5.4 *Papyri et inscriptiones graecae* – **Greek epigraphy.**

9956 **Abdalla** Aly, Graeco-Roman funerary stelae from Upper Egypt: Mg-ArchOr. Liverpool 1992, Univ. xviii-155 p.; 85 pl. 0-85323-125-7.

9957 *Aichinger* Anna, Zwei Arten des Provinzialcensus? Überlegungen zu neu publizierten israelischen Papyrusfunden [YADIN]: Chiron 22 (1992) 35-43.

9958 *Arata Mantovani* Piera, Gerico (Ketef-Jeriḫo), [ESHEL H. IsrEJ 38 (1958) 158-176], ritrovamenti epigrafici di età persiana ed ellenistica: RivB 40 (1992) 213-6.

9958* **Baccani** Donata, Oroscopi greci; documentazione papirologica: Ric-Papir 1. Messina 1992, Sicania. 192 p. 88-7268-032-8.

9959 ᴱBagnall Roger S., *al.,* Columbia papyri 8: AmStPapyrol 28, 1990 ➤ 6,9635*: ᴿCdÉ 66 (1991) 274-6 (J. D. *Thomas*).

9960 *Bagnall* Roger S., Military officers as landholders in fourth century [A.D.] Egypt: Chiron 22 (1992) 47-54.

9961 **Bernand** André, La prose sur pierre dans l'Égypte hellénistique et romain, I. Textes et traductions; II. Commentaires. P 1992, CNRS. 247 p.; 178 p. 2-222-04695-5.

9962 **Bernand** Étienne, Inscriptions grecques et latines d'Akôris 1988 ➤ 4, a582; 6,9637*: ᴿBO 49 (1992) 745-752 (H. *Heinen*).

9963 **Bertrand** Jean-Marie, Inscriptions historiques grecques traduites et commentées: La Roue à Livres. P 1992, BLettres. 273 p. 2-251-33915-8.

9964 **Bingen** Jean, *al.,* Mons Claudianus, ostraca graeca et latina I (O. Claud. 1 à 190): Documents de Fouilles 29. Le Caire 1992, IFAO. 198 p., 33 pl. 2-7247-0122-4 [OIAc 5,14].

9965 **Bingen** Jean, *Clarysse* Willy, Elkab III, les ostraca grecs 1989 ➤ 6,9639: ᴿAntClas 61 (1992) 526-8 (Jean A. *Straus*).

9966 **Bousquet** Jean, Corpus des inscriptions de Delphes 2. Les comptes du quatrième et du troisième siècle. P 1989, de Boccard. 322 p., 24 pl. –

ᴿGnomon 64 (1992) 360-2 (H. W. *Pleket*); ZSav-R 109 (1992) 599-602 (J. *Hengstl*).

9967 ᴱ**Clarysse** W., *al.*   Berichtigungsliste der griechischen Papyrusurkunden aus Ägypten; Konkordanz und Supplement zu Band I-VII, 1989 ⇒ 7, 9551: ᴿArPapF 38 (1992) 64-67 (G. *Poethke*).

9968 **Cotton** Hannah M., *Geiger* J.,   Masada II, Latin-Greek 1989 ⇒ 5, 9552 ... 7, also 9552: ᴿLatomus 51 (1992) 197s (A *Martin*).

9969 **Daniel** Robert W.,   *Maltomini* Franco, Supplementum magicum I-II: PapyrolColon 16,1s, AbhRhWfAkad.   Opladen 1990-2, Westdeutscher-V. xxvi-213 p.; 8 pl. / xiv-372 p.; 13 pl. 3-531-09926-4; -33-7.

9970 *Daris* Sergio, Scritti rari e scritti anonimi di Ossirinco: AevA 2 (1989) 47-95.

9971 *Diethart* Johannes, Lexikalisches in griechischen Papyri [... *anthēleios*, 'zur Rispe der Papyrusstaude gehörig'; sonst meist ablehnend]: Sprache 34 (1990) 190-194.

9972 **Ecker** Ute,   Grabmal und Epigramm; Studien zur frühgriechischen Sepulkraldichtung: Palingenesia 29.   Stu 1990, Steiner.   285 p. DM 76. – ᴿClasR 42 (1992) 410-2 (P. A. *Hansen*).

9973 **Fantoni** Georgina,   Greek papyri of the Byzantine period: Corpus Raineri 14, gr. 10, 1989 ⇒ 5,9559; 7,9557: ᴿBO 49 (1992) 405-411 (Ewa *Wipszycka*).

9974 *Feissel* Denis, Notes d'épigraphie chrétienne (VIII): BCH 116 (1992) 388-407.

9975 *Felle* Antonio E., Note su Sacra Scrittura ed epigrafia cristiana in margine a C. WESSEL [⇒ 6,9711]. Inscriptiones graecae christianae veteres occidentis [1989]: ⇒ 458, AnStoEseg 8,2 (1992) 467-482.

9976 **Frösén** Jakko, *Hagedorn* Dieter, Die verkohlten Papyri aus Bubastos 1, 1990 ⇒ 6,e705: ᴿCdÉ 67 (1992) 369-371 (Marie *Drew-Bear*); Gnomon 64 (1992) 517-520 (J. F. *Oates*, Eng.).

9976* *Gatier* Pierre-Louis, Répartition des inscriptions grecques en Jordanie; l'exemple des inscriptions métriques aux époques romaine et byzantine: ⇒ 740, Jordan 4 (1992) 291-4.

9977 *Haelst* J. van, Cinq textes provenant de Khirbet Mird (lettres etc.): AncSoc 22 (1991) 297-317; 7 pl.

9978 **Hanafi** Alia, Papyrus Hauniensis (P. Haun.) I: PapyrolB 6. Cairo 1989, Ain Shems Univ. Papyrol. Center. 92 p.; 13 pl.; ❹ 12 p. [OIAc 2,20]. – ᴿZSav-R 109 (1992) 592-9 (H.-A. *Rupprecht*, auch über 54-56).

9979 ᴱ**Haslam** M. W., *al.*, The Oxyrhynchus papyri 57: Memoir 77, 1990 ⇒ 7,9565. ᴿBO 49 (1992) 743-5 (J. A. *Straus*); ClasR 42 (1992) 413s (D. W. *Rathbone*); Gnomon 62 (1992) 293-9 (W. *Luppe*).

9980 **Hatzopoulos** M. B., Actes de vente d'Amphipolis: Meletemata 14. Athènes 1991. 111 p.; 19 fig. F 230. 960-7094-79-4. [RB 100, 448].

9981 *Hengstl* Joachim, Juristische Literaturübersicht 1983-1989: ArPapF 38 (1992) 89-154.

9982 **Horbury** William, *Noy* David, Jewish inscriptions of Graeco-Roman Egypt. C 1992, Univ. xxiv-378 p.; 32 pl. 0-521-41870-4 [OIAc 5,24; BL 93,32, L. L. *Grabbe*: replaces FREY CIJ]. ⇒ 9402.

9983 *Isaac* Benjamin, The Babatha archive [ᴱLEWIS N. 1989]: IsrEJ 42 (1992) 62-75.

9984 ᴱ**Kramer** Bärbel, Griechische Texte XIII: das Vertragsregister von Theogenis (P. Vindob. Gr 40618): Corpus Pap. Raineri 18. W 1991, Hollinek. xvi-228 p.; vol. pl. 1-XII + 2. – ᴿCdÉ 67 (1992) 341-359 (Andrea *Jördens*); REG 105 (1992) 616s (P. *Cauderlier*).

9985 **Kutzner** Edgar, Untersuchungen zur Stellung der Frau im römischen Oxyrhynchos: EurHS 3/392. Fra 1989, Lang. DM 42. 3-631-41847-7. – ᴿBO 49 (1992) 413-421 (Barbara *Anagnostou-Canas*).

9986 **Lalonde** Gerald V. (Horoi), *al.*, Inscriptions: Athenian Agora 19. Princeton 1991. xiii-245 p., 16 pl. – ᴿArchWsz 43 (1992) 131-3 (A. S. *Chankowski*, français).

9987 **Lewis** N., *al.* [Hever] Greek papyri 1989 → 6,9678, 7,9574: ᴿLatomus 51 (1992) 198-200 (A. *Martin*).

9988 ᵀᴱ**McKechnie** P. R., *Kern* S., Hellenica Oxyrhynchia [Eng.] 1988 → 5, 9574; £20; pa. £7.50. – ᴿMnemosyne 45 (1992) 109s (W *Luppe*).

9989 **McNamee** Kathleen, Sigla and select marginalia in Greek literary papyri: PapyrBrux 26. Bru 1992, Fond. Reine Élisabeth. 81 p. [OIAc 5,29].

9990 **Marengo** Silvia Maria, Lessico delle iscrizioni greche della Cirenaica: Studi 49. R 1991, Ist. Storia Antica. xxii-697 p.

9991 **Martín Vázquez** Lourdes, Inscripciones rodias: diss. 450/88. M 1988, Univ. Complutense. 492 p.; 675 p.; p. 677-1486. – ᴿÉtClas 60 (1992) 178s (C.-P.M.).

9992 *Masson* Olivier, Les lamelles de plomb de Styra [Eubée], IG XII 9,56; essai de bilan: BCH 116,1 (1992) 61-72; 4 fig.

9993 **Meimaris** Yiannis E. *al.*, Chronological systems in Roman-Byzantine Palestine and Arabia; the evidence of the dated Greek inscriptions: Meletemata 17. Athena / P 1992, Nat. Research / de Boccard. 433 p.; maps.

9994 **Messeri Savorelli** Gabriella, Griechische Texte XI. Papyri greci [sic] di Socnopaiu Neves e dell'Arsinoites: Corpus Pap. Raineri 16. W 1990, Hollinek. 135 p. + vol. 46 pl. – ᴿREG 105 (1992) 615s (P. *Cauderlier*).

9995 [**Migliardi**] **Zingale** Livia, I testamenti romani nei papiri e nelle tavolette d'Egitto; silloge di documenti dal I al IV secolo d.C.²ʳᵉᵛ. T 1991, Giappichelli. 157 p. Lit. 17.000. 88-348-0124-5.

9996 [**Migliardi**] **Zingale** Livia, Vita privata e vita pubblica nei papiri d'Egitto; silloge di documenti greci e latini dal I al IV secolo d.C. T 1992, Giappichelli. xi-211 p.; maps. 88-348-0113-X.

9997 **Pérez Molina** Miguel E., Index verborum in inscriptiones Corinthi / Megarae et coloniarum: Alpha-Omega A 117.121. Hildesheim 1990s, Olms-Weidmann. xii-174 p.; DM 98 / xii-396 p.; DM 198. 3-487-09364-2; 401-0. – ᴿAntClas 61 (1992) 525s (A. *Martin*).

9998 ᴱ**Pestman** P. W., *Rupprecht* H.-A., Berichtigungsliste der griechischen Papyrusurkunden aus Ägypten 8, ᴱ**Hoogendijk** F.A.J. Leiden 1992, Brill. x-626 p. 90-04-09621-3 [OIAc 5,31].

9999 **Pintaudi** Rosario, Papyri Prag. I. 1988 → 4,a632; 7,9579: ᴿAegyptus 72 (1992) 199s (Orsolina *Montevecchi*).

a1 **Pratesi** Alessandro, Frustula palaeographica: ScrCiv Bt 4. F 1992, Olschki. x-410 p. Lit. 95.000. 88-222-3929-6.

a2 [**Preisigke** F., *Bilabel* F., Berichtigungsliste der griechischen Papyrusurkunden aus Ägypten, 1-7], CLARYSSE W., *al.*, 1-7, — Konkordanz und Supplement. Lv 1991, Peeters. xiii-302 p. Fb 5000. 90-6831-205-7. – ᴿBO 49 (1992) 404s (Geneviève *Husson*).

a3 *Puech* Émile, Palestinian funerary inscriptions, ᵀ*Rosoff* Stephen: → 741, AnchorBD 5 (1992) 126-135 [143-6, *Pickering* S. R., Papyri, early Christian].

a4 ᴱ**Rea** J. R., Oxyrhynchus Papyri 58: Graeco-Roman Memoirs 78. L 1991, Egypt Expl. Soc. [British Acad.]. xxvii-155 p.; 8 pl. 0-85698-112-5 [OIAc 2,25].

a5 *Rebillard* Laurence,   La coupe d'Archiklès et Glaukytès; l'écrit dans l'image: BCH 116 (1992) 501-540; 10 fig.

a5* **Rupprecht** H. A., *Jördens* A.,   Wörterbuch der griechischen Papyrusurkunden Supp. 2 (Mainz.Akad).   Wsb 1991, Harrassowitz.   xi-335 p. DM 168.   3-447-03120-4. – ᴿZSav-R 109 (1992) 599-602 (J. *Hengstl*).

a6 **Şahin** Sencer,   Katalog der antiken Inschriften des Museums von İznik (Nikaia): Inschriften griechischer Städte aus Kleinasien 9. Bonn 1979, Habelt. – I. 328 p., xxvi pl.; II. 1981, 376 p., XXIX pl. 3-7749-1636-5; -87-X. – ᴿZSav-R 108 (1991) 651s (G. *Thür* über 22, 1990).

a7 *Schädler* Ulrich,   Attizismen an ionischen Tempeln Kleinasiens: IstMitt 41 (1991) 265-324; 1 fig.; pl. 38; Beilage 4-5.

a8 ᴱ**Schubert** Paul,   Les archives de Marcus Lucretius Diogenes et textes apparentés [Philadelphia NE Fayum, 500 years after Zeno]: PapyrTAbh 39. Bonn 1990, Habelt. xvii-278 p.; 24 pl. DM 124. – ᴿClasR 42 (1992) 166s (Dorothy J. *Thompson*).

a9 **SEG**: Supplementum epigraphicum graecum 37 for 1987 / 38 for 1988. Amst 1990s, Gieben. xxix-672 p. / xxxii-699 p. ƒ160 + 195. 90-5063-064-2; -73-1. – ᴿClasR 42 (1992) 482 (D. M. *Lewis*).

a10 **Seider** R.,   Paläographie der griechischen Papyri 3/1/1, [Vorgeschichte] Urkundenschrift. Stu 1990, Hiersemann. xii-422 p.; 109 fig. DM 480. 3-7772-8943-4 [BO 50, 151, B. *Boyaval*].

a11 **Shelton** John C.,   Greek and Latin papyri, ostraca, and wooden tablets in the collection of the Brooklyn Museum: PapyrolFlor 22. F 1992, Gonnelli. xvi-152 p.; XLV pl.

a12 ᴱ**Sirivianou** M. G.,   The Oxyrhynchus papyri **56:** Memoir 76, 1989 ➤ 6,9700*; 7,9581*: ᴿCdÉ 67 (1992) 175-182 (J. *Lenaerts*); Eikasmos 2 (1991) 387-391 (Rosa *Giannattasio Andria*, also on **57** ᴱHASLAM M.); Gnomon 64 (1992) 289-295 (W. *Luppe*).

a13 **Tracy** Stephen V.,   Attic letter-cutters of 229 to 86 B.C.; Hellenistic Culture and Society 6. Berkeley 1990, Univ. California. xvi-292 p.; 29 fig. $45. 0-520-06806-8. – ᴿAmJPg 113 (1992) 457-460 (M. B. *Walbank*); AntClas 61 (1992) 528s (A. *Martin*).

a14 **Tréheux** Jacques,   Inscriptions de Délos, Index, tome I, Les étrangers, à l'exclusion des Athéniens de la clérouchie et des Romains. P 1992, de Boccard. 113 p.

a15 **Wehrli** C.,   Les papyrus de Genève II Nᵒˢ 82-117, 1986 ➤ 3,9860; Fs 80: ᴿMnemosyne 45 (1992) 282-5 (Francisca A. J. *Hoogendijk*).

J5.5   Cypro-Minoa [➤ T9.1,4].

a16 ᶠ**BENNETT** Emmett L.:   Texts, tablets and scribes; studies in Mycenaean epigraphy and economy, ᴱ**Olivier** J.-P., *Palaima* T. G.: Minos supp. 10, S 1988 ➤ 7,21: ᴿKratylos 37 (1992) 191-3 (J. T. *Hooker*).

a17 **Best** Jan, *Woudhuizen* Fred,   Ancient scripts from Crete and Cyprus: Francfort Foundation 9. Leiden 1988, Brill. 148 p. $26. – ᴿSyria 68 (1991) 473-5 (Emilia *Masson*: peu plausible).

a18 *Best* Jan,   Linguistic evidence for a Phoenician pillar cult in Crete: JANES [14 (1982) 85, *Rendsburg* G. on his Talanta 12 *yaššaram* 1982] 20 (1991) 7-13; 3 fig.

a19 *Bile* Monique,   Les termes relatifs a l'initiation dans les inscriptions crétoises: ➤ 670, l'Initiation 1 (1991/2) 11-18.

a20 *a) Bile* Monique,   Dialectologie et cités crétoises; – *b) Duhoux* Yves,

Variations morphosyntaxiques dans les textes votifs Linéaires A: Cretan Studies 3 (Amst 1992) 55-63 / 65-88.

a21 **Chadwick** J., *al.*, Corpus of Mycenaean inscriptions from Knossos [I, 1986 ⇥ 4,a496; 5,9650] 2. C 1990, Univ. viii-243; ill. 0-521-32023-2. – ᴿRÉG 105 (1992) 612s (P. *Faure*).

a22 *Driessen* Jan, Homère et les tablettes en linéaire B; mise au point; ᵀ*Baurain* C.: AntClas 61 (1992) 5-37.

a23 *Dürr* Friedrich, Gibt es eine sprachliche Brücke, die von Kreta über Cypern zur Tarragona-Tafel [AJA 20, 1916] führt?: BibNot 56 (1991) 7-10; 2 fig.

a24 **Egetmeyer** Markus, [*Hintze* Almut, berücksichtigt], Wörterbuch zu den Inschriften im kyprischen Syllabar: Kadmos supp. 3. B 1992, de Gruyter. xvi-351 p. 3-11-012270-7 [OIAc 5,20].

a24* *a) Franceschetti* Adele, Le tazze ad iscrizione dipinta in Lineare A provenienti da Cnosso; – *b) Finkelberg* Margalit, Minoan inscriptions on libation-vessels: Minos 25s (1990s) 37-42 / 43-85.

a25 *a) Hutton* William F., The meaning of *qe-te-o* in Linear B; – *b) Himmelhoch* Leah, The use of the ethnics *a-ra-si-jo* and *ku-pi-ri-jo* in Linear B texts: Minos 25s (1990) 105-131 / 91-104.

a25* **Kazanskené** V.P., *Kazanskij* N.N., ❸ *Predmetnoponiatinii slovar*, Dictionnaire conceptuel de la langue grecque, période créto-mycénienne. Leningrad 1986, Nauka. 207 p. – ᴿBSLP 86,2 (1991) 143s (S. *Patri*) & 144s (A. *Christol*).

a26 **La Forse** Bruce M., The meaning of the Mycenean words *qa-si-re-u, qa-si-re-wi-ja*, and *ke-ro-si-ja*: M.A. diss. Austin 1989, Univ., Texas. iv-50 p. [OIAc 3,27].

a27 **Negri** Mario, PU.RO; tre lezioni di micenologia, ᴱ*Aloni* A.: QuadLing 2. Mi 1988, Unicopli. 50 p.; ill. – ᴿSalesianum 54 (1992) 782s (R. *Gottlieb*).

a27* *a) Olivier* Jean-Pierre, 'Cinq' en Linéaire A?; – *b) Panagl* Oswald, Mykenische Fossilien im Homertext? Zur Deutung von *harmatopāgós* und *harmatrochiē*; – *c) Doria* Mario, Schiavi in vendita nella Cnosso micenea: ⇥ 180*b*, ᶠSᴢᴇᴍᴇʀᴇ́ɴʏɪ O., Historical philology 1992, 135s / 137-144 / 127-133.

a28 *Ruijgh* C.J., L'emploi mycénien de –h– intervocalique comme consonne de liaison entre deux morphèmes: Mnemosyne 45 (1992) 433-472.

a29 *a) Woudhuizen* Fred C., Evidence of bilingualism in Cretan hieroglyphic; – *b) Zebisch* Herbert R., Die kretischen 'Linear-' Schriften und die iberische Sprachfamilie: Cretan Studies 3 (1992) 191-201 / 203-230.

J6 Indo-Iranica.

a30 **Abram** Michael, Nomina propria [iranica] in nummis 1986 ⇥ 4,a708: ᴿIndIranJ 34 (1991) 131-5 (P.O. *Skjærvø:* 'I see no justification for the Latin title').

a31 **Alavi** B., *Lorenz* M., Lehrbuch der persischen Sprache ⁵1988 ⇥ 6,9782; DM 49: ᴿWeltOr 23 (1992) 193-7 (I.K. *Soltani*).

a32 ᶠAsᴍᴜssɪɴ Jes P., A green leaf, ᴱ**Sundermann** W., *al.* 1988 ⇥ 4,6; 6,9783: ᴿOLZ 87 (1992) 565-9 (Gudrun S. *Jakobsdóttir*).

a33 ᴱ**Camps** A. *Muller* U.C., Sanskrit grammar of Rоᴛн H. 1988 ⇥ 4, a709 ... 7,9600*: ᴿIndIranJ 34 (1991) 152-4 (J.W. *De Jong*); ZMissRW 75 (1991) 8/s (H.-W. *Gensichen*). ⇥ 687.

a34 **Damerow** Peter, *Englund* Robert K., The proto-Elamite texts from Tepe Yahya: Harvard Peabody Bulletin 30, 1989 → 6,9785; $18: ᴿOrientalia 61 (1992) 10s (M. *Liverani*).

a34* *Dandamayev* M., The title *abšadrapānu* in Nippur: → 687, Nippur 1988/92, 29-32.

a35 ᴱ**Enderlein** Volkmar, *Sundermann* Werner, FIRDAWSI, (Shah Namah) Schāhnāme; das persische Königsbuch; Miniaturen und Texte der Berliner Handschrift von 1605. Lp 1988, Kiepenheuer. 207 p.; 8 pl. + color alternate p. 60-194. 3-378-00254-9.

a36 **Hinz** Walter, *Koch* Heidemarie, Elamisches Wörterbuch 1987 → 3,9960; 6,9789: ᴿJAOS 112 (1992) 340s (H. H. *Paper*).

a37 **Huyse** Philip, Iranische Namen in den griechischen Dokumenten Ägyptens: Iranisches Personennamenbuch V/6a. W 1990, Akad. 70 p. DM 24 [JAOS 112,726].

a38 *Huyse* Philip, 'Analecta iranica' [Iranian names] aus den demotischen Dokumenten von Nord-Saqqara: JEA 78 (1992) 287-293.

a39 **Lazard** Gilbert, (*Ghavam-Najad* Mehdi), Dictionnaire persan-français. Leiden 1990, Brill. xvii-482 p. 90-04-08549-1. – ᴿAulaO 10 (1992) 165s (R. *Lemosin*); ZDMG 142 (1992) 173 (G. *Herrmann*).

a40 **Mayrhofer** M., Iranische Ortsnamenstudien. W 1987, Österr. Akad. 100 p. – ᴿIndIranJ 34 (1991) 125-7 (P. *Huyse*).

a41 **Monchi-Zadeh** Davoud, Wörter aus Xurāsān und ihre Herkunft: Acta Iranica 29, TMém 15. Leiden 1990, Brill. vii-100 p.

a41* *Orsatti* Paola, Uno scritto ritrovato di Pietro DELLA VALLE [1633] e la polemica religiosa nella storia degli studi sul persiano: RSO 66 (1992) 267-274; 1 fig.

a42 ᴱ**Schmitt** Rüdiger, Compendium linguarum iranicarum 1989 → 7,9606: ᴿIndIranJ 34 (1991) 127-131 (P. *Huyse*).

a42* *Schmitt* Rüdiger, Epigraphisch–exegetische Noten zu Dareios' Bīsutūn-Inschriften: SzbW 561. W 1990, Akad. 88 p.; 12 pl. – ᴿJRAS (1992) 456s (D. N. *MacKenzie*).

a43 *Schmitt* Rüdiger, Zum Schluss von Dareios' Inschrift 'Susa c': ArchM-Iran 25 (1992) 147-154; 1 fig.

a44 **Stève** M.-J., Syllabaire élamite, histoire et paléographie: CivPrOr 2/1. Neuchâtel/P 1992, Recherches & Publ. [iv-] 172 p. [BO 49,587]. 2-940032-00-9.

a44* *Vittmann* Günther, Ein altiranischer Titel in demotischer Überlieferung: AfO 38s (1991s) 159s.

a45 **Weber** Dieter, Ostraca, Papyri und Pergamente: Corpus Inscriptionum Iranicarum 3/4s. L 1992. x-265 p., XLII pl., 2 maps. 0-7286-0198-2.

a46 *Zadok* Ran, Elamite onomastics: StEpL 8 (1991) 225-237.

J6.5 **Latina**.

a47 **Baratin** Marc, La naissance de la syntaxe à Rome. P 1989, Minuit. 540 p. – ᴿBSLP 86,2 (1991) 192-5 (F. *Kerlouégan*).

a48 **Bodelot** Colette, Termes introducteurs et modes dans l'interrogation indirecte au Latin de Plaute à Juvenal: BtVitaLat. Avignon 1990. 151 p. – ᴿRÉLat 70 (1992) 264s (J. *Dangel*).

a49 ᴱ**Egger** Karl, Lexicon recentis latinitatis: Soc. 'Latinitas'. Vaticano 1992, Editrice. I. A-L, 454 p. 88-209-1731-9.

a50 **Gaide** Françoise, Les substantifs masculins latins en –(i)ō 1988 → 7,9612: ᴿLatomus 51 (1992) 466s (M. *Fruyt*); Salesianum 54 (1992) 827s (R. *Della Casa*).

a50* — *Hamblenne* Pierre, Un nouveau corpus des substantifs masculins latins en ... (i)ō, ... (i)ōnis [GAIDE Françoise 1988]; compléments: RBgPg 70 (1992) 154-175.

a51 *a) García de la Fuente* Olegario, Sobre la colocación de los adverbios de cantidad en el latín vulgar y en el latín bíblico; – *b) Gaeng* P. A., La morphologie nominale des inscriptions chrétiennes de l'Afrique: ➤ 656*c*, Latin 1991/2, 143-157 / 115-131.

a52 **Mellet** Sylvie, L'imparfait de l'indicatif en latin classique; temps, aspect, modalité; étude synchronique dans une perspective énonciative [diss. d'État, Sorbonne]: BtInfGram. Lv 1988, Peeters. 357 p. – ᴿGnomon 64 (1992) 216-224 (H. *Pinkster*, Eng.).

a53 **Solin** Heikki, Namenpaare, ... zur römischen Namengebung. 1990. – ᴿMaia 44 (1992) 213s (G. *Mennella*).

J8.1 Philologia generalis.

a54 **Belardi** Walter, Filologia, grammatica e retorica nel pensiero antico. R 1985, Ateneo. 290 p. – ᴿLatomus 51 (1992) 462-6 (M. *Nasta*).

a55 *Best* Jan, *Woudhuizen* Fred, Lost languages from the Mediterranean: MeditHR 7,1 (1992) 101s (Margalit *Finkelberg*).

a56 *Biville* Frédérique, L'emprunt lexical, un révélateur des structures vivantes de deux langues en contact (le cas du grec et du latin): RPg 65 (1991) 45-58.

a57 *a) Blaensdorf* Jürgen, CRATÈS et les débuts de la philologie romaine; – *b) Biville* Frédérique, Tradition grecque et actualité latine chez les grammairiens latins; l'approche phonique de la langue; – *c) Moussy* Claude, *Signum* et les noms latins de la preuve; l'héritage de divers termes grecs: Ktema 13 (1988) 141-7 / 154-166 / 167-177.

a58 ꜰDELLA CORTE Francesco, Filologia e forme letterarie 1987 ➤ 3,45: ᴿAnzAltW 43 (1990) 129-154 (P. *Händel*: 8-line summary of each of the 184 art., 5 vols., with subject-index).

a59 ᴱFiaccadori Gianfranco, Autori classici in lingue del Vicino e Medio Oriente, Seminari 3-5, Brescia 1984, Roma 1985, Padova 1986: 1990 ➤ 6,733: ᴿOrChr 76 (1992) 272s (H. *Kaufhold*).

a60 *Huehnergard* John, Languages: ➤ 741, AnchorBD 4 (1992) 155-170; diagram [–229, *al.*, all the Bible-related languages in order, with p. 178-80, G. *Mendenhall* on the Byblos inscriptions].

a61 ꜰMACUCH R., ᴱMacuch M., *al.*, Studia semitica necnon iranica 1989 ➤ 5,126: ᴿHenoch 14 (1992) 185-7 (B. *Chiesa*, dettagliato; also on ERON mem. and other compilations).

a62 **Malkiel** Yakov, Prospettive della ricerca etimologica. N 1988, Liguori. 160 p. – ᴿArGlotIt 75 (1990) 249-255 (G. B. *Pellegrini*).

a63 *Nuessel* Frank, The study of names; a guide to the principles and topics. Westport CT 1992, Greenwood. xvii-152 p. 0-313-28356-7.

a64 *Renfrew* Colin, Archaeology and language: ParPass 47,244 (1992) 147-152.

a65 **Woudhuizen** Fred, The language of the Sea Peoples: Frankfort Found. Amst 1992, Najade. xii-237 p. 90-73835-02-X [OIAc 5,40].

a66 ᴱZgusta Ladislav, History, languages and lexicographers: Lexicographia 41. Tü 1992, Niemeyer. 155 p. 3-484-30941-5 [OIAc 5,40].

J8.2 Grammatica comparata.

a67 *Adrados* Francisco R., The new image of Indoeuropean; the history of a revolution: IndogF 97 (1992) 1-28.

a68 *Back* Michael,   Das Verhältnis von Aktionsarten und Tempus im In-
dogermanischen: HistSprF 104 (1991) 279-302.

a69 *Blau* Joshua,   Ⓔ On the problem of biliteral roots in Semitic languages
[VOIGT R. 1988]: Lešonenu 56 (1991s) 249-255; Eng. V-VI.

a70 **Campanile** Enrico,   La ricostruzione della cultura indoeuropea: Testi
Linguistici 16.   Pisa 1990, Giardini.   190 p. – ᴿBSLP 87,2 (1992) 134-9
(Francoise *Bader*).

a70* **Di Giovine** Paola,   Studio sul Perfetto indoeuropeo, 1.   La funzione
originaria del perfetto studiata nella documentazione delle lingue storiche:
BtRicLingFg 26.   R 1990, Univ. Dip. Glottoantrop.   399 p.; bibliog.
371-396.   88-85134-25-4.

a71 *Djahukian* Gevorg B.,   A variational model of the Indoeuropean consonant system: HistSprF 103 (1990) 1-16.

a72 *a) Dombrowski* F.A & B.W.W.,   Numerals and numeral systems in the
Hamito-Semitic and other language groups; – *b) Titov* E.G.,   On the
history of the study of the Semito-Hamitic (Afrasian) language family,
ᵀ*Perlman* Moshe;   – *c) Steiner* Richard C.,   Addenda to 'The case for
fricative-laterals in Proto-Semitic'; – *d) Dolgopolsky* A.,   Two problems of
Semitic; I. mimation and nunation; II. Akkadian reflexes of *V and *H:
↠ 118, ᶠLESLAU W., Semitic 1991, 340-381 / 1549-61 / 1499-1514 /
328-339.

a72* *Durand* Olivier,   La 'voyelle initiale' ou préfixe nominal d'état berbère;
implications chamito-sémitiques: RSO 66 (1992) 233-8.

a73 *Edzard* Lutz,   Polygenesis and entropy; an alternative model of linguistic
evolution applied to Semitic linguistics [... triradicalism]: diss. California,
ᴰ*Bloch* A.   Berkeley 1992.   170 p.   93-04903. – DissA 53 (1992s) 3509-A.

a74 *a)* Edzard Lutz,   Semitic philology and preference laws for syllabic
structure; – *b) Faber* Alice,   The diachronic relationship between negative
and interrogative markers in Semitic; – *c) Goshen-Gottstein* Moshe,   The
present state of comparative Semitic linguistics; – *d) Lipiński* E.,   Mono-
syllabic nominal and verbal roots in Semitic languages; – *e) Murtonen* A.,
On Proto-Semitic reconstructions: ↠ 118, ᶠLESLAU W., Semitic 1991,
397-410 / 411-429 / 558-569 / 927-930 / 1119-29.

a75 **Gamkrelidze** T.V., *Ivanov* V.V. Indoeuropejskii jazyk i indoeuropeicy.
Tbilisi 1984, Univ. 1328 p. (2 vol.). – ᴿAevum 65 (1991) 171 (G. *Bonfante*:
'regresso' anziche 'epoch-making' – PALMAITIS).

a76 ᴱ**Gvozdanović** Jadranka,   Indo-European numerals: TrendLing StMg 57.
B 1992, Mouton de Gruyter. x-943 p. 3-11-011322-8.

a77 *Jucquois* Guy,   Langages classiques et grammaire comparée I-II: ÉtClas
59 (1991) 205-229; 60 (1992) 101-111.

a78 **Lubotsky** A.M.,   The system of nominal accentuation in Sanskrit and
Proto-Indo-European.   Leiden 1988, Brill.   196 p. — ᴿBSLP 87,2 (1992)
145-155 (Françoise *Bader*).

a79 *a) Macuch* Rudolf,   Pseudo-Ethiopisms in Samaritan Hebrew and
Aramaic; – *b) Meltzer* Edmund S.,   *dr, k3, gr:* the intertwining of some
roots in Egyptian and Semitic; – *c) Rodgers* Jonathan,   The subgroupings
of the South Semitic languages: ↠ 118, ᶠLESLAU W., Semitic 1991,
966-976 / 1046-58 / 1323-36.

a80 **Mallory** J.P.,   In search of the Indo-Europeans 1989 ↠ 5,9719; 6,9821:
ᴿIndIranJ 34 (1991) 138-142 (J.W. de *Jong*); PraehZts 67 (1992) 132-6 (B.
Schlerath).

a81 ᴱ**Markey** T.L., *Greppin* John A.C.,   When worlds collide ... [Pre-]
Indo-Europeans 1988/90 ↠ 7,9631: ᴿKratylos 37 (1992) 53-57 (B.
Schlerath).

a82 *Masson* Michel, Étude d'un parallélisme sémantique; 'tresser' / 'être fort':
     Semitica 40 (991) 89-105 ...

a83 **Mayrhofer** Manfred, Etymologisches Wörterbuch des Altindoarischen
     1, [3s] ➤ 6,9823: Lfg. 7s/9. Heid 1990/1, Winter. p. 427-557-636-716:
     ᴿBSLP 86,2 (1991) 127-134 (Françoise *Bader*) & 87,2 (1992) 170; Ind-
     IranJ 34 (1991) 105-120 (F.B.J. *Kuiper*); Salesianum 54 (1992) 210s (R.
     Gottlieb).

a84 **Meid** Wolfgang, Archäologie und Sprachwissenschaft; Kritisches zu
     neueren Hypothesen der Ausbreitung der Indogermanen 1989 ➤ 5,9723:
     ᴿEmerita 60 (1992) 336-8 (F. R. *Adrados*); PraehZts 67 (1992) 137s (B.
     Schlerath).

a85 *Morani* Moreno, Sul vocativo singolare dei temi in -ā dell'indo-iranico:
     Aevum 65 (1991) 3-10.

a86 *a) Müller* Hans-Peter, Zur Theorie der historisch-vergleichenden Gram-
     matik dargestellt am sprachlichen Kontext des Althebräischen [➤ 7,9633];
     – *b) Segert* Stanislav, The use of comparative Semitic material in Hebrew
     lexicography; – *c) Zaborski* Andrzej, Biconsonantal roots and tricon-
     sonantal root variations in Semitic; solutions and prospects: ➤ 118,
     ꜰLESLAU W., Semitic 1991, 1100-1118 / 1426-34 / 1675-1703.

a87 *Rabin* Chaim, ❶ *Safot Shemiyot* ... Semitic languages, an introduction
     [< EnsM]: EnṣM Library. J 1991, Bialik. 163 p. 965-342-575-7 [OIAc
     5,32].

a88 *Renfrew* Colin, Before Babel; speculations on the origins of linguistic
     diversity: CamArch 1, (1991) 3-23.

a89 *Ricca* Davide, *Andare* e *venire* nelle lingue romanze e germaniche; dal-
     l'Aktionsart alla deissi: ArGlotIt 76 (1991) 159-192.

a90 **Saussure** Ferdinand de, Mémoires sur le système primitif des voyelles
     dans les langues indo-européennes. Hildesheim 1987 = 1879, Olms. –
     ᴿSalesianum 54 (1992) 825 (R. *Della Casa* nota senza titolo la versione
     italiana di G. C. *Vincenzi*, Bo 1978).

a91 **Schwink** Frederick W., Linguistic typology and the reconstruction of
     proto-languages [... Indo-European]; a study in methodology; diss. Texas,
     ᴰ*Polomé* E. Austin 1992. 212 p. 92-39346. – DissA 53 (1992s) 2789-A.

a92 **Villar** F., Los indoeuropeos y los orígenes de Europa; lenguaje y his-
     toria. M 1991, Gredos. 530 p. – ᴿAula0 10 (1992) 172s (X. *Ballester*).

a93 *Voigt* Rainer, Die Lateralreihe /ś ṣ ź/ im Semitischen: ZDMG 142
     (1992) 37-52.

J8.3 **Linguistica generalis.**

a94 **Aldridge** Maurice V., The elements of mathematical semantics: Trend-
     Ling StMg 66. B 1992, Mouton de Gruyter. xi-261 p. 3-11-012957-4.

a95 **Anderson** John M., Linguistic representation; structural analogy and
     stratification: TrendLing StMg 67. B 1992, Mouton-G. x-254 p. 3-11-
     013531-0.

a96 ᴱ**Andronov** M. S., *Mallik* Bhakti P., Linguistics; a Soviet approach.
     Calcutta 1988. – ᴿBSLP 87,2 (1992) 19-22 (R. *L'Hermitte*; chiefly farther
     Asia).

a97 **Atkinson** Martin, Foundations of general linguistics² [¹1982]. L 1991,
     Unwin Hyman. xv-437 p. 0-04-410005-1; pa. –9.

a98 **Baratin** Marc, *Desbordes* Françoise, L'analyse linguistique dans l'An-
     tiquité classique I. Les théories 1981 ➤ 65,8351: ᴿLatomus 51 (1992)
     200-4 (G. *Calboli*, ital.).

a99 ᴱBlack David A., *al.*, Linguistics and New Testament interpretation; essays on discourse analysis. Nv 1992, Broadman. 319 p. 0-8054-1509-2.

a100 ᶠBLANC Haim, Studia linguistica et orientalia, ᴱWexler P., *al.*, 1989 ⮞ 6,23: ᴿZDMG 141 (1991) 168 (E. *Wagner*).

a101 *Bodine* Walter R. [⮞ 343], Linguistics and biblical studies: ⮞ 741, AnchorBD 4 (1992) 327-333.

a102 **Botha** Rudolf P., Twentieth century conceptions of language; mastering the metaphysics market. Oxford 1992, Blackwell. xiv-439 p.

a103 **Brekle** Herbert E., Einführung in die Geschichte der Sprachwissenschaft 1985 ⮞ 3,a26: ᴿBSLP 86,2 (1991) 29-34 (P. *Swiggers*).

a104 **Cannon** Garland, The life and mind of Oriental Jones; Sir William JONES, the father of modern linguistics. C 1990, Univ. xix-409 p.; portr. 0-521-39149-0.

a104* **Chiesa** C., Semiosis – signes – symboles; introduction aux théories du signe linguistique de PLATON et d'ARISTOTE. Berne 1991, Lang. 374 p. [Elenchos 14, 168, G. *Sadun Bordoni*].

a105 ᴱConte Maria-Elisabeth, *Ramat* A. & P., Dimensioni della linguistica: Materiali linguistici 1. Mi 1990, F. Angeli. 239 p. – ᴿBSLP 87,2 (1992) 35-44 (P. *Kirtchuk*); Salesianum 54 (1992) 205 (R. *Gottlieb*).

a106 **Cotterell** P., *Turner* M., Linguistics and biblical interpretation 1989 ⮞ 5,9746...7,9649: ᴿRExp 89 (1992) 114 (D. S. *Dockery*).

a107 ᴱDavis Hayley G., *Taylor* Talbot J., Redefining linguistics 1990 ⮞ 6,9838; £35; pa. £10: ᴿBSLP 87,2 (1992) 31-33 (X. *Mignot*).

a107* **Denyer** Nicholas, Language, thought and falsehood in ancient Greek philosophy: Issues in Ancient Philosophy. L 1991, Routledge. xi-222 p. £35. – ᴿPhronesis 36 (1991) 319-327 (C. *Kirwan*).

a108 ᴱDowning Pamela, The linguistics of literacy: Typological Studies in Language 21. Amst 1992, Benjamins. xx-334. 90-272-2903-1; pa. -4-X / US 1-55619-406-4; pa. -7-2.

a109 ᴱDressler Wolfgang U., *al.*, Contemporary morphology: TrendLing StMg 49. B/NY 1990, Mouton-G. ix-317 p. 3-11-012349-5 / NY 0-89925-663-5.

a110 **Faarlund** Jan T., Syntactic change; toward a theory of historical syntax: TrendLing StMg 50. B 1990, Mouton-G. ix-219 p. 3-11-012651-6 / NY 0-89925-749-6.

a111 **Firbas** Jan, Functional sentence perspective in written and spoken communication: Studies in English language. C 1992, Univ. xv-239 p. 0-521-37308-5.

a112 **François-Geiger** Denise, À la recherche du sens; des ressources linguistiques aux fonctionnements langagiers. P 1990, Peeters / Société d'études linguistiques et anthropologiques de France. XV-279 p. – ᴿBSLP 87,2 (1992) 61-63 (C. *Hudelot*).

a113 *Gamkrelidze* Thomas V., The Indo-European glottalic theory in the light of recent critique, 1972-1991: Kratylos 37 (1992) 1-13.

a114 ᴱGerritsen Marinel, Internal and external factors in syntactic change [9th Hist. Linguistics Conference, Rutgers Univ., New Brunswick NJ, Aug. 1989]: TrendLing StMg 61. B 1992, Mouton-G. vi-482 p. 3-11-012747-4.

a115 *Güttgemanns* Erhardt, Elementare Fragen der Semiotik: LingB 67 (1992) 45-58; Eng. 58s.

a116 **Harris** Roy, Language, SAUSSURE and WITTGENSTEIN; how to play games with words. L 1988, Routledge. xv-136 p. – ᴿBSLP 86,2 (1991) 34-39 (P. *Swiggers*).

a117 ᴱIvir Vladimir, *Kalogjera* Damir, Languages in contact and contrast; essays in contact linguistics: Trends in Linguistics StMg 54. B 1991, Mouton-G. xi-502 p. 3-11-012574-9 / NY 0-89925-714-3.

a118 **Jahr** Ernst H., Language contact; theoretical and empirical studies [Symposium Univ. Tromsø, Sept. 1989]: TrendLingStM 60. [viii-] 243 p.; ill.; map. 3-11-012802-0.

a119 **Kreszowski** Tomasz P., Contrastive languages; the scope of contrastive linguistics: TrendLing StMg 51. B 1990, Mouton-G. viii-286 p. 3-11-012133-6 / NY 0-89925-590-6.

a120 *Loun* Johannes P., Semantics: ➤ 741, AnchorBD 5 (1992) 1077-81.

a121 **Lucy** John A., Grammatical categories and cognition; a case study of the linguistic relativity hypothesis: Studies in the Social and Cultural Foundations of Language 13. C 1992, Univ. xv-211 p. 0-521-38419-2.

a122 **Lucy** John A., Language diversity and thought: SocCult 12. C 1992, Univ. xi-328 p.; 12 fig. 0-521-38418-4; pa. –797-3.

a123 **Lyons** John, Languages and linguistics, an introduction. C 1992, Univ. xi-356 p.

a124 **Martin** Richard M., Logical semiotics and mereology: Foundations of Semiotics 16. Amst 1992, Benjamins. xiii-282 p. 90-272-3288-1.

a125 **Matthews** P. H., Morphology² [¹1974]. Textbooks in linguistics. C 1991, Univ. xii-251 p. 0-521-41043-6; pa. -2256-6.

a126 *Mazaudon* Martine, Lowe John B., Du bon usage de l'informatique en linguistique historique: BSLP 86,1 (1991) 49-87.

a127 **Merrell** Floyd, Sign, textuality, world: Advances in Semiotics. Bloomington 1992, Indiana Univ. xviii-264 p. 0-253-33748-8.

a128 **Muñiz Rodríguez** Vicente, Introducción a la filosofia del lenguaje [1. 1989] II. Barc 1992, Anthropos. 221 p. – ᴿBurgense 33 (1992) 582s (J. de *Sahagún Lucas*).

a129 **Nida** Eugene A., *Louw* Johannes P., Lexical semantics of the Greek New Testament; a supplement to the Lexicon based on semantic domains: SBL Resources 25. Atlanta 1992, Scholars. ix-157 p. $30. 1-55540-578-9 [NTAbs 36,414].

a130 **Noth** Winfried, Handbook of semiotics: Advances in Semiotics [ᴱSebeok T.]. Bloomington 1990, Indiana Univ. xii-576 p. 0-253-34120-5. – ᴿLingBib 66 (1992) 114-122 (W. *Schenk*).

a131 ᴱ**Payne** Doris L., Pragmatics of word order flexibility: Typological Studies in Language 22. Amst/Ph 1992, Benjamins. [vi-] 320 p. 90-272-2905-8; pa. -6-6 / US 1-55619-408-0; –9-9.

a132 ᴱ**Polomé** Edgar C., Research guide on language change [33 art.]: TrendsLingStMg 48. B/NY 1990, Mouton de Gruyter. 564 p. 3-11-012046-1 / NY 0-89925-579-5. – ᴿBSLP 87,2 (1992) 27-31 (X. *Mignot*).

a133 ᴱ**Polomé** Edgar C., *Winter* Werner, Reconstructing languages and cultures [Symposium Austin Nov. 1986, ᶠLEHMANN W. P.]: TrendLing StMg 58. B 1992, Mouton-G. ix-550 p. 3-11-012671-0.

a134 *Reichler-Béguelin* Marie-José, Motivation et remotivation des signes linguistiques: RPg 65 (1991) 9-30.

a136 ᴱ**Shopen** Timothy, Language typology and syntactic description. C 1990-3, Univ. I. Clause structure, x-399 p.; II. Complex constructions, x-317 p.; III. Grammatical categories and the lexicon, xii-427 p. 0-521-25700-X; –6858-3; –6859-1; pa. 0-521-27659-4; –31898-X; –31899-8.

a137 **Silva** Moisés, God, language, and Scripture; reading the Bible in the light of general linguistics: Foundations of Contemporary Interpretation 4, 1990 ➤ 6,9854: ᴿGraceTJ 12,1 (1991) 146-150 (B. L. *Woodard*).

a138 *Some* Joachim D.,   Bible et linguistique: RICAO 1 (1992) 55-68 [<
TContext 10/1, p. 20].
ᴱSvartvik Jan, 'Corpus [1.e. computerized] linguistics' 1991/2 ➤ 678.

a139 ᴱVentola Eija,   Functional and systemic linguistics; approaches and uses:
TrendLing StMg 55.   B 1991, Mouton-G.   xiii-493 p.   3-11-012740-7.

a140 ᴱWatts Richard J.,   *al.*,   Politeness in language; studies in its history,
theory and practice: TrendLing StMg 59.   B 1992, Mouton-G.   ix-381 p.
3-11-013184-6.

a141 **Wierzbicka** Anna,   Cross-cultural pragmatics; the semantics of human
interaction: TrendLing StMg 53.   B 1991, Mouton-G.   xiii-502 p.   3-11-
012538-2 / NY 0-89925-699-6.

a142 **Wierzbicka** Anna,   Semantics, culture, and cognition; universal human
concepts in culture-specific configurations.   NY 1992, Oxford-UP.   viii-
487 p.   0-19-507325-8; pa. –6-6.

J8.4   *Origines artis scribendi* – The origin of writing.

a143 *a*) *Bard* Kathryn A.,   Origins of Egyptian writing; – *b*) *Brink* Edwin
C. M. van den,   Corpus and numerical evaluation of the 'Thinite'
potmarks: ➤ 84, Mem. IIOFFMAN M. 1992, 297-306; 5 fig. / 265-281; 5
fig. (+ 6-17, the Corpus; + Table of 77 signs).

a144 **Bernal** Martin [grandson of Alan GARDINER],   Cadmean letters 1990
➤ 6,9859: ᴿBL (1992) 26 (W. *Johnstone*); ClasR 42 (1992) 159s (M. *Pope*);
Phoenix 46 (Toronto 1992) 270-4 (H. *Konishi*: 'thinks more powerfully
than B. POWELL' 1991).

a145 *Colless* Brian E.,   The Byblos syllabary and the proto-alphabet: Abr-
Nahr 30 (1992) 55-102.

a146 **Dietrich** Manfried, *Loretz* Oswald,   Die Keilalphabete ... 1988 ➤ 4,a801
... 7,9865:   ᴿOLZ 87 (1992) 133-6 (W. *Herrmann*); StEpL 7 (1990) 136
(Maria Giulia *Amadasi Guzzo*).

a147 **Fairservis** Walter A.,   The Harappan civilization and its writing; a model
for the decipherment of the Indus script. Leiden 1992, Brill.   viii-239 p.

a148 **Fales** Frederick L.,   Prima dell'alfabeto: Studi e Documenti 4, 1989
➤ 5,9781:   ᴿRelStR 18 (1992) 49 (J. M. *Sasson:* really a collection of
largely unpublished cuneiform, conveniently organized as a history of
writing, and with stunning photos of today's Iraq).

a149 **Gille-Maisani** Jean-Charles,   Psicologia de la escritura, ᵀ*Medrano* Luisa.
BtPsic 165. Barc 1991, Herder.   369 p. pt. 2000.   84-254-1705-8. – ᴿActuBbg 29 (1992) 291 (B. C.).

a150 **Haarmann** Harald,   Universalgeschichte der Schrift.   Fra 1990, Campus.
576 p.; ill. DM 78. – ᴿArOr 60 (1992) 80-82 (B. *Hruška*).

a151 **Harris** W. V.,   Ancient literacy 1989 ➤ 6,9869; 7,9681:   ᴿMnemosyne 45
(1992) 416-423 (H. W. *Pleket:* excellent; the last word).

a152 **Havelock** Eric A.,   Schriftlichkeit; das griechische Alphabet als kulturelle Revolution [about half of The literate revolution, Princeton 1982]ᵀ;
ᴱ*Assmann* Aleida & Jan.   Weinheim 1990, Acta Humaniora.   vi-169 p.
DM 42. – ᴿKratylos 37 (1992) 193-5 (Rüdiger *Schmitt*).

a153 **Hooker** J. T.,   Reading the past 1990 ➤ 6,9871:   ᴿJAOS 112 (1992) 691-3
(P. T. *Daniels*).

a154 **Immerwahr** Henry R.,   Attic script 1990 ➤ 6,9872:   ᴿAJA 96 (1992)
385s (R. S. *Stroud*, also on S. *Tracy*). RArchéol (1992) 144-7 (H. P. *Isler*).

a155 **Lemaire** André,   Writing and writing materials: ➤ 741, AnchorDB 6
(1992) 999-1008.

a156 *Németh* György, Sur l'histoire du théta: AcClas Debrecen 28 (1992) 17-24.
a157 **Powell** Barry,   HOMER and the origin of the Greek alphabet 1991
➤ 7,9686:   ᴿAmHR 97 (1992) 526 (W. C. *West*); CamArch 2 (1992)
115-8. 125s (ipse) & 118-120 (J. *Ray:* Phoenician connections?) & 120-2
(A. *Johnston*) & 122-4 (J. B. *Hainsworth:* the case for oral transmission) &
124s (J. *Whitley*); ClasR 42 (1992) 350-3 (D. *Ridgway*); ClasW 85 (1991)
735 (S. *Goins*); Kratylos 37 (1992) 69-73 (Rüdiger *Schmitt*).
a157* *Röllig* W., A re-examination of the early evidence of alphabetic script:
➤ 736, ᴱ*Shaath* S.,   Palestine 1981/5, 165-171.
a158 **Rossi-Landi** Ferruccio, ᴱ*Petrilli* Susan,   Between signs and non-signs:
Critical Theory 10.   Amst 1992, Benjamins.   xxix-322 p.   90-272-2419-6 /
Ph 1-55619-177-4.
a159 *Sandoz* Claude,   Le nom de la 'lettre' et les origines de l'écriture à Rome:
MusHelv 48 (1991) 216-9.
a160 **Sass** Benjamin, Studia alphabetica: OBO 102, 1991 ➤ 7,9688:   ᴿAfO 38s
(1991) 255s (K. *Jaroš*); BL (1992) 38 (W. *Johnstone*); Orientalia 61 (1992)
476-8 (Maria Giulia *Amadasi Guzzo*); RivB 40 (1992) 327s (Anna *Passoni
Dell'Acqua*); RSO 65 (1991) 131-5 (Fiorella *Scagliarini*).
a161 *Sauren* Herbert,   Une lance pour l'alphabet; le poignard de Lachish
[before 1500 (or 1700) B.C.E; known since 1936 C.E.]: Muséon 105 (1992)
213-232 + dessins p. 234-242.
a162 **Schmandt-Besserat** Denise,   Before writing, I. From counting to cuneiform; pref. *Hallo* William W.   Austin 1992, Univ. Texas.   xvii-269 p.
0-292-70782-5.

J9.1   *Analysis linguistica loquelae de Deo* – **God-talk**.

a163 **Arens** Edmund,   Christopraxis; Grundzüge theologischer Handlungstheorie [*Habermas* J., Kommunikatives Handeln]: QDisp 139.   FrB 1992,
Herder.   3-451-02139-0.
a164 *a*) *Basu* Arabinda,   Language of the absolute; a contemporary Indian
interpretation; *b*) *Amodio* Barbara A.,   The world made of sound;
WHITEHEAD and Pythagorean harmonics in the context of Veda and the
science of Mantra; – *c*) *Macquarrie* John,   The logic of religious and
theological language: JDharma 17,3 ('Religion and language' 1992) 203-9
/ 233-266 / 169-177.
a165 ᴱ**Braaten** Carl E.,   Our naming of God 1989 ➤ 5,637:   ᴿScotJT 45
(1992) 269s (D. *Hampson*).
a166 *Carter* C. Allen,   Logology and religion; Kenneth BURKE on the
metalinguistic dimensions of language: JRel 72 (1992) 1-18.
a167 *Chandler* Stuart,   When the world falls apart; methodology for em-
ploying chaos and emptiness as theological constructs: HarvTR 85 (1992)
467-491.
a168 **Chidester** David,   Word and light; seeing, hearing, and religious discourse.   Urbana 1992, Univ. Illinois.   xiv-168 p. $30.   0-252-01863-X
[TDig 40,57].
a169 *Clarkson* J. Shannon,   God-Talk; by what name do we call God?:
MethTStR 3,1 (1991) 121-6 [< ZIT 92,139].
a170 **Cooke** Bernard J.,   The distancing of God; the ambiguity of symbols in
history and theology 1990 ➤ 6,9884; 7,9698:   ᴿAmerica 165 (1991) 298-
300 (J. R. *Sachs*, also on HAIGHT R.) [N.B. p. 440s, A. *Greeley* on another
The distancing of God; Catholic bishops in American politics, by BYRNES
T. A.; Princeton, 177 p. $30]; – back to COOKE: ChrCent 108 (1991) 496s

(L. E. *Snook*); TLZ 117 (1992) 132-4 (W. *Schlüsser*: Anfragen); TTod 49 (1992s) 416.418 (Catherine M. *La Cugna*).

a171 **Cupitt** Don, Creation out of nothing [really about religious discourse] 1990 ➤ 6,2115: ᴿInterpretation 46 (1992) 332.334 (R. *Burke*); RelSt 27 (1991) 559-561 (S.R.L. *Clark*); TS 53 (1992) 158-160 (D. S. *Cunningham*).

a172 *Dalferth* Ingolf U., God and the mystery of words: JAAR 60 (1992) 79-104.

a173 *Domingues* Bernardo, Linguagem religiosa e comunicação da fé cristã: HumTeol 13 (1992) 43-56.

a174 **Franklin** Stephen T., Speaking from the depths; Alfred N. WHITE-HEAD's hermeneutical metaphysics of propositions, experience, symbolism, language, and religion. GR 1990, Eerdmans. xiv-410 p. $27.50. – ᴿCrit-RR 5 (1992) 401-3 (J. M. *Hallman:* defends Whitehead's understanding of language).

a175 **Frye** Northrop, The double vision; language and meaning in religion. Toronto 1991, Univ. xviii-88 p. – ᴿCritRR 5 (1992) 72-74 (E. V. *McKnight:* he wrote as a churchman ... United Church of Canada).

a176 *Gleeson* Gerald P., Deconstructing the concept of God [HART K. 1989]: Pacifica 5 (1992) 59-66.

a177 *a) Grasslé* Isabelle, La parole confessante, entre rite et vérité; un point de vue linguistique sur les confessions de foi; – *b) Mottu* Henry, La liturgie comme geste prophétique; – *c) Saussure* Thierry de, Archéologie du symbole, approche psychanalytique; – *d) Bourgeois* Henri, Que devient l'Évangile dans une culture médiatique?: BCentProt 43,8 ('La communication symbolique' 1991) 33-44 / 13-23 / 2-11 / 25-32.

a178 *Graf* Friedrich W., Religiöse Semantik in der Fortschrittskritik: Luth-Mon 31 (1992) 166-9 [< ᴢɪᴛ 92,229].

a179 **Grözinger** Albrecht, Die Sprache des Menschen; ein Handbuch, Grund-wissen für Theologinnen und Theologen. Mü 1991, Kaiser. 246 p. DM 49. 3-459-01880-1. – ᴿTsTKi 63 (1992) 76s (T. *Stordalen*); TvT 32 (1992) 205 (H. *Rikhof*).

a180 **Haglund** Dick, Tro — upplevelse — språk; till den religiösa erfaren-hetens fenomenologi: Religio 31. Lund 1990, Teologiska Institutionen. 102 p. – ᴿSvTKv 67 (1991) 97-99 (E. *Herrmann*).

a181 **Herholdt** Stephanus J., Grammatikale Teologie? 'n Kritiese beskrywing van George A. LINDBECK se kultuur-linguistiese model vir teologie: diss. ᴰ*Smit* D. J. Western Cape 1992. 222 p. – RTLv 24, p. 539.

a182 **Jones** Hugh O., Die Logik theologischer Perspektiven; eine Sprach-analytische Untersuchung: ForSysÖkT 42, ᴰ1985 ➤ 2,7912 ... 4,a834: ᴿTsTKi 63 (1992) 70s (T. *Wigen*).

a182* **Long** Charles H., Significations ... in religion 1986 ➤ 2,187 ... 7,9713: ᴿHistRel 31 (1991s) 60-68 (D. *Carrasco*).

a183 *McKenna* John, Symbol and reality; some anthropological considera-tions: Worship 65 (1991) 2-27.

a184 *Mondin* Battista, La expresión del misterio revelado en el lenguaje hu-mano: ScripTPamp 24 (1992) 813-836; lat. Eng. 837.

a185 *Moonan* Lawrence, Attributing things to God [... consistent with Nega-tive Theology]: ETL 68 (1992) 86-117.

a188 **Müller** W. M., Das Symbol in der dogmatischen Theologie; eine sym-boltheologische Studie anhand der Theorien bei K. RAHNER, P. TILLICH, P. RICOEUR und J. LACAN [Diss. München ➤ 5,9825]: EurHS 23/401, 1990 ➤ 7,9718; Fs 90. 3-631-43102-3: ᴿActuBbg 29 (1992) 81s (J. *Boada*); TvT 32 (1992) 326 (H. *Rikhof*).

a189 **Neville** Robert C.,   Behind the masks of God 1991 ➤ 7,7635:   ᴿAnglTR 74 (1992) 240-4 (O. C. *Thomas*).

a190 ᴱ**Noppen** J.-P. van,   Erinnern ... religiöse Sprache 1988 ➤ 4,a848 ... 7,9719:   ᴿRTLv 23 (1992) 248s (E. *Brito*).

a191 *Ochs* Peter,   Theosemiotics [M. RAPOSA coinage for C. PEIRCE] and pragmatism: JRel 72 (1992) 59-81.

a192 *a) Pellechia* Fausto, *al.* [raduno gen. 1991]. Le ragioni del simbolo; un colloquio fra filosofi e teologi; – *b) Schabert* Tilo,   Imagines imaginationis; – *c) Giorgi* Rubina,   Il simbolico e l'umano: FilT 5 (1991) 331-366 / 367-376 / 377-389 [391-433, *al.*].

a193 **Pereppadan** J.,   RICOEUR and postmodernity in debate; a study of Paul Ricoeur's hermeneutical principles in confrontation with postmodern deconstructionism; their relevance in ethico-theological reflection: diss. 1990, Lv, ᴰ*Schrijver* G. De.   xx-527 p. – TvT 32,87.

a194 *Robbins* J. Wesley,   'You will be like God'; Richard RORTY and Mark C. TAYLOR on the theological significance of human language use: JRel 72 (1992) 389-402.

a195 **Schaeffler** Richard,   Das Gebet und das Argument; zwei Weisen des Sprechen von Gott 1989 ➤ 6,9910; 7,9724: – ᴿColcT 62,1 (1992) 186s (L. *Balter*); LebZeug 45 (1990) 151s (E. *Biser*); ZMissRW 75 (1991) 250-2 (J. *Wohlmuth*).

a196 *Schlamm* Leon,   Numinous experience and religious language: RelSt 28 (1992) 533-551.

a197 **Short** Larry R.,   In a poetic fashion; an inquiry into language, world, and religion [... Religions as languages]: diss. Florida State, ᴰ*Swain* C. Tallahassee 1992. 347 p. 92-34248. – DissA 53 (1992s) 3420-A.

a198 *Tortorelli Ghidini* Marisa,   Semantica e origine misterica dei 'symbola': FilT 5 (1991) 391-5 [*al.* 331-433].

a199 **Tracy** D.,   Plurality and ambiguity 1987 ➤ 3,a117.a997 ... 7,9728: ᴿAnglTR 73 (1991) 339-342 (W. T. *Stevenson*); Gregorianum 73 (1992) 150 (R. *Fisichella*); ModT 7 (1991) 483-7 (G. *Loughlin*); SvTKv 66 (1992) 184-7 (A. *Rasmusson*).

a200 *a) Tracy* David,   L'herméneutique de la désignation de Dieu, ᵀ*Falandry* Maryse; – *b) Richard* Jean,   La théologie comme herméneutique chez C. GEFFRÉ et Paul TILLICH: ➤ 63, ᶠGEFFRÉ C., 49-67 / 69-101.

a201 **Vahanian** Gabriel,   Dieu anonyme ou la peur des mots 1989 ➤ 5,9815 ... 7,9730: ᴿRHE 87 (1992) 143s (M. Van *Overbeke*).

a202 *Veken* Jan van der,   De referent van het woord 'God': Bijdragen 53 (1992) 118-134; Eng. 134.

a203 **Whittaker** John H.,   The logic of religious persuasion: AmerUnivSt 7/71. NY 1990, Lang. 116 p. $29. – ᴿCritRR 5 (1992) 423-5 (C. *Creegan*).

a204 ᴱ**Wyschogrod** Edith, *al.*,   [Jacques] LACAN and theological discourse 1989 ➤ 5,528: ᴿJAAR 60 (1989) 825-7 (J. *Granger*: postmoderns with valuable interwoven commentary by David *Crownfield*).

a205 **Zimmer** C.,   'Deus'; logische Syntax und Semantik 1991 ➤ 7,9733: ᴿNedTTs 46 (1992) 260s (W. A. de *Pater*); TLZ 117 (1992) 300s (Ingolf U. *Dalferth*).

J9.2   *Hermeneutica paratheologica* – **wider linguistic analysis.**

a206 *Balmès* Marc,   Philosophie du langage et réalisme aristotélicien: RThom 92 (1992) 503-517.

a206* **Borella** Jean, Le mystère du signe; histoire et théorie du symbole. P 1989, Maisonneuve & L. – ᴿFilT 6 (1992) 180-2 (G. *Razzino*).

a207 **Bourdieu** Pierre, ᴱ*Thompson* John B., Language and symbolic power. C 1992, Polity. ix-302 p. 0-7456-0097-2; pa.-1034-X.

a208 **Bourgeois** Patrick L., *Schalow* Frank, Traces of understanding; a profile of HEIDEGGER's and RICŒUR's hermeneutics: Rodopi. ... 1990, Königshausen & N. 186 p. $30. – ᴿJAAR 60 (1992) 770-2 (J. R. *Wilson*).

a209 **Eco** Umberto (with *Rorty* Richard, *al.*), Interpretation and overinterpretation. C 1992, Univ. ix-151 p. 0-521-40227-1; pa.-2554-9.

a210 **Edwards** James C., The authority of language; HEIDEGGER, WITTGENSTEIN, and the threat of philosophical nihilism 1990 → 7,9737; 249 p. $29. – ᴿJAAR 60 (1992) 545-8 (G. C. F. *Beam*).

a211 **Ferrane** Mohamed Ali el-, Die Maʿna-Theorie bei ʿAbdalqāhir al-Ǧurǧani (gestorben 471/1079); Versuch einer Analyse der poetischen Sprache: HeidOrSt 17. Fra 1990, Lang. x-250 p. DM 74. 3-631-42794-8. – ᴿBO 49 (1992) 528-530 (G. J. van *Gelder: maʿnā l-maʿnā* somewhat anticipates OGDEN-RICHARDS 1923 Meaning of meaning).

a212 *Fitzgerald* William, CATULLUS and the reader; the erotics of poetry: Arethusa 25 (1992) 419-443.

a213 ᴱ**Greisch** Jean, *Kearney* Richard, [1-11 août 1988 rencontre avec] Paul RICŒUR, Les métamorphoses de la raison herméneutique. P 1991, Cerf. 414 p. F 175. – ᴿRTLv 23 (1992) 297s (É. *Gaziaux*).

a214 *Knobloch* Clemens, Überlegungen zur Theorie der Begriffsgeschichte aus sprach- und kommunikationswissenschaftlicher Sicht: ArBegG 35 (1992) 7-24.

a215 **Makolkin** Anna, Name, hero, icon; semiotics of nationalism through heroic biography: Approaches to Semiotics 105. B 1992, Mouton-G. xv-264 p. 3-11-013012-2.

a216 *Miccoli* Paolo, Abitare la parola: Studium 87 (R 1991) 51-69.

a217 **Sacks** Harvey, Lectures on conversation, ᴱ*Jefferson* Gail; pref. *Schegloff* Emanuel A. Ox 1992, Blackwell. I. lxv-818 p.; II. lll-580 p. 1-55786-358-X; -9-8.

a218 **Schleifer** Ronald, Rhetoric and death; the language of modernism and postmodern discourse theory. Champaign 1990, Univ. Illinois. x-252 p. $30; pa. $13. – ᴿTS 53 (1992) 183s (T. W. *Tilley*: 'seeks traces of the always-denied, Other of death').

a219 *Valenti* Rossana, La comunicazione nel mondo romano; un percorso tra filosofia, arte e retorica [ACHARD G. 1991; MORETTI G. 1990, *al.*]: BStLat 22 (1992) 289-296.

J9.4 **Structuralismus**, deconstructio.

a220 *Begley* John, Deconstruction and theology: AustralasCR 69 (1992) 335-342.

a221 **Dosse** François, Histoire du structuralisme, I. 1945-1966; II. P 1991s, Découverte. 480 p.; 588 p. F 230 + 250. – ᴿÉtudes 376 (1992) 711s (J. Y. *Calvez*: 'de déconstruction en déconstruction .. ').

a222 **Sarup** Madan, An introductory guide to post-structuralism and post-modernism. Athens GA 1989, Univ. Georgia. viii-171 p. 0-8203-1129-4; pa. -30-8.

a223 **Silverman** Hugh G., Inscriptions [i.e. inscribing or finding one's own place] between phenomenology and structuralism. NY 1987, Routledge-KP. xvi-390 p. 0-7100-9831-6.

J9.6 *Analysis narrationis* – **Narrative-analysis.**

a224 **Cupitt** Don, What is a story? [➤ 7,a428] L 1991, SCM. xiii-162 p. £9. 0-334-02419-6. – ᴿExpTim 103 (1991s) 285s (G. *Slater*; itself a master-story; implications for theology).

a225 **De Concini** Barbara, Narrative remembering. Lanham MD 1990, UPA. xv-292 p. $36,50. – ᴿJRel 72 (1992) 480s (W. A. *Kort*: clear but with three 'partialities').

a226 *Doherty* Lillian E., The internal and implied audiences of Odyssey II: Arethusa 24 (1991) 145-176.

a227 ᴱ**Foley** John M., Oral formulaic theory; a folklore casebook. NY 1990, Garland. 421 p. $51. 0-8240-8485-3. – ᴿClasW 85 (1991s) 51s (Julie *Williams*).

a228 **Grosser** Hermann, Narrativa; manuale/antologia: Leggere narrativa. Mi 1992 = 1985, Principato. xi-391 p.

a229 ᴱ**Lamberton** Robert, *Keaney* John J., HOMER's ancient readers; the hermeneutics of Greek epic's earliest exegetes: Magie Clas. Princeton 1992, Univ. xxv-195 p. 0-691-06984-4.

a230 **Pettersson** Anders, A theory of literary discourse: Studies in Aesthetics 2. Lund 1990, Univ. 275 p. 91-7966-128-9 / Chartwell-Bratt 0-86238-259-9.

a231 *Prince* Gerald, Remodeling narratology: Semiotica 90 (1992) 259-266.

a232 **Sturgess** Philip J. M., Narrativity; theory and practice. Ox 1992, Clarendon. x-322 p. 0-19-811954-2.

J9.8 *Theologia narrativa* – **Story-theology.**

a233 *Gascoigne* Robert, The relation between text and experience in narrative theology of revelation [THIEMANN R. 1985; LINDBECK G. 1984]: Pacifica 5 (1992) 43-58.

a234 **Hauerwas** S., *Jones* L. G., Why narrative? Readings in narrative theology 1989 ➤ 7,9762*: ᴿSalesianum 54 (1992) 385-7 (G. *Abbà*: dibattito difficile a seguire).

a235 *Oakes* Edward T., Apologetics and the pathos of narrative theology: JRel 72 (1992) 37-58.

a236 *Schoenborn* Ulrich, Narrative Theologie: ➤ 757, EvKL 3 (1992) 606-9.

a237 **Stegner** William R., Narrative theology in early Jewish Christianity 1990 ➤ 7,9763*: ᴿBtS 149 (1992) 124s (D. L. *Bock*).

(IV.) Postbiblica

K1 **Pseudepigrapha** [= catholicis 'Apocrypha'] .1 *VT, generalia.*

a238 **Charlesworth** J. H., Gli pseudepigrafi dell'AT e il NT ᵀ1990 ➤ 7,9768: ᴿCC 143 (1992,3) 198s (G. L. *Prato*).

a239 **Cimosa** Mario, La letteratura intertestamentaria: La Bibbia nella storia 6. Bo 1992, Dehoniane. 243 p. Lit. 28.000 [RHE 87, 370*].

a240 **Diez Macho** A., Apócrifos AT 5, 1987 ➤ 3,335 ... 6,9958: ᴿJSS 37 (1992) 96-99 (G. J. *Brooke*: editing largely by PIÑERO, closely following KEE for the Test. XII).
Evans C., Noncanonical writings 1992 ➤ 5134.

a242 **Lechner-Schmidt** Wilfried, Wortindex der lateinisch erhaltenen Pseudepigraphen zum AT: TANZ 3, 1990 ➤ 7,9770: ᴿStPhilonAn 136s (M. E. *Stone*: some problems); TLZ 117 (1992) 584s (E. *Reinmuth*).

a242* **Maier** Johann, Zwischen den Testamenten: NEchterEgb 3, 1990 ➤ 7, 9771: ᴿBijdragen 53 (1992) 324s (B. J. *Koet*); CritRR 5 (1992) 99-101 (J. *Kampen*).

a243 ᴱ**Pfabigan** A., Dic andere Bibel mit [= than] Altem und Neuem Testament [apocrypha selections]. Fra 1991, Eichborn. 206 + 177 p. DM 36 [RelStR 19, 86, J. R. *Mueller*: not for scholars].

a244 **Sacchi** P., Gli apocrifi dell'AT 1-2, 1989 ➤ 5,9893 ... 7,9774: ᴿLateranum 57 (1991) 219-223 (R. *Penna*); RÉJ 150 (1991) 179-182 (A. *Caquot*).

a245 **Stone** M. E., Selected studies in pseudepigrapha ... Armenian 1991 ➤ 7, 265a: ᴿRÉAug 38 (1992) 187s (L. *Leloir*).

a245* **Stone** Michael, Travaux actuels sur la littérature apocryphe arménienne: ➤ 470, Apocrypha 1 (1990) 303-311.

a246 *Walter* Nikolaus, [*Paulsen*] Henning], Pseudepigraphen AT [NT]: ➤ 757, EvKL 3 (1992) 1376-81 [-83].

a247 ᴱ**Weidinger** Erich, Gli apocrifi; l'altra Bibbia che non fu scritta da Dio, ᵀ*Jucci* Elio. CasM 1992, Piemme. 736 p.

K1.2   Henoch.

a248 **Albani** Matthias, Astronomie und Schöpfungsglaube; Untersuchungen zu Hen 72-82 unter Berücksichtigung der aramäischen Fragmente 4QEn-Astr. Diss. ᴰ*Seidel* H. Leipzig 1992. – RTLv 24, p. 544.

a248* *a*) *Black* Matthew, The messianism of the parables of Enoch; their date and contributions to Christological origins; *b*) *VanderKam* J. L., Righteous one, Messiah, Chosen One, and Son of Man in 1 Enoch 37-71: ➤ 463, Messiah 1987/92, 145-168 / 169-191.

a249 *Black* Matthew, A bibliography on 1 Enoch in the eighties: JPseud 5 (1989) 3-16.

a249* *Garcia Martinez* Florentino, *a*) Contribution of the Aramaic Enoch fragments to our understanding of the Books of Enoch [< EstB 45 (1987) 127-173],ᵀ; – *b*) The Book of Giants [< EstB 45 (1987) 175-192],ᵀ; – *c*) 4QMess Aram and the Book of Noah [< Salm 28 (1981) 195-232]: ➤ 244a, Qumran/Aramaic 1992, 45-96 / 97-115 / 1-44.

a250 **Kvanvig** Helge S., Roots of apocalyptic; the Mesopotamian background of the Enoch figure and of the Son of Man: WM 61, 1988 ➤ 5,3737; 6,9965: ᴿTsTKi 63 (1992) 305s (M. *Sæbø*).

a250* *Nickelsburg* George W. E., [1 Enoch 1-5] The Qumranic transformation of a cosmological and eschatological tradition (1 QH 4: 29-40): ➤ 498, MQumran 2 (1991/2) 649-659.

a251 *a*) *Segert* Stanislav, Parallelistic structures in the Aramaic Enoch fragments; – *b*) *VanderKam* James C., The birth of Noah [1 Enoch 106s ...]: ➤ 132, ᶠMILIK J. 1992, 187-203 / 213-231.

a251* *Sisson* Jonathan P., Intercession and the denial of peace in 1 Enoch 12-16: HebAnR 11 (1987) 371-386.

K1.3 Testamenta.

a252 *Puech* Émile, Fragments d'un apocryphe de Lévi et le personnage eschatologique; 4QTestLévi^cd et 4QAJa: ➤ 498, MQumran 2 (1991/2) 449-501; pl. 16-22.
a252* **Schenderling** J.G., Het Testament van Job; een document van joodse vroomheid uit het begin van onze jaartelling; *Cozijnsen* L., Het Testament van Salomo, een document van joodse magie uit de eerste eeuwen van onze jaartelling: Na de Schriften 6. Kampen 1990, Kok. 132 p. *f*29,50. 90-2422-030-0. – ᴿNedTTs 46 (1992) 243s (A. C. *Kooyman*).

K1.6 Jubilaea, Adam, Aḥiqar, Asenet.

a255 **VanderKam** James C., The book of Jubilees: CSOr 510s, Aethopici 88, 1989 ➤ 7,9797: ᴿJBL 111 (1992) 137 (J. J. *Collins*: DILLMANN's 1859 text was based on two ms., followed by CHARLES 1895 along with two others; VanderKam agrees with Charles that ms. 25 is the best; but his text uses 23 other newly identified ms., practically as in Zuurmond 1982 AmstCah, which however considers ms. 17 best).
a256 *VanderKam* J.C., *Milik* J.T., A preliminary publication of a Jubilees manuscript from Qumran Cave 4, 4QJub⁴ (4"219): Biblica 73 (1992) 62-83; franç. 83.
a257 *VanderKam* James, *a*) Jubilees; how it rewrote the Bible: BR 8,6 (1992) 33-39.60; ill.; – *b*) The Jubilees fragments from Qumran Cave 4: ➤ 498, MQumran 2 (1991/2) 635-648.
a258 **Stone** Michael E., A history of the literature of Adam and Eve: SBL Early Judaism and its Literature 3. Atlanta 1992, Scholars. x-163 p. $30; pa. $20. 1-55540-715-3; -6-1 [ZAW 105, 538, M. *Köckert*].
a259 **Sweet** Anne-Marie, A religio-historical study of the Greek 'Life of Adam and Eve': diss. ᴰ*Attridge* H. Notre Dame 1992. – RTLv 25, p. 544.
Kottsieper I., Die Sprache der Aḥiqarsprüche 1990 ➤ 3472.

K1.7 Apocalypses, ascensiones.

a261 **Frankfurter** David, Elijah in Upper Egypt; the Apocalypse of Elijah and early Egyptian Christianity [< diss. Princeton 1990]: StAnChr. Mp 1992, Fortress. xix-380 p. 0-8006-3106-4.
a262 *Lührmann* Dieter, [AscIsa, ApkEl...] Alttestamentliche Pseudepigraphen bei DIDYMOS von Alexandrien: ZAW 104 (1992) 231-249.
a263 *Geay* Patrick, L'Ascension d'Hénoch; imagination visionnaire et philosophie: RechSR 80 (1992) 187-202; Eng. 162.
a264 **Acerbi** Antonio, L'Ascensione di Isaia; cristologia e profetismo in Siria nei primi decenni del II secolo [contamination chrétienne d'une œuvre juive...]: StPatrMediolan 17, 1989 ➤ 5,9929 ... 7,9802: ᴿRHE 87 (1992) 564 (J.-C. *Haelewyck*).
a264* — *Norelli* Enrico, Interprétations nouvelles de l'Ascension d'Isaïe [ACERBI A. 1989]: RÉAug 37 (1991) 11-22.
a265 **Tromp** Johannes, The Assumption of Moses; a critical edition with commentary: diss. ᴰ*Jonge* M. de. Leiden 1992. 324 p. – TvT 33, 83; RTLv 24, p. 545.

a266 **Nieto Ibáñez** Jesús-María, El hexámetro de los Oráculos Sibilinos: ClasByzMg 25. Amst 1992, Hakkert. [x-] 421 p. 90-256-0638-3; -1004-8.

K2.1 Philo judaeus alexandrinus.

a268 **Alexandre** Manuel, Argumentação retórica em Filon de Alexandria: BtEuphrosyne 4. Lisboa 1990, Univ. Centro Class. 408 p. – ᴿStPhilonAn 4 (1992) 157s (J. P. *Martín*).

a269 *Borgen* Peder, Philo of Alexandria: ➤ 741, AnchorBD 5 (1992) 333-342 [Pseudo-Philo, 344s, *Harrington* D. J.; Philo of Byblos, 342-4, *Baumgarten* A. I.].

a270 **Daniel-Naṭaf** Suzanne, ❿ Philo 1. Historical, apologetical 1986 ➤ 7, 9811: ᴿRÉJ 150 (1991) 184-6 (Mireille *Hadas-Lebel*).

a271 *a*) *Decharneux* Baudouin, Apparitions et miracles des anges et démons chez Philon d'Alexandrie et PLUTARQUE; – *b*) *Tefnin* Roland, Miracles, merveilles et sortilèges en Égypte ancienne; – *c*) *Sansterre* Jean-Marie, Apparitions et miracles à Ménouthis; de l'incubation païenne à l'incubation chrétienne: ProbHistRel 2 (1991) 61-68 / 47-60 / 69-84 [< ZIT 92,68].

a272 *Graffigna* Paola, Osservazioni sull'uso del termine *phantasía* in Filone d'Alessandria: Koinonia 16,1 (1992) 5-19.

a273 *a*) *Hay* David M., Things Philo said and did not say about the Therapeutae; – *b*) *Sills* Deborah, Vicious rumors; Mosaic narratives in first-century Alexandria: ➤ 478, SBL Sem. 31 (1992) 673-683 / 684-694.

a274 **Horst** P. W. van der, De bijbelse geschiedenis van Pseudo-Philo, een joodse hervertelling van de Bijbel uit de ccrste eeuw van onze jaartelling: Na de Schriften 7. Kampen 1990, Kok. 174 p. ƒ34. 90-242-2020-3. – ᴿBijdragen 53 (1992) 433s (M. *Parmentier*).

a274* *u*) *Horst* Pictcr W. van der, Portraits of biblical women in...; – *b*) *Jacobson* Howard, Biblical quotation and editorial function in Pseudo-Philo's Liber antiquitatum biblicarum: JPseud 5 (1989) 29-46 / 47-61.

a275 *Martens* John W., Unwritten law in Philo: JJS [38 (1987) 165-186, *Cohen* Naomi G.] 43 (1992) 38-45.

a276 **Mendelson** Alan, Philo's Jewish identity: BrownJudSt 161, 1988 ➤ 5, 9947; 7,9818: ᴿStPhilonAn 4 (1992) 164-7 (Naomi G. *Cohen*).

a277 *Morris* Jenny, The Jewish philosopher Philo: ➤ a274a [*Schürer* E.] **Vermes** G., *al.*, History of the Jewish People (1987) 3/2, § 34, p. 809-889. – ᴿStPhilonAn 4 (1992) 137-140 (J. R. *Royse*: the opening lines curiously omit qualification 'next to Josephus', in Schürer's 'no Jewish Hellenist takes so prominent a position as Philo').

a278 **Pépin** Jean, La tradition de l'allégorie de Philon d'Alexandrie à Dante 2, 1987 ➤ 3,a282; 6,9997: ᴿRechSR 80 (1992) 139s (B. *Sesboüé*).

a279 **Radice** Roberto, Platonismo e creazionismo in Filone di Alessandria 1989 ➤ 5,9951; 6,9998: ᴿStPhilonAn 4 (1992) 159-164 (D. *Winston*).

a280 **Royse** J. R. The spurious texts of Philo of Alexandria; a study of textual transmission and corruption with index to the major collections of Greek fragments: ArbLGJ 22, 1991 ➤ 7,9822 [NTAbs 36,451]: ᴿVigChr 46 (1992) 296-9 (D. T. *Runia*).

a281 — *Runia* David T., Confronting the Augean stables; Royse's Fragmenta spuria philonica ... : StPhilonAn 4 (1992) 78-86.

a282 **Runia** David T., Exegesis and philosophy; studies on Philo 1991 ➤ 6,293: ᴿStPhilonAn 4 (1992) 146-153 (R. M. *Berchman*).

a283 *Runia* David T., An index to COHN-WENDLAND's apparatus testimoniorum: StPhilonAn 4 (1992) 87-96.
a284 **Runia** D. T., *Radice* R., *Satran* D., Philo of Alexandria, an annotated bibliography 1988-89: StPhilonAn 4 (1992) 97-116 with ten-line summary of each; 117-124 provisional 1990-92, titles without summary; 125-8, critical review of Radice-Satran 1937-86 bibliography VigChr supp. 8, 1988, by E. *Hilgert* and J. *Royse*.
a285 *Sandelin* Karl-Gustav, The danger of idolatry according to Philo of Alexandria: Temenos 27 (Helsinki 1991) 109-151 [< ZIT 92,350].
a286 *Sellin* Gerhard, Gotteserkenntnis und Gotteserfahrung bei Philo von Alexandrien: ➤ 573, QDisp 138, 1991/2, 17-40.
a287 **Sly** Dorothy, Philo's perception of women: BrownJudSt 209, 1990 ➤ 7,9825: ᴿStPhilonAn 4 (1992) 168-173 (R. S. *Kraemer*).
a288 **Vian** Giovanni Maria, Le Quaestiones di Filone [un solo testo, armeno, Venezia 1826 con traduzione latina di fronte]: ➤ 458, AnStoEseg 9,2 (1992) 365-386; Eng. 341.
a289 *a) Whittaker* John, Catachresis and negative theology; Philo of Alexandria and BASILIDES; – *b) Runia* David T., The language of excellence in PLATO's Timaeus and Later Platonism: ➤ 147, ᶠPLACES E. des, Platonism 1992, 61-82 / 11-37.
a289* **Winston** D., Logos and mystical theology in Philo 1985 ➤ 3,a290: ᴿJPseud 5 (1989) 118 (J. C. *VanderKam*).

K2.4 *Evangelia apocrypha* – Apocryphal Gospels.

a290 *Elliott* J. K., The apocryphal gospels: ExpTim 103 (1991s) 8-15.
a291 **Geerard** Maurice, Clavis Apocryphorum Novi Testamenti: CC. Turnhout 1992, Brepols. xiv-254 p. 2-503-50250-4; pa. 1-2.
a291* *Junod* É., 'Apocryphes du NT', une appellation erronée et une collection artificielle; discussion de la nouvelle définition proposée par W. SCHNEEMELCHER: Apocrypha 3 (1992) 17-46 [< RHE 88, 204*].
a292 ᵀᴱ**Klijn** A. F. J., Apokriefen van het Nieuwe Testament I-II. Kampen 1990, Kok. I. = 1984; 201 p.; II. = 1985; 253 p. 90-242-2804-6; -66-2.
a293 *Petterson* Stephen J. [*Charlesworth* James H.], Apocrypha NT [OT]: ➤ 741, AnchorBD 1 (1992) 294-7 [292-4].
a293* *a) Picard* Jean-Claude, L'apocryphe à l'étroit; notes historiographiques sur les corpus d'apocryphes bibliques; – *b) Kaestli* Jean-Daniel, Fiction littéraire et réalité sociale; que peut-on savoir de la place des femmes dans le milieu de production des Actes apocryphes des Apôtres; – *c) Drijvers* Han J. W., Apocryphal literature in the cultural milieu of Osrhoène: ➤ 470, Apocrypha 1 (1991) 69-117 / 279-302 / 231-247.
a294 **Rebell** Walter, Neutestamentliche Apokryphen und Apostolische Väter. Mü 1992, Kaiser. 287 p. DM 49. 3-459-01954-9 [TLZ 118, 625, G. *Haendler*].
a294* **Schneemelcher** Wilhelm, NT Apokryphen⁵ I-II, 1987-9 ➤ 3,a298* ... 7,9832: ᴿGeistL 64 (1991) 399s (H. *Brandt*); RHE 87 (1992) 144-7 (L. *Leloir*); ScripTPamp 24 (1992) 641-4 (G. *Aranda*).
a295 [*Hennecke* Edgar] ᴱ**Schneemelcher** Wilhelm, New Testament Apocrypha I⁶, Gospels and related writings, ᵀᴱ*Wilson* R. M.² 1991 ➤ 7,9833: ᴿNT 34 (1992) 406-409 (J. K. *Elliott*); TS 53 (1992) 342s (J. A. *Fitzmyer*).
a296 **Steimer** Bruno, Vertex traditionis; die Gattung der altchristlichen Kirchenordnungen [Pseudepigraphie]: BZNW 63. B 1992, de Gruyter. xvi-402 p. DM 148. – ᴿRechSR 80 (1992) 467-470 (P. *Vallin*).

a297 ᴱGiustolisi E., *Rizzardi* G., Il Vangelo di Barnaba; un Vangelo per i musulmani 1991 ➤ 7,9836*: ᴿRivB 40 (1992) 253-5 (G. *Corti*).

a298 **Moraldi** Luigi, Vangelo arabo apocrifo Gv 1991 ➤ 7,9837: ᴿETL 68 (1992) 168s (D. *Bundy*); Gregorianum 73 (1992) 347s (H. *Pietras*); StPatav 39 (1992) 467s (C. *Saccone*).

a298* *Norelli* Enrico, Situation des apocryphes pétriniens: ➤ 470, Apocrypha 2 (1991) 31-83.

a299 **Alcalá** Manuel, El Evangelio copto de Felipe: En torno al NT. Córdoba 1992, Almendro. 202 p. 84-8005-000-4.

a299* *Dubois* Jean-Daniel, Les 'Actes de Pilate' au quatrième siècle: ➤ 470, Apocrypha 2 (1991) 85-98.

a300 **Van Sickle** John, A reading of VIRGIL's Messianic Eclogue: Harvard DissClas. NY 1992, Garland. ix-183 p. 0-8153-0660-1.

a300* *a) Patlagean* Évelyne, Remarques sur la production et la diffusion des apocryphes [NT] dans le monde byzantin; – *b) Roquet* Gérard, La 'réception' de l'image et du texte à motifs d'apocryphes dans les chrétientés d'Égypte et de Nubie; quelques aperçus; – *c) Hudry* Marius, Les Apocryphes dans l'iconographie des églises et chapelles savoyardes: ➤ 470, Apocrypha 2 (1991) 155-163 / 181-215; pl. I-III / 249-259; pl. X-XIV.

K2.7 **Alia apocrypha NT.**

a301 **Kampen** L. van, Apostelverhalen; doel en compositie van de oudste apokriefe Handelingen der apostelen [Acta Petri, Pauli, Johannis, Andreae, Thomae; diss. Utrecht 1990]. Sliedrecht 1990. 338 p. ƒ45. – ᴿGerefTTs 92 (1992) 132-4 (J. *Helderman*).

a302 **Leloir** Louis, Écrits apocryphes [arméniens] 4. sur les Apôtres, 2. Philippe, Barthélemy, Thomas, Matthieu, Jacques frère du Seigneur, Thaddée, Simon, listes d'Apôtres: CCApocr 4. Turnhout 1992, Brepols. lx + p. 419-828 [RHE 87,193*]. Fb 5000. 2-503-41041-3; pa. -2-1.

a303 ᵀᴮLeloir Louis, Écrits apocryphes sur les apôtres ... armén: CCApocr 3, 1986 ➤ 2,8117 ... 5,9973: ᴿRivStoLR 27 (1991) 526-530 (W. *Schneemelcher*, 1, ital.).

a304 [*Hennecke* Edgar] ᴱ**Schneemelcher** Wilhelm, New Testament Apocrypha II⁵ [1989], Writings relating to the Apostles; Apocalypses and related subjects. Louisville 1992, W-Knox. [x-] 771 p.

a305 **MacDonald** Dennis R., Acts of Andrew 1990 ➤ 7,9840: ᴿCBQ 54 (1992) 579s (R. J. *Pervo*).

a305* *Bovon* François, Les paroles de vie dans les Actes de l'apôtre André: ➤ 470, Fable 1986, Apocrypha 2 (1991) 99-117.

a306 **Prieur** Jean-Marc, Acta Andreae: CCApocr 5s, 1989 ➤ 5,9975 ... 7, 9838: ᴿRB 99 (1992) 614-621 (J. *Taylor*); RechSR 80 (1992) 95-97 (B. *Sesboüé*); RHE 86 (1991) 350 (R. *Gryson*); RTPhil 124 (1992) 361s (J. *Borel*); ZKG 103 (1992) 122-8 (A. de *Santos Otero*: unvollständig).

a306* *Pervo* R. I., Johannine trajectories in the Acts of John; Apocrypha 3 (1992) 47-68 [< RHE 88, 204*].

a307 **Callahan** Allen D., The 'Acts of St. Mark' [late 4th c.]; an introduction and commentary: diss. Harvard. CM 1992. 149 p. 92-28326. – HarvTR 85 (1992) 494s; DissA 53 (1992s) 1546-A.

a308 *a)* *MacDonald* Dennis R., The Acts of Paul and the Acts of Peter; which came first?; – *b)* *Valantasis* Richard, Narrative strategies and Synoptic quandaries; a response to MacDonald; – *c)* *Stoops* Robert F.ᴶ, Peter, Paul, and priority in the apocryphal Acts: ➤ 478, SBL Sem. 21 (1992) 214-224 / 234-9 / 225-233.

a308* *Dinzelbacher* Peter, La 'Visio S. Pauli'; circulation et influence d'un apocryphe eschatologique: ➤ 470, Apocrypha 2 (1991) 165-180.

a309 *Perkins* Judith, The apocryphal Acts of Peter; a *Roman à thèse?*: Arethusa 25 (1992) 445-457.

a309* *Thomas* C. M., Word and deed; the Acts of Peter and orality: Apocrypha 3 (1992) 125-164.

a310 *Petterson* Stephen J., Sources, redaction and Tendenz in the Acts of Peter and the Twelve Apostles (NH VI, 1): VigChr 45 (1991) 1-17.

a311 ᵀᴱ*Starowieyski* Marek, ℗ Dzieje Pawła i Tekli: RuBi 44 (1991) 118-126.

a312 *Harris* M. R., The Occitan Epistle to the Laodiceans; towards an edition of MS PA 36 (Lyons, Bib.mun.): ➤ 62, ᶠGASCA QUEIRAZZA G. 1988 ...

a313 **Hills** J., Tradition and composition in the Epistula Apostolorum: HarvDissRel 24. Mp 1990, Augsburg. xvii-172 p. – ᴿSalmanticensis 39 (1992) 407-9 (R. *Trevijano*).

a313* *a)* *Desreumaux* Alain, La Doctrina Addaï; le chroniqueur et ses documents; – *b)* *Teyssèdre* Bernard, Les représentations de la fin des temps dans le chant V des Oracles sibyllins; les strates de l'imaginaire: ➤ 470, Apocrypha 1 (1990) 249-267 / 147-165.

K3 **Qumran** .1 *generalia.*

a314 **Baigent** Michael, Leigh Richard, The Dead Sea Scrolls deception 1991 ➤ 7,9854; also NY 1992, Summit. 268 p. $20. – ᴿBA 55 (1992) 107s (M. *Broshi*: pernicious); TS 53 (1992) 180s (J. A. *Fitzmyer*: 'much new information' and many errors).

a315 — **Baigent** M., *Leigh* R., Verschlusssache Jesu 1991 ➤ 7,9855*: ᴿHerdKor 46 (1992) 98s (K. *Nientiedt*); LuthTK 16 (1992) 55s (R. *Scheerer*); Orientierung 56 (1992) 44-46 (G. *Häfner*).

a316 *Bonani* Georges, *al.*, Radiocarbon dating of fourteen Dead Sea Scrolls: ➤ 723, Radiocarbon 34 (1992) 843-849; 2 fig.: 352 B.C. (Daliyeh!) 125 B.C. – 744 A.D. (Mird).

a317 CARMIGNAC J. mém., Études Qumraniennes: RQum 13 (1988) ➤ 4,22; 6,a31: ᴿFolOr 27 (1990) 223-235 (Z. J. *Kapera*).

a318 ᴱ**Charlesworth** James H., *al.*, Graphic concordance to the Dead Sea Scrolls 1991 ➤ 7,9857: ᴿJJS 43 (1992) 316 (G. *Vermes*: useless; but he plans a 'proper' concordance); Muséon 105 (1992) 385s (P.-M. *Bogaert*; difficultés d'usage; mais le mieux est l'ennemi du bien); NedTTs 46 (1992) 347s (P. W. van der *Horst*: very useful); NorTTs 93 (1992) 178s (A. S. *Kapelrud*); TLZ 117 (1992) 418-420 (P. von der *Osten-Sacken*); TüTQ 172 (1992) 329s (W. *Gross*).

a319 *Charlesworth* James H., Sense or sensationalism? [Behind] the Dead Sea Scrolls controversy: ChrCent 109 (1992) 92-98.

a320 *Collins* John J., Dead Sea Scrolls: ➤ 741, AnchorBD 2 (1992) 85-101.

a321 *Cothenet* É., Qumran, controverses et nouvelles publications [NEWSOM

(écrit Newson) C. 1985; PUECH E., Béatitudes]; EsprVie 102 (1992) 153-8; complément 176.
a322 *a) Cross* Frank M., Some notes on a generation of Qumran studies (*Tov* E. reply); – *b) Kapera* Zdzisław J., The present state of Polish Qumranology: ➤ 498, MQumran 1 (1991/2) 1-14 (-21) / 307-315.
a323 ᴱ**Dimant** Devorah, *Rappaport* Uriel, The Dead Sea Scrolls; forty years of research : Studies on the Texts of the Desert of Judah 10. Leiden 1992, Brill. viii-370 p. *f* 110 [TR 88,515].
a324 *Donceel* Robert, Reprise des travaux de publication des fouilles au Khirbet Qumran: RB 99 (1992) 557-573; Eng. 557.
a325 ᴱ**Eisenman** Robert H., *Robinson* James M., A facsimile edition of the Dead Sea Scrolls. Wsh 1992, BA[R]-Soc. I. xxii-907 pl.; II. pl. 908-1787. $210. 1-880317-01-X; -2-8. [BAR-W 18,1 (1992) 63; 18,2 p. 9, banned from use in 'Israel and elsewhere' by injunction of Israel district court].
a326 **Eisenman** Robert, *Wise* Michael, The Dead Sea Scrolls uncovered; the first complete translation and interpretation of 50 key documents withheld for over 40 years [British edition has 36 years]. Rockport MA 1992, Element. 286 p. $25 [BAR-W 19/1,60, A. *Segal*].
a327 *Eisenman* Robert, On 'go-slow' policies; the role of Paul and Carbon-14 dating [protesting BAR claim that he subscribed to 'conspiracy' theory]: BAR-W 18,2 (1992) 16s.
a328 **Fitzmyer** Joseph A., Responses to 101 questions on the DSS. NY 1992, Paulist. xviii-201 p. $9. 0-8091-3348-2 [RB 100, 632, J. *Murphy-O'Connor* adds Question 102: why is the scroll on the cover upside down?].
a329 **Fitzmyer** Joseph A., The Dead Sea Scrolls; major publications and tools for study[2] 1990 ➤ 6,a33; 7,9859: ᴿCBQ 54 (1992) 560s (C. *Bernas*); TLZ 117 (1992) 494s (S. *Holm-Nielsen*: 'Fitzmeyer' in Titel, richtig im Text).
a330 *Fitzmyer* Joseph A., What they found in the caves: Commonweal 119, 22 (1992) 13-16.
a331 **García Martínez** Florentino, Textos de Qumran, introducción y edición: Estructuras y Procesos, Religión. M 1882, Trotta. 526 p. 84-87699-44-8 [BL 93,30, P. R. *Davies*].
a331* *Burgos Núñez* Miguel de, Qumrán hoy, en el pensamiento y obra del Prof. F. GARCÍA MARTÍNEZ: ComSev 25 (1992) 255-268.
a332 *Greenfield* Jonas C., The texts from Naḥal Ṣeʿelîm (Wadi Seiyal): ➤ 498, MQumran 2 (1991/2) 661-5.
a333 *Haelst* J. van, Cinq textes provenant de Khirbet Mird: AncSoc 22 (1991) 297-317; 7 pl.; map. [< RHE 87, 357*].
a334 *Jucci* Elio, Qumran e dintorni; breve rassegna di studi qumranici: [CALLAWAY P., VIVIAN A. ...]: RivB 40 (1992) 467-477.
a335 *Kapera* Zdzisław J., Bibliography of Norman GOLB's hypothesis of the Jerusalem origin of the Dead Sea Scrolls: FolOr 27 (1990) 217-221.
a335* *Murphy-O'Connor* Jerome, Qumran, khirbet: ➤ 741, AnchorBD 5 (1992) 500-4.
a336 *Nebe* Gerhard W., Qumran: ➤ 757, EvKL 3 (1992) 1417-20.
a337 ᴱ**Reed** Stephen A., Dead Sea Scroll inventory project; lists of documents, photographs and museum plates; 14 fasc. [with National Foundation for the Humanities; Dorot Fund, Annenberg Inst.; Israel Antiquities authority]. Claremont 1991s, Bible Ms. Center. I, Cave 1, 44 p.; 2. minor caves, 33 p.; 3. Murabbaʿat, 37 p.; 4s, cave 4, 41 + 54 p. 7-10, 1992, also cave 4, 72 + 32 + 67 + 74 p.; 11, Mird, 25 p.; 12, Daliyah, 26 p.; 13, Seiyal/Ḥever 1992, 32 p.; 14, Masada 1992, 37 p. [OIAc 3.34s].

a338 *Safrai* Baruch, More scrolls lie buried; recollections from 40 years ago [at Naḥal Ḥever]: BAR-W 19,1 (1993) 50-57; (color.) ill.

a339 *Sanders* James A., Qumran update; what can happen in a year?: BA 55 (1992) 37-42.

a340 ᴱ**Shanks** Hershel, Understanding the Dead Sea Scrolls; a reader from the Biblical Archaeology Review. NY 1992, Random. xxxviii-337 p.; 41 fig. 0-679-41448-7.

a341 *Shanks* Hershel, Not so up-to-date in Kansas City [SBL-ASOR meeting Nov. 23-26, 1991, largely devoted to new norms for manuscript-find publication]: BAR-W 18,2 (1992) 54-56. – 18/5, Shanks on QIMRON lawsuit; 19/2, 68s, Qimron reply; 69s, Shanks.

a342 *a) Shanks* Hershel, What the monopolists have done right; – *b) Robinson* James M., What we should do next time great manuscripts are discovered [< Claremont OccP 28]: BAR-W 18,1 (1992) 65.70 / 66.68.

a343 — *Wright* John W., Another view of the 'Dead Sea Scrolls scandal' [SHANKS framed the issue rightly in 1984, despite his stereotyping rhetoric]: BAR-W 18,3 (1992) 64s.

a344 *Tov* Emanuel, The unpublished Qumran texts from Caves 4 and 11; *a)* [over 600, with names of assigned editors]: BA 55 (1992) 94-104; – *b)* JJS 43 (1992) 101-136.

a345 *a) Tov* Emanuel, The contribution of the Qumran scrolls to the understanding of the LXX; – *b) Ulrich* E. C., The Septuagint manuscripts from Qumran; a reappraisal of their value; – *c) Brooke* G. J., The Temple Scroll and LXX Exodus 35-40: ↠ 459, LXX 1990/2, 11-47 / 49-80 / 81-106.

a346 Video tapes: *a)* The Enigma of the Dead Sea Scrolls. Longmont CO c. 1992, Biblical Productions. $30; – *b)* Secrets of the Dead Sea Scrolls. Dallas c. 1992, Zola Levitt. $19 [BAR-W 19/1,63].

a347 **Wacholder** Ben Zion, *Abegg* Martin G., A preliminary edition of the unpublished Dead Sea scrolls; the Hebrew and Aramaic texts from cave four, 2. Wsh 1992, BA(R)S. xix-309 p. $67.50 [BAR-W 19/1,62, J. A. *Fitzmyer*].

a348 *Woude* Adam S. van der, Fünfzehn Jahre Qumranforschung (1974-1988) ... Handscriften aus Höhle 1; 4; 11 / Ursprung und Geschichte der Gemeinde: TRu 57 (1992) 1-57 / 225-253.

a349 YADIN Yigael memorial, Archaeology and history in the Dead Sea Scrolls, NYU conference, ᴱ**Schiffman** Lawrence H. 1985/90 ↠ 6,554: ᴿBA 55 (1992) 47s (J. C. *Moyer*); BO 49 (1992) 486-9 (M. *Delcor*: analyses); CBQ 54 (1992) 392s (J. C. *VanderKam*); JAOS 112 (1992) 322-4 (Devorah *Dimant*); JSS 37 (1992) 323-5 (P. R. *Callaway*).

a350 **Yadin** Yigael, The Message of the Scrolls [1962], ᴱ*Charlesworth* James H.: Christian Origins Library. NY 1992, Crossroad. viii-192 p. $17 pa. [CBQ 54,618].

K3.4   *Qumran,* **Libri biblici** [↠ singuli] **et pseudo-biblici.**

a351 *a) Haran* Menahem, ❸ 11QPsᵃ and the composition of the Book of Psalms; – *b) Brin* Gershon, ❸ Biblical prophecy in the Qumran scrolls: ↠ 181, Shaᶜarei TALMON 1992, 123*-128* / 101*-112*; Eng. xxi/xx.

a352 *García Martínez* Florentino, Las fronteras de lo 'bíblico': ScripT-Pamp 23 (1991) 759-784.

a352* *Greenstein* Edward L., Misquotation of Scripture in the Dead Sea Scrolls: ↠ 180c, Mem. TALMAGE F. 1 (1992s) 71-83.

a353 **Newsom** Carol, Songs of the Sabbath sacrifice 1985 ↠ 1,9793 ... 4,b36: ᴿJQR 83 (1992s) 235-9 (D. P. *McCarthy*).

a354 — *Maier* Johann, *Shîrê ʿolat hash-shabbat* [NEWSOM C., Songs of the Sabbath Sacrifice 1985]; some observations on their calendric implications and on their style: ➤ 498, MQumran 2 (1991/2) 543-560.

a355 **Schuller** Eileen, Non-canonical psalms from Qumran: HarvSemSt 28, 1986 ➤ 2,8145 ... 6,a52: ᴿSefarad 51 (1991) 213-6 (F. *Sen*).

a356 *Schuller* Eileen M., The psalm of 4Q372 1 within the context of Second Temple prayer: CBQ 54 (1992) 67-79.

a357 *Eshel* E. & H., *Yardeni* A., A Qumran composition containing part of Ps. 154 and a prayer for the welfare of King Jonathan and his kingdom [< ❶ ➤ 7,9871]: IsrEJ 42 (1992) 199-229; 1 fig.

a358 *a) Charlesworth* James H., An allegorical and autobiographical poem by the *Moreh ha-Ṣedeq* (1QH 8:4-11); – *b) Greenfield* Jonas C., Two notes on the apocryphal psalms; – *c) Rofé* Alexander, A neglected meaning of the verb κWL and the text of 1QS vi: 11-13; – *d) Sanders* James A., The Dead Sea Scrolls and biblical studies: ➤ 181, Shaʿarei TALMON 1992, 295-307 / 309-314 / 315-321 / 323-336.

a359 *Vegas Montaner* Luis, Some features of the Hebrew verbal syntax in the Qumran Hodayot: ➤ 498, MQumran 1 (1991/2) 273-286.

a360 *Williams* Gary R., Parallelism in the Hodayot from Qumran: diss. Annenberg, ᴰ*Geller* S. Ph 1991. 844 p. 92-34457. – DissA 53 (1992s) 2415-A.

a361 *Burgmann* Hans, 4 Q MMT [➤ 7,9873*]; Versuch einer historisch begründbaren Datierung: FolOr 27 (1990) 43-62.

a362 — **Dombrowski** Bruno W. W., An annotated translation of Miqsat Maʿaśeh ha-Torah (4Q MMT). Kraków-Weenzen 1992, Enigma. 44 p. [OIAc 5,19].

a362* — *Qimron* Elisha, Miqsat Maʿaśeh ha-Torah: ➤ 741, AnchorBD 4 (1992) 843-5.

a363 — *Flusser* David, ❶ Some of the precepts of the Torah from Qumran (4QMMT) and the benediction against the heretics: Tarbiz 61 (1991s) 333-374; Eng. II.

a364 *Stone* Michael E., *Eshel* Eather, An exposition on the Patriarchs (4Q 464) and two other documents (4Q 464a and 4Q 464b): Muséon 105 (1992) 243-262; 2 pl.

a365 *García Martínez* Florentino, *a)* The eschatological figure of 4Q246 [< ᶠ*Alonso Schökel* L., Misterio 1983, 229-244], ᵀ; – *b)* 'The new Jerusalem' and the future temple of the manuscripts from Qumran [< Mem. *Díez Macho* A., Salvación 1986, 563-590],ᵀ: ➤ 244, Qumran/Aramaic 1992, 162-179 / 180-213.

a366 *Puech* Émile, Fragment d'une apocalypse en Araméen (4Q 246 = pseudo Danᵈ) et le 'Royaume de Dieu': RB 99 (1992) 98-131; Eng. 98 (pre-Qumran expectation of a 'Messiah-King'; Qumran awaited also a 'Messiah-Priest').

a367 **Skehan** Patrick W. †, *Ulrich* Eugene, *Sanderson* Judith E., Qumran Cave 4 IV; Palaeo-Hebrew and Greek biblical manuscripts: DJD 9. Ox 1992, Clarendon. xiii-250 p.; XLVII pl. 0-19-326328-7.

к3.5 *Rotulus Templi* – **The Temple Scroll**, *al.*

a368 *Anderson* Gary A., The interpretation of the purification-offering (*ḥaṭaʾt*) in the Temple Scroll (11Q Temple) and rabbinic literature: JBL 111 (1992) 17-35.

a369 ᴱ**Brooke** George J.,   Temple scroll studies 1987/9 ➤ 5,568 ... 7,9879: ᴿBZ 36 (1992) 122s (J. *Maier*: tit. pp. comments).

a370 *a*) *García Martínez* Florentino,   11Q Templeᵇ; a preliminary publication [bibliog. 1985-91]; – *b*) *Schiffman* Lawrence H.,   The furnishings of the Temple according to the Temple Scroll: ➤ 498, MQumran 2 (1991/2) 363-391 [393-403]; pl. 9-15 / 621-634.

a371 *Milgrom* Jacob,   First day ablutions at Qumran [Temple scroll, Milgrom 1978]: ➤ 498, MQumran 2 (1991/2) 561-570.

a372 *Reeves* John C.,   The feast of the first fruits of wine and the ancient Canaanite calendar [Temple Scroll 19,11-21,10]:   VT 42 (1992) 350-361.

a373 **Vivian** Angelo,   Rotolo del Tempio 1990 ➤ 6,a65; 7,9882:   ᴿJBL 111 (1992) 331-3 (M. O. *Wise*); ParVi 36 (1991) 225-9 (A. *Rolla*); Protestantesimo 47 (1992) 137s (J. A. *Soggin*); ScuolC 120 (1992) 195-207 (Anna *Passoni Dell'Acqua*).

a374 **Wise** Michael O.,   A critical study of the Temple scroll ...: SAOC 49, 1990 ➤ 6,a66; 7,9884:   ᴿJBL 111 (1992) 329-331 (B. Z. *Wacholder*).

a375 **Schiffman** Lawrence H.,   The eschatological community of the DSS [Serek] 1989 ➤ 5,a30; 6,a69:   ᴿJQR 83 (1992s) 254s (L. J. *Prockter*); JRel 72 (1990) 99s (J. *VanderKam*: limited to one Serek appendix).

a375* *lśwḥ* in 1QS 7-15: JPseud 5 (1989) 83-94: not 'dig' nor related to excretion; as in Philo (Therapeutes) at meeting were to sit with their hands inside the robe.

a376 *Eshel* Esther & Hanan,   4Q471 fragment 1 and Maʿamadot in the War Scroll: ➤ 498, MQumran 2 (1991/2) 611-620; pl. 23.

a377 *a*) *Vermes* Geza,   The Oxford forum for Qumran research seminar on the Rule of War from Cave 4 (4Q285); – *b*) *Baumgarten* Joseph M.,   A [not-traceable] 'scriptural' citation in 4Q fragments of the Damascus Document: JJS 43 (1992) 85-94 / 95-98.

a378 *a*) *Kister* Menahem,   Some aspects of Qumranic halakhah; – *b*) *Baumgarten* Joseph,   The disqualifications of priests in 4Q fragments of the 'Damascus Document', a specimen of the recovery of pre-rabbinic Halakha: ➤ 498, MQumran 2 (1991/2) 571-588 / 503-513.

a379 *Albani* Matthias,   Die lunaren Zyklen im 364-Tage-Festkalender von 4QMischmerot/4QSe: KH-JudentumMitBeit (Lp 1992, 4) 48-56 [< TLZ 117,909].

a380 *Puech* Émile,   La pierre de Sion et l'autel des holocaustes d'après un manuscrit hébreu de la grotte 4 (4Q522): RB 99 (1992) 676-696; pl. XIX; Eng. 676.

a381 *a*) *Baumgarten* Joseph M.,   The Cave 4 versions of the Qumran penal code; – *b*) *Eshel* Esther, *Kister* Menahem,   A polemical Qumran fragment; – *c*) *Goranson* Stephen,   Sectarianism, geography, and the Copper Scroll; – *d*) *Vermes* G.,   Qumran Forum miscellanea I: JJS 43 (1992) 268-276 / 277-281 / 282-287 / 299-306.

a382 **García Martínez** F.,   Qumran and apocalyptic; studies on the Aramaic texts from Qumran: diss. Groningen 1992, ᴰ*Woude* A. S. van der.   xvi-233 p. (Leiden, Brill 90-04-09586-1). – TvT 32 (1992) 303.

a383 **McCarter** P. Kyleᴶ,   The mysterious copper scroll; clues to hidden Temple treasure?:   BR 8,4 (1992) 34-41 . 63s.

a384 *Wolters* Al, Literary analysis and the copper scroll: → 132, FMILIK J. 1992, 239-252 [131-3 misspellings, *Muchowski* P.].

K3.6 Qumran et NT.

a385 *Bockmuehl* Markus, A 'slain Messiah' in 4Q Serekh Milḥamah (4Q 285)?: TyndB 43,1 (1992) 155-169.

a386 — [*Shanks* Hershel, 4Q 285], The 'Pierced Messiah' text evaporates [other 'fragments' of news about current Scrolls research]: BAR-W 18,4 (1992) [70-] 72-82; further 18,5 (1992) 67s; 18,6 (1992) 56s; also 58-65, *Tabor* James & *Wise* Michael O. reopening 'Pierced Messiah' question; p. 59 *Vermes* G. on his own JJS paper]; 19/1, 66, *Eisenman, Vermes*.

a387 **Charlesworth** James H., *al.*, Jesus and the Dead Sea Scrolls: AnchorB Reference Library. NY 1992, Doubleday. xxxvii-370 p.; 13 fig. (p. 182, not 282 as p. xiii); 4 maps.

a388 *Copray* Norbert, War Jesus ein Essener? Warum die Schriftrollen vom Toten Meer eben doch brisant und katholische Abwimmelungsversuche unredlich sind: Publik-Forum (1992,1) 20-23 [< NSys 34 (1992) 327s: Fehlschluss, to identify religions because of parallels or mutual influences].

a389 *Ghiberti* Giuseppe, Marco a Qumran?: ParVi 37 (1992) 126-132.

a390 *Heutger* Nicolaus, Der Heilige Rest verstiess die Mehrzahl der Menschen; die Lehren der Gemeinde von Qumran stehen im Gegensatz zur Botschaft Jesu: LuthMon 31 (1992) 229s.

a391 EMayer Bernhard, Christen und Christliches in Qumran? [Tagung Eichstätt]: Eichstätter Studien NF 32. Rg 1992, Pustet. 268 p.; 23 fig. 3-7917-1346-9.

a392 *O'Callaghan* José, *a*) El papiro de Marcos en Qumrán: Gladius 8,25 (1992) 7-14 [AcPIB 9,778]; – *b*) Sobre el papiro de Marcos en Qumran: FgNt 5 (1992) 189-197; – *c*) L'ipotetico papiro di Marco a Qumran: CC 143 (1992,2) 464-473.

a393 *Quintens* Werner, Het Nieuwe Testament vijfenveertig jaar na de ontdekking van de Qumran-Rollen: CollatVL 22 (1992) 129-147.

a394 **Rohrhirsch** Ferdinand, Markus in Qumran? Wu 1990, Brockhaus. – RParVi 37 (1992) 129s (G. *Ghiberti*).

a395 *Spottorno* Maria Vittoria, [Za 7,4-5] Una nueva posible identificación de 7Q5 [punto clave en la teoría NT de O'CALLAGHAN]: → 155, FROMANO VENTURA D., Sefarad 52 (1992) 541-3.

a396 *Stegemann* Hartmut, Ein neues Bild des Judentums zur Zeit Jesu; zum gegenwärtigen Stand der Qumran- und Essenerforschung: HerdKor 46 (1992) 175-180.

a397 EStendahl Krister, (*Charlesworth* James H.), The Scrolls and the New Testament (1957); Christian Origins Library. NY 1992, Crossroad. xii-312 p. $17 pa. [CBQ 54,617].

a398 **Thiede** Carsten P., Die älteste Evangelien-Handschrift? Das Markus-Fragment von Qumran²ʳᵉᵛ [¹1986 → 2,8168] → 6,a79; Wu 1990, Brockhaus. 84 p.

a399 **Thiede** Carsten P., The earliest Gospel manuscript? The Qumran fragment 7Q5 and its significance for NT studies. L 1992, Paternoster. 80 p.; ill. [NTAbs 36,456]. – RActuBbg 29 (1992) 59s (J. *Pegueroles*).

a400 **Thiering** Barbara, Jesus & the riddle of the Dead Sea Scrolls; unlocking the secrets of his life story. SF 1992, Harper. 451 p. $24. – ᴿBAR-W 18,5 (1992) 69 (H. *Shanks*: 'Did Jesus really die on the Cross?'; the real mystery is how HarperSF division of HarperCollins decided to publish this volume); 19/1, 14s, letters, mostly disgusted; p. 17, Thiering reply.

a401 **Thiering** Barbara, Jesus the man; a new interpretation from the Dead Sea Scrolls. NY c. 1992, Doubleday. £17. – ᴿTablet 246 (1992) 1184-6 (G. *O'Collins*: 'selling Jesus; ignoring scholars').

a402 *VanderKam* James G., The Dead Sea Scrolls and early Christianity; what they share: BR 8,1 (1992) 16-22; 40.

к3.8　Historia et doctrinae Qumran.

a403 **Ausin Olmos** S., Moral y conducta en Qumran 1991 → 7,9895: ᴿScrip-TPamp 23 (1991) 1071s (J. M. *Casciaro*); StLeg 33 (1992) 265-7 (F. F. *Ramos*).

a404 *Blondet* Maurizio, La setta ebraica dei 'ricostruttori del Tempio': St-CattMi 35 (1991) 134-8.

a405 *Broshi* Magen, ❾ Visionary architecture and town planning in the Dead Sea Scrolls: → 18, ᶠBιʀᴀɴ A., ErIsr 23 (1992) 286-292; Eng. 155*.

a406 *a) Broshi* Magen, Anti-Qumranic polemics in the Talmud; – *b) Knohl* Israel, Post-biblical sectarianism and the priestly schools of the Pentateuch; the issue of popular participation in the Temple cult on festivals: → 498, MQumran 2 (1991/2) 589-600 / 601-9.

a407 **Burgmann** Hans, Weitere lösbare Qumranprobleme: Qumranica Mogilanensia 9. Kraków 1992, Enigma. viii-178 p. 83-800504-4-6.

a408 *Caquot* André, La secte de Qoumran et le Temple: → 36, ᶠCᴜʟʟᴍᴀɴɴ O., RHPR 72 (1992) 3-14; Eng. 125.

a409 **Davidson** Maxwell J., Angels at Qumran; a comparative study of 1 Enoch 1-36, 72-106 and sectarian writings from Qumran: JPseud supp 11. Sheffield 1992, JStOT. 164 p. [TR 88,338]. – £40; sb. 30. 1-85075-32-6. – ᴿExpTim 103 (1991s) 383 [C. S. *Rodd*]; Henoch 14 (1992) 332-4 (Liliana *Rosso Ubigli*).

a410 *a) Derrett* J. D. M., Discipline and betrayal in Qumran; – *b) Laperrousaz* Ernest-Marie, La chronologie de la Période I de l'occupation essénienne de Qumran et la datation des Manuscrits de la mer Morte: → 132, ᶠMιʟιᴋ J. 1992, 45-52 / 109-129.

a411 *García Martínez* F., Profeet en profetie in de geschriften van Qumran: → 503, Symposium A. van der Woude 1985/92, 119-132.

a412 *Newsom* Carol A., *a)* The case of the blinking I; discourse of the self at Qumran: → 370, Semeia 57 (1992) 13-23; – *b)* Knowledge as doing; the social symbolics of knowledge at Qumran: Semeia 59 (1992) 139-153.

a413 *Pines* S., Notes on the Twelve Tribes in Qumran, early Christianity and Jewish tradition: → 57, ᶠFʟᴜssᴇʀ D., Messiah 1992, 151-4.

a414 *a) Qimron* Elisha, Celibacy in the Dead Sea Scrolls and the two kinds of sectarians; – *b) Fröhlich* Ida, Pesher, apocalyptical literature and Qumran: → 498, MQumran 1 (1991/2) 287-294 / 295-305.

a415 **Rothstein** David, From Bible to Murabbaᶜat; studies in the literary, textual and scribal features of phylacteries and mezuzot in ancient Israel and early Judaism: diss. UCLA, ᴰSegert S. 554 p. 93-01560. – DissA 53 (1992s) 3252-A.

a415* *a) Schiffman* L. H., Messianic figures and ideas in the Qumran scrolls; – *b) Priest* J., A note on the messianic banquet; – *c) Talmon* S., The concept of mašiah and messianism in early Judaism: ➤ 463, Messiah 1987/92, 116-129 / 222-238 / 79-115.

a416 *Schiffman* Lawrence H., New light on the Pharisees; insights from the Dead Sea scrolls: BR 8,3 (1992) 30-33 . 54.

a416* *Sirat* Colette, Les rouleaux bibliques de Qumran au Moyen Âge [*sic*; tête de pages 'Qumrân']; du livre au Sefer Tora, de l'oreille à l'œil: CRAI (1991) 415-432; 2 pl.

a417 **Talmon** Shemaryahu, The world of Qumran from within [1951-88 reprints] 1989 ➤ 5,365; 6,a92: ᴿJAOS 112 (1992) 496 (B. A. *Taylor*).

a418 *VanderKam* James C., The people of the Dead Sea Scrolls; Essenes or Sadducees? [SCHIFFMAN: MMT a Sadducees document]: BR 7,2 (1991) 42-47 [cf. 7/1,4s, *Davies* W.].

a419 *Weinfeld* Moshe, Grace after meals in Qumran: JBL 111 (1992) 427-440.

a419* *Woude* A. S. van der, The Dead Sea Scrolls; some issues [... the 'Groningen hypothesis', a group split off from Essenes c. 140 B.C.; P. *Davies* skepticism unwarranted]: SvEx 57 (1992) 86-101.

к4.1 Esseni, Zelotae.

a420 **Beall** T. S, JOSEPHUS's description of the Essenes 1988 ➤ 4,b72 ... 6,a95: ᴿTsTKi 62 (1991) 75s (A. *Aschim*, also on VERMES-GOODMAN).

a421 *Bohrmann* Monette, La pureté rituelle; une approche de la communauté des Esséniens: DialHA 17,1 (1991) 307-330; deutsch 331.

a421* *Collins* J., Essenes: ➤ 741, AnchorBD 2 (1992) 619-626.

a422 *Delcor* Mathias, À propos de l'emplacement de la porte des Esséniens selon Josèphe [B 5,142] et de ses implications historiques, essénienne et chrétienne; examen d'une théorie [... PIXNER B.]: ➤ 132, ᶠMILIK J. 1992, 25-44.

a423 *Golb* Norman, The Qumran-Essene hypothesis; a fiction of scholarship· ChrCent 109 (1992) 1138-1143.

a424 *Hinson* E. Glenn, Essene influence on Roman Christianity [HIPPOLYTUS]; a look at the second-century evidence: ➤ 175, ᶠSMITH T., PerspRelSt 29,4 (1992) 399-407.

a425 *Oppenheimer* Aharon, Benevolent societies [*haburot*] in Jerusalem at the end of the Second Temple period [= ⊕ ᴱ*Oppenheimer* A., Perakin 1980, 178-190]: ➤ 132, ᶠMILIK J. 1992, 149-165.

a426 a) *Pixner* Bargil, The Jerusalem Essenes, Barnabas and the Letter to the Hebrews; – b) *Riesner* Rainer, Das Jerusalemer Essenerviertel; Antwort auf einige Einwände: ➤ 132, ᶠMILIK J. 1992, 167-178 / 179-186.

a427 *Rhoads* David, Zealots: ➤ 741, AnchorDB 6 (1992) 1043-1054.

a428 *Stegemann* Hartmut, The Qumran Essenes – local members of the main Jewish union in late Second Temple times: ➤ 498, MQumran 1 (1991/2) 83-166.

a428* **Stemberger** Günter, Pharisäer, Sadduzäer, Essener: SBS 144. Stu 1991, KBW. 144 p. DM 32,30. – ᴿIndTSt 29 (1992) 267s (L. *Legrand*).

к4.3 Samaritani.

a429 *Anderson* Robert T., Samaritans [*Waltke* Bruce K., Pentateuch]: ➤ 741, AnchorBD 5 (1992) 940-7 [932-40].

a430 **Bóid** I., Principles of Samaritan Halachah 1989 ➤ 5,a65; 7,9918: ᴿRHR 209 (1992) 74s (J. P. *Rothschild*).

a431 *Bowman* John, The Gospel of Barnabas and the Samaritans: AbrNahr 30 (1992) 20-33.

a432 ᴱ**Crown** Alan D., The Samaritans 1989 ➤ 5,389 ... 7,9920: ᴿBijdragen 53 (1992) 206s (P. C. *Beentjes*); IsrEJ 42 (1992) 125s (J. C. *Greenfield*, also on ROTHSCHILD-SIXDENIER); Muséon 105 (1992) 193-6 (J. M. Van *Cangh*).

a433 *Dexinger* Ferdinand, Der Ursprung der Samaritaner im Spiegel der frühen Quellen (ineditum) ➤ 349, WegFor 604 (1992) 67-142.

a434 **Egger** Rita, JOSEPHUS F. und die Samaritaner: NOrb 4, ᴰ1986 ➤ 2, 8195 ... 7,9921: ᴿJSS 37 (1992) 109-112 (G. J. *Brooke*).

a435 **Hall** B. W., Samaritan religion from John Hyrcanus to Baba Rabba; a critical examination of the relevant material in contemporary [to them] Christian literature, the writings of Josephus, and the Mishnah [diss.] Sydney 1987 ➤ 5,a68: ᴿHenoch 14 (1992) 294s (S. *Noja*); RelStR 18 (1992) 71 (J. D. *Purvis*).

a436 *a) Pummer* Reinhard, The Samaritans — a Jewish offshoot or a pagan cult?; – *b) Crown* Alan D., The Abisha scroll — 3,000 years old?: BR 7,5 (1991) 22-29 . 40 / 12-21 . 39; ill.

a437 **Rabello** Alfredo M., Giustiniano, Ebrei e Samaritani I. 1987 491 p. II. 1988 p. 492-979 ➤ 4,b89 ... 6,a109: ᴿRÉJ 151 (1992) 374-7 (Mireille *Hadas-Lebel*); ZSav-R 107 (1990) 704-7 (R. *Kerbl*).

a438 **Schur** Nathan, History of the Samaritans: BeitErfAJ 18, 1989 ➤ 5,a75; 6,a111: ᴿBAngIsr 11 (1991s) 38-40 (Joan F. *Taylor*); RelStR 18 (1992) 345 (J. D. *Purvis*).

κ4.5 *Ṣadoqitae, Qaraitae* – Cairo Genizah; Zadokites, Karaites.

a439 *a) Blau* Joshua, On a fragment of the oldest Judaeo-Arabic Bible translation extant; – *b) Khan* Geoffrey, The function of the shewa sign in vocalized Judaeo-Arabic texts from the Genizah; – *c) Wasserstrom* Steven F., The magical texts in the Cairo Genizah: ➤ 457, Genizah 1987/92, 31-39 / 105-111 / 160-6.

a440 ᴱ**Broshi** Magen, The Damascus Document reconsidered [*Qimron* Elisha, text with photos; *Baumgarten* J. M., 51-62; bibliog. 63-83; *García Martínez* F., 9-49]. J 1992, Israel Expl. Soc. 83 p. $20. 965-221-014-5. – ᴿBAR-W 18,4 (1992) 4.6 (H. *Shanks*); BbbOr 34 (1992) 190-2 (E. *Riboldi*); BR 8,5 (1992) 12 (J. *VanderKam*: 'the first Dead Sea Scroll'); Henoch 14 (1992) 195s (Liliana *Rosso Ubigli*).

a441 **Davis** Robert W., The history of the composition of the 'Damascus Document' statutes: diss. Harvard, ᴰ*Strugnell* J. CM 1992. 138 p. – 92-20158. – HarvTR 85 (1992) 495; DissA 53 (1992s) 528-A.

a442 *Dimant* Devorah, ⊕ The Hebrew Bible in the Dead Sea Scrolls; Torah quotations in the Damascus Covenant: ➤ 181, Sha'arei TALMON 1992, 113*-122*; Eng. xx.

a443 *Fenton* Paul B., La synagogue qaraïte du Caire d'après un fragment historique provenant de la Genizah: Henoch 14 (1992) 145-9; 150 texte judéo-arabe; ital. 151.

a444 **Khan** Geoffrey, Karaite Bible manuscripts from the Cairo Genizah 1990 ➤ 6,a116; 9,9929* ['of the CG']: ᴿÉTRel 67 (1992) 103 (J. *Margain*); JJS 43 (1992) 160-3 (S. *Hopkins*).

a444* *Lasker* Daniel J., Karaism and the Jewish-Christian debate [QIRQISANI; some 'Jesus was a good man and his way was the way of Zadok';

some 'Rabbanites conspired against him and killed him'...]: ➤ 180c,
Mem. TALMAGE F. 1 (1992s) 323-332.

a445 ᴱReif Stefan C., Published material from the Cambridge Genizah
collections; a bibliography 1896-1980: 1988 ➤ 6,a121; 7,9932: ᴿJQR 83
(1992s) 201-3 (M. R. *Cohen*).

a446 *Rosso Ubigli* Liliana, Il Documento di Damasco e l'etica coniugale; a
proposito di un nuovo passo qumranico: Henoch 14 (1992) 3-10; Eng. 11.

a447 **Schiffman** Lawrence H., *Swartz* Michael D., Hebrew and Aramaic
incantation texts from the Cairo Geniza ... Box K1: SemitTSt 1. Sheffield
1992, JStOT. 183 p. $42.50. 1-85075-265-0 [BL 93,158, P. W. *Coxon*;
RelStR 19, 88].

a448 **Schur** Nathan, History of the Karaites: BeitErfAJ 29. Fra 1992,
Lang. 207 p. 3-631-44435-4 [OIAc 5,34].

a449 **Trevisan-Semi** Emanuela, Les Caraïtes, un autre judaïsme, ᵀ*Kauders*
Simone. P 1992, A. Michel. 152 p. – ᴿRÉJ 151 (1992) 383s (J.-C. *Attias*).

K5 Judaismus prior vel totus.

a450 **Boccaccini** Gabriele, Middle Judaism: Jewish thought, 300 B.C.E. to
200 C.E. Mp 1991, Fortress. xxvii-289 p. – ᴿBR 8,4 (1992) 59 (J. *VanderKam*); CritRR 5 (1992) 354-6 (D. J. *Harrington*: if 'Judaism' includes
'Christianity', then why not 'Islam'?); Henoch 14 (1992) 334 341 (P.
Sacchi); Pacifica 5 (1992) 326-8 (R. A. *Anderson*).

a451 **Brewer** I., Techniques and assumptions in Jewish exegesis before 70 C.E.
[diss. Cambridge]: TStAJ 30. Tü 1992, Mohr. xiii-299 p. DM 198. 3-16-
145803-6 [BL 93,131, G. *Vermes*: if true, would be a bombshell, but...].

a452 **Cohen** Peter A., A motif-index of the Angel of Death in early rabbinic
literature: diss. Florida State 1992, ᴰ*Priest* J., 262 p. 93-09719. – DissA
53 (1992s) 3943-A.

a453 **Cohen** Raphaël, Le judaïsme en 70 thèmes. P c. 1991, Taleth. 499 p. –
ᴿRÉJ 151 (1992) 210 (G. *Nahon*).

a454 **Cohen** Stuart A., The three crowns; structures of communal politics in
early rabbinic Jewry. C 1990, Univ. xii-294 p. $49.50. – ᴿCritRR 5
(1992) 361-3 (T. *Zahavy*).

a455 **Eisenberg** Josy, Le Judaïsme: Ouverture. P 1989, Grancher. 204 p. –
ᴿRÉJ 151 (1992) 209 (G. *Nahon*).

a456 **Grabbe** Lester L., Judaism from Cyrus to Hadrian, 1. The Persian
and Greek periods; 2. The Roman period. Mp 1992, Fortress. ix-
722 p. $57. 0-8006-2620-6; -1-4 [BL 93,135, P. S. *Alexander*: an excellent
textbook].

a457 *Herrmann* K., Haggada / Halacha : ➤ 762, NBL II,6 (1991) 10-12 /
15-18.

a458 *Janowitz* Naomi, *Lazarus* Andrew, Rabbinic methods of inference and
the rationality debate: JRel 72 (1992) 491-511.

a458* **Johnson** P., Une histoire des juifs [Eng. 1987 ➤ 7,9947]. ᵀ*Quijano*
Jean-Pierre. Saint-Amand-Montront (Cher) 1989. 682 p. – ᴿHelmantica
42 sup (1991) 406s (S. *García-Jalón*).

a459 *a)* *Kraabel* A. T., The disappearance of the 'God-fearers' [< Numen 28
(1981) 113-126]; – *b)* *MacLennan* R. S., *Kraabel* A. T., The God-fearers, a
literary and theological invention [< BAR-W 12,5 (1986) 47-53]; – *c)*
Overman J. Andrew, The God-fearers; some neglected features [< JStNT
32 (1988) 17-26]: ➤ 107, ᶠKRAABEL A. T. 1992, 119-130 / 131-143 /
145-152.

a460 **Levine** Lee I., The rabbinic class of Roman Palestine in late antiquity 1989 ➤ 5,a103*; 7,9949: ᴿCritRR 5 (1992) 373-6 (J. *Neusner*: uncritical, incompetent).

a461 ᴱ**Levine** Lee I., The synagoque in late antiquity 1984/7 ➤ 3,551: ᴿSyria 68 (1991) 487-9 (E. *Will*).

a462 **McKnight** Scot, A light among the Gentiles; Jewish missionary activity in the Second Temple period 1991 ➤ 7,9953: ᴿBR 8,4 (1992) 59s (J. *VanderKam*); TS 53 (1992) 180 (A. J. *Saldarini*).

a463 **Maier** Johann [➤ a242*] Il giudaismo del Secondo Tempio; storia e religione: BtCuRel 59, 1991 ➤ 7,9954: ᴿÉTRel 67 (1992) 594s (Jeanne M. *Léonard*, aussi sur RUSSELL D. ital.); Helmantica 43 (1992) 450s (S. *García-Jalón*).

a464 **Maier** Johann, Storia del giudaismo nell'antichità [1989], ᵀ*Prach* Umberto: StBPaid 99. Brescia 1992, Paideia. 197 p. 88-394-0474-0.

a465 *Martínez* Teresa, Megillat Taʿanit, introducción, traducción y notas ➤ 144, ꟻDíAZ ESTEBAN F., Sefarad 52 (1992) 163-171: Eng. 171.

a466 *Murphy-O'Connor* Jerome, A first-century Jewish mission to Gentiles? [not as clear as W. DALTON supposed]: Pacifica [4 (1992) 51-61] 5 (1992) 32-42; 96-98, Dalton rejoinder.

a467 **Neusner** J., Formative Judaism [1982... ➤ 64,8866... 2,8238] 1985 ➤ 5, a113: ᴿRB 99 (1992) 623s (B. *Viviano*).

a468 **Neusner** Jacob, An introduction to Judaism; a textbook and reader. Louisville 1992, Westminster-Knox. xvi-476 p. $25 pa. 0-664-25348-2 [TDig 39,375].

a469 *Neusner* J., Judaism in the matrix of Christianity² [= ¹1986 ➤ 2,8239 + 67 p. updating]: SFLStHJud 8. Atlanta 1991, Scholars. lxxxv-148 p. $65. 1-55540-607-6 [NTAbs 36,297].

a470 **Neusner** Jacob, Judaism and story; the evidence of The Fathers according to Rabbi Nathan: StHistJud. Ch 1992, Univ. xxi-241 p. $49. 0-226-57630-2 [BL 93,140, Tessa *Rajak*].

a471 **Neusner** Jacob, A short history of Judaism; three meals, three epochs. Mp 1992, Fortress. xiii-235. $13. 0-8006-2552-8 [BL 93,141, H. A. *McKay* shows the difficulty of trying to find coherence in the meal-motif].

a472 *Neusner* Jacob, What we learn from studying religion — and Judaism in particular: BR 7,6 (1991) 40.42.

a473 **Nodet** Étienne, Essai sur les origines du Judaïsme; de Josué aux Pharisiens. P 1992, Cerf. 296 p. 2-204-04493-8. – ᴿRTLv 23 (1992) 472-481 (J.-C. *Haelewyck*: origine postexilique du sabbat ...).

a474 **Ognibeni** Bruno, Index biblique à la 'Ochlah w'ochlah' de S. FRENSDORFF: Henoch Quad 5. T 1992, Zamorani. [vi-] 114 p. Lit. 35.000 [BO 49,588].

a475 *Overman* J. Andrew, al., Judaism (Greco-Roman, Egypt etc.), various articles): ➤ 741, AnchorBD 3 (1992) 1057-1089 (1073-6 'Judaism in Rome' is by Romano *Penna*).

a476 *a) Overman* J. Andrew, The diaspora in the modern study of ancient Judaism; – *b) Neusner* Jacob, The two vocabularies of symbolic discourse in ancient Judaism: ➤ 107, ꟻKRAABEL A. 1992, 63-78 / 79-103.

a477 **Phillips** Elaine A., 'Mekhilta d'Rabbi ISHMAEL', a study in composition and context: diss. Annenberg. Ph 1991. 810 p. 92-30469. – DissA 53 (1992s) 2414-A.

a478 **Romero** E., La ley en la leyenda; relatos de tema bíblico en las fuentes hebreas [antología Hagada]. M 1989, Cons. Sup. Inv. 667 p. – ᴿComSev 24 (1991) 108 (M. de *Burgos*).

Roth Joel, The halakhic process, a systemic analysis 1986 ➤ 7362.

a479 **Sanders** E. P., Jewish law from Jesus to the Mishnah 1990 ➤ 6,295: ᴿCritRR 5 (1992) 382-4 (A. J. *Saldarini*: challenging debate with NEUSNER); JQR 83 (1992s) 405-7 (J. M. *Baumgarten*).

a480 **Sanders** E. P., Judaism, practice and belief, 63 BCE- 66 CE. L/Ph 1992, SCM/Trinity. 580 p. £20. − ᴿJJS 43 (1992) 307-310 (S. *Stern*); BtS 149 (1992) 380 (E. H. *Merrill*).

a481 *Schiffman* Lawrence H., From text to tradition; a history of Second Temple and Rabbinic Judaism 1991 ➤ 7,9970: ᴿBR 8,4 (1992) 15s (M. *Goodman*).

a482 **Schubert** Kurt, Die Religion des Judentums. Lp 1992, Benno. 298 p. DM 34. 3-7462-0509-9 [TLZ 118, 398, L. *Wächter*: Lob].

a483 **Schwarzwald** Ora, ⊕ Pirqe Abot Ladino: Edah wᵉ-Lašon 13, 1989 ➤ 7,9970*; ᴿJQR 83 (1992s) 290-3 (P. *Wexler*).

a484 **Stemberger** Günter, Il giudaismo classico; cultura e storia del tempo rabbinico (dal 70 al 1040) [1979], ᵀBarbieri Mariangela, ᵀᴱCattani Daniela & Luigi: Tradizione d'Israele 7. R 1991, Città Nuova. 348 p. 88-311-4914-8.

a485 *Wilcox* Max, Myth, legend and *midrash* in early Jewish thought: Prudentia 24,2 (1992) 6-31.

a486 **Will** Édouard, Orrieux Claude, 'Prosélytisme juif'?; histoire d'une erreur. P 1992, BLettres. 399 p. F 170. 2-251-38016-7. − ᴿRechSR 80 (1992) 471s (P. *Vallin*).

a487 *Wilson* Stephen G., Gentile Judaizers: NTS 38 (1992) 605-616.

a488 **Wylen** Stephen M., Settings of silver 1989 ➤ 6,a171; 7,9975: ᴿRRel 51 (1992) 151s (J. G. *Leies*).

K6 **Mišna**, *tosepta; Tannaim.*

a489 ᵀᴱCorrens D., Mischna: a) 3/5, Naschim/Gittin 1991 ➤ 7,9975*: ᴿArTGran 55 (1992) 434s (A. *Torres*); − b) 2/9 Taanijot, Fastentage, 1989 ➤ 5,a140: ᴿBO 49 (1992) 491-4 (W. *Zuidema*).

a490 **Destro** Adriana, In caso di gelosia; antropologia del rituale di Sotah. Bo 1989, Mulino. 236 p. Lit. 26.000. − ᴿBbbOr 34 (1992) 120 (E. *Jucci*).

a490* ᴱKuyt A., Uchelen N. A. van, History and form; Dutch studies in the Mishnah: Palache Inst. 4, Amst 1988, UvA. 1988 ➤ 7,9997 viii-107 p. [90-7139605-3]: ᴿNedTTs 46 (1992) 241s (P. W. van der *Horst*: '-04-5').

a491 *Lieberman* Abraham A., Again, the words of Gad the seer: JBL [109 (1990) 475-492, M. BAR-ILAN dates Mishnaic but without the expected indication of Greek vocabulary-influence] 111 (1992) 313s.

a492 **Neusner** J., A history of the Mishnaic law of damages I - 5, 1983-5 ➤ 64,8899 ... 6,a180: ᴿOLZ 87 (1992) 266-9 (L. *Wächter*).

a493 **Neusner** Jacob, Judaism without Christianity ... Mishnah 1991 ➤ 7, 9981: ᴿBLitEc 93 (1992) 401s (S. *Légasse*: son Evidence of the Mishnah 1981 ²1987 pour des non-spécialistes).

a494 **Neusner** Jacob, The Mishnah, introduction and reader. Ph 1992, Trinity. xii-226 p. $17. 1-56338-021-8 [TDig 40,178].

a495 **Neusner** Jacob, Rabbinic political theory; religion and politics in the Mishnah 1991 ➤ 7,9985: ᴿCritRR 5 (1992) 380-2 (R. A. *Kugler*: admits dependence on WEBER).

a496 **Neusner** Jacob, Sources of the transformation of Judaism; from philosophy to religion in the classics of Judaism; a reader: SFLStHJud 68. Atlanta 1992, Scholars. xiv-307 p. 1-55540-813-3.

a497 **Neusner** Jacob, The transformation of Judaism; from philosophy to religion. Urbana 1992, Univ. Illinois. xvi-345 p. $35. 0-252-01805-2 [TDig 40,78].

a497* — *Neusner* J., From Mishnaic philosophy to Talmudic religion; the transformation of Judaism between 200 and 400 A.D.: American Academy of Theology 58,4 (Miss 1990) 633-652.

a498 *Neusner* Jacob, Biblical exegesis and the formation of Judaism; Sifra [Lev] and the problem of the Mishnah: ➤ 181, Shaʿarei TALMON 1992, 345-363.

a499 *Neusner* Jacob, Méthode philosophique de la Mishna; le Judaïsme hiérarchique; classement dans le contexte gréco-romain, ᵀ*Bossy* Michel-André: RÉJ 150 (1991) 283-296.

a500 **Porton** Gary G., Goyim ... in Mishnah-Tosefta: BrownJudSt 155, 1988 ➤ 5,a155: ᴿRelStR 18 (1992) 155 (S. D. *Fraade*).

a501 **Urbach** Ephraim E. (*zal* July 1991), The Halakhah, its sources and development, ᵀ*Posner* Raphael, 1986 ➤ 2,8279: ᴿRB 99 (1992) 623 (B. T. *Viviano*).

K6.5 **Talmud; midraš.**

a502 *Becker* Hans-Jürgen, Verstreute Yerushalmi-Texte in MS Moskau 1133: FraJudBeit 19 (1991s) 31-61.

a503 **Bialik** Hayim N., *Ravnitzky* Yehoshua H., The book of legends, *Sefer ha-Aggadah*; legends from the Talmud and Midrash, ᵀ*Braude* William C. NY 1992, Schocken. xxii-897 p. 0-8052-4113-2 [OIAc 5,14].

a504 **Bietenhard** Hans, Midrasch Tanḥuma B[uber] 1980/2 ➤ 62,9552; 63, 8797: ᴿBijdragen 53 (1992) 91s (M. *Poorthuis*: commentary on some Pentateuch-texts).

a505 **Bokser** B. Z. & B. M., Talmud 1989 ➤ 6,a193: ᴿVidyajyoti 55 (1991) 117s (P. M. *Meagher*).

a506 **Boyarin** Daniel, Intertextuality and the reading of midrash [Ex 13-18] 1990 ➤ 6,a194; 7,9988: ᴿCritRR 5 (1992) 356-9 (T. *Zahavy*; nowhere deals with rabbinism); Salesianum 54 (1992) 156s (R. *Vicent*).

a507 *Boyarin* Daniel, On the status of the Tannaitic Midrashim [NEUSNER J. 1990]: JAOS 112 (1992) 455-465.

a508 *Cohen* Naomi G., Taryag [b Makkot 238 : 613 precepts?] and the Noahide commandments: JJS 43 (1992) 46-57.

a509 **Hauptmann** Judith, Development of the Talmudic sugya 1988 ➤ 5,a171: ᴿJQR 83 (1992s) 187-190 (N. *Aminoam*).

a510 *a) Herr* M. D., L'herméneutique juive et chrétienne des figures bibliques à l'époque du deuxième temple, de la Mishna et du Talmud; – *b*) *Fishbane* Michael, The 'measures' of God's glory in the ancient Midrash: ➤ 57, ᶠFLUSSER D., Messiah 1992, 99-109 / 53-74.

a511 ᵀᴱ**Hüttenmeister** Frowald G., Sheqalim/Scheqelsteuer: ᵀYerushalmi 2/5. Tü 1990, Univ. Inst. Judaicum. xviii-185 p. DM 128. 3-16-145607-6. – ᴿSalesianum 54 (1992) 376s (R. *Vicent*); TLZ 117 (1992) 502s (W. *Wiefel*).

a512 **Jacobs** Louis, Structure and form in the Babylonian Talmud. C 1991, Univ. xii-138 p. £25. 0-521-40345-6. – ᴿCritRR 5 (1992) 369-371 (J. *Neusner*: does not make clear just how he moves beyond HALIVNI); TvT 32 (1992) 310 (M. *Poorthuis*).

a513 **Kalmin** Richard, The redaction of the Babylonian Talmud; Amoraic or Sabaic? 1989 ➤ 6,a205: ᴿJRel 72 (1992) 136s (J. M. *Harris*).

a514 **Kraemer** David, The mind of the Talmud; an intellectual history of the Bavli 1990 → 7,9996: [R]CritRR 5 (1992) 371-3 (R. A. *Kugler*: mostly convincing); JAOS 112 (1992) 325-7 (J. *Neusner*).

a515 *Lerner* M. B., reconstruction of jHagiga 2,7 etc.: Lešonenu 53 (1989) 287s & 56 (1991s) 363-370 answering *Milikowsky* C., 361; all ⊙.

a516 **Lieberman** Saul, [all only ⊙] Studies in Palestinian Talmudic literature, [E]*Rosenthal* David. J 1991, Magnes. [x-] 667 p. 965-223-772-8.

a517 [TE]**Loopik** Marcus van, The ways of the Sages and the way of the world; the minor tractates of the Babylonian Talmud: Derekh 'Eretz Rabbah, Derekh 'Eretz Zuta, Pereq ha-Shalom; TStAJ 26, 1991 → 7, 9998: [R]AustralBR 40 (1992) 75s (J. S. *Levi*); BL (1992) 124 (A. P. *Hayman*: muddled and badly translated); CritRR 5 (1992) 376-8 (M. S. *Jaffee*: great labor marred by editing errors).

a518 **Manns** F., Le Midrash; approche et commentaire de l'Écriture 1990 → 7,9999: [R]NRT 114 (1992) 130s (D. *Luciani*).

a519 *Mayer* Günter, Midrasch/Midraschim: → 768, TRE 22 (1992) 614-724.

a520 **Milgrom** Jo, Handmade Midrash. Ph 1992, Jewish Publication Soc. xi-177 p. $25; pa. $16 [CBQ 54,835].

a521 **Neusner** J., The Bavli's one voice; types and forms of analytical discourse and their fixed order of appearance: SFLStHistJud 24. Atlanta 1991, Scholars xxix-536 p. $90. 1-55540-604-1 [NTAbs 36,297].

a522 **Neusner** J., The Bavli's own statement; the metapropositional program of Babylonian Talmud tractate Zebahim chapters One and Five: SFLStHistJud 30. Atlanta 1991, Scholars. xxviii-254 p. $70. 1-55540-637-8 [NTAbs 36,297: title 'Bavli's One', text 'Bavli's Own'].

a523 **Neusner** Jacob, The Bavli that might have been; the Tosefta's theory of Mishnah commentary compared with the Bavli's: SFLStJ 18. Atlanta 1990, Scholars. xv-215 p. [JAOS 112,359].

a524 **Neusner** J., Canonical history ... Sifra/Sifré 1990 → 7,a4: [R]Salesianum 54 (1992) 790s (R. *Vicent*).

a525 **Neusner** J., The rules of composition of the Talmud of Babylonia; the cogency of the Bavli's composite: SFLStHistJud 13. Atlanta 1991, Scholars. xxiv-253 p. $60. 1-55540-538-9 [NTAbs 36,298].

a527 **Neusner** Jacob, Symbol and theology in early Judaism. Mp 1991, Fortress. 242 p. $15. 0-8006-2456-4. – [R]ExpTim 103 (1991s) 382 (F. *Morgan*: new viewpoints on midrash).

a528 **Neusner** Jacob, Tradition as selectivity; Scripture, Mishnah, Tosefta and Midrash in the Talmud of Babylonia; the case of Tractate Arakhin. SFLStJud 9. Atlanta 1990, Scholars. xiv-231 p. [JAOS 112,359].

a529 **Neusner** Jacob, The Talmud; a close encounter. Mp 1991, Fortress. xi-186 p. $13. 0-8006-2498-X [TDig 39, 277].

a530 **Neusner** Jacob, The Talmud, an American translation 1990 31AB, Bekhorot 1-4; 5-9. xvi-166; xix-196 p. $55 + 60 Brown **219**s; 33, Temirah, xvi-221 $60, **218**; 1991 25AB, Abodah Zarah, xxv-196; xxv-204; $50, **227**s; 28C, Zebahim, 9-14; xiv-240; $65, **234**; 34, Keritot, xvi-202; $60, **223**; 36AB, Niddah 1-3; 4-10; xvi-189; xvi-236; $55; 60, **221**s; 14, Makkot, 1991, **238**. 1-55540 plus 553-3; 554-1; 521-5; 594-0; 595-9; 606-8; 546-0; 555-X; 556-8; -. [< NTAbs 36,298s].

a531 *Neusner* Jacob, Language as taxonomy; the rules for using Hebrew and Aramaic in the Babylonian Talmud [cf. → 7,a5]: → 132, [F]MILIK J. 1992, 327-342.

a532 *Niehoff* Maren, [bBer 55a] A dream which is not interpreted is like a letter which is not read: JJS 43 (1992) 58-84.

a533 **Ouaknin** Marc-Alain, [2rev] *Smilévitch* Éric, Chapitres de Rabbi Éliézer; midrach sur Genèse, Exode, Nombres, Esther: Les Dix Paroles. Lagrasse 1992, Verdier. 382 p. 2-86432-030-4.

a534 [TE]**Paperon** Bernard, Le Talmud, traité Makkot. Lagrasse c. 1990, Verdier. 288 p. – [R]RÉJ 151 (1992) 224 (G. *Nahon*).

a535 *Porton* Gary G., Talmud ➤ 741, AnchorBD 6 (1992) 510-515.

a536 *Samely* Alexander, Scripture's implicature; the midrashic assumptions of relevance and consistency: JSS 37 (1992) 167-205.

a537 **Schäfer** P., *Becker* H.-J., Ordnung Zera'im: Berakhot und Pe'a: Synopse zum Talmud Yerushalmi 1/1s: TStAntJ 31, 1991 ➤ 7,a7*; DM 348: [R]NRT 114 (1992) 776 (X. *Jacques*).

a538 **Schäfer** Peter, *Becker* Hans-Jürgen, *al.*, all **O**, Synopse zum Talmud Yerushalmi, Zeraim, Berakhot, I/3-5, Demai, Kil'aim, Shevi'it; 1/6-11, Terumot ... [bis] Bikkurim: TStAJud 33.35. Tü 1992, Mohr. v-321 p.; DM 318 / v-499 p. 3-16-145924-5; -6006-5 [BL 93,148, A.P. *Hayman*].

a539 *a) Schremer* Adiel, **O** Between text transmission and text redaction; fragments of a different recension of bMo'ed-Qaṭan from the Genizah; – *b) Naeh* Shlomo, **O** Did the Tannaim interpret the script of the Torah differently from the authorized reading?: Tarbiz 61 (1991s) 375-399 / 401-448; Eng. II-III.

a540 **Steinsaltz** Adin, The Talmud 4/4, Bava Metzia; 7/1 Ketubot. NY 1991, Random. xii-274 p. / xii-219 p. 0-394-58853-3 / 0-679-40769-3 [sic, OIAc 2,28].

a541 **Steinsaltz** Adin, Talmud 1989 Reference Guide ➤ 5,a190: [R]NTAbs 36 (1992) 303; Parabola 15,2 (1990) 94.98.100 (Judith *Hauptman*).

a542 **Stemberger** Günter, Einleitung in Talmud und Midrasch [8rev](first without *Strack* as prior author). Mü 1992, Beck. 367 p. 3-406-36695-3.

a543 [*Strack* H.L.], [E]**Stemberger** G., Introduction to the Talmud and Midrash, [T]*Bockmuehl* M. 1991 ➤ 7,a9*: [R]BL (1992) 130s (P.S. *Alexander*); BSO 55 (1992) 121s (S.B. *Leperer*); ExpTim 103 (1991s) 87s (F. *Morgan*: heavily influenced by NEUSNER; e.g. first chapter now 'The historical framework' instead of 'Definition of terms'); JTS 43 (1992) 225-7 (N. de *Lange*).

a544 **Stemberger** Günter, Midrasch; vom Umgang der Rabbinen mit der Bibel 1989 ➤ 5,a193; 7,a9: [R]Henoch 14 (1992) 341s (M. *Perani*); TLZ 117 (1992) 118s (S. *Schreiner*); TvT 32 (1992) 310 (W. *Weren*); ZkT 114 (1992) 94s (R. *Oberforcher*).

a545 **Stern** David, Parables in midrash 1991 ➤ 7,a12: [R]TS 53 (1992) 781s (A.J. *Saldarini*).

a546 **Taradach** Madeleine, Le Midrash 1991 ➤ 7,a13: [R]CBQ 54 (1992) 592s (B.L. *Visotsky*: 'la Midrash'; recommended to only-French readers); ETL 68 (1992) 160s (J. *Lust*: excellent).

a547 **Tilly** H.-P., Zur Formerhebung nicht-diskursiver Textstrukturen; ein Beitrag zur Formanalyse sequentieller Texte in jMoed Qatan [diss.]: FraJudBei 19/2 (1991) 1-29 [< ZAW 105, 286].

K7.1 **Judaismus mediaevalis,** *generalia.*

a549 **Abecassis** Armand, La pensée juive. P 1987, Librairie Générale Française. 331 + p. – [R]RÉJ 150 (1991) 176-9 (E. *Couteau*).

a550 *a) Assis* Yom Tov, Jewish attitudes to Christian power in medieval Spain; – *b) Carrete Parrondo* Carlos, *Morno Koch* Yolanda, 'Duelos os dé Dios ... se avrá christiandad'; nueva página sobre el criptojudaismo castellano: → 155, FROMANO VENTURA D., Sefarad 52 (1992) 291-304; castellano 304 / 369-379; Eng. 380.

a551 **Faur** José, In the shadow of history; Jews and conversos at the dawn of modernity [Maimonides to Ferdinand and Isabella]. Albany 1992, SUNY. x-311 p. $59.50; pa. $20. 0-7914-0801-9; –2-7 [TDig 39,361].

a552 *Goetschel* Roland, Nature et miracle dans la pensée juive du Moyen Âge: ProbHistRel 2 (Bru 1991) 167-184 [< ZIT 92,68].

a553 **Hayoun** Maurice-Ruben, La philosophie médiévale juive 1991 → 7,a22: RScripTPamp 24 (1992) 1087s (M. *Lluch-Baixauli*).

a554 **Newby** Gordon D., A history of the Jews of Arabia, from ancient times to their eclipse under Islam: St.Comp.Rel. 1988 → 7,a28: RRelStR 18 (1992) 179-187 (W. *Brinner*; 187-9 response).

a555 *a) Perani* Mauro, II. Congresso internazionale su L'inquisizione e gli ebrei in Italia (Livorno-Pisa, 9-10 nov. 1992); – *b) Capelli* Pietro, La cultura ebraica all'epoca di Lorenzo il Magnifico (Firenze, Accademia 29 nov. 1992): Henoch 14 (1992) 318-323 / 323s.

a556 **Rybár** C., Praga ebraica, glossa ad una storia e ad una cultura; la guida attraverso i monumenti. Praha 1991, Akropolis. – RHenoch 14 (1992) 368s (D. *Pelandi*).

a557 **Sáenz Badillos** A., *Targarona Borras* J., Gramáticos hebreos de Al-Andalus (siglos x-xii); filología y Biblia, 1988 → 5,a213: RHelmantica 43 (1992) 456s (S. *García-Jalón*).

a558 **Sirat** Colette, La filosofia ebraica medievale secondo i testi editi e inediti [1983], TCarena B., EChiesa B.: Philosophica 1. Brescia 1990, Paideia. 629 p. – RCC 143 (1992,3) 209 (G. *Pirola*); Henoch 14 (1992) 208-216 (M. *Zonta*); RivStoLR 28 (1992) 433-5 (Elena *Loewenthal*).

a559 **Stern** David, *Mirski* Mark J., Rabbinic fantasies; imaginative narratives from classical Hebrew literature. NY 1990, Jewish Publ. 376 p. $27.50. – RParabola 17,1 (1992) 106.108.110s (E. *Shore*).

a560 **Toaff** Ariel, Il vino e la carne; una comunità ebraica nel Medioevo. Bo 1989, Mulino. 324 p. – RSefarad 51 (1991) 216s (M. *Orfali*).

a561 *Vivacqua* Sonia, *a)* Gli Ebrei in Sicilia sino all'espulsione del 1492 (Palermo, 15-19 giugno 1992): – *b)* L'Ebraismo dell'Italia meridionale peninsulare dalle origini al 1541; società, economia, cultura; (Assoc. It. per lo studio del Giudaismo). – RHenoch 14 (1992) 309-312-315.

a562 *Wasserstein* David J., Jews, Christians and Muslims in medieval Spain: JJS 43 (1992) 175-186.

a563 **Wiesel** Elie, Sages and dreamers; biblical, Talmudic, and Hasidic portraits and legends. NY 1991, Summit. 443 p. $35. – RParabola 17,4 (1992) 103s (M. *Krassen*).

a564 *Zuidema* W., Het verschijnsel Leerhuis: Ter Herkenning 19,1 (1991) 1-13 [< GerefTTs 91,116].

K7.2 Maimonides.

a565 **Alexander** Tamar, *Romero* Elena, Érase una vez... Maimónides, cuentos tradicionales hebreos, antología: EstCulturaEbr 8. Córdoba 1988, Almendro. 282 p. – RSefarad 51 (1991) 459s (A. *Alba*).

a566 *Bertola* F., Mosé Maimonide e il problema del male: Archivio di Filosofia 59 (1991) 307-322 [< FilT 6,507].

a567 **Bruckstein** Almut S., Hermann COHEN's [1908] 'Charakteristik der Ethik Maimunis'; a reconstructive reading of Maimonides' ethics: diss. Temple, DSamuelson M. Ph 1992. 258 p. 92-27440. – DissA 53 (1992s) 1553-A.

a568 **Fox** M., Interpreting Maimonides 1990 → 6,a259; 7,a36; ᴿRÉJ 151 (1992) 184-7 (A. *Ages*).

a569 *Frank* Daniel, Maimonides survey: JJS 43 (1992) 232-7.

a570 *Harvey* Steven, Did Maimonides' letter to Samuel IBN-TIBBON determine which philosophers would be studied by later Jewish thinkers?: JQR 83 (1992s) 51-70.

a571 ᴱ**Hyman** Arthur, Maimonidean studies I, 1990 → 7,a38: ᴿJQR 83 (1992s) 429-432 (H. *Kreisel*: to be an ongoing journal).

a571* *Ivry* Alfred L., Strategies of interpretation in Maimonides' Guide of the Perplexed: → 180c, Mém. TALMAGE F. 2 (= Jewish History 6, 1992) 113-130.

a572 **Lazar** Moshe, Maimonides, Guide for the perplexed, a 15th century Spanish translation by PEDRO de Toledo 1989 → 7,a40*: ᴿSefarad 51 (1991) 465s (C. del *Valle*).

a572* **Leaman** Oliver, Moses Maimonides: Arabic thought and culture 1990 → 6,a572*: ᴿBSO 55 (1992) 319s (N. *Calder* compares to FOX M. 1990).

a573 **Leibovitz** Yechayahou, La foi de Maïmonide [❶], ᵀᴱ*Banon* David: Patrimoines Judaïsme. P 1992, Cerf. 113 p. 2-204-04592-6.

a574 **Niewöhner** Friedrich, Maimonides; Aufklärung und Toleranz im Mittelalter 1988 → 5,a229: ᴿRÉJ 150 (1991) 196s (G. *Freudenthal*).

a575 **Robelin** Jean, Maïmonide et le langage religieux: Pratiques théoriques. P 1991, PUF. 222 p. F 149. 2-13-043765-6. – ᴿÉTRel 67 (1992) 446s (Jeanne M. *Léonard*).

a576 *Starobinski-Safran* Esther, Le Roi-Messie et les temps messianiques dans la pensée de Maïmonide: NVFr 66 (1991) 149-160.

a577 ᴱ**Valle** Carlos del, Cartas y testamento de Maimónides (1138-1204) EstDoc 8. Córdoba 1989, Monte de Piedad. 360 p. – ᴿBO 49 (1992) 842-4 (W. M. *Reedijk*); Sefarad 51 (1991) 473s (L. *Díez Merino*).

a578 **Weiss** Raymond L., Maimonides' ethics; the encounter of philosophic and religious morality. Ch 1991, Univ. ix-224 p. $30. 0-226-89152-6 [TDig 39,293].

κ7.3 Alii magistri Judaismi mediaevalis.

a579 SAADYA: *Avishur* Yitzhak, Some new sources for the study of the text and language of Saadya's translation of the Pentateuch into Judaeo-Arabic: → 457, Genizah 1987/92, 5-13.

a580 *a*) *Klener* Ronald C., Saadia and the Sefer Yetzirah; translation theory in classical Jewish thought; – *b*) *Ross* Jacob J., The divine command theory in Jewish thought; a modern phenomenon: → 514, Interpretation 1992, 169-179 / 181-206.

a581 RASHI: *Dahan* Gilbert, Un dossier latin de textes de Rashi autour de la controverse de 1240: RÉJ 151 (1992) 321-336.

a582 IBN EZRA [→ 359]: ᴱ**Diaz Esteban** Fernando, A. ibn Ezra y su tiempo 1989/90 → 7,427*: ᴿBSO 55 (1992) 549-552 (J. A. *Abu-Haidar*); RÉJ 151 (1992) 182-4 (J.-C. *Attias*).

a583 *a*) *Brin* Gershon, ❶ Problems of composition and redaction in the Bible according to R. A. Ibn Ezra; – *b*) *Mondschein* Aaron, ❶ On the attitude of R. A. Ibn Ezra to the exegetical usage of the hermeneutic norm *gematria*; – *c*) *Orfali* Moisés, ❶ A. Ibn-Ezra and Jewish-Christian polemics: → 359, Teʿuda 8 (1992). 121-135; Eng. XVI / 137-151; Eng. XIV / 193-205; Eng. XIII.

a584 KIMḤI: *Chazan* Robert, Joseph Kimḥi's Sefer ha-Berit; pathbreaking medieval Jewish apologetics: HarvTR 85 (1992) 417-432.

a585 *Netzer* Nissan, ❻ Semantic studies in medieval Hebrew lexicography [... Kimḥi]: Tarbiz 61 (1991) 449-464; Eng. IV [not on specific words but on progress of scholarly interest].

a586 ABRAVANEL: **Attias** Jean-Christophe, Isaac Abravanel, La mémoire et l'espérance: Toledot-Judaïsmes. P 1992, Cerf. 302 p. 2-204-04651-5.

a587 FALAQUERA: **Harvey** Steven, Falaquera's 'epistle of the debate', an introduction to Jewish philosophy: HarvJudTS 8, 1987 ⇒ 7,a54*: ᴿJQR 81 (1990s) 437-440 (M. *Blaustein*).

a588 IBN DAUD: ᵀ**Samuelson** Norbert M., ᴱ*Weiss* Gordon. Abraham ibn Daud, The exalted faith [1160]. Cranbury NJ 1986, Assoc. Univ. Pr. 406 p. – ᴿRÉJ 150 (1991) 193-6 (G. *Freudenthal*).

a589 IBN ADRET: *Orfali* Moisés, La cuestión de la venida del Mesías en un responsum de Rabbí Šelomó ibn Adret al Cahal de Lérida [c. 1280]: Helmántica 43 (1992) 203-230.

a590 BEN-ISAAC 1110-1175: ᵀᴱ**Mutius** Hans-Georg, Ephraim von Regensburg, Hymnen und Gebete: JudTSt 10. Hildesheim 1988, Olms. xxi-171 p. 3 487-09086-4.

a591 BARHEBRAEUS (Gregorios 1226-86): **Zonta** Mauro, Fonti greche e orientali dell'economia di Bar-Hebraeus nell'opera 'La crema della scienza': AION 70,1 supp. to 52 (1992). [iv-] 135 p.

a592 ᴱ**Lazar** Moshe, Libro de las generaciones & The book of Yashar: Sephardic Classical Library 3. Culver City CA 1989, Labyrinthos. xxviii-516 p. – ᴿSefarad 51 (1991) 464s (C. del *Valle*).

K7.4 Qabbalâ, Zohar, Merkabâ — Jewish mysticism.

a593 *Fenton* Paul B., La 'tête entre les genoux'; contribution à l'étude d'une posture méditative dans la mystique juive et islamique: RHPR 72 (1992) 413-425; Eng. 522.

a594 *Goetschel* Roland, La troisième conférence internationale sur l'histoire de la mystique juive, 'Le Zohar et son époque' (Jérusalem 16-18 février 1988): RÉJ 150 (1991) 273-5.

a595 ᵀᴱ**Hansel** Joëlle, LUZZATTO Moïse H. [1707-c. 1743]. Le philosophe et le cabbaliste; exposition d'un débat: Les Dix Paroles 1991 ⇒ 7,a59*: ᴿÉTRel 67 (1992) 447 (Jeanne M. *Léonard*).

a596 *Huss* Boaz, ❻ *Sefer Poqeaḥ Ivrim* — new information on the history of Kabbalistic literature: Tarbiz 61 (1991s) 489-504; Eng. V.

a597 **Idel** Moshe, Kabbalah; new perspectives 1988 ⇒ 4,b248 ... 7,a60: ᴿJRel 72 (1992) 137-9 (E. R. *Wolfson*).

a598 **Janowitz** Naomi, The poetics of ascent 1989 ⇒ 5,a205 ... 7,a63: ᴿJQR 83 (1992s) 283s (M. *Verman*).

a599 **Lachower** Fischel, *Tishby* Isaiah, The wisdom of the Zohar, an anthology of texts [❻], ᵀ*Goldstein* David: Littman Library. Ox 1989, pa. 1991, UP. £120 / £60, 0-19-710076-7 [BL 93,152, A. G. *Auld* (1991, 149)].

a600 *Murray-Jones* C.R.A., Transformational mysticism in the apocalyptic-Merkabah tradition: JJS 43 (1992) 1-31.

a601 *Rohrbacher-Sticker* Claudia, Die Namen Gottes und die Namen Metatrons; zwei Geniza-Fragmente zur Hekhalot-Literatur: FraJudBei 19 (1991s) 95-168 [169-185, magische Traditionen].

a602 **Schäfer** Peter, The hidden and manifest God; some major themes in early Jewish mysticism [1991 ⇒ 7,a66],ᵀ: Judaica; hermeneutics, mysticism, and religion. Albany 1992, SUNY. xii-198 p. 0-7914-1043-9; pa. -4-7. [BL 93,147, A. P. *Hayman*].

a603 ᴱ**Schäfer** P., Übersetzung der Hekhalot-Literatur [→ 7,a65] 4. §§ 598-985: TStAntJud 29. Tü 1991, Mohr. xlv-208 p. DM 98. 3-16-145745-5 [NTAbs 36, 302]. – ᴿBL (1992) 129 (A. P. *Hayman*: last volume; first still awaited); NedTTs 46 (1992) 72s (P. W. van der *Horst*, 2).

a604 **Scholem** Gershom, On the mystical shape of the Godhead; basic concepts in the Kabbalah, [❶ 1976]; ᵀ*Neugroschel* Joachim, ²ʳᵉᵛ*Chipman* Jonathan]. NY 1991, Schocken. 328 p. $30. 0-8052-4082-9 [TDig 39,285].

a605 **Swartz** Michael D., Mystical prayer in ancient Judaism; an analysis of Maᶜaseh Merkavah [< diss. 1986 NYU, ᴰ*Schiffman* L.]: TStAntJ 28. Tü 1992, Mohr. x-268 p. DM 148. 3-16-145679-3 [NTAbs 36,455]. – ᴿRel-StR 18 (1992) 345 (M. S. *Jaffee*).

a606 **Verman** Mark, The books of contemplation; medieval Jewish mystical sources: Judaica. Albany 1992, SUNY. viii-270 p. $49.50; pa $17. 0-7914-0719-5; –20–9 [TDig 39,391].

a607 **Werses** Shmuel, ❶ Haskalah... and Sabbatianism; the story of a controversy. J 1988, Shazar Center. 276 p. – ᴿJQR 83 (1992s) 199s (E. *Carlebach*).

a607* **Wirszubski** Chaim, Pico della MIRANDOLA's encounter with Jewish mysticism 1989 → 6,a319: ᴿHeythJ 33 (1992) 457s (A. *Hamilton*, also on EDWARDS J., KIM H.-M.).

---

a608 ABULAFIA (1240-1292): **Idel** Moshe, Language, Torah, and hermeneutics in Abraham Abulafia 1989 → 6,a395: ᴿJQR 83 (1992s) 294-6 (E. R. *Wolfson*); Speculum 67 (1992) 159-162 (I. G. *Marcus*, also on CHIPMAN J.).

a609 QARA: **Brin** G., ❶ Studies in the biblical exegesis of R. Joseph Qara 1990 → 6,a298: ᴿZAW 104 (1992) 144 (I. *Kottsieper*).

K7.5 Judaismus saec. 14-18.

a610 **Attias** Jean-Christophe, Le commentaire biblique; Mordekhai KOMTINO [1402-82] ou l'herméneutique du dialogue: Patrimoines Judaïsme 1991 → 7,a74: ᴿÉTRel 67 (1992) 104s (J.-M. *Léonard*).

a611 *Blanco Martínez* Asunción, *Romano* David, Vidal (Ben) Saúl SATORRE, copista hebreo (1383-1411): Sefarad 51 (1991) 3-11; Eng. 11.

a612 **Bonfil** Robert, Rabbis and Jewish communities in Renaissance Italy (❶), ᵀ*Chapman* Jonathan: Littman Library. Ox 1990, UP. 366 p. – ᴿJSS 37 (1992) 338-340 (Joanna *Weinberg*).

a613 *Brague* Rémi, Deux livres récents sur Moïse de NARBONNE [HAYOUN M. 1986/9]: RechSR 80 (1992) 85-90.

a614 **Breuer** Edward, Politics, tradition, history; rabbinic Judaism and the eighteenth-century struggle for civil equality: HarvTR 85 (1992) 357-383.

a615 **Carpi** Daniel, ❶ Between Renaissance and ghetto; essays on the history of the Jews in Italy in the 14th [to] 17th centuries: Rosenberg Project. TA 1989, Univ. 308 p. – ᴿSefarad 51 (1991) 204-6 (A. *David*, ᵀM. *Orfali*).

a616 **Frakes** Harold C., The politics of interpretation; alterity and ideology in Old Yiddish studies. Albany 1989, SUNY. xv-283 p. – ᴿJQR 83 (1992s) 408-410 (J. *Biehl*).

a617 **Gampel** Benjamin R., The last Jews on Iberian soil; Navarrese Jewry, 1479-1498. Berkeley 1989, Univ. California. xi-226 p. – ᴿJQR 83 (1992s) 240s (Renée L. *Melammed*).

a618 GERSONIDES (Levi, 1288-1344): ᴱ**Dahan** Gilbert, Gersonide en son temps; science et philosophie médiévales, préf. *Touati* Charles: RÉJ coll. 11. Lv 1991, Peeters. 384 p.

a619 — **Weil** Gérard E., ᴱ*Chartrain* Frédéric, *al.*, La bibliothèque de Gersonide d'après son catalogue autographe: RÉJ coll. 10. Lv 1991, Peeters. 167 p.; 7 fig.

a620 **Kaplan** S., Les Falashas. Turnhout 1990, Brepols. [➤ 6,b233]: ᴿHelmantica 43 (1992) 465-7 (S. *Garcia-Jalón*).

a621 **Kaplan** Yosef, From Christianity to Judaism ... OROBIO [c. 1650] 1990 ➤ 7,a81: ᴿJRel 72 (1992) 294s (B. *David*).

a622 **Kirn** Hans-Martin, Das Bild vom Juden im Deutschland des frühen 16. Jahrhunderts dargestellt an den Schriften Johannes PFEFFERKORNS: TSt MedvModJudaism 3, ᴰ1989 ➤ 7,a180: ᴿJQR 83 (1992s) 221s (R. *Po-chia Hsia*); RelStR 18 (1992) 62 (R. *Kolb*: defends sincerity of converted Jews).

a623 **Koningsveld** P. S. van, *al.*, Yemenite authorities and Jewish Messianism; Aḥmad IBN NAṢIR al-Zaydī's account of the Sabbathian movement in seventeenth century Yamen and its aftermath. Leiden 1990, Univ. Theol. Fac. 206 p. *f* 36 pa. – ᴿJRAS (1992) 71-73 (R. B. *Serjeant*); JSS 37 (1992) 341-3 (A. *Shivtiel*).

a624 ᴱ**Lasker** Daniel J., a) ❺ CRESCAS Hasdai, *Sefer bittul iqqarei ha-Notzrim* (Refutation of the principles of Christianity) 1990 ➤ 7,a73: ᴿRelStR 18 (1992) 72 (Sara *Klein-Braslavy*). – b) Hasdai CRESCAS, The Refutation of the Christian principles, translated with an introduction and notes: Jewish Philosophy. Albany 1992, SUNY. x-156 p.

a625 ᴱ**Leoni** Daniela, La comunità chassidica; storie sul Baal Shem Tov: Tradizioni di Israele 1. R 1989, Città Nuova. 368 p. Lit. 38.000. – ᴿAsprenas 39 (1992) 415-429 (V. *Scippa*).

a626 ᴱ**Mechoulan** Henry, Hispanidad y judaismo en tiempos de Espinosa; PEREYRA Abraham, La certeza del camino [ed. 1666]. S 1987, Univ. 341 p. – ᴿJQR 83 (1992s) 445-7 (V. A. *Mirelman*); Sefarad 51 (1991) 209-211 (N. *Grimaldi*).

a627 [Basch] **Moreen** Vera, Iranian Jewry during the Afghan Invasion; the Kitab-i Sar Guzasht-i Kashan of Bahai ʙ. FARHAD: FreibIslamSt 14. Stu 1990, Steiner. 178 p. DM 98. – ᴿJAOS 112 (1992) 311-3 (E. *Spicehandler*: a model of good scholarship).

a628 *Nador* Georg, Bibliographisches und sachliches zu Rabbi Jonathan EIBESCHÜTZ' (1690-1764) Haggada-Kommentar: Sefarad 51 (1991) 175-8.

a629 *Nirenberg* David, A female rabbi in fourteenth century Zaragoza?: Sefarad 51 (1991) 179-182.

a630 **Ravitzky** Aviezer, [1310-1410, Hasday] CRESCAS' sermon on the Passover and studies in his philosophy. J 1988, Israel Academy. x-204 p. – ᴿJQR 83 (1992s) 226-8 (D. J. *Lasker*); Sefarad 51 (1991) 211s (M. *Orfali*).

a631 *Segal* Lester A., Historical consciousness and religious tradition in Azariah de' ROSSI's Me'or 'Einayim 1989 ➤ 7,a80: ᴿJQR 83 (1992s) 210-6 (E. *Gutwirth*); MeditHR 6 (1991) 117-9 (J. *Cohen*).

a632 *Stacey* Robert C., The conversion of Jews to Christianity in thirteenth-century England: Speculum 67 (1992) 263-283.

a633 **Yovel** Yirmiyahu, SPINOZA and other heretics, I. The Marrano of reason; II. The adventures of immanence 1989 ➤ 6,k823:   ᴿJQR 83 (1992s) 452-7 (D. *Schwartz*).

K7.7 **Hasidismus et Judaismus saeculi XIX.**

a634 **Barkai** Avraham, Jüdische Minderheit und Industrialisierung; Demographie, Berufe und Einkommen der Juden in Westdeutschland 1850-1914. Tü 1988, Mohr. xiv-177 p. – ᴿJQR 83 (1992s) 436s (S. *Lowenstein*).

a635 **Battenberg** Friedrich, Das europäische Zeitalter der Juden; zur Entwicklung einer Minderheit in der nichtjüdischen Umwelt Europas, I. bis 1650; II. bis 1945. Da 1990, Wiss. xvi-307 p., 16 pl., map; xiii-361 p., 26 pl., map: je DM 42. 3-534-11381-0; -2-9. – ᴿActuBbg 29 (1992) 112s (J. *Boada*).

a636 ᴱ**Beck** Wolfgang. Die Juden in der europäischen Geschichte [*Friedländer* Saul + 6]: Beck'sche Reihe 496. Mü 1992, Beck. 154 p. DM 16,80. 3-406-34088-1.

a637 **Beller** Steven, Vienna and the Jews, 1867-1938: a cultural history. C 1989, Univ. x-271 p. £27.50. 0-5213-5180-4. – ᴿNedTTs 46 (1992) 242s (P. W. van der *Horst*).

a638 **Berg** R., Histoire du rabbinat français (XVIᵉ-XXᵉ siècle): Patrimoines Judaïsme. P 1992, Cerf. 274 p.; 16 fig., map. F 199. – ᴿNRT 114 (1992) 780s (N. *Plumat*).

Berlin George L., Defending the faith; nineteenth-century American Jewish writings on Christianity and Jesus 1989 ➤ 4353.

a639 **Bernard** Gildas, Les familles juives en France, XVIᵉ s.-1815. P 1990, Archives Nationales. 281 p. – ᴿJQR 83 (1992s) 233-4 (Frances *Maling*).

e640 **Breuer** Mordechai, Jüdische Orthodoxie im Deutschen Reich 1871-1918; Sozialgeschichte einer religiösen Minderheit 1986 ➤ 7,a82*: ᴿBijdragen 53 (1992) 431 (F. De *Meyer*).

a640* **Cavignac** Jean, Les Israélites bordelais de 1780 à 1850; autour d'une émancipation [diss. Bordeaux 1986]: La France au fil des siècles. P 1991, Publisud. xii-463 p. F 228 [RHE 88,638s, J.-P. *Hendricks*].

a641 **Cheyette** Bryan H., An overwhelming question; Jewish stereotyping in English fiction and society, 1875-1914: diss. Sheffield 1986. 444 p. BRDX 95613. – DissA 53 (1992s) 156s-A.

a642 *Chouraqui* Jean-Marc, 'Échos de la chaire'; la prédication israélite en France d'après une rubrique des Archives Israélites (1892-1905): RÉJ 150 (1991) 71-105.

a643 **Fishbane** Simcha, The method and meaning of the Mishnah Berurah [commentary on first part of Šulḥan Aruk by Meir KAGAN (1838-1933)]. Hoboken 1991, KTAV. 183 p. $20 [RelStR 19,85, E. *Diamond*: useful but flawed].

a644 ᴱ**Gallingani** Daniela, Napoleone e gli Ebrei; Atti dell'Assemblea degli Israeliti di Parigi e verbali del Gran Sinedrio: BtEurRivoluzFr. 1. Bo 1991, Analisi. 669 p. [RHE 88,355, R. *Aubert*].

a645 **Harel** Yaron, Changes in Syrian Jewry 1840-1880: diss. Bar-Ilan. Ramat-Gan 1992. – RTLv 24, p. 544.

a646 **Hayoun** Maurice-Ruben, Mémoires de Jacob Emden [± 1697-1776] ou l'anti-Sabbataï Zewi: Patrimoines Judaïsme. P 1992, Cerf. vii-413 p. F 265. – ᴿNRT 114 (1992) 781s (N. *Plumat*).

a647 **Heilman** Samuel, Defenders of the faith; inside ultra-orthodox Jewry. NY 1992, Schocken. 407 p. $27.50. 0-8052-4095-0. – ᴿChrCent 109

(1992) 227 (N. *Kollar*); RelStR 18 (1992) 312 (J. *Boyarin*: Jerusalem's Ḥasidim).

a648 **Hertz** Deborah, Jewish high society in Old Regime Berlin [c. 1800]. NHv 1988, Yale. xvi-299 p. – ᴿHistJb 111 (1991) 512s (H. *Fenske*: only some 18 salons).

a649 ᴱ**Landau** Jacob M., ◑ The Jews in Ottoman Egypt, 1517-1914. J 1988, Misgav Y. 670 p. 14 art. – ᴿEngHR 107 (1992) 726s (D. S. *Katz*).

a650 *Lauer* Simon, *Luginbühl-Weber* Gisela, MENDELSOHN, Moses (1729-1786): → 768, TRE 22 (1992) 428-439.

a651 **Lubarsky** Sandra R., Tolerance and transformation; Jewish approaches to religious pluralism. Cincinnati 1990, HUC. 149 p. $25. – ᴿCrit-RR 5 (1992) 395 (Paul M. *Van Buren*: 'presumably Claremont' dissertation; treats *liberal* Jews BAECK, ROSENZWEIG, M. KAPLAN, and chiefly BUBER).

a652 **Lucas** Franz D., *Frank* Heike, Michael SACHS; der konservative Mittelweg; Leben und Werk des Berliner Rabbiners zur Zeit der Emanzipation. Tü 1992, Mohr. v-161 p.; ill. DM 98. 3-16-145888-5 [TLZ 118,487, S. *Schreiner*].

a653 **Lundgren** Svante, Moses HESS (1812-1875) on religion, Judaism and the Bible. Åbo 1992, Akademi. x-206 p. 952-9616-02-3 [TLZ 118,397, W. *Gericke*].

a654 **Malka** Victor, Ainsi parlait le Hassidisme: Toledot Judaïsmes. P 1990, Cerf. 174 p. – ᴿSalesianum 54 (1992) 373s (R. *Vicent*: el fundador, Baal Shem Tob 1700-1760 no tenía intención de fundar un movimiento).

a655 **Menasce** Jean de, Quand Israël aime Dieu; introduction au hassidisme: Patrimoines Judaïsme. P 1992, Cerf. 165 p.; p. 7-18, *Monnot* Guy, sur de Menasce. 2-204-04304-4.

a656 **Robberechts** Édouard, Les Hassidim: Fils d'Abraham 1990 → 6,a432*; 7,a91: ᴿHelmantica 43 (1992) 464s (S. *Garcia-Jalón*); RThom 92 (1992) 576-8 (D. *Cerbelaud*, aussi sur KAPLAN S., Falashas; TOLÉDANO J., Maghrébins).

a657 **Roland** Joan G., Jesus in British India; identity in a colonial era. Hanover NH 1989, Univ. P. New England (for Brandeis Univ.). xiii-355 p. £26.75. – ᴿEngHR 107 (1992) 1040 (H. *Tinker*: only 20,000, mostly in Cochin and after 1750 Bombay).

a658 *Schreiber* Jean-Philippe, Un rabbin dans le siècle; Élie-Aristide ASTRUC, Grand-Rabbin de Belgique de 1866 à 1879: Bijdragen 53 (1992) 3-22; Eng. 22.

a659 **Surasqi** Aharon, ◑ *Yᵉsod ha maᶜala*. Bene Baraq 1991, Ziyyuanim. 2 vol. – ᴿCHistEI 68,57-66, D. *Assaf*, ◑ 'a new chapter in the historiography of Hasidism in Eretz Israel'; Eng. 198: 111 letters 1778-1821).

K7.8 Judaismus contemporaneus.

a660 **Abitol** Michel, Les deux terres promises 1989 → 6,a343*: ᴿAmHR 96 (1991) 531 (M. *Burns*).

a661 **Bauer** Yehuda, Out of the ashes; the impact of American Jews on post-Holocaust European Jewry. Ox 1989, Pergamon. xxv-318 p. – ᴿJQR 83 (1992s) 422-5 (G. *Korman*).

a662 **Beit-Hallahmi** Benjamin, Despair and deliverance; private salvation in contemporary Israel: Israeli Studies. Albany 1992, SUNY. vii-221 p. 0-7914-0999-6; pa. -1000-5.

a663 **Beller** Steven, HERZL: Jewish Thinkers. L 1991, Halban. 164 p. £12; pa. £7. 1-870015-38-X; -9-4. – RExpTim 102 (1990s) 288 [C.S. *Rodd*: discerning, even if Herzl was neither a thinker nor really Jewish].

a664 **Ben Chlomo** Iosef, Introduction à la pensée de Rav KOOK [Isaac], TChalier Catherine. Patrimoines Judaïsme. P 1992, Cerf. 179 p. F 150. 2-204-04564-0.

a665 **Borowitz** Eugene B., Renewing the covenant [➤ 7,a92]; a theology for the postmodern Jew. Ph 1991, Jewish Publication. xiv-319 p. $25. – RTS 53 (1992) 774s (M. *Berenbaum*).

a666 *Bourel* Dominique, Bulletin du Judaïsme moderne: RechSR 80 (1992) 227-238; [No 1-17, histoire; No 18-29, Judaïsme moderne et contemporain].

a667 **Cohn-Sherbok** Dan, Issues in contemporary Judaism. L 1991, Macmillan. xv-175 p. £40. – RTLond 95 (1992) 151s (M.B. *Ettlinger*).

a668 **Danzger** Herbert M., Returning to tradition; the contemporary revival of orthodox Judaism 1989 ➤ 7,a94: RCritRR 5 (1992) 388-390 (Natalie *Isser*).

a669 **Ellis** Marc H., Towards a Jewish theology of liberation 1987 ➤ 3, a620 ... 7,a97: RCurrTMiss 19 (1992) 130 (J.E. *Ponet*).

a670 **Fackenheim** Emil L., The Jewish Bible after the holocaust; a re-reading. Bloomington 1990, Indiana Univ. 122 p. $27.50. 0-253-32097-8. – RInterpretation 46 (1992) 320.322 (W.E. *March*).

a671 **Frankel** Ellen, The classic tales; [300 from] 4,000 years of Jewish lore. Northvale NJ 1989, Aronson. xli-659 p. – RSalesianum 53 (1991) 584 (R. *Vicent*).

a672 **Friedman** Elias, Jewish identity. Highland NY 1987, Miriam. 231 p. 0-939409-00-3; pa. -2-1.

a673 **Gillman** Neil, Sacred fragments; recovering theology for the modern Jew 1990 ➤ 7,a101: RCritRR 5 (1992) 390-2 (T. *Weinberger*: asks all the tough questions; associates a particular sage with three of the five approaches).

a674 TEGlatzer Nahum N., The Judaic tradition; Jewish writings from antiquity to the modern age. Northvale NJ c.1987 [¹1961], Aronson. xviii-838 p. 0-87668-984-5.

a675 **Goldy** Robert C., The emergence of Jewish theology in America 1990 ➤ 6,7408: RJRel 72 (1992) 143 (A.J. *Wolf*).

a676 **Hartman** David, Conflicting vision; spiritual possibilities of modern Israel. NY 1990, Schocken. 292 p. $25. – RJRel 72 (1992) 297s (A. *Mittleman*).

a677 **Herring** Basil, Jewish ethics and halakhah for our time, sources and commentary [I]-II. Hoboken 1990, Ktav. 279 p. $20. 0-88125-045-7. – RExpTim 102 (1990s) 348 (Julia *Neuberger*: treats AIDS, brain-stem-death, and transplants without adverting to any less-traditional Jewish opinion).

a678 **Hertz** Aleksander, ⊕ Żydzi w kulturze polskiej. Wsz 1988, Znak. 304 p. – RAtKap 116 (1991) 538-540 (J. *Augustynowicz*, ⊕).

a679 **Hertzberg** Arthur, The Jews in America 1990 ➤ 7,a104: RJQR 83 (1992s) 433-5 (A.T. *Levenson*).

a680 EKatz David S., *Israel* Jonathan I., Sceptics, millenarians, and Jews: StIntelH 17, 1990 ➤ 6,349: RJQR 83 (1992s) 414s (T.M. *Endelman*).

a681 **Katz** J., The 'Shabbes Goy' 1989 ➤ 5,a302; 7,a106: RJQR 83 (1992s) 247-9 (D. *Novak*).

a682 *a) Kellner* Menachem, Messianic postures in Israel today [< Modern Judaism 6 (1986)]; – *b) Biale* David, Gershom SCHOLEM on Jewish messianism [< ^E*Biale* D., Scholem 1979 ²1982]: ➤ 365, Essential Messianic 1992, 505-518 / 521-550.

a683 **Leibowitz** Yeshayahu, Judaism, human values, and the Jewish state [27 art.], ^{TE}*Goldman* Eliezer. CM 1992, Harvard Univ. xxxiv-289 p. $40. 0-674-48775-3 [TDig 40,73].

a684 **Liebman** C. S., *Cohen* S. M., Two worlds of Judaism 1990 ➤ 6,a359: ^RCritRR 5 (1992) 392-4 (Bonny *Kraut*).

a685 *Margolis* Richard J., The Jewish experience in America; a religious perspective: ChSt 30 (1991) 127-144.

a686 **Mendes-Flohr** Paul, Divided passions; Jewish intellectuals and the experience of modernity. Detroit 1991, Wayne State Univ. 450 p. $40. – ^RJRel 72 (1992) 619s (M. L. *Morgan*).

a687 **Mittleman** Alan L., Between Kant and Kabbalah; an introduction to Isaac BRETTER's philosophy of Judaism 1990 ➤ 6,a362; 7,a118: ^RJRel 72 (1992) 467s (J. M. *Harris*).

a688 **Neusner** Jacob, The religious world of contemporary Judaism; observations and convictions: BrownJudSt 191. Atlanta 1989, Scholars. 201 p. – ^RRelStR 18 (1992) 342 (Mary Lee *Raphael*).

a689 *a) Neusner* Jacob, Worin besteht die Herausforderung des heutigen jüdischen Fundamentalismus? – *b) Karff* Samuel E., Wie soll man dem heutigen jüdischen Fundamentalismus begegnen? ➤ 384, IZT (Concilium) 28 (1992) 229-231 / 231-4; beide ^T*Albrecht* A.

a690 **Nini** Y., The Jews of the Yemen. Chur 1991, Harwood. xii-256 p. £30; sb. £18. – ^RJJS 43 (1992) 327-9 (P. J. L. *Frankl*).

a691 **Pinkus** Benjamin, The Jews of the Soviet Union; the history of a national minority 1988 ➤ 5,a336; £30: ^REngHR 107 (1992) 177s (L. *Kochan*).

a692 **Romanoff** Lena, Your people, my people; finding acceptance and fulfilment as a Jew by choice. Ph 1990, Jewish Publ. 280 p. $23. – ^RTTod 49 (1992s) 278 . 280 (M. J. *Glazer*).

a693 **Rubenstein** Richard L., After Auschwitz; history, theology, and contemporary Judaism² [¹1966]. Baltimore 1992, Johns Hopkins Univ. $48.50; pa. $15. 0-8018-4284-0; -5-9 [TDig 40,185: 9 chapters replaced by 10 new].

a694 **Schoem** David, Ethnic survival in America; an ethnography of a Jewish afternoon school: Brown Studies on Jews and their Societies 7. Atlanta 1989, Scholars. 157 p. – ^RJQR 83 (1992s) 217-220 (B. W. *Holtz*).

a695 **Schwartz** Shuly R., The emergence of Jewish scholarship in America; the publication of the Jewish Encyclopedia. ... 1991, Behrman 235 p. $35 [JAAR 59,884].

a696 **Shmueli** Efraim, Seven Jewish cultures 1990 ➤ 6,a163; 7,a124: ^RCritRR 5 (1992) 350-2 (Alice L. *Eckardt*).

a697 **Silverstein** Alan, Institutionalizing Reform Judaism; the accommodation of the UAHC and its affiliated congregations to America's environment, 1873-1930: diss. Jewish Theol. Sem., ^D*Schorsch* I. NY 1992. 466 p. 93-12995. – DissA 53 (1992s) 4365-A.

a698 *Vándor* Jaime, Orígenes y presente del fundamentalismo judío: ➤ 44, ^FDÍAZ ESTEBAN F., Sefarad 52 (1992) 253-260.

a699 **Vital** David, The future of the Jews; a people at the crossroads. CM 1990, Harvard Univ. ix-161 p. – ^RJQR 83 (1992s) 229-232 (I. S. *Lustick*).

a700 *Volkov* Shulamit, Die Erfindung einer Tradition; zur Entstehung des modernen Judentums in Deutschland: HZ 253 (1991) 603-628.

a701 *Webber* Jonathan,   Modern Jewish identities; the ethnographic complexities: JJS 43 (1992) 246-267.
a702 **Wlaschek** Rudolf M.,   Juden in Böhmen: Beiträge zur Geschichte des europäischen Judentums im 19. und 20. Jh.   Mü 1990, Oldenbourg. 236 p. DM 58. – ᴿEngHR 107 (1992) 518s (S. *Beller*).

к8   *Philosemitismus* – **Judeo-Christian rapprochement**.

a703 *Alexander* Philip S.,   Madam Eglentyne, Geoffrey CHAUCER and the problem of medieval anti-Semitism: BJRyL 74,1 (1992) 109-120.
a704 ᴱ**Amersfoort** J. van, *Oort* J. van,   Juden und Christen in der Antike 1989/90 ➤ 6,506*:   ᴿColcT 62,3 (1992) 185-8 (W. *Chrostowski*, ☻); KerkT 42 (1991) 171s (T. *Baarda*); NedTTs 46 (1992) 243 (A. C. *Kooyman*); TLZ 117 (1992) 437-9 (G. *Begrich*).
a705 *Apple* Raymond,   Australia and the Christian-Jewish encounter: AustralasCR 69 (1992) 446-461.
a706 *Bakker* Leo,   Herbezinning op de verhouding tot het joodse volk, 1. Over de voorlopigheid van de kerk; – 2. De aardse taak van de verrezen Christus: TvT 32 (1992) 272-296; Eng. 296s / 345-365; Eng. 366.
a707 **Bartolini** Elena, *Vasciaveo* Chiara, al.,   Gesù ebreo per sempre; proposta per una presentazione della rivelazione ebraico-cristiana a partire della Bibbia, testo sacro fondante, in riferimento al dialogo ebraico-cristiano: Grandi Religioni.   Bo 1991, Dehoniane.   128 p.   88-10-60405-9.
a707* **Beauchamp** Paul,   Le peuple juif et les nations à partir de l'AT: BDialRel 26 (1991) 43-60.
a708 **Betz** Hans Dieter,   Practicality or principle?   A memorable exchange of letters [1852; Jewish prof. J. BERNAYS; Christian ambassador J. von BUNSEN]: ➤ 57, ᶠFLUSSER D., Messiah 1992, 207-217.
a709 *a) Bramwell* Bevil,   The historicity of teaching theology; a Catholic perspective; – *b) Asbury* B. A.,   The revolution in Jewish-Christian relations; is it to be found in Christian theological seminaries?:   TEdn 28,2 (1991) 51-59 / 60-71.
a710 **Braybrooke** Marcus,   Children of one God; a history of the Council of Christians and Jews. ... 1991, Valentine Mitchell.   144 p. £15; pa. £9.50. 0-85303-242-4; -250-5. – ᴿExpTim 103 (1991s) 318 (C. *Middleburgh*).
a711 *Brittain* Teresa,   Mission and witness of the Jewish people: Month 253 (1992) 234-241 . 269-274.
a712 **Broer** Ingo,   Die Juden im Urteil der Autoren des Neuen Testaments; Anmerkungen zum Problem historischer Gerechtigkeit im Angesicht einer verheerenden Wirkungsgeschichte: TGʟ 82 (1992) 2-33.
a713 **Bunte** Wolfgang,   Religionsgespräche zwischen Christen und Juden in den Niederlanden (1100-1500): JudUmw 27, 1990 ➤ 7,a141; Fs 144; 3-631-42963-0:   ᴿBijdragen 53 (1992) 431 (L. *Bakker*); NRT 114 (1992) 780 (J. *Scheuer*); TGL 82 (1992) 470s (W. *Knoch*).
a714 ᴱ**Charlesworth** James H., al.,   Jews and Christians 1990 ➤ 6,396; 7,a142: ᴿCritRR 5 (1992) 264-8 (E. L. *Friedland*); IndTSt 28 (1991) 193s (L. *Legrand*).
a715 **Chazan** Robert,   Barcelona and beyond; the disputation of 1263 and its aftermath.   Berkeley 1992, Univ. California.   x-257 p. – ᴿRelStR 18 (1992) 311 (J. *Boyarin*).
a716 *a) Chilton* Bruce,   Jews in the NT; – *b) Wilson* Stephen G., Jewish-Christian relations 70-170 C.E.: ➤ 741, AnchorBD 3 (1992) 845-8 / 854-859.

a717 *a) Claude* Dietrich, GREGOR von Tours und die Juden; die Zwangs-bekehrungen von Clermont; – *b) Dreyer* Michael, Judenhass und Anti-semitismus bei Constantin FRANZ: HistJb 111 (1991) 137-147 / 155-172.

a718 *a) Coccopalmerio* Francesco, Ebrei e cristiani a 25 anni da 'Nostra Aetate'; – *b) Ben Horin* Natan, ... valutazione ebraica; – *c) Fumagalli* Pier Francesco, ... cristiana: Ambrosius 67 (1991) 528 / 529-542 / 543-550.

ᴱCohen, Essential papers on Judaism and Christianity in conflict 1991 ⇥ 346*b*.

a719 *a) Cohen* J., Towards a functional classification of Jewish anti-Christian polemic in the high Middle Ages; – *b) Berger* D., Christians, Gentiles, and the Talmud; a XIVth-cent. Jewish response to the attack on Rabbinic Judaism: ⇥ 581, Rel.-Gespräche 1989/92, 93-114 / 115-130.

a720 **Cohn-Sherbok** Dan, The crucified Jew. L 1992, Collins. xx-258 p. £18. 0-00-215994-5. – ᴿExpTim 103 (1991s) 381s (M. *Braybrooke* compares this account of bitter hostility, 'what has generally been believed in the Church rather than what was necessarily the case', with E. CHACOUR's on op-pression of Palestinians today, partly due to his own Melkite church); Month 253 (1992) 495s (D. *Howard*).

a721 **Comeau** Geneviève, Contribution au débat entre judaïsme et Église catholique, 2. Recueil de textes. P 1990, Médiasèvres. 122 + 77 p. – ᴿI.Vitae 47 (1992) 353 (L. *Partos*).

a722 **Conzelmann** Hans, Gentiles, Jews, Christians, polemics and apologetics in the Greco-Roman era, ᵀ*Boring* M. Eugene. Mp 1992, Fortress. xxxvii-390 p. $38 [CBQ 54,833].

a723 **Dahan** Gilbert, La polémique chrétienne contre le judaïsme au Moyen Âge: Présence du Judaïsme. P 1991, A. Michel. 152 p. – ᴿRÉJ 151 (1992) 403 (E. *Nicolas*).

a723* *a) Dautzenberg* Gerhard, Das christlich-jüdische Gespräch; – *b) Mechtenberg* Theo, Hoffnungszeichen eines polnisch-jüdischen Dialogs: Orientierung 56 (1992) 121-4 / 94-97.

a724 *a) Dietrich* Walter, Stefan HEYM und das jüdisch-biblische Erbe [Ehrendoktorat Bern 1990]; – *b) Heym* Stefan, Rede: EvT 52 (1992) 277-281 / 281-4.

a725 **Di Sante** Carmine, Parola e terra; per una teologia dell'ebraismo. Genova 1990, Marietti. xii-172 p. Lit. 28.000. – ᴿCC 143 (1992,1) 205s (S. M. *Katunarich*).

a725* *Drijvers* H. J. W., Christians, Jews and Muslims in northern Me-sopotamia in early Islamic times; the Gospel of the Twelve Apostles and related texts: ⇥ 682*, Syria 1990/2, 67-74.

a726 *Drummond* J. M. V., general director of The Church's Ministry among Jews, defends it against emotive terms of Bishop David SHEPPARD: ExpTim 102 (1990s) [131s] 374.

a727 **Dupuy** B., De relatie tussen Joden en Katholieken; monoloog of dialoog?: Ter Herkenning 20,1 (1992) 27-34 (35-38, *Levisson* R. A., comment) [< GerefTTs 92,197].

a728 **Falk** Gerhard, The Jew in Christian theology; Martin LUTHER's anti-Jewish Vom Schem Hamphoras, previously unpublished in English, and other milestones in Church doctrine concerning Judaism. Jefferson NC 1992, McFarland. viii-296 p. $30. 0-89950-716-6 [TDig 40,161].

a729 *Fisher* Eugene J., Catholics and Jews; face to face: Pacifica 4 (1991) 64-75.

a730 *Frankemölle* Hubert, Jüdisch-christlicher Dialog; interreligiöse und in-nerchristliche Aspekte: Catholica 46 (1992) 114-139.

a731 **Fuller** Roy D., Contemporary Judaic perceptions of Jesus; implications for Jewish-Christian dialogue: diss. Southern Baptist Theol. Sem. 1992, ᴰ*Johnson* J. 261 p. 93-10416. – DissA 53 (1992s) 3950-A.

a732 *Gager* John G., Jews, Christians and the dangerous ones in between: ➤ 514, Interpretation 1992, 259-282.

a733 *Graboïs* A., Le dialogue religieux au xiiᵉ s.; Pierre ABÉLARD et Jehudah HALÉVI: ➤ 581, Rel.-Gespräche 1989/92, 149-167.

a734 *Grondelski* John M., Auschwitz revisited... The Polish bishops on Christian-Jewish relations: America 164 (1991) 469-471.

a735 **Hägler** Brigitte, Die Christen und die 'Judenfrage', am Beispiel der Schriften OSIANDERS und ECKS zum Ritualmordentwurf [Diss. Frankfurt/M]: Erlanger Studien 92. Erlangen 1992, Palm & E. iii-274 p. DM 48 [TR 88,431].

a736 *Handy* Lowell K., The reconstruction of biblical history and Jewish-Christian relations: ScandJOT 5,1 (1991) 1-22.

a737 **Harrelson** Walter, *Falk* Randall M., Jews and Christians; a troubled family 1990 ➤ 7,a168: ᴿRelStR 18 (1992) 239 (A. J. *Everson*).

a738 **Harris-Shapiro** Carol A., Syncretism or struggle; the case of [U. S. Protestant] Messianic Judaism: diss. Temple, ᴰ*Raines* J. Ph 1992. 395 p. 92-27476. – DissA 53 (1992s) 1544-A.

a739 ᴱ**Haverkamp** A., *Ziwes* F.-J., Juden in der christlichen Umwelt während des späten Mittelalters: ZHistF Supp. 13. B 1992, Duncker & H. ii-102 p.; 2 maps. DM 48 [RHE 87,477*].

a740 *Haymel* Michael, Gottes Ja zu Israel; das Christusbekenntnis verbindet die Kirche und Israel: DPfarrB 91 (1991) 351-4 [< zit 91,677].

a741 *Heinen* Heinz, Ägyptische Grundlagen des antiken Antijudaismus; zum Judenexkurs des TACITUS, Historien V 2-13: TrierTZ 101 (1992) 124-149.

a741* a) *Heinrichs* Wolfgang, Das Bild vom Juden in der protestantischen Judenmission [... Zeitschrift]; – b) *Kremers-Sper* Thomas, Antijüdische und antisemitische Momente in protestantischer Kapitalismuskritik [1871]; – c) *Sonnenschmidt* Reinhard, Zum philosophischen Antisemitismus bei G. W. F. HEGEL; – d) *Klöcker* Michael, Das katholische Milieu [1871]: ZRGg 44 (1992) 195-220 / 221-240 / 289-301 / 241-262.

a742 **Hermle** Siegfried, Evangelische Kirche und Judentum—Stationen nach 1945: ArbKZG B-16. Gö 1990, Vandenhoeck & R. 422 p. DM 98. 3-525-55716-7 [TLZ 118,243, U. *Schröer*].

a743 **Hertzberg** Arthur, Jewish polemics. NY c. 1992, Columbia. 259 p. $28. – ᴿChrCent 109 (1992) 978s (J. R. *Preville*).

a744 **Hilberg** R., La destruction des Juifs d'Europe,ᵀ. P 1988, Fayard. 1099 p. [RHE 88,153].

a745 **Hoffmann** Christhard, Juden und Judentum im Werk deutscher Althistoriker des 19. und 20. Jh. 1988 ➤ 5,a389: ᴿRHR 209 (1992) 211s (S. *Schwarzfuchs*); ZSav-R 108 (1991) 565-571 (Helga *Botermann*).

a746 ᴱ**Houlden** Leslie, Judaism and Christianity [reprint of part of 1988 World's Religions]. L 1991, Routledge. 242 p. £17. – ᴿTLond 95 (1992) 312s (D. M. *Lindsay*: impressive but more neo-confessional than phenomenological as promised; p. 313s is on Tradition and new religion, another part).

a747 **Hsia Po-chia** R., Trent 1475; stories of a ritual murder trial. NHv/NY 1992, Yale/Yeshiva. xxvi-173 p.; 11 pl. $22.50. 0-300-05106-9 [TDig 40, 167: the trial record and other contemporary evidences, including efforts of Christian neighbors to help the 19 accused Jews].

a748 **Hsia Po-Chia** R., The myth of ritual murder 1988 ➤ 6,a406; 7,a173: ᴿRÉJ 150 (1991) 226-8 (J. *Shatzmiller*); RHR 209 (1992) 209s (S. *Schwarzfuchs*).

a749 **Ioly Zorattini** Pier Cesare, Processi del S. Uffizio di Venezia contro Ebrei e Giudaizzanti (1585-9) [3s, 1984s ➤ 5,a390] 7: Storia dell'Ebraismo in Italia 10. F 1989, Olschki. 220 p. – ᴿSefarad 51 (1991) 206s (M. *Orfali*).

a750 *a) Käsemann* Ernst, Protest! – *b) Traub* Helmut, Nein, Herr Seim! [Zur christlichen Identität im christlich-jüdischen Gespräch]; – *c) Seim* Jürgen, Vorläufige Antwort: EvT [51 (1991) 458-467] 52 (1992) 177s / 178-185 / 185-7.

a751 *a) Katz* Jacob, Les racines de l'antisémitisme moderne, 1. L'antisémitisme; un point de vue juif (*Dujardin* J., chrétien); – *b) Friedländer* Saul, 2. L'Église catholique dans l'engrenage nazi; – *c) Morley* John F., Réflexions historiques sur la Shoa (... *Wigoder* G., pensée juive; *Dupuy* B., théologie chrétienne): Istina 36 (1991) 231-6 (237-250) / 251-262 / 263-273 (275-290; 291-7).

a752 *Kinzig* Wolfram, 'Non-separation'; closeness and co-operation between Jews and Christians in the fourth century: VigChr 45 (1991) 27-53.

a753 **Kirchberg** Julie, Theo-logie in der Anrede als Weg zur Verständigung zwischen Juden und Christen [kath. Diss. Bochum, ᴰ*Pottmeyer* J.]: InnsbTSt 31. Innsbruck 1991, Tyrolia. 568 p. Sch 340. – ᴿTLZ 117 (1992) 503-5 (L. *Wächter*).

Kirn Hans-Martin, Das Bild vom Juden im Deutschland des frühen 16. Jahrhunderts, dargestellt an den Schriften Johannes PFEFFERKORNS 1989 ➤ a622.

a755 *Klein* Emma, Jews and missionaries: Tablet 245 (1991) 128s.

a756 *Kleinberg* Aviad M., HERMANNUS Judaeus's opusculum, in defence of its authenticity: RÉJ [147 (1988) 31-56, *Saltman* A.] 151 (1992) 337-353.

a757 **Küng** Hans, Das Judentum. Mü 1991, Piper. 907 p. DM 68 [TR 88,83]. – ᴿActuBbg 29 (1992) 183-5 (J. *Boada*); HerdKor 46 (1992) 48s (K. *Nientiedt*: Trilogie 'Die religiöse Situation der Zeit'); Orientierung 56 (1992) 146-8 (R. *Boschert-Kimmig*).

a758 **Küng** Hans, Judaism: [trilogy] The religious situation of our time. L/NY 1992, SCM/Crossroad. xxii-753 p.; maps. £35. 0-8245-1181-6 [TDig 49,368]. – ᴿAmerica 167 (1992) 332-4 (R. *Modras*: title 'Judaism between yesterday and tomorrow'); Tablet 246 (1992) 743 (M. *Braybrooke*) & 743s (I. *Levy*).

a759 *Kuschel* Karl-Josef, Die Kirche und das Judentum; Konsens- und Dissensanalyse auf der Basis neuerer kirchlicher Dokumente [*Rendtorff* R. 1988, al.]: StiZt 210 (1992) 147-162.

a759* *a) Lange* N.R.M. de, Jews and Christians in the Byzantine empire; problems and prospects; – *b) Biller* Peter, Views of Jews from Paris around 1300; Christian or 'scientific'?; – *c) d'Uzer* Vincenette, The Jews in the sixteenth-century homilies; – *d) Brearley* Margaret F., Jewish and Christian concepts of time and modern anti-Judaism; ousting the God of time: ➤ 638, C/Judaism 1992, 15-32 / 187-207 / 265-277 / 481-493.

a760 **Langmuir** Gavin I., Toward a definition of anti-Semitism 1991 ➤ 7,222a: ᴿAmHR 97 (1992) 838s (W.C. *Jordan*); CathHR 78 (1992) 90s (E.A. *Synan*); JIntdisc 22 (1991s) 498s (J.R. *Russell*: more readable than his HistRA); RRelRes 33 (1990s) 187s (O.M. *Nelson*).

a761 **Langmuir** Gavin J., History, religion, and antisemitism 1990 ➤ 6,a420;

7,a189:   ᴿChH 60 (1991) 586s (C. H. *Lippy*); ChrCent 108 (1991) 913-5 (F. *Sherman*); JEH 43 (1992) 293-5 (J. *Cohen*; p. 332, Anna S. *Abulafia* on Towards a definition); JRel 72 (1992) 295-7 (L. A. *Segal*).

a761* *a)* *Langmuir* Gavin J.,   The faith of Christians and hostility to Jews; – *b)* *Katz* David S.,   The phenomenon of philo-semitism; – *c)* *Moore* R. I., Anti-Semitism and the birth of Europe; – *d)* *Rubin* Miri,   Desecration of the host; the birth of an accusation; – *e)* *Stow* Kenneth R.,   The good of the Church, the good of the State; the Popes and Jewish money: ➤ 638, C/Judaism 1992, 77-92 / 327-361 / 33-57 / 169-185 / 237-252.

a762 **Liebeschütz** Hans,   Synagoge und Ecclesia... Hochmittelalter 1983 ➤ 64,9052... 1,a90:   ᴿTPhil 67 (1992) 599s (R. *Berndt*: nichts über warum jetzt).

a763 **Lodahl** Michael E.,   Shekinah/Spirit; divine presence in Jewish and Christian religion: Studies in Judaism and Christianity. NY c. 1992, Paulist.   vi-234 p. [TLZ 118,827, J. *Maier*: uses Judaic data at second-hand for 'higher goal' of holocaust-theology].

Lohfink Norbert,   La Alianza nunca derogada; reflexiones exegéticas para el diálogo entre judíos y cristianos 1992 + deutsch/Eng. ➤ 7320-7322.

a764 **Lubac** Henri de,   Christian resistance to anti-Semitism; memories from 1940-44, ᵀ*Englund* Elizabeth 1990 ➤ 7,a193:   ᴿHomP 91,10 (1990s) 68s (T. C. *Donlan*).

a765 **Manuel** Frank E.,   The broken staff; Judaism through Christian eyes [... how to cope with its continuing creativeness]. CM 1992, Harvard Univ.   ix-363 p. $35.   0-674-08370-9 [TDig 40,75].

a766 *Marquardt* F. W.,   De kerk tussen Israël en de volken: Ter Herkenning 18,3 (1990) 145-153 [< GerefTTs 91,63].

a767 *Marshall* Bruce D.,   Truth claims and the possibility of Jewish-Christian dialogue: ModT 8 (1992) 221-240.

a768 **Mussner** Franz,   Dieses Geschlecht wird nicht vergehen: Judentum und Kirche, 1991 ➤ 7,242:   ᴿTGgw 35 (1992) 73s (H. *Giesen*).

a769 **Neudecker** R.,   I vari volti del Dio unico [1989 ➤ 6,a435], ᵀ1990 ➤ 6,a436; 7,a195:   ᴿAsprenas 39 (1992) 256-268 (V. *Scippa*); Gregorianum 73 (1992) 541s (G. L. *Prato*).

a770 **Neudecker** Reinhard, Ⓜ Az egy Isten sok arca [Die vielen Gesichter des einen Gottes; Christen und Juden im Gespräch 1989 ➤ 6,a435],ᵀ. Budapest 1992, Merleg.   128 p. [AcPIB 9,777].

a771 *Neusner* Jacob,   Judaism and Christianity cannot both be right [progress of scholarship forced him to call 'unfortunate' in 1990 (BR 6,6) G. VERMES' 'Jesus the Jew' which he praised in 1974]: BR 7,3 (1991) 8s.

a772 *Niewöhner* Friedrich,   Philosemitismus: ➤ 757, EvKL 3 (1992) 1191-4.

a773 **Pakter** Walter,   Medieval canon law and the Jews: Abh. Rechtsw. GrundlF 68, ᴿHZ 253 (1991) 428-430 (F. *Lotter*).

a774 **Palardy** William B.,   The Church and the Synagogue in the sermons of Saint Peter CHRYSOLOGUS: diss. Catholic Univ. ᴰ*Eno* R. Wsh 1992. 513 p. 92-19876. – DissA 53 (1992s) 530-A.

a775 **Paul** André,   Leçons paradoxales sur les juifs et les chrétiens. P 1992, D-Brouwer.   237 p. F 135 [TR 88,347].

a776 **Polly** Stuart,   The portrayal of Jews and Judaism in current Protestant teaching materials: diss. Columbia Teachers' College, ᴰ*Kennedy* W. NY 1992.   452 p. 92-28514. – DissA 53 (1992s) 1467-A.

a776* *a)* *Popkin* Richard,   Jewish-Christian relations in the sixteenth and seventeenth centuries; the conception of the Messiah; – *b)* *Saperstein* Marc,   Christians and Christianity in the sermons of Jacob ANATOLI; – *c)*

Slow Kenneth R., The Papacy and the Jews; Catholic reformation and beyond: ⇥ 180c, Mem. TALMAGE F. 2 (= Jewish History 6, 1992) 163-177 / 225-242 / 257-279.

a777 *Raddatz* Alfred, Johann ECKS Widerlegung der Schrift OSIANDERS gegen die Blutbeschuldigung der Juden: ⇥ 163, ᶠSAUER G., Aktualität 1992, 177-186.

a778 ᵀᴱ**Robles Sierra** Adolfo, Ramón MARTÍ, Raimundi Martini Capistrum Iudaeorum I, texto crítico y traducción: Corpus Islamo-Christianum, 1990 ⇥ 7,a210: ᴿEstE 67 (1992) 227 (F. de P. *Solá*).

a779 **Rousmaniere** John, A bridge to dialogue; the story of Jewish-Christian relations, ᴱ*Carpenter* James A., *Klenicki* Leon. NY 1991, Paulist. v-149 p. $9. 0-8091-3284-2 [TDig 39,382].

a780 *Runia* David T., 'Where, tell me, is the Jew...?'; BASIL, PHILO and ISIDORE of Pelusium: VigChr 46 (1992) 172-189.

a781 *Salzano* Teresa, Ebrei e cristiani; chi siamo noi? La terra di Israele ci interpella; XII° colloquio ebraico-cristiano, Camaldoli (Arezzo) 4-8 dic. 1991: StPatav 39 (1992) 263-8.

a782 *a*) *Schaller* Berndt, Judenmission und christliches Zeugnis; Anmerkungen zu einem nötigen Streit; – *b*) *Stöhr* Martin, Geschwister im Glauben; Ökumene mit den Juden: EvKomm 25 (1992) 638-641 / 634-7.

a783 *a*) *Schandl* Felix M., 'Ich sah aus meinem Volk die Kirche wachsen'; Edith STEINS christliches Verhältnis zum Judentum und ihre praktischen Konsequenzen [... die Seligsprechung lass bedenklich die Reaktion der Kirche zu Auschwitz]; – *b*) *Gerl* Hanna-Barbara, 'Im Dunkel wohl geborgen'; die Mystik der Kreuzeswissenschaft [E. Stein]: Teresianum 43 (1992) 53-107 / 481-494.

a784 ᴱ**Schwemer** Ulrich, Christen und Juden; Dokumente der Annäherung: Siebenstern 790. Gü 1991, Mohn. 192 p. DM 24,80. 3-579-00790-4. [TLZ 118, 635, T. *Arndt*].

a785 *a*) *Siegele-Wenschkewitz* Leonore, The discussion of anti-Judaism in feminist theology — a new area of Jewish-Christian dialogue; – *b*) *Plaskow* Judith, Feminist anti-Judaism and the Christian God; – *c*) *Wacker* Marie-Theres, Feminist theology and anti Judaism ... Germany; *d*) *Dijk-Hemmes* Fokkelien van, ... Netherlands; – *e*) *Long* Asphodel P., ... Britain: JFemStRel 7,2 (1991) 95-98 / 99-108 / 109-116 / 117-124 / 125-134 [< ZIT 92,138s].

Siker Jeffrey S., Disinheriting the Jews; Abraham in early Christian controversy 1991 ⇥ 2343.

a786 **Simonsohn** Shlomo, The Apostolic See and the Jews [⇥ 7,a228] 2-5 [to 1555]: StT 99,104ss. Toronto 1990, Pont. Inst. Medv. vi-492 p.; vi-490 p.; vi-396 p.; vi-436 p. $49 each. – ᴿHZ 253 (1991) 187s (J. F. *Battenberg*); Speculum 67 (1992) 1045-8 (Mary *Stroll*: magisterial).

a787 **Smid** Marijke, Deutscher Protestantismus und Judentum 1932/33: 1990 ⇥ 7,a229: ᴿTR 88 (1992) 47-49 (K. *Nowak*).

a788 **Smiga** George M., Pain and polemic; anti-Judaism in the Gospels: Stimulus. NY 1992, Paulist. vii-210 p. $10. 0-8091-3355-5.

a789 **Sonderegger** Katherine, That Jesus Christ was born a Jew; Karl BARTH's doctrine of Israel. Univ. Park PA 1992, Penn State Univ. viii-191 p. $32.50. 0-271-00818-0 [TDig 40,187].

a790 *Steininger* Rolf, Katholische Kirche und NS-Judenpolitik: ZkT 114 (1992) 166-179.

a791 *Stolle* Volker, Der Staat Israel und die christliche Endzeiterwartung: LuthTK 16 (1992) 67-82.

a792 ᴱSwidler Leonard, Bursting the bonds? A Jewish-Christian dialogue on Jesus and Paul 1990 ➤ 7,560: ᴿCBQ 54 (1992) 591s (H. G. *Perelmuter*); HorBT 14 (1992) 87-89 (H. E. von *Waldow*); LvSt 17 (1992) 75 (R. F. *Collins*); Pacifica 5 (1992) 232s (B. *Byrne*).

a793 **Taylor** M. S., The Jews in the writings of the early Church Fathers (150-312); 'men of straw' or formidable rivals?: diss. Oxford 1992. – RTLv 24, p. 552.

a794 **Volkov** S., Jüdisches Leben und Antisemitismus im XIX. und XX. Jht., zehn Essays. Mü 1990, Beck. 233 p. DM 40. – ᴿHZ 255 (1992) 137s (R. *Erb*) [RHE 87,477*].

a795 **Weisbord** Robert G., *Sillanpoa* Wallace P., The Chief Rabbi [of Rome, E. Zᴏʟʟɪ baptized 1945], the Pope, and the holocaust; an era in Vatican-Jewish relations. New Brunswick ɴᴊ 1991, Transaction. ix-231 p. $35. 0-88738-416-1 [TDig 39,287, under Sillanpoa].

a796 *White* Robert, An early Reformed document [3-p. letter signed VFC] on the mission to the Jews: WestTJ 53 (1992) 93-108.

a797 **Willebrands** Johannes, Church and Jewish people; new considerations [articles and addresses]. NY 1992, Paulist. xvi-280 p. 0-8091-0456-3.

a798 **Wistrich** Robert S., Antisemitism, the longest hatred. NY 1992, Pantheon. xxvi-341 p. $25. 0-679-40946-7 [TDig 40,93].

a799 **Yardeni** Myriam, Anti-Jewish mentalities in early modern Europe 1990 ➤ 7,a236: ᴿSixtC 22 (1991) 859s (J. *Friedman*; p. 872 on 'Sceptics').

XVII,3 Religiones parabiblicae

ᴍ1.1 **Gnosticismus classicus.**

a800 *Beyer* Klaus, Das antireligiöse Fest im gnostischen Mythos: ➤ 7,465*, ᴱ*Assmann* J., Fest 1988/91, 157-9.

a801 **Couliano** I. P., The tree of Gnosis; gnostic mythology from early Christianity to modern nihilism [Les gnoses dualistes d'Occident 1990],ᵀ with *Wiesner* H. S. SF 1992, HarperCollins. xviii-296 p. $25. 0-06-061615-6 [NTAbs 36,443]. – ᴿChrCent 109 (1992) 817s (G. *Weekman*).

a802 *Dubois* Jean-Daniel, Les recherches gnostiques et l'exégèse du Nouveau Testament: ➤ 462, Naissance 1990/2, 175-185.

a803 **Filoramo** Giovanni, A history of Gnosticism [L'attesa della fine], ᵀ*Alcock* Anthony, 1990 ➤ 6,a474; 7,a244: ᴿCritRR 5 (1992) 296-8 (Karen *King*: refreshing introductory essays; only ch. 10 really history); Gnosis [A Journal of the Western Inner Traditions (occultism, spiritualism)] 23 (SF 1992) 64 (S. A. *Hoelber*); TS 52 (1991) 548s (Pheme *Perkins*).

a804 **Geisen** Richard, Anthroposophie und Gnostizismus; Darstellung, Vergleich und theologische Kritik [Diss. Paderborn]: PdTSt 22. Pd 1992, Schöningh. 584 p. DM 68 [TR 88,529].

a805 **Guillaumont** A. & C., Évᴀɢʀᴇ Le Gnostique: SChr 356, 1989 ➤ 5,a159; 7,a247: ᴿEsprVie 102 (1992) 610s (Y.-M. *Duval*); JbÖsByz 42 (1992) 357-9 (W. *Lackner*); LavalTP 48 (1992) 473s (Anne *Pasquier*).

a806 *Howe* Leroy T., Pʟᴏᴛɪɴᴜs and the Gnostics: SecC 9 (1992) 57-71.

a807 ᴱ**King** Karen L., Images of the feminine in Gnosticism 1988 ➤ 5,481*a*; 6,a480: ᴿBA 54 (1991) 174s (D. M. *Scholer*); TorJT 7 (1991) 293-5 (S. *Brown*). ➤ 9046.

a808 **Pearson** Birger A., Gnosticism, Judaism, and Egyptian Christianity [13 reprints] 1990 ➤ 6,281: ᴿCurrTMiss 19 (1992) 297s (E. *Krentz*); HeythJ

33 (1992) 335s (P. *Rousseau*); SecC 9 (1992) 120s (Pheme *Perkins*); St-
PhilonAn 4 (1992) 175-8 (G. E. *Sterling* adds an index).

a809 **Pétrement** Simone, A separate God; the Christian origins of gnosticism
[Le Dieu séparé; les origines du gnosticisme 1984], ᵀ*Harrison* Carol, 1990
➤ 7,a250; also L 1991, Darton-LT; 0-232-51874-2: ᴿCritRR 5 (1992)
300-3 (M. A. *Williams*: interesting probabilities; but 'possibility' taken for
'evidence' of Christian/Valentinian origin); ExpTim 102 (1990s) 380 (C.
Tuckett: bold and well argued; to be taken into account); HeythJ 33
(1992) 449-451 (M. J. *Edwards*); JAAR 60 (1992) 804-7 (Karen *King*); JTS
43 (1992) 657-661 (A. H. B. *Logan*); Parabola 17,2 (1992) 120 . 122-5 (J.
Carey).

a810 **Pokorný** Petr, Píseň o perle; tajne knihy starovékých gnostiků. Praha
1986, Vyšehrad. 280 p. 8 pl. kč 23. – ᴿArOr 60 (1992) 295s (S. *Segert*,
Eng.).

a811 ᶠROBINSON James M., Gnosticism/Gospel origins, ᴱ**Gochring** J. *al.*
1990 ➤ 6,152*ab*: ᴿCBQ 54 (1992) 392s (Adela Y. *Collins*: tit. pp.).

a812 **Rudolph** Kurt, Die Gnosis; Wesen und Geschichte einer spätantiken
Religion³ʳᵉᵛ [¹1977]: Uni-Tb 1577, 1990 ➤ 7,a251: ᴿBijdragen 53 (1992)
326s (A. van *Dijk*); TLZ 117 (1992) 22 (K.-W. *Tröger*).

a813 **Scopello** Madeleine, Les gnostiques: BREF 37. P 1991, Cerf. 127 p.
F 45. – ᴿCritRR 5 (1992) 306s (Deirdre *Good*: fine for its size but unduly
perpetuates IRENAEUS); ÉTRel 67 (1992) 471s (E. *Cuvillier*); LavalTP 48
(1992) 307s (Monique *Dumais*).

a814 *Scopello* Madeleine, Bulletin sur la Gnose [21 livres]: RechSR 80 (1992)
441-486. N⁰ 1-7, Nag Hammadi Studies.

a814* *Stroumsa* Gedaliahu G., Paradosis; traditions ésotériques dans le christianisme des premiers siècles: ➤ 470, Apocrypha 2 (1991) 133-153.

a815 **Voorgang** Dietrich, Die Passion Jesu und Christi in der Gnosis [Diss.
Kassel Gesamthochschule]: EurHSS 23/432. Fra 1991, Lang. 453 p.
DM 90 [TD 88,253].

M1.2 **Valentinus** – *Pistis sophia,* Elchasai.

a816 **Bader** Françoise, La langue des dieux, ou l'hermétisme des poètes
indo-européens: Testi linguistici 14. 1989 ➤ 7,a261: ᴿRHR 209 (1992)
65s (D. *Dubuisson*).

a817 **Bierwirth** Jill S., The ecclesiology of the Valentinians and its role in
their separation from orthodoxy: diss. Southern Baptist Theol. Sem. 1992,
ᴰ*Hinson* E. 321 p. – 92-28424. – DissA 53 (1992s) 1550s-A.

a817* *Cirillo* Luigi, L'apocalypse d'Elkhasaï; son rôle et son importance pour
l'histoire du judaïsme: ➤ 470, Apocrypha 1 (1990) 167-179.

a818 **Desjardins** Michael R., Sin in Valentinianism [diss. Toronto 1987,
ᴰ*Guenther* H.]: SBL diss. 108, 1990 ➤ 6,a496: ᴿCritRR 5 (1992) 291-3
(Deirdre *Good* recommends).

a819 **Good** Deirdre J., Reconstructing the tradition of sophia in Gnostic
literature [diss. 1983] 1987 ➤ 3,a785; 6,a497: ᴿAustral BR 40 (1992) 92s
(J. *Painter*).

a820 **Markschies** Christoph, Valentinus gnosticus? Untersuchungen zur va-
lentinischen Gnosis mit einem Kommentar zu den Fragmenten Valentins:
[Diss.Tü 1990; 546 p. –TLZ 117,881]: WUNT 65. Tü 1992, Mohr. xii-
516 p. 3-16-145993-8.

a821 **Procter** Everett L., The influence of BASILIDES, VALENTINUS, and
their followers on CLEMENT of Alexandria: diss. Univ. California, San-

ta Barbara 1992, ᴰ*Pearson* B. 246 p. 92-26576. – DissA 53 (1992s) 1969-A.

a822 ᴱ**Sloterdijk** Peter, *Macho* Thomas H., Weltrevolution der Seele; ein Lese- und Arbeitsbuch der Gnosis von der Spätantike bis zur Gegenwart. 1040 p. (2 vol.) DM 78. – ᴿTGL 82 (1992) 503s (K. *Hollmann*).

M1.3 **Corpus hermeticum; Orphismus.**

a823 **Ambrose** Elizabeth Ann, Self and cosmos in Thoth Hermes Trismegistus, Meister ECKHART and PARACELSUS: diss. Washington, ᴰ*Poag* J. Seattle 1992. 242 p. 92-34297. – DissA 53 (1992s) 2386-A.

a824 *Calame* Claude, Eros initiatique et la cosmogonie orphique: → 157, ᶠRUDHART J., Orphisme 1991, 227-247.

a825 *Mahé* Jean-Pierre, La voie d'immortalité à la lumière des Hermetica de Nag Hammadi et de découvertes plus récentes: VigChr 45 (1991) 347-375.

a826 *Minazzoli* Agnès, L'héritage du Corpus Hermétique dans la philosophie de Nicolas de CUÈS: CiuD 205 (1992) 101-122.

a827 *Quispel* Gilles, Hermes Trismegistus and the origins of Gnosticism: VigChr 46 (1992) 1-19.

M1.5 **Mani,** *dualismus;* **Mandaei.**

a828 *Adkin* Neil, 'Filthy Manichees' [JEROME, Ep. 22:38,7]: Arctos 26 (1992) 5-18.

a829 *a) Böhlig* Alexander, Manichäismus; – *b) Rudolph* Kurt, Mandäismus: → 768, TRE 22 (1992) 25-45 / 19-25.

a830 *Buckley* Jorunn J., The colophons in The canonical prayerbook of the Mandaeans [DROWER E. 1958]: JNES 51 (1992) 33-50.

a831 ᴱ**Cirillo** Luigi, Codex Manichaicus Coloniensis 1988/90: → 6,590: ᴿAnBoll 110 (1992) 417s (U. *Zanetti*).

a832 *Colditz* Iris, [Turfan] Hymnen an Šād-Ohrmezd; ein Beitrag zur frühen Geschichte der Dīnāwarīya in Transoxanien: AltOrF 19 (1992) 322-6; V pl.

a833 **Hutter** Manfred, Manis kosmogonische Sābuhragān-Texte; Edition, Kommentar und literaturgeschichtliche Einordnung der manichäisch-mittelpersischen Handschriften M 98/99 I und M 7980-7984: StOrRel 21. Wsb 1992, Harrassowitz. ix-175 p.; 30 pl. DM 98 [TR 88,526]. 3-447-03227-8.

a834 *Kasser* Rodolphe, Sagesse de Mani, célée ou manifestée: BSACopte 30 (1991) 29-41.

a835 **Klimkeit** Hans-Joachim, Hymnen und Gebete der Religion des Lichts; iranische und türkische liturgische Texte der Manichäer Zentralasiens: AbhRhW 79, 1989 → 5,a511; 7,a275: ᴿJAOS 112 (1992) 690s (J. C. *Reeves*).

a836 **Koenen** L., Römer C., Der Kölner Mani-Kodex; über das Werden seines Leibes [auf dem diplomatischen Text 1985 basiert]: Papyrol. Colon. 14. Opladen 1988, Westdeutscher-V. xxxii-120 p.; 2 pl. – 3-531-09924-8. – ᴿBO 49 (1992) 411-3 (J. *Helderman*); OLZ 87 (1992) 30-32 (H.-G. *Bethge*).

a837 **Lieu** Samuel N. C., Manichaeism in the later Roman Empire and medieval China²ʳᵉᵛ [¹1985]: WUNT 63. Tü 1992, Mohr. xxii-370 p.; maps [RelStR 18,55]. 3-16-145820-6.

a838 **Lindt** Paul Van, The names of Manichaean mythological figures; a comparative study on terminology in the Coptic sources [diss. Aarhus]: StOrRel 26. Wsb 1992, Harrassowitz. xxvii-347 p. DM 138 [TR 88,526].

a839 *McBride* Daniel, Egyptian Manichaeism: JSStEg 18 (1988) 80-98.

a840 **Macuch** Rudolf, (*Boekels* Klaus) Neumandäische Chrestomathie: Porta Ling.Or. 18, 1989 ➤ 5,a514; DM 68: ᴿBO 49 (1992) 838-840 (H. L. *Murre-Van den Berg*); BSO 55 (1992) 544-6 (O. *Jastrow*); JAOS 112 (1992) 339s (J. L. *Malone*).

a841 *Nägel* Peter, Mandaei / Manichäismus: ➤ 757, EvKL 3 (1992) 260-2 / 262-5.

a842 **Reeves** John C., Jewish lore in Manichaean cosmogony; studies in the Book of Giants traditions [diss.]: Mg. 14. Cincinnati 1992, HUC. 260 p. $50. 0-87820-413-X. – ᴿBR 8,5 (1992) 15.48 (J. *VanderKam*).

a843 *Römer* Cornelia, Zwei/Weitere neue Lesungen am Kölner Mani-Kodex: ZPapEp 93 (1992) 175s / 94 (1992) 101-3.

a844 **Runciman** Steven, Häresie und Christentum; der mittelalterliche Manichäismus, ᵀ*Jatho* Heinz. Mü 1988, Fink. 255 p. – ᴿZKG 102 (1991) 130s (C. *Capizzi*).

a845 **Stroumsa** Gedaliahu G., Savoir et salut; traditions juives et tentations dualistes dans le christianisme ancien: Patrimoines. P 1992, Cerf. 404 p. 2-204-04385-0.

a846 **Sunderman** Werner, The Manichaean hymn cycles Huyadagmān and Angad Rōšnān in Parthian and Sogdian; photo edition, transcription and translation of hitherto unpublished texts: Corpus Inscr. Iran. supp. 2. L 1990, School of Or.Afr.Studies. 42 p. 82 pl. 0-7286-0165-6. – ᴿBSO 55 (1992) 139s (Y. *Yoshida*); JRAS (1992) 84s (S.N.C. *Lieu*).

a846* *Tardieu* M., L'arrivée des Manichéens à al-Ḥira: ➤ 682*, Syrie 1990/2, 15-24; map.

a847 *Tubach* Jürgen, Mani und das 366-tägige Sonnenjahr: Muséon 105 (1992) 45-61.

a848 **Woschitz** Karl Matthäus, Das manichäische Urdrama des Lichtes; Studien zu koptischen, mitteliranischen und arabischen Texten. Wien 1989, Herder. 304 p. 3-210-24962-8. – ᴿRelCu 37 (1991) 742 (P. *Langa*).

M2.1 **Nagᶜ Ḥammadi,** *generalia.*

a849 **Charron** Régine, Concordances des textes de Nag Hammadi; le codex VII: BCNH-Conc 1. Saint Foy / Lv 1992, Univ. Laval / Peeters. xiv-785 p. 2-7637-7297-8 [OIAc 5,17].

a849* *Ménard* Jacques-É., [Tommaso, Filippo], *al.*, [Nag-Hammadi], L'Egitto agli inizi dell'era cristiana,ᵀ: Il mondo della Bibbia 3,13 (1992) 13-16 (1-42), 1120-7353.

a850 ᴱ**Parrott** D. M., NHC III,3-4 & V,1, 1991 ➤ 7,a287: ᴿNRT 114 (1992) 766s (X. *Jacques*).

a851 *Pearson* Birger A., Nag Hammadi: ➤ 741, AnchorDB 4 (1992) 982-993.

a852 ᴱ**Sieber** John H., Nag Hammadi Codex VIII: CGN (13th of the 17 awaited). Leiden 1991, Brill. xxxv-301 p. 90-04-09477-6. – ᴿJTS 43 (1992) 664-8 (R. M. *Wilson*: useful, not impeccable).

M2.2 *Evangelium etc. Thomae* – **The Gospel** (etc.) **of Thomas.**

a853 **Alcalá** Manuel, El evangelio copto de Tomás: BEB 67. S 1989, Sígueme. 113 p. – ᴿLumenVr 40 (1991) 528s (J. M. *Arroniz*); RET 52 (1992) 97 (M. *Gesteira*).

a854 *Arai* Sasagu, 'Drei Worte' Jesu im Logion 13 des EvTh: AnJap 18 (1992) 62-66.
a855 *Brown* Paterson, The sabbath and the week in Thomas 27 ['keep the sabbath (= entire week) as sabbath']: NT 34 (1992) 193 only.
a856 *Conick* April D. de, *Fossum* Jarl, 'Stripped before God', a new interpretation of Logion 37 in the Gospel of Thomas: VigChr 45 (1991) 123-130.
a857 *Davies* Stevan, The Christology and protology of the Gospel of Thomas: JBL 111 (1992) 663-682.
a858 *a) Dehandschutter* B., Recent research on the Gospel of Thomas; – *b) Carrez* M., Quelques aspects christologiques de l'Évangile de Thomas: ➤ 137, ꟷNEIRYNCK F., 1992, 2257-62 / 2263-76.
a859 *Desjardins* Michel, Where was the Gospel of Thomas written? [Antioch]: ➤ 74, ꟷGUENTHER H., TorJT 8 (1992) 121-133.
a860 **Eccles** Lance, Introductory Coptic reader; selections from the Gospel of Thomas with full grammatical explanations. Kensington MD 1991, Dunwoody. iv-80 p. – ᴿJSS 37 (1992) 326s (K. H. *Kuhn*).
a861 *Esbroeck* M. Van, Les actes apocryphes de Thomas en version arabe: ParOr 14 (1987) 11-78 [< ZIT 92,135].
a862 **Fieger** Michael, Das Thomasevangelium; Einleitung, Kommentar und Systematik: NTAbh NF 22, ᴰ1991 ➤ 7,a302: ᴿAntonianum 67 (1992) 435s (M. *Nobile*); Biblica 73 (1992) 288-292 (W. L. *Peterson*: fatally flawed); ÉTRel 67 (1992) 472s (M. *Bouttier* n'approuve pas la 'ségrégation'); JBL 111 (1992) 361-3 (S. *Patterson*); NRT 114 (1992) 756s (X. *Jacques*); Salesianum 54 (1992) 786s (R. *Farina*).
a863 **Figueiredo** Tomé Luis, Evangelho de S. Tomé; comparação com os livros bíblicos. Lisboa 1990, Vetorial. 70 p. – ᴿHumTeol 12 (1991) 301s (H. *Alves*).
a864 **Kloppenborg** John S., *al.*, Q-Thomas reader 1990 ➤ 6,a549: ᴿCBQ 54 (1992) 394s (F. J. *Matera*: queries tacit assumption that Q and Thomas belong to a single genre).
a865 *Layton* B., NH Codex II, 2-7, [Thomas, etc.] 1989 ➤ 6,a551; 7,a305: ᴿJbAC 34 (1991) 177-183 (H.-M. *Schenke*); VigChr 45 (1991) 78-87 (G. *Quispel*).
a866 ᵀᴱMeyer Marvin, The Gospel of Thomas, the hidden sayings of Jesus, with critical edition of the Coptic text and interpretation by *Bloom* Harold. SF 1992, Harper. [viii-] 130 p. $16. 0-06-065581-X [TDig 40,164].
a867 *Trevijano Etcheverría* Ramón, *a)* El anciano preguntará al niño (Evangelio de Tomás Log. 4): ➤ 135, ꟷMUÑOZ IGLESIAS S., EstB 50 (1992) 521-535; – *b)* Santiago el justo y Tomás el mellizo (Evangelio de Tomás, log. 12 y 13): Salmanticensis 39 (1992) 193-215; Eng. 215.

a868 **Kuntzmann** Raymond, Le livre de Thomas NH II,7; BCNH-T 10, 1986 ➤ 2,8614... 6,a541: ᴿCdÉ 67 (1992) 194-6 (M. K. H. *Peters*).

M2.3   *Singula scripta* – Nagᶜ Ḥammadi, various titles.

a869 *Barry* Catherine, La dynamique de l'histoire dans un traité gnostique de Nag Hammadi, La sagesse de Jésus-Christ: Muséon 105 (1992) 265-273.
a870 *Good* Deirdre J., Sophia in Eugnostos the Blessed and the Sophia of Jesus Christ (NHC III,3 and V,1; NHC III,4, and BG 8502,3): ➤ 690, Coptic 1984/90, 139-144.

a871 **Alcalá** M., El evangelio copto de Felipe. Córdoba 1992, Almendro. 208 p. – ᴿHelmantica 43 (1992) 452s (S. *García-Jalón*); REspir 51 (1992) 523 (F. *Antolín*).

a872 *Mantovani* Giancarlo, Illumination et illuminateurs; à la recherche des sources de l'Apocryphon de Jean: ➤ 690, 3d Coptic 1984/90, 227-231.

a873 *Bethge* Hans-Gebhard, Zu einigen literarischen, exegetischen und inhaltlichen Problemen der 'Epistula Petri ad Philippum' (NHC VIII,2): ➤ 690, 3d Coptic 1984/90, 65-69.

a874 **Zandee** J.†, The teaching of Sylvanus: EgUitg 6, 1991 ➤ 7,a324: ᴿJTS 43 (1992) 661-4 (M. *Smith*); NT 34 (1992) 309-311 (R. M. *Wilson*).

a875 *Schenke* Hans-M., Bemerkungen zur Apokalypse des Allogenes (NHC XI,3): ➤ 690, 3d Coptic 1984/90, 417-424.

a876 *Simonetti* Manlio, ERACLEONE, gli psichici e il trattato tripartito: RivStoLR 28 (1992) 3-33.

a877 ᴱ**Orlandi** Tito, Evangelium veritatis: TestiVOA 8. Brescia 1992, Paideia. 153 p. Lit. 33.000 [RHE 87,200*]. 88-394-0477-5.

a878 ᴱ**Gianotto** Claudio, La testimonianza veritiera NHC IX,3, 1990 ➤ 7, a316: ᴿAntonianum 67 (1992) 434s (M. *Nobile*); Asprenas 39 (1992) 111s (L. *Fatica*); RechSR 80 (1992) 462 (Madeleine *Scopello*, aussi sur son Melchisedek 1984).

a879 **Thomassen** E., *Painchaud* L., Le traité tripartite (NH I,5) 1989 ➤ 6, a569; 7,a319: ᴿRHPR 72 (1992) 330s (D. A. *Bertrand*).

a880 **Sevrin** J.-M., Le dossier baptismal séthien: BCNH-Ét 2, 1986 ➤ 1, a256… 6,a572: ᴿCdÉ 67 (1992) 196s (G. G. *Stroumsa*).

a881 *Vliet* J. van der, La Parrhésie anticosmique dans la Bibliothèque copte de Nag Hammadi: Muséon 105 (1992) 27-43.

M3,1   *Quid est religio? Inquisitiones speculativae.* – **What is religion?**

a882 **Adler** Mortimer J., Truth in religion; the plurality of religions and the unity of truth 1990 ➤ 7,a925: ᴿChrCent 109 (1992) 435s (M. *Novak*); LvSt 17 (1992) 69-71 (S. *Bucker*); RelStR 18 (1992) 124 (P. *Knitter*: rather simplistic).

a883 *Alessi* A., Filosofia della religione. R 1991, LAS. – ᴿAntonianum 67 (1992) 445-7 (L. *Oviedo*).

a884 *Antes* Peter, *al.*, Religion: ➤ 757, EvKL 3 (1992) 1543-5 (-65 *al.*, -sfreiheit, -skritik, -sgeschichte…) 1557-99.

a885 *Arthur* Chris, Religion as 'creative ignorance': Month 253 (1992) 160-4.

Baudler Georg, God and violence 1992 ➤ b142*.

a886 *Bermejo Barrera* José C., From the archaeology of religion to the archaeology of symbolic forms; theoretical and methodological foundations: DialHA 16,2 (1990) 211-230.

a887 *Brito* Emilio, Le sentiment religieux selon SCHLEIERMACHER: NRT 114 (1992) 186-211.

a888 *Caffiero* Marina, Sacro/Santo, una nuova collana di storia religiosa [ᴱ*Boesch Gajano* Sofia, *Scaraffia* L., T 1990, Rosenberg &S.]: RivStoLR 27 (1991) 465-474.

a889 ᴱ**Cancik** Hubert, *al.*, Handbuch religionswissenschaftlicher Grundbegriffe I-II, 1988/90 ➤ 5,897; 6,893: ᴿAnthropos 87 (1992) 255s (Ulla *Johansen*).

a890 ᴱ**Carman** John B., *Hopkins* Steven P., Tracing common themes; comparative courses in the study of religion. Atlanta 1991, Scholars. ix-318 p. $45; pa. $35 [RelStR 19,44, G. *Yocum*].

a891 *Cassese* Michele, Il dibattito sulla religione nel Protestantesimo contemporaneo: StEcum 9 (1991) 81-101.

a892 **Cunningham** Lawrence S., *al.*, The sacred quest, an invitation to the study of religion. NY 1991, Macmillan. v-218 p. $19 pa. – ᴿHorizons 19 (1992) 349s (M. A. *Lepain*).

a893 *a) Feifel* Erich, Religionsunterricht mit oder ohne Kirche? Die Zukunft des Religionsunterrichts in einer multikulturellen Gesellschaft; – *b) Simon* Werner, Religiöse Erziehung im Kontext gesellschaftlicher Individualisierung: TrierTZ 101 (1992) 262-279 / 281-301.

a894 *Floucat* Yves, La théologie de la religion selon le P. Labourdette: ➔ 114, ᶠLABOURDETTE M., RThom 92,1 (1992) 304-323.

a894* *Gaspar Pardo* Angelina, La religión en BERGSON: RelCu 38 (1992) 435-445.

a895 **Harrison** Peter, 'Religion' and the religions in the English enlightenment 1990 ➔ 7,a343: ᴿNRT 114 (1992) 282-4 (P. *Évrard*).

a896 **Hay** David, Religious experience today; studying the facts 1990 ➔ 7, a145: ᴿTablet 145 (1991) 338 (Renée *Haynes*).

a897 **Hill** Brennan R., *Knitter* Paul, *Madges* William, Faith, religion, and theology; a contemporary introduction 1990 ➔ 6,a590: ᴿRelStR 18 (1992) 218 (T. W. *Musser*).

a898 *Lüke* Ulrich, Religiosität — ein Produkt der Evolution?: StiZt 210 (1992) 125-133.

a899 **Meń** Alexandre [orthodoxe moscovite assassiné 1990], Les sources de la religion, ᵀ*Marichal* René. P 1991, Desclée. 274 p. F 129. 2-7189-0557-3. – ᴿEsprVie 102 (1992) 339s (M. *Delahoutre*); ÉTRel 67 (1992) 641s (A. *Gaillard*).

a900 *Osborn* Robert T., From theology to religion: ModT 8 (1992) 75-88.

a901 **Paden** William E., Interpreting the sacred; ways of viewing religion. Boston 1992, Beacon. ix-157 p. $25 [RelStR 19,44, H. L. *Carrigan*].

a902 **Pfleiderer** Georg, Theologie als Wirklichkeitswissenschaft; Studien zum Religionsbegriff bei Georg WOBBERMIN, Rudolf OTTO, Henrich SCHOLZ und Max SCHELER: BeitHistT 82. Tü 1992, Mohr. vii-265 p. DM 158. 3-16-145891-5. [Diss. Mü 1991 ➔ 7,a358; TLZ 118,213, F. *Wagner*].

a903 *Poland* Lynn, The idea of the holy and the history of the sublime: JRel 72 (1992) 175-197.

a904 **Richards** Glyn, Towards a theology of religions 1989 ➔ 7,a361: ᴿModT 7 (1990s) 487s (C. *Gillis*).

a905 *a) Schmidt* Werner H., Aspekte des Phänomens 'Religion' im AT; – *b) Salaquarda* Jörg, SCHOPENHAUER als Vorläufer und Anreger der Religionswissenschaft; ➔ 163, ᶠSAUER G., Aktualität 1992, 85-97 / 249-258.

a906 *Stone* Jim, A theory of religion: RelSt 27 (1991) 337-351.

a907 *a) Strenski* Ivan, What's 'rite? Evolution, exchange and the big picture; – *b) Raschid* M. Salman, Mysterium tremendum: Clark's Mysteries of Religion: Religion 21 (L 1991) 219-226 / 279-... [< ᴢIT 91,695].

a908 **Tessier** Robert, Le Sacré: Bref 34, 1991 ➔ 7,a368: ᴿMélSR 49 (1992) 59-61 (L. *Debarge*).

a909 **Vroom** Hendrik M., Religions and the truth 1990 ➔ 7,a273*b*: ᴿRelSt 28 (1992) 118-120 (J. *Hick*); ScripTPamp 23 (1991) 735s (F. *Conesa*).

M3.2 **Historia comparationis religionum:** *centra, scholae.*

a910 **Adams** Hannah, 1755-1831, A dictionary of all religions and religious denominations; Jewish, heathen, Mahometan, Christian, ancient and modern [⁶1817], ᴱ*Tweed* Thomas A.: AAR Classics in Religious Studies. Atlanta 1992, Scholars. xxxvii-376 p. $40; pa./sb. $25. 1-55540-727-7; -8-5 [TDig 40,49].

a910* **Belier** Wouter W., Decayed gods; origin and development of Georges DUMÉZIL's 'idéologie tripartie', ᵀ*Mason* Peter: Studies in Greek and Roman Religion 7. Leiden 1991, Brill. xv-254 p.; 26 fig. [RelStR 19,163, R. A. *Swanson*].

a911 *D'Souza* Felix, WHITEHEAD on the question of religion: IndTSt 29 (1992) 68-92.

a911* **Eliade** Mircea † 1986, Geschichte der religiösen Ideen 3/2, Vom Zeitalter der Entdeckungen bis zur Gegenwart, ᴱ*Culianu* Ioan P. FrB 1991, Herder. 496 p. DM 92. – ᴿTsTKi 62 (1991) 303-5 (N. O. *Breivik*); ZkT 114 (1992) 109s (R. *Oberforcher*).

a912 **Eliade** M., *Culianu* I. P., Handbuch der Religionen. Z 1991, Artemis. – ᴿTsTKi 62 (1991) 305 (N. O. *Breivik*).

a913 — **Ricketts** Mac L., Mircea ELIADE, the Romanian roots, 1907-1945; 1988 → 4,b586: ᴿJAAR 60 (1992) 174-7 (D. *Allen*).

a914 — *Spineto* Natale, La 'nostalgia del Paradiso'; religione e simbolo in Mircea ELIADE: FilT 6 (1992) 296-319; Eng. 296.

a915 **Feil** Ernst, Religio; die Geschichte eines neuzeitlichen Grundbegriffs 1986 → 3,a904; 4,b528. ᴿTsTKi 62 (1991) 305s (N. O. *Breivik*).

a916 ᴱ**Flew** Antony, David HUME, writings on religion: Carus Student Editions 2. La Salle IL, Open Court. xi-304 p. $7.50. 0-8126-9112-1 [TDig 40,167].

a917 **Godlove** Terry F.ᴶ, Religion, interpretation, and diversity of belief; the framework model from Kant to Durkheim to Davidson 1989 → 7,a381: ᴿHistRel 31 (1991s) 421-3 (R. F. *Campany*); JRel 72 (1992) 299s (S. *Davis*).

a918 *Godlove* Terry F.ᴶ, Respecting autonomy and understanding religion: RelSt 28 (1992) 43-60.

a918* *Götke-Hansen* Povl, Religionskritikken imødegået — om Peter L. BERGER: NorTTs 93 (1992) 107-124.

a919 **Goldman** Art L., The search for God at Harvard 1991 → 7,7009: ᴿAmerica 165 (1991) 148 (A. J. *Rudin*); ChrCent 109 (1992) 19s (C. *Kimball*); TrinJ 13 (1992) 249 (A. J. *Köstenberger*).

a920 ᴱ**Hinnells** John R., Who's who of world religions. NY 1991, Simon & S. xvi-560 p. $75 [CBQ 54,614].

a921 **Jaeschke** Walter, Reason in religion; the foundations of HEGEL's philosophy of religion [1986 → 3,a925; 7,a404], ᵀ*Stewart* J. Michael, *Hodgson* Peter C. Berkeley 1990, Univ. of California. 464 p. $50. – ᴿJAAR 60 (1992) 341-4 (D. M. *Schlitt*); RelSt 28 (1992) 280-2 (M. *Inwood*).

a922 **James** William, Die Vielfalt religiöser Erfahrung; eine Studie über die menschliche Natur [Gifford Lectures 1901s], ᵀᴱ*Herms* Eilert. Olten 1979, Walter. 597 p. DM 66. – ᴿMüTZ 43 (1992) 148s (A. *Kreiner*).

a923 — **Ruf** Frederick J., The creation of chaos; William JAMES and the stylistic making of a disorderly world: Rhetoric and Theology. Albany 1991, SUNY. xviii-185 p. $44.50; pa. $15. – ᴿTS 53 (1991) 588s (D. S. *Cunningham*).

a924 *Kamstra* J. H., De plaats van de godsdienstwetenschap in die theologie; samen op weg naar een klant gerichte theologie: NedTTs 46 (1992) 177-187; Eng. 226.

a925 *Keyserlingk* Alexander, Die Aneignung der Moral als das Thema der Religionsphilosophie KANTs: NSys 34 (1992) 17-29; Eng. 29.

a926 **Kitagawa** Joseph M., The quest for human unity 1990 → 7,a405: ᴿAnglTR 74 (1992) 255-7 (R.J. *Jones*); JRel 72 (1992) 468s (T.M. *Ludwig*).
a927 *Levine* Michael P., Deep structure and the comparative philosophy of religion [GREEN R. 1988]: RelSt 28 (1992) 387-399.
a928 ᴱ**Malony** H. Newton, Psychology of religion; personalities, problems, possibilities: Psychology and Christianity 5. GR 1991, Baker. 628 p. $30. 0-8010-6268-3 [TDig 39,380].
a929 *a) Mardones* José Maria, Religione e teoria critica; il potenziale critico della religione di fronte al progetto di J. HABERMAS; – *b) Conci* Domenico A., Segnali di un nuovo inizio? Il sacro nella postmodernità; – *c) Molinaro* Aniceto, La Chiesa il Santo il Sacro: FilT 6 (1992) 415-427 / 428-434 / 444-453; Eng. 415 etc.
a930 *Mürmel* Heinz, FRAZER oder MAUSS? Bemerkungen zu Magiekonzeptionen: ZMissRW 75 (1991) 147-154.
a931 *Ricœur* Paul, Une herméneutique philosophique de la religion, KANT: → 63, ᶠGEFFRÉ C., Interpréter 1992, 25-47.
a932 — ᴱ**Rossi** Philip J., KANT's philosophy of religion reconsidered. Bloomington 1991, Indiana Univ. xxiii-214 p. $25 [TR 88,526].
a933 **Rudolph** Kurt, Geschichte und Probleme der Religionswissenschaft: StHistRel 53. Leiden 1992, Brill. xix-443 p. ƒ220. 90-04-09503-9. – ᴿTsTKi 63 (1992) 309s (N. O. *Breivik*).
a934 **Sharpe** Erie J., Nathan SÖDERBLOM [1866-1931] and the study of religion 1990 → 6,a651*; $40. 0-8078-1868-2 [TDig 38,188]: ᴿRelSt 27 (1991) 422-4 (F. *Whaling*).
a935 **Smith** Malcolm C., MONTAIGNE and religious freedom; the dawn of pluralism: ÉtPgH 45. Genève 1991, Droz. 257 p. [TR 88,255].
a936 *Steunebrink* Gerrit A. J., Zur Notwendigkeit von Religion aus der Sicht DURKHEIMs und seiner Erben: TPhil 67 (1992) 536-557.
a937 **Terrin** A. N., Introduzione allo studio comparato delle religioni [< Credere Oggi]. Brescia 1991, Morcelliana. 282 p. Lit. 25.000. – ᴿStPatav 39 (1992) 666s (G. *Toffanello*).
a938 *Waardenburg* J. D. J., G. van der LEEUW [1890-1950] en de groei van de godsdienstwetenschap: NedTTs 46 (1992) 89-103.

M3.3 **Individui conspicui** in investigatione religionum.

a939 **Albanese** Catherine L., America, religions and religion². Belmont CA 1992, Wadsworth. xxv-548 p. $32.50 pa. 0-534-16488-9 [TDig 39,349].
a940 **Aldanov** Boris, The human predicament theory of religion. New Delhi 1988, Vikas. vi-550 p. – ᴿJDharma 16 (1991) 169 [P. *Kalluveettil*].
a941 **Alessi** Adriano, Filosofia della religione: BtScR 93. R 1991, LAS. 335 p. Lit. 30.000 [TR 88,170].
a942 **Alston** William P., Perceiving God; the epistemology of religious experience. Ithaca NY 1991, Cornell Univ. xiv-320 p. $37. – ᴿTS 53 (1992) 554-6 (T. W. *Tilley*).
a943 *Barnard* G. William, Explaining the unexplainable; Wayne PROUDFOOT's [1985] Religious experience: JAAR 60 (1992) 231-256.
a944 ᴱ**Blondeau** Anne-Marie, *Schipper* Kristofer, Essais sur le rituel I-II [colloque ÉPHÉR 1986/7]: BtÉPHÉR 92.95, 1988/90 → 7,470*; xiii-210 p.; 6 fig.; 20 phot. / xviii-236 p.; ill.: ᴿRHR 209 (1992) 181-4 (A. *Bareau*).
a945 **Bose** K. S., A theory of religious thought; the principles underlying forms of knowledge, behavior and social relationship in traditional

society. New Delhi 1991, Sterling. viii-134 p. rs 150. – ᴿRRelRes 33 (1990) 376s (W. H. *Swatos*: confused, repetitious).

a946 **Byrne** Peter, Natural religion and the nature of religion 1989 ➤ 6,a582: ᴿRelSt 27 (1991) 425s (J. *Hick*: important).

a947 ᴱ**Champion** Françoise, *Hervieu-Léger* Danièle, De l'émotion en religion; renouveaux et traditions. P 1990, Centurion. 253 p. [Bijdragen 53,179].

a948 *a) Chapman* Mark D., 'Theology within the walls'; Wilhelm HERR-MANN's religious reality; – *b) Brecht* Volker, Das Sittliche als Grundlage der Theologie W. Herrmanns: NSys 34 (1992) 69-84; deutsch 84 / 48-67; Eng. 68.

a949 **Couture** André, Sur la piste des dieux. Montréal 1990, Paulines. 241 p. – ᴿLavalTP 48 (1992) 137s (C. *Renauld*).

a950 *Dean* William, A present prospect for American religious thought: JAAR 60 (1992) 737-755.

a951 *Dhondt* U., Filosofie en godsdienst: Tijdschrift voor Filosofie 53,1 (1991) 3-22 [< RSPT 76,203].

a952 **Dupré** Louis, De symboliek van het heilige [selectie < The other dimension 1972], ᴱ*Visscher* Jacques de. Kampen/Kapellen 1991, Kok/Pelckmans. 165 p. Fb 590. – ᴿCollatVL 22 (1992) 728s (E. Vanden *Berghe*)

a953 **Faber** H., Het lichtend geheim; perspectieven in de godsdienstpsychologie. Baarn 1991, Ten Have. 191 p. *f* 27,50. 90-259-4459-0. – ᴿTvT 32 (1992) 218 (P. *Vandermeersch*).

a954 **Gay** Volney P., Understanding the occult. Mp 1989, Fortress. 211 p. 0-8006-237-X. – ᴿRExp 88 (1991) 101 (W. L. *Hendricks*).

a955 ᴱ**Grassi** Piergiorgio, Filosofia della religione; storia e problemi. Brescia 1988, Queriniana. – ᴿFilT 5 (1991) 164-8 (Giuseppina *De Simone*).

a956 ᴱ**Greisch** Jean, Penser la religion; recherches en philosophie de la religion: Philosophie 13. P 1991, Beauchesne. 430 p. F 180. – ᴿETL 68 (1992) 463s (E. *Brito*).

a957 ᴱ**Halder** Alois, *al.*, Religionsphilosophie heute: Chancen..., 1988 ➤ 6, 415: ᴿBijdragen 53 (1992) 102s (H. J. *Adriaanse*).

a958 *a) Harris* Walter S., Rendering unto Caesar; religion and nationalism; – *b) Augaard-Mogensen* Lars, Freedom, religion and socio-logic: ➤ 127, ꟻMATCZAK S., 1989, 35-50 / 1-27.

a959 **Heiler** Friedrich, ⁵*Goldammer* Kurt, Die Religionen der Menschheit. Stu 1991, Reclam. 672 p.; 98 fig. – ᴿSalesianum 54 (1992) 364 (R. *Sabin*: updated bibliog.).

a960 *Herzog* Markwart, Religionstheorie und Theologie René GIRARDS: KerDo 38 (1992) 105-136; Eng. 136s.

a961 **Hick** John, An interpretation of religion; human responses to the transcendent 1989 ➤ 5,a631 ... 7,a347: ᴿJTS 43 (1992) 800-4 (J. *Clayton*: 'a canny ability to identify the problems that really matter'); RelSt 27 (1991) 121-132 (P. *Byrne*); ScotJT 45 (1992) 403s (R. *Page*).

a962 — *Apczynski* John V., John HICK's theocentrism; revolutionary or implicitly exclusivist?: ModT 8 (1992) 39-52.

a963 — *Heim* S. Mark, The pluralistic hypothesis [HICK J. 1989], realism, and post-eschatology: RelSt 28 (1992) 207-219.

a964 — *Springsted* Eric O., Conditions of dialogue; John HICK and Simone WEIL: JRel 72 (1992) 19-36.

a965 **Hofmeister** Heimo E.M., Truth and belief; interpretation and critique of the analytical theory of religion [1978], ᵀ1990 ➤ 7,a403: ᴿTS 53 (1992) 564-6 (S. *Payne*: severe).

a965* **Hudson** Yeager, The philosophy of religion. Mountain View CA 1991, Mayfield. xvi-355 p. [TR 88,170].

a966 **Holl** Adolf, Im Keller des Heiligtums: Geschlecht und Gewalt in der Religion [In the basement of the sanctuary; sex and violence in religion]. Stu 1991, Kreuz. 222 p. DM 34 [TR 88,169].

a967 **Kerssemakers** J. H. N., Psychotherapeuten en religie; een verkennend onderzoek naar tegenoverdracht bij religieuze problematiek. Nijmegen 1990, auct. 207 p. *f* 29,70. 90-70713-23-3. – ᴿTvT 32 (1992) 218s (B. *Pattyn*).

a968 *Kippenberg* Hans G., The problem of literacy in the history of religions [8 books]: Numen 39 (1992) 102-107.

a969 **Krieger** D. J., The new universalism; foundations for a global theology. Mkn 1991, Orbis. 219 p. £13. 0-88344-727-4. – ᴿExpTim 103 (1991s) 191 (G. *D'Costa*: a genuine contribution, with help from Chicago).

a970 *La Fargue* Michael, Radically pluralistic, thoroughly critical; a new theory of religions [trying to reconcile HICK-W. C. SMITH approach with GEERTZ-WEBER]: JAAR 60 (1992) 693-716.

a971 **Langthaler** Rudolf, Kritischer Rationalismus; eine Untersuchung zu Aufklärung und Religionskritik in der Gegenwart: EurHS 20/218. Fra 1987, Lang. 542 p. Sch 965,40. – ᴿZkT 114 (1992) 445-8 (E. *Runggaldier*).

a972 **Lapointe** Roger, Socio-anthropologie du religieux 2. Le cercle enchanté de la croyance. Genève c.1991, Droz. 312 p. – ᴿScEsp 44 (1992) 380-2 (R. *Lemieux*).

a973 **Lawson** E. T., *McCauley* R. N., Rethinking religion; connecting cognition and culture. C 1990, Univ. 194 p. £32.50; pa. £13. 0-521-37370-0; -43806-3 [Numen 40,189, J. G. *Platvoet*].

a974 **Masih** Y., A comparative study of religions. New Delhi 1990, Motilal Banarsidass. xiv-400 p. rs. 200. – ᴿJDharma 17 (1992) 61-63 (Mari *Tom*).

a975 *Melchiorre* Virgilio, Dire il sacro: FilT 6 (1992) 59-83; Eng. 59.

a976 **Meslin** Michel, L'esperienza umana del divino; fondamenti di un'antropologia religiosa, [1988] ᵀ*Verdolin* A. R 1991, Borla. 401 p. – ᴿSapienza 45 (1992) 221-5 (Nora *Massa Gallucci d'Enrico*).

a977 **Milanesi** G., *Baizek* J., Sociologia della religione. T 1990, LDC. 176 p. Lit. 15.000. – ᴿProtestantesimo 47 (1992) 341 (C. *Tron*).

a978 **Mooren** Thomas, Auf der Grenze; die Andersheit Gottes und die Vielfalt der Religionen: EurHS 23/434. Fra 1991, Lang. 201 p. DM 63 [TS 88,170].

a979 **Nasr** Seyyed H., Knowledge and the sacred. Albany 1989, SUNY. 341 p. $34.50; pa. $13. 0-7914-0176-6; -7-4. – ᴿJRel 72 (1992) 284 (I. P. *Culianu*: for a pious public already agreed).

a980 **Neville** Robert C., Behind the masks of God; an essay toward comparative theology 1991 → 7,a478: ᴿTTod 49 (1992s) 550. 552s (J. H. *Chapman*).

a981 **Newport** John P., Life's ultimate questions; a contemporary philosophy of religion 1989 → 5,a667; $17: ᴿGraceTJ 12,1 (1991) 144s (J. D. *Morrison*).

ᴱ**Obayashi** Hiroshi, Death and afterlife; perspectives of world religions 1992 → 603.

a982 **Oberhammer** Gerhard, Begegnung als Kategorie der Religionshermeneutik: De Nobili 4. W 1989, Brill. 60 p. – ᴿZMissRW 75 (1991) 157-9 (H. *Waldenfels*, auch über sein Versuch 1987).

a983 **Oser** Fritz, *Gmuender* Paul, [T]*Ridez* Louis, L'homme, son développement religieux; étude de structuralisme génétique: Sciences humaines et religions. P 1991, Cerf. 352 p. F 147 [RTLv 24,257, P. *Weber*].

a984 **Paden** William E., Interpreting the sacred; ways of viewing religion. Boston 1992, Beacon. xi-157 p. $25. 0-8070-7706-2 [TDig 39,378].

a985 **Penner** Hans, Impasse and resolution; a critique of the study of religion 1989 → 6,a614: [R]JRel 72 (1992) 298s (T. M. *Vial*).

a986 *Pétursson* Pétur, Civilreligionen – ett svar på de yttersta frågorna? SvTKv 67 (1991) 170-181.

a987 **Phillips** D. Z., From fantasy to faith; the philosophy of religion and twentieth century literature. L 1991, Macmillan. xii-224 p. £35, pa. £10. 0-333-52956-1; -7-X. – [R]ExpTim 103 (1991s) 189 (G. *Pattison*); JTS 43 (1992) 788-790 (P. *Sherry*); TLond 95 (1992) 153s (D. *Cupitt*: £40, pa. £13).

a988 **Pruyser** Paul W., † 1987, Religion in psychodynamic perspective [12 art.], [E]*Maloney* H. Newton, *Spilka* Bernard. NY 1991, Oxford-UP. 233 p. 0-19-506234-5 [TDig 39,282]. – [R]RRelRes 33 (1990s) 381 (T. L. *Brink*).

a989 **Reat** N. Ross, *Perry* Edmund F., A world theology; the central spiritual reality of humankind. NY 1992, Cambridge-UP. xi-314 p. $50. 0-521-33159-5 [TDig 39,282].

a990 [E]**Ries** J., Trattato di antropologia del sacro I. 1989 → 7,a147; II, 1991: [R]StPatav 39 (1992) 206-211 (F. *Mora*).

a991 [F]Scott Nathan A.[J], Morphologies of faith; essays in religion and culture, [E]**Gerhart** Mary, *Yu* Anthony, 1990 → 6,162: [R]JRel 72 (1992) 313s (T. E. *Helm*).

a992 *Shaw* Patrick, On worshipping the same God: RelSt 28 (1992) 511-532.

a993 **Smith** Huston, The world's religions [= [2rev]Religions of man 1958, 1½ million sold]. SF 1991, Harper. xvi-399 p. $22; pa. $10. 0-06-250799-0; -811-3 [TDig 39,386].

a994 *Smith* Wilfred C., Reconsidérer l'Écriture à la lumière de la théologie et de l'étude de la religion, [T]*Basset* Jean-Claude: RTPhil 124 (1992) 369-388.

a995 [E]*Swidler* L., Toward a universal theology of religion 1987 → 3,a994 ... 6,a709: [R]LVitae 46 (1991) 355s (P. *Lebeau*).

a996 **Tambiah** Stanley J., Magic, science, religion and the scope of rationality (Morgan lectures 1984). C 1990, Univ. 187 p. – [R]HistRel 32 (1991s) 414-6 (D. *Gold*).

a997 **Taylor** James C., A new porcine history of philosophy and religion [[1]1972]. Nv 1992, Abingdon. 60 p. $5 [RelStR 19,70, D. R. *Janz*].

a998 *a*) *Turner* Paul R., Evaluating religions; – *b*) *Pickard* William M.[J], A universal theology of religions?: Missiology 19 (1991) 131-142 / 143-152.

a999 **Vergote** Antoine, Explorations de l'espace théologique; études de théologie et de philosophie de la religion [35, 1952-87]: BtETL 110, 1990 → 6,315*: [R]ActuBbg 29 (1992) 217s (J. *Boada*); LvSt 17 (1992) 89s (B. *Pattyn*); RTLv 23 (1992) 244s (P. *Weber*).

b1 **Waardenburg** Jacques, ❷ Religie i religia; systematyczne wprowadzenie do religioznawstwa, [T]*Bronk* Andrzej. Wsz 1991, Verbinum. 223 p. – [R]AtKap 119 (1992) 360-2 (S. *Pawlak*, ❷).

b2 [E]**Weger** Karl-Heinz, Religionskritik, [170] Texte zur Theologie; Fund-T 1. Graz 1991, Styria. 296 p. DM 40. 3-222-11999-6: [R]Gregorianum 73 (1992) 539s (R. *Fisichella*); TR 88 (1992) 310 (H. *Verweyen*); ZkT 114 (1992) 98 (K. H. *Neufeld*).

b3 **Weier** Wilfried,   Religion als Selbstfindung; Grundlegung einer existenz-analytischen Religionsphilosophie: AbhPh/Ök 45.   Pd 1991, Schöningh. 310 p. – ᴿZkT 114 (1992) 448-450 (E. *Coreth*).

b4 **Wuchterl** Kurt,   Analyse und Kritik der religiösen Vernunft; Grundzüge einer paradigmabezogenen Religionsphilosophie: Uni-Tb 1543.   Bern 1989, Haupt.   309 p. – ᴿTPhil 67 (1992) 134-7 (J. *Schmidt*).

b5 **Wulff** David M.,   Psychology of religion; classic and contemporary views. NY 1991, J. Wiley.   xxv-640 + [132] p. $40.   0-471-50236-7 [TDig 39,394].

b6 **Wuthnow** Robert,   Rediscoverung the sacred; perspectives on religion in contemporary society.   GR 1992, Eerdmans. v-178 p. $29; pa. $19. 0-8028-3697-6; -0633-3 [TDig 40,94]. – ᴿChrCent 109 (1992) 717 (L. S. *Cunningham*).

b7 **Wyss** Dieter,   Psychologie und Religion; Untersuchungen zur Ursprüng-lichkeit religiösen Erlebens.   Wü 1991, Königshausen & N.   174 p. DM 31. [RTLv 24,255, P. *Weber*].

b8 **Zdybicka** Zofia J., sr.,   Person and religion; an introduction to the philosophy of religion, ᵀ*Sandok* Theresa: Catholic Thought from Lublin. NY 1991, Lang.   xxv-418 p. $66.   0-8204-1447-6 [TDig 40,193].

b9 **Zirker** Hans,   Critica della religione 1989 ➤ 5,a728; 6,a631:   ᴿFilT 5 (1991) 168-171 (G. *Razzino*).

b10 **Zock** Hetty,   A psychology of ultimate concern; Erik H. ERIKSON's con-tribution to the psychology of religion.   Amst 1990, Rodopi.   258 p. $37.50 pa. – ᴿRRelRes 33 (1990) 95s (W. M. *Goldsmith*: Erickson in title, Erikson in text).

M3.4   **Aspectus particulares** *religionum mundi.*

b11 **Carmody** D. & J.,   Prayer in world religions 1990 ➤ 6,a660:   ᴿETL 68 (1992) 182 (V. *Neckebrouck*: danger de rapprochements illégitimes); RelStR 18 (1992) 124 (J. *Borelli*: rather on how Christians might reflect on other traditions similar to praying); Vidyajyoti 55 (1991) 117 (P. M. *Meagher*).

b12 **Coward** Howard,   Sacred word and sacred text; Scripture in world religions 1988 ➤ 4,b517 ... 6,a661:   ᴿCritRR 5 (1992) 271-4 (G. T. *Sheppard*).

b13 **De Falco Marotta** Maria,   Le grandi religioni oggi; storia, dottrina, culto, etica, libri sacri 1989 ➤ 7,a429:   ᴿAntonianum 67 (1992) 161s (T. *Larrañaga*).

b14 **Dickson** D. Bruce,   The dawn of belief; religion in the Upper Paleolithic of southwestern Europe.   Tucson 1990, Univ. Arizona.   264 p. $30.   0-8165-1076-8. – ᴿHistRel 32 (1992) 303-6 (B. C. *Ray*).

b15 ᴱ**Eathart** H. Byron,   Religious traditions of the world; a journey through Africa, Mesoamerica, North America, Judaism, Christianity, Islam, Hin-duism, Buddhism, China, and Japan [combined from ten volumes already published separately].   SF 1992, Harper.   xx-1204 p. $35. [TDig 40,184].

b16 *Filoramo* Giovanni,   La scienza della religione e il problema del plura-lismo: FilT 6 (1992) 106-118.

b17 **Haudry** Jean,   La religion cosmique des Indo-Européens [reprints dès 1982], ÉtIE, 1987 ➤ 5,a771; 6,a768:   ᴿLatomus 51 (1992) 439-444 (Francine *Mawet*).

b18 *a) Knitter* Paul F.,   Interreligious dialogue and the unity of humanity; – *b) Siddhashrama* B. P., *Nair* K. Ramachandran,   Swamy VIVEKANANDA's perspective of religion; its implications for war and peace; – *c) Narivelil*

Victor, Politics of Mandir-Masjid conflict; undoing of a secular and pluralistic society; – d) *Robinson* Leland W., The bases of anti-Bahá'i attitudes in Iran; – e) *Vageeshwari* S. P., Arab-Israeli wars; a historical analysis: JDharma 17,4 ('Religions; forces of unity or division?' 1992) 282-297 / 363-375 / 298-311 / 351-362 / 311-328 [-350 *al.*, Gulf; Ireland].

b19 **Lanczkowski** Günther, Geschichte der nichtchristlichen Religionen: Tb. Fra 1989, Fischer. 391 p. – ᴿTLZ 117 (1992) 21s (K.-W. *Tröger*).

b20 ᴱ**Meslin** M., Maître et disciples dans les traditions religieuses 1988/90 7,532: ᴿNRT 114 (1992) 284 (L.-J. *Renard*).

b21 **Rausch** David A., *Voss* Carl H., World religions; our quest for meaning. Mp 1989, Augsburg-Fortress. 208 p. $13. 0-8006-2331-2. – ᴿVidyajyoti 55 (1991) 438 (P. M. *Meagher*).

b22 **Smith** Wilfred C., Towards a world theology; faith and the comparative history of religion 1989 ➤ 61,k678 ... 7,a448: ᴿPacifica 4 (1991) 98s (P. *Rule*).

b23 **Staal** Fritz, Rules without meaning; rituals, mantras and the human sciences: TorStRel 4. NY 1989, Lang. xxii-490 p. – ᴿHistRel 31 (1991s) 412-4 (P. J. *Griffiths*).

M3.5 Religiones mundi ex conspectu christianismi.

b24 **Bernhardt** Reinhold, Der Absolutheitsanspruch des Christentums ᴰ1990 ➤ 7,a455: ᴿActuBbg 29 (1992) 62s (J. *Boada*); MüTZ 43 (1992) 116s (P. *Schmidt-Leukel*, auch über sein Horizontüberschreitung 1991); ZkT 114 (1992) 194-9 (W. *Kern*: unentbehrlich).

b25 ᴱ**Bernhardt** Reinhold, Horizontüberschreitung 1991 ➤ 7,340b: ᴿTGʟ 82 (1992) 360-2 (B. *Dieckmann*).

b26 **Braaten** Carl E., No other gospel? Christianity among the world's religions. Mp 1992, Fortress. 146 p. $11. 0-8006-2539-0 [TDig 39,353: Kɴɪᴛᴛᴇʀ/Hɪᴄᴋ unsatisfactory].

b27 ᴱ**Brunner-Traut** Emma, Die fünf grossen Weltreligionen⁵ [¹1974]: Spektrum 4006. FrB 1991, Herder. 144 p. DM 12,80. – ᴿZkT 114 (1992) 108s (K. H. *Neufeld*).

b28 *Carson* D. A., Reflections on Christian assurance: WestTJ 54 (1992) 1-29.

b29 **Catoir** John T., World religion; beliefs behind today's headlines; Buddhism, Christianity, Confucianism, Hinduism, Islam, Shintoism, Taoism. NY 1992, Alba. xxiv-119 p. $8. 0-8189-0640-5 [TDig 40,93].

b30 *Charpentier* Jean-Marie, Pluralismus: ➤ 757, EvKL 3 (1992) 1232-41.

b31 **Cox** Harvey, Many mansions 1989 ➤ 5,248: ᴿDoctLife 41 (1991) 217s (D. *Regan*).

b32 **Cracknell** Kenneth, Mission und Dialog; für eine neue Beziehung zu Menschen anderen Glaubens, ᵀ*Berger* Ulrike. Fra 1990, Lembeck. 160 p. DM 24 pa. – ᴿTR 88 (1992) 242-4 (B. *Doppelfeld*).

b33 *Culpepper* Robert H., The lordship of Christian and religious pluralism; a review article [Hɪᴄᴋ-Kɴɪᴛᴛᴇʀ 1987; D'Cᴏsᴛᴀ G. 1990]: PerspRelSt 19 (1992) 311-322 [Hick 141 from R. Rᴜᴇᴛʜᴇʀ 'the idea that Christianity, or even the biblical faiths, have a monopoly on religious truth is an outrageous and absurd chauvinism'].

b34 *D'Costa* Gavin, Christian uniqueness reconsidered; the myth of a pluralistic theology of religions 1990 ➤ 6,402*; 7,a461; also Gracewing 1990, £10; 0-88344-686-3; ᴿChrCent 108 (1991) 688-690 (S. M. *Heim*: crisscrossing the Rubicon); ETL 68 (1992) 466-8 (E. *Brito*); ExpTim 103

(1991s) 62 (M. *Forward*); Horizons 19 (1992) 346s (L. J. *Biallas*); ModT 8 (1992) 308s (D. *Burrell*, also on TRACY D., Inter-religious); NRT 114 (1992) 282 (J. *Masson*); SWJT 34,3 (1991s) 41s (H. N. *Smith*); Thomist 56 (1992) 361-3 (P. C. *Phan*).

b35 **Dallaporta-Xydias** Nicola, Cristianesimo e mondi tradizionali: Bt esoterica 4. Abano Terme 1991, Piovan. 344 p. Lit. 30.000. – ᴿStPatav 39 (1992) 636-640 (L. *Sartori*).

b36 **Dickson** Kwesi A., Uncompleted mission; Christianity and exclusivism. Mkn 1991, Orbis. x-180 p. $19. – ᴿETL 68 (1992) 468s (A. *Vanneste*).

b37 **DiNoia** J. A., The diversity of religions; a Christian perspective. Wsh 1992, Catholic University of America. xii-199 p. $30; pa. $18. 0-8132-0763-0; -9-X [TDig 40,60].

b38 **Dupuis** Jacques, Jesus Christ at the encounter of world religions [1989 ➔ 6,a684a], ᵀ*Barr* Robert R. 1991 ➔ 7,a464; also Gracewing. 301 p. £13. 0-88344-723-1. – ᴿExpTim 103 (1991s) 252 (P. D. *Bishop*: scholarly; conversion to Christianity not the primary aim); IndTSt 28 (1991) 369-374 (R. *Rossignol*, éd. franc.); TS 53 (1992) 178s (F. X. *Clooney*: perhaps the best comprehensive volume available today, despite some unproved concrete examples).

b39 **Dupuis** J., Gesù Cristo incontro alle religioni [1988] 1989 ➔ 6,a684b: ᴿCC 143 (1992,1) 364-375 (G. *de Rosa*).

b40 **Dupuis** J., Jesucristo al encuentro de las religiones: BtTeol 11. M 1991, Paulinas. 363 p. [NRT 115,595, P.-H. de *Bruyn*].

b41 *Dupuis* Jacques, Cristianesimo e religione: CC 143 (1992,3) 272-7.

b42 *Elders* Léon, La signification théologique des religions non chrétiennes: PeCa 251 (1991) 17-26.

b43 **Euler** Walter A., Unitas et pax; Religionsvergleich bei Raimundus LULLUS und Nikolaus von KUES: RelWSt 15, 1990 ➔ 7,a465: ᴿRTLv 23 (1992) 230s (J.-M. *Counet*); ZkT 114 (1992) 105s (K. H. *Neufeld*: durchaus aktuell).

b44 **Friedli** Richard, Le Christ dans les cultures; carnets de routes et de déroutes; un essai de théologie des religions. 1989 ➔ 6,a686*: ᴿLVitae 46 (1991) 115 (J. *Scheuer*); Spiritus 32 (1991) 94s (H. *Maurier*: déroutant).

b45 *Geffré* Claude, La singolarità del cristianesimo nell'età del pluralismo religioso, ᵀ*Tortolone* Gian M.: FilT 6 (1992) 38-58; Eng. 38 [119-123, commento *Vicari* Dario].

b46 **Gira** Dennis, Les religions: Parcours, 1991 ➔ 7,a469: ᴿChristus 39 (P 1992) 96s (J. B. *Baudin*).

b47 *Gisel* Pierre, Faire face aux pluralités religieuses: ➔ 63, ᶠGEFFRÉ C., Interpréter 1992, 193-210.

b48 *Goltz* Hermann, Kulturelle und konfessionelle Vielfalt in Europa heute: UnSa 46 (1991) 245-254.

b49 ᴱ**Gort** Jerald, *al.*, Dialogue and syncretism; an interdisciplinary approach 1989 ➔ 6,621: ᴿIntRMiss 80 (1991) 128s (A. *Race*, also on VROOM H.).

b50 *Greiner* Sebastian, Funktionale Religionstheorie und christlicher Glaube: MüTZ 43 (1992) 183-195.

b51 ᴱ**Griffiths** Paul J., Christianity through non-Christian eyes 1990 ➔ 7, a470: ᴿJRel 72 (1992) 128s (J. L. *Fredericks*).

b52 **Hardy** Gilbert G., Monastic quest and interreligious dialogue. NY 1990, Lang. x-285 p. Fs 62,40 [TR 88,171].

b53 ᴱ**Hick** J., Knitter P., The myth of Christian uniqueness 1989 ➔ 4,b546... 6,a690: ᴿÉTRel 67 (1992) 296s (A. *Gounelle*).

b54 ᴱHick J., *Meltzer* E., Three faiths — one God; a Jewish-Christian-Muslim encounter 1984. Albany 1989, SUNY. 224 p. $49.50; pa. $18. 0-7914-0042-5; -3-3. – ᴿRelSt 27 (1991) 133-5 (G. *D'Costa*).

b55 *Hogan* Kevin, The experience of reality; Evelyn UNDERHILL [1874-1941] and religious pluralism: AnglTR 74 (1992) 334-347.

b56 ᴱ**Holtrop** P.N., *Minnema* L., Voor Hem een ander? Ontwerpen voor een pluralistische theologie der religies [< Myth of Christian uniqueness ➤ b53 supra]. Haag 1990, Meinema. 152 p. *f* 27,50. – ᴿNedTTs 46 (1992) 262s (M.H. *Vroom*).

b57 **Immoos** Thomas, Ein bunter Teppich; die Religionen Japans. Graz 1990, Styria. 230 p.; ill. 3-222-11929-5. – ᴿActuBbg 29 (1992) 110s (J. *Boada*).

b58 **Kämpchen** Martin, Liebe auch den Gott deines Nächsten; Lebenserfahrungen beim Dialog der Religionen: Herder-Tb 1621, 1989 ➤ 6,345: ᴿZMissRW 75 (1991) 239s (P. *Antes*).

b59 **Knitter** Paul F., Ein Gott — viele Religionen; gegen den Absolutheitsanspruch des Christentums 1988 ➤ 4,b411 ... 7,a473: ᴿEstE 67 (1992) 466 (J.J. *Alemany*).

b60 ᴱ**Knitter** Paul, Pluralism and oppression; theology in world perspective: CTS Annual 34, 1988/90 ➤ 7,518: ᴿRelStR 18 (1992) 221 (L. *Richard*).

b61 *Knitter* Paul F., Religious pluralism in theological education [...locked within the house of authority]: AnglTR 74 (1992) 418-437 [-442-449-455, replies by *Braaten* C., *Schreiter* R., *Nishi* S.].

b62 **Küng** Hans, Projet d'éthique planétaire; la paix mondiale par la paix entre les religions. P 1991, Seuil. 247 p. F 120. 2-02-012777-6. – ᴿÉT-Rel 67 (1992) 600 (J.-D. *Causse*).

b63 *a) Ludwig* Theodore, Christianity and teaching about other faiths; – *b) Kyaw* Than, Relation between people of different faith commitments (toward a Christian paradigm); – *c) Braaten* Carl E., Christian theology and the history of religions: CurrTM 19 (1992) 14-20 / 21-28 / 5-13.

b64 *Marshall* I.H., Dialogue with non-Christians in the NT: EvRT 16,1 (1992) 28-47 [< NTAbs 36,380].

b65 **Moran** Gabriel, Uniqueness; problem or paradox in Jewish and Christian traditions: Faith meets faith. Mkn 1992, Orbis. $40; pa. $17. 0-88344-830-0; -29-7 [TDig 40,177; TContext 10/2,98, G. *Evers*].

b66 **Newbigin** Lesslie, The Gospel in a pluralist society 1989 ➤ 6,a697; 7, a479: ᴿHeythJ 33 (1992) 92s (J. *Sullivan*); IntRMiss 80 (1991) 130-2 (J.P. *Rajashekar*).

b67 *Ott* Heinrich, Reflexionen über ein Religionsgespräch: Dialog der Religionen 1,2 (München 1991) 179-186 [130-178, Tübinger Dialoggespräch].

b68 *a) Pagano* Maurizio, Filosofia e teologia di fronte alla sfida del pluralismo; – *b) Hick* John, Il Cristianesimo tra le religioni del mondo, ᵀ*Curry* Leslie C.; – *c) Pannenberg* W., Le religioni nella prospettiva della teologia cristiana e l'autocomprensione del cristianesimo nel suo rapporto con le religioni esterne alla Chiesa, ᵀ*Ravera* Marco: FilT 6 (1992) 1-12 / 13-24 / 25-37.

b69 **Panikkar** Raimon, Der neue religiöse Weg; im Dialog der Religionen leben 1990 ➤ 7,a480*: ᴿMüTZ 42 (1991) 295s (P. *Schmidt-Leukel*).

b70 **Panjikaran** Sebastian, Swami VIVEKANANDA's understanding of religious pluralism; a theological assessment from a Catholic view represented by Joseph NEUNER: diss. Pont. Univ. Gregoriana, ᴰ*Dhavamony* M. Roma 1992. 374 p.; Extr. 3889, 116 p. – RTLv 24, p. 567.

b71 a) *Pathrapankal* Joseph, Méditation universelle du Christ et pluralisme des religions; – b) *Dupuis* Jacques, Pluralisme religieux et mission évangélisatrice de l'Église: Spiritus 32 (1991) 3-14 / 63-76.

b72 ᴱ**Petit** Jean-Claude, *Breton* Jean-Claude, Jésus: Christ universel? Interprétations anciennes et appropriations contemporaines de la figure de Jésus [Soc. Canad. Théol. Montréal 27-29 oct. 1989]: Héritage et Projet 44. Saint-Laurent QUÉ 1990, Fides. 270 p. – ᴿETL 68 (1992) 474s (E. *Brito*).

b73 *Petri* Heinrich, Der Absolutheitsanspruch des Christentums und das Problem der Religionsfreiheit: MüTZ 43 (1992) 315-326.

b74 **Placher** William C., Unapologetic theology; a Christian voice in a pluralistic conversation. Louisville 1989, W-Knox. 178 p. $14. – ᴿModT 7 (1990s) 374s (P. *Lewis*).

b75 *Power* W. L., Religious experience and the Christian experience of God: IntJPhRel 31 (1992) 177-186 [+9 al. on the epistemic status of religious belief: < ZIT 92,277].

b76 **Richards** Glyn, Towards a theology of religions 1989 ➤ 7,a361: ᴿHeythJ 33 (1992) 209-212 (G. *Louglin* compares with W. H. SMITH).

b77 **Rosenstein** Gustav, Die Stunde des Dialogs; Begegnung der Religionen heute [Diss. Regensburg]: PädBeit 9. Ha 1991, Rissen. xiv-265 p. DM 38,60 [TR 88,171].

b78 **Rouner** Leroy S., To be at home; Christianity, civil religion, and world community. Boston 1991, Beacon. 151 p. $20. – ᴿJAAR 60 (1992) 815-8 (D. M. *Trimiew*: what exactly does he consider viable?).

b79 **Ruokanen** Miikka, The Catholic doctrine of non-Christian religions according to the Second Vatican Council: Studies in Christian Mission 7. Leiden 1992, Brill. 169 p. *f* 51,50 [TR 88,171].

b80 *Russo* Adolfo, Nel nome di chi siamo salvati? La cristologia non normativa di Paul KNITTER: Asprenas 39 (1992) 341-361.

b81 **Samartha** Stanley, One Christ — many religions; towards a revised Christology. Mkn 1991, Orbis. 190 p. $13. 0-88344-733-9. – ᴿExpTim 103 (1991s) 191 (G. *D'Costa*: on many things other than Christology).

b82 **Scheid** Edward G., Scripture and theology of the religions; on the theological interpretation of Sacred Scripture in Christian attitudes toward world religions [... RAHNER, HICK]: diss. Duquesne 1992, ᴰ*Thompson* W. 285 p. 92-22348. – DissA 53 (1992s) 855-A.

b83 *Seckler* Max, Wohin driftet man in der Theologie der Religionen? kritische Beobachtungen zu einer Dokumentation (MÜLLER K., PRAWDZIK W. 1991): TüTQ 172 (1992) 126-130.

b84 **Smith** Jonathan Z., Drudgery divine; the comparison of early Christianities and the religions of late antiquity 1990 ➤ 6,a706; 7,a486: ᴿChrCent 108 (1991) 695s (R. A. *Segal*); CritRR 5 (1992) 275-8 (L. H. *Martin*); HistRel 32 (1992) 301-3 (H. *Eilberg-Schwartz*); TorJT 7 (1991) 299-301 (J. S. *Kloppenborg*).

b84* *Smith* Joseph J., Christianity and world religions; Paul KNITTER's pluralistic perspective: Landas 4 (Manila 1990) 15-69.

b85 **Solomon** Norman, Judaism and world religion. L 1991, Macmillan. 295 p. £40. [RelSt 28,434].

b86 *Steenbrink* Karel, On the possibility of a creative and inspiring pluralism of religions: Mission Studies 9 (1992) 156-...

b87 *Stinnett* Timothy R., LONERGAN's 'critical realism' and religious pluralism: Thomist 56 (1992) 97-115.

b88 *a) Sutter* Jacques [*Bauberot* Jean], Pluralisme et minorités religieuses; – *b) Cohen* Martine, Identités et minorités religieuses; – *c) Bezeul* Y. [*Vincent* G.], L'identité des groupes religieux minoritaires; l'exemple protestant; – *d) Bensimon* Doris [*Schnapper* Dominique, *Azria* Régine], Les Juifs en France, leur émancipation; – *e) Whitol de Wenden* Catherine [al.], Islam...: → 510; Pluralisme 1989-91, 1-4 [153-9] / 51-62 / 63-71 [115-125] / 7-13 [73-79. 109-114] / 147s [...].

b89 **Swidler** L., After the absolute; the dialogical future of religious reflection 1990 → 7,a487: [R]Interpretation 46 (1992) 334s (W. C. *Placher*); NRT 114 (1992) 280s (J. *Masson*); RelStR 18 (1992) 44 (C. *Gillis*: his best).

b90 [E]**Swidler** L., *al.*, Death or dialogue 1990 → 6,a708: [R]IntRMiss 80 (1991) 127s (A. *Race*).

b91 **Thils** Gustave, L'État moderne 'non-confessionel' et le message chrétien: RTLv Cah hors série. Lv 1992, Peeters. 102 p. Fb 320. – [R]ETL 68 (1992) 484 (J. *Étienne*).

b92 **Türk** Hans-Joachim, Postmoderne (Unterscheidung; christliche Orientierung im religiösen Pluralismus). Stu/Mainz 1990, Quell/Grünewald. 140 p. – [R]TPhil 67 (1992) 142s (H. *Lenz*).

b93 **Vidal** Jacques †, L'Église et les religions ou le désir réorienté[2]: préf. *Jaigu* Yves: Foi vivante des Pères 301. P 1992, A. Michel (Cerf) ... F 42. – [R]EsprVie 102 (1992) 669s (M. *Delahoutre*).

b94 **Vroom** H. M., Van antithese naar ontmoeting; over de plaatsbepaling van christelijk geloof in een pluralistische cultuur: GerefTTs 91 (1991) 122-137.

b95 **Waldenfels** Hans, Begegnung der Religionen 1990 → 6,a711: [R]MüTZ 43 (1992) 114s (P. *Schmidt-Leukel*).

b96 **Wiles** Maurice, Christian theology and interreligious dialogue. L/Ph 1992, SCM/Trinity. viii-90 p. £6 [TR 88,171]. – [R]AnglTR 74 (1992) 522-4 (D. F. *Winslow*).

b97 **Zehner** Joachim, Kirche und Weltreligionen; Konzil und Ökumenischer Rat in der Herausforderung der Weltreligionen: Diss. Tübingen 1990. – TLZ 118,371.

M3.6 Sectae.

b98 **Allen** C. L., The cruciform Church; becoming a cross-shaped Church in a secular world [advice to a sect]. Abilene 1990, Christian Univ. Pr. $18; pa. $12. – [R]Mid-Stream 30 (1991) 402s (R. E. *Osborn*).

b99 *a) Anglarès* Michel, La religion du Nouvel Âge; – *b) Bastian* Bernard, [ses] Précurseurs et prophètes; – *c) Gira* Dennis, Entre christianisme et bouddhisme; réincarnation ou résurrection; – *d) Martin* Jean-M., Les eaux usées de l'Occident; pour une nouvelle lecture de l'Évangile; – *e) Cothenet* Édouard, Saint Paul et les puissances cosmiques; – *f) Maloney* George A., La conscience christique d'une nouvelle création; – *g) Lepoutre* Guy, L'effusion de l'Esprit; de quoi parle-t-on?: Christus 39,1 (P 1992) 8-18 / 19-28 / 29-41 / 51-60 / 61-66 / 67-78 / 114-120.

b100 **Baret** G., Le défi des Témoins de Jéhovah; comment les conduire à Christ. Genève 1992, Maison de la Bible. 132 p. F 12 [NRT 115,630, L.-J. *Renard*).

b101 **Bastian** Bernard, Le New Age, d'où vient-il, que dit-il? P 1991, O.E.I.L. 167 p. F 80. – [R]Christus 39 (P 1992) 98 (Régine du *Charlat*).

b102 **Baughmann** James, Social scientists study religion; a case study of the literature on religions with particular reference to the Unification

Movement: diss. Drew, ᴰ*Brown* K. Madison NJ 1991. – RTLv 24, p. 597.

b103 ᴱ**Beckford** James A., New religious movements and rapid social change. L 1986, Sage. 247 p. £25. 0-8039-8003-5. – ᴿRExp 88 (1991) 284 (R. D. *Cochran*).

b104 *Berzosa Martínez* Raúl, 'New Age', un nuevo reto a la teología: LumenVr 41 (1992) 266-289.

b105 **Blumhofer** Edith, The Assemblies of God; a chapter in the story of American Pentecostalism. Springfield MO 1989, Gospel. 464 p.; 242 p. $25. – ᴿWorship 65 (1991) 275s (J. *Gros*).

b106 **Bovon** François, Nouvel Âge et foi chrétienne; un dialogue critique à partir du Nouveau Testament. Aubonne 1992, Moulin. 85 p.

b107 *Breivik* Nils O. [in Norwegian] Phenomenon of 'neoshamanism' in Scandinavia: TsTKi 62 (1991) 1-15.

b108 **Bull** M., *Lockhart* K., Seeking a sanctuary... Adventism 1980 → 7,a492: ᴿChH 60 (1991) 579s (A. G. *Schneider*).

b109 **Chandler** Russell, Understanding the New Age ['nature mysticism']. Dallas 1988, Word. 360 p. $15. – ᴿSWJT 34 (1991s) 68 (S. *Lemke*).

b110 *Chauvet* Louis-M., Les nouvelles religiosités, un défi pour l'évangélisation: RICathP 43 (1992) 51-78.

b111 **Crocetti** G., L'interpretazione della Bibbia... falsa, Testimoni di Geova. T-Leumann 1990, L.D.C. 124 p. Lit. 8000. – ᴿParVi 36 (1991) 398s (C. *Ghidelli*).

b112 *Debarge* Louis, La scientologie [de Ron HUBBARD]: EsprVie 102 (1992) couv. 52-54.

b113 **Eidsmoe** John, Basic principles of New Age thought. Green Forest AR 1991, New Leaf. 157 p. $8. – ᴿBtS 149 (1992) 381 (J. A. *Witmer*).

b114 *Firyns* Ernest D., When the gods come marching in... The new religious movements; a missiological reflection: PhilipSa 26 (1991) 5-35.

b115 *Fizzotti* Eugenio, Aspetti psicologici dei nuovi culti: StCattMi 35 (1991) 587-592.

b116 **Garland** Robert, Introducing new gods. L 1992, Duckworth. xvi-234 p. ill. £30 [TR 88,169].

b117 **Gasper** Hans, *al.*, Lexikon der Sekten 1990 → 7,a493: ᴿAtKap 118 (1992) 339s (L. *Górka*, ☉); ZMissRW 75 (1991) 235s (F. *Usarski*).

b118 **Götz** Clemens, Heilssuche in 'New Age'; theologische Auseinandersetzung mit K. WILBER und H. M. ENOMIYA-LASSALLE S.J.; Diss. Pont. Univ. Gregoriana, ᴰ*Fuss* M. Roma 1992. 354 p.; Extr. 3839, 113 p. – RTLv 24, p. 564.

b119 **Gray** William D., Thinking critically about New Age ideas. Belmont CA 1991, Wadsworth. 164 p. $11.50 pa. – ᴿBtS 149 (1992) 105s (R. P. *Richard*).

b120 **Hesse** Nicolas, **Blanchet** Jean-François, Si des témoins de Jéhovah viennent vous voir. P 1991, Téqui. 120 p. F 29. – ᴿEsprVie 102 (1992) couv. 55 (M. *Trémeau*) répétée p. 127.

b121 *Hilhorst* H. W. A., De New Age-beweging als levensbeschouwelijk zingevingssysteem in de geseculariseerde samenleving: Praktische Theologie 19,1 [Zwolle 1992] 31-51 [< ZIT 92,403].

b122 *Jiménez Ortiz* Antonio, La increencia que nos acecha; el espejismo de una nueva religiosidad [Nueva Era ...]: EstE 67 (1992) 257-288.

b122* *Le Bar* James J., Cults, sects, and the New Age. Huntington 1989, Our Sunday Visitor. 288 p. – ᴿLandas 4 (1990) 246-9 (V. *Marasigan*).

b123 *Lovsky* Fadeiy, The Churches and the sects: OneInC 27 (1991) 222-233.

b124 **McConnell** D. R., A different Gospel; a historical and biblical analysis of the modern faith movement ['health and wealth gospel']. Peabody MA 1988, Hendrickson. 195 p. $8. – ᴿSWJT 34 (1991s) 67s (J. L. *Garrett*).

b125 *Mauss* Armand L., *Barlow* Philip L., Church, sect, and Scripture; the Protestant Bible and Mormon sectarian retrenchment: SocAnalysisRel 52 (1991) 397-... [< ZIT 92,140].

b126 ᴱ**Miller** Timothy, When prophets die; the postcharismatic fate of new religious movements. Albany 1991, SUNY. 241 p. $15 pa. [JAAR 59,889]. – ᴿChrCent 108 (1991) 1171.3 (R. B. *Mullin*).

b127 *Nichols* Aidan, The New Age movement: Month 253 (1992) 84-89.

b128 **Olivieri** A., Il mondo non è più per me [... comunità italiana pentecostale]. Castrovillari CS 1989, Teda. – ᴿStEv 2 (1990) 123-5 (P. *Bolognesi*).

b129 **Ossipow** Laurence, Le végétarisme, vers un autre art de vivre: Bref. P 1989, Cerf/Fides. 125 p. – ᴿMélSR 49 (1992) 209-211 (L. *Debarge*).

b130 *a*) *Richardson* James T., Reflexivity and objectivity in the study of controversial new religions; – *b*) *Jacobs* Janet L., Gender and power in new religious movements; a feminist discourse on the scientific study of religion: Religion 21 (L 1991) 305-318 / 345-356 [< ZIT 91,834].

b131 **Rightmire** R. David, Sacraments and the Salvation Army; pneumatological foundations [...BOOTH abandoned sacramental practice; < diss. Marquette]: Studies in evangelicalism 10. Metuchen 1990, Scarecrow. xii-327 p. $42.50. 0-8108-2396-9 [TDig 39,284]. – ᴿWorship 65 (1991) 274s (J. *Gros*).

b132 *Rudolph* Kurt, *a*) Wesen und Struktur der Sekte [< Kairos 21 (1979) 245-254]; – *b*) Das frühe Christentum als religionsgeschichtliches Phänomen [TU 120 (1977) 219-236; Eng. ᶠ*Koester* H. 1991, 39-58]; – *c*) Grundgedanke der religionsgeschichtlichen Schule [< FR 12 (1987) 293-6]: ⇒ 301, Geschichte 1992, 216-234 / 301-320 / 412-420.

b133 *Saliba* John A., Vatican response to the new religious movements [Les 'Sects', DocCath 69 (1986) 547-554]: TS 53 (1992) 3-39.

b134 **Schiwy** Günther, Lo spirito dell'Età Nuova; New Age e cristianesimo [Der Geist des Neuen Zeitalters 1987], ᵀ*De Filippi* Carlo: GdT 204. Brescia 1991, Queriniana. 128 p. Lit. 14.000. – ᴿETL 68 (1992) 478 (A. de *Halleux*).

b135 **Sudbrack** Josef, La nueva religiosidad; un desafío para los cristianos, ᵀ*Varona* Ezequiel: BtT 3. M 1990, Paulinas. 252 p. 84-285-1340-6. – ᴿActuBbg 29 (1992) 76s (J. *Boada*).

b136 *Tucker* Ruth A., New Age spirituality: RefR 45,1 (1991) 22-34 [< ZIT 92,18].

b137 **Vernette** Jules [prêtre, vicaire général], Le New Age: Que sais-je? ... P 1992, PUF. 128 p. – ᴿEsprVie 102 (1992) 668 (M. *Delahoutre*).

b138 *Waldenfels* Hans, Zwischen Dialog und Protest; religionstheologische Anmerkungen zu den Neuen Religiösen Bewegungen: StiZt 210 (1992) 183-198.

b139 **Wilson** Bryan R., The social dimensions of sectarianism; sects and new religious movements in contemporary society [13 art. 1975-90] 1990 ⇒ 7,a496: ᴿJRel 72 (1992) 596s (M. *Riesebrodt*); NRT 114 (1992) 425 (L.-J. *Renard*); RRelRes 33 (1990s) 286s (A. L. *Greil*).

b139* **Zinser** Hartmut, Ist das New Age eine Religion? Oder brauchen wir einen neuen Religionsbegriff: ZRGg 44 (1992) 33-50.

M3.8 **Mythologia.**

b140 **Baring** Anne, *Cashford* Jules, The myth of the goddess; evaluation of an image. L 1991, Viking. xv-779 p. £25. 0-670-83564-1. – ᴿMonth 253 (1992) 150s (C. A. M. *Wooding*); Tablet 246 (1992) 143 (Carolyn *Butler*).

b141 **Barsotti** Divo, Dal mito alla verità; EURIPIDE 'profeta' del Cristo. T 1991, Barsotti. 175 p. Lit. 20.000. 88-9152-308-3.

b142 **Baudler** Georg, Erlösung vom Stiergott 1989 ➤ 6,a971; 7,a727: ᴿLeb-Zeug 45 (1990) 231s (R. *Jungnitsch*).

b142* **Baudler** Georg, God and violence; the Christian experience of God in dialogue with myths and other religions [Erlösung vom Stiergott 1989 ➤ 6,a971; 7,a727], ᵀ*Lochner* Fabian C. Springfield ɪʟ 1992, Templegate. 366 p. $20. 0-87243-193-2 [TDig 39,253].

b143 **Benelli** Gian Carlo, Il mito e l'uomo; percorsi del pensiero mitico dall'antichità al mondo moderno: Oscar Saggi 267. Mi 1992, Mondadori. 348 p. 88-04-35628-6.

b144 **Champagne** Roland A., The structuralists on myth; an introduction: Theorists of myth 6. NY 1992, Garland. xiii-222 p. 0-6240-3447-3.

b145 **Conti** N., Mitología, ᵀᴱ*Iglesias* Rosa N., *Álvarez Morán* M. Consuelo. Murcia 1988, Univ. 790 p. – ᴿCiuD 204 (1991) 269s (J. *Gutiérrez*).

b146 **Downing** Christine, The goddess; mythological images of the feminine. NY 1992, Crossroad. xii-250 p. $12 pa. 0-8245-0091-1; pa. -624-3.

b147 **Dumézil** Georges, *a)* Le livre des Héros; légendes sur les Narses ᵀᴱ: Caucase. P 1989, Gallimard. F 36. – *b)* Mythe et épopée 3. Histoires romaines³ʳᵉᵛ: BtScHum. P 1990 = 1973. ³1981, Gallimard. 370 p. 2-07-071846-5; -28417-4. – *c)* Romans de Scythie et d'alentour: BtSc. P 1988 = 1978, Payot. 380 p. 2-228-88016-7.

b148 **Frankfort** Henri, Il dio che muore; mito e cultura nel mondo pre-classico, ᵀ*Scandone Matthiae* Gabriella. F-Scandicci 1992, Nuova. xxi-145 p.; 58 fig. 88-221-1122-2 [OIAc 5,21].

b149 **Grabner-Haider** Anton, Strukturen des Mythos 1989 ➤ 6,a734: ᴿZMiss-RW 75 (1991) 238s (H. *Waldenfels*).

b150 **Hatab** Lawrence J., Myth and philosophy; a contest of truths. La Salle ɪʟ 1990, Open Court. xiii-383 p. – ᴿJRel 72 (1992) 471s (A. W. H. *Adkins*).

b151 **Heinberg** Richard, Memories of paradise; exploring the universal myth of a lost golden age. LA 1989, Tarcher. xxxi-282 p. $19. – ᴿParabola 14,4 (1989) 110 ... 116 (C. *Zaleski*).

b152 **Hollenweger** Walter I., Umgang mit Mythen; interkulturelle Theologie: Tb 123. Mü 1992, Kaiser. 276 p. DM 22,80. 3-459-01946-8 [TLZ 118,214].

b153 **Isermann** Gerhard, Revitalisierung der Mythen? Gegen den Miss-brauch alter Geschichten für neue Interessen 1990 ➤ 7,a510: ᴿTLZ 117 (1992) 663s (P. *Heidrich*).

b154 **Lazenby** H. F., The mythical use of the Bible by evangelicals: JEvTS 34 (1991) 485-494 [< NTAbs 36,310: mythical means verified not by empirical evidence but by the individual's needs].

b155 **Leeming** David A., The world of myth; an anthology. NY 1990, Oxford-UP. xv-362 p. $25. 0-19-505601-9. – ᴿParabola 17,1 (1992) 120 . 122-4 (C. B. *Harvey*).

b156 **Leick** Gwendolyn, A dictionary of Ancient Near Eastern mythology 1991 ⇒ 7,a515: ᴿRÉAnc 94 (1992) 287 (P. *Lévêque*).

b157 ᴱ**Noel** Daniel C., Paths to the power of myth; Joseph CAMPBELL and the study of religion 1990 ⇒ 6,a742; $20: ᴿRExp 89 (1992) 422 (W. L. *Hendricks*).

b158 *Oden* Robert A., Myth and mythology, also OT [*Graf* Fritz, Greco-Roman]: ⇒ 741, AnchorDB 4 (1992) 946-960 [961-5].

b159 **O'Flaherty** Wendy D., Other people's myths. NY 1988, Collier Macmillan. 225 p. $20. – ᴿJAAR 60 (1992) 798-802 (R. A. *Segal*).

b160 **Restelli** Marco, Il ciclo dell'Unicorno; miti d'Oriente e d'Occidente: Saggi. Venezia 1992, Marsilio. xvi-177 p.; 24 fig. 88-317-5532-3.

b161 **Rue** Loyal D., Amythia; crisis in the natural history of western culture; pref. *Doty* William G., 1989 ⇒ 6,a744: ᴿZygon 27 (1992) 115-9 (W. B. *Gorlick*).

b162 **Samonà** Giuseppe A., Il sole la terra il serpente; antichi miti di morte, interpretazioni moderne e problemi di comparazione storico-religiosa: Chi Siamo 21. R 1991, Bulzoni. 522 p.; 2 fig. 88-7119-326-1.

b163 **Schelling** Friedrich W., Filosofia della mitologia [(1821 ... 1828) 1842-6], ᵀ*Procesi Xella* Lidia. Mi 1990, Mursia. – ᴿFilT 6 (1992) 481s (F. *Pellecchia*).

b164 **Schindler** Wolfgang, Mythos and Wirklichkeit in der Antike 1988 ⇒ 5, g753. ᴿBonnJbb 192 (1992) 599-607 (S. *Lehmann*).

b165 **Schlatter** Gerhard, Mythos; Streifzüge durch Tradition und Gegenwart 1989 ⇒ 6,a745: ᴿJRel 72 (1992) 300s (I. P. *Culianu*).

b166 **Stannard** Brendan, The cosmic contest; a systems study in Indo-European epic, myth, cult and cosmogony. Southport 1992, Carib. 304 p.

b167 **Wegman** H. A. J., Riten en mythen; liturgie in de geschiedenis van het christendom. Kampen 1991, Kok. 408 p. *f* 65 [TR 88,439].

M4 **Religio romana.**

b168 ᴱ**Beard** Mary, *North* John, Pagan priests 1990 ⇒ 6,389; 7,a535*: ᴿAmJPg 113 (1992) 476-9 (Frances V. *Hickson*); AntClas 61 (1992) 476-8 (J.-P. *Martin*); ClasW 85 (1991s) 55s (R. *Weigel*).

b169 *Biumonte* Giuseppe, Dal Segno pagano al simbolo cristiano: SMSR 16 (1992) 93-123.

b170 **Blázquez** José M., Religiones en la España antigua. M 1991, Cátedra. 445 p.; ill. – ᴿBSAA 58 (1992) 542s (G. *López Monteagudo*); RÉAnc 94 (1992) 517s (J. *D'Encarnação*); RÉLat 70 (1992) 374s (Nicole *Dupré*).

b171 *Bodel* John, Patrons and priests in Roman society [WALLACE HADRILL A. 1989; BEARD M., NORTH J., 1990]: ÉchMClas 36 (1992) 387-407.

b172 **Briard** Jacques, Mythes et symboles de l'Europe préceltique; les religions de l'Age du Bronze (2500-600 av. J.-C.): Hespérides. P 1987, Errance. 180 p. 2-903442-39-8.

b173 **Brouwer** H. H. J., Bona dea; the sources and a description of the cult: ÉPR 110, 1989 ⇒ 5,a758; 6,a752: ᴿRÉLat 70 (1992) 379-381 (Nicole *Boëls-Janssen*); StPatav 38 (1991) 192-4 (F. *Mora*).

b174 *Campanile* Enrico, Note sulle divinità degli Italici meridionali e centrali: StClasOr 41 (1991) 279-297.

b175 **Cancik** Hubert, Römische Religion: ⇒ 757, EvKL 3 (1992) 1698-1706 (-18 Reich, *Vollmer* Dankward).

b176 **Caranci Alfano** Luciana, Il mondo animato di LUCREZIO. N 1988, Loffredo. 196 p. – ᴿSalesianum 54 (1992) 410 (S. *Felici*).

b177 **Citroni Marchetti** Sandra, PLINIO il Vecchio e la tradizione del moralismo romano: BtMat 9. P 1991, Giardini. 308 p. – RRÉAnc 94 (1992) 490s (Lucienne *Deschamps*); RÉLat 69 (1991) 260s (J.-M. *André*).

b178 **Colish** M. L., The Stoic tradition from antiquity to the early Middle Ages[2] 1985 ⇒ 3,b52... 6,a757*: RBTAM 15,3 (1992) 146s (E. *Manning*).

b179 *Cristofani* Mauro, *Maggiani* Adriano, La religione degli Etruschi: Archeo 7,90 (1992) 61-111.

b180 **Del Ponte** Renato, La religione dei Romani; la religione e il sacro in Roma antica: Orizzonti della storia. Mi 1992, Rusconi. 301 p. 88-18-88029-2.

b181 **Deyts** Simone, Images des dieux de la Gaule: Hespérides. P 1992, Errance. 159 p., c. 150 fig. 2-877-72067-5.

b182 **Dorcey** Peter F., The cult of Silvanus; a study in Roman folk religion: Columbia Studies in the Classical Tradition 20. Leiden 1992, Brill. xiii-209 p.; 10 pl.; 6 maps. 90-04-09601-9.

b183 *Dovere* Elio, Occasioni e tendenze della normazione religiosa tardoantica: Labeo 38 (1992) 47-199.

b184 **Dubourdieu** Annie, Les origines et le développement du culte des Pénates à Rome 1989 ⇒ 5,a765: RGnomon 64 (1992) 25-30 (G. *Radke*); Latomus 51 (1992) 444-6 (G. *Freyburger*); RÉLat 70 (1992) 378s (Jacqueline *Champeaux*).

b185 **Dumézil** Georges, Feste romane [1976], TDel Ninno Maurizio: Itinera. Genova 1989, Melangolo. 284 p. 88-7018-291-3.

b186 **Fishwick** Duncan, The imperial cult in the Latin west [1, 1987 ⇒ 3,b57]; 2/Is: ÈPR 108. Leiden 1991s, Brill. vii + p. 375-625, pl. 74-113; p. 627-867. 90-04-09144-0; -495-4. – RClasR 42 (1992) 344s (J. F. *Drinkwater*).

b187 *Fishwick* Duncan, Sanctissimum numen, emperor or god: ZPapEp 89 (1991) 196-200: god.

b188 EGager John G., Curse tablets and binding spells from the ancient world. NY 1992, Oxford. xv-278 p. 0-19-506226-4.

b189 **Giancotti** Francesco, 'Religio, natura, voluptas'; studi su LUCREZIO 1989 ⇒ 7,a547: RLatomus 51 (1992) 426s (P. H. *Schrijvers*).

b190 *Gladigow* Burkhard, Roman religion, TMartin Dennis: ⇒ 741, Anchor-BD 5 (1992) 809-816.

b191 **Grimal** Pierre, Marc Aurel 1991 ⇒ 7,a548: RBBudé (1992) 101-7 (A. *Grandazzi*); RÉLat 70 (1992) 319-322 (M. *Testard*).

b192 **Hauken** Aage-Ignatius, The Greek vocabulary of the Roman Imperial Cult and the New Testament: diss. Pont. Univ. Angelicum, DParetsky A. Rome 1992, – RTLv 24, p. 547.

b193 **Heim** François, Virtus 1991 ⇒ 7,a550: RRHPR 72 (1992) 323s (P. *Maraval*).

b194 *Heinen* Heinz, Herrscherkult im römischen Ägypten und damnatio memoriae Getas; Überlegungen zum Berliner Severertondo und zu Papyrus Oxyrhynchus XII 1449: MiDAI-R 98 (1991) 263-298; pl. 68 (color.), 69.

b195 **Hijmans** B. L., al. SÉNÈQUE et la prose latine: Entretiens Hardt 36. Genève 1991. x-400 p.

b196 **Köves-Zulauf** Thomas, Römische Geburtsriten: Zetemata 87. Mü 1990, Beck. xxvi-420 p. DM 148. 3-406-33714-7. – RAnzAltW 45 (1992) 234-8 (G. *Radke*); ClasR 42 (1992) 92-4 (Jane F. *Gardner*); Gymnasium 99 (1992) 359s (I. *Stahlmann*); JRS 82 (1992) 238s (Gillian *Clark*); Latomus 51 (1992) 920-5 (G. *Radke*).

b197 **Lee** Owen, Death and rebirth in VIRGIL's Arcadia. NY 1989, SUNY. xii-140 p. – RLatomus 51 (1992) 188-191 (A. *Deremetz*).

b198 **Leopold** H. M. R.,   La religione di Roma [De ontwikkeling van het Heidendom in Rome 1918]. Genova 1988, Melita.   xv-239 p.; 2 fig. – ᴿHispania Antiqua 16 (1992) 297 (G. *Fernández*).

b199 *Lyapoustine* Boris,   Rites de passage dans le monde artisanal à Pompeii (Iᵉʳ s. ap. J.-C.): ⇥ 670, L'initiation 2 (1991/2) 19-25 + 2 fig.

b200 **Montero** S.,   Política y adivinación en el Bajo Impero Romano; emperadores y harúspices (193 d.C. - 408 d.C.): Coll. Latomus 211. Bru 1991. v-193 p. – ᴿBStLat 22 (1992) 83s (E. *Mastellone*); Gerión 10 (1992) 330-4 (S. *Perea Yebenes*).

b201 **Mora** Fabio,   Prosopografia Isiaca I-II: ÉPR 113.   Leiden 1990, Brill. xix-526 p.; 162 p.; 2 pl. *f* 240 + 90. 90-04-09232-3 (both). – ᴿBO 49 (1992) 756-8 (V. *Wessetzky*).

b202 *a) Negri* Angela M.,   La psyché chez VIRGILE; conceptions et terminologie; – *b) Dion* Jeanne,   L'expérience du sacré chez Virgile; l'exemple de l'*aegritudo*: BBudé (1992) 273-296 / 297-306.

b203 **O'Hara** James J.,   Death and the optimistic prophecy in VERGIL's Aeneid [the 'not-pathetic' half-lines left deliberately: SPARROW J. 1977]. Princeton 1990, Univ. xi-207 p. $32.50. – ᴿGnomon 64 (1992) 721-4 (W. A. *Krenkel*); Gymnasium 99 (1992) 175-7 (L. *Voit*).

b203* **Paladino** Ida,   Fratres arvales 1988 ⇥ 5,a785; 7,a567:   ᴿAnzAltW 45 (1992) 230-4 (G. *Radke*).

b204 *Perkins* Judith,   The 'self' as sufferer [A. ARISTIDES ... M. AURELIUS]: HarvTR 85 (1992) 245-272.

Romano Domenico,   LUCREZIO e il potere 1990 ⇥ 299.

b205 **Rüpke** Jörg,   Domi militiae; die religiöse Konstruktion des Krieges in Rom ᴰ1990 ⇥ 7,b725:   ᴿBonnJbb 192 (1992) 642-5 (L. *Burckhardt*: anregend); ClasR 42 (1992) 220s (J. *Briscoe*); JbAC 34 (1991) 187-193 (K. L. *Noethlichs*); JRS 82 (1992) 239s (A. *Erskine*); ZSav-R 109 (1992) 617-622 (K.-W. *Welwei*).

b206 *Rüpke* Jörg,   You shall not kill; hierarchies of norms in ancient Rome: Numen 39 (1992) 58-79.

b207 *Russello* Nicoletta,   Gli dèi di Archiloco: Acme 44,1 (1992) 99-116.

b208 **Rutherford** R. B.,   The meditations of MARCUS AURELIUS; a study 1989 ⇥ 6,a789; 7,a574:   ᴿGnomon 64 (1992) 313-7 (J. *Dalfen*); GrazBeit 18 (1992) 260-8 (R. *Schicker*); Mnemosyne 45 (1992) 122-6 (P. M. M. *Leunissen*).

b210 **Salem** Jean,   La mort n'est rien pour nous; LUCRÈCE et l'èthique. P 1990, Vrin. 302 p. [Elenchos 14, 106, G. *Giannantoni*].

b211 **Scheid** John,   Romulus et ses frères; le collège des frères arvales, modèle du culte public dans la Rome des empereurs: BÉF 275. R 1990, Éc. Française. – ᴿBonnJbb 192 (1992) 622-5 (P. *Herz*); ClasR 42 (1992) 341-4 (S. R. F. *Price*); ÉtClas 60 (1992) 295s (P. *Marchetti*); Gerión 9 (1991) 327s (S. *Montero*); Gymnasium 99 (1992) 54-56 (G. *Radke*); JRS 82 (1992) 263s (F. *Graf*, also on I. PALADINO); RÉLat 69 (1991) 281-3 (Annie *Dubourdieu*).

b212 **Schiesaro** A.,   Simulacrum et imago; gli argomenti analogi nel De rerum natura: BtMatClas 8. Pisa 1990, Giardini. 174 p. – ᴿJRS 82 (1992) 245s (P. *Hardie*).

b213 **Schmidt** J.,   LUCREZ, der Kepos und die Stoiker; Untersuchungen zur Schule EPIKURS und zu den Quellen von der 'De rerum natura': StKlasPg 53. Fra 1990, Lang. VII-283 p. £34. 3-631-43240-2. – ᴿJRS 82 (1992) 246 (M. R. *Gale*, also on SEGAL).

b214 *Seebold* Elmar, Der Himmel, der Tag und die Götter bei den Indogermanen: HistSprF 104 (1991) 29-45.

b215 **Segal** Charles, LUCRETIUS on death and anxiety; poetry and philosophy in De rerum natura 1990 ⇒ 6,a793; 7,a579: ᴿClasR 42 (1992) 299s (P. *Hardie*); ClasW 85 (1991s) 713s (H. B. *Evans*); ÉtClas 60 (1992) 93s (B. *Rochette*).

b215* **Setaioli** Aldo, SENECA e i Greci, citazioni e traduzioni nelle opere filosofiche: Testi Univ. Lat. 26, 1988 ⇒ 4,b795: ᴿRFgIC 120 (1992) 341-352 (G. *Mazzoli*).

b216 *Sfameni Gasparro* Giulia, Ruolo cultuale della donna in Grecia e a Roma; per una tipologia storico-religiosa: ⇒ 405, Donna e cultura 1989/ 91, 57-121.

b217 **Simon** Erika, Die Götter der Römer 1990 ⇒ 7,a580: ᴿGnomon 64 (1992) 397-402 (G. *Radke*); Salesianum 54 (1992) 156 (R. *Della Casa*).

b218 *Sinclair* Patrick, Deorum iniurias dis curae (TAC. Ann. I, 73,4): Latomus 51 (1992) 397-403 [no comment on the accusative epigram-subject].

b219 **Thurmond** David L., Felicitas; public rites of human fecundity in ancient Rome: diss. N. Carolina, ᴰ*Linderski* Jerzy. 228 p. 93-02569. – DissA 53 (1992s) 3257s-A.

b220 **Vanggaard** Jens H., The Flamen; a study in the history and sociology of the Roman religion 1988 ⇒ 5,a597*... 7,a583: ᴿGrazBeit 18 (1992) 287-290 (Claudia M. *Engelhofer*); Salesianum 54 (1992) 367s (R. *Sabin*).

b221 ᶠVITTINGHOFF Friedrich, Religion und Gesellschaft in der römischen Kaiserzeit, ᴱEck W. 1989 ⇒ 6,770: ᴿGymnasium 99 (1992) 58s (R. *Klein*).

b222 **Wacht** Manfred, Concordantia in LUCRETIUM: Alpha-Omega C-122. Hildesheim 1990, Olms-Weidmann. vii-845 p. DM 298. – ᴿRÉLat 70 (1992) 307s (J. *Hellegouarc'h*).

b223 *a*) *Wiśniewski* Bohdan, Le problème de la loi naturelle dans le De legibus de CICÉRON; - *b*) *Freyburger* G., Le droit d'asile à Rome: ÈtClas 60 (1992) 129-138 / 139-151.

b224 *Zuntz* Günther, Aion, Gott des Römerreichs: Univ. Abh ph/h 1989/2, 1989 ⇒ 5,a803; DM 36. 3-533-04170-0: ᴿAntClas 61 (1992) 485-8 (B. *Rochette*); ClasR 42 (1992) 212s (J. *Liebeschuetz*).

M4.5 **Mithraismus.**

b225 *Blomart* Alain, Les Cryphii, les Nymphi et l'initiation mithriaque: Latomus 51 (1992) 624-632.

b226 **Brashear** William M., A Mithraic catechism from Egypt, P. Berol. 21196: Tyche Supp. W 1992, Holzhausen. 70 p. 2 pl. 3-900518-07-6.

b227 — *Turcan* Robert, Un 'catéchisme' mithriaque? [*Brashear* W. 1990]: CRAI (1992) 549-564.

b228 **Clauss** Manfred, Cultores Mithrae; die Anhängerschaft des Mithras-Kultes: HeidAltHEpig 10. Stu 1992, Steiner. 335 p.; maps. 3-515-06128-2.

b229 **Clauss** Manfred, Mithras, Kult und Mysterien 1990 ⇒ 6,a802; 7,a587: ᴿAntClas 61 (1992) 492-4 (A. *Deman*).

b230 *Mitthof* Fritz, Der Vorstand der Kultgemeinden des Mithras; eine Sammlung und Untersuchung der inschriftlichen Zeugnisse: Klio 74 (1992) 275-290.

b231 *Tassignon* Isabelle, Les témoins des cultes romano-orientaux recueillis en Belgique et dans le Luxembourg [i. Mithra..]: ÉtClas 60 (1992) 39-54; 3 pl.

b232 *Tsetskhladze* Gocha R., The cult of Mithras in ancient Colchis: RHR 209 (1992) 115-124; franç. 115.

b233 **Ulansey** David, The origins of the Mithraic mysteries; cosmology and salvation in the ancient world 1989 → 5,a808... 7,a591: ᴿBCanadMesop 21 (1991) 101 (R. *Chadwick*; Eng.; fr. ᵀ*Fortin* M.); ClasPg 86 (1991) 48-63 (N. M. *Swerdlow*); GreeceR 39 (1992) 249 (P. *Walcot*); JRel 72 (1992) 301s (I. P. *Culianu*).

M5.1   *Divinitates Graeciae* – **Greek gods and goddesses.**

b234 *Alroth* Brita, Visiting gods [statues of one Greek deity dedicated to another]: → 701, ScAnt 3s (1989s) 301-310.

b235 **Antonetti** C., Les Étoliens, image et religion: Ann. Besançon 405. P 1990, BLettres. 470 p. – ᴿRÉG 105 (1992) 280s (J. N. *Corvisier*).

Arafat K. W., Classical Zeus, a study in art 1990 → d931.

b236 **Arlen** Shelley, The Cambridge ritualists 1989 → 6,a813; 7,a594: ᴿClasR 42 (1992) 236s (H. *Lloyd-Jones*: 406 items on Jane HARRISON; 1327 on Gilbert MURRAY, not a Cambridge man).

b237 — ᴱ**Calder** W. M.; Cambridge Ritualists reconsidered 1989/91 → 7,479: ᴿClasR 42 (1992) 419-421 (W. G. *Arnott*).

b237* *Arthur-Katz* Marilyn, Sexuality and the body in ancient Greece: Métis 4 (1989) 155-179.

b238 *Bader* Françoise, Autour de *wiris aellópos*; étymologie et métaphore [... messagers des dieux]: RPg 65 (1991) 31-44.

b239 **Bélis** Annie, Les [deux] hymnes à Apollon [étude épigraphique et musicale]: Corpus des Inscriptions de Delphes 3. P 1992, de Boccard. 187 p. ?-86958-051-7.

b240 *Bremmer* Jan N., Mythe en rite in het oude Griekenland; een overzicht van recente ontwikkelingen: NedTTs 46 (1992) 265-276.

b241 **Brulé** Pierre, La fille d'Athènes; la religion... 1987 → 4,b713; 5,a824: ᴿRPg 65,2 (1991) 53s (M. *Menu*).

b242 *a) Buchholz* Hans-Günter, Der Gott Hammon und Zeus Ammon auf Zypern; – *b) Kienast* Hermann J., Zum Heiligen Baum der Hera auf Samos: MiDAI-A 106 (1991) 85-128; 13 fig.; pl. 10-21 / 71-80; pl. 5-8.

b243 **Chaniotis** Angelos, Epigraphic bulletin for Greek religion 1988: Kernos 5 (1992) 265-306.

b244 **Crahay** Roland, La religion des grecs. Bru 1991 = 1966, Complexe. 180 p. – ᴿKernos 5 (1992) 348 (P. *Somville*).

b245 **Deforge** Bernard, Le commencement est un dieu; un itinéraire mythologique: Vérité des Mythes, 1990 → 7,a607: ᴿDialHA 18,1 (1992) 295s (P. *Lévêque*).

b246 **Delcourt** Marie, Légendes et cultes de héros en Grèce² [¹1942]: Dito. P 1992, PUF. viii-161 p. 2-13-044183-3.

b247 **Delcourt** Marie, Les grands sanctuaires de la Grèce² [¹1947]: Dito. P 1992, PUF. vii-145 p. 2-13-044184-X.

b248 *Desautels* Jacques, Dieux et mythes de la Grèce ancienne; la mythologie gréco-romaine 1988 → 6,a831; 7,a608: ᴿRBgPg 70 (1992) 258-260 (E. De *Waele*).

b249 *Dietrich* Bernard C., History and Greek religion: GrazBeit 18 (1992) 1-21.

b250 **Dowden** Ken [➤ b372] The uses of Greek mythology: Approaching the Ancient World. L 1992, Routledge. xi-204 p. 0-415-06134-2; pa. -5-0.

b251 **Faraone** Christopher A., Talismans and Trojan horses; guardian statues in ancient Greek myth and ritual. NY 1992, Oxford-UP. xiii-193 p. 0-19-506404-6.

b252 **Feeney** D. C., The gods in epic; poets and critics of the classical tradition 1991 ➤ 7,a612; £50: ᴿClasR 42 (1992) 61-63 (M. J. *Dewar*); ÉtClas 60 (1992) 168 (B. *Rochette*); JRS 82 (1992) 252-5 (P. *Hardie*: a critic of unusual authority).

b253 **Ferguson** J., Among the gods 1989 ➤ 6,a836; 7,a613: ᴿHeythJ 33 (1992) 212s (A. *Louth*).

b254 **Forbes** Irving P. M. C., Metamorphosis in Greek myths 1990 ➤ 7,a614; $69: ᴿClasPg 87 (1992) 258-260 (W. *Hanson*). ➤ b308.

b255 *Fuchs* Ottmar, Vom Unheimischen über die Erkenntnis zum Geheimnis; Gedanken im Horizont des delphischen Genius Loci: BibNot 64 (1992) 26-39.

b256 **Gärtner** Hannelore, Kleines Lexikon der griechischen und römischen Mythologie 1989 ➤ 6,a732: ᴿTLZ 117 (1992) 579-81 (M. *Hüneburg*).

b257 **Garland** Robert, Introducing new gods; the politics of Athenian religion. Ithaca NY/L 1992, Cornell Univ./Duckworth xvi-234 p.; 14 fig.; 30 pl. 0-8014-2766-5. – ᴿGreeceR 39 (1992) 246 (P. *Walcot*: Pan, Theseus, Asclepius; and much more); RÉG 105 (1992) 276s (Yvonne *Vernière*).

b258 *Gočeva* Zlatozara, Le culte d'Apollon [TAČEVA M.]: DialHA 18,2 (1992) 163-171; 3 fig.; map.

b259 **Goodison** Lucy, Death, women and the sun; symbolism of regeneration in early Aegean religion: BInstClas supp 53, 1989 ➤ 6,a839; 7, a616*: ᴿAntClas 61 (1992) 471s (R. *Laffineur*); ClasW 85 (1991s) 255 (Lois J. *Parker*; on early Aegean religious symbolism); RÉG 105 (1992) 275 (Yvonne *Vernière*).

b260 **Hans** James S., The origin of the gods. Albany 1991, SUNY. 227 p. $13 pa. [JAAR 59,887].

b261 *Harrell* Sarah E., Apollo's fraternal threats; language of succession and domination in the Homeric Hymn to Hermes: GrRByz 32 (1991) 307-330.

b262 **Höckmann** Ursula, Zeus besiegt Typhon: ArchAnz (1991) 11-23; 10 fig.

b263 *Hout* Philip, Herakles' apotheosis in lost Greek literature and art: AntClas 61 (1992) 38-59.

b264 **Hunger** Herbert, Lexikon der griechischen und römischen Mythologie[8rev]. W 1988, Hollinek. xi-557 p.; 115 fig. – ᴿDLZ 113 (1992) 323-7 (J. *Werner*).

b265 *Lévêque* Pierre, La naissance d'Erichthonios ou de quelques distorsions dans la Sainte Famille [déesse mère et fille néolithique-crétoise, enfant divin]: RÉAnc 94 (1992) 315-324.

b266 [Scalera] **McClintock** Giuliana, Il pensiero dell'invisibile nella Grecia arcaica. N 1989, Tempi moderni. – ᴿFilT 6 (1992) 151s (Elisabetta *Barone*).

b267 **Mikalson** Jon D., Honor thy gods; popular religion in Greek tragedy. Chapel Hill 1991, Univ. N. Carolina. xv-359 p. $44, pa. $16.45 [RelStR 19, 159, A. *Marmorstein*].

b268 **Neils** Jenifer [*Barber* E. J. W., al. exhibition catalogue], Goddess and polis; the Panathenaic festival in ancient Athens. Hanover NH/Princeton 1992, Hood Museum/Univ. 227 p.; 100 fig. 0-691-03612-8; pa. -0223-1.

b269 *Papachatzis* N.A., ⊚ Popular religion in post-archaic Greece [ancient Greece of historical times]: ArchEph 129 (1990) 1-80; Eng. 81.

b270 **Patton** Kimberley Christine, When the high gods pour out wine [into no recipient: vase-painting 510-450]; a paradox of ancient Greek iconography in comparative context: diss Harvard. CM 1992. 521 p. 93-07634. – DissA 53 (1992s) 3951-A.

b271 **Pötscher** Walter, Aspekte und Probleme der minoischen Religion; ein Versuch: RelWTSt 4, 1990 → 7,a633; DM 98. 3-487-09359-6: ᴿAntClas 61 (1992) 472-4 (J. *Driessen*); AnzAltW 45 (1992) 1-3 (E. *Simon*); ClasR 42 (1992) 85-87 (Nanno *Marinatos*); GrazBeit 18 (1992) 290-3 (B.C. *Dietrich*).

b272 **Pötscher** Walter, Hera; eine Strukturanalyse im Vergleich mit Athena. Da 1987, Wiss. ix-194 p. – ᴿAnzAltW 43 (1990) 39-41 (F. *Graf*).

b273 *Rudhardt* Jean, Rires et sourires divins; essai sur les sensibilités religieuses grecs [les dieux rient] et des premiers chrétiens [non, même Jésus]: RTPhil 124 (1992) 389-405.

b274 **Schachter** A., *al.*, Le sanctuaire grec, huit exposés suivis de discussions: Entretiens 37. Genève 1992, Fondation Hardt. [x-] 367 p.

b275 **Schachter** Albert, Cults of Boiotia, I. Acheloos to Hera; 2. Herakles to Poseidon: Bulletin Supp 38. L 1981/6, Univ. Inst. Classical Studies. I. xii-254 p.; II. v-225 p. 0-900587-41-5 both.

b276 **Schefold** Karl, (*Giuliani* Luca), Gods and heroes in late archaic Greek art [1978], ᵀ*Griffiths* Alan. C 1992, Univ. xiii-375 p.; 361 fig. 0-521- 32718-0.

b277 ᴱ**Schröder** Stephan, PLUTARCHS Schrift De Pythiae oraculis: BeitAltK 8. Stu 1990, Teubner. xxvii-474 p. DM 98. – ᴿClasR 42 (1992) 436s (B. *Hillyard*).

b278 *Seferis* Giorgio [Nobel 1963], *Panta pliri theōn*, tutto e piena di dèi [Atene, acropoli; Corinto], ᵀ*Pappalardo* Umberto: ArchViva 10,17 (1991) 18-33; color. ill.

b279 **Shapiro** H.A., Art and cult under the Tyrants in Athens. Mainz 1989, von Zabern. xiii-194 p.; 7 fig., 72 pl. ᴿAntClas 61 (1992) 558-562 (D. *Viviers*); Gnomon 64 (1992) 155-161 (Erika *Simon*); Hephaistos 11s (1992s) 207-213 (E. *Kluwe*).

b280 **Simon** Erika, Eirene et Pax; Friedensgöttinnen in der Antike 1988 → 4,b797; 6,a864: ᴿAnzAltW 43 (1990) 257-260 (Gerda *Schwarz*, auch uber ihr Augustus).

b281 *Sissa* Giulia, Greek virginity 1990 → 6,a947; 7,a645*: ᴿAmHR 97 (1992) 169s (Ann E. *Hanson*). Emerita 60 (1992) 354s (Ana *Iriarte*); MusHelv 48 (1991) 193 (W. *Burkert*: shows good knowledge of medical literature, but some typos crept into the translation).

b282 **Sørensen** Villy, Apolls Aufruhr; die Geschichte der Unsterblichen [1989; hisᵀ]. Mü 1991, Beck. 151 p. DM 28. 3-406-34922-6. – ᴿAntClas 61 (1992) 478s (P. *Somville*).

b283 *Sourvinou-Inwood* Christiane, Lire l'Arkteîa [Artémis à Brauron et à Mounichia] – lire les images, les textes, l'animalité: DialHA 16,2 (1990) 45-60 [61-90, *Brulé* Pierre, Retour à Brauron].

b284 **Stoneman** R., Greek mythology; an encyclopedia of myth and legend. L 1991, Aquarian. 192 p. $15 pa. 0-85030-934-4 [NTAbs 36, 455].

b285 *Suárez de la Torre* Emilio, Les pouvoirs des devins et les récits mythiques; l'exemple de Melampous: ÉtClas 60 (1992) 3-21.

b285* **Vernant** J.-P., Myth and society in ancient Greece, ᵀ*Lloyd* Janet 1988 → 6,316 [a866]: ᴿHistRel 31 (1991s) 69-74 (J. *Redfield*, also on her ᵀMyth and tragedy).

b286 **Versnel** H.S., Inconsistencies in Greek and Roman religion, I. Ter unus: Isis, Dionysos, Hermes; three studies in henotheism 1990 → 6,a867: ᴿClasR 42 (1992) 90-92 (J.G. *Griffiths*); CritRR 5 (1992) 307-9 (L.H. *Martin*); RÉLat 70 (1992) 375s (R. *Turcan*).

b287 **Veyne** Paul, Did the Greeks believe in their myths? 1988 → 6,a868: ᴿHistTheory 31 (1992) 65-81 (Marilyn A. *Katz*).

b288 *Vilatte* Sylvie, 'Hodos', le chemin; la genèse de la fonction oraculaire en Grèce ancienne: RHist 285 (1991) 209-234.

b289 *Vinogradov* Ju.G., The goddess Gē Mētēr Olybris; a new epigraphic evidence from Armenia: EWest 42,1 (1992) 13-26.

b290 *Wathelet* Paul, Arès chez HOMÈRE ou le Dieu mal aimé: ÉtClas 60 (1992) 113-128.

b291 **Watson** Lindsay, ARAE, the curse poetry of antiquity: Arca ClasMdv 26. Leeds 1991, Cairns. viii-263 p. 0-905205-75-8.

b292 *West* David B., Hekate, Lamashtu and *klbt 'ilm*: UF 24 (1992) 369-384.

b293 *Wolff* Christian, EURIPIDES' Iphigenia among the Taurians; aetiology, ritual, and myth: ClasAnt 11 (1992) 308-334.

b294 [Bruit] **Zaidman** Louise, Schmitt-Pantel Pauline, Religion in the ancient Greek city, ᵀ*Cartledge* Paul. C 1992, Univ. xxiv-278 p.; maps. 0-521-41261-5; pa. -2357-0.

b295 [Bruit] **Zaidman** Louise, *Schmitt-Pantel* Pauline, La religione greca [1989], ᵀ*Viano Maragna* Giorgia: Manuali 22. Bari 1992, Laterza. viii-233 p. 88-420-3929-2.

b296 *Żelazowski* Jerzy, Le culte et l'iconographie de Theòs mégas sur les territoires pontiques, ᵀ*Bartkiewicz* Katarzyna: ArchWsz 43 (1992) 35-51; 17 fig.

M5.2   *Philosophorum critica religionis;*   **Greek philosopher-religion.**

b297 **Alon** Ilai, Socrates in mediaeval Arabic literature: IslPhTSc 10. Leiden/ J 1991, Brill/Magnes. 198 p. ƒ95. – ᴿJAOS 112 (1992) 539s (F. *Rosenthal*).

b298 **Arieti** James A., Interpreting Plato; the dialogues as drama. Savage MD 1991, Rowman & L. x-270 p. $46.25; pa. $17. – ᴿClasR 42 (1992) 455s (G.B. *Kerferd*).

b299 **Aubriot-Sévin** Danièle, Prière et conceptions religieuses en Grèce ancienne jusqu'à la fin du Vᵉ siècle av. J.-C. Collection 22; lit/ph 5. Lyon 1992, Maison de l'Orient. 604 p. 2-903264-14-7.

b300 *Babut* Daniel, Hoútosi... Les procédés dialectiques dans le Gorgias et le dessein du dialogue: RÉG 105 (1992) 59-110.

b301 ᴱ**Billerbeck** Margarethe, Die Kyniker in der modernen Forschung; Aufsätze mit Einführung und Bibliographie: Bochumer Studien zur Philosophie 15. Amst 1991, Grüner. viii-324 p. ƒ80. – ᴿClasR 42 (1992) 210 (J. *Barnes*).

b302 *Blois* L. de, Bons J.A.E., Platonic philosophy and Isocratean virtues in PLUTARCH's Numa: AncSoc 23 (1992) 159-188.

b303 *Boter* G.J., EPICTETUS, Encheiridion 27 [there is no nature of evil in the world]: Mnemosyne 45 (1992) 473-481.

b304 **Brachet** Robert, L'âme religieuse du jeune ARISTOTE. P 1990, S. Paul. 207 p. – ᴿScripTPamp 24 (1992) 1081 (A. *Viciano*: rigor filosófico-filológico, estile elegante y sencillo).

b305 *Brancacci* Aldo, I *koinê aréskonta* dei cinici e la *koinōnía* tra cinismo e stoicismo nel libro VI (103-5) delle 'Vite' di Diogene LAERZIO: → 742, ANRW 2,36,6 (1992) 4049-4075.

b305* **Brandwood** Leonard, The [stylometric] chronology of Plato's dialogues [< diss. London 1958, already famous]. C 1990, Univ. x-256 p. £30. – ᴿPhronesis 36 (1991) 107-9 (the Editor compares with LEDGER G. 1989).

b306 **Brickhouse** Thomas C., *Smith* Nicholas D., Socrates on trial. Princeton 1989, Univ. = Ox 1990, Clarendon pa. xiv-337 p. £15 pa. – ᴿClasR 42 (1992) 71s (M. R. *Wright*).

b307 **Broek** R. van den, *al.,* Knowledge of God in the Graeco-Roman world: symposium Utrecht 1986 / ÉPR 112, 1988 → 4,b712 ... 7,a659: ᴿJTS 42 (1991) 317-320 (A. *Meredith*).

b308 ᴱ**Calame** C., Metamorphoses du mythe en Grèce antique 1988 → 4, b719 ... 6,a880: ᴿHistRel 32 (1992) 418-421 (R. *Garner*); RHR 209 (1992) 67-73 (Catherine *Darbo-Peschanski*). → b254.

b308* **Casey** John, Pagan virtue, an essay in ethics 1990 → 6,a883: ᴿThomist 56 (1992) 349-351 (Jean *Porter*).

b309 **Chen** Ludwig C. H., Acquiring knowledge of the Ideas; a study of PLATO'a methods in the Phaedo, the Symposium and the central books of the Republic: Palingenesia 35. Stu 1992, Steiner. x-284 p. 3-515-05862-1.

b310 ᵀᴱ**Clark** Gillian, IAMBLICHUS, On the Pythagorean life: Translated texts for historians 8. Liverpool 1989, Univ. xxi-122 p.; 2 maps. £8.50 pa. – ᴿClasR 42 (1992) 186s (J. *Dillon*).

b311 **Cohen** David, Law, sexuality and society; the enforcement of morals in classical Athens. C 1991, Univ. xi-250 p. 0-521-37447-2. – ᴿClasR 42 (1992) 345-7 (D. M. *MacDowell*); RÉG 105 (1992) 279s (Yvonne *Vernière*).

b312 **Corsano** Marinella, Themis; la norma e l'oracolo nella Grecia antica. Lecce-Galatina 1988, Congedo. 163 p. ᴿRivStorLR 27 (1991) 373s (F. *Trisoglio*).

b313 **Dal Pra** M., Lo scetticismo greco. Bari 1980, Laterza. viii-580 p. Lit. 42.000. – ᴿHelmantica 43 (1992) 248s (P. *Osorio*).

b314 *a)* *Döring* Klaus, Die Philosophie des Sokrates; – *b)* *Albert* Karl, Zum Philosophiebegriff Platons: Gymnasium 99 (1992) 1-16 / 17-33.

b315 **Dörrie** Heinrich †, Der hellenistische Rahmen des kaiserzeitlichen Platonismus, ᴱ*Baltes* M., *al.*: Bausteine 36-72. Stu-Bad Cannstatt 1990, Frommann-Holzboog. 547 p. – ᴿAnzAltW 45 (1992) 185-7 (M. *Erler*).

b316 **Dorandi** Tiziano, Ricerche sulla cronologia dei filosofi ellenistici: Beit-AltK 19. Stu 1991, Teubner. xvi-92 p. 3-519-07468-0.

b317 **Engberg-Pedersen** Troels, The Stoic theory of oikeiosis 1990 → 7, a661*: ᴿClasR 42 (1992) 77-79 (A. *Erskine*).

b317* **Engmann** Joyce, Cosmic justice in Anaximander [maybe our oldest surviving fragment of Greek literary prose]: Phronesis 36 (1991) 1-25.

b318 **Ferber** Rafael, Platos Idee des Guten. St-Augustin 1984, Richarz. 254 p. DM 39,50. 3-88345-523-9. – ᴿAntClas 61 (1992) 449-452 (O. *Ballériaux*).

b319 **Francioni** Antonio, Il 'topos' della lingua nella filosofia di Platone; l'emancipazione dell'empiria: IstItalStFilos Studi 10. N 1991, Bibliopolis. 192 p. 88-7088-181-4.

b320 ᵀᴱ**Frazier** Françoise, *Froidefond* Christian, PLUTARQUE, La fortune des Romains; La fortune ou la vertu d'Alexandre; La gloire des Athéniens:

Œuvres morales 5/1, Coll. Budé. P 1990, BLettres. 283 (d.) p. –
ᴿGnomon 64 (1992) 299-312 (S. *Schröder*).

b321 **Gadamer** Hans-Georg, Plato's dialectical ethics; phenomenological in-
terpretations relating to the *Philebus* [1931, ²1967, ³1982], ᵀ*Wallace* Robert
M. NHv 1991, Yale Univ. xxxv-240 p. £18. – ᴿClasR 42 (1992) 331s
(Pamela M. *Huby*).

b322 *Gerson* L. P., God and Greek philosophy; studies in the early history
of natural theology [➤ 7,a665]: Issues in Ancient Philosophy, 1991; $65:
ᴿClasW 85 (1991) 736 (J. E. *Rexine*).

b323 **Gigante** Marcello, Cinismo e epicureismo. N 1992, Bibliopolis. 128 p.
[Elenchos 14, 192, G. *Casertano*].

b324 *Gower* Dona S., Hero, healer, and martyr; Greek paradigms of the
teacher: Parabola 14,1 (1989) 44-50.

b325 *a*) *Hahm* David E., Diogenes Lᴀᴇʀᴛɪᴜs VII, On the Stoics [+indices]; –
b) *Gigante* Marcello, Das zehnte Buch des Diogenes Lᴀᴇʀᴛɪᴏs; Epikur
und der Epikureismus: ➤ 742, ANRW 2,36,6 (1992) 4076-4182 [4404-
4411] / 4302-7.

b326 **Herfort-Koch** Marlene, Tod, Totenfürsorge und Jenseitsvorstellungen
in der griechischen Antike; eine Bibliographie: QForAntW 9. Mü
1992, ᴛᴜᴅᴜᴠ. [xii-] 155 p. 3-88073-426-7.

b327 *Hershbell* Jackson P., Pʟᴜᴛᴀʀᴄʜ and Stoicism / Epicureanism: ➤ 742,
ANRW 2,36,5 (1992) 3336-52 / 3353-83.

b328 **Hossenfelder** Malte, Epikur: Grosse Denker 520, 1991 ➤ 7,a667; DM
24: ᴿDLZ 113 (1992) 289-292 (F. *Jürss*).

b328* *a*) *Ismardi Parente* Margherita, Sᴇsᴛᴏ, Pʟᴀᴛᴏɴᴇ, l'Accademia antica
e i Pitagorici; – *b*) *Classen* Carl J., L'esposizione dei Sofisti e della
Sofistica in Sesto Empirico; – *c*) *Sedley* David, Sextus Empiricus and
the atomist criteria of truth; – *d*) *Hülser* Karlheinz, Sextus Empiricus
und die Stoiker: ➤ 655, Elenchos 13 (1992) 119-167 / 57-79 / 19-56 /
233-276.

b329 **Janáček** Karel, Indice delle Vite dei filosofi di Diogene Lᴀᴇʀᴢɪᴏ:
Accad. Toscana Studi 123. F 1992, Olschki. viii-371 p. 88-222-3951-2.

b330 **Jones** Howard, The Epicurean tradition. L 1992, Routledge. vii-
276 p. 0-415-02069-7; – 7554-8.

b331 **Jordan** William, Ancient concepts of philosophy [...more geared to
right living]: Issues in Ancient Philosophy. L 1990, Routledge. xiii-
207 p. £35. – ᴿClasR 42 (1992) 204s (G. B. *Kerferd*).

b332 ᵀᴱ**Klaerr** Robert, *al.*, PʟᴜᴛᴀʀQᴜᴇ, Œuvres morales I/2: Coll. Budé. P
1989, BLettres, 358 (d.) p. – ᴿRBgPg 70 (1992) 208s (M. *Fiévez*).

b333 ᴱ**Kraye** Jill, *al.*, Pseudo-Aʀɪsᴛᴏᴛʟᴇ in the Middle Ages; the theology
and other texts: Surveys and Texts 11. L 1986, Univ. Warburg Inst.
310 p. £36 pa. – ᴿJAOS 112 (1992) 478-484 (E. K. *Rowson*).

b334 **Larsen** Öjvind, Ethik und Demokratie; die Entstehung des ethischen
Denkens im demokratischen Stadtstaat Athen: PhSozW 17. B 1990,
Argument. iv-151 p. – ᴿGnomon 64 (1992) 609-613 (Charlotte *Schubert*).

b335 *a*) *Lear* Jonathan, Inside and outside the Republic; – *b*) *Graham* Daniel
W., Socrates and Pʟᴀᴛᴏ: Phronesis 37 (1992) 184-215 / 141-165.

b335* **Ledger** G. R., Re-counting Plato; a computer analysis of Plato's style.
Ox 1989, Clarendon. xiv-254 p. £31.50 [Phronesis 36, 108].

b336 ᵀᴱ**Leroux** Georges, Pʟᴏᴛɪɴ, Traité sur la liberté et la volonté de l'Un
[Ennéade VI, 8 (39)]: HistDocAntClas 15. P 1990, Vrin. 449 p. 2-7116-
1027-6.

b337 **Lloyd** G. E. R., Magie, raison et expérience; origines et développement de la science grecque [1979], ᵀCarlier J., *Regnet* F. P 1990, Flammarion. 448 p. – ᴿRTPhil 124 (1992) 89s (S. *Imhoof*).

b338 **Luce** John V., An introduction to Greek philosophy. L 1992, Thames & H. 174 p.; map. 0-500-27655-2.

b339 **Magnaldi** Giuseppina, L'*oikeiosis* peripatetica in Ario Didimo e nel 'De finibus' di CICERONE: TSt Parini Chirio 2. T 1991, Lettere. x-108 p. – ᴿClasR 42 (1992) 459s (A. *Samuels*).

b340 **Manuwald** Bernd, Studien zum unbewegten Beweger in der Naturphilosophie des ARISTOTELES: Abh Mainz 1989 → 5,a868: ᴿClasR 42 (1992) 76s (J. D. G. *Evans*).

b341 *a*) *Mejer* Jørgen, Diogenes Laertius and the transmission of Greek philosophy; – *b*) *Brisson* Luc, Diogène LAËRCE, 'Vies et doctrines des philosophes illustres'; Livres III, structure et contenu [+indices]: → 742, ANRW 2,36,5 (1992) 3556-3602 / 3619-3760 [2*-25*].

b342 **Mitsis** Phillip, EPICURUS' ethical theory; the pleasures of invulnerability: StClasPG 48. Ithaca NY 1988, Cornell Univ. xi-184 p. 0-8014-2187-X.

b344 **Morgan** Michael L., Platonic piety; philosophy and ritual in fourth-century Athens. NHv 1990, Yale Univ. x-273 p. $28.50. – ᴿAmJPg 113 (1992) 630-3 (A. *Tulin*); ClasR 42 (1992) 72-74 (H. *Tarrant*); JRel 72 (1992) 443 (Elizabeth *Asmis*); TPhil 67 (1992) 424s (R. *Ficken*).

b345 **Navia** Luis E., *Katz* Ellen L., Socrates; an annotated bibliography: GarlandRefL 844. NY 1988, Garland. xxiv-536 p. $67. – ᴿGnomon 64 (1992) 252-4 (M. *Winiarczyk*: 'first' such work, but does not replace PATZER A. 1985).

b346 *North* Helen F., Death and afterlife in Greek tragedy and Plato: → 603, Death 1988/92, 49-64.

b347 *Obbink* Dirk, *Vander Waerdt* Paul A., DIOGENES of Babylon; the Stoic sage in the city of fools: GrRByz 32 (1991) 355-396.

b348 **Reesor** Margaret E., The nature of man in early Stoic philosophy. L 1989, Duckworth. ix-179 p. £24. – ᴿAmJPg 113 (1992) 115-9 (P. A. *Vander Waerdt*).

b349 **Roochnik** David, The tragedy of reason; toward a Platonic conception of Logos. NY 1990, Routledge. xv-223 p. £30. ᴿClasR 42 (1992) 205s (C. C. W. *Taylor*).

b350 **Rosen** S., PLATO's Sophist; the drama of original and image. NHv 1986, Yale Univ. x-341 p. $15 pa. – ᴿMnemosyne 45 (1992) 111-3 (H. *Oost*).

b351 **Rudhardt** J., Notions fondamentales de la pensée religieuse et actes constitutifs du culte dans la Grèce classique: Antiquité Synthèses. P 1991, Picard. 344 p. [TR 88,433]. – ᴿSMSR 58 (1992) 387-9 (S. *Ribichini*).

b352 *Rudhardt* Jean, De l'attitude des grecs à l'égard des religions étrangères: RHR 209 (1992) 219-238; Eng. 219, they knew that the gods were the same though names and rites varied.

b352* *Russell* Donald, *Ēthos* nei dialoghi di Platone: AnPisa 22 (1992) 399-429.

b353 **Schrödinger** Erwin, La nature et les Grecs [Shearman lectures, Dublin 1948], ᵀ; present. *Bitbol* Michel. P 1992, Seuil. 222 p. – ᴿParPass 47,266 (1992) 397-400 (N. *Minisse*).

b354 **Silvestre** Maria Luisa, Democritea; i documenti da EPICURO ad Aezio: BtScStoMor. R 1990, Cadmo. 171 p.

b355 **Sparisou** Mihai I., God of many names; play, poetry, and power in Hellenic thought from Homer to Aristotle. Durham 1991, Duke Univ. xix-246. $40; pa $18.50. – ᴿRelStR 18 (1992) 327 (R. A. *Swanson*).

b356 [Scarano] **Ussani** Vincenzo, Empiria e dogmi, la Scuola PROCULIANA fra Nerva e Adriano. T 1989, Giappichelli. 158 p. Lit. 20.000. – ᴿGnomon 64 (1992) 456-8 (W. *Waldstein*).

b357 **Velardi** Roberto, Enthousiasmós; possessione rituale e teoria della comunicazione poetica in PLATONE: FgCr 62. R 1989, Ateneo. 134 p. – ᴿAntClas 61 (1992) 452s (M. *Meulder*).

b358 **Vernant** Jean-Pierre, La mort dans les yeux; figures de l'Autre en Grèce ancienne: Textes du XXᵉ siècle. P 1985, Hachette. 96 p. – ᴿRHR 209 (1992) 55-64 (Annalisa *Paradiso*).

b359 ᴱ**Voelke** André-Jean, Le scepticisme antique 1988/90 ⮞ 6,771; 7,a681*: ᴿClasR 42 (1992) 458s (G. B. *Kerferd*).

b360 **Wisse** Jakob, Ethos and pathos, from ARISTOTLE to CICERO [De oratore the only first century work which follows the threefold approach of Aristotle: proofs-*ethos-pathos*]. Amst 1989, Hakkert. 370 p. – ᴿRÉLat 70 (1992) 304-6 (G. *Achard*).

b361 **Yunis** Harvey, A new creed; fundamental religious beliefs in the Athenian polis and Euripidean drama: Hypomnemata 91, 1988 ⮞ 5,a919; DM 45: ᴿÉtClas 60 (1992) 281s (M. *Huys*).

M5.3 *Mysteria Eleusinia; Hellenistica;* **Mysteries, Hellenistic cults.**

b362 **Annas** Julia E., Hellenistic philosophy of mind: Hellenistic Culture and Society 8. Berkeley 1992, Univ. California. ix-245 p. $35. 0-520-07554-4 [NTAbs 36,440].

b362* ᵀᴱ**Becchi** Francesco, PLUTARCO, La virtù etica: Corpus Plutarchi Moralium 5. N 1990, D'Auria. 249 p. – ᴿRFgIC 120 (1992) 461-3 (A. *Colonna*).

b363 ᴱ**Bilde** Per, *al.,* Religion and religious practice in the Seleucid Kingdom 1990 ⮞ 6,325*: ᴿJJS 43 (1992) 310-2 (S. *Stern*); MesopT 27 (1992) 307-9 (A. *Invernizzi*); TLZ 117 (1992) 819s (K. *Matthiae*).

b364 *Brashear* William, Zwei [Hermupolis] Zauberformulare: ArPapF 38 (1992) 19-26 [27-32, zu P. Berol. 11734, 36 (1990) 49-74].

b365 **Burkert** Walter, Antike Mysterien, Funktionen und Gehalt [= Harvard 1982] 1990 ⮞ 6,a934: ᴿGymnasium 99 (1992) 52-54 (Tanja S. *Scheer*).

b366 — *Casadio* Giovanni, I misteri di Walter BURKERT: QuadUrb 69,1 (1992) 155-160.

b367 *Carvalho* Silvia S. M. de, Les mystères d'Éleusis, ᵀ*Ralle* Michel: Dial-HA 18,2 (1992) 93-135.

b368 **Chuvin** P., Mythologie et géographie dionysiaques; recherches sur l'œuvre de NONNOS de Panopolis [diss. Sorbonne 1983]. Adosa 1991. 366 p. – ᴿRÉAnc 94 (1992) 487s (Danièle *Auserve-Berranger*).

b369 *Corsano* Marinella, Themis; la norma e l'oracolo nella Grecia antica. Galatina (Lecce) 1988, Congedo. 163 p. – ᴿRivStoLR 27 (1991) 373s (F. *Trisoglio*).

b370 **Dabdab Trabulsi** José Antonio, Dionysisme; pouvoir et société en Grèce jusqu'à la fin de l'époque classique [diss]: Ann. Univ. Besançon 412. P 1990, BLettres. 283 p. – ᴿRÉAnc 94 (1992) 512s (Marie-Christine *Villa-nueva-Puig*).

b371 **Dillon** J., *Hershbell* J., Iamblichus, On the Pythagorean way of life: SBL

TTr 29, GrRRel 1. Atlanta 1991, Scholars. ix-285p. $45; pa. $30. 1-55540-522-3; -3-1 [NTAbs 36,444].

b372 **Dowden** K., Death and the maiden; girls' initiation rites in Greek mythology 1989 → 6,a937; 7,a692: ᴿCritRR 5 (1992) 293-5 (Allaire *Brumfield*); HZ 253 (1991) 697-9 (F. *Graf*).

b373 **Eingartner** Johannes, Isis und ihre Dienerinnen in der Kunst der römischen Kaiserzeit: Mnemosyne supp. 115. Leiden 1991, Brill. xiii-198 p.; 98 pl. *f* 140. 90-0409312-5. – ᴿKernos 5 (1992) 329-346 (M. *Malaise*).

b374 *Elsas* Christoph, Mysterienreligionen / Mythos / Muttergottheit: → 757, EvKL 3 (1992) 565-570 / 586-592 / 562-5.

b375 *Espejo Muriel* Carlos, Una variante sexual en el rito de hospitalidad griego: Helmantica 43 (1992) 139-146.

b376 ᴱ**Faraone** C. A., *Obbink* D., Magika hiera 1991 → 7,392: ᴿClasR 42 (1992) 89s (S. *Pulleyne*); ClasW 86 (1992s) 259s (Sarah I. *Johnston*).

b377 *Faraone* Christopher, Binding and burying the forces of evil; the defensive use of 'voodoo dolls' [defixiones] in ancient Greece: ClasAnt 10 (1991) 165-220.

b378 *Gitler* Haim, New aspects on the Dionysiac cult in Nisa-Scythopolis: Schweizerische Numismatische Rundschau 70 (1991) 23-29; pl. 3-4.

b379 *Gosling* Anne, Political Apollo; from Callimachus to the Augustans: Mnemosyne 45 (1992) 501-512.

b380 **Gruen** Erich S., Studies in Greek culture and Roman policy [5 1985 Cincinnati Univ. lectures: Magna Mater, Bacchanalia ...]: CinciClasSt 7, 1990 → 6,241*; *f* 75: ᴿAntClas 61 (1992) 783s (J. *Poucet*).

b381 ᴱ**Halleux** Robert, [*Schamp* Jacques, Lithica, 774 hexamètres], Les Lapidaires grecs; Lapidaire orphique, Kérygmes lapidaires d'Orphée; Socrate et Denys; Lapidaire Nautique; Damigéron-Evax: Coll. Budé. P 1985, BLettres. xxxiv-349 (d.) p. – ᴿGnomon 64 (1992) 204-211 (E. *Livrea*).

b382 **Harrauer** Christine, Meliouchos; Studien zur Entwicklung religiöser Vorstellungen im griechischen synkrotistichen Zaubertexten: WienSt Beih 11, 1987 → 3,b133; 6,a941*: ᴿAnzAltW 45 (1992) 15-17 (H. J. *Thissen*); CdÉ 67 (1992) 375-7 (J. *Winand*).

b384 *Horsley* G. H. R., The mysteries of Artemis Ephesia in Pisidia; a new inscribed relief: AnSt 42 (1992) 119-150.

b385 **Kippenberg** Hans G., Die vorderasiatischen Erlösungsreligionen in ihrem Zusammenhang mit der antiken Stadtherrschaft [Heid Weber-Vorlesungen 1988]: TbWiss 917. Fra 1991, Suhrkamp. 604 p. DM 26 pa. [TR 88,169].

Kraemer Ross S., Her share of the blessings; women's religions among pagans, Jews, and Christians in the Greco-Roman world 1992 → 1490.

b387 *Kubińska* Jadwiga, Défense contre le mauvais œil en Syrie et en Asie Mineure: ArchWsz 43 (1992) 125-8; 4 fig.

b388 **Luck** Georg, Magie und andere Geheimlehren in der Antike, mit 112 neu übersetzten und einzeln kommentierten Quellentexten: Tb 489. Stu 1990. Kröner. xvii-499 p. 3-520-48901-5 [OIAc 2,23].

b389 **Malkin** Irad, Religion and colonization in ancient Greece [diss. Pennsylvania, ᴰ*Graham* A.] 1987 → 4,b762... 7,a700: ᴿGnomon 64 (1992) 683-7 (N. *Eberhardt*).

b390 *Malkin* Irad, What is an *Aphidruma* [transfer of cult... CLEMENT A., EUSEBIUS, BASIL]: ClasAnt 10 (1991) 77-93.

b391 ᴱ**Merkelbach** R., *Totti* M., Abrasax 1990 → 6,a945; 7,a701*: ᴿCdÉ 67 (1992) 373-5 (Michèle *Mertens*).

b392 *Pugliese Carratelli* Giovanni, I santuari panellenici e le *apoikíai* in Occidente: ParPass 47,267 (1992) 401-410.

b393 *Quet* Marie-Henriette, L'inscription de Vérone en l'honneur d'Aelius Aristide et le rayonnement de la seconde sophistique chez les 'Grecs d'Égypte': RÉAnc 94 (1992) 379-401.

b394 *Silvestre* Maria Luisa, L'initiation comme pratique politique dans les anciennes societés grecques selon les philosophes; Héraclite et les mystères d'Éphèse: ➤ 670, L'initiation 1 (1991/2) 237-250.

b396 [*Podemann*] **Sørensen** Jørgen, Rethinking religion; studies in the Hellenistic process 1984/9 ➤ 5,a902; 6,a948: ᴿLatomus 51 (1992) 722-4 (M. *Malaise*).

b397 *Wrede* Henning, Matronen im Kult des Dionysos; zur hellenistischen 'Genreplastik': MiDAI-R 98 (1991) 163-188; 2 fig.; pl. 39-48.

M5.5 **Religiones anatolicae.**

b398 *Archi* Alfonso, Funzioni economiche del tempio ittita: ➤ 701, ScAnt 3s (1989s) 119-124; Eng. 125.

b399 *Emets* I. A., *Maslennikov* A. A., ❸ New data about the religious ideas of antique Bosporus rural population: RossArkh (1992,4) 32-42; 2 fig.; Eng. 42.

b400 **Falco** Jeffrey L., The malediction in Indo-European tradition [including Hittite but not Bible]: diss. UCLA 1992, ᴰ*Puhvel* Jaan. 214 p. 92-30808. – DissA 53 (1992s) 1885-A.

b401 *a) Giorgieri* Mauro, Un rituale di scongiuro antico ittita per Labarna-Ḫattušili; – *b) De Martino* Stefano, Personaggi e riferimenti storici nel testo oracolore ittita KBo XVI 97: SMEA 29 (1992) 47-98 / 33-46.

b402 **Green** Tamara M., The city of the moon-god; religious traditions of Harran [half Islamic]; Religions in the Graeco-Roman world 114. Leiden 1992, Brill. viii-232 p. *f*95. 90-04-09513-6 [BL 93,120, L. L. *Grabbe*].

b403 ᵀ**Hoffner** H. A., ᴱ*Beckman* G. M., Hittite Myths: SBL Writings Anc-World. Atlanta 1990, Scholars. $20; pa. $13. 1-55540-481-2; pa. -2-0. – ᴿBL (1992) 117 (J. F. *Healey*); RB 99 (1992) 593s (J.-M. de *Tarragon*: all in all more useful for biblists than PECCHIOLI-DADDI).

b404 *Hout* T. P. J. van den, Some remarks on the third tablet of the Hittite KI.LAM festival: JbEOL 32 (1991s) 101-118.

b405 **Loon** Maurits N. van, Anatolia in the earlier first millennium B.C.: IconRel 15/13. Leiden 1991, Brill. xiii-49 p.; 48 pl. *f*60.

b406 *Lozano* Arminda, Festividades religiosas de ámbito local en Estratonicea de Caria: Gerión 10 (1992) 85-101.

b407 **McMahon** Gregory, The Hittite state cult of the tutelary deities 1991 ➤ 7,a716: ᴿAfO 38s (1991s) 209-213 (V. *Haas*); Orientalia 61 (1992) 468s (M. *Popko*).

b408 *Paz de Hoz* María, Theos hypsistos in Hierokaisareia [Teyenli, Lydia]: EpAnat 18 (1991) 75-77.

b409 *Watkins* Calvert, Le dragon hittite Illuyankas et le géant grec Typhôeus: CRAI (1992) 319-330.

b410 **Wegner** Ilse, *Salvini* Mirjo, Die hethitisch-hurritischen Ritualtafeln 1991 ➤ 7,a722; ᴿMesop-T 27 (1992) 304s (A. M. *Jasink*).

M6 **Religio canaanaea, syra.**

b411 **Ackerman** Susan, Under every green tree; popular religion in sixth-century Judah [diss. Harvard 1987, ᴰ*Cross* F.].: HarvSemMg 46. Atlanta 1992, Scholars. xiv-272 p. $36; pa. $24. 1-55540-273-9.

b412 **Albertz** Rainer, Religionsgeschichte Israels in alttestamentlicher Zeit, I. Von den Anfängen bis zum Ende der Königszeit: Grundrisse ATD 8. Gö 1992, Vandenhoeck &R. 373 p. DM 50 pa. – ᴿTüTQ 172 (1992) 325-7 (W. *Gross*).

b413 *Balzer* H. R., My God and your idols; political rivalry between human representatives of the divine in the OT: OTEssays 4 (1991) 257-271.

b414 **Barker** Margaret, The great angel; a study of Israel's second God. L 1992, SPCK. xvi-253 p. 0-281-04592-5. – ᴿBR 8,6 (1992) 14s (Elizabeth *Johnson*).

b415 **Barker** Margaret, The older testament 1987 → 3,b327 ... 7,a726: ᴿJAAR 60 (1992) 141-3 (V. K. *Robbins*); JJS 43 (1992) 143-5 (J. G. *Campbell*).

b416 *Barrick* W. Boyd, The bamoth of Moab: → 65, Mem. GEVIRTZ S., Maarav 7 (1991) 67-89.

b417 *Ben-Tor* Amnon, New light on cylinder seal impressions showing cult scenes from Early Bronze Age Palestine: IsrEJ 42 (1992) 153-164.

b418 **Block** Daniel I., The gods of the nations; studies in Ancient Near Eastern national theology: EvTS Mg 2, 1988 → 5,a939; 6,a973: ᴿRB 99 (1992) 767s (J. *Loza*); CBQ 54 (1992) 104-6 (R. A. *De Vito*: 'uniqueness' uncritically promoted).

b419 ᵀᴱ**Caquot** André, *al.*, Textes ougaritiques II. religieux et rituels: LAPO 14, 1989 → 5,a944 ... 7,a733: ᴿJTS 43 (1992) 155s (J. *Day*).

b420 *Casadio* Giovanni, A ciascuno il suo: otium e negotium del dio supremo della Siria [El] nella Mesopotamia: SMSR 58 (1992) 59-79.

b421 *Cross* Frank M., interview with *Shanks* Hershel, I. Israelite origins; II. The development of Israelite religion; III. How the alphabet democratized civilization: Bible Review 8 (1992) 4,20-33; 5,18-29; 6,18-31.58; ill.

b422 **Day** John, Molech 1989 → 5,a948; 7,a735: ᴿBA 55 (1992) 43 (J. A. *Dearman*); BZ 36 (1992) 295-7 (H. *Niehr*); IsrEJ 42 (1992) 119-121 (A. *Hurowitz*); IBL 111 (1992) 117-120 (W. B. *Barrick*); JSS 37 (1992) 321-3 (H. W. F. *Saggs*); OLZ 87 (1992) 264-6 (E. *Kellenberger*).

b423 *Day* Peggy L., Anat, Ugarit's 'mistress of animals': JNES 51 (1992) 181-190; 3 fig.

b424 **Dearman** J. Andrew, Religion and culture in ancient Israel. Peabody MA 1992, Hendrickson. xvi-281 p.

b425 *a*) *Dever* William G., Religion and cult in ancient Israel; social and economic implications; – *b*) *Baffi Guardata* Francesca, I Filistei; il culto alla luce dei dati archeologici: → 701, ScAnt 3s (1989s) 175-180 / 181-9; 5 fig.

b426 **Dietrich** Manfried, *Loretz* Oswald, 'Jahwe und seine Aschera'; anthropomorphes Kultbild in Mesopotamien, Ugarit und Israel; das biblische Bildverbot: UgBLit 9. Münster 1992, Ugarit-V. xi-206 p. 3-927120-08-1 [UF 23,450].

b427 **Dietrich** M, *Loretz* O., Mantik in Ugarit 1990 → 6,a984: ᴿOrientalia 61 (1992) 474-6 (E. *Lipiński*); ZAW 104 (1992) 145 (I. *Kottsieper*: von Mesopotamien abhängig).

b428 *a*) *Dietrich* M., *Loretz* O., Die Weisheit des ugaritischen Gottes El im Kontext der altorientalischen Weisheit; – *b*) *Niehr* H., Ein umstrittenes Detail der El-Stele aus Ugarit; – *c*) *Wyatt* N., The titles of the Ugaritic storm-god; – *d*) *Hübner* Ulrich, Der Tanz um die Ascheren: UF 24 (1992) 31-38 / 293-8 + 10 fig. / 403-424 / 121-130 + 3 fig.

b429 **Eilbert-Schwartz** Howard, The savage in Judaism ... religion 1990 → 6,a985; 7,a736: ᴿCritRR 5 (1992) 128-130 (F. E. *Greenspahn*: successful, though dubious that *zakar* 'remember/male' are kin); HistRel 32 (1992) 306-8 (M. *Fishbane*); JAAR 60 (1992) 153-8 (Ayala H. *Gabriel*);

JRel 72 (1992) 465-7 (G. A. *Anderson*); Numen 39 (1992) 148-150 (B. *Lang*).

b429* *Elliott* John H., The evil eye in the first testament; the ecology and culture of a pervasive belief: ➤ 7,67*, ᶠGOTTWALD N. 1991, 147-159 [< OTAbs 15, p. 143].

b430 *Feuillet* André, La religion d'Israël, préparation de celle du Christ: Divinitas 36 (1992) 222-230.

b431 **Fleming** Daniel E., The installation of Baal's high-priestess at Emar; a window on ancient Syrian religion [diss. Harvard 1989, ᴰ*Moran* W.]. HarvSemSt 42. Atlanta 1982, Scholars. $42; pa. $28. 1-55540-726-9 [TLZ 118, 497, W. von *Soden*].

b432 *a*) *Ford* J. N., The 'living Rephaim' of Ugarit; quick or defunct?; – *b*) *Loretz* Oswald, Die Teraphim alz 'Ahnen-Götter-Figur(inn)en' im Lichte der Texte aus Nuzi, Emar und Ugarit; Anmerkungen zu *ilānu/ilh, ilhm/ᵓlhym* und DINGIR / ERÍN / MEŠ / *inš ilm*: UF 24 (1992) 73-101 / 134-178.

b433 *Garbini* G., La dea de Tharros [Astarte]: RStFen 20 (1992) 99-110; pl. VII-XI.

b433* *a*) *Gawlikowski* Michael, Monotheism and polytheism in Roman Syria; – *b*) *Wright* G. R. H., Temple and Gate in Palestine; – *c*) *Seeden* Helga, The commerce of Palestine antiquities; a recent case of two metal figurines of a 'Canaanite god' from Jerusalem and Beirut: ➤ 736, ᴱ*Shaath*, Palestine 1981-5, 179-184 / 173-7 / 131-9.

Görg Manfred, Studien zur biblisch-ägyptischen Religionsgeschichte 1992 ➤ 244*.

b434 *Graf* David F., The 'god' of Ḥumayma [60 k N ᶜAqaba; Nabataean Aramaic graffiti]: ➤ 132. ᶠMILIK J., 1992, 67-76, pl. 3-4.

b435 **Haase** Ingrid, Cult prostitution in the Hebrew Bible? Ottawa 1990, Univ. [OIAc 3,23].

Halbertal Moshe, *Margalit* Avishai, Idolatry 1992 ➤ 7010.

b436 *Haran* Menahem, ❸ The 'incense altars' in the archaeological find and the worship of the host of heaven in the Judaean kingdom: Tarbiz 61 (1991s) 321-332; Eng. I.

b437 **Holloway** Steven W., The case for Assyrian religious influence in Israel and Judah; inference and evidence: diss. ᴰ*Ahlström* Gösta. Chicago 1992. xxiv-710 p. – OIAc 5,24; RTLv 24, p. 541.

b438 **Hvidberg-Hansen** Finn O., Kanaᶜanaeiske myter og legender: Bibel og historie 13s. Århus 1990, Univ. x-235 p.; xvi-247 p. Dk 268 pa. – ᴿTsTKi 63 (1992) 149s (T. *Stordalen*).

b439 **Keel** Othmar, *Uehlinger* Christoph, Göttinnen, Götter und Gottessymbole; neue Erkenntnisse zur Religionsgeschichte Kanaans und Israels aufgrund bislang unerschlossener ikonographischer Quellen: QDisp 134. FrB 1992, Herder. xiv-526 p. DM 58. – ᴿTüTQ 172 (1992) 323-5 (W. *Gross*).

b440 **Korpel** Marjo C. A., A rift in the clouds; Ugaritic and Hebrew descriptions of the divine 1990 ➤ 6,a995; 7,a744: ᴿBO 49 (1992) 462-4 (H. *Niehr*); ScandJOT 6 (1992) 150-2 (G. *Eidevall*).

b441 **Lewis** T. J., Cults of the dead in ancient Israel and Ugarit 1989 ➤ 5,a961; 7,a747: ᴿBZ 36 (1992) 298s (H. *Niehr*).

b441* **Loretz** Oswald, Ugarit und die Bibel; kanaanäische Götter und Religion im AT 1990 ➤ 6,a998: ᴿBO 49 (1992) 459-461 (K. *Spronk*); NorTTs 93 (1992) 48s (A. S. *Kapelrud*); TR 88 (1992) 186s (D. *Kinet*).

b442 **Moor** J. C. de, Rise of Yahwism 1990 ➤ 6,7022; 7,a748: ᴿRelCu 37 (1991) 556 (M. A. *Martín Juárez*).

b443 *Müller* Hans-Peter,   Kolloquialsprache und Volksreligion in den Inschriften von Kuntillet ʿA**ğ**rūd und Ḥirbet el-Qōm: ZAHeb 5 (1992)
15-51.
b444 **Niehr** Herbert,   Der höchste Gott ...: BZAW 190, 1990 → 6,b3; 7,a752:
ᴿArTGran 55 (1992) 335-9 (A. *Torres*); BL (1992) 109 (J. W. *Rogerson*);
CBQ 54 (1992) 120s (M. E. *Biddle*: materials ultimately only biblical).
b445 *Noy* David,   A Jewish place of prayer in Roman Egypt [inferred from a
text, Fox W., AJPg 38 (1917) 411]: JTS 43 (1992) 118-122.
b446 *Olmo Lete* Gregorio del,   Pervivencias cananeas (ugaríticas) en el culto
fenicio, III: Sefarad 51 (1991) 99-114; Eng. 114.
b447 **Patai** Raphael,   The Hebrew goddess³ ʳᵉᵛ [¹1967] 1990 → 7,a755:
ᴿParabola 16,3 (1991) 110. 112. 114 (Judith *Hauptmann*).
b448 **Podella** Thomas,   Ṣom-Fasten; kollektive Trauer um den verborgenen
Gott im AT [... auch Ugarit, Mesopotamien, Anatolien; Diss. Berlin
1988]: AOAT 224, 1989 → 3,6365; 5,7027: ᴿJBL 111 (1992) 513-5 (S. E.
Balentine).
b449 **Schmidt** B. B.,   Israel's beneficent dead; the origin and character of
Israelite ancestor cults and necromancy: diss. Oxford 1992. - RTLv 24,
p. 544.
b450 *Singer* Itamar,   Towards the image of Dagon, the god of the Philistines:
Syria 69 (1992) 431-450.
b451 **Smith** Mark S.,   The early history of God 1990 → 6,b11; 7,a761:
ᴿAndrUnS 30 (1992) 176s (A. J. *Greig*); BL (1992) 112 (J. R. *Porter*;
Ašera held to be not a goddess but maternal aspects of Yahweh); BR
7,3 (1991) 14s (R. S. *Hendel*); CBQ 54 (1992) 132s (also R. S. *Hendel*:
coverage exemplary, judgment often compelling); ChrCent 108 (1991) 87
(M. A. *Sweeney*); Interpretation 46 (1992) 196s (A. *Cooper*); JRel 72
(1992) 89s (Diana *Edelman*; some five dissatisfactions).
b452 *Spieckermann* Hermann,   Stadtgott und Gottesstadt; Beobachtungen im
Alten Orient und im Alten Testament: Biblica 73 (1992) 1-31; franç. 31.
b453 *Stieglitz* Robert R.,   Die Göttin Tanit im Orient: AntWelt 21 (1990)
106-9; 11 fig.
b454 *Toorn* Karel van der,   Anat-Yahu, some other deities, and the Jews of
Elephantine: Numen 39 (1992) 80-101.
b455 *Tzaferis* Vassilios,   Cults and deities worshipped at Caesarea Philippi-
Banias: → 19, ᶠBLENKINSOPP J. 1992, 190-201.
b456 *Uehlinger* Christoph,   Audienz in der Götterwelt; Anthropomorphismus
und Soziomorphismus in der Ikonographie eines altsyrischen Zylinder-
siegels: UF 24 (1992) 339-356+9 fig.
b457 *Wacker* Marie-Theres,   Kosmisches Sakrament oder Verpfändung des
Körpers? 'Kultprostitution' im biblischen Israel und im hinduistischen
Indien; religionsgeschichtliche Überlegungen im Interesse feministischer
Theologie: BibNot 61 (1992) 51-75.
b458 **Walls** Neal H.,   The goddess Anat in Ugaritic myth [diss. Johns
Hopkins, Baltimore 1991]: SBL diss. 135. Atlanta 1992, Scholars. xi-
256 p. $30; pa. $20.   1-55540-794-3 [OIAc 5,39].
b459 *Wenning* Robert,   Wer war der Paredros der Aschera? Notizen zu
Terrakottastatuetten in eisenzeitlichen Gräbern: BibNot 59 (1991) 89-97.
b460 *Worschech* Udo,   *a)* Der Gott Kemosch; Versuch einer Charakterisie-
rung; – *b)* Pferd, Göttin und Stier; Funde zur moabitischen Religion aus
el-Bālūʾ (Jordanien):   UF 24 (1992) 393-401 / 385-391.
b461 *a) Wyatt* Nicholas,   Of calves and kings; the Canaanite dimension in the
religion of Israel; – *b) Binger* Tilde, [Deity] Fighting the dragon; another

look at the theme in the Ugaritic texts: ScandJOT 6,1 (1992) 68-91 / 139-149.
b462 **Xella** Paolo, Baal Hammon 1991 → 7,a767: ᴿRStFen 20 (1992) 111-7 (F. O. *Hvidberg-Hansen*); ZAW 104 (1992) 317 (J. A. *Soggin*).

M6.5 **Religio aegyptia.**

b463 *a)* *Alfi* Mostafa El-, A sun hymn in the Fitzwilliam Museum [Cambridge]; – *b)* *Goedicke* Hans, The morning of the burial; pyramid spell 251: VarAeg 8,1 (1992) 3-5 / 7-16.
Arnold Dieter, Die Tempel Ägyptens 1992 → g13.
b464 *Assmann* Jan, *a)* Das ägyptische Prozessionsfest; – *b)* Der zweidimensionale Mensch; das Fest als Medium des kollektiven Gedächtnisses [*Löffler* Reinhold, Zur Diskussion]: → 7,465*, Fest 1988/91, 105-122 / 13-30 [-33].
b465 **Assmann** Jan, Maᶜat, Gerechtigkeit und Unsterblichkeit im Alten Ägypten 1990 → 6,b20: ᴿBiblica 73 (1992) 293-7 (V. A. *Tobin*); BL (1992) 115 (K. A. *Kitchen*); DiscEg 22 (1992) 79-90; 2 fig. (T. *DuQuesne*).
b466 *Assmann* Jan, Semiosis and interpretation in ancient Egyptian ritual: → 514, Interpretation 1992, 87-109.
b467 *Assmann* Jan, When justice fails; jurisdiction and imprecation in ancient Egypt and the Near East: JEA 78 (1992) 149-162.
b468 **Bartels** Jutta, Formen altägyptischer Kulte und ihre Auswirkungen im leiblichen Bereich [Diss. Bremen 1990]: EurHS 19B/29. Fra 1992, Lang. 202 p.; 65 fig. 3-631-44393-3 [OIAc 5,14].
b469 *Blumenthal* Elke, Vom Wesen der altägyptischen Religion [Koch K. 1989]: TLZ 117 (1992) 889-896.
b470 *Bolshakov* Andrey O., Princess ḤM-T-Rᶜ(w), the first mention of Osiris?: CdÉ 67 (1992) 203-210.
b471 **Bongioanni** Alessandro, *Tosi* Mario, Uomini e dèi nell'Antico Egitto. Parma 1991, Maccari. 230 p., ill.
b472 *Bresciani* Edda, Tipi di offerta per le divinità femminili nell'Egitto antico: → 701, ScAnt 3s (1989s) 191-6; Eng. 196.
b473 *Colin* Marie-Ève, Le symbolisme luni-solaire dans le Sanctuaire des Barques d'Edfou et de Dendara: → 113-8.
ᴱ**D'Auria** Sue, *al.,* Mummies and magic; the funerary arts of ancient Egypt → e279 [5,d608, not as Index].
b474 *Dunand* Françoise, *Zivie-Coche* Christiane, Dieux et hommes en Égypte, 3000 av. J.-C. -395 apr. J. C.; anthropologie religieuse. P 1991, Colin. 366 p. F 196. – ᴿAmHR 97 (1992) 1492s (W. *Davis*); CahHist 37 (1992) 175-7 (Michelle *Chermette*).
b475 *Dunand* Françoise, Le babouin Thot et la palme; à propos d'une terre cuite d'Égypte: CdÉ 66 (1991) 341-8; 4 fig.
b476 **DuQuesne** Terence, Jackal at the Shaman's gate; a study of Anubis lord of Ro-Setawe, with the conjuration to chthonic deities (PGM XXIII, pOxy 412). OxCommEg 3. Thame/Oxon 1991, Darengo. 135 p. £40; pa. £32. 1-0871-2613 [-0]. – ᴿDiscEg 24 (1992) 63s (A. *Roccati*: studio di un'invocazione copta).
b477 *Galán* José M., EA[marna] 164 and the god Amun: JNES 51 (1992) 287-291.
Godron Gérard, Études sur l'Horus Den [roi Iᵉ Dyn.] → b942.
b479 ᴱ**Haeckl** Anne E., *Spelman* Kate C., The gods of Egypt in the Graeco-Roman period [exhibition]. AA 1977, Kelsey Museum. 117 p. [OIAc 2,20].

b480 **Hart** George, Egyptian myths: The Legendary Past. Austin 1990, Univ. Texas. 80 p.; 20 fig.; map. $8 pa. 0-292-72076-9. – ᴿClasW 85 (1991) 734 (Shelly P. *Haley*).

b481 *a*) *Hassan* Fekri, Primeval goddess to divine king; the mythogenesis of power in the early Egyptian state; – *b*) O'Connor David, The status of early Egyptian temples; an alternate theory: ➤ 84, Mem. HOFFMAN M., 1992, 307-322; 5 fig. / 83-98; 6 fig.

b482 **Hornung** Erik, Die Nachtfahrt der Sonne; eine altägyptische Beschreibung des Jenseits 1991 ➤ 7,a799; DM 40: ᴿDiscEg 21 (1991) 83-88 (T. *DuQuesne* under title 'Twelve hours and an eternity').

b483 **Hornung** Erik, Gli dei dell'antico Egitto [Der Eine 1971 ➤ 52,6240: ⁴1990], ᵀ*Scaiola* Donatella: Profili NS 18. R 1992, Salerno. 286 p. 88-8402-106-5.

b484 **Jacq** C., Egyptian magic, ᵀ*Davis* Janet M. Wmr/Ch 1985 ➤ 1,a628*b* ...3,b316; Aris & P / Bolchazy-Carducci. 162 p.; 46 fig. 0-85668-299-3. – ᴿDiscEg 24 (1992) 59-61 (Geraldine *Pinch*).

b485 *Jansen-Winkeln* Karl, Zu einigen religiösen und historischen Inschriften: CdÉ 67 (1992) 240-259; 6 fig.

b486 **Johnson** Sally B., The cobra goddess of ancient Egypt; predynastic, early dynastic and Old Kingdom periods 1990 ➤ 7,a800; £70; 0-7103-0212-6: ᴿDiscEg 21 (1991) 101-8 (Angela M. J. *Tooley*). RSO 66 (1992) 401-3 (Adriana *Belluccio*).

b488 **Kákosy** László, Zauberei im Alten Ägypten 1989 ➤ 6,b51: ᴿArOr 60 (1992) 305s (L. *Bareš*).

b489 *Kákosy* László, Survivals of ancient Egyptian gods in Coptic and Islamic Egypt: ➤ 690, 3d Coptic 1984/90, 175-9.

b490 **Kruchten** Jean-Marie, Les annales des prêtres de Karnak... 1989 ➤ 7,a803: ᴿArOr 60 (1992) 307 (L. *Bareš*).

b490* *a*) *Kurth* Dieter, Über Horus, Isis und Osiris; – *b*) *Meeks* Dimitri, Le nom du dieu Bès et ses implications mythologiques; – *c*) *Heerma van Voss* Matthieu, Zur Göttin Hepetethor; – *d*) *Hubai* Peter, Eine literarische Quelle der ägyptischen Religionsphilosophie? Das Märchen vom Prinzon, der drei Gefahren zu überstehen hatte; – *e*) *Velde* Herman te, Some Egyptian deities and their piggishness; – *f*) *Ritner* Robert K., Religion vs. magic; the evidence of the magical statue bases: ➤ 96, ꜰKÁKOSY L. 1992, 373-383 / 423-436 / 265s; Pl. XVIII / 277-300 [297s, di⁵ esóptrou en ainígmati, 1 Kor 13,12] / 571-8 / 495-501.

b491 **Lapp** Günther, Die Opferformel des Alten Reiches 1986 ➤ 2,9034: ᴿCdÉ 67 (1992) 260-3 (M. *Valloggia*).

b492 **Leclant** J., *Clerc* G., Inventaire bibliographique des Isiaca 4: ÉPR 18. Leiden 1991, Brill. – ᴿBO 49 (1992) 755s (J. G. *Griffiths*).

b492* *a*) *Leclant* J., Diana nemorensis, Isis and Bubastis; – *b*) *Kákosy* L., Hermes and Egypt; – *c*) *Bresciani* E., Il simbolismo del 'cibo' nei dialoghi 'filosofici' del papiro demotico di Leida ('Mito dell'occhio del sole'); – *d*) *Smith* H. S., The death and life of the mother of Apis; – *e*) *Žabkar* L. V., A hymn to incense in the temple of Arensuphis at Philae: ➤ 72, ꜰGRIFFITHS J. G. 1992, 251-7 / 258-261 / 246-250 / 201-225 / 236-245.

b493 **Maystre** Charles, Les grands prêtres de Ptah de Memphis: OBO 113. FrS/Gö 1992, Univ./Vandenhoeck & R. xiv-465 p.; 2 pl. 3-7278-0794-6 / 3-525-53750-6 [OIAc 3,30].

b494 **Milde** H., The vignettes in the Book of the Dead of Neferrenpet [compared with the religious spells one by one]: EgUitg 7, 1991 ➤ 7,a808; DM 96: ᴿDiscEg 24 (1992) 47-50 (T. *DuQuesne*).

b495 *Moftah* Ramses, Das Spannungsverhältnis zwischen solaren und osi-
rianischen Vorstellungen [... Jenseits]: ASAE 67 (1988) 157-184 [< OLZ
88,103].

b496 **Montserrat** Dominic, The *klinē* of Anubis [Oxyrhynchus papyrus]: JEA
78 (1992) 301-7; 1 fig.

b497 **Morenz** Siegfried, Egyptian religion [1960, Eng. 1973], ᵀ*Keep* Ann E.
Ithaca NY 1992 (1st paperback), Cornell Univ. xxi-379 p. 0-8014-
8029-9 [OIAc 3,31].

b498 **Morschauser** Scott, Threat-formulae in ancient Egypt; a study of the
history, structure and use of threats and curses in ancient Egypt [diss.
Johns Hopkins, ᴰ*Goedicke* H.] Baltimore 1991, Halgo. xvi-268 p. $72.
0-9613805-5-1 [BO 49,584].

b499 *Murnane* William J., Taking it with you; the problem of death and
afterlife in ancient Egypt: ➤ 603, Death 1988/92, 35-48.

b500 **Naguib** Saphinaz-Amal, Le clergé féminin d'Amon Thébain à la 21ᵉ Dynastie: OrLovAnal 38. Lv 1990, Peeters/Univ. xiii-330 p.; 24 fig. (IX pl.).

b501 **Quirke** Stephen, Ancient Egyptian religion. L 1992, British Museum.
192 p.; ill. £13. 0-7141-0966-5.

Ringgren Helmer, Le religioni dell'Oriente antico [1979] ᵀ1991 ➤ b549.

b502 *Robiano* Patrick, Les gymnosophistes éthiopiens chez Philostrate et chez
Héliodore: RÉAnc 94 (1992) 412-428 [sophistes sì, nus non].

b503 **Sadek** Ashraf I., Popular religion in Egypt during the New Kingdom
1987 ➤ 4,b931: ᴿCdÉ 66 (1991) 164s (H. De *Meulenaere*); JEA 78 (1992)
338s (J. K. *Hoffmeier*).

b503* **Schoske** Sylvia, *Wildung* Dietrich, Gott und Götter im Alten Ägypten
[Katalog Ausstellung Sammlung Resandro B [Mü, Ha] 1992s. Mainz
1992, von Zabern, viii-240 p. 3-8053-1409-4 [OIAc 5,34].

b504 **Sellers** Jane B., The death of gods in ancient Egypt. L 1992, Penguin.
xxii-378 p.; 37 fig. 0-14-015307-1 [OIAc 5,34].

b505 ᴱ**Shafer** Byron E., Religion in ancient Egypt; gods, myths, and personal
practice [3 papers of 1987 Fordham University Annual Egyptological
Symposium] 1991 ➤ 7,625: ᴿCritRR 5 (1992) 66-69 (Susan T. *Hollis*:
excellent, well-illustrated).

b506 **Simpson** William K., The offering chapel of Kayemnofret in the Museum of Fine Arts. Boston 1992, Museum. x-33 p.; 16 fig.; 26 pl.+
foldouts. 0-87846-361-5.

b507 **Sternberg-El Hotabi** Heike, (*Kammerzell* Frank), Ein Hymnus an die
Göttin Hathor und das Ritual 'Hathor das Trankopfer darbringen' nach
den Tempeltexten der griechisch-römischen Zeit: Rites Égyptiens 7. Bru
1992, Fond. Ég. Reine Élisabeth. xi-157 p.; 48 pl. [OIAc 5,36].

b508 **Sternberg** Heike, Mythische Motive und Mythenbildung in den ägyptischen Tempeln und Papyri der griechisch-römischen Zeit 1985 ➤ 1,
a656 ... 6,b71: ᴿCdÉ 66 (1991) 177s (Sylvie *Cauville*).

b509 **Stricker** B. H., Het Zonne-offer. Amst 1989, Univ. 83 p.; 11 fig.; 1 pl.
– ᴿDiscEg 23 (1992) 83-92 (T. *DuQuesne*).

b510 **Tobin** Vincent A., Theological principles of Egyptian religion 1989
➤ 5,b47; 7,a814: ᴿBO 49 (1992) 705s (J. *Baines*); CritRR 5 (1992) 66s
(Susan T. *Hollis*, unfavoring).

b511 *Tobin* Vincent A., The creativity of Egyptian myth; wanderings in an
intellectual labyrinth: JSStEg 18 (1988) 106-118.

b511* *a) Tobin* Vincent A., Isis and Demeter; symbols of divine motherhood;
– *b) Spalinger* Anthony, Some revisions of temple endowments in the
New Kingdom: JAmEg 28 (1991) 187-200 / 21-39.

b512 **Traunecker** Claude, Les dieux d'Égypte: Que sais-je? 1194. P 1992, PUF. 127 p.; 9 fig. 2-13-044368-0 [BO 49,586].

b513 **Tremblay** Claude D., Athéna en Égypte; syncrétisme iconographique et religieux: diss. Laval, ^DTranTamTinh. 1992. 617 p. DANN 73609. – DissA 53 (1992s) 4365-A.

b514 *Valbelle* Dominique, Les métamorphoses d'une hypostase divine en Égypte: RHR 209 (1992) 3-21; Eng. 3: Montu becomes Bull.

b514* *Vernus* Pascal, Le mythe d'un mythe; la prétendue noyade d'Osiris; de la dérive d'un corps à la dérive du sens: StEgPun 9 (1992) 19-34.

b515 *Winand* Jean, Le serment de Paneb et de son fils; Papyrus Salt 124 V° 1, 6-8: BSocÉg 15 (Genève 1991) 107-113.

b516 *Youssef* Youhanna N., De nouveau, la christianisation de dates de fêtes de l'ancienne religion égyptienne: BSACopte 31 (1992) 109-113.

b517 **Žabkar** Louis V., Hymns to Isis 1988 ➤ 4,h940... 7,a815: ^ROLZ 87 (1992) 127s (L. *Kákosy*).

b518 **Zandee** Jan, Der Amunhymnus des Papyrus Leiden I 344 verso. Leiden 1992, Rijksmuseum. xxii-1106 p. [I.-405; II.-809: III.-1106, 38 pl.] 90-6255-046-0; all 90-71201-10-4 [OIAc 5,40].

b519 **Griggs** C. Wilfred, Early Egyptian Christianity: Coptic Studies 2, 1990 ➤ 7,a816. ^RBijdragen 53 (1992) 210 (M. *Parmentier*); JAOS 112 (1992) 490s (Susanna *Elm*); JTS 43 (1992) 229-231 (P. *Widdicombe*); Salmanticensis 39 (1992) 491-4 (R. *Trevijano*); VigChr 45 (1991) 205-7 (G. *Quispel*).

M7 **Religio mesopotamica.**

b520 *a) Abusch* Tzvi, Ritual and incantation; interpretation of textual history of Maqlu vii: 58-105 and ix: 152-59; – *b) Hallo* William W, Royal ancestor worship in the biblical world; – *c) Jacobsen* Thorkild, The spell of Nudimmud: ➤ 181, Sha'arei TALMON 1992, 367-380 / 381-401 / 403-416.

b520* *a) Alster* Bendt, The Manchester Tammuz; – *b) Beaulieu* Paul-Alain, Antiquarian theology in Seleucid Uruk; – *c) Selz* Gebhard J., Eine Kultstatue der Herrschergemählin Šaša; ein Beitrag zum Problem der Vergöttlichung; – *d) Szarzyńska* Krystyna, Names of temples in the archaic texts from Uruk: AcSum 14 (1992) 1-45+2 fig. / 47-75 / 245-268 / 269-287.

b521 **Balz-Cochois** Helgard, Inanna; Wesensbild und Kult einer unmütterlichen Göttin: Studien zum Verstehen fremder Religionen 4. Gü 1992, Mohn. 229 p. DM 78 [TR 88,433].

b522 **Black** Jeremy, **Green** Anthony, Gods, demons and symbols of ancient Mesopotamia; an illustrated dictionary. L 1992, British Museum. 1992 p.; 159 fig. 0-7141-1705-6 [OIAc 5,14].

b523 *Black* Jeremy A., Eme-sal cult songs and prayers: ➤ 32, ^FCIVIL M., Aula0 9,1 (1991) 23-36.

b524 **Bottéro** Jean, *Kramer* Samuel N., Uomini e dèi della Mesopotamia; alle origini della mitologia, ^TCellerino Alessandra, *Ruffa* Michele, ^EBergamini Giovanni. T 1992, Einaudi. 805 p.; 17 fig.; maps. Lit. 130.000. 88-06-12737-3. – ^RArcheo 7,90 (1992) 125 (S. *Moscati*).

b525 **Bottéro** Jean, Writing, reasoning and the gods [1987]. ^TBahrani Zeinab, *Mieroop* Marc Van de. Ch 1992, Univ. 326 p. $40 [BAR-W 19/1,10]. 0-226-06726-2 b525* **Braun-Holzinger** Eva A., Mesopotamische Weihgaben 1991 ➤ 7,a820: ᴿMesopT 27 (1992) 289-293 (P. *Brusasco*).

b526 *Casadio* Giovanni, A ciascuno il suo; otium e negotium del dio supremo dalla Siria alla Mesopotamia: SMSR 16 (1992) 59-79.

b527 **Charpin** Dominque, Le clergé d'Ur 1986 ➤ 2,9061 ... 6,b77*: ᴿOLZ 87 (1992) 526-531 (B. *Groneberg*); ZAss 82 (1992) 125s (P. *Attinger*).

b528 *Cooper* Jerrold S., The fate of mankind; death and afterlife in Ancient Mesopotamia: ➤ 603, Death 1988/92, 19-33.

b529 *Czichon* R., *Görg* M., Eine mittelassyrische Ritzzeichnung [Gott Šamaš vielleicht mit (*nā*)*ru* 'Musiker']: BibNot 61 (1992) 7; phot.; 2 fig.

b530 **de Martino** Stefano, Die mantischen Texte: Corpus der hurritischen Sprachdenkmäler 1/7, Boğazköy. R 1992, Bonsignori. xv-159 p.

b531 **Dijkstra** Klaas, Life and loyalty; a study of the socio-religious culture of Syria and Mesopotamia in the Greco-Roman period: diss. ᴰDrijvers H. Groningen 1992. 298 p. – TvT 33,92; RTLv 24, p. 566.

b532 *Fisher* Robert W., 'Secular' tendencies in the Neo-Assyrian period: BCanadMesop 24 (1992) 25-31; franç. 25.

b533 *Geller* M.J., CT 58, No. 70, a Middle-Babylonian *eršahunga* [MAUL S. 1988]: BSO 55 (1992) 528-532.

b534 *Heinshohn* Gunnar, The rise of blood sacrifice and priest-kingship in Mesopotamia; a 'cosmic decree'?: Religion 22 (L 1992) 109-134 [< ZIT 92,413].

b535 *Janssen* Caroline, Inanna-Mansum et ses fils; relation d'une succession turbulente dans les archives d'Ur-Utu: RAss 86 (1992) 19-51; 4 phot.; Eng. 52.

b536 **Jeyes** Ulla, Old Babylonian extispicy 1989 ➤ 5,b77; 7,a827: ᴿOrientalia 61 (1992) 482 (R. *Biggs*).

b537 *Jeyes* Ulla, Divination as a science in ancient Mesopotamia: JbEOL 32 (1991s) 23-41.

b538 **Kraus** F.R., The role of temples [Le rôle des temples 1953s]...ᵀ: MgANE. Malibu c. 1990, Undena. iv-20 p. [OLZ 88,509, R. *Dolce*, Eng.] 93-13.

b539 **Kuwabara** Toshikazu, The netherworld in Sumero-Akkadian literature: diss. Graduate Theol. Union, ᴰKilmer A. Berkeley 1990. – RTLv 24, p. 542; OIAc 2,22.

b539* *a*) *Lambert* W.G., Nippur in ancient ideology [city was in relation to its god(s)]; – *b*) *Glassner* Jean-Jacques, Inanna et les *me* [office ou qualité de justice/religion; p. 85 'discours théologique de très haute qualité']: ➤ 687, Nippur 1988/92, 119-126 / 55-86.

b540 **Lawson** Jack N., The concept of fate in ancient Mesopotamia of the first millennium; toward an understanding of *šimtu*: diss. HUC, ᴰWeisberg D. Cincinnati 1992. 224 p. 92-22537. – DissA 53 (1992s) 1244-A.

b541 **Ludwig** Marie-Christine, Untersuchungen zu den Hymnen des Išme-Dagan von Isin 1990 [< diss. Münster 1987, ᴰKrecher J.] ➤ 6,b89*; 8 pl. DM 112. 3-447-03097-6: ᴿBO 49 (1992) 780-2 (N. *Wassermann*).

b541* *MacGinnis* John, Neo-Babylonian prebend texts [income for Temple services] from the British Museum: AfO 38s (1991s) 74-100.

b542 *Margueron* J.G., Temples et pouvoirs en Mésopotamie; position du problème et étude de cas fournis par l'archéologie: Ktema 14 (1989) 7-17; 2 fig.

b543 **Maul** Stefan M., 'Herzberuhigungsklagen' 1988 ➤ 6,b91; 7,a829: ᴿBO 49 (1992) 777-780 (W. W. *Hallo*).

b544 *Maxwell-Hyslop* K. R., The goddess ['on a goose'] Nanše, an attempt to identify her representation: Iraq 54 (1992) 79-82.

b545 *Mayer* Werner R.,   Ein Hymnus auf Ninurta als Helfer in der Not: Orientalia 61 (1992) 17-54; 55-57 facsimiles.

b545* **Michel** Cécile,   Innāya dans les tablettes paléo-assyriennes: P 1991, ADPF. 294 p.; 440 p.   2-86538-221-4 [BO 49,587].

b546 **Osten-Sacken** Elisabeth von der,   Der Ziegen-'Dämon'; 'Obed- und Urukzeitliche Götterdarstellungen [Diss. Münster]: AOAT 230.   Neuk/ Kevelaer 1992, Neuk/Butzon & B.   x-287 p.   3-7666-9710-2 / 3-7887-1367-4 [OIAc 3,33].

b547 **Paul** Judith R.,   Mesopotamian ritual texts and the concept of the sacred in Mesopotamia: diss. UCLA 1992, ᴰ*Buccellati* G. 328 p. 93-01517. − DissA 53 (1992s) 3256-A.

b548 *Rawi* Farouk N. al-,   A new hymn to Marduk from Sippar: RAss 86 (1992) 79-83.

b549 **Ringgren** Helmer,   Le religioni dell'Oriente Antico [1979] 1991 ➤ 7,a836; ᵀ*Fantoma* Giovanna: ᴿAsprenas 39 (1992) 435s (A. *Rolla*, insoddisfatto della bibliografia italiana); ParVi 37 (1992) 398s (L. *Cagni*); Protestantesimo 47 (1992) 133 (J. A. *Soggin*).

b550 **Rochbert-Halton** Francesca,   Aspects of Babylonian celestial divination; the lunar eclipse tablets of Enūma Anu Enlil: AfO Beih 22, 1988 ➤ 7, a837:   ᴿArOr 60 (1992) 83-85 (A. *Livingstone*: reliable; some criticisms).

b551 *Römer* W. II. P.,   Sumerische Emesallieder: BO 49 (1992) 636-680.

b552 *Scurlock* J. A.,   K 164 (BA 2, P. 635); new light on the mourning rites for Dumuzi?:   RAss 86 (1992) 53-67; franç. 67.

b553 **Starr** Ivan,   The rituals of the diviner: BtMesop 12, 1983 [diss. Yale 1974] ➤ 65,9405 ...:   ᴿAulaO 10 (1992) 170s (R. *Biggs*).

b554 **Starr** I.,   Queries to the Sungod; divination and politics in Sargonid Assyria: SAA 4, 1990 ➤ 6,b102:   ᴿArOr 60 (1992) 304 (Jana *Pečírková*).

b555 *Thomsen* Marie-Louise,   The evil eye in Mesopotamia: JNES 51 (1992) 19-32.

b556 a) *Vivante* Anna,   Ex voto dai santuari mesopotamici protodinastici; − b) *Dolce* Rita,   Offerte votive alimentari e comportamenti economici nella Mesopotamia del III millennio a.C.; una proposta: ➤ 701, ScAnt 3s (1989s) 127-138; 10 fig.; Eng. 138 / 139-153; 3 fig.

b557 *Wasseman* Nathan,   CT 21,40-42, a bilingual report of an oracle with a royal hymn of Hammurabi [close affinity with his Law stela]: RAss 86 (1992) 1-18.

b557* a) *Westenholz* Joan G.,   The clergy of Nippur; the priestess of Enlil; − b) *Selz* Gebhard J.,   Enlil und Nippur nach präsargonischen Quellen; − c) *Robertson* John F.,   The temple economy of Old Babylonian Nippur; the evidence for centralized management: ➤ 687, Nippur 1988/92, 297-310; 3 fig. / 189-225; 3 maps / 177-188.

b558 **Wiggermann** F. A, M.,   Mesopotamian protective spirits; the ritual texts [diss. Amst 1986, Babylonian prophylactic ...]: Cuneiform Mg 1.   Groningen 1992, Styx. xiii-225 p.; 20 fig.   90-72371-52-6 [OIAc 5,39].

b559 **Zettler** Richard L.,   The Ur III temple of Inanna at Nippur; the operation and organization of urban religious institutions in Mesopotamia in the late third millennium B.C.: BBeitVO 11.   B 1992, Reimer.   xiv-303 p.; 21 fig.   3-496-00422-3.

M7.4   Religio persiana, *Iran.*

b560 **Ahn** Gregor,   Religiöse Herrscherlegitimation im achämenidischen Iran; die Voraussetzungen und die Struktur ihrer Argumentation: Acta Iranica 31.   Leiden 1992, Brill.   xiv-365 p.

b561 *Albrile* Ezio, Ahriman come 'demiurgo'; un'anomalia dualistica?: SMSR 58 = 16 (1992) 81-91.

b562 **Boyce** Mary, A Persian stronghold of Zoroastrianism [1975, Oxford-UP 1979 ➤ 58,d238*b*]. Lanham 1989, UPA. xv-284 p.; 8 pl. $39.75. – ᴿJRAS (1991) 293s (J. R. *Russell*).

b563 **Boyce** M., *Grenet* F., A history of Zoroastrianism 3. under Macedonian and Roman rule 1991 ➤ 7,a842*: ᴿJRS 82 (1992) 265-7 (A. D. H. *Bivar*).

b564 **Corbin** H., Corpo spirituale e terra celeste; dall'Iran mazdeo all'Iran sciita: Il Ramo d'Oro. Mi 1986, Adelphi. 335 p. Lit. 35.000. – ᴿStPatav 38 (1991) 460-3 (C. *Saccone*).

b565 *Corsten* Thomas, HERODOT I 131 und die Einführung des [persischen] Anahita-Kultes in Lydien: IrAnt 26 (1991) 163-180.

b566 **Firby** Nora K., European... perceptions of Zoroastrians ᴰ1988 ➤ 5, b101*: ᴿOLZ 87 (1992) 289-292 (A. V. *Williams*).

b567 **Gignoux** Philippe, Les quatre inscriptions du mage Kirdīr: Cah 9. P 1991, Assoc, Ét. Iraniennes. 108 p. Fb 720 [JAOS 112,726].

b568 *Khlopin* I. N., Zoroastrianism – location and time of its origins: IrAnt 27 (1992) 95-116; 4 fig.

b569 *Levit-Tawil* Dalia, The syncretistic goddess Anahita in light of the small bas relief at Darabgird; her imagery on early Sasanian rock reliefs and seals: IrAnt 27 (1992) 189-225; 15 fig.

b570 *Makkay* J., Funerary sacrifices of the Yamna-Complex and their Anatolian (Hittite) and Aegean (Mycenaean and Homeric) parallels: AcAHung 44 (1992) 213-237; 3 fig.

b571 *Shaked* Shaul, The myth of Zurvan; cosmology and eschatology: ➤ 57, ꟳFLUSSER D., Messiah 1992, 219-240.

b572 *a*) Shaked Shaul, Aspekte von Noruz. dem iranischen Neujahrsfest, ᵀGern Wolfgang; – *b*) *Löffler* Reinhold, Das Fest als das Unheilige; die Stammeshochzeit im iranischen Fundamentalismus: ➤ 7,465*, Fest 1988/ 91, 88-102 / 160-8.

b573 *Vértesalji* P. P., 'La déesse nue élamite' und der Kreis der babylonischen 'Lilû-Dämonen': IrAnt 26 (1991) 101-148; 12 fig.

b574 **Waldmann** Helmut, Der kommagenische Mazdaismus 1991 ➤ 7,a846: ᴿAnzAltW 45 (1992) 299s (P. W. *Haider*); BonnJbb 192 (1992) 618-622 (B. *Jacobs*: kritisch); ClasR 42 (1992) 340s (J. G. *Griffiths*).

b575 *Zaehner* R. C. †, Zoroastrian survivals in Iranian folklore: Iran [I. 3 (1965) 87-96] II. ᴱ*Kreyenbroek* Philip G, 30 (1992) 65-75.

M8.1   *Religio proto-arabica* – **Early Arabic religious graffiti.**

b576 *Avanzini* Alessandra, Alcune osservazoni sull'onomastica dell'Arabia meridionale preislamica: StEpL 8 (1991) 47-57.

b577 ᴱ**Fahd** M., L'Arabie préislamique 1987/9 ➤ 5,816: ᴿJRAS (1991) 266-273 (A. F. L. *Beeston*: detailed on each paper).

b578 *Grenet* Frantz [➤ 6,m374, rapport sur le colloque préislamique 1988] L'Asie centrale préislamique; bibliographie critique 1977-1986. Téhéran/P 1988, Inst. Français de Recherche en Iran. 179 p. [OIAc 3,22].

b579 *Khoury* Raif Georges, Du vocabulaire politico-religieux dans la plus vieille correspondance officielle en Islam: Ktema 14 (1989) 79-85.

b580 **Krone** Susanne, Die altarabische Gottheit al-Lāt: HeidOrSt 23. Fra 1992, Lang. 587 p.; 9 fig. 3-631-45092-3.

b581 *Macdonald* M. C. A., The seasons and transhumance in the Safaitic inscriptions: JRAS (1992) 1-11; 2 fig.

b582 **Trimingham** John S., Christianity among the Arabs in pre-Islamic times: Arab Background. Beirut 1990, Librairie du Liban. xiv-342 p. 0-582-78081-0.

M8.2   *Muḥammad et asseclae* – **Qurʾān and early diffusion of Islam.**

b583 *Bashear* Suliman †,   a) Apocalyptic and other materials on early Muslim-Byzantine wars; a review of Arabic sources: JRAS (1991) 173-207; – b) The images of Mecca; a case-study in early Muslim iconography: Muséon 105 (1992) 361-377.

b584 **Bell** Richard †, 1952   A commentary on the Qurʾān [microfilmed notes prepared to justify critical-edition features of his 1939 translation], E*Bosworth* C. Edmond, *Richardson* M. E. J.: JSS mg 14.   Manchester UK 1991, Univ. xxii-608 p.; 603 p. £60. 0-9516124-1-7. – RExpTim 103 (1991s) 190s (W. M. *Watt*: for the scholar, hopefully also Muslim); JAOS 112 (1992) 639-647 (A. *Rippin*).

b585 **Bello** Iysa,   The medieval Islamic controversy between philosophy and orthodoxy; *ijmāʾ* and *taʿwīl* in the conflict betwen al-GHAZĀLĪ and IBN RUSHD: Islamic PhT TSt 3.   Leiden 1989, Brill. 177 p. *f* 70. – RBO 49 (1992) 545s (R. M. *Frank*: unsatisfactory).

b586 TBerque Jacques, Le Coran... annoté; étude exégétique. P 1990, Sindbad. 848 p. – RRThom 92 (1992) 578-581 (J. *Jomier*).

b587 **Collins** Roger,   The Arab conquest of Spain, 710-797: History of Spain 3.   Ox 1989, Blackwell. xii-239 p. – RJRAS (1991) 273-6 (M. *Brett*).

b588 **Dall'Oglio** Paolo,   Speranza nell'Islam; interpretazione della prospettiva escatologica di Corano XVIII [diss. 1990 ↠ 7,a855]. R 1992, Pont. Univ. Gregoriana. xi-365 p.: ROrChrPer 58 (1992) 603s (V. *Poggi*).

b589 *Dero* Anne-Claude,   L'hagiographie miraculeuse de Muḥammad: Prob-HistRel 2 (1991) 153-166 [< ZIT 92,68].

b590 **Ess** Josef van,   Theologie und Gesellschaft im 2. und 3. Jahrhundert Hidschra; eine Geschichte des religösen Denkens im frühen Islam, 2. B/NY 1992, de Gruyter. xi-742 p. [TR 88,526, 'DM 400']. – RRSO 66 (1992) 223s (Blancamaria *Scarcia Amoretti*).

b590* *Fiema* Zbigniew T.,   The Islamic conquest of southern Jordan; a new research perspective: ADAJ 36 (1992) 325-331.

b591 **Gil** Moshe,   A history of Palestine, 634-1099 [☉], TBroido Ethel. C 1992, Univ. xxvi-968 p. £80. 0-521-40437-1 [OIAc 3,22]. – RIrénikon 65 (1992) 295 (E. *Lanne*); RHE 87 (1992) 584 (D. *Bradley*).

b592 **Gilliot** Claude,   Exégèse, langue et théologie en Islam; l'exégèse coranique de ṬABARI: Ét. Musulmanes 32, 1990 ↠ 7,b884: RBSO 55 (1992) 548s (J. *Barton*: excellent); Études 376 (1992) 139s (H. *Loucel*); RThom 92 (1992) 581s (J. *Jomier*).

b593 **Gimaret** D., La doctrine d'al-ASCHʿARI [874-935]: Patrimoines Islam. P 1990, Cerf. 601 p. F 295 [NRT 115, 606, J. *Scheuer*].

b594 **Gramlich** Richard,   Die Wunder der Freunde Gottes... Islam 1987 ↠ 5,b147: RArOr 60 (1992) 313s (L. *Kropáček*).

b595 **Jambet** Christian,   La grande résurrection d'Alamût [in northern Persia, refuge of breakaway Ismailiyas c. 1100]. Lagrasse 1990, Verdier. 418 p. F 180 pa. – RJAOS 112 (1992) 308-310 (F. *Daffary*).

b596 **Khoury** A. T.,   Der Koran   arabisch-deutsch,   wissenschaftlicher Kommentar I, 1990 ↠ 7,a864: RTLZ 117 (1992) 171s (H. *Preissler*).

b597 **Lewis** Bernard,   Race and slavery in the Middle East; an historical enquiry [< Race and color in Islam 1971]. NY 1990, Oxford-UP, xii-184 p.; 24 color. pl. $25. – RJRAS (1992) 69s (D. O. *Morgan*).

b598 **Madelung** Wilferd, Religious trends in early Islamic Iran: [five 1983] Columbia Lectures on Iranian Studies 4. Albany 1988, SUNY. x-128 p. $32.50; pa. $10. – RJAOS 112 (1992) 141s (Rosalind *Gwynne*); JNES 51 (1992) 158s (M. *Morony*).

b599 **Mandei** Gabriele, Il Corano senza segreti. Mi 1991, Rusconi. 276 p. Lit. 35.000. – RAsprenas 39 (1992) 311s (G. *Ragozzino*).

b600 **Mann** Michael, Hijri, a computer program to convert Hijri to Julian dates. L 1991, [J]RAS. IBM-compatible disk. £9.50. – RBSO 55 (1992) 328s (M. *Shokoohy*).

b601 **Mottahedeh** Roy P., Loyalty and leadership in an early Islamic society: StudiesNE. Princeton 1980, Univ. xi-209 p. 0-691-05296-4 [OIAc 2,24].

b602 **Motzki** Harald, Die Anfänge der islamischen Jurisprudenz; ihre Entstehung in Mekka bis zur Mitte des 2./8. Jahrhunderte: AbhKuM 50/2. Stu 1991, Steiner. x-292 p. DM 96. 3-515-05433-2. – RBO 49 (1992) 357-364 (G. H. A. *Juynboll*).

b603 **Newby** Gordon D., The making of the last prophet; a reconstruction of the earliest biography of Muhammad 1989 ➤ 5,b192: RRelStR 18 (1992) 179-187 (R. *Firestone, al.,* 187-9 response).

b604 **Noja** Sergio, L'Islam e il suo Corano. Mi 1990, Mondadori. vii-210 p. Lit. 10.000. – RStPatav 38 (1991) 222s (C. *Saccone*).

O'Shaughnessy Thomas J., Christian religious specialists in the Qur'ān 1991 ➤ b715.

b606 **Pentz** Peter, The invisible conquest; the ontogenesis of sixth and seventh century Syria. K 1992, Nat. Museum. 96 p.; 19 fig. 87-7288-504-1.

b607 **Powers** David S., Studies in Qur'ān and Hadīth; ... inheritance 1986 ➤ 5,b199: RBO 49 (1992) 543-5 (U. *Haarmann*).

b608 **Renard** John, In the footsteps of Muhammad; understanding the Islamic experience. NY 1992, Paulist. iv-173 p. $10. 0-8091-3316-4 [TDig 39,381].

b609 ERippin Andrew, *Knappert* Jan, Textual sources for the study of Islam. Ch 1990, Univ. [= Manchester 1986 ➤ 5,b202*] x-209 p. $15 pa. – RHorizons 19 (1992) 348 (D. B. *Burrell*); JAAR 60 (1992) 813 (W. M. *Brinner*: long introduction, then Quran & Hadith and their commentators; then later data on law, mysticism, Bahai, and Swahili, but little on Shiites or philosophy).

b610 **Rudolph** Ulrich, Der Doxographie des Pseudo-AMMONIOS; ein Beitrag zur neuplatonischen Überlieferung im Islam: AbhKUM 49,1. Stu 1989, Steiner (for DMG). 284 p. DM 128. – RJRAS (1991) 399s (J. N. *Mattock*).

b611 **Schimmel** Annemarie, Islam, an introduction: Albany 1992, SUNY. vii-166 p. $29.50; pa. $10. 0-7914-1327-6; -8-4 [TDig 40,185].

b612 **Schleifer** Aliah, A modified phenomenological approach to the concept and person of Maryam in Islam; diss. Exeter 1991. 334 p. BRDX-95862. – DissA 53 (1992s) 531s-A.

b613 **Serauky** Eberhard, Geschichte des Islam; Entstehung, Entwicklung und Wirkung von den Anfängen bis zur Mitte des XX. Jahrhunderts. B 1991, Deutscher Verlag Wiss. 523 p.; 21 fig.; 3 maps. DM 58. – RDLZ 113 (1992) 75s (T. *Nagel*); OLZ 87 (1992) 57-62 (U. *Haarmann*).

b614 TEThomas David, Anti-Christian polemic in early Islam; [M. Ibn-Harūn] Abu Isa al-WARRĀQ's 'Against the Trinity': Oriental Publ. 45. C 1992, Univ. viii-218 p. $75. 0-521-41244-7 [TDig 39,392]. – RTS 53 (1992) 783s (S. I. *Sara*: 9th century Shiite, Arabic-English on facing pages).

b615 **Ventura** Alberto. al-Fātiḥa — l'Aprente; la prima sura del Corano: Le voci della preghiera 4. Genova 1991, Marietti. 71 p.; ill. 88-211-6943-X.

b616 ᴱYoung M. J. L., al., Religion, learning and science in the Abbasid period: CHistArab Lit. C 1990, Univ. xxiii-587 p.; 10 fig. £60. [NRT 115,598, J. Scheuer].

b617 **Zakaria** Rafiq, Muhammad and the Quran. Penguin 1991. 443 p. £7. 0-14-014423-4. – ᴿExpTim 103 (1991s) 122s (O. Leaman: the liberal-Maududi wing of Islam).

b618 **Zepp** Ira G.ᴶ, A Muslim primer: Westminster MD 1992, Wakefield (Christian Classics). xl-292 p. $15 pa. [+ $3.50]. 0-87061-188-7 [TDig 40,94].

M8.3 **Islam**, evolutio recentior – later history and practice.

b619 ᴱ**Abrahamov** Binyamin, Al-Kāsim B. IBRĀHĪM on the proof of God's existence, Kitab al-Dalīl al-Kabīr: IslamPhTh 5. Leiden 1989, Brill. xiii-201 p. f 110. – ᴿBSO 55 (1992) 320s (Sarah Stroumsa); JRAS (1992) 267-270 (W. Madelung: unreliable).

b620 **Ahmad** Akbar S., Discovering Islam; making sense of Muslim history and society. L 1988, Routledge. 251 p. – ᴿJAAR 60 (1992) 1992) 537-9 (I. M. Abu-Rabi').

b621 **Ahmed** Leila, Women and gender in Islam; historical roots of a modern debate. NHv 1991, Yale Univ. viii-296 p. $30 [JAOS 112,728].

b622 **Amanat** Abbas, Resurection and renewal... Babi/Iran 1844-50: 1989 → 6,b162: ᴿJRAS (1991) 407-410 (D. MacEoin).

b623 **Arié** Rachel, L'Espagne musulmane au temps des Nasrīdes (1232-1492). P 1990 = 1973, de Boccard. 528 + 52 p. addenda; 12 pl. – ᴿJRAS (1992) 273-5 (A. Fernández-Puertas).

b624 **Arkoun** Mohammed, Le concept de sociétés du Livre-livre: → 63, ᶠGEFFRÉ C., Interpréter 1992, 211-223.

b625 **Baldick** Julian, Mystical Islam, an introduction to Sufism. L 1989, Tauris. viii-208 p. £8 pa. ᴿJRAS (1991) 289-292 (A. Knysh).

b626 ᴱ**Balmer** Heinz, Glaus Beat, Die Blütezeit der arabischen Wissenschaft. Z 1992, Fachvereine. 139 p. [JAOS 112,728].

b627 **Betts** Robert B., The Druze. NHv 1990, Yale Univ. 161 p. $9. – ᴿJAAR 60 (1992) 327s (Paul E. Walker).

b628 **Binder** Leonard, Islamic liberalism; a critique of development ideologies. Ch 1988, Univ. xiii-399 p. $60; pa $20. – ᴿJNES 51 (1992) 298s (R. Bianchi).

b629 **Bonaud** Christian, Le Soufisme; al-tasawwuf et la spiritualité islamique: Islam-Occident 8. P 1991, Maisonneuve & L. 155 p. 2-7068-1017-3. – ᴿÉTRel 67 (1992) 93 (Françoise Smyth); JSS 37 (1992) 129 (R. W. J. Austin).

b630 **Bürgel** Johann C., Allmacht und Mächtigkeit; Religion und Welt im Islam. Mü 1991, Beck. 416 p. 3-406-35374-6. – ᴿActuBbg 29 (1992) 263s (J. Boada).

b631 **Butt** Nasim, Science and Muslim Societies. ... 1991, Grey Seal. 136 p. £6. 1-85640-023-9. – ᴿExpTim 103 (1991s) 319 (O. Leaman).

b632 **Campo** Juan E., The other sides of Paradise... domestic space in Islam 1991 → 7,a879*: ᴿJRel 72 (1992) 622s (K. Kueny).

b633 **Clam** Jean, Das 'Paradoxon des Monotheismus' [Henri CORBIN 1981] und die Metaphysik des IBN ʿARABI: ZDMG 142 (1992) 275-286.

b634 **Daftary** Farhad, The Ismāʿīlīs; their history and doctrines 1990 → 6, b174 ['Deftery']: 0-521-370191. – ᴿBO 49 (1992) 552-4 (G. Hoffmann: based on 20 years' research, largely on primary sources in Tehran; but socio-economic activities only marginal); JAOS 112 (1992) 138s (P. E. *Walker*); JRAS (1992) 265s (R. *Irwin*: definitive).

b635 *Debarge* Louis, Mysticisme islamique et modernité: MélSR 48 (1991) 135-151; Eng. 151.

b636 **Fakhry** Majid, Ethical theories in Islam: Islamic philosophy 8. Leiden 1991, Brill. x-230 p. ƒ128. – ᴿJSS 37 (1992) 127s (I. R. *Netton*: essential for every Islamist).

b637 *Fierro* Maribel, The polemic about the *Karāmāt al-Awliyā* and the development of Sūfism in al-Andalus (fourth/tenth – fifth/eleventh centuries): BSO 55 (1992) 236-249.

b638 **Friedlander** Shems [= Ira], The whirling dervishes. Albany 1992, SUNY. xx-15+160 p.; ill. $13 pa. – [RelStR 19, 89, G. *Yocum*: unacknowledged reprint of Macmillan 1975].

b639 **Gramlich** Richard, Islamische Mystik; Sufische Texte aus zehn Jahrhunderten. Stu 1992, Kohlhammer. 320 p. 3-37-011772-6.

b640 ᵀᴱ**Gramlich** Richard, Schlaglichter über das Sufitum; Abū Naṣr as-SAR-RĀĞS Kitāb al-Lumaᶜ: Freiburger Islamstudien 13. Stu 1990, Steiner. 676 p. DM 270. – ᴿJRAS 270-2 (A. *Knysh*: flawless translation).

b641 **Guichard** Pierre, L'Espagne et la Sicile musulmanes aux XIᵉ et XIIᵉ siècles. Lyon 1990, Univ. 232 p. F 138. 2-7297-0384-5. – ᴿÉTRel 67 (1992) 122 (Dominique *Viaux*).

b642 ᴱ**Haddad** Yvonne Y., The Muslims of America: Religion in America. Ox 1991, UP. x-248 p. $40. 0-19-506728-2 [TDig 39,375]. – ᴿJAOS 112 (1992) 721s (Linda S. *Walbridge*: useful).

b643 **Halm** H., Shiism: Islamic Survey 18. E 1992, Univ. 218 p. £25. – [NRT 115, 606, J. *Scheuer*].

b644 **Harvey** L. P., Islamic Spain, 1250 to 1500. Ch 1990, Univ. xvi-370 p.; 2 maps. $47. – ᴿSpeculum 67 (1992) 976s (K. B. *Wolf*).

b645 **Hourani** Albert, A history of the Arab peoples [from the rise of Islam until the present day]. CM 1991, Harvard Univ. xx-551 p. $25. – ᴿJAOS 112 (1992) 307s (Z. *Lockman*: needed, standard); JRAS (1992) 414s (H. *Kennedy*: elegant and entertaining).

b646 *Jomier* Jacques, Le Coran et la liturgie dans l'Islam: MaisD 190 (1992) 121-6 [-141 *al.*, Sikhisme, Bouddhisme ...].

b647 *Livingston* John W., Science and the occult in the thinking of IBN QAYYIM al-Jawziyya [1292-1349, b. Damascus]: JAOS 112 (1992) 598-610.

b648 **Makdisi** George, The rise of humanism in Islam and the Christian west, with special reference to scholasticism. E 1990, Univ. xxi-431 p. $45. – ᴿBO 49 (1992) 538-540 (G. J. Van *Gelder*); JAOS 112 (1992) 135-7 (H. *Dabashi*); JRAS (1992) 272s (H. *Kennedy*).

b649 **Malti-Douglas** Fedwa, Woman's body, woman's world; gender and discourse in Arabic-Islamic writing. Princeton 1991, Univ. xi-206 p. $37.50; pa. $13 [JAOS 112,729].

b650 ᴱ**Mantran** Robert, Les grandes dates de l'Islam: Essentiels: Grandes Dates, 1990 ➤ 6,b193; 18 maps, F 98: ᴿJRAS (1992) 69 (D. O. *Morgan*: mixed merits; up to RUSHDIE 1989).

b651 *Melzer* Karl, Das Eigene und das Fremde; Überlegungen zur philosophischen Diskussion in arabischen Ländern seit etwa 1967: ZDMG 142 (1992) 287-298.

b652 **Nasr** Seyyed H., Islamic spirituality; manifestations: EWSp 20, 1991 ➤ 7,a891: ᴿExpTim 103 (1991s) 92 (W. M. *Watt*: 25 essays; GHAZALI's *Ihya* almost overlooked).

b653 ᴱNasr Seyyed H., *al.*, Shiʿism; doctrines, thought, and spirituality. Albany 1988, SUNY. xviii-402 p. $73.50; pa. $24.50. 0-88706-689-5; -90-9. – ᴿBO 49 (1992) 554s (J. G. J. *ter Haar*: anthology of published items to counter current view that it is political/violent; their 1989 Expectations of the Millennium is a continuation).

b654 **Nasr** Seyyed H., Ideali e realtà dell'Islam. Mi 1989, Rusconi. 203 p. Lit. 23.000. – ᴿStPatav 39 (1992) 673-5 (C. *Saccone*).

b655 **Netton** Ian R., Allah transcendent; studies in the structure and semiotics of Islamic theology, philosophy, and cosmology: Exeter ArIsl 5, 1989 ➤ 7,a892: ᴿJAOS 112 (1992) 527s (Thérèse-Anne *Druart*); JRAS (1991) 400s (J. *Baldick*).

b656 **Netton** Ian R., A popular dictionary of Islam. Atlantic Highlands NJ 1992, Humanities. 279 p. $17.50. 0-391-03756-0 [TDig 40,178].

b656* *Nielsen* J. S., *Muslimūn*; les Musulmans d'Europe: ➤ 756, Enc Islam² 7 (1992) 695-703.

b657 **Pasquier** Roger Du, Le réveil de l'Islam: Bref. P 1988, Cerf/Fides. 127 p. – ᴿMélSR 49 (1992) 63s (L. *Debarge*).

b658 **Poston** Larry, Islamic *daʿwah* and the west; Muslim missionary activity and the dynamics of conversion to Islam. NY 1992, Oxford-UP. 220 p. $30. 0-19-507227-8 [TDig 40,82].

b659 **Radtke** Bernd, Weltgeschichte und Weltbeschreibung im mittelalterlichen Islam: Beiruter Texte und Studien 51. Stu 1992, Steiner. xi-544 p. 3-515-05947-4 [BO 49,594].

b660 **Schimmel** Annemarie, *al.*, Der Islam [I. 1980; II. 1985]; III. Islamische Kultur — zeitgenössische Strömungen — Volksfrömmigkeit: Die Religionen der Menschheit 25/3, 1990 ➤ 7,a897: ᴿOLZ 87 (1992) 61-64 (D. *Sturm*); TR 88 (1992) 422s (A.-T. *Khoury*).

ᴱ**Tapper** Richard, Islam in modern Turkey; religion, politics, and literature in a secular state [1988 London conference; 11 art.] 1991 ➤ 695.

b662 **Tibi** Bassam, Islam and the cultural accommodation to social change [deutsch], ᵀ*Krojzl* Clare. Boulder CO 1990, Westview. xiv-272 p. $39.50; pa. $19. – ᴿJAOS 112 (1992) 716s (A. I. *Tayob*).

b663 ᴱ**Troll** Christian W., Muslim shrines in India; their character and significance: Islam in India 4. Delhi 1989, Oxford-UP. xvi-327 p.; 12 pl., 3 maps. £17.50. – ᴿJRAS (1992) 100 (P. *Jackson*).

b664 **Watt** W. M., Islamic fundamentalism and modernity 1988 ➤ 5,b223... 7,a899: ᴿJAAR 60 (1992) 362-5 (J. T. *Kenney*).

b665 **Watt** W. Montgomery, What is Islam?² [¹1968]: Arab Background. Beirut 1990, Librairie du Liban. x-262 p. 0-562-78302-X.

M8.4 *Alter philosemitismus* – Islamic-Christian rapprochement.

b666 **Akhtar** Shabbir, The light in the enlightenment; Christianity and the secular heritage. ...1990, Grey Seal. x-213 p. £25. 1-85640-001-8. – ᴿExpTim 102 (1990s) 351 (G. *McFarlane*: Muslim defence of natural theology).

b667 *Anawati* G. C., Islam et christianisme; la rencontre de deux cultures en Occident au moyen âge: MIDÉO 20 (Mélanges de l'Institut Dominicain d'Études Orientales 1991) 233-299 [< RSPT 76,528].

b668 **Anees** Munawar, *al.*, Christian-Muslim relations; yesterday, today, tomorrow. ...1991, Grey Seal. 96 p. £5. 1-85640-021-2. – ᴿExpTim 103 (1991s) 319 (O. *Leaman*).

b669 **Antes** Peter, *al.*, Der Islam; Religion, Ethik, Politik. Stu 1991, Kohlhammer. x-152. DM 29,80. – ᴿTR 88 (1992) 244s (P. *Heine*: aus früheren Sammelbänden).

b670 ᴱ**Antoun** Richard T., *Hegland* Mary E., Religious resurgence; contemporary cases in Islam, Christianity, and Judaism [11 art.] 1987 ➤ 4,415; 5,b109: ᴿCritRR 5 (1992) 263s (R. *Comstock*).

b671 *Arat* M. Kristin, Die nichtamtliche Religiosität als dialogisches Element der Religionen am Beispiel von Christentum und Islam: ZMissRw 75 (1991) 117-132 [274-297, *Kühn* Peter, Islamische Schulen].

b672 *Argyriou* Asterios, L'épopée de Digenis Akritas et la littérature de polémique et d'apologétique islamo-chrétienne: Byzantina 16 (1991) 7-34.

b673 **Armstrong** Karen, Muhammad; a western attempt at understanding [L 1992, Gollancz; £10; ? =] Muhammad, a biography of the Prophet. SF 1992, Harper. 290 p. $23. 0-06-250014-7 [TDig 39,350]. – ᴿTablet 246 (1992) 746 (Rana *Kabbani*).

b674 **Arnaldez** Roger, Réflexions chrétiennes sur la mystique musulmane 1989 ➤ 6,b210; 7,a906: ᴿArOr 60 (1992) 312s (L. *Kropáček*).

b675 **Barreau** Jean-Claude, De l'Islam en général et du monde moderne en particulier. ... 1991, La Pré aux Clercs-Belfond. 135 p. F 85. – ᴿEsprVie 102 (1992) 208 (M. *Henrie*: caricature, à cause de laquelle il a perdu sa présidence des Migrations Internationales).

b676 ᴱ**Basset** Jean-Claude, My neighbour is Muslim; a handbook for Reformed churches. Genève 1990, Knox Center. 111 p. Fs 10. 2-8843-0006-6. – ᴿNedTTs 46 (1992) 351s (K. *Steenbrink*).

b677 **Borrmans** Maurice, Orientamenti per un dialogo tra cristiani e musulmani [Eng. 1990 ➤ 7,a909] 1988 ➤ 5,b124: ᴿStPatav 38 (1991) 657s (C. *Saccone*).

b678 *Caspar* Robert, Une rencontre avec l'Islam; évolution personnnelle et vision actuelle: Spiritus 32 (1991) 15-25.

b679 Challenge of the Scriptures; the Bible and the Qur'ān [1978-82], ᵀ*Brown* Stuart E. Mkn 1989, Orbis. vii-101 p. $27, pa. $14. – ᴿChrCent 107 (1990) 943s (J. A. *Fogle*); Pacifica 4 (1991) 96-98 (D. *Madigan*: foredoomed by false parallels).

b680 ᴱ**Cohn-Sherbok** Dan, Islam in a world of diverse faiths [13 Birmingham Selly Oak papers]. NY 1991, St. Martin's. xvii-218 p. $45. 0-312-05348-7 [TDig 39,366].

b681 *Conrad* Robert, Points of tension; Christians and Muslims in northern Nigeria: CurrTMiss 19 (1992) 108-113.

b682 *Donohue* John J., Islam in Afrika (p. 1-57), Asien (*Michel* Thomas p. 59-141) und Europa (*Vöcking* Hans, p. 143-187); zum Verhältnis zwischen Christen und Muslimen: Beiträge zur Religions- und Glaubensfreiheit 5. Mü 1991, Kirche in Not/Priesterhilfe. 191 p.

b683 *Evers* Georg, Conferentie in Rome over Jezus Christus in de dialoog met de Islam [31 aug. - 6 sept. 1991]: TvT 32 (1992) 83s.

b684 **Fitzgerald** M. L., *Caspar* R., Signs of dialogue; Christian encounter with Muslims, ᴱ*Carzedda* Salvatore † V. 1992: Dialogue Forum 6. Zamboanga 1992, Silsilah. 245 p. [TContext 10/2, 104, G. *Evers*].

b685 **Gaudeul** J. M., Appelés... de l'Islam 1991 ➤ 7,a918: ᴿÉtudes 376 (1992) 284 (J. *Thomas*); LVitae 47 (1992) 353 [? L. *Partos*]

b686 ᴱ**Gervers** Michael, *Bikhazi* Ramzi J., Conversion and continuity; indigenous Christian communities in Islamic lands, eighth to eighteenth centuries: Papers in Mediaeval Studies 9. Toronto 1990, Pont. Inst. Medv. St. [xvii-] 559 p. $49.50. – ᴿBSO 55 (1992) 128s (H. T. *Norris*).

b687 *Gilliot* Claude, Bulletin d'Islamologie et d'etudes arabes: RSPT 76 (1991) 483-510.

ᴱGiustolisi E., *Rizzardi* G., Il Vangelo di Barnaba; un Vangelo per i musulmani? 1991 ⇥ a297.

b688 *Heine* Peter, Islam und Demokratie [... zwei unvereinbare Grössen?]: Orientierung 56 (1992) 165-8.

b689 **Hourani** Albert, Islam in European thought [+8 art.] 1991 ⇥ 7,a922: ᴿBSO 55 (1992) 329s (M. E. *Yapp*); JRAS (1992) 261 (D. O. *Morgan*); JRel 72 (1992) 621s (A. Al-*Azmeh*: his third collection of essays; gentle and sure touch).

b690 *Jansen* J. J. G., Islam en Jodendom; buren [neighbors], geestverwanten, cliënten, vijanden of vrienden: Ter Herkenning 19,2 (1991) 87-97 [< GerefTTs 91,188].

b691 *Jomier* Jacques, Bulletin d'Islamologie: RThom 92 (1992) 578-589 [ÉTIENNE B., LAROUI A., BEAUGÉ G., *al.*, plusieurs infra].

b692 **Kepel** Gilles, La revanche de Dieu (Chrétiens, Juifs et Musulmans à la reconquête du monde). P 1991, Seuil. 287 p. – ᴿSpiritus 32 (1991) 450s (M. *Borrmans*).

b693 **Kepel** Gilles, La revancha de Dios; cristianos, judios y musulmanes a la reconquista del mundo. M 1991, Muchnik. 313 p. – [deutsch 1991 ⇥ 7,a923]. – ᴿScripTPamp 24 (1993) 1097-9 (E. *Parada*).

b694 ᴱ**Kerber** Walter, Wie tolerant ist der Islam? [Symposium Mü, 5 S.J.+*al.*]: Fragen einer neuen Weltkultur 6. Mü 1991, Kindt. 147 p. DM 19,80. – ᴿZkT 114 (1992) 349s (K. H. *Neufeld*).

b695 *Khoury* Adel-T., Bekehrung in Islam NZMissW 47 (1991) 257-267.

b696 **Khoury** Adel T., *al.*, Islam-Lexikon; Geschichte-Ideen-Gestalten: 1, A-F; 2. G-N; 3. O-Z: Spektrum 4036. FrB 1991, Herder. 941 p. DM 78. – ᴿOLZ 87 (1992) 411-4 (D. *Bellmann*); TGL 82 (1992) 144s (W. *Beinert*).

b697 **Khoury** Adel T., Der Islam kommt uns näher, worauf müssen wir uns einstellen? FrB 1992, Herder. 157 p. DM 22,80. 3-451-22924-2 [TLZ 118,214].

b698 **Khoury** Paul, Matériaux pour servir à l'étude de la controverse théologique islamo-chrétienne de langue arabe du VIIIᵉ au XIIᵉ siècle [1, 1989 ⇥ 5,b174]; 2: RelWissSt 11/2. Wü/Altenberge 1991, Echter/Telos. ᴿCrNSt 13 (1992) 214-6 (M. *Borrmans*, 1); TR 88 (1992) 422 (P. *Heine*, 2).

b699 **Kimball** Charles, Striving together; a way forward in Christian-Muslim relations 1991 ▸ 7,a927: ᴿETL 68 (1992) 182s (V. *Neckebrouck*: 'à ceux qui ignorent tout du sujet, ce petit livre peut rendre service').

b700 *Kohlbrügge* Hanna, Die Stechmücke; über die schleichende Islamisierung des Westens: KerDo 38 (1992) 280-309; Eng. 309s '... underhand'.

b701 *Kruse* Martin, Toleranz genügt nicht; Christentum und Islam: DPfarrB 91 (1992) 354-7 [< ZIT 91,677].

b702 **Lazarus-Yafeh** Hava, Intertwined worlds; medieval Islam and Bible criticism. Princeton 1992, Univ. xiii-178 p. $30. 0-691-07398-8 [TDig 40,72]. – ᴿTarbiz 61 (1991s) 577-581 (S. *Harvey*, ❶).

b703 *Le Coz* R., Jean DAMASCÈNE, Écrits sur l'Islam: SChr 383. P 1992, Cerf. 272 p. F 196 [NRT 115, 434, V. *Roisel*].

b704 *Leimgruber* Stephan, Die Behandlung des Islam im christlichen Religionsunterricht: RpädB 28 (1991) 41-55 [< ZIT 91,683].

b705 ᴱ**Mabro** Judy, Veiled half-truths; western travellers' perceptions of Middle Eastern women. L 1991, Tauris. £20. – ᴿJRAS (1992) 453s (C. F. *Beckingham*, dubious).

b706 **McAuliffe** Jane D., Qur'ānic Christians 1991 → 7,a931: ᴿExpTim 103 (1991s) 184s (W. M. *Watt*: really on what 10 Muslims say about 7 Quranic mentions of Christians); JAAR 60 (1992) 345-7 (B. M. *Wheeler*); JSS 37 (1992) 331-3 (E. *Hulmes*: on the understanding of Christians in Qur'an and *tafsîr*).

b707 *a*) *McAuliffe* Jane D., An Islamic assessment of Christianity; – *b*) *Michel* Thomas, How Muslims view fundamental mideast issues; – *c*) *Borelli* John, Catholic-Muslim relations after the Gulf war: The Priest 47,7 ('Islam, the second world religion' 1991) 18-20 / 30-34 / 35-37.

b708 **Markowski** Rafał, ❷ Pojęcie... Notion de la société sunnite islamique (Umma) comparée avec la conception catholique contemporaine de l'Église: diss. ᴰ*Dajczer* T. Warszawa 1991. – RTLv 24, p. 597.

b709 *Michel* Thomas, Christian-Muslim dialogue in a changing world [36th Bellarmine Lecture, Saint Louis Univ. Sept. 30, 1992, unabridged]: TDig 39 (1992) 303-320.

b710 *Michel* Thomas F., I musulmani in Europa: CC 143 (1992, 4) 362-375.

b711 **Mooren** Thomas, Macht und Einsamkeit Gottes; Dialog mit dem islamischen Radikal-Monotheismus: WüForMRW 17, 1991 → 7,a913*: ᴿTR 88 (1992) 245s (P. *Heine*); TvT 32 (1992) 439 (J. *Peters*, also on 3 cognate books).

b712 **Moucarry** Georges C., Un Arabe chrétien face à l'Islam. P 1991, Bergers & Mages. 112 p. F 65. 2-85304-097-6. – ᴿÉTRel 67 (1992) 615s (J.-P. *Gabus*).

b713 **Nielsen** J. S., Muslims in western Europe. E 1992, Univ. x-186 p. £25. – ᴿNRT 114 (1992) 601s (P. *Evrard*).

b714 *Ocak* A. Yaşar, ❶ Influences réciproques du Christianisme et des Turcs en Anatolie aux siècles XIII.-XV., et le culte d'Aya Yorgi (Saint Georges): Belleten 55,214 (1991) 661-673; 1 fig.

b715 *O'Shaughnessy* Thomas J., Christian religious specialists on the Qur'ān: Landas 5 (Manila 1991) 189-200 [< TContexto 2/2, 71].

b716 *Palma* Francesco de, Dal pregiudizio al dialogo; la Civiltà Cattolica e l'Islam nel primo novecento: SMSR 58 (1992) 289-319.

b716*, *Papadopoulo* A., Moyen-Âge et monde musulman: → 52*, ᶠGAUSSIN P., Maisons 1992, 265-279.

b717 ᴱ**Piscatori** James, Islamic fundamentalism and the Gulf crisis. Ch 1991, Univ. xvii-267. $10. – ᴿTS 53 (1992) 792s (A. H. *Khan*: 'seems to assume the task of fundamentalist movements... is to accommodate democratic reforms rather than... Shari'a').

b718 *a*) *Sahas* Daniel J., ᴀɴᴀꜱᴛᴀꜱɪᴜꜱ of Sinai (c. 640-700) and 'Anastasii Sinaitae' on Islam; – *b*) *Savvides* Alexis, 7th-15th century Islamic history as portrayed in Greek Byzantine history manuals; a bibliographic survey: → 557*, Contacts 1990/2, 332-8 / 339-345.

b719 **Samir Khalil**, Alphonse MINGANA (1878-1937) and his contribution to early Christian-Muslim studies. Birmingham 1990, Selly Oak. 60 p. £10. – ᴿOrChr 76 (1992) 271s (H. *Kaufhold*).

b720 **Setton** Kenneth M., Western hostility to Islam and prophecies of Turkish doom: Mem 201. Ph 1992, AmPhilos. vi-64 p.; 5 pl. – ᴿRHE 87 (1992) 907s (G. *Basetti-Sani*); StPatav 39 (1992) 664s (G. *Fedalto*).

b721 **Shadid** W. A. R., *Koningsveld* P. S. van, Islam in Dutch society; current developments and future prospects [< Religion and emancipation of ethnic minorities in western Europe, Leiden 1990]. Kampen 1992, KokPharos. viii-205 p. 90-942-3047-0 [Numen 40, 196, L. P. van den *Bosch*].

b722 *Sheridan* Daniel P., Muslims and Islamic values in America: ChSt 30 (1991) 145-160.

b723 ᴱSwidler Leonard, Muslims in dialogue; the evolution of a dialogue [28 art. < JEcuSt]: Religions in Dialogue 3. Lewiston NY 1992, Mellen. xviii-536 p. $100. 0-88946-499-5 [TDig 40,178].

b724 *Teissier* Henri, *Stamer* Josef, Église d'Afrique et Islam; quelle évangélisation?: Spiritus 32 (1991) 165-179.

b725 **Thyen** Johann-Dietrich, Bibel und Koran; eine Synopse gemeinsamer Überlieferungen: Kölner Veröff.Rel.-Gesch. 19, 1989 → 5,b219; 7,a937: ᴿNRT 114 (1992) 288 (J. *Scheuer*); TLZ 117 (1992) 23s (H. *Preissler*).

b726 **Todt** Klaus-Peter, Kaiser Johannes VI. Kantakuzenus [† 1383]; politische Realität und theologische Polemik im paläologischen Byzanz: WüForMRW 16. Wü/Altenberge 1991, Echter/Oros. lix-705 p. DM 95. – ᴿTR 88 (1992) 69s (P. *Heine*).

b727 **Watt** W. Montgomery, Muslim-Christian encounters 1991 → 7,a939*: ᴿExpTim 103 (1991s) 185 (O. *Leaman*: a masterpiece); TContext 10/2, 104 (G. *Evers*).

b728 *Wessels* Anton, Die Herausforderung des Islams: TZBas 48 (1992) 276-289.

b729 *Yocum* Glenn, Notes on an Easter Ramadan: JAAR 60 (1992) 201-230.

b730 *Zannini* Francesco, The Bible in Islam: BToday 30 (1992) 303-7.

b731 **Zirker** Hans, Christentum und Islam; theologische Verwandtschaft und Konkurrenz 1989 → 5,b227; 7,a942: ᴿTGL 82 (1992) 143s (W. *Beinert*); TR 88 (1992)331s (A. T. *Khoury*).

b732 *Zirker* Hans, *a)* Unser Verhältnis zum Islam im Spiegel eines Lexikons [KHOURY A., *al.* 1991]: StiZt 210 (1992) 59-62; – *b)* Christentum und Islam – sind sie dialogfähig?: UnSa 47 (1992) 264-272.

M8.5 **Religiones Indiae** *et Extremi Orientis.*

b733 *a)* **Aasulv** Lande, Japans religionar. Oslo 1990, Norsk. 192 p. Nk 188. – *b)* **Lidin** Olof G., Japans religioner. 1985, Politikens. c. 300 p. – *c)* ᴱ**Andreasen** Esben, *Stefànsson* Finn, Japans religioner i fortid og nutid. K 1986, Gyldendal. – ᴿTsTKi 63 (1992) 157s (Dagfinn *Rian*).

b734 **Backianadan** Joseph F., Love in the life and [88 published] works of Mahatma Gandhi. Delhi 1991, Sterling. – ᴿJDharma 17 (1992) 53s (J. *Vazhappilly*).

b735 **Corless** Roger [not as ► 6,592 Corliss], The vision of Buddhism. NY 1989, Paragon. 224 p. $43. 1-55778-200-8. – ᴿJAAR 60 (1992) 525-536 (J. *Nattier*: refreshing style but countless errors).

b736 *Delahoutre* Michel, Le Nouvel Âge, un hindouisme mal inculturé à l'Occident? Réflexions d'un indianiste: EsprVie 102 (1992) 657-667.

b737 *Derrett* J. D. M., HOMER in India; the birth of the Buddha [... 'the prospect that Indian authors could have been inspired by Western authors is no longer alarming']: JRAS (1992) 47-57.

b738 ᵀᴱ**Desantis** Giovanni, Pseudo–PALLADIO, Le genti dell'India e i Brahmani: TPatr 99. R 1992, Città Nuova. 94 p. 88-311-3099-4.

b739 **Dhavamony** Mariasusai, L'induismo: Religioni e dialogo. Assisi 1991, Cittadella. 296 p. Lit. 25.000. 88-308-0480-0. – ᴿGregorianum 73 (1992) 495s (*ipse*).

b740 **Dumoulin** Heinrich, Zen Buddhism in the 20th Century, ᵀᴱO'*Leary* Joseph. NY 1992, Weatherhill. xii-173 p. $15 pa. 0-8348-0247-3 [TDig 40,159].

b741 **Dutt** Sukumar, Buddhist monks and monasteries of India; their history and their contribution to Indian culture. Delhi 1988, Motilal Banarsidass. 397 p. rs. 150. – ᴿJDharma 16 (1991) 302s (J. B. *Chethimattam*).

b742 **Fuller** Christopher J., The camphor flame; popular Hinduism and society in India. Princeton 1992, Univ. xii-306 p. $40; pa. $15. 0-691-07404-6; -2084-1 [TDig 40,163].

b743 **Girault** René, Introduction aux religions orientales; Hindouisme, Bouddhisme, Taoïsme: Repères N. Âge. P 1991, Droguet & A. 347 p. F 75. 2-7041-0590-1. – ᴿEsprVie 102 (1992) 669 (M. *Delahoutre*); ÉTRel 67 (1992) 445 (J. *Argaud*).

b744 *Gombrich* Richard, *Obeysekere* Gananath, Buddhism transformed / Sri Lanka 1988 ➤ 7,a947: ᴿJDharma 17 (1992) 155-7 (B. V. *Venkatakrishna*).

b745 *Hallisey* Charles, Recent work on Buddhist ethics: RelStR 18 (1992) 276-285.

b746 **Harvey** Peter, An introduction to Buddhism; teachings, history and practices. C 1990, Univ. 374 p. £35; pa. £11. 0-521-30815-1; -1333-3. – ᴿBSO 55 (1992) 142s (K. R. *Norman*); ExpTim 102 (1990s) 286 (D. V. *Krown*); JAOS 112 (1992) 65s (Collett *Cox*); JRAS (1992) 95s (P. J. *Griffiths*).

b747 **Herrenschmidt** Olivier, Les meilleurs dieux sont Hindous. Lausanne 1989, Âge d'Homme. 303 p. Fs 40. – ᴿAnthropos 87 (1992) 588s (P. van der *Veer*).

b748 **Immoos** Thomas, Ein bunter Teppich; die Religionen Japans. Graz 1990, Styria. 220 p.; 31 pl.; 2 maps. Sch 298. – ᴿWissWeis 54 (1991) 321-3 (W. *Dettloff*); ZkT 114 (1992) 351s (J. *Figl*).

b749 *Kitagawa* Joseph M., Dimensions of the East Asian religious universe [10 books 1987-9]: HistRel 31 (1991s) 181-209.

b750 **Klimkeit** Hans-Joachim, Der Buddha; Leben und Lehre: Urban-Tb 438. Stu 1990, Kohlhammer. 244 p. DM 22 [TLZ 118,211, K.-W. *Tröger*]. – ᴿZRGg 44 (1992) 369s (H.-P. *Hasenfratz*).

b751 **Kohn** Livia, Early Chinese mysticism; philosophy and soteriology in the Taoist tradition. Princeton 1992, Univ. ix-218 p. $45; pa. $15. 0-691-07381-3; -2065-5 [TDig 40,171].

b752 *McDermott* Rachel F. [5] New contributions to the study of Hindu goddesses: RelStR 18 (1992) 196-200.

b753 **Masson** J., Mystiques d'Asie, approches et réflexions. P 1992, D-Brouwer. 297 p. F 145 [NRT 115, 596, L.-J. *Renard*].

b753* *Moti Lal Pandit,* The mystical way to Nirvāṇa: IndTSt 29 (1992) 7-54.

b754 **Ortner** Sherry B., High religion; a cultural and biblical history of Sherpa Buddhism [20th century inauguration of celibacy in Nepal]. Princeton 1989, Univ. xxiv-245 p. $35; pa. $13. – ᴿJDharma 16 (1991) 303s (J. B. *Chethimattam*: 'big religion is the show of big power').

b755 *Panikkar* R., The silence of God; the answer of the Buddha 1989 ➤ 5,b269; 6,b261: ᴿParabola 15,2 (1990) 115s (F. *Franck*).

b756 *Pichard* Pierre, La composition architecturale des temples de Pagan: CRAI (1992) 357-373; 9 fig.

b757 **Raveri** Massimo, Il corpo e il paradiso; esperienze ascetiche in Asia Orientale: Saggi. Venezia 1992, Marsilio. vi-238 p. Lit. 35.000. 88-317-5523-4.

b758 **Reader** Ian, Religion in contemporary Japan. L c. 1991, Macmillan. £40; pa. £15. – ᴿTablet 246 (1992) 205s (C. *Veliath*: user-friendly).

b759 ᴱSanford James H., *al.*, [9 art.] Buddhism in the literary and visual arts of Japan. Princeton 1992, Univ. xii-275 p.; 37 fig. $39.50. 0-691-07365-1 [TDig 40,162].

b760 **Sharma** Arvind, A Hindu perspective on the philosophy of religion. L 1990, Macmillan. xi-180 p. $60. – ᴿRelSt 28 (1992) 279s (J. *Lipner*).

b761 **Shotaro** Iida, Facets of Buddhism. Delhi 1991, Motilal-B. 166 p. – ᴿJDharma 17 (1992) 51s (Pauline *Drouin* refers to the author as 'Dr. Iida').

b762 **Thursby** G. R., The Sikhs: IconRel 13/16. Leiden 1992, Brill. 42 p.; 48 pl. *f* 80 [NRT 115, 604, J. *Scheuer*]. 90-04-09554-5.

b763 **Vazeilles** Danièle, Les chamanes, maîtres de l'univers; persistance et exportations du chamanisme: Bref 33. P 1991, Cerf. 126 p. – ᴿMélSR 49 (1992) 61s (L. *Debarge*); ScEsp 44 (1992) 382s (A. *Couture*).

b764 **Wright** Arthur F., (1913-1976), Studies in Chinese Buddhism (1948-59). NHv 1990, Yale Univ. xii-204 p. £20. – ᴿOLZ 87 (1992) 90s (H. *Schmidt-Glintzer*).

b766 **Zotz** Volker, Der Buddha im Reinen Land; Shin-Buddhismus in Japan: Gelbe Reihe 92. Mü 1991, Diederichs. 152 p. DM 19,80 pa. – ᴿMüTZ 43 (1992) 252s (P. *Schmidt-Leukel*).

M8.7 *Interactio cum religione orientali;* Christian dialogue with the East.

b767 **Ariarajah** Wesley, Hindus and Christians; a century of Protestant ecumenical thought: Currents of Encounter 5. Amst/GR 1991, Rodopi/Eerdmans. x-244 p. *f* 45. – ᴿNRT 114 (1992) 598s (J. *Masson*).

b768 **Barnes** Michael, God East and West. L 1991, SPCK. vi-138 p. £8 pa. – ᴿTLond 95 (1992) 41s (G. *D'Costa*: sequel to his 1989 Religions in conversation).

b769 *Bretzke* James T., Minjung theology and inculturation in the context of the history of Christianity in Korea: EAPast 28 (1991) 108-130.

b770 **Brosse** Jacques, Zen et Occident: Spiritualités Vivantes. P 1992, A. Michel. 298 p. F 120. – ᴵᴵEsprVie 102 (1992) 671s (M. *Delahoutre*).

b771 ᴱ**Carter** Robert E., God, the self, and nothingness; reflections Eastern and Western: God, the contemporary discussion. NY 1990, Paragon. xxxix-291 p. $15 [RelStR 19, 45, C. *Ives*].

b772 **Ching** J., Konfuzianismsus und Christentum, ᴱ*Fürst* G.: Dialog der Religionen 1989 → 6,b268; 7,a967: ᴿNRT 114 (1992) 288 (J. *Scheuer*).

b773 *Clooney* Francis X., Extending the canon; some implications of a Hindu argument about Scripture: HarvTR 85 (1992) 197-215.

b774 ᶠ**Cobb** John B., *Ives* C. The emptying God; a Buddhist-Jewish-Christian conversation 1990 → 7,398: ᴿCritRR 5 (1992) 268-270 (D. J. *Fasching*); Interpretation 46 (1992) 104. 106 (T. G. *Dawe*); LvSt 16 (1991) 181-3 (Catherine *Cornille*).

b775 *a)* **Corless** Roger J., The hermeneutics of polemic; the creation of Hînayâna and Old Testament; – *b)* **Breckenridge** James, The salvific role of knowledge in a Buddhist and a Christian context; a comparative study of two parables: Buddhist Christian Studies 2 (1992) 59-[?74] / 75-84.

b775* **Cornille** Catherine, The Guru in Indian Catholicism 1991 → 7,a969: ᴿIndTSt 29 (1992) 379-381 (B. J. *Francis*).

b776 ᴱ**Coward** Harold, Hindu-Christian dialogue; perspectives and encounters 1989 → 7,a970: ᴿJDharma 17 (1992) 58-70 (A. *Thottakara*: all but one of the contributors are non-Indians; all but one or two are Christians).

b777 *Dal Ferro* Giuseppe, Buddhismo e via gnostica: StEcum 9 (1991) 285-300; Eng. 301.

b778 **Davis** Winston B., Japanese religion and society; paradigms of structure and change [8 reprints]. Albany 1992, SUNY. x-327 p. $49.50; pa. $17. 0-7914-0839-6; -40-X [TDig 39,358].

b779 **Ducornet** Étienne, Matteo RICCI, le Lettré d'Occident [Univ. Fribourg]. P 1992, Cerf. 185 p. F 92. – ᴿEsprVie 102 (1992) 670 (M. *Delahoutre*).

b780 *Fornberg* T., 'Jag är vägen...' Om Bibeln i indisk religionsteologi: Religion och Bibel 48 (Lund 1991) 23-37 [< NTAbs 36,151].

b781 *Fuchs* Martin, Hinduism; self-perception and assessment of tradition; Symposium in Tübingen, 29.X-4.XI.1990: ZMissRW 75 (1991) 300-309.

b782 *a) Gira* Dennis, Regard chrétien sur le Bouddhisme; réflexions sur le dialogue interreligieux; – *b) Sarpong* Peter K., Religion traditionnelle africaine; le dialogue est-il possible?: Spiritus 32 (1991) 26-38 / 39-50.

b783 **Goettmann** Alphonse, Dialogue on the [Zen Buddhism] path of initiation; an introduction to the life and thought of Karlfried Graf DÜRCKHEIM, ᵀ*Nottingham* Theodore & Rebecca; pref. *Maloney* George A. NY 1992, Globe. xv-168 p. $13 pa. 0-936385-26-X [TDig 39,359].

b784 ᴱ**Harskamp** A. van, Voorbij goed en kwaad; Christendom en Boeddhisme. Kampen 1990, Kok. 108 p. Fb. 398. – ᴿCollatVL 22 (1992) 219 (A. *Wullepit*).

b785 **Henderson** John B., Scripture/Confucius 1991 ⇒ 7,a977: ᴿGregorianum 73 (1992) 560s (J. T. *Bretzke*).

b786 **Huber** E., Die Bhagavadgita in der neueren indischen Auslegung und in der Begegnung mit dem christlichen Glauben: MgMissÖk 12. Erlangen 1991, Ev.-L. Mission. x-199 p. DM 56 [NRT 115, 604, J. *Masson*].

b786* *Huber* Friedrich, Die Reinkarnationsvorstellungen in den asiatischen Religionen und im Europa des 20. Jahrhunderts: ZRGg 44 (1992) 15-32.

b787 **Keenan** John P., The meaning of Christ; a Mahayana theology. Mkn 1989, Orbis. viii-312 p. – ᴿAntonianum 67 (1992) 543s (I. *Tonna*: coraggioso nuovo metodo di teologare).

b788 **Kitagawa** Joseph M., Understanding Japanese religions 1987 ⇒ 4,211*; 5,b256: ᴿParabola 15,1 (1990) 118.120 (R. S. *Ellwood*).

b789 **Kollaparambil** Jacob, The Babylonian origin of the Southists among the St. Thomas Christians: OrChrAnal 241. R 1992, Pont. Inst. St. Orientalium. xxviii-150 p.; map. 88-7210-289-8.

b790 *a) Lee* Peter H. K., Contextualization and inculturation of Christianity and Confucianism in the modern world; – *b) Tucker* Mary E., Confucianism and Christianity; resources for an ecological spirituality: Ching Feng 34,2 (1991) 84-93 / 94-99.

b791 **Le Saux** H., Sagesse hindoue, mystique chrétienne... 1991 [NRT 115, 601, J. *Masson*].

b792 *Magnin* Paul, Le vrai défi du bouddhisme à l'Occident chrétien: Études 376 (1992) 683-693.

b793 **Malpan** Varghese, A comparative study of the Bhagavad-Gītā and the Spiritual Exercises of St. IGNATIUS of Loyola on the process of spiritual liberation [diss. Pont. Univ. Gregoriana, ᴰ*Dhavamony* M.]: Documenta Missionalia 22. R 1992, Pont. Univ. Gregoriana. 442 p. 88-7652-648-X.

b794 **Manickam** T. M., Dharma according to Manu and Moses [including Pentateuch criticism and biblical theology themes]. Bangalore 1977, Dharmaram. xviii-358 p.

b795 **Mitchell** Donald W., Spirituality and emptiness; the dynamics of spir-

itual life in Buddhism and Christianity. NY 1991, Paulist. xvi-224 p.
$13. 0-8091-3266-4 [TDig 39,275].
b796 **Overzee** Anne H., The body divine; the symbol of the body in the
works of TEILHARD de Chardin and RAMANUJA [Hindu † 1137]: Studies
in Religious Tradition 2. C 1992, Univ. 220 p. £30. 0-521-38516-4. –
ᴿÉTRel 67 (1992) 445 (J. *Argaud*).
b797 **Panikkar** E., Der Weisheit eine Wohnung bereiten. Mü c. 1991, Kösel.
209 p. DM 36. 3-466-20334-1. – ᴿTvT 32 (1992) 119 (J. *Kamstra*).
b798 **Pushparajan** A., From conversation to fellowship; the Hindu Christian
encounter in the GANDHIAN perspective. Varanasi, Allahabad 1990, St.
Paul's. 350 p.; rs. 125, pa. 95. – ᴿJDharma 17 (1992) 53.
b799 **Puthenkalam** Xavier, Hindu Christian Bakhti, an Indian concept of
style and discipleship. Kottayam 1990, Oriental Inst. xv-172 p. rs. 40. –
ᴿBibleBhashyam 16 (1990) 270s (J. *Koikakudy*).
b800 **Raj** Joseph J., Grace in the Saiva Siddhāntham and in St. Paul; a
contribution to inter-faith cross-cultural understanding. Madras 1989,
South Indian Salesian. xxix-743 p. 81-90092-0-61. – ᴿGregorianum 73
(1992) 169s (M. *Amaladoss*).
b801 *Ryden* Edmond, ☉ From region of Jen to kingdom of Christ: Colc-
FuJen 92 (1992) 179-184 [< TContext 10/1, p. 26].
b802 *Schlette* Heinz R., Interreligiös/interkulturell; Marginalien zu einigen
Neuerscheinungen [Kyoto-Schule, WALDENFELS... KÜNG]: Orientierung
56 (1992) 55-58.
b803 **Schmidt-Leukel** Perry, 'Den Löwen brüllen hören'; zur Hermeneutik eines
christlichen Verständnisses der buddhistischen Heilsbotschaft [Diss. Mün-
chen]: BeitÖkT 23. Pd 1992, Schöningh. XVI-788 p. DM 98 [TR 88,171].
b804 *Schopen* Gregory, Archaeology and Protestant presuppositions in the
study of Indian Buddhism: HistRel 31 (1991s) 1-23.
b805 **Spink** Kathryn, A sense of the sacred... B. GRIFFITHS 1989 → 5,b279;
6,b296: ᴿNZMissW 41 (1991) 170s (J. *Baumgartner*).
b806 **Staffner** Hans, Jesus Christ and the Hindu community 1988 → 5,
b280... 7,a989: ᴿStudies 79 (1990) 216-9 (G. *Webb,* also on VEMPENY).
b807 *a) Tong* John, Confucian-Catholic dialogue in historical perspective; –
b) Raguin Yves, Dialogue with Chinese Buddhism: Tripod 12/68 (Hong
Kong 1992) 30-40 / 15-29 [< TContext 10/1, p. 28].
b808 **Tweed** Thomas A., The American encounter with Buddhism, 1844-1912;
Victorian culture and the limits of dissent. Bloomington 1992, Indiana
Univ. xxiv-242 p. $30. 0-253-36099-4 [TDig 39,390].
b809 *Waldenfels* Hans, Cristianesimo e Buddhismo Mahayana; un caso em-
blematico di incontro interreligioso, ᵀGuglielminetti Enrico: FilT 6 (1992)
85-105; Eng. 85.
b810 *Williams* Paul, Some dimensions of the recent work of Raimundo
PANIKKAR; a Buddhist perspective: RelSt 27 (1991) 511-521.
b811 **Yearley** Lee, MENCIUS and AQUINAS; theories of virtue and conceptions of courage. Albany 1990, SUNY. xiv-280 p. – ᴿHistRel 32 (1992)
309-312 (F. X. *Clooney*).
b812 *Zahniser* A. H. M., Ritual process and Christian discipling; contextualizing a Buddhist rite of passage: Missiology 19 (1991) 3-20.

M8.9   **Religiones Africae** (maxime → H8.6) **et Amerindiae.**

b813 *Kolig* Erich, Religious power and the all-father in the sky; monotheism in
an Australian aboriginal context reconsidered: Anthropos 87 (1992) 9-31.

b813* *Peelman* Achiel,   Christianisme et cultures amérindiennes: ÉglT 22 (1991) 131-156.

b814 **Turner** Daniel,   Return to Eden; a journey through the promised landscape of Amagalyuagba [... on Australian aborigine culture and religion]: Toronto Studies in Religion 9. NY 1989, P. Lang. xxiv-300 p. – ᴿSR 21 (1992) 96s (A. R. *Gualtieri*: a disconcerting book).

b814* *a) Vadakkumchery* Johnson,   Religion in the tribal eco-system; – *b) Tovagonze* Venance,   God-concept, 'supreme being' in African tribal religions: JDharma 17,2 ('Tribal Religions' 1992) 85-97 / 122-140.

XVII,1. Historia Medii Orientis Biblici

Q1   *Syria prae-islamica, Canaan,*   **Israel Veteris Testamenti.**

b815 **Blázquez** José M., *al.*, *a)* Historia de Oriente Antiguo.   M 1992, Cátedra. 648 p.   84-376-1044-3. – *b)* Los Hebreos [cap. 10 a parte].   M 1989, Akal. 64 p.; 31 fig. 84-7600-383-8 [-274-2, toda la serie]. – ᴿSyria 68 (1991) 471 (H. de *Contenson*).

b816 ᴱ**Brodersen** Kai,   APPIANS Abriss der Seleukidengeschichte (Syriake 45,232 - 70,369); Text und Kommentar: ArbAltG.   Mü 1989, Maris. 255 p. – ᴿGnomon 64 (1992) 667-670 (A. *Mastrocinque*, ital.).

b817 ᴱ**Canfora** L., *al.*,   I trattati 1990 ➤ 6,724:   ᴿAfO 38s (1991s) 201-6 (H. U. *Steymans*); JAOS 112 (1992) 683s (D. R. *Hillers*); ScuolC 119 (1991) 526-562 (Anna *Passoni dell'Acqua*: nuova luce sull'AT).

b817* *a) Chavalas* Mark W.,   Ancient Syria, a historical sketch; – *b) Owen* David I.,   Syrians in Sumerian sources from the Ur III period; – *c) Young* Gordon D.,   Wabash [College, Crawfordsville IN, tablet] I and a note on Ur III Syria: ➤ 705*, New Horizons 1991/2, 1-21 / 107-175 / 176.

b818 **Davies** Philip R.,   In search of 'Ancient Israel': JStOT supp 148. Sheffield 1992, JStOT. 204 p. £30; sb. £22.50. 1-85075-380-6.

b819 *Durand* Jean-Marie,   Unité et diversités au Proche-Orient [... Hourrite] à l'époque amorrite: ➤ 683, Circulation 1991/2, 97-128.

   Dus Jan,   Theokratische Demokratie des alten Israel; fünf Studien zur Geschichte Israels 1992 ➤ 237.

b819* **Giardina** A., *al.*, La Palestina 1987 ➤ 4,d95:   ᴿJNES 51 (1992) 224-6 (G. W. *Ahlström*).

b820 **Görg** Manfred,   Aegyptiaca – biblica; Notizen und Beiträge zu den Beziehungen zwischen Ägypten und Israel [< BibNot]: ÄgAT 11. Wsb 1991, Harrassowitz. [viii-] 368 p. 3-447-02670-2.

b821 **Grätz** Heinrich,   La construction de l'histoire juive [1846] + Gnosticisme et judaïsme [ᴰ1845],ᵀ: Passages.   P 1992, Cerf. 174 p. F 120. 2-204-04413-X [NTAbs 36,446].

b822 **Grant** Michael,   L'antica civiltà di Israele [History of Ancient Israel 1984 ➤ 65,9550], ᵀ*Osimo* Bruno: Popoli e civiltà.   Mi 1984, Bompiani. 333 p.

b823 **Hughes** Jeremy,   Secrets of the times; myth and history in biblical chronology (Or. Diss. Oxford 1986): JStOT supp 66, ᴰ1990 ➤ 6,b322; 7,b12:   ᴿCBQ 54 (1992) 323s (W. H. *Irwin*: refreshingly clearheaded); CritRR 5 (1992) 97-99 (L. K. *Handy*: insight).

   Johnson P., Une histoire des juifs 1989, ᵀ1989 ➤ a458*.

b824 **Kessler** Rainer,   Staat und Gesellschaft im vorexilischen Juda vom 8. Jahrhundert bis zum Exil [Hab.-Diss. Bethel, Bielefeld 1990 ➤ 7,b13]: VTS 47. Leiden 1992, Brill. 90-04-09646-9 [OIAc 5,27].

b825 **Klengel** Horst,   Syria 3000 to 300 B.C., a handbook of political history [1982],ᵀ. B 1992, Akademie. 275 p. DM 198. 3-05-001820-8 [OIAc 5,27; UF 23,450].

b826 *Klengel* Horst,   The political situation in Palestine and Syria as reflected in the Amarna tablets; a reconsideration: ➤ 736, ᴱ*Shaath* S.,   Palestine 1981/5, 77-84.

b827 *a) Knauf* Ernst A.   [Ismael ➤ 2350],   The cultural impact of secondary state formation; the cases of the Edomites and Moabites; – *b) Mattingly* Gerald L.,   The culture-historical approach and Moabite origins; – *c) Miller* J. Maxwell,   Early monarchy in Moab?; – *d) Dearman* J. Andrew,   Settlement patterns and the beginning of the Iron Age in Moab: ➤ 340, Early Edom 1991/2, 47-54 / 55-64; 2 fig. / 77-91 / 65-75; 4 fig.

b827* **Kreuzer** S.,   Die Frühgeschichte Israels: BZAW 178, ᴰ1989 ➤ 5,b304 ... 7,b15:   ᴿBLitEc 93 (1992) 329s (M. *Delcor*, aussi sur REINHOLD G.); GeistL 65 (1992) 153-5 (H. *Brandt*).

b828 *Larsson* Gerhard,   Ancient calendars indicated in the OT: JStOT 54 (1992) 61-76.

b828* **Lemaire** André,   Storia del popolo ebraico [1981 Que sais-je?]:   LoB 3.9, 1989 ➤ 5,b305:   ᴿParVi 36 (1991) 153-6 (G. *Marocco* propone ʿArjud non Ariaud per ʿAjrud).

b829 *Lemche* Niels P. [➤ 2735s],   Israel, history of premonarchic, ᵀ*Cryer* Frederick ➤ 741, AnchorBD 3 (1992) 526-545 (-558, Archaeological and the 'Conquest', *Dever* W. G.; 558-567, Monarchic period, *Hoppe* Leslie J.; 567-576 post-monarchic, *Carroll* Robert P.).

b830 *McFall* Leslie,   Some missing coregencies in THIELE's Chronology: AndrUnS 30 (1992) 35-58.

b831 **Mazzinghi** Luca,   Storia di Israele: Manuali di base 4, 1991 ➤ 7,b18: ᴿVivH 3 (1992) 431s (*ipse*).

b833 **Merrill** Eugene H.,   Kingdom of priests, a history of OT Israel 1987 ➤ 4,2101; 6,b330:   ᴿWestTJ 53 (1991) 145-7 (P. *Enns*: will hardly in fluence those who do not share his views).

b834 *Nagel* Wolfram, *Eder* Christian,   Altsyrien und Ägypten: DamaszM 6 (1992) 3-108; pl. 1-31.

b835 **Pixley** Jorge,   Biblical Israel; a people's history [1989 ➤ 7,b24ab],ᵀ by him.   Mp 1992, Fortress. 174 p. $9 pa. 0-8006-2551-X [BL 93,43, K. W. *Whitelam*: well written; but contentious issues presented as fact].

b836 *Redford* Donald B.,   Egypt, Canaan, and Israel in ancient times [Beer-Sheia 4 (1990)]: Princeton 1992, Univ. 511 p.; 40 fig. 36 pl. $40. 0-691-03606-3 [BAR-W 19/1, 6 & BL 93,43, K. A. *Kitchen*, severe on 2d half].

b837 **Reich** Bernard,   Historical dictionary of Israel: Asian Historical Dic tionaries 8.   Metuchen NJ 1992, Scarecrow. lxv-351 p. 0-8108-2535-X [OIAc 5,33].

b837* *Rogerson* J, W.,   Writing the history of Israel in the 17th and 18th centuries: ➤ 198, ᶠWOUDE A. van der, VTSupp 49 (1992) 217-227.

b838 **Schäfer** Peter,   Histoire des Juifs dans l'antiquité 1989 ➤ 5,b320 ... 7,b28:   ᴿRÉJ 150 (1991) 169-171 (Madeleine *Petit*).

b839 **Seebass** Horst,   Herrscherverheissungen im Alten Testament: BTSt 19. Neuk 1992. viii-95 p. 3-7887-1398-4.

b840 ᴱ**Shanks** H.,   Ancient Israel 1988 ➤ 4,326 ... 7,b29: ᴿIsrEJ 42 (1992) 127s (M. *Cogan*: A. LEMAIRE most judicious).

b841 *Singer* Ithamar,   How did the Philistines enter Canaan? a rejoinder [they were placed there as vassals, as the Egyptians claimed]: BAR-W [17,6 (1991)] 18,6 (1992) 44-46; ill.

b842 a) *Singer* Ithamar, Hittite cultural influence in the kingdom of Amurru;
    – b) *Izreʾel* Shlomo, Hatti and the kingdom of Amurru; linguistic
    influences: ➤ 683, Circulation 1991/2, 231-4 / 227-230.
b843 **Smelik** Klaas A. D., Historische Dokumente aus dem alten Israel 1987
    ➤ 3,b592... 6,b340: ᴿStPatav 38 (1991) 651s (M. *Milani*); TsTKi 63
    (1992) 220 (M. *Sæbø*).
b844 **Smelik** Klaas A. D., Writings from ancient Israel, ᵀ*Davies* G. 1991
    ➤ 7,b31: ᴿExpTim 103 (1991s) 281 (C. S. *Rodd*).
b845 **Soggin** J. Alberto, Einführung in die Geschichte Israels und Judas, von
    den Ursprüngen bis zum Aufstand Bar Kochbas 1991 ➤ 7,b32*: ᴿDielB
    27 (1991) 302 (B. J. *Diebner*: Vorw., 'eine Einführung in die Geschichte ist
    eben nicht die Geschichte').
b846 ṬABARI, SUNY translation: to the volumes noted in ➤ 7,b34, add now: **3.**
    ᵀᴱ**Brinner** William M., The children of Israel 1991, xii-194 p. – **7,** ᵀᴱ**Watt**
    W. M., *McDonald* M. V., The formation of the community, 1987;
    xxxviii-182 p. – **12,** ᵀᴱ**Friedman** Yohanan, The battle of al-Qadisiyya and
    the conquest of Syria and Palestine, 1992; xxii-237 p. – **33,** ᵀᴱ**Bosworth**
    C. E., Storm and stress along the northern frontiers of the Abbasid
    caliphate. 1991, 239 p. – **36,** ᵀᴱ**Waines** David, 1991, Revolt of the Zanj,
    xvii-229 p. 0-7914-0688-1; 0-88706-345-4; 0-7914-0; -734-9; — — [OIAc
    3s: 2,15.18.27; JAAR 59,888]. – ᴿBSO 55 (1992) 621s (Laila A. I. *Othman*,
    33); RelStR 17 (1992) 85 (D. P. *Little*, 20, 22, 24, 26).
b847 — *Juynboll* G. H. A., Some thoughts on early Muslim historiography
    [SUNY Tabari, I (of the 24 published) with F. ROSENTHAL's important
    introduction on his life and works]: BO 49 (1992) 685-691.
b848 **Thompson** Thomas L., Early history of the Israelite people; from the
    written and archaeological sources: Studies in the History of the Ancient
    Near East 4. Leiden 1992, Brill. xv-489 p. ƒ145. 90-04-09483-0 [BL 93,
    45, L. L. *Grabbe*: devastating even if inconclusive; updates his AnchorBD
    ➤ b908 below].
b849 *Winnicki* Jan K., Militäroperationen von Ptolemaios I. und Seleukos I.
    in Syrien in den Jahren 312-311 v.Chr.: AncSoc 22 (1991) 147-201.

Q2 **Historiographia** – *theologia historiae.*

b850 **Adler** William, Time immemorial... Africanus to Syncellus 1989 ➤ 6,
    b344: ᴿBO 49 (1992) 577-580 (L. de *Blois*: learned and useful).
b851 *Afinogenov* Dmitry E., Some observations on the genres of Byzantine
    historiography: ➤ 43, ᶠDELVOYE C., Byzantion 62 (1992) 13-33.
b852 *Aizpurua Donazar* Fidel, La Palabra; el diálogo de Dios con la historia:
    LumenVr 41 (1992) 419-428.
b853 ᵀᴱ**Arnaud-Lindet** Marie-Pierre, OROSE, Histoires contre les païens I
    (1-3), II (4-6), III (7, index): Coll. Budé. P 1990s, BLettres. ciii-302 (d.)
    p.; 282 p.; 218 p. 2-251-01347-0; -52-0; -53-9. – ᴿAntClas 61 (1991)
    408-410 (J. *Wankenne*); RÉLat 70 (1992) 278s (J.-C. *Richard*).
b854 **Assmann** Jan, Das kulturelle Gedächtnis; Schrift, Erinnerung und po-
    litische Identität in frühen Hochkulturen. Mü 1992, Beck. 344 p. 3-406-
    36088-2 [OIAc 3,11].
b855 **Bebbington** David, Patterns in history — a Christian perspective on
    historical thought² [= ¹1979]. Leicester 1990, Apollos. 219 p. £13 pa.
    0-85111-430-2. – ᴿEvangel 9,2 (1991) 32 (S. *Richards*).
b856 *Bermejo Barrera* José C., Des dimensions significatives de l'espace
    historique: DialHA 18,2 (1992) 29-49.

b857 **Boschi** B. G., Le origini di Israele nella Bibbia fra storia e teologia; la questione del metodo e la sfida storiografica: RivB supp 20, 1989 ➤ 5,b337; 7,b43: ᴿRivB 40 (1992) 95-100 (G. *Marocco*).

b858 *Bracke* Hilde, Il problema della libertà nella vita e nel pensiero di Arnaldo MOMIGLIANO: AncSoc 23 (1992) 297-323.

b859 **Brown** Donald E., Hierarchy, history and human nature; the social origins of historical consciousness. Tucson 1988, Univ. Arizona. x-384 p. $35. – ᴿEngHR 107 (1992) 691 (W. G. *Kiernan*: 'history flourished in mobile societies': Greece, Rome; Mesopotamia more than Egypt or Israel).

b859* *a) Bubner* Rudiger, Geschichtswissenschaft und Geschichtstheologie; – *b) Mommsen* Wolfgang J., Geschichte und Geschichten; über die Möglichkeit und Grenzen der Universalgeschichtsschreibung: Saeculum 43 (1992) 54-65 / 124-135.

b860 ᴱ**Buck** A., Humanismus und Historiographie; Rundgespräche, Deutsche Forschungsgemeinschaft. Weinheim 1991, Acta humaniora. 154 p. DM 68 [RHE 88,182*].

b861 ᴱ**Calder** W. M., *Demandt* A., Eduard MEYER, Leben und Leistung 1987/90 ➤ 6,b353*: ᴿBonnJbb 192 (1992) 782-5 (K. *Rosen*); JRS 82 (1992) 309s (B. *Meissner*).

b862 *Caviglia* Giovanni, Gesù Cristo 'punto focale dei desideri della storia e della civiltà' (Gaudium et spes 45); incontro misterioso e affascinante tra eternità e tempo: Salesianum 54 (1992) 41-78.

b863 *Certeau* M. de, The writing of history ᵀ: European Perspectives. NY 1988, Columbia Univ. xxix-368 p. [RHE 87,349*].

b864 **Christophe** P., La Chiesa nella storia degli uomini, dalle origini alle soglie del Duemila [1982, Droguet-Ardant], ᵀ*Colombani* e (dal XV secolo) *Traniello* Cecilia & Stefano. T 1989, SEI. 837 p. – ᴿSalesianum 54 (1992) 151 (O. *Pasquato*).

b865 **Colombo** J. A., An essay on theology and history; studies in PANNENBERG, METZ, and the Frankfurt school: AAR StRel, 1990 ➤ 7,b52: ᴿTS 53 (1992) 574-6 (S. *Schäfer*).

b865* **Cupitt** Don, The time being [relativism ...]. L/Ph 1992, SCM/Trinity. 208 p. $18.50. 0-334-025222-2. – ᴿExpTim 104 (1992s) 190s (J. C. A. *Gaskin*: easy reading; not about Christianity; erudite, uncritical).

b866 *Delcor* Mathias, Storia e profezia nel mondo ebraico: Fondamenti 13 (Brescia 1989) 3-33 [< OTAbs 15,4].

b866* **Dempf** A., Sacrum imperium; la filosofia della storia e dello stato nel medioevo e nella rinascenza politica [deutsch 1930]. F 1988 = 1933, Le Lettere. xxii-538 p. – ᴿSalesianum 54 (1992) 179s (O. *Pasquato*).

b867 *Diebner* B. J., Heilsgeschichte: ➤ 762, NBL II,6 (1991) 104-9.

b868 **Dunkel** Achim, Christlicher Glaube und historische Vernunft; eine interdisziplinäre Untersuchung über die Notwendigkeit eines theologischen Geschichtsverständnisses ᴰ1989 ➤ 6,b362; 7,b58: ᴿExpTim 102 (1990s) 335 (G. *Wainwright*: pupil of Pannenberg); Protestantesimo 47 (1992) 163s (F. *Ferrario*).

b869 **Forte** Bruno, Teologia della storia; saggio sulla rivelazione, l'inizio e il compimento: Simbolica ecclesiale 7, 1991 ➤ 7,b61: ᴿFilT 6 (1992) 172-6 (P. *Giustiniani*); Gregorianum 73 (1992) 546s (R. *Fisichella*); Lateranum 58 (1992) 526-9 (P. *Coda*).

b870 ᴱ**Forte** Bruno, Teologia e storia: 1992 ➤ 549*b*, p. 29-35; p. 9-20, *Vilanova* Evangelista; p. 59-67, *Pitta* Antonio, Storia ed esegesi; p. 69-92, *Russo* Adolfo, Rivelazione e storia.

b871 **Fukuyama** Francis,   The end of history [with capital H, overarching meaning to political endeavors, ended by the victory of liberal democracy and capitalist economics] and the last man. NY 1992, Free Press. Pp. xxiii-418. $25. – ᴿAmHR 97 (1992) 817-9 (P. *Fritzsche*: leaves obscure the 'last man' since births and private aspirations – small-h history – continue).

b872 **García Archilla** Aurelio A.,   The theology of history and apologetic historiography in Heinrich BULLINGER; truth in history: Mellen Research Univ. Lewiston NY 1992, Mellen.   337 p. $80.   0-7734-9828-1 [TDig 40,164].

b873 **Gilbert** F.,   History: politics or culture? Reflections on RANKE and BURCKHARDT. Princeton 1990, Univ. ix-109 p. $15 [RHE 87,167*].

b874 *Gill* David W. J.,   Authorized or unauthorized [LANE FOX R. 1991]; a dilemma for the historian: TyndB 43,9 (1992) 191-200.

b875 *González Radio* Vicente,   Semblanza historiográfica de Ramón OTERO PEDRAYO: RelCu 37 (1991) 521-551.

b876 **Hardtwig** Wolfgang,   Über das Studium der Geschichte.   Mü 1990, DTV-Wiss. 467 p. – ᴿHispania Antiqua 16 (1992) 395s (J. *Díez Asensio*).

b877 **Hinchliff** Peter,   God and history; aspects of British theology, 1875-1914. Ox 1992, Clarendon.   267 p. £32 [TR 88,524]. 0-19-826333-3. – ᴿExpTim 104 (1992s) 189 (B. M. G. *Reardon*: history not theology).

b878 **Hodgson** Peter C.,   God in history; shapes of freedom 1989 ► 5,b359; 7,b71: ᴿZygon 27 (1992) 119-121 (M. *Wiles*).

b879 *Hoffmeier* James K.,   The problem of 'history' in Egyptian royal inscriptions: ► 735, Sesto Eg. 1991/2, 291-9.

b880 *Hryniewicz* Wacław,   Gnade und Wahrheit in der Menschheitsgeschichte; die geschichtstheologische Sicht in den Schriften des Metropoliten ILARION, c. 1050:   OstkSt 421 (1992) 301-321.

b881 ᴱ**Iggers** George G.,   **Powell** James M.,   Leopold von RANKE and the shaping of historical discipline [14 art.]. Syracuse NY 1990, Univ. xxii-223 p. $29. – ᴿRBgPg 70 (1992) 558-560 (J. *Paquet*).

b882 *Inglebert* Hervé,   Un exemple historiographique au Vᵉ siècle; la conception de l'histoire chez QUODVULTDEUS de Carthage et ses relations avec la Cité de Dieu: RÉAug 37 (1991) 307-320.

b883 **Jameson** Fredric,   Postmodernism; or, The cultural logic of late capitalism. Durham NC 1991, Duke Univ. 438 p. $35. – ᴿJRel 72 (1992) 636s (M. *Krupnick*).

b884 **Kemp** Anthony,   The estrangement of the past; a study in the origins of modern historical consciousness. NY 1991, Oxford-UP. 228 + xi p. $32.50. – ᴿJRel 72 (1992) 600 (P. I. *Kaufman*).

b885 ᴱ**Le Goff** Jacques, *al.*,   Die Rückeroberung des historischen Denkens; Grundlagen der neuen Geschichtswissenschaft [1980, Tb. 1986], ᵀ*Kaiser* Wolfgang, 1990 ► 7,b74: ᴿHZ 253 (1991) 675s (L. *Raphael*).

b886 *Luirard* M.,   Réflexions sur les apports de l'histoire à l'ecclésiologie: ► 62*, ᶠGAUSSIN P., Maisons 1992, 207-219.

b887 **Maffeis** Gustavo,   Il piano di Dio nella storia 1989 ► 7,b77; Lit. 25.000: ᴿDocCom 44 (1991) 202 (D. *Vibrac*).

b887* **Marcus** R. A.,   Saeculum; history and society in the theology of St. Augustine²ʳᵉᵛ [¹1970]. C 1989, Univ. xxvi-254 p. $54.50; pa. $16. – ᴿChH 61 (1992) 234 (D. W. *Johnson*).

b888 **Martin** Raymond,   The past within us; an empirical approach to philosophy of history. Princeton 1989, Univ. xiii-163 p. – ᴿHistTheor 31 (1992) 200-8 (P. A. *Roth*).

b889 *Martínez Cavero* P., Los argumentos de OROSIO en la polémica pagano-cristiana: Antigüedad y Cristianismo 7 (Murcia 1990) 319-331 [< RHE 87,427*).

b890 **Meier** Christian, Il mondo della storia: Univ. pa. 257. Bo 1991, Mulino. 142 p. Lit. 14.000. 88-15-03233-9. – ᴿAntonianum 67 (1992) 438s (M. *Nobile*).

b891 **Mesure** Sylvie, DILTHEY et la fondation des sciences historiques: Sociologies. P 1990, PUF. 275 p. F 165. – ᴿRBgPg 70 (1992) 560s (Anne-Marie *Roviello*).

b892 **Momigliano** Arnaldo,   *a*) The classical foundations of modern historiography 1990 → 6,b386: ᴿClasR 42 (1992) 420s (A. *Cameron*; posthumous 1962 lectures); ÉtClas 60 (1992) 174s (C. *Baurain*); Gnomon 64 (1992) 462-4 (K. *Christ*); HistTheor 31 (1992) 224-230 (D. *Konstan*); Times Lit. Supp. (L 19.VII.1991) 35 (P. *Green*) [< NTAbs 36,15]. – *b*) Les fondations du savoir historique [The classical foundations, Sather lectures 1961s/1990], ᵀ*Rozenbaumas* Isabelle: Histoire 15. P 1992, BLettres. xv-198 p. F125 [RHE 88,202-5, J. L. *Quantin*]. 2-251-38014-0.

b893 **Mosès** Stéphane, L'ange de l'histoire [... sa nouvelle conception chez] ROSENZWEIG, BENJAMIN, SCHOLEM: La couleur des idées. P 1992, Seuil. 262 p. – ᴿArchivScSocR 78 (1992) 249s (M. *Löwy*: brillant).

b893* **Morrison** Karl F., History as a visual art in the twelfth-century renaissance: Princeton 1990, Univ. xxvi-262 p. – ᴿClıH 61 (1992) 238-240 (G. W. *Olsen*).

b894 **Müller** Christof, Geschichtsbewusstsein bei AUGUSTINUS; ontologische, anthropologische und universalgeschichtlich/heilsgeschichtliche Elemente einer augustinischen 'Geschichtstheorie': Diss. ᴰ*Mayer* C. Giessen 1992. 370 p. – RTLv 24, p. 552.

b895 **Murrmann-Kahl** Michael, Die entzauberte Heilsgeschichte; der Historismus erobert die Theologie 1880-1920 [Diss. München]. Gü 1992, Mohn. 515 p. DM 198 [TR 88,432].

b896 *Musti* Domenico, La storiografia del novecento sul mondo antico: RCuClasM 33 (1991) 99-113.

b896* *a*) *Myers* David N., The fall and rise of Jewish historicism; the evolution of the Akademie für die Wissenschaft des Judentums (1919-1934): HUCA 63 (1992) 107-144. – *b*) *Naor* Menahcm, ⏴ *Abot abelu*... in biblical historiography: BethM 37,129 (1991s) 150-6.

b897 *a*) *Pietri* Charles, Storia del cristianesimo e/o teologia della storia; – *b*) *Malgeri* Francesco, La storiografia religiosa: → Storia, Studium (R 1991) 889-902 / 903-922.

b898 *Pintos Peñaranda* M. L., La realidad histórica en I. ELLACURIA; fundamentación material para una filosofía de la historia comprometida: EstE 67 (1992) 331-360.

b899 **Pomeroy** Arthur J., The appropriate comment; death notices in the ancient historians: StKlPg 58. Fra 1991, Lang. – ᴿPrudentia 24,2 (1992) 75-79 (M. *Wilson*).

b900 *Räisänen* Heikki, The effective 'history' of the Bible; a challenge to biblical scholarship ['What effect has the Bible had?']: ScotJT 45 (1992) 303-324.

b901 **Sakellariou** Michael B., Between memory and oblivion; the transmission of early Greek historical traditions: Meletemata 12. Athenai 1990. 267 p. 960-7094-76-X. – ᴿDialHA 18,1 (1992) 306s (Claudia *Antonetti*).

b902 *Salvatierra* Ángel, La historia como lugar teológico inspirador de la catequesis: LumenVr 41 (1992) 201-236 [367-382, *Berzosa Martínez* Raúl].

b903 **Santini** Carlo, SILIUS Italicus and his view of the past [La Cognizione]: London Studies ClasPg 25. Amst 1991, Gieben. 123 p.

b904 **Schlaudraff** K. H., 'Heil als Geschichte?': BeitGbEx 29, 1988 ➤ 4, d161; 6,b398: ᴿStPatav 38 (1991) 203-5 (G. *Segalla*).

b905 ᴱ**Shapiro** Ann-Louise, History and feminist theory: HistTheor Beih 31. Middletown CT 1992, Wesleyan Univ. 137 p.; 8 art.

b906 *Silva* A. Eduardo, La significación teológica de los acontecimientos; el estatuto histórico de la teología según M.-D. CHENU: TVida 33 (1992) 269-297.

Smelik Klaas A. D., Converting the past 1992 ➤ 310.

b907 *Stegemann* Ekkehard W., Gottes Reich und seine Gerechtigkeit für die Erde; zur Geschichtstheologie von Leonhard RAGAZ: DielB 27 (1991) 237-252.

b908 **Thompson** Thomas L., Historiography (Israelite): ➤ 741, AnchorBD 3 (1992) 206-212 [... 211, collapse of 'salvation history']; *al.* Mesopotamian; Greco-Roman.

b909 *Troeltsch* Ernst, Historiographie [< Enc. Rel. Ethics 6 (1913) 716-723], ᵀ*Médevielle* Geneviève: RICathP 37 (1991) 143-170.

b910 *Trompf* G. W., RUFINUS and the logic of retribution in post-Eusebian church histories: JEH 43 (1992) 351-371.

b911 ᴱ**Verdin** H., *al.*, Purposes of history; studies in Greek historiography from the 4th to the 2d centuries B.C.; proceedings of the international colloquium Lv 24-26 May 1988: StHellenistica 30, 1990 ➤ 6,769; Fb 2250: ᴿAntClas 61 (1992) 581s (Véronique *Krings*).

b912 **Wells** Ronald A., History through the eyes of faith 1989 ➤ 6,b403; 7,b100: ᴿParadigms 8 (1992s) 38 (J. *Fea*).

b912* *Werner* Karl F., L'historien et la notion d'état: CRAI (1992) 709-721.

b913 **Wes** Marinus A., Michael ROSTOVTZEFF, historian in exile; Russian roots in an American context: HistEinz 65. Stu 1990, Steiner. xxxi-106 p.; 12 pl. – ᴿGnomon 64 (1992) 369-371 (K. *Christ*, Eng.).

b914 *Widmann* Peter, Die Hilfe der Historiker bei der Beältigung von Vergangenheit [ᴱ*Besier* G., *Wolf* S., Pfarrer... DDR 1991]: TLZ 117 (1992) 641-650.

b915 *Winkelmann* Friedhelm, Grundprobleme christlicher Historiographie in ihrer Frühphase (EUSEBIOS von Kaisareia und OROSIUS): JbÖsByz 42 (1992) 13-27.

b916 **Wood** Michael, Legacy; a search for the origins of civilization. L 1992, Network. 223 p.; (colour.) ill. 0-563-36429-7.

b917 **Woodman** Anthony J., Rhetoric in classical historiography; four studies. Portland OR / L 1988, Croom Helm/Areopagitica. xiii-236 p. – ᴿGGA 244 (1992) 33-40 (M. *Vielberg*).

b918 **Zimmer** Detlef, Der Mensch in der Geschichte und die Biographie; Entropie eines klassischen Streitpunktes: ZfG (1991) [sonst meist über dieses Jahrhundert].

Q3 *Historia Ægypti* – **Egypt.**

b919 **Anagnostou-Canas** Barbara, Juge et sentence dans l'Égypte romaine [2 awards 1983]: RechtsPhHSt 6. P 1991, Harmattan. xii-390 p. 2-7384-1153... [sic 3 times].

b920 *Arnold* Felix, New evidence for the length of the reign of Senwosret III?: GöMiszÄg 129 (1992) 27-31; 2 fig.

b921 *Bagnall* Roger S., Combat ou vide; christianisme et paganisme dans l'Égypte romaine tardive: Ktema 13 (1988) 285-296.

b922 *Barta* Winfried, Die Datierungspraxis in Ägypten unter Kambyses und Dareios I: ZäSpr 119 (1992) 82-90.

b923 *Beckerath* J. von, *a)* Ägypten und der Feldzug Sanheribs im Jahre 701 v.Chr.: UF 24 (1992) 3-8; – *b)* Zur Geschichte von Chonsemḥab und dem Geist: ZäSpr 119 (1992) 90-107.

b924 *a) Beckerath* J. von, Noch einmal Psusennes II.; – *b) Obsomer* Claude, Les lignes 8 à 24 de la stèle de Mentouhotep (Florenz 2540) érigée à Bouhen en l'an 18 de Sésostris Iᵉʳ: GöMiszÄg 130 (1992) 17-19 [Nachschrift 131 (1992) 11] / 130 (1992) 57-74.

b925 *a) Berg* David, Myth as history; the campaign of propaganda of Hatshepsut; – *b) Leprohon* Ronald J., La mythologie et le quotidien dans l'Égypte ancienne: BCanadMesop 22 (1991) 25-29; 1 fig. / 37-41.

b926 *a) Bietak* Manfred, Die Chronologie Ägyptens und der Beginn der MB-Zeit-Kultur; – *b) Helck* Wolfgang, Zur Chronologiediskussion über das Neue Reich; – *c) Beckerath* Jürgen von, Das Kalendarium des Papyrus Ebers und die Chronologie des ägyptischen Neuen Reiches [*Krauss* Rolf]; – *d) Luft* Ulrich, Remarks of a philologist on Egyptian chronology; – *e) Leitz* C. [*Mucke* H.], Bemerkungen zur astronomischen Chronologie: ➤ 702*b*, ÄgLev 3 (1990/2) 29-37 / 63-67 / 23-27 [75-96] / 109-114 / 97-102 [125-8].

b926* **Bilde** Per, *al.*, Ethnicity in Hellenistic Egypt: Studies in Hellenistic Civilization 3. Aarhus 1992, Univ. 210 p. 87-7288-359-6 [OIAc 5,14].

b927 ᴱ**Bloom** Harold: Cleopatra; Major Literary Characters. NY 1991, Chelsea. xv-269 p. $35. 0-7910-0915-7. – ᴿClasW 86 (1992s) 166 (S. *Bertman*).

b928 **Boorn** G. P. F. Van den, The duties of the vizier 1988 ➤ 4,d177... 7,b109: ᴿVarAeg 8,1 (1992) 57-62 (A. *Spalinger*).

b929 **Bowman** Alan K., Egypt after the Pharaohs 1990 = 1986 ➤ 2,9302... 6,b415: ᴿJAOS 112 (1992) 129-132 (D. B. *Spanel*).

b930 **Bryan** Betsy M., The reign of Thutmose IV, ᴰ1991 ➤ 7,b112; $63.50: ᴿOrientalia 61 (1992) 464-6 (K. A. *Kitchen*).

b931 *Burstein* Stanley M., HECATAEUS of Abdera's History of Egypt; – *b) Ray* J. D., Jews and other immigrants in late period Egypt; – *c) Hanson* Ann E., Egyptians, Greeks, Romans and *Ioudaioi* in the first century A.D. tax archive from Philadelphia; – *d) Smith* H. S., Foreigners in the documents from the sacred animal necropolis, Saqqara: ➤ 719, Life 1990/2, 45-49 / 273 only / 133-148 / 295-301.

b932 *a) Burstein* Stanley M., Pharaoh Alexander, a scholarly myth [Pseudo-Callisthenes unreliable]; – *b) Falivene* Maria R., Government, management, literacy; aspects of Ptolemaic administration in the Early Hellenistic period: AncSoc 22 (1991) 139-145 / 203-227.

b932* **Cesaretti** Maria Pia, Nerone e l'Egitto 1989 ➤ 7,b114: ᴿAegyptus 72 (1992) 203-5 (Patrizia *Piacentini*).

b933 ᴱ**Criscuolo** Lucia, *Geraci* Giovanni, Egitto e storia antica dall'Ellenismo all'età araba. Bo 1987/9 ➤ 6,795: ᴿCdÉ 67 (1992) 184s (J.-M. *Hannick*).

b934 *Dautzenberg* N., Plazierungsvorschläge zu zwei Königen der 13. Dynastie: GöMiszÄg 127 (1992) 17-19.

b935 **David** Rosalie & Antony E., A biographical dictionary of ancient Egypt. L 1992, Seaby. xxvi-179 p.; maps. 1-85264-032-4.

b936 *a) Depuydt* Leo, Der Fall des 'Hintersichschauers'; – *b) Wettenge*

Wolfgang, Zur Rubrengliederung der Erzählung von den zwei Brüdern: GöMiszÄg 126 (1992) 33-38 / 97-106.
b937 *Derchain* Philippe, Les débuts de l'histoire (rouleau de cuir Berlin 3029): RÉgp 43 (1992) 35-47.
b938 **Der Manuelian** Peter, Studies in the reign of Amenophis II, 1987 ⇨ 3,b667; 7,b117*: RCdÉ 67 (1992) 275-7 (M. *Deproost*); OLZ 87 (1992) 128-130 (J. *Lipińska*).
b939 **Ellis** Simon P., Graeco-Roman Egypt: Shire Egyptology. Princes Risborough, Bucks 1992, Shire. 56 p., 40 fig. 0-7478-0158-4.
b940 **Felde** Rolf, Ägyptische Könige und Königinnen. Wsb 1992. xxii-130 p. [OIAc 5,21].
b941 **Gestermann** Louise, Kontinuität und Wandel... Mitt. Reiches 1987 ⇨ 3, b675... 5,b398: RCdÉ 67 (1992) 73-76 (P. *Vernus*).
b942 **Godron** Gérard, Études sur l'Horus Den [roi Iᵉ Dyn.] et quelques problèmes de l'Égypte archaïque: CahOr 19, 1990 ⇨ 6,b40: RAfO 38s (1991s) 245-8 (J. *Kahl*); DiscEg 23 (1992) 95-98 (A. *Pérez Lagarcha*); Muséon 105 (1992) 385 (C. *Vandersleyen*); WeltOr 23 (1992) 158s (W. *Kaiser*).
b943 *Godron* Gérard, La politique extérieure de l'Egypte sous les deux premières dynasties: DialHA 16,2 (1990) 47-61.
b944 *Goedicke* Hans, The perimeter of Egypt's political interests in the (late?) Middle Kingdom: BSocÉg 15 (Genève 1991) 39-42.
b945 *Goldwasser* Orly, On the date of Seth from Qubeibeh [Tel Šalaf 128. 144]: IsrEJ 42 (1992) 47-51; 4 fig.
b946 *Grimal* Nicolas, A history of ancient Egypt [1982], TShaw Ian. Ox 1992, Blackwell. x-512 p.; 23 fig., 24 pl. 0-631-17472-9 [OIAc 5,23].
b947 *Hafemann* Ingelore, Stellung der Königssöhne und Entstehung des Titels z3-njswt: AltOrF 19 (1992) 212-8.
b948 *a) Helck* Wolfgang, Der Amtsbereich des Vezirs Ramose unter Amenophis III.; – *b) Dautzenberg* N., Seneferibre Sesostris IV. — ein König der 17. Dynastie?; – *c) Boochs* Wolfgang, Strafgrund und -zweck im altägyptischen Recht: GöMiszÄg 129 (1992) 53 / 43-48; 6 fig. / 39-41.
b949 *Henne* Willibald, Bemerkungen zum heliakischen Aufgang der Sothis: ZäSpr 119 (1992) 10-21.
b950 *Hölbl* Günther, Zum Titel ḥq3-ḥq3w des römischen Kaisers: GöMiszÄg 127 (1992) 49-52.
b951 *Husson* Geneviève, *Valbelle* Dominique, L'état et les institutions en Égypte, des premiers pharaons aux empereurs romains. P 1992, A. Colin. 368 p. 2-200-31310-1 [OIAc 5,25]. – RRÉAnc 94 (1992) 505s (C. *Orrieux*).
b952 *Jansen-Winkeln* Karl, Das Ende des Neuen Reiches: ZäSpr 119 (1992) 22-37.
EJohnson Janet H., Life in a multi-cultural society; Egypt from Cambyses to Constantine and beyond: SAOC 51, 1992 ⇨ 719.
b954 **Kemp** B., Ancient Egypt 1989 ⇨ 5,b409; 7,b129: RJAmEg 28 (1991) 227s (Diana C. *Patch*).
b955 **Kitchen** K.A., Ramesside inscriptions VIII,6-10. Ox 1990, Blackwell. 30 p. each (9 &10, 8 p.). – RBO 49 (1992) 174s (W. *Helck*).
b956 *Kitchen* K.A. (Chronology), *al.*, Egypt, history of: ⇨ 741, AnchorBD 2 (1992) 321-331 (-374), plus plagues, literature (378-399), relations with Canaan (399-408) religion (only 408-412).
b957 *Leahy* Anthony, Royal iconography and dynastic change, 750-525 BC; the blue and cap crowns: JEA 78 (1992) 223-240; pl. XXVI-XXVII.

b958 **Lichtheim** Miriam,   Ancient Egyptian autobiographies ... : OBO 84, 1988
➤ 4,d210* ... 7,b132:   ᴿIsrEJ 42 (122-4 (S. *Ahituv*); JEA 78 (1992) 330-2
(S. *Quirke*); WeltOr 23 (1992) 159s (E. *Graefe*).

b959 ᴱ**Lloyd** Alan B.,   ERODOTO, le storie, II.   L'Egitto 1989 ➤ 7,b133*b*;
ᵀ*Fraschetti* Augusto: ᴿAnzAltW 45 (1992) 199-203 (P. *Froschauer*).

b959* *a*) *Lloyd* Alan B.,   The great inscription of Khnumhotpe II at Beni
Hasan; – *b*) *Leahy* Anthony,   'May the king live'; the Libyan rulers in the
onomastic record; – *c*) *Brunner* Hellmut,   Vorbild und Gegenbild in
Biographien, Lehren und Anweisungen: ➤ 72, ᶠGRIFFITHS J.G. 1992,
21-36 / 146-163 / 164-8.

b960 *Meyer* Gudrun,   Hurija und Piphurija [Ende 18. Dynastie]: GöMiszÄg
126 (1992) 87-92.

b961 *Muller* Carl W.,   Das Schatzhaus des Rhampsinit oder die Überlistung
des Todes; zu HERODOTs ägyptischer Reise und der Authentizität seiner
Quellenangaben: ➤ 672, Fremdspr. 1987/92, 37-62.

b962 *Oosterhout* G.W. van,   The heliacal rising of Sirius [... absolute
chronology of ancient Egypt]: DiscEg 24 (1992) 71-111.

b963 **Palme** Bernhard,   Das Amt des *apaitetes* 1989 ➤ 7,b138:   ᴿJbÖsByz 42
(1992) 352-4 (J. *Gascou*); JEA 78 (1992) 344-6 (Ute *Wartenberg*).

b964 **Redford** D.B.,   Egypt and Canaan in the New Kingdom: Beer Sheva 4,
1990 ➤ 6,b454:   ᴿVT 42 (1992) 136 (J.D. *Ray*).

b965 **Rössler-Köhler** Ursula,   Individuelle Haltungen zum agyptischen Königtum der Spätzeit; private Quellen und ihre Königswertung im Spannungsfeld zwischen Erwartung und Erfahrung: GöOrF 4/21, 1991 ➤ 7,
b143; DM 148: ᴿLA 41 (1991) 569-571 (A. *Niccacci*).

b966 **Rowińska** Ewa, *Winnicki* Jan K.,   Staatsausdehunung (P 67-68) und
Massnahmen zur Verstärkung der Nordostgrenze (P 106-109) in der
'Lehre für den König Merikare': ZägSpr 119 (1992) 130-143.

b967 *a*) *Saady* Hassan El-,   The wars of Sety I at Karnak; a new
chronological structure; – *b*) *Spalinger* Anthony,   The date of the dream
of Nectanebo; – *c*) *Allam* Schafik,   *msw* = Kinder/Volksgruppe/Pro-
dukte/Abgaben: StAäK 19 (1992) 285-294 / 295-304 / 1-13.

b967* **Sabban** Sherif el-,   The temple calendars of ancient Egypt: diss.
Liverpool 1992. 332 p. BRDX-97755. – DissA 53 (1992s) 3331-A.

Schade-Busch Mechtilde,   Zur Königsideologie Amenophis' III; Analyse der
Phraseologie historischer Texte der Voramarnazeit [< Diss. Mainz 1989]:
Hildesheimer ÄgBeit 35, 1992 ➤ 9730.

b969 *Serrano Delgado* José M.,   Una época crítica de la historia de Egipto; el
primer período intermedio: Revista de Arqueología 13,140 (M 1992) ...
8-18.

b970 *a*) *Smith* Harry S.,   The making of Egypt; a review of the influence of
Susa and Sumer on Upper Egypt and Lower Nubia in the 4th millennium
B.C.; – *b*) *Majer* Joseph,   The Egyptian desert and Egyptian prehistory:
➤ 84, Mcm. HOFFMAN M., 1992, 235-246; 37 fig. / 227-234, map.

b971 **Springborg** Patricia,   Royal persons; patriarchal monarchy and the
feminine principle. L 1990, Unwin-H. xv-326 p.; 32 fig. £30. – ᴿCdÉ 67
(1992) 281s (B. Van *Hinsfeld*: délirant).

b972 **Strudwick** Nigel,   The administration of Egypt in the Old Kingdom 1985
➤ 3,b730:   ᴿJEA 78 (1992) 326-8 (N. *Kanawati*).

b972* *a*) *Thompson* Dorothy J.,   Literacy and the administration in Early
Ptolemaic Egypt; – *b*) *Ricketts* Linda †,   The administration of Late
Ptolemaic Egypt; – *c*) *Huss* Werner,   Some thoughts on the subject 'State'
and 'Church' in Ptolemaic Egypt; – *d*) *Lanciers* Eddy,   Die ägyptischen

Priester des ptolemäischen Königskultes: → 719, Life 1990/2, 323-6 / 275-281 / 159-163 / 207s (résumé).

b973 *Tobin* Vincent A., Myth and politics in the Old Kingdom of Egypt: BO 49 (1992) 605-636.

b974 *Trapani* Marcella, Il decreto regale e l'oracolo divino nell'antico Egitto (dalle origini alla XX dinastia, 2472-1070 a.C.): AION 52 (1992) 1-33.

b975 **Vercoutter** Jean, L'Égypte et la vallée du Nil I: NClio. P 1992, PUF. I. li-382 p. F 220. 2-13-044157-2.

b976 **Watterson** Barbara, Women in ancient Egypt. Stroud/NY 1991, Sutton/St. Martin's. xiv-201 p.; 13 color. pl. 0-86299-978-2 [OIAc 3,41].

b977 **Way** Thomas von der, Göttergericht und 'Heiliger' Krieg im Alten Ägypten; die Inschriften des Merneptah zum Libyerkrieg des Jahres 5 [Hab.-Diss. Heidelberg 1991]: StArchGAltÄg 4. Heid 1992, Orientverlag. xi-99 p., VI pl. 3-927552-06-2 [OIAc 5,39].

b978 **Way** Thomas von der, Die Textüberlieferung Ramses' II. zur Qadeš-Schlacht; Analyses und Struktur 1984 → 65,9677; 4,d229*: ᴿCdÉ 66 (1991) 163s (W. J. *Murnane*: a mine; some objections).

b979 **Wilson** Penelope, A lexicographical study of the Ptolemaic texts in the Temple of Edfu: diss. Liverpool 1991, 2350 p. BRDX-97039. – DissA 53 (1992s) 1885s-A.

b979* *a) Zadok* Ran, Egyptians in Babylonia and Elam during the 1st millennium B.C.; – *b) Baskakov* Alexej, Die Bibliothek eines ägyptischen Hofbeamten, wie Thomas MANN sie sich vorstellte: LAeg 2 (1992) 139-146 / 1-16.

b980 **Zibelius-Chen** Karola, Die ägyptische Expansion nach Nubien: TAVO B-78, 1988 → 4,g472; 6,b470: ᴿCdÉ 67 (1992) 273-5 (D. *Berg*); DiscEg 19 (1991) 93-97 (Renate *Müller-Wollermann*).

Griggs C. Wilfred, Early Egyptian Christianity from its origins to 451 C.E.: Coptic Studies 2, 1990 → b519.

Q4 Historia Mesopotamiae.

b982 **Beaulieu** Paul-Alain, The reign of Nabonidus 1989 → 5,b452; 7,b154: ᴿBA 55 (1992) 234s (D. W. *Suter*).

b983 *Beaulieu* Paul-Alain, New light on secret knowledge in Late Babylonian culture: ZAss 82 (1992) 98-111.

b984 **Boncquet** J., DIODORUS Siculus (II,1-34) over Mesopotamië; een historische kommentaar. Verh. 49/122, 1987 → 5,b453: ᴿBO 49 (1992) 801-4 (M. J. H. *Linssen*); Mnemosyne 45 (1992) 119-122 (E. Van der *Vliet*).

b985 **Bottéro** Jean, présent., Initiation à l'Orient ancien; de Sumer à la Bible [< L'Histoire]: Points, Histoire 170. P 1992, Seuil. 358 p. 2-02-018130-4 [OIAc 5,15].

b986 **Cabanes** Pierre, Introduction à l'histoire de l'Antiquité: Cursus. P 1992, 188 p. – ᴿDialHA 18,1 (1992) 305s (P. *Lévêque*).

b987 *Chadwick* Robert, Calendars, ziggurrats, and the stars: BCanadMesop 24 (1992) 7-24; 12 fig.; franç. 33 and figure-legends.

b988 *a) Charpin* Dominique, Immigrés, réfugiés et déportés en Babylonie sous Hammu-rabi et ses successeurs; – *b) Joannès* Francis, Une mission secrète à Ešnunna: → 683, Circulation 1991/2, 207-218 / 185-193.

b988* **Cooper** J.S., Reconstructing... The Lagash-Umma border conflict 1983 → 1,b93; 6,b480: ᴿZAss 82 (1992) 271 (H. *Steible*).

b989 **Crawford** Harriet,   Sumer and the Sumerians 1991 → 7,b156: ᴿBL (1992) 116 (T.C. *Mitchell*) [& 93,119, M.J. *Geller*]; TopO 2 (1992) 167-171 (Y. *Calvet*, aussi sur Huoᴛ J. 1989; Marguron J. 1991).

b990 *a*) *Edzard* Dietz O., Irikagina (Urukagina); – *b*) *Steinkeller* Piotr,   The reform of UruKAgina and an early Sumerian term for 'prison'; – *c*) *Yang Zhi*, King of Justice; – *d*) *Cooper* Jerrold S., Posing the Sumerian question; race and scholarship in the early history of Assyriology; – *e*) *Klein* Jacob, A new Nippur duplicate of the Sumerian King List in the Brockmon collection, University of Haifa: → 32, ꟳCɪᴠɪʟ M., AulaO 9,1 (1991) 77-79 / 227-232; 2 fig. / 243-9 / 47-66 / 123-9.

b991 **Fales** Frederico Mario,   Lettere dalla corte assira. Venezia 1992, Marsilio. 184 p. Lit. 14.000. – ᴿArcheo 7,91 (1992) 126 (S. *Pernigotti*).

b992 **Frame** Grant,   Babylonia 689-627 B.C., a political history: Uitgaven 69. İstanbul 1992, Nederlands Hist.-Arch. Instituut. xxxv-358 p.; 8 fig. 90-6258-069-6 [OIAc 5,21].

b993 **Gelb** I.J., *Kienast* B.,   Die altakkadischen Königsinschriften 1990 → 6, b489: ᴿZAss 81 (1991) 133-143 (M. *Krebernik*).

b994 ᴱ**Gibson** M., *Biggs* R.D.,   The organization of power 1983/7 → 3,781; 4,738: ᴿZAss 81 (1991) 144-6 (M.J. *Geller*).

b995 **Glassner** Jean-Jacques,   La chute d'Akkadé 1986 → 2,9373; 6,b462: ᴿBO 49 (1992) 433-9 (Sabina *Franke*).

b996 **Grayson** A. Kirk, *al.*,   Assyrian rulers 1987 → 3,b736... 7,b164: ᴿZAss 82 (1992) 274-6 (M. *Görg*).

b997 **Grayson** A. Kirk,   Mesopotamia; History of Assyria/Babylon: → 741, AnchorBD 4 (1992) 732-755-777 [714-732 *al.* (earlier) Mesopotamia].

b997* *Grzybek* Erhard,   Zu einer babylonischen Königsliste aus der hellenistischen Zeit (Keilschrifttafel BM 35603): Historia 41 (1992) 190-204.

b998 *a*) *Heimpel* Wolfgang,   Herrentum und Königtum im vor- und frühgeschichtlichen Alten Orient; – *b*) *Volk* Konrad,   Puzur-Mama und die Reise des Königs: ZAss 82 (1992) 4-21 / 22-29.

b999 ᴱ**Hrouda** B., *al.*, Der alte Orient 1991 → 7,b167: ᴿTyche 7 (1992) 241s (G. *Dobesch*).

d1 **Hrouda** Barthel,   L'Orient ancien, histoire et civilisations [1991], ᵀᴱ*Bottéro* Jean, *al.* 1991, Bordas. 464 p.; color. ill. 3-570-08578-3.

d2 **Huot** Jean-Louis,   Les Sumériens 1989 → 6,b494: ᴿRAss 86 (1992) 92-94 (P. *Amiet*).

d3 **Invernizzi** A., *a*) Sumeri e Accadi; – *b*) Babilonesi e Assiri: Dal Tigri all'Eufrate 1s. T 1992, Univ. 423 p.; 635 fig.; 65 col. pl. / 384 p.; 619 fig.; 54 col. pl. 88-7166-101-X; -2-8.

d4 *Kelly* Thomas,   The Assyrians, the Persians, and the sea: MeditHR 7,1 (1992) 5-28.

d5 ᴱ**Klengel** Horst,   Kulturgeschichte des alten Vorderasiens 1989 → 6,b498; 7,b168: ᴿDLZ 113 (1992) 73-75 (D. *Metzler*); ZDMG 142 (1992) 160-2 (W. *Schramm*).

d6 *Lackenbacher* Sylvie,   Un pamphlet contre Nabonide, dernier roi de Babylone: DialHA 18,1 (1992) 13-28; Eng. 28.

d7 *Lara Peinado* Federico,   La civilización sumeria: BtHistoria 16. M 1989, temi. 219 p. 84-7679-138-0 [OIAc 3,28 'Francisco'] 84-7679-138-0.

d8 *Maeda* Tohru,   The defence zone during the rule of the Ur III dynasty: AcSum 14 (1992) 135-172.

d9 **Margueron** J.-C.,   Les Mésopotamiens I-II, 1991 → 7,b173: ᴿBCanad-Mesop 22 (1991) 51s (M. *Fortin*); Syria 69 (1992) 234s (H. de *Contenson*).

d10 *Neumann* Hans,   Zur Problematik des subjektiven Faktors im Prozess po-

litischer Umwälzungen in Mesopotamien gegen Ende des 3. Jahrtausends v.u.Z.: ArOr 60 (1992) 234-250.
d11 **Nissen** Hans J., Mesopotamia before 5000 years [conference Rome 1986, not 1983 ➤ 64,a95; ital. 1990 ➤ 7,b175]: ScStor, Sussidi didattici 1. R. c. 1991, Univ. 188 p.; 3 pl.
d12 **Nissen** Hans J., The early history of the Ancient Near East [Grundzüge 1983 + new material], ᴿ*Lutzeier* Elizabeth, (*Northcott* Kenneth J.). Ch 1988, Univ. xiv-215 p.; 75 fig. $18. – ᴿÉglT 23 (1992) 134s (L. *Laberge*).
d13 **Pettinato** Giovanni, I Sumeri. Mi 1992, Rusconi. 423 p.; 12 pl. Lit. 40.000. 88-18-88018-7. – ᴿArcheo 7,90 (1992) 125 (S. *Moscati*).
d14 **Ponchia** Simonetta, L'Assiria e gli stati transeufratici nella prima metà dell'VIII sec. a.C.: History of the Ancient Near East, Studies 4-bis. Padova 1991, Sargon. xv-123 p. 1120-4680
d15 **Popko** Maciej, ⊕ Huryci. Wsz 1992, Inst. Or. Studies. 208 p.; 24 pl. 83-06-02114-2 [BO 49,587].
d16 *Powell* Marvin A., Naram-Sîn, son of Sargon; ancient history, famous names, and a famous Babylonian forgery: ZAss 81 (1991) 20-30.
d17 **Saggs** H. W. F., Civilization before Greece and Rome 1989 ➤ 5,b488; 7,b180: ᴿBA 55 (1992) 235 (G. *Alford*); JRAS (1991) 261s (D. J. *Wiseman*); Latomus 51 (1992) 210s (E. *Warmenbol*, deçu).
d18 **Saggs** H. W. F., The greatness that was Babylon²ʳᵉᵛ [¹1962]. NY 1991, St Martins = L 1988, Sidgwick. xvii-487 p.; ill. $45/£25 [RelStR 19, 153, D. I. *Owen*: revision inadequate].
d19 **Saporetti** Claudio, Fascino e bellezza; ideali maschili nell'Antichità preclassica. R 1992, Unesco Club. 47 p.
d20 *Vermaak* P. S., The relevance of administrative documents for writing ancient Mesopotamian history: JTydSem 3 (1991) 85-104.
d21 **Watanabe** Kazuko, Die *âde*-Vereidigung... Asarhaddons 1987 ➤ 3,b760 ... 6,b521: ᴿOrientalia 61 (1992) 326-8 (W. *Schramm*).
d21* *Watanabe* Kazuko, Nabû-uşalla, Statthalter Sargons II. in Tam(a)nūna: BaghMitt 23 (1992) 357-369; 1 fig.; pl. 70-71.
d22 *Weingerber* Gerd, Die Suche nach dem altsumerischen Kupferland Makan: Altertum 37 (1991) 76-90; 15 fig.
d23 *Weippert* Manfred, Die Feldzüge Adadnararis I. nach Syrien; Voraussetzungen, Verlauf, Folgen: ZDPV 108 (1982) 42-67; 2 fig. (map).
d24 *Weissert* Elnathan, The prologue to Ashurbanipal's Prism E: Orientalia 61 (1992) 58-77.
d25 *a)* *Weissert* Elnathan, Interrelated chronographic patterns in the Assyrian eponym chronicle and the 'Babylonian Chronicle'; a comparative view; – *b)* *Kottsieper* Ingo, Die literarische Aufnahme assyrischer Begebenheiten in frühen aramäischen Texten: ➤ 683, Circulation 1991/2, 273-282 / 283-9.
d26 *a)* *Wilcke* Claus, É-sağ-da-na Nibruᵏⁱ, an early administrative center of the Ur III empire; – *b)* *Steiner* Gerd, Nippur und die sumerische Königsliste; – *c)* *Lafont* Bernard, Quelques remarques sur Nippur à l'époque d'Ur III: ➤ 687, Nippur 1988/92, 311-324 / 261-279 / 113-8.
d27 **Zawadzki** Stefan, The fall of Assyria and Median-Babylonian relations in light of the Nabupolassar Chronicle 1988 ➤ 5,b498; 6,b525: ᴿJAOS 112 (1992) 163s (M. *Dandamayev*).

Q4.5 *Historia Persiae* – **Iran.**

d28 *Amiet* Pierre, Sur l'histoire élamite: IrAnt 27 (1992) 75-94.

d29 ᴱAsheri David, ERODOTO, Le Storie, I. Introduzione; + ᵀAntelami Virginio, Libro I, La Lidia e la Persia. Mi 1988, Mondadori. lxxvii-400 p. 88-04-30666-1 [OIAc 2,13].

d30 ᴱAsheri David, ᵀMedaglia Silvio M., ERODOTO, Le storie, libro III, la Persia: Scrittori greci e latini Valla. Mi 1990, Mondadori. lxvi-396 p. Lit. 45.000. – ᴿClasR 42 (1992) 276s (Stephanie West).

d31 Baliński Aleksander, 'Intercalations' of the 'Zoroastrian' calendar in ancient Iran: FolOr 27 (1990) 97-106.

d32 Briant Pierre, Darius, les Perses et l'Empire: Découvertes 159. P 1992, Gallimard. 176 p.; ill. 2-07-053166-X [OIAc 5,15].

d34 Dandamaev M. A., Lukonin V. G., The culture and social institutions of ancient Iran 1989 → 5,b504; 7,b194: ᴿÉtClas 60 (1992) 378s (T. Petit).

d35 Dandamaev M. A., A political history of the Achaemenid empire 1989 → 5,b503: ᴿBO 49 (1992) 453-6 (E. M. Yamauchi); CritRR 5 (1992) 65s (J. W. Wright).

d36 Dodgeon M. L., ᴱLieu S. N. C., The Roman eastern frontier and the Persian Wars AD 226-363; a documentary history 1990 → 7,b195: 0-415-00342-3. – ᴿRÉAnc 94 (1992) 504s (P. Arnaud); RÉLat 70 (1992) 363s (M. Sartre).

d37 Graziani Simonetta, Testi editi ed inediti datati al regno di Bardiya (522 a.C.): Supp. 67 ad AION 51,2 (1991). N 1991, Ist. Univ. Orientale. xxxvii-65 p.

d38 Högemann Peter, Das alte Vorderasien und die Achämeniden; ein Beitrag zur Herodot-Analyse: TAVO-B98. Wsb 1992, Reichert. xvi-430 p. 3-88226-563-9.

d39 Koch Heidemarie, Es kündet Dareios der König... Vom Leben im persischen Grossreich: KuGaW 55. Mainz 1992, von Zabern. 309 p.; ill.

d40 Lanfranchi Giovanni, I Cimmeri; emergenza delle élites militari iraniche nel Vicino Oriente (VIII-VII sec. a.C.): History of the Ancient Near East, Studies 2-bis. Padova 1990, Sargon. xviii-299 p. 1120-4680,

d41 Lang Mabel L., Prexaspes and usurper Smerdis: JNES 51 (1992) 201-7.

d42 Lipiński Edward, Les Mèdes, Perses et Arméniens de SALLUSTE, Jug. 18: AncSoc 23 (1992) 149-158.

d42* Marshak B. I., The historico-cultural significance of the Sogdian calendar: Iran 30 (1992) 145-154.

d43 Petit Thierry, Satrapes 1990 → 7,b196: ᴿClasR 42 (1992) 215 (S. Hornblower); Orientalia 61 (1992) 471-4 (M. Dandamayev); RPg 65,2 (1991) 33-39 (É. Will).

d44 Pirart Victor, Kayân Yasn (Yasht 19,9-96); l'origine avestique des dynasties mythiques d'Iran: AulaO supp 2. Barc 1992, AUSA. 127 p. 0212-5730 [OIAc 5,32].

d45 ᴱSancisi-Weerdenburg Heleen, al., Achaemenid History 4, 1986; 5, 1987: 1990 → 6,822*; [7. 1991 → 7,e875*] 6. Asia Minor and Egypt; old cultures in a new empire. Leiden 1991, Ned. Inst. xviii-367 p. ƒ140 [JAOS 112, 727]. – ᴿJAOS 112 (1992) 169-2 (R. H. Sack, 4s).

d46 Schottky Martin, Parther. Meder und Hyrkanier; eine Untersuchung der dynastischen und geographischen Verflechtungen im Iran des I. Jhs. n.Chr.: ArchMIran 24 (1991) 61-134; 17 fig. (maps).

d47 Vogelsang W. J., The rise and organisation of the Achaemenid empire; the Eastern Iranian evidence: Studies in the History of the ANE 3. Leiden 1992, Brill. xii-344 p.; 16 fig. 90-04-09682-5.

d48 Weiskopf Michael, The so-called 'Great Satraps' revolt'... 1989 → 5, b519; 6,b549:   ᴿHZ 253 (1991) 703s (J. *Wiesehöfer*); Mnemosyne 45 (1992) 129-132 (Heleen *Sancisi-Weerdenburg*).

d49 *Wolski* Józef, Sur l'authenticité des traités romano-perses: IrAnt 27 (1992) 169-187.

d50 **Yamauchi** Edwin M., Persia and the Bible 1990 ➤ 6,b553; 7,b200:   ᴿCBQ 54 (1992) 138s (D. L. *Smith*: useful beginning reference; conservative defenses debatable); CritRR 5 (1992) 109s (J. W. *Wright*: useful data and photos, but questionably conservative guidelines); Interpretation 46 (1992) 100s (S. P. *Brock*); JQR 83 (1992s) 256-261 (J. R. *Russell*: stops short of well-structured discussion); RExp 88 (1991) 98 (J. D. W. *Watts*: not ground-breaking but helpful).

Q5   *Historia Anatoliae:* **Asia Minor, Hittites** [➤ T8.2], **Armenia** [➤ T8.9].

d51 *a) Bryce* T. R.,   The role of Telepinu, the priest, in the Hittite kingdom; – *b) de Martino* Stefano,   I rapporti tra Ittiti e Hurriti durante il regno di Muršili I; – *c) Freu* J.,   Les guerres syriennes de Suppiluliuma et la fin de l'ère amarnienne: Hethitica 11 (1992) 5-18 / 19-37 / 39-101.

d51* *Cline* Eric,   A possible Hittite embargo against the Mycenaeans: Historia 40 (1991) 1-9.

d52 *a) Edel* Elmar,   Neues zur Schwurgötterliste im Hethitervertrag; – *b) Vittmann* Günter,   Lässt sich der mitannische Mitra hieroglyphisch nachweisen?:   ➤ 96, ᶠKÁKOSY L. 1992, 119-124 / 603-610.

d52* *McMahon* Gregory,   Hittites in the OT [5 references are to the Neo-Hittites of North Syria; earlier (Gn 23) references are to the Hattī]:   ➤ 741, AnchorDB 3 (1992) 231-3 [*al.* Hittite history, religion, texts 219-231].

d53 *a) Mora* Clélia,   Artistes, artisans et scribes entre Kargamiš et Ḫatti au XIIIᵉ siècle; – *b) Carruba* Onofrio,   Luwier in Kappadokien; – *c) Negri-Scafa* Paola,   Scribes locaux et scribes itinérants dans le royaume d'Arrapḫa; – *d) Gonnet* Hatice,   Un cas d'adaptation de l'écriture hiéroglyphique louvite à la langue hourrite: ➤ 683, Circulation 1991/2 241-9; 8 fig. / 251-7 / 235-240 / 267s; 4 fig.

d54 *a) Mora* Clelia,   KUB XXI 33 e l'identità di Muršili III; – *b) Hagenbuchner* Albertino,   War der ᴸᵁ*tuḫkanti* Neriqqaili ein Sohn Ḫattušilis III.?: SMEA 29 (1992) 127-148 / 111-126.

d55 ᵀᴱMurphy Edwin,   DIODORUS Siculus [II], The antiquities of Asia. New Brunswick 1989, Transaction. 130 p. 18 pl.

d57 **Rémy** Bernard,   Les fastes sénatoriaux des provinces romaines d'Anatolie au Haut-Empire (31 av.-284 apr. J.-C.) 1988 ➤ 3,b798... 5,b532 [index!]:   ᴿGnomon 64 (1992) 337-340 (H. *Halfmann*).

d58 *Şahim* Sencer,   Statthalter der Provinzen Pamphylia-Lycia und Bithynia-Pontus in der Zeit der Statusänderung beider Provinzen unter Mark Aurel und Lucius Verus: EpAnat 20 (1992) 77-89; pl. 3; p. 90 Özet.

d59 *Tybout* R. A.,   Barbarians in Phrygia; a new grave stele: EpAnat 20 (1992) 35-41; pl. 2; p. 42 Özet.

Q6.1   **Historia Graeciae classicae.**

d60 ᴱ**Acquaro** E., *al.*,   Momenti precoloniali nel Mediterraneo antico 1985/8 ➤ 5,811:   ᴿRPg 65,2 (1991) 29-33 (É. *Will*).

d61 *a) Bakhuizen* S. C.,   Carriers of the Mediterranean and Black Seas; an aspect of the relations between Greece and foreign countries in the archaic age; – b) *Blázquez* J. M., La colonisation grecque dans la Mer Noire et la péninsule ibérique; similitudes et différences, VII-V siècles av. J.-C.: ➤ 724, Black Sea 1987/90, 396-410 / 429-441.

d62 **Bauslaugh** Robert A., The concept of neutrality in classical Greece. Berkeley 1991, Univ. California. xxiii-305 p. $45. – ᴿClasR 42 (1992) 377s (H. D. *Westlake*).

d63 **Bengtson** Hermann † 2.XI.1989, Geschichte der alten Welt 1989 ➤ 7,214: ᴿHZ 253 (1991) 155s (D. *Vollmer*).

d64 **Bengtson** Hermann, History of Greece [⁵1977], ᵀᴱ*Bloedow* Edmond F., 1988 ➤ 5,b543; 6,b570: ᴿLatomus 51 (1992) 468s (B. *Rochette*).

d65 **Bleicken** Jochen, Die athenische Demokratie 1985 ➤ 3,b811; 4,d315: ᴿGrazBeit 18 (1992) 283-7 (W. *Nippel*).

d66 *Bouquiaux-Simon* Audette, **Mertens** Paul, Les papyrus de THUCYDIDE: CdÉ 66 (1991) 198-210.

d67 *Brodersen* Kai, Zur Überlieferung von DIODORs Geschichtswerk: ZPapEp 94 (1992) 95-100.

d68 **Bubel** Frank, HERODOT-Bibliographie 1980-1988: AltWTSt 20. Hildesheim 1991, Olms. 63 p. 3-487-09507-6 [OIAc 5,16].

d69 **Cabanes** Pierre, Introduction à l'histoire de l'Antiquité. P 1992, Colin. 187 p.; maps. – ᴿRÉAnc 94 (1992) 498 (Danièle *Auserne-Berranger*).

d70 **Carothers** Joan J., The Pylian kingdom; a case study of an early state: diss. UCLA 1992, ᴰ*Carter* Elizabeth. 427 p. 92-19151. – DissA 53 (1992s) 193-A.

d71 **Carter** L. B., The quiet Athenian 1986 ➤ 3,b817... 7,b221: ᴿGnomon 64 (1992) 321-5 (Elke *Stein-Hölkeskamp*).

Cohen David, Law, sexuality and society... Athens 1991 ➤ b311.

d73 **Cole** T., The origins of rhetoric in ancient Greece. Baltimore 1991, Johns Hopkins Univ. xiv-192. $30. – ᴿMnemosyne 45 (1992) 387-392 (D. M. *Schenkeveld*).

d74 **Detienne** Marcel, *Vernant* Jean-Pierre, Cunning intelligence in Greek culture and society [Les ruses de l'intelligence; la Métis des Grecs 1974], ᵀ*Lloyd* Janet. Ch 1991, Univ. [vi-] 337 p. 0-226-14347-3.

d74* **Drews** Robert, The coming of the Greeks 1988 ➤ 4,d330... 7,b224: AcAHung 44 (1992) 435s (J. *Makkay*); BASOR 285 (1992) 95s (N. *Yoffee*).

d75 **Ducat** Jean, Les hilotes: BCH supp 20. P 1990, ÉcFrAthènes / de Boccard. vii-212 p. 2-86958-034-7. – ᴿAntClas 61 (1992) 570s (J.-M. *Hannick*: plutôt ce que les Grecs en ont dit); ClasPg 87 (1992) 260-3 (P. *Cartledge*); ClasR 42 (1992) 358-360 (M. *Whitby*).

d76 **Ducat** Jean, ARISTOTE et la réforme de Clisthène: BCH 116 (1992) 37-51.

d77 **Due** Bodil, The Cyropaedia; XENOPHON's aims and methods. Aarhus 1989, Univ. 264 p. Dk 162. – ᴿClasR 42 (1992) 284s (C. *Tuplin*).

d78 **Ellis** J. R., The structure and argument of THUCYDIDES' archaeology ['ring-composition' of his apparently disordered Book I]: ClasAnt 10 (1991) 344-380.

d79 **Evans** J. A. S., HERODOTUS, explorer of the past; three essays. Princeton 1991, Univ. xi-166 p. – ᴿPhoenix 46 (Toronto 1992) 174-8 (D. *Konstan*, also on SHIMRON B. 1989 & ᴱ*Nenci* G.).

d80 **Fehling** Detlev, HERODOTUS and his sources; citation, invention and narrative art [1971], ᵀ*Howie* J. G. 1989 ➤ 6,b582: ᴿAnzAltW 43 (1990) 49-55 (R. *Bichler*).

d81 **Figueira** Thomas J.,   Athens and Aigina in the age of imperial colonization.   Baltimore 1991, Johns Hopkins Univ.   xii-274 p. $30. – ᴿAmHR 97 (1992) 1494s (T. W. *Gallant*).

d82 ᴱ**Foulon** Eric, livre X; *Weil* Raymond, livre XI: POLYBE, Histoires: Coll. Budé.   P 1990, BLettres. 195 (d.) p. – ᴿGnomon 64 (1922) 200-4 (J. M. *Moore*, Eng.).

d83 **Gehrke** Hans-J.,   Jenseits von Athen and Sparta 1986→ 2,9440; 4,d338: ᴿAnzAltW 45,1 (1992) 75-80 (C. *Ulf*).

d84 **Gould** John,   Give and take in HERODOTUS (15th Myres Lecture).   Ox 1991, Leopard's Head.   19 p. £3.50.   0-904920-22-4. – ᴿClasW 96 (1992s) 249s (D. *Lateiner*).

d85 **Gould** J.,   HERODOTUS: Historians on historians.   L 1989, Weidenfeld & N.   xii-164 p.; 2 maps. £15; pa. £6. – ᴿJHS 112 (1992) 182-4 (H. *Bowden*, also on FEHLING D., LATEINER D.).

d86 **Gray** Vivienne,   The character of XENOPHON's Hellenica 1989 → 5,b564: ᴿClasR 42 (1992) 281-4 (J. *Moles*).

d87 *Gschnitzer* Fritz,   Bemerkungen zum Zusammenwirken von Magistraten und Priestern in der griechischen Welt: Ktema 14 (1989) 31-38.

d88 **Hansen** Mogens H.,   The Athenian democracy in the age of Demosthenes; structure, principles and ideology.   Ox 1991, Blackwell. xvi-410 p.; 6 maps. £49.50; pa. £16. – ᴿClasR 42 (1992) 365-7 (P. J. *Rhodes*); GreeceR 39 (1992) 98s (J. *Salmon*).

d90 *Hansen* Mogens H.,   Athenian democracy; institutions and ideology [BLEICKEN J., Die athenische Demokratie 1985]: ClasPg 86 (1991) 137-148.

d91 **Hornblower** Simon,   A commentary on THUCYDIDES I (1-3).   Ox 1991, UP.   xi-548 p. £60.   0-19-814880-1. – ᴿClasR 42 (1992) 279-281 (P. J. *Rhodes*); ClasW 86 (1992) 243s (J. E. *Ziolkowski*); GreeceR 39 (1992) 237 (J. *Salmon*).

d92 **Karavites** P. P. (*Wren* Thomas),   Promise-giving and treaty-making; Homer and the Near East: MnemosyneBt. Leiden 1992, Brill. x-224 p. ƒ120. 90-04-09567-5 [BL 93,41, W. *Johnstone*].

d93 **Kearns** Emily,   The heroes of Attica: BInstClas supp 57, 1989 → 6,b598: ᴿJHS 112 (1992) 199 (R. G. *Osborne*); Phoenix 46 (Toronto 1992) 186-190 (R. *Develin*).

d94 *Kertész* István,   Schlacht und 'Lauf' bei Marathon — Legende und Wirklichkeit: Nikephoros 4 (1991) 155-160.

d95 ᴱ**Kinzl** K. H.,   Problems and method in Greek history = ÉchMC 32 (Calgary 1988) 285-450. – ᴿAnzAltW 45,1 (1992) 80-82 (H. *Grassl*).

d96 **Krawczuk** Aleksander,   Der Trojanische Krieg; Mythos und Geschichte. Lp 1990, Urania.   272 p.; 53 fig. – ᴿGymnasium 99 (1992) 60s (V. *Riedel*).

d97 **Lateiner** Donald,   The historical method of HERODOTUS; Phoenix Supp. 22, 1989 → 6,b600; 7,b239:   ᴿAnJPg 113 (1992) 99-103 (B. *Jordan* does not like his style).

d98 *a*) *Lévy* Edmond,   HÉRODOTE *philobarbaros* ou la vision du barbare chez Hérodote; – *b*) *Hodot* René,   Le vice, c'est les autres: → 665, ᴱLonis R., L'étranger dans le monde grec 1991/2, 193-244 / 169-183.

d99 **Ling** Roger,   The Greek world: Making of the Past. 1990, Bedrick. 160 p. $20; pa. $17.   0-87226-301-0; -229-4. – ᴿBA 54 (1991) 180 (C. P. *Lawrence*).

d100 *Littman* Robert J.,   Kinship and politics in Athens, 600-400 B.C.: Studia Classica 2.   NY 1990, P. Lang.   347 p. $61.   0-8204-1159-0. – ᴿClasR 42 (1992) 362s (C. *Tuplin*).

d102 **Long** Timothy,   Repetition and variation in the [7] short stories of HERODOTUS: BeitKLPg 179, 1987 ➤ 5,b590; 6,b604:   ᴿJHS 112 (1992) 184s (D. *Harvey*: based on false presuppositions; 200 of his contentions unconvincing).

d104 **Longo** Chiara, *Fuscagni* Stefania,   Fonti per la storia greca dall'età micenea all'ellenismo. F 1989, Sansone. viii-835 p. Lit. 50.000. – ᴿCC 143 (1992,1) 409s (P. P. *Rizzo*).

d107 **Loraux** Nicole,   Il femminile e l'uomo greco [Les expériences de Tirésias 1989 ➤ 5,b590*],ᵀ.   R 1991, Laterza.   377 p. Lit. 68.000.

d110 **Manville** Phillip B.,   The origins of citizenship in ancient Athens. Princeton 1990, Univ.   309 p. $35.   0-691-09442-X. – ᴿClasR 42 (1992) 360-2 (P. J. *Rhodes*).

d112 **Meier** Christian,   The Greek discovery of politics [1980], ᵀ. CM 1990, Harvard, ix-305 p. £26. – ᴿClasR 42 (1992) 99-101 (P. *Cartledge*).

d115 ᴱ**Meiggs** Russel, *Lewis* David,   A selection of Greek historical inscriptions to the end of the fifth century B.C.²ʳᵉᵛ [¹1971 = 1984]. Ox 1988, Clarendon. – ᴿGnomon 64 (1992) 359s (H. *Heinen*).

d116 **Meissner** Burkhard,   Lo storiografo emarginato; osservazioni sulla storiografia del primo ellenismo: RivCuClasMed 34 (1992) 191-222.

d117 **Meister** Klaus,   La storiografia greca, dalle origini alla fine dell'Ellenismo [1990 ➤ 7,b246*],   ᵀTosti Croce Mauro: Manuali 32.   R 1992, Laterza.   xi-298 p.   88-420-4061-4.

d118 *Morel* J. Paul,   Archéologie et textes; l'exemple de la colonisation grecque en occident: ➤ 724, Black Sea 1987/90, 356-368.

d119 ᴱ**Nenci** G., *Reverdin* O.,   HÉRODOTE et les peuples non grecs: Entretiens 35. Genève 1990, Fondation Hardt.   vii-350 p. Fs 68. – ᴿClasR 42 (1992) 277-9 (Stephanie *West*).

d120 **Ober** Josiah,   Mass and elite in democratic Athens 1989 ➤ 6,b607; 7,b248:   ᴿAmJPg 113 (1992) 110-5 (Cynthia *Patterson*); ClasPg 86 (1991) 67-74 (H. *Yunis*); HZ 253 (1991) 699s (Elke *Stein-Hölleskamp*).

d121 **Ostwald** Martin,   From popular sovereignty to the sovereignty of law... Athens 1986 ➤ 4,d371; 6,b601:   ᴿMnemosyne 45 (1992) 273-7 (H. W. *Pleket*).

d122 *Prachner* Gottfried,   Geschichtsdidaktische Ansätze in der Geschichtsschreibung des THUKYDIDES: ➤ 95, ꜰJEISMANN K. 1990, 18-36.

d124 **Prado** Jean-Jacques,   L'invasion de la Méditerranée par les peuples de l'Océan; XIIIᵉ siècle av. J.-C.; une réécriture de l'histoire antique. P 1992, Harmattan.   267 p.   2-7384-1234-3 [OIAc 2,34].

d125 **Romilly** Jacqueline de,   Pourquoi la Grèce?²   P 1992, Fallois.   311 p. F 130.   2-87706-155-8 – ᴿBBudé (1992) 320-5 (A. *Michel*).

d126 *a*) *Romilly* Jacqueline de,   Isocrates and Europe; – *b*) *Hansen* Mogens H., The tradition of the Athenian democracy A.D. 1750-1990:   GreeceR 39 (1992) 4-11 / 12-30.

d127 **Sagan** Eli,   The honey and the hemlock; democracy and paranoia in ancient Athens and modern America. NY 1991, Basic. ix-429 p. $27. 0-465-03058-0. – ᴿClasW 86 (1992s) 35 (D. *Lester*).

d128 **Samuel** Alan E.,   The promise of the west 1988 ➤ 4,d384... 7,b262: ᴿÉtClas 60 (1992) 176s (H. *Leclercq*).

d128* ᴱ**Schmitt-Pantel** Pauline,   *a*) L'antiquité [ᴱ**Duby** Georges, *Perrot* Michelle], Histoire des femmes en Occident 1 [ital. 1991 ➤ 7,b182] ➤ 7,b418:   ᴿClasR 42 (1992) 124-6 (Gillian *Clark*); JRS 82 (1992) 234s (S. *Treggiari*); RELat 70 (1992) 341s (Nicole *Boëls-Janssen*).

— *b*) From ancient goddesses to Christian saints: A history of woman in the west [ital. 1990 ➤ 7,b182], ᵀ*Goldhammer* A. CM 1992, Harvard Univ. xxiii-572 p. $30. 0-674-40370-3 [NTAbs 37, p. 316].

d129 **Sealey** Raphael, Women and law in classical Greece. Chapel Hill 1990, Univ. N. Carolina. 202 p. – ᴿRÉG 105 (1992) 607s (Hélène *Cassimatis*); ZSav-R 109 (1992) 588-591 (Éva *Jakab*).

d130 **Shapiro** Susan O., The role of advice in HERODOTUS' 'Histories': diss. Texas, ᴰ*Green* P. Austin 1992. 480 p. 92-25725. – DissA 53 (1992s) 1149-A.

d131 **Shimron** Binyamin, Politics and belief in HERODOTUS: HistEinz 58, 1989 ➤ 6,b620; 7,b265: ᴿHZ 253 (1991) 157s (J. *Cobet*).

d132 **Shrimpton** Gordon S., THEOPOMPUS the historian [c. 350 B.C., from the 409 surviving fragments]. Buffalo 1991, McGill-Queens Univ. xviii-346 p. $50. – ᴿAmHR 97 (1992) 827 (J. *Buckler*).

d133 **Stadter** Philip A., A commentary on PLUTARCH's Pericles. Chapel Hill 1989, Univ. N. Carolina. lxxxvii-419 p.; 3 fig.; front. $45. – ᴿClasR 42 (1992) 289-294 (J. *Moles*: major despite many criticisms).

d134 **Stanton** G. R., Athenian politics, c. 800-500 B.C.; a sourcebook. L 1990, Routledge. xiii-226 p.; map. £35; pa. £11. – ᴿClasR 42 (1992) 102s (J. L. *Marr*); Gymnasium 99 (1992) 61-63 (M. *Dreher*).

d135 **Stockton** David L., The classical Athenian democracy 1990 ➤ 7,b268: ᴿClasR 42 (1992) 364s (R. A. *Knox*); Gnomon 64 (1992) 557-7 (S. C. *Todd*: more balanced and readable than HIGNETT 1952, but without scholarly updating); JHS 112 (1992) 202s (Sitta von *Reden*: oversimplifies).

d136 *Swain* S., PLUTARCHAN synkrisis: Eranos 90 (1992) 101-111.

d137 **Tatum** James, XENOPHON's imperial fiction... Cyropaedia 1989 ➤ 6,b624: ᴿMnemosyne 45 (1992) 102-9 (Heleen *Sancisi-Weerdenburg*, Eng.).

d138 **Thomas** Rosalind, Literacy and orality in ancient Greece: Key Themes in Ancient History. C 1992, Univ. xii-201 p. 0-521-37346-8; pa. -742-0.

d139 **Thomas** Rosalind, Oral tradition and written record in classical Athens [her London dissertation]: Studies in Oral and Literate Culture 18, 1989 ➤ 5,b618... 7,b269: ᴿAmJPg 113 (1992) 96-99 (H. R. *Immerwahr*).

d140 ᶠTRENDALL Arthur D., Greek colonists and native populations, First Australian congress of classical archeology, Sydney 1985, ᴱ**Descoeudres** Jean-Paul. Canberra/Oxford 1990, Humanities/Clarendon. xxxviii-663 p.; [partly = MeditArch 2 (1989) ➤ 679] ➤ 5,196... 7,b344: ᴿRÉG 104 (1991) 255 (A. *Laronde*).

d141 **Vanoyeke** Violaine, La prostitution en Grèce et à Rome: Realia. P 1990, BLettres. 169 p. – ᴿTopO 2 (1992) 285-9 (F. *Picard*).

d142 ᴱ**Vernant** Jean-Pierre, L'uomo greco [8 art.], ᵀ*Baiocchi* Maria, al.: Storia e Società. R 1991, Laterza. [iv-] 292 p. Lit. 35.000. 88-420-3782-6. – ᴿArcheo 7,87 (1992) 126s (Giovanna *Quatrocchi*).

d143 **Vilatte** Sylvie, L'insularité dans la pensée grecque: Annales Univ. Besançon 446. 1991. 255 p. – ᴿRÉAnc 94 (1992) 500 (Patrice *Brun*).

d144 **Weeber** Karl-W., Smog über Attika 1990 ➤ 7,7267: ᴿAntClas 61 (1992) 502-4 (Liliane *Bodson*).

d145 **Wenskus** Otta, Astronomische Zeitangaben von Homer bis Theophrast: Hermes Heft 55. Stu 1990, Steiner. 212 p. DM 68. – ᴿAntClas 61 (1992) 509s (D. *Donnet*); WeltOr 23 (1992) 170-3 (J. *Koch*).

d146 **Winkler** J. J., The constraints of desire; the anthropology of sex and

gender in ancient Greece: The new ancient world, 1990 ➤ 7,b273:   ᴿJHS
112 (1992) 196-8 (S. *Goldhill* shows its superiority to REINBERG C.).

Q6.5   Alexander, Seleucidae; historia Hellenismi.

d147 **Adinolfi** M.,   Ellenismo e Bibbia [➤ 5592], 1991 ➤ 6,171:   ᴿAngelicum
69 (1992) 423-5 (D. *Mongillo*); NRT 114 (1992) (A. *Harvengt*); RB 99
(1992) 589, tit. pp.

d147* *a*) *Bianchi* Robert S.,   Alexander the Great as a kausia diadema-
tophoros from Egypt; – *b*) *Spalinger* Anthony,   The date of the death of
Alexander in Pseudo-Callisthenes; – *c*) *Chappaz* Jean-Luc,   Un bas-relief
fragmentaire au nom de Ptolémée-Césarion; – *d*) *De Salvia* Fulvio, 'Horo
sui coccodrilli' nella Roma costantiniana: ➤ 96, ᶠKÁKOSY L. 1992, 69-75
/ 527-533 / 95-99; 1 fig.; pl. VI-A / 509-517.

d148 *a*) *Bloedow* Edmund F.,   Alexander the Great and those Sogdianaean
horses; prelude to Hellenism in Bactria-Sogdiana; – *b*) *Fischer* Thomas,
Zur Seleukidischen Verwaltung Palästinas im 2. Jh. v.Chr.;   – *c*) *Orth*
Wolfgang,   Die frühen Seleukiden in der Forschung des letzten Jahr-
zehnts; – *d*) *Seibert* Jakob,   Zur Begründung von Herrschaftsanspruch
und Herrschaftslegitimierung in der frühen Diadochenzeit: ➤ 16, Hellenistische Studien, ᶠBENGTSON H., 1991, 17-32 / 33-40 / 61-74 / 87-100.

d149 *Bodson* Liliane,   Alexander the Great and the scientific exploration of
the oriental part of his empire; an overview of the background, trends and
results: AncSoc 22 (1991) 127-138.

d150 **Borza** Eugene N.,   In the shadow of Olympus; the emergence of
Macedon 1990 [= 1982] ➤ 6,b642; 0-691-05549-1; pa. -0880-9: ᴿClasPg
87 (1992) 169-173 (W. S. *Greenwalt*); ClasW 86 (1992s) 40 (Carolyn S.
Snively); Gnomon 64 (1992) 641-3 (R. M. *Errington*, deutsch); RPg 65,2
(1991) 45-50 (E. *Will*, also on HAMMOND N.).

d151 **Bowersock** G. W.,   Hellenism in late antiquity 1990 ➤ 6,b645; 7,b280:
ᴿClasR 42 (1992) 225 (R. *Browning*); Gymnasium 99 (1992) 371s (R.
Klein); HeythJ 33 (1992) 451s (Averil *Cameron*); JRS 82 (1992) 286s
(Polymnia *Athanassiadi*: brilliant, challenging); RÉLat 70 (1992) 383-5
(J.-P. *Callu*).

d152 **Bowersock** Glen W.,   L'ellenismo nel mondo tardoantico.   Bari 1992,
Laterza. 160 p. Lit. 28.000. – ᴿHelmantica 43 (1992) 425s (Inmaculada
Delgado); Protestantesimo 47 (1992) 323 (E. *Noffke*).

d153 ᴱ**Braccesi** Lorenzo,   Hesperia; studi sulla grecità di Occidente. R 1990s,
Bretschneider. I, 138 p.; 5 art.; II, 127 p.; 10 art. 88-7062-681-4 both.

d154 **Briant** Pierre, Alexander, Eroberer der Welt [De la Grèce à l'Orient,],ᵀ:
Abenteuer Geschichte 11. Ravensburg 1990, Maier. 176 s.; ill. 3-473-
51011-4 [OIAc 3,15].

d155 *a*) *Carney* Elizabeth,   The politics of polygamy; Olympias, Alexander
and the murder of Philip: Historia 41 (1992) 169-189; – *b*) *Cohen* Getzel
M.,   *Katoikiai, katoikoi* and Macedonians in Asia Minor: AncSoc 22
(1991) 41-50.

d155* **Cunliffe** Barry,   Greeks, Romans and barbarians 1988 ➤ 4,d580...
6,b647: ᴿGnomon 64 (1992) 640s (S. *Perlman*).

d156 ᴱ**Danien** Elin C.,   The world of Philip and Alexander 1990 ➤ 6,728:
ᴿMesop-T 26 (1991) 250s (A. *Invernizzi*).

d157 *Daumas* Michel,   Alexandre et la reine des Amazones: RÉAnc 94
(1992) 347-354.

d158 **Errington** Malcolm, Geschichte Makedoniens 1986 → 3,d333... 7,b285: ᴿClasPg 86 (1991) 160-5 (A. B. *Bosworth*).

d159 **Erskine** Andrew, The Hellenistic Stoa; political thought and action. Ithaca NY 1990, Cornell Univ. xii-233 p. 0-8014-2463-1.

d159* *Gabba* Emilio, Roma nel mondo ellenistico: IstLombR 126 (1992) 195-202.

d160 **Gehrke** Hans-Joachim, Geschichte des Hellenismus: Grundriss 1A, 1990 → 7,b287: ᴿGnomon 64 (1992) 68-70 (É. *Will*, franç.); Gymnasium 99 (1992) 65-67 (L. *Voit*).

d161 **Green** Peter, Alexander of Macedon, 356-323 B.C.; 1991 → 7,b289: ᴿClasW 86 (1992s) 179s (Sally A. *Rackley*: reprint of a 1974 limited-circulation documentation of his 1970 *Alexander*).

d162 **Green** Peter, Alexander to Actium; the historical evolution of the Hellenistic age 1990 → 6,b653; 7,b290: ᴿClasR 42 (1992) 105s (M. M. *Austin*); ClasW 85 (1991s) 730s (J. *Cargill*); JField 19 (1992) 239-243 (M. C. *McClellan*); JIntdisc 22 (1991s) 724s (D. *Kagan*: 'Hellenistic' invented by G. DROYSEN); Phoenix 46 (Toronto 1992) 284-7 (E. *Will*).

d163 **Grzybek** Erhard, Du calendrier macédonien au calendrier ptolémaïque 1990 → 7,b291: ᴿCdÉ 67 (1992) 143-171 (H. *Hauben*); ClasR 42 (1992) 371s (F. M. *Walbank*); MusHelv 48 (1991) 201s (T. *Gelzer*).

d164 **Hammond** N. G. L., The Macedonian State 1989 → 5,b570; 7,b293: ᴿHZ 253 (1991) 701-3 (M. *Errington*).

d164* *Hammond* Nicholas G. L., Alexander's charge at the battle of Issus in 333 B.C.: Historia 41 (1992) 395-406.

d165 **Högemann** Peter, Alexander und Arabien: Zetemata 82, 1985 → 2,9450 ... 6,b658: ᴿAnzAltW 43 (1990) 201-4 (P. W. *Haider*).

d166 **Lund** Helen S., Lysimachus; a study in early Hellenistic kingship [< diss. ᴰ*Kuhrt* A.]. L 1992, Routledge. xiv-287 p. 0-415-07061-9.

d167 *Meyers* Eric M., The challenge of Hellenism for early Judaism and Christianity: BA 55 (1992) 84-91; ill.

d168 *Milns* R. D., Alexander the Great: → 741, AnchorDB 1 (1992) 146-150.

d169 **O'Brien** John M., Alexander the Great; the invisible enemy. L 1992, Routledge. xx-336 p., 6 maps. 0-415-07254-9 [OIAc 5,31].

d170 *a) Oelsner* Joachim, Griechen in Babylonien und die einheimischen Tempel in hellenistischer Zeit; – *b) Guralnick* Eleanor, East to west; Near Eastern artifacts from Greek sites: → 683, Circulation 1991/2, 341-7 / 327-340; 10 fig.

d171 *Quass* Friedemann, Bemerkungen zur 'Honoratiorengesellschaft' in der griechischen Städten der hellenistischen Zeit: Gymnasium 99 (1992) 422-434.

d172 *Ramos Jurado* E. A., JÁMBLICO de Calcis y el género biográfico: Habis 22 (Sevilla 1991) 283-7.

d173 *Savalli-Lestrade* Ivana, Eumène (Iᵉʳ) et l'expansion de Pergame; à propos de IG XII suppl., n° 142: RÉG 105 (1992) 221-230.

ᴱ**Stadter** Philip A., PLUTARCH and the historical tradition 1989/92 → 677*.

Q7   Josephus Flavius.

d174 *Capelli* Piero, Associazione Italiana per lo studio del Giudaismo, International colloquium on Flavius Josephus in memory of Professor Morton SMITH, ᴰ*Parente* Fausto M., *Sievers* Joseph, San Miniato (Pisa) 2-5 nov. 1992: Henoch 14 (1992) 315-8.

d175 **Carras** George P., Paul, Josephus and Judaism; the shared Judaism of Paul and Josephus: diss. Oxford 1989. 372 p. BRD-97815. – DissA 53 (1992s) 3254-A.

d175* *a) Dexinger* F., Josephus Ant 18,85-87 und der samaritanische Taheb; – *b) Egger* R., Josephus Flavius and the Samaritans: ↠ 496*, Congress 1988/91, 49-59 / 109-114.

d176 *Edwards* Douglas R., Religion, power and politics; Jewish defeats by the Romans in iconography and Josephus: ↠ 107, ᴱKRAABEL A. T. 1992, 293-310.

d177 **Feldman** L., *Hata* G., *a)* Josephus, Judaism and Christianity 1987 ↠ 3,338; ... 6,b680: ᴿChH 59 (1990) 539s (A. J. *Springer*); JTS 43 (1992) 214-6 (W. *Horbury*). – *b)* Josephus, the Bible, and history 1989 ↠ 7,b304: ᴿJAOS 112 (1992) 315s (A. *Kamesar*: some titles of the 1987 volume fit this one better).

d178 *Feldman* Louis H., Josephus: ↠ 741, AnchorBD 3 (1992) 981-998.

d179 **Fenn** Richard K., The death of Herod [Josephus' account]: an essay in the sociology of religion. C 1992, Univ. x-200 p. $45; pa. $16. 0-521-41482-2; -2502-6 [TDig 40,162]. – ᴿExpTim 104 (1992s) 247 (A. D. H. *Mayes*: dialogue with RUNCIMAN).

d180 *Gerber* Frank, PLUT. Caes. 3,1: eine Korrektur des Flavius Josephus [Apion 2,255...]: RheinMus 134 (1991) 157-161.

d181 *Gnuse* Robert, The Temple experience of Jaddus in the Antiquities of Josephus [A 11,326s]: JQR 83 (1992s) 349-368.

d182 **Hadas-Lebel** Mireille, Flavius Josèphe, le Juif de Rome 1989 ↠ 5,b635; 6,b685: ᴿBO 49 (1992) 840-3 (G. *Mayer*).

d183 **Hayashi** Masateru, Moses in the 'Jewish Antiquities'; Josephus' political philosophy: diss. HUC, ᴰ*Rivkin* E. Cincinnati 1992. 241 p. 92-29042. – DissA 53 (1992s) 1960-A.

d184 *Horst* Pieter W. van der, Two short notes on Josephus [B 2,161; A 18,38]: StPhilonAn 4 (1992) 59-64.

d185 ᵀᴱ**Jossa** Giorgio, Flavio Giuseppe, Autobiografia: Studi sul Giudaismo e sul Cristianesimo Antico 3. N 1992, D'Auria. 211 p. 88-7092-089-5.

d186 *Krieger* Klaus-Stefan, Zur Frage nach der Hauptquelle über die Geschichte der Provinz Juda in den Antiquitates Judaicae des Flavius Josephus: BibNot 63 (1992) 37-41.

d187 **Mason** Steve, Josephus and the New Testament. Peabody MA 1992, Hendrickson. [viii-] 248 p. 0-943575-99-0.

d188 **Mason** Steve, Flavius Josephus on the Pharisees; a composition-critical study ᴰ1991 ↠ 7,b314: ᴿBL (1992) 126 (Tessa *Rajak*); JRS 82 (1992) 280s (N. *Kokkinos*); JTS 43 (1992) 216-220 (Rebecca *Gray*: source problem superficial; partly on an actual situation *not* confirmed from Josephus); NT 34 (1992) 303-7 (N. L. *Collins*); SR 21 (1992) 475s (Donna R. *Runnalls*).

d189 *Meier* John P., [A 18 (116-9) 5,2; Lk 3,10-14] John the Baptist in Josephus, philology and exegesis: JBL 111 (1992) 225-237.

d190 ᵀᴱ**Nodet** Étienne, (*Berceville* Gilles, *al.*), Flavius Josèphe, Les Antiquités Juives I-III, 2 vol. 1990: ↠ 6,b692; 7,b315: ᴿGregorianum 73 (1992) 139s (G. L. *Prato*); Latomus 51 (1992) 715 (J. *Schwartz* †); LavalTP 48 (1992) 453s (P. H. *Poirier*); RBgPg 70 (1992) 206-8 (J. *Klener*, Eng.: sensible, user-friendly); REJ 150 (1991) 220s (Mireille *Hadas-Lebel*); RTPhil 124 (1992) 94 (É. *Junod*); HoTheológos 10 (1992) 242-5 (P. *Iovino*).

d191 *Nodet* Étienne, Pourquoi Josèphe?: ↠ 462, Naissance 1990/2, 99-106.

d192 *Poehlmann* William, [B 2,119-166.647-654; 4,151-325...] The Sadducees as Josephus presents them, or The curious case of Ananus: ➤ 77, ᶠHARRISVILLE R., 1992, 87-100.

d193 **Robertson** Stuart D., The account of the ancient Israelite tabernacle and first priesthood in the 'Jewish Antiquities' of Flavius Josephus [3,99-207): diss. Annenberg, ᴰ*Feldman* L. Ph 1991. 327 p. 92-34456. – DissA 53 (1992s) 2504-A.

d194 **Rogers** Cleon L.ᴶ, The topical Josephus; historical accounts that shed light on the Bible. GR 1992, Zondervan. 238 p. $18. 0-310-57440-4 [TDig 40,84]. – ᴿBR 8,6 (1992) 15 (J. *VanderKam*).

d195 **Schreckenberg** Heinz [1. p. 141-307], *Schubert* Kurt [2. p. 141-307; 67 fig.], Jewish historiography and iconography in early and medieval Christianity; 1. Josephus in early Christian literature and medieval Christian art; 2. Jewish pictorial traditions in early Christian art: CompRerNT 3/2. Assen 1992, Van Gorcum. xviii-307 p. 90-232- 2653-4.

d196 **Schwartz** Seth, Josephus and Judaean politics: Columbia Studies in the Classical Tradition 18, ᴰ1990 ➤ 6,b695; 7,b320: ᴿBL (1992) 129 (L. L. *Grabbe*); BR 8,4 (1992) 60s (S. *Mason*); CiuD 205 (1992) 240s (J. *Gutiérrez*); ClasR 42 (1992) 107s (Margaret H. *Williams*: lacks solid evidence); GreeceR 39 (1992) 249 (P. *Walcot*); JBL 111 (1992) 708-710 (D. *Rhoads*); Pacifica 5 (1992) 226s (J. *McLaren*).

d197 ᴱTrost Klaus, Die Lexik der altrussischen Version des 'Jüdischen Krieges' des Flavius Josephus, 1. Belegstellenverzeichnis; 2. Rückläufiges Belegstellenverzeichnis; 3. Namen (1). Rg 1990s, Roderer. 232 p.; 319 p.; 328 p. DM 48 + 68 + 68. – ᴿKratylos 37 (1992) 215s (R. *Večerka*).

d198 ᵀᴱWiseman T. P., Flavius Josephus, Death of an emperor [A 19, 1-273, Caligula]. Exeter 1991, Univ. xviii-122 p.; 3 fig. £7. – ᴿClasR 42 (1992) 435 (A. A. *Barrett*); GreeceR 39 (1992) 238 (T. *Wiedemann*).

d199 **Williams** David S., Stylometric authorship studies in Flavius Josephus and related literature: Jewish Studies 12. Lewiston NY 1992, Mellen. xxiv-215 p.; bibliog. p. 205-211.

Q8.1   *Roma Pompeii et Caesaris* – **Hyrcanus to Herod.**

d200 ᴱBadali Renatus, Marcus Annaeus LUCANUS, Opera: SGL. R 1992, Poligrafico. lxx-475 p.

d201 **Bagnall** N., The Punic wars. L 1990, Hutchinson. xii-353 p.; 7 maps. £20. 0-09-174421-0. – ᴿJRS 82 (1992) 240 (J. W. *Rich*, also on DE-VIJVER).

d202 ᴱ[Shackleton] **Bailey** D. R., M. Annaei LUCANI De bello civili libri X: BtScrGR. Stu 1988, Teubner. xii-321 p. – ᴿGnomon 64 (1992) 15-20 (J. *Ramminger*).

d203 **Bleicken** Jochen, Zwischen Republik und Prinzipat 1990 ➤ 7,b324: ᴿClasR 42 (1992) 112-4 (J. W. *Rich*); Gymnasium 99 (1992) 67-69 (Z. *Hoffmann*); JRS 82 (1992) 251s (A. *Lintott*).

d204 *a) Brenk* Frederick E., PLUTARCH's life 'Markos Antonios'; a literary and cultural study [+ indices]; – *b) Blois* L. de, The perception of politics in Plutarch's Roman lives; – *c) Desideri* Paolo, La formazione delle coppie nelle 'Vite' plutarchee; – *d) Titchener* Frances B., Critical trends in Plutarch's Roman lives, 1975-1990; – *e) Podlecki* Anthony J., *Duane* Sandra, A survey of work on Plutarch's Greek lives, 1951-1988: ➤ 742, ANRW 2,33,6 (1992) 4347-4469 [4895-4915] / 4568-4615 / 4470-86 / 4128-53 / 4053-4127.

d204* *Brenk* F., Antony-Osiris, Cleopatra-Isis; the end of PLUTARCH's Antony: → 677*, Plutarch 1992, 159-182.

d205 **Brizzi** Giovanni, I sistemi informativi dei Romani; principi e realtà nell'età delle conquiste oltremare (218-168 a.C.): Historia 39. Wsb 1982, Steiner. xx-282 p. DM 78. – ᴿLatomus 51 (1992) 213s (Paula *Botteri*, ital.).

d206 ᵀᴱ**Carter** J. M., Julius CAESAR, The civil war I-II. Wmr 1991, Aris & P. vii-242 p. 3 maps. £32. – ᴿClasR 42 (1992) 446s (K. *Wellesley*); JRS 82 (1992) 248s (Carolyn *Hammond*).

d207 *Colombini* Simone, Roma, Cesare e l'Egitto nel 65 a.C. [SVETONIO Caes. 11]: RendLombardo 125,1 (1991) 141-150.

d208 **Dack** E. Van 't, *al.*, The Judean-Syrian-Egyptian conflict of 103-101 B.C. 1989 → 6,b704: ᴿBO 49 (1992) 752-4 (E. *Grzybek*); CdÉ 67 (1992) 185-188 (G. *Nachtergael*).

d209 *Dettenhofer* Maria H., Zur politischen Rolle der Aristokratinnen zwischen Republik und Prinzipat: Latomus 51 (1992) 775-795.

d210 ᴱ**Eder** Walter, Staat und Staatlichkeit in der frühen römischen Republik; Akten des Symposiums, 12.-15. Juli 1988, Freie Univ. Berlin, 1990 → 6,732: ᴿClasR 41 (1991) 144s (F. W. *Walbank*).

d211 **Edwards** M. J., PLUTARCH, the lives of Pompey, Caesar and Cicero; companion to Penguin tr. from Fall of the Roman Republic. L 1991, Bristol Classical. xv-155 p.; 7 maps. – ᴿGreeceR 39 (1992) 238 (T. *Wiedermann*).

d212 *Étienne* Robert, L'horloge de la civitas Igaeditanorum et la création de la province de Lusitanie [17 av. J.-C.]: RÉAnc 94 (1992) 355-362.

Fenn Richard, The death of Herod 1992 → d179 supra.

d213 *Ferrary* Jean-Louis, Philhellénisme et impérialisme 1988 → 7,b332: ᴿMemHistAnt 11s (Oviedo 1990s) 345s (J.-M. *Alonso-Núñez*).

d214 ᵀᴱ**Freyburger** Marie-Laure, *Roddaz* Jean Michel, DION Cassius, Histoire romaine 50s; Coll. Budé. P 1991, BLettres. ci-176 (d.) p., 2 maps. – ᴿClasR 42 (1992) 36s (J. *Carter*); RÉAnc 94 (1992) 484s (F. *Hinard*).

d215 **Grattarola** Pio, I cesariani dalle ide di marzo alla costituzione del secondo triumvirato. T 1990, Tirrenia. 366 p. Lit. 30.000. 88-77633-45-7. – ᴿLatomus 51 (1992) 939s (R. *Bedon*).

d216 **Habicht** Christian, CICERO the politician. Baltimore 1990, Johns Hopkins Univ. xiv-148 p. $26,50. 0-8018-3872-X. – ᴿLatomus 51 (1992) 660s (P. *Moreau*).

d217 *Hillman* Thomas P., PLUTARCH and the first consulship of Pompeius and Crassus: Phoenix 46 (Toronto 1992) 124-137.

d218 *Hoffmann* Zsuzsanna, Zur politischen Geschichte der späten römischen Republik [BLEICKEN J. und HistEinz 50.57.59]: Gymnasium 99 (1992) 42-48.

d219 **Huzar** Eleanor G., Mark Antony. L 1986 reprint, Croom Helm. 356 p. – ᴿAnzAltW 43 (1990) 219-221 (G. *Dobesch*).

d219* **Kasher** Aryeh, Jews and Hellenistic cities 1990 → 6,b717: ᴿGregorianum 73 (1992) 542-4 (G. L. *Prato*); Salesianum 54 (1992) 372s (R. *Vicent*: escasez de fuentes); JHS 112 (1992) 206-8 (B. *McGing*: some good work, some curious judgments).

d220 **Keppie** Lawrence, Understanding Roman inscriptions 1991 → 7,b336: ᴿAntiqJ 71 (1991) 285 (J. *Wilkes*).

d220* **Le Glay** Marcel, Rome, grandeur et déclin de la République 1990 → 7,b337: ᴿRÉLat 69 (1991) 286s (J.-C. *Richard*).

d221 **McLaren** James S., Power and politics in Palestine; the Jews and the governing of their land 100 BC-AD 70 [< diss. Oxford, ᴰSanders E. P.]: JStOT supp 63, 1991 → 7,b339: ᴿBR 8,5 (1992) 48s (J. W. *Wright*); JTS

43 (1992) 573-6 (R. A. *Burridge*: survey of 23 authors, then case-studies); TLZ 117 (1992) 906s (H. G. *Kippenberg*).

d221* *MacMullen* Ramsay, Hellenizing the Romans (2nd century B.C.): Historia 40 (1991) 419-438.

d222 **Maier** Johann, Zwischen den Testamenten; Geschichte und Religion in der Zeit des Zweiten Tempels: NEchter AT Egb 3, 1990 ➤ 6,b724; 7,b340: ᴿTLZ 117 (1992) 340-3 (N. *Walter*).

d223 *Marasco* Gabriele, Marco Antonio, 'Nuovo Dionisio' e il De sua ebrietate: Latomus 51 (1992) 538-548.

d224 ᵀᴱMeijer J. W., TACITUS, Jaarboeken (Ab excessu divi Augusti Annales). Baarn 1990, Ambo. 601 p. ƒ85. 90-263-1065-X. – ᴿBijdragen 53 (1992) 433s (M. *Parmentier*).

d225 **Mitchell** Thomas N., CICERO, the senior statesman. NHv 1991, Yale Univ. x-345 p. $22.50 [RelStR 19,162, Mary *Preus*]. – ᴿClasR 42 (1992) 110-2 (D. S. *Berry*: worthy successor to his 1979 'Ascending Years').

d226 **Nippel** Wilfried, Aufruhr und 'Polizei' in der römischen Republik 1988 ➤ 5,b701 ... 7,b377: ᴿAmJPg 113 (1992) 140-3 (M. C. *Alexander* compares BURCKHARDT L. 1988); Gnomon 64 (1992) 71-73 (L. *Schumacher*); Klio 74 (1992) 500 (K. *Wachtel*); Mnemosyne 45 (1992) 135s (P. J. J. *Vanderbroek*); ZSav 107 (1990) 476-480 (J. *Zlinsky*).

d226* *Petzold* Karl-Ernst, Griechischer Einfluss auf die Anfänge römischer Ostpolitik: Historia 41 (1992) 205-245.

d227 **Rosenstein** Nathan, Imperatores victi; military defeat and aristocratic competition in the Middle and Late Republic. Berkeley 1990, Univ. California. xii-234 p. $28. 0-520-06939-9. – ᴿAntClas 61 (1992) 588-590 (Monique *Dondin-Payre*).

d227* *Rubincam* Catherine, The nomenclature of Julius Caesar and the later Augustus in the triumviral period: Historia 41 (1992) 88-103.

d228 **Rüpke** Jörg, Wer las CAESARs *bella* als *commentarii?*: Gymnasium 99 (1992) 201-226.

d229 **Sacks** Kenneth S., DIODORUS Siculus [45-30 B.C.] and the first century. Princeton 1990, Univ. xii-242 p. $30. 0-691-03600-4 [NTAbs 36,302]. – ᴿAmHR 97 (1992) 528s (G. M. *Paul*); ClasJ 42 (1992) 34-36 (J. *Carter*); ClasPg 87 (1992) 383-8 (C. W. *Fornara*); JRS 82 (1992) 250s (F. W. *Walbank*); Prudentia 24,2 (1992) 72-75 (P. *McKechnie*).

d230 *Salza Prina Ricotti* Eugenia, L'amore a Roma nell'età di [cioè mogli e amanti di] Cesare e Augusto: Archeo 7,92 (1992) 55-99; ill.

d231 *a) Shotter* D. C. A., TACITUS' view of emperors and the principate; – *b) Benario* H. W., Tacitus' view of the Empire and the Pax Romana; – *c) Morford* M., How Tacitus defined liberty; – *d) Saddington* D. B., Tacitus and the Roman Army: ➤ 742, ARNW 2,33,5 (1991) 3263-3331 / 3332-3353 / 3420-50 / 3484-3555.

d232 **Sullivan** Richard D., Near Eastern royalty and Rome, 100-30 B.C.: Phoenix supp 24, 1990 ➤ 6,b741; 7,b351: ᴿSyria 68 (1991) 483-5 (E. *Will*).

d233 **Vollmer** Dankward, *Symploke* römische Expansion/gr. Osten 200 v.C. 1990 ➤ 7,b353: ᴿBonnJbb 192 (1992) 645-9 (R. *Werner*); Gnomon 64 (1992) 262-5 (Linda-Marie *Günther*).

d234 **Wallmann** Peter, Triumviri ... zur politischen [numismatischen] Propaganda im zweiten Triumvirat [41-30 v.Chr.]: EurHS 3/383. Fra 1989, Lang. 364 p. – ᴿNumC 151 (1991) 255s (Barbara *Levick*).

d235 *Wylie* Graham, The road to Pharsalus: Latomus 51 (1992) 557-565.

d236 *a) Yaginuma* Shigetake, PLUTARCH's language and style; – *b) Hardie* Philip R., Plutarch and the interpretation of myth; – *c) Buchler* John,

Plutarch and autopsy: ➤ 742, ANRW 2,33,6 (1992) 4726-42 / 4743-87 / 4788-4830.

Q8.4   Zeitalter Jesu Christi: particular/general.

d237 **Baar** Manfred, Das Bild des Kaisers Tiberius bei TACITUS, SUETON und Cassius DIO: BeitAltK 7. Stu 1990, Teubner. 257 p. DM 54. – [R]ClasR 42 (1992) 222s (B. *Levick*); Gnomon 64 (1992) 355-7 (S. *Borzsák*).

d238 *Bell* Brenda, The language of classical Latin poets as an indication of familiarity with Jewish institutions: AcClasSAf 35 (1992) 61-7 [50,000 Jews in Rome under Augustus!].

d239 **Belloni** G. G., Le 'res gestae divi Augusti'; … il nuovo regime e la nuova urbe 1987 ➤ 4,d441: [R]Helmantica 43 (1992) 262s (J. *Oroz*).

d240 **Blázquez Martínez** J. M., El nacimiento del cristianismo 1990 ➤ 7,b357: [R]Maia 44 (1992) 315s (Maria Carmen *Viggiani*); TLZ 117 (1992) 439 (Dorothea *Ortmann*).

d241 **Christ** Karl, Geschichte der römischen Kaiserzeit von Augustus bis zu Konstantin 1988 ➤ 4,d456; 6,b746: [R]AnzAltW 43 (1990) 72s (M. *Clauss*); HZ 253 (1991) 165-7 (W. *Dahlheim*); GGA 244 (1992) 55-65 (H. *Brandt*).

d242 *Ernst* Michael, Kurzgefasste neutestamentliche Zeitgeschichte Palästinas; die erzählte Welt der Evangelien: ProtokB 1,1 (1992) 23-43.

d243 *Fischer* Thomas, Ideologie in Schrift und Bild; Augustus als der 'Vater' seiner Söhne und des Vaterlandes: KLH-Münz 8. Bochum 1990, Brockmeyer. 24 p.

d244 [[E]**Giovannini** Adalberto], *Berchem* Denis van, Opposition et résistance à l'Empire d'Auguste à Trajan, 1986: Entretiens 33. Genève 1987, Hardt. 401 p. Fs 68. – [R]AnzAltW 43 (1990) 205-7 (K. *Christ*); Gnomon 64 (1992) 176-8 (H. *Grassi*); HZ 253 (1991) 167-9 (Angela *Pabst*).

d245 **Grimal** Pierre, TACITO [1990 ➤ 7,b362], [T]*Capra* Tuckeiy. Mi 1991, Garzanti. 357 p. [R]CivClasCr 13 (1992) 231s (R. *Strocchio*); Gerión 10 (1992) 306s (J. L. *Posadas Sánchez*); RÉLat 69 (1991) 262s (J.-M. *André*).

d245* **Kereszte** Paul, Imperial Rome and the Christians I-II, 1989 ➤ 6,b753; 7,b373: [R]ChH 61 (1992) 77s (H. *Rosenberg*); SR 21 (1992) 107s (M. *Eleanor Irwin*).

d246 **Linder** Amnon, The Jews in Roman imperial legislation 1987 ➤ 4,d504 … 6,b761: [R]Klio 74 (1992) 538 (F. *Winkelmann*).

d247 *Lossau* Manfred J., *Hamartía, anagnórisis, peripéteia*; TACITE sur Tibère: RÉLat 70 (1992) 37-42.

d248 **Marasco** Gabriele, Fra repubblica e impero. Viterbo 1992, Univ. Tuscia. 105 p.

d248* *Marasco* Gabriele, Tiberio e l'esilio degli Ebrei in Sardegna nel 19 d.C.: ➤ 726, L'Africa 1990/1 (2) 649-659.

d249 **Mette-Dittmann** Angelika, Die Ehegesetze des Augustus; eine Untersuchung im Rahmen der Gesellschaftspolitik des Princeps: HistEinz 67. Stu 1991, Steiner. 220 p. DM 68. – [R]ClasR 42 (1992) 386-9 (Jane F. *Gardner*, also on TREGGIARI S., RAWSON B.).

d250 *Osten-Sacken* Peter von der, Neutestamentliche Zeitgeschichte: ➤ 757, EvKL 3 (1992) 692-9.

d251 [E]**Raaflaub** Kurt A., *Toher* Mark, Between Republic and Principate; interpretations of Augustus and his principate […on SYME R., 18 essays] 1987/90 ➤ 6,764: [R]ClasR 42 (1992) 378-381 (F. *Millar*); ZSav-R 109 (1992) 622-9 (T. *Chaimowicz*).

d252 **Ramage** Edwin S., The nature and purpose of Augustus' 'Res gestae' 1987 ➤ 4,d519 ... 6,b766: ᴿZSav-R 108 (1991) 396-402 (W. *Waldstein*).

d253 ᵀᴱ**Rich** John, Cassius Dio, The Augustan settlement. Wmr 1990, Aris & P. xii-260 p.; 9 maps. £32; pa. £12.50. – ᴿClasR 42 (1992) 296s (Catharine *Edwards*); JRS 82 (1992) 258s (J. W. *Humphrey*).

Sanders E. P., Judaism, practice and belief 63 BCE - 66 CE, 1992 ➤ a480 supra.

d255 **Sartre** Maurice, L'Orient romain 1991 ➤ 7,b381: ᴿÉTRel 67 (1992) 283s (M. *Bouttier*); JRS 82 (1992) 284s (Polymnia *Athanassiadi*); Latomus 51 (1992) 479 (B. *Rochette*); TopO 2 (1992) 247-251 (H. I. *Macadam*).

d256 **Saulnier** Christiane, Storia d'Israele 3, 1988 ➤ 4,d531; 6,b769: ᴿStPatav 38 (1991) 194s (G. *Segalla*).

d257 **Schall** U., Augustus; Kaiser – Rächer – Komödiant. Pfungstadt 1990, Ergon. 388 p.; 13 pl. – ᴿGymnasium 99 (1992) 373 (I. *Stahlmann*).

d258 **Schrömbges** Paul, Tiberius und die res publica romana ᴰ1986 ➤ 4,d532; 6,b771: ᴿAnzAltW 43 (1990) 73s (H. *Grassl*).

d259 **Schwartz** Daniel R., Agrippa I [❶ ➤ 6,b773], ᵀ: TStAJ 23. Tü 1990, Mohr. xviii-233 p. DM 138. 3-16-145341-7. – ᴿCBQ 54 (1992) 587s (C. R. *Kazmierski*: largely defending Josephus); CritRR 5 (1992) 101-3 (H. W. *Hoehner*: judicious); JRS 82 (1992) 281s (N. *Kokkinos*); NT 34 (1992) 90-101 (Nina L. *Collins*); RB 99 (1992) 600-6 (J. *Taylor*).

d260 **Segalla** Giuseppe, Panorama storico del Nuovo Testamento³ʳᵉᵛ [¹1984]: LoB 3.5. Brescia 1992, Queriniana. 174 p. 88-399-1596-6.

d261 **Shaw** Millo L. G., Drusus Caesar, the son of Tiberius: diss. British Columbia 1990. 332 p. DANN-69792. – DissA 53 (1992s) 3331-A.

d262 **Shotter** David, Augustus Caesar: Lancaster Pamphlets. L 1992, Routledge-CH. x-98 p. $10 pa. 0-415-06048-6. – ᴿClasW 86 (1992s) 248 (K. *Gries*).

d263 **Simon** Marcel, *Benoît* André, Le Judaïsme et le Christianisme antique d'Antiochus Épiphane à Constantin³ʳᵉᵛ [¹1968 + bibliog. 1989]: Nouvelle Clio. P 1991, PUF. 360-xvii p. – ᴿBLitEc 93 (1992) 406s (H. *Hauser*: utile malgré les positions d'il y a 25 ans).

d264 **Tondo** Salvatore, Crisi della repubblica e formazione del principato in Roma. Mi 1988, Giuffrè. 299 p. – ᴿZSav-R 108 (1991) 390-6 (H. *Grziwotz*).

Q8.7 *Roma et Oriens,* **prima decennia post Christum.**

d265 ᴱ**Alexander** Loveday, Images of empire 1990/1 ➤ 7,412: ᴿBL (1992) 122 (R. J. *Coggins*); ClasR 42 (1992) 381-3 (B. M. *Levick*); JRS 82 (1992) 259s (V. *Nutton*: on the whole disappointing).

d266 *Amedick* Rita, Die Kinder des Kaisers Claudius: MiDAI-R 98 (1991) 375-395; 1 fig.; pl. 95-104.

d267 **Ayaso Martínez** José R., Iudaea capta; la Palestina romana entre las dos guerras judías (70-132 dC): BtMidrásica 10, 1990 ➤ 7,b389: ᴿREB 52 (1992) 485s (L. *Garmus*).

d268 **Barrett** Anthony A., Caligula; the corruption of power 1989 ➤ 6,b781; 7,b389*: ᴿAmJPg 113 (1992) 128-132 (C. J. A. *Talbert* compares with B. Levick's Claudius); Gymnasium 99 (1992) 182s (H. *Sonnabend*).

d269 **Baudy** Gerhard J., Die Brände Roms; ein apokalyptischer Motiv in der antiken Historiographie: Spudasmata 50. Hildesheim 1991, Olms. 76 p. DM 27,80. 3-487-09480-0. – ᴿJbAC 34 (1991) 171-5 (K. L. *Noethlichs*); Numen 39 (1992) 151s (P. W. van der *Horst*: Nero's, also 390 BC and Troy's, started on July 19, rising of Sirius and start of dog-days).

d270 **Bauman** R. A., Lawyers and politics in the early Roman empire; a study of relations between the Roman jurists and the emperors from Augustus to Hadrian: MüBeitPapRecht 82. Mü 1989 Beck. xxxi-336 p. DM 98. 3-406-33773-2. – ᴿJRS 82 (1992) 260-2 (P. *Birks*); ZSav-R 108 (1991) 432-447 (O. *Behrends*).

d271 *Cizek* Eugen, La poétique de l'histoire chez TACITE; RÉLat 69 (1991) 136-146.

Conzelmann Hans, Gentiles, Jews, Christians; polemics and apologetics in the Greco-Roman era, ᵀ*Boring* M. Eugene 1992 ➤ a722 supra.

d272 **Demougin** Ségolène, L'ordre équestre sous les Julio-Claudiens 1988 ➤ 7,b391*: ᴿLatomus 51 (1992) 219-221 (J. *Gascou*).

d273 **Ferrill** Arther, Caligula 1991 ➤ 7,b392: ᴿClasR 42 (1992) 114s (Catharine *Edwards*); GreeceR 39 (1992) 102 (T. E. J. *Wiedemann*).

d274 **Fischler** Susan S., The public position of the women of the imperial household in the Julio-Claudian period: diss. Oxford 1989. 388 p. BRD-98180. – DissA 53 (1992s) 3637-A.

d275 ᴱ**Frassinetti** Paolo, *Di Salvo* Lucia, Opera di C. SALLUSTIO Crispo² [¹1963]. T 1991, UTET. 595 p. – ᴿRÉLat 70 (1992) 295s (J. *Hellegouarc'h*: une édition de qualité, mais pas une véritable édition critique).

d276 *a)* *Girard* Jean-Louis, L'idée dynastique sous les Flaviens; – *b)* *Frézouls* Edmond, La politique dynastique de Rome en Asie Mineure: Ktema 12 (1987) 169-173 / 175-192.

d277 **González-Conde** María Pilar, La guerra y la paz bajo Trajano y Adriano. M 1991, Fund. Clásicos Pastor. 205 p. 84-404-9012-7. – ᴿClasR 42 (1992) 468s (A. R. *Birley*); ClasW 85 (1991) 748s (M. *Reinhold*).

d278 **Hadas-Lebel** Mireille, Jérusalem contre Rome [diss. 1987]: Patrimoines Judaïsme 1990 ➤ 6,b792; 7,b396: ᴿNRT 114 (1992) 129s (N. *Plumat*); RHPR 72 (1992) 317s (M. *Matter*: maigre conclusion, innombrables incorrections); Salesianum 54 (1992) 789 (R. *Vicent*).

d279 **Jakob-Sonnabend** Waltraud, Untersuchungen zum Nero-Bild der Spätantike: AltWTSt 18, ᴰ1990 ➤ 6,b794: ᴿHZ 253 (1991) 169-171 (K. L. *Noethlichs*).

d280 **Jones** Brian W., The emperor Domitian. L 1991, Routledge. xiv-301 p. £30. 0-415-04229-1 [BL 93, 121, J. *Lieu*: first in English].

d281 ᴱ**Kurfess** Alphonsus, Gaius SALLUSTIUS Crispus, Catilina, Ivgvrtha, fragmenta ampliora: BtSGR. Stu 1991 = 1957, Teubner. xxxii-200 p. 3-519-01763-6.

d282 **Levick** Barbara, Claudius 1990 ➤ 6,b794*; 7,b400: ᴿAntClas 61 (1992) 609-611 (Monique *Dondin-Payre*); Phoenix 46 (Toronto 1992) 199-201 (A. A. *Barrett*).

ᴱ**Lieu** Judith, *al.*, The Jews among the pagans and Christians in the Roman Empire 1992 ➤ 476.

d283 ᵀᴱ**McGushin** Patrick, SALLUST, The Histories I (1-2): AncH series. Ox 1992, Clarendon. xi-274 p. – ᴿRÉLat 70 (1992) 281s (J. *Hellegouarc'h*).

d284 **Martin** Ronald, TACITUS [... 'greatest of all Roman historians' p. 234]. L 1989, Batsford. 288 p. – ᴿArctos 26 (1992) 142s (Uta-Maria *Lierzt*).

d285 **Martin** R. H., *Woodman* A. J., TACITUS, Annals Book IV, 1989 ➤ 6,b796: ᴿLatomus 51 (1992) 171-3 (E. *Cizek*).

d286 **Mastellone Iovane** Eugenia, Paura e angoscia in TACITO; implicazioni ideologiche e politiche: Studi Latini 2, 1989 ➤ 7,b370: ᴱEmerita 60 (1992) 349s (Inés *Illán Calderón*); Gnomon 64 (1922) 354s (Elisabeth *Henry*); Helmantica 43 (1992) 264s (J. *Oroz*); Koinonia 15 (1991) 155s (U. *Criscuolo*).

d287 ᴱMellor Ronald, From Augustus to Nero; the first dynasty of imperial Rome [sources]. East Lansing 1990, Michigan State Univ. xv-393;
12 fig. $30; pa. $20. 0-87013-281-4; -63-6. – ᴿClasW 86 (1992s) 241s
(H. V. *Bender*).

d287* **Mendels** Doron, The rise and fall of Jewish nationalism: AnchorBRef.
NY 1992, Doubleday. xii-450 p.; ill.; maps. 0-385-26126-8 [OIAc 5,29].
0-385-26126-8.

d288 **Meyer** Kathryn E., Optima mater [of Nero, despite hostile portrayal in
TACITUS, SUETONIUS, and DIO]; the life of Agrippina the Younger: diss.
Washington State 1992, ᴰ*Williams* R. 328 p. 92-38411. – DissA 53 (1992s)
2937-A.

d289 **Mullins** Michael, Called to be saints; Christian living in first-century
Rome [diss.]. Dublin 1992, Veritas. ii-471 p. $20. – ᴿCathHR 78 (1992)
627 (S. *Benko*).

d290 ᴱ**Murison** Charles L., SUETONIUS; Galba, Otho, Vitellius [no tr.]. L
1991, Bristol Classical. xx-175 p. £10 pa. – ᴿGreeceR 39 (1992) 238 (T.
Wiedemann).

d291 **Paltiel** Eliezer, Vassals and rebels in the Roman Empire; Julio-Claudian policies in Judaea and the kingdoms of the East 1991 → 7,b402:
ᴿGymnasium 99 (1992) 471-3 (D. *Schmitz*); RÉLat 69 (1991) 297s (M.
Sartre).

d291* *Posadas* Juan-Luis, Mujeres en TÁCITO; retratos individuales y caracterización genérica: Gerión 10 (1992) 145-154.

d292 **Price** J. J., Jerusalem under siege; the collapse of the Jewish state 66-
70 C.E.: Jewish Studies 3. Leiden 1992, Brill. xiv-362 p. *f* 160. 90-04-
09471-7 [BL 93,143, J. R. *Bartlett*].

d293 *Saddington* D. B., Felix in Samaria — a note on TAC. *Ann.* 12,54,1
and SUET. Claud. 38.1: AcClasSAf c. 1992.

d294 **Salomies** Olli, Adoptive and polyonymous nomenclature in the
Roman Empire. Helsinki 1992, Akat. iv-179 p. – ᴿAnzAltW 45 (1992)
299 (H. *Schmeja*).

d295 **Shchukin** Mark B., Rome and the barbarians in central and eastern
Europe 1st c. B.C. - 1st c. A.D.: BAR-Int 542. Ox 1989. – ᴿRArchéol
(1992) 163-6 (M. *Kazanski*).

d296 **Schwier** Helmut, Tempel und Tempelzerstörung... 66-74: NOrb 11,
1989 → 5,b723 ... 7,b404: ᴿCBQ 54 (1992) 375-7 (D. E. *Oakman*: a rich
study, but overlooks Mary DOUGLAS, B. MALINA, J. NEYREY); CritRR
5 (1992) 384s (L. *Gaston*); NedTTs 46 (1992) 65s (P. W. van der *Horst*).

d297 **Strobel** Karl, Untersuchungen zu den Dakerkriegen Trajans: Antiquitas 1,33. Bonn 1984, Habelt. 284 p. DM 98. 3-7749-2021-4. – ᴿAnz-
AltW 43 (1990) 75s (G. *Dobesch*).

d298 **Wellesley** Kenneth, The long year A.D. 69², 1989 → 7,b407: ᴿHZ 253
(1991) 419s (K. *Strobel*).

d299 *Winkelmann* Friedhelm, Zur Stellung der Christen in der römischen
Gesellschaft: Altertum 37 (1991) 97-105.

d300 **Wischmeyer** W., Von Golgatha zum Ponte Molle; Studien zur Sozialgeschichte der Kirche im III. Jht.: ForKDgG 49. Gö 1992, Vandenhoeck & R. 256 p. [RHE 87,396*].

d301 *Yamauchi* Edwin, Christians and the Jewish revolts against Rome:
Fides et Historia 23,2 (1991) 11-30 [< ZIT 91,806].

          Q9.1   **Roma,** *historia generalis et* **post-christiana.**

d301* **Alföldy** Géza, Histoire sociale de Rome 1991 → 7,b411: ᴿCahHist
37 (1992) 73s (F. *Richard*).

d302 **Barzanò** Alberto, I cristiani nell'impero romano precostantiniano: PiccBtScR 12. Mi 1990, Àncora. 198 p. – RSalesianum 54 (1992) 775 (O. *Pasquato*).

d303 **Bettini** Maurizio, Anthropology and Roman culture; kingship, time, images of the soul [1988], TVan *Sickle* John: Ancient Society and History. Baltimore 1991, Johns Hopkins Univ. xiv-334 p. 0-8018-4104-6.

d304 **Birley** A., Marcus Aurelius[2] 1987 ➤ 5,b748: RAcAHung 44 (1992) 455s (B. *Lórincz*).

d305 EBriscoe John, Titi Livi, Ab urbe condita I (31-35), II (36-40). Stu 1991, Teubner. – RRÉLat 70 (1992) 279-281 (P. *Jal*).

d306 TECallu J.-P., *al.*, Histoire Auguste I: Coll. Budé. P 1992, BLettres. I/1, cxiv-176 p. [3/1, ETurcan R. 1993, xvi-241 p.] 2-251-01364-4 [-9-5].

d307 — **Bertrand-Dagenbach** Cécile, Alexandre Sévère et l'histoire Auguste: Coll. Latomus 208, 1990 ➤ 7,b414: RAntClas 61 (1992) 613-5 (J.-P. *Martin*).

d308 ECaltabiano Matilde, AMMIANO MARCELLINO, Storie. Mi 1989, Rusconi. 936 p. Lit. 98.000. – RKoinonia 15 (1991) 157-9 (U. *Criscuolo*); RÉLat 70 (1992) 301s (J. *Fontaine*).

d309 **Chastagnol** André, Le Sénat romain à l'époque impériale; recherches sur la composition de l'Assemblée et le statut de ses membres: Histoire. P 1992, BLettres. 484 p. F 250. 2-251-38018-3.

d310 *Cizek* Eugen, À propos de la poétique de l'histoire [chez TACITE 1991 ➤ 7,b359] chez Tite-LIVE: Latomus 51 (1992) 335-364.

d311 EComby Jean, *Lémonon* Jean-Pierre, Rome face à Jérusalem; regard des auteurs grecs et latins; textes: CahÉv supp. 42. P 1992, Cerf. 88 p.; map. 2-204-04525-X.

d312 *a) Cooper* Kate, Insinuations of womanly influence; an aspect of the Christianization of the Roman aristocracy; – *b) Braund* Susanna H., Misogynist or misogamist?: JRS 82 (1992) 150-164 / 71-86.

d313 *Crow* J.G., Through western eyes; a review of recent publications on Rome's eastern frontiers [ISAAC B., 1990; KENNEDY D. 1990; EFRENCH D. 1988/9]: Britannia 23 (1992) 335-9.

d314 **Dal Covolo** Enrico, I Severi e il cristianesimo ... 1989 ➤ 5,b659; 6,b825: RAtenRom 37 (1992) 118 (F. *Sartori*); FilT 5 (1991) 141-4 (G. *Visonà*); Salesianum 54 (1992) 151s (P. *Batesi*); VetChr 29 (1992) 221s (Silvia *Bettocchi*).

d315 **Doblhofer** Ernst, Exil und Emigration; zum Erlebnis der Heimatferne in der römischen Literatur: ImpulsFor 51. Da 1987, Wiss. viii-337 p. – RAnzAltW 43 (1990) 29s (K. *Abel*).

d316 **Dodds** E.R., Heiden und Christen in einem Zeitalter von Angst; Aspekte religiöser Erfahrung von Mark Aurel bis Konstantin, T: TbWiss 1024. Fra 1992, Suhrkamp. 197 p. DM 18 [RHE 88,232*].

Dodgeon M.L., ELieu S.N.C., The Roman eastern frontier and the Persian wars 1990 ➤ d36 supra.

d317 *Feichtinger* Barbara, Ad maiorem gloriam Romae; Ideologie und Fiktion in der Historiographie des LIVIUS: Latomus 51 (1992) 3-33.

d317* *Feldman* Louis H., Some observations on rabbinic reaction to Roman rule in third century Palestine: HUCA 63 (1992) 39-81.

d318 EFischer-Hansen Tobias, East and West cultural relations in the ancient world [København 22-24 April 1987]: Acta Hyperborea 1, 1988 ➤ 5,540: EAnzAltW 43 (1990) 186-8 (P.W. *Haider*).

d319 EFladerer Ludwig, T. LIVIUS IIIs: Universal-Bt 2033s. Stu 1988/91, Reclam. 263 p., map; 235 p., map. – RAnzAltW 45 (1992) 223s (O. *Schönberger*).

d319* *Fornara* Charles W., AMMIANUS' knowledge and use of Greek and Latin literature: Historia 41 (1992) 420-438.

d320 **Frey** Martin, Untersuchungen zur Religion/-spolitik... Elagabal 1989 ➤ 6,b832; 7,b419: ᴿGnomon 64 (1992) 459-461 (Bianca M. *Comucci Biscardi*, ital.); Latomus 51 (1992) 446-451 (E. *Lipiński*); Syria 69 (1992) 484s (E. *Will*); Tyche 6 (1991) 237s (G. *Dobesch*).

d321 ᵀᴱ**Fromentin** V., *Schnäbele* J., DENYS d'Halicarnasse, Les origines de Rome I-II: La Roue à livres. P 1990, BLettres. 303 p. [Pallas 39,220, D. *Briquel*].

d322 **Gabba** Emilio, DIONYSIUS [of Halicarnassus] and the history of ancient Rome (Sather classical lectures 56, 1980 revised). Berkeley 1991, Univ. California. xviii-253 p. $35. – ᴿGreeceR 39 (1992) 240 (T. *Wiedemann*); JRS 82 (1992) 257s (F. W. *Walbank*); RÉLat 70 (1992) 336s (Dominique *Briquel*).

d323 *Gascó* Fernando, Septimio Severo en Anazarbo [Cilicia]: Emerita 60 (1992) 235-9.

d324 *Gozalbes* Enrique, La conquista romana de la Mauritania: Studi Magrebini 20 (1991 for 1988) 1-43.

d325 **Grandazzi** Alexandre, La fondation de Rome: réflexion sur l'histoire, préf. *Grimal* P. P 1991, BLettres. 338 p. F 155 [Pallas 39,239, P. M. *Martin*].

d326 *Guarino* Antonio, Mecenate e Terenzia: Labeo 38 (1992) 137-146.

d327 **Gutsfeld** Andreas, Römische Herrschaft und einheimischer Widerstand in Nordafrika; militärische Auseinandersetzung Roms mit den Nomaden: Heid AltH 8. Stu 1989, Steiner. 216 p.; map. DM 48. – ᴿLatomus 51 (1992) 215-8 (M. *Euzennat*).

d328 **Haehling** Raban von, Zeitbezüge des T. LIVIUS Hist. 1-10, 1989 ➤ 6, b836; 7,b422: ᴿAnzAltW 45 (1992) 47-50 (W. *Kierdorf*); Latomus 51 (1992) 191-3 (P. *Jal*).

d329 **Ibarra** **Benlloch** M., Mulier fortis; la mujer en las fuentes cristianas (280-313). Zaragoza 1990, Univ. 396 p. – ᴿHelmantica 43 (1992) 285s (Rosa M. *Herrera*).

Isaac Benjamin, The limits of empire; the Roman army in the east 1990 ➤ d726 infra.

d331 **Jacques** François, *Scheid* John, Rome et l'intégration de l'Empire, I. Les structures... 1990 ➤ 7,b334: ᴿAntClas 61 (1992) 596-9 (R. *Duthoy*).

d332 *a)* *Jacques* François, Les *nobiles* exécutés par Septime Sévère selon l'Histoire Auguste; liste de proscription ou énumération fantaisiste; – *b)* *Baharal* Drora, The portraits of Julia Domna from the years 193-211 A.D. and the dynastic propaganda of L. Septimius Severus: Latomus 51 (1992) 119-144 / 110-8; 8 fig.

d333 ᵀᴱ**Jal** Paul, Tite-LIVE, Histoire romaine XVI, livre XXVI: Coll. Budé. P 1991, BLettres. lxxxii-153 (d.) p. – ᴿGnomon 64 (1992) 121-3 (E. *Burck*); RÉLat 70 (1992) 269-273 (R. *Adam*).

d334 **Kienast** Dietmar, Römische Kaisertabelle; Grundzüge einer römischen Kaiserchronologie 1990 ➤ 6,b838: ᴿAntClas 61 (1992) 599s (Marie-T. *Raepsaet-Charlier*); CdÉ 66 (1991) 366-373 (Erich *Kettenhofen*, deutsch).

d335 **Knoepfler** Denis, Diogène LAËRCE [2,126-144], Vie de Ménédème d'Érétrie; contribution à l'histoire et à la critique du texte des Vies des philosophes: SchweizBeitAltW 21. Ba 1991, Reinhardt. 214 p. – ᴿRÉAnc 94 (1992) 485-7 (D. *Babut*: admirant, sévère).

d336 **Kolb** Frank, Untersuchungen zur Historia Augusta 1987 ➤ 5,b691; 6,b754: ᴿLatomus 51 (1992) 437-9 (F. *Jacques*).

d337 *Kraabel* A. Thomas, *a)* The Roman diaspora; six questionable assumptions [< F*Yadin* Y., JJS 33 (1982) 454-464]; – *b)* Unity and diversity among diaspora synagogues [< E*Levine* L., Synagogue 1987, 49-60]; – *c)* *Synagoga caeca*; systematic distortion in Gentile interpretations of evidence for Judaism in the early Christian period [< E*Neusner* J., 'To see ourselves...' 1985, 219-246]: – *d)* Social systems of six diaspora synagogues [< E*Gutmann* J., Ancient synagogues 1981, 79-91, with illustrations 103-121]: → 107, F*Kraabel* A. T. 1992, 1-20 / 21-33 / 35-62 / 257-267.

d338 **Laudizi** G., SILIO Italico, il passato tra mito e restaurazione etica: Univ. Lecce 1989 → 6,b840; 7,b428: R*Maia* 44 (1992) 221-3 (Isabella *Bona*).

d339 **Lendon** Jon E., Perceptions of prestige and the working of Roman imperial government: diss. Yale, D*MacMullen* R. NHv 1991. 408 p. 92-18796. – DissA 53 (1992s) 589s-A.

d340 E**Lewis** Naphtali, *Reinhold* Meyer, Roman civilization; selected readings³ [¹c. 1950]. Ox 1990, Clarendon. I. The Republic; ix-674 p.; II. The Empire, ix-674 p. (also), $126; pa. $46. 0-231-07054-3; -5-1. – R*ClasR* 42 (1992) 108s (J. J. *Paterson*).

d341 **Lippold** A., Kommentar zur Historia Augusta I.: Maximini duo: Antiquitas 4,3. Bonn 1991. xv-740 p. – R*RÉLat* 70 (1992) 361s (J.-P. *Callu*).

d342 **MacMullen** Ramsay, Corruption and the decline of Rome 1988 → 4, d609 ... 7,b430: R*AnzAltW* 43 (1990) 237-241 (R. *Klein*); Hispania Antiqua 16 (1992) 396 (G. *Fernández*).

d343 **MacMullen** Ramsay, Le déclin de Rome et la corruption du pouvoir. P 1991, BLettres. – R*RÉLat* 70 (1992) 370-2 (J.-G. *Richard*).

d344 **MacMullen** R., La corruzione e il declino di Roma, T*Saletti* C. Bo 1991, Mulino. 449 p. – R*BStLat* 22 (1992) 79-81 (L. *Perelli*).

d345 **MacMullen** Ramsay, La diffusione del cristianesimo nell'impero romano, 100-400, T*Addumiano* S.: BtCuMod 968. R 1989, Laterza. 209 p. Lit. 27.000. – R*BbbOr* 34 (1992) 119s (F. *Jucci*).

d346 F**MacMullen** Ramsay, *Lane* Eugene N., Paganism and Christianity 100-425 C.E.; a sourcebook Mp 1992, Fortress. xiv-296 p. 0-8006-2647-1.

d347 **Matthews** John, The Roman Empire of AMMIANUS 1989 → 6,b842; 7,b431: R*Gnomon* 64 (1992) 182-4 (K. *Rosen*).

d348 *Meissner* Burkhard, Sum enim unus ex curiosis; Computerstudien zum Stil der Scriptores historiae augustae: RCuClasMdv 34 (1992) 47-79.

d349 **Mitchell** Richard E., Patricians and plebeians; the origin of the Roman state. Ithaca NY 1990, Cornell Univ. xvi-276 p. $29. – R*AmHR* 97 (1992) 1189s (W. V. *Harris*); ClasR 42 (1992) 464-6 (R. T. *Ridley*).

d350 **Peachin** Michael, Roman imperial titulature and chronology, A.D. 235-284: StAmstEpigPap 29. Amst 1990, Gieben. xxviii-515 p. 90-5063-034-0.

d351 *Pekary* Thomas, Unkonventionelle Gedanken zur römischen Geschichtsschreibung: → 95, F*Jeismann* K. 1990, 61-74.

d352 **Potter** D. S., Prophecy and history in the crisis of the Roman Empire; a historical commentary on the thirteenth Sibylline Oracle [→ 7,a571]. Ox 1990, Clarendon. xix-443 p. $110 [RHE 87,194*]. – R*JRS* 82 (1992) 296-8 (S. N. C. *Lieu*).

d353 *Poucet* Jacques, Les préoccupations étiologiques dans les traditions 'historiques' sur les origines et les rois de Rome: Latomus 51 (1992) 281-314.

d354 **Radke** Gerhard, Fasti romani; Beobachtungen zur Frühgeschichte des römischen Kalenders: Orbis antiquus 11. Münster 1990, Aschendorff.   xvi-105 p. – ᴿGnomon 64 (1992) 139-144 (J. *Rüpke*); Tyche 7 (1992) 732s (G. *Dobesch*).

d355 **Rapsch** Jürgen, *Najock* Dietmar,   Concordantia in corpus sallustianum. Hildesheim 1991, Olms. xii-1472 p. DM 596. – ᴿClasR 42 (1992) 316-8 (S. P. *Oakley*).

d356 *Reekmans* T.,   Verbal humour in PLUTARCH and SUETONIUS' Lives: AncSoc 23 (1992) 189-232.

d357 *Rinaldi* Giancarlo,   Giudei e pagani alla vigilia della persecuzione di Diocleziano; Porfirio e il popolo d'Israele: VetChr 29 (1992) 113-136.

d358 **Schmitzer** Ulrich,   Zeitgeschichte in OVIDs Metamorphosen; mythologische Dichtung unter politischem Anspruch: BeitAltK 4. Stu 1990, Teubner. viii-377 p. DM 78. – ᴿClasR 42 (1992) 303s (D. E. *Hill*).

d358* *Schwartz* Jacques,   L'Histoire Auguste utilisait-elle TACITE?: Historia 41 (1992) 251-3 [-5, *Lippold* Adolf].

d359 *Scuderi* Rita,   A proposito dell'inamovibilità e mobilità del confine nell'Impero Romano / confini naturali e artificiali: RendLombardo 125,1 (1991) 3-19; Eng. 3 / 41-60.

d360 ᴱ**Solin** H., *Kajava* M.,   Roman Eastern policy [*Millar* F. *al.*] 1987/70 ➤ 6,768*; 951-653-208-X: ᴿAntClas 61 (1992) 623-5 (Monique *Dondin-Payre*).

d361 *Sordi* Marta,   I rapporti fra i cristiani e l'impero da Tiberio ai Severi [risposta a JOSSA G. 1991]: HumTeol 13 (1992) 59-71.

d362 **Täubler** Eugen,   Der römische Staat. Stu 1985, Teubner. xxv-128 p.; 1 pl. – ᴿAnzAltW 43 (1990) 64-69 (R. *Rilinger*).

d363 **Thompson** Julia S.,   Aufstände und Protestaktionen im Imperium Romanum; die severischen Kaiser [193-235] im Spannungsfeld innenpolitischer Konflikte. Bonn 1990, Habelt. 257 p. – ᴿBonnJbb 192 (1992) 625-9 (P. *Herz*).

d364 **Turcan** Robert,   Vivre à la cour des Césars d'Auguste à Dioclétien: ÉtAnc 57. P 1987, BLettres. 321 p. F 130. – ᴿGnomon 64 (1992) 414-8 (A. *Winterling*).

d365 **Unruh** Frank,   Das Bild des Imperium Romanum im Spiegel der Literatur an der Wende vom 2. zum 3. Jahrhundert n.Chr. [Diss. Tübingen]: DissAlteG 29. Bonn 1991, Habelt. 210 p. – ᴿBonnJbb 192 (1992) 629-631 (R. *Klein*).

d366 ᴱ**Visala** Gayla,   After Jesus; the triumph of Christianity. Pleasantville NY 1992, Reader's Digest. 352 p. $24 + postage. 0-89577-392-9 [TDig 39,349].

d367 ᶠVITTINGHOFF Friedrich,   Religion und Gesellschaft in der römischen Kaiserzeit, ᴱEck W., 1985/9 ➤ 6,770: ᴿJbAC 34 (1991) 165-7 (W. H. C. *Frend*).

d368 **Wachter** Rudolf,   Altlateinische Inschriften; sprachliche und epigraphische Untersuchungen zu den Dokumenten bis etwa 150 v.Chr.: EurHS 15/38. Fra 1987, Lang. xxiv-551 p.; ill. Fs 89. – ᴿClasR 42 (1992) 162-4 (J. H. W. *Penney*).

d369 ᴱ**Walker** Susan, *Cameron* Averil,   The Greek renaissance in the Roman Empire 1989 ➤ 7,610: ᴿClasR 42 (1992) 120-2 (Helen M. *Parkins*).

d370 ᵀᴱ**Walsh** P. G., LIVY, Book XXXVI (191 B.C.). Wmr 1990, Aris & P. ix-134 p., 24 maps. £24; pa. £9.25. – ᴿGnomon 64 (1992) 123-5 (E. *Burck*); GreeceR 39 (1992) 102 (T. E. J. *Wiedemann*: good student text); RELat 70 (1992) 297-9 (R. *Adam*).

d371 **Wes** Marinus A.,   Michael ROSTOVTZEFF, historian in exile; Russian roots in an American context: HistEinz 65. Stu 1990, Steiner. xxxi-

106 p.; 13 pl. DM 40.   3-515-05664-5. – RJRS 82 (1992) 216-228 (B. D. *Shaw*, also on Rostovtzeff's Histoire Économique T1988).

d372 **Wesch-Klein** Gabriele,   Liberalitas in rem publicam... Afrika bis 284. Bonn 1990, Habelt.   iv-441 p. DM 120.   3-7749-2413-9. – RBonnJbb 192 (1992) 688-691 (H. *Freis*: nur ein Anfang).

d373 **Whittaker** C. R.,   Les frontières de l'Empire romain 1989 ➤ 6,b858; 7,b446*:   RGerión 9 (1991) 325 (M. *Ribagorda*).

d374 **Zuntz** Günther [➤ 9877],   Aion, Geist des Römerreichs: Abh P/h 1989/2. Heid 1989, Winter.   67 p. – RGnomon 64 (1992) 390-4 (W. *Pötscher*: Akribie).

Q9.5   Constantinus, Julianus, Imperium Byzantinum.

d375 **Athanassiadi** Polymnia,   Julian, an intellectual biography.   L 1992, Routledge.   xxii-249 p.   0-415-07763-X.

d376 *Barceló* Pedro,   Trajan [-relief auf dem Constantinsbogen], Maxentius und Constantin; ein Beitrag zur Deutung des Jahres 312:   Boreas 14s (1991s) 145-156.

d377 FBECK H.-G.,   Fest und Alltag in Byzanz, FPrinzing Günter, *al.*, 1990 ➤ 6,14:   RJbÖsByz 41 (1991) 313-6 (W. *Hörandner*).

d378 *a) Bertelli* Carlo,   Roma e Milano nell'ultimo conflitto col paganesimo; – *b) Pietri* Charles,   Aristocratie milanaise; païens et chrétiens au IVe siècle; – *c)* [Pani] *Ermini* Letizia,   Roma tra la fine del IV e gli inizi del V secolo: ➤ 706 (+ 677), Milano capitale 1990/2, 441-450 / 157-170 / 193-202.

d379 EBonamente Giorgio, *Nestori* Aldo,   I Cristiani e l'impero nel IV secolo; colloquio sul cristianesimo nel mondo antico, Macerata 17-18.XII.1987; Macerata 1988 ➤ 5,633; 6,b820:   RMaia 44 (1992) 202 (G. *Mannella*).

d380 *a) Brennecke* Hanns Christof,   Ecclesia est in re publica, id est in imperio Romano (OPTATUS III 3); das Christentum in der Gesellschaft an der Wende zum 'Konstantinischen Zeitalter'; – *b) Dassmann* Ernst,   Weltflucht oder Weltverantwortung; zum Selbstverständnis frühchristlicher Gemeinden und zu ihrer Stellung in der spätantiken Gesellschaft; – *c) Hamm* Brendt,   Reformation als normative Zentrierung von Religion und Gesellschaft?: ➤ 355, JbBT 7 (1992) 209-239 / 189-208 / 241-279.

d381 **Brown** Peter R. L.,   Power and persuasion in late antiquity; towards a Christian empire [1988 Curti Lectures]. Madison 1992, Univ. Wisconsin. x-182 p. $45, pa. $13.   0-299-13340-0; -4-3 [TDig 40,153].

d382 **Browning** Robert,   The Byzantine empire^{2rev} [11981] Wsh 1992, Catholic University of America. $25 pa.   0-8132-0754-1 [TDig 40,154].

d383 **Browning** Robert,   History, language and literacy in the Byzantine world [16 art. 1978-89]: CS 299, 1989 ➤ 6,203:   RJbÖsByz 41 (1991) 307s (J. *Koder*).

d384 EBryer Anthony, *Lowry* Heath,   Continuity and change in Late Byzantine and early Ottoman society 1982/6 ➤ 5,813:   RMeditHR 7,1 (1992) 103-5 (N. *Vatin*).

Cameron Averil,   Christianity and the rhetoric of empire 1991 ➤ k547*d*.

d385 **Cheikh-Saliba** Nadia M. el-,   Byzantium viewed by the Arabs: Diss. Harvard. CM 1992. 278 p.   92-28189. – DissA 53 (1992s) 1640s-A.

d386 **Chuvin** Pierre,   A chronicle of the last pagans, TArcher B. A.: Revealing Antiquity 4, 1990 ➤ 6,b865; 7,b448**b*:   RCahHist 37 (1992) 74-76 (F. *Richard*); CathHR 78 (1992) 269s (H. A. *Drake*); Gnomon 64 (1992) 82s (R. *Klein*); JRS 82 (1992) 285s (Polymnia *Athanassiadi*: naive and obsolete); TopO 2 (1992) 173-182 (P.-L. *Gatier*, aussi sur TARDIEU M., 1990; BOWERSOCK G. 1990).

d387 **Demandt** Alexander, Die spätantike römische Geschichte von Diocletian bis Justinian, 284-565 n.Chr.: HbAltW 3/6, 1989 ➤ 5,b757; 6,b869: ᴿRÉAnc 94 (1992) 283-6 (J. *Fontaine*).

d388 *a) Demandt* Alexander, Kaisertum und Reichsidee in der Spätantike; – *b) Waldstein* Wolfgang, Recht und Gesellschaftsordnung in der römischen Antike: ➤ 648* Spätantike 1992, 9-22 / 23-36.

d389 ᴱ**Dihle** Albrecht, L'Église et l'Empire au IVᵉ siècle, Colloque. 1987. Genève 1989, Hardt. 365 p. F 68. – ᴿAntClas 61 (1992) 620s (R. *Delmaire*).

d390 **Ducellier** Alain, L'Église byzantine; entre pouvoir et esprit (313-1204): BtHistChr 21. P 1990, Desclée. 279 p. – ᴱEglT 23 (1992) 139-141 (L. *Laberge*); RTLv 23 (1992) 235s (A. de *Halleux*: admirable).

d391 *Elders* Léon, Le christianisme et les religions païennes dans l'Empire romain: NVFr 67 (1992) 171-192.

d392 *Elliott* Thomas G., *a)* Constantine's explanation of his career [letter in EUSEBIUS. Life 2,24-42]: ➤ 43, ᶠDELVOYE C., Byzantion 62 (1992) 212-234; – *b)* Constantine and 'The Arian reaction after Nicaea': JEH 43 (1992) 169-194.

d393 *Gentili* Sara, Politics and Christianity in Aquileia in the fourth century A.D.: AntClas 61 (1992) 192-208.

Gil M., A history of Palestine, 634-1099: 1992 ➤ b591 supra.

d394 **Goffart** Walter, Rome's fall and after [13 reprints 1963-87] 1989 ➤ 6,238: ᴿBonnJbb 192 (1992) 746-9 (G. *Wirth*).

d395 **Grünewald** Thomas, Constantinus Max. Augustus, Herrschaftspropaganda in der zeitgenössischen Überlieferung: HistEinz 64. Stu 1990, Steiner. 320 p. DM 76. 3-515-05568-1. – ᴿAntClas 61 (1992) 617s (R. *Delmaire*).

d396 **Haldon** J. F., Byzantium in the seventh century [➤ 7,b452]; the transformation of a culture. C 1990, Univ. xxiii-485 p. £45. – ᴿEngHR 107 (1992) 114-6 (R. *Browning*: a sharp and original mind).

d397 *Haldon* John, The army and the economy; the allocation and redistribution of surplus wealth in the Byzantine state: MeditHR 7 (1992) 133-153.

d398 **Heim** François, Virtus; idéologie politique et croyances religieuses au IVᵉ siècle: EurHS 15/49. Fra 1991, Lang. 378 p. – ᴿRechSR 80 (1992) 290-2 (Y.-M. *Duval*).

d399 **Herrin** Judith, The formation of Christendom 1987 ➤ 3,d81 ... 7,b453: ᴿAevum 65 (1991) 319-331 (P. *Conte*).

d400 ᴱ**Jeffreys** Elizabeth, Studies in John MALALAS. 1990. – ᴿKoinonia 15 (1992) 76s (R. *Maisano*).

d401 **Jehel** Georges, La Méditerranée médiévale de 350 à 1450: Cursus. P 1992, A. Colin. 2-200-33091-X [OIAc 5,26].

d402 **Jerphagnon** Lucien, Julien 1986 ➤ 2,9669 ... 4,d599: ᴿLatomus 51 (1992) 917-920 (E. *Pack*).

d403 *Johnson* Mark J., Where were Constantius I and Helena buried? [York and Rome]: Latomus 51 (1992) 145-150.

d404 **Johnson** Stephen, Rome and its empire. L 1989, Routledge. vii-167 p.; 38 fig. $27.50. 0-415-03267-9. – ᴿJField 19 (1992) 243-281 (D. *Kennedy*: severe; it is rather on unsatisfactory archaeology).

d405 ᵀ**Keil** Volkmar, Quellensammlung zur Religionspolitik Konstantins des Grossen: TexteFor 54. Da 1989, Wiss. xi-244 p. – ᴿGnomon 64 (1992) 461s (P. *Barceló*).

d406 **Köprülü** M. Fuad, The origins of the Ottoman empire, TE*Leiser* Gary: SocEconME. Albany 1992, SUNY. xxviii-155 p. 0-7914-0820-5.

d407 **[Lane] Fox** Robin, De droom van Constantijn, heidenen en christenen in het romeinse rijk [1986 → 3,d87], T. Amst 1989, Agon. 742 p. 90-5157-025-2. – RBijdragen 53 (1992) 211 (Hanneke *Reuling*).

d408 **Leeb** Rudolf, Konstantin und Christus; die Verchristlichung der imperialen Repräsentation unter Konstantin dem Grossen als Spiegel seiner Kirchenpolitik und seines Selbstverständnisses als christlicher Kaiser [Diss. Wien]: ArbKG 58. B 1992, de Gruyter. xiv-223 p.; 46 fig. DM 144 [TR 88,520].

d409 **Lim** Richard, Public disputation, power, and social order in late antiquity: diss. D*Gager* J. Princeton 1991. – RTLv 24, p. 552.

d410 **Lorenz** Rudolf, Das vierte Jahrhundert 'der Osten': Die Kirche in ihrer Geschichte C-2. Gö 1992, Vandenhoeck & R. vi-158 p. DM 68 [TR 88,520].

d411 **Maier** Hans, Die christliche Zeitrechnung: Spektrum 4018. FrB 1991, Herder. 144 p. DM 15,80 pa. – RMüTZ 43 (1992) 126s (T. *Böhm*: his claim that the early Church had no special calendar requires attention to use of magistrate-eponyms and to Easter-strife).

d412 **Masaracchia** Emanuela, GIULIANO imp., Contra Galilaeos 1990 → 7, b459: RAnzAltW 45 (1992) 213-5 (R. *Klein*); Orpheus 13 (1992) 426-433 (U. *Criscuolo*); QuadUrb 69,2 (1992) 155-7 (M. *Di Marco*).

d413 **Meyendorff** John, Imperial unity and Christian divisions 1989 → 6, b887; 7,b461: RRTLv 23 (1991) 224-6 (A. de *Halleux*); TLZ 117 (1992) 549s (F. *Winkelmann*).

d414 TE**Muller-Rettig** Brigitte, Der Panegyricus des Jahres 310 auf Konstantin des Grossen: Palingencsia 31. Stu 1990, Steiner. ix-374 p.; 4 fig. DM 88. – RClasR 42 (1992) 318s (A. R. *Birley*); JRS 82 (1992) 302-5 (C. E. V. *Nixon*, also on GRÜNEWALD T.).

d415 **Nicol** Donald, A biographical dictionary of the Byzantine Empire. L 1991, Seaby. xxviii-156 p. £18.50. – RSpeculum 67 (1992) 732s (D. *Olster*).

d416 **Norwich** John J., Byzantium, the apogee. L c.1991, Viking. £20. – RTablet 246 (1992) 112s (C. *Mango*).

d417 **Pabst** Angela, Divisio regni; der Zerfall des Imperium Romanum in der Sicht der Zeitgenossen D1986 → 5,b780; 7,b463: RVizVrem 51 (1990) 222-6 (E. P. *Glushaniya*).

d417* *Peachin* Michael, [The Arabian] Philip's progress, from Mesopotamia to Rome in A.D. 244: Historia 40 (1991) 330-342.

d418 *Praet* Danny, Explaining the Christianization of the Roman Empire; older theories and recent developments: SacrEr 33 (1992s) 5-110; bibliog. 111-9.

d419 *Rougé* Jean †, Valentinien et la religion, 364-365: Ktéma 12 (1992) 285-297.

d420 *Sotinel* Claire, Autorité pontificale et pouvoir impérial, sous le règne de Justinien; le pape Vigile: MÉF-Ant 104,1 (1992) 439-463.

d421 **Stemberger** Günther, Juden und Christen im Heiligen Land; Palästina unter Konstantin und Theodosius 1987 → 3,d110 ... 7,b469: RJQR 83 (1992s) 413s (H. *Castritius*); RÉJ 151 (1992) 374s (Mireille *Hadas-Lebel*).

d422 **Thrams** Peter, Christianisierung des Römerreiches und heidnischer Widerstand. Heidelberg 1992, Winter. 225 p. DM 110 [TR 88,519]. – RGymnasium 99 (1992) 460s (R. *Klein*).

d423 **Treadgold** Warren, The Byzantine revival, 780-842. Stanford 1988, Univ. 504 p. $49,50. – ᴿEngHR 107 (1992) 426s (M. *Argold*: excellent, but the changes were subsurface); JNES 51 (1992) 72s (R. W. *Edwards*).

d424 *Ugenti* Valerio, Altri spunti di polemica anticristiana nel discorso Alla Madre degli dèi di GIULIANO imperatore: VetChr 29 (1992) 391-404.

d425 **Wilson** N. G., Filologi bizantini [1983 ➤ 64,1709], ᵀ*Gigante* Giulia: FgClas 5. N 1989, Morano. 425 p. – ᴿOrChrPer 58 (1992) 553-562 (C. *Capizzi*: primo manuale di filologia bizantina tradotto in italiano).

d426 *Wirth* Gerhard, Die Mission des Katholikos; zum Problem armenisch-römischer Beziehungen im 4. Jahrhundert: JbAC 34 (1991) 21-75.

| **XVIII. Archaeologia terrae biblicae** |

T1.1   **General biblical-area archeologies.**

d427 *a) Anikovich* M. V., On the definition of the term 'archaeological epoch'; – *b) Gening* V. F., A problem of creation of fundamental archaeological theory: SovArch (1992,1) 85-94; Eng. 94 / 69-83; Eng. 83s [88-86, *Zakharuk* Y. N., comment].

d428 ᴱ**Bapty** Ian, *Yates* Tim, Archaeology after structuralism 1990 ➤ 6,470: ᴿAntClas 61 (1992) 633-5 (F. *Verhaeghe*); PrPrehSoc 58 (1992) 417s (A. *Sherratt*, also on TILLEY c. 1991).

d429 **Beurdeley** Cécile, L'archéologie sous-marine; L'Odyssé des trésors. P 1991, Bibliothèque des Arts. 222 p.; ill.

d430 **Bienert** Wolfgang A., *Koch* Guntram, Christliche Archäologie 1989 ➤ 7,b474: ᴿTR 88 (1992) 199s (W. *Gessel*).

d431 *Biers* William R., Art, artefacts, and chronology in classical archaeology: Approaching the Ancient World. L 1992, Routledge. xiii-105 p. 0-415-06318-3; pa. -9-1.

d432 *Briend* Jacques [*al.*], Bible et archéologie; dialogue entre deux disciplines: MondeB 75 ('L'archéologie de l'an 2000' 1992) 34-40 [1-33].

d432* *Briquel* D., *al.*, Débat: C. RENFREW et les Indo-Européens, Lyon 20.I.1992: TopO 2 (1992) 69-130.

d433 ᴱ**Charlesworth** James H., *Weaver* Walter R., What has archaeology to do with faith? 1992 ➤ 705 supra: *Strange* James P., p. 23-59; *Miller* J. Maxwell, 60-74; *Willig* W. Weite, 75-111.

d433* ᴱ**Conkey** Margaret, *Hastorf* Christine, The uses of style in archaeology 1990 ➤ 6,b905; £25: ᴿAntiquity 66 (1992) 535 (T. *Taylor*); JField 19 (1992) 232-4 (C. C. *Coggins*).

d434 ᶠCORBO Virgilio C., Christian archaeology in the Holy Land, ᴱ**Bottini** G., *al.*: SBF 36, 1990 ➤ 6,39: ᴿRivB 40 (1992) 372-4 (G. *Ravasi*, dettagliato).

d435 **Courbin** Paul, What is archaeology? 1988 ➤ 6,b906; 7,b479: ᴿAJA 96 (1992) 164-6 (R. A. *Watson*: 'enormous fun to read', superb translation, but often inconsistently unfair).

d436 *Davis* Thomas W., Faith and archaeology; a brief history to the present: BAR-W 19,2 (1993) 54-59; 60s, rating of study Bibles.

d437 *Davis* Whitney, The deconstruction of intentionality in archaeology [... unthinking assumptions in trying to grasp the human meaning of the things found]: Antiquity 66 (1992) 334-347.

d438 **Dever** William G., Recent archaeological discoveries and biblical research 1990 ➤ 6,b908; 7,b480: ᴿBL (1992) 30 (K. W. *Whitelam*); BtS 149

(1992) 113s (R. D. *Ibach*); CBQ 54 (1992) 744s (P. F. *Jacobs*: his 'new archaeology' is 'biblical archaeology done sideways' since he does not recognize that Israel 'is a metaphysical construct invisible to the archaeologist'); Interpretation 46 (1992) 197s (M. E. *Biddle*); JJS 43 (1992) 140s (P. R. S. *Moorey*); Levant 24 (1992) 224s (J. R. *Bartlett*).

d439 *Dever* William G., Archaeology, Syro-Palestinian and biblical: ➤ 741, AnchorBD 1 (1992) 354-367: as in the 60-page 'Art and architecture', not a survey or history, nor anything at all outside Palestine; only a theoretical essay chiefly on how ALBRIGHT's 'probative' archeology 'has become unglued' (FREEDMAN).

d440 *a) Dommelen* Peter van, Blurred genres; archaeology as archaeology or...?; – *b) Kolen* Jan, Archaeology as hermeneutics; the science of ambiguity [TILLEY C., Material culture and text; the art of ambiguity 1991]: Helinium 32 (1992) 215-226 / 227-244.

d441 ᴱ**Edelman** Diana V., The fabric of history; text, artifact and Israel's past 1989/91 ➤ 7,428: ᴿETL 68 (1992) 402s (A. *Schoors*: 'should be compulsory reading in every theological study program'); JSS 37 (1992) 312s (J. *Van Seters*: MILLER clearer and less verbose than KNAUF or THOMPSON).

d442 **Finegan** Jack, The archaeology of the New Testament; the life of Jesus and the beginning of the early Church²ʳᵉᵛ [¹1969]. Princeton 1992, Univ. lviii-409 p.; 343 fig. $59; pa. $30. 0-691-03608; -0220-7 [TDig 40,162].

d443 **Free** Joseph P. [¹1950], ²ʳᵉᵛ*Vos* Howard F., Archaeology and Bible history. GR 1992, Zondervan. 314 p., ill., maps. 0-210-47961-4.

d444 **Fritz** V., Introduzione all'archeologia biblica, ᵀᴱ*Calabrese* M. V.; BtStoriogB 7, 1991 ➤ 7,b485: ᴿAsprenas 39 (1992) 269-271 (V. *Scippa*); ParVi 36 (1991) 476s (A. *Rolla*).

d445 **Gero** Joan M., *Conkey* Margaret W., Engendering archaeology; women and prehistory: Social archaeology. Ox 1991, Blackwell. xiii-418 p. $60; pa. $22. 0-631-16505-3, -7501-6. – ᴿAJA 96 (1992) 761s (Margaret C. *Nelson*: to expose bias); Helinium 32 (1992) 270-3 (W. *Prammel*).

d446 **Grant** Michael, The visible past; Greek and Roman history from archaeology 1960-1990: 1990 ➤ 6,b912; 7,b486: ᴿAcClasDebrecen 28 (1992) 133-5 (T. *Gesztelyi*).

d447 **Harris** Edward C., Principles of archaeological stratigraphy² [¹1979; ➤ 61,s23 = 1987] 1989 ➤ 6,b916: ᴿAntClas 61 (1992) 636 (G. *Raepsaet*).

d448 **Haydon** Brian, Archaeology, the science of once and future things. NY 1992, Freeman. x-484 p. 0-7167-2307-7 [OIAc 5,24].

d449 **Hölscher** Tonio, Bilderwelt, Formensystem, Lebenskultur; zur Methode archäologischer Kulturanalyse: ➤ 641, Pisane 1988, StItFgC 85 (1992) 460-483; ital. 483s.

d450 *a) Johansen* Ulla, Materielle oder materialisierte Kultur?; – *b) Schweizer* Thomas, Die Sozialstruktur als Problem der ethnologischen Forschung: ZEthnol 117 (1992) 1-15; Eng. 1 / 17-40; Eng. 17.

d451 **Kenyon** K., ⁴*Moorey* P. R. S., The Bible and recent archaeology 1987 ➤ 3,d143 ... 5,b490: ᴿBO 49 (1992) 498-500 (C. H. J. de *Geus*: 'a marvellous job', and admits many Kenyon views new outdated).

d452 *a) Klein* L. S., ❺ The methodological nature of archaeology; – *b) Zakharuk* Yu, N., ❺ On the discussion of status of archaeology: RossArkh (1992,4) 86-97 / 97-101.

d453 ᴱ**Knapp** A. Bernard, Archaeology, Annales [-ÉSC], and ethnohistory: New Directions in Archaeology. C 1992, Univ. xvi-152 p.; 29 fig. £2.50. 0-521-41174-2. – ᴿAntiquity 66 (1992) 542-6 (Catherine D. *Smith*).

d454 **Lance** H. Darrell, Archéologie et Ancien Testament [1981 ➤ 62,a899], T1990 ➤ 6,b923; 7,b492: RAntClas 61 (1992) 642s (F. J. De *Crée*); MondeB 75 (1992) 62 (J. L. *Huot*).

d455 **McRay** John, Archaeology and the NT 1991 ➤ 7,b495: RGraceTJ 12 (1991) 300-3 (B. L. *Woodard*: 'McRay'; BA 56,153 'Ray').

d456 **Malina** Jaroslav, *Vasicek* Zdenik, Archaeology yesterday and today; the development of archaeology in the sciences and humanities [1980], T1990 ➤ 6,b925: RJIntdisc 22 (1991s) 493s (B. *Fagan*).

d457 **Mantovani** P. A., Introduzione all'archeologia palestinese, dalla prima età del Ferro alla conquista di Alessandro Magno (1200 a.C.-332 a.C.): LoB 3.13. Brescia 1992, Queriniana. 142 p. Lit. 16.000. 88-399-1693-8 [BL 93,34, M. E. J. *Richardson*].

d458 *Matthews* Victor H., *Moyer* James C., Archaeological coverage in recent one-volume Bible dictionaries [Holman, EBUTLER T. 1991; Revell, ERICHARDS L.; & Mercer, EMILLS W. 1990; + 5]: BA 55 (1992) 141-150.

d459 **Mazar** Amihai, Archaeology of the Land of the Bible 10,000 - 586 B.C.E. 1990 ➤ 6,b927; 7,b497: RCBQ 54 (1992) 534s (P. J. *King*); Gregorianum 73 (1992) 339s (G. L. *Prato*); HeythJ 33 (1992) 329s (R. *Duckworth*); HomP 92,4 (1991s) 78s (W. G. *Most*: B. WOOD in BAR-W 1990 No. 3 found at Jericho what KENYON missed); SWJT 34 (1991s) 53s (G. L. *Kelm*).

d460 *a) Melucco Vaccaro* Alessandro, Conservazione e restauro presso Greci e Romani; – *b) Micheli* Mario, Il restauratore tra archeologia e scienza; – *c) Vidale* Massimo, Conservazione e archeometria: Archeo 7,83 (1992) 72-103 / 67-71 / 104-107; ill.

d461 **Millard** Alan, Discoveries from the time of Jesus 1990 ➤ 7,b498: RBAR-W 18,2 (1992) 4.6 (C. A. *Kennedy*).

d462 **Millard** Alan, Archeologia e Vangeli [1990 ➤ 7,b498], T*Mariani* Giuseppe, ERavasi Gianfranco: Guida alla Bibbia 9. CinB 1992, Paoline. 192 p.; color. ill. 88-215-2407-8.

d463 **Millard** A., Archeologia e Bibbia 1988 ➤ 4,d654 ... 6,b829: RParVi 35 (1992) 74 (G. *Biguzzi*).

d464 *Millard* Alan, *a)* How can archaeology contribute to the study of the Bible?; – *b)* Archaeology and the reliability of the Bible: Evangel 9,1 (1991) 9-12 / 9,2 (1991) 22-24.

d465 **Mitchell** T. C., Biblical archaeology; documents from the British Museum 1988 ➤ 4,d655 [cf. ➤ 4,d696]: RJNES 51 (1992) 223s (G. W. *Ahlström*: not about excavation).

d466 *Noort* Edward, Palästina (-kunde): ➤ 757, EvKL 3 (1992) 1002-6.

d467 *North* Robert, Archeologia e sociologia nella ricerca biblica di fronte al 2000 [conferenza per il 75° anno dell'emerito, 17.XII.1992, presente il Gran Cancelliere card. *Laghi* Pio]: AcPIB 9/8 (1992) 735-747 [645-7, *Stock* Klemens].

d468 *Ovadiah* Asher, Aspects of Christian archaeology in the Holy Land [FCORBO V. 1991]: LA 41 (1991) 469-481.

d469 **Pixner** Bargil, Wege des Messias... archäol. 1991 ➤ 7,248*: RRÉJ 151 (1992) 220-2 (S. *Mimouni*).

d470 **Prodhomme** J., La préparation des publications archéologiques; réflexions, méthodes et conseils pratiques: DocArchFranç. 8. P 1987, Maison de l'Homme. 184 p.; 156 fig. F 195. 2-7351-0187-8. – RHelinium 30 (1990) 123s (F. *Verhaeghe*); Latomus 51 (1992) 489s (Y. *Burnand*).

d471 **Rast** Walter E., Through the ages in Palestinian archaeology; an introductory handbook. Ph 1992, Trinity. xiii-221 p. 1-56338-055-2.

d472 **Renfrew** Colin, *Bahn* Paul, Archaeology; theories, methods and practice 1991 ➤ 7,b500: ᴿGreeceR 39 (1992) 108 (B. A. *Sparkes*); JField 19 (1992) 77-80 (B. *Fagan*); PrPrehSoc 58 (1992) 418s (P. J. *Fowler*).

d473 *Saitta* Dean J., Radical archaeology and mid-range methodology: Antiquity 66 (1992) 886-892.

d474 [*Shanks* Hershel], 1992 excavation opportunities; a spirit of discovery: BAR-W 18,1 (1992) 38-45, with data on current situation of mostly Israel sites; tabulated p. 46-49 in order of dates of excavation in 1992.

d475 **Thompson** Henry O., Biblical archaeology 1987 ➤ 3,d167; 5,b851: ᴿPEQ 124 (1992) 159 (J. R. *Bartlett*).

d476 **Trigger** Bruce G., A history of archaeological thought 1989 ➤ 5,b852... 7,b504: ᴿAJA 96 (1992) 163s (D. B. *Small*); BASOR 285 (1992) 94s (S. A. *Rosen*); RossArkh (1992,3) 251-262 (I. B. *Vishnyatsky, al.* ❸).

d477 **Tubb** Jonathan N., *Chapman* Rupert L., *Dorrell* Peter G., Archaeology and the Bible 1990 ➤ 6,b951; £8; 60 fig.; 3 maps: ᴿBAR-W 18,4 (1992) 6.8 (K. N. *Schoville*); PEQ 124 (1992) 159s (K. D. *Politis*).

d478 *Velde* Pieter van de, Archaeology is archaeology and philology is philology and never the twain shall meet?: Babesch 67 (1992) 183-9.

d479 *a)* *Will* Ernest, L'Église biblique et la découverte archéologique; – *b)* *Humbert* Jean-Baptiste, La chaise de PASCAL ou l'archéologie comme prétexte: ➤ 462, Naissance 1990/2, 339-346 / 107-114.

T1.2 **Musea, organismi, expositiones.**

d480 *Abou-Ghazi* Dia, [7 art. on] History of the Egyptian Museum: ASAE 67 (1988) 1-77, ill. [< OLZ 88,102].

d481 *a)* *Barnea* Alexandru, Chronique des recherches archéologiques effectuées en 1989/1990/1991 par l'Institut d'Archéologie dc Bucarest; – *b)* *Petolescu* Constantin C., Chronique épigraphique de la Roumanie X,1990 / XI,1991 (en roumain): ScIstVArh (a) 41 (1990) 315-323; 42 (1991) 255-264; 43 (1992) 433-440 / (b) 42 (1991) 265-8; 43 (1992) 441-6.

d482 ᴱ**Bayer-Niemeier** Eva, Liebighaus Fra., Museum Alter Plastik, Bildwerk der Sammlung Kaufmann, I. Griechisch-römische Terrakotten. Melsungen 1988, Gutenberg. 304 p.; 131 pl. 3-87290-044-2 [OIAc 5,14].

d482* ᴱ*Beck* H., *al.*, Polyklet, der Bildhauer der griechischen Klassik; Austellung im Liebighaus, Museum Alter Plastik; Katalog, 215 Objekte. Mainz 1990, von Zabern. 678 p.; 275 fig.; 8 pl. DM 98. 3-8053-1175-3. – ᴿNikephoros 5 (1992) 282-9 (M. *Oppermann*).

d483 **Besques** Simone, Catalogue raisonné des figurines et reliefs en terre-cuite grecs, étrusques et romains 4/2, Époques hellénistique et romaine, Cyrénaïque, Égypte ptolémaïque et romaine, Afrique du Nord et Proche-Orient. P 1992, Réunion Musées. 182 p.; vol. of 1161 pl. 2-7118-2386-5 [OIAc 5,14].

d484 **Bienkowski** P., *Southworth* E., Egyptian antiquities in the Liverpool Museum I., 1986 ➤ 2,9750; 3,d175: ᴿCdÉ 67 (1992) 291s (Jeanne *Bulté*).

d485 ᴱ**Bienkowski** P., Treasures from... Jordan [in Liverpool] 1991 ➤ 7,k13: ᴿLevant 24 (1992) 225-7 (P. R. S. *Moorey*); PEQ 124 (1992) 152s (K. D. *Politis*).

d486 **Borowski** Elie, Bible Lands museum, Jerusalem, opened May 10, 1992: BAR-W 18,2 (1992) 46-53; ill. (S. F. S.) [18,4 (1992) 22.85, letter of D. *Ilan* claims the contents 'completely ... stolen property'].

d487 **Bothmer** Bernard V., [Eg.] *al.*, Antiquities from the collection of C. C. Bastis 1987 ➤ 4,d674... 7,b515: ᴿCdÉ 66 (1991) 184-6 (C. *Vandersleyen*).

d487* *Brashear* William M., Ein neues Zauberensemble in München: StAäK 19 (1992) 79-109; pl. 9-12.

d488 *Bury* M., *Smailes* E., *al.*, Copies [moulages], Albacini collection [18th c. Rome; originally 255 pieces; 154 survive], Edinburgh National Gallery: Journal of the History of Collections 3,2 (Ox 1991). 294 p.; ill. – ᴿRÉAnc 94 (1992) 473s (Nathalie de *Chaisemartin*).

d488* *Caquot* André, Rapport sur l'état et les activités de l'École Biblique et Archéologique Française pendant l'année 1990-1991: CRAI (1991) 701-6.

d489 **Careddu** Giorgio, Museo Barracco ... scultura ... egizia 1985 ➤ 1,b469: ᴿCdÉ 67 (1992) 292s (A. *Mekhitarian*).

d490 **Caubet** A., *Bernus-Taylor* M., The Louvre, Near Eastern Antiquities. L 1991, Scala. 96 p.; 155 fig. (50 Islamic). £13. 1-870248-80-5 [BL 93,29, A. R. *Millard*).

d490* *Chamoux* François [*Fontaine* Jacques], Rapport sur l'état et l'activité de l'École française d'Athènes [de Rome]: CRAI (1992) 739-751 / 753-763.

d491 Cleopatra's Egypt, Age of the Ptolemies [exposition catalogue, also Detroit, Munich]. NY 1988, Brooklyn Museum. 293 p. $29.50. 0-87273-113-8. – ᴿBO 49 (1992) 422-8 (Herwig *Maehler*).

d492 [Déchelette] Catalogue des antiquités égyptiennes du Musée Joseph Déchelette [*Moinet* Éric, conservateur]. Roanne 1990. 317 p.; 25 fig.

d493 ᴱ*Doron* Ganya, Fakes and forgeries from collections in Israel. TA 1989, Eretz-Israel Museum. ❶ 118 + 26* p. Eng.; 21 fig.

Fitton Lesley, Heinrich SCHLIEMANN and the British Museum 1991 ➤ d554.

d495 *Guarducci* Margherita, Per la storia dell'Istituto Archeologico Germanico: MiDAI-R 99 (1992) 307-327.

d496 ᴱ**Gubel** Eric, Exposition 1991 catalogue, Van Nijl tot Scheldt / Du Nil à l'Escaut. Bru 1991, Bank Lambert. 296 p.; 367 objects [OIAc 3,22].

d497 ᴱ**Harper** Prudence O., *al.*, The royal city of Susa; ancient Near Eastern treasures in the Louvre: NY Met exhibition 1992s. NY 1992, Metropolitan Museum of Art. xx-316 p.; 62 fig.; 195 phot. [OIAc 5,24].

d498 **Head** Raymond, Catalogue of paintings, drawings, engravings and busts, in the collection of the Royal Asiatic Society. L 1991, RAS. xxiii-229 p.; 180 pl. + 30 colour. £55. – ᴿJRAS (1992) 427-9 (J. *Carswell*).

d499 ᴱ**Hornung** Erik, *Staehlin* Elisabeth, Ein Pharaonengrab: Univ. Äg. Sem. Ausstellung. Basel 1991, Antikenmuseum(sfreunde). 112 p.; 68 fig. + 51 color. [OIAc 3,25].

d500 **Hudson** Kenneth, *Nicholls* Ann, The Cambridge guide to the museums of Europe. C 1991, Univ. xxvi-509 p. 0-521-37175-9 [OIAc 3,25].

d501 ᴱ**Jakob-Rost** Liane, *al.*, Das Vorderasiatische Museum: Staatliche Museen zu Berlin, Preussischer Kulturbesitz. Mainz 1992, von Zabern. 256 p., 196 color. ill. 3-8053-1188-5 [OIAc 3,25].

d502 *Kakovkin* Aleksander, L'art copte de l'Ermitage: ➤ 690, 3d Coptic 1984/90, 179-186; 8 fig.

d503 *King* Philip J., American Schools of Oriental Research, history of the: ➤ 741, AnchorBD 1 (1992) 186-8.

d504 **Klose** Dietrich O. A., Von Alexander zu Kleopatra, Herrscherporträts der Griechen und Barbaren: Mü 1992, Staatliche Münzsammlung, Katalog. – ᴿJbNumG 40 (1990!) 121 (Margret K. *Nollé*).

d505 **Kozloff** Arielle P., *al.*, Egypt's dazzling sun; Amenhotep III and his world: Cleveland 1992, Museum (Indiana Univ. Press). xxiv-476 p. £65 [BL 93,122, K. A. *Kitchen*].

d506 **Kunze** Max, *al.*, Die Antikensammlung im Pergamonmuseum und in

Charlottenburg; Staatliche Museen zu Berlin.   Mainz 1992, von Zabern.
315 p.; 168 fig.   3-8053-1187-7.

d507 ᴱLéclant J.,   L'Égypte en Périgord, dans les pas de Jean CLÉDAT, exposition 1991 ➤ 7,b528*: ᴿCdÉ 67 (1992) 387 (Marguerite *Rassart-
Debergh*).

d508 **Liverani** Paolo,   Museo Chiaramonti: Guide Cataloghi Musei Vaticani 1.
R 1989, Bretschneider. 137 p.; 10 fig. 88-7062-665-2.

d509 **Merrillees** Robert S.,   Living with Egypt's past in Australia; Gold of the
Pharaohs Exhibition seminar.   Melbourne 1990, Museum of Victoria.
viii-78 p.; 48 fig.; 6 colour. pl.   0-7241-9673-0 [OIAc 3,30].

d510 *Meyer* Laure,   Archéologie au pays de la Bible [British Museum 1991]:
Archéologia 265 (1991) 32-43; color. ill.

d511 **Pasini** Paolo, *al.*,   L'Eufrate e il tempo; Rimini 28.III-31.VIII.1993:
Meeting 11,9 (Rimini 1992) 3-14.

d512 **Patch** Diana C.,   Reflections of greatness; ancient Egypt at the Carnegie
Museum of Natural History [600 out of 6000 objects]. Pittsburgh 1990.
x-118 p. [OLZ 88,129, R. S. *Bianchi*].

d513 **Peltenburg** E.,   Glasgow Museum Burrell Collection, Western Asiatic antiquities. E 1991, Univ. 156 p. £65. 0-7846-0224-0 [BL 93,35, T.C. *Mitchell*].

d514 *Platelle* E.,   [Expositions 4.] Dieu en son royaume; la Bible dans la
France d'autrefois (XIIIᵉ-XVIIIᵉ s.):   MélSR 49 (1992) 200-2.

d515 **Priese** Karl-Heinz,   Das Gold von Meroe; B-Charlottenburg Ausstellung.   Mainz 1992, von Zabern. 49 p.; 47 fig. [OIAc 5,32].

d516 *Priese* Karl-Heinz, *al.*,   Antike Welt auf der Berliner Museuminsel:
AntWelt 21, Sdb 1 (1990). 144 p.; (color.) ill.

d517 ᴱ**Quirke** Stephen, *Spencer* Jeffrey,   The British Museum book of ancient Egypt.   L 1992, BM. 240 p.; 173 fig. 0-500-01550-3 [OIAc 5,32
'Quircke'; 'Thames & Hudson'].

d518 Rediscovering Pompeii IBM exposition. [ᴱ*Franchi Dell'Orto* L., *Varone*
A.]. 1990. – ᴿAntClas 61 (1992) 739-741 (Christiane *Delplace*); JRS 82
(1992) 274 (Penelope *Allison*); RArchéol (1992) 156 (Hélène *Eristov*)

d519 [Nota] **Santi** Maresita, *Cimino* Maria Gabriella,   Museo Barracco, Roma, R 1991, Ist. Poligrafico. 121 p.; 90 fig. Lit. 15.000, 88-240 0213-7.

d520 **Shechtory** Itai,   Rock engravings from the Negev; Mount Karkom and
Timna [Eng. I ⊕]; exhibition. TA 1990, Univ. Schreiber Art Gallery.
38 p.; ill. [OIAc 3,37].

d521 ᴱ**Schmauder** Michael, *Wisskirchen* Rotraut,   Spiegel einer Wissenschaft;
zur Geschichte der Christlichen Archäologie vom 16. bis 19. Jahrhundert,
Ausstellung 1991. Bonn 1991, Univ.-Bt. viii-130 p. – ᴿRömQ 87 (1992)
110-5 (H. R. *Seeliger*).

d522 ᴱ**Seipel** Wilfried,   Gott, Mensch, Pharaoh; viertausend Jahre Menschen-
bild in der Skulptur des Alten Ägypten [Ausstellung Künstlerhaus 1992].
W 1992, Kunsthistorisches Museum. 511 p.; 211 fig. 3-900- 32522-7
[OIAc 5,34].

d523 *Sigal-Klagsbald* Laurence,   Vers un nouveau musée juif en France; le
Musée d'Art et d'Histoire du Judaïsme: RÉJ 151 (1992) 429-440.

d524 ᴱ**Steiner** Ann,   Corpus vasorum antiquorum, Joslyn Art Museum 1.
Omaha 1986, Joslyn Museum. xii-51 p.; 148 fig. DM 128. – ᴿDLZ 113
(1992) 123s (E. *Paul*).

d525 *a) Trensky* Michael,   Das Deutsche Evangelische Institut für Alter-
tumswissenschaft des Heiligen Landes; – *b) Strobel* August, Heiliges
Land — vom Institut aus gesehen / Zur Geschichte des lutherischen
Hospizes in Jerusalem / Der Lehrkurs 1987 in Jordanien und Syrien

[Taiyibe]: JbEvHL 1 (1989) 9-14; map / 15-19. 78-99; 133-172 [177-183]. 7 fig. (*Krüger* E. W.).
Tubb J. N., *Chapman* R. L., Archaeology and the Bible [British Museum 1990s] ➤ d477.

d526 *Vassilika* Eleni, Museum acquisitions 1990; Egyptian, UK: JEA 78 (1992) 267-272.

d526* *Will* Ernest [< Sigrist M.], Rapport sur l'état et les activités de l'École biblique et archéologique française de Jérusalem: CRAI (1992) 765-7; ➤ d488* supra.

d527 *Zatelli* Ida, [➤ 7,b542] La Bibbia a stampa da Gutenberg a Bodoni; mostra Biblia/BtMedicea Firenze ott.-nov. 1991: AnStoEseg 9 (1992) 278-281; BL (1992) 25 (R. P. R. *Murray*).

T1.3   *Methodi*, **Science in archeology.**

d528 *Angeletti* C., *Bonincontro* I., L'apporto delle moderne tecniche di analisi atomiche allo studio di materiale numismatico: RitNum 94 (1992) 265-278.

d529 **Clark** Anthony, Seeing beneath the soil 1990 ➤ 6,d12: RHelinium 32 (1992) 264-6 (Karin *Anderson*).

d530 **Cronyn** J. M., The elements of archaeological conservation 1990 ➤ 7, b548: RAntClas 61 (1992) 636-9 (P. *Verhaeghe*).

d531 **Dorrell** P. G., Photography in archaeology and conservation: Manuals in Archaeology. C 1989, Univ. 262 p.; 90 pl. £30. [PEQ 125,78, R. *Pitt*].

d532 *Fábregas Valcarce* Ramón, ¿'Tercera revolución del radiocarbono'? Una perspectiva arqueológica del C-14: BSAA 58 (1992) 9-24.

d533 **Herold** Karl, Konservierung von archäologischen Bodenfunden; Metall, Keramik, Glas: Szb 565. W 1990, Österr. Akad. 236 p.; 42 color. pl. – RBonnJbb 192 (1992) 557 (G. *Eggert*, ganz negativ).

d534 *Jansma* Esther, Dendrochronological methods to determine the origin of oak timber; a case study of wood from 's-Hertogenbosch: Helinium 32 (1992) 195-214; 4 fig.

d535 *Manning* Sturt W., *Weninger* Bernhard, A light in the dank; archaeological [radiocarbon] wiggle matching and the absolute chronology of the close of the Aegean Late Bronze Age: Antiquity 66 (1992) 636-663; 12 fig.

d536 *Mellars* Paul, *Grün* Rainer, A comparison of the electron spin resonance and thermoluminescence dating methods; the results of ESR dating at Le Moustier (France): CamArch 1 (1991) 269-276; 4 fig.

d537 *Nakhla* Shawki M., Relative and absolute dating with respect to ancient Egyptian chronology [reliability of C-14]: ASAE 67 (1988) 131-155; 1 pl. [< OLZ 88,102].

d538 *Peterman* Glen L., Geographic information systems [database]; archaeology's latest tool: BA 55 (1992) 162-7; ill., mostly black-white; nothing is said of the brilliant red-yellow, green-black of the photo beside an all-azure one of the same spot.

d539 *a) Babes* Mircea, ODOBESCU [1834-95], arheologul; – *b) Avram* Alexandru, Grigore G. TOCILESCU (1850-1909) arheolog și epigrafist: ScIstVArh 43 (1992) 119-126 / 139-143; franç. 126; 143.

T1.4   *Exploratores* – **Excavators, pioneers.**

d540 **Bauer** Karl J., Alois MUSIL, Wahrheitssucher in der Wüste: Perspektiven der Wissenschaftsgeschichte 5. Wien 1989, Böhlau. 402 p.; pl. 3-205-05128-9 [OIAc 5,14].

d540* **Dostal** Walter, Eduard GLASER, Forschungen im Yemen [1884-86-88]; eine quellenkritische Untersuchung in ethnologischer Sicht: Szb p/h 545, Arab. Komm. 4. W 1990, Österr. Akad. 280 p. Sch. 420. – [R]Anthropos 87 (1992) 260s (P. *Schröder*).

d541 *Eyice* Semavi, Hittitologues et byzantinistes à la découverte de l'Asie Mineure: Belleten 56,215 (1992) 243-260.

d542 [E]**Fales** F. M., *Hickey* B. J., Austen H. LAYARD tra l'Oriente e Venezia 1983/87 ► 5,849; 7,b571: [R]RSO 65 (1991) 351-3 (R. *Contini*); ZSav-R 109 (1992) 748s (G. *Ries*).

d543 **Fraser** Robert, The making of [FRAZER J. G.] the Golden Bough; the origins and growth of an argument. NY 1990, St. Martin's. xiii-240 p. $40. 0-312-04205-1. – [R]ClasW 85 (1991s) 54 (R. A. *Hornsby*).

d544 *Gehrke* Hans-Joachim, Karl Otfried MÜLLER und das Land der Griechen: MiDAI-A 106 (1991) 9-35 [1-7, 150. Gb., *Fittschen* Klaus].

d545 **Grinsell** L. V., An archaeological autobiography. Gloucester 1989, Sutton. 134 p.; 16 pl. 0-86299-658-9 [OIAc 5,23].

d546 **James** Thomas G. H., Howard CARTER, the path to Tutankhamun. L 1992, Kegan Paul. xv-443 p.; portr. [OIAc 5,25]. 0-7103-0425-0.

d547 *Kakovkin* Alexander, Vladimir de BOK (1850-1899) [Hermitage Coptic collection]: GöMiszÄg 131 (1992) 61-66 + 10 pl.

d548 **Kettel** Jeannot, J.-F. CHAMPOLLION le Jeune, répertoire de bibliographie analytique, 1806-1989; CRAI Mém. NS 10 1990 ► 6,d37: [R]BO 49 (1992) 364-7 (M. *Christina Guidotti*).

d549 — [E]**Bresciani** Edda, Jean-François CHAMPOLLION, Lettres à Zelmire: Champollion et son temps 1. P 1978, Asiathèque. 116 p.

d549* *Leclant* Jean, Aux sources de l'Égyptologie européenne: CHAMPOLLION, [Thomas] YOUNG, [Ippolito] ROSSELLINI, [Karl-K,] LEPSIUS: CRAI (1991) 743-762.

d550 LEKA František 1876-1960 [appreciation by Czech colleagues] Praha 1989. – [R]DiscEg 19 (1991) 75-77 (S. *Allam*).

d551 *a) Moorey* P. R. S., British women in Near Eastern Archaeology; K. KENYON and the pioneers; – *b) Prag* Kay, K. Kenyon and Archaeology in the Holy Land: PEQ 124 (1992) 91-100 / 109-123.

d552 *Ramage* Nancy H., Goods, graves, and scholars; 18th century archaeologists in Britain and Italy: AJA 96 (1992) 653-661.

SCHLIEMANN:

d553 [E]**Calder** William M.[III], *Cobet* Justus, Heinrich Schliemann nach hundert Jahren, Symposium Reimers-Stiftung, Bad Homburg, Dez. 1989/90 ► 6,792; DM 148: [R]ClasR 42 (1992) 178-180 (W. G. *Arnott*).

d554 **Fitton** Lesley, Heinrich Schliemann and the British Museum: Occas. Papers 83. L 1991, BM. 51 p. 0-86159-083-X [OIAc 3,20].

d555 *Gigante* Marcello, Schliemann e WILAMOWITZ; tra leggenda e scandalo, Schliemann dilettante o bugiardo?: AtenRom 37 (1992) 33-41 [in 1929 before his death Wilamowitz published a hostile reaction to the 'Tesoro].

d556 *a) Bloedow* Edmund, The authenticity and integrity of 'Priam's treasure'; – *b) Traill* David A., Schliemann's trips 1841-1867 and a detailed record of his movements 1868-1890: Boreas 14s (1991s) 197-206 / 207-214.

d557 *a) Herrmann* Joachim, Heinrich Schliemann — forschungsgeschichtliche Leistung, wissenschaftsmethodischer Neuansatz und zentenare Wirkung; – *b) Schindler* Wolfgang †, Werk und Leben Heinrich Schliemanns; – *c) Hertel* Dieter, Zum Problem der Historizität der Sage vom Trojanischen

Krieg; – d) Goldmann Stefan, Der Mythos von Trojas Untergang in Schliemanns Autobiographie; – e) Goldmann Klaus, Der Schatz von Priamos; zum Schicksal von S's 'Sammlung trojanischer Altertümer'; – f) Traill David A., 'Priam's treasure'; further problems: ➤ 715, Schliemann 1990/2, 93-102 / 15-21 / 177-181 / 37-48 / 377-390 al. [-401 al.] / 183-189 [-198-204, Easton D., Makkay J.].

d558 **Hazirlayan** Yayına, Esin Ufuk, Heinrich Schliemann, ❼ Selection of excavation reports and letters: Sandoz Kultur Yayınları 13. Istanbul 1991, Güzel Sanatları. 88 p. 975-95545-1-8 [OIAc 3,23].

d559 **Herrmann** Joachim, al., Die Korrespondenz zwischen Heinrich Schliemann und Rudolf VIRCHOW [1821-1902, identifier of leukemia and thrombosis, opponent of Bismarck] 1876-1890. B 1990, Akademie. 619 p.; 4 fig.; 20 pl. DM 58. – ᴿClasR 42 (1992) 236s (W. G. Arnott: both were vain; Virchow's 'snub' rankled).

d560 **Schindler** Wolfgang, An archaeologist on the Schliemann controversy: ILCL 17 (1992) 135-151.

d561 **Siebler** Michael, a) Troia – Homer – Schliemann; Mythos und Wahrheit; KgAW 46. Mainz 1990, von Zabern. 248 p.; 81 fig.; 5 pl. + 25 color. DM 50. 3-8053-1129-0. – b) Schliemann 100. Todestag: AntWelt 21 (1990) 222-4.

d562 **Waardenburg** J. D. G., Mustashrikun, Orientaliste: ➤ 756, EncIslam² 7 (1992) 736-754.

d563 **Winstone** H. V. F., WOOLLEY of Ur. L 1990, Secker & W. 314 p. – ᴿBCanadMesop 22 (1991) 52s (M. Fortin).

d563* **Wright** G. R. H., [W.] Brede KRISTENSEN [1867-1953] on the religion of ancient Egypt: JPrehRel 5 (1991) 24-35.

T1.5   Materiae primae – **metals, glass.**

d564 **Ehrenreich** Robert M., Metals in society; theory beyond analysis: MASCA Paper 8/2. Ph 1992, Univ. Museum. 92 p. 1048-5325.

d564* **Görg** Manfred, Sinai und Zypern als Regionen der Erzgewinning; Beobachtungen zur Namengabung nach Mineralien in Ägypten und im Alten Orient: ➤ 96, ᶠKÁKOSY L. 1992, 215-221.

d565 **Pozzi** Dora, Wickershan John, Il metallo, mito e fortuna nel mondo antico. XII-300 p., 273 fig. (color). – ᴿREG 105 (1992) 277 (Yvonne Vernière).

d566 **Aes, BRONZE:** Jacobson D. M., Weitzman M. P., What was Corinthian bronze? [an alloy of gold and silver, as PLINY says; not 'any bronze from Corinth', as J. MURPHY-O'CONNOR]: AJA 96 (1992) 237-247.

d567 **[Pirzio] Biroli** Stefanelli L., Il bronzo dei Romani 1990 ➤ 7,b688: ᴿGerión 9 (1991) 357s (J. L. Posadas Sánchez).

d568 **Alabastrum:** Casanova Michèle, La vaisselle d'albâtre de Mésopotamie, d'Iran et d'Asie centrale aux III et II millénaires av.J.-C.: Mém. Asie Centrale 4. P 1991, RCiv. 112 p.; 11 pl. 2-86538-217-6. – ᴿMesopT 27 (1992) 285-9 (P. Brusasco).

d569 **Amber: Mastrocinque** Attilio, L'ambra e l'Eridano. Este 1991, Zielo. 163 p. – ᴿDialHA 18,2 (1992) 379-383 (J. Kolendo).

d570 **Aurum, GOLD:** Éluère Christiane, Les secrets de l'or antique. P 1990, Bt. Arts. 239 p.

d571 **Bitumen:** Lackenbacher Sylvie, Le bitume [de Hît sur l'Euphrate], un enjeu à l'époque de Hammurabi; RÉAnc 94 (1992) 325-336.

d572 *Ebur,* IVORY: **Krzyszkowska** Olga,   Ivory and related materials; an illustrated guide: BInstClas supp. 59. L 1990.   xvi-109 p.; 30 fig.; 32 pl.; map; foldout. £12. – ᴿDiscEg 23 (1992) 23-37 (Helen *Hughes-Brook*).

d573 GALÈNE: **Castel** G., *Soukiassian* G.,   Gebel el-Zeit I.   Les mines de galène [lead sulphide] IFAO, Fouilles 35, 1989 ➤ 5,467: ᴿBO 49 (1992) 721s (Rosemarie *Klemm*).

d574 **Lapis Lazuli:** *Brown* Stuart C.,   Lapis lazuli and its sources in ancient West Asia: BCanadMesop 22 (1991) 5-13.

d574* *Marmor: a) Holtzmann* Bernard,   Les marbres de la Grèce archaïque et classique; – *b) Waelkens* Marc,   Carrières et marbres de l'Asie mineure: DossA 173 ('Le marbre dans l'Antiquité' 1992) 2-7 / 22-29; color. ill.

d575 OBSIDIAN: *Cauvin* Marie-Claire, *al.*,   Nouvelles analyses d'obsidiennes du Proche-Orient: Paléorient 17,2 (1991) 5-20.

d576 *Yellin* Joseph, *Gopher* Avi,   The origin of the obsidian artefacts from Mujahiya — a PPNB site in the Golan Heights: TAJ 19 (1992) 94-99.

d577 *Vitrum,* GLASS: *a) Bailey* Donald M.,   A grave group from Cyzicus; – *b) Jacobson* Gusta L.,   Greek names on prismatic jugs: JGlass 34 (1992) 27-34 / 35-43; 14 fig.

d578 ᴱ**Bimson** M., *Freestone* I. C.,   Early vitreous materials [symposium 2-3 Nov. 1984]: British Museum, Occas. Paper 56, 1987 ➤ 3,d294; 4,d808: £10: ᴿJNES 51 (1992) 71s (Eleanor *Guralnik*).

d579 **Engle** Anita, *a)* Luxury glass of the Roman period: Readings in Glass History 21, 1988; – *b)* An intelligent woman's guide to glass history: 23, 1991; – *c)* The ubiquitous trade bead: 22, 1990. Jerusalem 1988-91, Phoenix. 100 p., 60 fig.; 103 p., 76 fig.; 100 p., 29 fig. [OIAc 3,20].

d580 **Kaczmarczyk** A., *Hodges* R. E. M.,   Ancient Egyptian faience 1983 ➤ 64,a586:   ᴿRossArkh (1992,4) 217-220 (Yu. A. *Falkovich*).

d581 **Meyer** Caroli,   Glass from Quseir al-Qadim and the Indian Ocean trade: SAOC 53. Ch 1992, Univ. Or. Inst. xxvi-201 p.; 6 fig.; 21 pl. 0-918986-87-7 [OIAc 5,29].

d582 *Spaer* Maud,   The Islamic glass bracelets of Palestine; preliminary findings: JGlass 34 (1992) 44-62; 29 fig.

T1.6   *Silex, os:* **'Prehistory' flint and bone industries.**

d583 **Austin** Shaun J.,   An analysis of architectural variability in Levantine settlements during the Late Pleistocene and Early Holocene: diss. ᴰ*Schroeder* H.   Toronto 1990.   vii-274 p.   0-315-59841-7 [OIAc 5,13].

d583* *Bahat* Dan,   Dolmens in Palestine: ➤ 48, Mem. DUNAYEVSKY I. 1992, 91-93; 3 fig.

d584 *Bar-Yosef* Ofer,   Palestine, archaeology of (prehistoric): ➤ 741, Anchor-BD 5 (1992) 99-109.

d585 *Bednarik* Robert G.,   Palaeoart and archaeological myths: CamArch 2,1 (1992) 27-43; 7 fig. response *Chase* P. & *Dibble* H. 43-51; 2 fig.; *Davidson* J., 52-57.

d586 *Bednarik* Robert G.,   Developments in rock art dating: AcArchK 63 (1992) 141-155; 4 fig.

d587 *Bettinger* Robert L.,   Hunter-gatherers; archaeological and evolutionary theory.   NY 1991, Plenum.   xv-257 p.; 14 fig. – ᴿAJA 96 (1992) 557s (P. J. *Crabtree*).

d588 **Blázquez Martínez** José M.,   Prehistoria y primeras culturas: Historia Universal 1. Barc 1991, Inst. Gallach. [xvi-] 448 p.; color. ill.   84-7764-521-3.

d589 *Bradley* Richard, Rock art and the perception of landscape: CamArch 1,1 (1991) 77-101; 17 fig.; 4 pl.

d590 *Chase* Philip G., *a*) What were the Ice Ages?; – *b*) Language in the Ice Ages; when did Europeans first speak?: Expedition 34,3 (Ph 1992) 4-13 / 52-61.

d591 **Cziesla** Erwin, Siedlungsdynamik auf steinzeitlichen Fundplätzen; methodische Aspekte zur Analyse latenter Strukturen: Studies in Modern Archaeology 2. Bonn 1990, Holos. 465 p.; 254 fig. – ᴿBonnJbb 192 (1992) 560-2 (K. *Valoch*).

d592 ᴱ**Dibble** Harold L., *Mellars* Paul, The Middle Paleolithic; adaptation, behavior, and variability: Symposium 4, Mg 78. Ph 1992, Univ. Museum. x-217 p.; ill. 0-924171-073.

d593 *Duff* Andrew I., *al.*, Symbolism in the Early Palaeolithic; a conceptual odyssey: CamArch 2 (1992) 211-229.

d594 **Ehrenberg** Margaret, Women in prehistory. L 1992 = 1989, British Museum. 192 p. £10. 0-7141-1388-3.

d595 *Fagan* Brian, A sexist view of prehistory [*Gimbutas* M., 1992; *Hastorf* C. in ᴱGᴇʀᴏ J. 1990 better]: Archaeology 45,2 (1992) 14s. 18. 66.

d596 **Gopher** Avi, The flint assemblages of Munbāqa 1989 ➤ 6,e149 [not Muntaḥa]: ᴿSyria 69 (1992) 233s (H. de *Contenson*).

d596* **Greene** Mott T., Natural knowledge in preclassical antiquity [... i. prehistory]. Baltimore 1992, Johns Hopkins Univ. xix-182 p.; 9 fig. £18. 0-8018-4292-1. – ᴿAntiquity 66 (1992) 533s (T. *Taylor*).

d597 *Grooth* Marjorie E. de, Socio-economic aspects of neolithic flint mining: Helinium 31 (1991) 153-189.

d598 ᴱ**Guilaine** Jean, Prehistory, the world of early man, ᵀ*Bunson* Stephen. NY 1991, Facts on File. vii-192 p.; (color.) ill. $40. 0-8160-2432-4. – ᴿClasW 86 (1992s) 152 (A. *McPherron*).

d599 **Herrmann** B., *al.*, Prähistorische Anthropologie; Leitfaden der Feld- und Labormethoden. B 1990, Springer. 445 p.; 222 fig. – ᴿBonnJbb 192 (1992) 557-560 (W. *Henke*).

d600 **Isaac** Glynn, The archaeology of human origins [20 art.], ᴱ*Isaac* Barbara. c. 1989, Univ. – ᴿCamArch 1 (1991) 277-283 (S. *Mithen*, also on R. Pᴏᴛᴛs 1988 Olduvai).

d601 *Kardulias* P. Nick, The ecology of Bronze Age flaked stone tool production in southern Greece; evidence from Agios Stephanos and the southern Argolid: AJA 96 (1992) 421-442; 2 fig. + 2 maps.

d602 *Lee* Phyllis C., Biology and behaviour in human evolution: CamArch 1 (1991) 207-226.

d603 *Mellars* Paul, Cognitive changes and the emergence of modern humans in Europe: CamArch 1 (1991) 63-76 [&140-4, review of his Human Revolution (1989 ➤ 6,d92*; 7,b624) by P. *Rowley-Conwy*].

d604 **Midant-Reynes** Béatrix, Préhistoire de l'Égypte des premiers hommes aux premiers pharaons; préf. *Leclant* Jean. P 1992, A. Colin. 288 p. 2-86538-221-4 [OIAc 3,31].

d605 *Moser* Stephanie, The visual language of archaeology; a case study of the Neanderthals: Antiquity 66 (1992) 831-844; 2 fig.

d606 *Mottura* Alberto, Adamo in Piemonte; l'età della pietra in Italia; come si lavora la pietra: ArchViva 10,10 (1991) 48-58; color. ill.

d607 Le peuplement magdalénien; paléogéographie physique et humaine; Actes du colloque de Chancelade, 10-15 oct. 1988. P 1992, C.T.H.S. 451 p. 2-7355-0255-4. – ᴿAcArLov 31 (1992) 95s (P. van *Peer*).

d608 **Muhesen** S., Bilan sur la préhistoire de la Syrie: Syria 69 (1992) 247-305; map.

d609 **Schyle** Daniel, Near Eastern Upper Palaeolithic cultural stratigraphy; an evaluation of evidence: TAVO B-59. Wsb 1992, Reichert. [vi-] 150 p. 3-88226-552-3 [OIAc 5,34].

d610 **Tangri** D., A reassessment of the origins of the Predynastic in Upper Egypt: PrPrehSoc 58 (1992) 111-125; 5 fig.

d610* **Thomas** Julian, Rethinking the [... Britain] neolithic. C 1991, Univ. xvi-212 p.; 60 fig. £35. 0-521-40377-4. – RAntiqJ 71 (1991) 268s (P. *Ashbee*).

d611 ᴱ**Trinkaus** Erik, The emergence of modern humans; biocultural adaptations in the later pleistocene: School of American Research seminar. C 1989, Univ. 385 p.; 10 fig. $49.50. 0-521-37241-0. – RJField 19 (1992) 80-83 (J. J. *Shea*).

d612 ᴱ**Valla** François R., Bar-Yosef Ofer, The Natufian culture in the Levant: MgPreh, arch. 1. AA 1991, Int. Mg. Prehistory. vi-644 p. 1-879621-01-1 [OIAc 5,37].

d613 **Wright** Katherine I., Ground stone assemblage variations and subsistence strategies in the Levant [22 Jordan sites] 22,000 to 5500 b.p.: diss. Yale ᴰ*Hole* F. NHv 1992. 718 p. 93-06982. – DissA 53 (1992s) 3575-A.

T1.7 Technologia antiqua.

d614 **Baer** Eva, Ayyubid metalwork with Christian images: Muqarnas supp. 4. Leiden 1989, Brill. xiii-55 p.; 128 fig. – RJRAS (1991) 287-9 (J. W. *Allan*).

d615 ᴱ**Bonghi Jovino** Maria, Artigiani e botteghe nell'Italia preromana. R 1990, Bretschneider. 353 p.; 38 pl. Lit. 200.000. – RArcheo 7,88 (1992) 127 (S. *Moscati*); Babesch 67 (1992) 201-3 (R. R. *Knoop*); RArchéol (1992) 152s (Marie-Françoise *Briquet*).

d616 **Brentjes** Burchard, Bergbau im Altertum; einige Grundzüge und Tendenzen: Altertum 37 (1991) 133-9; 5 fig. [140-154 Ägypten, *Weisgerber* Gerd].

d617 **Frontisi-Ducroux** Françoise, Die technische Intelligenz des griechischen Handwerkers, ᵀ*Rappl* Werner: Hephaistos 11s (1992s) 93-105.

d618 **Hassan** Ahmad el-, **Hill** Donald R., Islamic technology, an illustrated history. C 1992 [=] 1986, Univ. xv-304 p.; ill. 0-521-42239-6 [OIAc 5,24].

d619 **Lavenex Vergès** Fabienne, Bleus égyptiens; de la pâte auto-émaillé au pigment bleu synthétique [diss.]. Lv 1992, Peeters. 86 p.; ill. 90-6831-392-4.

d620 **McNutt** Paula M., The forging of Israel ᴰ1990 → 5,b998; 6,d116: RBA 55 (1992) 153s (J. D. *Muhly*); BL (1992) (K. W. *Whitelam*); JAOS 112 (1992) 697-701 (also J. D. *Muhly*: competent); JBL 111 (1992) 510s (J. A. *Dearman*); TLZ 117 (1992) 112-4 (E. A. *Knauf*: from 3d-4th-hand sources).

d621 *a)* **Moores** Robert G.ᴶ, Evidence for use of a stone-cutting drag saw by the Fourth Dynasty Egyptians; – *b)* **Isler** Martin, The gnomon [measuring-pole in Egyptian antiquity]: JAmEg 28 (1991) 139-148; 11 fig. / 155-185; 37 fig.

d622 **Neumann** Hans, Handwerk in Mesopotamien ᴰ1987 → 3,d330 ... 6,d121: RJAOS 112 (1992) 336-8 (D. C. *Snell*).

d623 **Rickenbach** Judith, Magier mit Feuer und Erz; Bronzekunst der frühen Bergvölker in Luristan, Iran: OBO 117. FrS/Gö 1992, Univ./

Vandenhoeck & R.   xi-138 p.; 13 pl.   3-7278-0813-6 / 3-525-53751-4 [OIAc 3,36].

d624 ᴱRothenberg B., The ancient metallurgy of copper, 2, 1990 ➤ 7,b643: ᴿPEQ 124 (1992) 158s (G. *Philip*).

d625 *Rothenberg* Beno, *Glass* Jonathan, The beginnings and the development of early metallurgy... western Arabah: Levant 24 (1992) 141-157; map.

d626 **Saladino** V., Arte e artigianato in Grecia; dall'età del bronzo alla fine dell'età classica: StT 9. F 1988, Univ. Dip. Antich. 352 p. Lit. 30.000. – ᴿMaia 44 (1992) 116-8 (Bianca Maria *Giannattasio*).

d627 **Schneider** Helmuth, Einführung in die antike Technikgeschichte: AltW. Da 1992, Wiss. xii-258 p.

d628 **Tallon** Françoise, Métallurgie susienne I. De la fondation de Suse au XVIIIᵉ s. av.J.-C.: NDocMusF 15, 1987 ➤ 3,e674; 7,b646: ᴿJNES 51 (1992) 67-70 (E. *Pernicka*); ZAss 82 (1992) 290-2 (J. *Curtis*).

d629 **Tripathi** D. N., Bronzework of mainland Greece from c. 2600 B.C. to c. 1450 B.C. [diss. Cambridge c. 1978]: SIMA 69. Göteborg 1988, Åström. – ᴿJHS 112 (1992) 210s (K. *Branigan*: outdated; short on economic-social influence).

d630 *Whitehouse* David, A glassmaker's workshop at Rome? [STERNINI Mara, 1989]: JRomArch 4 (1991) 385s.

d631 **Zimmer** Gerhard, Griechische Bronzegusswerkstätten; zur Technologieentwicklung eines antiken Kunsthandwerks. Mainz 1990, von Zabern. ix-225 p.; ill. DM 34,50. 3-7785-1445-8. – ᴿClasR 42 (1992) 398-400 (Carol C. *Mattusch*); Gnomon 64 (1992) 706-712 (C. *Reinholdt*).

T1.8 **Architectura.**

d632 **Arnold** Dieter, Building in Egypt 1991 ➤ 7,b651; $69: ᴿAntiqJ 71 (1991) 267s (I. *Shaw*); ClasW 85 (1991s) 718 (Karen P. *Foster*); JField 19 (1992) 228-230 (G. T. *Martin*).

d633 *Barański* Marek, 'Opus palmyrenum': DamaszMi 5 (1991) 59-63; 1 fig.; pl. 27-28.

d634 ᴱ**Barton** I. M., Roman public buildings 1989 ➤ 6,d138: ᴿClasR 42 (1992) 480s (Susan *Walker*).

d635 **Beacham** Richard C., The Roman theatre and its audience. L 1991, Routledge. 267 p.; ill. – ᴿRÉAnc 94 (1992) 489s (Lucienne *Deschamps*).

d635* *a*) *Ben-Tor* Amnon, Early Bronze Age dwellings and installations; – *b*) *Kempinski* Aharon, Fortifications, public buildings, and town planning in the Early Bronze Age; – *c*) *Beit-Arieh* Itzhaq, Buildings and settlement patterns at EB II sites in southern Israel and southern Sinai; – *d*) *Cohen* Rudolf, Architecture in the Intermediate EB-MB; – *e*) *Ben-Dov* Meir, MB/LB dwellings; – *f*) *Mazar* Amihai, Temples: ➤ 48, Mem. DUNAYEVSKY I. 1992, 60-67; 10 fig. / 68-80; 12 fig. / 80-83; 2 fig. / 85-90; 6 fig. / 99-104; 9 fig. / 161-187; 35 fig.

d636 **Bouyer** Louis, Architecture et liturgie [1967], ᵀLecourt G.: Foi vivante 276. P 1991, Cerf. 108 p. – ᴿEsprVie 102 (1992) 106-8 (J. *Rocacher*: thème bon, mais trop fondé sur les exagérations 1964-7).

d636* **Bretschneider** Joachim, Architekturmodelle in Vorderasien und der östlichen Ägäis vom Neolithikum bis in das 1. Jahrtausend; Phänomene in der Kleinkunst an Beispielen aus Mesopotamien, dem Iran, Anatolien, Syrien, der Levante und dem ägäischen Raum unter besonderer Berücksichtigung der Bau- und religionsgeschichtlichen Aspekte: AOAT

229. Kevelaer/Neuk 1991, Butzon & B./Neuk. x-263 p.; 157 pl. 3-7666-0765-X / 3-7887-1383-6. – ᴿOTAbs 15 (1992) 268s (A. *Fitzgerald*).

d637 **Brodribb** Gerald, Roman brick and tile. Wolfeboro 1989, Sutton. xi-164. – ᴿPhoenix 46 (Toronto 1992) 82-84 (J. J. *Rossiter*: Roman Britain part more successful).

d638 **Brödner** Erika, Wohnen in der Antike [meist römische Kaiserzeit] 1989 ➤ 7,b655: ᴿGnomon 64 (1992) 272s (W. *Hoepfner*).

d640 **Clarke** John R., The houses of Roman Italy, 100 B.C. - A.D. 250; ritual, space, and decoration. Berkeley 1991, Univ. California. lvi-411 p.; 227 fig.; 24 pl.; 3 maps. $65. 0-520-07267-7 [NTAbs 36,442].

d641 **Cooper** Nancy K., The development of roof revetement in the Peloponnese: SIMA pocket 88, 1988 ➤ 7,b656: ᴿGnomon 64 (1992) 374s (J. *Heiden*).

d642 **Currid** John D., Rectangular storehouse construction during the Iron Age: ZDPV 108 (1992) 99-121; 8 fig.

d643 **Damerji** Muayad S. B., The development of the architecture of doors and gates in ancient Mesopotamia, 1987 ➤ 4,d864: ᴿJNES 51 (1992) 228-230 (Sally *Dunham*).

d644 **Danner** Peter, Griechische Akrotere der archaischen und klassischen Zeit: RdA supp. 5, ᴰ1989 ➤ 7,b657: ᴿAcAHung 44 (1992) 439s (M. *Szabó*); AnzAltW 45,1 (1992) 98-100 (A. *Bammer*).

d645 ᴱ**Darcque** Pascal, *Treuil* René, L'habitat égéen préhistorique: CNRS, Univ. Paris / ÉcFrRome 23-25.VI.1987: BCH supp. 19. P 1990, de Boccard. ix-495 p. F 700. 2-86958-031-2. – ᴿAJA 96 (1992) 706-8 (Carol *Hershenson*).

d646 *Denissen* Sabine, The history of brick-making... still a rich field for archaeological and historical research: AcArLov 31 (1992) 1-7.

d647 *Dentzer-Feydy* Jacqueline, Les linteaux aux figures divines en Syrie méridionale: RArchéol (1992) 65-103; 39 fig.

d648 *Downey* Susan B., Mesopotamian religious architecture, Alexander... Parthians 1988 ➤ 4,d866; 5,d26 [not 7 (as index)]: ᴿJNES 51 (1992) 227s (Ann C. *Gunter*); Syria 68 (1991) 485-7 (E. *Will*).

DUNAYEVSKY mem., The architecture of ancient Israel, from the prehistoric to the Persian periods, ᴱKempinski A., Reich R., 1992 ➤ 48.

d649 **Eichmann** Ricardo, Aspekte prähistorischer Grundrissgestaltung in Vorderasien... 9.-4. Jahrtausend: BaghFor 12, 1991 ➤ 7,b613; DM 110: ᴿMesop-T 27 (1992) 278-280 (A. *Invernizzi*).

d650 **Fagerström** Kåre, Greek Iron Age architecture: SIMA 81, 1988 ➤ 4, d868; 6,d145: ᴿAntAltW 45 (1992) 264-8 (S. *Hiller*); JHS 112 (1992) 214s (Catherine *Morgan*).

d651 ᴱ**Fleury** Philippe, VITRUVE [➤ 711], De l'architecture, I: Coll. Budé 1990 ➤ 7,b660: ᴿRArchéol (1992) 425-9 (G. *Hallier*).

d652 — ᴱ**Gros** P., VITRUVE, De l'architecture III: Coll. Budé. P 1990, BLettres. xcii-324 (d.) p.; 43 fig. 2-251-01350-4. – ᴿLatomus 51 (1992) 926-8 (L. *Callebat*).

d653 *Frey* Louis, Pour un modèle du chapiteau ionique vitruvien: RArchéol (1992) 37-63; 9 fig.

d654 **Freyberger** Klaus S., Stadtrömische Kapitelle 1990 ➤ 7,b662: ᴿAntClas 61 (1992) 709s (Cécile *Evers*); RArchéol (1992) 424s (P. *Gros*).

d655 **Fritz** V., Haus: ➤ 762, NBL II,6 (1991) 53-57; fig. 3-6.

Golvin Jean-Claude, L'amphithéâtre romain 1988 ➤ d794.

d656 **Grandjean** Yves, Recherches sur l'habitat thasien à l'époque grecque: ÉtThas 12, 1988 ➤ 6,d151: ᴿMusHelv 48 (1991) 190s (D. *Knoepfler*).

d657 **Hellmann** Marie-Christine, Recherches sur le vocabulaire de l'architecture grecque, d'après les inscriptions de Délos: BtÉcFAR 278. Athènes 1992, École Française. 475 p.; 24 pl. 2-86958-045-2.

d658 *Hellmann* Marie-Christine, Caves et sous-sols dans l'habitat grec antique: BCH 116 (1992) 259-266; 4 fig.

d659 **Helms** Svend, *al.*, Early Islamic architecture of the desert; a bedouin station (Rīsha) in eastern Jordan. E 1990, Univ. xi-188 p. £25. – ᴿBSO 55 (1992) 127s (A. *Northedge*).

d660 **Hiesel** Gerhard, Späthelladische Hausarchitektur; Studien zur Architekturgeschichte des griechischen Festlandes in der späten Bronzezeit 1990 ➤ 7,b664*; 3-8053-1005-6: ᴿAntClas 61 (1992) 650-2 (R. *Laffineur*); BonnJbb 192 (1992) 572-5 (S. *Hiller*).

d661 **Hirschfeld** Yizhar, ✪ Dwelling houses in Roman and Byzantine Palestine [M.A. diss. J]. J 1987, Yad Ben Zvi. 222 p.; 197 fig. – ᴿLA 41 (1991) 587-591 (L. *Di Segni Campagnano*).

Hoepfner W., Hermogenes/Architektur 1988/90 ➤ 717.

d661* *Holladay* John S.ᴶ, House, Israelite: ➤ 741, AnchorDB 3 (1992) 308-318; 4 fig.

d662 *Jung* Michael, La decorazione architettonica dell'Arabia del Sud alla luce delle scoperte recenti; progetto di ricerca: AION 52 (1992) 473-7.

d662* ᴱ**Kent** Susan, Domestic architecture and the use of space; an interdisciplinary cross-cultural study: New Directions. C 1990, Univ. vii-192 p. 0-521-38160-6. – ᴿAJA 96 (1992) 764s (Alexandra *Kalogirou*); BonnJbb 192 (1992) 563-6 (Ulrike *Sommer* mentions two items on ancient Greece).

d663 *Lara* Salvador, El trazado vitruviano como mecanismo abierto de implantación y ampliación de los teatros romanos: ArEspArq 65 (1992) 151-179; 14 fig.

d664 **Lendle** Otto, Vitruv als Übersetzer aus dem Griechischen: ➤ 672, Fremdspr. 1989/92, 189-200; 2 fig.

d664* ᴱ**Linders** Tullia, *Hellström* Pontus, Architecture and society in Hecatomnid Caria 1987/9 ➤ 5,852; 6,e814: ᴿAnzAltW 45,1 (1992) 101-3 (A. *Bamme*).

d665 *Liphschitz* Nili, *Biger* Gideon, ✪ Secondary and tertiary use of Cedrus Libani (cedar of Lebanon) timber in construction: Qadmoniot 25 (1992) 19-21; 4 fig.

d666 ᴱ**Macready** Sarah, *Thompson* F.H., Roman architecture in the Greek world 1985/7 ➤ 4,454... 6,d165: ᴿSyria 68 (1991) 489-491 (E. *Will*).

d667 — *Yegül* Fikret K., 'Roman' architecture in the Greek world [ᴱ**Macready** S., *Thompson* F. 1989]: ᴿJRomA 4 (1991) 345-355.

d668 [Deuterman] **Maguire** Eunice, *al.*, Art and holy powers in the early Christian house 1990 ➤ 7,b671; 251 p. 53 fig.; 151 phot. + 2 color. pl.: ᴿBAR-W 18,4 (1992) 8 . 10 (J. F. *Strange*).

d669 **Martin** Susan D., The Roman jurists and the organisation of private building in the late Republic and early Empire: Coll. Latomus 204, 1989 ➤ 7,b672: ᴿGymnasium 99 (1992) 80s (A. *Poláček*).

d670 **Mersereau** Rebecca, Prehistoric architectural models from the Aegean: diss. Bryn Mawr, ᴰ*Wright* J. Ph 1991. xix-396 p., 207 fig. 91-28585. – OIAc 3,30.

d670* *Moretti* J.-C., L'architecture des théâtres en Asie Mineure (1980-1989): TopO 2 (1992) 9-32: books and articles by general regions, subdivided by locality.

d671 **Oren** Eliezer D., ◑ Ashlar masonry in the western Negev in the Iron Age: ➤ 18, ᶠBIRAN A., ErIsr 23 (1992) 94-105; 17 fig.; Eng. 149*s.

d672 ᴱ**Parsegian** Vasken L., Armenian architecture. Leiden c. 1991, Inter-Documentation. 7 vol. microfiches, 42.000 photos. ƒ9100 [JbÖsByz 43, 487, H. *Buschhausen*].

d673 **Ruggieri** V., Byzantine religious architecture (582-867); its history and structural elements [= OrChrAnal 237] ᴰ1991 ➤ 7,b679: ᴿOrChrPer 58 (1992) 579-582 (C. *Capizzi*).

d674 **Pietilä-Castrén** Leena, Magnificentia... victory monuments [Punic era Rome] 1987 ➤ 6,d175 [Index !]: ᴿGnomon 64 (1992) 737-9 (T. *Hölscher*).

d674* *a) Reich* Ronny, Building materials and architectural elements in ancient Israel; – *b) Netzer* Ehud, Massive structures; processes in construction and deterioration; – *c) Bar-Yosef* Ofer, Building activities in the prehistoric periods until the end of the Neolithic; – *d) Porath* Yosef, Domestic architecture of the chalcolithic period; – *e) Kempinski* Aharon, Chalcolithic and Early Bronze Age Temples: ➤ 48, DUNAYEVSKY I. mem. 1992, 1-16; 22 fig. / 17-26; 13 fig. / 31-39; 8 fig. / 40-48; 2 fig. / 53-59; 14 fig.

d675 *Seigne* Jacques, Le château royal de Shabwa [S. Yemen]; architecture, techniques de construction et restitutions: Syria 68 (1991) 111-164 [-227, al. décor, histoire].

d676 **Steible** Horst, Die neusumerischen Bau- und Weihinschriften, 1. Inschriften der II. Dynastie von Lagaš; 2. Kommentar zu den Gudea-Statuen; Inschriften der III. Dynastie von Ur; Inschriften der IV. und 'V.' Dynastie von Uruk; Varia: FreibAltorSt 9. Stu 1991, Steiner. xv-430 p.; vii-359 p., xxiv pl. [JAOS 112,727].

d677 *Strommenger* Eva, The earliest architecture in Syria and in Palestine: ➤ 736, ᴱ*Shaath*, Palestine 1981/5, 43-48; 10 fig.

d678 **Tadgell** Christopher, The history of architecture in India, from the dawn of civilization to the end of the Raj. L 1990, Architecture Design. 336 p.; 55 pl. – ᴿBSO 55 (1992) 150s (G. H. H. *Tillotson*).

d679 *Tarditi* Chiara, Architettura come propaganda; esame dell'attività edilizia degli Antigonidi in Grecia e nuove proposte di attribuzione: AevA 3 (1990) 43-67 + 7 fig.

d680 **Thornton** M.K. & R.L., Julio-Claudian building programs; a quantitative study in political management 1989 ➤ 6,d185; 7,b681: ᴿAIONclas 44 (1992) 360-4 (M. *Munzi*).

d681 **Tybout** Rolf A., Aedificiorum figurae; Untersuchungen zu den Architekturdarstellungen des frühen zweiten [pompejanischen] Stils [Diss. Leiden]: DutchMgHA 7. Amst 1989, Gieben ix-462 p.; 21 fig.; 112 pl. – ᴿBonnJbb 192 (1992) 681-4 (W. *Wohlmayr*); Gnomon 64 (1992) 433-8 (B. *Wesenberg*).

d682 **Weber** Marga, Baldachine und Statuenschreine [< Diss. Fra 1982 on statue-shelters of all kinds from all over the ancient world]: Archaeologica 87. R 1990, Bretschneider. xviii-260 p.; 58 pl. – ᴿRArchéol (1992) 399s (Anne *Jacquemin*); RÉAnc 94 (1992) 294s (R. *Étienne*); RÉLat 70 (1992) 389s (R. *Adam*: 280 objets).

d683 *Wenning* Robert, Herodianische Architektur, eine Bibliographie: Boreas 14s (1991s) 109-129.

d684 **White** L. Michael, Building God's house ᴰ1990 ➤ 6,d189; 7,b684: ᴿAJA 96 (1992) 776s (P. C. *Finney*); CritRR 5 (1992) 255-7 (R. F. *Hock*: despite scarce data, mostly under later churches, shows early Christianity less sectarian and proletarian than formerly assumed); JAOS 112 (1992) 165s (S.*Goranson*); JRS 82 (1992) 283 (Janet *Huskinson*).

d685 **Wright** G. R. H., Ancient building in Cyprus: HbOr 7/1/2B/8. Leiden 1992, Brill. xxviii-557 p.; vol. of xviii-343 fig. 90-04-09545-4; -6-2 (-7-0 both) [BL 93,46, G. I. *Davies*, splendid].
d686 **Wright** G. H. R., Ancient building in South Syria and Palestine 1985 ➤ 1,b709 ... 6,d190: ᴿSyria 69 (1992) 229-231 (Corinne *Castel*: utile).

T1.9 *Supellex;* **furniture; objects of daily life.**

d687 [Pirzio] **Biroli Stefanelli** Lucia, Il bronzo dei romani, arredo e supel-lettile 1990 ➤ 7,b688: ᴿLatomus 51 (1992) 234s (S. *Boucher*); RÉG 105 (1992) 272s (Mary-Anne *Zagdoun*).
d688 *Bruwier* Marie-Cécile, Du caractère individuel du siège mobile en Égypte pharaonique: CdÉ 66 (1991) 89-107; 13 fig.
d689 **Cholidis** Nadja, Möbel in Ton; Untersuchungen zur archäologischen und religionsgeschichtlichen Bedeutung der Terrakottamodelle von Ti-schen, Stühlen und Betten aus dem Alten Orient [Diss. Münster 1990]: AltKVO 1. Münster 1992, Ugarit-V. xii-323 p.; 46 pl. [OIAc 5,17]. 3-927120-10-3. – ᴿUF 24 (1992) 498 (M. *Dietrich*).
d690 **Daviau** Paulette M. M., Artifact distribution and functional analysis in Palestine domestic architecture of the second millennium B.C.: diss. Toronto 1990, ᴰ*Holladay* J. 813 p. DANN-65798. – DissA 53 (1992s) 538-A; OIAc 5,18).
d691 **Dupont** Florence, *a*) La vie quotidienne du citoyen romain sous la République: La Vie Q. P 1989, Hachette. 336 p. – ᴿCahHist 35 (1990) 165s (F. *Richard*); – *b*) La vita quotidiana nella Roma repubblicana ᵀ. R 1990, Laterza. vii-324 p. – ᴿOrpheus 13,1 (1992) 180s (Antonella *Borgo*).
d692 **Faust** Sabine, Fulcra; figürlicher und ornamentaler Schmuck an antiken Betten: MiDAI-R Ergh. 30. Mainz 1989, von Zabern. 248 p.; 11 fig.; 80 pl.; 2 maps. DM 135. – ᴿBabesch 67 (1992) 191-3 (S. *Mols*, ᵀ*Buylinckx* F.); ClasR 42 (1992) 150s (R. *Jackson*).
d693 **Gardner** Jane F., *Wiedemann* T., The Roman household 1991 ➤ 7,b689: ᴿClasR 42 (1992) 389s (S. *Currie*); ClasW 85 (1991) 736s (Sheila K. *Dickison*).
d694 **Gower** Ralph, Usi e costumi dei tempi della Bibbia [The new Manners 1985, ¹1953]. T 1990, LDC. 396 p.; ill. Lit.42.000. – ᴿCC 143 (1992,1) 307s (G. L. *Prato*); ParVi 36 (1991) 311s (F. *Mosetto*).
d695 **Gubel** E., Phoenician furniture ᴰ1987 ➤ 4,d915 ... 7,b691: ᴿIsrEJ 42 (1992) 121s (E. *Stern*); Qadmoniot 25 (1992) 123 (also E. *Stern*, ⊕).
d696 **Jahn** Birgit, Bronzezeitliches Sitzmobiliar ... griechisch.: EurHS 38/31, ᴰ1990 ➤ 6,d195; DM 90; 3-631-42430-2: ᴿAntClas 61 (1992) 654s (Frieda *Vandenabeele*).
d697 **Janssen** Rosalind M. & Jac. J., Growing up in ancient Egypt 1990 ➤ 6,d196: ᴿDiscEg 21 (1991) 77s (H. *Brunner*).
d698 **Klengel** Horst, Hammurapi und der Alltag Babylons². Da 1992, Wiss [= Z 1991, Artemis ➤ 7,b692]. 280 p. – ᴿUF 24 (1992) 508 (M. *Dietrich*).
d698* ᴱ**Laiou** A. E., Byzantine family and household: Dumbarton Oaks 1989/90 ➤ 7,647*: ᴿJTS 43 (1992) 720s (A. *Louth*).
d699 **Schäfer** Thomas, Imperii insignia; sella curulis und fasces; zur Re-präsentation römischer Magistrate: MiDAI-R Ergh 29. Mainz 1989, von Zabern. 457 p.; 12 fig.; 122 pl. DM 198. – ᴿClasR 42 (1992) 155-7 (Glenys *Davies*).
d700 **Strouhal** Eugen, Life in ancient Egypt [1989],ᵀ. C 1992, Univ. 279 p.; photos *Forman* Werner. 0-521-44093-9.

d701 **Thompson** J. A., Hirten, Händler und Propheten; die lebendige Welt der Bibel. Giessen 1992, Brunnen. 384 p. DM 59 [ZAW 105,538, D. *Vieweger*].

d702 *Wallace-Hadrill* Andrew, Houses and households; sampling Pompeii and Herculaneum: ➤ 674, ᴱ*Rawson* B., Marriage 1992, 191-227; pl. 7-8.

T2.1   *Res militaris;* **weapons, army activities.**

d702* *Bahn* Paul G., Letters from a Roman garrison [rather *to* a soldier in Britain]: Archaeology 45,1 (1992) 61-65.

d703 *Barkworth* Peter R., The organization of Xerxes' army: IrAnt 27 (1992) 149-167; 2 fig. (page-headings 'organisa-').

d704 **Beal** Richard H., The organisation of the Hittite military: Texte der Hethiter 20. Heid 1992, Winter. xiv-594 p. 3-533-04562-5 [BeiNam 27,3s cover adv.].

d705 **Bol** Peter C., Argivische Schilde: DAI Olympische For. 17. B 1989, de Gruyter. xi-176 p.; 92 pl. DM 198. 3-11-011587-5. – ᴿBabesch 67 (1992) 193s (Maria *Stoop*).

d706 *Brentjes* Burchard, Ḥumuṭ-ṭabal ('nimm schnell hinweg') – ein Wunschname für eine Waffe?: ArchMIran 24 (1991) 3-11; 7 fig.; pl. 1s.

d707 **Brentjes** Helga & Burchard, Die Heerscharen des Orients. B 1990, Brandenburg. 196 p.; ill. 3-327-01075-7 [OIAc 3,15].

d708 *Brizzi* Giovanni, al., Le grandi battaglie nell'antichità: Archeo 7,88 (1992) 59-115.

d709 *Cagniart* Pierre, Victori receptaculum, victo perfugium; notes à propos des camps de marche de l'armée romaine: ÉtClas 60 (1992) 217-234.

d710 *Castel* Corinne, Armes et armement; des premiers guerriers à l'armée de métier: DossiersArch 160 ('La guerre au Proche-Orient dans l'Antiquité' 1991) 48-53 (-55 *Parayre* Dominique, La symbolique des armes); 1-91 al., Mari, Qadesh.

d711 *Ciałowicz* Krzysztof M., L'étude des armes égyptiennes dans les époques prédynastique et archaïque; la typologie des pointes de flèches et de javelots: FolOr 27 (1990) 63-77 + 11 fig.

d712 *Cordente Vaquero* Félix, La toma de Masada, ejemplo de eficacia de la técnica poliorcética en el ejército romano [< dis. Complutense 1991, en prensa]: Gerión 10 (1992) 155-169; plan 170.

d713 **Davidson** David P., The barracks of the Roman army: BAR-Int 472, 1989 ➤ 6,d214; 7,h701: ᴿBonnJbb 192 (1992) 653-7 (J. K. *Haalebos*).

d714 ᴱ**Driel-Murray** Carol van, The sources of evidence... Roman military equipment: BAR-Int 476, 1987/9 ➤ 6,798: ᴿBonnJbb 192 (1992) 658-663 (M. *Junkelmann*).

d715 **Dumézil** Georges, Heur et malheur du guerrier; aspects mythiques de la fonction guerrière chez les Indo-Européens. P 1992 = 1985, Flammarion. 236 p. F 125. 2-08-211158-X.

d715* *Dupuis* Xavier, L'armée romaine en Afrique; l'apport des inscriptions relevées par J. MARCILLET-JAUBERT: AntAfr 28 (1992) 147-160; 3 fig.

d716 *Federspiel* Michel, Sur le mouvement des projectiles (ARISTOTE, Du ciel, 228 a 22): RÉAnc 94 (1992) 337-345.

d717 **Flemberg** Johan, Venus armata; Studien zur bewaffneten Aphrodite in der griechisch-römischen Kunst [Diss. Uppsala 1989]: Svenska Institutet i Athen 10. Sto 1991, Åström. 128 p. – ᴿRÉAnc 94 (1992) 516s (Claire *Muckensturm-Poulle*).

d718 **Gabriel** Richard A., *Metz* Karen S., From Sumer to Rome; the military capabilities of ancient armies: Contributions in Military Studies 108 (0883-6884). NY 1991, Greenwood. xxi-182 p. 0-313-27645-5 [OIAc 3,21].

d719 *Greenewalt* Crawford H., *Heywood* Ann M., A helmet of the sixth century B.C. from Sardis: BASOR 285 (1992) 1-31; 27 fig.

d719* *Grew* Francis, *Griffiths* Nick, The pre-Flavian military belt; the evidence from Britain: Archaeologia 109 (1991) 47-84 [< AnPg 62, p. 980].

d720 **Hanson** Victor D., Hoplites 1991 ➤ 7,b711: ᴿClasR 42 (1992) 374s (J. *Hackett*); ClasW 86 (1992s) 235 (J. *Cargill*); Gerión 10 (1992) 312 (C. *Fornis & J. M. Casillas*); RÉG 105 (1992) 604s (J.-N. *Corvisier*).

d721 **Hanson** V. D., The western way of war; infantry battle in classical Greece 1990 ➤ 6,d225: ᴿJHS 112 (1992) 203s (J. F. *Lazenby*: original, good).

d722 **Healy** Mark, (ill.) *McBride* Angus: New Kingdom Egypt: [military] Élite 40. L 1992, Osprey. 64 p. 1-85532-208-0 [OIAc 5,24].

d723 *Hinds* Stephen, Arma in OVID's Fasti, 1. Genre and Mannerism; 2. Genre, Romulean Rome and Augustan ideology: Arethusa 25,1 (1992) 81-112. 113-153.

d724 *Hockey* Marilyn, *al.*, An Illyrian helmet in the British Museum: AnBritAth 87 (1992) 281-291; pl. 19-27.

d725 *Holmes* Diane, Analysis and comparison of some prehistoric projectile points from Egypt: BInstArch 28 (1991) 99-132; 4 fig.

d725* **Horsmann** Gerhard, Untersuchungen zur militärischen Ausbildung im republikanischen und kaiserzeitlichen Rom: Wehrwissenschaftliche Forschungen 35. Boppard/Rhein 1991. 260 p. 3-7646-1897-3. – ᴿNikephoros 5 (1992) 290s (M. *Hainzmann*).

d726 **Isaac** Benjamin, The limits of empire; the Roman army in the east. Ox 1990 [²1992, xiv-520 p., £50], Clarendon. 0-19-814926-3. – ᴿBonnJbb 192 (1992) 649s (M. P. *Speidel*); JbAC 34 (1991) 193-200 (G. *Wirth*); JRomA 5 (1992) 467-472 (S. T. *Parker*, also on KENNEDY-RILEY), 473-9 (Kennedy on Parker); Latomus 51 (1992) 672-5 (Y. *Le Bohec*); Qadmoniot 25 (1992) 60s (Y. *Tsafrir,* **Ⓗ**).

d727 *Kazanski* Michel, À propos des armes et des éléments de harnachement 'orientaux' en Occident à l'époque des Grandes Migrations (IVᵉ-Vᵉ s.): JRomA 4 (1991) 123-139; 9 fig.

d728 *Kennedy* David, Roman army: ➤ 741, AnchorBD 5 (1992) 789-798.

d729 **Le Bohec** Yves, L'armée romaine sous le Haut-Empire. P 1989, Picard. 287 p. F 250. – ᴿGnomon 64 (1992) 328-337 (K. *Strobel*).

d730 **Le Bohec** Yann, La Troisième Légion Auguste ᴰ1989 ➤ 7,b717: ᴿLatomus 51 (1992) 675-7 (P. *Trousset*).

d731 *Le Roux* Patrick, L'armée romaine dans la péninsule ibérique sous l'Empire; bilan pour une décennie: RÉAnc 94 (1992) 231-257 + 2 fig.

d732 **Link** Stephen, Konzepte der Privilegierung römischer Veteranen: HeidAltH 9, 1989 ➤ 7,b721; 3-515-05193-7: ᴿAntClas 61 (1992) 536-9 (Margaret M. *Roxan*).

d733 **Lissarrague** François, L'autre guerrier; archers, peltastes, cavaliers dans l'imagerie attique: Images à l'appui 3, 1990 ➤ 7,b722; F 265: ᴿAntClas 61 (1992) 567-9 (D. *Viviers*, aussi sur HANSON H., Hoplites).

d734 *Malbran-Labat* F., Military organization in Mesopotamia, ᵀ*Davis* Jennifer L.: ➤ 741, AnchorBD 4 (1992) 826-831 [no similar art. on Israel, Egypt ...].

d735 *Nikonorov* Valeri P., *Savchuk* Serge A., New data on ancient Bactrian body-armour (in the light of finds from Kampyr Tepe): Iran 30 (1992) 49-54; 5 fig.

d736 **North** Tony, An historical guide to arms and armour. L 1991, Cassell. 224 p.; ill.

d737 *Pétrin* Nicole, Philological notes on the crossbow and related missile weapons: GrRByz 33 (1992) 265-291.

d738 *Picard* Gilbert-Charles, L'idéologie de la guerre et ses monuments dans l'Empire romain: RArchéol (1992) 111-141; 17 fig.

d739 **Pollard** Nigel D., Nota et familiaria castra; soldier and civilian in Roman Syria and Mesopotamia: diss. Michigan, ᴰ*Potter* D. AA 1992. 421 p. 93-08424. – DissA 53 (1992s) 4042-A.

d739* *Pongratz-Leisten* Beate, *Deller* Karlheinz, *Bleibtreu* Erika, Götterstreitwagen und Götterstandarten; Götter auf dem Feldzug und ihr Kult im Feldlager: Bagh Mitt 23 (1992) 291-356; pl. 50-69.

d740 ᵀᴱ**Poznański** Lucien, ASCLÉPIODOTE, Traité de tactique: Coll. Budé. P 1992, BLettres. xxix-63 (d.) p. 2-251-00394-3.

d740* *Primas* Margarita, Waffen aus Edelmetall: Jb des Römisch-Germanischen Zentralmuseums 35 (1988) 161-185 [< AnPg 62, p. 981].

d741 **Pritchett** W. Kendrick, Ancient Greek military practices [1.1971- 3.1979] 4. The Greek State at war. Berkeley 1985, Univ. California. → 3,d400; 0-520 02758-2. ix-278 p.

d742 **Pritchett** W. Kendrick, The Greek state at war, 5 [p. 1-68, slings; the rest, booty]. Berkeley 1991, Univ. California. x-578 p. – ᴿClasR 42 (1992) 375-7 (N. G. L. *Hammond*: a magnificent series); Prudentia 24,2 (1992) 67s (P. *McKechnie*).

Rüpke Jörg, Domi militiae; die religiöse Konstruktion des Krieges in Rom ᴰ1990 → b205.

d743 **Shatzmann** I., The armies of the Hasmonaeans and Herod; from Hellenistic to Roman frameworks: TStAJ 25, 1991 → 7,b728: ᴿZAW 104 (1992) 460 (J. *Zangenberg*).

d744 **Shaw** Ian, Egyptian warfare and weapons: Shire Egyptology 16. Princes Risborough 1991, Shire. 72 p.; 52 fig. 0-7478-0142-8 [OIAc 5,34].

d745 **Speidel** Michael P., Roman army studies 2: Mavors 8. Stu 1992, Steiner. 430 p., 112 fig. – ᴿMünstHand 11,1 (1992) 108-117 (O. *Stoll*).

d745* *Swan* Vivien G., Legio VI and its men; African legionaries in Britain: JPot 5 (1992) 1-33; 6 fig.

d746 *Taracha* Piotr, Wagenkämpfer aus Knossos und Dendra; zur Rolle der Bogenwaffen im späthelladischen Griechenland: ArchWsz 43 (1992) 121-3.

d746* **Wees** Hans van, Status warriors; war, violence and society in HOMER and history: Dutch MgHA 9. Amst 1992, Gieben. x-455 p. 90-5063- 075-8.

d747 *Wilkinson* Richard H., The representation of the bow in the art of Egypt and the Ancient Near East: JANES 20 (1991) 83-99; 17 pl.

d748 **Worley** Leslie J., The cavalry of ancient Greece: diss. Washington, ᴰ*Ferrill* A. Seattle 1992. 286 p. 92-30457. – DissA 53 (1992s) 2059-A.

T2.2   *Vehicula,* **transportation.**

d748* *Alfi* Mostafa el-, Means of transport in neolithic Egypt: → 703, Nile Delta 1990/2, 339-344.

d749 a) *Amiet* Pierre, Les chars d'Ugarit: ⇢ 179, ᶠSTROMMENGER Eva 1992, 23-27. – b) *Bernabé* A. al., Estudios sobre el vocabulario micénico, I. términos referidos a las ruedas [de carros]: Minos 25s (1990s) 133-173; 3 fig.

d749* **Heizer** Robert F.†, ᴱ*Hester* Thomas R., al., All'era dei giganti; i trasporti pesanti nell'antichità. Venezia 1990, ²1991, Marsilio. 286 p.; (color.) ill. 88-517-5397-5.

d750 **Liebowitz** Harold, Terra cotta figurines and model vehicles... Selenkahiye 1988 ⇢ 5,d114... 7,b737: ᴿZAss 82 (1992) 162s (E. *Strommenger*).

d751 *Palágyi* Sylvia, Der Inotaer Grabstein — der richtige Inhalt der Wagendarstellungen: ⇢ 729*, MittGraz 3s (1989s) 153-161; pl. 44-47.

d752 **Piggott** Stuart, Wagon, chariot and carriage; symbol and status in the history of transport. L 1992, Thames & H. 184 p.; 16 fig.; 17 pl. £19. 0-500-25114-2. – ᴿAntiquity 66 (1992) 980s (C. *Thomas*: 'transports of delight').

d753 *Voyatzis* Mary, Votive riders seated side-saddle at early Greek sanctuaries: An BritAth 87 (1992) 259-279; 14 fig.

T2.3 **Nautica.**

d754 *Auffray-Guillerm* Danièle, Les premiers bateaux de guerre en Méditerranée [plutôt des cales sèches de Paros destinées à les abriter]: Archéologia 269 (1991) 66-75.

d755 a) *Avilia* Filippo, Appunti per uno studio delle navi greche dell'VIII secolo a.C.; – b) *Frost* Honor, Les constructeurs puniques; – c) *Corretti* Alessandro, Contributo alla discussione sulle strutture del commercio arcaico; le navi: ⇢ 713, PACT 20 (1987/90) 205-210; 1 fig. / 211-225; 11 fig. / 241-258; 5 fig.

d756 *Bonfante* Giuliano, Gli Indoeuropei e la navigazione: RFgIC 120 (1992) 257-9.

d757 *Bound* Mensun, A Roman amphora wreck (Pélichet 47) off the island of Montecristo, Italy – preliminary report: IntJNaut 21 (1992) 329-336.

d758 **Casson** Lionel, The ancient mariners² [¹1959] 1991 ⇢ 7,b746: ᴿClasR 42 (1992) 461s (J.S. *Morrison*); RÉLat 70 (1992) 330s (A. *Dubourdieu*).

d759 ᴱ**Casson** Lionel, *Steffy* J. Richard, The Athlit ram [Haifa 1981]: NautArch 3. Texas A & M 1991. xiii-91 p.; 83 fig. $72.50. – ᴿClasR 42 (1992) 476s (J.S. *Morrison*).

d760 *Chevereau* Pierre-Marie, Contribution à la prosopographie des titres militaires du Moyen-Empire, B. Titres nautiques: RÉgp 43 (1992) 11-34.

d761 *Clarysse* W., *Idion* and *idiotikon ploion*: ZPapEp 89 (1991) 69s.

d762 a) *Diakonoff* I. M., The naval power and trade of Tyre; – b) *Raban* Avner, A nautical scene from ʿAkko: IsrEJ 42 (1992) 168-193 / 194-8; 5 fig.

d762* a) *Effenterre* Henri van, Le 'port des cerfs' de la tablette pylienne An 657,12; – b) *Hocker* Fred, *Palaima* Thomas J., Late Bronze Age Aegean ships and the Pylos tablets Vn 46 and Vn 879: Minos 25s (1990s) 87-90 / 297-317.

d763 *Fischer* Henry G., Boats in non-nautical titles of the Old Kingdom: GöMiszÄg 126 (1992) 59-78; 4 fig.

d764 **Garland** Robert, The Piraeus 1987 ⇢ 4,d973... 7,b749: ᴿMnemosyne 45 (1992) 132s (H.T. *Wallinga*).

d765 **Göttlicher** Arvid, Kultschiffe und Schiffskulte im Altertum. B 1992, Mann. 185 p.; ill. 3-7861-1679-2.

d767 *Hadas* Gideon,   Stone anchors from the Dead Sea [off En-Gedi 1989]: ꜥAtiqot 21 (1992) 55-57; 3 fig.; map [58-62, *al*., ancient anchor ropes].

d768 **Jones** Dilwyn, [35] Model boats from the tomb of Tut'ankhamūn 1990 ⇥ 6,d269:   ᴿArOr 60 (1992) 202 (B. *Vachala*); DiscEg 21 (1991) 91-94 (S. E. *Mark*).

d769 *Leospo* Enrichetta, *Fossati* Luigi,   I modelli navali del Museo Egizio di Torino; prospettive per un'indagine storico-antropologica: ⇥ 735, Sesto Eg. 1991/2, 391-6; 8 color. pl.

d769* *Lilliu* Giovanni,   La Sardegna e il mare durante l'età romana: ⇥ 726, L'Africa 1990/1, (2) 661-694; 1 fig.; X pl.

d770 *Linder* Elisha,   Excavating an ancient merchantman; Maꜥagan Michael shipwreck [20 k S Haifa, 400 B.C.E.]: BAR-W 18,6 (100th issue, 1992) 24-35.

d771 *Moutsos* Demetrios,   Greek *chelandion* and Latin *celundria* [kind(s) of boat]: ⇥ 43, ᶠDELVOYE C., Byzantion 62 (1992) 402-413.

d772 *Raveh* Kurt, *Kingsley* Sean A.,   The wreck complex at the entrance to Dor harbour, Israel; preliminary details (4 or 5 c. 600 C.E.; 4 others 1650: 1991 survey): IntJNaut 21 (1992) 309-315; 7 fig.

d773 *Rougé* Jean †,   Transports maritimes et transports fluviaux dans les provinces occidentales de l'Empire: Ktema 13 (1988) 87-93.

d774 *Salies* Gisela H.,   Der antike Schiffsfund von Mahdia [Tunis 1907, von c. 100 v.C.]; Bericht zur Table Ronde vom 4. bis 7. Juni 1992 [Bonn]: BonnJbb 192 (1992) 507-536; 33 fig.

d775 **Starr** Chester G.,   The influence of sea power on ancient history 1989 ⇥ 5,d163...7,b765:   ᴿGnomon 64 (1992) 258s (D. *Kienast*); HZ 253 (1991) 409s (O. *Höckmann*); JHS 112 (1992) 198s (J. S. *Morrison*: inaccurate data).

d776 *Tilley* Alec,   Three men to a room — [Olympias] a completely different trireme: Antiquity 66 (1992) 599-610; 10 fig.

d777 *Vann* Robert L.,   A survey of classical harbors in Cilicia (Turkey), AIA 1991: ⇥ 699, AJA 96 (1992) 337.

d777* *Verner* Miroslav,   Funerary boats of Neferirkare and Raneferef: ⇥ 96, ᶠKÁKOSY L., Heritage of Egypt 1992, 587-602; 9 fig.; pl. XXXVI-XL.

d778 **Wachsmann** Shelley, *al*.,   The excavations of an ancient boat in the Sea of Galilee 1990⇥ 6,d288; 7,b767:   ᴿBAR-W 18,2 (1992) 4 (L. *Casson*).

d779 **Wright** Edward,   The Ferriby boats; seacraft of the Bronze Age [carbon-14 1300 B.C., near Hull]. NY 1991, Routledge. xxi-206 p.; 174 fig. $160.   0-415-02599-0. – ᴿClasW 86 (1992s) 33 (L. *Casson*: momentous).

d780 *Zimmermann* Martin,   Die lykischen Häfen und die Handelswege im östlichen Mittelmeer; Bemerkungen zu PMich I 10: ZPapEp 92 (1992) 201-217.

T2.4   *Athletica,* **sport, games.**

d781 **André** Jean-Marie, *al*.,   Jouer dans l'Antiquité: Marseille Musée d'Archéologie Méditerranée, exposition 1991s.   Marseille 1991, Réunion Musées Nationaux. 205 p. 2-7118-2499-3 [OIAc 3,11].

d782 ᴱ**Arrigoni** Giampiera, (p. 55-201) Donne e sport nel mondo greco. Bari 1985, Laterza [⇥ 3,482].   Lit. 36.000. 88-420-2651-4. – ᴿNikephoros 4 (1991) 266-8 (Barbara *Mauritsch-Bein*).

d783 *Blázquez* J. M., *García Gelabert* M. P.,   El origen funerario de los juegos olímpicos: RevArq 13,140 (M 1992) 28-39.

d784 **Blum** Richard, *Golitzin* Alexander,   The sacred athlete; on the mystical experience and Dionysios [Ps.-Areop.], its westernworld fountainhead. Lanham NY 1991, UPA.   503 p. $36.50 [RelStR 19,160, W. G. *Rusch*: deficient in every way].

d785 *Caldelli* Maria Letizia,   Curia athletarum, *iera xystike synodos* e organizzazione delle terme a Roma: ZPapEp 93 (1992) 75-87; 2 plans.

d786 **Carter** John M.,   *Krüger* Arnd,   Ritual and record; sports records and quantification in pre-modern societies.   NY 1990. – ᴿStadion 17 (1991) 307-310 (R. *Renson*).

d787 *Crowther* Nigel B.,   *a*) Second-place finishes and lower in Greek athletics (including the Pentathlon): ZPapEp 90 (1992) 97-102; – *b*) Slaves and Greek athletics: QuadUrb 69 (1992) 35-42.

d788 **Davis** Whitney,   Masking the blow; the scene of representation in late prehistoric Egyptian art: Studies in the History of Art 30.   Berkeley 1992, Univ. California.   xvii-299 p.; 53 fig.   0-520-07488-2.

d789 **Decker** Wolfgang,   Sport und Spiel im alten Ägypten 1987 ↠ 3,d463 ... 6,d306:   ᴿDiscEg 19 (1991) 78-82 (S. *Allam*).

d790 **Decker** Wolfgang,   Sports and games of ancient Egypt,   ᵀ*Guttmann* Allan: Sport and History. NHv 1992, Yale Univ.   xi-212 p.   0-300-04463-1 [OIAc 3,17].

d791 **Decker** Wolfgang, *Herrmann* Werner,   Jahresbibliographie zum Sport im Altertum 1992:   Nikephoros 5 (1992) 219-245.

d791* **Di Donato** Michele, *Teja* Angela,   Agonistica e ginnastica nella Grecia antica 1989 ↠ 5,d175; 7,b772:   ᴿStCattMi 35 (1991) 379 (Maria Teresa *de Martino*).

d792 *Flobert* Pierre,   Quelques survivances de la gladiature [... dans l'imaginaire chrétien]: Voces 1 (1990) 71-76; Eng. 122 [< AnPg 62, p. 982].

d793 **Fuchs** H. (fem.),   Lusus Troiae: Diss. Köln 1990. 111 p.; 5 pl. – ᴿNikephoros 4 (1991) 281-3 (L. *Bouke van der Meer*).

d793* *Golub* Ivan,   Homo ludens – imago Dei: BogSmot 61 (Dei Verbum 25 Anniv. 1991) 46-60 croatice.

d794 **Golvin** Jean-Claude,   L'amphithéâtre romain 1988 ↠ 5,d30 ... 7,b776: ᴿBonnJbb 192 (1992) 667-672 (W. K. *Kovacsovics*); Latomus 51 (1992) 228-230 (P. *Gros*); JRomA 4 (1991) 272-281 (Katherine *Welch*, also on Toulouse colloquium 1987).

d795 **Golvin** Jean-Claude, *Landes* Christian,   Amphithéâtres et gladiateurs 1990 ↠ 7,b775:   ᴿJRS 82 (1992) 267s (Hazel *Dodge*, also on three cognates); Nikephoros 4 (1991) 292-5 (Augusta *Hönle*).

d795* *Herrmann* Monika,   Zur Frau als Zuschauerin bei Wettkämpfen in römischer Zeit; – *b*) *Dolch* Martin,   Wettkampf, Wasserrevue oder diätetische Übungen? Das Mosaik mit den zehn Mädchen in der römischen Villa bei Piazza Armerina auf Sizilien: Nikephoros 5 (1992) 85-102; 6 fig.; pl. p. 323 / 153-181; fig. 1; pl. 10-13.

d796 ᴱ**Hoffman** Shirl J.,   Sport and religion [reprints].   ... c. 1991, Human Kinetics.   289 p. $28. – ᴿChrCent 109 (1992) 167.

d797 **Hübner** Ulrich,   Spiele und Spielzeug im antiken Palästina: OBO 121. FrS/Gö 1992, Univ./VR.   229 p.; 60 fig.   3-7278-0847-0 / 3-525-53755-7.

d797* *Janssen* Rosalind M.,   Rectification; a case of moveable arms [on doll; not weapons; > Growing up in Ancient Egypt 1991]: GöMiszÄg [123 (1991) 101-111, *Tooley* J.] 126 (1992) 83-86.

d798 *Knobloch* Johann,   *Skapérda*; eine sportliche Kraftprobe der Griechen, mit dem Versuch einer etymologischen Deutung: IndogF 97 (1992) 65-67.

d798* **Kyle** Donald E.,   Athletics in ancient Athens: Mnem supp. 95, 1987
→ 3,d471 ... 6,d323:   ᴿEirene 27 (1990) 174-6 (— *Oliva*).

d799 *Langenfeld* Hans,   Artemidors Traumbuch als sporthistorische Quelle:
Stadion 17 (1991) 1-26.

d800 **Laser** Siegfried,   Sport und Spiel: Archaeologia Homerica T.   Gö 1987,
Vandenhoeck & R. 204 p.; 8 pl.   3-525-25426-1. – ᴿBabesch 67 (1992)
199s (J. M. *Hemelrijk*).

d801 **Lavrencic** Monika,   Diskos; sporthistorischer Kommentar,   ᵀ*Doblhofer*
Georg, *Mauritsch* Peter: QDokGymnastik I.   W 1991, Böhlau.   vi-172 p.

d802 *Lavrencic* Monika,   Krieger und Athlet? Der militarische Aspekt in der
Beurteilung des Wettkampfes der Antike: Nikephoros 4 (1991) 167-175.

d803 **Lippolis** Enzo,   Gli eroi di Olimpia; lo sport nella società greca e ma-
gnogreca.   Taranto 1990, Scorpione.   119 p.; ill.

d804 *Lohmann* Dieter,   Homer als Erzähler; die Athla im 23. Buch der Ilias:
Gymnasium 99 (1992) 289-319.

d805 *Looy* Herman Van,   Le sport dans la Grèce antique: Archéologia 281
(1992) 24-39; ill.

d806 *Lorenz* Thuri,   Der Doryphoros des Polyklet; Athlet, Musterfigur, poli-
tisches Denkmal oder mythischer Held?:   Nikephoros 4 (1991) 177-190.

d807 *Muróti* Egon,   Zur Problematik des Gladiatorenkampfes zur Ehrung des
Andenkens des Crixus: AcClasDebrecen 28 (1992) 41-44.

d808 *Marrero Rodríguez* G.,   Psicologia del juego: Almogaren 3,3 (1990)
103-142 [< RET 51,408].

d809 *Matoušová* Marie,   Tanzschulen im alten Vorderen Orient [Siegelabrol-
lungen]:   ArOr 60 (1992) 167-9 + 9 fig.

d810 **Matz** David,   Greek and Roman sport; a dictionary of athletes and
events from the eighth century B.C. to the third century A.D.   Jefferson NC
1991, McFarland.   181 p. $30.   0-89950-558-9. – ᴿClasW 85 (1991s) 733s
(W. W. *Briggs*); ClasR 42 (1992) 391s (H. W. *Pleket*); Nikephoros 5
(1992) 249-257 (Ingomar *Weiler*).

d810* **Maul-Mandelartz** Elsbeth,   Griechische Reiterdarstellungen in agoni-
stischem Zusammenhang [Diss. Bochum 1989]. EurHS 38/32.   Fra 1990,
Lang.   280 p.; 50 pl.   DM 77.   3-631-42881-2. – ᴿHelmantica 42 sup
(1991) 340 (J. *Mazas*); Nikephoros 5 (1992) 278-281 (P. *Stefanek*).

d811 *u*) *Mehl* Andreas,   Erziehung – zum Hellenen – Erziehung zum Weltbürger; Bemerkungen zum Gymnasium im hellenistischen Osten; – *b*)
Catenacci Carmine,   Il tiranno alle Colonne d'Eracle; l'agonistica e le
tirannidi arcaiche: Nikephoros 5 (1992) 43-78 / 11-36.

d811* **Miller** Stephen G.,   *Aretē*; Greek sports from ancient sources²
[doubling ¹1979]. Berkeley 1991, Univ. California.   239 p.; 16 fig. $37.50,
pa. $13.   0-520-07508-0; -9-9. – ᴿClasW 86 (1992s) 161 (J. *Rutter*: the
best); GreeceR 39 (1992) 247 (P. *Walcot*, also on *Matz*, 'patronizing');
Nikephoros 5 (1992) 258-260 (W. *Decker*).

d812 *Moretti* Gabriella,   L'arena, Cesare e il mito; appunti sul De spectaculis
di MARZIALE [per l'inaugurazione del Colosseo 80 d.C.]:   Maia 44 (1992)
55-63.

d813 **Morgan** Catherine,   Athletes and oracles; the transformation of Olympia
and Delphi in the eighth century B.C., 1990 → 6,d329; 7,b791:   ᴿGnomon
64 (1992) 317-320 (Ingomar *Weiler*); JHS 112 (1992) 200 (H. *Bowden*);
Nikephoros 4 (1991) 260-5 (H.-V. *Herrmann*).

d813* **Nielsen** Inge,   Thermae et balnea; the architecture and cultural history
of public Roman baths. Aarhus 1990, Univ.   194 p.; 212 p., 260 fig.
87-7288-212-3. – ᴿNikephoros 5 (1992) 292-8 (W. *Heinz*).

d814 **Panagiotopoulos** D. P., Ⓖ *Dikaio*... Legal status of the Olympic Games: diss. Athens 1991, Sakkoula. 425 p. – ᴿNikephoros 5 (1992) 264-270 (K. D. *Frangandreas*).

d814* *Papalas* Anthony J., Boy athletes in ancient Greece: Stadion 17 (1991) 165-192.

d815 *Petzold* Joachim, Entstehung und Symbolbedeutung des Schachspiels: Altertum 37 (1991) 38-47; 7 fig.

d816 **Poliakoff** Michael B., Kampfsport in der Antike 1989 → 7,b796: ᴿNikephoros 4 (1991) 249-256 (M. *Herb*).

d817 *a) Raubitschek* Anthony E., Sport und Zivilisation; – *b) Ulf* C., Die Frage nach dem Ursprung des Sports, oder weshalb und wie menschliches Verhalten anfängt, Sport zu sein: Nikephoros 4 (1991) 9-11 / 13-30.

d818 *Rauh* Nicholas K., Was the [Delos] Agora of the Italians an établissement de sport? [yes]: BCH 116 (1992) 293-333; 8 fig.

d819 *Rollefson* Gary O., A neolithic game board from ʿAin Ghazal, Jordan: BASOR 286 (1992) 1-5; 1 fig.

d819* *a) Siewert* Peter, Zum Ursprung der Olympischen Spiele; – *b) Raubitschek* A., Wo war der erste Dromos der Panathenäen?; – *c) Luppe* Wolfgang, Das Kottabos-Spiel mit den Essignäpfchen (Kratinos fr. 124 K/A): Nikephoros 5 (1992) 7s / 9s / 37-42.

d820 *a) Sinn* Ulrich, Olympia; die Stellung der Wettkämpfe im Kult des Zeus Olympios; – *b) Crowther* Nigel B., The Olympic training period: Nikephoros 4 (1991) 31-54 / 161-6.

d821 *Speidel* Michael P., [Soranus in 118] Swimming the Danube under Hadrian's eyes; a feat of the emperors' Batavi horse guard: AncSoc 22 (1991) 277-282.

d822 *Tracy* Stephen V., The Panathenaic festival and games; an epigraphic inquiry: Nikephoros 4 (1991) 133-153.

d823 **Tzachou-Alexandri** O., Mind and body; athletic contests in ancient Greece, ᵀ*Binder* J., *al.* Athens 1989, Ministry of Culture. 352 p.; 235 pl. – ᴿJHS 112 (1992) 223 (S. *Instone*).

d824 **Vanoyeke** Violaine, La naissance des Jeux Olympiques et le sport dans l'Antiquité: Realia. P 1992, BLettres. 195 p.; 10 plans. F 100. 2-251-33812-8.

d825 *Ward* Roy B., Women in Roman baths: HarvTR 85 (1992) 125-147.

d825* *a) Weber-Hiden* Ingrid, Wettkampfdarstellungen auf Terra Sigillata; – *b) Pausz* Ralf-Dieter, *Rettinger* Walter, Das Mosaik der gymnischen Agone von Batten Zammour, Tunesien: Nikephoros 5 (1992) 103-117 / 119-133; pl. 2-3.

d826 *Weeber* Karl-Wilhelm, Die unheiligen Spiele; das antike Olympia zwischen Legende und Wirklichkeit. Z 1991, Artemis & W. 220 p.; 18 fig. DM 40. – ᴿClasR 42 (1992) 390s (H. W. *Pleket*); Nikephoros 5 (1992) 261-3 (Sabine *Schmidt*).

d827 **Wiedemann** Thomas, Emperors and gladiators. L 1992, Routledge. xvii-198 p.; 17 fig. 0-415-00005-X.

d827* *a) Yoyotte* Jean, Les jeux des enfants et des adolescents en Égypte; – *b) Bellessort* Marie-Noël, Le jeu de serpent; – *c) May* Roland, Les jeux de table dans l'antiquité; – *d) Finkel* Irving, Le jeu royal d'Ur; – *e) Durand* Agnès, Jeux et jouets de l'enfance en Grèce et à Rome; – *f) André* Jean-Marie, Jeux et divertissements dans le monde gréco-romain; – *g) Poplin* François, Les jeux d'osselets antiques; – *h) Manson* Michel,

Les poupées antiques: DossA 168 (1992) 2-7 / 8s / 18-34 / 34s / 10-17 / 36-45 / 46s / 48-57; color. ill.

T2.5 Musica, dance.

d828 (Oyedele) *Abe* Gabriel, The influence of Nigerian music and dance on Christianity: AsiaJT 5 (1991) 296-310 [< ZIT 91,558].

d829 **Adams** Doug, *Apostolos-Cappadona* Diane, Dance as religious studies. NY 1990, Crossroad. 256 p. $18 pa. 0-8245-0988-9. – [R]RExp 88,2 (1991) 237 (W. L. *Hendricks*: M. GRUBER gives 'ten dance-derived expressions in the Hebrew Bible').

d830 *Arndt-Jeamart* Joachim, Zur Konstruktion und Stimmung von Saiteninstrumenten nach den musikalischen Keilschrifttexten: Orientalia 61 (1992) 425-447.

d831 *Bauer* J. B., *al.*, Horn: → 764, RAC 125 (1992) 524-574.

Bélis Annie, Les hymnes à Apollon, étude... musicale 1992 → b239.

d832 *Bélis* Annie, *a*) À propos de la coupe CA 482 du Louvre [femme avec deux cithares]: BCH 116 (1992) 53-59; 7 fig. – *b*) L'aulète et le jeu de l'oie: BCH 116 (1992) 497-500; 1 fig.

d833 **Bourcier** Paul, Danser devant les dieux: La recherche en danse. P 1989, Univ.-IV Sorbonne. 448 p. – [R]ArchivScSocR 78 (1992) 268s (Françoise *Lautman*: en sanctuaires d'occident, surtout macabre).

d834 [TE]**Bower** Calvin M., A. M. S. BOETHIUS, Fundamentals of music: Music Theory Translations. NHv 1989, Yale Univ. xliv-205 p. $32.50. 0-300-03943-3. – [R]ClasW 85 (1991s) 712s (J. C. *Relihan*).

d835 **Brunner-Traut** Emma, Der Tanz im alten Ägypten, nach bildlichen und inschriftlichen Zeugnissen[3rev] [[1]1937]: ÄgF 6. Glückstadt 1992, Augustin. 101 p.; 42 fig. → d809.

d836 **de Martino** Stefano, La danza nella cultura ittita: Eothen 2. F 1989, ELITE [Ed. Librerie Italiane Estere]. 103 p. [OIAc 3,17 'danta'].

d836* *Fischer-Elfert* Hans-W., Amun als Harfner: GöMiszÄg 127 (1992) 38-40.

d837 **Flender** Reinhard, Der biblische Sprechgesang und seine mündliche Überlieferung in Synagoge und griechischer Kirche 1988 → 5,d217; 6,d363*: [R]RÉJ 150 (1991) 171-6 (Denise *Jourdan-Hemmerdinger*).

d837* **Foley** Edward, Foundation of Christian music; the music of pre-Constantinian Christianity. Bramcote Notts/Wsh 1992, Grove / Pastoral. 84 p. £7.50. 1-85174-218-2. – [R]TBR 5,3 (1992s) 43 (W. F. *Clocksin*).

d838 *Gersh* Stephen, PORPHYRY's commentary on the 'Harmonics' of PTOLEMY and Neoplatonic musical theory: → 147, [F]PLACES E. des, Neoplatonism 1992, 141-155.

d839 *Green* L., Asiatic musicians and the court of Akhenaten: → 557*, Contacts 1990/2, 215-9; 3 fig.

d840 **Haïk-Vantoura** Suzanne, The music of the Bible revealed [[2]1978], [T]*Weber* Dennis, [E]*Wheeler* John, 1991 → 7,b813: [R]BAR-W 18,4 (1992) 6 (P. *Jeffery*; her claim is untrue; she argues in a circle); JAOS 112 (1992) 499 (P. T. *Daniels*: the system is arbitrary and need have nothing to do with the music of the Masoretes, but she is a gifted composer).

d841 *Jones* Ivor H., Music and musical instruments: → 741, AnchorDB 4 (1992) 950-9.

d842 *Kilmer* Anne D., Musical practice at Nippur: → 687, Nippur 1988/92, 101-112; 3 fig.

d843 **Krah** Karen, Die Harfe im pharaonischen Ägypten; ihre Entwicklung und Funktion [< MA Diss. Göttingen 1984]: Orbis Musicarum. Gö 1991, Ramaswamy. 230 p.; 68 fig. 3-927636-10-X [OIAc 3,27].

d844 **Manniche** Lise, Music and musicians in ancient Egypt. L 1991, British Museum. 142 p., 80 fig.; 20 pl. 0-7141-0949-5 [OIAc 3,29].

d845 *Milanese* Guido, Tradizione varroniana e tradizioni grammaticali nei libri II-V del De musica di AGOSTINO: AevA 2 (1989) 273-297.

d846 *Mitchell* T.C., The music of the Old Testament reconsidered: PEQ 124 (1992) 124-143.

Musicians/acrobats 1989/92 ➤ k242c *Maul*; k209d *Blocher*.

d847 **Pizzani** Ubaldo, *Milanese* Guido. Commento al 'De Musica' di AGOSTINO 1990 ➤ 7,b823: ᴿOrpheus 13,1 (1992) 162-5 (G. *Boccuto*); RTPhil 124 (1992) 99s (R. *Petraglio*); Salesianum 54 (1992) 395s (T. *Porzycki*); ScripTPamp 24 (1992) 686s (P. *Fernández-Navajas*).

d848 **Pöhlmann** Egert, Beiträge zur antiken und neueren Musikgeschichte 1988 ➤ 7,b824: ᴿAnzAltW 43 (1990) 265s (W. *Salmen*); RÉLat 70 (1992) 347 (D. *Porte*).

d849 **Ravasi** G. (*Turoldo* D.M.), Il canto della rana; musica e teologia nella Bibbia 1990 ➤ 7,b825: ᴿNRT 113 (1992) 929 (S. *Hilaire*).

d850 *a)* **Ravasi** Gianfranco, 'Cantate a Dio con arte'; il teologico e il musicale nella Bibbia; – *b)* **Troia** Pasquale, '...Musicalmente parlando, Babele è una benedizione'; – *c)* **Rainoldi** Felice, La Bibbia nel canto liturgico medievale; – *d)* **Costa** Eugenio, Bibbia, liturgia e musica: ➤ 455, Musica 1990/2, 65-110 / 1-55 (245-255; bibliog. 395-476) / 137-169 / 189-202.

d851 **Rossin** Thomas D., The Calov Bible of Johann Sebastian Bach; an analysis of the composer's markings: diss. (music.) Minnesota, ᴰSchultz S. Mp 1992. 315 p. 92-31075. – DissA 53 (1992s) 1720-A.

d852 *Sarti* Susanna, Gli strumenti musicali di Apollo: AnnArchSto 14 (1992) 95-104; pl. 17-20.

d853 **Schelika** Renata von, Vom Wettkampf der Dichter; der musische Agon bei den Griechen. Amst 1987, Castrum Peregrini. 158 p. DM 36. 90-603-4061-2. – ᴿNikephoros 4 (1991) 269-273 (Ingomar *Weiler*).

d854 *Schuster* Sabine., Musikinstrumente in der Situlenkunst: ➤ 167, SCHÜLE W. 1991, 311-5; 12 fig. Eng. 315.

d855 *Seidel* Hans, Musik in Altisrael [ᴰ1970] 1989 ➤ 6,d379; 7,b831: ᴿTsTKi 63 (1992) 150s (T. *Stordalen*); VT 42 (1992) 276s (L.R. *Wickham*).

d855* *Seidel* H., Hiob, der Patron der Musiker, ➤ 149, ᶠPREUSS 1992, 225-232.

d856 *Sequeri* Pierangelo, Convegno di 'Bibbia' su La musica e la Bibbia (Siena, 24-26.VIII.1990) [< Il sole 16.IX.1990]: ParVi 36 (1991) 56-59.

d857 *a)* *Somville* Pierre, Le signe d'extase et la musique; – *b)* *Moutsopoulos* E., Prévenir ou guérir? Musique et états orgiastiques chez Platon: ➤ 671, Kernos 5 (1991/2) 173-181 / 141-151.

d858 ᴱWallace Robert W., *MacLachlan* Bonnie, Harmonia mundi; musica e filosofia nell'Antichità [Symposium Rome, American Acad. 1989]: QuadUrb Bt 5, R 1991, Ateneo. vii-153 p. – ᴿAntClas 61 (1992) 467-9 (F. *Duysinx*).

d859 **West** M.L., Ancient Greek music. Ox 1992, Clarendon. xiii-410 p.; 12 fig.; 35 pl. 0-19-814897-6.

d860 *West* M.L., *a)* Analecta musica; 1. On the text of the Greek musical documents; 2. Alcidamas (?), *Katà tôn harmonikôn*; 3. Observations on other texts relating to music; 4. The origins of the notation systems: ZPapEp 92 (1992) 1-15.16-23.23-35.36-54. – *b)* An alleged musical inscription [two rather; against D. *Themelis*, Die Musikforschung 42 (1989) 307-324]: ZPapEp 93 (1992) 27s.

d861 **Zanoncelli** Luisa, La manualistica musicale greca [8 autori]: Ricerche. Mi 1990, Guerini. 508 p. Lit. 60.000. 88-7802-156-3. – ᴿAntClas 61 (1992) 504-6 (F. *Duysinx*); RPg 65,2 (1991) 60s (Annie *Bélis*).

T2.6 Textilia, *vestis*, clothing.

d862 **Barber** E. J. W., Prehistoric textiles 1991 ➤ 7,b836: ᴿClasR 42 (1992) 393-5 (J. P. *Wild*).

d863 *Coquin* R.-G., À propos des vêtements des moines égyptiens [MORFIN-GOURDIER; INNEMÉE K.]: BSArCopte 31 (1992) 3-24.

d864 *Edwards* Douglas R., Dress and ornamentation: ➤ 741, AnchorBD 2 (1992) 232-8.

d865 **Germer** Renate, Die Textilfärberei und die Verwendung gefärbter Textilien im alten Ägypten: ÄgAbh 53. Wsh 1992, Harrassowitz. x-151 p.; 10 color. phot. 3-447-03183-2.

d866 **Goette** Hans R., Studien zu römischen Togadarstellungen: Beiträge zur Erschliessung hellenistischer und kaiserzeitlicher Skulptur und Architektur 10, Mainz 1989 ➤ 6,d387: ᴿBonnJbb 192 (1992) 674-7 (H. *Gabelmann*).

d867 *Gropp* Gerd, Clothing of Sasanian Persians from Egyptian tombs: ➤ 557*, Contacts 1990/2, 274-6.

d868 *Jacoby* D., Silk in western Byzantium before the Fourth Crusade: ByZ 84s (1991s) 452-500.

d868* *Janssen* J. J., Pictorial clothing lists on Deir El-Medina ostraca: GöMiszÄg 131 (1992) 55-60.

d869 *Janssen* Rosalind M., The 'ceremonial garments' of Tuthmosis IV reconsidered: StAäK 19 (1992) 217-224; pl. 15.

d869* *Kakovkine* Alexandre, Le tissu copte des VIIᵉ-VIIIᶜ siècles du Musée Métropolitain: GöMiszÄg 129 (1992) 55-58 + 1 fig.

d870 *Klochko* I. S., ❻ The Scythian foot-wear: SovArch (1992,1) 28-33; 4 fig.; Eng. 33.

d871 ᴱ**Kühnel** Harry, Bildwörterbuch der Kleidung und Rüstung, vom Alten Orient bis zum ausgehenden Mittelalter: Tb 453. Stu 1992, Kröner. lxxxi-334 p. DM 42 [ErbAuf 68,255]. 3-520-45301-0.

d871* *Madigan* Brian, An [Egyptian textile] Orpheus among the animals at Dumbarton Oaks: GrOrByz 33 (1992) 405-416.

d872 **Martiniani-Reber** Marielle [*al.*], *a*) Tissus coptes; 1. Textes et catalogue; 2. Planches. Genève 1991, Musée d'Art et d'Histoire. – *b*) Les textiles: DossA 176 ('L'art byzantin' 1992) 44-53; color. ill.

d873 *Nauerth* Claudia, Evidence for a David cycle on Coptic textiles: ➤ 690, 3d Coptic 1984/90, 285-297; 12 fig.

d874 *Niehr* H., *śimlah* 'Mantel': ➤ 770, TWAT 7,6s (1992) 822-8.

d875 *Osborne* John, Textiles and their painted imitations in early medieval Rome: PBritSR 60 (1992) 309-351; 12 fig.; ital. 425.

d876 **Pekridou-Gorecki** Anastasia, Mode im antiken Griechenland; Textile-Fertigung und Kleidung 1989 ➤ 7,b844: ᴿGnomon 64 (1992) 53-56 (Christine *Schnurr*).

d877 **Renner** Dorothee, Die spätantiken und koptischen Textilien ... in Darmstadt 1985 ➤ 3,d520: ᴿCdÉ 67 (1992) 199s (Jacqueline *Lafontaine-Dosogne*).

d878 **Renner-Volbach** Dorothee, Spätantike und koptische Textilien im erzbischöflichen Diözesanmuseum in Köln. Wsb 1992, Harrassowitz. 84 p.; 11 pl. + 2 color. 3-447-03242-1 [OIAc 5,33].

d879 **Renner-Volbach** Dorothee, Die koptischen Textilien... Vat. 1988 → 7, b847: ᴿBonnJbb 192 (1992) 693-6 (D. *Willers*).

d880 *Sanmartín* J., Tejidos y ropas en ugarítico; apuntes lexicográficos: AulaO 10 (1992) 95-103.

d880* *Savage* Paula, Ancient footwear: BIL 16,1 (1989) 49-55 [< OTAbs 15,15].

d881 a) *Schick* Tomas, Early neolithic twined basketry and fabrics from the Nahal Hemar cave, Israel [6 k W Dead Sea]; – b) *Grilletto* Renato, Double panier en jonc pour une sépulture de l'Ancien Empire...; – c) *Leospo* Enrichetta, *al.*, Deux tuniques égyptiennes d'Assiout [Ancien-Moyen Empire] conservées dans le Musée Égyptien de Turin: → 710e, Tissage Antibes 1988/9, 41-52; 16 fig. / 71-74; 2 fig. / 75-80; 2 fig.

d881* **Seagrott** Margaret, Coptic weaves. Liverpool..., Merseyside Museums. 43 p.; 45 fig.

d882 **Stauffer** Annemarie, Textiles d'Égypte de la collection Bouvier; antiquité tardive, période copte, premiers temps de l'Islam / Textilien... [FrS Musée exposition 1991s]. FrS 1991, Benteli-Werg. 231 p.; 116 fig. 3-7165-0827-6 [OIAc 3,39].

d882* a) *Stordeur* Danielle, Vannerie et tissage au Proche-Orient néolithique; – b) *Maréchal* Claudine, ... d'El Kowm (Syrie, VIᵉ millénaire); – c) *Le Brun* Alain, Un fragment de tissu recueilli sur le site néolithique précéramique de Khirokitia (Chypre): → 710e Tissage Antibes 1988/9, 19-39 / 53-68; 9 fig. / 69s; 1 fig.

d883 *Vogelsang-Eastwood* G. M., Deciphering a pictorial clothing-list: GöMiszÄg 128 (1992) 105-111; 8 fig.

d884 *Vogelsang-Eastwood* G. M., *Haeringen* J. van, The so-called boy spinners of Beni Hasan: GöMiszÄg 126 (1992) 95s; 2 fig.

d885 **Walters** Elizabeth J., Attic grave... dress of Isis 1988 → 5,d543; 7,b851; ᴿJEA 78 (1992) 346-8 (J. G. *Griffiths*).

d886 **Weir** Shelagh, Palestinian costume [mostly since 1920]. L/Austin 1989, British Museum / Univ. Texas. 288 p.; 100 fig. + 200 color. $40. – ᴿJAOS 112 (1992) 166s (Jeanette *Wakin*).

d887 **Zoffoli** Ermanno, Costume e cultura dell'antico Egitto, da Narmer a Cleopatra, ᴱClayton Peter A., pref. *Curto* Silvio. Mi 1991, Fabbri. 255 p.; ill. 88-450-4011-9 [OIAc 3,43].

T2.7 *Ornamenta corporis,* jewelry, mirrors.

d888 [Pirzio] **Biroli Stefanelli** Lucia, L'oro dei Romani; gioielli di età imperiale: Il metallo, mito e fortuna nel mondo antico. R 1992, Bretschneider. 294 p.; ill. 88-7062-773-X.

d888* *Emmanuel-Rebuffat* Denise, Pourquoi un corpus des miroirs étrusques?: DossA 175 ('Les Étrusques' 1992) 66-71; color. ill.

d889 **Fay** Biri, Altägyptischer Goldschmuck – Ancient Egyptian jewelry. Mainz 1990, von Zabern. 81 p. DM 16,80 [BO 50,150].

d890 **Formigli** E., *Heilmeyer* W.-D., Tarentiner Goldschmuck in Berlin: Winckelmannsprogramm 130s. B 1990, de Gruyter. 100 p.; 52 fig.; 7 pl. DM 75. – ᴿJHS 112 (1992) 223s (R. *Higgins*).

d891 **Henig** M., *Whiting* M., Engraved gems from Gadara 1987 → 3,d753: ᴿLA 41 (1991) 597-9 (S. *Amorai-Stark*).

d892 **Heres** G., Corpus speculorum etruscorum, Berlin/Dresden. B 1986s, Akademie. 64 p., 7 fig., 161 pl.; 47 p., 4 fig., 73 pl. DM 75 + 50. 3-

05-000130-5; -1-3. – ᴿAJA 96 (1992) 386-8 (R. D. *DePuma*, also on R. LAMBRECHTS Bru).

d893 **Limper** Klaudia, Uruk, Perlen... 1988 → 5,d256; 6,d417*: ᴿAfO 38s (1991s) 220-2 (D. T. *Potts*).

d893* *Lohwasser* Angelika, Versuch einer Terminologie der Perücken im Relief des Neuen Reiches: GöMiszÄg 131 (1992) 77-84 + 1 pl.

d894 **Megow** Wolf-R., Kameen 1987 → 5,d259... 7,b865: ᴿAnzAltW 43 (1990) 91-94 (Erika *Simon*).

d895 *Miller* M. C., The parasol, an oriental status symbol in late archaic and classical Athens: JHS 112 (1992) 91-105.

d896 **Musche** Brigitte, Vorderasiatischer Schmuck von den Anfängen bis zur Zeit der Achämenider (ca. 10.000-330 v.Chr.): HbOr 7/1/2B/7. Leiden 1992, Brill. xii-306 p.; 116 pl. 90-04-09491-1 [OIAc 3,31: 'Musch', '-33 v.Chr.']. – ᴿAfO 38s (1991s) 231-3 (J. *Curtis*).

d897 *Pászthory* Emmerich, Salben, Schminken und Parfüme im Altertum; Herstellungsmethoden und Anwendungsbereiche im östlichen Mediterraneum: AntWelt 21 Sdb. 2 (1990), 64 p.; ill.

d898 *a) Phillips* Jacke, Reworked and reused Egyptian jewellery; – *b) Ertman* Earl L., The search for the significance and origin of Nefertiti's tall blue crown; – *c) Quaegebeur* Jan, Les pantoufles du dieu Thot; – *d) Chiotasso* L., al., La parrucca di Merit: → 735, SestoEg 1991/2, 497-502; 4 fig. / 189-193 / 521-7; 6 fig. / 99-103; 6 fig.

d899 *Platt* Elizabeth E., Jewelry, ancient Israelite: → 741, AnchorBD 3 (1992) 823-834.

d899* **Rehm** Ellen, Schmuck der Achämeniden [Diss. Münster 1991]. Münster 1992 Ug-V. xii-468 p.; 200 + 120 fig. 3-927120-11-1. – ᴿUF 24 (1992) 514s (M. *Dietrich*).

d900 **Spier** Jeffrey, Ancient gems and finger rings; catalogue. Malibu 1992, Getty Museum. xiii-184 p. 0-89236-215-4 [OIAc 5,36].

d901 Il tesoro ritrovato; mulierum ornamenta: Complesso monumentale di San Michele. R 1991, Ministero Beni Culturali. 55 p., ill.

d902 **Zwierlein-Diehl** Erika, Die antiken Gemmen des kunsthistorischen Museums in Wien III. Mu 1991, Prestel. 362 p.; 253 pl. – ᴿMusHclv 48 (1991) 191 (K. *Schefold*).

T2.8   Utensilia.

d903 *Bolshakov* Andrey O., Addenda to [J.] MÁLEK's list of ointment-slabs: GöMiszÄg 131 (1992) 21-23.

d904 *Cassimatis* Hélène, Le strigile dans l'iconographie italiote: Nikephoros 4 (1991) 191-5 [197-209, fig. 11-17, féminin, *Massa-Pairault* F.-H.].

d905 *Courbin* Paul, Une fibule gauloise à Bassit [N Ugarit]: Syria 69 (1992) 211-9.

d906 **de Tommaso** Giandomenico, Ampullae vitreae; contenitori in vetro di unguenti e sostanze aromatiche dell'Italia romana (I sec. a.C.-III sec. d.C.): Archaeologica 94. R 1990, Bretschneider. 134 p.; ill. – ᴿRÉLat 70 (1992) 391s (R. *Adam*).

d907 *Fischer-Elfert* Hans-W., Der Vorsteher und sein Stab: GöMiszÄg 127 (1992) 40-43.

d907* *Goldwasser* Orly, The Narmer Palette and the 'Triumph of Metaphor': LAeg (1992) 67-82 + 5 fig.

d908 **Hayes** John W., Ancient metal axes and other tools in the Royal

Ontario Museum; European and Mediterranean types 1991 ⇥ 7,b873*: ᴿRÉAnc 94 (1992) 293s (A. *Coffyn*).

d909 **Klein** Harald, Untersuchungen zur Typologie bronzezeitlicher Nadeln in Mesopotamien und Syrien [Diss. Saarbrücken 1990]: SchrVorderasArch 4. Saarbrücken 1992, Drückerei. 388 p., 198 pl. 3-925036-68-7 [OIAc 5,27].

d910 *Maeir* Aron M., *Garfinkel* Yosef, Bone and metal straw-tip beer-strainers from the Ancient Near East: Levant 24 (1992) 218-223; fig. 12-16.

d911 **Muscarella** O. W., Bronze and iron 1988 ⇥ 5,d281*... 7,b878: ᴿJNES 51 (1992) 65-67 (P. R. S. *Moorey*).

d912 *Pászthory* Emmerich, Die Alabasterpaletten für die 'Sieben Heiligen Salböle' im Alten Reich: AntWelt 23 (1992) 129-132; 4 fig.

d913 *Poulsen* Erik, Römische Bronzeeimer; Typologie der Henkelattachen mit Frauenmaske, Palmette und Tierprotomen: AcArchK 62 (1991) 209-230; 25 fig.

d914 **Riz** Anna E., Bronzegefässe in der römisch-pompejanischen Wandmalerei: DAI-R Sond. 7, 1990 ⇥ 7,b880: ᴿGnomon 64 (1992) 530-540 (W. *Ehrhardt*).

d915 *Schorsch* Deborah, Copper ewers of Early Dynastic and Old Kingdom Egypt — an investigation of the art of smithing in antiquity: MiDAI-K 42 (1992) 145-159; 5 fig. pl. 31-36.

d915* *Sievertsen* Uwe, Das Messer vom Gebel el-Arak [Nag Hamadi]: Bagh-Mitt 23 (1992) 1-75; 45 fig.; pl. 1-9.

d916 *Stibbe* Conrad M., Archaic bronze hydriai: Babesch 67 (1992) 1-62; 70 fig.

d917 *Vertesalji* Peter P., Le manche de couteau [saturé de figures humaines et animales] de Gebel el-Arak ['on dit', près de Nagᶜ Ḥammadi: du Caire au Louvre 1914] dans le contexte des relations entre la Mésopotamie et l'Égypte: ⇥ 683, Circulation 1991/2, 29-41; 4 fig.

d918 *Wynn* Thomas, Tools, grammar, and the archaeology of cognition: ComArch 1 (1991) 191-206: 'there is no sound basis for inferring grammatical abilities from prehistoric stone tools'.

d919 *Zwickel* W., Einige [4] neue Räuchergeräte aus Palästina: JbEvHL 3 (1991) 29-34.

T2.9   *Pondera et mensurae*   – **Weights and measures.**

d920 *Ali* Mohammed S., *T̠ᶜr* – eine Masseinheit im Papyrus Boulaq 19: GöMiszÄg 131 (1992) 7-10.

d921 *Elayi* Josette, Nouveaux poids nord-ouest sémitiques: ⇥ 132, ᶠMᴵᴸᴵᴷ J., 1992, 285-8, pl. 5-6.

d922 *Gatier* Pierre-Louis, Poids inscrits de la Syrie hellénistique et romaine, I: Syria 68 (1991) 433-444; 2 fig.

d923 *Geiger* Joseph, Jᵁᴸᴵᴬᴺ of Ascalon [on metrology, known in four versions not recognized as identical]: JHS 112 (1992) 31-43.

d924 ᴱ**Gyselen** Rika, Prix, salaires, poids et mesures: Res Orientales 2. P 1990, Étude Civilisation Moyen-Orient. 161 p. 1142-2831 [OIAc 3,22].

d925 *Jonas* Peter, *Wendt* Sylvia, Masse und Gewichte der Industal-Kultur: Altertum 37 (1991) 14-20; 6 fig.

d926 **Lefort** J., *al.*, Géométries de fisc byzantin: Réalités byzantines 4. P 1991, Lethielleux. 295 p.; 8 pl. F 270. – ᴿBAnglsr 12 (1992s) 74-79 (C. *Dauphin*: instructive data on ropes used).

d927 *Naveh* Joseph, The numbers of *bat* in the Arad ostraca: IsrEJ 42 (1992) 52-54.

d928 *Powell* Marvin A., Weights and measures: ➤ 741, AnchorBD 6 (1992) 897-908.

d929 *Seidel* Matthias, Gewichte in Tiergestalt aus dem Alten Ägypten; eine Neuerwerbung des Hildesheimer Pelizaeus-Museums: AntWelt 23 (1992) 190s; 6 color. fig.

T3.0 **Ars antiqua,** *motiva, picturae* [icones ➤ T3.1 infra].

d930 *Albenda* Paulina, Symmetry in the art of the Assyrian empire: ➤ 683, Circulation 1991/2, 297-309; 9 fig.

d931 **Arafat** K.W., Classical Zeus 1990 ➤ 6,814.d471; 7,b895: ᴿAntClas 61 (1992) 680s (C. *Delvoye*); ClasR 42 (1992) 148s (B.A. *Sparkes*); JHS 112 (1992) 219s (Susan *Woodford*); RÉAnc 94 (1992) 515s (P. *Lévêque*).

d932 **Belting** Hans, Bild und Kult; eine Geschichte des Bildes vor dem Zeitalter der Kunst 1990 ➤ 6,d478; 7,b898: ᴿByZ 84s (1991s) 533-9 (J. *Gaus*).

d933 *Biamonte* Giuseppe, [corona] Dal segno pagano al simbolo cristiano: SMSR 58 (1992) 93-123; 7 fig.

d934 **Blocher** Felix, Untersuchungen zum Motiv der nackten Frau in der altbabylonischen Zeit 1987 ➤ 3,d586; 5,d315: ᴿJNES 51 (1991) 308-310 (Elise *Auerbach*); Syria 68 (1991) 176s (P. *Amiet*).

d935 *Boardman* John, The phallos-bird in archaic and classical Greek art: RArchéol (1992) 227-242; 12 fig.

d936 **Böhm** Stephanie, Die 'nackte Göttin'; zur Ikonographie und Deutung unbekleideter weiblicher Figuren in der frühgriechischer Kunst. Mainz 1990, von Zabern. xv-192 p.; 42 pl. 3-8053-1085-4 [OIAc 3,14]. – ᴿTopO 2 (1992) 183-7 (Λ. *Hermary*).

d937 **Brilliant** Richard, *a)* Visual narratives; storytelling in Etruscan and Roman art. Ithaca NY 1984, Cornell Univ. 200 p.; ill. – *b)* Narrare per immagini; racconti di storie nell'arte etrusca e romana, ᵀ*Draghi* B. F 1987, Giunti. 200 p.; ill. – ᴿAION-clas 44 (1992) 329-336 (L. *Bianchi*: 'Brillant' in titolo solo).

d938 *Calmeyer* Peter, Zur Genese altiranischer Motive XI. 'eingewebte Bildchen' von Städten: ArchMIran 25 (1992) 95-124; 14 fig. (27 coins); pl. 19-28.

d939 **Carpenter** T.H., Art and myth in ancient Greece: World of Art 1990 ➤ 7,b903; 0-500-02236-2: ᴿClasW 85 (1991s) 716s (Frances van *Keuren*); JHS 112 (1992) 217 (Susan *Woodford*).

d940 **Castriota** David, Myth, ethos, and actuality; official art in fifth-century B.C. Athens. Madison 1992, Univ. Wisconsin. xii-337 p.; 39 fig.; 2 maps. 0-299-13350-8.

d941 ᴱ**Châtelet** A., *Groslier* B.P., Storia dell'arte, I. Dalla preistoria all'arte romana [1988], ᵀ*Puccinelli* F. R 1992, Gremese. 285 p. Lit. 25.000. 88-7605-647-8 [BL 93,118, W.G.E. *Watson*: densely printed, no pictures; but 'at a non-technical level this is the work to consult'].

d942 *Cohon* Robert, HESIOD and the order and naming of the Muses in Hellenistic art: Boreas 14s (1991s) 67-83; 5 fig.

d942* *Collon* Dominique, The scroll cross: ➤ 179, ᶠSTROMMENGER Eva 1992, 45-50; pl. 15 [27 examples of a design formed by four c-shaped curlicues, only no. 10 looking at all like a cross; and nothing related to any scrolls of Qumran or elsewhere].

d943 *Cristofani* Mauro, Über die Anfänge der 'römischen Kunst'; die Zeit der Tarquinier: MiDAI-R 99 (1992) 123-138; 4 fig. pl. 31-33.

d944 **Davis** Whitney, The canonical tradition in ancient Egyptian art 1989 ➤ 7,b907: ᴿJAOS 112 (1992) 328-330 (R. S. *Bianchi*: careful use of evidence).

d945 *Dierichs* Angelika, Es muss nicht immer Timotheos sein; Leda und der Schwan in Wandmalereien aus den Vesuvstädten: KölnJb 25 (1992) 51-64; 20 fig.

d946 **Dillenberger** Jane, Image and spirit in sacred and secular art, ᴱ*Apostolos-Cappadona* Diane. NY 1990, Crossroad. xiii-217 p. $30. – ᴿParabola 17,3 (1992) 121-4 (D. *Thorpe*); TTod 49 (1992s) 420. 422 (T. *Buser*).

d947 **Dochniak** Craig C., Kingship festival iconography in the Egyptian archaic period: diss. Arizona 1991, ᴰ*McElroy* K. [vi-] 82 p. 13-46418.

d948 **Eingartner** Johannes, Isis und ihre Dienerinnen in der Kunst der römischer Kaiserzeit: Mnemosyne supp. 115. Leiden 1991, Brill. ix-197 p. $71.79 [RelStR 19,160, M. T. *Gustafson* praises; suggests R. E. *Witt* (for WILD ?) Isis in the G-R world]. – ᴿClasR 42 (1992) 409s (J. *Gwyn Griffiths*).

Erffa Hans M. von, Ikonologie der Genesis: Die christlichen Bildthemen aus dem AT und ihre Quellen 1, 1989 ➤ 2024.

d949 **Fleischer** Robert, Studien zur seleukidischen Kunst, 1. Herrscherbildnisse. Mainz 1991, von Zabern. xiv-106 p.; 88 pl. 3-8053-0991-0 [BO 49,590]. – ᴿArchWsz 43 (1992) 134s (Z. *Kiss*).

d950 **Fowler** Barbara H., The Hellenistic aesthetic. Madison WI / Bristol 1989, Univ. ➤ 7,b914; also Bristol Press. xix-213 p.; 27 fig. £20, pa. £10. – ᴿGnomon 64 (1992) 377s (Christine M. *Havelock*: poetry dominates, art exemplifies).

d951 **Francis** E. David †1987, Image and idea in fifth century Greece; art and literature after the Persian Wars [Oxford Magdalen College Waynflete lectures 1983], ᴱ*Vickers* Michael. L 1990, Routledge. x-156 p.; 40 fig. £25. 0-415-01914-1. – ᴿAntClas 61 (1992) 681s (P. *Somville*).

d952 **Fresco** M. F., Filosofie en Kunst. Assen 1988, Van Gorcum. xiii-284 p.; 38 fig. *f* 49.50. – ᴿMnemosyne 45 (1992) 427-9 (R. *Ferwerda*).

d953 **Hachlili** Rachel, Ancient Jewish art 1988 ➤ 4,e193; 6,d516: ᴿJRomA 5 (1992) 440-4 (Susan *Weingarten*, M. *Fischer*).

d954 **Haussperger** Martha, Die Einführungsszene; Entwicklung eines mesopotamischen Motivs ... ᴰ1991 ➤ 7,b922: ᴿSyria 69 (1992) 474s (P. *Amiet*); ZAss 82 (1992) 157s (D. *Collon*).

d955 **Hebert** Bernhard, Schriftquellen zur hellenistischen Kunst; Plastik, Malerei und Kunsthandwerk der Griechen vom 4. zum 2. Jh.: Grazer-Beit Supp 4. Horn 1989, Berger. 314 p. – ᴿAnzAltW 45 (1992) 294-7 (W. *Wohlmayr*).

d956 *Hesberg* Henner von, Publica magnificentia; eine antiklassistische Intention der frühen augusteischen Baukunst: JbDAI 107 (1992) 125-147; pl. 49-52.

d957 *Hurwit* Jeffrey M., A note on ornament, nature, and boundary in Greek art: Babesch 67 (1992) 63-72; 10 fig.

d958 **Immerwahr** Sara A., Aegean painting in the Bronze Age 1990 ➤ 6,d519; 7,b925: ᴿAJA 96 (1992) 383s (Karen P. *Foster*); AntClas 61 (1992) 652-4 (Frieda *Vandenabeele*).

d959 *Isager* Jacob, PLINY on art and society; the elder Pliny's chapters on the history of art [books 33-37] 1991 ➤ 7,b926 ('255 p.') £40: ᴿGreeceR 39 (1992) 105 (B. A. *Sparkes*; '355 p.').

d960 *Jacoby* Ruth, ❺ The Jew in ancient art from the 12th century B.C.E. to the 3d century C.E.: Qadmoniot 25 (1992) 116-122; 17 fig.

d961 *Klagsbald* Victor, 'Comme un lis entre les chardons; de la symbolique de la fleur de lis aux origines du Magen Dawid: RÉJ 150 (1991) 133-143 + 7 fig. [photo fig. 6 shows a half-open fleur de lis in exactly the form of a Star of David].

d962 **Leach** Eleanor W., Rhetoric of ... landscape 1988 ➤ b936: ᴿGnomon 64 (1992) 637s (R. *Jenkins*: intriguing, intractable); JRomA 4 (1991) 262-7 (D. O. *Ross*); Latomus 51 (1992) 231-4 (J.-M. *Croisille*).

d963 *Leach* Eleanor W., Reading signs of status; recent books on Roman art in the domestic sphere [GAZDA E., LING R., BLANCKENHAGEN P.]: AJA 96 (1992) 551-7.

d964 **Ling** Roger, Roman painting. C 1991, Univ. xii-245 p.; 236 pl. + 16 color.; 2 maps. $80; pa. $28. 0-521-30614-0; -1595-6. – ᴿAntiqJ 71 (1991) 284s (C. *Vermeele*); BonnJbb 192 (1992) 678-681 (E. M. *Moormann*); ClasW 85 (1991s) 724s (Elizabeth *Bartman*).

d965 *Mendecki* Norbert, ⊕ De arte Israelitarum [in the century of origins of Palestine archeology]: RuBi 44 (1991) 99-103.

d966 *Moon* Warren G. † 22.VI.1992, Nudity and narrative; observations on the frescoes from the Dura synagogue: JAAR 60 (1992) 587-617 + 37 fig.; bibliog. 634-8; nudeness = non-Jewishness, e.g. Pharaoh's daughter.

d967 **Morris** Sarah P., Daidalos and the origins of Greek art. Princeton 1992, Univ. xxx-413 p.; 62 fig.; map. 0-691-03599-7.

d968 **Otto** Gunter & Maria, Auslegen; ästhetische Erziehung als Praxis des Auslegens in Bildern und des Auslegens von Bildern. Seelze 1987, Friedrich. [II. 384 p. 3-617-32242-9]. – ᴿBijdragen 53 (1992) 338 (J. *Besemer*).

d969 *Pairault Massa* Françoise-Hélène, Iconologia e politica nell'Italia antica; Roma, Lazio, Etruria dal VII al I secolo a.C.: BtArcheologia 18. Mi 1992, Longanesi. 259 p.; 229 fig. Lit. 80.000. 88-304-1112-4.

d970 **Pollitt** J. J., The art of ancient Greece; sources and documents²ʳᵉᵛ [¹1965]. C 1990, Univ. xiv-298 p.; 9 fig. £35; pa. £13. – ᴿGreeceR 39 (1992) 104s (B. A. *Sparkes*).

d971 *Pomerantseva* Natalia, The grid of squares as the mechanical device of proportions in ancient Egyptian art: DiscEg 21 (1991) 21-47; 11 fig.

d972 *Pomorska* Irena, Les flabellifères à la droite du roi en Égypte ancienne 1987 ➤ 3,d636... 6,d548: ᴿOLZ 87 (1992) 130-2 (B. *Menu*).

d973 **Ramage** Nancy H. & Andrew, Roman art, Romulus to Constantine. NY / ENJ 1991, Abrams / Prentice Hall. $49.50 / pa. $36.75. 0-8109-3755-7 / 0-13-782947-7. – ᴿAJA 96 (1992) 773s (Susan *Wood*); ClasW 85 (1991s) 722 (C. *Parslow*).

d974 **Ramage** Nancy H. & Andrew, The Cambridge history of Roman art 1991 ➤ 7,b955; 373 fig. £20. 0-521-40297-2. – ᴿAntClas 61 (1992) 688-690 (Cécile *Evers*); JRS 82 (1992) 235s (V. *Huet*, also on LING).

d974* *Robins* Gay, Composition and the artist's squared grid: JAmEg 28 (1991) 41-54; 12 fig.

d975 *Rocacher* Jean, L'art et le sacré [... fondements bibliques du sacré]: EsprVie 102 (1992) 97-103.

d976 *Rosenthal-Heginbottom* Renate, Herakles' goldene Keulen: DielB 27 (1991) 181-5 + 3 fig.

d977 **Rouveret** Agnès, Histoire et imaginaire de la peinture ancienne 1989 ➤ 6,d552; 7,b656: ᴿAJA 96 (1992) 183-6 (Eleanor W. *Leach*).

d977* *Saporetti* Claudio, Fascino e bellezza; ideali maschili nell'Antichità preclassica [< convegno]. R 1992, Unesco Club. 47 p.

d978 **Schefold** Karl, *Jung* Franz, Die Sagen von den Argonauten, von Theben und Troia in der klassischen und hellenistischen Kunst. Mü 1989,

Hirmer. 427 p.; 341 fig. 3-7774-4690-4. – RAntClas 61 (1992) 682s (C. *Delvoye*: dernier des 5 volumes): ➤ 6,d556.

Schreckenberg H. (on Josephus); *Schubert* K. (pictorial traditions), Jewish historiography and iconography 1991 ➤ d195.

d979 *Shaheen* Alaael-din M., The palm [of hand] painting motif; an interpretation of a continuing tradition: GöMiszÄg 130 (1992) 79-93 + 4 maps; 16 fig.

d980 *Shapiro* H. A., Theseus in Kimonian Athens; the iconography of empire; MeditHR 7,1 (1992) 29-49.

d981 *Small* Jocelyn P., The Etruscan view of Greek art: Boreas 14s (1991s) 51-65.

d982 *Strange* John, Theology and politics in architecture and iconography: ScandJOT 5,1 (1991) 23-44.

d982* ESweeney Jane, *al.*, The human figure in early Greek art [US exhibition]. Athens 1988, Greek Ministry of Culture. 183 p.; 67 items ill. 0-89468-1079.

d983 **Vercoutter** Jean, *al.*, L'image du noir dans l'art occidental, I. Des Pharaons à la chute de l'Empire romain. P 1991, Gallimard. xi-350 p.

d984 **Weitzmann** Kurt, *Kessler* Herbert L., The frescoes of the Dura Synagogue and Christian art: DumbO St 28, 1990 ➤ 7,b962; xiv-202 p.; $68: RBASOR 287 (1992) 94-96 (D. *Kinney*); BonnJbb 192 (1992) 697-705 (Petra *Sevrugian*); Speculum 67 (1992) 502-4 (J. *Gatmann*: unconvincing).

d985 *Whitley* James, The explanation of form; towards a reconciliation of archaeological and art historical approaches: Hephaistos 11s (1992s) 7-33; 11 fig.

d986 *Wilkinson* Richard H., New Kingdom astronomical paintings and methods of finding and extending direction: JAmEg 28 (1991) 149-154; 4 fig.

T3.1 *Theologia iconis,* **ars postbiblica.**

d987 *Avenarius* Alexander, Der Geist der byzantinischen Ikonodulie und seine Tradition: JbÖsByz 42 (1992) 41-54.

d988 **Babolin** Sante, Icona e conoscenza; preliminari d'una teologia iconica 1990 ➤ 7,b968: RAngelicum 69 (1992) 432s (G. *Grasso*); Lateranum 57 (1991) 613s (O. *Pasquato*); Marianum 54 (1992) 502s (G. M. *Vasina*); Salesianum 54 (1992) 797-9 (O. *Pasquato*); HoTheológos 10 (1992) 109-115 (C. *Scordato*).

d989 *Barber* Charles, The Koimesis church, Nicaea; the limits of representation on the eve of iconoclasm: JbÖsByz 41 (1991) 43-60; 1 pl.

d990 **Begbie** Jeremy S., Voicing creation's praise; towards a theology of the arts [diss.]. E/McLean VA 1991, Clark / Books Int. xix-286 p. £12.50. 0-567-29188-X. – RExpTim 103 (1991s) 188 (M. J. *Townsend*: his own views are fresh and stimulating, but too subordinated to TILLICH and KUYPER); RefTR 51 (1992) 65 (D. *Peterson*); TS 53 (1992) 584-6 (J. J. *Feeney*).

d991 *Blättner* Martin, Kein Bildnis Gottes mehr; wie christliche Kunst war und wie sie verging: LuthMon 31 (1992) 130-2.

d992 **Brend** Barbara, Islamic art. L 1991, British Museum. 240 p.; 60 ill. + 102 colour. £15 pa. – RJRAS (1992) 449s (T. *Falk*: a good job for the public; not for the art-historian).

d993 **Buechner** Frederick, The faces of Jesus. NY/SF 1989, Stearn/Harper. 256 p.; 154 photos (*Boltin* Lee). $20 pa. – ᴿBR 7,3 (1991) 15.52 (Jane *Dillenberger*).

d993* *Carle* P. L., Le mystère de Dieu et le culte des images dans la liturgie de la Nouvelle Alliance; l'enseignement conciliaire, le Concile de Trente: DivThom 94 (1991) 67-95.

d994 **Chenis** Carlo, Fondamenti teorici dell'arte sacra; Magistero postconciliare: BtScRel 94. S 1991, Sígueme. 220 p. – ᴿSalmanticensis 39 (1992) 317-9 (J. A. *Rivera de las Heras*).

d995 *Cottin* Jérôme, Bible et art: ÉTRel 67 (1992) 259-264: MENOZZI D. 1991, PRIGENT P. 1990, TOUBERT H. 1990, RIGAUX D. 1989...

d996 *Criscuolo* Ugo, Iconoclasmo bizantino e filosofia delle immagini divine nel neoplatonismo: → 147, ꜰPLACES E. des, Platonism 1992, 83-102.

d997 **Dalferth** Ingolf U., Kombinatorische Theologie [mit Kunstlehre]; Probleme theologischer Rationalität. FrB 1991, Herder. 158 p. – ᴿTZBas 48 (1992) 299s (J.-C. *Wolf*).

d998 **Donadeo** M., El ícono, imagen de lo invisible. M 1989, Narcea. 128 p. – ᴿRelCu 37 (1991) 344 (P. *Langa*).

d999 *a) Donadeo* Maria, Teologia delle icone; – *b) Fabris* Rinaldo, Il Cristo, parola e immagine di Dio; – *c) Bertoli* Bruno, La Bibbia nei mosaici di San Marco; – *d) Melczer* William, Immagine e compromesso; il problema della rappresentazione pittorica nelle Bibbie ebraiche del Medioevo; – *e) Hartt* Frederick, Tippi, *Hurth* Dietrich, Gruenewald: Arte 1988/92, 111-118 / 103-110 / 121-132 / 151-165 / 166-177-189.

e1 ᴱ**Dowley** Tim, The Bible in stained glass. Harrisburg PA 1990, Morehouse. 160 p.; photographs by *Halliday* Sonia, *Lushington* Laura. $40. – ᴿBR 8,3 (1992) 12s (J. *Limburg*).

e1* *Durand* Jannic, *a)* Icones et iconoclasme; – *b)* L'orfèvrerie à Constantinople: DossA 176 ('L'art byzantin' 1992) 10s / 76-87.

e2 ᴱ**Duval** Noël, *al.*, Naissance des arts... paléochrétiens de la France. P 1991, Imprimerie Nationale. 434 p.; 210 fig. + 364 color. – ᴿBLitEc 93 (1992) 343s (J. *Rocacher*).

e3 **Effenberger** Arne, Frühchristliche Kunst und Kultur, von den Anfängen bis zum 7. Jahrhundert 1986 → 3,d595; 4,e183: ᴿVizVrem 51 (1990) 227s (A. P. *Kakovkin*).

c4 **Flavathingal** Sebastian, Inculturation and Indian art; an Indian perspective. R 1990, Urbaniana Univ. 342 p. – ᴿJDharma 17 (1992) 54s (J. *Nandikkara*).

e5 **Feld** Helmut, Der Ikonoklasmus des Westens 1990 → 7,b977: ᴿBtHumRen 54 (1992) 807s (J. *Wirth*); OstKSt 41 (1992) 339-341 (E. C. *Suttner*); RelStR 18 (1992) 335 (T. F. X. *Noble*).

c6 ᴱ**Grabar** Oleg, Muqarnas, annual on Islamic art and architecture 5 (1988): ᴿJRAS (1992) 450-2 (J. *Carswell*: Grabar's prefatory essay condemns recent ceramic studies by both SOUSTIEL and KINGERY/VANDIVER, along with wildly exaggerated spurning of Arthur LANE, whose approach is the very one he commends).

e7 *Griffiths* Richard, Religion and the arts; BAUDELAIRE and R. S. THOMAS: TLond 95 (1992) 5-10.

e8 **Hamburger** Jeffrey F., The Rothschild canticles; art and mysticism in Flanders and the Rhineland circa 1300. NHv 1991, Yale Univ. 336 p. $60. 0-300-04308-2. – ᴿExpTim 103 (1991s) 89 (A. *Henry*: by 'a nun under Dominican supervision?'; ideas idiosyncratic; 46 miniatures and 160 vignettes creative).

e9 ᴱHuber Rudolf, *Rieth* Renate, Glossarium artis, 2. Kirchengeräte, Kreuze und Reliquiare der christlichen Kirchen³. Mü 1992, Saur. 365 p.; 267 fig. 3-598-11079-0. – ᴿBLitEc 93 (1992) 426-8 (J. *Rocacher*).

e10 **Humfrey** Peter, *Kemp* Martin, The altarpiece in the Renaissance. C 1991, Univ. 273 p. £35. 0-521-36061-7. – ᴿExpTim 103 (1991s) 88 (J. B. *Bates*: mostly Italy and Netherlands; tells much about patrons' attitudes).

e11 ⓖ L'icône dans la théologie et l'art; ÉtT Chambésy 9. Genève 1990, Patriarcat orthodoxe. 323 p.; 18 pl. – ᴿÉTRel 67 (1992) 631s (J. *Cottin*).

e12 *Jones* Tom D., Art - theology - Church; a survey, 1940-1990, in Britain: TLond 95 (1992) 360-370.

e13 *Kakovkin* A., Un monument copte de la peinture et de la littérature de l'Ermitage: GöMiszÄg 128 (1992) 95-103; 1 fig.

e14 *Keel* Othmar, Iconography and the Bible: ⇒ 741, AnchorBD 3 (1992) 358-374; 21 fig.

e15 *Kötzsche* Liselotte. Das herrscherliche Christusbild: ⇒ 648*, ᴱ*Colpe*, Spätantike 1992, 99-123; 14 fig.

e16 **Kühnel** Gustav, Wall painting in the Latin Kingdom of Jerusalem: Fra-ForKunst 14. B 1988. xiv-242 p.; 142 pl. + 155 color. 3-8761-1489-7 [JbÖsByz 43,482, H. *Buschhausen*].

e17 *Leeb* Rudolf, Zum Ursprung des Kaiserbildes im Kreuz [DEÉR J. 1955]: JbÖsByz 41 (1991) 1-14; pl. 1-4.

e18 **Limouris** G., Icons, windows 1990 ⇒ 6,d532: ᴿHorizons 19 (1992) 177s (Diane *Apostolos-Cappadona*); IndTSt 29 (1992) 273 (B. J. *Francis*); TsTKi 62 (1991) 218s (D.-E. *Hansen*).

e19 **Menozzi** Daniele, Les images; l'Église et les arts visuels [Textes], 1991 ⇒ 7,b987; F 129. 2-204-04220-X: ᴿRivStoLR 28 (1992) 659-661 (G. C. *Sciolla*).

e20 ᵀᴱ*Mondzain-Baudinet* Marie-José, NICÉPHORE, Discours contre les iconoclastes: Coll. Esthétique 52. P 1989, Klincksieck. 380 p. 2-252-02669-3. – ᴿJbÖsByz 41 (1991) 338-341 (J. *Declerk*, franç.).

e21 **Pattison** George, Art, modernity and faith. Basingstoke 1991, Macmillan. 193 p. £35. 0-333-52954-5. – ᴱExpTim 103 (1991s) 253s (J. B. *Bates*: iconoclasm, icons, Zen, 'death of art'); TLond 95 (1992) 232s (C. *Pickstone*).

e22 **Pelikan** Jaroslav, Imago Dei 1987/90 ⇒ 6,d544; 7,b991: ᴿChrCent 108 (1991) 337s (T. A. *Idinopulos*); CritRR 5 (1992) 343-5 (D. J. *Sahas*); CurrTMiss 19 (1992) 218s (P. *Rorem*); JEH 43 (1992) 298-300 (J. *Shepard*).

e23 *Plank* Peter, Die Wiederaufrichtung des Adam und ihre Propheten; eine neue Deutung der Anastasis-Ikone: OstkSt 41 (1992) 34-49.

e24 *Rassart-Debergh* Marguerite, Trois icônes romaines du Fayoum: CdÉ 66 (1991) 349-355; 5 fig.

e25 **Raw** Barbara C., Anglo-Saxon Crucifixion iconography and the art of the monastic revival: Anglo-Saxon England 1. C 1990, Univ. xii-296 p. $60. 0-521-36370-5 [TDig 38,185]. – ᴿJAAR 60 (1992) 607-9 (Cynthia *Hahn*).

e26 **Roberts** Helene E., Iconographic index to Old Testament subjects represented in photographs and slides of paintings in the visual collections, Fine Arts Library, Harvard University: RefLibHum 729. NY 1987, Garland. xvii-197 p.; 6 fig. 0-8240-8345-8.

e27 *Samir* Khalil Samir, Le traité sur les icônes d'ABŪ QURRAH mentionné par EUTYCHIUS: OrChrPer 58 (1992) 461-474.

e28 **Schaffer** Christa, Koimesis, der Heimgang Mariens; das Entschlafungsbild in seiner Abhängigkeit von Legende und Theologie 1985 → 1,8440; 2,6980: ᴿMarianum 53 (1991) 324-6 (L. *Gambero*).

e29 *Schmitt* J.-C., La question des images dans les débats entre juifs et chrétiens au XIIᵉ s.: → 68, ᶠGRAUS F., Spannungen 1992, 245-254 [< RHE 88,35*].

e30 **Steck** Paul, Ich bin's nicht, Kaiser Konstantin ist es gewesen; die Legenden vom Einfluss des Teufels, des Juden und des Moslem auf den Ikonoklasmus: Poikila Byz 10. Bonn 1990, Habelt. 719 p. 3-7749-2419-8 [JbÖsByz 43,430, E. *Gamillscheg*].

e31 **Stock** Alex, Zwischen Tempel und Museum; theologische Kunstkritik: Positionen der Moderne. Pd 1991, Schöningh. 368 p. 3-506-78830-2: ᴿOrientierung 56 (1992) 214-6 (A. *Heuser*); TPhil 67 (1992) 622-4 (J. *Splett*); TvT 32 (1992) 438 (L. *Goosen*).

e32 *Stock* Alex, Katholisches Kunstgespräch? Stationen der ersten Jahrhunderthälfte: Orientierung 56 (1992) 235-9.

e33 **Temple** Richard, Icons and the mystical origins of Christianity. Shaftesbury 1990 → 7,d1; also Longmead 1991, Element. 198 p. $16 pa. – ᴿParabola 16,3 (1991) 106. 108. 110 (J. *George*).

e34 **Thérel** Marie-Louise, Les symboles de l' 'Ecclesia' dans la création iconographique de l'art chrétien du IIIᵉ au VIᵉ siècle; préf. *Daniélou* Jean. R 1973, Storia Letteratura. xii-185 p.; xlvi pl.

e35 **Thümmel** Hans Georg, Die Frühgeschichte der ostkirchlichen Bilderlehre; Texte und Untersuchungen zur Zeit vor dem Bilderstreit: TU 139. B 1992, Akademie. 399 p.

e36 ᴱTolkemitt B., *Wohlfeil* R., Historische Bildkunde; Probleme, Wege, Beispiele: Zeitschrift für Historische Forschung, supp. 12. B 1991, Duncker & H. 261 p.; 51 fig. [RHE 87,292*].

e37 **Toubert** Hélène, Un art dirigé; réforme grégorienne et iconographie. P 1990, Cerf. 495 p. F 305. 2-204-04105-X [ÉTRel 67,262].

e38 **Ugolnik** Anthony, The illuminating icon. GR 1989, Eerdmans. 290 p. $19. 6-8028-3652-6. – ᴿRExp 88 (1991) 288s (B. *Leonard*).

e39 **Ulmer** Renate, Passion und Apokalypse; Studien zur biblischen Thematik in der Kunst des Expressionismus: EurHS 28/144. Fra 1992, Lang. 241 p.; 82 fig. 3-631-42557-0.

e40 **Urbaniak-Walczak** Katarzyna, Die 'conceptio per aurem'; Untersuchungen zum Marienbild in Ägypten unter besonderer Berücksichtigung der Malereien in el-Bagawat: ArbSpätKÄg 2. Altenberge 1992, Oros. xv-233 p.; 33 fig. 3-89375-047-9 [OIAc 5,37].

e41 **Zaloscer** Hilde, Zur Genese der koptischen Kunst; Ikonographische Beiträge [1942-1967]: Stichwort Kunstgeschichte. W 1991, Böhlau. 128 p. [OIAc 3,42].

T3.2 Sculptura.

e42 *Akurgal* Ekrem, Zur Entstehung der ostgriechischen Klein- und Grossplastik: IstMit 42 (1992) 67-81; 11 fig.

e42* **Amedick** Rita, Die Sarkophage mit Darstellungen aus dem Menschenleben, 4. Vita privata: DAI, Die antiken Sarkophagreliefs 1/4. B 1991, Mann. 186 p.; 120 pl. DM 240. 3-7861-1642-3. – ᴿNikephoros 5 (1992) 299-304 (Friederike *Sinn*).

e43 *Amiet* Pierre, Bronzes élamites de la collection George Ortiz: ArchMIran 25 (1992) 81-89; 5 fig.; pl. 15-17.

e44 **Baer** Eva, Ayyubid metalwork with Christian images: Muqarnas 4 supp. Leiden 1989, Brill. xiii-55 p.; 128 pl. *f* 65. – ᴿJAOS 112 (1992) 533s (Linda *Komaroff*).

e45 *a*) *Barra Bagnasco* Marcella, Bes-Sileno; un'iconografia tra mondo egizio e greco; nuovi documenti; – *b*) *Robins* Gay, Masculine and feminine traits in male figures in Egyptian two-dimensional art from the late 4th dynasty to the 26th dynasty: ➤ 735, Sesto Eg 1991/2, 41-49; 2 fig.; color. pl. II / 534-540 + 14 fig.

e46 *Beach* Eleanor F., The Samaria ivories, *marzeaḥ* and biblical texts: BA 55 (1922) 130-9; ill.

e47 *a*) *Bentz* Martin, Zum Porträt des Pompeius; – *b*) *Tomei* Maria Antonietta, Statue di terracotta del Palatino: MiDAI-R 99 (1992) 229-246; pl. 64-69 / 171-228; 2 fig.; pl. 48-63.

e48 **Bergemann** Johannes, Römische Reiterstatuen ᴰ1990 ➤ 7,d12: ᴿAJA 96 (1992) 390s (F. S. *Kleiner*); AntClas 61 (1992) 719-722 (J.-C. *Balty*, aussi sur CALCANI G. 1989); ArchWsz 43 (1992) 137s (J. *Żelazowski*, ●).

e49 *Blome* Peter, Funerärsymbolische Collagen auf mythologischen Sarkophagreliefs: ➤ 641, StItFgC 85 (1992) 1061-1073; 5 fig.; Eng. 1073.

e50 **Bonghi Jovino** Maria, Artigiani e botteghe nell'Italia preromana; studi sulla coroplastica di area etrusco-laziale-campana: StArch 56. R 1990, Bretschneider. 252 p.; 12 fig.; 38 pl. Lit. 200.000. – ᴿClasR 42 (1992) 405-7 (F. R. *Serra Ridgway*).

e51 **Boschung** D., Bildnisse des Caligula 1989 ➤ 6,d583: ᴿDLZ 113 (1992) 271-3 (W. *Schindler* †); JRS 82 (1992) 272s (R. R. R. *Smith*).

e52 *Bricault* Laurent, Isis dolente [statue laissée par A. RODIN]: BIFAO 92 (1992) 37-49; pl. 11-13.

e53 *Brilliant* Richard, Roman myth / Greek myth; reciprocity and appropriation on a Roman sarcophagus in Berlin: ➤ 641, StItFgC 85 (1992) 1030-1041; 1 fig.; ital. 1041.

e54 **Bruneau** Philippe, *al.*, La Sculpture; le prestige de l'antiquité du 8ᵉ siècle av.J.C. au 3ᵉ s. ap.J.C. Genève 1991, Skira. 253 p.; ill.

e55 *Croissant* Francis, Anatomie d'un style colonial; les protomés féminines de Locris [BARRA BAGNASCO Marcella 1986]: RArchéol (1992) 103-110; 8 fig.

e56 **Czichon** Rainer M., Die Gestaltungsprinzipien der neuassyrischen Flachbildkunst und ihre Entwicklung vom 9. zum 7. Jahrhundert v.Chr. [Diss. Mü 1992]: MüVorderasSt 13. Mü 1992, Profil. 210 p.; 77 pl. 3-89109-308-0 [OIAc 3,17].

e57 **D'Ambrosio** Antonio, *Borriello* Mariarosaria, Le terracotte figurate di Pompei: Soprintendenza Catalogo 4. R 1990, Bretschneider. 122 p.; 40 pl. – ᴿSalesianum 54 (1992) 778 (S. *Maggio*).

e58 **Donohue** Alice A., Xoana 1988 ➤ 5,d401 ... 7,d22: ᴿAntClas 61 (1992) 657s (Didier *Viviers*); RBgPg 70 (1992) 294s (R. *Chevallier*); RFgIC 120 (1992) 445-451 (Antonella L. *Santarelli*).

e59 *a*) *Dwyer* Eugene J., The temporal allegory of the Tazza Farnese; – *b*) *Pollini* John, The Tazza Farnese; Augusto imperatore 'redeunt Saturnia regna': AJA 96 (1992) [249-254 pl. 1-6] 255-282; 3 fig. / 283-300.

e60 *Evers* Cécile, Propagande impériale et portraits officiels; le type de l'adoption d'Antonin le Pieux: MiDAI-R 98 (1991) 249-262; 2 fig.; pl. 62-67.

e61 *Eygun* Guilmine, Les figurines humaines et animales du site néolithique de Ganj Dareh (Iran): Paléorient 18,1 (1992) 109-117; 2 fig.

Faraone Christopher A., Talismans and Trojan horses: guardian statues in ancient Greek myth and ritual ᴰ1992 ➤ b251.

e62 **Firatlı** Nezih († 1979), ᴱ*Metzger* G., *al.*,   La sculpture byzantine figurée au Musée archéologique d'Istanbul 1990 ➤ 6,d595:   ᴿRivArCr 68 (1992) 366s (A. *Iannello*).

e63 **Fleischer** Robert,   Studien zur seleukidischen Kunst, I. Herrscherbildnisse [besonders auf Münzen]: DAI, Mainz 1991, von Zabern.   xiv-160 p.; 58 pl. − ᴿRArchéol (1992) 410 (F. *Queyrel*).

e64 **Floren** Josef,   Die geometrische und archaische Plastik: HbArch 1, 1987 ➤ 7,d25:   ᴿGGA 244 (1992) 1-19 (H. v. *Steuben*).

e65 **Frontisi-Ducroux** Françoise,   Le dieu-masque, une figure du Dionysos d'Athènes: Images à l'appui 4. P/R 1991, Découverte/Éc.Fr.   288 p.; 120 fig. − ᴿRArchéol (1992) 397-9 (Marie-Christine *Villanueva-Puig*).

e66 **Fullerton** Mark D.,   The archaistic style in Roman statuary: Mnemosyne supp. 110, 1990 ➤ 6,d597; 7,d27; *f*72:   ᴿAntClas 61 (1992) 715-8 (J.-C. *Balty*, aussi sur ZAGDOUN M. 1989).

e67 *Gauer* Werner,   Der argivische Heros mit dem Pferd; Überlegungen zum Deutung des polykletischen Doryphoros: ArchWsz 43 (1992) 7-14; 4 fig.

e67* **Himmelmann** Nikolaus,   Laokoon: AntKu 34 (1991) 97-115; franç. 115; pl. 11-14.

e68 **Hintzen-Bohlen** Brigitte,   Herrscherrepräsentation im Hellenismus; Untersuchungen zu Weihgeschenken, Stiftungen und Ehrenmonumenten in den mutterländischen Heiligtümern Delphi, Olympia, Delos und Dodona [Diss. Köln 1991]. Köln 1992, Böhlau.   252 p.

c69 **Hundsalz** Brigitte,   Das dionysische Schmuckrelief: StArchäol 1.   Mü 1987, Iuduv.   328s; 32 pl. DM 53.   3-88073-236-1. − ᴿAJA 96 (1992) 187 (Sheila *McNally*).

e70 *Imhof* Paul,   Paulus und Petrus; zu drei romanischen Skulpturen: GeistL 65 (1992) 142-9; 3 fig.

e71 **Jongste** Peter F. B.,   The twelve labours of Hercules on Roman sarcophagi: Stud. Archaeol. 59. R 1992, Bretschneider.   157 p.; 88 fig   88-7062-730-6.

e72 **Knell** Heiner,   Mythos und polis; Bildprogramme griechischer Bauskulptur. Da 1990, Wiss.   xii-497 p.; 305 fig. 3-534-11025-0. − ᴿAJA 96 (1992) 708s (F. *Van Keuren*); BonnJbb 192 (1992) 607-611 (T. *Hölscher*).

e73 *Koenig* Yvan,   Les patèques inscrits du Louvre: RÉgp 43 (1992) 122-132; 6 fig.; Eng. 132 leaves untranslated Patèque, which on p. 123 seems to mean an image of Ptaḥ put on the prow of Phoenician ships; but this article deals with the pre-rabbinic hermeneutic character of the inscriptions.

e74 *Laubscher* Hans-Peter,   Ptolemäische Reiterbilder: MiDAI-A 106 (1991) 223-238 pl. 46-51.

e75 **Maderna** Caterina,   Iuppiter, Diomedes und Merkur als Volbilder für römische Bildnisstatuen 1988 ➤ 5,d421; 6,d613*:   ᴿBonnJbb 192 (1992) 673s (H. G. *Niemeyer*).

e76 **Malbon** Elizabeth S.,   The iconography of the sarcophagus of Junius Bassus 1990 ➤ 7,d42:   ᴿCritRR 5 (1992) 79 (J. *Gutmann*); GreeceR 39 (1992) 116 (P. *Walcot*: 'Roman tradition affirmed but as subordinate to Christian' unconvincing); JRS 82 (1992) 305s (J. *Curran*: too sure); JTS 43 (1992) 685-690 (Mary C. *Murray*: relevance to typological exegesis); RelStR 18 (1992) 146 (Sarah *Guberti Bassetti*, severe); RivArCr 68 (1992) 350-2 (Anna *Campese Simone*).

e77 *Mattusch* Carol C.,   A bronze warrior from Corinth [1925]: Hesperia 61 (1992) 79-84; pl. 20-22.

e78 *Maurach* Gregor, Der vergilische und der vatikanische Laokoon: Gymnasium 99 (1992) 227-247; Pl. I-VIII.

e79 **Morales** Vivian B., Figurines and other clay objects from Sarab and Cayönü: OIC 25. Ch 1990, Univ. Or. Inst. 92 p.; 30 fig. – ᴿBASOR 288 (1992) 86 (A. M. T, *Moore*); PEQ 124 (1992) 153s (Ellen *McAdam*).

e80 *a) Moreno* Paolo, La scultura ellenistica da Alessandro ad Augusto; – *b) Andreae* Bernard, L'altare di Pergamo: Archeo 7,85 (1992) 63-107 / 44-53; ill.

e81 **Moser** Karin von *Filseck*, Kairos und eros, zwei Wege zu einem Neuverständnis griechischer Bildwerke. Bonn 1990, Habelt. 87 p., 7 pl. DM 28. 3-7749-2449-X. – ᴿBabesch 67 (1992) 200s (L. B. van der *Meer*).

e82 *Myśliwiec* Karol, *Szymańska* Hanna, Les [350] terres cuites de Atrib [Benha]: CdÉ 67 (1992) 112-132; 10 fig.

e83 **Neudecker** Richard, Die Skulpturen-Ausstattung römischer Villen in Italien [Diss. München 1981s, ᴰ*Zanker* P.]: Beiträge zur Erschliessung hellenistischer und kaiserzeitlicher Skulptur und Architektur 9. Mainz 1988, von Zabern. x-276 p.; 28 pl.; 5 Beilagen. 3-8053-0937-6. – ᴿJRS 82 (1992) 270s (R. R. R. *Smith*).

e84 **Ozyar** Ash, Architectural relief sculpture [orthostats] at Karkamish, Malatya, and Tell Halaf; a technical and iconographic study: diss. Bryn Mawr. Ph 1991, 383 p. 92-25200. – DissA 53 (1992s) 1983-A.

e85 *Parlasca* Klaus, Einige Meisterwerke syrischer Kleinkunst des Hellenismus und der frühen Kaiserzeit: DamaszMi 5 (1991) 49-58; pl. 20-26.

e86 *Pirelli* Rosanna, La cosiddetta Dama di Napoli e il problema delle statue arcaiche egiziane: AION 51 (1991) 1-15; 2 pl.

e86* *Porada* Edith, A man with serpents [Cincinnati museum, thought by A. Pᴀʀʀᴏᴛ to have been filched from Tello]: → 179, ᶠSTROMMENGER Eva 1992, 171-5; fig. 72-78.

e87 **Posener** Georges, Cinq figurines d'envoûtement 1987 → 3,d699; 5,d432: ᴿCdÉ 67 (1992) 263-5 (B. van de *Walle* †).

e88 **Putter** Thierry De, *Karlshausen* Christina, Les pierres utilisées dans la sculpture et l'architecture de l'Égypte pharaonique: Étude 4. Bru 1992, Connaissance de l'ÉgAnc. 176 p.; 54 (color.) pl.; map. 2-87268-003-9 [OIAc 5,18].

e89 **Ridgway** Brunilde S., Hellenistic sculpture, I. The styles of ca. 331-200 B.C. 1990 → 6,d628; 7,d52; $35: ᴿClasW 85 (1991s) 122 (Anne *Weis*: first of three).

e90 **Schlögl** Hermann A., *Brodbeck* Andreas, Ägyptische Totenfiguren: OBO arch 7, 1990 → 6,d631: ᴿArOr 60 (1992) 201s (B. *Vachala*); RB 99 (1992) 592s (J. M. de *Tarragon*).

e91 **Schulman** Alan R., Ceremonial execution and public rewards... NK stelae; OBO 75, 1988 → 6,d635; 7,d50: ᴿJNES 51 (1992) 152-5 (W. A. *Ward*).

e92 **Schulz** Regine, Die Entwicklung und Bedeutung des kuboiden Statuentypus; eine Untersuchung zu den sogenannten 'Würfelhockern' [< Diss. München 1984s]: HildÄgBeit 33s. Hildesheim 1992, Gerstenberg. xi-544 p., 51 fig.; p. 547-815, fig. 52-111, 147 pl. 3-8067-8125-7; -6-5 [OIAc 5,34].

e93 *Shubert* Steven B., Realistic currents in portrait sculpture of the Saite and and Persian periods in Egypt: JSStEg 19 (1989) 27-47.

e94 *Smith* R. R. R., Hellenistic royal portraits [coins and other Kleinplastik] 1988 → 4,e315... 7,d62: ᴿGnomon 64 (1992) 34-45 (R. *Fleischer*); JRS 82 (1992) 243-5 (Lori-Ann *Touchette*).

e95 **Smith** R. R. R., Hellenistic sculpture; a handbook; World of Art. L 1991, Thames & H. 287 p.; 387 fig. £7. – RGreeceR 39 (1992) 244 (B. A. *Sparkes*).

e96 **Spycket** Agnès, Les figurines de Suse, 1. Les figurines humaines IVe-IIe millénaires av.J.-C.; Ville Royale de Suse 6, MémDélIran 52. P 1992, Gabalda. x-283 p.; 161 pl.; 8 plans. 2-85021-053-6 [OIAc 3,38].

e97 **Spycket** Agnès, al., EDannheimer H., Hrouda B., Eine frühdynastische Frauen-Statuette in der prähistorischen Staatssammlung München: Mü-VorderasSt 7. Mü 1990, Profil. 32 p.; 5 pl. 3-89019-261-0.

e98 *Tanner* Jeremy J., Art as expressive symbolism; civic (sculpture) portraits in classical Athens: CamArch 2 (1992) 167-183; 5 fig.; 183-7 comments, *Renfrew* C., *Hodder* I., *Schnapp* A.; 187s reply; 189s bibliog.

e99 FTHOMPSON Dorothy, EUhlenbrock Jerome P., The coroplast's art 1990 (exhibition catalogue) ➤ 7,f154.b536: RAJA 96 (1992) 771-5 (J. F. *Kenfield*, also on U.'s Protomai).

e100 *Weber* Marga, Das früheste Homerporträt als Kunstkopie und als römisches Gerät: MiDAI-R 98 (1991) 199-221; pl. 50-52.

e101 *Wildung* Dietrich, Gehemnisvolle Gesichter [... ägypt. Sarkophage]: Ant-Welt 21 (1990) 206-221; 34 (color.) fig.

e102 **Zanker** P., Augustus und die Macht der Bilder 1987 ➤ 4,c251; 5,d385*: RAtenRom 35 (1990) 209-212 (V. *Saladino*).

e103 **Zimmermann** Jean-Louis, Les chevaux de bronze dans l'art géométrique grec (diss. Genève DDeuchler F.). Mainz/Genève 1989, von Zabern/Univ. 388 p.; 80 pl. – RAnzAltW 45 (1992) 280-6 (S. *Hiller*).

T3.3 *Glyptica:* **stamp and cylinder seals,** scarabs, amulets.

e104 *a) Antonova* E., Images on seals and the ideology of the state formation process; – *b) Lombardi* Alessandra, Alcune osservazioni sul motivo del vaso zampillante: Mesop-T 27 (1992) 77-87 / 119-147; 14 fig.

e105 *Aruz* Joan, The stamp seals from Tell esh-Sheikh (Açana): AnSt 42 (1992) 15-28.

e106 **Avigad** Naḥman, Hebrew Bullae 1986 ➤ 2,a264... 6,d75: RZDPV 108 (1992) 189-193 (F. *Israel*; p. 190, brief rejection of G. GARBINI's 'only discordant' denial of authenticity).

e107 **Ben Tor** Amnon, *a)* ✪ New light on [two kinds of] cultic cylindric seal impressions from the Early Bronze Age in [northern] Eretz Israel: ➤ 18, FBIRAN A., ErIsr 23 (1992) 38-44; 10 fig.; Eng. 146*. – *b)* New light on cylinder seal impressions showing cult scenes from Early Bronze Age Palestine: IsrEJ 42 (1992) 153-164; 10 fig.

e108 **Ben-Tor** Daphna, The scarab, a reflection of ancient Egypt 1989 ➤ 7, d76: RDiscEg 19 (1991) 84s (Irène *Gautier-Vodoz*).

e109 **Blocher** Felix, Siegelabrollungen auf frühbabylonischen Tontafeln im British Museum, Vorw. *Mitchell* T. C.: MüVorderasSt 10. Mü 1992, Profil. 157 p.; 92 fig.; 3 pl. 3-89019-311-0 [OIAc 5,15].

e110 **Blocher** Felix, Siegelabrollungen auf frühbabylonischen Tontafeln in der Yale Babylonian collection; ein Katalog, Vorw. *Hallo* W. W.: MüVorderasSt 9. Mü 1992, Profil. 94 p.; 47 fig.; 4 pl. 3-89019-310-2 [OIAc 5,15].

e111 *Bloedow* Edmund F., Minoan talismanic goats: JPrehR 6 (1992) 15-23; 13 fig.

Boehmer Rainer M., *Güterbock* Hans G., Glyptik aus dem Stadtgebiet von Boğazköy I-II, 1987s ➤ g313.

e112 **Boussac** Marie-Françoise, Les sceaux de Délos 1-2; Sceaux publics, Apollon, Hélios, Artémis, Hécaté: Recherches Franco-Helléniques 2. P 1992, de Boccard. I. xv-193 p.; 71 pl. II. 287 p.; LXVII pl. 2-86958-052-5; -3-3.

e113 *Brenne* Stefan, *Willemsen* Frans, Verzeichnis der [8653] Kerameikos-Ostraka; Mi-DAI-A 106 (1991) 147-156.

e114 *Bulté* Jeanne, Talismans égyptiens d'heureuse maternité; 'faience' bleu-vert à pois foncés. P 1991, CNRS. 138 p.; 33 pl. F 270. 2-222-04538-X [BO 49,583].

e114* *Charpin* D., Les légendes de sceaux de Mari; nouvelles données: → 739, Mari 1992, 59-76.

e115 *Charvát* Petr, The token of the covenant; stamp seals of the ancient Near East [WICKEDE A. von, ᴰ1990]: ArOr 60 (1992) 279-284.

e116 *Colbow* Gudrun, Einige Abrollungen aus der Zeit Ammiditanas bis Samsuditanas im Louvre: RAss 86 (1992) 121-157; 63 fig.

e117 **Collon** D., Near Eastern seals, BM 1990 → 6,d662; 7,d81: ᴿClasW 86 (1992s) 48s (Sherill L. *Spaar*).

e118 *Crawford* Harriet, Seals from the first season's excavation at Saar, Bahrein: CamArch 1 (1991) 255-262; 14 fig.

e119 *Dijk* Jacobus van: The authenticity of the Arslan Tash amulets [now in Aleppo; perhaps filched from the excavation]: Iraq 54 (1992) 65-68, against TEIXIDOR-AMIET unwarranted skepticism.

e120 *Dinçol* Ali M., A hieroglyphic seal impression from Samsat: Belleten 56,215 (1992) 3-6; 2 phot.; ❶ 1s.

e121 *Dolce* Rita, Some remarks about Kassite glyptic art in the period of the relation between Palestine and Mesopotamia: → 736, ᴱShaath S., Palestine 1981/5, 85-92; 7 fig.

e122 **Doumet** Claude, Sceaux et cylindres orientaux, la collection Chiha; préf. *Amiet* P.; OBO arch. 9. FrS/Gö 1992, Univ./VR. 210 p.; 400 fig. 3-7278-01816-0 / 3-525-53659-3 [OIAc 5,19].

e123 *Fischer* Claudia, Siegelabrollungen im British Museum auf neusumerischen Tontafeln aus der Provinz Lagaš; Untersuchungen zu den Tierkampfszenen: ZAss 82 (1992) 60-91; 5 + 29 fig.; 2 pl.

e124 **Franke-Vogt** Ute, Die Glyptik aus Mohenjo-Daro; Uniformität und Variabilität in der Induskultur; Untersuchungen zur Typologie, Ikonographie und räumlichen Verteilung [Diss. Berlin FU 1990]: BaghFor 13. Mainz 1992, von Zabern. xlix-227 p.; p. 228-569; 57 pl. 3-8053-1350-0 [OIAc 3,21].

e124* a) *Frontisi-Ducroux* F., *Lissarague* F., Vingt ans de vases grecs; tendances actuelles des études; – b) *Bažant* Jan, The case for a complex approach to Athenian vase-painting; – c) *Davies* Mark J., Asses and rams; Dionysiac release in Aristophanes' Wasps and Attic vase-painting: Métis 5 (1990) 205-234 / 93-112 / 169-181.

e125 **Giveon** R., *Kertesz* Trude, Egyptian scarabs and seals from Acco 1986 → 2,e286 ... 7,89: ᴿDiscEg 19 (1991) 83-85 (Irène *Gautzier-Vodoz*).

e126 **Giveon** R., *al.*, Scarabs from ... Israel: OBO 83, 1988 → 4,e356 ... 7,d88: ᴿJNES 51 (1992) 155-7 (W. A. *Ward*).

e127 *Gladigow* Burkhard, Schutz durch Bilder; Bildmotive und Verwendungsweisen antiker Amulette; → 713*, ᴱ*Hauck* K., Der historische Horizont der Götterbild-Amulette 1988/92, 13-31.

e128 *Gorelick* Leonard, *Gwinnett* A. John, Minoan versus Mesopotamian seals; comparative methods of manufacture: Iraq 54 (1992) 57-64.

e129 *Haarlem* Willem M. van, A functional analysis of ancient Egyptian amulets: ➤ 735, Sesto Eg. 1991/2, 237-240; 1 fig.; color. pl. VII.

e130 *Harrauer* Hermann, Soubrom, Abrasax, Jahwe u.a. aus Syrien: Tyche 7 (1992) 39-45.

e131 **Herbordt** Suzanne, Neuassyrische Glyptik des 8.-7. Jh. v.Chr. unter besonderer Berücksichtigung der Siegelungen auf Tafeln und Tonverschlüssen [Diss. Mü 1991]: SAA Studies 1 (ISSN 1235-1032). Helsinki 1992, Neo-Assyrian Project. xix-276 p.; 12 fig.; 36 pl.; map. 951-45-6047-7 [OIAc 3,24].

e132 *Kaim* Barbara, Das geflügelte Symbol in der achämenidischen Glyptik: ArchMIran 24 (1991) 31-34; pl. 7-10.

e133 **Keel** Othmar, Studien zu den Stempelsiegeln 2: OBO 88,1989 ➤ 5,d475; 6,d681: ᴿBO 49 (1992) 733-9 (W. A. *Ward*, under 'Pharaonic Egypt'); JAOS 112 (1992) 492-4 (E. *Porada*).

e134 ᴱ**Keel** O., *Shuval* M., *Uehlinger* C., Studien zu den Stempelsiegeln 3, OBO 100, 1990 ➤ 6,d682; 7,d92: ᴿÉTRel 67 (1992) 274 (Françoise *Smyth*, aussi sur Miniaturkunst); ExpTim 103 (1991s) 297 (R. J. *Coggins*); RivB 40 (1992) 115s (A. *Bonora*); TLZ 117 (1992) 821-3 (D. *Vieweger*); ZDPV 108 (1992) 92-97 (W. *Zwickel*, 1-3).

e135 **Keel-Leu** H., Vorderasiatische Stempelsiegel: OBO 110, 1991 ➤ 7,d94: ᴿRStFen 20 (1992) 189 (E. *Acquaro*).

e135* *Koenig* Yvan, Un gri-gri égyptien?: ➤ 96, ᶠKÁKOSY L. 1992, 355-362; 3 fig., pl. XX-B.

e136 *Kunath* Siegward, Ein Skarabäus vom Tel Rechov (Beth-Shan): BibNot 64 (1992) 14-16; 1 fig.

e137 *Lang* M. L., Athenian Agora 25, Ostraca. Princeton 1990, U. xix-188 p. 41 pl. $55. – ᴿJHS 112 (1992) 220s (D. M. *Lewis*).

e138 *Leinwand* Nancy, Regional characteristics in the styles and iconography of the seal impressions of Level II at Kültcpe: ➤ 730, JANES 21 (1989/ 92) 141-172; 27 fig.

e139 *Lemaire* André, Cinq nouveaux sceaux inscrits ouest-sémitiques; StEpL 7 (1990) 97-109.

e140 *Mühner* Sibylle, Ein Namen- und Bildsiegel aus 'En Šems (Beth Schemesch): ZDPV 108 (1992) 68-81; 14 fig.; 1 pl.

e141 **Maltsberger** Charles D., Glyptic remains from Timnah; geopolitical and socioeconomic implications for the Shephelah during the Amarna period: diss. SW Baptist Theol. Sem. 1992. 257 p. 92-31665. – DissA 53 (1992s) 1983-A; OIAc 5,29.

e142 **Matthews** Donald M., Principles of composition in Near Eastern Glyptic of the late second millennium B.C.; OBO arch. 8, ➤ 1990 ➤ 6,d686; Fs 75: ᴿBL (1992) 118 (W. G. *Lambert*); RB 99 (1992) 594 (J.-M. de *Tarragon*).

e143 *Matthews* Donald M., (*Lambert* W. G., inscriptions), The Kassite glyptic of Nippur: OBO 116. FrS/Gö 1992, Univ./VR. [viii-] 153 p.; 210 fig. 3-7278-0807-1 / 3-525-53750-6 [OIAc 3,30].

e144 *Matthews* Donald, The random Pegasus; loss of meaning in Middle Assyrian seals: CamArch 2 (1992) 191-204; 18 fig.; 204-210 comments (*Collon* D., *Porada* E., al.), reply, bibliography.

e145 **Merrillees** Parvine H., Cylinder and stamp seals in Australian collections: OccasP 3. Burwood 1990, Victoria College. [vi-] 168 p.; 40 pl.; map. 0-909184-31-3.

e146 *Møller* Eva, Ancient Near Eastern seals in a Danish collection: CNI 11. K 1992, Mus. Tusc. 94 p.; 143 fig. 87-7289-080-0. – ᴿAfO 38s (1991s) 230s (D. *Collon*); Mesop-T 27 (1992) 284s (A. *Invernizzi*).

e147 **Müller-Winkler** Claudia, Die ägyptischen Objekt-Amulette: OBO arch 5, 1987 ⇢ 3,d767 ... 6,d689: ᴿBASOR 285 (1992) 83 (Diana C. *Patch*); Orientalia 61 (1992) 146-8 (G.T. *Martin*).

e148 ᴱ**Palaima** Thomas G., Aegean seals: Univ. Texas Aegean Scripts conference, Austin Jan. 11-13, 1989; Liège 1990, Univ. 250 p.; 40 pl. – ᴿAJA 96 (1992) 176-9 (J. *Bennet*).

e149 **Pittman** Holly, The glazed steatite glyptic style; the structure and function of an image: Diss. Columbia, ᴰ*Porada* E. NY 1990. xxv-943 p. 91-02449. – OIAc 5,32.

e150 **Rashad** Mahmoud, Die Entwicklung der vor- und frühgeschichtlichen Stempelsiegel in Iran im Vergleich mit Mesopotamien, Syrien und Kleinasien: DAI-T, ArchMIranEgb 13. B 1990, Reimer. 304 p. 48 pl. 3-496-00392-8. – ᴿBO 49 (1992) 847-9 (P. *Amiet*: trop rapide); RAss 86 (1992) 188s (aussi P. *Amiet*); ZAss 82 (1992) 283-5 (E. *Porada*).

e151 **Richards** Fiona V., Scarab seals from a Middle to Late Bronze Age tomb at Pella in Jordan: OBO 117. FrS/Gö 1992, Univ./Vandenhoeck & R. xi-139 p. DM 45. 3-7278-0813-6 / VR 3-525-537751-4 [BL 93,36, A.R. *Millard*].

e152 **Salje** Beate, Der 'common style' der Mitanni-Glyptik 1990 ⇢ 7,d108: ᴿMesop-T 27 (1992) 293-7 (G. *Bergamini*); ZAss 82 (1992) 285-290 (D.M. *Matthews*).

e153 *Salje* Beate, Der Einfluss des 'common style' der Mitanni-Glyptik auf die Glyptik der Levante in der späten Bronzezeit: ⇢ 683, Circulation 1991/2, 259-265; 14 fig.

e154 *Scandone Matthiae* G., Khentiamenti-Horus [large cylinder seal from Abydos]; the dead king during the Early Dynastic period of Egypt: JPrehR 6 (1992) 31-37.

e154* *a*) *Schulman* Alan E., Still more Egyptian seal impressions from 'En Beşor; – *b*) *Kaplony* Peter, Archaische Siegel und Siegelabrollungen aus dem Delta; die Arbeit an den Siegeln von Buto: ⇢ 703, Nile Delta 1990/2, 395-418 / 23-30.

e155 ᴱ**Shah** Sayid G. M., *Parpola* Asko, Corpus of Indus seals and inscriptions, 2. Collections in Pakistan: AnnAcadScGFennicae B-240. Helsinki 1991, Tiedeakatemia. xxxii-448 p. [OIAc 5,34].

e156 *Śliwa* Joachim, Egyptian scarabs and magical gems 1989 ⇢ 6,d695: ᴿDiscEg 23 (1992) 93s (Irène *Gautier-Vodoz*).

e157 *Tushingham* A.D., New evidence bearing on the two-winged LMLK stamp: BASOR 287 (1992) 61-65.

e158 *a*) *Tushingham* A.D., A 'Neo-Babylonian' seal from Tell Taanach; – *b*) *Garfinkel* Yosef, al., A late neolithic seal from Herzliya: BASOR 286 (1992) 15-18; 2 fig. / 7-13; 3 fig.

e159 **Veenhof** Klaas R., *Klengel-Brandt* Evelyn, Altassyrische Tontafeln aus Kültepe: Texte und Siegelabrollungen: B StaatMus VorderasSchr 26. B 1992, Mann. 60 p.; 51 pl. 3-7861-1668-7 [OIAc 5,38].

e160 *Vincentelli* Irene, A group of figurated clay sealings from Jebel Barkal (Sudan): Orientalia 61 (1992) 106-121; 3 fig.; pl. I-IV.

e161 **Weingarten** Judith, The Zakro master: SIMA pocket 26, 1983 ⇢ 64, a998 ... 4,e381: ᴿAnzAltW 45 (1992) 277-280 (S. *Hiller*).

e162 *Weingarten* Judith, The multiple sealing system of Minoan Crete and its possible antecedents in Anatolia: OxJArch 11 (1992) 25-37; 13 fig.

e163 *Weiss* Peter, Bleietiketten mit Warenangaben aus dem Umfeld von Rom: Tyche 6 (1991) 211-220; pl. 16.

e164 **Wickede** Alwo von,   Prähistorische Stempelglyptik in Vorderasien [Diss. München]: MüVorderasSt 6. Mü 1990, Profil. 334 p.; 43 fig.; 630 pl. DM 128.   3-89019-249-1. – ᴿAfO 38s (1991s) 228-230 (D. *Collon*: a classic); ArOr 60 (1992) 279-284 (P. *Chervát*); ZAss 82 (1992) 298-302 (E. *Porada*).

e165 *Wickede* Alwo von,   Chalcolithic sealings from Arpachiyah: BInstArch 28 (1991) 153-196; 6 fig.; VI pl.

e166 **Wiese** André,   Zum Bild des Königs auf ägyptischen Siegelamuletten: OBO 96, 1990 ➤ 7,d116:   ᴿBO 49 (1992) 394s (J. *Śliwa*).

e166* *Wittmann* Beatrice,   Babylonische Rollsiegel des 11.-7. Jahrhunderts v.Chr.:   BaghMitt 23 (1992) 169-289; pl. 16-49.

e167 *Zanetti* Ugo,   Amulettes éthiopiennes chez les Bollandistes: AnBoll 110 (1992) 28-30.

T3.4   Mosaica.

e168 [*Ben Abed-*]**ben Khader** Aïcha,   Corpus des mosaïques de Tunisie II, Région de Zaghouan, 3. Thuburbo Majus, les mosaïques de la région ouest, 1987 ➤ 6,d707; 135 p.; 10 fig.; 54 pl. + 12 color.; 13 foldout plans. – ᴿBMosAnt 13 (1990s) 397-400 (J.-P. *Darmon*).

e169 **Daszewski** Wiktor A.,   *Michaelides* Demetrios,   a) Mosaic floors in Cyprus: Bt Felix Ravenna. Ravenna 1988, Girasole. 166 p.; 67 fig. – b) Guide des mosaïques de Paphos. Nicosia 1989.   73 p.; 51 fig. – ᴿBMosAnt 13 (1990s) 413-8 (Suzanne *Gozlan*).

e169* **Desreumaux** Alain, *Gatier* Pierre-Louis,   Inscription bilingue grecque et syriaque d'une mosaïque paléochrétienne [...'provenance de Beyrouth']: Semitica 41s (1991) 173-181; 2 fig.

e170 **Donderer** Michael,   Die Mosaizisten der Antike 1989 ➤ 7,d121:   ᴿAJA 96 (1992) 186s (D. *Parrish*); AntClas 61 (1992) 732s (Janine *Balty*).

e171 *Ghedini* Francesca,   Iconografie urbane e maestranze africane nel mosaico della piccola caccia di Piazza Armerina: MiDAI-R 98 (1991) 323-335; pl. 75-79.

e172 *Goette* Hans R.,   Alpheios in Syrien — zu einem Mosaik in Ṭarṭūs: DamaszMi 5 (1991) 71-80; 1 fig.; pl. 31s.

e173 **Guimier-Sorbets** Anne-Marie, La mosaïque dans le monde grec. ᴰ1989: ᴿBMosAnt 13 (1990s) 383s (R. *Ginouvès*).

e174 *Guimier-Sorbets* Anne-Marie, *Nenna* Marie-Dominique,   L'emploi du verre, de la faïence et de la peinture dans les mosaïques de Délos: BCH 116 (1992) 607-631; 2 fig.; IV color. pl. [727-732 *al.*, Délos 1991].

c175 **Henderson** Priscilla,   The Christian mosaics of Byzantine Palestine; towards an interpretation: diss. Canberra 1989. – BMosAnt 13 (1990s) 387.

e176 **Jeddi** Nabiha,   Les mosaïques de Thaenae (Thina en Tunisie); étude descriptive et analytique: diss. Paris-IV Sorbonne 1990. 570 p.; CV pl. – ᴿBMosAnt 13 (1990s) 385s (Suzanne *Gozlan*).

e177 **Kondoleon** Christine,   The mosaics of the house of Dionysos at Paphos; a contribution to the study of Roman provincial art: diss. Harvard, ᴰ*Kitzinger* E. – BMosAnt 13 (1990s) 388 [> Ithaca NY 1991, Cornell Univ.].

e178 **Lancha** Janine,   Muses, poètes, philosophes, scènes littéraires ét dramatiques dans les mosaïques des provinces occidentales de l'Empire romain (Iᵉʳ-IVᵉ s.): diss. d'État, Paris-X Nanterre 1989. – BMosAnt 13 (1990s) 389s.

e179 *Lange* Judith,   Scene di vita africana... Scuola di mosaico: ArchViva 10,16 (1991) 10-23; color. ill.

e180 *Netzer* Ehud, *Weiss* Zeev, New mosaic art from Sepphoris: BAR-W 18,6 (100th issue, 1992) 36-43.78; ill.; ... [19/2, 10, letter of R.B. *Six* deplores failure to recognize cockfighting origins; an onyx cock from Mizpah is 'for Jaazaniah', probably of 2 Kgs 25,23; Jer 40,8].

e181 **Ovadiah** Ruth & Asher, Hellenistic, Roman, and early Byzantine mosaic pavements in Israel 1987 ➤ 4,e396... 6,d718: ᴿWeltOr 23 (1992) 211-5 (H.P. *Kuhnen*).

e182 **Roussin** Lucille A., The iconography of the figural mosaic pavements of early Byzantine Palestine: diss. Columbia, ᴰ*Frazer* A. NY 1985. – BMosAnt 13 (1990s) 391.

e183 *Schlatter* Fredric W., Interpreting the mosaic of Santa Pudenziana: VigChr 46 (1992) 276-295; 1 pl.

e184 **Wisskirchen** Rotraut, Das Mosaikprogramm von S. Prassede in Rom...: JbAC Egb 17, 1990 ➤ 7,d133: ᴿGymnasium 99 (1992) 278-280 (R. *Sörries*); TLZ 117 (1992) 455s (H.G. *Thümmel*).

e185 *Wisskirchen* Rotraut, Die Mosaiken der Kirche Santa Prassede in Rom: AntWelt 23-Sond. (1992). 70 p., 65 (color.) fig. (Schlechter F.).

T3.5 *Ceramica*, **pottery** [➤ *singuli situs*, infra].

e186 **Adams** Barbara, Sculptured pottery from Koptos in the [London University College] Petrie collection 1986 ➤ 3,d807; 5,d512: ᴿCdÉ 66 (1991) 186-8 (C.A. *Hope*).

e187 *Adan-Bayewitz* David, *Wieder* Moshe, Ceramics from Roman Galilee; a comparison of several techniques for fabric characterization: JField 19 (1992) 189-205; 14 fig.

e187* *Balensi* Jacqueline, L'archéologie palestinienne; une science du tesson [sherd]?: MondeB 75 (1992) 30-33 [20s; 34-40, *Briend* J.].

e188 ᴱ**Barlow** Jane A., *al.*, Cypriot ceramics; reading the prehistoric record: Mg 74. Ph 1991, Univ. Museum. xx-258 p.; ill. 0-924171-10-3.

e189 ᴱ**Barrelet** M.T., *Gardin* J.C., À propos... poterie, questions ouvertes: RCiv mém 64, 1984/6 ➤ 2,a335... 7,d137: ᴿAulaO 10 (1992) 158-160 (E. *Olávarri*); Syria 68 (1991) 477-9 (J.-L. *Huot*: 'charabia à la mode' de A. GALLAY n'a pas diminué le plaisir de lire).

e190 *Biers* William R., Archaic plastic [i.e. *plastós* 'formed or molded'] vases from Corinth: Hesperia 61 (1992) 227-238; pl. 53-60.

e191 *Bourriau* J.D., *Nicholson* P.T., Marl clay pottery fabrics of the New Kingdom from Memphis, Saqqara and Amarna: JEA 78 (1992) 29-91; 5 fig.; pl. 1-4 (colour) + V-XVII.

e192 *Breniquet* Catherine, À propos [de la peinture] du vase halafien de la tombe G2 de Tell Arpachiyah: Iraq 54 (1992) 69-78; 3 fig.

e193 **Burow** Johannes, Der Antimenesmaler 1989 ➤ 6,d737; 7,d146: ᴿRBg-Pg 70 (1992) 289s (Christiane *Delplace*).

e194 **Cahier** ceramique ég 1,1987: ᴿArOr 60 (1992) 197s (E. *Strouhal*).

e195 **Clark** Andrew J., Attic black-figured *oirai* and *oinochoai*: diss. ᴰ*Bothmer* D. von. NYU 1992. 1077 p. 92-22871. – DissA 53 (1992s) 861-A.

e196 *a) Crouwel* J.H., Mycenaean pictorial pottery from Cyprus in Oxford; – *b) Lemos* Irene S., *Hatcher* Helen, Early Greek vases in Cyprus; Euboean and Attic; – *c) Cook* B.F., Attic red-figured lekythoi, secondary types, class 6L: OxJArch 10 (1991) 45-55: 11 fig. / 197-208; 17 fig. / 209-230; 19 fig.

e197 *Epstein* Claire, ❹ Chalcolithic 'Golan pottery' in Galilee: ➤ 18, ᶠBIRAN A., ErIsr 23 (1992) 1-4; 7 fig.; Eng. 144*.

e198 **Ettlinger** Elisabeth, *al.*, Conspectus... terrae sigillatae: Materialien röm.-germ. Keramik 10, 1990 ➔ 7,d149; 3-7749-2456-2: ᴿAJA 96 (1992) 190 (Andrea M. *Berlin*); RArchéol (1992) 161-3 (Ariane *Bourgeois*).

e199 Firenze, museo [ᴱ*Bresciani* E.]: L'argilla e il tornio; la produzione fittile dell'Egitto Antico [esposizione 1991s] Firenze, Museo Archeologico. R 1992, Ateneo. 99 p.; 121 color. fig.

e199* *Frange* Mathias, Der Raub der Leukippiden auf einer Vase des Achilleusmalers: AntKu 35 (1992) 3-17; 4 pl.; franç. 17.

e200 **Frank** Susanne, Attische Kelchkratere; eine Untersuchung zum Zusammenspiel von Gefässform und Bemalung: EurHS 38/24. Fra 1990, Lang. 306 p.; 18 pl. DM 75. 3-631-41647-4. – ᴿAntClas 61 (1992) 673s (Athéna *Tsingarida*).

e201 **Frontisi-Ducroux** Françoise, Le dieu masque; une figure du Dionysos d'Athènes [lécythes, stamnoi]; diss. d'État]: Images à l'appui 4. P 1991, Découverte. 288 p. – ᴿRÉAnc 94 (1992) 513-5 (Colette *Jourdain-Annequin*).

e202 *Gabler* D., *Vaday* A. H., Terra sigillata im Barbaricum zwischen Pannonien und Dazien, 2: AcArchH 44,1 (1992) 83-160; 30 fig.

e203 *Gal* Zvi, Two kernoi from Lower Galilee: 'Atiqot 22 (1993) 121-4; 3 fig.

e204 *García Heras* Manuel, *Olastxea* Carlos, Métodos y análisis para la caracterización de cerámicas arqueológicas; estado actual de la investigación en España: ArEspArq 65 (1992) 263-289.

e205 **Gibson** Alex, *Woods* Ann, Prehistoric pottery for the archaeologist 1990 ➔ 7,d152: ᴿBInstArch 28 (1991) 201s (C. *Orton*).

e206 *Gilmour* Garth A., Mycenaean III A and III B pottery in the Levant and Cyprus: RepCyp (1992) 113-128; 2 maps.

e206* *Guéry* Roger, Les marques de potiers sur terra sigillata découvertes en Algérie 4/1 (italique): AntAfr 28 (1992) 15-95 + 36 fig.

e207 *Hoffmann* Herbert, 'Crocodile love' [6 vases show a black being devoured by a crocodile near a sex-scene] (the Dionysian connection); further studies in the iconology of Athenian vase-painting: Hephaistos 11s (1992s) 133-169; 20 fig.

e207* *Holbrook* Neil, *Bidwell* Paul T., *al.*, Roman pottery from Exeter 1980-1990: JPot 5 (1992) 35-80; 19 fig. [p. 123, J. *Monaghan*'s review of their 1991 Roman finds from Exeter).

e208 **Holmberg** Erik J., The red-liner painter and the workshop of the Acheloos painter: SIMA pocket 87, 1990 ➔ 6,d746; 107 p.; 70 fig. 91-86098-73-X: ᴿAntClas 61 (1992) 674s (Athéna *Tsingarida*).

e209 *Jones* Olwen T., Chalkidic painted ware; three Stamnoid craters from Torone: ArchEph 129 (1990) 177-189; 8 fig.

e210 **Kearsley** Rosalinde, The pendent semi-circle skyphos; a study of its development and chronology and an examination of it as evidence for Euboean activity at Al Mina; BInstArch supp 44, ᴰ1989 ➔ 7,d160: ᴿAnzAltW 45 (1992) 262-273 (S. *Hiller*); Gnomon 64 (1992) 152-5 (M. *Popham*, Irene *Lemos*: hallmark of Euboean).

e211 *Kolbus* Susanne, Von Knickwandschalen und Schalenmauern; Bemerkungen zu Palästina und Mesopotamien im dritten vorchristlichen Jahrtausend [< Diss. Münster, ᴰ*Mayer-Opificius* R.]: ➔ 683, Circulation 1991/2, 43-51; 4 fig.

e212 **Kossatz** Anne-Ulrike, Funde aus Milet [1899], 5/1. Die megarischen Becher: DAI. B 1990, de Gruyter. xi-144 p.; 46 fig.; 55 pl., 10 foldouts. DM 320. – ᴿClasR 42 (1992) 227s (Susan I. *Rotroff*: data on Delian moldmade bowls).

e213 *Lapp* Nancy L., Pottery: ➤ 741, AnchorBD 5 (1992) 428-444.

e214 **Lezzi-Hafter** Adrienne, Der Eretria-Maler; Werke und Weggefährten: Kerameus 6, 1988 ➤ 6,d752; 7,d161: ᴿAntClas 61 (1992) 675-7 (Didier *Martens*).

e215 *Majidzadeh* Yousef, The Arjan bowl [c. 700 B.C., Assyrian; five concentric registers with figures as on Phoenician bowls]: Iran 30 (1992) 131-144.

e216 *Malagardis* Nassi, Note sur un peintre athénien novateur ou du bon usage de la passion chez les dieux: ArchEph 128 (1989) 105-114; 8 fig.

e217 *Mayerson* Philip, The Gaza 'wine' jar (*gazition*) and the 'lost' Ashkelon jar (*askalônion*): IsrEJ 42 (1992) 76-80; 3 fig.

e218 *Mazzoni* Stefania, The diffusion of Palestine combed jars: ➤ 736, ᴱ*Shaath* S., Palestine 1981/5, 145-158; 32 fig.; 2 pl.

e219 **Neeft** C.W., Addenda et corrigenda to D.A. AMYX, Corinthian vase-painting 1988. Amst 1991, A. Pierson Museum. 168 p. – ᴿRArchéol (1992) 402s (H.P. *Isler*: book-review of a masterpiece).

e220 *Neils* Jenifer, The Morgantina phormiskos [... Corinthianizing in style]: AJA 96 (1992) 225-235; 15 fig.

e221 **Noll** Walter, Alte Keramiken und ihre Pigmente; Studien zu Material und Technologie. Stu 1991, Schweizerbart. vi-334 p. 3-510-65145-6 [OIAc 5,31].

e222 **Oakley** John H., The Phiale painter: Kerameus 8, 1990 ➤ 6,d758; 7,d163: ᴿGnomon 64 (1992) 276-8 (Adrienne *Lezzi-Hafter*); RBgPg 70 (1992) 288s (Christiane *Delplace*).

a222* *Paice* Patricia, The pottery of daily life in ancient Egypt: JSStEg 19 (1989) 50-88; 16 fig.

e223 *Perpillou* Jean-Louis, 'Badly miswritten' ou de la manière d'écrire des peintres de vases: RÉG 105 (1992) 557-560.

e224 **Prange** Mathias, Der Niobidenmaler und seine Werkstatt... frühklassischer Zeit: EurHS 38/25. Fra 1989, Lang. xiv-215 p.; 16 fig.; 54 pl. Fs 85. – ᴿGnomon 64 (1992) 30-34 (Kalinka *Huber*).

e225 ᴱ**Rasmussen** Tom, *Spivey* Nigel, Looking at Greek vases. C 1991, Univ. xvii-282 p.; 110 fig. 0-521-37521-X. – ᴿAJA 96 (1992) 709s (W.E. *Biers*).

e226 **Rombos** Theodora, The iconography of Attic Late Geometric II pottery [with thanks to N. COLDSTREAM]: SIMA pocket 68. Jonsered 1988, Åström. 178 p.; 74 pl. – ᴿGnomon 64 (1992) 236-240 (S. *Hiller*).

e227 *a*) *Roux* Charles, Bulletin archéologique; céramique; – *b*) *Empereur* J.-Y., *Garlan* Y., Amphores et timbres amphoriques: RÉG 105 (1992) 121-175 / 176-230.

e228 **Roux** Valentine, (*Corbetta* Daniela), Le tour du potier; spécialisation artisanale et compétences techniques: MgCRechArch 4. P 1990, CNRS. 155 p.; 30 fig.; 25 pl. F 140. 2-222-04474-X. – ᴿAntClas 61 (1992) 639 (G. *Raepsaet*).

e229 *a*) *Shaheen* Alaa el-Din M., A possible synchronization of EB IV C / MB I ceramic ware in Syro-Palestinian and Egyptian sites; – *b*) *Wessetzky* Vilmos, Das Wort š als Opferschale: GöMiszÄg 131 (1992) 101-106 + 3 fig. / ill.

e230 **Simantoni-Bournia** Eva, *a*) Ⓖ Anaskaphes Naxou, oi anaglyphoi pithoi; – *b*) La céramique à reliefs au musée de Chios: Bt SocArchéol Athènes 113.125. Athenai 1990/1992. 165 p., 11 pl. / 117 p., 29 pl. – ᴿDialHA 18,2 (1992) 349-351 (P. *Lévêque*).

e231 *Singer-Avitz* Lily, *Levi* Yossi, Ⓗ Nahal Soreq MB II A pottery kiln: ᶜAtiqot 21 (1992) 9*-14*; Eng. 174.

e232 *Sinopoli* Carla M., Approaches to archaeological ceramics 1991 ➤ 7, d172: ᴿAJA 96 (1992) 763s (C. C. *Kolb*).

e233 *Smith* Robzrt H., 'Bloom of youth', a labelled Syro-Palestinian unguent jar [purchased in Palestine 'many years ago']: JHS 112 (1992) 163-7; 2 fig.

e234 **Sparkes** B. A., Greek pottery; an introduction. Manchester 1991, Univ. xiii-186 p.; ill. £35; pa. £10. – ᴿGreeceR 39 (1992) 215 (N. *Spivey*).

e235 *Tenwolde* C., Myrtos [Crete] revisited; the role of relative function ceramic typologies in Bronze Age settlement analysis: OxJArch 11 (1992) 1-24; 20 fig.

e236 *Tournavitou* Iphigeneia, Practical use and social function; a neglected aspect of Mycenaean pottery: AnBritAth 87 (1992) 181-210; 6 fig.

e237 *Villanueva Puig* Marie-Christine, Les représentations de ménades dans la céramique antique à figures rouges de la fin de l'archaïsme: RÉAnc 94 (1992) 125-141 + 19 fig.

e238 **Williams** Bruce, Decorated pottery and the art of Naqada III, 1988 ➤ 4,e460: ᴿJEA 78 (1992) 318-322 (C. A. *Hope*).

e239 **Wood** Bryant G., The sociology of pottery in ancient Palestine; the ceramic industry and the diffusion of ceramic style in the Bronze and Iron ages: JStOT supp 103, ᴰ1990 ➤ 6,d777: ᴿBL (1992) 39s (K. W. *Whitelan*); JAOS 112 (1991) 705-7 (Gloria A. *London*: some unanswered questions); JBL 111 (1992) 317-9 (J. A. *Dearman*: by sociology he means 'the relationship between pottery and its cultural and economic environment'); VT 42 (1992) 575 (Joan *Oates*: needs more analyses and less unfounded speculation).

e240 *Worschech* Udo, Collared-rim jars aus Moab; Anmerkungen zur Entwicklung und Verbreitung der Krüge mit 'Halswulst': ZDPV 108 (1992) 149-155; 3 fig.

T3.6 Lampas.

e241 *Baily* Donald M., Lamps metal, lamps clay; a decade of publication [Roman lamps, 37 books; SUSSMAN V. 1982 on Jewish lamps]: JRomA 4 (1991) 51-62.

e242 **Beaune** Sophie A. de, Lampes et godets au Paléolithique: Gallia Préhistoire supp. 23. P 1987, CNRS. 278 p.; 93 fig.; 16 pl. – ᴿSCIstVArh 43 (1992) 93s (M. *Cârciumaru*).

e242* *Bussière* Jean, Lampes à canal courbe de Maurétanie césarienne: Ant Afr 28 (1992) 187-222; 51 fig.

e243 *Ciceroni* Marina, Iside protettrice della navigazione; la testimonianza delle lucerne a forma di barca: ➤ 701, ScAnt 3s (1989s) 793-801; Eng. 801.

e244 **Conticello De Spagnolis** M., *Carolis* E. de, Le lucerne di bronzo di Ercolano e Pompei. R 1988, Bretschneider. 244 p.; 16 pl. – ᴿLatomus 51 (1992) 259 (L. *Lerat*).

e245 *Gill* D. W. J., *Hedgecock* Deborah, Debris from an Athenian lamp workshop of the Roman period [55 relief disci fragments purchased by Fitzwilliam Museum in 1969]: AnBritAth 87 (1992) 411-421; 30 fig.

e246 *Kakovkin* Alexander, The Coptic bronze lamp of the 8-9th c. from the Hermitage collection: GöMiszÄg 130 (1992) 25-30 + 1 fig.

e247 *Lapp* Eric C., Jüdische Tonlampen aus der Spätantike im Landesmuseum Mainz: ZDPV 108 (1992) 171-3; pl. 2.

e248 **Loffreda** Stanislao, Lucerne bizantine: SBF 35, 1989 ➤ 5,d571... 7,d181: ᴿAJA 96 (1992) 198s (Anna M. *Macdonnell*).

e249 a) *Loffreda* Stanislao, Ancora sulle lucerne bizantine con iscrizioni; – b) *Waliszecki* T., Acclamatio crucis sur une lampe romaine tardive: LA 42 (1992) 313-329 / 305-312; Eng. 337.

e250 *Manns* Frédéric, Le symbole de l'échelle sur les lampes baptismales de Terre Sainte: EphLtg 106 (1992) 68-74 [< RSPT 76,517].

e251 *Pétridis* Platon, Les lampes corinthiennes de Kritika [N. Paléocorinthe]: BCH 116 (1992) 649-671; 23 fig. (maps).

e252 *Sussman* Varda, [late Byzantine lamp of unknown provenance] *eis theos*, 'one God': BAnglIsr 12 (1992s) 32-37; 2 fig.

               T3.7   **Cultica** [→ M4-7 et singuli situs].

e253 *Bienert* Hans-Dieter, Skull-cult in the prehistoric Near East: JPrehRel 5 (1991) 9-23; 19 fig.

      Braun-Holzinger E., Mesopotamische Weihgaben 1991 → b525*.

e254 **Chalkia** Eugenia, Le mense paleocristiane; tipologia e funzioni delle mense secondarie nel culto paleocristiano: diss. ^D*Fasola* U.: StAntichità-Cr 47. Vaticano 1991, Pont. Ist. Archeologia Cristiana. xxxviii-259 p.; 19 disegni; 79 fot. Lit. 120.000. 88-85991-02-5. – ^RCC 143 (1992,3) 342s (A. *Ferrua*).

e255 **Chen** D., The design of the ancient synagogues in Judaea; Eshtemoa and Horvat Susiya: LA 42 (1992) 297-303; Eng. 337.

e256 **Donceel-Voûte** Pauline, Les pavements des églises byzantines de Syrie et du Liban 1988 → 7,d186: ^RLA 41 (1991) 591s (I. *Peña*).

e257 a) *Hägg* Robin, Cult practice and archaeology; some examples from early Greece; – b) *La Genière* Juliette De, Réflexions sur les sanctuaires de la Mère des dieux au Péloponnèse: → 641, Pisane 1989, StItFgC 85 (1992) 79-95; 4 fig.; ital. 95 / 96-103; franç. 103.

e258 **Hancock** Graham, The sign and the seal; the quest for the lost ark of the covenant. NY 1992, Crown. viii-600 p.; maps. 0-517-57813-1.

e259 [*Kempinski* A., *Avigad* N. controversy] The pomegranate scepter head — from the Temple of the Lord [for which Israel Museum in 1988 paid $550,000 relying on Avigad] or from a temple of Asherah?: BAR-W 18,3 (1992) 42-45 [*Shanks*], with two appreciations of Avigad p. 46-49, F. *Cross*, H. *Shanks*.

e260 **Kraus** F. R., The role of temples, ^T*Foster* B.: MANE 2/4. Malibu 1990, Undena. 20 p. – ^RMesop-T 27 (1992) 302s (L. *Cagni*).

e261 **Malki** Abdo J., A case study in computer applications to archaeology; Byzantine churches in Syria and Palestine: diss. UCLA 1992, ^D*Bierman* Irene. 1816 p. 92-15732. – DissA 52 (1991s) 4381s-A; OIAc 5,28.

e262 a) *Ma'oz* Zvi U., ❻ The synagogue in the Second Temple period — architectural and social interpretation; – b) *Weiss* Zeev, ❻ The synagogue at Hammat Tiberias: → 18, ^FBIRAN A., ErIsr 23 (1992) 331-344; 2 fig. / 320-6; 5 fig.; Eng. 156*s.

e263 **Parry** D. W., *al.*, A bibliography on temples of the Ancient Near East and Mediterranean world: ANE TSt 9. Lewiston NY 1991, Mellen. xii-311 p. £40. 0-7734-9775-7 [BL 93,126, L. L. *Grabbe*].

e264 **Platon** L., *Pararas* Y., Pedestalled offering-tables in the Aegean world: SIMA pocket 106. Jonsered 1991, Åström. 54 p.; 22 fig.; 16 pl. – ^RJPreh-R 6 (1992) 545 (J. van *Leuven*).

e265 **Reden** Sibylle von, (*Neubert* Sigrid) Die Tempel von Malta; das Mysterium der Megalithbauten. Bergisch Gladbach 1988, Lübbe. 159 p.

e266 — *Reinecke* Andreas, Steinzeittempel auf Malta: Altertum 37 (1991) 69-75; 9 fig.

e267 *Ribichini* Sergio, I luoghi del sacro: Archeo 7,89 (1992) 62-110.

e268 **Tchalenko** G., Églises syriennes à bēma: IFA-BAH 105. P 1990, Geuthner. 336 p., ill. – ᴿJTS 43 (1992) 263-6 (C. *Mango*).

e269 *Vermaak* P. S., Die posisie van die tempel in Mesopotamië: JTydSem 4 (1992) 51-80; Eng. 51.

e269* *Wasilewska* Ewa, Archaeology of religion; colors as symbolic markers dividing sacred from profane: JPrehRel 5 (1991) 36-41.

e270 *Wimmer* Stefan, Ägyptische Tempel in Kanaan und im Sinai: JbEvHL 1 (1989) 29-55; 3 fig.; map.

T3.8 **Funeraria**; *Sindon*, **the Shroud.**

e270* **Abdalla** Aly, Graeco-Roman funerary stelae from Upper Egypt: MgArch. Liverpool 1992, Univ. xviii-153 p.; 85 pl. £35 [OLZ 88,259, K. *Parlasca*].

e271 *Bachelet* Luc, Iconographie et pratiques funéraires en Mésopotamie au troisième millénaire av.J.C.: ➤ 683, Circulation 1991/2, 53-59 + 8 fig.

e272 **Baima Bollone** Pier Luigi, Sindone o no. T 1990, SEI. 334 p. Lit. 35.000. – ᴿStCattMi 35 (1991) 183 (L. *Fossati*).

e272* *a) Balut* P.-Y., Le funéraire et l'histoire; – *b) Dunand* F., *Lichtenberg* R., Exploration de la nécropole de Douch; problèmes méthodologiques; – *c) Étienne* R., Comment faire parler les morts? [MORRIS I. 1987]: TopO 2 (1992) 131-140 / 141-150 / 151-6.

e273 **Bertrand** Doris, Les dimensions sociales des pratiques funéraires à Chypre (7500-750 av.J.-C.): diss. Laval, ᴰ*Fortin* M. 1992. 487 p. DANN 71612. – DissA 53 (1992s) 4434-A.

e274 **Binant** Pascale, La préhistoire de la mort; les premières sépultures en Europe: Hespérides. P 1991, Errance. 170 p.; ill. 2-87772-045-4.

e275 **Bloch-Smith** Elizabeth, Judahite burial practices and beliefs about the dead [diss.]: JStOT supp 123. Sheffield 1992. 314 p.; ill. [BL 93,27, J. *Day*]. £40; sb. £30. 1-85075-335-0. – ᴿExpTim 104 (1992s) 185 (J. F. *Healey*).

e276 **Caillet** Jean-Pierre, *Loose* Helmuth Nils, La vie d'éternité; la sculpture funéraire dans l'Antiquité chrétienne 1990 ➤ 7,d197: ᴿAntClas 61 (1992) 770-2 (C. *Delvoye*).

e277 **Celier** O., Le signe du linceul; le Saint Suaire de Turin, de la relique à l'image: Théologies. P 1992, Cerf. 247 p.; 32 pl. F 148 [RHE 87,436*].

c278 **Colvin** Howard, Architecture [classical burial-patterns] and the after-life. NHv 1991, Yale Univ. xii-418 p.; 358 fig. $75. 0-300-05093-1. – ᴿAntiquity 66 (1992) 815s (M. *Vickers*: good).

e278* *Compostella* Carla, Banchetti pubblici e privati nell'iconografia funeraria romana del I secolo d.C.: MÉF 104 (1992) 659-689; 22 fig.

e279 ᴱ**D'Auria** Sue, *al.*, Mummies and magic; the funerary arts of ancient Egypt 1988 ➤ 5,d608 (Index!): ᴿArOr 60 (1992) 200 (E. *Strouhal*).

e280 **Dodson** Aidan, Egyptian rock-cut tombs: ShireEg 14. Princes Risborough 1991, Shire. 64 p.; 62 fig. 0-7478-0128-2 [OIAc 5,19].

e280* *Dodson* Aidan, On the burial of Prince Ptahshepses: GöMiszÄg 129 (1992) 49-51.

e281 **Dunand** Françoise, *Lichtenberg* Roger, Les momies; un voyage dans l'Antiquité: Découvertes. P 1991, Gallimard. – ᴿDialHA 18,1 (1992) 297 (G. *Tate*).

e281* **Fedak** Janos, Monumental tombs of the Hellenistic age; a study of selected tombs from the pre-classical to the imperial era: Phoenix supp. 24, 1990 → 6,d822: ᴿPhoenix 46 (1992) 287-290 (H. *Williams*).

e282 *Fiaccadori* Gianfranco, The tomb of Alexander the Great: ParPass 47,244 (1992) 128-131.

e283 *Fossati* Luigi, Sindone e sacri volti [... gli errori del carbonio]: StCattMi 36 (1992) 30-33.

e284 Getty Museum, Roman funerary monuments 1 [8 art. in German. 1 Eng.]: OccasP 6. Malibu CA 1990, J. Paul Getty Museum. 144 p. 0-89226-151-4.

e285 *Goette* Hans Rupprecht, Attische Klinen-Riefel-Sarkophage: MiDAI-A 106 (1991) 309-338; pl. 89-112.

e286 **Gonen** Rivka, Burial patterns and cultural diversity in Late Bronze Age Canaan [diss.Jerusalem 1979]: ASOR diss. 7. WL 1992, Eisenbrauns. viii-168 p. $25. 0-931464-68-4 [BL 93,31, T. C. *Mitchell*].

e287 *Gramaglia* Pier Angelo, Ancora la Sindone di Torino: RivStoRL 27 (1991) 85-114: reazioni di cattolici di paura e insicurezza.

e288 **Haarløv** Britt, The half-open door; a common symbolic motif within Roman sepulchral sculpture [diss. 1974]: ClasSt 10. Odense 1977, Univ. 174 p.; 62 fig. 87-7492-213-0.

e288* *Helck* W., Begräbnis Pharaos: → 96, ᴱKÁKOSY L. 1992, 267-276.

e289 *Janssen* J.J., Gear for the tombs [continuing ČERNÝ J. 1973] O. Turin 57366 and O. BM. 50733+O. Petrie 30): RÉgp 43 (1992) 107-122; pl. 2.

e290 **Kieser** Julius A., Human adult odontometrics; the study of variations in adult tooth size: Biological Anthropology 4. C 1990, Univ. xii-194 p.; 28 fig. $54.50. 0-521-35390-4. – ᴿAJA 96 (1992) 762s (M.J. *Becker*, also on HOWELLS W., Skull shapes: both for libraries].

e291 ᴱ**Ladu** Tarquinio, La datazione della Sindone; Atti del V. Congresso Nazionale della Sindone [Siracusa 13.X.1988]. Cagliari 1990, Edicar. 560 p.; ill. – ᴿStCattMi 35 (1991) 665s (L. *Fossati*).

e291* ᴱ**Laffineur** Robert, Thanatos; les coutumes funéraires en Égée à l'âge du Bronze, Liège 1986/7 → 4,752; 5,d619: ᴿJPrehRel 5 (1991) 84-89 (H.-G. *Buchholz*).

e292 **McCane** Byron B., Jews, Christians, and burial in Roman Palestine: diss. Duke, ᴰ*Meyers* E. Durham NC 1992. 268 p. 93-03525. – DissA 53 (1992s) 3249-A.

e292* *Marcozzi* Vittorio, La sacra sindone di Torino: Vita Consacrata 28 (1992) 261-8.

e293 **Morris** Ian, Death-ritual and social structure in classical antiquity: Key themes in ancient history. C 1992, Univ. xvii-264 p.; 48 fig. 0-521-37611-4 [OIAc 5,30].

e294 *Morris* Ian, *a*) The archaeology of ancestors; the Saxe-Goldstein hypothesis revisited [on the emergence of formal cemeteries]: CamArch 1 (1991) 147-169; 5 fig.; – *b*) Law, culture and funerary art in Athens, 600-300 B.C.: Hephaistos 11s (1992s) 35-50.

e295 *Pernigotti* S., Una nuova statuetta funeraria a nome di Potasimto di Pharbaithos [famoso per l'iscrizione greca di Abu Simbel]: StEgPun 9 (1991) 1-9+3 pl.

e296 *Rahmani* L.Y., Five lead coffins from Israel: IsrEJ 42 (1992) 81-102; 17 fig.

e297 *Reeder* Jane C., Typology and ideology in the mausoleum of Augustus; tumulus and tholos: ClasAnt 11 (1992) 265-304+6 fig.

e298 *Roth* Ann M., The *pss̆-kf* and the 'opening of the mouth' ceremony; a ritual of birth and rebirth: JEA 78 (1992) 113-147; 11 fig.

e299 **Sanders** François G., Lapides memores; païens et chrétiens face à la mort; le témoignage de l'épigraphie funéraire latine: Epigrafia e Antichità 11. Faenza 1991, Lega. 527 p. – ᴿRHE 87 (1992) 441-4 (M. *Carrias*).

e300 *Schoen* Edward L., David HUME and the mysterious shroud of Turin: RelSt 27 (1991) 209-222.

e301 **Stewart** H. M., Mummy-cases and inscribed funerary cones in the Petrie collection 1986 → 2,a442 ... 5,d638: ᴿCdÉ 66 (1991) 188-190 (J.-L. *Chappaz*).

e302 *Valenza-Mele* Nazarena, Vita dell'aldilà e corredi funerari; evoluzioni comparate: DialHA 17,2 (1991) 149-174.

e303 **Walker** Susan, Catalogue of Roman sarcophagi in the British Museum 1990 → 7,d214: ᴿGnomon 64 (1992) 568s (F. *Baratte*, franç.); RArchéol (1992) 55s (R. *Turcan*).

T3.9   *Numismatica*, coins.

e304 *a) Acquaro* E., *Manfredi* L. I., Rassegna di numismatica punica 1989-1991; – *b) Viola* Mauro R., Monete puniche; mercato antiquario 1989-1991: StEgPun 10 (1992) 7-70 / 71-189; ill.

e305 *Bukhoum* Sohein, Signification de l'image d'Apis sur le monnayage d'Alexandrie: CdÉ 67 (1992) 133-141 + 16 fig.

e306 **Bar** M., Monnaies grecques et assimilées trouvées en Belgique: Travaux 11. Bru 1991, CercleÉtNum. 303 p.; 9 pl. – ᴿRStFen 20 (1992) 196-8 (Lorenza-Ilia *Manfredi*).

e307 *Beldiman* Corneliu, Coins from the Second Iron Age discovered in eastern Transylvania (in Rumanian): (Sc)IstVArh 41 (1990) 111-3; Eng. 113.

e308 **Bérend** Denyse, Sylloge nummorum graecorum, Amer. Numismatic Soc. 5/3, Sicily/Syracusa. NY 1988, American Numismatic Soc. 45 pl. with facing text. 0-89722-224-5. – ᴿAJA 96 (1992) 188 (E. Ross *Holloway*).

e309 **Berman** Allen G., Papal coins. South Salem NY 1991, Attic [with Imprimatur]. 257 p.; 77 pl. 0-915018-43-8.

e310 *Betlyon* John W., Coinage: → 741, AnchorBD 1 (1992) 1076-1089; 15 fig.

e311 *a) Bland* Roger, A hoard of Syrian tetradrachms of the third century A.D. from Trans-Jordan; – *b) Rosenberger* Meir, Unpublished and rare city coins (Decapolis) [*Barkay* R., Canatha]: IsrNumJ 11 (1990s) 81-83 / 77-80; pl. 12 [72-76].

e312 *a) Bland* Roger, Six hoards of Syrian tetradrachms of the third century AD; – *b) Oddy* Andrew, Arab imagery on early Umayyad coins in Syria and Palestine; evidence for falconry: NumC 151 (1991) 1-34; pl. 1-12 / 59-66; 1 fig.; pl. 19-20.

e313 **Burnett** Andrew, La numismatique romaine [Coinage 1987 → 4,e458], ᵀ*Depeyrot* Georges. P 1988, Errance. 119 p.; ill. 2-903442-69-2.

e314 *Butcher* Kevin, The Roman coinage of Thessalonica [TOURATSOGLOU I. 1988]: JRomA 5 (1992) 434-9.

e315 *a) Butcher* Kevin, Rhodian drachms at Caesarea in Cappadocia; – *b) Ashton* Richard, The pseudo-Rhodian drachms of Mylasa; – *c) Gautier* Georges, An unpublished nummus of Constantine I of the mint of London: NumC 152 (1992) 41-48 / 1-39; pl. 1-10 / 157-160.

e316 **Buttrey** T. V., *al.*, Morgantina 2. Coins 1989 → 7,d226: ᴿAJA 96 (1992) 188-190 (Carmen *Arnold-Biucchi*).

e317 **Carson** R. A. G., Coins of the Roman Empire 1990 ➤ 6,d867; 7,d228: $200. 0-415-01591-X: ᴿClasW 86 (1992s) 145s (H. C. *Boren*); NumC 151 (1991) 247-250 (H. B. *Mattingly*).

e319 **Christiansen** Erik, Coins of Alexandria and the nomes; supplement to R. POOLE 1892 BM Catalogue. L 1991, British Museum. vii-151 p.; 12 pl.

e320 **Cribb** Joe, *al.*, The coin atlas; the world coinage from its origins down to the present day. NY 1990, Facts on file. 337 p.; ill. $40. – ᴿNumC 152 (1992) 183-5 (R. G. *Doty*: useful despite peculiar presentation).

e321 **Davesne** A., *Le Rider* G., Gülnar 2, Le trésor de Meydancıkkale 1989 ➤ 6,d874; 7,d234: ᴿNumC 151 (1991) 241-4 (M. J. *Price*).

e322 *Deutsch* Robert, Six unrecorded 'Yehud' silver coins: IsrNumJ 11 (1990s) 4-6; pl. 1.

e323 *Eshel* Hanan, A Philisto-Arabian coin from Sha'albim: IsrNumJ 11 (1990s) 7s; pl. 6,1s.

e324 *a) Foraboschi* Daniele, Civiltà della moneta e politica monetaria nell'ellenismo; – *b) Christiansen* Erik, The Roman coins of Alexandria during the reign of Claudius; – *c) Lacam* Guy, La main de Dieu; son origine hébraïque, son symbolisme monétaire durant le Bas Empire romain: RivItNum 94 (1992) 53-63 / 91-111 / 143-154 + 7 pl.

e325 **Foss** Clive, Roman historical coins 1990 ➤ 6,d878: ᴿNumC 151 (1991) 251-3 (K. *Butcher*).

e326 **Giard** J. B., Catalogue des monnaies de l'Empire Romain II. De Tibère à Néron, 1988 ➤ 5,d666; F 400: ᴿNumC 152 (1992) 203-5 (H.-M. von *Kaenel*).

e327 *Gitler* Haim, Numismatic evidence on the visit of Marcus Aurelius [c. 175 C.E.]: IsrNumJ 11 (1990s) 36-51; pl. 7.

e328 *Grünert* Hans, Vom allgemeinen Äquivalent zum Münzgeld: Altertum 37 (1991) 5-13; 8 fig.

e329 *Hackens* Tony, Sources monétaires et histoire économique de l'époque archaïque en Méditerranée occidentale; un bilan: ➤ 713, PACT 20 (1987/90) 495-500.

e329* ᴱ**Hahn** Wolfgang, *Metcalf* William E., Studies in early Byzantine gold coinage: AmN 17. NY 1988, American Numismatic. 144 p. $75. 0-89722-225-3. – ᴿByZ 84s, 1 (1991s) 148-151 (S. *Maciej*).

e330 *Houghton* Arthur, *a)* The revolt of Tryphon and the accession of Antiochus VI at Apamea [mints of both there]: Schweizerische Numismatische Rundschau 71 (1992) 119-141; pl. 16-18; – *b)* Two late Seleucid lead issues from the Levant: IsrNumJ 11 (1990s) 26-31.

e331 **Jenkins** G. K., Ancient Greek coins[2rev] [[1]1972]: Coins in history. L 1990, Seaby. x-182 p.; 439 fig.; 8 pl. £35. – ᴿClasR 42 (1992) 477s (N. K. *Rutter*).

e332 **Johnston** Ann, The coinage of Metapontum [I-II = *Noe* S. P., [2rev]1984] III: NumNMg 164, 1990 ➤ 7,d245: ᴿRÉG 105 (1992) 273s (G. *Le Rider*).

e333 **Kaenel** Hans-M. von, Münzprägung und Münzbildnis des Claudius 1986 ➤ 3,d970 ... 7,d247: ᴿNumC 151 (1991) 257-260 (C. L. *Clay*).

e334 *Kagan* Jonathan H., [*Thompson* M. 1973 Inventory of Greek coin hoards] IGCH 1185 [Brussels] reconsidered: RBgNum 138 (1992) 1-24; pl. 1-V.

e335 *a) Kindler* A., The coins of Antipatris; – *b) Hendin* David, New discovery on a coin of Herod I [helmet, not censer]; – *c) Amit* D., *Eshel* H., A tetradrachm of Bar Kokhba from a cave in Naḥal Ḥever: IsrNumJ 11 (1990s) 61-71; pl. 1-11 / 32; pl. 6,3 / 33-35; map; pl. 6,4.

e336 **Klose** Dietrich O. A., Die Münzprägung von Smyrna in der römischen Kaiserzeit ᴰ1987 ➤ 4,e577... 7,d250: ᴿBonnJbb 192 (1992) 714-7 (R. *Ziegler*).

e337 *Knoepfler* Denis, La chronologie du monnayage de Syracuse sous les Deinoménides; nouvelles données et critères méconnus: Schweiz. Num. Rundschau 71 (1992) 5-40 + 3 pl.; foldout.

e338 **Koch** Heidemarie, A hoard of coins from eastern Parthia 1990 ➤ 7, d251: ᴿBSO 55 (1992) 563s (A. D. H. *Bivar*).

e339 ᴱ**Lightfoot** C. S., Recent Turkish coin hoards and numismatic studies: British Inst. Ankara Mg. 12. Oxford 1991, Oxbow. vii-347 p.

e340 **Lindgren** Henry C., Ancient Greek bronze coins; European mints 1989 ➤ 7,d259: ᴿNumC 151 (1991) 230-2 (J. *Morcom*, Jennifer *Warren*).

e341 **Martin** Thomas R., Sovereignty and coinage in classical Greece 1985 ➤ 2,a479... 7,d261: ᴿGnomon 64 (1992) 687-693 (B. *Smarczyk*).

e342 *Meshorer* Yoʿaqov, *Qedar* Shraga, The coinage of Samaria in the fourth century BCE. Fine Arts. 84 p.; 542 pl. – ᴿQadmoniot 25 (1992) 58s (E. *Stern*, ◐).

e344 *Meshorer* Yaʿakov, Ancient Jewish coinage (1982), Addendum I: Isr-NumJ 11 (1990s) 104-132; 2 fig.; pl. 17-32.

c345 *Meyer* Marion, Mutter, Ehefrau und Herrscherin; Darstellungen der Königin auf seleukidischen Münzen: Hephaistos 11s (1992s) 107-132, 21 fig.; Eng. 125.

e346 *Mildenberg* Leo, Notes on the coin issues of Mazday [345-331 B.C. Transeuphratene satrap]: IsrNumJ 11 (1990s) 9-23; pl. 2-3.

e347 **Mitchiner** Michael, Indo-Greek and Indo-Scythian coinage. L 1975s, Hawkins. IX. 1976, p. 785-924, XX pl.

e348 **Mørkholm** Otto †, Early Hellenistic coinage from the accession of Alexander to the peace of Apamea (336-188 B.C.), ᴱ*Grierson* Philip, *Westermark* Ulla, 1991 ➤ 7,d265: ᴿClasR 42 (1992) 403-5 (I. *Carradice*); RÉG 105 (1992) 274 (G. *Le Rider*); RitNum 94 (1992) 343 (D. *Foraboschi*).

e349 **Morrisson** Cécile, La numismatique: Que sais-je? 2638. P 1992, PUF. 128 p.; 21 fig. 2-13-044261-7.

e350 *Munro-Hay* S. C. H., The coinage of Shabwa (Hadhramawt) and other ancient South Arabian coinage in the National Museum, Aden: Syria 68 (1991) 393-418.

e351 **Price** Martin J., The coinage in the name of Alexander the Great and Philip Arrhidaeus: British Museum Catalogue. Z 1991, Swiss Numismatic Asn. with BM. 637 p. 159 pl. [vol. 1, introd., catalogue; 2, concordances, plates].

e352 *Price* Martin, A hoard of tetradrachms from Jericho [before 300 B.C.]: IsrNumJ 11 (1990s) 24s; pl. 4.

e353 *Raeder* Joachim, Herrscherbildnis und Münzpropaganda; zur Deutung des 'Serapistypus' des Septimius Severus: JbDAI-107 (1992) 175-196; pl. 61-72.

e353* [Panvini] *Rosati* Franco, La zecca di Mediolanum nell'ambito delle zecche imperiali del IV-V secolo: ➤ 706, Milano capitale 1990/2, 61-64.

e354 *Sari* Sālīh K., ʿ*Amr* Abdel-Jalil, Ayyubid and Saljukid dirhams and fulus from Rujm al-Kursi [wadi Sîr]: LA 41 (1991) 459-468; pl. 53s.

e354* *Sheedy* Kenneth, Greek coins in the Museum of Applied Arts and Sciences, Sydney: MeditArch 5s (1992s) 143-160.

e355 *a*) *Sutherland* C. H. V., Roman history and coinage 1987 ➤ 3,d995 ...7,d272: ᴿHZ 253 (1991) 416-8 (M. R. *Alfoldi*).

— *b*) *Tačeva* Margarita, On the problems of the coinages of Alexander I

Sparadokos and the so-called Thracian-Macedonian tribes: Historia 41 (1992) 58-74.

— c) *Tekin* Oğuz, The coins from Üçtepe [Diyarbakır] with a problematic emission of Tigranes the Younger: EpAnat 43; pl. 5-6; p. 54 Özet.

e356 **Visona** Paolo, Punic bronze coinage: diss. Michigan, ᴰ*Buttrey* Theodore V. AA 1986. xxiii-487 p. 86-00568. – OIAc 3,41.

e357 *Weiser* Wolfram, Quintus Corellius Rufus und Marcus Maecius Rufus in Asia; flavische Münzen aus Hierapolis und Ephesos: EpAnat 20 (1992) 117-124; pl. 8; p. 125 Özet (summary ⊕).

T4   *Situs,* **excavation-sites** .1   *Chronica,* **bulletins.**

e360 Excavations: IEJ 42 (1992) 252-272; map; signed articles.

e362 *Delvoye* Charles †, Chronique archéologique: ➤ 43, Byzantion 62 (1992) 474-544 [*Deichmann* F. 1983; *Weitzmann-Galavaris* 1991; *Caillet-Loose* 1990; *Piccirillo* M. 1986].

e364 *Folmer* M. L., Actualiteiten: Israël: PhoenixEOL 38,1 (1992) 47-52; 2 fig. [Egypte 5-13, *Loose* A., *Willems* H., Mesopotamië 14-31, *Veenhof* K., *Soldt* W. van; Anatolië 32-46, *Hout* T. van den].

e364* *Nixon* C. E. V., Recent Australian and New Zealand field work in the Mediterranean region: MeditArch 5s (1992s) 160-187; 10 fig.

T4.2   *Situs effossi,* **syntheses.**

e365 **Bierling** Neal, Giving Goliath his due; new archaeological light on the Philistines. GR 1992, Baker. 281 p. $15. 0-8010-1018-7 [TDig 40,152].

e366 **Briard** Jacques, L'âge du Bronze en Europe (2000-800 av.J.-C.): Hespérides. P 1985, Errance. 211 p.; ill.; maps. 2-903-442-10-X.

e367 *Dever* William G., Palestine, archaeology of (Bronze-Iron ages): ➤ 741, AnchorBD 5 (1992) 109-114 [-116 Persian, *Stern* Ephraim; -118 NT, *Strange* John].

e367* a) *Dever* William G., The chronology of Syria-Palestine in the second millennium B.C.; – b) *Kempinski* Aharon, The MB in northern Israel; local and external synchronisms; – c) *Loon* Maurits van, The beginning of the MB in Syria; – d) *Thomas* Homer L., Historical chronologies and radiocarbon dating; – e) *Åström* Paul, Implications of an ultra low chronology: ➤ 702b, Bronze Age 1990, ÄgLev 3 (1992) 39-51 / 69-73 / 103-7 / 143-155 / 19-21.

e368 a) *Dever* William G., The chronology of Syria-Palestine in the second millennium B.C.E.; a review of current issues; – b) *Weinstein* James M., The chronology of Palestine in the early second millennium B.C.E.; – c) *Merrillees* Robert S., The absolute chronology of the Bronze Age in Cyprus; a revision; – d) *Ward* William A., The present state of Egyptian chronology: BASOR 288 (1992) 1-25; 4 fig. / 27-46 [correction to p. 32 in 289 (1993) 54] / 47-52 / 53-66.

e368* **Dothan** Trude & Moshe, People of the sea; the search for the Philistines. NY 1992, Macmillan. xiii-276 p.; 32 color pl. 0-02-532261-3 [OIAc 5,19].

e369 ᴱ**Ehrich** Robert W., Chronologies in Old World Archaeology³. Ch 1992, Univ. x-515 p.; 588 p. 0-226-19447-7 [OIAc 5,20].

e370 **James** Peter, Centuries of darkness; a challenge to the conventional chronology of Old World archaeology [just dropping some 250 years around 1000 BC] 1991 ➤ 7,d293: ᴿBL (1992) 34 (G.I. *Davies*); BO 49

(1992) 699-701 (G. W. van *Oosterhout*: 'light at the end of the tunnel', C. RENFREW); ExpTim 103 (1991s) 81s (J. R. *Bartlett*: justifiably forces re-examining our assumptions); JHS 112 (1992) 213s (J. D. *Ray*: important questions, unconvincing answers); JTS 43 (1992) 141s (A. G. *Auld*: lucidly written; Bible-chronology stays the same, an island in a sea of change; good to keep questions open, but better evidence is needed); PrPrehSoc 58 (1992) 432-5 (Susan *Sherratt*).

e371 *James* Peter, *al.*, Centuries of darkness [1991 → 7,d293]; a reply to critics: CamArch [1 (1991) 235-251 'disappointing'] 2 (1992) 127-130.

e372 **Kuhnen** Hans-Peter, Palästina in griechisch-römischer Zeit: HbArch 2/2, 1990 → 6,d926; 7,d296: RMesop-T 27 (1992) 310-313 (A. *Invernizzi*); PEQ 124 (1992) 156s (D. M. *Jacobson*); TR 88 (1992) 106-8 (M. *Zenger*); ZkT 114 (1992) 225s (R. *Oberforcher*).

e373 *Lindemeyer* Elke, Traditionen und Innovationen in der Siedlungsge-schichte Syriens zur Zeit der Auflösung der Urgesellschaft und der Her-ausbildung der frühen Klassengesellschaft [bis 2000 v.C.]: AltOrF 19 (1992) 259-265.

e374 *Marinescu-Bîlcu* Silvia, Stratigraphie et typologie dans l'étude du Néolithique et Énéolithique (en roumain): ScIstVArh 42 (1991) 112-119; franç. 119.

e374* *Na'aman* Nadav, Israel, Edom and Egypt in the 10th century B.C.E : TAJ 19 (1992) 71-93.

e375 *Negbi* Ora, Were there Sea Peoples in the central Jordan Valley at the transition from the Bronze Age to the Iron Age? AIA 1991: → 699, AJA 96 (1992) 344s.

EPorada Edith, Chronologies in Old World Archaeology; archaeological seminar at Columbia University 1989/92 → 730.

e375* *Vinitzky* Lipaz, The date of the dolmens in the Golan and the Galilee — a reassessment [EB]: TAJ 19 (1992) 100-112, map.

e376 *Watkins* Trevor, The beginning of the Neolithic; searching for meaning in material culture change: Paléorient 18,1 (1992) 63-75; 3 fig.

c377 **Weippert** Helga, Palästina in vorhellenistischer Zeit 1988 → 4,e639 ... 7,d301: RAfO 38s (1991s) 253s (K. *Jaroš*); BO 49 (1992) 506-10 (C. H. J. de *Geus*); GGA 244 (1992) 158-171 (W. *Zwickel*) / 171-3 (V. *Fritz* über KUHNEN), RTLv 23 (1992) 377s (J.-C. *Haelewyck*); VT 42 (1992) 569s (G. I. *Davies*).

T4.3 **Jerusalem,** *archaeologia et historia.*

e377* *Abu Khalaf* Marwan, The religious factors in settlement patterns in Jerusalem in the early Islamic period [*King* Geoffrey (*al.*), Umayyad-Abbasid era settlement patterns]: → 740, Jordan 4 (1992) 347-350 [369-375 (351-415)].

e378 *Ariel* Donald T. [Qedem 30,1990 → 6,d932], given in first place as contributor, but in second place as editor, after **Groot** A. → c395 infra.

e379 EAsali K. J., Jerusalem in history [9 invited art. from 8 countries]. Essex 1989 → 6,468*.d933; 7,d304: £14; 0-905906-70-5: RBL (1992), 41 (A.G. *Auld*: the former director of Jordan University has done debate a service, sought to counter a flow of writings on Jerusalem more favourable to Israeli perspectives); JRAS (1992) 66-69 (R. *Irwin*: critical FRANKEN and casual MENDENHALL hardly seem to be writing about the same place).

e380 **Auxentios** Bishop, A study of the rite of the [Greek Orthodox] Holy Fire at the Church of the Holy Sepulchre in Jerusalem: diss. Graduate

Theological Union, ᴰ*Baldwin* J. Berkeley 1992, 286 p. 93-05968. – DissA
53 (1992s) 3948-A.
e381 *Aziz* Mohammed A., The status of Jerusalem and the rise of Islamic
fundamentalism: ➤ 557*, Contacts 1990/2, 52-57.
e382 **Bahat** Dan, Illustrated Atlas of Jerusalem 1990 ➤ 6,d934; 7,d305: ᴿLA
41 (1991) 577-9 (S. *Loffreda*).
e383 *Barag* Dan, Some rare and unpublished coins of Aelia Capitolina:
IsrNumJ 11 (1990s) 52-60; pl. 8s.
e384 *Baumgarten* Jean, Jerusalem in seventeenth-century traveller's accounts
in Yiddish, ᵀ*Roumani* Judith: MeditHR 7 (1992) 219-226.
e385 *Berder* Michel, *al.*, Gerusalemme al tempo di Gesù: Il mondo della
Bibbia 10 (1992).
e386 *Biddle* Mark E., The figure of Lady Jerusalem; identification, deification
and personification of cities in the Ancient Near East: ➤ 7,334*: Canon
1990/1, 173-194.
e387 **Borgehammar** Stephan, How the Holy Cross was found; from event to
medieval legend 1991 ➤ 7,d309: ᴿBAngllsr 12 (1992s) 52-60 (Joan E.
Taylor, also on *Drijvers* J.); RHE 87 (1992) 150-4 (P. *Maraval*); TPhil 62
(1992) 275-7 (H. J. *Sieben*).
e388 *Brentjes* B., Jerusalem in pictorial records by Christian artists in pre-
Osmanic times: ➤ 736, ᴱ*Shaath* S., Palestine 1981/5, 185-9; fig. p. 246-9.
e389 **Drijvers** Jan W., Helena Augusta; the mother of Constantine the Great
and the legend of her finding of the True Cross: StIntellH 27. Leiden
1992, Brill. viii-217 p.; 1 frontispiece; p. 189-194 'portraits of Helena'
only described.
e390 *Fleckenstein* Karl-Heinz, La tomba di famiglia di Caifa, ᵀ*Bichler*
Martin: TerraS 68 (1992) 233-5.
e391 **Franken** H. J., *Steiner* M. L., [KENYON] Excavations in Jerusalem 1961-7,
II. The Iron Age extramural quarter 1990 ➤ 6,d949; 7,d318: ᴿZAW 104
(1992) 147s (Ulrike *Schorn*).
e392 *Franken* H. J., *Steiner* M. L., Urusalim and Jebus; ZAW 104 (1992)
110s [no Amarna-era finds].
e393 *Greenhut* Zvi, The 'Caiaphas' tomb in North Talpiot, Jerusalem [3 km S
Jerusalem S wall, E of Hebron road; 1990]: 'Atiqot 21 (1992) 63-71; 10
fig. (72-79, *Reich* R., inscriptions; 81-87, *Flusser* D., Caiphas in NT).
e394 *a*) *Greenhut* Zvi, Burial cave of the Caiaphas family; – *b*) *Reich* Ronny.
Caiaphas name inscribed on bone boxes; – *c*) *Horst* Pieter W. van der,
Jewish funerary inscriptions; most are in Greek; – *d*) *Fitzmyer* Joseph A.,
Did Jesus speak Greek? [some, yes; the more difficult question is whether
he sometimes taught in Greek]; – *e*) *Shanks* Hershel, The dangers of
dividing disciplines: BAR-W 18,5 (1992) 28-34.76; ill. / 38-64.76; ill. /
46-57 / 58-63.76s / 64.
e395 ᴱ**Groot** A., *Ariel* Donald T., Excavations in the City of David 1978-1985
[➤ 6,d932]; 2. Imported stamped amphora handles, coins, worked bone
and ivory and glass: Qedem 30. J 1990, Univ. Institute of Archaeology.
xx-188 p.; 33 fig.; 6 pl.; 0333-5844: ᴿJBL 111 (1992) 509s (W. G. *Dever*);
LA 41 (1991) 582-6 (P. *Kaswalder*); VT 42 (1992) 132s (J. A. *Emerton*).
e395* *Gunneweg* Antonius H. J., 3000 Jahre Jerusalem [Vortrag Bonn 1988,
unveröffentlicht]: ➤ 249, Sola Scriptura II (1992) 175-190.
e396 *Heid* Stefan, EUSEBIUS von Cäsarea über die Jerusalemer Grabeskirche:
RömQ 87 (1992) 1-28.
e396* **Jeremias** Joachim, Gerusalemme al tempo di Gesù [¹1923-37, ³ʳᵉᵛ1962],
ᵀ1989 ➤ 5,d746; 6,d951: ᴿLateranum 57 (1991) 596s (R. *Penna*).

e397 *King* Philip J., Jerusalem: ⇥ 741, AnchorBD 3 (1992) 747-766.

e398 *Küchler* M., Jerusalem: ⇥ 762, NBL II,7 (1992) 291-314; fig. 10-12.

Langer Gerhard, Von Gott erwählt — Jerusalem Dt 12 1989 ⇥ 2700.

e399 *Leonardi* Giovanni, Ritrovata la tomba di Caifa: ParVi 37 (1992) 456-461.

e400 **Lerch** Wolfgang G., Jerusalem, Stadt der Weltreligionen; Vorw. *Ben-Chorin* Schalom. Z 1992, Benziger. 104 p. [phot. *Dornhege* Hermann]. 3-545-34107-0.

e401 *Maeir* A. M., al., A re-evaluation of the red and black bowl from PARKER's excavations in Jerusalem: OxJArch 11 (1992) 39-53; 7 fig.

e402 *Magness* Jodi, A reexamination of the archaeological evidence for the Sasanian Persian destruction of the Tyropoeon Valley [< 1989 diss.]: BASOR 287 (1992) 67-74.

e402* *Margalit* S., Jerusalem zur Zeit des Zweiten Tempels; ein geschichtlicher und archäologischer Überblick: JbEvHL 2 (1990) 22-49 [< JStJud 24,355].

e403 *Mazar* Benjamin, Jerusalem, — 'royal sanctuary and seat of the monarchy' [< Judah and Jerusalem (1957) 25-32], T: ⇥ 283, Biblical Israel 1992, 88-99.

e404 **Millgram** Abraham E., Jerusalem curiosities. Ph 1990, Jewish Publ. xiv-349 p. 0-8276-0358-4 [OIAc 3,31].

e405 *Nu'uman* Nadav, Canaanite Jerusalem and its central hill country neighbours in the second millennium B.C.: UF 24 (1992) 275-291.

e406 *Nicholson* Oliver, Holy Sepulcher, church of the: ⇥ 741, AnchorBD 3 (1992) 258-260.

e407 *Palmer* Andrew, The history of the Syrian Orthodox in Jerusalem: OrChr 75 (1991) 16-43; 76 (1992) 74-94.

e409 *Rose* R. B., The native Christians of Jerusalem, 1187-1260: ⇥ 692, Horns 1987/92, 250-260.

e410 **Rosen-Ayalon** Myriam, The early Islamic monuments of al-Haram al-Sharif: Qedem 28, 1989 ⇥ 5,d777 ... 7,d338: RBSO 55 (1992) 324s (G. R. D. *King*).

e411 **Rosovsky** Nitza, Jerusalemwalks². NY 1992, Holt. 272 p.; 40 fig.; 7 maps. $15. – RBAR-W 18,5 (1992) 16s (W. *Zanger*).

e412 *Rosovsky* Nitza, A thousand years of history in Jerusalem's Jewish quarter: BAR-W 18,3 (1992) 22-40 . 78; ill.

e412* *Schleicher* Wolfgang, Auf den Spuren König Davids [Ausgrabungen Davidstadt), in memoriam Prof. Yigal SCHILOH: JbEvHL 1 (1989) 23-29.

e413 *Storme* Albert, Luoghi del Calvario e del S. Sepolcro; che c'è di autentico? TBarbetta Bernardino: TerraS 68 (1992) 67-76 . 96.

e414 *Strange* John, Jerusalems topografi i hasmonæisk tid; Akra-problemet: DanTTs 54 (1991) 81-94 [< ZIT 91,771].

e415 *Testini* Pasquale, EGERIA e il S. Sepolcro di Gerusalemme; qualche appunto per il traduttore: ⇥ 676, Egeria 1987/90, 215-230; 6 fig.

e416 EWalker P. W. L., Jerusalem past and present in the purposes of God. C 1992, Tyndale. xi-210 p. 0-9518356-1-0.

e417 **Walker** P. W. L., Holy city, holy places? 1990 ⇥ 7,d350: RAmHR 97 (1992) 167s (M. *Maas*: 'Eusebian solution': Christians should for the sake of Christ deny any inherent holiness of Jerusalem); JbAC 34 (1991) 204-210, map (S. *Heid*); JJS 43 (1992) 323s (Tessa *Rajak*).

e418 **Walls** Archie G., Geometry and architecture in Islamic Jerusalem; a study of the Ashrafiyya: World of Islam Festival Trust. Buckhurst Hill,

Essex 1991, Scorpion. 207 p.; 20 pl.; 150 plans; map. – ᴿJRAS (1992) 284s (G. *Goodwin*).

e419 *Werblowski* R. J. Zwi, *al.*, Jérusalem, 5000 ans d'histoire: DossArch 165s (1991) 6-13 (-138); 78-87, *Murphy-O'Connor* J., Chrétiens; 88-99, *Bahat* Dan, Croisés ...

e420 *Wharton* Annabel J., The baptistery of the Holy Sepulcher in Jerusalem and the politics of sacred landscape: ➤ 100, ᶠKᴀᴢʜᴅᴀɴ A., DumbO 46 (1992) 313-325; 9 fig.

e421 **Wightman** G. J., The Damascus Gate excavations by C. M. Bᴇɴɴᴇᴛᴛ and J.-B. Hᴇɴɴᴇssʏ, 1964-6: BAR-Int 519, 1989 ➤ 5,d790; 6,d981: ᴿBASOR 287 (1992) 96 (J. *Magness*); RB 99 (1992) 287-290 (J. *Murphy-O'Connor*).

e422 *Zanger* Walter 18/5; *Reich* Ronny, The great Mikveh debate BAR-W 19/2, 52s.

e423 ᴱ**Zarzecki** Anabel, Arqueología de Jerusalén, desde los inicios de la ciudad hasta el período musulmano temprano; selección de artículos y fragmentos de libros. J 1990. Univ. Hebrea. iv-140 p.; ill.

---

e424 **Arnold** Patrick M., Gibeah 1990 ➤ 6,d988; 7,d354: ᴿBA 55 (1992) 161 (P. E. *McMillion*); CBQ 54 (1992) 309s (Patricia M. *Bikai*: really on the Hosea references); JAOS 112 (1992) 164 (J. A. *Soggin*).

e425 **Langston** Scott M., The religious and political role of the tribe of Benjamin; a study of Iron Age cultic sites [Gibeah, Ramah; bamah] and activities: diss. SW Baptist theol. sem. 1992, ᴰ*Kent* D. 268 p. 92-23539. – DissA 53 (1992s) 843s-A.

ᴛ4.4 *Situs alphabetice:* **Judaea, Negeb.**

e426 **Applebaum** Shimon, Judaea in Hellenistic and Roman times: StJLA 40, 1989 ➤ 5,225: ᴿSyria 69 (1992) 482-4 (E. *Will*).

e427 *Hirschfeld* Y., Les laures du désert judéen; les monastères cénobitiques: MondeB 68 ('Desert de Juda' 1991) 10-32 (33-40 *Maraval* P., *al.*).

e428 *Patrich* Joseph, The Sabaite monastery of the cave (spelaion) in the Judean desert: LA 41 (1991) 429-448; 12 fig.; pl. 47-52.

e429 **Leonard** Albert, The Jordan valley survey [1953, Mᴇʟʟᴀᴀʀᴛ James]; some unpublished soundings: AASOR 50. WL 1992, Eisenbrauns. viii-199 p. 0-931464-72-2.

e430 *Nevo* Yehuda D., Sde Boqer and the central Negev, 7th-8th century ᴀ.ᴅ. [< 3d colloquium From Jahiliyya to Islam, J 1985]. J 1985, Publication Services. 51 p. [OIAc 3,32].

e431 *Arad:* ᴱ**Amiran** Ruth, *Ilan* Ornit, Arad, eine 5000 Jahre alte Stadt in der Wüste Negev: Hamburger Museum für Archäologie, Ausstellung-Katalog. Neumünster/J 1992, Wacholtz / Israel Museum. 115 p.; 96 fig. 3-529-01842-2 [OIAc 5,13].

e432 *Ascalon:* *Stager* Lawrence, Un veau d'argent découvert à Ashqelôn: MondeB 70 (1991) 50-52.

e432* *Mendecki* Norbert, ❾ The silver calf from Ascalon: RuBi 45 (1992) 44.

e433 *Bata* (Carmiel) 178.257: 1976s, mosaic church: ʿAtiqot 21 (1992) 109-128; 25 fig. (Z. *Yeivin*; 129-134, *Tzaferis* V., Greek inscriptions; 135s, *Sharabani* M., coins).

e434 *Beersheba:* **Commenge-Pellerin** Catherine, La poterie de Safadi (Beer-shéva) au IVᵉ millénaire avant l'ère chrétienne: Cah. Centre Rech. Fr. Jérusalem 5, 1990 ➤ 7,d361*: ᴿSyria 68 (1991) 480 (H. de *Contenson*).

e435 *Jericke* Detlef, Tell es-Sebaᶜ Stratum V [c. 900]: ZDPV 108 (1992) 122-148; 11 fig.

e436 *a) Levy* Thomas E., Radiocarbon chronology of the Beersheba culture and predynastic Egypt; – *b) Amiran* Ruth, *Gophna* Ram, The correlation between Lower Egypt and Southern Canaan during the Early Bronze period: ➤ 703, Nile Delta 1990/2, 345-356 / 357-360 [-394].

e437 *Beer Shemaᶜ: Gazit* Dan, *Lender* Yešiyahu, ❸ St. Stephan's church at Beer Shemaᶜ, northern Negev: Qadmoniot 25 (1992) 33-40; 4 fig. + mosaic color-spread + Eng. cover.

e438 *Beit-ᶜAnun* Byz. church: Qadmoniot 25 (1992) 40-44; 8 fig. (I. *Magen*, ❸).

e439 *Beit-Gemal* può essere il luogo di sepoltura di Santo Stefano?: Salesianum 54 (1992) 453-478; 3 fig. (A. *Strus*).

e440 *Beth-Zur: Reich* Ronny, The Beth-zur citadel II — a Persian residency?: TAJ 19 (1992) 113-123; 5 fig.

e441 *Beyudat:* Ḥizmi Ḥananya, ❸ Ḥ. Bᵉyudat/Archelais [1525.1945; ᶠCORBO V. 1990, 245], the village of Archelaus: Qadmoniot 25 (1992) 27-33; 10 fig.

e442 *Eitun* 18 k SW Hebron 1968-85: ᶜAtiqot 21 (1992) 10-48 (V. *Tzaferis, al.*).

e443 *Erani: Kempinski* Aharon, Reflections on the role of the Egyptians in the Shefelah of Palestine, in the light of recent soundings at Tel Erani: ➤ 703, Nile Delta 1990/2, 419-426 [-476 *al.*].

e444 *Gaza:* **Sadek** Mohammed-Moain, Die mamlukische Architektur der Stadt Gaza: IslamkU 144. B 1991, Schwarz. 700 p.; 401 fig.; foldout plan. 3-922968-76-X. – ᴿZDPV 108 (1992) 194 (E. A. *Knauf*: useful but with some lacks).

e445 *Gezer:* **Seger** J. D., Gezer V. The Field I Caves 1988 ➤ 5,d812: ᴿBO 49 (1992) 849-851 (K. J. H. *Vriezen*).

e446 *Ḥalif:* **Dessel** J. P., Ceramic production and social complexity in fourth millennium Canaan; a case study from the Halif terrace: diss. Arizona, ᴰ*Dever* W. Tucson 1992. 544 p. 92-00047. – OIAc 3,18.

e447 *Handumah* ḫ (Ḥ. Aḥmar, w. Qilt) Byz: LA 42 (1992) 279-287; Eng. 336 (O. *Sion*).

c448 *Hebron:* **Chadwick** Jeffrey R., The archaeology of biblical Hebron in the Bronze and Iron Ages [Rumcide excavation 1963-6]: diss. Utah 1992, ᴰ*Hammond* P. 202 p. 92-26191. – DissA 53 (1992s) 1201 A.

e449 *Herodium:* **Corbo** V. C., Herodion I, gli edifici della Reggia-Fortezza: SBF Pub 20. J 1989. – ᴿIsrEJ 42 (1992) 241-5 (J. *Patrich*).

e450 *Strobel* A., *a)* Das Herodeion im arabischen Gebirge [JosF B. 1,419 = Qaṣr Riyaj im Sēl Hēdān]; Bericht über einen Survey in unbekannter Landschaft am Toten Meer; – *b)* Das Versteck der Qumranhöhle 1 in der Zeit des jüdisch-arabischen Krieges: JbEvHL [2 (1990) 73-77] 3 (1991) 82-84 / 85s.

e451 *Ḥesi:* **Bennett** W. J., *Blakely* Jeffrey A., Tell el-Hesi, The Persian period (Stratum V): ASOR Hesi 3. WL 1989, Eisenbrauns. 483 p.; 242 fig.; 23 foldouts. $95. 0-931464-54-4. – ᴿJAOS 112 (1992) 684s (W. G. *Dever*); JField 19 (1992) 234-9 (Gloria A. *London*).

e452 *Horeš* ḥorvat, frescoes: Qadmoniot 25 (1992) 44-47 (Y. *Tepper*, Y. *Shahar*).

e453 *Ira* t : ➤ 741, AnchorBD 3 (1992) 446-8; plan (I. *Beit Arieh*).

e454 **Jemameh** 1208.1012 18 k E Gaza, Byzantine monastery: ʿAtiqot 22 (1993) 97-108; 16 fig.; plan (R. *Gophna*, N. *Feig*).

e455 **Jericho:** ➤ 741, AnchorDB 3 (1992) 723-737; 4 plans (*Holland* T.A.; 737-9 Roman, *Netzer* Ehud).

e455* *Benton* J.N., *al.*, Jericho tomb 47; a Palestinian Middle Bronze Age tomb in the [Sydney] Nicholson Museum: MeditArch 5s (1992s) 59-109; 43 fig.

e456 *Holland* T.A., Jericho in the proto-urban period: ➤ 736, ᴱ*Shaath*, Palestine 1981/5, 17-25; 4 fig.; 2 pl.

e457 *Bienkowski* Piotr, [*al.*] Jéricho... le rempart: MondeB 69 (1991) [3-] 15-24 [41].

e458 *Geus* C.H.J. de, Het Jericho-graf in het Rijksmuseum van Oudheden te Leiden: PhoenixEOL 38,2 (1992) 4-15; 4 fig.

e460 **Lachish:** *Schoville* Keith N., Literacy at Lachish ➤ 696, As.-Af. 32 (1986/92) 1s.

e461 **Ussishkin** David, Lachish: ➤ 741, AnchorBD 4 (1992) 114-122; 6 fig. (Letters, 126-8, *DeVito* Robert A.).

e462 **Mampsis**-Kurnub: **Negev** A., The architecture of Mampsis 2: Qedem 27, 1988 ➤ 3,d838 ... 7,d376: ᴿByZ 84s,1 (1991s) 139-143 (P. *Grossmann*); JQR 83 (1992s) 204-7 (S. *Dar*).

e463 **Masada:** ᴱ*Aviram* Joseph, Masada, the Yigael YADIN excavation 1963-1965, final reports [I-II] III. **Netzer** Ehud, The buildings; stratigraphy and architecture. J 1991, Israel Expl. Soc. & Hebrew Univ. 683 p.; 945 fig.; 78 plans. $144: ➤ 7,d379: ᴿBAR-W 18,5 (1992) 4.6.8.10 (K.G. *Holum*, on background of all 3); Qadmoniot 25 (1992) 59s (J. *Patrich*, ❶ 3).

e464 *Foerster* Gidéon, La vie des rebelles / la chute de Massada: MondeB 79 (1992) 23-32 [3-22 al.].

e465 *Magness* Jodi, Masada; arms and the man; the technology of Roman warfare helps to explain the fall of Masada: BAR-W 18,4 (1992) 58-67.

e466 **Miqne:** *Gitin* Seymour, New [four-horned] incense altars from [Miqne-] Ekron; context, typology and function: ➤ 18, ᶠBIRAN A., ErIsr 23 (1992) 43*-49*; 1 fig. [50*-53*, the LB 'city', *Gittlen* Barry M.].

e466* *Dothan* T., *Gitin* S., Ekron, tell Miqne: ➤ 741, AnchorBD 2 (1992) 414-422.

e467 *Negeb:* **Haiman** Mordechai, Cairn burials and cairn fields in the Negev: BASOR 287 (1992) 25-45; 19 fig.

e468 **Shereshevski** Joseph, Byzantine urban settlements in the Negev Desert: Beer-Sheva 5. Beersheba 1991, Ben-Gurion Univ. xvi-277 p.; 70 pl.; 7 foldout maps. 0334-2255 [OIAc 3,37].

e469 **Oboda:** *Castritius* Helmut, Zu zwei Ortsnamen in der Palästina Tertia, Oboda und Idiota: ZDPV 108 (1992) 82-91.

e470 **Qanah:** **Gopher** Avi, *Tsuk* Tasvita, Ancient gold; rare finds from the Nahal Qanah cave. J 1991, Israel Museum. xxxvi-36 p. 965-278-118-X.

e471 **Qiṭmit:** *Finkelstein* Israel, Ḥorvat Qiṭmit and the southern trade in the Late Iron II: ZDPV 108 (1992) 156-170.

e472 **Timna:** **Rothenberg** Beno, The Egyptian mining temple at Timna 1988 ➤ 4,e742; 7,d390: 0-906-18302-2. – ᴿAJA 96 (1992) 171s (J.M. *Weinstein*).

e473 ᴱ**Rothenberg** Benno, The ancient metallurgy of copper: Researches in the Arabah 1959-1984, 2. L 1990, Thames & H. 191 p.; 118 pl. £48 [BAR-W 19/1, 8.10.12, Martha *Goodway*].

e474 **Umm Qatafa:** *Perrot* Jean, Umm Qatafa and Umm Qalaʿa; two 'Ghassulian' caves in the Judean desert: ➤ 18, ᶠBIRAN A., ErIsr 23 (1992) 100*-111*; 8 fig.

e475 **Yarmut** 140.160), 9th 1992: IsrEJ 42 (1992) 265-272; 4 fig. (P. de *M-iroschedji*).
e476 **Yarmuth**: MondeB 70 (1991) 55-59 (P. de *Miroschedji*).
e477 **Yavne'el** 1980, EB-IV tombs: ʿAtiqot 21 (1992) 1-7; 1 fig. (H. *Liebowitz*, P. *Porat*).

T4.5 **Samaria, Sharon.**

e478 **Ai:** ➤ 741, AnchorBD 1 (1992) 125-130; map (J. A. *Calloway*).
e479 **Caesarea** M., Byz city wall 1985s: ʿAtiqot 21 (1992) 137-170; 26 fig. (M. *Peleg*, R. *Reich*; p. 171s, N. *Amitai-Preiss*, Fatimid gold-bead: 2 fig. p. 171 and 2 in color as frontispiece).
e480 **Levine** Lee I., *Netzer* Ehud, Excavations at Caesarea M.: Qedem 21, 1986 ➤ 2,a629 ... 6,e75*: ᴿJNES 51 (1992) 220s (E. *Krentz*).
e481 *Holum* Kenneth G., Archaeological evidence for the fall of Byzantine Caesarea [against L. *Toombs* (1978) destructions in 614 and 641]: BASOR 286 (1992) 73-85; 5 fig.
e482 **Holum** K. G., *al.*, King Herod's dream; Caesarea on the sea 1988 ➤ 4,e753; 7,d397: ᴿJNES 51 (1992) 157s (E. *Krentz*).
e483 *McGuckin* J. A., Caesarea Maritima as ORIGEN knew it: ➤ 531, Origeniana V, 1989/92, 3-25.
e484 **Raban** A., The harbours of Caesarea Maritima I, 1989 ➤ 5,d862: ᴿJRomA 5 (1992) 445-9, 3 fig. (Y. *Hirschfeld*).
e485 *Carmelus* mons: *Mazar* Benjamin, Carmel the holy mountain [< ErIsr 14 (1979) 39-41] ᵀ: ➤ 283, Biblical Israel 1992, 127-133.
e485* *Friedman* Elias, Christian legends of the terrace of Mount Carmel: Teresianum 43 (1992) 251-284.
e486 *Dor* 1991: IsrEJ 42 (1992) 34-46; 9 fig. (E. *Stern, al.*).
e487 *Stern* Ephraim, Dor [ḫ. Burj, 13 k N Césarée], les maîtres de la mer: MondeB 79 (1992) 33-40, ill.
e488 *Fischer* Thomas, Tryphons verfehlter Sieg von Dor [GERA D., IsrEJ 35 (1985) 153-163, mehr oder weniger richtig]: ZPapEp 93 (1992) 29s.
e489 *Ebal*: **Mechlin** Milt, Joshua's altar; the [ZERTAL A.] dig at Mount Ebal. NY 1991, Morrow. 256 p. $23. – ᴿBAR-W 18,5 (1992) 17 (G. L. *Kelm*: Zertal's achievement superb; Mechlin [in title; Machlin in text] unfortunate).
e490 *Far'ah-N*: **Mallet** Joël, Tell el-Farʿah II,1s 1987s ➤ 4,a763 ... 7,d406: ᴿAfO 38s (1991s) 254s (K. *Juroš*); ArOr 60 (1992) 79 (P. *Charvát*).
e491 *Gezer*: **Gitin** S., Gezer III, ceramic typology, 1990 ➤ 6,a86; 7,d409: ᴿAndrUnS 30 (1992) 167-9 (D. *Merling*).
e492 *Ḥirāf*: *Hirschfeld* Yizhar, Khirbet Khiraf, a 2nd-c.[C.E.] fort in the Jordan valley [37 k N Jericho]: JRomA 4 (1991) 170-183; 15 fig. (map).
e493 *Jaffa-Tel Aviv*: **Kaplan** Haya R., The Tell Qasile inscriptions once again: IsrEJ 42 (1992) 246-9; 2 fig.
e494 **Ḥoršim** (Yarqon 147.171) EMB tombs: ʿAtiqot 21 (1992) ⊕ 1-8 (2. *Gilboa*, E. *Yannai*), Eng. 174.
e495 **Lydda:** **Schwartz** Joshua J., Lod (Lydda) from its origins through the Byzantine period, 5600 B.C.E. - 640 C.E.: BAR-Int 571. Ox 1991, Tempus Reparatum. 212 p.; 15 fig. (maps); 16 phot. 0-86054-721-3 [OIAc 3,37].
e496 *Michal* [Herzliya]: **Herzog** Z., *al.*, Excavations 1977-80: 1988 ➤ 7,d413*: ᴿBASOR 287 (1992) 93s (G. W. *Van Beek*).
e497 *Modiin:* Ehud givʿat, (Modiin), Byz, farmhouse: LA 42 (1992) 289-295; Eng. 336 (H. *Hizmi*).

e498 **Ramat ha-Nadiv** (5 k S Zikhron Yaʿaqov), tumulus field, 1988-91: IsrEJ
      42 (1992) 129-152; 20 fig. (R. *Greenberg*).
e499 **Samaria** - Sabasṭiya: *Purvis* James D., Samaria, city [*al.* ostraca, region,
      papyri]: ➤ 741, AnchorBD 5 (1992) 914-921 [-932].
e500 **Tappy** Ron E., The archaeology of Israelite Samaria, I. Early Iron Age
      through the ninth century BCE: HarvSemSt 44. Atlanta 1992, Scholars.
      xix-295 p. $45; pa. $30. 1-55540-770-6.
e501 **Goedicke** Hans, Amenophis II in Samaria: StAäK 19 (1992) 133-150.
e502 **Magen** Isaac, ❻ Samaritan synagogues: Qadmoniot 25 (1992) 66-90; 51
      fig. + 2 color (Ḥ. *Samra*).
e503 **Šekem:** *Mazar* Benjamin, Shechem – a city of the patriarchs [< his ❻
      Canaan and Israel, p. 144-151], T: ➤ 283, Biblical Israel 1992, 42-54.
e504 **Adamthwaite** Murray R., Lab'aya's connection with Shechem reassessed
      [Amarna 289,20]: AbrNahr 30 (1992) 1-19.
e505 **Piccirillo** Michele, Il tempio [Garizim] e la città dei Samaritani: TerraS
      67 (1991) 124-6.
e506 **Toombs** Lawrence E., Shechem: ➤ 741, AnchorBD 5 (1992) 1174-86; 4 fig.
e507 **Šīlōh:** **Schley** D. G., Shiloh 1989 ➤ 5,886; 7,d425: RVT 42 (1992) 143
      (J. A. *Emerton*: hard to refute).

T4.6 **Galilaea; pro tempore** *Golan.*

e508 **Frankel** Rafael, Galilee (pre-hellenistic): ➤ 741, AnchorBD 2 (1992)
      879-895, map (895-9, *Freyne* Seán, Roman).
e509 **Lee** Marjorie, *al.*, Mamluk caravanserais in Galilee [Tujjār, SW Tiberias
      near Tabor; Jubb Yusif, N Tiberias toward Rosh Pinna]: Levant 24 (1992)
      55-94; 63 fig.
e510 **Oppenheimer** Aharon, Galilee in the Mishnaic period. J 1991, Shazar.
      204 p. § 35. 965-227-070-9 [RB 100,436-446, E. *Nodet*].
e511 ᴱ**Levine** Lee I., The Galilee in Late Antiquity. NY 1992, Jewish Theol.
      Sem. xxiii-410 p. 0-674-34113-9 [OIAc 5,28].
e512 **Tassin** Claude [*al.*], Voyage dans la Galilée de Jésus: MondeB 72 (1991)
      3-14 [-39].
e513 — **Daoust** J. [< *Tassin* Claude, MondeB 72, 1991], Dans la Galilée de
      Jésus: EsprVie 102 (1992) 313-5.

e514 **Acco:** ➤ 741, AnchorBD 1 (1992) 50-53 (M. *Dothan*).
e515 **Banyas:** **Jaki** Stanley, Et sur ce roc; témoignage d'une terre et de deux
      Testaments. P c. 1990 [après une viste à la falaise de Banias], Téqui. –
      RPeCa 250 (1991) 26-30 (Y. *Daoudal*).
e516 **Tzaferis** Vassilios, *a)* The 'god who is in Dan' and the cult of Pan at
      Banias in the Hellenistic and Roman periods: ➤ 18, ꟻBIRAN A., ErIsr 23
      (1992) 128*-135*; 5 fig. – *b)* Cults and deities worshipped at Caesarea
      Philippi-Banias: ➤ 19a, ꟻBLENKINSOPP J., Priests 1992, 190-201.
e517 **Bethsaida** 1992 (Omaha consortium): IsrEJ 42 (1992) 252-4; 2 fig.; plan
      (R. *Arav*).
e517* **Kuhn** Heinz-W., *Arav* Rami, The Bethsaida excavations; historical and
      archaeological approaches: ➤ 104, ꟻKOESTER H., Future of Early Chris-
      tianity 1991, 77-106.
e518 **Capharnaum:** **Tzaferis** V., *al.*, Excavations at Capernaum 1989 ➤ 6,
      e122; 7,d432: RCritRR 5 (1992) 104-7 (D. R. *Edwards*: fine; includes J.
      Wilson on Islamic gold coin hoard and J. *Blenkinsopp* on the literary
      evidence).

e519 *Mendecki* Norbert, ⊕ Synagoga z Kafarnaum w świetle ostatnich badań: RuBi 45 (1992) 104-6.

e520 **Dan:** *Gunneweg* J., *al.*, On the origin of a Mycenaean III-A chariot krater and other related Mycenaean pottery from Tomb 387 at Laish/Dan (by neutron activation analysis): ➤ 18, ᶠBIRAN A., ErIsr 23 (1992) 54*-63*; 18 fig.

e521 **Gamla:** *Syon* Danny, Gamla [6 k NE Lake Tiberias], portrait of a rebellion: BAR-W 18,1 (1992) 20-37.72; (color) ill.

e522 **Golan:** *Dauphin* Claudine, *Gibson* Shimon, Ancient settlements and their landscapes; the results of ten years of survey on the Golan Heights (1978-1988): BAnglIsr 12 (1992s) 7-31; 14 fig.

e523 *a) Kochavi* Moshe, *al.*, Rediscovered! the land of Geshur [2 Sam 13, 20-38; Golan, t. Hadar]; – *b) Mizrachi* Yonathan, Mystery circles; newly discovered walls (Golan Rujm Hiri): BAR-W 18,4 (1992) 30-44.84s; ill. / 46-57.84; ill.

e524 **Guš Halav** *(Jiš)*: **Meyers** E. & C., *Strange* J., Excav. Synagogue Gush-Halav 1991 ➤ 7,d436: ᴿBL (1992) 37 (P. *Alexander*); CritRR 5 (1992) 107-9 (D.R. *Edwards*).

e525 **Hazor** 3d 1992: IsrEJ 42 (1992) 254-260; 5 fig. (A. *Ben-Tor*).

e526 **Qedah**-Hazor: ➤ 741, AnchorDB 5 (1992) 578-581 (W.G. *Dever*).

e527 *Rubiato Díaz* María Teresa, Volver a Hatsor (I campaña de excavaciones arqueológicas 'in memoriam Y. Yadin'): Sefarad 51 (1991) 183-195; 7 fig.

e528 *Horowitz* Wayne, *Shaffer* Aaron, A fragment of [an administrative cuneiform] letter from Hazor: IsrEJ 42 (1992) 21-23; 5 fig.; 17-20, pref. *Ben-Tor* A. / 166; 2 fig. [167, additions to p. 21-33, Hazor tablet].

e529 **Hazorea** [12 k N Megiddo]: **Meyerhof** E. I., The Bronze Age necropolis at Kibbutz Hazorea, Israel: BAR-Int 534. Ox 1989. vi-174 p.; 27 fig.; 42 pl. £12 [PEQ 125,81, Kay *Prag*].

e530 **Hermon:** **Ehrl** Friedrich, Das Höhenheiligtum am Mount Hermon: ➤ 184, ᶠTRENTINI J.-B., Echo 1990, 123-9; 3 fig.; 3 pl.

e531 **Jezreel** tel, 1990s: TAJ 19 (1992) 3-55; 38 fig. (D. *Ussishkin*, J. *Woodhead*; 57-70; 9 fig. pottery (Orna *Zimhoni*).

e532 *Gal* Zwi, The period of the Israelite settlement in the lower Galilee and the Jezreel valley [< ⊕ 1990]: ➤ 65, Mcm. GEVIRTZ S., Maarav 7 (1991) 101-115; 2 maps: *after* destruction of the Canaanite cities.

e533 *Goedicke* Hans, Where did Sinuhe stay in Asia? (Sinuhe B 29-31) [perhaps Jezreel plain]: CdÉ 67 (1992) 28-40.

e533* *a) Oeming* Manfred, Der Tell Jesreel (Hirbet Zerʿīn); Studien zur Topographie, Archäologie und Geschichte; – *b) Goren* Haim, Erste Siedlungsversuche der deutschen Templer in der Jesreel-Ebene im 19. Jahrhundert: JbEvHL 1 (1989) 56-78; 5 fig.; map; pl. 1-4 / 100-130; 4 fig. (maps); pl. 5-10.

e534 **Kabri** (Akko coast): 6th, 1991: IsrEJ 42 (1992) 260-4; 4 fig. (A. *Kempinski*, W.-D. *Niemeier*).

e534* ᴱ**Kempinski** Aharon, *Niemeyer* W.-D., ⊕ Excavations at Kabri, preliminary report of 1989 season 1/4. TA 1990, Univ. lii p. (Eng.) + ⊕ 53 p.; 23 fig. [OIAc 5,26].

e535 **Keisan:** *Humbert* J.-B., Keisan, tell: ➤ 741, AnchorBD 4 (1992) 14-16.

e536 **Khirbet Kerak:** *Reich* Ronny, The Bet Yerah 'synagogue' reconsidered: ʿAtiqot 22 (1993) 137-144; 6 fig.; plan.

e537 — *Beth Yerah:* **Esse** Douglas L., Subsistence, trade, and social change in Early Bronze Age Palestine [Delougaz-Kantor materials 1953-64 plus surveys: < diss. Chicago]: SAOC 50, 1989 ➤ 7,d289; $26:   ᴿJAOS 112 (1992) 495s (W. G. *Dever*).

e538 — *Milson* David, The design of the ancient synagogues in Galilee [I-IV by D. *Chen*] V, Beth Yerach, Horvat Shemaᶜ, and ᶜEn Neshut: LA 41 (1991) 449-454; pl. 55s.

e539 *Magdala: Reich* Ronny, A note on the Roman mosaic at Magdala on the Sea of Galilee: LA 41 (1991) 455-8; pl. 53s.

e540 *Megiddo: a)* ➤ 741, AnchorBD 4 (1992) 666-679; 5 fig. (D. *Ussishkin*); – *b)* ➤ 768, TRE 22 (1992) 365-8 (V. *Fritz*).

e541 **Kempinski** Aharon, Megiddo, a city-state and royal centre in North Israel. Mü 1991, Beck. 262 p.; 14 plans. DM 118 [BAR-W 19/1, 8, N. A. *Silberman*]. – ᴿRB 99 (1992) 753 (E. *Puech*).

e542 *Briend* J., *al.*, Meghiddo, città regale da Salomone a Giosia: Il mondo della Bibbia 9 (T 1992).

e543 **Currid** John D., Puzzling public buildings [Megiddo 'stables', Hazor parallel, and six smaller similar buildings]: BAR-W 18,1 (1992) 52-57. 60s; ill. [p. 58s 'Storehouses or stables?' insert].

e544 *Esse* Douglas L., The collared pithos at Megiddo; ceramic distribution and ethnicity: JNES 51 (1992) 81-103; 4 fig.

e545 *Naḥal Beṣet: Gopher* Avi, *al.*, The pottery assemblage of Naḥal Beṣet I, a neolithic site in the Upper Galilee: IsrEJ 42 (1992) 4-16; 4 fig.

e546 *Nazareth:* **Monelli** Nanni, La Santa Casa a Loreto — La Santa Casa a Nazareth: Collana del Centenario 8. Loreto 1992, Congregazione Universale della Santa Casa. 123 p.; 13 fig.; XIV (color.) pl.

e547 — **Santarelli** Giuseppe, La Santa Casa di Loreto — tradizione e ipotesi 1988 ➤ 5,d942: ᴿFranzSt 72 (1990) 372s (L. *Lehmann*, auch über Santarelli, Kunst 1984).

e548 *Palmarea: Hiestand* Rudolf, Palmarea – Palmarium; eine oder zwei Abteien in Galiläa im 12. Jahrhundert? ZDPV 108 (1992) 174-188 (zwei).

e549 *Quneitra:* **Goren-Inbar** Nama, Quneitra, a Mousterian site on the Golan Heights: Qedem 31. J 1990, Hebrew Univ. xv-239 p.; 120 fig.; 43 pl. 0333-5844. – ᴿJField 19 (1992) 85-89 (A. *Marks*).

e550 *Roš Zayit: Gal* Zvi, Hurbat Rosh Zayit and the early Phoenician pottery: Levant 24 (1992) 173-186; 10 fig.

e551 *Sepphoris:* **Batey** Richard A., Jesus and the forgotten city; new light on Sepphoris and the urban world of Jesus 1991 ➤ 7,d456: ᴿBA 55 (1992) 105s (L. *Schiffman*: a tissue of assumptions) + 106s (E. M. *Meyers*: J. R. *Teringo*'s illustrations anti-Semitic); ExpTim 104 (1992s) 56 (C. *Tuckett*: 'hypocrites' were the stage-actors of Sepphoris theatre); GraceTJ 12 (1991) 299s (R. *Ibach*).

e552 *Batey* Richard A., Sepphoris, an urban portrait of Jesus: BAR-W 18,3 (1992) 50-62.

e553 *Meyers* Eric M., *al.*, Sepphoris. WL 1992, Eisenbrauns. [viii-] 63 p.; (color.) ill. 0-9602-6869-3.

e554 *Miller* Stuart S., Sepphoris, the well remembered city: BA 55 (1992) 74-83; ill.

e555 *Tiberias: Harrison* Timothy P., The early Umayyad settlement at Ṭabariyah; a case of yet another *Miṣr* ?: JNES 51 (1992) 51-59.

T4.8 *Transjordania:* **East-Jordan.**

e556 *a) Bartlett* John R., Biblical sources for the Early Iron Age in Edom; – *b) Kitchen* Kenneth A., The Egyptian evidence on ancient Jordan; –

c) Millard Alan,   Assyrian involvement in Edom: ➤ 340, Early Edom 1991/2, 13-19 / 21-34; 2 maps / 35-39.

e557 *De Vries* Bert,   Archaeology in Jordan: AJA 96 (1992) 503-542; 35 fig.; map.

e558 *Finkelstein* Israel,   *a)* ❶ Edom in Iron Age I: ➤ 18, ᶠBIRAN A., ErIsr 23 (1992) 224-9; 2 fig.; Eng. 153*s; – *b)* Edom in the Iron I: Levant 24 (1992) 159-166 [167-9 reply, *Bienkowski* P.; rejoinder 171s].

e559 **Gubser** Peter,   Historical dictionary of the Hashemite Kingdom of Jordan: Asian historical dictionaries 4.   Metuchen NJ 1991, Scarecrow. xxx-140 p.   0-8108-2449-3 [OIAc 5,23].

e560 **Homès-Fredericq** Denyse, *Hennessy* J.B.,   Archaeology of Jordan 2. Field reports, survey and sites; A-K, I-Z: Akkadica supp. 7s, 1989 ➤ 5,d960: ᴿBonnJbb 192 (1992) 706s (R. *Wenning*).

e561 *a) Homès-Fredericq* Denyse,   General introduction to the theme 'Sites and settlements in Jordan'; – *b) Prag* Kay,   Bronze Age settlement patterns in the South Jordan Valley; archaeology, environment and ethnology; – *c) Schaub* R.   Thomas,   A reassessment of Nelson GLUECK on settlement on the Jordan Plateau in Early Bronze III & IV; – *d) Sapin* Jean, [*Braemer* Frank],   De l'occupation à l'utilisation de l'espace à l'aube de l'âge de bronze... Jerash; – *e) Herr* Larry G., [*McGovern* Patrick]; Shifts in settlement patterns of Late Bronze and Iron Age Ammon. ➤ 740, Jordan 4, 1992, 37-46 / 155-160 / 161-8 / 169-174 [191-9] / 175-7 [179-183].

Kasher Aryeh,   Jews and Hellenistic cities 1990 ➤ d219*.

e561* *Miller* J. Maxwell,   Moab: ➤ 741, AnchorDB 4 (1992) 882-893.

e562 *a) Parr* Peter J.,   Edom and the Hejaz; – *b) Hart* Stephen,   Iron Age settlement in the land of Edom; – *c) Zeitler* John P.,   'Edomite' pottery from the Petra region; – *d) Lindner* Manfred / *MacDonald* Burton / *Adams* Russell, Petra-area / Hasa-Ghor / Fidan surveys: ➤ 340, Early Edom 1991/2, 41-46 / 93-98 / 167-175, 6 fig. / 143-166; 29 fig. . 113-142; 13 fig. / 177-186; 9 fig.

e563 *Piccirillo* Michele,   Nuove [antiche] chiese nella Giordania settentrionale: TerraS 68 (1992) 11-13 (315-9, la chiesa del prete Waᵓil); 67 (1991) 229-231, villaggio di Macheronte. ➤ e603.

e564 **Timm** S.,   Moab zwischen den Mächten 1989 ➤ 5,d963; 7,d467: ᴿBO 49 (1992) 821-4 (B. *Becking*); TLZ 117 (1992) 500-2 (K.-D. *Schunck*).

---

e565 *'Abata,* Deir ᶜain, 3d 1991: ADAJ 36 (1992) 281-6; 4 pl. (K.D. *Politis*).

e566 Deir ᶜAin 'Abata (SE Dead Sea) 3d 1991: LA 41 (1991) 517s; pl. 70s (K.D. *Politis*).

e567 *'Amman* Citadel: ➤ e557, AJA 96 (1992) 526-541; fig. 21-28 (Christine *Nelson*, R.H. *Dornemann*, M. *Najjar*).

e568 *Greene* Joseph A., ᶜ*Amr* Khairieh, *al.,*   Deep sounding on the lower terrace of the Amman citadel [1987s, EB to Umayyad]; final report: ADAJ 36 (1992) 113-144; 10 fig.

e569 *Humbert* J.-B., *Zayadine* F.,   Trois campagnes de fouilles à Amman (1988-1991); troisième terrasse de la citadelle (mission franco-jordanienne): RB 99 (1992) 214-260; Eng. 214; 16 fig.; pl. IV-XIV; dépliant A.

e569* *a) Humbert* Jean-Baptiste,   L'occupation de l'espace à l'âge du fer en Jordanie; – *b) Lemaire* André, ... Ammon, Moab, Édom 850-800; ➤ 740, Jordan 4 (1992) 199-208 / 209-214.

e570 *Hübner* Ulrich, Supplementa ammonitica I: BibNot 65 (1992) 19-28 (zwei Siegel).

e571 *Azraq* Basin 1989: Levant 24 (1992) 1-31; 19 fig. (D. *Baird, al.*).

e572 *Bab/Ḍra: Rast* Walter E., Tombs, kinship indicators, and the biblical ancestors [... Bab/Ḍraᶜ]: ➤ 18, ᶠBIRAN A., ErIsr 23 (1992) 112*-119*; 3 fig.

e573 **Schaub** R. Thomas, *Rast* Walter E., Bāb edh Dhrāʿ... cemetery 1965-7: 1989 ➤ 5,d974; 7,d479: JAOS 112 (1992) 491s (K. N. *Schoville*).

e574 *Balūʾ* 3d 1991: ADAJ 36 (1992) 167-172; 4 fig.; 2 pl. (U. *Worschech*, F. *Ninow*). ➤ e624*b.

e575 *Burquᶜ*, NE Jordan, neo, 1989: Levant 24 (1992) 33-54; 24 fig. (Carole *McCartney*).

e576 *Helms* Svend, A new architectural survey of Qasr Burquᶜ, eastern Jordan: AntiqJ 71 (1991) 191-215; 13 fig.

e577 *Deir ʿAlla:* ᴱ**Kooij** Gerrit van der, *Ibrahim* M. M., Picking up the threads; a continuing review of excavations at DeirʿAlla, Jordan. Leiden 1989, Univ. 112 p. $29.50 pa. [BAR-W 19/2, 4.6, R. W. *Younker*].

e578 *Vilders* Monique M. E., The stratigraphy and pottery of Phase M at DeirʿAlla and the date of the plaster texts: Levant 24 (1992) 187-200; 5 fig.

e579 *Dibon:* ᴱ**Dearman** Andrew, Studies in the Mesha inscription and Moab 1989 ➤ 5,392.9256*... 7,d484: ᴿAustralBR 40 (1992) 64s (H. A. *Stamp*).

e579* *Smelik* Klaas A. D., King Mesha's inscription; between history and fiction: ➤ 310, Converting 1992, 59-92 [< OTAbs 15, p. 358].

e580 *Dohaleh*/Nuʿaymah 2d 1991: ADAJ 36 (1992) 398-387 (sic); 14 fig.; 10 pl. (S. *Sari*, ◎).

e581 Dohaleh 1st 1990: LA 42 (1992) 259-278; Eng. 336 (S. *Sari*).

e582 *Fukhar* (2 k NW Ramtha); ➤ e557, AJA 96 (1992) 516-8, 3 fig. (M. *Ottosson*).

e582* *Ottosson* Magnus, Tell el-Fukhar, den skandinaviska expeditionen till norra Jordanien: SvEx 57 (1992) 7-23 + 6 fig.

e583 *Gadara* Umm Qeis: ➤ e557, AJA 96 (1992) 534-7; fig. 31-32 (T. *Weber*, S. *Kerner*).

e584 *Künzl* E., *Weber* T., Das spätantike Grab eines Zahnarztes zu Gadara in der Dekapolis: DamaszMitt 5 (1991) 81-118.

e585 *Gassul: Hennessy* John B., Ghassul, Tuleilat el-: ➤ 741, AnchorBD 7 (1992) 1003-1006 [does not acknowledge any disparity or problem in dating 4600-3600 by radiocarbon (formerly c. 3600-3200) though citing North's relevant 1982 article].

e586 *Gazal: Rollefson* Gary O., *al.*, Neolithic cultures at ʿAin Ghazal, Jordan: JField 19 (1992) 443-470; 20 fig.

e587 *Gerasa:* Jerash, restauration porte sud 1988-90: ADAJ 36 (1992) 241-254; 8 fig.; 5 pl. (J. *Seigne*, C. *Wagner*); 261-273; 7 fig.; 4 pl. (M. *Smadeh*, nécropole NW).

e588 *Kehrberg* Ina, Flaked glass and pottery sherd tools of the Late Roman and Byzantine periods from the hippodrome at Jerash: Syria 69 (1992) 451-464; 11 fig.

e588* *Gatier* Pierre-Louis, *al.*, La Pompei d'Oriente, Jerash, ᵀ*Saraceno Luridiana* Lama, *Cavallaro Montagna* Silvana: Il mondo della Bibbia 3,12 (1992) 5-9 (-45).

e589 *Ḥarana:* Urice Stephen K., Qasr Kharana in the Transjordan 1987 ➤ 3,e285; 5,d987: ᴿSyria 68 (1991) 495-7 (E. *Will*).

e589* *Haraz:* *Fischer* Peter M., A possible Late Bronze Age sanctuary at Tell Abu al-Kharaz, Transjordan: JPrehRel 5 (1991) 42-47; 5 fig.

e590 *Hasa* paleolithic 3d 1992: ADAJ 36 (1992) 13-21 + 1 pl. (G.A. *Clark, al.*).

e591 **MacDonald** Burton, Wadi el Hasa archaeological survey 1988 ➤ 4,e861: ᴿBASOR 285 (1992) 90-94 (A. H. *Joffe*).

e592 *Hešbon:* *Lemaire* André, Heshbôn – Hisbân?: ➤ 18, ᶠBIRAN A., ErIsr 23 (1992) 64*-70* [yes with caution].

e593 *Hibr* (250 k E Diban in Bâdiya desert), rock shelter c. 3200: BASOR 287 (1992) 5-23; 7 fig. (A. V. G. *Betts*).

e594 *Iktanu* 1966, 87, 89s: ➤ AJA 96 (1992) 515s; 1 fig. (Kay *Prag*, also on nearby t. Hammam).

e595 *Iotabâ:* *Mayerson* Philip, The island of Iotabê in the Byzantine sources; a reprise [not Tiran (ABEL) nor Faraʿûn (AHARONI)]: BASOR 287 (1992) 1-4; map [286,87s, E. *Banning* on earlier Mayerson].

e596 *Iskender* ḫ 223.107 EB: ➤ 741, AnchorBD 3 (1992) 523-6 (Suzanne *Richard*).

e597 *Jawa* (t, 'Madaba' not as ➤ e604) 2d, 1991, ADAJ 36 (1992) 145-157; 7 fig.; 2 pl. (M. *Daviau*).

e598 ᴱ**Betts** A. V. G., Excavations at Jawa [East] 1972-1986; stratigraphy, pottery and other finds. E 1991, Univ. xii-397 p.; 241 fig.; 7 pl. 0-7486-0307-7 [OIAc 3,13].

e599 *Jilat,* w: *Garrard* Andrew N., *Byrd* Brian F., New dimensions to the epipalaeolithic of the Wadi el-Jilat in central Jordan: Paléorient 18,1 (1992) 47-62; 5 fig.

e600 *Kerak,* ard: **Worschech** U., Die Beziehungen Moabs 1990 ➤ 6,e208; 7,d501: ᴿZAW 104 (1992) 316 (Ulrike *Schorn,* auch über Das Land jenseits, 1991 ➤ 7,d467*a).

e600* *a) Worschech* Udo, ... Ard al-Karak; – *b) Rollefson* Gary O., ... neolithic; – *c) Helms* Svend, ... Zarqa; – *d) Muheisen* Mujahed, ... paléolithique; [*ul.*], Stone Age: ➤ 740, Jordan 4, 1992, 83-88, map / 123-7 / 129-136 / 97-103 [47-143].

e601 *Lehun* [E ʿAroʿer, N Mojib/Arnon] LB-Iron Age 1986-8: ➤ 340, Early Edom 1991/2, 187-202 (Denyse *Homès-Fredericq*).

e602 *Mabrak* (E Amman), LB-Iron: ADAJ 36 (1992) 408-401 (sic); 4 fig.; 2 pl. (M. *Waheeb,* ❹).

e603 *Machaerus:* *Piccirillo* Michele, Une église dans le village de Machéronte en Jordanie: MondeB 69 (1991) 50s; ill.

e604 *Madaba:* *Piccirillo* Michele, Madaba 1989 ➤ 6,e214; 7,d504: ᴿBAnglIsr 12 (1992s) 63-74 (C. *Dauphin,* also on ᶠCORBO); BMosAnt 13 (1990s) 428-434 (J.-P. *Sodini*).

e605 *Di Segni* L., The date of the Church of the Virgin in Madaba: LA 42 (1992) 251-7; Eng. 336.

e606 *Midian*-Dedan: Riyadh 1975, Dept. Antiquities. 12 p. (Eng. + ❹) [OIAc 3,18, noting four cognates].

e607 *Nebo* Mount: *Piccirillo* M., *a)* ➤ 471, AnchorBD 4 (1992) 1056-8; – *b)* Il pellegrinaggio di Egeria al Monte Nebo in Arabia: ➤ 676, Egeria 1987/90, 193-214. – *c)* L'église du diacre Thomas au Mont Nébo: MondeB 68 (1981) 56-60.

e609 *Nimrin* 2d 1990: ADAJ 36 (1992) 89-107; 1 pl. (J. W. *Flanagan*).

e610 *Pella* 14th 1992: MeditArch 5s (1992s) 161-3 (S. *Bourke*).

e611 Pella-Fahil: ➤ e557, AJA 96 (1992) 539-541; plan (A. *Walmsley*).

e612 *Petra, Nabataea:* *Freyberger* Klaus S., Zur Datierung des Grabmals des Sextius Florentinus in Petra: DamaszMi 5 (1991) 1-8; pl. 1-4.

e613 *Graf* D. F.,   Nabat: ➤ 756, EncIslam² 7 (1992) 835-7 (unchanged from ed. 1).
e613* *a) Hammond* Philip C.,   Nabataean settlement patterns inside Petra; – *b) Graf* David F., ... in Arabia Petraea; – *c) Lindner* Manfred, Abu Khusheiba; – *d) Dentzer-Feydy* Jacqueline,   Le décor architectural ... hellénistique; – *e)* ᶜ*Amr* Khairieh,   Islamic or Nabataean? 100 AD cream ware; – *f) Villeneuve* François,   Le peuplement nabatéen de la Gobolitide: ➤ 740, Jordan 4 (1992) 211s / 253-262 / 263-7; 9 fig. / 227-232; 4 fig. / 221-5; 5 fig. / 277-290.
e614 **McKenzie** Judith,   The architecture of Petra 1990 ➤ 6,e235: ᴿAntiqJ 71 (1991) 286s (T. F. C. *Blagg*); GreeceR 39 (1992) 106s (B. A. *Sparkes*: excellent); JRS 82 (1992) 280 (N. *Kokkinos*); Mesop-T 27 (1992) 313-6 (A. *Invernizzi*); OLZ 87 (1992) 16-19 (K. *Matthiae*); Qadmoniot 25 (1992) 124 (A. *Segal*, **⊙**).
e614* *Stucky* Rolf A.,   Das nabatäische Wohnhaus und das urbanistische System der Wohnquartiere in Petra: AntKu 35 (1992) 129-142; 9 fig.; pl. 26-28.
e615 — *Beidha:* **Byrd** Brian,   The Natufian encampment at Beidha; late pleistocene adaptation in the Southern Levant: Publ. 23, 1989 ➤ 6,e230; 87-7288-054-6: ᴿAntiqJ 71 (1991) 267 (Lorraine *Copeland*).
e616 — *Sabra* 6 k S Wadi Musa, 1990 survey: ADAJ 36 (1992) 193-204; 4 fig.; 12 pl. (M. *Lindner*).
e617 — *Zantur* 3d 1991: ADAJ 36 (1992) 175-186; 10 fig., 6 pl. (R. A. *Stucky, al.*).
e618 *Zayadine* Fawzi,   L'espace urbain du Grand Pétra; les routes et les stations caravanières: ADAJ 36 (1992) 217-230; 4 fig.; 9 pl.
e619 *Zayadine* Fawzi, *al.*,   Pétra et le royaume des Nabatéens: DossiersArch 163 (1991) 2-45 (-88).
e620 **Wenning** Robert,   Die Nabatäer – Denkmäler und Geschichte ...: NOrb 3, 1987 ➤ 3,a317 ... 7,d519: ᴿOLZ 87 (1992) 160-2 (J. *Conrad*).
e621 **Negev** Avraham,   Personal names in the Nabatean realm: Qedem 32. J 1991, Univ. Inst. Archeol. vii-228 p. 0333-5844.
Patrich Joseph,   The formation of Nabatean art 1990 ➤ 2560.

e622 *Pounon:* Feinan copper production: ➤ e557, AJA 96 (1992) 510-2; 2 fig. (A. *Hauptmann*).
e623 *Samra*, Khirbet es-; ➤ 741, AnchorBD 5 (1992) 949s (J.-B. *Humbert*).
e624 *Sarbut*, t, abū, 2d 1989, 3d 1990: ADAJ 36 (1992) 333-9; 10 fig.; 3 pl. (H. de *Haas, al.*).
e624* *a) Snesla:* *Kerner* Susanne, *al.*,   Excavations in Abu Snesleh; Middle Bronze Age and Chalcolithic architecture in central Jordan; – *b) Worschech* Udo,   El-Baluᶜ, a Moabite city in central Jordan: NEA 3 (1992) 43-54; 13 fig. / 9-17; 4 fig.
e625 *Šuna*-N 1st 1991: ADAJ 36 (1992) 71-86; 8 fig. + 2 pl. (D. *Baird*, G. *Philip*).
e626 *Tabaqat al Būma* (wadi Ziqlāb) Kebaran-Neo 1990: ADAJ 36 (1992) 43-64 + 5 pl. (E. B. *Banning*).
e627 *Tiwāl*, lower w. Zerqa: **Tubb** J. N.,   Excavations at the Early Bronze Age cemetery of Tiwal esh-Sharqi. L 1990, British Museum. 111 p. 61 fig.; 14 pl. + foldout. £14 [PEQ 125,81s; Kay *Prag*].
e628 *Um el-Hedamus* (wadi Yabis) 1990: ADAJ 36 (1992) 35-39 + 3 phot. (G. *Palumbo*).
e629 *Umm el-Muqur*, 60 k E Aqaba: *Jobling* William J., *Tangeri* Daniel,   A prepottery neolithic site in the Hisma basin, southern Jordan: Paléorient 17,2 (1991) 141-147; 4 fig. (map).

e630 **Umm Rasas:** TerraS 67 (1991) 77-80 (M. *Piccirillo*).

e630* *Piccirillo* Michele, a) Les problèmes résolus et les questions posées par les trois premières campagnes de fouilles à Umm er-Rasas-Kastron Méfaa; la fin de la civilisation urbaine en Jordanie: ➤ 740, Jordan 4, 1992, 343-6; – b) Les églises paléo-chretiennes d'Umm er-Rasas (Jordanie); cinq campagnes de fouilles: CRAI (1991) 273-294; 11 fig.

e631 *Umm Raṣaṣ,* églises géminées: ADAJ 36 (1992) 291-9; 1 fig.; 4 pl. (J. *Bujard,* M.-P. *Haldimann*); 300s (M. *Piccirillo*).

e632 a) *Piccirillo* Michele, La chiesa dei Leoni a Umm al-Rasas – Kastron Mefaa; – b) *Alliata* Eugenio, Ceramica e piccoli oggetti dallo scavo della chiesa dei Leoni a Umm al-Rasas: LA 42 (1992) 199-226 / 227-250; Eng. 335.

e633 *Piccirillo* Michele, Kastron Mefaa; i mosaici di Giordania: ArchViva 10,20 (1991) 10-25; color. ill.

e634 **Bujard** Jacques, *Schweizer* François, Entre Byzance et Islam; Umm er-Rasas et Umm el-Walid; fouilles genevoises en Jordanie. Genève 1992, Musée Fond. van Berchem. 32 p. 2-8306-0092-4 [OIAc 5,16].

e635 **Yasileh** 1991: LA 41 (1991) 514-7; pl. 69 (Z. al-*Muheisin*).

e635* **Zara:** *Strobel* August, Die Grabungskampagne in ez-Zara (Kallirhöe) am Toten Meer (Jordanien): JbEvHL 1 (1989) 173-6.

T5.1 **Phoenicia – Libanus, Lebanon.**

e636 **Briquel-Chatonnet** F., Les relations entre les cités de la côte phénicienne et les royaumes d'Israël et de Juda [diss. Paris]: OrLovAnal 46. Lv 1992, Peeters / Univ. Dep. Oriëntalistiek. xviii-448 p. Fb 3900. 90-767831-379-7 [BL 93,38, K. W. *Whitelam*].

e637 *Elayi* Josette, a) Les cités phéniciennes, entre liberté et sujétion: DialHA 16,2 (1990) 93-113; – b) La présence grecque dans les cités phéniciennes sous l'empire perse achéménide: RÉG 105 (1992) 305 327.

e638 **Grainger** John D., Hellenistic Phoenicia 1991 ➤ 7,d533: RClasR 42 (1992) 369s (F. W. *Walbank*); Prudentia 24,2 (1992) 69-72 (P. *McKechnie*).

e639 *Peckham* Brian, Phoenicia, history of: ➤ 741, AnchorBD 5 (1992) 349-357 [religion 357-363, *Schmitz* Philip C.].

e639* *Seeden* Helga, Archaeology in Lebanon today: NEA 2 (1991) 143-159; 7 fig.

e640 *Steppat* Fritz, Libanon: ➤ 757, EvKL 3 (1992) 83-86.

c641 **Baalbeck** (Heliopolis): ESolin Heikki, Roman Eastern policy, Tvärminne 1987/90 ➤ 6,768*: 951-653-208-X [*Miller* F., Berytus, Heliopolis... Caesarea, Aelia]: RAntClas 61 (1992) 623-5 (Monique *Dondin-Payre*); RÉLat 69 (1991) 288s (R. *Chevallier*).

e642 **Byblos:** *Saghieh* Muntaha, Byblos in the third millennium B.C., 1983 ➤ 64,b514: RJNES 51 (1992) 141-3 (D. L. *Esse*).

e643 *Scandone Matthiae* Gabriella, Da Athribis a Biblo; modi di contatto tra Egitto e costa siriana: StEpL 7 (1990) 39-42.

e644 **Kamīd/Loz:** *Echt* Rudolf, Kamīd el-Loz 5, die Stratigraphie: SaarbBeitA 34, 1984 ➤ 1,d732b; 3,e344: RZAss 82 (1992) 292-5 (D. *Warburton*).

e645 **Metzger** Martin, Kamīd el-Loz 7; die spätbronzezeitlichen Tempelanlagen; Stratigraphie, Architektur und Installationen: SaarbBeitAltK 35. Bonn 1991, Habelt. 260 p.; vol. of 45 pl. 3-7749-2108-3 [OIAc 3,30].

e646 *Arnaud* Daniel, Une lettre de Kamid-el-Loz: Semitica 40 (1991) 7-16; 2 phot.

e647 **Ksar ʿAqil:** *Kersten* Annemie M.P., Rodents and insectivores from the palaeolithic rock shelter of Ksar ʿAkil (Lebanon) and their palaeoecological implications: Paléorient 18,1 (1992) 27-45; 3 pl.

e648 **Sarafand: Anderson** W.P., Sarepta I 1988 ↠ 6,e264; 7,d546: ᴿOrientalia 61 (1992) 152-7 (A.J. *Frendo*).

e649 **Khalifeh** Issam A., Sarepta II 1988 ↠ 6,a264: ᴿOrientalia 61 (1992) 329-354 (A.J. *Frendo*).

e650 **Pritchard** James B. [IV], *al.*, Sarepta I-IV 1985-8 ↠ 5,e38 ... 7,d547: ᴿJAOS 112 (1992) 504-8 (J.A. *Greene*: high standard, some reserves).

e651 **Tyrus: Schmeling** Gareth, Historia Apollonii regis Tyri 1988 ↠ 4,e942 ... 7,d554: ᴿAmJPg 113 (1992) 470-473 (D. *Konstan*, M. *Roberts*); Mnemosyne 45 (1992) 560-576 (G.A.A. *Kortekaas*: very severe).

e651* *Diakonoff* I.M., Naval power and trade of Tyre: IsrEJ 42 (1992) 168-193.

e652 *Abramenki* Andrik, Die zwei Seeschlachten vor Tyros; zu den militärischen Voraussetzungen für die makedonische Eroberung der Inselfestung (332 v.Chr.): Klio 74 (1992) 166-178.

T5.2   *Situs mediterranei* **phoenicei et punici.**

e653 **Amadasi Guzzo** Maria Giulia, *al.*, Dizionario della civiltà fenicia. R 1992, Gremese. 222 p. Lit. 25.000 pa. 88-7605-638-0 [BL 93,118, W.G.E. *Watson*: a first; handy].

e654 *Amadasi Guzzo* Maria Giulia, *Bonnet* Corinne, Anthroponymes phéniciens et anthroponymes grecs; remarques sur leurs correspondances: StEpL 8 (1991) 1-21.

e655 **Baurain** Claude, *Bonnet* Corinne, Les phéniciens, marins des trois continents. P 1992, A. Colin. 250 p.; ill. 2-200-21223-2.

e656 **Blázquez** José María, Fenicios, griegos y cartagineses en Occidente: Historia, serie menor. M 1992, Cátedra. 648 p. 88-376-1044-3 [OIAc 5,15].

e657 *Briese* Christoph, *Docter* Roald, Der phönizische Skyphos; Adaptation einer griechischen Trinkschale: MadMitt 33 (1992) 25-69; 15 fig.

e658 ᴱ**Delz** J. SILII Italici Punica, Teubner 1987 ↠ 5,e49 ... 7,d557: ᴿAnz-AltW 45 (1992) 50-52 (M. *Fussl*).

e659 — *Delarue* Fernand, Sur l'architecture des Punica de SILIUS Italicus: RÉLat 70 (1992) 149-165.

e660 — **Spaltenstein** François, Commentaire des Punica de SILIUS Italicus: Lausanne Fac. Lett. 28*b*. Genève 1990, Droz. 526 p. – ᴿRPg 65,2 (1991) 73-75 (P. *Jal*).

e661 **Gehrig** Ulrich, *Niemeyer* Hans Georg, Die Phönizier im Zeitalter Homers. Mainz 1991, von Zabern. 260 p. DM 50 [JAOS 112,357].

e662 **Gras** Michel, *al.*, L'univers phénicien 1989 ↠ 5,e51 ... 7,d559: ᴿSyria 69 (1992) 475s (F. *Bron*).

e663 *a) Hoz* Javier de, Graffites mercantiles puniques; – *b) Bisi* Anna Maria, Continuità e innovazioni nel sistema di scambi fenicio-punici: ↠ 713, PACT 20 (1987/90) 101-113 / 273-289.

e664 ᴱ**Lipiński** E., *al.*, Dictionnaire de la civilisation phénicienne et punique. Turnhout 1992, Brepols. xxii-502 p.; ill. 2-503-50033-1.

e664* *Lipiński* E., Vestiges et survivances du droit phénico-punique: AncSoc 22 (1991) 5-24.

e665 a) *Markoe* Glenn E., Phoenician art and the emergence of 'orientalizing' in Greek pottery; – b) *Esse* Douglas J., Phoenician and Greek ivories [Carthage c. 750]; AIA 1991; ⇢ 699, AJA 96 (1992) 339 (both).

e666 ᴱMoscati Sabatino, The Phoenicians 1988/9 ⇢ 5,e59: ᴿBA 55 (1992) 43-45 (G. E. *Markoe*).

e667 a) *Moscati* Sabatino, Die phönikische Expansion im westlichen Mittelmeerraum [< ᴱNiemeyer H., Phönizier im Westen 1982, 5-12], ᵀZimmermann K.; – b) *Bondi* Sandro F., Zu einigen Aspekten der phoinikisch-punischen Durchdringung Siziliens [< Rend. Lombard. 1977, 237-248], ᵀBignami R.; – c) *Amadasi Guzzo* Maria Giulia, Die epigraphischen Zeugnisse aus dem Tofet von Motye und das Problem des Molk-Opfers [< Studia Phoenicia 4 (Namur 1986) 199-207], ᵀBignami-Zimmermann; ⇢ e696, Karthago 1992, 11-25 (124-181 Sardinien; 341-352 Kunst) / 109-123 / 370-393; 1 fig.

e668 *Negbi* Ora, Early Phoenician presence in the Mediterranean islands; a reappraisal: AJA 96 (1992) 599-615; 3 fig. (map).

e669 *Wagner* Carlos G., En torno al supuesto carácter incruento e iniciático del *molk* [Phoenician, really infanticide]: Gerión 10 (1992) 11-22.

e670 **Hispania:** a) *Brown* Shelby, Perspectives on Phoenician art; – b) *Treumann-Watkins* Brigette, Phoenicians in Spain: BA 55 (1992) 6-24 / 28-35; ill.

c671 *Cruz Andreotti* G., *Wulff* Alonso M., Fenicios y griegos en la historiografía ilustrada española: [los] Masdeu: RStFen 20 (1992) 161-180.

e672 *Cunchillos* Jesús-Luis, Las inscripciones fenicias del Tell de **Doña Blanca** II/IV: Sefarad 51 (1991) 13-22; Eng. 22 / 52 (ᶠDíaz Esteban F. 1992 ⇢ 44) 75-83.

e673 *Aubet Semmler* María Eugenia, Die phönizische Niederlassung vom **Cerro del Villar** (Guadalhorce, Málaga); die Ausgrabungen von 1986-9: MadMitt 32 (1991) 29-51; 18 fig.; pl. 9-22.

e674 ᴱGran-Aymerich Jean, al., **Málaga** phénicienne et punique; recherches franco-espagnoles 1981-1988 P 1991. 328 p., 97 fig.; 8 pl. 2-86538-223-0. – ᴿRStFen 20 (1992) 199 (S. *Moscati*).

e675 **Harrison** Richard, Spain at the dawn of history; Iberians, Phoenicians and Greeks 1988 ⇢ 5,e66; 6,e278: ᴿAJA 96 (1992) 181s (W. E. *Mierse*).

c676 *López Castro* José Luis, El imperialismo cartaginés y las ciudades fenicias de la Península Ibérica entre los siglos VI-III a.C.: StEgPun 9 (1991) 87-107.

e677 *Padilla Monge* Aurelio, Aproximación a la economía de Asido (Medina Sidonia, **Cádiz**) y su comarca en época orientalizante: Habis 22 (Sevilla 1991) 7-17.

c678 *Moscati* S., Il 'barocco' [punico] spagnolo: RStFen 20 (1992) 137-141.

e679 **Ramos Sainz** Maria Luisa, Estudio sobre el ritual funerario en las necrópolis fenicias y púnicas de la Península Ibérica. M 1990, Univ. Autónoma. 151 p.; 164 pl. 84-7477-252-4. – ᴿBO 49 (1992) 522s (E. *Gubel*).

e680 **Melita:** Hölbl Günther, Ägyptisches Kulturgut auf Malta und Goza in phönikischer und punischer Zeit 1989 ⇢ 5,e74; 7,d572: ᴿArOr 60 (1992) 306s (L. *Bareš*).

e681 **Sardinia:** Balmuth Miriam S., Archaeology in Sardinia: AJA 96 (1992) 663-697; 33 fig. (map).

e682 *Bartoloni* P., Recipienti rituali fenici e punici dalla Sardegna: RStFen 20 (1992) 123-140 + 10 fig.; pl. IX-XV.

e683 *Moscati* Sabatino,   Arte popolare nella Sardegna punica: StEgPun 9 (1991) 65-80.
e684 *a*) *Moscati* Sabatino,   Nuovi studi sull'artigianato tardo-punico in Sardegna; – *b*) *Bernardini* P.,   La Sardegna e i Fenici; appunti sulla colonizzazione: RStFen 20 (1992) 83-98 / 29-81; pl. I-VI.
e685 *Garbini* G.,   *Magomadas* [S Bosa, al nuraghe di S. Nicola, Sardegna]: RStFen 20 (1992) 181-7; 1 fig.; pl. XVI.
e686 **Barnett** R. D.,   *Tharros*... British Museum 1987 → 3,e391... 7,d581: ᴿJNES 51 (1992) 149-151 (S. R. *Wolff*).
e687 **Acquaro** Enrico, *al.*, Tharros, la collezione Pesce: CollStFen 31.   R 1990, Cons. Naz. Ric.   121 p.; 31 pl.

T5.3   **Carthago.**

e688 *Baurain* Claude,   La place des littératures grecque et punique dans les bibliothèques de Carthage: AntClas 61 (1992) 158-177.
e689 *Bertrandy* F.,   Les représentations du 'signe de Tanit' sur les stèles votives de Constantine [Hofra, anc. Cirta]:   RStFen 20 (1992) 3-22 + 6 fig.
e689* *Beschaouch* Azedine,   Topographie de Carthage romaine; sur la localisation du temple d'Isis: CRAI (1991) 323-330; 4 fig.
e690 **Brown** Shelby,   Late Carthaginian child sacrifice and sacrificial monuments in their Mediterranean context [< diss.]: JStOT/ASOR mg 3, 1991 → 7,d586:   ᴿBA 55 (1992) 45s (Mary Joan Winn *Leith*); PEQ 124 (1992) 154s (T. *Axe*).
e691 ᴱ**Ennabli** Abdelmajid,   Pour sauver Carthage: exploration et conservation de la cité punique, romaine et byzantine. Tunis 1992, UNESCO. 252 p. 92-3-202782-8 [OIAc 3,20].
e692 **Ennabli** L.,   Les inscriptions funéraires chrétiennes de Carthage, 3. Carthage 'intra' et 'extra muros': Coll. Éc. Fr. 151.   R 1991, École Française.   vii-397 p.; 615 fig.; foldout plan. [RHE 87,183*].
e693 *Fantar* Muḥammad H., ⓐ From Palestine and Canaan to Carthage: → 736, ᴱ*Shaath* S., Palestine 1981/5, 79-84; 3 pl.
e694 **Holst** J., *al.*,   Die deutschen Ausgrabungen in Karthago 1991 → 7,d589: ᴿAntClas 61 (1992) 747s (J. *Debergh*).
e695 **Humphrey** John H.,   The circus and a Byzantine cemetery at Carthage I, 1988 → 7,d590:   ᴿLatomus 51 (1992) 256s (J. *Debergh*).
e696 *a*) ᴱ**Huss** Werner,   Karthago: WegF 654.   Da 1992, Wiss.   xi-462 p.; map; 3-534-04236-0; – *b*) *Bunnens* Guy, Die Gründung; Chronologie [< ÉtPg 17 (1979) 315-328], ᵀ*Zimmermann* Klaus; – *c*) *Rakob* Friedrich, Die internationalen Ausgrabungen in Karthago [< Gymnasium 92 (1985) 480-513]; – *d*) *Picard* Gilbert C.,   Die Territorialverwaltung Karthagos [< ᶠ*Piganiol* A. 1966, 1257-65], ᵀ*Zimmermann*; – *e*) *Stager* Lawrence E., Carthage, a view from the tophet [< ᴱ*Niemeyer* H., Phönizier im Westen 1982, 155-165]; 26-45 / 46-75; 15 fig. / 291-303 / 353-369.
e697 **Lancel** S., *al.*,   Histoire et archéologie de l'Afrique du Nord (Strasbourg 5-9 avril 1988) I, Carthage et son territoire dans l'antiquité 1990 → 7,648: ᴿJRS 82 (1992) 276s (J. B. *Rives*).
e698 *Lancel* Serge,   Carthago: → 743, AugL 1,5s (1992) 761-771 (en français); plan.
e699 **Niemeyer** H. G.,   Das frühe Karthago und die phönizische Expansion im Mittelmeerraum 1989 → 6,e297:   ᴿGymnasium 99 (1992) 79s (P. *Barceló*).
e700 *Niemeyer* Hans G.,   Karthago, Stadt der Phönizier am Mittelmeer: AntWelt 21 (1990) 89-105; 25 (color.) fig.

e701 *Ørsted* Peter, *al.*, Town and countryside in Roman Tunisia (Oued R'mel basin): JRomA 5 (AA 1992) 69-96.

e702 *Rakob* Friedrich, *a*) Ein punisches Heiligtum in Karthago und sein römischer Nachfolgebau: MiDAI-R 98 (1991) 33-80; 17 (foldout) fig.; pl. 3-27; – *b*) Neue Ausgrabungen in Karthago; ein punisches Heiligtum und das Stadtcentrum der punischen und römischen Metropole: AntWelt 23 (1992) 158-174; 59 (color.) fig.

e703 *Sznycer* Maurice, Un texte carthaginois relatif aux constructions (C.I.S. I,5523): Semitica 40 (1991) 69-81; 1 fig.

e704 *Teixidor* Javier, Le miracle phénicien: L'Histoire 157 ('Paix et guerre en Méditerranée' 1992) 18-22.

T5.4   **Ugarit** – *Ras Šamra.*

e705 **Amiet** Pierre, Ras Shamra – Ougarit IX, Corpus des cylindres 2, Sceaux-cylindres en hématite et pierres diverses: PublRSOu. P 1992, RCiv. 231 p.; 98 fig. 2-86538-234-6.

e706 *a*) *Arnaud* Daniel, *Salvini* Mirjo, Le divorce du roi Ammistamru d'Ougarit; un document redécouvert; – *b*) *Bordreuil* Pierre, *Pardee* Dennis, Textes ougaritiques oubliés et 'transfuges': Semitica 41s (1991s) 7-22 / 23-58; 6 fig.

e707 *Bordreuil* Pierre, Recherches ougaritiques, 1. Où Baal a-t-il remporté la victoire contre Yam? [Mt. Ṣapon]; 2. La mention du mois d'Adaru dans une lettre du roi de Tyr au roi d'Ougarit (RS 18.59, L. 14): Semitica 40 (1991) 17-27; 7 fig. / 28-30.

e708 **Bordreuil** Pierre, Une bibliothèque au sud de la ville; les textes de la 34e campagne (1973): RSOu 7. P 1991, RCiv. 210 p. F 128. 2-86538-219-2 [BO 49,587].

e709 *Caquot* A., Information sur la campagne Ougarit 1992 (*Yon* Marguerite): CRAI (1992) 461s.

e710 **Contenson** Henri de, (*Blot* Jacques, *al.*), Préhistoire de Ras Shamra; les sondages stratigraphiques de 1955 à 1976: RSOu 8. P 1992, RCiv. I. 283 p.; II. 421 p. (= 240 fig., 169 pl.). 2-86538-232-X.

e711 **Cunchillos** Jesús-Luis, Manual de estudios ugaríticos I [Arbeitsinstrumente; Geographie; Geschichte der Ausgrabung; Schrift und Sprache]: Textos universitarios 12. M 1992. 435 p. 84-00-07214-6 [UF 23,449].

e712 *Cunchillos* Jesús-Luis, Realizaciones informáticas del Sistema integrado de análisis morfológico de textos ugaríticos (SIAMTU) [< IV Simposio Bíblico Español, Granada 1992]: Bíblica 73 (1992) 547-559.

e713 *a*) *Jobling* W. J., Canaan, Ugarit and the Bible; some problems of relationship; – *b*) *Healey* John F., The Rephaites of ancient Palestine and Ugarit: ➤ 736, ᴱ*Shaath*, Palestine 1981/5, 93-110; 3 fig. / 159-164.

e714 *Lipiński* Édouard, Arcanes et conjonctures du marché immobilier à Ugarit et à Emar au XIIIe siècle av.n.è.: AltOrF 19 (1992) 40-43.

e715 *Loretz* Oswald, [➤ b441*] Ugariter, 'Kanaanäer' und 'Israeliten' [ALBERTZ R. 1992]: UF 24 (1992) 249-258.

e716 *Olmo Lete* Gregorio del, Yarḫu y Nikkalu; la mitología lunar sumeria en Ugarit: ➤ 32, ᶠ*Civil* M., AulaO 9,1 (1991) 67-75.

e717 *Pardee* D., *Bordreuil* P., Ugarit texts: ➤ 741, AnchorBD 6 (1992) 706-721 (excavation 695-706 *Yon* Marguerite, ᵀ*Rosoff* Stephen).

e718 **Reden** Sibylle von, Ugarit und seine Welt; die Entdeckung einer der ältesten Handelsmetropolen am Mittelmeer. Bergisch Gladbach 1992,

Lübbe. 376 p., 43 fig.+35 Zeichnungen; 48 color. pl. 3-7857-0634-0. – ᴿUF 23 (1991!) 446s (Nadja *Cholidis*).

e719 *Ribichini* Sergio, *Xella* Paolo, Problemi di onomastica ugaritica; il caso dei teofori: StEpL 8 (1991) 149-170.

e720 ᴱYon Marguerite, RS-Ougarit III, Le centre de la ville, 38ᵉ-44ᵉ, 1978-84: RCivMém 72, 1987 ➤ 4,g3; 6,e311*: ᴿSyria 69 (1992) 471-3 (D. *Collon*).

e721 **Yon** M., Arts et industries RS 6; bibliothèque au sud RS 7 1991 ➤ 7,d605: ᴿRSO 66 (1992) 403s (G. *Garbini*).

e722 *Yon* Marguerite, Ugarit, the urban habitat; the present state of the archaeological picture; ᵀ*Pardee* Dennis: BASOR 286 (1992) 19-34; p. 21, Courtois grid correcting North's [ZDPV 90,97; 68,113] is not topographically valid.

т5.5 Ebla.

e723 ᴱ**Archi** Alfonso, Eblaite personal names... symposium 1985/7 ➤ 4,718; 7,d609: ᴿJAOS 112 (1992) 159s (M. *Heltzer*).

e724 *Archi* Alfonso, The city of Ebla and the organization of its rural territory: AltOrF 19 (1992) 24-28.

e725 *a*) *Archi* Alfonso, The relevance of Ebla's discovery of the 3d millennium B.C. for the cultures of western Syria and Palestine; – *b*) *Scandone-Matthiae* Gabriella, The mace of Pharaoh Hotepibra and the connections between Egypt and Syria-Palestine in the XIIIth Dynasty; – *c*) *Pinnock* Frances, The lapis-lazuli in the royal palace of Ebla: ➤ 736, ᴱ*Shaath*, Palestine 1981/5, 59-63 / 49-58; 12 fig. / 65-71; 3 fig.

e726 *a*) *Astour* Michael C., The date of the destruction of Palace G at Ebla; – *c*) *Hallo* William W., The Syrian contribution to cuneiform literature: ➤ 705, New Horizons 1991/2, 23-28; map / 63-68 / 69-88.

e727 **Baldacci** Massimo, Partially published Eblaite texts: StAsiatMin 40. N 1992, Ist. Univ. Orientale. xvii-517 p.

e728 *Biggs* Robert D., Ebla texts: ➤ 741, AnchorBD 2 (1922) 263-7; bibliog. 267-270.

e729 *Bonechi* Marco, Onomastica dei testi di Ebla; nomi propri come fossili-guida?: StEpL 8 (1991) 59-78; 79 map.

e730 *Elayi* J., Deux 'ateliers' de coroplastes nord-phéniciens et nord-syriens sous l'empire perse [Arwad; Ebla...]: IrAnt 26 (1991) 181-206+X pl.

e731 ᴱ**Fronzaroli** Pelio, Literature and literary language at Ebla: Quad-Semitist. F 1992, Univ. Dept. Linguistica. x-326 p.

e732 ᴱ**Gordon** C., *al.*, Eblaitica 1, 1987 ➤ 3,491; 4,g10: ᴿSyria 68 (1991) 471-3 (P. *Talon*).

e733 *Gordon* Cyrus H., *a*) The Ebla incantations and their affinities with Northwest Semitic magic: ➤ 65, Mem. Gevirtz S., Maarav 7 (1991) 117-129; – *b*) The Eblaite language: ➤ 557*, Contacts 1990/2, 101-7.

e734 *a*) *Gordon* Cyrus H., Eblaite; – *b*) *Fronzaroli* Pelio, Niveaux de langue dans les graphies Eblaites: ➤ 118, ᶠLeslau W., Semitic 1991, 550-7 / 461-476.

e735 ᴱ**Gordon** C. H., *Rendsburg* G. A., Eblaitica 2, 1990: ➤ 6,e319: ᴿBSO 55 (1992) 542s (W. G. *Lambert*, including some partly-reply comments on Gordon).

e735* *a*) *Gordon* Cyrus H., The Ebla exorcisms; – *b*) *Rendsburg* Gary A., Eblaite sa-su-ga-lu = Hebrew ssᶜgar [bird smaller than eagle]; – *c*) *Hallo* William W., Ebrium at Ebla; – *d*) *Astour* Michael C., An outline of the history of Ebla I; – *e*) *Buccellati* Giorgio, Ebla and the Amorites / The Ebla electronic corpus; onomastic analysis: ➤ 433*c*, Eblaitica 3 (1992) 127-137 / 151-3 / 139-150 / 3-82 / 83-104 . 105-126.

e736 *Matthiae* Paolo, L'art du III*e* millénaire à Ebla: Archéologia 278 (1992) 60-66; ill.

e737 *Matthiae* Paolo, High Old Syrian royal statuary from Ebla: ➤ 179, F*Strommenger* Eva 1992, 111-128; pl. 48-53.

e738 **Mazzoni** Stefania, Le impronte su giara eblaite e siriane nel Bronzo Antico: MStArchEbla 1. R 1992, Univ. Missione Siria. [iv-] 267 p.; 51 pl.

e738* *a*) *Mazzoni* Stefania, Ebla e la formazione della cultura urbana in Siria; – *b*) *Archi* Alfonso, Ebla, la formazione di uno Stato del III millennio a.C.; – *c*) *Matthiae* Paolo, Architettura e urbanistica di Ebla paleosiriana: ParPass 258ss (1991) 163-194; 9 fig. / 195-219 / 304-345 + 21 fig.

e739 *Milano* Lucio, Luoghi di culto in Ebla; economia e sistema delle offerte: ➤ 701, ScAnt 3s (1989s) 155-173.

e740 *Millard* Alan, Ebla and the Bible; what's left (if anything)?: BR 8,2 (1992) 18-31 . 60; color. ill. (*Lessing* Erich).

e741 **Pettinato** Giovanni, Ebla, a new look at history [Nuovi orizzonti 1986 ➤ 2,a841], T1991 ➤ 7,d621; $37: RAJA 96 (1992) 559s (B. R *Foster*); BAR-W 18,3 (1992) 4 . 6 (A. *Millard*); DL (1992) 37 (J. F. *Healey*).

e742 **Pettinato** Giovanni, Il rituale per la successione al trono di Ebla; appendici *D'Agostino* Franco, *Pisi* Paola: StSem NS 9. R 1992, Univ. xv-363 p. XII pl.

e743 *Sanmartín* Joaquín, Isoglosas morfoléxicas eblaítico-ugaríticas; la trampa lexicográfica: ➤ 32, F*Civil* M., AulaO 9,1 (1991) 165-217.

e744 E*Wetzoldt* Hartmut, *Hauptmann* Harald, Wirtschaft und Gesellschaft von Ebla 1986/8 ➤ 4,707 ... 7,d622: ROLZ 87 (1992) 148-150 (L. *Cagni*).

T5.8 Situs effossi Syriae *in ordine alphabetico*

e745 F*Bounni* A., Resurrecting the past, E*Matthiae* P., *al.* 1990 ➤ 6,28: ROLZ 87 (1992) 32-35 (M. *Heinz*: Analysen ohne Tit. pp.).

e746 E*Dentzer* J., *Orthmann* W., Archéologie et histoire de la Syrie I 1989 ➤ 6,481; 7,d624: RAJA 96 (1992) 379s (Susan B. *Downey*).

e747 **Elayi** Josette, *Sapin* Jean, Nouveaux regards sur la Transeuphratène [= Syrie/Palestine perse]: Mémoire première. Turnhout 1991, Brepols. 223 p. Fb 725. – RRHE 87 (1992) 559 (A. de *Halleux*).

e748 ʾ*Abr:* *Hammade* Hamido, *Koike* Yayoi, Syrian archeological excavation in the Tishreen Dam basin excavations at Tell al-ʾAbr 1990 and 1991: DamaszM 6 (1992) 109-137 + 50 fig.; pl. 32-35.

e749 *Aḥmar*/Euphrates 1989-92: Akkadica 79s (1992) 1-7 + 19 fig. (G. *Bunnens*).

e750 E**Bunnens** Guy, Tell Aḥmar 1988 Season: Abr-Nahrain supp. 2, 1990 ➤ 7,d632: RZAss 82 (1992) 160s (U. *Seidl*).

e751 A*la;* **Peña** I., *al.*, Inventaire Jebel Aʿla: SBF min 31, 1990 ➤ 6,a342; 7,d634: RRB 99 (1992) 595 (J. M. de *Tarragon*).

e752 **Peña** Ignacio, La straordinaria vita dei monaci siri, secoli IV-VI, T*Ferrero* Grazia & Luigi. CinB 1990, Paoline. 190 p.; 18 pl. – RLA 41 (1991) 593-7 (L. *Di Segni Campagnano*).

e753 **Aleppo:** Bonechi Marco, Aleppo in età arcaica; a proposito di un'opera recente [ARM 26]: StEpL 7 (1990) 15-37.

e754 ᴱ**Ohta** Keiko, IBN ASH-SHIḤNA, The history of Aleppo: Studia culturae islamicae 40. Tokyo 1990, Inst. AsAfr. 422 p. – ᴿJRAS (1991) 396s (P. M. Holt: rather a topographical survey incorporating historical data of various periods).

e755 Quack Joachim F., Eine Erwähnung des Reiches von Aleppo in den Ächtungstexten?: GöMiszÄg 130 (1992) 75-78.

e756 **Amarna/Tašrin** [10 k S Carchemish; N Euphrates Tabqa dam] 1991: Akkadica 79 (1992) 14s (1992) 14s. 24-31 (Ö. Tunca); 32-35, terrescuites, Joëlle Horlait-Lecocq: 36-38, timbre grec, J. Winand; p. 39-46, maps; 8 pl.

e757 **Amrit:** Jourdain-Annequin Colette, Héraclès-Melqart à Amrith; recherches iconographiques: BAH 142. P 1992, Geuthner. 93 p.; 20 pl. 2-7053-0677-3 [dans le livre 777-3].

e758 **Apameia:** Houghton Arthur, The revolt of Tryphon and the accession of Antiochus VI at Apamea; the mints and chronologies of Antiochus VI and Tryphon: Schw.Num.Rundschau 71 (1992) 119-141 + pl. 16-18.

e759 **Bāra:** Fourdrim Jean-Pascal, Église E.5 d'El Bāra: Syria 69 (1992) 171-210; 74 fig.

e760 **Biᶜa:** Krebernik Manfred, Schriftfunde aus Tell Biᶜa 1990: MDOG 123 (1991) 41-70 [< UF 24 (1992) 508-510 (M. Dietrich)].

e761 **Brak:** Oates David & Joan, A human-headed bull statue from Tell Brak [1990]: CamArch 1,1 (1991) 131-5; 1 fig.; 4 pl.

e762 **Damascus:** Blanquais T., Damas et la Syrie sous la domination fatimide (359-468 / 969-1076); essai d'interprétation de chroniques arabes médiévales. Damas 1986, Inst. Français. xxii-804 p.; 5 maps. – ᴿPEQ 124 (1992) 152 (D. S. Richards).

e763 **Pouzet** Louis, Damas au VIIᵉ/XIIIᵉ siècle; vie et structures religieuses 1988 ⇥ 4,g37; 6,e355: ᴿOLZ 87 (1992) 555-8 (C. E. Bosworth; very successful).

e764 **Sack** Dorothée, Damaskus 1989 ⇥ 5,e128*... 7,d651: ᴿGnomon 64 (1992) 652s (M. Scharabi).

e765 **Dura-Europos** 1988-1990: Syria 69 (1992) 1-28 (P. Leriche) -120 al.; 121-140, 10th 1936s (Yale-AIBL; Susan B. Mattheson); 141-151, Frank BROWN's notes (Susan Downey).

e766 **Weitzmann** K., Kessler H. L., The frescoes of Dura 1990 ⇥ 7,d653: ᴿJRS 82 (1992) 283s (J. Huskinson).

e767 **Emar** [-Meskéné; 80 k E Aleppo; across the Euphrates from Munbaqa]: Wilcke C., Aḫ, die 'Brüder' von Emar; Untersuchungen zur Schreibtradition am Euphratknie: AulaO 10 (1992) 115-127; 128-150, charts with key.

e768 **Arnoud** D., Recherches au pays d'Aštata: Emar 6/4, 1987 ⇥ 2,a870 ... 6,e362: ᴿÉtClas 60 (1992) 174 (C. Bonnet).

e769 **Bonneterre** Daniel, Un aperçu des découvertes épigraphiques d'Émar [VI (1972-8; Syro-Hittite XIVᵉ-XIIIᵉ s.), ARNAUD D. 1986s]: BCanad-Mesop 24 (1992) 41-45.

e770 **Fleming** Daniel E., The rituals from Emar; evolution of an indigenous tradition in second millennium Syria: ⇥ 705, New horizons 1991/2, 51-61.

e771 a) **Fleming** Daniel E., A limited kingship; Late Bronze Age Emar in ancient Syria; – b) Yamada Masamichi, Reconsidering the letters from the 'King' in the Ugarit texts; royal correspondence of Carchemish?: UF 24 (1992) 59-71 / 431-446.

e772 **Gudeda:** Fortin Michel, a) Tell Gudeda, un site 'industriel' du IIIème millénaire av. J.-C., dans la moyenne vallée du Khabour? – b) Récentes recherches archéologiques dans la moyenne vallée du Khabour (Syrie): BCanadMesop 21 (1991) 63-78; 14 fig. / 5-15.

e773 **Habûba Kabira:** *Lindemeyer* Elke, Traditionen und Innovationen in der Siedlungsgeschichte Syriens zur Zeit der Auflösung der Urgesellschaft und der Herausbildung der frühen Klassengesellschaft: AltOrF 19 (1992) 259-265.

e774 **Habûr:** *McCorriston* Joy, The Halaf environment and human activities in the Khabur Drainage, Syria: JField 19 (1992) 315-333; 9 fig.

e775 **Hafûr:** *Koliński* Rafal, *Lawecka* Dorota, Report of Polish excavations at Tell Abū Hafūr, North Syria 1988-9, Area A: DamaszM 6 (1992) 177-228 (+) 24 fig.; pl. 36-39.

e776 **Hama: Riis** P. J., *Buhl* Marie-Louise, Hama 1931-8, 2/2, Les objets de la période dite Syro-Hittite (âge du fer), 1990 → 6,e368: ᴿOrientalia 61 (1992) 151s (Maria Giulia *Amadasi Guzzo*).

e777 **Hamidiyya:** ᴱ**Eichler** S., Tall al-Hamidiya [Upper Khabur] 2. Symposium Berne 1986 + Vorbericht 1985-7: OBO arch 6, 1990 → 6,e369: ᴿAfO 38s (1991s) 222-5 (Ö. *Tunca*).

e778 **Hammam/Turkman:** **Loon** M. N. Van, Hammam et-Turkman I-II, 1988 → 6,e370: ᴿBelleten 56 (1992) 1101 (A. *Özfırat*).

e779 **Haradum:** ᴱ**Kepinski-Lecomte** Christine, Haradum I, une ville nouvelle sur le Moyen-Euphrate (XVIIIᵉ-XVIIᵉ s. av. J.-C.). P 1992, RCiv. 456 p. + ❹ 21; 176 fig ; 23 (foldout) pl. 2-86538-229-X.

e780 **Hauran:** *Graf* David F., The Syrian Hauran [ᴱDENTZER J. 1986]: JRomA 5 (1992) 450-466.

e781 **Ory** Solange, Cimetières et inscriptions du Hawran et du Ğabal al-Durūz 1989 → 6,e372: ᴿJRAS (1991) 277s (J. M. *Rogers*).

e782 **Homs**-Emesa: *Strobel* Karl, Jüdisches Patriarchat, Rabbinentum und Priesterdynastie von Emesa; historische Phänomene innerhalb des Imperium Romanum der Kaiserzeit: Ktema 14 (1989) 39-77.

e783 *Woods* David, The regii emeseni indaei [Not. Dig. Or vi, 49]: Latomus 51 (1992) 404-7.

e784 **Huarte: Canivet** P. & M. T., Huarte... Apamène: BAH 122, 1987 → 3,e486: ᴿSyria 68 (1991) 491-3 (J. M. *Spieser*).

e785 **Hujayra** 20 k NW Hassake: *Martin* Lutz, *Tietze* Christian, Ausgrabungen auf dem Tell Abu Hğaira [1987-90]: AltOrF 19 (1992) 247-258; 5 fig. (map).

e786 **Hurayra:** *Molleson* Theya, al., A neolithic painted skull from Tell Abu Hureyra, Northern Syria: CamArch 2 (1992) 231-6; 4 fig.

e787 **Jabala** [30 k S Ladiqiya]: **Tsugitaka** Sato, The Syrian coastal town of Jabala — its history and present situation. Tokyo 1988, Univ. of Foreign Studies. 89 p. + ❹ 121; 50 fig. – ᴿArOr 60 (1992) 79s (P. *Charvát*).

e788 **Khalid** jabl [5 k S Qitar-Ahmar dam]: *Clarke* Graham, a) Greek graffiti from North Syria; – b) with *Hillard* Tom, A limestone altar from North Syria: MeditArch 5s (1992s) 117-120, 1 fig.; pl. 40:9 / 111-5; 3 fig.; pl. 38-39.

e789 **Leilan** [20 k NE Brak]: *Parayre* Dominique, *Weiss* Harvey, Cinq campagnes de fouilles à Tell Leilan dans la Haute Jezireh (1979-1987); bilan et perspectives: JSav (1991) 3-26; 19 fig.

e790 **Schwartz** G. M., A ceramic chronology from Tell Leilan 1988 → 6, e379: ᴿBO 49 (1992) 500-5 (Stefania *Mazzoni*).

e791 **Mari: Anbar** M., Les tribus amurrites de Mari (❺ 1985)ᵀ: OBO 108, 1991 → 7,d669: ᴿBL (1992) 40 (A. R. *Millard*); ZAW 104 (1992) 441 (H.-C. *Schmitt*); ZAss 82 (1992) 272 (D. O. *Edzard*).

e792 *Astour* Michael C., Sparagmos, omophagia, and ecstatic prophecy at Mari [ARMT 26/1,206]: UF 24 (1992) 1s.

e793 *Charpin* Dominique, Mari entre l'est et l'ouest; politique, culture, religion [conférence Bru 25.III.1992]: Akkadica 78 (1992) 1-10.

e794 *a) Dornemann* R., Early second millenium ceramic parallels between Tell Hadidi-Azu and Mari; – *b) Hoskisson* P., The nīšum oath in Mari: ➤ 739, Mari 1992, 77-112 / 203-210.

e795 ᴱ**Durand** Jean M. / *Charpin* D. *al.*, Archives epistolaires. I,1/2; ARM 26, 1988 ➤ 4,g55 ... 7,d670: ᴿJNES 51 (1992) 311s (R. D. *Biggs*).

e796 **Heintz** J.-G., *al.*, Bibliographie de Mari, archéologie et textes (1933-1988) ➤ 6,e384: ᴿBL (1992) 32 (J. F. *Healey*); ZAss 82 (1992) 144s (D. O. *Edzard*).

e797 *Heintz* Jean-Georges, *al.*, Bibliographie de Mari, supplément I (1989-1990): Akkadica 77 (1992) 1-37.

e798 *a) Lafont* Bertrand, Messagers et ambassadeurs dans les archives de Mari; – *b) Abrahami* Philippe, La circulation militaire dans les textes de Mari; la question des effectifs; – *c) Villard* Pierre, Le déplacement des trésors royaux, d'après les archives royales de Mari: ➤ 683, Circulation 1991/2, 167-183 / 157-166 / 195-205.

e799 **Malamat** A., ❿ Mari and Israel, two West-Semitic cultures. J 1991, Magnes. 233 p. – ᴿQadmoniot 25 (1992) 122s (N. *Naʾaman*, ❿).

e799* *Malamat* Abraham, Mari and Hazor; the implication for a MB chronology: ➤ 702b, ÄgLev 3 (1990/2) 121-3.

e800 **Malamat** Abraham, Mari and the early Israelite experience (Schweich 1984) 1989 ➤ 5,b307 ... 7,d675: ᴿBASOR 287 (1992) 92s (V. H. *Matthews*); OLZ 87 (1992) 54s (L. *Wächter*); Syria 68 (1991) 469-471 (H. de *Contenson*: rapprochements avec Ebla et Ugarit).

e801 *a) Malamat* A., The divine nature of the Mediterranean Sea in the foundation inscription of Yaḫdunlim; – *b) Fisher* R., The Mubassiru messengers at Mari; – *c) Pack* M. D., ᴸᵁ*ebbum* as a professional title at Mari; – *d) Safran* J. D., He restoreth my soul; a biblical expression and its Mari counterpart: ➤ 739, Mari 1992, 211-5 / 113-120 / 249-264 / 265-271.

e802 **Margueron** Jean-Claude, Mari, l'Euphrate, et le Khabur au milieu du IIIe millénaire [complete symposium lecture, with Eng. complete ᵀ*Whiting* L. S.]: BCanadMesop 21 (1991) 79-100; 9 fig. (map.); further on Mari: 6 (1990) 102-4 (M. *Fortin*, archéologie) & 104-7 (D. *Bonnetière*, épigraphie); both ᵀ*Wilding* L.

e803 *Margueron* Jean-C., Mari: ➤ 741, AnchorBD 4 (1992) 525-9 (-536, texts, *Durand* Jean-M.).

e804 *a) Michalowski* P., Mari, the view from Ebla; – *b) Astour* M. C., The North Mesopotamian kingdom of Ilānṣūra; – *c) Gelb* I. J., Mari and the Kish civilization; – *d) Mendenhall* George, The Amorite migrations: ➤ 739, Mari 1992, 243-8 / 1-34 / 121-202 / 233-241.

Young Gordon D., Mari in retrospect; fifty years of Mari and Mari studies 1992 ➤ 739; cfr. ➤ 56, ᶠFLEURY,

e806 *Mozan:* Milano Lucio, *al.*, Mozan 2. The epigraphic finds of the sixth season: Syro-MesopSt 5/1. Malibu 1991, Undena. 34 p.; 11 fig. – ᴿMesop-T 27 (1992) 300-2 (L. *Cagni*).

e807 *Munbāqa:* Mayer Walter, Eine Urkunde über Grundstückkaufe aus Ekalte / Tall Munbāqa: UF 24 (1992) 263-274; 1 fig.

e808 *Nebi Mend* 1990: MeditArch 5s (1992s) 168-170; fig. 4 (A. *Sagona*, C. *Haymes*).

e809 **Palmyre** 1981-7: ÉtTrav 16 (Wsz 1992) 325-335; 7 fig. (M. *Gawlikowski*).
e810 *Briquel-Chatonnet* Françoise, Un petit autel votif palmyrénien: Semitica 40 (1991) 83-87; 2 fig.
e811 *Equini Schneider* Eugenia, Scultura e ritrattistica onorarie a Palmira; qualche ipotesi: AION-Clas 44 (1992) 111-145; 20 fig.
e812 *Gawlikowski* Michel, *As'ad* Khaled, Le péage [toll] à Palmyre en 11 après J.-C.: Semitica 41s (1991s) 163-172; 1 fig.
c812* *Gawlikowski* Michel, Fouilles récentes à Palmyre: CRAI (1991) 399-410; 9 fig.
e813 *Parlasca* Klaus, *a)* Die palmyrenische Grabkunst in ihrem Verhältnis zur römischen Gräbersymbolik: ➤ 729*, MittGraz 3s (1989s) 112-136; pl. 22-32; – *b)* Palmyrenische Skulpturen in Museen an der amerikanischen Westküste: ➤ 738, Getty 1990, 133-144; 18 fig.
e814 *a)* *Parlasca* Klaus, Auswärtige Beziehungen Palmyras im Lichte archäologischer Funde; – *b)* *Saliby* Nasib, L'hypogée de Sassan fils de Malê à Palmyre: DamaszM 6 (1992) 257-265 (290-2); pl. 41-44f / 267-289; 8 fig. (I foldout); pl. 44g-58.
e815 **Stoneman** Richard, Palmyra and its empire; Zenobia's revolt against Rome. AA 1992, Univ. Michigan. 246 p.; 27 fig. 0-472-10387-3 [OIAc 5,36].
c816 *Teixidor* Javier, Remarques sur l'onomastique palmyrénienne: StEpL 8 (1991) 213-223.
e817 *Will* Ernest, *Teixidor* Javier, *Gawlikowski* M., al., Palmyre: MondeB 74 (1992) 3-46; ill.

e818 **Qara Qūzāq** 2d 1990, MB [Univ. Barcelona, dir. G. *del Olmo Lete*]: AulaO 10 (1992) 5-43; 18 fig. (E. *Olávarri*).

e819 **Reṣāfa:** *a)* *Konrad* Michaela, Flavische und spätantike Bebauung unter der Basilika B von Resafa-Sergiupolis; – *b)* *Ulbert* Thilo, Beobachtungen im Westhofbereich der Grossen Basilika von Resafa; – *c)* *Logar* Nuša, Die Kleinfunde aus dem Westhofbereich der Grossen Basilika von Reṣafa: DamaszM 6 (1992) 313-383 (+) 22 fig.; pl. 67-71 / 403-416; 4 fig.; pl. 72-76 / 417-460 + 18 fig.; pl. 77-78.
c820 **Mackensen** Michael, Resafa I 1984 ➤ 65,b159 ... 5,e170: ᴿClasR 42 (1992) 481 (N. *Christie*).
e821 **Ulbert** Thilo, Resafa II. Basilika 1986 ➤ 2,a898 ... 6,e406: ᴿRBgPg 70 (1992) 279s (M. *Rassart-Debergh*).
Ulbert Thilo, Rasafa 3, Silberschatz 1990 ➤ k490.

e822 **Sabi Abyad:** *Ahkermans* Peter, *Le Mière* Marie, The 1988 excavations at Tell Sabi Abyad, a Later Neolithic village in Northern Syria: AJA 96 (1992) 1-22; 22 fig.
e823 **Šamseddin:** **Meyer** Jan-Waalke, Gräber des 3. Jahrtausends v. Chr. im syrischen Euphrattal; 3. Ausgrabungen in Šamseddin und Djerniye: SchrVorderasArchäol 3. Saarbrücken 1991, Druckerei. 170 p.; 25 pl. a parte. 3-925036-48-2 [OIAc 3,30].
e824 **Šeh Ḥamad** Dur Katlimmu 1988: AnASyr 37s (1987s) 142-157 (H. *Kühne*: Syrian Antiquities Dept.).
e825 **Kühne** H., al., Die rezente Umwelt von Tall Šeḫ Ḥamad [Ḫabur 1983-9] und Daten zur Umweltsrekonstruktion der assyrischen Stadt Dur-Katlimmu: Berichte 1. B 1991, Reimer. 193 p.; 6 loose maps. DM 188. 3-496-00499-1. – ᴿBCanadMesop 23 (1992) 46s (français/English, both unsigned); ZAss 82 (1992) 297s (D. O. *Edzard*).

e826 **Shahba** [90 k S Damascus]: *Freyberger* Klaus S., Die Bauten und Bildwerke von Philippopolis; Zeugnisse imperialer und orientalischer Selbstdarstellung der Familie des Kaisers Philippus Arabs: DamaszM 6 (1992) 293-311; pl. 59-66.

e827 **Slīm:** *Freyberger* Klaus S., Der Tempel in Slīm [auch 90 k S Damaskus; ant. Selaima], ein Bericht: DamaszMi 5 (1991) 9-38; 6 fig.; pl. 5-16.

e828 **Sūkās:** **Lund** John. Sūkās VIII. The habitation quarters 1986 ⇝ 3,e527 ... 7,d690: ᴿGnomon 64 (1992) 648-650 (H. G. *Niemeyer*).

e829 **Oldenburg** Evelyn, Sūkās IX, 1991 ⇝ 7,d691: ᴿSyria 69 (1992) 473s (H. de *Contenson*).

e830 **Suweidaᶜ:** **Dentzer** J.-M., *Dentzer-Feydy* J., Le Djébel al-Arab; histoire et patrimoine au musée de Suweidaᶜ: IFAPO Guides Archéologiques 1. P 1991, CNRS. x-155 p.; 26 pl. + 8 color. 3-86538-213-X [OIAc 3,18].

e831 **Wastani** jebel: *Khouri* Wedad, *Castellana* Pasquale, Frühchristliche Städte im nördlichen Jebel Wastani (Syrien) [NE Laḍiqiya]: AntWelt 21 (1990) 14-25; 26 fig.

e832 **Yabroud** 1987: AnASyr 37s (1987s) 9-50 (R. *Solecki*).

e833 **Ziyāda:** *a)* Buccellati Giorgio, *al.*, Tell Ziyada; the first three seasons of excavation (1988-1990); – *b)* *Hole* Frank, Middle Khabur settlement and agriculture in the Ninevite 5 period: BCanadMesop 21 (1991) 31-61; 15 fig. / 17-29; 3 fig. (map).

T6.1   **Mesopotamia:** *generalia.*

e834 ꟳARTZI Pinḥas, Bar-Ilan Studies in Assyriology, ᴱKlein J., *Skaist* A. 1990 ⇝ 6,7: ᴿJAOS 112 (1992) 686-690 (Stephen J. *Lieberman, zal.*).

e835 **Baffi Guardata** Francesca, *Dolce* Rita, Archeologia della Mesopotamia; l'età cassita e medio-assira: Arch 88. R 1990, Bretschneider. xvi-296 p. 25 fig.; 40 pl. – ᴿOLZ 87 (1992) 537-541 (R. *Dittmann*).

e836 *Bottéro* Jean, La Mésopotamie et la Bible; cent ans de découvertes: ⇝ 462, Naissance 1990/2, 303-318.

e837 *a)* Chadwick Robert, Calendars, Ziggurrats and the stars; – *b)* *Fisher* Robert W., 'Secular' tendencies in the Neo-Assyrian period; – *c)* *Henrickson* Elizabeth F., Early everyday economics; distribution of trash and interpretation of activity patterns in an ancient village: BCanadMesop 24 (1992) 7-24 / 25-31 / 33-40. ⇝ gl.

e838 *Caretto* G., *al.*, Dalla Mesopotamia all'Iraq. Mi 1991, Jaca. 160 p. 88-16-42002-2 [OIAc 3,16].

e839 *Curtis* John, Recent British Museum excavations in Assyria [Barnett memorial lecture 1990]: JRAS (1992) 147-165; 16 fig.

e840 *a)* Durand Jean-Marie, Le roi d'Assyrie dans son palais; – *b)* *Bachelot* Luc, Les palais assyriens; – *c)* *Joannès* Francis, Des palais construits avec les richesses de l'univers; – *d)* *Parayre* Dominique, Fastes et splendeurs des cours assyriennes: DossA 171 (1992) 2-7 / 10-17 / 24-31 / 38-43; color. ill.

e841 *Frame* Grant, [170] Assyrian clay hands: BaghMit 22 (1991) 337-381; fig. 1 [looks somewhat like a foot] -3; pl. 43-47.

e842 ꟳGARELLI Paul, Marchands, diplomates et empereurs; études sur la civilisation mésopotamienne, ᴱCharpin D., *Joannès* F. 1991 ⇝ 7,61: ᴿAfO 38s (1991s) 168-171 (W. von *Soden*).

e843 **Guest** John S., The Euphrates expedition. L 1992, Kegan Paul. xiv-182 p. 52 fig. 0-7103-0429-3 [OIAc 3,22].

e844 ᴱHenrickson Elizabeth F., *Thuesen* Ingolf, Upon this foundation; the ʿUbaid reconsidered 1988/9 ➤ 6,804; 7,d700:   ᴿJAOS 112 (1992) 685s (T. L. *McClellan*); Syria 69 (1992) 465s (Y. *Calvet*).

e845 **Invernizzi** Antonio,   Dal Tigri all'Eufrate; 1. Sumeri e Accadi; 2. Babilonesi e Assiri: Univ. Torino, StMArch 5s.   F 1992, Lettere.   I. 421 p.; 635 fig.; 65 color. pl.; II. 384 p.; 619 fig.; 54 color. pl.   88-7166-101-X; -2-8.

e846 **Lackenbacher** Sylvic,   Le palais sans rivale; le récit de construction 1990 ➤ 7,d701:   ᴿRBgPg 70 (1992) 261s (E. De *Waele*).

e847 *Nashef* Khaled,   Archaeology in Iraq: AJA 96 (1992) 301-323; 28 fig.

e848 *Neumann* Hans,   Bemerkungen zum Problem der Fremdarbeit in Mesopotamien (3. Jahrtausend v.u.Z.): AltOrF 19 (1992) 266-275.

e849 **Roux** Georges,   Ancient Iraq³ [¹1964].   L 1992, Penguin.   xxii-547 p.; ill. 0-14-012523-X.

e850 *a)* *Stepniowski* Franciszek M.,   'Upper temples' on [the seven known] Assyrian ziqqurats — did they ever exist? [unlikely]; – *b)* *Schmid* Hansjörg, Zur inneren Organisation früher mesopotamischer Palastbauten: ➤ 179, ᶠSTROMMENGER Eva,   Von Uruk nach Tuttul 1992, 197-202 / 185-192; pl. 82-83.

e851 *a)* *Thuesen* Ingolf,   Information exchange in the ʿUbaid period in Mesopotamia and Syria; – *b)* *Forest* Jean-Daniel,   La circulation des idées et le niveau d'intégration politique; l'exemple des systèmes de mesures: ➤ 683, Circulation 1991/2, 13-17 + 4 fig. / 21-25; 3 fig.

e852 *Tunca* Önhan,   Ausgrabungen im Irak: AfO 38s (1991s) 269-281.

e853 *a)* *Watkins* Trevor,   Pushing back the frontiers of Mesopotamian prehistory; – *b)* *Campbell* Stuart,   The Halaf period in Iraq; old sites and new: BA 55 (1992) 176-181 / 182-7; ill.

e854 *Zarins* Juris,   The early settlement of southern Mesopotamia; a review of recent historical, geological, and archaeological research [NISSEN H. 1983, ᵀ1988]: JAOS 112 (1992) 55-77; 6 fig. (maps).

T6.3   *Mesopotamia, scripta effossa* – **Excavated Tablets.**

e855 **Archi** A., *Pomponio* F., [103] Tavolette cconomiche neo-sumeriche dell'Univ. Pont. Salesiana 1989 ➤ 5,e180:   ᴿBO 49 (1992) 439s (H. *Limet*); JAOS 112 (1992) 338s (D. C. *Snell*).

e856 **Archi** Alfonso, *Pomponio* Francesco,   Testi cuneiformi neo-sumerici di Drehem.   Mi 1990, Cisalpino.   216 p.; 69 pl. Lit. 95.000.   – ᴿOLZ 87 (1992) 245-8 (D. I. *Owen*).

e857 **Arnaud** Daniel,   Altbabylonische Rechts- und Verwaltungsurkunden 1989 ➤ 6,e430:   ᴿAfO 38s (1991s) 198s (M. Van De *Mieroop*); Orientalia 61 (1992) 324s (Stephanie *Dalley*).

e858 *Brown* Stuart G.,   A Neo-Assyrian stele inscription recently discovered in the Lowie Museum of the University of California, Berkeley [how Albiri ... kirka, the 'éminence grise', a competent scribe-decipherer, hurled heavy clay tablets at the heads of the shekel-dispensers in Babylon, and further threatened them until they allotted enough shekels to fill the library to the RIM]: BCanadMesop 24 (1992) 43s (49s, correction or spoof by *Grayson* A. K.).

e859 **Cagni** L.,   Briefe aus dem Iraq Museum: AltbB 8, 1980 ➤ 61,t178 ... 5,e181:   ᴿZAss 82 (1992) 141s (D. O. *Edzard*).

e860 *Cavigneaux* Antoine [*al.*], Texte, Uruk 33/34 [1977-8]: BaghMit 22 (1991) [1-33] 33-56, facsimiles 57-123 / 124-135, facsimiles 137-163.

e861 **Donbaz** Veysel, Keilschrifttexte... Stamboul 2, 1989 ⇒ 5,e184...7,d709: ᴿJAOS 112 (1992) 333-5 (W. C. *Gwaltney*: better with some obscurities than never).

e862 **Eidem** Jesper, The Shemshāra archives 2. The administrative texts: HFilSkr 15. K 1992. 165 p., 146 facsimiles, 33 fot. 87-7304-227-7. – ᴿMesop-T 27 (1992) 303s (C. *Saporetti*).

e863 ᴱ**Fales** Frederick M., *Postgate* J. N., Imperial administrative records, 1. Palace and temple administration: SAA 7. Helsinki 1992, Univ. xliii-261 p.; 42 fig.; XI pl. 951-570-112-0; pa. -1-2 [OIAc 5,20].

e864 **Frayne** Douglas R., Royal Inscriptions of Mesopotamia, Early Periods 4, Old Babylonian period, 2003-1595 B.C. Toronto 1990, Univ. xxxi-853 p.; 7 microfiches. $195. – ᴿBSO 55 (1992) 538-540 (A. R. *George*; 30 queries); RAss 86 (1992) 88-91 (D. *Charpin*).

e865 *Freydank* Helmut, Das Archiv Assur 18764 [W. ANDRAE 1911]: AltOrF 19 (1992) 276-321.

e866 **Fuller** Russell T., Cuneiform Texts [British Museum 48], a transliteration and translation with philological notes, commentary, and indices: diss. HUC, ᴰ*Greengus* S. Cincinnati 1992. 467 p. 92-30558. — DissA 53 (1992s) 1885-A.

e867 **Gehlken** E., Uruk, Spätbabylonische Wirtschaftstexte aus dem Eanna-Archiv, 1. Texte verschiedenen Inhalts: Endb 5. Mainz 1990, von Zabern. 215 p. DM 110. 3-8053-1116-8 [BL 93,31, W. G. *Lambert*].

e868 **Gelb** I. J., *Kienast* B., Die altakkadischen Königsinschriften 1990 ⇒ 6, e443; 7,d712: ᴿJAOS 112 (1992) 619-638 (D. R. *Frayne*).

e870 **Gross** Katarzyna, The archive of the Wullu family 1988 ⇒ 4,g96 [Arraphe-Kirkuk]: ᴿJNES 51 (1992) 232-6 (Martha A. *Morrison*).

e871 *Hallo* William W., *Weisberg* David B., A guided tour through Babylonian history; cuneiform inscriptions in the Cincinnati art museum: JANES 21 (1992) 49-67; 69-90, facsimiles.

e872 ᴱ**Hunger** Hermann, Astrological reports to Assyrian kings: SAA 8. Helsinki 1992, Univ. xxix-385 p.; 15 pl. [ᴱ*Reade* J., *Parpola* S.]. 951-570-130-9 [OIAc 5,25].

e873 **Joannès** Francis, Les tablettes néobabyloniennes de la Bodleian 1990 ⇒ 6,e448: ᴿBSO 55 (1992) 540-2 (J. A. *Brinkman*).

e874 **Joannès** Francis, Archives de Borsippa; la famille Ea-ilûta-bâni: ÉPHÉH Or. 25, 1989 ⇒ 5,e190...7,d718: ᴿAfO 38 (1991s) 199-201 (M. *Stol*); ArOr 60 (1992) 85s (J. *Pečirková*); RAss 86 (1992) 87 (Brigitte *Lion*); ZAss 82 (1992) 145s (M. *Strack*).

e875 **Kutscher** Raphael, The Brockmon tablets 1989 ⇒ 5,e191...7,d720: ᴿBSO 55 (1992) 120s (S. *Tinney*); OLZ 87 (1992) 385-392 (H. *Neumann*).

e876 **Kwasman** T. Neo-Assyrian legal: StPohl 14, 1988 ⇒ 4,g101...7,d722: ᴿWeltOr 23 (1992) 167s (K. *Kessler*).

e877 **Lacheman** Ernest R. †, *Maidman* Maynard P., Joint Expedition... Nuzi 7, miscellaneous texts ⇒ 5,e192; 7,d724: ᴿAfO 38s (1991s) 174-9 (C. *Zaccagnini*, Eng.); WeltOr 23 (1992) 165-67 (Jeanette *Fincke*); ZAss 82 (1992) 143s (D. O. *Edzard*).

e879 **Lafont** B., *Yıldız* F., Tablettes cunéiformes de Tello au musée d'Istanbul... III Ur 1, 1989 ⇒ 5,e194: ᴿAulaO 10 (1992) 163-5 (M. *Sigrist*: un modèle); BO 49 (1992) 441-8 (D. I. *Owen*); Orientalia 61 (1992) 162 (F. *Pomponio*); ZAss 82 (1992) 137s (W. *Sallaberger*).

e880 *Lafont* Bertrand, Quelques nouvelles tablettes dans les collections américaines [4, all from Philadelphia]: RAss 86 (1992) 97-105 + facsimiles.

e881 **Lambert** Wilfred G., Catalogue of the cuneiform tablets in the Kouyounjik collection of the British Museum, 3d supp. L 1992. BM. xvi-95 p. 0-7141-1131-7 [OIAc 5,28].

e882 **Lanfranchi** G. B., *Parpola* S., The correspondence of Sargon II, 2: SAA 5, 1990 ➤ 6,e454: ᴿZAW 104 (1992) 299 (O. *Kaiser*).

e883 **Leichty** E., *al.*, Catalogue of the Babylonian tablets in the British Museum 6-8, Sippar 1986-8 ➤ 4,g103 ... 7,d525: ᴿJNES 51 (1992) 143-7 (J. *Oelsner*).

e884 **Lerberghe** Karel van, *al.*, Old Babylonian legal and administrative texts from Philadelphia: OrLovAnal 21, 1986 ➤ 3,e569: ᴿJAOS 112 (1992) 503s (R. A. *Veenker*); ZAss 82 (1992) 273s (D. O. *Edzard*).

e885 ᵀᴱ**Livingstone** Alasdair, Court poetry and literary miscellanea: SAA 3, Helsinki 1989 ➤ 5,e197; xxxvii-183 p.; 16 pl. [ᴱ*Reade* J.]; 4 microfiche texts: ᴿArOr 60 (1992) 82s (B. *Hruška*); JAOS 112 (1992) 500s (Barbara N. *Porter*); OLZ 87 (1992) 36-39 (J. *Black*, Eng.).

e886 **Marzahn** Joachim, Altsumerische Verwaltungstexte aus Girsu/Lagaš: Vorderasiatische Schriftdenkmäler der Staatlichen Museen zu Berlin 25. B 1991, Akademie. 23 p.; 50 fig. [BO 49,586]. 3-05-000747-8.

e887 **Maul** Stefan M., Die Inschriften von Tell Bderi [KÜHNE H., 1985-90; 25 k S Ḥasaka]: Berliner Beiträge VO Texte 2. B 1992, Reimer. 79 p. DM 68 [BO 49,586]. 3-496-00410-X.

e888 *Molina Martos* Manuel, *a*) Tablillas sargónicas del museo de Montserrat, Barcelona: ➤ 32, ᶠCIVIL M., AulaO 9,1 (1991) 137-147; 148-154, photos with facing facsimiles. – *b*) Tablillas neosumerias de la Universidad de Santiago de Compostela: AulaO 10 (1992) 87-92 + 16 facsimiles.

e889 **Postgate** J. N., The archive of Urad-Šerūa 1988 ➤ 6,e461; 7, d734: ᴿBSO 55 (1992) 120s (R. *Jas*); JESHO 35 (1992) 101-3 (W. F. *Leemans* †).

e890 *Rawi* Farouk N. H. al-, More royal inscriptions from Babylon: AnRIM 9 (1991) 1-10.

e891 *a*) *Rawi* F. N. H. Al-, *George* A. R., Enūma Anu Enlil XIV and other early astronomical tables; – *b*) *Koch* Johannes, Zu einigen astronomischen 'Diaries': AfO 38s (1991s) 52-69 + 7 fig. / 101-9 [110-124 *Neumann* Hans, zu Kochs Fixsternhimmel; 125-130, Antwort Kochs].

e892 *Sanati-Müller* Shirin, Texte aus dem [Warka] Sinkašid-Palast, IV: BaghMit 22 (1991) 313-330.

e893 **Snell** Daniel C., *Lager* Carl H., Economic texts from Sumer: Yale Babylonian 18. NHv 1991, Yale Univ. ix-70 p., LXXXV pl. $50 [JAOS 112,727; BO 49,587]. 0-300-04945-5.

e894 ᴱ**Spar** Ira, Cuneiform texts in the Met I, 1988 ➤ 4,g112 ... 7,d739: ᴿAfO 38 (1991s) 182-7 (H. *Hirsch*).

e895 **Steinkeller** Piotr, Sale documents of the Ur-III-period: FrbOrSt 17, ᴰ1989 ➤ 5,e207 ... 7,d739*: ᴿJAOS 112 (1992) 118-122 (D. S. *Snell*: excursus with tables of prices).

e896 **Steinkeller** Piotr, Third-millennium legal and administrative texts in the Iraq Museum, Baghdad (+ copies, *Postgate* J. N.): Mesopotamian Civilizations 4. WL 1992, Eisenbrauns. xv-125 p.; 32 pl. 0-931464-60-9.

e897 **Weiher** E. von, Spätbabylonische Texte 3: Ausgrabungen in Uruk-Warka 12, 1988 ➤ 4,g117; 7,d741: ᴿAfO 38s (1991s) 179-182 (M. J. *Geller*, Eng.).

e898 **Yıldız** Fatma, *Gomu* Tohru, Puzriš-Dagan-Texte 1988 ➤ 4,g119 ... 7,d745:

ᴿJESHO 35 (1992) 206s (B. *Lafont*); ZAss 82 (1992) 131 (W. *Sallaberger*).

T6.5   **Situs effossi ʿIraq** in ordine alphabetico.

e899 *Abada:* **Jasim** S. A., The Ubaid period in Iraq; recent excavation in the Hamrin region: BAR-Int 267. Ox 1985. viii-247 p.; xiii p.; 279 fig.; 19 pl. £25. – ᴿBASOR 286 (1992) 91-94 (R. *Dittmann*).

e900 *Agadé:* **Glassner** Jean-Jacques, La chute d'Akkadé; l'événement et sa mémoire: BBVO 5, 1986 ➤ 6,a475; 7,d747: ᴿAfO 38s (1991s) 171-4 (J. S. *Cooper*); JAOS 112 (1992) 503 (P. *Michalowski*); OLZ 87 (1992) 39-47 (A. *Westenholz*, Eng.).

e901 *Ana:* **Northedge** A., *al.*, Excavations et ʿAna, Qalā island 1988 ➤ 7, d748: ᴿAfO 38s (1991s) 226s (Ö. *Tunca*).

e902 *Aššur:* **Donbaz** Veysel, **Grayson** A. Kirk, Royal Inscriptions on clay cones from Ashur now in Istanbul: RIM Sup I, 1984 ➤ 65,b183...4,g92: ᴿAfO 38s (1991s) 104s (H. *Hirsch*).

e903 **Jakob-Rost** Liane, **Marzahn** Joachim, Assyrische Königsinschriften auf Ziegeln aus Assur 1985 ➤ 1,d962...4,g98: ᴿAfO 38s (1991s) 196 (H. *Hirsch*).

e904 **Pedersén** Olof, Archives and libraries in the city of Assur 1985s ➤ 1, d981...7,d751: ᴿAfO 38s (1991s) 193s (H. *Hirsch*).

e905 *Vera Chamaza* Galo W., Sanheribs letzte Ruhestätte [Keilschrifttexte der zwei Grabinschriften aus Aššur]: BZ 36 (1992) 241-9.

e906 *Babylon:* **Becker** Andrea & Udo, 'Altes' und 'Neues' Babylon?: Bagh-Mit 22 (1991) 501-511.

e907 *Bassorah:* **Denton** [Branwen] Elizabeth, The late second millennium B.C. in the Arab-Iranian gulf: diss. Bryn Mawr, ᴰ*Ellis* R. Ph 1992. xiv-323 p. 92-12994. – OIAc 3,18.

e908 *Borsippa:* **Allinger-Csollich** Wilfrid, Birs-Nimrud I. Die Baukörper der Ziqqurrat von Borsippa: BaghMit 22 (1991) 383-499; 48 fig.; pl. 48-55.

e909 *Deylam:* **Armstrong** James A., West of Edin: Tell al-Deylam and the Babylonian city of Dilbat: BA 55 (1992) 219-226; ill. [Edin (also p. 169) does not occur in the text].

e910 *Diyala:* **Hill** Harold H., *al.*, Old Babylonian public buildings in the Diyala region: OIP 98, 1990 ➤ 6,e492 (Iščali): ᴿOLZ 87 (1992) 258-261 (J. *Börker-Klähn*).

e911 *Fara:* **Visicato** Giuseppe, Some aspects of the administrative organization of Fara: Orientalia 61 (1992) 94-99.

e912 *Ḥafaja:* **Deblauwe** Francis, A study of accessibility and circulation patterns in the Sīn temple of Ḥafaǧi from the third millennium B.C.: MesopT 27 (1992) 89-99; plans p. 100-118.

e913 *Hamad Aǧa* aṣ-Ṣaǧîr 1990: BaghMitt 23 (1992) 87-105 + 20 fig. (P. Z. *Spanos*).

e914 *Ḥatra* 3d 1989: Mesop-T 27 (1992) 189-198 (Roberta *Venco Ricciardi*).

e915 **Aggoula** B., Inventaire des inscriptions Ḥatréennes. P 1991, Geuthner. ix-195 p.; XXXVII pl. – ᴿAION 52 (1992) 221s (R. *Bertolino*).

e916 *Hiba* 6th 1990: ➤ e852, AfO 38s (1991s) 269-271; 2 fig. (D. P. *Hansen*).

e917 *Imlihiya:* **Boehmer** R., *al.*, Tell Imlihiye *al.* 1985 ➤ 1,g1...6,e491: ᴿJNES 51 (1992) 230-2 (R. L. *Zettler*: valuable).

e918 *Isin:* **Hrouda** B., Isin – Išān Bahrīyāt 4, die Ergebnisse der Ausgrabungen 1986-1989: Abh ph/h 105. Mü 1992, Bayerische Akademie. 213 p.; 67 pl.; foldout plans. 3-7696-0100-9.

e919 **Jamdat Naṣr:** *Matthews* Roger J., *a)* Jemdet Nasr; the site and the period: BA 55 (1992) 196-203; ill.; – *b)* Defining the style of the period: Jemdet Nasr 1926-28: Iraq 54 (1992) 1-34; 14 fig. pl. I.

e920 **Karhasan:** *Tucker* David, A Middle Assyrian hoard from Khirbet Karhasan [on Tigris 75 k NW Mosul], Iraq [faience beads; rosettes for bridle]: Iraq 54 (1992) 157-177 (-182 shells, *Reese* D.).

e921 **Kiš:** *Clayden* T., Kish in the Kassite period (c. 1650-1150 B.C.): Iraq 54 (1992) 141-155.

e922 **Kissik:** *Beaulieu* Paul-Alain, [S. Babylonia] Kissik, Dūru and Udannu: Orientalia 61 (1992) 400-424.

e923 **Lagaš:** *Hansen* Donald R., Royal building activity at Sumerian Lagash in the Early Dynastic period: BA 55 (1992) 206-211.

e924 **Larsa,** Oueili: **Huot** J.-L., Larsa 10e, Oueili 4e: RCiv mém 73, 1987 ➤ 4,g139; 6,e497: ᴿAulaO 10 (1992) 160-3 (R. L. *Zettler*).

e925 ᴱ**Huot** J.-L., Larsa, travaux de 1985: Dél. Iraq 5. P 1989, RCiv. 196 p. + ❹ 82. F 280. 2-86538-198-6. – ᴿBO 49 (1992) 496-8 (Ö. *Tunca*).

e926 **Oueili** 1987, 1989: ➤ e852, AfO 38s (1991s) 274-6; fig. 9-11 (J.-D. *Forest*).

e927 Larsa/Sinkara 1987, 1989: ➤ e852, AfO 38s (1991s) 276-9; fig. 12-14 (Y. *Calvet, al.*).

e928 *Huot* Jean-Louis, The first farmers at Oueili: BA 55 (1992) 188-195.

e929 **Maškan-Šapir** (northernmost navigable Tigris-Euphrates confluence); *Stone* Elizabeth C., *Zimansky* Paul, Mashkan-shapir and the anatomy of an Old Babylonian city: BA 55 (1992) 212-8; ill.

e930 **Nimrud**/ Balawat: ➤ e852, AfO 38s (1991s) 272-4; fig. 5-8 (J. *Curtis*).

e931 **Herrmann** Georgina, The small collections from Fort Shalmaneser: Ivories from Nimrud 5. L 1992, British School Iraq. xiv-146 p.; 104 pl. 0-903472-12-0.

e932 **Herrmann** Georgina, Ivories ... Nimrud 1986 ➤ 2,a973 ... 7,d766: ᴿJNES 51 (1992) 135-140 (Irene J. *Winter*).

e933 *Herrmann* Georgina, The Nimrud ivories [1. Iraq 51 (1989) 85-109] 2. A survey of the traditions: ➤ 179, ᶠSTROMMENGER Eva 1992, 65-79, pl. 20-34.

e935 **Ninive:** *Stronach* David, *Lumsden* Stephen, UC-Berkeley's excavations at Nineveh: BA 55 (1992) 227-233; ill.

e936 *Charpin* Dominique, Les bibliothèques des palais de Ninive: DossA 171 (1992) 68-71; color. ill.

e937 **Nippur:** *a)* Gibson* McGuire, Patterns of [site-] occupation at Nippur [his stratigraphic programs 1972-87]; – *b)* Westenholz* Aage, The early excavators of Nippur: ➤ 687, Nippur 1988/92, 33-54; 14 fig. / 291-5.

e938 *a)* Spek* R.J. van der, Nippur, Sippar, and Larsa in the Hellenistic period; – *b)* Tuman* V.S., Astronomical dating of the Nebuchadnezzar Kudurru found in Nippur in February, 1896: ➤ 687, Nippur 1988/92, 235-260 / 281-290; 4 fig.

e938* **Zettler** Richard L., The Ur III temple of Inanna at Nippur; the operation and organization of urban religious institutions in Mesopotamia in the late third millennium B.C. [< diss. Chicago 1984: BBeitVO 11. B 1992, Reimer. xiv-303 p.; 21 fig. 3-496-00422-3 [OIAc 5,40].

e939 *a)* Zettler* Richard L., Excavations at Nippur, the University of Pennsylvania, and the University's Museum; – *b)* Myer* Charles F.,ᴶ, Joseph A. Meyerᴶ, architect at Niffer: ➤ 687, Nippur 1988/92, 325-334 + 4 fig. / 137-9; 10 handwritten-page photos.

e940 *Zettler* Richard L., Nippur under the third dynasty of Ur; area TB: ➤ 32, ᴱCIVIL M., AulaO 9,1 (1991) 251-274 + 7 plans.

e941 *Nuzi:* *Negri-Scafa* Paola, *a*) Nuzologia; – *b*) La radice hurrica *ḫan*- nei testi di Nuzi; – *c*) Osservazioni sull'espressione *Šinapšumma epēšu* nei testi di Nuzi: SMEA 29 (1992) 255-8 / 183-7 / 189-202.

e942 **Stein** Diana L., Khabur ware and Nuzi ware; their origin, relationship and significance: Assur 4/1, 1984 ⇒ 1,e14: ᴿBO 49 (1992) 494-6 (H. *Curvers*).

e944 *Raqaʾi:* *Schwartz* Glenn M., *Curvers* Hans H., Tell al-Raqāʾi 1989 and 1990; further investigations at a small rural site of early urban northern Mesopotamia: AJA 96 (1992) 397-419; 29 fig. (map).

e945 *Rijjim,* Raffân (Eski Mosul) 1984-6: ÉtTrav 16 (Wsz 1992) 273-288; 11 fig. (P. *Bieliński*).

e946 *Rubeidha:* ᴱ**Killick** R. G., Excavations at Tell Rubeidheh, an Uruk village in the Jebel Hamrin: BrtSch 2, Hamrin Salvage 7, 1988 ⇒ 7,d769; $46 pa.: ᴿAfO 38s (1991s) 325s (Ö. *Tunca*); JAOS 112 (1992) 327s (Zainab *Bahrani*).

e947 *Sabra:* **Tunca** Ö., Tell Sabra, Hamrin Report 7, Akkadica supp. 5, 1987 ⇒ 6,e514: ᴿSyria 68 (1991) 480s (J.-L. *Huot*).

e948 *Salabiḫ* 1988s: ⇒ e852, AfO 38s (1991s) (J. N. *Postgate*).

e949 *Pomponio* Francesco, I nomi personali dei testi amministrativi di Abu Ṣalābīḫ: StEpL 8 (1991) 141-147.

e950 *Sawwan* 10 k S Samarra, 2s, 1988s: Mesop-T 27 (1992) 5-30; 13 fig.; pl. 1-5 (Catherine *Breniquet*); 31-46; 8 fig., silex (E. *Coqueugniot*); 63-70, faune, c. 5000 a.C. (P. *Ducos*).

e951 *Sippar:* **Joannès** Francis, Les temples de Sippar et leurs trésors à l'époque néo-babylonienne: RAss 86 (1992) 159-184.

e952 *Umma:* *Pomponio* Francesco, Lukalla of Umma: ZAss 82 (1992) 169-179.

e953 *Ur:* **Karstens** Karsten, Typologische Untersuchungen an Gefässen aus altakkadischen Gräbern des Königsfriedhofes in Ur; ein Beitrag zur modernen archäologischen Methodik. Mü 1987, Profil. 246 p.; 78 fig.; 283 pl. – ᴿOLZ 87 (1992) 49-51 (L. *Martin*); Syria 69 (1992) 235-7 (J.-L. *Huot*).

e954 **Mieroop** Marc van de, Society and enterprise in Old Babylonian Ur: BBeitVO 12. B 1992, Reimer. xviii-328 p.; 29 fig. 3-496-00438-X [OIAc 5,37].

e955 *Mieroop* Marc van de, Old Babylonian Ur; portrait of an ancient Mesopotamian city: ⇒ 730, JANES 21 (1989/92) 119-130; 2 fig.

e956 *Pollock* Susan, Of priestesses, princes and poor relations; the dead in the royal cemetery of Ur: CamArch 1 (1991) 171-189; 9 fig,

e957 *Warka/Uruk* 1989: ⇒ e852, AfO 38s (1991s) 279-281; fig. 15-19 (R. M. *Boehmer*).

e958 **Boehmer** R. M., Uruk 38, 1985: Endb. 1, 1987 ⇒ 6,e525; 7,d775: ᴿZAss 82 (1992) 276s (U. *Seidl*).

e959 *Boehmer* Rainer M., *a*) Lugalzagesi, der Bauherr des Stampflehmgebäudes in Uruk; – *b*) ¹⁴C-Daten aus Uruk und Abydos — Ägyptisches (?) im frühen Nordsyrien, Sumer und Elam: BaghMit 22 (1991) 165-174 / 223-230; 5 fig.

e960 **Eichmann** R., Uruk, Die Stratigraphie 1912-77 Eanna/Anu 1989 ⇒ 6, e526; 7,d776: ᴿAfO 38s (1991s) 213-220 (R. *Hachmann*: endet mit Zusammenfassung ... der ungelösten Probleme).

e961 **Finkbeiner** Uwe, Uruk, Kampagne 35-37, 1982-4; die archäologische Oberflachenuntersuchung: Endb. 4, 1991 ⇒ 7,d776*: ᴿMesop-T 27 (1992) 281-4 (A. *Invernizzi*).

e962 *Finkbeiner* Uwe, Keramik der seleukidischen und parthischen Zeit aus den Grabungen in Uruk-Warka, I.: BaghMit 22 (1991) 537-637; 352 fig.

e963 **Ess** Margarete van, *Pedde* Friedhelm, Uruk, Kleinfunde 2, Metall und Asphalt, Farbreste, Fritte/Fayence, Glas, Holz, Knochen/Elfenbein, Leder, Muschel/Perlmutt/Schnecke, Schilf, Textilien: Endb 7. Mainz 1992, von Zabern. xvii-314 p.; 157 pl. 3-8053-1223-7 [OIAc 5,37].

e964 *Dandamayev* Muhammad, Was Eanna destroyed by Darius I?: ArchMIran 25 (1992) 169-171: no, because it continued its normal functions during his reign.

e965 *Frame* Grant, Nabonidus, Nabû-Šarra-Uṣur, and the Eanna temple: ZAss 81 (1991) 37-86; 2 facsimiles.

e966 *a) Rigillo* Maira T., Sealing systems on Uruk doors; – *b) Damerji* Muayad S., Die Tür nach Darstellungen in der altmesopotamischen Bildkunst von der 'Ubaid- bis zur Akkad-Zeit: BaghMitt 22 (1991) 175-222; pl. 26-32 / 231-296 + 194 fig.; pl. 35-38.

e967 *a) Salje* Beate, Keramik der neubabylonischen Zeit...; – *b) Finkbeiner* Uwe, Keramik der seleukidischen und parthischen Zeit (II) aus den Grabungen in Uruk-Warka: BaghMitt 23 (1992) 371-420 + fig. p. 421-464; pl. 72-100 / 473-539 + fig. p. 540-580; pl. 101-120.

e968 *a) Sanati-Müller*, Texte aus dem Sinkašid-Palast 5/2 [*Waetzoldt* Hartmut, eine neue Inschrift]; – *b) Böck* Barbara, *Boehmer* Rainer M., Zwei neusumerische Tontafeln aus Uruk (Kampagne 39, 1989): BaghMitt 23 (1992) 119-161 mit Faksimiles; pl. 12-13 [p. 163-5 + 2 fig.; pl. 14-15] / 77-86; 1 fig.; pl. 10-11.

T6.7   **Arabia.**

e969 *Bauzou* Thomas, Les fastes de la province d'Arabie et les inscriptions des milliaires: Syria 68 (1991) 445-457; 4 fig.

e970 *Costa* Paolo M., Arabia; la civiltà della scure: Archeo 7,90 (1992) 44-52.

e971 *de Maigret* Alessandro, Arabia felix... altopiano yemenita i re sabaei: ArchViva 11,26 (1992) 24-35; ill.

e972 *Müller* Walter W., Südarabien im Altertum; ausgewählte und kommentierte Bibliographie des Jahres 1990: AfO 38s (1990s) 463-6.

e973 **Potts** Daniel T., The Arabian Gulf in antiquity 1990 ⮕ 7,d783:   RAfO 38s (1991s) 239-244 (W. W. *Müller*, auch über sein Abraq ⮕ 7,d787); AJA 96 (1992) 378s (K. *Randsborg*); BA 55 (1992) 234 (J. *Zarins*); Orientalia 61 (1992) 157-161 (M. *Liverani*); RAss 86 (1992) 186-8 (P. *Amiet*); TopO 2 (1992) 195-9 (P. *Lombard*, I) & 201-235 (J.-F. *Salles*, II).

e974 *Salles* Jean-François, Découvertes du golfe arabo-persique aux époques grecque et romaine: RÉAnc 94 (1992) 79-96; map.

e975 **Shahîd** Irfan, Byzantium and the Arabs 1989 ⮕ 7,b467:   RJbÖsByz 41 (1991) 326-9 (K. *Belke*); Speculum 67 (1992) 482-4 (S. T. *Parker*).

e976 *Failaka:* **Højlund** F., Failaka/Dilmun 2, 1987 ⮕ 4,g186:   RSyria 69 (1992) 237s (Y. *Calvet*).

e977 **Jeppesen** Kristian, Ikaros, the Hellenistic settlements 1, 1989 ⮕ 7,d790* ('Kirsten', 'Failaka... sacred enclosure'):   RGnomon 64 (1992) 469-471 (R. A. *Stucky*).

e978 *Hasa:* **Potts** D. T., Miscellanea Hasaitica 1989 ⮕ 5,e259:   RBO 49 (1992) 517-521 (Elizabeth C. L. *During-Caspers*).

e979 *Qatar:* **Inizan** M.-L., Préhistoire à Qatar: Mission française. P 1988, RCiv. – RSovArch (1992,1) 285-7 (K. *Amirkhanov*).

e980 **Shabwa,** Hadramawt S. Yemen (1974-) 1987: Syria 68 (1991) 1-431, ill. (J.-F. *Breton,* al.).
e981 **Pirenne** Jacqueline, Les témoins écrits de la région de Shabwa et l'historie: BAH 134, 1990 ➤ 7,d792: ᴿSyria 68 (1991) 459-462 (F. *Bron*).

T6.9 **Iran,** *Persia;* Asia centralis.

e982 **Gall** Hubertus von, Das Reiterkampfbild in der iranischen und iranisch beeinflussten Kunst parthischer und sasanidischer Zeit: DAI-Teheran 6, 1990 ➤ 7,d800: ᴿMesop-T 27 (1992) 251-7 (A. *Invernizzi*).
e983 **Gunter** Ann C., **Jett** Paul, Ancient Iranian metalwork in Sackler and Freer galleries. Wsh 1992, Smithsonian. 271 p.; ill. [OIAc 5,23].
e984 *Kleiss* Wolfram, *a)* Rechteckige und quadratische Befestigungen in Nordiran; – *b)* Qadjarische Festungen in Nord- und Zentraliran: Arch-MIran 24 (1991) 155-185; 41 fig.+62 fig. Keramik; pl. 24-27 / 269-286; 22 fig.; pl. 47-52.
e985 *Kleiss* Wolfram, *a)* Rechteckige Befestigungen und befestigte Plätze in Iran-II.; – *b)* Siedlungen mit Zitadellenbildung in Iran: ArchMIran 25 (1992) 117-189; 14 fig.; pl. 44-47 / 277-292; 17 fig.+Keramik 29 fig.; pl. 66-70.
e986 *Medvedskaya* Inna, The question of the identification of 8th-7th century Median sites and the formation of the Iranian architectural traditions: ArchMIran 25 (1992) 73-79; 1 fig.
e987 ᶠPERROT Jean, Contribution... Iran, ᴱ**Vallat** F., 1990 ➤ 6, 138: ᴿAfO 38s (1991s) 206-9 (Heidemarie *Koch*).

———

e988 **Darabgird:** *Levit-Tawil* Dalia, The Sasanian rock-relief at Darabgird — a re-evaluation: JNES 51 (1992) 161-180; 13 fig.
e989 **Haft:** *Negahban* E. O., Excavations at Haft Tepe, Iran: MuseumMg 70, 1991 ➤ 7,d807: ᴿPaléorient 18,1 (1992) 141s (J. *Perrot*).
e990 **Hamadan:** *Brodersen* Kai, Ein Weltwunder der Antike in Iran [Ecbatana in C.I. HYGINUS 2. Jh. nicht Persepolis wie in einer Ausstellung]: Arch-MIran 24 (1991) 53-55.
e991 **Hasanlu:** *Kroll* Stephan, Ein 'triple road system' oder 'Stallbauten' in Hasanlu IV B?: ArchMIran 25 (1992) 65-72; 4 fig.
e992 **Khar o Tauran:** *Horne* Lee C., The spatial organization of rural settlement in Khar o Tauran, Iran; an ethnoarchaeological case study: diss. Pensylvania, ᴰ*Dyson* R. Ph 1988. xii-286 p. 89-08341, – OIAc 5,24.
e993 *Horne* Lee, Reading village plans; architecture and social change in northeastern Iran: Expedition 33,1 ('Ethnoarchaeology' 1991) 44-52.
e994 **Lahīru:** *Dandamayev* M. A., Achemenid estates in Lahīru (eastern Babylonia): IrAnt 27 (1992) 117-123.
e995 **Luristan:** **Schmidt** Erich F., († 1964) The Holmes expedition to Luristan [1934-8]: OIP 108, 1989 ➤ 5,e282: ᴿAJA 96 (1992) 179s (R. C. *Henrickson*)
e996 **Marguš:** **Sarianidi** V. I., ⊕ *Drevnosti...* Antiquities of old Marguš. Ašhabal 1990, Vilim. 205 p.; 108 pl. – ᴿMesop-T 27 (1992) 258-265 (G. A. *Košelenko*).
e997 **Pengan:** *Huff* Dietrich, Zum Problem zoroastrischer Grabanlagen in Fars II. Das Säulenmonument von Pengan: ArchMIran 25 (1992) 207-217; fig.; pl. 48-51.

e998 *Persepolis:* Jamzadeh Parivash, *a)* Persepolis, the Achaemenid capital: ➤ 557*, Contacts 1990/2, 267-273; – *b)* The Apadana stairway reliefs and the metaphor of conquest [< diss. California 1991 'The Achaemenid throne']: IrAnt 27 (1992) 125-147; 4 fig.

e999 *Kleiss* Wolfram, Beobachtungen auf dem Burgberg von Persepolis: ArchMIran 25 (1992) 155-167; 15 fig.; pl. 39-43.

g1 *Šeḥ Gabi* (Kangavar, W. Iran) 1971-3: *Henrickson* Elizabeth F., Early everyday economics; distribution of trash and interpretation of activity patterns in an ancient village: BCanadMesop 24 (1992) 33-40; 8 fig.; franç. 33.

g2 *Susa:* Alizadeh Abbas, Prehistoric settlement patterns and cultures in Susiana, southwestern Iran: Gremliza Survey collection; pref. *Wright* Henry T.: Museum of Anthropology, Technical 24. AA 1992, Univ. Michigan. xiv-175 p.; 73 fig. 0-915703-29-7 [OIAc 5,13].

g3 *Grillot-Susini* Françoise, Les textes de fondation du palais de Suse: JAs 278 (1990) 213-222; Eng. 222.

ᴱHarper Prudence O., *al.,* The royal city of Susa 1992 ➤ d497.

Spycket Agnès, Figurines de Suse 1992 ➤ e96.

g5 *Stolper* Matthew W., The Murašû texts from Susa: RAss 86 (1992) 69-77 [likelier Susa in Elam than a village near Nippur].

g6 *Tureng:* Boucharlat Rémy, *al.,* Les fouilles de Tureng Tepe [DESHAYES J. 1960-77]: Mém. 74, 1987 ➤ 4,g221 ... 6,c553; 2-86538-182-X: – ᴿAJA 96 (1992) 380s (D. *Whitehouse*).

---

g7 *Bernard* Paul, *al.,* Fouilles de la mission Franco-Ouzbèque à l'ancienne Samarkand, 2ᵉ, 3ᵉ, 1990s: CRAI (1992) 275-311; 25 fig.

g8 *Hiebert* Fredrik T., *Lamberg-Karlovsky* C.C., Central Asia and the Indo-Iranian borderlands: Iran 30 (1992) 1-15; 4 fig.

g9 Parpola Asko, The coming of the Aryans to Iran and India and the cultural and ethnic identity of the Dasas: StOr 5/64. Helsinki 1988. 83 p. – ᴿRossArkh (1992,3) 249-251 (T. N. *Trunaeva*).

g10 Pitschikjan Igor R., Oxos-Schatz und Oxos-Tempel; achämenidische Kunst in Mittelasien: Antike in der Moderne. B 1992, Akademie. xii-155 p.; 41 fig. 3-05-002145-4 [OIAc 3,33].

g11 *Vidale* Massimo, *Kenoyer* Jonathan M., La civiltà della valle dell'Indo [Mohenjo-Daro, Harappa]: Archeo 7,91 (1992) 55-99.

g12 Zieme Peter, Die Geschichte Zentralasiens in einer neuen Gesamtschau: OlZ 87 (1992) 117-125.

T7.1 Aegyptus, *generalia.*

g13 Arnold D., Die Tempel Ägyptens; Götterwohnungen, Kultstätten, Baudenkmäler. Z 1992, Artemis & W. 239 p. 120 fig. + 80 color. DM 128. [ZAW 105, 518, M. *Köckert*].

g14 Beaucour Fernand, *al.,* The discovery of Egypt, ᵀBallard Bambi. P 1990, Flammarion. 272 p., ill. 2-08-013506-6 [OIAc 3,13, excerpted].

g15 ᴱBerman Lawrence M., The art of Amenhotep III; art historical analysis [Symposium Cleveland Nov. 20-21; 1987]. 1990 ➤ 6,790; ᴿArOr 60 (1992) 201 (B. *Vachala*).

g16 Bonhême Marie-Ange, L'art égyptien? Que sais-je? Nᵒ 1909. P 1992, PUF. 128 p. 2-13-044760-0.

g17 **Bucaille** Maurice,   Mummies of the Pharaohs 1990 ➤ 6,e564; $20: RBAR-W 18,1 (1992) 6 (F. J. *Yurco*).

g18 **Dochniac** Craig C.,   Kingship festival iconography in the Egyptian archaic period: M. A. diss. Arizona, DMcElroy K. Tucson 1992. 82 p. 13-46418. – OIAc 3,19.

g19 **Dunand** Françoise, *Lichtenberg* Roger,   Les momies; un voyage dans l'éternité: Découvertes 118. P 1991, Gallimard. 128 p.; ill. 2-07-053167-8 [OIAc 5,19].

g20 **Goyon** J-C., *Josset* P.,   Un corps pour l'eternité; autopsie d'une momie 1988 ➤ 6,e572: RArOr 60 (1992) 199s (E. *Strouhal*).

g21 **Healy** Mark,   New Kingdom Egypt: [battle] Elite 40. L 1992, Osprey. 64 p.; *McBride* Angus ill.

g22 **Hillinger** Richard, *Loeben* Christian E.,   Obelisken [16 Städte: Stadtresidenz 1992 Ausstellung] Landshut 1992, Stadt. 60 p. 3-927-61206-5 [OIAc 3,24].

g23 **Hope** Murry,   Ancient Egypt; the Sirius connection. Longmead 1990, Element. x-244 p. 1-85230-177-5 [OIAc 3,24].

g24 EHornung Erik,   Zum Bild Ägyptens... Vorträge Konstanz: OBO 95; 1986/90 ➤ 7,645:   RWeltOr 23 (1992) 160-5 (Johanna *Schmitz*).

  James P., *al.*,   Centuries of darkness; a challenge to the conventional chronology of Old World archeology [events assigned since PETRIE to the years 1200-950 must be relocated and the gap closed] 1991 ➤ e370.

g25 **James** T. G. H.,   Egypt: The Living Past. L 1992, British Museum. 208 p.

g26 **Janssen** Rosalind M.,   The first hundred years; Egyptology at University College, London, 1892-1992. L 1992, Univ. College. xvii-105 p.; 29 fig. 0-902137-33-6 [OIAc 5,25].

g27 *Kákosy* László,   King Bocchoris and the Uraeus serpent: AcClas Debrecen 28 (1992) 3-5; 1 fig.

g28 **Kemp** Barry,   Ancient Egypt 1989 ➤ 5,e307; 6,e578:   RJEA 78 (1992) 313-7 (J. J. *Janssen*).

g29 *Kemp* Barry, *Rose* Pamela,   Proportionality in mind and space in ancient Egypt: CamArch 1 (1991) 103-129; 11 fig.

g30 *Lalouette* Claire,   L'Art et la vie dans l'Égypte pharaonique. P 1992, A. Fayard. 330 p., 63 fig. 3-213-02920-2 [OIAc 5,28].

g31 *Leclant* Jean, *Clerc* Gisèle,   Fouilles et travaux en Égypte et au Soudan, 1990-1991:   Orientalia 61 (1992) 214-322; pl. VII-XL; 96 + 26 sites.

g32 *a) Leclant* Jean,   Archaeological activities in Egypt (en français); – *b) Nicholson* Paul T.,   The relation between excavation, ethnoarchaeology and experiment in Egyptology; – *c) Majewska* Aleksandra,   Some remarks on the exhibiting value of ancient Egyptian civilisation in the light of Polish museological studies: ➤ 735, Sesto Eg. 1991/2, 3-9 / 473-9; 1 fig. / 307-311.

g33 **Metwally** Emad El-,   Entwicklung der Grabdekoration in den altägyptischen Privatgräbern; ikonographische Analyse der Totenkultdarstellungen von der Vorgeschichte bis zum Ende der 4. Dynastie: GöOrF 4/24. Wsb 1992, Harrassowitz. xxvi-251 p.; 193 fig. 3-447-03270-7 [OIAc 5,20 'El-Matwally'].

g34 **Michalowski** Kazimierz,   Art of ancient Egypt, TGuterman Norbert. NY c. 1990, Abrams. 600 p., 968 (color.) fig.

g34* *Mortensen* Bodil,   Change in the [Egypt] settlement pattern and population in the beginning of the historical period: ÄgLev 2 (1991) 11-37; 3 fig. (maps).

g35 *Nibbi* Alessandra, The two lands, the black and the red: DiscEg 22 (1992) 9-23.

g36 *Oenbrink* Werner A., Prädynastische Keramik im Archäologischen Museum der Universität Münster: Boreas 14s (1991s) 223-233.

g36* **Osing** Jürgen, Aspects de la culture pharaonique; quatre leçons au Collège de France (1989): AIBL Mém. 12. P 1992, de Boccard. 60 p.; 11 (foldout) fig.

g37 *Pamminger* Peter, Ägyptische Kleinkunst aus der Sammlung Gustav MEMMINGER. Wsb 1991, auct. 216 p. 3-927068-04-7 [BO 50, 136, Magdalena *Stoof*].

g38 ᴱ**Pernigotti** Sergio, L'Egitto antico. Imola 1992, Mandragora. 232 p.; ill. Lit. 40.000. – ᴿArcheo 7,93 (1992) 118 (S. F. *Bondi*).

g38* *Pirelli* Rosanna, Le scene di battaglia nel Nuovo Regno: AION 52 (1992) 353-373.

g39 **Putter** Thierry De, *Karlshausen* Christina, Les pierres utilisées dans la sculpture et l'architecture de l'Égypte pharaonique: Étude 4. Bru 1992, Connaissance de l'Égypte Ancienne. 176 p.; 54 (color.) pl. 2-87268-003-9.

g40 ᴱ**Quirke** Stephen, *Spencer* Jeffrey, The British Museum Book of Ancient Egypt. L 1992, Thames & H. 240 p.; 173 fig. 0-500-01550-3 [OIAc 5,32 'Quircke'].

g41 **Russmann** Edna R., Egyptian sculpture, Cairo and Luxor [92 photos by D. *Finn*] BM 1989 ➤ 6,e590; 7,d850: ᴿBO 49 (1992) 395-8 (Elisabeth *Delange*).

g42 **Scott** Gerry D.ᴵᴵᴵ, Temple, tomb and dwelling; Egyptian antiquities from the Harer family trust collection [154 objects]. San Bernardino 1992, California State Univ. Art Gallery. xv-207 p.; ill. 0-945486-08-1 [OIAc 3,37].

g43 *Siliotti* Alberto, La memoria dell'Egitto... CHAMPOLLION... Quel giorno a Rosetta: ArchViva 10,16 (1991) 36-47; color. ill.

g44 **Smith** G. Elliot, *Dawson* Warren R., Egyptian mummies. L 1991 = 1924, Kegan Paul. £8 pa. – ᴿDiscEg 21 (1991) 79s (A. R. *David* speaks of a 'new edition' but with no indication of changes, and 'some statements made in this work have now been superseded').

g45 **Sourdive** Claude, La main dans l'Égypte pharaonique 1984 ➤ 4,c237: ᴿCdÉ 66 (1991) 148-155 (Nicole *Genaille*).

g46 **Syndram** Dirk, Ägypten-Faszination; Untersuchungen zum Ägyptenbild im europäischen Klassizismus 1990 ➤ 6,e593: ᴿDLZ 113 (1992) 273-5 (B. *Brentjes*).

g47 **Syriani** Samuel al-, *Habib* Badri, Guide to ancient Coptic churches and monasteries in Upper Egypt 1990 ➤ 6,e594; 7,d854: – ᴿBSACopte 30 (1991) 145 (M. A. *Roy*).

g48 **Tefnin** Roland, Éléments pour une sémiologie de l'image égyptienne: CdÉ 66 (1992) 60-88; 5 fig.

g49 **Valbelle** Dominique, L'Égyptologie: Que sais-je? 1312. P 1991, PUF. 127 p. F 32. – ᴿMondeB 72 (1991) 61 (J.-L. *Huot*).

g50 **Vercoutter** Jean, L'Égypte ancienne[13]: Que sais-je? P 1990, PUF. 127 p. 2-13-043516-5. – ᴿDiscEg 21 (1991) 81 (A. *Dodson*).

g51 **Vercoutter** Jean, The search for ancient Egypt [1986],ᵀ, NY 1992, Abrams. 208 p. 0-8109-2817-5 [OIAc 3,41].

g52 **Vercoutter** Jean, L'antico Egitto; archeologia di una civiltà. T 1992, Electa/Gallimard. 192 p.; color. ill. Lit. 18.000. 88-445-0001-9. – ᴿArcheo 7,91 (1992) 125s (S. *Pernigotti*).

g53 **Vivian** Cassandra, *a*) Father of rivers; a traveler's companion to the Nile Valley; – *b*) Islands of the Blest, a guide to the oases and western desert of Egypt; – *c*) (with *Ryan* Nigel), Siwa Oasis; its history, sites and crafts: Monessen PA 1989, Trade Route. 290 p. / 309 p. / 1991, 28 p. 977-5100-00-3; -2-0; -2-X [OIAc 3,41].

g53* *West* Stephanie, Sesostris' stelae (HERODOTUS 2, 102-106): Historia 41 (1992) 117-120.

g54 **Wilkinson** Charles K., Egyptian wall paintings; the Metropolitan Museum of Art's collection of facsimiles. NY 1983, Met. 165 p.; ill. 0-87099-325-9.

g55 **Wilkinson** Richard H., Reading Egyptian art; a hieroglyphic guide to ancient Egyptian painting and sculpture. L 1992, Thames & H. 224 p. 0-500-05064-3 [OIAc 3,42].

g56 **Ziegler** Christiane, [Louvre] Catalogue des stèles, peintures, et reliefs ... 1990 ➤ 6,d5: ᴿOrientalia 61 (1992) 142-6 (H. G. *Fischer*).

T7.2 **Luxor,**   *Karnak* [East Bank] -   **Thebae** [West Bank].

g57 **Lalouette** Claire, Thèbes ou la naissance d'un empire 1986 ➤ 2,b45: ᴿCdÉ 67 (1992) 76-78 (E. *Maraite*).

g58 *Saghir* Mohammed El-, Das Statuenversteck im Luxortempel: Bildbände Archäologie 6. Mainz 1992, von Zabern. 76 p.; 165 fig. 3-8053-1259-8 [OIAc 5,20].

g59 *Saghir* Mohammed El-, The great processional way of Thebes (the avenue of sphinxes of Luxor): ➤ 735, Sesto Eg. 1991, 2, 181-3 + 14 phot.

g60 **Saleh** Mohammed, Luxor temple; a brief guide[2] [[1]1987]. Giza 1989, Prism. 6 p.; 50 pl. 977-1495-11-9. – ᴿDiscEg 19 (1991) 87s (J. *Malek*).

g61 *Albouy* M., *al.,* Il tempio di Karnak vive ancora: ArchViva 10,22 (1991) 32-51; color. ill., 40s & 44s, splendid bird's eye drawings with identifications.

g62 *Alfi* Mostafa El-, La liste de rois de Karnak: DiscEg 19 (1991) 29-36.

g63 *a*) Karnak Temple C, 1st 1986; 2d 1987: JSStEg 18 (1988) 1-23; 18 fig. D. B. *Redford,* al.) – *b*) East Karnak Akhenaten Temple project 20th 1991: JSStEg 18 (1988!) 24-48; 10 fig. pl. XIV-XXI (D. *Redford,* al.) – *c*) East Karnak excavations, 1987-9: JAmEg 28 (1991) 75-106; 27 fig. (D. *Redford, al.*).

g63* *Dégardin* Jean-Claude, Khonsou et ses compagnes dans son temple de Karnak: ➤ 96, ꟻKÁKOSY L., 1992, 101-112.

g64 **Murnane** W. J., The road to Kadesh ... Sety/Karnak: SAOC 42, [2]1990 ([1]1985) ➤ 6,e601: ᴿOLZ 87 (1992) 522s (K. A. *Kitchen*: much better printed).

g65 *Eaton-Krauss* Marianne, *Murnane* William J., Tutankhamun, Ay, and the avenue of sphinxes between Pylon X and the Mut precinct at Karnak: BSocEg 15 (Genève 1991) 31-38.

g66 **Gohary** Jocelyn, Akhenaten's Sed-festival at Karnak: StEg. L 1992, Kegan Paul. x-238 p.; 110 (foldout.) fig. 0-7103-0380-7.

g67 **Golvin** J.-C., *Goyon* J.-C., Les bâtisseurs de Karnak 1987 ➤ 3,e718; 5,e330: ᴿCdÉ 67 (1992) 83-86 (R. *Tefnin*).

g68 **David** A. R., *Tapp* E., The mummy's tale; the scientific and medical investigation of Natsef-Amun, priest in the temple of Karnak. L 1992, O'Mara, 176 p., 69 fig. 1-85479-135-4 [OIAc 5,18].

g69 **Hornung** E., The tomb of Pharaoh Seti I / Das Grab Sethos' I. Z 1991, Artemis. 264 p.; 234 phot. + 8 color. (*Burton* H.) [BO 49,585]. – ᴿTyche 7 (1992) 243s (G. *Dobesch*).

g70 ᴱ**Hornung** Erik, *Staehelin* Elisabeth, Sethos, ein Pharaonengrab; Dokumentation zu einer Ausstellung des Ägyptologischen Seminars der Universität Basel im Antikenmuseum 1991s. Ba 1991s, Freunde. 112 p.; 68 fig.

g71 **Jong** Willem J. de, Thebe, Wachtkamer van de eeuwigheit. Amst 1992, Djedoetimes. 198 p.; 199 fig. 90-80-10171-5 [OIAc 5,18].

g72 **Abitz** Friedrich, Ramses III. in den Gräbern seiner Söhne: OBO 72, 1986 ⇒ 5,e339... 7,d866: ᴿCdÉ 66 (1991) 180s (W. J. *Murnane*).

g73 **Abitz** Friedrich, Baugeschichte und Dekoration des Grabes Ramses' VI: OBO 89, 1989 ⇒ 5,a338... 7,d867: ᴿArOr 60 (1992) 307s (L. *Bareš*).

g74 — *Stricker* B. H., The enemies of Re', 1. The doctrine of ascesis [Ramses VI tomb vignettes, *Piankoff* A. 1953]: DiscEg 23 (1992) 45-76; 16 fig.

g75 *Smith* Stuart T., Intact tombs of the seventeenth and eighteenth dynasties from Thebes and the New Kingdom burial system: MiDAI-K 42 (1992) 193-231; 9 fig.

g76 **Reeves** Nicholas, The complete Tutankhamun; the king, the tomb, the royal treasure 1990 ⇒ 6,e627; 7,d869*: ᴿAJA 96 (1992) 560s (Nancy *Serwiny*); DiscEg 21 (1991) 109-112 (C. *Walters*).

g77 ᴱ**Reeves** Carl Nicholas, After Tut'ankhamūn; research and excavation in the royal necropolis at Thebes [Carnavaron meeting, 15 June 1990; 13 art]: Studies in Egyptology. L 1992, Kegan Paul. xv-211 p.; 40 fig.; 24 pl. 0-7103-0406-4.

g78 **Beinlich** Horst, *Saleh* Mohamed, Corpus der hieroglyphischen Inschriften aus dem Grab des Tutanchamun 1989 ⇒ 5,e342 .. 7,d869. 145. 0-9004-1653-X: ᴿJEA 78 (1992) 333-6 (M. *Eaton-Krauss*).

g79 **Eaton-Krauss** M., *Graefe* E., The small golden shrine from the tomb of Tutankhamun 1985 ⇒ 1,c138... 5,e348: ᴿCdÉ 66 (1991) 181-4 (C. *Vandersleyen*).

g80 **Johnson** W. Raymond, An Asiatic battle scene of Tutankhamun from Thebes; a Late Amarna antecedent of the Ramesside battle-narrative tradition; diss. ᴰ*Wente* E. Chicago 1992. viii-194 p. – OIAc 3,25.

g81 **Reeves** C. N., Valley of the Kings; the decline of a royal necropolis [diss Durham 1984, ᴰ*Harris* J.]: StEg, 1990 ⇒ 6,e626: ᴿBO 49 (1992) 706-717 (M. *Eaton-Krauss*: imperative but exasperating).

g82 *Siliotti* Alberto, Il risveglio di Nefertari [Tebe valle delle regine]: Arch-Viva 10,18 (1991) 32-51; color. ill.

g83 **Barthelmess** Petra, Der Übergang ins Jenseits in den thebanischen Beamtengräbern der Ramessidenzeit: StAGAä 2. Heid 1992, Orient. xvi-201 p. 3-927552-04-6.

g84 **Bay-Grab** (KV 13) 1.-4., Vorb. 2.: StAäK 19 (1992) 15-36; 7 fig. (H. *Altenmüller*).

g84* **Dorman** Peter F., The tombs of Senenmut; the architecture and decoration of tombs 71 and 353 [?Thebes]: EgExped 24. NY 1991, Metropolitan Museum. 181 p.; 96 pl. 0-87099-620-7 [OIAc 3,19].

g85 *Kákosy* L., Seventh preliminary report on the Hungarian excavation in Theban tomb 32 (season 1990): AcAHung 44 (1992) 193-212; 12 fig.

g86 **Assmann** Jan, *al.,* Das Grab des Amenemope TT 41: Theben 3. Mainz 1991, von Zabern. I. x-299 p.; II. LXXXIV pl.; 76 Beilagen. 3-8053-1091-9.

g87 **Dziobek** Eberhard, Das Grab des Ineni Theben Nr. 81 [< Diss. Heid 1985]: DAI-K ArchVeröff 68. Mainz 1992, von Zabern. 149 p.; 71 pl. 3-8053-0975-9 [OIAc 3,19].

g88 **Dziobek** Eberhard, *al.,* Eine ikonographische Datierungsmethode für thebanische Wandmalereien der 18. Dynastie: StAGAä 3. Heid 1992, Orient. ix-85 p.; 8 pl. 3-927552-05-4 [OIAc 5,20].

g89 **Seyfried** Karl, *al.,* Das Grab des Amonmose (TT373): Theben 4. Mainz 1990, von Zabern. ix-324 p., 276 fig., 28 pl.; 65 pl. + 4 color.; 12 maps. 3-8053-1089-7. – ᴿArOr 60 (1992) 202s (B. *Vachala*).

g90 *a) Vandersleyen* Claude, The sculpture in the round of Amenhotep III; types and purposes; – *b) Kozloff* Ariel P., Theban tomb paintings from the reign of Amenhotep III; problems in iconography and chronology; – *c) Bothmer* Bernard V., Eyes and iconography in the splendid century; King Amenhotep III and his aftermath; → 700c, Amenhotep 1987/90, 1-8 / 55-64; pl. 14-17 / 84-88; pl. 20-27.

g91 **Wachsmann** S., Aegeans in the Theban tombs 1987 → 3,e746... 7,d885: ᴿBASOR 285 (1992) 86s (A. F. *Rainey*).

g92 **Manniche** Lise, Lost tombs (diss. C 1985) 1988 → 6,e624: ᴿCdE 67 (1992) 86-89 (A. *Mekhitarian*).

g93 *Niwinski* Andrzej, Studies on the illustrated Theban funerary papyri of the 11th and 10th centuries B.C.: OBO 86, 1989 → 6,e625: ᴿBL 49 (1992) 375-9 (Irmtraud *Munro*).

g94 **Shedid** Abdel-Ghaffar, *Seidel* Matthias, Das Grab des Nacht; Kunst und Geschichte eines Beamtengrabes der 18. Dynastie in Theben-West. Mainz 1991, von Zabern. 83 p.; ill. 3-8053-1332-2 [OIAc 5,34].

g95 *Deir el-Bahari* 1982-5, 1986-8: ÉtTrav 16 (Wsz 1992) 435-485; 41 fig. (Z. *Wysocki*).

g96 *Szafrański* Zbigniew E., Pottery from the time of construction of the Hatshepsut temple: DiscEg 22 (1992) 54-59 (-78), 12 fig.

g97 *Wysocki* Zygmunt, The temple of Queen Hatshepsut at Deir el Bahari; the raisng of the structure in view of architectural studies [two phases of differing spatial plan, each executed in several stages]: MiDAI-K 42 (1992) 233-254; 2 fig.; pl 42-47.

g98 *Donohue* V. A., The goddess of the Theban mountain [Deir el-Bahri cliff colossal-statue group]: Antiquity 66 (1992) 871-885; 9 fig.

g99 *Ramesseum:* ᴱ**Goedicke** Hans, Perspectives on the battle of Kadesh 1985 → 1,e428: ᴿDiscEg 20 (1991) 107-112 (E. P. *Uphill*).

g100 *a) Kitchen* K. A., The vintages of the Ramesseum; – *b) Broadhurst* Clive, Religious considerations at Qadesh, and the consequences for the artistic depiction of the battle; – *c) Donohue* V. A., A gesture of submission [Ramesside portrayals of sea-peoples siege ...]: → 72, ᶠGRIFFITHS J. G. 1992, 115-123; 1 fig. / 77-81 / 82-92 + 22 fig., key p. 113s.

g102 *Bietak* Manfred, An iron age four-room house in Ramesside Egypt [within Thebes Aya-Horemheb temenos]: → 18, ᶠBIRAN A., ErIsr 23 (1992) 10*-12*; 1 fig.

g103 **Medinet Habu:** *Essche-Merchez* Éric van, La syntaxe formelle des reliefs et de la grande inscription de l'an 8 de Ramsès III à Médinet Habou: CdÉ 67 (1992) 211-239; 10 fig.

g104 **Ventura** Raphael,   Living in a city of the dead...: OBO 69, 1986 ➤ 3,e752 ... 7,d887: ᴿCdÉ 67 (1992) 277-281 (C. J. *Eyre*).

g105 **Deir/Medina:** **McDowell** A., Jurisdiction in the workmen's community of Deir el Medina: Eg.Uitgaven 5. Leiden 1990, Ned.Inst.Nab. Oosten. xii-308 p. *f*65. 90-6258-205-2; ➤ 6,e633: ᴿBO 49 (1992) 379-386 (S. *Allam*, unfavoring: ᴰ*Silverman* D. 'in reality *Janssen* J.'); DiscEg 23 (1992) 99-109 (D. *Lorton*).

g106 a) *Bierbrier* M. L., [Deir el-Medina, Valley of Kings/Queens workmen's village] Genealogy and chronology; theory and practice; – b) *McDowell* Andrea, Awareness of the past in Deir el-Medīna; – c) *Häring* B., Libyans in the late twentieth dynasty / Bibliography 1980-90: ➤ 684, Village voices 1991/2, 1-7 / 95-109 / 71-80 . 111-140.

g107 **Gurna:** *Dupont* Pierre, *Goyon* Jean-Claude,   Amphores grecques archaïques de Gurna; à propos d'une publication récente [Mʏꜱʟɪᴡɪᴇᴄ K. 1987]: ➤ 735, Sesto Eg 1991/2, 153-165 + 3 fig.

g108 *Bickel* Susanne,   Blocs d'Amenhotep III réemployés dans le temple de Merenptah à Gourna, une porte monumentale: BIFAO 92 (1992) 1-13; 6 fig.

g109 *Jaritz* Horst,   Der Totentempel des Merenptah in Qurna, 1. Grabungsbericht (1.-6. Kampagne) [Schweiz. Inst. 1971-1991]: MiDAI-K 48 (1992) 65-91; 4 fig.; pl. 11-15.

g110 **Dra⁰ Abul-Naga,** Theben-West, 1st 1991: MiDAI-K 42 (1992) 109-130; 12 fig.; pl. 22-27 (D. *Polz*).

T7.3   **Amarna.**

g111 *Boddens Hosang* F. J. E.,   Two Amarna collections in the Netherlands: OMRO 72 (1992) 15-38 + 15 pl.

g112 *Bolshakov* Andrey O.,   Two Amarna objects in the Hermitage museum: GöMiszÄg 126 (1992) 23-27; 2 pl.

Gohary Jocelyn, Akhenaten's Sed-festival at Karnak 1992 ➤ g66.

g113 a) *Holthoer* Rostislav,   Hittite origin of the [Amarna] 'Syrian winejars'; – b) *Dodson* Aidan, KV 55 and the end of the reign of Akhenaten: ➤ 735, Sesto Eg. 1991/2, 313-321 + 8 fig. / 135-8 + 4 fig.; Nefertiti's crown ➤ d898b.

g114 *Karcher* Chris,   The sun disk's horizon; life in the city of Akhenaten and Nefertiti [San Antonio exhibition 1992]: VarAcg 8 (1992) 65-68; 3 fig.

g115 *Karlshausen* C., *Putter* T. de,   Why did Akhenaten forsake the use of pink granite?: GöMiszÄg 130 (1992) 21-23: for religious considerations.

g116 **Kemp** Barry J.,   Amarna reports V, 1989 ➤ 7,d895b: ᴿOLZ 87 (1992) 26s (M. *Mode*).

g117 **Khouli** A. El-, *Kanawati* N.,   Quseir el-Amarna, tombs... 1989 ➤ 5,e379; 6,e644: ᴿDiscEg 20 (1991) 75-87 (Robyn A. *Gillam*).

g118 *Loeben* Christian E.,   No evidence of coregency; zwei getilgte Inschriften aus dem Grab von Tutanchamun: BSocÉg 15 (Genève 1991) 81-90; 4 fig.

g119 *Loose* A. A.,   Woonhuizen in Amarna en het domein van de vrouwen: PhoenixEOL 38,2 (1992) 16-29; 3 fig + 1 color.

g120 **Martin** Geoffrey T.,   The royal tomb at El-ᶜAmarna [1. 1974] 2, The reliefs, inscriptions, and architecture: RockTombs 7, Mem. 39, 1987 ➤ 6, e646: ᴿArOr 60 (1992) 203s (B. *Vachala*).

g121 **Martin** Geoffrey T., A bibliography of the Amarna period 1991
➤ 7,d898: ᴿDiscEg 21 (1991) 97-100 (Angela P. *Thomas* adds a few).

g122 ᵀᴱ**Moran** William L., The Amarna letters [français 1987 ➤ 3,a766...
7,d899]. Baltimore 1992, Johns Hopkins Univ. xlvii-393 p.; map. $78.
0-8018-4251-4.

g123 *Naʾaman* Nadav, Amarna letters: ➤ 741, AnchorBD 1 (1992) 174-181
(-2, Tell el-, *Redford* D. B.).

g124 **Osman** Ahmed, Pharaoh of Egypt; the mystery of Akhenaten resolved.
L 1990, Grafton. 262 p. 0-246-13665-0 [OIAc 3,32].
Reeves N., The complete Tutankhamun 1990 ➤ g76.

g125 *Robins* G., The mother of Tutankhamun: DiscEg 20 (1991) 71-73
[could have been Nefertiti rather than Kiya as REEVES N. 1990]; 22 (1992)
25-28 notes Kiya wrongly cited as 'born to Kiya' and adds further data.

g126 **Schlögl** Hermann A., Echnaton-Tutanchamun, Fakten und Texte²ʳᵉᵛ
[¹1983 ➤ 64,b862]. Wsb 1989, Harrassowitz. x-88 p. DM 30. – BO 49
(1992) 431.

g127 *Shaw* Ian, [Amarna] Ideal homes in ancient Egypt; the archaeology of
social aspiration: CamArch 2 (1992) 147-166; 13 fig.

g128 *Vries* Hilbert G. de, Amarna en de polytheistische traditie: GöMiszÄg
129 (1992) 109-112.

g129 *Weatherhead* Fran, Painted pavements in the great palace at Amarna:
JEA 78 (1992) 179-194; 6 fig.; pl. XXIV-XV.

T7.4 **Memphis**, *Ṣaqqara* – **Pyramides**, *Giza* (Cairo).

g130 *Abdalla* Aly, The cenotaph of the Sekwaskhet family from Saqqara:
JEA 78 (1992) 93-111; 6 fig.; pl. XIX-XXIII.

g131 *Allen* James B., Menes the Memphite: GöMiszÄg 126 (1992) 19-22.

g132 **Cherpion** Nadine, Mastabas et hypogées de l'Ancien Empire 1989 ➤ 5,
e387; 7,d906: ᴿDiscEg 20 (1991) 93-98 (J. *Malek*); JEA 78 (1992) 324-6
(N. *Kanawati*).

g133 *Giddy* Lisa, *Jeffreys* David, Memphis 1991: JEA 78 (1992) 1-11; 5 fig.;
2 pl. (13-18 epigraphy, *Malek* Jaromir, *Quirke* Stephen).

g134 *Malek* Jaromir, A meeting of the old and new; Saqqāra during the
New Kingdom: ➤ 72, ᶠGRIFFITHS J. G. 1992, 57-76; 3 fig.; pl. V-VI.

g135 **Khouli** A. El-, *Kanawati* N., Excavations at Saqqara, II. north-west of
Teti's pyramid 1988 ➤ 5,e391: ᴿDiscEg 20 (1991) 89-92 (Diana *Magee*,
with an index to the private names and titles).

g136 *Martin* G.T., The Memphite tomb of Horemheb, I. 1989 ➤ 5,e349;
6,e660: ᴿArOr 60 (1992) 308s (B. *Vachala*); JEA 78 (1992) 336-8 (M.
Eaton-Krauss).

g137 — **Arnst** Caris-Beatrice, Die Aussagekraft unscheinbarer Motive; vier
memphitische 'NN'-Reliefs aus der Zeit Tutanchamuns und ihre mögliche
Zuordnung zum Grab des Haremheb: BSocÉg 15 (Genève 1991) 5-30;
17 fig.

g138 **Martin** Geoffrey T., The hidden tombs of Memphis 1991 ➤ 7,d910:
ᴿDiscEg 21 (1991) 95s (S. *Snape*); JField 19 (1992) 409-413 (J. *Taylor*).
Maystre Charles, Les grands prêtres de Ptah de Memphis: OBO 113, 1992
➤ b493.

g139 *Dijk* Jacobus van, Hieratic inscriptions from the tomb of Maya at
Saqqara; a preliminary survey: GöMiszÄg 127 (1992) 23-32.

g140 **Giddy** Lisa L., The Anubieion at Saqqāra, II. The cemeteries: Excav-
Mem 56. L 1992, Egypt Explor. xx-103 p.

g141 *Prévot* Pierre, Observations sur des stèles du Sérapéum de Memphis: RÉgp 43 (1992) 215-221.

g142 *Bourriau* Janine, The Memphis pottery project: CamArch 1 (1991) 263-8; 2 fig.

g143 **Thompson** Dorothy J., Memphis under the Ptolemies 1988 → 4,g340 ... 7,d915: ᴿBonnJbb 192 (1992) 615-8 (W. *Huss*); HZ 253 (1991) 704s (H. *Sonnabend*).

g144 **Simpson** William K., The mastabas of Qar and Idu / of the western cemetery: Giza Mastabas 2.4. Boston 1976/80, Museum of Fine Arts (with Ph/Yale). vi-31 p.; 43 fig.; XXXIV pl. / vii-37 p.; 52 fig.; LXI pl. 0-87846-093-4; -156-6.

g145 **Lauer** Jean-Philippe, Les pyramides de Sakkara⁶ʳᵉᵛ. Le Caire 1991, IFAO. 145 p.; 90 fig. 2-7247-0099-6.

g146 **Goyon** Georges, Le secret des bâtisseurs des grandes pyramides; Khéops²ʳᵉᵛ. P 1990, Pygmalion. 316 p.; 103 fig.; 16 pl. 2-85704-315-5.

g147 **Hart** George, Pharaohs and pyramids; a guide through Old Kingdom Egypt; pref. *Cunliffe* Barry. L 1991, Herbert. 240 p.; 50 fig.; 101 phot. 1-871-56936-2 [OIAc 5,24].

g148 **Kerisel** Jean, La pyramide à travers les âges: Art et Religions. P 1991, École Ponts et Chaussées. 213 p.; 120 fig. 2-85978-166-8 [OIAc 5,26].

g149 ᴱ**Haarman** Ulrich, Das Pyramidenbuch des Abū Ǧaʿfar al-IDRĪSĪ (649/1251): BeirutTSt 38. Stu 1991, Steiner. xi-94 p. + ⊕ 283. DM 98 [JAOS 112,728].

g150 **Stadelmann** Rainer, Die grossen Pyramiden van Giza 1990 → 6,e686: ᴿBO 49 (1992) 386-392 (J. *Brinks*: about the pyramids, only half at Giza; some confusion about step-by-step construction).

g151 *Abitz* Friedrich, Der Bau der grossen Pyramide mit einem Schrägaufzug: ZäSpr 119 (1992) 61-82; 11 fig.

g152 *a) Hönig* Werner, Die Cheopspyramide, 'Grosser Gang' zur Galerie; – *b) Legon* J. A. R., On pyramid dimensions and proportions; – *c) Pomerantseva* Natalia, The geometrical basis of the proportional canon in ancient Egyptian art: DiscEg 20 (1991) 19-23 / 25-34 / 45-70; 12 fig.

g153 *Pitlik* Herbert, Ing., Baustelle Cheops Pyramide: *a)* Auszug Bau- und Nutzholz-Wasser-Transporte: GöMiszÄg 127 (1992) 81-86; 3 fig.; – *b)* Auszug Rampen und Materialtransporte: GöMiszÄg 129 (1992) 83-86; 1 fig.

g154 *Stierlin* Henri, La barque royale de Khéops: Archéologia 267 (1991) 26-33; color. ill.

g155 *a) Deaton* J. C., On the Egyptian origin for the legend of an island under the Great Pyramid; – *b) Rousseau* Jean, Analyse dimensionnelle de la Pyramide de Chéops; – *c) Testa* Pietro, Il progetto del sarcofago del re Khefren: DiscEg 22 (1992) 5s / 29-52 / 23 (1992) 77-81.

g156 *Neumann* Claudio, The sarcophagus in Khephren's pyramid; its design and construction: DiscEg 19 (1991) 47-52; 4 fig.

g157 **Sers** Jean-François, Le secret de la pyramide de Khephren: L'homme et l'univers. P 1992, Rocher. 144 p.; 39 fig. 2-268-01247-6 [OIAc 5,34].

g158 *Heick-Hansen* Bent, The Sphinx temple: → 735, Sesto Eg. 1991/2, 243-5 + 2 plans.

g159 *Lehner* Mark, [Computer-] Reconstructing the Sphinx: CamArch 2 (1992) 3-26.

g160 **Arnold** Dieter, The south cemeteries of Lisht, 1. The pyramid of Senwosret I 1988 ► 5,e415: ᴿJEA 78 (1992) 328-330 (M. *Verner*).
g161 **Arnold** Dieter, *al.*, The pyramid complex of Senwosret I: South cemeteries of Lisht 3. NY 1992, Metropolitan Museum. 118 p.; 133 pl.; foldout plans. 0-87099-612-6.
g162 *Deaton* John C., The evidence for a second pyramid complex for Cheops near El-Lisht [GOEDICKE H. 1971]: DiscEg 21 (1991) 7s.; 22 (1992) also 7s. Goedicke, 'the so-called evidence'.
g163 [*Dahšur*]: *Dorner* Josef, Die Form der Knickpyramide: GöMiszÄg [116 (1990) 65-72, *Legon* J.] 126 (1992) 39-45.
g164 *Legon* J.A.R., The problem of the bent pyramid: GöMiszÄg 130 (1992) 49-56.

g165 *Moussa* Ahmed M., A lintel of Ramesses II from Atfih [Giza]: Orientalia 61 (1992) 92; 93, fig.; pl. V.
g166 *Abusir* 1990s: ZäSpr 119 (1992) 108-116-124 (*Bareš* L., shaft tomb; *Verner* M., survey).

g167 **Kubiak** Władisław, Al-Fustat ᴰ1987 ► 5,e419...7,d927: ᴿBO 49 (1992) 558s (D. *Whitehouse*: of archeological interest though entirely from written evidence).

т7.5 **Delta Nili.**

g168 *Alexandrie* 1986/7: ÉtTrav 16 (Wsz 1992) 337-351; 9 fig. (Z. *Kiss*).
g169 *Altheim-Stiehl* Ruth, Wurde Alexandreia im Juni 619 n. Chr. durch die Perser erobert? Bemerkungen zur zeitlichen Bestimmung der sāsānidi-schen Besetzung Ägyptens unter Chosrau II. Parwez: Tyche 6 (1991) 3-16.
g170 *Burkhalter* Fabienne, Le gymnase d'Alexandrie [STRABON 17,1,10], cen-tre administratif de la province romaine d'Égypte: BCH 116 (1992) 345-373; 14 fig.
g171 **Canfora** Luciano, The vanished [Alexandria] library [1990 franç. ► 5, e424; ital. 1990 ► 7,d935]; Hellenistic Culture and Society 7. Berkeley 1989, Univ. California. ix-205 p. $20. – ᴿClasW 85 (1991s) 247s (Victoria *Foertmeyer*); CurrTMiss 19 (1992) 139s (E. *Krentz*).
g172 **Delia** Diana, Alexandrian citizenship during the Roman principate [< diss. 1983, Columbia]: AmClasSt 33. Atlanta 1991, Scholars. 210 p. [NewsAmEg 158s, 20]. 1-55540-526-8.
g173 *Frankfurter* David, Let Egypt's city be deserted; religion and ideology in the Egyptian response to the Jewish revolt (116-117 C.E.): JJS 43 (1992) 203-219.
g174 **Kiss** Zsolt, Les ampoules de Saint Ménas découvertes à Kôm al-Dikka (1961-1981): Alexandrie 5; Centre polonais méditerranéen. Wsz 1989, PWN. 83-01-08718-8. – ᴿBO 49 (1992) 421s (K. C. *Innemée*).
g175 *a*) *Kołodziejczyk* Kamila, Remarques sur les thermes privés à Kôm el-Dikka (Alexandrie); – *b*) *Kiss* Zsolt, Un sphinx sur un plat romain tardif à KD-A; – *c*) *Lichocka* Barbara, Un 'trésor' de monnaies

byzantines à KD-A: ÉtTrav 16 (Wsz 1992) 57-65; 4 fig. / 29-34; 3 fig. / 67-79; 7 fig.

g176 *Abou el-Atta* Hussein,   The relation between the Egyptian tombs and the Alexandrian hypogea: ÉtTrav 16 (Wsz 1992) 11-19.

g177 ᶠMONDÉSERT C.,   Alexandrina 1987 ➤ 3,117; 7,d933:   ᴿTR 88 (1992) 30-32 (M.-Barbara von *Stritzky*).

g178 *Rodenbeck* John,   Alexandrian literature: NewsAmEg 156s (1992) 1-19.

g178* *Spencer* A. J.,   [10] Roman sites in the northwest Delta: ➤ 96, ᶠKÁ-KOSY L. 1992, 535-8 + map.

g179 *a) Thaezow* Barbara,   Archaeological sources for the earliest churches in Alexandria; – *b) Parandowski* Piotr,   Coptic terra-cotta figurines from Kôm el-Dikka: ➤ 690, 3d Coptic 1984/90, 431-5; plan / 303-7; 4 fig.

g180 *Buto*-Faraʿin 1987: ➤ 703, Nile Delta 1990/2, 1-10 (T. von der *Way*; 11-22 pottery, Christiana E. *Köhler*).

g180* *Thanheiser* Ursula,   Untersuchungen zur Landwirtschaft der vor- und frühdynastischen Zeit in Tell-el-Faraʿin-Buto: ÄgLev 2 (1991) 39-45.

g181 *Ibrahim Awad* 1988-90: ➤ 703, Nile Delta 1990/2, 43-68 (E. van den *Brink*); 79-96, lithic (K. *Schmidt*); 97-110, fauna (J. *Boessneck*, Angela von den *Driesch*); 111-126, flora (G. de *Roller*, al.); 69-78, a temple (D. *Eigner*).

g182 *Mendes*, t. Rubʿa, 1st 1991: JSStEg 18 (1988!) 49-79; 9 fig., pl. I-XIII ᵖ (D. *Redford*, al.).

g183 Rubʿa (Mendes): NewsAmEg 155 (1991) 1-4 (D. B. *Redford*).

g184 Mendes 1990: ➤ 703, Nile Delta 1990/2, 191-206 (D. *Brewer*, al.).

g185 *Minshat Abu Omar:* ➤ 703, Nile Delta 1990/2, 127-170 (Karla *Kroeper*, al.).

g186 *Pithom:*   *Paice* Patricia,   The Punt relief, the Pithom stele, and the periplus of the Erythraean Sea [page-headings: Trade in the Nile Delta]: ➤ 557*, Contacts 1990/2, 227-235.

g187 *Qanṭîr*-Dabʿa: *a) Hein* Irmgard, Two excavation areas from Tell el-Dabʿa; *b) Jánosi* Peter,   Recent excavations of the Austrian Archaeological Institute at the village of ʿEzbet/Helmi/Tell el-Qirqafa near Tell el-Dabʿa: ➤ 735, Sesto Eg. 1991/2, 249-251 + 2 plans / 345-9; 1 plan.

g187* *Bietak* Manfred,   Der Friedhof in einem Palastgarten aus der Zeit des späten Mittleren Reiches und anderc Forschungsergebnisse aus dem östlichen Nildelta (Tell el-Dabʿa 1984-7): ÄgLev 2 (1991) 47-75 + 33 pl. [111-8, 2 color. pl., *Walberg* Gisela, gold pendant; finds and Minoan chronology].

Boessneck J., *Driesch* A. v.d., Tell el-Dabʾa VII, Tiere 1992 ➤ g852.

g188 *Dever* William G.,   Tell el-Dabʿa and the Levantine Middle Bronzc Age chronology; a rejoinder to Manfred BIETAK: BASOR 281 (1991) 73-79.

g189 *Saft el-Henna* + 5:   **Snape** S. R.,   Liverpool University Delta Survey; six archaeological sites in Sharqiyeh province 1986 ➤ 5,e434 [ʾZagazigʾ]: ᴿCdÉ 67 (1992) 82s (H. De *Meulenaere*).

g190 *Tanis:*   *Geoffroy* Bérénice, Tanis, ʾles pharaons de lʾincertitudeʾ: Archéologia 272 (1991) 32-37; color. ill.

T7.6   *Alii situs Aegypti* **alphabetice**

g191 *Abu Mina* (1989): BSACopte 30 (1991) 65-75; 3 fig.; 3 pl. (P. *Grossmann*, J. *Kosciuk*).

g192 Abû Mînâ (... Quft) 1990: BSACopte 31 (1992) 25-30 (P. *Grossmann*; 31-41 sundial, J. *Kosciuk*).

g193 *Abu Sha‘ar* (Red Sea coast) 1990: NewsAmEg 153 (1991) 1-6.

g194 *Abydos:* O'Connor David,   Boat graves and pyramid origins: Expedition 33,3 (Ph 1991) 5-17.

g195 *Dreyer* Günter,   Recent discoveries in the U-cemetery at Abydos: ➤ 703, Nile Delta 1990/2, 293-300.

g196 *Perdu* Olivier,   Socle d'une statue de Neshor à Abydos [inscription]: RÉgp 43 (1992) 145-162.

g197 *Zayed* ‘Abd el-Hamid,   The inscriptions on the exterior of the southern wall of the Temple of Ramesses II at Abydos: ASAE 67 (1988) 79-114 [< OLZ 88,102].

g198 *Adaima* 1990, prédyn.: BIFAO 92 (1992) 133-146; 7 fig. (Béatrix *Midant-Reynes, al.*).

g199 *Akoris:* [8th 1988 ➤ 7,d945*; 9th 1989 ➤ 6,e718] [E]**Kawanashi** Hiroyuki, *Tsujimura* Sumiyo.   Preliminary report; 10th season of the investigations at the site of Akoris, Egypt, 1990.   Tokyo 1991, Paleological Society of Japan. iii-22 p.; 8 pl. [OIAc 3,26].

g200 *Ašmunayn:* **Spencer** A. J., *al.*,   Excavations at El-Ashmunein 1. L 1989, British Museum [2, 1989 ➤ 5,e445]. – [R]JEA 78 (1992) 341-3 (G. *Dreyer*, deutsch).

g201 *Barański* Marek, *al.*,   Polish-Egyptian archaeological and preservation mission at El-Ashmunein 1987-1990; Report 2. Wsz 1992. PKZ. 47 p. 83-85004-27-2.

g202 **Bailey** D. M.,   Excavations at El-Ashmunein IV. Hermopolis Magna; buildings of the Roman period. L 1991, British Museum. 82 p.; 116 pl. (graphics *Bird* S.). 0-7141-0958-4 [OIAc 3,12].

g203 **Aswan:** *Abdel Wareth* Usama, *Zignani* Pierre,   Nag al-Hagar [Aswan], a fortress with a palace of the late Roman Empire [1st-5th, 1984-9]: BIFAO 92 (1992) 185-210; pl. 22 (foldout) - 34.

g204 **Junge** Friedrich,   Elephantine XI, Funde und Bauteile 1.-7. Kampagne, 1969-1976: 1987 ➤ 4,g396; 6,e721:   [R]CdÉ 67 (1992) 289-291 (P. De *Meulanaere* critique les transcriptions).

g205 *Seidlmayer* Stephan J., *Ziermann* Martin,   Eine Friesinschrift von einem Mastaba-Grab des Alten Reiches aus Elephantine: MiDAI-K 42 (1992) 161-176; 3 fig. pl. 37-38.

g206 *Beni Hasan:* *Hölzl* Christian,   The rock tombs of ~; architecture and sequence: ➤ 735, Sesto Eg. 1991/2, 279-283.

g206* *Dair Abu Fana* [Oberäg.] 1989: ÄgLev 2 (1991) 121-146 + 16 pl. (H. *Buschhausen, al.*).

g207 *Dakhleh* oasis project, Ismant el-Kharab 1991-2: JSStEg 19 (1989!) 1-26; 5 fig.; XX pl. (C. A. *Hope, al.*).

g208 — *Balat* 1991s (1. ‘Ayn Asil; 2. Qila al-Dabba): BIFAO 92 (1992) 213-225; 3 fig. (N. *Grimal*).

g209 **Soukiassian** Georges, *al.*,   Balat III. Les ateliers de potiers d'‘Ayn-Aṣil; *Ballet* Pascale, *Picon* Maurice, La céramique. Le Caire 1990, IFAO. xiv-174 p.; 52 fig.; 46 pl. 2-7247-0089-9. – [R]BO 49 (1992) 717-721 (S. *Hendrickx*); JAOS 112 (1992) 404s (Gloria A. *London*).

g210 **Minault-Gout** Anne, *al.*,   Balat II, Le Mastaba d'Ima-Pepi; fin de l'Ancien Empire: Fouilles 33. Le Caire 1992, IFAO. xii-241 p.; 51 pl.; foldout plan [*Deleuze* P.]. 2-7247-0112-7 [OIAc 5,29].

g211 *McDonald* Mary M. A.,   The roots of Egyptian civilization as seen from the Dakhleh oasis in the Western Desert: ➤ 557*, Contacts 1990/2, 257-261.

g212 — **Kellia:** *Rassart-Debergh* Marguerite,   Les peintures des Kellia (missions de 1981 et 1983): ➤ 690, 3d Coptic 1984/90, 343-354; 14 fig. (2 maps).

g213 **Dendera:** a) *Cauville* Sylvie,   Les prêtres 'spécifiques' de Dendera; – b) *Pezin* Michel, Hor, fils de Labys, *phrontistēs* / *swrd* d'Hathor de Dendera [p. 210 en grec *phrontistēz*, p. 214 *phrogtistēs*]: RÉgp 43 (1992) 195-202 / 210-4.

g214 **Douch** 1991, porte de Trajan: BIFAO 92 (1992) 232-241; fig. 8 (N. *Grimal*).

g215 **Dunand** Françoise, *al.*,   Douche I, la nécropole, exploration archéologique; tombes 1-72, structures sociales, économiques, religieuses de l'Égypte romaine: Fouilles 24. Le Caire 1992, IFAO. xi-389 p., iv + 93 pl. 2-7247-0111-9 [OIAc 3,19].

g216 **Fatira** [désert E], mons Claudianus 5th-6th, 1991s: BIFAO 92 (1992) 15-36 + 10 pl. (J. *Bingen*, S. *Jensen*) + 250-4 (N. *Grimal*).

g217 **Fayûm:** *Garbrecht* Günther, *Jaritz* Horst,   Neue Ergebnisse zu altägyptischen Wasserbauten im Fayum: AntWelt 23 (1992) 238-254; 23 fig.

g217* a) *Bianchi* Robert S.,   The cultural transformation of Egypt as suggested by a group of enthroned male figures from the Faiyum; – b) *Corcoran* Lorelei H.,   A cult function for the so-called Faiyum mummy portraits?: ➤ 719, Life 1990/2, 15-26; 13 pl. / 57-60; 2 fig.

g218 **Halfia Gibli** (Nag Hammadi) 1991: NewsAmEg 158s (1992) 11-15 (Kathryn A. *Bard*, *al.*).

g219 **Haridi**, gebel (Sohag, 350 k S Cairo), 1st 1991s: JEA 78 (1992) 19-27; 1 fig.; pl. IV (C. J. *Kirby*).

g220 **Heracleopolis:** *Padró* J.,   La tumba de Sehu en Heracleópolis Magna [1985s]: AulaO 10 (1992) 105-7 + 4 fig.

g221 **Hierakonpolis:** **Adams** Barbara,   The fort cemetery 1987 ➤ 3, e835 ... 6, g413: RJEA 78 (1992) 322-4 (R. F. *Friedman*).

g222 **Idfu:** *Murnane* William J., *Yurco* Frank J.,   Once again the date of the New Kingdom pylon at Edfu: ➤ 84, Mem. HOFFMAN M. 1992, 337-346; 8 fig. [possibly as late as Amenhotep III; hardly (mid-) 19th dynasty].

g223 **Labrique** Françoise,   Stylistique et théologie à Edfou; le rituel de l'offrande de la campagne; étude de la composition: OrLovAnal 51. Lv 1992, Peeters/Univ. ix-369 p.; 24 pl. 90-6831-461-0.

g224 F*Kurth* Dieter,   Edfu, Studien zu Ikonographie, Textgestaltung, Schriftsystem, Grammatik und Baugeschichte: InschTempelsEdfu Begleithefte 1. Wsb 1990, Harrassowitz. viii-83 p.

g225 **Cauville** S.,   Essai sur... Edfou 1987 ➤ 3, b296; 6, b33: RCdÉ 67 (1992) 282-9 (P. *Germond*: de grande qualité).

g226 **Derchain-Urtel** Maria-Theresia,   Priester im Tempel... Edfu, Dendera 1989 ➤ 5, a996: RCdÉ 66 (1991) 178-180 (H. De *Meulenaere*).

g227 **Germond** Philippe,   Les invocations à la Bonne Année au temple d'Edfou: AegHelv 11, 1986 ➤ 2, b155 ... 4, g415: RCdÉ 66 (1991) 175-7 (Sylvie *Cauville*).

g228 **Goyon** Jean-Claude,   Les dieux-gardiens et la genèse des temples d'après les textes égyptiens d'époque gréco-romaine); les Soixante d'Edfou et les Soixante-dix-sept dieux de Pharbaethos 1985 ➤ 5, b9: RCdÉ 66 (1991) 166-175 (P. *Germond*).

g229 *Kharga:* Kuth Dieter, Einige Anmerkungen zum oberen Tempel von Nadura in der Oase Charga: DielB 27 (1991) 172-180; 4 fig.

g230 *Kom Ombo:* Jones Michael, An unusual foundation deposit at Kom Ombo: BSACopte 31 (1992) 97-107; pl. X-XI.

g231 *Koptos:* Traunecker C., Coptos; hommes et dieux sur le parvis de Geb: OrLovAnal 43. Lv 1992, Univ./Peeters. xvii-425 p.; 30 fig. 90-6831-405-X [OIAc 5,37].

g232 **Pantalacci** Laure, **Traunecker** Claude, Le temple d'El-Qal'a [Koptos] I: IFAO 698, Le Caire 1990. – ᴿBO 49 (1992) 392s (Maria T. *Derchain-Urtel*).

g233 *Malqata:* Nishimoto Shin-Ichi, The ceiling paintings of the harem rooms of the [NK] palace of Malqata: GöMiszÄg 127 (1992) 69-75 + 8 fig.

g234 *Merimde:* Eiwanger Josef, Merimde-Benisalāme III. Die Funde der jüngeren Merimde-Kultur: DAI ArchVeröff 59. Mainz 1992, von Zabern. 143 p.; 106 + 6 pl. 3-8053-0614-8 [OIAc 3,19].

g235 *Nagaᶜ/Der:* Podzorski Patricia Y., Their bones shall not perish 1990 → 6,e748: ᴿBO 49 (1992) 728-731 (L. *Morimoto*); CdÉ 67 (1992) 295s (A. *Leguèbe*).

g236 *Oxyrhynchus:* Krüger Julian, Oxyrhynchos in der Kaiserzeit 1990 → 6, e749; 7,d964: ᴿCdÉ 67 (1992) 377-9 (Paola *Pruneti*); Gnomon 64 (1992) 700-2 (P. J. *Sijpesteijn*); WienerSt 105 (1992) 252s (H. *Harrauer*).

g237 *Porphyrius* mons: Johannes Dieter, Eine Kirche im 'mons porphyrius' [östliche Wüste, 50 k N Claudianus]: DielB 27 (1991) 198-202; 7 fig.

g238 *Qarat Hilwa:* Gosline Sheldon L., Bahariya oasis expedition season report for 1988, part 1. survey of Qarat Hilwah: VarAeg supp 3. San Antonio 1990, Van Siclen. ix-45 p., XXIX fig.; 5 maps. 0-933175-25-6.

g239 *Qasr Sagha* (N. Qarun-See), 1987s: MiDAI-K 42 (1992) 177-191; 11 fig. pl. 39-41 (J. *Śliwa*).

g240 *Rizeikat:* Beinlich Horst, Eine Stele des Nebseni und des Sobekmose von Er-Rizeikat: StAäK 19 (1992) 37-77; 5 fig.; pl. 1-8.

g241 *Šārūna* Kōm/Aḥmar 6th 1989: GöMiszÄg 127 (1992) 89-108; 9 fig. (Louise *Gestermann, al.*).

g242 *Sohag:* Kanawati Naguib, Sohag in Upper Egypt; a glorious history. Giza 1990, Prism. xiv-82 p.; 23 fig., 57 pl. [phot. *Scannell* Reece]. 977-235-002-5. – ᴿDiscEg 19 (1991) 89-92 (J. *Malek*).

g243 *Tôd,* 25k S Luxor; historique du site et des fouilles [Louvre 1979 ...]: → 690, 3d Coptic 1984/90, 59-64; 5 fig.

g244 *Zawyet Sulṭān:* Osing Jürgen, *al.,* Das Grab des Nefersecheru in Zawyet Sulṭān: DAI ArchVeröff 88. Mainz 1992, von Zabern. 82 p.; 48 pl. 3-8053-1012-9.

T7.7 **Antiquitates Nubiae et alibi.**

g245 **Affholder-Gérard** Brigitte, Cornic Marie-Jeanne, Angers, musée Pincée, collections égyptiennes: Inventaire 35. P 1990, Réunion Musées. 216 p. F 180. 2-7118-2293-1. – ᴿBO 49 (1992) 398s (G. *Hölbl*).

g246 **Corzo** Miquel Angel, *al.,* In the tomb of Nefertari; conservation of the wall paintings. Santa Monica 1992, Getty Trust. 88 p.; 39 fig. 0-89236-229-4 [OIAc 5,17].

g247 **Fleur-Lobban** Carilyn, Lobban Richard A.ᴶ, Voll John O., Historical dictionary of the Sudan²: African Historical Dictionaries 53. Metuchen 1992, Scarecrow. cvii-409 p. 0-8108-2547-3 [OIAc 5,21, 'Fleuhr'].

g248 **Simonse** Simon, Kings of disaster; dualism, centralism, and the scapegoat king in southeastern Sudan. Leiden 1992, Brill. xv-477 p.; 2 maps [CoV&R 6,12, J. *Williams*].

g249 **Simpson** William K., The offering chapel of Kayemnofret in the Museum of Fine Arts, Boston. Boston 1992, Museum Dept.EgNE. x-32 p.; 26 pl.; 7 loose facsimile drawings. 0-87846-361-5 [OIAc 5,35].

---

250 *Abu Simbel:* [*El-Achirie*] *Jacquet* J., *al.*, Le grand temple d'Abou Simbel I/1, architecture. Le Caire / P 1984, Organisation Égyptienne des Antiquités / Institut Géographique National. vii-39 p.; 123 pl. [OIAc 5,20].

g251 *Aethiopia:* **Fattovich** Rodolfo, Lineamenti di storia dell'archeologia dell'Etiopia e della Somalia: AION supp 71 al 52,2 (1992). N 1992, Ist.Univ.Orientale. [iv-] 89 p.

g252 *Akša: Daneri de Rodrigo* Alicia, Further notes on the war reliefs at Aksha (Serra West): JSStEg 18 (1988) 99-105; pl. XXIII-XXV.

g253 *Berenice:* **Kenrick** P. M., Excavations at Sidi Khrebish Benghazi (Berenice) 3/1, The fine pottery. Libyan Ant. Supp. 5. Tripoli 1985, Dept. Antiquities. xviii-516 p.; 24 pl. – ᴿAJA 96 (1992) 191s (Kathleen W. *Slane*).

g254 *Rozzi* Alessandra, Berenice Berenice [... tre città di Toledo II Filadelfo per sua madre]: ArchViva 10,17 (1991) 10-18; color. ill.

g255 *Cyrene: White* Donald [*al.*], Excavations at the extramural sanctuary of Demeter and Persephone at Cyrene, 1969-1981: Expedition 34,1s (Ph 1992) 3-15 [-85].

g256 ᴱ**Gentili** B., Cirene [SISAC Urbino 3.VII.1989]. Urbino 1990, Quattro Venti. iii-151 p.; 9 pl.; 7 plans. Lᵐ 20. – ᴿClasR 42 (1992) 215s (J. M. *Reynolds*).

g257 *Cameron* Alan, Synesius and Late Roman Cyrenaica [ROQUES D. 1987 & 1989]: JRomA 5 (1992) 419-430.

g258 *Chamoux* François, Un pigeonnier antique près d'Apollonia en Cyrénaïque: CRAI (1992) 623-641; 11 fig.

g259 *Babraj* Krzysztof, La symbolique des lettres [grecques: G] et H dans l'abside de la Cathédrale de Faras et leur lien avec l'art copte: → 690, 3d Coptic 1984/90, 27-40; 10 fig.

---

g260 *Kerma: Bonnet* Charles, Excavations at the Nubian royal town of Kerma, 1975-91: Antiquity 66 (1992) 611-625; 18 fig. [626-635 *al.*, end of Meroe].

g261 *Kûš: Damiano-Appia* Maurizio, Cercando il regno di Kush: ArchViva 11,26 (1992) 36-51; 11,27 (1992) 52-65; 11,34 (1992) 10-23 ...

g262 *a) Sabbahy* Abdul-Fattah al-, Kings' sons of Kush under Hatshepsut; – *b) Pamminger* Peter, Nochmals zum Problem der Vizekönige von Kusch unter Hatschepsut: GöMiszÄg 129 (1992) 99-102 / 131 (1992) 97-100.

g263 *Damiano-Appia* Maurizio, Le plus ancien royaume chrétien d'Afrique noire ['L'Éthiopie dont parlent les auteurs anciens porte aujourd'hui le nom de Nubie']: MondeB 74 (1992) 62-67 [> EsprVie 102 (1992) 305 (J. *Daoust*)].

g264 *Leptis: Segal* Arthur, ⊕ Leptis Magna, caravan city and port in Roman Africa: Qadmoniot 25 [not 24 as Eng. contents] (1992) 2-14; ill. (also ⊕ cover).

g265 *Melita:* **Hölbl** G., Äg. Kulturgut auf Malta 1989 → 5,e74; 7,d980: ᴿOLZ 87 (1992) 381s (K. *Parlasca*).

g266 *Meroë:* ᶠHINTZE Fritz, Studia ᴱApelt D., *al.*: Meroitica 12, 1990 ➤ 6,78: ᴿOLZ 87 (1992) 515-7 (U. *Luft*).

g267 *Nagᶜ/Šeyma*; 180 k S Aswan: Bietak Manfred, *Schwarz* Mario, Nagᶜ el-Scheima I. 1987 ➤ 3,e893 ... 6,e790: ᴿBO 49 (1992) 428-430 (P. van *Moorsel*); CdÉ 67 (1992) 197-9 (Marguerite *Rassart-Debergh*).

g268 *Nubia:* Haynes Joyce L., Nubia: Ancient Kingdoms of Africa. Boston 1992, Museum of Fine Arts. 64 p.; 61 fig. 0-87846-362-3 [OIAc 3,23].

g269 Hein Irmgard, Die ramessidische Bautätigkeit in Nubien: GöOrF 4/22. Wsb 1991, Harrassowitz. xiv-202 p.; 23 pl.; 8 maps. 3-447-03080-1 [OIAc 3,23].

g270 ᴱSäve-Söderberg Torgny, Middle Nubian Sites: Scandinavian Expedition to Sudanese Nubia 4,1s. Partille 1989, Åström. I. xvi-293 p.; II. 101 p. + 173 pl. 91-70810-00-1 both.

g271 Säve-Söderberg T., *Troy* Lana, New Kingdom pharaonic sites; Uddevall 1989, Scandinavian Nubian Expedition 1991. xv-293 p., 57 fig.; II. 110 p., 173 pl. – ᴿRÉgp 43 (1992) 223-7 (J. *Vercoutter*, aussi sur Middle Nubian sites 1989).

g272 Taylor John H., Egypt and Nubia. CM 1991, Harvard. 72 p. $12 [BAR-W 19/1,10]. – ᴿAfO 38s (1991s) 248s (Karola *Zibelius-Chen*).

g273 Török László, Late antique Nubia 1988 ➤ 4,g467; 5,e493*: ᴿOLZ 87 (1992) 28-30 (I. *Hofmann*).

g274 *Qustul:* Williams Bruce B., Excavations ... 1A Qustul cemetery L, 1985 ➤ 3,e877; 4,g473: ᴿCdÉ 67 (1992) 89-96 (Brigitte *Gratien*).

g275 Williams Bruce B., 2-4 cemeteries: Nubian Exp. 4, 1989 ➤ 5,e495: ᴿBO 49 (1992) 399-403 (A. *Vila*).

g276 Williams Bruce B., Qustul IV.VII, 1989s ➤ 6,e769: ᴿBO 49 (1992) 231-3 (I. *Hofmann*, 7); JAOS 112 (1992) 133s (K. *Grzymski*).

g277 Williams Bruce B., ... Qustul 9, 1991 ➤ 7,d986: ᴿOrientalia 61 (1992) 466-8 (W. Y. *Adams*).

g278 Williams Bruce B., Meroitic remains from Qustul cemetery Q, Ballana cemetery B, and a Ballana Settlement: Excavations between Abu Simbel and the Sudan frontier 8. Ch 1991, Univ. Or. Inst. xlvii-458 p.; xiii-293 + 114 pl. [JAOS 112,727].

g279 *Roma:* Alföldy G. Der Obelisk auf dem Petersplatz 1990 ➤ 6,e755: ᴿGymnasium 99 (1992) 275s (R. *Klein*).

g280 *Sabratha:* Dore John, *Keay* Nina, Excavations at Sabratha 1948-1951, 2/1, The amphorae, coarse pottery and building materials 1989 ➤ 7,d987: ᴿAION-Clas 44 (1992) 352-4 (A. *Martin*).

g281 Taborelli Luigi, L'area sacra di Ras Almunfakh presso Sabratha; le stele: RStFen 20 supp. R 1992, Cons. Naz. Ricerche. 198 p.; 30 pl. [OIAc 5,36].

g282 *Tabo:* Maystre Charles, Tabo I, statue 1986 ➤ 4,g478 ... 6,e794: ᴿJNES 51 (1992) 300s (B. *Williams*).

g283 *Ukma:* Vila André, Cimetière kermaïque d'Ukma Ouest 1987 ➤ 3, e895; 5,e511: ᴿJNES 51 (1992) 302-4 (B. *Williams*).

T7.9 **Sinai.**

g284 Bailey Clinton, Bedouin poetry from Sinai and the Negev; mirror of a culture [113 poems recorded 1968-88]; pref. *Thesiger* Wilfred, 1991

➤ 7,d995b; $125: ᴿJAOS 112 (1992) 718s (Heikki *Palva*); Parabola 17,4 (1992) 105.107 (D. F. *Reynolds*).

g285 *Chartier-Raymond* Maryvonne, Les exploitations minières des anciens Égyptiens au Sinaï: MondeB 69 (1991) 42-48.

g286 *Grossmann* Peter, *Reichert* Andreas, Report on the season in *Fayran* (March 1990): GöMiszÄg 128 (1992) 7-20 (+) 16 fig.

g287 *Hinz* Walther, Zu den Sinai-Inschriften: ZDMG [141 (1991) 16-32] 142 (1992) 262-274.

g288 **Kamil** Jill, The monastery of Saint Catherine in Sinai; history and guide. Cairo 1991, American University. xiv-99 p. $12 [JAOS 112,726].

g289 **Kontogiannes** Spyridon D., ⑥ The Sinai problem [*zētēma*], struggle of the monastery for independence from Alexandria and/or Jerusalem [16-19 cent.] Athena 1987. 421 p. – ᴿZKG 103 (1992) 270s (G. *Podskalsky*).

g290 *a) Rubin* Zeev, Sinai in the Itinerarium Egeriae; – *b) Di Nino* Antonella M., Sul Sinai con Egeria: ➤ 676, Egeria 1987/90, 177-191 / 343-353; 8 fig.

g291 **Solzbacher** Rudolf, Mönche... Sinai 1989 ➤ 5,e20; 7,d994: ᴿEstE 67 (1992) 120 (A. *Borràs i Felix*); ZKG 103 (1992) 119s (K. S. *Frank*).

g292 *Stewart* Frank H., Texts in Sinai Bedouin law [mostly oral recorded, only 2% of his 1976-82 fieldwork]: TA Univ MeditLangCu 5. Wsb 1988, Harrassowitz. 1. Eng. xvii-232; 2. ❹ xix-349 p. DM 78 + 112. – ᴿJAOS 112 (1992) 524s (Heikki *Palva*).

g293 ᶠZENGER E., Vom Sinai zum Horeb, ᴱHossfeld F. 1989 ➤ 5,220: ᴿBO 49 (1992) 477 (C. *Houtman*: detailed analyses).

T8.1 **Anatolia,** *generalia.*

g294 *Algaze* Guillermo, *al.*, The Tigris-Euphrates archaeological reconnaissance project 1989-90; Anatolica 17 (1991) 175-211 + 34 fig.

g295 *Anabolu* Mükerrem (Usman), ❶ Temples [Sardis Artemis, Hierapolis Apollo ...] à plusieurs nefs en Anatolie occidentale: Belleten 56,215 (1992) 7-12; 15 fig.

g295* *Aslan* Rodolfo, *Boccalaro* Giorgio, Itinerari di viaggi geo-archeologici 3. La Cappadocia: Geo-Archeologia (1991,2) 129-157; 14 fig.

g296 *Beal* Richard H., The location of Cilician Ura: AnSt 42 (1992) 65-73.

g297 **Brandes** Wolfram, Die Städte Kleinasiens im 7. und 8. Jh. 1989 [Diss. 1984] ➤ 6,e808: ᴿJRS 82 (1992) 300s (M. *Whittow*).

g298 **Briquel** Dominique, L'origine lydienne des Étrusques; histoire de la doctrine dans l'Antiquité: Coll. ÉcFr 139. R 1991, École Française. x-575 p. – ᴿRÉLat 70 (1992) 329-331 (R. *Adam*).

g299 *Darrouzès* Jean, Notes de littérature et de géographie ecclésiastiques [Asie Mineure]: RÉByz 50 (1992) 87-112.

g300 **De Frankovich** Géza, Santuari e tombe rupestri dell'antica Frigia e un'indagine sulle tombe della Licia: Mediaevalia 3. R 1990, Bretschneider. 210 p.; vol. of 512 fig. – ᴿSalesianum 54 (1992) 778 (S. *Maggio*).

g301 **Hellenkemper** Hans-Gerd, **Hild** Friedrich, Neue Forschungen in Kilikien; Denkschrift ph/h 186. W 1986, Österr. Akad. 144 p.; 24 + 201 fig. – ᴿBelleten 56,215 (1992) 307-310 (L. *Zoroğlu*, ❶).

g302 **Hild** Friedrich, *Hellenkemper* Hansgerd, Kilikien und Isaurien: Tabula imperii byzantini 5, W 1990, Österr. Akad. 465 p.; volume of 96 p., 402 phot., 3 foldout maps. DM 260. ➤ g693. – ᴿRÉByz 50 (1992) 307s (J.-C. *Cheynet*).

g302* **Iplikçioğlu** Bülent, *Çelgin* Gület & A. Vedat, Neue Inschriften aus Nord-Lydien: Szb ph/h 584. W 1992, Österr. Akad. v p.; 12 facsimiles, 26 phot.; map.

g303 **Lloyd** Seton, Ancient Turkey 1989 ↠ 5,e533 ... 7,e13: RBA 55 (1992) 155s (R. *Gorny*).

g304 *McMahon* Gregory, [*Gorny* Ronald L.,] Anatolia: ↠ 741, AnchorBD 1 (1992) 233-240 [prehistory 228-233].

g305 *Mellink* Machteld J., Archaeology in Anatolia [1990]: AJA 96 (1992) 119-150; 43 fig.

g306 **Rémy** Bernard, Pontica I. Recherches sur l'histoire du Pont dans l'Antiquité: Centre Palerme Mém 9. Istanbul 1991, Inst. Franç. Ét. Anatol., *al.* 125 p.; ill.; maps. 2-906053-19-1 – RAntClas 61 (1992) 575s (C. *Delvoye*); RÉAnc 94 (1992) 504 (M. *Sartre*).

g307 *Rozen* Minna, A survey of Jewish cemeteries in western Turkey: JQR 83 (1992s) 71-110 + 30 phot.

g308 **Taksöz** Cemil, Ancient cities of Lycia, TMill Adair, İstanbul 1988, auct. 160 p.; ill.

g309 **Trebilco** Paul, Jewish communities in Asia Minor SNTS Mg 69, 1991 ↠ 7,e24: RAntClas 61 (1992) 579s (J. A. *Straus*); BL (1992) 132s (C. J. A. *Hickling*); ClasR 42 (1992) 384s (J. *Geiger*); ÉtClas 60 (1992) 161s (H. *Leclercq*); JRS 82 (1992) 287s (M. *Goodman*); JTS 43 (1992) 564-6 (D. E. *Noy*); NT 34 (1992) 410s (Nina L. *Collins*); RÉG 105 (1992) 609s (P. *Nautin*); RHR 209 (1992) 303s (F. *Blanchetière*).

g310 *a) Woronoff* Michel, Villages d'Asie Mineure et promenade militaire dans l'Anabase de XÉNOPHON; – *b) Coyaud* L.-M., Approches géographiques du village; – *c) Cadell* Hélène, Les noms du village dans les papyrus grecs d'Égypte: Ktema 12 (1987) 11-18 / 3-9 / 19-27.

g311 **Yakar** Jak, Prehistoric Anatolia; the neolithic transformation and the early chalcolithic period: Nadler Mg 9. TA 1991, Univ. Inst. Arch. x-361 p.; ill. 965-440-000-6.

T8.2	**Boğazköy,** *Hethaei* – **The Hittites.**

g312 *a) Beckman* Gary M., Hittite administration in Syria in the light of the texts from Ḫattuša, Ugarit and Emar; – *b) Hoffner* Harry A., Syrian cultural influence in Hatti: ↠ 705*, New Horizons 1991/2, 41-49 / 89-106.

g313 **Boehmer** Rainer M., *Güterbock* Hans G., Boğazköy-Ḫattusa 14, Glyptik: 1987 ↠ 3,e926; 7,e27; 2. 1988: RAJA 96 (1992) 172-4 (Edith *Porada*, 1); Athenaeum 80 (1992) 255-262 (Clelia *Mora*); JNES 51 (1992) 73s (G. *Beckman*, 2); ZAss 82 (1992) 281s (U. *Seidl*, 2).

g314 *a) Güterbock* Hans G., Bemerkungen über die im Gebäude A auf Büyükkale gefundenen Tontafeln; – *b) Heinhold-Krahmer* Susanne, Zur Bronzetafel aus Boğazköy und ihrem historischen Inhalt: AfO 38s (1991s) 132-7 / 138-158.

g315 *Houwink ten Cate* Philo H. J., The bronze tablet of Tudhaliyas IV and its geographical and historical relations [*Otten* H., 1988]: ZAss 82 (1992) 233-270.

g316 **Klengel** H., Texte verschiedenen Inhalts: KaB 60, 1990 ↠ 6,e832: ROrientalia 61 (1992) 470s (M. *Popko*).

g317 **Košak** Silvin, Konkordanz der Keilschrifttafeln I. Die Texte der Grabung 1931; Einl. *Otten* Heinrich: StBoḡT 34. Wsb 1992, Harrassowitz. xi-116 p.; ill. 3-447-03280-4.

g318 *Mellink* M., Boğazköy-Nişantepe 1990: AJA 96 (1992) 127-9; fig. 12-19.

g319 *Neu* Erich, Zu einigen graphischen Varianten in der hurritischen Fassung der hurritisch-mittelhethitischen Bilingue aus Ḫattuša: SMEA 29 (1992) 203-216.

g320 **Parzinger** Hermann, *Sanz* Rosa, Die Oberstadt von Ḫattuša; hethitische Keramik aus dem zentralen Tempelviertel; Funde aus den Grabungen 1982-1987: B-Ḫattuša 15. B 1992, Mann. xii-155 p.; 80 pl. 3-7861-1656-3 [OIAc 5,31].

g321 *Sürenhagen* Dietrich, Untersuchungen zur Bronzetafel und weiteren Verträgen mit der Sekundogenitur in Tarḫuntašša [Boğazköy 1986]: OLZ 87 (1992) 341-371.

g322 **Wilhelm** Gernot, Literarische Texte in sumerischer und akkadischer Sprache: KeilsTBoğ 36. B 1991, Mann. xiii-29 pl. (114 facsimiles). 3-7861-1664-4 [OIAc 3,42].

g323 **Gürsan-Salzmann** Aysa, Alaca Höyük; a reassessment of the excavation and sequence of the Early Bronze Age settlement: diss. Pennsylvania, DDyson R. Ph 1992. 491 p. 92-27671. – DissA 53 (1992s) 1565-A; OIAc 5,23.

T8.3 **Ephesus.**

g324 *a) Alzinger* Wilhelm, Ziele der Ephesusforschung von 1863 bis heute; – *b) Bammer* Anton, Bronzen aus dem Artemision von Ephesos; – *c) Vetters* Hermann, Ein weiterer Schlangengott in Ephesos; – *d) Wiplinger* Gilbert, Restaurierungsprojekte in Ephesos; – *e) Karwiese* Stefan, Keine Kaiserhochzeit in Ephesos: ➤ 184, FTRENTINI J. B., Echo 1990, 17-19 / 21-35; 22 fig. / 315-320; 3 fig. / 329-334 + 5 fig. / 171-8.

g325 **Aurenhammer** Maria, Die Skulpturen von Ephesus, Bildwerke aus Stein, Idealplastik I: ForEphesos 10/1, 1990 ➤ 7,e35: RBabesch 67 (1992) 219-221 (E. M. *Moormann*); Gnomon 64 (1992) 422-6 (A. *Linfert*).

g325* *a) Domitilla Campanile* M., Contese civiche ad Efeso in età imperiale: StClasOr 42 (1992) 215-223. – *b) Bammer* Anton, *al.*, Efeso, la città di Artemide.T· Il mondo della Bibbia 3,14 (1992) 8-33 (4-48). 1120-7353.

g326 *Engelmann* H., Beiträge zur ephesischen Topographie [KFIL J. 1920]: ZPapEp 89 (1991) (273-) 275-295.

g327 *Hall* Margaretha D., The reluctant rhetor; a recently published inscription from Late Imperial Ephesus: ZPapEp 91 (1992) 121-8.

g328 *Hill* Andrew E., Ancient art and Artemis; toward explaining the polymastic nature of the [Ephesus] figurine: JANES 21 (1992) 91-94.

g329 *Horsley* G. H. R., The inscriptions of Ephesos and the New Testament: NT 34 (1992) 105-168.

g330 *Lang-Auinger* Claudia, *Outschar* Ulrike, Ephesos/Hanghaus, I. Vorläufiger Grabungsbericht 1990/91: AnzW 128 (1991) 129-154; 25 fig. (2 foldout plans).

g331 *LiDonnici* Lynn R., The images of Artemis Ephesia and Greco-Roman worship; a reconsideration: HarvTR 85 (1992) 389-411 + 6 fig.

g332 *Mastrocinque* Attilio, Nel segno di Artemide ... Efeso: ArchViva 11,27 (1992) 10-21; ill.

g333 **Padovese** L. [➤ 485], Atti del I/II simposio di Efeso su S. Giovanni Apostolo : Turchia, la Chiesa e la sua storia 2s. R 1991/2, Antonianum / S. L. Brindisi, 152 p. 328 p. – ROrChrPer 58 (1992) 586-8 (E. G. *Farrugia*) & 588s (V. *Ruggieri*).

g334 **Rogers** Guy M., The sacred identity of Ephesus 1991 ➤ 7,e44: ᴿClasR 42 (1992) 383s (A. J. S. *Spawforth*); ClasW 86 (1992s) 369s (T. H. *Watkins*).

g335 *Rogers* G. M., *a*) The assembly of imperial Ephesos: ZPapEp 94 (1992) 224-8; – *b*) The constructions [public building projects] of women at Ephesos: ZPapEp 90 (1992) 215-223.

g335* *Sobel* Christa, *a*) Ephesus; – *b*) Efeso italiano. Istanbul 1992, Hitit Color. 111 p. 975-7487-07-4 (Eng.).

g336 *Tschäpe* Ruth, Die Artemis Ephesia in Sir John Soane's Museum [London Nº 613 M]; auf der Suche nach ihrem Aussehen im Cinquecento: Boreas 14s (1991s) 179-195; 5 fig.

T8.4 **Pergamum.**

g337 ᴱ**Andreae** Bernard, Phyromachos-Probleme, mit einem Anhang zur Datierung des grossen Altars von Pergamon: 1990 ➤ 7,e48: ᴿRArchéol (1992) 367-380 (F. *Queyrel*).

g338 *Andreae* Bernard, Vom Pergamonaltar bis Raffael; Vorbilder, Eigenart und Wirkung der römischen Sarkophage: AntWelt 23 (1992) 41-64; 71 (color.) fig. (65, Phyromachos – Schöpfer des P-Altars).

g339 *a*) *Brize* Philip, Göttin oder Kaiserin? Zu einem späthellenistischen Frauenkopf aus Pergamon; – *b*) *Meyer-Schlichtmann* Carsten, Ein Reiterrelief aus Pergamon: IstMitt 40 (1990) 179-194; pl. 31-36 / 167-177; pl. 30; Beilage 3.

g340 **Filgis** M. N., *Radt* W., Altertümer von Pergamon 15/1, Das Heroon 1986 ➤ 3,e951 ... 7,e40: ᴿAnzAltW 43 (1990) 85-89 (H. *Vetters*).

g341 *de Luca* Gioia, Zur Hygieia von Pergamon, ein Beitrag: IstMitt 41 (1991) 325-362; 1 fig. pl. 39-45.

g342 *Deubner* Otfried, *a*) Eine pergamenische Architekturordnung?: ➤ 184, ᶠTRENTINI J. B., Echo 1990, 89-97; 8 fig. – *b*) Eine hellenistische Bronzefigur aus dem Asklepieion von Pergamon: ➤ 93, ᶠINAN J. 1989, 13-16; pl. 12.

g343 *a*) *Hintzen-Bohlen* Brigitte, Die Prometheus-Gruppe im Athenaheiligtum zu Pergamon; ein Beitrag zur Repräsentation der Attaliden; – *b*) *de Luca* Gioia, Hellenistische Kunst in Pergamon im Spiegel der megarischen Becher; ein Beitrag zur pergamenischen Ornamentik (nicht Keramik wie Index): IstMitt 40 (1990) 145-156; pl. 22-23 / 157-166; pl. 24-29.

g344 *a*) *Kertész* István, Zur Sozialpolitik der Attaliden; – *b*) *Sonnabend* Holger, Polybios, die Attaliden und die Griechen: Tyche 7 (1992) 133-141 / 207-216.

g345 *Radt* W., Pergamon 1990: ➤ g305, AJA 96 (1992) 144-6; fig. 33-42.

g346 *a*) *Radt* Wolfgang, Die frühesten Wehrmauern von Pergamon und die zugehörigen Keramikfunde; – *b*) *Meyer-Schlichtmann* C., ... Heroon; – *c*) *Rheidt* Klaus, Obere Agora; – *d*) *Rumscheid* Frank, Demeter-Tempel: IstMitt 42 (1992) 163-234; 8 fig.; pl. 24-31 / 287-306; 4 fig. / 235-286; 20 fig.; pl. 32-39 / 347-351; pl. 42.

g347 **Schalles** Hans-Joachim, Untersuchungen zur Kulturpolitik der pergamenischen Herrscher im 3.Jh.v.Chr.: IstFor 36, 1985 ➤ 3,b860.e960; 4,d387.g534: ᴿRÉG 105 (1992) 281 (Mary-Anne *Zagdoun*).

g348 **Meyer-Schlichtmann** Carsten M., Die pergamenische Sigillata aus der Stadtgrabung von Pergamon: PergFor 6, B 1988, de Gruyter. xvii-

265 p.; 27 fig.; 48 (foldout) pl. 3-11-011351-1. – ᴿAION-clas 44 (1992) 347-9 (A. *Martin*).

T8.6 *Situs Anatoliae,* **Turkey sites** in alphabetical order.

g349 *Alalaḫ:* **Heinz** Marlies, Tell Atchana / Alalakh; die Schichten VII-XVII: AOAT 41. Kevelaer / Neuk 1992, Butzon & B. xii-229 p.; 44 fig., 47 plans + Katalog 91 pl. 3-7666-9711-0 [OIAc 3,23].

g350 *a) Hess* Richard S., Observations on some unpublished Alalakh texts, probably from Level IV [... SA,GAZ]; – *b) Zeeb* Frank, Studien zu den altbabylonischen Texten aus Alalaḫ II; Pfandurkunden: UF 24 (1992) 113-5 / 447-480 [481-498 zu RS 34.153].

g351 *Alaşehir: Petzl* Georg, Zum neupythagoreischen Monument aus Philadelpheia [lydischem, Alaşehir]: EpAnat 20 (1992) 1-5; pl. Ia; ❶6.

g352 *Amorium* [E. Phrygia] 4th, 1991; AnSt 42 (1992) 207-222; 6 fig. (R. M. *Harrison, al.*).

g353 *Ancyra: Martels* Z. von, The discovery of the inscription of the Res Gestae Divi Augusti [Ancyra, BUSBEQUIUS A. and others around 1579; portions found also at Apollonia and Pisidian Antioch, 19th & 20th c.]: ResPublica Litterarum 13 (Kansas U. 1990) 147-156.

g354 *Antiochia: Kennedy* Hugh, Antioch; from Byzantium to Islam and back again: ➤ 675, City 1986/92, 181-198.

g355 *Aphrodisias:* **Campbell** Sheila, The mosaics of Aphrodisias in Caria: Corpus of mosaic pavements in Turkey 18. Toronto 1991, Pont. Inst. Medv. St. ix-47 p.; 90 pl.

g355* *Brooten* Bernadette J., Iael *prostátēs* in the Jewish donative inscription from Aphrodisias: ➤ 104, ᶠKOESTER H. 1991, 149-162.

g356 *a) Isık* Fahri, Ein späthellenistisches Grabrelief aus Aphrodisias; *b) Erim* Kenan T., *Reynolds* Joyce, Sculptors of Aphrodisias in the inscriptions of the city: ➤ 93, ᶠİNAN J. 1989, 429-438; pl. 167-8 / 517-538; pl. 199-206.

g357 **Roueché** Charlotte, Aphrodisias in late antiquity: JRS Mg 5. L 1989, Soc. Prom. Rom. St. xxvii-371 p.; 48 pl.; 2 maps. £35. 0-907764-09-0. – ᴿJRS 82 (1992) 299s (C. *Foss*).

g358 *Williams* Margaret H., The Jews and Godfearers inscription from Aphrodisias; a case of patriarchal interference in early 3d century Caria?: Historia 41 (1992) 297-310.

g359 *Arpas: Marchese* R., Ancient remains in Caria; the watchtower at Arpas: AnSt 42 (1992) 47-51; 1 fig.

g360 *Belkis: Horst* Pieter W. van der, A new altar of a Godfearer? [Belkis in Pamphylia: not made with hands]: JJS 43 (1992) 32-37.

g361 *Burdur: Duru* Refik, Höyücek excavations, 1989: Belleten 56 (1992) 551-566; 27 pl. (plan).

g362 *Mitchell* Stephen, The Hadrianic forum and basilica at Cremna [15 k E Bucak (Burdur)]: ➤ 93, ᶠİNAN J. 1989, 279-245; 3 fig.; pl. 103-106.

g363 *Carchemish: Kupper* J.-R., Karkémish aux IIIème et IIème millénaires avant notre ère: Akkadica 79s (1992) 16-23.

g364 *Chios: Bresson* Alain, Chios de Carie: DialHA 16,1 (1990) 97-113.

g365 *Commagene:* Şahin Sencer [*Jacobs* Bruno], Forschungen in Kommagene, I. Epigraphik; II. Topographie [III. Archäologie]: EpAnat 18 (1991)

99-111; map. 113; pl. 10-13; Özet 112 / 114-131; 5 fig.; pl. 14-17; Özet p. 132 / [133-9; pl. 15-17; Özet 140].

g366 **Daskyleion: Nollé** Margret, Denkmäler vom Satrapensitz Daskyleion; Studien zur graeco-persischen Kunst: Antike in der Moderne. B 1992, Akademie. xvi-179 p.; 15 pl. 3-05-002146-2 [OIAc 3,32].

g367 **Demirci**-Sarıket 1990: ⊁ g305, AJA 96 (1992) 131-3; fig. 22-24 (M. *Mellink*).

g368 Demirci-Sarıket Nekropole 1991: IstMit 42 (1992) 5-19; 9 fig.; pl. 1-2 (J. *Seeher*).

g369 **Didyma: Polt** Stefan, Untersuchungen zur kaiserzeitlichen Bauornamentik von Didyma 1989 ⊁ 7,e70: ᴿBonnJbb 192 (1992) 707-715 (R. *Köster*).

g370 **Erzurum:** *Sagona* Antonio, *al.*, Excavations at Büyüktepe Höyük, 1991 (Erzurum-Melbourne), Second preliminary report: AnSt 42 (1992) 29-46; 10 fig.; XVI pl.

g371 **Euxinus** pontus: ᴱ**Lordkipanidze** Otar, *Lévêque* Pierre, Le Pont-Euxin vu par les grecs 1987/90 ⊁ 7,596: ᴿAntClas 61 (1992) 574 (D. *Viviers*); RÉG 104 (1991) 272s (A. *Laronde*).

g372 *Nadel* Benjamin, The Euxine Pontos as seen by the Greeks : DialHA 17,2 (1991) 115-126 [127-133, nouvelles monographies, *Wasowicz* Aleksandra: 17,1 (1991) 425-445].

g373 **Girikihaciyan: Watson** Patty Jo, *Le Blanc* Steven, Girikihaciyan, a Halafian site in southeastern Turkey: Inst. Arch. Mg. 33. LA 1990, UCLA. 146 p. 0-917956-69-9. – ᴿJField 19 (1992) 515-7 (S. *Campbell*).

g374 **Göreme:** *Bernardini* Lisa, Les donateurs des églises de Cappadoce: ⊁ 43, ᶠDELVOYE C., Byzantion 62 (1992) 118-140; 3 (foldout) tables; 8 pl.

g375 **Jolivet-Lévy** Catherine, Les églises byzantines de Cappadoce; le programme iconographique de l'abside et de ses abords. P 1991. 341 p.; 169 pl. + 16 color. – ᴿByZ 84s (1991s) 543-5 (Jenny *Albani*); RivArCr 68 (1992) 365s (Basema *Hamarneh*).

g376 **Thierry** Nicole, L'illustration des apocryphes dans les églises de Cappadoce: ⊁ 470, Apocrypha 2 (1991) 217-247; pl. III-IX.

g377 **Thierry** Nicole, *Jolivet-Lévy* Catherine, *al*, Monastères et ermitages, Tokalı Kilise à Göreme / Le renouveau artistique du Xᵉ siècle: MondeB 70 ('La Cappadoce' 1991) [2-] 20-46; ill.

g378 **Gordion** 1990: ⊁ g305, AJA 96 (1992) 136s, fig. 25s (M. *Mellink*).

g379 **Gunter** A. C., Gordion excavation final reports III. the Bronze Age: Museum Mg 73. Ph 1991, Univ. XIX-113 p.; 31 fig.; 32 pl.; 12 plans; map. $65. – ᴿJHS 112 (1992) 209s (A. B. *Knapp*).

g380 *Schaus* Gerald P., Imported West Anatolian pottery at Gordion: AnSt 42 (1992) 151-177; 5 fig.

g381 **Hassek:** ᴱ**Behm-Blancke** M. R. [+ 29 *al.*], Hassek Höyük; naturwissenschaftliche Untersuchungen und lithische Industrie: IstFor 38. Tü 1992, Wasmuth. xii-261 p.; 51 fig.; 3 pl. 3-8030-1759-9.

g381* **Hierapolis** [Phrygia]: **Bejor** Giorgio, Hierapolis, scavi e ricerche 3. Le statue [46 sin dal 1957]: Archaeologica 99. R 1991, Bretschneider. xvi-104 p.; 44 pl. [RBgPg 71, 209, F. *Baratte*].

g382 **Hierapolis** in Cilicia: **Sayar** M. *al.*, Inschriften aus Hierapolis-Kastabala [Ost-Kilikien, nicht Pamukkale oder andere in Phrygien] 1989 ⊁ 7,e77: ᴿLatomus 51 (1992) 431s (A. *Martin*).

g383 İstanbul: **Demicheli** Anna Maria, La megálē ekklēsía [S. Sophia] nel lessico e nel diritto di Giustiniano: MgVocabG 3. Mi 1990, Giuffrè. 108 p.; 3 pl. Lit. 15.000. – ᴿGnomon 64 (1992) 166s (F. Tinnefeld).

g384 **Harrison** M., Ein Tempel für Byzanz; die Entdeckung und Ausgrabung von Anicia Julianas Palastkirche in İstanbul [1989 ➤ 6,e878], ᵀWeitbrecht Brigitte. Z 1990, Belser. 160 p.; 180 fig.; map. – ᴿJbÖsByz 41 (1991) 367s (J. Koder).

g385 Rebenich Stefan, Zum Theodosiusobelisken in Konstantinopel: IstMitt 41 (1991) 447-476; pl. 51-53.

g386 İzmir-Smyrna: **Goffman** Daniel, Izmir and the Levantine world: Near-East 5. Seattle 1990, Univ. Washington. xv-236 p., 31 fig.; 3 maps. $25. – ᴿBSO 55 (1992) 337s (Caroline Finkel); JRAS (1992) 276s (C. Imber); SixtC 23 (1992) 364s (W. F. Cook).

g387 İzmit: **Özbek** Metin, ❶ Squelettes d'enfants trouvés au théâtre romain de Nicomédie: Belleten 55,213 (1991) 315-322 + 9 pl.

g388 Klazomenai: **Beek** René van, **Beelen** Jos, Excavations on Karantina island in Klazomenai [coast 40k W İzmir]: Anatolica 17 (1991) 31-45 + 23 fig.

g389 Kültepe: **Özgüç** Tahsin, Kültepe-Kaniş 2. ❶ New researches at the trading center of the ancient Near East. Ankara 1986, Tarih Kurumu. 123 p.; 136 pl.

g390 Bayram Sebahattin, ❶ Nouveaux documents [cunéiformes] de Kültepe sur les immeubles: Belleten 55,213 (1991) 297-314; 10 facsimiles.

g391 **Bilgiç** Emin, Ankara Kültepe tabletleri: Yayınları 6,1. Ankara 1990, Türk Tarih.

g392 Michel Cécile, Le décès d'un contractant (Kaniš): RAss 86 (1992) 113-9.

g393 a) Özgüç Tahsin, New glazed faience objects from Kanish; – b) Emre Kutlu, Two imported bottle shaped jars from Karum Kanish; – c) Özgüç Nimet, The Uruk culture at Samsat: ➤ 179, ꜰSTROMMENGER Eva, 1992, 159-162; pl. 70-71 / 51-56; pl. 17 / 151-162; pl. 62-69.

g394 Sever Hüseyin, Anadolu'da Nişanın bozulması hakkinda verilmiş Kaniş Karumu karari [... decision sur des fiançailles rompues]: Belleten 56 (1992) 667-675; 1 cuneiform facsimile.

g395 Kurban: **Wilkinson** T. J., Town and country in southeastern Anatolia, Kurban Höyük, I. Settlement and land use [➤ 7,e92a], II. ᴱAlgaze Guillermo, Stratigraphic sequence [➤ 7,e92b]: OIP 109s. Ch 1990, Univ. Or. Inst. 315 p.; 104 fig., 6 pl.; 438 p., 139 fig., vol. of 169 pl. 0-918986-64-8; -5-6. – ᴿAfO 38s (1991s) 233-8 (Karin Bartl); JField 19 (1992) 98-100 (P. Zimansky).

g396 Kurkh: **Conradie** F. A., The Kurkh [30 k S Diyarbakır 1861] monolith of Ashurnasirpal II: JTydSem 3 (1991) 1-10.

g397 Kyaneai (Kaş, Yavu-Bergland) 1989: IstMitt 41 (1991) 187-264; 30 fig.; pl. 29-37 (F. Kolb, al.).

g398 Lukka: **Bryce** Trevor R., Lukka revisited: JNES [1974] 51 (1992) 121-130: near Miletus as well as in Lycaonia, but a vaguely single population.

g399 Lycia: **Borchhardt** Jürgen & (-Birbaumer) Brigitte, Zum Kult der Heroen, Herrscher und Kaiser in Lykien: AntWelt 23 (1992) 99-116; 37 (color.) fig.

g400 Milet 1989/1990 Vorbericht: IstMitt 40 (1990) 37-78; pl. 5-16 / 41 (1991) 125-186; 18 fig.; pl. 20-28 (V. von Graeve, al.).

g401 Miletus 1991: IstMit 42 (1992) 97-154 (V. von *Graeve*).
g402 **Kossatz** Anne-Ulrike, Milet V,1.1 Die megarischen Becher: DAI. B
   1990, de Gruyter. xii-144 p.; 10 fig.; 55 pl. – ᴿRArchéol (1992) 149s
   (Catherine *Abadie-Reynal*).
g403 *Nimrud Dağ*: **Dörner** Friedrich K., ❶ Nimrud Dağ, ᵀ*Ülkü* Vural.
   Ankara 1990, Türk Tarih. viii-255 p.; 70 fig.; 22 pl. 075-16-0227-0
   [OIAc 5,19].
g404 *Ouranion*: *Varinlioğlu* E., *al*., Ouranion en Carie: RÉAnc 94 (1992)
   155-174; 6 fig. (map.).
g405 *Perge* 1979-87: *Akıllı* Hüseyin ➤ 93, ᶠİNAN J. 1989, 259-265; pl.
   109-112.
g406 *Schmidt-Colinet* Andreas, Eine severische Priesterin aus Syrien in Perge:
   IstMitt 41 (1991) 439-445; 1 fig.; pl. 49-50.
g407 *Porsuk*-Ulukışla 1986-9: Syria 69 (1992) 305-348; 40 fig.; 2 foldout plans
   (O. *Pelon*); 349-377; 54 fig. (Catherine *Abadie-Reynal*, 1989 chantier est);
   379-388 (*al.*, dendrochronology).
g408 *Râvendân*: **Demirkent** Işın, ❶ Râvendân, une des forteresses de
   l'époque des Croisades : Belleten 56 (1992) 371-389; 6 color. pl.
g409 *Sagalassos*: *Waelkens* Marc, *al.*, The excavations at Sagalassos [Bur-
   dur] 1991: AnSt 42 (1992) 75-98; 7 fig. [99-117 *Vandeput* Lutgarde,
   theatre-façade].

g410 *Sardis* 1990: ➤ g305, AJA 96 (1992) 143s; plan (M. *Mellink*).
g411 **Crawford** J. Stephens, The Byzantine shops at Sardis; Mg 9. CM 1990,
   Harvard Univ. xx-156 p.; 610 fig. 0-674-08968-5. – ᴿAJA 96 (1992) 575
   (Jodi *Magness*).
g412 *Kraabel* A.T., Impact of the discovery of the Sardis synagogue [<
   ᴱ*Hanfmann*, Sardis 1983) 178-190 . 284s]: ➤ 107, ᶠKRAABEL 1992, 269-
   291, plus five other reprints of his Sardis research.
g413 **Ratté** Christopher J., *a*) Lydian masonry and monumental architecture
   at Sardis [diss. California, Berkeley 1989] ➤ 5,e907; 395 p. – *b*) The
   'Pyramid Tomb' at Sardis: IstMit 42 (1992) 135-161; 16 fig.; pl. 21-23.

g414 *Seleucia*: **Erol** O., *Pirazzoli* P. A., Seleucia Pieria, an ancient harbour
   submitted to two successive uplifts: IntJNaut 21 (1992) 317-327; 8 fig.
g415 *Sidé*: *Nollé* Johannes, Sidé [Perge]; zur Geschichte einer kleinasiatischen
   Stadt in der römischen Kaiserzeit im Spiegel ihrer Münzen: AntWelt 21
   (1990) 244-265; 21 (color), fig.
g416 *Tanais*: *Ustinova* Julia, The Thiasoi of Theos Hypsistos in Tanais
   [Bosporus]: HistRel 31 (1991s) 150-180; 6 fig.
g417 *Toprakkale*: **Wartke** Ralf-Bernhard, Toprakkale [Rusaḫinili] 1990 ➤ 6,
   e907; 7,e102: ᴿZAss 82 (1992) 277-281 (U. *Seidl*).
g418 *Trapezous*: *a*) *Huxley* George, EUSEBIOS on the founding of Trapezous;
   – *b*) *Bouzek* J., Five notes on the Pontic relations with Greece during the
   archaic and classical times: ➤ 724, BlackSea 1987/90, 195-201 / 464s.

g419 *Troja*: **Schliemann** Heinrich, Bericht über die Ausgrabungen in Troja in
   den Jahren 1871 bis 1873 [1874] mit 70 Abbildungen und 48 Tafeln aus
   dem 'Atlas trojanischer Alterthümer' [1874], ᴱ*Korfmann* Manfred 1990
   ➤ 7,e104: ᴿWeltOr 23 (1992) 209-211 (G. *Gamer*).
g419* **Fehling** Dieter, Die ursprüngliche Geschichte vom Fall Trojas, oder
   Interpretationen zur Troja-Geschichte: InBeitKuW 75, Innsbruck 1991,
   Univ. Inst. Sprachw. 96 p. Sch 480 [ClasR 43, 418, J. B. *Hainsworth*].

g420 ᴱGamer-Wallert Ingrid, Troia, Brücke zwischen Orient und Okzident. Tü 1992, Attempto. 289 p. 3-89308-150-X [OIAc 5,22].

g421 ᴱKorfmann Manfred, Studia Troica [I. Troad 1982-, II. Troy itself from 1987]. Mainz 1991, von Zabern. 182 p.; 102 fig.; 8 pl. DM 148 [ClasR 43, 368, P. *Warren*: good].

g421* *Goldman* Klaus, ᴱ*Steiner* Andreas M., Cos'è successo al tesoro di Priamo?: Archeo 7,83 (1992) 38-41 [in Russia; non ho potuto avere testimonianze dirette]; poi 7,93 (1992) 20s: 'Novità' (10 soggetti mancavano all'arrivo a Mosca) [meanwhile on exposition in Moscow].

g422 *Meyer* Laure, Troie, de Schliemann aux dernières découvertes : Archéologia 267 (1991) 34-43; color. ill.

g423 *Schmidt-Doumas* Barbara, Zur Datierung der Metopen des Athena-Tempels von Ilion: IstMitt 41 (1991) 363-415; 1 fig.; pl. 46-48.

g424 *Ṭur Abdin*: **Palmer** Andrew, Monk and mason... Ṭur Abdin 1990 ➤ 6,e915; 7,e111: ᴿClasW 85 (1991s) 254s (W. E. *Fahey*); HeythJ 33 (1992) 337s (S. *Brock*); OrChrPer 58 (1992) 575-8 (V. *Ruggieri*); PrOrChr 41 (1991) 193s (J. M. *Fiey*); Speculum 67 (1992) 734s (J. *Rosser*).

g425 *Urfa*: *Donbaz* Veysel, A brick inscription of Nabonidus from Harran: AnRIM 9 (1991) 11s.

g426 **Green** Tamara M., The city of the moon god; religious traditions of Harran: RelGrWorld 114. Leiden 1992, Brill. viii-232 p. ƒ110 [TR 88,526].

g427 *Harrak* Amir, The ancient name of Edessa [Adme]: JNES 51 (1991) 209-214.

g428 *Xanthos*: *Christol* Michel, *Drew-Bear* Thomas, Un sénateur de Xanthos: JSav (1991) 195-226; 2 fig.; 5 pl.

g429 *Keen* Antony G., The dynastic tombs of Xanthos; who was buried where?: AnSt 42 (1992) 53-63; 1 fig.

g430 *Yaraşli* Cevre Kala, aerial survey: AnSt 42 (1992) 179-206; 11 fig. (G. D. *Summers*).

т8.9 **Armenia, Urarţu.**

g431 **Arat Mari** Kristin, Die Wiener Mechitaristen; Armenische Mönche in der Diaspora: BoBeitKG. W 1990, Böhlau. 286 p. DM 98. 3-205-05230-7. – ᴿBO 49 (1992) 576s (J. J. S. *Weitenberg*: Venice/Vienna groups of Roman Catholic monks; informative, reliable).

g432 *a*) *Dedeyan* Gérard, Histoire de l'Arménie et des Arméniens des origines au Moyen-Age; – *b*) *Hintlian* Kévork, La communauté arménienne de Jérusalem: DossA 177 (1992) 10-21 / 112-131 [*al.* Turquie, France, USA...].

g433 *Diakonoff* Igor M., Sacrifices in the city of Teišebâ (UKN 448) — lights on the social history of Urarţu: ArchMIran 24 (1991) 13-21.

g434 *Kalantarian* Aram, *al.*, Armenische und sasanidische Bautätigkeit in Dvin [Erivan, near Ararat peak]: ArchMIran 25 (1992) 219-233; 11 fig.; pl. 52-57.

g435 **Kellner** Hans-Jörg, Gürtelbleche aus Urartu: Präh.Bronzefunde 12/3. Stu 1991, Steiner. vii-87 p.; 23 fig.; 89 pl. – ᴿBonnJbb 192 (1992) 592s (Imma *Kilian*).

g436 **Kleiss** Wolfram, Zur Ausbreitung Urartus nach Norden: ArchMIran 25 (1992) 91-94; 2 fig.

g437 *Tonikian* Armen, The layout of Artashat and its historical development: Mesop-T 27 (1992) 161-187; 8 fig.

g438 **Traina** Giusto, Il complesso di Trimalcione; Movsēs KORENAC'I e le origini del pensiero storico armeno: Eurasiatica 27. Venezia 1991, Univ. 127 p.

g439 **Lordkipanidze** Otar, Archäologie in Georgien von der Altsteinzeit zum Mittelalter. Weinheim 1991, V.C.H. 202 p.; 46 pl. + 12 color. – ᴿBonnJbb 192 (1992) 593-8 (Annegret *Plontke-Lüning*).

g440 *Lordkipanidze* Otar, Vani, an ancient city of Colchis: GrRByz 32 (1991) 151-195.

T9.1 **Cyprus.**

g441 ᴱ**Barlow** Jane A., *al.*, Cypriote ceramics; reading the prehistoric record: Mg 74. Ph 1992, Univ. Museum. xvi-258 p. 0-924171-10-3 [OIAc 3,12].

g442 **Connelly** Joan B., Votive sculpture of Hellenistic Cyprus. Nicosia 1988, Dept. Ant. xi-128 p.; 54 pl. 9963-36-413-6. – ᴿJPrehRel 5 (1991) 89s (P. *Åström*).

g443 *a) Demakopoulou* K., Mycenaean vases from Cyprus in the National Archaeological Museum of Athens; – *b) Bikai* Patricia M., Cyprus and Phoenicia; literary evidence for the Early Iron Age; – *c) Masson* Emilia, Le dieu guerrier à Enkomi; est-il debout sur un lingot?; – *d) Wright* G. R. H., The Cypriot rural sanctuary: → 99, ᶠKARAGEORGHIS V. 1992, 141-150, pl. XXIII-XXVI / 241-8 / 155s; pl. XXVIII / 269-283.

g444 **Demetriou** Andreas, Cypro-Aegean relations in the early Iron Age [< diss.]: SIMA 83. Göteborg 1989, Åström. xvi-114 p.; 230 fig. 91-86098-75-6 [OIAc 3,18].

g445 [Palma] **di Cesnola** Louis, Cyprus, its cities, tombs, and temples [1877; NY Met collection classified by J. *Myres* in 1909]. 1991 = 1878 [+foreword etc.]; C£30: ᴿAfO 38s (1991s) 161-7 (G. R. H. *Wright*); RArchéol (1992) 413s (O. *Masson*).

g446 **Held** Steven O., Pleistocene fauna and holocene humans; a gazetteer of paleontological and early archaeological sites on Cyprus: SIMA 95. Jonsered 1992, Åström. 195 p.; 3 maps. 91-7081-025-7 [OIAc 5,24].

g447 **Hermary** Antoine, Musée du Louvre ... Chypre 1989 → 6,e928; 7,e123*: ᴿGnomon 64 (1992) 626-9 (Veronica *Tatton-Brown*, Eng.): Syria 69 (1992) 476-9 (E. *Gubel*).

g448 **Karageorghis** Vassos, Les anciens Chypriotes, entre Orient et Occident: Néréides. P 1991, Errance. 218 p.; ill. [OIAc 5,26]. – ᴿRArchéol (1992) 415.

g449 **Karageorghis** Vassos, The coroplastic art of ancient Cyprus, I. Chalcolithic — Late Cypriote I. Nicosia 1991, Leventis. xii-219 p.; 151 fig.; 151 pl.; map. C£35 [ClasR 43, 128, H. W. *Catling*].

g449* **Karageorghis** V., End of late bronze in Cyprus [lecture Trier 1988]. Nicosia 1990, Pierides. 36 p.; 18 fig.; 20 pl. – ᴿSyria 69 (1992) 240s (Valérie *Cook*).

g450 **Niklasson** Karin, Early prehistoric burials in Cyprus: SIMA 96, 1991 → 7,e126*; Sk 500: ᴿAJA 96 (1992) 766s (K. *Randsborg*); JPrehR 6 (1992) 51-54 (E. *Peltenburg*).

g451 *Orphanides* Andreas G., The Bronze Age terracotta anthropomorphic figurines from Cyprus; their interpretation: → 557*, Contacts 1990/2, 221-6.

g452 ᴱ**Peltenburg** Edgar J., Early society in Cyprus 1988/9 → 5,861 ... 7,e128: ᴿSyria 69 (1992) 241-4 (H. de *Contenson*).

g453 **Walberg** Gisela, The Nelson and Helen Glueck collection of Cypriote antiquities, Cincinnati: SIMA pocket 111. Jonsered 1992, Åström. ii-66 p.; 36 pl. 91-7081-029-X [OIAc 5,38].

g454 *Amathonte* 1991: BCH 116 (1992) 755-791; 62 fig. (Emmanuelle *Du Bouetiez, al.*) [793-831, fouilles: à Chypre 1991, D. *Christou*]. – TEuph 4 (1991) 9-20 (T. *Petit*).

g455 ᴱ**Karageorghis** V., *al.*, La nécropole d'Amathonte: ÉtChyp 14. Nicosia 1992, Éc. Fr. Athènes / Leventis. 174 p.; 20 fig.; 36 pl. [RStFen 21, 246, Annachiara *Fariselli*].

g456 *Aupert* Pierre, Progrès de l'archéologie et de l'histoire de l'étéochypriote Amathonte depuis OHNEFALSCH-RICHTER: FolOr 27 (1990) 81-88; 4 fig. (plan).

g457 *Hala Sultan Tekke*: *Åström* Paul, Hala Sultan Tekke et l'Égypte: CRAI (1992) 877-882; 4 fig.

g458 *Idalion* 1987: RepCyp (1992) 167-178; 10 fig.; pl. LII-LIV (Pamela *Gaber*); 179-183 ceramics (R. S. *Marris*).

g459 *Masson* Olivier, Les fouilles américaines à Idalion (1971-1980) et leurs résultats épigraphiques: Kadmos 31 (1992) 113-123; IV pl.

g460 *Kataliontas*: *Buchholz* Hans-Günter, *Ender* Wolfgang, Kataliontas-Kourvellos, eine präkeramische Siedlung im Zentrum Zyperns: Praeh-Zts 67 (1992) 163-182; 12 fig.

g461 *Katydhata*: *Åström* Paul, Katydhata ...: SIMA 86, 1989. [excav. 1916]: ᴿBO 49 (1992) 512s (D. *Bolger*).

g462 *Kissonerga-Mosphilia* 8th 1990: Levant 24 (1992) 209-211; 2 fig. (E. *Peltenburg*).

g463 *Kourion*: **Sinos** S., *al.*, The temple of Apollo Hylates at Kourion. Athens 1990, Leventis. 301 p. ᴿClasR 42 (1992) 141-3 (H. W. *Catling*).

g464 *Kouris*: **Flourentzos** Pavlos, Excavations in the Kouris Valley, I. The tombs. Nicosia 1991, Dept. Antiquities. ix-71 p.; 13 fig.; 48 pl. [ClasR 43, 126, H. W. *Catling*].

g465 *Maroni* 1990s: RepCyp (1992) 271-283; 8 fig.; pl. XCIII-XCIV (S. W. *Manning*, D. H. *Conwell*).

g466 *Nicosia*: **Merrillees** Robert S., Nicosia before Nicosia: Leventis Lectures 2. Nicosia 1992, Leventis. 15 p.; 9 fig. 9963-560-13-X [OIAc 5,29].

g467 *Palaipaphos* 1991: RepCyp (1992) 285-317; 14 fig. (D. W. *Rupp, al.*).

g468 **Karageorghis** Vassos, Tombs at Palaepaphos 1/2, 1990 ➙ 7,e142*: ᴿClasR 42 (1992) 139-141 (H. W. *Catling*).

g469 Nea Paphos 1985/6/8: ÉtTrav 16 (Wsz 1992) 269-323; 33 fig. (W. A. *Daszewski*).

g470 *Mikocki* Tomasz, Essai de reconstruction du Mur Ouest de la Salle I dans la 'Maison d'Aion' à Nea Paphos: ÉtTrav 16 (Wsz 1992) 135-150; 9 fig. [2-4 à lire palais de Thésée; 6 bol de bronze; 7 phot. renversée; 9 Maison d'Aion].

g471 **Nicolaou** J., Paphos II. The coins from the house of Dionysos. Nicosia 1990, Dept. Antiq. 227 p.; 41 pl. – ᴿNumC 152 (1992) 199s (K. *Butcher*).

g472 *Olzewski* Marek E., L'allégorie, les mystères dionysiaques et la mosaïque de la maison d'Aiôn de Nea Paphos à Chypre: BMosAnt 13 (1990s) 444-462; 2 fig.

g473 *Soloi*: **Ginouvès** René, Soloi, dix campagnes de fouilles (1964-74), La 'ville basse' 1989 ➙ 7,e142*: ᴿPhoenix 46 (Toronto 1992) 80-82 (M. *Lebel*).

g473* **Toumba** S.: **Vermeule** Emily D. T., *Wolsky* Florence Z., Toumba tou Skourou, a Bronze Age potters' quarter on Morphou Bay in Cyprus. CM 1990, Harvard Univ. (1971-3 excavation). xxxix-442 p.; 46 fig.; 11 + 183 pl. £80. – [ClasR 43, 366-8, P. *Warren*].

T9.3 *Graecia*, **Greece** – mainland sites in alphabetical order.

g474 Archaiologikon deltion ☉ 42 (for 1987: 1992) B 1-2 Chronika. xii-348 p., 194 pl.; p. 349-713; pl. 195-395.

g475 **Archibald** Zofia, Discovering the world of the ancient Greeks. NY 1991, Facts on File. 192 p.; ill. $30. 0-8160-2614-9. – ᴿClasW 86 (1992s) 146s (G. *O'Sullivan*).

g476 *Brunet* M., Campagnes de la Grèce antique; le danger du prisme athénien [... R. OSBORNE]: TopO 2 (1992) 33-51.

g477 **Burkert** Walter, The orientalizing revolution; Near Eastern influence on Greek culture in the early archaic age, ᵀwith *Pinder* Margaret E. CM 1992, Harvard Univ. ix-225 p. 0-674-64363-1 [OIAc 5,16].

g478 **Étienne** Roland et Françoise, La Grèce antique; archéologie d'une découverte 1990 ➤ 7,e144; 2-07-05304-34: ᴿAntClas 61 (1992) 674s (G. *Raepsaet*).

g479 *Loucas* Ioannis, *Loucas-Durie* Éveline, Chronique des fouilles: Kernos 5 (1992) 307-317.

g480 **Ridgway** David, The first western Greeks. C 1992, Univ. xix-180 p.; 38 fig.; 14 pl. 0-521-30882-8; pa. -42164-0.

g481 **Rouillard** Pierre, Les Grecs et la péninsule ibérique du VIIIᵉ au IVᵉ s. av. J. C.: Casa Velázquez 21. P 1991, De Boccard, 467 p.; 48 fig.; 16 pl., 16 maps, 10 microfiches. F 600. 0339-1736. – ᴿAJA 96 (1992) 770s (M. *Dietter*: impressive).

g482 **Snodgrass** Anthony M., An archaeology of Greece 1987 ➤ 3,f86 ... 5,e667: ᴿGnomon 64 (1992) 147-152 (H. G. *Niemeyer*).

g483 **Whitley** James, Style and society in Dark Age Greece; the changing face of a pre-literate society 1100-700 B.C.: New Studies in Archaeology. C 1991, Univ. xx-225 p.; 21 fig.; 39 pl. £32.50. – ᴿClasR 42 (1992) 400s (M. J. *Alden*); GreeceR 39 (1992) 104 (B. A. *Sparkes*); PrPrehSoc 58 (1992) 435s (O. *Dickinson*).

---

g484 *Argos* 1991: BCH 116 (1992) 673-6 (-684) 4 fig. (M. *Piérart*).

g485 *Antonaccio* Carla M., Terraces, tombs, and the early Argive Heraion: Hesperia 61 (1992) 85-105; 6 fig.; pl. 23-26 [491-500 al., Mycenaean pictorial pottery].

g486 *Viret Bernal* Francine, Argos, du palais à l'Agora [licence Lausanne 1987, ᴰBérard C.]: DialHA 18,1 (1992) 61-88; 4 pl.; Eng. 88.

g487 **Dietz** Søren. The Argolid at the transition to the Mycenaean Age ... 1991 ➤ 7,e149: ᴿClasR 42 (1992) 395s (R. A. *Tomlinson*).

g488 *Athenae*: **Bohen** Barbara, Die geometrischen Pyxiden: Kerameikos 13. B 1988, de Gruyter. ix-153 p.; 29 fig.; 44/20 pl. – ᴿGnomon 64 (1992) 273s (J. *Bouzek*).

g489 **Kovacsovics** Wilfried K., Kerameikos XIV. Die Eckterrasse 1990 ➤ 7, e153: ᴿRArchéol (1992) 142-4 (Marie-Thérèse *Le Dinahet*).

g490 **Knigge** Ursula, The Athenian Kerameikos; history, monuments, excavations. ᵀBinder Judith. Athens 1991, Krene. 196 p.; 164 (color.) fig. [1988].

g491 *Gadbery* Laura M., The sanctuary of the twelve gods in the Athenian agora; a revised view: Hesperia 61 (1992) 447-489; 13 fig.; pl. 105-111.

g492 **Grandjouan** Clairève †, ᴱ*Markon* Eileen, *Rotroff* Susan I., Hellenistic [terracotta] relief molds from the Athenian agora: Hesperia supp. 23. Princeton 1989, Amer. Sch. Athens. xvii-71 p.; 2 fig.; 34 pl. – ᴿClasR 42 (1992) 402s (H. W. *Catling*); Gnomon 64 (1992) 629-632 (Carola *Reinsberg*).

g493 *Harrington* Spencer P. M., Shoring up the temple of Athens; the Western World's most cherished monument gets a much-needed face-lift [scaffolding for 10 more years]: Archaeology 45,1 (1992) 30-43; ill.

g494 *Harris* Diane, Bronze statues on the Athenian acropolis; the evidence of a Lycurgan inventory: AJA 96 (1992) 637-652, 7 fig.

g495 **Lang** Mabel L., Ostraka; The Athenian agora 25, 1990 ➤ 7,e156: ᴿClasR 42 (1992) 160-2 (A. *Johnston*); RÉAnc 94 (1992) 292s (A. *Bresson*).

g495* **Rotroff** Susan I., *Oakley* John H., Debris from a public dining place in the Athenian Agora [1972]: Hesperia supp. 25. Princeton 1992, Amer. School Athens. xiii-154 p.; 26 fig.; 64 pl. $35 [ClasR 43, 371, B. A. *Sparkes*].

g496 *Nagy* Blaise, Athenian officials on the Parthenon frieze: AJA 96 (1992) 55-69; 14 fig.

g497 *Papachatzis* N. A., Ⓖ Chthonic Athena and associated chthonic deities at the Athens acropolis: ArchEph 128 (1989) 1-14.

g498 *Tölle-Kastenbein* Renate, Die Athener Akropolis-Koren; Ort, Anlässe und Zeit ihrer Aufstellung: AntWelt 23 (1992) 133-148; 19 fig.

g499 **Waele** Jos de, The propylaea of the Akropolis in Athens; the project of Mnesikles. Amst 1990, Gieben. xx-86 p.; 39 fig.; 5 pl. ƒ95. 90-5063-059-6. – ᴿAntClas 61 (1992) 658 (C. *Delvoye*); GreeceR 39 (1992) 106 (B. A. *Sparkes*).

g500 *Weidauer* Liselotte, *Krauskopf* Ingrid, Urkönige in Athen und Eleusis; neues zur 'Kekrops'-Gruppe des Parthenonwestgiebels: JbDAJ 107 (1992) 1-16; 4 pl.

g501 **Willers** Dietrich, Hadrians panhellenisches Programm ... Athen 1990 ➤ 7,e163: ᴿBonnJbb 192 (1992) 718-722 (S. *Mitchell*, Eng.); ClasR 42 (1992) 372-4 (A. J. S. *Spawforth*).

g502 — *Étienne* Roland, La nouvelle Athènes d'Hadrien: RÉAnc 94 (1992) 269-271.

g503 *Boeotia:* ᶠLAUFFER Siegfried, Boiotika (Kolloq.) ᴱReister H., *Buckler* J., 1989/9 ➤ 6,746: ᴿAnzAltW 45 (1992) 71-73 (G. *Dobesch*); Gymnasium 99 (1992) 285-7 (H. *Matthäus*).

g503* **Effenterre** Henri van, Les Béotiens; aux frontières de l'Athènes antique: Civilisations. P 1989, A. Colin. 217 p.; ill. 2-200-21244-5.

g504 *Snodgrass* Anthony, The Boeotia project: CamArch 1,1 (1991) 136-9; map.

g505 *Corinthus:* **Engels** Donald, Roman Corinth; an alternative model for the classical city 1990 ➤ 7,e164: ᴿAJA 96 (1992) 573s (M. C. *Hoff*); BibTB 22 (1992) 39s (R. L. *Rohrbaugh*: revisionist description of the classical city to counter left-wing bias); ClasR 42 (1992) 119s (A. J. *Spawforth*).

g507 *Hannestad* Lise, Athenian pottery in Corinth, c. 600-470 B.C.: AcArchK 62 (1991) 151-163.

g508 **Dickey** Keith, Corinthian burial customs, ca. 1100 to 550 B.C.: diss. Bryn Mawr, ᴰWright J. Ph 1992. 418 p. 92-25195. – DissA 53 (1992s) 1201-A.

g509 **Pemberton** Elizabeth G., The sanctuary of Demeter and Kore : Corinth 18/1, 1989 ➤ 7,e166: ᴿAION-clas 44 (1992) 357-9 (F. *Canciani*) & 390-4 (A. *Martin* on 18/2, K. SLANE); ClasW 85 (1991s) 57 (G.P. *Schaus*); Gnomon 64 (1992) 734 (Christiane *Dehl-von Kaenel*); JHS 112 (1992) 216s (K.W. *Arafat*).

g510 — **Slane** Katherine W., The sanctuary of Demeter and Kore, the Roman pottery and lamps; Corinth 18/2. Princeton 1990, Amer. School Athens. xvi-160 p.; 33 fig. 18 pl.; 3 plans. $65. – ᴿClasR 42 (1992) 479s (D.M. *Bailey*); ClasW 86 (1992s) 68s (Ann *Steiner*); RArchéol (1992) 411-3 (Catherine *Abadie-Reynal*).

g511 *Romano* David G., The planning of Roman Corinth, AIA 1991: ➤ 699, AJA 96 (1992) 336.

g512 *Steiner* Ann, Pottery and cult in Corinth; oil and water at the sacred spring: Hesperia 61 (1992) 385-408; 6 fig.; pl. 87.

g513 *Gebhard* Elizabeth R., *Hemans* Frederick P., Chicago excavations at Isthmia 1989, I: Hesperia 61 (1992) 1-77; 19 fig.; pl. 1-19 [133-191 *al.*, Frankish Corinth 1991].

g514 *Delphi*: Delphes 1991: BCH 116 (1992) 685-711; 33 fig. (plan) (F. *Lefèvre, al.*) [833-954, Anne *Pariente*, fouilles en Grèce 1991].

g515 a) *Amandry* Pierre, Delphes oublié; – b) *Marcadé* Jean, Delphes retrouvé: CRAI (1992) 793-800 / 801-9.

g516 **Daux** Georges, *Hansen* Erik, Le trésor de Siphnos 2. Topographie et architecture: Fouilles de Delphes, 1987 ➤ 4,g693; 5,e692: ᴿGnomon 64 (1992) 244-250 (W. *Koenigs*).

g517 **Bommelaer** J.-F., *al.*, Guide de Delphes; le musée, le site 1991 ➤ 7,e170: ᴿNikephoros 5 (1992) 271-7 (W. *Decker*); RÉAnc 94 (1992) 518-520 (M. *Brunet*).

g518 *Jacquemin* Anne, *Laroche* Didier, La terrasse d'Attale Iᵉʳ revisitée: BCH 116 (1992) 229-258; 16 fig.

g519 ᴱPicard Olivier, La redécouverte de Delphes. P 1992, de Boccard. 295 p.; 181 (color.) fig. 2-86958-050-9.

g520 *Lacroix* Léon, À propos des offrandes à l'Apollon de Delphes et du témoignage de PAUSANIAS [Periégèse X, 8-14...]; du réel à l'imaginaire: BCH 116,1 (1992) 157-176 (177-196, *Bousquet* Jean, Inscriptions de Delphes).

g521 *Maass* Michael, Die wirtschaftlichen und politischen Umstände der delphischen Tempelbauten: Ktema 13 (1988) 5-11.

g521* *Malkin* Irad, Delphoi and the founding of social order in archaic Greece: Métis 4 (1989) 129-153.

g522 *Müller* Sylvie, Delphes et sa région à l'époque mycénienne: BCH 116 (1992) 445-496; 18 fig.

g523 *Swain* Simon, PLUTARCH, Hadrian and Delphi: Historia 40 (1991) 318-330.

g523* **Vatin** Claude, Monuments votifs de Delphes: Arch 100 (perusina 10). R 1991, Bretschneider. iv-267 p.; 115 fig.; 11 pl. [ClasR 43, 458s, Catherine *Morgan*].

g524 *Goritsa*: **Bakhuizen** S.C., A Greek city of the fourth century B.C. by the Goritsa team: BtArchaeol 10. R 1992, Bretschneider. 329 p.; 113 fig.; 207 phot.; 5 foldouts. 88-7062-720-9.

g525 *Halai* [E. Lokris, today Theologos N of Boeotia] 1990s: Hesperia 61 (1992) 265-289; 5 fig.; pl. 69-74 (J. E. *Coleman*).

g526 *Macedonia*: *Zahlhaas* Giselo,   Ein makedonischer Grabfund und verwandte Bronzen aus Makedonien: ➤ 101, [F]KELLNER H., Spursuchen 1991, 31-54; 27 fig.

g527 *Mycenae*: **McDonald** W. A., [2] *Thomas* Carol G., Progress into the past... Mycenaean 1990 ➤ 7,e178: [R]ClasR 42 (1992) 226 (Mervyn *Popham*).

g528 *a*) *Darcque* Pascal,   Les fortifications mycéniennes; – *b*) *Snodgrass* Antony M., Les premières fortifications grecques; DossA 172 (1992) 12-19 / 20-27; color. ill.

g528* *Laffineur* Robert, Material and craftsmanship in the Mycenae shaft graves; imports vs. local production: Minos 25s (1990s) 245-295.

g529 *Niemeier* Wolf-Dieter, La struttura territoriale della Grecia micenea : ➤ 673, Geog. Gr. 1989/91, 123-149.

g530 **Ozanne** Isabelle, Les Mycéniens; pillards, paysans et poètes: Néréides. P 1990, Errance. 255 p.

g530* **Ruipérez Martín** S., *Melena* José L., Los griegos micénicos: BtHistoria 16. M 1990. 267 p. pl 850.   [R]Minos 25s (1990s) 465-7 (Kathleen A. *Cox*: much new information).

g531 *Nemea*: **Miller** S. G. *al.*, Nemea, guide 1990 ➤ 7,e181: [R]AJA 96 (1992) 563s (Donna B. *Wescoat*); Nikephoros 4 (1991) 274-280 (W. *Decker*).

g531* **Birge** Darick E., *al.*, Excavations at Nemea... the Sacred Square, the Xenon, and the Bath. Berkeley 1992, Univ. California. xxx-319 p.; 496 fig.; 6 maps. $70 [ClasR 43, 372-4, Catherine *Morgan*].

g532 *Olympia*: **Hitzl** Konrad, Die kaiserzeitliche Statuenausstattung des Metroon: OlympFor 19, 1991 ➤ 7,e183: [R]ArchWsz 43 (1992) 140-2 (Z. *Kiss*, français).

g533 *Siewert* Peter, *a*) Staatliche Weihungen von Kesseln und anderen Bronzegeräten in Olympia; – *b*) Die frühe Verwendung und Bedeutung des Ortsnamens 'Olympia'; MiDAI-A 106 (1991) 81-84; pl. 9 / 65-69; pl. 4.

g534 *Sinn* Ulrich, Bericht über das Forschungsprojekt 'Olympia während der römischen Kaiserzeit', I. Die Arbeiten von 1987-1992: Nikephoros 5 (1992) 75-84; 3 fig.

g535 *Pylos*: *Popham* Mervyn, Pylos; reflections on the date of its destruction and of its Iron Age reoccupation: OxJArch 10 (1991) 315-324; 6 fig.

g535* *Jasink* Anna M., Funzionari e lavoranti nel palazzo di Pilo: Minos 25s (1990s) 203-243.

g536 *Sparta*: *Bonnefond-Coudry* M., Mythe de Sparte et politique romaine; les relations entre Rome et Sparte au début du IIe siècle av. J.-C.: Ktema 12 (1987) 81-110.

g537 **Cartledge** P., *Spawforth* A., Hellenistic and Roman Sparta 1989 ➤ 6, e988; 7,e187: [R]JHS 112 (1992) 206 (S. *Hodkinson*); JRomA 4 (1991) 231-4 (J. J. *Wilkes*).

g538 *Sunium*: *Sinn* Ulrich, Sunion; das befestigte Heiligtum der Athena und des Poseidon an der 'Heiligen Landspitze Attikas': AntWelt 23 (1992) 173-190; 20 fig.

g539 **Thessalia: Decourt** J.-C., La vallée de l'Enipeus en Thessalie, étude de topographie et de géographie antique: BCH suppl. 20. P 1990, Éc. Fr. Athènes/Boccard. 252 p.; 42 pl. – ᴿRArchéol (1992) 407-410 (D. *Rousset*); RÉG 105 (1992) 281s (J.-N. *Corvisier*).

g540 **Tiryns: Weisshaar** Hans-Joachim, *al.*, Tiryns 11: DAI-A. Mainz 1990, von Zabern. vii-171 p.; 58 pl.; 8 maps. DM 148. – ᴿClasR 42 (1992) 397s (O. *Dickinson*: largely animal remains).

T9.4 **Creta.**

g541 **Alexiou** Stylianos, Minoische Kultur: Sternstunden der Archäologie [1964], ᵀ*Liebich* Werner. Gö 1976, Musterschmidt. 163 p.; 28 pl. 3-7881-1508-4.

g542 *a)* **Carinci** Filippo, *D'Agata* Anna Lucia, Aspetti dell'attività cultuale a Creta nel III e nel II millennio a. C.; – *b)* **Curti** Susanna, I 'santuari d'altura' minoico-micenei nel contesto dell'età del bronzo nell'Egeo: → 701, ScAnt 3s (1989s) 221-242; Eng. 242 / 263-270; Eng. 270.

g543 **Castleden** Rodney, Minoans; life in Bronze Age Crete 1990 → 6,e995; £19: ᴿAntClas 61 (1992) 648 (Frieda *Vandenabeele*).

g544 **Chaniotis** A., Habgierige Götter, habgierige Städte; Heiligtumsbesitz und Gebietsanspruch in den kretischen Staatsverträgen: Ktema 13 (1988) 31-39.

g545 **Dierckx** Heidi M. C., Aspects of Minoan technology, culture, and economy; the Bronze Age stone industry of Crete: diss. Pennsylvania, ᴰ*Muhly* J. Ph 1992, 439 p. 92-27650. – DissA 53 (1992s) 1565-A.

g546 *Eliopoulos* Theodore, The earliest Minoan ritual hammer? Notes on the emergence of a Cretan emblem: JPrehRel 5 (1991) 48-61; 8 fig.

g547 *Empereur* Jean-Yves, *al.*, Recherches sur les amphores crétoises (III): BCH 116 (1992) 633-648; 11 fig. (maps).

g548 *Godart* Louis, *a)* I minoici: Archeo 7,86 (1992) 49-103; – *b)* I signori di Apodoulou; scavi a Creta: ArchViva 11,26 (1992) 10-23.

g549 **Godart** Louis, *Tzedakis* Yannis, Témoignages archéologiques et épigraphiques en Crète occidentale du Néolithique au Minoen Récent III B: Incunabula Graeca 93. R 1992, Gruppo Ed. Int. 356 p.; 173 pl.

g550 **Kirsten** Ernst, Die Insel Kreta in vier Jahrtausenden. Amst 1990, Hakkert. 126 p. 90-256-0943-0. – ᴿAntClas 61 (1992) 666 (Didier *Viviers*).

g551 ᴱ**Marangou** Lila, Minoan and Greek civilization from the Mitsotakis collection. Athens 1992, Goulandris Museum of Cycladic Art. 332 p.; color. ill.

g552 **Mastorakis** Michael, *Effenterre* Micheline van, Les Minoens; l'âge d'or de la Crète 1991 → 7,e196*; 2-87772-054-3: ᴿCretan Studies 3 (1992) 231s (R. F. *Willetts*); RÉAnc 94 (1992) 408s (Michèle *Brunet*).

g553 **Walberg** Gisela, Middle Minoan III — a time of transition: SIMA 97. Jonsered 1992, Åström. 166 p.; 14 pl. — 91-7081-037-0 [OIAc 5,38].

___

g554 *Atsipadhes: Peatfield* Alan, Rural ritual in Bronze Age Crete; the peak sanctuary at Atsipadhes [farthest east of the 25 shown on a map of Crete]: CamArch 2 (1992) 59-87; 25 fig.; with comments of P. *Warren*, C. *Renfrew*, Joyce *Marcus*, J. *Cherry*, R. *Hägg*.

g555 *Knossos: a) Branigan* Keith, The early keep, Knossos; a reappraisal; – *b) Momigliano* Nicoletta, The 'proto-palatial façade': AnBritAth 87 (1992) 153-163 / 165-175, pl. 8-10.

g556 **Driessen** Jan, An early destruction in the Mycenaean palace of Knossos: AcArchaeolLv Mg 2. Lv 1990, Univ. vi-151 p.; 19 fig.; 41 ill. Fb 1500. – ᴿClasR 42 (1992) 137-9 (P. *Warren*).

g557 *a) Momigliano* Nicoletta,   MMIA pottery from Evans' excavations at Knossos; a reassessment; – *b) Paton* Sara,   A Roman Corinthian building at Knossos; – *c) Warren* P. M.,   A new Minoan deposit from Knossos, c. 1600 B.C., and its wider relations: AnBritAth 86 (1991) 149-271; 39 fig; pl. 17-57 / 297-318; 14 fig.; pl. 62-74 / 319-340; 10 fig.; pl. 75-80.

g558 **Niemeier** Wolf-Dietrich,   Die Palaststilkeramik von Knossos; Stil, Chronologie und historischer Kontext: ArchFor 13, 1985 → 7,e202: ᴿIstVArh 43 (1992) 329s (M. *Simon* †).

g559 *Palmer* Leonard R. †,   Die letzten Riten im Thronraum von Knossos: → 184, ᶠTRENTINI J. B., Echo 1990, 279-287.

g560 **Sackett** L. H., *Branigan* K., *al.*,   Knossos from Greek city to Roman colony; excavations at the Unexplored Mansion II: BritAth supp 21.   L 1992, British School at Athens.   I. xii-498 p.; II. vii-353 p.   0-0904887-081 [sic, in both].

g561 **Sjöquist** Karl-Erik, *Åström* Paul, Knossos; keepers and kneaders: SIMA 82.   Jonsered 1991, Åström.   129 p.; 29 pl.   91-86098-95-0 [BO 49,591]. – ᴿMinos 25s (1990s) 434-6 (T. G. *Palaima*).

g562 **Tiemann** I.,   Die Deutung des Minotaurus von den ältesten Quellen bis zum frühen Mittelalter: Diss. Utrecht, ᴰ*Broek* R. van den, 1992. 274 p. – TvT 32 (1992) 305; RTLv 24, p. 597.

g563 **Weingarten** Judith,   The transformation of Egyptian Taweret into the Minoan genius; a study of cultural transmission in the Middle Bronze Age: SIMA 88.   Partille 1991, Åström.   24 p.; 8 pl.   91-7081-028-1. – ᴿJPrehR 6 (1992) 55s (N. *Marinatos*).

g564 *Whitelaw* T. M.,   Lost in the labyrinth? Comments on BROODBANK's 'Social change at Knossos before the Bronze Age' [1983]: JMeditArch 5 (1992) 225-238.

g565 *Kommos,* Crete: **Betancourt** Philip P.,   Kommos, The final neolithic through Middle Minoan III pottery.   Princeton 1990, Univ.   X V-262 p.; 70 fig.; 109 pl. $150. – ᴿAJA 96 (1992) 174s (J. S. *Soles*); ClasR 42 (1992) 135-7 (P. *Warren*); JHS 112 (1992) 211s (Carol *Zerner*).

g566 *Malia* 1991: BCH 116 (1992) 733-753; 44 fig. (J.-C. *Poursat, al.*).

g567 *Farnoux* Alexandre,   Malia et la Crète à l'époque mycénienne: → 703*, RArchéol (1992) 201-216; 18 fig.

g568 **Hue** Michel, *Pelon* Olivier,   La Salle à Piliers du palais de Malia et ses antécédents: BCH 116 (1992) 1-36; 40 fig.

g569 *Mochlos* island 1989: Hesperia 61 (1992) 413-445; 15 fig.; pl. 89-104 (J. S. *Soles, C. Davaris*).

g569* **Soles** Jeffrey S.,   The prepalatial cemeteries at Mochlos and Gournia and the house tombs of Bronze Age Crete: Hesperia supp. 24.   Princeton 1992, Amer.Sch.Athens.   xxi-266 p.; 40 pl.; 3 plans; map. $35 [ClasR 43, 365s, C. *Mee*].

g570 *Nerokouro:* **Kanta** A., *Rochetti* L., *al.*,   Scavi a Nerokouro, Kydonias I; ricerche greco-italiane in Creta occidentale: Incunabula Graeca 91.   R 1989. 339 p. – ᴿMinos 25s (1990s) 460s (J. *Driessen*).

g570* *Palaikastro:* *MacGillivray* J. A., *Sackett* I. A., *al.*,   Excavations at [Minoan] Palaikastro, 1990: AnBritAth 86 (1991) 121-147; 22 fig.; pl. 6-16.

T9.5   Insulae graecae.

g571 ᴱ**Acquaro** E.,   Momenti precoloniali nel Mediterraneo antico 1985/8 → 5,811: ᴿOrLovPer 22 (1991) 235s (F. van *Wonterghem*).

g571* **Burdajewicz** Mariusz, The Aegean sea peoples and religious architecture in the eastern Mediterranean at the close of the Late Bronze Age: BAR-Int 558. Ox 1990. ix-196 p.; 60 fig. – ᴿJPrehR 6 (1992) 45-50 (Y. *Pararas*: challenging).

g572 *Cline* Eric H. & Martin J., 'Of shoes...' International trade and the Late Bronze Age Aegean: Expedition 33,3 (Ph 1991) 46-54; 11 fig.

g573 **Cosmopoulos** Michael B., The Early Bronze 2 in the Aegean [diss, Washington U. 1989]: SIMA 98. Jonsered 1991, Åström. XII-327 p.; 12 pl. 91-7081-019-2 [OIAc 5,17 'Cosmopolous'].

g574 **Crowley** Janice L., The Aegean and the east: SIMA pocket 51, 1989 ➤ 5,d321; 7,e212: ᴿJSStEg 18 (1988!) 117s (R.H. *Wilkinson*: a serious attempt); RAss 86 (1992) 185 (P. *Amiet*); Syria 69 (1992) 239 (aussi P. *Amiet*).

g575 *Davis* Jack L., Review of Aegean prehistory, I. The islands of the Aegean: AJA 96 (1992) 699-756; 25 fig.

Drews Robert, The coming of the Greeks ... Aegean and Near East 1988 ➤ 4,d330 ... 7,b224.

g576 **Lambrou-Phillipson** C., Hellenorientalia; the Near Eastern presence in the Bronze Age Aegean ca. 3000-1100 B.C.; interconnections based on the material record and written evidence plus Orientalia, a catalogue ... [< diss.]: SIMA pocket 95. Göteborg 1990, Åström. 503 p.; 81 fig.; 4 maps. Sk 250. ᴿAntClas 61 (1992) 649s (F.-J. *DeCree*).

g577 **Treuil** René, *al.*, Les civilisations égéennes du Néolithique et de l'Âge de Bronze: NClio 1, 1989 ➤ 6,503; 7,e213: ᴿClasR 42 (1992) 132-5 (R.L.N. *Barber*); ÉtClas 60 (1992) 177s (J. *Vanschoenwinkel*); Syria 69 (1992) 466-9 (Corinne *Castel*).

---

g578 *Chios*: **Lemos** Anna A., Ancient pottery of Chios; the decorated styles : Mg 30. Ox 1991, Committee Arch.

g579 *Keos*: **Overbeck** John C., Ayia Irini period IV,1: Keos 7, 1989 ➤ 5, e734; 7,e224: ᴿAJA 96 (1992) 175s (Susan H. *Allen*); AntClas 61 (1992) 655s (R. *Laffineur*); Gnomon 64 (1992) 371-4 (S. *Hiller*).

g580 *Cherry* John F., The Ptolemaic base at Koressos on Keos: AnBritAth 86 (1991) 9-28; map.

g581 *Lemnos*: a) **Messineo** Gaetano, Gli scavi di Achille ADRIANI a Lemno (1928-1930); – b) *Bonacasa* Nicola, Un inedito di A. Adriani sulla tomba di Alessandro: ➤ 640b, Giornate 1984/91, 3-19; 5 fig. VI pl. / 141-154; 10 fig.

g582 *Lesbos*; **Stos-Gale** Zofia, The origin of metal objects from the Early Bronze Age site of Thermi on the island of Lesbos [Siphnos island and Troad]: OxJArch 11 (1992) 155-177; 3 fig.

g583 *Naxos*: **Lentini** Maria C., C'era una volta Naxos: ArchViva 10,17 (1991) 34-49; color. ill.

g584 ᴱ**Marangou** Lila, Cycladic culture; Naxos in the 3rd millennium BC. Athens 1990, Goulandris. 179 p.; ill.; 2 maps. £15. – ᴿGreeceR 39 (1992) 104 (B.A. *Sparkes*, also p. 242 on RENFREW 1991).

g585 *Paros*: **Overbeck** John C., The Bronze Age pottery from the Kastro at Paros [RUBENSOHN O. c. 1900): SIMA pocket 78. Jonsered 1989, Åström: vii-36 p.; 84 fig.; 12 pl. 91-85058-09-2. – ᴿAntClas 61 (1992) 656s (R. *Laffineur*).

g586 **Schuller** Manfred, Der Artemistempel im Delion auf Paros: DAI-Denkmäler 18,1, 1991 ➤ 7,e226: ᴿRArchéol (1992) 400-2 (M.C. *Hellmann*).

g587 **Rhodus: Benzi** Mario, Rodi e la civiltà micenea: Incunabula Graeca 94. R 1992, Gruppo Ed. Int. I. testi, xxiii-482 p.; II. 186 pl.

g588 *Catling* H. W., A late Cypriot import in Rhodes: AnBritAth 86 (1991) 1-7; 2 fig.

g588* *Gabrielsen* Vincent, The status of Rhodioi in ancient Rhodes: ClasMedv 43 (1992) 43-69.

g589 **Samos: Shipley** Graham, History of Samos 1987 ➤ 4,g773; 5,e741 (6,g750): ᴿClasR 42 (1992) 355s (R. *Osborne*).

g590 **Samothrace: Dinsmoor** Anastasia N., Red-figured pottery from Samothrace: Hesperia 61 (1992) 501-515; 4 fig.; pl. 117-120.

g591 **Frazer** Alfred, Samothrace, the Propylon of Ptolemy II; Bollingen 60/10. Princeton 1990, Univ. xxi-244 p.; v-88 p. (184 fig.); 88 pl. $130. 0-691-09922-7. – ᴿClasW 85 (1991s) 147s (Susan H. *Auth*).

g592 **Tenos: Étienne** Roland, Ténos II 1990 ➤ 7,e231 ['*Roland* E.']: ᴿAJA 96 (1992) 564s (N. K. *Bauh*); AntClas 61 (1992) 661-5 (G. *Schepens*, Eng.: magnificent); RPg 65,2 (1991) 54-59 (É. *Will*).

g593 **Teos: Graham** A. J., Abdera and Teos: JHS 112 (1992) 44-73.

g594 *Riejko* Francis, Antiochus III and Teos reconsidered [HERRMANN P., Anadolu 9 (1965) 29-159, in general excellent]: Belleten 55, 212 (1991) 13-69.

g595 **Thasos: Grandjean** Yves, Contribution à l'établissement d'une typologie des amphores thasiennes; le matériel amphorique du quartier de la Porte du Silène: BCH 116 (1992) 541-584; 16 fig. [721-6 *al.*, Thasos 1991].

g595* **Duchêne** Hervé, La stèle du port; fouilles du port, I. recherches sur une nouvelle inscription thasienne: ÉtThas 14. Athènes/P 1992, Éc. Française / de Boccard. 157 p.; 20 pl.; 1 plan. [ClasR 43, 402, D. M. *Lewis*].

g596 *Holtzmann* Bernard, L'habitat grec et les fouilles de Thasos: RÉAnc 94 (1992) 261-7.

g597 **Thera: Forsyth** P. Y., After the big bang; eruptive activity in the caldera of Greco-Roman Thera: GiRByz 33 (1992) 191-204; pl. 3.

g598 ᴱ**Hardy** D. A., *al.*, Thera and the Aegean world III, 1989. L 1990, Thera Foundation ➤ 7,642: I. Archaeology, 511 p.; II. Earth Sciences, 487 p.; III. Chronology, 242 p. 0-9506133-7-1. – ᴿJField 19 (1992) 92-95 (C. *Runnels*); JHS 112 (1992) 212s (R. L. N. *Barber*).

g599 *Knapp* A. Bernard, Bronze Age Mediterranean island cultures and the Ancient Near East [... Thera, Rhodes]: BA 55 (1992) 52-72, 112-129; ill.

g600 **Marinatos** Nanno, Art and religion in Thera 1984 ➤ 65,b663 ... 3,f174: ᴿRBgPg 70 (1992) 269-271 (J. *Vanschoonwinkel*).

T9.6   Urbs Roma.

g601 **Almar** Knud P., Inscriptiones latinae; eine illustrierte Einführung in die lateinische Epigraphik: ClasSt 14. Odense 1990, Univ. 569 p. Dk 328. – ᴿArctos 26 (1992) 147-9 (O. *Salomies*: more ambitious than KEPPIE).

g602 *Amedick* Rita, Die Tychen des Silberschatzes vom Esquilin und der Wagen des Praefekten von Rom: JbAC 34 (1991) 107-114; 1 fig.; pl. 1.

g603 **Amici** Carla Maria, Il foro di Cesare. F 1990, Olschki. 169 p. + album. Lit. 95.000. – ᴿArcheo 7,83 (1992) 126 (D. *Manacorda*).

g604 *Bergemann* Johannes, Marc Aurel als Orientsieger? Noch einmal zur Ikonographie der Reiterstatue auf dem Kapitol in Rom: ArchMIran 24 (1991) 135-140; pl. 19-23.

g605 [de Angelis] *Bertolotti* Romana, Contributo per un'aggiornamento della forma urbis: MiDAI-R 98 (1991) 111-120; 4 fig.; pl. 28.

g606 **Broise** Henri, *Scheid* John, Recherches archéologiques à la Magliana, le 'balneum' des Frères Arvales: Roma antica 1. R 1987, Éc. Fr. / Surintendance. 186 p.; 236 fig.; 3 pl. – ᴿRArchéol (1992) 157s (V. *Jolivet*).

g607 *Casavola* Franco, Il concetto di 'urbs Roma'; giuristi e imperatori romani: Labeo 38 (1992) 20-29.

g607* [Fine] **Licht** Kjeld de, *al.*, Sette Sale, Untersuchungen zu den Trajansthermen in Rom, 2: Inst. Dan. Rom. Anal. supp. 19. R 1990, Bretschneider. 125 p.; 146 pl. – ᴿAthenaeum 80 (1992) 521-3 (Elena *Calandra*).

g608 *Fishwick* Duncan, *a*) The statue of Julius Caesar in the Pantheon: Latomus 51 (1992) 329-336; – *b*) On the temple of Divus Augustus: Phoenix 46 (Toronto 1992) 232-255.

g609 *Galinsky* Karl, Venus, polysemy, and the Ara Pacis Augustae: AJA 96 (1992) 457-475; 21 fig.

g610 *Garbrecht* Günther, *Manderscheid* Hubertus, 'Etiam fonte novo Antoniniano'; l'acquedotto antoniniano alle Terme di Caracalla: AION-clas 44 (1992) 193-234; 30 (color.) fig.

g611 *Grandazzi* A., Contribution à la topographie du Palatin: RÉLat 70 (1992) 28-34.

g612 **Hinard** François, *Royo* Manuel, Rome; l'espace urbain et ses représentations [P. BIGOT model, Caen 1937]; préf. *Nicolet* Claude. P/Tours 1991, Univ. 286 p.; 74 fig. F 250 pa. [ClasR 43, 205, R. *Laurence*].

g613 **Jashemski** Wilhelmina F., *Salza Prina Ricotti* Eugenia, Preliminary excavations in the gardens of Hadrian's villa; the Canopus area and the Piazza d'Oro: AJA 96 (1992) 579-597; 18 fig.

g614 **Keppie** Lawrence, Understanding Roman inscriptions. L 1991, Batsford. 158 p. £15 pa. – ᴿArctos 26 (1992) 146-9 (O. *Salomies*, also on ALMAR).

g615 *Kleiner* Fred S., The Trajanic gateway to the Capitoline sanctuary of Jupiter optimus maximus: JbDAI 107 (1992) 149-174; pl. 53-60.

g616 *a*) *Köppel* Gerhard M., Der Fries der Trajanssäule in Rom, 2. Der zweite dakische Krieg, Szenen LXXIX-CLV; – *b*) *Bode* Reinhard, Interpretationsversuch; – *c*) *Chrysos* Evangelos, Von der Räumung der Dacia Traiana zur Entstehung der Gothia: BonnJbb 192 (1992) 61-121, 56 fig. / 123-174 / 175-194.

g617 **Leander Touati** Anne-Marie, The great Trajanic frieze 1987 ⮕ 4,e290 ... 6,d613: ᴿAION-clas 44 (1992) 339-342 (S. *Tortorella*); AnzAltW 45,1 (1992) 112-4 (N. *Hannestad*).

g617* *Levi* Mario A., Augusto e l'Urbe (rassegna): Athenaeum 79 (1991) 579-583.

g618 **Meyer** Hugo, Antinoos; die archäologischen Denkmäler unter Einbeziehung der numismatischen und epigraphischen Materials sowie der literarischen Nachrichten [Hab. Diss. Mü 1985s]. Mü 1991, Fink, 278 p.; 147 pl.

g619 *Murgatroyd* P., The porticus vipsania and contemporary poetry: Latomus 51 (1992) 79-100.

g620 *Muzzioli* Maria Pia, Fonti per la topografia della IX regione di Roma; alcune osservazioni: PBritSR 60 (1992) 179-211; 14 fig.; Eng. 424: Campus Martius from Tiber to Pantheon and towards Flaminia.

g621 **Neumeister** Christoff, Das antike Rom, ein literarischer Stadtführer 1991 ⮕ 7,e256: ᴿRÉAnc 94 (1992) 520s (F. *Hurlet*); RÉLat 70 (1992) 346s (R. *Chevallier*).

g622 *Packer* James E., Trajan's forum in 1989 [PENSABENE Patrizia, *al.* ArchClas 41 (1989) 27-291]: AJA 96 (1992) 151-162; 3 fig.

g623 *Packer* James E., *Sarring* Kevin L., *al.*, Il foro di Traiano: Archeo 7,93 (1992) 63-93; ill.

g624 **Palmer** Robert E. A., Studies of the northern Campus Martius in ancient Rome: AmPhTr 80/2, 1990 ➤ 7,e257; $12. 0-87169-802-1: ᴿClasW 85 (1991s) 61 (P. *Harvey*).

g625 *Patterson* John R., The city of Rome, from republic to empire: JRS 82 (1992) 186-215; 5 fig.

g626 *Poulter* A. G., Trajan's column and the Dacian wars [LEPPER F. 1988; SETTIS A. 1988]: Britannia 23 (1992) 331-3.

g627 **Richardson** Lawrence, A new topographical dictionary of ancient Rome. Baltimore 1992, Johns Hopkins Univ. xxxvi-458 p.; 92 fig. 0-8018-4300-6.

g628 **Ridley** Ronald T., The eagle and the spade; archaeology in Rome during the Napoleonic era. C 1992, Univ. xxviii-328 p.; 78 pl. 0-521-40191-7.

g629 **Settis** Salvatore, La colonne Trajane; l'empereur et son public. Bru 1990, Féd. Prof. Gr. Lat. 27 p.; 21 pl. – ᴿLatomus 51 (1992) 269s (A. *Malissard*).

g630 *Simpson* C. J., On the unreality of the Parthian arch [19 B.C., DIO 54,8,3]: Latomus 51 (1992) 835-842.

g630* *Turcan* Robert, Les *tondi* d'Hadrien sur l'arc de Constantin: CRAI (1991) 53-80; 15 fig.

g631 **Vance** William L., America's Rome 1989 ➤ 6,g63: ᴿRelStR 17 (1992) 186 (W. G. *Rusch*).

g632 **Velestino** Daniela, La collezione epigrafica dei Musei Capitolini: Comune di Roma, Centro di coordinamento didattico 44. R 1991, Palombi. 35 p. 0394-9753.

g633 **Yarden** Leon *zal.*, The spoils of Jerusalem on the Arch of Titus: Acta Inst. Rom. Sueciae 8/16. Sto 1991, Åström. 137 p.; 32 fig.; 67 pl.; foldout plan. Sk 275. 91-7042-138-7. – ᴿAJA 96 (1992) 775s (F. S. *Kleiner*).

T9.7 *Roma,* Catacumbae.

g633* **Bargebuhr** Frederick P., The paintings of the 'new' catacomb of the Via Latina and the struggle of Christianity against paganism, ᴱ*Utz* Joachim: Abh Heid Ak p/h 1991/2. Heid 1991, Winter. 107 p.; 48 pl.

g634 **Baruffa** A., Catacombe S. Callisto ²1989 ➤ 6,g65; 7,c262: ᴿEsprVie 102 (1992) 432 (M. *Noirot*).

g635 *Carletti* Carlo, Gli affreschi della cripta di Milziade nel cimitero di S. Callisto; interventi di restauro: RivArCr 68 (1992) 141-168 (-171); 14 fig. [+ p. 329-331].

g636 La catacomba anonima di via Anapo; repertorio delle pitture. Vaticano 1991, Pont. Ist. Arch. Cr. 3 vol. 120 p. ognuno; 24 color. pl. Lit. 200.000. – ᴿArcheo 7,91 (1992) 127 (F. *Bisconti*).

g637 **Deckers** Johannes G., *al.* Die Katakombe Ss. Marcellino e Pietro 1987 ➤ 3,f211 ... 6,g68: ᴿVigChr 45 (1991) 404-7 (P. van *Moorsel*).

g638 *Deckers* J. G., Wie genau ist eine Katakombe zu datieren? Das Beispiel SS. Marcellino e Pietro: ➤ 164, ᴲSAXER V., Memoriam 1992, 217-238; 1 plan.

g639 **Duval** Yvette, Auprès des saints corps et âme; l'inhumation 'ad sanctos' dans la chrétienté d'Orient et d'Occident du IIIᵉ au VIIᵉ siècle 1988 ➤ 5,e774 ... 7,e264: ᴿJbAC 34 (1991) 211-3 (Sible de *Blaauw*); LavalTP 48 (1992) 466s (L. *Painchaud*); Latomus 51 (1992) 487-9 (Brigitte *Beaujard*); RechSR 80 (1992) 290-3 (Yves-M. *Duval*: ample enquête épigraphique mais sans Index).

g640 **Eisner** Michael, Zur Typologie der Grabbauten im Suburbium Roms [< Diss. Marburg 1968]. M 1986, von Zabern. 254 p.; 60 pl.; 9 foldouts. – ᴿGnomon 64 (1992) 345-8 (V. *Kockel*).

g641 **Farmer** W. R., *Kereszty* R., Peter and Paul in the church of Rome 1990 ➤ 6,g52; 7,e265: ᴿRelStR 18 (1992) 130 (J. T. *Ford*).

g642 **Guyon** J., Le cimetière 'Aux deux lauriers' 1987 ➤ 4,g814 ... 7,e268*: ᴿByZ 84s, 1 (1991s) 146-8 (E. *Jastrzebowska*).

g643 **Hertling** Ludwig, *Kirschbaum* Engelbert, Le catacombe romane e i loro martiri⁴ [¹1941]. R 1992, Pont. Univ. Gregoriana. – ᴿCC 143 (1992,3) 341s (A. *Ferrua*).

g644 *Isman* Fabio (incontro con *Zevi* Tullia), Un tesoro nascosto; le catacombe ebraiche a Roma: Archeo 7,91 (1992) 108-117.

g645 ᴱ**Kolendo** Jerzy, *Bianchini* Francesco, Camera ed iscrizioni sepulcrali dei liberti, servi ed ufficiali della casa di Augusto scoperta nella via Appia [1727]: Antiqua 60. N 1991, Jovene. xl-87 p. – ᴿRÉLat 70 (1992) 456 (J.-C. *Richard*).

g646 **Konikoff** Adia, [22] Sarcophagi from the Jewish catacombs of ancient Rome² 1990 ➤ 7,d269*: ᴿRHPR 72 (1992) 212 (P. *Prigent*: rapprochements avec Bet Shearim).

g647 *Mazzoleni* Danilo, *Bisconti* Fabrizio, I martiri cristiani: Archeo 7,87 (1992) 53-97.

g648 *Pergola* Philippe, [*al.*], Rome; à la découverte des catacombes: MondeB 73 (1991) [3-] 13-35; ill.

g648* **Ruggeri** Costantino, Stenografie dell'anima; simboli epigrafici delle catacombe. CasM 1991, Piemme. 168 p.; ill. Lit. 75.000. – ᴿLetture 47 (1992) 373-5 (G. A. *Dell'Acqua*).

g649 *Rutgers* Leonard V., Archaeological evidence for the interaction of Jews and non-Jews in late antiquity [Rome catacombs]: AJA 96 (1992) 101-118; 7 fig.

g650 *Spera* Lucrezia, Un cubicolo monumentale nella catacomba di Pretestato: RivArCr 68 (1992) 271-307; 18 fig.

T9.8 *Roma,* **Ars palaeochristiana.**

g651 *Bejaoui* Fathi, Découvertes paléochrétiennes récentes en Tunisie; monuments et décors du sol: RivArCr 68 (1992) 317s (résumé).

g652 *Brandenburg* Hugo, La chiesa di S. Stefano Rotondo a Roma; nuove ricerche e risultati; un rapporto preliminare: RivArCr 68 (1992) 201-232; 4 fig. + foldout.

g653 —— *Martin* Archer, Sondages under S. Stefano Rotondo (Rome); the pottery and other finds: Boreas 14s (1991s) 157-178; 48 fig.
Chalkia Eugenia, La mensa paleocristiana 1991 ➤ e254.

g654 **Duval** Noël, *al.*, Naissance des arts chrétiens; Atlas des monuments paléochrétiens de la France: Atlas archéologiques de la France. P 1991, Imprimerie nationale. 434 p.; 210 fig. + 364 en couleurs; maps. F 890. – ᴿEsprVie 102 (1992) 109s (J. *Rocacher*: 19 spécialistes, commencé 1983 par Duval).

g655 **Ferrua** Antonio,   La polemica antiariana nei monumenti 1991 ➤ 7,e875: ^RRHPR 72 (1992) 327s (P. *Maraval*).

g656 *Monfrin* Françoise,   À propos de Milan chrétien; siège épiscopal et topographie chrétienne IVe-VIe siècles: CahArch 39 (1991) 7-46; 28 fig.

g657 **De Rossi**, Giovanni Battista [1822-94],   ^E*Mazzoleni* Danilo, *Carletti* Carlo: Inscriptiones christianae vrbis Romae septimo saecvlo antiqviores NS.   Vaticano 1992, Pont. Inst. Archaeologiae Christianae.   [viii-] 262 p.; XXXVII pl.   88-85991-03-3.

Zanker P. Pompeji, Stadtbilder 1988 ➤ k269.

T9.9   *(Roma) Imperium occidentale*, **Europa**.

g658 *Barberi* Franco, *al.*,   Riscoprire Pompei; informatica ed archeologia: ArchViva 10,15 (1991) 26-40; color. ill.
Rediscovering Pompeii 1990 ➤ d518.

g660 — **Carocci** Francesco, *al.*,   Le insule 3 e 4 della Regio VI di Pompei; un'analisi storico-urbanistica: Arch 89, Perusina 5.   R 1990, Bretschneider.   245 p.; 60 pl.; 27 foldouts in case.   Lit. 550.000.   ^RGnomon 64 (1992) 185-7 (V. *Kockel*: consists of four doctoral dissertations).

g661 *a) Cuporusso* Donatella,   Alcuni elementi per la topografia di Milano in età romana; – *b)* [Pani] *Ermini* Letizia,   Roma tra la fine del IV e l'inizio del V secolo; – *c)* [Farioli] *Campanati* Raffaello,   Ravenna capitale: ➤ 706, Milano capitale 1990/2, 45-60; 10 fig. / 193-202; 2 fig. / 375-380; 2 fig.

g662 *Fiocchi Nicolai* Vincenzo, [*al.*],   Scavi nella catacomba di S. Senatore ad Albano Laziale: RivArCr 68 (1992) 7-70 [-140]; 45 fig.; 3 foldouts.

g663 **Fröhlich** Thomas,   Lararien- und Fassadenbilder in den Vesuvstädten; Untersuchungen zur 'volkstümlichen' pompejanischen Malerei: MiDAI-R, Egh. 32.   Mainz 1991, von Zabern.   370 p.; 11 fig.; 41 pl. + 23 color.   DM 198 [ClasR 43,139, R. *Ling*].

g664 **Greco** Emanuele,   Archeologia della Magna Grecia: Manuali 29.   R 1992, Laterza.   xi-398 p.; ill.   2-200-21244-5.

g665 **Greenhalgh** Michael,   The survival of Roman antiquities in the Middle Ages 1989 ➤ 6,g93: ^RAntClas 61 (1992) 774-6 (F. *Verhaeghe*).

g665* **Heuze** Philippe,   Pompéi ou le bonheur de peindre: Antiques. P 1990, de Boccard.   166 p.; 19 fig. F 190.   2-7018-0057-9 [Latomus 52,526, R. *Chevallier*].

g666 **Kind** Richard de,   Huizen in Herculaneum [blok 3s], een analyse van de stadebouw en de maatvoering: diss. Nijmegen 1992, auct.   iii-390 p.; 16 fig.

g667 **Laidlaw** Anne,   The first style in Pompeii; painting and architecture 1985 ➤ 3,f238; 5,e800:   ^RLatomus 51 (1992) 230s (Hélène *Eristov*).

g668 *a) Lavagne* Henri,   Chronique Gallo-Romaine; – *b) Bémont* Colette,   Chronique de céramologie de la Gaule: RÉAnc 94 (1992) 429-443 / 445-453.

g669 *Long* Charlotte R.,   The [Naples museum 18] Pompeii calendar medallions: AJA 96 (1992) 477-501; 5 fig.

g669* **Millett** Martin,   The Romanization of Britain; an essay in archaeological interpretation. 1990.   £35.   0-521-36084-6. – ^RLatomus 52 (1993) 939s (R. *Chevallier*).

g670 **Moscati Castelnuovo** Luisa,   Siris; tradizione storiografica e monumenti della storia di una città della Magna Grecia: Coll. Latomus 207. Bru 1989.   175 p.; 3 maps. – ^RAntClas 61 (1992) 577-9 (P. *Desy*); Athenaeum 80 (1992) 267-9 (D. *Asheri*).

Neudecker Richard, Die Skulpturenausstattung römischer Villen in Italien 1988 ➤ e83.
g671 Pompei, the vanished city. Lost Civilizations. Alexandria VA 1992, Time-Life. 168 p.; ill.
g672 **Pontrandolfo** Angela, *Rouveret* Agnès, Le tombe dipinte di Paestum. Modena 1992, (Cosimo) Panini. 487 p.; 82 fig. color. ill.; maps.
g672* *Quattrocchi* Giovanna, Ercolano e Pompei: Archeo 7,94 (1992) 3-120.
ᴱ**Randsborg** Klaus, The birth of Europe 1987/9 ➤ 732.
g673 *Russo* Eugenio, 'Ravenna, Hauptstadt des spätantiken Abendlandes' di Friedrich W. DEICHMANN [1991]: VetChr 29 (1992) 137-160.
g674 *Warden* P. Gregory, The sculptural program of the [Herculanum] Villa of the Papyri [NEUDECKER R., 'römische Villen in Italien' 1988]: JRomA (1991) 257-261.
g674* **Watts** Dorothy, Christians and pagans in Roman Britain. L 1991, Routledge. XIV-302 p.; 29 fig. £35. 0-415-05071-5 [Latomus 52,718, S. S. *Frere*: archaeological traces].
Zanker Paul, Pompeji, Stadtbilder 1988 ➤ k269.

XIX. Geographia biblica

U1 **Geographies.**

g675 **Ahrweiler** Hélène, Géographie historique du monde méditerranéen: ByzSorbon 7. P 1988, Sorbonne. 312 p.; 3 foldout maps. F 180. 2-85944-152-2. – ᴿJbÖsByz 42 (1992) 347s (F. *Hild*).
g676 *Chrostowski* Waldemar, ❷ 'Terra fluens lacte et melle'; meditacja nad geografią historyczną Palestyny: RuBi 44 (1991) 131-8.
g677 ᴱ**Corna Pellegrini** G., *Bianchi* E., Varietà delle geografie; limiti e forza della disciplina [Seminario Univ. Mi 28.XI.1989]: Acme quad 14. Mi 1992, Cisalpino. 211 p. 88-205-06694-7.
Decourt Jean-Claude, La vallée de l'Enipeus en Thessalie; études de to-pographie antique: BlCH supp 21, 1990 ➤ g359.
g679 **Ehlers** Eckart, *al.*, Der islamische Orient; Grundlagen zur Länderkunde eines Kulturraums I.: Köln, Islamische Akademie Wechselbeziehung. Fra 1990, Diesterweg. xv-417 p.; 51 fig.; maps. DM 48. – ᴿJRAS (1992) 260 (W. *Madelung*: mainly regional environment; vol. 2-3 will treat history and religion).
g680 **Gać** Jan, ❷ Moja ziemia święta. Łódź 1992, Klio. 272 p. – ᴿColcT 62,3 (1992) 193s (W. *Chrostowski,* ❷).
g681 **Gomaà** Farouk, *al.*, Mittelägypten zwischen Samalūt und dem Gabal Abu Svi; Beiträge zur historischen Topographie der pharaonischen Zeit: TAVO B-69. Wsb 1991, Reichert. xx-288 p.; 96 pl. 3-88226-467-5 [BO 49,584].
g682 **González Echegaray** J., El creciente fertil y la Biblia 1991 ➤ 7,e302: ᴿRB 99 (1992) 766s (J. *Loza*: does not always cite latest or available Spanish edition); RBiArg 53 (1991) 170s (P. *Andiñach*); Salmanticensis 39 (1992) 292s (M. *García Cordero*, también sobre Entorno 1).
g684 **Gyselen** Rika, La géographie administrative de l'Empire Sassanide; les témoignages sigillographiques: Res Orientales 1. P 1989, Ét.Civ. Moyen-Orient. xx-166 p.; 3 pl. 1142-2831.
g685 **Haag** Herbert, El país de la Biblia; geografía, historia, arqueología [Das Land], ᵀ*Villanueva Salas* Marciano. Barc 1992, Herder, pb. 1509. 243 p.

84-254-1764-3. – ᴿActuBbg 29 (1992) 199s (J. *O'Callaghan*); LumenVr 41 (1992) 398 (F. *Ortiz de Urtaran*); REspir 51 (1992) 361s (S. *Castro*).

g686 ᴱ**Kark** Ruth, The land that became Israel 1990 ➤ 7,347: ᴿPEQ 124 (1992) 156 (B. S. J. *Isserlin*).

g687 **Marshall** Bruce, The real world. Boston 1991, Houghton-M. £20. 0-395-52450-4. – ᴿMonth 253 (1992) 33 (C. *Hunt*: the New Geography).

g688 **Nicolet** Claude, Space, geography, and politics in the early Roman empire (Jerome Lectures 19). AA 1991, Univ. Michigan. xii-230+34p. – ᴿClasPg 87 (1992) 183-5 (E. S. *Gruen*).

g689 **Ogden** D. K., Where Jesus walked; the land and culture of NT times. Salt Lake City 1991, Deseret. viii-171p.; 7 maps. 0-87579-530-7 [NTAbs 36,299].

g690 **Pritchett** W. Kendrick, Studies in ancient Greek topography [1. 1965; 2. 1969; 3. 1980; 4. 1982; 5. 1985; 6. Berkeley 1989, Univ. California. ix-142p.; 4 fig.; 244 pl. $37. – 7. Amst 1991, Gieben. x-228p.; 10 fig.; 173 pl. *f*160 [ClasR 43,131-4, G. *Shipley*].

g691 *Raphael* G. Nicholas, Geography and the Bible (Palestine): AnchorDB 2 (1992) 964-977 (Early Jewish, 977-988, Philip S. *Alexander*).

g691* **Samsari** Dimitri K., Ⓖ *Historikē geōgraphía tēs romaikēs eparchias Makedonias*. Thessaloniki 1989, Soc. Macedonian Studies. VII-328p.; XXXVI pl. 96-0726-501-7 [Latomus 52,488, D. *Marcotte*].

g692 ᴱ**Scott** J., *Simpson-Housley* P., Sacred places 1991 ➤ 7,328: ᴿRelStR 18 (1992) 310 (M. S. *Jaffee*).

g693 **Soustal** Peter, Thrakion (Thrakē, Rodope and Haimimontos): Tabula imperii byzantini 6. W 1991, Österr. Akad. 579p.; 2 foldout maps. DM 280. ➤ g302. – ᴿRÉByz 50 (1992) 321s (J.-C. *Cheynet*).

u1.2 Historia geographiae.

g494 *Alercrombie* Thomas J., IBN BAṬṬUṬA, prince of travelers: NatGeog 180 (1991) 4-49.

g695 *a) André-Sulvini* Béatrice, Une carte topographique des environs de la ville de Girsu (pays de Sumer); – *b) Salvini* Mirjo, Il canale di Se-miramide: GeogAnt 1 (1992) 57-62+8 fig. / 67-77+8 (color) fig.

g696 *Arafat* K. W., PAUSANIAS' attitude to antiquities: AnBritAth 87 (1992) 387-409.

g697 *a) Arnaud* Pascal, Les relations maritimes dans le Pont-Euxin d'après les données numériques des géographes anciens; – *b) Lévêque* Pierre, Recherches nouvelles sur le Pont-Euxin: RÉAnc 94 (1992) 57-74; 3 maps / 49-56; 3 fig.

g698 **Bernecker** Annemarie, Die Feldzüge des Tiberius und die Darstellung der unterworfenen Gebiete in der 'Geographie' des PTOLEMAEUS 1989 ➤ 6,g115: ᴿGnomon 64 (1992) 265-7 (O. A. W. *Dilke*, Eng.).

g699 *Bonnafé* Annie, Texte, carte et territoire; autour de l'itinéraire d'Io dans le Prométhée [ESCHYLE, 2 cartes p. 168] (partie I): JSav (1991) 133-193 ...

g700 **Bradshaw** Joseph, The imperishable stars of the northern sky in the Pyramid Texts. L c. 1991, auct. – ᴿVarAeg 8 (1992) 115-8 (C. *Leitz*: 'die einzige und wahre Initiation in die Pyramidentexte').

g701 **Bultrighini** U., PAUSANIA e le tradizioni democratiche; Argo ed Elide. Padova 1990, Programma. 286p. – ᴿAevum 65 (1991) 179-181 (Cinzia *Bearzot*).

g702 ᵀᴱ**Burstein** Stanley M., AGATHARCHIDES, On the Erythraean Sea: Hakluyt 2/172, 1989 ➤ 7,e318: ᴿJAOS 112 (1992) 500 (A. A. *Mosshammer*: fine).

g703 *Caballero Sánchez* Raul, Excursus geografici nella Vita Alexandri di
PLUTARCO: → 654, Convegno 4, 1991/2, 91-97.

g704 ᴱCasevitz Michael, *al.*, PAUSANIAS, Description de la Grèce I, L'Attique,
ᵀ*Pouilloux* J.: Coll. Budé. P 1992, BLettres. xlvi-313 (d.) p. – ᴿRÉG 105
(1992) 631s (A. *Wartelle*).

g704* **Casson** Lionel, The periplus maris erythraei 1989 → 5,e819*; 7,e319:
ᴿOriento 33,2 (1990) 139-145 (Y. *Shitomi*, ◑).

g705 *Chadwick* Robert, Celestial episodes and celestial objects in ancient
Mesopotamia: BCanadMesop 22 (1991) 43-49; 3 fig.

g706 *Citroni Marchetti* Sandra, Filosofia e ideologia nella 'Naturalis historia'
di PLINIO: → 742, ANRW 2,36,5 (1992) 3248-3306.

g707 **Cardano** Federica, La geografia degli antichi. R 1992, Laterza. viii-
216 p.; p. 60 fig. Lit. 33.000. 88-420-3906-3. – ᴿArcheo 7,88 (1992) 128
(P. G. *Guzzo*).

g708 *a)* *Couloubaritsis* Lambros, Cosmogonies et cosmologies présocratiques;
– *b)* *Donnay* Guy, La révolution des orbes célestes d'Anaximandre à
Copernic: → 693, D'Imhotep 1989/92, 141-158 / 13-22.

g709 *a)* ᴱ*Cuntz* Otto, Itineraria ANTONINI Augusti et Burdigalense [1929]; –
b) ᴱ**Schnetz** Joseph, RAVENNATIS anonymi Cosmographia et GUIDONIS
Geographica [1940]: Itineraria romana 1s. Stu 1990, Teubner. xv-139 p.,
map; DM 75 / x-214 p.; DM 115. 3-519-04273-8; -4-6. – ᴿAntClas 61
(1992) 522 (Marie-T. *Raepsaet-Charlier*).

g710 **Dankoff** Robert, *Krieser* Klaus, Materialien zu Evliya Çelibi: II. A
guide to the Seyaḥat-Name of Evliya Çelibi: TAVO B-90/2. Wsb 1992,
Reichert. 200 p. 3-88226-535-3 [OIAc 3,17].

  Delano-Smith C., *Ingram* E. M., Maps in Bibles 1991 → g753.

g711 **Döring** Klaus, *Wöhrle* Georg, Antike Naturwissenschaft und ihre Rezeption. Bamberg 1992, Collibri. viii-313 p.; 38 fig. [ClasR 43,413,
G. E. R. *Lloyd*: WOLF ARMIN on whether Homer had a map; several
others on sky-maps].

g712 **Donner** Herbert, The Mosaic Map of Madaba, an introductory guide:
Palaestina antiqua 7. Kampen 1992, Kok Pharos. 182 p.; 1 loose map.
90-390-0011-5.

g713 *Dubler* C. E. †, Al-Andalus en la geografía de al-IDRĪSĪ: Studi
Maghrebini 20 (1988) 113-151 [45-112, chapters on Egypt, *Monés* Husein].

g714 **Ekschmitt** Werner, Weltmodelle; griechische Weltbilder von Thales
bis PTOLEMÄUS: KuGAW 43, 1989 → 6,g122; DM 34. 3-8053-1092-7. –
ᴿAntClas 61 (1992) 508 (Monique *Mund-Dopchie*).

g715 *a)* *Fabre* Paul, Les Grecs à la découverte de l'Atlantique; – *b)* *Briard*
Jacques, Les relations atlantiques protohistoriques: → SOPHAU 1991,
RÉAnc 94 (1992) 11-20, map / 7s; 2 fig. (map).

g716 *a)* *Funke* Peter, STRABONE, la geografia storica e la struttura etnica della Grecia nord-occidentale; – *b)* *Koder* Johannes, Sopravvivenza e trasformazione delle concezioni geografiche antiche in età bizantina: → 673,
Geografia 1989-91, 174-193 / 46-66.

g717 ᴱ*Fusillo* Massimo, Antonio DIOGENE; le incredibili avventure al di là
di Tule 1990 → 7,e322: ᴿClasR 42 (1992) 184 (G. *Anderson*); Maia 44
(1992) 204-6 (C. *Bevegni*).

g718 *a)* *Gehrke* Hans-Joachim, Die wissenschaftliche Entdeckung des Landes
Hellás; – *b)* *Aujac* Germaine, Napoléon, [Diamantios] CORAY, et la
première traduction française de la Géographie de STRABON: GeogAnt 1
(F 1992) 15-36; pl. I-II / 37-49 + 6 pl.

g719 *González Ponce* F.-J., Revisión de la opinión de A. PERETTI [1961]

sobre el orígen cartográfico del Periplo del Ps.-ESCÍLAX: Habis 22
(Sevilla 1991) 151-5.
g720 *Grant* Robert M., Early Christian geography: VigChr 46 (1992) 105-111.
g721 **Guzmán** Carmen, *Pérez* Miguel E., Concordantia in libros POMPONII
MELAE De chorographia 1989 ➤ 7,e324:   ᴿGnomon 64 (1992) 59-61 (D.
Najock).
g722 ᵀᴱ**Healy** John F., PLINY the Elder, Natural History – a selection. NY
1991, Penguin. xliii-400 p.; $10 pa. 0-14-044413-0. – ᴿClasW 86 (1992s)
249 (C. F. *Natunewicz*).
g723 ᵀᴱ**Hewsen** Robert H., The geography of ANANIAS of Širak
(Ašxarhacʿoucʿ); the long and the short recensions: TAVO B-77. Wsb
1992, Reichert. xii-467 p. 3-88226-485-5 [OIAc 5,24].
g724 *a*) *Hind* G., HERODOTUS' Geography of Scythia; the rivers and the
'rugged peninsula'; – *b*) *Boardman* J., Perceptions of Colchis: ➤ 724,
Black Sea 1987/90, 127-138 / 195-197 [202-214 *al.*].
g726 **Koch** Johannes, Neue Untersuchungen zur Topographie des babylonischen Fixsternhimmels 1989 ➤ 5,e834:   ᴿWeltOr 23 (1992) 168-170
(D. *Pingree*).
g727 **Kunitzsch** Paul, C. PTOLEMAEUS, Der Sternkatalog des Almagest [1,
1986 ➤ 4,g884 ... 7,e333]: II. Die lateinische Übersetzung GERHARDS von
Cremona; III. Gesamtkonkordanz der Sternkoordinaten. Wsb 1990s,
Harrassowitz. [viii-344 p.] viii-174 p.; viii-200 p. 3-447-02[581-6] -984-6;
-985-4. – ᴿJAOS 112 (1992) 708-710 (G. *Saliba*); Scriptorium 46 (Bru
1992) 151 (E. *Poulle*).
g728 *Lafond* Yves, PAUSANIAS historien dans le livre VII de la Périégèse:
JSav (1991) 27-45.
g729 **Laut** Jens P., Materialien zu Evliya Çelebi [Reisender 1611-1684]:
TAVO map B IX 6, Beih 90/1, 19 ➤ 5,e836:   ᴿOLZ 87 (1992) 284s (H.
Stein).
g730 **Le Bœuffle** A., Le ciel des Romains [astronomy, varia]. P 1989, de
Boccard. – ᴿJRS 92 (1992) 238s (Tamsyn *Barton*)
g731 **Leitz** Christian, Studien zur ägyptischen Astronomie: ÄgAbh 49, 1989
➤ 5,c837 ... 7,e335:   ᴿBO 49 (1992) 723-8 (R. A. *Wells*: should have been
reviewed before publication rather than after): OLZ 87 (1992) 23-26 (A.
Spalinger).
g732 *Levrero* Roberta, La géographie de l'Égypte selon HÉRODOTE; les
expéditions de Cambyse contre les Éthiopiens et les Ammoniens: ➤ 735,
Sesto Eg. 1991/2, 397-408.
g733 **Licini** Patrizia, La regione armena nella 'Mappa mundi' medievale di
tradizione occidentale: OrChrPer 58 (1992) 515-525; 8 fig.
g733* *Liebmann* M., Die Heiligland-Karte Lucas CRANACHs des Älteren, ein
kunstgeschichtlicher Bericht: Wiener JbKunstG 45 (1992) 195-9; 8 fig.
[< RHE 88,305*]. ➤ m338.
g734 **Madathil** Commen John, Die Theologie des Kosmas INDIKOPLEUSTES;
zum Standort zwischen alexandrinischer und antiochenischer Tradition:
Diss. ᴰ*Hofrichter* P. Salzburg 1992. 187 p. – RTLv 24, p. 552.
g735 **Pichot** André, La naissance de la science; 1. Mésopotamie, Égypte; 2.
Grèce présocratique: Folio/Essais 154s. P 1991, Gallimard. 313 p.;
474 p. 2-07-032603-9; -4-7 [OIAc 5,32].
g736 *Rengakos* Antonios, Zur Biographie des APOLLONIOS von Rhodos
[Argonautica]: WienerSt 105 (1992) 39-67.
g737 *Robin* Christian, L'Arabie du sud et la date du Périple de la Mer
érythrée (nouvelles données): JAs 279,1s (1991) 1-29; Eng. 29s.

g738 ᴱRocha Pereira Maria Helena, PAUSANIAE Graeciae descriptio 2s²ʳᵉᵛ.
[¹1977, 1981]: BtScrGR. Stu 1990, 1989, Teubner. v-338 p.; v-329 p. -
ᴿGnomon 64 (1992) 102-111 (H.-W. Nörenberg).

g739 Romm James S., The edges of the earth in ancient thought. Princeton
1992, Univ. xvi-228 p. $30. 0-691-06933-6. - ᴿClasW 86 (1992s) 254 (M.
Hammond).

g740 Sachs A. J., Hunger H., Astronomical diaries... from Babylon I, 1988
➤ 4,g110 [II. 1989 ➤ 6,e462]: ᴿZAss 81 (1991) 153-5 (W. H. van Soldt).

g741 Simek R., Erde und Kosmos im Mittelalter; das Weltbild vor Ko-
lumbus. Mü 1992, Beck. 219 p.; 32 fig.; 3 maps [RHE 87,361*].

g742 Sturm Dieter, Die Darstellung der byzantisch-islamischen Verhältnisse
bei den arabischen Geographen des 10. Jahrhunderts: ByzFor 18 (1992)
147-166.

g743 Tsavari Isabelle O., Histoire du texte de la Description de la terre de
DENYS le Periégète 1990 ➤ 7,e350: ᴿEikasmos 2 (1991) 413-5 (E. De-
gani); JbÖsByz 42 (1992) 405s (E. Gamillscheg); RFgIC 120 (1992) 478-
483 (R. Nicolai).

g744 Wajntraub E. & G., Medieval Hebrew manuscript maps: Imago mundi
44 (L 1992) 99-105; 6 fig.

g745 Warland Rainer, Die Mosaikkarte von Madaba und ihre Kopie in der
Sammlung des Archäologischen Instituts der Universität Göttingen:
AntWelt 23 (1992) 287-296; 20 (color.) fig.

U1.4   Atlas - maps.

g746 Aharoni Yohanan, Avi-Yonah Michael, La Bible par les cartes; la
Palestine de 3000 av.J.-C. [-à?] 1991 ➤ 7,e351*; F325: ᴿEsprVie 102
(1992) 605s (É. Cothenet); RBiArg 53 (1991) 168s (P. Andiñach).

g747 Atlas biblijny. Wsz 1990, 324 p. - ᴿAtKap 116 (1991) 531-4 (S. Pisarek
❺: this first Bible atlas ever to appear in Polish gives no indication
whatever of its author).

g748 ᴱBaladier Charles, Le grand Atlas des religions 1989 ➤ 7,e352:
ᴿZMissRW 75 (1991) 232 (P. Antes).

g749 ᴱBarnavi Eli, A historical atlas of the Jewish people from the time of
the patriarchs to the present, ᵀᴱEliav-Feldon Miriam; maps Opatowski
Michel. NY 1992, Knopf. xii-299 p. 0-679-40332-9 [OIAc 5,14].

g749* Bertrán Lloris F., Marco Simón F., Atlas de historia antigua.
Zaragoza 1987, Portico. 127 p. - ᴿFaventia 14,2 (1992) 112 (M. Mayer).

g750 Biscione Raffaele, D'Amore Paola, Elam e l'altipiano iranico, c.
2500-1500: Atlante Storico VO Antico 2/5. R 1992, Univ. Scienze
Storiche. 17 loose maps + 6 p. [OIAc 5,14].

g751 ᴱBurkhardt Helmut, al., Der neue Bibelatlas. Wu/Giessen 1992,
Brockhaus/Brunnen. 128 p.; (color.) ill.; maps. 3-417-24634-2 / 3-7655-
5729-3.

g752 Conti Anna Maria, Serangeli Flavia, Palestina; la preistoria fino al
2000: Atlante Storico del Vicino Oriente Antico 5/3. R 1991, Univ. 34
loose p., 23 pl. [OIAc 3,16].

g753 Delano-Smith Catherine, [Morely] Ingram Elizabeth, Maps in Bibles,
1500-1600; an illustrated catalogue: TravHumRen 256. Genève 1991,
Droz. xxxviii-202 p.; ill. Fs85 [RHE 88,603, J.-F. Gilmont]. - ᴿJEH 43
(1992) 686s (P. D. A. Harvey).

g754 Friesel Evyatar, Atlas of modern Jewish history 1990 ➤ 7,e356: ᴿBSO
55 (1992) 621 (L. Glinert).

g755 **Galbiati** E. R., *Aletti* A., Atlas histórico da Bíblia e do Antigo Oriente 1991 ➤ 7,e357: ᴿEstudosB 32 (1991) 107-9 (V. da *Silva*).

g756 **Hartmann** Karl, Atlas-Tafel-Werk zur Geschichte der Weltreligionen, 1, fernöstliche; 2. Islam; 3. Judentum. 1987-90 ➤ 7,e359: ᴿZRGg 44 (1992) 91s (W. *Beltz*).

g757 **Jedin** H., *al.*, Atlante universale di storia della Chiesa (le chiese cristiane ieri e oggi) [1987 ➤ 6,g149],ᵀ. Vaticano/CasM 1991, éd. Vaticano/Piemme. 280 p. Lit. 120.000. – ᴿEsprVie 102 (1992) 192 (M. *Noirot*).

g758 **Oliphant** Margaret, The atlas of the ancient world; charting the great civilizations of the past. NY 1992, Simon &S. 220 p. 0-671-75103-4 [OIAc 5,31].

g758* ᴱ**Pritchard** James B. Harper Atlas 1987 ➤ 3,e869... 7,e363: ᴿRBiArg 53 (1991) 169s (P. *Andiñach*).

g759 **Pritchard** J. B., ᵀᴱ*Keel* O., *Küchler* M., Herders grosser Bibelatlas 1989 ➤ 5,e870; 6,g154: ᴿGeistL 65 (1992) 155s (H. *Brandt*).

g760 **Rasmussen** Carl G., NIV atlas of the Bible 1989 ➤ 5,e871; 6,g155: ᴿCalvaryB 7,1 (1991) 68 (G. H. *Lovik*); RelStT 11,2 (1991) 90-92 (I. G. *Herr*).

g761 *Roaf* Michael, Cultural atlas of Mesopotamia and the Ancient Near East 1990 ➤ 6,g156; 7,e365: ᴿClasW 86 (1992s) 67 (J. M. *Russell*).

g762 **Roaf** M., Atlas de la Mésopotamie et du Proche-Orient ancien [Cultural Atlas 1990 ᵀ*Talon* Philippe] 1991 ➤ 7,e336: ᴿTopO 2 (1992) 167-171 (Y. *Calvet*).

g763 **Strange** John, Atlante biblico 1990 ➤ 6,g157*b: ᴿProtestantesimo 47 (1992) 134s (C. *Tron*).

g764 *Talbert* Richard J. A., Mapping the classical world; major atlases and map series 1872-1990: JRomA 5 (Ann Arbor 1992) 5-38; 1 fig.

g765 **Wajntraub** E. & G., Hebrew maps of the Holy Land. W 1992, Hollinek. xxiv-277 p.; 104 pl. 3-85119-248-6 [OIAc 5,38].

U1.5 Photographiae.

g766 **Andreae** Bernard, Die Kunst des alten Rom. FrB 1989, Herder. 244 p. – ᴿNZMissW 46 (1990) 158 (J. *Amstutz*: Bildband).

g767 *Franke* Detlef, Das Photoarchiv H. W. Müller der Universitätsbibliothek Heidelberg: GöMiszÄg 131 (1992) 33-53.

g768 *Harer* W. Benson,ᴶ, [1859] Bible illustrated by David ROBERTS [whose paintings of the Holy Land were probably the most popular of all times]: BR 7,6 (1991) 34-39.

g769 **Kennedy** D., *Riley* D., Rome's desert frontier from the air 1990 ➤ 6,g164; 7,e370: ᴿClasW 86 (1992s) 43s (Liane *Houghtalin*); Gerión 9 (1991) 324s (M. *Ribagorda*); Gnomon 64 (1992) 278s (Margot *Klee*).

g770 *Lebert* Marie France, Jérusalem et la photographie ancienne: RB 99 (1992) 544-556; Eng. 545 [photography was invented in 1839; the first examples are daguerrotypes; several of Jerusalem from 1839; (and yet) the first photo of Jerusalem dates from 1849?!].

g771 ᴱ**McManners** John. The Oxford illustrated history of Christianity [19 authors]. Ox 1990, UP. 704 p.; 350 (colour.) fig. $45. 0-19-822928-3. – ᴿRExp 88 (1991) 464 (W. L. *Hendricks*).

g772 **Perez** Nissan N., Focus past; early photography in the Near East (1839-1885). NY 1988, Abrams (with J. Domino & Israel Museum). 256 p.; ill. 0-8109-0924-3 [OIAc 3,33].

g773 *Racanicchi* Piero, *al.*, Fotografie in terra d'Egitto; immagini dell'archivio del Museo di Torino 1991 ➤ 7,e373: ᴿArcheo 7,86 (1992) 126 (S. *Pernigotti*).

g774 **Rossi** Guido A., *Rodenbeck* Max, Egypt, gift of the Nile; an aerial portrait. NY 1992, Abrams. 208 p.; ill. 0-8109-3254-7 [OIAc 5,33].

g775 *a*) **Strange** James F., Galilee archaeology slide set. Wsh 1989, BA[R]Soc. 34 p. + 140 slides. $119.50. – *b*) **Pratico** Gary, Egypt-Sinai-Negev slide set 1987. 43 p. + 142 slides. $119.50. – ᴿCurrTMiss 19 (1992) 63s (E. *Krentz*: 4-5 in the series).

g776 **Taylor** J., Jordanien; biblische Stätten im Luftbild 1990 ➤ 6,g169b; 7,e376: ᴿCiuD 205 (1992) 243s (J. *Gutiérrez*).

g777 *Tomlinson* R. A., Ten early photographs of Athens: AnBritAth 87 (1992) 447-453; pl. 28-37.

g778 **Vercoutter** Jean, présent.; L'Égypt à la chambre noire; Francis FRITH, photographe de l'Égypte retrouvée. P 1992, Gallimard. 168 p. 2-07-056661-7 [OIAc 5,38].

U1.6 **Guide books**, *Führer*.

g779 **Bizzetti** Paolo [➤ 6,173], *Pratesi* Marco, La Turchia, guida per i cristiani. Bo 1990, Dehoniane. 170 p. Lit. 30.000. – ᴿRivScR 5 (1991) 285s (A. *Resta*).

g780 ᵀᴱ**Brodersen** Kai, Reiseführer zu den Sieben Weltwundern; PHILON von Byzanz und andere antike Texte: Insel-Tb 1392. Fra 1992, Insel. 173 p. 11 fig. DM 16 [ClasR 43,179, O. A. W. *Dilke*].

g781 **Díez Fernández** F., Guía de Tierra Santa 1990 ➤ 6,g175; 7,e379: ᴿRelCu 37 (1991) 335 (M. A. *Martín Juárez*).

g782 **Faber** Gustav, Auf den Spuren des Paulus [Reise-Erfahrungen]. Mü 1989, List. 120 p. DM 39,80. – ᴿGeistL 65 (1992) 156s (P. *Imhof*).

g783 **Lyk-Jensen** Per, Jordan – en kulturhistorisk rejsefører ... 1988, Safra. 158 p. – ᴿSvEx 56 (1991) 151s (M. *Ottosson*).

g784 *Mackowski* Richard M., 4-page retrospect on his ongoing career as tour guide. R 1992, auct. (P. S. M. Maggiore 7) [CBQ 54,511].

g785 **Murphy-O'Connor** Jerome, The Holy Land, an archaeological guide from earliest times to 1700³ [¹1980]. NY 1992, Oxford-UP. 471 p. $15 [BAR/W 19/1,12, J. *Laughlin*].

g786 **Pixner** Bargil, Mit Jesus durch Galiläa nach dem fünften Evangelium. Rosh Pina 1992, Corazin. 136 p. DM 32. – ᴿGeistL 65 (1992) 477s (P. *Imhof*).

U1.7 **Onomastica.**

g787 *Astour* Michael C., The location of Ḥaṣurā of the Mari texts: ➤ 65, GEVIRTZ S. mem., Maarav 7 (1991) 51-65: not Hazor but Ḥaṣur 24 k S Maysaf in NW Syria.

g788 *Billot* Marie-Françoise, Le [gymnase de] Cynosarges, Antiochos et les tanneurs; questions de topographie: BCH 116 (1992) 119-156.

g788* *Diament* H., Altérité des noms de lieu ou d'adaptation rencontrés par les croisés en Proche-Orient; modes de compréhension ou d'adaptation: CahCivMedv 35,1 (1992) 143-6 [< RSPT 77,139].

g789 **Frayne** Douglas R., The Early Dynastic list of geographical names: AmOrSeries 74. NHv 1992, American Oriental Soc. xiii-161 p.; 13 maps. 0-940490-74-9.

g790 **George** A. R., Babylonian topographical texts: OrLovAnal 40. Lv

1992, Univ. Dep. Orientalistiek / Peeters. xvii-504 p.; 8 fig.; 58 pl.; addendum. 90-6831-410-6 [OIAc 5,22].

g791 *Habermann* Wolfgang, Kerkeosiris/Kerkeusiris in Arsinoites: CdÉ 67 (1992) 101-111.

g792 ᴱ**Hakkert** Adolf M., *Branigan* K., *al.*, Lexicon of the Greek and Roman cities and place names in antiquity ca 1500 B.C. - ca A.D. 500. Amst 1992, Hakkert. Fasc. 1, A-Ad Novas, 160 col., with many copies of portions of maps.

g793 *Hoch* James, The supposed *hgr* 'fort' in Negeb place names of the Shishak toponym list: ➤ 557*, Contacts 1990/2, 262-6.

g794 *a) Kaper* Olaf E., Egyptian toponyms of Dakhla oasis; – *b) Cauville* Sylvie, Les inscriptions géographiques relatives au nom tentyrite: BIFAO 92 (1992) 117-132 / 67-99; 2 fig.

g795 *Liebig* Michael, Zur Lage einiger im Bericht über den 8. Feldzug Sargons II. von Assyrien genannten Gebiete [Urmia ... Diyala]: ZAss 81 (1991) 31-36.

g796 **Liverani** Mario, Studies on the Annals of Ashurnasirpal II/2, topographical analysis: QuadGeogStor 4. R 1992, Centro Stampa d'Atenco. 181 p.; 29 (color) maps. Lit. 35.000.

g797 **Maʿani** Sultan al-, Nordjordanische Ortsnamen; eine etymologische und semantische Untersuchung: TStOrientalistik 7. Hildesheim 1992, Olms. [xiv] 326 p. 3-487-09632-3.

g798 *Quirke* S., The Egyptological study of placenames [GOMAÁ F., Besiedlung 1986]: DiscEg 21 (1991) 59-71.

g799 **Smadi** Taleb A., The Umayyad presence in the Bilād al-Sham; a toponymic study: diss. Pennsylvania, ᴰ*Holod* Renata. Ph 1991. 400 p. 92-12005. – DissA 53 (1992s) 280-A.

g799* **Stavrianopoulou** E., Untersuchungen zur Struktur des Reiches von Pylos; die Stellung der Ortschaften im Lichte der Linear-B-Texte: SIMA pocket 77. Göteborg 1989, Åström. ii-252 p. + 35 p. of tables. – ᴿMinos 25s (1990s) 460-4 (Cynthia W. *Shelmerdine*: also treats animal husbandry, flax and textiles, cult ...).

g800 *Thissen* Heinz J., Zwischen Theben und Assuan; onomastische Bemerkungen: ZPapEp 90 (1992) 202-6.

g801 *Thirion* Michelle, Notes d'onomastique [anthroponymie théophore/topophore]; contribution à une révision du Ranke PN, 8: RÉgp 43 (1992) 163-8.

g802 *Zadok* Ran, Onomastic, prosopographic and lexical notes: BibNot 65 (1992) 47-54.

u2.1   **Geologia:** soils, mountains, volcanoes, earthquakes.

g803 *Buxton* Richard G.A., Imaginary Greek mountains: JHS 112 (1992) 1-15.

g804 *Dever* W. G., A case-study in biblical archaeology ['what can *legitimately* be called that']; the earthquake of ca. 760 B.C.E.: ➤ 18, ᶠBIRAN A., ErIsr 23 (1992) 27*-35*; 4 fig.

g805 *Lax* Elliott, *Strasser* Thomas F., Early holocene extinctions on Crete; the search for the cause: JMeditArch 5 (1992) 203-224.

g806 *Tsafrir* Yoram, *Foerster* Gideon, The dating of the 'earthquake of the sabbatical year' of 749 C.E. in Palestine [date inferred from 748 of a Cairo Geniza lament; 749 being a Sabbatical year 'according to current calculation' p. 233]: BSO 55 (1992) 231-235; pl. I-II: confirmed by Beth-Shan gold dinar.

g807 *Wright* G. A.^{J}, Earthquakes in ancient Palestine: BIL 16,3 (1990) 35-37 [< OTAbs 15,20].

U2.2 *Hydrographia:* **rivers, seas, salt.**

g808 *Alföldy* Géza, Die Inschrift des Aquäduktes von Segovia; ein Vorbericht: ZPapEp 94 (1992) 231-248; pl. VIII-X.

g809 *Armstrong* Pamela, *al.*, Crossing the river; observations on routes and bridges in Laconia from the Archaic to Byzantine periods: AnBritAth 87 (1992) 293-310.

g810 **Ashby** Thomas, Gli acquedotti dell'antica Roma [1935], ^{T}*Aiosa Gambardetti* A. R 1991, Quasar. 403 p.; 103 fig.; 7 maps. – ^{R}Archeo 7,92 (1992) 127 (R. A. *Staccioli*).

g811 *Barta* Winfried, Die Bedeutung der Personifikation Huh ['Endlosigkeit des Wassers', SETHE] im Unterschied zu den Personifikationen Hah und Nun: GöMiszÄg 127 (1992) 7-32.

g812 *Brinker* Werner, Zur Wasserversorgung von Resafa-Sergiupolis: DamaszMi 5 (1991) 119-146; 15 fig.; pl. 40-49 (p. 147-162, 6 fig.; pl. 50-53, Keramik, *Logar* Nuše; 169-79 Türsturzinschrift, *Gatier* P., *Ulbert* T.).

g813 *Brodsky* Harold, The Jordan, symbol of spiritual transition: BR 8,3 (1992) 34-43 . 52; ill.

g814 **Bruun** Christer. The water supply of ancient Rome; a study of Roman imperial administration: CommHumLitt 93. Helsinki 1991, Soc. Scientiarum. viii-456 p.; 4 fig. – ^{R}AntiqJ 71 (1991) 296 (Janet *Delaine*); ArchWsz 43 (1992) 138s (Malgorzata *Biernacka-Lubańska*, **℗**); ClasR 42 (1992) 392s (O. F. *Robinson*); Gerión 10 (1992) 328-340 (J. M. *Casillas*); RÉLat 70 (1992) 358-360 (L. *Callebat*).

g815 **Calvet** Yves, *Geyer* Bernard, Barrages antiques de la Syrie: CollMOM 21. Lyon 1992, Maison de l'Orient Méditerranéen. 144 p.; 66 fig. 2-903264-13-9 [OIAc 5,16].

g816 *Calvet* Yves, *Geyer* Bernard, La maîtrise de l'eau en Syrie [... barrage de Khanouqa]: Archéologia 280 (1992) 42-49; ill.

g817 **Caulier** B., L'eau et le sacré; les cultes thérapeutiques autour des fontaines en France du Moyen Âge à nos jours 1990 ⮕ 7,e405: ^{R}NRT 114 (1992) 284s (A. *Toubeau*).

g818 **Gentelle** Pierre, *al.*, Prospections archéologiques en Bactriane orientale (1974-1978), I. Données paléographiques et fondements de l'irrigation: Mém MissArFr en Asie centrale 3. P 1989, de Boccard. 217 p.; 16 pl.; foldouts. 2-907431-01-3.

g819 *Gentelle* Pierre, Les irrigations antiques à Shabwa [S. Yemen]: Syria 68 (1991) 5-54 [-57, *Audoin* R.].

g820 **Gerbrecht** Günther, *Jaritz* Horst, Untersuchung antiker Anlagen zur Wasserspeicherung [Pergamon 1987 ⮕ 5,e561; Jericho 1991 ⮕ 6,g215...] im Fayûm 1990: ^{R}ArPapF 38 (1992) 72-74 (U. *Buske*).

g821 **Giddy** Lisa L., Egyptian oases ^{D}1986 ⮕ 3,f389... 7,e408: ^{R}JNES 51 (1992) 304s (W. L. *Murnane*).

g822 *Grewe* Klaus, Lugdunum/Lyon; der Aquädukt aus dem Fluss Gier: AntWelt 23 (1992) 82-86; 16 (color.) fig.

g823 **Heymeyer** *Ingrid, Schmidt* Jürgen, Antike Technologie – die Sabäische Wasserwirtschaft von Marib: ArchBYemen 5/1. Mainz 1991, von Zabern. viii-112 p.; 12 pl. 3-8053-1215-6 [BO 49,590].

g824 **Hodge** A. Trevor, Roman aqueducts and water supply. L 1992, Duckworth. viii-504 p.; 241 fig. 0-7156-2194-7.

g825 *Hofmann* Inge, Das Wasserschöpfrad und die meroitische Landwirt-schaft: → 735, Sesto Eg. 1991/2, 301-6.

g826 *Isserlin* B. S. J., The [Athos] canal of Xerxes [HERODOTUS 7,22-24. 37. 122]; facts and problems: AnBritAth 86 (1991) 83-91; 2 fig.; pl. 4.

g827 *Kleiss* Wolfram, Wasserschutzdämme und Kanalbauten in der Um-gebung von Pasargadae: ArchMIran 24 (1991) 23-30; 7 fig. (*map*).

g828 *Kleiss* Wolfram, Dammbauten aus achämenidischer und aus sasanidi-scher Zeit in der Provinz Fars: ArchMIran 25 (1992) 131-145; 19 fig. (map; foldout plan.); pl. 29-38.

g829 **Kreiger** Barbara, Living waters; myth, history, and politics of the Dead Sea. NY 1988, Continuum. 226 p. $25. – ᴿBR 7,1 (1991) 36 (H. *Brodsky*).

g829* *Luft* Ulrich, Neîlos; eine Anmerkung zur kulturellen Begegnung der Griechen mit den Ägyptern: → 96, ᶠKÁKOSY L. 1992, 403-410.

g830 *Malamat* Abraham, The divine nature of the Mediterranean Sea in the foundation inscription of Yaḥdunlim: → 739, Mari in retrospect 1983/92, 211-5.

g830* *Manakidou* Eleni, Athenerinnen in schwarzfiguren Brunnenhausszenen: Hephaistos 11s (1992s) 51-97; 21 fig. (only fig. 19 seems clearly a bath and fig. 6 a toilet).

g831 *Oleson* John P., Water works: → 741, AnchorBD 6 (1992) 883-893.

g831* *Oleson* John P., The water-supply system of ancient Auara; pre-liminary results of the Ḥumeima hydraulic survey: → 740, Jordan 4 (1992) 269-275.

g832 **Owens** Waylan B., The theological significance of *mayim* in the OT: diss. Baptist Theol. Sem., ᴰ*Bailey* D. New Orleans 1992. 317 p. 92-27157. – DissA 53 (1992s) 1547s-A.

g833 **Psychoyos** Olga, Déplacements de la ligne de rivage et sites archéo-logiques dans les régions côtières de la mer Égée, au Néolithique et à l'Âge de Bronze [diss. 1986, Paris-1, Panthéon-Sorbonne]: SIMA pocket 62. Jonsered, Åström. vi-323 p.; 72 fig. – ᴿGnomon 64 (1992) 83-85 (M. *Kunst*).

g833* *Sanlaville* Paul, al., Il Giordano: Il mondo della Bibbia 3,15 (1992) 1-7 (-47).

g834 **Stevenson** D. W. W., A proposal for the irrigation of the hanging gardens of Babylon [water-wheels on five levels: for an Iraqi government sponsored competition, announced 1989 but suspended owing to Gulf war]: Iraq 54 (1992) 35-55; 11 fig.

g835 *Thompson* Henry O., Jordan River: → 741, AnchorBD 3 (1992) 953-8 (-960, Jordan Valley, excavation data, *Ibrahim* M. W.).

g836 *Traina* Giusto, Sale e saline nel Mediterraneo antico: ParPass 47,266 (1992) 363-378.

U2.3 **Clima**, pluvia.

g837 *Bohrmann* Monette, La pluie dans le Judaïsme antique et l'inondation en Égypte: DialHA 18,2 (1992) 175-184 + 1 fig.; deutsch 186.

g838 a) *Driel* G. van, Weather; between the natural and the unnatural in first millennium cuneiform inscriptions; – b) *Loon* M. van, The rainbow in ancient West Asian iconography; – c) *Houwink ten Cate* P., The Hittite storm god: → 727*, ᴱ*Meijer* D., Natural phenomena 1989/92, 39-52 / 149-156; 20 fig. / 83-148 [53-77, 4 pl. *Hawkins* J. D.].

g839 *Frick* Frank S., Palestine, climate of: ➤ 741, AnchorBD 5 (1992) 118-126; 11 fig.

g840 *Manning* Sturt W., Thera, sulphur, and climatic anomalies: OxJArch 11 (1992) 245-253; 3 fig.

g841 *Sanlaville* Paul, Changements climatiques dans la péninsule arabique durant le Pléistocène supérieur et l'Holocène: Paléorient 19,1 (1992) 5-26; 11 fig.

U2.5   *Fauna;* Animals.

g842 **Abdel-Hamid** Hussam E., Study of animal bones from Mit-Rahena: Travaux 31. Wsz 1990, Polish Acad. ii-66 p. 83-900-0964-1 [BO 49,583].

g842* *Adly* Sanaa A. El-, Amun und seine Nilgans: GöMiszÄg 126 (1992) 47-57.

g843 *a) Amorosi* Thomas, Icelandic archaeofauna, a preliminary review; – *b) Adalsteinsson* Stefan, Importance of sheep in early Icelandic agriculture: AcArchK 61 ('The Norse of the North Atlantic', conference Bowdoin, Apr. 18-22, 1988/1991) 272-284 / 285-291.

g844 *Anthony* David W., Horses and prehistoric chronology of Eastern Europe and Western/Central Asia: ➤ 730, JANES 21 (1990/2) 131-3.

g845 *a) Bagnera* Alessandra, 'Delfinus non longe ab Aquila' (TOLOMEO-Almagesto); una rara iconografia della protomaiolica e la sua probabile derivazione dall'Islam; – *b) Roccati* Alessandro, A proposito di bipedi e quadrupedi [Benedizione di Ptah di Ramesse II]: RSO 65 (1991) 247-267; 19 fig. / 339s.

g846 ᴱBalme D.M. (*Gotthelf* Allan), ARISTOTLE, History of animals VII-X; Loeb 439. CM/L 1991. Harvard Univ. /   605 p. £10.50. – ᴿÉtClas 60 (1992) 283 (Hélène *Perdicoyianni*).

g847 *Barkay* Gabriel, 'The prancing horse' — an official seal impression from Judah of the 8th century BCE: TAJ 19 (1992) 124-130; 3 fig.

g848 **Barton** Bruce B., *al.*, [70] Bible animals [for ages 8-12 (and up!)]. Wheaton IL 1992, Tyndale. 64 p. $13. 0-8423-1006-1 [TDig 39,253].

g849 *Bernand* Étienne, Le culte du lion en Basse Égypte d'après les documents grecs: DialHA 16,1 (1990) 63-94.

g849* *Böhme* Wolfgang, Mensch und Tier: Zeitwende 63 (Karlsruhe 1992) 129-131 [< ZIT 92,508].

g850 *Boessneck* Joachim †, *Driesch* Angela von den, *al.*, Eine Eselbestattung der 1. Dynastie in Abusir [N Saqqâra]: MiDAI-K 48 (1992) 1-10; 3 fig.

g851 *a) Boessneck* Joachim, *Driesch* Angela von den, Besprechung der Tier-knochenfunde aus dem Grabkomplex des Horus Aha in Umm el-Qaab bei Abydos; – *b) Engelhardt* Bernd, Eine vollplastische Tierdarstellung der ältesten Linienbandkeramik aus Ton [Rg]: ➤ 167, ᶠSCHÜLE W. 1991, 55-60; 2 fig.; Eng. 59 / 127s; 2 fig.; Eng. 128.

g852 **Boessneck** Joachim, *Driesch* Angela von den, Tell el-Dabʿa VII: Tiere und historische Umwelt im Nordost-Delta im 2. Jahrtausend v.Chr. anhand der Knochenfunde der Ausgrabungen 1975-1986: Denkschr 11. W 1992, Österr. Akad. 137 p.; 3 pl.; 8 plans. 3-7001-1922-4 [OIAc 5,15: ÖsAI-K 10].

g853 *Bonneau* Danielle, Le sacrifice du porc et *liloition* en Pachôn: CdÉ 66 (1991) 330-340.

g854 **Brewer** Douglas J., *Friedman* Renee F., Fish and fishing in ancient Egypt: Natural History of Egypt 2, 1989 ➤ 5,e957; 7,e433: ᴿDiscEg 19 (1991) 103-5 (G. *Robins*).

g855 *Cardoso Cunha* A., Os animais na religiosidade popular [i. na Biblia...]: HumTeol 12 (1991) 283-300.

g856 **Charbonneau-Lassay** Louis, The bestiary of Christ 1991 → 7,e437: ᴿScripTPamp 24 (1992) 203s (A. de *Silva*).

g857 **Chouliara-Raïos** Hélène, L'abeille et le miel en Égypte d'après les papyrus grecs 1989 → 6,g255; 7,e438: ᴿAegyptus 72 (1992) 211s (Or-solina *Montevecchi*); AntClas 61 (1992) 549s (J. A. *Straus*); ClasR 42 (1992) 471s (K. D. *White*: about bees in the economy); RÉAnc 94 (1992) 506 (C. *Orrieux*).

g858 **Cialowicz** Krzysztof M., Les palettes égyptiennes aux motifs zoomorphes et sans décoration; études de l'art prédynastique: St.Anc.Art 3. Kraków 1991, Univ. 85 p. 83-233-04963 [BO 49,584].

g859 *a*) *Ciałowicz* Krzysztof M., La composition, le sens et la symbolique des scènes zoomorphes prédynastiques en relief; les manches de couteaux; – *b*) *Adams* Barbara, Two more lions from Upper Egypt, Hierakonpolis and Koptos; – *c*) *McArdle* John E., Preliminary observations on the mammalian fauna from predynastic localities at Hierakonpolis: → 84, Mem. HOFFMAN M. 1992, 247-258; 9 fig. / 69-76; 7 fig. / 53-56.

g860 *Ciccarese* Maria Pia, Il simbolismo dell'aquila; Bibbia e zoologia nell'esegesi cristiana antica: CivClasCr 13 (1992) 295-333.

g861 *Cline* Eric, Monkey business in the Bronze Age Aegean; the Amenhotep II faience figurines at Mycenae and Tiryns: AnBritAth 86 (1991) 29-43; pl. 1-2.

g862 **Clutton-Brock** Juliet, Horse power; a history of the horse and the donkey in human societies. CM 1992, Harvard Univ. 192 p. 0-674-40646-X [OIAc 5,17].

g863 **Crabtree** Pamela J., *Ryan* Kathleen, Animal use and culture change: MASCA 8-supp. (1992) 96 p. 1048-5325 [OIAc 3,16].

g864 ᴱ**Crabtree** P. J., *Campana* D., *Ryan* K., Early animal domestication and its cultural context: MASCA 6 supp. Ph 1989, Univ. Pennsylvania. 134 p. – ᴿPaléorient 18,1 (1992) 137-9 (P. *Ducos*).

g865 *Crocker* P. T., *a*) Ancient horse training [Hittite Kikkuli]; – *b*) Oxen and donkeys – beasts of burden?: BurHist 27 (1991) 107-9 / 21-23 [< OTAbs 15, p. 326. 142].

g866 *Curtis* John, The dying lion [Assyrian relief cut from a larger panel, excavated in Syria; 1880 Mansell photograph (here pl. XV) often reproduced; there was also a drawing by W. Boutcher made earlier, sometimes reproduced in reverse; then the original disappeared, but a Boutcher heiress has now given it to the British Museum]: Iraq 54 (1992) 113-7.

g867 *Czernohaus* Karola, Delphindarstellungen von der minoischen bis zur geometrischen Zeit: SIMA pocket 67, 1988 → 6,g262: ᴿGnomon 64 (1992) 464-6 (I. *Pini*).

g868 **Delporte** Henri, L'image des animaux dans l'art préhistorique. P 1990, Picard. 256 p.; 289 fig. F 550. 2-7084-0404-0. – ᴿÉTRel 67 (1992) 91 (J. *Argaud*, sous 'science des religions').

g869 **Domagalski** Bernhard, Der Hirsch...: JbAC Egb 15, ᴰ1990 → 7,a443: ᴿRivArCr 68 (1992) 372-4 (Luciana *Tulipani*); Salesianum 54 (1992) 413s (B. *Amata*).

g870 *Dor* Menahem, ❿ [Lev 11,1... 'chewing the cud'] in Bible and Mishnah: BethM 37,129 (1991s) 122-130.

g871 *Duhard* Jean-Pierre, Images de la chasse au paléolithique: OxJArch 10 (1991) 127-157; 15 fig.

g872 *Durken* Daniel, The Bible is for the birds! BToday 30 (1992) 160-3.

g873 **Eisenstein** Herbert, Einführung in die arabische Zoographie; das tierkundliche Wissen in der arabisch-islamischen Literatur. B 1991, Reimer. 306 p. DM 48. – ᴿJSS 37 (1992) 130s (Remke *Kruk*); OLZ 87 (1992) 280 (C. *Toll*).

g874 **Epstein** Marc M., Medieval Jewry and the allegorization of the animal world; a textual and iconographic study: diss. Yale, ᴰ*Ruderman* D. New Haven ... – RTLv 24, p. 544 sans date.

g875 *Finet* A., Colloque international, L'histoire de la connaissance du comportement animal, Liège 11-14 mars 1992, avec résumé de Finet, Le comportement du chien, facteur de son ambivalence en Mésopotamie; *Trokay* M., Le comportement du chien illustré dans l'iconographie mésopotamienne du 4ᵉ millénaire av.J.-C.; *Limet* H., L'observation des animaux dans les présages en Mésopotamie ancienne: Akkadica 78 (1992) 52-54.

g875* **Feucht** Erika, Fishing and fowling with the spear and the throw-stick reconsidered: ➤ 96, ᶠKÁKOSY L. 1992, 157-169; 7 fig.

g876 *Firmage* Edwin, Zoology [i. generalia, animal bone (col. 1117; 'bore' 1108) archaeology; butchering; – ii. Profiles: 'ordinary' animals described and located at excavations; Appendix I, animal names in biblical Hebrew and cognate languages; appendix 2, index of sites treating faunal remains]. All animal-names in the Bible occur in AnchorDB only as a renvoi to this zoology article: ➤ 741, AnchorDB 6 (1992) 1109-1167.

g877 *Gasse* Annie, Une nouvelle stèle d'Horus sur les crocodiles: RÉgp 43 (1992) 207-210; 2 fig.

g878 **Georgoudi** Stella, Des chevaux et des bœufs dans le monde grec; réalités et représentations animalières à partir des livres XVI et XVII des Géoponiques [gr. franç. + comm.]; préf. *Detienne* Michel. P 1990, Daedalus. 391 p.; 10 pl. – ᴿRÉG 105 (1992) 637 (J.-N. *Corvisier*).

g879 *Gómez Pallarès* Josep M., Del simbolisme eròtic de la imatge del cavall: Faventia 14,1 (1992) 7-33.

g880 *Halstead* Paul, *a)* Dimini and the 'DMP'; faunal remains and animal exploitation in Late Neolithic Thessaly: AnBritAth 87 (1992) 29-59; – *b)* Lost sheep? On the Linear B evidence for breeding flocks at Mycenaean Knossos and Pylos: Minos 25s (1990s) 343-365.

g881 *Hendrickx* S., Une scène de chasse dans le désert sur le vase prédynastique Bruxelles, M.R.A.H. E.2631: CdÉ 67 (1992) 5-27; 7 fig.

g882 **Hofmann** Inge, Hase, Perlhuhn und Hyäne; Spuren meroitischer Oralliteratur: BeitSud Beih 4. Wien/Mödling 1988. 152 p. – ᴿBO 49 (1992) 403s (P. L. *Shinnie*).

g883 **Hyland** Ann, Equus, the horse in the Roman world 1990 ➤ 6,g290: ᴿBonnJbb 192 (1992) 663-7 (M. *Junkelmann*); ClasR 42 (1992) 122-4 (K. D. *White*).

g884 *a) Indelli* Giovanni, PLUTARCO, Bruta animalia ratione uti; qualche riflessione; – *b) Barigazzi* Adelmo, Implicanze morali nella polemica plutarchea sulla psicologia degli animali: ➤ 654, Convegno 4, 1991/2, 317-352 / 297-315.

g885 *Irwin* Robert, The Arabic beast fable: JWarb 55 (1992) 36-50.

g886 *Kersten* Annemie M.P., Birds from the paleolithic rock shelter of Ksar ᶜAkil, Lebanon: Paléorient 17,2 (1991) 99-116.

g887 *Kertsch* Manfred, Notizen zur Formulierkunst des Johannes CHRYSOSTOMOS und ihrem Nachwirken bei ISIDOR von Pelusion und NEILOS von Ankyra; das Vorbild der (wilden) Tiere für naturgemässes, korrektes Verhalten: JbÖsByz 42 (1992) 29-39.

g888 **Knoefel** Peter K., *Covi* Madeline C., A Hellenistic treatise on poisonous animals (the 'Theriaca' of NICANDER of Colophon), a contribution to the history of toxicology. Lewiston NY 1991, Mellen. xiv-173 p.; 28 fig.; 18 pl. [ClasR 43,166, A. A. *Richmond*: unreliable].

g889 *Knox* Peter E., Love and horses in VIRGIL's Georgics: Eranos 90 (1992) 43-53.

g890 *Krauss* Rolf, Zur Pelikanszene und damit zusammenhangenden Darstellungen in den Reliefs der sog. 'Jahreszeitenkammer': BSocÉg 15 (Genève 1991) 69-80.

g891 **Laurens** Pierre, L'abeille dans l'ambre; célébration de l'épigramme de l'époque alexandrine à la fin de la Renaissance: Coll. ÉtAnc. 59. P 1989, BLettres. 571 p. F 245. – ᴿClasR 42 (1992) 325s (P. *Howell*); Latomus 51 (1992) 929s (P.-J. *Dehon*).

g892 *a*) *Lauwerier* R., *Hessing* W., Men, horses and the Miss Blanche effect [few details, suggesting others, in a drawing]: Roman horse burials in a cemetery at Kesteren, The Netherlands; – *b*) *Prummel* Wietske, Early medieval dog burials among the Germanic tribes: ₋ Helinium 32 (1992) 78-109; 6 fig. / 132-194; 2 fig. + 8 maps.

g893 *Leclerc* Marie-Christine, L'épervier et le rossignol d'HÉSIODE [202-212]; une fable à double sens: RÉG 105 (1992) 37.44.

g894 **Leiderer** Rosmarie, Anatomie der Schafsleber im babylonischen Leberorakel, eine makroskopisch-analytische Studie 1990 ↠ 6,g298; DM 74: ᴿOLZ 87 (1992) 248-255 (T. *Richter*).

g895 **Leviton** Alan E., *al.*, Handbook to Middle East amphibians and reptiles: Contributions to Herpetology 8. Ox 1992, SocStAmphRep. vii-252 p.; 33 pl. 0-916984-23-0 [OIAc 3,28].

g896 *Lion* Brigitte, La circulation des animaux exotiques au Proche-Orient antique: ↠ 683, Circulation 1991/2, 357-365.

g897 **Lonsdale** Steven H., Creatures of speech; lion, herding and hunting similes in the Iliad 1990 ↠ 7,c458: ᴿGnomon 64 (1992) 632-4 (T. *Krischer*).

g898 *Loth* Heinz-Jürgen, Hund: ↠ 764, RAC 125s (1992) 773-800.

g899 **Mahmoud** Osama, Die wirtschaftliche Bedeutung der Vögel im Alten Reich [Diss. Hamburg 1989]: EurHS 38/35. Fra 1992, Lang. 312 p. 3-631-43038-8 [OIAc 3,29].

g899* *Mane* Perrine, Images médiévales de la pêche en eau douce: JSav (1991) 227-249; 6 fig.; + 12 pl., y comprises 2 de la pêche miraculeuse des Évangiles.

g900 *Megally* Mounir, À propos des chèvres et d'un chevrier de la nécropole thébaine [Ostracon Mond nᵒ 171]: CdÉ 66 (1991) 108-128; 2 fig.

g901 *Milburn* Mark, *Wunderlich* Gisela, A probable game-trap complex of the central Sahara: DiscEg 24 (1992) 25-28.

g902 **Miquel** Pierre, Dictionnaire symbolique des animaux; zoologie mystique. P 1992, Léopard d'Or. 286 p. F 245. – ᴿEsprVie 102 (1992) couv.-123 (J. *Rocacher*).

g903 *Myers* K. Sara, The lizard and the owl; an etymological pair in OVID, Metamorphoses Book 5 (446-61; 534-50): AmJPg 113 (1992) 63-68.

g904 *Pardee* Dennis, Some brief remarks on hippiatric methodology: AulaO 10 (1992) 154s.

g905 *Parker* Holt N., Fish in trees and tie-dyed sheep; a function of the surreal in Roman poetry: Arethusa 25 (1992) 293-321.

g906 **Paz** Uzi, The birds of Israel. Lexington 1987, S. Greene. viii-264 p.; 60 color. pl. (*Eshbol* Yossi). 0-8289-0621-1 [OIAc 3,33].

g906* *Peruzzi* Emilio, Il nome latino del leone: ParPass 46,261 (1991) 417-429.

g907 *Péter-Contesse* René, Quels animaux Israël offrait-il en sacrifice? Étude de lexicographie hébraïque: ➤ 491, ᴱSCHENKER A., Opfer 1990/2, 67-76; deutsch 77.

g908 *Popovič* Ivana, Observations sur le plat d'argent à scènes de chasse du trésor de Seuso: Latomus 51 (1992) 611-623.

g909 **Prieur** Jean, Les animaux sacrés dans l'antiquité: ArtRelMédit 1988 ➤ 5,g11: ᴿLatomus 51 (1992) 481-3 (R. *Chevallier*: érudition assimilable).

g910 *Rössler-Köhler* Ursula, Zur Darstellung der Fliege in Ägypten: DielB 27 (1991) 170+3 fig.

g911 **Rommelaere** Catherine, Les chevaux du Nouvel Empire égyptien 1991 ➤ 7,e473: ᴿNikephoros 4 (1991) 257-9 (W. *Decker*).

g912 **Schelvis** Jaap, Mites and archaeozoology: diss. Groningen 1992. 116 p.; 28 fig. – ᴿHelinium 32 (1992) 266s (T. *Hakbijl*).

g913 *Schwab* Eckart, Die Tierbilder und Tiervergleiche des Alten Testaments; Material und Problemanzeigen: BibNot 59 (1991) 37-44.

g914 *Scott* Alan, Notes and observations; Pseudo-ARISTOTLE's Historia Animalium 9 in ORIGEN: HarvTR 85 (1992) 235-9.

g915 *Sergent* Bernard, Ethnozoonymes indo-européens: DialHA 17,2 (1991) 9-55.

g916 *Shaheen* Alaa el-din M., Royal hunting scenes on scarabs: VarAeg 8,1 (1992) 17-28 . 33-47.

g917 *Simotas* Panagiotis, ⊖ Old Testament narratives about speaking animals: TAth 63 (1992) 611-647.

g918 **Smith** Stephen M., HERODOTUS' use of animals; a literary, ethnographic, and zoological study: diss. Ohio State 1992. ᴰ*Allison* June W. 222 p. 92-19027. – DissA 53 (1992s) 488-A.

g919 **Stampfli** Hans Rudolf, *Schibler* Jörg, Bibliography of archaeozoology. Basel 1991, Seminar Ur/FGesch. 37 p.+ 6 microfiches.

g920 *Staubli* T., Kamel: ➤ 762, NBL II,8)1992) 433-5; 6 fig.

g921 *a) Sweydan* Nabil, Buffles et taureaux au prédynastique; – *b) Kemna* Claudia, Bemerkungen zu den Darstellungen der Wildeseljagd; – *c) Menu* Bernadette, Les échanges portant sur du betail (26ème-30ème dynasties); – *d) Györy* Hedvig, Une amulette représentant Néfertoum-sur-le-lion à Budapest: ➤ 736, Sesto Eg. 1991/2, 585-591+map; 7 fig. / 365-370 / 459-463 / 233-6; pl. VI.

   Tamulénas J., Fågellistorna (lists of birds) in Lev 11,13-19; Dt 14,11-18 1992 ➤ 2633c.

g922 *Tchernia* André, Le dromadaire des Peticii et le commerce oriental: MÉF-Ant 104,1 (1992) 293-301; 2 fig.

g923 ᵀᴱ**Terian** A., PHILON, Alexander... animalia 1988 ➤ 4,h64 ... 7,e479: ᴿLavalTP 48 (1992) 452s (P.-H. *Poirier*); VigChr 46 (1992) 194s (J. C. M. van *Winden*).

g924 *a) Tripodi* Bruno, Il fregio della *caccia* della II tomba reale di Vergina e le cacce funerarie d'Oriente; – *b) Briant* Pierre, Chasses royales macédoniennes et chasses royales perses; le thème de la chasse au lion sur la *chasse* de Vergina; – *c) Prestiani Giallombardo* Anna Maria, Recenti testimonianze iconografiche sulla *kausia* in Macedonia e la datazione del fregio della *caccia* della tomba reale II di Vergina: DialHA 17,1 (1991) 143-209; Eng. 209 / 211-255 / 257-294+14 fig.; Eng. 294.

g925 *Tuplin* Christopher, The 'Persian' bird; an ornithonymic conundrum: ArchMIran 25 (1992) 125-129.

g926 *Viré* F., *a) Naḥl*, abeille, bee; – *b) Naml*, fourmis, ant; ➤ 756, EncIslam² 7 (1992) 906-910 / 951-3.

g927 *Waschke* E.-J., a) *śæh* 'Kleinvieh'; – b) *Maiberger* P., *śᵉlāw* 'Wachtel':
→ 770, TWAT 7,6s (1992) 718-721 . 802-4.

g928 *Watson* Janet,   A lexicon of Cairene horse terminology: JJS 37 (1992)
247-303.

g929 *Wolterman* Charles,   On the names of birds and hieroglyphic sign-list
G 22, G 35 and H 3:   JbEOL 32 (1991s) 119-130.

U2.7   **Flora;** *plantae biblicae et antiquae.*

g930 *Amigues* Suzanne,   Hyakinthos; fleur mythique et plantes réelles: RÉG
105 (1992) 19-36.

g931 **Barakat** Hala N., *Baum* Nathalie,   Douch II. La végétation antique; une
approche macrobotanique: DocFouilles 27.   LeCaire 1992, IFAO. x-
106 p.; aussi 106 fig.   2-7247-0113-5 [OIAc 3,12].

g932 *Baum* Nathalie,   La végétation antique de Douch: → 735, Sesto Eg.
1991/2, 51-53.

g933 **Beaux** Nathalie,   Le cabinet de curiosités de Thoutmosis III; plantes et
animaux du 'Jardin botanique' de Karnak ᴰ1990 → 6,g339:   ᴿCdÉ 67
(1992) 60-65 (Nathalie *Baum*); StEgPun 9 (1991) 35-49 (R. *Fattovich*).

g934 **Bikai** Pierre M.,   The cedar of Lebanon; archaeological and dendrochronological perspectives; diss. California, ᴰ*Stronach* D. Berkeley 1991.
424 p. 92-28575. – DissA 53 (1992s) 2863-A.

g935 *Bower* Mini,   Cereal pollen dispersal; a pilot study: CamArch 2 (1992)
236-241; 8 fig.

g936 *Diethart* Johannes, *Kislinger* Ewald,   [Oreibasios, Collectiones medicae,
ᴱ*Raeder* J. 1928-33] Aprikosen und Pflaumen: JbÖsByz 42 (1992) 75-81.

g937 **Ferrara Pignatelli** Marina,   Viaggio nel mondo delle essenze; aromi e
rimedi di ieri e di oggi: Il corvo e la colomba.   Padova 1991, Mozzio.
xv-413 p.

g938 **Frey** Wolfgang, *Kürschner* Harald,   Die Vegetation im Vorderen Orient;
Erläuterungen zur Karte A VI 1 VO;   TAVO Reih A-30.   Wsb 1989,
Reichert. [viii-] 92 p.   3-88226-449-7 [OIAc 5,21].

g939 *Graindorge* Catherine,   Les oignons de Sokar [rencontre entre le monde
végétal et animal, faucon Sokar]:   RÉgp 43 (1992) 87-105; pl. I; Eng. 105.

g940 **Greppin** John A. C.,   On Arabic *qunābarā* and Greek *kinnabari(s)*: → 43,
ᶠ*Delvoye* C., Byzantion 62 (1992) 254-263.

g941 *Guillaume-Coirier* Germaine,   Arbres et herbe; croyances et usages rat-
tachés aux origines de Rome: MÉF-Ant 104,1 (1992) 339-371.

g942 ᴱ**Gyselen** Rika, (*David* J.-C., al.),   Jardins d'Orient: Res Orientales 3. P
1991, Groupe ÉtCiv Moyen-Orient.   75 p.   1142-2831 [OIAc 3,22: '1990'].

g943 ᴱ**Hackens** Tony, al.,   Bois et archéologie 1987/8 → 5,b892 ('Wood &...'):
ᴿAntClas 61 (1992) 639-641 (F. *Verhaeghe*).

g946 **Hareuveni** Nogah,   Nature in our biblical heritage.   Kiryat Ono 1991,
Neot Kedumim.   142 p. – ᴿRBibArg 54,47 (1992) 170s (P. *Andiñach*).

g947 **Hansen** J. M.,   The palaeoethnobotany of Franchthi Cave: Excavations
7, 1991.   280 p.; 75 fig. – ᴿPaléorient 18,1 (1992) 135-7 (S. *Bottema*).

g948 **Hepper** F. Nigel,   Illustrated encyclopedia of Bible plants, flowers and
trees, fruits and vegetables, ecology.   Leicester/GR 1992, Inter-Varsity/
Baker. 182 p.; (color.) ill.   0-85110-643-9 / GR 0-8010-4361-1.

g949 **Hepper** F. Nigel,   Pharaoh's flowers; the botanical treasures of Tutankhamun 1990 → 6,g151:   ᴿPEQ 124 (1992) 154s (D. *Samuel*).

g950 **Jacob** Irene,   Biblical plants.   Pittsburgh 1989, Rodef Shalom.   60 p. $5.
– ᴿBR 7,1 (1991) 36 (S. *Feldman*).

g951 *Jacob* Irene & W., Flora: ➤ 741, AnchorBD 2 (1982) 803-816, lists all the known edible and other plants found in or near Palestine, and ends with a useful list of 50 purely fanciful 'biblical' plant-names 'Aaron's beard', 'rose of Sharon').

g952 *Koemoth* Pierre P., *a)* L'arbre *im3* vénérable de 'l'île-dans-le-fleuve' à Soumenou: VarAeg 8 (1992) 93-109; 2 fig.; – *b) Sub*, le papyrus ou le cordon en papyrus de Pé: GöMiszÄg 130 (1922) 33-43.

g953 *Lev-Yadun* Simcha, The origin of the cedar beams from Al-Aqsa mosque; botanical, historical and archaeological evidence: Levant 24 (1992) 201-8; 7 fig.

g954 *Lev-Yadun* Simcha, *Gophna* Ram, Exportation of plant products from Canaan to Egypt in the Early Bronze Age I; a rejoinder to William A. WARD: BASOR [281 (1991) 11-26] 287 (1992) 89s.

g955 *Lion* Brigitte, Jardins et zoos royaux [assyriens]: DossA 171 (1992) 72-79; color. ill.

g956 **Mandaville** James P., Flora of Eastern Saudi Arabia [with Riyadh Wildlife Conservation]. L 1990, Kegan Paul. 482 p.; 268 color. phot. 0-7103-0949-5 [OIAc 3,29].

g957 **Manniche** Lise, An ancient Egyptian herbal. Austin 1989, Univ. Texas. 176 p.; ill. $20. – ᴿJAOS 112 (1992) 541s (Marie-Francine *Moens*).

g958 ᴱ**Mastroroberto** Marisa, Archeologia e botanica 1989/90 ➤ 6,811*: ᴿAntClas 61 (1992) 743s (Claire De *Ruyt*).

g959 *Moftah* Ramses, Le défaut et le palmier-doum: GöMiszÄg 127 (1992) 63-5 + 3 fig.

g960 *Nibbi* Alessandra, The so-called plant of Upper Egypt: DiscEg 19 (1991) 53-68; 4 fig.; 20 (1991) 35-38 postscript.

g961 *Nielsen* Kjeld, Ancient aromas, good and bad: BR 7,3 (1991) 26-33.

g961* *Paulis* Giulio, Le piante dei Sardi, dei Romani e dei Punici: ➤ 726, L'Africa 1990/1, (2) 827-854.

g962 *Volke* Klaus, Die Ölwahrsagung der Babylonier aus chemischer Sicht: Altertum 37 (1991) 115-120; 6 fig.

g963 **Weber** Steven A., Plants and Harappan subsistence; an example of stability and change from Rojdi [< diss. Pennsylvania 1989]. Boulder 1991, Westview. xii-200 p. 0-8133-1379-1 [OIAc 3,41].

g964 *Wettengel* Wolfgang, Zu den Darstellungen des Papyrusraschelns [*zšš* 'ausreissen', nicht wie MONTET 'verehren']: StAäK 19 (1992) 323-338; 4 fig.

g965 *Willcox* George, Exploitation des espèces ligneuses au Proche-Orient; données anthracologiques: Paléorient 17,2 (1991) 117-126.

g965* *Witztum* Allan, *Gruber* Mayer L., ❿ *qurnit*... Hebrew, Aramaic and Arabic names for plants in the mint family: Lešonenu 56 (1991s) 147-151; 4 fig.; Eng. iii.

g966 **Zahran** M. A., *Willis* A. J., The vegetation of Egypt. L 1992, Chapman & H. xvi-242 p. 0-412-31510-6 [OIAc 5,40].

g967 *Zeist* Willem Van, *Bottema* Sytze, Late quaternary vegetation of the Near East: TAVO Beih. A-18. Wsh 1991, Reichert. 156 p.; 49 fig. 3-88226-530-X [OIAc 5,37; BO 49,591].

g968 ᴱ**Zeist** W., van, *al.*, Progress in Old World palaeoethnobotany. Rotterdam 1991, Balkema. ix-350 p. 52 fig.; 36 pl. – ᴿSyria 68 (1991) 481s (H. de *Contenson*).

U2.8   **Agricultura,** *alimentatio.*

g969 **Abdel-Hamid** Hussam El Din, Study of animal bones from Mit-Rahena: Travaux Médit. 31. Wsz 1990, Akad. ii-66 p. 83-900096-4-1 [BO 49,583].

g970 *Benco* Nancy L., Manufacture and use of clay sickles from the Uruk mound, Abu Salabikh, Iraq: Paléorient 18,1 (1992) 119-134; 10 fig.

g970* *Bergqvist* Stig, Consideration on yields, the distribution of crops and the size of estates; three Roman agricultural units: ClasMedv 43 (1992) 111-139.

g971 *Betancourt* Philip P., *Simpson* Richard H., The agricultural system of Bronze Age Pseira: Cretan Studies 3 (1992) 47-54.

g972 *Blažek* Václav, *Boisson* Claude, The diffusion of agricultural terms from Mesopotamia [... of likely Sumerian origin]: ArOr 60 (1992) 16-37.

g973 **Blázquez** J. M., Agricultura y minería romanas durante el alto imperio: Roma 54. M 1991, Akal. 71 p.; 13 colour. pl. – ᴿClasR 42 (1992) 407-9 (K. *Greene*, also on PONSICH M., RODRÍGUEZ ALMEIDA E.).

g974 *Blázquez* J. M., The latest work on the export of Baetican olive oil to Rome and the army [Rome Testaccio excavations]: GreeceR 39 (1992) 173-188; 6 phot.

g975 *Böcher* Otto, *al.*, Honig: ➤ 764, RAC 123s (1992) 433-473.

g976 *a)* *Bonora* Antonio, La simbologia biblica del mangiare e del bere; gioia e sapienza; – *b)* *Garrone* Daniele, Il vino nella Bibbia; – *c)* *De Benedetti* Paolo, Videro Dio e mangiarono e bevvero; – *d)* *Sierra* Sergio, La cucina della Bibbia; – *f)* *Natale Terrin* Aldo, Il pasto sacro e il pasto sacrificale nella storia comparata delle religioni: ➤ 454, ᴱ*Marenghi* F, Il cibo e la Bibbia 1992, 76-87 / 65-74 / 9-20 / 52-64 / 105-115 / 22-37 [120-4 ricette (ebraiche)].

g977 *Borowski* Oded, Agriculture: ➤ 741, AnchorBD 1 (1992) 95-98.

g978 *Broshi* Magen, Agriculture and economy in Roman Palestine [... Babatha]: IsrEJ 42 (1992) 230-240.

g979 ᴱ**Cauvin** M.-C., Rites et rythmes agraires [seminari] 1987-9, paleoagricultura Vicino Oriente]: Travaux 20, 1991 ➤ 7,632*: ᴿRStFen 20 (1992) 143s (Lorenza-Ilia *Manfredi*: 22 tit. pp.).

g980 *a)* *Cavigneaux* Antoine, Nouveaux fragments des Géorgiques ['Farmer's Instructions', Tell Haddad/Meturan]; – *b)* *Powell* Marvin A.ᴶ, Epistemology and Sumerian agriculture; the strange case of sesame and linseed: ➤ 32, ᶠCIVIL M., AulaO 9,1 (1991) 37-47, incl. facsimiles / 155-164.

g981 *Chambon* Alain, *Strus* André, Une installation agricole byzantine à 'Ain Fattir [non loin de Beth Shemesh]: RB 99 (1992) 425-435; Eng. 425; 2 fig.; pl. XVII-XVIII; 435-9, *Alpi* Frédéric, L'inscription.

g982 ᴱ**Chevallier** Raymond, Archéologie de la vigne et du vin 1988/90 ➤ 7,633: ᴿRArchéol (1992) 153s (J.-P. *Thuillier*).

g983 *Chic García* Genaro, Los Aelii en la producción y difusión del aceite bético: MünstHand 11,2 (1992) 1-21; Eng. franç. 22.

ᴱ**Cowan** C., Origins of agriculture 1985/92 ➤ 709.

g984 *Cribiore* Raffaella, The happy farmer; a student composition from Roman Egypt [... usefulness of such exercises for history]: GrRByz 33 (1992) 247-263; pl. I, the wooden tablet.

g985 *Dalby* Andrew, Greeks abroad; social organisation and food among the ten thousand [XENOPHON]: JHS 112 (1992) 16-30.

g986 *a)* *Delwen* Samuel, Ancient Egyptian baking and brewing; – *b)* *Simon* Claire, Râpes, siphons ou filtres pour pailles; développement égyptien d'un art de boire; – *c)* *Guidotti* Maria Cristina, Studio preliminare sulle forme da pane del tempio funerario di Tutmosi IV: ➤ 735, Sesto Eg. 1991/2, 129-134 / 555-560 + 15 fig. / 227-230 + 4 fig.

g987 **Durliat** J., De la ville antique à la ville byzantine; le problème des subsistances: Coll. ÉcFrR 136. R 1990, Éc.Française. xii-642 p. F 153. 2-7283-0190-5. – ᴿJRS 82 (1992) 301s (O. F. *Robinson*).

g988 *Easley* Kendell H., Ancient winepresses: BIL 16,1 (1989) 65-69 [<
OTAbs 15,37].

g989 *Fischer-Eifert* Hans-W., Amenemope und der Spucknapf oder 'Die
Kultivierung des Appetits': GöMiszÄg 127 (1992) 33-37.

g990 **Flach** Dieter, Römische Agrargeschichte 1990 → 7,e517: ᴿTyche 7
(1992) 242s (G. *Dobesch*).

g991 **Forsén** Björn, Lex Livinia Sextia de modo agrorum, fiction or reality:
Comm. Hum. Litt. 96. Helsinki 1991, Soc. Scientiarum Fennica. 88 p. –
ᴿRÉLat 70 (1992) 343s (J.-C. *Richard*).

g992 *Frankel* Rafael, Some oil presses from western Galilee: BASOR 286
(1992) 39-71: 35 fig.

g993 **Gallant** Thomas W., Risk and survival in ancient Greece; reconstructing
the rural domestic economy. Stanford 1991, Univ. xxi-267 p. $39.50. 0-
8047-1857-1. – ᴿAmHR 97 (1992) 1189 (R. *Garland*); ClasR 42 (1992)
103-5 (R. *Osborne*); ClasW 86 (1992s) 167s (V. D. *Hanson*); GreeceR 39
(1992) 98s (J. *Salmon*).

g994 *Gargola* Daniel J., Grain distributions and the revenue of the temple of
Hera on Samos: Phoenix 46 (Toronto 1992) 12-28.

g995 *a*) **Garnsey** Peter, Mass diet and nutrition in the city of Rome; – *b*)
Virlouvet Catherine, La plèbe frumentaire à l'époque d'Auguste; une
tentative de définition; – *c*) *Ungern-Sternberg* Jürgen von, Die politische
und soziale Bedeutung der spätrepublikanischen *leges frumentariae*; – *d*)
Frézouls Edmond, L'évergétisme 'alimentaire' dans l'Asie Mineure romaine: → 645, ᶠBERCHEM D. van, Nourrir la plèbe 1989/91, 67-99 (-101)
/ 43-62 (-65) / 19-42 / 1-18.

g996 *a*) *Geller* Jeremy, From prehistory to history; beer in Egypt; – *b*) Mills
James O., Beyond nutrition; antibiotics produced through grain-storage
practices; their recognition and implications for the Egyptian predynastic;
– *c*) *Wendorf* Fred, *Close* Angela, Early neolithic food economies in the
eastern Sahara: → 84, Mem. HOFFMAN M. 1992, 19-26; 4 fig. / 27-35; 3
fig. / 155-162; 3 fig.

g997 **Hadjisavvas** Sophocles, Olive oil processing in Cyprus from the Bronze
Age to the Byzantine period: SIMA 99. Jonsered 1992, Åström. xvi-
133 p. 91-7081-033-8 [OIAc 5,23].

g998 **Hamel** Gildas, Poverty and charity in Roman Palestine, first three
centuries C.E. 1989 → 6,g407: ᴿGnomon 64 (1992) 561-3 (H. *Kloft*).

g999 *Hansen* Julie, The introduction of agriculture into Greece; the Near
Eastern evidence; AIA 1991: → 699, AJA 96 (1992) 340s.

k1 **Hruska** P., Tradični obilnářsvi staré Mezopotámie (Der traditionelle
Ackerbau im alten Mesopotamien). Praha 1990, CŠAV. 618 p. (2 vol.).
DM 77. – ᴿArOr 60 (1992) 87s (J. *Pečirková*: up to 2000 B.C.).

k2 *Husson* Geneviève, Sur quelques termes du grec d'Égypte désignant des
bâtiments agricoles: RPg 65 (1991) 89-94.

k2* *Jaïdi* Houcine, L'Afrique et le blé de Rome aux IVᵉ et Vᵉ siècles [diss.
1984]. Tunis 1990, Fac. Sciences Humaines, hist. 34. 240 p. 99-73922-00-0
[Latomus 52,495, J. *Debergh*].

k3 *Janssen* J.J., Rations with riddles [grain-distribution ostraca]: GöMiszÄg
128 (1992) 81-86 [87-93, additions and queries (mathematics), *Spalinger*
Anthony].

k4 *Jenks* Alan W., Eating and drinking in the OT (no NT!): → 741, Anchor-
BD 2 (1992) 250-4.

k5 **Juengst** S. C., Breaking bread; the spiritual significance of food. Louisville 1992, W-Knox. 113 p. $9. 0-664-25383-0 [NTAbs 36,437].

k6 *Kruit* Nico,   The meaning of various words related to wine; some new interpretations [*apoiētos, ozarion, kallonē, lēnós, paramonē, rhýsis*]: ZPap-Ep 90 (1992) 265-276 [94, 167].

k7 *Lerstrup* Annette,   The making of wine in Egypt: GöMiszÄg 129 (1992) 61-77 + 27 fig.

k8 *a*) *Lieberman* Stephen J.,   Nippur, city of decisions [... we may learn best what 'the daily bread of the people' was by dissecting the gods' dinner]; – *b*) *Nashef* Khaled,   The Nippur countryside in the Kassite period: ➤ 687, Nippur 1988/92, 127-136 / 151-159.

k9 **Lissarague** François,   The aesthetic of the Greek banquet; images of wine and ritual [Un flot d'images 1987 ➤ 4,e446], T*Szegedy-Maszak* Andrew, 1990 ➤ 6,g424:   RClasR 42 (1992) 224s (J. *Boardman*).

k10 *Los* Andrzej,   Les intérêts des affranchis dans l'agriculture italienne: MÉF 104 (1992) 709-753.

k11 *a*) *Loupiac* Annie,   Le *labor* chez VIRGILE; essai d'interprétation; – *b*) *Briquel* Dominique,   Virgile et les aborigènes: RÉLat 70 (1992) 92-106 / 69-91.

k12 **Mabry** Jonathan B.,   Alluvial cycles and early agricultural settlement phases in the Jordan Valley: diss. Arizona, D*Olsen* J. 1992. 393 p. 93-10595. – DissA 53 (1992s) 3964-A.

k13 **McCorriston** Joy,   The early development of agriculture in the Ancient Near East; an ecological and evolutionary study: diss. Yale, D*Hole* F. NHv 1992. x-425 p. 92-35550. – OIAc 5,29.

k14 *McDowell* Andrea,   Agricultural activity by the workmen of Deir el-Medina: JEA 78 (1992) 195-206.

k15 *Maekawa* Kazuya,   *a*) The agricultural texts of Ur III Lagash of the British Museum (VIII); – *b*) The shape and orientation of the domain units in the 'round tablets' of Ur III Girsu [LIVERANI M., BSumAg 1990]: AcSum 14 (1992) 175-224: 225-243, facsimiles / 407-423.

k16 *Mason* C. Graham,   The agrarian role of coloniae maritimae, 338-241 B.C.:   Historia 41 (1992) 75-87.

k16* *a*) *Migliario* E.,   Terminologia e organizzazione agraria tra tardo antico e alto medioevo; ancora su *fundus* e *casalis/casale*; – *b*) *Hermon* E.,   Le mythe des Gracques dans la législation agraire du Ier siècle av.J.-C.: Athenaeum 80 (1992) 371-384 / 97-131; 4 fig.

k17 *Milevski* I.,   Nota sobre sistemas de almacenamiento [food-storage] en Palestina y el Próximo Oriente: AulaO 10 (1992) 69-76 + 16 fig.

k18 *Miller* Naomi F.,   The origins of plant cultivation in the Near East ➤ 709, Origins 1985/92, 39-58.

k19 **Mrozek** Stanisław,   Les distributions d'argent et de nourriture: Coll. Latomus 198, 1987 ➤ 4,h184; 6,g437:   RAntClas 61 (1992) 605-9 (R. *Duthoy*).

k19* *Muheisin* Zeidoun al-,   Modes d'installations agricoles nabatéennes dans la région de Pétra et dans le wadi Arabah: ➤ 740, Jordan 4 (1992) 215-9.

k20 EMurray Oswyn,   Sympotica 1990 ➤ 6,758*; 7,e537:   RClasR 42 (1992) 128-130 (B. A. *Sparkes*).

k21 **Oehme** Marlis,   Die römische Villenwirtschaft D1988 ➤ 6,g440:   RAnz-AltW 43 (1990) 266-9 (P. *Panitschek*); Latomus 51 (1992) 475s (J. *Kolendo*); RÉLat 70 (1992) 354-6 (G. *Hentz*).

k22 *Papayiannopoulos* John G., Ⓖ Information in the Pentateuch concerning the diet of the ancient Israelites: TAth 63 (1992) 729-735.

k23 *Plácido* Domingo,   La ley olearia de Adriano; la democracia ateniense y el imperialismo romano: Gerión 10 (1992) 171-179; 5 fig.

k24 *Pomponio* Francesco, Antiche sementi [Sumer]: RSO 65 (1991) 161-3.

k25 **Pullen** Daniel J., Ox and plow in the Early Bronze Age Aegean: AJA 96 (1992) 45-59; 4 fig.

k26 *Sáez Fernández* Pedro, El lugar de la ganadería en los tratados de agricultura de época romana-republicana; el tratado de los Sasernae: Latomus 51 (1992) 549-556.

k27 **Sallares** Robert, The ecology of the ancient Greek world [really an updating of L. GERNET's 'approvisionnement d'Athènes en blé' 1909, especially in its last third]. Ithaca NY 1991, Cornell Univ. x-588 p. $75. – ᴿAmHR 97 (1992) 826s (Nancy *Demand*).

k28 *Schuller-Götzburg* Thomas, Did Egypt give food-aid to Nubia?: Gö-MiszÄg 126 (1992) 93s.

k29 **Sirks** Boudewijn, Food for Rome; the legal structure of the transportation and processing of supplies for the imperial distributions in Rome and Constantinople: StAmstEpig 31, 1991 ⇾ 7,e545: ᴿAmHR 97 (1992) 1496s (B. W. *Frier*); GreeceR 39 (1992) 102 (T. E. J. *Wiedemann*); JRS 82 (1992) 301s (O. F. *Robinson*).

k29* *Sirks* A. J. B., The size of the grain distributions in Rome and Constantinople: Athenaeum 79 (1991) 215-237.

k30 **Spurr** M. S., Arable cultivation in Roman Italy 1986 ⇾ 4,h197... 7,e548: ᴿGnomon 64 (1992) 73s (J. *Kolendo*, franç.).

k31 *Stager* Lawrence E., The rise of horticulture in the Levant: ⇾ 736, ᴱ*Shaath*, Palestine 1981/5, 27-41.

k32 *Talmon* Shemaryahu, Prophetic rhetoric and agricultural metaphors: ⇾ 7,141, ᶠSOGGIN J. A., Storia 1991, 267-279.

k33 *a) Thelamon* Françoise, Ascèse et sociabilité; les conduites alimentaires des moines d'Égypte au IVᵉ siècle; – *b) Dihle* Albrecht, La fête chrétienne: RÉtAug 38 (1992) 295-321 / 323-335.

k34 **Vleeming** S. P., The gooseherds of Hou (Pap. Hou); a dossier relating to various agricultural affairs from provincial Egypt of the early fifth century B.C.: Studia Demotica 3. Lv 1991, Peeters. xii-278 p.; 16 p. + 14 pl. apart. 90-6831-360-6 [OIAc 5,38].

k35 **Wilhelm** Gernot, Rationenlisten: Das Archiv des Šilwa-teššup 3/2, 1985 ⇾ 6,g463: ᴿSMEA 29 (1992) 259s (M. *Salvini*).

k36 *a) Willcox* G., La culture inventée, la domestication inconsciente; le début de l'agriculture au Proche Orient; – *b) Sigaut* F., Les techniques de récolte des grains; identification, localisation, problèmes d'interprétation; – *c) Yon* M., Réalités agraires et mythologie d'Ougarit: ⇾ g979, Rites agraires 1987/91, 9-29 / 31-43 / 53-68.

k37 *Wyatt* N., The pruning of the vine in KTU 1.23: UF 24 (1992) 425-7 [428-430 on his 12 (1980), F. *Renfroe* comment].

k38 ᴱ**Zaccagnini** C., Production and consumption in the Ancient Near East [< Dialoghi 3/3, 1961], ᵀ1989 ⇾ 5,877: ᴱBO 49 (1992) 695-7 (N. *Yoffee*: *Liverani* on farms; L. *Milano* on diet in Syria...); JAOS 112 (1992) 159 (M. *Heltzer*: important; many typos); OLZ 88 (1993) 134-7 (H. *Limet*).

k39 *Zaffagno* E., Sul capitolo introduttivo del 'De cibis iudaicis' di No-VAZIANO: GitPg 44 (1992) 59-66.

U2.9 **Medicina** *biblica et antiqua.*

k40 *Adams* J. N., The use and meaning of *stratum* and *scordiscus* in Latin veterinary texts [saddle-bandage / soft leather under saddle]: Latomus 51 (1992) 159-168.

k41 **André** Jacques,   Le vocabulaire latin de l'anatomie: Coll.Ét.Anc. 59.
282 p. – ᴿRÉLat 69 (1991) 299 (D. *Gourévitch*).

k42 **Bäumer** Anne,   Geschichte der Biologie 1. von der Antike bis zur Renaissance [2. Zoologie der Renaissance — Renaissance der Zoologie]:
Fra 1991, Lang. x-266 p. [xvii-472 p.]. – ᴿGnomon 64 (1992) 715s (G. *Wöhrle*).

k43 *Baines* John,   Merit by proxy; the biographies of the dwarf Djeko and his
patron Tjaiharpta: JEA 78 (1992) 241-257, mentioning *Dasen* Véronique,
awaited ᴰDwarfs in Egypt and Greece.

k44 **Barkai** Ron,   Les infortunes de Dinah ou la gynécologie juive au Moyen
Âge (Sefer ha-toledet, ᵀ*Garel* Michel). P 1991, Cerf. 300 p. F 245. –
ᴿRHR 209 (1992) 311-3 (J.-C. *Attias*).

k45 *Barras* Gabriel (médecin),   Notre corps et nous [rapport exprimé le plus
clairement dans la souffrance et la maladie, p. 22]: Échos de Saint-
Maurice 22,2 (Valais 1992) 18-37; 2 fig.

k46 *Biggs* Robert D.,   Ergotism and other mycotoxicoses in ancient Mesopotamia?: → 32, ꟻCIVIL M., AulaO 9,1 (1991) 15-21.

k47 ᵀᴱ**Burguière** P., *al.*, SORANOS, Maladies des femmes I-II, 1988s → 4,
h215 ... 6,g479: ᴿKoinonia 15 (1991) 77-79 (I. *Mazzini*).

k48 ᴱ**Bush** Helen, *Zvelebil* Marek,   Health in past societies; biocultural
interpretations of human skeletal remains in archaeological contexts:
BAR-Int 567. Ox 1991, Tempus Reparatum. vii-145 p. 0-86054-716-7
[OIAc 3,15].

k49 **Curtis** Robert L.,   Garum and salsamenta ... materia medica 1991 → 7,
e562: ᴿClasR 42 (1992) 487 (Vivian *Nutton*); MünstHand 11,2 (1992)
81-85 (P. *Herz*).

k50 **Di Benedetto** Vincenzo,   Il medico e la malattia; la scienza di IPPOCRATE
1986 → 3,f596 ... 5,g168: ᴿGnomon 64 (1992) 251s (P. *Demont*, franç.);
WienerSt 105 (1992) 269s (E. *Dönt*).

k51 *Donini* P I., GALENO e la filosofia: → 712, ANRW 2,26,5 (1992)
3484-3504 (-3554, al.).

k52 *Estes* J. Worth,   The medical skills of ancient Egypt 1989 → 5,g161;
7,e565: ᴿJAmEg 28 (1991) 229-231 (W. B. *Harer*); JEA 78 (1992) 317s (J.
Nunn: strong on pharmacy despite use of unreliable translations).

k53 *Filer* Joyce M.,   Head injuries in Egypt and Nubia; a comparison of
skulls from Giza and Karma: JEA 78 (1992) 281-5.

k54 **Gil Modrego** Ángel,   Estudio de *lēb/ab* en el Antiguo Testamento; análisis
sintagmático y paradigmático: diss. Univ. Complutense, ᴰ*Piñero* Antonio.
Madrid 1992.

k55 *a*) *Gourévitch* Danielle,   La pratique méthodique, définition de la maladie,
indication et traitement; – *b*) *Hanson* Ann E.,   The restructuring of female
physiology at Rome: → 729, Les écoles médicales 1986/91, 57-81 /
255-268.

k56 *Goyon* Jean-Claude,   Chirurgie religieuse ou thanatopraxie? Données
nouvelles sur la momification en Égypte et réflexions qu'elles impliquent:
→ 735, Sesto Eg. 1991/2, 215-224; 1 facsimile.

k57 ᵀ**Hankinson** R.J., GALEN, On the therapeutic method I-II. Ox 1991,
Clarendon. xxxix-269 p. $72. 0-19-824494-0. – ᴿClasW 86 (1992s) 162
(P. *De Lacy*).

k58 ᴱ**Hart** Gerald D.,   Disease in ancient man 1979/83 → 65,638* ... 6,g502:
ᴿHistory and Philosophy of the Life Sciences 11 (N 1989) 129s (P.
Thillaud) [< AnPg 62, p. 970].

k59 **Hogan** Larry P.,   Healing in the Second Temple period: NOrb 21

['Tempel' on cover and title-page]. FrS/Gö 1992, Univ/Vandenhoeck & R. [xiv-] 337 p. Fs 88. 3-7278-0728-2 / VR 3-525-53922-3 [TLZ 118,499, W. *Herrmann*].

k60 **Holzmair** Eduard, Medicina in nummis, Sammlung Dr. Josef Brettauer: Numismatische Kommission 22. W 1989 = 1937 + Vorw. *Göbl* Robert, Österr. Akad. xv-384 p.; 25 pl. 3-7001-1487-7. – ᴿAnzAltW 45,1 (1992) 138-140 (J. *Benedum*).

k61 **Honda** Gisho, *al.*, Herb drugs and herbalists in Syria and North Yemen 1990 ⇥ 6,g504: ᴿJAOS 112 (1992) 167s (D. M. *Varisco*).

k62 *Isaacs* Haskell D., Medical texts in Judaeo-Arabic from the Genizah: ⇥ 457, Genizah 1987/92, 100-4.

k63 **Jenner** K. A., A study of GALEN's 'Commentary' on the 'Prognostikon' of HIPPOCRATES I, 1-26: diss. Oxford 1989, 406 p. BRD-97262. – DissA 53 (1992s) 2356-A.

k64 *Jones* Richard N., Paleopathology: ⇥ 741, AnchorBD 5 (1992) 60-69.

k65 **Jouanna** Jacques, HIPPOCRATE. P 1992, Fayard. 648 p. – ᴿRÉG 105 (1992) 292s (P. *Demont*); RFgIC 120 (1992) 451-6 (Amneris *Roselli*).

k66 **Jouanna** J., HIPPOCRATE, Des vents 1988 ⇥ 5,g186; 6,g512: ᴿHelmantica 42 sup (1991) 304 (Rosa M. *Herrera*).

k67 *Kee* Howard C., Medicine and healing: ⇥ 741, AnchorBD 4 (1992) 659-664 [3,88, *Hamm* M. D., Healing, gifts of].

k68 ᴱ**König** R., PLINIUS Maior, 29./30. Medizin und Pharmakologie; Heilmittel aus dem Tierreich. Mü 1990, Artemis. 335 p. ᴅᴍ 58. 3-7608-1610-X.

ᴱ**Konstan** D., Women and ancient medicine 1988/9 ⇥ 659*.

k69 **Kudlien** Fridolf, Die Stellung des Arztes 1986 ⇥ 2,b781 ... 7,e577: ᴿAnz-AltW 43 (1990) 105-8 (D. *Nickel*).

ᴱ**Kudlien** Fridolf, *Durling* Richard J., GALEN's method of healing: 1982 Symposium: Stud. Anc. Med. 1, 1991 ⇥ 660; **López-Férez** J. 1988/91 ⇥ 666*.

k71 **Langholf** Volker, Medical theories in HIPPOCRATES; early texts and the 'Epidemics': UntAntLG 34, 1990 ⇥ 7,e578; DM 166: ᴿClasR 42 (1992) 167s (J. T. *Vallance*): Gnomon 64 (1992) 546-9 (W. D. *Smith*); Gymnasium 99 (1992) 71s (G. *Wöhrle*).

k72 *Langslow* David, The development of Latin medical terminology; some working hypotheses: PrPgS 37 (1991) 106-130.

k73 **Larchet** Jean-Claude, Théologie de la maladie: Théologie. P 1991, Cerf. 149 p. F 85. 2-204-04290-0. – ᴿÉTRel 67 (1992) 613s (J. *Ansaldi*); RechSR 80 (1992) 470s (P. *Vallin*).

k74 **Larchet** Jean-Claude, Thérapeutique des maladies mentales; l'expérience de l'Orient chrétien des premiers siècles: Théologies. P 1992, Cerf. 184 p. F 98. 2-204-04518-7 [RTLv 24,515, P. *Weber*].

k75 **Lloyd Davies** Margaret & T. A., The Bible; medicine and myth. C c. 1992, Silent Books. 288 p. £12 pa. 1-85183-053-7.

k76 **Lorenz** Günther, Antike Krankenbehandlungen in historisch-vergleichender Sicht; Studien zum konkret-anschaulichen Denken [PLATO Rep. 405d-406d]: BtKlAltW 2/81, 1990 ⇥ 6,g521: DM 130; pa. 96. 3-533-04140-9; -1-7: ᴿAntClas 61 (1992) 520-2 (A. *Touwaide*); AnzAltW 45,1 (1992) 121-3 (V. *Langholf*); Salesianum 54 (1992) 780 (R. *Bratky*).

k77 *Maisano* Maria Rosaria, IPPOCRATE e Perdicca II: esame storico di un *tópos* medico-letterario: AnPisa 22 (1992) 71-83.

k78 *a) Manchester* Keith, Leprosy; the origin and development of the disease in antiquity; – *b) Bardinet* Thierry, Des guérisons immédiates dans les textes médicaux de l'Égypte ancienne; – *c) Byl* Simon, Néologismes et premières attestations de noms de maladies, symptômes et syndromes dans le Corpus Hippocraticum: ➤ 73, FGRMEK M., Maladie et maladies 1992, 31-49 / 51-75 / 77-94.

k79 *Marganne* Marie-Hélène, Un témoignage antérieur à CELSE sur l'opération du coloboma; P. bibl. univ. Giss. IV,44: CdÉ 66 (1991) 227-236; 3 fig.

k80 *Matthäus* Harmut, Medizinische Instrumente der römischen Kaiserzeit in Zypern; Untersuchungen zu einem Neufund aus Kourion: ➤ 99, FKARAGEORGHIS V. 1992, 313-332.

k81 *Mazzini* Innocenzo, Caratteri della lingua del De medicina di A. Cornelio CELSO: RCuClasMdv 34 (1992) 17-46.

k82 EMeier Levi, Jewish values in health and medicine. Lanham MD 1991, UPA. xvii-201 p. $16.75 [RelStR 19,85, L. E. *Newman*].

k83 *Mikat* Paul, Ethische Überlegungen zum hippokratischen Ethos: ➤ 105, FKORFF W., Markierungen 1992, 215-228.

k84 *Morens* David M., *Littman* Robert J., Epidemiology of the plague of Athens: AmPgTr 122 (1992) 271-304.

EMudry Philippe, *Pigeaud* Jackie, Les écoles médicales à Rome; Actes du 2ème Colloque International sur les textes médicaux latins antiques 1986/91 ➤ 729.

k85 *Müller-Dürr* Marianne, Sogenannte medizinische Instrumente im Tiroler Landesmuseum Ferdinandeum zu Innsbruck: ➤ 184, FTRENTINI J. B., Echo 1990, 227-244; 4 pl.

k86 *Mull* Kenneth V. & Carolyn S., Biblical leprosy; is it really?: BR 8,2 (1992) 22-39; 62.

k87 *Neufeld* Edward, The earliest document of a case of contagious disease in Mesopotamia (Mari tablet ARM X,129): JANES 18 (1986) 53-66.

k88 **Papayiannopoulos** Ioannis Y., Ⓖ *Thémata*... Themes of the history of medicine [... OT; from articles 1977-92]. Ioannina 1992. 445 p. – RTAth 63 (1992) 873-5 (P. *Simotas*).

k88* **Parry** Hugh, Thelxis; magic and imagination in Greek myth and poetry. Lanham MD 1992, UPA. xi-332 p. $44.50 [ClasR 43,443s, S. *Goldhill* finds relevant to ancient medicine].

k89 *Pearcy* Lee T., Diagnosis as narrative in ancient literature: AmJPg 113 (1992) 595-616.

k89* *a) Pigeaud* Jackie, L'esthétique de GALIEN; – *b) Petzil* Georg, LUKIANs podagra und die Beichtinschriften Kleinasiens; – *c) Kahn* Pierre, La mort dans les yeux; questions à Jean-Pierre VERNANT: Métis 6 (1991) 7-42 / 131-145 / 285-299.

Pigeaud J., *Gourévitch* D., *Thivel* A., *al.*, Les écoles médicales à Rome 1986/91 ➤ 729.

k90 *Pilch* John, Understanding healing in the social world of early Christianity: BibTB 22 (1992) 26-33.

k90* **Pinault** Jody R., Hippocratic lives and legends: Studies in Ancient Medicine 4. Leiden 1992, Brill. x-159 p.; front. *f*100 [ClasR 43,408, K.-H. *Leven*].

k91 **Pisani** Giuliano, PLUTARCO, Moralia I, 'La serenità interiore' e altri testi sulla terapia dell'anima: Il Soggetto e la Scienza 6. Pordenone 1991 = 1989, Bt. dell'Immagine. lix-512 p.

k92 EPotter Paul, *al.*, La maladie et les maladies 1987/90 ➤ 7,599: RClasR 42 (1992) 168-170 (J. T. *Vallance*); ÉtClas 60 (1992) 86s (T. *Ory*).

k93 **Reeves** Carole, Egyptian medicine: Shire Egyptology 15. Princes Risborough, Bucks 1992, Shire. 72 p.; 63 fig. 0-7478-0127-4.

k94 *Rengen* Johannes, Kranke, Krüppel, Debile — eine Randgruppe im Alten Orient? ➤ 691, Aussenseiter 1989/92, 113-126.

k94* **Riddle** J. M., Quid pro quo; studies in the history of drugs: CS 367. Aldershot 1992, Variorum. xi-341 p.; 2 fig. [ClasR 43,409, R. *French*].

k95 *Rouanet-Liesenfelt* Anne-Marie, Les plantes médicinales de Crète à l'époque romaine: Cretan Studies 3 (1992) 173-190.

ᴱSabbah G., Le latin médical 1989/91 ➤ 675c.

k97 **Sanford** John A., Healing body and soul; the meaning of illness in the New Testament and in psychotherapy. Leominster/Louisville 1992, Gracewing/W-Knox. [vi-] 136 p. 0-852-44228-9 / US 0-664-25351-2.

k98 *Sauser* Ekkart, [Mk 2,17; HARNACK 'als Arzt ist Jesus in der Mitte seines Volkes getreten'] Christus medicus — Christus als Arzt und seine Nachfolger im frühen Christentum: TrierTZ 101 (1992) 101-123.

k99 *Scheid* Jean, Épigraphie et sanctuaires guérisseurs en Gaule: MÉF-Ant 104,1 (1992) 25-40.

k100 **Sheridan** Susan G., Minor and trace element distributions in bone; reconstruction of diagnostic, dietary and disease patterns in an ancient Nubian population: diss. Colorado. Boulder 1992. xvii-167 p. 92-32733. – OIAc 5,34.

k101 ᴱ**Smith** Wesley D., HIPPOCRATES pseudepig. 1990 ➤ 7,e596: ᴿClasR 42 (1992) 287-9 (P. *Potter*).

k102 **Staden** Heinrich von, HEROPHILUS 1989 ➤ 5,g222; 6,g544: ᴿMnemosyne 45 (1992) 547-550 (P. J. van der *Eijk*).

k103 *a) Staden* Heinrich von, Women and dirt [in Greek laws and poetry, and Hippocratica]; – *b) Pinault* Jody R., The medical case for virginity in the early second century C.E.; SORANUS of Ephesus, Gynecology 1.32: ➤ 659*, Helios 19 (1992) 7-30 / 123-139 [+ articles on medical views of female sexual appetite].

k104 *Steiner* Richard C., Northwest Semitic incantations in an Egyptian medical papyrus [London; WRESZINSKI W. 1912] of the fourteenth century B.C.: JNES 51 (1992) 191-200.

k105 *Stol* M., Diagnosis and therapy in Babylonian medicine: JbEOL 32 (1991s) 42-65.

k106 *Sussman* Max, Sickness and disease; ➤ 741, AnchorDB 6 (1992) 6-15.

k107 **Temkin** Owsei, Hippocrates in a world of pagans and Christians 1991 ➤ 7,e599: ᴿClasR 42 (1992) 232s (Helen *King*: could a Christian take the Hippocratic oath invoking Apollo? — Hippocrates was neither god nor miracle-worker, so Aesculapius became Christ's rival); ClasW 86 (1992s) 65s (Ann E. *Hanson*).

k108 *Villard* Laurence, Les vases dans la Collection Hippocratique; vocabulaire et usage: BCH 116,1 (1992) 73-96 (97-117, *Blondé* Francine, Sur quelques vases, 13 fig.).

k109 *Volpe Cacciatore* Paola, Un problema plutarcheo di medicina: ➤ 654, Convegno 4, 1991/2, 375-383.

k110 **Westendorf** W., Erwachen der Heilkunst; die Medizin im Alten Ägypten. Z 1992, Artemis & W. 297 p. DM 44 [ZAW 105,540, M. *Köckert*].

k111 *Winkworth* Laurence E., A request for purgatives: P. Oxy. I 187: ZPapEp 91 (1992) 85-87.

k112 **Wöhrle** Georg, Studien zur Theorie der antiken Gesundheitslehre: Hermes Einz 56, 1990 ➤ 7,e602: ᴿGnomon 64 (1992) 717s (I. *Mazzini*, ital.); RFgIC 120 (1992) 456-460 (Daniela *Manetti*).

k113 *Wöhrle* Georg, CATO und die griechischen Ärzte: Eranos 90 (1992) 112-125.

k114 *Wolska-Conus* Wanda, Les commentaires de STÉPHANOS d'Athènes au Prognostikon et aux Aphorismes d'HIPPOCRATE; de GALIEN à la pratique scolaire alexandrine: RÉByz 50 (1992) 5-86.

k115 *Wright* David P., *Jones* Richard N., Leprosy: ⇒741, AnchorBD 4 (1992) 277-282.

k116 *Zaghloul* El-Hussein, An eye-disease (amblyopia) mentioned in a private letter from Tuna El-Gebel (Pap. Mallawi Inv. no. 484): MiDAI-K 42 (1992) 255-260; 1 fig.; pl. 48.

U3   *Duodecim Tribus:* **Israel Tribes;** Land-Ideology.

k117 ᴱ**Cahen** Joel, *al.* [*Eyul* Eli, present.], Beyond the sambatyon; the myth of the ten lost tribes. TA 1991, Beth Hatefutsoth. 98 p., ❺ 32 p. + (color.) pl.; Eng. 98-63 (sic.). 965-425-000-4.

k118 *Davies* W.D., Reflections on territory in Judaism: ⇒181, Sha'arei TALMON 1992, 339-343.

k119 *Dequeker* L., Christoffel Columbus; op kruistocht of op zoek naar de tien Joodse stammen?: Ter Herkenning 19,4 (1991) 254-270 [217-296 on Jews in Spain: < GerefTTs 92,58].

k120 *a*) *Dieckhoff* Alain, Terre rêvée, terre convoitée, Israel; – *b*) (Nederveen) *Pieterse* Jan, The history of a metaphor; Christian Zionism and the politics of apocalypse: ArScSocR 36,75 (1991) 69-74 / 75-104 [< ZIT 92,66].

k121 *Janzen* W., Land: ⇒741, AnchorDB 4 (1992) 143-154.

k122 **Langston** Scott M., The religious and political role of the tribe of Benjamin; a study of Iron Age cultic sites and activities: diss. SW Baptist Sem., ᴰ*Kent* D. Fort Worth 1992. viii-256 p. 92-23539. – OIAc 5,28.

k123 *a*) *Lux* Richard C., Biblical land traditions; – *b*) *Neher* André, The land as locus of the sacred, ᵀ*Burrell* David; *c*) *Dubois* Marcel I., Living in Jerusalem; the meaning for Jews and for Christians; – *d*) *Goldstein* Marie, The Jerusalem HOPE center for interfaith understanding; – *e*) *Stransky* Thomas F., The Tantur dialogue on the land: Catholic World 234,1 (1991) 4-10 / 11-16 / 27-30 / 38-41 / 44-46.

k124 **Wilken** Robert L., The land called holy; Palestine in Christian history and thought. NHv 1992, Yale Univ. xviii-355 p.; 7 fig. map. 0-300-05491-2.

k124* **Wolff** Katherine E., 'Geh in das Land ...' Das Land Israel in der frühen rabbinischen Tradition und im NT [diss. Fra St-Georgen] 1989 ⇒ 6,g564: ᴿÉglT 22 (1991) 368s (L. *Laberge*).

U4   *Limitrophi,* **adjacent lands.**

k125 *Adamo* David T., ❺ Aethiopia in the Bible: DeltioVM 11,1 (1992) 101-112 [< ZIT 92,576].

k125* **Bartlett** J., Edom 1989 ⇒ 5,g242; 6,g565: ᴿBO 49 (1992) 816-820 (B. *Becking*); BZ 36 (1992) 304 (H. *Engel*); JAOS 112 (1992) 543 (D.B. *MacKay*: cautious, good; but no synthesis).

k126 *Bianchetti* Serena, Aethiopes in Africa; aspetti della storia di un nome: ⇒ 726, L'Africa 1990/1, 117-125.

k126* *Borchhardt* Jürgen, Skythen in der griechischen Kunst: ⇒ 93, ᶠİNAN J., 1989, 337-349; pl. 139-142.

k127 **Gutsfeld** A., Römische Herrschaft und einheimischer Widerstand in Nordafrika; militarische Auseinandersetzungen Roms mit den Nomaden [Diss. Heidelberg, ᴰ*Alföldy* G.]: HeidAlthBeit 3. Stu 1989, Steiner. 215 p. map. DM 48. 3-515-05549-5. – ᴿJRS 82 (1992) 278s (D. F. *Graf*).

k128 **Haider** Peter W., Griechenland – Nordafrika [Ägypten, Keftiu, Sea-Peoples, Cyrenaica...]; ihre Beziehungen zwischen 1500 und 600 v. Chr.: ImpFor 53, 1988 → 4,h294:   ᴿAnzAltW 43 (1990) 63s (B. *Brentjes* wants more on climate and Phoenicians); Gnomon 64 (1992) 171-3 (J. M. *Cook*, Eng.).

k129 **Karttunen** Klaus, India in early Greek literature. StOr 65. Helsinki 1989, Finnish Oriental Soc. iv-296 p. 3 maps. Fm 150. – ᴿIndIranJ 35 (1992) 63-66 (J. W. de *Jong*); JAOS 112 (1992) 515-7 (A. K. *Narain*).

k130 **Kazanski** Michel, Les Goths (Iᵉʳ-VIIᵉ s. ap. J.-C.); Hespérides. P 1991, Errance. 148 p. 2-87772-062-4.

k131 **Rolle** Renate, The world of the Scythians [Stutenmelker und Pferdebogner 1980] ᵀ*Walls* F. G. Berkeley 1989, Univ. California. 160 p. $35 → 6,g572. – ᴿAthenaeum 74 (1991) 653s (Laura *Boffo*); BA 55 (1992) 155 (K. S. *Rubinson*); RBgPg 70 (1992) 265 (Anne *Francis*).

k132 *a)* **Szabo** Miklos, Les Celtes de l'Est; le second âge du fer dans la cuvette des Karpates; – *b)* **Brun** Patrice, Princes et princesses de la Celtique; le premier âge du fer en Europe 850-450 av. J.-C.: Hespérides. P 1991/1987, Errance. 206 p. / 219 p. 2-87772-065-9 / 2-903442-46-0.

k132* *Tavares* Antonio A., Des Indoeuropéens aux Peuples de la Mer; reflets sur la péninsule ibérique: Orpheus-Thrax 2 (1992) 37-44.

ᴜ4.5 *Viae* – **Routes, roads.**

k133 *Beitzel* Barry J. (*al.*), *a)* Roads and highways; – *b)* Travel and communication (OT World): → 741, AnchorBD 5 (1992) 776-782 (-787) / 6 (1992) 644-8 (- 653, *Bruce* F., NT).

k133* — *Deblauwe* F., Old South Arabian trade routes: OrLovPer 22 (1991) 133-152 + 6 maps.

k134 *a)* *Beitzel* B. J., The Old Assyrian caravan road in the Mari royal archives; – *b)* *Fisher* Robert W., The *mubassirū* messengers at Mari: → 740, Mari in retrospect 1992, 35-57 / 113-120.

k135 *Cloppet* Christian, Les voies romaines du Rhône au Rhin et dans l'est de la Gaule: les sources écrites: Ktema 14 (1989) 95-104.

k135* **Cuntz** Otto, Itineraria romana 1. Antonini Augusti et Burdigalense; 2. (ᴱ**Schnetz** Joseph) Ravennatis anonymi cosmographia et Guidonis geographica. Stu 1990 = 1929/40, Teubner. xvi-140 p.; xii-214 p. 3-519-04273-8; -4-6 [Latomus 52,723, Y. *Janvier*].

k136 **Dorsey** David A., The roads and highways of ancient Israel [diss. Dropsie 1981, ᴰ*Rainey* A.]. Baltimore 1991, Johns Hopkins Univ. xviii-300 p. – ᴿBAR-W 18,6 (1992) 6.8 (B. J. *Beitzel*); RelStR 18 (1992) 326 (R. S. *Hanson*); WestTJ 54 (1992) 367s (R. B. *Dillard*).

k137 *Ercenk* Giray, ❶ The ancient road system of Pamphylia region and environs: Belleten 56 (1992) 361-370; map.

k138 *Frézouls* Edmond, Sᴛʀᴀʙᴏɴ et les voies d'Agrippa: Ktema 13 (1988) 275-284.

k139 ᴱ**Haellquist** Karl R., Asian trade routes, continental and maritime: Scandinavian Institute of Asian Studies 13. L 1991, Curzon. xi-292 p. 0-7007-0212-1 [OIAc 3,23].

k140 ᴱ**Kase** Edward W. †, *Szemler* George J., *al.*, The great Isthmus corridor route: Minnesota Univ. Phokis-Doris expedition I, 1991 ➤ 7,e633; 49 fig.; 199 pl. $30 pa.: ᴿClasR 42 (1992) 145s (R. *Osborne*: 'the road from Lamia to Amphissa').

k141 *a*) *Kleiss* Wolfram, Brücken aus Zentral- und Südiran - IV; – *b*) *Brentjes* Burchard, Karawanenwege durch Mittelasien: ArchMIran 25 (1992) 235-245; 12 fig.; pl. 58-66 / 247-266; 9 maps; + 18 fig.

k142 **Nashef** Khaled, Rekonstruktion der Reiserouten der altassyrischen Handelsniederlassungen: TAVO B-83, 1987 ➤ 3,f706... 6,g583 (*der Reis*...!): ᴿZAss 81 (1991) 146-150 (A. *Harrak*).

k143 *Sayar* Mustafa H., Strassenbau in Kilikien unter den Flaviern nach einem neugefundenen Meilenstein: EpAnat 20 (1992) 57-61; pl. 4; p. 62 Özet (summary).

k144 **Tardieu** Michel, Les paysages reliques... routes et haltes syriennes 1990 ➤ 6,g585; 7,d878*: ᴿAfO 38s (1991s) 256s (É. *Kettenhofen*); BO 49 (1992) 510s (M. *Stol*); RÉAnc 94 (1992) 506s (P. *Arnaud*).

k145 *Varinlioğlu* Ender, *French* David H., A new milestone from Ceramus [Sek]: RÉAnc 94 (1992) 404-412; 2 facsim.; 3 phot.

U5 *Ethnographia*, **sociologia** [servitus ➤ E3.5; G6.5].

k146 *a*) *Ackerman* Robert, J. G. FRAZER and the Jews; – *b*) *Segal* Robert A., Joseph CAMPBELL on Jews and Judaism: Religion 22 (L 1992) 135-150 / 151-170 [< ZIT 92,413].

k147 **Adams** Matthew D., Community and societal organization in early historic Egypt [Abydos 1991s]: NewsAmEg 158s (1992) 1-9.

k148 **Alföldy** Géza, Histoire sociale de Rome [1975, ³1984 + bibliog. française 1971-86], ᵀ*Évrard* Étienne. P 1991, Picard. 219 p. – ᴿRÉLat 69 (1991) 270 (J.-C. *Richard*).

k149 *Auffarth* Christoph, Protecting strangers; establishing a fundamental value in the religions of the Ancient Near East and ancient Greece: Numen 39 (1992) 193-216.

k150 **Berger** Klaus, Historische Psychologie des NTs: SBS 146s. Stu 1991, KBW. 303 p. DM 50,20. – ᴿIndTSt 29 (1992) 265-7 (I. *Legrand*).

k151 *Berger* Klaus, Innen und Aussen in der Welt des NTs, in: ᴱASSMANN J., Die Erfindung des inneren Menschen (Gü, Mohn) 161-7 [< TLZ 118,936, ohne Datum].

k152 **Bernal** Martin, Black Athena, the Afroasiatic roots of classical civilization [I ➤ 7,b214] II. The archaeological and documentary evidence. New Brunswick 1991, Rutgers Univ. 736 p. $60, pa. $17. 0-8135 1583-1. – ᴿAJA 96 (1992) 381-3 (J. M. *Weinstein*: sloppy and manipulative); BAR-W 18,5 (1992) 14.16 (R. L. *Pounder*: myopic, inaccurate); Gerión 9 (1991) 309-315 (J. L. *López Castro*); GrecccR 39 (1992) 78s (P. *Walcot*).

k153 **Bernal** Martin, Atena nera; le radici afroasiatiche della cultura classica. Parma 1991, Pratiche. 675 p. Lit. 70.000. – ᴿArcheo 7,90 (1992) 127 (S. *Moscati*).

k154 — *Hall* Edith, When is a myth not a myth? BERNAL's 'Ancient Model' [Black Athena I]: Arethusa 25 (1992) 181-201; Bernal response, 204-215.

k155 — *a*) *Levine* Molly M., The use and abuse of [BERNAL M. 1987] Black Athena; – *b*) *Pounder* Robert L., Black Athena 2; history without roles: AmHR 97 (1992) 440-460 / 461-4.

k156 **Bettini** Maurizio, Anthropology and Roman culture; kinship, time, images of the soul, ᵀ*Van Sickle* John. Baltimore 1991, Johns Hopkins Univ. xi-334 p. $37. – ᴿRelStR 18 (1992) 326 (J. H. *Elliott*: brilliant).

k157 **Bouvrie** Synnøve des, Women in Greek tragedy; an anthropological approach: Symbolae Osloenses supp. 27. Oslo 1992 = 1990, Norwegian Univ. Press. 394 p. 82-00-21125-8.

k158 *Bowler* Peter J., From 'savage' to 'primitive'; Victorian evolutionism and the interpretation of marginalized peoples: Antiquity 66 (1992) 721-729.

Bradley Keith R., Discovering the Roman family; studies in Roman social history 1991 ➤ 217a; ➤ Krause bibliog. 967.

k159 *a*) **Bradley** K. R., Slavery and rebellion 1989 ➤ 5,6293: ᴿAthenaeum 80 (1992) 535-540 (G. *Traina*).

— *b*) ᴱ*Bradley* Keith R., Child labor in the Roman world [< Historical Reflections 12 (1985) 311-330] ➤ 217, Roman Family 1991, 103-124.

k160 *Brulé* Pierre, Infanticide et abandon d'enfants; pratiques grecques et comparaisons anthropologiques: DialHA 18,2 (1992) 53-90.

k161 **Capriglione** Jolanda C., La passione amorosa nella città 'senza' donne; etica e prassi politica: BtFilosofia 16. N 1990, Tempi Moderni. 227 p. Lit. 23.000. – ᴿAntClas 61 (1992) 409s (E. *Borza*: savoureux).

k162 ᴱ**Clements** R. E., The world of ancient Israel; social, anthropological and political perspectives 1989 ➤ 5,387 ... 7,e651: ᴿBibTB 22 (1992) 38s (Claudia V. *Camp*); Bijdragen 53 (1992) 86 (P. C. *Beentjes*); EvQ 64 (1992) 259s (I. H. *Marshall*); HeythJ 33 (1992) 206s (J. *Mulrooney*); JRel 72 (1992) 90s (A. *Dearman*).

k163 **Cole** Thomas, DEMOCRITUS and the sources of Greek anthropology: AmPgMg 25. Atlanta 1990 = 1967, Scholars. xii-243 p. $27; pa. $22. 1-55540-501-0; -14-2. – ᴿClasAnt 61 (1992) 448s (Evelyne *Scheid-Tissinier*).

k165 **Coote** R. & M., Power, politics, and the making of the Bible 1990 ➤ 6,g608; 7,e652*: ᴿCBQ 54 (1992) 318s (J. M. *Kennedy*); CritRR 5 (1992) 85s (D. L. *Smith*: fascinating, provocative); IndTSt 28 (1991) 323-6 (A. R. *Ceresko*: rigid consistency confines their perspective); Interpretation 46 (1992) 100s (B. *Lang*); TorJT 8 (1992) 328s (D. J. *Reimer*).

k166 *Corbier* Mireille, Construire sa parenté à Rome: RHist 284 (1990) 3-36.

k166* *Craffert* P. F., More on models and muddles in the social-scientific interpretation of the New Testament; the sociological fallacy reconsidered: Neotestamentica 26 (1922) 217-239.

k167 *Curchin* Leonard A., Responses to wealth-diferentiation in ancient Mesopotamia: ➤ 557*, Contacts 1990/2, 1-6.

k168 **Dabdab Trabulsi** José A., Dionysisme, pouvoir et société en Grèce jusqu'à la fin de l'époque classique [diss. Besançon]: Univ. Ann. Litt. 412. P 1990, BLettres. 288 p. 2-251-60412-1. – ᴿAntClas 61 (1992) 480-2 (G. *Casadio*).

k169 *David* Ephraim, Sparta's social hair [coiffure as clue to code of behaviour]: Eranos 90 (1992) 11-21.

k170 *Decourt* J.-C., Territoires des cités grecques: Table Ronde ÉcFrAth 31 oct. - 3 nov. 1991: TopO 2 (1992) 301-4.

k171 **Dixon** Suzanne, The Roman family. Baltimore 1992, Johns Hopkins Univ. xiv-279 p. $38.50; pa. $14. 0-9018-4199-2; -200-X. – ᴿClasW 86 (1992s) 371 (Natalie B. *Kampen*).

k172 **Dixon** Suzanne, The Roman mother 1988 ➤ 4,h340 ... 7,e656: ᴿAmJPg 113 (1992) 132-4 (Marie-T. *Raepsaet-Charlier*, franç.).

k173 *du Bois* Page, Torture and truth [evidence from slaves]: The New Ancient World. L 1991, Routledge. viii-162 p. £10 pa. [ClasR 43,125, Edith *Hall*].

k174 **Dunston** Alfred G., The black man in the Old Testament and its world; a study of the facts that are revealed in the Authorized (King James) version of the Holy Bible during the days in which the OT was lived. Trenton 1992, Africa World. xi-153 p. 0-86543-304-6; pa. -5-4.

k175 **Eichenauer** Monika, Untersuchungen zur Arbeitswelt der Frau in der römischen Antike: EurHS 3/360. Fra 1988, Lang. 344 p. – ᴿBonnJbb 192 (1992) 639-642 (K. *Thraede*).

k176 **Evans** John K., War, women and children in ancient Rome. NY 1991, Routledge. xvi-263 p. $45. – ᴿAmHR 97 (1992) 1190 (Susan *Treggiari*); ClasR 42 (1992) 126s (Jane F. *Gardner*).

k177 *Ewald* Janet J., Slavery in Africa and the slave trades from Africa [mostly to Islamic societies, from long before the Atlantic trade into the twentieth century: review of seven books]: AmHR 97 (1992) 465-485.

k178 *Eyre* C. J., The adoption papyrus in social context: JEA 78 (1992) 207-221.

k179 *Fales* Frederick M., West Semitic names in the Assyrian empire; diffusion and social relevance: StEpL 8 (1991) 99-117.

k180 **Felder** Cain H., Troubling biblical waters; race, class and family: Turner Black Rel. 3. Mkn 1989, Orbis. xix-233 p. $16 pa. – ᴿCritRR 5 (1992) 88s (H. C. *Waetjen*).

Fenn Richard, The death of Herod, an essay in the sociology of religion 1992 → d179.

k181 **Fiensy** D. A., The social history of Palestine in the Herodian period; the land is mine: StBeC 20. Lewiston NY 1991, Mellen. ix-195 p.; 4 fig.; 3 maps. $70. 0-88946-272-0 [NTAbs 36,445].

k181* **Forster** Peter G., T. Cullen YOUNG, missionary and anthropologist 1991 → 7,e661: ᴿMissiology 19 (1991) 487s (Kathleen A. W. *Dillman*).

k182 **Fraser** David A., **Campolo** Tony, Sociology through the eyes of faith. 1992, Apollos. 316 p. – ᴿExpTim 104 (1992s) 283 (R. J. *Elford*: clear, good).

k182* **Francisi** G., Famiglia e persona in Roma antica dall'età arcaica al Principato. T 1989, Giappichelli. 228 p. – ᴿIvra 40 (1989) 102-7 (A. *Corbino*).

k183 *Frölich* Eric, Mariage indo-européen et mariage naturel: Divinitas 36 (1992) 160-179.

k184 **Furnham** Adrian, The Protestant work-ethic; the psychology of work-related beliefs and behaviors. L 1990, Routledge. 305 p. $17 pa. – ᴿJScStR 30 (1991) 342s (M. L. *Stackhouse*).

k185 **Gilli** G. A., Origini dell'eguaglianza; ricerche sociologiche sull'antica Grecia 1988 > 6,b585: ᴿQuadUrb 68 (1991) 141-6 (R. *Campagner*: 'un volume sulle *téchnai*').

k186 *Gismondi* Gualberto, Il dialogo fra teologia e sociologia; problematiche, limiti, possibilità: Antonianum 67 (1992) 3-38; Eng. 3.

k187 **Golden** Mark, Children and childhood in classical Athens: Ancient Society and History. Baltimore 1990, Johns Hopkins Univ. 288 p. $30. 0-8018-3980-7. – ᴿPhoenix 46 (Toronto 1992) 294-6 (G. *Raepsaet*).

k188 *a) Golden* Mark, The uses of cross-cultural comparison in ancient social history; – *b) Hallett* Judith P., Heeding our native informants; the uses of Latin literary texts in recovering elite Roman attitudes toward age, gender and social status: EchMClas 36 (1992) 309-331 / 333-355.

k189 *a) Gottwald* Norman K., Sociology, ancient Israel; – *b) Garrett* Susan R., ...early Christianity: → 741, AnchorDB 6 (1992) 79-88-99.

k189* **Greeley** Andrew M., The Catholic myth — the behavior and beliefs of American Catholics 1990 → 7,e668: ᴿCCurr 42 (1992s) 119s (R. *Quillo*).

k190 **Gronemeyer** R., Die Entfernung vom Wolferudel; über den drohenden Krieg der Jüngen gegen die Alten. Dü 1989. 178 p. – ᴿDielB 27 (1991) 281 (B. J. *Diebner*).

k191 *Grumelli* Antonio, Per un'analisi fenomenologica dei movimenti ecclesiali: EuntDoc 44 (1991) 143-6.

k192 **Günther** Rosmarie, Frauenarbeit – Frauenbindung ᴰ1987 ➤ 5,g308; 6,g634: ᴿBonnJbb 192 (1992) 633-8 (K. *Thraede*).

k193 *Gustafsson* Göran, Religionssociologin i Sverige — bakgrund och utveckling: SvTKv 67 (1991) 153-9.

k194 **Hall** Edith, Inventing the barbarian; Greek self-definition through tragedy. Ox 1989, pa. 1991. xvi-277 p. £15. – ᴿHephaistos 11s (1992s) 215-223 (D. *Metzler*).

k195 *Harrod* Howard L., Reflections on the sociology of American religion [Peyote; Mainline; GREELEY A. 1989...]: RelStR 18 (1992) 301-7.

k196 *Hilhorst* H. W. A., Ontwikkelingen in de godsdienstsociologie in Nederland: NedTTs 46 (1992) 10-22.

k197 **Holmberg** Bengt, Sociology and the NT, an appraisal 1990 ➤ 6,g639; 7,e672: ᴿBA 55 (1992) 157 (D. M. *May*); CBQ 54 (1992) 353s (Carolyn *Osiek*); Interpretation 46 (1992) 82s (D. C. *Duling*); NorTTs 92 (1991) 59-61 (H. *Moxnes*); RB 99 (1992) 461-3 (J. *Murphy-O'Connor*); RelStR 18 (1992) 140 (H. C. *Kee*: effectively challenges THEISSEN, MEEKS, GAGER, MOLINA); TR 88 (1992) 293s (R. *Pesch*).

k198 **Hooff** Anton J. L., From autothanasia to suicide. L 1990, Routledge. xv-306 p.; 7 fig.; Gill. £35. – ᴿClasR 42 (1992) 130-2 (Miriam *Griffith*).

k199 **Horsley** Richard, Sociology and Jesus-movement 1989 ➤ 7,e673: ᴿJAAR 60 (1992) 788-791 (R. A. *Ramsaran*).

k200 **Jamieson-Drake** David W., Scribes and schools in monarchic Juda: JStOT supp 109, ᴰ1991 ➤ 7,e676: ᴿÉTRel 67 (1992) 99 (Françoise *Smyth*); JAOS 112 (1992) 707-8 (A. *Lemaire*, franç.); JTS 43 (1992) 145-7 (B. A. *Mastin*); PEQ 124 (1992) 155s (P. *Darrell*).

k201 *Karttunen* Klaus, Distant lands in classical ethnography: GrazBeit 18 (1992) 195-205.

k202 **Kaster** R. A., Guardians of language 1988 ➤ 5,g321... 7,e680: ᴿByZ 84s (1991s) 515-7 (C. *Theodoridis*); EngHR 107 (1992) 423s (A. C. *Dionisotti*).

k203 **Kaufmann** Franz-X., Religion und Modernität; sozialwissenschaftliche Perspektive. Tü 1989, Mohr. 286 p. DM 58. – ᴿLuthMon 30 (1991) 378s (H. *Grosse*).

k204 **Kee** Howard C., Knowing the truth; a sociological approach to NT interpretation 1989 ➤ 5,g322... 7,e681: ᴿRelStT 11,2 (1991) 114s (S. *Mason*).

k204* *Kee* Howard C., A sociological approach to New Testament interpretation: Drew Gateway 61,2 (1992) 3-...

k205 *a*) *Kee* Howard C., Changing modes of leadership in the NT period; – *b*) *Ebertz* Michael N., Le stigmate du mouvement charismatique autour de Jésus de Nazareth; – *c*) *Bloomquist* L. Gregory, al., Prolegomena to a sociological study of early Christianity; – *d*) *Wackenheim* Charles, Trois initiateurs; ENGELS, WEBER, TROELTSCH; – *e*) *Duhaime* Jean, L'univers social des premiers chrétiens d'après J. G. GAGER / Early Christianity and the social sciences; a bibliography: Social Compass 39,2 (1992) 241-254 / 255-273 / 221-239 / 183-205 / 207-219 . 290.

k206 **Keim** Paul A., When sanctions fail; the social function of curse in ancient Israel [Mary DOUGLAS approach]: diss. Harvard, ᴰCross F. CM

1992. 167 p. 92-28343. – DissA 53 (1992s) 1547-A (mentions only failed cases, Jg 21; 1 Sam 14).

k207 **Kessler** Rainer, Staat und Gesellschaft im vorexilischen Juda, vom 8. Jh. bis zum Exil [diss. Bethel 1990, ᴰ*Crüsemann* F.]: VTSup 47. Leiden 1992, Brill. xi-246 p. *f*140. 90-04-09646-9.

k207* *Kessler* Rainer, Sozialgeschichtliche Bibelauslegung: Junge Kirche 53 (1992) 636-8 [< ZIT 92,686].

k208 **Kleijwegt** Marc, Ancient youth 1991 ➤ 7,e685: ᴿAmHR 97 (1992) 527s (R. *Saller*: significant but incomplete, as also BRADLEY K. 1991); AntClas 61 (1992) 495-7 (Marie-Thérèse *Isaac*).

k209 *a) Klengel* Horst, Soziale Differenzierung und Randgruppen der Gesellschaft im Alten Orient; – *b) Haas* Volkert, Soziale Randgruppen und Aussenseiter altorientalischer Gesellschaften; – *c) Wilcke* Claus, Diebe, Räuber und Mörder; – *d) Blocher* Felix, Gaukler im AO: ➤ 691, Aussenseiter 1989/92, 15-27 / 29-51 / 53-78 / 79-111 + 45 fig. (Akrobate, Musikanten).

k209* **Kudlien** Fridolf, Sklavenmentalität im Spiegel antiker Wahrsagerei: ForAntSkl 23. Stu 1991, Steiner. 189 p. DM 58 [ClasR 43,360-2, Sitta von *Reden*: exceptionally, how the slaves themselves bore their lot].

k210 **Kutzner** Edgar, Untersuchungen zur Stellung der Frau im römischen Oxyrhynchus: EurHS 3/392, 1989 ➤ 6,c750: ᴿCBQ 54 (1992) 358-360 (Janet *Timbie*: women's rights often had to be exercised through male relatives).

k211 *Lamberti* Francesca, L'antichità e Max WEBER [CAPOGROSSI COLOGNESI L. 1990]: Labeo 38 (1992) 347-361: una sorta di nuova edizione di M. Weber 1988.

k211* *Lassen* Eva Maria, The ultimate crime, parricidium and the concept of family in the late Roman Republic and early Empire: ClasMedv 43 (1992) 147-161.

k212 *Lategan* Bernard, NT anthropological perspectives in a time of reconstruction: JTSAf 76 (1991) 86-94; response 95s, *Kruger* M A.

Lemche N.P., Early Israel 1985 ➤ 2,1955; Ancient Israel ... society 1988 ➤ 4,d98; The Canaanites and their land 1991 ➤ 7,b17.

Leutzsch Martin, Die Wahrnehmung sozialer Wirklichkeit im 'Hirten des Hermas' [Diss. Bochum, ᴰ*Wengst* K.]: FRL 150, 1989 ➤ k643.

k213 ᶠLIENHARDT Geoffrey: Vernacular Christianity; essays in the social anthropology of religion, ᴱ**James** Wendy, *Johnson* Douglas H., 1988 ➤ 5,119; $44: ᴿChH 60 (1991) 584s (N. Q. *King*).

k214 **Lightstone** Jack N., Society, the sacred, and Scripture in ancient Judaism 1988 ➤ 4,h384 ... 7,e687: ᴿJQR 83 (1992s) 208s (M. *Goodman*); RelStR 18 (1992) 155 (H. C. *Kee*).

k215 ᴱ**Lincoln** C. Eric, *Mamiya* Lawrence H., The Black Church in the African American experience. Durham NC 1990, Duke Univ. 519 p. $19. – ᴿTTod 49 (1992s) 266.268 (P. J. *Paris*).

k216 **Liverani** M., Antico oriente; Storia, società, economia 1988 ➤ 4,h385; 5,g331: ᴿParVi 36 (1991) 387-9 (A. *Rolla*).

k217 *López* Ediberto, The earliest traditions about Jesus and social stratification: diss. Drew, ᴰ*Doughty* D. Madison NJ 1992. 291 p. 92-33188. – DissA 53 (1992s) 1961-A.

k218 *López Martín* Julián, Situación, perspectiva y objeto de la antropología litúrgica: Salmanticensis 39 (1992) 349-377; Eng. 377, 'mutual rapprochement between (cultural) anthropology and liturgical science'.

k219 **Love** John R., Antiquity and capitalism; Max WEBER and the sociological foundations of Roman civilization 1991 ⮕ 7,e688: ᴿGreeceR 39 (1992) 103 (T. E. J. *Wiedemann*).

Maier Henry O., The social setting of the ministry ... HERMAS ᴰ1991 ⮕ k644.

k220 **Malina** Bruce, *Rohrbaugh* Richard L., Social science commentary on the Synoptic Gospels. Mp 1992, Fortress. viii-422 p.; ill. 0-8006-2562-5.

k221 **Marx** R., Ist Kirche anders? Möglichkeiten und Grenzen einer soziologischen Betrachtungsweise: AbsSozialethik 29. Pd 1990, Schöningh. 476 p. DM 84. 3-506-70229-7. – ᴿTvT 32 (1992) 334 (R. *Houdijk*).

k222 *Matthews* Victor H., *Benjamin* Don C., The virgin and the prince [biblical sexual violence often a matter of honor/shame]: BToday 30 (1992) 42-46.

k223 *Maurer* Michael, Feste und Feiern als historische Forschungsgegenstand [GEBHARDT W. 1987; *al*.]. HZ 253 (1991) 101-130.

k224 **May** David M., Social scientific criticism of the New Testament; a bibliography: Nat. Baptist Bibliog. 4. Macon 1991, Mercer Univ. xvi-91 p. $19 [CBQ 55,210].

k225 **Mayes** Andrew, The Old Testament in sociological perspective 1989 ⮕ 5,g137; 7,e690: ᴿInterpretation 46 (1992) 88 (R. B. *Coote*); JAAR 60 (1992) 348-350 (L. W. *Countryman*); JTS 43 (1992) 153s (W. D. *Stacey*: too much a review of other people's work).

k226 **Meeks** W. A., Los primeros cristianos urbanos; el mundo social del apóstol Pablo [1986 ⮕ 2,b908], 1988 ⮕ 4,5884: ᴿRET 51 (1991) 107s (M. *Gesteira*).

Mieroop Marc Van de, Society and enterprise in Old Babylonian Ur 1992 ⮕ e954.

k227 **Milbank** John, Theology and social theory; beyond secular reason 1990 ⮕ 7,e693: ᴿScotJT 45 (1992) 125s (L. *Ayres*: an important book with a grand scope).

k228 *Morgan* Catherine, Ethnicity and early Greek states; historical and material perspectives: PrPgS 37 (1991) 131-163.

k229 *Neesen* Lutz, Zur Rolle und Bedeutung der produzierenden Gewerbe in antiken Städten: AncSoc 22 (1991) 25-40.

k230 *Neumann* Hans, Bemerkungen zum Problem der Fremdarbeit in Mesopotamien (3. Jahrtausend v.u. Z.): AltOrF 19 (1992) 266-275.

k231 ᴱ**Nicolet** Claude, Du pouvoir dans l'Antiquité; mots et réalités: Centre Glotz 1983-4, ÉPHÉ 3/16, 1990 ⮕ 6,760: ᴿAntClas 61 (1992) 555s (P. *Simelon*).

k233 **Nippel** Wilfried [⮕ d226], Griechen, Barbaren und 'Wilde' 1990 ⮕ 7, e698: ᴿClasR 42 (1992) 219 (Edith *Hall*).

k234 *O'Connor* M., Northwest Semitic designations for elective social affinities: JANES 18 (1986) 67-80.

k235 *Oesch* Josef M., Sozialgeschichtliche Auslegung des Alten Testaments; ein forschungsgeschichtlicher Überblick: ProtokB 1,1 (1992) 3-22.

k236 **Osiek** Carolyn, What are they saying about the social setting of the New Testament? ²ʳᵉᵛ [¹1984 ⮕ 65,d131]. NY 1992, Paulist. iv-127 p. $8. 0-8091-3339-3.

k237 *a)* Osiek Carolyn, The social sciences and the Second Testament; problems and challenges; – *b)* *Malina* Bruce J., Is there a circum-Mediterranean person? Looking for stereotypes: ⮕ 500, BibTB 22 (1992) 88-95 / 66-87.

k238 **Pailin** David A., The anthropological character of theology 1990 ⮕ 7,e702: ᴿHorizons 19 (1992) 158 (J. J. *Buckley*); JAAR 60 (1992) 802-4 (L. *Malcolm*); JRel 72 (1992) 457s (C. M. *Wood*).

k239 **Perepelkin** Jurij J., Privateigentum ... des Alten Reichs 1986 ➤ 2,d1; 4,b401: ᴿCdÉ 67 (1992) 80-82 (I. *Harari* †).

k240 **Petrocelli** Corrado, La stola e il silenzio; sulla condizione femminile nel mondo romano: Prisma. Palermo 1989, Sellerio. 480 p. Lit. 38.000.

k241 *Pomeroy* Arthur J., Status and status-concern in the Greco-Roman dream books: AncSoc 22 (1991) 51-74.

k242 *a) Prechel* Doris, Fremde in Mesopotamien; – *b) Klinger* Jörg, Fremde und Aussenseiter in Ḫatti; – *c) Maul* Stefan M., *kûr garrû* und *assīnnu* [cultic performer, musician] und ihr Stand in der babylonischen Gesellschaft; – *d) Lambert* Wilfried G., Prostitution [Eng.]: ➤ 691, Aussenseiter 1989/92, 173-185 / 187-212 / 159-171 / 127-157 + 2 facsim.

k243 *Rawson* Beryl, Adult-child relationships in Roman society: ➤ 674, Marriage, divorce, and children in ancient Rome 1988/92, (1-) 7-30.

k244 *Reden* Sitta von, Arbeit und Zivilisation; Kriterien der Selbstdefinition im antiken Athen: MünstHand 11,1 (1992) 1-31; 7 fig.; franc. Eng. 31 'toil and achievement, rather than production'.

k245 **Reviv** Hanoch, The Elders 1989 ➤ 5,g356; 7,e709: ᴿBL (1992) 44 (A. D. H. *Mayes*); JAOS 112 (1992) 320-2 (R. G. *Boling*).

k246 **Richards** Janet E., Mortuary variability and social differentiation in Middle Kingdom Egypt: diss. Pennsylvania, ᴰ*O'Connor* D. Ph 1992. 362 p. 92-35189. DissA 53 (1992s) 2865-A.

k247 **Rilinger** Rolf, Humiliores – honestiores 1988 ➤ 6,g676; 7,e710: ᴿAnzAltW 45 (1992) 260-4 (J.M. *Rainer*); ClasR 42 (1992) 349s (O.F. *Robinson*).

k248 *a) Ritner* Robert K., Implicit models of cross-cultural interaction; a question of noses, soap, and prejudice; – *b) Clarysse* Willy, Some Greeks in Egypt; – *c) Quaegebeur* Jan, Greco-Egyptian double names as a feature of a bi-cultural society; the case *Psosneús ho kaì Triádelphos*; – *d) Thomas* Thelma K., Greeks or Copts; documentary and other evidence for artistic patronage during the Late Roman and Early Byzantine periods at Herakleopolis Magna and Oxyrhynchus: ➤ 719, Life 1990/2, 283-290 [defective p. 287 supplied apart] / 51-56 / 265-272 / 317-320; 2 pl.

k249 **Saldarini** A., Pharisees 1989 ➤ 4,h410* ... 7,e711: ᴿArchivScSocR 80 (1992) 289s (J.-D. *Dubois*); AustralBR 40 (1992) 76-78 (J. *Painter*).

k249* **Salzman** Michele R., On Roman time; the codex-calendar of 354 and the rhythms of urban life in late antiquity 1991 ➤ 7,e713: ᴿClasW 85 (1991s) 719 (L. P. *Schrenk*).

k250 **Schluchter** Wolfgang, Rationalism, religion, and domination; a Weberian perspective, ᵀ*Solomon* Neal. Berkeley 1990, Univ. California. 618 p. $75. – ᴿHistRel 32 (1992) 193-5 (M. *Riesebrodt*, also on SWATOS).

k251 *a) Schreiter* Robert A., Anthropology and faith; challenges to missiology; – *b) Tienou* Tite, The invention of the 'primitive' and stereotypes in mission: Missiology 19 (1991) 283-294 / 295-303.

k252 **Schweyer** François-Xavier, Autopsie d'une manipulation; analyse des procédés d'orientation et d'interprétation des sondages religieux. P 1991, Fleurus. 240 p. – ᴿEsprVie 102 (1992) 96 (S. *Bonnet*).

k253 *Séguy* Jean, WEBER et TROELTSCH... encore [... FREUND J. 1990, *al.*]: ArchivScSocR 78 (1992) 191-7.

k253* **Sicari** A., Prostituzione e tutela giuridica della schiava; un problema di politica legislativa nell'Impero romano: Univ. Fac. Giur. 99. Bari 1991, Cacucci. 175 p. – ᴿAthenaeum 80 (1992) 540-2 (D. *Mantovani*).

k254 **Stambaugh** J. E., *Balch* D. L., Das soziale Umfeld des NTs, ᵀ*Lüdemann* G.: Grundrisse NT 9. Gö 1992, Vandenhoeck & R. 179 p. DM 34 pa. 3-525-51376-3 [NTAbs 36,454].

k255 **Stone** Elizabeth C., *Owen* David I., Adoption in Old Babylonian Nippur: Mesop. Civ. 3: WL 1991, Eisenbrauns. x-149 p. $36.50. 0-931-46453-6 [OLZ 88,500, J. *Oelsner*].

k256 ᴱ**Sundermeier** Theo, Den Fremden wahrnehmen; Bausteine für eine Xenologie [Kolloquium St. Augustin April 1991]: Studien zum Verstehen fremder Religionen 5. Gü 1992, Mohn. 231 p. [OLZ 88,477, P. *Heine*].

k257 **Theissen** G., The social setting of Pauline Christianity, ᵀᴱ*Schütz* John H., 1990 ⇒ 63,270 ... 7,e731: ᴿNedTTs 46 (1992) 238s (H. W. *Hollander*).

k257* **Theissen** Gerd, Sociologia del cristianesimo primitivo 1987 ⇒ 5,g373; 6,g701: ᴿParVi 35 (1990) 384-6 (S. *Migliasso*).

k258 **Theissen** Gerd, Social reality and the early Christians; theology, ethics and the world of the NT [Studien zur Soz. des Urchr. 1992 + *al.*], ᵀ*Kohl* Margaret. Mp 1992, Fortress. xvi-303 p. £20. 0-8006-2560-9.

k259 **Thompson** Lloyd A., Romans and Blacks 1989 ⇒ 5,g375 ... 7,e732*: ᴿMnemosyne 45 (1992) 424-7 (E. Van der *Vliet*).

k260 *Thorp* John, The social construction of homosexuality: Phoenix 46 (Toronto 1992) 54-61.

k261 *Tyrell* Hartmann, 'Das Religiöse' in Max WEBERs Religionssoziologie: Saeculum 43 (1992) 172-224 (-230 Bibliog.).

k262 *Utzschneider* Helmut, Patrilinearität im alten Israel — eine Studie zur Familie und ihrer Religion: BibNot 56 (1991) 60-97.

k263 **Vanderhooft** David S., Kinship organization in ancient Israel: diss. North York 1990, ᴰ*Halpern* B. viii-270 p. 0-315-60924-9 [OIAc 5,37, not mentioning Canada (or UK)].

k264 ᴱ**Wallace-Hadrill** Andrew, Patronage in ancient society 1989 ⇒ 5,808; 6,g710: ᴿGnomon 64 (1992) 129-135 (J. *Nichols*); RPg 65,2 (1991) 42-45 (E. *Will*).

Wees Hans Van, Status warriors; war, violence and society in Homer and history 1992 ⇒ d746*.

k265 *Weiss* Johannes, TROELTSCH, WEBER und das Geschichtsbild des Kulturprotestantismus: ⇒ 410, ᴱ*Müller* Hans M., Kulturprot. 1992, 230-244.

k266 **Whitley** James, Style and society in Dark Age Greece; the changing face of a pre-literate society 1100-700 B.C. [Knossos ...; 'the social use to which pots were put']. C 1991, Univ. xx-225 p.; 21 fig.; 39 pl. $54.50. 0-521-37383-2. – ᴿClasW 86 (1992s) 70 (Lee T. *Pearcy*).

k267 **Wiedemann** T., Adults and children in the Roman Empire 1989 ⇒ 5,g383 ... 7,e745: ᴿAmJPg 113 (1992) 134-7 (Susan D. *Martin*); ChH 60 (1991) 85s (L. W. *Countryman*).

k268 *Winter* J. Alan, Religious belief and managerial ideology; an exploratory study of an extrapolation from the WEBER thesis: RRelRes 33 (1990s) 169-175.

Wood B. G., The sociology of pottery in ancient Palestine 1990 ⇒ e239.

Wood Forrest G., The arrogance of faith; Christianity in America 1990 ⇒ m513.

k269 *Zanker* Paul, Pompeji; Stadtbilder als Spiegel von Gesellschaft und Herrschaftsform: Trierer Winckelmannsprogramme 9. Mainz 1988, von Zabern. viii-60 p.; 18 fig.; 8 pl. – ᴿGnomon 64 (1992) 426-433 (A. *Hoffmann*).

U5.3 Commercium, oeconomica.

k270 *Bayram* Salahattin, *Veenhof* Klaas R., Unpublished Kültepe texts on real estate [with which only a few of the 15,000 texts deal]: JbEOL 32 (1991s) 87-100.

k271 **Beer** Moshe, ✪ The Babylonian Amoraim; aspects of economic life. Ramat-Gan 1982, Bar-Ilan Univ. 446 p. 965-226-026-6.

k272 *Berchem* Denis van, Commerce et écriture; l'exemple de Délos à l'époque hellénistique: MusHelv 48 (1991) 129-143.

k273 *Bogaert* Raymond, *a)* Les banques à Alexandrie aux époques gréco-romaine et byzantine: AncSoc 23 (1992) 31-42. – *b)* Zénon et ses banquiers: CdÉ 66 (1991) 308-315.

k274 *Bondì* Sandro F., Anmerkungen zur phönikischen Wirtschaft; private Unternehmertätigkeit und die Rolle des Staates [< EgVO 1 (Pisa 1978) 139-149], ᵀ*Bignami* Renato, *Zimmermann* Klaus: → e596a, Karthago 1992, 304-320.

k275 *Bopearachchi* Osmand, Le commerce maritime entre Rome et Sri Lanka d'après les données numismatiques: RÉAnc 94 (1992) 107-117; 4 pl.

k276 **Capogrossi Colognesi** Luigi, Economie antiche e capitalismo moderno; la sfida di Max WEBER: BtCuMod 981. Bari 1990, Laterza. 391 p. – ᴿRÉLat 69 (1991) 304s (J.-C. *Richard*).

k277 *Casey* P. J., The monctization of a third world economy; money supply in Britain in the first century AD: → 680, Romanization 1989/92. 95-99.

k278 *Castle* Edward W., Shipping and trade in Ramesside Egypt: JESHO 35 (1992) 239-277.

k279 **Chakrabarti** Dilip K., The external trade of the Indus civilization. ix-183 p.; 2 maps [OLZ 88,78, R. D. *Jung*].

k280 **Clark** Grahame, L'economia della preistoria. Bari 1992, Laterza. 352 p. Lit. 45.000. – ᴿArcheo 7,92 (1992) 125 (C. *Zaccagnini*).

k280* *Cline* Eric H., Contract and trade or colonization? Egypt and the Aegean in the 14th-13th centuries B.C.: Minos 25s (1990s) 7-36.

k281 *Corbier* Mireille, Cité, territoire et fiscalité: → 7,583, ᶠDEGRASSI A., 1988/91, 629-665.

k282 **Cozzo** Andrea, Le passioni economiche nella Grecia antica. Palermo 1991, Sellerio. 138 p. – ᴿMaia 44 (1992) 316s (Nicoletta *Marini*).

k283 *a) Crawford* Harriet, An Early Dynastic trading network in North Mesopotamia? – *b) Foster* Benjamin R., A Sargonic itinerary; – *c) Neumann* Hans, Nochmals zum Kaufmann in neusumerischer Zeit; die Geschäfte des Ur-DUN und andere Kaufleute aus Nippur: → 683, Circulation 1991/2, 77-82 / 73-76; 1 fig. / 83-93.

k283* *Criniti* Nicola, La tabula alimentaria di Veleia. Parma 1991, Storia Patria. 345 p.; 12 fig.; map. [ClasR 43,404, J. R. *Sallares*: deals not with food but with 'the operation of the *alimenta*' as financial).

k284 ᴱ*Descat* R., L'or perse et l'histoire grecque 1989 = RÉAnc 91,1s (1989) → 5,782*: ᴿNumC 151 (1991) 229s (I. A. *Carradice*).

k285 **Drexhage** Raphaela, Untersuchungen zum römischen Osthandel [Diss.] 1988 → 5,g403...7,g733: ᴿGnomon 64 (1992) 643-5 (S. F. *Sidebotham*: Palmyra caravan-trade).

k286 *Driel* G. van, Uit het leven van een Nieuw-Babylonische handelaar: PhoenixEOL 38,2 (1992) 30-45; 2 fig.

k287 **Duncan-Jones** Richard, Structure and scale in the Roman economy 1990 → 6,g734; 7,e764: ᴿAthenaeum 80 (1992) 277-280 (Alessandra *Gara*); Hispania Antiqua 16 (1992) 400s (G. *Fernández*); NumC 152 (1992) 202s (C. J. *Howgego*); RÉLat 69 (1991) 295s (J.-C. *Richard*); RelStR 18 (1992) 54 (R. L. *Den Adel*: sequel to his Economy ²1982).

k288 *Eichler* Eckhard, POLANYI – KEYNES – WARBURTON; zur Rekonstruktion des altägyptischen Wirtschaftssystems: GöMiszÄg 131 (1992) 25-31.

k289 **Freyberg** Hans-Ulrich von,   Kapitalverkehr und Handel im römischen Kaiserreich (27 v.Chr.-235 n.Chr.): Univ. Inst. WirtschF.   FrB 1980, Haufe.   198 p. – ᴿGnomon 64 (1992) 418-422 (J. *Andreau*, franç.).

k290 *Gagos* Traianos, *Minnen* Peter van,   Documenting the rural economy of Byzantine Egypt; three papyri from Alabastrine [Kom al Aḥmar, opposite Minya and SE]: JRomA 5 (1992) 186-202.

k291 *Going* C.J.,   Economic 'long waves' in the Roman period? A reconnaissance of the Romano-British ceramic evidence (as at Samos, correlates with silver coinage circulation 1st-3d cent.): OxJArch 11 (1992) 93-117; 5 fig.

k292 **Gras** Michel,   Trafics tyrrhéniens archaïques 1985 ↠ 2,b970 ... 7,e771: ᴿGnomon 64 (1992) 135-9 (W. V. *Hassis*, Eng.).

k293 *Gras* Michel,   L'apport des amphores à la connaissance des commerces archaïques en mer Tyrrhénienne: ↠ 713, PACT 20 (1987/90) 291-303.

k294 **Griswold** William A.,   Imports and social status; the role of long-distance trade in predynastic Egyptian state formation: diss. Harvard, ᴰ*Lamberg-Karlovsky* C.   CM 1992.   420 p. 92-28334. – DissA 53 (1992s) 1565-A.

k295 *a) Hallo* W. W.,   Trade and traders in the Ancient Near East; some new perspectives; – *b) Dandamayev* M. A.,   Egyptians in Babylonia in the 6th-5th centuries B.C.: ↠ 683, Circulation 1991/2, 351-6 / 321-5.

k296 *Halstead* Paul,   The Mycenaean palatial economy; making the most of gaps in the evidence: PrPgS 38 (1992) 57-86.

k297 *Helck* Wolfgang,   Städtischer Handel im Alten Ägypten?: AltOrF 19 (1992) 3-7.

k298 ᴱ**Heltzer** M., *Lipiński* E.,   Society and economy in the eastern Mediterranean 1985/8 ↠ 4,742: ᴿColcT 62,1 (1992) 173s (W. *Chrostowski*, ❷).

k299 *a) Herz* Peter,   Organisation und Finanzierung der spätantiken *annona*; – *b) Millar* Fergus,   Les congiaires à Rome et la monnaie: ↠ 645, Nourrir la plèbe 1989/91, 161-188 / 143-157.

k299* *Hladik* Joe,   Geld(ver)leih im Imperium Romanum zur Zeit Jesu; seine Praxis und die dadurch verursachte Not der Schuldnerinnen: ProtokB 1 (1992) 115-133.

k300 *a) Howgego* Christopher,   The supply and use of money in the Roman world 200 B.C. to A.D. 300; – *b) Speidel* M. Alexander,   Roman army pay scales; – *c) Bagnall* Roger S.,   Landholding in Late Roman Egypt; the distribution of wealth: JRS 82 (1992) 1-31 / 87-106 / 128-149.

k301 **Ismail** Farouk,   Altbabylonische Wirtschaftsurkunden aus Tall Leilan (Syrien): Diss. Tübingen 1991. xvii-182 p. – OIAc 5,25.

k302 **Jongman** Willem,   The economy and society of Pompeii; Dutch MgA 4, 1988 ↠ 5,g416 ... 7,e775: ᴿAnzAltW 45,1 (1992) 82-85 (H. *Grassl*).

k303 **Kehoe** Dennis P.,   Management and investment on estates in Roman Egypt during the Early Empire: PapTAbh 40. Bonn 1992, Habelt. xiv-188 p. 3-7749-2532-1 [OIAc 2,22].

k303* **Kloft** H.,   Die Wirtschaft der griechisch-römischen Welt; eine Einführung.   Da 1992, Wiss. xvi-266 p.: 16 fig.; 9 maps; DM 44 [ClasR 43,321, Sitta von *Reden*].

k304 **Koch** Heidemarie,   Verwaltung und Wirtschaft im persischen Kernland zur Zeit der Achämeniden [Hab. Marburg 1986, ᴰ*Hinz* W.]: TAVO B-89. Wsb 1990, Reichert.   428 p.; maps. 3-88226-468-3.

k304* *Krasilnikoff* Jens A.,   Aegean mercenaries in the fourth to second centuries B.C. — a study in payment, plunder and logistics of ancient Greek armies: ClasMedv 43 (1992) 23-36.

k305 **Manning** Joseph G. D., The conveyance of real property in Upper Egypt during the Ptolemaic period; a study of the Hauswaldt Papyri and other related demotic instruments of transfer: diss. ᴰ*Johnson* Janet. Chicago 1992, Univ. xiii-388 p. (2 vol.) – OIAc 3,29.

k306 *Manning* J. G., The transfer of landed property in Upper Egypt in the Ptolemaic period: NewsAmEg 152 (1990) 1s.

k307 **Marasco** Gabriele, Economia e storia. Viterbo 1992, Univ. Tuscia. 133 p.; 3 pl.

k308 **Meijer** Fik, *Nijf* Onno van, Trade, transport and society in the ancient world; a sourcebook L 1992, Routledge. xxii-201 p. £35; £11. 0-415-00344-X; -5-8 [BL 93,125, L. L. *Grabbe*].

k309 **Michel** Cécile, Innāya [marchand] dans les tablettes paléo-assyriennes [< diss.]. P 1991, RCiv. 294 p.; 440 p. F 141 + 183. 2-86538-221-7; -2-2. – ᴿBO 49 (1992) 790-800 (J. G. *Dercksen*).

k310 *Michel* Cécile, Transporteurs, responsables et propriétaires de convois dans les tablettes paléo-assyriennes; réflexions sur les expressions *šép NP et ellat NP:* ➤ 683, Circulation 1991/2, 137-156.

k311 ᴱ**Miller** Naomi F., Economy and settlement in the Near East; analyses of ancient sites and materials; MASCA 7 supp. Ph 1992, Univ. 88 p. 1048-5325 [OIAc 3,31, excerpted].

k312 **Millett** Paul, Lending and borrowing in ancient Athens 1991 ➤ 7,e784; £40: ᴿGreeceR 39 (1992) 235s (J. *Salmon*).

k313 **Nadjo** Léon, L'argent et les affaires à Rome... 1989 ➤ 7,e791: ᴿOrpheus 13 (1992) 403-8 (Elena *Scuotto*).

k314 **Needleman** Jacob, Money and the meaning of life. NY 1991, Doubleday. 321 p. £20. – ᴿTTod 49 (1992s) 268.270 (F. O. *Bonkovsky*: an ill-connected file-case of quotable quotes).

k315 *a) Neumann* Hans, Zur privaten Geschäftstätigkeit in Nippur in der Ur III-Zeit; – *b) Skaist* Aaron, Pre- and post-Hammurapi loan contracts from Nippur: ➤ 687, Nippur 1988/92, 161-176 / 227-233.

k316 **Nissen** Hans J., al., Frühe Schrift und Techniken der Wirtschaftsverwaltung im alten Vorderen Orient [Ausstellung] 1990/91 ➤ 7,e794. ᴿBO 49 (1992) 761-3 (B. R. *Forster*).

k317 **Obermark** Peter R., Adoption in the Old Babylonian period [99 contracts: the aging adopted adults to care for them and inherit their property]: diss. HUC. Cincinnati 1992. 299 p. 92-30559. – DissA 53 (1992s) 2059-A.

k318 **Ørsted** Peter, Roman imperial economy and Romanization 1985 ➤ 4, h491: ᴿAnzAltW 45 (1992) 247-251 (R. *Rilinger*).

k319 **Ohrenstein** Roman A., Economic analysis in Talmudic literature; rabbinic thought in the light of modern economics: StPostB 40. Leiden 1992, Brill. xviii-152 p. 90-04-09540-3.

k320 **Pérez** Christine, La monnaie de Rome à la fin de la République; un discours politique en images: Coll. Numismatiques. P 1989, Errance. 132 p.; 149 fig. 2-903443-97-5.

k321 *Perlès* Catherine, Systems of exchange and organization of production in neolithic Greece: JMeditArch 5 (1992) 115-164.

k322 *Polfer* Michel, Der Transport über den Landweg — ein Hemmschuh für die Wirtschaft der römischen Kaiserzeit: Helinium 31 (1991) 273-295.

k323 **Postgate** J. Nicholas, Early Mesopotamia; society and economy at the dawn of history. L 1992, Routledge. xxiii-367 p. 0-415-00843-3 [OIAc 3,34]. – ᴿBCanadMesop 24 (1992) 51-53 (Elizabeth *Coopera*, franç. à côté).

k324 **Rathbone** Dominic, Economic rationalism and rural society in third-century A.D. Egypt; The Heroninos Archive and the Appianus estate [< diss. Cambridge 1986]. C 1991, Univ. xix-489 p. 0-521-40149-6 [OIAc 3,34].

k325 *Römer* Malte, Der Handel und die Kaufleute im Alten Ägypten: StAäK 19 (1992) 257-284.

k326 **Schmitz** Winfried, Wirtschaftliche Prosperität... Athens (ᴰ1985) 1988 → 4,h499... 7,e806: ᴿAnzAltW 45 (1992) 238-241 (W. *Hameter*).

k327 *Schottroff* W. & H., Handel AT/NT; → 762, NBL II,6 (1991) 28-31.

k328 **Schreiner** Peter, Texte zur spätbyzantinischen Finanz- und Wirtschaftsgeschichte in Handschriften der Bibliotheca Vaticana: ST 344. Vaticano 1991, Bibliotheca. 528 p.; 10 pl.; 2 maps. 88-210-0637-9.

k329 **Silver** Morris, Taking ancient mythology economically. Leiden 1992, Brill. 354 p. 90-0409-7066 [OIAc 5,35].

k330 **Snell** Daniel C., **Lager** Carl H., Economic texts from Sumer: Babylonian Texts 18. NHv 1991, Yale. x-70 p., 85 pl. $50. 0-300- 04945-5 [OIAc 3,38; RelStR 19,153, D. I. *Owen*: texts only in facsimile, but largely translated in AcSum 11 (1989) 155-224].

k331 *a) Snell* Daniel E., [*Sidebotham* Steven F.], Trade and commerce ANE [Roman]; – *b) Betlyon* J. W., Money in the Hebrew Bible (p. 1076-8; ANE 1078s): in Coinage: → 471, AnchorBD 6 (1992) 624-9 [-633] / 1076-89.

k332 *Soggin* J. Alberto, Tre opere storico-economiche sul Vicino Oriente antico [LIVERANI M., 1988; 1990; ᴱKLENGEL H. 1989]: Henoch 14 (1992) 181-3.

k333 **Stenger** Werner, 'Gebt...' Besteuerung Palästinas 1988 → 4,h510... 6,g782: ᴿRÉJ 150 (1991) 187s (A. *Caquot*).

k334 **Stöver** Hans D., Macht und Geld im alten Rom 1989 → 5,g447; 7,e808: ᴿHZ 253 (1991) 705s (T. *Pekáry*).

k334* **Tortorici** Edoardo, Argiletum; commercio, speculazione edilizia e lotta politica dall'analisi topografica di un quartiere di Roma in età repubblicana. R 1991, Bretschneider. 128 p.; 63 fig.; 2 foldout plans. 88-7062-668-7 [Latomus 52,485, R. *Chevallier*].

k335 ᶠTRÉHEUX J., Comptes... ᴱKnoepfler D. 1986/8 → 4,698... 7,e809: ᴿAntClas 61 (1992) 529-531 (J.-M. *Hannick*).

k336 **Tsetskhladze** Gocha R., Kolchis im System des antiken Handels (6.-2. Jh. v.u. Z.): MünstHand 11,1 (1992) 80-107; 2 maps; Eng. franç. 107.

k337 ᴱ**Vittinghoff** Friedrich, *al.*, Europäische Wirtschafts- und Sozialgeschichte in der römischen Kaiserzeit: HbEurWs 1. Stu 1990, Klett-Cotta. 805 p.

k338 **Wesch-Klein** G., Liberalitas in rem publicam; private Aufwendungen im römischen Afrika: Antiquitas 1/40. Bonn 1990, Habelt. 441 p. – ᴿRÉLat 70 (1992) 344 (Y. *Le Bohec*).

k339 *Westhuizen* J. P. Van der, To pay or not to pay interest in ancient Nippur: JTydSem 4 (1992) 22-34.

U5.7 Nomadismus; ecology.

k340 ᴱ**Bar-Yosef** Ofer, **Khazanov** Anatoly, Pastoralism in the Levant; archaeological materials in anthropological perspective: Mg World Archaeology (1055-2316). Madison WI 1992, Prehistory. 269 p., ill. [OIAc 3,12].

k341 *Bernbeck* Reinhard, Migratory patterns in early nomadism; a reconsideration of Tepe Tula'i: Paléorient 18,1 (1992) 77-88; 2 fig.

k342 **Bradley** Rebecca J., Nomads in the archaeological record; case studies in the northern provinces of the Sudan [< diss. Cambridge 1985]:

Meroitica 13. B 1992, Akademie. 237 p. 3-05-001819-4 [OIAc 5,15; BO 49,583].

k343 **Cribb** Roger, Nomads in archaeology 1991 ➤ 7,e817: ᴿAntiquity 66 (1992) 794-6 (T. *Ingold*); JRAS (1992) 431s (M. *Roaf*: by 'nomads' he means seasonal pastoralists; by 'archaeology' modern campsites in SE Turkey).

k344 *Gates* Marie-Henriette, Nomadic pastoralists and the chalcolithic hoard from Nahal Mishmar: Levant 24 (1992) 131-9; 6 fig.

k345 **Hareuveni** Nogah, Desert and shepherd in our biblical heritage, ᵀ*Frenkley* Helen. Lod 1991, Neot Kedumim. 159 p.; (color) ill. 965-233-017-5.

k346 *Kaufman* Daniel, Hunter-gatherers of the Levantine epipalaeolithic; the socioecological origins of sedentism: JMeditArch 5 (1992) 165-201.

k347 *Kolendo* Jerzy, Les 'déserts' dans les pays barbares; représentations et réalités: DialHA 17,1 (1991) 35-60.

k348 **Levi** Mario A., I nomadi alla frontiera 1989 ➤ 6,g991: ᴿJRS 82 (1992) 277-9 (D. F. *Graf*).

k349 *Milburn* Mark, Nomads and religion in the context of Christian Nubia and Coptic Egypt; an enquiry: ➤ 690, 3d Coptic 1984/90, 261-6; 2 fig.

k350 **Neu** Rainer, Von der Anarchie zum Staat; Entwicklungsgeschichte Israels vom Nomadentum zur Monarchie im Spiegel der Ethnosoziologie Neuk 1992, Neuk.-V. 350 p. 3-7887-1347-X [OIAc 3,32].

k351 *Rosen* Steven A., Nomads in archaeology; a response to FINKELSTEIN and PEREVOLOTSKY: BASOR [279 (1990) 67-88] 287 (1992) 75-85; 2 fig.; 87s Finkelstein rejoinder, 'Invisible nomads'.

k352 **Sallares** Robert, The ecology of the ancient Greek world 1991 ➤ 7, e821: ᴿClasPg 87 (1992) 376-381 (S. *Hodkinson*); ClasW 86 (1992s) 46s (Anne *Foley*: grain supply of Athens! replacing GERMET 1909); RelStR 18 (1992) 227 (J. M. *Balcer*: unduly polemical).

k353 ᴱ**Scholz** Fred, Nomaden; zur gegenwärtigen Lage von Nomaden und zu den Problemen und Chancen mobiler Tierhaltung. B 1991, Das Arabische Buch. ix-420 p. DM 78. – ᴿAnthropos 87 (1992) 625-8 (M. *Bollig*).

k354 **Staubli** Thomas, Das Image der Nomaden... OBO 107, 1991 ➤ 7,e822: ᴿJBL 111 (1992) 693-5 (J. A. *Dearman*); TütQ 172 (1992) 143-5 (W. *Gross*, auch über ANBAR M. OBO 108 = ◉ 1985); ZAW 104 (1992) 461s (H. C. *Schmitt*).

k355 *Thompson* Thomas J., Palestinian pastoralism and Israel's origins: ScandJOT 6,1 (1992) 1-13.

U5.8 **Urbanismus.**

k356 **Audring** Gerd, Zur Struktur des Territoriums griechischer Poleis in archaischer Zeit (nach den schriftlichen Quellen): SchrGKAnt 29. B 1989, Akademie. 108 p. – ᴿAnzAltW 45 (1992) 73-75 (K. *Tausend*); Athenaeum 79 (1991) 650s (Laura *Boffo*).

Baldovin John F., The urban character of Christian worship 1987 ➤ 7,8178*.

k357 ᴱ**Baud** Michel, Cités disparues: MondeHS 55. P 1991, Autrement. 237 p. 2-86260-334-1 [OIAc 3,13].

k357* **Benevolo** Leonardo, Die Geschichte der Stadt.⁶ Fra 1991, Campus. 1072 p.; 1649 fig. DM 99. – ᴿBiKi 47 (1992) 54 (D. *Bauer*).

k358 **Burnham** B. C., *Wacher* J., The 'small towns' of Roman Britain. L 1990, Batsford. xii-388 p.; 127 fig. £45. 0-7134-6175-6. – ᴿJRS 82 (1992) 293s (I. M. *Barton*).

k359 **Cahill** Nicholas D., Olynthus; social and spatial planning in a Greek city: diss. California, Berkeley 1991. 541 p. 92-28589. – DissA 53 (1992s) 1564-A.

k359* [Domingos] *Cassonatto* Odalberto, Visão bíblica da pastoral urbana: RBBras 7 (1990) 126-132 [p. 298 'Cassanatto'].

k360 *Cook* R. M., Towns (*astu*) before the *polis*: OxJArch 10 (1991) 385 only.

k361 **Corsini** E. present. [*Sartori* F., *al.*], La polis e il suo teatro² [¹1986 ➤ 4,h528]: Saggi e materiali universitari 7. Padova 1988, Programma. 304 p. Lit. 40.000.

k362 **Cox** Harvey, The secular city; secularization and urbanization in theological perspective. NY 1990, Collier. 255 p. $10 pa. – ᴿHomP 91,11s (1990s) 84s (G. W. *Rutler*).

k363 **Demont** P., La cité grecque 1990 ➤ 6,g805; 7,e825: ᴿClasR 42 (1992) 98s (E. J. *Owens*); RBgPg 70 (1992) 235s (L. *Jerphagnon*); RÉLat 69 (1991) 244s (C. *Lévy*).

k364 **Domínguez Monedero** Adolfo J., La polis y la expansión colonial griega (siglos VIII-VI): HistUnivAntigua 6. M 1991, Síntesis. 287 p. 84-7738-108-9. – ᴿGerión 10 (1992) 310-2 (J. *Martínez-Pinna*) [315: in Sicilia, ᴿ*Plácido* D.].

Durliat Jean, De la ville antique à la ville byzantine; le problème des subsistances 1990 ➤ g997.

k365 **Fritz** Volkmar, Die Stadt im alten Israel 1990 ➤ 6,g807; 7,e827: ᴿTZBas 48 (1992) 291s (M. *Keller*).

k366 **Frosini** Giordano, Babele o Gerusalemme? Per una teologia della città. CinB 1992, Paoline. 312 p. – ᴿVivH 3 (1992) 438s (*ipse*).

k367 **Grainger** John D., The cities of Seleukid Syria 1990 ➤ 7,e829: ᴿRivCuClasMedv 34 (1992) 309-315 (T. *Gnoli*).

k368 **Greco** E., *Torelli* M., Storia dell'urbanistica; il mondo greco 1983 ➤ 64, d825: ᴿHelmantica 43 (1992) 250s (P. *Orosio*).

k368* a) *Hadidi* Adnan, Amman-Philadelphia; aspects of Roman urbanism; – b) *Seigne* Jacques, Jérash romaine et byzantine; développement urbain d'une ville provinciale orientale; – c) *Bentzer* Jean-Marie, *Zayadine* Fawzi, L'espace urbaine de Pétra; – d) *Mare* William H., Internal settlement patterns in Abila: ➤ 740, Jordan 4 (1992) 295-8; 2 fig. / 337-341; 9 fig. / 233-249; 10 fig. / 309-313.

k369 **Huot** Jean-Louis, *al.*, Naissance des cités 1990 ➤ 6,g813: ᴿSyria 69 (1992) 469-471 (G. *Tate*).

k370 ᵀᴱ**Jacques** François, Les cités de l'Occident romain, du Iᵉʳ siècle avant J.-C. au VIᵉ siècle après J.-C.; documents 1990 ➤ 7,e831: ᴿHabis 22 (1991) 477-9 (J. M. *Serrano Delgado*); Latomus 51 (1992) 669s (J. *Gascou*).

k371 *Janssen* J. J., A New Kingdom settlement; the verso of Pap. BM 10068: AltOrF 19 (1992) 8-23.

k372 a) *Kempinski* Aharon, Urbanization and town plans in the MB II (...forts); – b) *Baumgarten* Jacob J., Urbanization in LB; – c) *Herzog* Zeev, Settlement and fortification planning in the Iron Age; – d) *Oren* Eliezer D., Patrician and plebeian houses MB-LB; – e) *Stern* Ephraim, The Phoenician architectural elements in Palestine during the Late Iron Age and the Persian period: ➤48, Mem. DUNAYEVSKY I. 1992, 121-6 (-142); 3 + 29 fig. / 143-150; 3 fig. / (223-) 231-274; 32 fig. / 105-120; 23 fig. / 302-9; 9 fig.

k373 *Köberle* Claudia, *Rohweder* Christine, Die 'Dunklen Jahrhunderte' von der Unterwelt aus gesehen; eine Auseinandersetzung mit Ian MORRIS, Burial and ancient society; the rise of the Greek city-state (1987): Boreas 14s (Münster 1991s) 5-13.

k374 **Kolb** Frank, Die Stadt im Altertum 1984 → 65,d248... 6,g815: ᴿZkT 114 (1992) 224s (R. *Oberforcher*).

k375 **Kubba** Shamil A. A., Mesopotamian architecture and town planning 1987 → 3,d354: ᴿBASOR 285 (1992) 87-90 (Sally *Dunham*).

k376 *London* Gloria Anne, Tells; city center or home?: → 18, ꟳBIRAN A., ErIsr 23 (1992) 71*-79*.

k377 **McKechnie** Paul, Outsiders in the Greek cities 1989 → 7,e835: ᴿGnomon 64 (1992) 514-7 (K.-W. *Welwei*).

k378 **Maisels** C. K., The emergence of civilization; from hunting and gathering to agriculture, cities, and the state in the Near East 1990 → 7,e836: ᴿBCanadMesop 22 (1991) 50 (M. *Fortin*).

k379 ᴱ**Malkin** Irad, *Hohlfelder* Robert L., Mediterranean cities; historical perspectives [all but 2 = MeditHR 3,1, 1986 meeting in Israel] 1988 → 5,g497: ᴿPhoenix 46 (Toronto 1992) 203ss (G. M. *Woloch*).

k380 **Manville** Philip B., The origins of citizenship in ancient Athens. Princeton 1990, Univ. xiv-265 p. $35. – ᴿClasPg 87 (1992) 65-71 (Cynthia *Farrar*, also on MEIER C. 1990).

k381 ᴱ**Meadow** Richard H., Harappa excavations 1986-1990; a multidisciplinary approach to third millennium urbanism: Mg World Archaeology 3. Madison WI 1991, Prehistory. x-262 p.; 136 fig. 0-9629-1101-1.

k382 *Moggi* M., STRABONE interprete di OMERO (contributo al problema della formazione della *polis*): An Pisa 21 (1991) 537-532.

ᴱ**Molho** Anthony, al., City-States in classical antiquity... 1989/91 → 669*.

k383 *Morin* A., La ciudad en la Biblia: Medellín 16 (1990) 362-395 [< Stromata 47,443].

k384 ᴱ**Murray** O., *Price* S., The Greek city 1990 → 6,759; 7,e840: ᴿAthenaeum 80 (1992) 269-292 (Laura *Boffo*); ClasW 85 (1991) 747s (S. *Scully*); Gymnasium 99 (1992) 367 (K.-W. *Welwei*, tit. pp.).

k385 *Oliva* Pavel, The polis in early Greek society: → 641, Pisane 1989, StItFgC 85 (1992) 105-121; ital. 118 (153-160, *Jameson* Michael).

k385* *Olsen* Glenn W., The city in Christian thought: Thought 66 (1991) 259-278.

k386 **Owens** E. J., The city in the Greek and Roman world → 7,e844; also NY 1991, Routledge. xi-210 p. $52.50. 0-415-01896-X. – ᴿClasW 85 (1991s) 728 (Karelisa *Hartigan*); ÉtClas 60 (1992) 175s (B. *Rodette*).

k386* **Papazoglou** F., Les villes de Macédoine à l'époque romaine: BCH supp 16. Athènes 1988, École Française. xvii-528 p. F 850. 2-86958-014-2. – ᴿAthenaeum 79 (1991) 282s (Laura *Boffo*).

k387 **Patch** Diana C., The origin and early development of urbanism in ancient Egypt: diss. Pennsylvania, ᴰ*O'Connor* D. Ph 1992. xix-592 p. 92-00380. – OIAc 3,33.

k388 **Pozzi** Dora, *Wickersham* – Myth and the polis. Ithaca NY 1991, Cornell Univ. ix-232 p. – ᴿRÉG 105 (1992) 277s (Yvonne *Vernière*).

k389 ᴱ**Rich** John, *Wallace-Hadrill* Andrew, City and country in the ancient world: Leicester-Nottingham Studies Anc. Society. L 1991, Routledge. xvii-306 p. £12. 0-415-08223-4. – ᴿClasR 42 (1992) 218 (G. E. *Rickman*).

k390 **Robinson** Olivia F., Ancient Rome; city planning and administration. L 1992, Routledge. x-256 p.; foldout map. 0-415-02234-7.

k391 **Sakellariou** M. B., The polis-state 1989 ➤ 5,g505; 7,e850: [R]AmJPg 113 (1992) 107-110 (R. *Drewe*: uneven).

k392 *Schneider* Thomas, DOURRIOT [Félix,   Recherches sur la nature du génos; étude d'histoire sociale athénienne, périodes archaïque et classique I-II 1976] und ROUSSEL [Denis, Tribu et cité; études sur les groupes sociaux dans les cités grecques aux époques archaïque et classique, 1976] in der althistorischen Forschung der Jahre 1977-1989]: Boreas 14s (1991s) 15-31.

k393 **Schofield** Malcolm, The Stoic idea of the city. C 1991, Univ. xii-164 p. £28 [ClasR 43,92, A. *Erskine*].

k394 **Scully** Stephen, HOMER and the sacred city [... without existence in the archaeological record]: Myth and poetics 4.   Ithaca NY 1990, Cornell Univ. xi-230 p. $33. – [R]ClasR 42 (1992) 252s (M. J. *Alden*).

k395 *Stambaugh* John F.,   Cities: ➤ 741, AnchorBD 1 (1992) 1031-1048; 10 plans.

k396 **Stein-Hölkeskamp** Elke,   Adelskultur und Polis-Gesellschaft; Studien zum griechischen Adel in archaischer und klassischer Zeit,   1989 ➤ 7, e857: [R]AmJPg 113 (1992) 137-140 (W. *Donlan*).

k397 *Stone* Elizabeth E.,   The spacial [sic] organization of Mesopotamian cities: ➤ 32, [F]CIVIL M., AulaO 9,1 (1991) 235-242.

k398 **Tomlinson** Richard,   From Mycenae to Constantinople; the evolution of the ancient city.   L 1992, Routledge. xiii-238 p.; ill.   0-415-05997-6; pa. -8-4 [NTAbs 37, p. 477].

k399 [Cantino] *Wataghin* Gisella,   Urbanistica tardoantica e topografia cristiana; termini di un problema; ➤ 706, Milano capitale 1990.2, 171-192; 7 fig.

k399* *Welwei* Karl-Wilhelm,   Polisbildung, Hetairos-Gruppen und Hetairien: Gymnasium 99 (1992) 481-500.

k400 **Welwei** Karl-W., Die griechische Polis 1983 ➤ 64,a190... 1,f295: [R]Anz-AltW 43 (1990) 55-57 (C. *Ulf*).

k400* *a) Winter* Urs,   Städte unseres Gottes; zur Urbanisation in Israel und ihrer Deutung im AT; – *b) Staubli* Thomas,   Das Image der Stadt auf dem Lande; alttestamentliche und jesuanische Kritik an der Stadt; – *c) Schmeller* Thomas,   Der Weg der Jesusbotschaft in die Städte; – *d) Schwarz* Roland, Bürgerliches Christentum in den Städten am Ende des ersten Jahrhunderts?: BiKi 47 (1992) 2-9 / 10-17 / 18-24 / 25-29 [54-56, *Bauer* Dieter, 11 Bücher, die Stadt].

U5.9   *Demographia,* **population-statistics.**

k401 *Bagnall* Roger S.,   Census declarations from Tebtunis [< awaited Demography of Roman Egypt]: Aegyptus 72 (1992) 61-84.

k402 *Broshi* Magen, *Finkelstein* Israel,   The population of Palestine in Iron Age II: BASOR 287 (1992) 47-60; 4 fig.

k402* **Carter** Charles E.,   A social and demographic study of post-exilic Judah; diss. Duke, [D]*Meyers* E.   Durham NC 1992. 429 p. 92-27042. – DissA 53 (1992s) 1958-A.

k403 **McCarthy** Justin,   The population of Palestine; population statistics of the late Ottoman period and the Mandate: Inst. Pal. St.   NY 1990, Columbia Univ. xxvii-242 p. $63.50. – [R]BSO 55 (1992) 130s (M. E. *Yapp*: refutes Joan PETERS claim that most Arab inhabitants immigrated after Zionists).

k404 *Sekunda* N. V., Athenian demography and military strength 338-322 BC: AnBritAth 87 (1992) 311-355.

k405 **Storey** Glenn R., Preindustrial urban demography; the ancient Roman evidence: diss. Pennsylvania, ᴰ*Sanders* W. Ph 1992. 670 p. 92-26782. – DissA 53 (1992s) 1567-A.

k406 **Suder** Wieslaw, Census populi; bibliographie de la démographie romaine 1988 ➤ 6,g846: ᴿLatomus 51 (1992) 249s (P. *Salmon*).

k406* *Vestergaard* Torben, *al.*, The age-structure of Athenian citizens commemorated in sepulchral inscriptions: ClasMedv 43 (1992) 5-21 [many non-citizens died young].

U6   **Narrationes peregrinorum et exploratorum;** *Loca sancta.*

k407 ᵀᴱ**Arrowsmith-Brown** J. H., *Pankhurst* Richard, PRUTKY's travels in Ethiopia and other countries: Series II, 174. L 1991, Hakluyt. xxviii-546 p. 0-904180-30-1 [OIAc 3,11].

k408 *Augé* Matias, La asamblea litúrgica en el 'Itinerarium Egeriae': EcOrans 7 (1990) 41-60.

k409 **Barber** Richard, Pilgrimages. Rochester NY 1991, Boydell. vii-159 p.; 20 fig. $34. – ᴿRelStR 18 (1992) 311 (G. *Yocum*: unconventional).

k410 **Bausinger** Hermann, *Beyer* Klaus, Reisekultur; von der Pilgerfahrt zum modernen Tourismus. Mü 1991, Beck. 409 p. DM 68. – ᴿStiZt 210 (1992) 213 (R. *Bleistein*).

k411 ᴱ**Betrò** M. C., Racconti di viaggio e di avventura dell'antico Egitto: TestiVOA. Brescia 1990, Paideia. 83 p. Lit. 13.000. – ᴿParVi 36 (1991) 68s (Λ. *Rolla*).

k412 ᴱ**Bianchini** Walter, Faostino DA TOSCOLANO [1595-1679], Itinerario di Terra Santa [1633]: Univ. Perugia Centro Medv/Um 6. Spoleto 1992, Centro Alto Medioevo. xi-613 p.

k413 **Bilt** Edwardus F. van de, Proximity and distance; American travellers in the Middle East 1819-1918. diss. Cornell. Ithaca NY 1985. v 264 p. 85-25688. – OIAc 5,37.

k414 ᴱ**Büttner** Manfred, *al.*, Grundfragen der Religionsgeographie, mit Fallstudien zum Pilgertourismus: Geographia Religionum 1 [2. Religion und Siedlungsraum]. B 1985[s], Reimer. 288 p. DM 48 [268 p. DM 38]. – ᴿTR 88 (1992) 454-6 (R. *Haas*).

k415 *a) Busi* Giulio, Realtà e finzione negli itinerari ebraici del medioevo; – *b) Perani* Mauro, Il viaggio di Nachmanide in Terra Santa; – *c) Ochoa* José Λ., El imperio bizantino en el viaje de Benjamín de Tudela: ➤ 681, Viaggiatori ebrei 1991/2, 13-23 / 67-79 / 81-98.

k416 *a) Cardini* Franco, La Gerusalemme di EGERIA e il pellegrinaggio dei Cristiani d'Occidente in Terrasanta fra IV e V secolo; – *b) Maraval* Pierre, Égérie et GRÉGOIRE de Nysse, pèlerins aux Lieux Saints de Palestine; – *c) Tafi* Angelo, Egeria e la Bibbia: ➤ 676, Egeria 1987/90, 333-341 / 315-331 / 167-176.

k417 ᴱ**Cervani** Giulio, Il 'Voyage en Égypte' (1861-1862) di Pasquale REVOLTELLA. Trieste 1962, ALUT. 337 p.; 97 fig.; 29 color. pl. – ᴿAnzAltW 45 (1992) 300 (P. W. *Haider*: worth noting even so late).

k418 **Davies** Robert, Warriors and gentlemen; the occidental context of the Arabian travel narratives of [Richard] BURTON, [Wilfrid S.] BLUNT and [T. E.] LAWRENCE: diss. Loughborough 1991. 410 p. BRDX-35699. – DissA 53 (1992s) 158-A.

k418* *Derogy* J., *Hesi* C., Bonaparte en Terre Sainte. P 1982, A. Fayard. 495 p. [RHE 88,243*].

k419 ᴱ**Eade** John, *Sallnow* Michael J., Contesting the sacred; the anthropology of Christian pilgrimage 1988/91 ➤ 7,e871: ᴿJRel 72 (1992) 633-5 (Karen *Pechilis*: a marvelous book).

k420 **Eisner** Robert, Travelers to an antique land; the history and literature of travel to Greece. AA 1991, Univ. Michigan. xiv-304 p.; 16 fig.; map. $28. 0-472-10241-9. – ᴿClasW 86 (1992s) 151s (S. E. *Sidebotham*).

k421 *a*) **Fabbrini** Fabrizio, La cornice storica della 'Peregrinatio EGERIAE'; – *b*) *Campana* Augusto, La storia della scoperta del codice aretino nel carteggio GAMURRINI-DE ROSSI; – *c*) *Melani* Lapo, Sul ms. 405 della Biblioteca di Arezzo; – *d*) *Smiraglia* Pasquale, Il testo di Egeria; problemi di struttura: ➤ 676, Egeria 1987/90, 21-75 / 77-84 / 85-91 / 93-108.

k422 **Faroqhi** Suraiya, Herrscher über Mekka; die Geschichte der Pilgerfahrt. Mü 1990. Artemis. 350 p.; 12 fig.; 2 maps. – ᴿJRAS (1992) 444-6 (J. M. *Rogers*); WeltOr 23 (1992) 197-202 (Rita *Stratkötter*).

k423 *Filal* Abdellah, La région thébaine dans les relations des voyageurs anciens de 1600 à 1799 [SICARD P., 1718; POCOCKE 1738]: DialHA 18,1 (1992) 29-32; Eng. 33.

k424 **Ganz-Blättler** Ursula, Andacht und Abenteuer; Berichte europäischer Jerusalem- und Santiago-Pilger (1320-1520): Jakobus-Studien 4. Tü 1990, Narr. viii-425 p.; 18 fig. – ᴿRHE 87 (1992) 187-191 (C. *Cannuyer*).

k425 ᵀᴱ**Garzaniti** Marcello, DANIËL Egumeno, Itinerario in Terra Santa [12º s.]. R 1991, Città Nuova. 208 p. Lit. 20.000. – 88-311-1009-8. – ᴿCC 143 (1992,3) 352 (A. *Ferrua*).

k426 *Gehrke* Hans-J., Le strutture regionali della Grecia antica nei resoconti di viaggio del XVIII e XIX secolo: ➤ 873, Geog. Gr. 1989/91, 3-23.

k427 *Geoffroy* Bérénice, Le voyage en Orient; Athènes , Le Caire, Jérusalem [19ᵉ siècle; exposition Louvre 1992]: Archéologia 278 (1992) 48-53; ill.

k428 **González Tejero** Pedro, A journey through the Gospel lands. San Juan Manila 1989, Life Today. 136 p. – ᴿPhilipSa 26 (1991) 160s (J. *Gonzalez*).

k429 ᴱ**Grivaud** Gilles, Excerpta Cypria nova 1. Voyageurs occidentaux à Chypre au XVᵉᵐᵉ siècle: StHistC 15. Nicosia 1990, CRS. 212 p. – ᴿJRAS (1992) 442-4 (C. F. *Beckingham*; notes helpful; some printing oddities).

k431 **Hamilton** R. W., Letters from the Middle East by an occasional archaeologist. E 1992: Pentland. xi-240 p.

k432 *Hinkel* Friedrich W., Otto F. von RICHTERs Reise in Unternubien im Jahre 1815: AltOrF 19 (1992) 230-246; 6 fig.

k433 **Hughes** Gerard W., Walk to Jerusalem [a Jesuit priest's 1700 mile trek]. L 1991, Darton-LT. 244 p. £8. 0-232-51917-X. – ᴿExpTim 103 (1991s) 87 (K. G. *Greet*: 'there is not a page in this book that does not reward the reader' including strictures on far-right 'apparition piety').

k434 **Kalfatovic** Martin R., Nile notes of a howadji; a bibliography of travelers' tales from Egypt, from the earliest times to 1918. Metuchen NJ 1992, Scarecrow. xxxvi-425 p. 0-8108-2541-4 [OIAc 5,26].

k435 ᴱ**Kreuer** W., *Staigerwallder* Friderich, Tagebuch der Heilig-Land-Reise des Grafen Gaudenz von KIRCHBERG 1470: Essener Geog. Arb. 20. Pd 1990, Schöningh. viii-336 p.; 25 pl.; 10 maps [RHE 87,376*].

k436 **Ledegang** F., Als pelgrim naar het Heilige Land; de pelgrimage van Egeria in de vierde eeuw; Christliche Bronner 4. Kampen 1991, Kok. 106 p. ƒ 22,50. – ᴿStreven 59 (1992s) 853 (R. *Beentjes*).

k437 **López Pereira** X. E., EXERIA, viaxe a Terra Santa. Vigo 1991, Xerais. – ᴿCompostellanum 36 (1991) 243-4 (J. *Precedo Lafuente*).

k438 **Magdalena Nom de Deu** J.R., Relatos de viajes y epistolas de peregrinos judíos a Jerusalén 1987 ➤ 4,h590... 6,g878: ᴿHelmantica 43 (1992) 460s (S. *GarciaJalón*).

k439 *Malečková* Jitka, European travel books about the Ottoman Empire in the late eighteenth and early nineteenth centuries as historical sources: ArOr 60 (1992) 147-156.

k440 *Manns* Frédéric, L'Anonyme de Plaisance 30,3 à la lumière d'un texte caraïte: CrNSt 13,1 (1992) 165-8; Eng. 169.

k441 **Maraval** Pierre, Lieux saints et pèlerinage d'Orient 1985 ➤ 1,f342... 6,g879: ᴿTLZ 117 (1992) 196s (J. *Irmscher*).

k442 *Maraval* Pierre, L'attitude des Pères du IVᵉ siècle devant les lieux saints et les pèlerinages: Irénikon 65 (1992) 5-23; Eng. 23.

k443 **Melman** Billie, Women's Orients; English women and the Middle East 1718-1918. AA 1992, Univ. Michigan. xix-417 p.; 24 fig. 0-472-10332-6 [OIAc 3,30].

k444 **Niebuhr** Carsten, Reisebeschreibung nach Arabien und andern umliegenden Ländern [1774-1837 ed.], Vorw. *Rasmussen* Stig; Biog. *Niebuhr* Barthold G.: BtWeltgeschichte. Z 1992, Manasse. 943 p.; maps.

k445 *O'Loughlin* Thomas, The exegetical purpose of ADOMNÁN's De locis sanctis [... Jerusalem; Mambre]: Cambridge Medieval Celtic Studies 24 (1992) 37-53.

k446 ᴱ**Ousterhout** Robert, The blessings of pilgrimage [Christians to East Mediterranean, by 9 authors]: ILByzSt 1. Urbana 1990, Univ. Illinois. xi-149 p.; 54 fig. $25 [RelStR 18,143, G. *Weckman*].

Piccirillo M., Il pellegrinaggio di Egeria al Monte Nebo in Arabia 1987/90 ➤ e607*b*.

k448 **Pixner** Bargil, Wege des Messias und Stätten der Urkirche; Jesus und das Urchristentum im Licht neuer archäologischer Erkenntnisse, ᴱ*Riesner* Rainer: StBArchZg 2. Giessen 1991, Brunnen. 434 p. DM 48. – ᴿErb-Auf 68 (1992) 74 (B. *Schwank*).

k449 **Sackville-West** V., Passenger to Teheran [1926], introd. *Nicholson* Nigel. NY 1992, HarperCollins. 155 p.; ill. 0-06-097458-3 [OIAc 3,36].

k450 **Schreiner** S., Jüdische Reisen im Mittelalter; Benjamin von TUDELA, Petachja von REGENSBURG: Sammlung Dieterich 416. Lp 1991, Dieterich. 236 p. DM 24 [RHE 87,375*].

k451 ᴱ**Vatin** Jean-Claude, DENON Vivant, Voyage dans la basse et la haute Égypte, pendant les campagnes du général Bonaparte. Cairo 1989s = 1802, IFAO. xii-323 p.; vol. of xvii-141 pl. [OLZ 88,380s, R. S. *Bianchi*].

k451* *Wallis* Gerhard, Luther und die Wallfahrt: ➤ 149, ᶠPREUSS H. 1992, 352-361.

k452 *Wasser* B.A.J., Die Peregrinatie van Iherusalem; pelgrimsverslagen van Nederlandse Jerusalemgangers in de xvde, xvide en xviide eeuw; ontstaan en ontwikkeling: De gulden Passer 69 (Antwerpen 1991) 5-72; 7 facsim. [< RHE 87,376*].

k453 *Weigert* Gideon, ⓰ An eighteenth-century travel diary from Damascus to Jerusalem: CHistEI 68 (1993) 49-56; Eng. 198, Mustapha al-BAKRI 1710, copied 1902.

U7 *Crucigeri* – The Crusades.

k454 **Amouroux-Mourad** M., Le Comté d'Édesse 1098-1150: BAH 129. P 1988, Geuthner. xii-172 p.; 8 pl., foldout. F 280. – ᴿSyria 69 (1992) 244s (J.-P. *Sodini*).

k455 *Cannuyer* Christian, Visions d'Égypte; continuité et ruptures du Moyen Âge aux débuts de l'égyptologie [... croisades]: CdÉ 66 (1991) 136-147.

k456 **Cole** Penny J., The preaching of the Crusades to the Holy Land: Medv-Ac 98, 1991 ➤ 7,e887: ᴿSpeculum 67 (1992) 129-132 (C. W. *Connell*). Crusade toponymy ➤ g788*.

k457 **Edbury** Peter W., The kingdom of Cyprus and the Crusades 1191-1374: 1991 ➤ 7,e889: ᴿAmHR 97 (1992) 1200s (J. M. *Powell*); JEH 43 (1992) 339s (N. *Housley*); JRAS (1992) 70s (C. F. *Beckingham*); MeditHR 7 (1992) 230s (B. *Arbel*).

k458 **Edbury** Peter W., *Rowe* John G., WILLIAM of Tyre, historian of the Latin East 1988 ➤ 4,h606 ... 6,g909: ᴿEngHR 107 (1992) 163s (C. J. *Tyerman*).

k459 *Failler* Albert, L'occupation de Rhodes par les hospitaliers: RÉByz 50 (1992) 113-135.

k460 **Favreau-Lilie** Marie-Luise, Die Italiener im Heiligen Land vom ersten Kreuzzug bis zum Tode Heinrichs von Champagne (1098-1197). Amst 1989, Hakkert. xlix-586 p. – ᴿSpeculum 67 (1992) 141-3 (D. *Abulafia*: Levant trade; how others would have written it).

k461 *Flori* J., *a)* Une ou plusieurs 'première croisade'? Le message d'Urbain II et les plus anciens pogroms d'Occident: RHist 285 (1991) 3-27. – *b)* L'Église et la Guerre Sainte; de la Paix de Dieu à la Croisade: Annales 47 (1992) 453-466 [< RHE 88,351*].

k462 **Forey** Alan, The military orders; from the twelfth to the early fourteenth centuries. Buffalo 1992, Univ. Toronto. xiv-278 p. $60; pa. $19. 0-8020-2805-5; -7680-7 [TDig 39,362]. – ᴿAmHR 97 (1992) 1502 (W. *Urban*).

k462* ᴱ**Gervers** M., The IId Crusade and the Cistercians. NY 1992, St. Martin's. xxi-266 p. $45 [RHE 88,237*].

k463 *Grégoire* R., Esegesi biblica e 'militia Christi': ➤ 694a, Militia 1989/92, 21-45.

k464 **Grousset** René, Histoire des Croisades et du Royaume franc de Jérusalem. P 1991 = 1934-6, Perrin. 702 p.; 924 p.; 876 p.; ill. – ᴿÉtudes 376 (1992) 127s (P. *Vallin*).

k465 **Housley** Norman, The later Crusades, 1274-1580, from Lyons to Alcazar. Ox 1922, UP. xxiv-528 p.; 14 maps. £45; pa. £15 [RHE 87,229*].

k466 *Jotischky* Andrew T., The breath of the dove; hermits and eremitical monasticism in the Holy Land, 1095-1291: diss. Yale. NHv 1991. 323 p. 92-24353. – DissA 53 (1992s) 1244s-A.

k467 *Kenaan-Kedar* Nurith, A neglected series of Crusader sculpture; the ninety-six corbels of the Church of the Holy Sepulchre: IsrEJ 42 (1992) 103-114; 13 fig.

k468 *Kolia-Dermitzaki* Athina, Die Kreuzfahrer und die Kreuzzüge im Sprachgebrauch der Byzantiner: JbÖsByz 41 (1991) 163-188.

k469 **Lewis** Archibald R., Nomads and Crusaders 1988 ➤ 7,e896: ᴿEngHR 107 (1992) 437s (J. *Shepard*).

k470 **Luttrell** Anthony, The Hospitallers of Rhodes and their Mediterranean world: CS 360. Brookfield VT 1992, Variorum/Aldgate. $98. 0-86078-307-3 [TDig 40,172].

k471 *Madden* T. F., The fires of the Fourth Crusade in Constantinople, 1203-1204; a damage assessment: ByZ 84s,1 (1991s) 72-93; map.

k472 **Maleczek** Werner, Petrus CAPUANUS; Kardinal, Legat am vierten Kreuzzug, Theologe († 1214). W 1988, Österr. Akad. 350 p. Sch 350. – ᴿEngHR 107 (1992) 174s (P. W. *Edbury*).

k473 *Marshall* C. J., The crusading motivations of the Italian city republics in the Latin East, c. 1096-1104: Rivista di Bizantinistica 1,2 (Bo 1991) 41-68 [< RHE 87,401*].

k474 **Miethke** Jürgen, L'engagement politique; la seconde croisade, ᵀ*Bertrand* D.: ⇥ 513, Bernard: SChr 380 (1992) 475-503.

k475 *Murray* Alan V., The army of Godfrey of Bouillon, 1096-1099; structure and dynamics of a contingent on the First Crusade: RBgPg 70 (1992) 301-329.

k476 *Nastase* Dimitri, Le Mont Athos et l'Orient chrétien et musulman au Moyen Âge: ⇥ 557*, Contacts 1990/2, 324-331.

k477 **Pernoud** Régine, La mujer en el tiempo de las Cruzadas [1990 ⇥ 7, e900], ᵀ*Garcia Martin* Pilar. M 1991, Rialp. 370 p.; 12 pl. 84-321-2819-8. – ᴿActuBbg 29 (1992) 117 (A. *Borràs*).

k478 ᴱ**Powell** James M., Muslims under Latin rule 1100-1300 [... mostly Spain] 1990 ⇥ 7,e902: ᴿBSO 55 (1992) 126s (B. *Hamilton*).

k479 **Prawer** Joshua, The history of the Jews in the Latin Kingdom of Jerusalem 1988 ⇥ 5,g585 ... 7,e903: ᴿRHR 209 (1992) 309s (S. *Schwarzfuchs*).

k480 *Queller* D. E., *Madden* T. F., Some further arguments in defense of the Venetians on the fourth crusade [Queller 1977]: Byzantion 62 (1992) 433-473.

k481 **Richard** J., a) St. Louis, crusader king of France, ᵀᴱ*Lloyd* S. C/P 1992, Univ./Sciences de l'Homme. xxix-354 p.; 4 maps. £40 [RHE 87,58*]. – b) Le crociate: Il mondo della Bibbia [1120-7353] 3,11 (1992) 13-20 (3-44).

k481* ᴱ**Sargent-Baur** N., Journeys toward God; pilgrimage and crusade. Kalamazoo 1992, Medieval Institute. xii-229 p.; 12 fig. [RHE 88,234*].

k482 *Sarnowsky* Jürgen, Die Johanniter und Smyrna (1344-1402), Teil 2. Quellen: RömQ [86 (1991) 215-251] 87 (1992) 47-98.

k483 **Schein** Sylvia, 'Fideles crucis'; the papacy, the west, and the recovery of the Holy Land, 1274-1314: 1991 ⇥ 7,e911a; $82: ᴿAmHR 97 (1992) 536 (W. C. *Jordan*).

k484 [*Setton* K. M., History of the Crusades 5s] ᴱ**Hazard** H. W., **Zacour** N. P., Impact of the Crusades in the Near East / on Europe 1985/9 ⇥ 2,d146 ... 7,e891*: ᴿSpeculum 67 (1922) 221-4 (J. A. *Brundage*: the brilliant chapters outnumber the awful ones).

k485 *Sivan* E., Islam and the Crusades; antagonism, polemics, dialogue: ⇥ 581, Rel.-Gespräche 1989/92, 207-215.

k485* *Slack* C. K., The Premonstratensians and the Crusader Kingdoms in the twelfth and thirteenth centuries: AnPraem 67 (1991) 207-231; 68 (1992) 76-110.

k486 *Thomas* R. D., Anna COMNENA's account of the First Crusade; history and politics in the reigns of the emperors Alexius I and Manuel I Comnenus: ByzModGk 15 (Birmingham 1991) 269-312 [< RHE 88,209*].

k487 **Thorau** Peter, The lion of Egypt; Sultan Baybars I and the Near East in the thirteenth century, ᵀ*Holt* P. M. L 1992, Longman. xiii-321 p. [JAOS 112,730].

k488 **Tyerman** Christopher, England and the Crusades 1988 ⇥ 5,g593; 6, g937: ᴿEngHR 107 (1992) 449s (A. *Macquarrie*).

k489 a) *Tyerman* C., Who went on crusade to the Holy Land?; – b) *Housley* N., Jerusalem and the development of the Crusade idea: ⇥ 692, Horns 1987/92, 13-26 / 27-40.

k490 **Ulbert** Thilo, Der kreuzfahrerzeitliche Silberschatz aus Resafa-Sergiupolis: Resafa 3. Mainz 1990, von Zabern. xii-115 p.; 48 fig.; 138

pl. + 24 color. – ᴿBonnJbb 192 (1992) 778-781 (V. H. *Elbern*); Syria 69 (1992) 487-9 (J. P. *Sodini*).

k491 *West* Delno C., Christopher Columbus, lost biblical sites, and the last crusade: CathHR 78 (1992) 519-541.

U8   *Communitates Terrae Sanctae* – **The Status Quo.**

k492 **Abdel-Sayed** Edris, Les coptes d'Égypte: les premiers chrétiens du Nil: Courants Universels. P 1992, Publisud. 72 p. 0298-2153 [OIAc 5,13].

k493 **Abu Mokh** François, évêque melkite (entretiens avec *Chabert* Joëlle, *Mourvillier* François), Les confessions d'un Arabe catholique. P 1991, Centurion. 255 p. F 45. – ᴿEsprVie 102 (1992) 207s (M. *Henri*).

k494 *Appleby* R. Scott, The Arab problem and the Islamic solution: Chr-Cent 109 (1992) 188-192.

ᴱ**Ateek** Naim S., *al.*, Faith and the Intifada 1990/1 ➤ 507*c*.

k495 **Ateek** Naim S., Justice and only justice 1989 ➤ 5,g595 ... 7,e914: ᴿSv-TKv 67 (1991) 101-3 (S. *Norin*).

k496 *Barnavi* Élie, Israël, face au passé et au présent: Notre Histoire 89 (1992) [< EsprVie 102 (1992) 644-6, J. *Daoust*).

k497 **Bat Ye'or**, Les chrétientés d'Orient entre Jihād et Dhimmitude, VII-XX siècle: préf. *Ellul* Jacques: L'Histoire à vif. P 1991, Cerf. vi-529 p. [TR 88,519]. – ᴿRÉJ 151 (1992) 379-381 (G. *Nahon*).

k498 **Benbassa** Esther, Le Sionisme ou la politique des alliances dans les communautés juives ottomanes (début XXᵉ siècle): RÉJ 150 (1991) 107-131.

k499 ᴱ**Carmel** Alex, *al.*, The Jewish settlement in Palestine 634-1881: TAVO B-88. Wsb 1990, Reichert. 184 p. – ᴿRÉJ 151 (1992) 225-8 (G. *Nahon*).

k500 **Chroniques** [Liban, synode; .. relations interconfessionelles/Égypte, Irak, Jérusalem]: PrOrChr 41 (1991) 103-176 / 362-434 [299-339, *Lingot* Jean-Louis, Le synode de l'espérance].

k501 ᴱ**Cohen** Mark R., *Udovitch* Abraham L., Jews among Arabs; contacts and boundaries 1986/9 ➤ 7,614: ᴿJQR 83 (1992s) 242s (Vera B. *Moreen*).

k502 **Cohn-Sherbok** Dan, Israel, the history of an idea. L 1992, SPCK. 192 p. £13. 0-281-04577-1. – ᴿExpTim 104 (1992s) 223 (F. *Morgan*).

k502* ᴱ**Colombo** Furio, Per Israele. Mi 1991, Rizzoli. 269 p. Lit. 28.000. – ᴿProtestantesimo 47 (1992) 239s (J. A. *Soggin*).

k503 **Cragg** K., The Arab Christian; a history in the Middle East 1991 ➤ 7,e925; also L 1992, Mowbray. 136 p. £9.50. – ᴿProtestantesimo 47 (1992) 240s (J. A. *Soggin*); Tablet 246 (1992) 204s (A. *Hourani*); TLond 95 (1992) 566s (H. *Wybrew*).

k504 *Daoust* J. [< *Klein* T., Revue des Deux Mondes mai 1992)] Israéliens-Palestiniens; le devoir de l'Europe: EsprVie 102 (1992) 581-3.

k505 *de Brul* Peter, The crisis of Palestinian Christians: CathW 234 (1991) 31-34.

k506 **Desbiens** Jean-Paul, Jérusalem (terra dolorosa). Montréal 1991, Bef-froi. 225 p. – ᴿLavalTP 48 (1992) 131s (L.-A. *Richard*).

k507 *Dieckhoff* Alain, Le Sionisme est-il le dernier projet colonial?: L'Histoire 157 (1992) 114-8.

k508 **Ellis** Marc H., Beyond innocence and redemption; confronting the holocaust and Israeli power; creating a moral future for the Jewish people. NY 1990, Harper. 214 p. $22. – ᴿJRel 72 (1992) 620 (A. *Mittleman*: Jewish ethics has been compromised by both Israeli and Diaspora attitude to Palestinians); RExp 89 (1992) 134s (E. G. *Hinson*: raises hopes).

k509 **Ellisen** Stanley A., Who owns the land? The Arab-Israeli conflict. Portland OR 1991, Multnomah. 248 p. $10, – ᴿBtS 149 (1992) 247s (R. P. *Lightner*); GraceTJ 12 (1991) 324-6 (H. A. *Kent*).

k510 **Ferrari** Silvio, Vaticano e Israele dal secondo conflitto mondiale alla guerra del Golfo. F 1991, Sansoni. 348 p.; ill. Lit. 50.000. – ᴿCC 143 (1992,2) 415s (G. *Martina*).

k511 **Firro** Kais M., A history of the Druzes: HbOr I, Egb 9. Leiden 1992, Brill. xv-395 p. ƒ195. 90-04-09437-7 [OIAc 5,21].

k512 **Fishman** Aryei, Judaism and modernization on the religious kibbutz. C 1992, Univ. 202 p. £32.50. 0-521-40388-X. – ᴿExpTim 104 (1992s) 222s (F. *Morgan*).

k513 **Gerber** Haim, The social origins of the modern Middle East [Ottoman land-tenure policies]. Boulder/L 1987, Rienner/Mansell. ii-224 p. £26.50. / 0-7201-1844-1 [BO 50,281, A. H. de *Groot*].

k514 ᴱ**Garvers** Michael, *Bikhazi* Ramzi J., Conversion and continuity; indigenous Christian communities in Islamic lands, eighth to eighteenth centuries. Toronto 1990, Pont. Inst. Medieval St. xviii-559 p. – ᴿSR 21 (1992) 224s (Sheila *McDonough*).

k515 ᴱ**Gilbar** Gad G., Ottoman Palestine, 1800-1914; studies in economic and social history. Leiden 1990. Brill. xv-348 p. ƒ150. – ᴿBSO 55 (1992) 334 (M. E. *Yapp*).

k516 *Giustiniani-Bandini* Maria C. † 1951, Les droits de la chrétienté sur la terre du Christ [1950], ᵀ: PeCa 256 (1992) 9-24.

k517 *a) Haddid* Munim, Contacts between Palestinian Arab traditional culture and western culture in Israel; – *b) Ali* Sheikh R., The superpowers and self-determination for Palestine: → 557*, Contacts 1990/2, 477-480 / 91-99.

k518 **Imber** C., The Ottoman empire 1300-1481. İstanbul 1990, Isis. xiii-288 p., 3 maps. – ᴿByZ 84s,1 (1991s) 130s (E. A. *Zachariadou*. an indispensable manual).

k519 *Jaeger* David M. A., Il cristianesimo in Terra Santa: → 383, Communio 122 (1992) 37-44 (52-63).

k520 **Khalaf** Samir, Lebanon's predicament. NY ..., Columbia Univ. xvi-328 p. $30. 0-231-06378-4. – ᴿBO 49 (1992) 563-9 (F. *Smit*: also on SALIBI K. & ZAMIR M. 1988).

k521 *Kühtopf-Gentz* Michael, 'Israel geht vor Zion': Nathan BIRNBAUM und die Palästinafrage: ZRGg 44 (1992) 118-139.

k522 **Laskier** Michael M., The Jews of Egypt 1920-1970, in the midst of Zionism, anti-Semitism, and the Middle East conflict. NYU 1992. xiv-326 p. – ᴿRelStR 18 (1992) 346 (Rachel *Simon*).

k523 **Laurens** Henry, *a)* Le royaume impossible; la France et la genèse du monde arabe; – *b)* Le grand jeu; Orient arabe et rivalités internationales. P 1990s, A. Colin. 210 p.; 447 p. [BO 50,279, R. G. *Khoury*: superb].

k523* **Martlin** Carl H., Gud i Orienten; om de orientaliska kyrkornas framväxt och egenart. Sto 1990, Verbum. 239 p. Sk 198. – ᴿNorTTs 92 (1991) 55s (N. E. *Bloch-Hoell*).

k524 **Minerbi** Sergio J., The Vatican and Zionism; conflict in the Holy Land, 1895-1925: 1991 → 7,e942: ᴿAmerica 164 (1991) 543s (D. *Neiman*); CathHR 78 (1992) 135s (G. E. *Irani*).

k525 **O'Brien** William V., Law and morality in Israel's war with the P[alestine]L[iberation]O[rganization]. NY 1991, Routledge. ix-342 p. $45; pa. $16. – ᴿTS 53 (1992) 370-2 (J. E. *Dougherty*).

k526 **Ovendale** Ritchie, Britain, the United States, and the end of the Palestine Mandate, 1942-1948: Royal Studies in History 57. Rochester NY 1989, Boydell (for London Royal Historical Soc.). 332 p. $71. – ᴿAmHR 97 (1992) 162s (I. *Abu-Lughod*).

k527 **Palmer** Alan, The decline and fall of the Ottoman empire. L c. 1992, J. Murray. £25. – ᴿTablet 246 (1992) 1403 (E. C. *Hodgkin*).

k528 **Peterson** Paul C. R., The Church's ministry of reconciliation in the Holy Land: diss. Fuller, ᴰ*Anderson* R. Pasadena 1992. 238 p. 92-25160. – DissA 53 (1992s) 2410-A.

k529 **Pfisterer** Rudolf, Israel oder Palästina? Perspektiven aus Bibel und Geschichte. Wu 1992, Brockhaus. 224 p. 3-417-24124-3.

k530 *Pleins* J. David, Is a Palestinian theology of liberation possible? AnglTR 74 (1992) 133-143.

k531 **Raheb** Mitri, Das reformatorische Erbe unter den Palästinensern 1990 ➤ 7,e946: ᴿLuthMon 30 (1991) 564s (C. *Meyer*).

k532 *Reilly* James A., Property, status, and class in Ottoman Damascus; case studies from the nineteenth century: JAOS 112 (1992) 9-21.

k533 **Roshwald** Aviel, Estranged bedfellows; Britain and France in the Middle East during the Second World War. NY 1990, Oxford-UP. xii-315 p. – ᴿAmHR 97 (1992) 161 (W. I. *Shorrock*).

k534 *Sabbah* Michael, *al.*, La présence chrétienne en Orient; témoignage et mission; lettre pastorale adressée collégialement par les Patriarches Catholiques d'Orient à leurs fidèles. Le Caire, Pâques 1992 [< CC 143 (1992,2) 493-501 (G. *Caprile*)].

k534* *Sabella* Bernard, Palestinian Christian emigration from the Holy Land: PrOrChr 41 (1991) 74-85; franç. 85.

k535 **Sharkansky** Ira, Ancient and modern Israel — an exploration of political parallels. Albany 1991, SUNY. 194 p. $11. – ᴿAustralBR 40 (1992) 66s (J. S. *Levi*).

k536 **Shlaim** Avi, The politics of partition; King Abdullah, the Zionists and Palestine (1921-1951). Ox 1990, UP. 465 p. – ᴿRÉJ 151 (1992) 251-3 (A. *Boyer*).

k537 *Soetens* Claude, Origine et développement de l'Église copte catholique: Irénikon 65 (1992) 42-62; Eng. 62.

k538 *Sonyel* Salâhi R., The fifth centenary of the first Jewish migrations to the Ottoman Empire: Belleten 56,215 (1992) 207-211; ❶ 201-6.

k538* **Stillman** Norman A., The Jews of Arab lands in modern times 1991 ➤ 7,e954: ᴿJAOS 112 (1992) 718s (J. *Jankowski*: companion to his 1979 History).

k539 **Stofferengen-Pedersen** Kirsten, Les Éthiopiens: Fils d'Abraham 1990 ➤ 7,e955: 2-503-5000-48: ᴿÉTRel 67 (1992) 119 (J.-M. *Prieur*, aussi sur Les Coptes).

k539* *Szulc* Tad, Who are the Palestinians?: NatGeog 181 (1992) 84-113.

k540 ᵀᴱ**Thackston** Wheeler M.ᴶ, Mikhayil MISHĀQA [1873: AUB ms 956; abbreviated edition 1955], Murder, mayhem, pillage, and plunder; the history of the Lebanon in the 18th and 19th centuries. Albany 1988, SUNY. xix-309 p. $49.50; pa. $17. – ᴿJAOS 112 (1992) 523s (R. *Schulze*).

k541 **Vatikiotis** P. J., Among Arabs and Jews; a personal experience 1936-1990. L 1991, Weidenfeld & N. ix-166 p. £18. – ᴿBSO 55 (1992) 334-6 (H. T. *Norris*).

k542 **Wilson** Mary C., King Abdullah, Britain, and the making of Jordan 1988 ➤ 6,g981; 7,e958: ᴿAmHR 97 (1992) 590s (Janice J. *Terry*).

k543 ᴱWilson Rodney, Politics and the economy in Jordan [School of Oriental and African studies conference, London 17 May 1987]. NY 1991, Routledge. xiv-243 p. £35. – ᴿBSO 55 (1992) 131 (J. *Rudd*).

k543* *Winther* J., The Hebrew revolution and the revolution of the Hebrew language between the 1880s and the 1930s: Nordisk Judaistik 11 (Åbo 1990) 73-80 [< Judaica 47,179].

k544 **Yadlin** Rivka, An arrogant oppressive spirit; anti-Zionism as anti-Judaism in Egypt: Studies in Antisemitism. Ox 1989, Pergamon. x-135. – ᴿJQR 83 (1992s) 426-8 (M. *Kramer*: Egyptian press clippings since 1979 treaty).

k545 **Yapp** M. F., The Near East [since 1792: 1987] since the First World War. L 1991, Longman. xviii-526 p. £15. ᴿBSO [52 (1989) 140] 55 (1992) 136s (M. S. *Anderson*).

XX. Historia Scientiae Biblicae

Y1   **History of Exegesis .1 General.**

k545* *Bartnik* Czesław, ⊕ *a*) L'apport du Christianisme à la culture; – *b*) L'Église et la parole: ➤ 43*, ᶠDᴇᴍʙᴏᴡsᴋɪ B. AtKap 119 (1992) 80-92 / 6-17.

k546 *Bertrand* Dominique, Die Rückkehr zu den Vätern; eine Weg zur Erneuerung der Theologie; das Beispiel der 'Sources Chrétiennes' [Gastvorlesung Tü 14.X.1991]: TüTQ 172 (1992) 295-306.

k546* ᴱBosio Guido, *al.*, Introduzione ai Padri della Chiesa, secoli I e II: Corona Patrum Strum 1, 1990 ➤ 6,g987; 7,e969: ᴿCC 143 (1992,3) 96s (F. *Bergamelli*); EuntDoc 45 (1992) 115s (C. *Noce*); Gregorianum 73 (1992) 562s (H. *Pietras*); Lateranum 58 (1992) 502-4 (anche F. *Bergamelli*); Orpheus 13,1 (1992) 159s (A. *Gallico*); Salesianum 54 (1992) 165s (anche F. *Bergamelli*).

k547 *a*) **Brown** Colin, Christianity and western thought I, 1990 ➤ 7,e969*: ᴿEvangel 10,1 (1992) 30 (S. *Williams*: unstinting praise). — *b*) **Brown** Harold O.J., Heresies: Doubleday 1984 = GR 1988, Baker ➤ 65,d381 ... 6,g998: ᴿCurrTMiss 19 (1992) 53s (K. *Killinger*). — *c*) ᴱ**Burini** Clara, *al.*, Epistolari cristiani (sec. I-V) 1-3. R 1990, Benedictina ➤ 7,e970: xxviii-132 p.; xxii-158 p.; xxii-208 p. Lit. 22.000 + 25.000 + 28.000. – ᴿCC 143 (1992,1) 201s (A. *Ferrua*). — *d*) **Cameron** Averil, Christianity and the rhetoric of empire; the development of Christian discourse: Sather Classical Lectures, 1991 ➤ 7, e971: ᴿAmHR 97 (1992) 1188s (T. D. *Barnes*); ChH 61 (1992) 437s (C. A. *Volz*); CathHR 78 (1992) 435s (R. D. *Sider*); ClasR 43 (1993) 356s (Gillian *Clark*); JAAR 60 (1992) 332s (Kathryn *Argetsinger*); JTS 43 (1992) 701-5 (R. A. *Markus*: courageous, suggestive, elliptical); TS 53 (1992) 782 (M. J. *Hollerich*).

k548 ᶠCʜᴀᴅᴡɪᴄᴋ Henry, The making of orthodoxy, ᴱWilliams Rowan 1989 ➤ 5,38*: ᴿRTLv 23 (1992) 105-8 (A. de *Halleux*: tit. pp., analyses détaillées; aussi p. 204-8 sur ᶠSᴄʜɴᴇᴇᴍᴇʟᴄʜᴇʀ).

k549 **Comby** Jean, Deux mille ans d'évangélisation; histoire de l'expansion chrétienne: BtHist Christianisme 29. P 1992, Desclée. 327 p. F 189 [TR 88,344].

k550 **Contreras** E., *Peña* R., Introducción al estudio de los Padres, periodo pre-niceno 1991 ➤ 7,a973: ᴿPhase 32 (1992) 83s (R. *Alberdi*); RBiArg

54,45 (1992) 56-58 (A. *Zorzin*); RÉAug 38 (1992) 192s (P. *Mattei*); Salmanticensis 39 (1992) 399-402 (R. *Trevijano*); StPatav 39 (1992) 242s (C. *Corsato*).

Conzelmann Hans, Gentiles, Jews, Christians; polemics and apologetics in the Greco-Roman era 1992 → a722.

k550* ᴱ**Culbertson** Philip I., *Shippee* Arthur B., The Pastor 1990 → 7,e974: ᴿIrBSt 14 (1992) 150-2 (J. R. *Boyd*).

k551 ᴱ**Dal Covolo** Enrico, *Triacca* Achille M., Lo studio dei Padri della Chiesa oggi: BtScR 96, 1991 → 7,426*: ᴿBLitEc (1992) 408s (H. *Crouzel*); CC 143 (1992,3) 448s (G. *Cremascoli*); ETL 68 (1992) 446s (A. de *Halleux*: commentent l'instruction 'précipitée' de janv. 1990).

k551* *Dal Covolo* Enrico, La 'Corona Patrum'; un contributo al progresso degli studi patristici in Italia: FilT 6 (1992) 321-330.

k552 **Dassmann** E., Kirchengeschichte, I., Ausbreitung, Leben und Lehre der Kirche in den ersten drei Jahrhunderten: StBTheol 10, → 7,e976 [-0-1]. – ᴿTvT 32 (1992) 417s (A. *Davids*).

k552* **Deedy** John, Retrospect; the origins of Catholic beliefs and practices. ...1992, Mercier. 330 p. £10. 0-85342-990-1. – ᴿExpTim 103 (1991s) 378 (R. *Butterworth*: will reassure aging readers).

k553 **Dekkers** Eligius, De Kerkvaders, hun wegen en grenzen: CollatVL 22 (1992) 149-161.

k554 [**Denzinger** Heinrich] **Hünermann** Peter (*Hoping* Helmut), Enchiridion symbolorum definitionum et declarationum de rebus fidei et morum[37], jetzt mit deutscher Übersetzung. FrB 1991, Herder. 1706 p. DM 158. – ᴿMüTZ 43 (1992) 251s (G. L. *Müller*); TGL 82 (1992) 263-6 (W. *Beinert*); TR 88 (1992) 99-101 (H. *Vorgrimler*); TrierTZ 101 (1992) 239s (R. *Weier*); ZkT 114 (1992) 215s (H. B. *Meyer*).

k555 **Droge** Arthur J., Homer or Moses? 1989 → 5,g629... 7,e978*: ᴿJbAC 34 (1991) 183s (G. J. M. *Bartelink*); RÉJ 150 (1991) 188-191 (A. Le *Boulluec*).

k556 **Evans** G. R., *Wright* J. Robert, The Anglican tradition, a handbook of sources: L/Mp 1991, SPCK/Fortress. 620 p. £20. 0-281-04496-1 / 0-8006-2483-1. – ᴿExpTim 103 (1991s) 157s (S. G. *Hall*: an Anglican-style Denzinger approved by Canterbury; EGERIA gets 8 pages, JULIAN of Norwich 7).

k557 **Faivre** A., Ordonner la fraternité; pouvoir d'innover et retour à l'ordre dans l'Église ancienne: Histoire. P 1992, Cerf. 555 p. F 299 [RHE 87,395*].

k558 ᴱ**Feri** Roberta, Prontuario patristico; sussidio per la consultazione della collana 'Testi Patristici' (Testi 1-100). R 1992, Città Nuova. 166 p. 88-311-7246-6.

k558* **Figueiredo** Fernando A., La vida de la Iglesia primitiva [A vida da Igreja], ᵀ: ColSemLAm 2. Bogotá 1991, Consejo Episcopal. 452 p. 958-625-208-6. – ᴿGregorianum 73 (1992) 170-2 (C. I. *González*: autor ahora obispo).

k559 **Gibert** Pierre, Petite histoire de l'exégèse biblique: Lire la Bible 94. P 1992, Cerf.. 268 p. F 110. 2-204-04483-0. – ᴿArchivScSocR 80 (1992) 265 (É. *Poulat*); EsprVie 102 (1992) 411 (É. *Cothenet*).

k560 *Gould* G., Women in the writings of the Fathers; language, belief and reality: → 6,692*, ᴱ*Sheils* W., *al.*, Women in the Church 1989/90, 1-13.

k561 [ᴱ**Greschat** M.] 'Nimm und lies'; Christliche Denker von Origenes bis Erasmus [10 < Gestalten der KG 1981+3]. Stu 1991, Kohlhammer. 388 p. – ᴿTPhil 67 (1992) 285 (H. J. *Sieben*).

k562 *a)* **Hall** Stuart G., Doctrine and practice in the early Church 1991 ➤ 7,e983; also GR 1992, Eerdmans. x-262 p. $17 [TR 88,519]. – ᴿTLond 95 (1992) 286 (H. *Chadwick*).
— *b)* ᴱ**Hamman** A., Les Pères dans la foi 38-43. P 1990s, Association J.-P. Migne. – ᴿEsprVie 102 (1992) 59-62 (Y.-M. *Duval*: peu différent des volumes précédents 'Ichtys').
— *c)* ᴱ**Herrmann** Joachim, Griechische und lateinische Quellen zur Frühgeschichte Mitteleuropas bis zur Mitte des I. Jahrtausends u.Z.: Schriften und Quellen zur Alten Welt 37. B 1988-92, Akademie. I. Homer-Plutarch 1988; 632 p.; foldout maps. – II. Tacitus 1990; 291 p. – III. Tacitus-Ausonius, 1991; 723 p. – IV. Ammianus-Zosimus 1992, 656 p. 3-05-000348-0; -349-0; -571-9; -591-2.
— *d)* *Hoornaert* Eduardo, La memoria del pueblo cristiano; una historia de la Iglesia. BA 1986, Paulinas. 305 p. – ᴿTArg 27 (1990) 73-93 (H. E. *Lona*).

k563 **Jantsch** Johanna, Die Entstehung des Christentums bei A. v. HARNACK und E. MEYER [Diss. Marburg] 1990 ➤ 6,4192.b752: ᴿAthenaeum 79 (1991) 694-6 (Beat *Näf*); ZkT 114 (1992) 232-4 (K. H. *Neufeld*).

k564 *Koester* Helmut, Jesus the Victim [SBL presidential address, Kansas City 23.XI.1991]: JBL 111 (1992) 3-15: in the 'New Quest' (KÄSEMANN, J. M. ROBINSON) focuses the early Christian proclamation that Jesus was victim of the age whose end he had announced, 'the age of Augustus as realized eschatology'.

k565 **Karpp** H., Schrift, Geist und Wort Gottes; Geltung und Wirkung der Bibel in der Geschichte der Kirche, von der Alten Kirche bis zum Ausgang der Reformationszeit. Da 1992, Wiss. xxiii-270 p. DM 54. 3-534-10862-9 [BL 93,109, R. P. R. *Murray*: concentrated; Orientals overlooked].

Kirchschläger Walter, Die Anfänge der Kirche, eine biblische Rückbesinnung 1990 ➤ 5517.

k566 **Kraft** Heinrich, Einführung in die Patrologie 1991 ➤ 7,e989: ᴿScripTPamp 24 (1992) 1090s (A. *Viciano*).

k566* *Làconi* Mauro, Storia della Chiesa dalle origini (rassegna): ParVi 35 (1990) 212-6 . 304-9.

k567 **McGinn** Bernard, The foundations of mysticism, origins to the fifth century [first of four volumes: The presence of God; a history of Western Christian mysticism]. NY 1991, Crossroad. xxii-494 p. $39.50. – ᴿTS 53 (1992) 552-4 (H. D. *Egan*).

k568 **Mason** Steve, *Robinson* Tom, An early Christian reader. Toronto 1990, Canadian Scholars. xiv-605 p. – ᴿSR 21 (1992) 483 (S. G. *Wilson*).

k569 *Meyer* B. F., The Church in earliest Christianity; identity and self-definition: McMasterJT 2,2 (Hamilton 1991) 1-19 [< NTAbs 36,380].

k570 *Morales* José, La vocación cristiana en la primera patrística: ScripTPamp 23 (1991) 837-889.

k571 ᴱ**Norelli** E., La Bibbia nell'antichità cristiana: Bo 1992, Dehoniane. 2 vol. [VivH 3,428].

k572 **Olivar** Alexandre, La predicación cristiana antigua: Bt 189. Barc 1991, Herder. 1000 p. – ᴿCiuD 205 (1992) 251s (J. M. *Ozaeta*); ScripTPamp 24 (1992) 314-6 (D. *Ramos-Lissón*).

k573 **Padovese** Luigi, Introduzione alla teologia patristica. CasM 1992, Piemme. 237 p. Lit. 35.000 [NRT 115,747, A. *Harvengt*].

k573* **Padovese** Luigi, Lo scandalo della croce; la polemica anticristiana nei primi secoli 1988 ➤ 5,7768*: ᴿLateranum 57 (1991) 599s (V. *Grossi*).

k574 *a*) **Pelikan** Jaroslav, The Christian tradition, a history of the development of doctrine, Ch 1971-89 ⇥ ... 6,k850: ᴿRelStR 18 (1992) 1-4 (M. F. *Wiles*) & 4-6 (J. O. *Duke*).

— *b*) **Pierrard** Pierre [⇥ 7,e998*], Histoire de l'Église catholique³ [¹1972, ²1978]. P 1991, Desclée. 352 p. F 125. – ᴿEsprVie 102 (1992) 15s (J.-C. *Meyer*); ScEspr 44 (1992) 237-9 (P.-H. *Poirier*).

— *c*) **Prudhomme** Claude, Histoire des chrétiens: Parcours. P c. 1991, Centurion/Paulines. 186 p. F 69. – ᴿEsprVie 102 (1992) 553 (R. *Epp*).

k575 **Quacquarelli** A., Complementi interdisciplinari di Patrologia 1989 ⇥ 5,503 ... 7,g1: ᴿAsprenas 39 (1992) 430-4 (L. *Fatica*); CC 143 (1992,2) 519s (C. *Capizzi*); RÉAug 37 (1991) 160-2 (P. *Mattei*); ScripTPamp 24 (1992) 343s (D. *Ramos-Lissón*); VigChr 46 (1992) 98-100 (L. *Van Rompay*).

k576 **Reventlow** H., Epochen der Bibelauslegung I, 1990 ⇥ 6,k10; 7,g2: ᴿAntClas 61 (1992) 412 (J. *Wankenne*); TsTKi 62 (1991) 152-4 (Terje *Stordalen*); ZkT 114 (1992) 88s (R. *Oberforcher*).

k577 **Ruggiero** Fabio, La follia dei cristiani; su un aspetto della 'reazione pagana' tra I e V secolo; pref. *Simonetti* Manlio: La Cultura. Mi 1992, Mondadori. xvi-250 p. Lit. 45.000 [TR 88,341].

k577* *a*) *Ryan* Patrick, The influence of the Fathers on modern theology; – *b*) *Chryssavgis* John, The Church Fathers; insight into the theology of the Eastern Church: AustralasCR 69 (1992) 267-277 / 291-308.

k578 *Sæbø* Magne, Hebrew Bible / Old Testament; the history of its interpretation; report on a new international project [begun at 1983 Salamanca IOSOT]: Biblica 73 (1992) 137-143.

k579 **Sawicki** Marianne, The Gospel in history... origins of Christian education 1988 ⇥ 4,h691; 6,k13: ᴿCathHR 78 (1992) 86s (M. M. *Mulcahey*: popular rather than scholarly).

k579* **Schnusenberg** Christine C., The relationship between the Church and the theatre, exemplified by selected writings of the Church Fathers and by liturgical texts until AMALARIUS of Metz — 775-852 A.D. [diss. Ch. 1976, deutsch 1981]. Lanham MD 1988, UPA. xxiv-428 p. $34.50. – ᴿLatomus 51 (1992) 661-3 (J. *Meyers*).

k580 ᴱ**Sfameni Gasparro** G., *al.*, La coppia nei Padri: Letture Iº millennio 9. CinB 1991, Paoline. 474 p. Lit. 35.000. – ᴿAsprenas 39 (1992) 274s (L. *Fatica*).

k581 **Sieben** Hermann J., Kirchenväterhomilien, Repertorium 1991 ⇥ 7,g7: ᴿRÉAug 38 (1992) 203s (J. *Doignon*).

k581* **Spanneut** Michel [*Liébart* J. ⇥ 7,e991], Les Pères de l'Église [1. Iᵉʳ-IVᵉ s., ᴱ*Liébaert* J. 1986] II. IVᵉ-VIIIᵉ s.: BtHistChr 22. P 1990, Desclée. 357 p. – ᴿMélSR 48 (1991) 249s (G. H. *Baudry*).

k582 **Stead** Christopher, Philosophie und Theologie, I. Die Zeit der Alten Kirche: Theologische Wissenschaft 14/4. Stu 1990, Kohlhammer. 182 p. DM 36. 3-17-008924-2. – ᴿJTS 43 (1992) 234 (A. *Meredith*: contentious work by a distinguished English patristic scholar); TPhil 67 (1992) 278s (F. *Ricken*).

k583 **Tanner** Norman P., Decrees of the ecumenical councils 1990 ⇥ 6,k18; 7,g12: ᴿExpTim 104 (1992s) 58 (H. *Chadwick*: worth the high price); JRel 72 (1992) 642 (M. *Cameron*: 'a major publishing achievement'); NRT 114 (1992) 429s (A. *Toubeau*).

k584 *Tanner* Norman, The African Church and the first five ecumenical councils: AfER 33 (1991) 201-213.

k585 La terminologia esegetica nell'antichità 1984/7: VetChr Quad 20.   Bari
1987, Edipuglia.   v-177 p. – ᴿRivStoLR 27 (1991) 532-5 (Giuliana *Iacopino*).
k586 **Thiede** Carsten,   The heritage of the first Christians [1992 Brockhaus],
ᵀ*Hein* Knut.   Ox 1992, Lion.   157 p.; color. ill.
k586* *Treu* Ursula,   Formen und Gattungen in der [post-NT] frühchristlichen
Literatur: ➤ 648*, Spätantike 1992, 125-139.
k587 **Vilanova** E.,   Historia de la teología cristiana 1-3, 1987-92 ➤ 3,g125 ...
7,g13:   ᴿPhase 32 (1992) 533s (J. *Llopis*); StPatav 39 (1992) 217-9 (L.
Sartori).
k587* **Vilanova** Evangelista,   Storia della teologia cristiana, I. Dalle origini
al XV secolo, ᵀ*Chiecchi* Carlo.   R 1991, Borla.   776 p.   Lit. 100.000. –
ᴿLetture 47 (1992) 271s (G. *Ravasi*); RasT 33 (1992) 231s (A. *Barruffo*).
k588 *Vogt* Hermann J.,   Neuausgabe christlicher Quellen [Fontes Christiani
1-5 & 7, 1990-2]: TüTQ 172 (1992) 310-7.
k588* **Young** Frances,   The making of the creeds 1991 ➤ 7,g17: ᴿFurrow 43
(1992) 642s (M. *Howlett*); ScotJT 45 (1992) 124s (L. R. *Wickham*).

Y1.4   *Patres apostolici et saeculi II*   **First two centuries.**

k589 **Bertrand** Dominique, présente, Les écrits des Pères apostoliques.   P
1991, Cerf.   548 p. – ᴿBLitEc 93 (1992) 409s (H. *Crouzel*); EsprVie 102
(1992) 599s (Y.-M. *Duval*: prix loué sans être mentionné).
k590 *Dal Covolo* E.,   La letteratura cristiana a Roma nell'età dei Severi:
RivStoLR 27 (1991) 213-222 [< ᴢɪᴛ 92,42].
k591 *Fredouille* Jean-Claude,   L'apologétique chrétienne antique; naissance
d'un genre littéraire: RÉtAug 38 (1992) 219-234.
k592 [*Funk* F.X., *Bihlmeyer* K. neu] ᵀᴱ**Lindemann** Andreas, *Paulsen* Henning.
Die Apostolischen Väter; griechisch-deutsche Parallclausgabe.   Tü 1992,
Mohr.   viii-574 p.   3-16-145887-7.
k593 **Grant** Robert M.,   Greek apologists of the second century 1988
➤ 4,h708 ... 7,g29.   ᴿGregorianum 73 (1992) 150s (R. *Fisichella*).
k594 **Grant** Robert M.,   Jesus after the Gospels; the Christ of the second
century (Seabury-Western Hale lectures) 1990 ➤ 6,k25; 7,g21:   ᴿCBQ 54
(1992) 153s (Pheme *Perkins*: disjointed confusion of random topics instead
of what would be expected from such an expert); chH 60 (1991) 372s
(D. F. *Winslow*).
k595 *a*) *MacLennan* Robert S.,   Christian self-definition in the *Adversus
Judaeos* preachers in the second century; – *b*) *Kraemer* Ross S.,   On the
meaning of the term 'Jew' in Greco-Roman inscriptions [< HarvTR 92
(1989) 35-53]: ➤ 107, ᶠ*Kraabel* A.T. 1992, 209-224 / 311-329.
k595* **Neymeyr** Ulrich,   Die christlichen Lehrer im zweiten Jahrhundert; ihre
Lehrtätigkeit, ihr Selbstverständnis und ihre Geschichte: VigChr supp 4,
ᴰ1989 ➤ 6,k30; 7,g23:   ᴿZKG 103 (1992) 111s (W. A. *Bienert*).
k596 **Orbe** Antonio,   Introducción a la teología de los siglos II y III: AnGreg
248, 1987 ➤ 3,g128 ... 7,g24:   ᴿOrChrPer 58 (1992) 624-7 (J. D. *Baggarly*:
some resemblances to less technical *González* 1989).
k597 **Pilhofer** Peter,   Presbyteron kreitton ᴰ1990 ➤ 6,k32; 7,g25:   ᴿCritRR 5
(1992) 303-6 (G. E. *Sterling*); JbAC 34 (1991) 184-7 (C. *Scholten*); NedTTs
46 (1992) 239-241 (P. W. van der *Horst*, ook over *Droge* A. 1989); TS 53
(1992) 345-7 (M. A. *Schatkin*).
k598 **Rebell** Walter,   Neutestamentliche Apokryphen [+ Nag-Hammadi 21-62]
und Apostolische Väter.   Mü 1992, Kaiser.   287 p.   3-459-01954-9.

k599 *Simonetti* Manlio, Ortodossia ed eresia tra I e II secolo [BAUER W. 1934 ²1964]: VetChr 29 (1992) 359-389.

---

k601 ARISTIDES: ᵀᴱ**Alpigiano** Carlotta, Aristide di Atene, Apologia: BtPatr 11. F 1988, Nardini. 216 p. – ᴿSalesianum 54 (1992) 379s (S. *Felici*: 'il più antico scritto apologetico'; greco con italiano a fronte).

k602 ATHENAGORAS: **Marcovich** M., Athenagoras, Legatio 1990 ➤ 6,k27; 7,g27: ᴿJbAC 34 (1991) 175s (S. G. *Hall*).

k603 ᵀᴱ**Pouderon** Bernard, Athénagore, Supplique au sujet des Chrétiens et sur la résurrection des morts: SChr 379. P 1992, Cerf. 360 p. [NRT 115,429, A. *Harvengt*]. 3-204-04447-4.

k604 **Pouderon** Bernard, Athénagore ᴰ1989 ➤ 5,g667; 6,k38: ᴿCrNSt 13 (1992) 205s (L. W. *Barnard*, Eng.); LavalTP 48 (1992) 457s (Anne *Pasquier*): TR 88 (1992) 388s (H. E. *Lona*); VigChr 46 (1992) 190s (G. J. M. *Bartelink*).

k605 *Pouderon* Bernard, Les éditions d'Athénagore imprimées aux XVIᵉ et XVIIᵉ siècles: BtHumRen 52 (1990) 641-661.

k606 *Runia* David T., Verba philonica, *agalmatophoreîn*, and the authenticity of the De resurrectione attributed to Athenagoras: VigChr 46 (1992) 313-327.

k607 *Ruprecht* Louis A.ᴶ, Athenagoras the Christian, PAUSANIAS the travel guide, and a mysterious Corinthian girl: HarvTR 85 (1992) 35-48.

k608 *Zeegers-Vander Vorst* Nicole, La paternité athénagorienne du De resurrectione: RHE 87 (1992) 333-373; Eng. deutsch 374.

k609 BARNABAS: *a*) *Horbury* William, Jewish-Christian relations in Barnabas and JUSTIN Martyr; – *b*) *Birdsall* J. Neville, Problems of the Clementine Literature: ➤ 467, Parting of the Ways 1989/92, 315-345 / 347-361.

---

k610 CLEMENS A.: **Hoek** Annewies van den, Clement of Alexandria and his use of PHILO in the 'Stromateis'; an early Christian reshaping of a Jewish model: VigChr supp 3, 1988 ➤ 4,a982; 6,k45: ᴿAustralBR 38 (1990) 94s (E. *Osborn*); RechSR 80 (1992) 109s (B. *Sesboüé*).

k611 ᴱ**Hamman** A.-G., ᵀ*Tron* B., *Gauriat* P., Clément d'Alexandrie, Le Pédagogue; Les Pères dans la Foi 'Migne' 44s. P 1991, Brepols. 350 p. F 160. – ᴿEsprVie 102 (1992) 601s (Y.-M. *Duval*).

k612 **Faivre** Alexandre, The emergence of the laity in the early Church [1984], ᵀ*Smith* David. NY 1990, Paulist. iii-242 p. $12 pa. – ᴿCathHR 78 (1992) 433s (P. *Granfield*: already in CLEMENT, ORIGEN, TERTULLIAN for a Christian not deacon etc.).

k613 *Fernández-Ardanaz* Santiago, 'Ratio et sapientia'; el problema del método en la escuela de Alejandria [... Clemente] y el desarrollo de la metodología 'sapiencial': Compostellanum 36 (1991) 43-79.

k614 ᵀᴱ**Nardi** C., Clemente A., Quale ricco si salva? Il cristiano e l'economia: CuCrAnt. R 1991, Borla. L 20.000. – ᴿAsprenas 39 (1992) 442s (L. *Fatica*).

Procter Everett L., Influence of VALENTINUS & BASILIDES on Clement A. ᴰ1992 ➤ a821.

---

k615 CLEMENS R.: **Bowe** Barbara E., A Church in crisis... Clement R. ᴰ1989 ➤ 4,h716... 7,g33: ᴿChH 60 (1991) 87s (J. S. *Jeffers*).

k616 ᴱLindemann Andreas, Die Clemensbriefe: HbNT 17/1. Tü 1992, Mohr. vi-277 p. DM 59 pa. [TR 88,519]. 3-16-145824-9; -3-0. – ᴿExpTim 104 (1992s) 270s (E. *Best*: replaces KNOPF R.); SNTU A-17 (1992) 276-9 (F. *Weissengruber*: 42 typos); SvEx 58 (1993) 189-192 (L. *Koen*). **Jeffers** J., Conflict at Rome 1991 ➤ 4892.

k617 ᴱJambet Christian, Les homélies clémentines 1991 ➤ 7,g37: ᴿRechSR 80 (1992) 91-93 [É. *Poulat*: sévère].

k618 *Di Donna* Antonio, Il linguaggio della catechesi nelle pseudo-clementine: Asprenas 39 (1992) 199-230. 382-396.

k619 **Birdsall** J.N., Problems of the Clementine literature: ➤ 467, Jews & C 1989/92, 347-351.

k620 ᴱRehm Bernhard [¹1952], ²ʳᵉᵛ*Strecker* Georg, Die Pseudoklementinen I. Homilien: GChrSchrS. B 1992, Akademie. xxix-287 p. 3-05-000575-0.

k621 ᴱStrecker Georg, Die Pseudoklementinen III. Konkordanz II. B 1989, Akademie. 554 p. DM 185. – ᴿJTS 43 (1992) 252s (R. *Vaggione*); ZkG 103 (1992) 120s (A. *Lindemann*, I, 1986).

k622 *Wehnert* J., Abriss der Entstehungsgeschichte des pseudo-klementinischen Romans: Apocrypha 3 (1992) 211-235 [237-257, *Jones* F.S.; < RHE 88,204*].

k623 *Didache* etc.: **Niederwimmer** Kurt, Die Didache 1989 ➤ 6,k62; 7,g41: ᴿRechSR 80 (1992) 97-99 (B. *Sesboüé*).

k624 ᴱAyán Calvo J.J., Didaché / Pseudo-Bernabé. 1992: ᴿSalmanticensis 39 (1992) 402-4 (R. *Trevijano*); StPatav 39 (1992) 638s (C. *Corsato*).

k624* *Rordorf* Willy, Does the Didache contain Jesus tradition independently of the Synoptic Gospels?: ➤ 7,460b, Jesus and the oral Gospel tradition 1989/91, 394-423.

k625 ᵀᴱSchöllgen Georg, Didache / *Geerlings* Wilhelm, Traditio apostolica: Fontes Christiani 1, 1991: ➤ 7,g42: ᴿMüTZ 43 (1992) 121-4 (T. *Böhm*); StiZt 210 (1992) 142s (H. *Frohnhofen*); VigChr 46 (1992) 90-94 (J.C.M. van *Winden*).

k625* Steimer Bruno, Vertex traditionis; die Gattung der altchristlichen Kirchenordnungen [Didache; Trad./Const. Ap.; Diss. Regensburg, ᴰ*Brox* N.]: BZNW 63. B 1992, de Gruyter. xvi-402 p. 3-11013-460-8.

k626 **Harnack** Adolf von, *al.*, Die Lehre der zwölf Apostel nebst Untersuchungen zur ältesten Geschichte der Kirchenverfassung und des Kirchenrechts [1886]: TU 2. B 1991, Akademie. iv-719 p. DM 280. 3-05-001823-2 [NTAbs 36,446].

k627 **Jefford** C.N., The sayings of Jesus in the Teaching of the Twelve Apostles: VigChr supp. 11, 1989 ➤ 6,k161; 7,g43: ᴿCBQ 54 (1992) 354 (J.S. *Kloppenborg*: some merits, but poorly organized); Salmanticensis 38 (1991) 238-240 (R. *Trevijano*).

k628 *Draper* Jonathan A., Christian self-definition against the 'hypocrites' in Didache 8: ➤ 478, SBL Sem. 31 (1992) 362-377.

k629 *Henderson* Ian H., *Didache* and orality in synoptic comparison: JBL 111 (1992) 283-306.

k630 **Harnack** Adolf von, *al.*, Die Überlieferung der griechischen Apologeten des zweiten Jahrhunderts in der Alten Kirche und im Mittelalter [1882s]: TU 1. B 1991, Akademie. xiii-731 p. DM 280. 3-05-001822-4 [NTAbs 36,446].

k631 *a*) *Faivre* Alexandre, Apostolicité et pseudo-apostolicité dans la Constitution ecclésiastique des apôtres; l'art de faire parler les origines; – *b*)

Metzger Marcel, À propos des règlements ecclésiastiques et de la prétendue Tradition Apostolique: RevSR 68 (1992) 19-67 / 249-261.

k632 AD DIOGNETUM: ᵀᴱ**Morelli** Enrico, A Diogneto: Letture Cristiane del Primo Millennio 11. T 1991, Paoline. 180 p.

k633 **Rizzi** M., La questione dell'unità dell'"Ad Diognetum' 1989 ➤ 5,g681 ... 7,g45: ᴿAsprenas 39 (1992) 441 (L. *Fatica*); Athenaeum 79 (1991) 689s (F. *Gasti*); Mnemosyne 45 (1992) 257-9 (J.J. *Thierry*); Salesianum 54 (1992) 170-3 (C. M. *Mukesyali*); TR 88 (1992) 204s (H. E. *Lona*).

k634 *Rizzi* Marco, Tre lettori dell'Ad Diognetum nel XX secolo; BUONAIUTI, PELLEGRINO, LAZZATI: RivStoLR 27 (1991) 483-495.

k635 HERMAS: ᴱ**Brox** Norbert, Der Hirt des Hermes KeK Egb 7, 1991 ➤ 7,g46: ᴿErbAuf 68 (1992) 79 (B. *Schwank*: klarer Kommentar zu einem der schwierigsten Bücher der frühchristlichen Literatur); ExpTim 103 (1991s) 275 (E. *Best*);Neotestamentica 26 (1992) 535s (H. F. *Stander*); SNTU A-17 (1992) 279-281 (F. *Weissengruber*).

k636 ᴱ**Carlini** Antonio, (*Giacone* Luigi), Erma, Bodmer 38, 1991 ➤ 7,g47: ᴿAnnTh 6 (1992) 215-7 (M. *Bandini*); Biblica 73 (1992) 135s (J. O'Callaghan); NT 34 (1992) 302s (A. *Kirkland*); RÉG 105 (1992) 614s (P. *Nautin*); RHE 87 (1992) 147-150 (P. *Henne*).

k637 *Carlini* Antonio, Testimone e testo; il problema della datazione di PI and I 4 del Pastore di Erma: StClasOr 42 (1992) 17-30; 2 pl.

k639 **Henne** Philippe, L'unité du Pasteur d'Hermas, tradition et rédaction: CahRB 31. P 1992, Gabalda. 196 p. F 190. 2-85021-054-4.

k640 *Henne* Philippe, Un seul 'Pasteur', un seul Hermas: RTLv 23 (1992) 482-8; Eng. 607.

k641 ᴱ**Jardine** William, Shepherd of Hermas; the gentle apocalypse. Redwood City CA 1992, Proteus. xi-159 p. $10 pa. [CBQ 54,834].

k642 *Kirkland* Alastair, The literary history of the Shepherd of Hermas visions I to IV: SecC 9 (1992) 87-102.

k643 **Leutzsch** Martin, Die Wahrnehmung sozialer Wirklichkeit im 'Hirten des Hermas': FRL 150, 1989 ➤ 5,g686 [ind.!] ... 7,g69: ᴿCBQ 54 (1992) 575-7 (Carolyn *Osiek*: good); Gregorianum 73 (1992) 766s (M. *Chappin*); TR 88 (1992) 123s (Maria-Barbara von *Stritzky*).

k644 **Maier** Harry O., The social setting of the ministry as reflected in the writings of Hermas, CLEMENT and IGNATIUS ᴰ1991 ➤ 7,g50: ᴿJTS 43 (1992) 668-670 (W. A. *Meeks*); TS 53 (1992) 383s (M. *Hollerich*).

k645 **Osiek** Carolyn, Rich and poor in the Shepherd of Hermas; CBQ Mg 15, 1983 ➤ 64,d724 ... 1,f113: ᴿRB 99 (1992) 581-6 (P. *Henne*).

k646 *Osiek* Carolyn, The social function of female imagery in second century prophecy [Hermas Visions 1-4; the church as woman who becomes progressively younger; Panarion 49,1]: VetChr 29 (1992) 55-74.

k647 IGNATIUS A.: ᴱ**Ayán Calvo** J.J., Ignacio de Antioquía, Cartas; POLICARPO de Esmirna. Carta; Carta de la Iglesia de Esmirna a la Iglesia de Filamelio 1991 ➤ 7,g51: ᴿBLitEc 93 (1992) 258-260 (J.-P. *Houdret*); ComSev 24 (1991) 425s (M. *Sánchez*); Helmantica 43 (1992) 422-4 (J. *Mazas*); RÉAug 38 (1982) 188-191 (A. *Viciano*); ScripTPamp 23 (1991) 1029-1033 (también A. *Viciano*); StPatav 38 (1991) 446s (C. *Corsato*).

k648 **Bleynberg** Ursula, Die Gegenwart Christi in der Kirche; eine theologische Untersuchung zu den Briefen des hl. Ignatius von Antiochien: diss. S. Croce. R 1991. 244 p. – ᴿScripTPamp 24 (1992) 1092s (A. *Viciano*).

k649 **Legarth** Peter V., Guds tempel; tempelsymbolisme og kristologi hos Ignatius af Antiokia: Menighedsfak. 3. Århus 1992, Kolon [SvEx 58,187, L. *Koen*].

k650 **Patrick** Mary W., Ethos in epistles; rhetorical analyses of Ignatius' epistles: diss. Lutheran School of Theology 1992, ᴰ*Krentz* E. 447 p. 92-33423. – DissA 53 (1992s) 2357-A.

k650* *Wilkins* Michael J., The interplay of ministry, martyrdom, and discipleship in Ignatius of Antioch: ➤ 126, ᶠWILKINS R., 1992, 294-315.

k651 ᵀᴱ*Rius-Camps* Josep, L'epistolari d'Ignasi d'Antioquia (IV), Carta espúria als Filadelfis; segona part de la primitiva carta d'Ignasi als Magnesis: RCatalT 17 (1992) 43-84.

k652 **Trevett** Christine, A study of Ignatius of Antioch in Syria and Asia: StBeC 29. Lewiston NY 1992, Mellen. 248 p. $70 [TR 88,519].

k653 IRENAEUS: **Balthasar** H. v., The scandal of the Incarnation; Irenaeus against the heresies. Harrison NY 1991, Ignatius. 111 p. $11. – ᴿHomP 92,5 (1991s) 75s (J. R. *Sheets*: enriching).

k654 **Fantino** Jacques G. D., La théologie de saint Irénée; lecture trinitaire des Écritures en réponse à l'exégèse gnostique: diss. ᴰ*Derousseaux* L. Lille 1992. 420 p. – RTLv 24, p. 551.

k655 **Fantino** Jacques, L'homme image de Dieu... IRÉNÉE ᴰ1986 ➤ 2,1454; 3,1957: ᴿBijdragen 53 (1992) 330s (Heleen van de *Reep*).

k656 **Orbe** Antonio, Espiritualidad de S. Ireneo: AnGreg 256, 1989 ➤ 5, g698...7,g58: ᴿTLZ 117 (1992) 610 (J. *Irmscher*).

k657 **Orbe** Antonio, Teología de San Ireneo V/3, 1988 ➤ 5,g697; 6,k81: ᴿRechSR 80 (1992) 106s (B. *Sesboüé*, aussi sur sa Spiritualité 1989).

k658 **Romero Posé** E. [< *Orbe* A.], Ireneo de Lión, Demostración de la predicación apostólica: Fuentes Patrísticas 2. M 1992, Ciudad Nueva. 262 p. – ᴿSalmanticensis 39 (1992) 409-411 (R *Trevijano*).

k659 **Torisu** Yoshifumi, Gott und Welt; eine Untersuchung zur Gotteslehre des Irenäus von Lyon [Diss. Wien 1990]: StudVD 52, 1992 ➤ 7,g59, DM 54,80; 3-8050-0286-6: ᴿForKT 8 (1992) 311 (M. *Hauke*); MüTZ 43 (1992) 373-5 (R. *Hanig*).

k660 ᵀᴱ**Unger** Dominic J., St. Irenaeus of Lyons, Against the heresies: AncChrW 55. NY 1992, Paulist. I. vii-300 p. 0-8091-0454-7.

k661 JUSTINUS: *a*) *Hengel* M., Die Septuaginta als von den Christen beanspruchte Schriftensammlung bei Justin und den Vätern vor Origenes; – *b*) *Horbury* W., Jewish–Christian relations in BARNABAS and Justin Martyr: ➤ 467, Jews & C 1989/92, 39-84 / 315-345.

k662 *Hirshman* Marc, Polemic literary units in the classical midrashim and Justin Martyr's Dialogue with Trypho: JQR 83 (1992s) 369-384.

k663 *Keith* Graham, Justin Martyr and religious exclusivism: TyndB 43,1 (1992) 57-80.

k664 *Marcovich* Miroslav, Notes on Justin Martyr's Apologies: ILCL 17 (1992) 323-335.

k665 *a*) *Nahm* Charles, The debate on the 'Platonism' of Justin Martyr; – *b*) *Guerra* Anthony J., The conversion of Marcus Aurelius and Justin Martyr; the purpose, genre, and content of the first apology: SecC 9 (1992) 129-151 / 171-187.

k666 *Rizzi* Marco, 'Iustitia' et 'veritas'; l''exordium degli scritti apologetici di Giustino, ATHENAGORA, TERTULLIANO: Aevum 65 (1991) 125-149.

k667 *Wartelle* A., Le traité De la résurrection de S. Justin ou le destin d'une œuvre: ➤ 124, [F]MARCHASSON 1992, 3-10.

Y1.6 **Origenes.**

k668 *Amphoux* Christian, *Mēdeìs prositō pepaideuménos*, un écho de la devise de l'Académie de Platon chez CELSE?: RÉG 105 (1992) 247-252.

k669 **Clark** Elizabeth A., The Origenist controversy; the cultural construction of an early Christian debate. Princeton 1992, Univ. xii-287 p. $45. 0-691-03173-8 [TDig 40,157].

k670 **Crouzel** Henri, Origen, [T]*Worrall* A. S., 1989 ➤ 5,g707 ... 7,g70: [R]RExp 89 (1992) 131s (E. G. *Hinson*: grand! despite poor proofreading).

k671 *Crouzel* H., Chronique origénienne: BLitEc 93 (1992) 225-230.

k672 *Crouzel* Henri, Ekklesiastikós et Ecclesiasticus dans l'œuvre d'Origène: ➤ 164, [F]SAXER V., Memoriam sanctorum 1992, 147-169: as noun, a member of the Church; 'cleric' only secondarily.

k673 [TE]**Daly** R. J., Origen, treatise on the Passover and dialogue with Heraclides and his fellow bishops on the Father, the Son, and the soul: Ancient Christian Writers 54. NY 1992, Paulist. vi-121 p. $17. 0-8091-0452-0 [BL 93,92, R. P. R. *Murray*].

k674 *Dillon* J., Origen and PLOTINUS; the Platonic influence on early Christianity: ➤ 547, Neoplatonism 1990/2, 7-26.

k675 *Edwards* M. J., Origen no gnostic; or, on the corporeality of man: JTS 43 (1992) 23-37.

k676 *Évieux* Pierre, Christianisme et religions païennes [FÉDOU M. 1988]: RechSR 80 (1992) 409-418.

k677 **Fédou** Michel, Christianisme et religions païennes dans le Contre CELSE d'Origène 1989 ➤ 5,g708 ... 7,g74: [R]LavalTP 48 (1992) 458-460 (Anne *Pasquier*); RÉAug 37 (1991) 163-5 (A. *Le Boulluec*: rigueur et maîtrise); RTPhil 124 (1992) 343s (É. *Junod*); Spiritus 32 (1991) 96-98 (M. *Oger*); TvT 32 (1992) 96 (A. *Davids*).

k678 **Galluccio** G. A., Origene 'l'Adamanzio' e il Papa; Storia ecclesiastica aversana 1. Giugliano 1990, Aurani. 153 p. Lit. 23.000. – [R]Asprenas 39 (1992) 276 (L. *Fatica*).

k679 *Hällström* Gunnar af, Probleme der Bibelauslegung bei Origenes: ➤ 475*b*, Bibelauslegung 1992, 36-44.

k680 **Hauck** R., More divine proof... Origen 1989 ➤ 5,g708; 7,g77: [R]ChH 61 (1992) 394s (Antonía *Tripolitis*).

k681 *Heither* Theresia, 'Gotteserfahrung' in der Theologie des Origenes: Erb-Auf 68 (1992) 265-278.

k682 *Jackson* Howard M., The setting and sectarian provenance of the fragment of the 'celestial dialogue' preserved by Origen from CELSUS's *Alēthēs lógos*: HarvTR 85 (1992) 273-305.

k683 *Junod* Eric, Origenismus, [T]*Buttkus* I.: ➤ 757, EvKL 3 (1992) 934-8.

k684 *a*) *Junod* Éric, L'auteur de l'Apologie pour Origène traduite par RUFIN; – *b*) *Jourjon* Maurice, De trois banalités origéennes [sic]; – *c*) *Brésard* Luc, AELRED de Rievaulx et Origène; – *d*) *Cabié* Robert, Le dimanche et le temps pascal au temps d'Origène: ➤ 35, [F]CROUZEL H., Recherches 1992, 165-179 / 153-163 / 21-46 / 47-60.

k685 [E]**Kannengiesser** C., Petersen W. L., Origen... legacy 1986/8 ➤ 5,683 ... 7,g79: [R]ChH 60 (1991) 88-90 (Elizabeth A. *Clark*).

k686 *Kranitz* Mihaly, La fonction de la conscience et de l'ange gardien chez Origène: BLitEc 93 (1992) 199-208; Eng. 208.

k687 **Lies** Lothar, Origenes' 'Peri archon', eine undogmatische Dogmatik; Einführung und Erläuterung: Werkinterpretationen. Da 1992, Wiss. xi-218 p. DM 40 [TR 88,429].

k688 *Lies* Lothar, Zur Exegese des Origenes: TR 88 (1992) 89-96.

k688* *McGuckin* John A., Origen on the Jews: ➤ 638, C/Judaism 1992, 1-13.

k689 *a) Meis W.* Anneliese, La preeminencia de Jesús; interrelación filosófica-teológica en la obra de Orígenes; – *b) Ossandón* Pedro, *Rodríguez* Pedro, El método de Orígenes: TVida 33 (1992) 65-79 / 185-191.

k690 **Neuschäfer** Bernhard, Origenes als Philologe 1987 ➤ 3,g177 ... 7,g82: ᴿGnomon 64 (1992) 394-7 (Herwig *Görgemanns*).

k691 **Nevis** Fernando Leonard, Origen's presentation of Christianity among other religions: diss. Innsbruck 1991s, ᴰ*Lies* L. – ZkT 114 (1992) 499.

k692 **Pietras** Henryk, L'amore in Origene 1988 ➤ 4,h761 ... 6,k116: ᴿRÉ-Aug 37 (1991) 166 (A. *Le Boulluec*).

k692* *Ricken* Friede, Origenes über Sprache und Transzendenz: ➤ 108, ᶠKREMER K. 1992, 75-92 [115-192 *al.*, AUGUSTINUS, SCOTUS, CUSANUS].

k693 **Rowe** J. Nigel, Origen's doctrine of subordination; a study in Origen's Christology; EurUnivSt 23/279, 1987 ➤ 4,h762: ᴿChH 61 (1992) 76 (J. W. *Trigg*).

k694 *Rubenson* Samuel, The letters of St. Anthony, Origenist theology ... 1990 ➤ 7,g86: ᴿOrChr 76 (1992) 255-8 (C. D. G. *Müller*); RÉAug 37 (1991) 171s (G. J. M. *Bartelink*).

k695 **Schockenhoff** Eberhard, Zum Fest der Freiheit; Theologie des christlichen Handelns bei Origenes: TüTSt 33, 1990 ➤ 7,g87: ᴿJTS 43 (1992) 239-241 (M. J. *Edwards*); RTLv 23 (1992) 222s (A. de *Halleux*); Salesianum 54 (1992) 808s (G. *Abbà*); TvT 32 (1992) 97 (F. van de *Paverd*).

k696 **Scott** Alan, Origen and the life of the stars 1991 ➤ 7,g88: ᴿExpTim 103 (1991s) 218 (G. *Bostock*).

k697 **Smith** J. C., The ancient wisdom of Origen. Lewisburg PA 1992, Bucknell Univ. 372 p. £35 [RHE 87,254*; TDig 40,187].

k698 **Torjesen** Karen Jo, Hermeneutical procedure and theological method in Origen's exegesis 1986 ➤ 2,d316 ... 6,k119: ᴿJbAC 34 (1991) 200-3 (R. *Gögler*); RExp 89 (1992) 137s (C. J. *Scalise*).

k699 *Williams* Rowan, METHODIUS von Olympus [Gegner Origenes'], ᵀ*Schnitker* Thaddäus: ➤ 768, TRE 22 (1992) 680-4.

Y1.8 **Tertullianus.**

k700 *Aland* Barbara, MARCION: ➤ 768, TRE 22 (1992) 89-101.

k701 ᴱ**Azzali Bernardelli** Giovanna, Tertulliano, Scorpiace: BtPatr 14. F 1990, Nardini. 338 p. – ᴿRivStoLR 27 (1991) 535-552 (P. A. *Gramaglia*, dettagliatissimo).

k702 ᵀᴱ**Braun** René, Tertullien, Contre Marcion I-II: SChr 365.368, 1990s ➤ 6,k122; 7,g92: ᴿAntClas 61 (1992) 422-5 (H. *Savon*, 1); BLitEc 93 (1992) 261 (H. *Crouzel*); EsprVie 102 (1992) 600s (Y.-M. *Duval*); ÉtClas 60 (1992) 173 (F. X. *Druet*); Gregorianum 73 (1992) 363-5 (G. *Pelland*); JTS 43 (1992) 238s (M. *Winterbottom*: 'outguns EVANS'); MélSR 49 (1992) 49s (M. *Spanneut*); NRT 114 (1992) 758 (V. *Roisel*); RÉAnc 94 (1992) 492s (Simone *Deléani*: présentation impeccable); RÉLat 70 (1992) 291-3 (F. *Chapot*: grand progrès, mais sans index surtout scripturaire); RTPhil 124 (1992) 195s (É. *Junod*, 1).

Braun René, Approches de Tertullien (2 inédits + 24) 1992 ➤ 217b.

k703 **Hagendahl** Harald, Cristianesimo latino e cultura classica, da Tertulliano a Cassiodoro [Von Tertullian 1983], ᵀ*Gianotti* Daniele; intr. *Siniscalco* Paolo: CuCrAnt, 1988 ➤ 5,g869; 7,g96: ᴿLatomus 51 (1992) 193s (J. *Doignon*); Salesianum 54 (1992) 830s (S. *Felici*).

k704 ᵀᴱ**Heine** Ronald E., The Montanist oracles and testimonia: NAm PatrMg 14, 1989 ➤ 5,g732... 7,g98: ᴿCathHR 78 (1992) 99 (K. B. *Steinhauser*: excellent); ChH 61 (1992) 75s (R. M. *Grant*); ScotJT 45 (1992) 416-8 (J. *McGuckin*).

k705 *Kaufman* Peter I., Tertullian on heresy, history and the reappropriation of revelation: ➤ ᶠ(dedicated to) BRAUER J., ChH 60 (1991) 167-179.

k706 ᵀᴱ**Mattei** Paul, Tertullien, Le mariage unique: SChr 343, 1988 ➤ 4, b769... 7,g101: ᴿRÉLat 70 (1992) 290s (S. *Deléani*); MélSR 48 (1991) 247s (M. *Spanneut*).

k707 ᵀᴱ**Micaelli** Claudio, Tertulliano, La risurrezione dei morti. R 1990, Città Nuova. 217 p. Lit. 20.000. – ᴿCC 143 (1992,2) 206s (G. *Cremascoli*).

k708 *Orbe* Antonio, Hacia la pneumatología de Marcion: Compostellanum 36 (1991) 7-42.

k709 **Quellet** Henri, Concordance verbale du De exhortatione castitatis de Tertullien: Alpha-Omega A-131. Hildesheim 1992, Olms-Weidmann. [iv-] 236 p. 3-487-09501-7.

k710 *Schneider* André, O testimonium animae naturaliter christianae! (Tertullien, Apol. 17,6) [en français]: MusHelv 48 (1991) 320-8.

k711 ᵀ**Steely** John E., *Bierma* Lyle D., Adolf von HARNACK, Marcion, the Gospel of the Alien God [1924] 1990 ➤ 7,g97*: ᴿExpTim 103 (1991s) 347 (S. N. C. *Lieu*); PerspRelSt 19 (1922) 97-100 (E. G. *Hinson*).

k712 *Vassileiou* Alain, Les éponges des rétiaires [n'existaient pas: contre TURCAN, Tertullien Spect. SChr 332, 1986]: DialHA 18,2 (1992) 137-162.

k713 *Veltri* Giuseppe, Dalla tesi giudeo-ellenistica del 'plagio' dei greci al concetto rabbinico del verus Israel; disputa sull'appartenenza della *sofia* [... Tertulliano]: RCatalT 17 (1992) 85-104; Eng. 104.

Y2 *Patres graeci* – **The Greek Fathers.**

k714 *a) Alonso Díaz* José, La espiritualización del 'Reino' en la línea de la 'aculturación' del Cristianismo dentro del Imperio Romano; – *b) Dorival* G., Hellénisme et patristique grecque, continuité et discontinuité; – *c) Spanneut* M., L'impact de l''apatheia' stoïcienne sur la pensée chrétienne jusqu'à S. Augustin: Antigüedad y Cristianismo 7 (Murcia 1990) 73-89 / 27-37 / 39-52 [< RHE 87,496*].

k715 **Armstrong** A. H., Hellenic and Christian studies: CS 321, 1990 ➤ 6,197: ᴿClasR 42 (1992) 94-6 (R. M. *Atkins*).

k716 **Aubin** Paul, PLOTIN et le christianisme; triade plotinienne et Trinité chrétienne: ArchPh Bt 55. P 1992, Beauchesne. 238 p. F 180. 2-7010-1258-9.

k717 **Betz** Hans-Dieter, Hellenismus und Urchristentum [16 reprints] 1990 ➤ 6,199: ᴿGnomon 64 (1992) 212-6 (F. *Siegert*).

k718 ᴱ**Camelot** P., al., Les conciles œcuméniques 1s, 1988 ➤ 6,g990a: ᴿÉglT 23 (1992) 280-2 (J. K. *Coyle*).

k719 **Chrestos** Panagiotis K., Ⓖ Greek patrology 5, pre-Byzantine. Thessaloniki 1992, Kyromanos. 728 p. – ᴿTAth 63 (1992) 870-3 (P. *Simotas*).

k720 *Contreras* Enrique, 'Guia' de traducciones castellanas de los Padres prenicenos (siglos I-IV), Padres Griegos: Salmanticensis 39 (1992) 277-295.

k721 **Dillon** John,   The golden chain; [28] studies in the development of Platonism and Christianity CS 33,   1990 → 6,220; £43.50.   0-86078-286-7. – ᴿJTS 43 (1992) 817s (C. *Stead*).

k721* *Gasti* Fabio,   L'oro degli Egizi; cultura classica e paideia cristiana: Athenaeum 80 (1992) 311-329.

k722 **Geyer** Carl-Friedrich,   Religion und Diskurs; die Hellenisierung des Christentums aus der Perspektive der Religionsphilosophie ᴰ1990; → 6, k140; 7,g107; DM 48: ᴿActuBbg 29 (1992) 207s (J. *Boada*); MüTZ 43 (1992) 466-8 (T. *Böhm*); RSPT 76 (1992) 637-9 (G.-M. de *Durand*).

ᴱ**Heim** S. Mark,   Faith to creed; ecumenical perspectives on the affirmation of the apostolic faith in the fourth century 1991 → 7719.

k723 *Hult* Karin,   Mᴀʀɪɴᴜs [Neoplatonist, successor of Pʀᴏᴄʟᴜs] the Samaritan; a study of Dᴀᴍᴀsᴄɪᴜs Vit. Isid. fr. 141: ClasMedv 43 (1992) 163-178.

k724 **Ivanka** Endre von,   Pʟᴀᴛᴏ christianus; la réception [1964] ᵀ1990 → 7,g109: ᴿLavalTP 48 (1992) 470s (L. *Painchaud*).

k725 *a*) *Lutz-Bachmann* Matthias,   Hellenisierung des Christentums? – *b*) *Honnefelder* Ludger,   Christliche Theologie als 'wahre Philosophie'; – *c*) *Schwenk* B.,   Hellenistische Paideia und christliche Erziehung; – *d*) *Irmscher* Johannes,   Inhalte und Institutionen der Bildung in der Spätantike; – *e*) *Berger* Klaus,   Antike Rhetorik und christliche Homiletik: → 648*, *Colpe* Spätantike 1992, 77-98 / 55-75 / 141-158 / 159-172 / 173-187.

k726 *a*) *Marcovich* Miroslav,   Platonism and Church Fathers; three notes; – *b*) *Mortley* Raoul,   The alien God in Arius; – *c*) *Armstrong* A. Hilary,   Plotinus and Christianity; – *d*) *Dillon* John,   Plotinus and the Chaldean Oracles: → 147, ᶠPʟᴀᴄᴇs E., des, Platonism 1992, 189-203 / 205-215 / 115-130 / 131-140.

k727 **Mazza** Enrico,   Mystagogy; a theology of liturgy in the patristic age, ᵀ. NY 1989, Pueblo.   xii-228 p. $14.50. – ᴿHeythJ 33 (1992) 91 (K. *Stevenson*: OT in preaching; ColMn has taken over Pueblo, and is represented by Columbia, Dublin).

k728 ᴱ**Murphy** Francis X., *Sherwood* Polycarp,   Konstantinopel II und III: (ᴱ*Dumeige* G., *Bacht* H.) Geschichte der Ökumenischen Konzilien 3, 1990 → 7,g112: ᴿTüTQ 172 (1992) 53-57 (H. J. *Vogt*, auch über 4,1985 und 5,1975).

k729 ᴱ**Oort** J. van, *Wickert* U.,   Christliche Exegese zwischen Nicaea und Chalcedon.   Kampen 1992, Kok Pharos.   226 p.

k730 **Panagopoulos** Johannes, ⓖ *Hermeneia* ... Interpretation of the Holy Scriptures in the Church of the Fathers 1-3 cent. and Alexandrian tradition till 5 cent., I: Orthodoxē martyría 38, 1991 → 7,e997: ᴿOstkSt 41 (1992) 62 (H. M. *Biedermann*); RHPR 72 (1992) 324s (A. *Papaconstantinou*).

k730* *Panagopoulos* Johannes,   Christologie und Schriftauslegung bei den griechischen Kirchenvätern: ZTK 89 (1992) 41-58.

k731 ᴱ**Riedlinger** Rudolf,   Concilium Constantinopolitanum 3, 680s, 2. Actiones XII-XVII, epistulae, indices: AcCOec 2/2.   B 1992, de Gruyter. xxxiv + p. 514-962.   DM 495 [TR 88,520].

k732 *Romanides* John S., ⓖ Church councils and civilization: TAth 63 (1992) 423-450.

k733 *Schmidt* Thomas E.,   Should Jerusalem honor Athens?: ChrSchR 21 (GR 1992) 249-253 [< zɪᴛ 92,353].

k734 *Sesboüé* Bernard, Bulletin de théologie patristique grecque [61 écrits, plusieurs ici]: RechSR 80 (1992) 95-156.

k735 **Stead** Christopher, Philosophie und Theologie [Verhältnisse], I. Die Zeit der Alten Kirche: TWiss 14/4, 1990 ➤ 7,g115: ᴿTR 88 (1992) 119-123 (B. *Studer*).

k736 **Tsirpanlis** Constantine N., Introduction to eastern patristic thought and Orthodox theology: Theology & Life 30, 1991 ➤ 7,g115*: ᴿTAth 63 (1992) 360s (E. D. *Moutsoulas*, Ⓖ).

k737 *Wyller* Egil A., The Platonic concept of rhetoric in 'Phaedrus' and its effect upon Christian rhetoric: TsTKi 63 (1992) 241-252 [in Norwegian; Eng. 252].

k737* *Wyrwa* Dietmar, Über die Begegnung des biblischen Glaubens mit dem griechischen Geist: ZTK 88 (1991) 29-67.

---

k738 APOLLINARIUS: **Spoerl** Kelley M., A study of the 'Katà méros pístis' by Apollinarius of Laodicea: diss. Toronto 1991. 428 p. DANN-65927. – DissA 53 (1992s) 534-A.

k739 ARIUS: **Hanson** R. P. C., The search for the Christian doctrine of God; the Arian controversy 1988 ➤ 4,8475 ... 7,7436: ᴿEvQ 64 (1992) 155-164 (T. A. *Hart*); RÉAug 37 (1991) 167s (J. *Doignon*); ScotJT 45 (1992) 101-111 (R. *Williams*).

k740 *Gliściński* Jan, ⊕ Apogeum Arianizmu (359-360 r.): ColcT 62,1 (1992) 43-55.

k741 *Runia* David T., A note on PHILO and Christian heresy ['father of Arianism' to moderns but not to Fathers]: StPhilonAn [3 (1991) 302] 4 (1992) 65-74.

k742 **Williams** R., Arius, heresy and tradition 1987 ➤ 3,g216 ... 7,g120: ᴿCrNSt 13 (1992) 209-212 (R. *Lorenz*, deutsch).

---

k743 ATHANASIUS: **Arnold** Duane W., The early episcopal career of Athanasius of Alexandria ᴰ1991 ➤ 7,g122: ᴿAnglTR 74 (1992) 389-391 (C. *Badger*); CathHR 78 (1992) 100s (T. D. *Barnes*); TS 51 (1992) 181s (G. H. *Ettlinger*: not a gangster).

k744 **Boulos** Washib H. K., St. Athanasius of Alexandria's doctrine of grace: diss. ᴰDragas G. Durham UK 1992. 336 p. – RTLv 24, p. 551: > Cairo Patristic Centre.

k745 *Devos* Paul, Les cinq premières lettres festales de saint Athanase d'Alexandrie, un test: AnBoll 110 (1992) 5-19.

k746 *Henne* Philippe, Athanase avait-il une version complète du Pasteur d'HERMAS?: RevSR 66 (1992) 69-76.

k747 **Kannengiesser** C., Athanase...: THist 70, 1983 ➤ 64,e45 ... 5,g760: ᴿÉglT 22 (1991) 225-7 (J. K. *Coyle*).

k748 *Piras* Antonio, Kritische Bemerkungen zur Schrift De Athanasio des LUCIFER von Calaris: VigChr 46 (1992) 57-74.

---

k749 BASILIUS: **Backus** Iréna, Lectures humanistes de Basile de Césarée; traductions latines (1439-1618): ÉtAugAntiquités 125, ➤ 7,g129: ᴿBt-HumRen 54 (1992) 551-3 (J. *Chomarat*); RÉByz 50 (1992) 297s (J. *Wolinski*); TLZ 117 (1992) 517s (K.-H. *Kandler*).

k750 **D'Alessandro** Angelo, L'unità della Chiesa nell'epistolario di Basilio di Cesarea: Vivere-In. R 1991, Monopoli. 83 p. Lit. 15.000. – ᴿRivScR 5 (1991) 497 (S. *Ramírez*).

k750* *Daoust* J., Monachisme et liturgie au temps des Pères cappadociens [*Gain* B., MondeB 70 (1991)]: EsprVie 102 (1992) 56-58.

k751 **Davies** Oliver, Gateway to Paradise; Basil the Great (T*Witherow* Tim): Spirituality of the Fathers 1. NY 1991, New City. 125 p. $8 pa. [CBQ 54,613].

k752 TE**Ducatillon** Jeanne [texte de *Neri* U. 1976], Basile de Césarée, Sur le baptême: SChr 357, 1989 ➤ 6,k169; 7,g131: RRivStoLR 27 (1991) 552-5 (Clementina *Mazzucco*).

k754 **Fenwick** John R. K., The anaphoras of St. Basil and St. James; an investigation into their common origin: OrChrAnal 240. R 1992, Pont. Inst. Orientale. xxvi-315 p.

k755 **Girardi** Mario, Basilio di Cesarea e il culto dei martiri nel IV secolo; [fondamento nella] Scrittura e tradizione: VetChrQuad 21. Bari 1990, Univ. 317 p. – RRÉAug 38 (1992) 202s (J.-N. *Guinot*).

k756 *Girardi* Mario, Note sul lessico esegetico di Basilio di Cesarea: VetChr 29 (1992) 19-53.

k757 **Maietta** Francesco, Il 'Discorso ai Giovani' di Basilio Magno; il cristianesimo e la cultura classica: diss. D*Longobardo* L. Napoli 1992. 200 p. – RTLv 24, p. 548.

k758 **Pouchet** Robert, Basile le Grand et son univers d'amis d'après sa correspondance; une stratégie de communion: StEphAug. 36. R 1992, Inst. Patristicum Augustinianum. 802 p.; 2 facsim.; 5 maps [RHE 87,255*]. – RAnBoll 110 (1992) 164-6 (P. *Devos*); BLitEc 93 (1992) 410s (H. *Crouzel*); EsprVie 102 (1992) 609s (Y.-M. *Duval*); ScripTPamp 24 (1992) 1093s (L. F. *Mateo-Seco*); TPhil 67 (1992) 586-8 (H. J. *Sieben*).

k759 *Pouchet* Jean-Robert, La date de l'élection épiscopale de saint Basile [370] et celle de sa mort [378]: RHE 87 (1992) 5-33.

k759* *Scholten* Clemens, Der Chorbischof bei Basilius [< Kolloquium 'Das kirchliche Amt im dritten und vierten Jht', 18.-19. Febr. 1991, Bonn, Univ. InstKG]: ZKG 103 (1992) 149-171 + 2 maps.

k760 TE**Risch** Franz Xaver, Pseudo Basilius, Adversus Eunomium IV-V: VigChr supp 16. Leiden 1992, Brill. vii-234 p. 90-04-09558-6.

k761 CHRYSOSTOMUS: *Aubineau* Michel, Restitution de quatorze folios du codex hiérosolymitain Photios 47, au codex Saint Sabas 32 [the three homilies (on Isaiah …) of Chrysostom thus complete a sequence of homilies 19-44]: JTS 43 (1992) 528-544.

k762 **Christofis** Gus G., The Church's identity established through images according to St. John Chrysostom: diss. Durham UK 1992. 499 p. BRD-97680. – DissA 53 (1992s) 3260-A.

k763 *a) Dupleix* André, Jean Chrysostome; un évêque social face à l'Empire; – *b) Cattenoz* Jean-Pierre, La philanthropie divine dans l'œuvre de Jean Chrysostome: ➤ 35, FCROUZEL H., Recherches 1992, 119-139 / 61-76.

k764 **Hall** Christopher A., John Chrysostom's 'On Providence'; a translation and theological interpretation: diss. Drew, D*Oden* T. Madison NJ 1991. – RTLv 24, p. 551.

k764* **Klasvogt** Peter, Leben zur Verherrlichung Gottes; Botschaft des Johannes Chrysostomos; ein Beitrag zur Geschichte der Pastoral: Hereditas 7. Bonn 1992, Borengässer. xxii-258 p. [RSPT 77,632, G.-M. de *Durand*: not 'patriarch'].

k765 **Krupp** Robert A., Shepherding the flock of God; the pastoral theology of John Chrysostom: AmerUnivSt 7/101. NY 1991, P. Lang. xviii-294 p. $50. 0-8204-1515-4 [TDig 39,368].

k766 *Leduc* Francis, Penthos et larmes dans l'œuvre de saint Jean Chrysostome: PrOrChr 41 (1991) 220-257; Eng. 219.

k767 ᵀᴱ**Malingrey** Anne-Marie, PALLADIOS, Dialogue sur la vie de Jean Chrysostome: SChr 341s, 1988 ➤ 4,h812... 7,g138: ᴿBijdragen 53 (1992) 443s (M. *Parmentier*, Eng.); RechSR 80 (1992) 131-3 (B. *Sesboüé*)

k768 **Malingrey** A. M., Indices chrysostomici II. De sacerdotio 1989 ➤ 5, g770: ᴿScripTPamp 24 (1992) 345s (D. *Ramos-Lissón*).

k769 ᴱ**Piédagnel** Auguste, Jean Chrysostome, Trois catéchèses baptismales: SChr 366, 1990 ➤ 6,k176; 7,g141: ᴿEstE 67 (1992) 124 (C. *Granado*).

k770 **Pleasants** Phyllis R., Making Antioch Christian; the city in the pastoral vision of John Chrysostom: diss. Southern Baptist Theol. Sem. 1991, ᴰ*Hinson* E. 206 p. 92-10176. – DissA 53 (1992s) 263-A.

k771 ᴱ**Schatkin** Margaret A., *al.*, Jean Chrysostome, Discours sur Babylas...: SChr 362, 1990 ➤ 6,k178; 7,g142 (non SChr 562): ᴿEsprVie 102 (1992) 612s (J.-M. *Duval*); JTS 43 (1992) 677-680 (J. N. D. *Kelly*); RHPR 72 (1992) 333 (P. *Maraval*); SMSR 16 (1992) 169-171 (S. *Zincone*).

k772 *Staats* Reinhart, Chrysostomus über die Rhetorik des Apostels Paulus; makarianische Kontexte zu 'De sacerdotio IV,5-6': VigChr 46 (1992) 225-240.

k773 **Taft** Robert F., A history of the liturgy of St. John Chrysostom, 4. (second to appear) The Diptychs: OrChrAnal 238, 1991 ➤ 7,g142*: ᴿIrénikon 65 (1992) 151 (B. *Lanne*); JTS 43 (1992) 716-8 (B. D. *Spinks*: challenging); TS 53 (1992) 592 (J. F. *Baldovin*).

k774 *Taft* R., The fruits of communion in the anaphora of St. John Chrysostom: ᶠPINELL J., Psallendum 1992, 275-302.

k775 *Voicu* Sever, Note su un'omelia pseudocrisostomica per il natale (CPG 5068; BHG 1920q): Orpheus 13 (1992) 354-363.

k776 **Wenk** Wolfgang, Zur Sammlung der 38 Homilien des Chrysostomus Latinus (mit Edition der Nr. 6, 8, 27, 32 und 33): WSt Beih 10, 1988 ➤ 7,g143: ᴿGnomon 64 (1992) 63s (J.-P. *Bouhot*, franç.).

k777 CYRILLUS A.: ᵀᴱ**Évieux** Pierre, *al.* [texte *Burns* W. H.], Cyrille d'Alexandrie, Lettres festales I (1-6): SChr 372, 1991 ➤ 7,g145: ᴿETL 68 (1992) 452-4 (A. de *Halleux*); JTS 43 (1992) 680-685 (L. R. *Wickham*: a fine book); RÉByz 50 (1992) 269s (J. *Wolinski*).

k778 *Halleux* André de, Les douze chapitres cyrilliens au concile d'Éphèse (430-433): RTLv 23 (1992) 425-58; Eng. 607.

k779 CYRILLUS S.: ᵀ**Price** R. M., ᴱ*Binne* John, Cyril of Scythopolis [c. 524-558], The lives of the monks of Palestine [Euthymius, Sabas]. Kalamazoo 1991, Cistercian. lii-306 p. $35; pa. $18. – ᴿTS 53 (1992) 782s (F. G. *McLeod*).

k780 DAMASCENUS: *Backus* Iréna, Jean Damascène, Dialogus contra Manichaeos; les traductions de M. MARGUNIOS (1572), de M. HOPPER (?) (1575), de J. de BILLY (1577) et de J. LEUNCLAVIUS (1578): RÉAug 38 (1992) 154-167.

k781 ᵀᴱ**Le Coz** Raymond, Jean Damascène, Écrits sur l'Islam: SChr 383. P 1992, Cerf. 272 p. 2-204-04676-0.

k781* *Montana* Fausto, Dal glossario all'esegesi; l'apparato ermeneutico al canone pentecostale attribuito a Giovanni Damasceno nel ms. Ottob. Gr. 248: StClasOr 42 (1992) 147-153; 154-164 testo greco.

k782 DIONYSIUS ALEX.: *Pietras* Henryk, L'unità del mondo secondo Dionigi Alessandrino; sviluppo di una tradizione: RasT 33 (1992) 363-386.

k783 DIONYSIUS PSEUD.-AREOP: ᵀᴱHeil Günter, Ps. Dionysius A., Über die himmlische Hierarchie; Über die kirchliche Hierarchie: BtGLit 22, 1986 ➤ 7,g152: ᴿTüTQ 172 (1992) 62-65 (H.J. *Vogt*, auch über SUCHLA B., Die Namen Gottes 1988).

k783* ᵀᴱMartín Teodoro H., Obras completas del Pseudo Dionisio Areopagita: BAC 551, 1990 ➤ 7,g154: ᴿScripTPamp 24 (1992) 342s (A. *Viciano*).

k784 ᴱSuchla Beate R. [I.; Heil G., *Ritter* A. II. ➤ 7,g152] Corpus Dionysiacum: PatrTSt 33.36, 1990s ➤ 7,g151: ᴿJTS 43 (1992) 266-8 (A. *Louth*: dazzling clarity).

k785 EPIPHANIUS: *a*) ᵀᴱAmidon Philip R., The 'Panarion' of St. Epiphanius, bishop of Salamis; selected passages 1990 ➤ 6,k192: ᴿRHE 87 (1991) 251s (D. *Bradley*: useful but no introd. or bibliog.).

— *b*) **Williams** Frank, The Panarion of Epiphanius of Salamis I (sects 1-46) 1987 ➤ 4,h824; 5,g783: ᴿJPseud 5 (1989) 113-7 (W. *Adler*).

k785* **Pourkier** Alain, L'hérésiologie chez Épiphane de Salamine: Christianisme antique 4. P 1992, Beauchesne. 539 p. F 570 [RSPT 77,627-630, G.-M. de *Durand*].

k786 **Dechow** Jon F., Dogma and mysticism... Epiphanius/ORIGEN 1988 ➤ 4,h821... 7,g155: ᴿHeythJ 33 (1992) 336s (A. *Louth*).

k786* **Stewart** Columba, 'Working...' [Epiphanius, *al.*] Messalian 1991 ➤ 7, g156: ᴿOstkSt 41 (1992) 343 (E. C. *Suttner*).

k787 *Kazhdan* Alexander, Epiphanios of Catania, a panegyrist of the council in Nicaea of 787 ?: Koinonia 15 (1991) 145-153.

k788 EUSEBIUS C.: ᶠGressmann Hugo [¹1904], ²ʳᵉᵛLaminski Adolf, Eusebius Pamphili, Werke 3/2: GrChrSchrSt. B 1992, Akademie. lxvii-277 p. 3-05-000871-7.

k789 ᴱPlaces Édouard des, Eusèbe, Préparation IX + VIII & X avec *Schroeder* G.: SChr 369, 1991 ➤ 7,g160: ᴿBLitEc 93 (1992) 412-4 (H. *Crouzel*: aussi 370-9); EsprVie 102 (1992) 604 (Y.-M. *Duval*); JEH 43 (1992) 502 (G. *Bonner*: paean for des Places at 90... 95 in 1995); JTS 43 (1992) 248s (H. *Chadwick*: the whole eighth book asserts the superiority of Hebrew to Greek culture); NRT 114 (1992) 758 (V. *Roisel*); RÉByz 50 (1992) 292s (J. *Wolinski*); RÉG 105 (1992) 632s (P. *Nautin*); RHPR 72 (1992) 331s (D. A. *Bertrand*); VigChr 46 (1992) 94s (J. C. M. van *Winden*); ZkT 114 (1992) 230s (K. H. *Neufeld*).

k790 ᴱAttridge Harold W., *Hata* Gohei, Eusebius, Christianity and Judaism: StPostB 42. Leiden 1992, Brill. 802 p. ƒ165. 90-0409-688-4. 30 art., mostly new ad hoc.

k790* *Backus* Irena, CALVIN's judgment of Eusebius of Caesarea; an analysis: SixtC 22 (1991) 419-437.

k791 *Hollerich* Michael J., Religion and politics in the writings of Eusebius; reassessing the first 'court theologian': ChH 59 (1990) 309-325.

k792 *Nautin* Pierre, La continuation de l'«Histoire ecclésiastique» d'Eusèbe par GÉLASE de Césarée: RÉByz 50 (1992) 163-183.

k793 **Christensen** Torben, RUFINUS of Aquileia and the History VIII-IX of Eusebius 1989 ➤ 5,g793... 7,g159: ᴿRHPR 72 (1992) 332 (P. *Maraval*); SvTKv 67 (1991) 138 (P. *Beskow*).

k794 *Norderval* Øyvind, Eusebius' Vita Constantini som kilde til forståelsen av splittelsene i Øst-kirken som følge av den arianske strid: NorTTs 93 (1992) 120-148.

k795 **Verheyden** Jozef, De vlucht van de Christenen naar Pella ... Eus. Epiph.
1988 ➤ 4,h833 ... 7,g163: ᴿRechSR 80 (1992) 120s (B. *Sesboüé*).

k796 EVAGRIUS [➤ 9878]: ᵀᴱ**Bunge** Gabriel, Evagrios Pontikos, Praktikos
oder Der Mensch; hundert Kapitel über das geistliche Leben: Koinonia
Oriens 32. Köln 1989, Luthe. 287 p. – ᴿFreibZ 39 (1992) 237-9 (G.
Descœudres).

k797 *O'Laughlin* M., The Bible, the demons and the desert; evaluating the
Antirrheticus of Evagrius Ponticus: StMonast 34 (1992) 201-215 [< RHE
88,30*].

k798 GREGORIUS NAZ.: *Demoen* Kristoffel, Biblical vs. non-biblical vocabulary in Gregorius Nazianzenus; a quantitative approach: ➤ 450,
Informatique 2, 1988/9, 243-253.

k799 *Kertsch* Manfred, Gregor von Nazianz und Johannes CHRYSOSTOMUS
bei NILUS dem Asketen: GrazBeit 18 (1992) 149-153; Lat. vi.

k800 ᴱMoreschini C., ᵀGallay P., Grégoire de Nazianze, Discours 38-41:
SChr 358, 1990 ➤ 6,k213: ᴿJbÖsByz 41 (1991) 324-6 (M. *Kertsch*); RasT
33 (1992) 595-7 (U. *Criscuolo*); RHPR 72 (1992) 335s (T. *Ziegler*).

k800* ᵀᴱ**Bernardi** Jean, Grégoire de Nazianze, Discours 42-43: SChr 384. P
1992, Cerf. 325 p. F 226. 2-204-04595-0 [NRT 115,432, V. *Roisel*].

k801 ᴱMoreschini Claudio, *Costa* Ivano, Niceta DAVID, Commento ai Carmina Arcana di Gregorio Nazianzeno: Storia e Testi 1. N 1992, D'Auria.
195 p. 88-7092-093-3.

k802 *Mattera* Lucia, LIBANIO, or. 17 e Gregorio di Nazianzo, or. 4: Koinonia 15 (1991) 139-143.

k803 **Norris** Frederick F., Faith gives fullness to reasoning; the five theological orations of Gregory Nazianzen: VigChr supp. 13; 1991 ➤ 7,g168:
ᴿAnglTR 74 (1992) 237-240 (T. A. *Kopecek*); RSPT 76 (1992) 625-8
(G.-M. de *Durand*).

k804 **Russell** Paul, Two replies to the Arians; a comparison of the theological
orations of Gregory of Nazianzus and the hymns and sermons on the
faith of EPHRAEM of Nisibis: diss. Catholic Univ., ᴰ*Darling* R. Washington D.C. 1992. – RTLv 24, p. 552.

k806 GREGORIUS NYSS.: **Harrison** Verna E. F., Grace and human freedom
according to St. Gregory of Nyssa [< diss. Berkeley GTU]: StBeC 30.
Lewiston NY 1992, Mellen. ii-286 p. $70. 0-7734-9542-8 [TDig 40,67].

k808 *Borrego* Enrique M., Aspectos plotinianos del conocimiento en la
exégesis bíblica de Gregorio de Nisa: EstE 67 (1992) 3-17.

k809 *Hart* Mark D., Gregory of Nyssa's ironic praise of the celibate life:
HeythJ 33 (1992) 1-19.

k810 ᵀᴱ**Lozza** Giuseppe, Gregorio di Nissa, Discorso sui defunti: Corona
Patrum, 1991 ➤ 7,g174; Lit. 40.000: ᴿGregorianum 73 (1992) 563s (G.
Pelland).

k811 ᵀᴱ**Maraval** Pierre, Grégoire de Nysse, Lettres: SChr 363, 1990 ➤ 6,
k219; 7,g175: ᴿAntClas 61 (1992) 415-8 (J. *Schamp*); JTS 43 (1992) 253s
(A. *Meredith*).

k812 **Meissner** Henriette M., Rhetorik und Theologie; der Dialog Gregors
von Nyssa De anima et resurrectione: Patrologie 1. Fra 1992, Lang. –
ᴿVigChr 46 (1992) 417-422 (J. C. M. van *Winden*).

k813 *Moreschini* Claudio, Il BESSARIONE e il testo dei Cappadoci; due note
[G. Nyss.; Basil.]: Koinonia 15 (1991) 71-74.

k814 GREGORIUS THAUMATURGUS: **Valantasis** Richard, Spiritual guides of the third century: diss. Harvard. Ph 1991, Fortress. 155 p. $17 pa. – RSecC 9 (1992) 189-191 (B. *Leyerle*).

k815 LEONTIUS N.: **Krueger** Derek, Cynics, Christians, and Holy Fools; the late antique contexts of Leontius of Neapolis' 'Life of Symeon the Fool': diss. DGager J. Princeton 1991. – RTLv 24, p. 551.

k816 MARCELLUS A.: **Feige** Gerhard, Die Lehre Markells von Ankyra in der Darstellung seiner Gegner [Diss. 1987] 1991 ➤ 7,g182: RJTS 43 (1992) 675s (M. *Slusser*); TPhil 67 (1992) 271s (H. J. *Sieben*).

k817 *Feige* Gerhard, Markell von Ankyra und das Konzil von Nizäa (325): ➤ 52, FErfurt 1992, 277-296.

k818 *Logan* Alastair H. B., Marcellus of Ancyra and the councils of AD 325; Antioch, Ancyra and Nicaea: JTS 43 (1992) 428-446.

k819 *Seibt* Klaus, Marcell von Ancyra (c. 280-374): ➤ 768, TRE 22 (1992) 83-89.

k820 MAXIMUS C. ELaga C., Steel C., Maximi confessoris Quaestiones ad Thalassium II, q. LVI-LXV una cum latina interpretatione Ioannis Scoti ERIUGENAE iuxtaposita: CCG 22. Turnhout/Lv 1990, Brepols/Univ. lxii-363 p. – RFreibZ 39 (1992) 515s (D. *O'Meara*).

k821 **Blowers** Paul M., Exegesis and spiritual pedagogy in Maximus the Confessor; an investigation of the 'Quaestiones ad Thalassium': Chr-JudAnt 7. ND 1992, Univ. xiv-288 p. $30 [TR 88,520; TDig 39,352].

k822 *Blowers* Paul M., Maximus the Confessor, GREGORY of Nyssa, and the concept of 'perpetual progress': VigChr 46 (1992) 151-171.

k823 **Gatti** Maria Luisa, Massimo, bibliog. 1987 ➤ 3,g256; 6,k222: RSalesianum 54 (1992) 363s (S. *Felici*).

k824 *Tollefsen* Torstein, Maximos Bekjennerens kristosentriske kosmologi: NorTTs 93 (1992) 189-198.

k825 *Vocht* Constant de, Maximus Confessor, TSchäferdiek K.: ➤ 768, TRE 22 (1992) 298-304.

k826 MELITO S.: **Angerstorfer** Ingeborg, Melito und das Judentum: kath. Diss. Rg. 1986 ➤ 4,b295: RSecC 9 (1992) 188s (Lynn *Cohick*).

k827 *Hall* Stuart G., Melito von Sardes, TSchäferdiek K.: ➤ 768, TRE 22 (1992) 424-8.

k828 PAULUS S.: *Perrone* Lorenzo, L'enigma di Paolo di Samosata; dogma, chiesa e società nella Siria del III secolo; prospettive di un ventennio di studi: CrNSt 13 (1992) 253-326; Eng. 327.

k829 ROMANOS M.: *Schork* R. J., [Romanos the Melodist] Sung sermons; melodies, morals and biblical interpretations in Byzantium: BR 7,2 (1991) 20-27 . 48.

k830 SERAPION: *a)* **Fitschen** Klaus, Serapion von Thmuis, echte und unechte Schriften sowie die Zeugnisse des ATHANASIUS und anderer [Diss. Kiel]: PatrTSt 36. B 1992, de Gruyter. xi-226 p. DM 108 [TR 88,520].
— *b)* **Johnson** Maxwell E., The prayers of Serapion of Thmuis [c. 339-360; 11th c. ms.]: diss. Notre Dame 1992, DBradshaw P. 400 p. 92-31406. – DissA 53 (1992s) 1965-A.
— *c)* *Wainwright* Geoffrey, A fresh look at the prayers of Sarapion of Thmuis: StLtg 22 (1992) 163-183 [< ZIT 92,666].

k830* SINAITA: *Olivar* Alexandre, Anastasi Sinaíta [segle VII] i el seu sermo sobre la sagrada sinaxi: RCatalT 16 (1991) 227-235; Eng. 235.

k831 SYNESIUS C.: *Long* Jacqueline, Dating an ill-fated journey; Synesius, ep. 5: AmPgTr 122 (1992) 351-380.

k832 *Lacombrade* Christian, Synésios de Cyrène, *nautikòs anēr*: Koinonia 15 (1991) 41-47.
k833 **Roos** Bengt-Anne, Synesius of Cyrene, a study on his personality: StGrLat. 2, 1991 ➤ 7,g190: Sk 180; 0-86238-277-7: ᴿAntClas 61 (1992) 418-421 (J. *Schamp*).
k834 **Roques** Dennis, Études sur la correspondance de Synésios de Cyrène: Coll. Latomus 205, 1989 ➤ 7,g191: ᴿGymnasium 99 (1992) 350s (J. *Gruber*).
k835 TATIANUS S.: ᵀᴱ**Di Cristina** Salvatore, Taziano il Siro, Discorso ai Greci; apologetica cristiana e dogmi della cultura pagana. R 1991, Borla. 170 p. Lit. 20.000. – ᴿCC 143 (1992,3) 204s (A. *Orazzo*).
k836 THEODORETUS C.: **Viciano Vives** Alberto, Cristo el autor de nuestra salvación... Teodoreto / Paulinas 1990 ➤ 7,5184: ᴿBurgense 33 (1992) 306s (F. *Pérez Herrero*); RÉAug 38 (1992) 202-4 (J.-N. *Guinot*); ScEspr 44 (1992) 102s (B. de *Margerie*); SMSR 16 (1992) 171-3 (S. *Zincone*); TGL 82 (1992) 256-8 (H. R. *Drobner*). ➤ 6195.
k837 ᵀᴱ**Halton** Thomas, Theodoret of Cyrus, On divine providence: AncChrW 49. NY 1988, Newman. vii-230 p. 0-8091-0430-2.
k838 THEODORUS M.: **Zaharopoulos** Dimitri Z., Theodore of M. on the Bible 1989 ➤ 5,g818 ... 7,g196: ᴿCalvinT 26 (1991) 235-8 (J. R. *Payton*); RechSR 80 (1992) 136-8 (B. *Sesboüé*).
k839 THEODOTUS A.: *Lo Castro* Giovanni, Osservazioni su un'omelia greca sul battesimo confrontata con omelie di Teodoto d'Ancira [... autore diverso]: Orpheus 13 (1992) 295-314 [364-8 citazione di un Ps.-Teodoto].

---

k840 G. PALAMAS: ᵀᴱ**Sinkewicz** Robert E., St. Gregory Palamas (1296-1359), The 150 chapters: StT 83. Toronto 1988, Pont. Inst. Medieval Studies. xi-283 p. – ᴿScEsp 44 (1992) 375s (J. *Lison*).
k841 CABASILAS N.: **Congourdeau** Marie-Hélène, N. Cabasilas (c. 1400), La vie en Christ: SChr 355.361, 1989s: ᴿAntClas 61 (1992) 437-9 (J. *Schamp*); Bijdragen 53 (1992) 435s (M. *Parmentier*, also on 320.336.363.356); EsprVie 102 (1992) 565s (Y.-M. *Duval*); JbÖsByz 42 (1992) 398-401 (J. A. *Munitiz*, Eng.); LavalTP 48 (1992) 474s (P.-H. *Poirier*); Speculum 67 (1992) 388s (M. *Philippides*).
k842 ᵀᴱ**Touraille** J., Philocalie des Pères Neptiques 10s, 1990s: ᴿEsprVie 102 (1992) 564s (Y.-M. *Duval*).
k842* **Touraille** Jacques, Nouvelle petite Philocalie; extraits thématiques de la Grande Philocalie Grecque: Perspective Orthodoxe 10. Genève 1992, Labor et Fides. 195 p. 2-8309-0657-8.
k843 *Paschos* P. B., Ⓖ The mystic-neptic Fathers and contemporary man: TAth 63 (1992) 94-116.

Y2.4 Augustinus.

k844 ᵀᴱ**Alici** Luigi, S. Agostino d'Ippona, La dottrina cristiana: Lett. Cr.I.Millen. 7. Mi 1989, Paoline. 392 p. – ᴿAthenaeum 80 (1992) 299s (F. *Gasti*); Orpheus 13,1 (1992) 197s (B. *Clausi*); Salesianum 54 (1992) 378s (O. *Pasquato*).
k845 *Ayres* Leuris, Between Athens and Jerusalem; prolegomena to anthropology in [Aug.] De trinitate: ModT 8 (1992) 53-73.
k846 ᴱ**Babcock** William S., The ethics of St. Augustine: JRelEth-St. Atlanta 1991, Scholars. 194 p. $45; pa. $30. 1-55540-660-2; -1-0. – ᴿVigChr 46 (1992) 427s (J. van *Oort*).

k846* *Bori* Pier Cesare, Figure materne e Scrittura in Agostino [*Destro* Adriana, commento]: ➤ 458, AnStoEseg 9,2 (1992) 397-420 [421-4]; Eng. 342.

k847 *Bray* Gerald, The doctrine of the Trinity in Augustine's De civitate Dei: European Journal of Theology 1,2 (Devon 1992) 141-150 [< ZIT 92,661].

k847* ᴱ**Carr** Thomas M.ᴶ, ARNAULD Antoine, Réflexions sur l'éloquence des prédicateurs (1695); GOIBAUT DU BOIS Philippe, Avertissement en tête de sa traduction de Saint Augustin (1694): Textes Littéraires Français. Genève 1992, Droz. 230 p. [RBgPg 71,770, F. *Deloffre*].

k848 **Ceriotti** Giancarlo, La pastorale delle vocazioni in S. Agostino. Palermo 1991, Augustinus. 152 p. Lit. 19.000. – ᴿVigChr 46 (1992) 1985s (J. den *Boeft*: piety based on solid scholarship; also CLERICI); ViPe 75 (1992) 394-7 (Elisabetta *Zambruno*).

k849 ᵀᴱ**Chadwick** Henry, Saint Augustine, Confessions. Oxford 1991, UP. xxviii-311 p. £17.50. 0-19-281779-5. – ᴿExpTim 103 (1991s) 56 (G. *Huelin*: hints Monica drank); JEH 43 (1992) 459-462 (G. *Bonner*: masterly among so many rivals); Manuscripta 35 (1991) 229-231 (V. J. *Bourke*).

k850 *Claussen* M. A., 'Peregrinatio' and 'peregrini' in Augustine's 'City of God': Traditio 46 (1991) 33-75.

k851 **Clerici** Agostino, Ama e fa' quello che vuoi; carità e verità nella predicazione di Sant'Agostino: Quaerere Deum 8. Palermo 1991, Augustinus. 208 p. – ᴿOrpheus 13 (1992) 426-433 (Paola *Santorelli*); ScuolC 120 (1992) 674-8 (Elisabetta *Zambruno*).

k853 ᴱ**Coyle** J. Kevin, *al.*, Agostino, De moribus... Manichaeorum 1991 ➤ 7,461: ᴿCC 143 (1992,3) 318s (G. *Cremascoli*); ETL 68 (1992) 456s (A. de *Halleux*); VigChr 46 (1992) 428-432 (J. van *Oort*).

k854 *Doignon* Jean, 'Les arts, appelés vertus, de bien vivre et de parvenir à une félicité immortelle' (Aug. ciu. 22,24,3); de l'usage de l'"exemple" des Romains: RÉAug 37 (1991) 79-86.

k855 *Dolbeau* François, Nouveaux sermons de saint Augustin pour la conversion des païens et les donatistes: RÉAug 37 (1991) 37-78 . 261-306.

k856 *Duval* Yves-Marie, Bulletin de patrologie latine: RechSR 80 (1992) 265-313; 42 livres, plusieurs infra; Nᵒ 13-20 (+ 42), Augustin.

k857 ᴱ**Eckermann** Willigis, *Krümmel* Achim, Repertorium annotatum operum et translationum S. Augustini: Cassiciacum 43/1. Wü 1992, Augustinus. xxxv-552 p.; 8 pl. DM 150, pa. 138. ᴿNRT 114 (1992) 907 (V. *Roisel*); TüTQ 172 (1992) 250 (R. *Reinhardt*).

k858 *Engelen* Eva-Maria, Erkennen und Glauben; die Zeit bei Augustin: ArBegG 35 (1992) 39-53.

k858* *Feiertag* Jean-Louis, Les Consultationes Zacchaei et Apollonii [peut-être d'Afrique c. 412 dans quelque rapport avec Augustin], étude d'histoire et sotériologie [tirée de son édition critique en préparation]: Paradosis 30. FrS 1990. 280 p. 3-8271-0495-4. – ᴿRechSR 80 (1992) 274-6 (Y.-M. *Duval*).

k859 *Fischer* Norbert, Übereinkunft und Überstieg; philosophische Betrachtungen zum Naturverständnis Augustins: TGL 82 (1992) 393-413.

k860 *Fuhrer* Thérèse, Das Kriterium der Wahrheit in Augustins Contra academicos: VigChr 46 (1992) 257-275.

k861 *Greer* Rowan A., The transition from death to life [Augustine in the decline of Rome]: Interpretation 46 (1992) 240-9.

k862 **Grier Smith** David E., The idea of justice in Augustine's criticism of Manicheism; diss. Dalhousie Univ. 1991. 260 p. DANN 71449. – DissA 53 (1992s) 4366-A.

k863 **Harrison** Carol, Beauty and revelation in the thought of Saint Augustine: TheolMg. Ox 1992, Clarendon. xi-289 p. $65. 0-19-826342-2 [TDig 40,166].

k864 *Jonge* H.J. de, Augustine on the interrelations of the Gospels: ➤ 137, ᶠNEIRYNCK F. 1992, 2409-2417.

k865 *Joubert* Catherine, Le livre XIII et la structure des Confessions de saint Augustin: RevSR 66 (1992) 77-117.

k866 *Keller* Miguel-Ángel, Para una lectura del pensamiento de San Agustín desde América Latina; práctica de inculturación; pasado, presente, futuro: CiuD 205,25 ('Presencia religioso-cultural de los Agustinos in América' 1992) 677-697.

k867 *Kienzler* Klaus, Der Aufbau der 'Confessiones' des Augustinus im Spiegel der Bibelzitate: RechAug 24 (1989) 123-164.

k867* **Kowalczyk** S., ❷ *Czlowiek i Bóg* [Man and God in St. Augustine] 1987 ➤ 7,g221 [.7168 titre français]: ᴿDivThom 94 (1991) 149-160 (I. *Kolodziejczyk*).

k868 **La Bonnardière** A.M., S. Augustin et la Bible: BTT 1986 ➤ 2,391 ... 5,g838: ᴿÉglT 22 (1991) 104-7 (J.K. *Coyle*).

k869 **Lanzi** Nicola, La Chiesa nella conversione di S. Agostino. Vaticano 1989. 53 p. – ᴿColcT 62,1 (1992) 182s (J. *Gliściński*, ❷).

k870 ᵀᴱ**Leinenweber** John, Letters of Saint Augustine. Tarrytown NY 1992, Triumph. 255 p. $10 [CBQ 54,615].

k871 **Lossano** M. (*Gorp* A. Van), Catalogus verborum quae in operibus S. Augustini inveniuntur XI, De sermone Domini in monte 1990, CCSL 35(+46). vi-167 p.; ƒ80 [XII De doctrina christiana, CCSL 32; De vera religione 32A; 1992; iii-116 p.; ƒ65]. Eindhoven, Thesaurus Ling. Aug. – ᴿNRT 114 (1992) 907s (V. *Roisel*).

k872 **McMahon** Robert, Augustine's prayerful ascent; an essay on the literary form of the Confessions. Athens 1989, Univ. Georgia. xxiv-175 p. $27.50. – ᴿAugSt 21 (1990) 177-186 (J.C. *Cavadini*); Speculum 67 (1992) 191-3 (K.F. *Morrison*).

k873 ᴱ**Madec** Goulven, *al.*, AGOSTINO d'Ippona 'De libero arbitrio': Settimana pavese 6. [5. De musica ➤ k886] 1990 ➤ 7,543c ('ᴱ*Pizzolato* L.F.'): ᴿTR 88 (1992) 483s (C. *Müller*).

k874 ᵀᴱ**Marcos Casquero** Manuel A., Escritos bíblicos 3º: Obras completas de San Agustín 27. M 1991, BAC. 566 p. – ᴿSalesianum 54 (1992) 599 (S. *Maheshe*).

k875 ᴱ**Mayer** Cornelius, *Chelius* Karl-Heinz, Internationales Symposium über den Stand der Augustinus-Forschung [Univ. Giessen, 12.-16. April 1987]: Cassiciacum 39/1, 1989 ➤ 5,707; 6,k267: ᴿRechSR 80 (1992) 280-2 (Y.-M. *Duval*).

k876 *Mayer* Cornelius, Caro-spiritus: ➤ 743, AugL 1,5s (1992) 743-759.

k877 ᴱ**Meynell** H.A., Grace, politics and desire; essays on Augustine. Calgary 1990, Univ. x-194 p. $20. 0-919813-55-0. – ᴿLatomus 51 (1992) 933-5 (F. *Capponi*, ital.).

k877* ᵀ**Mourant** John A., ᴱ*Collinge* William J., St. Augustine, Four anti-Pelagian writings; On nature and grace, On the proceedings of Pelagius, On the predestination of the saints, On the gift of perseverance: Fathers of the Church 86. Wsh 1992, Catholic University of America. xix-351 p. 0-8132-0086-3.

k878 *Nauta* R., De verloren zoon; enkele psychologische aspecten van Augustinus' bekering: NedTTs 46 (1992) 199-211; Eng. 226s.

k879 **Nazzaro** Antonio V., QUODVULTDEUS [corrispondente di Agostino], Promesse e predizioni di Dio: TPatr. R 1989, Città Nuova. 349 p. – RMaia 44 (1992) 124s (Nicoletta *Pavia*).

k880 ENicolosi Mauro, [*Pizzolato* L., ➤ g239] AGOSTINO a Milano; il battesimo: Agostino nelle terre di Ambrogio (II) [22-24.IV.1987]: Augustiniana Testi e Studi 3. Palermo 1988, Augustinus. 111 p. Lit. 28.000. – RHeythJ 32 (1991) 294-7 (B. R. *Brinkman*); TPQ 139 (1991) 216 (U. G. *Leinsle* menziona SORDI Marta, MARTINI Carlo M.).

k881 **O'Donnell** James J., Augustine, Confessions, I. Introduction and text; II. Commentary on books 1-7; III. books 8-13; indexes. Ox 1992, Clarendon. lxii-205 p.; xiii-484 p.; ... $85+115+110. 0-19-814378-8; 0-074-6; -075-4 [TDig 40,50].

k882 **Oort** Johannes van, Jerusalem and Babylon; a study into Augustine's City of God and the sources of his doctrine of the two cities [diss. Utrecht DQuispel G.], T: VigChr supp. 14, 1991 ➤ 7,g234; $103: RJEH 43 (1992) 116s (H. *Chadwick*); JTS 43 (1992) 258-260 (R. A. *Markus*: thorough; search for sources old-fashioned); TS 53 (1992) 347-9 (K. B. *Steinhauser*: bold).

k883 *Pani* Giancarlo, Il Contra Iulianum di Agostino nella Römerbrief-vorlesung di M. LUTERO: SMSR 58 (1992) 125-146.

k884 **Paronetto** V., Augustinus; de boodschap van een leven [1981],T. Averbode/Helmond 1991, Altiora/Helmond. 192 p. f29,90. 90-317- 0882-8. – RTvT 32 (1992) 315s (M. *Lamberigts*).

k885 **Pérez Paoli** Ubaldo Ramón, Der plotinische Begriff von *hypóstasis* und die augustinische Bestimmung Gottes als subiectum: Cassiciacum 41. Wü 1990, Augustinus. xxiv-236 p. DM 116. – RJbAC 34 (1991) 203s (C. *Stead*).

k886 EPizzani U., Milanese G., De musica: Lectio Aug. 5, 1990 ➤ 6,d372: RGregorianum 73 (1992) 567s (F.-A. *Pastor*, también sobre 6. MADEC G., y 7. COYLE J.).

k887 **Poque** Suzanne, Le langage symbolique ... d'Augustin 1984 ➤ 1,f622: RLatomus 51 (1992) 194s (Y.-M. *Duval*).

k888 **Prestel** Peter, Die Rezeption der ciceronischen Rhetorik durch Augustinus in 'De doctrina christiana' [Diss. Heid 1991, DAlbrecht M. v.]: StKlasPg 69. Fra 1992, Lang. 307 p. 3-631-44694-2.

k889 **Pucci** Joseph, The dilemma of writing; Augustine, Confessions 4,6 and HORACE Odes 1,3: Arethusa 24,2 (1991) 257-281.

k890 ERees B. R., The letters of Pelagius and his followers. Woodbridge 1991, Boydell. vi-355 p. £35. 0-85115-282-1. – RExpTim 103 (1991s) 218s (G. *Bonner*).

k891 *Schenker* Anton, Entzauberter Augustinus? [TSchäfer Walter, EFlasch Kurt, Logik des Schreckens, Div. Q. ad Simplicianum 1/2, Mainz 1990]: TR 88 (1992) 97-100.

k891* *Schmitt* E., Le 'sacramentum' dans la théologie augustinienne du mariage; analyse sémantique: Revue de Droit Canon 42,2 (1992) 173-195 [< RSPT 77,337].

k892 ESchnaubelt J. C., Fleteren F. Van, Collectanea 'Augustine, second founder of the faith' 1987/90 ➤ 6,688*a: RTPhil 67 (1992) 273-5 (H. J. *Sieben*).

k893 *Shanzer* Danuta, Latent narrative patterns, allegorical choices, and literary unity in Augustine's Confessions: VigChr 46 (1992) 40-56.

k894 **Starnes** C., Augustine's conversion ... Conf. I-IX, 1990 ➤ 6,k286: RVig-Chr 46 (1992) 303-5 (J. den *Boeft*).

k894* *Teske* Roland J., Augustine's Epistula X; another look at *deificari in otio*: AugR 32 (1992) 289-299.
k895 *a) Teske* Roland J., 'Homo Spiritualis' in the Confessions of St. Augustine; – *b) O'Meara* J. J., Augustine's Confessions; elements of fiction: ➤ 588, Rhetor 1992, 67-76 / 77-95.
k896 Thesaurus Augustinianus: CCThesA. Turnhout... Brepols. lxx-700 p. + microfiches. Fb 35.000. 2-303-60279-7. – ᴿBijdragen 53 (1992) 92s (M. *Parmentier*: includes Migne and CSEL as well as CCSL).
k897 *Tilley* Maureen A., Dilatory Donatists or procrastinating Catholics; the trial at the Conference of Carthage: ChH 60 (1991) 7-19.
k898 *Todisco* Orlando, Parola e verità; Agostino e la filosofia del linguaggio: MiscFranc 92 (1992) 436-493.
k899 **Vannier** M., Creatio/Aug. 1991. – ᴿArTGran 55 (1992) 358s (A. *Segovia*); WienerSt 105 (1992) 275-8 (Hildegund *Müller*).
k900 ᵀᴱ**Watson** Gerard, Saint Augustine, Soliloquies and Immortality of the soul: ClasTexts. Wmr 1990, Aris & P. x-213 p. £30; pa. 10.75. – ᴿGnomon 64 (1992) 726 (J. *Doignon*, franç.).
k901 *a) Zocca* Elena, Sapientia e libri sapienziali negli scritti agostiniani prima del 396; – *b) Studer* Basil, Agostino d'Ippona e il Dio dei libri sapienziali; – *c) Harrison* Carol, 'Who is free from sin?' The figure of Job in the thought of St. Augustine: ➤ 457*, LettureSap 1991/2, 97-114 / 115-125 / 483-8.

Y2.5 Hieronymus.

k902 *Adkin* Neil, *a)* Hieronymus ciceronianus; the Catilinarians in Jerome: Latomus 51 (1992) 408-420; – *b)* Jerome as centoist: Epist 22 [de virginitate], 38,7: RivStoLR 28 (1992) 461-471; – *c)* 'Oras, loqueris ad sponsum; legis, ille tibi loquitur' (Jerome, Epist. 22,25,1): VigChr 46 (1992) 141-150; – *d)* Some features of Jerome's compositional technique in the Libellus de virginitate servanda (Epist. 22): Philologus 136 (1992) 234-255; – *e)* 'Taceo de meis similibus' (Jerome, epist. 53,7): VetChr 29 (1992) 261-8.
k903 **Allegri** Giuseppina, I damna della mensa in San Girolamo 1989 ➤ 6,k295: ᴿLatomus 51 (1992) 246 (C. *Rambaux*); RÉAug 37 (1991) 168s (G. J. M. *Bartelink*).
k904 *Augustijn* Cornelis, Hieronymus in Luther 'De servo arbitrio': ➤ 22, ᶠBRACHT M., Luthers Wirkung 1992, 193-208.
k905 *Blázquez* José M., Aspectos de la sociedad romana del Bajo Imperio en las cartas de San Jerónimo: Gerión 9 (1991) 263-288.
k906 **Brown** Dennis, Vir trilinguis; a study in the biblical exegesis of Saint Jerome. Kampen 1992, Kok Pharos. 229 p. 90-390-0031-X.
k907 *Calabuig* Ignazio M., L'appellativo 'Stella maris' da Girolamo a Bernardo; schede per un repertorio: ➤ 519, Maria in S. Bernardo 1991, Marianum 54 (1992) 411-428.
k908 *Catellani* Cristina, *a)* Il buon uso delle ricchezze nell'epistolario di san Girolamo: CrNSt 13,1 (1992) 47-72; Eng. 72; – *b)* Immagini di 'servi' nell'epistolario di S. Gerolamo: StPatav 39 (1992) 557-568.
k909 ᵀᴱ**Ceresa-Gastaldo** Aldo, Gerolamo, Gli uomini illustri: BtPatr 12, 1988 ➤ 4,h883 (not 4883 as) 6,k298: ᴿOrpheus 13,1 (1992) 161s (F. *Corsaro*); Salesianum 54 (1992) 828 (S. *Felici*).
k910 *Ceresa-Gastaldo* Aldo, Figure e motivi femminili nell'epistolario di Gerolamo: Orpheus 13,1 (1992) 77-83.

k911 **Clark** Elizabeth A., Jerome, Chrysostom and [women] friends 1979
➤ 61,9338 ... 63,7495 ...: RBijdragen 53 (1992) 445 (M. *Parmentier*, Eng.:
'a sorry picture of patristic attitudes towards sex and society'); ÉglT 23
(1992) 279s (J. K. *Coyle*).

k912 ᵀᴱ**Cola** Silvano, Omelie sui Vangeli e su varie ricorrenze liturgiche:
TestPatr 88, 1990 ➤ 6,k301: RCC 143 (1992,2) 215 (E. *Cattaneo*);
Teresianum 43 (1992) 519 (M. *Diego Sánchez*).

k913 ᴱ**Duval** Yves-M., Jérôme entre l'Occident et l'Orient 1986/8 ➤ 5,e577*
... 7,g249: RBTAM 15,3 (1992) 153-8 (P. *Hamblenne*) & 180-4 (H. *Silvestre* sur C. J. *Mews* sur Abelard).

k914 *Frye* David, A mutual friend of Athaulf and Jerome [Orosius; could
have been Olympiodorus' Rustic(i)us]: Historia 40 (1991) 507s.

k915 **Gorce** Denys, La Lectio divina nell'ambiente ascetico di san Girolamo: Cammini dello Spirito 1990 ➤ 7,g252: RRivB 40 (1992) 375s (C.
Ghidelli); Teresianum 43 (1992) 300 (M. *Diego Sánchez*).

k916 *Guttilla* Giuseppe, Paolino di Nola e Girolamo: Orpheus 13 (1992)
278-294.

k916* *a) Hennings* Ralph, Rabbinisches und Antijüdisches bei Hieronymus;
Ep. 121,10; – *b) Horbury* William, Jews and Christians on the Bible;
demarcation and convergence (325-451): ➤ 484*, ᴱ*Oort* J. van, 1991/2,
49-71 / 72-103.

k917 **Larbaud** Valery, Sotto la protezione di san Girolamo [Sous l'invocation,
Gallimard 1946], ᵀ*Zanetello* Anna: La memoria 203. Palermo 1989,
Sellerio. [VivH 3,244].

k918 **Mirri** Luciana, La vita ascetica femminile in S. Girolamo: diss. Pont.
Univ. Angelicum, ᴰ*Degorski* B. Roma 1992. 217 p. – RTLv 24, p. 564.

k919 ᴱ**Moreschini** C., Hieronymus, Dialogus adversus pelagianos 1990
➤ 7,g254: RCiuD 204 (1991) 274 (J. M. *Ozaeta*); Maia 44 (1992) 317-9
(S. *Rocca*); RÉLat 70 (1992) 285s (Y.-M. *Duval*).

k920 *O'Loughlin* Thomas, [HebQQGn; Ginzberg Legends 1937 = 1909]
Adam's burial at Hebron; some aspects of its significance in the Latin
tradition: PrIrB 15 (1992) 66-88.

k921 *Polanski* Tomasz, Jerome as a translator of Hebrew poetry I. Grammar
and lexicography; II. Poetics; discussion: GrazBeit 18 (1992) 155-170; 19
(199 ...) ...

k922 *Rebenich* Stefan, Der heilige Hieronymus und die Geschichte — zur
Funktion der Exempla in seinen Briefen: RömQ 87 (1992) 29-46.

k923 *Taisne* A.-M., Saint Cyprien et saint Jérôme, chantres du Paradis:
BBudé (1992) 47-61.

k924 *Trisoglio* Francesco, La personalità di san Girolamo attraverso l'epistolario: ScuolC 120 (1992) 575-612.

Y2.6 **Patres latini** in ordine alphabetico.

k925 *Dal Covolo* Enrico, La letteratura cristiana a Roma nell'età dei Severi:
RivStoLR 27 (1991) 213-221.

k926 ᴱ**Herrmann** Joachim, Griechische und lateinische Quellen zur Frühgeschichte Mitteleuropas bis zur Mitte des I. Jahrtausends u. Z.: Schriften
und Quellen der Alten Welt 37. B 1988-92, Akademie.

k927 **Margerie** Bertrand de, Introduction à l'histoire de l'exégèse, 4. L'occident latin de Léon le Grand à Bernard de Clairvaux 1990 ➤ 6,k312;
7,g259: RLavalTP 48 (1992) 449s (L. *Painchaud*); RÉAug 37 (1991) 177-9

(F. I. *Rigolot*); RHPR 72 (1992) 325s (D. A. *Bertrand*); ScEspr 44 (1992) 100s (M. *Girard*).

k928 AMBROSIUS: *Capponi* Filippo, *a*) Per uno studio sulle fonti naturalistiche dell'omiletica ambrosiana: RCuClasMdv 34 (1992) 81-103; – *b*) Note a testi di patristica latina [Ambros. Hexaem. 5,1,2; 5,4,11]: Koinonia 15 (1991) 49-60; – *b*) Ambrosiana, note di lettura: Koinonia 16 (1992) 137-145.

k929 *a*) *Cappa* Giovanni, Istanze formative e pastorali del presbitero nella vita e nelle opere di S. Ambrogio; – *b*) *Janssen* Jos, La verecundia nel comportamento dei chierici secondo il 'De officiis ministrorum' di Sant'Ambrogio: ➤ 545, Formazione 1990/2, 95-132 / 133-143.

k930 *Demeglio* Paolo, Città e territorio in Emilia sullo scorcio del IV secolo; la testimonianza di Ambrogio: RivStoLR 27 (1991) 3-26.

k931 **Fontaine** Jacques, *al.*, Ambroise de Milan, Hymnes: Patrimoines Christianisme. P 1992, Cerf. 703 p. F 150. 2-204-04330-3. – ᴿBBudé (1992) 326-9 (A. *Michel*).

k932 **Jacob** Christoph, 'Arkandisziplin', Allegorese, Mystagogie... Ambrosius ᴰ1990 ➤ 6,k314; 7,g263: ᴿETL 68 (1992) 454-6 (J. *Verheyden*, Eng.); Gnomon 64 (1992) 125-9 (H. *Savon*, franç.); TS 53 (1992) 143s (L. J. *Swift*); ZKG 103 (1992) 118s (W. A. *Bienert*).

k933 **McLynn** N. B., St. Ambrose and ecclesiastical politics in Milan, 374-397: diss. Oxford 1988. 577 p. BRD-96851. – DissA 53 (1992s) 1631-A.

k934 **Mazzarino** Santo, Storia sociale del vescovo Ambrogio: ProbRicStoAnt 4, 1989 ➤ 6,k316; 7,g265: ᴿGnomon 64 (1992) 144-7 (K. L. *Noethlichs*).

k935 **Oberhelman** Steven M., Rhetoric and homiletics in fourth-century Christian literature; prose rhythm, oratorical style, and preaching in the works of Ambrose [complete], Jerome, and Augustine [both selective]: AmPgClasSt 26. Atlanta 1991, Scholars. v-199 p. $30; pa. $20. – ᴿClasR 42 (1992) 450 (I. J. *Davidson*).

k936 **Pasini** Cesare, Le fonti greche su sant'Ambrogio 1990 ➤ 6,k317; 7,g266: ᴿBenedictina 39 (1992) 246s (G. *Spinelli*).

k937 ᵀᴱ**Schmitz** Josef, Ambrosius, De sacramentis; De mysteriis: Fontes Christiani 3, 1990 ➤ 7,g266*: ᴿBijdragen 53 (1992) 440s (M. *Parmentier*).

k938 *Springer* Carl P. E., Ambrose's Veni redemptor gentium; the aesthetics of antiphony: JbAC 34 (1991) 76-87.

k939 ᵀᴱ**Testard** Maurice, Saint Ambroise, Les devoirs [I. 1984] II: Coll. Budé. P 1992, BLettres. 269 (d.) p. 2-251-013 [26-1] 62-8.

k940 **Williams** Daniel H., Nicene Christianity and its opponents in northern Italy; ... the early career of Ambrose of Milan: Diss. ᴰBarnes T. Toronto 1990. – RTLv 24, p. 552.

k941 CASSIODORUS: **Macpherson** Robin, Rome in involution; Cassiodorus's Variae in their literary and historical setting: FgKlas 14, 1989 ➤ 6,k321; 7,g269: ᴿAnzAltW 45,1 (1992) 94s (A. *Lippold*); Emerita 60 (1992) 350s (J. M. *Díaz de Bustamante*); JbÖsByz 42 (1992) 344-6 (Michaela *Zelzer*); WienerSt 105 (1992) 278s (K. *Zelzer*).

k942 CYPRIANUS: ᵀᴱ**Clarke** G. W., The letters of St. Cyprian of Carthage III (letters 55-66), IV (67-82): AncChrW 46s. NY 1986/9, Newman. III. vi-345 p., 0-8091-0369-9; IV. also vi-345 p.

k943 *Gramaglia* Pier Angelo, Cipriano e il primato romano: RivStoLR 28 (1992) 185-213.

k944 ᵀ**Pascual Torres** J., S. Cipriano, La unidad de la Iglesia: BtPatr 12. M 1990, Ciudad Nueva. 143 p. – ᴿScripTPamp 24 (1992) 339s (M. *Merino*).

k945 FACUNDUS: *Fatica* Luigi, La Defensio di Facondo di Ermiane; saggio antologico-critico: Asprenas [38 (1991) 359-374] 39 (1992) 35-55.

k946 GREGORIUS M.: *Bammel* E., Gregor der Grosse und die Juden: ⇒ 7, 501, Gregorio [9-12.V.1990] 1991, 283-291: ᴿTPhil 67 (1992) 280-2 (S. C. *Kessler*).

k948 **Clark** Francis, The pseudo-Gregorian dialogues 1987 ⇒ 3,g342 ... 6, k327: ᴿCC 143 (1992,1) 302-4 (G. *Cremascoli*).

k949 — *Cracco* Giorgio, Francis CLARK e la storiografia sui 'Dialoghi' di Gregorio Magno: RivStoLR 27 (1991) 115-124: non accetta ma ringrazia.

k949* ᵀᴱ**Gildea** Joseph, PETER of Waltham, Remediarium conversorum [Cranbury NJ 1984], Source-book of self-discipline; a synthesis of Moralia in Job by Gregory the Great: AmerUnivSt 7/117.˙ NY 1991, Lang. vii-371 p. $55. 0-8204-1650-9 [TDig 39,379].

k950 **Godding** Robert, Bibliografia di Gregorio Magno (1890/1989): Opere, Complementi 1, 1990 ⇒ 6,k333; 7,g276: ᴿSpeculum 67 (1992) 150 (G. A. *Zinn*).

k951 *Godding* Robert, Saint Grégoire le Grand à travers quelques ouvrages récents [STRAW Carole; ... congrès de Rome, avec mention de CLARK F.]: AnBoll 110 (1992) 142-157.

k952 ᴱ**Judic** Bruno (texte *Rommel* Floribert), ᵀ*Morel* Charles, Grégoire le Grand, Règle pastorale: SChr 381s. P 1992, Cerf. I. 257 p.; II. p. 258-564; 3 maps. 2-204-04733-3; -4-1.

McCready William, Signs of sanctity; miracles / Gregory 1989 ⇒ 4804.

k953 **Markus** Robert A., The end of ancient Christianity [Gregory] 1990 ⇒ 6,g379: ᴿAmHR 97 (1992) 530 (B. A. *Krupp*); DowR 110 (1992) 69-77 (D. *Foster*); JRS 82 (1992) 307s (J. *Curvan*); JTS 43 (1992) 705-712 (G. *Bonner*); RÉAnc 94 (1992) 501-3 (J. *Fontaine*); RechSR 80 (1992) 299 301 (Y.-M. *Duval*); TLZ 117 (1992) 757s (H. G. *Thümmel*); TvT 32 (1992) 198s (L. *Goosen*).

k954 *Portalupi* E., Gregorio Magno nell'Index Thomisticus: Bulletin de philosophie mediévale 31 (1989) 112-146 [< BTAM 15,3 (1992) 163-5, R. *Quinto*].

k955 **Straw** Carole, Gregory ... perfection in imperfection 1988 ⇒ 5,g888 ... 7,g282: ᴿBTAM 15,3 (1992) 161s (E. *Manning*); EngHR 107 (1992) 162s (Judith *McLure*); HeythJ 33 (1992) 339 (F. *Clark*: also on MCCREADY 1989, more relevant to his own recent claim).

k956 HILARIUS: *Williams* Daniel H., The anti-Arian campaign of HILARY of Poitiers and the 'Liber contra Auxentium': ChH 61 (1992) 7-22.

k957 HIPPOLYTUS: *Beylot* Robert, Hippolyte de Rome, Traité de l'Antéchrist traduit de l'éthiopien: Semitica 40 (1991) 107-139.

k958 **Mansfeld** Jaap, Heresiography in context; Hippolytus' Elenchos as a source for Greek philosophy: Philosophia Antiqua 56. Leiden 1992, Brill. xvii-391 p. 90-04-09616-7.

k959 [Martinelli] *Tempesta* Stefano, A proposito di un passo controverso di Ippolito (Ref. 1 7,7): IstLombR 126 (1992) 11-18.

k960 *a) Mueller* Ian, Heterodoxy and doxography in Hippolytus' 'Refutation of all heresies'; – *b) Mouraviev* Serge N., Hippolyte, Héraclite et Noët (Ref. IX 8-10): ⇒ 742, ANRW 2,36,6 (1992) 4309-4374 / 4375-4402.

k961 LACTANTIUS: ᵀᴱMonat Pierre [Is], *Perrin* Michel [Épitomé], Lactance, Institutions divines: SChr 326.337 / 335, 1986s ➤ 2,d449 ... 6,k354: ᴿGnomon 64 (1992) 592-600 (E. *Heck*); RivStoLR 27 (1991) 377s (E. *Gallicet*).

k962 ᵀᴱMonat Pierre, Lactance, Institutions divines IV: SChr 377. P 1992, Cerf. 277 p. F 237. 2-204-04572-1 [Latomus 52,681, M. *Perrin*]. – ᴿRÉAnc 94 (1992) 495s (C. *Ingremeau*).

k963 LEO M.: **Marelli** Silvana, Cristo Signore e Salvatore nella Chiesa in san Leone Magno: diss. Roma S. Anselmo N⁰ 163, ᴰ*Studer* B. Genova, 1992 Edisigma (excerptum 88 p.).

k964 MACARIUS: *Desprez* Vincent, L'Eucharistie d'après le pseudo-Macaire et son arrière-plan syrien: EcOrans 7 (1990) 191-222.

k965 MAXIMUS T.: **Cervellin** Luigi, Rassegna bibliografica su Massimo di Torino: Salesianum 54 (1992) 555-565 [perhaps not entirely by chance just after a lengthy bibliography of Maximus Confessor (➤ k820) as a footnote on pp. 551-3].

k966 ᵀᴱRamsey Boniface, The sermons of St. Maximus of Turin: Ancient Christian Writers 50. NY 1989, Paulist. 388 p. $23. 0-8091-0423-7. – ᴿCurrTMiss 19 (1992) 138 (J. *Zell*).

k967 OPTATUS: ᵀᴱDattrino Lorenzo, Ottato di Milevi, La vera chiesa: TPatr 71, 1988 ➤ 4,8894 ... 6,7881: ᴿRivStoLR 28 (1992) 646-655 (Clementina *Mazzucco*).

k968 PERPETUAE PASSIO: **Habermehl** Peter, Perpetua und der Ägypter; oder, Bilder des Bösen im frühen afrikanischen Christentum; ein Versuch zur Passio Sanctarum Perpetuae et Felicitatis: TU 140. B 1992, Akademie. [viii-] 280 p. 3-05-001998-0.

k969 PRUDENTIUS: **Kah** Marianne, 'Die Welt der Römer mit der Seele suchend ...' Prudentius 1990 ➤ 6,k259; 7,g295: ᴿGnomon 64 (1992) 676-680 (Danuta R. *Shanzer*, Eng.); GrazBeit 18 (1992) 301-3 (L. *Vanyó*: adds 6 items); Gymnasium 99 (1992) 358s (F. X. *Herrmann*); JTS 43 (1992) 692s (Anne-Marie *Palmer*); RÉAug 37 (1991) 169-171 (W. *Evenepoel*); RÉLat 70 (1992) 382 (J.-L. *Charlet*); VigChr 46 (1992) 202-4 (J. den *Boeft*); ZKG 103 (1992) 109s (R. *Klein*).

k970 **Malamud** Martha A., Poetics of ... Prudentius 1989 ➤ 6,k360: ᴿClasR 42 (1992) 51-53 (J. B. *Hall*).

Y2.8 Documenta orientalia.

k971 *Albertine* Richard, 'Theosis' according to the Easter[n] Fathers, mirrored in the development of the Epiclesis: EphLtg 105 (1991) 393-417; lat. 393.

k972 **Beggiani** Seely, An introduction to Eastern Christian spirituality; the Syriac tradition. L/Toronto 1991, Univ. Scranton/UPA. 124 p. £22. 0-940866-12-9. – ᴿJEH 43 (1992) 297s (S. *Brock*).

k973 **Coulie** Bernard, Les manuscrits arméniens de Jérusalem; notes sur le volume X du catalogue de N. BOGHARIAN [(I. 1966 ... IX. 1979) X. 1990, J. Gulbenkian Foundation; xvi-674 p.]: Muséon 105 (1992) 159-171.

k974 *Esbroeck* Michel Van, Les signes des temps dans la littérature syriaque: RICathP 39 (1991) 113-149.

k974* **Fenwick** John R. K., The anaphoras of St. Basil and St. James, an investigation into their common origin [diss. ᴰ*Cuming* G. (Bristol)]: OrChrAn 240. R 1992, Pontificium Institutum Orientale. xxvi-315 p. 88-7210-295-2.

k975 *Fiey* Jean Maurice, Christologie et Mariologie de l'Église syriaque orientale d'après ses anciens synodes: PrOrChr 41 (1991) 3-9; Eng. 9.

k976 *Ghattas* Michael, Jesus Christus in den Hymnen und im liturgischen Beten der koptischen Kirche: UnSa 47 (1992) 130-7 (138-141, Christologie-Konsens, *Hassab Alla* Waheeb).

k977 *Habbi* Joseph, La Chiesa d'Oriente in Mesopotamia: Mesop-T 27 (1992) 207-224; fot. 17-40.

k978 **Hage** Wolfgang, Syriac Christianity in the east: Mōrān 'Eth'ō 1. Kottayam 1988, St. Ephrem Ecumenical Research Inst. ii-93 p. – RRSO 65 (1991) 354-7 (R. *Contini*).

k979 EHaile G., *Amare* M., Beauty of the creation: JSS Mg 16, 1991 ➤ 7, g305: RBL (1992) 823s (M.A. *Knibb*); JTS 43 (1992) 823s (also M.A. *Knibb*).

k980 **Kannookadan** Pauly, The East Syrian lectionary; an historico-liturgical study. R 1991, Mar Thomas Centre. xxxi-215 p. – RETL 68 (1992) 479-481 (A. de *Halleux*).

k981 *Teixidor* Javier, L'apôtre d'après la littérature syriaque: ➤ 470, Apocrypha 1 (1990) 269-277.

k982 **Zanetti** Ugo, Les lectionnaires coptes annuels, Basse-Égypte: LvPubl. 33, 1985 ➤ 2,7655 ... 4,a542: RBSAComptc 30 (1991) 143s (A.Y. *Sidarus*).

---

k983 ABRAHAM, mar: *Alichoran* Joseph, Quand le [mont] Hakkari penchait pour le catholicisme; Nemrod, Mar Abraham et le parti catholique dans le pays 'Nestorien': PrOrChr 41 (1991) 34-55; Eng. 55.

k984 ABU QURRAH: *Lamoreaux* John C., An unedited tract against the Armenians by Theodore Abu Qurrah [c. 725-829; Arabic text with translation on facing pages]: Muséon 105 (1992) 327-333.

k984* *Samir Khalil* Samir, Abū Qurrah et les Maronites: PrOrChr 41 (1991) 25-33; Eng. 33.

k985 ADDAI: **Gelston** Anthony, The eucharistic prayer of Addai and Mari. Ox 1992, Clarendon 134 p. £30. 0-19-826737-1. – RExpTim 103 (1991s) 380s (S.P. *Brock*); JTS 43 (1992) 670-3 (B.D. *Spinks*); TR 88 (1992) 296s (P. *Bruns*).

k986 AITHALLAHA: *Bruns* Peter, Aithallahas Brief über den Glauben; ein bedeutendes Dokument frühsyrischer Theologie: OrChr 76 (1992) 46-73.

k987 APHRAATES: TBruns Peter, Aphrahat, Unterweisungen: Fontes Christiani 5, 1s, ➤ 7,g315; 629 p. DM 44 + 53: RColcT 62,4 (1992) 186-9 (W. *Myszor*); TLZ 117 (1992) 608s (G. *Haendler*); ZkT 114 (1992) 229s (L. *Lies*).

k988 EPierre M.J., Aphraate, Les Exposés: SChr 349.359, 1988s ➤ 4,h935 ... 7,g317: REsprVie 102 (1992) 561s (Y.-M. *Duval*).

k989 BARDESANES: **Teixidor** J., Bardesane d'Édesse; la première philosophie syriaque: Patrimoines-Chr. P 1992, Cerf. 159 p. F 151 [NRT 115,750, V. *Roisel*].

k990 DIOSCORUS: **MacCoull** L.S.B., Dioscorus of Aphrodito 1988 ➤ 7,g321: RJRS 82 (1992) 308s (D. *Montserrat*).

k991 EPHRAEM: **Brock** Sebastian, Ephrem, L'œil de lumière; La harpe de l'Esprit; florilège de poèmes; T Spiritualité Orientale 50, 1991 ➤ 7,g383: RBLitEc 93 (1992) 340s (L. *Monloubou*: 'surpris puis conquis'); NRT 114 (1992) 908 (V. *Roisel*); RHPR 72 (1992) 334s (J.-C. *Larchet*); RThom 92 (1992) 946s (D. *Cerbelaud*).

k992 ᵀᴱ**Brock** Sebastian, Ephrem, Hymns on Paradise 1990 ⇾ 6,k390:
ᴿInterpretation 46 (1992) 330 (F.R. *Kellog*); TR 88 (1992) 205s (P.
Bruns).

k993 **Bouwhorst** H. G. A. M., Les hymnes pascales d'Éphrem de Nisibe; analyse théologique et recherche sur l'évolution de la fête pascale chrétienne à
Nisibe et à Édesse et dans quelques églises voisines au quatrième siècle:
VigChr supp. 7. Leiden 1992, Brill. xiv-224 p.; 140 p. – ᴿLavalTP 48
(1992) 460-2 (P.H. *Poirier*).

k994 [Javier] *Martínez* Francisco, Los himnos 'sobre la perla' de San Efrén
de Nisibe (De fine, lxxxi-lxxxv): Salmanticensis 38 (1991) 5-32; Eng. 32.

k995 **Perniola** Erasmo, Sant'Efrem Siro, dottore della Chiesa e cantore di
Maria 1989 ⇾ 5,g924: ᴿAngelicum 69 (1992) 274-6 (B. *Degórski*:
puramente divulgativo).

k996 Israel K.: **Holmberg** Bo, A treatise on the unity and trinity of God
by Israel of Kashkar 1989 ⇾ 7,g333: ᴿOLZ 87 (1992) 166-8 (T. *Nagel*);
OrChr 76 (1992) 266-270 (S.K. *Samir*); TLZ 116 (1991) 171s (E.A.
Knauf).

k997 Johannes D.: **Beulay** Robert, L'enseignement spirituel de Jean de Da-
lyatha 1990 ⇾ 6,k403; 7,g335: ᴿLavalTP 48 (1992) 468s (P.-H. *Poirier*);
RSPT 76 (1992) 129-31 (G.-M. de *Durand*); RTLv 23 (1992) 226s (A. de
Halleux); Teresianum 43 (1992) 293s (M. *Diego Sánchez*); TvT 32 (1992)
98 (A.J. van der *Aalst*).

k998 Johannes E.: **Harvey** Susan A., Asceticism and society in crisis; John
of Ephesus and the lives of the Eastern saints. Berkeley 1990, Univ.
California. xvi-226 p. $35. – ᴿChH 61 (1992) 395s (G. *Frazee*); CritRR 5
(1992) 325-7 (J. *Meyendorff*).

k999 Johannes S.: **Martikainen** Jouko, Johannes I. Sedra, syr.: GöOrF 1/
34, 1991 ⇾ 7,g336: ᴿOstkSt 41 (1992) 63s (M. *Breydy*).

m1 Nerses: **Gugerotti** Claudio, Interazione dei ruoli in una celebrazione
come mistagogia; il pensiero di Nerses Lambron[ac'i = 'di' (Edessa)
1152-98] nella spiegazione del sacrificio: Caro salutis cardo 8. Padova
1991, Messaggero. 204 p. Lit. 28.000. 88-250-0072-7. – ᴿHoTheológos
10 (1992) 233-8 (P. *Sorci*).

m2 Petrus A.: *Pearson* Birger A., Two homilies attributed to St. Peter of
Alexandria: ⇾ 690, 3d Coptic 1984/90, 309-313 [no text].

m3 Simeon N.: **Jaoudi** Maria M., God-consciousness in Simeon the New
Theologian [b. 949 A.D.]: diss. Fordham, ᴰ*Cousins* D. NY 1992. 194 p.
92-15349. – DissA 52 (1992s) 4371-A.

Y3 **Medium aevum**, generalia.

m4 ᴱ**Affeldt** Werner, Frauen in Spätantike und Frühmittelalter 1987/90 ⇾ 6,
715: ᴿTLZ 117 (1992) 292-4 (Hanna-Barbara *Gerl*); TR 88 (1992) 297s
(Gisela *Muschiol*).

m5 **Angenendt** Arnold, Das Frühmittelalter; die abendländische Christenheit
von 400 bis 900: 1990 ⇾ 7,g340: ᴿTLZ 117 (1992) 515-7 (Angelika
Dörfler-Dierken).

m6 **Angenendt** Arnold (p. 7-44), *Schieffer* Rudolf (p. 45-70), Roma – caput et
fons; zwei [G. *Henkel*-] Vorträge über das päpstliche Rom zwischen Antike und Mittelalter. Opladen 1989, RhWf Akademie. – ᴿZKG 103
(1992) 128s (Martina *Stratmann*).

m7 **Banniard** Michel, Viva voce: communication écrite et communication orale du IVᵉ au IXᵉ s. en Occident latin [diss. ᴰ*Fontaine* J.]: Coll.Ét.Aug

MA-Mod 25. P 1992, Inst.Ét.Aug. 596 p. 2-85121-112-9. – ᴿRÉAug 37 (1992) 427 (G. *Madec*).

m8 *a*) **Banniard** Michel, Chronique d'antiquité tardive; langage et communication; – *b*) *Gauthier* Nancy, L'épigraphie latine chrétienne, 1980-1992: RÉAnc 94 (1992) 455-9 / 461-472.

m9 ᴱ**Bertini** F., Medioevo al femminile 1989 ⮞ 7,g344: ᴿGitFg 44 (1992) 315-7 (Germana *Eichberg*).

m10 ᴱ**Bianchi** Luca, *Randi* Eugenio, Filosofi e teologi; la ricerca e l'insegnamento nell'università medievale: Quodlibet 4. Bergamo 1989, Lubrina. 279 p. – ᴿRTPhil 124 (1992) 436s (R. *Imbach*).

m11 **Bloch** R. Howard, Medieval misogyny and the invention of western romantic love. Ch 1991, Univ. 298 p. $45; pa. $18. – ᴿTS 53 (1992) 784 (Sandra R. *O'Neal*).

m12 **Brieskorn** Norbert, Finsteres Mittelalter? Über das Lebensgefühl einer Epoche. Mainz 1991, Grünewald. 301 p. DM 42. – ᴿStiZt 210 (1992) 574s (O. *Köhler*).

m13 **Brooke** C., The medieval idea of marriage 1989 ⮞ 5,g946; 6,k420: ᴿTorJT 7 (1991) 288s (P. J. *Fedwick*).

m14 **Brundage** James A., Law, sex, and Christian society in medieval Europe 1987 ⮞ 4,h959 ... 7,g347. – ᴿÉglT 22 (1991) 236s (A. *Guindon*).

m15 **Brunhölzl** F., Histoire de la littérature latine du Moyen Âge I. De Cassiodore à la fin de la Renaissance carolingienne 1-2 [1976 mis à jour], ᵀ*Rochais* H.; bibliog. *Bouhot* J.-P., 1990s ⮞ 7,g348: ᴿRÉAnc 94 (1992) 496-8 (M. *Banniard*).

m16 **Bumke** Joachim, Courtly culture; literature and society in the high Middle Ages, ᵀ*Dunlap* Thomas. Berkeley c. 1991, Univ. California. 770 p. $50. – ᴿChrCent 109 (1992) 101s (T. K. *Lerud*).

m17 **Camille** Michael, The Gothic ideal; ideology and image-making in medieval art. C 1989, Univ. 407 p. $59.50. – ᴿJRel 72 (1992) 108-110 (J. *Hamburger*: original).

m18 **Cantor** N. F., Inventing the Middle Ages; the lives, works, and ideas of the great medievalists of the twentieth century. NY 1991, Morrow. 477 p. $27 [RHE 88,182*]. – ᴿAmHR 97 (1992) 1499s (B. D. *Hill*).

m19 **Casagrande** Carla, *Vecchio* Silvana, Les péchés de la langue; discipline et éthique de la parole dans la culture médiévale, ᵀ*Baillet* Philippe; préf. *Le Goff* J.: Histoire. P 1991, Cerf. 345 p. F 195 [RTLv 24,93, J.-M. *Counet*].

m19* *Cavallo* G., La circolazione dei testi greci nell'Europa dell'alto medioevo: ⮞ 656*b*, ᴱ*Hamesse* J., Rencontres/traducteurs 1990, 47-64.

m20 *Cereti* Giovanni, Il concilio di Ferrara-Firenze [1439] e la riconciliazione fra Oriente e Occidente: ScuolaC 120 (1992) 377-401.

m21 **Chelini** Jean, L'aube du Moyen Âge; naissance de la chrétienté médiévale. P 1991, Picard. 548 p. F 350. 2-7094-043-2. – ᴿÉTRel 67 (1992) 284s (Dominique *Viaux*).

m22 *Chiffoleau* Jacques, Pour une histoire de la religion et des institutions médiévales du XIIème au XVème siècle: CahHist 36 (1991) 3-21.

m23 **Dahan** Gilbert, Les intellectuels chrétiens et les juifs au Moyen Âge 1990 ⮞ 6,k430; 7,g254: ᴿMélSR 49 (1992) 59 (J. *Heuclin*); NRT 114 (1992) 133 (B. *Joassart*); RThom 92 (1992) 574-6 (D. *Cerbelaud*).

m24 *Dahan* Gilbert, La connaissance de l'hébreu dans les correctoires de la Bible du XIIIᵉ siècle; notes préliminaires: RTLv 23 (1992) 178-190; Eng. 296 [RHE 87,896, R. *Aubert*].

m25 *Depreux* Philippe, Empereur, empereur associé et pape au temps de Louis le pieux: RBgPg 70 (1992) 893-906.

m26 **Döpmann** Hans-Dieter, Die Ostkirchen vom Bilderstreit bis zur Kirchenspaltung von 1054: KG Einz 1/8. Lp 1990, Ev-VA. 138 p. 3-374-01195-0. – ᴿOstkSt 41 (1992) 218s (H. *Röhling*).

m26* *d'Onofrio* Giulio, Theological ideas and the idea of theology in the early Middle Ages (9th-11th centuries): FreibZ 38 (1991) 273-297.

m27 **Du Boulay** F.R.H., The England of Piers Plowman; William LANGLAND and his vision of the fourteenth century. Rochester 1991, Boydell & B. 147 p. $59. – ᴿTS 53 (1992) 785 (J.F.R. *Day*).

m28 ᴱ**Duby** Georges, *Perrot* Michelle, Histoire des femmes en occident, 2. ᴱKlapisch-Zuber Christiane. Le Moyen Âge. P 1991, Plon. 567 p. – ᴿAmHR 97 (1992) p. 1193s (Caroline W. *Bynum*).

m29 **Dupuigrenet-Desroussilles** F., Dieu en son royaume; la Bible dans la France d'autrefois (xiiiᵉ-xviiiᵉ s.). P 1991, Bt.Nat./Cerf. 176 p.; ill. [RSPT 76,165].

m30 **Emmerson** Richard K., *Herzman* Ronald B., The apocalyptic imagination in medieval literature: Middle Ages. Ph 1992, Univ. Pennsylvania. xi-244 p. $28. 0-8122-3122-8 [TDig 40,160].

m31 **Ennen** Edith, The medieval woman 1989 ➤ 7,g361: ᴿRHist 285 (1991) 412s (Dominique *Barthélemy*).
Fälschungen im Mittelalter 1986/8 ➤ 1702.

m32 ᴱ**Fossier** Robert, The Cambridge illustrated history of the Middle Ages I. 350-950, ᵀ*Sondheimer* Janet. C 1989, Univ. xxiii-556 p. $49.50. – ᴿChH 61 (1992) 398s (G. *Christianson*).

m33 **Fossier** R., Hommes et villages d'Occident au Moyen Âge. P 1992, Sorbonne. 526 p. [RHE 88,233*].

m34 **Fuhrmann** Horst, Einladung ins Mittelalter³ [¹1987 ➤ 6,k436; 7,g362]. Mü 1988, Beck. 327 p. DM 39,50. 3-406-32052-X. – ᴿBijdragen 53 (1992) 328 (A. van der *Helm*).

m35 **Goodich** Michael E., From birth to old age; the human life cycle in medieval thought, 1250-1350. Lanham MD 1989, UPA. x-215 p. $29.50. – ᴿChH 60 (1991) 530s (Clarissa W. *Atkinson*).

m36 *Guenée* Bernard, Le religieux et les docteurs; comment le religieux [Michel PINTOIN] de Saint-Denis voyait les professeurs de l'Université de Paris: CRAI (1992) 675-686.

m37 **Haas** Alois M., Todesbilder im Mittelalter; Fakten und Hinweise in der deutschen Literatur. Da 1989, Wiss. 299 p. – ᴿFreibZ 39 (1992) 522-8 (R. *Blumrich*).

m38 **Haye** Thomas, Der catalogus testium veritatis des Matthias FLACIUS Illyricus — eine Einführung in die Literatur des Mittelalters: ArRefG 83 (1992) 31-48.

m39 ᶠHÖDL Ludwig, Renovatio et reformatio; wider das Bild vom 'finsteren' Mittelalter, ᴱGerwing Manfred, *Ruppert* Godehard 1985 ➤ 65,68... – ᴿTPhil 67 (1992) 598s (R. *Berndt*).

m40 *Hunter* Erica C.D., Syriac Christianity in [12th century] central Asia: ZRGg 44 (1922) 362-8.

m41 *Imbach* Ruedi, Notabilia I; Hinweise auf wichtige Neuerscheinungen aus dem Bereich der mittelalterlichen Philosophie [...MARTINI R. Capistrum 1990; MADEC C. BONAVENTURE 1990]: FreibZ 39 (1992) 180-194.

m42 **Johnson** Penelope D., Equal in monastic profession; religious women in medieval France 1991 ➤ 7,g370*: ᴿTS 53 (1992) 184 (L. *Örsy*).

m43 *Kahane* H.†. & R., JUSTINIAN's Credo in western medieval literature: ByZ 84s,1 (1991s) 37-42.

m44 *Keller* Hagen, Vom 'heiligen Buch' zur 'Buchführung'; Lebensfunktionen der Schrift im Mittelalter: FrühMaS 26 (1992) 1-31.

m45 **Kieckhefer** Richard, Magic in the Middle Ages 1990 → 7,g372: RChH 60 (1991) 537-9 (R. C. *Finucane*); JRel 72 (1992) 305s (I. P. *Culianu*).

m46 *Kieckhefer* Richard, The land of lost discontent; classics of late medieval spirituality [ROLLE G., *al*.; Paulist 1988s]: JRel 72 (1992) 82-88.

m47 *Koterski* Joseph W., Messianic expectations in the fourteenth century: Thought 65,1 ('Dante' 1990) 47-58.

m48 *La Riviere* Randall P., The imperial library of Charlemagne: Eranos 90 (1992) 82-96.

m49 **Leclercq** Jean, L'amour des lettres et de désir de Dieu; initiation aux auteurs monastiques du Moyen Âge³ 1990 → 7,g374: RRTLv 23 (1992) 202-4 (M. *Testard*: aucunement vieilli, après 40 ans).

m50 **Leclercq** Jean, Esperienza spirituale e teologia; alla scuola dei monaci medievali: BtCuMdv. Mi 1990, Jaca. 195 p. – RScripTPamp 24 (1992) 353s (M. J. *Cano*).

m51 *Leclercq* Jean, Naming the theologies of the early twelfth century [i. For a sociology of theologies ...]: MedvSt 53 (1991) 327-336.

m52 *Le Goff* Jacques, Le travail au Moyen Âge: CahPhRel 6 (1989) 9-28.

m53 ELeonardi C., La Bibbia nel medioevo.

m54 ELevy Bernard S., The Bible in the Middle Ages; its influence on literature and art [conference Binghamton 1985]: MedvRenTSt 89. Binghamton 1992, SUNY. xvi-208 p. $25. 0-86698-101-2 [TDig 40,151]. 6 art.

m55 **Libera** Alain de, Penser au Moyen Âge: Chemins de pensée. P 1991, Seuil. 408 p. F 145. 2-02-013199-4. – RNVFr 67 (1992) 70-72 (F.-X. *Putallaz*).

m56 *a*) *Lobrichon* Guy, La Bible des maîtres du XIIᵉ s.; – *b*) *Figuet* Jean, La Bible de Bernard; données et ouvertures: → 513, Bernard, SChr 380 (1992) 209-236 / 237-269.

m57 EMachielsen John, Clavis patristica pseudepigraphorum Medii Aevi: CCLat, 1990 → 6,k456: RRBén 102 (1992) 375 [L. *W(ankenne?)*]; JTS 43 (1992) 273 (G. R. *Evans*); ZkT 114 (1992) 223s (S. C. *Kessler*).

m58 EMcKitterick Rosamond, The uses of literacy in early medieval Europe. C 1990, Univ. xvi-345 p.; 14 fig. $60; pa. $20. – RSpeculum 67 (1992) 1003-7 (R. E. *Reynolds*; also on her Carolingians 1989).

m59 *McLaughlin* R. Emmet, The Word eclipsed? Preaching in the early Middle Ages: Traditio 46 (1991) 77-122.

Markus Robert A., The end of ancient Christianity [... GREGORY] 1990 → k953.

m60 **Martin** Hervé, Le métier de prédicateur en France septentrionale à la fin du Moyen Âge 1988 → ? 7,g380: RBijdragen 53 (1992) 333s (J. *Besemer*).

m61 *Muzal* Otto, Byzanz und das Abendland: Biblos 40 (1991) 1-17.

m62 *Menache* Sophia, *Horowitz* Jeannine, 'Au commencement était le Verbe'; propagatio fidei et propagande au Moyen Âge: RBgPg 70 (1992) 330-356.

m63 **Milis** Ludo J. R., Angelic monks and earthly men; monasticism and its meaning in medieval society. Rochester NY 1992, Boydell. xiv-170 p. $50. 0-85115-303-8 [TDig 40,176].

m64 EMollat du Jourdin M., *Vauchez* A., Die Geschichte des Christentums; Religion – Politik – Kultur, 6. [EMayeur J. M., *al*.] Die Zeit der Zerreisproben [1274-1499: Lyon II – Ferrara], TOschwald M., ESchimmelpfennig B. FrB 1991, Herder. xx-912 p. DM 198. 3-451-22256-6

[-62-0]. – ᴿTvT 32 (1992) 316s (J. van *Laarhoven*: 14 equal-size volumes to appear 'tegelijk' in French & English).

m65 El monasterio... cultural 1989/90 ⇥ 7,537*a*: ᴿRivStoLR 27 (1991) 340-343 (Rita *Lizzi*).

m66 *Mondin* Battista, La prima scolastica; BOEZIO, CASSIODORO, Scoto ERIUGENA: EuntDoc 44 (1991) 5-30.

m67 **Moulin** Léo, La vita degli studenti nel Medioevo [La vie... 1991 ⇥ 7,g183], ᵀ*Tombolini* Antonio. Mi 1992, Jaca. xv-284 p. Lit. 25.000. – ᴿLetture 47 (1992) 944s (Paola *Müller*).

m68 **Muralt** André de, L'enjeu de la philosophie médiévale; études thomistes, scotistes, occamiennes et grégoriennes: StTGgMA. Leiden 1991, Brill. xvi-448 p. – ᴿNVFr 67 (1992) 155s (F.-X. *Putallaz*).

m69 **Nichols** Aidan, Rome and the Eastern Churches; a study in schism. E 1992, Clark. xiv-338 p. 0-567-29206-1.

m70 **Paxton** Frederick S., Christianizing death; the creation of a ritual process in medieval Europe 1990 ⇥ 7,8994: ᴿClasW 85 (1991s) 723s (Gail P. *Corrington*); RExp 89 (1992) 122s (E. G. *Hinson*).

m71 **Peters** Edward, Inquisition 1988 ⇥ 5,g982... 7,g389: ᴿHomP 91,5 (1990s) 75-77 (P. T. *MacCarthy*).

m72 **Pigulewska** N. W., ❷ Syrian culture in the early Middle Ages, ᵀ*Mazur* C. Wsz 1989, Pax. 310 p.; 25 fig. – ᴿColcT 62,3 (1992) 192s (J. *Gliściński*).

m73 *Price* B. B., Medieval thought; an introduction. Ox 1992, Blackwell. ix-261 p. [RHE 87,167*].

m74 *Prinz* Friedrich, Hagiographie als Kultpropaganda; die Rolle der Auftraggeber und Autoren hagiographischer Texte des Frühmittelalters: ZKG 103 (1992) 174-194.

m75 *Raba* J., The biblical tradition in the old Russian chronicles: Forschungen zur osteuropäischen Geschichte 46 (B 1992) 9-20 [< RHE 87,376*].

m76 *Reinburg* Virginia, Liturgy and the laity in Late Medieval and Reformation France: SixtC 23 (1992) 526-547; 8 fig.

m77 **Richards** Jeffrey, Sex, dissidence, and damnation; minority groups in the Middle Ages 1991 ⇥ 7,g392*: ᴿAmHR 97 (1992) 836s (R. C. *Stacey*: R. MOORE 1987 did it better); JAAR 60 (1992) 809-812 (Carolyn P. *Schriber*).

m78 ᴱ*Riché* R., *al.*, Lo studio della Bibbia nel Medioevo latino [BTT 4 (Riché, *Chatillon, Verger*) 1984 ⇥ 1,308], ᵀ*Rigo* C. ⇥ 5,g984; 7,k489; ᴱ*Chiesa* Bruno: StBPaid 87. Brescia 1989, Paideia. 153 p. – ᴿTeresianum 43 (1992) 292s (M. *Diego Sánchez*).

m79 **Rubin** Miri, Corpus Christi; the Eucharist in late medieval culture 1991 ⇥ 7,g394: ᴿEngHR 107 (1992) 386-8 (N. *Orme*); TLond 95 (1992) 145s (J. L. *Houlden*: excellent though spelling and translations flawed).

m80 **Schimmelpfennig** Bernhard, The papacy, ᵀ*Sievert* James: [up to the Renaissance: Das Papsttum, Da ³1988, Wiss.; ix-370 p. DM 24,80; 0-534-80024-9]. NY 1992, Columbia Univ. ix-330 p. $60; pa. $20. 0-231-07514-6; -5-4 [TDig 40,186].

m81 ᶠSCHMALE Franz-Josef: Ecclesia et Regnum; Beiträge zur Geschichte von Kirche, Recht und Staat im Mittelalter, 65. Gb. ᴱ*Berg* Dieter, *Goetz* Hans Werner, 1989 ⇥ 5,171: ᴿColcFran 61 (1991) 685s (B. de *Armellada*).

m82 **Schmidinger** Heinrich (70. Gb.), Patriarch im Abendland; Beiträge zur Geschichte des Papsttums, Roms und Aquileias im Mittelalter, [seine] ausgewählte[n] Aufsätze, ᴱ*Dopsch* Heinz, *al.* Salzburg 1986, St. Peter. xxiv-464 p. – ᴿZKG 103 (1992) 130-2 (U. *Nonn*).

m83 *Schneider* Jakob H. J.,   Scientia sermocinalis/realis; Anmerkungen zum Wissenschaftsbegriff im Mittelalter und in der Neuzeit: ArBegG 35 (1992) 54-92.

m84 *Schulthess* Peter,   Satztheorien; Texte zur Sprachphilosophie und Wissenschaftstheorie im 14. Jahrhundert: FreibZ 39 (1992) 501-512.

m85 **Sims-Williams** Patrick,   Religion and literature in western England, 600-800.   C 1990, Univ.   xvi-448 p.   £40. – ᴿEngHR 107 (1992) 954-6 (R. *Sharpe*).

m85* *Small* Carola,   The Fourth Lateran Council of 1215; a turning point in the history of medieval Europe: RelStT 11,2s (1991) 66-78.

m86 *Speer* Andreas, *Schneider* Jakob H. J., [*al.*] Das Mittelalter im Spiegel neuerer Literatur: TüTQ 172 (1992) [162-] 221-237.

m87 *Struve* Tilman,   Die Wende des 11. Jahrhunderts; Symptome eines Epochenwandels im Spiegel der Geschichtsschreibung: HistJb 112 (1992) 324-365.

m87* *Stuard* Susan M., [*al.*], From women to woman; new thinking about gender, c. 1140:   Thought 64,3 ('Gender and the moral order in medieval society' 1989) 208-219 [-309].

m88 **Taylor** Larissa,   Soldiers of Christ; preaching in late medieval and reformation France.   NY 1992, Oxford-UP.   xiv-352 p. $55. – ᴿTS 53 (1992) 568s (T. *Worcester*: not adequate on Protestants, but shows in Franciscans and Dominicans a constructive and consoling trend disproving Hᴜɪᴢɪɴɢᴀ, Dᴇʟᴜᴍᴇᴀᴜ, antisemitism misogyny).

m89 *Thomson* Francis J.,   SS. Cyril and Methodius and a mythical western heresy, trilinguism; a contribution to the study of patristic and mediaeval theories of sacred languages: AnBoll 110 (1992) 67-122.

m90 **Uytfanghe** Marc van, Stylisation biblique et condition humaine dans l'hagiographie mérovingienne 1987 ➤ 5,g993; 6,k477:   ᴿSpeculum 67 (1992) 494-6 (R. A. *Gerberding*: ground-breaking, a joy, though a bit overweight like most of us these days).

m91 *Van Hove* Brian,   Oltre il mito dell'Inquisizione: CC 143 (1992,4) 458-467. 578-588.

m92 **Vernet** André, (*Genevois* Anne-Marie), La Bible au Moyen Age, Bibliographie 1989 ➤ 5,g996; 7,g401*:   ᴿBtHumRen 52 (1990) 695s (E. *Beltram*, 983 items).

Y3.4   Exegetae mediaevales [hebraei ➤ K7].

m95 Aʙᴇʟᴀʀᴅᴜs: **Allegro** Giuseppe,   La teologia di Pietro Abelardo fra lettura e pregiudizi: QuadMdv 9, 1990 ➤ 7,g407:   ᴿScripTPamp 24 (1992) 354 (M. J. *Cano*).

m95* *Knoch* Wendelin,   Der Streit zwischen Bᴇʀɴʜᴀʀᴅ von Clairvaux und Petrus Abaelard — ein exemplarisches Ringen um verantworteten Glauben: FreibZ 38 (1991) 299-315.

m96 Aʟʙᴇʀᴛᴜs: *Prestipino* Carlo A.,   S. Alberto Magno e il suo tempo: SacDoc 37 (1992) 35-59.

m97 Aɴᴅʀᴇᴀs S. V.:   *Berndt* Rainer,   Les interprétations juives dans le Commentaire de l'Heptateuque d'André de Saint-Victor: RechAug 24 (1989) 199-240.

m98 **Berndt** Rainer,   André de Saint-Victor († 1175) exégète et théologien: Bt. Victorina 2, 1991 ➤ 7,g410; Fb 3048:   ᴿRHE 87 (1992) 803s (A. *Haquin*); TPhil 67 (1992) 594-7 (K. *Reinhardt*).

m99 ANGELOMO: **Cantelli** S., Angelomo e la scuola esegetica di Luxueil, I-II: Bt Medioevo Latino 1. Spoleto 1990. 530 p.; 22 p. + 250 pl. – ᴿAn-StoEseg 9 (1992) 617-620 (R. *Savigni*).

m100 ANSELMUS: ᴱ**Corbin** Michel, L'Œuvre de saint Anselme IV. La conception virginale... 1990 ➤ 7,g412: ᴿRICathP 39 (1991) 185-190 (Coloman E. *Viola*).

m101 **Corbin** Michel, Prière et raison de la foi; introduction à l'œuvre de S. Anselme de Cantorbéry. P 1992, Cerf. 478 p. F 150. 2-204-04423-7 [RTLv 24,390, R. *Guelluy*].

m102 *Jacobs* Klaus, Begründen in der Theologie; Untersuchungen zu Anselm von Canterbury: PhJb 99 (Mü 1992) 225-244 [< ᴢɪᴛ 92,589].

m103 **Southern** Richard W., St. Anselm, a portrait in a landscape 1990 ➤ 7,g416; 0-521-36262-8: ᴿDowR 110 (1992) 150-3 (J.J.F. *Williams*); EngHR 107 (1992) 119-121 (M. *Brett*); JEH 43 (1992) 309-311 (C.H. *Lawrence*: superb); JTS 43 (1992) 279-281 (Marjorie *Chibnall*); RBén 102 (1992) 239s (L. *Wankenne*); TvT 32 (1992) 98s (J. van *Laarhoven*).

m104 AQUINAS: *Bonino* Serge-Thomas, (*al.*), Bulletin; Thomistica: RThom 92 (1992) 892-914 (-929).

m105 *Coggi* Roberto, Le caratteristiche fondamentali dell'esegesi biblica di S. Tommaso: SacDoc 35 (1990) 533-544.

m106 **Davies** Brian, The thought of Thomas Aquinas. Ox 1992, Clarendon. xv-391 p. £45. 0-19-826458-5 [TDig 40,60]. – ᴿExpTim 103 (1991s) 347 (Susan J. *Smalley*; fresh perspectives); NBlackf 73 (1992) 288s (G.R. *Evans*: a remarkable achievement).

m107 *Duquoc* Christian, De l'actualité de saint Thomas: ➤ 63, ᶠGEFFRÉ G., Interpréter 1992, 13-24.

m108 **Elders** L., The philosophical theology of St Thomas Aquinas: StMA 26. Leiden 1990, Brill. ix-332 p. ƒ145. 90-04-09156-4. – ᴿTvT 32 (1992) 909s (H. *Rikhof*).

m108* **Gaboriau** F., Thomas d'Aquin penseur dans l'Église. P 1992, FAC. F 198 [RSPT 77,528, É.-H. *Wéber*].

m109 **Geisler** Norman L., Thomas Aquinas, an evangelical appraisal 1991 ➤ 7,g420: ᴿCurrTMiss 19 (1992) 130s (P.J. *Wadell*); ExpTim 103 (1991s) 247 (N. *Tanner*: 'Should old Aquinas be forgot?' No, says this Baptist to evangelicals); WestTJ 54 (1992) 385-8 (K.S. *Oliphint*).

m110 **Janz** Denis R., LUTHER on Aquinas 1989 ➤ 5,k65; 7,g424: ᴿChH 60 (1991) 542s (E.W. *Gritsch*); Speculum 67 (1992) 430s (A.E. *McGrath*).

m111 **Michalik** Andrzej M., L'aspetto apologetico del metodo esegetico di S. Tommaso d'Aquino: diss. Santa Croce, ᴰ*Cirillo* A. R 1992. – RTLv 24, p. 540.

m112 **Mondin** Battista, Dizionario enciclopedico del pensiero di S. T. d'Aquino 1991 ➤ 7,735*b*; 88-7094-092-6: ᴿAnnTh 6 (1992) 475-481 (A. *Cirillo*); CC 143 (1992,3) 444s (M.L. *Ciappi*); CiVit 47 (1992) 225-234 (C. *Ruini*).

m113 **Pesch** Otto H., Tomás de Aquino; límite y grandeza de una teología medieval [1988 sin 'una' ➤ 4,k6], ᵀ*Moll* Xavier, *Gancho* Claudio. Barc 1992, Herder. 546 p. pt. 3585. 84-254-1806-2. – ᴿActuBbg 29 (1992) 232s (J. *Boada*); CiuD 205 (1992) 762s (J.M. *Ozaeta*); ComSev 25 (1992) 435-7 (M. de *Burgos*); LumenVr 41 (1992) 481s (U. *Gil Ortega*).

m114 *Porter* Jean, Rethinking religious classics: Aquinas and public disputation: ChrCent 109 (1992) 1100-03.

m115 *Prete* Benedetto, La Bibbia nella Somma Teologica: SacDoc 36 (1991) 5-27.

m116 **Valkenburg** Wilhelmus G. B. M., 'Did not our heart burn?' Place and function of Holy Scripture in the theology of St. Thomas Aquinas [diss. Utrecht]: Thomas Instituut 3. Utrecht 1990, Kath. Univ. x-440 p. 90-9003235-5. – RBijdragen 53 (1992) 216 (J. van den *Eijnden*).

m117 BACON R.: *Tonna* Yvo, La concezione del sapere in Ruggero Bacone (1214-1292) [prolusione 9.XI.1992]: Antonianum 67 (1992) 461-471; Eng. 461.

m118 BEDA V.: TESimonetti **Abbolito** Giuseppina, Beda, Omelie sul Vangelo: TPatr 90. R 1990, Città Nuova. 542 p. – RSalesianum 54 (1992) 611 (S. *Felici*).

m119 **Sims-Williams** Patrick, [Bede...] Religion and literature in western England 600-800: Studies in Anglo-Saxon England 3. C 1990, Univ. xiii-448 p.; 2 maps. £40. 0-521-38325-0. – RJTS 43 (1992) 721-4 (Clare *Stancliffe*).

m120 **Ward** Benedicta, The Venerable Bede 1990 → 7,g426: RHeythJ 33 (1992) 454s (G. *Bonner*); JEH 43 (1992) 338s (J. C. *Crick*).

m121 BERNARDUS C.: **Bell** Theo, Divus Bernhardus; Bernhard von Clairvaux in M. LUTHERS Schriften: Inst EurGesch Veröff 148. Mainz 1992, von Zabern. xi-418 p. [TR 88,523].

m122 *a*) *Bell* Theo M., Testimonium Spiritus Sancti; an example of Bernard-reception in Luther's theology; – *b*) *Pranger* M. B., Perdite vixi; Bernard de Clairvaux et Luther devant l'échec existentiel: Bijdragen 53 (1992) 62-72 / 46-60; Eng. 60s.

m123 **Diers** Michaela, Bernhard von Clairvaux; elitäre Frömmigkeit und begnadetes Wirken: BeitGPhTMA 34. Münster 1991, Aschendorff. 436 p. DM 110. – RErbAuf 68 (1992) 163s (J. *Schaber*).

m124 *Biffi* Inos, *a*) La cristologia di san Bernardo, 'pellegrino' in Terra Santa; – *b*) Pubblicazioni su san Bernardo: ScuolaC 120 (1992) 14 47 / 113-125.

m125 *a*) *Figuet* J., La Bible de Bernard; données et ouvertures; – *b*) Lobrichon G., La Bible des maîtres du XIIᵉ siècle: → 513, Bernard 1991/2, 237-269 / 209-236.

m126 **Heller** Dagmer, Schriftauslegung und geistliche Erfahrung bei Bernhard von Clairvaux [Diss.]: Studien zur systematischen und spirituellen Theologie 2, 1990 → 7,g427; 3-429-01332-1: RBijdragen 53 (1992) 95s (T. *Bell*).

m127 *Hendrix* Guido, Le centenaire de saint Bernard... une belle récolte: RHE 87 (1992) 132-139.

m128 *Izard* Camille, Jean CALVIN à l'écoute de saint Bernard: ÉTRel 67 (1992) 19-41.

m129 **Leclercq** Jean, Women and St. Bernard of Clairvaux [1982], TSaïd Marie-B.: Cistercian Studies 104. Kalamazoo 1989. 171 p. – RÉglT 22 (1991) 227s (K. C. *Russell*).

m130 *Leclercq* J., L'écrivain: → 513, Bernard: SChr 380, 1991/92, 529-556.

m131 *a*) *Louf* André, Saint Bernard était-il iconoclaste?; – *b*) *Rocacher* Jean, Existe-t-il un art cistercien?; – *c*) *Leclercq* Jean, Le moi, la compassion et la contemplation: → 512c, S. Bernard 1991/2, 49-64 / 65-70 / 39-48.

m132 **McGuire** Brian, The difficult saint; Bernard of Clairvaux and his tradition. Kalamazoo 1991, Cistercian. 317 p. $30. – RTS 53 (1992) 593 (L. S. *Cunningham*).

m133 BONAVENTURA: **Keck** David A., The angelology of Saint Bonaventure and the harvest of medieval angelology: diss. Harvard, ᴰ*Ozment* S. CM 1992. 500 p. 93-07563. – DissA 53 (1992s) 4044-A.

m133* ᵀᴱ**Madec** Goulven, Le Christ maître... Bonaventure, 'Unus est...'. P 1990, Vrin. 144 p. – ᴿFreibZ 39 (1992) 187s (R. *Imbach*).

m134 **You Hae Yong**, Bonaventure and John CALVIN; the restoration of the image of God as a mode of spiritual consummation: diss. Fordham, ᴰ*Cousins* E. NY 1992. 281 p. 92-23829. – DissA 53 (1992s) 1197-A.

m135 CUSANUS: ᵀᴱ**Sigmund** Paul E., Nicholas of Cusa, The Catholic Concordance [a treatise, not a concordance; Heidelberg Academy text 1968]: Texts in the History of Political Thought. C 1991, Univ. xlvii-326 p. £45. 0-521-40207-7. – ᴿJTS 43 (1992) 746 (G. R. *Evans*).

m135* **Haubst** Rudolf, Streifzüge in die cusanische Theologie: CusGes, 1991 ➤ 7,g431; DM 74; 3-402-03494-8: ᴿJTS 43 (1992) 744s (G. R. *Evans*: a lifetime's work, deeply matured).

ᶠWATANEBE M., Nicholas of Cusa, in search of God and wisdom 1981/91 ➤ 7,a23.

m136 DANTE A.: **Morgan** Alison, Dante and the medieval other world. C 1990, Univ. ix-255 p.; 4 fig.; 22 pl. £10. – ᴿJTS 43 (1992) 286-9 (Marjorie *Reeves*).

m137 ECKHART M.: **Davis** Olivier, Meister Eckhart, mystical theologian. L 1991, SPCK. 257 p. £13. 0-281-04520-8. – ᴿExpTim 103 (1991s) 192 [C. S. *Rodd*, with no comment on his use of Scripture].

m138 ᴱ**Stirnimann** Heinrich, *Imbach* R., Eckardus Theutonicus, homo doctus et sanctus; Nachweise und Berichte zum Prozess gegen Meister Eckhart: Dokimion 11. FrS 1992, Univ. 312 p. Fs 39 [TR 88,254].

m139 ERIUGENA: **Moran** Dermot, The philosophy of John Scotus Eriugena; a study of idealism in the Middle Ages. C 1989, Univ. xviii-333 p. £35. – ᴿHeythJ 33 (1992) 214s (A. *Louth*).

m139* ᴱ**Beierwaltes** Werner, Begriff und Metapher bei Eriugena 1989/91 ➤ 6,574*: ᴿBeiNam 27 (1992) 417-9 (E. *Meineke*).

m140 *Moran* D., ORIGEN and Eriugena; aspects of Christian gnosis: ➤ 547, Platonism 1990/2, 27-53.

m141 *López Silonis* Raphael, ❶ Images and symbols in the theology of Eriugena: KatKenk 31 (1992) 211-239; Eng. iv-v.

m142 *O'Loughlin* Thomas, Unexplored Irish influence on Eriugena: RTAM 59 (1992) 23-40.

m143 GERSON J.: **Burrows** Mark S., Jean Gerson... biblical and reforming theology ᴰ1991 ➤ 7,g442: ᴿJTS 43 (1992) 282s (G. R. *Evans*); TS 53 (1992) 754s (D. Catherine *Brown*).

m144 GILBERTUS P.: **Nielsen** Lauge O., Theology and philosophy in the twelfth century; a study of Gilbert Porreta's thinking and the theological expositions of the doctrine of the Incarnation during the period 1130-1180: AcTDanica 15. Leiden 1982, Brill. 396 p. – ᴿTPhil 67 (1992) 597s (R. *Berndt*: 'mit Verspätung').

m145 GIUSTINIANI: **Massa** Eugenio, L'eremo, la Bibbia e il Medioevo in umanisti veneti del primo Cinquecento [... T/P. Giustiniani, riformatore dei Camaldolesi]. N 1992, Liguori. 405 p. Lit. 45.000 [RHE 88,671, S. *Tramontin*].

m146 GODEFRIDUS A.: ᵀᴱ**Rochais** H., Geoffroy d'Auxerres, Entretien de Simon-Pierre avec Jésus: SChr 364. P 1990, Cerf. 328 p. – ᴿRÉAug 38 (1992) 216-8 (G. de *Martel*).

m147 GULIELMUS S. T.: **Piazzoni** Ambrogio, Guglielmo di Saint-Thierry; il declino dell'ideale monastico nel XII secolo: Studi Storici 181-183, 1988 ➤ 7,g444: ᴿRivStoLR 27 (1991) 555-8 (A. *Bodrato*).

m148 HARTMANN von Aue: **Dahlgrün** Corinna, Hoc fac et vives (Lk 10,28) im Gregorios und ~ : HaBeitGermanistik 14. Fra 1991, Lang. viii-277 p. 3-631-44036-7 [TLZ 118,37, G. *Haendler* ohne Datum].

m149 HILDEGARD B.: **Hart** Columba, *Bishop* Jane, Hildegard of Bingen,... 'Scivias'. NY 1990, Paulist. $18. – ᴿHeythJ 33 (1992) 343-5 (F. *Bowie*).

m150 *a*) *Kirby-Fulton* Kathryn, Hildegard of Bingen; two recent studies [FLANAGAN Sabina, 1989; NEWMAN Barbara, 1988]; – *b*) *Gertz* Sunhee K., Modern views of medieval women: MedHum 18 (1992) 189-197 / 199-208.

m151 HUGO S. V.: **Illich** Ivan, Du lisible au visible, la naissance du texte; un commentaire du Didascalicon de Hugues de Saint-Victor, ᵀ*Mignon* Jacques, ᴱ*Sissung* Maud, 1991 ➤ 7,g499; 2-204-04334-6: ᴿRTLv 23 (1992) 390s (J.-M. *Counet*).

m152 ᵀᴱ**Lemoine** Michel, Hugues de Saint-Victor, L'art de lire; Didascalicon: Sagesses chrétiennes. P 1991, Cerf. 243 p., F 125. 2-204-04369-9. – ᴿÉTRel 67 (1992) 122s (H. *Bost*, aussi sur ILLICH); RTLv 23 (1992) 227s (J.-M. *Counet*).

m153 ᵀᴱ**Sicard** Patrice, Hugues de Saint-Victor et son école, choix de [54] textes: Témoins de notre histoire 1991 ➤ 7,g450; 2-503-50073-0: ᴿJEH 43 (1992) 678s (Margaret *Gibson*); RHE 87 (1992) 459 (J. *Longère*).

m154 **Zwieten** J. van, The place and significance of literal esegesis in Hugh of St. Victor: diss. Amsterdam 1992, ᴰ*Laarhoven* J. van. 207 p. – TvT 32 (1992) 301; RTLv 24, p. 554.

m155 HUGOLIN: *Schrama* Martijn, 'Studere debemus eam viriliter et humiliter'; theologia affectiva bei Hugolin von Orvieto († 1373): Bijdragen 53 (1992) 135-150; Eng. 151.

m156 JOACHIM F.: **McGinn** Bernard, L'Abate calabrese; Gioacchino da Fiore nella storia del pensiero occidentale [1985 ➤ 1,f740], ᵀ*Di Giulio* P. & E.; Opere di G. Strumenti. Genova 1990, Marietti. 265 p. Lit. 35.000. 88-211-7251-1. – ᴿRivStoLR 28 (1992) 434 (G. I. *Potesta*).

m157 ᴱ**Potesta** G. L., Il profetismo gioachimita 1989/91 ➤ 7,544: ᴿScrip-TPamp 24 (1992) 357s (M. *Lluch-Baixauli*).

m158 JULIANA N.: *Nuth* Joan M., Wisdom's daughter; the theology of Julian of Norwich 1991 ➤ 7,g453*: ᴿTS 53 (1992) 593s (E. *Dreyer*).

m158* **Palliser** Margaret Ann, Christ, our mother of mercy; divine mercy and compassion in the theology of the Shewings of Julian of Norwich [diss. Pont. Univ. Gregoriana, Rome]. B/NY 1992, de Gruyter. xiii-262 p. DM 168. 3-11-013558-2 [TDig 39,378].

m159 LULLUS: **Euler** Walter A., Unitas et pax; Religionsvergleich bei Raimundus Lullus und Nikolaus von KUES: RelWSt 15. Altenberge 1990, Oros. 296 p. DM 44. 3-89375-029-0. – ᴿGeistL 65 (1992) 399s (J. *Sudbrack*);TPhil 67 (1992) 285-7 (J. *Splett*).

m160 *Artus* Walter W., *a*) Three indicators of the Christian character and spirit revealed in Ramón Llull's writings; – *b*) Ramón Llull's approach and answers to atheism: Antonianum 67 (1992) 330-359; ital. 330 / 520-8; ital. 520.

m161 *Hillgarth* J. N., Ramón Lull's early life; new documents: MedvSt 53 (1991) 337-347.

m161* MECHTILD: **Heimbach** Marianne, 'Der ungelehrte Mund' als Autorität; mystische Erfahrung als Quelle kirchlich-prophetischer Rede im

Werk Mechthilds von Magdeburg. Stu 1989, Frommann-Holzboog.
202 p. – ᴿFreibZ 38 (1991) 175-191 (Beatrice A. *Zimmermann*).

m162 OCKHAM W.: **Adams** Marilyn M., William Ockham. ND 1987, Univ.
1402 p. (2 vol.). $40. – ᴿPerspRelSt 19 (1992) 227s (M. *Arges*).

m163 **Beckmann** Jan P., Ockham-Bibliographie 1900-1990. Heid 1992,
Meiner. 107 p. DM 120 [TR 88,513].

m163* ᴱ**Vossenkuhl** Wilhelm, *Schönberger* Rolf, Die Gegenwart Ockhams
[München März 1988]: Acta Humaniora. Weinheim 1990, VCH. ix-
419 p. – ᴿFreibZ 38 (1991) 513-6 (D. *Perler*).

m164 PÉREZ DE V.: **Peinado Muñoz** Miguel, Jaime Pérez de Valencia
(1408-1490) y la Sagrada Escritura [diss. Granada]: BtTGran 26. Granada 1992, Fac. Teol. xx-280 p. 84-85653-52-1.

m165 PETRARCA: **Boyle** Marjory O., Petrarch's genius; pentimento and
prophecy. Berkeley 1991, Univ. California. ix-216 p. $35. – ᴿTS 53
(1992) 784s (Florinda M. *Iannace*: 'rhetorical theology deserving of
appreciation' thesis brilliant but difficult to accept).

m166 PETRUS C.: *Zier* Mark A., Preaching by distinction; Petrus Comestor
and the communication of the Gospel: EphLtg 105 (1991) 301-329.

m167 PETRUS DAMIANI: **Reindel** K., Die Briefe des Petrus Damiani 3,
91-150; MonGHist. 1989 ➤ 7,g460: ᴿAevum 65 (1991) 355-360 (A.
Granata).

m168 ᵀᴱ**Blum** Owen J., St. Peter Damian, letters 61-90: Fathers. MedvCont
3. Wsh 1992, Catholic University of America. xxvi-397 p. $43. 0-
8132-0750-9 [TDig 40,284].

m169 **Wünsch** Thomas, Spiritalis intellegentia; zur allegorischen Bibelinter-
pretation des Petrus Damiani [Diss. Regensburg]: Theorie und Forschung
190, Ph/Th 14. Rg 1992, Roderer. 196 p. DM 46 [TR 88,522].

m170 PETRUS V.: **Leclercq** Jean, Pietro il Venerabile [Pierre... 1094-1156]:
Di fronte e attraverso 300. Mi 1991, Jaca. 297 p. Lit. 38.000. 88-
16-40300-4. – ᴿGregorianum 73 (1992) 570-2 (Maria C. *Zaffi*).

m171 DE REIGNY: **Friedlander** C., *Leclercq* J., *Raciti* G., Galand de Reigny
[12ᵉ s.], Parabolaire: SChr 378. P 1992, Cerf. 471 p. F 296 [NRT 115,435,
A. *Harvengt*].

m172 DE RIEVAULX (1110-1167): **TePas** Katherine M., Aelred of Rievaulx;
the correlation between human friendship and union with God: diss.
Catholic Univ. ᴰ*Wiseman* J. Wsh 1992. 463 p. 92-39769. – DissA 53
(1992s) 3262-A.

m173 RUPERTUS T.: **Arduini** M. Lodovica, Rupert von Deutz (1076-1129)
und der 'status christianitatis' seiner Zeit; symbolisch-prophetische Deutung der Geschichte 1987 ➤ 5,k41; 6,k544: ᴿEngHR 107 (1992) 170s
(H. E. J. *Cowdrey*).

m174 SCOTUS: ᵀᴱ**Boulnois** Olivier, Duns SCOT, Sur la connaissance de Dieu
et l'univocité de l'étant: 1,3,1; 1,8,1, Collatio 24. P 1988, PUF. 496 p. –
ᴿSalmanticensis 38 (1991) 89s (L. *González Montes*).

m175 DE TAIBOTHEH (c. 1200): ᵀᴱ**Bettiolo** Paolo, Simone de Taibotheh,
Violenza e grazia; la coltura del cuore: TPatr 102. R 1992, Città Nuova.
188 p. Lit. 18.000. 88-311-3102-8.

Y4.1 **Luther.**

m176 *Arnold* Matthieu, Luther imitateur de Paul; ses lettres aux communautés évangéliques: ➤ 36, ᶠCULLMANN O., RHPR 72 (1992) 99-112;
Eng. 126.

m177 *a) Asendorf* Ulrich, Luthers Theologie nach seinen Katechismuspredigten; – *b) Wendebourg* Ernst-Wilhelm, Die Reformulierung der lutherischen Zweireiche-Lehre in Trutz RENDTORFFs Ethik — der Versuch einer theologischen Bewertung: KerDo 38 (1992) 2-19; Eng. 19 / 199-229; Eng. 229.

m177* *a) Beutel* Albrecht, Erfahrene Bibel; Verständnis und Gebrauch des verbum Dei scriptum bei Luther; – *b) Schwarz* Reinhard, Der hermeneutische Angelpunkt in Luthers Messreform: ZTK 89 (1992) 302-339 / 340-364.

m178 ᴱBrecht Martin, Martin Luther und das Bischofsamt [7. Kongress Oslo 1988]. Stu 1990, Calwer. 145 p. DM 48. – ᴿNorTTs 93 (1992), 56 (1992) 56 (O. *Tjørhom*).

m179 **Brecht** Martin, M. Luther, 2. Shaping and defining the Reformation, ᵀ*Schaaf* J. L. 1990 ➤ 7,g474: ᴿAnglTR 74 (1992) 506-8 (R. C. *Zachman*); CathHR 78 (1992) 110s (E. L. *Saak*); ÉTRel 67 (1992) 124s (H. *Bost*: iconographie remarquable); ExpTim 103 (1991s) 186 (J. K. *Cameron*); RelStR 18 (1992) 63 (R. *Kolb*); SixtC 23 (1992) 164s (J. W. *Zophy*); TTod 49 (1992s) 116s (M. E. *Osterhaven*).

m180 **Brendler** Gerhard, Martin Luther, theology and revolution, ᵀ*Foster* Claude R., 1991 ➤ 7,g476: ᴿExpTim 103 (1991s) 247s (J. K. *Cameron*: Luther for the onetime DDR); JTS 43 (1992) 823 (A. *McGrath*: one of the better centenary products); RelStR 18 (1992) 63 (R. *Kolb*); SixtC 23 (1992) 601s (S. *Hendrik*); TS 53 (1992) 387 (M. U. *Edwards*: no reason for translating such a Marxist outlook).

m181 **Buchholz** Armin, Schrift Gottes im Lehrstreit; M. Luthers Schriftverständnis und Schriftauslegung in seinen drei grossen Lehrstreitigkeiten der Jahre 1521-28: Diss. ᴰ*Fischer* H. Hamburg 1992s. – RTLv 24, p. 554.

m182 *Cottin* Jérôme, Luther théologien de l'image: ÉTRel 67 (1992) 561-7.

m182* *Ebeling* Gerhard, Todesangst und Lebenshoffnung; ein Brief Luthers: ZTK 88 (1991) 181-210.

Ebeling G., Lutherstudien; Disputatio de homine 1-3, 1977-89 ➤ 7168.

m183 **Emme** Dietrich, Martin Luthers Weg ins Kloster; eine wissenschaftliche Untersuchung in Aufsätzen 1991 ➤ 7,g479: ᴿTLZ 117 (1992) 678s (M. *Treu*).

m184 *Goffi* Tullo, M. Lutero, teologo spiritualista: StEcum 8 (1990) 313-322; Eng. 322.

m185 *Green* Lowell C., Welchen Luther meinen wir? Der Gegensatz zwischen der Rechtfertigungslehre des frühen und des reformatorischen Luther und seine Rezeption im Konkordienbuch, ᵀ*Martens* Gottfried: LuthTK 15 (1991) 2-19; p. 83, fehlender Teil der Anm. 5 p. 4.

m186 *Hampton* Daphne, Luther on the self, a feminist critique: Word & World 8 (St. Paul 1988) 334-342 [< LuJb 59, p. 231].

m187 **Haustein** Jörg, M. Luthers Stellung zum Zauber- und Hexenwesen: MüKhSt 2. Stu 1990, Kohlhammer. 208 p. DM 69. 3-17-010769-0. – ᴿLuthTK 15 (1991) 45s (J. *Schröter*); Protestantesimo 47 (1992) 247s (U. *Eckert*); RBgPg 70 (1992) 1044s (R. *Crahay* †); TvT 32 (1992) 101s (P. J. A. *Nissen*); ZKG 103 (1992) 262s (H. *Lehmann*).

m188 **Hell** Silvia, Die Dialektik des Wortes bei M. Luther; die Beziehung zwischen Gott und dem Menschen [Diss. Innsbruck 1992, Tyrolia. 195 p. DM 44 [TR 88,523].

m189 ᴱ**Junghans** H., Luthers Theologie als Weltverantwortung; Absichten und Wirkungen... 7. Kongress Oslo 14.-20. Aug. 1988: LuJb 57. Gö 1990, Vandenhoeck & R. 373 p. DM 88. – ᴿTLZ 117 (1992) 442-4 (E. *Koch*).

m190 **Lage** Dietmar, Martin Luther's Christology and ethic 1990 ➤ 6,k560: ᴿSixtC 22 (1991) 502 (W. R. *Russell*).

m191 **Lienhard** Marc, Au cœur de la foi de Luther: Jésus-Christ: JJC 48, 1991 ➤ 7,g486: ᴿÉTRcl 67 (1992) 124 (H. *Bost*: ne rend pas caduc son Luther 1973).

m192 **Lienhard** Marc, L'évangile et l'Église chez Luther: CogF 153, 1989 ➤ 5,k75... 7,g487: ᴿÉglT 22 (1991) 110-2 (A. *Peelman*); RTLv 23 (1992) 232s (J.-F. *Gilmont*: une foule d'informations, un jugement équilibré).

m193 *a) Lüpke* Johannes von, Theologie als 'Grammatik zur Sprache der heiligen Schrift'; eine Studie zu Luthers Theologieverständnis; – *b) Koch* Traugott, Die Vernunft in der Theologie — in Auseinandersetzung mit Luther geörtert; – *c) Barth* Ulrich, Luthers Verständnis der Subjektivität des Glaubens: NSys 34 (1992) 227-250; Eng. 250 / 251-268; Eng. 268 / 269-290; Eng. 291.

m194 **McGoldrick** James E., Luther's Scottish connection 1989 ➤ 6,k565; 7,g491: ᴿChH 60 (1991) 551s (W. F. *Graham*); GraceTJ 12,1 (1991) 151s (R. T. *Clutter*).

m195 **Moda** Aldo, M. Lutero, un decennio di studi 1989 ➤ 5,k83*; 7,g492: ᴿGregorianum 73 (1992) 174s (J. *Wicks*).

m196 *a) Möller* Christian, Luthers Seelsorge und die neueren Seelsorge-konzepte; – *b) Bohren* Rudolf, CALVIN als Seelsorger: TBeit 23,2 (Wu 1992) 75-92 / 62-74 [< ᴢɪᴛ 92,301s].

m197 *Müller* Gerhard, Ein Vierteljahrhundert Luther-Forschung: TRu 57 (1992) 337-391.

m198 *Nestingen* James A., Luther's Heidelberg disputation; an analysis of the argument [redimensioning Catholic J. VERCRUYSSE 1976]: ➤ 77, ꜰHARRISVILLE R. 1992, 147-154.

m198* *Nilsen* Else-Britt, Luthers oppgjør med klostervesenet i 'De votis monasticis' vurdert med henblikk på forholdet mellom kirke og samfunn i dag: NorTTs 92 (1991) 15-28.

m199 **Oberman** Heiko A., Luther, man between God and the devil 1989 ➤ 6,k572; 7,g494: ᴿChH 60 (1991) 383-5 (E. W. *Gritsch*); JRel 72 (1992) 112s (T. J. *Wengert*); SixtC 22 (1991) 126s (R. B. *Barnes*); Speculum 67 (1992) 459s (G. *Strauss*).

m200 ᴱ**Peura** Simo, *Raunio* Antti, Luther und Theosis 1989/90 ➤ 6,669*; 7,g495: ᴿTLZ 117 (1992) 444-6 (R. *Mau*); TvT 32 (1992) 100 (T. H. M. *Akerboom*).

m201 ᵀᴱ**Pin** Italo, pref. *Quinzio* Sergio, *a)* Martin Lutero, le 95 tesi; della libertà del cristiano; sulla prigionia babilonese della Chiesa [= 1984]; – *b)* ERASMO da Rotterdam, Sul libero arbitrio; – *c)* ENRICO VIII, Contro Lutero: Collezione Biblioteca 20.75.76. Pordenone 1989, Studio Tesi. 185 p., Lit. 20.000 / 95 p., Lit. 22.000 / 163 p., Lit. 25.000 [VivH 4,192-5, C. *Nardi*].

m202 ᴱ**Ronchi de Michelis** L., M. Lutero, Replica ad Ambrogio CATARINO sull'Anticristo 1521: 1989 ➤ 6,k575: ᴿAnStoEseg 9 (1992) 620-2 (Ottavia *Niccoli*, also on four cognate Luther-books, with no pp. for any).

m203 **Rothen** B., Die Klarheit der Schrift, 1. Luther [1990 ➤ 7,1055]; 2. BARTH 1990 [➤ m776 infra]: ᴿProtestantesimo 47 (1992) 339-341 (F. *Ferrario*); TsTKi 62 (1991) 215-7 (T. *Stordalen*).

m204 *Schloemann* Martin, Maria – Mutter – Kirche? lutherische Asso-ziationen zum Schlussstein 'Jesu Schulgang' im Chor der Nürnberger Frauenkirche: ➤ 19*b*, ꜰBLOTH P., 'Vor Ort' 1991 [< LuJb 59, p. 165] p. 67-76.

m205 **Schmidt** Axel, Die Christologie in M. Luthers späten Disputationen: Diss. Theol. 41, 1990 ➤ 6,7481*: ᴿForKT 8 (1992) 77 (W. *Brandmüller*).

m206 *Vercruysse* Jos E. sᴊ, Eine rechte Weise in der Theologie zu studieren; oratio – meditatio – tentatio; Luthers Vorrede von 1539: ➤ 52, ꟳErfurt 1992, 297-307.

m207 *White* Graham, Luther's view on language; LitTOx 3 (1989) 188-218 [< LuJb 59, p. 228].

m208 **Wicks** Jared, Luther's Reform; studies on conversion and the Church: Mainz EurG Beih 35. Mainz 1992, von Zabern. viii-351 p. [TR 88,343].

m209 *zur Mühlen* Karl-Heinz, Lutherforschung: ➤ 757, EvKL 3 (1992) 191-4 (-209 Kirchen, *al.*); 211-220, *Hendrix* Scott, Luthers Theologie; 220-8, *Hauschild* Wolf-Dieter, Luthertum.

Y4.3   Exegesis et controversia saeculi XVI.

m210 **Allison** A. F., *Rogers* D. M., The contemporary [to them] printed literature of the English Counter-Reformation between 1558 and 1640, I. Works in languages other than English 1989 ➤ 5,k98; 7,g499: ᴿEphLtg 105 (1991) 182s (A. *Ward*).

m211 *Andrés Martín* Melquiades, La teología española en el siglo XVI: RET 52 (1992) 129-153.

m212 ᴱ**Backus** Irena, *Higman* Francis, Théorie et pratique de l'exégèse, XVIᵉ s. 1988/90 ➤ 6,511: ᴿJEH 43 (1992) 318-321 (J. C. *Paget*: role of LXX and Fathers not stressed).

m213 **Barnes** Robin B., Prophecy and gnosis... Apocalypticism, Reformation 1988 ➤ 4,k80... 6,k581: ᴿAndrUnS 30 (1992) 159-160 (D. *Augsburger*).

m214 ᵀᴱ**Baylor** Michael G., [13 tracts] The radical Reformation. C 1991, Univ. 295 p. $44.50. – ᴿSixtC 23 (1992) 607s (E. J. *Furcha*).

m215 ᴱ**Bedouelle** G., *Roussel* B., Le temps des Réformes et la Bible: BTT 5, 1989 ➤ 5,k101... 7,g504: ᴿBtHumRen 52 (1990) 733-5 (M. *Grandjean*), SixtC 22 (1991) 115-7 (J. D. *Willis*).

m216 **Berriot-Salvadore** Evelyne, Les femmes dans la société française de la Renaissance: Histoire des idées 285. Genève 1990, Droz. 592 p. – ᴿBt-HumRen 54 (1992) 607-610 (Catherine *Magnien-Simonin*).

m217 ᴱ**Birmelé** André, *Lienhard* Marc, La foi des églises luthériennes; confessions et catéchismes, ᵀ*Jundt* A. & P., *al.* 1991 < 7,g505: ᴿRThom 92 (1992) 589s (G.-T. *Bedouelle*).

m218 ᵀᴱ**Blanco** Cesare, Il sommario della Santa Scrittura e l'ordinario dei cristiani (< nederl. 1523), intr. *Trapman* Johannes: Testi della Riforma 16. T 1988, Claudiana. – ᴿRTLv 23 (1992) 96s (J.-F. *Gilmont*).

m219 **Blickle** Peter, Communal reformation; the quest for salvation in sixteenth-century Germany, ᵀ*Dunlap* Thomas: StGermanHist. Atlantic Highlands ɴᴊ 1992, Humanities. xix-219 p. $45. 0-391-03730-7 [TDig 40,53].

m220 **Brigden** Susan, London and the Reformation. Ox 1990, Clarendon. 696 p. £55; pa. $30. 0-19-822774-4; -0256-2. – ᴿArchivScSocR 78 (1992) 217s (Viviane *Barrie-Currien*: comble un vide flagrant); RTLv 23 (1992) 233s (J.-F. *Gilmont*); TrinJ 13 (1992) 108-110 (T. *Beougher*).

m221 **Bujanda** J. M. de, *al.*, Index des livres interdits, 7. Anvers 1569, 1570, 1571: 1988 ➤ 6,k589; 7,g507: ᴿRBgPg 70 (1992) 1039-42 (R. *Crahay* †); RHE 87 (1991) 298 (J.-F. *Gilmont*).

m222 **Bujanda** J. M. de, *al.*, Index de Rome 1537, 1559, 1564; les premiers index romains et l'index du concile de Trente: Index des livres interdits

8. Sherbrooke/Genève 1990, Univ./Droz. 435 p. Fs 98. – ᴿRHE 87 (1992) 920 (J.-F. *Gilmont*).

m223 **Cameron** Euan, The European reformation. Ox 1991, Clarendon. xv-564 p.; 2 fig.; 6 maps. £45, pa. £13. 0-19-8739094-2; -3-4. – ᴿEngHR 107 (1992) 131-4 (T. *Scott*); JTS 43 (1992) 392-4 (A. *McGrath*: with 2000 publications a year on Luther alone, a book like this is impossible, but does its best); Month 253 (1992) 201s (L. *Warren*); SixtC 23 (1992) 864s (Larissa *Taylor*).

m224 **Campi** Emidio, Protestantesimo nei secoli, fonti e documenti, 1. Cinquecento e seicento 1991 → 7,g509; 88-7016-142-0: ᴿÉTRel 67 (1992) 476 (H. *Bost*).

m225 **Caponetto** Salvatore, La riforma protestante nell'Italia del cinquecento: Studi Storia. Torino 1992, Claudiana. 526 p.; ill.; maps. Lit. 54.000 [TR 88,522].

m226 ᴱ**Chaunu** Pierre, The Reformation, ᵀ*Arland* V. 1989 → 7,6510: ᴿScot-JT 45 (1992) 261-4 (E. *Cameron*).

m227 **Couliano** Ioan P., Eros and magic in the Renaissance [Eros et Magie], ᵀ*Cook* Margaret. Ch 1987, Univ. 296 p. $35; pa. $14. 0-226-12315-4; -6-2. – ᴿActuBbg 29 (1992) 114s (A. *Malet*).

m228 **Davidson** N.-S., La Contre-Réforme: Bref, 1989 → 6,k593 [non 'Le ...']: ᴿMélSR 48 (1991) 193s (G.-H. *Baudry*).

m229 *Decot* Rolf, Die Entstehung des modernen Erd- und Weltbildes im 15./16. Jahrhundert; theologische Voraussetzungen und Folgen: TGgw 35 (1992) 265-279.

m230 **Dittrich** Christoph, Die vortridentinische katholische Kontroverstheologie und die Täufer, Cochläus, Eck, Fabri. Fra 1991, Lang. 457 p. $67. – ᴿSixtC 23 (1992) 592s (W. *Harrison*).

m231 **Doran** Susan, **Durston** Christopher, Princes, pastors, and people; the Church and religion in England 1529-1689. NY 1991, Routledge. vii-216 p. – ᴿTS 53 (1992) 594 (H. J. *Ryan*: views of the revisionists).

m232 **Duffy** Eamon, The stripping of the altars; traditional religion in England, c. 1400-c. 1580. NHv 1992, Yale Univ. xii-654 p. $45. 0-300-05342-8 [TDig 40,159].

m233 *Dowse* Edgar, The teaching of the English Reformers on ministry and worship: Churchman 106 (1992) 102-110 [< ZIT 92,483].

m234 **Evans** Gilliam R., Problems of authority in the Reformation debates. C 1992, Univ. 328 p. £35. 0-521-41686-8. – ᴿExpTim 104 (1992s) 253 (J. K. *Cameron*).

m235 **Forster** Marc R., The Counter-Reform in the villages; religion and reform in the bishopric of Speyer, 1560-1720. Ithaca NY 1992, Cornell Univ. xii-272 p. $37.50. 0-8014-2566-2 [TDig 49,62].

m236 **Garstein** Oskar, Rome and the counter-reformation in Scandinavia; *a*) Jesuit educational strategy, 1553-1622; – *b*) the age of Gustavus Adolphus and Queen Christina of Sweden 1622-1656: StChrTht 47. Leiden 1992, Brill. xii-462 p. *f*220; xviii-533 p. *f*220 [TR 88,523]. – ᴿEngHR 107 (1992) 961-4 (M. *Roberts*).

m237 *Gentilcore* D., Methods and approaches in the social history of the Counter-Reformation in Italy: SH 17 (1992) 73-98 [< RHE 87,258*].

m238 **George** Timothy, Theology of the Reformers 1988 → 4,k102 ... 7,g520: ᴿChH 60 (1991) 387-9 (J. W. *Baker*); SAfBap 2 (1992) 104s (D. L. *Morcom*).

m239 ᴱ**Gilmont** Jean-François, La Réforme et le livre 1990 → 6,411*; 7,g521: ᴿRHE 87 (1992) 201s (Monique *Mund-Dopchie*).

m240 *Giombi* Samuele, *a*) Lo studio umanistico dell'antichità cristiana nella Riforma cattolica; rassegna storiografica e ipotesi interpretative: RivStoLR 28 (1992) 143-162; – *b*) Riforma protestante e cinquecento italiano: StPatav 39 (1992) 605-615.

m241 **Gmiterek** Henryk, Antitrinitaires polonais 2s: Bibliotheca dissidentium 13s. Baden-Baden 1991s, Koerner. 204 p.; 143 p. je DM 120 [TR 88,522].

m242 **Grafton** Anthony, Defenders of the text; the traditions of scholarship in an age of science, 1450-1800. CM 1991, Harvard Univ. ix-330 p.; 2 fig. £28 [ClasR 43,136, M. D. *Reeve*].

m243 *Günther* Hartmut, 'Allein die Schrift'; nötige Bemerkungen zum Verständnis der Heiligen Schrift und zum Umgang mit ihr: LuthTK 16 (1992) 58-66.

m244 **Hall** B., Humanists and Protestants 1500-1900. E 1990, Clark. 180 p. £20. – [R]Protestantesimo 47 (1992) 334s (V. *Bernardi*).

m244* *a*) *Huber* Wolfgang, Ökumenische Situation und protestantisches Prinzip; eine Problemanzeige; – *b*) *Graf* Friedrich W., Ist bürgerlich-protestantische Freiheit ökumenisch verallgemeinerbar? Zum Streit um das protestantische Verständnis von Freiheit: ZTK 89 (1992) 98-120 / 121-138.

m245 *Iserloh* Erwin, Compendio di storia e teologia della Riforma [Geschichte und T. im Grundriss, 1969 [3]1985] ➤ 7,g525; [T]*Poletti* Gianni. Brescia 1990, Morcelliana. 308 p.; 2 color. pl. Lit. 30.000. – [R]Angelicum 69 (1992) 295-7 (A. *Kordel*); Protestantesimo 47 (1992) 328-330 (P. *Ribet*).

m246 *Junghans* Helmer, Reformation: ➤ 757, EvKL 3 (1992) 1470-92 (-1520, *al.*).

m247 **King** Margaret L., Women of the Renaissance. Ch 1991, Univ. 333 p. – [R]BtHumRen 54 (1992) 803-5 (Régine *Reynolds-Cornell*).

m248 **Kirk** James, Patterns of reform 1989 ➤ 5,k120; 7,k528: [R]ScotJT 45 (1992) 259-261 (E. *Cameron*).

m249 **Klötzer** Ralf, Die Täuferherrschaft von Münster; Stadtreformation und Welterneuerung [Diss. Hamburg]: 230 p.; ill. DM 78 [TR 88,523].

m250 *Koch* Kurt, Tragik oder Befreiung der Reformation? Unzeitgemässe Überlegungen aus ökumenischer Sicht: StiZt 210 (1992) 234-246.

m251 **Köhler** Hans-J., Bibliographie der Flugschriften des 16. Jahrhunderts I/1, 1501-1530 A-G. Tü 1991, BtAcademica. xlvii-620 p. – [R]ArRefG 83 (1992) 315-9 (B. *Moeller*).

m252 **Köster** Beate, Evangelienharmonien im frühen Pietismus: ZKG 103 (1992) 195-225.

m253 *Laberge* Léo, La Bible dans le temps [BTT 5-8]: ÉglT 23 (1992) 113-121.

m254 **Leader** Damien R., A history of the University of Cambridge, I. to 1546. C 1988, Univ. xxi-399 p. $65. – [R]SixtC 23 (1992) 179s (C. G. *Nauert*).

m255 *Le Cointe* Jean, Structures hiérarchiques [de pensée] et théorie critique de la Renaissance: BtHumRen 52 (1990) 529-560.

m256 *Lienhard* Marc, La Réformation et l'Europe: ÉTRel 67 (1992) 541-555.

m257 *Llin Cháfer* Arturo, La reforma de la Iglesia en el siglo XVI: RelCu 37 (1991) 73-102.

m258 *Lorenz* S., Studium generale Erfordense; neue Forschungen zum Erfurter Schulleben: Traditio 46 (1991) 261-289. ➤ m279.

m259 **Lortz** Joseph, zum Gedenken, Beiträge zur Reformationsgeschichte und Ökumene, [E]**Decot** R. 1989 ➤ 6,120: [R]ZKG 103 (1992) 259-261 (S. *Skalweit*).

m260 **McGrath** Alister E., Reformation thought; an introduction 1988
➤ 4,k107* ... 7,g529: ᴿChH 60 (1991) 116-8 (E. W. *Gritsch*).

m261 **McGrath** Alister E., Il pensiero della Riforma: PiccBtT 24, 1991
➤ 7,g530: ᴿSalesianum 54 (1992) 807s (M. *Müller*).

m262 **McGrath** Alister, Roots that refresh; a celebration of Reformation
spirituality. L 1992, Hodder & S. 202 p. £7. 0-340-55803-2. – ᴿExpTim
104 (1992s) 58s (G. S. *Wakefield*).

m263 **Martin** A. Lynn, The Jesuit mind; the mentality of an elite in early
modern France. Ithaca 1988, Cornell Univ. xvi-256 p. $33. – ᴿEngHR
107 (1992) 462s (J. *Bergin*: from the 5000 letters of superiors to Rome).

m264 *Navarro Sorni* Miguel, Problemas históricos y teológicos en torno a 'Il
beneficio di Cristo' [Venezia 1543; ᴱ*Da Mantova* B. 1972]: AnVal 17
(1991) 49-114.

m265 *Nestingen* James A., Challenges and responses in the Reformation:
Interpretation 46 (1992) 250-261.

m266 **Olim** John C., Catholic reform; from Cardinal Ximenes to the Council
of Trent 1495-1563; 1990 ➤ 7,g536: ᴿChH 60 (1991) 390s (R. *Keen*);
SixtC 22 (1991) 854-6 (M. R. *Forster*).

m267 **O'Malley** John W., Catholicism in early modern history; a guide to
research: Reformation Guides to Research 2, 1989 ➤ 6,1054; 0-910345-
02-3: ᴿJEH 43 (1992) 102-9 (D. *Fenlon*).

m268 *Ottati* Douglas F., The spirit of reforming Protestantism: ChrCent 109
(1992) 1163-6.

m269 **Ozment** Steven, Protestants, the birth of a revolution. NY 1992,
Doubleday. xiv-270 p. $20. 0-385-42172-9 [TDig 39,378]. – ᴿChrCent
109 (1992) 847s (M. L. *Wagner*).

m269* *Pastoureau* Michel, La Réforme et la couleur: BProtFr 138 (1992)
323-342 [< ᴢɪᴛ 92,649].

m270 **Pettegree** Andrew, Emden [a place] and the Dutch revolt; exile and
the development of Reformed Protestantism. Ox 1992, Clarendon. xii-
350 p.; ill. [RHR 88,563, J.-F. *Gilmont*].

m271 ᴱ**Rodríguez** Pedro, Catechismus romanus ... Tridentini, ed. crítica. Va-
ticano/Pamplona 1989, Editrice/Univ. Navarra. lxxx-1378 p.; 26 fig. Lit.
260.000. – ᴿETL 68 (1992) 173-5 (M. *Simon*).

m272 **Romeo** Giovanni, Inquisitori, esorcisti e streghe nell'Italia della Controriforma. F 1990, Sansoni. x-332 p. – ᴿRivStoLR 27 (1991) 348-352
(E. *Stumpo*).

m273 **Rublack** Hans-Christoph, ... hat die Nonne den Pfarrer geküsst?: Aus
dem Alltag der Reformationszeit: Siebenstern 1113. Gü 1991, Mohn.
160 p.; 6 fig. DM 19,80. 3-579-01113-8. – ᴿTLZ 117 (1992) 613 (S.
Bräuer).

m274 *Rummel* Erika, Et cum theologo bella poeta gerit; the conflict between
humanists and scholastics revisited: SixtC 23 (1992) 713-728.

m275 **Sáenz-Badillos** Ángel, La filología bíblica en los primeros helenistas de
Alcalá 1990 ➤ 7,g664: ᴿBtHumRen 54 (1992) 847s (D. *Barthélemy*);
Helmantica 42 sup (1991) 393 (C. *Carrete Parrondo*).

m276 *Schmid* Vincent, Cathares et Protestants, persistance d'un reflet: BCent-
Prot 43,3 (1991) 3-22.

m277 *Schulte Herbrüggen* Hubertus, A hundred new humanists' letters;
MORE, ERASMUS, VIVES, CRANEVELT, GELDENHOUWER and other Dutch
humanists [Bundle auctioned 21.VI.1989 to Belgium for £280,000]: Bt-
HumRen 52 (1990) 65-76.

m278 **Sieben** Hermann J., Die katholische Konzilsidee von der Reformation

bis zur Aufklärung [1984 ➤ 1,f721] 1988 ➤ 6,k635: ᴿTPhil 67 (1992) 290s (H. J. *Pottmeyer*).
m279 **Sönke** Lorenz, Studium generale Erfordense; zum Erfurter Schulleben im 13. und 14. Jahrhundert. MgGMA 34. Stu 1989, Hiersemann. xvi-403 p. DM 298. – ᴿColcFran 61 (1991) 353s (P. *Maranesi*).
m280 **Sommerville** C. John, The secularization of early modern Europe; from religious culture to religious faith. NY 1992, Oxford-UP. 227 p. $40. 0-19-507427-0 [TDig 39,386].
m281 **Spykman** Gordon J., Reformational theology, a new paradigm for doing dogmatics. GR 1992, Eerdmans. xiii-584 p. $40. 0-8028-3701-8 [TDig 39,386].
m282 **Stayer** James M., The German peasants' war and Anabaptist community of goods: StHistRel 6. Montreal 1991, McGill-Queen's Univ. x-227 p.; 12 fig.: 2 maps. £27. 0-7735-0842-2. – ᴿJTS 43 (1992) 297s (A. *McGrath*).
m283 ᴱ**Steinmetz** David C., The Bible in the sixteenth century 1982/90 ➤ 6,556b: ᴿJRel 72 (1992) 434s (E. *McKee*); SixtC 23 (1992) 351 (S. G. *Burnett*); VT 42 (1992) 284 (J. A. *Emerton*).
m284 **Strehle** Stephen, Calvinism, Federalism, and scholasticism; a study of the Reformed doctrine of covenant: BaBSt 58. NY 1988, Lang. Fs 69,70. – ᴿJTS 43 (1992) 298-300 (J. *Platt*).
m285 *Strehle* Stephen, Calvinism, Augustinianism, and the will of God: ➤ 38, ᶠCULLMANN O., TZBas 48 (1992) 221-237.
m286 *Sunnes* Kjell O., Recent research on the Augsburg Confession: TsTKi 63 (1992) 141-7.
m287 ᴱ**Venard** Marc, Le temps des confessions (1530-1620/30): Histoire du christianisme 8. P 1992, Desclée. 1236 p.; ill. [RHE 88,562, J.-F. *Gilmont*].
m289 **Weir** David A., The origins of federal theology in sixteenth-century Reformation thought 1990 ➤ 6,k643; 7,g544: ᴿJRel 72 (1992) 597s (R. A. *Muller*); RTPhil 124 (1992) 102s (K. *Blaser*).
m290 **Whiting** Robert, The blind devotion of the people; popular religion and the English Reformation 1989 ➤ 6,k645: ᴿChH 60 (1991) 549-551 (B. *Tipson*).
m291 **Wright** William J., Capitalism, the State, and the Lutheran Reformation; sixteenth-century Hesse. Athens 1988, Ohio Univ. xiv-326 p. $38. – ᴿEngHR 107 (1992) 184s (K. von *Greyerz*: valuable, irritating).
m292 **Wuthnow** Robert, Communities of discourse; ideology and social structure in the Reformation, the Enlightenment, and European socialism. CM 1989, Harvard Univ. 739 p. $49.50. – ᴿJRel 72 (1992) 588s (M. *Riesebrodt*: if he is right, publications are a social process and 'meaning' is irrelevant).
m293 **Zapalac** Kristin E. S., 'In his image and likeness'; political iconography and religious change in Regensburg 1500-1600. Ithaca NY 1990, Cornell Univ. xv-279 p. $30. – ᴿJRel 72 (1992) 436s (V. *Reinburg*).
m294 *Zimmermann* Gunter, Prinzipielle Anliegen der reformierten Theologie nach dem Staffortschen Buch von 1599: TZBas 48 (1992) 243-267.
m295 ᴱ**Zinguer** Ilana, L'Hébreu au temps de la Renaissance: Jewish Studies 4. Leiden 1992, Brill. 252 p. 90-04-09557-8. 11 art.

Y4.4   Periti aetatis reformatoriae.

m296 ANDREWES: **Lossky** Nicholas, Lancelot Andrewes, the preacher 1555-1626; the origins of the mystical theology of the Church of England,

ᵀ*Louth* Andrew. Ox 1991, Clarendon. 377 p. £45. 0-19-826185-3. –
ᴿExpTim 103 (1991s) 159 (G. S. *Wakefield*: Arminian leader of great
erudition and poetic richness).

m297 ARMINIUS: *Cameron* Charles M., Arminius – hero or heretic?: EvQ
64 (1992) 213-227.

m298 **Muller** Richard A., God, creation and Providence in the thought of
Jacob Arminius; sources and directions of scholastic Protestantism in
the era of early orthodoxy 1991 → 7,g549: ᴿRelStR 18 (1992) 149
(J. L. *Farthing*); TrinJ 13 (1992) 98-104 (M. J. *Klauber*).

m299 **Witt** William, Creation, redemption and grace in the theology of
Jacobus Arminius: diss. ᴰ*Burrell* D. Notre Dame 1992. – RTLv 24,
p. 556.

m300 BARTILIUS: *Darowski* Roman, ℗ Wawryniec Bartilius SJ (1569-
1635) filozof i teolog: Bobolanum 3 (1989) 101-111 (bibliog. 109-111);
franç. 111.

m301 BELLARMINO: **Biersack** Manfred, Initia Bellarminiana [Diss. Tü 1980
ᴰ*Oberman* H.] 1989 → 7,g553: ᴿGregorianum 73 (1992) 371-3 (J. E.
Vercruysse); TLZ 117 (1992) 851-3 (E. *Koch*).

m302 ᴱ**Galeota** Gustavo, R. Bellarmino, convegno 1988/90 → 7,e496*: ᴿCC
143 (1992,1) 298-300 (G. *Mellinato*); CrNSt 13 (1992) 452-5 (U. *Parente*);
Gregorianum 73 (1992) 370s (M. *Delmirani*); RTLv 23 (1992) 393s (J.-F.
Gilmont); Salesianum 54 (1992) 277s (E. *Semeraro*); TPhil 67 (1992) 600s
(H. J. *Sieben*).

m303 BEZA: **Brice** Derek C., Theodore Beza; the image and the man: Exp-
Tim 104 (1992s) 35-38.

m304 *Jinkins* Michael, Theodore Beza; continuity and regression in the Reformed tradition: EvQ 64 (1992) 131-154.

m305 BRAUN: **Rössner** Maria B., Konrad Braun (ca. 1495-1563) — ein
katholischer Jurist, Politiker, Kontroverstheologe und Kirchenreformer
im konfessionellen Zeitalter [Diss. Bonn]: RefGStT 130. Münster 1991,
Aschendorff. 435 p. DM 98. 3-402-03778-5 [TLZ 118,417, T. *Kaufmann*].

m306 BUCER: **Burnett** Amy N., Church discipline and moral reformation in
the thought of Martin Bucer: SixtC 22 (1991) 438-456; portr.

m307 *Brooks* Peter N., Martin Bucer, oecuméniste and forgotten Reformer:
ExpTim 103 (1991s) 231-5.

m308 **Greschat** M. M. Bucer 1990 → 7,g557: ᴿBtHumRen 54 (1992) 560-3
(R. *Bodenmann*).

m309 **Joisten** Harmut, Martin Bucer, un Réformateur européen, ᵀ*Joch* C.
Strasbourg 1991, Oberlin. 162 p. F 92. 3-85369-110-1. – ᴿÉTRel 67
(1992) 287s (H. *Bost*: excellente petite biographie).

m310 **Kroon** M. de. Martin Bucer en Johannes Calvin; reformatorische
perspectieven. Zoetermeer 1991, Meinema. 222 p. ƒ 39,50. 90-211-
3560-4. – ᴿTvT 32 (1992) 200 (W. van 't *Spijker*).

m311 **Kroon** Marijn de, M. Bucer und J. CALVIN; reformatorische Perspektiven, Einleitung und Texte, ᵀ*Rudolph* H. Gö 1991, Vandenhoeck &
R. 285 p. DM 58 pa. 3-525-55337-4 [TLZ 118,39, J. *Rogge*].

m312 *Lienhard* Marc, Martin Bucer, le Réformateur européen: BSocHist-
ProtFr 138 (P 1992) 161 (-180?).

m312* a) *Wright* David, Martin Bucer in England; – b) *McGrath* Alister E.,
The European roots of evangelism: Anvil 9 (1992) 249-... / 239-248
[< ZIT 92,677].

m313 BULLINGER: *Biel* Pamela, Heinrich Bullinger's death and testament; a
well-planned departure: SixtC 22 (1991) 3-14.

m314 **McCoy** Charles S., *Baker* J. Wayne, Fountainhead of federalism; Heinrich Bullinger and the Covenantal tradition 1990 ➤ 7,g561: ᴿWestTJ 54 (1992) 396-400 (M. W. *Karlberg*).

m315 CAJETANUS: *Gunten* A. F. von, Cajetan et Luther; foi et sacrement dans la justification: NVFr 67 (1992) 259-288.

m316 CALVIN: ᵀᴱ**Beaty** Mary, *Farley* Benjamin W., Calvin's ecclesiastical advice [from hitherto un-Englished letters and bits of exegesis]. E 1991, Clark. 184 p. £9. 0-567-29196-0. – ᴿExpTim 103 (1991s) 186 (Claire *Cross*: 'Christian common sense').

m316* *Böttger* Paul C., Gott, der Brunnenquell aller Guter — gibt es einen 'mystischen' Grundzug in der Theologie Calvins? ➤ 120, ᶠLOCHER G., Zwingliana 19,2 (1992) 59-72.

m317 **Böttger** Paul C., Calvins Institutio als Erbauungsbuch; Versuch einer literarischen Analyse. Neuk 1990, Neuk.-V. 148 p. DM 48 pa. – ᴿTLZ 117 (1992) 43s (J. *Rogge*).

m317* **Carter** Ben M., The depersonalization of God; a consideration of soteriological difficulties in High Calvinism. Lanham MD 1989, UPA. 72 p. $23.75. – ᴿSixtC 22 (1991) 372s (M. I. *Klauber* disagrees).

m318 *Compier* Don H., The independent pupil; Calvin's transformation of ERASMUS' theological hermeneutics: WestTJ 54 (1992) 217-233.

m319 ᴱ**Gamble** Richard C., [256 1899-1989] Articles on Calvin and Calvinism. Hamden CT 1992, Garland. 14 vols. $775 [RelStR 19,172, D. R. *Janz*].

m320 ᴱ**George** Timothy, John CALVIN and the Church, a prism of reform [colloquia 1982-8] 1990 ➤ 6,616*; 7,g567: ᴿCritRR 5 (1922) 324s (Charmarie J. *Blaidell*); Interpretation 46 (1992) 187-9 (J. C. *Goodloe*).

m321 **Greef** W. de, Johannes Calvijn, zijn werk en geschriften 1989 ➤ 5,k160; 90-61401-76-3: ᴿNedTTs 46 (1992) 74 (C. *Graafland*).

m322 **Helleman** Adrian A., John Calvin on papal primacy: diss. St. Michael, ᴰ*McSorley* H. Toronto 1992, 473 p. – RTLv 24, p. 555.

m323 **Kelly** Douglas F., The emergence of liberty in the modern world; the influence of Calvin on five governments from the 16th through 18th centuries. Phillipsburg NJ 1992, P & R. xii-156 p. [RHE 88,659, J.-F. *Gilmont*: Calvin se reconnaîtrait-il?].

m324 *Klauber* Martin I., Calvin on fundamental articles [not like 1900s US fundamentalism's] and ecclesiastical union: WestTJ 54 (1992) 341-8.

m325 **McGrath** Alister E., A life of John Calvin 1990 ➤ 6,k666; 7,g571: ᴿCritRR 5 (1992) 339-341 (Elsie *McKee*); EvQ 64 (1992) 372s (T. *Lane*); SixtC 23 (1992) 358s (D. K. *McKim*); TTod 49 (1992s) 116s (M. E. *Osterhaven*); WestTJ 54 (1992) 197s (D. W. *Hall*).

m326 *Monheit* Michael L., 'The ambition for an illustrious name'; humanism, patronage, and Calvin's doctrine of the Calling: SixtC 23 (1992) 267-287.

m327 *a) Oberman* Heiko A., 'Subita conversio'; the 'conversion' of John Calvin; – *b) Blaser* Klauspeter, Le combat de l'Église selon Calvin; – *c) Hesselink* I. John, Governed and guided by the Spirit — a key issue in Calvin's doctrine of the Holy Spirit; – *d) Lange van Ravenswaay* J. Marius, Calvin und die Juden — eine offene Frage [*Augustijn* Cornelis, Philipp von Hessen/Juden]: ➤ 129, ᶠLOCHER G., Zwingliana 19,2 (1992) 279-295 / 43-57 / 161-171 / 183-194 [1-11].

m327* *Oberman* Heiko A., John Calvin and condign merit: AnRefG 83 (1992) 73-110; deutsch 110s.

m328 **Olson** Jeannine E., Calvin and social welfare; deacons and the Bourse française 1989 → 6,k670: ᴿRHE 87 (1992) 204-7 (J.-F. *Gilmont*).

m329 **Parker** Thomas H. L., Calvin's preaching. Louisville 1992, W-Knox. xiii-202 p. $23. 0-664-25309-1 [TDig 40,283]. – ᴿExpTim 104 (1992s) 285 (P. N. *Brooks*).

m330 **Ruler** Arnold A. van, Calvinist Trinitarianism and theocentric politics [essays since 1947], ᵀ*Bok* John: Studies in theology 38. Lewiston 1989, Mellen. xliv-228 p. $60. – ᴿWestTJ 53 (1991) 165-7 (R. E. *Otto*).

m330* *Saarinen* Risto, Christus als Lehrer bei FICINO und Calvin; ein Beitrag zur Entstehung der Dreiämterlehre: ZTK 89 (1992) 197-221.

m331 **Schreiner** Susan E., The theater of his glory; nature and the natural order in the thought of John Calvin [diss.]: Studies in historical theology 3. Durham 1991, Labyrinth. ix-164 p. 0-939464-51-9. – ᴿÉTRel 67 (1992) 602s (H. *Bost*).

m332 **Torrance** Thomas F., The hermeneutics of John Calvin 1988 → 4,k151; 5,k168: ᴿHeythJ 33 (1992) 348s (A. HAMILTON: shows better than GANOCZY the influence of John MAJOR).

m333 **Van Hamersveld** Michael D., The concept of *suspensio* in Calvin's interpretation of the Gospel: diss. Aberdeen 1991. 284 p. BRDX-95661. – DissA 53 (1992s) 185-A.

m334 CAMERARIUS: ᴱ**Harms** Wolfgang, *Kuechen* Ulla-Britta, Joachim Camerarius, Symbola et Emblemata (Nürnberg 1590-1604): Naturalis historia Bibliae, Schriften zur biblischen Naturkunde des 16.-18. Jahrhunderts 2. Graz 1986, Akad-VA. 438 p.; 63 pl. – ᴿZKG 103 (1992) 266-8 (Monica *Mutzbauer*).

m335 CASTELLION: **[Gallicet] Calvetti** Carla, S. Castellion... contro Calvino 1989 [4 dialogues posthumesᵀ] → 7,g566: ᴿAsprenas 39 (1992) 303s (U. *Dovere*); BtHumRen 52 (1990) 205-7 (A. *Dufour*).

m336 *Guggisberg* Hans R., [Sebastian] Castellio auf dem Index: ArRefG 83 (1992) 112-128; Eng. 129.

m337 CORTESE: **Cesareo** Francesco C., Humanism and Catholic reform; the life and work of Gregorio Cortese (1483-1548): RenBaroque 2. NY 1990, P. Lang. xviii-203 p. → 6,k682; $45.50. 0-8204-0907-3 [TDig 38,351]. – ᴿRivStoLR 27 (1991) 567-9 (M. *Firpo*); SixtC 23 (1992) 139-141 (R. E. *Delph*).

m338 CRANACH: **Tacke** Andreas, Der katholische Cranach ['lutherischer' Maler der Reformation]: Berliner Schriften zur Kunst 2. Mainz 1992, von Zabern. 289 p.; 172 fig. DM 120 [ErbAuf 68,520]. → g733*.

m339 CRANMER: **Brooks** Peter N., Cranmer in context 1989 → 4,k683; 7,g577*: ᴿChH 60 (1991) 543s (P. F. *Vieson*).

m340 ECK: **Ziegelbauer** Max, J. Eck 1987 → 6,k688: ᴿAtKap 116 (1991) 191s (L. *Balter*, ❷).

m340* *Bagchi* David, Catholic Anti-Judaism in Reformation Germany; the case of Johann Eck: → 638, C/Judaism 1992, 253-263.

m341 ERASMUS: **Augustijn** Cornelis, Erasmus; his life, works, and influence [1986 → 3,g587], ᵀ*Grayson* J. C.: Erasmus Studies 10, 1990 → 7,g579*; $40: ᴿCathHR 78 (1992) 651-3 (N. H. *Minnich*); ExpTim 103 (1991s) 256 [C. S. *Rodd*].

m342 ᴱ**Chomarat** J., *al.*, Colloque Érasme 1986/90 → 6,725: ᴿNRT 114 (1992) 769 (S. *Hilaire*).

m343 **Coogan** Robert, Erasmus, [Edward] LEE and the correction of the Vulgate; the shaking of the foundations: TravHumRen 261. Genève 1992, Droz. 125 p. – ᴿRHPR 72 (1992) 364s (M. *Arnold*).

m344 **D'Ascia** L., Erasmo e l'umanesimo romano: RivStoLR Bt 2. F 1991, Olschki. 226 p. Lit. 44.000. – ᴿStPatav 39 (1992) 243-6 (S. *Giombi*).

m345 *Estes* James M., Officium principis christiani; Erasmus and the origins of the Protestant state church: ArRefG 83 (1992) 49-72; deutsch 72.

m346 **Halkin** L. E., Erasmo, ital. [Erasme parmi nous 1988],ᵀ. Bari 1989, Laterza. xiv-406 p. Lit. 45.000. – ᴿHelmantica 43 (1992) 277 (J. *Oroz*).

m347 *Halkin* Léon-E., Érasme et la troisième voie: RHE 87 (1992) 405-415; Eng. deutsch 416: neither a crypto-Lutheran nor avid of Catholic power, but a patient (and unsuccessful) searcher for reconciliation.

m348 *Kinowaki* Etsuro, *Philosophia* in the writings of Erasmus: ➤ 74, ᶠGUENTHER H., TorJT 8 (1992) 134-147.

m348* ᴱKnott Betty I., De duplici copia verborum ac rerum commentarii: Erasmus Opera 1/6. Amst 1988, North-Holland. vii-314 p. – ᴿGnomon 64 (1992) 20-25 (R. *Jakobi*).

m349 **McConica** James, Erasmus: Past Masters, 1991 ➤ 7,g383: ᴿRHE 87 (1992) 287s (J. *Warrilow*); TLond 95 (1992) 58s (Anne J. *Duggan*: Luther's views were like a striking manuscript variant, interesting but needing to await a devout critical consensus, p. 80); TrinJ 13 (1992) 221-5 (T. P. *Scheck*).

m350 *Margolin* Joan-Claude, Marcel BATAILLON, Érasme et l'Espagne: BtHumRen 54 (1992) 427-439.

m351 **Pabel** Hilmar M., Prayer in Erasmus; pastoral ministry through the printing press: diss. Yale, ᴰPelikan J. NHv 1992. 370 p. 93-08996. – DissA 53 (1992s) 4044-A.

m352 **Reese** Alan W., Erasmus [an Augustinian Canon] and the ascetic tradition: diss. Saskatchewan 1991. 287 p. DANN 72991. – DissA (1992s) 4435s-A.

m353 ᴱ**Rummel** Erika, The Erasmus reader. Toronto 1990, Univ. 376 p. $20. – ᴿSixtC 23 (1992) 387s (W. R. *Russell*).

m354 **Rummel** Erika, Erasmus and his Catholic critics 1989 ➤ 6,k693; 7,g585*: ᴿBtHumRen 52 (1990) 729-732 (E. V. *Telle*); CrNSt 13 (1992) 445-7 (S. *Giombi*); SixtC 22 (1991) 401s (R. L. *De Molen*); TLZ 117 (1992) 287-9 (C. *Augustijn*).

m355 **Schoeck** R. J., Erasmus grandescens 1988 ➤ 5,k183; 7,g586: ᴿRBgPg 70 (1992) 1046s (J.-C. *Margolin*); TLZ 117 (1992) 134s (C. *Augustijn*).

m356 **Screech** M. A., Érasme, l'extase et l'Éloge de la folie [Ecstasy 1980], ᵀChambert J.: BtT. P 1991, Desclée. 364 p. F 195 [RTLv 24,391, J.-F. *Gilmont*].

m357 **Seidel Menchi** Silvana, Erasmus als Ketzer; Reformation und Inquisition im Italien des 16. Jahrhunderts [Erasmo in Italia 1987 ➤ 4,k163; Hab.-Diss. Heidelberg 1990: RHE 88,674, J.-F. *Gilmont*]: StMdvRefT 49. Leiden 1992, Brill. x-505 p. ƒ230 [TR 88,522].

m358 **Shantz** Douglas H., CRAUTWALD and Erasmus; a study in humanism and radical reform in sixteenth-century Silesia [diss. Waterloo ON]: BtDiss 4. Baden-Baden 1992, Koerner. 254 p.; ill.; maps [TR 88,255].

m359 **Walter** Peter, Theologie/Rhetorik ... Schriftauslegung/Erasmus 1991 ➤ 7,g387: ᴿBtHumRen 54 (1992) 559s (R. *Coogan*); JTS 43 (1992) 294-7 (Irena *Backus*); RömQ 87 (1992) 338 (A. *Schmid*).

m360 FAREL: **Heyer** Henri, Guillaume Farel [chiefly 1521-55], an introduction to his theology, ᵀ*Reynolds* Blair: TStRel 54. Lewiston NY 1990, Mellen. 103 p. $50. − ᴿWestTJ 54 (1992) 389s (D. W. *Hall*: important).

m361 FISCHER A.: **Liechty** Daniel, Andreas Fischer and the Sabbatarian Anabaptists; an early Reformation episode in East Central Europe: AnabMennonHist 29. Scottdale 1990, Herald. 192 p. $30. 0-8361-1293-8. − ᴿEngHR 107 (1992) 461s (B. *Scribner*).

m362 FISHER J.: **Rex** Richard, The theology of John Fisher. C 1991, Univ. xii-293 p. £30. 0-521-39177-6. − ᴿCathHR 78 (1992) 650s (W. S. *Stafford*: deeply researched and clearly written); ExpTim 103 (1991s) 120 (P. N. *Brooks*: condemned not for his 'Augustinian orthodoxy' or 'developing patristic orientation' but for questioning the King's authority); JEH 43 (1992) 650-4 (A. *Kenny*, also on MARTZ's More); SixtC 23 (1992) 582s (T. F. *Mayer*).

m363 FLORIMOND: **Tinsley** B. C., History and polemics in the Reformation, Florimond, defender of the Church. Selinsgrove/L 1992, Susquehanna Univ./Assoc. Univ. 238 p.; 3 fig. $38.50 [NRT 115,613, P. *Evrard*].

m364 FRANCKE: **Peschke** Erhard, Die frühen Katechismuspredigten August H. Franckes, 1693-5: ArbPietismus 28. Gö 1992, Vandenhoeck & R. 235 p. DM 80. 3-525-55812-0 [TLZ 118,46, J. *Wallmann*].

m365 HENRICUS VIII: ᴱ**Fraenkel** Pierre, Heinrich VIII., Assertio septem sacramentorum adversus Martinum LUTHERUM: CCath 43. Münster 1992, Aschendorff. vi-250 p.; portr. 3-402-93457-3.

m366 HOFFMAN M.: *Bailey* Richard G., Melchior Hoffman; proto-Anabaptist and printer in Kiel, 1527-1529: ChH 59 (1990) 175-190.

m367 HUBMAIER: ᵀᴱ**Pipkin** Wayne H., *Yoder* John H., Balthasar Hubmaier [complete writings]: Classics of the Radical Reformation 1991 → 7,g591a: ᴿSixtC 22 (1991) 776-8 (K. R. *Davis*).

m368 KLINGE: *Rickauer* Hans-Christian, Glaube und Heilshandeln; zur theologischen Auseinandersetzung des Erfurter Franziskaners Konrad Klinge mit der reformatorischen Lehre: → 52, ᶠErfurt 1992, 55-70.

m369 KNOX: *Kyle* Richard, John Knox, a man of the Old Testament: WestTJ 54 (1992) 65-78.

m370 LAS CASAS: *Köpcke-Duttler* Arnold, Las Casas — ein Gewissen des Abendlandes?: Junge Kirche 53 (Bremen 1992) 401-4 [< ZIT 92,492].

m371 **Mahn-Lot** Marianne, Bartolomé de Las Casas, De l'unique manière d'évangéliser le monde entier [1522-7]: Sagesses chrétiennes. P 1990, Cerf. 145 p. − ᴿBtHumRen 52 (1990) 767s (F. *Lestringant*).

m372 **Las Casas** Bartolomé de, The devastation of the Indies, a brief account, ᵀ*Briffault* Herma. Baltimore c. 1992, Johns Hopkins. 152 p. $12. − ᴿChrCent 109 (1992) 655s (R. M. *Brown*, also on two cognates).

m373 *Milhou* Alain, Las Casas, prophétisme et millénarisme: Études 376 (1992) 393-404.

m374 *Nonis* Pietro, 'La distruzione delle Indie' di Bartolomé de Las Casas: ViPe 75 (1992) 578-589.

m375 *Orhant* Francis, Bartolomé de Las Casas: Mémoire d'hommes, mémoire de foi. P c. 1991, Ouvrières. F 78 [Études 376,392 adv.].

m375* *Peter* Antón, Bartolomé de Las Casas y el tema de la conversión en la teología de la liberación: Páginas 17,116 (1992) 49-63 [118,82-85, *Guchtenberg* Pedro de, Congreso sobre Las Casas, Lima 25-28,VIII.1992].

m376 LEUNCLAVIUS: *Burtin* Marie-Pierre, Un apôtre de la tolérance, l'humaniste allemand Johannes Löwenklau, dit Leunclavius (1541-1593?): BtHumRen 52 (1990) 561-570.

m377 L. DE GRANADA: *Llin Cháfer* Arturo, Fray Luis de Granada y la democratización de la oración: AnVal 17 (1991) 247-270.

m378 L. DE LEÓN: *Folgado Flórez* S., Fray Luis de León como teólogo y escriturario: AnVal 17 (1991) 193-216.

m379 MAROT: *Defaux* Gérard, *Lestringant* Frank, [Clément] Marot et le problème de l'Évangélisme; à propos de trois articles récents de C. A. MEYER ['depasse les limites...']: BtHumRen 54 (1992) 125-130.

m380 MELANCHTHON: *Neuser* Wilhelm, Luther und Melanchthon; ein Herr, verschiedene Gaben: ➤ 22, FBRECHT M., Luthers Wirkung 1992, 47-61.

m381 *Scheible* Heinz, Melanchthon, Philipp (1497-1560): ➤ 768, TRE 22 (1992) 371-395; bibliog. 395-410!

m382 [Simons] MENNO: *Goertz* Hans-J., Menno/-niten: ➤ 768, TRE 22 (1992) 444-457.

m383 MORE: *Yoder* Jay T., Thomas More and the Anabaptists: Mennonite-QR 66,1 (1992) 47-56 [< ZIT 92,132].

m384 MÜNTZER: EBräuer Sigfried, *Junghans* Helmar, Der Theologe Thomas Müntzer; Untersuchungen zu seiner Entwicklung und Lehre. Gö 1989, Vandenhoeck & R. 386 p. – RProtestantesimo 47 (1992) 155-7 (E. *Campi*).

m384* a) *Duch* Lluis, Thomas Müntzer, una alternativa radical a l'ortodòxia luterana: RCatalT 16 (1991) 307-325; Eng. 325. – b) *Battafarano* Italo M., Wider das vergiftete Wort; zur Metaphorik bei T. Müntzer: ➤ 375*, Begrifflichkeit 1992, 87-113 [-195, *al.*, über Müntzer].

m385 **Friesen** A., T. Muentzer, a destroyer of the godless 1990 ➤ 7,g608: RChH 60 (1991) 539-542 (J. L. *Irwin* compares with GRITSCH E.); JEH 43 (1992) 151s (E. *Cameron*).

m386 **Goertz** Hans-Jürgen, T. Müntzer 1989 ➤ 6,k727; 7,g609: RTLZ 117 (1992) 45s (R. *Mau*); TvT 32 (1992) 102 (E. *Honée*).

m387 **La Rocca** T., Es ist Zeit; Apocalisse e storia; studio su Thomas Müntzer 1988 ➤ 6,729* [RasT 32,532 ➤ 7,5028]. RFilT 6 (1992) 154-7 (G. *Campana*).

m388 ELa Rocca Tommaso, Thomas Müntzer e la rivoluzione dell'uomo comune [Colloquio Univ. Ferrara, 5-6.V.1989]. T 1990, Claudiana. 208 p. RArchivScSocR 78 (1992) 238 (J. *Séguy*); Protestantesimo 47 (1992) 152s (C. *Tron*).

m389 a) *Lohse* Bernhard, Thomas Müntzer, der Prophet mit dem Schwert; – b) *Beintker* Horst J. E., Jesu Nachfolge im Zeichen des Kreuzes bei Müntzer und Luther: Luther 61 (1990) 1-20 / 80-91.

m390 **Seidemann** Johann K., Thomas Müntzer und der Bauernkrieg: Kleine Schriften zur Reformationsgeschichte (1842-1880), I, EKoch E. Lp 1990, Zentralantiquariat. vii-481 p. – RTLZ 117 (1992) 46s (S. *Bräuer*).

m391 OETINGER: **Weyer-Menkhoff** Martin, Christus, das Heil der Natur... Oetingers 1990 ➤ 6,k738*; 7,g616: RTLZ 117 (1992) 446-9 (E. *Pältz*); ZKG 103 (1992) 402-4 (K. *Gottschick*).

m392 PETRI O.: **Gardemeister** Christer, Den suveräne Guden; en studie i Olavus Petris teologi. Lund 1989. – RSvTKv 67 (1991) 49-51 (C.-A. *Aurelius*).

m393 PFLUG Julius: ENeuss E., *Pollet* J. V., Pflugiana 1985/90 ➤ 6,670; 7,g617: RZKG 103 (1992) 263s (R. *Bäumer*).

m394 PHILIPS: TEDyck Cornelius J., *al.*, The writings of Dirk Philips, 1504-1568 [second to Menno Simons]. Scottdale PA 1992, Herald. 701 p.; foldout map. $45. 0-8361-311-8 [TDig 39,379].

m395 POLE: ᴱPagano Sergio M., Ranieri Concetta, Nuovi documenti su Vittoria COLONNA e Reginald Pole: Collectanea Archivi Vaticani 24. Vaticano 1989, Archivio. 178 p. Lit. 30.000. 88-85042-13-9. – ᴿJEH 43 (1992) 102-9 (D. Fenlon).

m396 REITZ: Schrader Hans-Jürgen. Literaturproduktion und Büchermarkt des radikalen Pietismus; Johann H. Reitz' 'Historie der Wiedergebohrnen' und ihr geschichtlicher Kontext [Diss. Göttingen 1979, ᴰSchöne A.]: Palestra 283. Gö 1989, Vandenhoeck & R. 635 p. – ᴿZKG 103 (1992) 404-7 (R. Mohr).

m397 SCHATZGEYER: ᵀᴱSchäfer Philipp, Kasper Schatzgeyer, Von der waren ... freyheit: CCath 40, 1987 ➤ 4,k180 ... 7,g618*: ᴿAnHConc 23 (1991) 408-410 (R. Decot).

m398 SPENER: Aland Kurt, Spener und Luther; zum Thema Rechtfertigung und Wiedergeburt: ➤ 22, ᶠBRECHT M., Luthers Wirkung 1992, 209-232.

m399 Osculati Roberto, Vero cristianesimo; teologia e società moderna nel pietismo luterano [... Spener]. R 1990, Laterza. 424 p. – ᴿCC 143 (1992,3) 94-96 (M. Fois); RivStoLR 27 (1991) 579-581 (Anna Chiarloni); Salesianum 54 (1992) 599-601 (M. Müller).

m400 TERESA: Williams Rowan, Teresa of Avila: Outstanding Christian Thinkers. L 1991, Chapman. 177 p. £15; pa. £8. 0-225-66579-4; -47-6. – ᴿExpTim 103 (1991s) 160 (C. S. Rodd: born of the line of a Jewish converso).

m401 VALDÉS: Firpo Massimo, Tra alumbrados e 'spirituali'; studi su Juan de Valdés e il valdesianesimo nella crisi religiosa del '500 italiano. F 1990. Olschki. 191 p. – ᴿProtestantesimo 47 (1992) 330-3 (T. Fanlo y Cortés).

m402 James Frank A.ᴵᴵᴵ, Juan de Valdés before and after Peter Martyr VERMIGLI; the reception of Gemina praedestinatio in Valdés' later thought: ArRefG 83 (1992) 180-208; deutsch 208.

m403 VALIER: Pullapilly Cyriac K., Agostino Valier [1531-1606] and the conceptual basis of the Catholic reformation: HarvTR 85 (1992) 307-333.

m404 VERMIGLI: ᴱDonnelly John P., Kingdon Robert M., A bibliography of the works of Peter Martyr Vermigli 1990 ➤ 7,g629: ᴿCathHR 78 (1992) 111s (F. A. James: first-rate scholarship); SixtC 22 (1991) 410s (J. C. McLelland); WestTJ 54 (1992) 388s (R. Letham).

m405 WHITGIFT: Horie Hirofumi, The origin and the historical context of Archbishop Whitgift's 'Orders' of 1586: ArRefG 83 (1992) 240-257; deutsch. 257.

m406 ZWINGLI: Pollet J. V., H. Zwingli et le Zwinglianisme [DTC 1951 + updating] 1988 ➤ 7,g638: ᴿChH 61 (1992) 404-6 (J. A. Templin).

m406* a) McKee Elsie Ann, The defense of SCHWENKFELD, Zwingli, and the Baptists, by Katharina Schütz ZELL; – b) Pipkin H. Wayne, 'They went out from us, for they were not of us'; Zwingli's judgment of the early Anabaptists; ➤ 120, ᶠLOCHER G., Zwingliana 19,1 (1991) 245-264 / 279-292.

m407 Stephens W. Peter, Zwingli; an introduction to his thought. Ox 1992, Clarendon. xiii-174 p. $45. 0-19-826329-5 [TDig 40,88]. – ᴿExpTim 104 (1992s) 122s (P. N. Brooks).

m408 Wandel Lee P., 'Always among us'; images of the poor in Zwingli's Zurich 1990 ➤ 7,g640: ᴿJEH 43 (1992) 660-3 (Carlos M. N. Eire); JRel 72 (1992) 113s (Maureen Flynn); RelStR 18 (1992) 64 (D. K. McKim).

m408* *a*) *Winzeler* Peter, Zwinglis sozialökonomische Gerechtigkeitslehre – heute wiedergelesen; – *b*) *Hollenweger* Walter, Zwinglis Einfluss in England; – *c*) *Furcha* Edward J., Women in Zwingli's world; – *d*) *Morita* Yasukazu, Zürich und die Reichsstädte; Zwinglis Bundnispläne; – *e*) *Aschenbacher* Gerhard, Zwingli und die Musik im Gottesdienst: → 120, ᶠLOCHER G., Zwingliana 19,1 (1991) 427-444 / 171-186 / 131-142 / 265-278 / 1-11.

Y4.5   *Exegesis post-reformatoria* – **Historical criticism to 1800.**

m409 **Ahearn** Marie L., The rhetoric of war [Puritan New England]; training day, the militia, and the military sermon: CtrbAmerSt 95. NY 1989, Greenwood. ix-217 p. $40. – ᴿChH 61 (1992) 107s (Louise A. *Breen*).

m410 ᴱ**Armogathe** J. R., Le grand siècle [XVII]: BTT 6,1989 → 6,k767; 7,g641: ᴿIndTSt 28 (1991) 191-2 (L. *Legrand*); RTPhil 124 (1992) 350s (Maria-Cristina *Pitassi*).

m411 **Baird** William, History of New Testament research, I. [of 2] From Deism to Tübingen. Mp 1992, Fortress. xxii-450 p. $42. 0-8006-2626-5 [TDig 39,351].

m412 **Bavaud** Georges, Lorsque l'accès de l'Écriture était rendu difficile aux laïcs; la sévérité des prescriptions de l'Église catholique [Rome XVI XVII s.]: ÉchSM 22,1 (1992) 39-48.

m413 ᴱ**Besier** Gerhard, *Gestrich* Christof, 450 Jahre evangelische Theologie in Berlin [Univ. nur seit 1810] 1989 → 6,k769; 20 fig.: ᴿSvTKv 67 (1991) 200 (B. *Hägglund*).

m414 *Bost* Charles, Histoire des Protestants de France⁹ [¹1924]. Carriè-res-sous-Poissy 1992, La Cause. 253 p. F 75. 2-87657-005-X. – ᴿÉTRel 67 (1992) 603s (H. *Bost*: bon, mais peu de titres après 1960).

m415 *Bost* Hubert, Protestantisme; une naissance sans faire-part (xvɪᵉ-xvɪɪᵉ s., rupture entre Réforme et protestantisme, précipitée par la révocation de l'Édit de Nantes]: ÉTRel 67 (1992) 359-373.

m416 *Bozeman* Theodore D., Federal theology and the 'National Covenant'; an Elizabethan Presbyterian case study: ChH 61 (1992) 394-407.

m417 **Bradley** James E., Religion, revolution, and English radicalism; nonconformity in eighteenth-century politics and society 1990 → 7,g644: ᴿCritRR 5 (1992) 315-7 (B. P. *Levack*).

m417* **Butler** Jon, Awash in a sea of faith 1990 → 6,k770; 7,g646: ᴿJRel 72 (1992) 593s (R. E. *Wentz*); RExp 89 (1992) 290s (R. J. *Leonard*); WestTJ 54 (1992) 208s (J. R. *Muether*).

m418 *Chamberlain* Ava, The theology of cruelty; a new look at the rise of Arminianism in eighteenth-century New England. HarvTR 85 (1992) 335-356.

m419 *Cottret* Bernard, Les 'fils des hommes'; christologie et révolution en Angleterre (vers 1642-vers 1660): ÉTRel 67 (1992) 43-66.

m420 *Doriani* Daniel, The Puritans, sex, and pleasure: WestTJ 53 (1991) 125-143.

m421 **Driancourt-Girod** Janine, Ainsi priaient les luthériens; la vie religieuse, la pratique et la foi des luthériens de Paris au 18ᵉ siècle; préf. *Delumeau* Jean. P 1992, Cerf. 237 p. F 110 [RHE 88,574, Y. *Krumenacher*].

m422 **Elderen** R. J. van, Toekomst voor Israël; een theologie-historisch on-derzoek naar de visie op de bekering der Joden en de toekomst van Israël bij Engelse Protestanten in de periode 1547-1670, tegen de achter-grond van hun eschatologie [...mistakenly considered philosemitism]:

geref. diss. ᴰ*Hartvelt* G. Kampen 1992, Mondiss. x-314 p. 90-5337-013-7. – TvT 32 (1992) 303s; RTLv 24, p. 556.

m423 **Gaustad** Edwin S., Faith of our fathers; religion and the new nation 1988: ᴿRExp 89 (1992) 130s (B. J. *Leonard*) [Our index 5,76 and 6,k843 wrongly refer a Gaustad; and 4,846b gives title A documentary history of religion in America, 2. since 1865).

m424 **Gericke** Wolfgang, Theologie und Kirche im Zeitalter der Aufklärung: KGEinz 3/2. B 1989, Ev.-V. 139 p. – ᴿTLZ 117 (1992) 47-50 (W. *Sommer*).

m425 ᴱ**Graf** Friedrich W., Profile des neuzeitlichen Protestantismus I. Aufklärung – Idealismus – Vormärz: Siebenstern 1430. Gü 1990, Mohn. 329 p.; 12 phot. DM 40. 3-579-01430-7. – ᴿEvKomm 24 (19921) 493. 495 (M. *Wolfes*).

m426 *Gres-Gayer* Jacques M., The magisterium of the faculty of theology of Paris in the seventeenth century: TS 53 (1992) 424-450.

m427 **Gross** Hanns, Rome... post-Tridentine syndrome 1990 ⇝ 7,g652: ᴿJRel 72 (1992) 586s (B. *Dooley*).

m429 **Harrison** Peter, 'Religion' and the religions in the English enlightenment. C 1990, Univ. x-277 p. £30. 0-521-38530-X. – ᴿExpTim 103 (1991s) 155 (J. A. *Newton*: the Deists and Christian 'Platonists' were a step toward making religion more scientific and ethical); JAAR 60 (1992) 553-5 (J. S. *Preus*); JTS 43 (1992) 304-6 (C. *Cunliffe*); RelSt 28 (1992) 122s (P. *Byrne*); TvT 32 (1992) 319 (T. *Merrigan*).

m430 **Hughes** R., *Allen* C., Illusions of innocence 1988 ⇝ 4,k348... 6,k843: ᴿChH 60 (1991) 406-8 (J. *Butler*).

m431 *Hunwick* A., Nouvelles remarques critiques sur le NT, un manuscrit clandestin inédit: Dix-huitième siècle 24 (P 1992) 239-266 [< RHE 87,389*].

m432 *Hutzing* Klaas, [Die heilige Schrift als] Wächserne Nase: NSys 34 (1992) 200-218; Eng. 218: expression used in several authors between Reformation and Lessing-Goeze.

m433 ᴱ**Kroll** Richard, al., Philosophy, science and religion in England 1640-1700. C 1992, Univ. 287 p. £37.50. 0-521-41095-2. – ᴿExpTim 104 (1992s) 29 (J. H. *Brooke*).

m434 *a*) *Laplanche* François, La marche de la critique biblique d'Érasme à Spinoza; – *b*) *Armogathe* J.-R., Les études bibliques au xVIIIᵉ siècle; de la lettre à la figure; – *c*) *Dupruigrenet-Desroussilles* François, La production de Bibles imprimées en France au xVIIᵉ siècle: ⇝ 462, Naissance 1990/2, 29-39 / 41-48 / 117-124.

m435 *Nash* Jerry C., The Christian-humanist meditation on man [1553 Nicolas] DENISOT, MONTAIGNE, RABELAIS, RONSARD, SCÈVE: BtHumRen 54 (1992) 353-371.

m436 **Olmo Lete** G. del, Semitistas catalanes del siglo XVIII, 1988 ⇝ 6,k779: ᴿHelmantica 43 (1992) 462s (S. *García Jalón*).

m437 **Packer** James J., Among God's giants; the Puritan vision of the Christian life. ... 1991, Kingsway. 447 p. £10 pa. – ᴿTLond 95 (1992) 62s (A. *McGrath*: fine).

m437* **Pelikan** Jaroslav, [Christian tradition 5:] Christian doctrine and modern culture (since 1700) 1989 ⇝ 7,g661: ᴿChH 59 (1990) 594-6 (C. *Welch*); TLond 95 (1992) 449s (T. *Williams*).

m438 **Podskalsky** Gerhard, Griechische Theologie in der Zeit der Türkenherrschaft (1453-1821) 1988 ⇝ 3,g633... 6,k781: ᴿCrNSt 13 (1992) 443s

(A. *Rigo*); Istina 36 (1941) 426s (G. L.); JbÖsByz 41 (1991) 356-9 (Dorothea *Wendebourg*); ZKG 103 (1992) 398-401 (P. *Hauptmann*).

m439 *Prieur* Jean-Marc, Minorité et multitudinisme [des Églises protestantes: ces caractères ne sont pas contradictoires, mais se complètent fructueusement]: ÉTRel 67 (1992) 433-444.

m440 *Reinhardt* Rudolf, Katholizismus ['practices and attitudes loosely related to the authoritative Church', RAHNER LTK] und Katholizismen; zur Deutung der Kirchengeschichte des 17. und 18. Jahrhunderts: ZKG 103 (1992) 361-5.

m440* **Schwarke** Christian, Jesus kam nach Washington 1991 → 7,g666: ᴿActuBbg 29 (1992) 74s (J. *Boada*).

m441 *Schwarzbach* Bertram E., L'étude de l'hébreu en France au XVIIIe siècle; la grammaire d'Étienne FOURMONT: RÉJ 151 (1992) 43-75.

m442 **Sell** Alan P. F., Dissenting thought and the life of the Churches; studies in an English tradition. SF 1990, Mellen Research Univ. xvi-713 p. – ᴿSR 21 (1992) 483 (E. J. *Furcha*: varied essays: the reviewer's 'Cherburty' believed in the author's 'immorality').

m443 **Sluger** Debora K., Habits of thought in the English renaissance [HERBERT, DONNE, HOOKER, ANDREWES]; religion, politics, and the dominant culture. Berkeley 1990, Univ. California. x-284 p. $35. – ᴿAnglTR 74 (1992) 110-2 (J. N. *Wall*, also on J. LULL).

m444 **Smith** A. J., Metaphysical wit [the mid-17th century quietly assimilated it to the laws of natural science]. C 1992, Univ. 270 p. £35. 0-521-34027-6. – ᴿExpTim 104 (1992s) 223 (M. J. *Townsend*).

m445 **Spurr** John, The restoration of the Church of England 1646-1689. NHv 1991, Yale Univ. 445 p. $45. 0-300-05071-2. – ᴿExpTim 103 (1991s) 248 (Claire *Cross*: expert).

m446 **Stam** E. P. van, The controversy over the theology of Saumur, 1635-1650; disrupting debates among the Huguenots in complicated circumstances [diss. Amst VU]. Nijmegen Inst. Bayle 19. Amst 1988, APA. xiv-497 p. – ᴿWestTJ 54 (1992) 392-6 (R. *Nicole*).

m447 *Stolle* Volker, Zur [spärlichen] missionarischen Perspektive der lutherischen Theologie im 17. Jahrhundert: LuthTK 15 (1991) 21-35.

m448 **Vilanova** Evangelista, Historia de la teología cristiana [I. 1987 → 3, g125; 2. 1984 → 3,g553... 6,k641] 3. siglos XVIII, XIX y XX, ᵀLlopis Juan: BtHerder 182. Barc 1992, Herder. 1059 p. 84-254-1569-1. – ᴿActuBbg 29 (1992) 235 (J. *Boada*); ComSev 25 (1992) 433-5 (H. *Sánchez*); EstE 67 (1992) 477s (E. *Franco*); LumenVr 41 (1992) 395-7 (F. *Ortiz de Urtaran*); RET 52 (1992) 357-361 (M. *Andrés Martín*).

m449 **Ward** William R., Methodistische Kirche, ᵀ*Marquardt* Manfred: → 768, TRE 22 (1992) 666-680.

Y4.7 Auctores 1600-1900 alphabetice.

m450 ARNAULD: *Ginsburg* Lisa, *a*) La sinossi evangelica di Antoine Arnauld [1653]; – *b*) Ancora su Arnauld e GALILEO: → 481, AnStoEseg 9 (1992) 77-86 / 239-245; Eng. 4 / 6.

m451 BAYLE: **Whelan** Ruth, The anatomy of superstition; a study of the historical theory and practice of Pierre Bayle; StVoltaire 259, 1989 → 6,k285: ᴿRTPhil 124 (1992) 351s (M.-Cristina *Pitassi*).

m452 BUNYAN: **Hill** Christopher, A turbulent, seditious, and factious people; John Bunyan and his church 1628-1688: 1988 → 5,k241*a*: ᴿHZ 253 (1991) 759s (P. *Wende*).

m453 COMENIUS: *Engelhardt* Klaus, *al.*, Zur 400. Wiederkehr des Geburt-stages von [Jan Amos] Comenius: EvErz 44,2 (Fra 1992) 86s [-163, 7 art.: < ZIT 92,399].

m454 DIDEROT: *Garnier* André, À propos de Diderot le philosophe et de son frère ecclésiastique [LEPAPE P., Diderot (P 1991, Flammarion) 446 p.]: EsprVie 102 (1992) 44-47.

m455 DOBROVSKY: *Segert* Stanislaw, Josef Dobrovsky's contribution to Hebrew studies [b. 1753, d. 1829; his attempts to introduce new material and methods remain in manuscript form]: ZAHeb 5 (1992) 52-56.

m456 EDWARDS: *Haykin* Michael A. G., Jonathan Edwards (1703-58) and his legacy: Evangel 9,3 (1991) 17-23.

m457 FOX: **Bailey** Richard G., New light on George Fox and early Quakerism; the making and unmaking of a god [1624-1691]. SF 1992, Mellen Univ. xvii-340 p. $80. 0-7734-9829-X [TDig 40,254 cites: 'a magus and an avatar; more than a miracle worker; by his own account he was the Son of God'].

m458 HAMANN: **Velduis** Henri, Een verzegeld boek; het natuurbegrip in de theologie van J. G. Hamann (1730-1788) [diss. Utrecht, ᴰ*Knijff* H. de]. Sliederecht 1990, Merwedeboek. 396 p. *f* 55. 90-7186-423-5. – ᴿGeref-TTs 91 (1991) 246-256 (J. T. *Bakker*); NedTTs 46 (1992) 250s (G. E. *Meuleman*).

m459 HOBBES: **Martinich** Aloysius P. The new gods of Leviathan; Thomas Hobbes on religion and politics [... his principles of biblical interpretation were compatible with views held by responsible Scripture scholars today]. C 1992, Univ. xiv-430 p. $60. 0-521-41849-6 [TDig 40,174].

m460 JANSENIUS: *Ceyssens* Lucien, Innocent XII et le jansénisme: Antonia-num 67 (1992) 39-66; Eng. 39.

m461 **Ceyssens** L.: Le sort de la bulle Unigenitus; 90ᵉ anniv.; présent. *Lamberigts* M. Lv 1992, Univ./Peeters. xxvi-641 p.; portr. Fb 2000 [RHE 88,96*].

m462 **Grès-Gayer** Jacques M., Théologie et pouvoir en Sorbonne; la Facul-té de Théologie de Paris et la bulle Unigenitus 1714-1721: Mélan-gesBtSorbonne 22. P 1991, Klincksieck. 391 p. F 300. – ᴿEsprVie 102 (1992) 553s (R. *Epp*).

m463 **Hildesheimer** F., Le jansénisme; l'histoire et l'héritage. P 1992, D-Brouwer. 150 p. [RHE 88,96*].

m464 *Spiertz* M. G., Jansenisme in en rond de Nederlanden 1640-1690: Trajecta 1 (1992) 144-167 [< TR 88,431].

m465 KANT: *Galbraith* Elizabeth, Was Kant a closet theologian? [though called the great 18th century sceptic of religion]: TLond 95 (1992) 245-254.

m466 *Palmquist* Stephen, Kant's appropriation of [his old servant] Lampe's God: HarvTR 85 (1992) 85-108.

m466* LAVATER b. 1741: *Ebeling* Gerhard, Genie des Herzens unter dem ge-nius saeculi; Johann Caspar Lavater als Theologe: ZTK 89 (1992) 59-97.

m467 L'EMPEREUR: **Rooden** Peter T. van, Theology, biblical scholarship and rabbinical studies in the seventeenth century (C. L'Empereur): StHist-LeidenUniv 6, 1989 → 5,k257; *f* 86: ᴿJTS 43 (1992) 300-2 (B. *Hall*).

m468 LOCKE: **Pitassi** Maria Cristina, Le philosophe de l'écriture; John Locke exégète de saint Paul: RTPhil Cah 14. Genève 1990. 99 p. – ᴿProtestantesimo 47 (1992) 152s (E. *Campi*).

m469 MICHAELIS: *Wiefel* Wolfgang, Michaelis, Johann David (1717-1791):
→ 768, TRE 22 (1992) 712-4.

m470 PASCAL Blaise, Briefe in die Provinz; die Schriften der Pfarrer von
Paris: Werke 111. Heid 1990, Schneider. ciii-524 p. – RTPhil 67 (1992)
602-5 (A. *Raffelt*).

m471 ROUSSEAU: **Lefebvre** P., Les pouvoirs de la parole; l'Église et Rousseau (1762-1848): Histoire. P 1992, Cerf. 491 p.; ill. F 195 [NRT
118,615, S. *Hilaire*].

m472 SMYTH: **Coggins** James R., John Smyth's Congregation, English
separatism, Mennonite influence and the elect nation. Scottdale 1991,
Herald. 240 p. 0-8361-3109-6. – RExpTim 104 (1992s) 123 (B. R. *White*:
the first Baptists).

m473 SOUTH: **Reedy** Gerard, Robert South (1634-1716), an introduction to
his life and sermons: Eighteenth century lit. 12. C 1992, Univ. xiii-
171 p.; 6 fig.; 1 facsim. £30 [RHE 87,90*]. 0-521-40164-X. – RExpTim 104
(1992s) 24 (H. D. *Rack*).

m474 SPINOZA: *Vedder* Ben, De verhouding tussen geloven en denken in
de hermeneutiek van Baruch de Spinoza: Bijdragen 53 (1992) 350-370;
Eng. 370s.

m475 *Matheron* Alexandre, Philosophie et religion chez Spinoza: → 594,
Raison/foi, RSPT 76,1 (1992) 56-72; Eng. 72.

m475* *Walther* Manfred, Spinozas Kritik der Wunder — ein Wunder der
Kritik? Die historisch-kritische Methode als Konsequenz des reformatorischen Schriftprinzips: ZTK 88 (1991) 68-80.

m476 TOLAND: *Schmidt* Francis, John Toland, critique déiste de la littérature apocryphe: Apocrypha 1 (1990) 119-145.

m477 TRONCHIN: *Klauber* Martin L., Reason, revelation, and cartesianism;
Louis Tronchin and enlightened orthodoxy in late seventeenth-century
Geneva: ChH 59 (1990) 326-339.

m478 TURRETTINI F.: TGIger George M., EDennison James T., François
Turrettini 1623-1687, Institutes of eclectic theology, I first through tenth
topics. Phillipsburg NJ 1992, Presbyterian &R. xiii-685 p. $40. 0-87552-
451-6 [TDig 40,180].

m479 **Meijering** E. P., Reformierte Scholastik und patristische Theologie; die
Bedeutung des Väterbeweises... F. Turretins... Christologie: BtHumRen
50. Nieuwkoop 1991, De Graaf. 508 p. *f* 150. – RVigChr 46 (1992) 195s
(J. C. M. Van *Winden*).

m480 TURRETTINI J.-A.: *Klauber* Martin L., The drive toward Protestant
union in early eighteenth-century Geneva; Jean-Alphonse Turrettini on
the 'fundamental articles' of the faith: ChH 61 (1992) 334-349.

m481 *Klauber* Martin I., Jean-Alphonse Turrettini and the abrogation of the
formula consensus in Geneva: WestTJ 53 (1991) 325-338.

m482 VICO: **Botturi** F., La sapienza della storia; Giambattista Vico e la
filosofia pratica. Mi 1991, ViPe. 512 p. – REuntDoc 45 (1992) 136s (P.
Miccoli).

m483 *Lollini* Massimo, La Sapienza, l'Ermeneutica e il Sublime in G. B.
Vico: → 481, AnStoEseg 9 (1992) 101-140; Eng. 4.

m484 *Miccoli* Paolo, Fantasia politeista; gli 'universali fantastici' di Vico e gli
'dei' di SCHELLING: EuntDoc 45 (1992) 55-72.

m485 WESLEY: *Campbell* Ted A., Christian tradition, John Wesley, and
evangelicalism: AnglTR 74 (1992) 54-67.

m486 *English* Donald, Revisitazione di Aldersgate; storia e teologia della
missione metodista: Protestantesimo 47 (1992) 82-95.

m486* **Gordon** J. M., Evangelical spirituality from the Wesleys to John
STOTT. L 1991, SPCK. 340 p. £12.90. – ᴿIrBSt 14 (1992) 147-9 (R. B.
Knox: informative, challenging).

m487 **Rataboul** Louis J., John Wesley, un Anglican sans frontières (1703-
1791) 1991 ➤ 7,g705: ᴿÉTRel 67 (1992) 127s (H. *Bost*).

m488 DE WETTE: **Rogerson** John, M. de Wette, founder of modern biblical
criticism; an intellectual biography: JStOT supp 126. Sheffield 1992,
JStOT. 313 p. £35; sb. 26.25. 1-85075-330-X. – ᴿExpTim 103 (1991s)
384 [C. S. *Rodd*].

Y5 *Saeculum XIX* – **Exegesis** – **19th Century.**

m489 **Addinall** Peter, Philosophy and biblical interpretation... 19th c. conflict
ᴰ1991 ➤ 7,1006. g706: ᴿCritRR 5 (1992) 80s (C. *Brown*); ExpTim 103,
co-starred in fasc. 4 (1991s) 97s (C. S. *Rodd*); TS 53 (1992) 781 (J.
Reuscher: scholarship at its best, except for ch. 9s claiming 'KANT laid a
firm foundation for religious belief'; his critical philosophy is directly
relevant to the theology of a science-dominated culture); TvT 32 (1992)
425s (T. *Merrigan*: really on science-threat).

m490 *a*) **Barrios-Auscher** Dominique, La Bible en France aux xixᵉ et xxᵉ
siècles; – *b*) **Savart** Claude, Connaissance et méconnaissance de la Bible en
France au xixᵉ siècle: ➤ 462, Naissance 1990/2, 137-145 / 131-6.

m491 **Bebbington** David W., Evangelicalism in modern Britain 1730-1980:
1988 ➤ 5,k292... 7,g707: now also GR 1992, Baker. xi-364 p. $20 pa.
0-8010-1028-4 [TDig 40,51].

m492 **Camroux** Martin, The case for liberal theology: ExpTim 103 (1991s)
168-173.

m493 **Cashdollar** Charles D., The transformation of theology, 1830-1890 ... :
1989 ➤ 5,k295... 7,g709: ᴿEngHR 107 (1992) 1044s (G. *Rowell*); JAAR
60 (1992) 333-7 (E. B. *Holifield*).

m494 **Cholvy** Gérard, Deux siècles d'histoire des mouvements de laïcs dans le
catholicisme français: EsprVie 102 (1992) 273-285.

m495 **Edgar** William, Face à la modernité; la pensée apologétique protestante de langue française de 1815 à 1848: diss. Genève 1992. – RTLv
24, p. 557.

m496 **Fitzer** J., Romance and the Rock; nineteenth century Catholics on faith
and reason 1989 ➤ 6,607: ᴿChH 61 (1992) 111s (J. P. *Gaffey*).

m497 **Flegg** Columba G., 'Gathered under Apostles'; a study of the [1851
London-founded; since 1901 and especially 1945 reduced to a remnant]
Catholic Apostolic Church [< diss.]. Ox 1992, Clarendon. xvi-524 p.
£50. 0-19-826335-X. – ᴿExpTim 104 (1992s) 250s (W. *Ferguson*).

m498 **Fogarty** Gerald P., American Catholic Biblical Scholarship 1989
➤ 4,k245... 7,g711: ᴿCCurr 42 (1992s) 268s (J. *Jensen*).

m498* ᴱ**Frerichs** Ernest S., The Bible and Bibles in America 1988 ➤ 4,300...
7,g712: ᴿRelStT 11,2 (1991) 81-83 (G. T. *Sheppard*).

Goldman Art L., The search for God at Harvard 1991 ➤ a919.

m500 *Graf* Friedrich W., Liberale Theologie: ➤ 757, EvKL 3 (1992) 86-98.

m501 *Groot* Aart de, Het negentiende-eeuwse Nederlandse protestantisme in
recente publikaties; een overzicht: NedTTs 46 (1992) 212-225; Eng. 226
[100 of the 1600 publications 1975-90].

m502 **Hamilton** Ian, The erosion of Calvinist orthodoxy; seceders and subscription in Scottish Presbyterianism [1730-1879]. E 1990, Rutherford.
216 p. – ᴿWestTJ 54 (1992) 390-2 (D. W. *Hall*).

m503 **Hurley** Mark J., The unholy ghost; anti-Catholicism in the American experience: N° 429. Huntington IN 1992, Our Sunday Visitor. 320 p. $20 [Priest adv. 48/9, 55].

m504 **Lawton** William J., The better time to be; Utopian [... eschatological] attitudes to society among Sydney Anglicans 1885 to 1914 [< diss.]. Sydney 1990, NSW Univ. 200 p. $25 [RefTR 51,37].

m505 **Litwack** Leon F., *Meier* August, Black leaders of the nineteenth century. Champaign 1988, Univ. Illinois. 344 p. $25. 0-252-01506-1. – ᴿRExp 89 (1992) 127s (B. J. *Leonard*: includes Richard ALLEN, founder of African Methodist Episcopal Church).

m506 ᴱ**Marsden** George M., *Longfield* Bradley J., The secularization of the Academy: Religion in America. NY 1992, Oxford-UP. x-323 p. $35. 0-19-507351-7; pa. -2-5 [TDig 40,290].

m507 **Marshall** David B., Secularizing the faith; Canadian Protestant clergy and the crisis of belief, 1850-1940. Toronto 1992, Univ. viii-325 p. $55; pa. $20. 0-8020-5938-4; -6879-0 [TDig 40,173].

m508 **O'Neill** J. C., The Bible's authority... Lessing to Bultmann 1991 → 7,g718*: ᴿAustralBR 40 (1992) 71s (R. *Houghton*); IrBSt 14 (1992) 146s (R. B. *Knox*: does he mean to include BARTH in the Barth-like verdict?); JTS 43 (1992) 306s (R. *Morgan*: all guilty of making it a source about humanity, not God); RefTR 51 (1992) 113-5 (R. *Gaffin*); TLond 95 (1992) 295s (A. C. *Thiselton*: Germanophile; no others need apply).

m509 **Poole** Thomas G., What country have I? Nineteenth-century African-American theological critiques of the nation's birth and destiny: JRel 72 (1992) 533-548.

m510 **Smend** Rudolf, Deutsche Alttestamentler in drei Jahrhunderten 1989 → 5,358 ... 7,g721: ᴿCBQ 54 (1992) 546s (D. F. *Morgan*: limited aim); ComSev 24 (1991) 419 (M. de *Burgos*).

m511 **Vidmar** John, English Catholic historians and the English reformation 1793-1954: diss. Pont. Univ. Angelicum. Roma 1992. Extr. 93 p. – RTLv 24, p. 559.

Vilanova Evangelista, Historia de la teologia cristiana 3. (siglos XVIII, XIX y XX), ᵀ*Llopis* Juan: 1992 → m448.

m512 **Westfall** William, Two worlds; the Protestant culture of nineteenth-century Ontario: HistRel 2. Montréal 1989, McGill-Queen's Univ. 288 p. $35. – ᴿTorJT 7 (1991) 302s (B. J. *Fraser*).

m513 **Wood** Forrest G., The arrogance of faith; Christianity and race in America from the colonial era to the twentieth century. Boston 1991, Northeastern Univ. xxii-517 p. $17. – ᴿJRel 72 (1992) 118s (R. *Hatch*); RelStR 18 (1992) 349 (G. P. *McKenny*).

---

m513* BAUR: *Köpf* Ulrich, Ferdinand C. Baur als Begründer einer konsequent historischen Theologie: ZTK 89 (1992) 440-461.

m514 BRAUN: *Angel* Hans-Gerd, Katholisch und doch vernünftig? Die Moraltheologie des Trierer [Georg] HERMESschulers Godehard Braun [1798-1861]: TrierTZ 101 (1992) 150-9.

m515 BRIGGS: **Christensen** Richard L., The ecumenical orthodoxy of Charles Augustus Briggs; critical scholarship in the service of Church unity: Diss. Union Theol. Sem. 1992. 313 p. 92-23637. – DissA 53 (1992s) 1186-A.

m516 **Massa** M. S., Charles A. Briggs and the crisis of historical criticism: HarvDissRel 25, 1990 → 6,k859: ᴿCrNSt 13 (1992) 242s (J. *Hennesey*);

JAAR 60 (1992) 169-171 (W. *Baird*); TTod 49 (1992s) 138s (B. J. *Longfield*); WestTJ 54 (1992) 198-200 (D. W. *Hall*).

m517 BRUNN: *Threinen* Norman J., Friedrich Brunn [1819-1895], Erweckung und konfessionelles Luthertum: LuthTK 16 (1992) 29-47.

m517* CAREY: **George** Timothy, Faithful witness; the life and mission of William Carey [c. 1800 'father of modern missions']. Birmingham 1991, New Hope. 202 p. – ᴿTrinJ 13 (1992) 241-5 (Ruth A. *Tucker*).

m518 CHANTEPIE D.: *Veldhuis* H., Vanuit het midden; hoofdlijnen van de theologie van Daniël Chantepie de la Saussaye (1818-1874): NedTTs 46 (1992) 109-123.

m519 DELITZSCH: **Wagner** Siegfried, Franz Delitzsch, Leben und Werk²ʳᵉᵛ [¹1978]: MgStBü 369. Giessen 1991, Brunnen. 510 p. 3-7655-9369-9. – ᴿLuthTK 15 (1991) 181 (V. *Stolle*).

m520 DREY: *Schreurs* Nico, International symposium over de theologie van Johann S. Drey [Stu 19-22.III.1992]: TvT 32 (1992) 185s.

m521 **Tiefensee** Eberhard, Die religiöse Anlage... Drey 1988 ➤ 5,k316... 7,g728: ᴿBijdragen 53 (1992) 223s (U. *Hemel*).

m522 EMERSON: **Gelpi** Donald L., Endless seeker... Emerson 1991 ➤ 7,g729: ᴿCritRR 5 (1992) 403-5 (A. D. *Hodder*).

m523 **Hodder** Alan D., Emerson's rhetoric of revelation; 'nature', the reader, and the apocalypse within. ... 1989, Penn. State Univ. 170 p. $23.50. – ᴿJAAR 60 (1992) 786-8 (L. S. *Person*).

m524 FEUERBACH: **Meyer** Matthias, Feuerbach und ZINZENDORF; Lutherus redivivus und die Selbstauflösung der Religionskritik [Diss. Tü 1991 ➤ 7, g731]: ThTSt 1. Hildesheim 1992, Olms. xx-242 p. DM 50. 3-487-09599-8 [TLZ 118,756, H. *Grose*].

m525 FINNEY: **Hardman** Keith J., C. G. Finney 1990 ➤ 5,k318... 7,g733: ᴿEvQ 64 (1992) 184-6 (A. S. *Wood*).

m526 **Hewitt** Glenn A., Regeneration and morality... Finney al. 1991 ➤ 7,g734: ᴿChH 61 (1992) 419s (E. B. *Holifield*).

m527 *Smith* Jay E., The theology of Charles Finney; a system of self-reformation: TrinJ 13 (1992) 61-93.

m528 GRATRY: **Giurovich** Giancarlo, La teodicea di Alfonso Gratry [1805-1873], un Oratoriano contro i sofisti. L'Aquila 1989, Japadre. 190 p. – ᴿDivinitas 36 (1992) 277-9 (D. *Composta*).

m529 GRUNDTVIG: *Iversen* Hans R., Becoming a Christian in a non-Christian age; an attempt to answer an old question from a modern Grundtvigian standpoint [Nikolaj F. S. Grundtvig 1783-1872, 'the greatest Dane who has ever lived']: ST 46 (1992) 133-146.

m530 GÜNTHER: **Osswald** Bernhard, Anton Günther; theologisches Denken im Kontext einer Philosophie der Subjektivität: AbhPhPs 43. Pd 1990, Schöningh. 288 p. DM 68. 3-506-70193-2. – ᴿTPhil 67 (1992) 444-7 (J. *Reikerstorfer*); TvT 32 (1992) 103s (A. J. *Leijen*, also on KRONABEL C. 1989).

m531 HEGEL: **Brito** Emilio, Dieu et l'être d'après Thomas d'AQUIN et Hegel 1991 ➤ 7,g418: ᴿTLZ 117 (1992) 292-4 (K. H. *Neufeld*); TS 53 (1992) 752s (J. M. *McDermott*: such queries as are inevitable for so erudite an undertaking).

m531* *Dierken* Jörg, Theologie im Anschluss an Hegel; Überlegungen zu einer religions-philosophischen Zweideutigkeit: ZTK 88 (1991) 247-271.

m532 **Fessard** Gaston, Hegel, le christianisme et l'histoire 1990 ➤ 6,k873; 7,g738: ᴿRTLv 23 (1992) 242s (E. *Brito*); TLZ 117 (1992) 937s (K. H. *Neufeld*).

m533 *Stepelevitch* Lawrence S., Hegel and Roman Catholicism: JAAR 60 (1992) 673-691.

m534 HESS J.: **Ackva** Friedhelm, Johann Jakob Hess (1741-1828) und seine Biblische Geschichte: ev. Diss. ᴰ*Benrath* D. Mainz 1992. – RTLv 24, p. 554.

m535 HESS M.; **Lundgren** Svante, Moses Hess on religion, Judaism and the Bible. Åbo 1992, Akademi. x-206 p. 952-9616-02-3.

m536 HUG: **Müller** Gerald, Johann L. Hug (1765-1846) ... NT Wissenschaft: ErlangerSt 85, 1990 ➤ 6,k881; DM 46: ᴿTLZ 117 (1992) 603s (C.-P. *März*).

m537 IRELAND: **O'Connell** Marvin R., John Ireland and the American Catholic Church. St. Paul 1988; Minnesota Historical Soc. xiii-610 p. $35. – ᴿWorship 65 (1991) 177-180 (R. *Taft*).

m538 IRVING: *Allen* David, A belated bouquet; a tribute to Edward Irving (1792-1834) [condemned for Christological heresy in the Church of Scotland]: ExpTim 103 (1991s) 328-331.

m539 JÄSCHKE: *Kolmaš* Josef, Jäschkeana [Jäschke Heinrich A., 1837-1883] (a contribution to the bibliography of Tibetan and biblical studies): ArOr 60 (1992) 113-127; 2 phot.

m540 KEIL: **Siemens** Peter, Carl Friedrich Keil, Studien zu Leben und Werk: ev. Diss. ᴰ*Raeder* S. Tübingen 1990. – RTLv 24, p. 561; TLZ 118,370 [Keil's dates and specialty not mentioned; the exegete-'archeologist' Keil is Carl F., but LTK² gives only a J. F. Karl Keil, 1807-1888, exegete].

m541 KIERKEGAARD: *Cannistra* Saverio, Storia e fede nell''interludio' delle Briciole filosofiche di S. Kierkegaard [ital. *Spera* S., 1987: 'Si può costruire su una conoscenza storica una beatitudine eterna?']: Teresianum 43 (1992) 241-250.

m542 KUHN: **McCready** Douglas, Jesus Christ for the modern world: the Christology of the Catholic Tübingen school [KUHN J., MÖHLER J., ... KASPER W.]: AmerUnivSt 7/77. NY 1991, P. Lang. x-353 p. $53. 0-8204-1337-2 [TDig 39,370: also H. KÜNG 'who was attracted to the school but is in conflict with recent members'].

m543 **Wolf** Hubert, Ketzer oder Kirchenlehrer? Der Tübinger Theologe Johannes von Kuhn (1806-1887) in den kirchenpolitischen Auseinandersetzungen seiner Zeit: kath. Diss. ᴰ*Reinhardt* R. Tü 1990. 395 p. – RTLv 24, p. 559.

m544 LIGHTFOOT: *Hengel* Martin, Bischof Lightfoot und die Tübinger Schule: TBeit 23 (1992) 5-33 [< ZIT 92,91].

m545 MIGNE J. P. (1803-75): ᴱ**Langlois** Claude, *Laplanche* François, La science catholique; l'Encyclopédie théologique de Migne (1844-1873) entre apologétique et vulgarisation: Histoire. P 1992, Cerf. 276 p. 2-908-96503-8.

m546 NIETZSCHE: *Cadello* James P., The last Pope; George Burman FOSTER's [early 20th century] reading of Friedrich Nietzsche: JRel 72 (1992) 512-532.

m547 **Valadier** Paul, Nietzsche e la critica radicale 1991 (fr. 1974) ➤ 7,g755: ᴿEuntDoc 45 (1992) 473s (P. *Miccoli*); Lateranum 58 (1992) 548-550 (G. *Lorizio*); FilT 6 (1992) 466s (M. *Vannini*).

m548 **Nietzsche** Friedrich, Unmodern observations [I. David STRAUSS, writer and confessor, ᵀ*Golder* Herbert], 1875, ᴱ*Arrowsmith* William. NHv 1990, Yale Univ. xix-402 p. $40. – ᴿCritRR 5 (1992) 417-9 (J. F. *Humphrey*).

m549 REUSS: **Vincent** Jean-Marcel, Leben und Werk des frühen E. Reuss ᴰ1990 ➤ 6,k897; 7,g760: ᴿTsTKi 62 (1991) 71-73 (Terje *Stordalen*).

m550 SCHEEBEN: [**Stimpfle** J., *al.*,] M.J. Scheeben 1988 ⇥ 4,k289 (.8178!);
5,k335: ᴿSalmanticensis 39 (1992) 171s (A. *González Montes*).

m551 SCHLEIERMACHER: *Brito* Emilio, L'apologétique de Schleiermacher:
BLitEc 93 (1992) 379-400.

m552 *Crouter* Richard, Schleiermacher [Gesamtausgabe, 8 vol. 1980-90;
Archiv, 8 vol. 1984-90; 5 translations + ᴱ*Duke* J. 1985]: RelStR 18 (1992)
20-27.

m553 **Junker** Maureen, Das Urbild des Gottesbewusstseins... Schleiermacher
ᴰ1990 ⇥ 7,g770: ᴿZkT 114 (1992) 98s (K. H. *Neufeld*).

m554 ᴱ**Meckenstock** Günter, (*Ringleben* Joachim), Schleleiermacher und die
wissenschaftliche Kultur des Christentums: ThBtTöpelmann 51. B 1991,
de Gruyter. xv-521 p. DM 198. 3-11-012857-8. – ᴿZkT 114 (1992) 340-3
(K. H. *Neufeld*).

m555 **Meier-Dörken** Christoph, Die Theologie der frühen Predigten Schleier-
machers; Bt. Töpelmann 45. B 1988, de Gruyter. xii-288 p. DM 108.
3-11-011352-X. – ᴿGerefTTs 91 (1991) 61s (W. *Stoker*).

m556 **Ohst** Martin, Schleiermacher und die Bekenntnisschriften; eine Untersuchung zu seiner Reformations- und Protestantismusdeutung: BeitHistT
77, 1989 ⇥ 7,g771: ᴿNedTTs 46 (1992) 87s (H. J. *Adriaanse*).

m557 ᴱ**Penzo** G., *Farina* F., F. D. E. Schleiermacher (1768-1834) tra teologia e filosofia: Trento 11-13.IV.1985. Brescia 1990, Morcelliana. 486 p.
– ᴿEuntDoc 45 (1992) 121s (P. *Miccoli*).

m558 *Pöttner* Martin, Theologie als semiotische Theorie [PEIRCE C. S.] bei
Schleiermacher: NSys 34 (1992) 182-199; Eng. 199.

m559 ᴱ**Sachs** Walter, Schleiermacher, Theologische Enzyklopädie 1987 ⇥ 5,
k344; 6,k906: ᴿTüTQ 172 (1902) 155 (M. *Seckler*).

m560 ᵀᴱ**Shelley** John C., Friedrich Schleiermacher, Introduction to Christian
ethics [... 1 Cor 13; Gal 5,16-24]. Nv 1989, Abingdon. 108 p. 0-687-
19500-4. – ᴿExpTim 103 (1991s) 125 (W. D. *Hudson*).

m561 *Thandeka* [sic], Schleiermacher's Dialektik; the discovery of the self that
KANT lost: HarvTR 85 (1992) 433-452.

m562 STEPHENS: *Edwards* M. S., Joseph R. Stephens (1805-1879) [Evangelical
social gospel]: ExpTim 104 (1992s) 136-140.

m563 WELLHAUSEN: *Spieckermann* H., Exegetischer Individualismus; Julius
Wellhausen 1844-1918: in ᶠGRAF F. W., Profile der neuzeitlichen Protestantismus (Gü 1991, Mohn) 231-250 [< ZAW 105,534].

Y5.5 *Crisis modernistica* – **The Modernist era.**

m564 **Appleby** R. Scott, 'Church and age unite!': The modernist impulse in
American Catholicism. ND 1992, Univ. viii-296 p. $30. 0-268-00782-9
[TDig 40,50].

m565 *Berzosa Martínez* Raúl, La teología en el período pre-conciliar; de la
crisis modernista a la teología de la revelación: ScripV 39 (1992) 55-83.

m566 *a*) *Bourgeois* Daniel, Essai d'analyse théologique de 'l'intégrisme catholique'?; – *b*) *Étienne* Bruno, Intégrisme; vous avez dit intégriste?:
RRéf 43,4 (1992) 39-48 / 59-68 [< ZIT 92,498].

m566* *Bressolette* Claude, Ultramontanisme et gallicanisme engagent-ils deux
visions de la société?: FreibZ 38 (1991) 3-25.

m567 **O'Meara** Thomas F., Church and culture; German Catholic theology,
1860-1914. ND 1992, Univ. x-260 p. $40. 0-268-00783-7 [TDig 39,377:
sequel to his 1982 Romantic Idealism; modern rather than scholastic

approach of SCHEEBEN and four others; afterward, 'some Catholics advocated freedom' during the campaign against modernism].

m568 *Rutler* George W., The modernist spirit ['synthesis of all heresies' (but) a mood, not religion]: HomP 91,4 (1990s) 9-14.

m569 *Weinzierl* Erika, Modernismus: ➤ 757, EvKL 3 (1992) 508-513.

m570 BLONDEL: **Favraux** Paul, Une philosophie du Médiateur, M. Blondel 1986 ➤ 3,g759; 6,k928: ᴿRechSR 80 (1992) 427-430 (P. *Olivier*).

m571 **Izquierdo** Cesar, Blondel y la crisis modernista; análisis de 'Historia y dogma': ColTeol 71, 1990 ➤ 7,g783: ᴿActuBbg 29 (1992) 71 (J. *Boada*); RCatalT 16 (1992) 429s (S. *Pié y Ninot*).

m572 *Texier* Roger, Maurice Blondel; le défi de l'Action à l'athéisme actuel: NRT 114 (1992) 708-725.

m573 **Blondel** Maurice, Lettera sull'apologetica [Lettre sur les exigences... 1896; P 1956, PUF],ᵀ: GdT 196. Brescia 1990, Queriniana. 146 p. Lit. 16.000. 88-399-0696-7. – ᴿGregorianum 73 (1992) 547s (R. *Fisichella*).

m574 BRANDI: **Ciani** John L., Across a wide ocean; Salvatore M. Brandi S.J. and the 'Civiltà Cattolica' from Americanism to Modernism, 1891-1914: diss. Virginia, ᴰ*Fogarty* G. 1992, 429 p. 92-37522. – DissA 53 (1992s) 3255-A.

m575 DÖLLINGER: *Weiss* Otto, Das Gedächtnis des 100. Todestages J.J. Ignaz von Döllingers; ein Forschungsbericht: HistJb 112 (1992) 482-495.

m576 *Wolf* Hubert, Rekonziliation Döllingers durch Johann Heinrich FLOSS? ... Brief an Nuntius MASELLA 1877: TüTQ 172 (1992) 121-5.

m577 DUCHESNE: *Sesboüé* B., Avant le modernisme; Louis Duchesne et Alfred LOISY à la faculté de l'Institut Catholique de Paris: ➤ 537, ᴱ*Doré* J., Les cent ans 1990/2, 99-139.

m578 FARLEY: *Shelley* Thomas J., John Cardinal Farley and modernism in New York: ChH 61 (1992) 350-361.

m579 HECKER: ᴰ**Farina** John, Isaac T. Hecker, the Diary; romantic religion in ante-bellum America [1842-5]: Sources of American Spirituality NY 1988, Paulist. v-456 p. $15. 0-8091-0391-5. – ᴿChH 59 (1990) 574s (J. *McShane*; 6 volume series).

m580 O'**Brien** David J., Isaac Hecker, an American Catholic. NY 1992, Paulist. ix-446 p.; 25 phot. $25. 0-8091-0397-4 [TDig 40,180].

m581 LE ROY: **Schmitz** Rudolf M., Dogma und Praxis; der Dogmenbegriff des Modernisten Édouard Le Roy kritisch dargestellt: Studi Tomistici 51. Vaticano 1992, Editrice. 130 p. [TR 88,524].

m582 LOISY: *a) Dianich* Severino, La questione dell'essenza del cristianesimo; una critica storica [HARNACK]; – *b) Forni* Guglielmo, Storia e dogma; il secondo piccolo libro di Loisy: FilT 5 (1991) 12-22 / 23-34 [35-93 al.].

m583 MANNING: *Gilley* Sheridan, Manning, Henry Edward (1808-1892), ᵀ*Schwöbel* C. ➤ 768, TRE 22 (1992) 60-63.

m584 NEWMAN, OXFORD MOVEMENT: *Buck* P.L., Tractarian doctrine in KEBLE's The Christian year [against J.R. GRIFFIN and J.C. SHAIRP]: DowR 110 (1992) 239-258.

m585 **Chadwick** Owen, The spirit of the Oxford Movement 1990 ➤ 6,211; 7,g798: ᴿChH 60 (1991) 560-2 (L. *Barmann*); CritRR 5 (1992) 319-321 (Nadia M. *Lahutsky*).

m586 **Ching Yao-Shan,** Unity of opposites; a Chinese interpretation of Newman: Cardinal Bea Studies. Manila 1987, Ateneo. – ᴿRechSR 80 (1992) 430s (P. *Olivier*).

m587 **Dessain** Charles S., Vida y pensamiento del Cardenal Newman [1966], ᵀ*Boix* Aureli: Testigos 12. M 1990, Paulinas. 238 p. – ᴿScripTPamp 23 (1991) 729 (J. *Morales*).

m588 **Forrester** David, Young Doctor Pusey 1989 → 6,k962; 7,g801: ᴿHeythJ 33 (1992) 224s (P. *Butler*: editor of 1983 SPCK compilation which he admits was unsatisfactory).

m589 **Ffinch** Michael, Newman; towards the Second Spring. SF 1992, Ignatius. x-220 p. $13 pa. 0-89870-388-3 [TDig 39,361].

m590 ᴱ**Gaffney** James, Conscience, consensus, and the development of doctrine; [four] revolutionary texts by J. H. Newman. NY 1992, Doubleday Image. xiii-464 p. $15. 0-385-42280-6 [TDig 40,79].

m591 **Gauthier** Pierre, Newman et BLONDEL...: CogF 147, 1988 → 4,k335... 6,k964: ᴿFilT 5 (1991) 539-541 (S. *Sorrentino*); RechSR 80 (1992) 414-6 (P. *Olivier*).

m592 *a) Gauthier* Pierre, Un ami de Newman, Richard Hurrell FROUDE (1803-1836); – *b) Lazcano González* Raphael, J. H. Newman en la cultura de la lengua castellana ... (1890-1990); – *c) Monzón Arazo* August, Newman y el personalismo: RAg 31 (1990) 839-866 / 905-929 / 889-901.

m593 **Gilley** Sheridan, Newman and his age 1990 → 6,k966; 7,g805: ᴿAmerica 167 (1992) 191s (F. L. *Fennell*); Commonweal 119,20 (1992) 26s (J. A. *Komonchak*); HeythJ 33 (1992) 462-5 (S. *Thomas*); LavalTP 48 (1992) 308s (T. R. *Potvin*); RHE 87 (1992) 211-3 (D. *Lloyd*).

m594 **Grave** S. A., Conscience in Newman's thought. Ox 1989, Clarendon. viii-191 p. £22.50. – ᴿJTS 43 (1992) 307-9 (B. *Mitchell*).

m595 **Honoré** Jean, abp., The spiritual legacy of Newman [1988 → 5,k384], ᵀ*Ludden* sr. M. Christopher. NY 1992, Alba. ix-251 p. $15. 0-8189-0654-5 [TDig 40,272].

m596 *Hummel* Thomas C., John Henry Newman and the Oriel Noetics: AnglTR 74 (1992) 203-215.

m597 ᴱ**Jenkins** Arthur H., J. H. Newman and modernism 1983/90 → 7,516: ᴿJEH 43 (1992) 491-4 (N. *Sagovsky*, also on GILLEY and KER).

m598 **Jost** Walter, Rhetorical thought in J. H. Newman. Columbia 1989, Univ. S. Carolina. 278 p. $35. 0-87249-620-1. – ᴿJRel 72 (1992) 282 (G. *Magill*: originality with strength).

m599 **Ker** Ian, The achievement of J. H. Newman 1990 → 6,k973; 7,g811; pa. 1991, £7, 0-00-599276-1: ᴿExpTim 103 (1991s) 315 (B. M. G. *Reardon*: lavish quoting, expository rather than critical); JRel 72 (1992) 446s (G. *Magill*).

m600 ᴱ**Ker** Ian, *Hill* Allan G., Newman after a hundred years (22 essays) 1990) → 6,422*; 7,g814: ᴿCritRR 5 (1992) 334s (D. W. *Johnson*); Furrow 42 (1991) 128-130 (J. F. *Flynn*); HeythJ 33 (1992) 465s (M. C. *Barber*: best of the centenary collections; D. BROWN's also good, but 'lighter in tone').

m600* *Knox* R. Buick, J. H. Newman: IrBSt 14 (1992) 154-169.

m601 *Langa* Pedro, El Vaticano II, el concilio del Cardenal Newman: RAg 31 (1990) 781-819.

m602 *Magill* Gerard, Moral imagination in theological method and Church teaching: J. H. Newman: TS 53 (1992) 451-475.

m603 *Mann* Josef, Seelsorge an Studenten und Akademikern im Denken und Wirken J. H. Newmans im Umkreis der Universitäten Oxford und Dublin: → 52, ᶠErfurt 1992, 308-319.

m604 **Merrigan** Terrence, Clear heads and holy hearts; the religious and theological ideal of J. H. Newman 1991 → 7,818: ᴿTS 53 (1992) 572-4 (G. *Magill*: mastery of Newman's writings but not enough dialogue).

m605 **Morales Marín** J., Newman 1990 ➤ 7,g819: ᴿBurgense 32 (1991) 590-2 (A. *Pacho*); Gregorianum 73 (1992) 373s (F. de *Lasala*); Lateranum 57 (1991) 622s (M. *Semeraro*).

m606 *Morales* José, Religión, hombre, historia; estudios newmanianos [5 de 1978-88 + 1 inédito] 1989 ➤ 6,276: ᴿRTLv 23 (1992) 245 (A. de *Halleux*); Lateranum 57 (1991) 620s (M. *Semeraro*); Salmanticensis 39 (1992) 430s (F. *Martín Hernández*).

m607 *Morrone* Fortunato, L'incarnazione nel pensiero cristologico di Newman: RasT 33 (1992) 315-332.

m608 ᴱ**Murray** Placid, J.H. Newman, Sermons on the liturgy and the sacraments [43 uncorrected mss. in this first of 5 volumes of 246 unpublished sermons 1824-1843]. Ox 1991, Clarendon. xx-384 p. $89. – ᴿTS 53 (1992) 787s (M.X. *Moleski*: superb edition for scholars; for others the 217 Anglican sermons revised and published by Newman will serve better).

m609 *a) Neuner* Peter, Newmans Bedeutung für die Theologie heute; – *b) Wiedmann* Franz, J.H. Newman – ein Philosoph der Gegenwart?; – *c) Biemer* Günter, 'Niebuhrisieren?' [NIEBUHR Berthold G., 1776-1831; 12-mal bei Newman erwähnt]; Newmans Verständnis der Geschichtsschreibung als Rekonstruktion von Leben; – *d) Biemer*, Die Gläubigen in Dingen der Lehre befragen; Newmans Auffassung...: MüTZ 43 (1992) 391-408 / 409-419 / 421-435 / 437-448.

m610 **Newman**, *a) Les Ariens du quatrième siècle,* ᵀ*Veyriras* Paul, *Durand* Michel. P 1988, Téqui. 360 p. – *b)* Choix de lettres, ᵀ*Billioque* Andrée, *Clais* Jacqueline, intr. *Bordeaux* André. P 1990, Téqui. 360 p. – ᴿRThom 92 (1992) 590s (G.-T. *Bedouelle*).

m611 ᴱ**Nicholls** David, *Kerr* Fergus, J.H. Newman; reason, rhetoric and romanticism 1991 ➤ 7,g821; also Duckworth-Bristol, £25: ᴿTablet 246 (1992) 931s (R. *Strange*: some unusual accusations); TLond 95 (1992) 63s (C.C. *O'Gorman*).

m612 **Nichols** Aidan, From Newman to Congar... doctrinal development 1990 ➤ 6,k976: ᴿFurrow 43 (1992) 450s (J. *Macken*); JRel 72 (1992) 589-591 (B.R. *Hinze*); JTS 43 (1992) 309s (N. *Sagovsky*); NBlackf 73 (1992) 572s (G. *Rowell*); Pacifica 5 (1992) 100-2 (J. *Wilcken*).

m613 *Olivier* Paul, Newman, BLONDEL, LE ROY et le modernisme [10 livres]: RechSR 80 (1992) 419-440.

m614 **Pattison** Robert, The great dissent; J.H. Newman and the liberal heresy 1991 ➤ 7,g824: ᴿJTS 43 (1992) 764-7 (I. *Ker*: wrong-headed, eccentric; absurdly holds Newman minor and moribund); TLond 95 (1992) 288 (B.L. *Horne*: persuasive, irritating); TS 53 (1992) 596 (J. *Gaffney*).

m615 *a) Pereiro* J., S.F. WOOD and an early theory of development in the Oxford Movement; – *b) Foster* S., 'Dismal Johnny', a companion of Newman recalled: Recusant History 20 (1991) 524-553 / 21 (1992) 99-110 [< RHE 88,359*].

m616 *Quinn* John F., Newman, FABER and the Oratorian separation; a reappraisal: Recusant History 20 (1990s) 106-126.

m617 **Selén** Mats, The Oxford Movement and Wesleyan Methodism in England 1833-1882; a study in religious conflict: Diss. Lund 1992. 438 p. – RTLv 24, p. 558.

m618 *Streater* David, Newman's doctrine – development or deviation?: Churchman 106,1 (1992) 5-19 [< ZIT 92,282].

m619 **Thomas** Stephen, Newman and heresy [...the nature of revelation]: the Anglican years 1991 ➤ 7,g828; 0-521-39208-X: ᴿExpTim 103 (1991s)

315 (B. M. G. *Reardon*: weighty); JTS 43 (1992) 752-4 (R. *Strange*: resists the blandishments of Newman's story-telling).

m620 *Velocci* Giovanni, a) Aspetti della coscienza nel pensiero di J.H. Newman; – b) La spiritualità di J.H. Newman: SacDoc 37 (1992) 677-701 / 36 (1991) 72-87.

m621 ᴱWeaver Mary Jo, Newman and the Modernists 1985 ➤ 2,d844 ... 6,k982: ᴿRechSR 80 (1992) 422s (P. *Olivier*).

m622 ᴱWeidner H. D., J. H. Newman, The via media of the Anglican Church 1990 ➤ 6,k983: ᴿRHE 87 (1991) 310 (D. *Bradley*).

m623 NOCEDAL: *Magaz Fernández* José M., El pensamiento integrista de Ramón Nocedal: RET 52 (1992) 447-479.

m624 PIUS IX: **Martina** G., Pio IX [3.] (1867-1878) 1990 ➤ 6,k985; 7,g829: ᴿRHE 87 (1992) 848-854 (R. *Aubert*).

m624* **Polverani** Alberto, Vita di Pio IX, II. Vaticano 1987, Postulazione. 271 p. – ᴿGregorianum 73 (1992) 175s (Josef *Wicki*).

m625 PIUS X: **Romanato** Gianpaolo, Pio X; la vita di papa Sarto. Mi 1992, Rusconi. 346 p. – ᴿRHE 87 (1992) 858-862 (R. *Aubert*).

m626 TYRRELL: ᴱLivingston James C., Tradition and the critical spirit; [some of Tyrrell's] Catholic modernist writings: Texts in Modern Theology 1990; $16; 0-8006-3210-9: ➤ 7,g837: ᴿExpTim 103 (1991s) 315 (R. *Butterworth*: 'Tyrrell's Catholicism was simply non-Roman'); RelStR 18 (1992) 131 (J. R. *Sachs*: fine selection).

m627 **Sagovsky** Nicholas, On God's side ... Tyrrell 1990 ➤ 6,k996; 7,g835: ᴿHeythJ 33 (1992) 225-7 (S. *Gilley*: warts and all; despite his eloquence, he was often hard to defend); TvT 32 (1992) 202s (T. *Schoof*).

m628 *Schultenover* David G., George Tyrrell, 'devout disciple of Newman' [Tyrrell's claim, perhaps justified; here only the beginnings of Newman's influence examined]: HeythJ 33 (1992) 20-44.

Y6   *Saeculum XX* –   **20th Century Exegesis**

m629 a) *Caquot* André, L'exégèse et l'épigraphie sémitique à l'École biblique; – b) (*Cusin* Miche), *Defois* Gérard, Ouverture du colloque Centenaire de l'École biblique et archéologique française de Jérusalem; – c) *Tournay* R.-J., La Revue biblique depuis sa création jusqu'à nos jours; – d) *Sigrist* Marcel, Bibliothèque de l'École biblique; – e) *Barthélemy* Dominique, Actualité de la Bible dans le monde d'aujourd'hui: ➤ 462, Naissance 1990/2, 331-8 / (21s) 23-25 / 89-92 / 93-98 / 287-301.

m630 **Epp** E., *MacRae* G., NT & its modern interpreters 1989 ➤ 5,394 ... 7,g840: ᴿSvTKv 67 (1991) 43s (E. *Lövestam*).

m631 ᴱFabris Rinaldo, La Bibbia nell'epoca moderna e contemporanea: La Bibbia nella storia 17. Bo 1992, Dehoniane. 412 p. [... Nell'antichità, 2 vol. ᴱ*Norelli* E.; nel Medioevo ᴱ*Leonardi* C.]. – ᴿVivH 3 (1992) 420-2 (L. *Mazzinghi*).

m632 ᴱFelder Cain H., Stony the road we trod; African American biblical interpretation 1991 ➤ 7,433: ᴿExpTim 103 (1991s) 201 (R. F. *Carroll*: fascinating); NewTR 5,2 (1992) 109-111 (Dianne *Bergant*); RExp 89 (1992) 569-571 (T. J. *Johnson*).

m633 *Ghiberti* Giuseppe, Biblische Exegese in Italien zwischen Vaticanum I und Vaticanum II: NTS 38 (1992) 1-14.

m634 **Graffard** Sylvio, *Tristan* Léo, Les Bibelforscher [Jehovah's Witnesses] et le nazisme (1933-1945), ces oubliés de l'histoire². P 1990, Tiresias. 234 p. F 110. – ᴿRHR 209 (1992) 215 (S. *Schwarzfuchs*).

m635 *La Verdiere* Eugene, Evangelization and the Bible in the United States today: CathW 234 (1991) 67-71.

m636 *Rendtorff* Rolf, The image of postexilic Israel in German biblical scholarship from WELLHAUSEN to von RAD: → 181, Sha'arei TALMON 1992, 165-173.

m637 **Sperling** S. David, *al.*, Students of the Covenant; a history of Jewish biblical scholarship in North America; SBL Confessional Perspective. Atlanta 1992, Scholars. xii-216 p. $55; pa. $35. 1-55540-655-6; -6-4. – ᴿOTAbs 15 (1992) 488s (F. E. *Greenspahn*).

m638 ALTHAUS: **Meiser** Martin, Paul Althaus als Neutestamentler, dargestellt auf der Grundlage seiner Veröffentlichungen, seiner Briefe und seiner unveröffentlichten Manuskripte und Rundbemerkungen: Diss. ᴰ*Merk* O. Erlangen-Nürnberg 1992. 457 p. – RTLv 84, p. 548.

m639 BEA: **Schmidt** Stjepan, Augustin Bea, the cardinal of unity [1987 → 3,g812], ᵀ*Wearne* Leslie. New Rochelle 1992, New City. 806 p. $49. 1-56548-016-3 [TDig 40,186].

m640 BROWN R. E.: *Walsh* John E., Illogic and impression in the writings of Fr. Raymond Brown: HomP 92,8 (1992) 44-49 [< ZIT 92,400].

m641 BUBER: ᴱ**Glatzer** Nahum M., *Mendez-Flohr* Paul, The letters of Martin Buber, a life of dialogue [1972-5; 753 letters, ᴱ*Schoeder* Grete], ᵀ*Winston* Richard & Clara, *Zohn* Harry. NY 1991, Schocken. xiii-722 p. $45. 0-8052-4109-4 [TDig 40,54].

m642 *Jaberg* E. C., Buber, theologian of the dialogue: → 40, ᴱDAVID C., Arasaradi 5 (1992) 33-41.

m643 **Buber** Martin, La regalità di Dio, pref. *Soggin* J. A. Genova 1989, Marietti. xii-216 p. 1 it 32,000. – ᴿCC 143 (1992,4) 103s (G. L. *Prato*).

m644 **Buber** Martin, Encontro; fragmentos autobiográficos, ᵀ*Sofia* I. Albornoz Stein. Petrópolis 1991, Vozes. 86 p. [REB 52 (1992) 257].

m645 BULTMANN: **Baasland** Ernst, Theologie und Methode; eine historiographische Analyse der Frühschriften Rudolf Bultmanns [Hab.-Diss. Oslo]: MgStR. Wu 1992, Brockhaus. xvi-532 p. DM 88 [TR 88,524].

m646 *a) Bayer* Oswald, Entmythologisierung? Christliche Theologie zwischen Metaphysik und Mythologie im Blick auf Rudolf Bultmann: – *b) Jaspert* Bernd, Existenz–Mythos–Theologie; fünfzig Jahre nach R. Bultmanns Entmythologisierungsprogramm; – *c) Rosenau* Hartmut, Die Mythos-Diskussion im Deutschen Idealismus; – *d) Körtner* Ulrich H. J., Arbeit am Mythos?: NSys 34 (1992) 109-134; Eng. 134 / 135-148; Eng. 148 / 149-162; Eng. 162 / 163-181; Eng. 181.

m647 **Fergusson** David, Bultmann: Outstanding Christian thinkers. L 1992, Chapman. xvi-154 p. 0-225-66626-X; pa. -3-5 [TDig 40,80 gives publ. (also) ColMn. Liturgical/Glazier, 0-8146-5053-8].

m649 *Moda* Aldo, La recezione della teologia di Rudolf Bultmann in Italia: StPatavina 39 (1992) 283-353 (-362 bibliog.).

m650 *Hauschild* Eberhard, Was heisst 'lutherisch'? erörtert am Beispiel der Theologie R. Bultmanns: Luther 61 (1990) 20-36.

m651 **Jones** Gareth, Bultmann, towards a critical theology 1991 → 7,g855: ᴿJTS 43 (1922) 317-9 (A. C. *Thiselton*: solidly maintains that Historie and the God question take precedence over human existence in a way

overlooked by KÄSEMANN, EBELING, FUCHS); TTod 49 (1992s) 288s
(J. F. *Kay*).
m652 *Pesce* Mauro, L'odierna recezione cattolica dell'ermeneutica di Bultmann: FilT 5 (1991) 117-120.
m653 *Weier* Reinhold, Christsein als 'eschatologische Existenz' [Bultmann]:
TrierTZ 101 (1992) 161-171,

m654 CADBURY: ᴱParsons Mikeal C., *Tyson* Joseph B., Cadbury, Knox and
Talbert; American contributions to the study of Acts [Cadbury, p. 7-51,
Gaventa B., *al.*: Knox 55-130, Tyson *al.*; Talbert 133-251, Parsons *al.*]:
SBL, Biblical Scholarship in North America 18. Atlanta 1992, Scholars.
x-264 p. 1-55540-653-X.
m655 CULLMANN: *a*) *Agourides* S., Oscar Cullmann, the theologian and
Church leader; – *b*) *Rigopoulos* George, ... his retrospection: ➤ 37,
DeltioVM 21,11 (1992) 5-7 / (9-) 14-22 [-41, *al.*].
m656 *Moessner* David P., Oscar Cullmann, scholar of early Christianity;
doctor of the contemporary Church; the significance of his contribution
[< Dictionary of Bible Interpretation 1992]: ➤ 38, ᶠCULLMANN O.,
TZBas 48 (1992) 238-242.
m657 DALMAN G.: *Männchen* J., G. Dalman als erster Direktor [† 1941]:
JbEvHL 3 (1991) 15-28 [< ZAW 105,507].
m658 HARNACK: *Hübner* Thomas, Adolf von Harnacks Vorlesungen über
das Wesen des Christentums unter besonderer Berücksichtigung der Me-
thodenfragen als sachgemässer Zugang zu ihrer Christologie und Wirkungsgeschichte: Diss. ᴰ*Honecker* M. Bonn 1992. 400 p. – RTLv 24,
p. 557.
m659 JACKSON: *Redcliffe* Gary, A pastoral perspective in the Jackson- [A.]
Carman controversy, 1908 [George Jackson's Higher Criticism at Toronto
Victoria Univ. split Methodists]: ➤ 74, ᶠGUENTHER H., TorJT 8 (1992)
161-173.
m660 KAUFMANN: **Krapf** Thomas, Yehezkel Kaufmann, ein Lebens- und
Erkenntnisweg zur Theologie der Hebräischen Bibel: Studien zu Kirche
und Israel 11, 1990 ➤ 6,m31; 7,g862: DM 17,80. 3-923095-62-7. – ᴿBO
49 (1992) 471-3 (M. J. *Mulder*); RelStR 18 (1992) 137 (M. A. *Sweeney*).

m661 LAGRANGE: **Gilbert** M., M.-J. Lagrange, L'Écriture en l'Église 1990
➤ 6,m35; 7,g863: ᴿÉTRel 67 (1992) 113 (C.-B. *Amphoux*: le présentateur
'était' et est SJ); Salesianum 54 (1992) 373 (R. *Vicent*).
m662 **Gilbert** Maurice, M.-J. Lagrange, Exégète à Jérusalem; nouveaux mélanges d'histoire religieuse (1890-1931): CahRB 29, 1991 ➤ 7,g684: ᴿBL
(1992) 20 (A. G. *Auld*: also on AT/NT Cent Ans ÉcB 1990); RB 99 (1992)
624 (R. J. *Tournay*).
m663 *Gilbert* Maurice, Vingt-cinq lettres de M.-J. Lagrange à Robert
DEVREESSE (1928-1936): RB 99 (1992) 471-498; Eng. 471.
m664 *Kourie* C. E. T., Leading lights in twentieth century Roman Catholic
biblical scholarship: M.-J. Lagrange (1855-1938): TEv 24,3 (Pretoria 1991)
37-43 [< NTAbs 36,320].
m665 *Montagnes* Bernard, L'ascendant du Père Lagrange; documents:
➤ 114, ᶠLABOURDETTE M., RThom 92,1 (1992) 52-58.
m666 *Montagnes* P., Le Père Lagrange ou la miséricorde de la vérité: VSp
146 (1992) 191-200 [< NTAbs 36,320].
m667 *Raurell* Frederic, [en catalán] Nota crítico-bibliogràfica, 'Portrait du
Père Lagrange' de Jean GUITTON: EstFranc 93 (1992) 369-404.

m667* — **Guitton** Jean,   Portrait du Père Lagrange.   P 1991, Laffont.   266 p.
F 100. – ᴿEsprVie 102 (1992) 206s (M. *Trémeau* réfléchit sur sa douleur à
la perte de vocations brillantes).

m668 *Refoulé* François,   La méthode historico-critique et le père Lagrange:
RSPT 76 (1992) 553-587; Eng. 587.

m669 *a*) *Théobald* Christoph,   Le père Lagrange et le modernisme; – *b*)
Montagnes Bernard,   La méthode historique; succès et revers d'un
manifeste: ➤ 462, Naissance 1990/2, 49-64 / 67-88.

m670 MARTI: *Mathys* Hans-Peter,   Karl Marti 1855-1925:   TZBas 48 (1992)
356-368.

m671 MARTINI Carlo M.,   Nel cuore della Chiesa e del mondo; dialogo con
Antonio *Balletto* e Bruno *Musso*.   Genova 1991, Marietti.   113 p. –
ᴿArchivScSocR 80 (1992) 277 (J.-D. *Durand*: di meno valore dei suoi
discorsi, Educare 1990).

m672 NYBERG: **Kahle** Sigrid,   H. S. Nyberg, en vetenskapsmans biografi.
Norstedts 1991, Ev. Akad.   584 p. – ᴿSvTKv 67 (1991) 193s (S. *Hidal*).

m673 O'HARA: **Dolan** Timothy M.,   'Some seed fell on good ground'; the life
of Edwin V. O'Hara [CBA founder: CBQ 17 (1955)].   Wsh 1992, Catholic
University of America.   xxv-301 p. $30 [CBQ 54,833].

m674 QUINZIO: *Mucci* Giandomenico,   Sergio Quinzio tra storicismo e
fideismo: CC 143 (1992,4) 258-270.

m674* **Quinzio** Sergio,   La sconfitta di Dio [... si è persa la fiducia].   R 1992,
Adelphi.   104 p. – ᴿRCatalT 16 (1991) 421-3 (F. *Raurell*: esdevé una
paraula profètica).

m675 ROBINSON: **Taylor** T. F.,   J. Armitage Robinson, eccentric, scholar
[Eph.] and churchman 1858-1933:   1991 ➤ 7,g870: ᴿJEH 43 (1992) 159s
(C. N. L. *Brooke*).

m676 ROSENZWEIG: **Görtz** Heinz-Jürgen,   Franz Rosenzweigs neues Denken; eine Einführung aus der Perspektive christlicher Theologie: Bonner
DogmSt 12.   Wü 1992, Echter.   151 p.   DM 39 [TR 88,524].

m677 SCHMITHALS: **Boshoff** Petrus B.,   The unity of Walter Schmithals's
historical and theological interpretation of the New Testament: [Afri-
kaans] diss. ᴰ*Aarde* A. G. van.   Pretoria 1992. – DissA 53 (1992s) 1556-A.

m678 SCHWEITZER: **Pleitner** Henning,   Das Ende der liberalen Hermeneutik
am Beispiel Albert Schweitzers: TANZ 5.   Tü 1992, Francke.   xi-281 p.
DM 78.   3-7720-1884-X [TLZ 118,1050-2, H.-H. *Jensen*].

Y6.3   *Influxus Scripturae saeculo XX* – surveys of current outlooks.

m679 **Alberigo** Giuseppe,   Il cristianesimo in Italia 1989 ➤ 7,g882:   ᴿRET 52
(1992) 102s (M. *Gesteira*); Salesianum 54 (1992) 367s (C. *Semeraro*).

m680 *Allan* J. D.,   The evangelicals; the story of a great Christian movement.
Exeter 1989, Paternoster.   154 p. £6 [RefTR 51,35].

m681 **Bacik** James J.,   [20] Contemporary theologians [Rahner to Gandhi]. ...
1992, Mercier.   270 p. £10.   0-85342-992-8. – ᴿExpTim 103 (1991s) 383
[C. S. *Rodd*].

m682 **Bloom** Harold,   The American religion; the emergence of the post-
Christian nation.   NY 1992, Simon &S.   228 p. $22. – ᴿTTod 49 (1992s)
542-4 (Cleo M. *Kearns*).

m683 **Carcel Ortí** V.,   ¿España neopagana? Análisis de la situación y
discursos del Papa en las visitas 'ad limina'.   Valencia 1992, EDICEP.
301 p. – ᴿBurgense 33 (1992) 593s (N. *López Martínez*).

m684 **Cholvy** Gérard, La religion en France de la fin du XVIIIe siècle à nos jours: Carré Histoire. P 1991, Hachette. 219 p. F 79. 2-01-015958-6. – ^REsprVie 102 (1992) 78s (J.-C. *Meyer*); ÉTRel 67 (1992) 292 (L. *Gambarotto*).

m685 ^ECoalter Milton J., *al.*, The diversity of discipleship: Presbyterian presence [7 vols.] 1991 → 7,g587*: ^RTTod 49 (1992s) 283s (C. *Ocker*).

m686 ^ECoreth Emerich, *al.*, Christliche Philosophie im katholischen Denken des 19. und 20. Jahrhunderts, 3. Moderne Strömungen im 20. Jahrhundert. Graz 1990, Styria. 920 p. – ^RFreibZ 39 (1992) 550-6 (P. *Secretan*).

m687 **D'Antonio** William, *al.*, American Catholic laity in a changing Church. KC 1989, Sheed &W. 193 p. $16. – ^RThought 66 (1991) 95-7 (T. P. *Rausch*).

Davis Cyprian, The history of black Catholics in the U. S. 1990 → 8814.

m688 **Dembowski** Bronisław, ℗ O filozofii chrześciańskiej w Ameryce Północnej. 231 p. – ^RAtKap 118 (1992) 328-331 (J. *Krokos*).

m689 *a*) *Doré* Joseph, Les courants de la théologie française depuis Vatican II; – *b*) *Alberigo* Giuseppe, Critères herméneutiques pour une histoire de Vatican II; – *c*) *Metz* Johann-B., Esprit de l'Europe, esprit du christianisme; – *d*) *Jossua* Jean-Pierre, La théologie devant l'incroyance: → 63, ^FGEFFRÉ C., Interpréter 1992, 227-259 / 261-275 / 277-287 / 289-300.

m690 *Dulles* Avery, Theological orientations; American Catholic theology, 1940-1962: CrNSt 13 (1992) 361-382.

m691 **Dyrness** William A., How does America hear the Gospel? GR 1990, Eerdmans. 168 p. $12. 0-8028-0437-3. – ^RWestTJ 53 (1991) 171-3 (W. *Edgar*: friendly criticisms).

m692 **Eagleton** Terry, The ideology of the aesthetic. Ox 1990. Blackwell. 426 p. £11. – ^RHeythJ 33 (1992) 94 (H. *Meynell*: hardly on aesthetics; refreshing insights from the not so dead horse of Marxism).

m693 **Ferm** Deane W., Contemporary American theologies² [¹1980]. SF 1990, Harper & R. 184 p. $15 pa. – ^RInterpretation 46 (1992) 419.422 (D. L. *Migliore*).

m694 ^EFord David F., The modern theologians 1989 → 5,k461 ... 7,g888: ^RGregorianum 73 (1992) 755s (R. *Fisichella*).

m695 **Frei** Hans W., † 1988, ^EHunsinger George, *Placher* William C., Types of Christian theology [KAUFMANN G.: TRACY D.: SCHLEIERMACHER F.: BARTH K.: PHILLIPS J.]. NHv 1992, Yale Univ. xi-180 p. $26.50. 0-300-05104-2 [TDig 40,62].

m696 **Garelli** Franco, Religione e chiesa in Italia. Bo 1991, Mulino. 271 p. – ^RArchivScSocR 80 (1992) 263s (J.-D. *Durand*).

m697 **Gastaldi** Ugo, I movimenti di risveglio nei mondo protestante; dal 'Great Awakening' (1720) ai 'revivals' del nostro secolo. T 1989, Claudiana. 200 p. – ^RSTEv 3 (1991) 136s (N. *Ciniello*).

Gauly Thomas M., Katholiken; Machtanspruch 1991 → 8611.

m698 **Gaustad** Edwin S., A religious history of America³rev [¹1966]. SF 1990, Harper & R. xvi-391 p. 0-06-063092-2. – ^RAsbTJ 47,1 (1992) 104s (D. *Bundy*).

m699 *Grenz* Stanley J., *Olson* Roger E., 20th century theology; God and the world in a transitional age. DG 1992, InterVarsity. 393 p. $20. 0-8308-1761-1 [TDig 40,65]. – ^RChrCent 109 (1992) 943-5 (J. G. *Stackhouse*).

m700 *Greschat* Martin, Neuzeitliche Kirchengeschichte: → 757, EvKL 3 (1992) 704-720 (-739, *al.*).

m701 ᶠHANDY R.T.: Altered landscapes; Christianity in America, ᴱLotz David W., 1989 ➤ 6,82*: ᴿChH 60 (1991) 580-2 (R. Scott *Appleby*: an unconventional Festschrift).

m702 **Hastings** Adrian, A history of English Christianity 1920-1990³ [= ¹1986 for 1920-85 + update]. ➤ 7,g893; L/Ph 1991, SCM/Trinity. xxix-720 p. £7.50. 0-334-02496-X / 1-56338-003-X. – ᴿTvT 32 (1992) 104s (R. *Bunnik*).

m703 **Hatch** Nathan O., Democratization of American Christianity 1989 ➤ 6,m69; 7,g894: ᴿJAAR 60 (1992) 778-791 (T. E. *Fulop*); RelStR 18 (1992) 99-105 (R. L. *Moore*, also on 3 cognates).

m704 **Hellwig** Monika K., What are the theologians saying now? A retrospective on several decades. Dublin 1992, Gill &M. xvii-170 p. £7. 0-7171-2091-0.

m704* **Hornsby-Smith** Michael P., Roman Catholic beliefs in England; customary Catholicism and transformation of religious authority 1991 ➤ 7,g896: ᴿNBlackf 73 (1992) 192-4 (B. R. *Wilson*).

m705 **Hummel** Gert, Die Begegnung zwischen Philosophie und evangelischer Theologie im 20. Jahrhundert 1989 ➤ 6,m70; 7,g597: DM 108. 3-534-00599-6: ᴿActuBbg 29 (1992) 69s (J. *Boada*).

m706 ᴱHutchison William R., Between the times; the travail of the Protestant establishment in America 1900-1960. 1989 ➤ 5,679; 7,g898: ᴿCritRR 5 (1992) 327-9 (D. N. *Williams*); TTod 49 (1992s) 250-2 . 254 (R. K. *Fenn*).

m707 **Jones** W. Paul, Theological worlds; understanding the alternative rhythms of Christian belief [TILLICH, CONE, HARTSHORNE, BARTH, KIERKEGAARD]. Nv 1992, Abingdon. 255 p. – ᴿRelStR 18 (1992) 39 (L. J. *Biallas*).

m708 **Jung** Friedhelm, Die deutsche evangelikale Bewegung; Grundlinien ihrer Geschichte und Theologie [Diss, Marburg]: EurHS 23/461. Fra 1992, Lang. 430 p. DM 98 [TR 88,529].

m709 **Kaiser** Jochen-Christoph, Sozialer Protestantismus in 20. Jahrhundert; Beiträge zur Geschichte der Inneren Mission 1914-1945. Mü 1989, Oldenbourg. xi-506 p. DM 128. – ᴿTR 88 (1992) 49-51 (W.-D. *Hauschild*).

m709* *Knox* J. Buick, Presbyterianism: ᶠBARKLEY J., IrBSt 13 (1991) 17-32.

m710 **Larère** Philippe, L'essor des Églises évangéliques. P 1992, Centurion. 116 p. F 94. – ᴿEsprVie 102 (1992) 570 (P. *Jay*).

m711 **Leach** Kenneth, Subversive orthodoxy [... Church renewal rather than comfort]. Toronto 1992, Anglican. 64 p. $7. 0-921846-49-5. – ᴿExpTim 104 (1992s) 23s (G. *Patrick*).

m712 **Leimgruber** S., *Schoch* M., Gegen die Gottvergessenheit [Schweiz 19.-20. Jh.] 1990 ➤ 6,m71: ᴿTZBas 48 (1992) 391s (T. K. *Kuhn*).

m713 **Luker** Ralph E., The social gospel in black and white; American racial reform, 1885-1912. Chapel Hill 1991, Univ. N. Carolina. xiv-445 p. $40. – ᴿChrCent 109 (1992) 197s (G. H. *Shriver*); TS 53 (1992) 580-2 (J. H. *Fichter*: rectifies SCHLESINGER-style astigmatism restricting both Protestant and Catholic social reform to the working class).

m714 **McDonough** Peter, Men astutely trained; a history of the Jesuits in the American century, NY 1991, [Maxwell-Macmillan] Free Press. $25. 0-02-920527-1 [BR 8/3,51 adv.].

m715 **Manzke** Karl H., Ewigkeit und Zeitlichkeit; Aspekte für eine theologische Deutung der Zeit [ev. Diss. München 1989: 'die Suche nach einem Standort im Denken des 20. Jahrhunderts']: ForSysÖkT 63. Gö 1992, Vandenhoeck &R. 541 p. DM 148. 3-525-56270-5 [TLZ 118,434-7, U. *Körtner*].

m716 **Marchasson** Y., Les papes du XXᵉ siècle: BtHistChr 26. P 1990, Desclée. 154 p. F 95. – ᴿRTLv 23 (1992) 99-101 (C. *Soetens*).

m717 **Marty** Martin M., Modern American religion 2. The noise of conflict, 1919-1941: 1991 ➤ 7,g902: ᴿCCurr 42 (1992s) 250s (D. H. *Watt*); ChH 61 (1992) 427s (L. I. *Sweet*: some few flecks); ChrCent 108 (1991) 552-9 (M. A. *Noll*); Interpretation 46 (1992) 216s (D. *Jodock*); JRel 72 (1992) 591s (P. A. *Carter*); RRelRes 33 (1990s) 189 (A. A. *Preisinger*); TS 53 (1992) 358s (J. *Hennesey*).

m718 **Michelat** Guy, *al.*, Les Français sont-ils encore catholiques? Analyse d'un sondage d'opinion: Sciences humaines et religions. P 1991, Cerf. 332 p. F 240. 2-204-04346-X. – ᴿArchivScSocR 78 (1992) 246-8 (R. *Lambert*); ÉTRel 67 (1992) 538-40 (J.-M. *Prieur*: 81% se déclarent catholiques; les autres demandes sont trop contraignantes); RechSR 80 (1992) 471s (P. *Vallin*).

m719 ᴱ**Müller** Hans Martin, Kulturprotestantismus; Beiträge zu einer Gestalt des modernen Christentums. Gü 1991, Mohn. 384 p. DM 98. 3-579-00275-9 [TLZ 118,426, K. *Nowak*].

m720 **Munson** James, The nonconformists; in search of a lost culture. L 1991, SPCK. vii-360 p. £17.50 pa. – ᴿNBlackf 73 (1992) 464-6 (J. *Kent*); TLond 95 (1992) 64s (G. S. *Wakefield*: 1890-1914 Nonconformity *was* England; but a story without saints).

m721 **Myers** Kenneth A., All God's children and blue suede shoes; Christians and popular culture. ... 1989, Crossway. 224 p. $11 pa. 0-89107-538-0. – ᴿWestTJ 53 (1991) 377-380 (W. *Edgar*: long overdue Christian analysis of popular culture; art, rock music, TV...).

m722 *Navone* John, Tendenze religiose negli Stati Uniti: CC 143 (1992.1) 453-7 [(1992,2) 30-41, *Madelin* Henri].

m723 **Noll** Mark A., A history of Christianity in the United States and Canada. GR 1992, Eerdmans. xvi-576 p. $40; pa. $30. 0-8028-2703-4; -0651-1 [TDig 40,179: this Wheaton prof centers on the rise and decline of Protestantism, but with full attention to Catholics].

m724 **O'Brien** David, Public Catholicism; Bicentennial History 1989 ➤ 5, k466; 6,m73: ᴿJAAR 60 (1992) 355s (P. H. *McNamara*).

m725 *Orsi* Robert A., Beyond the mainstream in the study of American religious history [BROWN A. V., Grail; ᴱHUTCHISON W. R.: ᴱLACEY M. J., all 1989]: JEH 43 (1992) 287-292.

m726 **Pelikan** Jaroslav, The idea of the university, a reexamination. NHv 1992, Yale Univ. x-238 p. $30. – ᴿCathHR 78 (1992) 621-3 (T. M. *Hesburgh*: enormously positive, like NEWMAN, and unlike Mark ANDERSON's 'Imposters in the temple').

m727 **Pinnock** Clark H., *Brown* Delwin, Theological crossfire; an evangelical/liberal dialogue. GR 1991, Zondervan. 261 p. $13 pa. – ᴿChrCent 108 (1991) 815s (J. G. *Stackhouse*).

m728 **Pinnock** Clark, Tracking the maze 1990 ➤ 6,m74; 7,g903*b*: ᴿCurrTMiss 19 (1992) 60s (K. *Sawyer*); Interpretation 46 (1992) 106 (D. G. *Bloesch*).

m729 **Ruthven** Malise, The divine supermarket; shopping for God in America. NY 1989, Morrow. x-317 p. $19. – ᴿChH 61 (1992) 276s (P. W. *Williams*).

m730 **Selby** Peter, Belonging; challenge to a tribal church. L 1991, SPCK. viii-79 p. £6 pa. – ᴿTLond 95 (1992) 65 (M. *Wharton*: on the Church of England by its bishop of Kingston).

m731 **Simons** Ed, *Winkeler* Lodewijk, Het verraad der clercken; Intellectuelen en hun rol in de ontwikkelingen van het Nederlandse katholicisme na

1945 [diss. 1987]. Baarn 1987, Arbor. 504 p.; ill. 90-5158-005-3. – RBijdragen 53 (1992) 96-98 (J. *Jacobs*, also on Winkeler's 1989 Gegronde twijfel).

m732 **Sparr** Arnold,   To promote, defend and redeem; the Catholic literary revival and the cultural transformation of American Catholicism, 1920-1960: Westport CT 1990, Greenwood.   xiv-240 p. $40. – RCritRR 5 (1992) 347-351 (J. M. *McShane*).

m732* **Tamney** Joseph B.,   The resilience of Christianity in the modern world: Religion, Culture, Society.   Albany 1992, SUNY.   x-178 p. $49.50; pa. $17. 0-7914-0821-3; -2-1 [TDig 39,290].

m733 *Tiryakian* Edward A.,   L'exceptionnelle vitalité religieuse aux États-Unis; une relecture de 'Protestant-Catholic-Jew': Social Compass 38 (1991) 215-238.

m734 EWeinrich Michael,   Theologiekritik in der Neuzeit ... Texte 18.-19. Jh.: 1988 ► 6,465:   REstE 66 (1991) 108 (J. J. *Alemany*).

m735 **Wentz** Richard E.,   Religion in the New World; the shaping of religious traditions in the United States 1990 ► 7,g907*b: RTS 53 (1992) 169-171 (E. G. *Ernst*: grand, but overlooks Baptists as well as Hispanics).

m736 *Wentz* Richard E.,   'Under the spell of Don Marquis' worm' in the study of American religion: CritRR 5 (1992) 39-59.

m737 **Wuthnow** Robert,   The struggle for America's soul 1989 ► 7,g909: RChH 60 (1990) 421-3 (J. H *Dorn*: as a good sociologist should); Thought 66 (1991) 107s (J. R. *Kelly*).

Y6.5   **Theologi influentes** *in exegesim saeculi XX.*

m738 ADAM K.: *Reinhardt* Rudolf,   Karl Adam in altkatholischer Sicht; ein Brief aus dem Jahre 1923; zugleich ein Beitrag zu den Beziehungen von Joseph Burkard LEU (Luzern) zu Johann Adam MÖHLER: TüTQ 172 (1992) 117-121.

m739 ALTIZER Thomas J.J.,   Genesis and apocalypse; a theological voyage toward authentic Christianity.   Louisville 1991, W-Knox.   198 p. $19. 0-664-21932-2 [TDig 39,45]. – RRelStR 18 (1992) 317 (R. *Feeru*), TS 53 (1992) 562-4 (S. *Duffy*); TTod 49 (1992s) 132s (R. S. *Corrington*).

m740 **Taylor** Mark C.,   Tears [uninformative title of a lively book on Altizer and BARTH]. Albany 1989, SUNY.   263 p. $54.50; pa. $18.   RJRel 72 (1992) 453s (J. D. *Caputo*).

m741 BALTHASAR: **Beaudin** Michel,   Obéissance et solidarité; essai sur la christologie de H. U. v. Balthasar [diss. Montréal 1978]: Héritage et projet 42, 1989 ► 7,7452: RÉglT 22 (1991) 378-380 (A. *Peelman*).

m742 **Guerriero** Elio,   H. U. v. Balthasar 1991 ► 7,g916:   RLateranum 58 (1992) 519-521 (R. *Fisichella*).

m743 **Konda** Jutta,   Das Verhältnis von Theologie und Heiligkeit im Werk Balthasars: DogmSt 9.   Wü 1991, Echter.   384 p. – RTPhil 67 (1992) 606s (W. *Löser*).

m744 **Krenski** Thomas R.,   Passio caritatis; trinitarische Passiologie ... Balthasars [Diss. FrB 1989] 1990 ► 7,g917:   RFreibZ 39 (1992) 225-8 (G. *Dorneger*); TLZ 116 (1991) 759-762 (M. *Lochbrunner*); TPhil 67 (1992) 302s (W. *Löser*).

m745 **Lehmann** K., Kasper W.,   H. U. v. Balthasar, Gestalt und Werk 1989 ► 6,10; 7,g918: RForumKT 7 (1991) 153-5 (J. *Auda*).

m746 ELehmann K., Kasper W.,   H. U. v. Balthasar, figura e opera [1990 ► 6,10; 7,g918],T.   CasM 1991, Piemme.   467 p. Lit. 45.000. – RAsprenas 39 (1992) 121s (R. *Russo*).

m747 **Naduvilekut** James, Christus der Heilsweg... Balthasar 1987 ➤ 4,8756*; 5,k481: TPhil 67 (1992) 606 (W. *Löser*).

m748 *O'Connor* James T., Von Balthasar et le salut [< HomP July 1989]ᵀ: PeCa 247 (1990) 42-56.

m749 **O'Donnell** John, Hans Urs von Balthasar: Outstanding Christian thinkers. ColMn 1992, Glazier/Liturgical. x-166 p. $13. 0-8146-5039-2 [TDig 40,80].

m750 *a) Ros García* Salvador, La estética teológica de Hans Urs von Balthasar; – *b) Castro* Secundino, La belleza en la Biblia: REspir 51 (1992) 295-325 / 253-270.

m751 **Balthasar** Hans U. v., Mein Werk, Durchblicke [5, aus 1945, 1955, 1965, 1975, 1988]. Einsiedeln 1990, Johannes. 113 p. DM 23 pa. – ᴿGregorianum 73 (1992) 178s (J. M. *McDermott*); MüTZ 42 (1991) 282s (M. *Tiator*).

m752 **Balthasar** H. U. v., Spouse of the Word [14 essays 1939-61 relating to ecclesiology, partly in 1967 Church and World]: Explorations in Theology 2. SF 1991, Ignatius. 513 p. – ᴿTS 53 (1992) 763-5 (A. *Dulles*: useful, though source and date not supplied, and translation uneven).

m753 **Balthasar** Hans Urs von, The realm of metaphysics in the modern age: Glory 5 [ᵀ*Davies* O., *al.*; ᴱ*Fessio* J., *Riches* J.]. SF/E 1991, Ignatius/Clark. 624 p. £28. -/0-567-09576-2. – ᴿDowR 110 (1992) 77-81 (Francesca *Murphy*: worst translated and proofread of the 5); 146-50 (on 1s); ExpTim 103 (1991s) 90 (G. *Newlands*: final section 'Our inheritance and the Christian task'); JTS 43 (1992) 324s (D. *MacKinnon*: high praise, also for the translators of this great work); NBlackf 73 (1992) 516-8 . 573s (J. *O'Donnell*); TS 53 (1992) 359-361 (W. M. *Thompson*).

m754 **Balthasar** Hans U. v., La dramatique divine 2/1s, 1988 ➤ 4,k409*; 6,m87: ᴿÉglT 22 (1991) 229s (A. *Peelman*); RTLv 23 (1992) 91s (É. *Gaziaux*).

m755 **Balthasar** H. v., La dramatique divine 3; ᵀ*Givord* E., *Dumont* Camille: Horizon. (P)/Namur 1990, (Lethielleux)/Culture et Vérité. 477 p. Fb 1975. – ᴿRTLv 23 (1992) 374-6 (E. *Gaziaux*).

m756 BARTH: **Anzinger** Herbert, Glaube und kommunikative Praxis; eine Studie zur vordialektischen Theologie Karl Barths: BeitEvT 110, 1991 ➤ 7,g924: ᴿTR 88 (1992) 470s (E. *Arens*).

m757 **Barth** Karl, Introduzione alla teologia evangelica²; ital.² *Bof* Giampiero *al.* (¹1968 *Riverso* E.): Classici del Pensiero Cristiano 5, 1990 ➤ 7,g928: ᴿLateranum 57 (1991) 608-611 (B. *Gherardini*).

m758 **Chung Sueng-Hoon**, Karl Barth und die Hegelsche Linke; die Revolution Gottes bei Karl Barth in Auseinandersetzung mit der politisch-ökonomischen Anthropologie bei Karl MARX: Diss. Basel 1992, ᴰ*Lochman* J. M. – TLZ 118,691.

m759 **Frey** Christofer, Die Theologie Karl Barths, eine Einführung 1988 ➤ 4,k424*; 7,g935: ᴿRTLv 23 (1992) 346s (E. *Brito*: solide, vivant).

m760 *Frey* Christofer, Der Zuspruch Gottes; die Aktualität der Theologie Karl Barths: EvKomm 24 (1991) 15-18.

m761 **Haga** Tsutomu, Theodizee und Geschichtstheologie; ein Versuch der Überwindung der Problematik des Deutschen Idealismus bei Karl Barth [Diss. Heidelberg]: ForSysÖkT 59. Gö 1991, Vandenhoeck & R. 289 p. DM 74 [TLZ 118,954, C. *Frey*).

m762 **Hunsinger** George, How to read Barth 1991 ➤ 6,m100*; 7,g939: ᴿCCurr 42 (1992s) 405-7 (J. J. *Buckley*); ChrCent 108 (1991) 566 (P.

Stroble); JAAR 60 (1992) 791-6 (F. D. *Molnar*); JRel 72 (1992) 447s (P. E. *Stroble*); Month 253 (1992) 199s (J. *Hanvey*); TLond 95 (1992) 42s (C. *Gunton*).

m763 **Johnson** William S.[J], God the center of theology; a reinterpretation of Karl Barth: diss. Harvard. CM 1992. 336 p. 93-07630. – DissA 53 (1992s) 3954-A.

m764 **Kelso** Adelia, God alongside us; Karl Barth's reform of John CALVIN's theological method and the doctrine of divine providence: diss. Edinburgh 1992. 386 p. – RTLv 24, p. 539.

m765 **Kim Jae Jin**, Die Universalität der Versöhnung im Gottesbund; zur biblischen Begründung der Bundestheologie in der Kirchlichen Dogmatik Karl Barths [Diss. Münster]: StSysTE 2. Münster 1992, Lit. 220 p. DM 48 [TR 88,524].

m766 **Kirschstein** Helmut, Der souveräne Gott und die heilige Schrift; die Grundrelation der biblischen Hermeneutik Karl Barths als kontinuierliches Zentrum seiner Theologie: ev. Diss. [D]*Moltmann* J. Tübingen 1992. 355 p. – RTLv 24, p. 574; TLZ 118,459.

m767 *Klimek* N., Der Begriff 'Mystik' in der Theologie Karl Barths [Diss. Bochum 1989]: KkKSt 56, 1990 ➤ 7,g941; 3-87088-641-2: [R]TvT 32 (1992) 421s (R. J. *Peeters*).

m768 **MacGlasson** Paul, Jesus and Judas; biblical exegesis in Barth 1991 ➤ 7,g947: [R]TTod 49 (1992s) 129 (J. A. *Wharton*).

m769 *Machen* J. Gresham, Karl Barth and 'the Theology of Crisis': WestTJ 53 (1991) 191-207 [189-196, *Hart* D. G., recently uncovered paper: 209-225, legacy of Machen]; 54 (1992) 404, A. *MacRae* protest.

m770 **Matheny** P. D., Dogmatics and ethics; the theological realism and ethics of Karl Barth's Church Dogmatics: StIntcult 63, 1990 ➤ 7,g949: [R]TvT 32 (1992) 320 (R. J. *Peeters*).

m771 **Molendijk** Arie L., Aus dem Dunklen ins Helle; Wissenschaft und Theologie im Denken von Heinrich Scholz [Diskussionspartner Barths; Diss.]: AmstSiT 8. Amst 1991, Rodopi. 390 p. ƒ120. 90-5183-247-8. – [R]TR 88 (1992) 56-59 (G. *Pfleiderer*); TvT [31,188] 32 (1992) 421 (A. *Brants*).

m772 *Molendijk* Arie L., Ein 'heidnischer' Wissenschaftsbegriff? Der Streit zwischen Heinrich SCHOLZ und Karl Barth um die Wissenschaftlichkeit der Theologie: EvT 52 (1992) 527-545. [549-554, *Eicher* Peter zu *Frey* Christofer].

m773 **Mueller** David L., Foundation of Karl Barth's doctrine of reconciliation; Jesus Christ crucified and risen: Toronto StT, 1990 ➤ 7,g950: [R]TS 53 (1992) 762s (G. *Fackre*).

m774 [E]**Reiffen** Hannelotte, Barth, The Göttingen Dogmatics [1924], instruction in the Christian religion I, [T]*Bromiley* Geoffrey 1991 ➤ 7,g926: [R]ChrCent 109 (1992) 227 (P. E. *Stroble*); ExpTim 103 (1991s) 312s (K. W. *Clements*); TLond 95 (1992) 291 (G. *Ward*: fills a blank).

m775 **Roberts** Richard, [Barth] A theology on its way? E 1992, Clark. xvi-208 p. £18. 0-567-09585-1. – [R]ExpTim 104 (1992s) 25 (C. *Gunton*: sociological milieu; warnings of monism).

m776 **Rothen** Bernhard, Die Klarheit der Schrift [➤ 7,1055], 2. Karl Barth, eine Kritik. Gö 1990, Vandenhoeck &R. 211 p. DM 38 pa. – [R]CritRR 5 (1992) 486s (G. *Hunsinger*: Luther grasped it, Barth missed it completely).

m777 [E]**Stoevesandt** Hinrich, K. Barth - K. H. MISKOTTE, Briefwechsel 1924-1968. Z 1991, Theol.-V. 195 p. DM 38. – [R]LuthMon 31 (1992) 42 (H.-J. *Kraus*).

m778 **Süss** René, Een genadeloos bestaan; Karl Barth over het Joodse volk. Kampen 1991, Kok. 198 p. ƒ39,50. – ᴿStreven 59 (1992s) 1235s (P. *Beentjes*).

m779 **Thompson** John, The Holy Spirit in the theology of Karl Barth: PrincetonTMg. Allison Park PA 1991, Pickwick. 211 p. $24. – ᴿTS 53 (1992) 391 (G. *Fackre*).

m780 **Torrance** Thomas F., Karl Barth, biblical and evangelical theologian 1990 ⇥ 6,m100*a*; 7,g953: ᴿNBlackf 73 (1992) 462s (T. *Williams*); RefTR 50 (1991) 75s (R. C. *Doyle*); ScotJT 45 (1992) 253s (B. L. *McCormack*).

Wallace Mark I., The second naiveté; Barth, RICŒUR and the New Yale theology 1990 ⇥ b2.

m781 **Watzek** Margaret M., The Christocentrism of Karl Barth and Karl RAHNER; a re-examination of transcendental theology: diss. Emory, ᴰ*Lowe* W. Atlanta 1992. 323 p. 92-24434. – DissA 53 (1992s) 1196s-A; RTLv 24, p. 578.

m781* ᴱ**Widmann** Peter, *Jørgensen* Theodor, Karl Barth og den lutherske tradition; et teologisk opgør i nordisk perspektiv, elleve afhandlinger; mit einer deutschen Zusammenfassung. Århus 1990, Aarhus Univ. 206 p. – ᴿNorTTs 92 (1991) 242-5 (K. M. *Hansen*).

m782 **Wildi** Hans M., ᴱ*Osthof* Matthias, Bibliographie Karl Barth 2/1, Veröffentlichungen über KB, A-Z; 2/2 Register. Z 1992, Theol.-V. xxii-1778 p.; vi-362 p. DM 1500 [TR 88,518].

m783 **Winnefske** Ned, Our natural knowledge of God; a prospect for natural theology after KANT and Barth. NY 1990, Lang. 168 p. $52. – ᴿCritRR 5 (1992) 495s (S. H. *Webb*).

m784 BENJAMIN: *Wohlmuth* Josef, Walter Benjamin [100. Gb.] und die christliche Theologie: WAntw 33 (1992) 119-123.

m785 BOFF Leonardo, To my companions on the journey of hope [after leaving the priesthood; ᵀ*Pimenzel-Pinto* C. & F.]: Tablet 246 (1992) (827s) 882s.

m786 *Sobrino* Jon, Reflexiones sobre la decisión de Leonardo Boff [abandona el sacerdocio, non la Iglesia]: SalT 80 (1992) 749-757.

m787 BONHOEFFER: *Feil* Ernst, Aspekte der Bonhoefferinterpretation; ein Rückblick auf das vergangene Jahrzehnt: TLZ 117 (1992) 1-16.81-99.

m788 *Ciola* Nicola, Il Dio di Gesù Cristo crocifisso chiave interpretativa delle ermeneutiche di D. Bonhoeffer; per un discernimento critico: Lateranum 57 (1991) 27-53 [311-410].

m789 **Dinger** Jörg, Bonhoeffer in der deutschsprachigen Theologie der 50er Jahre; eine theologische Untersuchung: Diss. ᴰ*Huber*. Heidelberg 1992. – RTLv 24, p. 557.

m789* *a*) D'*Isanto* Luca, Bonhoeffer's hermeneutical model of community; – *b*) *Green* Clifford, Bonhoeffer, modernity and liberation theology; – *c*) *Harvey* Barry A., A post-critical approach to a 'religionless Christianity': ⇥ 547*, UnSemQ 46 (1992) 135-148 / 117-131 / 39-58.

m790 **Kodalle** K. M., D. Bonhoeffer/Theologie 1991 ⇥ 7,g958: ᴿLuthMon 31 (1992) 281 (E. *Feil*: eine Kritik, die nicht trifft).

m791 *Rochelle* Jay C., Mystery and relationship as keys to the Church's response to secularism [... Bonhoeffer]: CurrTMiss 19 (1992) 267-276.

m792 **Soosten** Joachim von, Die Sozialität der Kirche; Theologie und Theorie der Kirche in D. Bonhoeffers 'Sanctorum Communio' [Diss. Heidelberg]: Öffentliche Theologie 2. Mü 1992, Kaiser. 301 p. DM 68 [TR 88,532].

m793 *Trowitzsch* Michael, 'Auf die Anfänge des Verstehens zurückgeworfen'; Bemerkungen zu Dietrich Bonhoeffers Hermeneutik: NSys 34 (1992) 292-314; Eng. 314.

m794 BULGAKOV: *Coda* Piero, Per una rivisitazione teologica della sofiologia di S. Bulgakov: FilT 6 (1992) 216-235; 253-265; 191-215. 236-252 *al.*, su di lui.

m795 CASALIS: *a*) **Sölle** Dorothée, Parteilichkeit und Evangelium; Grundzüge der Theologie von Georges Casalis. 1990. – *b*) ᴱ**Casalis-Thurneysen** Dorothée, Von Basel nach Managua; Georges Casalis, ein Leben im Widerstand [séminaire Bad Boll 1988 + textes]. B 1990, Alector. 130 p. DM 15,80. 3-88425-049-3. – ᴿÉTRel 67 (1992) 144 (J. *Cottin*).

m796 COHEN H.: **Edel** Geert, Von der Vernunftkritik [KANTs] zur Erkenntnislogik; die Entwicklung der theoretischen Philosophie Hermann Cohens. FrB 1988, Alber. 545 p. – ᴿTPhil 67 (1992) 447-451 (H. L. *Ollig*).

m797 CONGAR: **Nichols** A., Yves Congar [1989 → 5,k529], ᵀ*Lustri* Felicia: I teologi del XX secolo 1. CinB 1991, Paoline. 296 p. Lit. 33.000. – ᴿAsprenas 39 (1992) 122-4 (B. *Forte*); Lateranum 58 (1992) 533-6 (P. *Scabini*).

m798 CUPITT: *Cowdell* Scott, All this, and God too? Postmodern alternatives to Don Cupitt: HeythJ 33 (1992) 267-282.
Cupitt Don, The time being. 1992 → b865*.

m799 CURRAN: **Grecco** Richard, A theology of compromise; a study of method in the ethics of Charles E. Curran [diss. 1982]: AmerUnivSt. NY 1991, Lang. xi-273 p. $46. – ᴿTS 53 (1992) 788s (R. M. *Gula*: Curran has meanwhile abandoned the compromise here called inconsistent).

m800 DANIÉLOU: *Rondeau* M.-J., Les travaux conciliaires du Père Daniélou; le décret sur l'apostolat des laïcs: Bulletin des Amis du card. D. 18 (1992) 3-39 [< RHE 88,364].

m801 DERRIDA: *Ward* Graham, Why is Derrida important for theology?: TLond 95 (1992) 263-270.

m802 DIEKMANN: **Hughes** Kathleen, The monk's tale; a biography of Godfrey Diekmann, O.S.B. ColMn 1991, Liturgical. xxiv-383 p. $19 pa. – ᴿCathHR 78 (1992) 479 (A. *Kavanagh*); RelStR 18 (1992) 313 (J. T. *Ford*).

m803 DÜRCKHEIM: **Ottemann** Christian, Initiatisches Christentum; Karlfried Graf Dürckheims Lehre vom 'initiatischen Weg' als Herausforderung an die evangelische Theologie [Diss. Hamburg 1989]: EurHS 23/402, 1990 → 6,m125: ᴿTLZ 117 (1992) 135-7 (P. *Heidrich*).

m804 EBELING: **Gelder** Katrin, Glaube und Erfahrung; eine kritische Auseinandersetzung mit Gerhard Ebelings 'Dogmatik des christlichen Glaubens' im Kontext der gegewärtigen ev.-theol. Diskussion [Diss. Erlangen]: BeitSysT 11. Neuk 1992, Neuk.-V. xi-209 p. DM 54 [TR 88,524].

m805 ESCRIVÁ DE BALAGUER J.: *a*) *Garofalo* Salvatore, El valor perenne del Evangelo [Escrivá de Balaguer J.]; – *b*) *Mateo-Seco* Lucas F., El misterio de la Cruz en los escritos de EB: ScripTPamp 24 (1992) 13-39 / 419-438.

m806 FARRER: ᴱ**Houlden** J. L., Austin Farrer, The essential sermons. L 1991, SPCK. 211 p. £13. 0-281-04464-3. – ᴿExpTim 103 (1991s) 190 (R. *Lunt*: 52 gems of 'scintialling' wit, for a year's reflection, not for the harassed pastor's tomorrow's sermon).

m807 FLOROVSKY: **Künkel** Christoph, Totus Christus; die Theologie Georges V. Florovskys: ForSysÖkT 62, 1991 → 7,g979*; 3-525-56269-1: ᴿActuBbg 29 (1992) 228s (J. *Boada*).

m808 Fox Matthew [procedure for his dismissal from the Dominicans, which he claims was dictated by RATZINGER]: ChrCent 109 (1992) 183s [J. Wall].

m808* Fox Matthew, Sheer joy; conversations with Thomas AQUINAS on creation spirituality. NY 1992, HarperCollins. xviii-532 p. $18. – ᴿNBlackf 73 (1992) 514-6 (B. Davies).

m809 GUARDINI: **Borghesi** Massimo, Romano Guardini, dialettica e antropologia. R 1990, Studium. 310 p. [RTLv 24,233, E. Brito).

m810 **Zucal** Silvano, Romano Guardini e la metamorfosi del 'religioso' tra moderno e post-moderno; un approccio ermeneutica a HÖLDERLIN, DOSTOEVSKIJ e NIETZSCHE: BtHermeneutica. Urbino 1990, Quattro venti. – ᴿFilT 6 (1992) 165-9 (Sabina Moser); 163-6 (M. Gargano su GOLDONI D. su Hölderlin).

m811 HABERMAS: Giustiniani Pasquale, L'ultimo Habermas e la teologia; in margine a due recenti pubblicazioni [ᵀCalloni M. 1991; ᴱArens A. 1989 ᵀ1992]: Asprenas 39 (1992) 407-414.

m812 HÄRING Bernhard, (Licheri Gianni) Fede, storia, morale 1989 ➤ 5, 1375; 7,g984: ᴿRHE 87 (1992) 334s (R. Aubert).

m813 **Häring** Bernard [Licheri Gianni, interview], My witness for the Church, ᵀSwidler L. NY 1992, Paulist. iv-236 p. $15. – ᴿTS 53 (1992) 788 (R. A. McCormick: TROMP-HURTH machinations; Häring's own 'worse than Nazi' trial by 'ignorant and arrogant' Holy Office personnel coupled with tribulations of LYONNET-ZERWICK, GUTIÉRREZ, CURRAN).

m814 HALDANE: **Haldane** Alexander, The lives of Robert (1764-1842) and James Haldane. E 1990 = 1852, Banner of Truth. xvii-706 p. £13. – ᴿEvQ 64 (1992) 373-5 (A. S. Wood).

m815 HEIDEGGER: Ronchi Sergio, Heidegger e la teologia: Protestantesimo 47 (1992) 103-125.

m816 JENKINS David, Still living with questions. L/Ph 1990, SCM/Trinity. 240 p. $17. / 0-334-02439-0. – ᴿFurrow 41 (1990) 663s (G. Daly, favoring).

m817 JOHANNES XXIII: **Kaufmann** Ludwig, Klein Nikolaus, Johannes XXIII. Prophetie im Vermächtnis². Brig 1990, Exodus. 159 p. Fs 23,80. – ᴿZkT 114 (1992) 242s (A. Batlogg).

m818 JOHANNES PAULUS II: **Di Schiena** Luca, Karol Wojtyla: I grandi leaders. R 1991, Editalia. viii-414 p. Lit. 18.000. – ᴿCC 143 (1992,4) 319-321 (G. Caprile).

m819 O'Collins Gerald, The Pope's theology: Tablet 246 (1992) 801.

m820 Ricca Paolo, Une évaluation protestante de l'encyclique Centesimus annus: BCentProt 44,1 (1992) 3-27.

m821 JÜNGEL: **Paulus** E., Liebe – das Geheimnis der Welt; formale und materiale Aspekte der Theologie Eberhard Jüngels: BonnDogmStud 7. Wü 1990, Echter. ix-434 p. DM 56. – ᴿMüTZ 43 (1992) 140-3 (M. Schulz).

m822 **Jüngel** E., Theological essays, ᵀᴱWebster J. B. 1989 ➤ 5,287*: ᴿPacifica 4 (1991) 102-5 (M. Owen).

m823 KING M. L.: **Cone** James H., Martin [L. King] and Malcolm [X.] and America; a dream or a nightmare 1991 ➤ 7,k1*; $23: ᴿCCurr 42 (1992s) 131s (J. D. Cato); JRel 72 (1992) 595s (R. M. Franklin); JScStRel 31 (1992) 552 (E. D. Smith).

m824 **Molla** Serge, Les idées noires de Martin Luther King: Lieux théologiques 20. Geneve c. 1991, Labor et Fides. 336 p. [RTPhil 124,427].

m825 KÜNG: **Nowell** Robert, Hans Küng – Leidenschaft für die Wahrheit; Leben und Werk [1981], ᵀSchäfer U., Dierlamm H. Z 1993, Benziger. 400 p. DM 44. 3-545-34110-0 [TLZ 118,818, W. Schöpsdau].

m826 **Küng** Hans, FREUD and the problem of God²ʳᵉᵛ [1987 ➤ 3,h69],ᵀ. NHv 1990. 161 p. – ᴿPerspRelSt 19 (1992) 232-6 (Ulrike *Wiethaus*: 'lacks both depth and thoughtfulness'; also on GALIPEAU S. 1990).

Küng Hans, Projekt Weltethos 1990 ➤ 8525.

m828 LASH: *Lamadrid* Lucas, Is there a system in the theology of Nicholas Lash? [... he favors NEWMAN and WITTGENSTEIN precisely as 'unsystematic']: HeythJ 33 (1992) 399-414.

m829 LEFEBVRE: **Perrin** Luc, Il caso Lefebvre, ᵀᴱ*Menozzi* Daniele. Genova 1991, Marietti. 184 p. Lit. 20.000. – ᴿCC 143 (1992,4) 434s (G. *Caprile*: non citata CC né il suo 'Ragioni' 1977).

m830 LEWIS: **Duriez** Colin, The C. S. Lewis handbook 1990 ➤ 7,k7*: ᴿGraceTJ 12 (1991) 323s (M. A. *Van Horn*).

m831 LINDBECK: **Marshall** Bruce D., Theology and dialogue; essays [of D. *Tracy*, D. *Burrell*, N. *Lash* + 6] in conversation with George Lindbeck 1990 ➤ 7,k9: ᴿChrCent 108 (1991) 915s (H. P. *Santmire*); CritRR 5 (1992) 478-480 (L. H. *Jones*); ModT 8 (1992) 401s (M. I. *Wallace*); TS 53 (1992) 167-9 (J. E. *Thiel*).

m831* LOGSTRUP K. E.: *Jensen* Ole, Skabelse og kritik: NorTTs 92 (1991) 65-82 [83-104 *Andersen* Svend; 105-117, *Christoffersen* Svein A.: all on HANSEN Karstein M. ᴰ1990].

m832 LOMBARDI [& PIO XII ➤ 7,k38]: **Zizola** G. C., Il microfono di Dio... Lombardi 1990: ᴿCrNSt 13 (1992) 415-420 (G. *Alberigo*: due decenni di notorietà, poi eclissi totale).

m833 LONERGAN: **Crowe** Frederick E., Lonergan: Outstanding Christian thinkers. ColMn 1992, Liturgical/Glazier. xiv-146 p. $13 pa. 0-8146-5052-X [TDig 40,80].

m834 **Dobroczyński** Grzegorz, Einsicht und Bekehrung; Ausgangspunkt der Fundamentaltheologie bei Bernard Lonergan [Diss. Innsbruck]: EurHS 23/441. Fra 1992, Lang. 385 p. DM 99 [TR 88,258],

m835 **Doran** Robert M., Theology and the dialectics of history [Lonergan] 1990 ➤ 7,b56: ᴿThomist 56 (1992) 160s (M. *Vertin*).

m836 ᴱ**Gregson** Vernon, Desires ,,, Lonergan 1988 ➤ 5,k884; 6,m170: ᴿLvSt 16 (1991) 180s (G. *Boodoo*).

m837 **McEvenue** S., *Meyer* B., Lonergan's hermeneutics 1986/90 ➤ 6,650*. ᴿNRT 114 (1992) 770s (L. *Renwart*); TorJT 9 (1993) 295s (D. *Trevan*).

m838 **Mooney** Hilary A., The liberation of consciousness; Bernard Lonergan's theological foundations in dialogue with the theological aesthetics of Hans Urs von BALTHASAR [Diss. Frankfurt St. Georgen ➤ 7,k14]: FraTSt 41. Fra 1992, Knecht. xi-284 p. DM 58 [TR 88,524].

m839 **Lonergan** Bernard, Insight; a study of human understanding⁵: Works 3 (ᴱ*Crowe* F. E., *Doran* R. M.). Toronto 1992, Univ. xxvi-875 p. $105; pa. $38. 0-8020-3454-3; -5-1. – ᴿExpTim 104 (1992s) 159 (R. *Butterworth*: the definitive edition).

m840 DE LUBAC: **Berzosa Martínez** Raul, La teología del sobrenatural en... de Lubac ᴰ1991 ➤ 7,k17: ᴿActuBbg 29 (1992) 77s (J. M. *Fondevila*).

m841 *Geffré* Claude, Nouvelle théologie, (La), deutsch, ᵀ*Buttkus* I.: ➤ 757, EvKL 3 (1992) 798-800.

m842 **Russo** Antonio, Henri de Lubac, teologia e dogma nella storia; l'influsso di BLONDEL [diss. Tübingen 1989]; pref. ᴰ*Kasper* W. R 1990, Studium. 440 p. Lit. 42.000. – ᴿCC 143 (1992,1) 410s (X. *Tilliette*); JEH 43 (1992) 498 (P. *McPartlan*); RasT 33 (1992) 354s (E. *Cattaneo*); ScripTPamp 24 (1992) 367s (C. *Izquierdo*).

m843 **Lubac** Henri de, Mémoire sur ... mes écrits 1989 ➤ k594; 7,k19: ᴿGregorianum 73 (1992) 176-8 (M. *Chappin* names names of the Rome and Gregorian clique, and associates ZERWICK and LYONNET with de Lubac).

m844 **Lubac** Henri de, Surnaturel, études historiques, ² *Sales* Michel, avec la traduction intégrale des citations latines et grecques: Théologie. P 1991, D-Brouwer. xvi-634 p. F 160. – ᴿZkT 114 (1992) 59-64 (K. H. *Neufeld*).

m845 LUSTIGER Jean-Marie, [ᴱ*Missika* J.-L., *Wolton* D.] Gotteswahl; jüdische Herkunft, Übertritt zum Katholizismus, Zukunft von Kirche und Gesellschaft [1991 ➤ 7,k24], ᵀ. Mü 1992, Piper. 470 p. DM 58. – ᴿStiZt 210 (1992) 501s (O. *Köhler*).

m846 MACINTYRE: *Stackhouse* Max L., Alasdair MacIntyre; an overview and evaluation: RelStR 18 (1992) 203-8.

m847 MACQUARRIE: *Begley* John, The dialectical theism of John Macquarrie: AustralasCR 69 (1992) 462-472.

m848 MANSON: *Bruce* Frederick F., Manson, Thomas W. (1893-1958); ᵀ*Schnitker* T.: ➤ 768, TRE 22 (1992) 63-65.

m849 **MARTY** M. E., How my mind has changed: ChrCent 108 (1991) 703.

m850 MIEGGE: *a) Spini* Giorgio, Giovanni Miegge, l'ambiente politico-culturale al tempo in cui si formò il suo pensiero; – *b) Rostagno* Sergio, La linea teologica [Giuseppe] Gangala-Miegge: Protestantesimo 47 (1992) 2-11 / 12-25 [-80, *al.*].

m850* **MILBANK** John [lay Anglican], Theology and social theory; beyond secular reason. Ox 1990, Blackwell ➤ 7,e693: ᴿNBlackf 73,861 (1992) 306-340 (the whole issue, F. *Kerr* and 4 others), 341-352 Milbank's reply [ModTheol also devotes its whole Oct. 1922 issue to this book ➤ 8641]: *Burrell* David B., An introduction to Theology and social theory: ModT 8,4 ('Focus on Milbank' 1992) 319-330 (-384 *al.*).

m851 MOLTMANN Jürgen, Il Protestantesimo come 'religione della libertà': HumBr 47 (1992) 9-27.

m852 MOODY: **Butler** Jonathan M., Softly and tenderly Jesus is calling [D. L. Moody's shift from Great Awakening terror tactics]: Chicago Studies in the History of American Religion 3 (of 21). Brooklyn 1991, Carlson. 196 p. – ᴿTrinJ 13 (1992) 253 (T. J. *Nettles*).

m853 MURRAY: ᴱ**Hunt** Robert P., *Grasso* Kenneth L., John Courtney Murray and the American civil conversation. GR 1992, Eerdmans. x-298 p. $22 pa. [CBQ 55,210].

m854 **McElroy** Robert W., The search for an American public theology... J. C. Murray 1989 ➤ 6,m183: ᴿTPhil 67 (1992) 295s (J. M. *McDermott*, Eng.).

m855 NEILL: ᴱ**Jackson** E. M., God's apprentice; the autobiography of Bishop Stephen Neill. L 1992, Hodder & S. 349 p. £17. – ᴿProtestantesimo 47 (1992) 254 (J. A. *Soggin*); SAfBap 2 (1992) 110s (D. T. *Williams*); TLond 95 (1992) 473s (R. *Woods*).

m856 NEWBIGIN: *Brink* G. van den, Lesslie Newbigin als postmodern apologeet: NedTTs 46 (1992) 302-319.

m857 *Hamersma* Harry, Lesslie Newbigin; kan het Westen wel bekeerd worden?: Streven 59 (1991s) 291-7.

m858 **Newbigin** Lesslie, Truth to tell. L 1991, SPCK. 90 p. £6. 0-281-04566-6. – ᴿExpTim 103 (1991s) 284 (M. J. *Townsend*).

m859 NIEBUHR H. R.: ᴱ**Thiemann** Ronald F., The legacy of H. Richard Niebuhr. Mp 1991, Fortress. 148 p. $14. 0-8006-7084-1. – ᴿExpTim 103 (1991s) 347s (R. J. *Elford*).

m860 NIEBUHR Reinhold: *Watts* Craig M., The problem of universal love in the thought of Reinhold Niebuhr: JRelSt 17 (1989) 44...

m861 **Brown** Charles C., Niebuhr and his age; Reinhold Niebuhr's prophetic role in the twentieth century. Ph 1992, Trinity. xiii-217 p. $35. 1-56338-042-0 [TDig 40,153].

m862 ᴱNiebuhr Ursula M., Remembering Reinhold Niebuhr; letters. SF 1991, Harper. 432 p. $30. – ᴿTTod 49 (1992s) 257s. 260 (D. J. *Hall*).

m863 NYGREN: *Hall* Thor, The continuing significance of Anders Nygren's early philosophical and methodological works in the late 20th century theological debate: ST 45 (1991) 149-170.

m864 **Brohed** Ingemar present., Anders Nygren som teolog och filosof. Lund 1990/1, Teol. Inst. 146 p. – ᴿTsTKi 63 (1992) 235s (G. *Heiene*).

m865 ONG: *Neilsen* Mark, A bridge-builder; Walter J. Ong at 80: America 167 (1992) 404-6. 415.

m866 OTT: **O'Connell** Colin B., A study of Heinrich Ott's theological development; his hermeneutical and ontological programme; foreword by Ott. NY 1991, Lang. xxii-262 p. $46 [RelStR 19,60, J. S. *Scott*: Ott known for his Reality and faith on BONHOEFFER].

m867 PANNENBERG: **Grenz** S., Reason for hope... Pannenberg 1990 ⭢ 7, k28: ᴿJRel 72 (1992) 606s (M. *Kolden*).

m867* *Mortensen* Viggo, Gud – menneske – natur: NorTTs 92 (1991) 129-142 [143-156, *Hafstad* Kjetil: both on Hans-Olav HENRIKSEN's 1990 doctorate on Pannenberg].

m868 *Schulz* Michael, Zur Hegelkritik Wolfhart Pannenbergs und zur Kritik am 'Antizipationsgedanken' Pannenbergs im Sinne HEGELS: MüTZ 43 (1992) 197-227.

m869 **Pannenberg** W., Metaphysics and the idea of God, ᵀ*Clayton* P. 1990 ⭢ 7,k30: ᴿJRel 72 (1992) 285s (R. E. *Olson*); WestTJ 53 (1991) 370-2 (R. E. *Otto*).

m870 *Pannenberg* Wolfhart, Un'ermeneutica storico-filosofica del cristianesimo [< TPhil 86 (1991) 481-492], ᵀ*Materzanini* Francesca: HumBr 47 (1992) 638-653.

m870* *Pannenberg* Wolfhart, Die Rechtfertigungslehre im ökumenischen Gespräch: ZTK 88 (1991) 232-246.

m871 PAULUS VI: **Dorn** Luitpold A., Pablo VI, el reformador solitario, ᵀ*Gancho* Claudio. Barc 1990, Herder. 352 p. – ᴿLumenVr 40 (1991) 533-5 (U. *Gil Ortega*).

m872 **Gloder** Giampiero, Carattere ecclesiale e scientifico della teologia in Paolo VI: diss. Pont. Univ. Gregoriana, ᴰ*Antón* A. Roma 1992. 394 p. – RTLv 24, p. 557.

m873 PAVAN: **Biffi** Franco, Prophet of our times; the social thought of Cardinal Pietro Pavan, ᵀ(abridged) *Goldie* Rosemarie. New Rochelle 1992, New City. viii-136 p. $9. 1-56548-010-4 [TDig 40,152].

m874 PETERSON Erik, 1890-1960: *Loeser* Werner, *a*) Un converti en dialogue avec la théologie protestante de son temps; – *b*) Une contribution déroutante à la théologie politique: RICathP 43 (1992) 7-21 / 22-35.

m875 PIUS XI: **D'Orazi** Lucio, Il coraggio della verità; vita di Pio XI: Protagonisti 5. R 1989, Logos. Lit. 24.000. – ᴿBenedictina 39 (1992) 269-271 (L. *Crippa*: tema che quasi nessuno ha osato toccare).

m876 POHIER: *Krikilion* Walter, De theologie van Jacques Pohier [Quand je dis Dieu 1977; Dieu fractures 1985 ...]; tussen contingentie en transcendentie: TvT 32 (1992) 388-407; Eng. 407.

m878 PRZYWARA Erich, Analogia entis, ᵀSecretan P.: Théologies, 1990
➤ 7,k38*: ᴿLavalTP 48 (1992) 309s (M. St. Pierre).

m879 RAHNER: Cavalcoli Giovanni, L'antropologia di Karl Rahner: SacDoc
36 (1991) 28-55.
m880 a) Colombo J.A., Rahner and his critics: Lindbeck and Metz; – b)
Phillips Winfred G., Rahner's transcendental deduction of the Vorgriff:
Thomist 56 (1992) 71-96 / 257-290.
m880* Di Noia Joseph A., Nature, grace and experience; Karl Rahner's
theology of human transformation: PhTh 7,2 (1992) 115-126 [-228 al.;
229-43 annual Rahner bibliography update].
m881 Dych William V., Karl Rahner: Outstanding Christian thinkers. ColMn
1992, Liturgical/Glazier. viii-168 p. $13 pa. 0-8146-5053-8 [TDig 40,80].
m882 Knoepffler Nikolaus, Der Begriff 'Transzendental' bei Karl Rahner;
zur Frage seiner Kantischen Herkunft: Diss. Pont. Univ. Gregoriana,
ᴰHenrici P. Roma 1992, 219 p. – RTLv 24, p. 558.
m883 RAMSEY: Chadwick Owen, Michael Ramsey, a life 1990 ➤ 6,m292*;
7,k45*: ᴿChH 61 (1992) 475s (W. L. Sachs); Mid-Stream 30 (1991) 400-2
(P. A. Crow).
m884 Ramsey Michael, The Anglican spirit [1979 Nashotah lectures], ᴱColeman
Dale, CM 1991, Cowley. vi-176 p. $12 pa, – ᴿAnglTR 74 (1992) 116-8
(D. F. Winslow).
m885 RATZINGER Joseph, Mirar a Cristo; ejercicios de fe, esperanza y amor,
ᵀSerra Xavier: Nuevos Horizontes 6. Valencia 1990, Edicep. 138 p. –
ᴿLumenVr 40 (1991) 196s (U. Gil Ortega).
m886 Ratzinger Joseph, a) Les conditions de la liberté [à l'Institut de France,
en succession à SAKHAROV]; – b) Le primat de Pierre et l'unité de l'Église:
PeCa 261 (1992) 21-25 / 250 (1991) 11-25.
m887 RAUSCHENBUSCH: Beckley Harlan, Passion for justice; retrieving the
legacies of Walter Rauschenbusch, John A. RYAN, and Reinhold NIE-
BUHR. Louisville 1992, W-Knox. 391 p. 0-664-21944-6 [TDig 40,256].
m887* Moore Rebecca, Social redemption and individual liberty; Walter
Rauschenbusch's challenge to Henry GEORGE: AmBapQ 11 (1992) 259-
280 [< ZIT 92,611].
m888 RICŒUR: Dornisch Loretta, Faith and philosophy in the writings of
Paul Ricœur: Problems in Contemporary Philosophy 29. Lewiston NY
1990, Mellen. 400 p. $80. 0-88946-737-4 [TDig 39,359].
m889 RITSCHL: McCulloh Gerald W., Christ's person and life-work, in the
theology of A. Ritschl, with special attention to Munus Triplex. Lanham
1990, UPA. 234 p. $44.50. 0-8191-7885-3. – ᴿChH 61 (1992) 460s (D.
Jodock).
m890 ROUSSELOT: McCool Gerald A., From unity to pluralism; the internal
evolution of Thomism [Rousselot... GILSON]. NY 1992, Fordham. 248 p.
$20 pa. – ᴿRelStR 18 (1992) 340 (M. J. Kerlin: excellent); Thomist 55
(1991) 301-319 (M. Lauder), criticized 56 (1992) 701-710 (R. Cessario).
m891 Rousselot Pierre, The eyes of faith, ᵀDonceel J., ᴱDulles A. NY 1990,
Fordham Univ. 117 p. $27.50. – ᴿThomist 56 (1992) 145-9 (G. A.
McCool).
m892 RUNCIE: Hastings A., R. Runcie 1991 ➤ 7,k51: ᴿAnglTR 74 (1992)
248-250 (R. Kollar).
m893 SCHARF: Zimmermann Wolf-Dieter, Kurt Scharf [Bischof in West-
Berlin], ein Leben zwischen Vision und Wirklichkeit. Gö 1992, Vandenhoeck & R. 219 p. DM 34. 3-525-55421-4 [TLZ 118,819, G. Forck].

m894 SCHILLEBEECKX: *Brambilla* Franco G., Uomini come storia di Dio; una 'summa' dell'itinerario teologico di Schillebeeckx?: TItSett 17 (1992) 33-72; Eng. 72.

m895 *Borgman* Erik,   Gods Geest over de wateren; sporen van God temidden van de bedreigende moderniteit [... Schillebeeckx]: TvT 32 (1992) 143-163; Eng. 164.

m896 **Lee** Randall R., The use of experience in the theology of Edward Schillebeeckx from the perspective of a Lutheran understanding of the doctrine of justification; diss. 1992, Lutheran School of Theology, *D Braaten* C. 216 p. 92-30462. – DissA 53 (1992s) 1973-A.

m897 ᴱ**Schreiter** R., *Hilkert* Mary C., Praxis of ... Schillebeeckx 1989 ➤ 5,514; 7,k53:   ᴿHorizons 19 (1992) 148s (J.P. *McCarthy*); JRel 72 (1992) 122 (Anne *Clifford*).

m898 SCHMIDLIN: **Müller** Karl, Josef Schmidlin (1876-1944) — Papsthistoriker und Begründer der katholischen Missionswissenschaft: SIM 47. Nettetal (Steyler) 1989. 441 p. – ᴿZKG 103 (1992) 421s (H.-W. *Gensichen* vergleicht mit der G. WARNECK-Biographie 1990).

m899 SLIPYJ: **Pelikan** Jaroslav, Confessor between East and West; a portrait of Ukrainian cardinal Josyf Slipyj. GR 1990, Eerdmans. xix-249 p. $30. – ᴿChII 60 (1991) 583s (C.A. *Frazee*: massive research in Vatican documents).

m900 SÖHNGEN: **Graf** Josef, Gottlieb Söhngens (1892-1971) Suche nach der 'Einheit in der Theologie.' ein Beitrag zum Durchbruch des heilsgeschichtlichen Denkens [Diss. Gregoriana, ᴰ*O'Collins* G.]: RgStT 39. Fra 1991, Lang. 417 p. DM 99. 3-631-43304-2. – ᴿTGL 82 (1992) 258s (G. *Fuchs*); TvT 32 (1992) 422 (A. *Brante*).

m901 TEILHARD: *Ballweg* John M., Undergraduates discover Pierre Teilhard de Chardin: Horizons 19 (1992) 277-287.

m902 **Carles** Jules, *Dupleix* André, Teilhard de Chardin. P 1991, Centurion. 286 p. F 135. – ᴿÉtudes 376 (1992) 415s (F. *Russo*).

Overzee Anne Hunt, The body divine ... in Teilhard and Rāmānuja 1992 ➤ 7190.

m903 *Vale* Carol Jean, Teilhard de Chardin, Ontogenesis vs. Ontology: TS 53 (1992) 313-337.

m904 TILLICH: *Fischer* Hermann, Tillichs philosophisch-theologisches Werk und das Problem seiner 'Werke' [ᴱ*Ratschow* C.H., 1-6, 1987-92]: TLZ 117 (1992) 803-816.

m905 **Gilkey** [Langdon] on Tillich 1990 ➤ 6,236; 7,k65:   ᴿJRel 72 (1992) 452s (R.P. *Scharlemann*); WestTJ 54 (1992) 400-3 (R.E. *Otto*).

m906 **Irwin** Alexander C., Eros toward the world; Paul Tillich and the theology of the erotic. Mp 1991, Fortress. 204 p. 0-8006-2494-7. – ᴿÉT-Rel 67 (1992) 605 (O. *Abel*).

m907 **Scharlemann** R.P., Paul Tillich, Hauptwerke 5. B 1988, de Gruyter. xiv-325. DM 98. – ᴿJTS 43 (1992) 311-6 (J.H. *Thomas*: also on 1/1 G. WENZ 1989; 4 J. CLAYTON 1987; ISBN faulty).

m908 **Schüssler** W., Jenseits ... Tillich 1989 ➤ 6,m220:   ᴿActuBbg 29 (1992) 73s (J. *Boada*).

m909 TRACY: ᴱ**Jeanrond** Werner G., *Rike* Jennifer L., Radical pluralism and truth; David Tracy and the hermeneutics of religion. NY 1991, Crossroad. xxvii-296 p. $34.50. – ᴿTLond 95 (1992) 382 (J.L. *Houlden*).

m909* **Boodoo** Gerald M., Development and consolidation; the use of theological method in the works of David Tracy: diss. ᴰ*Schrijver* G. De Lv 1991. xxv-267 p. – ETL 68 (1992) 212.

m910 TROELTSCH: **Drescher** Hans-Georg, Ernst Troeltsch, Leben und Werk. Gö 1991, Vandenhoeck & R. 558 p.; portr.; 12 fig. DM 98. – ᴿDLZ 113 (1992) 402-4 (G. *Wendelborn*).

m911 ᴱ**Gisel** Pierre, Histoire et théologie chez Ernst Troeltsch [Lausanne mars 1991]: LieuxTh 22. Genève 1992, Labor et Fides. 430 p. Fs 54. 2-8309-0668-3. 17 art. [TLZ 118,1046-8, M. *Suda*].

m912 *Jacobs* Manfred, Das religiöse Apriori bei Ernst Troeltsch: ➤ 95, ꟳJEISMANN K. 1990, 492-534.

m913 **Rendtorff** Trutz, Theologie in der Moderne; Über Religion im Prozess der Aufklärung: Troeltsch-Studien 5. Gü 1991, Mohn. 340 p. DM 78. – ᴿTLZ 117 (1992) 532s (G. *Wenz*, kaum etwas über Troeltsch).

m914 ᴱ**Tétaz** J.-M., ᵀ*Fink* Anne-Lise, E. Troeltsch, Religion et histoire; esquisses philosophiques et théologiques: LieuxT 18, 1990 ➤ 7,k70; F 125. 2-8309-0598-9: ᴿETL 67 (1991) 453s (E. *Brito*); LavalTP 48 (1992) 297-9 (A. *Dumais*).

m915 **Vermeil** Edmond, La pensée religieuse de Troeltsch [= RHPR 1921], ᴱ*Ruddies* Hartmut; Histoire et Société 18, 1990 ➤ 7,k70*b*: ᴿETL 67 (1991) 454s (E. *Brito*); MélSR 48 (1991) 254s (L. *Debarge*).

m917 **Troeltsch** Ernst, Protestantisme et modernité [4 art. 1906-1913], ᵀ*Launay* M. de: BtScHum. P 1991, Gallimard. 167 p. F 92. 2-07-072326-7. – ᴿÉTRel 67 (1992) 477s (H. *Bost*).

m918 **Troeltsch** Ernst, The Christian faith [1894; written down by Gertrud von LE FORT 1911s], ᵀ*Paul* Garrett E.: Texts in Modern Theology. Mp 1991, Fortress. xli-310 p. 0-8006-3209-5. – ᴿJTS 43 (1992) 767-772 (M. D. *Chapman*).

m919 VINAY: *Selge* Kurt-Victor, Valdo Vinay [1906-1990], storico della Riforma e della Chiesa Evangelica in Italia: Protestantesimo 47 (1992) 178-201 [-229, al., convegno Roma 29-30.XI.1991].

m920 WEIGEL: **Collins** Patrick W., Gustave Weigel, S.J., a pioneer of reform. ColMn 1992, Liturgical. 287 p. $20 pa. – ᴿCathHR 78 (1992) 478s (A. *Dulles*); RelStR 18 (1992) 317 (J. T. *Ford*).

m921 WEIZSÄCKER: **Görnitz** Thomas, Carl Friedrich von Weizsäcker, ein Denker an der Schwelle zum neuen Jahrtausend: Spektrum 4125. FrB 1992, Herder. 191 p. DM 16,80. 3-451-04125-1 [TLZ 118,1011, H. *Genest*].

m922 WINGREN: *Vance-Welsh* Mary C., Gustaf Wingren [b. 1910]; creation faith and its call for full incarnation: CurrTMiss 19 (1992) 259-266.

m923 WITTGENSTEIN: **Barrett** Cyril, Wittgenstein on ethics and religious belief. Ox 1991, Blackwell. xiv-285 p. £45. 0-631-16815-X. – ᴿExpTim 103 (1991s) 250s (W. D. *Hudson*: what did W. really believe? 'late' not so different from 'early').

m924 **Kerr** Fergus, La théologie après Wittgenstein; une introduction à la lecture de W. [1986], ᵀ*Letourneau* Alain: CogF 162, 1991 ➤ 7,k74; F 198; 2-204-04286-2: ᴿActuBbg 29 (1992) 210s (J. *Boada*); ETL 68 (1992) 469s (E. *Brito*); ÉTRel 67 (1992) 295 (J. *Ansaldi*); RThom 92 (1992) 766-8 (A. *Reix*); ScEspr 44 (1992) 240 (M. *Maesschalck*).

m925 WOOD: **Bevans** Stephen, John Wood [b. 1860] and the doctrine of God. C 1992, Univ. 175 p. £28. 0-521-41059-2. – ᴿExpTim 104 (1992s) 32 (C. S. *Rodd*).

m926 YODER: *Zimbelman* Joel, The contribution of John H. Yoder to recent discussions in Christian social ethics: ScotJT 45 (1992) 367-399.

m927 ZUBIRI: Llenín Iglesias Fernando,   La teología en la filosofía de Xavier Zubiri: RET 52 (1992) 69-86.

Y6.8   Tendentiae exeuntis saeculi XX – **Late 20th Century Movements.**

m928 **Abbruzzese** Salvatore,   Comunione e liberazione; identità religiosa e disincanto laico [... identité catholique et disqualification du monde 1989 ⇒ 7,k76]. R 1991, Laterza. xi-248 p. – ᴿRivStoLR 27 (1991) 581-4 (P. Scoppola).

m929 Alberigo Giuseppe,   Dinamiche e procedure nel Vaticano II; verso la revisione del regolamento del Concilio (1962-1963): CrNSt 13,1 (1992) 115-164; Eng. 164.

m930 a) Alberigo Giuseppe,   Il Vaticano II nella tradizione conciliare; – b) Melloni Alberto, Tipologia delle fonti per la storia del Vaticano II; – c) Chadwick Henry,   Un concetto per la storia dei concili; la recezione, ᵀTurbanti Giovanni; – d) Soetens Claude,   Impulsions et limites dans la réception du Concile: ⇒ 505, CrNSt 13,3 (1992) 593-612 / 493-514 / 475-492 / 613-641.

m931 **Allen** Diogenes,   Christian belief in a postmodern world 1989 ⇒ 5,k667; 6,m228:   ᴿJAAR 60 (1992) 539-542 (G. Fendt).

m932 **Alterman** Urs,   Katholizismus und Moderne; Zur Sozial- und Mentalitätsgeschichte der Schweizer Katholiken im 19. und 20. Jh.   Z 1989, Benziger.   468 p. – ᴿForKT 8 (1992) 157-9 (A. Kolping).

m933 Balasuriya Tissa,   Right relationships, de-routing and re-rooting of Christian theology [... traditional theology is off the track]: Logos 3s. Colombo 1992.   248 p. – ᴿTContexto 2 (1992) 138 (G. Evers).

m934 **Ballestreros** Jesús,   Postmodernidad; decadencia o resistencia.   M 1989, Tecnos.   158 p. – ᴿEuntDoc 44 (1991) 464s (L. Clavell).

m935 **Bayer** Oswald,   Leibliches Wort; Reformation und Neuzeit im Konflikt. Tü 1992, Mohr.   xii-372 p. DM 69 [TR 88,518].

m936 Breton Stanislas,   Culture et super-marché culturel: RICathP 38 (1991) 165-189.

m937 **Bühlmann** Walbert,   Wer Augen hat 1989 ⇒ 7,k84a; ᴿZMissRW 75 (1991) 232s (M. Hakenes).

m938 **Bühlmann** Walbert,   With eyes to see; Church and world in the third millennium, ᵀBarr Robert R. 1990 ⇒ 6,m235*; 7,k84*:   ᴿCritRR 5 (1992) 317-9 (A.F. McGovern); Gregorianum 73 (1992) 157s (J. Dupuis: insightful); Horizons 19 (1992) 146s (C. McEnroy); Pacifica 5 (1992) 105s (L. Nemer); Tablet 246 (1992) 1019s (A. Shorter).

m939 **Carr** Wesley,   Manifold wisdom; Christians in the New Age. L 1991, SPCK.   xiii-144 p. £10.   0-281-04550-X. – ᴿExpTim 103 (1991s) 284 (D.G. Deeks).

m940 **Centore** F.F.,   Being and becoming; a critique of post-modernism, 1991 ⇒ 7,86:   ᴿTS 55 (1992) 165-7 (M.J. Kerlin: 'modern' is an umbrella term for tendencies involving objectivity, distinction, autonomy and control; 'postmodern' is the rejection of these tendencies).

m941 Cholvy Gérard,   De la déchristianization et de son histoire: EsprVie 102 (1992) 476-8.

m942 ᴱCoalter Milton J., al.,   The Presbyterian predicament; six perspectives 1990 ⇒ 7,k87*:   ᴿInterpretation 46 (1992) 217s (Shirley Guthrie); RRel-Res 33 (1990s) 283s (R.E. Beckley).

m943 [19 anonymes] Le Concile en 75 questions.   P 1990, Dubigeon.   282 p. – ᴿScEsp 44 (1992) 373s (A. Naud: trop simplifié).

m944 **Delhaye** Philippe †, Inventaire du fonds [1000 interventions de lui-même, aussi dans la commission préparatoire; 3000 papiers de la Commission Théologique, pas encore accessibles aux chercheurs], ᴱ*Famerée* J., *Hulsbosch* I..: Concile Vatican II ct Église contemporaine 3. LvN c. 1992, Fac.Théol. 81 p. [RHE 88,603s, C. *Soetens*].

m945 Le deuxième Concile du Vatican: Coll. Éc. Franç. Rome 113, 1986/9 ➤ 5,652 ... 7,k92: ᴿRivStoLR 27 (1991) 364-371 (Bruna *Bocchini Camaiani*).

m946 **Doyle** Dennis M., The Church emerging from Vatican II; a popular approach to contemporary Catholicism. Mystic CT 1992, Twenty-Third. vii-349 p. $15 pa. 0-89622-507-0 [TDig 40,264].

m947 ᴱ**Ducret** R., *al.*, Christianisme et modernité 1987/90 ➤ 7,491*: ᴿNRT 114 (1992) 295s (J.-B. *Prévost*).

m948 *Falbo* Elvira, L'epoca dello zapping [cambiare canale TV usando telecomando]: Presbyteri 26 (1992) 411-420.

m949 **Fausti** Silvano, Lettera [pseudopaolina] a Sila; quale futuro per il cristianesimo². CasM 1991, Piemme. 80 p. Lᵐ 12. – ᴿCC 143 (1992,3) 104s (D. *Scaiola*: riflessioni su esperienze di diverse comunità odierne).

m950 *Fortin-Melkevik* Anne, Relecture du rapport théologie/philosophie; le statut du paradigme esthétique dans la théologie postmoderne: SR 21 (1992) 381-394.

m951 **Fox** Matthew [➤ m808], Vision vom Kosmischen Christus [1988], ᵀ*Wichmann* Jörg 1991 ➤ 7,k97; 3-7831-1073-4: ᴿActuBbg 29 (1992) 35-38 (J. *Boada*).

m952 **Gabriel** Karl, Christentum zwischen Tradition und Postmoderne: QDisp 141. FrB 1992, Herder. 220 p. 3-451-02141-2.

m953 **Girardi** Giulio, La túnica rasgada (La identidad cristiana, hoy, entre liberación y restauración). Sdr 1991, Sal Terrae. 486 p. – ᴿREB 52 (1992) 232-5 (E. F. *Alves*).

m954 *Glebe-Møller* Jens, The possibility of theology in a postmodern world: ST 46 (1992) 29-39.

m955 **Griffin** David R., God and religion in the postmodern world 1989 ➤ 5,k679; 6,m244: ᴿTPhil 67 (1992) 141s (T. M. *Schmidt*).

m956 **Griffin** David R., *al.*, Varieties of postmodern theology 1989 ➤ 5,k681: ᴿThought 66 (1991) 97s (R. R. *Viladesau*).

m957 **Griffin** David R., *Smith* Huston, Primordial truth and postmodern theology ➤ 5,k680; 7,k98: ᴿCritRR 5 (1992) 471-3 (B. L. *Whitney*).

m958 ᴱ**Hastings** A., Modern Catholicism, Vatican II and after: 1990 ➤ 7, 358*a*.k100: ᴿArTGran 55 (1992) 412s (R. *Franco*); CathHR 78 (1992) 261s (J. *Hitchcock*: liberal triumphalism, like GANNON); HeythJ 33 (1992) 469-471 (F. M. *Perko*: thoughtful, important); RelStR 18 (1992) 43 (J. R. *Sachs*: superb); TLond 95 (1992) 148s (M. *Santer*: E. *Norman*'s postscript, 'Was the council simply a symptom of changes which were going to happen anyway?').

m959 *Jacobs* J. Y. H. A., L'aggiornamento' est mis en relief; les 'vota' des évêques néerlandais pour Vatican II; ᵀ*Famerée* J.: CrNSt 12 (1991) 323-340; Eng. 340.

m960 *Jiménez Sánchez Mariscal* José D., Posmodernidad; ¿el encanto desilusionado o la ilusión del desencanto?: RelCu 38 (1992) 367-388.

m961 *a) Jones* Arthur, The New World grows older; – *b) McBrien* Richard, Theologians at large: Tablet 246 (1992) 100-2 / 105s [+ 2, on The Church in the US].

m962 **Jorstad** Erling, Holding fast / pressing on; religion in America in the

1980s. Westport CT 1990, Greenwood (pa. NY Praeger). xiv-195 p. $45 ($15). – ᴿCritRR 5 (1992) 331s (K. J. *Christiano*).

m963 *Junkin* Edward D., Up from the grassroots; the Church in transition: Interpretation 46 (1992) 271-280.

m964 **Kaufmann** Franz-Xaver, Religion und Modernität; sozialwissenschaftliche Perspektiven 1989 ➤ 6,255*: ᴿNorTTs 92 (1991) 63s (Ola *Tjørhom*); TPhil 67 (1992) 615s (H.-J. *Höhn*).

m965 **Kerckhove** Derrick De, La civilisation vidéo-chrétienne. P 1990, Retz. 187 p. 2-7256-1383-3. – ᴿÉTRel 67 (1992) 632 (J. *Cottin*: rien sur le Christ ou la Bible, mais p. 107-117, 'Le Pape', doté d'un 'corps bionique' et d'une 'aura électronique').

m966 **Kew** Richard, *White* Roger J., New millennium, new Church; trends shaping the Episcopal Church for the twenty-first century. Boston 1992, Cowley. xiv-177 p. $13 pa. 1-56101-062-6 [TDig 40,277].

m967 **Kobler** J. F., Vatican II, theophany and the phenomenon of man; the Council's pastoral servant leader theology for the third millennium 1991 ➤ 7,k106; 'Lang Highlights': ᴿRelCu 38 (1992) 617s (J. *Tejedor*).

m968 *Koch* Robert, Das 'neue Pfingsten' in der nachkonziliaren Kirche: TGegw 35 (1992) 53-61.

m969 **Küng** Hans, Theology for the third millennium; an ecumenical view [Theologie im Aufbruch], ᵀ*Heinegg* Peter, 1991 ➤ 7,k109: ᴿTLond 95s (J. *Macquarrie*: pretentious American title for 'A new start in theology'); Way 32 (1992) 77 (S. *Barrow*).

m970 **Küng** H., Reforming the Church today; keeping hope alive ➤ 6,259; 7,221*.k108* ᴿChrCent 108 (1991) 599s (L. A. *Green*); CurrTMiss 19 (1992) 134s (A. *Garcia Rivera*); Pacifica 5 (1992) 236s (J. *Wilcken*).

m971 **Küng** Hans, Garder espoir; écrits sur la réforme de l'Église [1990 ➤ 7,221* k108], ᵀ: Théologies. P 1991, Cerf. 263 p. F 136. – ᴿEsprVie 102 (1992) 673-5 (P. *Jay*); VSp 146 (1992) 567.

m972 *Lamberigts* M., The 'vota antepraeparatoria' of the Facultics of Theology of Louvain and Lovanium (Zaire): À la veille Vat II 1992 [< RHE 87,48*], p. 146-168.

m973 **Laurentin** René, La Iglesia del futuro más allá de sus crisis, ᵀ*Gancho* Claudio. Barc 1991, Herder. 303 p. – ᴿCarthaginensia 8 (1992) 948 (F. *Oliver Alcón*); CiuD 205 (1992) 248 (J. M. *Ozaeta*).

m974 **Liechty** Daniel, Theology in postliberal perspective 1990 ➤ 7,k116: ᴿChrCent 108 (1991) 975s (W. W. *Urffer*); TTod 49 (1992s) 142s (M. P. *Ford*).

m975 a) *Link* Christian, Kirche in der Krise der Moderne; – b) *Klinger* Elmar, Das Volk Gottes auf dem Zweiten Vatikanum; die Revolution in der Kirche; – c) *Fuchs* Ottmar, Volk Gottes im Horizont der Befreiung; – d) *Weth* Rudolf, Diakonische Kirche und sozialer Staat; – e) *Reiher* Dieter, Kirche und Gesellschaft am Beispiel der Kontroverse 'Religionsunterricht – Christenlehre' in den evangelischen Kirchen in Ostdeutschland: ➤ 355, JbBT 7 (1992) 283-303 / 305-319 / 321-342 / 343-368 / 369-383.

m975* **Lucas** J. R., The future; an essay on God, temporality and truth. Ox 1989, Blackwell. x-245 p. $74. – ᴿRelStT 11,2 (1991) 83s (W. *Sweet*).

m976 **McBrien** Richard P., Report on the Church; Catholicism after Vatican II [< syndicated column]: NY c. 1992, Harper Collins. 263 p. $19. – ᴿAmerica 167 (1992) 409s (Kathleen E. *McVey*).

m977 *McBrien* Richard P., Re-imagining the Church in the year 2000: Furrow 42 (1991) 679-691.

m978 **Martelli** Stefano, La religione nella società post-moderna tra seco-larizzazione e de-secolarizzazione. Bo 1990, Dehoniane. 496 p. Lit. 45.000. – ᴿRClerIt 72 (1991) 619-621 (G. *Ambrosio*).

m978* *a) Metz* Johann B., Suchbewegungen nach einem neuen Gemein-debild; – *b) Fuchs* Ottmar, Kirchliche Gemeinde – wohin? – *c) Spohr* Michael, Zukunft der Gemeinde – Gemeinde der Zukunft; Über-legungen entlang des Stichwortes Identität: BLtg 65 (1992) 3-9 / 9-14 / 21-31.

m979 *Miccoli* Paolo, Eros – thanatos; discorso antropologico per gli anni Novanta: EuntDoc 44 (1991) 43-73.

m980 *Morey* Ann-Janine, Margaret ATWOOD and Toni MORRISON; Re-flections on postmodernism and the study of religion and literature: JAAR 60 (1992) 493-513.

m981 **Müller** Alois, Der dritte Weg zu glauben; Christen zwischen Rückzug und Auszug. Mainz 1990, Grünewald. 108 p. DM 19,80. – ᴿRTLv 23 (1992) 116s (P. *Weber*).

m982 *O'Donoghue* John O. / *Kelly* Anne F. / *Jeanrond* Werner G., The agenda for theology in Ireland today: Furrow 42 (1991) 692-8 / 698-703 / 704-710.

m983 **Poupard** Paul, card., Christianisme et culture en Europe; mémoire – conscience – projet [Symposium pre-synodal, Vatican 28-31 oct. 1991]: EsprVie 102 (1992) 25-31.

m984 *Reijen* Willem van, Postmoderne: ➤ 757, EvKL 3 (1992) 1276-82.

m985 *Schenk* Richard, Evangelisierung und Religionstoleranz; Thomas von AQUIN und die Gewissenslehre des II. Vatikanums: ForTK 8 (1992) 1-17.

m986 **Secondin** B., Nuovi cammini dello Spirito; la spiritualità alla soglia del terzo millennio: Problemi e dibattiti 15. CinB 1990, Paoline. 296 p. Lᵐ 18. – ᴿStPatav 38 (1991) 220 (G. *Segalla*: di piacevole lettura).

m987 **Smith** David L., A handbook of contemporary theology: Bridgepoint. Wheaton IL 1992, Victor. 394 p. $20. 0-89693-699-6 [TDig 39,288].

m988 *Tavard* George H., Vatican II, understood and misunderstood: One-InC 27 (1991) 209-221.

m989 *Thornhill* John, Popular religion and post-conciliar Catholicism: Aus-tralasCR 69 (1992) 3-13.

m990 **Unsworth** Tim, The last priests in America; conversations with [44] remarkable men. NY 1991, Crossroad. 281 p. $20. – ᴿTTod 49 (1992s) 433.4.6 (J. F. *Devine*: there are 17,000 resigned and about 30,000 active priests).

m991 *Verhack* Ignace, Terugkeer van de religie ?: Bijdragen 53 (1992) 152-180; 180s 'A reappearance of religion?'.

m992 **Villa-Vicencio** Charles, A theology of reconstruction [... should be more concerned with the building of emerging nations]. C 1992, Univ. 300 p. £37.50; pa. £12. 0-521-41625-6; -2628-6. – ᴿExpTim 104 (1992s) 221 (G. J. *Warnock*).

m993 **Ward** Keith, A vision to pursue; beyond the crisis in Christianity 1991 ➤ 7,k134; 0-334-02411-0: ᴿExpTim 103,6 1st choice (1991s) 161-3 (C. S. *Rodd*: superb, exciting; basically a defense of the En-lightenment, but it is now past; we need a map like this toward a present stance); NBlackf 73 (1992) 520 (M. *Wynn*); TvT 32 (1992) 440s (A. *Lascaris*: Christ-centered).

m994 *a) Webb* Eugene, Religion, modernity, and the humanities; – *b) Coward*

Harold, Multiculturalism and religious freedom: RelStT 11,2s (1991) 18-35 / 50-56.

Y7 *(Acta) Congressum* .2 *biblica:* **nuntii,** rapports, Berichte.

m995 *Ayoun* Richard, Le dixième congrès mondial des études juives (Jérusalem, 16-24 août 1989): RÉJ 150 (1991) 297-303.

m996 *Berger* Teresa, 'Bibel und Liturgie'; XIII. Internationaler Kongress der Societas Liturgica in Toronto 12.-17. August 1991: LtgJb 42 (1992) 70-78.

m997 Documento final de la cuarta asamblea plenaria de la federación bíblica católica, Bogotá, Colombia, 27.VI-6.VII.1990: RBiArg 53 (1991) 231-249.

m998 *Focant* C., The Synoptic Gospels; source criticism and the new literary criticism; Colloquium Biblicum Lovaniense XLI (1992) [Aug. 18-20]: ETL 68 (1992) 494-9.

m998* a) *Herman* Zvonimir, Radni sastanak... Symposion exegetarum NT linguae germanicae (Trier 13.-17.III.1989); – b) *Rebić* Adalbert, XIII. kongres. int. studiorum VT (Lv 1989): BogSmot 60 (1990) 124-7 / 128-131.

m999 *Gerhardsson* Birger, Symposion om Paulus och hans hellenistiska bakgrund [K 19-22.VI.1991]: SvTKv 67 (1991) 151s.

r1 *Gilmont* Jean-François, La Bible imprimée dans l'Europe moderne, xvᵉ-xviiiᵉ siècles [P. Bibliothèque Nationale, 21-23 nov. 1991]: RTLv 23 (1992) 277s.

r1* *Grasso* Santi, Il IV convegno di studi neotestamentari, Perugia 11-14 settembre 1991: RivB 40 (1992) 121-4 [Santi non cognome come nell'Indice].

r2 a) *Keler* Konrad, ⊕ IV sesja plenaria katolickiej federacji biblijnej (Bogotá 1990); – b) ᵀ*Wodecki* Bernard, *Kantor* Maria, ⊕ Komunikat końcowy IV sesji plenarnej katolickiej federacji biblijnej (Bogotá 1990); – c) *Kapera* Zdzisław J, ⊕ III Międzynarodowe kolokwium qumranologiczne (Kraków-Mogilany 1991); – d) *Kempiak* Ryszard, ⊕ Sympozjum 'Młodzi [young people] i Biblia' (Rzym 1992): RuBi 45 (1992) 39-41 / 24-38 / 41-43 / 43.

r3 a) *Legrand* L., Towards an ecological hermeneutic; XV conference of the Society for Biblical Studies [Hyderabad, Jeevan Jyothi, Jan. 2-4, 1992]; – b) *Keerancheri* George; Annual meeting of the Indian Theological Association 1991: IndTSt 29 (1992) 150s / 151-5.

r4 *März* Claus-Peter, 46th General Meeting der Studiorum NT Societas vom 29. Juli bis 2. August in Bethel bei Bielefeld: BZ 36 (1992) 158s.

r5 *Marocco* Giuseppe, L'epoca di Ezechia (Perugia 9-11.IX.1991): ParVi 37 (1992) 212-4.

r6 a) *Pisarek* Stanisław, ⊕ 46. Zjazd Studiorum Novi Testamenti Societatis (1991) [Bielefeld 29.VII-2.VIII]; – b) *Kempiak* Ryszard, ⊕ 'Biblia i ewangelizacja młodzieży', biblijne spotkanie Salezjańskie w Lyonie (1991) [26-31.VIII]; – c) [*Chmial* Jerzy] ⊕ Biblia w Europie dzisiaj [13-15.IX.1991, Warszawa: for 175th year of British and Foreign Bible Society in Poland]: RuBi 44 (1991) 146s / 147s / 150s.

r7 *Milani* Marcello, VII convegno neotestamentaristi (Perugia 9-11 sett. 1991); l'epoca di Ezechia, alle origini della letteratura religiosa di Israele: StPatav 39 (1991) 665-9 [671-3 NT e anticocristiani, Perugia 12-14 sett.: *Cilia* Lucio].

r8 *Salvarini* Bruno,   Biblia [con 6 simili organizzazioni]: Il libro assente; Bibbia, cultura e scuola in Italia, Bologna 20 ott. 1991: AnStoEseg 9 (1992) 274-8.

r10 *a) Segalla* Giuseppe,   47° congresso della Studiorum Novi Testamenti Societas (Madrid, 27-31 luglio 1992); – *b) Milani* Marcello,   12ª settimana biblica nazionale (Roma, 14-18 settembre 1992), 'Miti di origine, miti di caduta e presenza del femminismo nella loro tradizione interpretativa': StPatav 39 (1992) 679-684 / 685-694.

r11 *Tuckett* C.M.,   Studiorum Novi Testamenti Societas, the forty-sixth general meeting [Bielefeld-Bethel] 29 July-2 August 1991: NTS 38 (1992) 298s; 301-320, membership list with addresses (residence).

r12 *Walsh* Jerome T.,   Report of the Fifty-Fifth General Meeting of the Catholic Biblical Association of America [Wsh Aug 15-18, 1992]: CBQ 54 (1992) 726-731 (-735, participants); p. 729, A. *Cody* replaces J. *Kselman* as CBQ editor.

r13 *Woude* A.S. van der,   The book of Daniel in the light of recent findings; Colloquium biblicum lovaniense XL (1991): ETL 68 (1992) 194-8.

Y7.4 *(Acta) theologica:* **nuntii.**

r14 *a) Alcalá* Manuel,   II encuentro internacional sobre teologías de la liberación [Fe y Secularidad, Madrid-Escorial 30.VI-4.VII.1992]; – *b) Corral* Carlos,   El patrimonio cultural de la Iglesia y la nueva evangelización [XII Jornadas, Escorial 15-18.VI.1992]: EstE 67 (1992) 449-454 / 455-9.

r15 American Academy of Religion / Society of Biblical Literature annual meeting program, Washington D.C. Nov. 20-23, 1993. 348 p. [175-288 new book ads].

r16 *Antón* Ángel,   Santo Domingo, IV Conferencia General del episcopado latinoamericano; su status teológico y el valor magisterial de su documento conclusivo: Gregorianum 73 (1992) 437-466; Eng. 466-7.

r17 *Bortolin* Valerio,   Il 'movimento di Gallarate'; i convegni [filosofici] dal 1945 al 1985: TItSett 17 (1992) 73-100. 182-202; Eng. 202.

r18 *a) Brok* Jan,   Congres over christologie en context in Tilburg [13-14 mei 1992]; – *b) Evers* Georg,   Algemene conferentie van derde-wereld-theologen in Nairobi [6-13 jan. 1992]; – *c) Hoeben* Harry,   Conferentie van afrikaanse theologen in Harare, Zimbabwe [6-11 Jan. 1991]: TvT 32 (1992) 299s / 298s / 298.

r19 *Cacciotti* Alvaro,   Simposio interecumenico su 'preghiera e contemplazione' (Accademia Ortodossa, Colimbari, Creta, 7-11.IX.1992): Antonianum 67 (1992) 551s: non spiega la differenza che vede fra 'ecumenico' e 'interecumenico'.

r20 *Chrostowski* Waldemar, ℗ Colloquium of the International Council of Christians and Jews (ICCJ), Southampton, 14-18.VII.1991: ColcT 62,2 (1992) 175-8.

r21 *Collins* R.F.,   8 U.S. meetings: ETL 68 (1992) 218s.

r22 *Courth* Franz,   Maria in der Evangelisierung: Tagung Augsburg 27.-29. März 1992: ForKT 8 (1992) 215-7.

r23 *Cozzi* Alberto,   'La creazione; antropocentrismo in questione'; XIV congresso nazionale dell'A.T.I. [Pisa]: ScuolC 120 (1992) 657-672.

r24 *Dal Covolo* Enrico,   Laici e teologia nei Padri della Chiesa; il XIV Convegno di Catechesi Patristica [Roma 14-16 marzo 1991]: Lateranum 57 (1991) 583-594.

r25 *Dupuy* Bernard, La VIIe Assemblée du Conseil œcuménique des Églises à Canberra (7-20 février 1991): Istina 36 (1991) 363-378.

r26 *Federici* Tommaso, La Chiesa in missione e il dialogo con le religioni; le difficili ottiche moderne [La salvezza oggi, V Congresso di Missiologia, Roma Urbaniana 3-6.X.1988]: EuntDoc 44 (1991) 137-201.

r27 *Gąsiorek* Jarosław, ℗ Le sacerdoce à l'époque de l'antiquité chrétienne (Symposium patristique Lublin 29-30.X.1991): AtKap 119 (1992) 163-6.

r28 *Gaziaux* Éric, Colloque 'Destin, prédestination, destinée' [LvN 28-29.X.1991]: RTLv 23 (1992) 279-283.

r29 *Gesteira* Manuel, *Alemany* José J., La aportación de la fe cristiana a la construcción de Europa; I congreso de la Asociación Europea de Teólogos Católicos [4-9.IV.1992 Stu]: EstE 67 (1992) 91-99.

r30 *Giannoni* Paolo, Il XIV Congresso dell'ATI (Pisa 7-11.IX.1992): VivH 3 (1992) 385-390.

r30* *Green* Thomas H., Spirituality in [Plenary Council of the Philippines] PCP II [Jan. 20-Feb. 17, 1991]; integrated, Scripture-based, communitarian: Landas 6 (Manila 1992) 133-144 [180-202 on ecumenism, *Achutegui* P. S. de).

r31 *Johnstone* Brian V., The European Synod (Rome 28.XI-14.XII.1991); the meaning and strategy of evangelization: Gregorianum 73 (1992) 469-486; franç. 487.

r32 *Keshavjee* Shafique, Manille, Lausanne, San Antonio et nous [1974, 1989 'L'évangélisation du monde exige que toute l'Église apporte l'évangile dans sa totalité au monde entier']: Hokhma 46s (1991) 1-8 (-173, contributions de Manille).

r33 *Konecki* Krzysztof, *Przybyłowski* Jan, Sympozja józefologiczne w Kaliszu [25-26.IV.1990 / 10-11.IV.1991; 29-30. IV.1992]: AtKap 118 (1992) 503-7-9 / 119,342-4.

r34 *Kremers* Helmut, Fine lose Maske der Theologie; Loccumer Tagung zum christlichen Absolutheitsanspruch [5.-10.III.]. LuthMon 30 (1991) 160-3.

r35 *Lamberigts* M., Colloque sur le thème 'martyrium' [Leuven, Inst. Ét. Paléochrétiennes et Byzantines, 13-15.V]: ETL 68 (1992) 501s.

r36 *Madonia* Nicolò, Forum ATI... L'ecclesiologia contemporanea, Roma 2-4 gennaio 1990: RasT 33 (1992) 89-98 [217-222; 338-344, La creazione, Pisa 7-11 sett. 1992, G. L. *Prato*; G. *Barbaglio*; 445-462. 575-582. 694-702].

r37 *Martin* John H., Reflections on the New Zealand symposium [Christ and context, Dunedin 13-18 May 1991]: Pacifica 4 (1991) 337-340.

r38 a) *Matras* Tadeusz, ℗ XXIX sesja sekcji biblistów polskich, Siedlce – Nowe Opole 1991; b) *Romanek* Michał, ℗ Sympozjum 'Biblia a kultura Europy' Łódź 26-28.V.1992]: RuBi 45 (1992) 99-101 (102s, addresses of 56 Polish biblical scholars) / 103s.

r39 *Moutsoulas* Elias D., Ⓖ The eleventh international conference of patristic studies, Oxford 19-24 Aug. 1991: TAth 63 (1992) 349-352.

r40 *Nickel* Edgar, Spiritualität für unsere Zeit – für unsere Kirche – für unsere Welt; ein Bericht über die 29. Internationale Altkatholische Theologiekonferenz, Morschach 26.-31. Aug. 1991: IkiZ 82 (1992) 1-9.

r41 *Paiano* Maria, Vatican II commence; la première période (Lyon 27-29 mars 1992): CrNSt 13 (1992) 643-658.

r42 *Peerlinck* Frans, Het eerste Congres van de europese vereniging voor katholieke Theologie (Stuttgart/Hohenheim, 4-9 april 1992): CollatVL 22 (1992) 295-304.

r43 *Ries* J., Premier congrès mondial des directeurs de pèlerinages et des recteurs de sanctuaires; Rome, 26-29 février 1992: EsprVie 102 (1992) 251s.

r44 *Rostagno* Sergio, Congresso teologico sull'antropocentrismo nella creazione [ATI, Pisa 7-11.IX.1992]: Protestantesimo 47 (1992) 319-322.

r45 *Schreiter* Robert, Symposium in Kansas City over het werk van Charles DAVIS [AAR, 19 nov. 1991]: TvT 32 (1992) 84s.

r46 *Soetens* C., Le colloque de Chevetogne [2-6.IX.1991] sur les dimensions historiques de l'uniatisme: RTLv 23 (1992) 137-9.

r47 *Soetens* C., 3e colloque sur l'histoire du Concile Vatican II, Lyon-Arbresle/Univ. 27-29 mars 1992, 'Vatican II commence; la première période 1962', org. *Fouilloux* É.: RHE 87 (1992) 611-6.

Y7.6   *Acta congressuum philologica:* **nuntii.**

r48 *Ankum* Hans, *Michel* Jacques-Henri, La XLVe session de la société De Visscher pour l'histoire des droits de l'Antiquité: RIDA 39 (1992) 415-449.

r49 *Arcellaschi* A., sécr., Compte-rendu des séances [Liste des membres]: RÉLat 69 (1991) 1-23 [ix-xxix]; 70 (1992) aussi 1-23 [ix-xxix].

r50 ᴱBois H., *Roegiers* J., The contribution of the Jews to the culture in the Netherlands: SourcesDocHistIdeas 16,2 (1989) 159-362 [< Henoch 14 (1992) 206 (B. *Chiesa*)].

r51 *Bouwen* Frans, Un symposium 'Pro Oriente' au Wadi Natroun [26-28 oct. 1991]: PrOrChr 41 (1991) 340-361.

r52 *Chamoux* François, Rapport sur la 66e session annuelle de l'Union Académique Internationale [Bruxelles c. 16 juin 1992]: CRAI (1992) 481-4.

r53 *Davaris* Costas, The seventh international conference for Cretan studies, Rethymnon 1991: Kadmos 31 (1992) 164-170.

r54 *Diethart* Johannes, 20. Internationaler Kongress der Papyrologen, Kopenhagen, 23. bis 29. August 1992: Biblos 41 (1992) 232-4.

r55 *Heilporn* Paul, Quatrième Séminaire international de papyrologie, Strasbourg, 15-20 juillet 1991: CdÉ 66 (1991) 364s.

r56 Manuscript studies, 18th conference, St. Louis 11-12 Oct. 1991 / 9-10 Oct. 1992: Manuscripta 35 (1991) 163-181 / 36 (1992) 163-177.

r57 *Motte* André, *Loucas-Durie* Éveline, Chronique des rencontres scientifiques: Kernos 5 (1992) 319-328 [352-4 Actes (tous les titres) des colloques].

Y7.8   *Acta congressuum orientalistica et archaeologica:* **nuntii.**

r58 Archaeological conference 18: TA Univ. 12-13 Feb. 1992: IsrEJ 42 (1992) 117s.

r59 *Billot* Marie-Françoise, Les grands ateliers d'architecture dans le monde égéen du VIe siècle av.-J.C., Colloque int. Inst. Fr. Ét. Anatoliennes, Istanbul 23-25 mai 1991: TopO 2 (1992) 295-300.

r60 *Devauchelle* Didier, Journées d'Études en hommage à Étienne DRIOTON (1889-1961), 'L'Égyptologie et ses publics' [*Heintz* J.-G., Prov.]: RICathP 38 (1991) 195.

r61 *Farnoux* A., *Driessen* J., La Crète mycénienne: Table Ronde ÉcFAth, 26-28.III.1991: TopO 2 (1992) 291-3.

r62 *Hackens* Tony, *Moucharte* Ghislaine, Le XIe Congrès international de numismatique, Bruxelles 8-13 septembre 1991: RBgNum 138 (1992) vii-lxxi; 21 fig.; Tables rondes, lxxv-ciii.

r63 *Mauritsch* Peter, *Schmidt* Sabine,   Ursprungstheorien des Sports; Symposion vom 25.-27. September 1991 in Alpl/Steiermark: Nikephoros 4 (1991) 301-7.

r64 *a) Mylonas* Georges, 1987; – *b) Petrakos* Vassilios 1988: Ⓖ *Ekthesē* of the Secretary of the Archeological Society in Athens: Praktika Arch. Etaireias (Athenai 1991) 29-31 / 29-38.

r65 *Pergola* Philippe,   Seminari di archeologia cristiana; [18 relazioni] sedute 1991s: RivArCr 68 (1992) 309-344.

r66 *Phoungas* A.,   Primero coloquio nacional de conservación de mosaicos, Palencia 1989 [Actas 150 p.; 49 fig.]: BMosAnt (AIEMA) 13 (1990s) 378-380.

r67 Rencontre assyriologique 38ᵉ, Paris 1991: participants (ordre alphabétique) et leurs titres: Akkadica 76 (1992) 1-3 [-42, 'Coopération', projets en progrès].

r68 *Thompson* Dorothy J.,   Thebes in the Graeco-Roman period (colloquium Leiden, 9-11 September 1992): CdÉ 67 (1992) 56-59.

r68* *Tikhonov* I. L., *Platonova* N. I., Ⓡ Scientific seminar: The problems of history and historiography of archeological science [Sept. 1988]: RossArkh (1992,3) 276-8.

Y8   *Periti,* Scholars, Personalia, organizations.

r69 *Alonso Díaz* José,   Cien años de estudios bíblicos en Comillas: Misc-Comillas 50 (I centenario de la Universidad, 1992) 45-79.

r70 Annuaire du Collège de France 1991-1992; résumé des cours et travaux. P 1992. 928 p. Ⲅ 100. 625-47, *Yoyotte* Jean, Égyptologie; 647s, *Garelli* Paul, Assyriologie; 649-654, *Caquot* André, Hébreu et Araméen ...

r71 **Arnold** Matthieu,   La Faculté de Théologie Protestante de l'Université de Strasbourg de 1919 à 1945: Travaux 2, 1990 ➤ 7,k210:   ᴿTZBas 48 (1992) 395s (K. *Hammer*); ZKG 103 (1992) 423-5 (M. *Greschat*: von M. LIENHARD & O. CULLMANN empfohlene Diss).

r72 ᴱ**Brinkman** M. E.,   100 jaar theologie; aspecten van een eeuw theologie in de gereformeerde kerken in Nederland (1892-1992). Kampen 1992, Kok. 344 p. ƒ 55. 90-242-8561-5. – ᴿTvT 32 (1992) 422s (G. P. *Hartvelt*: in 1892 were united the 1834 Afscheiding and 1886 Doleantie Reformed groups).

r73 *Ceresko* A.,   Report on the post-graduate programme in biblical theology at St. Peter's Pontifical Institute, Bangalore: IndTSt 29 (1992) 362-6.

r74 *Conti* Martino,   Relazione del Rettore Magnifico sul Pontificio Ateneo 'Antonianum': Antonianum 67 (1992) 553-576.

r75 ᴱ**Doré** Joseph,   Les cent ans de la Faculté de Théologie; UER de théologie et de sciences religieuses; Institut catholique de Paris: ScThRel 1. P 1992, Beauchesne. 392 p. F 198. – ᴿEsprVie 102 (1992) 383s (E. *Cothenet*); RTLv 23 (1992) 495s (C. *Focant*).

r76 *Drobner* Hubertus R.,   Die Oswald-Stiftung und die Preisausgaben der Theologischen Fakultät Paderborn 1871-1983: TGL 82 (1992) 95-137.

r77 Facultat de Teologia de Catalunya, Memòria del curs acadèmic 1990-1: RCatalT 16 (1991) 433-443.

r77* *González Novalín* José L., Cien años de estudios eclesiásticos en España [*Carcel Orti* Vicente, a Roma] p. 15-49 [-201]: Estudios, seminarios y pastoral en un siglo de historia de la Iglesia en España (1892-1992). R 1992, Pontificio Colegio español. 277 p.

r78 **Hunt** Keith & Gladys,   For Christ and the university; the story of

InterVarsity Christian Fellowship of the U.S.A., 1940-1990. DG 1992, InterVarsity. 454 p. $20. 0-8308-4996-3 [TDig 39,365].

r79 **Lindquist** Eric N., The origins of the center for Hellenic studies. Princeton 1990, Univ. viii-88 p.

r80 *Magnani* Giovanni, I 25 anni dell'Istituto di Scienze Religiose dell'Università Gregoriana: CC 143 (1992,3) 43-54.

r81 *Munier* Charles, La patristique à la Faculté de Théologie Catholique de l'Université de Strasbourg 1902-1940: *a)* RevSR 66 (1992) 319-332; *b)* RHPR 72 (1992) 381-390; Eng. 522.

r82 **Murphy-O'Connor** Jerome, (*Taylor* Justin), Le Nouveau Testament, cent ans d'exégèse à l'École Biblique 1990 → 6,m401; 7,k216: ᴿAngelicum 69 (1992) 269s (S. *Jurić*); AustralasCR 69 (1992) 131s (J. *McSweeney*); CritRR 5 (1992) 235s (Barbara E. *Bowe*) & 536 French; HeythJ 338 (1992) 444-6 (R. C. *Fuller*); NedTTs 46 (1992) 241 (P. W. van der *Horst*); RThom 92 (1992) 541-3 (L. *Devillers*); TLZ 117 (1992) 604-6 (W. *Wiefel*).

r83 New Testament Society of South Africa, list of members 1992: Neotestamentica 26 (1992) 551-8, with addresses.

r84 Princeton Seminary Catalogue 16,1 (1992) 243 p., with photos of faculty.

r84* Pubblicazioni e attività accademica della Pontificia Facoltà Teologica della Sardegna 1990-1 / 1991-2: TSard 1 (1992) 299-302 / 359-364.

r85 **Rogerson** J. W., The Society for Old Testament Study, a short history, 1917-1992: Leeds 1992, Maney. 16 p.; phot. – Members List, apart, 9 p.

r86 Society of Biblical Literature, membership directory and handbook. Atlanta 1992, Scholars. vi-234 p. [OIAc 5,35].

r87 *Swetnam* James, [segr.; *Valentino* Carlo, assist.], Acta Pontificii Instituti Biblici 9/8 (1992) 629-748; 639-644, prolusione del Rettore *Stock* Klemens, 14.X.1991.

r88 ᴱVesco J. V., L'Ancien Testament, cent ans d'exégèse à l'École Biblique 1990 → 6,m408: ᴿAngelicum 69 (1992) 367-9 (J. *Garcia Trapiello*); CBQ 54 (1992) 773 (L. *Laberge*: de Vᴀᴜx taller than 'limited vision of historical and exegetical problems'); RBén 102 (1992) 227s (D. *Misonne*); RThom 92 (1992) 543-5 (L. *Devillers*).

r88* *White* Robert A., Centre for interdisciplinary study of communications; an institution at the Pontifical Gregorian University in Rome; – *b)* Sassi Silvio, sᴘɪᴄs, Internationales Studio der Pauliner für soziale Kommunikation; – *c)* Lever Franco, Das Institut der Wissenschaften der sozialen Kommunikation; ein Institut der Päpstlichen Universität der Salesianer in Rom: Communicatio socialis 25,4 (Pd 1992) 383-7 / 388-393 / 394-7 [< ᴢɪᴛ 93,44s].

Y8.5 Periti, in memoriam.

r89 Nécrologies: AnPg 62, p. 1001-1010, amid Collected Studies; – REB 52 (1992) 217-226 . 476-484 . 752-761 . 989-1001; – RHE 87 (1992) 116*s. 289*s . 457*.

r90 Ahlström. Gösta Werner, 27.VIII.1918-17.I.1992: BAR-W 18,3 (1992) 21 (Diana *Edelman*).

r91 Akhinzhanov, Sergian Musatnyevich, 3.IX.1939-16.VIII.1991: RossArkh (1992,3) 297s, phot. (E. A. *Smagulov*, ⓡ).

r92 Aldred, Cyril, 19.II.1914-20.VI.1991; Egyptology popularizer: JEA 78 (1992) 259-266; phot. (T. G. H. *James*).

r93 Alexeev, Valery Pavlovich, 22.VIII.1929-7.XI.1991: RossArkh (1992,3) 67-70, phot. (K. A. *Amirkanov*, ⓡ); bibliog. 70-84, 544 items.

r94 Andrewes, Antony, 1910-1990: Memorias de Historia Antigua 11s (Oviedo 1990s) 343s (J.-M. *Alonso-Núñez*).

r95 Andrianopoli, Luigi, mons.: 21.I.1906-3.IX.1991: RivLtg 79 (1992) 896-9 (R. *Dalla Multa*; 899s bibliog. < RivLtg).

r96 Andronikos, Manolis, X.1919-30.III.1992: Vergina excavator: AJA 96 (1992) 757, phot. (E. N. *Borza*).

r97 Angershausen, Julius, Bischof, → 7,k224*; 3.I.1911-22.VIII.1990: ZMiss-RW 75 (1991) 155s (H. *Waldenfels*).

r98 Ardley, Gavin, † 12.III.92; co-founder: Prudentia 24,2 (1992) 1-5 (J. *Morton, al.*).

r99 Athol Gill, William, 5.IX.1937-9.III.1992; Baptist, NT: Pacifica 5,2 (1992) ii.

r100 Auboyer, Jeannine, 6.IX.1912-6.II.1990: conservateur du Musée Guimet; JAs 78 (1990) 195-204 (A. *Rosu*; bibliog.).

r101 Avigad, Nahman, 25.IX.1905-28.I.1992; epigraphist: BAR-W 18,3 (1992) 46.48.78 (F. M. *Cross*) & 47-49 (H. *Shanks*); BAngllsr 12 (1992s) 83 (S. *Gibson*); IsrEJ 42 (1992) 1-3; phot.; RÉJ 151 (1992) 451-3 (E.-M. *Laperrousaz*).

r101* Balducci, Ernesto, padre, 1922-1992: Religioni e società 7,13 (R 1992) 99s (L. *Martini*).

r102 Balil Illana, Alberto [→ 5,k836], 1928 - 23.VIII.1989: BMosAnt 13 (1990s) VII-X; bibliog.

r103 Baraschi, Silvia, 1.XI.1942-16s.III.1991: IstVArh 42 (1991) 109-111, phot., bibliog. (P. *Diaconi*).

r104 Baron, Salo Wittmayer [→ 6,m424], 1895-1989: RÉJ 151 (1992) 455-8 (J. *Shatzmiller*).

r105 Barschel, Bernd, 28.VI.1937- 1990: HistSprF 104 (1991) 1-8 (B. *Forssman, Bibliog.*).

r106 Barta, Winfred, 20.VIII.1938-27.X.1992: GöMiszÄg 131 (1992) 5 (D. *Kessler, Regine Schulz*)

r107 Bartlett, Francis, † 12.II.1992; 30 years chaplain at Westminster Cathedral: Tablet 246 (1992) 259 (bp. W. G. *Wheeler*).

r108 Bartoletti, Vittorio, StClasOr 42 (1992) 13s senza date.

r109 Bausani, Alessandro: RSO 66 (1992) 197-9 (S. *Moscati*) & 200-6 (V. *Poggi*) [per la presentazione del volume commemorativo Yad Nama (R 1992)].

r109* Behnam, Gregorius Būlus, 1916-1969, metropolitan: Aram 3 (1991) 287-291 (I. *Shahīd*).

r110 Ben-Dor, Stella, 2.XII.1899- IV.1951: IsrNumJ 11 (1990s) 1-3; phot.

r111 Bernardi, Aurelio, 1912-1989: Athenaeum 68 (1990) xiii-xiv (E. *Gabba*, D. *Magnino*) [< AnPg 62, p. 1002].

r112 Bischoff, Bernhard, [→ 7,k237] 20.XII.1906-17.IX.1991; codices latini: Gnomon 64 (1992) 474-7; portr. (Johanne *Autenrieth*); Bayr. Akad. Ehre [89 p. hors commerce; tit. pp. RHE 88,378]; ScrCiv 16 (1992) 331-340 (also Johanne *Autenrieth*); Phoenix 46 (Toronto 1992) 298.

r113 Bisi, Anna-Maria, 1938-1988: AntAfr 27 (1991) 13 (G. C. *Picard*); RStFen 17 (1989) I-XV (S. *Moscati*).

r114 Bittel, Kurt, [→ 7,k238] 5.VII.1907-30.I.1991: Ausgrabungen Boğazköy, Dir. DAI: AfO 38s (1991s) 359s, portr. (R. M. *Boehmer*); CRAI (1991) 167s; IstMitt 41 (1991) 5-12 (Halet *Çambel*).

r115 Blanckenhagen, Peter Heinrich, von, [→ 7,k239] 21.III.1909-6.III.1990: NY Institute of Fine Arts: Gnomon 64 (1992) 283-5 (Dela von *Boeselager*).

r116 Blanco Freijeiro, Antonio [➤ 7,k240], 6.IX.1923-6.I.1991: MadMitt 32 (1991) 232-241; phot. (W. *Trillmich*).

r117 Bloesch, Hansjörg, 1.VII.1912-21.I.1992: Klas. Archäol.: AntKu 35 (1992) 146 (H. P. *Isler* < Univ. Z Jahresbericht 1991s, 122s).

r118 Boessneck, Joachim, 26.II.1925-1.III.1991 [AnPg 62, p. 1002 < M. *Kokabi*].

r118* Bonifacio, Francesco Paolo, 1923 - 14.III.1989: Ivra 40 (1989) 180-3 (F. *Casavola*; bibliog.).

r119 Bonjour, Edgar, 21.VIII.1898-26.V.1991, Schweizerische Neutralität: HZ 254 (1992) 223-8 (H. R. *Guggisberg*).

r120 Boriskovsky, Pavel Iosefovich, 27.V.1911-27.IX.1991: RossArkh (1992,3) 288-290; phot. (N. D. *Praslov,* ⑬); bibliog. 290-6; 230 items.

r121 Bortignon, Girolamo, mons., 1905-12.III.1992, promotore di cultura: StPatav 39 (1992) 275-282 (L. *Sartori*).

r122 Bosch, David J., 1929-16.IV.1992; auto accident: IntRMiss 81 (1992) 362; KerkT 43 (1992) 248 (J. A. B. *Jongeneel*); Missiology 20 (1992) 453-6 (J. A. *Scherer*).

r123 Brauer Jerald C.: ChH 60,2 (1991) 163-270; bibliog. 263-270 (Kenneth *Sawyer*).

r124 Braun, Benedikta (Maria Lätizia), Äbtissin, 27.IX.1895-17.XI.1991: ErbAuf 68 (1992) 242-5 (Anastazija *Čizmin*).

r125 Broneer, Oscar Theodore, 28.XII.1894-22.II.1992 (in Corinth): AJA 96 (1992) 543-6; 2 phot. (Elizabeth R. *Gebhard*).

r126 Browne, Michael, 1910-1.IV.1992: Iran 30 (1992) vi (Mary *Gueritz*).

r127 Brusselmans, Christiane, [➤ 7,k246] 1.XI.1930-c.1991: LvSt 17 (1992) 3-9 (Susan K. *Roll*, T.P. *Ivory*); Commonweal 119,2 (1992) 19-21 (J. *Parker*).

r128 Burrus, Ernest Joseph, S.J., 20.IV.1907-11.XII.1991: CathHR 78 (1992) 499-501 (C. E. *O'Neil*); RHE 87 (1992) 949 (R. *Aubert*).

r128* Cahen, Claude, 1909 - 18.XI.1991: CRAI (1991) 763s (F. *Chamoux*).

r129 Cambier, Jules-Marie, SDB, 1915 - 15.VIII.1992: NT (à Kinshasa...): ETL 68 (1992) 503 [A. *Vanneste*].

r129* Carpenter, Philip, † 5.VI.1992, University chaplain: NBlackf 73 (1992) 356s (T. *Radcliffe*).

r130 Carthy, Margaret, (Mother Mary Peter, O.S.U.) aet. 80, 21.VI.1992; president of New Rochelle college; collaborator of New Catholic Encyclopedia: CathHR 78 (1992) 715s (Alice *Gallin*).

r131 Colombo, Giovanni, card., 1902-20.V.1992; arcivescovo di Milano: ScuolC 120 (1992) 419-421; Ambrosius 68 (1992) 391-407 (card. G. *Biffi*) & 408-457 (*al.*); TItSett 17 (1992) 209-215 (Giuseppe *Colombo*: '22.V'; 'letteratura e teologia') [216-235, un suo articolo, Fonti della Teologia Spirituale < RivAscM 34 (1965) 443-461].

r132 Corbo, Virgilio Canio, O.F.M. [➤ 7,k253*] 8.VII.1918-6.XII.1991, scavatore di Cafarnao: Antonianum 67 (1992) 168-171 (A. *Niccacci*); RivB 40 (1992) 124-7 (anche A. *Niccacci*); ADAJ 36 (1992) 9-11 (ᵀS. *Mausholt*); IsrEJ 42 (1992) 116; ParVi 37 (1992) 118-120 (G. C. *Bottini*).

r133 Courtois, Jean-Claude [➤ 7,k255 'Jacques-Claude'], 1.III.1931-18.III.1991; fouilles de Ras Shamra: Syria 68 (1991) 467s (H. de *Contenson*).

r134 Crahay, Roland, aet. 76, 11.III.1992; hist. rel.: RHE 87 (1992) 325 (J.-F. *Gilmont*).

r135 Culianu, Ioan, aet. 41, 21.V.1991: HistRel 31 (1991s) i.

r136 Dadoun-Canoui Joële, 1949-c.1992: RÉJ 151 (1992) 459s (Eliane *Roos*).

r137 Dahlmann, Hellfried, 8.VII.1905-7.VII.1988; Latinist: Gnomon 64 (1992) 281-3 (C. *Zintzen*).

r138 Darricau, Raymond, † 24.VIII.1992: RHE 87 (1992) 957s (J. *Gadille*).

r139 Darrouzès, Jean, A.A., [➤ 6,m457; 7,k257] 3.IV.1912-26.VI.1990, byzantiniste: RHE 87 (1992) 622 (R. *Aubert*).

r140 Della Corte, Francesco [➤ 7,k239], † 24.IX.1991: Orpheus 13,1 (1992) 1s.

r141 Delvoye, Charles, [➤ 43] 18.IV.1917-9.XII.1991: Byzantion 62 (1992) 5-11; phot. (Lydie *Hadermann-Misguich*, bibliog.); art grec/byzantin: Ant-Clas 61 (1992) 3.

r142 Demus, Otto, [➤ 7,k260] 4.XI.1902-17.XI.1990: Byzantine mosaics: JbÖsByz 42 (1992) 431-3 (H. *Hunger*).

r143 Dooling, Dorothea Matthews, 1.XI.1910-4.X.1991; founder: Parabola 17,1 (1992) 2s; phot. (Ellen D. *Draper*).

r143* Dürig, Walter, 1913-1922; Liturgiewissenschaftler: Klerusblatt 72 (Mü 1992) 265s (T. *Maas-Eward*).

r144 Dumitrescu, Vladimir, 20.X.1920-11.IV.1991: IstVArh 42 (1991) 105-8, phot. (S. *Morintz*).

r144* Dumont, Christophe-Jean, O.P., 22.VI.1897- 1991: Istina 37 (1992) 57-64 (B. *Dupuy*).

r145 Eichhorn, Werner, 1.VII.1899-1.II.1991; chinesische Religion: ZDMG 142 (1992) 3-11 (K. *Flessel*; Bibliog.).

r146 Elert, Werner: Lutherische Kirche in der Welt 39 (Erlangen 1992) 29-58 (K. *Beyschlag*) [< ZIT 92,408].

r147 Ellis, John Tracy, 1905, † aet. 87, 16.X.1992: 'dean of American Catholic historians': Tablet 246 (1992) 1585s (G. *Fogarty*); America 167 (1992) 340 (T. J. *Shelley*); RHE 87 (1992) 950 (also T. J. *Shelley*).

r148 Engelsen, Nils J., 29.VII.1914-15.II.1991; Baptist seminary rector: Ts-TKi 63 (1992) 65s (E. *Larsson*).

r149 Esse, Douglas L., 1.XII.1949-13.X.1992: OIAc 3s (1992) 7.

r149* Fazzari, Anna, 1912-1991: PBritSR 60 (1992) vii (Margaret *Ward-Perkins*, Susanna *Spurr*).

r150 Ferenczy, Endre, 25.II.1912-11.III.1990; Althistoriker: Ivra 41 (1990) 225-234 (F. *Sturm*; Bibliog.).

r151 Février Paul-A., [➤ 7,k275] 1931-10.IV.1991, BMosAnt 13 (1990s) XI-XIII (Michèle *Blanchard-Lemée*); ArEspArq 65 (1992) 291-4 (N. *Duval*); AntAfr 28 (1992) 9-14, phot. (aussi N. *Duval*).

r152 Finkelstein, Louis, aet. 96, 29.XI.1991; Jewish Theological Seminary director 1940-72: ETL 68 (1992) 221 (R. F. *Collins*).

r153 Flesseman-van Leer E., 17.VII.1912-18.VI.1991: KerkT 42 (1991) 347-9.

r154 Flint, Hildebrand, O.S.B. [➤ 7,k276], 1921-10.I.1991: EphLtg 105 (1991) 180 (Edith *Barnecut*).

r155 Fletcher Joseph F., aet. 86, 28.X.1991; 'Situation ethics' 1966: ETL 68 (1992) 220s (R. F. *Collins*).

r156 Forni, Giovanni, 28.V.1922-2.V.1991; storia militare romana: Gnomon 64 (1992) 187-9 (G. *Susini*); Athenaeum 80 (1992) 251-3 (M. G. *Angeli Bertinelli*).

r157 Franchon, Lisette, 1916-1992: RICathP 43 (1992) 175 (P. *Guiberteau*).

r158 Fusella, Luigi, 16.III.1914-12.VII.1992: RasEtiop 34 (1990) 229-232; fot. (L. *Ricci*).

r159 García. Ruben Dario, O.S.B., 2.IV.?1990: hist. eccl.: TArg 27 (1990) 95-57 (J. C. *Maccarone*).

r160 Glock, Albert E., 1925-19.I.1992; 16 years professor at Bir Zeit, killed by a masked gunman there: ChrCent 109 (1992) 123 & 179 (J. *Wall*); BAR-W 18,3 (1992) 21 (Nancy *Lapp*: '20.I').

r161 Goldberg, Arnold, 18.II.1928-19.IV.1991, 'Die ägyptischen Elemente in der Sprache des ATs' 1957: ZDMG 142 (1992) 247-255; portr. (F. *Böhl*; Bibliog.); FraJudBeit 19 (1991s) i-v, phot. (Margarete *Schlüter*).

r162 Gómez Canedo, Lino, OFM, 24.VI.1908-24.XII.1990; Archivio Ibero-Americano: RHE 87 (1992) 322 (R. *Aubert*).

r163 Gonda, Jan, 14.IV.1905-28.VII.1991: Indologist: IndIranJ 34 (1991) 281-6 (H. W. *Bodewitz*).

r164 Goshen-Gottstein Moshe, aet. 66, 14.IX.1991: Hebrew Univ. Bible project: ETL 68 (1992) 223 (R. F. *Collins*).

r165 Graham, James Walter, 5.VIII.1906-22.VIII.1991; Olynthus, Crete: AJA 96 (1992) 325s, portr. (J. W. *Shaw*).

r166 Greimas, Algirdas Julien, 9.III.1917-27.II.1992: ZSemiot 14 (1992) 433-6 (S. E. *Larsen*, 'La sémiotique est devenue veuve', deutsch, ᵀ*Oligschläger* Martina); SémBib 67 (1992) 3-12 (J. *Delorme*); FgNt 5 (1992) 119-121 (aussi J. *Delorme*).

r167 Gutiérrez Morán, David, 22.III.1903-15.II.1992: CiuD 205 (1992) 204-229 (M. *González Velasco*; bibliog. 148 títulos).

r168 Haberland, Eike, 18.V.1924-6.VI.1992; Westafrika: BeitVgAr 11 (1991) 11; phot. (K. H. *Striedter*).

r169 Hackman, George Gottlob, 10.II.1901-21.III.1991: cuneiform copying technique: AfO 38s (1991s) 261s, phot. (B. R. *Foster*).

r170 Hanley, Thomas O'Brien, S.J., 8.VI.1918-29.IX.1991: biographer of Charles Carroll: CathHR 78 (1992) 157 (N. *Varga* says he died in Omaha but went to high school at Gonzaga in D.C.); RHE 87 (1992) 949 (R. *Aubert*).

r171 Hawkes, Christopher, aet. 86, 29.III.1992: OxJArch 11 (1992) iii, phot.

r172 Hintze, Fritz, 18.IV.1915-30.III.1993 (traffic accident), Herausgeber 1962-86: OLZ 88 (1993) 237s.

r173 Hinz, Walther, 19.XI.1901-12.IV.1991: ArchMIran 25 (1992) iii.

r174 Hombert, Marcel, 20.III.1900-21.III.1992; papyrologie: AntClas 61 (1992) 3; Aegyptus 72 (1992) 214.

r175 Honselmann, Klemens, 1.XI.1900-19.XII.1991: Bibliothekar: TGL 82 (1992) 173-7 (H. R. *Drobner*).

r176 Horedt, Kurt, 39.III.1914-1.XII.1991: IstVArh 43 (1992) 241-3, phot. (R. *Popa*).

r177 Jobert, Ambroise, 8.VII.1904-28.V.1988; dir. 1969-76: CahHist 35 (1990) 55-57, phot. (V. *Chomel*) & 58-60 (P. *Bolle*).

r178 Joset, Camille-Jean, S.J., 26.II.1912-28.X.1992: RHE 87 (1992) 947s (P. *Wynants*).

r179 Joubert H. L. N.: Neotestamentica 26 (1992) 551.

r180 Karmiris John N., 1903-5.I.1992: TAth 63 (1992) 7-17; portr. (E. D. *Theodorou, al.* ☺).

r181 Karstensen, Per Karsten, 7.XI.1936-24.V.1991; Menighetsfakultet: TsTKi 62 (1991) 214 (O. *Skjevesland*).

r182 Kelly, John M., 1932-24.I.1991; Irish politician and historian of law: ZSav-R 109 (1992) 785s (P. B. H. *Birks*).

r183 Kerr, Hugh Thomson, 1.VII.1909-27.III.1992: editor, TTod 49 (1992s) 147-151; 449; 516-8-523 (F. W. *Dillistone*; J. M. *Mulder*).

r184 Kilian, Klaus, 27.II.1939-28.V.1992; erster Direktor AVA: BeitVgArch 11 (1991) 1-5; phot. (H. *Kyrieleis*); 6-8, Bibliog.

r185 Klíma, Josef, [➤ 7,k301] 16.XI.1909-30.XI.1989; Assyriologie: Ivra 40 (1989) 183-5 (Dagmar *Klímová*); ZSav-R 108 (1991) 672-5 (G. *Ries*).

r186 Kłoniecki, Felicjan, 28.V.1909-27.X.1990; De catalogis apostolorum; parabolis talentorum et minarum (Roma); doct. PIB 1939: RuBi 44 (1991) 151-6 (M. *Wolniewicz*; bibliog.).

r186* Kniazev, Alexis, 1913 - 8.II.1991: Istina 37 (1992) 65s.

r187 Kowalski, Georges Wierusz, 20.XII.1931-16.IX.1990; théologien; RICathP 40 (1991) 5-17, 2 phot. (J. *Doré*; bibliog. 157-164; 23-102 témoignages; 105-156, 'Un itinéraire de recherche' par lui; 167-273, Anthologie.

r188 Kraus, Fritz Rudolf [➤ 6,m515; 7,k306], 21.III.1910-19.I.1991: Assyriologie: AfO 38s (1991s) 262-5, phot. (K. R. *Veenhof*).

r189 Kruse, Hans, 26.IX.1921-1.V.1990; Islamkunde: ZDMG 142 (1992) 237-246; portr. (H.-G. *Migeod*; Bibliog.).

Kuss, Otto, S.I. 1905 - 7.II.1991 ➤ 112*.

r190 Kutscher, Raphael, 4.IV.1938-29.I.1989, Sumerologist: AfO 38s (1991s) 265-7, phot. (J. *Klein*).

r191 Lackner, Wolfgang, 11.VI.1937-9.I.1992, Byz. Hagiographie – Philosophie: JbÖsByz 42 (1992) 435s (H. *Hunger*).

r193 Laroche, Emmanuel [➤ 7,k309], 10.VII.1914-16.VI.1991: CRAI (1991) 435s (F. *Chumoux*, '11.VII.'); SMEA 29 (1992) 9-11 (O. *Carruba*).

r194 Lassus, Jean, [➤ 6,m519], 17.VI.1903-9.X.1990; premier dir.: AntAfr 27 (1991) 7-9; phot. (M. *Le Glay*); BMosAnt 13 (1990s) xiv-xv (P.-A. *Février*); art byzantin: Syria 68 (1991) 466s (J.-P. *Sodini*).

r195 Latimer, John F., 1903-29.X.1991: ClasW 85 (1991s) 687s, phot. (J. E. *Ziolkowski*).

r196 Lazzaro, Luciano: DialHA 18,2 (1992) 7-10; foto, sans dates (Monique *Clavel-Lévêque*).

r197 Leemans, Wilhelmus François [➤ 7,k311], 1912-28.VI.1991: PhoenixEOL 38,1 (1992) 3 (M. *Heerma van Voss*).

r198 Le Gall, Joël, 1913-1991; RÉAnc 94 (1992) 429s (H. *Lavagne*).

r199 Le Glay, Marcel, 1920-14.VIII.1992; dir. ant. Algérie: AntAfr 28 (1992) 7 (G. *Souville*); RÉAnc 94 (1992) 429 (H. *Lavagne*).

r200 Leloir Louis, 1911-15.VIII.1992: RHE 87 (1992) 610s (J. *Leclercq*).

r201 Lengeling, Emil Joseph, 26.V.1916 - 18. (nicht 19.).VI.1986: ArLtgW [28 (1986) 488 '19'] 34 (1992) 154-167 (K. *Richter*), 168-198 Bibliog. (B. *Kranemann*).

r202 Lenger, Marie-Thérèse, 28.VI.1920-2.II.1992; papyrologie juridique: RIDA 39 (1992) 9-18 (J. *Bingen*; bibliog. 19-24).

r203 Lepore, Ettore, † 24.III.1990: ➤ 713, PACT 20 (1990) 7s (A. *Stazio*, T. *Hackens*).

r204 Lieberman, Stephen J., 1943-1985; Assyriologist: AfO 38s (1991s) 267 (T. *Jacobsen*).

r205 Livingstone, James, 1912-4.X.1991, treasurer: Iran 30 (1992) v, phot. (D. *Wright*).

r206 Llaguno Farias, José A., S.I., obispo, 7.VIII.1925-26.II.1992: Christus 57,3 (1992) 52-54; foto.

r207 Löfgren, Oscar, † 23.IV.1992: RasStEtiop 34 (1990!) 233-5 (L. *Ricci*).

r208 Lubac, Henri de [➤ 7,k317], 20.II.1896-4.IX.1991: AnStoEseg 9 (1992) 269-274 (M. *Pesce*); Commonweal 119,2 (1992) 14-17 (J. A. *Komonchak*); PrPeo 6 (1992) 343-6 (P. *McPartlan*); HumBr 47 (1992) 321-351 (J. Y. *Calvez*) [< Études 1991, 371-8], ᵀ*Iamoni* Daniela; RClerIt 73 (1992) 435-447 (X. *Tilliette*); RHE 87 (1992) 624s (R. *Aubert*); TAth 63 (1992) 175-180 (E. D. *Moutsoulas*).

r209 Luschey, Heinz, 3.XII.1910-1.I.1992: ArchMIran 25 (1992) iii.
r209* McCord, James I., 1919 - 19.II.1990; past president of Princeton Sem.
    and Reformed World Alliance: RefW 41 (1990s) 1.
r210 McDonald, D. M., † 26.II.1991: CamArch 1,1 (1991) 1.
r211 McKenzie, John L. [➤ 7,k320], 9.X.1910-2.III.1991: ChrCent 108 (1991)
    321; ETL 68 (1992) 219s (R. F. *Collins*).
r212 Maiberger, Paul, 18.IV.1941-21.I.1992 [Hab. 1983 'Topographische und
    historische Untersuchungen zum Sinaiproblem']: OrChr 76 (1992) 238 (J.
    Assfalg).
r213 Manns, Peter, 10.III.1923-23.III.1991, Rel/Kirchengeschichte: LuthTK
    15 (1991) 82s (W. *Klän*); Ökumeniker: LuJb 59 (1992) 7-10 (R. *Vinke*:
    '23.IV').
r214 Marchasson, Yves, mgr., 6.V.1920-16.II.1992; hist. eccl. moderne; DSpir:
    RHE 87 (1992) 326s (J. *Gadille*); RICathP 43 (1992) 168-173.
r215 Marcillet-Jaubert, Jean, 28.X.1924-18.IX.1987: AntAfr 27 (1991) 11s (M.
    Euzennat; bibliog., X. *Dupuis*).
r216 Marot, Pierre, 15.XII.1900-28.XI.1992: CRAI (1992) 847-852.
r217 Mastagli, Pierre, s.J., 24.VII.1908-13.XII.1990; chimie: RICathP 39
    (1991) 207-211 (M. *Riquet, al.*).
r218 Meyendorff, John, aet. 66, 22.VII.1992; hist. religieuse byzantine: RHE
    87 (1992) 611 (R. *Aubert*); ChrCent 109 (1992) 837 (J. *Pelikan*).
r219 Meyer, Rudolf, [➤ 7,k326], 8.IX.1909-2.IV.1991: TLZ 117 (1992) 137s (J.
    Conrad).
r219* Mihailov, Georgi, 16.X.1915-21.XI.1991; helléniste: CRAI (1991) 764
    (F. *Chamoux*).
r220 Molinari, Franco, mons., 1928-1991, collaboratore: RHE 87 (1992) 332
    (R. *Aubert*); ScuolaC 120 (1992) 287s (A. *Rimoldi*; bibliog. da ScuolaC).
r221 Moody, Dale, aet. 76, 22.I.1992, Baptist prof., once TILLICH's assistant
    and Gregorian Univ. prof.: ChrCent 109 (1992) 123.
r222 Moon, Warren G., 2.III.1945-22.VI.1992 (accidental fall), classical art
    history: AJA 96 (1992) 759s (Brunilde S. *Ridgway*).
r223 Moretti, Luigi, 1922-8.VIII.1991: Nikephoros 4 (1991) 5s (W. *Decker*).
r224 Müller, Hans Wolfgang, 16.VIII.1907-6.II.1991: ZägSpr 119,2 (1992)
    I-III; portr. (P. *Munro*).
r225 Müller-Wiener, Wolfgang [➤ 7,k230], 17.V.1923-25.III.1991: IstMitt 41
    (1991) 13-16 (W. *Koenigs*); bibliog. 17-24 (M. *Dennert*, O. *Feld*).
r226 Murray, Gregory, osb., 1905 - 19.I.1992: DowR 110 (1992) 159s.
r227 Musiolek, Peter, aet. 64, 28.XI.1991; klassische Ökonomie: Gnomon 64
    (1992) 572s (H.-J. *Gehrke*, Isolde *Stark*).
r228 Nell-Breuning, Oswald von, [➤ 7,k332] 1890 - 21.VIII.1991: ZkT 114
    (1992) 66-70 (B. *Kuppler*); Gregorianum 73 (1992) 329-335 (auch B.
    Kuppler).
r229 Nishitani, Keiji, 1900-23.XI.1990 [but 1901 in title]; SvTKv 67 (1991)
    81-86 (H. *Eilert*: en tänkare mellan öst och väst).
r230 O'Brien, Thomas C., aet. 67, 17.VI.1991?, editor of 60-volume English
    Aquinas Summa: ETL 68 (1992) 220 (R. F. *Collins*).
r231 Ocaña Jiménez, Manuel, 21.II.1914-18.I.1990: MadMitt 32 (1991)
    242-256; phot. (K. *Brisch*; Bibliog.).
r232 Ojihara, Yutaka, 16.III.1923-8.II.1991, Japan's chief Indologist: Ind-
    IranJ 34 (1991) 277-280 (M. *Hara*, bibliog.).
r233 Opelt, Ilona, † 30.IX.1991: ➤ 457*, Sapienza p. 5; p. 265.
r234 Orcibal, Jean, 10.V.1913-18.XII.1991, catholicisme moderne: RHE 87
    (1992) 625-9 (I. *Noye*, J.-R. *Armogathe*).

r235 Orlinsky, Harry M.,   17.III.1908-21.III.1992: Septuaginta; BAR-W 18,4 (1992) 27 (S. D. *Sperling*; with Orlinsky's 1974 essay on how he became an undercover agent); IsrEJ 42 (1992) 116s.

r236 Outler, Albert C.,   17.X.1908-1.IX.1989; patristics, early Christianity; co-founder: SecC 9 (1992) 1-4 (E. *Ferguson*).

r236* Petit, François [Camille], 20.VI.1894-28.VIII.1990: AnPraem 67 (1991) 120-137, portr. (Martine *Plouvier*); al., bibliog.

r237 Paul-David, Madeleine, † 12.III.1989, art japonais/coréen: JAs 277 (1989) 221-5 (Daisy *Lion-Goldschmidt*).

r237* Pelegri i Valls, Joan, 27.VII.1927-28.XI.1991; Hist. filos.; RCatalT 16 (1991) 225s (J. M. *Via*).

r238 Peter, Carl J., † 20.VIII.1991: Catholic U. Religious Studies dean: ETL 68 (1992) 220 (R. F. *Collins*).

r239 Petrenko, Valeri Petrovich, 1943-9.IX.1991: RossArkh (1992,4) 260, phot. ℗; 261s bibliog.

r240 Petschov, Herbert, 26.XII.1909-28.VI.1991: babylonisches Recht: ZSav-R 109 (1992) 787-790 (G. *Ries*); ZAss 82 (1992) 1-3 (J. *Oelsner*).

r241 Petuchowski, Jakob J., [➤ 7,k341], 1925-12.XI.1991: ETL 68 (1992) 221 (J. F. *Collins*).

r242 Picard, Jean-Charles, aet. 50, 3.VII.1992: RHE 87 (1992) 956s (P. *Riché*).

r243 Piétri, Charles [➤ 7,k342], 19.IV.1932-7.VIII.1991· ArEspArq 65 (1992) 294-7 (N. *Duval*); MondeB 73 (1991) 48 (A. *Mandouze*: historien de la Rome chrétienne).

r244 Pinès, Shlomo, 1908-10.I.1990, judaïsme arabe: JAs 278 (1990) 205-211 (Sarah *Stroumsa*).

r245 Pirenne, Jacqueline, 1918-8.XI.1990; épigraphie sud-arabe: Syria 68 (1991) 465s (E. *Will*).

r246 Pólay, Elemér, 1915-1988: ZSav-R 107 (1990) 739-741 (G. *Härtel, al.*).

r247 Polotsky, Hans Jakob [➤ 7,k347], 1905-10.VIII.1991; Orientalia 61 (1992) 208-213; portr. (Ariel *Shisha-Halevy*); IsrEJ 42 (1992) 115 ➤ 735, 6th Eg. 1991/2, xxxiii-xxxiv (M. *Lichtheim*).

r248 Prenter, Regin, 6.XI.1907-15.XII.1990: TsTKi 62 (1991) 55-57 (T. *Austad*).

r248* Provera, Giuseppe, 12.X.1919-3.IX.1990: Ivra 41 (1990) 235-241 (S. *Romano*).

r249 Ravdina, Tamara Vladimirovna, 1919-1991: RossArkh (1992,4) 263s, phot. (T. I. *Makarova*).

r249* Reggi, Roberto, 1923 - V.1990: Ivra 41 (1990) 242-5 (F. *Pastori*).

r250 Reuschel, Wolfgang,   16.XI.1924-18.IX.1991; Arabist: ZDMG 142 (1992) 256-261.

r251 Řezáč, Jan, 8.V.1914-4.I.1990; secretary [35 years] and minister of the Pontifical Oriental Institute: OrChrPer 58 (1992) 353-5 (E. G. *Farrugia*; bibliog. 361-6).

r252 Robert, Fernand, 1908-25.VII.1992; ancien président: BBudé (1992) 117-121 (J. *Bompaire*) & 122s (J. *Jouanna*, avec bibliogr. hippocratique).

r253 Rosenfeld, Irina Gabrielovna, 23.V.1923-10.VIII.1991: RossArkh (1992,4) 265s; photo (K. A. *Smirnov*).

r254 Rossano, Pietro, mons. [➤ 7,k354], 25.IV.1923-15.VI.1991; rettore della Pont. Univ. Lateranense: Lateranum 57 (1991) 307-310.

r255 Rothenberg, Meir: Lešonenu 56,1 (1991s) 9.

r256 Rouillard, Édouard, O.S.B., 17.VI.1920-18.IX.1992; Basile sur les Psaumes: RHE 87 (1992) 958 (B. *Gain*).

r257 Ruyt Franz De, 5.IX.1907-7.II.1992: archéologie classique: AntClass 61 (1992) 4.
r258 Rychner, Jean, 1916 - 5.VI.1989: BtHumRen 52 (1990) 385s (Geneviève Hasenohr).
r259 Salleron, Louis, aet. 86, 20.I.1992: PeCa 257 (1992) 79s (Y. Daoudal, avec trois récensions).
r260 Salo, Yişḥaq: Lešonenu 56,1 (1991s) 7.
r261 Sandbach, F. Harry, 23.II.1903-18.IX.1991, classics: Gnomon 64 (1992) 473s (R. D. Dawe).
r262 Schmökel, Hartmut, 1906-6.VIII.1991: Geschichte AO/AT: AfO 38s (1991s) 268 (R. Borger).
r263 Schneider-Herrmann Gisela, 1.IX.1893 - 1992: Babesch 67 (1992) vi-vii, phot. (A. D. Trendall; bibliog. ix-xi, R. Scheurleer).
r264 Schulek, Tibor, 3.II.1904-31.V.1989: JbLtgHymn 33 (1990s) vi (I. Botta).
r265 Sermoneta, Giuseppe, 25.XII.1924-2.X.1992: filosofia medievale (Enc. Hebraica), Univ. Ebraica: Henoch 14 (1992) 307s (M. Perani).
r266 Sevenster J. N., 1900 - 30.XI.1991; NT, Philo: NedTTs 46 (1992) 150s (P. Smit Sibinga).
r267 Simms, George Otto, 1910 - 15.XI.1991, abp. Armagh: Studies 81 (1992) 212-216 (M. Hurley).
r268 Simon, Mihai, 1.II.1954-10.II.1992: IstVArh 43 (1992) 227-9; phot; bibliog. (A. Avram).
r269 Simon, Monique, 1924-1991: RICathP 40 (1991) 315-9 (E. Marcus, homélie).
r270 Skydsgaard, Kristen Ejner, 1902 - 9.II.1990: TsTKi 62 (1991) 57s (I. Asheim).
r271 Smith, Morton, 28.V.1915-11.VII.1991, 'most erudite and controversial figure of the U. S.'; Episcopalian priest till 1948: Gnomon 64 (1992) 382-4 (W. M. Calder^III); 'secret Mark': ChrCent 108 (1991) 714.
r272 Sorge, Giuseppe, † 12.IX.1992; storico; SMSR 58 (1992) 381-3 (Mariam de Ghantuz Cubbe; bibliog.).
r273 Spuler, Bertold, 1911-6.III.1990, Islamologe: ZDMG 142 (1992) 1s (H. Göckenjan).
r274 Stenger, Werner, [→ 7,k369] 14.XI.1938-7.VI.1990; NT: BiKi 45 (1990) 159s (P.-G. Müller).
r275 Stern, Henri, 1902-1988: BMosAnt 13 (1990s) xvi-xviii [X. Barral i Altet < CahCivMédv 33,1 (1990) 97-99].
r276 Stern, Menahem [→ 5,k974; 6,m597], 5.III.1925-22.VI.1989 (assassiné): RÉJ 150 (1991) 281s (Mireille Hadas-Lebel).
r277 Stucchi, Sandro, 1922-1991; AION-Clas 44 (1992) vi-ix; portr. (Maria Floriani Squarciapino).
r278 Sullivan, Richard D., aet. 52, † 1988; Judaean history, Toronto [Syria 68 (1991) 483].
r279 Swanton, Robert, 1910-30.III.1992; editor: RefTR 51 (1992) 41 (A. M. Harman).
r280 Tabasz, Zbigniew, mgr., 3.XII.1928-28.VIII.1992: ArchWsz 43 (1992) 145, phot. (J. Wielowiejski); bibliog. 146.
r280* Tacik, Felicitas, aet. 50, 21.I.1991: HLand 123,1 (1991) 1 (H. Michel).
r281 Thompson, Margaret, 22.II.1911-29.II.1992; Athens agora; first woman president of AIA: AJA 96 (1992) 547-9, phot. (W. E. Metcalf).
r282 Tibesar, Antonine, O.F.M., c. 22.III.1907-4.III.1992; ed. 1970-88, The Americas [44 (1988) 343-362]: CathHR 78 (1992) 501-3 (R. Trisco).

r283 Treu, Kurt [→ 7,k377], 15.IX.1928-6.VI.1991: ArPapF 38 (1992) 4-6, phot. (W. *Müller*).
r283* Turčinović, Josip, † 3.X.1990: BogSmot 60 (1990) ante 141; phot. (A. *Rebić*).
r284 Unversagt, Wilhelm, 21.V.1892-17.III.1971: PraehZts 67 (1992) 1-14.
r285 Valgiglio, Ernesto, † 22.VII.1990: → 653c, Convegno plutarcheo 4 (1991) 15-18 (I. *Gallo*).
r286 Verbraken, Pierre-Patrick, O.S.B., 26.II.1926-22.II.1992: RHE 87 (1992) 321 (C. *Soetens*); dir.: RBén 102 (1992) 7s; RÉtAug 38 (1992) 3-5 (G. *Folliet*).
r287 Vergote Joseph, 1910- † aet. 82, 8.I.1992; Grammaire copte: OrChr 76 (1992) 238 (J. *Assfalg*); PhoenixEOL 38,2 (1992) 2s, phot. (M. *Heerma van Voss*).
r287* Via i Boada, Lluis, 23.X.1910-14.XI.1991; filosofia, geologia: RCatalT 16 (1991) 323-5 (F. *Nicolau*).
r288 Villers, Robert, 1912-1989: Ivra 40 (1989) 185-9 (F. *Sturm*).
r288* Visser, Jan, C.Ss.R. (1912-1991): StMor 30,1 (R 1992) 129...
r289 Vogt, Heinrich, 19.XI.1910-9.V.1990: ZSav-R 108 (1991) 679-682 (R. *Knütel*).
r290 Wahba, Magdi, 19.X.1925-4.X.1991: BSArCopte 31 (1992) 1s, phot. (W. *Boutros-Ghali*).
r291 Weinberg, Saul S., 1912-24.X.1992; Aegean archaeology [BAR-W 19/1,21].
r292 Weitzmann, Kurt: ByZ 48s (1991s) 656s (H. L. *Kessler*, no * †).
r292* Wornon, Herman E., 1902-1992: RelEdn 87 (Ch 1992) 497-505 [< ZIT 93,52].
r293 Zamora Sánchez, Germán, 11.IX.1933-13.II.1992: Inst. Hist.: ColcFran 62 (1992) 349-363; portr. (I. de *Villapadierna*; bibliog.).
r294 Zandee, Jan [→ 7,k386], 9.IX.1914-23,I.1991: Egyptologie: NedTTs 46 (1992) 51 (D. van der *Plas*).
r295 Zedda, Silverio, S.J., 1913-14.VI.1992: TSard 1 (1992) 7-10.

Index Alphabeticus: Auctores – *Situs (omisso al-, tel, abu etc.)*
Ddiss./dir. Eeditor FFestschrift Mmentio, de eo Rrecensio Ttranslator † in mcm.

Ddiss./dir. Eeditor FFestschrift Mmentio, de eo Rrecensio Ttranslator † in mem.
Sub de, van etc.: cognomina americana (post 1979) et italiana (post 1984); non reliqua.

Cognomina **italiana** et **americana** *sola* sub praefixo separato *da* etc.

Cognomina **italiana** et **americana** *sola* sub praefixo separato *da* etc.

Cognomina **italiana** et **americana** *sola* sub praefixo separato *da* etc.

Cognomina **italiana** et **americana** *sola* sub praefixo separato *da* etc.

Cognomina **italiana** et **americana** *sola* sub praefixo separato *da* etc.

Cognomina **italiana** et **americana** *sola* sub praefixo separato *da* etc.

Cognomina **italiana** et **americana** *sola* sub praefixo separato *da* etc.

Cognomina **italiana** et **americana** *sola* sub praefixo separato *da* etc.

ᴰdiss./dir. ᴱeditor ꟻFestschrift ᴹmentio, de eo ᴿrecensio ᵀtranslator † in mem.
Sub **de**, **van** etc.: cognomina *americana* (post 1979) et *italiana* (post 1984); **non** reliqua.

ᴰdiss./dir. ᴱeditor ꟳFestschrift ᴹmentio, de eo ᴿrecensio ᵀtranslator † in mem.
Sub de, van etc.: cognomina americana (post 1979) et italiana (post 1984); non reliqua.

ᴰdiss./dir. ᴱeditor ꜰFestschrift ᴹmentio, de eo ᴿrecensio ᵀtranslator † in mem.
Sub **de**, **van** etc.: cognomina *americana* (post 1979) et *italiana* (post 1984); **non** reliqua.

Ddiss./dir. Eeditor FFestschrift Mmentio, de eo Rrecensio Ttranslator † in mem.
Sub de, van etc.: cognomina americana (post 1979) et italiana (post 1984); non reliqua.

ᴰdiss./dir. ᴱeditor ᶠFestschrift ᴹmentio, de eo ᴿrecensio ᵀtranslator † in mem.
Sub de, van etc.: cognomina americana (post 1979) et italiana (post 1984); non reliqua.

ᴰdiss./dir. ᴱeditor ꜰFestschrift ᴹmentio, de eo ᴿrecensio ᵀtranslator † in mem.
Sub **de**, **van** etc.: cognomina *americana* (post 1979) et *italiana* (post 1984); **non** reliqua.

Ddiss./dir. Eeditor FFestschrift Mmentio, de eo Rrecensio Ttranslator † in mem.
Sub de, van etc.: cognomina americana (post 1979) et italiana (post 1984); non reliqua.

Ddiss./dir. Eeditor FFestschrift Mmentio, de eo Rrecensio Ttranslator † in mem.
Sub de, van etc.: cognomina *americana* (post 1979) et *italiana* (post 1984); non reliqua.

Ddiss./dir. Eeditor FFestschrift Mmentio, de eo Rrecensio Ttranslator † in mem.
Sub de, van etc.: cognomina americana (post 1979) et italiana (post 1984); non reliqua.

ᴰdiss./dir. ᴱeditor ᶠFestschrift ᴹmentio, de eo ᴿrecensio ᵀtranslator † in mem. Sub **de, van** etc.: cognomina *americana* (post 1979) et *italiana* (post 1984); **non** reliqua.

ᴰdiss./dir. ᴱeditor ᶠFestschrift ᴹmentio, de eo ᴿrecensio ᵀtranslator † in mem.
Sub **de, van** etc.: cognomina *americana* (post 1979) et *italiana* (post 1984); **non** reliqua.

Ddiss./dir. Eeditor FFestschrift Mmentio, de eo Rrecensio Ttranslator † in mem.
Sub de, van etc.: cognomina *americana* (post 1979) et *italiana* (post 1984); **non** reliqua.

R7330 7852 8190 8328
R M6297 W 8664
R1318 a199
Stewart C 2267 k786* D
R1063a 1430c 3218 F
g292 H e301 J Ta921
Steyl C 9595
Steymans H Rb817
Stibbe C d916 M 5724
R5741
Sticca S 5042
Stichele C D6414
Stickler A F177
Stidsen C 8017*
Stiebing W M2728
Stiefel R 1382
Stieglitz R b453 R9545
Stier F 1902 J R9160
Stierlin H g154
Stiglmair A R2508
Stille P R252c
Stillman N k538* R1379
Stiltner B R7677
Stimpfle A 5740 5899
m550
Stine P 1929 E8900
Stinnett T b87
Stipp H D3809
Stirnemann A E109 H
9006
Stirnimann H Em138
Stjörn 1951
Stjordalen T Rm549
Stobbe H 1306b
Stock A e31 e32 E
M8921R K 4638 5182
5183 5319ab 5378 5943
8392 d467 D4639
Stockhausen C 5271b
6564 R6137
Stockmann-Köckert F
R8083
Stockton D d135 E 8901
Stoddart W E168a
Stoebe H 4777e R2885
Stoeger W 2197c
Stöhr M 1407 a782b
Stöver H k334
Stoevesandt H Em777
Stofferengen-Pedersen K
k539
Stogre M R8841
Stojkovic J M8009
Stoker W Rm555
Stol M 9634b k105
Re874 k144

Stoldt H 4233
Stoll D 8777 M8739 E
4592 O Rd745 V a791
m447 R6116 6281
m519
Stolper M g5
Stolz A M620
Stone B 3729 E 2608
e929 k255 k397 J a906
M 2269a 2428 3064
3080d a245 a245* a258
a364 E1051 9420
M4121 Ra242 R E7409
Stoneman R b284 e815
Stoof M Rg37
Stookey L 1382*
Stoop M Rd705
Stoops R a308c
Stordalen T 1528 1680
2270a 2281 R772 1075
1108 1112 1226 2198*
2250*a 2589 3500 7318
a179 b438 d855 k576
m203
Stordeur D d882*a
Storey G Dk405
Storfjell J D1976
Stork D 3134
Storme A e413
Storniolo I 4706
Stortz P R6137
Stos-Gale Z g582
Stott J 4735 5502 F177*
M1524 8339 m486*
Stotz G 7205
Stoutenburg D R5738
6075
Stow K 776*c a761*a
Stowasser M D5633
Stowers S 6055 6597b
Straarup J 7291*
Strabo g716a M668 g170
g718b k138 k382
Strack H a542 a543 M
Re874
Straeten J van der R748
Strahm D E9178*
Strain C R8610
Stramare T R2754
Strand K 8276 R5901
Strange B Rm619 J d433
d982 e367 e414 e524
g763 g775a Rd668 M
R9093 Rm611 W 5503
5607
Stransky T k123e

Strasser T g805
Stratkötter R Rk422
Stratman M Rm6
Straus J R6651 9965
9979 g309 g857
Strauss D M4226 9342
m548 G F178 Rm199 H
2709b 7420 L M2015*R
Straw C k955 Mk951
Strayer J E751
Streater D m618
Strecker G 4192 4193
4211c 5882 6018ab
6479b 6482 Ek620 k621
R5876 5885
Strehle S m284 m285
Strenski I a907a
Streza S D3562
Striano Corrochano A
R9820
Stricker B b509 g74
Strickland D R7688*
Striedter K 1168
Strijp R 989
Stringer C E728
Stringhini P 6754
Stritzky M v 4775 Rg177
k643
Strobel A d525a e450ab
e635* R48 K 6523 d297
e728 Rd298 d729 R
E9178*
Strober M F9106
Stroble P Rm762 m774
Strocchio R Rd245
Ströter-Bender J 2428*
Strohmaier-Wiederan-
ders G R191 9170
Stroker W 4454
Stroll M Ra786
Strommenger E d677
Rd750
Stronach D e935 Dg934
Strong B D7609 LD6160
Strop F R8888
Strotmann A 7077
Stroud R Ra154
Strouhal E d700 Re194
e279 g20
Stroumsa G 316 1169b
2388 2504 3238 4505c
a814* a845 E57 Ra880
S r244 Rb619
Strudnick N b972

ᴰdiss./dir. ᴱeditor ᶠFestschrift ᴹmentio, de eo ᴿrecensio ᵀtranslator † in mem.
Sub de, van etc.: cognomina americana (post 1979) et italiana (post 1984); non reliqua.

VOCES

ordine **graeco**

Abba 7059
aga 9872
agápē 5422 9873
ángelos 5610
agroikía 9874
adelphótēs 9875 7933
âthlon d804
aítion 9876
aiōn 9877
akēdía 9878
halískō 9888
hamartía d247
Amazōn 9889
Ambakoum 4074
amēn 8340
anaginōskō 9890
ānagnōrísis d247
anámnēsis 9891
anaphorá 8369*
ánemos 9892
anoigō 4904
apeithéō 9893
ápistos 6474
apoíētos k6
apoikía b392
apokatástasis 5550 5551
aretē d811
arketós 9894
harmathrochiē a27*b*
arrabōn 6155 6470
archē 5888 7635
arsenokoîtai 6404
askalónion e217
-assō 9896
Assyría 9895
ástu k360
auktoritas 9897
autós 9905
aphídruma b390
aphíēmi 5411

Bēma e268
bíblos 4635*c*
bíos 4635*c*

Gazítion e217
gár 5426 5799 9835
geláō 9898
gymnasíarchos 9926

Dé 9899
déxios 9900
deutereúō 9901
diathēkē 6765
diakonía 8203 8280 9902
diákonos 6464
díkaios 9935
dikē 9903

diōkō 6552
dískos d801
dýnamis 7583 9904

Eimí, éstai 5429
eirēnē 371
ekeînos 9905
eklektoì ángeloi 6718
éleos 9951
eleuthería 6368 6409
endiáthetos lógos 4498
enthousiasmós b357
entolē 4601*e*
entós 5455
epílogos 5870
éraze 9932
éschaton 7927
heterozygōn 6474
euangélion 4635*c*
eumarēs 9906

Ētoi 9908
ēthos 9907 b352 b352*

Thánatos 9229 m979
theios anēr 5121
thelxis k88*
thémis b312
theosebēs 9909
Theotókos 8974
theōsis k971 m200
thlîpsis 9910 9911
thymós 9955ᴿ 9912

Idios d761
Italía 9914
Ioudaîos 9913

-ka 9115
katheleîn 5044
kathexēs 5260*d*
kaí 9835*a*
kairós 9916 e81
kálamos 9917
kallonē k6
kántharos 4078
Káranos 9918
karmatopāgós a27*b*
katápausis 6762
katà sôma 6265
katáchrēsis a289*a*
kátoikos, -ía d155*b*
kausía g924*d*
ker 9955ᴿ
kephas 6525
kinnabaris g940

perôt 3676
Purim 3083 3088
tafsîr °b706
pᵉtîgîil 3677

ṣade
ṣedeq 9479 9480
ṣaddîq 3256
ṣôm b448
ṣûr 9482
ṣāpôn 9483
ṣᵓṣᵓym 3704b

qoph
qᵉdēšâ 3721
qôs 9566
maqlūta *2630
qamūṣ 2512
qunābarā °g940
qînīta *2630
qēn 9484
QRB 9485
qurnit g965*

rêš
arbuʿîm šanāh 2900
ruaḥ 2061 7076 9486
marzeaḥ e46
rḥmt 9537
rāḥôq 9486*
rîb 4104ᴿ 9487
rāṣaḥ 9491
rᵉpāᵓîm 9488 b432a
e713b
teraphim b432b
raqîaᶜ 2061bc
RQM 9489
rāṣāᶜ 9495

rāṣāh 9490
rṣp ṣprm ‡9492
rāṣas 9493
rāqad 9494
raš 9425
eršahunga *b533
rešep 9495*
rešet 9496

śin
śāba 9497
śābāh 9503
śābar 9498
śāgab 9499
śādeh 9500
śdrt, śdbt 2923
śeh g927
śôṣ 9501
śāḥaq 9502
śāṭām 2250*
śîhāh 9504
śîm 9505
śākal maśkîl 9506
śākār 9507
Issachar 2416
śelāw g927b
śᵉmôᵓl 9508
śimḥâ 9509
śimḥat Tôrâh 7343
śanēᶜ 9510
śāpāh 9511
śuq 9512
śar 9513
śārîd 9514
śārap 9515

šin
šaᵓab 9516

Voces hebr.-S. Scr. – 1253

šāᵓag 9517
šāᵓāh 9518
šāᵓal 9519
šᵉᵓôl 7424a 7425
7426c 7428*
šaᵓᵃnān 9520
šāᵓap 9521
šāᵓar 9522
šābaᶜ 9526
šebaᶜ 9527
šebeṭ 9525
šᵉbî 9523
šᵉbût 9524
šibbolet 2792
šdmt 9528
šwy 2845
šwb 3974
šoḥad 2946
škm 9529
šākan *muškēnum
9530
miškan 2605*
šᵉkînâ 7013 a763
šālôm 371
muslimūn °b656*
šālîšîm 2905
šnh 5406
mšᶜy 3877
mustašrik °d562
šN- šᵉtayim 9605a
šūpān 9530*

tau
tophet e667c c696a
taryag a508
Thummîm 2606*

Genesis	2,4-3,24: 2117	5,21: 2301	12,3: 2351
	2,4: 2281	5,28: 2299	12,10-20: 2353
–: 1812 2000-2036	2,7: 2281* 2282	6-9: 2303 2325	12,10: 2352
7181	2282*	6,1-4: 2301*	14: 2358-2360
1-11: 148b 2039	2,8s: 2286b	6,3: 2297 2302	14,1-11: 2357*
2041a 2055 2077	2,18-25: 2284	6,14: 9484	14,18-29: 2360*
2276 7245	2,23: 1489	10s: 2326	14,18-20: 2361
1-6: 2061bd	2,23: 2062	10: 2328	15: 2363-2368
1-3: 6413	3: 2285	10,9: 2328*	15,1: 2368
1: 2037-2057*	3,5: 2285*	11: 2329-2330	15,20: 2368
1,1-3: 2058	3,19: 2286*a	11,26-25,11: 2341	16s: 2370-2372
1,2: 2058*	4,1-16: 2288-2294	11,27-32: 2331	16,12: 2373
1,26: 2063-2074	4,1: 2297	12-36: 2342	17s: 2374
1,27: 2282*	4,19-21: 2300	12s: 2347b	17,10-14: 2375
1,28: 2075	4,22: 2298	12: 1952* 2332-	17,17: 2375*
1,29: 2079	4,23: 2299	2356	18: 2383

1-11: 6254
1-8: 6256 6257
1-5: 6227
1,1-5,21: 6258
1-4: 6259
1,1-17: 6261a 6262
1,3s: 6263
1.13: 6265
1,16-3,26: 6266
1,17: 6267 6268
1,18-4,25: 6261b
1,18-32: 6262 6269
1,20: 6270
1,24-27: 6271
1,26s: 6273
2,1-29: 6274
2,1-16: 6262
2,13: 6275 6276
  6539
2,17-3,8: 6262
3: 6277
3,3: 6278
3,9-23: 6262
3,20: 6279
  6539
3,21-26: 6280
3,25: 6281
3,31: 6278
4: 6282
5: 6445*
5,1-11: 6283
5,12-21: 6284-
  6288
6,1-14: 7864b
6,1s: 6289
6,5: 6290
7s: 6291 6292
7: 6293-6295
7,14-25: 6296
7,14-23: 6297
7,15: 6298a
8: 6249 6299
8,1-11: 6300
8,1-4: 6301
8,15: 6302a
8,18-27: R6303
8,19-27: 6304
8,28: 6302b
9,32: 6298
9-11: 6305-6335
10,5-10: 6545
10,6-17: 6336
11,1: 6142R
11,25-32: 6337
11,30-32: 6338
  6339a

12-15: 6340
12: 6341-6343
12,2: 6344
12,9-21: 6345
12,12: 6346
13: 6347
13,1-7: 6348-6350
14,1-15,13: 6351
14,19: 8246
15,14-16,24:
  6261a
15,18-21: 63654a
15,25-31: 6353
16: 6355
16,1s: 6356
16,17: 8524a
16,22: 6057

1 Ad Corinthios

–: 6357-6375 6569
1-6: 6359 6376
1-4: 6377
1s: 6380
1,2: 6381
1,18-31: 6382
1,18-25: 2958
1,20: 6383
2,1: 6381
2,6-16: 6384
2,10: 6381
3s: 6385
3,5-4,5: 6386
4: 6164
5s: 6387
5: 6388
5,1-15: 4905
5,1: 6389
5,5: 6390
5,9-13: 8524a
6-11: 6399
6,9: 6273
6,12-7,40: 6392
6,12-10: 6393
6,18: 6391
7: 6400
7,1-7: 6394
7,7: 139*R
7,8-16: 4748
7,15: 6367
7,21-24: 6396
7,25-40: 6397
8-10: 6401
8: 6403
8,1-13: 6402
8,9: 6404
8,10: 6367

9,1: 6089
9,9-11: 6406
9,19-23: 6407
9,22: 8362R 6408a
10: 6403
10,16: 6409a
10,18: 6410
10,22: 6411
10,25: 6412
11s: 6413
11,2-16: 6414
11,2s: 6443*
11,4s: 6415
11,10: 6416
11,12-16: 6376
12-14: 6440*
12s: 6416-6440
12: 6343 6630R
12,14-26: 6367
13: 1570 6442
13,7: 6441*
13,12: b490*d
14,1-25: 6442*
14,33-38: 6443
14,33-35: 6396
14,33s: 6447
14,34s: 6715
14,34: 6444
15: 6445 6445*
15,12s: 6446
15,22: 6446*
15,50: 6447
15,54: 6447*
15,56: 6448
16,1s: 6448*
16,9: 5606

2 Ad Corinthios

: 6449-6459
2,12: 6544b
2,14-7,4: 6460
2,14-4,6: 6461
2,14-3,3: 6462
2,17: 6463
3-6: 6464
3,6: 6465
3,7: 6544b
3,7-14: 6467
3,12-18: 6466
4,4: 6468
5,5: 6469
5,11-6,10: 6461
5,14-21: 6470
5,16: 6471
5,21: 6472
6,10: 6473

Ind. (➔ Rom) – 1261

6,14: 6474
8: 6475-6477
9: 6476
10-13: 477* 6464
  6480-6482
10s: 6481b
10,17: 6478
11,15: 6483
11,16-29: 6484
11,22s: 6142R
11,32s: 6485
12,1-13: 6486a
12,7: 6487
12,9: 6488
13,5: 6489

Ad Galatas

–: 2336 6371 6498-
  6524
1s: 6525
1,6: 6526
1,10-2:21: 6526
1,13s: 6142R
1,15s: 4901
1,16: 6527
2: 6529
2,1-15: 6530
2,7-9: 6531
2,7s: 6532
2,11-14: 6534 6535
2,11: 6536
2,14: 6537
2,15: 6539
2,16: 6279
3: 6583R
3,1-14: 6540
  6541
3,1-6: 6542
3,6-14: 6542
3,10-13: 6543
3,11s: 6545
3,23-29: 6546
3,24: 6544b
3,28: 6547
4,3.9: 6548
4,4: 309
4,9s: 6549
4,21-5,1: 6549b
5,1: 6551
5,6: 6550a
5,11: 6552
5,13-6,10: 6550bc
5,13-25: 6551
5,13-16: 6544b

PONTIFICIO ISTITUTO BIBLICO
EDIZIONI 1995

NOVITÀ

ANALECTA BIBLICA

133. MINISSALE ANTONINO: *La versione greca del Siracide. Confronto con il testo ebraico alla luce dell'attività midrascica e del metodo targumico.*
pp. X-334.   ISBN 88-7653-133-5.   Lit. 65.000

134. MAZZINGHI LUCA: *Notte di paura e di luce. Esegesi di Sap 17,1-18,4.*
pp. XXXII-360 + pieghevole.
ISBN 88-7653-134-3.   Lit. 65.000

135. BORGONOVO GIANANTONIO: *La notte e il suo sole. Luce e tenebre nel Libro di Giobbe. Analisi simbolica.*
pp. XIV-498.   ISBN 88-7653-135-1.   Lit. 56.000

SUBSIDIA BIBLICA

18. FITZMYER JOSEPH A.: *The Biblical Commission's Document «The Interpretation of the Bible in the Church». Text and Commentary.*
pp. XVI-212.   ISBN 88-7653-605-1.   Lit. 30.000

RISTAMPE

ANALECTA ORIENTALIA

33. VON SODEN WOLFRAM - MAYER WERNER R.: *Grundriss der Akkadischen Grammatik.* 3ª edizione aggiornata.
pp. XXXII-328-56*.   ISBN 88-7653-258-7.   Lit. 90.000

BIBLICA ET ORIENTALIA

19/A. FITZMYER JOSEPH A.: *The Aramaic Inscriptions of Sefire.* 2ª edizione riveduta.
pp. 252 + 19 tav.   ISBN 88-7653-347-8.   Lit. 54.000

Ordini e pagamenti a:

AMMINISTRAZIONE PUBBLICAZIONI PIB/PUG

Piazza della Pilotta, 35 – 00187 Roma – Italia
Tel. 06/678.15.67 – Fax 06/678.05.88
Conto Corrente Postale n. 34903005 – Compte Postal n. 34903005
Monte dei Paschi di Siena – Sede di Roma – c/c n. 54795.37

Pubblicazioni periodiche dell'Editrice
Pontificio Istituto Biblico

BIBLICA

rivista trimestrale di Studi Biblici
abbonamento 1996: L. 75.000 – US $ 70.00

ORIENTALIA

rivista trimestrale di Studi sull'Antico Oriente
abbonamento 1996: L. 110.000 – US $ 100.00

Pubblicazioni periodiche dell'Editrice
Pontificia Università Gregoriana

ARCHIVUM
HISTORIAE PONTIFICIAE

rivista annuale di Storia Ecclesiastica
abbonamento vol. 33/1995: L. 110.000 – US $ 100.00

GREGORIANUM

rivista trimestrale di Teologia e Filosofia
abbonamento 1996: L. 80.000 – US $ 75.00

PERIODICA
DE RE CANONICA

rivista trimestrale di Diritto Canonico
abbonamento 1996: L. 80.000 – US $ 75.00

Amministrazione: Piazza della Pilotta 35 – 00187 Roma
Tel. 06/678.15.67 – Fax 06/678.05.88 – ccp 34903005

ISBN 88-7653-603-5